Hammer's *German* Grammar and Usage

Hammer's *German* Grammar and Usage

MARTIN DURRELL

FOURTH EDITION

McGraw-Hill

Chicago   New York   San Francisco   Lisbon   London   Madrid   Mexico City
Milan   New Delhi   San Juan   Seoul   Singapore   Sydney   Toronto

McGraw-Hill

A Division of The **McGraw-Hill** *Companies*

This edition published in 2002 by The McGraw-Hill Companies

Originally published by Edward Arnold, a member of the Hodder Headline Group.

10 9 8

ISBN 978-0-07-139654-7

Cover design by Jenny Locke

This book is printed on acid-free paper

Contents

List of tables   xi
List of abbreviations and points for the user   xiii
Preface to the second edition   xv
Preface to the third edition   xix
Preface to the fourth edition   xxi

1.	**Nouns**	**1**
1.1	Gender	1
	A: Gender and meaning	2
	B: Gender and form	7
1.2	Noun plurals	15
1.3	Noun declension	26
2.	**Case**	**34**
2.1	The nominative case	34
2.2	The accusative case	36
2.3	The genitive case	37
2.4	Genitive case or *von*?	39
2.5	The dative case	41
2.6	Apposition	45
2.7	Measurement phrases: genitive, *von* or apposition?	46
3.	**Personal pronouns**	**49**
3.1	The forms of the personal pronouns	49
3.2	Reflexive and reciprocal pronouns	51
3.3	Pronouns of address	53
3.4	Third person pronouns	55
3.5	Third person pronoun or prepositional adverb?	56
3.6	Special uses of the pronoun *es*	58
4.	**The articles**	**64**
4.1	The declension of the articles	65
4.2	The use of articles with abstract nouns	67
4.3	The use of articles in generalisations	71

4.4	The use of articles with geographical and other proper names	72
4.5	The use of articles in time expressions	74
4.6	Definite article or possessive?	75
4.7	Miscellaneous uses of the definite article	76
4.8	Miscellaneous uses of the zero article	77
4.9	Article use with prepositions	79
5.	**Other determiners and pronouns**	**82**
5.1	Demonstratives	83
5.2	Possessives	89
5.3	Interrogatives	92
5.4	Relative pronouns	96
5.5	Indefinites, quantifiers and other determiners and pronouns	103
6.	**Adjectives**	**125**
6.1	Declension of adjectives	126
6.2	The use of the strong and weak declensions	127
6.3	Irregularities in the spelling of some adjectives	132
6.4	Adjectives used as nouns	133
6.5	Cases with adjectives	136
6.6	Adjectives with prepositions	139
7.	**Adverbs**	**143**
7.1	Adverbs of place	144
7.2	Adverbs of direction: *hin* and *her*	146
7.3	Adverbs of manner, viewpoint, attitude and reason	150
7.4	Adverbs of degree	156
7.5	Interrogative adverbs	157
8.	**Comparison of adjectives and adverbs**	**159**
8.1	Regular formation of the comparative and superlative	159
8.2	Irregularities in the formation of comparatives and superlatives	160
8.3	The use of the comparative and other types of comparison	164
8.4	Types and uses of the superlative	167
9.	**Numerals**	**171**
9.1	Cardinal numbers	171
9.2	Ordinal numbers	177
9.3	Fractions and decimals	179
9.4	Other numerical usages	181
9.5	Addresses	183
10.	**Modal particles**	**184**
10.1	*aber*	185
10.2	*allerdings*	186

10.3	*also*	186
10.4	*auch*	187
10.5	*bloß*	189
10.6	*denn*	189
10.7	*doch*	190
10.8	*eben*	193
10.9	*eh*	194
10.10	*eigentlich*	194
10.11	*einfach*	195
10.12	*erst*	195
10.13	*etwa*	197
10.14	*freilich*	198
10.15	*gar*	198
10.16	*gleich*	199
10.17	*halt*	199
10.18	*immerhin*	199
10.19	*ja*	199
10.20	*jedenfalls*	201
10.21	*lediglich*	201
10.22	*mal*	202
10.23	*man*	202
10.24	*noch*	203
10.25	*nun*	204
10.26	*nur*	204
10.27	*ohnehin*	206
10.28	*ruhig*	206
10.29	*schließlich*	206
10.30	*schon*	207
10.31	*sowieso*	209
10.32	*überhaupt*	209
10.33	*übrigens*	210
10.34	*vielleicht*	210
10.35	*wohl*	211
10.36	*zwar*	212
11.	**Expressions of time**	**213**
11.1	Times of the clock	213
11.2	Days of the week, months and public holidays	215
11.3	Dates	216
11.4	The accusative and genitive cases used in time adverbials	217
11.5	Adverbial time phrases with prepositions	219
11.6	Adverbs of time	227
12.	**Verbs: conjugation**	**231**
12.1	Verb conjugation	232
12.2	The simple present and past tenses, the non-finite forms and the imperative	238

12.3	The compound tenses	244
12.4	The passive	248
12.5	The subjunctive	250

13.	**The infinitve and the participles**	**261**
13.1	Forms of the infinitive	261
13.2	The use of the infinitive with *zu*	263
13.3	The use of infinitive without *zu*	273
13.4	Infinitives used as nouns	277
13.5	The present and past participles	280
13.6	Clauses with participles	284
13.7	German equivalents of English constructions with the 'ing'-form	285

14.	**Uses of the tenses**	**291**
14.1	The German tenses: general	291
14.2	The present tense	292
14.3	The past tense and the perfect tense	295
14.4	The future tense and the future perfect tense	300
14.5	The pluperfect tense	302
14.6	German equivalents for the English progressive tenses	304

15.	**The passive**	**307**
15.1	The *werden*-passive	308
15.2	The *sein*-passive	312
15.3	*von, durch* and *mit* with the passive	315
15.4	Other passive constructions	317
15.5	The use of active and passive in German	321

16.	**Mood: the imperative and the subjunctive**	**323**
16.1	Indicative, imperative and subjunctive	323
16.2	Commands and the imperative	324
16.3	The subjunctive mood: general	327
16.4	Forms and tenses of the subjunctive	327
16.5	Conditional sentences	330
16.6	Indirect speech	335
16.7	Other uses of the subjunctive	343

17.	**The modal auxiliaries**	**348**
17.1	The modal auxiliaries: common features of form and syntax	348
17.2	*dürfen*	352
17.3	*können*	353

17.4 *mögen*   356
17.5 *müssen*   358
17.6 *sollen*   360
17.7 *wollen*   363

18. Verbs: valency   **365**

18.1 Valency, complements and sentence patterns   365
18.2 The subject   368
18.3 The accusative object   374
18.4 The dative object   379
18.5 Genitive objects   384
18.6 Prepositional objects   386
18.7 Place and direction complements   394
18.8 Predicate complements   395

19. Conjunctions and subordination   **397**

19.1 Coordinating conjunctions   398
19.2 Noun clauses   402
19.3 Conjunctions of time   406
19.4 Causal conjunctions   411
19.5 Conjunctions of purpose and result   412
19.6 Concessive conjunctions   415
19.7 Conjunctions of manner and degree   417

20. Prepositions   **421**

20.1 Prepositions governing the accusative case   421
20.2 Prepositions governing the dative case   428
20.3 Prepositions governing the accusative or the dative case   442
20.4 Prepositions governing the genitive case   458
20.5 German equivalents for English 'to'   464

21. Word order   **468**

21.1 Clause structure and the position of the verb   469
21.2 Initial position in main clause statements   473
21.3 The order of other elements in the sentence: general principles   480
21.4 The position of the pronouns   480
21.5 The position of noun subject and objects   483
21.6 The place and order of adverbials   485
21.7 The position of *nicht* and other negative elements   488
21.8 The position of complements   490
21.9 Placing elements after the end of the verbal bracket   491

22. Word formation   **495**

22.1 Methods of word formation   495
22.2 The formation of nouns   497

22.3	The formation of adjectives	503
22.4	The formation of verbs: inseparable prefixes	508
22.5	The formation of verbs: separable prefixes	511
22.6	The formation of verbs: variable prefixes	514
22.7	Verb formation by means other than prefixes	519
23.	**Spelling and punctuation**	**521**
23.1	The use of capital letters	521
23.2	One word or two	524
23.3	*ss* or *ß*?	526
23.4	Other points of spelling	526
23.5	The use of the comma	527
23.6	Other punctuation marks	529
List of sources		**531**
Bibliography and references		**533**
Glossary		**539**
Index		**549**

Tables

1.1	Gender and meaning	2
1.2	Gender and endings	8
1.3	How nouns form their plural in German	15
1.4	Plurals and gender	16
1.5	Case endings of regular nouns	27
1.6	Declension of weak masculine nouns	27
1.7	Declension of irregular nouns	29
2.1	Chief uses of the cases in German	35
3.1	Forms of the personal pronouns	49
3.2	Forms of the reflexive pronoun	52
4.1	Declension of the definite article	65
4.2	Declension of the indefinite article *ein* and negative *kein*	67
5.1	Declension of *der* used as a pronoun	83
5.2	Declension of *dieser*	85
5.3	Declension of *derjenige* and *derselbe*	86
5.4	Base forms of the possessive pronouns and determiners	89
5.5	Declension of the possessive determiners	90
5.6	Declension of the possessive pronouns	90
5.7	Declension of *wer*	94
5.8	Declension of the relative pronoun *der*	96
5.9	Indefinites, quantifiers and determiners	103
5.10	Declension of the pronoun *einer*	108
5.11	Declension of *jemand, niemand*	116
6.1	The endings of adjectives in the strong and weak declensions	126
6.2	Strong adjective declension, with no determiner	127
6.3	Weak adjective declension, with the definite article	127
6.4	Mixed adjective declension, with the indefinite article	128
6.5	Declension of adjectives used as nouns	134
7.1	Main types of adverb	143
8.1	Regular formation of comparative and superlative	160
9.1	The forms of the cardinal numbers	171
9.2	The forms of the ordinal numbers	178

10.1 German modal particles 185

11.1 Clock times 213
11.2 The twenty-four-hour clock 214
11.3 The days of the week 215
11.4 The months of the year 215

12.1 Vowel changes in strong verbs 234
12.2 Conjugation of the verb in the simple tenses 239
12.3 Conjugation of *sein, haben, werden* 243
12.4 Conjugation of the modal auxiliary verbs and *wissen* 244
12.5 Compound tenses of strong and weak verbs 245
12.6 The forms of the *werden*-passive 249
12.7 The forms of the *sein*-passive 250
12.8 The forms of *Konjunktiv I* and *Konjunktiv II* 250
12.9 The simple forms of *Konjunktiv I* and *Konjunktiv II* 251
12.10 The pluperfect subjunctive and conditional forms of *Konjunktiv II* 252
12.11 Formation of the simple form of *Konjunktiv II* (past subjunctive) 253
12.12 Principal parts of strong and irregular verbs 254

14.1 German and English tenses 292

15.1 Active and passive sentences 308

16.1 The forms of *Konjunktiv I* and *Konjunktiv II* 328
16.2 Conditional sentences 330
16.3 *Konjunktiv I* and *Konjunktiv II* in indirect speech – standard rules 336
16.4 Indirect speech in spoken German 338

17.1 The tenses and moods of *können* with an infinitive 349

18.1 Verb complements in German 366
18.2 German sentence patterns 367

19.1 Coordinating conjunctions 398
19.2 Conjunctions of time 406
19.3 Causal conjunctions 411
19.4 Conjunctions of purpose and result 413
19.5 Conjunctions of manner and degree 417

20.1 German prepositions and their cases 422

21.1 Basic order of the elements in the German sentence 481

Abbreviations and points for the user

Points

1 Lists of words are in general alphabetical, although occasionally a deviation from this has seemed more helpful.
2 Where required, the plural of a noun is indicated in brackets after the noun, e.g. *das Lager (-)*, i.e. *die Lager; der Hut (¨e)*, i.e. *die Hüte*, etc. *(-en, -en)* or *(-n, -n)* indicate a weak masculine noun, see 1.3.2.
3 If necessary, a stressed syllable in a word is indicated by the mark ` placed before the stressed syllable, e.g. *die Dok`toren, unter`schreiben*. Where it is required, a stressed word in context is shown by underlining, e.g. *Wie bist du denn gekommen?*
4 Sentences used for illustration which are ungrammatical in German are indicated by an asterisk, e.g. **Jedoch dann ist er nicht gekommen.*

Abbreviations

In principle, abbreviations have been kept to a minimum. The following have been used where required by considerations of space.

abbrev.	abbreviated	indic.	indicative
acad.	academic	inf.	informal
A., acc.	accusative	jd.	jemand
arch.	archaic	jdm.	jemandem
Austr.	Austrian	jdn.	jemanden
aux.	auxiliary	lang.	language
Bav.	Bavarian	lit.	literary
ch.	chapter	masc.	masculine
cl.	clause	N., nom.	nominative
coll.	colloquial	neut.	neuter
conj.	conjunction	N.G. ¨	north German
D., dat.	dative	obs.	obsolete
elev.	elevated	occ.	occasionally
esp.	especially	o.s.	oneself
etw.	etwas	part.	participle
fem.	feminine	pej.	pejorative
form.	formal	pl.	plural
G., gen.	genitive	prep.	preposition

S.G.	south German	Sw.	Switzerland
sb.	somebody	techn.	technical
sg., sing.	singular	vb.	verb
sub. cl.	subordinate clause	vulg.	vulgar
sth.	something		

PREFACE *to the second edition*

Since the appearance of the first edition in 1971, Hammer's grammar has been an indispensable source of information about modern German grammar and usage for teachers and students of German. Its acknowledged strength lay above all in the wealth of well chosen examples, but also in its comprehensiveness and its sheer reliability. However, much has changed in the intervening twenty years, and it became clear that a thoroughgoing revision which retained the essential virtues of Mr Hammer's work had become necessary. For, if the basic structure of the language remains unaltered, the needs of language students and sixth-formers learning German are now rather different, as is the range of German with which they must cope and the methods by which they are taught, and it is these needs which this revised edition is intended to address.

In preparing the revision, I have attempted to bear a few central principles in mind, given that the work is intended to be a comprehensive descriptive grammar of standard German for the use of the foreign learner whose native or first language is English. First, if it is to be used by advanced learners of German in sixth forms and on university courses, it can no longer be taken for granted that they will be fully familiar with grammatical terminology and notions. I have thus added a certain amount of explanatory material to help the user to understand the points of grammar and usage being treated. In general, I have used familiar and traditional grammatical terminology where possible, and thus refer, for example, to 'subordinating conjunctions' rather than 'complementizers'. However, where I consider more recent and perhaps less familiar terms and ideas to be a help to the potential user in understanding the structures of the language, as is the case with 'determiners' (Chapter 5) or the 'valency' of verbs (Chapter 18), I have adopted them and explained them fully.

Secondly, I have retained the range of examples which constituted one of the principal strengths of the original edition. In practice, I have kept a large proportion of Mr Hammer's examples, but checked them again with native speakers to confirm that they fully reflect current usage. Where I have substituted new examples, it has been with the aim of extending the range of registers covered (in particular to represent everyday spoken usage more fully) or updating the material.

Thirdly, it is taken as a basic principle that the work should be as comprehensive as possible and serve as a reference work which may be consulted on any point of grammar and usage. To this end, all the individual sections have been checked to confirm that the information is as full as necessary for the English learner and that it is as accurate as possible. A substantial body of research has been completed in the last twenty years which has increased our knowledge and understanding of current usage in German – there have, for example, been two completely new editions of the standard DUDEN grammar since 1971 – and this has been consulted at every stage. The reviser's debt to this original research on the modern language may be seen in the bibliography.

Fourthly, the changed needs of the present-day learner have been borne in mind by including information on all forms of the modern language. Thus, more attention has been paid to registers other than formal writing or literature and details given on spoken usage to reflect the greater emphasis paid to communicative skills in modern language teaching. Thus, where spoken and written usage diverge, this is clearly explained, as are forms which, though they may be regarded as grammatically 'correct', are felt to be stilted outside the most formal written registers. Similarly, forms which are frequently heard in everyday speech but widely thought of as substandard or incorrect are included here, as the foreign learner will encounter them every day, but with a clear indication of their status. In general, the foreign learner is counselled to avoid such forms as they sound particularly unacceptable when spoken with a foreign accent. Important regional variants within standard German are also included and marked accordingly, but purely dialectal forms have been ignored.

Finally, the structure of the work has been totally recast to simplify the user's task in finding his or her way to the required information. In practice, this has meant that the bulk of the text is quite new to this revised edition. Although the basic sequence of chapters is much the same as in the original edition, the layout has been simplified, longer chapters have been split up (that on verbs, which constituted almost a quarter of the whole book, has been divided into seven separate chapters), related information which was scattered in different parts has been brought together (even where this has involved a certain amount of repetition) and cross-references have been radically simplified and eliminated where unnecessary. The index has been expanded to include as many words and topics as possible, and to facilitate access to the material it has been divided into a German word index, an English word index and a topic index.

Acknowledgements

It is with sincere gratitude that I acknowledge the assistance I have been fortunate enough to receive during the preparation of the revised edition, first and foremost to those German speakers, unfortunately too numerous to mention, who have answered questions, given advice and, often unwittingly, provided me with examples and other linguistic data. I am especially indebted to those friends and colleagues in Britain who have been kind enough to comment on draft chapters, provide me with material, let me see their own notes resulting from their use of the first edition and advise me in other ways, in particular Dr J.S. Barbour, Dr C. Beedham, Mr P.A. Coggle, Dr D. Duckworth, Dr J.L. Flood, Dr C. Hall, Mr W. Hanson, Mr P. Holgate, Mr D.H.R. Jones, Prof. W.J. Jones, Dr K.M. Kohl, Mr D.G. McCulloch, Dr G.D.C. Martin, Dr D. Rösler, Ms M. Schwab, Dr R.W. Sheppard, Prof. H.G. Siefken, Dr J.K.A. Thomaneck, Mrs A. Thompson, Dr B. Thompson, Mr M.R. Townson, Mr B.A. Watson, Dr J. West and Dr D.N. Yeandle. I must also express my thanks to the German Academic Exchange Service, who made it possible for me to spend a month at the Institut für deutsche Sprache in Mannheim, where I was able to check many aspects of usage and points of grammar in its computerised corpus of modern spoken and written German and use its inestimable library facilities. I am very grateful to all colleagues there for their help, particularly to Mr Tobias Brückner, Prof. U. Engel, Prof. G. Stickel, Mrs Eva Teubert, Prof. R. Wimmer and Dr Gisela Zifonun. Last but not least, I must acknowledge my debt to Royal Holloway and Bedford New College, University of London, which granted me an invaluable term's leave of absence to work on this revision and to all my colleagues in the German Department at RHBNC for their continued support whilst I was engaged on this task.

Martin Durrell
1991

PREFACE *to the third edition*

The principal aim of the revised second edition of Hammer's grammar was to make the excellent material of the original version accessible to a new generation of students by providing more detailed explanations, improving the layout and presentation and providing a more comprehensive system of access to the material. In short, it was to be more up-to-date and user-friendly, whilst retaining the basic ordering of the original and much of its wealth of examples. Reactions from users and practical experience in working with the new edition suggest that these aims were welcome and that they were fulfilled to a certain extent, but that further improvements were possible and necessary. The present revised third edition is intended to achieve these.

After some hesitation, it was decided that the basic, relatively traditional layout based on the parts of speech should be retained. If there is much in favour of a presentation which systematically uses longer authentic texts as the basis for an account of grammatical structures and usage (like Weinrich (1993)), such an approach would probably be unfamiliar to most potential users and could detract from the usefulness of the work for everyday reference. Similarly, considerations of the user prevailed in the decision to retain a separate chapter on expressions of time, although consistency would suggest that the material dealt with there really belongs elsewhere, e.g. in the chapter on adverbs or the chapter on prepositions.

It was clear, though, that there was scope for the essential information in each chapter to be presented in the form of easily consulted tables. This has been done systematically in this new edition, so that almost every chapter or section has a table summarising basic points or presenting inflectional paradigms. Similarly, an innovation in the second edition was that each chapter has a short introduction explaining the subject matter of the chapter and any relevant grammatical terminology. These have been made more consistent and aim more deliberately to summarise the contents of each chapter so that the user can find his/her way more easily to the relevant material. In practice, all explanatory material has been subjected to close scrutiny from the point of view of the potential user and revised where necessary, with the aim of simplifying and clarifying explanations wherever possible. The opportunity was also taken to review all the language examples, substituting better or newer material where required.

Naturally, all information about specific points of grammar and usage was checked fully against my own database of modern German, the corpus of spoken and written German at the Institut für deutsche Sprache in Mannheim and the most recent academic research, as reflected (selectively) in the bibliography. This has resulted in substantial revision of some chapters and sections, notably the account of adverbs (Chapter 7), of the subjunctive mood (in particular the analysis of the *würde*-form in the light of Thieroff (1992)) and of the gender of foreign words in section 1.1. A number of sections have been added on points which were dealt with sketchily or inadequately in the second edition, for instance on verb agreement (section 12.1.4), on commands and the imperative (section 16.2) and on complement clauses (section 19.2). And, of course, information had to be given on the reformed spelling which will be implemented from summer 1998 onwards (section 23.7).

As for the second edition, I owe an immense debt of gratitude to a large number of friends, colleagues and acquaintances in the English- and German-speaking countries without whose help this revision would have been impossible. In addition to those who already helped me for the second edition, I must offer particular thanks to Dr Paul Bennett, Dr Carol Chapman, Dr Bruce Donaldson, Mr Piklu Gupta, Prof. Randall Jones, Dr John Manton, Ms Victoria Martin, Prof. Ulrike Meinhof, Dr Michael Minden, Prof. Hugh Ridley, Ms Susan Tebbutt and Dr Sheila Watts. I am particularly grateful, too, for the continuous collaborative help and support of Prof. David Brée and his colleagues and postgraduates at the Department of Computer Science, University of Manchester.

Martin Durrell
1996

PREFACE *to the fourth edition*

The primary motivation for a new edition of Hammer's grammar is naturally the reform of German spelling which was introduced just after the appearance of the third edition, where a brief indication of the proposed changes was given. Despite the ensuing controversies, which have not completely died down, it now appears clear that the reforms have been largely accepted in principle, and the vast majority of new publications in the German-speaking countries have adopted its prescriptions, as have new editions of textbooks for foreign learners. As today's learners will be confronted predominantly with German written according to the reformed spelling and expected to conform to it themselves, it was evident that a new edition of the present work was required which did not simply give an indication of the changes but incorporated the new rules for spelling and punctuation consistently throughout the text. In line with this, all examples of grammatical points have been revised according to the new rules (even where the original publication conformed to the norms valid at the time of publication), and all information given throughout the work now relates exclusively to the new prescriptions (with reference to the major differences where necessary). Among other things, the simplifications introduced by the new rules, in particular in respect of the placement of commas, have meant that Chapter 23, 'Spelling and Punctuation', is somewhat shorter than in previous editions.

The need to revise the work also presented an opportunity to incorporate a number of changes and improvements which have been suggested by various users who were kind enough to contact me. The basic principle of the work remains that it aims to be a comprehensive descriptive account of modern German for the use of the advanced learner whose first language is English. However, it became clear that it needed to be somewhat more accessible for those who might be less familiar with general grammatical notions and modern linguistic methods and terminology. The third edition already made a step in this direction by incorporating tables in each chapter summarising basic points and an introduction to each chapter explaining its subject matter and all the relevant grammatical terminology. These have all been totally revised and much expanded in this edition, so that the introduction to each chapter provides a full summary of its contents and accessible explanations of the material: by turning to the first page of each chapter, users can find their way easily and quickly to the points about which they require information. The number of summarising tables has also been increased considerably, assisted by work in collaboration with Dr Katrin Kohl and Ms Gudrun Loftus on *An Essential Grammar of German* (Arnold: London 2002), which is intended as a companion work for less advanced English-speaking learners. I am inordinately grateful to these colleagues for their many suggestions on the present revision. The layout of the sections has also been altered to facilitate consultation, with essential information made more prominent. The three separate indexes had proved clumsy and confusing for many users, and they have here been combined into a single index. Furthermore, since the indexes relate to section numbers, rather than to pages, the section numbers have also been incorporated into the running heads of each page to facilitate finding the relevant sections. Following the model of other recent grammars published by Arnold, in particular Martin Maiden and Cecilia Robustelli, *A Reference Grammar of Modern Italian* (London 2000), a glossary of major grammatical terms is also provided, with reference to the sections or chapters where they are exemplified more fully.

The opportunity was also taken to update linguistic examples where necessary and incorporate the result of recent research. This is, however, no longer referred to directly in the text, as this was felt to be distracting, but the bibliography has been re-organised so that, aside from giving the major general works on German which have been consulted, the principal sources and major recent work on individual points are given for each chapter separately to assist those who wish to consult more detailed studies. In order to facilitate cross-reference between this and the third edition, changes in the numbering and content of individual sections and subsections have been kept to a minimum. In practice, the basic material presented in the body of the text is largely the same as in the third edition, with the exception of necessary individual amendments and corrections effected in consultation with my own database of modern German, the corpora of spoken and written German at the Institut für Deutsche Sprache in Mannheim and recent research.

As for the third edition, I owe an immense debt of gratitude to a large number of friends, colleagues and acquaintances throughout the world without whose help this revision would have been impossible. I am particularly grateful to Dr Bruce Donaldson in Melbourne for his continued unflagging attention to detail and helpful queries and suggestions, but I must also offer particular thanks, in addition to those who had already helped me for previous editions, to Prof. Vilmos Ágel, Prof. John Ole Askedal, Dr Wiebke Brockhaus, Dr Philippa Cook, Prof. Peter Eisenberg, Prof. Christoph Gutknecht, Dr Gregor Hens, Prof. Ewald Lang and an anonymous reviewer for Arnolds.

Martin Durrell
2002

1

Nouns

NOUNS are words which name living creatures, things, places, ideas or processes. In German they are distinguished by being written with an initial capital letter (see 23.1). A noun is often preceded by an article or other determiner (see Chapters 4 and 5), and often also by one or more adjectives or a longer adjectival phrase (see Chapter 6). Together, these form the NOUN PHRASE:

Determiner	Adjective/adjectival phrase	Noun
die das ein	 ultramoderne vom Kultbuchautor Adams erfundenes	Gott Erde Raumschiff Computerspiel

This chapter gives you details about the three grammatical categories which relate to nouns and which are marked by inflections on the noun or the other words within a noun phrase:

- the **gender** of nouns (section 1.1)
- how nouns form their **plural** (section 1.2)
- how the form of nouns changes to show **case** (section 1.3)

1.1 Gender

Every German noun is assigned to one of the three genders: MASCULINE, FEMININE or NEUTER. GENDER, in grammar, is a system for classifying nouns. It differs from 'natural' gender (i.e. 'males', 'females' and 'things', as in English). In this way, the names of the genders are misleading and the classification can seem arbitrary, especially as words for 'things' can have any of the three genders.

MASCULINE: **der** Tisch, FEMININE: **die** Wand, NEUTER: **das** Fenster

Gender differences only affect the singular of nouns in German, not the plural:

die Tische, **die** Wände, **die** Fenster

Foreign learners are always recommended to learn German nouns together with their gender as shown by the relevant definite article. In practice, though, the meaning or the form (especially the ending) of a noun often gives a useful clue to its gender, as does the way the plural is formed. The gender of 80% of German nouns can be recognised in this way, and a knowledge of these, even if there are some exceptions, is a valuable assistance in learning the gender of nouns. This section shows:

- How gender can relate to the meaning of nouns (sections 1.1.1–1.1.4)
- How gender can be recognised from the form or ending of nouns (sections 1.1.5–1.1.8)
- The gender of compound words and abbreviations (section 1.1.9)
- The gender of loan-words from English (section 1.1.10)
- Nouns with varying or double gender (sections 1.1.11–1.1.12)
- Problems with gender agreement (section 1.1.13)

A: Gender and meaning

Sections 1.1.1–1.1.4 give detail on where the meaning of a noun is relevant for its gender. The most important cases are summarised in Table 1.1.

TABLE 1.1 *Gender and meaning*

Masculine	Examples
male humans and animals	**der** Arzt, **der** Hahn, **der** Löwe, **der** Bock
seasons, months, days of the week	**der** Sommer, **der** Januar, **der** Montag
winds, weather, points of the compass	**der** Föhn, **der** Nebel, **der** Schnee, **der** Norden
rocks, minerals	**der** Granit, **der** Diamant,
alcoholic and plant-based drinks	**der** Gin, **der** Kakao
makes of car	**der** BMW, **der** Audi, **der** Mercedes
rivers outside Germany	**der** Ganges, **der** Nil, **der** Severn
monetary units	**der** Euro, **der** Dollar, **der** Franken
mountains, mountain ranges	**der** Brocken, **der** Spessart
Feminine	
female humans and animals	**die** Frau, **die** Henne, **die** Löwin, **die** Sau
aeroplanes, motor-bikes, ships	**die** Boeing, **die** BMW, **die** „Bismarck"
rivers inside Germany	**die** Weser, **die** Donau, **die** Maas, **die** Memel
names of numerals	**die** Eins, **die** Vier, **die** Milliarde
Neuter	
young humans and animals	**das** Baby, **das** Kind, **das** Ferkel, **das** Lamm
metals, chemicals, scientific units	**das** Gold, **das** Eisen, **das** Aspirin, **das** Volt
letters of the alphabet, musical notes	**das** A, **das** Ypsilon, ein großes D, **das** hohe C
other parts of speech used as nouns	**das** Stehen, **das** Aber, **das** moderne Deutsch
hotels, cafés, restaurants, cinemas	**das** „Hilton", **das** „Kranzler", **das** „Kapitol"
continents, countries, towns	**das** alte Europa, **das** neue Polen, **das** geteilte Berlin

1.1.1 Nouns with these meanings are masculine:

(a) Male persons and male animals
(see also 1.1.4)

> der Arzt, der Ingenieur, der König, der Student, der Vater, der Bock, der Eber, der Hahn

NB: Diminutives in *-chen* and *-lein* are neuter (see 1.1.7), e.g.: *das Büblein, das Karlchen, das Kerlchen.*

(b) Seasons, months and days of the week

> der Frühling, der Sommer, der Herbst, der Januar, der Mai, der Mittwoch, der Sonnabend

NB: (i)   Compounds, e.g. *das Frühjahr, die Jahreszeit,* have the gender of the second element, see 1.1.9.
　　(ii) Exceptions: *die Nacht, die Woche, das Jahr.*

(c) Points of the compass and words referring to winds and kinds of weather

der Norden, der Osten, der Süden, der Westen
der Föhn, der Passat, der Taifun, der Wind
der Frost, der Hagel, der Nebel, der Regen, der Schnee, der Sturm, der Tau

NB: Exceptions: *die Brise, das Eis, das Gewitter* (see 1.1.8c), *die Graupel, das Wetter, die Witterung* (see 1.1.6).

(d) Rocks and minerals

der Diamant, der Granit, der Lehm, der Quarz, der Ton

NB: Exceptions: *das Erz, die Kohle, die Kreide, das Mineral.*

(e) Alcoholic drinks and plant-based drinks

der Cocktail, der Gin, der Kirsch, der Schnaps, der Wein, der Wodka
der Kakao, der Kaffee, der Most, der Saft, der Tee

NB: Exception: *das Bier.*

(f) Makes of car

der Audi, der BMW, der Citroën, der Polo, der Rolls-Royce, der Trabant

NB: *der BMW* is a car made by BMW, but *die BMW* is a motor-bike made by BMW (see 1.1.2b).

(g) Rivers outside Germany

(see 1.1.2c for those within Germany)

der Ganges, der Jordan, der Kongo, der Mississippi, der Nil, der Po, der Shannon, der Severn

NB: Those ending in *-a* or *-e* are feminine, e.g.: *die Seine, die Themse* 'the Thames', *die Wolga*. Also: *die Liffey*.

(h) Monetary units

der Cent, der Dollar, der Euro, der Franken, der Pfennig, der Rappen, der Schilling

NB: There are several exceptions, notably: *die Mark, das Pfund.*

(i) Mountains and mountain ranges

der Ätna, der Brocken, der Montblanc, der Mount Everest, der Säntis
der Balkan, der Harz, der Himalaja, der Jura, der Spessart, der Taunus

NB: There are some exceptions, e.g.:
(i)   compounds: *das Erzgebirge, das Matterhorn, die Zugspitze.*
(ii)   *die Eifel, die Haardt, die Rhön, die Sierra Nevada.*

1.1.2 Nouns with these meanings are feminine:

(a) Female persons and animals
(see also 1.1.4)

die Frau, die Gans, die Henne, die Köchin, die Kuh, die Mutter, die Sau, die Tante

NB: Exceptions: *das Weib, das Fräulein, das Mädchen* (and other diminutives in *-chen* and *-lein*, see 1.1.7).

(b) Aeroplanes, motor-bikes and ships

die Boeing, die Cessna, die Tu-154
die BMW (see 1.1.1f), die Honda
die „Bismarck", die „Bremen"

NB: Some names retain the gender of the base word, e.g.: *der Airbus, der Storch; der „Albatros", das „Möwchen"*.

(c) Native German names of rivers

die Donau, die Elbe, die Ems, die Fulda, die Isar, die Lahn, die Maas, die Memel, die Mosel, die Neiße, die Oder, die Ruhr, die Saale, die Spree, die Weichsel, die Weser

NB: The most important exceptions are: *der Inn, der Lech, der Main, der Neckar, der Rhein.*

(d) Names of numerals

die Eins, die Vier, die Tausend, die Million, die Milliarde

NB: Note, as quantity expressions: *das Dutzend, das Hundert, das Tausend* (see 9.1.5b).

1.1.3 Nouns with these meanings are neuter:

(a) Young persons and animals
(see also 1.1.4)

das Baby, das Ferkel, das Fohlen, das Junge (but see 1.1.12), das Kalb, das Kind, das Lamm

(b) Metals and chemical elements

das Blei, das Eisen, das Gold, das Kobalt, das Kupfer, das Messing, das Uran, das Zinn

NB: Exceptions: *die Bronze, der Phosphor, der Schwefel, der Stahl* (and compounds such as *der Sauerstoff* 'oxygen', see 1.1.9).

(c) Scientific units

das Ampere, das Atom, das Elektron, das Molekül, das Pfund, das Volt, das Watt

NB: *Liter* and *Meter* may be masculine or neuter, see 1.1.11b.

(d) Letters of the alphabet and musical notes

das A, ein großes D, das Ypsilon
das hohe C, das Cis, das Ges

NB: In Swiss usage letters are masculine, e.g.: *der A.*

(e) Other parts of speech used as nouns
This includes verb infinitives, colours, languages and English *ing*-forms, e.g.:

das Ach, das Blau des Himmels, das vertraute Du, das Inkrafttreten, das Jenseits, das Kommen, sein ewiges Nein, das moderne Spanisch, das Doping, das Meeting

(f) Hotels, cafés, restaurants and cinemas

das Hilton, das „Kranzler", das „Roxy"

(g) Names of continents, countries, provinces and towns

For the use of the article with these neuter names, see 4.4.1c.

> das gärende Afrika, das viktorianische England, das alte Bayern,
> das zerstörte Frankfurt, das historische Neustadt (*despite*: die Stadt)

NB: Exceptions:
   (i)   Some names of countries and provinces are **feminine**; they are always used with the definite article, see
        4.4.1b. The commonest are: *die Arktis, die Antarktis; die Lausitz, die Pfalz, die Schweiz* and all ending in *-a, -e, -
        ei* and *-ie* (except *Afrika, China*), e.g.: *die Riviera, die Bretagne, die Türkei, die Normandie.*
  (ii) A few are **masculine**; they are also often used with the definite article, see 4.4.1a: *der Irak, der Iran, der Jemen,
        der Kongo, der Libanon, der Sudan.*

1.1.4 The gender of nouns for humans and animals: special cases

(a) Professions, occupations, nationality, etc.

(i) For many names denoting professions, occupations or nationality the basic designation is masculine, and a feminine may be formed from it with the suffix *-in* (see 22.2.1f):

> der Engländer – die Engländer**in**   der Lehrer – die Lehrer**in**
> der Koch – die Köch**in**   der Türke – die Türk**in**

or by replacing *-mann* with *-frau*, e.g.:

> der Kaufmann – die Kauf**frau**
> der Milchmann – die Milch**frau**
> der Amtmann – die Amt**frau** (the form *Amtmännin* is obsolete)

(ii) These forms are used where appropriate to refer to female persons:

> Sie gilt als die beste **Kundin**   *She is considered our best customer*
> von unserem Geschäft
> Heute Abend habe ich deine   *I saw your friend Anna this evening*
> **Freundin** Anna gesehen

On the other hand, the masculine form is often used in a general sense to refer to either sex, especially with titles and 'newer' professions (including those which were previously predominantly or exclusively male), or when the profession itself is emphasised, e.g.:

> Sie ist Ingenieur, Autoschlosser, Informatiker
> der damalige Minister für Volksbildung Margot Honecker
> Frau Professor Dr. Hartmann, Frau Bundestagspräsident Rita Süßmuth

NB: The feminine form is usual if *Frau* is omitted, e.g.: *Bundestagspräsidentin Rita Süßmuth.*

This usage is particularly common after the verb *sein*, and it was predominant in the former GDR.

(iii) Usage nowadays is in practice variable and uncertain. The use of undifferentiated masculine nouns to refer to women (or men and women) is often considered discriminatory, although it is quite common in practice, even with younger speakers. Indeed, some speakers (male and female) feel that terms like *Professorin* are derogatory because they suggest that the masculine term is more basic. In general:

> • The feminine form is used if it is considered relevant in context:

> Die neue **Lehrerin** scheint sehr beliebt zu sein
> (*Der neue Lehrer* would be odd if a woman is referred to)

- The feminine forms are usual to refer back to a woman (or women) already mentioned:

Meine beiden Schwestern sind Ärzt**innen** (NOT: Ärzte)
Hanne Frisch, die Ärzt**in** (NOT: der Arzt), die ihn behandelt hatte
Sie wurde die erste Professor**in** an einer deutschen Universität

In advertisements, both forms are now commonly given:

Wir suchen ab sofort eine(n) Musiklehrer(in)	*We have an immediate vacancy for a music teacher*
Wir brauchen eine/n Mitarbeiter/in für Gemeinde- und Jugendarbeit	*We have a vacancy for a social and youth worker*

When no feminine form is available, the masculine is used despite the anomaly:

der Säugling hieß Anna
der Teenager war schwanger
unser werter Gast, Frau Dr. Schilling

In written German, the feminine form is sometimes used to refer to feminine nouns denoting things:

Die Sowjetunion ist die größte Produzent**in** von Personenwagen im Ostblock (*NZZ*)	*The Soviet Union is the largest producer of private cars in the eastern block*

In such contexts the masculine form (e.g. *der größte Produzent*) would be equally acceptable.

(iv) In the plural, to refer to both men and women, various possibilities are current.

It is not uncommon for the masculine form to be used:

Der Bürgermeister begrüßte **die Besucher** aus der Hauptstadt Wien

However, this may be considered discriminatory, especially where the feminine form is in common usage. Both forms may then be given:

liebe Zuschauer und Zuschauerinnen; die Studenten und Studentinnen

A recent option is the use of the feminine form with a capital *I* (sometimes spoken as long [iː]) to indicate both sexes:

die **StudentInnen** der Westfälischen Wilhelmsuniversität Münster

(b) Animals

The names of species of animals can be masculine, feminine or neuter, e.g.:

der Fisch, **die** Ratte, **das** Pferd, etc.

Many familiar or domesticated animals have different masculine and feminine forms:

der Fuchs – **die** Füchsin
der Gänserich – **die** Gans
der Hahn – **die** Henne
der Kater – **die** Katze

NB: **die** Drohne *drone,* **der** Weisel *queen bee.*

Usually, one of these designates the species (e.g. *der Fuchs, die Gans, die Katze*) and the other is only used if the sex is known or relevant in context. In the absence of a specific term, male or female animals and birds can be indicated by *das Männchen* or *das Weibchen*, e.g.:

das Zebra**männchen**; das Frosch**weibchen**

(c) Anomalous genders of names of human beings

die Geisel	*hostage*
das Genie	*genius*
das Haupt	*head* (of state, family)
das Individuum	*individual*
das Mannequin	*mannequin*
das Mitglied	*member*
das Mündel	*ward*
(in legal language masculine)	
die Person	*person*
die Wache	*sentry*
die Waise	*orphan*
das Weib	*woman, wife* (pej. or arch.)

In addition, all nouns in *-chen* and *-lein* are neuter, irrespective of sex, e.g.: *das Bübchen, das Fräulein,* etc. (see 1.1.7).

NB: *zum Waisen machen* 'to orphan'.

Problems of agreement if grammatical and natural gender are in conflict are dealt with in 1.1.13.

B: Gender and form

Sections 1.1.5–1.1.8 give detail on where the form, in particular the ending of nouns, indicates gender. The most frequent cases are summarised in Table 1.2.

1.1.5 The form of some nouns shows that they are masculine

(a) Nouns with the following endings are masculine:

-ant	der Konsonant	**-ig**	der Essig	**-or**	der Motor
-ast	der Kontrast	**-ismus**	der Idealismus	**-us**	der Rhythmus
-ich	der Teppich	**-ling**	der Feigling		

NB: Common exceptions: *das Labor, das Genus* 'gender', *das Tempus* 'tense'.

(b) Nouns formed from strong verbs without a suffix are masculine

der Betrieb, der Biss, der Fall, der Gang, der Sprung, der Wurf

NB: Common exceptions: *das Band, das Grab, das Leid* 'harm, sorrow', *das Maß* 'measurement', *das Schloss, das Verbot.*

TABLE 1.2 *Gender and endings*

Masculine endings			
-ant	der Konsonant	-ismus	der Sozialismus
-ast	der Kontrast	-ling	der Liebling
-ich	der Teppich	-or	der Motor
-ig	der Honig	-us	der Rhythmus
Feminine endings			
-a	die Pizza	-in	die Freundin
-anz/-enz	die Eleganz	-schaft	die Herrschaft
-ei	die Bücherei	-sion/-tion	die Explosion
-heit/-keit	die Krankheit	-tät	die Universität
-ie	die Biologie	-ung	die Bedeutung
-ik	die Panik	-ur	die Natur
Neuter endings			
-chen	das Mädchen	-tel	das Viertel
-lein	das Büchlein	-tum	das Eigentum
-ma	das Drama	-um	das Album

1.1.6 The form of some nouns shows that they are feminine

(a) Nouns with the following endings are feminine

-a	die Villa	**-ik**	die Panik	**-tion**	die Revolution
-anz	die Eleganz	**-in**	die Freundin	**-tät**	die Universität
-ei	die Bücherei	**-keit**	die Heiterkeit	**-ung**	die Bedeutung
-enz	die Existenz	**-schaft**	die Botschaft	**-ur**	die Natur
-heit	die Gesundheit	**-sion**	die Explosion		
-ie	die Biologie	**-sis**	die Basis		

NB: Common exceptions are words in *-ma* (see 1.1.7), chemical terms in *-in* (see 1.1.7) and the following: *das Sofa, das Genie, der Atlantik, der Katholik, das Mosaik, der Pazifik, das Abitur, das Futur, das Purpur.*

(b) Most nouns ending in *-t* from verbs are feminine

die Ankunft, die Fahrt, die Flucht, die Macht, die Schlacht, die Sicht

NB: Some common exceptions are: *der Dienst, der Durst, der Frost, das Gift, der Verdienst, der Verlust.*

1.1.7 Nouns with the following endings are neuter

-chen	das Mädchen	**-lein**	das Büchlein	**-tel**	das Viertel
-icht	das Dickicht	**-ma**	das Schema	**-tum**	das Eigentum
-il	das Ventil	**-ment**	das Appartement	**-um**	das Album
-it	das Dynamit				

Chemical terms in *-in* are also neuter: *das Benzin, das Protein*

NB: Common exceptions: *der Profit, der Granit, die Firma, der Zement, der Irrtum, der Reichtum, der Konsum.*

1.1.8 Some other noun endings or prefixes give a clue to gender

The endings *-el, -er* and **-en**; *-e*; *-nis* and *-sal*; and the prefix *Ge-* tend to be associated with particular genders and it is helpful to be aware of this. However, this is a matter of tendency rather than firm rule.

(a) Nouns in *-el*, *-er* and *-en* are predominantly (60%) masculine

der Flügel, der Schatten, der Fehler

All nouns in *-er* from verbs are masculine: *der Bäcker, der Bettler, der Lehrer*

The rest fall into three groups:

(i) All nouns from verb infinitives in *-en* are neuter (see 1.1.3e): *das Essen, das Kaffeetrinken*

(ii) About 25% of those in *-el* and *-er* (but none in *-en*) are feminine: *die Butter, die Regel, die Wurzel*

(iii) Remaining nouns in *-el*, *-en* and *-er* (some 15%) are neuter: *das Fieber, das Segel, das Zeichen*

(b) Nouns in *-e* are mainly (90%) feminine

die Biene, die Blume, die Bühne, die Garage, die Liebe, die Sahne

There are five major groups of exceptions:

(i) Names of male persons and animals (see 1.3.2): *der Affe, der Bote, der Junge, der Löwe*

(ii) Eight irregular masculines (see 1.3.3): *der Buchstabe, der Friede, der Funke, der Gedanke, der Glaube, der Name, der Same, der Wille*

(iii) Two other masculine nouns: *der Charme, der Käse*

(iv) Most nouns with the prefix *Ge-* are neuter (see 1.1.8c): *das Gebirge, das Gefälle, das Gemüse*

(v) A few other neuter nouns: *das Auge, das Ende, das Erbe* 'inheritance' (see 1.1.12), *das Finale, das Image, das Interesse, das Prestige, das Regime, das Repertoire*

(c) Most nouns with the prefix *Ge-* [gə] are neuter

das Geäst, das Gebäude, das Gebot, das Gelübde, das Gesetz, das Gespräch

The exceptions fall into three groups:

(i) Names of male or female humans:

der Gehilfe/die Gehilfin	*assistant*
der Gemahl/die Gemahlin (elev.)	*spouse*
der Genosse/die Genossin	*comrade*
der Gevatter (arch.)	*godfather*

(ii) Eleven other masculines:

der Gebrauch	*use*	der Gehorsam	*obedience*	der Geschmack	*taste*
der Gedanke	*thought*	der Genuss	*enjoyment*	der Gestank	*stink*
der Gefallen	*favour*	der Geruch	*smell*	der Gewinn	*profit*
der Gehalt	*content*	der Gesang	*singing*		

NB: *Gefallen* and *Gehalt* are neuter in other meanings, see 1.1.12.

(iii) Eleven other feminines:

die Gebärde	*gesture*	die Gefahr	*danger*	die Gestalt	*figure*
die Gebühr	*fee*	die Gemeinde	*community*	die Gewähr	*guarantee*
die Geburt	*birth*	die Geschichte	*history; story*	die Gewalt	*force, violence*
die Geduld	*patience*	die Geschwulst	*tumour*		

(d) Nouns with the suffixes -*nis* and -*sal* are mainly (about 70%) neuter

das Bedürfnis, das Ereignis, das Erlebnis, das Scheusal, das Schicksal

About 30% are feminine, including:

(i) all those in -*nis* from adjectives: *die Bitternis, die Finsternis*

(ii) all those in -*nis* from verbs denoting a state of mind: *die Besorgnis, die Betrübnis*

(iii) a few other common feminines: *die Erkenntnis, die Erlaubnis, die Kenntnis, die Mühsal*

(e) Nouns with certain endings are most often neuter if they refer to things
These endings are mainly of foreign origin:

-al	das Lineal	**-at**	das Sekretariat	**-iv**	das Adjektiv
-an	das Organ	**-ent**	das Talent	**-o**	das Büro
-ar	das Formular	**-ett**	das Etikett	**on**	das Mikrophon
-är	das Militär	**-ier**	das Papier		

Nouns with these endings referring to persons are masculine, see 1.1.1.

NB: The most common exceptions are: *der Kanal, die Moral, der Skandal, der Altar, der Kommentar, der Apparat, der Automat, der Salat, der Senat, die Manier, der Kanton, die Person.*

1.1.9 The gender of compound words and abbreviations

(a) Compound nouns usually have the gender of the last component

der Fahr**plan**, **die** Bushalte**stelle**, **das** Hallen**bad**

There are a few exceptions to this rule:

(i) Some compounds of *der Mut* are feminine: *die Anmut, die Armut, die Demut, die Großmut, die Langmut, die Sanftmut, die Schwermut, die Wehmut*

(ii) For the compounds of *der/das Teil*, see 1.1.11c.

(iii) Others:

das Gift	BUT die Mitgift *dowry*
der Grat	BUT das Rückgrat
die Scheu	BUT der Abscheu (cf. 1.1.11)
das Wort	BUT die Antwort
die Woche	BUT der Mittwoch

(b) The gender of abbreviations is determined by the base word

der HSV (der Hamburger Sportverein)
die CDU (die Christlich-Demokratische Union)
das BAFöG (das Bundesausbildungsförderungsgesetz)

(c) Shortened words have the gender of the full form

> der Akku (Akkumulator)
> der Krimi (Kriminalroman)
> das Labor (Laboratorium)
> die Lok (Lokomotive)
> die Uni (Universität)

NB: *das Foto* (despite: *die Fotografie*). In Switzerland, though, *die Foto* is usual.

1.1.10 The gender of English loan-words

Large-scale borrowing of words from English is a feature of modern German. These need to be given a gender, and this is determined by the following principles (which sometimes conflict):

(a) Many English words adopt the gender of the nearest German equivalent

> der Airbag (der Sack) die Band (die Kapelle)
> der Airport (der Flughafen) die Box (die Büchse)
> der Bob (der Schlitten) die E-Mail (die Post)
> der Lift (der Aufzug) das Baby (das Kind)
> der Shop (der Laden) das Bike (das Fahrrad)
> der Smog (der Nebel) das Handy (das Telefon)

NB: This principle can result in a word having two genders in different meanings, e.g.: *der Service* 'service' (by analogy with *der Dienst*); *das Service* '(dinner/tea) service' (by analogy with *das Geschirr*).

(b) The ending or the form of some English words can determine the gender
(i) Words with endings similar to German endings adopt the gender associated with that ending:

> der Broiler, der Container, der Computer, der Dimmer (-*er* is a masculine ending)
> der Agitator, der Konduktor, der Rotor (-*or* is a masculine ending)
> die Animation, die Supervision (-*sion* and -*tion* are feminine endings)
> die City, die Lobby, die Publicity, die Party, die Story (-*ie* is a feminine ending)
> das Klosett, das Pamphlet, das Ticket (-*ett* is a neuter ending)
> das Advertisement, das Realignment, das Treatment (-*ment* is a neuter ending)

(ii) Monosyllabic nouns from verbs are often masculine (cf. 1.1.5b):

> der Hit, der Look, der Raid, der Rock, der Streik, der Strip, der Talk

(iii) Nouns from phrasal verbs or English *ing*-forms are usually neuter, see 1.1.3e:

> das Blow-up, das Check-up, das Handout, das Teach-in
> das Dumping, das Floating, das Meeting, das Merchandising

NB: There are some exceptions: *der Fallout, die Holding* (company).

(c) If there is no other indication, monosyllabic nouns are most often masculine

> der Chip, der Choke, der Lunch, der Sex, der Spot, der Trend

However, feminines and neuters are not uncommon:

> die Bar, die Couch, die Farm, das Match, das Steak, das Team

(d) No gender has yet become firmly established in a good number of cases

Common examples are:

der/das Blackout	der/das Deal	der/das Ketchup	der/das Plaid
der/das Break	der/die Forehand	der/das Looping	der/das Radar
der/das Cartoon	der/das Go-slow	der/die Parka	die/das Soda
der/das (coll. also: die) Jogurt			

1.1.11 Nouns with varying gender

The gender of a few nouns is not fixed, although the variation is often linked to regional or register differences.

(a) Some common examples

Abscheu *abhorrence*	**der** (occ. **die**)	Mündel *ward*	**das** (legal **der**)
Aperitif *aperitif*	**der** (Sw. **das**)	Puff *brothel*	**der** (Au. **das**)
Backbord *port side*	**das** (Au. **der**)	(vulg.)	
Barock *Baroque*	**der** or **das**	Pyjama *pyjamas*	**der** (Au./Sw. **das**)
Dotter *yolk*	**der** or **das**	Radio *radio*	**das** (S.G. **der**)
Dschungel *jungle*	**der** (occ. **das**,	Sakko *jacket*	**der** (Au. **das**)
	obs. **die**)	Sims	**der** or **das**
Fakt *fact*	**der** or **das**	*(window-)sill,*	
Filter *filter*	**der** (techn. **das**)	*mantelpiece*	
Foto *photo*	**das** (Sw. **die**)	Soda *soda*	**die** or **das**
Gelee *jelly*	**das** or **der**	Spargel	**der** (Sw. **die**)
Gischt *spray*	**der** or **die**	*asparagus*	
Katapult *catapult*	**das** or **der**	Steuerbord	**das** (Au. **der**)
Kehricht *sweepings*	**der** or **das**	*starboard*	
Keks *biscuit*	**der** (Au. **das**)	Taxi *taxi*	**das** (Sw. **der**)
Knäuel *ball (wool)*	**der** or **das**	(NB: also	**die** *Taxe*)
Kompromiss	**der** (Au. **das**)	common:	
compromise		Virus *virus*	**der** (medic. **das**)
Match *match*	**das** (Au./Sw. **der**)	Zubehör	**das** or **der**
Meteor *meteor*	**der** (astronom. **das**)	*accessories*	

(b) *Liter* and *Meter*

Both these words (and their compounds, e.g. *Zentimeter*) are officially neuter, i.e. *das Liter*, *das Meter*. However, they are regularly masculine in colloquial speech, and not infrequently in print, i.e. *der Liter*, *der Meter*. Written Swiss usage **always** prefers the masculine.

(c) *Teil*

Teil is most often masculine, *der Teil*, in all meanings:

dieser Teil von Deutschland; er behielt den größten Teil für sich

However, it may be neuter in a few set phrases:

ich für mein (*or* meinen) Teil; das bessere (*or* den besseren) Teil wählen;
sie trug ihr (*or* ihren) Teil dazu bei; er hat sein (*or* seinen) Teil getan

The neuter *das Teil* is also usual in technical language, to refer to a detached part:

jedes einzelne Teil, ein defektes Teil

Compounds of *Teil* are mostly masculine, with the following exceptions:

das Abteil *compartment*   das Gegenteil *opposite*
das (*legal* der) Erbteil *inheritance*   das/der Oberteil *upper part*
das Einzelteil *separate part*   das Urteil *verdict*
das Ersatzteil *replacement part*

1.1.12 Double genders with different meanings

A number of words have two meanings differentiated by gender:

der Band (ˉe) *volume, book*   das Band (ˉer) *ribbon, tape*
                                   das Band (-e) *bond, fetter* (see 1.2.8)
   NB: also: *die Band (-s)* (pron. [bɛnt]) *band, (pop) group.*
der Bulle (-n, -n) *bull; cop* (coll.)   die Bulle (-n) (*papal*) *bull*
der Bund (ˉe) *union; waistband*   das Bund (-e) *bundle, bunch*
der Ekel (no pl.) *disgust*   das Ekel (-) (coll.) *nasty person*
der Erbe (-n, -n) *heir*   das Erbe (no pl.) *inheritance, heritage*
der Flur (-e) *entrance hall* (N.G.)   die Flur (-en) *meadow* (elev.)
der Gefallen (-) *favour*   das Gefallen (no pl.) *pleasure*
der Gehalt (-e) *content*   das Gehalt (ˉer) *salary*
   NB: Au. *der Gehalt* also = 'salary'.
der Golf (-e) *gulf*   das Golf (no pl.) *golf*
der Gummi (-s) *eraser*   das Gummi (no pl.) *rubber (as material)*
der Harz *Harz (mountains)*   das Harz (no pl.) *resin*
der Heide (-n) *heathen*   die Heide (-n) *heath*
der Hut (ˉe) *hat*   die Hut (no pl.) *guard*
                (e.g.: *auf der Hut sein* 'to be on one's guard')
der Junge (-n, -n) *boy*   das Junge (adj.) *young (of animals)*
der Kiefer (-) *jaw*   die Kiefer (-n) *pine*
der Kunde (-n, -n) *customer*   die Kunde (no pl.) *knowledge, news* (elev.)
der Lama (-s) *lama*   das Lama (-s) *llama*
der Laster (-) *lorry* (coll.)   das Laster (-) *vice*
der Leiter (-) *leader*   die Leiter (-n) *ladder*
der Mangel (ˉ) *lack*   die Mangel (-n) *mangle*
die Mark ( ) *mark (coin)*   das Mark (no pl.) *marrow (bone)*
die Marsch (-en) *fen* (N.G.)   der Marsch (ˉe) *march*
der Mensch (-en, -en) *human being*   das Mensch (-er) *slut* (coll., pej.)
der Messer (-) *surveyor; gauge*   das Messer (-) *knife*
der Militär (-s) *military man*   das Militär (no pl.) *the military*
der Moment (-e) *moment*   das Moment (-e) *(determining) factor*
der Otter (-) *otter*   die Otter (-n) *adder*
  (also: *der Fischotter*)   (also: *die Kreuzotter*)
der Pack (-e or ˉe) *package*   das Pack (no pl.) *mob, rabble*
der Pony (no pl.) *fringe (of hair)*   das Pony (-s) *pony*
der Schild (-e) *shield*   das Schild (-er) *sign, plate*
der See (-n) *lake*   die See (no pl.) *sea*
die Steuer (-n) *tax*   das Steuer (-) *steering-wheel, helm*
der Stift (-e) *pen, stripling* (coll.)   das Stift (-e) *foundation, home (e.g. for aged)*
der Tau (no pl.) *dew*   das Tau (-e) *rope, hawser*
der Tor (-en, -en) *fool* (lit.)   das Tor (-e) *gate*
der Verdienst (no pl.) *earnings*   das Verdienst (-e) *merit, achievement*
die Wehr (no pl.) *defence*   das Wehr (-e) *weir*

1.1.13 Problems of gender agreement

Difficulty with gender agreement arises most often when grammatical gender and natural gender do not correspond, as in the nouns treated in 1.1.4.

(a) In formal written German, pronouns normally agree with the grammatical gender of the noun, irrespective of natural gender

Wir suchen eine männliche Fachkraft. **Sie** muss im Besitz eines Führerscheins sein	*We are looking for a skilled male worker. He must have a clean driving licence*
ein**es** der Mitglieder dieses Vereins	*one of the members of this club*
Ich kann mich jedoch an keine Person erinnern, **die** in dem so benannten Vorort wohnte (*Grass*)	*However, I cannot remember any person who lived in the suburb of that name*
Es war einmal ein Mädchen aus Alaska, **das** war Sängerin in einem Club in San Diego. Vor drei Jahren, mit 19, nahm **es seine** erste CD auf (*Kurier*)	*There was once a girl from Alaska, she was a singer in a club in San Diego. Three years ago, at the age of 19, she recorded her first CD*

This rule is rarely adhered to consistently. In practice, the relative pronoun almost always agrees for grammatical gender, but personal pronouns usually have the form appropriate to the natural gender of the person referred to (i.e. *sie* or *er*), especially in spoken German:

Das Mädchen da drüben? **Sie** hat doch rotes Haar!	*That girl over there? But she's got red hair!*

Even in writing natural gender tends to predominate if the pronoun is some distance from the noun it refers to, especially if it is in a different clause or sentence:

Das junge Mädchen ist gestern Abend angekommen. **Sie** ist sehr liebenswürdig	*The young girl arrived last night. She's very kind*
Sie stürzten sich auf das Mädchen, **das** in der Ecke stand, und drohten **ihr** mit Erschießen (*Quick*)	*They rushed upon the girl standing in the corner and threatened to shoot her*

Fräulein is treated in this way, i.e. as a neuter noun, when it is used on its own, e.g. *das Fräulein, **das** ihn bediente*. But when followed by a name, feminine pronouns are used: *Fräulein Müller, **die** mich gestern bediente*.

(b) Neuter singular pronouns are used to refer to male and female persons

Sie stehen eine Weile schweigend, **jedes** die Hand auf der Schulter des anderen (*Fallada*)	*They stand silent for a while, each with their hand on the other's shoulder*

(c) Adjectives and determiners always agree for grammatical gender

> **ein** jung**es** Mädchen, **das** unartige Bübchen, ein**e** männliche Person

This also applies with *Fräulein* followed by a name, for instance at the start of a letter: *Liebes Fräulein Müller* (although, in practice, very few people use the address *Fräulein* nowadays).

(d) Personal names in *-chen* and *-lein* are treated as neuter

> Unser klein**es** Fritzchen spielt mit seiner Modelleisenbahn
> **Das** Mariechen konnte gestern nicht schlafen. **Es** dachte an **seine** kranke Mutter

In speech the pronouns appropriate to natural gender are often used.

NB: In colloquial south German speech neuter pronouns were often used to refer to a younger girl, whatever her name, and this usage may still be encountered in rural areas. It is considered to be a mark of affection.

1.2 Noun plurals

In English, most nouns simply add *-s* to form their plural. There is no similar general rule in German, and foreign learners should learn the plural of each noun with the noun. This section gives details on all aspects of plural formation and use in German, as follows:

- The formation of noun plurals (section 1.2.1)
- The regular plural of masculine, feminine and neuter nouns (sections 1.2.2–1.2.4)
- Plurals with the ending *-s* (section 1.2.5)
- Unusual plural forms (sections 1.2.6–1.2.7)
- Words with two plurals with different meanings (section 1.2.8)
- Differences between English and German in the use of the plural (sections 1.2.9–1.2.13)
- The use of the plural with nouns of weight, measurement and value (section 1.2.14)

1.2.1 Seven regular ways of forming noun plurals in German

These are shown in Table 1.3.

TABLE 1.3 *How nouns form their plural in German*

Formation of plural	Singular	Plural
no ending (-)	der Lehrer das Segel	die Lehrer die Segel
no ending, with Umlaut (¨)	der Vogel der Bruder	die Vögel die Brüder
add -e (-e)	der Arm das Jahr	die Arme die Jahre
add -e, with Umlaut (¨e)	der Stuhl die Hand	die Stühle die Hände
add -er, with Umlaut if possible (-er)/(¨er)	das Tal das Kind	die Täler die Kinder
add -n or -en (-n)/(-en)	die Frau die Wiese	die Frauen die Wiesen
add -s (-s)	der Streik das Auto	die Streiks die Autos

In practice, the gender of a noun gives clues as to how it forms its plural, as shown in Table 1.4.

TABLE 1.4 *Plurals and gender*

Plural formation	Masculine	Feminine	Neuter
no ending (-)	Those ending in *-el, -en, -er*	**none**	Those ending in *-el, -en, -er, -chen, -lein* Those in *Ge...e*
no ending, with Umlaut (¨)	About **20** ending in *-el, -en, -er*	**two**: *Mutter, Tochter*	**one**: *Kloster*
add –e (-e)	**most**	Those in *–nis* *Kenntnis –nisse*	**most**
add -e, with Umlaut (¨e)	Many **monosyllables** that can have *Umlaut*	about **30**	**one**: *Floß*
add -er, with Umlaut if poss. (-er)/(¨er)	About **12**	**none**	Many **monosyllables**
add -n or –en (-n)/(-en)	All in *-e*, and a few others, mainly	**most**	About **12**

1.2.2 The plural of masculine nouns

(a) Most masculine nouns have a plural in (-e) or (¨e)

<table>
<tr><td>der Arm – die Arme</td><td>der Bart – die Bärte</td></tr>
<tr><td>der Hund – die Hunde</td><td>der Bock – die Böcke</td></tr>
<tr><td>der Punkt – die Punkte</td><td>der Fuß – die Füße</td></tr>
<tr><td>der Versuch – die Versuche</td><td>der Stuhl – die Stühle</td></tr>
</table>

Umlaut is found with nearly half the nouns where it would be possible. The following list gives some common masculine nouns which have a plural in (-e) without *Umlaut* even though the vowel could have *Umlaut*:

der Aal	*eel*	der Huf	*hoof*	der Schuh	*shoe*
der Arm	*arm*	der Hund	*dog*	der Star	*starling*
der Beruf	*profession*	der Laut	*sound*	der Stoff	*material*
der Besuch	*visit*	der Monat	*month*	der Tag	*day*
der Dolch	*dagger*	der Mond	*moon*	der Takt	*beat (music)*
der Dom	*cathedral*	der Ort	*place*	der Thron	*throne*
der Druck	*pressure*	der Pfad	*path*	der Verlag	*publishing house*
der Erfolg	*success*	der Punkt	*point*	der Verlust	*loss*
der Grad	*degree*	der Ruf	*call*	der Versuch	*attempt*
der Gurt	*belt*	der Schluck	*gulp*		

Nouns ending in stressed *-al, -an, -ar, -on* and *-or* also usually have the plural ending (-e), without *Umlaut*:

der Bibliothekar – die Bibiothekare
der Major – die Majore

However, the following do have *Umlaut* in the plural:

der Altar – die Altäre	*altar*	der Kardinal – die Kardinäle	*cardinal*
der Kanal – die Kanäle	*canal*	der Tenor – die Tenöre	*tenor*

NB: (i)   *der General, der Korporal* and *der Kran* have either (¨e) or (-e).
    (ii)   *der Erlass* has (-e) in Germany, but (¨e) in Austria and Switzerland.
    (iii)   *der Rest* usually has the pl. (-e), but (-er) is frequent in coll. and commercialese, and (-en) in Swiss usage.
    (iv)   *der Pastor* (usual pl. (-en)) may have (¨e) in north German usage.
    (v)   The plural of *der Saal* is *die Säle*, see 23.4.2.

(b) Most masculine nouns ending in *-el*, *-en* or *-er* form their plural without an ending or *Umlaut*

der Onkel – die Onkel	der Bäcker – die Bäcker
der Haken – die Haken	der Computer – die Computer

NB: Exceptions are the words dealt with in section 1.2.2c and the following:

der Bauer (-n, -n) *farmer, peasant*	der Pantoffel (-n) *slipper*
der Bayer (-n, -n) *Bavarian*	der Stachel (-n) *thorn; sting*
der Charakter (-e) *character*	der Vetter (-n) *cousin*
der Muskel (-n) *muscle*	

(c) About twenty masculine nouns ending in *-el*, *-en* or *-er* form their plural solely by umlauting the stressed vowel

der Apfel – die Äpfel	der Bogen – die Bögen

These are:

der Acker	*field*		der Magen	*stomach*
der Apfel	*apple*		der Mangel	*lack*
der Boden	*floor*		der Mantel	*coat*
der Bogen	*arch*		der Nagel	*nail*
der Bruder	*brother*		der Ofen	*stove*
der Faden	*thread*		der Sattel	*saddle*
der Garten	*garden*		der Schaden	*damage*
der Graben	*ditch*		der Schnabel	*beak*
der Hafen	*harbour*		der Schwager	*brother-in-law*
der Hammer	*hammer*		der Vater	*father*
der Kasten	*box*		der Vogel	*bird*
der Laden	*shop; shutter*			

NB: (i)   *der Bogen* and *der Kasten* may have the plural (-) in north German. The compound *der Ell(en)bogen* always has (¨).
    (ii)   *der Laden* sometimes has the plural (-) in north German usage in the meaning 'shutter'.
    (iii)   In spoken south German *der Kragen* and *der Wagen* may have the plural (¨). This usage appears to be spreading to the north, but it is considered incorrect in written German.

(d) About a dozen masculines have a plural in (¨er)/(-er)

The vowel takes *Umlaut* if possible. These are:

der Bösewicht	*villain* (arch.)		der Rand	*edge*
der Geist	*spirit*		der Reichtum	*wealth*
der Gott	*god*		der Ski	*ski*
der Irrtum	*error*		der Strauch	*shrub*
der Leib	*body*		der Wald	*forest*
der Mann	*man*		der Wiking	*viking*
der Mund	*mouth*		der Wurm	*worm*

NB: (i)   For the plural of compounds in *-mann*, see 1.2.7.
    (ii)   *Der Bösewicht* has an equally used alternative plural in (-e).

(e) A number of masculine nouns have the plural (-en)/(-n)

These fall into three groups, depending on the declension of the singular:

(i) The so-called 'weak' masculines which have *-(e)n* in the accusative, genitive and dative singular as well as in the plural. Full details about these are given in **1.3.2**.

der Affe – die Affen   der Mensch – die Menschen

der Bär – die Bären   der Student – die Studenten

(ii) Some irregular masculines, see **1.3.3**. The following occur in the plural:

der Buchstabe	*letter* (of alphabet)	der Gedanke	*thought*
der Friede	*peace*	der Name	*name*
der Funke	*spark*	der Same	*seed*

(iii) A few other masculines with a regular singular:

der Dorn	*thorn*	der Schmerz	*pain*
der Fasan	*pheasant*	der See	*lake*
der Fleck	*spot*	der Staat	*state*
der Lorbeer	*laurel*	der Stachel	*prickle*
der Mast	*mast*	der Strahl	*ray*
der Muskel	*muscle*	der Typ	*bloke, guy*
der Nerv	*nerve*	der Untertan	*subject*
der Pantoffel	*slipper*	der Vetter	*cousin*
der Pfau	*peacock*	der Zeh	*toe*

Words in unstressed *-on* and *-or* also belong to this group, but shift the stress in the plural:

der `Dämon – die Dä`monen   der Pro`fessor – die Profes`soren

NB: (i)   *der Bau* 'building' and *der Sporn* 'spur' have the irregular plurals *die Bauten* and *die Sporen*.
      (ii)   *die Seen* is pronounced *See-en* [zeːən], see 23.4.1.
      (iii) *der Fleck* has an alternative singular form *der Flecken*.
      (iv) *der Zeh* has the alternative (mainly north German) singular *die Zehe*.
      (v)   *der Typ* may have the 'weak' singular declension in colloquial speech, see 1.3.2c.

1.2.3 The plural of feminine nouns

(a) Over 90% of all feminine nouns have the plural (-en)/(-n)

The ending *-n* is used with nouns ending in *-e*, *-el* or *-er*.

die Arbeit – die Arbeiten   die Regel – die Regeln

die Last – die Lasten   die Wiese – die Wiesen

Nouns in *-in* double the consonant in the plural:

die Studentin – die Studentinnen

NB: *die Werkstatt* has an irregular plural with *Umlaut* **and** the suffix *-en*: *die Werkstätten*.

(b) About a quarter of feminine monosyllables have a plural in (¨e)

die Hand – die Hände   die Nuss – die Nüsse

The following are the most common. Note that over half end in -*t*:

die Angst	*fear*	die Haut	*skin*	die Nacht	*night*
die Axt	*axe*	die Kraft	*strength*	die Naht	*seam*
die Bank	*bench*	die Kuh	*cow*	die Not	*need, distress*
die Braut	*fiancée*	die Kunst	*art*	die Nuss	*nut*
die Brust	*breast*	die Laus	*louse*	die Sau	*sow*
die Faust	*fist*	die Luft	*air; breeze*	die Schnur	*string*
die Frucht	*fruit*	die Lust	*desire*	die Stadt	*town, city*
die Gans	*goose*	die Macht	*power*	die Wand	*wall*
die Gruft	*vault, tomb*	die Magd	*maid*	die Wurst	*sausage*
die Hand	*hand*	die Maus	*mouse*	die Zunft	*guild*

Compounds of -*brunst*, -*flucht* and -*kunft* also have a plural in (¨e):

die Feuersbrunst – die Feuersbrünste   die Auskunft – die Auskünfte
die Ausflucht – die Ausflüchte

NB: *die Sau* and *die Schnur* can have the plural ending (-en) in technical usage.

(c) Feminine nouns in -*nis* and -*sal* have the plural (-e)

In practice few of these nouns have a plural. Those in -*nis* double the consonant in the plural:

die Kenntnis – die Kenntnisse   die Mühsal – die Mühsale

(d) Two feminine nouns have the plural (¨)

die Mutter – die Mütter (see 1.2.8); die Tochter – die Töchter

(e) No feminine nouns have plurals in (-) or (¨er).

1.2.4 The plural of neuter nouns

(a) Roughly three quarters of neuter nouns have the plural (-e)

das Bein – die Beine   das Schaf – die Schafe
das Gefäß – die Gefäße   das Ventil – die Ventile
das Jahr – die Jahre   das Verbot – die Verbote

This group includes most neuters of more than one syllable, especially foreign words, with the exceptions listed under other groups.

NB: Nouns ending in -*nis* double the consonant in the plural: *das Zeugnis – die Zeugnisse*
das Knie has the plural *die Knie*, pronounced *Knie-e* [kniːə], see 23.4.1.

(b) About a quarter of neuter nouns have the plural (¨er)/(-er).

Umlaut is used if possible. The majority are monosyllabic, e.g.:

das Blatt – die Blätter   das Kind – die Kinder
das Dorf – die Dörfer   das Tal – die Täler

A few polysyllabic neuters also have this ending. The following are common:

das Gehalt *salary*   das Gesicht *face*
das Gemach *chamber* (elev.)   das Gespenst *ghost*
das Gemüt *mood*   das Regiment *regiment*
das Geschlecht *sex*   das Spital *hospice*

In addition, all nouns in -*tum* take this plural:

>   das Altertum – die Altertümer

NB: (i)   *das Ross* 'steed' (usual pl. *die Rosse*) commonly has the plural (¨er), i.e. *die Rösser*, in Austria and Bavaria,
        where it is the everyday word for 'horse'.

    (ii)   A number of words are used colloquially with an (-er/¨er) plural in a derogatory or facetious sense, e.g.:
        die Dinger, die Scheusäler.

(c) Neuter nouns ending in -*el*, -*en*, -*er*, diminutives in -*chen* and -*lein* and words in *Ge...e* have the plural (-)

das Segel – die Segel	das Mädchen – die Mädchen
das Kissen – die Kissen	das Büchlein – die Büchlein
das Messer – die Messer	das Gebäude – die Gebäude

NB: The only exceptions are the two nouns dealt with in 1.2.4d.

(d) Two neuter nouns have plurals in (¨)

>   das Kloster – die Klöster; das Wasser – die Wässer

das Wasser has the alternative plural *die Wasser* (though neither plural form is common in practice). Its compounds, e.g. *das Abwasser* 'effluent', always have the plural with *Umlaut*, e.g. *die Abwässer*.

(e) A few neuter nouns have the plural (-en)/(-n)

>   das Auge – die Augen   das Hemd – die Hemden

The following are the most frequent:

das Auge	*eye*	das Hemd	*shirt*	das Juwel	*jewel*
das Bett	*bed*	das Herz	*heart*	das Ohr	*ear*
das Ende	*end*	das Insekt	*insect*	das Statut	*statute*
das Fakt	*fact*	das Interesse	*interest*	das Verb	*verb*

Scientific terms in -*on* also belong to this group, with a shift of stress in the plural: *das E`lektron – die Elek`tronen*.

NB: (i)   *das Herz* has an irregular singular, i.e.: *das Herz, des Herzens, dem Herzen* (see 1.3.4).
    (ii)   *das Kleinod* 'jewel' has the unusual plural *die Kleinodien*.

(f) One neuter noun has the plural (¨e)

>   das Floß *raft* – die Flöße

1.2.5 The plural ending (-s)

The plural ending -*s* occurs with nouns of all three genders, but it is restricted to a few special cases.

(a) (-s) is used with many recent loan-words from English or French

das Atelier – die Ateliers	der Scheck – die Schecks
der Chef – die Chefs	das Sit-in – die Sit-ins
das Detail – die Details	der Streik – die Streiks
das Hotel – die Hotels	das Team – die Teams
das Labor – die Labors	der Tunnel – die Tunnels
der Park – die Parks	der Waggon – die Waggons

This ending has sometimes been frowned on as 'un-German', and attempts have been made to foster the use of 'native' German plurals with foreign words, recommending forms like *die Parke, die Streike*, which many dictionaries and German grammar books still list. However, few such forms are widely used in practice. Only with English words in *-er* (e.g.: *der Computer – die Computer*), which tend to have the regular endingless plural, is a plural formation other than *-s* common with loan-words from English.

English loan-words in *-y* have a plural in *-ys*, e.g.: *die Babys, die Rowdys,* and this has been prescribed for all such words by the spelling reform, even for those which formerly used the English plural, e.g.: *die Lobbys, die Partys,* NOT *die Lobbies, die Parties.*

(b) (-s) is used with most words ending in a vowel other than unstressed -e

das Auto – die Autos
das Genie – die Genies
der Ossi – die Ossis
der Uhu – die Uhus

(c) (-s) is used with abbreviations and shortened words

der PKW – die PKWs
die Lok – die Loks

NB: This ending is often omitted in speech, especially in south Germany: *die PKW.*

(d) (-s) is used with some north German seafaring words
The most frequent are:

das Deck – die Decks
das Dock – die Docks
der Kai – die Kais
das Wrack – die Wracks

(e) (-s) is used in colloquial speech with some words referring to persons

die Bengels, die Doktors, die Fräuleins, die Jungs (older: die Jungens), die Kerls, die Kumpels, die Mädels, die Onkels

This usage is typical of substandard north German speech, where some of them are very frequent. The standard plural form (*die Jungen, die Kumpel, die Mädel,* etc.) is always preferred in writing.

(f) (-s) is used with family and other names

die Müllers, die Buddenbrooks, zwischen den beiden Deutschlands (*Zeit*)

1.2.6 Unusual plural forms

A number of words, particularly those borrowed into German from the classical languages or Italian, have retained unusual plural forms. Some of the more unusual ones are in practice restricted to formal written language.

(a) Most words in *-us* or *-um* replace this by *-en* in the plural

der Genius – die Genien
der Organismus – die Organismen
der Rhythmus – die Rhythmen
der Zyklus – die Zyklen
das Album – die Alben (coll.: Albums)
das Museum – die Museen
das Visum – die Visen (or: Visa)
das Zentrum – die Zentren

There are a few exceptions, mainly of unusual words, but note *der `Kaktus – die Kak`teen*, pronounced [kakteːən] (colloquial: *die Kaktusse*); *das Tempus* 'tense' – *die Tempora*; *der Terminus* 'term' – *die Termini*. Some words in *-us* have adopted a native plural:

der Bonus – die Bonusse
der Bus – die Busse
der Globus – die Globusse
   (rare: die Globen)

der Krokus – die Krokusse
   (rare: die Krokus)
der Zirkus – die Zirkusse

(b) Most words in *-ma* have a plural in *-men*

das Aroma – die Aromen (*or:* Aromas)
das Dogma – die Dogmen
das Drama – die Dramen
die Firma – die Firmen

das Paradigma – die Paradigmen
   (acad.: Paradigmata)
das Thema – die Themen
   (acad.: Themata)

A few have a plural in *-mata*:

das Dilemma – die Dilemmata
   (now commoner: Dilemmas)
das Klima – die Klimata
   (less common: Klimas)

das Komma – die Kommata
   (in speech usually: Kommas)
das Schema – die Schemata
   (*also:* Schemen *or* Schemas)

(c) A few other words replace *-a* with *-en*

die Pizza – die Pizzen
   (*or:* die Pizzas)
die Razzia – die Razzien
   (*or:* die Razzias)

die Regatta – die Regatten
die Skala – die Skalen
die Veranda – die Veranden
die Villa – die Villen

(d) Other frequent words
Many of these have alternatives, with the foreign plural being most used in more formal registers.

das Adverb – die Adverbien
der Atlas – die Atlanten
   (*also* coll.: Atlasse)
die Basis – die Basen
das Cello – die Celli (*or:* Cellos)
das Epos – die Epen
das Examen – die Examina
   (commoner: Examen)
der Espresso – die Espressi
   (*or:* Espressos)
das Fossil – die Fossilien
das Fresko – die Fresken
der Index – die Indices
   (*or:* Indexe)
das Konto – die Konten
   (*also:* Konti *or* Kontos)
das Lexikon – die Lexika
   (*also:* Lexiken, Lexikons)
das Material – die Materialien

das Mineral – die Mineralien
   (*or:* Minerale)
der Mythos – die Mythen
die Praxis – die Praxen
das Prinzip – die Prinzipien
das Privileg – die Privilegien
das Reptil – die Reptilien
das Risiko – die Risiken
   (coll.: Risikos)
der Saldo – die Salden
   (*also:* Saldos *or* Saldi)
das Solo – die Soli
   (*or:* Solos)
das Stadion – die Stadien
das Tempo – die Tempi
   (*or:* Tempos)
das Textil – die Textilien
das Utensil – die Utensilien

1.2.7 The plural of nouns in -*mann*

Compounds of -*mann* usually replace this by -*leute* in the plural when they refer to the occupation as such or to the group as a whole:

> der Fachmann – die Fachleute   der Kaufmann – die Kaufleute

In cases where we think more in terms of individuals than a group, or where we are not dealing with persons, the plural is in -*männer*, e.g.:

> die Ehrenmänner, Froschmänner, Schneemänner, Staatsmänner

In some cases both are used:

> die Feuerwehrleute/-männer   die Kameraleute/-männer

There is a slight difference between these in that plurals in -*männer* refer to a set of male individuals, whereas those in -*leute* can be used to refer to a collection of people which possibly includes females. A similar distinction applies with the following, where the forms in -*leute* typically denote groups including females:

> die Ehemänner *husbands*, BUT: die Eheleute *married couples* (i.e. *Ehemänner + Ehefrauen*)
> die Seemänner *seamen* (as individuals), BUT: die Seeleute *seafaring folk* (general)

1.2.8 A few nouns have two plurals with different meanings

The following are the most common:

der Abdruck	die Abdrucke *offprints*
	die Abdrücke *impressions*
das Band	die Bande *bonds* (elev.)
	die Bänder *ribbons*
die Bank	die Bänke *benches*
	die Banken *banks*
das Ding	die Dinge *things*
	die Dinger *things* (coll.); *girls* (coll.)
der Effekt	die Effekte *effects* (i.e. *results*)
	die Effekten *effects* (i.e. *valuables*)
das Land	die Länder *countries, provinces*
	die Lande *regions* (esp. in *historical contexts*)
der Mann	die Männer *men*
	die Mannen *vassals* (hist.)
die Mutter	die Mütter *mothers*
	die Muttern *nuts* (for bolts)
der Rat	die Räte *councils, officials*
	die Ratschläge *pieces of advice*
der Stock	die Stöcke *sticks*
	die Stockwerke *storeys* (sg. also: das Stockwerk)
der Strauß	die Strauße *ostriches*
	die Sträuße *bunches* (of flowers)
das Wort	die Wörter *words* (in isolation)
	die Worte *words* (connected words, i.e. *sayings*)

The distinction between *die Wörter* and *die Worte* is sometimes ignored in practice, with *Wörter* being widely used in both senses, especially in less formal German. However, there are contexts, especially after *sprechen* and its synonyms, where only *Worte* is possible, e.g. *Am Grabe seines Vorgängers sprach der Bürgermeister einige Worte des Gedenkens.*

1.2.9 In some instances the usual equivalent of a German singular noun is an English plural noun

The following are frequent:

das Archiv	*archives*	die Politik	*politics*
die Asche	*ashes*	das Protokoll	*minutes (of meeting)*
das Aussehen	*looks*	der Pyjama	*pyjamas*
das Benehmen	*manners*	der Reichtum	*riches*
der Besitz	*possessions*	im Rückstand	*in arrears*
der Bodensatz	*dregs*	der Schadenersatz	*damages (legal)*
die Brille	*spectacles*	die Schere	*scissors*
der Dank	*thanks*	das Schilf	*reeds*
das Fernglas	*binoculars*	die Treppe	*(flight of) stairs, steps*
der Hafer	*oats*	die Umgebung	*surroundings*
das Hauptquartier	*headquarters*	die Waage	*scales*
die Hose	*trousers*	die Wahl	*elections*
der Inhalt	*contents*	das Werk	*works (factory)*
die Kaserne	*barracks*	die Zange	*tongs*
der Lohn	*wages*	der Ziegenpeter	*mumps*
das Mittel	*means*	der Zirkel	*(pair of) compasses*
das Mittelalter	*the Middle Ages*		

Many of these German words can be used in the plural in appropriate contexts:

Die meisten Löhne sind erhöht worden	*Most wages have been raised*
Er wohnt zwei Treppen hoch	*He lives on the second floor*

1.2.10 Some German nouns are used only, or predominantly, in the plural

Usually, this corresponds to English usage, e.g.: die Ferien *holidays*, die Leute *people*.

(a) With a few nouns German and English usage differs

die Flitterwochen	*honeymoon*	die Naturalien	*natural produce*
die Geschwister	*brothers and sisters*	die Pocken	*smallpox*
die Immobilien	*real estate*	die Ränke	*intrigue* (elev.)
die Kosten	*cost(s)*	die Trümmer	*rubble*
die Kurzwaren	*haberdashery*	die Wirren	*turmoil*
die Lebensmittel	*food*	die Zinsen	*interest* (on a loan)
die Möbel	*furniture*		

Note that *die Eltern* has no commonly used singular corresponding to English 'parent', although *ein Elternteil* is used in officialese).

(b) Usage with the names of festivals is different in German.
Ostern, *Pfingsten* and *Weihnachten* are generally treated as plurals:

Frohe Weihnachten!	Sie hat uns letzte Ostern besucht

However, *Weihnachten* and *Ostern* can occur as neuter singulars, particularly with an indefinite article, e.g.:

Wir haben ein stilles Weihnachten verbracht	*We had a quiet Christmas*
Hast du ein schönes Ostern gehabt?	*Did you have a nice Easter?*

All are followed by a verb in the singular:

> Weihnachten steht vor der Tür *Christmas is almost here*
> Pfingsten fällt dieses Jahr spät *Whitsun is late this year*

1.2.11 Some English nouns have plurals, but their German equivalents do not

In such cases a plural has to be expressed through other forms:

> der Atem *breath* – die Atemzüge *breaths*
> das Essen *meal* – die Mahlzeiten *meals* (occ.: die Essen)
> die Furcht *fear* – die Befürchtungen *fears*
> der Käse *cheese* – die Käsesorten *cheeses* (occ.: die Käse)
> der Kohl *cabbage* – die Kohlköpfe *cabbages*
> die Liebe *love* – die Liebschaften *loves* (occ.: die Lieben)
> der Luxus *luxury* – die Luxusartikel *luxuries*
> das Obst *fruit* – die Obstsorten *fruits*
> der Rasen *lawn* – die Rasenflächen *lawns*
> der Raub *robbery* – die Raubüberfälle *robberies*
> der Sport *sport* – die Sportarten *sports*
> der Tod *death* – die Todesfälle *deaths* (occ.: die Tode)
> das Unglück *accident* – die Unglücksfälle *accidents*

The following words are used in the singular only in German, and this corresponds to both singular and plural in English:

> der Kummer *care(s)*   die Sehnsucht *longing(s)*   der Verdacht *suspicion(s)*

1.2.12 Some German nouns have singular and plural forms but their English equivalents do not

> die Auskunft *(piece of) information* – die Auskünfte *information*
> das Brot *bread, loaf* – die Brote *loaves*
> der Blitz *(flash of) lightning* – die Blitze *flashes of lightning*
> der Fortschritt *advance* – die Fortschritte *progress*
> die Hausaufgabe *(piece of) homework* – die Hausaufgaben *homework*
> die Information *(piece of) information* – die Informationen *information*
> die Kenntnis *(piece of) knowledge* – die Kenntnisse *knowledge*
> die Nachricht *(piece of) news* – die Nachrichten *news*
> der Rat *(piece of) advice* – die Ratschläge *(pieces of) advice*
> der Schaden *damage* – die Schäden *(instances of) damage*

1.2.13 German normally uses a singular noun for items of clothing and parts of the body if each individual possesses only one of each

> Alle hoben **die rechte Hand**   *They all raised their right hands*
> Ihnen klopfte **das Herz**   *Their hearts were beating*

To use the plural *die Herzen* in the last example could suggest that each person had more than one heart. Nevertheless, exceptions to this rule are not unknown, especially if the possessive is used rather than the definite article (see **4.6.1**), e.g.:

> Die Passagiere drehten **ihre Köpfe** (*Frisch*)   *The passengers turned their heads*

1.2.14 Masculine and neuter nouns of weight, measurement or value, preceded by a numeral, have the singular form, not the plural

zwei **Pfund** Kirschen, zwei **Sack** Kartoffeln, drei **Dutzend** Eier, zwei **Paar** Schuhe, zehn **Fass** Wein, zwanzig englische **Pfund**, um ein paar **Dollar** mehr

zwei, drei, mehrere **Glas** Bier	*two, three several glasses of beer*
ein paar **Schluck** (Kaffee)	*a few mouthfuls (of coffee)*
Wir hatten zehn **Grad** Kälte	*We had ten degrees of frost*
zehn **Schritt**	*ten paces*
3 **Schuss** – ein Euro 50	*3 shots for one euro fifty*

The singular is typically used when shopping or ordering in restaurants:

Diese hier sind gerade das Richtige. Geben Sie mir bitte drei **Stück**!
Bringen Sie mir bitte drei **Erdbeereis** und zwei Glas **Bier**!

Masculine and neuter nouns of measurement do have plural endings if they are seen as individual objects:

Auf dem Hof lagen zehn **Fässer**   *There were ten barrels in the yard*

Feminine nouns of measurement do take the plural form:

zehn **Flaschen** Wein   zwei **Ladungen** Holz   vier **Tassen** Kaffee

However, *die Mark* never has a plural ending: *zwanzig Mark*.

NB: For the agreement of the verb with measurement phrases, see **12.1.4f**.

1.3 Noun declension

Case shows the relationship of a noun or noun phrase to the sentence as a whole (see Chapter 2). It is marked most clearly in German by inflections on the other words in the noun phrase, i.e. the determiner and adjectives, rather than on the noun itself. However, there are one or two forms where German nouns have inflections for case, and these are explained in this section:

- Case endings for regular nouns (section 1.3.1)
- Case endings for 'weak' masculine and irregular nouns (sections 1.3.2–1.3.4)
- The dative singular ending -*e* (section 1.3.5)
- The genitive singular ending -*(e)s* (sections 1.3.6–1.3.7)
- The declension of names (section 1.3.8)

1.3.1 Case endings with regular nouns in German

The majority of German nouns have only two endings which signal case. These are added to the basic singular or plural forms, giving the regular declension patterns summarised in Table 1.5, where the declension of two typical regular nouns of each gender is given, with the definite article.

TABLE 1.5 *Case endings of regular nouns*

	Masculine Singular	Masculine Plural	Feminine Singular	Feminine Plural	Neuter Singular	Neuter Plural
Nom.	der Vater	die Väter	die Frau	die Frauen	das Kind	die Kinder
Acc.	den Vater	die Väter	die Frau	die Frauen	das Kind	die Kinder
Gen.	des Vaters	der Väter	der Frau	der Frauen	des Kindes	der Kinder
Dat.	dem Vater	den Vätern	der Frau	den Frauen	dem Kind	den Kindern
Nom.	der Park	die Parks	die Hand	die Hände	das Jahr	die Jahre
Acc.	den Park	die Parks	die Hand	die Hände	das Jahr	die Jahre
Gen.	des Parks	der Parks	der Hand	der Hände	des Jahres	der Jahre
Dat.	dem Park	den Parks	der Hand	den Händen	dem Jahr	den Jahren

These endings are:

(a) Masculine and neuter nouns add -*s* or -*es* in the genitive singular

> des Bahnhofs, des Busch**es**, des Fensters, des Mann(**e**)s, des Tal(**e**)s

For the use of -*s* and -*es* see 1.3.6. For the occasional omission of this ending, see 1.3.7.

(b) -*n* is added in the dative plural if possible

> den Kinder**n**, den Fenster**n**, den Hunde**n**, den Stühle**n**, den Töchter**n**

However, if the plural form of the noun ends in -*n* or -*s*, no ending can be added in the dative plural:

> den Gärten, den Frauen, den Autos, den Müllers

Other notes on the dative plural of nouns:

(i) Nouns of measurement often drop the -*n* after numerals: *eine Entfernung von zweihundert Kilometer(n)*.

(ii) In colloquial German this dative plural -*n* is sometimes omitted, and one may even see notices such as *Eis mit Früchte*. This is considered substandard.

(iii) No -*n* is used in the set phrase *aus aller Herren Länder* 'from the four corners of the earth'

1.3.2 'Weak' masculine nouns

A small group of masculine nouns, most of which denote living beings, have the ending -*n* or -*en* throughout the plural and in all singular cases except the nominative. These are called (for no good reason) 'weak' masculine nouns. Table 1.6 shows their declension:

TABLE 1.6 *Declension of weak masculine nouns*

	Singular	Plural	Singular	Plural	Singular	Plural
Nom.	der Junge	die Jungen	der Student	die Studenten	der Herr	die Herren
Acc.	den Jungen	die Jungen	den Studenten	die Studenten	den Herrn	die Herren
Gen.	des Jungen	der Jungen	des Studenten	der Studenten	des Herrn	der Herren
Dat.	dem Jungen	den Jungen	dem Studenten	den Studenten	dem Herrn	den Herren

In general, nouns ending in *-e* or *-er* have the ending *-n*, like *der Junge*, nouns ending in another consonant have the ending *-en*, like *der Student*. The noun *der Herr*, however, has the ending *-n* in the singular but *-en* in the plural.

(a) Most of these 'weak' masculine nouns refer to male humans and animals
The following nouns belong to this group:

(i) those which end in *-e* in the nominative singular:

> der Affe, der Bote, der Chinese, der Franzose, der Schwabe

NB: A few masculine nouns in *-e* follow other declension patterns. *der Käse* and *der Charme* are regular. The eight nouns which decline like *der Name* are irregular and explained in 1.3.3.

(ii) a large number of foreign nouns, in particular those ending in stressed *-and*, *-ant*, *-aph*, *-arch*, *-at*, *-ent*, *-et*, *-ist*, *-krat*, *-log*, *-nom*, *-on*:

> der Diamant, der Monarch, der Automat, der Student, der Komet, der Komponist, der Demokrat, der Psycholog(e), der Astronom, der Dämon

Also a number with other endings:

> der Barbar, der Chirurg, der Kamerad, der Katholik, der Prinz, der Tyrann

(iii) a few native nouns which do not end in *-e* in the nominative singular. The most frequent are:

der Bär	*bear*	der Hirt	*shepherd*
der Bauer	*peasant*	der Mensch	*human being*
der Bayer	*Bavarian*	der Nachbar	*neighbour*
der Bub	*lad* (S.G.)	der Narr	*fool*
der Fink	*finch*	der Oberst	*colonel*
der Fürst	*prince*	der Ochs	*ox*
der Graf	*count*	der Papagei	*parrot*
der Held	*hero*	der Spatz	*sparrow*
der Herr	*gentleman*	der Tor	*fool* (lit.)

(b) Weak masculine nouns have no ending in the singular if they are used without a determiner
This avoids the possibility of ambiguity between singular and plural:

Die Situation war für Arzt und **Patient** kritisch	*The situation was critical for doctor and patient alike*
Ich schrieb an Christian Schulze, **Präsident** des Gesangvereins	*I wrote to Christian Schulze, the president of the choral society*

However, the noun *der Herr* always keeps the ending *-n* in the singular even if used without a determiner, e.g. (when addressing an envelope): *Herrn Alfred Bletzer*.

(c) The singular endings of weak masculine nouns are often dropped in colloquial German
i.e. they have the 'regular' forms: *den Bauer, des Bauers, dem Bauer*. For most of these nouns, this usage is regarded as substandard and avoided in formal writing. However, it has come to be accepted with a few of them which are now in practice

found as frequently with the 'regular' endings as with the 'weak' endings. This is the case with the following:

> der Magnet, der Oberst, der Papagei, der Partisan, der Spatz;
> (*also, less frequently, with* der Bauer *and* der Nachbar).

On the other hand, *der Typ* 'bloke, chap' (see 1.2.2e) is often heard with the 'weak' singular endings in colloquial speech: *den Typen, des Typen, dem Typen*.

(d) 'Weak' masculine nouns should not be confused with adjectives used as nouns

e.g. *der Beamte, der Vorsitzende*. These seem to have similar endings, but in fact they are the endings of adjectives, see 6.4.

1.3.3 Irregular masculine nouns

Eight masculine nouns are irregular. They have the ending *-n* in the plural and in the accusative and dative singular, but *-ns* in the genitive singular, as shown in Table 1.7.

TABLE 1.7 *Declension of irregular nouns*

	Masculine		Neuter	
	Singular	Plural	Singular	Plural
Nom.	der Name	die Namen	das Herz	die Herzen
Acc.	den Namen	die Namen	das Herz	die Herzen
Gen.	des Namens	der Namen	des Herzens	der Herzen
Dat.	dem Namen	den Namen	dem Herzen	den Herzen

The following nouns belong to this group:

der Buchstabe	*letter* (of alphabet)	der Glaube	*belief*
der Friede	*peace*	der Name	*name*
der Funke	*spark*	der Same	*seed*
der Gedanke	*thought*	der Wille	*will*

The form of a number of these words is variable: *der Friede, der Funke, der Glaube* and *der Same* are often used with *-n* in the nominative singular, making them quite regular, i.e. *der Frieden, der Funken, der Glauben, der Samen*. Of these *der Frieden, der Funken* and *der Samen* are now commoner in practice than the forms without *-n*, especially in speech, but *der Glaube* is far more frequent than *der Glauben*.

1.3.4 The irregular neuter *das Herz*

The neuter noun *das Herz* has forms which look like those of the irregular masculine nouns, as Table 1.7 shows, with the ending *-ens* in the genitive singular and *-en* in the dative singular. However, regular singular forms (*des Herzes, dem Herz*) often occur in colloquial speech and medical writing.

1.3.5 Dative singular in -e

In older German, regular masculine and neuter nouns, particularly those of one syllable, regularly added -*e* in the dative singular, e.g.:

dem Flusse, dem Manne, dem Tage, dem Tale

This 'dative -*e*' is now uncommon. It is occasionally used in formal writing, but even there it can sound old-fashioned or facetious. However, it is still current in a few set phrases:

das Kind mit dem Bade ausschütten	*to throw out the baby with the bathwater*
im Falle, dass	*if/in the event that*
bis zu einem gewissen Grade	*to a certain extent*
im Grunde genommen	*basically*
jdm. zum Halse heraushängen	*to be sick of sth.*
jdm. im Halse stecken bleiben	*to stick in sb.'s throat*
nach Hause	*home*
zu Hause	*at home*
im Jahre 2005	*in 2005*
auf dem Lande	*in the country*
im Laufe des Tages	*in the course of the day*
bei Lichte betrachtet/besehen	*seen in the (cold) light of day*
in gewissem Maße	*to a certain extent*
jdn. zu Rate ziehen	*to consult sb.*
in diesem Sinne	*in this sense*
am Tage	*by day*
unter Tage arbeiten	*to work below ground*
(nicht) zum Zuge kommen	*(not) to get a look-in*

Many of these phrases are used equally commonly without the -*e*, e.g. *im Lauf des Tages, am Tag*.

1.3.6 Genitive singular in -es or -s?

Regular masculine and neuter nouns have the ending -*s* or -*es* in the genitive singular. The choice between these depends on style, rhythm and ease of pronunciation. The ending -*es* is often felt to be more formal and tends to be preferred with monosyllabic words, words with a stressed final syllable and those ending in more than one consonant. However, in some cases usage is more fixed:

(a) -*es* **MUST be used with nouns ending in -*s*, -*ß*, -*x* or -*z***

des Krebses, des Maßes, des Reflexes, des Kreuzes, etc.

It is also commonly used with nouns in -*sch*, -*st* or -*zt*:

des Tisches, des Dienstes, des Arztes, etc.

NB: (i) Neuter nouns in -*nis* have genitive singular -*nisses*, e.g. *des Ereignisses*.
(ii) Foreign nouns in -*s* and -*x* usually lack the ending (see 1.3.7g).

(b) -*s* **is normal:**

(i) with polysyllabic words ending in an unstressed syllable:

des Abends, des Königs, des Lehrers, des Schicksals

(ii) with words ending in a vowel (or vowel + *h*):

> des Schnees, des Schuhs, des Uhus

(iii) with names and foreign words:

> Schillers Dramen, des Hotels, des Klubs

1.3.7 Lack of inflection in the genitive singular

In some instances (apart from names, see 1.3.8) the ending -(*e*)*s* is omitted in the genitive singular of masculine and neuter nouns:

(a) Frequently with the names of the months and seasons

> am Morgen des zehnten Januar(s)
> die kräftigste Zyklone des beginnenden Herbst (NZZ)

The months in -*er* more often keep the -*s*: *in den ersten Tagen des Oktobers*. The -*s* is also often omitted with the names of the weekdays, e.g. *am Morgen des folgenden Mittwoch*, although this is considered incorrect.

(b) Often with names of artistic styles and epochs

> des Barock(s), des Empire(s), des Rokoko(s), etc.

(c) Optionally with abbreviations and other parts of speech used as nouns

> ein Stück des eignen Ich(s) des Lkw(s)
> eines gewissen Jemand(s) die Aussprache des modernen Deutsch(s)
> meines Gegenüber(s)

(d) With many foreign nouns (and several native German words)

This is particularly prevalent with words seen as technical terms or specific names:

> des Dativ, des Dynamo, des Establishment, des Gulasch, des Holunder, des Interesse, des Islam, des Parlament, des Parterre, des Radar

This usage has increased markedly in recent years although many standard authorities consider it incorrect.

(e) Frequently after prepositions when the noun has no accompanying adjective or determiner

> laut Bericht wegen Schnee geschlossen trotz Geldmangel

Compare (illustrating the absence and presence of -*s* dependent on the absence or presence of article or adjective):

> eine Agrar-Reform, die aber wegen *an agricultural reform which is proceeding*
> **Geldmangel** und **gebremsten Eifers** *only slowly because of a lack of money*
> nur langsam vorankommt (*Zeit*) *and moderated zeal*

However, usage is variable on this point, and the genitive ending is still by no means unusual in written German:

eine Strafuntersuchung gegen mehrere
   Stadtpolizisten wegen **schwerer**
   Körperverletzung und **Amtsmissbrauchs**
   (NZZ)

a criminal investigation against several
   city police officers for grievous bodily
   harm and abuse of office

(f) Foreign nouns ending in -s and -x usually have no ending in the genitive:

des Atlas, des Chaos, des Index, des Globus, des Sozialismus, des Zirkus

However, several foreign words such as *der Bus* and *der Kongress* have been fully assimilated and are treated as German words, e.g. *des Busses, des Kongresses.*

1.3.8 Declension of proper names and titles

(a) Proper names without titles and geographical names add -*s* in the genitive singular

Helmut Kohls Politik	Elisabeths Bücher
die Werke Johann Sebastian Bachs	der Tod Friedrichs des Großen
die Straßen Deutschlands	Deutschlands Straßen

Personal names ending in -*s*, -*ß*, -*x*, -*z* do not add -*s* in the genitive. In writing an apostrophe may be used:

Fritz' Schwester, Agnes' Hut, Perikles' Tod, Marx' Einfluss

In speech, a construction with *von* is usual and may be used in writing as an alternative to the apostrophe:

der Hut von Agnes, der Tod von Perikles, der Einfluss von Marx

With geographical names in -*s*, -*ß*, -*x*, -*z*, only a phrase with *von* is possible:

die Straßen von Paris   die Geschichte von Florenz

NB: In colloquial north German, the generic names of members of the family are treated as names, e.g.: *Tantes Haus, Mutters Kleid, Vaters Anzug.*

(b) Proper names rarely have the ending -*s* in the genitive singular if they are used with an article

die Rolle des Egmont	die Gedichte des alten Goethe
die Werke eines Johann Sebastian Bach	die Briefe dieses Schmidt

(c) Geographical names used with an article

(i) With German names, the ending -(*e*)*s* is optional:

eines vereinigten Europa(s)   die Einwohner des geteilten Berlin(s)

However, if the article is part of the name (e.g. with rivers), the ending *is* normally used, e.g. *an den Ufern des Rheins* (less frequent: *des Rhein*).

(ii) Foreign geographical names usually lack the ending -*s*:

an den Ufern des Nil   die Berge des High Peak

(d) Proper names with titles in the genitive singular

(i) If there is no article, only the name is declined:

König Heinrichs Politik   die Politik König Heinrichs
Onkel Roberts Haus   Bundeskanzler Kohls Amtsantritt

(ii) If there is an article, only the title is declined:

die Siege des Kaisers Karl   die Hauptstadt des Landes Niedersachsen

(iii) If the title is a weak masculine noun, the ending *-n* is optional:

Wir bedauern Genosse(n) Schmidts Versetzung nach Bautzen

However, *Herr* is always declined (see 1.3.2b), and a following title may then lack the ending *-s*: *der Vortrag des Herrn Generaldirektor(s) Kramer.*

(iv) *Doktor* and *Fräulein*, used as titles, are never declined:

die Erfolge unseres Doktor Meyer   die Mutter dieses Fräulein Sauer

(e) Titles and names of books, plays, newspapers, hotels, companies

(i) These are normally fully declined:

ein Lied aus Schillers „Räubern", aus Brechts „kaukasischem Kreidekreis"
Sie las es in der „Süddeutschen Zeitung", im „Spiegel"
Ich wohne im „Goldenen Apostel"

(ii) After a word which describes what kind of thing it is, a full title in quotation marks remains in the nominative.

in Brechts Drama „Der kaukasische Kreidekreis"
im Hotel „Goldener Apostel"
in der Wochenzeitschrift „Der Spiegel"

(iii) A short title in the genitive with an article may drop the *-(e)s*:

in der letzten Strophe des Erlkönig(s)

(iv) Names of companies should always be declined in full:

der Überschuss bei der Süddeutschen Zucker AG
die ehemalige Verwaltung der Deutschen Reichsbahn

2

Case

The grammatical category of CASE relates to the inflection of a noun, pronoun or noun phrase which serves to indicate its role in the sentence or clause and thus its relationship to the rest of the clause or sentence. German has four cases: NOMINATIVE, ACCUSATIVE, GENITIVE and DATIVE.

In English, which has kept few case forms – they occur only in the possessive in -*s* and some pronouns like *I* – *me*, *he* – *him*, etc. – these relationships are shown in other ways, chiefly through word order (e.g. *My brother* [subject] *gave his friend* [indirect object] *the book* [direct object]) or by using prepositions (e.g. *My brother gave the book* **to** *his friend*).

Inflection for case plays an essential part in showing the structure of a German sentence. This is particularly apparent in relation to verb valency (see Chapter 18) and word order (see Chapter 21). All the German cases have a variety of uses, as summarised in Table 2.1. Details are given in the remainder of this chapter, as follows:

- the uses of the **nominative** case (section 2.1)
- the uses of the **accusative** case (section 2.2)
- the uses of the **genitive** case and its replacement by a phrase with *von* (sections 2.3–2.4)
- the uses of the **dative** case (section 2.5)
- case use in **apposition** and **measurement phrases** (sections 2.6–2.7)

2.1 The nominative case

2.1.1 The nominative is the neutral case

It is used with nouns or pronouns in isolation:

> **Ein schöner Tag** heute, nicht?
> Und **dein Onkel**, wann siehst du ihn wieder?
> Und **du**, was meinst du dazu?

Similarly for persons and things addressed and in exclamations:

> Was beunruhigt dich, **mein Lieber**?   **Herr Müller**, Telefon für Sie!
> Ach **du liebe Zeit**!   **Der unverschämte Kerl**!

It can be used in so-called 'absolute' phrases, where the noun phrase is placed outside the main framework of the clause:

> als er an den Mann dachte, zu dem er   *when he thought of the man he now*
> jetzt gehen musste, **dieser Mann aus**   *had to go to, that man from Röder's*
> **Röders Abteilung** (*Seghers*)   *company*

TABLE 2.1 *Chief uses of the cases in German*

Nominative	Examples
marks the subject of the verb	**Der Fußballspieler** schoss ein Tor.
	The football player shot a goal.
marks the complement of copular verbs like *sein*	Brecht ist **ein großer Dichter.**
	Brecht is a great writer.
used with the noun in isolation	**Dein Freund**, wann siehst du ihn wieder?
	Your friend, when will you see him again?
Accusative	
marks the direct object of the verb	Ich kaufe **einen kleinen Fernseher.**
	I'm buying a small television.
used after some prepositions	Sie tat es für **ihren Bruder.**
	She did it for her brother.
used in many adverbials (e.g. to mark length of time)	Anita blieb **den ganzen Tag** zu Hause.
	Anita stayed at home the whole day.
used in conventional greetings and wishes	**Guten Tag! Herzlichen Glückwunsch!**
	Good morning/afternoon! Congratulations!
Genitive	
links nouns (especially to show possession)	Der Ton **des Radios** ist furchtbar.
	The sound of the radio is awful.
used after a few prepositions	Sie lief trotz **ihres hohen Alters** schnell.
	She ran fast despite her advanced age.
Dative	
marks the indirect object of the verb	Ich gebe **dem Hamster** sein Futter.
	I'm giving the hamster its food.
marks the sole (dative) object of some verbs	Sie will **ihrem Freund** helfen.
	She wants to help her friend.
can show possession, esp. with clothing and parts of the body	Sie zogen **dem Verletzten** die Hose aus.
	They took the injured man's trousers off.
used after some prepositions	Wir suchten überall nach **dem Geld.**
	We looked everywhere for the money.
used with many adjectives	Dieses Gespräch war **mir** sehr nützlich.
	This conversation was very useful for me.

Er saß am Feuer, **der Hund zu seinen Füßen**	*He sat by the fire, (with) the dog at his feet*

The type of absolute phrase seen in the last example is found mainly in formal, especially literary German; other registers generally prefer a construction with *mit*, e.g. *mit dem Hund zu seinen Füßen*.

2.1.2 The main function of the nominative case is to mark the SUBJECT of the FINITE VERB

Der Zug war nicht pünktlich	Heute war ausnahmsweise **der Mittagszug** nicht pünktlich
Heute war **der Zug** nicht pünktlich	

For further details see 18.2. As the subject is shown through case marking it does not have to precede the verb, as it does in English, cf. 21.2.3.

2.1.3 The nominative is used in the PREDICATE COMPLEMENT of COPULAR VERBS

i.e. after the verbs *sein, werden, bleiben, heißen, scheinen* and with the passive of *nennen*

Karl ist, wird, bleibt **mein Freund**   Ich will **ein Schuft** heißen
Er scheint **ein großartiger Turner**   Er wurde **der Weise** genannt

Further details about these verbs is given in 18.8.

2.2 The accusative case

2.2.1 The main function of the accusative case is to mark the DIRECT OBJECT of TRANSITIVE VERBS

Ich habe **einen Stein** geworfen   Die Putzfrau hat **den Fußboden** gebohnert
Sie hat mir **den Inhalt** erklärt   Er hat **die Tauben** im Park vergiftet

Full details are given in 18.3. A very few verbs, e.g. *kosten* and *lehren*, take two objects in the accusative, see 18.3.3.

2.2.2 Some intransitive verbs can be used with a 'cognate' accusative noun

This is a noun whose meaning is related to that of the verb and which thus repeats or explains more fully the idea expressed by the verb:

Er starb **einen schweren Tod**   Sie schlief **den Schlaf** der Gerechten

2.2.3 Most conventional greetings and wishes are in the accusative case

Guten Morgen, Tag, Abend   Gute Nacht   Guten Rutsch (ins neue Jahr)
Schönen Sonntag   Besten Dank   Herzlichen Glückwunsch
Viel Vergnügen   Gute Besserung   Angenehme Reise.

In effect this is an elliptical construction, with a verb such as *wünschen* being understood.

2.2.4 A few adjectives are used with the accusative case

e.g. *etwas gewohnt sein*. Details are given in 6.5.2.

2.2.5 The accusative case is found in a number of adverbial phrases

(a) To denote length of time or a point in time

Es hat **den ganzen Tag** geschneit   Ich war **einen Monat** in Stuttgart
Ich sah ihn **letzten Freitag**   Er kommt noch **diesen Monat** zurück

For further detail on usage, see 11.4.1. The accusative is also used in dates in letters: *Essen, den 4. August.*

(b) To express a measurement or value

This is particularly frequent with adjectives of measurement:

Das ist **keinen Pfennig** wert   Der Tisch ist **ein(en) Meter** breit
Das Kind ist **vier Jahre** alt   Der Sack wiegt **einen Zentner**

(c) To express the distance covered with verbs and adverbs denoting motion

> Ich bin **den ganzen Weg** zu Fuß gegangen   Sie kam **den Berg** herauf
> Wir sind **die Straße** heruntergekommen   Sie kam **die Treppe** herunter

This **adverbial accusative** is particularly common with the direction adverbs formed with *hin-* and *her-* (see 7.2.4).

2.2.6 The accusative case is sometimes used in 'absolute' phrases

This usage without a verb is mainly restricted to formal literary German:

> Wilhelmine, **den Kopf geneigt**, erlaubt   *Wilhelmine, her head bowed, allows*
>   ihm, ihr Haar zu lösen (*Wolf*)   *him to untie her hair*
> **Den Bauch voller Fracht,** fliegt der Jet   *Its belly full of freight, the jet flies to*
>   nach Fernost (*Spiegel*)   *the Far East*

This construction is uncommon even in literary German, and a construction with *mit* is often used, as is usual in other registers, e.g.: *mit dem Bauch voller Fracht*.

2.2.7 The accusative case is used with a number of prepositions

(a) Some prepositions are <u>always</u> followed by the accusative case

e.g. *bis, durch, für, gegen, ohne, um.*

See section 20.1 for full details.

(b) Ten prepositions are followed by the accusative case if they express movement in a particular direction

an, auf, entlang, hinter, in, neben, über, unter, vor, zwischen.

See section 20.3 for full details.

2.3 The genitive case

In modern German the genitive case is mainly restricted to registers (especially in writing). This section outlines its current uses with this general proviso. In some contexts a phrase with *von* may be preferred, especially in colloquial speech (see 2.4). For the genitive forms of personal pronouns see 3.1.2; for the genitive of the relative pronoun, see 5.4.1c.

2.3.1 The main function of the genitive case is to link nouns or noun phrases

For this, English typically uses the preposition *of*. We often think of the genitive as the 'possessive' case, but its range is wider, since it can be used:

(a)	**to express possession:**	das Haus meines Bruders
(b)	**as a partitive:**	die Hälfte des Kuchens
(c)	**for the subject of a verbal noun:**	die Abfahrt des Zuges
(d)	**for the object of a verbal noun:**	der Umbau des Hauses

(e) **to qualify a noun:**   ein Strahl der Hoffnung
(f) **to define a noun:**   die Pflicht der Dankbarkeit

For the use of the genitive case in measurement phrases, see 2.7.

2.3.2 A noun phrase in the genitive case usually follows the noun phrase on which it depends

die Gefahr **eines Erdbebens**   das Rauschen **der Bäume**

The main exception to this rule is that proper names in the genitive may come first:

Karls Freund	**Annas** Stereoanlage	**Frau Benders** Haus
Heinrich Bölls Werke	**Figaros** Hochzeit	**Deutschlands** Grenzen

However, in written German, personal names without a title, and geographical names may also follow:

ein Freund **Karls**   die Werke **Heinrich Bölls**   die Grenzen **Deutschlands**

Otherwise, the genitive comes first only in old-fashioned literary style or set phrases:

seiner Vorfahren großes altes Haus   *the large old house of his ancestors*
     (*Th. Mann*)
Undank ist **der Welt** Lohn   *Never expect thanks for anything*

In other contexts this order sounds facetious:

da wir **des Postministers** Kabelpläne   *as we reject the post minister's plans for*
     verwerfen (*Zeit*)   *cable television*

2.3.3 A few verbs take an object in the genitive case

e.g. *bedürfen, gedenken, sich ermächtigen* For details on this construction, see 18.5.

2.3.4 A noun phrase in the genitive case may be used as the PREDICATE COMPLEMENT of the verb *sein*

This is restricted in practice to a few set expressions, e.g.:

Wir sind gleichen Alters	*We are of the same age*
Ich bin der Ansicht, dass ...	*I am of the view that ...*
Ich bin der Auffassung, dass ...	*I am of the opinion that ...*
Hier ist meines Bleibens nicht (lit.)	*I cannot remain here*
Er ist guter Dinge	*He is in good spirits*
Wir waren guter Laune	*We were in a good mood*
Sie ist der Meinung, dass ...	*She is of the opinion that ...*
Er wurde anderen Sinnes (lit.)	*He changed his mind*
Dann sind wir des Todes	*Then we are doomed*
Sie sind der festen Überzeugung, dass ...	*They are firmly convinced that ...*
Das Wort ist griechischen Ursprungs	*The word is of Greek origin*

2.3.5 The genitive case is found in a few adverbial phrases

In the main these are set expressions or fixed idioms.

(a) A noun or noun phrase in the genitive case can denote habitual or indefinite time

(see also 11.4.2 for further details):

> eines Tages, eines schönen Sommers, eines Sonntagabends, montags, wochentags, werktags

(b) other adverbial genitives

unverrichteter Dinge	*without achieving anything*
letzten Endes	*after all*
meines Erachtens (abbrev.: m.E.)	*in my view*
allen Ernstes	*in all seriousness*
stehenden Fußes (lit.)	*immediately*
gesenkten/erhobenen Hauptes	*with one's head bowed/raised*
leichten/schweren Herzens	*with a light/heavy heart*
Hungers sterben (lit.)	*to die of starvation*
Sie fährt erster Klasse	*She is travelling first class*
aller Orten (lit.)	*everywhere*
seines Weges gehen (lit.)	*to go on one's way*
meines Wissens (abbrev.: m.W.)	*to my knowledge*

2.3.6 A few adjectives are used with the genitive case

A frequent English equivalent is a construction with *of*. Full details are given in 6.5.3.

> Er ist **einer solchen Tat** nicht fähig   *He is not capable of such a deed*

2.3.7 The genitive case is used with a number of prepositions

e.g. *innerhalb, statt, trotz, während, wegen*. Full details of these are given in 20.4.

2.4 Genitive case or *von*?

A PREPOSITIONAL PHRASE with *von* is often used rather than a genitive. The genitive is widely used in writing, especially in technical registers, but, except with names in north German usage (e.g. *Ruths Buch, Peters Fahrrad*), it tends to be avoided entirely in colloquial speech, where a paraphrase with *von* is usually preferred, e.g.:

colloquial speech:	das Dach **vom Haus**, der Ring **von seiner Frau**
usual written German:	das Dach **des Hauses**, der Ring **seiner Frau**

However, even in written German there are contexts where the genitive is not possible and where the paraphrase with *von* <u>must</u> be used. There are other written contexts where this paraphrase <u>may</u> be used, i.e. where it is an acceptable alternative to the genitive. This section explains those contexts where the paraphrase with *von* must or may be used in written German rather than a genitive. In other contexts a prepositional phrase with *von* is normally used in colloquial speech only.

2.4.1 The genitive case is not usual in written German

i.e. a phrase with *von* is used instead:

(a) if a noun stands by itself or is used with an indeclinable word

der Bau **von Kraftwerken**	*the building of power stations*
die Wirkung **von wenig Wein**	*the effect of a little wine*
der Preis **von fünf Fahrrädern**	*the price of five bicycles*
ein Strahl **von Hoffnung**	*a ray of hope*

(b) with a descriptive phrase

eine Frau **von bezaubernder Höflichkeit**	*a woman of enchanting politeness*
ein Ereignis **von weltgeschichtlicher Bedeutung**	*an event of global historical significance*

(c) with personal pronouns

The genitive forms of personal pronouns are rarely used, see 3.1.2:

fünf **von euch**	*five of you*
ein Freund **von ihr**	*a friend of hers*

(d) in partitive constructions with *viel, wenig* and indefinite pronouns

viel/wenig **von dem**, was sie sagte	*much/little of what she said*
etwas **von ihrem Charme**	*something of her charm*
welches **von diesen Büchern**?	*which of those books?*
nichts **von diesem Zauber**	*nothing of this magic*

2.4.2 In some contexts it is equally acceptable to use a phrase with *von* or the genitive case in written German

(a) to avoid consecutive genitive noun phrases in -(e)s

der Turm **von dem Palast** des Königs	*the tower of the king's palace*
der Turm **des Palastes** des Königs	

Consecutive genitive noun phrases are considered stylistically poor, but they are not unknown in practice, e.g. *die Existenz **eines Verdachts eines Verstoßes** gegen den Atomsperrvertrag* (SZ).

(b) if a noun is qualified by an adjective alone

der Bau **von modernen Kraftwerken**	*the building of modern power stations*
der Bau **moderner Kraftwerke**	

There is a clear preference for a phrase with *von* in these contexts if the first noun is qualified by an indefinite article, e.g. *ein fader Geruch **von aufgewärmten Speisen*** (*Zweig*).

(c) with nouns qualified by indefinite pronouns

die Ansicht **von vielen Politikern**	*the view of many politicians*
die Ansicht **vieler Politiker**	

(d) in most partitive constructions

i.e. following number words (except those listed at 2.4.1d above):

eines **von den wenigen alten Häusern** eines **der wenigen alten Häuser**	*one of the few old houses*
viele **von meinen Freunden** viele **meiner Freunde**	*many of my friends*
zwei **von seinen Kindern** zwei **seiner Kinder**	*two of his children*

(e) With geographical names which have no article:

die Zerstörung **von Dresden** die Zerstörung **Dresdens**	*the destruction of Dresden*
die Hauptstadt **von Deutschland** die Hauptstadt **Deutschlands**	*the capital of Germany*

2.5 The dative case

The dative case has the widest range of all the German cases, with many idiomatic uses. It is used

- as the indirect or sole object of a verb (sections 2.5.1–2.5.2)
- as a 'free' dative with other verbs where it is not a grammatical requirement (section 2.5.3)
- to indicate possession (section 2.5.4)
- with many adjectives (section 2.5.5)

In all these contexts it typically marks a person (rather than a thing) in some way concerned or affected, if not necessarily very directly, by the action or the event expressed through the verb.

2.5.1 The dative case marks the indirect object of transitive verbs

For full details see 18.4.2. It is used typically with verbs of giving and receiving, etc., and it often corresponds to an English indirect object indicated by the word order or a phrase introduced by *to* or *for*:

Ich zeigte **dem Polizisten** meinen Führerschein	*I showed the policeman my driving-licence/* *I showed my driving-licence to the policeman*
Ich habe **meinem Freund** ein Buch gebracht	*I brought my friend a book/I brought a book to/* *for my friend*

2.5.2 Many verbs take a sole object in the dative case

e.g.: *danken, dienen, folgen, gratulieren, helfen, schmeicheln.*

Full details about these are given in 18.4.1:

2.5.3 The dative case often marks a person affected in some way by the action or event expressed by the verb

In these uses the dative case is not necessarily a grammatical requirement of the verb (although opinions differ on this) and it is often referred to as a **'free' dative**. They are often idiomatic and lack a clear English equivalent.

Various subgroups of 'free' datives have been identified, but there are similarities between them all (and between them and the possessive dative, see 2.5.4). 'Free' datives are most common with verbs which express an activity, especially moving and making things, or which indicate a change of state.

(a) The dative case can indicate a person on whose behalf the action is done

(i) This is sometimes referred to as the **'dative of advantage'** or **'benefactive' dative** and often corresponds to an English phrase with 'for':

Sie schrieb **mir** seine Adresse auf	*She wrote his address down for me*
Ich öffnete **ihr** die Tür	*I opened the door for her*
Er füllte **meinem Vater** das Glas	*He filled the glass for my father/my father's glass*

(ii) It is sometimes used with things, especially things being altered, repaired or improved:

Sie setzt **dem Auto** einen neuen Motor ein	*She's putting a new engine in the car*

(iii) In this 'benefactive' sense a dative reflexive pronoun is common in idiomatic colloquial speech if a physical action is involved:

Ich will **mir** das Buch anschauen	*I want to go and look at that book*

(iv) A phrase with *für* is a frequent alternative to the dative case in this sense, especially in spoken German:

Er will **mir/für mich** Blumen kaufen	*He's going to buy some flowers for me*
Ich habe **ihm die Tür/die Tür für ihn** geöffnet	*I opened the door for him*

The construction with *für* may be preferred if the dative is ambiguous. For instance, *Er hat **seinem Vater** einen Brief geschrieben* could mean 'to his father' or 'for his father', whereas *Er hat **für seinen Vater** einen Brief geschrieben* is quite clear.

(b) The dative case can indicate a person who is disadvantaged by the action

This **'dative of disadvantage'** characteristically indicates a person who is affected by something undesirable happening to the person or thing which is the subject or direct object of the verb:

Mir ist Großmutters Vase kaputtgegangen	*Grandmother's vase broke on me*

(c) The dative case can mark a person from whose standpoint an action or event is judged or in respect of whom the statement holds good

This usage typically involves an adjective qualified by *zu* or *genug*:

Mir verging die Zeit zu schnell	*I felt that the time passed too quickly*
Fährt sie **dir** schnell genug?	*Is she going fast enough for you?*

A similar dative of the person concerned is frequent with the verb *sein* and a noun. In such cases, English uses a phrase with 'to' or 'for':

Das Wiedersehen mit dir war **mir** ein Vergnügen	*It was a pleasure for me to see you again*
Dem Schüler war diese Zensur ein Trost	*This mark was a consolation to/for the schoolboy*

(d) The 'ethic dative' shows the speaker's emotional involvement

It is only usual with the first person in commands or exclamations:

Dann soll **mir** mal so einer vorbeikommen!	*Just let me catch one like that coming past!*
Seid **mir** doch nett!	*Be nice, for my sake!*

2.5.4 The dative of possession

(a) The dative case often indicates possession

This is especially frequent with parts of the body or articles of clothing, but it is also found with close relatives and prized possessions (like vehicles or houses). The definite article is used rather than a possessive determiner, see 4.6; the dative usually precedes the item possessed:

Einem Mann ist das Bein gebrochen worden (*FR*)	*One man's leg was broken*
Mir muss der Mund offen geblieben sein (*Borst*)	*My mouth must have hung open*
Dem Alten ist gerade die Frau gestorben	*The old man's wife has just died*
Das Kind ist **mir** vors Auto gelaufen	*The child ran in front of my car*

If the possessor is the subject of the sentence, a reflexive pronoun in the dative case is used. This may be optional if no ambiguity is involved:

Er wischte **sich** den Schweiß von der Stirn	*He wiped the sweat from his brow*
Willst du (**dir**) den grünen Pullover anziehen?	*Are you going to put your green pullover on?*

It is difficult to give hard and fast rules as to when the possessive dative **must** be used and when it **cannot** be used. In general the following tendencies may be observed·

(i) It is **not** used if no-one else could possibly do it to or for one:

Er machte die Augen auf	*He opened his eyes*
Sie hob den Arm	*She raised her arm*
Er nickte mit dem Kopf	*He nodded his head*

(ii) It **must** be used if the body part or article of clothing is used with a preposition (other than *mit*):

Ich habe **mir** in den Finger geschnitten	*I've cut my finger*
Die Mütze fiel **mir** vom Kopf	*The cap fell off my head*
Regen tropfte **mir** auf den Hut	*Rain was falling on my hat*

(iii) It **must** be used where reference is not to the subject of the sentence:

Die Mutter wäscht **ihm** die Hände	*His mother is washing his hands*
Wir zogen **dem Verletzten** die Hose aus	*We took the injured man's trousers off*

(b) If the dative is used rather than a possessive construction, the person is seen as affected by the action as well

Possession can also be indicated by using a genitive phrase or a possessive like *sein* or *mein*. However, using these often has a different meaning to that of the possessive dative. Compare:

Regen tropfte **ihm auf den Hut**	(he was wearing it and getting wet)
Regen tropfte **auf seinen Hut**	(he wasn't necessarily wearing it)
Sie strich **dem Jungen übers Gesicht**	(normal for: 'she ran her hand over the boy's face')
Sie strich **über das Gesicht des Jungen**	(only possible if the boy is dead or unconscious)
Er zog **ihr die** Jacke an	*He helped her on with her jacket*
Er zog **sich ihre** Jacke an	*He put her jacket on*

(c) With some verbs the accusative case is an alternative to the dative case to indicate possession of parts of the body

If the accusative is used, the whole person is seen as more directly affected:

Der Hund biss **ihm/ihn** ins Bein   Ich klopfte **ihm/ihn** auf die Schulter
Alle Glieder schmerzten **ihm/ihn**

In practice, accusative and dative are equally common and usual with the following verbs:

beißen   küssen   schmerzen   stechen   stoßen   zwicken

With some verbs, the accusative occurs, but the dative is more common:

hauen   klopfen   schießen   schlagen   schneiden   treten

(d) In colloquial speech a phrase in the dative case may be used rather than a genitive to indicate possession

This construction is common but it is universally considered to be a substandard colloquialism:

Das ist **meiner Mutter** ihr Hut   *That's my mother's hat*
Meinem Onkel sein Garten ist ganz groß   *My uncle's garden is quite big*
Dem Huck Finn sein Vater (*Andersch*)   *Huck Finn's father*

The use of the dative case with *sein* to indicate possession is a substandard regionalism, mainly heard in the west and south-west:

Ist der Hut **dir**?   *Is that your hat?*

Standard German would use: *Gehört der Hut dir?*

2.5.5 The dative case with adjectives

(a) The dative is the most common case governed by adjectives

e.g.: *Er ist **seinem Bruder** sehr ähnlich*. Full details are given in section 6.5.1.

(b) Adjectives with *zu* or *genug* may govern a dative case or a phrase with *für*

The latter may come before **or** after the adjective, whereas the dative always precedes:

Diese Uhr ist **mir** zu teuer/**für mich** zu   *That watch is too expensive for me*
   teuer/zu teuer **für mich**
Dieser Mantel ist **mir** nicht warm   *That coat is not warm enough for me*
   genug/**für mich** nicht warm genug/nicht
   warm genug **für mich**

(c) The dative case is used in impersonal constructions with *sein* and *werden* with certain adjectives expressing sensations

The person in the dative is experiencing the sensation; it corresponds to a simple subject in English:

> Es ist **mir** kalt/**Mir** ist kalt   *I am cold*

For the omission of *es*, see 18.2.4e. This construction occurs with the following adjectives:

bange	heiß	schlecht	übel	(un)wohl
gut	kalt	schwindlig	warm	

2.6 Apposition

A NOUN PHRASE is said to be **'in apposition'** to another noun phrase if it immediately follows and expands it by giving some additonal information about it, e.g.

> Wilhelm, der letzte deutsche Kaiser
> Berlin, die Hauptstadt der Bundesrepublik Deutschland

Comparative phrases introduced by *als* and *wie* are also commonly considered to be 'in apposition' to the noun they qualify, e.g. *ein Tag **wie jeder andere**, er gilt **als großer Staatsmann**, Jürgen ist größer **als du**.*

Apposition in measurement phrases is dealt with in section 2.7.

2.6.1 A noun phrase in apposition usually has the same case as the noun which it follows

Es spricht Herbert Werner, **der Vorsitzende des Vereins**	*The speaker is Herbert Werner, the chairman of the society*
6,8 Prozent der Frauen empfinden die Arbeitslosigkeit als **einen Makel** (*LV*)	*6.8% of women feel that being unemployed is a stigma*
der „Mythos der Schweiz" als **eines Landes mit vier Landessprachen** (*NZZ*)	*The 'myth of Switzerland' as a country with four national languages*
in Michelstadt, **einem kleinen Städtchen im Odenwald**	*in Michelstadt, a little town in the Odenwald*
für Heinrich Böll als **gläubigen Katholiken**	*for Heinrich Böll as a devout Catholic*
nach einem Tag wie **diesem**	*after a day like this*

2.6.2 There are some exceptions to the general rule for case use in apposition

The rule given in 2.6.1 is followed in over 90% of instances in both spoken and written German. However, a few exceptions are found:

(a) Exceptions are particularly common in two contexts

(i) After a genitive, an unqualified noun in apposition is usually in the nominative:

nach dem Tode meines Onkels, **Bürgermeister** der Stadt Krefeld	*after the death of my uncle, the mayor of the city of Krefeld*

(ii) In dates a weekday introduced by *am* may be followed by the date in the dative **or** the accusative:

> am Montag, **dem** 2. Juli 2001   *or:*   am Montag, **den** 2. Juli 2001

(b) Other exceptions to the general rule are occasionally encountered

These are in practice much less common alternatives, i.e.:

(i) the nominative or dative case is sometimes used after a noun phrase in the genitive case:

> nach dem Tode meines Onkels, **der/dem früheren Bürgermeister dieser Stadt**
> die Wirtslaute des „Birnbaumes", **einem kleinen Dorfhaus** (*BZ*)

(ii) the genitive case is sometimes used after a phrase with *von*:

> Sacramento ist die Hauptstadt von Kalifornien, **des reichsten Bundesstaates**

Despite what is sometimes claimed, these and similar exceptions are neither common nor becoming more frequent.

2.6.3 German often uses appositional constructions with geographical names

> die Insel Rügen   die Universität Hamburg   die Stadt Bremen

In most such constructions English has 'of': 'the University **of** Hamburg', etc.

NB: German uses *bei* with battles, e.g. *die Schlacht bei Lützen* 'the battle of Lützen'.

2.7 Measurement phrases: genitive, *von* or apposition?

There is much variation and uncertainty in respect of case usage in measurement phrases. The most widely accepted current usage is given in this section.

NB: For the use of singular nouns in measurement phrases, e.g. *zwei Pfund Kirschen*, see 1.2.14.

2.7.1 Nouns and noun phrases after a noun of measurement are most commonly in the same case as the noun of measurement

In this way the two phrases are in apposition, see 2.6:

eine Flasche **Wein**	*a bottle of wine*
eine Flasche **deutscher Wein**	*a bottle of German wine*
er kauft zwei Flaschen **deutschen Wein**	*he is buying two bottles of German wine*
mit einer Tasse **heißem Tee**	*with a cup of hot tea*
von vier Kilo **grünen Erbsen**	*of four kilograms of green peas*

NB: In spoken German it is not uncommon to hear datives for accusatives and vice versa, e.g. *Er kauft zwei Flaschen deutschem Wein, mit einer Tasse heißen Tee*. This is considered incorrect in writing.

2.7.2 The genitive case is sometimes used in measurement phrases

eine Flasche sommerabendlichen Dufts (*Süßkind*)	*a bottle of the perfume of a summer evening*
zehn Jahre treuer Mitarbeit	*ten years' faithful service*

This alternative **only** occurs in the sequence: noun of measurement + adjective + noun. In the masculine and neuter singular it can sound stilted and is restricted to formal writing, but it is not uncommon in speech in the plural.

2.7.3 Usage with words of rather vague quantity

e.g.: *die Anzahl, die Gruppe, der Haufen, die Schar, die Reihe, die Sorte*

Usage with these varies according to whether the following noun has an adjective with it:

(a) If the following noun has an adjective with it (or is an adjective used as a noun)

In these contexts the following noun may be in the genitive case or (especially in speech) in a phrase with *von*:

zwei Gruppen **junger Arbeiter**	*or* zwei Gruppen **von jungen Arbeitern**
große Mengen **neuer Platten**	*or* große Mengen **von neuen Platten**
eine Reihe **ernsthafter Probleme**	*or* eine Reihe **von ernsthaften Problemen**
die wachsende Anzahl **Ausreisewilliger**	*or* die wachsende Anzahl **von Ausreisewilligen**

(b) If these words are followed by a single noun

Normal usage is a phrase with *von*, although simple apposition is also possible (cf. 2.7.1):

eine Art **(von) Museum**	eine große Menge **(von) Schallplatten**
eine Anzahl **(von) Touristen**	

2.7.4 Usage with nouns of number

i.e.: *das Dutzend, das Hundert, das Tausend, die Million, die Milliarde.* If these are used in the plural without a preceding numeral, they are followed by a phrase with *von*:

Dutzende **von Anfragen**	Tausende **von Briten**	Millionen **von Menschen**

If the following noun has an adjective with it, they are followed by a phrase with *von*, or by a phrase in the genitive case, or by a phrase in apposition.

Tausende/tausende **von jungen Arbeitern** *or* Tausende/tausende **junger Arbeiter** *or* Tausende/tausende **junge Arbeiter**

NB: In such contexts, *Dutzend, Hundert* and *Tausend* can be spelled with an initial capital **or** small letter, see 9.1.5.

If they are used in the singular **or** the plural with a numeral, the following noun is usually in apposition, less commonly in the genitive:

zwei Millionen **hungernde(r) Menschen**	*two million starving people*
ein Dutzend **Eier**	*a dozen eggs*
Allein im Bahnhof kam es im Februar zu mehr als einem Dutzend **Taschendiebstählen** (*MM*)	*In the station alone there were more than a dozen pickpocket thefts in February this year*

2.7.5 Usage in contexts where the noun of measurement is in the dative case

Here usage is particularly uncertain and variable. The following alternatives are current:

(a) with nouns of measurement in -*er*

e.g.: *Zentner* 'hundredweight', *Liter*, *Meter*, etc. The dative plural ending -*n* may be attached to these rather than to the following noun:

> mit zwei Zentner**n** Äpfel *or* mit zwei Zentner Äpfel**n**

(b) If the following noun is plural, it may be in the nominative

i.e. it may lack the usual -*n* of the dative plural:

> mit einem Haufen **Butterbrote(n)**   *with a pile of sandwiches*
> mit einem Dutzend **Kühe(n)**   *with a dozen cows*
> mit einem Dutzend **saure(n) Äpfel(n)**   *with a dozen sour apples*

However, the dative should be used if the case is not otherwise clear from the measurement noun or its articles, adjectives, etc.:

> von drei Kilo **Äpfeln**   *of three kilos of apples*
> mit zwei Tüten **Nüssen**   *with two bags of nuts*

(c) An adjective preceding the second noun can have the 'weak' adjective ending -*en* or the expected 'strong' ending -*em*:

> von einem Pfund **gekochten** Schinken   *of a pound of cooked ham*
> von einem Pfund **gekochtem** Schinken

2.7.6 Usage in contexts where the noun of measurement is in the genitive case

In such contexts a phrase with *von* is <u>always</u> used, e.g. *der Preis **von einem Pfund** gekochtem/gekochten Schinken* to avoid a stilted construction like *der Preis **eines Pfundes** gekochten Schinkens*.

3

Personal pronouns

PRONOUNS **are a limited ('closed') set of small words which can stand in place of** NOUNS **or** NOUN PHRASES.

In particular they stand for nouns or noun phrases which have already been mentioned or which are so well known to the speaker and the listener that they do not need to be repeated in full. Pronouns are used in the same grammatical contexts as nouns or noun phrases and thus, in German, they can also change their form to indicate the same grammatical categories as nouns, i.e. CASE, PLURAL and GENDER.

There are a number of different classes of pronouns, most of which are treated in Chapter 5. Here we explain the forms and uses of the personal pronouns, which refer to:

- the speaker(s) (the FIRST PERSON)
- the person(s) addressed (the SECOND PERSON)
- other person(s) or thing(s) mentioned (the THIRD PERSON)

In particular, this chapter deals with

- the forms of the **personal pronouns** (section 3.1)
- **reflexive** and **reciprocal** pronouns (section 3.2)
- the use of the **second person pronouns** *du*, *ihr* and *Sie* (section 3.3)
- the uses of the **third person pronouns** (sections 3.4–3.5)
- special uses of the **pronoun** *es* (section 3.6)

3.1 The forms of the personal pronouns

The personal pronouns have distinct forms to indicate PLURAL, CASE and, in the third person, GENDER. These forms are given in Table 3.1.

TABLE 3.1 *Forms of the personal pronoun*

	Person		Nominative		Accusative	Genitive	Dative
Singular	1st		ich	*I*	mich	meiner	mir
	2nd		du	*you*	dich	deiner	dir
	3rd	masculine	er	*he/it*	ihn	seiner	ihm
		feminine	sie	*she/it*	sie	ihrer	ihr
		neuter	es	*it*	es	seiner	ihm
Plural	1st		wir	*we*	uns	unser	uns
	2nd	familiar	ihr	*you*	euch	euer	euch
		polite (sg/pl)	Sie	*you*	Sie	Ihrer	Ihnen
	3rd		sie	*they*	sie	ihrer	ihnen

3.1.1 The declension of the personal pronouns

Some notes on the forms of the personal pronouns given in Table 3.1

(a) In everyday speech, personal pronouns are reduced and weakly stressed

'ch soll's 'm geben	*for:*	Ich soll **es ihm** geben
Jetzt kannste'n sehen	*for:*	Jetzt kannst **du ihn** sehen

These reductions are seldom used in written German, with the exception of *'s* for *es*, which is quite common in written dialogue and poetry.

(b) In rapid colloquial speech, the subject pronouns *ich*, *du* and *es* are often omitted entirely

Such omissions are never found in written German, except to represent colloquial speech.

(Ich) Weiß es nicht   Kannst (du) morgen kommen?   (Es) Scheint zu klappen

(c) In South Germany *mir* is commonly heard for *wir*

This usage, although widespread, is considered substandard.

Mir gehen jetzt ins Kino   *for:*   **Wir** gehen jetzt ins Kino

3.1.2 The genitive of the personal pronouns

(a) The genitive forms of the personal pronouns are only used in formal registers

They practically never occur in everyday speech, but only in writing:

mittels einer Passbildaufnahme **seiner** selbst (*Grass*)	*by means of a passport photograph of himself*
Ist die Politik erst einmal auf die Straße verlegt, dann wird sich die Straße **ihrer** annehmen (*OH*)	*If politics is moved onto the streets, the streets will take it over*

Even in writing, they sound rather stilted and awkward, and their use is avoided in a number of ways:

(i) With verbs, an alternative construction or a different verb can be used (for further information, see 18.5):

Erinnern Sie sich **an mich** (*rarely:* meiner)
Er braucht **mich** nicht (*rarely:* Er bedarf meiner nicht).

(ii) After most prepositions the dative case is used in speech and is now acceptable in writing:

wegen **uns**, trotz **ihnen**, statt **ihm** (*or:* an seiner Stelle)

To refer to things, the adverbs *stattdessen*, *trotzdem*, *währenddessen* and *deswegen* are used rather than the preposition with a pronoun.

(iii) After the prepositions which have alternative constructions with *von* (see 20.4.2b) the prepositional adverb *davon* (see 3.5) is used rather than a pronoun in the genitive, e.g.: *innerhalb davon, unweit davon.* Alternatively, the prepositions may be used on their own, as adverbs: *außerhalb* 'outside (it)', *jenseits* 'on the other side (of it)'.

(iv) In other contexts, *von* is used (see 2.4.1c):

> sechs **von ihnen**, drei **von euch**, ein Freund **von mir**

(b) The genitive personal pronouns usually only refer to persons or animals

> Ich bedarf **seiner** nicht   *I don't need him*

The demonstratives *dessen* or *deren* are used to refer to things:

> Ich bedarf **dessen** nicht   *I don't need it*

Nevertheless, this usage is not absolutely fixed, and personal pronouns are sometimes used to refer to things:

> Er lässt seinen Autoschlüssel im Küchenschrank, so dass andere Familienmitglieder sich **seiner** bedienen können (*MM*)
>
> *He leaves his car key in the kitchen cupboard so that other members of the family can use it*

(c) Special forms of the genitive pronouns (with -(e)t-) are used with the prepositions *wegen, um ... willen* and *-halben*

(see also 20.4). They are compounded with the preposition as illustrated:

> **meinet**wegen, **deinet**wegen, um **ihret**willen, um **unsert**willen, **seinet**halben

(d) The genitive forms *mein, dein* and *sein* (for *meiner, deiner, seiner*) are archaic

They are occasionally still used for stylistic effect:

> Man gedachte **sein** (*for. seiner*) nicht mehr

3.2 Reflexive and reciprocal pronouns

3.2.1 Forms of the reflexive pronoun

The **reflexive pronoun** is a personal pronoun which refers back to the subject of the sentence or clause, e.g. *Ich wasche **mich*** 'I wash myself', *Sie wäscht **sich*** 'She washes herself'. In German it has a special form *sich* which is used for the third person (singular and plural) and for the 'polite' second person, in the accusative and dative cases. In the first and second persons, the personal pronouns given in Table 3.1 are used as reflexive pronouns.

The German reflexive pronoun is used much more widely than English forms in *-self*, in particular with certain verbs which are occur exclusively or predominantly with a reflexive pronoun – the so-called **reflexive verbs** (see 18.3.6 and 18.4.3). Table 3.2 shows the forms of the reflexive pronoun in the accusative and dative cases, as used in the present tense and imperative of the reflexive verbs *sich setzen* 'sit down' and *sich (das) einbilden* 'imagine (that)'.

TABLE 3.2 *Forms of the reflexive pronoun*

	Accusative		Dative	
ich setze	mich	ich bilde	mir	das ein
du setzt	dich	du bildest	dir	das ein
er/sie/es setzt	sich	er/sie/es bildet	sich	das ein
wir setzen	uns	wir bilden	uns	das ein
ihr setzt	euch	ihr bildet	euch	das ein
Sie setzen	sich	Sie bilden	sich	das ein
sie setzen	sich	sie bilden	sich	das ein
setz	dich!	bilde	dir	das ein!
setzt	euch!	bildet	euch	das ein!
setzen Sie	sich!	bilden Sie	sich	das ein!

3.2.2 The genitive pronoun is sometimes used reflexively in formal written German

It mainly occurs in conjunction with certain adjectives (see 6.5.3). To avoid ambiguity, it always occurs with *selbst*:

Er ist **seiner selbst** sicher	*He is sure of himself*
Sie war **ihrer selbst** nicht mehr mächtig	*She had lost control of herself*

3.2.3 The reflexive pronoun is used after a preposition to refer back to the subject of the sentence

Er hatte kein Geld bei **sich**	*He had no money on him*
Sie schlossen die Tür hinter **sich**	*They closed the door behind them*

3.2.4 Usage in infinitive constructions without *zu*

It is not always clear in these constructions who the reflexive pronoun refers to. Normal usage is as follows:

(a) A reflexive pronoun is normally taken as referring back to the OBJECT of the finite verb

Er hörte seinen Freund **sich** tadeln	*He heard his friend blaming himself*
Er ließ den Gefangenen **sich** ausziehen	*He made the prisoner get undressed*

(b) A non-reflexive pronoun refers back to the SUBJECT of the finite verb

Er hörte seinen Freund **ihn** tadeln	*He heard his friend blaming him*
Er ließ den Gefangenen **ihn** ausziehen	*He made the prisoner undress him*

(c) A reflexive pronoun after a preposition refers back to the SUBJECT of the finite verb

Peter sah eine dunkle Gestalt **vor sich** auftauchen	*Peter saw a dark shape appear in front of him*
Eva ließ mich **bei sich** wohnen	*Eva let me live at her place*

3.2.5 In infinitive clauses with *zu*, the choice of pronoun depends on who is understood to be the subject of the infinitive

(see also 13.2.4b):

Karl versprach Peter, **sich** zu entschuldigen	(Karl is to apologise)
Karl versprach Peter, **ihn** zu entschuldigen	(Karl is excusing Peter)
Karl bat Peter, **sich** zu entschuldigen	(Peter should apologise)
Karl bat Peter, **ihn** zu entschuldigen	(Peter is asked to excuse Karl)

3.2.6 *selbst* or *selber* is used together with a pronoun as the equivalent of emphatic 'myself', 'yourself', etc.

These are always stressed:

Ich habe **selbst/selber** mit dem Minister darüber gesprochen	*I spoke to the minister about it myself*
Er hat **selbst/selber** den Brief gelesen	*He's read the letter himself*

NB: Unstressed *selbst* has the meaning 'even' and always precedes the pronoun (or noun) which it qualifies, e.g.: *Selbst er hat den Brief gelesen.*

3.2.7 Reciprocal pronouns

These are the equivalent of English 'each other'. For these, German uses either the reflexive pronoun or *einander*. The latter is less common in speech than writing, but it is the only possible alternative after prepositions, when it is written together with the preposition (*durcheinander, miteinander*, etc.):

Sie sahen **sich** (*or* **einander**) oft	*They often saw each other*
Wir gehen **uns** (*or* **einander**) aus dem Wege	*We avoid each other*
Wir verlassen **uns** aufeinander	*We rely on each other*
Sie sprachen **voneinander**	*They were talking about each other*
NB: Sie sprachen von **sich**	*They were talking about themselves*

If the reflexive pronoun could be ambiguous, *selbst* can be added to confirm that the sense is reflexive or *gegenseitig* to show that it is reciprocal:

Sie widersprachen **sich selbst**	*They contradicted themselves*
Sie widersprachen **sich gegenseitig** (*or:* Sie widersprachen **einander**)	*They contradicted each other*

3.3 Pronouns of address

For English 'you', German distinguishes between the **familiar** pronouns *du* and *ihr*, and the **polite** pronoun *Sie*.

English lacks this distinction in the second person pronoun, and English-speaking learners of German need to establish which is appropriate in context. Since the late 1960s the use of *du* and *Sie* (commonly referred to as *duzen* and *siezen*) has shifted with changing social attitudes. The use of *du* has become more widespread, particularly among younger people, and Germans can nowadays sometimes feel insecure about which one to use in unfamiliar surroundings. However, consciousness of the need to use the 'right' one is still <u>very</u> strong.

Essentially, *du* signals intimacy, affection and solidarity. People who use *du* to one another are conscious of belonging to the same group or standing together, whereas *Sie* signals a degree of social distance (rather than simply 'politeness'). Thus, in the 'wrong' situation *du* sounds familiar and even offensive (in extreme cases it can be such a gross insult that people have been prosecuted for using it), whilst *Sie* in the 'wrong' situation sounds stand-offish or pompous.

Outside school or university, when talking to fellow pupils or fellow students (where the use of *du* is universal), non-native speakers are advised to let native speakers take the initiative in proposing the use of *du*. It is very important for English speakers to be aware that the use of *du* (and first names) is still <u>much</u> less frequent or acceptable between adults than is the use of first names in the English-speaking countries, especially between colleagues at work and casual acquaintances. It has a quite different social meaning to the use of first names in English and very often indicates lack of respect rather than friendliness.

3.3.1 The uses of *du*, *ihr*, and *Sie*

(a) *du* is used

(i) when speaking to children (up to about the age of fourteen – in schools to the 10th class), to animals and inanimate objects, to oneself and to God.

(ii) between relatives and close friends, between schoolchildren and students, predominantly between blue-collar workmates, between non-commissioned soldiers and between members of clubs, interest groups and (especially left-wing) political parties.

The use of *du* to persons regarded as of lower social status – with the expectation that they should use *Sie* back – is now obsolete. When it resurfaces it is offensive, often deliberately so; it is particularly reprehensible (and racist) when used indiscriminately to non-Europeans.

(b) *ihr* is used to address two or more people whom the speaker would individually address with *du*

As *ihr* is unambiguously plural, whereas *Sie* can be singular or plural, it is sometimes used to address a group, even if one is not *per du* with every single one of them, e.g. (at work):

> Ich wollte **euch** doch alle zum Kaffee einladen

Occasionally, *ihr* may be used to any group to stress plurality, even if all would normally be addressed individually as *Sie*. In this way, *ihr* can sometimes function as a kind of neutral compromise to mask the speaker's uncertainty about whether to use *du* or *Sie*.

(c) *Sie* is used in all other cases

It is used especially to adult strangers and generally in middle-class professions (e.g. to colleagues in an office or a bank).

Usually, the use of *du* is linked to that of first names, that of *Sie* to formal titles (*Herr Engel, Frau Kallmeyer*, etc.). However, the use of *Sie* and first names is not uncommon from adults to older teenagers and in 'trendy' circles (in the latter case possibly in imitation of American usage of first names).

3.3.2 *du* and *ihr* and their forms (*dich, dein, euch*, etc.) are no longer spelled with initial capitals in letter-writing

Ich danke **dir** recht herzlich für deinen Brief

The prescription that capitals should be used was eliminated in the spelling reform. In practice, though, many people still use capitals in private correspondence.

3.3.3 Other forms of address

(a) Titles are often used in shops, restaurants, etc. to address customers

Was wünscht **der Herr**? Was möchten **die Herrschaften** zu Mittag essen?

NB: The use of singular titles of rank with a plural verb (e.g. *Was wünschen gnädige Frau, Herr Major?*) is now archaic or facetious.

(b) In older German the singular pronouns *Er* and *Sie* (spelled with capitals) were used to address people of a lower social standing

This usage is now obsolete (except facetiously), but it persisted into the early twentieth century, especially in Austria.

3.4 Third person pronouns

3.4.1 The third person singular pronouns agree in gender with the noun to which they refer

In this way, *er, sie* or *es* can thus all correspond to English *it* when referring to things.

Dein Bleistift? Ach, **er** lag vorhin auf dem Tisch, aber ich muss **ihn** jetzt verloren haben	*Your pencil? Oh, it was lying on the table a little while ago, but I must have lost it now*
Er hörte meine Meinung und stimmte **ihr** bei	*He heard my opinion and agreed with it*
Darf ich Ihr Buch noch eine Woche behalten? Ich habe **es** noch nicht gelesen	*May I keep your book another week? I haven't read it yet*

NB: Possible conflicts between grammatical and natural gender in the agreement of the pronoun are explained in 1.1.13.

3.4.2 In informal colloquial speech, the demonstrative pronouns *der, die, das* are often used rather than a third person personal pronoun

Der kommt wohl nicht mehr	*for:*	**Er** kommt wohl nicht mehr
Ich hätt' **die** nicht wieder erkannt	*for:*	Ich hätte **sie** nicht wieder erkannt

Although common, this usage is considered substandard, and even in speech it is avoided (and considered rude) if the person referred to is present. It is usually avoided in written German, especially to refer to people, but it may occur if there is a possible ambiguity or a need for emphasis:

Sie hatte die Fernsehanstalten massiv unter Druck gesetzt, als **die** sich in Gibraltar umtaten (*Zeit*)	*She had put massive pressure on the television companies when they were nosing around in Gibraltar*

3.4.3 Third person pronouns are used in comparative clauses with *wie*

This makes it absolutely clear what is being compared:

Das waren Reichtümer, wie **sie** Fürsten nicht besaßen (*Süßkind*)	*These were riches such as princes did not possess*
Ein Kuchen, wie **ihn** deine Mutter backt, ist was Besonderes	*A cake like your mother makes is something special*

3.5 Third person pronoun or prepositional adverb?

The PREPOSITIONAL ADVERB (sometimes called the 'pronominal adverb') is formed by prefixing *da(r)-* to a PREPOSITION, e.g. *damit, daran, darüber*.

3.5.1 The prepositional adverb is often used rather than a preposition followed by a third person pronoun

The general rule is that the personal pronoun is used when referring to people (e.g. *Ich spiele **mit ihr**,* i.e. *mit meiner Schwester*) whereas the prepositional adverb is used when referring to things (e.g. *Ich spiele **damit**,* i.e. *mit der Puppe*). There are variations, however, and modern usage is broadly as follows.

(a) The pronoun *es* is not normally used after prepositions

Here the prepositional adverb is the norm, although occasional exceptions may be encountered.

Da steht mein neues Auto. Ich habe lange **darauf** (NOT: auf es) warten müssen	*There's my new car. I had to wait a long time for it*

(b) Preposition plus personal pronoun is always used to refer to individual persons

(but **not** groups of people, see 3.5.1d):

Du darfst nicht **mit ihr** spielen	*You mustn't play with her*
Ich kann mich nicht **an ihn** erinnern	*I can't remember him*

(c) When reference is to a specific thing (or things), either preposition plus pronoun or the prepositional adverb may be used

Ich habe diese Geschirrspülmaschine seit drei Wochen und bin sehr zufrieden **damit/mit ihr**	*I've had this dishwasher for three weeks and am very satisfied with it*

In practice, the prepositional adverb is more frequent.

(d) The prepositional adverb is used to refer to abstracts and to groups of people

Wie findest du den Vorschlag? Bist du **damit** einverstanden?	*What do you think of the suggestion? Do you agree with it?*
Ich erwarte zehn Gäste, **darunter** einige sehr alte Bekannte	*I am expecting ten guests, among them some very old acquaintances*

(e) The prepositional adverb is always used to refer to whole sentences

Ihr Mann hat eine neue Stelle gekriegt. **Darüber** freut sie sich sehr	*Her husband has got a new job. She's very pleased about it*

(f) If motion is involved, separable prefixes with *hin-* or *her-* are used rather than the prepositional adverb

(see 7.2.4):

Wir fanden eine Hütte und gingen **hinein**	*We found a hut and went into it*
Sie kam an einen langen Gang und eilte **hindurch**	*She came to a long passage and hurried through it*

3.5.2 Four common prepositions do not form a prepositional adverb

i.e.: *außer, gegenüber, ohne, seit*

These are used with pronouns with reference to people *or* things:

Außer ihm ist keiner gekommen	*Nobody came apart from him*
Vor uns ist das Rathaus, und ihm **gegenüber** liegt der Dom	*In front of us is the town hall and opposite it is the cathedral*
Ohne es wäre unser Erfolg nicht möglich gewesen	*Without it our success wouldn't have been possible*

With reference to things, the pronoun is usually omitted after *gegenüber* and *ohne*, e.g.: *(ihm) gegenüber liegt der Dom; ohne (es) wäre es nicht möglich gewesen*, and *außer* and *seit* are not used with a pronoun, the adverbs *außerdem* 'besides (that)' and *seither* 'since (then)' being used instead.

NB: The prepositions which govern the genitive do not form prepositional adverbs. For the use of pronouns with them, see 3.1.2.

3.5.3 Further notes on the use of the prepositional adverb

(a) In colloquial speech the prepositional adverb is often split

Da weiß ich nichts **von**   **Da** kann ich nichts **mit** anfangen

This usage was originally typical of north Germany, but it has recently become more widespread.

(b) When the prepositional adverb replaces preposition plus pronoun, the second syllable is usually stressed

da`durch, da`mit, dar`an

In spoken German the first syllable may be reduced, e.g.: *dran, drauf, drin, drunter*. However, if the prepositional adverb replaces a preposition plus a demonstrative, (i.e. = 'with **that**', 'in **that**', etc., cf. 5.1.1i), then the **first** syllable is stressed, e.g.: `dadurch, `damit, `daran.

(c) The prepositional adverb is often used to anticipate a following *dass*-clause or infinitive clause

Ich verlasse mich **darauf**, dass sie rechtzeitig kommt

Details are given in 6.6.2, 18.6.14 and 19.2.5b.

3.6 Special uses of the pronoun es

The pronoun *es* has an extended range of uses beyond simply referring back to a neuter noun. In many constructions it functions as a grammatical particle (sometimes called a 'clitic').

es cannot be stressed. If emphasis is needed *es* is replaced by *das* for most of the uses given in this section, e.g.:

Sind **das** Ihre Handschuhe?   **Das** bist du.   Ich mache **das** schon.

3.6.1 *es* can refer to elements other than neuter nouns

(a) *es* can refer to a whole phrase, sentence or situation

Willst du die Brötchen holen? Angela macht **es** schon	*Will you get the rolls? Angela is already doing it*
Ich weiß, dass sie gestorben ist, aber Uwe weiß **es** noch nicht	*I know that she is dead, but Uwe doesn't know it yet*

(b) *es* can refer back to the predicate complement of *sein* or *werden*

In English nothing equivalent or a different equivalent is required:

Er soll zuverlässig sein, und ich bin sicher, dass er **es** ist	*He is said to be reliable and I am sure he is*
Ist Jürgen ein guter Schwimmer? Ja, er ist **es**	*Is Jürgen a good swimmer? Yes, he is (one)*
Sein Vater ist Arzt, und er wird **es** auch	*His father is a doctor and he's going to be one, too*

3.6.2 Impersonal and other uses of *es* as the subject of a verb

(a) *es* is used as a formal subject in many impersonal constructions

(i) With all kinds of impersonal verbs or verbs used in impersonal constructions:

es regnet   **es** klingelt   **es** fehlt mir an Geld   **es** bedarf noch einiger Mühe

Details on the use of *es* as an impersonal subject are given in 18.2.4.

(ii) As an indefinite subject, communicating the idea of a vague, impersonal agent:

Ringsum war alles still, dann schrie **es**	*Round about everything was quiet, then there was a cry*
Ihn trieb **es** in die schottischen Hochlande (*Zeit*)	*He felt a desire to go the Highlands of Scotland*

(iii) In impersonal reflexive constructions, often with the force of a passive, see 15.4.3b:

Es schreibt sich so leicht mit diesem Filzstift	*It's so easy to write with this felt-tip pen*

(iv) In impersonal passive constructions and in passive constructions with verbs which do not govern the accusative (see 15.1.3–4):

Es wurde in dieser Zeit viel gearbeitet	*A lot of work was done at this time*
Es wurde im Nebenzimmer geredet	*There was talking in the next room*
Es kann ihm doch nicht geholfen werden	*He can't be helped, though*

es is always omitted in this construction if it is not in first position in a main clause, e.g.: *In dieser Zeit wurde viel gearbeitet. Wir wissen doch, dass in dieser Zeit viel gearbeitet wurde*

(b) *es* **can be used as an indeterminate subject with the verbs** *sein* **and** *werden* **followed by a noun or an adjective**

(i) This corresponds to the English use of *it*:

Es ist der Briefträger, ein Polizist	*It's the postman, a policeman*
Es wurde spät	*It got late*
Es ist Mittag	*It's midday*
Es ist Sonntag heute	*It's Sunday to-day*

es can be omitted in non-initial position in time phrases, e.g.: *Jetzt ist (es) Mittag. Er weiß, dass (es) heute Sonntag ist.*

ii) *es* can be used with a plural verb, corresponding to English 'they':

Es sind Ausländer	*They're foreigners*
Sind **es** Ihre Handschuhe?	*Are they your gloves?*
Was sind **es**?	*What are they?*

(iii) In this indeterminate function, *es* can refer back to a non-neuter or plural noun, as an alternative to the expected masculine, feminine or plural pronoun:

Seine Mutter lebt noch. **Es/Sie** ist eine alte Frau	*His mother is still alive. She's an old woman*
Siehst du die Kinder dort? **Es/Sie** sind meine	*Do you see the children there? They're mine*

(c) *es* **with** *sein* **and a personal pronoun (= English 'It's me', etc.)**

(i) The German construction differs from the English one, with *es* following the verb:

Du bist **es**. Ich bin **es**	*It's you. It's me*
Seid ihr **es** gewesen?	*Was it you?*
Sie werden **es** wohl sein	*It will probably be them*

(ii) 'Cleft sentence' constructions with relative clauses (like English 'It was you who rang the bell') are based on this construction in German:

Er war **es**, der es mir sagte	*It was him who told me*
Du warst **es** also, der geklingelt hat	*So it was you who rang the bell*

Other cleft sentence constructions, especially those corresponding to the English type 'It was this morning that I saw her', are unusual in German (see 21.2.3a).

(d) *es* **is often used as a 'dummy subject' in initial position in order to permit the 'real' subject to occur later in the sentence**

(i) This construction is particularly frequent if the 'real' subject is a noun phrase with an indefinite article or an indefinite quantifier. It gives more emphasis to the 'real' subject, see 21.2.2d. With *sein*, this *es* corresponds to 'there' in 'there is/are', see 18.2.5b:

Es ist ein Brief für Sie da	*There's a letter for you*
Es waren viele Wolken am Himmel	*There were a lot of clouds in the sky*

This *es* is omitted if it is not in first position in a main clause, e.g.: *Viele Wolken waren am Himmel. Ich weiß, dass ein Brief für mich da ist.*

NB: For *es ist/sind* and *es gibt* for English 'there is/are', see 18.2.5.

(ii) *es* may be used in this construction with any verb in German. The verb agrees with the 'real' subject, not with the *es*:

Es saß eine alte Frau am Fenster	*There was an old woman sitting at the window*
Es hatte sich auch ihr Verhältnis zu den Nachbarn verändert	*Their relationship to their neighbours had changed, too*
Es liegen zwei Briefe für Sie auf dem Schreibtisch	*There are two letters for you lying on the table*

This construction is particularly frequent with verbs of happening:

Es ist gestern ein schwerer Unfall **passiert**	*A serious accident happened yesterday*

In spoken German *da* is a common alternative to *es* in this function: **Da** *hat eine alte Frau am Fenster gesessen.*

(e) *es* **can be used to anticipate a following subordinate or infinitive clause which is the real subject of the verb**

Es freut mich, **dass** du dein Examen bestanden hast	*I am pleased that you have passed your examination*
Es fällt mir ein, **dass** ich ihn schon gesehen haben muss	*It occurs to me that I must already have seen him*
Es war mir nicht möglich, früher **zu** kommen	*It wasn't possible for me to come earlier*
Es liegt mir fern, Schwierigkeiten **zu** machen	*The last thing I want is to make difficulties*

If the clause precedes the verb there is no need for the *es*, e.g.: *Dass du dein Examen bestanden hast, freut mich.*

This 'anticipatory' *es* is often omitted if it is not in first position in a main clause:

Dann fiel (**es**) auf, **dass** er kein weißes Hemd trug	*Then it was noticed that he wasn't wearing a white shirt*
Ihm steht (**es**) nicht zu, ein Urteil **zu** fällen	*It's not up to him to pass judgement*

Usage is variable as to when *es* is omitted, and there are no hard and fast rules. Nevertheless, the following general tendencies reflect current usage:

(i) The omission of *es* is very common with the following verbs:

auffallen	sich erweisen	gelten *to be valid*	hinzukommen
aufgehen	sich ergeben aus	sich herausstellen	vorschweben
dazukommen	feststehen	hervorgehen	sich zeigen
einfallen	folgen aus		

(ii) With many verbs, especially those expressing feelings and emotions, *es* can be omitted before a following *dass*-clause if the main clause begins with a pronoun:

Ihn interessiert (**es**) nur, dass ihr Vater viel Geld hat	*The only thing that interests him is that her father's got a lot of money*
Damit hängt (**es**) natürlich zusammen, dass er im Gefängnis sitzt	*Of course, that's connected with the fact that he's in prison*

(iii) *es* can be omitted with the verb *sein* if the main clause begins with the noun or adjective complement of *sein*:

Wichtig ist (**es**), dass er es weiß	*It's important for him to know it*
Wichtig ist (**es**), diesen Satz richtig zu verstehen	*It is important to understand this sentence correctly*
Ein Glück ist (**es**), dass du kommst	*It's fortunate you're coming*

With *klar, leicht, möglich, schwer* and *wichtig*, *es* can be omitted in these constructions if the main clause begins with a pronoun:

Ihm war (**es**) völlig klar, dass er jetzt springen musste	*It was quite clear to him that he had to jump now*

NB: *es* is not omitted before *wenn*-clauses: *Mir ist es recht, wenn sie jetzt kommt.*

3.6.3 es as the object of a verb

(a) An accusative *es* is often used to anticipate a following infinitive or *dass*-clause which is the object of the verb

Ich konnte **es** kaum ertragen, ihn so leiden zu sehen	*I could hardly endure to see him suffer like that*
Ich habe **es** erlebt, dass Riemann die beste Rede gehalten hat	*I have known Riemann to give the best speech*

(i) The use of this 'anticipatory' *es* is variable, and there are no hard and fast rules as to when it is used and when not. It is particularly common with the following verbs:

ablehnen	erleben	leiden	verantworten
angewöhnen	ermöglichen	leisten	verdienen
aufgeben	ertragen	leugnen	vergessen
aushalten	fertig bringen	lieben	vermeiden
bedauern	genießen	merken	versäumen
begrüßen	gönnen	mögen	vertragen
bemerken	halten für	schaffen	verzeihen
bereuen	hassen	schätzen	wagen
betrachten als	hindern	übel nehmen	zulassen
dulden	hinnehmen	überlassen	
erfahren	lassen	unterlassen	

The phrases *nicht erwarten können* and *nicht wahrhaben wollen* are also usually found with an anticipatory *es*, as is *finden* followed by an adjective, e.g.: *Ich finde es schön, dass du da bist.*

(ii) Verbs of saying, thinking and knowing, e.g.: *ahnen, denken, erzählen, fühlen, glauben, hören, sagen, wissen* are also often used with an anticipatory *es* in conjunction with certain adverbs and particles, in particular *bereits, deutlich, doch, genug, ja, oft* and *schon*, or when there is an appeal to the listener's prior knowledge, e.g.:

Ich habe (es) ihm deutlich gesagt, dass er schreiben muss	*I've told him clearly enough that he's got to write*
Ich ahnte (es) schon, dass sie schwanger ist	*I already suspected she was pregnant*
Ich weiß (es) ja selber, dass die Ampel rot war	*I know myself that the lights were red*

(b) *es* corresponds to English 'so' as the object of a few verbs, especially *sagen* 'say' and *tun* 'do'

Er hat **es** gesagt	*He said so*
Warum hast du **es** getan?	*Why did you do so?*

es can also be used with *glauben* and *hoffen*, but it is not essential:

Kommt sie? – Ich glaube/hoffe (es)	*Is she coming? – I think/hope so*

(c) *es* is used as an object in a number of idiomatic verbal phrases

A selection of the most frequent:

es auf etwas absehen	*to be after sth.*
es auf etwas ankommen lassen	*to take a chance on sth.*
es jdm. antun	*to appeal to sb.*
sie hat es ihm angetan	*he fancies her*
es mit jdm./etwas aufnehmen können	*to be a match for sb./sth.*
es bei etwas belassen	*to leave it at sth.*
es weit bringen	*to go far*
es zu etwas bringen	*to attain sth. (esp. a position)*
er hat es zum Oberst gebracht	*he got to be a colonel*
es an etwas fehlen lassen	*to be lacking in sth.*
es eilig haben	*to be in a hurry*
es gut/schlecht haben	*to be (un)fortunate*
es in sich haben	*to be a tough nut to crack*
es sich leicht/schwer machen	*to make it easy/difficult for oneself*

es gut mit jdm. meinen	*to mean well with sb.*
es mit etwas genau nehmen	*to be punctilious with sth.*
es mit jdm. zu tun haben	*to have to deal with sb.*
es sich mit jdm. verdorben haben	*to have fallen out with sb.*
es mit etwas (dat.) versuchen	*to try (one's hand at) sth.*

3.6.4 *es* is used with a few adjectives in constructions with the verb(s) *sein* and/or *werden*

in particular with adjectives which govern the genitive of nouns (see 6.5.3), e.g.: *Ich bin es nun überdrüssig*. The following adjectives occur in this construction:

los   müde   satt   teilhaftig   überdrüssig   wert   würdig   zufrieden

Also:

Ich bin **es** gewohnt	*I am used to it*
Ich wurde **es** gewahr (lit.)	*I became aware of it*

NB: When *gewohnt sein* and *wert sein* are used with a following *dass*-clause, the *es* may optionally be used to anticipate the subordinate clause: *Ich bin (es) nicht mehr gewohnt, am frühen Morgen aufzustehen.*

4

The articles

German, like English, has a definite and an indefinite article.

The ARTICLES belong to a closed set of small words known as DETERMINERS. These are used with NOUNS to link them to a particular context or situation. Besides the articles, the determiners include all those words, like the DEMONSTRATIVES (*dieser, jener*, etc.), the POSSESSIVES (*mein, sein*, etc.) and INDEFINITES (*einige, etliche*, etc.), which are used to determine nouns and typically have first position in a NOUN PHRASE, before any adjectives, as the chart below shows.

Determiner	Adjective/adjectival phrase	Noun
der	runde	Tisch
ein	schnelles	Auto
eine	sehr langweilige	Stunde
das	in der bayrischen Hauptstadt gebraute	Bier

Only the form and use of the articles are explained in this chapter; the other determiners are dealt with in chapter 5.

The definite and indefinite articles change their form ('decline') to indicate the grammatical categories of the nouns they are used with, i.e. CASE, PLURAL and GENDER. In practice the forms of the article are the main way these categories of the noun are shown in German, and mastering them is an essential stage in being able to use German competently.

In most instances (85%) German and English agree on whether the definite, indefinite or no ('zero') article is used with a noun in a particular context. However, as the articles are very frequent words, the instances where the two languages do not correspond are quite significant, in particular where German uses a definite article when English has none.

This chapter deals with the **forms** and **uses** of the **articles** as follows:

- The **declension** of the definite and indefinite articles (section 4.1)
- The use of the articles with **abstract nouns**, **generalisations** and **names** (sections 4.2–4.4)
- The use of the articles in **time expressions** (section 4.5)
- The use of the definite article to indicate **possession** (section 4.6)
- Other contexts where **German and English differ** in the use of the articles (sections 4.7–4.8)
- The use of the articles with **prepositions** (section 4.9)

4.1 The declension of the articles

4.1.1 The forms of the DEFINITE ARTICLE

The declension of the definite article *der/die/das* is given in Table 4.1, with further information on these forms given in the remainder of this section.

TABLE 4.1 *Declension of the definite article*

	Masculine	Feminine	Neuter	Plural
Nominative	der	die	das	die
Accusative	den	die	das	die
Genitive	des	der	des	der
Dative	dem	der	dem	den

(a) In spoken German the definite article is relatively unstressed and reduced forms are usual

der: [dɐ]	*die*: [dɪ]	*das*: [d(ə)s] or [s]
den: [d(ə)n] or [n]	*dem*: [d(ə)m] or [m]	*des*: [d(ə)s]

These reductions are rarely reflected in writing, but they are the norm in unaffected everyday speech, since the full forms, e.g. [deːm], have the force of a demonstrative (i.e. = 'this' or 'that', see 5.1.1). Compare:

Ich habe **'n** Tisch gekauft	*I bought the table*
Ich habe **den** [deːn] Tisch gekauft	*I bought that table*

(b) The definite article cannot be omitted in pairs of words if a different gender or number is involved

In English we can say 'the house and garden(s)' or 'the son(s) and daughter(s)', with the definite article being understood to refer to the second noun as well. This is only possible in German if the two nouns have the same gender or number. In other contexts the second article with its different form **must** be included:

das Haus und **der** Garten/**die** Gärten   **der** Sohn und **die** Tochter/**die** Töchter

On the other hand, *die Söhne und Töchter* is correct, since both nouns are plural and would have the same article.

NB: This rule naturally applies to all the other determiners, and to adjectives used with nouns, e.g.: **sein** *Sohn und* **seine** *Töchter* but **seine** *Söhne und Töchter*; **guter** *Wein und* **gutes** *Bier* but **alte** *Männer und Frauen*.

(c) Contracted forms of the definite article are used with some prepositions

We can distinguish:

(i) Contractions which are usual in speech and writing, i.e.:

ans = an + das	**am** = an + dem	**beim** = bei + dem	**ins** = in + das
im = in + dem	**vom** = von + dem	**zum** = zu + dem	**zur** = zu + der

With these the uncontracted forms are only used if the article is relatively stressed. This often depends on style and sentence rhythm, although many Germans consider the uncontracted forms to be 'better style' in formal writing. Uncontracted forms are also particularly frequent to refer back to something recently mentioned in order to make it clear that it is the one meant. Note the difference between:

> Er ging **zu der** Hütte (i.e. the one we were just talking about)
> Er ging **zur** Hütte (i.e. the one we all know about).

Where the force of *der* is demonstrative (i.e. = 'that', see 5.1.1), only the uncontracted form is possible:

> Einer der Affen war besonders lebhaft.   *One of the monkeys was particularly*
>   Klaus wollte unbedingt eine Aufnahme   *active. Klaus really wanted to take*
>   **von dem** Affen machen   *a picture of that monkey*

Similarly, where the noun is particularised, e.g. by a following relative clause, the uncontracted form is usual:

> **an dem** Nachmittag, an dem sie anrief   *on the afternoon when she called*
> Er geht **zu der** Schule, wo sein Vater früher war   *He goes to the school where his*
>   *father used to be*

On the other hand, only the contracted forms are used in set phrases and expressions, e.g.:

am Dienstag	**am** 10. Mai	**am** einfachsten
im Frühling	**im** Freien	**im** Gang
zum Frühstück	**zur** Zeit	**im** Vertrauen
Ich nahm ihn **beim** Wort	Sie war **beim** Kochen	

Compare:

> **Am** Dienstag kam er spät zur Arbeit   *On Tuesday he came to work late*
> **An dem** Dienstag kam er spät zur Arbeit   *That Tuesday he came to work late*

NB: With some phrases, the contraction has to be understood as including the indefinite article, e.g *Das Haus liegt* **am** *Hang* 'The house is situated on a slope'.

(ii) Contractions which are common in speech and sometimes used in writing. These are:

aufs = auf + das	**durchs** = durch + das	**fürs** = für + das
übers = über + das	**ums** = um + das	**unters** = unter + das

Written German prefers the uncontracted forms of these, using the contracted ones chiefly only in set phrases, e.g.:

aufs Land fahren	**übers** Herz bringen
fürs Leben gern	**ums** Leben kommen

(iii) Contractions which are usual in spoken German, but only very occasionally found in writing, usually in set phrases. These are:

außerm	hinterm	hintern	hinters	überm
übern	unterm	untern	vorm	vors

(iv) Other contractions are regular in everyday colloquial speech but not normally used in writing, e.g.:

an'n	bei'n	durch'n	in'n	mit'm	nach'm	seit'm

4.1.2 The forms of the INDEFINITE ARTICLE

The declension of the indefinite article *ein* and its negative counterpart *kein* is given in Table 4.2, with further information provided in the remainder of this section.

TABLE 4.2 *Declension of the indefinite article* ein *and negative* kein

	Masculine	Feminine	Neuter	Masculine	Feminine	Neuter	Plural
Nominative	ein	eine	ein	kein	keine	kein	keine
Accusative	einen	eine	ein	keinen	keine	kein	keine
Genitive	eines	einer	eines	keines	keiner	keines	keiner
Dative	einem	einer	einem	keinem	keiner	keinem	keinen

(a) The indefinite article has no plural

Indefinite plural nouns are used without an article, as in English:

    Hier gibt es gute Weine   *There are good wines here*

(b) In spoken German the indefinite article is relatively unstressed and reduced forms are frequent

ein· [n]	*eine*: [nə]	*einen*: [nən]
einem: [nəm]	*einer*: [nɐ]	*eines*: [nəs]

These reductions are rare in writing (except to render the flavour of colloquial dialogue) but they are the norm in unaffected speech, where the full forms, e.g. [aɪn], [aɪnən], etc., would be interpreted as the numeral *ein* 'one'. Compare:

    Ich habe **'n** Buch gekauft   *I bought a book*
    Ich habe **ein** [aɪn] Buch gekauft   *I bought **one** book*

(c) The indefinite article *ein* has a negative form *kein*

Unlike *ein*, *kein* has a plural form, and its declension is given in Table 4.2. It is used chiefly where a corresponding positive sentence would have an indefinite article or no article, and it is thus usually the equivalent of English *not ... a, not ... any* or *no*. Further details on its use are given in **5.5.16**:

    Es war ein angenehmer Anblick   Es war **kein** angenehmer Anblick
    Kennst du einen Arzt?   Kennst du **keinen** Arzt?
    Hier gibt es gute Weine   Hier gibt es **keine** guten Weine
    Ich habe Geld   Ich habe **kein** Geld

4.2 The use of articles with abstract nouns

4.2.1 German frequently uses the definite article with abstract nouns where English often has no article

This is particularly the case where the reference is to a specific and definite whole, known and familiar to the speaker and listener, e.g.:

(a) abstract nouns

Er fürchtet **das Alter**	*He is afraid of old age*
Er liebte **die Demokratie** (*K. Mann*)	*He loved democracy*
Wir hängen von **der Industrie** ab	*We depend on industry*
Die Zeit vergeht	*Time passes*
Das Volk lebt **im Elend** (*Spiegel*)	*The people are living in misery*
Die Menschheit braucht nichts nötiger	*Humanity needs nothing more*
als **den Frieden**	*urgently than peace*

(b) infinitives used as nouns

Er hat **das Schwimmen** verlernt	*He has forgotten how to swim*
Das Kaffeetrinken kam im 17.	*Coffee-drinking came to Europe in*
Jahrhundert nach Europa	*the 17th century*

4.2.2 In certain contexts abstract nouns are used with no article

Clear rules are difficult to formulate precisely, but the following generalisations are broadly valid:

(a) No article is used in contexts where the idea is referred to not as a whole, but in a vaguely general, indefinite and partial sense, which comes as a new idea in the context

Typically in such contexts *some* or *any* can often be inserted in the corresponding English sentence without changing its essential meaning:

Zu dieser Aufgabe gehört **Mut**	*This task demands (some) courage*
Es war nicht das erste Mal, dass	*It was not the first time that (some)*
Verrat seinen Lebensweg gekreuzt	*treachery had crossed his path*
hatte (*Hermlin*)	
Unentschlossenheit wäre jetzt	*(Any) indecision now would be fatal*
verhängnisvoll	
Bewegung ist gesund	*(Any) exercise is healthy*

Compare the following sentences:

Unter seinen Anhängern entstand	*(Some) distrust arose among his*
Misstrauen	*followers*
Das Misstrauen wächst unter seinen	*Distrust is growing among his followers*
Anhängern	

In the first sentence 'distrust' is a new concept of a rather vague, general and indefinite nature. In the second it is a specific notion, already known and familiar from the context.

In practice such a partial or indefinite sense is often present when an abstract noun, particularly one denoting a human quality or emotion, is used with an adjective. In such contexts no article is used in German:

Ich verachte **kleinliche Eifersucht**	*I despise (any) petty jealousy*
Im Heer wuchs **neuer Mut**	*In the army new courage was growing*
Er neigt zu **unnötiger Verschwendung**	*He tends to unnecessary extravagance*

(b) In proverbs, sayings and set phrases:

Alter schützt vor **Torheit** nicht	*There's no fool like an old fool*
Not kennt kein Gebot	*Necessity knows no law*
Stolz ist keine Tugend	*Pride is not a virtue*

(c) In a few other contexts

- in general statements, see 4.3.1.
- in pairs of words and enumerations, see 4.8.1.
- in some constructions with the verbs *sein* and *werden*, see 4.8.2.
- in many phrasal verbs, see 4.2.3.

4.2.3 The use of the article with abstract nouns in phrasal verbs

e.g.: *Abschied nehmen, in Druck geben, in Erfahrung bringen*

The use of a definite or no article with these is often a matter of individual idiom, e.g.: *zum Abschluss bringen* but *zu Ende bringen*. However, the following general rules usually apply:

(a) Infinitives used as nouns have a definite article in phrasal verbs with prepositions

ins Rollen kommen, **zum** Kochen bringen

(b) Feminine nouns in phrasal verbs with *zu* have a definite article

zur Kenntnis bringen, **zur** Verfügung stehen

(c) Phrasal verbs with *außer* and *unter*, and most of those with *in* have no article

außer Gefahr sein, jdn. **unter** Druck setzen, jdn. **in** Verlegenheit bringen

NB: Those with *in* followed by an infinitive used as a noun do have an article, see (a) above.

(d) Most phrasal verbs with *gehen*, *halten* and *setzen* have no article with the noun

in Erfüllung gehen, **in** Gang halten, **in** Brand setzen

(e) Abstract nouns used with *haben* have no article

Aufenthalt haben, Angst haben, Durst haben, Geduld haben, Mut haben

(f) Most phrasal verbs consisting of a verb and an object noun with no preposition have no article

Anspruch erheben, Antwort geben, Abschied nehmen, Rücksicht üben, Krieg führen, Not leiden, Zeit sparen

(g) An article is used with phrasal verbs if the noun is qualified by an adjective

This applies even if the phrasal verb normally lacks an article:

jdn. in Gefahr bringen	*lead sb. into danger*
jdn. in (eine) große Gefahr bringen	*lead sb. into great danger*
jdn. in die größte Gefahr bringen	*lead sb. into the greatest danger*

4.2.4 The use of the article with some other groups of nouns is similar to that with abstract nouns

(a) Names of substances

These have a definite article if they are understood as general concepts, but no article if they are used in an indefinite or partial sense:

Die Butter kostete sechs Mark das Pfund	*Butter cost six marks a pound*
Faraday hat **die Elektrizität** erforscht	*Faraday investigated electricity*
Die Bauern bauen hier **Roggen** an	*The farmers grow rye here*
Wir importieren **Kaffee** aus Afrika	*We import coffee from Africa*

NB: (i) The definite article occurs in some set phrases, e.g.: *beim Bier sitzen; Das steht nur auf dem Papier; Man kann nicht von der Luft leben.*
   (ii) Usage is optional in generalisations, see 4.3, e.g.: *(Die) Elektrizität ist eine wichtige Energiequelle.*

(b) Names of meals

A definite article is used if they are referred to as known quantities, but the article is optional if the reference is indefinite or partial:

Das Mittagessen wird um 13 Uhr eingenommen	*Lunch is taken at 1 p.m.*
Wir sollen uns vor **dem Frühstück** treffen	*We are to meet before breakfast*
Ich habe **(das) Mittagessen** bestellt	*I have ordered lunch*
Wann bekommen wir **(das) Frühstück**?	*When are we getting breakfast?*

(c) Names of sicknesses and diseases

These have a definite article when they are referred to in general as known quantities, but there is no article when they are referred to in an indefinite or partial sense, or as a new idea in the context, particularly after *haben*:

Er ist an **der Schwindsucht** gestorben	*He died of consumption*
Sie ist an **den Masern** erkrankt	*She fell ill with measles*
Die Grippe hat Tausende weggerafft	*Influenza carried off thousands*
Ich habe **Kopfschmerzen, Gelbsucht**	*I've got a headache, jaundice*

Singular names of specific illnesses are used with the indefinite article to refer to a bout of that disease. This is in particular the case when the noun is modified by an adjective:

Er ist an **einer Lungenentzündung** gestorben	*He died of (a bout of) pneumonia*
Er hat **einen Schnupfen, eine Erkältung**	*He's got a cold*

(d) Names of languages

These nouns from adjectives (see 6.4.6a) have two forms:

(i) an inflected one, always used with the definite article, which refers to the language in a general sense:

Das Spanische ist **dem Portugiesischen** sehr nahe verwandt	*Spanish is very closely related to Portuguese*
eine Übersetzung aus **dem Russischen** ins **Deutsche**	*a translation from Russian into German*

(ii) an uninflected form, which refers to the language in a specific context. With this, article use is similar to that in English:

das **Deutsch** der Auswanderer	*the German of the emigrants*
Luthers **Deutsch**	*Luther's German*
Sie kann, versteht, lernt **Deutsch**	*She knows, understands, is learning German*
Sie kann **kein Deutsch**	*She doesn't know any German*
eine Zusammenfassung **in Deutsch**	*a summary in German*

4.2.5 A definite article is usual in German with some other nouns which often lack an article in English

(a) historical periods, literary and philosophical movements, religions

der deutsche Expressionismus	*German Expressionism*
Diese Auffassung ist charakteristisch für **den Islam**	*This view is characteristic of Islam*
Marx begreift **den Feudalismus** als notwendige Stufe der historischen Entwicklung (*Knaur*)	*Marx considers feudalism to be a necessary stage in the process of history*

(b) arts and sciences

Ich erwarte von **der Literatur** mehr Anregung als **vom Leben** (*Grass*)	*I expect more stimulus from literature than from life*
Darüber schweigt **die Geschichte**	*History is silent about that*
ein Lehrbuch **der Astronomie**	*a textbook of astronomy*
Sie liebt **die Musik**	*She loves music*

NB: No article is used for school or university subjects, e.g.: *Sie hat eine Zwei in Geschichte aber eine Vier in Mathe. Elke studiert Astronomie in Göttingen.*

(c) institutions, company titles and buildings

Sie geht in **die Schule**	*She goes to school*
Er wurde **ins Parlament** gewählt	*He was elected to parliament*
Die Bundesrepublik gehört **der NATO** an	*The Federal Republic belongs to NATO*
Er arbeitet bei **der BASF**	*He works for BASF*
im Kölner **Dom, das** Ulmer **Rathaus**	*in Cologne cathedral, Ulm town hall*

NB: No article is used with names of buildings with a proper name in apposition, e.g.: *Schloss Sanssouci, Burg Gibichstein, Kloster Beuron.*

4.3 The use of articles in generalisations

4.3.1 Generalisations about people and things can be expressed in different ways

Compare the following possibilities in German and English:

(a) Die Tanne ist ein Nadelbaum   *The fir is a conifer*
(b) Die Tannen sind Nadelbäume   [English equivalent not used]
(c) Eine Tanne ist ein Nadelbaum   *A fir is a conifer*
(d) Tannen sind Nadelbäume   *Firs are conifers*

German tends to use constructions like (a) above, especially in writing, whereas English has a clear preference for sentences like (d), so that the following example illustrates a very common type of equivalence:

Das Auto ist der Fluch der modernen   *Cars are the curse of modern cities*
    Stadt (*Zeit*)

Construction (b), with a definite article and a plural noun, is quite common in German, but it is only used in English with a limited number of nouns (especially nouns of nationality). Compare:

Die Beschwerden vermehren sich   *Complaints are increasing*
Die Steuern waren drückend (*Brecht*)   *Taxes were oppressive*
Die Italiener lieben die Musik   *The Italians love music*

English 'man; in the sense 'human being' is usually found with no article, whilst *der Mensch*, with a definite article, is regular in German in general statements of type (a) above, e.g.:

Der Mensch ist ein seltsames Geschöpf   *Man is a strange animal*

4.3.2 Nouns which have no plural can be used either with the definite article or with no article in general statements

This applies in particular to abstract nouns and names of substances:

(Der) Frieden ist das höchste Gut der   *Peace is man's greatest good*
    Menschen
(Das) Rauchen schadet der Gesundheit   *Smoking is injurious to health*
(Das) Eisen ist ein Metall   *Iron is a metal*

4.4 The use of articles with geographical and other proper names

4.4.1 Usage with geographical and astronomical names

(a) Masculine names of countries
With these, the definite article is usual, but optional:

(der) Libanon   **(der)** Iran   **in/im** Sudan

With masculine names of regions or provinces the use of the definite article is the norm, e.g.: *der Balkan, der Bosporus*.

(b) Feminine and plural names of countries and regions
These are **always** used with a definite article:

die Schweiz	**die** Türkei	**die** Ukraine
die Lausitz	**die** Normandie	**die** Steiermark
die USA	**die** Niederlande	

(c) Neuter names of countries and cities

No article is used with most of these:

> Deutschland Norwegen Spanien Leipzig London Ulm

However, a few neuter names of regions and provinces are normally used with the article:

> **das** Elsass **das** Engadin **das** Ries **das** Wallis *Valais*
> **das** Rheinland **das** Vogtland (and all others in -*land*)

The definite article is always used with neuter nouns from adjectives for German regions. These are frequent in colloquial German: *Jetzt kommen wir **ins** Bayrische; Das Dorf liegt **im Thüringischen**.*

NB: Use of the article is optional with *Tirol*: *in/im Tirol*.

(d) Other geographical and astronomical names have a definite article

This is so even where English has no article:

> **der** Mont Blanc **der** Genfer See **der** Bodensee *Lake Constance*
> **der** Mars **die** Venus **der** Jupiter

(e) The definite article is used to refer to street names

> Ich wohne in **der** Goethestraße
> Wir treffen uns auf **dem** Schlossplatz
> **Der** Alexanderweg ist die zweite Querstraße **zur** Humboldtstraße

However, no article is used in addresses: *Frau Gerlinde Haarmann, Weserstraße 247, 34125 Kassel.*

4.4.2 In standard German there is usually no article with personal names

There are some exceptions to this rule:

(a) In colloquial speech a definite article is frequent with names

> Ich sehe **die** Monika Gestern war ich bei **der** Frau Schmidt

This usage is particularly characteristic of south German speech, but it has been spreading into north Germany in recent years.

(b) To clarify case or gender

(see also **4.7.1**):

> der Vortrag **des** Klaus Müller Das hat Klaus **dem** Wolfgang Pedersen gesagt
> Ich habe eben mit **der** Rupp (i.e. **Frau** Rupp, NOT **Herr** Rupp) gesprochen

(c) To individualise the person concerned more strongly

> **Der** Lehmann hat einen ausgezeichneten Vortrag gehalten
> die Briefe Leopold Mozarts an **das** Nannerl (*Hildesheimer*)

(d) to refer to characters in plays

Er hat in der vorigen Saison **den** Hamlet gespielt

4.4.3 All geographical and proper names are used with a definite article when qualified by an adjective

das heutige Deutschland	**das** kalte Moskau
das viktorianische England	**der** junge Heinrich
das zerstörte Dresden	**der** alte Doktor Schulze

This applies also to saints' names: *der heilige Franziskus* 'Saint Francis'.

4.5 The use of articles in time expressions

4.5.1 Names of months and seasons usually have the definite article

Der April war verregnet	**Der Frühling** war dieses Jahr spät
Wir fahren **im August** nach Italien	**Im Winter** friert der Bach zu

The names of the months have no article after prepositions other than *an, bis zu* and *in*, see 4.5.3, or after *Anfang, Mitte, Ende*:

Es war kalt für April	Ende Februar hat es geschneit
Der Fahrplan gilt von Mai bis Oktober	Er kommt erst Anfang Mai

No article is used with these words after *sein* and *werden*, see **4.8.2c**, e.g.: *Es ist, wird Sommer; Es ist Januar*, or when the name is qualified by *nächsten, letzten, vorigen, vergangenen*: *nächsten Oktober, letzten Herbst*.

4.5.2 The major festivals have no article

Weihnachten	Silvester	Neujahr	Pfingsten	Ostern

Note though: *der Heilige Abend* 'Christmas Eve', *der Karfreitag* 'Good Friday'

4.5.3 All time nouns are used with the definite article after the prepositions *an, bis zu* and *in*

am Mittwoch	am 27. Januar	bis zum Montag
am Tag *by day*	in der Nacht *at night*	in der vorigen Woche
in der Gegenwart *at present*	im Jahre 1945	

After other prepositions in time expressions there is normally no article, see 11.5.

4.6 Definite article or possessive?

4.6.1 The definite article is used to refer to parts of the body and articles of clothing

(a) This is usual in German, whereas in English a possessive determiner is used

Hast du **die** Zähne geputzt?	*Have you cleaned your teeth?*
Sie hat **das** Bein gebrochen	*She has broken her leg*
Sie strich **den** Rock glatt	*She smoothed her skirt*

Das Mädchen zog **den** rötlichen Kamm aus **dem** Haar, nahm ihn in **den** Mund und fing an, mit **den** Fingern **die** Frisur zurechtzuzupfen (*Böll*)

A possessive dative is frequent in such constructions, and it is essential when the relevant person is not the subject of the verb, see 2.5.4, e.g.:

Sie nahm es **(sich)** in den Mund	*She put it in her mouth*
Die Mütze fiel **mir** vom Kopf	*My cap fell off my head*
Wir zogen **dem Verletzten** die Hose aus	*We took the injured man's trousers off*

(b) However, a possessive determiner is normal rather than the definite article in a few contexts

(i) when the owner has been named in a previous sentence, or when the part of the body or article of clothing is the first element in the sentence:

Ein Fremder erschien. **Seine** Stirn glänzte. **Sein** Anzug war altmodisch	*A stranger appeared. His forehead glistened. His suit was old-fashioned*
Meine Beine sind nicht krumm (*Brecht*)	*My legs aren't crooked*

(ii) when the owner must be specified, but the verb does not permit the use of a possessive dative:

Ich erblickte eine Wespe auf **meinem** Ärmel	*I caught sight of a wasp on my sleeve*
Sie legte **ihre** Hand auf **seine** Hand (*Wendt*)	*She put her hand on his hand*

(iii) to emphasise the owner or avoid ambiguity:

Langsam hob sie **ihre** rechte Hand	*Slowly, she raised her right hand*
Hast du **deine** Zähne geputzt?	*Have you cleaned your teeth?*
Zieh (dir) lieber **deinen** Mantel an!	*Put your coat on (i.e. not mine!)*
Ich zog mir **seine** Hose an	*I put his trousers on*

4.6.2 The definite article is used rather than a possessive with some abstract nouns

This is particularly frequent with nouns denoting human attributes and emotions, which are thus seen as 'part' of the person concerned. A possessive dative may occur under the same conditions as with body parts:

Du musst versuchen, **die/deine** Angst zu überwinden	*You must try to overcome your fear*
Ich werde ihm **die Faulheit** austreiben	*I shall rid him of his laziness*
Der Appetit ist mir vergangen	*I've lost my appetite*

4.6.3 The definite or indefinite article is commonly used with the adjective *eigen*

The appropriate one of these can be an alternative to using a possessive determiner

Er hat **den/seinen** eigenen Sohn erschlagen	*He has killed his own son*
Jetzt haben wir **eine/unsere** eigene Wohnung	*We've got our own flat/a flat of our own now*

Note, as a set phrase with no article: *Das haben wir **mit eigenen Augen** gesehen.*

4.7 Miscellaneous uses of the definite article

4.7.1 The definite article is sometimes used to make the case of a noun clear

i.e. in contexts where an article would not usually be expected. This applies in particular in the genitive and dative cases

(a) Examples of the definite article used to mark genitive case

der Geruch **des** Seetangs	*the smell of seaweed*
ein Ausdruck **des** Erstaunens	*an expression of surprise*

In practice it is not possible for a noun (other than a proper name) to be used in the genitive without a determiner or an adjective to show the case. In this way, the article is essential in the first of the sentences below to show that the noun is in the genitive case:

Sie bedarf **der** Ruhe } Sie braucht Ruhe }	*She needs rest*

If ambiguity could arise from the use of a definite article, then a phrase with *von* must be used (see 2.4). Thus 'the smell of wild boar' has to be given with *der Geruch von Eber* if *der Geruch des Ebers* could be understood in the context to mean 'the smell of the wild boar'.

(b) Examples of the definite article used to mark dative case

Ich ziehe Kaffee **dem** Tee vor	*I prefer coffee to tea*
Dieses Metall gleicht **dem** Gold	*This metal resembles gold*
Er hat sich **der** Physik gewidmet	*He devoted himself to physics*

4.7.2 The definite article can be used in a distributive sense

In such contexts English commonly uses the indefinite article or 'per':

Die Butter kostete sechs Mark **das** Pfund	*The butter cost six marks a/per pound*
Sie komm zweimal **die** Woche zu uns (*or:* zweimal in der Woche)	*She comes to us twice a week*
Wir fuhren 80 Kilometer **die** Stunde	*We were doing 80 kilometres per hour*

pro and (with measurements) *je*, both without an article, are common alternatives to the definite article:

Wir zahlten 2 Euro **pro/je** Meter	*We paid 2 euro a/per metre*
Es kostet 20 Euro **pro** Stunde	*It costs 20 euro an hour*

4.7.3 The definite article is always used with *meist*

Er hat **das meiste** Geld	*He has (the) most money*
die meisten Jungen	*most of the boys*
die meisten meiner Freunde	*most of my friends*

4.8 Miscellaneous uses of the zero article

In a number of contexts no article is used in German where the usual English equivalent construction has a definite or indefinite article.

4.8.1 Nouns used in pairs or enumerations often lack the definite article

This can even be the case when a single noun in the same construction would require an article. In many cases these are conventional or set phrases:

Form und Inhalt	*(in) form and content*
Tag und Nacht	*day and night*
mit Müh und Not	*with great difficulty*
Es geht um Leben und Tod	*It's a matter of life and death*
in Hülle und Fülle	*in plenty*
Rhein, Main und Donau sind schiffbare Flüsse	*The Rhine, the Main and the Danube are navigable rivers*
Sie ließ Schale und Rest im Esszimmer liegen (*Baum*)	*She left the skin and the remains lying in the dining-room*
In Industrie und Handwerk bleiben Tausende von Arbeitsplätzen unbesetzt (*Spiegel*)	*In industry and trade thousands of job vacancies remain unfilled*

4.8.2 No article is used in some constructions in the predicate complement of the verbs *sein, werden, bleiben*

(a) With nouns denoting professions, nationality, origins or classes of people in general

Er ist **Arzt, Bäcker, Installateur**	*He is a doctor, a baker, a plumber*
Ich bin **Deutscher, Engländer, Schwede**	*I am a German, an Englishman, a Swede*

Franz ist **gläubiger Katholik**	*Franz is a devout catholic*
Helmut blieb **Junggeselle**	*Helmut remained a batchelor*
Danach wurde er **Marxist**	*After that he became a Marxist*

But the indefinite article is used if the noun refers to a specific individual, not to a class of person:

Sie ist **eine bekannte Anwältin**	*She is a well-known lawyer*
Er ist **ein richtiger Schauspieler**	*He's a real actor*

The indefinite article is also used in descriptive constructions with professions and positions, e.g.:

Er hatte den Titel **eines Professors**, die Stelle **eines Untersuchungsrichters**	*He had the title of professor, the position of examining magistrate*

(b) With certain nouns used mainly in formal writing

i.e. *Bedingung, Fakt, Gegenstand, Grundlage, Sache, Schwerpunkt, Tatsache, Voraussetzung, Ziel.* These usually precede the verb:

Tatsache ist, dass ...	*It is a fact that ...*
Bedingung dafür ist, dass er den Vertrag unterschreibt	*The condition for this is that he signs the contract*
Grund meines Schreibens ist der Artikel „Unser Garten" (*HA*)	*The reason I am writing is the article 'Our Garden'*

(c) With names of months and seasons, and abstract nouns used in a general sense

This runs counter to the usual rule with these, see 4.2 and 4.5:

Es war schon **April**	*It was already April*
Jetzt ist **Sommer**	*It's summer now*
Heute Abend ist **Tanz**	*There's a dance on tonight*
Das ist **Geschmackssache**	*That is a matter of taste*

4.8.3 No article is used in phrases introduced by *als* 'as'

Ich kannte ihn **als Junge**	*I knew him when I was a boy*
Er sprach **als Franzose**	*He spoke as a Frenchman*
die Bedeutung des Passes **als wichtige(r) Handelstraße**	*the significance of the pass as an important trade route*
Als überzeugter Demokrat kann ich das nicht gutheißen	*As a convinced democrat, I cannot approve of that*
Er gilt **als bester Tenor** der Neuzeit	*He is reckoned to be the best tenor of modern times*

NB: (i) An article can be used with verbs which are usually followed by *als*, e.g. *ansehen, betrachten, fühlen, gelten*: *Er gilt als* (**der**) *beste Tenor der Neuzeit.*

    (ii) The article can be used in the genitive case, e.g.: *mit der Verhaftung des Generals als* (**des**) *eigentlichen Putschführers.*

4.8.4 The article can be omitted in appositional phrases in formal writing

Zunächst kamen wir nach Florenz, **(der) Hauptstadt der Toskana**	*First we arrived in Florence, the capital of Tuscany*
dieses Zürich, **(der) Treffpunkt der Kaufleute** (*Frisch*)	*this Zurich, the meeting place of businessmen*
Neil Armstrong, **(der) amerikanischer Astronaut**, betrat als erster Mensch den Mond (*Zeit*)	*Neil Armstrong, the American astronaut, was the first man to set foot on the moon*

4.8.5 No article is used in a few formulaic expressions referring to people

This usage is restricted to formal, especially official registers, e.g.:

Angeklagter hat gestanden, dass …	*The accused confessed that …*
Unterzeichneter bittet um rasche Entscheidung seiner Angelegenheit	*The undersigned requests a speedy decision in the matter concerning him*
Verfasser behauptet, das Problem gelöst zu haben	*The author claims to have solved the problem*

4.8.6 Articles are often omitted for stylistic effect in headlines and advertisements

Verbrechen gestanden. Münchner Kaufmann vom Geschäftspartner erschlagen (*HA*)	*Crime admitted. Munich businessman killed by partner*
Wohnung mit Bad gesucht möglichst nahe Stadtzentrum	*Flat with bathroom required as close as possible to city centre*

4.8.7 The most usual equivalent in German for the English indefinite determiners 'some' or 'any' is to use the noun without an article

Ich möchte **Suppe**	*I should like some soup*
Brauchen Sie **Marken**?	*Do you need any stamps?*
Ich habe **(rote) Äpfel** gekauft	*I bought some (red) apples*
wenn du noch **Schwierigkeiten** hast	*if you have any more difficulties*
Hast du **Geld** bei dir?	*Have you got any money on you?*

For further information on German equivalents for *some* and *any*, see 5.5.9b.

4.8.8 No article is used with adverbial genitives

e.g.: *schweren Herzens* 'with a heavy heart', see 2.3.5b.

4.9 Article use with prepositions

Article use with prepositions can be very idiomatic. Usage in phrasal verbs and time phrases is dealt with in sections 4.2.3 and 4.5.3. More detail, in particular concerning differences between English and German use of articles in set phrases with prepositions, can be found in Chapter 20 under the individual prepositions. In this section we deal with those special cases where general rules can be stated.

4.9.1 The indefinite article is often omitted in adverbial or adjectival phrases consisting of preposition, adjective plus noun

This is common where a set phrase is extended by an adjective and is characteristic of formal registers:

ein fahrender Virtuose **mit italienischem Namen** (*Th. Mann*)	*a travelling virtuoso with an Italian name*
ein Mann, der **solchem Rat** nicht folgte und **zu schrecklichem Ende** kam (*Hildesheimer*)	*a man who failed to follow such advice and met a terrible end*
Wir erhielten den Betrag **in frei konvertierbarer Währung**	*We received the sum in a freely convertible currency*

This usage is also the norm in phrases with *mit* which are alternatives to adverbial genitives (see 2.3.5b):

Sie ging **mit schnellem Schritt** (= schnellen Schrittes) über die Straße	*She crossed the road at a fast pace*

4.9.2 The definite article can be omitted in prepositional phrases if the following noun is qualified by a genitive or another prepositional phrase

auf Anraten des Arztes	*on the advice of a doctor*
in Gegenwart von zwei Kollegen	*in the presence of two colleagues*
die Studie, die Smith noch **in Diensten** der Bank verfasste, ... (*Spiegel*)	*the study which Smith wrote in the service of the bank ...*
unter Ausnutzung aller Möglichkeiten	*by exploiting all possibilities*

4.9.3 A few prepositions are used with no article in some or all of their uses

The most noteworthy (because of the differences to English) are:

(a) *mit* **is often used with no article when a part-whole relationship is involved**

ein Zimmer **mit Bad**	ein Opel **mit Schiebedach**
ein Hut **mit breitem Rand**	eine Suppe **mit Wursteinlage**

(b) *ohne* **is used with no article in German in cases where English has an indefinite article**

Er geht gern **ohne Hut**	Sie trat **ohne Brille** auf
Ich übersetzte den Text **ohne Wörterbuch, ohne Mühe**	Wie hast du die Tür **ohne Schlüssel** aufgemacht?

(c) A few other prepositions are used without a following article

Most of these belong to formal written registers. More information is given under the individual prepositions in Chapter 20:

ab:	ab ersten/erstem Mai; ab Bahnhof; Preise ab Fabrik *ex works*
gemäß:	Die Angelegenheit wurde gemäß Verordnung entschieden

NB: An article is normally used if *gemäß* follows the noun, e.g.: *den geltenden Verordnungen gemäß*.

infolge:	Die Straße ist infolge schlechten Wetters gesperrt
kraft:	Er handelte kraft Gesetzes
laut:	Der Fahrer wurde laut Gesetz verurteilt
mangels:	Der Angeklagte wurde mangels Beweises freigesprochen
per:	per Einschreiben *by registered mail*; per Anhalter fahren *to hitch-hike*
pro:	pro Stück; der Preis pro Tag *per day*, pro männlichen Angestellten
von ... wegen:	Diese Angelegenheit muss von Amts wegen geklärt werden
zwecks:	Junge Dame möchte netten, gebildeten Herrn zwecks Heirat kennen lernen (*FAZ*)

5

Other determiners and pronouns

DETERMINERS **are a limited set of small words used with** NOUNS **to relate them to a particular context or situation.**

They typically occupy the first position in a noun phrase, before any adjectives.

Determiner	Adjective/adjectival phrase	Noun
dieser	heidnische	Gott
einige	fleißige	Studenten
sein	ultramodernes	Raumschiff
jedes	vom Kultbuchautor Adams erfundene	Computerspiel

The determiners include the definite and indefinite ARTICLES, which are dealt with in Chapter 4, and all other words used to determine nouns, like the DEMONSTRA-TIVES (*dieser, jener,* etc.), the POSSESSIVES (*mein, sein,* etc.), the INTERROGATIVES (e.g. *welcher*) and INDEFINITES (*einige, etliche,* etc.).

PRONOUNS **are a limited set of small words which stand in place of** NOUNS **or noun** PHRASES.

In particular they stand for nouns or noun phrases which have already been mentioned or which do not need to be repeated in full. They include the PERSONAL PRONOUNS, which are dealt with in Chapter 3, DEMONSTRATIVE PRONOUNS, POSSESSIVE PRONOUNS, INTERROGATIVE PRONOUNS, the RELATIVE PRONOUNS (the 'who' and 'which' words) and INDEFINITE PRONOUNS.

Determiners and pronouns qualify or stand in place of nouns. Thus, in German, they typically change their form ('decline') to indicate the same grammatical categories as nouns, i.e. CASE, PLURAL and GENDER. In German, many of the same basic forms can be used either as determiners or pronouns, e.g.:

> **Mein** Auto fährt sehr schnell (determiner) – **Meines** fährt aber schneller (pronoun)

A few of them (like *mein/meines* in the example) have different sets of endings depending on whether they are being used as determiners or pronouns, which is why it is important to distinguish between these.

This chapter deals with the following sets of determiners and pronouns:

- **demonstratives** (section 5.1)
- **possessives** (section 5.2)
- **interrogatives** (section 5.3)
- the **relative pronouns** (section 5.4)
- **indefinites**, **quantifiers** and other determiners and pronouns (section 5.5)

5.1 Demonstratives

5.1.1 der 'that'

der is the most frequent demonstrative in spoken German. It can be used to point in a general way to something distant or something near at hand and thus it can be the equivalent of both 'this' and 'that'.

(a) *der*, **when used as a determiner, has exactly the same written forms as the definite article**

i.e. as given in Table 4.1. It differs from the definite article in speech because it is always stressed, e.g. *den* [deːn], *der* [deːɐ], etc. It is thus quite distinct from the definite article, whose spoken forms are always unstressed and reduced, e.g. *'n, d'n* or *d'r*, etc., see 4.1.1. Compare:

Ich möchte ein Stück von **d'r** Wurst	*I would like a piece of the sausage*
Ich möchte ein Stück von **der** [deːɐ] Wurst	*I would like a piece of this/that sausage*

In written German the demonstrative force of *der* may sometimes be clear from the context, especially when a relative clause follows, e.g.:

Ich kann dir **die** Hefte der Zeitschrift schicken, die dir noch fehlen	*I can send you those issues of the journal which you haven't got yet*
Bei **der** Lehrerin würde ich auch nichts lernen	*I wouldn't learn anything from that teacher either*

In many cases, though, it would be difficult to tell the demonstrative *der* apart from the definite article in writing, and *dieser* or *derjenige* is preferred. In colloquial speech the demonstrative force of *der* can be strengthened by adding *da* or *hier* after the noun, e.g. *der Mann hier* 'this man', *der Mann da* 'that man'. These forms are not used in writing.

(b) **The declension of demonstrative *der* used as a pronoun**

This is the same as the declension of the determiner, except in the **genitive** and the **dative plural**. The forms are given in Table 5.1.

TABLE 5.1 *Declension of der used as a pronoun*

	Masculine	Feminine	Neuter	Plural
Nominative	der	die	das	die
Accusative	den	die	das	die
Genitive	dessen	deren	dessen	deren/derer
Dative	dem	der	dem	denen

NB: The genitive forms *dessen* and *deren* are compounded with a following *-halben, -wegen* or *-willen*, with *-t-* inserted, e.g. *dessentwegen, um derentwillen*.

(c) **The use of *der* as a pronoun**

When it is being used as a pronoun, *der* cannot be confused with the definite article, as there is no noun following, and it is used freely in writing. It often corresponds to English 'the one'/'this one'/'that one':

mein Wagen und **der** meines Bruders	*my car and my brother's*
Die Sache ist nämlich **die**: Er ist schon verheiratet	*It's like this: he's already married*
Diese Seife ist besser als **die**, die ich gebrauche	*This soap is better than the one I use*
Wir können **dem** nicht so viel Bedeutung beimessen	*We cannot attach so much importance to that*
Die sind mir zu teuer	*Those (ones) are too expensive for me*
Das Buch liegt auf dem Tisch. Ja, auf **dem** da drüben	*The book's lying on the table. Yes, on that one over there*

(d) Pronominal *der* is often used instead of a third person pronoun

This usage is mainly colloquial, especially to refer to persons, see 3.4.2:

Ist der Teller kaputt? Ja, **den** hat Astrid fallen lassen	*Is the plate broken? Yes, Astrid dropped it*
Keine Möwen. **Die** waren weiter draußen (*Grass*)	*No gulls. They were further offshore*

(e) *der* can be strengthened by the addition of *da* or *hier*

This makes it more clear whether '**this** one (here)' or '**that** one (there)' is being referred to, e.g. *das da* 'that one', *das hier* 'this one'. This usage is limited to informal colloquial speech.

(f) The genitive of the pronoun *der* can be used for a possessive pronoun to avoid ambiguity

Sie war die Tochter des Schriftstellers Thomas Mann und **dessen** viertes Kind (*Spiegel*)	*She was the daughter of the writer Thomas Mann and his fourth child*
Dennoch wurden sie alle geprägt von ihrer Stadt und **deren** geistiger Tradition	*Nevertheless they were all moulded by their city and its intellectual tradition*
Erboste Bauern nahmen britische LKW-Fahrer gefangen und plünderten **deren** Konvois (*Zeit*)	*Angry farmers held some British lorry-drivers captive and plundered their (i.e. the lorry-drivers') convoys*

In colloquial German, the genitive of *der* can be used instead of a possessive for emphasis, e.g.: *Ich kann **deren** Mann nicht leiden.*

(g) In the genitive plural *derer* can be used rather than *deren* to refer forwards

It is most frequent with a following relative clause:

die Zahl **derer**, die seit 1950 die Westzone verlassen haben (*ND*)	*the number of those who have left the Western zone since 1950*

(h) The pronoun *das* is used as an emphatic form of *es*

Like *es* (see 3.6), it can be used with either singular or plural forms of the verb *sein*. In the corresponding English constructions we distinguish between 'that' and 'those':

Das sind meine Bücher	*Those are my books*
Das ist mein Arm, meine Hand, mein Knie	*That is my arm, my hand, my knee*

(i) A form of the prepositional adverb is normally used rather than a preposition followed by the demonstrative pronoun
e.g. *damit* 'with that', *darin* 'in that'. The stress is on the first syllable (see 3.5.3b):

> `Damit kann man die Büchse doch nicht aufmachen, oder? *You can't open the can with that, can you?*

To refer to something near or something just mentioned, a prepositional adverb with *hier-* can be used, e.g. *hiermit* 'with this', *hierin* 'in this':

> **Hierüber** lässt sich nichts mehr sagen *There is nothing more to be said about this*

However, a preposition followed by the demonstrative pronoun is used with a following relative clause in written German (although the prepositional adverb may sometimes be heard in speech). See 5.4.3c:

> Ich richtete meine ganze Aufmerksamkeit **auf das** (NOT darauf), was er erklärte *I focused my whole attention on what he was saying*

5.1.2 *dieser* 'this'

The declension of *dieser* is given in Table 5.2. It is the same whether *dieser* is used as a pronoun or as a determiner. Many other determiners and pronouns have the same set of endings.

TABLE 5.2 *Declension of* dieser

	Masculine	Feminine	Neuter	Plural
Nominative	dieser	diese	dieses	diese
Accusative	diesen	diese	dieses	diese
Genitive	dieses	dieser	dieses	dieser
Dative	diesem	dieser	diesem	diesen

There is an increasing tendency to use the form *diesen* in the genitive singular masculine and neuter of the determiner rather than *dieses* if the noun has the ending *-(e)s*, e.g. *im Februar diesen Jahres* (MM) (for: *dieses Jahres*). However, this usage is considered to be substandard.

(a) As a determiner and a pronoun *dieser* refers to something near at hand, corresponding to English 'this'
As a determiner, *dieser* occurs in both spoken and written German, but as a pronoun it is mainly used in writing:

> **Diese** Erklärung ist unbefriedigend *This explanation is unsatisfactory*
> **Dieser** Junge arbeitet aber gut *That boy really does work well*
> Er hat den roten Wagen nicht gekauft, weil ihm **dieser** (spoken: der hier) viel besser gefallen hat *He didn't buy the red car, because he liked this one much better*

dieser is often used simply to point to an object or person in contexts where the difference between near and distant is not crucial. In such contexts it often corresponds to English 'that', e.g. *Warum hast du dieses Top gekauft?* 'Why did you buy this/that top?'

(b) The short pronoun form *dies* is commonly used for *dieses*
It refers to something close by or recent and its use corresponds closely to that of English 'this':

> **Dies** geschieht nicht oft
> Gerade **dies** hatte ich vergessen

dies, like *das*, can be used irrespective of gender or number, with a plural verb where appropriate: *Dies sind meine Schwestern; Dies ist meine Frau.*

NB: In formal writing, *dies* is occasionally used as a determiner for *dieses*, e.g. **Dies** *Werk malte Konrad Witz aus Basel* (*Borst*).

5.1.3 *jener* 'that'

jener declines like *dieser*, see Table 5.2. As a determiner or a pronoun it is largely restricted to a few special uses in formal written German, i.e.:

(a) to contrast with *dieser*

> Herr Schröder wollte nicht dieses Bild   *Mr Schröder did not want to sell this*
> verkaufen, sondern **jenes**   *picture, but that one*
> Wir sprachen über dieses und **jenes**   *We talked about this and that*
> (less formal: über dies und das)

(b) to refer to something distant, but well-known

> Werfen wir einen kurzen Blick über den   *Let us cast a short glance at the Iron*
> Eisernen Vorhang **jener** Zeit   *Curtain of those times*
> (*Sonnenberg*)

(c) with a following relative clause

> Sein linker Arm war mit dicken   *His left arm had thick material wrapped*
> Tüchern umwickelt, wie es bei **jenen**   *round it, as is the custom with those who*
> Brauch ist, die Hunde zum Anpacken   *train dogs to attack*
> einüben (*Dürrenmatt*)

5.1.4 *derjenige* 'that'

TABLE 5.3 *Declension of* derjenige *and* derselbe

	Masculine	**Feminine**	**Neuter**	**Plural**
Nominative	derjenige	diejenige	dasjenige	diejenigen
Accusative	denjenigen	diejenige	dasjenige	diejenigen
Genitive	desjenigen	derjenigen	desjenigen	derjenigen
Dative	demjenigen	derjenigen	demjenigen	denjenigen
Nominative	derselbe	dieselbe	dasselbe	dieselben
Accusative	denselben	dieselbe	dasselbe	dieselben
Genitive	desselben	derselben	desselben	derselben
Dative	demselben	derselben	demselben	denselben

Both parts of *derjenige* decline, as shown in Table 5.3. It is an emphatic demonstrative determiner or pronoun and is typically used with a following restrictive

relative clause, corresponding to English 'that (one), which/who'. It is now quite
frequent in spoken registers as well as in writing.

Wir wollen **diejenigen** Schüler herausfinden, die musikalisch begabt sind	*We want to find those pupils who are musically gifted*
Dieses neue Denken ist für **denjenigen**, der ein bisschen Bildung hat, ein sehr altes Denken gewesen (*Heuss*)	*This new way of thinking is an old way for those who have a little education*

5.1.5 *derselbe* 'the same'

Both parts of *derselbe* decline, like *derjenige* (see Table 5.3). However, unlike *derjenige*, it can be used with a contracted preposition, e.g. *am selben Tag, zur selben Zeit*. It corresponds to English 'the same':

Er besucht **dieselbe** Schule wie dein Bruder	*He goes to the same school as your brother*
Sind das **dieselben**?	*Are those the same?*
Sie wohnt **im selben** Haus	*She lives in the same house*
Es läuft auf (ein und) **dasselbe** hinaus	*It all comes to the same thing*

The difference between *derselbe*, i.e. 'the very same', and *der gleiche*, i.e. 'one which is similar' (cf. *Er trägt den gleichen Hut* 'He is wearing the same (i.e. a similar) hat'), is often ignored in spoken German, either being used in both senses. It is widely felt, though, that this distinction should be upheld, at least in writing.

5.1.6 *solch* and other equivalents of 'such'

solch- occurs in a number of forms, i.e.:

- inflected *solcher*, which declines like *dieser* (Table 5.2), except that in the genitive singular masculine and neuter it usually has the ending *-en* if the noun has the ending *-(e)s*, e.g. *Der Vorzug solchen Spieles* (*Th.Mann*).
- endingless *solch*, used with an indefinite article: *solch ein Unsinn*
- *solch-* used after the indefinite article *ein* or another determiner, with the endings of an adjective: *ein solches Buch, jeder solche Gedanke, alle solchen Frauen*

The use of these forms is as follows:

(a) The commonest variants for the determiner are *ein solcher* in the singular and inflected *solche* in the plural
This applies to both written and spoken German:

Eine solche Auflockerung könnte dem politischen Diskurs gut bekommen (*Zeit*)	*Such a relaxation of tension could benefit the political debate*
Einen solchen Wagen würde ich nie kaufen	*I would never buy a car like that*
Solchen Leuten kann man alles erzählen	*You can tell people like that anything*
solche großen Häuser	*such big houses*

NB: In colloquial speech, *so ein* is also current in the singular for 'such a', e.g. *in so einer Stadt, so ein Geschenk*. In the plural, simple *so* may be used, e.g. *Das sind so Sachen*, but this is considered clearly substandard.

(b) Inflected *solcher* as a determiner in the singular is found principally in formal, especially literary registers

bei **solchem** Wetter	*in such weather*
ein Mann, der **solchem** Rat nicht folgte (Hildesheimer)	*a man who failed to follow such advice*

(c) Usage as a determiner with a following adjective

(i) the most usual equivalent with singular count nouns for English 'such a' followed by an adjective is *ein so* (more colloquial *so ein*):

ein so großes Haus ⎱ **so ein** großes Haus ⎰	*such a big house*

(ii) In spoken German *so* is also used with plural count nouns and singular mass nouns, but the written language prefers inflected *solcher*:

so große Häuser (spoken) ⎱ **solche** großen Häuser (written) ⎰	*such big houses*
bei **so** gutem Wetter (spoken) ⎱ bei **solchem** guten Wetter (written) ⎰	*in such good weather*

(iii) In formal registers uninflected *solch* is not uncommon if an adjective follows. It also occurs in a few set phrases:

Der Westen ließ sich von **solch** verfehlter Ablehnung allen Verhandelns leiten (*Zeit*)	*The West allowed itself to be guided by such a mistaken rejection of any negotiations*
mit **solch** unermüdlichem Eifer	*with such tireless enthusiasm*
Solch dummes Gerede!	*Such stupid gossip!*

(d) In formal registers uninflected *solch* can be used as a determiner with a following indefinite article

This is more emphatic than if the article comes first:

Solch einem Experten sollte das nicht passieren	*That shouldn't happen to **such** an expert*

NB: Uninflected *solch* is sometimes used <u>without</u> *ein* before a singular neuter noun, e.g.: *solch Wetter*. This has a very old-fashioned sound.

(e) Pronoun usage

(i) The most usual variants are *solche* (plural) and *so einer* (singular):

Ich habe **solche** oft gesehen	*I've often seen ones like that*
So eines kann ich mir nicht leisten	*I can't afford one like that*

(ii) Singular *solcher* is used after *als*:

Der Fall als **solcher** interessiert mich	*The case as such interests me*

(iii) Singular (*k*)*ein solcher* is restricted to literary registers. In the singular it sounds rather stilted:

Sie hatte auch **einen solchen**	*She had one like that, too*
Leider haben wir **keine solchen** mehr	*I'm afraid we haven't got any more like that*

(f) The adjective *derartig* is a common, more emphatic alternative to *solch-*
It is used with *ein* in the singular, or with no article in either singular or plural:

Er fuhr mit **einer derartigen** Geschwindigkeit gegen die Mauer, dass ...	*He drove into the wall at such a speed, that ...*
Erfahrung im Umgang mit **derartiger** Kälte hat niemand (*Bednarz*)	*Nobody has experience in dealing with that degree of cold*
Derartige Gerüchte hören wir oft	*We often hear rumours like those*

NB: If another adjective follows, *derartig* may be uninflected, e.g.: *Er fuhr mit einer derartig(en) hohen Geschwindigkeit gegen die Mauer, dass* ... In some contexts, though, there can be a difference in meaning. Compare *ein derartig dummes Geschwätz* (i.e. 'gossip which is stupid to such an extent') and *ein derartiges dummes Geschwätz* (i.e. 'such gossip which is stupid').

(g) *dergleichen* **and** *derlei*
dergleichen and *derlei* do not decline. They are used as determiners or pronouns meaning 'suchlike', 'that kind/sort of':

Dergleichen Behauptungen stören mich	*Assertions like that bother me*
nichts **dergleichen**	*nothing of the kind*
und **dergleichen** mehr (abbrev.: u.dgl.m.).	*and so forth*
Er hatte ein langes Messer oder **dergleichen** in der Tasche	*He had a long knife or something of the kind in his pocket*
Die rotblonde Miss Leclerc hatte **derlei** Tricks nicht nötig (*BILD*)	*The strawberry blond Miss Leclerc didn't need tricks like that*
Sie sah **derlei** nicht ungern (*Jacob*)	*She wasn't averse to that kind of thing*

5.2 Possessives

5.2.1 The possessives have distinct base forms for each grammatical person

These are given in Table 5.4 together with the personal pronoun to which they relate.

TABLE 5.4 *Base forms of the possessive pronouns and determiners*

Singular			Plural		
ich	**mein**	*my*	wir	**unser**	*our*
du	**dein**	*your*	ihr	**euer**	*your*
er	**sein**	*his/its*	Sie	**Ihr**	*your (polite)*
sie	**ihr**	*her/its*	sie	**ihr**	*their*
es	**sein**	*its*			

NB: (i) To refer back to indefinites, the masculine form *sein* is used: *Wer hat seine Zahnbürste vergessen? Niemand hatte sein Heft mit.*

(ii) A demonstrative is sometimes used instead of a third person possessive to avoid ambiguity, see 5.1.1f.

5.2.2 When used as DETERMINERS the possessives have the same endings as the indefinite article

Table 5.5 gives the forms of *mein* 'my' and *unser* 'our'.

TABLE 5.5 *Declension of the possessive determiners*

	Masculine	Feminine	Neuter	Plural
Nominative	mein	meine	mein	meine
Accusative	meinen	meine	mein	meine
Genitive	meines	meiner	meines	meiner
Dative	meinem	meiner	meinem	meinen
Nominative	unser	unsere	unser	unsere
Accusative	unseren	unsere	unser	unsere
Genitive	unseres	unserer	unseres	unserer
Dative	unserem	unserer	unserem	unseren

The following is to be noted in relation to these declensions:

(a) The -er of *unser* and *euer* is part of the root and <u>not</u> an ending
As Table 5.5 shows, the endings are attached to this root.

(b) When *unser* and *euer* have an ending, the -e- of the root is often dropped
e.g. *unsrer, unsren, eurer, euren.* Alternatively, the *-e-* of the endings *-en* or *-em* may be dropped, e.g. *unsern, unserm, euern, euerm.*
  With *unser*, the full forms, as given in the table, are the more usual ones in written German, although the reduced forms, which are the norm in speech, are quite permissible.
  With *euer*, the forms with no *-e-* in the root, i.e. *euren, eurer, eures, eurem,* are by far the most common in both spoken and written German.

5.2.3 When used as PRONOUNS, the possessives have the endings of *dieser*

Table 5.6 gives the full forms of *meiner* 'mine' and *unserer* 'ours'.

TABLE 5.6 *Declension of the possessive pronouns*

	Masculine	Feminine	Neuter	Plural
Nominative	meiner	meine	meines	meine
Accusative	meinen	meine	meines	meine
Genitive	meines	meiner	meines	meiner
Dative	meinem	meiner	meinem	meinen
Nominative	unserer	unsere	unseres	unsere
Accusative	unseren	unsere	unseres	unsere
Genitive	unseres	unserer	unseres	unserer
Dative	unserem	unserer	unserem	unseren

(a) The forms of the possessive pronouns
(i) Note in particular that, unlike the possessive determiners, the possessive pronouns have endings in the nominative singular masculine and the nominative/accusative singular neuter (i.e *meiner, meines*). Compare:

> Das ist nicht **mein** Hut, sondern **deiner**
> Hast du **dein** Fahrrad? Ich sehe **mein(e)s** nicht
> Seine Sammlung ist größer als **meine**
> **Ihr** Garten ist größer als **uns(e)rer**
> Er sprach mit **meinen** Eltern, ich mit **seinen**
> Ich nehme **uns(e)ren** Wagen. In **seinem** habe ich immer Angst

(ii) The -*e*- of the nominative/accusative neuter ending -*es* is often dropped in writing and almost always in speech, i.e. *meins, deins*. With *unseres* and *eueres* the -*e*- of the ending is dropped, i.e. *unsers, euers*. Otherwise, *unserer* and *euerer* can drop the -*e*- of the root or the ending as with the possessive determiner, see 5.2.2 above.

(iii) Endingless forms of the possessive are occasionally found in set phrases, archaic expressions or poetic language:

> **Dein** ist mein Herz! Die Welt ist **unser**
> Die Rache ist **mein**

(b) Alternative forms of the possessive pronoun

The following types of phrase are sometimes used instead of *meiner, deiner, unserer*, etc. The possessive forms are used as adjectives after a definite article, and they have the endings of adjectives. They can be spelled with a small or a capital initial letter (see 23.1.1b):

(i) *der meinige/Meinige* 'mine', *der deinige/Deinige* 'yours', *der uns(e)rige/Uns(e)rige* 'ours', etc.

(ii) *der meine/Meine* 'mine', *der deine/Deine* 'yours', *der uns(e)re/Uns(e)re* 'ours', etc.

> Seine Sammlung ist größer als **die meine/die meinige**.

These forms are much less common than *meiner*, etc., and are found mainly in formal written German. Type (ii) is rather more emphatic than *meiner*, etc., whilst type (i) is current mainly in set phrases, e.g.: *die Deinigen* 'your people' (i.e. your family); *Ich habe das Meinige getan* 'I've done my bit'.

5.2.4 Differences between German and English in the use of the possessives

(a) A definite article is often used rather than a possessive to refer to parts of the body and articles of clothing

e.g.: *Sie hat sich **den** Arm gebrochen* 'She has broken her arm'. Details are given in 4.6.

(b) Some idiomatic equivalents

Das gehört mir. Gehört das dir?	*That's mine. Is that yours?*
ein Freund von mir/einer meiner Freunde	*a friend of mine*
Freunde von mir	*friends of mine*
Das ist eins von meinen Büchern	*That's a book of mine*
Mein Vater und meine Mutter (see 4.1.1b)	*My father and mother*

5.3 Interrogatives

5.3.1 *welcher* 'which'

(a) *welcher* can be used as a determiner or a pronoun
It has the same endings as *dieser*, see Table 5.2. The forms are the same whether it is used as a determiner or a pronoun.

Welches Bier willst du trinken?	*Which beer do you want to drink?*
Welchen Zug nehmen wir denn?	*Which train shall we take?*
Aus **welchem** Land kommt sie denn?	*Which country does she come from?*
Welcher berühmte Schriftsteller hat diesen Roman geschrieben?	*Which famous author wrote this novel?*
Hier sind zwei gute Romane. **Welchen** möchtest du zuerst lesen?	*Here are two good novels. Which one would you like to read first?*
Er fragte mich, **welchen** (Roman) ich zuerst lesen wollte	*He asked me which (novel) I wanted to read first*

(b) Some special uses of *welcher*
(i) Before an adjective the endingless form *welch* is sometimes used, in formal written German only, as an alternative to the declined form:

Welch berühmter Schriftsteller hat diesen Roman geschrieben?
Die Künstler zeigten, **welch** reiches Kulturgut sie mitbrachten (*MM*)

(ii) In the genitive singular masculine and neuter the determiner can have the ending *-en* rather than *-es* if the following noun has the ending *-(e)s*:

Welch**en**/Welch**es** Kindes Buch ist das?
Innerhalb welch**en** Zeitraumes müssen nicht bestandene Prüfungen wiederholt werden? (*Uni Innsbruck*)

In practice, the genitive tends to be avoided if possible.

(iii) *welcher* can have the neuter singular form *welches* when it is used as a pronoun in an indefinite sense with the verb *sein*, irrespective of the gender and number of the noun it refers to:

Welches ist die jüngere Schwester?   **Welches** sind die besten Zeitungen?
Welches ist der längste Fluss in Amerika?

Using endings in agreement with the following noun would be equally possible in these examples: *Welche ist die jüngere Schwester?* etc.

(c) *welcher* is used in exclamations (= 'What (a) ...!')

Welcher Unterschied!	**Welcher** schöne Tag!
Welche Überraschung!	**Welchen** unglaublichen Unsinn hat er geredet!

Endingless *welch* can be used for declined *welcher* in exclamations if *ein* or an adjective follows:

Welch ein Unterschied!	**Welch (ein) schöner** Tag!
Welch eine Überraschung!	**Welch unglaublichen** Unsinn hat er geredet!

Der Smogalarm machte erneut deutlich, in **welch hohem** Maße die Luft mit Giftstoffen verseucht ist (*MM*)	*The smog alarm made it clear once again to what high degree the air is polluted with poisonous substances*

This exclamatory use of *welch(er)* is mainly found in formal German. *was für (ein)* (see 5.3.2), is more current in speech.

NB: The form *welcher* has a number of other uses, i.e.
    (i)   as a relative pronoun (= 'who', 'which'), see 5.4.2.
    (ii)   as an indefinite (= 'some', 'any'), see 5.5.26.

5.3.2 *was für (ein[er])* 'what kind of (a)'

(a) *was für (ein[er])* **can be used as a determiner or a pronoun**
(i) Used as a determiner, *ein* in *was für ein* declines like the indefinite article, see Table 4.2. Simple *was für*, without *ein*, is used in the plural and before mass nouns in the singular:

Aus **was für einer** Familie stammt er?	*From what kind of a family does he come?*
Sie können sich denken, in **was für einer** schwierigen Lage ich mich befand	*You can imagine in what an awkward situation I found myself*
Was für ausländische Marken haben Sie?	*What kinds of foreign stamps do you have?*
Was für Käse soll ich kaufen?	*What kind of cheese shall I buy?*

The case of *ein* depends on the role of the noun phrase in the sentence, i.e. it is not dependent on *für* and is not automatically in the accusative.

(ii) When used as a pronoun, *was für einer* 'what kind (of a one)' has the endings of the pronoun *einer* given in Table 5.10. In the plural *was für welche* is used:

Er hat sich ein neues Auto gekauft. **Was für ein(e)s?**	*He has bought a new car. What kind?*
Ich habe Blumen gebracht. **Was für welche?**	*I have brought some flowers. What kind?*

NB: (i)   *was für welcher* is used in place of *was für einer* in the singular in colloquial north German speech, e.g.: *Er hat einen neuen Wagen gekauft. Was für welchen?*
     (ii) *was für (ein)* is also used in concessive clauses, see 19.6.2c.

(b) *was* **is often separated from** *für (ein[er])*
This is especially frequent in speech, but the construction is used in writing, too:

Was hast du denn **für ein** Auto gekauft?
Was sind das **für** Vögel?

(c) *was für (ein[er])* **is used in exclamations (= 'What (a) ...!')**
It is in practice commoner than *welcher*, see 5.3.1 (c), especially in less formal registers. In this usage the separated form is more frequent:

Was für eine Chance!	*What a chance!*
Was für herrliche Blumen!	*What lovely flowers!*
Er ist ein Schauspieler – und **was für einer**!	*He's an actor- and what an actor!*
Was sind das **für** wunderschöne Häuser!	*What lovely houses these are!*

NB: If there is a verb in these exclamations, it may, alternatively, go to the end, like in a subordinate clause: *Was für wunderschöne Häuser das **sind**!*

(d) In colloquial speech *was für* (*ein[er]*) **is often used for** *welcher* **'which'**
see 5.3.1. This usage is considered substandard:

    Was für ein Kleid ziehst du an?   *Which dress are you going to wear?*

5.3.3 wer, was 'who, what'

(a) *wer* **and** *was* **are used only as pronouns**
(i) *wer*, like English 'who', only refers to persons. It does not distinguish gender
and it has the case forms given in Table 5.7:

TABLE 5.7 *Declension of* wer

Nominative	wer
Accusative	wen
Genitive	wessen
Dative	wem

Examples of use:

Wer hat diesen Brief geschrieben?	*Who wrote this letter?*
Wen hast du heute gesprochen?	*Who(m) did you speak to today?*
Wem wollten sie vorhin helfen?	*Who(m) did they want to help just now?*
Mit **wem** hast du gespielt?	*Who(m) did you play with?*
Wessen Bücher sind das?	*Whose books are those?*
Ich kann Ihnen sagen, **wer** spielte	*I can tell you who was playing*

(ii) *was*, like English 'what', refers only to things. Its only case form is the genitive
wessen:

Was bewegt sich dort im Gebüsch?	*What is moving there in the bushes?*
Was hat sie dir zum Geburtstag geschenkt?	*What did she give you for your birthday?*
Wessen schämst du dich?	*What are you ashamed of?*
Weißt du, **was** er getan hat?	*Do you know what he did?*

The genitive form *wessen*, whether referring to people or things, is felt to be clumsy
and tends to be avoided nowadays, even in written German. Thus *Wem gehören
diese Bücher?* is used rather than *Wessen Bücher sind das?* and *Warum schämst du
dich?* rather than *Wessen schämst du dich?*

    As *was* has no dative, a paraphrase has to be used in contexts where it would be
needed, e.g.:

Welcher Ursache kann man seinen Erfolg zuschreiben?	*To what can one ascribe his success?* (Literally: 'To what cause …?')

(b) Nominative *wer* **and** *was* **are usually followed by a singular verb**
(i) Compare the examples in (a) above and the following:

Wer **kommt** denn morgen?	*Who's coming tomorrow?*
Was **liegt** dort in der Ecke?	*What's that lying there in the corner?*

(ii) However, with *sein* the appropriate singular or plural form of the verb is used,
as in English:

Wer **ist** das an der Tür?	*Who's that at the door?*
Wer **sind** diese Leute?	*Who are those people?*
Was **ist** der Vogel da?	*What's that bird there?*
Was **sind** die längsten Flüsse der Welt?	*What are the longest rivers in the world?*

(iii) To emphasise quantity, *alles* is often added to sentences with *wer* and *was*. This usage is chiefly colloquial:

Wen kennen Sie hier **alles**?	*What people do you know here?*
Was hat er denn alles **gefragt**?	*What were the things he asked?*

(c) *was* is not used in combination with most prepositions

The compound forms *wo(r)*+preposition, e.g. *woran, womit, wozu*, etc., are used instead.

(i) These forms are like those of the prepositional adverb with *da(r)-*, see 3.5:

Womit schreibst du?	*What are you writing with?*
Worüber sprechen Sie?	*What are you talking about?*
Weißt du, **worauf** wir warten?	*Do you know what we are waiting for?*

NB: Some prepositions are not used in the form with *wo(r)-*, i.e.: *außer, gegenüber, hinter, neben, ohne, seit, zwischen*.

(ii) The forms *wodurch, wonach, wovon* and *wozu* can only be used if there is no idea of movement involved, e.g.:

Wodurch weiß er das?	*How is it that he knows that?*
Wonach soll man sich denn richten?	*By what is one to be guided?*
Wovon sollen wir leben?	*What are we to live on?*
Wozu gebraucht man das?	*What is that used for?*

Compare: *durch was?* 'through what?', *von wo?* or *woher?* 'where ... from?', *wohin?* 'where ... to?'.

(iii) In colloquial German *was* (irrespective of case) is often heard with a preposition instead of *wo(r)*+preposition, e.g.: *Von was sollen wir leben?* This usage is considered substandard.

(d) *wer* and *was* are commonly used in exclamations

Wer hätte so was erwartet!	*Who would have expected such a thing!*
Wem hat er nicht alles geholfen!	*Who(m) hasn't he helped!*
Was haben wir gelacht!	*How we laughed!*
Was er nicht alles tut!	*The things he does!*

(e) *was* can be followed by an adjective used as a noun, with the neuter ending *-es*

See 6.4 for further details on these forms. The adjective is separated from *was* and placed later in the sentence:

Was haben sie **Wichtiges** besprochen?	*What important matters did they discuss?*
Was ist **Komisches** dran?	*What's funny about it?*
Was könnt ihr hier **anderes** erwarten?	*What else can you expect here?*
(*Fallada*)	

(f) *was* **can be used in the sense of 'why?' or 'what for?'**
This usage is restricted to colloquial German:

> **Was** sitzt ihr da rum? *What are you doing just sitting around?*

was in this usage often carries a tone of reproach.

(g) Idiomatic differences between German and English
In a few contexts German has *wie* where English uses 'what'.

> **Wie** ist Ihr Name, bitte? *What is your name, please?*
> **Wie** heißt Ihr Bruder? *What's your brother called?*
> **Wie** ist das Buch? *What's the book like?*

(h) Other uses of *wer* **and** *was*
(i) *wer* and *was* are used as relative pronouns (= 'who', 'which', 'that') in some contexts, see 5.4.3 and 5.4.5.

(ii) *wer* and *was* are used in some concessive clauses (i.e. = 'whoever', 'whatever'), see 19.6.2.

(iii) For the colloquial use of *wer* as an indefinite (i.e. = 'someone'), see 5.5.27.

5.4 Relative pronouns

RELATIVE PRONOUNS introduce subordinate clauses (called '**relative clauses**') which describe or qualify nouns, e.g. *die Frau,* **die** *heute kommt* 'the woman **who** is coming today'; *das Buch,* **das** *ich gerade lese* 'the book **which** I am just reading'. In this way relative clauses have the same function in a sentence as adjectives.

In English, we often drop a relative pronoun, especially in speech (*The book (which) I am just reading*), but in German it can **never** be left out in this way.

5.4.1 *der* 'who', 'which', 'that'

(a) *der* **is the most commonly used relative pronoun in German**
der declines for the categories of gender, plural and case. Its forms, which are almost identical to that of the demonstrative pronoun *der*, are given in Table 5.8.

TABLE 5.8 *Declension of the relative pronoun* der

	Masculine	Feminine	Neuter	Plural
Nominative	der	die	das	die
Accusative	den	die	das	die
Genitive	dessen	deren	dessen	deren
Dative	dem	der	dem	denen

der takes its **gender** and **number** from the noun it refers to, e.g.

> **der Mann, der** heute zu uns kommt **das Kind, das** heute zu uns kommt
> (masculine) (neuter)
> **die Frau, die** heute zu uns kommt **die Leute, die** heute zu uns kommen
> (feminine) (plural)

Its **case** is determined by the role it plays in the relative clause:

der Mann, **der** zu uns kommt (**subject** of *kommt*)	der Mann, **dem** ich helfen musste (**dative object** of *helfen*)
den Mann, **den** ich kenne (**accusative object** of *kenne*)	der Mann, mit **dem** sie gekommen ist (after **preposition** *mit* governing the **dative** case)

(b) Relative clauses are less frequent in spoken German than in writing

In speech a construction with a main clause (and the verb in second place) and the demonstrative pronoun *der* is often used rather than a subordinate relative clause (with the verb at the end). This is usually considered to be poor style in writing, unless colloquial speech is being imitated, as in the following examples:

Er trug ein Heft bei sich, **in dem** standen die Namen der fünfzig Verräter (*E.W. Heine*)	*He had a little book with him in which the names of the fifty traitors were written down*
Es gibt Leute, **die** freuen sich über die Fahrt (*Bichsel*)	*There are people who are pleased about the trip*

(c) The genitive of *der*

(i) The genitive forms of *der* correspond to English 'whose' or 'of which':

die Frau, **deren** Namen ich immer vergesse	*the woman whose name I always forget*
Sie blickten auf das Mietshaus gegenüber, in **dessen** Erdgeschoss sich eine Schreibwarenhandlung befand	*They looked out on the apartment house opposite, on the ground floor of which there was a stationer's*
ein Mann, von **dessen** Erfolg ich hörte	*a man of whose success I heard*

NB: It is incorrect (though a common mistake by Germans) to decline *dessen* and *deren*, i.e.: *ein Mann, von dessem* (correct: *dessen*) *Erfolg ich hörte.*

(ii) In the genitive plural and the genitive singular feminine *derer* is sometimes used rather than *deren*:

ein Zusammenhang ausgebildeter Verfahrensweisen, innerhalb **derer** der einzelne Wissenschaftler seine besondre Aufgabe erfüllt (*Bollnow*)	*a framework of established procedures within which the individual scientist carries out his own particular task*
die ungewöhnliche Autorität, **derer** sich die katholischen Bischöfe in Polen erfreuen (*Spiegel*)	*the extraordinary authority which is enjoyed by the Catholic bishops in Poland*

This usage is considered incorrect by the standard authorities, but *derer* is in practice more frequent than *deren*, especially in the genitive plural. However, *deren* is preferred if a noun follows: *die Frau, **deren** Tochter du kennst.*

(iii) After prepositions, the shorter form *der* also occurs for *deren*:

eine lange Übergangszeit von sechs Jahren, innerhalb **der** die Länder die Juristenausbildung umstellen können (*Zeit*)	*a long transitional period of six years, within which the Länder can reorganise the training of lawyers*

(iv) Constructions of the type 'one of whom', 'most of which', 'some of which' correspond to constructions with *von denen* in German:

die Studenten, **von denen** ich **einen** nicht kenne	*the students, one of whom I don't know*
eine Anzahl Jungen, **von denen** ich **die meisten** kenne	*a number of boys, most of whom I know*
viele Bilder, **von denen einige** ganz gut sind	*a lot of pictures, some of which are quite good*

(v) *dessen* and *deren* are compounded with *-halben*, *-wegen* and *-willen* with the insertion of a *-t-*, e.g. *derentwegen, um dessentwillen*:

das Außenhandelsgesetz, **dessentwegen** Nixon so lange mit dem Kongress kämpft (*Welt*)	*the foreign trade bill, because of which Nixon has been battling so long with Congress*

(d) Relative pronouns with first and second person personal pronouns
Normally, the pronoun is repeated in the relative clause, e.g.:

du, **der/die du** ja nicht alles wissen kannst	*you, who cannot know everything*
für mich, **die ich** noch gar nicht ordentlich lesen konnte (*Dönhoff*)	*for me, who couldn't read properly yet*
ich, **der ich** seit 20 Jahren seinem Volke diene	*I, who have been serving my people for 20 years*

The alternative construction with a third person verb, e.g.: *ich, **der** seit 20 Jahren seinem Volke **dient*** (*FAZ*), is possible, but less frequent in practice.

5.4.2 *welcher* 'who, which, that'

(a) *welcher* **is chiefly used as a stylistic variant of** *der*
It has the same endings as *dieser*, see Table 5.2, but it is not normally used in the genitive. It is restricted to formal written German, and even there it can be considered clumsy and is much less frequent than *der*.

die Gerüchte, **welche** über die wirtschaftliche Lage meines Vaters am Orte umgelaufen waren (*Th. Mann*)	*the rumours which had been circulating in the town about my father's financial situation*
Der Herr tat doch immer so, als umgäbe ihn eine vielköpfige Familie, **welcher** er Anweisungen zu geben hätte (*Grass*)	*The gentleman always acted as if he was surrounded by a large family to which he had to give instructions*

It is frequent (although never necessary) to avoid repeating forms of *der*, e.g.: *Die, welche zuletzt kamen, waren erschöpft*. But compare, as perfectly acceptable (see 5.4.5b): *Die, **die** gingen, haben in der DDR mehr verändert, als die, **die** geblieben sind* (*FR*).

(b) *welcher* **is used in formal German before a noun which refers back to part or whole of the preceding clause**
This use corresponds to that of English 'which'. In this construction *welcher* agrees with the following noun for case, number and gender:

Er wurde zum Stadtdirektor ernannt, **welches Amt** er gewissenhaft verwaltete	*He was appointed town clerk, which office he administered conscientiously*
Er sagte ihr, sie müsse den Betrag sofort zurückzahlen, **welcher Forderung** sie dann auch nachging	*He told her she had to repay the amount immediately, which request she then complied with*

5.4.3 *was* is used as a relative pronoun in some contexts

The only case form of *was* in this usage is the genitive *wessen*, which tends to be avoided. *was* is used:

(a) After neuter indefinites
i.e. *alles, einiges, etwas, folgendes, manches, nichts, vieles, weniges:*

✓ Nichts/Etwas/Alles, **was** er sagte, war mir neu	*Nothing/Something/Everything (that) he said was new to me*
Sie mieden alles, **was** ihre Unabhängigkeit einschränken könnte (*Walser*)	*They avoided anything which could restrict their independence*

After *etwas*, *das* may be used as an alternative to *was* if something specific is referred to:

✓ Gerade in diesem Moment fiel ihr etwas ein, **das** sie erstarren ließ: Die Gasrechnung (*Baum*)	*Just then she remembered something that made her go rigid: the gas bill*
Ich erinnere mich an etwas Merkwürdiges, **das** er sagte	*I remember something strange that he said*

das is occasionally found after other indefinites, but this usage is considered incorrect.

NB: (i)   After prepositions, forms of *was* are replaced by the prepositional adverb in *wo(r)*, see 5.4.4b
          (ii)   *was* is often heard for *das* to refer to a neuter noun, e.g.: *das Buch, **was** er mir geliehen hat*. This usage is considered substandard.   *Should be das ✓ Wrong!*

(b) After a neuter adjective used as a noun referring to something indefinite
This usage is particularly frequent with superlatives:

✓ Das Richtige, **was** man sich ansehen müsste, finden wir nie (*Fallada*)	*The right things [in museums] that one ought to look at, we never find*
✓ Das Erste, **was** Evelyn sah, waren Mariannes Augen (*Baum*)	*The first thing Evelyn saw was Marianne's eyes*

If the adjective refers to something specific, *das* can be used: *Das Gute, **das** er getan hat, wird ihn überdauern*, although the difference in meaning can be very slight. However, *was* is always used after superlatives.   *Das Beste, was er (im Leben) getan hat*

(c) After the indefinite demonstrative *das*

Eben **das**, **was** uns fehlte, hat er uns verweigert	*He denied us just what we were lacking*

If *das* is in the genitive or dative, or after a preposition, it cannot be omitted. In English, by contrast, only 'what' may be needed. Compare:

Ich hörte nichts von **dem**, **was** er mir sagte	*I didn't hear anything of what he said to me*
eine Antwort auf **das**, **was** er gerade dachte (*Walser*)	*an answer to what he was just thinking*
ein eifriger Leser **dessen**, **was** neu auf den Markt kommt (*Zeit*)	*a keen reader of what is new on the market*

(d) To refer back to a whole clause

Er hat sein Examen bestanden, **was** mich sehr erstaunt	*He has passed his examination, which surprises me very much*
Er sagte, er hätte mich damals gesehen, **was** ich nicht glauben konnte	*He said he had seen me then, which I couldn't believe*

5.4.4 Relative pronouns after prepositions

(a) Normal usage is the appropriate form of *der* after the preposition

The construction corresponds more closely to that of written English than to that with a 'stranded' preposition typical of spoken English (compare the alternative translations of the first example):

die Frau, **auf die** Sie warten	{ *the woman for whom you are waiting* { *the woman (who) you are waiting for*
der Stuhl, **auf den** du dich setzen wolltest	*the chair you wanted to sit down on*
der Stuhl, **auf dem** du sitzt	*the chair you are sitting on*
der Bleistift, **mit dem** sie schreibt	*the pencil she is writing with*
die Stadt, **in der** ich wohne	*the town I live in*

(b) The form *wo(r)*+preposition as a relative pronoun

The forms of the prepositional adverb in *wo(r)*- (e.g. *worauf, woran, wovon*, etc., see 5.3.3c) are used as relative pronouns in some constructions.

(i) *wo(r)*+preposition is used in all contexts where *was* is used as a relative pronoun (see 5.4.3), since *was* is not used after a preposition:

Das, **woran** du denkst, errate ich nie	*I'll never guess what you're thinking of*
Es kam etwas, **womit** kein Mensch auf der Welt hätte rechnen können (*Süßkind*)	*Something came which nobody on earth could have reckoned with*
Er hat sein Examen bestanden, **worüber** ich mich freue	*He has passed his examination, which I am very pleased about*

If *etwas* refers to something specific, preposition + *das* can be used instead of *wo(r)* + preposition:

Ich spürte, dass noch etwas geschehen war ... etwas, **für das** sich nur ein Anlass ergeben hatte (*Lenz*)

(ii) *wo(r)*+preposition used to be a common alternative to the preposition followed by *der* to refer to things, e.g.: *das Heim, worin ich geboren wurde (Th. Mann)*.

This usage is now unusual even in formal registers, and the standard authorities advise against it.

NB: The use of prepositional adverb with *da(r)*- (e.g. *darauf, daran,* cf. 3.5) as a relative pronoun to refer to things, e.g.: *das Heim,* **darin** *ich geboren wurde,* is now wholly obsolete.

5.4.5 'the one who', 'he/she who', 'that which'

There are a number of German equivalents for these English constructions.

(a) *wer* and *was* can be used in generalisations

Wer viele Freunde hat, ist glücklich	*He who has many friends is happy*
Wer wagt, gewinnt	*Who dares wins*
Und **was** noch schlimmer ist, er merkt es selber nicht	*And what is worse, he doesn't realise it himself*
Was du sagst, stimmt nicht	*What you say is not right*

If there is a difference in case or construction between the two clauses, an appropriate demonstrative pronoun can be added to begin the main clause:

Wen es zum Lehrerberuf hinzieht, **der** bevorzugt eher die philosophischen Fächer	*Those who are attracted to the teaching profession favour Arts subjects*
Was wir getan haben, **darüber** müssen wir auch Rechenschaft ablegen	*What we have done we shall also have to answer for*

Often, though, no such clarifying demonstrative pronoun is used:

Wen es zum Lehrerberuf hinzieht, bevorzugt eher die philosophischen Fächer (*Zeit*)

(b) Relative pronouns used after a demonstrative pronouns
The following alternatives are found

(i) demonstrative *der* followed by relative *der*. Despite the repetition, this is the commonest alternative:

Die, die gingen, haben in der DDR mehr verändert, als **die, die** blieben (*FR*)	*Those who left have changed more in the GDR than those who stayed*

(ii) in more elevated styles, demonstrative *der* followed by relative *welcher*:

Die, welche ich kaufen wollte, waren mir zu teuer	*The ones I wanted to buy were too expensive for me*

(iii) demonstrative *derjenige* followed by relative *der* (or, in elevated style, *welcher*). This is frequent in both speech and writing:

Diejenigen, die (welche) in den hinteren Reihen saßen, konnten nichts sehen	*Those who were sitting in the back rows couldn't see anything*

(iv) demonstrative *jener* followed by relative *der* (or *welcher*). This is not uncommon in formal writing:

Der deutsche Zug darf nicht aufgehalten werden von **jenen, die** sich hinter Europa verstecken, um Deutschland zu verhindern (*ARD*)	*The train called Germany mustn't be held up by those people who are hiding behind Europe in order to prevent a (united) Germany*

(v) *der* can be used as a compound relative (e.g. 'he who'). This is common in speech:

Die hier sitzen, sind Verfluchte (*Wolf*)	*Those who are sitting here are cursed*
Der ihm Brötchen und Bockwurst verkaufte, kam aus Winsen an der Luhe (*Surminski*)	*The man who sold him rolls and sausage came from Winsen an der Luhe*

5.4.6 Other forms of the relative pronoun

(a) To refer to a place, *wo* can be used as a relative pronoun as an alternative to *der* with a preposition

die Stadt, **wo** (*or:* in der) ich wohne	*the town where I live*

If motion to or from a place is involved, *wohin* or *woher* are used:

die Stadt, **wohin** (*or:* in die) ich ging	*the town to which I went*
das Dorf, **woher** (*or:* aus dem) er kam	*the village from which he came*

NB: The use of *wo* as a general relative pronoun (e.g.: *die Frau, **wo** jetzt kommt*) is a substandard regionalism.

(b) Usage with time words

In such contexts English often uses 'when' as a relative. A number of alternatives exist in German, depending on register:

(i) Preposition with *der* is the most widely accepted form for writing:

Den Tag, **an dem** er ankam, werde ich nie vergessen	*I shall never forget the day when he arrived*
in einer Zeit, **in der** die Jugend immer unabhängiger wird	*at a time when young people are becoming more and more independent*

(ii) *als* (for past time) or *wenn* (for present or future time) are possible alternatives. In formal (especially literary) German *da* is often used:

In dem Augenblick, **als** der Hund aufsprang, schrie er (*Valentin*)	*At the moment when the dog jumped up, he cried out*
an seinem nächsten Geburtstag, **wenn** er volljährig wird	*on his next birthday, when he comes of age*
Ach, wo sind die Zeiten, **da** Pinneberg sich für einen guten Verkäufer hielt? (*Fallada*)	*Alas, where are the days when Pinneberg considered himself a good salesman?*

(iii) The use of *wo* as a relative indicating time is common, especially in speech, and it is also widely used in writing. However. many Germans consider it to be colloquial and prefer other alternatives in formal registers:

im Augenblick, **wo** er die Tür aufmachte	*at the moment when he opened the door*

Wir leben in einer Zeit, **wo** Verkaufen arm macht (*Remarque*)	*We live in a time when selling makes one poor*
jetzt, **wo** ich das weiß	*now that I know that*

(c) *wie* is used to indicate manner, principally after *die Art*

die Art, **wie** er zu mir sprach	*the manner in which he spoke to me*
so, **wie** ich es gewohnt bin	*just as I am used to*

(d) *warum* is used to indicate cause, chiefly after *der Grund*
weshalb is an alternative in formal registers:

der Grund, **warum** (weshalb) ich nach Aachen ging	*the reason why I went to Aachen*

5.5 Indefinites, quantifiers and other determiners and pronouns

This section deals with the meaning and use of the remaining determiners and pronouns, in alphabetical order. A list of them, with their most frequent English equivalents, is given in Table 5.9. The declension of adjectives after these determiners is explained in 6.2.3.

TABLE 5.9 *Indefinites, quantifiers and determiners*

aller, alle	*all (the)*	folgende(r)	*the following*	manch(er)	*some*
ander	*(the) other*	irgend(-)	*some-*	mehrere	*several*
beide(s)	*both*	jeder	*each, every*	meinesgleichen	*people like me*
einer	*one*	jedermann	*everyone*	nichts	*nothing*
ein bisschen	*a little*	jedweder	*each, every*	sämtlich(e)	*all (the)*
ein paar	*a few*	jeglicher	*each, every*	unsereiner	*someone like me*
ein wenig	*a little*	jemand, niemand	*someone, no-one*	viel, viele	*much, many*
einige(r)	*some*	kein(er)	*no, none*	wenig, wenige	*a little, a few*
etliche	*some*	lauter	*nothing but*	welcher	*some*
etwas	*something*	man	*one*	wer	*someone*

5.5.1 *aller, alle* 'all (the)'

(a) *all-* 'all (the)', used as a DETERMINER, has various alternative forms
(i) Inflected *aller*, with the endings of *dieser* (see Table 5.2), used on its own:

Alle Kinder spielen gern	*All children like playing*
Alle Schüler waren gekommen	*All the pupils had come*
mit **allen** denkbaren Mitteln	*with all conceivable means*
alles Glück dieser Erde	*all the happiness of this world*

This is the commonest alternative in the plural, especially in the nominative and accusative. In the singular it is largely restricted to formal registers and set phrases. Plural *alle* may correspond to English 'all the' or 'all (of) the', e.g. *alle Schüler* 'all the pupils'/'all of the pupils'. *alle* is **never** followed by a genitive.

NB: In the genitive singular masculine and neuter, the ending *-en* is used rather than *-es* if the noun has the ending *-(e)s*, e.g.: *solch verfehlte Ablehnung allen* (less frequent: *alles*) *Verhandelns* (*Zeit*).

(ii) Inflected *aller* followed by the definite article:

alle die Bücher	*all the books*
alle die Mühe	*all the trouble*

This is quite common in the plural, especially in colloquial speech, and with feminine nouns in the nominative and accusative singular.

(iii) Uninflected *all* followed by the definite article:

all das schlechte Wetter	*all the bad weather*
all die Schüler	*all the pupils*
mit **all dem** Geld	*with all the money*

This is the most frequent alternative in the singular, and it is quite frequent in the plural. Attempts to establish a consistent difference of meaning between inflected and uninflected forms are unconvincing.

NB: The most idiomatic equivalent of English *all* with a singular noun is often a phrase with *ganz*, see (g) below.

(b) *all-* is often used in conjunction with another determiner
In the plural both inflected and uninflected forms are found, in the singular only uninflected *all*:

all mein Geld
von **all diesem** Brot
all/alle meine Brüder
nach **all ihrer** Mühe
mit **all/allen diesen** Schwierigkeiten

NB: Only the inflected form is used before *solch*, which then has the endings of an adjective, e.g.: *alle solchen Frauen*.

(c) *all-* used as a PRONOUN declines like *dieser*
(see Table 5.2), but it has no genitive singular forms. The neuter singular *alles* is used for 'everything', the plural *alle* for 'everyone':

Alles ist bereit	*Everything is ready*
Ich bin mit **allem** einverstanden	*I agree to everything*
Alle waren anwesend	*Everybody was present*
Sind das **alle**?	*Is that all (of them)?*

(d) Plural *alle* 'all' is often used with a personal pronoun

Sie hat uns **alle** beleidigt	*She insulted us all*
Ich habe mit ihnen **allen** gesprochen	*I have spoken to all of them*
Das ist unser **aller** Hoffnung	*That is the hope of all of us*

alle usually follows the pronoun, but in the nominative it can be separated from it. In this case it has slightly less emphasis. Compare:

Sie **alle** sind gekommen	*They have all come*
Sie sind **alle** gekommen	

(e) Uninflected *all* and inflected *alles* are commonly used with the demonstratives *das* and *dieses*

This corresponds to English 'all that' or 'all this'. Uninflected *all* always precedes the demonstrative, but inflected *alles* may precede or follow the demonstrative, or, with less emphasis, be separated from it:

Ich habe **all das/alles das/das alles** ⎫ schon gesehen **Das** habe ich **alles** schon gesehen ⎭	*I've already seen all that*
Ich bin mit **all dem/dem allen/allem** dem einverstanden	*I agree to all that*
Mit all diesem werde ich nicht fertig	*I can't cope with all this*

NB: In the dative singular, when *all-* follows the demonstrative, it can have the ending *-en* as an alternative to *-em*, e.g.: *dem/diesem allen* or *dem allem*.

(f) A noun can be qualified by a following inflected *all-*

all- follows the verb if the noun comes first. This usage is most common in the plural:

> **Die Kinder** spielen **alle** im Garten
> **Die Semmeln** sind **alle** trocken

In the singular this construction is colloquial and restricted to the nominative and accusative singular feminine and neuter:

> **Das Brot** ist **alles** trocken
> Ich habe **die Milch alle** verschüttet

Singular *alles* is often used with a plural noun after the verb *sein* in the sense 'nothing but': *Das sind **alles** Lügen.*

(g) The use of *ganz* for English 'all'

In practice, the adjective *ganz* is often the most idiomatic equivalent of English 'all', particularly with singular nouns. Thus, English 'all my money' may correspond in German to *mein ganzes Geld* or *all mein Geld*, with the former being rather more frequent. Compare also:

Der **ganze** Wein war schlecht	*All the wine was bad*
diese **ganze** Unsicherheit	*all this uncertainty*
mit seiner **ganzen** jugendlichen Energie	*with all his youthful energy*

With collective nouns, time expressions and geographical names *ganz* is often the only possible equivalent for English 'all':

Die **ganze** Familie kommt	*all of the family is coming*
den **ganzen** Tag (lang)	*all day (long)*
der **ganze** Januar war kalt	*all January it was cold*
ganz Europa, **ganz** Schweden, **ganz** München	*all (of) Europe, all (of) Sweden, all (of) Munich*
in der **ganzen** Schweiz	*in all of Switzerland*

The use of *ganz* with a plural noun is colloquial, e.g.: *Nach dem Sturm waren die ganzen Fenster kaputt*. In such cases *sämtliche* (see 5.5.23) is a common alternative in formal registers, e.g.: *Nach dem Sturm waren **sämtliche** Fenster* ('all the windows') *kaputt*.

(h) Other uses of *all-*

(i) *alles* can be used to emphasise a large number of people or things with the interrogatives *wer* and *was*, cf. 5.3.3b, e.g.: *Wer kommt denn **alles**? Was hast du dort **alles** gekauft?*

(ii) In regional colloquial speech in the south and west, *all(e)s* (often spelled *als*) is used to emphasise the continuous nature of an action (= English 'to keep on doing sth.'), e.g.: *Er hat **als** geflucht* 'He kept on cursing'

(iii) In colloquial North German *alle* is used in the sense of 'all gone': *Die Butter ist jetzt **alle**. Meine Geduld ist **alle**.*

(iv) *alle* is compounded with the demonstrative pronoun in the phrases *bei alledem* 'for all that', *trotz alledem* 'in spite of all that'.

(v) *alles* occurs frequently with an adjective used as a noun, see 6.4.5, e.g.: *alles Wichtige* 'all (the) important things'.

5.5.2 *ander* 'other'

(a) In most contexts *ander* is used simply as an adjective
However, it has a few special forms and uses which resemble those of a determiner or pronoun. The following examples illustrate the range of its most common uses:

der **and(e)re** Student	*the other student*
mein **anderes** Auto	*my other car*
der **and(e)re**	*the other one*
irgendein **and(e)rer**	*some/any other one*
die drei **anderen**	*the three others*
alle **anderen**	*all the others*
alles **and(e)re**	*everything else*

(b) Notes on the spelling and forms of *ander*
(i) The first *-e-* is often dropped in writing, e.g. *andre, andrer, andres*. With the endings *-en* and *-em*, though, it is more usual to drop the second *-e-*, e.g. *ander(e)m, ander(e)n* (less common: *andrem, andren*).

(ii) When used with a preceding determiner, it differs from other adjectives in not normally being spelled with a capital letter: *der and(e)re, alles and(e)re*, etc. However, an initial small or capital letter can be used after *etwas* and *nichts*: *etwas and(e)res/And(e)res, nichts and(e)res/And(e)res*.

(iii) When *ander* is used without a preceding article or other determiner, a following adjective has the same ('strong') endings as those of *ander*, <u>except</u> that *-en* is the norm in the dative singular masculine and neuter:

anderes dumm**es** Gerede	mit anderer moderner Musik
andere italienische Maler	aus anderem wertvollen Material

NB: (i) 'another cup of tea' = *noch eine Tasse Tee*.
(ii) For the adverb *anders* 'else', see 7.3.5.

5.5.3 *beide* 'both'

(a) *beide* **'both' can be used as a determiner or a pronoun**
It has the same endings as the plural of *dieser* (see Table 5.2):

Ich habe **beide** Bücher gekauft	*I bought both books*
Beide Brüder sind gekommen	*Both brothers came*
Seine Brüder sind **beide** gekommen	*His brothers both came*
Beide sind gekommen	*Both came*

When used as a pronoun, *beide* can be strengthened by *alle*:

Alle beide sind gekommen	*The two of them came*

(b) *beide* **can also be used as a simple adjective**
after a definite article or another determiner. It then has the endings of an adjective ('weak' declension) and often corresponds to English 'two':

Seine **beiden** Brüder sind gekommen	*His two brothers came*
Die **beiden** Brüder sind gekommen	*The two brothers came*

(c) **Used with a personal pronoun,** *beide* **usually has the endings of** *dieser*

wir **beide**, sie **beide**, von euch **beiden**, unser **beider**

There is some variation in usage with *wir* and *ihr*:

(i) In isolation *wir beiden* can be used rather than *wir beide*. It is generally less common, but it is usual if a noun follows, e.g.: *wir beiden Freunde*.

(ii) *ihr beiden* is more usual than *ihr beide* in isolation, e.g.: *Ihr **beiden**, wollt ihr mitkommen?* Within a clause either is usual, e.g.: *Wollt ihr **beide(n)** schon mitkommen?*

(iii) If *beide* is separated from the pronoun, only the ending *-e* is usual:

Wir wollen **beide** schon mitkommen.	Ihr wolltet **beide** mitkommen, oder?

Beide halten sie ein Wahlergebnis für möglich, das eine große Koalition erzwänge (*Zeit*)	*They **both** consider an election result possible which would force a grand coalition*

(d) **The neuter singular** *beides* **is used collectively to refer to two things:**

Sie hatte einen Hut und einen Regenschirm mit und ließ **beides** im Zug liegen	*She had a hat and an umbrella with her and left both on the train*
Sprechen Sie Deutsch oder Englisch? – **Beides**	*Do you speak German or English? – Both.*
Beides ist möglich	*Either is possible*

If *beides* is the subject of *sein*, the verb can be singular or plural:

Das Hotel und die Landschaft: **beides ist/sind** schön	*The hotel and the scenery: both are lovely*

NB: The use of *beides* to refer to people is purely colloquial, e.g.: *Ich habe mit den Brüdern Schmid zu Mittag gegessen. **Beides** ist/sind* (in writing: *Beide sind*) *Vegetarier.*

(e) Other uses of *beide* and other equivalents of English 'both'

Einer von beiden könnte uns helfen	*One/Either of the two could help us*
An beiden Enden des Ganges hängt ein Bild	*At either end of the corridor there is a picture*
in beiden Fällen	*in either case*
Keiner von beiden ist gekommen	*Neither of them came*
Sowohl seine Frau **als (auch)** seine Tochter sind krank	*Both his wife and his daughter are sick*

5.5.4 *einer* 'one'

(a) The pronoun *einer* declines like the possessive pronoun *meiner*

The forms are given in Table 5.10. The pronoun *einer* has different endings from those of the indefinite article *ein* in the nominative singular masculine (*einer*) and the nominative/accusative singular neuter (*eines*).

TABLE 5.10 *Declension of the pronoun* einer

	Masculine	Feminine	Neuter
Nominative	einer	eine	eines
Accusative	einen	eine	eines
Genitive	eines	einer	eines
Dative	einem	einer	einem

The genitive forms of *einer* are not in common use. A paraphrase with *von* (see 2.4) is usually preferred, e.g.: *die Empfehlung **von einem** ihrer Freunde*, rather than: *die Empfehlung **eines** ihrer Freunde* 'the recommendation of one of her friends'.

NB: (i) *eines* is often written *eins*, reflecting its usual pronounciation.
(ii) For the use of *eins* as a numeral 'one', see **9.1.2**.

(b) *einer* corresponds to English pronoun 'one'

einer der Männer, **eine** der Frauen, **ein(e)s** der Kinder	*one of the men, one of the women, one of the children*
Ein Fenster war offen und **ein(e)s** war zu	*One window was open and one was shut*
Ich sprach mit **einer** der Damen	*I spoke to one of the ladies*
eines der Themen, die der slowenische Außenminister angesprochen hat (*Presse*)	*one of the topics which the Slovenian foreign minister touched on*

Unstressed *einer* has the negative *keiner*, see 5.5.16, stressed *einer* has the negative *nicht einer*. Compare: *Ich habe **keinen** gesehen* 'I haven't seen one' and: *Ich habe **nicht einen** gesehen* 'I haven't seen a single one'.

(c) *einer* often has the sense of 'someone', 'anyone'

Einer muss es getan haben	*Someone must have done it*
einer, der ihn kannte	*a person/someone who knew him*
Mit so **einem** will ich nichts zu tun haben	*I don't want anything to do with anyone like that*
Da kam **einer** durch die Glastür	*Someone came through the glass door*

This is common in spoken German. It is often equivalent to *jemand*, see **5.5.15**, although this more clearly refers to an indefinite 'somebody' whose identity is quite unknown. *jemand* is also generally more polite, whereas *einer* can sound offensive, particularly in the feminine, e.g.: *Da war gerade **eine** mit sechs Kindern*.

The case forms of *einer* are used for those which *man* lacks (principally the accusative and dative, see **5.5.18**), but using *einer* for *man* in the nominative (e.g.: *Und das soll **einer** wissen!* for: *Und das soll man wissen!*) is restricted to colloquial speech.

(d) *ein-* can be used as an adjective with the definite article, the demonstratives or the possessives

It then has the 'weak' adjective endings (see Table 6.3), but it never has an initial capital letter, even when there is no noun following:

Der **eine** deutsche Tourist beschwerte sich	*One German tourist complained*
das **eine**, das ich brauche	*the one thing I need*
Mein **einer** Sohn ist gestorben (coll.)	*One of my sons has died*
Dieser **eine** Schnaps wird dich nicht gleich umwerfen	*This one schnupps won't knock you out*

Particularly common is *der eine* linked to a following *der andere*, corresponding to English '(the) one ... the other', etc. In German, though, the definite article is usually present, whereas it can be lacking in English, and the plural *die einen* can occur, in the meaning 'some':

Das eine Buch habe ich gelesen, **das andere** aber noch nicht	*I've read one of the books, but not the other one yet*
Die einen sangen, **die anderen** spielten	*Some were singing, others were playing*

(e) Some idiomatic uses of *einer*

Das ist aber **einer**!	*He's quite a lad*
Du bist mir **einer**! (see 2.5.3e)	*You're a nice one!*
Eins wollte ich noch sagen	*There's one more thing I wanted to say*
Trinken wir noch **eins**?	*Shall we have another (drink)?*
Es ist mir alles **eins**	*It's all the same to me*
Er redet **in einem** fort	*He talks without stopping*

5.5.5 *ein wenig, ein bisschen* 'a little'

(a) *ein wenig* corresponds to English 'a little'

The *ein* does <u>not</u> decline. A phrase with *von* (see 2.4) is used rather than a genitive:

Ich hatte noch **ein wenig** deutsches Geld	*I still had a little German money*
Der Zug hatte sich **ein wenig** verspätet	*The train had got a little late*
Der Saal war **ein wenig** ruhiger geworden	*The room had become a little more quiet*
mit **ein wenig** männlicher Eitelkeit	*with a little male vanity*

(b) *ein bisschen* can replace *ein wenig* in most contexts

It could be used in all the examples in (a) without any difference in meaning, but it can sound more colloquial. Unlike *ein wenig*, it can, optionally, be declined in the dative singular, e.g. *mit ein(em) bisschen Geld*. This is normal when it is used as a pronoun, e.g. *Mit einem bisschen wäre ich schon zufrieden*. It also differs from *ein wenig* in that it can occur with a preceding adjective:

ein winziges **bisschen** Käse	*a tiny little bit of cheese*
mit einem ganz kleinen **bisschen** gesundem Verstand	*with a very little bit of common sense*

NB: In spoken south German usage the form *ein bisse(r)l* is a frequent variant for northern *ein bisschen*.

(c) *bisschen* may also be used with a demonstrative, a possessive or *kein*

mit **dem bisschen** Verstand, den er hat	*with that little sense he has*
mit **ihrem bisschen** Talent	*with her bit of talent*
Er hat **kein bisschen** Humor	*He hasn't got the least sense of humour*

5.5.6 *ein paar* 'a few'

The *ein* of *ein paar* does not decline. A phrase with *von* (see 2.4) is used rather than a genitive. *ein paar* is close in meaning to *einige*, see 5.5.7, but it sounds more colloquial:

Ein paar Flaschen Wein haben wir noch im Keller	*We've still got a few bottles of wine in the cellar*
Willst du **ein paar** haben?	*Do you want a few?*
mit der Hilfe von **ein paar** alten Freunden	*with the help of a few old friends*

The *ein* can be replaced by another determiner, which <u>is</u> declined. Such combinations can sound disparaging or pejorative:

Was soll ich mit den **paar** Mark anfangen?	*What am I supposed to do with these lousy few marks?*
der Wert meiner **paar** Möbel	*the value of my few bits of furniture*
Die Straßenbahn kommt alle **paar** Minuten	*The tram comes every few minutes*

NB: *ein paar* should not be confused with *ein Paar* 'a pair'. Compare *ein paar Schuhe* 'a few shoes' but *ein Paar Schuhe* 'a pair of shoes'.

5.5.7 *einiger, einige* 'some'

einig- refers to a limited amount or number. It corresponds to English unstressed 'some', (or 'a few', as it is close in meaning to *ein paar*, see 5.5.6). It declines like *dieser* (see Table 5.2) except that the genitive singular masculine and neuter form (which is little used) is *einigen*.

(a) The use of *einiger* in the singular is limited

The usual German equivalents of English unstressed *some* in the singular are *etwas* (see 5.5.9), or, most commonly, simply no article or determiner at all (see 4.8.7), e.g.: *Ich habe heute (etwas) Butter gekauft* 'I bought some butter today'.

When *einig-* is used in the singular it implies a rather unusual or unexpected quantity and often comes close to English 'no little'. It is most frequent with mass and abstract nouns (especially *Entfernung* and *Zeit*), adjectives used as nouns and collectives:

mit **einigem** Glück	*with some degree of luck*
bei **einigem** guten Willen (*Th. Mann*)	*with a certain degree of good will*
vor ihm in **einiger** Entfernung	*some distance in front of him*
vor **einiger** Zeit schon	*some time ago now*
nach **einigem** Überlegen	*after some consideration*
Diese Schlangen, die ihr Gift spucken, zielen bis drei Meter weit noch mit **einiger** Treffsicherheit (*Grzimek*)	*These snakes, which spit their venom, can aim up to three metres with no little accuracy*

Singular *einig-* is mainly used as a determiner rather than as a pronoun, but the neuter singular *einiges* does occur as a collective indefinite pronoun:

einiges davon	*some of it*
Ich habe noch **einiges** zu tun	*I've still got a few things to do*

(b) *einige* is widely used both as a determiner and a pronoun in the plural

Sie wollte **einige** Ansichtskarten von Rothenburg kaufen	*She wanted to buy some postcards of Rothenburg*
In der Stadt gibt es **einige** Friseure	*There are a few hairdressers in the town*
unter Verwendung **einiger** technischer Mittel	*by using some technical methods*
Einige mussten stehen	*Some/A few had to stand*
Sie hat schon **einige** mitgebracht	*She's already brought some/a few*

German often uses no determiner in contexts where English uses unstressed 'some' to refer to a number of things. Thus, a common alternative to the first example above would be: *Sie wollte Ansichtskarten von Rothenburg kaufen.*

NB: *einige* is often used with numerals to mean 'a few', e.g. *einige tausend Bücher* 'a few thousand books'.

5.5.8 *etliche* 'some'

etliche is similar in meaning to *einige*. However, it typically implies 'more than the expected number'. In this way, it approaches English 'several' or 'a fair number of'. It declines like *dieser* (see Table 5.2) and it is almost only used in the plural, as a determiner (much less commonly as a pronoun).

It is quite widely used, with its special meaning, in both spoken and written German, and it is by no means obsolete or old-fashioned, as some authorities maintain:

Warum ist die Bahn so unpünktlich geworden? Da gibt es **etliche** Ursachen (*Spiegel*)	*Why have the railways become so unpunctual? There are several/ a (good) number of reasons for this*
Etliche dieser Stücke sind auch für Anfänger relativ leicht zu bewältigen (*SWF*)	*Some/A number of these pieces are relatively easy to manage, even for a beginner*

5.5.9 etwas 'something', 'anything'

etwas is used as an **indefinite pronoun**, to **qualify nouns**, and as an **adverb**. It has no case forms and is not used in genitive constructions, a phrase with *von* (see 2.4) being used if necessary.

(a) As an indefinite pronoun, *etwas* corresponds to English 'something' or 'anything'

Etwas störte mich	*Something bothered me*
Ich habe **etwas** für Sie	*I've got something for you*
Hast du **etwas** gesagt?	*Did you say anything?*

In this use, *etwas* is commonly reduced to *was* in colloquial speech unless it occupies first position in the sentence, e.g. *Ich habe **was** für Sie; Hast du **was** gesagt? etwas* is often used with *von* in a partitive sense, i.e. 'some (of)':

Ich möchte **etwas** von diesem Kuchen	*I would like some of this cake*

etwas can be omitted in such contexts: *Ich möchte von diesem Kuchen.*

(b) Qualifying a noun, *etwas* has the sense of 'some', 'any' or 'a little'
It is used chiefly with mass and abstract nouns in the singular. However, as an equivalent to unstressed English 'some' or 'any', German very commonly does not use any determiner at all (see 4.2.2a, 4.8.7 and 5.5.7b), and *etwas* could be omitted in all the examples below:

Ich brauche **etwas** frisches Fleisch	*I need some fresh meat*
Er hat kaum **etwas** Geld	*He has hardly any money*
Bringen Sie mir bitte **etwas** Brot	*Please bring me some bread*
Sie muss **etwas** Geduld haben	*She needs a little patience*
Etwas mehr Aufmerksamkeit wäre nützlich gewesen	*A little more attention would have been useful*

etwas is commonly used with a following adjective used as a noun, (see 6.4.5). The adjective has the 'strong' adjective endings:

etwas ganz Neu**es**	*something quite new*
Er hat von **etwas** ganz Neu**em** gesprochen	*He spoke of something quite new*

(c) As an adverb, *etwas* means 'somewhat', 'a bit'

Er ist **etwas** nervös	*He is somewhat/rather/a bit nervous*
Es geht ihm **etwas** besser	*He is somewhat/a bit better*
Er zögerte **etwas**	*He hesitated somewhat/a bit*

5.5.10 folgend '(the) following'

folgend can be used as a simple adjective, but it has some special forms and uses which resemble those of a determiner or pronoun. Unlike English 'following', it is often used without a preceding article or other determiner. In these contexts a following adjective usually has 'weak' endings in the singular and 'strong' endings in the plural, see 6.2.3:

alle **folgenden** Bemerkungen	*all the following remarks*
Sie machte **folgende** Bemerkungen	*She made the following remarks*
Sie machte **folgende** treffende Bemerkungen	*She made the following apposite remarks*
folgender interessante Gedanke	*the following interesting thought*
mit **folgender** nachdrücklichen Warnung	*with the following firm warning*
Sie sagte mir **Folgendes**: ...	*She said the following to me: ...*
Im **Folgenden** wird diese Frage näher erläutert	*In the following this question will be clarified more precisely*
Aus **Folgendem** lässt sich schließen, dass ...	*From the following it may be deduced that ...*

When *folgend* is used as a pronoun meaning 'the following', as in the last three examples, it has an initial capital letter.

5.5.11 *irgend* 'some ... or other'

(a) The principal use of *irgend* is to emphasise indefiniteness
It occurs in combination with many indefinite pronouns, adverbs and determiners, giving them the sense of 'some ... or other' or 'any ... at all'. All these compounds of *irgend* are nowadays written as single words, e.g. *irgendetwas*, *irgendjemand*, *irgendwo*.

(b) *irgend* can be compounded with most interrogative adverbs to form indefinite adverbs
(see 7.5 for the basic forms of these interrogative adverbs), i.e.:

irgendwann 'sometime or other, any time'; *irgendwie* 'somehow, anyhow'; *irgendwo* 'somewhere, anywhere'; *irgendwohin* '(to) somewhere, anywhere'; *irgendwoher* 'from somewhere, anywhere':

Du musst es **irgendwie** machen	*You'll have to do it somehow*
Er fährt heute Nachmittag **irgendwohin**	*He's going somewhere this afternoon*
Gehst du heute Abend **irgendwohin**?	*Are you going anywhere tonight?*

(c) With *einer*, *(et)was*, *jemand* and *wer*, *irgend* stresses indefiniteness
irgendeiner, *irgendjemand* and *irgendwer* correspond to English 'somebody, anybody', *irgendetwas* to 'something, anything'. In practice, *irgendeiner* and *irgendwer* are commoner than simple *einer* and *wer* (see 5.5.4 and 5.5.27) to mean 'somebody, anybody':

Irgendwann wurden von **irgendwem** diese Briefe aus dem Kasten genommen (*Böll*)	*At some time or other someone (or other) took these letters out of the letter-box*
Versteht er **irgendetwas** vom Wein?	*Does he know anything (at all) about wine?*
Irgendeiner soll es gesagt haben	*Someone (or other) is supposed to have said it*
Hat denn **irgendjemand** angerufen?	*Did anybody phone?*

Note that only *irgendjemand* and *irgendetwas*, <u>not</u> simple *jemand* or *etwas*, are possible in response to a question:

Wer hat eben geklopft? – **Irgendjemand**	*Who just knocked? – Someone or other*
Was willst du denn kaufen? – **Irgendetwas**	*What are you going to buy, then? – Something or other*

In colloquial north German, *irgend* can be compounded with the prepositional adverb with *wo(r)-* (see **5.3.3c**), in place of *irgendetwas* with a preposition:

Ich habe mich **irgendworan** gestoßen (written: *an irgendetwas*)	*I knocked against something or other*

(d) irgendein(er) and irgendwelcher

These correspond to 'some (or other), any (whatsoever)', often with the sense of 'no matter which/who'. They are used as determiners or pronouns.

(i) The determiner *irgendein* has the endings of the indefinite article *ein*, see Table 4.2. It is used in the singular with countable nouns:

Er zeigte mir **irgendeine** Broschüre	*He showed me some brochure or other*
Hat er **irgendeine** Bemerkung gemacht?	*Did he make any remark (at all)?*
Die Selbstmordquote soll höher sein als in **irgendeinem** anderen Ort der Welt (*Bednarz*)	*The suicide rate is supposed to be higher than in any other place in the world*

(ii) The pronoun *irgendeiner*, which declines like *einer* (see Table 5.10) has only singular forms and can only refer to countable nouns. The masculine and feminine forms are used in the sense of 'somebody, anybody':

Irgendeiner muss dich gesehen haben	*Someone or other must have seen you*
Wenn du wirklich einen neuen Tisch suchst, musst du hier im Geschäft **irgendeinen** gesehen haben, der dir gefällt	*If you're really looking for a new table, you must have seen one here in the shop which you like*
Ich habe ein paar Bücher über Berlin. Sie können sich **irgendeins** ausleihen	*I've got a few books on Berlin. You can borrow any one you like*

(iii) *irgendwelcher*, which declines like *dieser* (see Table 5.2), is used as a determiner in the singular with mass and abstract nouns, and in the plural. The genitive is rarely used in the singular:

Er zeigte mir **irgendwelche** neue Bücher	*He showed me some new books or other*
Er hat **irgendwelches** dumme(s) Zeug geredet	*He was talking some stupid rubbish or other*
Wenn Sie **irgendwelche** Probleme haben, wenden Sie sich an uns (*Bednarz*)	*If you have any problems (at all), turn to us*

NB: Colloquially, *irgendwelcher* is often used for *irgendein*, e.g. *Er zeigte mir* **irgendwelche** *Broschüre*.

(c) *irgend so ein* (plural: *irgend solche*) corresponds to English 'one/some of those', 'any/some such'

It often has a pejorative tone:

Wer war es? – Es war **irgend so ein** Vertreter für Doppelfenster	*Who was it? – It was one of those men who sell double glazing*
Er machte **irgend solche** komische Bemerkungen	*He made some such odd remarks*

(f) *irgend* **is used as an independent adverb with the sense of** *irgendwie* i.e. 'somehow, anyhow, in some way':

wenn **irgend** möglich	*if at all possible*
Ich würde mich freuen, wenn es **irgend** geht	*I would be pleased if it's possible somehow*

5.5.12 *jeder* 'each', 'every'

(a) *jeder* **is only used in the singular, as a determiner or a pronoun**
When used as a determiner, *jeder* corresponds to English 'each', 'every', when used as a pronoun to English 'everyone', 'everybody'. It declines like *dieser* (see Table 5.2), except that *jeden* (rather than *jedes*) is frequent in the genitive singular masculine and neuter if the following noun has the ending -(e)s, e.g. *am Ende jeden/jedes Abschnitts*. It is not used in the genitive as a pronoun.:

Sie hat **jedem** Kind einen Apfel gegeben	*She gave each child an apple*
nach **jedem** solchen Versuch	*after each such attempt*
Er kam **jeden** Tag zur selben Zeit	*He came every day at the same time*
In diesem kleinen Ort kennt **jeder jeden**	*In this little place everyone knows everybody else*

jeder often has an individualising sense (i.e. 'no matter which/who'), in which case it can be the equivalent of English 'any':

Das weiß doch **jeder** gebildete Bürger	*Any/Every educated citizen knows that, though*
Die industrielle Revolution verwandelte die Lebensbedingungen der Menschen radikaler als **jeder** andere Ereigniszusammenhang der neueren Geschichte (*Jaeger*)	*The Industrial Revolution changed people's living conditions more radically than any other set of events in recent history*

NB: The neuter *jedes* can refer back to both sexes. *Seine Eltern waren sehr tüchtig, jedes auf seine Weise.*

(b) The combination *ein jeder* **is more emphatic than** *jeder*
It is used chiefly as a pronoun and is particularly frequent in the individualising sense of stressed 'any', i.e. 'no matter which/who'. In this combination, *jeder* has same endings as a simple adjective:

Ein jeder wollte was sagen	*Everyone wanted to say something*
Das könnte doch **ein jeder** machen	*But everybody/anybody (at all) could do that*
Das kannst du doch nicht **einem jeden** erzählen	*But you can't tell that to just anybody*
Die Wünsche **eines jeden** werden berücksichtigt	*The wishes of every individual are taken into account*

5.5.13 jedermann 'everybody', 'everyone'

jedermann is only used in elevated, formal registers and set phrases. Its meaning is the same as that of *jeder*, which is much more commonly used. Its only case form is the genitive *jedermanns*.

Jedermann wusste, dass Michael den Wehrdienst verweigert hatte	*Everyone knew that Michael had refused to do military service*
Das ist nicht **jedermanns** Sache	*That's not everyone's cup of tea*

5.5.14 jedweder, jeglicher 'each', 'every'

jedweder and *jeglicher* decline like *dieser* (see Table 5.2). They are used as determiners or pronouns as alternatives to *jeder*, but they are both largely restricted to formal written language.

(a) *jedweder* is rather more emphatic than *jeder*
It has a rather old-fashioned ring and is used sparingly, even in formal registers:

Er weist seine Sekundanten an, auf **jedwede** Bedingung der Gegenseit einzugehen (*Frevert*)	*He instructs his seconds to agree to his opponent's each and every condition*

(b) *jeglicher* stresses the individuality of the items in question
It is most often used in the sense of stressed 'any' (i.e. 'no matter who/what'). It is most frequent nowadays with abstract nouns and in negative contexts. Unlike *jeder*, it can also be used in the plural:

Das entbehrt **jeglicher** Grundlage	*That is completely unfounded*
Gorbatschow lehnte **jegliche** Änderung der Grenzziehungen in der Sowjetunion ab (*FR*)	*Gorbachov turned down any alteration of the frontiers in the Soviet Union*
die vollkommen unbefangene Ablehnung **jeglicher** demagogischer Attraktionen (*Pörtner*)	*the completely natural rejection of all kinds of attractive demagogery*

5.5.15 jemand 'somebody', 'someone', niemand 'nobody', 'no-one'

(a) Declension and use of *jemand* and *niemand*
jemand 'somebody', 'someone' and *niemand* 'nobody', 'no-one' have the case forms shown in Table 5.11.

TABLE 5.11 *Declension of* jemand, niemand

Nominative	jemand	niemand
Accusative	jemanden	niemanden
Genitive	jemandes	niemandes
Dative	jemandem	niemandem

In the accusative and dative, forms without endings are at least as common as the forms with endings in both speech and writing:

Ich habe **niemand/niemanden** gesehen
Ich habe **jemand/jemandem** das Paket gegeben

The genitive forms tend to be avoided by paraphrasing, i.e. *Hat jemand diese Aktentasche liegen lassen?* rather than: *Ist das jemands Aktentasche?*

Pronouns and determiners referring back to *jemand* and *niemand* have the masculine singular form: *Niemand, der es weiß; Jemand hat seine Tasche vergessen*

NB: (i) In colloquial speech, *einer* and *wer* are common alternatives to *jemand*, see 5.5.4 and 5.5.27, as is *keiner* for *niemand*, see 5.5.16.

(ii) The indefiniteness of *jemand* may be emphasised by combining it with *irgend*, see 5.5.11c.

(b) *jemand* and *niemand* with a following adjective

When followed by an adjective, *jemand* and *niemand* are usually endingless in the accusative and dative. The adjective is treated as a noun (see 6.4), and it can have the ending *-es* in all cases, or, alternatively, the endings *-en* in the accusative and *-em* in the dative cases.

> Jemand Fremdes ist gekommen
> Ich habe jemand Fremdes/en gesehen
> Ich habe mit jemand Fremdes/em gesprochen

jemand and *niemand* can be used in a similar way with *ander*, which, unlike other adjectives, always has a small initial letter in all these forms:

> Jemand anders ist gekommen
> Ich habe jemand anders/anderen gesehen
> Ich habe mit jemand anders/anderem gesprochen

NB: The endings *-en* and *-em* are more typical of south German usage. Here, too, the ending *-er* is used in the nominative case, e.g. *jemand anderer, jemand Bekannter*. However, this is regarded as a substandard regionalism.

5.5.16 *kein, keiner* 'no', 'not … any', 'none'

(a) *kein* is the negative form of the indefinite article

See 4.1.2. Its forms are given in Table 4.2. It is used typically where a corresponding positive sentence would have an indefinite or no article, and it thus usually corresponds to English 'not a', 'not … any' or 'no':

Sie hat ein Auto	Sie hat **kein** Auto
Wir haben frische Brötchen	Wir haben **keine** frischen Brötchen
Ich habe Zeit	Ich habe **keine** Zeit

(b) *kein* or *nicht* in negation?

It sometimes seems difficult to know whether to use *kein* or *nicht* in negation. In general, *kein* is used to negate an indefinite noun (i.e. one with an indefinite article or no article), as in the examples given under (a) above. *nicht* is used in other cases, notably to negate a whole sentence, e.g. *Sie will heute mitkommen – Sie will heute nicht mitkommen*. However, there are contexts where the choice is not completely obvious, i.e.:

(i) German phrases with an indefinite noun (and thus negated with *kein*) which have rather different English equivalents:

Ich bin Deutscher	Ich bin **kein** Deutscher
Ich spreche Deutsch	Ich spreche **kein** Deutsch
ein Problem von großer Bedeutung	ein Problem von **keiner** großen Bedeutung

(ii) Phrasal verbs with nouns, e.g. *Atem holen, sich Mühe geben, Freude empfinden* and all those with *haben*, e.g. *Angst, Durst, Hunger haben*, etc. are generally negated with *kein*:

Er hat sich **keine** Mühe gegeben   Ich habe **keinen** Durst, Hunger
Dabei hat er **keine** Freude empfunden   Sie hatten **keine** Angst

Phrasal verbs with *nehmen* have *kein* **or** *nicht*:

Er hat **keine/nicht** Rücksicht auf mich genommen
Sie wollen **keine/nicht** Rache nehmen
Sie hat **keinen/nicht** Abschied von ihm genommen

nicht occurs with phrasal verbs where the noun is so closely linked to the verb that it is felt to be the equivalent of a separable prefix:

Er spielt **nicht** Klavier   Er hat **nicht** Wort gehalten
Sie läuft **nicht** Schi   Er kann **nicht** Auto fahren
Sie haben in Berlin **nicht** Wurzel gefasst   Sie schreibt **nicht** Maschine

Similarly: *Schritt fahren, Gefahr laufen*, etc.

(c) *kein* and *nicht ein*

kein is the usual equivalent of English 'not a' (and using *nicht ein* for *kein* is typical of English learners' German). Nevertheless, there are a few contexts where *nicht ein* is used:

(i) if *ein* is stressed, i.e. 'not one/a (single)':

Die TAP besitzt **nicht ein** Flugzeug,   *TAP doesn't own a single aeroplane, as all*
  denn alle 38 Maschinen sind geleast   *38 planes are leased*
  (NZZ)

(ii) for direct contrasts:

Das ist eine Ulme, **nicht eine** Eiche   *That's an elm, not an oak*

(iii) *nicht ein* is more usual than *kein* after *wenn* 'if': *Man hätte ihn kaum bemerkt, wenn ihm **nicht ein** Schnurrbart etwas Distinguiertes verliehen hätte.*

(d) Some idiomatic uses of *kein* as a determiner

Sie ist noch **keine** zehn Jahre alt   *She's not yet ten years old*
keine zwei Stunden vor meiner Abreise   *within two hours of my departure*
Es ist noch **keine** fünf Minuten her   *It is less than five minutes ago*
Sie ist schließlich **kein** Kind mehr   *After all, she's no longer a child*

(e) The form *keiner* is used as a pronoun

It has endings like those of *einer*, see Table 5.10. It is rarely used in the genitive:

Keiner von uns hat es gewusst   In **keinem** dieser neuen Häuser möchte
Zum Schluss hat sie **kein(e)s** der Bücher   ich wohnen
  gekauft   **kein(e)s** von beiden *neither of them*
Haben Sie einen Farbfernseher? – Nein,
  wir haben **keinen**

NB: (i) The neuter form *kein(e)s* is used to refer to people of different sex: *Ich fragte meine Eltern, aber* **keins** *(von beiden) wusste es.*

(ii) The use of *keiner* for *niemand* to mean 'no-one', 'nobody' (see 5.5.15a) is frequent in speech but considered to be substandard.

5.5.17 *lauter* 'only', 'nothing but'

lauter is indeclinable. It is used only as a determiner, i.e. before nouns:

Dort lag **lauter** Eis und Schnee	*Nothing but ice and snow lay there*
Es kamen **lauter** junge Leute	*Only young people came*
Er hat **lauter** solchen Unsinn geredet	*He only talked rubbish like that*

5.5.18 *man* 'one'

(a) The indefinite pronoun *man* corresponds to English 'one'

However, unlike 'one', it is not restricted to elevated speech. Rather, it corresponds to the general use of 'you' in spoken English, or, frequently, to 'we', 'they' or 'people' (and overusing *Leute* in contexts where *man* would be appropriate is typical of English learners' German). It is also often used in contexts where English would most naturally use a passive construction, e.g. *Man sagt* 'It is said', see 15.4.1. The corresponding pronouns are possessive *sein* and reflexive *sich*:

Als **man** sich zum Abendessen setzte, fehlte der alte Herr	*When they/we sat down to dinner the old gentleman was missing*
Man hat sich nach dir erkundigt	*People were asking after you*
Man sollte seinen Freunden helfen	*One ought to help one's friends*
Hier spricht **man** meistens Plattdeutsch unter sich	*People mainly speak Low German here amongst themselves*

man is sometimes used, for reasons of politeness, to refer to the speaker, e.g.: *Darf* **man** *fragen, wohin Sie fahren?* In certain situations this can acquire a note of sarcasm. This is always so when it is used to refer to the listener, e.g.: *Hat* **man** *schon wieder zu tief ins Glas geguckt?*

NB: (i) *man* should **never** be referred back to with *er*, e.g.: *Wenn man müde ist, muss* **man** (not: *er*) *sich setzen.*

(ii) The form *frau* has recently gained some currency in feminist circles as a substitute for *man*, calling attention to the gender discrimination felt to be inherent in the form *man*.

(b) *man* only has a nominative case form

In the accusative and dative *einen* and *einem* (see 5.5.4) are used:

Man weiß nie, ob er **einen** erkannt hat	*You never know whether he has recognised you*
So Leid es **einem** tut, man muss manchmal hart sein	*However much you regret it, you have to be hard sometimes*

NB: The use of the nominative form *einer* for *man* (see 5.5.4) is considered to be a substandard colloquialism.

5.5.19 *manch* 'some', 'many a'

manch always has the rather special sense of stressed 'some', i.e. 'a fair number, but by no means all'. This may be equivalent to English by 'many a' and in certain contexts comes close to the sense of English 'several'. *manch* has a number of alternative forms.

(a) As a determiner, *manch* is most often used in the inflected form *mancher* i.e. with the endings of *dieser*, see Table 5.2.

In the genitive singular masculine and neuter, the form *manchen* is occasionally found besides the more frequent *manches* if the following noun has the ending -(*e*)*s*, (e.g. *manches Mannes* or *manchen Mannes*).

mancher can be used in the singular or the plural. The singular form (like English 'many a') may put more emphasis on the individual items, whereas the plural (like English stressed 'some') stresses the collectivity. In practice, however, the difference between, for example, *mancher schöne Tag* and *manche schöne Tage* is slight.

An **manchen** Tagen blieb er lange im Bett	*Some days he stayed in bed a long time*
der Stoßseufzer **mancher** deutschen Frau, die von der bisherigen Pille enttäuscht ist (*BILD*)	*the deep sigh of many a German woman who has been disappointed by the present pill*
ein überhöhter Preis, wie er in **manchen** Reparaturwerkstätten seit Jahren üblich ist (*BILD*)	*an exorbitant price, such as has been usual in some garages for years*

(b) Uninflected *manch* is quite commonly used as a determiner especially in the following constructions:

(i) before the indefinite article *ein*. This is a less common alternative to inflected *manch*, and it is mainly used in formal written German. The individual items are emphasised rather more strongly:

Da gibt es mancherlei Grund zum Zweifeln – **manch ein** Zeitgenosse wird sagen: zum Verzweifeln (*Zeit*)	*There are many kinds of reasons for doubt – many contemporaries will say: for despair*

(ii) before an adjective, where the uninflected form is a widespread and frequent alternative to the inflected one, especially in the singular:

Sie konnten dem Kanzler **manch** guten Tipp geben (*MM*)	*They were able to give the Chancellor many a good tip*
... um neben **manch** Komischem auch etliches Entlarvende bieten zu können (*MM*)	*... to be able to present quite a few revealing things besides much that is comical*

(iii) before neuter nouns. This alternative sounds rather old-fashioned, but it has become fashionable again recently:

manch Wörtchen der Verwunderung (*Th. Mann*)	*many a word of amazement*

(c) As a pronoun *mancher* declines like *dieser*
See Table 5.2. It is not used in the genitive:

Mancher hat es nicht geglaubt	*Not many believed it*
Das ist schon **manchem** passiert	*That has happened to quite a few people*
Manche trinken Tee, andere lieber Kaffee	*Some people drink tea, others prefer coffee*
manche meiner Bekannten	*a fair number of my acquaintances*

manch einer is a fairly frequent alternative to inflected *mancher*:

Manch einer musste auf die Mittagspause verzichten (*MM*)	*Some had to give up their lunch hour*

5.5.20 *mehrere* 'several'

mehrere is used, as a determiner or a pronoun, in the plural only. It has the same endings as *dieser*, see Table 5.2:

Ich habe **mehrere** Bücher darüber gelesen	*I have read several books about it*
Mehrere standen draußen und warteten	*Several people were standing outside waiting*
Es ist doch viel spannender, mit **mehreren** Jungen auszugehen, als immer an einem zu kleben (*BILD*)	*But it's much more exciting to go out with several boys than always to stick with one*

5.5.21 *meinesgleichen* 'people like me'

meinesgleichen is indeclinable. Parallel forms can be formed for the other persons, i.e. *deinesgleichen, seinesgleichen, ihresgleichen, unsresgleichen, euresgleichen*. If they are used as the subject of a verb, it has the endings of the third person singular. They now sound rather old-fashioned:

Ich und **meinesgleichen** interessieren uns für so etwas nicht	*I and people like me aren't interested in things like that*
Euresgleichen hat es wirklich leicht	*People like you really have it easy*
Dieser Wagen hat nicht **seinesgleichen**	*This car has no equal*

5.5.22 *nichts* 'nothing', 'not ... anything'

nichts does not decline:

Aus **nichts** wird **nichts** (Proverb)	*Nothing comes of nothing*
Nichts gefiel ihr dort	*She didn't like anything there*
nichts als Schwierigkeiten	*nothing but difficulties*

nichts is often used with a following adjective used as a noun, which has the strong endings, see 6.4.5:

nichts Neues	*nothing new*
Er hat von **nichts Neuem** gesprochen	*He didn't speak of anything new*

It is also common with *von* in partitive constructions, i.e. 'nothing (of)':

Ich möchte **nichts von** dem Essen	*I don't want any of the food*
nichts von alledem	*nothing of all that*

NB: In colloquial speech *nichts* is almost invariably pronounced *nix*.

5.5.23 *sämtlich* 'all (the)'

sämtliche inflects like *dieser*, see Table 5.2. It is used, as a determiner or a pronoun, in the plural only, as an emphatic alternative to *alle*:

Wir haben nicht den Ehrgeiz, **sämtliche** Pflanzen zu sammeln, die in der Serengeti vorkommen (*Grzimek*)	*We have no ambition to collect all the plants which occur in the Serengeti*
die Anschriften **sämtlicher** neuen Mitglieder	*the addresses of all the new members*

sämtliche is rather more limited than *alle*, since it can refer to all the members of a subgroup of persons or things, but not to all those which are in existence. Thus, one can say *Sämtliche* (OR: *Alle*) *Bäume in dem Wald wurden gefällt*, but only: *Alle* (NOT: *Sämtliche*) *Menschen sind sterblich*.

sämtliche can also be used with a preceding definite article or other determiner, in which case it has the endings of an adjective:

Meine **sämtlichen** Verwandten haben mir geschrieben	*All my relatives wrote to me*

As an adverb, *sämtlich* is used in the meaning 'without exception':

Sämtlich waren sie dem Staat eigen (*Johnson*)	*They all belonged to the state*

5.5.24 *unsereiner* 'someone like me', 'one of us'

unsereiner declines like *dieser*, see Table 5.2. There are parallel forms for the other persons, i.e. *eurereiner*, *ihrereiner*, although these are less frequent in practice:

Unsereiner kann das nicht wissen	*Someone like me can't know that*
Mit **unsereinem** spricht sie nie	*She doesn't talk to the likes of us*

NB: In the nominative and accusative, the neuter form *unsereins* is a common alternative to the masculine, especially in colloquial speech.

5.5.25 *viel* 'much', *viele* 'many', *wenig* 'a little', *wenige* 'a few'

The various forms and uses of *viel* 'much', 'many', 'a lot of' and *wenig* '(a) little', '(a) few', 'not many' are broadly similar. Both occur as a determiner, a pronoun, or an adverb. Both have alternative uninflected and inflected forms, in the latter case with the endings of *dieser* (see Table 5.2). In certain constructions and uses the uninflected forms are more usual, in others the inflected, without any identifiable difference in meaning.

NB: (i) *ein wenig* 'a little' is invariable, see 5.5.5.
(ii) For the comparatives of *viel* and *wenig*, see 8.2.4.

(a) Used as pronouns, *viel* and *wenig* most often have no endings in the singular, but they do have an ending in the plural

They are not used in the genitive singular:

Sie hat **viel/wenig** versucht	Ich bin mit **viel/wenig** von dem einverstanden, was du sagst
Er will **viel/wenig** haben	
Viel/Wenig von dem Kuchen	**Viele/Wenige** von diesen Büchern
Sie hat **viel/wenig** verraten	Ich habe **viele/wenige** gesehen

The inflected neuter singular forms nominative/accusative **vieles**, dative **vielem** are occasionally used, chiefly in formal writing:

Sie hat **vieles** versucht	*She has tried a lot of things*
Mit **vielem** bin ich nicht einverstanden	*There's much I don't agree with*

Inflected forms of *wenig* (i.e. *weniges, wenigem*) are rare.

(b) Used as determiners, *viel* and *wenig* usually have no endings in the singular, but they do have endings in the plural

The genitive singular is scarcely ever used, a phrase with *von* being preferred:

Dazu ist **viel** Mut nötig	*Much courage is needed for that*
Ich trinke **wenig** Milch	*I don't drink much milk*
Er handelte mit **viel** Geschick	*He acted with a lot of skill*
Sie ist mit **wenig** Geld ausgekommen	*She managed with little money*
die Wirkung von **wenig** Wein	*the effect of not much wine*
der Genuss von **viel** Obst	*eating a lot of fruit*
Viele Probleme wurden besprochen	*Many problems were discussed*
Gestern waren **wenige** Zuschauer im Stadion	*There weren't many spectators at the ground yesterday*
Er hat **viele/wenige** Freunde	*He has a lot of/few friends*
die Reden **vieler** Politiker	*the speeches of a lot of politicians*
mit **vielen/wenigen** Ausnahmen	*with a lot of/few exceptions*

There are some common exceptions to this usage:

(i) Inflected singular forms are sometimes used in formal registers with a following adjective used as a noun (see 6.4.5), e.g.: *Er hat **vieles/weniges** Interessante gesagt* (for everyday *Er hat **viel/wenig** Interessantes gesagt*).

(ii) Inflected forms are quite common in the dative singular masculine and neuter, e.g.: *Mit **viel/vielem** Zureden konnten wir einiges erreichen.*

(iii) Uninflected plural forms are occasionally found, mainly in colloquial speech: *Im Grunde interessieren mich furchtbar **wenig** Dinge außer meiner eigenen Arbeit* (*Langgässer*).

(iv) Inflected singular forms are found in a few set phrases, notably *vielen Dank.*

(c) *viel* and *wenig* can be used with a preceding definite article or other determiner

They then have the usual adjective endings:

Ich staunte über das **viele** Geld, das er ausgab	*I was amazed at the large amount of money that he spent*
der Mut dieser **vielen/wenigen** Frauen	*the courage of these many/few women*
Sie hat ihr **weniges** Geld verloren	*She lost her little bit of money*
die **wenigen**, die ihn erkannten	*the few who recognised him*

(d) *wenig* in constructions like *wenig gutes Fleisch* can be ambiguous

It could mean 'not much good meat' or 'not very good meat'. If the context does not resolve the ambiguity, the first meaning can be made clear by replacing *wenig* by *nicht viel*, i.e. *nicht viel gutes Fleisch*, the second by using *nicht sehr*, i.e. *nicht sehr gutes Fleisch*.

Similarly, *weniger gutes Fleisch* could mean 'meat which was less good' or 'a smaller amount of good meat' (English 'less good meat' shows similar ambiguity). This ambiguity can also be resolved if necessary by paraphrasing, i.e. *nicht so gutes Fleisch* or *nicht so viel gutes Fleisch*.

(e) The spelling of *so viel, wie viel, zu viel,* **etc.**
Compounds with *viel* and *wenig* are now spelled as separate words: *so viel, wie viel, zu viel, zu wenig.*

5.5.26 *welcher* 'some', 'any'

When it is used as an indefinite pronoun *welcher* has the endings of *dieser*, see Table 5.2. It is typical of colloquial speech, other alternatives (i.e. *einige, manche, etwas*) usually being preferred in formal registers.

It is used without restriction in the plural, but in the singular it can only refer to a mass noun. It refers back to a noun which has just been mentioned or to 'some people' identified by a following relative clause:

Hast du Käse? – Ja, ich habe **welchen**	*Have you got any cheese? Yes, I've got some*
Wenn kein Wein da ist, hole ich uns **welchen**	*If there's no wine left, I'll get us some*
Ich brauche Marken. Kannst du mir **welche** geben?	*I need some stamps. Can you give me some/any?*
Hier sind **welche** vom Westfernsehen (Bednarz)	*Here are some people from Western television*

NB: For the use of *welcher* as an interrogative, see 5.3.1, as a relative pronoun, see 5.4.2.

5.5.27 *wer* 'someone', 'somebody'

wer is used as a pronoun in colloquial speech, where formal registers prefer *jemand* (see 5.5.15):

Dich hat wieder **wer** angerufen	*Someone's been on the phone for you again*
Die hat wohl wieder **wen** angelächelt	*It looks as if she's picked some bloke up again*
Hast du wenigstens **wem** Bescheid gesagt?	*Have you at least told someone about it?*

NB: For the use of *wer* as an interrogative pronoun, see 5.3.3.

6

Adjectives

ADJECTIVES are words which describe, modify, or qualify NOUNS and PRONOUNS. They do this in two main ways:

- either on their own or as part of a longer adjectival phrase. They then form part of a NOUN PHRASE, and they come immediately before the noun, after any determiners. This is termed the **attributive** use of the adjective:

Determiner	Adjective/adjectival phrase	Noun
	kaltes	Wasser
eine	hohe	Wand
das	ultramoderne	Raumschiff
ein	vom Kultbuchautor Adams erfundenes	Computerspiel

- or by being used as a COMPLEMENT to a noun which is the subject or object of a verb. This is termed the **predicative** use of the adjective:

Helga ist aber **klein**   Er isst die Würstchen **warm**
Das Mädchen lag **krank** im Bett   Sie strich die Wand **gelb**

In German, **attributive adjectives** (and only attributive adjectives) have endings which indicate the same grammatical categories as nouns, i.e. CASE, PLURAL and GENDER. They are said to decline in agreement with the noun. There are two main sets of adjective endings in German, the so-called STRONG and WEAK declensions. Which one is used depends on whether or not there is also a determiner in the noun phrase, and what kind of ending it has (if any). **Predicative adjectives** have no endings.

This chapter deals with the forms and uses of adjectives in German:

- the **strong** and **weak declension** of adjectives (sections 6.1–6.3)
- adjectives used as **nouns** (section 6.4)
- the use of **cases** with adjectives (section 6.5)
- the use of **prepositions** with adjectives (section 6.6)

We can compare the extent to which a particular person or thing possesses the quality expressed by an adjectives by using special endings, e.g. *schön – schöner – schönst*. This is called the COMPARISON of adjectives, and it is dealt with in detail in Chapter 8.

6.1 Declension of adjectives

6.1.1 In German, adjectives are only declined when they are used attributively

ein gut**er** Mensch   diese schön**en** Tage   frisch**es** Brot

When used **predicatively**, or in phrases separated from the noun, they have **no endings**:

Der Mensch war **gut**   Er trat **ungeduldig** in das Zimmer
Er fühlte sich **gesund**   Wir essen die Möhren **roh**
Mein Vater, in Hamburg **tätig**, ...   Das Klima machte ihn **krank**
Sie hielt ihn für **dumm**   Das gilt als **sicher**

Optimistisch wie immer, sie ließ sich von ihrem Vorhaben nicht abhalten
ein erstklassiger Kellner, **rasch**, nicht **schwerhörig** (*Wohmann*)
Das Gewehr gehörte zu ihm wie eine Frau zu einem Mann, **schweigsam**, **schön** und **zuverlässig** (*E.W.Heine*)

The use of an endingless adjective after the noun is typically poetic: *O Täler weit, o Höhen!* (*Eichendorff*), but it has become quite frequent as a stylistic device in advertising and technical language:

Henkel **trocken**   Schrankwand in Eiche **rustikal** oder Kiefer **natur**
Whisky **pur**   700 Nadelfeilen **rund** nach DIN 8342

6.1.2 There are two basic declensions of adjectives in German

These are usually called the STRONG and WEAK declensions. The endings of these declensions are shown in Table 6.1, and they are illustrated in full noun phrases in Tables 6.2, 6.3 and 6.4. These tables are all arranged with the neuters next to the masculines to show the overlap between the endings more clearly.

TABLE 6.1 *The endings of adjectives in the strong and weak declensions*

Strong	Masc.	Neut.	Fem.	Plural
Nom.	-er	-es	-e	-e
Acc.	-en	-es	-e	-e
Gen.	-en	-en	-er	-er
Dat.	-em	-em	-er	-en

Weak	Masc.	Neut.	Fem.	Plural
Nom.	-e	-e	-en	-en
Acc.	-en	-e	-en	-en
Gen.	-en	-en	-en	-en
Dat.	-en	-en	-en	-en

(a) The STRONG declension has relatively more distinctive endings
They are identical to those of *dieser* (see Table 5.2), except that the genitive singular masculine and neuter ends in *-en*:

ein Stück international**en** Gewässers (*Presse*)
die Perfektion rein**en** Klanges (*hifi ad*)

However, with **weak masculine nouns** which have the ending *-en* in the genitive singular (see 1.3.2), the strong adjective has the ending *-es*, e.g. *der **Gesuch** obiges Adressaten*. This form rarely occurs in practice.

(b) The WEAK **declension has only two endings,** *-e* **and** *-en*
-*e* is used in the **nominative singular** of all genders and the **accusative singular feminine and neuter**. -*en* is used in all other combinations of case, plural and gender.

TABLE 6.2 *Strong adjective declension, with no determiner*

	Masculine		Neuter		Feminine		Plural	
Nom.	guter	Wein	gutes	Brot	gute	Suppe	gute	Weine
Acc.	guten	Wein	gutes	Brot	gute	Suppe	gute	Weine
Gen.	guten	Weines	guten	Brotes	guter	Suppe	guter	Weine
Dat.	gutem	Wein	gutem	Brot	guter	Suppe	guten	Weinen

TABLE 6.3 *Weak adjective declension, with the definite article*

	Masculine		Neuter		Feminine		Plural	
Nom.	der	gute Wein	das	gute Brot	die gute	Suppe	die	guten Weine
Acc.	den	guten Wein	das	gute Brot	die gute	Suppe	die	guten Weine
Gen.	des	guten Weines	des	guten Brotes	der guten	Suppe	der	guten Weine
Dat.	dem	guten Wein	dem	guten Brot	der guten	Suppe	den	guten Weinen

6.2 The use of the strong and weak declensions

The underlying principle governing the use of the strong and weak declensions is as follows:

The **strong** endings (which are more distinct) are used if there is no determiner in the noun phrase with an ending which indicates the case, gender and number of the noun as clearly as possible.

The **weak** endings are used if there is a determiner with an ending in the noun phrase.

6.2.1 The STRONG declension is used in the following contexts

in accordance with this principle, and as illustrated in Table 6.2

(a) When there is no determiner in the noun phrase

frische Milch	frisch**es** Obst	durch genau**e** Beobachtung
mit neu**em** Mut	aus deutsch**en** Landen	das Niveau französisch**er** Filme

This also applies to adjectives used after **numerals** (including the genitives *zweier* and *dreier*, see 9.1.3a), after preceding **genitives**, and after the **genitive** of the **relative pronoun**:

zwei schön**e** Pfirsiche	*two fine peaches*
Karls unermüdlich**er** Eifer	*Karl's tireless zeal*
in Astrids klein**em** Arbeitszimmer	*in Astrid's little study*
mein Freund, dessen ältest**er** Sohn krank war	*my friend, whose eldest son was ill*

(b) When the determiner in the noun phrase has no ending

ein älterer Herr	unser kleines Kind	kein schöner Tag
mein neues Kleid	viel indischer Tee	ein paar grüne Äpfel
manch reiches Land	welch herrliches Wetter!	mit was für englischen Büchern
lauter faule Äpfel	bei solch herrlichem Wetter	

An important effect of this rule is that strong endings are used after the endingless forms of the indefinite articles *ein* and *kein* and of the possessives (i.e. *mein, dein, unser*, etc.). The declension of adjectives after these determiners, which seems to mix strong and weak endings, is sometimes called the mixed declension. For reference, it is illustrated in full in Table 6.4.

TABLE 6.4 *Mixed adjective declension, with the indefinite article*

	Masculine			Neuter			Feminine		
Nom.	ein	guter	Wein	ein	gutes	Brot	eine	gute	Suppe
Acc.	einen	guten	Wein	ein	gutes	Brot	eine	gute	Suppe
Gen.	eines	guten	Weines	eines	guten	Brotes	einer	guten	Suppe
Dat.	einem	guten	Wein	einem	guten	Brot	einer	guten	Suppe

6.2.2 The WEAK declension is used after most major determiners which have endings clearly indicating the case, number and gender of the noun

This rule follows the principle given above and is illustrated in Table 6.3. It applies, in particular:

(a) After the definite article and demonstrative *der*

der weiße Wein	den weißen Wein	des weißen Weines	die weißen Weine

(b) After the indefinite articles *ein* and *kein* and the possessives, if they have an ending

i.e. except in the nominative singular masculine and the nominative/accusative singular neuter, where the strong endings are used (see 6.2.1b). This is illustrated in Table 6.4:

einen weißen Wein	seinem weißen Wein	ihrer weißen Weine

(c) After *dieser, jener, jeder* and *welcher*

dieser weiße Wein	diesen weißen Wein	diesen weißen Weinen
jenes weißen Weines	jedem weißen Wein	von welchem weißen Wein?

6.2.3 There is some variation in the use of the strong and weak endings after certain determiners

In general, following the principle given above, the adjective has **weak** endings following any determiner which itself has an ending showing the case, number and gender of the noun clearly. However, usage is not fixed after some of the indefinites and quantifiers given in section 5.5. The following summarises general current practice:

(a) Weak endings are always used in the SINGULAR

mancher brave Mann	mit folgender nachdrücklichen Warnung
durch irgendwelchen puren Unsinn	mit einigem bühnentechnischen Aufwand
mit allem möglichen Fleiß	(*Zeit*)
von vielem kalten Wasser	aus wenigem schlechten Wein
solches dumme Gerede	

NB: As a solitary exception, *jeglicher* is most often followed by strong endings, e.g. *jegliches* **organisches** *Leben* (*Grzimek*).

(b) Usage in the PLURAL varies for different determiners

(i) After *alle, beide* and *sämtliche* the weak endings are usual:

alle fremden Truppen	sämtliche schönen Bücher
beide bekannten Politiker	aller interessierten Zuschauer

NB: Strong endings are occasionally found, especially with *beide*, e.g. *beide bekannte Politiker*.

(ii) After *irgendwelche* and *solche* either weak or strong endings are used. The weak endings are more frequent:

solche schönen (less common: *schöne*) Tage
irgendwelcher interessierten (less common: *interessierter*) Zuschauer

(iii) After *manche* either weak or strong endings are used. The strong endings are more frequent:

manche schone (less common: *schönen*) Aussichten

(iv) After *einige, etliche, folgende, mehrere, viele, wenige* the strong endings are the general rule:

einige neue ICE-Verbindungen	etliche fremde Besucher
folgende bezeichnende Beispiele	mehrere große Städte
vieler nichtbeamteter Österreicher (*Kurier*)	weniger günstiger Zeiten

NB: Weak endings are occasionally found, most often in the genitive plural, e.g. *einiger* **großen** *ausländischen Firmen* for (much more frequent) *einiger* **großer** *ausländischer Firmen*.

(v) For adjective endings after *ander*, see 5.5.2.

(c) Some indefinites and quantifiers may themselves be preceded by one of the major determiners

i.e. by a definite or indefinite article, by one of the demonstratives *dieser* or *jener*, or by one of the possessives *mein, dein*, etc. They are then treated like adjectives and have a weak or strong adjective ending as appropriate:

eine **solche** interessante Nachricht	aller **solchen** guten Wünsche
mit der **folgenden** krassen Behauptung	diese **vielen** alten Dörfer
mit seinem **wenigen** deutschen Geld	mein **sämtliches** kleines Vermögen

(d) Some indefinites and quantifiers have alternative endingless forms

The conditions under which these occur are explained under the relevant determiner in section 5.5. These endingless forms are followed by adjectives with strong endings, following the general principle explained above:

viel deutsches Geld	manch schöner Tag	solch dummes Gerede

6.2.4 Two or more adjectives qualifying the same noun all have the same ending

dieser schöne, große Garten	mein lieber alter Vater
gutes bayrisches Bier	die Lösung wichtiger politischer Probleme

An occasional deviation from this rule is that in the dative singular masculine or neuter, a second (or subsequent) adjective may, optionally, have the weak ending *-en* rather than the strong ending *-em*:

mit dunklem bayrischem/bayrischen Bier
nach langem beunruhigendem/beunruhigenden Schweigen
nach wochenlangem politischen Tauziehen (*Presse*)

Using the weak ending *-en* in such contexts is considered 'incorrect' by some authorities. However, although it is less frequent the strong ending *-em*, it is by no means unusual in all kinds of written German, and it is the norm with adjectives used as nouns, see 6.4.2b.

6.2.5 The adjective is still declined if a noun is understood

'one' often has to be supplied in the equivalent English construction:

Welches Kleid hast du gewählt? –	*Which dress did you choose? –*
Das **rote**	*The red one*
Ich habe mein Taschenmesser verloren.	*I've lost my penknife. I'll have*
Ich muss mir ein **neues** kaufen	*to buy myself a new one*
Deutsche Weißweine sind süßer als	*German white wines are sweeter than*
französische	*French ones*

NB: Adjectives used in this way with a noun understood are spelled with a <u>small</u> initial letter, not a capital, since they are not adjectives being used as nouns, see 6.4 and 23.1.1.b.

6.2.6 Adjectives governing more than one noun with a different gender cannot be understood

In English an adjective (with or without a determiner) can be understood in a series of linked noun phrases, e.g. *my old aunt and uncle, dear Ruth and Martin, the new table and chairs*. This is <u>not</u> possible in German if the nouns involved are of a different gender or number. The adjective (and determiner) <u>must</u> be repeated, with the appropriate different endings:

mein alter Onkel und meine alte Tante	liebe Ruth, lieber Martin
der neue Tisch und die neuen Stühle	

6.2.7 In a few special cases an attributive adjective has no ending

(a) In older German adjectives sometimes lacked the strong ending *-es* before a neuter singular noun in the nominative or accusative

This usage is retained in a few idioms and set phrases, e.g.:

etwas auf gut Glück tun	*to take a chance*
sich lieb Kind machen	*to ingratiate oneself*
Gut Ding will Weile haben	*Nothing good is done in a hurry*

Ruhig Blut bewahren!	*Keep calm!*
Kölnisch Wasser	*eau de Cologne*
ein gehörig/gut Stück	*a substantial/good piece*
ein gut Teil	*a large proportion*
ein ander Mal	*another time*

(b) Some foreign adjectives ending in a full vowel do not take endings

Many of these are colour terms, i.e.: *lila, rosa*:

eine **klasse** Idee	ein **lila** Mantel	die **orange** Farbe (*MM*)
ein **rosa** Kleid	eine **prima** Ware	eine **super** Schau

In writing a suffix such as *-farben* or *-farbig* is an acceptable alternative for the colour terms, e.g. *ein rosafarbenes Kleid*. In substandard speech, an *-n-* is sometimes inserted as a base for the usual endings, e.g. *ein rosanes Kleid*. This is widespread but regarded as incorrect in written German.

(c) An adjective used as an adverb to qualify a following adjective has no ending

Compare the difference between the following:

ein unheilbar**er**, fauler Junge	*an incurable, lazy boy*
ein unheilbar fauler Junge	*an incurably lazy boy*

However, this distinction is not always clear-cut, and the first of a pair of adjectives is sometimes left uninflected even if it is not being used as an adverb. This is a common stylistic device in modern writing:

ein reingebürtiger Pole von **traurig** edler Gestalt (*Grass*)	*a pure-bred Pole with a sad, noble figure*
seine **hochrot** abstehenden Ohren (*Grass*)	*his deep red, protuberant ears*

einzig may regularly have no ending if it can be considered as qualifying a following adjective e.g. *die einzig(e) mögliche Lösung*. For similar usage with *derartig*, see 5.1.6f.

(d) Adjectives in *-er* from town names do not add endings

die Leipziger Messe, die Lüneburger Heide, der Kölner Dom

(e) Adjectives in *-er* from numerals do not add endings

die neunziger Jahre	*the nineties*

(f) Endingless adjectives are used with names of letters and numerals

groß *A*, klein *z*, römisch *IV*, arabisch *4*

(g) *halb* and *ganz* have no endings before geographical names used without an article

halb Berlin, ganz Deutschland, ganz Europa

NB: See 9.3.2 for details on the use of *halb*.

6.2.8 Adjectives used after a personal pronoun usually have strong endings

ich arm**er** Deutscher
Wer hat dich dumm**en** Kerl gesehen?
Wer konnte euch treulos**en** Verrätern helfen?
Wer kümmert sich um uns früher**e** Kollegen?

However, weak endings are found in a few contexts:

(i) In the (rarely used) dative singular, weak or strong endings can be used in the masculine and neuter, e.g.: *mir mittellosem/mittellosen Mann*, but the feminine almost always has weak endings, e.g.: *Er hat mir alten* (rarely: *alter*) *Frau geschmeichelt.*

(ii) Weak endings are more usual in the nominative plural: *wir jungen Kollegen; ihr hilflosen Kerle.* However, for 'we Germans' *wir Deutsche* and *wir Deutschen* are equally common.

6.3 Irregularities in the spelling of some adjectives

6.3.1 The spelling of inflected adjectives in -el, -en, -er

(a) Adjectives in -el always drop the -e- when there is an ending

ein **dunkler** Wald, eine **respektable** Leistung

NB: When used as a noun, *dunkel* drops the *-e-* of the ending, e.g. *im Dunkeln* 'in the dark'.

(b) Adjectives in -en can drop the -e- when there is an ending
This is usual in everyday speech, but uncommon in writing: *eine **metallene*** (rarely written: *metallne*) *Stimme, ein **seltener*** (rarely written: *seltner*) *Vogel.*

(c) Adjectives in -er
Foreign adjectives and those with *-au-* or *-eu-* before the *-er* always drop the *-e-*:

eine **makabre** Geschichte, mit **teuren** Weinen, durch **saure** Milch

The others usually keep it in written German, although it is usually dropped in speech: *eine **muntere*** (rarely written: *muntre*) *Frau.*

NB: (i)   The *-e-* of the comparative ending *-er* (see 8.1) is rarely omitted in writing, e.g.: *eine **bessere*** (rarely in writing: *bessre*) *Lösung.*
(ii)   For the spelling of declined *ander*, see 5.5.2.

(d) The -e- is quite often left out in -el- or -er- in the middle of an adjective which has endings

neb(e)lige Tage, eine **wäss(e)rige** Suppe, etc.

6.3.2 *hoch* 'high'

hoch has the special form *hoh-* to which the usual endings are added: *der Berg ist hoch*, but *ein **hoher** Berg.*

6.3.3 A few adjectives have alternative base forms with or without final -e

e.g.: *Er ist feig* or *feige* 'He is cowardly'. They are:

blöd(e)	bös(e)	fad(e)	irr(e)	leis(e)	mild(e)
müd(e)	öd(e)	träg(e)	trüb(e)	vag(e)	zäh(e)

With all except *blöd(e)*, *mild(e)* and *zäh(e)*, the alternative with -*e* tends to be preferred in written German. In speech the form without -*e* is more frequent unless the adjective is stressed.

6.4 Adjectives used as nouns

6.4.1 All adjectives and participles can be used as nouns in German

They are written with a capital letter:

der **Alte** *the old man*	die **Alte** *the old woman*
das **Alte** *old things*	die **Alten** *the old people*

English cannot turn adjectives into nouns as easily, except in a few restricted cases ('the young, 'the old', 'the Dutch', 'the good, the bad and the ugly', etc.). and we usually have to supply a dummy noun like 'man', 'woman', 'thing(s)', 'people' to be used with the adjective. The overuse of the corresponding German words like *Ding* or *Leute* is a characteristic feature of the German of English learners.

Idiomatic German exploits fully the possibilities of concise expression offered by the fact that adjectives can readily be used as nouns. In particular, they are often used where full clauses would be needed in English:

Die Farbe dieser Vögel war das für mich **Interessante**	*The colour of these birds was what interested me*
Er hat sich über das **Gesagte** aufgeregt	*He got annoyed about what had been said*
Das **Erschreckende** an diesem Vorfall war seine scheinbare Unabwendbarkeit	*What was terrifying about this occurrence was its apparent inevitability*
Die gerade **Eingestiegenen** waren ein älterer Herr und eine elegante Dame	*The people who had just got in were an elderly man and an elegant lady*
ein Ort, wo das irgendwie zu denkende **Konkrete** unwiederbringlich in **Abstraktes** umschlägt	*a point where concrete reality, however it may be imagined, becomes irrevocably abstract*

NB: Adjectives used as nouns in this way are different from adjectives being used with a preceding noun understood. These are spelled with a **small** initial letter, see 6.2.5. Compare *Kennst du den Alten? '*Do you know the old man?' with *Hast du einen neuen Wagen gekauft? – Nein, einen alten (Wagen* understood). 'Did you buy a new car? – No, an old one.'

6.4.2 The declension of adjectives used as nouns

(a) Adjectives used as nouns decline like attributive adjectives

They have weak or strong endings according to the rules given in 6.2. They thus have the same endings as any preceding adjective, e.g.: *ein zuverlässiger Angestellter, von einer unbekannten Fremden*. The declension with the definite and indefinite articles of a typical masculine adjective used as a noun, *der Angestellte* 'employee', is shown in Table 6.5.

NB: *der Angestellte* is naturally only used of a <u>male</u> employee. A female employee will be *die Angestellte*, *eine Angestellte*, with the appropriate endings, see 6.4.3.

TABLE 6.5 Declension of adjectives used as nouns

Declension with:		Definite article		Indefinite article	
Singular	Nominative	der	Angestellte	ein	Angestellter
	Accusative	den	Angestellten	einen	Angestellten
	Genitive	des	Angestellten	eines	Angestellten
	Dative	dem	Angestellten	einem	Angestellten
Plural	Nominative	die	Angestellten		Angestellte
	Accusative	die	Angestellten		Angestellte
	Genitive	der	Angestellten		Angestellter
	Dative	den	Angestellten		Angestellten

Adjectives used as nouns in this way should not be confused with 'weak' masculine nouns, whose declension looks quite similar, see Table 1.6. Note the difference between the endings of adjectives used as nouns and 'weak' masculine (or other regular) nouns:

Adjective used as noun	**'Weak' masculine (or other) noun**
der Deutsche, des Deutschen *German*	der Franzose, des Franzosen *Frenchman*
NB: ein Deutsch**er**	NB: ein Franzos**e**
das Junge *young of an animal*	der Junge, des Jungen *boy*
NB: ein Jung**es**	NB: ein Jung**e**
die Fremde *female stranger*	die Fremde *foreign parts*
NB: mit der Fremd**en**	NB: in der Fremd**e** *abroad*

(b) In a few contexts adjectives used as nouns decline in a different way from other adjectives

(i) In the dative singular the adjective used as a noun usually has the weak ending *-en* if preceded by an adjective with the strong endings *-em* or *-er*:

    Ich sprach mit Karls alt**em** Bekannt**en**, mit Helmuts englisch**er** Bekannt**en**

(ii) In apposition (see 2.6), the weak ending is used in the dative singular even if there is no determiner:

    Er sprach mit Karl Friedrichsen, Angestellt**en** (rarely: Angestellt**em**) der BASF in
       Ludwigshafen
    Er sprach mit Heike König, Angestellt**en** (never: Angestellt**er**) der BASF in
       Ludwigshafen

In practice, such contexts are avoided. The nominative case is used: *mit Karl Friedrichsen, Angestellter der BASF,* or an article is added: *mit Karl Friedrichsen, dem/einem Angestellten der BASF.*

(iii) The neuters *das Äußere, das Ganze* and *das Innere* can have the weak or the strong endings in the nominative/accusative singular after the indefinite article or the possessives if another adjective comes first:

    sein schlichtes Äußer**e(s)**   ein einheitliches Ganz**e(s)**   mein eigenes Inner**e(s)**

6.4.3 Masculine and feminine adjectival nouns usually refer to people

(a) The gender is indicated by using the appropriate article

e.g. *der Fremde* 'the (male) stranger', *die Fremde* 'the (female) stranger'. Many common ones correspond to simple nouns in English:

der Adlige *aristocrat*
der Abgeordnete *representative*
der Angestellte *employee*
der Beamte *civil servant*
der Bekannte *acquaintance*
der Deutsche *German*
der Erwachsene *adult*
der Freiwillige *volunteer*
der Fremde *stranger*
der Gefangene *prisoner*
der Geistliche *clergyman*
der Gesandte *emissary*

der Heilige *saint*
der Industrielle *industrialist*
der Jugendliche *young person*
der Obdachlose *homeless person*
der Reisende *traveller*
der Staatsangehörige *citizen*
der Überlebende *survivor*
der Verlobte *fiancé*
der Verwandte *relative*
der Vorgesetzte *superior*
der Vorsitzende *chairman*

(b) A few feminine adjectival nouns represent special cases

(i) A few referring to things are always feminine, i.e.:

die Elektrische *tram* (old south German)
die Rechte, Linke *right, left (hand)*;
  (political) *right, left*

die Gerade *straight line*
die Variable (mathematical) *variable*

e.g.: *überdrüssig des Terrors einer revolutionären Linken* (SZ)

(ii) Some **feminines** which were originally adjectival nouns are now treated as regular feminine nouns:

die Brünette *the brunette*
die Parallele *the parallel (line)*

die Vertikale *the vertical*
die Horizontale *the horizontal* (e.g.: *aus der Horizontale* (no longer: *Horizontalen*)

After a numeral, though, *drei Parallele* is still used as well as the more usual *drei Parallelen*.

(iii) *die Illustrierte* 'the magazine' is usually still treated as an adjectival noun, e.g.: *in dieser Illustrierten.* In the plural, though, it may have the endings of an adjective or of a regular feminine noun, e.g.: *Wir haben zwei Illustrierte/Illustrierten gekauft.*

(iv) Exceptionally, the feminine form corresponding to *der Beamte* is *die Beamtin.* This is treated as a regular feminine noun, with the plural *die Beamtinnen.*

6.4.4 Neuter adjectival nouns usually denote abstract or collective ideas

Es ist schon **Schlimmes** passiert
Er hat **Hervorragendes** geleistet
der Schauer des **Verbotenen** und
  Versagten (*Zweig*)
... zugleich immer aufbauend auf
  das **Erreichte** (*Mercedes advert*)

Bad things have already happened
He has achieved outstanding things
the frightening fascination of what
  is forbidden or denied
... at the same time always building
  on what has been achieved

NB: *das Junge* 'the young' (of an animal), see 1.1.12.

Especially in spoken German, the names of regions within the German-speaking countries often take the form of neuter adjectival nouns, e.g.:

Jetzt kommen wir ins **Hessische**   Hier sind wir im **Thüringischen**
Der Baron von Münchhausen kam im **Braunschweigischen** zur Welt (*Kästner*)

6.4.5 Neuter adjectival nouns are frequently used after indefinites

especially after *alles, nichts, viel(es), wenig*, see 5.5. These have weak or strong endings depending on whether the indefinite itself has an ending, e.g.:

alles Gute	nichts Neues
von allem Guten	von nichts Neuem
weiteres Interessante	lauter Neues
folgendes Neue	viel/wenig Interessantes
vieles Interessante	von viel Interessantem
von vielem Interessanten	

6.4.6 Words denoting languages and colours have the form of neuter adjectival nouns

(a) Names of languages
For the use of the article with these nouns, see 4.2.4d.

(i) The most common form, used to refer to the language in a specific context, or when an adjective precedes, is a neuter adjective. It has no endings, except that, optionally, *-s* can be added in the genitive (see 1.3.7c):

Wir lernen **Spanisch, Französisch, Russisch, Englisch**
Die Aussprache des modernen **Deutsch(s)**
eine Übersetzung aus **dem amerikanischen Englisch**

(ii) To refer to the language in a general sense, a declined adjectival neuter noun is used. It **always** has the definite article. This form cannot be used with a preceding adjective.

Das Englische ist **dem Deutschen** verwandt
eine Übersetzung aus **dem Tschechischen**

(b) Names of colours
These usually have the form of an endingless neuter adjectival noun which has no endings, except that *-s* is usually added in the genitive singular. The plural is endingless in written German, though *-s* is sometimes used in speech:

das **Grün** der Wiesen	dieses hässlichen **Gelbs**
von einem glänzenden **Rot**	die beiden **Blau** (spoken: Blaus)
in **Schwarz** gekleidet	

In a few set phrases with the definite article this noun is declined:

ins **Grüne** fahren	Es ist das **Gelbe** vom Ei
ins **Schwarze** treffen	das **Blaue** vom Himmel herunter versprechen

6.5 Cases with adjectives

Many adjectives can be used with a noun dependent on them, which then takes a particular case (we say that the adjective 'governs' a noun in that case). The case varies depending on the individual adjective, e.g.:

- dative: *Sie ist ihrem Bruder sehr ähnlich* (section 6.5.1)
- accusative: *Ich bin den Lärm nicht gewohnt* (section 6.5.2)
- genitive: *Sie ist der deutschen Sprache mächtig* (section 6.5.3)

6.5.1 Adjectives which govern the DATIVE

(a) The dative is the most common case used with adjectives

Sie waren **ihrem Freund** beim Umzug behilflich	*They helped their friend when he moved house*
Dieses Gespräch war **mir** sehr nützlich	*This conversation was very useful for me*
Er war **seinem Gegner** überlegen	*He surpassed his opponent*
Ein **ihr** unbekannter Mann trat herein	*A man she didn't know walked in*

The following list gives a selection of frequent adjectives which govern the dative.

ähnlich* *like, similar*
angenehm[†] *agreeable*
begreiflich *comprehensible*
behilflich *helpful*
bekannt *known, familiar*
bequem *comfortable*
bewusst *known*
beschwerlich[†] *arduous*
böse *angry*
dankbar *grateful*
• eigen *peculiar*, *saját*
entbehrlich[†] *unnecessary*
ergeben *devoted, attached*
erwünscht *desirable*
fern *distant*
fremd *strange*
gefährlich[†] *dangerous*
gefällig *obliging*
nicht geheuer *scary*
gehorsam *obedient*
geläufig *familiar*
gemeinsam *common*
gerecht *just*
gesinnt *inclined*
gewogen (lit.) *well-disposed*

günstig *favourable*
heilig *holy, sacred*
hinderlich *awkward*
klar *obvious*
lästig[†] *troublesome*
leicht[†] *easy*
möglich[†] *possible*
nahe* *near, close*
nötig *necessary*
nützlich[†] *useful*
peinlich[†] *embarrassing*
schädlich[†] *injurious, harmful*
schuldig *owing*
schwer *difficult*
teuer *expensive*
treu* *faithful*
überlegen *superior*
verhasst *hateful*
verständlich[†] *comprehensible*
wichtig[†] *important*
widerlich *repugnant*
willkommen *welcome*
zugänglich[†] *accessible*
zuträglich *beneficial*

NB: The adjective usually **follows** the noun (or pronoun) dependent on it, but those marked with an asterisk in the above list may come first. Those marked with † may alternatively be used with *für* (before or after the adjective), e.g.: *Das war für mich unangenehm/unangenehm für mich* (see also 6.6). *böse* can also be used with *auf* or *mit* (see 6.6).

(b) Some adjectives which govern the dative are only used predicatively

Sie ist **mir** zuwider	*She is repugnant to me*

These are:

abhold (arch., lit.) *ill-disposed*
feind (arch., lit.) *hostile*
freund (lit.) *friendly*
gram (lit.) *angry (with)*

hold (arch., lit.) *favourably disposed*
untertan *subordinate*
zugetan *well-disposed*
zuwider *repugnant*

This group also contains all the adjectives meaning 'all the same', e.g.: *Das ist **mir** gleich* 'That's all the same to me', i.e.: *einerlei, egal* (coll.), *gleich, piepe* (coll.), *schnuppe, wurs(ch)t* (coll.). *zugetan* is occasionally used predicatively: *Die mir sonst sehr zugetane Oberschwester.*

(c) Some adjectives expressing sensations are used in the predicate of *sein*
with a dative of the person experiencing the sensation
e.g.: *Es ist mir heiß, kalt, schlecht, übel, warm.* More detail on these is given in 2.5.5c.

6.5.2 Adjectives which govern the ACCUSATIVE

These occur mainly in verbal constructions with *sein* or *werden*, although some can
be used with a following *dass*-clause or an infinitive clause with *zu*.

jdn./etwas *****gewahr** werden (lit.)	*to become aware of sth./sb.*
Wir wurden unseren Irrtum gewahr	*We realised our mistake*
etwas **gewohnt** sein	*to be used to sth.*
Ich bin den Lärm nicht gewohnt	*I'm not used to the noise*
etwas/jdn. **los** sein/werden	*to be/get rid of sth/sb.*
Endlich bin ich den Schnupfen los	*At last I've got rid of the cold*
etwas/jdn.***** **satt** sein/haben	*to be sick of sb./sth.*
Er ist/hat es gründlich satt	*He's thoroughly sick of it*
jdm. etwas **schuldig** sein	*to owe sb. sth.*
Sie ist ihm eine Erklärung schuldig	*She owes him an explanation*
etwas *****wert** sein	*to be worth sth.*
Es ist das Papier nicht wert, auf	*It's not worth the paper it's*
dem es steht (*MM*)	*printed on*

NB: (i) The adjectives asterisked can be used with a genitive in formal registers, see 6.5.3; in the case of *satt* this is
only possible in conjunction with *sein*, not with *haben*.

(ii) *schuldig* is used with a genitive in the sense of 'guilty', e.g.: *Er ist des Verbrechens schuldig* 'He is guilty of the
crime'.

6.5.3 Adjectives which govern the GENITIVE

(a) The genitive with adjectives is mainly restricted to formal German
A number of the adjectives concerned have alternative constructions in less formal
registers. With the exception of *bar*, they follow the noun:

bar *devoid of*	Seine Handlungsweise war bar **aller Vernunft**
	His action was devoid of all reason
bewusst *conscious of*	Ich war mir **meines Irrtums** bewusst
	I was conscious of my mistake
fähig *capable of*	Er ist **einer solchen Tat** nicht fähig
(or with *zu* + noun)	*He is not capable of such a deed*
froh *pleased at*	Sie war **seines Erfolges** froh
(usually: *über*)	*She was pleased about his success*
gewahr *aware of*	Wir wurden **unseres Irrtums** gewahr
(more often with acc.)	*We became aware of our mistake*
gewiss *certain of*	Sie können **meiner Unterstützung** gewiss sein
	You can be certain of my support
mächtig *master of*	Sie ist **des Deutschen** absolut mächtig
	She has a complete command of German
müde *tired of*	Sie waren **des langen Streites** müde (*Döblin*)
	They were tired of the long quarrel
schuldig *guilty of*	Der Angeklagte ist **des Hochverrats** schuldig
(see 6.5.2)	*The accused is guilty of high treason*
sicher *sure of*	Er ist sich **seiner Sache** noch nicht sicher (*Zeit*)
	He is not quite sure of his ground
überdrüssig *tired of*	Er war **des Herumhockens** überdrüssig (*Pinkwart*)
(or, rarely, with acc.)	*He was tired of sitting around*

wert *worthy of*	etwas, das **jeder Anstrengung** wert ist (*Th. Mann*)
(often with acc.)	*something which is worth any effort*
würdig *worthy of*	Er ist **dieser Ehre** nicht würdig
	He is not worthy of this honour

NB: A relative pronoun is always inserted when *bewusst* and *sicher* are used with a genitive.

(b) *voll* and *voller* are used in a number of alternative constructions

(i) *voll* and *voller* are used with the genitive in formal written language: *Das Theater war voll* **aufmerksamer Zuschauer**, *ein Korb voller* **grüner Äpfel**. Alternatively, *voll* and *voller* are used with the dative singular *ein Korb voll* **grünem Obst**, *mit einer Schüssel voller* **warmem Wasser** (*Grass*).

(ii) With a noun standing alone, *voll* or *voller* is used with a nominative: *ein Korb voll* **Obst**, *voll(er)* **Äpfel**.

(iii) With a noun qualified by an adjective, *voll von* can be used: *ein Korb* **voll von** *herrlichem Obst, roten Äpfeln*

(iv) *voll mit* is also frequent, particularly in spoken registers: *ein Korb* **voll mit** *herrlichem Obst, roten Äpfeln*

(c) A few adjectives governing the genitive are largely restricted to predicate use after *sein, bleiben* and/or *werden*

These are used only in the most formal (particularly legal) written German:

ansichtig	bedürftig	eingedenk	geständig	gewärtig	habhaft
(un)kundig	ledig	teilhaftig	verdächtig	verlustig	

An example from official legal language:

Er ist **der Bürgerrechte** für	*He has been deprived of his civic*
verlustig erklärt worden	*rights*

6.6 Adjectives with prepositions

6.6.1 Many adjectives can be linked to a noun by means of a preposition

We speak of the adjective governing a particular preposition:

Das ist **von** dem Wetter **abhängig**   die um ihre Kinder **besorgte** Mutter
Er war **mit** meinem Entschluss **einverstanden**

Which preposition is used depends on the individual adjective, and the preposition often retains little of its full meaning. A selection of adjectives governing prepositions is given below, especially those which are frequent or which have a construction different from their usual English equivalents.

The prepositional phrase may precede or follow the adjective. If it contains a noun it commonly comes first but may come second; if it contains a pronoun it almost invariably comes second, i.e.:

either:	Er ist **über den neuen Lehrling** verärgert
or (less usual):	Er ist verärgert **über den neuen Lehrling**
but always:	Er ist verärgert **über ihn**

NB: *arm* and *reich* usually precede a phrase with *an*, even if it has a noun, e.g. *Das Land ist arm/reich an Bodenschätzen.*

(a) Frequently used adjectives governing a preposition

abhängig von	*dependent on*
angewiesen auf etwas/jdn. sein	*to have to rely on sth./sb.*
Wir waren **auf uns selber** angewiesen	
ärgerlich auf/über	*annoyed with*
arm an	*poor in*
aufmerksam auf	*aware of*
Sie machte mich **auf meinen Irrtum** aufmerksam	
begeistert von/über	*enthusiastic about*
berechtigt zu	*justified in*
Sie sind **zu diesem Vorwurf** berechtigt	
bereit zu	*ready for*
Die Truppen waren **zum Einsatz** bereit	
besorgt um	*anxious about*
bezeichnend für	*characteristic of*
blass, bleich vor	*pale with*
Er war völlig blass/bleich **vor Entsetzen**	
böse auf/mit	*cross with*
Bist du böse **auf mich/mit mir**? (**or**: Bist du **mir** böse, see 6.5.1)	
charakteristisch für	*characteristic of*
dankbar für	*grateful for*
Ich war ihm **für seine gütige Hilfe** dankbar	
durstig nach	*thirsty for*
eifersüchtig auf	*jealous of*
einverstanden mit	*in agreement with*
Bist du **mit diesem Vorschlag** einverstanden?	
empfänglich für	*susceptible, receptive to*
Sie ist sehr empfänglich **für Schmeichelei**	
empfindlich gegen	*sensitive to*
Sie ist sehr empfindlich **gegen Kälte**	
ersichtlich aus	*obvious, clear from*
Das ist **aus seiner letzten Bemerkung** ersichtlich	
fähig zu	*capable of*
Sie ist **zu einer solchen Tat** nicht fähig (or genitive, see 6.5.3a)	
fertig mit etwas sein	*to have finished sth.*
Bist du **mit dem Essen** schon fertig?	
geeignet für/zu	*suitable for*
Er ist **für diese/zu dieser Arbeit** nicht geeignet	
gefasst auf	*ready, prepared for*
Mach dich gefasst **auf seine Reaktion**!	
gespannt auf	*extremely curious about*
Ich bin **auf diesen Film** sehr gespannt	*I am dying to see that film*
gewöhnt an	*accustomed/used to*
Ich bin jetzt **an diesen Kaffee** gewöhnt	
gierig nach	*greedy for*
gleichgültig gegen/gegenüber	*indifferent to(wards)*
höflich zu/gegenüber	*polite to(wards)*
hungrig nach	*hungry for*
interessiert an	*interested in*
müde von	*tired from*
Er war müde **von der schweren Arbeit** (see also 6.5.3a)	
neidisch auf	*envious of*
neugierig auf	*curious about*
reich an	*rich in*
scharf auf (coll.)	*keen on*
Er ist scharf **auf seine Rechte**	
schuld an etwas sein/haben	*to be blamed for sth.*

Wer war/hatte **an dem Streit** schuld?

sicher vor	*safe from*
stolz auf	*proud of*
stumm vor	*dumb with*
typisch für	*typical of*
überzeugt von	*convinced of*
unabhängig von	*independent of*
verheiratet mit	*married to*
verliebt in	*in love with*

Sie ist **in den Bruder** ihrer Freundin verliebt

verschieden von	*different to/from*
versessen auf	*(very, mad) keen on*

Er ist versessen **auf alte Sportwagen**

verwandt mit	*related to*
vorbereitet auf	*prepared for*
wütend auf	*mad at, furious with*

Er war wütend **auf seine Chefin**

zornig auf	*angry with*
zuständig für	*responsible for*

NB: If they depend on adjectives, *auf* and *über* are always followed by the accusative case.

(b) *über* (with the accusative) is used with many adjectives to mean 'about'

Sie war erfreut, erstaunt, froh, verwundert über seinen Erfolg

Frequent adjectives which govern *über* (see also 20.3.12e):

aufgebracht *outraged*	erfreut *delighted*
beschämt *ashamed*	erstaunt *amazed*
bestürzt, betroffen *full of consternation*	froh *glad* (see 6.5.3a)
empört, entrüstet *indignant*	glücklich *happy*
entzückt *delighted*	traurig *sad*
erbittert *bitter*	verwundert *astonished*
erbost *infuriated*	

6.6.2 Many adjectives governing prepositions can be used with a following *dass*-clause or an infinitive clause with *zu*

These clauses are often anticipated by the prepositional adverb (i.e. *da(r)* + preposition, e.g. *daran, damit*, see 3.5):

Er ist **davon** abhängig, dass ihm sein Bruder hilft	He is dependent on his brother's helping him
Er ist **davon** abhängig, das Geld zu erhalten	He is dependent on receiving the money
Wir sind **dazu** bereit, Ihnen darüber Auskünfte zu geben	We are prepared to give you some information about this
Sie war **darüber** froh, dass sie ihn noch sehen würde	She was pleased that she would still see him

There are no hard and fast rules for when the prepositional adverb is used in these constructions and when it is not. With a number of the adjectives given in section 6.6.1 it is quite optional and pairs of sentences like the following are equally acceptable and grammatical:

> **Ich bin gewöhnt,** jeden Tag eine Stunde zu üben
> **Ich bin daran gewöhnt,** jeden Tag eine Stunde zu üben

Using the prepositional adverb seems to focus emphasis on the content of the dependent clause or infinitive phrase. In practice it is more commonly used than left out, even where it is optional, especially in written German.

6.6.3 Extended phrases with adjectives can be used attributively

In German extended adjectival phrases can be used attributively, i.e. before the noun, in a way quite unknown in English. Such phrases include a noun phrase (in the case governed by the adjective) or a prepositional phrase (with the preposition governed by the particular adjective), and they can be very long. This **extended attribute** construction is very common in formal German, especially in technical and official registers:

dieses **seinem Vorgestezten äußerst nützliche** Gespräch	*this conversation which was very useful to his superior*
zum Einsatz bereite Truppen	*troops ready to be deployed*
eine von rhetorischen Effekten freie Rede	*a speech free of rhetorical devices*
eine für sie ganz typische Haltung	*an attitude quite typical of her*

This construction is also very common with participles, see 13.5.3.

7

Adverbs

The traditional term ADVERB covers a range of words with a variety of uses. Typically, adverbs are words which do not decline and which express relations like time, place, manner and degree. They can be used:

- to qualify verbs: *Sie hat ihm **höflich** geantwortet*
- to qualify adjectives: *ein **natürlich** eleganter Stil*
- they often relate to the sentence as a whole, e.g. *Er hat ihr **sicher** geholfen*

In practice all authorities differ, sometimes quite radically, on what are to be considered as adverbs in German and how they are to be classified in terms of their function. In this chapter we use a simplified classification for practical purposes, and this is summarised in Table 7.1.

TABLE 7.1 *Main types of adverb*

Adverbs	Use	Examples
time	*answering the question when*	damals, lange, oft, gestern, heute
place	*answering the question where*	hier, dort, oben, draußen, überall
direction	*answering the question where to/from*	dahin, daher, hinüber, herein
attitude/viewpoint	*commenting on what is said, or answering a yes/no question*	hoffentlich, leider, wahrscheinlich, natürlich, psychologisch
reason/cause	*answering the question why*	dadurch, daher, deshalb, folglich, trotzdem
manner	*answering the question how*	irgendwie, anders, telefonisch
degree	*answering the question how much/small . . . (often with adjectives)*	sehr, außerordentlich, relativ, etwas, ziemlich
interrogative	*w-words introducing questions*	wann?, weshalb?, wieso?

Phrases, often with a preposition, can have the same function as an adverb in a sentence. Compare:

> Sie hat **heute** gearbeitet – Sie hat **den ganzen Tag** gearbeitet
> Sie ist **trotzdem** gekommen – Sie ist **trotz des Regens** gekommen
> Sie blieb **dort** – Sie blieb **in der alten Stadt am Rhein**

The term ADVERBIAL is commonly used to refer to both single words (i.e. ADVERBS) and phrases like the above (traditionally called **adverbial phrases**) which function adverbially. This chapter only deals with adverbs proper (i.e. single words) and concentrates on those adverbs of German and their uses which present significant differences to their most usual English equivalents, in particular:

- adverbs of **place** (section 7.1)
- adverbs of **direction** (section 7.2)

- adverbs of **manner, viewpoint, attitude** and **reason** (section 7.3)
- adverbs of **degree** (section 7.4)
- interrogative **adverbs** (section 7.5)

Adverbs of **time** are dealt with in Chapter 11 with other time expressions (i.e. in section 11.6). **Modal particles** like *doch, schon* and *wohl* are treated in Chapter 10. The **comparative** and **superlative** forms of adverbs (e.g. *Sie fährt schneller, am schnellsten*) are explained in Chapter 8.

7.1 Adverbs of place

This section deals with those adverbs which indicate position.

7.1.1 *hier, dort, da*

(a) *hier* **refers to a place close to the speaker**
(= English 'here'):

> Ich habe deine Tasche **hier** im Schrank gefunden

(b) *dort* **refers to a place away from the speaker**
(= English 'there'):

> Ich sah deine Schwester **dort** an der Ecke stehen

(c) *da* **is a less emphatic alternative to** *dort*
It is used more frequently than *dort* and usually refers to a place away from the speaker:

> Ich sah ihn **da** an der Ecke stehen

da is often used to point in a general, unemphatic way when the difference between 'here' and 'there' is not crucial. In such contexts it can in some contexts correspond to English 'here':

> Herr Meyer ist momentan nicht **da**   *Mr Meyer is not here at the moment*

7.1.2 *oben, unten*

German lacks noun equivalents for 'top 'and 'bottom 'and often uses phrases with *oben* and *unten* in contexts where these would be used in English:

oben auf dem Turm	*at the top of the tower*
Sie stand ganz **oben** auf der Treppe	*She was standing right at the top of the stairs*
unten auf dem Bild	*at the bottom of the picture*
Bis unten sind es noch zwei Stunden zu Fuß	*It's another two hours' walk to the bottom*
Die Säule wird **nach unten hin** breiter	*The column broadens out towards the bottom*
Sein Name steht **unten** auf der Liste	*His name is at the bottom of the list*
ganz **unten** im Kasten	*right at the bottom of the chest*
auf Seite 90 **unten**	*at the bottom of page 90*
von **oben** bis **unten**	*from top to bottom*

7.1.3 The adverb *mitten* is the most usual equivalent for the English noun 'middle'

It is usually followed by a preposition. In some contexts *mitten* has other English equivalents:

Mitten im Garten ist ein Teich	*In the middle of the garden there is a pond*
Sie stellte die Vase **mitten** auf den Tisch	*She put the vase in the middle of the table*
mitten in der Nacht	*in the middle of the night*
mitten in der Aufregung	*in the midst of the excitement*
Ich war **mitten** unter den Leuten auf der Straße (*Zuckmayer*)	*I was in the midst of the people in the street*
Er bahnte sich **mitten** durch die Menge einen Weg	*He forced his way through the middle of the crowd*
mitten auf der Leiter	*halfway up/down the ladder*

7.1.4 *außen, draußen, innen, drinnen*

außen and *innen* mean '**on** the outside', '**on** the inside', i.e. they refer to the outer or inner surface of the object. *draußen* and *drinnen*, on the other hand, mean 'outside' and 'inside', i.e. away from the object or contained within it:

Die Tasse ist **außen** schmutzig	*The cup is dirty on the outside*
Ich musste **draußen** warten	*I had to wait outside*
Die Äpfel sind **innen** faul	*The apples are rotten inside*
Drinnen ist es aber schön warm	*Indoors it's nice and warm, though*
Dieses Fenster geht **nach innen** auf	*This window opens inwards*
Wir kommen **von draußen**	*We are coming from outside*
Er schloss die Tür **von außen** zu	*He shut the door from the outside*
von außen/innen gesehen	*seen from the outside/inside*

NB: The use of *außen* and *innen* to mean 'outside' and 'inside' is now archaic or regional (especially Austrian).

7.1.5 Indefinite place adverbs

i.e. the equivalents of English 'somewhere', 'anywhere', 'everywhere', 'nowhere'.

(a) *irgendwo* corresponds to 'somewhere' or, in questions, 'anywhere'

Ich habe es **irgendwo** liegen gelassen	*I've left it somewhere*
Hast du Paula **irgendwo** gesehen?	*Have you seen Paula anywhere?*

In spoken German simple *wo* is commonly used for *irgendwo* if unstressed: *Ich habe es wohl wo liegen gelassen.*

(b) *überall* corresponds to 'everywhere', or to 'anywhere' in the sense of 'no matter where'

Erika hat dich **überall** gesucht	*Erika was looking for you everywhere*
Sie dürfen hier **überall** parken	*You can park anywhere here*

(c) *nirgendwo, nirgends* correspond to 'nowhere', 'not . . . anywhere'

Er war **nirgendwo/nirgends** zu sehen	*He was nowhere to be seen*
Ich habe dich gestern **nirgends** gesehen	*I didn't see you anywhere yesterday*

(d) *anderswo, woanders* **correspond to 'somewhere else', 'elsewhere'** (in questions also = *anywhere else*):

Sie müssen ihn **anderswo/woanders** suchen	*You'll have to look for him somewhere else*
Hast du ihn **anderswo/woanders** gesehen?	*Have you seen him somewhere/anywhere else?*

7.2 Adverbs of direction: *hin* and *her*

By using the adverbs *hin* and *her*, German can express direction away from or towards the speaker more consistently than is possible in English. These adverbs have a wide range of uses and can occur alone or linked with another word. In general, *hin* denotes **motion away from** the speaker (or the person concerned), whilst *her* denotes **motion towards** the speaker.

7.2.1 *hin* and *her* are compounded with position adverbs to form direction adverbs

By using these compound forms, German differentiates consistently between **position**, **movement away from the speaker** and **movement towards the speaker**. This can be illustrated by the interrogative adverbs:

Wo wohnen Sie?	*Where do you live?*
Wohin gehen Sie?	*Where are you going (to)?*
Woher kommen Sie?	*Where are you coming from?*

The other adverbs of position given in section 7.1.1 and 7.1.5 compound in a similar way with *-hin* and *-her* to indicate direction to/from:

Sie wohnt **hier**	*She lives here*
Sie kommt **hierher**	*She's coming here*
Leg das Paket **hierhin**!	*Put the parcel down here*
Sie wohnt doch **da/dort**	*She lives there*
In den Ferien fahren wir **dorthin/ dahin**, wo wir voriges Jahr waren	*In the holidays we're going where we were last year*
Sie kommt **dorther**	*That's where she comes from*
Er stand **dort** an der Ecke	*He was standing there on the corner*
Wie wollen wir **dorthin** kommen?	*How are we going to get there?*
Er geht heute Nachmittag **irgendwohin**	*He's going somewhere this afternoon*
Sie geht **überallhin**	*She goes everywhere*
Morgen fahren wir **anderswohin**	*We're going somewhere else tomorrow*

wohin, woher, dahin and *daher* are often split, especially in spoken German, with *hin* and *her* being placed at the end of the clause (and written together with the verb):

Wo kommt deine Mutter **her**?	**Wo** gehört dieses Buch **hin**?
Da gehe ich praktisch nie **hin**	Da kommt er doch nicht **her**, oder?
ein kleines, gutes Restaurant, wo keine Amerikaner **hin**kamen (*Baum*)	

NB: (i) *von wo* and *von da/dort* are common alternatives in spoken German to *woher, daher/dorther*: **Von wo** *kommt er? Er kommt* **von da/dort**.

(ii) *dahin* is used with *sein* in the meaning 'finished, lost', e.g.: *Sein Leben ist* **dahin**; *Mein ganzes Geld war* **dahin**.

(iii) If these words are used in an extended sense they cannot be split, e.g. *woher* in: **Woher** *weißt du das?* 'How do you know that?' and *daher* in the meaning 'that is why', e.g.: **Daher** *hat sie sich aufgeregt*.

7.2.2 *hin* and *her* combine with many verbs as a separable prefix

(a) With most verbs they indicate the direction of movement

In such contexts they do not need a specific 'here' or 'there' element. The English equivalents (if any) can be idiomatic, especially if the verb does not primarily denote movement:

Heute ist eine Wahlversammlung, und ich gehe **hin**	*There's an election meeting today and I'm going there/to it*
Ich hielt ihm die Zeitung **hin**	*I held out the newspaper to him*
Ich hörte einen Ruf und sah **hin**	*I heard a cry and looked over in that direction*
Komm mal **her**!	*Come here*
Gib den Schlüssel **her**!	*Give me the key*
Er hat mich mit dem Auto **her**gefahren	*He drove me here*
Halt den Teller **her**!	*Hold out your plate*
Setz dich **her** zu mir!	*Come and sit down over here by me*

(b) Some verbs compounded with *hin-* and *her-* have a derived, abstract or figurative meaning

sein Leben für etwas **hingeben**	*to sacrifice one's life for sth.*
Das wird schon **hinhauen** (coll.)	*It'll be OK in the end*
Nach dem Interview **war** ich völlig **hin**	*After the interview I was shattered*
Die Burschen **fielen** über ihn **her**	*The youths attacked him*
Das Thema **gibt** doch nicht viel **her**	*There's not a lot to this topic*
Es **ging** recht lustig **her**	*It was good fun*
Sie hat ein Zimmer für ihn **hergerichtet**	*She got a room ready for him*
Mit der Qualität der Abiturienten **ist** es nicht mehr weit **her** (*Spiegel*)	*The quality of school-leavers isn't up to much any more*

7.2.3 *hin* and *her* can emphasise direction with a preceding prepositional phrase

(a) In such contexts they are usually optional

Wir wanderten bis zu den Bergen (**hin**)	Er blickte zur Decke (**hin**)
Wir fuhren nach Süden (**hin**)	Er ging zum Fenster (**hin**)
Wir wanderten durch das Tal (**hin**)	Sie flogen über den Berg (**hin**)
Eine Stimme kam von oben (**her**)	Rings um ihn (**her**) tobte der Sturm

NB: (i) The combination *an ... hin* (see 20.3.2a) means 'alongside'. The noun is in the dative case: *Der Weg führt an der Wiese hin* 'along the meadow'.

(ii) *von ... her* is commonly used to mean 'in respect of': *Das war schon verfehlt von der Zielsetzung her* (see 20.2.8a).

(b) With *hinter, neben, vor* and *zwischen, her* is used to indicate relation of movement to another person or thing moving in the same direction. The noun in this construction is always in the dative case, see 20.3:

Er ging **hinter** ihr **her**	*He was walking behind her*
Der Hund lief **neben** mir **her**	*The dog was running beside me*
Ein deutscher Wagen fuhr **vor** ihm **her**	*A German car was driving in front of him*
Sie ging **zwischen** uns **her**	*She was walking between us*

The adverbs *hinterher* and *nebenher* are used in a similar sense, e.g.: *Er lief hinterher, nebenher* 'He was running behind, alongside'.

(c) Phrases with *auf* giving reasons or causes can be strengthened by *hin*
See also 20.3.5d:

Das tat er **auf** meinen Vorschlag **hin**	*He did it at my suggestion*
auf die Gefahr **hin**, erkannt zu werden	*at the risk of being recognised*

7.2.4 *hin-* and *her-* combine with prepositions to form directional adverbs

e.g. *hinab, herab, hinauf, herbei,* etc. These occur mainly as separable verb prefixes. In general they link the direction indicated by the preposition with the notion **away from** or **towards** the speaker.

(a) Six prepositions form pairs of compounds with *hin-* and *her-*:

hinab, herab *down*	hinein, herein *in*
hinauf, herauf *up*	hinüber, herüber *over*
hinaus, heraus *out*	hinunter, herunter *down*

They are characteristically used in conjunction with a preceding prepositional phrase or a noun phrase in the accusative case (see 2.2.5c):

Wir stiegen die Treppe **hinauf**	*We climbed up the stairs*
Wir kamen die Treppe **herab/herunter**	*We came down the stairs*
Er ging in das Haus **hinein**	*He went into the house*
Er kam in das Zimmer **herein**	*He came into the room*

NB: (i) *hin/herab* and *hin/herunter* have identical meanings. Those with *-unter* are more usual in spoken registers.
(ii) *hinaus* and *heraus* are used with a preceding phrase with *zu* to indicate movement or vision out of or through doors, windows etc., e.g.: *Er blickte **zur** Tür **hinaus**; Sie warf es **zum** Fenster **heraus**.*

(b) Other prepositions or adverbs combine with only one of *hin-* or *her-*:

With *hin-*: **hindurch** *through*	**hinweg** *away*	**hinzu** *in addition*	
With *her-*: **heran** *along; up (to)*	**herbei** *along*	**herum** *round*	**hervor** *forth, out*

Er drang durch die Menge **hindurch**	*He pushed through the crowd*
Die Rollbahn sauste unter uns **hinweg**	*The runway sped away beneath us*
Sie legte einige Papiere **hinzu**	*She put down some papers in addition*
Sie trat an den Tisch **heran**	*She stepped up to the table*
Einige Polizisten kamen **herbei**	*A few policemen came along*
Er kam um die Ecke **herum**	*He came round the corner*
Die Bücher lagen auf dem Tisch **herum**	*The books were lying around on the table*
Er zog einen Revolver unter dem Tisch **hervor**	*He pulled a revolver out from under the table*

NB: Formal German used to make a distinction between *herum* 'round in a circle' and *umher* 'criss-crossing; higgledy-piggledy'. Nowadays, though, *herum* is commonly used in both senses in both speech and writing.

(c) The adverb with *hin-* or *her-* often repeats the direction given by a previous preposition

Der Vogel flog **in** das Zimmer **hinein**	Er kam **um** die Ecke **herum**
Wir kamen **aus** dem Wald **heraus**	Sie gingen **durch** das Tal **hindurch**

These constructions can seem tautologous, but if the adverb is omitted, the effect is usually that the verb is emphasised rather than the direction and the adverb should thus be used **unless** the verb is to be stressed. Compare:

> Der Vogel ist in das Zimmer **geflogen** (i.e. it flew rather than hopped)
> Der Vogel ist in das Zimmer **hinein**geflogen (i.e. it didn't fly **out**)
> Wir wollen die Truhe in dein Zimmer **tragen** (i.e. carry, not push)
> Wir wollen die Truhe in dein Zimmer **hinüber**tragen (i.e. take it **across** – not up or down)

If another word in the sentence bears the main stress, the adverb is optional:

> Der **Vogel** ist in das Zimmer (hinein)geflogen
> Wir wollen die **Truhe** in dein Zimmer (hinüber)tragen

(d) Verbs with the simple prefixes, e.g. *ab-*, *an-*, *auf-*, etc. usually have a derived, extended or other non-literal sense

(see also 22.5.1) This is because simple direction is indicated by using the forms in *hin-* or *her-*. Compare:

Er ist (in das Zimmer) **hineingegangen**	*He went in(to the room)*
Die Zeitung ist **eingegangen**	*The newspaper went bust*
Er hat den Koffer **hereingebracht**	*He brought the suitcase in*
Das **bringt** nichts **ein**	*That's not worth it*
Er **kam** (aus dem Haus) **heraus**	*He came out (of the house)*
Mit 100 Euro **kommen** wir nicht **aus**	*We won't manage on 100 euros*
Ich **ging** zu ihm **hinüber**	*I went over to him*
Er ist zur SPD **übergegangen**	*He went over to the SPD*

(e) Some verbs with *hin-* and *her-* compounds have figurative meanings

sich zu etwas **herablassen**	*to condescend to (do) sth.*
Er **gibt** eine Zeitschrift **heraus**	*He edits a journal*
Es **kommt** auf dasselbe **heraus**	*It all comes to the same thing*
Er **leierte** die Predigt **herunter**	*He reeled off the sermon*
Die Verhandlungen **zogen sich hinaus**	*The negotiations dragged on*

(f) In colloquial German, both *hin-* and *her-* are often reduced to *r-* in compound forms

(irrespective of the direction involved). This is especially frequent in north German usage:

> Wollen wir jetzt **raus**gehen (written: *hinausgehen*)
> Wollen wir die Jalousien **runter**lassen? (written: *herunterlassen*)

These forms are occasionally found in writing if informal usage is being suggested, e.g.: *Ich ging morgens Bahnhofstreppen **rauf** und **runter** und nachmittags Bahnhofstreppen **runter** und **rauf*** (Böll)

7.2.5 Some special meanings and uses of *hin-* and *her-*

(a) *hin-* often has the sense 'down':

> Sie legte sich **hin**   Der Junge fiel **hin**   Er setzte den Stuhl **hin**

(b) *vor sich hin* **means 'to oneself' (see 20.3.16b):**

Das murmelte er so **vor sich hin**   Sie las **vor sich hin**

(c) *hin und her* **means 'to and fro', 'back and forth':**

Er ging auf der Straße **hin und her**

(d) *hin und wieder* **means 'now and again':**

Hin und wieder sehe ich ihn in der Stadt

(e) *her* **is used in the sense of 'ago' in time phrases (see 11.5.13):**

Das ist schon lange **her**

7.3 Adverbs of manner, viewpoint, attitude and reason

A large number of adverbs fall into these categories, or into related subgroups which are not dealt with specifically. It is convenient to deal with them all together here.

7.3.1 Adverbs of manner and viewpoint

(a) Adverbs of manner typically answer the question *Wie?*

Wie ist sie gefahren?	Sie ist **schnell** gefahren
Wie hat sie gesungen?	Sie hat **gut** gesungen
Wie hat er es gemacht?	Er hat es **anders** gemacht

When they occur in a sentence with *nicht*, the *nicht* always refers specifically to the manner adverb:

Sie hat **nicht deutlich** gesprochen (she did speak, but not clearly)
Werder Bremen hat gestern Abend in Leverkusen **nicht gut** gespielt (they played, but not well)

(b) Adverbs of viewpoint indicate a context in which the statement is to be understood

They can be paraphrased by 'seen from a … point of view' or ' …-ly speaking', e.g.:

Die Stadt liegt **verkehrsmäßig** ungünstig
   (i.e. in terms of road and rail communications)
Finanziell war diese Entscheidung eine Katastrophe
   (i.e. financially speaking)
Deutschland ist **wirtschaftlich** stärker geworden
   (i.e. from an economic point of view)

(c) Most adjectives (and participles) can be used as adverbs

Most of these are in practice adverbs of manner or viewpoint. In English such adverbs are usually marked by the suffix '-ly', but German has no such ending, and these words have exactly the same form whether they are being used as adjectives or adverbs. Compare:

Er hat die Sache **überraschend schnell** erledigt	*He settled the matter surprisingly quickly*
Ein Dokument zeigt doch, dass er **mäßigend** und **bremsend** zu wirken versuchte (*Zeit*)	*A document nevertheless shows that he tried to exercise a moderating and calming influence*

An adverb qualifying an adjective before a noun is marked as such by having no ending. Compare:

ein **schön** geschnitzter Schrank	*a beautifully carved cupboard*
ein **schöner,** geschnitzter Schrank	*a beautiful carved cupboard*

NB: This distinction is not always maintained in practice, see 6.2.7c.

These adjective–adverbs can be very widely and flexibly used in German, often with compounding, in a way which lacks a direct English equivalent:

Er hat mir **brieflich** mitgeteilt, dass er anderer Meinung sei	*He informed me by letter that he was of a different opinion*
Widerrechtlich geparkte Fahrzeuge werden **kostenpflichtig** abgeschleppt	*Illegally parked vehicles will be removed at the owner's expense*
Das Mitbringen von Hunden ist **lebensmittelpolizeilich** verboten	*Bringing dogs (into the shop) is forbidden by order of the food inspectorate*

7.3.2 Adverbs of attitude

Adverbs of attitude express the speaker's comment on the content of the statement, i.e. whether he or she thinks it is probable, likely, welcome, well-known or the like. In many ways their function overlaps with that of the modal particles (see Chapter 10). Because they relate to the sentence as a whole they are sometimes called *Satzadverbien* in German.

Anscheinend ist sie erst um sieben gekommen
(i.e. it appears to the speaker that she only arrived then)
Er fährt **leider** schon heute ab
(i.e. the speaker thinks it is unfortunate that he's going)
Natürlich/Selbstverständlich darfst du das machen
(i.e. the speaker's opinion is that it goes without saying)
Sie wird uns **sicher(lich)** helfen
(i.e. the speaker thinks that it is certain)

These adverbs of attitude have a number of characteristic features. In particular, although they can occur in a negative sentence, they cannot themselves be negated:

Sie kommen **hoffentlich** noch heute
(one can't say *nicht hoffentlich*)
Er fährt **leider** nicht weg
(*nicht leider* is not possible)
Sie ist **wahrscheinlich** nicht gekommen
(*nicht wahrscheinlich* ... does not make sense)

Unlike adverbs of manner, they cannot answer the question *Wie?*, but they **can** be used to answer a yes/no question:

Singt sie heute? Ja, **bestimmt/leider/vielleicht/zweifellos**, etc.
(None of these words can answer the question *Wie singt sie?*)

7.3.3 Adverbs of reason

A large group of adverbs indicate cause, circumstance, condition, purpose or reason. The most frequent members of this group are:

allenfalls *at most*	deswegen *therefore*
andernfalls *otherwise*	folglich *consequently*
dabei *at the same time*	gegebenenfalls *if necessary*
dadurch *thereby*	gleichwohl (elev.) *nevertheless*
daher *therefore*	infolgedessen *consequently*
dann *in that case*	jedenfalls *in any case*
darum *therefore*	mithin (elev.) *consequently*
dazu *to that end*	nichtsdestoweniger *nevertheless*
demnach *therefore*	somit *consequently*
demzufolge (elev.) *therefore*	sonst *otherwise* (see 7.3.5b)
dennoch *nevertheless*	trotzdem *nevertheless*
deshalb *therefore*	

7.3.4 Many German adverbs have a verb or a subordinate clause construction as their only or most natural idiomatic English equivalent

The most frequent equivalent of English 'to like', for example, is to use the German adverb *gern* with *haben* or another verb, e.g.: *Ich esse gern Käsekuchen* 'I like cheese-cake'; *Sie hat Ihren Lehrer ganz gern* 'She quite likes her teacher'. A number of the most useful of these adverbs are given below. In some cases a construction with a verb is also possible in German, so that 'It must be admitted that it isn't easy' could correspond to *Man muss zugeben, dass es nicht einfach ist* or to *Es ist freilich nicht einfach*. In general, the equivalents with adverbs sound more idiomatic and concise:

Das Problem ist **allerdings** schwierig	*I must admit that the problem is difficult*
Er wurde **allmählich** rot im Gesicht	*He began to get red in the face*
Er hat **andauernd** gespielt	*He kept on playing*
Er ist **angeblich** arbeitslos	*He claims to be unemployed*
Er ist **anscheinend** nicht gekommen	*He seems not to have come*
Wir können Ihnen **bedauerlicherweise** nicht weiter behilflich sein	*We regret that we can be of no further assistance to you*
Er ist **bekanntlich** ein hervorragender Linguist	*Everyone knows that he is an outstanding linguist*
Hier können Sie **beliebig** lange bleiben	*You can stay here as long as you wish*
Am besten behalten Sie das für sich	*You'd better keep that to yourself*
Thomas kommt **bestimmt** mit	*I'm sure Thomas is coming with us / Thomas is sure to be coming with us*
Wir haben **erfreulicherweise** das Spiel gewonnen	*I'm glad to say that we won the game*
Es ist **freilich** nicht einfach	*It must be admitted that it isn't easy*
Gegebenenfalls kann man auch eine andere Taste wählen	*If the need should arise, another key may be selected*
✓ Im Sommer spielt er **gern** Tennis	*He likes playing tennis in summer*
Dienstags hat er **gewöhnlich** Tennis gespielt	*He used to play tennis on Tuesdays*
Hoffentlich erreichen wir die Hütte vor Sonnenuntergang	*I hope we shall reach the cabin before sunset*
Sie kann **leider** nicht kommen	*I'm afraid she can't come*
Im Winter spielt er **lieber** Fußball	*He prefers playing football in the winter*
Ich habe Reiten **lieber** als Radfahren	*I prefer riding to cycling*

Er kommt **möglicherweise** noch vor dem Abendessen	*It is possible that he will be coming before dinner*
Sie erschien **nicht**	*She failed to appear*
Die Firma stellt diese Ersatzteile **nicht mehr** her	*The company has ceased/stopped making these spare parts*
Nimm dir **ruhig** noch etwas zu trinken	*Don't be afraid to help yourself to another drink*
Alle Insassen sind **vermutlich** ums Leben gekommen	*It is presumed that all the passengers lost their lives*
Er las **weiter**	*He continued to read/went on reading*
Ich habe sie **zufällig** in der Stadt gesehen	*I happened/chanced to see her in town*
Zweifellos wird auch dieses Jahr sehr wenig Schnee im Allgäu fallen	*There is no doubt that very little snow will fall in the Allgäu this year either*

7.3.5 *anders* and *sonst*

(a) *anders* means 'else' or 'differently'

In origin, *anders* is the genitive of the adjective *ander*, see 5.5.2. It usually has the written form *anders* (very occasionally *anderes*), which differentiates it from the nominative/accusative singular neuter of *ander*, which is normally written *andres* or *anderes*. It is used as follows:

(i) In the meaning 'else' with *jemand* and *niemand*:

Es ist jemand **anders** gekommen	*Somebody else came*
Der Schirm gehört jemand **anders**	*The umbrella belongs to somebody else*
Ich habe mit niemand **anders** gesprochen	*I didn't talk to anybody else*
Sie hat niemand **anders** als dich gesucht	*She wasn't looking for anyone else but you*

NB: In standard German, *jemand, niemand* do not inflect in combination with *anders*, see 5.5.15b. In south German usage, inflected forms of *ander* sometimes occur rather than invariable *anders*, most commonly in the accusative and dative, e.g. *jemand/niemand anderer* (rare), *jemand/niemand anderen, jemand/niemand anderem*.

(ii) *anders* is used in the meaning 'else' with *wo, wohin, woher, (n)irgendwo*. Note the various alternative combinations:

woanders/anderswo/irgendwo anders	*somewhere else/elsewhere*
Ich gehe irgendwo anders hin/ woandershin/anderswohin	*I'm going somewhere else*
Er kommt anderswoher, nicht aus Hamburg	*He comes from somewhere else, not from Hamburg*
nirgendwo anders	*nowhere else*
Ich gehe nirgendwo anders hin	*I'm not going anywhere else*

(iii) *anders* also means 'different(ly)', 'in a different way':

Er ist ganz **anders** als sein Bruder	*He is quite different to his brother*
Du musst es irgendwie **anders** anpacken	*You'll have to tackle it differently*
Es ist etwas **anders**	*It is rather different*
Compare:	
Es ist etwas and(e)res	*It is something else*
Das klingt jetzt anders	*That sounds different now*

(b) *sonst* **means 'else' or 'otherwise'**

(i) In some contexts *sonst* can overlap with the meaning of *anders* 'else' or *ander* 'other', 'different' (see (a) above). Compare the following possible alternatives:

Kannst du **etwas anderes/sonst (noch) etwas** vorschlagen?	*Can you suggest anything else?*
War **noch jemand anders/sonst noch jemand** da?	*Was anyone else here?*
Niemand anders/Niemand sonst hat mir geholfen	*Nobody else helped me*
sonst wo/sonst irgendwo/irgendwo sonst/anderswo, etc. (see (ii) above)	*somewhere/anywhere else*
Ich muss **noch sonst wohin/ anderswohin**	*I've got to go somewhere else*
Wenn **noch andere Probleme/sonst noch** Probleme auftauchen …	*If any other problems arise, …*
Wer anders kann es gesagt haben?/ (more common: **Wer** kann es **sonst** gesagt haben?)	*Who else can have said it?*

(ii) However, if the sense is clearly 'different' or 'other', only *ander* or, where appropriate, *anders*, can be used. Compare:

Da ist Professor Niebaum und **niemand anders**	*That's Professor Niebaum and nobody else* (i.e. not a different person)
Da ist Professor Niebaum und **sonst niemand**	*That's Professor Niebaum and nobody else* (i.e. he's the only one there)

(iii) If the meaning is clearly 'in addition', 'apart from that', 'otherwise', then only *sonst* is possible:

Wer kommt **sonst** noch?	*Who else is coming?*
Mit wem haben Sie **sonst** noch gesprochen?	*Who else did you talk to?*
Was hat sie **sonst** noch gesagt?	*What else did she say?*
sonst irgendwann	*some/any other time*
Sonst geht alles gut	*Otherwise all is well*
Wir müssen uns beeilen, **sonst** verpassen wir den Zug	*We'll have to hurry, otherwise we'll miss the train*
länger als **sonst**	*longer than usual*

7.3.6 Adverbs in *-weise*

The suffix *-weise* is very productive for the formation of adverbs of manner or attitude. It is most often added to nouns or adjectives.

(a) Adverbs formed from a noun or a verb + *weise* are in the main manner adverbs with the meaning 'by way of', 'in the form of'

andeutungsweise *by way of a hint*	bruchstückweise *in the form of fragments*
ausnahmsweise *by way of exception*	
beispielsweise *by way of example*	dutzendweise *by the dozen*
beziehungsweise *or, as the case may be* (see 19.1.3b)	familienweise *in families*
	gruppenweise *in groups*

massenweise *on a massive scale*
paarweise *in pairs*
pfundweise *by the pound*
probeweise *on approval*
ruckweise *by jerks*
schrittweise *step by step*

stückweise *piecemeal*
stundenweise *by the hour*
teilweise *partly*
versuchsweise *tentatively*
zeitweise *temporarily*
zwangsweise *compulsorily*

Die Flüchtlinge strömten **massenweise** über die ungarische Grenze	*The refugees were flooding in hordes across the Hungarian border*
Sein neues Buch ist **stellenweise** ganz gut	*His new book is quite good in places*
Er wird **stundenweise** bezahlt	*He is paid by the hour*

These forms, which were originally only adverbs, are increasingly used as adjectives as well:

eine **probeweise** Anstellung
eine **ruckweise** Bewegung
der **stückweise** Verkauf
eine **schrittweise** Verminderung der Streitkräfte in Europa (SZ)

die **teilweisen** Verbesserungen
eine **stundenweise** Bezahlung
die **stufenweisen** Fortschritte

Predominantly, though, they are used with nouns which denote a process, chiefly those which are derived from verbs, as in the examples above. Combinations like *der stückweise Preis* or *eine auszugsweise Urkunde* are not (yet?) generally regarded as acceptable.

(b) Adverbs of attitude are very commonly formed from adjectives or participles with the suffix -*weise* and the linking element -*er*
e.g. *möglicherweise* from *möglich*, *bezeichnenderweise* from *bezeichnend*. Similarly:

bedauerlicherweise *regrettably*
begreiflicherweise *understandably*
dummerweise *foolishly*
erstaunlicherweise *astonishingly*
fälschlicherweise *erroneously*
glücklicherweise *fortunately*
interessanterweise *interestingly*
komischerweise *funnily*

liebenswürdigerweise *obligingly*
möglicherweise *possibly, perhaps*
natürlicherweise *of course*
normalerweise *normally*
überflüssigerweise *superfluously*
unglücklicherweise *unfortunately*
unnötigerweise *unnecessarily*
unvermuteterweise *unexpectedly*

As these are adverbs of **attitude**, indicating a comment by the speaker on the statement, their meaning is different from that of the adjective-adverb of **manner** from which they are derived, and from that of the corresponding phrase with *Weise*:

Er war **merkwürdig** müde	*He was strangely tired*
Er war **merkwürdigerweise** müde	*Strange to say, he was tired*
Er war **in merkwürdiger Weise** müde	*He was tired in an unusual way*
Er hat **vernünftig** geantwortet	*He replied sensibly*
Er hat **vernünftigerweise** geantwortet	*Sensibly enough, he replied*
Er hat **auf vernünftige Weise** geantwortet	*He replied in a sensible way*

NB: These adverbs in -*erweise* are <u>never</u> used as adjectives.

7.4 Adverbs of degree

7.4.1 Adverbs of degree (or 'intensifiers') are used to emphasise, amplify or tone down another part of speech

Their main use is to modify adjectives or other adverbs.

(a) A selection of the most frequent adverbs of degree in German

außerordentlich *extraordinarily*	mäßig *moderately*
äußerst *extremely*	nahezu *virtually*
beinahe *almost, nearly*	recht *really*
besonders *especially*	relativ *relatively*
durchaus *absolutely, thoroughly*	sehr (see 7.4.3) *very*
etwas *a little*	überaus *extremely*
fast *almost, nearly*	verhältnismäßig *relatively*
ganz *quite*	völlig *completely*
genug *enough*	vollkommen *completely*
geradezu *virtually*	wenig *little*
höchst *extremely, highly*	ziemlich *fairly*
kaum *hardly, scarcely*	zu *too*

This list is not exhaustive; many more occur, particularly in colloquial speech, e.g. *echt, enorm, irrsinnig, ungeheuer, unheimlich, verdammt.*

eine **durchaus** selbstkritische Einsicht	*a thoroughly self-critical understanding*
Der Kaffee ist **etwas** süß	*The coffee is a little sweet*
Er fährt schnell **genug**	*He's driving fast enough*
Das ist **geradezu** lächerlich	*That is little short of ridiculous*
Die Suppe war nur **mäßig** warm	*The soup was (only) moderately warm*
eine **nahezu** optimale Lösung des Problems	*a virtually optimal solution to the problem*
Er arbeitet **recht** gut	*He works really well*
ein **überaus** ehrliches Geschäft	*a thoroughly honest transaction*
Dieser Schriftsteller ist **wenig** bekannt	*This author is little known*

(b) *hoch* 'highly' is used with a small number of abstract adjectives

It is usually compounded with them: *hochempfindlich, hochfrequent, hochinteressant, hochgeschätzt, hochqualifiziert.*

(c) *lange* and *längst* are used before a negative to indicate a considerable difference in degree

lange is often preceded by *noch*:

Das ist **noch lange nicht** gut genug	*That is not nearly good enough*
Dieses Buch ist **lange/längst nicht** so gut wie sein letztes	*This book isn't nearly as good as his last one*

7.4.2 Some adverbs of degree are used only or principally with adjectives in the comparative or superlative

bedeutend *significantly*:
Die Donau ist **bedeutend** länger als der Rhein

beträchtlich *considerably*:
> Die Zugspitze ist **beträchtlich** höher als die anderen Gipfel in den
> bayrischen Alpen

denkbar *possible*:
> Sie hat den **denkbar** schlechtesten Eindruck gemacht

entschieden *decidedly*:
> Er hat **entschieden** schlechter gespielt als vor einem Jahr

viel *much*:
> Diese Schule ist **viel** größer als meine

weit *far*:
> Der Wagen ist **weit** schneller, als ich dachte

bei weitem *(by) far*:
> Er ist **bei weitem** besser als Jochen
> Er ist **bei weitem** der Beste in der Klasse

weitaus *(by) far*:
> Isabella ist **weitaus** reifer, als man ihrem Alter nach schließen dürfte
> Der neueren Geschichte ist das **weitaus** größte Gewicht beizumessen

wesentlich *substantially*:
> Er hat heute **wesentlich** besser gespielt

7.4.3 *sehr* is chiefly used as an adverb of degree (= 'very')

Er weiß es **sehr** gut.   Das ist **sehr** nett von dir.

However, it has a wider range of use than English *very*:

(a) It can modify a verb or phrase, corresponding to English 'very much'

Ich bewundere sie **sehr**   Er ist **sehr** dafür   Das interessiert mich **sehr**
Das ist **sehr** nach meinem Geschmack   Er hat sich **sehr** verändert

(b) After *so*, *wie* or *zu*, it can denote degree, like English 'much'

Nicht **so sehr** die Handlung wie der Stil hat mich gefesselt
Wie sehr ich es bedaure, dass sie durchgefallen ist!
Er hat es sich **zu sehr** zu Herzen genommen

7.5 Interrogative adverbs

The German interrogative adverbs correspond to the English *wh*-words, and like them they introduce questions. They fall into similar groups to other adverbs:

Time:

> wann? *when?*: **Wann** kommt der Zug in Gelsenkirchen an?
> bis wann? *until when?*, *how long?*: **Bis wann** bleibt ihr hier?
>   *by when?*: **Bis wann** seid ihr damit fertig?
> seit wann? *since when?*, *how long?*: **Seit wann** spielen Sie Tennis?
> wie lange? *how long?*: **Wie lange** wollt ihr heute noch spielen?
> wie oft? *how often?*: **Wie oft** fährt ein Bus nach Eberbach?

Place and direction (see also 7.2.1):

> wo? *where?*: **Wo** steckt die Angelika jetzt?
> wohin? *where (to)?*: **Wohin** fahrt ihr heute?/**Wo** fahrt ihr heute **hin**?
> woher? *where from?*: **Woher** kommt der Wagen?/**Wo** kommt der Wagen **her**?
> von wo? *where from?*: **Von wo** kommt der Wagen?

Manner:

> wie? *how?*: **Wie** habt ihr das nur gemacht?

Reason:

> warum? *why?*: **Warum** wollt ihr nicht gehen?
> was? (coll.) *why?*: **Was** rennst du denn so schnell? (see 5.3.3f)
> wieso? (coll.) *why?*: **Wieso** wollt ihr nicht gehen?
> weshalb? (formal) *why?*: **Weshalb** wollt ihr nicht gehen?
> wozu? *what … for?*: **Wozu** benutzt man das?

These interrogative adverbs can also introduce indirect questions (see 16.6.4a and 19.2.4):

> Er hat mich gefragt, **wann** ich morgen komme
> Ich habe dir doch gesagt, **wie** man das macht

NB: For the interrogative pronouns *was* and *wer*, see 5.3.3. For the interrogative determiner *welcher*, see 5.3.1.

8

Comparison of adjectives and adverbs

Qualities can be compared using special forms of adjectives (and adverbs). These are called the COMPARATIVE and SUPERLATIVE forms. Thus, for the adjective *groß*:

positive degree:	Mein Haus ist **groß**	*My house is big*
comparative degree:	Dein Haus ist **größer**	*Your house is bigger*
superlative degree:	Ihr Haus ist **das größte**	*Her house is the biggest*

Naturally, some adjectives or adverbs, such as *sterblich*, *einmalig* or *absolut*, have a meaning which excludes any possibility of comparison, and there are a number of other ways of indicating degree, for example by modifying the adjective or adverb by an adverb of degree like *sehr*, see 7.4.

The **comparative** is normally used to compare two items, the **superlative** more than two:

der **größere** der beiden Brüder
Von den zwei Büchern über Berlin hat er das **billigere** gekauft
der **größte** von acht Jungen
Von diesen vielen Büchern hat er das **billigste** gekauft

As in English, this rule is not universally observed in everyday speech.

This chapter deals with the formation and use of the comparative and superlative degree of adjectives and adverbs, and other various means of comparison in German:

- the **formation** of comparatives and superlatives (sections 8.1–8.2)
- the **uses** of the **comparative** and other means of comparison (section 8.3)
- the **uses** of the **superlative** (section 8.4)

8.1 Regular formation of the comparative and superlative

8.1.1 The comparative and superlative of adjectives are formed by adding the endings -er and -st to the positive form

This is shown for some common adjectives in Table 8.1. As the superlative almost always occurs in a declined form, with the definite article, *das* is included with all examples. The few exceptions to this regular pattern are explained in section 8.2.

TABLE 8.1 *Regular formation of comparative and superlative*

Positive	Comparative	Superlative
tief *deep*	tiefer	(das) tiefste
schön *beautiful*	schöner	(das) schönste
langsam *slow*	langsamer	(das) langsamste
freundlich *friendly, kind*	freundlicher	(das) freundlichste
unwiderstehlich *irresistible*	unwiderstehlicher	(das) unwiderstehlichste

In English we form comparatives and superlatives in two ways. With short adjectives, we use the endings '-er' and '-est', with longer adjectives we use 'more' and 'most'. In German, the endings *-er* and *-st* are used **no matter how long the adjective is**; *mehr* and *meist* are not normally used in comparatives and superlatives (for the few special cases, see 8.2.7).

Comparative and superlative forms decline in the same way as any adjective when used before a noun, with the same weak or strong endings (see 6.1–6.2).

> ein schneller**er** Zug, der schnellst**e** Zug, in der tiefst**en** Schlucht der Erde

8.1.2 Comparative and superlative of adverbs

The comparative of adverbs is formed with the ending *-er*, exactly like that of adjectives:

> Schumacher fährt aber schnell**er**   Kannst du bitte etwas laut**er** sprechen?

For the superlative of adverbs, a phrase is used formed using the stem in *-st*, with the ending *-en*, together with *am*

Schumacher fährt **am schnellsten**	*Schumacher drives fastest*
Von der Burg aus sieht man es **am klarsten**	*You can see it most clearly from the castle*

For further details about the form *am . . . sten*, see 8.4.1.

8.2 Irregularities in the formation of comparatives and superlatives

8.2.1 Adjectives in *-el, -en, -er* can drop the *-e-* of the stem in the comparative

dunkel – **dunkler** – das dunkelste	bitter – **bitt(e)rer** – das bitterste
trocken – **trock(e)ner** – das trockenste	teuer – **teurer** – das teuerste

(a) Those in *el* regularly drop the *-e-*

> dunkel – dunk**l**er   edel – ed**l**er

(b) Those in *-en* and *-er* usually drop the *-e-* if they have an inflectional ending

> trocken – der trock**n**ere Wein   bitter – ein bitt**r**erer Geruch

If there is no ending, the *-e-* is usually retained in writing, although it often drops in speech:

Dieser Wein ist trock**ener**   Dieser Geruch war bitt**erer**

If the comparative ending *-er* is preceded by a diphthong, the *-e-* of the stem is always dropped:

teuer – Diese Tasche ist teu**rer** – die teu**rere** Tasche

8.2.2 Some adjectives add -est in the superlative

i.e. an *-e-* is added to the ending to aid pronunciation.

(a) Those whose stem ends in -*haft*, -*s*, -*sk*, -*ß*, -*x* and -*z* always have -*est*

boshaft – der boshaft**este**   süß – der süß**este**
lieblos – der lieblos**este**   fix – der fix**este**
brüsk – der brüsk**este**   stolz – der stolz**este**

(b) Those with a stem ending in -*d*, -*t* and -*sch* usually add -*est*

mild – der mild**este**   berühmt – der berühmt**este**
sanft – der sanft**este**   rasch – der rasch**este**

However, longer words ending in these consonants have the ending *-st* if the last syllable is unstressed:

spannend – der spannend**ste**   komisch – der komisch**ste**

(c) Those with a stem ending in a long vowel or diphthong can have the ending -*est* or -*st*

früh – der frühste/früh**este**   treu – der treuste/treu**este**

8.2.3 A few adjectives and adverbs have *Umlaut* on the root vowel in the comparative and superlative, in addition to the ending

arm – ärmer – der ärmste   klug – klüger – der klügste

Most of these adjectives are very common.

(a) The following adjectives always have *Umlaut* in the comparative and superlative

alt *old*   fromm *pious*
arg *bad*   gesund *healthy*
arm *poor*   grob *coarse*
dumm *stupid*   hart *hard*

jung *young*	rot *red*
kalt *cold*	scharf *sharp*
klug *clever*	schwach *weak*
krank *sick*	schwarz *black*
kurz *short*	stark *strong*
lang *long*	warm *warm*
oft *often*	

NB: (i) *groß, hoch* and *nah* also always have *Umlaut* in the comparative and superlative, but they are otherwise irregular, see 8.2.4.

(ii) *fromm* and *gesund* quite often lack *Umlaut* in the comparative and superlative in written German.

(b) A few adjectives have alternative forms with or without *Umlaut*

e.g.: *nass – nässer/nasser – der nässeste/nasseste.* These are:

bang *scared*	krumm *crooked*
blass *pale*	nass *wet*
glatt *smooth*	schmal *narrow*
karg *sparse*	zart *tender*

In general, the forms without *Umlaut* are more frequent in writing, whereas those with *Umlaut* are more typical of spoken German, especially in the south.

8.2.4 Some adjectives and adverbs have irregular comparative and superlative forms

bald	**eher**	am **ehesten**	*soon*
gern	**lieber**	am **liebsten**	*willingly, gladly*
groß	**größer**	das **größte**	*big, large*
gut	**besser**	das **beste**	*good*
hoch	**höher**	das **höchste**	*high*
nah	**näher**	das **nächste**	*near*
viel	**mehr**	das **meiste**	*much, many*
wenig	**weniger/minder**	das **wenigste/das mindeste**	*little, few*
wohl	wohl**er/besser**	am wohl**sten/am besten**	*well*

Further notes on these irregular forms:

(a) *mehr* and *weniger*

As these are adverbs, they do not decline even when used with a following noun: *Er hat **weniger** Geld als ich; Sie hat **mehr** Verstand als du; der Verlust von **weniger** Stunden.*

(b) *minder* and *mindest*

minder is restricted to formal written German. It is only used to qualify adjectives, most commonly with a preceding *nicht*:

Anderswo zwischen Ostsee und Erzgebirge ist die Lage der Denkmalpflege nicht **minder** prekär (*Spiegel*)

mindest can be used for 'least' in the sense 'slightest':

Er hatte nicht die **mindesten** Aussichten zu gewinnen.

(c) *wohl*

wohl has the comparative and superlative forms *wohler* and *am wohlsten* in the meaning 'at ease, (physically) well', e.g. *sich wohler fühlen*. *besser* and *am besten* are used in the meaning 'well', i.e. the adverb from 'good', e.g.: *Sie haben gestern* **besser** *gespielt*.

(d) *nichts weniger als* **normally means 'anything but'**
i.e. the same as *alles andere als*:

> Er ist **nichts weniger als** klug   *He is anything but clever*

For 'nothing less than', German often uses a positive statement: *Das ist* **wirklich** *katastrophal* 'That is nothing less than catastrophic'. However, some Germans <u>do</u> now use *nichts weniger als* in the sense of 'nothing less than', and ambiguity is possible.

8.2.5 Eight adjectives denoting position only have comparative and/or superlative forms

das äußere *outer, external*	das äußerste *outermost, utmost*
das innere *inner, internal*	das innerste *innermost*
das obere *upper*	das oberste *uppermost*
das untere *lower*	das unterste *lowest, bottom*
das vordere *front*	das vorderste *foremost, front*
das hintere *back*	das hinterste *back(most)*
das mittlere *central, middle; medium*	das mittelste *central, middle*
das niedere *low, inferior (mainly of social rank)*	(superlative not used)

These adjectives are only used attributively, i.e. before a noun:

> seine **äußere** Erscheinung   seine **innersten** Gedanken
> mit der **äußersten** Höflichkeit   in der **vorderen**, **vordersten** Reihe

As equivalents for English 'external(ly)' and 'internal(ly)' in other contexts, i.e. after *sein* or as adverbs, German uses *äußerlich* and *innerlich*.

> Seine Verletzungen sind nicht   Sie blieb **äußerlich**, **innerlich** ganz
> **äußerlich**, sondern **innerlich**   ruhig

8.2.6 The comparative and superlative of compound adjectives

(a) Compound adjectives are treated as single words and form their comparative and superlative in the usual way
This is always the case with those written as a single word:

altmodisch *old-fashioned*	altmodisch**er**	das altmodisch**ste**
schwerwiegend *serious, weighty*	schwerwiegend**er**	das schwerwiegend**ste**
vielsagend *meaningful*	vielsagend**er**	das vielsagend**ste**
vielversprechend *promising*	vielversprechend**er**	das vielversprechend**ste**

(b) However, if both parts are felt to retain their original meaning, they are written as separate words and only the first has the comparative or superlative form

The superlative is in the adverbial form *am . . . -sten*

> die dicht bevölkerte Stadt *the densely populated city*
> die **dichter bevölkerte** Stadt   die **am dichtesten bevölkerte** Stadt

> die leicht verdauliche Speise *the easily digested food*
> die **leichter verdauliche** Speise   die **am leichtesten verdauliche** Speise

A few frequent idiomatic combinations have **superlative** forms which are written as single words:

> der hoch gelegene Ort *the place situated high up*
> ein **höher gelegen**er Ort   der **höchstgelegen**e Ort

> nahe liegende Gründe *obvious reasons*
> **näher liegend**e Gründe   **nächstliegend**e Gründe

> die weit gehende Übereinstimmung *the far-reaching agreement*
> die **weiter gehende** Übereinstimmung die **weitestgehende** Übereinstimmung

Compound comparative forms of such adjectives with the suffixes added to the second part (*weitgehender, das weitgehendste*) are regarded as incorrect, although they are not uncommon.

8.2.7 *mehr* and *meist* in comparison

(a) A very few adjectives form their comparative and superlative by means of a preceding *mehr* or *am meisten*

This is restricted to use with participles which are not normally used as adjectives, a few adjectives which are only used predicatively (like *zuwider*, see 6.5.1b), and some unusually long and complex adjectives like *bemitleidenswert*:

> Er verrichtet jetzt eine ihm **mehr zusagend**e Tätigkeit
>
> *He is now performing a job which appeals to him more*
>
> Dresden ist die durch den Krieg **am meisten zerstört**e deutsche Stadt
>
> *Dresden is the German city most completely destroyed in the war*
>
> Er ist mir noch **mehr zuwider** als sein Bruder
>
> *He is even more repugnant to me than his brother*
>
> Er ist der **am meisten bemitleidenswert**e Kranke
>
> *He is the most to be pitied of all the patients*

With past participles a prefixed *meist-* can be used rather than *am meisten*, e.g.: *die meistzerstörte Stadt, der meistgekaufte Geschirrspülautomat Deutschlands.*

(b) *mehr* is also used if two qualities of the same object are being compared

i.e. in the sense 'rather': *Diese Arbeit ist **mehr** langweilig als schwierig.* In more formal German, *eher* is an alternative to *mehr* in this meaning.

8.3 The use of the comparative and other types of comparison

8.3.1 The comparative particle (= 'than') is usually *als*

> Peter ist älter **als** Thomas   Mein Wagen fährt schneller **als** deiner

(a) Alternatives to *als*

wie (or *als wie*) is common for *als* in colloquial speech, e.g. *Peter ist älter **(als) wie** Thomas*. This usage, although very old, is regarded as a substandard regionalism.

The use of *denn* instead of *als* is archaic, although it can be used in formal registers to avoid the sequence *als als*:

Die Mauer erscheint eher als Kunstwerk denn als Grenze (*Schneider*)	*The wall appears rather as a work of art than as a frontier*

NB: (i) *denn* is commonly used in a couple of set phrases: *mehr denn je* 'more than ever', *Geben ist seliger denn nehmen* 'It is better to give than to receive'.
   (ii) Noun phrases after *als* and *wie* are in apposition to the noun they refer to, i.e. they are in the same case, see 2.6.

(b) Degree of difference is expressed by *um . . . als*, or by a noun phrase in the accusative case

Eine Fahrt im TGV-Atlantique kann **um** bis zu 50 Prozent teurer kommen **als** in einem herkömmlichen Schnellzug (*FR*)	*A trip on the TGV-Atlantique can work out up to 50% more expensive than in an ordinary express train*
Er ist (**um**) **einen Monat** jünger **als** ich	*He is a month younger than me*

(c) To express a greater degree (= 'even') *noch* is used with the comparative

London ist eine **noch schmutzigere** Stadt als Amsterdam	*London is an even dirtier city than Amsterdam*
Er hat gestern **noch weniger** gearbeitet	*He worked even less yesterday*
Es regnete **noch stärker**	*It was raining even harder*

8.3.2 Lower degrees of comparison are expressed by *weniger*, *am wenigsten*

These correspond to English 'less tall than', 'least tall', etc.:

Er war **weniger optimistisch** als sein Bruder	*He was less optimistic than his brother*
Er arbeitet **weniger fleißig** als ich	*He works less hard than me*
der **am wenigsten talentierte** Spieler	*the least talented player*
Er arbeitet **am wenigsten fleißig** von allen	*He works the least hard of all*

In practice, *am wenigsten* is little used for 'least', and other constructions tend to be preferred wherever possible. Compare:

die **uninteressanteste** Rede	*the least interesting speech*
der **billigste/preiswerteste** Wagen	*the least expensive car*
die **einfachste** Methode	*the least difficult method*
möglichst geringe Kosten	*the least possible expenditure*

NB: In formal German, *minder* is an occasional alternative to *weniger*, see 8.2.4b, e.g.: *Angesichts der Aktenlage eine nicht* **minder** *verwegene Behauptung* (*Spiegel*).

8.3.3 The 'absolute comparative'

The comparative of some common adjectives or adverbs is used not to signal a direct comparison, but to indicate a fair degree of the relevant quality, e.g. *ein älterer Herr* 'an elderly gentleman', *eine größere Stadt* 'a fair-sized town'. This so-called 'absolute comparative' is possible with the following adjectives:

alt	dick	dünn	gut	jung	kurz	neu
bekannt	dunkel	groß	hell	klein	lang	oft

eine **bessere** Wohngegend	*a fairly good neighbourhood*
seit **längerer** Zeit	*for a longish time now*
ein **neueres** Modell	*a fairly new model*
Kommen Sie **öfter** (coll. also: öfters) hierher?	*Do you come here quite often?*

8.3.4 Progression is expressed by using *immer* with the comparative

This corresponds to English 'more and more':

Er lief **immer schneller**	*He ran faster and faster*
Das Benzin wird **immer teurer**	*Petrol is getting dearer and dearer*
Meine Arbeit wird **immer schwieriger**	*My work is getting more and more difficult*

NB: A construction like that of English, e.g. *Er lief schneller und schneller* is occasionally found, but it is much less frequent than that with *immer*.

8.3.5 Proportion (i.e. 'the more . . . the more')

Proportion is expressed in German by using a subordinate clause introduced by the conjunction *je*, followed by a main clause beginning with *umso* or (especially in formal written German) *desto*:

Je länger man Deutsch lernt, **desto/umso** leichter wird es	*The longer you learn German, the easier it gets*
je eher, **desto/umso** besser	*the sooner the better*
Je besser das Wetter, **desto/umso** mehr können wir wandern	*The better the weather, the more we can go hiking*

NB: (i) In older German, a second *je* could be used rather than *desto* or *umso*. This survives in a few set phrases such as *je länger, je lieber* and *je länger, je mehr*.
(ii) As an equivalent to 'all the more because', German uses *umso mehr, als/da/weil* . . . (see 19.4.3b).
(iii) In colloquial German the combination *umso . . . umso* is common, e.g. *umso größer, umso besser* 'the bigger, the better'.

8.3.6 Equality is expressed by *so . . . wie* (= 'as . . . as')

Peter ist **so** alt **wie** Thomas	Mein neuer Wagen fährt nicht **so** schnell **wie** deiner
Er arbeitet **so** fleißig **wie** ich	Er ist nur halb **so** alt **wie** seine Schwester

A number of variations on this construction occur:

(a) In colloquial German, *als* is often used for *wie*

Peter ist **so** alt **als** Thomas   Ich bin doch **so** groß **als** du

This is not usually acceptable in written registers, except in the following contexts:

(i) 'as well as' can be *sowohl wie* or *sowohl als* (see also 19.1.4b), e.g.: *Ich will **sowohl** Anna **als/wie (auch)** Helga einladen*

(ii) 'as soon/little as possible' can be *so bald/wenig wie möglich* or *so bald/wenig als möglich*.

(iii) 'twice as ... as' can be *doppelt so ... wie* or *doppelt so ... als*: *Die Ernte ist **doppelt so groß als/wie** im vorigen Jahr*

NB· The combination *als wie*, e.g. *Ich bin doch so groß **als wie** du* is common in speech, but it is generally considered to be a substandard regionalism.

(b) *so* can be omitted in some common phrases and idioms

Er ist (so) hart wie Stahl   Er ist (so) schlau wie ein Fuchs

(c) 'just as ... (as)' is expressed by *ebenso* ... *(wie)* or *genauso* ... *(wie)*

Peter ist **ebenso/genauso** alt **wie** Thomas
Dort können wir **genauso** gutes Fleisch kaufen

(i) *ebenso* is also used to indicate equivalence between two qualities:

Er ist **ebenso** fleißig wie geschickt   *He is (just) as industrious as he is skilful*

(ii) *ebenso sehr* is used adverbially to indicate degree (= 'just as much'):

Die Brücke ist **ebenso sehr** ein Teil der   *The bridge is just as much part of the*
   Landschaft wie der Fluss   *scenery as the river*

(iii) *nicht so sehr ... wie* is used for 'not so much ... as':

Er ist **nicht so sehr** dumm **wie** faul   *He is not so much stupid as lazy*

(d) *gleich* can be used to indicate equality

Peter und Thomas sind **gleich** alt   *Peter and Thomas are the same age*
Diese Städte sind etwa **gleich** groß   *These towns are about the same size*

8.4 Types and uses of the superlative

8.4.1 The superlative form *am ... sten*

This form (see 8.1.2) is used in the following contexts:

(a) Always for adverbs

Von allen Gästen sprach er **am wenigsten**	*Of all the guests he spoke least*
Ich arbeite **am besten** nachts	*I work best at night*
Am einfachsten faxen Sie es ihr durch	*The simplest thing is to fax it to her*
Helmut läuft **am schnellsten**	*Helmut runs fastest*
Das hasse ich an den Schulmeistern **am meisten** (*Valentin*)	*That's what I hate most about schoolmasters*

(b) After the verb *sein*

Both superlative forms are found predicatively after *sein*, e.g.: *Welcher Junge ist* **am stärksten**? and *Welcher Junge ist* **der stärkste**?

(i) If a noun is understood, either can be used:

Diese Blume ist **die schönste/am schönsten**	*This flower is the most beautiful*
Unter den deutschen Flüssen ist die Donau **der längste/am längsten**	*Of the German rivers the Danube is the longest*

(ii) If there is no noun to be be understood or if something is being compared with itself (= 'at its most . . . '), only the form with *am* can be used:

Ein Mercedes wäre **am teuersten**	*A Mercedes would be the dearest*
Für meinen Geschmack ist eine Nelke schöner als eine Tulpe, aber eine Rose ist natürlich **am schönsten**	*For my taste a carnation is nicer than a tulip, but a rose is the nicest*
Hier ist die Donau **am tiefsten**	*The Danube is (at its) deepest here*
Der Garten ist **am schönsten** im Juni	*The garden is (at its) nicest in June*

8.4.2 Any superlative may be used in an absolute sense

i.e. not as a comparison but in the sense 'extremely'. This is known as the 'elative' use of the superlative:

in **höchster** Erregung	*in great excitement*
mit **größter** Mühe	*with the greatest difficulty*
Es ist **höchste** Zeit, dass . . .	*It is high time that . . .*
Es herrschte das **rauheste** Wetter	*The weather was extremely raw*
Modernste Kureinrichtungen stehen zu Ihrer Verfügung (*FAZ*)	*You will have the use of the most up-to-date spa treatment*

8.4.3 An absolute adverbial superlative can be formed in *aufs . . . ste*

e.g. *aufs einfachste*, *aufs genaueste*, etc. The form can be spelled with a small or a capital letter: *aufs einfachste/aufs Einfachste*, and the preposition and definite article can be written out in full if emphasis is needed: *auf das einfachste/Einfachste*. It is common in formal writing:

Der große runde Tisch war **aufs festlichste/Festlichste** geschmückt (*Dürrenmatt*)	*The large round table was decorated in a most festive way*
Herr Naumann war **aufs äußerste/Äußerste** gereizt (*MM*)	*Mr Naumann was exceedingly irritated*
Lange Zeit hat der Ministerpräsident jeden Verdacht **auf das heftigste/Heftigste** dementiert	*For a long time the Prime Minister denied all suspicions most vehemently*

8.4.4 Some adverbial superlatives are formed in -st, -stens and zu- ... -st

Generally, only a few of each type are common, usually with an absolute or idiomatic meaning. New formations on these patterns are limited.

(a) Adverbial superlatives in -st

These consist simply of the superlative stem, whether regular or irregular. Some are in common use in speech and writing, often with special meanings:

äußerst *extremely*	meist *mostly*
höchst *highly, extremely*	möglichst *as ... as possible; if at all possible*
jüngst (elev.) *recently*	
längst *for a long time, a long time ago*	unlängst *recently*

Examples of use:

Die Situation ist **höchst** problematisch	*The situation is highly problematical*
Er ist **längst** gestorben	*He died a long time ago*
Du musst einen **möglichst** guten Eindruck machen	*You must make the best possible impression*
Sie ist **unlängst** zurückgekehrt	*She got back recently*

Others are quite frequent in formal registers, often in formulaic idioms:

eiligst *as quickly as possible*	höflichst *respectfully*
freundlichst *friendly*	schleunigst *as promptly as possible*
gefälligst, gütigst *kindly*	sorgfältigst *most carefully*
herzlichst *most cordially*	tunlichst *absolutely*

Examples of use:

Ich danke Ihnen **herzlichst**	*I thank you most cordially*
Sie werden **höflichst** gebeten, diesen Irrtum ohne Verzug zu berichtigen	*You are respectfully requested to rectify this mistake without delay*
Wir machten uns **schleunigst** aus dem Staube (*Dönhoff*)	*We quickly got up off the floor*
Jeder Lärm ist **tunlichst** zu vermeiden	*Any noise is absolutely to be avoided*

These forms are widely used in both writing and speech. Although they can sound overdone or stilted, they are now common, and new formations on this model are often encountered, especially in journalism:

Die Böhmendeutschen sind nicht ausgesiedelt, sondern **brutalst** vertrieben worden (*Presse*)	*The Germans of Bohemia were not resettled, but driven out in the most brutal fashion.*

Some forms in -*st*, i.e. *best-, größt-, höchst-, kleinst-, kürzest-* can be compounded with *möglich* to mean 'the best possible', etc.:

die **bestmögliche** Lösung   die **kleinstmögliche** Summe
der **größtmögliche** Schaden   der **kürzestmögliche** Weg

(b) A few in -*stens* are still widely used
Most are idiomatic:

bestens *very well*   schnellstens *as quickly as possible*
frühestens *at the earliest*   spätestens *at the latest*
höchstens *at the most*   strengstens *strictly*
meistens *mostly*   wärmstens *most warmly*
mindestens *at least*   wenigstens *at least*
nächstens *shortly, soon*

Es kommen **höchstens** dreißig Gäste   *At most thirty guests are coming*
Ich stehe **meistens** früh auf   *I mostly get up early*
Ich brauche **mindestens** dreitausend   *I need at least three thousand euros for this*
  Euro für diese Reise   *trip*
Wir kommen **spätestens** um sechs an   *We'll arrive at six at the latest*
Rauchen ist **strengstens** verboten   *Smoking is strictly prohibited*
Er könnte **wenigstens** anrufen   *He might at least ring up*

wenigstens and *mindestens* are often interchangeable, but *mindestens* emphasises the idea of the absolute minimum possible rather more strongly. It is used less often when no actual figure is mentioned, in which case *zumindest* (see (c) below) is a possible, rather more emphatic alternative to *wenigstens*.

(c) A few forms in *zu-* ... -*st* are still current, with idiomatic meanings

zumindest *at (the very) least*   zutiefst *(very) deeply*
zunächst *at first, in the first place*   zuvorderst *(right) at the front*
zuoberst *(right) on top*

Some examples of use in context:

Er hätte uns **zumindest** grüßen können   *He could at least have said hello*
Das Angebot sah **zunächst** verlockend   *The offer looked attractive at first*
  aus
Sie nahm das Buch, das **zuoberst** lag   *She took the book which was lying on top*
In seinem Brief erklärt Solschenizyn, er   *In his letter Solzhenitsyn declares that he*
  sei **zutiefst** bewegt von dem Angebot   *was deeply moved by the Swedish*
  der schwedischen Akademie (FR)   *Academy's offer*

9

Numerals

This chapter deals with all words for NUMBERS and NUMERALS in German and their associated forms and uses:

- **Cardinal numbers**, such as 'one', 'two', 'three', etc. (section 9.1)
- **Ordinal numbers**, such as 'first', 'second', 'third', etc. (section 9.2)
- **Fractions** and **decimals** (section 9.3)
- Other **numerical usages** (section 9.4)
- **Addresses** (section 9.5)

9.1 Cardinal numbers

CARDINAL NUMBERS are the numerals used in counting. Their form in German is shown on Table 9.1.

TABLE 9.1 *The forms of the cardinal numbers*

0	null	10	zehn	20	zwanzig	30	dreißig
1	eins	11	elf	21	einundzwanzig	40	vierzig
2	zwei	12	zwölf	22	zweiundzwanzig	50	fünfzig
3	drei	13	dreizehn	23	dreiundzwanzig	60	sechzig
4	vier	14	vierzehn	24	vierundzwanzig	70	siebzig
5	fünf	15	fünfzehn	25	fünfundzwanzig	80	achtzig
6	sechs	16	sechzehn	26	sechsundzwanzig	90	neunzig
7	sieben	17	siebzehn	27	siebenundzwanzig	91	einundneunzig
8	acht	18	achtzehn	28	achtundzwanzig	92	zweiundneunzig
9	neun	19	neunzehn	29	neunundzwanzig	93	dreiundneunzig

100	(ein)hundert	1000	(ein)tausend
101	hundert(und)eins	1099	tausend(und)neunundneunzig
102	hundertzwei	1100	(ein)tausendeinhundert/elfhundert
151	(ein)hunderteinundfünfzig	2305	zweitausenddreihundertfünf
200	zweihundert	10 000	zehntausend
535	fünfhundertfünfunddreißig	50 000	fünfzigtausend
999	neunhundertneunundneunzig	100 000	hunderttausend

564 297   fünfhundertvierundsechzigtausendzweihundertsiebenundneunzig

1 000 000	eine Million	1 000 000 000	eine Milliarde
2 000 000	zwei Millionen	1 000 000 000 000	eine Billion

5 276 423   fünf Millionen zweihundertsechsundsiebzigtausendvierhundertdreiundzwanzig

9.1.1 Notes on the forms of the cardinal numbers

(a) Long numbers are rarely written out in full
i.e. those with more than one element, like *zweiunddreißig, hundertzwanzig*. In practice, complex numbers are rarely written fully except on cheques, and, in general, figures are used in written German more often than is usual in English.

(b) Numbers higher than a thousand can be written with spaces every three digits
i.e. <u>not</u> commas as in English, i.e. *564 297*, <u>not</u> *564,297*. The comma is used in German for the English decimal point (see 9.3.3). Confusingly, a point is sometimes used instead of a space in German to separate thousands: *564.297*.

(c) *hundert* or *einhundert*?
There is a difference of emphasis between *hundert* 'a hundred', *tausend* 'a thousand' and *einhundert* '**one** hundred', *eintausend* '**one** thousand'. However, *ein* is normally inserted in complex numbers, e.g. 101 100 *hunderteintausendeinhundert*.

(d) *und* can be used between *hundert* and *eins*
This is wholly optional, e.g. *hundert(und)eins, zweihundert(und)eins*, as also between *tausend* and tens or units, e.g. *tausend(und)eins, viertausend(und)elf, zwanzigtausend(und)zweiunddreißig*.

(e) *eine Million, eine Milliarde* and *eine Billion* are treated as separate nouns
They have a plural ending where necessary: *zwei Millionen; fünf Millionen vierhunderttausend*. Numbers higher than *eine Milliarde* are rare in normal use, so that, for instance, *tausend Milliarden* is more usual than *eine Billion*.

NB: The plural form is used when **one** million is followed by a decimal: *1,4 Millionen Mark*. This is spoken as *einskommavier Millionen Mark*.

(f) The old form *zwo* is often heard for *zwei*
This helps to avoid the possibility of confusion with *drei*. This usage is particularly frequent on the telephone, but it has become common in other spoken contexts and is extended to 2 in complex numbers, e.g. *zwounddreißig*, and the ordinal *der zwote*.

(g) The numbers from 2 to 12 have alternative forms with an additional *-e*
e.g. *sechse, neune, elfe*. These are common in spoken colloquial German (especially in the south) for emphasis, particularly when stating the time: *Ich bin um fünfe aufgestanden*.

(h) Longer numbers are often stated in pairs
e.g. *4711* (a brand of eau de Cologne), spoken *siebenundvierzig elf*. This usage is regular with telephone numbers (less frequently the dialling code), e.g. *(0621) 54 87 23*, which is typically given as *null sechs zwo eins – vierundfünfzig siebenundachtzig dreiundzwanzig*.

(i) Years from *1100* to *1999* are usually stated in hundreds
This is in fact similar to everyday English usage, e.g. *1996*: *neunzehnhundert-sechsundneunzig.*

(j) *beide* is used in some contexts where English uses the numeral 'two'
This is particularly the case where it is a question of 'two and only two' of the relevant items, see 5.5.3b, e.g. *Ich möchte diese beiden Hemden* 'I would like these two shirts'.

(k) *fünfzehn* and *fünfzig*
These are regularly pronounced *fuffzehn* and *fuffzig* in colloquial speech.

(l) As an indefinite large number, corresponding to English 'umpteen', colloquial German uses *zig*

Ich kenne sie schon **zig** Jahre	*I've known her umpteen years*
Die ist mit **zig** Sachen in die Kurve gefahren	*She took the bend at a fair old speed*

The compounds *zigmal* 'umpteen times', *zigtausend* 'umpteen thousand', etc. are also frequently used. All these forms can be written with an initial hyphen: *-zig*, *-zigmal*, etc.

(m) Cardinal numbers used as nouns
Where these refer to the numeral, they are feminine (see 1.1.2) and have a plural in *-en* if required:

Die Sieben ist eine Glückszahl   In Mathe habe ich nie eine **Fünf** gehabt
Die Hundert ist eine dreistellige Zahl
Im Abitur hat er **drei Zweien** und **eine Eins** gekriegt

The feminine nouns *die Hundert* and *die Tausend*, referring to the numbers as such, as illustrated above, are to be distinguished from the neuters *das Hundert* and *das Tausend*, which refer to quantities, see 9.1.5h.

(n) The numeral 7 is usually written in handwriting with a stroke
i.e. 7. This helps to distinguish it from 1, which Germans write with an initial sweep, i.e. 1.

9.1.2 *eins, ein, einer* 'one'

(a) The form *eins* is used in isolation as a numeral
i.e. in counting and the like:

Wir müssen mit der (Linie) eins zum Bahnhof fahren	*We've got to take the number one (i.e. tram, bus) to the station*

This form is also used with decimals (see also 9.3.3): *einskommasieben*

(b) The form *ein* is used with a following noun
It agrees with the following noun for case and gender and has the same endings as the indefinite article, see Table 4.2.

ein Tisch	*one table*
eine Kirche	*one church*
ein Buch	*one book*
durch **einen** Fehler	*by one mistake*
aus **einem** Grund	*for one reason*

The **numerical** sense of *ein* (i.e. 'one') is distinguished from the **indefinite article** *ein* (i.e. 'a, an') in speech by *ein* always being pronounced in full, see 4.1.2b. In writing, if there is a possibility of ambiguity in context, the numerical sense can be made clear typographically, e.g.:

éin Buch   *ein* Buch   <u>ein</u> Buch   **ein** Buch   e i n Buch

In practice this is only necessary in exceptional cases.

After *hundert* and *tausend*, e.g. *301, 2001*, there is considerable uncertainty as to how or whether to decline forms of *ein*. The combinations *hundertundeine Mark* and *Tausendundeine Nacht* 'The 1001 Nights' are well established idiomatically. However, few Germans are sure whether this construction can be used in other contexts, i.e. *?ein Buch mit dreihundertundeiner Seite*. However, the alternative of undeclined *-ein*, with a plural noun, e.g. *?ein Buch mit dreihundertein Seiten*, is felt by many speakers to be equally odd.

(c) The form *einer* is used as a pronoun
Its declension is given in Table 5.10.

> Wir haben einen Rottweiler, und ihr habt auch **einen**, nicht?
> **einer** der Männer *one of the men*   **ein(e)s** der Häuser *one of the houses*

Further details on the use of *einer* are given in 5.5.4.

(d) After a determiner *ein-* declines like an adjective
e.g. *der eine* ... , 'the one ...'

> Das Dorf hatte bloß **die eine** Straße
> Mit **seinem einen** Auge sieht er schlecht

(e) *ein* has no ending in a few constructions
(i) When followed by *oder* or *bis* and another number, e.g. *ein oder zwei, ein bis zwei*:

> Ich pflückte **ein oder zwei** Rosen   Wir müssen **ein bis zwei** Tage warten
> Er kam vor **ein oder zwei** Wochen   Ich sprach mit **ein oder zwei** anderen

(ii) When linked with *andere* or *derselbe*, the alternatives of declining *ein* or leaving it endingless are equally acceptable:

> **Ein(er)** oder der andere machte eine   *One or other made a brief remark*
>   kurze Bemerkung
> An **ein(em)** und demselben Tag   *On one and the same day three firms went*
>   machten drei Firmen Pleite   *bankrupt*

With *mehrere*, *ein* is more commonly inflected: *vor einem* (rarely: *ein*) *oder mehreren Monaten* 'one or more months ago'.

(iii) *ein* is not inflected in *ein Uhr* 'one o'clock', see Table 11.1. (Compare *eine Uhr* 'a/one clock').

9.1.3 Declension of cardinal numbers

Apart from *ein* 'one', which is declined as explained in 9.1.2, cardinal numbers do not normally decline to show case or gender in German. Thus:

gegen sechs Kinder	die sechs Kinder
mit sechs Kindern	mit den sechs Kindern
wegen sechs Kindern	wegen der sechs Kinder

However, endings are found in one or two special contexts:

(a) *zwei* and *drei* have the GENITIVE forms *zweier* and *dreier*
These are quite frequent in formal written German, e.g.:

Der Taufe **zweier** Kinder aus der Ehe stimmte er zu (*MM*)	*He agreed to the baptism of two children of the marriage*
die vielerlei Eindrücke **dreier** anstrengender Tage (*Zeit*)	*the various impressions from three strenuous days*

A following adjective has the strong ending *-er* (see 6.2.1a), as in the second example above, but an adjective used as a noun most often has the weak ending *-en*: *die Seligkeit zweier **Verliebten**. In less formal German a phrase with *von* is used, e.g. *die Eindrücke von drei anstrengenden Tagen.*

(b) The numbers from 2 to 12 can have a DATIVE in *-en* when used in isolation
i.e. when no noun follows:

> Nur einer von **zweien** ist als gesund zu bezeichnen (*Zeit*)
> als sich die Tür hinter den **dreien** geschlossen hatte (*Welt*)

This is a common alternative to the endingless form (i.e. *einer von zwei*, etc.), even in spoken German, especially with the numbers 2, 3 and 4. It is most frequent for added emphasis and in set phrases such as *auf allen vieren* 'on all fours', *mit dreien* 'with three (Jacks)' (in the card game *Skat*), and in the formula *zu zweien, dreien, vieren* etc. 'in twos, threes, fours', e.g.: *dieser Spaziergang **zu zweien** (Th. Mann)*
A rather more frequent alternative here is a form in *-t* (using the stem of the ordinal, see 9.2.1), e.g. *zu zweit, zu dritt, zu viert*. However, a distinction can be made between *zu zweien* 'in pairs' and *zu zweit* 'as a pair' (i.e. when there are only two). Compare:

Sie gingen **zu zweien** über die Straße	*They crossed the road in pairs*
Sie gingen **zu zweit** über die Straße	*The two of them crossed the road together*

9.1.4 Cardinals have an adjectival form in *-er*

e.g. *fünfer, zehner*. This is used to denote value and measurement, or with reference to years. When they are used as adjectives, they do not decline (see 6.2.7e). When they are used as nouns, they have the dative ending *-n*:

Ich habe zwei Zehner und einen Hunderter	*I've got two ten-euro notes and a hundred-euro note*
zwei Fünfziger	*two fifty-cent pieces* **or** *two fifty-euro notes*
zehn achtziger Marken	*ten 80-cent stamps*
eine Achtziger	*an 80-cent stamp*
die Zehner und die Einer	*tens and units*

eine Sechserpackung	*a six-pack*
in den neunziger Jahren des 20. Jahrhunderts	*in the 1990s*
ein Mann in den Vierzigern	*a man in his forties*
eine Mittfünfzigerin	*a woman in her mid-fifties*
ein Dreitausender	*a mountain (over) 3000 metres high*
ein vierundneunziger Heppenheimer Krötenbrunnen	*a 94 Heppenheimer Krötenbrunnen* (i.e. a wine vintage 1994)

9.1.5 hundert, tausend, Dutzend

(a) *hundert* and *tausend* are used as normal numerals

They are not declined:

hundert, zweihundert Häuser	*a hundred, two hundred houses*
tausend Bücher, **sechstausend** Bücher	*a thousand books, six thousand books*

(b) *das Hundert, das Tausend* and *das Dutzend* are used as nouns of quantity

das zweite **Dutzend, Hundert, Tausend**	*the second dozen, hundred, thousand*
ein halbes **Dutzend,** ein halbes **Hundert**	*half a dozen, half a hundred* (i.e. fifty)
zwei **Dutzend** Eier	*two dozen eggs*
Hunderttausende von Menschen	*hundreds of thousands of people*
Die Menschen verhungerten zu **Hunderten** und **Tausenden**	*People were starving in hundreds and thousands*

(c) If these words refer to an indefinite quantity, they can be spelled with an initial capital or small letter

i.e. when they are used in the plural, especially after quantifiers such as *einige, mehrere, viele*, etc. In such contexts it is not clear whether they are nouns or numerals. They have a plural ending if the following phrase is introduced by *von* or is in the genitive (see 1.2.14 and 2.7.4):

In dem Stadion warten **Tausende/ tausende** von Menschen auf den Spielbeginn	*In the stadium thousands of people are waiting for the start of the match*
Mehrere **Hundert/hundert** Kinder waren an Typhus gestorben	*Several hundred children had died of typhus*
Diesen Stoff verkauft man in einigen **Dutzend/dutzend** Farben	*This material is sold in a few dozen shades*

In the genitive plural, they have the ending *-er* if no determiner precedes. A following adjective has the strong endings:

ein Dokumentation in der Form **Hunderter/hunderter** ausschließlich deutscher Zeugnisse (*Spiegel*)	*a documentation in the form of hundreds of exclusively German pieces of evidence*
die Flucht **Tausender/tausender** DDR-Bewohner (*Spiegel*)	*the flight of thousands of inhabitants of the GDR*

However, they have the ending *-e* if a preceding determiner has the genitive plural ending *-er: die Ersparnisse vieler Tausende/tausende.*

NB: (i) *Dutzend* does not take a plural ending when used as a measurement noun in constructions such as *drei Dutzend (Eier)* 'three dozen (eggs)', see 1.2.14.

(ii) For the use of the genitive, apposition or a phrase with *von* after the nouns *Dutzend, Hundert, Tausend* see 2.7.4.

9.1.6 Qualification of cardinal numbers

(a) Numerals may be modified by a number of adverbs of degree

bis zu *up to*	knapp *barely*	über *over*
unter *under*	zwischen *between*	

gegen, rund, um, ungefähr, circa/zirka (abbrev.: ca.) *about, approximately*

Although most of these are prepositions which would be expected to require a particular case (dative or accusative), when they are used in these constructions with a following numeral they have no influence on the case of the following noun phrase:

Bis zu zehn Kinder können mitfahren	*Up to ten children can come with us*
Sie ist **zwischen 30 und 40 Jahre** alt	*She is between 30 and 40 years old*

However, when they are used as prepositions, the following noun phrase is in the case normally required by the preposition (dative or accusative):

Kinder **unter sieben Jahren** zahlen die Hälfte	*Children under seven years old pay half-price*
Kinder **über sechs Jahre** zahlen voll	*Children over six years old pay the full price*
geeignet für Kinder **zwischen sieben und zwölf Jahren**	*suitable for children between the ages of seven and twelve*

It is quite straightforward to work out whether these words are being used as **adverbs** (when they do not influence the selection of case) or **prepositions** (when they do), since in contexts where they are being used as adverbs the sentence would still be grammatically correct if they were left out: *Zehn Kinder können mitfahren*. But prepositions cannot be omitted: **Kinder sieben Jahren zahlen die Hälfte* is not a grammatical sentence.

(b) Other adverbials used with numbers:

Es dauert gut drei Stunden	*It lasts a good three hours*
Er gab mir **ganze** fünf Euro	*He gave me all of five euro*

9.2 Ordinal numbers

9.2.1 The formation of ordinal numbers

ORDINAL NUMBERS are those used as adjectives like English 'first', 'second', 'third', etc. The forms of ordinal numbers in German are given in Table 9.2. Most are formed by adding the suffix *-te* to the cardinals *2–19* and *-ste* to the cardinals from *20* upwards, but *der erste* 'first', *der dritte* 'third' and *der siebte* 'seventh' are exceptions to this pattern. All ordinal numbers are declined like adjectives.

TABLE 9.2 *The forms of the ordinal numbers*

1	der erste	20	der zwanzigste
2	der zweite	21	der einundzwanzigste
3	der dritte	27	der siebenundzwanzigste
4	der vierte		
5	der fünfte	30	der dreißigste
6	der sechste	40	der vierzigste
7	der siebte	50	der fünfzigste
8	der achte	60	der sechzigste
9	der neunte	70	der siebzigste
10	der zehnte	80	der achtzigste
11	der elfte	90	der neunzigste
12	der zwölfte		
13	der dreizehnte	100	der hundertste
14	der vierzehnte	101	der hundert(und)erste
15	der fünfzehnte	117	der hundertsiebzehnte
16	der sechzehnte		
17	der siebzehnte	1000	der tausendste
18	der achtzehnte		
19	der neunzehnte	1 000 000	der millionste

5437   der fünftausendvierhundertsiebenunddreißigste

There are a few special forms and uses;

(a) *der x-te* **and** *der zigste* **are used as indefinite ordinals**
i.e. as equivalents of English 'the umpteenth', e.g.: *Das war mein* **x-ter/zigster** *Versuch*.

NB: *x-te* is pronounced [ɪkstə]. For the form *zig*, see 9.1.2l.

(b) **The form** *der wievielte* **can be used to enquire about numbers**

Das **wievielte** Kind ist das jetzt?	*How many children is that now?*
Den **Wievielten** haben wir heute?	*What's the date today?*
Zum **wievielten** Mal bist du schon hier?	*How many times have you been here?*

(c) **The ordinal stems can be compounded with superlatives**

die **zweitbest**e Arbeit   die **drittgröß**te Stadt   der **vierthöchst**e Berg

(d) **Ordinal numbers are indicated in writing by using a full stop after the numeral**

am 14. Mai   das 275. Regiment   die 12. Klasse

This is nowadays the <u>only</u> usual means of indicating ordinal numbers; abbreviations (e.g. *am 5ten Mai*) are no longer current.

(e) **Ordinal numbers can be used as nouns**
In this respect they are like other adjectives, and they are written with initial capitals:

jeder **Dritte**   Er kam als **Erster**   Wer ist der **Zweite**?

NB: As with other adjectives, a small initial letter is used if the noun is understood, e.g. *Anke war die erste Frau in unserem Kreis, aber wer war die zweite?* (see 6.2.5).

9.2.2 Equivalents for English 'to be the first to'

For 'to be the first to', German uses either *als Erster*, or *der Erste* followed by a relative clause:

Die Russen **waren die Ersten**, die einen künstlichen Erdsatelliten um den Globus schickten; sie brachten **als Erste** einen Menschen in den Weltraum (*Zeit*)	*The Russians were the first to send an artificial satellite round the earth; they were the first to put a man into space*
Dann musste Konstantin **als Erster** über den Graben (*Dönhoff*)	*Then Konstantin had to be the first to cross the ditch*

9.2.3 Equivalents for English 'first(ly)', 'secondly', etc.

For these, German uses the stem of the ordinal with the suffix *-ens*, e.g. *erstens* 'first(ly)', *zweitens* 'secondly', *drittens* 'thirdly', etc. Alternatively, the forms *zum Ersten, zum Zweiten, zum Dritten*, etc. are used.

9.3 Fractions and decimals

9.3.1 Fractions (*die Bruchzahlen*) are formed by adding *-el* to the ordinal stem

These are neuter nouns:

　　ein Drittel　　ein Viertel　　ein Fünftel　　ein Achtel　　ein Zehntel

They have an endingless plural, e.g. *zwei Drittel*. The ending *-n* is optional in the dative plural:

　　Die Prüfung wurde von **vier Fünftel(n)** der Schüler bestanden

If a fraction is the subject of a verb, then it takes a singular or plural ending as appropriate:

　　Ein Drittel ist schon verkauft　　　Zwei Drittel sind schon verkauft

When followed by a noun of measurement they are spelled with a small letter and an accompanying indefinite article takes its case and gender from the noun:

　　mit einer **drittel** Flasche　　　mit einem **viertel** Liter

They can also be written together with measurement words, e.g. *ein Viertelliter, fünf Achtelliter, vier Zehntelgramm* and (especially) *eine Viertelstunde*. The following alternatives are thus all acceptable:

　　Er verfehlte den Rekord um **drei Zehntel einer Sekunde**
　　Er verfehlte den Rekord um **drei zehntel Sekunden**
　　Er verfehlte den Rekord um **drei Zehntelsekunden**

drei Viertel can be used in the same way, as a noun phrase: *der Topf ist zu drei Vierteln voll*, or, with a small letter, as an adverb: *der Topf ist drei viertel voll*. It can be compounded with *Stunde*, e.g. *in einer Dreiviertelstunde* 'in three-quarters of an hour' (alternatively: *in drei Viertelstunden*).

　　When used with full integers, fractions are read out as written, with no *und*: 3⅝ *drei fünfachtel*, 1⁷⁄₁₀ *eins siebenzehntel*.

9.3.2 'half' corresponds to the adjective *halb* and the noun *die Hälfte*

These are used as follows:

(a) 'half', used as a noun, is normally *die Hälfte*

Er hat mir nur **die Hälfte** gegeben	*He only gave me half*
die größere **Hälfte**	*the bigger half*

However, the form *das Halb*, from the adjective, is used in order to refer to the number as such:

(Ein) **Halb** ist mehr als ein Drittel	*Half is more than a third*

(b) 'half a': the usual equivalent is the indefinite article with *halb*

Ich aß einen **halben** Apfel	*I ate half an apple*
ein **halbes** Dutzend	*half a dozen*
ein **halbes** Brot	*half a loaf*

(c) 'half the/this/my'
The usual equivalent is *die Hälfte* with a following genitive, but the appropriate determiner can be used with *halb* if the reference is to a whole thing which can be divided cleanly in two:

Die Hälfte der/dieser Äpfel ist schlecht	*Half the/these apples are bad*
die **Hälfte** meines Geldes	*half my money*
Ich aß **die Hälfte des Kuchens**	*I ate half the cake*
Ich aß **den halben Kuchen**	

NB: The use of *halb* with a plural noun in such contexts, i.e. *die halben Äpfel* 'half the apples', is considered to be substandard colloquial usage.

(d) English adverbial 'half 'corresponds to German *halb*

halb angezogen	*half dressed*
Er weiß alles nur **halb**	*He only half knows things*

(e) German equivalents for English 'one and a half'
German uses either *eineinhalb* or (in more informal usage) *anderthalb*. 2½, 3½, etc. are *zweieinhalb*, *dreieinhalb*, etc. These are not declined:

Bis Walldürn sind es noch **eineinhalb/anderthalb** Stunden	*It's another hour and a half to Walldürn*
Sie wollte noch **sechseinhalb** Monate bleiben	*She wanted to stay another six and a half months*

(f) Some other phrases and idioms:

Er hatte **halb so viel** wie ich	*He had half as much as me*
Kinder fahren **zum halben Preis**	*Children travel half price*
Er ist mir **auf halbem Wege** entgegengekommen	*He met me halfway* (literal and figurative sense)
Ich nehme noch **ein Halbes**	*I'll have another half*

Das ist **nichts Halbes** und nichts Ganzes	*That's neither flesh nor fowl*
Die Besucher waren **zur Hälfte** Deutsche	*Half the visitors were German*
nach der ersten **Halbzeit**	*after the first half* (sport)
halb Europa, **halb** München (see 6.2.7g)	*half Europe, half Munich*

9.3.3 Decimals are written with a comma

i.e. <u>not</u> with a point, e.g.:

0,7	nullkommasieben	4,75	vierkommasiebenfünf
1,25	einskommazweifünf	109,1	hundertneunkommaeins
3,426	dreikommavierzweisechs		

In colloquial speech, two places of decimals may be read out in terms of tens and units, e.g. *4,75 vierkommafünfundsiebzig.*

9.4 Other numerical usages

9.4.1 Numerically equal distribution is expressed by *je*

Ich gab den Jungen **je** zehn Euro	*I gave each of the boys ten euro*
A. und B. wurden zu **je** drei Jahren verurteilt	*A and B were each sentenced to three years*
Sie erhielten **je** fünf Kilo Reis	*They each received five kilograms of rice*

9.4.2 Multiples

(a) German suffixes -*fach* to the cardinal number to form multiples
e.g. *einfach* 'single', *zweifach* 'twofold', *dreifach* 'threefold', etc.:

eine **einfach**e Karte	*a single ticket*
ein **vierfach**er Olympiasieger	*a four-time gold-medal winner*
... stiegen die Grundstückspreise zunächst aufs **Zehnfache** (*Böll*)	*... the price of land first went up tenfold*

(b) *zweifach* and *doppelt*
zweifach is sometimes interchangeable in meaning with *doppelt* 'double', but more often refers to two <u>different</u> things, whilst *doppelt* refers to two of the same, e.g.: *ein zweifaches Verbrechen* 'two kinds of crime' but *Der Koffer hat einen doppelten Boden* 'the suitcase has a double bottom'. *zweifach* has the variant form *zwiefach* in older literary usage.

(c) -*fach* can also be suffixed to a few indefinites
e.g. *vielfach* or *mehrfach* 'manifold', 'frequent(ly)', 'repeatedly', *mannigfach* 'varied', 'manifold'.

(d) Forms in -*fältig* can also be used as multiples
e.g. *zweifältig, dreifältig, vielfältig*, etc. These are rather less common than forms in -*fach*. Note too (without *Umlaut*!) *mannigfaltig*, which is more frequent than *mannigfach*, and *die (heilige) Dreifaltigkeit* 'the (Holy) Trinity'. *einfältig* most often has the meaning 'simple(-minded)'.

(e) Equivalents for English *single*
When it is used in the sense 'individual', 'separate', *single* corresponds to *einzeln*, e.g. *Die Bände werden **einzeln** verkauft* 'The volumes are sold singly/separately'. In the sense 'sole', it corresponds to *einzig*, e.g. *Er hat keinen **einzigen** Freund* 'He hasn't got a single friend'.

9.4.3 *einmal, zweimal*, etc.

(a) Adverbs made up from *-mal* suffixed to the cardinals express the number of occasions
e.g. *einmal* 'once', *zweimal* 'twice', *dreimal* 'three times', *zehnmal* 'ten times', *hundertmal* 'a hundred times', *x-mal*, *zigmal* 'umpteen times', *dutzendmal* 'a dozen times', etc.

Ich habe ihn diese Woche **dreimal** gesehen	*I've seen him three times this week*
Ich habe es **hundertmal** bereut	*I've regretted it a hundred times*
Also, Herr Ober, **zweimal** Gulasch, bitte	*Right, waiter, goulash for two, please*
anderthalbmal so groß wie der andere Luftballon	*half as big again as the other balloon*

Adjectives are formed from these adverbs by suffixing *-ig*, e.g. *einmalig, zweimalig*:

eine **einmalige** Gelegenheit	*a unique opportunity*
nach **dreimaligem** Durchlesen seines Briefes	*after reading his letter three times*

Formed in a similar way is *mehrmalig* 'repeated'.

(b) Forms and phrases with *-mal* and *Mal*
Mal (plural *Male*) is a neuter noun, and it is in most contexts written separately from any preceding adjectives or determiners, with an initial capital letter:

das erste **Mal**, das ich ihn sah	Das letzte **Mal** war das schönste
kein einziges **Mal**	ein um das andere **Mal** *time after time*
Ich werde es nächstes **Mal** tun	Das vorige **Mal** war es schöner
Zum wievielten **Mal bist du hier**?	Beim vorletzten **Mal** war sie schwer krank
Jedes **Mal** bist du zu spät gekommen	Er war nur ein paar **Mal** dort gewesen
Beide **Male** bin ich durchgefallen	viele (hundert) **Male**
Ich habe ihn oft besucht; das eine **Mal** zeigte er mir seine Sammlung	
Dieses **Mal** wird sie mich anders behandeln müssen	
Die letzten paar **Male** war sie nicht zu Hause	

The form *-mal* can be compounded in a few phrases:

diesmal *this time*   ein **paarmal** *a few times*   ein **andermal** *another time*

This possibility has been considerably limited in the reformed spelling. Only those given above are now accepted, and forms like *jedesmal* and *zum erstenmal* have been replaced by the full phrases, with each word written separately, as shown above.

(c) *vielmals* 'many times' is used in a few set constructions:

Ich danke Ihnen **vielmals** ⎫	*Many thanks*
Danke **vielmals** ⎭	
Ich bitte **vielmals** um Entschuldigung	*I do apologise*
Sie lässt Sie **vielmals** grüßen	*She sends you her kindest regards*

Cf. also *erstmals* 'for the first time', *mehrmals* 'repeatedly'.

9.4.4 The suffix *-erlei*

-erlei is added to the cardinal numbers to give forms which mean 'x kinds of', e.g. *zweierlei* 'two kinds of', *dreierlei* 'three kinds of', *vielerlei* 'many kinds of', etc. They can be used as nouns or adjectives and do not decline:

Ich ziehe **zweierlei** Bohnen	*I grow two kinds of beans*
Er hat **hunderterlei** Pläne	*He's got hundreds of different plans*
Ich habe ihm **dreierlei** vorgeschlagen	*I suggested three different things to him*

einerlei is most often used in the sense 'all the same' (i.e. = *egal, gleich,* etc.), e.g. *Das ist mir alles einerlei.*

9.4.5 Mathematical terminology

The common arithmetic and mathematical functions are expressed as follows in German. In some cases the symbols used in the German-speaking countries are slightly different from those current in the English-speaking countries:

$4 + 5 = 9$	vier und/plus fünf ist/gleich neun
$8 - 6 = 2$	acht weniger/minus sechs ist/gleich zwei
$3 \times 4 = 12$ $3 \cdot 4 = 12$	drei mal vier ist/gleich zwölf
$8 : 2 = 4$	acht (geteilt) durch zwei ist/gleich vier
$3^2 = 9$	drei hoch zwei (drei zum Quadrat) ist/gleich neun
$3^3 = 27$	drei hoch drei ist/gleich siebenundzwanzig
$\sqrt{9} = 3$	Quadratwurzel/zweite Wurzel aus neun ist/gleich drei
$5 > 3$	fünf ist größer als drei

9.5 Addresses

These are typically written in the following form:

Herrn	Firma	Herrn und Frau
Dr. Ulrich Sievers	Eugen Spengel	Peter und Eva Specht
Sichelstraße 17	Rossgasse 7–9	Stelnweg 2½
54290 Trier	07973 Greiz	35037 Marburg/Lahn
Familie	Frau	An das
Karl (und Ute) Schulz	Maria Jellinek	Katasteramt Westfalen
Königsberger Straße 36	Maximiliansgasse 34	Bismarckallee 87
64711 Erbach/Odw.	1084 Wien	48151 Münster

Especially in printed addresses, a clear line is left above the name of the postal town or city. The post code is regarded as essential, and when writing from outside the country, the appropriate country code, i.e. *A* (Austria), *CH* (Switzerland), *D* (Germany), is prefixed to it.

On private letters the sender's name and address are written in a single line on the back of the envelope, preceded by *Abs.* (i.e. *Absender*), e.g.: *Abs.: Indermühle, Strohgasse 17, CH-8600 Düsendorf.*

10

Modal particles

MODAL PARTICLES **are words which express the speaker's attitude to what is being said.**

They are words like *aber, doch, ja, mal, schon*, etc., which alter the tone of what is being said and make sure that the speaker's intentions and attitudes are clearly understood They can typically

- appeal for agreement
- express surprise or annoyance
- tone down a blunt question or statement
- sound reassuring

There is no full agreement as to which words can be classified as modal particles (called in German *Abtönungspartikeln* or *Modalpartikeln*). Their function is quite like that of adverbs of attitude (see 7.3.2), and like them they cannot be negated. In general, though, they are less independent and they cannot normally occur in first position in a main clause, before the main verb.

German has a far richer repertoire of these words than English, but English speakers have other ways of expressing their attitude to what is being said, especially intonation and tag questions like 'isn't it?' There is, though, a very marked tendency for German to use downtoners much more extensively than English. We have tried to give some idea of the flavour of each of the German modal particles in the translations by using equivalents like this, but they can only be a rough guide to usage.

True modal particles relate to the clause or sentence as a whole, whereas scalar or focus particles (called *Gradpartikeln* in German), like *sogar*, focus attention on a particular word or phrase.

However, these distinctions are not clear-cut, and many of these words can be used in more than one way. *auch* and *nur*, for example, can be used both as modal and as focus particles, whereas *eigentlich* and *freilich* can function as adverbs of attitude as well as modal particles.

This chapter aims to give a practical account of the use in modern German of all those words which might be considered to be modal particles. They are listed in Table 10.1, which gives the section in which they are dealt with in this chapter. Many of these words have a range of uses besides those of modal particles; to avoid confusion, all their uses are explained here.

TABLE 10.1 *German modal particles*

aber	10.1	eigentlich	10.10	ja	10.19	ruhig	10.28
allerdings	10.2	einfach	10.11	jedenfalls	10.20	schließlich	10.29
also	10.3	erst	10.12	lediglich	10.21	schon	10.30
auch	10.4	etwa	10.13	mal	10.22	sowieso	10.31
bloß	10.5	freilich	10.14	man	10.23	überhaupt	10.32
denn	10.6	gar	10.15	noch	10.24	übrigens	10.33
doch	10.7	gleich	10.16	nun	10.25	vielleicht	10.34
eben	10.8	halt	10.17	nur	10.26	wohl	10.35
eh	10.9	immerhin	10.18	ohnehin	10.27	zwar	10.36

10.1 *aber*

10.1.1 In statements, *aber* expresses a surprised reaction

In effect, *aber* converts such statements to exclamations:

Das war aber eine Reise!	*That was quite a journey, wasn't it?*
Der Film war aber gut!	*The film was good*
Der Kaffee ist aber heiß!	*Oh! The coffee is hot*

aber can be given greater emphasis by adding *auch*. Compare:

| Das war aber auch eine Reise! | *That really was some journey!* |

ja is also used to express surprise (see 10.19.2), but surprise resulting from a difference in kind, where *aber* indicates a difference in degree. Compare:

| Der Kaffee ist **aber** heiß | (i.e. hotter than you had expected) |
| Der Kaffee ist **ja** heiß | (you had expected *cold* coffee) |

In this sense, *aber* can be replaced by *vielleicht* (see 10.34.1): *Der Tee ist vielleicht heiß!*

10.1.2 *aber* is used within a clause to express a contradiction

In such contexts, *aber* has much the same sense it would have at the beginning of the clause (i.e. = English 'but', see 19.1.1). This sense is close to that of *doch* (see 10.7.1):

Mein Freund kam aber nicht	*My friend didn't come, though*
Sie muss uns aber gesehen haben	*But she must have seen us*
Jetzt kannst du etwas schneller fahren ... Pass aber bei den Ampeln auf!	*You can go a bit quicker now ... Look out at the lights, though!*

Used with *oder*, *aber* has the sense of 'on the other hand':

| Seine Befürwortung könnte der Sache helfen oder aber (auch) schaden | *His support might help the affair or on the other hand it might harm it* |

10.1.3 When used initially in exclamations, *aber* stresses the speaker's opinion

aber can sound scolding or reassuring, depending on the context:

Hast du was dagegen? – Aber nein!	*Have you any objection? – Of course not!*
Aber Kinder! Was habt ihr schon wieder angestellt?	*Now, now, childen! What have you been doing?*
Aber, aber! Was soll diese Aufregung?	*Oh now! What's all the excitement about?*

10.1.4 *aber* is also used as a coordinating conjunction

i.e. corresponding to English 'but', see 19.1.1.

10.2 *allerdings* (= *dmbdr*)

allerdings most often expresses a reservation about what has just been said. It usually corresponds to English 'admittedly', 'of course', 'to be sure', 'all the same', etc. *freilich* has a very similar meaning, see 10.14.

10.2.1 Within a sentence, the sense of *allerdings* is close to that of *aber*

However, *allerdings* is rather less blunt:

Es ist ein gutes Buch, allerdings gefallen mir seine anderen etwas besser	*It's a good book. Even so, I like his others rather better*
Wir haben uns im Urlaub gut erholt, das Wetter war allerdings nicht sehr gut	*The holiday was a good rest for us. All the same, the weather wasn't very good*
Ich komme gern, allerdings muss ich zuerst der Rita Bescheid sagen	*I want to come, of course I'll have to tell Rita first*

10.2.2 On its own in answer to a question, *allerdings* expresses a strongly affirmative answer

There can be a hint of a reservation of some kind which the speaker isn't making explicit:

Kennst du die Angelika? –Allerdings!	*Do you know Angelika? – Of course!* (I know what she's like, too!)
Ist der Helmut schon da? –Allerdings!	*Is Helmut here yet? – Oh, yes!* (and you should see who he's come with!)

10.3 *also*

10.3.1 *also* confirms something as the logical conclusion from what has just been said

also often corresponds to English 'so', 'thus' or 'then':

Du wirst mir also helfen können	*You're going to help me, then*
Wann kommst du also genau?	*So, when are you coming precisely?*
Sie meinen also, dass wir uns heute entscheiden müssen	*So you think we're going to have to make a decison today*

10.3.2 Used in isolation, *also* links up with what has just been said

also can introduce a statement or a question:

Also, jetzt müssen wir uns überlegen, wie wir dahinkommen	*Well then, now we've got to think about how we're going to get there*
Also, besuchst du uns morgen?	*So, are you going to come to see us tomorrow?*
Also, gut!	*Well all right then!*
Also, so was!	*Well I never!*

10.4 *auch*

10.4.1 In statements, *auch* stresses the reasons why something is or is not the case

auch can be used to correct a false impression and is often used with *ja*:

Günther sieht heute schlecht aus	*Günther's not looking well today*
– Er ist (ja) auch lange krank gewesen	*– Well, he's been ill for a long time*
Jetzt möchte ich schlafen gehen	*I'd like to go to bed now*
– Es ist (ja) auch spät	*– Well, after all, it is late*
Das hättest du nicht tun sollen	*You ought not to have done that*
– Ich habe es (ja) auch nicht getan	*– But I didn't do it, you know*

10.4.2 In yes/no questions, *auch* asks for confirmation of something which the speaker thinks should be taken for granted

The English equivalent is very often a tag question:

Kann ich mich auch darauf verlassen?	*I can rely on that, can't I?*
Hast du auch die Rechnung bezahlt?	*You did pay the bill, didn't you?*
Bist du auch glücklich mit ihm?	*You're happy with him, aren't you?*

10.4.3 *auch* turns w-questions into rhetorical questions

auch confirms that nothing else could be expected:

Was kann man auch dazu sagen?	*Well, what can you say to that?*
Ich bin heute sehr müde	*I'm very tired today*
– Warum gehst du auch immer so spät ins Bett?	*– Well, why do you always go to bed so late?*

These questions can be turned into exclamations which emphasise the speaker's negative attitude:

Was war das auch für ein Erfolg?!	*Well, what sort of success do you call that?!*
Wie konnte er auch so schnell abreisen?!	*How could he have left as quickly as that?!*

10.4.4 *auch* reinforces commands

This is similar to the use of English 'Be/Make sure ... !':

| Bring mir eine Zeitung und vergiss es auch nicht! | *Bring me a paper and be sure you don't forget!* |
| Sei auch schön brav! | *Be sure you behave!* |

10.4.5 Further uses of *auch*

(a) Before a noun *auch* has the force of English 'even'

It is an alternative to *sogar* or *selbst* as a focus particle:

Auch der beste Arzt hätte ihr nicht helfen können	*Even the best doctor wouldn't have been able to help her*
Auch der Manfred kann sich ab und zu mal irren	*Even Manfred can be wrong now and again*
Und wenn auch!	*even so, no matter*

NB: The usual equivalent for English 'not even' is *nicht einmal*.

(b) As an adverb, *auch* has the meaning 'too', 'also', 'as well'

Der Peter will auch mit	*Peter wants to come too*
Die Gisela ist auch nett	*Gisela's nice as well*
In Potsdam sind wir auch gewesen	*We also went to Potsdam*

(c) The combination *auch nur* expresses a restriction

It corresponds to English 'even', 'as/so little/much as', etc.:

wenn ich auch nur zwei Freunde hätte	*if I only had just two friends*
ohne auch nur zu fragen	*without even so much as asking*
Es war unmöglich, auch nur Brot zu kaufen	*You couldn't buy so much as a loaf of bread*

(d) *oder auch* has the sense 'or else', 'or even'

| Du kannst Birnen kaufen oder auch Pfirsiche | *You can buy pears or else peaches* |

(e) *auch nicht, auch kein* and *auch nichts* are often used for 'nor', 'neither', etc.

See 19.1.3d for details on German equivalents of 'neither' and 'nor':

Ich habe nichts davon gewusst – Ich auch nicht	*I didn't know anything about it – Nor me/Neither did I*
Sie kann nicht nähen und stricken kann sie auch nicht	*She can't sew, and neither can she knit*
Das wird ihm auch nichts helfen	*That won't help him either*
Er liest keine Zeitungen und auch keine Bücher	*He doesn't read any newspapers or books*

(f) *auch* occurs in many concessive constructions

Its force is similar to that of English 'ever', e.g.: *Wer es auch sein mag* 'Whoever that may be'. Full details are given in 19.6.2.

10.5 *bloß*

bloß usually has a restrictive sense (= English 'only', 'simply', 'merely'). In all its uses it is a rather less formal alternative to *nur*, see 10.26:

Störe mich bloß nicht bei der Arbeit	*You'd better not disturb me while I'm working*
Wie spät ist es bloß?	*I wonder just what the time is?*
Wenn er bloß bald käme!	*If only he would come soon!*
Sie hatte bloß 100 Euro bei sich	*She only had 100 euro on her*
Sollen wir Tante Mia einladen?	*Shall we invite aunt Mia?*
– Bloß nicht!	*– No way!*

10.6 *denn*

10.6.1 As a modal particle, *denn* is used exclusively in questions

(a) *denn* most often serves to tone down the question

denn refers back to what has just been said, or to the general context, and makes the question sound rather less blunt and more obliging. In practice it is almost automatic in *w*-questions:

Hast du denn die Renate geschen?	*Tell me, have you seen Renate?*
Geht der Junge denn heute nicht in die Schule?	*Isn't the boy going to school today, then?*
Ach, der Bus hält. Sind wir denn schon da?	*Oh, the bus is stopping. Are we already there, then?*
Warum muss er denn in die Stadt?	*Tell me, why has he got to go to town?*
Wie bist denn du gekommen?	*Tell me, how did **you** get here?*
Wie geht es dir denn?	*How are you then?*

NB: In colloquial speech, *denn* is often reduced to *'n* and suffixed to the verb, e.g. *Hast'n du die Renate gesehen? Wie bist'n du gekommen?*

(b) If there is a negative element in the question, *denn* signals reproach

The negative element may not be explicit. The question itself expects a justification rather than an answer:

Hast du denn keinen Führerschein?	*Come on, haven't you got a driving licence?*
Bist du denn blind?	*Come on now, are you blind?*
Wo bist du denn so lange geblieben?	*Where on earth have you been all this time?*
Was ist denn hier los?	*What on earth's going on here?*

(c) *denn* can convert *w*-questions into rhetorical questions

A negative answer is expected:

Wer redet denn von nachgeben?	*Who's talking of giving in?* (prompting the answer: nobody!)
Was haben wir denn damit erreicht?	*And what have we achieved by that?* (prompting the answer: nothing!)

Adding *schon* makes it absolutely clear that the question is rhetorical:

Was hat er denn schon damit gewonnen?	*And what did he gain by that?* (prompting the answer: nothing!)

(d) Yes/no questions with *denn* can be used as exclamations of surprise
They often begin with *so*:

Ist das Wetter denn nicht herrlich?	*How lovely the weather is!*
So hat er denn die Stellung erhalten?	*So he did get the job!*

(e) The combination *denn noch* is used to recall a fact

Wie heißt er denn noch?	*What is his name again?*

NB: The force of *denn noch* is similar to that of *doch gleich* in section 10.7.4.

10.6.2 Further uses of *denn*

(a) The combination *es sei denn, (dass)* is a conjunction meaning 'unless'
e.g.: *Sie kommt gegen ein Uhr, es sei denn, sie wird aufgehalten.* It is used chiefly in formal German; for further details see 16.5.3d.

(b) *geschweige denn* means 'let alone', 'still less':

Er wollte mir kein Geld leihen, geschweige denn schenken	*He wouldn't even <u>lend</u> me any money, let alone give me any*

(c) *denn* is often used in place of *dann* 'then'
e.g.: *Na, **denn** geht es eben nicht.* This usage is common in north German colloquial speech, but is considered to be substandard.

(d) *denn* is used as a coordinating conjunction indicating a cause or reason
It corresponds to English 'for', 'because', e.g.: *Er kann uns nicht verstehen, denn er spricht kein Deutsch.* For details, see 19.1.2.

(e) *denn* is sometimes used in formal German and set phrases for *als* 'than'
e.g. *mehr denn je* 'more than ever'.
For details, see 8.3.1a.

10.7 *doch*

doch is used typically in an attempt to <u>persuade the listener of the speaker's point of view</u>. It usually expresses a <u>contradiction or disagreement</u> and often corresponds to English 'though' or a <u>tag question</u>. The element of persuasion is given more force if *doch* is stressed.

10.7.1 In statements, *doch* indicates disagreement with what has been said

If *doch* is stressed, it clearly contradicts, and its meaning is close to that of *dennoch* or *trotzdem*. If it is unstressed, it appeals politely for agreement or confirmation:

Gestern hat es **doch** geschneit	*All the same, it <u>did</u> snow yesterday*
Gestern hat es doch geschneit	*It snowed yesterday, didn't it?*
Ich habe **doch** Recht gehabt	*All the same, I <u>was</u> right*
Ich habe doch Recht gehabt	*I was right, wasn't I?*
Wir müssen **doch** morgen nach Bremen	*All the same, we <u>have</u> got to go to Bremen tomorrow*
Ich habe ihm abgeraten, aber er hat es **doch** getan	*I advised him against it, but he did it all the same*
Du hast doch gesagt, dass du kommst	*You did say you were coming, didn't you?*

Unstressed *doch* may also mildly point out a reason for disagreement. In such contexts it is interchangeable with *aber*, see 10.1.2:

Wir wollten doch heute Abend ins Theater gehen	*Surely we were going to go to the theatre tonight(, weren't we?)*
Die Ampel zeigt doch rot, wir dürfen noch nicht gehen	*But the lights are red, we can't go yet*

In literary German *doch* can be used with the verb first in the clause. This is used principally to explain a preceding statement:

War ich doch so durch den Lehrbetrieb beansprucht, dass ich dafür keine Zeit fand (*Grass*)	*After all, I was so busy with my lessons that I didn't have any time for that*

NB: For the difference in meaning between *doch* and *ja* in statements appealing for the listener's agreement, see 10.19.1b.

10.7.2 Unstressed *doch* can turn a statement into a question expecting a positive answer

doch is then the equivalent of a following *oder?* or *nicht (wahr)?*, and one of these may be used as well:

Den Wagen kann ich mir doch morgen abholen?	*I can collect the car tomorrow, can't I?*
Du kannst mir doch helfen(, oder)?	*You can help me, can't you?*
Du glaubst doch nicht, dass ich es getan habe?	*Surely you don't think I did it?*

10.7.3 *doch* in commands

The force of *doch* in commands can vary depending on the context. Sometimes it adds a note of impatience or urgency, and in this sense it can be strengthened by *endlich* or, in a negative sentence, by *immer*:

Reg dich doch nicht so auf!	*For heaven's sake, don't get so excited*
Bring den Wagen doch (endlich) in die Werkstatt!	*For goodness' sake, take the car to the garage*
Mach doch nicht (immer) so ein Gesicht!	*Don't keep making faces like that*
Freu dich doch!	*Do cheer up*

In other sentences, *doch* can moderate the force of the command, making it sound more advisory or encouraging. This can be made even more clear by adding *mal* or *ruhig*:

Lassen Sie mich doch (mal) das Foto sehen!	*Why don't you just let me see the photograph?*
Kommen Sie doch (ruhig) morgen vorbei!	*Why not drop by tomorrow?*

10.7.4 In w-questions, *doch* asks for confirmation of an answer or the repetition of information

doch can be strengthened by adding *gleich* (see 10.16), and its force is then similar to that of *denn noch*, see 10.6.1e:

Wie heißt doch euer Hund?	*What did you say your dog is called?*
Wer war das doch (gleich)?	*Who was that again?*
Wohin fahrt ihr doch auf Urlaub?	*Where did you say you were going on holiday?*

10.7.5 In exclamations, *doch* emphasises the speaker's surprise

In such sentences the force of *doch* is close to that of *ja*, see 10.19.2:

Wie winzig doch alles von hier oben aussieht!	*But how tiny everything looks from up here!*
Du bist doch kein kleines Kind mehr!	*You're not a baby any more, you know!*
Das ist doch die Höhe!	*That really is the limit!*

10.7.6 In wishes expressed with *Konjunktiv II*, *doch* emphasises the urgency of the wish

See also 16.7.6b. In such sentences *doch* is the equivalent of *nur* and may be used together with it, see 10.26.1c:

Wenn er doch jetzt käme!	*If only he would come now!*
Wäre ich doch zu Hause geblieben!	*If only I'd just stayed at home!*

10.7.7 Further uses of *doch*

(a) In reply to a question, *doch* contradicts a negative or emphasises an affirmative reply

Bist du nicht zufrieden? – Doch!	*Aren't you satisfied? – Yes, I am*
Kommt er bald? – Doch!	*Is he coming soon? – Oh, yes*

Er hat nie etwas für uns getan.
  – Doch, er hat mir einmal 100 Mark geliehen
	He's never done anything for us.
	  – Oh, yes he has, he once lent me a hundred marks

When used with *nein* or *nicht*, *doch* emphasises a negative reply:

Mutti, kann ich ein Stück Schokolade haben? – Nein doch, du hast jetzt genug gegessen	*Mummy, can I have a piece of chocolate? – Certainly not, you've had enough to eat*

(b) As a conjunction, *doch* is an alternative to *aber* 'but'

e.g.: *Sie wollten baden gehen, **doch** es hat geschneit.* Further details are given in 19.1.1.

10.8 *eben*

10.8.1 As a modal particle, *eben* typically expresses a confirmation that something is the case

eben often corresponds to English 'just'.

(a) In statements, *eben* emphasises an inescapable conclusion

Das ist eben so	*But there, that's how it is*
Ich kann ihn nicht überreden. Er ist eben hartnäckig	*I can't convince him. He's just obstinate*
Er zeichnet ganz gut	*He draws quite well*
– Nun, er ist eben ein Künstler	*– Well, he is an artist*
Ich mache es, so gut ich eben kann	*I'll do it as well as I can (given the circumstances)*

(b) In commands, *eben* emphasises that there is no real alternative
These commands are often introduced by *dann*:

(Dann) bleib eben im Zug sitzen!	*Well, just stay on the train, then*
(Dann) fahr eben durch die Stadtmitte!	*Well, just drive through the town centre, then*

halt is a frequent alternative to *eben*, see 10.17. It was originally restricted to south Germany, but it has become more widely used recently.

10.8.2 Further uses of *eben*

(a) *eben* can be used in the sense of 'exactly', 'precisely', 'just'
In this meaning it can be used as a focus particle before another word, or as a response to a statement or a question. *genau* is a common alternative:

Eben dieses Haus hatte mir zugesagt	*It was just this house which attracted me*
Das wäre mir eben recht	*That would be just what I'd like*
Eben daran hatte ich nie gedacht	*That's the one thing I hadn't thought of*
Das wird sie doch kaum schaffen.	*She won't manage it, will she?*
– Eben!	*– Precisely!*

(b) Used with *nicht* before an adjective, *eben* lessens the force of *nicht*
gerade is a common alternative:

Sie ist nicht eben fleißig	*She's not exactly hard-working*
Der Zug war nicht eben pünktlich	*The train wasn't what you'd call on time*

(c) As an adverb, *eben* means 'just (now)'
gerade is a common alternative:

Wir sind **eben** (erst) angekommen   **Eben** geht mir ein Licht auf
Mit zweitausend Euro im Monat kommen wir **eben** (noch) aus

(d) As an adjective, *eben* means 'level'
e.g.: *Die Straße ist hier nicht **eben***

10.9 *eh*

eh is an alternative to *ohnehin* or *sowieso*. Like them, it is an equivalent of English 'anyway' or 'in any case', but it is used predominantly in colloquial south German, especially in Austria and Bavaria, although its use has recently spread to other areas:

Wenn ich arbeite, brauche ich eh immer mehr zum Essen (*Kroetz*)	*When I'm working I need more to eat anyway*
Für eine Markenpersönlichkeit wie Sie ist das neue Magazin der Süddeutschen eh ein Muss (*SZ*)	*It goes without saying that the new magazine of the "Süddeutsche Zeitung" is a must for a person of quality like you*

10.10 *eigentlich*

eigentlich emphasises that something is actually the case, even if it appears otherwise. It is often used to change the topic of conversation.

10.10.1 *eigentlich* in questions

(a) *eigentlich* can tone a question down and makes it sound more casual
In such cases it is relatively lightly stressed. It comes close to the sense of English 'actually' and is often used in conjunction with *denn*:

Sind Sie eigentlich dieses Jahr schon in Urlaub gewesen?	*Tell me, have you been on holiday yet this year?*
Wohnt die Eva eigentlich schon lange in Hameln?	*Has Eva actually been living a long time in Hamelin?*

(b) In *w*-questions, *eigentlich* implies that the question has not yet been answered fully or satisfactorily
In such contexts it is rather more heavily stressed and very close in meaning to *im Grunde genommen*, *tatsächlich* or *wirklich*, with the sense of 'at bottom', 'in actual fact', 'in reality':

Wie heißt er eigentlich?	*What's his real name?*
Warum besuchst du mich eigentlich?	*Why, basically, did you come to visit me?*

10.10.2 *eigentlich* in statements

(a) *eigentlich* indicates that something actually is the case, despite appearances
It moderates a refusal, an objection or a contradiction by indicating how strong the reasons are:

Er scheint manchmal faul, aber er ist eigentlich sehr fleißig	*He appears lazy sometimes, but in actual fact he's very hard-working*
Ich wollte eigentlich zu Fuß gehen	*In actual fact, I did want to walk*
Ich trinke eigentlich keinen Kaffee mehr	*Well, actually, I don't drink coffee now*

(b) Sometimes *eigentlich* can signal that the matter is still a little open

Wir haben eigentlich schon zu	*Well, actually, we're already closed* (hinting that an exception might not be wholly out of the question)
Das darf man hier eigentlich nicht	*Strictly speaking, that's not allowed here* (but, possibly, …)

10.10.3 As an adjective, *eigentlich* means 'real', 'actual', 'fundamental'

Was ist die **eigentliche** Ursache?	Er nannte nicht den **eigentlichen** Grund

10.11 *einfach*

einfach emphasises that alternative possibilities are excluded. It usually corresponds to English 'simply' or, especially in commands, 'just'. In commands it is frequently used in conjunction with *doch* and/or *mal* and in exclamations with *ja*:

Ich bin einfach weggegangen	*I simply walked away*
Ich werde ihm einfach sagen, dass es nicht möglich ist	*I'll simply tell him it's not possible*
Warum gehst du nicht einfach ins Bett?	*Why don't you simply go to bed?*
Leg dich (doch) einfach hin!	*Why don't you just go and lie down?*
Geh doch einfach mal zum Zahnarzt!	*Why not just simply go to the dentist?*
Heute ist das Wetter (ja) einfach herrlich!	*The weather is simply lovely today!*

einfach is used as a true adverb, as well as a particle, but there is a clear difference in meaning. As an adverb, *einfach* is always stressed and means 'in a simple manner'. Compare:

Sie macht es **einfach**	*She is doing it simply* (in an uncomplicated way)
Sie **macht** es einfach	*She's simply doing it* ('just', 'without further ado')
Du musst **einfach** anfangen	*You have to begin simply*
Du musst einfach **anfangen**	*You simply have to begin*

10.12 *erst*

10.12.1 As a modal particle, *erst* has intensifying force

(a) In statements and exclamations

Here *erst* implies that something really is the absolute limit and perhaps more than expected or desirable. It is often strengthened by adding *recht*:

Dann ging es erst (recht) los	*Then things really got going*
Das konnte sie erst recht nicht	*That she really couldn't manage*
Das macht es erst recht schlimm	*That really does make it bad*
Sie hat schon Hunger, aber das Kind erst (recht)!	*She may be hungry, but that's nothing to how hungry the kid is*

(b) In wishes

Here, *nur* or *bloß* are alternatives to *erst* (and may be used with it):

Wäre er doch erst zu Hause! (*Fallada*)	*If only he were at home!*
Wenn er (bloß) erst wieder arbeiten könnte!	*If only he could start work again!*

10.12.2 As a focus particle, *erst* indicates that there are/were less or fewer than expected

(a) Before a number or an expression of quantity it corresponds to 'only'

Ich habe erst zehn Seiten geschrieben	*I've only written ten pages*
Er ist erst sieben Jahre alt	*He's only seven years old*
Ich habe erst die Hälfte fertig	*I've only got half of it finished*

Before other nouns the sense is 'nothing less than':

Erst mit einem Lehrstuhl in Bonn wird er sich zufrieden geben	*He'll only be satisfied with a professorship in Bonn*

(b) In time expressions, *erst* implies that it is later than expected or desirable

It usually corresponds to English 'only', 'not before', 'not until' or, in certain contexts, 'as late as':

Er kommt erst (am) Montag	{ *He's not coming till Monday* { *He's only coming on Monday*
Es ist erst acht Uhr	*It's only eight o'clock*
Ich kam erst im Sommer nach Heidelberg	*I didn't get to Heidelberg until the summer*
erst wenn/als (see 19.3.2b)	*not until, only when*
wenn er erst zu Hause ist, ...	*once he's home ...*
Es hatte eben erst zu schneien aufgehört (*Jünger*)	*It had only just stopped snowing*
Ich kann den Wagen erst Anfang nächste Woche abholen	*I shan't be able to collect the car till the beginning of next week*

(c) *erst* 'only' must be carefully distinguished from *nur*
(see 10.26.2)

(i) With numbers, as in the examples in (a) above, *erst* implies that more are to follow. In English this can be made clear by adding 'as yet' to the sentence. *nur*, on the other hand, sets a clear limit, i.e. that number and no more. Compare:

Ich habe **erst** drei Briefe bekommen	*I've only received three letters (as yet)* (more are expected)
Ich habe **nur** drei Briefe bekommen	*I've only received three letters* (i.e. three and no more)

(ii) In time expressions, like the examples in (b) above, *erst* has the sense 'not before', etc., but *nur* means 'on that one occasion'. Compare:

Sie ist erst (am) Montag gekommen	*She only came on Monday* (i.e. not before Monday)
Sie ist nur (am) Montag gekommen	*She only came on Monday* (i.e. on no other day)

NB: (i) The opposite of *erst* 'only' as a focus particle is *schon*, see 10.30.5.
(ii) The distinction between *erst* and *nur* is not always consistently maintained in substandard colloquial speech.

10.13 *etwa*

10.13.1 In yes/no questions, *etwa* implies that something is undesirable and suggests that the answer ought to be *nein*

A common English equivalent is a negative statement followed by a positive tag question or an exclamation beginning with 'Don't tell me …':

Hast du die Zeitung etwa schon weggeworfen?	*You haven't thrown the paper away already, have you?*
Ist das etwa dein Wagen?	*That's not your car, is it?*
Habt ihr etwa geschlafen?	*Don't tell me you've been asleep!*

Such questions with *etwa* can be in the form of statements, in which case they also contain *doch nicht*:

Sie wollen doch nicht etwa nach Paderborn umziehen?	*You don't want to move to Paderborn, do you?*

10.13.2 In negative sentences, *etwa* intensifies the negation

Sie müssen nicht etwa denken, dass ich ihn verteidigen will	*Now don't go and think I want to defend him*
Komm nicht etwa zu spät zum Flughafen!	*Make sure you don't get to the airport too late!*

10.13.3 In conditional sentences *etwa* stresses the idea of a possibility

Wenn der Zug etwa verspätet sein sollte, dann verpassen wir den Anschluss nach Gera	*If the train should be delayed we'll miss our connection to Gera*
Wenn das Wetter etwa umschlagen sollte, müssen wir die Wanderung verkürzen	*If the weather were to change, we'll have to shorten our walk*

10.13.4 Uses of *etwa* before a noun or noun phrase

In such contexts *etwa* is used as a focus or scalar particle.

(a) Before a number or expression of size or quantity, *etwa* expresses approximation

Ich komme etwa um zwei	*I'll come at about two*
Es kostet etwa dreißig Euro	*It costs about thirty euro*
Er ist etwa so groß wie dein Vater	*He is about as tall as your father*
Wir haben es uns etwa so vorgestellt	*We imagined it to be something like that*

(b) Before a noun or list of nouns, *etwa* suggests a possibility

It is often close in meaning to English 'for instance' or 'for example':

Er begnügte sich mit etwa folgender Antwort	*He was satisfied with, for instance, the following answer*
Bist du sicher, dass du den Jürgen gesehen hast, und nicht etwa seinen Bruder Thomas?	*Are you sure you saw Jürgen, and not perhaps his brother Thomas?*
Er hat viele Hobbys, (wie) etwa Reisen, Musik und Sport	*He has a lot of hobbies, for example travelling, music and sport*
Willst du etwa (am) Sonntag kommen?	*You're not thinking of coming on Sunday, are you?*

10.14 *freilich*

freilich usually has a concessive sense and its force is very similar to that of *allerdings*, see 10.2. It was originally typically south German, but it is coming to be used more widely.

10.14.1 Within a clause *freilich* means 'admittedly', 'all the same'

Es scheint freilich nicht ganz so einfach zu sein	*Admittedly, it doesn't appear to be that simple*
Wir nehmen ihn mit, freilich muss er pünktlich am Treffpunkt sein	*We'll take him with us, even so he'll have to get to the meeting place on time*

10.14.2 In answer to a question, *freilich* stresses that the answer is yes

freilich is often used in conjunction with *ja*. It lacks the hint that there is some kind of reservation or qualification to the answer which is sometimes present with *allerdings*:

Kennst du die Angelika?	*Do you know Angelika?*
– (Ja,) freilich (kenne ich sie)!	*– Of course (I know her)!*
Kannst du auch alles besorgen?	*Can you see to it all?*
– (Ja,) freilich!	*– Certainly I can!*

NB: *freilich* can <u>never</u> mean 'freely', which is *frei* in most contexts.

10.15 *gar*

gar is used in a number of ways with an intensifying sense.

(a) The commonest use of *gar* is to intensify a negative
In these contexts *gar* is an alternative to *überhaupt*:

Sie hatte gar nicht gewusst, ob er abfahren wollte (*Johnson*)	*She hadn't even known whether he wanted to leave*
Ich habe doch heute gar keine Zeit	*I really haven't got any time at all today*

Less commonly, *gar* can intensify *so* or *zu* with an adjective (*allzu* is a more frequent alternative):

Du darfst das nicht gar so ernst nehmen	*You really mustn't take that quite so seriously*
Es waren gar zu viele Leute auf der Straße	*There were far too many people in the street*

(b) *gar* can be used to emphasise the following word and indicate surprise

In such contexts *gar* is the equivalent of English 'even' or 'possibly' and is a less frequent alternative to *sogar*, used mainly in literary registers:

Eher würde ich einem Habicht oder gar Aasgeier eine Friedensbotschaft anvertrauen als der Taube (*Grass*)	*I would rather entrust a message of peace to a hawk or even a vulture than to a dove*

10.16 *gleich*

As a modal particle *gleich* is used in *w*-questions to politely request the repetition of information. It is often used with *doch*, see 10.7.4:

Wie war Ihr Name (doch) gleich?	*What was your name again?*
Was hast du gleich gesagt?	*What was it you said?*

gleich is also used as a time adverb in the sense of 'immediately', e.g.: *Ich werde ihn **gleich** fragen*, or to mean 'at once' or 'at the same time', e.g. *Er hat **gleich** zwei Hemden gekauft.*

10.17 *halt*

halt is an alternative to *eben* in some senses (see 10.8). It was originally characteristic of south German speech, but its use has recently become more widespread:

Da kann man halt nichts machen	*There's just nothing to be done*
Dann nimm halt die U-Bahn!	*Just take the underground, then!*

10.18 *Immerhin*

immerhin indicates that something might not have come up to expectations, but is acceptable at a pinch. It corresponds most often to English 'all the same' or 'even so' and can be used within a sentence or (very frequently) as a response:

Du hast immerhin tausend Euro gewonnen	*All the same, you won a thousand euros*
Wir haben uns immerhin ein neues Videogerät anschaffen können	*Even so, we were able to buy a new video recorder*
Das Wetter im Urlaub war miserabel, aber wir hatten ein schönes Zimmer – (Na,) immerhin!	*The weather was lousy on holiday, but we did have a nice room.* *– Well, that was something, at least!*

10.19 *ja*

10.19.1 In statements, *ja* appeals for agreement

(a) By using *ja* the speaker insists that what s/he is saying is correct

A common English equivalent is the 'do' form of the verb:

Wir haben ja gestern davon gesprochen	*We did talk about that yesterday (you know)*
Ihr habt ja früher zwei Autos gehabt	*Of course, you used to have two cars*
Ich komme ja schon	*It's all right, I'm on my way*
Der katastrophale Zustand des Landes ist ja gerade das Erbe der Diktatur (*Spiegel*)	*Of course, the catastrophic state of the country is precisely the legacy of dictatorship*

(b) *ja* **has a distinct meaning from** *doch* **when used to appeal for agreement**
doch (see 10.7.1), implies that the listener may hold a different opinion, but *ja* always presupposes that speaker and listener are agreed. Compare:

Du könntest dir **ja** Karls Rad leihen	*You could borrow Karl's bike, of course (we both know you can)*
Du könntest dir **doch** Karls Rad leihen	*Surely, you could borrow Karl's bike (you might have thought you couldn't)*
Das ist es **ja** eben	*Why, of course, that's the point*
Das ist es **doch** eben	*Don't you see, that's just the point*
Er kann unmöglich kommen, er ist **ja** krank	*He can't possibly come, he's ill, as you know*
er ist **doch** krank	*he's ill, don't you know*

10.19.2 In exclamations, *ja* expresses surprise

Heute ist es ja kalt!	*Oh, it is cold today!*
Er hat ja ein neues Auto!	*Why, he's got a new car!*
Das ist ja unerhört!	*That really is the limit!*
Da kommt ja der Arzt!	*Oh (good), here comes the doctor!*

By using *ja* (or *doch*, which has a very similar force in exclamations, see 10.7.5), the speaker can express surprise that something is the case at all. When *aber* or *vielleicht* are used in exclamations, though, surprise is expressed at the extent of a quality, see 10.1.1 and 10.34.1. Thus *die Milch ist **ja/doch** sauer!* would be said if the milk had been expected to be fresh, whilst *die Milch ist **aber/vielleicht** sauer* expresses surprise at <u>how</u> sour the milk is.

10.19.3 *ja* intensifies a command

There is often an implied warning or threat, especially if *ja* is stressed:

Bleib ja hier!	*Be sure to stay here!*
Geht ja nicht auf die Straße!	*Just don't go out onto the street!*
Er soll j̲a̲ nichts sagen	*He really must not say anything (or else)*

NB: *nur* is an alternative to *ja* to intensify commands and sound a note of warning, see 10.26.1a.

10.19.4 *ja* can be used as a focus particle

In a string of nouns, verbs or adjectives, *ja* (sometimes in combination with *sogar*) emphasises the importance of the one (usually the last) before which it is placed. This often corresponds to English *indeed*, *even* or *nay*:

Es war ein Erfolg, ja ein Triumph	*It was a success, indeed a triumph*
Es war ein unerwarteter, ja ein sensationeller Erfolg	*It was an unexpected, indeed a sensational success*
Sie konnte die Aussage bestätigen, ja (sogar) beeiden	*She was able to confirm the testimony, even on oath*

10.19.5 *ja* is the affirmative particle

It corresponds to English 'yes', e.g.: *Kommst du morgen? – Ja!* It can also be used as a tag:

Es geht um acht los, ja?	*We're starting at eight, aren't we?*

10.20 *jedenfalls*

The phrases *auf jeden Fall* and *auf alle Fälle* are possible alternatives to the particle *jedenfalls*.

10.20.1 In statements *jedenfalls* stresses the reason why something should be the case

(or why something is not as bad as it may seem). In these contexts, *jedenfalls* corresponds to 'at least' or 'at any rate':

Vielleicht ist er krank, er sieht jedenfalls schlecht aus	*Perhaps he's ill, at least he doesn't look well*
Er ist nicht gekommen, aber er hat sich jedenfalls entschuldigt	*He didn't come, but at least he did apologise*

wenigstens or *zumindest* are alternatives to *jedenfalls* in this sense, see 8.4.4b.

10.20.2 In commands *jedenfalls* indicates that something should be done in any event

jedenfalls corresponds to English 'anyhow' or 'in any case':

Bei schönem Wetter gehen wir morgen baden. Bring jedenfalls deinen Badeanzug mit	*If it's fine we'll go swimming tomorrow. Bring your costume along anyhow*

10.21 *lediglich*

lediglich is used before another word to indicate a restriction or a limit. It is an emphatic alternative to *nur* in the sense 'only', 'no more than'. It is used mainly in formal registers and can sound stilted:

Er hat lediglich zwei Semester in Münster studiert	*He only studied two semesters in Münster*
Ich verlange lediglich mein Recht	*I am only asking for what's due to me*

10.22 *mal*

10.22.1 *mal* moderates the tone of a sentence, making it sound less blunt

mal is frequent in commands, requests and questions. It can correspond to English 'just', (although in practice this is used less than German *mal*):

Lies den Brief mal durch!	*Just read the letter through (will you?)*
Hol mal schnell den Feuerlöscher!	*Just quickly go and get the fire extinguisher*
Das sollst du mal probieren	*You just ought to try that*
Ich will sie schnell mal anrufen	*I just want to ring her up quickly*
Würden Sie mir bitte mal helfen?	*Could you just help me?*
Hältst du mir mal die Tasche?	*Just hold my bag for me, will you?*

mal is almost automatically added to a command in colloquial speech, especially if there is nothing else in the sentence apart from the verb:

Sieh mal her!   Hör mal zu!   Komm mal herüber!   Sag mal!

The tone of a request or a command may be moderated further by adding *eben*:

Reich mir eben mal das Brot!	*Just pass me the bread, would you?*
Lies den Brief eben mal durch!	*Won't you please just read the letter through?*

The combination *doch mal* makes a command sound more casual:

Nimm doch mal ein neues Blatt!	*Why don't you get another piece of paper?*
Melde dich doch mal beim Chef!	*Why not just arrange to see the boss?*

10.22.2 The particle *mal* is quite distinct from the adverb *einmal* 'once'

(see 9.4.3). In other words, *mal* is not simply a shortened form of *einmal*, which cannot be used for *mal* in any of the contexts explained in 10.22.1. However, in some contexts *einmal* is often shortened to *mal* in colloquial speech, e.g.:

(a) *noch einmal* '(once) again', 'once more'

Ich habe ihn noch (ein)mal gewarnt   *I warned him once again*

(b) *nun einmal* 'just'
This combination emphasises the lack of alternatives. It is a rather more forceful equivalent to *eben* or *halt*, see 10.8.1a:

Es wird nun (ein)mal lange dauern   *It's just going to take a long time*

(c) *nicht einmal* 'not even':

Er hat sie nicht (ein)mal gegrüßt   *He didn't even say hello to her*

10.23 *man*

man is a colloquial north German equivalent to *mal* in commands and requests

Geh du man vor!	*You just go ahead*
Seien Sie man bloß ruhig! (*Fallada*)	*Just keep calm*

10.24 noch

10.24.1 noch indicates something additional

In this sense *noch* can be used as a focus particle preceding a noun or pronoun, or as a modal particle within the clause:

Er hat noch drei Stunden geschlafen	*He slept another three hours*
Ich trinke noch eine Tasse Kaffee	*I'll have another cup of coffee*
Das wird sich noch herausstellen	*That will remain to be seen, too*
Wer war noch da?	*Who else was there?*
Und es hat auch noch geregnet!	*And apart from that, it rained too*

10.24.2 noch in time expressions

(a) noch can indicate that something is going on longer than expected

noch can be strengthened by *immer* and corresponds to English 'still 'or 'yet':

Angela schläft (immer) noch	*Angela's still asleep*
Franz ist (immer) noch nicht gekommen	*Franz hasn't come yet/Franz still hasn't come*
Sie wohnen noch in Fritzlar	*They're still living in Fritzlar*
Ich habe sie noch nie gesehen	*I've never seen her (yet)*
Sie ist doch noch jung	*She's still young, isn't she?*

(b) If a particular point in time is indicated, noch indicates that an event took place or will take place by then

The implication may be that this is contrary to expectations:

Ich habe ihn noch vor zwei Tagen gesehen	*I saw him only two days ago*
Noch im Mai hat sie ihre Dissertation abgegeben	*She managed to hand her thesis inby the end of May*
Ich werde noch heute den Arzt anrufen	*I'll ring the doctor before tomorrow*

In this sense, *noch* can come after short time words and phrases rather than before them, e.g. *Ich werde heute noch den Arzt anrufen.*

10.24.3 Further uses of noch

(a) In w-questions, noch asks for the listener to jog the speaker's memory

i.e. suggesting that something has just slipped his/her mind:

Wie hieß er noch?	*Oh now, what was his name?*
Wann war das Spiel noch?	*Oh now, when was the game?*

(b) noch is used with comparatives in the sense of 'even'

e.g.: *Er ist noch größer als du.* For further details, see 8.3.1c.

(c) noch is used with weder as the equivalent of English 'neither … nor'

e.g.: *Er liest weder Bücher noch Zeitungen* (see 19.1.3d).

(d) *noch* **is used with** *so* **and an adjective in a concessive sense**
e.g.: *Wenn sie (auch) **noch** so fleißig ist, sie wird die Prüfung doch nicht bestehen* (see 19.6.2b).

10.25 *nun*

10.25.1 In questions, *nun* signals dissatisfaction with a previous answer

By using *nun* the speaker insists that the correct or complete information should be provided:

Wann kommt der Zug nun an?	When <u>does</u> this train get in, now?
Stimmt es nun, dass sie verheiratet ist?	Now, is it really true that she's married?

nun is commonly used on its own as a question to push the other speaker to give more information, cf. *Nun?* 'Well?', *Nun ... und?* 'And then what?'

10.25.2 *nun* signals that the speaker considers the topic exhausted

In this sense *nun* occurs characteristically in isolation at the beginning of a sentence. It often corresponds to English 'well':

Nun, das ist alles schon wichtig, aber ich glaube, wir müssen zunächst das Wahlergebnis besprechen	Well, of course that's all very important, but I think we've got to discuss the election results first
Nun, natürlich hat er die besten Erfahrungen	Well, of course he's got the widest experience
Nun, wir werden ja sehen	Well, we shall see
Nun, meinetwegen!	All right then

10.25.3 *nun* is used as an adverb of time to mean 'now'

nun is rather less definite than *jetzt* and it is used less frequently to refer simply to the present moment as such:

Nun wollen wir umkehren	Now we'll turn back
Nun hat er mehr Zeit als früher	Now he's got more time than he used to have
Geht es dir nun besser?	Are you better now?
als es nun Winter wurde, ...	now when it turned to winter ...

10.26 *nur*

nur is used as a modal particle with an intensifying sense, and as a focus particle with a restrictive sense (= 'only'). *bloß*, see 10.5, is a frequent alternative to *nur* in all its uses except where indicated below. It tends to be slightly more emphatic, and more colloquial.

10.26.1 As a modal particle, *nur* usually has intensifying force

(a) In a command, *nur* intensifies the basic meaning
Depending on the sense of the command, i.e. whether it is an urgent instruction or a request, *nur* can make it sound more of a threat <u>or</u> more reassuring respectively.

(i) 'threatening' or 'warning' *nur* is more common in negative commands or when *nur* is stressed. This sense is similar to that of *ja* (see 10.19.3):

Komm nur nicht zu spät!	*You'd better not be late!*
Nimm dich nur in Acht!	*You'd better be careful!*
Geh nur nicht in diesen Laden!	*Whatever you do, don't go into that shop*
Sehen Sie nur, was Sie gemacht haben!	*Just look what you've done!*

In this sense, *nur* (but <u>not</u> *bloß*) can be used initially in a positive or negative command using the infinitive or with no verb at all:

Nur nicht so schnell laufen!	*Just don't run so fast!*
Nur aufpassen!	*Just be sure to look out!*
Nur immer schön langsam!	*Take it nice and slow!*

(ii) The 'reassuring' sense of *nur* is close to that of *ruhig* (see 10.28):

Lass ihn nur reden!	*Just let him speak, do!*
Kommen Sie nur herein!	*Do come in!*
Hab nur keine Angst!	*Don't be afraid, will you!*
Nur weiter!	*Just carry on!* (implying: *It's all right so far*)

bloß is <u>not</u> used in this 'reassuring' sense, and commands with *bloß* always have a 'warning' tone. Compare *Lass ihn bloß reden!* 'Just let him speak (and you'll suffer the consequences)' with the first example in (ii) above.

(b) *nur* intensifies *w*-questions and makes them sound more urgent

Wie kann er nur so taktlos sein?	*How on earth can he be so tactless?*
Was können wir nur tun, um ihr zu helfen?	*Whatever can we do to help her?*
Wo bleibt sie nur?	*Where on earth is she?*

Such questions can be used as exclamations of reproach or astonishment, as no real answer is possible or expected:

Wie siehst du nur wieder aus?!	*What on earth do you look like?!*
Warum musste er nur wegfahren?!	*Why on earth did he have to go away?!*

(c) *nur* intensifies a wish in the form of a *wenn*-clause
See also 16.7.6b. The force of *nur* similar to that of *doch*, see 10.7.6, and they are often used together to add an even greater intensity to the wish:

Wenn sie (doch) nur anrufen würde!	*If only she would ring up!*
Hätte ich nur mehr Zeit!	*If only I had more time!*
Wenn er mir nur geschrieben hätte!	*If only he had written me!*

10.26.2 *nur* is used as a focus particle to express a restriction

i.e. with the force of English 'only'. *nur* is used in all kinds of sentences to qualify nouns, verbs or adjectives:

Ich wollte nur Guten Tag sagen	*I only/just wanted to say Hello*
Die Mittelmeerküste ist sehr schön, sie ist leider nur etwas dreckig	*The Mediterranean coast is very nice, only I'm afraid it's rather dirty*
Er geht nur bei schönem Wetter spazieren	*He only goes for a walk when it's fine*
Ich vermute nur, dass er gestern in Urlaub gefahren ist	*I'm only assuming that he went on holiday yesterday*
Man kann es nur dort kaufen	*You can only buy it there*
Dort kann man nicht nur Bücher kaufen, sondern auch allerlei Zeitschriften	*You can not only buy books there, but also magazines of all kinds*

NB: (i) For the difference between *erst* and *nur* as an equivalent of English 'only', see 10.12.2c.
   (ii) *nur dass* is used as the equivalent of the English conjunction 'only' (see also 19.7.6), e.g. *Die Zimmer waren in Ordnung,* **nur dass** *die Duschen fehlten.*
   (iii) *lediglich*, see 10.21, is a more formal alternative to *nur*.

10.27 *ohnehin*

ohnehin indicates that something is correct irrespective of any other reasons given or implied. A typical English equivalent is 'anyway' or 'in any case'. It is a more formal alternative to (southern) colloquial *eh* (see 10.9), or *sowieso* (see 10.31):

Er trinkt ohnehin zu viel	*He drinks too much anyway*
Der Zug hat ohnehin Verspätung	*The train's late anyway*
Du musst sofort zum Arzt – Ich hätte ihn ohnehin morgen besucht	*You'll have to go to the doctor right away – I would have gone to see him tomorrow in any case*

10.28 *ruhig*

ruhig lends a reassuring tone to what the speaker is saying. This meaning is clearly related to that of the adjective *ruhig* 'quiet'. It is used in commands (where it is an alternative to *nur*, see 10.26.1a), and in statements, especially with a modal auxiliary:

Bleib ruhig sitzen!	*Don't get up for me*
Arbeite ruhig weiter!	*Just carry on* (i.e. don't let me disturb you)
Auf dieser Straße kannst du ruhig etwas schneller fahren	*It's all right, you can go a bit faster on this road*
Sie dürfen ruhig hier im Zimmer bleiben	*You can stay here in this room, I don't mind*

10.29 *schließlich*

schließlich indicates that the speaker accepts the validity of a reason. It usually corresponds to English 'after all':

Es liegt schließlich nicht genug Schnee auf der Piste	*After all, there's not enough snow on the piste*
Wir wollen ihn schließlich nicht zu sehr reizen	*We don't want to annoy him too much, after all*
Schließlich kann das einem jeden passieren	*After all, it can happen to anybody*

10.30 *schon*

schon has the widest range of meaning of all the German particles.

10.30.1 The use of *schon* as a modal particle in statements

(a) In statements generally, *schon* expresses agreement or confirmation in principle, but with slight reservations

This sense is in practice concessive. *schon* often has (or implies) a following *aber*, *nur* or the like. *zwar* or, especially in north Germany, *wohl* are possible alternatives, see 10.35.3 and 10.36.1:

Das ist schon möglich(, aber ...)	*That's quite possible (but ...)*
Ich wollte schon kommen	*Well, I did want to come*
Das stimmt schon, aber es könnte auch anders kommen	*That may be true, but things might turn out differently*
Ja, ich glaube schon(, aber ...)	*Well, I think so(, but ...)*
Der Film hatte schon wunderschöne Aufnahmen, nur war er etwas langweilig	*The movie may have had some lovely shots, only it was a bit boring*

In a response, *schon* corrects what has just been said and indicates why it was wrong:

Niemand fährt über Ostern weg – Mutter schon!	*Nobody's going away over Easter – But mother is*
Heute waren keine deiner Freunde da – Der Kurt aber schon!	*None of your friends came today – But Kurt did*
Er hat da ein sehr schönes Haus gekauft – (Das) schon, aber ...	*He's bought himself a nice house there – Well yes, but ...*

(b) In statements referring to the future, *schon* emphasises the speaker's confidence that something will happen

schon usually sounds reassuring, but in some contexts and situations it may take on a more threatening tone. English 'all right' has similar force:

Er wird uns schon helfen	*He'll help us all right*
Es wird schon gehen	*It'll be all right, don't worry*
Ich krieg's schon hin	*I'll manage it all right*
Dem werde ich's schon zeigen!	*I'll show him all right!*

10.30.2 *schon* gives persuasive force to a *w*-question which expects a negative answer or where the speaker has a negative attitude

Was sagt die Regierung zu Ungarn? – Nichts. Was sollen sie schon sagen? (Horbach)	*What does the government say about Hungary? – Nothing. But then, what are they to say?*
Wer kann diesem Angebot schon widerstehen?	*Who can refuse this offer?* (i.e. 'nobody')
Warum kommt der schon wieder?	*What's he coming again for?* (implying: 'he's up to no good')
Na, und wenn schon?	*So what?*

10.30.3 In conditional sentences *schon* emphasises the condition

In addition, *schon* may point to the inescapability of the conclusion. It is normally used only in open conditions, with the indicative, see 16.5.2:

Wenn ich das schon mache, dann muss ich über alle Probleme informiert sein	*If I am going to do it, I'll need to be told about all the problems*
Wenn du schon ein neues Auto kaufst, dann aber keinen so teueren	*If you are going to buy a new car, then don't get one that's as expensive*
Wenn sie schon ans Meer fährt, dann will sie auch baden	*If she's going to the seaside, she will want to go swimming*

10.30.4 In commands, *schon* adds an insistent note

The sentence often begins with *nun*:

(Nun,) beeile dich schon!	*Do hurry up(, then)!*
Fang schon an!	*Do make a start!*
Sag mir schon, was du denkst! Ich werde es dir nicht übel nehmen	*Do tell me what you think. I shan't take it amiss*

10.30.5 *schon* is used as a focus particle to express a restriction

erst is the opposite of *schon* in the contexts dealt with under (a) and (b) below, see 10.12.2.

(a) Referring to time, *schon* indicates that something is happening or has happened sooner than expected or desirable
In some contexts, *schon* can stress that something actually has happened. In this meaning, it can correspond to English 'already', but its use is wider:

Er war schon angekommen	*He had already arrived*
schon am nächsten Tag	*the very next day*
Da bist du ja schon wieder	*There you are back again*
Sind Sie schon einmal in Köln gewesen?	*Have you been to Cologne before?*
Ich habe ihn auch schon in der Bibliothek gesehen	*I've sometimes seen him in the library*
Das habe ich schon 1996 geahnt	*I suspected that as early as 1996*
Es war schon 7 Uhr, als sie aufstand	*It was already 7 o'clock when she got up*

(b) Before a number or an expression of quantity, *schon* indicates that this is more than expected or desirable

Sie hat schon drei Briefe bekommen	*She has already received three letters*
Ich habe schon die Hälfte des Buches gelesen	*I've already read half the book*
Er wartet schon eine Stunde auf dich	*He's already been waiting for you for an hour*

(c) When used to qualify most nouns, *schon* expresses a restriction
schon can occasionally be used to qualify another part of speech:

Schon der Gedanke ist mir unsympathisch schon ihrer Kinder wegen	*The very thought is repugnant to me if only because of their children*
Das geht schon daher nicht, weil ...	*That's impossible, not least because ...*
Schon vor dem Krieg war die Eisenbahn in Schwierigkeiten geraten	*Even before the war the railways had run into difficulties*

10.31 *sowieso*

sowieso indicates that something is correct irrespective of any other reasons given or implied. It usually corresponds to English 'anyway' or 'in any case'. It is a rather more colloquial alternative to *ohnehin*, see 10.27:

Ich kann heute sowieso nicht arbeiten	*I can't work today anyway*
Der ist sowieso scharf auf sie	*He fancies her anyway*
Ich wäre sowieso nach Nürnberg gefahren	*I would have gone to Nuremberg in any case*

10.32 *überhaupt*

10.32.1 *überhaupt* makes statements and commands more general

The English equivalent is often 'at all' or 'anyhow':

Duisburg ist überhaupt eine grässliche Stadt	*Duisburg is a dreadful city anyhow*
Das ist überhaupt eine gefährliche Angelegenheit	*That's a risky business in any case*
Er liebte die italienische Sprache, ja die Sprachen überhaupt (*Goes*)	*He loved the Italian language, indeed, languages in general*
Seinen Mut müsste man haben, dachte ich. Oder überhaupt Mut (*Walser*)	*One ought to have his courage, I thought. Or any courage at all*
Ihr sollt überhaupt besser aufpassen!	*You ought anyway to pay more attention*

10.32.2 In questions, *überhaupt* casts doubt on the basic assumption

Er singt nicht besonders gut – Kann er denn überhaupt singen?	*He doesn't sing particularly well – Can he sing at all?*
Wie konntest du überhaupt so was tun?	*How could you do such a thing at all?*
Der Brief ist nicht da. Wo kann er überhaupt sein?	*The letter's not there. Wherever can it be?*
Was will er denn überhaupt?	*What the dickens does he want?*

10.32.3 *überhaupt* intensifies a negative

gar is a frequent alternative, see 10.15a:

Du hättest es überhaupt nicht tun sollen, und besonders jetzt nicht	*You ought not to have done it at all, and particularly not now*
Sie hat überhaupt keine Ahnung	*She's got no idea at all*
Ich weiß überhaupt nichts von seinen Plänen	*I don't know anything about his plans*

10.33 *übrigens*

übrigens is used in statements and questions to indicate a casual remark which is incidental to the main topic of conversation. It corresponds to English 'by the way', etc.:

Ich habe übrigens erfahren, dass er eine neue Stelle bekommen hat	*Incidentally, I've found out he's got a new job*
Sie hat übrigens vollkommen Recht	*She's perfectly right, by the way*
Wo wollt ihr übrigens dieses Jahr hin?	*By the way, where are you going this year?*

10.34 *vielleicht*

10.34.1 In exclamations unstressed *vielleicht* expresses surprise

These exclamations can have the form of statements or questions.

Siehst du vielleicht schlecht aus! ⎫ Du siehst vielleicht schlecht aus! ⎭	*Oh, you really do look awful!*
Die Kiste ist vielleicht schwer!	*How heavy the crate is!*
Du bist vielleicht ein Idiot!	*You really are stupid!*
Das hat vielleicht gegossen!	*It really did pour!*
Ich habe vielleicht gestaunt!	*I wasn't half surprised!*

Like *aber* (see 10.1.1), *vielleicht* expresses surprise at a difference in **degree** from the speaker's expectation, whereas *ja* (see 10.19.2) relates to a difference in **kind**.

10.34.2 In yes/no questions, *vielleicht* signals that the speaker expects a negative answer

The sense of *vielleicht* is close to that of *etwa*, see 10.13.1. The English equivalent is often an exclamation beginning with 'Don't tell me ...' or a negative statement followed by a positive tag question:

Willst du mir vielleicht erzählen, dass ...?	*You don't mean to tell me that ... , do you?*
Soll ich vielleicht bis 7 Uhr abends hier sitzen?	*I'm not supposed to sit here till seven at night, am I?*
Arbeitet er vielleicht?	*Don't tell me he's working?*

10.34.3 *vielleicht* is used as an adverb of attitude

i.e. corresponding to English 'perhaps':

Sie ist vielleicht 30 Jahre alt	*She is perhaps thirty years old*
Sie wird vielleicht morgen kommen	*She may come tomorrow*
Wird sie uns vielleicht morgen besuchen?	*Will she come to see us tomorrow, perhaps?*

vielleicht has a quite different meaning when it is used as an adverb from when it is used as a particle:

Die Kiste ist vielleicht schwer	*Perhaps the case is heavy*
Die Kiste ist vielleicht schwer!	*How heavy the case is!*

In requests in the form of a question, *vielleicht*, like English 'perhaps', expresses polite reserve on the part of the speaker:

Könnten Sie mir vielleicht sagen, wo es zum Bahnhof geht?	*Could you perhaps tell me the way the way to the station?*
Würden Sie mir vielleicht helfen?	*Would you perhaps help me?*

10.35 *wohl*

10.35.1 In statements, *wohl* signals a fair degree of probability

The force of *wohl* is very similar to that of the future tense, see 14.4.3, and it is often used in conjunction with it. It corresponds to the English future tense or a positive statement followed by a negative tag question, or to formulae like 'I suppose', 'probably':

Das wird wohl der Briefträger sein	*That'll be the postman*
Sie sind wohl neu hier	*You're new here, aren't you?*
Sie hat wohl ihr Auto schon verkauft	*I suppose she's already sold her car*
Diese Probleme versteht er wohl nicht	*He probably doesn't understand these problems*
Ich habe ihn nie gesprochen, wohl aber oft gesehen	*I've never spoken to him, but I have often seen him*

The combination *ja wohl* sounds rather more certain, corresponding to English '(pretty) certainly' or 'no doubt':

Sie wird ja wohl noch in Potsdam sein	*She's pretty certainly still in Potsdam*
Das weißt du ja wohl	*No doubt you know that*

The combination *wohl doch* (or, for some speakers, *doch wohl*) sounds rather less certain, though the speaker hopes that it is the case:

Er hat wohl doch noch einen Schlüssel	*Surely he's got another key, hasn't he?*
Die Antje wird doch wohl noch das Abitur schaffen	*Antje's surely going to get through her Abitur, isn't she?*

10.35.2 In questions *wohl* signals uncertainty on the part of the speaker

wohl can make the question sound tentative, as if the speaker doubts whether the other can give a clear answer. The question can be in statement form.

Wer hat den Brief wohl geschrieben?	*Who can possibly have written the letter?*
Wie spät ist es wohl?	*I wonder what time it is*
Ist der Peter wohl schon zu Hause?	*Peter is at home, isn't he?*
Darf ich wohl bei Ihnen telephonieren?	*Might I use your telephone?*
Horst ist wohl gestern Abend angekommen?	*Horst arrived last night, didn't he?*

10.35.3 In statements, stressed *wohl* has a concessive sense

wohl expresses agreement or confirmation in principle, but tinged with a slight reservation. It often has (or implies) a following *aber*, *nur* or the like. *zwar* or, especially in south Germany, *schon* are possible alternatives, see 10.30.1a and 10.36.1:

Er ist wohl mein Freund, aber ich kann ihm nicht helfen	*He may be my friend, but I can't help him*
Das ist wohl möglich(, aber ...)	*That may be possible(, but ...)*
Herbert ist wohl nach Basel gefahren, aber nur für eine Woche	*Herbert did go to Basle, but only for a week*

10.35.4 *wohl* intensifies a command, making it sound urgent, insistent and rather abrupt

wohl is often used with *werden* or *wollen*:

Hebst du wohl das Buch wieder auf!	*Pick that book up again right away!*
Wirst du wohl sofort wieder ins Bett gehen!	*Will you go straight back to bed!*
Wollt ihr wohl endlich still sein!	*Once and for all, will you be quiet!*

10.35.5 As an adverb, usually stressed, *wohl* has the sense 'well', 'fully'

wohl often strengthens an affirmative response (i.e. *jawohl!* 'yes, indeed'):

Ich fühle mich wohl	*I feel well*
Er hatte es sich wohl überlegt	*He had considered it fully*
Er weiß sehr wohl, daß er Unrecht hat	*He knows full well that he's wrong*
Schlaf wohl!	*Sleep well!*
Leb wohl!	*Farewell!*
Und er war so geartet, dass er solche Erfahrungen wohl vermerkte (*Th. Mann*)	*And his nature was such that he took full note of such experiences*

10.36 *zwar*

10.36.1 *zwar* can be used in a concessive sense

zwar is normally followed by a clause with *aber* (or one is implied), and the combination *zwar ... aber* can have the force of English '(al)though', see also 19.6.1b:

Er ist zwar krank, aber er kommt heute Abend noch mit	*Although he's ill, he's still coming with us tonight*
Er stand nach Kinkels Aussage „zwar in der Mitte, aber doch mehr nach rechts als nach links" (*Böll*)	*According to Kinkel he was 'politically in the centre, but tending all the same to the right rather than the left'*

In north Germany *wohl* is a possible alternative to *zwar* in this concessive sense, see 10.35.3, whilst in south and central Germany *schon* is used, see 10.30.1a.

10.36.2 *und zwar* is used in the sense of English 'namely' to specify what has just been mentioned

Mein Entschluss fiel auf dem neuen Flugplatz in Mexico-City, und zwar im letzten Augenblick (*Frisch*)	*My decision was taken at the new airport in Mexico City, (in actual fact) at the very last minute*
Ich habe die wichtigsten Museen besucht, und zwar das kunsthistorische, das naturhistorische und die Albertina	*I visited the most important museums, namely the Museum of Art History, the Museum of Natural History and the Albertina*

Expressions of time

Usage in TIME EXPRESSIONS is characteristically idiomatic in all languages, involving special uses and meanings. German usage can differ quite markedly from that of English in the way in which various aspects of time are referred to, and particular attention is paid to these differences in this chapter, where we treat the following aspects of time expressions in detail:

- **clock times** (section 11.1)
- the **days of the week**, **months** and **public holidays** (section 11.2)
- dates (section 11.3)
- the use of **cases** (i.e. the accusative and the genitive) in time adverbials (section 11.4)
- the use of **prepositions** in time adverbials (section 11.5)
- simple time **adverbs** (section 11.6)

11.1 Times of the clock

11.1.1 In everyday speech the twelve-hour clock is the norm

As in English, the twelve-hour clock is used in normal conversation, when reference is not being made to public events, official timetables and the like. The relevant forms are given in Table 11.1.

TABLE 11.1 *Clock times*

1.00	Es ist ein Uhr	*It's one (o'clock)*
	Es ist eins	
3.00	Es ist drei (Uhr)	*It's three (o'clock)*
3.05	fünf (Minuten) nach drei	*five (minutes) past three*
3.07	sieben Minuten nach drei	*seven minutes past three*
3.10	zehn (Minuten) nach drei	*ten (minutes) past three*
3.15	Viertel nach drei	*quarter past three*
	viertel vier (*south and east Germany*)	
3.20	zwanzig nach drei	*twenty past three*
	zehn vor halb vier	
3.25	fünf vor halb vier	*twenty-five past three*
3.30	halb vier	*half past three/half three*
3.35	fünf nach halb vier	*twenty-five to four*
3.40	zwanzig vor vier	*twenty to four*
	zehn nach halb vier	
3.45	Viertel vor vier	*quarter to four*
	dreiviertel vier (*south and east Germany*)	
3.47	dreizehn Minuten vor vier	*thirteen minutes to four*
3.50	zehn (Minuten) vor vier	*ten (minutes) to four*
3.55	fünf (Minuten) vor vier	*five (minutes) to four*

Note the striking difference between English and German when referring to the half hour: *halb vier* 'half past **three**'.

11.1.2 In official contexts the twenty-four-hour clock is used

This is the norm in timetables, for television and radio programmes, theatrical performances, official meetings, business hours, and in all other official contexts. Examples are given in Table 11.2:

TABLE 11.2 *The twenty-four-hour clock*

0.27	null Uhr siebenundzwanzig	*12.27 a.m.*
5.15	fünf Uhr fünfzehn	*5.15 a.m.*
10.30	zehn Uhr dreißig	*10.30 a.m.*
13.07	dreizehn Uhr sieben	*1.07 p.m.*
21.37	einundzwanzig Uhr siebenunddreißig	*9.37 p.m.*
24.00	vierundzwanzig Uhr	*12.00 midnight*

When these are used in speech, the word *Uhr* is only omitted in giving the full hours between 1 a.m. and noon, e.g. *Ihr Zug kommt um 9.00 an* (spoken: *um neun (Uhr)*). Otherwise the full forms, with *Uhr*, are used, e.g. *Die Vorstellung beginnt um 20.00* (spoken: *um zwanzig Uhr*), *um 20.15* (*um zwanzig Uhr fünfzehn*), *Der Zug fährt um 9.17* (spoken: *um neun Uhr siebzehn*), etc.

Even in everyday conversation, though, it is quite common for 'official' times to be given using the twenty-four hour clock. Thus one would say *Mein Zug fährt um 19.35* (i.e. *um neunzehn Uhr fünfunddreißig*), but it would be odd to say *Tante Käthe hat uns für fünfzehn Uhr dreißig zum Kaffee eingeladen* – you would say: *halb vier*.

11.1.3 Further phrases with clock times

Wie viel Uhr ist es?	*What's the time?*
Wie spät ist es? (coll.)	
Wie viel Uhr haben Sie?	*What time do you make it?*
Um wie viel Uhr kommt sie?	*What time is she coming?*
Sie kommt um halb drei	*She's coming at half-past two*
um drei Uhr nachts	*at three in the morning*
um neun Uhr vormittags	*at nine in the morning*
um zwölf Uhr mittags	*at twelve noon*
um drei Uhr nachmittags	*at three in the afternoon*
um sieben Uhr abends	*at seven in the evening*
um Mitternacht	*at midnight*
Es ist Punkt/genau neun (Uhr)	*It is exactly nine (o'clock)*
Es ist gerade halb	*It is just half-past*
Es ist ungefähr neun (Uhr)	*It's about nine (o'clock)*
Es ist (schon) neun Uhr vorbei	*It's gone nine o'clock*
Er kommt ungefähr um neun Uhr	*He's coming at about nine o'clock*
Er kam gegen neun (Uhr) an	*He came at about nine/just before nine*

NB: *gegen* is ambiguous with clock times, see 11.5.6.

11.2 Days of the week, months and public holidays

11.2.1 The days of the week

The names of the days of the week in German are shown in Table 11.3.

TABLE 11.3 *The days of the week*

Sonntag	Sunday	Donnerstag	Thursday
Montag	Monday	Freitag	Friday
Dienstag	Tuesday	Samstag/Sonnabend	Saturday
Mittwoch	Wednesday		

As the equivalent for 'Saturday', *Samstag* was originally the southern word and *Sonnabend* northern (roughly to the north of Frankfurt am Main). Since 1949 *Samstag* has come to be known and used more widely, especially in the former West Germany.

NB: For English 'on Sunday', etc. German uses *am Sonntag*, etc., see **4.5.3** and **11.5.1**.

11.2.2 The months

The German names of the **months** are shown in Table 11.4.

TABLE 11.4 *The months of the year*

Januar	January	Mai	May	September	September
Februar	February	Juni	June	Oktober	October
März	March	Juli	July	November	November
April	April	August	August	Dezember	December

NB: (i) In Austria, *Jänner* is always used for *Januar*, and, less commonly, *Feber* for *Februar*.
(ii) *Juni* and *Juli* are sometimes pronounced *Juno* and *Julei* to avoid confusion, especially on the telephone.
(iii) For English 'in January', etc., German has *im Januar*, etc., see 4.5.3 and 11.5.7

11.2.3 The major public holidays and religious festivals

Neujahr(stag)	*New Year's Day*
Dreikönigsfest/-tag	*Epiphany*
Rosenmontag	*Carnival Monday* (the day before Shrove Tuesday)
Aschermittwoch	*Ash Wednesday*
Gründonnerstag	*Maundy Thursday*
Karfreitag	*Good Friday*
Ostersonntag	*Easter Sunday*
Ostern	*Easter*
Ostermontag	*Easter Monday*
Fronleichnam	*Corpus Christi*
Pfingsten	*Whitsun*

Pfingstsonntag	*Whit Sunday*
Pfingstmontag	*Whit Monday*
(Christi) Himmelfahrt	*Ascension Day*
Mariä Himmelfahrt	*Assumption of the Virgin Mary (15th August)*
Tag der Deutschen Einheit	*Day of German Unity (3rd October)*
Allerheiligen	*All Saints' Day (1st November)*
Buß- und Bettag	*Day of Penitence and Prayer (Wednesday before the last Sunday before Advent)*
der Heilige Abend *or* Heiligabend	*Christmas Eve*
Weihnachten	*Christmas*
Erster Weihnachts(feier)tag	*Christmas Day*
Zweiter Weihnachts(feier)tag	*Boxing Day*
Silvester	*New Year's Eve*

NB: *Ostern*, *Pfingsten* and *Weihnachten* are usually treated as plurals, see 1.2.10b.

11.3 Dates

11.3.1 Ordinal numbers are used for the days of the month

i.e. *der fünfte April* 'the fifth of April'. This usage is similar to that in English, although there is no equivalent to English 'of'. In practice numbers are always used for them in writing, i.e. they are never written out as words:

Der Wievielte ist heute? ⎫	*What's the date today?*
Den Wievielten haben wir heute? ⎭	
Heute ist der 8.(*spoken:* achte) Mai ⎫	*Today is the eighth of May*
Wir haben heute den 8. (achten) Mai ⎭	
Er kam am 5.(*spoken:* fünften) Juni, 1993	*He came on the fifth of June, 1993*
am 5.6.93 (*spoken:* am fünften, sechsten, dreiundneunzig)	*on 5.6.93*

NB: As the last example shows, the day is given **before** the month in German. This corresponds to usage in British English, but it is the reverse of American practice.

11.3.2 Usage where the day of the week precedes the date

i.e. equivalents of 'Monday, the fifth of June'. There are three alternative ways of expressing this in German.

(i) with the day of the week and the date in the accusative case:

Wir fliegen **Montag, den 5. Juni**(,) nach Australien

(ii) with the day of the week preceded by *am* and followed by the date in the accusative case:

Wir fliegen **am Montag, den 5. Juni**(,) nach Australien

(iii) with the day of the week preceded by *am* and followed by the date in the dative case:

Wir fliegen **am Montag, dem 5. Juni**(,) nach Australien

11.3.3 Usage in letter headings

In private correspondence (i.e. where the address is not printed on the notepaper), the writer's address is not usually written out in full at the head of the letter, as is the usual British practice. Instead, just the town is given, followed by the date, which may be written in various ways, i.e.:

Siegen, **(den)** 5.6.02	Siegen, **am** 5.6.02
Siegen, **(den/d.)** 5. Juni 2002	Siegen, **im Juni 2002**

When writing a formal letter to an unknown person, especially for the first time, some Germans put their full name and address in the top left-hand corner of the letter and the town and date, as given above, in the top right-hand corner.

11.4 The accusative and genitive cases used in time adverbials

In certain contexts the **accusative** and **genitive** cases of nouns can be used adverbially, without a preposition, to express ideas of time.

11.4.1 Adverbial time phrases with the ACCUSATIVE

A noun denoting time can be used in the accusative case to express duration of time or a specific point in time or period of time.

(a) The accusative can be used to indicate a length of time

The period of time lies entirely in the past, present or future, and the accusative usually corresponds to English 'for '(see 11.5.5b). The word or phrase in the accusative may optionally be followed by *lang*, or, emphasising the duration, *über* or *hindurch*:

Ich war **einen Monat/drei Monate** (lang) in Kassel	*I was in Kassel for a month/for three months*
Dort blieb sie **viele Jahre** (lang)	*She stayed there for many years*
Jahre hindurch blieb er im Gefängnis	*He stayed in prison for years (on end)*
Ich bin jede Woche **einen Tag** (lang) in Kaiserslautern	*I am in Kaiserslautern one day every week*
Er lag **den ganzen Tag** (lang/über) im Bett	*He lay in bed the whole day/all day (long)*
den ganzen Sommer (lang)	*all summer, for the whole of the summer*
den ganzen Winter hindurch/über	*throughout the winter*
sein ganzes Leben (lang)	*all his life/for his whole life*
Wo warst du **die ganze Zeit**?	*Where were you the whole time?*
eine ganze Weile	*for quite a while*

(b) The accusative can be used to indicate a specific time

(i) Particularly in phrases denoting a period of time, corresponding to English 'last week', 'next year', etc.:

Einen Augenblick zuvor hätte sie ihn noch retten können	*A moment before she could still have saved him*
Er kommt **jeden Tag/jede Woche**	*He comes every day/every week*
Sie fährt **alle vierzehn Tage/alle paar Jahre** in die Schweiz	*She goes to Switzerland every two weeks/every few years*
Jede halbe Stunde kommt er vorbei	*Every half hour he comes past*
Wir besuchen sie **nächsten Dienstag/ kommenden Dienstag**	*We are visiting her next Tuesday*
Wir besuchen sie **kommende/nächste Woche**	*We are visiting her next week*
Wir werden **dieses Jahr** nicht verreisen	*We're not going away this year*
Sie ist **2001** wieder zur Vorsitzenden des Vereins gewählt worden	*In 2001 she was elected chair of the society again*
Ich sah sie **letzten Freitag/vorigen Freitag/vergangenen Freitag**	*I saw her last Friday*
Ich sah sie **letzte/vorige/vergangene Woche/den 5. Juni**	*I saw her last week/on the 5th of June (see 11.3.1)*

In many contexts a prepositional phrase (see 11.5) can be used as an alternative to a phrase in the accusative case, and the phrases below illustrate typical alternatives to the examples above:

am nächsten/kommenden Dienstag	*next Tuesday*
am letzten/vorigen/vergangenen Freitag	*last Friday*
in der nächsten/kommenden Woche	*next week*
in diesem Jahr	*this year*
im Jahre 2001	*in 2001*

In general, phrases with the accusative case are more frequent in everyday speech, whereas those with a preposition are rather commoner in writing. Further examples, with other prepositions:

Ich bin **Mittag** (for: um Mittag) wieder zu Hause	*I'll be back home at noon*
Fährst du **Ostern** (for: zu Ostern) zu deinen Eltern?	*Are you going to your parents at Easter?*
Sind Sie **das erste Mal** (for: zum ersten Mal) hier?	*Is this the first time you've been here?*

(ii) *Anfang*, *Mitte* and *Ende*, unlike their English equivalents, are used without a preposition, i.e. in the accusative, in time phrases:

Er ist **Anfang Januar**, **Mitte Januar**, **Ende Januar** gestorben	*He died at the beginning of January, in the middle of January, at the end of January*
Ich fahre schon **Anfang, Ende** nächster Woche	*I'm leaving at the beginning, at the end of next week*
Anfang 1990 fanden in der DDR die ersten freien Wahlen statt	*At the beginning of 1990 the first free elections took place in the GDR*

Note that if *Anfang* and *Ende* are used without a following time phrase, they are preceded by *am*, e.g. *am Anfang* 'at the beginning', *am Ende* 'at the end'.

11.4.2 Adverbial time phrases with the GENITIVE

The genitive case of nouns denoting time can refer to indefinite or habitual time.
These are now mainly set expressions, and only in formal literary language are
they commonly extended by adjectives:

eines Tages	*one day*
eines schönen Tages	*one fine day*
eines schönen Sommers (*Frisch*)	*one fine summer*
eines Sonntags	*one Sunday*
eines Morgens	*one morning*
eines Sonntagmorgens	*one Sunday morning*
eines nebligen Morgens (*Kolb*)	*one foggy morning*
eines Nachts	*one night*
dieser Tage	*in the next/last few days*

NB: Note the form *eines Nachts*, although *die Nacht* is feminine.

Some genitive phrases have become simple adverbs, and they are written with a
small initial letter:

morgens, vormittags	*in the mornings*
nachmittags, abends	*in the afternoons, in the evenings*
tags, nachts	*by day, at night*
dienstags, freitags	*on Tuesdays, on Fridays*
wochentags, werktags	*on weekdays, on working days*
donnerstagabends/donnerstags abends	*on Thursday evenings*
von morgens bis abends	*from morning till night*
morgens und abends	*morning and evening*

These adverbs are sometimes used to refer to single occasions, (e.g. *nachmittags* for
am Nachmittag), especially in south German usage:

Wir kamen dort **sonntags** auf dem Spaziergang vorüber (*Gaiser*)	*We came past there on Sunday during our walk*

NB: The adverbs *morgens*, *abends*, etc. originated from noun phrases in the genitive with the definite article, e.g. *des Morgens*, *des Abends*. These full phrases are still sometimes used in formal written German.

11.5 Adverbial time phrases with prepositions

This section treats the most common prepositions used with nouns denoting time.
Other uses of all prepositions are explained fully in Chapter 20.

11.5.1 *an* (+ dative)

an is used with nouns denoting days and parts of the day. It is always followed by
a noun in the dative case when referring to time, and the definite article is always
used with nouns in the singular, see 4.5.3. In most contexts it corresponds to

English 'in' or 'on':

am Tag	*in the daytime*
am Montag, **am** Dienstag, ...	*on Monday, on Tuesday, ...*
an Wochentagen	*on weekdays*
an besonderen Tagen	*on particular days*
am Morgen, **am** Nachmittag, **am** Abend	*in the morning, in the afternoon, in the evening*
am 31. Oktober (see 11.3.1)	*on the 31st of October*

Combinations of the days of the week and nouns denoting parts of the day are written together, e.g. *am Donnerstagabend*.

an is used with *Tag*, etc. even in contexts where English has no preposition:

am Tag nach seinem Tod	*the day after his death*
An diesem Morgen war er schlecht gelaunt	*That morning he was in a bad mood*
am anderen Tag, **am** anderen Morgen	*the next day, the next morning*

an occurs in a few other contexts:

Es ist **an** der Zeit, dass ...	*It is about time that ...*
am Anfang, **am** Ende (see **11.4.1b**)	*at the beginning, at the end*
gleich **am** Anfang	*at the very beginning*

NB: (i) *in* is used with *Nacht*, see 11.5.7a.
(ii) An accusative time phrase is often an alternative to a phrase with *an*, especially in spoken German, see 11.4.1b.

11.5.2 *auf* (+ accusative)

auf indicates a period of time from 'now', corresponding to English 'for'. It is always used with a following accusative case in time phrases. In this sense it is a less common alternative to *für*, see 11.5.5, found mainly in formal registers and set phrases:

Sie fährt **auf** vier Monate in die Schweiz	*She is going to Switzerland for three months*
auf unbestimmte Zeit	*indefinitely*
auf ewig, **auf** immer	*for ever, for good*

NB: *auf* is used idiomatically in *auf die Minute (genau)* '(precisely) to the minute'.

11.5.3 *bei*

bei is used chiefly with nouns which do not of themselves express time to indicate the 'time when x took/was taking/will take place':

bei seiner Geburt	*at his birth*
bei dieser Gelegenheit	*on this occasion*
bei der Probe	*during the rehearsal*

It is also used in a similar meaning in a few set phrases with nouns expressing time:

Paris **bei** Tag, London **bei** Nacht	*Paris by day, London by night*
bei Tagesanbruch	*at daybreak*
bei Einbruch der Nacht	*at nightfall*
bei Sonnenuntergang	*at sunset*

11.5.4 *bis*

bis indicates an end-point in time and can correspond to English 'until' <u>or</u> 'by'. It can only be used on its own with adverbs and simple time phrases like dates and the days of the week, and it is <u>never</u> followed by a definite article:

Bis 1945 lebte er in Wien	*Until 1945 he lived in Vienna*
Das Geschäft ist von 9 Uhr **bis** 18.30 Uhr durchgehend geöffnet	*The shop is open continuously from 9 a.m. until 6.30 p.m.*
Ich werde es **bis** heute Abend, **bis** Montag fertig haben	*I'll have it finished by tonight, by Monday*
bis nächste Woche, nächstes Jahr	*until next week, next year*
bis dahin/**bis** dann	*by then, until then*
bis jetzt, **bis** anhin (Sw.)	*up to now*
Bis dahin bin ich längst zurück	*I'll be back long before then*

With days of the week, months and dates, *bis* can be used with or without a following *zu* (<u>and</u> the definite article):

bis (zum) Freitag	*by/until Friday*
bis (zum) 11. Juni	*by/until the 11th of June*
Bis (zum) kommenden Montag kannst du mich hier erreichen	*You can reach me here till next Monday*

In other contexts *bis* <u>must</u> be followed by *zu* (or another appropriate preposition) with the definite article:

bis zum 18. Jahrhundert	*until/by the 18th century*
bis zu seinem Tode	*until his death*
bis zu den Ferien	*until the holidays*
bis vor kurzem	*until recently*
Bis vor zwei Wochen war er hier	*He was here until two weeks ago*
Ich arbeite **bis gegen** Mittag im Büro	*I'm working at the office until about noon*
Wir wollen es **bis auf** weiteres verschieben	*We'll postpone it for the present*
bis auf weiteres	*until further notice*
bis tief/spät **in** die Nacht hinein	*till late at night*

A date following a phrase with *bis* and a weekday is in the accusative, e.g. *bis Montag, **den** 5. September*. In other contexts, the date is in the dative, e.g. *bis morgen, **dem** 11. November*.

NB: (i)   *erst* is used for 'not until', e.g. *Er kommt erst am Montag*, see 10.12.2.
     (ii) *bis* is frequently used in colloquial leave-taking phrases, e.g. *Bis gleich! Bis bald! Bis morgen! Bis nächste Woche!*

11.5.5 *für* and English 'for'

(a) *für* indicates a period of time extending from 'now'
In this sense, it corresponds to English 'for':

Ich habe das Haus **für** sechs Monate gemietet	*I've rented the house for six months*
Am nächsten Tag fuhren wir **für** einen Monat in den Schwarzwald	*The next day we went to the Black Forest for a month*

√B: (i) *auf* (+ accusative) is a less common alternative in this meaning, used chiefly in formal registers and set expressions, see 11.5.2.
(ii) The use of *für* is idiomatic in *Tag für Tag* 'day by day'.

(b) English 'for' has the following main German equivalents
(i) a phrase in the accusative case, used to denote a period of time lying entirely in the past or future, e.g. *Er blieb **einen Monat (lang)** in Berlin* 'He remained in Berlin for a month'. See 11.4.1a for further details.

(ii) *seit* refers to a period of time which began in the past and extends up to the present, e.g. *Ich warte **seit einer Stunde** auf dich* 'I've been waiting for you for an hour'. See 11.5.9 for further details.

(iii) *für* (or more formal *auf*) to refer to a period of time extending from the present, as illustrated in (a) above.

In colloquial speech a phrase in the accusative is sometimes used instead of *für* to refer to a period of time extending from the present, e.g.: *Ich gehe **eine halbe Stunde (lang)** ins Cafe*. On the other hand, *für* is not unknown in the place of an accusative phrase to refer to a period of time lying entirely in the past or future, e.g. *Nur während der Wintermonate blieb er für längere Zeit an einem Ort (Bumke)*.

11.5.6 *gegen*

gegen means 'about' or 'towards'. It can be ambiguous, especially with clock times, as some Germans understand *gegen zwei Uhr* to mean 'at about two o'clock', while others interpret it as 'just before two o'clock'. In other phrases it usually has the meaning 'towards'. It is normally used without an article in time expressions:

gegen Mittag, **gegen** Abend	*towards noon, towards evening*
gegen Monatsende	*towards the end of the month*
gegen Ende des Jahrhunderts	*towards the end of the century*

11.5.7 *in* (+ dative)

in can refer to a specific period of time or a length of time. It is always used with the dative case in time expressions.

(a) *in* is used with most words denoting periods of time
It is used with all such words except those with which *an* is used (see 11.5.1), i.e. especially with the names of the months and seasons (<u>always</u> with a definite article, see 4.5.3), and with the following nouns:

der Augenblick	der Monat
die Epoche	die Nacht
das Jahr	die Woche
das Jahrhundert	das Zeitalter
die Minute	

Examples of use:

im Augenblick, **im** letzten Augenblick	*at the moment, at the last moment*
in der Frühe (*south German*)	*early in the morning*
im Jahre 2002	*in 2002*
in den letzten paar Jahren	*in the last few years*
in letzter Minute	*at the last moment*
im Mittelalter	*in the Middle Ages*
in der Nacht	*at night*
in der Nacht von Sonntag auf Montag	*during the night from Sunday to Monday*
in der Nacht zum/auf Montag	
zweimal **in** der Woche	*twice a week*
in der Woche vor Weihnachten	*in the week before Christmas*
in der Vergangenheit	*in the past*
in Zukunft	*in future*

The normal equivalent for English 'in 1988' in German is either *im Jahre 1988* or simply *1988*, with no preposition. However, the form *in 1988* is becoming widely used, in imitation of English usage, although many Germans consider this to be quite incorrect.

NB: For the use of *in* or *zu* with *Zeit* and *Stunde*, see 11.5.14b.

(b) *in* indicates a period of time within which something happens

Ich habe die Arbeit **in** zwei Stunden gemacht	*I did the work in two hours*
In zwei Jahren ist der Umsatz um 40 Prozent gestiegen	*In two years the turnover rose by 40%*
im Lauf(e) der Zeit	*in the course of time*
Das kann man **in** zwei Tagen schaffen	*You can do that in two days*

NB: *Das kann man an einem Morgen, Nachmittag, Abend schaffen.*

(c) *in* can indicate the time after which something happens or is done

Er kommt **in** einer halben Stunde zurück	*He's coming back in half an hour*
heute **in** acht Tagen	*a week today, in a week's time*
Sie fliegt **in** ein paar Tagen nach Sydney	*She's flying to Sydney in a few days (time)*

In some contexts, *in* can be ambiguous, like English 'in', so that *in drei Tagen* can mean 'in the course of three days' or 'in three days' time'. This ambiguity can be avoided by using *binnen* or *innerhalb*, which clearly mean 'within', e.g. *Der Rhein hat zum zweitenmal binnen 13 Monaten die Kölner Altstadt überschwemmt (SZ)*.

11.5.8 *nach*

nach usually corresponds to English 'after' or 'later':

Nach vielen Jahren ließen sie sich scheiden	*After many years they got divorced*
Einen Monat nach seiner Verhaftung wurde er freigelassen	*A month after his arrest he was released*
Nach Ostern studiert sie in Erlangen Chemie	*After Easter she's going to study chemistry in Erlangen*
bald nach Anfang des 17. Jahrhunderts	*soon after the beginning of the 17th century*
nach einer Weile	*after a while*
nach Wochen, Jahren	*weeks, years later*

11.5.9 *seit*

seit marks a period of time beginning in the past and continuing to the present or a more recent point in the past. It corresponds to English 'since' or 'for', see 11.5.5b:

Er ist **seit** drei Wochen hier	*He's been here for three weeks*
Ich wartete **seit** einer halben Stunde auf dem Marktplatz	*I had been waiting in the market-place for half an hour*
Seit wann bist du wieder zu Hause?	*Since when have you been back home?*
Seit seiner Krankheit habe ich ihn nicht mehr gesehen	*I haven't seen him again since his illness*
Erst **seit** kurzem gibt es Sondertarife nach Spanien	*There have only been special fares to Spain for a short while*

NB: (i) For the use of tenses with *seit* 'for', see 14.2.2 and 14.3.4a.
(ii) An accusative phrase with *schon* is a possible alternative to *seit* 'for', e.g. *Er ist schon drei Wochen hier*, see 10.30.5a.

11.5.10 *über* (+ accusative)

über occurs in a few time expressions in the sense of 'over'. It is always used with the accusative case in time expressions:

Sie ist **über** Nacht, **übers** Wochenende geblieben	*She stayed overnight, over the weekend*
über kurz oder lang	*sooner or later*

It can be used **after** a noun in the accusative (see 11.4.1a) to emphasise duration:

Sie blieb die ganze Nacht **über**	*She stayed the whole night*
die Schwäne, die den Winter **über** geblieben waren (*Surminski*)	*The swans which had stayed the whole winter*

11.5.11 *um*

um is used with clock times (= 'at') and to express approximation.

(a) *um* **corresponds to English 'at' with clock times**
e.g. *um vier Uhr* 'at four o'clock', etc., see 11.1.3.

(b) With other time words *um* expresses approximation

It corresponds to English 'around' or 'about' and is often used with *herum* following the noun:

um Mitternacht (herum)	*around midnight*
um Ostern (herum)	*round about Easter time*
um 1890 (herum)	*around 1890*
die Tage **um** die Sommersonnenwende (herum)	*the days either side of the summer solstice*

NB: *um diese Zeit* is ambiguous. It can mean 'at this time' or 'around this time'. Adding *herum*, i.e. *um diese Zeit herum*, makes it clear that the second meaning is intended.

(c) Idiomatic time phrases with *um*

Stunde **um** Stunde	*hour after hour*
einen Tag **um** den anderen	*one day after the other*

11.5.12 *von*

von indicates a starting-point in time. It corresponds to English 'from' and is often linked with a following *an*:

Von 1976 an lebte sie in Rostock	*From 1976 she lived in Rostock*
Von kommendem Montag an kostet das Benzin 10 Cent mehr pro Liter	*From next Monday petrol will cost 10 cents a litre more*
von Anfang an	*(right) from the start*
von neun Uhr an	*from nine o'clock (on)*
von nun an	*from now on*
von der Zeit an	*from then on*
von Anfang bis Ende	*from beginning to end*
von heute auf morgen	*from one day to the next, overnight*
von vornherein	*from the outset, from the first*
von jeher/**von** alters her	*from time immemorial, always*
von Jugend auf	*from his (my, etc.) youth on*
von Zeit zu Zeit	*from time to time*

NB: *ab* can be used in the sense 'from' in time expressions, e.g. *ab Montag den/dem 5. August, ab nächste(r) Woche*, see 20.2.10a.

11.5.13 *vor* (+ dative)

vor corresponds to English 'ago' or 'before'. It is always used with the dative case in time expressions:

vor einem Jahr, **vor** mehreren Jahren	*a year ago, several years ago*
vor langer Zeit, **vor** einiger Zeit	*a long time ago, some time ago*
vor kurzem	*not long ago, recently* (see 11.6.5)
gestern **vor** acht Tagen	*a week ago yesterday*
die Verhältnisse **vor** der Krise	*the conditions before the crisis*

In many contexts *her* can be used in the sense of English 'ago', e.g. *Es ist schon lange, einen Monat her* 'It's a long time, a month ago'. *Wie lange ist es (schon) her?* 'How long ago is it?', see 7.2.5e.

11.5.14 *während*

während usually corresponds to English 'during':

Sie hat **während** der Aufführung geschlafen	*She slept during the performance*
während der Wintermonate (*Bumke*)	*during the winter months*
während des letzten Urlaubs, den sie in Italien verbracht hatten (*Walser*)	*during the last holiday which they had spent in Italy*

Unlike English 'during', *während* is not used with time words like *Tag*, *Abend*, *Nacht* or *Jahr* if these simply have a definite article with them. Compare:

am Tag, **am** Abend, **in** der Nacht	*during the day, during the evening, during the night*

However, *während* can be used with these nouns if there is an adjective with them, or if they are used with a determiner other than the definite article:

Während der letzten Nacht ist der Junge zweimal aufgewacht	*During the previous night the boy woke up twice*
während eines einzigen Tages	*during/in the course of a single day*

In effect, *während* indicates a period rather than simply duration, and it can be used in this sense in contexts where 'during' is not possible (or would be unusual) in English:

während der ganzen Nacht	*throughout the night*
Andere Vogelarten wie der Star können **während** mindestens zweier Jahre Neues dazulernen (*NZZ*)	*Other species of birds like starlings can learn new things over the course of at least two years*
Während dreier Jahre verbrachten sie den Urlaub auf Sylt	*Three years running they spent their holidays on Sylt*

11.5.15 *zu*

zu is used with a number of time words, i.e.:

(a) *zu* with the major festivals

zu Weihnachten	zu Pfingsten
zu Ostern	zu Neujahr

NB: In south German, *an* is often used rather than *zu* with these festivals. In colloquial speech, there may be no preposition, e.g. *Sie kommt Weihnachten*.

(b) Both *zu* and *in* are used with *Zeit* and *Stunde*

(i) *zu* is used in contexts denoting one or more specific points or limited periods of time:

zur Zeit der letzten Wahlen	*at the time of the last election*
zu der Zeit, **zu** dieser Zeit	*at that time*
zu der Zeit, als du hier warst	*at the time when you were here*
zu einer anderen Zeit	*at some other time*
zu jeder Zeit	*at all times, at any time*

zu jeder Tageszeit	*at any time of the day*
zu gewissen Zeiten	*at certain times*
zur gewohnten Zeit	*at the usual time*
gerade noch **zur** rechten Zeit	*in the nick of time*
zu gleicher Zeit	*at the same time, simultaneously*
Zu meiner Zeit war das alles anders	*In my time that was all different*
zu dieser Stunde	*at this hour*
zu jeder Stunde	*at any time*
zur selben Stunde	*at the same hour*
zu später Stunde (lit.)	*at a late hour*

NB: (also) *zu diesem Zeitpunkt* 'at this point in time'.

(ii) *in* is used to denote a period within or after which something occurs, or in phrases which are felt to denote duration rather than a point or limited period in time:

In all **der** Zeit (or: In der ganzen Zeit) haben wir sie nicht gesehen	*In all that time we didn't see her*
In kurzer Zeit war er wieder da	*In a short time he was back again*
In unserer Zeit tut man das nicht mehr	*In our times that is no longer done*
in einer Zeit, in der die Städte wachsen	*at a time when towns are growing*
in einer solchen Zeit wie heute	*at a time like the present*
in früheren Zeiten	*in earlier times*
in künftigen Zeiten	*in times to come*
in der ersten Zeit	*at first*
in ruhigen Stunden	*in peaceful hours*
in elfter Stunde	*at the eleventh hour*

(c) *zu* **is used with** *Mal*

e.g.: *zum ersten Mal, zum zehnten Mal,* etc. (see 9.4.3)

11.6 Adverbs of time

Adverbs of time can indicate a **point in time** (e.g. *damals*), **duration** (e.g. *lange*) or **frequency** (e.g. *oft*). A selection of commonly used German time adverbs listed in terms of these categories is given in 11.6.1. Sections 11.6.2–11.6.5 deal with some time adverbs where German and English usage does not correspond.

11.6.1 Commonly used adverbs of time

Further information on some of these adverbs is given where indicated. Note that the 'present' in terms of time adverbs can sometimes be a point of reference in the past or future rather than the actual present moment.

(a) indicating a point in time
(i) referring to the present:

augenblicklich	*at the moment*	jetzt	*now*
derzeit	*at present*	momentan	*at present*
gegenwärtig	*at present, currently*	nun (10.25)	*now*
gleichzeitig	*at the same time*	vorerst	*for the moment*
heuer (S. G.)	*this year*	zugleich	*at the same time*
heute (11.6.2)	*today*	zurzeit	*at present*
heutzutage	*nowadays*		

(ii) referring to the past (or 'previously'):

damals (11.6.3a)	*then,*	kürzlich (11.6.5)	*a short time ago*
	at that time	neuerdings,	*recently*
ehedem (arch.)	*formerly*	neulich (11.6.5)	
ehemals (form.)	*formerly*	seinerzeit	*at the time*
einst	*once*	soeben	*just (now)*
früher	*formerly,*	unlängst (11.6.5)	*recently*
	previously	vordem (lit.)	*in olden times*
gerade	*just (now)*	vorher (11.6.4)	*before(hand)*
gestern (11.6.2)	*yesterday*	vorhin	*just now*
jüngst (elev.)	*lately*	zuvor (11.6.4)	*before(hand)*

(iii) referring to the future (or 'subsequently'):

alsbald (lit.)	*straightway*	hernach (form.)	*after(wards)*
augenblicklich	*at once*	morgen (11.6.2)	*tomorrow*
bald	*soon*	nachher (11.6.4)	*after(wards)*
danach (11.6.4)	*afterwards*	nächstens (8.4.4)	*shortly*
darauf (11.6.4)	*after that*	sofort, sogleich	*at once, immediately*
daraufhin	*after that*	später	*later*
demnächst	*soon*	vorher, zuvor	*before(hand)*
einst	*once*	(11.6.4)	
gleich (10.16)	*at once*		

(b) indicating duration

bisher, bislang	*up to now, hitherto*	nunmehr (elev.)	*from now/then on*
fortan (elev.)	*henceforth*	seither, seitdem	*since then*
indessen (form.),	*meanwhile*	solange	*meanwhile*
inzwischen		unterdessen	*in the meantime*
künftig	*in future*	vorerst,	*temporarily, for the*
kurz	*for a short time*	vorläufig,	*time being, for the*
lange	*for a long time*	vorübergehend	*moment*
längst (8.4.4a)	*for a long time*	währenddem (inf.),	*meanwhile*
mittlerweile	*in the meantime*	währenddessen	
momentan	*for an instant*	zeitweilig	*temporarily*

lang can be suffixed to other time words to indicate duration, e.g. *stundenlang, monatelang, jahrelang*'for hours, months, years (on end)', see also 11.4.1a.

(c) indicating frequency

abermals	*once more*	nochmals	*again*
bisweilen (elev.)	*now and then*	oft, öfters	*often*
gelegentlich	*occasionally*	selten	*seldom, rarely*
häufig	*frequently*	ständig	*continually*
immer	*always*	stets	*always*
irgendwann (5.5.11b)	*sometime*	unaufhörlich	*incessantly*
je	*ever*	wieder, wiederum	*again*
jederzeit	*at any time*	(elev.)	
manchmal	*sometimes*	zeitweise	*at times*
mehrmals	*repeatedly*	zuweilen	*from time to time*
meistens (8.4.4b)	*mostly*	zwischendurch	*in between times*
mitunter	*now and then*		
nie, niemals,	*never*		
nimmer (lit.)			

11.6.2 *gestern*, *heute* and *morgen*

These are used in conjunction with words indicating periods of the day to give the equivalent of English 'last night', 'this afternoon', etc.:

gestern Morgen	*yesterday morning*
gestern Abend	*last night* (before bedtime)
vorgestern	*the day before yesterday*
heute Nacht	*tonight* (after bedtime), *last night* (after bedtime)
heute Morgen/heute früh	*this morning*
heute Vormittag	*this morning* (after breakfast)
heute Nachmittag	*this afternoon*
heute Abend	*this evening, tonight* (before bedtime)
morgen früh	*tomorrow morning*
morgen Vormittag	*tomorrow morning* (after breakfast)
übermorgen	*the day after tomorrow*

11.6.3 German equivalents of English 'then'

(a) *damals* **refers to past time**
i.e. meaning 'at that time':

Sie war **damals** sehr arm	*She was very poor, then*
damals, vor dem großen Kriege (*Roth*)	*at that time, before the Great War*

(b) *dann* **is used for other meanings of 'then' referring to time**
especially in the sense of 'after that' with a series of actions or events:

Dann fuhr er weg	*Then he left*
Erst bist du an der Reihe, **dann** ich	*First it's your turn, then mine*
Wenn er dir schreibt, **dann** musst du es deiner Mutter sagen	*If he writes to you, then you'll have to tell your mother*
Und wenn sie kommt, was machst du **dann**?	*And if she comes, what will you do then?*

dann is not used after a preposition, cf.: *bis dahin* 'till then, by then', *seither, seitdem* 'since then', *von da an* 'from then on', *vorher, zuvor* 'before then' (see also 11.6.4a).

(c) **To intensify a question, the German equivalent is** *denn*
e.g. *Was ist* **denn** *daran so komisch?* See 10.6.1 for further details.

11.6.4 German equivalents of English 'before' and 'after'

(a) *vorher* and *zuvor* **are the commonest equivalents of 'before'**
Both can be used with reference to past **or** future time:

Ich war ein Jahr **vorher/zuvor** da gewesen	*I had been there a year before*
Ich muss **vorher/zuvor** noch telephonieren	*I've got to make a phone call before then*
Er hatte uns am Tag **vorher/zuvor** besucht	*He had been to visit us the day before*
einige Zeit **vorher/zuvor**	*some time previously*

Referring to time up to the present moment, *früher* or *zuvor* is used (or, in a negative context, *noch*):

Sie hätten es mir **früher/zuvor** sagen sollen	*You ought to have told me before*
Ich habe sie **nie zuvor/noch nie** gesehen	*I've never seen her before*

(b) *danach* **or** *nachher* **are the usual equivalents for 'after' (or 'later')**
darauf is also often used after words expressing a period of time:

Ich habe sie einen Monat **danach/nachher** gesehen	*I saw her a month after/later*
Kurz **danach**/Kurz **nachher**/Kurz **darauf** sah ich sie wieder	*I saw her a short time after/ shortly afterwards*
Am Tag **darauf/danach** gingen wir ins Theater	*The day after we went to the theatre*
Das werde ich dir **nachher** erzählen	*I'll tell you that afterwards*

im Nachhinein and *hinterher* are also frequently used for 'afterwards'.

11.6.5 German equivalents for English 'recent(ly)'

German has no single word with the range of meaning of English 'recent(ly)'. The following are the main equivalents, and the choice depends on the precise meaning to be expressed:

vor kurzem/kürzlich	*at a point in time not long ago*
unlängst/jüngst (*both* elev., southern)	
neulich/letztens (elev.)	*at a point in time not long ago* (recalled well by speaker and relevant to the present)
neuerdings	*up to and including the present* (sth. which started recently)
letzthin	*recently* (a point in the recent past or during a period up to the present)
in letzter Zeit	*latterly* (over a period of time up to and including the present)
seit kurzem	*not for very long* (continuing to the present)

As the above are all adverbial, they have to be used in paraphrases, etc. to give German equivalents for the English adjective 'recent', e.g.:

auf der **kürzlich stattgefundenen** Konferenz	*at the recent conference*
bei unserer Begegnung **neulich**	*at our recent meeting*
als er **vor kurzem** krank war	*during his recent illness*
eine **erst kürzlich eingeführte** Neuerung	*a (very) recent innovation*
sein **neuestes** Buch	*his most recent book*

Some other equivalents:

bis vor kurzem	*until recently*
Ich habe ihn noch später gesehen als Sie	*I have seen him more recently than you*
Kurt hat sie zuletzt gesehen	*Kurt has seen her most recently/just recently*

12

Verbs: conjugation

Chapters 12–18 deal with the forms of VERBS in German and their uses:

- Chapter 12: the forms of verbs (their CONJUGATION)
- Chapter 13: the uses of the INFINITIVE (e.g. *machen, schlafen*) and the PARTICIPLES (e.g. *machend, schlafend; gemacht, geschlafen*)
- Chapter 14: the uses of the TENSES
- Chapter 15: the uses of the PASSIVE
- Chapter 16: the uses of the MOODS (the *imperative* and the *subjunctive*)
- Chapter 17: the MODAL AUXILIARY verbs (e.g. *dürfen, können, müssen*)
- Chapter 18: the VALENCY of verbs (i.e. which complements they need to make up a sentence)

Verbs typically express actions (like *gehen, schreiben, stehlen*), processes (like *gelingen, sterben, wachsen*) or states (like *bleiben, leben, wohnen*). They constitute the core of the sentence and are usually accompanied by one or more noun phrases, i.e. the subject and the other complements of the verb:

Subject	Verb	Complement(s)
Der Lehrer	redet	Unsinn
Ihre Freundin	unterrichtet	die deutsche Sprache
Die Mutter	gibt	ihrer Tochter die Mappe
Der alte Mann	wartet	auf seine Frau

In German, verbs change their form (typically adding endings or changing the vowel) to express various grammatical ideas like TENSE, e.g. present and past; MOOD, e.g. the imperative and the subjunctive; and PERSON and NUMBER, e.g. *du* (second person singular), *wir* (first person plural). These are known as the grammatical categories of the verb. All the different forms of each verb make up its CONJUGATION. This chapter gives details on the conjugation of all regular and irregular verbs in German, as follows:

- Basic principles of the **conjugation** of verbs in German (section 12.1)
- The conjugation of the simple **present** and **past** tenses and the imperative (section 12.2)
- The conjugation of the compound tenses: **future** and **perfect** (section 12.3)
- The conjugation of the **passive** (section 12.4)
- The conjugation of the **subjunctive** (section 12.5)

The forms of all STRONG and IRREGULAR verbs are given in Table 12.12, at the end of the chapter.

12.1 Verb conjugation

12.1.1 The forms and grammatical categories of German verbs

German verbs are usually given in dictionaries in the form of the INFINITIVE, which ends in *-en* or *-n*, e.g. *kaufen, singen, wandern*. If we take off this *-(e)n*, we obtain the basic core of the verb, which is called the ROOT, e.g. *kauf-, sing-, wander-*. The root carries the basic meaning of the verb (i.e. 'buy', 'sing' 'wander', etc.). By adding endings to this root, or by changing the vowel, we can show different grammatical categories, i.e.:

(a) Indicate the person and number of the SUBJECT of the verb
There is a particularly close link between a verb and its subject. This is indicated in German by adding special endings to the verb for each PERSON (i.e. **first**, **second** or **third** person, see Chapter 3) in the **singular** and **plural**.

	First person	Second person	Third person
Singular	**ich** kaufe	**du** singst	**er/sie/es** wandert
Plural	**wir** kaufen	**ihr** singt	**sie** wandern

In this way verbs are said to **agree** with the subject. Those forms of verbs which have an ending in AGREEMENT with the subject like this are known as FINITE VERBS. For further details on the agreement between subject and verb, see 12.1.4.

(b) Indicate the time of the action, process or event expressed by the verb
We can add endings to the root of the verb (or change the vowel of some verbs) to show time:

Present tense	Past tense
ich kaufe	ich kaufte
du singst	du sangst
er wandert	er wanderte

The various forms of the verb which express time relationships are known as the TENSES of the verb. German, like English, has two SIMPLE TENSES (i.e. with a single word), the PRESENT tense and the PAST tense, as illustrated above. The formation of these simple tenses is explained in section 12.2.

The other tenses are COMPOUND TENSES, formed by using the AUXILIARY VERBS *haben, sein* or *werden*, together with the PAST PARTICIPLE or the INFINITIVE of the verb:

Perfect tense	Pluperfect tense	Future tense
ich **habe** gekauft	er **hatte** gekauft	sie **werden** kaufen
ich **habe** gesungen	er **hatte** gesungen	sie **werden** singen
ich **bin** gewandert	er **war** gewandert	sie **werden** wandern

The formation of the compound tenses is explained in section 12.3, and the use of the tenses in German is treated in detail in Chapter 14.

(c) Show whether we are dealing with a fact, a possibility or a command
This is shown by the MOOD of the verb. German has three moods:

(i) The INDICATIVE mood states a **fact**
(ii) The SUBJUNCTIVE mood indicates a **possibility** or a **report**
(iii) The IMPERATIVE mood expresses a **command**

Indicative	Subjunctive	Imperative
Sie kauft	Sie kauft	kaufe!
Sie singt	Sie sänge	singt!
Sie sind gewandert	Sie würden wandern	wandern Sie!

The indicative is the usual mood for statements or questions, and all the information about verb conjugation in sections 12.2–12.4 relates to the indicative mood. The formation of the subjunctive in German is explained in section 12.5, and its use is dealt with in Chapter 16. The use of the imperative is explained in section 16.2, together with other ways of expressing commands.

(d) Change the relationship between the elements in the sentence
Using a different VOICE of the verb, i.e. the ACTIVE VOICE or the PASSIVE VOICE, allows different elements to appear as the subject of the verb and thus relates the action from a different perspective. German has two forms of the passive voice, formed by using the past participle with the auxiliary verb *werden* (the *werden*-passive), or the auxiliary verb *sein* (the *sein*-passive):

Active	werden-passive	sein-passive
Sie **zerstören** die Stadt	Die Stadt **wird zerstört**	Die Stadt **ist zerstört**
Er **kaufte** das Buch	Das Buch **wurde gekauft**	Das Buch **war gekauft**

The conjugation of the passive forms is treated in section 12.4, and their uses are explained in Chapter 15.

(e) Construct the non-finite forms of the verb
Some forms of the verb do not show agreement with the subject of the verb, unlike the finite forms dealt with in (a) above. These are called the NON-FINITE forms of the verb, i.e. the INFINITIVE, the PRESENT PARTICIPLE and the PAST PARTICIPLE.

Infinitive	Present participle	Past participle
kaufen	kaufend	gekauft
singen	singend	gesungen
wandern	wandernd	gewandert

The non-finite parts of the verb can be combined with auxiliary verbs to form the compound tenses and the passive voice (see 12.3–4). They also have some other uses which are treated in Chapter 13.

12.1.2 How a verb is conjugated depends on whether it is weak or strong

There are two main types of conjugation for verbs in German, which are called WEAK and STRONG. The main difference between them is the way in which the **past tense** is formed:

(a) WEAK verbs form their past tense by adding *-te* to the root:

kauf-en → kauf-**te**
mach-en → mach-**te**
wander-n → wander-**te**

(b) STRONG verbs form their past tense by changing the vowel of the root:

greif-en → gr**i**ff
flieg-en → fl**o**g
sing-en → s**a**ng

Most German verbs are weak; they are the regular verbs. There are far fewer strong verbs, but most of them are very common. There is no way of telling from the infinitive of a verb whether it is weak or strong, so that a foreign learner needs to remember which verbs are strong, and learn their most important forms, the principal parts, i.e. the infinitive, the past tense and the past participle. All the other forms can be built up from these three basic forms.

Infinitive	Past tense	Past participle
bleiben	blieb	geblieben
singen	sang	gesungen
fahren	fuhr	gefahren

The principal parts of all strong and irregular verbs are given in Table 12.12.

In practice, the vowel changes in most strong verbs (called *Ablaut* in German) follow a small number of recurrent patterns. It is useful to be aware of these patterns, which are shown in Table 12.1.

TABLE 12.1 *Vowel changes in strong verbs*

Vowel change	Example
ei – ie – ie	bleiben – blieb – geblieben
ei – i – i	greifen – griff – gegriffen
i – a – u	singen – sang – gesungen
i – a – o	schwimmen – schwamm – geschwommen
ie – o – o	fliegen – flog – geflogen
e – a – o	helfen – half – geholfen
e – a – e	geben – gab – gegeben
e – o – o	fechten – focht – gefochten
a – u – a	fahren – fuhr – gefahren
a – ie – a	fallen – fiel – gefallen

12.1.3 There are a few other irregular verbs

They can be divided into four groups:

(a) A few irregular weak verbs have vowel changes (and sometimes also consonant changes) in the past tense and the past participle
These changes are in addition to the usual endings of weak verbs:

kennen – k**a**nnte – gek**a**nnt   rennen – r**a**nnte – ger**a**nnt
bringen – br**ach**te – gebr**ach**t   denken – d**ach**te – ged**ach**t

The principal parts of these irregular weak verbs are given in Table 12.12.

(b) A few irregular strong verbs have consonant changes as well as vowel changes in the past tense and the past participle

> gehen – **g**ing – geg**ang**en   leid-en – **litt** – ge**litt**en
> stehen – **st**and – gestand**en**   zieh-en – z**og** – gez**og**en

The principal parts of these irregular strong verbs are given in Table 12.12.

(c) The modal auxiliary verbs and *wissen*

The six modal auxiliary verbs *dürfen, können, mögen, müssen, sollen, wollen* and the verb *wissen* 'know' have an irregular present tense with no ending *-t* in the third person singular and, in most cases, a different vowel in the singular and plural. Most of them also change the vowel in the past tense and the past participle:

> **können** – er kann, wir können – konnte – gekonnt
> **müssen** – er muss, wir müssen – musste – gemusst
> **wissen** – er weiß, wir wissen – wusste – gewusst

All the forms of these verbs in the indicative tenses are given in Table 12.4.

(d) The verbs *haben, sein* and *werden*

These three verbs are wholly irregular. Aside from their basic meanings, i.e. *haben* 'have', *sein* 'be', *werden* 'become', they are used as AUXILIARY VERBS to form the compound tenses and the passives. All the indicative forms of these verbs are given in Table 12.3.

12.1.4 Agreement of subject and finite verb

As explained in 12.1.1a, the finite verb has endings in agreement with the person and number (i. .e. singular or plural) of the subject.

	First person	Second person	Third person
Singular	ich kaufe	du singst	er/sie/es wandert
Plural	wir kaufen	ihr singt	sie/Sie wandern

NB: The 'polite' form of the second person (with *Sie*) always has the same ending as the third person plural.

In some constructions there can be uncertainty about what the verb agrees with.

(a) If the subject of the verb is a clause, the verb has the third person singular endings
The clause can be a subordinate clause (see Chapter 19) or an infinitive clause (see 13.2.3):

> Dass sie nichts tut, **ärgert** mich sehr   *I'm very annoyed that she isn't doing anything*
> Sie wiederzusehen **hat** mich gefreut   *I was pleased to see her again*

(b) If the verb *sein* is followed by a noun in the plural, the verb has a plural ending even if the subject is singular

> Mein Lieblingsobst **sind** Kirschen   *My favourite fruit is cherries*

This is in particular the case with *es, das* and other neuter pronouns (see 3.6.2b, 5.1.1h and 5.3.1a):

Was **sind** das für Vögel?	*What kind of birds are those?*
– Es **sind** Storche	*– They are storks*
Sind es deine Handschuhe?	*Are they your gloves?*
Welches **sind** deine Handschuhe?	*Which are your gloves?*

(c) If the subject consists of a series of linked nouns, the verb is usually plural

Helmut und sein Bruder **sind** gekommen	*Helmut and his brother have come*
Vater, Mutter, Tochter **saßen** beim Essen	*Father, mother and daughter were sitting down to a meal*

However, there are some constructions where it is possible to use a singular ending (although this is still less common than the plural ending):

(i) if the subject follows the verb:

Im Osten **winkte** das Völkerschlacht-denkmal, die Türme und die Essen von Leipzig	*In the east, the war memorial, the towers and chimneys of Leipzig beckoned*

(ii) if the parts of the subject are seen as separate or distinct (this is especially the case if the nouns are qualified by *jeder* or *kein*):

Wenig später **wurde** heiße Suppe und Weißbrot ausgeteilt	*A little later hot soup and white bread were distributed*
Ihm **konnte** kein Arzt und kein Apotheker mehr helfen	*No doctor and no chemist could help him now*

(iii) if the linked nouns are felt to form a single whole:

Diese Haltung und Miene **war** ihm eigentümlich (*Th. Mann*)	*This attitude and facial expression were peculiar to him*

(iv) with the conjunctions *sowie* and *sowohl . . . als/wie* (*auch*):

Sowohl Manfred als auch seine Frau **war** einverstanden	*Both Manfred and his wife agreed*

(d) If the subject consists of nouns linked by a disjunctive conjunction (= 'or') the verb is usually in the singular

(i) This applies in particular to (*entweder . . .*) *oder* and *nicht (nur) . . ., sondern (auch)*

Entweder Hans oder Karl **wird** mir helfen	*Either Hans or Karl will help me*
Mit dieser Lösung **wäre** nicht nur die Mehrheit der Partei, sondern auch Erhard selbst zufrieden gewesen (*Spiegel*)	*Not only the majority of the party but Erhard too would have been satisfied with this solution*

A plural verb is sometimes used with these, especially if the nearest noun is plural, e.g.: *Entweder Karl oder seine Brüder* **werden** *mir helfen*

(ii) With *weder … noch*, either singular or plural is possible, but the plural is more frequent:

> In Bonn **waren** sich weder Kabinett   *In Bonn neither the cabinet nor the*
> noch Regierungsfraktionen einig   *governing parties were agreed*
> (*Zeit*)

(e) If a coordinated subject includes a pronoun, the verb has the ending which corresponds to the combination
(i) This applies in particular with the conjunction *und* and its synonyms:

> Mein Mann und ich (= wir) **trennten**   *My husband and I separated in the spring*
> uns im Frühjahr (*Spiegel*)
> Du und sie (= ihr) **könnt** damit   *You and she can be satisfied with that*
> zufrieden sein
> Sowohl sie als auch er (= sie) **haben**   *Both she and he were pleased about it*
> sich darüber gefreut

These combinations can sound artificial, especially if the second person plural *ihr* is involved, and they are often avoided by adding the appropriate plural pronoun, e.g.: *Ihr könnt damit zufrieden sein, du und sie.*

(ii) With disjunctive conjunctions, the verb usually agrees with the nearest pronoun, whether this precedes or follows:

> Entweder du oder ich **werde** es ihnen sagen
> Nicht ich, sondern ihr **sollt** es ihnen sagen
> Dann **werden** nicht nur sie, sondern auch ihr es ihnen sagen
> Ich, nicht du, **sollst** es ihnen sagen

These, too, can sound unnatural, and can be avoided by repeating the verb or splitting one pronoun off, e.g.:

> Entweder du **sagst** es ihnen, oder ich **sage** es ihnen
> Entweder du **sollt** es ihr sagen **oder ich**

(f) Usage with expressions of measure or quantity
(i) With singular nouns of indefinite quantity followed by a plural noun, the verb is normally plural:

> Ein Dutzend Eier **kosten** 2 Euro   *A dozen eggs cost 2 euro*
> Es **waren** eine Menge Leute da   *There were a lot of people there*
> Eine Gruppe von Studenten **standen**   *A group of students were standing in front*
> vor dem Bahnhof   *of the station*
> Die Hälfte meiner Gedanken **waren** bei   *Half my thoughts were with her*
> ihr (*Grass*)

This is the predominant usage in speech and common in writing. Some authorities continue to insist that the use of the singular (e.g. *ein Dutzend Eier* **kostet** *2 Euro*) is still current, but it is in practice unusual.

(ii) With singular measurement words followed by a plural noun, the verb can be either singular or plural:

> Ein Kilogramm Kartoffeln **reicht/reichen** aus
> Ein Kubikmeter Ziegelsteine **wiegt/wiegen** fast zwei Tonnen

(iii) With nouns of measurement used with a numeral or with a plural determiner, the verb is normally in the plural, although in such cases, masculine and neuter nouns of measurement have no plural ending (see 1.2.14):

Mehrere Liter Benzin **waren** verschüttet	*Several litres of petrol were spilled*
Fünf Kilo **kosten** fünfzehn Euro	*Five kilograms cost 15 euro*
Dafür **wurden** mir tausend Euro angeboten	*I was offered a thousand euros for it*
80 Prozent der Bevölkerung **waren** dagegen	*80% of the population was opposed to it*

However, a singular ending is often used in such contexts, especially in spoken German, as the quantity is envisaged as a single whole: *Zwanzig Euro **ist**/**sind** zu viel; 80 Prozent der Bevölkerung **war**/**waren** dagegen*.

(g) Singular collective nouns are used with a singular verb
This contrasts strongly with English usage, where the plural is the norm or at least frequent:

Die ganze Familie **ist** verreist	*The whole family have/has gone away*
Unsere Mannschaft **hat** wieder verloren	*Our team have/has lost again*
Die Polizei **kommt** gleich	*The police are coming straight away*
Die Regierung **hat** es beschlossen	*The government have/has decided it*

12.2 The simple present and past tenses, the non-finite forms and the imperative

These forms make up the basic conjugation of the German verb. They are all single words, formed by adding different prefixes or suffixes to the verb root, or by changing the form of the root, especially by altering the vowel.

12.2.1 Weak and strong verbs

WEAK and STRONG verbs differ mainly in the way in which they form the PAST TENSE and the PAST PARTICIPLE (their 'principal parts'). Weak verbs have the ending *-te* in the past tense and *-t* in the past participle, whilst strong verbs change the vowel of the root in the past tense and have the ending *-en* (sometimes with a further change of vowel) in the past participle.

Otherwise, both weak and strong verbs have the same endings marking person and number in the two simple tenses and in the imperative mood, and the same affixes in the non-finite forms. Table 12.2 gives these forms for typical weak and strong verbs. The principal parts of all strong and irregular verbs are given in Table 12.12.

There are a few regular variations to the pattern of endings for strong and weak verbs as given in Table 12.2:

(a) Verbs whose root ends in *-d* or *-t*, or in *-m* or *-n* after a consonant
These verbs add *-e-* before the endings *-t*, *-st*, and the *-te* of the past tense of weak verbs: *du arbeitest, er arbeitet, er arbeitete, gearbeitet*, etc. The full forms of *warten* 'wait' are given in Table 12.2 as illustration. Other examples:

TABLE 12.2 *Conjugation of the verb in the simple tenses*

		Weak		**Strong**
Infinitive	kaufen	warten	wandern	singen
Present participle	kaufend	wartend	wandernd	singend
Past participle	gekauft	gewartet	gewandert	gesungen
Present tense	ich kaufe	ich warte	ich wand(e)re	ich singe
	du kaufst	du wartest	du wanderst	du singst
	es kauft	es wartet	es wandert	es singt
	wir kaufen	wir warten	wir wandern	wir singen
	ihr kauft	ihr wartet	ihr wandert	ihr singt
	Sie kaufen	Sie warten	Sie wandern	Sie singen
	sie kaufen	sie warten	sie wandern	sie singen
Past tense	ich kaufte	ich wartete	ich wanderte	ich sang
	du kauftest	du wartetest	du wandertest	du sangst
	es kaufte	es wartete	es wanderte	es sang
	wir kauften	wir warteten	wir wanderten	wir sangen
	ihr kauftet	ihr wartetet	ihr wandertet	ihr sangt
	Sie kauften	Sie warteten	Sie wanderten	Sie sangen
	sie kauften	sie warteten	sie wanderten	sie sangen
Imperative				
singular	kauf(e)!	warte!	wand(e)re!	sing(e)!
plural (familiar)	kauft!	wartet!	wandert!	singt!
plural (polite)	kaufen Sie!	warten Sie!	wandern Sie!	singen Sie!

finden *find*:	du findest, er findet, ihr findet; ihr fandet
regnen *rain*:	es regnet, es regnete, geregnet
atmen *breathe*:	du atmest, sie atmet, ihr atmet, ich atmete, geatmet

These verbs also always have the ending *-e* in the imperative singular: *arbeite!*, *finde!*, *warte!*

NB. (i) *e-* is not added in the second person singular of the past tense of strong verbs: *du fandst*.
(ii) Verbs with *l* or *r* before *m* or *n* do not need the linking *-e-*: *sie filmt* 'she is filming', *er lernt* 'he is learning'.
(iii) Some strong verbs with a vowel change do not add *-t* in the third person singular of the present tense, see (e) and (f) below.

(b) Verbs whose root ends in *-s*, *-ß*, *-x* or *-z*

These drop the *-s-* of the ending *-st* in the second person singular of the present tense:

rasen *race* – du **rast**	grüßen *greet* – du **grüßt**
faxen *fax* – du **faxt**	sitzen *sit* – du **sitzt**

The use of the ending *-est* with these verbs, e.g. *du sitzest*, is archaic, except in Swiss usage.

(c) Verbs whose root ends in *-el* and *-er*

These verbs have some differences from the general pattern of endings, as illustrated by the forms of *wandern* given in Table 12.2.

They have the ending *-n* in the infinitive, and the first and third person plural of the present tense, e.g. *klingeln* 'ring', *wandern* 'wander'.

In the first person singular of the present tense and the imperative singular, the *-e-* of the root is always dropped with verbs in *-el* and frequently with verbs in *-er* (more commonly in speech than in writing), e.g.: *ich klingle, ich wand(e)re*.

NB: In spoken German hear forms are heard where the *-e-* of the root is kept, but the *-e* of the ending dropped, e.g. *ich klingel, ich wander*, etc.

(d) Verbs whose root ends in a long vowel or diphthong
These sometimes drop *-e-* in their endings, in particular:

(i) The present tense and infinitive of *tun* 'do': *ich tue, du tust, es tut, wir tun, ihr tut, sie tun*

(ii) The present tense of *knien* [kniːə n] 'kneel' is as follows:

> ich knie [kniːə], du kniest [kniːst], er kniet [kniːt],
> wir knien [kniːən], ihr kniet [kniːt], sie knien [kniːən].

The past tense of the strong verb *schreien* 'shout, scream' is similar, i.e.: *ich/er schrie, wir/sie schrien* [ʃriːə n]. The past participle is *geschrieen* or *geschrien*.

(iii) Other such verbs generally lose the *-e-* of the ending *-en* in spoken German, and these forms are occasionally found in writing, e.g.: *schaun, gehn, gesehn* (for *schauen, gehen, gesehen*).

(e) Most strong verbs with *-e-* in the root change this to *-i-* or *-ie-* in the second and third person singular present, and in the imperative singular
In general, verbs in **short** *-e-* [ɛ] change this to *-i-*, whilst those in **long** *-e-* [eː] usually change this to *-ie-*:

essen *eat*:	du isst, es isst, iss!
helfen *help*:	du hilfst, es hilft, hilf!
lesen *read*:	du liest, es liest, lies!
stehlen *steal*:	du stiehlst, es stiehlt, stiehl!

There are some exceptions and further irregularities with these verbs, and full details are given for each verb in Table 12.12. However, the following general points may be noted:

(i) The following strong verbs in *-e-* do **not** change the vowel to *-i-* or *-ie-*:

bewegen *induce*	melken *milk*
gehen *go*	scheren *shear*
genesen *recover*	stehen *stand*
heben *lift*	weben *weave*

(ii) *erlöschen* 'go out' (of lights, fires) changes *-ö-* to *-i-*: *es erlischt*

(iii) Three strong verbs which have long *-e-* in their root change this to short *-i-* in these forms:

geben *give*:	du gibst, es gibt, gib!
nehmen *take*:	du nimmst, es nimmt, nimm!
treten *step*:	du trittst, es tritt, tritt!

(iv) Verbs with this vowel change whose root ends in *-d* or *-t* do **not** add *-et* in the third person singular of the present tense (see (a) above):

gelten *be worth*:	es gilt
treten *step*:	es tritt

(v) In colloquial speech, imperative forms without the vowel change are commonly heard: *ess!, geb!, nehm!* These are considered incorrect.

(f) Most strong verbs with -a- or -au- in their root have *Umlaut* in the second and third person singular of the present

fahren *go*:	du fährst, es fährt
lassen *let*:	du lässt, es lässt
wachsen *grow*:	du wächst, es wächst
laufen *run*:	du läufst, es läuft

There are some exceptions and further irregularities with these verbs:

(i) *stoßen* 'push' has *Umlaut* of -o-: *du stößt, es stößt*

(ii) *schaffen* 'create' and *saugen* 'suck' do **not** have *Umlaut*: *du schaffst, saugst; er schafft, saugt.*

(iii) Verbs whose root ends in -d or -t and which have *Umlaut* in these forms do **not** add -et in the third person singular (see (a) above):

halten *hold*:	es hält
laden *load*:	es lädt
raten *advise*:	es rät

Full details are given for each verb in Table 12.12.

NB: In spoken south German, *Umlaut* is often lacking with these verbs, and one hears, for example, *sie schlaft* instead of *sie schläft*. This is considered substandard.

(g) The ending -e of the imperative singular

(i) With most weak or strong verbs, this ending is optional: *Komm(e) in den Garten! Setz(e) dich! Stör(e) mich nicht!*. It is usually dropped in speech, but quite commonly used in written German.

(ii) The verbs with a vowel change of -e- to -i- or -ie- in the imperative (see (e) above) never have the ending: *Lies! Gib! Nimm!*

(iii) Verbs with roots ending in -ig, and -m or -n after another consonant (see (a) above) normally keep the ending -e: *Entschuldige bitte! Segne mich!*

(iv) Verbs in -el (see (c) above) drop the -e- of the root, but keep the ending: *Klingle laut!*.

(h) Some verbs lack the prefix *ge-* in the past participle
All these are verbs which are not stressed on the first syllable, i.e.:

(i) Verbs with inseparable prefixes (see 22.4):

bedeuten *mean*:	bedeutet	zerbrechen *smash*:	zerbrochen
erfinden *invent*:	erfunden	überlegen *consider*:	überlegt
gelingen *succeed*:	gelungen	unterdrücken *suppress*:	unterdrückt
misslingen *fail*:	misslungen	anvertrauen *entrust*:	anvertraut

(ii) Verbs in -ieren:

gratulieren *congratulate*:	gratuliert	studieren *study*:	studiert

(iii) A few other verbs which are not stressed on the first syllable:

frohlocken *rejoice*:	frohlockt	posaunen *bellow*:	posaunt
interviewen *interview*:	interviewt	recykeln *recycle*:	recykelt
offenbaren *reveal*:	offenbart	schmarotzen *sponge*:	schmarotzt
prophezeien *prophesy*	prophezeit	stibitzen *nick, pinch*:	stibitzt

NB: Some of these verbs can, alternatively, be pronounced with the first syllable stressed. In this case the past participle has the prefix *ge-*: `*frohlocken – ge`frohlockt*; `*offenbaren – ge`offenbart*.

(i) Separable verbs

Separable verbs are made by adding a PREFIX to a simple verb to form a new verb
with a distinctive meaning (as explained in 22.5 and 22.6). These verbs are called
SEPARABLE VERBS because this prefix is separated from the main verb in certain
contexts.

Separable verbs have exactly the same endings and forms, whether weak or
strong, as the simple verbs from which they are derived. Thus, *ankommen* 'arrive'
conjugates like *kommen*, *zumachen* 'shut' like *machen*.

(i) In main clauses, the prefix is separated from the verb and is placed at the end
of the clause (see also 21.1.2):

ankommen *arrive*:	Ich komme morgen um zwei Uhr **an**. Ich kam gestern **an**
ausgehen *go out*:	Sie geht heute Abend **aus**.
nachahmen *imitate*:	Sie ahmten seine Bewegungen **nach**
totschlagen *kill*:	Er schlug das Tier mit einer Keule **tot**

(ii) The prefix remains joined to the verb in all the non-finite forms. The *ge-* of the
past participle is inserted between the prefix and the verb:

ankommen – ankommend – an**ge**kommen
ausgehen – ausgehend – aus**ge**gangen
ausmachen – ausmachend – aus**ge**macht
vorstellen – vorstellend – vor**ge**stellt

If the simple verb has no *ge-* in the past participle (see (h) above), it is also lacking
in all corresponding separable verbs:

einstudieren *rehearse*:	einstudiert
anerkennen *recognise*:	anerkannt

The *zu* of the expanded infinitive is also added between the prefix and the verb
(see 13.1.4b):

ankommen – an**zu**kommen
ausgehen – aus**zu**gehen
anerkennen – an**zu**erkennen

(iii) In subordinate clauses, the prefix rejoins the finite verb in final position:

Ich weiß, dass sie heute Abend **ausgeht**
Er sah, wie sie seine Bewegungen **nachahmten**

(j) Usage in colloquial speech differs in some cases from that in writing

Although widespread in the spoken language, these forms are considered to be
substandard colloquialisms and they are rarely used in writing.

(i) Final *-e* tends to be dropped in all endings, e.g.: *ich kauf, ich fall, ich/es sucht* for
ich kaufe, ich falle, ich/es suchte.

(ii) The ending *-en* tends to be reduced to *-n*, e.g. *wir kaufn, sie falln, wir kauftn, sie
botn, getretn* for standard German *wir kaufen, sie fallen, wir kauften, sie boten, getreten*.
In western and south-western regions, on the other hand, *-en* is often reduced to *-e*:
wir kaufe, sie falle, getrete.

(iii) In Austria and Bavaria the second person plural is often -*ts* rather than-*t*: *ihr kaufts, ihr kommts.*

(iv) *brauchen* is sometimes heard without the ending -*t* in the third person singular of the present tense, e.g. *er, sie brauch.*

12.2.2 Irregular verbs

The verbs *sein* 'be', *haben* 'have', *werden* 'become', the six modal auxiliary verbs *dürfen, können, mögen, müssen, sollen, wollen* and the verb *wissen* 'know' are wholly irregular in their conjugation. The conjugation of *sein, haben* and *werden* is given in full in Table 12.3 and that of the modal auxiliaries and *wissen* in Table 12.4. Some specific points about the forms of these verbs should be noted:

(a) Reduced forms of *sein* and *haben* are usual in colloquial speech
e.g.: *es is* for *es ist; wir/sie sin, ham* for *wir/sie sind, haben; simmer, hammer* for *sind wir, haben wir.*

(b) Special forms of *werden*
(i) The old form *ich/es ward* was sometimes used for *ich/es wurde* in elevated styles into the twentieth century, and it is still occasionally found in deliberately archaicising (especially biblical) contexts.

(ii) The past participle of *werden* has no *ge-* when used as an auxiliary to form the passive, see 12.4.2a, e.g.: *Er ist gelobt* **worden**. Compare its use as a full verb meaning 'become': *Er ist Schauspieler* **geworden**.

(c) The past participle of the modal auxiliaries is rarely used
When these verbs are used in the perfect tenses in conjunction with a main verb, the infinitive is used rather than the past participle (see 13.3.2):

Ich habe es machen **müssen**   Sie hatte es sehen **können**
Wir haben ihn lehren **sollen**   Sie hatten es uns sagen **wollen**

TABLE 12.3 *Conjugation of sein, haben, werden*

Infinitive	sein		haben		werden	
Present participle	seiend		habend		werdend	
Past participle	gewesen		gehabt		geworden	
Present tense	ich	bin	ich	habe	ich	werde
	du	bist	du	hast	du	wirst
	es	ist	es	hat	es	wird
	wir	sind	wir	haben	wir	werden
	ihr	seid	ihr	habt	ihr	werdet
	Sie	sind	Sie	haben	Sie	werden
	sie	sind	sie	haben	sie	werden
Past tense	ich	war	ich	hatte	ich	wurde
	du	warst	du	hattest	du	wurdest
	es	war	es	hatte	es	wurde
	wir	waren	wir	hatten	wir	wurden
	ihr	wart	ihr	hattet	ihr	wurdet
	Sie	waren	Sie	hatten	Sie	wurden
	sie	waren	sie	hatten	sie	wurden
Imperative						
singular	sei!		hab!		werde!	
plural (familiar)	seid!		habt!		werdet!	
plural (polite)	seien Sie!		haben Sie!		werden Sie!	

TABLE 12.4 Conjugation of the modal auxiliary verbs and wissen

Infinitive		dürfen	können	mögen	müssen	sollen	wollen	wissen
Present tense	ich	darf	kann	mag	muss	soll	will	weiß
	du	darfst	kannst	magst	musst	sollst	willst	weißt
	es	darf	kann	mag	muss	soll	will	weiß
	wir	dürfen	können	mögen	müssen	sollen	wollen	wissen
	ihr	dürft	könnt	mögt	müsst	sollt	wollt	wisst
	Sie	dürfen	können	mögen	müssen	sollen	wollen	wissen
	sie	dürfen	können	mögen	müssen	sollen	wollen	wissen
Past tense	ich	durfte	konnte	mochte	musste	sollte	wollte	wusste
	du	durftest	konntest	mochtest	musstest	solltest	wolltest	wusstest
	es	durfte	konnte	mochte	musste	sollte	wollte	wusste
	wir	durften	konnten	mochten	mussten	sollten	wollten	wussten
	ihr	durftet	konntet	mochtet	musstet	solltet	wolltet	wusstet
	Sie	durften	konnten	mochten	mussten	sollten	wollten	wussten
	sie	durften	konnten	mochten	mussten	sollten	wollten	wussten
Past part.		gedurft	gekonnt	gemocht	gemusst	gesollt	gewollt	gewusst

(d) The present participle and imperative of the modal auxiliaries are not used

Those of *wissen* are regular, i.e. present participle: *wissend*. Imperative: *wisse! wisst! wissen Sie!*

12.3 The compound tenses

12.3.1 The conjugation of the verb in the compound tenses

(a) The perfect and future are formed with the auxiliary verbs *sein*, *haben* and *werden*

The perfect tenses are formed with the past participle and *haben* or *sein*, and the future tense is constructed using *werden* and the infinitive, e.g.:

perfect:	ich habe gekauft *I have bought*
pluperfect:	ich hatte gekauft *I had bought*
future:	ich werde kaufen *I shall/will buy*
future perfect:	ich werde gekauft haben *I shall have bought*

Full forms of all these tenses are given in Table 12.5 for the weak verb *machen* 'make' and the strong verb *singen* 'sing', which form their perfect tenses with the auxiliary *haben*, and for the strong verb *bleiben* 'remain' which forms its perfect tenses with the auxiliary *sein* (see 12.3.2). The uses of the tenses are explained in detail in Chapter 14.

(b) The non-finite parts of compound tenses are placed at the end of the clause in main clauses

i.e. they constitute the final part of the 'verbal bracket', see 21.1.2, e.g. *Ich **habe** sie gestern in der Stadt **gesehen***. In subordinate clauses the auxiliary usually follows the non-finite part at the end of the clause, see 21.1.3, e.g. *Sie wissen, dass ich sie gestern in der Stadt **gesehen habe***.

TABLE 12.5 *Compound tenses of strong and weak verbs*

Perfect

	with haben		with sein
ich	habe gemacht	habe gesungen	bin geblieben
du	hast gemacht	hast gesungen	bist geblieben
es	hat gemacht	hat gesungen	ist geblieben
wir	haben gemacht	haben gesungen	sind geblieben
ihr	habt gemacht	habt gesungen	seid geblieben
Sie	haben gemacht	haben gesungen	sind geblieben
sie	haben gemacht	haben gesungen	sind geblieben

Pluperfect

	with haben		with sein
ich	hatte gemacht	hatte gesungen	war geblieben
du	hattest gemacht	hattest gesungen	warst geblieben
es	hatte gemacht	hatte gesungen	war geblieben
wir	hatten gemacht	hatten gesungen	waren geblieben
ihr	hattet gemacht	hattet gesungen	wart geblieben
Sie	hatten gemacht	hatten gesungen	waren geblieben
sie	hatten gemacht	hatten gesungen	waren geblieben

Future

	with haben		with sein
ich	werde machen	werde singen	werde bleiben
du	wirst machen	wirst singen	wirst bleiben
es	wird machen	wird singen	wird bleiben
wir	werden machen	werden singen	werden bleiben
ihr	werdet machen	werdet singen	werdet bleiben
Sie	werden machen	werden singen	werden bleiben
sie	werden machen	werden singen	werden bleiben

Future perfect

	with haben		with sein
ich	werde gemacht haben	werde gesungen haben	werde geblieben sein
du	wirst gemacht haben	wirst gesungen haben	wirst geblieben sein
es	wird gemacht haben	wird gesungen haben	wird geblieben sein
wir	werden gemacht haben	werden gesungen haben	werden geblieben sein
ihr	werdet gemacht haben	werdet gesungen haben	werdet geblieben sein
Sie	werden gemacht haben	werden gesungen haben	werden geblieben sein
sie	werden gemacht haben	werden gesungen haben	werden geblieben sein

12.3.2 *haben* **or** *sein* **in the perfect?**

Whether the perfect tenses are constructed with *haben* or *sein* depends on the meaning of the verb.

(a) The following groups of verbs form their perfect with *sein*

All these verbs are INTRANSITIVE, i.e. they do not have a direct object in the accusative case (see 18.3):

(i) Intransitive **verbs of motion**:

Ich **bin** in die Stadt gegangen   Sie **war** zum Boden gefallen
Wir **sind** aus dem Haus entkommen   Ihr **wart** auf die Mauer geklettert
✓ Um die Zeit werden wir schon angekommen **sein**

NB: Some verbs of motion take *sein* **or** *haben* in different contexts, see (c) below.

(ii) Intransitive verbs expressing a **change of state**. This group includes a large number of verbs which point to the beginning or end of a process, notably those with the prefixes *er-* and *ver-* (see 22.4):

Sie **ist** schon eingeschlafen   Die Blumen **sind** verwelkt
Die Bombe **ist** um zwei Uhr explodiert   Der Reifen **war** geplatzt
Das Licht **ist** ausgegangen   Der Schnee **war** schon geschmolzen
Mein Buch **ist** verschwunden   Sie werden gleich danach ertrunken **sein**
Die Glocke **ist** erklungen

NB: In colloquial North German, *anfangen* and *beginnen* form their perfect with *sein*. One thus hears *ich bin angefangen, begonnen* for standard German *ich habe angefangen, begonnen*.

(iii) Most verbs meaning **'happen', 'succeed', 'fail'**, i.e.:

begegnen *meet* (by chance)   misslingen *fail*
fehlschlagen *fail*   passieren *happen*
gelingen *succeed*   vorgehen *happen*
geschehen *happen*   vorkommen *occur*
glücken *succeed*   zustoßen *happen*
missglücken *fail*

Ich **bin** ihr gestern begegnet   Das **war** schon einmal vorgekommen
Der Plan **ist** fehlgeschlagen   Was wird mit ihr passiert **sein**?
Es **war** mir gelungen, ihn zu überzeugen

NB: The colloquial verb *klappen* 'succeed' takes *haben*, e.g. *Hat's mit den Karten geklappt?* 'Did you manage to get the tickets?'

(iv) The verbs *bleiben* and *sein*:

Sie **ist** früher Lehrerin gewesen   Wir **sind** in Dessau geblieben
War er mal Diplomat gewesen?   Sie wird dort geblieben **sein**

(b) All other verbs form their perfect tenses with *haben*

This includes the majority of German verbs. The most important fall into the following groups:

(i) Transitive verbs, i.e. those taking an accusative object (see 18.3):

Ich **habe** sie gesehen
Er **hat** die Wohnung geputzt

Der Hund **hatte** die Mülltonne umgeworfen
Sie **hatte** mich geschlagen
Ich werde den Brief bis morgen früh geschrieben **haben**

A few compounds of *gehen* and *werden* are exceptions to this rule, e.g.:

Er ist die Strecke abgegangen	*He paced the distance*
Sie ist die Arbeit mit dem Schüler durchgegangen	*She went through the work with the pupil*
Er ist die Wette eingegangen	*He made the bet*
Ich bin ihn endlich losgeworden	*I have finally got rid of him*

(ii) Reflexive verbs:

Sie **hat** sich sehr gefreut	Ich **hatte** mir alles eingebildet
Ich **habe** mich schon erholt	Sie wird sich müde gelaufen **haben**
Ich **hatte** mich aus dem Zimmer gestohlen	

When verbs which normally form their perfect with *sein* are used with a reflexive pronoun in the dative (= 'each other', see 3.2.7), the perfect is still constructed with *sein*, e.g.:

Sie sind sich ausgewichen	*They avoided each other*
Wir sind uns in der Stadt begegnet	*We met (each other) in town*

(iii) Intransitive verbs which do not express motion or a change of state, (see (a) above). Most of these verbs denote a **continuous action** or **state**, e.g.:

Ich **habe** gestern lange gearbeitet	Sie **hatte** dabei gepfiffen
Hast du in der Nacht gut geschlafen?	Sie **hatten** in Münster studiert
Dort **hat** jemand auf der Bank gesessen	Sie wird dort lange gewartet **haben**
Oben **hat** vorhin das Licht gebrannt	

The verbs *liegen*, *sitzen* and *stehen* form their perfect tenses with *haben* in standard German, e.g. *ich habe gelegen, gesessen, gestanden*. However, in south German, *sein* is commonly used (i.e. *ich bin gelegen*, etc.) and this usage is accepted in writing in Austria and Switzerland.

(iv) Most **impersonal verbs**:

Es **hat** geregnet, geschneit, gehagelt	Es **hatte** nach Benzin gerochen
An der Tür **hat** es geklopft	Da **hatte** es einen Krach gegeben

Impersonal expressions with verbs which usually form their perfect tenses with *sein* form an exception to this rule, e.g.: *Es ist mir kalt geworden; Wie war es Ihnen in Berlin gegangen?*

(v) The **modal auxiliaries**:

Ich **habe** es hinnehmen müssen	Wir **haben** es nicht gekonnt
Sie **hat** ihn besuchen wollen	Sie **hat** ihn nie gemocht

(c) The use of *haben* and *sein* with the same verb
(i) The choice of *haben* or *sein* depends on meaning, i.e. it is <u>not</u> an automatic feature of a particular verb. Several verbs which have more than one meaning can be used with *haben* or *sein* in the perfect if they have one meaning of the kind which requires *haben* for the perfect tense, and another which requires *sein*, as explained in (a) and (b) above. This variation between *haben* and *sein* is most

common with verbs which can be used transitively or intransitively. Thus, *fahren*, used as an intransitive verb of motion (= 'go'), forms its perfect with *sein*:

Sie **ist** nach Stuttgart gefahren   Wir **sind** zu schnell gefahren

But when it is used transitively (= 'drive'), it takes *haben*:

Sie **hat** einen neuen Porsche gefahren   Ich **habe** ihn nach Hause gefahren

Some further examples with other verbs:

Ich **habe** einen Brief bekommen	*I have received a letter*
Das Essen **ist** mir gut bekommen	*The meal agreed with me*
Er **hat** das Rohr gebrochen	*He has broken the pipe*
Das Rohr **ist** gebrochen	*The pipe has broken*
Sie **hat** auf Zahlung gedrungen	*She has pressed for payment*
Wasser **ist** in das Haus gedrungen	*Water has penetrated into the house*
Er **hat** ihr gefolgt	*He has obeyed her*
Er **ist** ihr gefolgt	*He has followed her*
Es **hat** in der Nacht gefroren	*There was a frost in the night*
Der See **ist** gefroren	*The lake has frozen*
Da **haben** Sie sich geirrt	*You have made a mistake*
Er **ist** durch die Straßen geirrt	*He roamed through the streets*
Sie **hat** ihn zur Seite gestoßen	*She pushed him to one side*
Ich **bin** an den Schrank gestoßen	*I bumped into the cupboard*
Du **hast** mir den Spaß verdorben	*You have spoilt my fun*
Das Fleisch **ist** verdorben	*The meat has gone bad*
Ich **habe** die Vase zerbrochen	*I have broken the vase*
Die Vase **ist** zerbrochen	*The vase has broken*

(ii) A few verbs of motion can form their perfect with *sein* if they express movement from one place to another, but *haben* if they just refer to the activity as such, without any idea of getting somewhere, e.g.:

Ich **habe** als junger Mann viel getanzt	*I danced a lot when I was a young man*
Er **ist** aus dem Zimmer getanzt	*He danced out of the room*
Sie **hat** den ganzen Morgen gesegelt	*She's been sailing the whole morning*
Sie **ist** über den See gesegelt	*She sailed across the lake*

This usage is more frequent in north Germany, and it is restricted to a few verbs, i.e. *flattern*, 'flutter', *paddeln* 'paddle', *reiten* 'ride', *rudern* 'row', *schwimmen* 'swim', *segeln* 'sail', *tanzen* 'dance', *treten* 'step'.

12.4 The passive

12.4.1 There are two passives in German, the *werden*-passive and the *sein*-passive

They are formed by combining the auxiliary verbs *werden* or *sein* with the past participle:

werden-passive:	Die Stadt **wird zerstört**	Ich **wurde verletzt**
sein-passive:	Die Stadt **ist zerstört**	Ich **war verletzt**

The *werden*-passive is usually referred to as the *Vorgangspassiv* in German, and the *sein*-passive as the *Zustandspassiv*. The uses of both passives are dealt with in Chapter 15. The forms of the *werden*-passive are given in Table 12.6, and those of the *sein*-passive which are actually used are given in Table 12.7.

TABLE 12.6 *The forms of the werden-passive*

Present

ich	werde	gelobt
du	wirst	gelobt
es	wird	gelobt
wir	werden	gelobt
ihr	werdet	gelobt
Sie	werden	gelobt
sie	werden	gelobt

Perfect

ich	bin	gelobt	worden
du	bist	gelobt	worden
es	ist	gelobt	worden
wir	sind	gelobt	worden
ihr	seid	gelobt	worden
Sie	sind	gelobt	worden
sie	sind	gelobt	worden

Future

ich	werde	gelobt	werden
du	wirst	gelobt	werden
es	wird	gelobt	werden
wir	werden	gelobt	werden
ihr	werdet	gelobt	werden
Sie	werden	gelobt	werden
sie	werden	gelobt	werden

Past

ich	wurde	gelobt
du	wurdest	gelobt
es	wurde	gelobt
wir	wurden	gelobt
ihr	wurdet	gelobt
Sie	wurden	gelobt
sie	wurden	gelobt

Pluperfect

ich	war	gelobt	worden
du	warst	gelobt	worden
es	war	gelobt	worden
wir	waren	gelobt	worden
ihr	wart	gelobt	worden
Sie	waren	gelobt	worden
sie	waren	gelobt	worden

Future perfect

ich	werde	gelobt	worden	sein
du	wirst	gelobt	worden	sein
er	wird	gelobt	worden	sein
wir	werden	gelobt	worden	sein
ihr	werdet	gelobt	worden	sein
Sie	werden	gelobt	worden	sein
sie	werden	gelobt	worden	sein

TABLE 12.7 *The forms of the* sein-*passive*

Present			Past			Imperative
ich	bin	verletzt	ich	war	verletzt	
du	bist	verletzt	du	warst	verletzt	Sei gegrüßt!
es	ist	verletzt	es	war	verletzt	
wir	sind	verletzt	wir	waren	verletzt	
ihr	seid	verletzt	ihr	wart	verletzt	Seid gegrüßt!
Sie	sind	verletzt	Sie	waren	verletzt	Seien Sie gegrüßt!
sie	sind	verletzt	sie	waren	verletzt	

12.4.2 The formation of the passive

(a) the *werden*-passive

(i) In the perfect tenses of the passive the past participle of *werden* has no prefix *ge-*, i.e. *worden*: *Das Haus ist 1845 gebaut worden.*

(ii) Imperative forms of the *werden*-passive, e.g. *werde gelobt!* are rare. If a passive imperative is needed, the form with *sein* is used, see (b) below.

(b) the *sein*-passive

In practice, only the present and past tenses of the *sein*-passive, and the imperative, are at all frequently used. Other tenses, e.g. the perfect (*ich bin verletzt gewesen*, etc.) or the future (*ich werde verletzt sein*, etc.) are only used occasionally.

(c) The participle is placed at the end of the clause in main clauses (as in other compound verb forms, see 21.1.2):

    Das Haus wurde 1845 **gebaut**   Das Kind war schwer **verletzt**

In subordinate clauses the participle comes at the end, before the auxiliary, see 21.1.3:

    Ich weiß, dass das Haus voriges Jahr **gebaut** wurde

12.5 The subjunctive

In general the SUBJUNCTIVE mood presents what the speaker is saying as **not necessarily true**, whereas the INDICATIVE presents what is said as a **fact**. Most modern German grammars and textbooks divide the forms of the German subjunctive into two major groups, which they refer to as *Konjunktiv I* and *Konjunktiv II*, since dividing the forms up in this way makes it simpler to explain their use. There are no English equivalents for these terms, and the German ones are used here. Table 12.8 shows how these groupings are made up in terms of the traditional 'tenses' of the subjunctive:

TABLE 12.8 *The forms of* Konjunktiv I *and* Konjunktiv II

Konjunktiv I	present subjunctive	es gebe
	perfect subjunctive	es habe gegeben
	future subjunctive	es werde geben
Konjunktiv II	past subjunctive	es gäbe
	pluperfect subjunctive	es hätte gegeben
	conditional	es würde geben

The subjunctive has the same compound tenses and passive forms as the indicative, formed in the same way, with the auxiliaries *haben, sein* and *werden.* In this section we give information about the various forms of the subjunctive. Their uses are treated in detail in Chapter 16.

12.5.1 *Konjunktiv I*

(a) The simple form of *Konjunktiv I* is regular for all verbs except *sein*
For all verbs except *sein* the endings are added to the root of the verb without any other changes or irregularities, as illustrated for a range of typical regular and irregular verbs in Table 12.9.

TABLE 12.9 *The simple forms of* Konjunktiv I *and* Konjunktiv II

		sein	haben	können	werden	geben	machen
Konjunktiv I	ich	sei	habe	könne	werde	gebe	mache
(present subjunctive)	du	sei(e)st	habest	könnest	werdest	gebest	machest
	es	sei	habe	könne	werde	gebe	mache
	wir	seien	haben	können	werden	geben	machen
	ihr	seiet	habet	könnet	werdet	gebet	machet
	Sie	seien	haben	können	werden	geben	machen
	sie	seien	haben	können	werden	geben	machen
Konjunktiv II	ich	wäre	hätte	könnte	würde	gäbe	machte
(past subjunctive)	du	warest	hättest	könntest	würdest	gäbest	machtest
	es	wäre	hätte	könnte	würde	gäbe	machte
	wir	wären	hätten	könnten	würden	gäbe	machten
	ihr	wäret	hättet	könntet	würdet	gäbet	machtet
	Sie	wären	hätten	könnten	würden	gäben	machten
	sie	wären	hätten	könnten	würden	gäben	machten

Points to note about the simple form of *Konjunktiv I*:

(i) The second person singular and plural forms in -*est* and -*et* (e.g. *du sagest, ihr saget*), are felt to be artificial and are rarely used.

(ii) For most verbs except *sein*, the only difference in practice between the simple form of *Konjunktiv I* and the present indicative is in the third person singular, which has the ending -*e* as opposed to the ending *t* of the indicative.

(iii) There are no vowel changes with any strong or irregular verbs. Compare subjunctive: *er gebe, er fahre,* with indicative: *er gibt, er fährt.*

(iv) The verbs with a root in -*el* (see 12.2.1c) usually drop the -*e*- of the root before the ending -*e*, e.g. *es segle, es lächle,* etc.

(b) Compound forms of *Konjunktiv I*
Compound perfect and future tenses of *Konjunktiv I*, and the *werden*- and *sein*-passive, are constructed in exactly the same way as in the indicative, using subjunctive forms of the appropriate auxiliary verb, i.e. *haben, sein* or *werden*, together with the past participle or the infinitive. Examples are given in the third person singular, which is in practice the only form used.

perfect subjunctive with *haben*:	es **habe gekauft**
perfect subjunctive with *sein*:	es **sei gekommen**
future subjunctive:	es **werde kaufen**
werden-passive (present):	es **werde gekauft**
werden-passive (perfect):	es **sei gekauft worden**
werden-passive (future):	es **werde gekauft werden**
sein-passive:	es **sei gekauft**

12.5.2 *Konjunktiv II*

(a) There are three important and frequently used forms of *Konjunktiv II*

(i) The **simple form**, in one word, traditionally called the past subjunctive. Table 12.9 gives typical examples of its forms and endings with some common verbs. It is formed from the past indicative, as explained in paragraph (b) below and illustrated in Table 12.11.

(ii) The **pluperfect subjunctive**, formed from the past subjunctive of the auxiliary verbs *haben* or *sein* and the past participle, as illustrated in Table 12.10.

(iii) The **conditional**, formed from the past subjunctive of the auxiliary verb *werden* and the infinitive, as illustrated in Table 12.10.

TABLE 12.10 *The pluperfect subjunctive and conditional forms of* Konjunktiv II

	Pluperfect subjunctive (with *haben*)		Pluperfect subjunctive (with *sein*)		Conditional	
ich	hätte	gekauft	wäre	geblieben	würde	kaufen
du	hättest	gekauft	wärest	geblieben	würdest	kaufen
es	hätte	gekauft	wäre	geblieben	würde	kaufen
wir	hätten	gekauft	wären	geblieben	würden	kaufen
ihr	hättet	gekauft	wäret	geblieben	würdet	kaufen
Sie	hätten	gekauft	wären	geblieben	würden	kaufen
sie	hätten	gekauft	wären	geblieben	würden	kaufen

(b) The simple form of *Konjunktiv II* is formed from the past tense of the indicative

This is done in the following ways, as illustrated in Table 12.11. The forms are listed for each individual strong or irregular verb in Table 12.12.

(i) For regular weak verbs it is identical with the past indicative.

(ii) For regular strong verbs, it is formed by taking the form of the past tense, umlauting the vowel if possible, and adding *-e* to the endings if possible (although this *-e* of these endings is often dropped in everyday speech).

(iii) A few strong verbs have an irregular *Konjunktiv II* form with a different vowel from that of the past tense. Only those given in Table 12.11 are in commonly use nowadays.

(iv) Some other irregular verbs also have *Umlaut* in the simple *Konjunktiv II*. The most frequent are given in Table 12.11.

NB: In colloquial (especially south German) speech, *brauchen* 'need' also often has a *Konjunktiv II* form with *Umlaut*, e.g. *ich bräuchte*. This usage is regarded as substandard, but it is widespread, and increasingly common in writing.

TABLE 12.11 *Formation of the simple form of* Konjunktiv II *(past subjunctive)*

	Verb	Past tense	*Konjunktiv II*
Regular weak verbs	kaufen	kaufte	kaufte
	machen	machte	machte
Regular strong verbs	bleiben	blieb	bliebe
	brechen	brach	bräche
	fahren	fuhr	führe
	gehen	ging	ginge
	kommen	kam	käme
	lassen	ließ	ließe
	sprechen	sprach	spräche
	tragen	trug	trüge
	tun	tat	täte
	ziehen	zog	zöge
Strong verbs with irregular past subjunctive	helfen	half	hülfe
	stehen	stand	stünde
	sterben	starb	stürbe
Irregular verbs	sein	war	wäre
	haben	hatte	hätte
	werden	wurde	würde
	dürfen	durfte	dürfte
	können	konnte	könnte
	mögen	mochte	möchte
	müssen	musste	müsste
	wissen	wusste	wüsste
	bringen	brachte	brächte
	denken	dachte	dächte

(c) The simple form of *Konjunktiv II* and the compound form with *würde*

The compound conditional form with *würde* is often used rather than the simple 'past subjunctive' form of *Konjunktiv II*, so that, for example, *ich würde kommen* is often used rather than *ich käme*. Which form is used depends on register and the individual verb involved. Current usage is explained fully in 16.4.4, but it can be summarised briefly here as follows:

(i) The simple forms of the weak verbs and those of many less frequent strong verbs are only used in formal writing. Indeed, several simple forms of strong verbs (e.g. *ich flöge, ich röche*) are felt to be stilted and avoided entirely. These are indicated in Table 12.12.

(ii) On the other hand, with the most common verbs, in particular *haben, sein, werden* and the modal auxiliaries, the simple form is much more common than the compound form in both writing and everyday speech.

(d) Passive forms of *Konjunktiv II*

The *werden-* and *sein*-passive of *Konjunktiv II* are constructed in exactly the same way as in the indicative, using subjunctive forms of the auxiliary verb *werden* or *sein* and the past participle:

werden-passive (past):	es **würde gekauft (werden)**
werden-passive (pluperfect):	es **wäre gekauft worden**
sein-passive:	es **wäre gekauft**

Notes on Table 12.12

Table 12.12 gives the principal parts, i.e. the infinitive, the past tense and the past participle, of all strong and irregular verbs (with the exception of the wholly irregular verbs whose forms are given in Tables 12.3 and 12.4).

(i) The third person singular of the present tense is given for those verbs which have vowel changes (see 12.2.1e/f).

(ii) The simple past subjunctive form of *Konjunktiv II* (see 12.5.2) is given for all verbs listed, but it is given in **italics** if it is obsolete, archaic or rarely used.

(iii) The auxiliary used to form the perfect tenses (i.e. *haben* or *sein*, see 12.3.2) is indicated by *hat* or *ist* alongside the past participle.

(iv) Less common alternative forms are given in brackets after the commoner ones.

(v) In principle, simple verbs (i.e. without prefixes) are given if they exist, even in cases when they are less frequent than compound verbs. As a rule, compound verbs conjugate in the same way as the simple verb from which they are derived; exceptions to this are given in the table.

TABLE 12.12 *Principal parts of strong and irregular verbs*

Infinitive	Past tense	Past participle
3rd person singular present	*Konjunktiv II*	
backen *bake*	**backte** (buk)	hat **gebacken**
es bäckt (backt)	*büke*	
befehlen *command*	**befahl**	hat **befohlen**
es befiehlt	*beföhle (befähle)*	
NB: *fehlen* 'lack' is a weak verb, i.e. *fehlte, gefehlt.*		
beginnen *begin*	**begann**	hat **begonnen**
	begänne (begönne)	
beißen *bite*	**biss**	hat **gebissen**
	bisse	
bergen *rescue; hide*	**barg**	hat **geborgen**
es birgt	*bärge*	
bersten *crack, burst*	**barst**	hat **geborsten**
es birst (berstet)	*bärste*	
bewegen *induce*	**bewog**	hat **bewogen**
	bewöge	
NB: *bewegen* 'move' is weak, i.e. *bewegte, bewegt*		
biegen *bend; turn*	**bog**	hat **gebogen**
	böge	
bieten *offer*	**bot**	hat **geboten**
	böte	
binden *bind*	**band**	hat **gebunden**
	bände	
bitten *ask, request*	**bat**	hat **gebeten**
	bäte	
blasen *blow*	**blies**	hat **geblasen**
es bläst	*bliese*	
bleiben *stay, remain*	**blieb**	ist **geblieben**
	bliebe	
braten *fry, roast*	**briet**	hat **gebraten**
es brät (bratet)	*briete*	
brechen *break*	**brach**	hat/ist **gebrochen**
es bricht	bräche	
brennen *burn*	**brannte**	hat **gebrannt**
	brennte	
bringen *bring*	**brachte**	hat **gebracht**
	brächte	
denken *think*	**dachte**	hat **gedacht**
	dächte	

TABLE 12.12 *Principal parts of strong and irregular verbs – continued*

Infinitive	Past tense	Past participle
3rd person singular present	*Konjunktiv II*	
dreschen *thresh*	drosch	hat **gedroschen**
es drischt	*drösche*	
dingen *hire, engage*	dingte (dang)	hat **gedungen**
(e.g. servant)	*dingte/dänge*	

NB: Simple *dingen* is archaic, but the compound *sich (etwas) ausbedingen* 'make (sth.) a condition' is still used in formal registers. It always has strong forms, i.e. *bedang sich . . . aus, ausbedungen.*

dringen *penetrate*	drang	hat/ist **gedrungen**
	dränge	
empfehlen *recommend*	empfahl	hat **empfohlen**
es empfiehlt	*empföhle (empfähle)*	
erkiesen *choose*	erkor	hat **erkoren**
	erköre	

NB: Only the past tense and the past participle are now used, in elevated registers.

erlöschen *go out* (lights)	erlosch	ist **erloschen**
es erlischt	*erlösche*	

NB: Transitive *löschen* 'extinguish' is weak, i.e. *löschte, gelöscht*

erschrecken *be startled*	erschrak	ist **erschrocken**
es erschrickt	*erschräke*	

NB: Transitive *erschrecken* 'frighten' is weak, i.e. *erschreckte, erschreckt*.

essen *eat*	aß	hat **gegessen**
es isst	*äße*	
fahren *go, drive*	fuhr	ist/hat **gefahren**
es fährt	*führe*	
fallen *fall*	fiel	ist **gefallen**
es fällt	*fiele*	
fangen *catch*	fing	hat **gefangen**
es fängt	*finge*	
fechten *fight, fence*	focht	hat **gefochten**
es ficht	*föchte*	
finden *find*	fand	hat **gefunden**
	fände	
flechten *plait, braid*	flocht	hat **geflochten**
es flicht	*flöchte*	
fliegen *fly*	flog	ist/hat **geflogen**
	flöge	
fliehen *flee*	floh	ist **geflohen**
	flöhe	
fließen *flow*	floss	ist **geflossen**
	flösse	
fragen *ask*	fragte (*lit.* frug)	hat **gefragt**
er fragt (S.G. frägt)	*fragte*	
fressen *eat (of animals)*	fraß	hat **gefressen**
es frisst	*fräße*	
frieren *freeze*	fror	hat/ist **gefroren**
	fröre	
gären *ferment*	gor/gärte	hat/ist **gegoren/gegärt**
	göre/gärte	

NB: Strong forms are usual when *gären* is used literally, the weak ones when it is used figuratively.

gebären *give birth*	gebar	hat **geboren**
es gebärt (gebiert)	*gebäre*	
geben *give*	gab	hat **gegeben**
es gibt	*gäbe*	
gedeihen *thrive*	gedieh	ist **gediehen**
	gediehe	
gehen *go*	ging	ist **gegangen**
	ginge	
gelingen *succeed*	gelang	ist **gelungen**
	gelänge	

NB: *misslingen* 'fail' has similar forms, i.e. *misslang, misslungen*.

TABLE 12.12 *Principal parts of strong and irregular verbs – continued*

Infinitive	Past tense	Past participle
3rd person singular present	*Konjunktiv II*	
gelten *be valid*	**galt**	hat **gegolten**
es gilt	*gälte (gölte)*	
genesen *recover* (elev.)	**genas**	ist **genesen**
	genäse	
genießen *enjoy*	**genoss**	hat **genossen**
	genösse	
geschehen *happen*	**geschah**	ist **geschehen**
es geschieht	geschähe	
gewinnen *win*	**gewann**	hat **gewonnen**
	gewänne/gewönne	
gießen *pour*	**goss**	hat **gegossen**
	gösse	
gleichen *resemble*	**glich**	hat **geglichen**
	gliche	
gleiten *glide, slide*	**glitt**	ist **geglitten**
	glitte	
NB: *begleiten* 'accompany' is weak, i.e. *begleitete, begleitet*		
glimmen *glimmer* (elev.)	**glomm/glimmte**	hat **geglommen/geglimmt**
	glömme/glimmte	
graben *dig*	**grub**	hat **gegraben**
es gräbt	*grübe*	
greifen *grasp*	**griff**	hat **gegriffen**
	griffe	
halten *hold; stop*	**hielt**	hat **gehalten**
es hält	hielte	
NB: The compound verbs *beinhalten* 'comprise' and *haushalten* 'be economical' are weak		
hängen *hang*	**hing**	hat **gehangen**
(intrans.)	hinge	
NB: The transitive verb *hängen* 'hang' is weak, i.e. *hängte, gehängt.*		
hauen *hew, cut*	**haute** (*hieb*)	hat **gehauen** (*coll.* gehaut)
	haute (*hiebe*)	
NB: The strong past form *hieb* is used in literary German in the meaning 'hew, cut (with a sword)'.		
heben *lift*	**hob** (*hub*)	hat **gehoben**
	höbe (*hübe*)	
NB: The forms *hub* and *hübe* are archaic, but they are still occasionally used in formal literary registers, particularly with the compound *anheben* 'commence'.		
heißen *be called*	**hieß**	hat **geheißen**
	hieße	
helfen *help*	**half**	hat **geholfen**
es hilft	hülfe (hälfe)	
kennen *know*	**kannte**	hat **gekannt**
	kennte	
klimmen *climb*	**klomm** (klimmte)	hat **geklommen** (geklimmt)
	klömme	
klingen *sound*	**klang**	hat **geklungen**
	klänge	
kneifen *pinch*	**kniff**	hat **gekniffen**
	kniffe	
kommen *come*	**kam**	ist **gekommen**
	käme	
kriechen *creep, crawl*	**kroch**	ist **gekrochen**
	kröche	
küren *choose*	**kürte** (*elev.* kor)	hat **gekürt** (*elev.* gekoren)
	kürte/köre	
laden *load; invite*	**lud**	hat **geladen**
es lädt (ladet)	*lüde*	
NB: *ladet* is regional, and only used in the sense 'invite', or with the compound *einladen*.		
lassen *leave; let*	**ließ**	hat **gelassen**
es lässt	ließe	
NB: *veranlassen* 'cause' is weak, i.e. *veranlasste, veranlasst.*		

TABLE 12.12 *Principal parts of strong and irregular verbs – continued*

Infinitive 3rd person singular present	Past tense *Konjunktiv II*	Past participle
laufen *run* es läuft	lief liefe	ist/hat **gelaufen**
leiden *suffer*	litt litte	hat **gelitten**
NB: *verleiden* 'spoil' is weak, i.e. *verleidete, verleidet.*		
leihen *lend; borrow*	lieh liehe	hat **geliehen**
lesen *read* es liest	las läse	hat **gelesen**
liegen *lie*	lag läge	hat **gelegen**
lügen *tell lies*	log *löge*	hat **gelogen**
mahlen *grind*	**mahlte** *mahlte*	hat **gemahlen**
meiden *avoid*	**mied** miede	hat **gemieden**
melken *milk* es melkt (milkt)	**melkte** (molk) melkte	hat **gemolken** (gemelkt)
messen *measure* es misst	**maß** *mäße*	hat **gemessen**
nehmen *take* es nimmt	**nahm** nähme	hat **genommen**
nennen *name, call*	**nannte** *nennte*	hat **genannt**
pfeifen *whistle*	**pfiff** *pfiffe*	hat **gepfiffen**
preisen *praise*	**pries** priese	hat **gepriesen**
quellen *gush, well up* es quillt	**quoll** *quölle*	ist **gequollen**
raten *advise* es rät	**riet** riete	hat **geraten**
reiben *rub*	**rieb** *riebe*	hat **gerieben**
reißen *tear*	**riss** *risse*	hat/ist **gerissen**
reiten *ride (a horse)*	**ritt** *ritte*	hat/ist **geritten**
rennen *run*	**rannte** *rennte*	hat/ist **gerannt**
riechen *smell*	**roch** *röche*	hat **gerochen**
ringen *wrestle*	**rang** *ränge*	hat **gerungen**
rinnen *flow, trickle*	**rann** *ränne (rönne)*	ist **geronnen**
rufen *call, cry*	**rief** riefe	hat **gerufen**
salzen *salt*	**salzte** *salzte*	hat **gesalzen** (gesalzt)
saufen *drink (of animals); booze* es säuft	**soff** *söffe*	hat **gesoffen**
saugen *suck*	**saugte/sog** *saugte/söge*	hat **gesaugt/gesogen**
NB: In technical language, only weak forms are used, especially in the compound *staubsaugen* 'vacuum'.		
schaffen *create*	**schuf** *schüfe*	hat **geschaffen**
NB: *schaffen* is weak (*schaffte, geschafft*) in the meaning 'manage', 'work'.		

TABLE 12.12 *Principal parts of strong and irregular verbs – continued*

Infinitive	Past tense	Past participle
3rd person singular present	*Konjunktiv II*	
scheiden *separate; depart*	schied / schiede	hat/ist **geschieden**
scheinen *seem; shine*	schien / schiene	hat **geschienen**
scheißen *shit (vulg.)*	schiss / *schisse*	hat **geschissen**
schelten *scold* es schilt	schalt / *schölte*	hat **gescholten**
scheren *shear, clip*	schor / *schöre*	hat **geschoren**

NB: *scheren* is weak (i.e. *scherte, geschert*) in the meaning 'concern', as is the reflexive *sich scheren* 'bother about; clear off'.

schieben *push, shove*	schob / *schöbe*	hat **geschoben**
schießen *shoot*	schoss / *schösse*	hat/ist **geschossen**
schinden *flay, ill-treat*	schindete (*not used*)	hat **geschunden**
schlafen *sleep* es schläft	schlief / schliefe	hat **geschlafen**
schlagen *hit, beat* es schlägt	schlug / schlüge	hat **geschlagen**
schleichen *creep*	schlich / schliche	ist **geschlichen**
schleifen *grind, sharpen*	schliff / *schliffe*	hat **geschliffen**

NB: *schleifen* is weak (i.e. *schleifte, geschleift*) in the meaning 'drag'.

schließen *shut*	schloss / schlösse	hat **geschlossen**
schlingen *wind, wrap*	schlang / *schlänge*	hat **geschlungen**
schmeißen *chuck* (coll.)	schmiss / schmisse	hat **geschmissen**
schmelzen *melt* (geschmelzt) es schmilzt (schmelzt)	schmolz (schmelzte) / schmölze	hat/ist **geschmolzen**

NB: The weak forms only occur if *schmelzen* is used transitively, and are less frequent even then.

schneiden *cut*	schnitt / schnitte	hat **geschnitten**
schreiben *write*	schrieb / schriebe	hat **geschrieben**
schreien *shout, scream*	schrie / schriee	hat **geschrie(e)n**
schreiten *stride*	schritt / schritte	ist **geschritten**
schweigen *not speak*	schwieg / schwiege	hat **geschwiegen**
schwellen *swell* es schwillt	schwoll / *schwölle*	ist **geschwollen**

NB: *schwellen* is weak (i.e. *schwellte, geschwellt*) when used transitively

schwimmen *swim*	schwamm / *schwömme (schwämme)*	ist/hat **geschwommen**
schwinden *disappear*	schwand / schwände	ist **geschwunden**
schwingen *swing*	schwang / *schwänge*	hat **geschwungen**
schwören *swear*	schwor (*lit.* schwur) / *schwüre (schwöre)*	hat **geschworen**
sehen *see* es sieht	sah / sähe	hat **gesehen**

TABLE 12.12 *Principal parts of strong and irregular verbs – continued*

Infinitive	Past tense	Past participle
3rd person singular present	Konjunktiv II	

senden *send* — sendete/sandte — hat **gesendet/gesandt**
sendete

NB: The weak forms *sendete, gesendet* are used in technical senses, (i.e. = 'broadcast'). Otherwise the irregular forms are commoner.

sieden *boil (elev.; S.G.)* — siedete/sott — hat **gesotten** (gesiedet)
siedete (sötte)

singen *sing* — sang — hat **gesungen**
sänge

sinken *sink* — sank — ist **gesunken**
sänke

sinnen *meditate (elev.)* — sann — hat **gesonnen**
sänne (sönne)

sitzen *sit* — saß — hat **gesessen**
säße

spalten *split, cleave* — spaltete — hat/ist **gespaltet** (gespalten)
spaltete

NB: The strong past participle *gespalten* is used mainly as an adjective, e.g. *das gespaltene Deutschland*.

speien *spit, spew (elev.)* — spie — hat **gespie(e)n**
spiee

spinnen *spin; be stupid* — spann — hat **gesponnen**
spönne (spänne)

sprechen *speak* — sprach — hat **gesprochen**
es spricht — *spräche*

sprießen *sprout (elev.)* — spross — ist **gesprossen**
sprösse

springen *jump* — sprang — ist **gesprungen**
spränge

stechen *prick, sting* — stach — hat **gestochen**
es sticht — *stäche*

stehen *stand* — stand — hat **gestanden**
stünde (stände)

stehlen *steal* — stahl — hat **gestohlen**
es stiehlt — *stähle (stöhle)*

steigen *climb; rise* — stieg — ist **gestiegen**
stiege

sterben *die* — starb — ist **gestorben**
es stirbt — *stürbe*

stieben *fly up (like dust) (elev.)* — stob (stiebte) — ist **gestoben** (gestiebt)
stöbe

stinken *stink* — stank — hat **gestunken**
stänke

stoßen *bump; push* — stieß — ist/hat **gestoßen**
es stößt — *stieße*

streichen *stroke* — strich — ist/hat **gestrichen**
striche

streiten *quarrel* — stritt — hat **gestritten**
stritte

tragen *carry; wear* — trug — hat **getragen**
es trägt — *trüge*

NB: *beantragen* 'apply' and *beauftragen* 'commission' are weak.

treffen *meet; hit* — traf — hat **getroffen**
es trifft — *träfe*

treiben *drive; drift* — trieb — ist/hat **getrieben**
triebe

treten *step* — trat — ist/hat **getreten**
es tritt — *träte*

triefen *drip (elev.)* — triefte/troff — hat **getrieft** (getroffen)
tröffe

trinken *drink* — trank — hat **getrunken**
tränke

TABLE 12.12 *Principal parts of strong and irregular verbs – continued*

Infinitive 3rd person singular present	Past tense *Konjunktiv II*	Past participle
trügen *deceive*	**trog** *tröge*	hat **getrogen**
tun *do*	**tat** *täte*	hat **getan**
verbleichen *fade*	**verblich** verbliche	ist **verblichen**

NB: Simple *bleichen* 'bleach' is weak (i.e. *bleichte, gebleicht*), as is *erbleichen* 'turn pale'.

verderben *spoil* es verdirbt	**verdarb** *verdürbe*	hat/ist **verdorben**
verdrießen *vex (elev.)*	**verdross** verdrösse	hat **verdrossen**
vergessen *forget* es vergisst	**vergaß** vergäße	hat **vergessen**
verlieren *lose*	**verlor** verlöre	hat **verloren**
verschleißen *wear out*	**verschliss** verschlisse	ist/hat **verschlissen**
verzeihen *excuse*	**verzieh** verziehe	hat **verziehen**
wachsen *grow* es wächst	**wuchs** wüchse	ist **gewachsen**
wägen *weigh (one's words)*	**wog/wägte** *wöge*	hat **gewogen/gewägt**

NB: Simple *wägen* is archaic. The compound *erwägen* 'consider' only has strong forms, *erwog, erwogen*.

waschen *wash* es wäscht	**wusch** *wüsche*	hat **gewaschen**
weben *weave*	**webte** (wob) webte	hat **gewebt** (gewoben)

NB: Usually weak, but the strong forms are used in literary German in figurative senses.

weichen *yield, give way*	**wich** wiche	ist **gewichen**

NB: The weak verb *weichen* (*weichte, geweicht*) means 'soften'. It has the compounds *einweichen* 'soak' and *aufweichen* 'make soft'.

weisen *point*	**wies** wiese	hat **gewiesen**
wenden *turn*	**wandte/wendete** wendete	hat **gewandt/gewendet**

NB: The irregular forms *wandte, gewandt* are generally more frequent, except in the sense 'turn over', 'turn round' (e.g. *das Auto, das Heu wenden*) and in the compounds *entwenden* and *verwenden*.

werben *recruit; advertise* es wirbt	**warb** *würbe*	hat **geworben**
werfen *throw* es wirft	**warf** *würfe*	hat **geworfen**
wiegen *weigh*	**wog** *wöge*	hat **gewogen**

NB: *wiegen* is weak (*wiegte, gewiegt*) in the meaning 'rock' (cradle, etc.)

winden *wind, twist* (elev.)	**wand** *wände*	hat **gewunden**
winken *wave*	**winkte** winkte	hat **gewinkt** (*coll.* gewunken)
wringen *wring (N.G.) (clothes)*	**wrang** *wränge*	hat **gewrungen**
ziehen *pull; move*	**zog** *zöge*	hat/ist **gezogen**
zwingen *force*	**zwang** *zwänge*	hat **gezwungen**

13

The infinitive and the participles

This chapter deals with the main uses of the NON-FINITE forms of the verb, i.e. the infinitive and the present and past participles:

Infinitive	Present participle	Past participle
kaufen	kaufend	gekauft
wandern	wandernd	gewandert
singen	singend	gesungen
aufmachen	aufmachend	aufgemacht
bestellend	bestellend	bestellt

As explained in 12.1.1e, these forms of the verb do not have endings to show agreement with the subject, or to express other categories of the verb such as tense and mood. They are used to form the compound tenses and the passive (see 12.3 and 12.4), and they occur in a number of constructions which depend on an element in a full clause with a finite verb. The formation of the infinitive and the participles of regular verbs is shown in Table 12.2.

Despite certain similarities, German differs quite markedly from English in respect of some non-finite constructions and their use, especially those with the present participle. The various uses and forms of these non-finite forms are explained in this chapter as follows:

- The **forms of the infinitive**: the compound infinitive; the infinitive with and without *zu* (section 13.1)
- The uses of the **infinitive with** *zu* (section 13.2)
- The uses of the **infinitive without** *zu* – the bare infinitive (section 13.3)
- Infinitives used **as nouns** (section 13.4)
- The uses of the **present** and **past participles** (section 13.5)
- **Clauses** with participles (section 13.6)
- Equivalents of the **English 'ing'-form** in German (section 13.7)

13.1 Forms of the infinitive

13.1.1 The simple infinitive

The simple INFINITIVE is the basic form under which verbs are listed in dictionaries, see 12.1. For most verbs it ends in *-en* (e.g. *kommen, machen, sehen*), but a few verbs have an infinitive ending in *-n*, i.e. *sein, tun* and verbs with a stem ending in *-el* and *-er*, see 12.2.1c.

13.1.2 The compound infinitive

The infinitive of the auxiliaries *haben, sein* and *werden* can be combined with the past participle of a verb to form compound infinitives:

perfect infinitive (with *haben* or *sein*):	gesehen haben	angekommen sein
passive infinitive (with *werden* or *sein*):	verletzt werden	verletzt sein
perfect passive infinitive:	verletzt worden sein	

The German perfect infinitive is used to show that an action took place before that of the main verb. This is similar to English:

Sie muss das Buch **lesen**	She must **read** the book
Sie muss das Buch **gelesen haben**	She must **have read** the book

13.1.3 The infinitive with and without *zu*

In some constructions in German, the infinitive is accompanied by the particle *zu*, whilst in others a so-called **bare infinitive** is used, without *zu*:

Ich riet ihr zum Arzt **zu gehen**	I advised her **to go** to the doctor
Ich konnte nicht zum Arzt **gehen**	I couldn't **go** to the doctor

Constructions with *zu* (which are more frequent) are explained in section 13.2. Constructions with the bare infinitive are treated in section 13.3.

13.1.4 The form of the infinitive with *zu*

(a) With simple verbs and verbs with inseparable prefixes
zu comes immediately before the verb and is separated from it in writing:

Sie fing an **zu schreiben**	Wir kamen auf dieses Thema **zu sprechen**
Ich war bereit **zu verhandeln**	Es gefiel mir mich mit ihr **zu unterhalten**

negotiate

(b) With verbs with a separable prefix
zu is placed between the prefix and the verb. The whole is written as a single word (see 12.2.1i and 22.5):

Sie hatte vor ihn **anzurufen**	Es war schön euch **wiederzusehen**
Es wäre wohl besser ihr davon **abzuraten**	Sie wusste mit diesem Mann **umzugehen**

warn   *deal with*

Similarly, if a separable prefix precedes an inseparable one:

Es fällt mir nicht ein mich ihm **anzuvertrauen**

NB: Although the verb *missverstehen* is inseparable, the *zu* is placed **after** the prefix, i.e. *misszuverstehen*. This is an alternative, if less frequent, possibility with a few other verbs with the prefix *miss-*, e.g. *zu missachten* or (less commonly) *misszuachten*, see 22.6.3.

(c) With compound infinitives
zu precedes the auxiliary *haben, sein* or *werden*:

Er verleugnet es sie betrogen **zu** haben	He denies having deceived her
Ihr gefällt es nicht betrogen **zu** werden	She doesn't like being deceived
Sie behauptete betrogen worden **zu** sein	She claimed to have been deceived

Similarly, *zu* comes between the main verb and a modal auxiliary:

Es freut mich Sie hier begrüßen	*It is a pleasure to be able to welcome*
zu dürfen	*you here*

13.2 The use of the infinitive with *zu*

13.2.1 The infinitive with *zu* occurs in a reduced clause

In German this is called the *Infinitivsatz*. It can depend on a noun, verb or adjective in a full clause within the same sentence. The infinitive with *zu* comes at the end of its clause, i.e. in the same position as the finite verb in a subordinate clause (see 21.1.1c):

Er fing an **heftig zu weinen**	*He began to cry bitterly*
Er gab mir die Erlaubnis in	*He gave me permission to stay in*
Berlin zu bleiben	*Berlin*
Es ist nicht schwer **eine fremde**	*It is not difficult to learn a foreign*
Sprache zu lernen	*language*

13.2.2 The position of the infinitive clause with *zu*

(a) The infinitive clause is usually quite separate from the main clause
i.e. it is <u>not</u> normally enclosed inside the clause it depends on (see 21.9.2), coming after whatever part of the verb comes in last position in that clause.

Sie hatten beschlossen **vor dem Rathaus zu warten**
  (NOT: *Sie hatten vor dem Rathaus zu warten beschlossen)
Wir hatten vor **im Urlaub nach Rom zu fliegen**
  (NOT: *Wir hatten im Urlaub nach Rom zu fliegen vor)
... weil er sich bemüht hat **rechtzeitig fertig zu sein**
  (NOT: *... weil er sich rechtzeitig fertig zu sein bemüht hat)

(b) In a few contexts the infinitive clause can be (or must be) enclosed within the main clause it depends on
These constructions are exceptions to the general rule given under (a), and the infinitive clause comes inside the main clause.

(i) Enclosure is the rule with the **semi-auxiliary verbs** (see 13.2.5):

... bevor sein Duft ihn **zu ersticken drohte** (*Süßkind*)
Seine Brutalität ist nicht mehr **zu ertragen gewesen** (*Wickert*)

(ii) Enclosure is possible with some other common verbs, although it is **never obligatory**. It is more common in subordinate clauses than with the compound tenses:

Dass sie ihn **entdeckt zu haben** glaubte, war ein Beweis dafür, dass ... (*Süßkind*)
  (**or**: Dass sie glaubte ihn entdeckt zu haben, ...)
Du hast mir **das zu tun** versprochen
  (**or**: Du hast mir versprochen das zu tun)

Verbs which are frequently used like this are *anfangen, beginnen, hoffen, meinen, trachten, vermögen, versuchen, wagen, wünschen*. In very formal registers enclosed infinitive clauses may be found with other verbs and phrases, but such constructions can sound rather stilted.

(c) Incorporation of infinitive clause and main clause

If there is only the finite verb and its subject in the main clause, the infinitive clause can be incorporated with the main clause by splicing the object of the infinitive into it:

Er wagte **die Reise** aus diesem Grunde nicht **abzubrechen**	*He didn't dare to break his journey for this reason*
Diesen Vorgang wollen wir zu **erklären** versuchen	*We want to try to explain this series of events*

This construction is restricted to formal registers. It is usual only with those verbs which regularly enclose an infinitive clause, see (b) above.

(d) Infinitive clauses depending on relative clauses

The German equivalent of English constructions such as 'a man whom I tried to kill' typically has the infinitive clause enclosed within the relative clause, e.g. *ein Mann, den ich zu töten versuchte*. Other examples:

... die Person, **deren Gesicht** ich zu **erraten** versucht hatte (*Frisch*)	*... the person whose face I had tried to recognise*
... kein Mann, **den zu beseitigen** eine Revolution gelohnt hätte (*Spiegel*)	*... not a man whom it would have been worth a revolution to get rid of*

Alternatively, if there is only a simple infinitive clause (i.e. one consisting only of *zu* plus the infinitive), it can follow the finite verb, e.g. *ein Mann, den er versuchte zu töten*.

13.2.3 An infinitive clause with *zu* can be the subject of a verb

(a) A German infinitive clause used as the subject of a verb can correspond in English to an infinitive clause or to a clause with an 'ing'-form

In many contexts a choice exists in English which is lacking in German, since German does not use present participles in the way the 'ing'-form is used in English (see 13.7.1). The finite verb has the ending of the third person singular:

Ihn zu überzeugen wird nicht leicht sein	*To convince him/Convincing him won't be easy*
So etwas zu erlauben ist unerhört	*To allow/allowing that kind of thing is outrageous*
Ihr Ziel ist **einen Roman zu schreiben**	*Her aim is to write/writing a novel*

(b) If a subject infinitive clause is short, it can, optionally, lack *zu*

This is most frequent with the verb *sein* and in set phrases:

Lange Auto (zu) fahren ist sehr anstrengend	*Driving a car for long periods is very strenuous*
Irren ist menschlich	*To err is human*

(c) A subject infinitive clause which follows the main verb is often anticipated by *es* in the main clause

(see 3.6.2e for further details of when this *es* is used):

Es war mir nicht möglich **früher**	It wasn't possible for me to come
zu kommen	earlier
Ihm steht **(es)** nicht zu **ein Urteil**	It's not up to him to pass judgement
zu fällen	

13.2.4 Many verbs can have an infinitive clause with *zu* as their object

(a) A German infinitive clause used as the object of a verb can correspond to an English infinitive clause <u>or</u> a clause with an 'ing'-form

In English the choice of infinitive or 'ing'-form depends on the individual verb used:

Ich hoffe **dich bald wiedersehen zu**	I hope to be able to see you again soon
können	
Ich gebe zu **das gesagt zu haben**	I admit having said that
Ich habe vor **sie morgen zu besuchen**	I intend to visit them/visiting them tomorrow

(b) In some contexts, it is the subject of the main verb which is taken as the subject of the infinitive clause, but in other contexts it is the object

Compare the following sentence, where the **subject** of *versprechen* is understood as the subject of *mitzunehmen*:

| Christian versprach Ellen **sie** | Christian promised Ellen to take |
| mitzunehmen | her with him |

with this one, where the **object** of *bitten* is understood as the subject of *mitzunehmen*:

| Christian bat Ellen **ihn** mitzunehmen | Christian asked Ellen to take him with her |

What is understood to be the subject of the infinitive depends on the sense of the verbs involved and the context. In practice English and German generally agree on whether the subject or object of the main verb is to be understood as the subject of the infinitive. More examples:

Er gab zu **sich geirrt zu haben**	He admitted having made a mistake
Sie hat **ihm** geraten die Ausstellung	She advised him to see the exhibition
zu besuchen	

However, there are one or two constructions where there are significant differences between the two languages:

(i) There are fewer verbs in German than English which allow an object to be taken as the subject of a following infinitive clause. In particular, it is not possible with verbs of **wishing, desiring, saying, knowing, thinking** and the like. With these a *dass*- or *wenn*-clause has to be used in German, <u>not</u> an infinitive clause:

Sie will, **dass ich mit ihr gehe**	She wants me to go with her
Ich möchte nicht, **dass es irgendein**	I don't want there to be any
Missverständnis gibt	misunderstanding
Ich erwarte, **dass sie bald nach**	I expect her to move to Flensburg soon
Flensburg umzieht	
Mir wäre es lieber, **wenn Sie hier**	I would prefer you not to smoke here
nicht rauchen würden	
Sage ihm doch, **dass er warten soll**	Tell him to wait, though
Ich wusste, **dass es ein Irrtum war**	I knew it to be a mistake

It is not possible, either, to use these verbs in the passive with a following infinitive clause. Thus, there is no direct equivalent in German for English constructions of the type, and subordinate clause has to be used:

Man erwartet, **dass sie bald nach**   *She is expected to move to Flensburg*
   Flensburg umzieht   *soon*
Man sagte uns/Uns wurde   *We were told to wait*
   gesagt, **dass wir warten sollten**

(ii) With some verbs the subject of the infinitive has to be understood as indefinite (i.e. = *man*):

Der Präsident hat angewiesen alle   *The president has instructed that all the*
   Universitäten zu schließen   *universities should be closed*
Er ordnete an die Gefangenen zu   *He ordered the prisoners to be released*
   entlassen
Helmut befahl früh aufzubrechen   *Helmut ordered an early start*

Other verbs commonly used this way are *anregen, auffordern, beantragen, befür-worten, bitten, drängen, eintreten, empfehlen, ersuchen, fordern, plädieren, raten, veranlassen, verlangen, warnen.*

(iii) With a few verbs, the subject **or** the object (or both) can be taken to be the subject of the infinitive:

Er schlug mir vor das Zimmer   *He suggested that I/he/we should*
   aufzuräumen   *tidy the room up*

Other verbs which can be used like this are *anbieten, einreden, zusichern.*

(c) An infinitive clause can be used in German after some verbs denoting mental processes
The English equivalents usually require a subordinate clause:

Er behauptete (glaubte, meinte, war   *He maintained (believed, thought, was*
   überzeugt) **mich gesehen zu haben**   *convinced) that he had seen me*

This construction is more usual in writing than in speech, where a subordinate clause will often be preferred, e.g. *Er meinte, er hätte mich gesehen/dass er mich gesehen hätte.*

(d) A following object infinitive may be anticipated by *es*
(see 3.6.3a for details of when this *es* is used):

Ich konnte **es** kaum ertragen **ihn**   *I could hardly bear to see him suffer*
   so leiden zu sehen   *like that*
Sie hat **(es)** versäumt **die Miete**   *She failed to pay the rent*
   zu zahlen

(e) When verbs which govern a prepositional object are followed by an infinitive clause, it is frequently anticipated by a prepositional adverb
(i.e. *da(r)*+preposition. See 18.6.14 for further details of when this is used):

Ich verlasse mich **darauf** ihn zu Hause zu finden	*I am relying on finding him at home*
Ich erinnere mich (**daran**) sie voriges Jahr in Bremen gesehen zu haben	*I remember having seen her in Bremen last year*

13.2.5 Infinitive clauses with 'semi-auxiliary' verbs

Some verbs have a closer link with a following infinitive clause than others. Their main role is to modify the meaning of the verb used in the infinitive in some way, like a modal auxiliary verb (see Chapter 17), and it is useful to think of them as **'semi-auxiliary'** verbs.

English has a much wider range of such 'semi-auxiliary' verbs than German. The natural German equivalent to many of these English verbs is a construction with an adverb, e.g. *Ich spiele **gern** Tennis* 'I **like** to play tennis', *Ich sah sie **zufällig** in der Stadt* 'I **happened** to see her in town'. A survey of these equivalences is given in 7.3.4.

A feature of these semi-auxiliary verbs in German is that they <u>always</u> enclose the infinitive in dependent clauses or compound tenses (see 13.2.2b):

> ... da er den eben Angekommenen **zu erkennen schien**
> ... als das Boot **zu kentern drohte**
> Sie hat uns **zu verstehen gegeben**, dass sie morgen kommt

These verbs are also often incorporated with a dependent infinitive clause, see 13.2.2c. The most important verbs which can be used as semi-auxiliaries in German are listed below. Many of them have other uses and meanings.

bekommen 'get':

Und wenn ich dich **zu fassen bekomme** ...	*And if I lay hands on you,* ...

belieben 'like, wish'. Nowadays archaic except in an ironic sense:

Sie **belieben zu scherzen**	*You must be joking*

bleiben 'remain' The following infinitive has a passive force:

Die Gesetzesvorlage **bleibt** noch **zu diskutieren**	*The draft bill still remains to be discussed*

NB: For the use of *bleiben* with a **bare infinitive**, see 13.3.1f.

brauchen 'need'. In this sense it only occurs with a negative (or with *nur* or *bloß*). This the most common negative to *müssen* (see 17.5.1c):

Du **brauchst** nur **anzurufen**, und ich komme sofort	*You only need to call and I'll come straight away*
eine Sprache, die sie nie **zu erlernen brauchten** (*Spiegel*)	*a language which they never needed to learn*

NB: (i) In colloquial speech, *brauchen* is commonly used without *zu* (see 13.3.1a): *Ich brauche nicht hingehen.*
(ii) The infinitive is used rather than the past participle in the perfect tenses (see 13.3.2a): *Du hättest nicht hinzugehen brauchen.*

drohen 'threaten'. The subject is usually inanimate in this use:

> Oskars Herz **drohte** zu Stein **zu** | *Oskar's heart threatened to turn to*
> **werden** (*Grass*) | *stone*

geben 'give'. Used mainly with *denken, erkennen, verstehen*:

> ... weil sie uns **zu verstehen gab**, dass | ... *because she gave us to understand that*
> sie bald kommen würde | *she would be coming soon*

NB: *es gibt* 'there is' (see 18.2.5) is also used as a semi-auxiliary, e.g. *... weil es hier wenig* **zu trinken gibt**.

gedenken 'propose'. It is restricted to elevated, formal registers:

> die Zahl der Truppen, die die Nato nach | *the number of troops which NATO proposes*
> Bosnien **zu schicken gedenkt** (*Presse*) | *to send to Bosnia*

gehen 'go'. The use of *gehen* as a semi-auxiliary is colloquial. It expresses a possibility and the infinitive has passive force (see 15.4.5):

> Die Uhr **geht zu reparieren** | *The clock can be repaired*

NB: For the use of *gehen* with a bare infinitive, see 13.3.1e.

haben 'have' expresses necessity or obligation. It is a (rather less frequent) alternative to *müssen* or *sollen*:

> Was **habe** ich **zu bezahlen**? | *What have I got to pay?*
> Ich **habe** mehrere Briefe **zu schreiben** | *I have several letters to write*
> Sie **haben** hier nichts **zu suchen** | *You have no business here*

With some verbs (especially *tun*), this use of *haben* is idiomatic and there is little sense of obligation or necessity:

> Das **hat** mit dieser Sache nichts **zu tun** | *That's got nothing to do with this matter*
> Das **hat** wenig **zu bedeuten** | *That doesn't mean very much*

NB: For the use of *haben* with a bare infinitive, see 13.3.1f.

kommen 'come' expresses a (chance) result:

> Es war nicht meine Absicht, dass wir | *It was not my intention for us to get onto*
> auf dieses Thema **zu sprechen kamen** | *this subject*
> Wir arrangierten es so, dass ich neben | *We arranged it so that I came to sit next to*
> ihr **zu sitzen kam** | *her*

NB: For the use of *kommen* with a bare infinitive, see 13.3.1e.

pflegen 'to be accustomed to' is restricted to literary registers:

> Dann **pflegte** ich öfters zwischen den | *Then I often used to go through the heavy*
> schweren Eisenstangen hindurch in | *iron bars into Katharina's pen*
> Katharinas Stall **einzutreten** (*Grzimek*)

scheinen 'seem'

> Ihm **schien** es **zu gefallen** | *He seemed to like it*
> Das Dorf Lidiče, wohin die Spuren der | *The village of Lidiče, where the tracks of the*
> beiden Attentäter **zu führen** | *two assassins seemed to lead, was*
> **schienen**, wurde zerstört (*Presse*) | *destroyed*

sein 'be', as a semi-auxiliary, is the equivalent of *können* (or sometimes *müssen* or *sollen*). The following infinitive has passive force, see 15.4.5:

Ist der Direktor heute **zu sprechen**?	*Can I see the manager today?*
Die Fahrausweise **sind** auf Verlangen **vorzuzeigen**	*The tickets are to be shown on demand*
Das Haus **ist zu verkaufen**	*The house is for sale*

NB: For the use of *sein* with a bare infinitive, see 13.3.1e.

stehen has a similar sense to *sein*, and the following infinitive also has passive force. It is used chiefly with *befürchten, erwarten* and *hoffen*:

Es **steht zu erwarten**, dass er bald nachgibt	*It can be expected that he will soon give in*

suchen 'try, seek' is restricted to formal registers:

eine Ordnung, die die selbständige militärische Betätigung des Adels **einzuschränken suchte** (*Bumke*)	*a decree which sought to limit the independent military activities of the nobility*

versprechen 'promise'. In this sense, *versprechen* refers to an involuntary action with something desirable in the offing. The subject is normally **inanimate**:

Das Wetter **verspricht schön zu werden**	*The weather promises to be nice*
Wir sind froh, weil das Unternehmen **zu gedeihen verspricht**	*We are happy because the enterprise promises to prosper*

NB: As a full verb, in the sense of 'make a promise', *versprechen* is used with a separated infinitive clause and the subject is always **animate**, e.g. *Der Arzt versprach mir sofort zu kommen.*

verstehen 'be able to', 'know how to':

Sie war in Verhältnisse geschleudert worden, mit denen sie nicht **umzugehen verstand** (*Fleißer*)	*She had been catapulted into circumstances which she didn't know how to cope with*

wissen 'know how to'. In this sense *wissen* is similar to *verstehen*:

Er **weiß mit den Leuten umzugehen**	*He knows how to deal with people*
Wie soll zurechtkommen, wer sich in das Gegebene nicht **zu schicken weiß**? (*Wolf*)	*How is anyone going to manage who doesn't know how to come to terms with reality?*

13.2.6 The infinitive with *zu* after adjectives

In some infinitive constructions after *sein* used with an adjective the **subject** of *sein* has to be understood as the **object** of the infinitive:

Diese Aufgabe ist **einfach zu lösen**	*This problem is simple to solve*
Er ist **leicht zu überzeugen**	*He is easy to convince*
Diese Frage ist **schwer zu beantworten**	*This question is difficult to answer*

This construction is common in English, but it is only possible with very few adjectives in German, i.e.: *einfach, interessant, leicht, schwer, schwierig*. In German, too, the construction is only possible if the verb takes an accusative object, i.e. it cannot occur with verbs like *helfen*. These other English constructions have quite different German equivalents:

Es war schön, sie zu kennen   *She was nice to know*
  (i.e. NOT **Sie war schön zu kennen*)
Meiner Schwester zu helfen war schwierig   *My sister was difficult to help*
  (i.e. NOT **Meine Schwester war schwierig zu helfen*)
Zum Trinken war der Kaffee zu heiß   *The coffee was too hot to drink*
  (i.e. NOT **Der Kaffee war zu heiß zu trinken*)

In English we can also use these adjectives attributively (i.e. in front of a noun), with an infinitive depending on them, e.g. 'That is a **difficult** question **to answer**'. This construction does not exist in German, and other constructions must be used:

Diese Frage zu beantworten
  ist schwer
Das ist eine schwer zu   *That is a difficult question to answer*
  beantwortende Frage
Es ist ein leicht erreichbarer Ort   *It's an easy place to reach*
Es war dumm diese Frage gestellt   *That was a silly question to have asked*
  zu haben

13.2.7 The infinitive with *zu* after prepositions

An infinitive with *zu* can be used after a few prepositions, i.e. *um, ohne, (an)statt* and *außer*. Such constructions have special meanings and are the equivalent of adverbial clauses.

(a) The construction *um . . . zu*
This has a number of different uses:

(i) It can express **purpose**, often corresponding to English 'in order to'. It is the equivalent of a clause introduced by *damit* (see 19.5.1):

Ich konnte nichts tun **um** ihn **zu**   *I couldn't do anything to reassure him*
  beruhigen
Er zündete das Haus an **um** die   *He set fire to the house (in order) to*
  Versicherung **zu** kassieren   *collect on the insurance*
Da war kein Wasser **um** das Feuer   *There was no water to put the fire out*
  zu löschen

NB: The *um* is sometimes omitted, in elevated **and** colloquial registers, e.g. *Ich konnte nichts tun ihn zu beruhigen.*

(ii) It is used after an **adjective qualified by** *zu* **or** *genug*:

Er ist **zu jung um** alles **zu** verstehen   *He is too young to understand everything*
Er ist alt **genug um** alles **zu** verstehen   *He is old enough to understand everything*

NB: *um* is sometimes omitted, especially in colloquial speech, e.g. *Er ist zu jung alles zu verstehen.*

If the subject of the two clauses is different, the conjunction *als dass* is used, e.g. *Er ist zu jung/nicht alt genug,* **als dass wir es ihm erklären können**. See 19.5.3 for further details.

(iii) It can be used simply to **link clauses**, as an equivalent to *und*:

Er betrat die Gaststätte **um** sie nach kurzer Zeit wieder **zu** verlassen	*He went into the restaurant, only to leave it again after a short time*

NB: This construction is limited to formal writing and has been criticised by stylists, as it might be misunderstood to imply purpose, e.g. *Karl ging nach Australien, um dort von einem Auto überfahren zu werden.*

(b) *ohne ... zu*

This corresponds to English 'without 'followed by an 'ing'-form:

Wir konnten nie mehr Karten spielen **ohne** an Henriette **zu** denken (*Böll*)	*We could never play cards again without thinking of Henriette*
Er verließ das Haus **ohne** gesehen **zu** werden	*He left the house without being seen*

With a change of subject, the conjunction *ohne dass* (see 19.7.7) is used, e.g.: *Er verließ das Haus, ohne dass ich ihn sah.*

(c) *(an)statt ... zu*

This corresponds to English 'instead of' followed by an 'ing'-form:

Er hat gespielt **(an)statt zu** arbeiten	*He played instead of working*

A clause with *(an)statt dass*, e.g. *Er hat gespielt, (an)statt dass er gearbeitet hat*, is an alternative to this construction. No change of subject is possible with either *(an)statt zu* or *(an)statt dass*.

(d) *außer ... zu*

This corresponds to English 'except', 'apart from' or 'besides 'with an infinitive:

Was konnten sie tun **außer** **zu** protestieren? (*Zeit*)	*What could they do except protest?*

The use of *außer* with a following infinitive is quite recent. A common alternative is to use the preposition *außer* with an infinitive noun, e.g. *Sie tat nichts außer Schlafen*. With a different subject, a clause with the conjunction *außer dass* is used (see 19.7.2a).

(e) German equivalents for other English constructions with prepositions and a following infinitive

In German only the prepositions *um, ohne, (an)statt* and *außer* can be used with a following infinitive. English can use other prepositions, notably 'for 'and 'with', with a following infinitive. These correspond to different constructions in German.

(i) English 'for 'followed by a noun or a pronoun and an infinitive.

In a few contexts this corresponds in German to a noun with *für*, or a noun in the dative in the main clause:

Es ist Zeit für uns loszugehen	*It is time for us to leave*
Es war ihm unmöglich, das auch nur zu verstehen	*It was impossible for him even to understand that*

However, the most usual German equivalent is a construction with a subordinate clause, with the conjunction used depending on the sense:

Ihr lag es sehr daran, dass er die Stelle annahm	*She was very keen for him to take the job*
Hier sind ein paar Formulare, die Sie ausfüllen sollen	*Here are a few forms for you to fill in*
Er wartete darauf, dass sie ankam	*He was waiting for her to arrive*
Sie bringt die Fotos, damit wir sie uns ansehen können	*She's bringing the photographs for us to look at*
Sie muss schon sehr krank sein, wenn ihre Mutter ein Telegramm schickt	*She must be very ill for her mother to send a telegram*

(ii) English 'with 'followed by a noun or a pronoun and an infinitive:
Depending on the sense, the German equivalent for this can be a subordinate clause with *da* or *weil*, a main clause with *und*, or a relative clause:

Da ich so viele Briefe schreiben muss, werde ich wohl nicht ins Kino gehen können	*With so many letters to write, I probably shan't be able to go to the cinema*
Sie waren nur auf der Durchreise in München und konnten dort nur ein paar Stunden verbringen	*They were just passing through Munich, with no more than an hour or two to spend*
Auch der Sonntag, an dem sie nicht ins Büro ging, verging irgendwie	*Even Sunday, with no office to go to, passed somehow*

13.2.8 English uses infinitives in several constructions where an infinitive with *zu* is not used in German

Some of these are explained in 13.2.4 and 13.2.6-7, but there are some others:

(a) English infinitives in indirect statements and questions
e.g. 'He told me **how to do** it'. In German a subordinate clause (often with *sollen*, *müssen* or *können*) is used:

Er sagte mir, wie ich es machen soll	*He told me how to do it*
Ich weiß nicht, was ich tun soll/muss	*I don't know what to do*
Woher weiß man, welchen Knopf man drücken soll?	*How do you tell which button to press?*

(b) English infinitives used after a noun as attributes
e.g. 'the person **to apply to**'. A relative clause is used in German:

Ich möchte ein Paar Handschuhe, die zu meinem Wintermantel passen	*I want a pair of gloves to go with my winter coat*
das Einzige, was man tun kann	*the only thing to do*

These constructions are especially common after superlatives:

Er war der Erste (der Letzte, der beste Spieler), **der gekommen ist**	*He was the first (the last, the best player) to come*

13.2.9 Other uses of the infinitive with *zu*

(a) In comparative phrases with *als*

zu can be omitted, although it is more usual for it to be included:

> Du kannst nichts Besseres tun **als zu Hause (zu) bleiben**
> Man sollte lieber erst alles gründlich besprechen **als sofort (zu) streiten**

(b) In exclamations

These are very similar to the corresponding English constructions:

Und zu denken, dass es ihr nichts bedeutet hat!	*And to think it didn't mean anything to her!*
Ach, immer hier zu bleiben!	*Oh, to stay here for ever!*

(c) In small ads

Zwei-Zimmer-Wohnung ab 1. Mai zu vermieten	*Two-room flat to let from May 1st*

13.3 The use of the infinitive without *zu*

The **bare infinitive,** without *zu,* is used in fewer constructions than the infinitive with *zu,* but many of these are very frequent.

13.3.1 A few verbs are followed by an infinitive without *zu*

Such infinitives are placed at the end of the clause: *Sie will diese Briefe morgen schreiben.* They are enclosed in subordinate clauses and compound tenses: *Ich weiß, dass sie diese Briefe morgen schreiben will* or *Sie hat diese Briefe heute schreiben wollen.* For further details see 21.1. The infinitive without *zu* is used with a small number of common verbs:

(a) The modal auxiliaries

i.e. *dürfen, können, mögen, müssen, sollen, wollen* (see Chapter 17):

Sie **darf** heute nicht **ausgehen**	Ich **musste** heute früh **aufstehen**
Wir **können** es nicht **verhindern**	Er wird mir nicht **helfen wollen**

In colloquial German *brauchen* is often treated as a modal auxiliary and used with a bare infinitive, e.g. *Sie brauchen heute nicht hingehen.* However, many German speakers consider this to be substandard, and *brauchen* is normally used <u>with</u> *zu* in writing: *Sie brauchen heute nicht hinzugehen.*

(b) A few verbs of perception

i.e. *fühlen, hören, sehen, spüren,* e.g.:

Ich **sah** ihn ins Zimmer **kommen**	*I saw him come into the room*
Sie **hörte** das Kind **weinen**	*She heard the child crying*
Er **fühlte** sein Herz **klopfen**	*He felt his heart beat(ing)*
Ich **spürte** seinen Einfluss **wachsen**	*I sensed how his influence was growing*

With these verbs, a clause with *wie* is an alternative to the infinitive construction, e.g.:

> Ich **hörte**, **wie** das Kind weinte   Ich **spürte**, **wie** sein Einfluss wuchs
> Ich **sah**, **wie** der Polizist sich nach dem alten Mann umsah

This tends to be more frequent than the infinitive construction in certain contexts, in particular if the sentence is long or complex, with the verbs *fühlen* and *spüren*, and in colloquial registers.

(c) *lassen*

lassen with a bare infinitive has two principal meanings:

(i) 'let', 'allow':

> Er **ließ** mich das Buch **behalten**   *He let me keep the book*
> **Lass** sie doch **hereinkommen**!   *Do let her come in!*

In this sense *lassen* is often used reflexively with a similar force to a passive construction (see 15.4.6):

> Das **lässt sich** leicht **ändern**   *That can easily be changed*
> Das Buch **lässt sich** leicht **lesen**   *The book is easy to read*

(ii) 'cause', 'make':

> Sie **ließ** den Schlosser die Tür   *She had the locksmith fix the door*
> **reparieren**
> Die Nachricht **ließ** ihn **erblassen**   *The news made him turn pale*
> Er **ließ** sich die Haare **schneiden**   *He had his hair cut*

lassen is never followed by a passive infinitive, but in both meanings the infinitive after *lassen* can have passive force:

> Er **lässt** die Bäume **fällen**   *He has the trees felled*
> Er **ließ** sich **sehen**   *He allowed himself to be seen*
> Sie **ließen** die Brücke **von den**   *They had the bridge built by the*
> **Gefangenen bauen**   *prisoners*

(d) *tun*

The use of *tun* with a bare infinitive is typical of colloquial speech:

> Er **tut** ja immer noch **essen**   *He's still eating*
> **Tust** du mich auch **verstehen**?   *Do you understand me?*
> Ich **täte** gern ins Kino **gehen**   *I would like to go to the cinema*

This usage is generally considered substandard and not normally acceptable in writing. It is, however, permissible in written German to use *tun* in order to allow an emphasised verb to be placed first in the sentence:

> **Bewundern tu** ich ihn nicht, aber   *I don't admire him, but he does*
> er imponiert mir doch   *impress me*
> Aber **schmerzen tat** es darum   *But it was no less painful for all that*
> nicht weniger (*Reuter*)

(e) Certain verbs of motion

i.e. *gehen, kommen, fahren, schicken*. The verb in the infinitive expresses the purpose of going:

Während ich **öffnen ging**, … (*Andersch*)	*While I went to open the door, …*
Kommst du heute **schwimmen**?	*Are you coming swimming today?*
Er **fährt** immer vormittags **einkaufen**	*He always goes shopping in the mornings*
Sie hat den Großvater **einkaufen geschickt**	*She sent grandfather shopping*

This usage is typically (but not only) colloquial. In everyday speech, too, the past tenses of *sein* can be used with a bare infinitive to mean 'go':

Ich **war** heute Morgen **schwimmen**	*I went swimming this morning*
Er **ist einkaufen gewesen**	*He went/has been shopping*

NB: *schicken* can alternatively be used with *zu* and an infinitive: *Sie hat den Großvater geschickt, Kartoffeln und Gemüse zu kaufen.* This is most usual if the infinitive clause is fairly long.

(f) *bleiben, finden* and *haben* followed by a verb of position

Er **blieb** im Zimmer **sitzen**	*He stayed sitting in the room*
Sie **ist** an den Ampeln **stehen geblieben**	*She stopped at the lights*
Er **hat** sein Auto vor der Tür **stehen**	*He's got his car at the door*
Sie **hat** einen Bruder in Köln **wohnen**	*She's got a brother living in Cologne*
Sie **fand** das Buch auf dem Boden **liegen**	*She found the book lying on the floor*

NB: (i) *stehen bleiben* 'stop' and *sitzen bleiben* 'repeat a year' (at school) have developed a distinct lexical meaning.
(ii) For *finden* with the present participle, see 13.7.5c.
(iii) *haben* is used with a bare infinitive in a few set constructions with adjectives, i.e. *Du hast gut/leicht reden* 'It's all very well for you to talk'.

(g) *heißen* 'command', *helfen, lehren, lernen*

These verbs can be followed by a bare infinitive or an infinitive with *zu*:

Sie **hieß** ihn **schweigen**	*She bade him be silent*
Er **hieß** seine Truppen die Burg bis zum letzten Mann **zu verteidigen**	*He ordered his troops to defend the castle to the last man*
… und jetzt **hilf** mir **anpacken** (*Remarque*)	*… and now give me a hand*
Er **half** Carla die Weinflaschen **zu öffnen** (*Horbach*)	*He helped Carla to open the wine-bottles*
Sie **lehrte** mich **kochen**	*She taught me to cook*
Sie **lehrte** mich Suppe **zu kochen**	*She taught me how to make soup*
Er **lernte** beim Militär Russisch **sprechen/zu sprechen**	*He learnt to speak Russian in the army*

NB: (i) This sense of *heißen*, i.e. 'command', is restricted to older literary language. In the sense 'mean', *heißen* is always followed by an infinitive without *zu*, see (h) below.
(ii) *kennen lernen* 'meet', 'get to know' has developed a distinct lexical meaning.

The construction with *zu* tends to be used with longer and more complex infinitive clauses. However, the bare infinitive is preferred if the alternative is an awkward construction, e.g.:

Es geht darum, die seit vierzig
   Jahren geforderte Freiheit der
   osteuropäischen Völker
   verwirklichen zu helfen (*FR*)
   (i.e. NOT **zu verwirklichen zu helfen*)

*It is a matter of helping the peoples of
Eastern Europe to realise the freedom
which they have been demanding for
forty years*

(h) A few other verbs in certain constructions or idioms

(i) With *machen* in a couple of idioms, i.e. *von sich reden machen* 'become a talking point' and *jdn. etwas glauben machen* 'convince sb. of sth.', and with a few other verbs, i.e. *jdn. gruseln, lachen, schwindeln, weinen, zittern machen* 'make sb. have the creeps, laugh, feel dizzy, cry, tremble'.

(ii) A bare infinitive is used as the complement of *heißen* 'be (the equivalent of)', 'mean' and *nennen* 'call', e.g.:

Das **heißt lügen**   *That amounts to lying*
Das **hieße** wieder von vorne   *That would mean starting again*
   anfangen   *from scratch*
Das **nennst** du höflich **sein**!   *You call that being polite!*

NB: *heißen* in the meaning 'command' is followed by a bare infinitive **or** an infinitive with *zu*, see (g) above.

(iii) *legen* is followed by a bare infinitive in the idiom *sich schlafen legen* 'go to bed', e.g. *Ich legte mich schlafen.*

13.3.2 The use of the infinitive for a past participle

The infinitive is used rather than a past participle in the perfect tenses of some verbs used with a bare infinitive, e.g. *Sie hat kommen **wollen*** (NOT: *gewollt*), see 17.1.3. This is the case with the following verbs:

(a) the modal auxiliaries

Er hat heute ausgehen **dürfen**   Wir hätten Ihnen helfen **können**
Er hat ihn sehen **müssen**   Sie hätte es machen **sollen**
Karl hatte Sie sehen **wollen**

brauchen also forms its perfect tenses with the infinitive rather than the past participle, whether used with an infinitive with *zu* or with a bare infinitive (see 13.3.1a), e.g.: *Wir haben nicht (zu) warten **brauchen**.*

NB: The past participle is occasionally used with these verbs in spoken German, e.g. *Sie hat arbeiten gemusst, gekonnt, gewollt* etc. These forms are regarded as incorrect.

(b) *lassen*

Sie hat den Schlosser die Tür **reparieren lassen**
Er hat sich die Haare **schneiden lassen**
Er hat sie in das Zimmer **kommen lassen**

The infinitive of *lassen* is generally used rather than the past participle, but it is occasionally heard in the sense of 'leaving something somewhere', e.g. *Ich habe Kaffee und Kuchen stehen gelassen* (more usual: *stehen lassen*), and with the combinations *fallen lassen, liegen lassen*, etc.

(c) *sehen, hören* **and other verbs of perception**
With *sehen* and *hören*, the norm is to use the infinitive:

Ich habe sie hereinkommen **sehen**	*I have seen her come in*
Sie hatte ihn nicht kommen **hören**	*She hadn't heard him come*

In colloquial speech, the past participle is sometimes used with these verbs, e.g. *Sie hatte ihn nicht kommen gehört*. This is usually regarded as substandard, but it is occasionally encountered in writing. However, *fühlen* and *spüren* are now used almost exclusively with a past participle, e.g. *Sie hat die Katastrophe kommen gefühlt*.

(d) *helfen, heißen* **and other verbs used with a bare infinitive**
Both the infinitive and the past participle are accepted with all these verbs, but there are differences in frequency of usage.

(i) With *helfen* the infinitive is more usual than the past participle:

Sie hat ihn den Koffer **tragen helfen** (less common: **tragen geholfen**)

(ii) With *heißen* the infinitive and the past participle are equally common:

Wer hat dich **kommen heißen/geheißen**?

(iii) With other verbs, i.e. *lehren, lernen, machen*, the infinitive is now very rarely used, and the past participle is the norm:

Er hat sie **lachen gemacht** (unusual: **lachen machen**)

NB: In subordinate clauses the auxiliary precedes these double infinitives: *Er sagte, dass sie es hätte machen sollen/…, dass sie den Koffer hat tragen helfen*, etc. (see also 17.1.4c and 21.1.3b).

13.3.3 Other uses of the bare infinitive

(a) in commands, in place of an imperative
The use of the infinitive with the force of a command is particularly frequent in official language and instructions, see also 16.2.2a:

Nicht rauchen! Bitte anschnallen!   *No smoking. Fasten seat-belts*

(b) in isolation, especially in elliptical questions, wishes and similar

Wie? Alles vergessen und vergeben?	*What? (Am I supposed to) forgive and forget?*
Wozu sich weiter bemühen?	*Why (should we) bother further?*
Was möchtest du jetzt?	*What would you like to do now?*
– Schlafen bis Mittag!	*– Sleep till lunchtime!*

13.4 Infinitives used as nouns

13.4.1 The infinitive of almost any verb can be used as a noun in German

(a) Infinitival nouns often correspond to English 'ing'-forms used as nouns
Such nouns from infinitives are neuter, see 1.1.3e, and they are spelled with a capital letter:

Ich hörte das laute **Bellen** eines Hundes	*I heard the loud barking of a dog*
Nach monatelangem **Warten** erhielt sie die Nachricht von seinem Erfolg	*After waiting for months she received news of his success*
Das **Mitnehmen** von Hunden ist polizeilich verboten	*Bringing dogs in is forbidden by law*
die Kunst des **Schreibens**	*the art of writing*

(b) With reflexive verbs, the pronoun *sich* is usually omitted
(i) This is especially the case if the use of the infinitive as a noun is well established and frequent, e.g. *das Benehmen* 'behaviour' (from *sich benehmen* 'behave').

(ii) However, it may be included to avoid ambiguity, e.g. *die Kunst des Sichäußerns* 'the art of expressing oneself', where *das Äußern* could mean something different.

(iii) Increasingly, *sich* tends to be included with forms which have not yet become established usage, e.g. *dieses ständige Sichumschauen* 'this continual looking round', *das meditative Sichannähern an Gott* 'coming closer to God through meditation', *das Sichnichtbegnügenkönnen (Süßkind)* 'not being able to be satisfied'.

NB: The spelling of nouns from reflexive verbs produces uncertainties, and spellings like *das sich Äußern* are not unusual, if incorrect.

(c) Infinitival nouns cannot normally be used in the plural
This is because, like the English 'ing'-form, they simply express the action denoted by the verb. However, one or two established forms, with extended meanings, are commonly used in the plural, see 13.4.4.

(d) They can be compounded with the object or another part of the clause
e.g. *das Zeitunglesen* 'reading the newspaper', *das Rückwärtsfahren* 'reversing', *das Schlafengehen* 'going to bed'. If there are several words in these additional elements, they are normally written with hyphens, e.g. *dieses ständige Mit-sich-selbst-Beschäftigen (SWF)*, *das Auf-die-lange-Bank-Schieben*. The first word, the infinitive, and any nouns in the combination are all spelled with capital letters.

13.4.2 Wide use of infinitival nouns is typical of written German

They are especially frequent in technical registers, e.g.:

In der Bundesrepublik beginnt sich diese Basis humanen **Miteinanderlebens, Untereinanderaussprechens** und **Miteinanderwirkens** aufzulösen (*FAZ*)	*In the Federal Republic this foundation of humane living together, freely exchanging ideas and cooperating is beginning to dissolve*

But they are used in literary prose, too, e.g.:

Dann kam das Schiff, und ich beobachtete, wie so viele Male schon, das vorsichtige **Längsfahren, Stoppen, Zurückweichen** in dem **Sprudeln** und **Rauschen** und **Räderklatschen**, das **Taueschleudern** und **Festbinden** (*Strauß*).

13.4.3 Infinitival nouns used with prepositions

The preposition is usually fused with the appropriate form of the definite article in these constructions (see 4.1.1c).

(a) *beim* + infinitival noun
This usually corresponds to English 'on 'with an 'ing'-form, or an adverbial time clause with 'when' or 'as':

Beim Erwachen am Morgen erschrak ich eine Sekunde lang (*Frisch*)	*On waking up/When I woke up in the morning I was frightened for an instant*
Die Brücke war so dicht mit vierstöckigen Häusern bebaut, dass man **beim Überschreiten** den Fluss nicht zu Gesicht bekam (*Süßkind*)	*The bridge was so densely built up with four-storey houses that you couldn't see the river as you crossed it*

(b) *zum* + infinitival noun
(i) This combination expresses purpose. It often corresponds to English 'for 'with an 'ing'-form or an infinitive with 'to':

Zum Fußballspielen ist der Garten viel zu klein	*The garden is much too small for playing football in*
Ich gebrauche das Messer **zum Kartoffelschälen**	*I use the knife for peeling potatoes*
Der Kaffee ist zu heiß **zum Trinken**	*The coffee is too hot to drink*

(ii) Some combinations of infinitival nouns with *zum* are idiomatic:

Das ist doch **zum Lachen, zum Kotzen, zum Verrücktwerden**	*But that's laughable, enough to make you sick, enough to drive you mad*

(iii) *bis zum* with an infinitival noun is used for 'until':

Bitte bewahren Sie den Fahrschein **bis zum Verlassen** des Bahnhofs	*Please retain your ticket until you leave the station*

(iv) Combinations of infinitival nouns with *zum* are used with *bringen* or *kommen* to form phrasal verbs expressing the completion of an action:

zum Halten bringen/kommen	*bring/come to a stop*
zum Kochen bringen/kommen	*bring/come to the boil*

(c) *ins* + infinitive
This combination is frequent with *geraten* or *kommen* to form phrasal verbs denoting the beginning of an action, e.g.:

Der Ball geriet/kam **ins Rollen**	*The ball started rolling*
Der Turm kam/geriet **ins Schwanken**	*The tower started to sway*
Der Wagen kam **ins Schleudern**	*The car went into a skid*

13.4.4 Some infinitival nouns have extended meanings

In effect, they have become independent nouns, isolated from the verb they come from and no longer merely expressing the action denoted by it. The following is a selection of the most frequent:

das Andenken	*souvenir*	das Schrecken	*terror*
das Benehmen	*behaviour*	das Unternehmen	*enterprise*
das Dasein	*existence*	das Verbrechen	*crime*
das Einkommen	*income*	das Vergnügen	*pleasure*
das Essen	*meal*	das Vermögen	*wealth*
das Gutachten	*reference*	das Versprechen	*promise*
das Guthaben	*credit balance*	das Vorhaben	*intention*
das Leben	*life*		

Such nouns are sometimes used in the plural, and plural forms of most of the above may be encountered (except for *das Benehmen* and *das Dasein*).

13.5 The present and past participles

Aside from the use of the past participle to form the perfect tenses and the passive (see 12.3–4), the German participles are chiefly employed as adjectives (see 13.5.2–4) or in participial clauses (see 13.6).

13.5.1 The names and meanings of the participles

In English terminology, the two participles are usually called the **present participle** (e.g. *lesend*, *überwältigend*, etc.), and the **past participle** (e.g. *gestellt*, *geworfen*, etc.). These terms are rather misleading, as the participles do not necessarily refer to present or past time, and they are often referred to as *das erste Partizip* and *das zweite Partizip* in German.

(a) The present participle usually indicates an action which is taking place at the same time as that of the finite verb

Den Schildern **folgend**, fanden sie das Krankenhaus (*Walser*)	*Following the signs, they found the hospital*

(b) The meaning of the past participle differs according to the verb
(i) With **intransitive verbs**, the past participle has an active (i.e. not passive) sense, and refers to an action which has taken place before that indicated by the finite verb:

Der neue Lehrer, in Freiburg **angekommen**, suchte das Humboldt-Gymnasium auf	*Having arrived in Freiburg, the new teacher went to the Humboldt Secondary School*

(ii) With **transitive** verbs, the past participle has a passive sense. If the verb denotes a continuous action, the participle refers to an action simultaneous with that of the main verb:

Der Zug, von zwei Lokomotiven **gezogen**, fuhr in den Bahnhof ein	*The train, which was being pulled by two engines, came into the station*

With transitive verbs which denote a momentary action, the past participle refers to an action which has taken place before that of the main verb:

Der Flüchtling, von seinen Freunden **gewarnt**, verließ sein Versteck	*The fugitive, who had been warned by his friends, left his hiding-place*

13.5.2 The adjectival use of the participles

(a) Most German present and past participles can be used as adjectives
This is in fact their most frequent type of use outside compound tenses:

die **schreienden** Vögel	mein **verlorener** Schirm
das **kochende** Wasser	der **gehasste** Feind

(b) Like other adjectives, they can be used as nouns
See 6.4 for more information on the use of adjectives as nouns.

die **Streikenden**	*the people on strike*	die **Gehasste**	*the detested woman*
der **Sterbende**	*the dying man*	das **Hervorragende**	*the outstanding thing*

ein bitterer Kampf zwischen **Habenden** und Habenichtsen, zwischen **Überfütterten** und **Zukurzgekommenen** (*Zeit*)	*a bitter struggle between the haves and the have-nots, between the overfed and those who have come off badly*

Many such participles used as nouns have taken on special meanings, e.g. *der/die Abgeordnete* 'member of parliament', *der/die Vorsitzende* 'chairperson', etc. More of these are given in 6.4.3.

(c) Like many other adjectives, they can be used as adverbs
They mainly become adverbs of manner or viewpoint, see 7.3.1c:

Er hat die Sache **überraschend** schnell erledigt	*He settled the matter surprisingly quickly*
Sie rannten **schreiend** davon, als sie ihn sahen (*Süßkind*)	*They ran off screaming when they saw him*
Die alte Frau ging **gebückt** zum Rathaus hin	*The old woman was walking with a stoop towards the town-hall*

(d) They are often compounded, especially in written German
These compounds can then also be used as nouns or adverbs in the same way as simple participles:

Vancouver ist eine Stadt von **atemberaubender** Schönheit	*Vancouver is a breathtakingly beautiful city*
die **Arbeitsuchenden**	*the people looking for work*
ein **weichgekochtes** Ei	*a soft boiled egg*
Tiefgefrorenes	*frozen food*

(e) Present participles can be used adjectivally with an accompanying *zu*
e.g. *das abzufertigende* Gepäck 'the baggage for checking'. This is an adjectival form of the construction with *sein* and an infinitive with *zu* expressing possibility or necessity (see 13.2.5). As in that construction the participle has passive force:

ein nicht **zu übersehender** Fehler	*a mistake which cannot be overlooked*
ihre **anzuerkennende** Leistung	*her achievement which must be acknowledged*
ein **Auszubildender**	*a trainee*

As the last example shows, these forms, too, can be used as nouns. This construction is common in official written registers, but it is rare in informal speech.

13.5.3 The extended participial phrase

In German, a participle used adjectivally can be expanded leftwards by adding objects and/or adverbials. In this way, what in English would be a phrase or a subordinate clause placed **after** the noun can appear in German as an extended adjectival phrase placed **before** the noun:

Die **um ihre eigenen Arbeitsplätze fürchtenden** Stahlarbeiter wollten nicht streiken (*FR*)	*The steelworkers, who were afraid for their own jobs, did not want to strike*
Ich habe dieses von meinem Vetter **warm empfohlene** Buch mit Genuss gelesen	*I enjoyed reading this book which was strongly recommended to me by my cousin*
Wegen Überproduktion entlassene Arbeiter demonstrierten im Fabrikhof	*Workers who had been laid off on account of overproduction were demonstrating in the factory yard*
eine **von allen echten Demokraten zu begrüßende** Entwicklung	*a development which must be welcomed by all true democrats*

These extended adjectival phrases can be made into nouns, e.g. *das wirklich Entscheidende* 'what is really decisive', *die soeben Angekommenen* 'the people who have just arrived', etc.

This construction is common in formal written German, especially in non-literary registers (journalism, officialese, non-fiction, etc.), but it is not common in everyday speech. The following example shows that there can be a considerable distance between article and noun in these phrases:

> Zwar gilt **der** in den vergangenen vier Jahren auf der Basis einer deutsch-amerikanischen Regierungsvereinbarung für bislang 552 Millionen Mark entwickelte **Panzer** als Spitzenmodell seiner Klasse (*Spiegel*)

Although such constructions typically occur with participles, they are used with other adjectives, too: *eine für sie ganz typische Haltung* (see 6.6.3).

13.5.4 Lexicalisation of participles used as adjectives

Many participles used as adjectives have become **lexicalised**, i.e. they have developed a meaning distinct from that of the original verb, so that they are now felt to be independent adjectives rather than simply the participles of a particular verb. A clear indication of this happening is that lexicalised participles can be used with the usual comparative and superlative endings, e.g. *spannender, am spannendsten* 'more, most exciting'. With true participles, *mehr* and *meist* are used, see 8.2.7. Another indication of lexicalisation is the possibility of using the prefix *un-* with them, e.g. (*un*)*bedeutend* '(in)significant', (*un*)*angebracht* '(in)appropriate', etc. A selection of those most frequently used is given below.

(a) Lexicalised present participles

abstoßend	*repulsive*	auffallend	*conspicuous*	drückend	*oppressive*
abwesend	*absent*	aufregend	*exciting*	einleuchtend	*reasonable*
ansteckend	*infectious*	bedeutend	*significant*	empörend	*outrageous*
anstrengend	*strenuous*	beruhigend	*reassuring*	entscheidend	*decisive*
anwesend	*present*	dringend	*urgent*	glühend	*glowing*

reizend	*charming*	überraschend	*surprising*	verblüffend	*amazing*
rührend	*touching*	überzeugend	*convincing*	verlockend	*tempting*
spannend	*exciting*	umfassend	*extensive*	wütend	*furious*

These can be used not only before an adjective, but also after *sein*:

ein **spannender** Film	*an exciting film*
der Film war **spannend**	*the film was exciting*

True present participles cannot be used like this in German, and English speakers must beware of confusing these lexicalised participles with the 'ing'-forms of the English progressive tenses. Compare:

die **brennenden** Lichter	*the burning lights*
die Lichter **brannten**	*the lights were burning*

i.e. NOT: *die Lichter waren brennend*. German present participles <u>cannot</u> be used with *sein* to form progressive tenses as can the English 'ing'-form with the verb 'be' (see also 14.6).

(b) Lexicalised past participles

angebracht	*appropriate*	ausgezeichnet	*excellent*	gelehrt	*scholarly*
angesehen	*respected*	bekannt	*famous*	geschickt	*clever*
aufgebracht	*outraged*	belegt	*occupied*	verliebt	*in love*
aufgeregt	*excited*	erfahren	*experienced*	verrückt	*insane*

Some lexicalised past participles are archaic and are no longer used as the past participle of the verb in question, e.g.:

erhaben *illustrious*	(*erheben* 'raise' – modern past participle *erhoben*)
gediegen *solid, upright*	(*gedeihen* 'prosper' – modern past participle *gediehen*)
verhohlen *secret*	(*verhehlen* 'conceal' – modern past participle *verhehlt*)
verworren *confused*	(*verwirren* 'confuse' – modern past participle *verwirrt*)

A few adjectives which look like past participles are in fact not from verbs at all, e.g. *beleibt* 'portly' and *benachbart* 'neighbouring' These come directly from the nouns *der Leib* 'body' and *der Nachbar* 'neighbour' – there are no such verbs as *beleiben* or *benachbaren*.

13.5.5 Other uses of the past participle

(a) Elliptical use of the past participle
The past participle is sometimes used in isolation as an exclamation or a depersonalised command. Many such forms have become idiomatic:

Verdammt! Verflucht (noch mal)!	*Blast!*
Frisch gewagt!	*Let's get on with it!*
Aufgepasst!	*Watch out!*

For further details, see 16.2.2b.

(b) The past participle after *finden*
This corresponds closely to the English construction:

Ich **fand** sie vor dem Ofen **zusammengesunken**	*I found her slumped in front of the stove*
Du wirst ihn dort **aufgebahrt finden**	*You will find him laid out there*

NB: For the use of *finden* with a present participle, see **13.7.5c**.

(c) The past participle after *kommen*

This corresponds to an English 'ing'-form:

Er **kam** ins Zimmer **gelaufen**	*He came running into the room*
Sie **kam herbeigeeilt**	*She came hurrying along*

(d) The past participle after *bleiben* and *scheinen*

These are similar to English constructions, e.g. *Ihr Brief blieb unbeantwortet* 'Her letter remained unanswered'; *Die Tür schien geschlossen* 'The door seemed/ appeared closed'. The participle with these verbs has a similar force to that of the *sein*-passive, see 15.2.2c.

13.6 Clauses with participles

13.6.1 Both participles can be used to construct non-finite clauses

These can have the force of an adjective, qualifying a noun or pronoun, or of an adverb, giving the circumstances of the action. The participle is usually placed last in the clause, but, exceptionally, it may come earlier:

Ich putzte **auf dem Brett stehend** das Fenster von außen (*Spiegel*)	*I was cleaning the window from the outside, standing on the plank*
eine ständige Verbesserung des Automobils nach den Möglichkeiten der Zeit, **doch zugleich immer aufbauend auf das Erreichte** (*Mercedes advert*)	*a continuous improvement of the car according to the possibilities of the time, but at the same time always building on what has been achieved*
Zwar hatte dieses Mal der Dolch, **durch ein seidenes Unterkleid abgelenkt,** das Opfer nicht sogleich tödlich getroffen (*Heyse*)	*Although this time the dagger, deflected by a silk petticoat, had not immediately wounded the victim fatally*
Von der Wucht seiner Rede hingerissen, brachen die Zuhörer immer wieder in Beifall aus	*Carried away be the force of his speech, the audience continually broke out into applause*
Da saß eine zarte Dame mit einem zarten Gesicht, **umrahmt von einem blonden Pagenkopf**	*There sat a delicate lady with a delicate face, which was framed by blond hair cut in the page-boy style*

Participial clauses like these are restricted to formal written registers in German. In particular, those with present participles can sound stilted and they are used much less frequently than clauses with 'ing'-forms in English. In practice, English learners are best advised to avoid them entirely in German and use instead one of the alternatives detailed in 13.7.

13.6.2 Comparative clauses can be formed with *wie* and a past participle

eine Betonburg, **wie** von einem anderen Stern in diesen Wald **gefallen** (*Walser*)	*a castle made of concrete, as if it had fallen into this forest from another star*

In general, this construction is also typical of formal registers, but some have become established idioms and are more widely used:

Also, wie ausgemacht: Wir treffen uns um acht	*Well, then, as arranged, we'll meet at eight o'clock*
wie gesagt, wie erwartet, wie vorausgesehen	*as I said, as expected, as foreseen*
wie gehabt (coll.)	*as before, as usual*

13.6.3 A clause with a past participle can be introduced by *obwohl*

This is similar to the English construction with '(al)though':

Obwohl von seinen Kollegen geachtet, war er nicht sehr beliebt	*Although respected by his colleagues, he was not very popular*

No other conjunction can introduce a participial clause in German.

13.7 German equivalents of English constructions with the 'ing'-form

The English 'ing'-form is used much more widely than the German present participle, which is found mainly as an adjective (see 13.5). In other contexts, different constructions are usually preferred in German. In particular, the German present participle is not often used in participial clauses (see 13.6.1). English learners are advised to avoid clauses with the present participle entirely in German. In general, the equivalents given below for constructions with the English 'ing'-form represent more idiomatic German usage.

13.7.1 The English 'ing'-form used as a noun

The usual German equivalent is one of the following. Often, more than one alternative is possible, as the examples in (a), (b) and (c) below show.

(a) An infinitive used as a noun, or another noun derived from a verb (see 13.4 and 22.2):

Aufmerksames **Zuhören** ist wichtig	*Attentive listening is important*
die Freuden des **Skilaufens**	*the pleasures of skiing*
Warum hat man die **Eröffnung** der neuen Schule aufgeschoben?	*Why has the opening of the new school been delayed?*
Er ist einer solchen **Tat** nicht fähig	*He is not capable of doing such a thing*

(b) An infinitive clause with *zu*

Es ist wichtig aufmerksam zuzuhören	*Attentive listening is important*
Er gab zu das Fenster zerbrochen zu haben	*He admitted having broken the window*
Ich verlasse mich darauf ihn zu Hause zu finden	*I rely on finding him at home*

(c) A *dass*-clause

Es ist wichtig, dass man aufmerksam zuhört	*Attentive listening is important*
Er gab zu, dass er das Fenster zerbrochen hatte	*He admitted having broken the window*
Ich verlasse mich darauf, dass ich ihn zu Hause finde	*I rely on finding him at home*

This alternative <u>must</u> be used if the English 'ing'-form has a different subject from that of the main verb:

Ich kann es mir nicht vorstellen, **dass sie ihren Ring verkauft**	*I can't imagine her selling her ring*
Ich verlasse mich darauf, **dass er alles arrangiert**	*I rely on his/him arranging everything*

NB: After verbs (or nouns and adjectives) governing a preposition, the infinitive clause or *dass*-clause of alternatives (b) and (c) above is often anticipated by a prepositional adverb (e.g. *darauf*), as the relevant examples show. For details see 6.6.2 and 18.6.14.

(d) A finite verb

Wer **kocht** bei Ihnen zu Hause?	*Who does the cooking at your house?*

The subjectless passive (see 15.1.4) can be used for an English 'ing'-form after 'there is/are':

Überall **wurde** laut **gesungen**	*There was loud singing everywhere*

For 'there is/are' followed by 'no 'and an 'ing'-form, a construction with *sich lassen* (see 15.4.6) is often possible, e.g.:

Das **lässt sich** nicht leugnen	*There's no denying that*

13.7.2 The English 'ing'-form after prepositions

(a) 'by '(or 'through') + 'ing'-form

This construction usually corresponds to a clause with *dadurch, dass* or *indem* (see 19.7.3), or to *durch* followed by an infinitival noun. Thus the following are possible equivalents for the English sentence 'He escaped by jumping out of the window':

Er rettete sich **dadurch, dass er aus dem Fenster sprang**
Er rettete sich, **indem er aus dem Fenster sprang**
Er rettete sich **durch einen Sprung aus dem Fenster**

(b) 'for '+ 'ing'-form

The commonest equivalents are (*um*) ... *zu* (see 13.2.7a), or *zum* with an infinitival noun (see 13.4.3b):

Sie hat keine Zeit mehr **(um) zu üben** } Sie hat keine Zeit mehr **zum Üben** }	*She no longer has any time for practising*
Es ist zu kalt **zum Schwimmen**	*It's too cold for swimming*

(c) 'instead of' + 'ing'-form

For this, (an)statt ... zu or (an)statt dass is used (see 13.2.7c):

> Er spielt, **anstatt zu arbeiten/**   *He is playing instead of working*
> **anstatt dass er arbeitet**

(d) 'on '+ 'ing'-form

This usually corresponds to a clause with *als* or *wenn*, or *beim* followed by an infinitival noun (see 13.4.3a):

> **Als sie den Brief las**, wurde sie rot ⎫
> **Beim Lesen des Briefes** wurde sie rot ⎬   *On reading the letter, she blushed*

(e) 'with '+ 'ing'-form

This construction has a variety of possible equivalents in German, similar to those for participial clauses with 'ing'-forms (see 13.7.3):

> Wenn der Berg nur als ein unbestimmtes Gebilde erscheint, **wobei** sich die Baumgruppen bloß als blasse Schatten zeigen, ...
>
> *If the hill only appears as an indefinite shape with the groups of trees showing only as faint shadows, ...*
>
> Es ist schön hier, **wenn** die Sonne durch die Bäume scheint
>
> *It's lovely here with the sun shining through the trees*
>
> Wir sahen die alte Stadt, **über die** die zerfallene Burg emporragte
>
> *We could see the old town with the ruined castle towering above it*
>
> **Da** der Fluss rasch stieg, mussten Notmaßnahmen getroffen werden
>
> *With the river rising rapidly, emergency measures had to be taken*
>
> Der Bürgermeister eröffnete die Sitzung **unter** Ausschluss der Öffentlichkeit
>
> *The mayor opened the meeting, with the public being excluded*
>
> Sie eilte durch die Stadt, **und dabei** wehten ihre Haare nach hinten
>
> *She raced through the town with her hair streaming behind her*

(f) 'without' + ing'-form

This corresponds to *ohne ... zu* or *ohne dass* (see 13.2.7b):

> Der Zug fuhr durch, **ohne zu halten**   *The train went through without stopping*
> Er bot uns seine Hilfe an, **ohne dass wir**   *He offered us his help without our/us*
> **ihn darum bitten mussten**   *having to ask him for it*

(g) Other prepositions followed by 'ing'-forms

These correspond most often to a German subordinate clause or an appropriate preposition with an infinitival noun:

> **Nach** seiner Ankunft/**Nachdem** er angekommen war, ging er sofort zum Rathaus
>
> *After arriving he went straight to the town hall*
>
> **Vor** dem Einschlafen/**Bevor** er einschlief, las er schnell die Zeitung
>
> *Before going to sleep he read the newspaper quickly*
>
> **Trotz** seiner Hilfe/**Obwohl** er mir geholfen hatte, kam ich zu spät an
>
> *In spite of his/him having helped me, I arrived late*

NB: 'ing'-forms after prepositions governed by nouns, verbs or adjectives (e.g. 'I rely on finding him at home') are dealt with in 13.7.1.

13.7.3 Participial clauses with 'ing'-forms

The German equivalent depends on the sense of the clause.

(a) The participial clause and the main verb refer to consecutive or simultaneous actions
(i) The simplest German equivalent is to use main clauses joined by *und. dabei* can be used in the second to stress the simultaneity of the actions:

Sie öffnete die Schublade **und** nahm das Testament heraus	*Opening the drawer, she took out the will*
Ich saß an seinem Tisch **und** schrieb einen Brief	*I was sitting at his table writing a letter*
Er erzählte seine Geschichte **und** machte (**dabei**) nach jedem Satz eine Pause	*He told his story, pausing after each sentence*

NB: In modern German, clauses with *indem* do NOT correspond to English participial clauses like those above, despite what some English handbooks of German claim. For the use of *indem*, see 19.7.3.

(ii) A clause introduced by *wobei* can be used if the actions in the two clauses are simultaneous:

Er erzählte seine Geschichte, **wobei** er nach jedem Satz eine Pause machte.

(iii) If the action of the English participial clause precedes that of the main clause, the German equivalent is a clause with *als, wenn* or *nachdem*:

Als wir zum Fenster hinausschauten, sahen wir einen Polizeiwagen heranfahren	*Looking out of the window, we saw a police car approaching*
Wenn man oben auf dem Kirchturm steht, sieht man das ganze Dorf	*Standing on top of the church tower, you can see the whole village*
Nachdem ich die Briefe beantwortet hatte, ging ich spazieren	*Having answered the letters, I went for a walk*

(b) Participial clauses which give a reason or cause
In German, a subordinate clause with *da* or *weil* can be used:

Da es schon spät war, gingen wir nach Hause	*It being late, we went home*
Weil ich wusste, dass sie verreist war, habe ich sie nicht angerufen	*Knowing that she was away, I didn't call her*

(c) Participial clauses introduced by a conjunction
Subordinate clauses with the appropriate conjunction are used in German:

Während ich auf dich wartete, habe ich einen schweren Unfall gesehen	*While waiting for you, I saw a bad accident*

13.7.4 Clauses with 'ing'-forms used to qualify nouns

These correspond in German to a relative clause or, especially in formal written German, to an extended participial phrase (see 13.5.3):

Er sah ein **in entgegengesetzter
  Richtung kommendes** Auto
Er sah ein Auto, **das in
  entgegengesetzter Richtung kam** } *He saw a car coming in the opposite
  direction*

Einige Minuten später eilte der Arzt,
  der einen kleinen Koffer trug, zum
  Krankenhaus hin | *A few minutes later the doctor, carrying a
  small suitcase, was hurrying towards the
  hospital*

13.7.5 English 'ing'-forms after some verbs

The usual German equivalent of English 'ing'-forms after verbs is an infinitive with *zu* or a clause, see 13.7.1. However, a few verbs are special cases.

(a) verbs of perception
i.e. 'see', 'hear', 'feel'. The English 'ing'-form corresponds to a bare infinitive or a clause with *wie* (see 13.3.1b):

Ich höre die Vögel laut **singen**
Ich höre, **wie die Vögel laut singen** } *I can hear the birds singing loudly*

(b) verbs of motion
e.g. 'go', 'come', 'send', etc. If the 'ing'-form expresses purpose, a bare infinitive is used in German (see 13.3.1e):

Wir gehen heute **schwimmen** — *We're going swimming today*
Kommst du heute mit **schwimmen**? — *Are you coming swimming with us today?*
Sie schickte ihn **einkaufen** — *She sent him shopping*

The past participle is used after *kommen*, e.g. *Sie kam herangelaufen* 'She came running up', see 13.5.5c.

(c) *ing*-form expressing position
i.e. *standing, sitting*, etc. after *find, have, remain, stay*.

(i) German uses a bare infinitive after *bleiben, finden, haben* and *lassen* (see 13.3.1):

Sie **blieb** neben dem Ofen **sitzen** — *She remained sitting by the stove*
Ich **fand** ihn am Fenster **stehen** — *I found him standing by the window*
Haben Sie einen Mantel in der
  Garderobe **hängen**? — *Have you got a coat hanging in the
  wardrobe?*
Sie **ließ** ihre Sachen **herumliegen** — *She left her things lying about*

(ii) *finden* can also be used with the present participle of most verbs, e.g. *Sie fand ihn schlafend. Er fand sie Pilze suchend im Wald.* This construction is also possible with verbs of place, as an alternative to the infinitive: *Sie fand das Buch auf dem Boden liegend.*

(d) 'keep '+ 'ing'-form
A frequent equivalent is *lassen* with a bare infinitive, see 13.3.1:

Sie **ließ** uns **warten** — *She kept us waiting*

(e) 'keep'/'go on' + 'ing'-form
The simplest idiomatic equivalent is *weiter* with the verb (see 7.3.4):

> Sie sang **weiter**   *She kept/went on singing*

(f) 'need', 'want '+ 'ing'-form
These most often correspond to *müssen*, see 17.5.1b:

> Das muss noch erklärt werden   *That still needs/wants explaining*
> Man muss sich um sie kümmern   *She needs/wants looking after*

(g) 'can't help' + 'ing'-form
einfach müssen is the commonest German equivalent, see 17.3.6:

> Sie musste einfach lachen   *She couldn't help laughing*

14

Uses of the tenses

The grammatical category of TENSE involves the indication of time through special forms of the verb (see 12.1.1b). This chapter deals with the uses of the tenses of the INDICATIVE MOOD (i.e. not the subjunctive) in German:

- General notes on the **German tenses** (section 14.1)
- The **present tense** (section 14.2)
- The uses of the **past** and the **perfect tenses** (section 14.3)
- The **future tenses** (section 14.4)
- The **pluperfect tense** (14.5)
- German equivalents for the **English progressive tenses** (section 14.6)

The conjugation (i.e. the forms) of the tenses in German is explained in Chapter 12 and shown in full in the following tables:

- Table 12.2: the **simple tenses** of **regular verbs**
- Table 12.3: the **simple tenses** of the irregular verbs *haben, sein* and *werden*
- Table 12.4: the **simple tenses** of the **modal auxiliary** verbs and *wissen*
- Table 12.5: the **compound tenses**

14.1 The German tenses: general

14.1.1 There are six tenses in German

These are illustrated for the verb *kaufen* 'buy' in Table 14.1 (see also section 12.1.1b). There are, exactly as in English:

- two SIMPLE TENSES, with a single word: the PRESENT tense and the PAST tense
- four COMPOUND TENSES, formed with the AUXILIARY VERBS *haben, sein* and *werden*: the PERFECT tense, the PLUPERFECT tense, the FUTURE tense, and the FUTURE PERFECT tense.

In general, the forms and uses of the tenses in German and English are quite similar, as shown in Table 14.1. For this reason this chapter concentrates on those aspects of the use of German tenses which differ significantly from those of the corresponding English tenses.

Table 14.1 illustrates the tenses of the active voice of *kaufen*. Exactly the same set of tenses are also found in the passive voice, with the same meanings, as shown in Chapter 15. This chapter only deals with the tenses of the indicative mood, which signal a fact. The subjunctive mood also has tense forms, but these are used in a rather different way, as explained in Chapter 16.

TABLE 14.1 *German and English tenses*

Present	ich kaufe	*I buy*
Past	ich kaufte	*I bought*
Perfect	ich habe gekauft	*I have bought*
Pluperfect	ich hatte gekauft	*I had bought*
Future	ich werde kaufen	*I shall/will buy*
Future perfect	ich werde gekauft haben	*I shall/will have bought*

14.1.2 The German past tense

What in this book is referred to as the **past tense** is sometimes called the **imperfect tense.** However, unlike the imperfect tense of some languages (e.g. French and Latin), but like the English past tense, this German tense does <u>not</u> convey the idea of an incomplete or continuous action, but simply indicates that the action or event took place at some time in the past. For this reason, the less misleading term 'past tense' is preferable.

14.1.3 There are no progressive tenses in German

ich kaufe, for instance, normally corresponds to <u>both</u> English 'I buy' and 'I am buying'. However, in some contexts the difference in meaning between these English forms can (or must) be made clear in German in other ways, by using additional words or different constructions. Details are given in section 14.6.

14.2 The present tense

14.2.1 The present tense is used to relate present, habitual or 'timeless' actions or events

This corresponds to the normal use of the present tense (simple or progressive) in English:

Sie **singt** gut	*She sings/is singing well*
Ich **lese** die Zeitung von gestern	*I'm reading yesterday's newspaper*
Dankend **bestätigen** wir den Empfang Ihres Schreibens vom 30. Juni	*We gratefully acknowledge receipt of your letter of 30th June*
Ursula **spricht** ein wenig Spanisch	*Ursula speaks a little Spanish*
In Irland **regnet** es viel	*It rains a lot in Ireland*

14.2.2 The present tense indicates an action or state which began in the past and is still going on at the moment of speaking

Such sentences usually contain an adverb (*schon* or *bisher*), an adverbial phrase with *seit*, or an adverbial clause with *seit(dem)* or *solange*. These express the idea of 'up to now'.

(a) In 'up-to-now' contexts the present tense is used in German

This is quite different to English, where we use the **perfect** tense, typically the perfect progressive (e.g. 'have been doing', etc.):

Ich **stehe** schon lange hier vor dem Bahnhof	*I've been standing in front of the station for a long time*
Seit wann **wohnen** Sie in Rendsburg?	*How long have you been living in Rendsburg?*
Hier im Ngorongoro-Krater **darf** schon seit Jahrzehnten nicht mehr geschossen werden (*Grzimek*)	*Shooting hasn't been allowed here in the Ngorongoro crater for decades*
Seitdem die Europäer Tanganjika **verwalten**, hat sich eine solche Hungersnot nur noch in Kriegszeiten ereignet (*Grzimek*)	*Since the Europeans have been governing Tanganyika a famine like that has only occurred in wartime*
Er **wohnt** in Hamburg, solange ich ihn kenne	*He's lived in Hamburg as long as I've known him*

(b) In a few 'up-to-now' contexts German uses the perfect tense

i.e. the perfect tense, rather than the present tense. These constitute exceptions to the general rule given in (a) above. There are two main types of such contexts:

(i) in **negative statements**:

Ich **habe** ihn seit Jahren nicht **gesehen**	*I haven't seen him for years*
Seitdem ich ihn kenne, **haben** wir uns nie **gestritten**	*Since I've known him, we have never quarrelled*

However, the present tense is used, even in negative statements, if there has been a continuous action or state lasting up to the present time:

Seit Weihnachten **arbeitet** er nicht mehr	*He hasn't worked since Christmas*
Seitdem ich im Dorf wohne, **bin** ich nie einsam	*Since I've been living in the village, I've never been lonely*

(ii) when referring to a **series** of repeated actions or states

Er **ist** seit Weihnachten mehrmals krank **gewesen**	*He's been ill several times since Christmas*
Seit ihrer Erkrankung/Seitdem sie krank ist, **hat** sie viele Bücher **gelesen**	*Since she's been ill, she has read a lot of books*

However, the present tense is used to refer to a habit or state which has continued up to the present. English uses a different tense here, too, as can be seen by comparing this example with the one above:

Seit ihrer Erkrankung/Seitdem sie krank ist, **liest** sie viele Bücher	*Since she's been ill, she's been reading a lot of books*

(c) The present tense of *kommen* is often used to refer to the immediate past

Again, the idea is of an action continuing up to the present moment. English normally uses the perfect tense:

Ich **komme**, die Miete zu bezahlen	*I've come to pay the rent*

14.2.3 The present tense can refer to future time

(a) A present tense is often quite usual in German in contexts where a future tense is needed in English

This applies whether English uses a future tense with 'will/shall/'ll' or 'be going to':

In zwei Stunden **bin** ich wieder da	*I'll be back in two hours*
Wir **finden** es nie	*We're never going to find it*

In practice, the present tense is much more frequent than the future tense in German to refer to future time as long as future reference is clear from the context. This is especially the case if there is an adverbial in the sentence pointing to the future:

Ich **schreibe** den Brief heute Abend	*I'll write the letter tonight*
Morgen um diese Zeit **bin** ich in Wien	*This time tomorrow I'll be in Vienna*

But a present tense can always be used in German to refer to future time even when no adverbial is present, as long as the context points unambiguously to the future:

Sigrid **holt** uns von der Bahn ab	*Sigrid is going to meet us from the station*
Ich erwarte, dass sie **kommt**	*I expect she'll come*
Weitere Einzelheiten **erteilt** Ihnen unser Fachpersonal	*Our specialist staff will give you further information*
Vielleicht **sage** ich es ihm	*Perhaps I'll tell him*

The only contexts where a future tense needs to be used in German are those where the present tense could be taken simply to refer to the present, i.e. if the rest of the context does not make it clear that reference is to the future. Compare the following pairs of sentences, where we must use the future tense in German if we want to make it clear that the future is meant, because the present tense can only be understood to refer to the present moment:

Er **wird** wieder bei der Post **arbeiten**	*He's going to work for the post office again*
Er **arbeitet** wieder bei der Post	*He's working for the post office again*
Ich **werde** auf euch **warten**	*I'll be waiting for you*
Ich **warte** auf euch	*I'm waiting for you*
Sie weiß, was **geschehen wird**	*She knows what will happen*
Sie weiß, was **geschieht**	*She knows what is happening*

(b) If the future tense is used where it would be possible to use the present tense, it often emphasises the idea of a prediction, an intention or a supposition

This is particularly the case where reference to the future is clear, e.g. through an adverbial:

Es **wird** morgen wieder **regnen**	*It is going to rain again tomorrow*
Ich **werde** den Brief heute Abend **schreiben**	*I shall write the letter tonight*
Wir aber fliegen dorthin, wo die Sonne scheint, und keine Wolken **werden** uns jetzt noch **stoppen** (*Grzimek*)	*But we're flying to where the sun shines, and no clouds are going to stop us now*

14.2.4 The present tense is sometimes used to refer to the past

This so-called **'historic present'** is used more often in writing in German than English. It makes the past seem more immediate and it is a common stylistic device in narrative fiction and historical writing:

> Mit zuckenden Nerven **marschieren** sie näher, noch immer **versuchen** sie sich gegenseitig zu täuschen, so sehr sie alle schon die Wahrheit **wissen**: dass die Norweger, dass Amundsen ihnen zuvorgekommen **ist**. Bald **zerbricht** der letzte Zweifel . . . (*Zweig*)

Similarly in newspaper headlines:

> 40-Tonner **zermalmt** Trabi – 2 starben   *Forty-ton lorry squashes Trabi – two dead*
> (*BILD*)

It is also a typical feature of colloquial speech, as in English:

> Gestern Abend **geh** ich ins Café und **seh**   *Last night I go down the pub and see Horst*
> den Horst Brunner dort an der Theke   *Brunner sitting there at the bar*
> sitzen

14.3 The past tense and the perfect tense

14.3.1 The uses of the past and the perfect tenses in German: summary

In English there is a clear difference in meaning between the past and the perfect tenses, and the sentences 'I broke my leg' and 'I have broken my leg' are quite distinct in meaning. The English past tense simply tells us that something happened in the past, so that 'I broke my leg' tells us that it happened at some time in the past – and it's probably mended now. The English perfect tense, on the other hand, usually indicates that what happened in the past still has some relevance at the present. When we say 'I have broken my leg', for instance, it usually means that it is still broken at the moment of speaking.

The German sentences *Ich* **brach** *mir das Bein* and *Ich* **habe** *mir das Bein* **gebrochen** are deceptively similar to the English ones. However, there is no such clear cut difference in meaning as in English, and in many contexts we can use the one or the other without there being any real distinction between them. Which one is used is often a matter of style or register rather than meaning. The main differences between the two German tenses can be summarised as follows:

- The PERFECT tense is used principally:

  to refer to a past action or event which has relevance to the present

  in spoken German, to refer to past actions and events

- The PAST tense is used principally:

  in written German, to refer to past actions and events

More details on specific usage are given in the remainder of this section.

14.3.2 **The use of the perfect and past tenses to refer to a past action or event which has continuing relevance in the present**

(a) The PERFECT tense is usual in both spoken and written German to indicate a past action or event whose effect is relevant or apparent at the moment of speaking

Linking the past with the present is the typical function of the English perfect tense, as explained in 14.3.1, and the perfect tense is used in both English and German in such contexts. Specifically, we find the perfect in German:

(i) where the result of a past action or event is still evident at the moment of speaking:

Es **hat** in der Nacht **geschneit** (there's snow on the ground)	*It has snowed in the night*
Sie **hat** sich das Bein **gebrochen** (her leg is still in plaster)	*She's broken her leg*
Meine Tante **ist** gestern **angekommen** (and she's still here)	*My aunt arrived last night*

As the last example above shows, the perfect tense is used in German to express the present relevance of a past action even if there is a past time adverbial in the sentence. By contrast, English always uses the past tense in sentences which contain adverbials expressing past time.

(ii) to refer to something which happened in the immediate past:

Jetzt **hat** Klinsmann den Ball **eingeworfen**	*Klinsmann has just thrown the ball in*
Damit **haben** wir diese kleine Führung **beendet**	*With this we have come to the end of this short guided tour*

(iii) to refer to states or repeated actions which have lasted up to the moment of speaking:

Ich **habe** immer **gefunden**, dass es nützlich ist, viel zu wissen	*I've always found it useful to know a lot*
Ich **habe** ihm wiederholt **gesagt**, dass er ihr schreiben sollte	*I've told him repeatedly that he ought to write to her*
Das Paket **ist** noch nicht **angekommen**	*The parcel hasn't arrived yet*

NB: The **present** tense is used in German to refer to activities or states which began in the past and continue into the present, where English typically uses a perfect progressive, see 14.2.2.

(b) The PAST tense is occasionally used to indicate a past action or event which has relevance for the present

i.e. in the kind of contexts given under (a) above. This use of the past tense is mainly restricted to the following contexts, almost exclusively in written German:

(i) in newspaper headlines and short announcements. In these contexts the past tense, with its single word, can sound neater and snappier:

Lastwagenfahrer **gaben** Blockade am Brenner nach einer Woche auf (*FR*)	*Lorry drivers have given up their blockade on the Brenner pass after a week*
Sie **sahen** soeben einen Bericht von unserem Korrespondenten in Moskau	*You have just been watching a report from our Moscow correspondent*

(ii) with common verbs, especially the auxiliary verbs, and in the passive:

In der letzten Zeit **war** sie sehr krank	*She has been very ill recently*
Er **musste** heute kommen	*He has had to come today*
Noch nie **wurde** ein Auto so oft gebaut (*VW advert*)	*No car has ever been produced in such numbers*

(iii) in relative clauses:

Das sind die ersten Bilder der Unruhen in Beijing, die uns **erreichten**	*These are the first pictures which have reached us of the disturbances in Beijing*

In all the above examples the perfect tense would be equally possible.

14.3.3 The use of the past and perfect tenses to relate past actions or events

Narrations of past actions and events are typically in the past tense in written German and in the perfect tense in spoken German. In English, we typically use the past tense to relate an action or event lying entirely in the past. In German, however, while the past tense is usual in such contexts in the written language, the perfect predominates in everyday speech, especially in south Germany.

The characteristic use of the past tense for a written narrative can be seen in the following passage from Bernhard Schlink's best-selling novel *Der Vorleser*:

> Den Sommer nach dem Prozess **verbrachte** ich im Lesesaal der Universitäts-bibliothek. Ich **kam**, wenn der Lesesaal **öffnete**, und **ging**, wenn er **schloss**. An den Wochenenden **lernte** ich zu Hause. Ich **lernte** so ausschließlich, so besessen, dass die Gefühle und Gedanken, die der Prozess betäubt hatte, betäubt **blieben**. Ich **vermied** Kontakte. Ich **zog** zu Hause aus und **mietete** ein Zimmer. Die wenigen Bekannten, die mich im Lesesaal oder bei gelegentlichen Kinobesuchen **ansprachen**, **stieß** ich zurück

In Franz Xaver Kroetz's *Chiemgauer Geschichten*, by contrast, where ordinary people (from south Germany) are telling their stories to the author, the narrative is in the perfect tense:

> Ja, und dann **hats** wieder ein bisschen **gedauert**, bis sie wieder eine Arbeit **gekriegt hat**, also Lohn von ihr **ist** praktisch nichts **eingegangen**. **Hab** ich alles selbst verdienen **müssen**. Da wo wir dann **geheiratet haben**, da **hab** ich zwei Monate so noch **gearbeitet** auf Montage, und dann **bin** ich gekündigt **worden**.

There are some exceptions to this general tendency for the past tense to be used in written narrative and the perfect tense in spoken narrative:

(a) The past tense in spoken German

In south Germany (and Austria and Switzerland) the past tense is practically never used in everyday speech. However, this is much less true in north Germany (i.e. north of the river Main), where the past tense is not uncommon in everyday speech in the following contexts:

(i) with **commonly used verbs**, i.e.:

- *sein, haben, bleiben, gehen, kommen, stehen* and *es gibt*
- the modal auxiliaries
- verbs of saying, thinking and feeling

In this way, the following would be equally frequent in north German speech:

Ich **war** vorige Woche in Bremen	Ich **bin** vorige Woche in Bremen **gewesen**
Sie **konnte** gestern nicht kommen	Sie **hat** gestern nicht kommen **können**
Was **sagten** Sie?	Was **haben** Sie **gesagt**?

The past tense of other verbs does occur in spoken North German, but, in general, it is used rather less often than the perfect tense.

(ii) with the **passive**, e.g. *Das alte Haus* ***wurde*** *abgerissen* or *Das alte Haus* ***ist*** *abgerissen* ***worden***

(iii) in clauses introduced by *als* or *wie*, and in any sentence with the adverb *damals*:

Ich habe sie gemerkt, als sie aus der Straßenbahn **ausstieg**	*I noticed her when she got out of the tram*
Ich habe gehört, wie sie die Treppe **herunterkam**	*I heard her coming down the stairs*
Damals **mussten** wir alle Ersatzkaffee trinken	*At that time we all had to drink coffee substitute*

(iv) to record a **state**, or a **habitual** or **repeated action** in the past:

Die Rechnung **lag** auf dem Balkon	*The bill was lying on the balcony*
Bei uns in der alten Heimat **dauerten** die Sommerferien länger als hier	*In our old homeland the summer holidays used to last longer than they do here*
Ich habe gewusst, dass sein Vater **trank**	*I knew his father used to drink*

(b) There is a tendency for a longer narrative to start with a perfect tense, and then continue in the past tense
The perfect is used to set the scene, as it were. This usage is especially frequent in newspaper reports:

> 10 Tage nach der Jumbo-Katastrophe in Japan **ist** schon wieder eine Boeing **explodiert**. 54 Urlauber **starben** gestern in einem flammenden Inferno auf dem Flughafen Manchester (England). Als ihr Jet nach Korfu (Griechenland) starten **wollte**, **wurde** das linke Triebwerk krachend zerfetzt. Sofort **brannte** die Maschine wie eine Riesenfackel. Im Rumpf eingeschlossene Urlauber **trampelten** andere tot. (*BILD*)

(c) The perfect is sometimes used as a narrative tense in written German
The perfect tense is sometimes used deliberately to give a more colloquial tone. However, particularly outside fiction, it is often treated simply as an alternative to the past and used for reasons relating to style, emphasis and sentence rhythm, as in the following text from Grzimek's *Serengeti darf nicht sterben*:

> Ein tüchtiger Mann namens Rothe, der Verwalter bei den Siedentopfs **war**, **hat** 1913 die Reste einer uralten Siedlung und eines Friedhofs aus der Jungsteinzeit am Nordende des Kraters **entdeckt**. Schon diese Leute, die einige Jahrhunderte vor

Christus **gelebt haben, weideten** als Hirten ihr Vieh wie heute die Massai. Rothe **hieß** eigentlich anders, er **war** 1905 bei der ersten finnischen Revolution kurze Zeit Minister **gewesen**, . . . In Ägypten **stellte** ihm die russische Geheimpolizei nach, und so **kam** er als Tierpfleger mit Maultieren nach Deutsch-Ostafrika.

In practice, the past tense could be substituted for any of the perfect tenses in this passage, or vice versa, without any real difference in meaning.

14.3.4 Other uses of the past tense

The perfect tense cannot be used in any of these contexts.

(a) to relate a state or activity which began in the past and was still in progress at a more recent point in the past

This is the equivalent in past time of the use of the present with *seit* phrases, etc. (see 14.2.2). In English the pluperfect tense (especially the pluperfect progressive) is used in such contexts:

Seitdem ich ihn **kannte, besuchte** ich ihn jeden Sonntag	*Since I had known him, I had visited him every Sunday*
Ich **wartete** schon zwei Stunden/seit zwei Stunden auf sie	*I had been waiting for her for two hours*

However, as with the use of the perfect tense rather than the present (see 14.2.2), the pluperfect tense, not the past tense, is used in **negative statements** or when referring to a **series** of actions or states:

Seitdem ich ihn kannte, **hatten** wir uns nie **gestritten**	*Since I had known him, we had never quarrelled*
Ich **hatte** ihm seit Jahren **zugeredet**, sein Haus zu verkaufen	*I had been urging him for years to sell his house*

(b) with the sense of a future-in-the-past

In such contexts, the past tense is an uncommon alternative to the *würde*-form of *Konjunktiv II* (the 'conditional', see 16.4.5):

Nachdem er sicher war, dass der Vorgang nicht mehr **hochging** (more usual: *hochgehen würde*), verließ er das Theater	*When he was sure that the curtain would not go up again, he left the theatre*

(c) to refer to the present moment

This is a special usage to recall information which has already been given in the past:

Wie **war** ihr Name doch gleich?	*What was your name again?*
Wer **erhielt** das Eisbein?	*Who is getting the knuckle of pork?*
Herr Ober, ich **bekam** noch ein Bier	*Waiter, I did order another beer*

14.3.5 Further uses of the perfect tense

The past tense cannot be used in any of these contexts.

(a) as an alternative to the future perfect tense
(i) The perfect tense is frequently used with the sense of a future perfect:

Bis morgen um diese Zeit **habe** ich alles **geregelt**	*By this time tomorrow I shall have settled everything*
Bald **habe** ich den Brief **geschrieben**	*I'll have written the letter soon*

As with the use of the present tense to refer to future time (see 14.2.3), the perfect tense can only substitute for a future perfect tense if it is clear from the context (e.g. from a time adverbial) that the reference is to the future. There is no comparable usage in English, where the future perfect tense is always used in such contexts. When the future perfect tense is used in such sentences in German, e.g. *Bis morgen um diese Zeit **werde** ich alles **geregelt haben**,* there is often an additional sense of a prediction or a supposition, see 14.4.2.

(ii) The perfect is the usual tense in subordinate time clauses with future reference. In these contexts English and German correspond in the use of the perfect tense.

Wenn ich von ihm **gehört habe**, werde ich dir schreiben	*When I've heard from him, I shall write to you*

Very occasionally a future perfect is used in such sentences in written German:

Ich will fortgehen, wenn ich genug **gelesen haben werde** (*Andersch*)	*I intend to leave when I have read enough*

(b) to indicate a characteristic state
As the perfect can signal the present result of a past action, it can be used in German to indicate an action whose completion can be taken to define a particular person or thing. This usage, which is particularly common in technical and legal language, has no equivalent in English.

Ein Unglück **ist** schnell **geschehen** (i.e. they are over before you realise)	*Accidents happen quickly*
Ein Akademiker **hat studiert**	*A graduate is a person who has completed a course of studies*
Die Mannschaft, die zuerst 50 Punkte **erreicht hat**, ist Sieger	*The first team to reach 50 points is the winner*

14.4 The future tense and the future perfect tense

The FUTURE tense in German is formed with the auxiliary verb *werden* and the **infinitive** (e.g. *Ich werde sie am Montag sehen*). The FUTURE PERFECT is formed with *werden*, the **past participle** of the main verb, and the **infinitive** of the auxiliary verb *haben* or *sein* (depending on what main verb is involved, e.g. *Ich werde den Brief geschrieben haben; Sie wird schon gegangen sein*) The conjugation of these tenses is explained and shown in detail in 12.3.1 and Table 12.5.

The English future has two forms, one with the auxiliary *will* (in some contexts *shall*), which is usually reduced to *'ll* in speech (e.g. *I'll probably see her on Monday*), and one with the phrase *be going to* (e.g. *I'm going to see her on Monday*). There is little practical difference in meaning between these English forms, but there is no comparable form to the latter in German; the verb *gehen* is never used with another verb to indicate futurity in German.

14.4.1 The basic uses of the future tense and the future perfect tense are to refer to future time

The **future tense** (referred to as *Futur I* in German) relates an action or event which will happen at a point subsequent to the time of speaking:

Ich **werde** sie nicht mehr **sehen**	*I won't/shan't see her again*
Wirst du ihr helfen **können**?	*Will you be able to help her?*

The **future perfect** tense (referred to as *Futur II* in German) is a 'relative' tense; it indicates an action or event which will take place **before** another action or event in the future:

Gewiss **wird** sie den Brief bis morgen Abend **geschrieben haben**	*She will certainly have written the letter by tomorrow evening*

However, if the reference to future time is otherwise clear from the context, German tends to prefer the present tense to the future (see 14.2.3), and the perfect tense to the future perfect (see 14.3.5a). However, there are contexts where these tenses must be used simply to indicate futurity, since the present or the perfect would have their basic meaning:

Ich mag sie nicht und **werde** sie nie **mögen**	*I don't like her and I'll never like her*
Hat er Ihnen nicht gesagt, dass er Sie **besuchen wird**?	*Didn't he tell you that he's going to visit you?*
Am Montag **wird** sie den Gipfel **erreicht haben**	*On Monday she'll have reached the summit*

14.4.2 The future and future perfect tenses often convey the idea of an intention or an assumption

This is generally the case when future time reference is otherwise clear from the context, and the present or the perfect tense could be used rather than the future tenses:

Morgen **wird** es bestimmt **schneien**	*It will definitely snow tomorrow*
Ich **werde** es heute Abend noch **erledigen**	*I am going to finish it tonight*
Morgen **wird** er die Arbeit **beendet haben**	*He'll have finished the work tomorrow*

14.4.3 The future tenses often simply express an assumption

In these contexts these tenses do not refer to future time at all; the future refers to the present and the future perfect to the past. English uses its future tenses in a similar way:

Sie **wird** bereits zu Hause **sein**	*She'll be home already*
Er ist nicht gekommen. Er **wird** wieder zu viel zu tun **haben**	*He hasn't come. He'll have too much to do again*
Sie **wird** den Zug **verpasst haben**	*She'll have missed the train*
Er **wird** sich gestern einen neuen Hut **gekauft haben**	*He'll have bought a new hat yesterday*

When used like this to express a supposition, these tenses are often accompanied by the particle *wohl* (see 10.35.1):

Sie wird **wohl** bereits zu Hause sein   Sie wird **wohl** den Zug verpasst haben

NB: This sense of the future and future perfect is very similar to the meaning of *dürfte* (see 17.2.2), so that *Sie wird wohl bereits zu Hause sein* means much the same as *Sie dürfte bereits zu Hause sein*.

14.5 The pluperfect tense

The German PLUPERFECT tense is formed with the **past tense** of one of the auxiliary verbs *haben* or *sein* (depending on the verb involved) and the **past participle**: *Ich hatte sie nicht gesehen; Ich war schon gegangen*, see 12.3 and Table 12.5. This closely parallels the formation of the pluperfect in English (e.g. 'I hadn't seen her').

14.5.1 The German pluperfect tense mainly indicates a past within the past

(a) **The German pluperfect tense is a relative tense**
Like the English pluperfect, it places an action or event further back in the past than the time of the context. It is characteristically used in clauses introduced by *nachdem* (see 19.3.4):

Nachdem sie **gegangen war**, fiel ihr ein, was sie **vergessen hatte**	*After she had gone she remembered what she had forgotten*
Das bemerkte man erst, nachdem man Platz **genommen hatte** (Morgner)	*You only noticed that after you had sat down*

But it is used in other contexts where it is necessary to indicate a more **remote** past:

Wir warteten, bis der Zug **abgefahren war**	*We waited until the train had left*
Sie kamen zu spät, denn das Hochwasser **hatte** den Damm schon **überflutet**	*They came too late, as the high water had already flooded over the embankment*

(b) The perfect tense is occasionally used where one would expect a pluperfect

This may emphasise the immediacy of a state or an action. The effect is rather similar to that of the 'historic present', see 14.2.4:

> Dann seufzte sie auf eine Weise, die mir deutlich machte, wie alt sie **geworden ist** (*Böll*)
>
> *Then she sighed in a way which made it clear to me how old she had become*

This usage is fairly frequent in writing, and increasingly common in everyday speech.

(c) The past tense is sometimes used for an expected pluperfect

This usage is predominantly literary and is usually motivated by stylistic reasons, the one-word form being preferred in context:

> . . . doch ergab der Befund jene hoffnungslose Krankheit, die man **vermutete** (*Dürrenmatt*)
>
> *. . . but the investigation revealed the terminal disease which had been suspected*

14.5.2 The pluperfect tense is sometimes used in colloquial German simply to refer to the past

i.e. the pluperfect occurs where a past or perfect tense would be expected:

> Eva **hatte** dich **gesucht**
> Wer **war** das **gewesen**?
>
> *Eva was looking for you*
> *Who was that?*

This 'pseudopluperfect', is increasingly common in everyday speech. Standard authorities still consider it to be substandard.

14.5.3 Complex pluperfect tense forms

In south Germany the **pluperfect** tense is commonly formed with the **perfect** tense of the auxiliaries *haben* or *sein*. For example, *Ich* **habe ihn gesehen gehabt**, is used for standard German *Ich hatte ihn gesehen*. Forms like this are now widespread in spoken German and no longer restricted to the south. Indeed, if an extra dimension of remoteness in time is needed, the **pluperfect** tense of the auxiliary is sometimes used, e.g.: *Sie* **hatte ihn gesehen gehabt**, *bevor er sie bemerkt hatte*. This form is particularly common in speech if the action has been reversed again, e.g.:

> Sie hatte ihren Schlüssel vergessen gehabt
>
> *She had forgotten her key*
> *(but she's remembered it again now)*

These complex pluperfects are chiefly <u>colloquial</u> and generally regarded as <u>non-standard</u>. However, they are not unknown in formal writing:

Er dachte: Du kannst jetzt nichts gesehen haben, du kannst wegdrücken ... und **hast** bloß den Anschluss **verloren gehabt** und bist kein Jäger (*Gaiser*)	*He thought 'You can't have seen anything now, you can sneak off ... You had just got left behind and you're not a rifleman*
Wir **haben** uns alle schon daran **gewöhnt gehabt**, dass nichts geschieht, aber immer etwas geschehen soll (*Musil*)	*We had all got used to the idea that nothing was going to happen but that something always ought to happen*

14.6 German equivalents for the English progressive tenses

14.6.1 There are <u>no</u> progressive tenses in German

The distinction between the English **progressive present** tense 'He is singing well' (i.e. at the moment) and the **simple present** tense 'He sings well '(i.e. usually) cannot be expressed by using different forms of the verb in German. In most contexts the distinction is simply ignored in German and 'Er singt gut' is used for both these English sentences.

NB: The English perfect progressive can indicate that an action beginning in the past is still going on at the moment of speaking, e.g. *I have been waiting here for an hour*. German uses the simple present tense in these contexts, see 14.2.2.

14.6.2 Indicating continuous action in German

Nevertheless, there are contexts where we need to make it clear in German that we are dealing with a continuous action. For instance, an English sentence like 'He was reading *War and Peace* yesterday' implies that he didn't finish reading it, whereas to say in German *Gestern las er „Krieg und Frieden"* or *Gestern hat er „Krieg und Frieden" gelesen* could imply that he <u>did</u> finish it (which is unlikely in a single day). In such contexts, German has a number of possibilities for indicating that the action was continuous or unfinished, i.e.:

(a) By using an appropriate adverb
(i) especially *eben* or *gerade*:

Ich schreibe **eben** Briefe	*I'm writing letters*
Er rasiert sich **gerade**	*He's shaving*

(ii) With verbs of motion, *schon* or *gleich* can often be used:

Ich fahre **schon**	*I'm leaving*
Sie kommt **gleich**	*She's coming*

(iii) Other adverbs or particles may serve in other contexts:

Ich habe ihn **letzthin** zweimal in der Woche gesehen	*I've been meeting him twice a week (recently)*
Ich kümmere mich **eben mal** darum	*I'm seeing to it now*

(iv) The sense of habitual or repeated action expressed by a simple tense in English can be indicated by an adverb in German:

Ich stehe **immer** um sechs auf	*I always get up at six*
Sie spielt **meistens** gut	*She (usually) plays well*

(b) By using *(gerade/eben) dabei sein* followed by an infinitive with *zu*

Ich bin **gerade dabei**, das Zimmer ein bisschen aufzuräumen	*I'm just tidying the room up a bit*
Gestern war er **gerade dabei**, „Krieg und Frieden" zu lesen	*He was reading* War and Peace *yesterday*

(c) By using a construction with an infinitival noun

(i) In standard German *beim* is used with an infinitival noun (see 13.4.3a):

Als seine Frau zurückkam, war er **beim Kochen**	*When his wife returned, he was cooking*
Wir waren **beim Kartenspielen**, als er klingelte	*We were playing cards when he rang the bell*

(ii) In north-west Germany, *am* can be used with an infinitival noun to express continuous action:

Wir sind **am Arbeiten**	*We are working*
In Köln ist es immer **am Regnen**	*It's always raining in Cologne*

This originally regional usage has recently become much more widely used in colloquial speech, but it is still considered non-standard.

(d) by using a noun with a prepositional phrase

Wir sind **an der Arbeit**	*We're working*
Er liest **in der Zeitung**	*He's reading the newspaper*
Sie strickte **an einem Strumpf**	*She was knitting a stocking*

(e) by using a different verb

Some German verbs, especially those with prefixes, imply the completion of an action. The corresponding unprefixed verbs do not necessarily imply that the action has finished and can in certain contexts correspond more closely to the sense of an English progressive tense:

Sie **erkämpften** die Freiheit ihres Landes *(kiharcolták)*	*They fought for their country's freedom* (i.e. they were successful)
Sie **kämpften** für die Freiheit ihres Landes	*They were fighting for their country's freedom*
Wir **aßen** die Würste **auf**	*We ate the sausages (up)*
Wir **aßen** die Würste	*We were eating the sausages*
Sie **erstiegen** den Berg *(megmászták)*	*They climbed the mountain*
Sie **stiegen** auf den Berg	*They were climbing the mountain* (i.e. in the process of climbing, or only part of the way)

15

The passive

We typically express actions by using the active voice, both in English and in German. The active sentence tells us what is happening and who or what is doing it. But we can present a different perspective on an action by using the PASSIVE VOICE. This places the emphasis on what is going on, without necessarily saying who or what is doing it.

> **active voice:** Die Schlange frisst **den Frosch**
> **passive voice:** **Der Frosch** wird (von der Schlange) gefressen

Most active sentences with a TRANSITIVE VERB (i.e. a verb which has an accusative object, see 18.3) can be turned into passive sentences. The **accusative object** of the **active sentence** becomes **the subject** of the **passive sentence**. The subject of the active sentence (the person or thing carrying out the action, called the **agent**) is often left out altogether, but it can also appear in a phrase using *von* or *durch* (= English 'by').

There are two passive forms in German, using the auxiliary verbs *werden* or *sein* together with the past participle:

- The *werden*-passive (e.g. *die Stadt wurde zerstört*) expresses a process (German: *Vorgangspassiv*) and is closely related to the corresponding active voice.
- The *sein*-passive (e.g. *die Stadt war zerstört*) expresses a state (German *Zustandspassiv*). Its use is more restricted than that of the *werden*-passive (which is three or four times more frequent).

The use of these, and other German constructions which are the equivalent of passives, is explained in this chapter:

- The *werden*-passive (section 15.1)
- The *sein*-passive, and the differences between it and the *werden*-passive (section 15.2)
- The use of *von* and *durch* for English 'by' with the passive (section 15.3)
- Other German constructions with **passive meaning** (section 15.4)
- The use of the active and passive voice in German and English (section 15.5)

The conjugation of the *werden*-passive is given in Table 12.6, and the *sein*-passive in Table 12.7. Forms of the passive in the subjunctive mood are explained in section 12.5.

15.1 The *werden*-passive

15.1.1 The *werden*-passive has the same range of tenses and moods as the active voice

The conjugation of these tenses in the indicative is given in Table 12.6. For passive forms in the subjunctive mood, see section 12.5. Table 15.1 shows the relationship between the tenses of the active and passive voice.

TABLE 15.1 *Active and passive sentences*

Tense	Active	Passive
Present	Der Arzt **heilt den Patienten** *The doctor **heals the patient***	Der Patient **wird** (vom Arzt) **geheilt** *The patient **is healed** (by the doctor)*
Past	Die Bauleute **rissen das Haus ab** *The builders **pulled down the house***	Das Haus **wurde** (von den Bauleuten) **abgerissen** *The house **was pulled down** (by the builders)*
Perfect	Die Firma **hat den Angestellten entlassen** *The company **has sacked the employee***	Der Angestellte **ist** (von der Firma) **entlassen worden** *The employee **has been sacked** (by the company)*
Future	Der Computer **wird das Buch verdrängen** *The computer **will replace the book***	Das Buch **wird** (vom Computer) **verdrängt werden** *The book **will be replaced** (by the computer)*

(a) The use of the passive tenses is in general the same as in the active (see Chapter 14). There is slight variation in use in a few instances:

(i) The **future** tense is little used in the passive, and the present tense is always preferred unless there is a risk of being misunderstood (see 14.4):

| Das Buch **wird** nächste Woche **gelesen werden** | *The book will be read next week* |
| Es **werden** große Anforderungen an Sie **gestellt werden** (*Kafka*) | *Great demands will be placed on you* |

In the first example above, normal usage would prefer the present tense *Das Buch wird* nächste Woche *gelesen* rather than the future, and this is possible because the phrase *nächste Woche* makes the time reference clear. In the second example, however, we cannot replace the future tense by the present tense without changing the meaning. *Es werden* große Anforderungen an Sie *gestellt* can only mean 'Great demands are being placed on you'.

(ii) The **past** tense of the passive is quite commonly used in both written and spoken German, even in contexts where the perfect tense might be expected in the active voice (see 14.3.2). *i, e, past action, related to present* *

(b) The *werden*-passive is hardly ever used in commands
To give commands in the passive, the *sein*-passive is used, e.g. *Sei gegrüßt! Sei beruhigt!* (see 15.2.1).

15.1.2 The *werden*-passive can be formed from most transitive verbs

i.e. verbs which are used with a direct object in the accusative case, see 18.3.1.

continued until present of result in pres.

(a) The ACCUSATIVE OBJECT of the active verb becomes the SUBJECT of the corresponding passive construction

> Mein Vater liest **diesen Roman** → **Dieser Roman** wird von meinem Vater gelesen
> *My father is reading this novel*   *This novel is being read by my father*

Further examples are shown in Table 15.1.

(b) A few transitive verbs cannot be used in the *werden*-passive

Verbs of knowing, containing, possessing and receiving, i.e. *bekommen, besitzen, enthalten, erhalten, haben, kennen, kriegen, umfassen, wissen* are not used in the passive in German. Other constructions occur as the equivalent of English passives with such verbs, in particular active forms of another verb or a construction with *man*:

> Dieses Schloss gehört dem Grafen von Libowitz   *This palace **is owned** by Count von Libowitz*
> (i.e. NOT **wird ... besessen*)
>
> Ihr Brief traf gestern ein   *Your letter **was received** yesterday*
> (i.e. NOT **wurde ... erhalten*)
>
> Man wusste nicht, wie viele Kinder kommen würden   *It **was not known** how many children would come*

NB: (i)   *enthalten* can be used with *sein*, e.g. *Wieviel Essig ist in diesem Gefäß enthalten?* but this is not really a passive construction.
      (ii)   A passive of *erhalten* can be formed with *bleiben*, see 15.2.2c.

(c) No passive can be formed with the verbs of perception followed by a bare infinitive

(see 13.3.1). These verbs can be used in the passive with an 'ing'-form in English, but the equivalent sentences in German must use alternative constructions, usually with the active voice:

> Man hörte ihn singen   *He was heard singing*
> Ein Vorbeigehender sah ihn in das Haus einbrechen   *He was seen breaking into the house by a passer-by*

15.1.3 Passive constructions with verbs governing a dative object, a genitive object or a prepositional object

In German only the **accusative (direct) object** of a transitive verb can become the **subject** of a passive construction. This is an important restriction which does not apply in English. It means that the dative object, the genitive object or the prepositional object of a verb can never become the subject of a passive construction in German:

(a) If a verb which takes a dative object is used in the passive, the dative object remains in the dative case

This is the case with all those verbs which govern the dative case, and have no accusative object (see 18.4.1).

> Astrid dankte **ihm** für seine Hilfe   →   **Ihm** wurde für seine Hilfe gedankt
> *Astrid thanked him for his help*   *He was thanked for his help*

er'halten (inn) = get, receive, keep, preserve
ent'halten (inn) = contain, hold

As the dative object remains in the dative, the verbs in these passive constructions are **subjectless** (or **impersonal**) and the verb has the endings of the third person singular. Further examples:

Die Zigeuner können **Ihnen** helfen → **Ihnen** kann geholfen werden
   The gypsies can help you   *You can be helped*
Er empfahl **mir**, eine Kur zu nehmen → **Mir** wurde empfohlen, eine Kur zu nehmen
   He recommended me to take a course   *I was recommended to take a course*
    of treatment at a spa   *of treatment at a spa*

The dative object does not need to be placed before the verb, but if it is placed later in the sentence the pronoun *es* (see 3.6.2a) is inserted before the verb. Compare the following (equally acceptable) alternatives to the examples above:

Es kann Ihnen geholfen werden
Es wurde mir empfohlen, eine Kur zu nehmen

(b) With verbs which have both an accusative object and a dative object, the dative object remains in the dative in the passive

Details on these *einem etwas* verbs are given in 18.4.2. In German, only an accusative object can be converted into the subject of a passive verb. This differs from English, where, with many verbs which have two objects, either can become the subject of the passive:

Er gab **dem alten Mann** das Geld   → **Dem alten Mann** wurde das Geld
                                   gegeben
   He gave the old man the money   *The old man was given the money*
Sie hatten **ihr** ein Fahrrad versprochen → **Ihr** war ein Fahrrad versprochen worden
   They had promised her a bike   *She had been promised a bike*

NB: A dative object can become the subject of a passive construction with *bekommen* or *kriegen*, see 15.4.2.

(c) The passive infinitive of a verb which governs the dative case cannot be used in an infinitive clause with *zu*

Sentences like 'He could not hope to be helped' are quite usual in English. In German, though, we cannot say **Er konnte nicht hoffen geholfen zu werden*, since *helfen* governs a dative and its object cannot be used as the subject of a passive construction. We have to use a *dass*-clause in these contexts:

Er konnte nicht hoffen, dass ihm   *He could not hope to be helped*
  geholfen wurde
Er besteht darauf, dass ihm geantwortet   *He insists on being answered*
  wird

(d) Subjectless passives are also used with verbs which govern a genitive object or a prepositional object

See 18.5 and 18.6 for details on these verbs. Genitive objects and prepositional objects also remain in the same form in the passive:

Sie gedachten **der Toten**   →   **Der Toten** wurde gedacht
   They remembered the dead   *The dead were remembered*
Meine Mutter sorgt **für die Kinder**   →   **Für die Kinder** wird gesorgt
   My mother is taking care of the children   *The children are being taken care of*

With these verbs, too, the genitive or the prepositional phrase can be placed later in the sentence rather than at the beginning, but, similarly, *es* then has to be inserted before the verb:

> Es wurde der Toten gedacht   Es wird für die Kinder gesorgt

NB: In practice, *gedenken* is the only verb governing the genitive which is used in the passive in modern German.

15.1.4 The 'subjectless' *werden*-passive

(a) The *werden*-passive can be used without a subject to denote an activity in general

A sentence like *Es wird getanzt* simply means 'There is dancing going on' without any indication of who is doing it. No comparable construction exist in English. The verb has the third person singular endings:

Sie hörten, wie im Nebenzimmer **geredet wurde**	*They heard someone talking in the next room*
Hier darf nicht **geraucht werden**	*Smoking is not allowed here*
Vor Hunden **wird gewarnt**	*Beware of dogs*
Heute **ist** mit den Bauarbeiten **begonnen worden** (*ARD*)	*They started building today*

(b) A subjectless passive can be formed from any verb which expresses an activity

This construction can be used not only with transitive verbs, but also with verbs which otherwise cannot form a passive, i.e. intransitive verbs and, in colloquial German, even reflexive verbs:

Dann **wurde** auf den Straßen **getanzt**	*Then there was dancing in the streets*
An dem Abend **wurde** viel **gesungen**	*There was a lot of singing that evening*
Hier **wird gelegen, gestöhnt, geliebt, gestorben** (*Goes*)	*Here men lie, moan, love, die*
Jetzt **wird sich gewaschen**	*It's time to get washed*

NB. This is basically the same construction as that used with verbs which do not govern an accusative object (and which, strictly speaking, are also intransitive), see 15.1.3.

(c) The pronoun *es* is inserted in a main clause if there is no other word or phrase before the verb

(see 3.6.2a for further details on this use of *es*):

Es wurde auf den Straßen getanzt	*There was dancing in the streets*
Es wird besonders rücksichtslos geparkt (*ARD*)	*People are parking in a particularly inconsiderate way*

(d) The subjectless passive is often used to give commands

(see 16.2 for further details on commands):

Jetzt wird gearbeitet!	*Let's get down to work now*
Jetzt wird nicht gelacht!	*No laughing now!*

15.2 The *sein*-passive

15.2.1 Forms of the *sein*-passive

The conjugation of verbs in the *sein*-passive is given in Table 12.7 (for the indicative mood). Subjunctive forms are explained in section 12.5. In practice, only a restricted range of tenses and moods is in use:

Present tense:	Ich **bin** beruhigt
Past tense:	Ich **war** beruhigt
Konjunktiv I:	Ich **sei** beruhigt
Konjunktiv II:	Ich **wäre** beruhigt
Imperative:	**Sei** beruhigt

The past tense tends to be used rather than the perfect tense, although the perfect tense is sometimes heard in spoken German and may occasionally be found in writing:

Vierzig Lehrer **sind** gestern als krank **gemeldet gewesen** (*Zeit*)	*Forty teachers were reported sick yesterday*

The future tense (e.g. *Die Bilder **werden** morgen entwickelt **sein***) is very rare.

15.2.2 The *sein*-passive and the *werden*-passive

(a) The *sein*-passive indicates the state which the subject of the verb is in as the result of a previous action
This is reflected in its German name: *Zustandspassiv*. The *werden*-passive, on the other hand, relates an action or process, hence its German name: *Vorgangspassiv*.

(i) The following sentence illustrates the difference between the two passives:

Als ich um fünf kam, **war** die Tür **geschlossen**, aber ich weiß nicht, wann sie **geschlossen wurde**	*When I came at five the door was shut, but I don't know when it was shut*

In the first case, someone had **already shut** the door by the time I arrived, i.e. it was in a shut **state**, and for this reason the *sein*-passive is used. In the second case I am referring to the time when the **action** of shutting the door occurred, and the *werden*-passive has to be used.

(ii) As with the *werden*-passive, see 15.1.3, only the accusative object of a transitive verb can become the subject of a *sein*-passive. With verbs which take a dative, genitive or prepositional object, a 'subjectless' construction must be used in the *sein*-passive too:

Damit ist **den Kranken** nicht geholfen	*The patients have not been helped by that*
Für die Verletzten ist gesorgt	*The wounded have been taken care of*

NB: In practice few intransitive verbs are used in the *sein*-passive, chiefly *dienen, helfen, nützen, schaden, sorgen für*.

(iii) The *werden*-passive is used more widely than the *sein*-passive. It can occur with more verbs and, overall, it is three or four times more frequent in both speech and writing. Nevertheless, the *sein*-passive can be quite common in some registers, e.g. in newspaper reports, which often have reason to refer to states or to the results of actions:

> Deutschland **ist** fest in die NATO **eingebunden** (*Welt*)
> Dass die Wahlergebnisse in der DDR **gefälscht waren**, bestreitet auch Modrow nicht (*Spiegel*)

(b) Examples of the difference between the *sein*-passive and the *werden*-passive

A constant source of confusion for English learners is that the English passive, which uses the auxiliary 'be', <u>looks</u> like the *sein*-passive. The examples below show that the two passives have distinct meanings and are rarely interchangeable:

Der Tisch **wird gedeckt**	*The table is being laid* (i.e. someone is performing the action of laying the table)
Der Tisch **ist gedeckt**	*The table is laid* (i.e. someone has already laid it)
Die Stadt **wurde** 1944 **zerstört**	*The town was destroyed in 1944* (i.e. the action took place in 1944)
Die Stadt **war zerstört**	*The town was destroyed* (i.e. someone had already destroyed it)
Die Stadt **wurde** allmählich von Truppen **umringt**	*The town was gradually (being) surrounded by troops* (i.e. the troops were in the process of surrounding it)
Die Stadt **war** von Truppen **umringt**	*The town was surrounded by troops* (i.e. the troops were already in position round the town)

(c) Indicators pointing to the use of the *werden*-passive or the *sein*-passive

In practice, there are a number of indicators which can prove helpful in determining whether to use the *sein*-passive or the *werden*-passive:

(i) The *werden*-passive often corresponds to an **English progressive** tense, whilst this is never the case with the *sein*-passive. As the examples in (b) above show, this is especially the case in the present tense.

(ii) As the *sein*-passive relates the state resulting from a previous action, its meaning is close to that of the **perfect tense,** since the perfect tense often presents a **result** (see 14.3.2). This means, for example, that the difference between the following pairs of sentences is slight:

> Das Haus **ist gebaut**   Das Haus **ist gebaut worden**
> Die Stadt **war zerstört**   Die Stadt **war zerstört worden**

As a consequence, the idiomatic English equivalent of a German *sein*-passive is often a perfect or pluperfect tense rather than a present or a past tense:

Das Auto **ist repariert**	*The car has been repaired*
Rund 2500 Polizeibeamte riegelten die Stadt ab, über die ein umfassendes Demonstrationsverbot **verhängt war** (*Welt*)	*About 2500 police officers cordoned off the city, which had been made subject to a comprehensive ban on demonstrations*

(iii) In the *sein*-passive, the past participle is essentially **descriptive**, being used with the force of an **adjective** describing the state of the subject of the verb. For example, *geöffnet* in the sentence *Die Tür ist geöffnet* has much the same function as *offen* in *Die Tür ist offen*. Compare also:

Der Brief **ist geschrieben**   Der Brief ist fertig
Die Stadt **war zerstört**   Die Stadt war kaputt

The past participles of many reflexive verbs (which cannot form a passive) can similarly be used with *sein* with the force of an adjective:

Das Mädchen **ist verliebt**   (compare: *Das Mädchen hat sich verliebt*)
Ich **bin erholt**   (compare: *Ich habe mich erholt*)

The past participle can be used in a similar manner, with the force of an adjective, with the verbs *bleiben* and *scheinen*:

Das Museum **bleibt geschlossen**   *The museum remains closed*
Der Wagen **schien** leicht **beschädigt**   *The car seemed slightly damaged*
Nur Bruchstücke dieser Skulptur **sind**   *Only fragments of this sculpture have been*
  erhalten geblieben   *preserved*

(iv) As the *sein*-perfect expresses a **state resulting from a previous action**, it can only be used with verbs whose action produces a clear result, e.g. *bauen, begraben, beunruhigen, brechen, öffnen, reparieren, schreiben, verletzen, waschen, zerstören*, etc. Compare the following examples:

Meine Hand ist verletzt   *My hand is injured*
                      (and you can see the resulting injury)
Mein Wagen ist beschädigt   *My car is damaged*
                      (and you can see the resulting damage)

By contrast, verbs whose action produces no tangible or visible result, like *bewundern* or *zeigen*, cannot be used in the *sein*-passive at all, as admiring or showing do not involve any kind of result. Other verbs which are not used in the *sein*-passive include:

anbieten	*offer*	brauchen	*need*
begegnen	*meet*	erinnern	*remind*
bemerken	*notice*	loben	*praise*
betrachten	*look at*	sehen	*see*

(d) The *sein*- and *werden*-passive with *geboren*
Current usage with this verb is as follows:

(i) *Ich bin geboren* is used when no other circumstances or only the place of birth are mentioned:

Wann **sind** Sie **geboren**?
Ich **bin** in Hamburg **geboren**

(ii) *Ich wurde geboren* is used if further circumstances, or the date, are mentioned:

Ich **wurde** im Jahre 1965 in Hamburg **geboren**
Als ich **geboren wurde**, schneite es

(iii) Referring to people who are dead, either passive may be used:

Goethe **wurde/war** im Jahre 1749 in Frankfurt **geboren**

15.2.3 The *sein*-passive can indicate a continuing state

Diese Insel **ist** von Kannibalen **bewohnt**	*The island is inhabited by cannibals*
Die Oberrheinebene **ist** durch ihre Randgebirge vor rauhen Winden **geschützt** (*Brinkmann*)	*The Upper Rhine plain is protected from harsh winds by the hills which fringe it*
Die Häuser **sind** nur durch einen Drahtzaun von der Müllverbrennungsanlage **getrennt**	*The houses are only separated from the incinerating plant by a wire fence*
Das Esszimmer **ist** von einem großen Kronleuchter **beleuchtet**	*The dining-room is lit by a large chandelier*
Die Bücher in der alten Bibliothek **sind** mit Staub **bedeckt**	*The books in the old library are covered with dust*

Here we are not dealing with the result of a process, but with a lasting state, often a permanent one. In such sentences, the *werden*-passive and the *sein*-passive are interchangeable as long as the *werden*-passive cannot be interpreted as referring to an action. Thus, the following are alternatives to the first four examples above:

Diese Insel **wird** von Kannibalen bewohnt
Die Oberrheinebene **wird** durch ihre Randgebirge vor rauhen Winde geschützt
Die Häuser **werden** nur durch einen Drahtzaun von der Müllverbrennungsanlage getrennt
Das Esszimmer **wird** von einem großen Kronleuchter beleuchtet

But NOT: *Die Bücher in der alten Bibliothek **werden** mit Staub bedeckt*, as this would mean someone is covering them with dust.

15.3 *von, durch* and *mit* with the passive

A major motivation for using the passive rather than the active is to avoid mentioning who is performing the action. However, if required, the **agent** (i.e. the person or thing carrying out the action) can be included in a passive construction by adding a prepositional phrase introduced by *von* or *durch*, which correspond to English *by*.

The traditional rule of thumb is that *von* is used with persons, *durch* with things. This is a useful guideline, but it is not fully reliable, as it simplifies the real meaning of the two prepositions in passive contexts, and usage is not wholly consistent. Phrases with the agent occur chiefly with the *werden*-passive. With the *sein*-passive they only occur when it is a matter of a continuing state, as in 15.2.3.

15.3.1 *von* indicates the AGENT who actually carries out the action

This is usually a person, but can be an inanimate force:

Ich war **von meinem Onkel** gewarnt worden	*I had been warned by my uncle*
Sie wurde **von zwei Polizeibeamten** verhaftet	*She was arrested by two police officers*
Die Stadt wurde **von einem großen Waldbrand** bedroht	*The city was threatened by a huge forest fire*

15.3.2 *durch* indicates the MEANS by which the action is carried out

This is most often a thing which is the involuntary cause of the occurrence, but it can be a person acting as an intermediary. Thus, we would say *Ich wurde **durch einen Boten** benachrichtigt* 'I was informed by a messenger', not *von einem Boten*, because the messenger was bringing a message from someone else.

Die Ernte wurde **durch den Hagel** vernichtet	*The crop was destroyed by hail*
Ich wurde **durch den starken Verkehr** aufgehalten	*I was held up by the heavy traffic*
Die Hühnerpest wird **durch ein mikroskopisch nicht nachweisbares Virus** verursacht (*ND*)	*Fowl pest is caused by a virus which is not detectable under the microscope*

15.3.3 The distinction between *von* and *durch* is not always upheld

(a) In practice there is considerable hesitation between *von* and *durch*
It is often not wholly clear whether we are dealing with the 'agent' or the 'means'. *von* is always usual for persons who obviously carried out the action themselves. However, when this might be a matter of interpretation, or with 'things' (like storms and earthquakes) which people might think of as actually carrying out an action, either *von* or *durch* can be acceptable, as in the following sentences:

Die Brücke ist **von Pionieren/durch Pioniere** gesprengt worden	*The bridge has been demolished by sappers*
Der Baum ist **von dem Blitz/durch den Blitz** getroffen worden	*The tree has been struck by lightning*

(b) The difference between *von* and *durch* is most clear when both are used in the same sentence

Ich war v**on meinem Onkel durch seinen Sohn** gewarnt worden	*I had been warned by my uncle through his son* (My uncle is doing the warning, his son is the intermediary)
Die Kaserne wurde **von Terroristen durch einen Sprengstoffanschlag** zerstört	*The barracks were destroyed by terrorists in a bomb attack* (Terrorists destroyed it, the bombs were the means)

15.3.4 A phrase with *mit* is used to indicate the INSTRUMENT used to perform an action

Das Schiff wurde **mit einem Torpedo** versenkt	*The ship was sunk by a torpedo*
Das Schloss musste **mit einem Hammer** geöffnet werden	*The lock had to be opened with a hammer*
Dieser Brief ist **mit der Hand** geschrieben	*This letter was written by hand*

durch can replace *mit* when inanimate instruments are involved, so that, for instance, *Das Schiff wurde **durch ein Torpedo** versenkt* is a possible alternative for the first example above.

15.4 Other passive constructions

German has a wide range of alternative means of expressing the passive.

15.4.1 *man* is often used in German where English naturally uses a passive

See 5.5.18 for details on the use of *man*:

Man sagt, dass ...	*It is said that ...*
Man hatte ihn davor **gewarnt**	*He had been warned about it*
Das **macht man** nicht	*That's not done*

15.4.2 A passive construction is possible with *bekommen* and *kriegen*

(a) By using the verbs *bekommen* or *kriegen* a dative object can be made into the subject of a passive construction
As explained in 15.1.3, a dative object cannot be turned into the subject of the *werden*-passive. However, if *bekommen* or *kriegen* is used with the past participle of another verb, a dative object can be converted into the subject:

Ich schenke **meinem Bruder** das Buch	→ **Mein Bruder kriegt/bekommt** das Buch (von mir) **geschenkt**
Ich widerspreche **meinem Bruder**	→ **Mein Bruder kriegt/bekommt** (von mir) **widersprochen**

This construction is chiefly found in speech (especially with *kriegen*), and not all Germans accept it as correct in writing, although it is increasingly frequent. The conditions under which it is possible are not fully clear, but in general it appears that it can only be used with verbs which express an action and where the original dative object can be interpreted in some way as receiving something.

NB: Less commonly, the verb *erhalten* is used rather than *bekommen* or *kriegen*, e.g. *Sie **erhält** die Kosten **erstattet**.*

(b) The *bekommen/kriegen*-passive can be formed from various kinds of dative
Specifically:

(i) from the dative object of a verb which governs both a dative and an accusative object (see 18.4.2). The English equivalent may be a passive, or a construction with 'have' and a past participle:

Ich **bekomme/kriege** das Geld regelmäßig **ausgezahlt**	*I am paid the money regularly/I have the money paid to me regularly*
Wir haben viel **gezeigt bekommen/ gekriegt**	*We were shown a lot/We had a lot shown to us*
Dort wartet die Oma, um **erzählt** zu **bekommen**, was sie in den nächsten Tagen sehen wird (*Böll*)	*Granny is waiting there to be told what she is going to see in the next few days*

This construction is possible with most such verbs, **except** *geben*.

(ii) from the dative object of verbs which only govern a dative object (see 18.4.1):

Sie bekam gratuliert	*She was congratulated*
Vera bekommt von dir geholfen	*Vera is being helped by you*
Er bekam von niemandem widersprochen	*He was contradicted by nobody*

This construction is not possible with verbs which do not denote an activity or whose dative object cannot be interpreted as a recipient, e.g. *ähneln*, *begegnen*, *gefallen*, *gehören* or *schaden*.

(iii) from the dative of advantage or the dative of possession (see 2.5.3 and 2.5.4). This often corresponds to an English construction with 'get':

Sie **kriegte** den Wagen **repariert**	*She got her car repaired*
Man **bekommt** den Schlips **abgeschnitten** (*Grzimek*)	*You get your tie cut off*
Er **bekam** von mir die Wohnung **renoviert**	*He got his flat renovated by me*
Das Haus **bekam** einen Balkon **angebaut**	*The house got a balcony built on*

(c) In a few instances, the subject of a construction with *kriegen/bekommen* does not relate to a dative

(i) It can be used with verbs which take two accusatives, e.g. *lehren* 'teach' and *schimpfen* 'tell off, bawl out' (see 18.3.3). The conditions are the same, i.e. that the verb denotes an action and the subject of the *kriegen/bekommen* construction is a recipient:

Er **bekommt** (von mir) **geschimpft**	*He's getting told off (by me)*
Der Junge **bekommt** die Vokabeln **gelehrt**	*The boy is getting the words taught him*

(ii) It can be used in other contexts where English can use a construction with 'get':

Ich **kriege** den Brief bis heute Abend **geschrieben**	*I'll get the letter written by tonight*

15.4.3 A reflexive verb can often be an alternative to a passive

With verbs which denote accomplishments or activities a verb can be used with *sich* to give the sense of a passive, e.g. *Das erklärt sich leicht* 'That is easily explained' (see 18.3.6 for further details on reflexive verbs). A sense of ability (= *können*) is often implied, but not with all verbs.

(a) Reflexive constructions from transitive verbs
In most instances an adverbial of manner is needed to complete the sense:

Das **lernt sich** rasch	*That is/can be quickly learned*
Das Buch **verkaufte sich** in Rekordauflagen	*The book was sold in record numbers*
Mein Verdacht **hat sich bestätigt**	*My suspicions have been confirmed*

(b) Reflexive constructions from intransitive verbs

An adverbial of manner **and** an adverbial of place or time are usually needed to complete the sense. These are impersonal constructions:

Es fährt sich gut auf der Autobahn	*You can drive well on the motorway*
In der Hauptstadt **lebt es sich** besser als anderswo (*Zeit*)	*You can live better in the capital than anywhere else*

(c) A reflexive verb is the natural German equivalent of many English passives or constructions which look like passives

sich ärgern	*be annoyed*	sich schämen	*be ashamed*
sich freuen	*be pleased*	sich verbinden	*be associated*

15.4.4 Many phrasal verbs have a passive meaning

Such phrasal verbs comprise a verbal noun (especially in *-ung*) and a verb which has little real meaning in the context. The following verbs are frequently used to form such complex verb phrases with a passive sense: *erfahren, erhalten, finden, gehen, gelangen, kommen, stehen*:

eine große Vereinfachung erfahren (= sehr vereinfacht werden)	*be greatly simplified*
seine Vollendung finden (= vollendet werden)	*be completed*
in Vergessenheit geraten (= vergessen werden)	*be forgotten*
zur Anwendung kommen (= angewendet werden)	*be used*
Unsere Arbeit hat **Anerkennung gefunden**	*Our work was appreciated*
Der Wunsch **ging in Erfüllung**	*The wish was fulfilled*
Das Stück **gelangte/kam zur Aufführung**	*The play was performed*
Diese Frage **steht zur Diskussion**	*This question is being discussed*

Such phrasal verbs are characteristic of modern written German. They have been criticised by stylists as verbose, but they have nuances lacking in the simple verb. For example, *Das Stück gelangte zur Aufführung* emphasises the start of the action, whilst *Das Stück wurde aufgeführt* simply records that the action took place.

15.4.5 The infinitive with *zu* with some semi-auxiliary verbs has the force of a passive

This has been termed the 'modal infinitive' construction, and further details are given in 13.2.5. Depending on the verb, these constructions can express possibility, obligation or necessity, i e. have the sense of *können, müssen* or *sollen* followed by a passive infinitive. The following verbs occur in this construction.

(a) *sein*: **the construction has the sense of** *können, müssen* **or** *sollen*

Die Anträge **sind** im Rathaus **abzuholen** (= Die Anträge können/müssen im Rathaus abgeholt werden)	The applications may/must be collected from the town hall/are to be collected from the town hall
Diese Frage **ist** noch **zu erörtern** (= Diese Frage muss/soll noch erörtert werden	This question must still be discussed/is still to be discussed
Dieser Text **ist** bis morgen **zu übersetzen** (= Dieser Text muss/soll bis morgen übersetzt werden)	This text must be translated by tomorrow/ This text is to be translated by tomorrow

This construction can be turned into an extended adjective using a present participle, e.g. *diese noch zu erörternde Frage* (see 13.5.2e).

(b) *bleiben*: **the construction has the sense of** *müssen*

Vieles bleibt noch zu erledigen (= Vieles muss noch erledigt werden)	Much still remains to be done

(c) *gehen*: **the construction has the sense of** *können*

Das Bild geht nicht zu befestigen (= Das Bild kann nicht befestigt werden)	The picture cannot be secured

This construction is colloquial and considered substandard.

(d) *stehen*: **the construction has the sense of** *müssen*
It is only used impersonally, with a limited number of verbs, principally *befürchten* and *erwarten*:

Es **steht zu befürchten**, dass sich diese Vorfälle häufen (= Es muss befürchtet werden, dass sich diese Vorfälle häufen)	It is to be feared that these incidents will occur increasingly

(e) *es gibt*: **the construction has the sense of** *müssen*

Es **gibt** noch vieles **zu tun** (= Vieles muss noch getan werden)	There's still a lot to be done

15.4.6 *sich lassen* with a following infinitive can have the force of a passive

It expresses possibility and thus means much the same as using *können* with a passive infinitive. This construction is frequent in all registers, with transitive verbs:

Das lässt sich aber erklären (= Das kann aber erklärt werden)	But that can be explained
Das Problem lässt sich leicht lösen (= Das Problem kann leicht gelöst werden)	The problem can be solved easily
Das ließe sich aber ändern (= Das könnte geändert werden)	That might be altered, though
Ein Ende lässt sich nicht absehen (*Lenz*)	There is no end in sight

This construction can be used impersonally with transitive or intransitive verbs. The impersonal subject *es* can be omitted if it is not in initial position in a main clause:

Es **lässt sich** dort gut **leben**	*It's a good life there*
Darüber **lässt** (es) **sich streiten**	*We can argue about that*

In general, this construction is only possible if the subject is a thing rather than a person. Reflexive *lassen* with a person as subject usually has the sense of 'cause' or 'permit', see 13.3.1c.

15.4.7 *gehören* with a past participle has passive force and the sense of obligation or necessity

This construction is mainly colloquial and southern:

Dieser Kerl **gehört eingesperrt** (= Dieser Kerl sollte eingesperrt werden)	*That bloke ought to be locked up*
Dem **gehört** das deutlich **gesagt** (= Ihm sollte das deutlich gesagt werden)	*He ought to be told that clearly*

15.4.8 Adjectives in *-bar* from verbs can be used with *sein* to express a possibility with a passive sense

They correspond to English adjectives in '-able'/'-ible', see 22.3.1a:

Diese Muscheln sind nicht **essbar** (= Diese Muscheln können nicht gegessen werden)	*These shellfish are not edible/ cannot be eaten*
Das Argument ist nicht **widerlegbar** (= Dieses Argument kann nicht widerlegt werden)	*The argument is irrefutable/cannot be refuted*
Man ist einfach **unerreichbar** (*Frisch*)	*One simply cannot be reached*

Adjectives with the suffixes *-lich* (from some verbs, see 22.3.1f) or *-fähig* (from some verbal nouns) can have similar force:

Seine Antwort war **unverständlich** (= Seine Antwort konnte nicht verstanden werden)	*His answer was incomprehensible/ could not be understood*
Dieser Apparat ist nicht weiter **entwicklungsfähig** (= Dieser Apparat kann nicht weiter entwickelt werden)	*This apparatus cannot be developed further*

15.5 The use of active and passive in German

The passive is commonly used in German, particularly in formal writing (especially in technical registers and journalism), and it is certainly <u>not</u> to be 'avoided' as a matter of course, as some English manuals and handbooks of German suggest. However, it does tend to be rather less frequently used than in English. One reason for this is that we often use a passive in English to manoeuvre something other than the subject to the beginning of the sentence. In German, with its more flexible word order, this can be achieved simply by shifting the elements in the sentence round. Thus, the following sentences probably represent the most natural equivalents in the two languages:

Diesen Roman hat Thomas Mann während eines Aufenthaltes in Italien **geschrieben**	*This novel **was written by Thomas Mann** during a stay in Italy*

In German, the accusative object can be placed before the verb and the subject after it, in order to change the emphasis of the sentence, without needing to use a passive construction, as in English. Clearly, this is only possible if the agent (i.e. the subject of the verb in the active) is mentioned. For a more detailed explanation, see 21.2.3b.

16

Mood
The imperative and the subjunctive

The grammatical category MOOD makes it possible for speakers to signal their attitude to what they are saying, in particular to indicate whether what they are saying is to be understood as a fact, a possibility or a command. The different moods of the verb are shown by special endings or forms. German has three moods:

- The INDICATIVE mood states a **fact**
- The SUBJUNCTIVE mood indicates a **possibility** or a **report**
- The IMPERATIVE mood expresses a **command**

Indicative	Subjunctive	Imperative
sie ist	sie sei	sei!
sie kauft	sie kaufe	kaufe!
sie kam	sie käme	kommt!
sie ist gewandert	sie würde wandern	wandern Sie!

The forms of the indicative and the imperative are given in the active voice in Tables 12.2–12.5, and in the passive in Tables 12.6 and 12.7. The formation of the subjunctive mood is explained in section 12.5 and the most important forms are shown in Tables 12.9–12.11.

This chapter gives details on the use of the moods in German as follows:

- The three moods of German (section 16.1)
- The **imperative** mood and other means of expressing commands (section 16.2)
- The **subjunctive** mood, its forms and tenses (sections 16.3–16.7)

16.1 Indicative, imperative and subjunctive

16.1.1 The INDICATIVE mood presents what the speaker is saying as a fact

The **indicative** is the most frequent mood, used in all kinds of statements and in questions – in effect in all contexts where speakers do not want to give a command or to signal that what they are saying may not be the fact. As it is the 'normal' or default mood, its use is not treated specifically here.

16.1.2 The IMPERATIVE mood is used in commands and requests

As we normally address these to the person we are talking to, the **imperative** mood is restricted to the second person (i.e. the 'you'-form). The uses of the imperative in German are treated in section 16.2, together with the other ways of giving commands and requests.

16.1.3 The SUBJUNCTIVE mood presents what the speaker is saying as not necessarily true

If we use the **subjunctive**, we are characterising an activity, an event or a state as unreal, possible or, at best, not necessarily true (hence its old German name of *Möglichkeitsform*). English has very few distinct subjunctive forms, and we express these ideas in other ways, most often by using a 'modal auxiliary' verb like 'may' or 'should', or an adverb of attitude like 'perhaps' or 'presumably'. German has these possibilities too, with modal auxiliaries like *können* or *müssen* (see Chapter 17), adverbs of attitude like *vielleicht* and *vermutlich* (see 7.3.2) or modal particles (see Chapter 10). But the subjunctive mood is widely used in German, in particular to signal a hypothetical possibility and in indirect speech. Full information is given in sections 16.3 to 16.7.

16.2 Commands and the imperative

16.2.1 The imperative mood is used in all kinds of commands and requests

(a) The imperative mood only has special forms for the second person
i.e. the person to whom the request or command is being directly addressed. For its forms, see Tables 12.2 and 12.3:

> Hans, **sei** doch nicht so dumm!
> Angela, **stell(e)** dich nicht so an!
> Kinder, **bringt** mal die Stühle zu uns in den Garten!
> **Kommen Sie** doch bitte herein und **nehmen Sie** Platz, Frau Meier!

In colloquial speech the imperative is characteristically used with the modal particles *mal* (see 10.22.1) and/or *doch* (see 10.7.3). Without one of these, a spoken command can sound insistent or harsh. Other modal particles which are commonly used with the imperative and alter the tone of a command are *ja* (10.19.3), *nur* (10.26.1a), *ruhig* (10.28) and *schon* (10.30.4).

(b) Stressed *du* or *ihr* is sometimes added to the simple imperative form
A pronoun is normally only present in the *Sie* form of the imperative, but the other pronouns are occasionally added to give strong emphasis:

> Bestell <u>du</u> inzwischen das Frühstück!   *Meanwhile, you order breakfast*
> (*Wendt*)
> Kinder, wir kommen gleich. **Geht <u>ihr</u>**   *Children, we're just coming. You go first.*
> **schon vor!**

16.2.2 Other ways of expressing commands and requests

German has a range of constructions besides the imperative which express commands, requests, instructions and the like.

(a) The infinitive is commonly used in official commands and instructions

Using the infinitive makes the command sound more general and less directed at a particular person or group (see also 13.3.3a):

Nicht **rauchen**! Bitte **anschnallen**!	*No smoking. Fasten seat belts*
Erst **gurten**, dann **starten**!	*Fasten your safety belt before setting off*
(official advice to motorists)	
Bitte **einsteigen** und die Türen **schließen**!	*Please get in and close the doors*
(railway announcement)	
4 Eiweiß zu sehr steifem Schnee **schlagen**	*Beat 4 egg whites until stiff*
(cooking instruction)	

With reflexive verbs, the reflexive pronoun is omitted, e.g. *Nicht* **hinauslehnen**! (from *sich* hinauslehnen 'lean out')

(b) The past participle is sometimes used for depersonalised commands

In practice, this construction is limited to idiomatic usage with a small number of verbs (see also 13.5.5a):

Abgemacht!	*Agreed!*
Aufgepasst!	*Look out!*
Stillgestanden!	*Attention!* (military command)

(c) The subjectless passive can have the force of a command

See also 15.1.4d. The speaker can include him/herself in the instruction:

Jetzt wird gearbeitet!	*Let's get down to work now*
Hier wird nicht geraucht!	*No smoking here!*

(d) Statements or questions in the present or future can serve as commands

i.e. by being given the characteristic intonation of a command, as in English. These always sound more blunt than the simple imperative. In this way, any of the following could be used for English 'Are you going to listen now?!' or 'You're going to listen now!':

Hörst du jetzt zu?!	Du hörst jetzt zu!
Wirst du jetzt zuhören?!	Du wirst jetzt zuhören!

(e) The modal auxiliary *sollen* can be used with the force of a command

This usage is linked to the basic meaning of *sollen*, which expresses obligation, see 17.6.1b:

Du **sollst** das Fenster zumachen	*(I want you to) shut the window*
Sie **sollen** ihr sofort schreiben	*(You should) write to her at once*

sollen is often used to repeat a command to someone who appears not to have heard the first time: *Du* **sollst** *sofort nach Hause kommen!*

Commands in indirect speech are most often given with *sollen*, e.g. *Sie sagte ihm, dass er sie am Dienstag anrufen* **sollte** 'She told him to call her on Tuesday'. For details see 16.6.4b. *sollen* is also commonly used in third person commands (see (g) below).

(f) Commands and requests in the first person plural
In English, these are typically in the form 'Let's …'. German has a number of equivalents for this, i.e.:

(i) the first person plural form of *Konjunktiv I*, with the verb first:

Na, also, **gehen wir** ganz langsam (*Fallada*)	*Well then, let's walk quite slowly*
Seien wir dankbar, dass nichts passiert ist!	*Let's be thankful that nothing happened*
Also, **trinken wir** doch noch ein Glas Wein!	*All right, let's have another glass of wine then*

Only the verb *sein* shows that a subjunctive is used in this construction, as this is the only verb with a distinctive first person plural *Konjunktiv I* form.

(ii) the imperative of *lassen*. This construction is rather formal:

Lass uns jetzt ganz langsam gehen!   **Lasst uns** dankbar sein!
Lassen Sie uns doch noch ein Glas Wein trinken!

(iii) the modal auxiliary *wollen*:

Wir wollen doch noch ein Glas Wein trinken!

Questions with *wollen*, e.g. *Wollen wir jetzt nach Hause gehen?* have the force of a suggestion, rather like English 'Shall we …?' (see 17.7.1b).

(g) Commands and requests in the third person
We use these, for instance, to ask someone else to tell a third person to do something, as in English 'Let/Have her come in', or when issuing general instructions to anyone concerned.

(i) Third person commands are most often expressed using the modal auxiliary *sollen*, see 17.6.1b:

Er **soll** hereinkommen	*Let him come in/Tell him to come in*
Sie **sollen** draußen bleiben	*Tell them to stay outside*
Man **soll** hier nicht parken	*There's no parking here*

(ii) *Konjunktiv I* is sometimes used in third person commands (see 16.7.6d):

Es **sage** uns niemand, es gebe keine Alternative mehr (*Augstein*)	*Let nobody tell us that there is no longer any alternative*
Er **komme** sofort	*Let him come at once*

A generalised command (i.e. 'to whom it may concern') can be expressed by using *Konjunktiv I* with the pronoun *man*:

Man **schlage** 4 Eiweiß zu sehr steifem Schnee	*Beat 4 egg whites until stiff*

These constructions with *Konjunktiv I* now sound stilted and old-fashioned. *sollen* is preferred for third person commands, and the infinitive for generalised commands and instructions (see (a) above).

(iii) *Konjunktiv I* of the modal auxiliary *mögen* can also express a command to a third person: *Er möge sofort kommen* (see 17.4.4). This usage is formal and rather old-fashioned.

(h) A *dass*-clause in isolation can be used as a command
These are emotive in tone and are normally heard exclusively with the particle *ja* (see 10.19.3) and/or with an 'ethic' dative (see 2.5.3d):

Dass du **mir** **(ja)** gut aufpasst!	*Be careful for my sake*
Dass ihr **ja** der Mutter nichts davon erzählt!	*Just don't tell your mother anything about it*

16.3 The subjunctive mood: general

Although the subjunctive mood is widely used in modern German, some forms and uses are nowadays restricted to formal written German, whilst others have become obsolete. Even educated native speakers are often uncertain about what is 'good' or 'correct' usage, and there is often a gulf between what people think they ought to say or write and what they actually do say or write. No other aspect of German grammar has attracted so much attention from self-appointed guardians of the language and sundry pedants. This does not make it easy to describe modern usage clearly for the foreign learner, but we concentrate here on those usages which are most likely to be encountered in practice or needed when speaking and writing German, as follows:

- The forms and tenses of the subjunctive: *Konjunktiv I* and *Konjunktiv II* (section 16.4)
- The use of the subjunctive in **conditional** sentences (section 16.5)
- The use of the subjunctive in **indirect speech** (section 16.6)
- **Other uses** of the subjunctive (section 16.7)

16.4 Forms and tenses of the subjunctive

16.4.1 The German subjunctive has two main sets of forms: *Konjunktiv I* and *Konjunktiv II*

The forms of the subjunctive are traditionally referred to by the names of the tenses, e.g. present subjunctive (*er komme*), past subjunctive (*er käme*), perfect subjunctive (*er sei gekommen*), etc. However, the six forms of the subjunctive do not correspond to time differences in the same way as the tenses of the indicative, and these traditional terms are misleading. Many modern German grammars group the subjunctive forms into two sets which they call *Konjunktiv I* and *Konjunktiv II* as set out in Table 16.1, and these terms will be adopted here since they make it easier to explain how the subjunctive is used in German.

TABLE 16.1 *The forms of* Konjunktiv I *and* Konjunktiv II

Konjunktiv I	present subjunctive perfect subjunctive future subjunctive	es gebe es habe gegeben es werde geben
Konjunktiv II	past subjunctive pluperfect subjunctive conditional	es gäbe es hätte gegeben es würde geben

16.4.2 *Konjunktiv I* and *Konjunktiv II* have largely distinct uses

These have nothing to do with time or tense, and the so-called 'present subjunctive' and 'past subjunctive' can both refer to the present time, as the following examples show:

(a) present subjunctive

> Gisela sagt ihrer Mutter, sie **komme** *Gisela is telling her mother that she is*
> um sechs in Berlin an *arriving in Berlin at six*

The main use of the present subjunctive – and all the other *Konjunktiv I* forms – is to mark indirect speech, see 16.6.

(b) past subjunctive

> Wenn ich es jetzt **wüsste, könnte** *If I knew it now, I would be able to*
> ich es dir sagen *tell you*

The main use of the past subjunctive – and all the other *Konjunktiv II* forms – is to indicate an unreal condition or a possibility, see 16.5.

16.4.3 Time differences are indicated by using compound forms

Within both *Konjunktiv I* and *Konjunktiv II* we can express past time by using the corresponding compound tenses:

(a) The perfect subjunctive functions as a past tense in *Konjunktiv I*

> Gisela sagt ihrer Mutter, sie **sei** um *Gisela is telling her mother that she arrived*
> sechs in Berlin **angekommen** *in Berlin at six*

(b) The pluperfect subjunctive functions as the past tense of *Konjunktiv II*

> Wenn ich es damals **gewusst hätte,** *If I had known it then, I would have been*
> **hätte** ich es dir sagen **können** *able to tell you*

16.4.4 The CONDITIONAL form with *würde* often replaces the simple past subjunctive

Konjunktiv II has three forms:

f o r m s

Past subjunctive	Pluperfect subjunctive	Conditional
ich hätte	ich hätte gehabt	ich würde haben
ich wäre	ich wäre gewesen	ich würde sein
ich käme	ich wäre gekommen	ich würde kommen
ich schliefe	ich hätte geschlafen	ich würde schlafen
ich machte	ich hätte gemacht	ich würde machen

The compound CONDITIONAL form is often used instead of the simple past subjunctive, in exactly the same meanings and contexts, so that people say or write *ich würde schlafen* rather than *ich schliefe*. Which one is used depends on the individual verb involved and on register (i.e. whether we want to sound formal or informal). The use of the simple forms is often encouraged by German school teachers and stylists as a mark of good style, but in practice they often sound stilted or archaic, and they are avoided. Modern usage can be summarised as follows:

(a) **With weak verbs the simple form is only used if the subjunctive meaning is otherwise clear from the context**
This is because their past subjunctive form is exactly the same as the past indicative. For example:

> Wenn ich das Fenster **aufmachte**, **hätten**   *If I opened the window, we would have*
> wir frische Luft im Zimmer   *some fresh air in the room*

Although *aufmachte* could be ambiguous (in isolation we would have no way of knowing whether it is indicative or subjunctive), the clear *Konjunktiv II* form *hätte* in the other half of the sentence makes it clear that the whole sentence is to be understood as expressing possibility.

However, the past subjunctive forms of weak verbs are not normally used in everyday speech, which usually prefers the conditional: *Wenn ich das Fenster aufmachen würde, hätten wir frische Luft im Zimmer.*

Even in writing, the conditional is used <u>if</u> the subjunctive meaning is not otherwise clear from the context:

> In diesem Fall **würde** ich das Fenster   *In that case I would open the window*
> **aufmachen**

(b) **With the common irregular verbs only the past subjunctive form is usual**
This applies in particular to *sein, haben, werden* and the modal auxiliaries. With these, the past subjunctive forms *wäre, hätte, würde, könnte, müsste,* etc. are used, in both spoken and written German. The conditional forms *würde sein, würde haben,* etc. are quite infrequent in any register, unless there is a sense of 'future-in-the-past', see 16.4.5.

*sein
haben
werden
+ würde auxiliaries*

(c) **The past subjunctive forms of a few other common strong or irregular verbs are quite frequent**
With the following verbs the past subjunctive forms and the conditional forms are roughly equally frequent in written German:

finden	geben	gehen	halten	heißen	kommen	lassen	stehen	tun	wissen
fände	**gäbe**	**ginge**	**hielte**	**hieße**	**käme**	**ließe**	**stünde**	**täte**	**wüsste**

käme, *täte* and *wüsste* are also quite common in spoken German, as well as in writing, and those of the others in this group are sometimes heard, too.

(d) The past subjunctive forms of the other strong or irregular verbs are infrequent

In practice, they only ever occur in formal written German, and even there they are less common than the conditional forms, so that, for example, *sie würde schlafen* is significantly more frequent than *sie schliefe*.

In fact, many past subjunctive forms of less common strong verbs, in particular most of the irregular ones and others in -ö- and -ü- (e.g. *begönne*, *flösse*, *verdürbe*), are felt to be impossibly archaic and stilted. Many Germans do not even know the forms, and they are generally avoided even in writing. The forms which are no longer used in practice are given in italics in Table 12.12.

(e) Pluperfect forms with *würde . . . haben/sein* are unusual

The pluperfect subjunctive normally has *hätte* or *wäre* (depending on whether the verb forms its perfect tenses with *haben* or *sein*) together with a past participle:

Ich **hätte geschlafen**	*I would have slept*
Ich **wäre gekommen**	*I would have come*

The longer forms (e.g.: *ich würde geschlafen haben, ich würde gekommen sein*) do occasionally occur, but they are much less common than the shorter forms with *hätte* or *wäre*, especially in writing.

16.4.5 The conditional is often used in the sense of a future-in-the-past

i.e. where the writer is looking forward within a narrative in the past tense, e.g.:

Er wusste viel besser als Chénier, dass er keine Eingebung **haben würde**; er hatte nämlich noch nie eine gehabt (*Süßkind*)	*He knew much better than Chénier that he would not have an inspiration; because he had never had one*
Ich beschloss, sobald ich groß **sein würde**, Spengler zu lesen (*Dönhoff*)	*I decided I would read Spengler as soon as I was grown up*
Ich dachte auch an die Gossen, in denen ich einmal **liegen würde** (*Böll*)	*I thought also of the gutters I would some day lie in*

The simple past subjunctive is <u>not</u> normally used in contexts of this type.

16.5 Conditional sentences

Typical CONDITIONAL SENTENCES consist of a subordinate clause, introduced by the conjunction *wenn* (= English 'if'), expressing a condition, and a main clause, expressing the consequence, as shown in Table 16.2:

TABLE 16.2 *Conditional sentences*

Condition	Consequence
Wenn ich genug Zeit hätte, *If I had enough time*	käme ich gern mit *I would gladly come with you*
Wenn sie mich fragen würde, *If she asked me*	würde ich ihr alles sagen *I would tell her everything*
Wenn ich gewonnen hätte, *If I had won*	wäre ich nach Amerika gefahren *I would have gone to America*

16.5.1 *Konjunktiv II* is used in sentences which express unreal conditions

(a) The past subjunctive or conditional form of *Konjunktiv II* is used to express an unreal condition relating to the present

Wenn wir Zeit **hätten**, **könnten** wir einen Ausflug machen *believe*	*If we had time, we would be able to go on an excursion*
Die Europäer **wären** erleichtert, wenn England wieder **austreten würde** (*Zeit*) *kreip*	*The Europeans would be relieved if England pulled out again*
Wenn ich 20 000 Euro im Lotto **gewinnen würde**, **würde** ich sofort nach Teneriffa **fliegen**	*If I won 20,000 euro in the lottery I would fly to Tenerife immediately*

Konjunktiv II is used in both the *wenn*-clause and the main clause in German. This contrasts with English, which uses the past tense in the 'if'-clause, and the conditional (with 'would') in the main clause. Either form – past subjunctive or conditional – may be used in either of the clauses. Which one is used depends on register and on the individual verb used, as explained in 16.4.4.

Stylists have long argued that sentences with two *würde*-forms should be avoided. However, this prescription is widely ignored in both spoken and written German, especially if the simple forms of the verbs involved are obsolete, as in the last example above and the following:

Mein Vater **würde** sich im Grabe **umdrehen**, wenn ich jetzt nicht seine Ansprüche **weiterfolgen würde** (*Spiegel*)	*My father would turn in his grave if I didn't continue to keep to the standards he set*

(b) Conditional sentences with the pluperfect subjunctive express a *Past condit.* **hypothetical possibility in the past**
The pluperfect subjunctive is used in both the *wenn*-clause and the main clause:

Wenn ich es nicht mit eigenen Augen **gesehen hätte**, **hätte** ich es nicht geglaubt	*If I hadn't seen it with my own eyes, I wouldn't have believed it*
Wenn mich jener Anruf nicht mehr **erreicht hätte**, **wären** wir einander nie **begegnet** (*Frisch*)	*If that call hadn't reached me, we would never have met*
Es **wäre** besser für mich **gewesen**, wenn ich **hätte** absagen **können** (*Böll*)	*It would have been better for me if I had been able to refuse*

refuse
lemond

(c) Time differences between the main clause and the *wenn*-clause can be indicated by using the past subjunctive/conditional forms or the pluperfect forms as appropriate

Wäre de Gaulle schon im ersten Wahlgang **gewählt worden**, **würde** die französische Bevölkerung schon jetzt das Datum **kennen** (*FAZ*)	*If de Gaulle had been elected in the first ballot the French people would already know the date*
Ich **säße** hier nicht auf demselben Stuhl, wenn wir bisher diesen Punkt nicht **erreicht hätten** (*Zeit*)	*I wouldn't be sitting here in the same chair if we hadn't already reached this point*

(d) Other auxiliary verbs used in sentences expressing unreal conditions

(i) The *Konjunktiv II* of *sollen* is often used in the *wenn*-clause. These normally point to the future, and the meaning is similar to using 'should' or 'were to' in English:

Wenn sie mich **fragen sollte**, würde ich ihr alles sagen	*If she were to ask me, I would tell her everything*
Er hält sich bereit, aus der Bodenluke zu springen, wenn sich nachts ein Auto der Sägemühle **nähern sollte** (*Strittmatter*)	*He is ready to jump out of the skylight if a car should approach the sawmill at night*

(ii) The *Konjunktiv II* of *wollen* also occurs frequently in the *wenn*-clause, often with only a faint suggestion of its basic meaning of 'want, intend':

Wenn du schneller **arbeiten wolltest**, könntest du mehr verdienen	*If you worked a bit faster you could earn more*
Wie wäre es, wenn wir ihr **helfen wollten**?	*What about us helping her?*

It is particularly common in formal written German if the conjunction *wenn* is omitted (see 16.5.3a):

Es würde uns zu lange aufhalten, **wollten wir** alle diese Probleme ausführlich behandeln	*It would detain us too long if we were to treat all these problems in detail*

(iii) Especially in south Germany, the *Konjunktiv II* of *tun* is common in substandard colloquial speech instead of *würde*, see 13.3.1d:

Wenn ich jetzt **losfahren täte**, so könnte ich schon vor zwölf in Augsburg sein	*If I set off now, I could be in Augsburg by twelve*

16.5.2 The indicative is used in conditional sentences which express 'open' conditions

i.e. where there is a real possibility of the conditions being met. These correspond to conditional sentences without 'would' in English:

Wenn sie immer noch krank **ist, muss** ich morgen allein kommen	*If she's still ill, I'll have to come on my own tomorrow*
Wenn ich ihr jetzt **schreibe, bekommt** sie den Brief morgen	*If I write to her now, she'll get the letter tomorrow*
Wenn wir jetzt **losfahren, werden** wir schon vor zwölf in Augsburg **sein**	*If we set off now, we'll be in Augsburg by twelve*

With the past tense, the sense is that the conditions have been met:

Wenn meine Eltern mir Geld **schickten**, **kaufte** ich mir sofort etwas zum Anziehen	*If my parents sent me money I immediately bought something to wear*

16.5.3 Alternative forms for conditional sentences

A typical conditional sentence has a *wenn*-clause and a main clause, as shown in Table 16.2, but there are a few possible variations on this pattern.

(a) The conjunction *wenn* can be omitted

If this is done, the subordinate clause begins with the verb:

Hätte ich Zeit, käme ich gern mit	*If I had time, I should like to come with you*
Ist sie krank, muss ich morgen allein kommen	*If she's ill, I'll have to come on my own tomorrow*
Sollte ich nach Berlin kommen, würde ich sie sicher besuchen	*If I should get to Berlin I'd be sure to visit her*

This construction can be compared to the similar, rather old-fashioned English construction, e.g. 'Had I time, ...'. In German it is commoner in formal writing than in speech. Occasionally, the main clause comes first:

Das Bild wäre unvollständig, **würden** nicht die vielen Gruppen erwähnt, die den Einwanderern das Leben leichter machen (*FR*)	*The picture would be incomplete if the many groups were not mentioned who make life easier for the immigrants*

(b) If the *wenn*-clause comes first in the sentence, it can be picked up by *so* or *dann* at the start of the main clause

This 'correlating' *so* or *dann* is optional, but quite common:

Wenn ich Zeit hätte, (**so/dann**) käme ich gern mit
Wenn ich ihr heute schreibe, (**so/dann**) bekommt sie den Brief morgen

It is particularly frequent if *wenn* is omitted (compare (a) above):

Hätte ich Zeit, (**so**) käme ich gern mit
Ist sie krank, (**so**) muss ich morgen allein kommen
Sollte ich nach Berlin kommen, (**so**) würde ich sie sicher besuchen

(c) The condition may appear in another form than in a *wenn*-clause

e.g. in an adverbial or another kind of clause. A form of *Konjunktiv II* is used to signal a hypothetical condition:

Dieser Unbekannte würde mich **wahrscheinlich** besser verstehen (*Böll*)	*This stranger would probably understand me better*
Ohne die Notlandung in Tamaulipas wäre alles anders gekommen (*Frisch*)	*But for the emergency landing in Tamaulipas everything would have turned out differently*
Wer diese Entwicklung vorausgesehen hätte, hätte viel Geld verdienen können	*Anyone foreseeing this development would have been able to make a lot of money*

In some sentences the condition is implicit:

Lieber **bliebe** ich zu Hause (i.e. wenn ich die Wahl hätte)	*I would rather stay at home*
Ich **hätte** dasselbe **getan** (i.e. an deiner Stelle)	*I would have done the same*

(d) Other conjunctions used in conditional sentences

wenn is the predominant conjunction in conditional sentences, but there are one or two other possibilities:

(i) *falls* 'if' unambiguously introduces a condition.

This contrasts with *wenn*, which can also mean 'when(ever)' (see 19.3.1e). It can be useful to make the sense clear in contexts where a misunderstanding would be possible. A sentence like:

> **Wenn** ich nach Berlin komme, besuche ich sie

could mean 'When(ever) I get to Berlin I visit her' or 'If I get to Berlin I shall visit her'. But *Falls ich nach Berlin komme, besuche ich sie* can only mean 'If I get to Berlin I shall visit her'.

falls is most often used to introduce 'open' conditions, with the indicative (see 16.5.2), although it does occasionally occur with *Konjunktiv II*, and it is particularly frequent with *sollte*:

Sie kann niemanden ins Oberhaus befördern lassen, **falls** er einen unsicheren Wahlkreis vertritt (*FAZ*)	*She cannot elevate anybody into the Upper House if he hasn't got a safe seat*
Falls diese Hinweise zuträfen, wäre das eine eindeutige Verletzung der Abmachungen (*MM*)	*If these indications were correct, that would be a clear infringement of the agreements*
Man hielt eine Ratskonferenz für denkbar, jedoch nur, **falls** Frankreich dem Haushalt die Zustimmung verweigern sollte (*FAZ*)	*A meeting of the Council was considered conceivable, but only if France should refuse to give its consent to the budget*

Even if it is used with the subjunctive, it still leaves the possibility open that the consequence can be realised – unlike *wenn*, which can indicate a completely hypothetical and unfulfillable condition.

(ii) *angenommen, dass …, vorausgesetzt, dass …* 'assuming that', 'provided that' mainly introduce open conditions.

Angenommen, dass er den Brief erhalten hat, wird er bald hier sein	*Assuming he got the letter, he'll be here soon*
Vorausgesetzt, dass nichts dazwischen kommt, ziehen wir im Frühjahr nach Graz um	*Provided that all goes well, we'll be moving to Graz in the spring*

The *dass* can be omitted, and then the following clause has the word order of a main clause, e.g. *Angenommen, er hat den Brief erhalten, wird er bald hier sein.*

(iii) *sofern* and *soweit* are used in the sense of 'if' or 'provided that' in open conditions:

Sofern/Soweit es die Witterungsbedingungen erlauben, findet die Aufführung im Freien vor der alten Abtei statt	*If weather conditions permit, the performance will take place in the open air in front of the old abbey*

(iv) *selbst wenn, auch wenn, sogar wenn, wenn … auch* all correspond to English 'even if'. For example, the German equivalent of 'Even if I wrote to him today, he wouldn't get the letter until Tuesday', could be any of the following:

> **Selbst wenn** ich ihm heute schriebe,
> **Auch wenn** ich ihm heute schriebe
> **Sogar wenn** ich ihm heute schriebe,
> **Wenn** ich ihm **auch** heute schriebe,

würde er den Brief erst Dienstag bekommen

or with *wenn* omitted, in formal written German only (often with an optional *doch* in the main clause):

Schriebe ich ihm **auch** heute, würde er den Brief (**doch**) erst Dienstag bekommen

(v) *es sei denn, (dass)* ... 'unless' is chiefly used in 'open' conditions.
The *dass* can be omitted, and then the following clause has the word order of a main clause:

Ich komme um zwei, **es sei denn**, ich werde aufgehalten/dass ich aufgehalten werde	*I'll come at two, unless I'm held up*

In old-fashioned literary usage *denn* on its own can have this meaning:

„Ich lasse dich nicht fort", rief sie, „du sagst mir **denn**, was du im Sinn hast" (*Wiechert*)	*'I shan't let you go', she cried, 'unless you tell me what you have in mind'*

(vi) *wenn ... nicht* is the most frequent equivalent for English 'unless'. It is used with open **or** unreal conditions, in the latter case with *Konjunktiv II*:

Wenn er **nicht** bald kommt, wird es zu spät sein	*Unless he comes soon, it will be too late*
Er hätte es nicht gesagt, **wenn** er **nicht** schuldig wäre	*He wouldn't have said it unless he was guilty*

In some contexts, *wenn ... nicht* can mean 'if not'. Compare:

Du brauchst die Suppe nicht zu essen, **wenn** du sie wirklich **nicht** magst	*You needn't eat the soup if you really don't like it*

16.6 Indirect speech *See p. 341*

16.6.1 Indirect and direct speech

(a) In indirect speech we report what someone said by putting it into a sentence of our own

This is sometimes called 'reported speech'. It contrasts with direct speech, where we quote what someone said in the original spoken form. Compare the following English examples:

Direct speech:	She said, 'I am writing a letter'
Indirect speech:	She said **that she was writing a letter**

There are marked differences in English between direct and indirect speech. In particular, we put what was said in a subordinate clause of its own, often introduced by 'that', the pronoun can be altered (especially from the first person to the third person) and the tense is shifted to the past.

(b) In German, instead of shifting the tense, forms of *Konjunktiv I* mark indirect speech

Direct speech:	Sie sagte: „Ich schreibe einen Brief"
Indirect speech:	Sie sagte, **dass sie einen Brief schreibe**

This is the most important use of *Konjunktiv I* – so much so that *Konjunktiv I* on its own is often enough to indicate indirect speech.

However, the use of the subjunctive to mark indirect speech varies considerably. It is used much less in informal registers, and there is much uncertainty among native speakers about correct usage. The remainder of this section explains current usage.

The conjunction *dass*, like English 'that', can be left out after the verb of saying, see 19.2.1b. In this case, the following clause has the order of a main clause, with the verb in second place (see 21.1.1a), e.g. *Sie sagte, sie **schreibe** einen Brief.*

16.6.2 Standard rules for the use of the subjunctive in indirect speech

All modern grammars of German prescribe the following standard rules as correct in formal writing. They are summarised with examples in Table 16.3.

TABLE 16.3 Konjunktiv I *and* Konjunktiv II *in indirect speech – standard rules*

Rule	Tense of direct speech	Direct speech	Indirect speech
Rule 1: Use *Konjunktiv I* in indirect speech, keeping the same tense as in the original direct speech	present	„Sie weiß es" *'She knows it'*	Er sagte, sie wisse es *He said she knew it*
	past	„Sie wusste es" *'She knew it'*	Er sagte, sie habe es gewusst *He said she had known it*
	perfect	„Sie hat es gewusst" *'She knew/has known it'*	Er sagte, sie habe es gewusst *He said she had known it*
	future	„Sie wird es wissen" *'She will know it'*	Er sagte, sie werde es wissen *He said she would know it*
Rule 2: If the *Konjunktiv I* form is the same as the indicative, use *Konjunktiv II*	present	„Sie wissen es" *'They know it'*	Er sagte, sie wüssten es *He said they knew it*
	past	„Sie wussten es" *'They knew it'*	Er sagte, sie hätten es gewusst *He said they had known it*
	perfect	„Sie haben es gewusst" *'They knew/have known it'*	Er sagte, sie hätten es gewusst *He said they had known it*
	future	„Sie werden es wissen" *'They will know it'*	Er sagte, sie würden es wissen *He said they would know it*

(a) Rule 1: *Konjunktiv I* is used to mark indirect speech wherever possible
i.e. as long as the forms of *Konjunktiv I* are clearly distinct from those of the present indicative tense.

(i) In practice, for all verbs except *sein*, this is the case only in the third person singular, where the *-e* ending of *Konjunktiv I* (e.g. *sie schreibe*) contrasts with the present indicative ending *-t* (e.g. *sie schreibt*)

(ii) The crucial principle is that the same tense of *Konjunktiv I* is used for the indirect speech as was used in the indicative in the original direct speech, as shown in the examples in Table 16.3.

The only exception to this principle is that if the original direct speech was in the past or the pluperfect tense, the perfect subjunctive is used in indirect speech. In this way the following sentences of direct speech:

> „Ich **wusste** es nicht"   „Ich **habe** es nicht **gewusst**"   „Ich **hatte** es nicht **gewusst**"

would all be converted into indirect speech as *Sie sagte, sie **habe** es nicht gewusst.*

NB: Complex pluperfect forms are sometimes used if the original direct speech was in the pluperfect, e.g: *Sie sagte, sie habe es nicht **gewusst gehabt**.* This construction is not considered correct.

(iv) If the present tense of the original direct speech refers to the future (see 14.2.3), the future subjunctive is often used in indirect speech, as an alternative to the present subjunctive. In this way, there are two possibilities for converting the following sentence into indirect speech:

> „Sie **heiratet** bald" → Sie sagte, sie **heirate** bald *or* Sie sagte, sie **werde** bald **heiraten**

(b) Rule 2: If the form of *Konjunktiv I* is the same as that of the indicative, *Konjunktiv II* is used

The principle underlying this **replacement rule** is that indirect speech should be marked by a distinct subjunctive form if possible. This is typically needed in the third person plural, where only *sein* has a *Konjunktiv I* form (*sie seien*) which differs from the form of the present indicative (see Table 12.9).

For example, to turn the sentence „*Wir wissen es nicht*" into indirect speech, we cannot use the *Konjunktiv I* form *sie wissen*, because it is not different from that of the present indicative. It is replaced by the *Konjunktiv II* form: *Sie sagten, sie wüssten es nicht.* Table 16.3 gives more examples of the application of this rule for the other tenses.

(c) The standard rules for the use of the subjunctive in indirect speech are adhered to with particular consistency in newspapers

By using *Konjunktiv I* we can indicate that we are simply reporting what someone else said, without committing ourselves to saying whether we think it is true or not. This makes it a handy device for journalists (especially when reporting politicians?!) and newspapers make wide use of it:

Der Bundespressechef verwies darauf, dass in den kommenden Gesprächen noch manches verfeinert werden **könne** (*FAZ*)	*The Federal information officer pointed out that some things could be refined in future discussions*
Auf seine Eindrücke über den Stand des Bürgerkrieges – der besser **verliefe**, als es die Presse **darstelle**, erklärte Johnson – sollen sich die Beschlüsse stützen (*Welt*)	*The decisions ought to be based on his impressions of the state of the civil war – which, Johnson declared, was going better than portrayed by the press*

Konjunktiv I is such a clear indication of indirect speech that it can be used on its own to show that a statement is simply reported. This means that in German we can often dispense with the repeated cues like 'He said that . . .', 'He went on to say that . . .' which we usually need in English. Almost any report in a serious newspaper will provide examples of how this possibility is exploited:

> Die Bundesregierung **verhalte** sich „widerrechtlich", wenn sie DDR-Bürgern in ihrer Botschaft Aufenthalt **gewähre**, sagte der Sprecher des Ostberliner Ministeriums am Abend. Diese „grobe Einmischung in die souveränen Angelegenheiten der DDR" **könne** ebenso wie „Kampagnen, die bis zur versuchten Erpressung anderer Staaten ausarten, zu folgenreichen Konsequenzen führen". Bundesdeutsche Medien **führten** eine Kampagne, in die sich Berichten zufolge nun auch das Auswärtige Amt in Bonn **eingeschaltet habe**. (*SZ 8.8.1989*)

Note the alternation of *Konjunktiv I* and *Konjunktiv II* forms according to the 'replacement rule' and that, even in a main clause without any verb of saying, as in the last sentence above, the subjunctive on its own is enough to signal indirect speech.

16.6.3 Alternative current usage in indirect speech

The standard rules given in 16.6.2 still represent dominant usage in formal writing, and recent surveys have confirmed that they are still adhered to consistently in that register. However, there is a fair range of alternative usage, particularly in colloquial speech. This section surveys these alternatives and explains where they occur most commonly. A summary is given for quick reference in Table 16.4.

TABLE 16.4 *Indirect speech in spoken German*

Formal writing *Konjunktiv I*	Everyday speech Indicative or *Konjunktiv II*
Er sagte, sie wisse es	Er hat gesagt, sie weiß es Er hat gesagt, sie wüsste es
Er sagte, sie habe es gewusst	Er hat gesagt, sie hat es gewusst Er hat gesagt, sie hätte es gewusst

(a) *Konjunktiv II* is used rather than *Konjunktiv I*, even where a distinct *Konjunktiv I* form is available

i.e. in contexts – notably in the third person singular of most verbs except *sein* – where it is not required by the 'replacement rule' explained in 16.6.2b. This occurs:

(i) in everyday speech:

Sie hat gesagt, sie **käme** heute nicht	*She said she wasn't coming today*
Sie hat gesagt, sie **hätte** es verstanden	*She said she had understood it*
Sie hat gesagt, sie **würde** den Brief noch heute schreiben	*She said she'd get the letter written today*

In spoken German *Konjunktiv II* is an alternative to the indicative (see (c) below), but it sounds less informal and it is preferred when the main verb is in the past tense. *Konjunktiv II* also tends to be used if there is a longer stretch of indirect speech covering more than one sentence:

Er sagt, er hat eben einen neuen Wagen gekauft. Der **hätte** über 80 000 Euro gekostet und **hätte** eine Klimaanlage	*He says he's just bought a new car. It cost more than 80,000 euro and it's got air-conditioning*

Konjunktiv I is rarely used in indirect speech in colloquial German, as it sounds stilted and affected in informal registers. However, forms of *sein* are occasionally heard, but then it usually implies that the speaker has doubts. If someone says *Gertrud hat mir gesagt, sie sei heute krank* it often indicates that s/he thinks that Gertrud might not have been telling the whole truth.

(ii) in writing. *Konjunktiv II* is less usual than *Konjunktiv I*, but it does occur occasionally, especially in fiction written by north Germans:

Sie sagte, ihr Vater **schliefe** erst gegen morgen richtig ein und **würde** bis neun im Bett **bleiben**, und sie müsse den Laden aufmachen (*Böll*)	*She said that her father didn't get to sleep properly till the morning and he would stay in bed till nine and that she had to open the shop*
Tante Sissi schrieb uns, es gehe Onkel Heinrich nicht gut und sie **säße** oft an seinem Bett (*Dönhoff*)	*Aunt Sissi wrote telling us that Uncle Heinrich wasn't well and she often sat at his bedside*

('Standard' usage in the above examples would be *schlafe*, *bleibe* and *sitze*)

(b) The conditional with *würde* is used in place of the past subjunctive form of *Konjunktiv II*

For English speakers, the use of *würde* in indirect speech as a substitute for the one-word past subjunctive is potentially confusing, as they need to be careful not to interpret it as equivalent to an English conditional with 'would'.

(i) The use of *würde* is particularly common in colloquial spoken German, especially since the use of the past subjunctive is restricted to a few common verbs (see 16.4.4):

Er sagte, ich **würde** zu schnell **reden**	*He said I talk too fast*
Sie sagte, ihr Hund **würde** kein Fleisch **fressen** *Subj. II future*	*She said that her dog didn't eat meat*

(ii) In writing the use of the conditional is frowned on by purists, but it does occur, most often with those strong verbs whose simple *Konjunktiv II* forms are obsolete, or with weak verbs (see 16.4.1). It can:

be used for a *Konjunktiv II* required by the 'replacement rule':

Immer häufiger, berichtet Professor N. von der Uni Hamburg, **würden** Studenten abends oder nachts **jobben.** Tagsüber seien sie dann furchtbar erschöpft (*Spiegel*)	*Professor N from the University of Hamburg reports that more and more often students take on casual work in the evenings or at night. During the day they are then terribly exhausted, he said*
Sieben Leser gaben an, sie **würden** regelmäßig Fachzeitschriften **lesen** (*MM*)	*Seven readers declared that they regularly read specialist journals*

(The conditionals are used here rather than the ambiguous past subjunctive of *jobben* (i.e. *jobbte*) or the obsolescent *läsen*.)

be used even where a distinct *Konjunktiv I* form is available:

Gleichzeitig informierte man die Presse, die Polizei **würde** auch die Namen zweier Komplizen **kennen** (*Horizont*)	*At the same time the press was informed that the police also knew the names of two accomplices*

(The past subjunctive _kennte_ is obsolete, but by the standard rule one would expect the unambiguous *Konjunktiv I* form *kenne*.)

- be used in place of the *Konjunktiv I* form *werde* if the meaning is 'future-in-the-past' (see 16.4.5):

Er glaubte, er **würde** schon eine Lösung **finden**	*He thought he would surely find a solution*

In practice, this last usage is very frequent, and it is accepted in formal writing even by the most fastidious stylists.

(c) The indicative is used rather than the subjunctive

If the main verb is in the past tense, the verb in indirect speech is usually in the tense of the original direct speech. However, it is sometimes shifted to the past tense, as in English. The indicative is used:

(i) in spoken German:

Sie hat gesagt, sie **weiß** es schon	*She said she knew it already*
Sie hat gesagt, sie **hat** es verstanden	*She said she had understood it*
Sie hat gesagt, sie **wird** den Brief noch heute schreiben	*She said she'd write the letter today*

In practice, the indicative is the most frequent alternative in informal registers, although *Konjunktiv II* also occurs (see (a) above).

(ii) in writing. There are a few contexts where the indicative is fairly regular in indirect speech in written German, as a permissible alternative to the subjunctive, i.e.:

- if the indirect speech is in a clause introduced by *dass*:

Der Kanzler erklärte, dass er zu weiteren Verhandlungen bereit **ist/war**	*The Chancellor declared that he was prepared to enter into further negotiations*
Es wurde erzählt, dass der Verwalter ihnen persönlich das Mittagessen **auftrug** (*Wiechert*)	*It was recounted that the administrator served them lunch in person*

If *dass* is included, the indicative is almost as frequent as the subjunctive even in written German. However, if *dass* is omitted (see 19.2.1b), then the subjunctive is essential in writing: *Der Kanzler erklärte, er **sei** zu weiteren Verhandlungen bereit.*

- if a **first** or **second person** is involved:

Er sagte ihr, von wo ich gekommen **bin**	*He told her where I had come from*
Er hat mir erzählt, dass der Fluss hier tief **ist**	*He told me that the river was deep here*
In deinem letzten Brief hast du mir geschrieben, seine Tochter **studiert** schon vier Semester in Hamburg	*In your last letter you wrote that his daughter had already been studying in Hamburg for four semesters*

The function of *Konjunktiv I* is to distance the speaker from what is being reported, i.e. to make it clear that s/he isn't willing to vouch for whether it is true or not. For this reason it may not make sense to use it in contexts the speaker or the listener is directly involved in.

- if the 'replacement rule' (see 16.6.2b) is ignored:

Die Verfügung des letzten deutschen Kaisers besagte, dass im Ruhrgebiet weder Universitäten noch Kasernen gebaut werden **dürfen** (*v. d. Grün*)	*The decree by the last German emperor declared that neither universities nor barracks were allowed to be built in the Ruhr*

The standard rule would require *dürften*, as the form *dürfen* is identical with the indicative and not a clear subjunctive. However, these ambiguous third person plurals are not unusual. They are sometimes used, too, if the 'replacement rule' produces an obsolete past subjunctive form, as in the following newspaper example:

Der Unterhändler sagte, er hoffe, dass die Vernunft siege und Verhandlungen **beginnen**	*The negotiator said he hoped that reason would prevail and talks would begin*

Applying the replacement rule would result in the obsolete form *begönnen*.

- for stylistic reasons, to render the flavour of colloquial speech:

Seit der Wende denken die Nazis, sie **bestraft** ohnehin keiner	*Since unification the Nazis have thought that nobody would punish them anyway*

(d) There is no consistent distinction in meaning between *Konjunktiv I*, *Konjunktiv II* and the indicative when used in indirect speech

It is sometimes claimed that there is a difference between the three possible forms, i.e.:

(i) Manfred sagte, dass er krank **gewesen sei** *Subj. I*

(ii) Manfred sagte, dass er krank **gewesen wäre** *Subj. II*

(iii) Manfred sagte, dass er krank **gewesen ist** *indicative*

According to this theory, (i) *Konjunktiv I* is used merely to report Manfred's statement neutrally, without offering any personal opinion as to whether it is true or false. Using (ii) *Konjunktiv II*, on the other hand, would make it clear that the speaker thinks Manfred's statement is untrue, whilst in (iii) the speaker's use of the indicative would acknowledge that it is a fact that he had been ill.

However, although some writers may try to operate with such a distinction, it is never consistently maintained. In practice the use of the three forms is determined not by meaning, but by register, stylistic considerations and norms of usage, as outlined in this section.

16.6.4 Indirect questions and commands

(a) Usage in indirect questions follows the same pattern as in indirect statements

i.e. as outlined in 16.6.2 and 16.6.3:

(i) In written German *Konjunktiv I* (or *Konjunktiv II*, by the 'replacement rule') is used:

Sie fragte ihn, wie alt sein Vater **sei**	*She asked him how old his father was*
Der Lehrer fragte uns, ob wir **wüssten**, was das **bedeute** (*Böll*)	*The teacher asked us if we knew what that meant*
Die Dame fragte, ob denn die Typen einer bestimmten Sorte von Schreibmaschinen alle ununterscheidbar gleich **wären** (*Johnson*)	*The lady asked whether the characters of a particular make of typewriter were all the same and indistinguishable from each other*

As in statements, *Konjunktiv II* is sometimes used even if a distinct *Konjunktiv I* form is available: *Sie fragte ihn, wie alt sein Vater **wäre**.*

The indicative occasionally occurs in indirect questions in formal writing, although it is less frequent than the subjunctive:

Warum ich nicht fragte, ob Hanna noch **lebt**, weiß ich nicht (*Frisch*)	*I don't know why I didn't ask whether Hanna was still alive*

(ii) In spoken German either the indicative or *Konjunktiv II* is used:

Sie hat ihn gefragt, wie alt sein Vater **ist/wäre**
Tante Emma hat sie gefragt, ob sie Hunger **hat/hätte**
Der Lehrer hat gefragt, ob sie es **wissen/wüßten**

(b) Commands are reported in indirect speech by using a modal verb
Konjunktiv I is used in writing, but both *Konjunktiv II* and the indicative are quite frequent, and they are usual in spoken German.

(i) *sollen* is the most frequent verb in indirect commands. Thus the direct command *Rufe mich morgen im Büro an!* would correspond to the indirect command:

Herr Hempel sagte ihr, sie **solle/sollte/ soll** ihn morgen im Büro anrufen	*Mr Hempel told her to call him at the office tomorrow*

(ii) *müssen* indicates a rather more forceful command, e.g. *Herr Hempel sagte ihr, sie **müsse/müsste/muss** ihn (unbedingt) morgen im Büro anrufen*

(iii) *mögen* sounds less peremptory. It is most often used in the *Konjunktiv II* form *möchte*: *Herr Hempel sagte ihr, sie **möchte** ihn morgen im Büro anrufen.* The *Konjunktiv I* form *möge* is occasionally still found, but it sounds old-fashioned and stilted (or facetious):

Bitte richten Sie Herrn Schnier aus, die Seele seines Bruders sei in Gefahr, und er **möge**, sobald er mit dem Essen fertig ist, anrufen (*Böll*)	*Please inform Mr Schnier that his brother's soul is in peril and he should call as soon as he has finished his meal*

16.7 Other uses of the subjunctive

16.7.1 Hypothetical comparisons: 'as if'-clauses

(a) Clauses expressing a hypothetical comparison are typically introduced by *als ob* in German
This corresponds to English clauses with 'as if':

Er tat, **als ob** er krank wäre	*He acted as if he was/were ill*
Das Kind weint, **als ob** es Schmerzen hätte	*The child is crying as if it is in pain*

There are one or two alternatives to using **als ob**:

(i) The *ob* can be left out. The finite verb then moves into the position immediately after the *als*:

Er tat, **als wäre** er krank   Das Kind weint, **als hätte** es Schmerzen

This is more frequent than **als ob** in writing, but it is rare in speech.

(ii) *als wenn* and *wie wenn* are less frequent alternatives to *als ob*:

Er tat, **als wenn/wie wenn** er krank wäre
Das Kind weint, **als wenn/wie wenn** es Schmerzen hätte

(b) The verb in German 'as if'-clauses is usually in a form of *Konjunktiv II*
(i) If the action in the 'as if'-clause is simultaneous with the action in the main clause, the simple past subjunctive is used:

Er tat, als ob er krank **wäre**   Das Kind weint, als ob es Schmerzen **hätte**

The conditional can be used if the simple past subjunctive is obsolete or unusual (see 16.4.4). See also (c) below:

Sie hatten den Eindruck, als **würde** sich Diana um die Rolle in einem Kostümfilm **bewerben** (*Spiegel*) (Simple *bewürbe* is obsolete)	*They got the impression that Diana was trying for a part in a period film*

(ii) If the action in the 'as if'-clause took place before the action in the main clause, the pluperfect subjunctive is used:

Sie sieht aus, als ob sie seit Tagen nicht **gegessen hätte**	*She looks as if she hasn't eaten for days*
Er tat, als ob nichts **passiert wäre**	*He acted as if nothing had happened*

(iii) If the action in the 'as if'-clause will take place after the action in the main clause, the conditional is used:

Es sieht aus, als ob es **regnen würde**	*It looks as if it will rain*
Es sah aus, als ob er gleich **hinfallen würde**	*It looked as if he was about to fall down*

(c) In written German *Konjunktiv I* can be used in 'as if'-clauses
It is less frequent than *Konjunktiv II* even in writing, and some Germans even consider it incorrect. It can be used **if** its form is distinct from that of the present indicative:

Er tat, als ob er krank **sei**   Es sah aus, als **werde** er hinfallen
Sie sieht aus, als ob sie seit Tagen nicht gegessen **habe**

There is no difference in meaning between using *Konjunktiv I* and *Konjunktiv II* in 'as if'-clauses. *Konjunktiv I* is sometimes used, rather than a conditional (see (b) above), to avoid an obsolete or unusual past subjunctive form (see 16.4.4):

Der Eindruck, als **befände** sich die Partei auf dem Weg zurück in ihre beschwerliche Vergangenheit – als **kämpfe** sie nicht für die Überwindung akuter Probleme (*Zeit*)	*The impression that the party was on the road back to its problematic past, that it wasn't fighting to overcome immediate problems*

The *Konjunktiv II* form *kämpfte* is not distinguishable from the past tense, and so the writer has preferred to use *Konjunktiv I* – although s/he **did** use the past subjunctive *befände* earlier in the same sentence.

(d) In spoken German the indicative is commonly used in 'as if'-clauses

The indicative is probably at least as frequent as the subjunctive in spoken German, especially in the North (Austrians consider it a 'Prussianism') but it is much less common in writing. The *ob* is never omitted (see (a) above) if the verb is in the indicative.

Er tat, als ob er krank **war**   Es ist mir, als ob ich hinfallen **werde**
Sie sieht aus, als ob sie seit Tagen nicht gegessen **hat**

16.7.2 The subjunctive in clauses of purpose

(a) Clauses with *damit* 'so that' sometimes have a verb in the subjunctive

Konjunktiv I or *Konjunktiv II* is used without any difference in meaning:

Konstantin musste als Erster über den Graben, um die Flinte in Empfang zu nehmen, damit sie nicht womöglich mir ins Wasser **fiele** (*Dönhoff*)	*Konstantin had to cross the ditch first to take hold of the shotgun so that I shouldn't let it drop into the water*
Einmal schickte Dionysos dem Aristippos drei Mädchen, damit er sich eine davon als Geliebte aussuchen **könne** (*SZ*)	*Dionysus once sent three girls to Aristippos so that he could choose one of them as a lover*

This usage is now restricted to formal German and can sound old-fashioned. The indicative is nowadays more frequent in all registers, e.g.:

Ich habe ihm auch Bücher gebracht, damit er sich nicht **langweilte** und nicht immer gezwungen **war**, an seine Verschwörungen zu denken (*Bergengruen*)	*I brought him some books too, so that he didn't get bored and wasn't always compelled to be thinking of his plots*

The modal verbs *können* or *sollen* are often used in *damit*-clauses, especially (but not only) in spoken German, e.g. *Er zog sich zurück, damit wir ihn nicht sehen* **konnten/sollten**.

(b) The conjunction *auf dass* 'so that'

auf dass is an alternative to *damit* which is used only in formal written German. It sounds archaic and solemn and is usually followed by a subjunctive (usually *Konjunktiv I* if the form is unambiguous):

Der Häuptling eines Eingeborenenstammes verfluchte sie, auf dass ihnen nichts von allem, was sie dem Boden und den Gewässern abgewinnen würde, je zum Nutzen **gereiche** (*Spiegel*)	*The chief of a native tribe cursed them, that they might never derive benefit from anything they gained from the soil or the waters*

16.7.3 *Konjunktiv II* can moderate the tone of an assertion, a statement, a request or a question

It sounds less blunt than the indicative. This usage is very frequent, especially in spoken German, and the conditional is often used in similar contexts with a similar effect in English. The simple past subjunctive of the common verbs is used, or the conditional form of others (see 16.4.4):

Ich **wüsste** wohl, was zu tun **wäre**	*I think I know what's to be done*
Eine Frage **hätte** ich doch noch (*Valentin*)	*There's one more thing I'd like to ask*
Da **wäre** er nun aufgewacht (*Dürrenmatt*)	*He seems to have woken up*
Ich **würde** auch **meinen**, dass es jetzt zu spät ist	*It seems a little late to me, too*
Diese Sache **hätten** wir also geregelt	*That would appear to be sorted out*
Das **wär**'s für heute	*I think that's enough for today*
Hätten Sie sonst noch einen Wunsch?	*Is there anything else you would like?*
Würden Sie bitte das Fenster **zumachen**?	*Would you be so kind as to shut the window?*
Könnten Sie mir bitte sagen, wie ich zum Bahnhof **komme**?	*Could you please tell me how to get to the station?*

16.7.4 *Konjunktiv II* is sometimes used in time clauses

Especially in clauses introduced by *bis*, *bevor* or *ehe*, this use is restricted to formal written German and is an optional alternative to the indicative. It can stress that it was still in doubt whether the action or event in question would actually take place:

Sie beschlossen zu warten, bis er **käme**	*They decided to wait till he came*
Er weigerte sich, den Vertrag zu unterzeichnen, bevor wir ihm weitere Zugeständnisse **gemacht hätten**	*He refused to sign the contract before we had made further concessions*

16.7.5 The subjunctive in negative contexts

Konjunktiv II can be used in contexts where an event, action or state was possible, but in fact did not take place or was not the case. The indicative is in most cases a possible alternative, especially in speech, but it can sound less tentative. Such contexts are:

(a) After the conjunctions *nicht dass, ohne dass* and *als dass*

Nicht, dass er faul **wäre** (*or:* ist), aber er kommt in seinem Beruf nicht voran	*Not that he's lazy, but he's not getting on in his career*
Vukovar ist in den letzten drei Monaten pausenlos beschossen worden, ohne dass klar geworden **wäre**, warum dies geschah (*NZZ*) (**ist** would sound more definite)	*Vukovar has been shelled incessantly over the last three months without it becoming clear why this was happening*
Die Auswahl war zu klein, als dass ich mich **hätte** schnell entscheiden mögen (*Grass*)	*The choice was too small for me to have wanted to decide quickly*

NB: The set phrase *nicht dass ich (es) wüsste* 'not that I know of' is <u>always</u> used with a subjunctive.

(b) In other subordinate clauses where the main clause and/or the subordinate clause have a negative element

So gab es keine menschliche Tätigkeit, die nicht von Gestank begleitet gewesen **wäre** (*Süßkind*)	*So there was no human activity which was not accompanied by stench*
Es gibt nichts, was schwieriger **wäre** (*or:* ist), als der Gebrauch des Konjunktivs	*There's nothing more difficult than the use of the subjunctive*
nicht eine einzige Großstadt, die nicht ihr Gesicht in zwei Jahrzehnten gründlich gewandelt **hätte** (*Zeit*) (**hat** would sound much more positive)	*not a single city that has not changed its appearance totally in twenty years*

(c) In sentences with *fast* or *beinahe*
In these the pluperfect subjunctive can be used to emphasise that something almost happened, but didn't:

Er **wäre** (*or:* ist) **beinahe hingefallen**	*He almost fell down*
Ich **wäre** (*or:* bin) **fast nicht gekommen**	*I nearly didn't come*
Wir **hätten** (*or:* haben) das Spiel **beinahe gewonnen**	*We almost won the match*

16.7.6 The subjunctive in wishes, instructions and commands

(a) *Konjunktiv I* can be used in the third person to express a wish
In modern German this is largely restricted to set phrases, e.g.:

Gott **segne** dich/dieses Haus!	*God bless you/this house!*
Es **lebe** die Freiheit!	*Long live freedom!*
Gott **sei** Dank!	*Thank God!*
Behüte dich Gott!	*God protect you!*

NB: (i) *Behüte dich Gott* is often heard in Bavaria and Austria in the contracted form *Pfiati (Gott)!* 'goodbye'.
(ii) The use of the *Konjunktiv I* of *mögen* in wishes, e.g. *Möge er glücklich sein!* 'May he be happy!' is now archaic.

(b) A conditional clause with *Konjunktiv II* can express a wish
The clause can have the form with or without *wenn*, see 16.5.3a. The force of the wish is often strengthened by adding *doch* and/or *nur* or *bloß* (see 10.7.6 and 10.26.1c):

Wenn er doch nur **käme**!	*If only he would come*
Wenn er bloß fleißiger **arbeiten würde**!	*If only he would work harder!*
Wenn ich bloß/nur/doch zu Hause **geblieben wäre**!	*If only I'd stayed at home!*
Hätte mein Vater doch dieses Haus nie **gekauft**!	*If only my father hadn't bought this house!*

(c) The *Konjunktiv I* of *sein* or the *sein*-passive can be used in technical German to express a proposition

Gegeben **sei** ein Dreieck ABC	*Given a triangle ABC*
In diesem Zusammenhang **sei** nur darauf verwiesen, dass diese Hypothese auf Einstein zurückgeht	*In this context we merely wish to point out that this hypothesis goes back to Einstein*

NB: In mathematical contexts the indicative is nowadays at least as common as the subjunctive, e.g. *Gegeben **ist** ein Dreieck ABC*.

(d) *Konjunktiv I* is used for commands or instructions in the third person and the first person plural

Also, **spielen** wir jetzt Karten!	*Well, let's play cards*
Im Notfall **wende** man sich an den Hausmeister!	*In case of emergency please apply to the caretaker*

Details are given in 16.2.2f/g.

17

The modal auxiliaries

Six verbs are usually referred to as MODAL AUXILIARY verbs:

dürfen	**mögen**	**sollen**
können	**müssen**	**wollen**

They are given this name because they indicate the attitude of the speaker with regard to what is being said, and this meaning is very similar to that of the modal PARTICLES (see Chapter 10) and the category of MOOD (see Chapter 16). They are called auxiliary verbs because they are mainly used with other verbs, and they express ideas like ability, possibility, permission, necessity, obligation and volition.

The modal auxiliary verbs are all irregular in similar ways (see 12.1.3c), and their conjugation is given in full in Table 12.4.

This chapter explains the uses of the modal auxiliaries:

- Common features of all the modal auxiliary verbs (section 17.1)
- Individual modal auxiliary verbs, treated in alphabetical order (sections 17.2–17.7)

17.1 The modal auxiliaries: common features of form and syntax

The modal auxiliary verbs have several special features which distinguish them from other German verbs, and from their English equivalents. The most important of these are listed briefly below and explained in the sections indicated:

- Their forms are quite **irregular** in similar ways (see 12.1.3c and Table 12.4)
- They have a full range of **tense** and **mood** forms (see 17.1.1)
- They are used with a **'bare' infinitive**, without *zu* (e.g. *Ich kann ihn **sehen**, see 13.3.1a and 17.1.2)
- Their **perfect tenses** are constructed with the **infinitive**, not with the past participle (e.g. *Ich habe ihn sehen **können***, see 13.3.2a and 17.1.3)

17.1.1 The German modal auxiliaries have a full range of tense and mood forms

In this they differ from the corresponding English verbs (*can, may, must,* etc.), which have at most only a present tense and a past tense (which often has conditional meaning). German *können*, for example, can be used in the future tense:

Er **wird** es morgen nicht machen können　　　*He won't be able to do it tomorrow*

English 'can' is impossible here, as it has no future tense, and we have to use the paraphrase 'be able to'. Similarly, there is a clear difference in German between the past tense *konnte*, which means 'was able to', and the subjunctive *könnte*, which means 'would be able to'. English 'could', on the other hand, is often used in either sense, depending on the context:

Ich **konnte** sie gestern nicht besuchen, weil ich keine Zeit hatte	*I couldn't visit her yesterday, as I didn't have time*
Ich **könnte** sie morgen besuchen, wenn ich das Auto nehmen dürfte	*I could visit her tomorrow if you let me take the car*

Because of this, the German modal auxiliaries can seem complicated for the English learner. But they are easy to master if the various combinations of tense and mood with a following simple or compound infinitive are treated independently and learned with their usual English equivalents. The examples in sections 17.2 to 17.7 are set out to facilitate this, and Table 17.1 illustrates the various possible combinations with *können*.

TABLE 17.1 *The tenses and moods of* können *with an infinitive*

Tense	Infinitive type	Example	
present	+ infinitive	Er kann es machen.	*He can do it.*
	+ perfect infinitive	Er kann es gemacht haben.	*He can have done it.*
future	+ infinitive	Er wird es machen können.	*He will be able to do it.*
past	+ infinitive	Er konnte es machen.	*He was able to do it.*
perfect	+ infinitive	Er hat es machen können.	*He has been able to do it.*
pluperfect	+ infinitive	Er hatte es machen können.	*He had been able to do it.*
past subj.	+ infinitive	Er könnte es machen.	*He could do it.*
past subj.	+ perfect infinitive	Er könnte es gemacht haben.	*He could have done it.*
pluperf. subj.	+ infinitive	Er hätte es machen können.	*He would have been able to do it.*

⊗ Subj. II Present ⊞ Subjunct II Past

17.1.2 The modal verbs are followed by a 'bare' infinitive, without *zu*

(see 13.3.1a). This is quite similar to the typical English equivalents of these verbs. As Table 17.1 shows, they can be followed by a simple or a compound infinitive:

Ich kann **schwimmen**	*I can swim*
Darf ich **gehen**?	*May I go?*
Sie muss es **gesehen haben**	*She must have seen it*

kellett, hogy lássa

17.1.3 In the perfect tenses, the infinitive of the modal verbs is used instead of the past participle

Wir haben meinen Onkel nicht besuchen **können**	*We weren't able to visit my uncle*
Ich habe es ihr versprechen **müssen**	*I had to promise her*
Sie hätte das Buch lesen **sollen** ✳	*She ought to have read the book*

The past participle is used, however, if the modal auxiliary is used on its own, without another verb, see 13.3.2 and 17.1.5, e.g. *Ich habe es nicht gewollt.* ⊗

NB: The use of the past participle if the modal auxiliary has another infinitive with it, e.g. *Herbert hat arbeiten gemusst*, is not unknown in colloquial speech, but it is considered substandard.

✳ cf. Sie sollte das Buch lesen. Ich habe nie Fisch gemacht.

17.1.4 The position of the modal auxiliary and the infinitive

For more general information on word order and the modals, see 21.1.

(a) In MAIN CLAUSES the infinitive of the main verb is in final position

Darf ich heute Tennis **spielen**?	*May I play tennis today?*
Ich möchte das Buch gern **lesen**	*I would like to read that book*

In compound tenses, the infinitive of the modal verb comes **after** the infinitive of the main verb at the end of the clause:

Sie wird morgen nicht **kommen können**	*She won't be able to come tomorrow*
Sie hätte ihrem Mann doch **helfen sollen**	*She really ought to have helped her husband*

(b) In INFINITIVE CLAUSES with *zu*, the modal verb comes after the infinitive of the main verb

i.e. at the **end** of the infinitive clause, with the infinitive particle *zu* coming between the main verb and the modal verb:

Es scheint **regnen zu wollen**	*It looks as if it's going to rain*
Sie gab vor, meine Handschrift **nicht lesen zu können**	*She claimed not to be able to read my handwriting*

(c) In SUBORDINATE CLAUSES, the modal verb comes after the infinitive of the main verb at the end of the clause

Wenn Sie diesen Ring nicht **kaufen wollen,** ...	*If you don't want to buy this ring, ...*
Obwohl ich gestern Abend **ausgehen durfte,** ...	*Although I was allowed to go out last night, ...*
die Frau, die ich **besuchen sollte**	*the woman I ought to visit*

If a modal verb is used in a compound tense in a subordinate clause, the tense auxiliary *werden* or *haben* comes **before** the two infinitives:

Obwohl ich ihn morgen **werde** besuchen können, ...	*Although I'll be able to visit him tomorrow*
Es war klar, dass er sich **würde** anstrengen müssen	*It was clear that he would have to exert himself*
Das Buch, das ich **hätte** kaufen sollen, kostete dreißig Mark	*The book I ought to have bought cost thirty marks*
Sie hat mir gesagt, dass sie es **hat** machen müssen	*She told me she had had to do it*

NB: In Austrian usage, the tense auxiliary is commonly placed between the main verb and the modal verb, e.g. *Das Buch, das ich kaufen hätte sollen,* ...

17.1.5 The omission of the main verb after the modal auxiliaries

In certain contexts the infinitive of the main verb can be left understood and omitted. This is particularly the case in the following contexts:

(a) The main verb is a verb of motion

(i) If there is an adverbial or, very commonly, a separable prefix in the sentence which conveys the idea of movement, a specific verb of motion can be omitted after the modal verbs. This usage is especially common in colloquial speech, but it is found in writing, too: *Wo bist du denn hin? Hova igyekszel?* ✓✓

Wo wollen Sie morgen hin?	*Where do you want to go tomorrow?*
Ich will nach Frankfurt	*I want to go to Frankfurt*
Ich sollte zu meinem Onkel	*I ought to go to my uncle's*
Ich kann heute Abend nicht ins Kino	*I can't go to the cinema tonight*
Sie will ihm nach	*She wants to go after him*
Ich möchte jetzt fort	*I'd like to leave now*

If the modal is at the end of the clause, a separable prefix is written together with it, e.g. *Sie wissen ja, dass Sie jetzt zu Fuß nach Elberfeld* **zurückmüssen**.

(ii) The verb understood is usually *gehen, kommen* or *fahren*, as in the above examples, but other verbs can be omitted if the idea of movement is sufficiently clear from the adverbial or the prefix:

Er wollte über die Mauer [klettern]	*He wanted to climb over the wall*
Die Strömung war so stark, dass er nicht bis ans Ufer [schwimmen] konnte	*The current was so strong that he couldn't swim to the bank*
Er musste in den Krieg [ziehen] (*Böll*)	*He had to go to the war*

(iii) The omission of a verb of motion is most common with simple tenses of the modals, but it can be found with the future and perfect tenses of *können* and *müssen*:

Er hat ins Geschäft gemusst	*He's had to go to work*
Ich glaube, ich werde vorbeikönnen	*I think I'll be able to get past*

(b) The main verb is *tun*

Das kann ich nicht	*I can't do that*
Das darfst/sollst du nicht	*You mustn't/ought not to do that*
Was soll ich damit?	*What am I supposed to do with it?*
Ich kann nichts dafür	*I can't help it*
Er kann was	*He is very able*

(c) The main verb has just been mentioned

This usually corresponds to English usage. Optionally, *es* can be added to make it clear that a previous phrase is being referred to, see 3.6.1a:

Ich wollte Tennis spielen, aber ich konnte/durfte (es) nicht	*I wanted to play tennis, but I couldn't/wasn't allowed to*
Der junge Herr Leutnant könnte niemanden erkennen, auch wenn er es wollte (*Wolf*)	*The young lieutenant couldn't recognise anyone even if he wanted to*

(d) In some idiomatic phrases

Ich kann nicht mehr [weitermachen]	*I can't go on*
Was soll das eigentlich [bedeuten]?	*What's the point of that?*
Sie hat nicht mehr gewollt	*She didn't want to go on*
Er kann mich [am Arsch lecken] (vulg.)	*He can get stuffed*
Mir kann keiner [was antun]	*No-one can touch me*

17.1.6 In German two modals can be used in the same sentence

This is not usual in standard English:

Rechnen **muss** doch jeder **können**	*But everyone has to be able to add up*
Wir **müssten** hier spielen **dürfen**	*We should be allowed to play here*
Wie **kannst** du das nur machen **wollen**?	*How can you want to do that?*

17.2 *dürfen*

17.2.1 *dürfen* most often expresses permission

(a) In this sense *dürfen* corresponds to English 'be allowed to' or 'may'

Sie dürfen hereinkommen	{ *They may/can come in* { *They are allowed to come in*
Sie durfte ausgehen, wenn sie wollte	*She was allowed to go out when she wanted to*
Endlich durfte er die Augen wieder aufmachen	*At last he could open his eyes again*
Sie wird erst heute Nachmittag mit uns spielen dürfen	*She won't be allowed to play with us till this afternoon*

In English, 'can' often expresses permission and is often preferred to 'may', which can sound affected. *können* is sometimes heard for *dürfen* in everyday speech (see 17.3.4), but it is less common in this sense than English 'can'.

(b) Negative *dürfen* has the sense of English 'must not'
i.e. it expresses a prohibition (= 'not be allowed to'):

Sie **dürfen nicht** hereinkommen	{ *They mustn't come in* { *They're not allowed to come in*
Aber ich **darf** mich **nicht** loben (*Langgässer*)	*But I mustn't praise myself*
Wir **dürfen** es uns **nicht** zu leicht machen (*Brecht*)	*We mustn't make it too easy for ourselves*

Note that *nicht müssen* usually means 'doesn't have to', 'needn't', not 'mustn't', see 17.5.1c.

(c) *Konjunktiv* II forms of nicht dürfen often correspond to English 'shouldn't', 'ought not to'
dürfen keeps its basic sense of permission in such contexts and sounds more incisive than *sollen*, see 17.6.4a:

Das **dürfte** sie doch gar **nicht** wissen (it shouldn't be allowed)	*She ought not to know that*
Er **hätte** so etwas **nicht** machen **dürfen** (someone should have forbidden it)	*He ought not to have done anything like that*

(d) *dürfen* is commonly used in polite formulas
It usually corresponds to English 'can' in such contexts. The tone is that of a polite request or a tentative suggestion:

Das **darf** als Vorteil betrachtet werden	*That can/may be seen as an advantage*
Was **darf** sein? (in shop)	*How can/may I help you?*
Der Wein **dürfte** etwas trockener sein	*The wine could just be a bit drier*
Dürfte ich Sie um das Salz bitten?	*Could I ask you to pass the salt?*
Wir freuen uns, Sie hier begrüßen zu **dürfen**	*We are pleased to be able to welcome you here*

17.2.2 *dürfen* can express probability

The *Konjunktiv II* of *dürfen* expresses an assumption that something is likely:

Das **dürfte** reichen	*That'll be enough*
Rapid **dürfte** unser bisher schwerster Gegner im Europacup werden (*BILD*)	*Rapid will probably be our most difficult opponent so far in the European Cup*
Das **dürfte** ein Vermögen gekostet haben	*That'll have cost a fortune*

This sense of *dürfen* is very close to that of the future tense with *werden* (see 14.4), or that of the modal particle *wohl* (see 10.35.1).

17.3 *können*

17.3.1 *können* is most often used to express ability

Its usual English equivalents are 'can' or 'be able to':

Sie **kann** ihn heute besuchen	*She can/is able to visit him today*
Ich **konnte** sie nicht besuchen ⎫	*I couldn't visit her/I wasn't able to visit*
Ich **habe** sie nicht besuchen **können** ⎭	*her*
Ich **werde** sie morgen besuchen **können**	*I'll be able to visit her tomorrow*
Ich **könnte** sie morgen besuchen, wenn ich Zeit hätte	*I could visit her tomorrow if I had time*
Ich **hätte** sie gestern besuchen **können**, wenn ich Zeit gehabt hätte	*I would have been able to/could have visited her yesterday, if I'd had time*

17.3.2 *können* can have the sense of possibility

In this sense *können* usually corresponds to English 'may':

Das **kann** sein	*That may be*
Ich **kann** mich irren	*I may be wrong*
Er **kann** krank sein	*He may be ill*

(a) The use of *können* to express possibility is limited
In general können can only be used in this sense in contexts where it cannot be understood to mean 'be able to'. This is most frequently the case:

(i) with a perfect infinitive:

Er kann den Schlüssel verloren haben	*He may have lost the key*
Die Straße kann gesperrt sein	*The road may be blocked*
Er kann krank gewesen sein	*He may have been ill*

(ii) in the *Konjunktiv II* form *könnte* (= English 'might' or 'could'), to indicate a remote possibility:

Sie **könnte** jetzt in Wien sein	*She could be in Vienna now*
Wir **hätten** umkommen **können**	*We might/could have been killed*
Er **könnte** krank sein	*He might/could be ill*
Er **könnte** krank gewesen sein	*He might/could have been ill*

könnte can also be used to express a tentative request (see 16.7.3):

Könnten Sie mir bitte helfen?	*Could you please help me?*

(b) Other German equivalents for English 'may, might'

Since *können* can only be used in the sense of possibility in contexts where it could not be taken to mean 'be able to', we often need to express the idea of possibility in German in other ways, i.e.:

(i) The adverbs *vielleicht* or *möglicherweise*, or a paraphrase (e.g. *Es ist möglich, dass ...*) are often possible alternatives:

Vielleicht arbeitet er im Garten	*He may be working in the garden*
(Compare: *Er kann im Garten arbeiten*)	*(He is able to work in the garden)*
Es ist möglich, dass er jetzt im Garten arbeitet	*He may be working in the garden now*
(Compare: *Er kann jetzt im Garten arbeiten*)	*(He can work in the garden now)*
Möglicherweise kommt sie heute Abend	*She may come tonight*
(Compare: *Sie kann heute Abend kommen*)	*(She can come tonight)*

(ii) In sentences with a negative, the phrasings given under (i) above can be used, or the sense of possibility can be made clear by adding *auch* to *nicht können* (see 10.4.1). *nicht* is stressed in these contexts:

Sie **kann auch** <u>**nicht**</u> kommen	*She may not come*
(Möglicherweise kommt sie nicht)	
Er **kann auch** <u>**nicht**</u> krank gewesen sein	*He may not have been ill*
(Vielleicht ist er gar nicht krank gewesen)	
Sie **kann** das Auto **auch** <u>**nicht**</u> gesehen haben	*She may not have seen the car*
(Vielleicht hat sie den Wagen gar nicht gesehen)	

17.3.3 *können* is used in the meaning 'know' of things learnt

especially languages, school subjects, the rules of games, etc. *können* is effectively being used as a full verb in these contexts, not as an auxiliary:

Er **kann** Spanisch	*He can speak Spanish*
Ich **kann** die Melodie der österreichischen Nationalhymne	*I know the tune of the Austrian national anthem (i.e. I've learnt it)*
Kann der Manfred Skat?	*Does Manfred know how to play Skat?*
Ich **kann** den Trick	*I know that trick*

(i.e. 'I can do it'. Compare *Ich **kenne** den Trick* 'I've seen it before')

17.3.4 *können* is used to express permission

i.e. in the sense of *dürfen* (see 17.2.1) This usage is primarily colloquial:

Kann ich herein?	*Can I come in?*
Du **kannst** den Bleistift behalten	*You can keep the pencil*

Even in colloquial German *können* is less frequent to express permission than is 'can' in English.

17.3.5 *können* is used less often than English 'can' with verbs of sensation

The verbs 'see', 'hear', 'feel 'and 'smell' are often used with 'can' in English without any real idea of being able. In such contexts *können* is frequently not necessary in German:

Ich sehe die Kirche	*I can see the church*
Ich höre Musik	*I can hear music*
Sie sahen die Stadt im Tal liegen	*They could see the town lying in the valley*

17.3.6 German equivalents for English 'I couldn't help ...'

There are a number of alternative possibilities, e.g., for English 'I couldn't help laughing':

(i) Ich **musste einfach** lachen
(ii) Ich **konnte nicht anders, ich musste** lachen
(iii) Ich **konnte nichts dafür, ich musste** lachen
(iv) Ich **konnte nicht umhin zu** lachen

Alternative (i) is the simplest and most usual in speech, although (ii) and (iii) are quite current. Alternative (iv) is restricted to formal registers.

17.3.7 *könnte ... gemacht haben* and *hätte ... machen können*

These two constructions have different meanings in German. The English equivalents for both are 'could have done' or 'might have done', but German makes distinctions here which we ignore in English, e.g.:

Sie **könnte** den Brief nicht **geschrieben haben**	*She couldn't have written the letter*
(i.e. it isn't possible that it was she who wrote it)	
Sie **hätte** den Brief nicht **schreiben können**	*She couldn't have written the letter*
(i.e. she wouldn't have been able to)	
Er **könnte umgekommen sein**	*He might have been killed*
(i.e. it is possible that he was killed)	
Er **hätte umkommen können**	*He might have been killed*
(i.e. it was possible, but he wasn't)	

17.4 *mögen*

17.4.1 The most frequent sense of *mögen* is to express liking

(a) It most commonly occurs in the *Konjunktiv II* form *möchte*
This expresses a polite request and usually corresponds to English 'would like' or 'want'. It is often linked with the adverb *gern*:

Sie **möchte** (gern) nach Rom fahren	*She would like to go to Rome*
Ich **möchte** nichts mehr davon hören	*I don't want to hear any more about it*
Ich **möchte** ihr Gesicht gesehen haben	*I would have liked to see her face*
Ich **möchte** nicht, dass er heute kommt	*I don't want him to come today*

The pluperfect subjunctive is also used occasionally in this sense, e.g.:

Baldini **hätte** ihn erwürgen **mögen** (*Süßkind*)	*Baldini would have liked to strangle him*

In general, though, German more often uses *gern* with the pluperfect subjunctive of the verb than this, e.g., for 'I would have liked to read the book', *Ich **hätte gern** dieses Buch **gelesen**.*

(b) Other tenses of *mögen* are used in the sense of English 'like'
(i) As a full verb, on its own, it occurs most often (although not exclusively) in the negative, chiefly with reference to people, places and food:

Sie **mag** keinen Tee	*She doesn't like tea*
Mögt ihr den neuen Lehrer?	*Do you like the new teacher?*
Ich **mag** ihn nicht	*I don't like him*
Sie **hat** ihn nie **gemocht**	*She never liked him*

(ii) With a following infinitive it is only used in the negative:

Wie es im Winter werden soll, daran **mag** er noch gar nicht denken (*Zeit*)	*He doesn't want to think about what it's going to be like in winter*
Ich **mag** das Wort gar nicht aussprechen	*I don't even like saying that word out loud*
Ich **mag** diese Fragen nicht beantworten (*BILD*)	*I don't want to answer these questions*
Er **mochte** nicht allein an der Straße stehen (*Johnson*)	*He didn't want to stand on the street alone*

17.4.2 *mögen* sometimes expresses possibility or probability

The use of *mögen* to express possibility is largely limited to formal written registers and set phrases (although it is more widely used in spoken south German). When it is used it tends to express a rather higher degree of probability than *können*, see 17.3.2.

(a) When indicating possibility *mögen* often has a concessive sense
i.e. there is an expected qualification by a following *aber* (which may or may not be present). This usage is similar to English 'That may well be (, but . . .)':

Das **mag** vielen nicht einleuchten, (aber ...)	*That may not be clear to many, (but ...)*
Das Tief **mag** über Italien weiterwandern und den Balkan einnässen. Wir aber fliegen dorthin, wo die Sonne scheint (*Grzimek*)	*The low may drift over Italy and make the Balkans wet. But we're flying to where the sun shines*
Eine Zeitlang **mochte** es scheinen, dass es gelänge, das Absinken der deutschen Währung abzubremsen, doch schien es nur so (*Heuss*)	*For a time it might have appeared that the attempt to stop the German currency falling would be successful, but that appearance was deceptive*

(b) In other contexts *mögen* indicates a reasonable degree of probability

i.e. somewhere between 'possible' and 'probable':

Sie **mag/mochte** etwa sechzig sein	*She is/was probably about sixty*
Jetzt **mögen** über 1000 DDR-Bürger sich in der Botschaft aufhalten (*ARD*)	*There are now probably more than a thousand GDR citizens in the embassy*
An einem Sonntag im März – es **mochte** etwa ein Jahr seit seiner Ankunft in Grasse vergangen sein (*Süßkind*)	*On a Sunday in March – a year or so had probably gone by since his arrival in Grasse*

(c) Some idiomatic phrases with *mögen* express possibility

The following set phrases are used in spoken German as well as in formal writing:

Das mag (wohl) sein	*That may well be*
Wer mag das (schon) sein?	*Who can that be?*
Wie mag das (nur) gekommen sein?	*How can that have happened?*

A few phrases with *möchte* convey a **doub**t or a supposition:

Ich möchte meinen, dass ...	*I should think that ...*
Dabei möchte man verrückt werden	*It's enough to drive you mad*

könnte can be used for *möchte* in such contexts, but it sounds less tentative.

17.4.3 *mögen* in concessive clauses

i.e. the German equivalent of English clauses like 'whatever/whoever that may be', etc. (see also 19.6.2). *mögen* can be used in these clauses in German:

Wann er auch ankommen mag, ...	*Whenever he may arrive ...*
Was auch immer geschehen mag, ...	*Whatever happens ...*
Wer er auch sein mag, ...	*Whoever he may be ...*

Alternatively, the main verb can simply be used on its own, and in practice this is more frequent in less formal registers, especially in spoken German:

Wann er auch **ankommt**, ...   Was auch immer **geschieht**, ...   Wer er auch **ist**, ...

However, *mögen* is <u>always</u> used in the set phrase *Wie dem auch sein mag* 'However that may be'.

17.4.4 *mögen* in wishes and commands

(a) *Konjunktiv I* of *mögen* can express a wish or a command in the third person

Möge er glücklich sein!	*May he be happy!*
Die Herren **mögen** bitte unten warten	*Would the gentlemen be so kind as to wait downstairs?*

This usage is limited to formal German and sounds old-fashioned, see 16.2.2g.

(b) The subjunctive of *mögen* is used in indirect commands

Sagen Sie ihr, sie **möchte** zu mir kommen	*Ask her to be kind enough to come and see me*
Er sagte mir, ich **möchte** einen Augenblick auf ihn warten	*He asked me to wait for him a moment*

The *Konjunktiv I* of *mögen* (e.g. . . ., *sie **möge** zu mir kommen*) is also used in indirect commands in very formal registers. For further details, see 16.6.4b.

17.5 *müssen*

17.5.1 *müssen* most often expresses necessity or compulsion

(a) The most frequent English equivalent is 'must, have (got) to'

Wir **müssen** jetzt abfahren	*We must leave now/ We have (got) to leave now*
Wir **werden** bald abfahren **müssen**	*We'll have to leave soon*
Ich **musste** um acht abfahren	*I had to leave at eight*
Ich **habe** um acht abfahren **müssen**	
Ich **muss** den Brief bis heute Abend **geschrieben haben**	*I've got to have the letter written by tonight*
Wir **mussten** die Anträge bis zum 15. Januar **abgegeben haben**	*We had to have the applications handed in by the 15th of January*
Sie **muss** sich beeilen, wenn sie den Zug erreichen will	*She'll have to hurry if she wants to catch the train*

(b) With a passive infinitive or a passive equivalent, 'need' is sometimes a more natural English equivalent for *müssen*

Das **muss** gut überlegt werden	*That needs thinking about properly*
Man **muss** sich um sie kümmern	*She needs looking after*

(c) Negative *müssen* keeps the sense of necessity
(i) It usually has the sense of English 'needn't' or 'don't have to':

Wir **müssen** noch **nicht** gehen	*We needn't go yet/ We don't have to go yet*
Er **hat** es **nicht** tun **müssen**	*He didn't need to/didn't have to do it*
Du **musst nicht** hier bleiben, du kannst auch gehen	*You needn't stay here, you can leave*

In practice *nicht brauchen* (see 13.2.5) is at least as frequent as *nicht müssen* in this meaning, e.g. *Du brauchst nicht hier zu bleiben*.

(ii) English 'mustn't' expresses a prohibition, and usually corresponds in German to *nicht dürfen*, see 17.2.1b. *nicht müssen* is sometimes used in this sense in speech, e.g. *Sie müssen hier nicht parken* 'You mustn't park here', but this is usually considered to be non-standard and regional (northern).

17.5.2 *müssen* can express a logical deduction

(a) This corresponds to English 'must' or 'have to'

Sie spielt heute Tennis, also **muss** es ihr besser gehen	*She's playing tennis today, so she must be better*
Das **muss** ein Fehler sein	*That must/has to be a mistake*
Sie **muss** den Unfall gesehen haben	*She must have seen the accident*

If *müssen* could be taken in context to express necessity where logical deduction is intended, the meaning can be made clear by using the adverb *sicher* rather than *müssen*, e.g.:

Er ist heute **sicher** in Frankfurt	*He must be in Frankfurt today*

Er muss heute in Frankfurt sein would naturally be understood to mean 'He has to be in Frankfurt today'.

(b) German uses the past tense *musste* with a simple infinitive to express a logical deduction in the past

In such contexts English uses 'must' with a compound infinitive:

Er schuftete, dass ihm heiß sein **musste** (*Grass*)	*He was working hard, so he must have been hot*

(c) A logical deduction can be queried by *nicht brauchen*

This is commoner than *nicht müssen*, e.g.: *Er war heute nicht im Büro, aber er* **braucht** **nicht** *deshalb* krank zu sein (less often: *aber er muss nicht ...*)

(d) A negative logical deduction is expressed by *nicht können*

This corresponds to English 'can't':

Sie spielt heute Tennis, also **kann** sie **nicht** krank sein	*She's playing tennis today, so she can't be ill*

17.5.3 The *Konjunktiv II* of *müssen*

(a) The *Konjunktiv II* form *müsste* can express a possible compulsion or necessity
In this sense it can correspond to English 'would have to/need to':

Er weiß ja nicht, was er tut – ich **müsste** ja sonst meine Hand von ihm zurückziehen (*Böll*)	*He doesn't know what he's doing – otherwise I would have to disown him*
Es sind Felsen, Gestein, wahrscheinlich vulkanisch, das **müsste** man nachsehen und feststellen (*Frisch*)	*They are rocks and stones, probably volcanic, that would need to be checked and established*

In negative sentences the *Konjunktiv II* of *nicht brauchen* is more usual than that of *nicht müssen*, see 17.5.2:

Du hättest **nicht** hinzugehen **brauchen**, wenn ...	*You wouldn't have had to go there if ...*

(b) *müsste* **can express a logical probability or necessity**
(i) In this sense, 'should' or 'ought to' are the usual English equivalents:

Deutschlands Kohle ist teurer, als sie sein **müsste** (*Zeit*)	*Coal in Germany is dearer than it ought to be/should be*
Das **müsste** eigentlich reichen	*That really ought to be enough*
Es **müsste** viel mehr Prügel in der Schule geben (*Böll*)	*There should be a lot more beatings in school*
Ich **hätte** mich vielleicht anders ausdrücken **müssen**	*Perhaps I ought to/should have expressed myself differently*

(ii) This sense of *müsste* is close to that of *sollte*, which also corresponds to English 'should, ought to', see 17.6.4. There is a difference, though, as *sollte* always expresses an obligation (often laid on a person by someone else), whereas *müsste* expresses a logical probability or necessity. Compare:

Sie **sollte** heute im Büro sein	*She ought to be at the office today*
(i.e. she is obliged to be if she doesn't want to get into trouble)	
Sie **müsste** heute im Büro sein	*She ought to be at the office today*
(i.e. I assume that is the most likely place for her to be)	
Das **hätte** er eigentlich wissen **sollen**	*He ought to have known that*
(i.e. he was obliged to – it could have stopped him making a mistake)	
Das **hätte** er eigentlich wissen **müssen**	*He ought to have known that*
(i.e. I would have thought it was a pretty fair assumption that he did)	
Wo ist der Brief? – Er **müsste** in dieser Schublade sein	*Where's the letter? – It ought to be/should be in this drawer*
(A logical deduction: *sollte* would not be possible)	

müsste nicht is not normally used as an equivalent for English 'shouldn't, ought not to'; we usually find *sollte nicht* or *dürfte nicht*, see 17.6.4.

(c) *müsste ... gemacht haben* **and** *hätte ... machen müssen*
The English equivalent for both these constructions is usually 'should/ought to have done', but there is often a clear distinction between them in German. Compare, for English *He ought to have written the letter yesterday*:

Er **müsste** den Brief schon gestern **geschrieben haben**
(i.e. it is a fair deduction that he did)
Er **hätte** den Brief schon gestern **schreiben müssen**
(i.e. he had to, but he didn't)

17.6 *sollen*

17.6.1 *sollen* most commonly expresses an obligation

(a) This corresponds to 'be to', 'be supposed to' or (occasionally) 'shall'

Um wie viel Uhr **soll** ich kommen?	*What time am I to/shall I come?*
Ich **soll** nicht so viel rauchen	*I'm not supposed to smoke so much*
Was **soll** ich in Greifswald tun?	*What am I (supposed) to do in Greifswald?*
Sie wusste nicht, was sie tun **sollte**	*She didn't know what to do*
Wir **sollten** uns gestern treffen	*We were (supposed) to meet yesterday*

The meaning of *sollen* is close to that of *müssen*, and 'must', 'have to' is often a possible English equivalent. However, *sollen* always conveys the idea that some other person is making an obligation. Compare:

Ich **soll** hier bleiben	*I am to/have (got) to stay here*
	(i.e. someone's told me to)
Ich **muss** hier bleiben	*I've got to stay here*
	(i.e. it is necessary for me)

In questions, the past tense of *sollen* can be used to prompt a strong reaction (negative or positive, depending on the context). It can sound ironic:

Wie **sollte** ich das wissen?	*How was I (supposed) to know that?*
Sollte das nun fertig sein?	*Is that supposed to be finished?* (ironic)
Sollte er wirklich nichts davon wissen?	*Is he really supposed not to know anything about it?*

(b) *sollen* often has the force of a command

See also 16.2.2e. This use is related to the basic sense of obligation:

Du **sollst** nicht stehlen	*Thou shalt not steal*
Du **sollst** das Fenster zumachen	*(I want you to) shut the window*
Man **soll** sofort den Saal verlassen	*Everyone has to leave the room immediately*
Das **soll** dir eine Warnung sein	*Let that be a warning to you*
Er **soll** sofort kommen	*He is to/has got to come at once/Tell him to come at once*

sollen is the most frequent modal auxiliary in indirect commands (see 16.6.4b):

Er sagte ihr, sie **solle/sollte** unten warten	*He told her to wait downstairs*
Ich habe ihm gesagt, er **soll** seinem Vater helfen	*I told him to help his father*

17.6.2 *sollen* can express an intention or prediction

(a) In this sense *sollen* corresponds to 'be to', 'be supposed/meant to'

Eine zweite Fabrik **soll** bald hier gebaut werden	*A second factory is to be built here soon*
Soll das ein Kompliment sein?	*Is that meant as a compliment?*
Es **sollte** eine Überraschung sein	*It was intended to be a surprise*
XWas **soll** das heißen?	*What's that supposed to mean?*
Es **soll** nicht wieder vorkommen	*It won't happen again*
XDas **sollst** du noch bereuen	*You're going to regret that*

(b) The sense of intention is common in first person plural questions

In such contexts *sollen* is an alternative to *wollen*, although there is a slight difference of meaning, see 17.7.1b:

Was **sollen wir** uns heute in der Stadt ansehen?	*What are we going to look at in town today?*
Sollen wir heute Abend ins Kino gehen?	*Shall we go to the cinema tonight?*

(c) The past tense of *sollen* can indicate what was destined to happen

This sense is essentially that of a 'future-in-the-past':

Diese Meinung **sollte** sie noch oft zu hören bekommen	*She would often hear this opinion again*
Er **sollte** früh sterben	*He would/was (destined) to die young*
Er **sollte** niemals nach Deutschland zurückkehren	*He would never return to Germany*

In these contexts *sollte* differs slightly from *würde* (see 16.4.5), since it indicates that this is a prediction by the speaker.

17.6.3 *sollen* can express a rumour or report

i.e. 'It is said that ...'. Only the present tense of *sollen* is used in this sense, with a compound infinitive to refer to past time if necessary:

Er **soll** steinreich (gewesen) sein	*He is said to be (have been) enormously rich*
Bei den Unruhen **soll** es bisher vier Tote gegeben haben (*FAZ*)	*So far four people are reported to have been killed in the course of the riots*
Eine solche Bombe **soll** die Katastrophe von Lockerbie ausgelöst haben (*ARD*)	*A similar bomb is assumed to have caused the Lockerbie disaster*

17.6.4 The *Konjunktiv II* of *sollen*

(a) The *Konjunktiv II* of *sollen* conveys the idea of a possible obligation
These forms are the most frequent equivalents to English 'should (have)', 'ought to (have)':

Warum **sollte** ich denn nicht ins Theater gehen?	*Why shouldn't I go to the theatre?*
Das **solltest** du mal probieren	*You ought just to try that*
Das **sollte** ihm inzwischen klar geworden sein	*He ought to have realised that by now*
Das **hätten** Sie mir aber gestern sagen **sollen**	*You ought to have told me that yesterday*

NB: (i) For negative 'shouldn't, ought not to', *dürfte nicht* can be used as a more incisive alternative to *sollte nicht*, see 17.2.1b.

(ii) For the distinction between *sollte* and *müsste* as equivalents of English 'should/ought to', see 17.5.3b.

(b) *sollte ... gemacht haben* and *hätte ... machen sollen*
The English equivalent for both these constructions is usually 'should/ought to have done', but German can make a distinction between them. Thus, for English 'He ought to have written the letter yesterday':

Sie **sollte** den Brief gestern **geschrieben haben** (i.e. I would expect her to have done so)	
Er **hätte** den Brief gestern **schreiben sollen** (i.e. he ought to have done, but he didn't)	

(c) In questions, *sollte* is often used as an alternative to *könnte*
There is no real difference in meaning:

Wie **sollte/könnte** ich das wissen?	*How could I know that?*
Warum **sollte/könnte** er nicht einmal in London gewesen sein?	*Why shouldn't he have been to London some time?*

(d) *sollte* is often used in conditional sentences and clauses of purpose
(i) In 'if'-sentences it corresponds to 'should' or 'were to', see 16.5.1d:

Wenn/Falls es regnen **sollte**, so komme ich nicht	*If it should rain, I shan't come*
Sollten Sie ihn sehen, dann grüßen Sie ihn bitte von mir	*If you were to see him, please give him my regards*

(ii) *sollen* is commonly used in clauses of purpose with *damit* (see 19.5.1a):

Ich trat zurück, damit sie mich nicht sehen **sollten** (ne lásson)	I stepped back, so that they shouldn't see me

For alternative usage in clauses of purpose see 16.7.2.

17.7 wollen

17.7.1 wollen most often expresses desire or intention

(a) In many contexts it expresses a wish
(i) It usually corresponds to English 'want/wish (to)':

Sie **will** ihn um Geld bitten	She wants to ask him for money
Sie **wollte** ihn um Geld bitten	She wanted to ask him for money
Sie **hat** ihm um Geld bitten **wollen**	
Hättest du kommen **wollen**?	Would you have wanted to come?
Willst du nicht deinem Vater helfen?	Don't you want to help your father?

(ii) In this sense, *wollen* is often used without a dependent infinitive, as a full v

Was **wollen** Sie von mir?	What do you want from me?
Der Arzt will, dass ich mehr Bewegung mache	The doctor wants me to take more exercise
Mach, was du **willst**	Do what you like

(iii) The sense of 'wish' is often given by *Konjunktiv II*:

Ich **wollte**, ich hätte sie nicht so beleidigt	I wish I hadn't offended her like th
Ich **wollte**, ich wäre zu Hause	I wish I was at home

(iv) *wollen* can correspond to English 'will', 'would':

Er **will** es nicht zugeben	He won't admit it
Ich bat sie, es zu tun, aber sie **wollte** nicht	I asked her to do it, but she woul
Willst du mir helfen? – Ja, ich **will** dir helfen	Will you help me? – Yes, I will h

wollen in this sense is distinct in meaning from the future tense. **Wirst** du
– Ja, ich **werde** dir helfen, sounds more impersonal and lacks the sens
willingness conveyed by *wollen*.

(v) *wollen* is common in second person questions with the sense of a
request:

Willst du bitte noch mal nachsehen?	Will you have another look, pl
Wollen Sie bitte die Frage wiederholen?	Will you repeat the question,

In such requests, *Konjunktiv II* (e.g. **Würden** Sie bitte noch mal nachsehe
sounds less blunt and direct than *wollen*.

(b) *wollen* can express intention
(i) In such contexts it often corresponds to English 'be going to', but
the notion of intention more forcefully than the future with *werden*

wollen uns bald einen neuen
rnseher anschaffen

We're going to buy ourselves a new TV set soon

ie future *Wir **werden** uns bald einen neuen Fernseher anschaffen* would have more
ie sense of a prediction than a definite intention)

ɔllen Sie ihm das klarmachen? — *How are you going to explain that to him?*

'lte Sie darüber fragen — *I was going to ask you about it*

llen Sie damit sagen? — *What do you mean by that?*

nicht viel sagen — *That doesn't mean much*

ie erst morgen anrufen — *I don't intend phoning her till tomorrow*

regnen zu **wollen** — *It looks as if it's going to rain*

ɔn plural questions *wollen* has the sense of English 'Shall we …?':

ine Tasse Kaffee trinken? — *Shall we/Let's have a cup of coffee*

vir heute machen? — *What shall we do today?*

'en wir mal (anfangen)? — *Well then, let's get on with it!*

ve to *wollen* in such constructions, see 17.6.2b. However, there
ɔ in meaning. *wollen* clearly indicates that the speaker is in
ɔsal, but *sollen* leaves the decision entirely to the other

erb:

subject, *wollen* corresponds to English 'need'

hese contexts is similar to that in (a) and (b) above, but
' are not normally used with an inanimate subject:

ɔnne — *Tomatoes need a lot of sun*

Zeit haben — *A piece of work like that needs time*

ɔrden — *That needs proper consideration*

will gelernt — *Working like that as an interpreter needs*
ɡlauben (*Frisch*) — *to be learnt, believe me*

nate subject has the sense of 'refuse':

hen — *The suitcase refused to/wouldn't close*

hr — *My legs won't carry me any further*

f — *I can't grasp that*

dn't
elp you

mir helfen
of active

n insistent

sense of 'claim'

ed with a perfect infinitive. The implication is

ɪ — *He claims to have shot down a Mosquito*

ben — *They say they saw you in Berlin*

to — *At the same time at which I said I had*
) — *seen the car with the Jews, …*

ease?
please?

?, see 16.7.3)

sense of *wollen*:

No-one admits doing it
Go on as if I hadn't said anything
I'll go on as if I hadn't heard/
seen/noticed anything

wollen stresses

18

Verbs: Valency

Different verbs need different elements to make a grammatical sentence. The el
ments which a particular verb needs to form a grammatical sentence are called t
COMPLEMENTS of the verb, and the type and number of complements required
a particular verb to construct a grammatical sentence is known as the VALENCY
the verb.

The valency of verbs can involve significant differences between English
German. In particular, German typically shows the relationship between the c
plements and the verb through the use of the various CASES (see Chapter 2). En
noun phrases do not have endings to show case, and the relationship of the
plements to the verb is indicated more often by their position (see Chapter 2

This chapter explains about the valency and the complements of verbs, p
attention to those verbs and constructions which are most different from
nearest English equivalents:

- verb **valency**, **complements** and **sentence patterns** (section 18.1)
- the **subject** of the verb, in the nominative case (section 18.2)
- the **accusative** or direct object of the verb (section 18.3)
- verb objects in the **dative** case (section 18.4)
- verb objects in the **genitive** case (section 18.5)
- **prepositional** objects (section 18.6)
- **place** and **direction** complements (section 18.7)
- **predicate complements** (section 18.8)

18.1 Valency, complements and sentence patterns

18.1.1 The COMPLEMENTS of the verb

The complements of a particular verb are the elements it needs to const
matical sentence. Different verbs need different elements – the action o
instance, involves a person handing a thing over to another person. Th
therefore, needs three elements to form a sentence: a **subject** (in the nom
a **direct object** (in the accusative case) and an **indirect object** (in the c

> Gestern hat **mein Vater** (NOM) **seinem Bruder** (DAT) **das Geld** (ACC) g

If we omitted any of these, the sentence would be ungrammatica
like *telefonieren*, only need one element, i.e. a subject:

> **Ich** habe eben telefoniert   *I've just made a phone cal*

s, like *schlagen*, need two, i.e. a subject and a direct object:

den Ball geschlagen   *She hit the ball*

have other types of construction, for example with a subject and a particular preposition (a 'prepositional object'), like *warten*:

ange **auf dich** gewartet   *I waited a long time for you*

major types of complement in German, and these are shown on of them is explained further in detail in sections 18.2 to 18.8 as able.

complements in German

Para.	Form of complement	Example
18.2	a noun phrase in the nominative case	**Der Bäcker** trinkt zu viel Das hast **du** mir doch versprochen!
.3	a noun phrase in the accusative case	Er trinkt **schwarzen Tee** **Diesen Mann** sah er in der Stadt
	a noun phrase in the dative case	Sie verkaufte **mir** zwei CDs **Ihrem Mann** teilte sie es nicht mit
	a noun phrase in the genitive case	Er bedurfte **ihrer Hilfe** Er erinnerte sich **des Vorfalls**
	a phrase introduced by a preposition determined by the verb	Sie warnte mich **vor dem Polizisten** Er starb an **einer Lungenentzündung**
	phrase indicating place with a verb of position	Sie wohnt **in Heiligenhafen** **Dort** blieb sie einen Monat
	phrase indicating direction a verb of motion	Gestern ist sie **in die Stadt** gefahren Er legte das Buch **auf den Tisch**
	n phrase in the native case or an ve with a copular	Er ist **ihr Betreuer** Das Heft war **teuer**

is the type and number of complements
construct a grammatical sentence

cific number of complements of a particular a subject, an accusative object and a dative a subject (see 18.1.1). This property of each nplements of a particular type is the valency

tly, we have to know its valency. This can seem to be the equivalent English verb:

He informed me of that yesterday
I'm afraid of the dentist
He advised her against (making) this
journey

uct a gram-
f giving, for
e verb *geben*,
inative case),
ative case):

egeben

Other verbs,

lency of each verb in order to be able
d practice to learn German verbs in
ber of verbs, especially the most

frequent, are used with different valencies. This is often associated with differences in meaning:

jemanden achten	*respect somebody*
auf jemanden achten	*pay attention to somebody*

Further examples are given in the remainder of this chapter.

18.1.3 German sentence patterns

All German verbs require one, two or three of the complements listed in Table 18.1 to form a complete clause or sentence. How many there are, and of what type, is determined by the valency of the verb.

There are a limited number of combinations of complements which occur commonly with German verbs, since many verbs have the same valency. In this way, we can say that German possesses a restricted number of possible sentence structure types or **sentence patterns** (the German term is *Satzbaupläne*). For example, many verbs are *einem etwas* verbs, like *geben*, requiring an accusative object and a dative object besides a subject.

The most frequent sentence patterns of German are given in Table 18.2. They are explained in sections 18.2 to 18.8 under the heading of the chief complements.

TABLE 18.2 *German sentence patterns*

A	SUBJECT + Der Mann	VERB schwimmt		
B	SUBJECT + Der Mann	VERB + kauft	ACCUSATIVE OBJECT den Fernseher	
C	SUBJECT + Der Mann	VERB + hilft	DATIVE OBJECT seinem Bruder	
D	SUBJECT + Der Mann	VERB + gibt	DATIVE OBJECT + seinem Bruder	ACCUSATIVE OBJECT den Fernseher
E	SUBJECT + Der Mann	VERB + bedarf	GENITIVE OBJECT der Ruhe *(szükségel)*	
F	SUBJECT + Der Mann	VERB + würdigt	ACCUSATIVE OBJECT + seinen Kollegen	GENITIVE OBJECT keines Blickes *(appreciate)*
G	SUBJECT + Der Mann	VERB + wartet	PREPOSITIONAL OBJECT auf seinen Bruder	
H	SUBJECT + Der Mann	VERB + hindert	ACCUSATIVE OBJECT + seinen Bruder	PREPOSITIONAL OBJECT an seiner Arbeit
I	SUBJECT + Der Mann	VERB + dankte	DATIVE OBJECT + seinem Bruder	PREPOSITIONAL OBJECT für seine Hilfe
J	SUBJECT + Der Mann	VERB + wohnt	PLACE COMPLEMENT in einem Hausboot	
K	SUBJECT + Der Mann	VERB + fährt	DIRECTION COMPLEMENT in die Stadt	
L	SUBJECT + Der Mann	VERB + bringt	ACCUSATIVE OBJECT + seinen Bruder	DIRECTION COMPLEMENT in die Stadt
M	SUBJECT + Der Mann	VERB + ist	PREDICATE COMPLEMENT nett/ein netter Mensch	

18.1.4 Complements and adverbials

The complements are those elements which are required by the verb to form a complete grammatical sentence. However, a sentence can contain other elements:

> Mein Vater hat seinem Bruder **gestern** das Geld gegeben
> **Heute** habe ich diesen Mann **in der Stadt** gesehen
> Sie wohnte **lange** in Halle
> **Gestern** ging sie **schnell** in die Stadt

Words and phrases like those in bold type provide additional information or circumstantial detail, often about the time, manner or place of the action or event. They may be important in context, but they are not closely bound up with the basic meaning of the verb like the complements. If we leave them out, the sentence is still grammatical. These elements are called ADVERBIALS (in German *freie Angaben*). They can be single words (adverbs) or adverb phrases, and they can be classified into types as shown in Table 7.1.

As a rule, **complements are necessary** to make a complete grammatical sentence, whilst **adverbials are optional**. But the distinction is not always as clear-cut as this. Certain complements of some verbs can be omitted without this resulting in an ungrammatical sentence. Compare:

Er trinkt **viel Kaffee**	Er trinkt
Sie fährt **in die Stadt**	Sie fährt

We still have grammatical sentences even when the phrases in bold are left out. However, the action of *trinken* must involve consuming some liquid (the direct object), and the action of *fahren* always implies going somewhere (the direction complement). These elements are so closely bound up in meaning with the action of the verb that, even if we can leave them out in some contexts, we have to take them as complements rather than as adverbials. They are not simply extra pieces of information about the circumstances of the action.

It can happen that the same word or phrase is a complement in some contexts, but an adverbial in others. Compare:

Sie wohnte **in Köln**:	*in Köln* is a **place complement** to the verb of position *wohnen*; it cannot be omitted
Sie starb **in Köln**:	*in Köln* can be omitted; it is a **place adverbial** adding extra information to the sentence

18.2 The subject

18.2.1 Most German verbs require a subject complement

Characteristically, the **subject** of verbs in the active voice is the agent, i.e. the animate being carrying out the action, e.g. *der Räuber* hat das Geld gestohlen, *die Soldaten* singen, *der Bär* frisst das Fleisch.

(a) If the subject is a noun phrase, it is in the nominative case
The finite verb agrees with the subject, see 12.1.4:

> **Ich** reise nach Italien
> Das hat uns **die Geschichte** gelehrt
> **Wer** ruft mich?
> Kommen **deine Geschwister** morgen?

NB: For the use of *es* as a 'dummy subject' in order to permit the real subject to occur later, e.g. *Es saß eine alte Frau am Fenster*, see 3.6.2d.

(b) The subject can be a subordinate clause or an infinitive clause
The finite verb has the third person singular ending, see 12.1.4a.

> **Dass du hier bist**, freut mich
> **Dich wiederzusehen** hat mich gefreut

Subordinate subject clauses are introduced by *dass* or an interrogative, see 19.2. For further information on subject infinitive clauses see 13.2.3. If such a clause is not in first position in the sentence, it can be anticipated by *es*, e.g. *Es freut mich, dass du hier bist*, see 3.6.2e.

(c) The subject can be 'understood' in certain contexts
In German as in English, we can leave out the subject of the verb in some contexts. In particular, if the verbs in two (or more) main clauses linked by the coordinating conjunctions *und* and *oder* (see 19.1) have the same subject, the second (or subsequent subject) is usually omitted. We say that the subject is 'understood' in the second clause:

> Er kam herein und sah seine Frau in der Ecke sitzen — *He came in and saw his wife sitting in the corner*
> Meine Schwester geht ins Theater oder besucht ein Konzert — *My sister is going to the theatre or attending a concert*

18.2.2 A few verbs do not need a subject complement

i.e. they just have an **accusative** or a **dative object** (depending on the verb), but **no subject**. The verb is in the third person singular form, e.g. *mich hungert, mir bangt*. Most of these verbs express an emotion or a sensation, and almost all are now limited to formal or literary registers, or to regional usage (especially southern). A selection of those still used is given below (with more currently used equivalents where appropriate):

> Mir **bangt** vor etwas (dat.) — *I am afraid of sth.*
>   (More usual: *Ich habe Angst um etwas*)
> Mich **dürstet, hungert** — *I am thirsty, hungry*
>   (More usual: *Ich habe Durst, Hunger*)
> Mich/Mir **ekelt** vor etwas (dat.) — *I am disgusted at sth.*
>   (More usual: *Es ekelt mich/Ich ekele mich vor etwas* or: *Etwas ekelt mich*)
> Mich **friert** — *I am cold*
>   (More usual: *Es friert mich* or, more colloquially: *Ich friere*)
> Mir **graut** vor jdm./etwas (dat.) — *I have a horror of sb./sth.*
>   (More usual: *Es graut mir vor etwas*)
> Mich/Mir **schaudert** vor etwas (dat.) — *I shudder at sth.*
>   (More usual: *Es schaudert mich vor etwas*)
> Mich/Mir **schwindelt** — *I feel dizzy*
>   (More usual: *Mir ist schwindlig*)
> Mir **träume** von etwas (dat.) — *I dream of sth.*
>   (More usual: *Ich träumte von etwas*)
> Mich **wundert**, dass ... — *I am surprised that ...*
>   (Frequent, but there are common alternatives: *Es wundert mich/Ich wundere mich, dass ...*)

18.2.3 German is more restrictive than English in respect of the noun which can occur as the subject of the verb

In English nouns which do not denote an agent can often be used as the subject of the verb. This is less frequent in German, where the subject of the verb must usually be the agent actually performing the action. Typically, the noun which is the subject in English appears in a prepositional phrase in German:

In diesem Hotel sind Hunde verboten	*This hotel forbids dogs*
In diesem Zelt können vier schlafen	*This tent sleeps four*
Mit dieser Anzeige verkaufen wir viel	*This advertisement will sell us a lot*
Wir können **mit dem Prozess** nicht fortfahren	*The trial cannot proceed*
Damit haben wir den besten Mittelstürmer verloren	*This loses us the best centre-forward*
In Berlin wird es wieder ziemlich heiß sein	*Berlin will be rather hot again*

Logically, things like 'hotels' cannot really 'forbid'. Neither do 'tents' actually 'sleep' or 'advertisements' do any 'selling', etc., and, in the last example, Berlin is <u>where</u> 'it' is hot rather than a person or thing feeling the heat. The German constructions reflect this more clearly than do the corresponding English sentences.

18.2.4 The impersonal subject *es*

Many verbs are exclusively or commonly used impersonally, with the indefinite subject *es*, (see also 3.6.2a), which corresponds to English 'it' or 'there'. The *es* cannot be omitted in these constructions except in the cases indicated under (e) and (f) below.

(a) Verbs referring to weather (which are only used impersonally)

Es regnet, hagelt, schneit	*It is raining, hailing, snowing*
Es blitzte	*There were flashes of lightning*
Es dämmert	*It is growing light/dusk*

(b) Verbs used with impersonal *es* to refer to an indefinite agent

These are verbs which **can** be used with a specific subject, but are used impersonally if the agent is vague or unknown:

(i) verbs referring to natural phenomena:

Es zieht	*There's a draught*
Es brennt	*Something's burning*
Da riecht **es** nach Teer	*There's a smell of tar there*

(ii) verbs denoting noises:

Es läutet, klingelt	*Someone's ringing the bell*
Es klopfte an der Tür	*There was a knock at the door*
Es kracht, zischt, knallt	*There is a crashing, hissing, banging noise*

Many other verbs can be used with an impersonal *es* to bring out the idea of a vague impersonal agent, see 3.6.2a.

(c) Verbs denoting sensations and emotions

Many verbs denoting sensations can be used with an impersonal *es* as subject to give the idea of an unspecified force causing the sensation. The person involved appears as an accusative object:

Es juckt mich	*I itch*
Es überlief mich kalt	*A cold shiver ran up my back*
Es zog mich zu ihr	*I was drawn to her*
Es hält mich hier nicht länger	*Nothing's keeping me here any more*

Most verbs which can be used without a subject in formal or older German are now more usually constructed like this, e.g.: *Es friert mich, Es wundert mich*, etc. See 18.2.2 for details.

(d) Impersonal *es* with *sein* or *werden* followed by a noun or an adjective
This usually corrresponds to English 'it':

Es ist, wurde spät	*It is, got late*
Es ist dein Vater	*It's your father*

Further details on this use of *es* are given in 3.6.2b. The use of *es ist* in the sense of English 'there is/are' is treated in detail in 18.2.5.

(e) *sein* and *werden* can be used impersonally with a personal dative and some adjectives expressing a sensation

> **Es** ist mir heiß, kalt, schwindlig, übel, warm, etc.

For details see 2.5.5c. *es* is usually omitted if it is not in initial position in a main clause.

> Ist (es) dir kalt? – Ja, mir ist (es) kalt
> Ich merkte, dass (es) mir schwindlig wurde.

(f) Impersonal passive and reflexive constructions

> **Es** lebt sich gut in dieser Stadt
> **Es** wurde im Nebenzimmer geredet

es is usually deleted unless it is in initial position in a main clause. Details are given in 3.6.2a and 15.1.3–4.

(g) Other impersonal verbs and constructions
Many of these are idiomatic and the verbs involved are also used in other constructions with a definite subject. A selection of the most common:

Es bedurfte keiner anonymen Briefe (*Th. Mann*)	*No anonymous letters were needed*
Es fehlt mir an etwas (dat.) (see also 18.4.1d)	*I lack sth.*
Es gefällt mir in Heidelberg (see also 18.4.1d)	*I like it in Heidelberg*
Es gibt	*There is/are*

(For *es gibt* and *es ist* as equivalents of 'there is/are', see 18.2.5)

Es geht	*It can be done; OK* (in answer to *Wie geht es (dir/Ihnen)?*)
Wie geht es (dir/Ihnen)?	*How are you?*
Es geht um Leben und Tod	*It's a matter of life and death*
Es gilt, etwas zu tun	*The thing is to do something*
Es geschah ihm recht	*It served him right*
Es handelt sich um etwas (acc.)	*It is a question of sth.*
Es heißt, dass ...	*It is said that ...*
Es kommt auf etwas (acc.) an	*It depends on sth.*
Es kommt zu etwas (dat.)	*Something occurs*
e.g.: Am Abend **kam es zu** neuen Zusammenstößen	*There were fresh clashes in the evening*
Es liegt an etwas (dat.)	*It is due to sth.*
e.g.: **Woran liegt es**, dass ...?	*Why is it that ...?*
Es macht/tut nichts	*It doesn't matter*
Es steht schlecht/besser um ihn	*Things look bad/better for him*
Wie steht es mit ihr?	*How's she doing?*
Es verhält sich so	*Things are like that*
e.g.: Ähnlich **verhält es sich** an der Universität Münster	*Things are similar at the University of Münster*

18.2.5 es ist/sind and es gibt as equivalents of English 'there is/are'

es ist/sind and *es gibt* have rather different meanings. The following is a guide to choosing the correct one for the context.

(a) *es gibt* **indicates existence in general**
It is a real impersonal construction, and the *es* is never omitted.

(i) *es gibt* is typically used in **broad, general statements**, denoting existence in general, without necessarily referring to a particular place:

Es gibt Tage, wo alles schief geht	*There are days when everything goes wrong*
So etwas **gibt es** nicht	*There's no such thing*
Es gibt verschiedene Gründe dafür	*There are various reasons for that*
Es **hat** immer Kriege **gegeben** (*Valentin*)	*There have always been wars*
Unglückliche **gibt es** in allen Häusern, in jedem Stand (*Walser*)	*There are unhappy people in every kind of home, in every walk of life*

(ii) *es gibt* is used to point in a general way to **permanent existence in a large area** (i.e. a city or a country):

Es gibt drei alte Kirchen in unserer Stadt	*There are three old churches in our town*
In Trier **gibt es** ja so viel zu sehen	*There's so much to see in Trier*
Es dürfte in der Bundesrepublik wenige **geben**, die so gut wie er informiert sind (*Zeit*)	*There are probably not many people in the Federal Republic who are as well informed as he is*

(iii) *es gibt* records the **consequences** of some event:

Wenn du das tust, **gibt's** ein Unglück	*If you do that, there'll be an accident*
Bei den Unruhen **soll es** bisher vier Tote **gegeben haben** (*FAZ*)	*It is reported that there have been four killed in the disturbances so far*

NB: In everyday speech in south-west Germany, *es hat* is used for *es gibt*. This is a substandard regionalism.

(b) *es ist/sind* **indicates the presence of something at a particular time and place**
The *es* of *es ist/sind* is a 'dummy' subject (see 3.6.2e), allowing the real subject of the verb to occur later in the sentence, and it drops out when it is not in initial position in a main clause. Compare:

Es war eine Maus in der Küche	*There was a mouse in the kitchen*
BUT: In der Küche **war** eine Maus	*In the kitchen there was a mouse*
Er hat gemerkt, dass eine Maus in der Küche **war**	*He noticed that there was a mouse in the kitchen*

Given this, *es ist/sind* is used:

(i) to refer to **permanent or temporary presence in a definite and limited place**, or **temporary presence in a large area**:

Es war eine kleine Gastwirtschaft im Keller (*Baum*)	*There was a little bar in the cellar*
Schade, dass hier im Haushalt keine Nähmaschine **ist** (*Fallada*)	*It's a shame there isn't a sewing machine here in the house*
Es ist irgendjemand an der Tür	*There's someone at the door*
Es waren noch viele Menschen auf den Straßen	*There were still a lot of people in the streets*
Es waren Wolken am Himmel	*There were clouds in the sky*

Sentences with *es ist/sind* **must** contain an indication of place. This is often quite simply *da*:

Es ist ein Brief für Sie **da**	*There's a letter for you*

es gibt is occasionally used in such contexts. It emphasises the thing rather than the place and underlines its distinctive character:

In dieser Diele **gab es** gegenüber der Tür einen offenen Kamin (*Wendt*)	*In this lounge there was an open fireplace opposite the door*

(ii) to **record events** and when speaking of **weather conditions**:

Letzte Woche **war** in Hamburg ein Streik	*There was a strike in Hamburg last week*
Im Fernsehen **war** eine Diskussion darüber (*Valentin*)	*There was a discussion about that on the television*
In Mainz **war** ein Aufenthalt von fünf Minuten	*There was a five-minute stop in Mainz*
Am nächsten Morgen **war** dichter Nebel	*Next morning there was thick fog*
Gestern **war** ein Gewitter in Füssen	*There was a thunderstorm in Füssen yesterday*

Usage varies in this type of context, and *es gibt* is often used:

Letzte Woche **gab es** einen Streik in Hamburg
In Mainz **gab es** einen Aufenthalt von fünf Minuten
Gestern **gab es** ein Gewitter in Füssen

es gibt is particularly frequent when a need is felt to emphasise the exceptional nature of the event or to refer to the future:

Es gab eine Explosion in der Fabrik	*There was an explosion in the factory*
Morgen **wird es** wieder schönes Wetter **geben**	*It will be fine again tomorrow*

18.3 The accusative object

18.3.1 Transitive verbs govern a direct object in the accusative as one of their complements

Verbs which govern an accusative object are called TRANSITIVE VERBS. This accusative object is called the DIRECT OBJECT. With many of these verbs, the accusative is the only complement apart from the subject (sentence pattern B in Table 18.2):

> Er hat **sie** besucht
> Christian hat **seine Freundin** besucht
> Seine Worte haben **mich** verletzt
> **Den Arzt** hat sie nicht gesehen

Table 18.2 shows that some transitive verbs can have other complements in addition to the accusative object, i.e. a dative object (sentence pattern D), a genitive object (sentence pattern F), a prepositional object (sentence pattern H) or a direction complement (sentence pattern L). Details about verbs with these sentence patterns are given in the sections dealing with these other complements.

Verbs which do not have a direct object in the accusative case (i.e. those in all the other sentence patterns in Table 18.2) are called INTRANSITIVE VERBS.

NB: The accusative case is used in some time and place phrases, e.g.: *Es hat **den ganzen Tag** geschneit* (see 2.2.5). These are **not** complements of the verb, but adverbials.

18.3.2 The direct object can have the form of a clause

(a) Many verbs can have a clause as their direct object
Because these clauses function as complements of the verb, they are called COMPLEMENT CLAUSES. These clauses can be:

(i) A **subordinate clause** with *dass*, *ob* or an interrogative (see 19.2):

> Ich bedauerte, **dass ich nicht kommen konnte**
> Sie fragte mich, **ob ich dort übernachten wollte**

(ii) An **infinitive clause** with *zu* (see 13.2.4):

> Ich hoffe **dich bald wiedersehen zu können**
> Ich habe vor **sie morgen zu besuchen**

Many verbs which have a clause as object can have <u>either</u> a subordinate clause <u>or</u> an infinitive clause, depending on context. However, a few verbs only allow an infinitive clause (especially verbs denoting an intended action, like *versuchen, vorhaben, wagen, sich weigern, zögern*), whereas others only allow a subordinate clause (especially verbs of saying and hearing, e.g. *erleben, fragen, mitteilen, verfügen*). In practice usage in German is similar to that with the nearest English equivalents; exceptions are detailed in 13.2.4.

(b) A direct object clause is sometimes anticipated by *es*
This can be the case whether the complement is a subordinate clause or an infinitive clause, e.g.:

> Sie sah **es** als gutes Zeichen an, dass keine Leute mehr vorbeikamen
> Ich konnte **es** kaum ertragen, ihn so leiden zu sehen

Details on the use of this 'anticipatory' *es* are given in 3.6.3a.

18.3.3 A handful of verbs are used with two accusative objects

In general, only one accusative (direct) object is possible in a sentence. However, a small number of verbs allow two accusative complements.

(a) Verbs with two accusative objects
(i) *kosten* and *lehren* are normally used with two accusatives:

Der Flug hat **meinen Vater 5000 Euro** gekostet	*The flight cost my father 5000 euro*
Sie hat **mich Deutsch** gelehrt	*She taught me German*

In colloquial German both these verbs are commonly used with a dative of the person, e.g. *Sie hat **mir** Deutsch gelehrt; Das hat **mir** viel Geld gekostet*. This is considered substandard, but it is acceptable with *kosten*, as an alternative to the accusative, in figurative contexts:

Das kann **ihn/ihm** den Hals kosten	*That may cost him his life*

(ii) *abfragen* and *abhören* 'test sb. orally' can be used <u>either</u> with two accusative objects <u>or</u> a dative of the person and an accusative:

Der Lehrer hat **ihn/ihm** die englischen Vokabeln abgefragt/abgehört	*The teacher tested him on his English vocabulary*

If only the person is mentioned in the sentence, only the accusative is used, e.g. *Der Lehrer hat **ihn** abgefragt/abgehört*

(iii) *bitten* and *fragen* can be used with two accusatives. One denotes the person asked, the other is an indefinite pronoun or a subordinate clause:

Hast du **ihn etwas** gefragt?	*Did you ask him something?*
Das möchte ich **dich** bitten	*I would like to request that of you*
Sie fragte **ihn, ob er mitkommen wollte**	*She asked him if he wanted to come with her*

NB: *bitten* is more commonly used with a prepositional object introduced by *um*, see 18.6.10, e.g. *Ich möchte dich **darum** bitten*.

(iv) *angehen* is used with an accusative of the person and an indefinite expression of quantity, e.g.:

Das geht **dich nichts** an	*That doesn't concern you at all*

Similarly: *Das geht mich viel, wenig, einen Dreck an*. The use of *angehen* with a dative of the person (e.g. *Das geht **dir** nichts an*) is considered a substandard north German regionalism.

(b) A few verbs have a predicate complement in the accusative
i.e. an additional element which relates back to the accusative object, describing or identifying it:

Er nannte **mich einen Lügner**	*He called me a liar*

This construction is restricted in German to verbs of calling, i.e. *heißen, nennen* and *schimpfen*. A similar construction is used with more verbs in English; the corresponding contexts in German usually have a phrase with *als* in apposition (see 2.6) or a prepositional complement, usually with *zu*, although some verbs select other prepositions:

Ich sehe es **als eine Schande** an	*I consider it a shame*
Er erwies sich **als Feigling**	*He proved himself a coward*
Er machte sie **zu seiner Frau**	*He made her his wife*
Man erklärte ihn **zum Verräter**	*He was declared a traitor*
Wir hielten ihn **für einen Idioten**	*We considered/thought him an idiot*

18.3.4 Some German transitive verbs have English equivalents with different constructions

Common examples are:

etwas beantragen	*to apply for sth.*
jemanden beerben	*to inherit from sb.*
etwas bezahlen	*to pay for sth.*
etwas ekelt mich (see also 18.2.2)	*I am disgusted at sth.*
etwas dauert mich	*I regret sth.*
etwas freut mich	*I am pleased/glad about sth.*
jemanden/etwas fürchten	*to be afraid of sb./sth.*

18.3.5 Fewer verbs can be used both transitively and intransitively in German than in English

German verbs are often less flexible syntactically than their nearest English counterparts and more restricted to use in certain constructions only. A few German verbs can be used both transitively and intransitively, e.g.:

Ich brach den Zweig	*I broke the branch*
Der Zweig brach	*The branch broke*

Far fewer German than English verbs have this facility, and the transitive and intransitive uses of many English verbs have different German equivalents. These can take a number of forms:

(a) The transitive and intransitive uses of some English verbs can correspond to quite different verbs in German

grow	
Er **züchtet** Blumen	*He grows flowers*
Die Blumen **wachsen** im Garten	*The flowers grow in the garden*
leave	
Sie **verließ** das Haus	*She left the house*
Ich **ließ** den Brief im Fach (**liegen**)	*I left the letter in the pigeonhole*
Der Zug **fährt** schon **ab**	*The train is already leaving*
Er **ging** früher als ich (**weg**)	*He left before me*
open (see also (c) below)	
Ich **machte** die Tür **auf**	*I opened the door*
Die Tür **ging auf**	*The door opened*

(b) The transitive and intransitive uses of some English verbs can correspond to related verbs in German

The prefix *be-* (see 22.4.1) often forms transitive verbs from intransitive verbs, but other prefixes (e.g. *er-* and *ver-*) can sometimes have this function, and there are some pairs of verbs with vowel changes:

answer
Sie **beantwortete** die Frage	*She answered the question*
Sie **antwortete**	*She answered*

climb
Ich **bestieg** den Berg	*I climbed the mountain*
Ich **erstieg** den Berg	*I climbed the mountain (to the top)*
Die Maschine **stieg**	*The plane climbed*

drown
Man **ertränkte** die Hexe	*The witch was drowned*
Die Matrosen **ertranken**	*The sailors drowned*

sink
Wir **versenkten** das Schiff	*We sank the ship*
Das Schiff **sank**	*The ship sank*

(c) Some transitive German verbs can be used reflexively as the equivalent of the intransitive use of the corresponding English verb

change
Das hat nichts **geändert**	*That has changed nothing*
Das hat **sich geändert**	*That has changed*

feel
Sie **fühlte** etwas unter ihren Füßen	*She felt something under her feet*
Sie **fühlte sich** unwohl	*She felt unwell*

open (see also (a) above)
Ich **öffnete** die Tür	*I opened the door*
Die Tür **öffnete sich**	*The door opened*

turn
Ich **drehte** das Rad	*I turned the wheel*
Das Rad **drehte sich**	*The wheel turned*

(d) A construction with *lassen* and a German intransitive verb can correspond to the transitive use of the verb in English

For this 'causative' use of *lassen*, see 13.3.1c:

drop
Ich **ließ** den Stein **fallen**	*I dropped the stone*
Der Stein **fiel**	*The stone dropped*

fail
Sie **haben** den Kandidaten **durchfallen lassen**	*They failed the candidate*
Der Kandidat **ist durchgefallen**	*The candidate failed*

run
Ich **habe** das Wasser in die Badewanne **laufen lassen**	*I've run the bathwater*
Der Wasserhahn **läuft**	*The tap's running*

(e) A construction with *sich lassen* and a German transitive verb sometimes corresponds to the intransitive use of the verb in English

For this construction with *sich lassen*, see 15.4.6:

cut

| Sie **hat** das Papier **geschnitten** | *She cut the paper* |
| Das Papier **lässt sich** leicht **schneiden** | *The paper cuts easily* |

18.3.6 Reflexive verbs

Many German verbs are always used with a reflexive pronoun in the accusative case (see 3.2), e.g. *sich beeilen* 'hurry', *sich erkälten* 'catch a cold'. These REFLEXIVE VERBS have no direct equivalent in English – reflexive pronouns like 'myself' in English are used in a quite different way – and they can correspond to a variety of English verb constructions and verb types.

A number have English equivalents quite different from the simple verb (and the English equivalent is often an intransitive verb), e.g. *sich setzen* 'sit down' (cf. *setzen* 'put'), etc. In many instances the nearest English equivalent is a passive (or passive-like) construction (see 15.4.3).

Many verbs used with a reflexive accusative also have other complements, e.g. a dative, genitive or prepositional object. They are treated in the sections dealing with these other complements.

It is helpful to distinguish two types of reflexive verb in German:

(a) 'True' reflexive verbs, which are only used with a reflexive pronoun
With these, the reflexive pronoun is an integral part of the verb:

sich bedanken	*say 'thank you'*	sich erholen	*recover*
sich beeilen	*hurry*	sich erkälten	*catch a cold*
sich befinden	*be (situated)*	sich irren	*be mistaken*
sich benehmen	*behave*	sich verabschieden	*say 'goodbye'*
sich eignen	*be suited*	sich verneigen	*bow*
sich entschließen	*decide*	sich weigern	*refuse*

(b) Other transitive verbs used reflexively, with the accusative object appearing as a reflexive pronoun
(i) Many transitive verbs can be used with a reflexive pronoun. The agent is then performing the action on him-/herself. Compare:

non-reflexive	**reflexive**
Das habe ich **meinen Bruder** gefragt	Das habe ich **mich** gefragt
Ich setzte **den Koffer** auf den Stuhl	Ich setzte **mich** auf den Stuhl
Ich habe **den Hund** gewaschen	Ich habe **mich** gewaschen
Ich habe **ihn** nicht überzeugen können	Ich habe **mich** nicht überzeugen

(ii) Many transitive verbs denoting activities and accomplishments can be used reflexively with a subject which is not the person carrying out the action. These usually correspond to English passive constructions:

| Das **erklärt sich** leicht | *That is easily explained* |
| Mein Verdacht **hat sich bestätigt** | *My suspicions were confirmed* |

Intransitive verbs denoting activities and accomplishments can also be used in a similar way with a reflexive pronoun. These constructions are always impersonal and have a sense similar to a construction with *man* (see also 15.4.3).

Dort **wohnt** es **sich** gut	*One can live well there*
Hier **arbeitet** es **sich** bequem	*One can work comfortably here*

(iii) A few verbs have reflexive and non-reflexive forms where the reflexive variant is a 'true' reflexive, with a rather different meaning, see also 18.3.5c:

Das erinnert mich an etwas	*That reminds me of something*
Ich erinnere mich an etwas	*I remember something*
Das hat mich gefreut	*That pleased me*
Ich habe mich gefreut	*I was pleased*
Das habe ich ihr versprochen	*I promised her that*
Ich habe mich versprochen	*I made a slip of the tongue*

18.4 The dative object

A DATIVE OBJECT occurs in three main sentence patterns (see Table 18.2), and these are explained in the sections indicated:

- C: Subject + verb + dative object (section 18.4.1)
- D: Subject + verb + accusative object + dative object (section 18.4.2)
- I: Subject + verb + dative object + prepositional object (section 18.4.1)

The prepositions used with individual verbs in sentence pattern I are treated in 18.6. Verbs with a dative reflexive are dealt with in 18.4.3. The dative case has a wide range of other uses in German, as detailed in 2.5. As explained in 15.1.3, the dative object can <u>never</u> be converted into the subject of a corresponding passive sentence.

18.4.1 Verbs governing the dative

A fair number of German verbs have a dative object, but no accusative object. These have no direct equivalent in English, and English learners need to learn these verbs with their constructions. No general rules can be given as to which verbs govern a dative object, but it is helpful to be aware that these dative objects often relate to persons who are advantaged or disadvantaged in some way through the action expressed by the verb.

(a) Common verbs which govern a dative object

abraten *advise against*	
Sie hat **ihm** davon abgeraten	*She advised him against it*
ähneln *resemble, look like*	
Er ähnelt **seinem Bruder**	*He looks like his brother*
applaudieren *applaud*	
Sie applaudierten **dem Solisten**	*They applauded the soloist*
ausweichen *get out of the way of, evade, avoid*	
Er ist **der Gefahr** ausgewichen	*He avoided the danger*
begegnen *meet* (by chance)	
Ich bin **ihr** in der Stadt begegnet	*I met her in town*
bekommen *agree with one* (of food)	
Fleisch bekommt **mir** nicht	*Meat doesn't agree with me*

NB: *bekommen* with an accusative object means 'receive', e.g. *Er bekam **einen langen Brief** von seinem Vater.*

danken *thank*

    Ich dankte **ihnen** sehr dafür   *I thanked them very much for it*

dienen *serve*

    Er diente **dem König von Italien**   *He served the king of Italy*

drohen *threaten*

    Sie drohte **ihm** mit einem Stock   *She threatened him with a stick*

einfallen *occur*

    Das ist **mir** nicht eingefallen   *That didn't occur to me*

erliegen *succumb to*

    Er **erlag** seinen Wunden   *He succumbed to his injuries*

folgen *follow*

    Er ist **ihr** ins Exil gefolgt   *He followed her into exile*

        NB: *folgen* is used with *auf* (acc.) in the sense 'succeed, come after': **Auf den Sturm** *folgten drei sonnige Tage*

gehorchen *obey*

    Sie gehorcht **ihrem Vater**   *She obeys her father*

gehören *belong*

    Der Mercedes gehört **mir** nicht   *The Mercedes doesn't belong to me*

        NB: (i) In the sense 'be part of, be one of', *gehören* is used with *zu*: *Das gehört zu meinen Aufgaben*. See
            18.6.13b.
           (ii) In the sense 'be a member of', *angehören* is used. It also takes a dative: *Ich gehöre dem Verein an*.

gelten *be meant for, be aimed at, be for*

    Gilt diese Bemerkung **mir**?   *Is that comment meant for me?*

    der Beifall galt **den Schauspielern**   *The applause was for the actors*

gleichen *be equal to, resemble*

    Jeder Tag glich **dem anderen**   *One day was like the next*

gratulieren *congratulate*

    Sie haben **ihr** zum Geburtstag   *They congratulated her on her birthday*
       gratuliert

helfen *help*

    Er half **seinem Vater** in der Küche   *He helped his father in the kitchen*

imponieren *impress*

    Sie hat **ihm** sehr imponiert   *She impressed him a lot*

kündigen *fire, give notice*

    Der Chef hat **ihm** gestern gekündigt   *The boss gave him notice yesterday*

        NB: In spoken German, *kündigen* is used with an accusative object, e.g. *Sie hat* **ihn** *gekündigt*. In the meaning
           'cancel', it is <u>always</u> used with an accusative, e.g. *Er hat* **den Vertrag** *gekündigt*.

nutzen/nützen *be of use*

    Das nutzt **mir** doch gar nichts   *But that's no use to me*

passen *suit*

    Das neue Kleid passt **dir** gut   *The new dress suits you*

        NB: *zu jdm./etwas passen* 'go with sb./sth.' (see 18.6.13b)

schaden *harm*

    Rauchen schadet **der Gesundheit**   *Smoking is harmful to your health*

schmeicheln *flatter*

    Der Student wollte **dem Professor**   *The student wanted to flatter the professor*
       schmeicheln

trauen *trust*

    Ich traute **meinen Augen** nicht   *I couldn't believe my eyes*

        NB: *misstrauen* 'distrust' also governs a dative object.

trotzen *defy*

    Er trotzte **der Gefahr**   *He defied, braved the danger*

unterliegen *be defeated by, be subject to*

    Er unterlag **seinem Gegner**   *He lost to his opponent*

vertrauen *have trust in*

    jemandem blind vertrauen   *have a blind trust in somebody*

wehtun *hurt*

    Der Wespenstich hat **ihm** wehgetan   *The wasp sting hurt him*

(b) Most verbs with the meaning 'happen', 'occur' govern a dative

Es wird **dir** doch nichts geschehen	*But nothing will happen to you*
Was ist **ihm** gestern passiert?	*What happened to him yesterday?*
So etwas ist **mir** noch nie vorgekommen	*Nothing like that has ever happened to me*

Similarly: *bevorstehen, widerfahren, zustoßen,* etc.

(c) Verbs with certain prefixes usually take a dative

i.e. those with *bei-, ent-, entgegen-, nach-, wider-, zu-*:

Er ist **der SPD** beigetreten	*He joined the SPD*
Das entsprach **meinen Erwartungen**	*That came up to my expectations*
Sie kam **mir** entgegen	*She approached me*
Er eilte **ihr** nach	*He hurried after her*
Das Kind widersprach **seiner Mutter**	*The child contradicted its mother*
Er hat **dem Gespräch** zugehört	*He listened to the conversation*

Similarly (among many others):

beistehen	*give support to*	nachlaufen	*run after*
beiwohnen	*be present at*	nachstellen	*follow, pester*
entsagen	*renounce*	nachstreben	*emulate*
entstammen	*originate from*	sich widersetzen	*oppose*
entgegengehen	*go to meet*	widerstehen	*resist*
entgegenwirken	*counteract*	zulaufen	*run up to*
nachgeben	*give way to*	zustimmen	*agree with*
nachkommen	*follow*	zuvorkommen	*anticipate*

The verbs prefixed with *ent-* meaning 'escape' (*entgehen, entfliehen, entkommen, entrinnen, entwischen,* etc.) also all govern a dative.

NB: A few verbs with these prefixes have a dative and an accusative object (see 18.4.2), e.g. *jemandem etwas beibringen* 'teach somebody something', *jemandem etwas zutrauen* 'credit somebody with something'.

(d) The dative object of some verbs corresponds to the subject of the usual English equivalent

Etwas fällt mir auf	*I notice something*
Etwas entfällt mir	*I forget something*
Es fällt mir leicht, schwer	*I find something easy, difficult*
Etwas fehlt, mangelt mir/Es fehlt, mangelt mir an etwas	*I lack something*
Etwas gefällt mir	*I like something*
Etwas geht mir auf	*I realise something*
Etwas gelingt mir	*I succeed in something*
Etwas tut mir Leid	*I am sorry about something*
Das leuchtet mir nicht ein	*I don't understand that*
Es liegt mir viel an etwas (dat)	*I am keen on something*
Etwas liegt mir	*I fancy something*
Das genügt, reicht mir	*I have had enough of that*
Etwas schmeckt mir	*I like something* (i.e. food)

NB: With these verbs, there is a marked tendency for the dative object to precede the verb in main clauses, e.g. *Mir hat das nicht gefallen.*

18.4.2 Verbs governing a dative and an accusative object

These are transitive verbs with two complements aside from the subject, i.e. an accusative (direct) object, which is usually is a thing, and a dative object, called the indirect object, which is usually a person. It is helpful to remember them as *einem etwas* **verbs**.

The German dative commonly corresponds to an English prepositional phrase with 'to' or 'from', or to an English indirect object (e.g. *He gave me the book*). In German, though, the indirect object is indicated solely by the dative case. Unlike English, no preposition is used with these verbs, so that 'He gave the money to his uncle' is *Er gab **seinem Onkel** das Geld*, NOT **Er gab das Geld zu seinem Onkel*.

With many verbs (e.g. *geben*) the dative object is essential to construct a grammatical sentence, with others (e.g. *beweisen*) it can be dropped in some contexts.

(a) Verbs of giving and taking (in the widest sense) govern a dative and an accusative object

There are a large number of such verbs:

Sie haben **mir eine Stelle** angeboten	*They offered me a job*
Das wollte er (**mir**) beweisen	*He wanted to prove that (to me)*
Er brachte (**ihr**) **einen Blumenstrauß**	*He brought (her) a bunch of flowers*
Ich kann (**dir**) **diesen Roman** empfehlen	*I can recommend this novel (to you)*
Er hat **dem Lehrer einen Bleistift** gegeben	*He gave the teacher a pencil*
Sie will **mir** jetzt **etwas Ruhe** gönnen	*She is now willing to let me have some peace and quiet*
Kannst du **mir zehn Franken** leihen?	*Can you lend me ten francs?*
Wir haben (**ihr**) **die Tasche** genommen	*We took the bag (from her)*
Ich habe (**ihr**) **das Paket** geschickt	*I've sent (her) the parcel*
Du schuldest **mir** noch **hundert Euro**	*You still owe me a hundred euros*
Er verkaufte (**mir**) **seinen alten Opel**	*He sold (me) his old Opel*
Er zeigte **ihr seine Kupferstiche**	*He showed her his etchings*

(b) Most verbs involving an act of speaking are used with a dative and an accusative object

(i) With most of these verbs the accusative object can only be either a neuter or indefinite pronoun (e.g. *es, das, etwas, nichts*) or a clause (a subordinate clause introduced by *dass, ob* etc., or an infinitive clause). The equivalent English verbs often have quite different constructions:

Sie hat (mir) geantwortet, dass sie morgen kommen wollte	*She answered me, and said she was going to come tomorrow*
Wer hat (dir) befohlen, die Geiseln zu erschießen?	*Who gave (you) the order to shoot the hostages?*
Das habe ich ihm schon gestern erzählt	*I already told him that yesterday*
Er hat mir geraten, mein Haus zu verkaufen	*He advised me to sell my house*
Er versicherte mir, dass er alles erledigt hätte	*He assured me he had taken care of everything*
Das wird er (dir) nie verzeihen können	*He'll never be able to forgive you that*

NB: With *antworten*, the dative is only used for persons. Cf.: *Er hat **auf** meinen Brief, **auf** meine Frage geantwortet.*

sagen is normally used in this way, with an optional dative of the person:

Was wollen Sie (ihm) sagen?	*What do you want to say (to him)?*
Sie sagte mir, dass sie es auf keinen Fall machen würde	*She told me that on no account would she do that*

However, it is used with *zu* when introducing direct speech or for a person addressing himself:

„Nun komm doch!" sagte sie zu Christian	*'Come along now', she said to Christian*
„Wie kannst du das nur machen" sagte er zu sich selbst	*'How on earth can you do that?', he said to himself*

(ii) With a few verbs the accusative object **or** the dative object can be omitted, as the context requires. This is not possible with all the nearest equivalent verbs in English:

Die irakische Regierung erlaubte (der Delegation) die Einreise	*The Iraqi government allowed the delegation into the country*
Sie hat mir (einen langen Brief) geschrieben	*She wrote me (a long letter)*

(iii) *glauben* has a dative of the person and/or an accusative of the thing:

Er glaubt **dem Lehrer**
Er glaubt **jedes Wort**
Er glaubt **dem Lehrer jedes Wort**

NB: *glauben an* (acc.) (see 18.6.2b), is used for 'believe in', e.g. *Ich glaube an seinen Erfolg.*

(c) With some verbs the German dative and accusative construction differs from the construction used with the nearest equivalent English verb
The following are common:

Man merkt ihm die Anstrengung an	*One notices the effort he's making*
Sie fügte es dem Brief bei	*She enclosed it with the letter*
Das hat ihm das Studium ermöglicht, erschwert	*That made it possible, difficult for him to study*
Das hat sie mir gestern mitgeteilt	*She informed me of that yesterday*
Die Polizei konnte ihm nichts nachweisen	*The police couldn't prove anything against him*
Das hat sie mir aber verschwiegen	*She didn't tell me about that, though*
Das hätte ich ihr nicht zugetraut	*I wouldn't have believed her capable of that*

(d) With verbs of sending or transferring, a phrase with *an* can be a common alternative to a noun phrase in the dative
The effect is to emphasise the recipient more strongly:

Ich habe ein Paket **an meinen Vater** geschickt
Ich habe einen Brief **an deinen Vater** geschrieben
Er hat seinen alten Opel **an seinen Vater** verkauft

(e) A few reflexive verbs have a dative object
With these the reflexive pronoun is the accusative object:

Sie mussten sich **dem Feind** ergeben	*They had to surrender to the enemy*
Sie näherten sich **der Stadt**	*They approached the city*

18.4.3 Some verbs are used with a dative reflexive pronoun

(a) Many verbs governing a dative may be used with a dative reflexive pronoun if the action refers back to the subject
Both types of verbs governing the dative can be used in this way, i.e.:

(i) Verbs where the dative is the sole object (see 18.4.1):

Ich habe **mir** mehrmals widersprochen	*I contradicted myself several times*
Du schadest **dir** mit dem Rauchen	*You're harming yourself by smoking*

(ii) *einem etwas* verbs (see 18.4.2):

Ich erlaubte **mir**, ihm zu widersprechen	*I allowed myself to contradict him*
Ich muss **mir** Arbeit verschaffen	*I must find work*
Ich habe **mir** zu viel zugemutet	*I've taken on too much*

(b) A few other verbs occur with a dative reflexive pronoun
These are 'true' reflexive verbs (see 18.3.6), where the reflexive pronoun is an integral part of the verb. All also have an accusative object:

Das habe ich **mir** angeeignet	*I acquired that*
Das habe ich **mir** eingebildet	*I imagined that*
Das verbitte ich **mir**	*I refuse to tolerate that*
Ich habe **mir** vorgenommen, das zu tun	*I have resolved to do that*
Das kann ich **mir** gut vorstellen	*I can imagine that well*
Ich habe **mir** eine Grippe zugezogen	*I contracted flu*

Similarly: *sich etwas anmaßen* 'claim sth. for oneself', *sich etwas ausbedingen* 'make sth. a condition'.

18.5 Genitive objects

A small number of verbs have an object in the genitive case. With a very few this is the only object, i.e. they are intransitive verbs with no accusative object (sentence pattern E in Table 18.2). Others are transitive verbs with an accusative object and a genitive object (sentence pattern F in Table 18.2). Many of the latter are reflexive verbs.

All these verbs are uncommon in modern German and restricted to formal writing. A few more are used only in set phrases. In listing those verbs which are still used with a genitive more widely used alternatives are given wherever possible.

18.5.1 Non-reflexive verbs with a noun phrase in the genitive case as the only object

bedürfen *need* (more common: *brauchen, benötigen*)
Er bedurfte **meiner Hilfe** nicht	*He didn't need my help*

entbehren *lack* (more commonly used with an accusative object)

Der Staat konnte **eines kraftvollen Monarchen** nicht entbehren (*v. Rimscha*)	*The state could not do without a powerful monarch*

ermangeln *lack* (more usual *fehlen*, see 18.4.1d)

Sein Vortrag ermangelte **jeglicher Sachkenntnis**	*His lecture was lacking in any kind of knowledge of the subject*

gedenken *remember* (elev. for *denken an* (acc.), with reference to the dead)

Lech Walensa hat **der Opfer** des Nationalsozialismus gedacht (*FR*)	*Lech Walensa remembered the victims of National Socialism*

harren *await* (elev. for *warten auf* (acc.). It has a biblical ring)

Wir harren **einer Antwort** (*Zeit*)	*We are awaiting an answer*

18.5.2 Reflexive verbs with a genitive object

Most of these are 'truc' reflexive verbs, with an accusative reflexive pronoun (see 18.3.6)·

sich annehmen *look after, take care of* (more usual: *sich kümmern um*)

Er hätte sich **dieses Kindes** angenommen (*Walser*)	*He would have looked after that child*

sich bedienen *use* (more usual: *benutzen, gebrauchen, verwenden*)

Die Firma bediente sich nur **schmutziger Schiffe** (*Böll*)	*The firm only used dirty ships*

sich bemächtigen *seize* (various alternatives, e.g. *ergreifen, nehmen*)

Sie bemächtigten sich **des Bürgermeisters** von Le Mans (*Zeit*)	*They seized the mayor of Le Mans*

sich entsinnen *remember* (more usual: *sich erinnern an* (acc.), see 18.6.2b)

Ich entsann mich **des Anblicks** der langgestreckten Baracken (*Andersch*)	*I remembered the sight of the long huts*

sich erfreuen *enjoy* (more usual: *genießen, sich freuen über* (acc.))

Sie erfreuten sich **des schönen Sommerwetters** (*OH*)	*They were enjoying the fine summer weather*

sich erinnern *remember* (more usual: *sich erinnern an* (acc.), see 18.6.2b)

Ich erinnere mich **bestimmter Details** noch (*Böll*)	*I still remember certain details*

sich erwehren *refrain from* (more usual: *abwehren*)

Ich konnte mich **eines Lächelns** kaum erwehren	*I could scarcely refrain from a smile*

sich rühmen *boast about/of* (more usual: *stolz sein über*)

Die meisten Länder Europas rühmen sich **einer tausendjährigen Geschichte** (*Haffner*)	*Most European countries can boast of a thousand years of history*

sich schämen *be ashamed of* (more usual: *sich schämen für/wegen*, see 18.6.5)

Er schämte sich seines Betragens   *He was ashamed of his behaviour*

sich vergewissern *make sure* (more usual: *nachprüfen, überprüfen*)

Sie vergewisserte sich **der**   *She made sure about this man's reliability*
Zuverlässigkeit dieses Mannes

18.5.3 Verbs used with a genitive and an accusative object

anklagen *accuse* (outside formal legal parlance: *anklagen wegen*)

Man klagte ihn der fahrlässigen   *He was accused of manslaughter through*
Tötung an   *culpable negligence*

berauben *rob* (more commonly: *einem etwas rauben*)

Er beraubte ihn der Freiheit   *He robbed him of his freedom*

versichern *assure* (more commonly: *einem etwas zusichern*)

Ich versichere Sie meines   *I assure you of my absolute trust*
uneingeschränkten Vertrauens

The following verbs are used with a genitive in legal language, but with a following clause in everyday speech:

jdn. einer Sache beschuldigen/bezichtigen   *accuse sb. of sth.*
jdn. einer Sache überführen   *convict sb. of sth.*
jdn. einer Sache verdächtigen   *suspect sb. of sth.*

18.5.4 Set phrases with a genitive object

Many more verbs were used with a genitive object in older German, and some of these still occur in idiomatic phrases, although they, too, are mainly used in formal writing:

der Gefahr nicht **achten**   *pay no heed to danger*
jemanden eines Besseren **belehren**   *teach someone better*
sich eines Besseren **besinnen**   *think better of something*
jeder Beschreibung **spotten**   *beggar description*
jemanden des Landes **verweisen**   *expel someone from a country*
seines Amtes **walten**   *discharge one's duties*
jemanden keines Blickes **würdigen**   *not to deign to look at someone*

18.6 Prepositional objects

18.6.1 Many verbs are followed by an object introduced by a preposition

The PREPOSITION used in prepositional objects is wholly idiomatic and determined by the individual verb. The fact that German has *Ich warte **auf** Sie* for English 'I am waiting **for** you', for example is not related in any way to the usual meaning of the preposition 'auf'. For this reason, the foreign learner has to treat each combination of verb and preposition separately and remember them as a whole.

There are three main sentence patterns with prepositional objects, see Table 18.2, i.e.:

- Verbs with a prepositional object as their only object (sentence pattern G)

- Transitive verbs with an accusative object and a prepositional object (sentence pattern H)
- Verbs with a dative object and a prepositional object (sentence pattern I).

A few verbs even have two prepositional objects. All prepositional objects are treated in this section under the individual prepositions, with other complements governed by the verb indicated in appropriate cases.

18.6.2 *an*

an most often occurs with a following dative case in prepositional objects, but a few verbs govern *an* with the accusative case.

(a) Used in prepositional objects with the DATIVE case, *an* often conveys the idea of 'in respect of, in connection with'

Ich erkannte sie **an ihrem knallroten Haar**	*I recognised her by her bright red hair*
Er ist **an einer Lungenentzündung** gestorben	*He died of pneumonia*
Ich zweifle **an seiner Ehrlichkeit**	*I doubt his honesty*

A selection of other verbs:

arbeiten an	*work at*	mitwirken an	*play a part in*
erkranken an	*fall ill with*	teilnehmen an	*take part in*
gewinnen an	*gain (in)*	verlieren an	*lose (some)*
(e.g.: *an Bedeutung gewinnen*)		(e.g.: *an Boden verlieren*)	
leiden an	*suffer from*		
sich an jdm./etwas freuen	*take pleasure in sb./sth.*		

> NB: *sich freuen auf* (acc.) 'look forward to' (18.6.3a), *sich freuen über* 'be glad/pleased about' (18.6.9).

jdn. an etwas hindern	*prevent sb. from (doing) sth.*
Es fehlt mir an etwas	*I lack sth.* (see 18.4.1d)
Es liegt mir viel an etwas	*I am very keen on sth.* (see 18.4.1d)
sich an etwas orientieren	*orientate oneself by sth.*
etwas an jemandem rächen	*avenge sth. on sb.*
sich an jemandem für etwas rächen	*take revenge on sb. for sth.*

(b) Most of the few verbs which govern a prepositional object with *an* and a following ACCUSATIVE case denote mental processes

Du erinnerst mich **an ihn**	*You remind me of him*
Ich erinnere mich **an ihn**	*I remember him* (see 18.5.2)
Ich glaube **an den Fortschritt**	*I believe in progress* (see 18.4.2b)

Also:

denken an	*think of*
sich an etwas halten	*stick to sth.*
sich an etwas gewöhnen	*get used to sth.*

18.6.3 *auf*

auf most often occurs with the accusative case in prepositional objects. Very few verbs govern *auf* with the dative.

(a) *auf* with the ACCUSATIVE case is the commonest preposition in prepositional objects

Ich werde **auf deine Kinder** aufpassen	*I'll mind your children*
Seine Bemerkung bezog sich **auf dich**	*His comment related to you*
Das läuft **auf das Gleiche** hinaus	*It amounts to the same thing*
Er wies (mich) **auf die Schwierigkeiten** hin	*He pointed the difficulties out (to me)*

Other verbs:

achten, Acht geben auf	*pay attention to*
sich berufen auf	*refer to*
drängen auf	*press for*
sich erstrecken auf	*extend to*
folgen auf	*follow (see 18.4.1a)*
sich freuen auf	*look forward to (see 18.6.2a, 18.6.9a)*
hoffen auf	*hope for*
sich konzentrieren auf	*concentrate on*
pfeifen auf (coll.)	*not care less about*
pochen auf	*insist on*
reagieren auf	*react to*
rechnen auf	*count on*
schimpfen auf/über	*curse about*
schwören auf	*swear on/by*
sich spezialisieren auf	*specialise in*
sich stützen auf	*lean, count on*
sich verlassen auf	*rely on*
sich verstehen auf	*be expert in*
(jdn.) verweisen auf	*refer (sb.) to*
verzichten auf	*do without*
warten auf	*wait for*
zählen auf	*count on*
zurückkommen auf	*come back to, refer to*

Es kommt (mir) auf etwas an	*sth. matters (to me)*
etwas auf etwas beschränken	*limit/restrict/confine sth. to sth.*
sich auf etwas beschränken	*limit oneself/be limited to sth.*
etwas auf etwas zurückführen	*put sth. down to sth.*

(b) A few verbs which convey the idea of not moving govern *auf* with the DATIVE case

Er beharrte **auf seiner Meinung**	*He didn't shift from his opinion*
Ich bestehe **auf meinem Recht**	*I insist on my right*

NB: *bestehen aus* 'consist of' (18.6.4), *bestehen in* 'consist in' (18.6.6b).

Similarly *basieren auf, beruhen auf, fußen auf*, which all mean 'be based on', 'rest on'. Note, however, *sich gründen auf* (**acc.**) 'be based on', e.g. *Der Vorschlag gründet sich auf diese Annahme*.

18.6.4 *aus*

aus usually has the meaning 'of', 'from' in prepositional objects.

Ihr Essen bestand **aus trockenem Brot**	*Their food consisted of dry bread*

Other verbs:

etwas aus etwas entnehmen, ersehen	*infer, gather sth. from sth.*
sich aus etwas ergeben	*result from sth.*
etwas aus etwas folgern, schließen	*conclude sth. from sth.*

NB: (i) *bestehen auf* 'insist on' (see 18.6.3), *bestehen in* 'consist in' (18.6.6b).
    (ii) *entnehmen* can alternatively be constructed with a dative, e.g. *Ich entnehme (aus) Ihrem Brief, dass Sie das Geschäft aufgeben wollen.*
    (iii) *sich in etwas ergeben* 'submit to sth.' (see 18.6.6a), *sich jemandem/etwas ergeben* 'surrender to sb./sth.' (see 18.4.2e).

18.6.5 *für*

für usually has the meaning 'for' in prepositional objects.

Ich habe ihm **für seine Mühe** gedankt	*I thanked him for his trouble*
Ich habe mich **für den Audi** entschieden	*I decided on the Audi*
Ich halte deine Freundin **für hochbegabt**	*I consider your friend to be very gifted*

Other verbs:

sich (bei jdm.) für etwas bedanken	*give thanks for sth. (to sb.)*
sich für etwas begeistern	*be enthusiastic about sth.*
sich für jdn./etwas eignen	*be suitable for sb./sth.*
sich für jdn./etwas interessieren	*be interested in sb./sth.*
sich für jdn./etwas schämen	*be ashamed of sth./for sb.*
für jdn./etwas sorgen	*take care of/look after sb./sth.*

NB: (i) Non-reflexive *interessieren* is used with *für* or *an* (dat.), e.g. *Er interessierte sie für das/an dem Unternehmen.*
    (ii) *sich eignen zu/als* means 'be suitable as' (see 18.6.13).
    (iii) *sich (wegen) jemandes/etwas schämen* (see 18.5.2) 'be ashamed of sb./sth.', *sich vor jemandem schämen* 'feel ashamed in front of sb.' (see 18.6.12a).
    (iv) *sich um jdn./etwas sorgen* 'be worried about sb./sth.'.

18.6.6 *in*

(a) *in* is most often used with the ACCUSATIVE case in prepositional objects

Sie willigte **in die Scheidung** ein	*She agreed to the divorce*
Er verliebte sich **in sie**	*He fell in love with her*

Other verbs:

jdn. in etwas einführen	*introduce sb. to sth.*
sich ergeben in	*submit to (see 18.6.4)*
sich mischen in	*meddle in*
sich vertiefen in	*become engrossed in*

(b) A very few verbs govern *in* with the DATIVE case

Meine Aufgabe besteht **in der Erledigung** der Korrespondenz (see also 18.6.3b)	*My duties consist in dealing with the correspondence*
Ich habe mich nicht **in ihr** getäuscht	*I was not mistaken in (my judgement of) her*

NB: (i) *bestehen auf* 'insist on' (18.6.4), *bestehen aus* 'consist of' (18.6.5).
    (ii) *sich täuschen über* 'to be mistaken about' (18.6.9a).

18.6.7 *mit*

mit usually has the sense of 'with' in prepositional objects.

Sie hat **mit ihrer Arbeit** angefangen	*She made a start on her work*
Willst du bitte **damit** aufhören?	*Please stop doing that*
Sie hat ihm **mit der Faust** gedroht	*She threatened him with her fist*
Ich habe gestern **mit ihm** telefoniert	*I spoke to him on the telephone yesterday*

sich abfinden mit	*be satisfied with*
sich befassen mit	*deal with*
sich begnügen mit	*be satisfied with*
sich beschäftigen mit	*occupy o.s. with*
rechnen mit	*count on*
sprechen mit (*or:* jdn. sprechen)	*speak to/with*
übereinstimmen mit	*agree with*
sich unterhalten mit	*converse with*
vergleichen mit	*compare with*
sich verheiraten mit	*marry*
versehen mit	*provide with*
zusammenstoßen mit	*collide with*

18.6.8 *nach*

(a) *nach* **often has the sense of English 'after', 'for' with verbs of calling, enquiring, longing, reaching, etc.**

Haben Sie sich nach seinem Befinden erkundigt?	*Have you enquired how he is?*
Plötzlich griff das Kind nach der Katze	*Suddenly the child made a grab for the cat*
Sie schrie nach ihrem Cousin	*She yelled for her cousin*
Ich telefonierte nach einem Arzt	*I rang for a doctor*

Other verbs:

fragen nach	*ask after, for*
hungern nach	*hunger after, for*
rufen nach	*call after, for*
sich sehnen nach	*long for*
streben nach	*strive for*
suchen nach	*search for*
verlangen nach	*ask, long for; crave*

NB: *sich erkundigen über* 'enquire about'; *fragen über* 'ask about'.

(b) *nach* **often has the sense of English 'of' with verbs of smelling, etc.**

Es riecht **nach Teer**	*It smells of tar*
Es schmeckte **nach Fisch**	*It tasted of fish*

Similarly: *duften nach, stinken nach*, etc. Cf. also: *Es sieht nach Regen aus* 'It looks like rain'.

18.6.9 *über*

über always governs the **accusative** case in prepositional objects.

(a) *über* corresponds to English 'about' with verbs of saying, etc.

Ich habe mich sehr **über sein Benehmen** geärgert	I was very annoyed at his behaviour
Sie musste lange **darüber** nachdenken	She had to think it over for a long time
Ich sprach gestern mit dem Chef **über diese Bewerbung**	I talked to the boss about this application yesterday

Many verbs can be used with *über* in this sense, e.g.:

sich bei jdm. über etwas beklagen/ beschweren	complain to sb. about sth.
sich über jdn./etwas freuen	be pleased about sth. (see 18.6.2a, 18.6.3a)
jdn. über etwas informieren	inform sb. about sth.
über jdn./etwas spotten	mock sb./sth.
sich täuschen über etwas	be mistaken about sth. (see 18.6.6b)
über etwas urteilen	judge sth.
sich über jdn./etwas wundern	be surprised at sb./sth.

Some verbs, i.e. *denken, erzählen, hören, lesen, sagen, schreiben, sprechen* and *wissen* can be used with *über* or *von* in the sense of 'about'. *über* tends to refer to something more extensive than *von*. Compare:

Was denken Sie **darüber**?	What is your view of that?
Was denken Sie **von ihm**?	What do you think of him?
Er wusste viel **über Flugzeuge**	He knew a lot about aeroplanes
Er wusste nichts **von ihrem Tod**	He knew nothing of her death

(b) Other verbs governing a prepositional object with *über*

es über sich bringen, etwas zu tun	bring o.s. to do sth.
sich über etwas hinwegsetzen	disregard sth.
über etwas verfügen	have sth. at one's disposal

18.6.10 *um*

um usually has the meaning 'concerning', 'in respect of' in prepositional objects.

Sie hat sich **um ihre Schwester** in Dresden geängstigt	She was worried about her sister in Dresden
Es handelte sich **um eine Wette**	It was a question of a bet
Ich kümmerte mich **um meine Enkelkinder**	I took care of my grandchildren

Other verbs:

sich um etwas bemühen	take trouble over sth.
jdn. um etwas beneiden	envy sb. sth.
jdn. um etwas betrügen	cheat sb. out of sth.
jdn. um etwas bitten, ersuchen (elev.)	ask sb. for sth., request sth. from sb.
jdn. um etwas bringen	make sb. lose sth.
Es geht um etwas (see 18.2.4g)	Something is at stake
um etwas kommen	lose sth., be deprived of sth.
sich um jdn./etwas sorgen	be worried about sth.
sich um/über etwas streiten	argue about/over sth.

NB: *sich ängstigen vor* 'be afraid of' (18.6.12).

18.6.11 *von*

von usually has the sense of English 'of' or 'from' in prepositional objects.

Ich will dich nicht **von der Arbeit** abhalten	*I don't want to keep you from your work*
Wir müssen **davon** ausgehen, dass ...	*We must start by assuming that ...*
Ich muss mich **von meinem Kollegen** distanzieren	*I have to dissociate myself from my colleague*
Das Kind träumte **von einer schönen Prinzessin**	*The child was dreaming of a beautiful princess*

Other verbs:

etwas hängt von jdm./etwas ab	*sth. depends on sb./sth.*
jdm. von etwas abraten	*advise sb. against sth.*
von etwas absehen	*refrain from sth., disregard sth.*
jdn. von etwas befreien	*liberate sb. from sth.*
sich von etwas erholen	*recover from sth.*
von etwas herrühren	*stem from sth.*
jdn. von etwas überzeugen	*convince sb. of sth.*
jdn. von etwas verständigen	*inform sb. of sth.*
von etwas zeugen	*show, demonstrate sth*

18.6.12 *vor*

vor is always used with the **dative** case in prepositional objects.

(a) *vor* **often corresponds to English 'of' with verbs of fearing, etc.**

Ich ekele mich **vor diesen großen Spinnen**	*I have a horror of these big spiders* (see 18.2.2)
Er fürchtete sich **vor dem Rottweiler**	*He was afraid of the Rottweiler*
Er warnte mich **vor dem Treibsand**	*He warned me about the quicksand*

Other verbs:

sich vor jdm./etwas ängstigen	*be afraid of sb./sth.* (see 18.6.10)
Angst vor jdm./etwas haben	*be afraid, scared of sb./sth.*
sich vor etwas drücken (coll.)	*dodge sth.*
vor jdm./etwas erschrecken	*be scared by sb./sth.*
sich vor jdm./etwas hüten	*beware of sb./sth., be on one's guard against sb./sth.*
sich vor jdm. schämen	*feel ashamed in front of sb.* (see 18.6.5)
sich vor etwas scheuen	*be afraid of, shrink from sth.*

(b) *vor* **often corresponds to English 'from' with verbs of protecting, etc.**

Sie bewahrte ihn **vor der Gefahr**	*She protected him from danger*
Sie flohen **vor der Polizei**	*They fled from the police*

Other verbs:

jdn. vor jdm./etwas beschützen, beschirmen (elev.)	*protect sb. from sb./sth.*
jdn. vor etwas retten	*save sb. from sth.*
sich vor jdm./etwas verbergen	*hide from sb./sth.*

18.6.13 zu

(a) zu often corresponds to English '(in)to' with verbs of empowering, leading, persuading, etc.

All these verbs are transitive, i.e. they have an accusative object besides the prepositional object with zu:

Er ermutigte sie **zum Widerstand**	*He encouraged them to resist*
Er trieb sie **zur Verzweiflung**	*He drove her to despair*
Er überredete mich **zu einem Glas Wein**	*He talked me into having a glass of wine*
Er zwang mich **zu einer Entscheidung**	*He forced me into a decision*

Other verbs used similarly:

autorisieren	*authorise*	herausfordern	*challenge*
berechtigen	*entitle*	nötigen	*invite*
bewegen	*induce*	provozieren	*provoke*
einladen	*invite*	veranlassen	*cause*
ermächtigen	*empower*	verführen	*seduce*

(b) Some other verbs have a prepositional object with zu

Das hat **zu seinem Erfolg** sehr beigetragen	*That contributed a lot to his success*
Sie entschloss sich **zur Teilnahme**	*She decided to take part*
Ich rechne, zähle ihn **zu meinen Freunden**	*I count him among my friends*

Other verbs:

es zu etwas bringen	*attain sth.* (see 3.6.3c)
zu etwas dienen	*serve as sth.*
sich zu etwas eignen	*be suitable as sth.* (see 18.6.5)
zu etwas führen	*lead to sth.*
zu etwas gehören	*be part of sth., be one of sth.* (see 18.4.1a)
jdm. zu etwas gratulieren	*congratulate sb. on sth.*
zu etwas neigen	*tend to sth.*
zu jdm./etwas passen	*go with sb./sth.* (see 18.4.1a)
jdm. zu etwas raten	*advise sb. to (do) sth.*
sich zu etwas verhalten	*stand in a relationship to sth.*
jdm. zu etwas verhelfen	*help sb. to (do) sth.*

18.6.14 If a prepositional object is in the form of a CLAUSE it is usually anticipated by a prepositional adverb

i.e. the form *da(r)*+**preposition**, see 3.5. The prepositional object can be a subordinate clause (usually introduced by *dass*), or an infinitive clause with *zu*, for example:

Sie hat ihm **dafür** gedankt, **dass er ihr geholfen hatte**
Ich verlasse mich **darauf, dass er alles arrangiert**
Er hinderte mich **daran, den Brief zu schreiben**
Ich verlasse mich **darauf, ihn zu Hause zu finden**

The prepositional adverb is optional with some verbs, e.g.:

> Ich ärgerte mich (**darüber**), dass er so wenig getan hatte
> Sie haben (**damit**) angefangen, die Ernte hereinzubringen

There are no precise rules for contexts when the prepositional adverb is used or not, and it is often left out with some common verbs. If it is used, it tends to emphasise the following clause more strongly. In general, it is more commonly included than omitted in written German, whilst omission is more typical of everyday speech.

The following list gives the common verbs with which the prepositional adverb is often left out:

abhalten von	sich ekeln vor	raten zu
abraten von	sich entscheiden für	sich scheuen vor
Acht geben auf	sich entschließen zu	sich schämen über
anfangen mit	sich erinnern an	sich sehnen nach
(sich) ärgern über	fragen nach	sorgen für
aufhören mit	sich freuen auf/über	sich sorgen um
aufpassen auf	sich fürchten vor	sich streiten über
beginnen mit	glauben an	träumen von
sich beklagen über	hindern an	überzeugen von
sich bemühen um	hoffen auf	urteilen über
sich beschweren über	sich hüten vor	sich wundern über
bitten um	klagen über	zweifeln an

In addition, the prepositional adverb can be omitted with all the transitive verbs used with *zu* (see 18.6.13a).

18.7 Place and direction complements

Place and direction complements differ from adverbials, even if they can be left out, because they are closely linked with the meaning of the verb, as explained in 18.1.4. The difference between them and adverbials is particularly important in respect of word order, see 21.8.1.

18.7.1 A few verbs denoting position have a place complement

PLACE COMPLEMENTS are words or phrases denoting place or position which are used with verbs of position (sentence pattern J in Table 18.2). These complements indicate where someone or something is located, and they typically have the form of a prepositional phrase or an equivalent word:

Sie wohnte lange **in der Pfeilgasse**	*She lived a long time in the Pfeilgasse*
Der Brief befand sich **dort**	*The letter was there*
Nach der Party übernachtete er **bei ihr**	*He spent the night with her after the party*
Sie hielt sich **in Hamm** auf	*She stayed in Hamm*

The place phrases in bold in these examples are clearly complements, since the sentences would be ungrammatical if they were omitted. Common verbs which require place complements are:

sich aufhalten	*stay*	stattfinden	*take place*
bleiben	*stay, remain*	stehen	*stand*
hängen	*hang*	übernachten	*spend the night*
leben	*live*	sich verlieren	*get lost*
liegen	*lie, be lying*	wohnen	*live, dwell*
parken	*park*	zelten	*camp*
sitzen	*sit*		

18.7.2 Verbs which express motion can occur with a direction complement

DIRECTION COMPLEMENTS are words or phrases used with verbs of motion which indicate where someone or something is moving. A direction complement usually takes the form of a prepositional phrase or an equivalent word. It can be omitted with many verbs.

Some verbs of motion – typically verbs of coming and going – are INTRANSITIVE and only have a direction complement with them (sentence pattern K in Table 18.2).

> Gestern fuhr sie **nach Italien**
> Der Junge fiel **hinein**

Other verbs of motion – typically verbs of putting – are TRANSITIVE and have an accusative object as well as the direction complement (sentence pattern L in Table 18.2):

> Ich warf den Ball **dorthin**
> Sie legte das Buch **auf den Tisch**

18.8 Predicate complements

PREDICATE COMPLEMENTS are used with very few verbs, but these are common and important, like *sein* and *werden*. These verbs typically have a noun phrase or an adjective with them which describes the subject in some way (sentence pattern M in Table 18.2):

> Er ist **mein Freund**
> Das Buch ist **langweilig**
> Sie ist **blass** geworden

> Das scheint mir **ratsam**
> Er wurde **Katholik**
> Du bist ganz **der Alte** geblieben

These verbs are known as COPULAR (i.e. 'linking') VERBS, because the verb simply links the subject with the noun phrase or adjective which is the predicate complement. Because the complement simply describes the subject, it is in the **nominative** case if it is a noun. The following verbs are used with a predicate complement:

bleiben	*remain*	sein	*be*
heißen	*be called*	werden	*become*
scheinen	*seem*		

werden is used in two sentence patterns. When used with the predicate complement it has the meaning 'become' and is typically used with nouns denoting professions and beliefs, etc. (e.g. *Er wurde Katholik, Kommunist; Sie werden Soldaten*). When used with a prepositional object introduced by *zu*, it means 'change, develop, turn into', e.g.:

Die Felder waren **zu Seen** geworden	*The fields had turned into lakes*
Das ist mir **zur Gewohnheit** geworden	*That has become a habit of mine*
Es wurde **zur Mode**	*It became a fashion*
Er wurde **zum Verbrecher**	*He became a criminal*

19

Conjunctions and subordination

If sentences contain more than one clause, the clauses can be related to one another in two ways.

- There may be two (or more) parallel clauses of equal status. Typically, MAIN CLAUSES (German *Hauptsätze*) with, in German, the finite verb in second position, are linked by a **coordinating conjunction** like *und* or *aber*.
- Alternatively, one or more clauses can be embedded inside another. These are SUBORDINATE CLAUSES (sometimes also called 'embedded clauses' or 'dependent clauses': German *Nebensätze*). In German they have the finite verb in final position and they are introduced by a **subordinating conjunction**.

SUBORDINATE CLAUSES form part of another clause, and we can distinguish three main types of subordinate clause according to their function in the clause which they are part of:

(i) **Noun clauses** play the same part as a noun phrase, for example as the subject or object of a verb, e.g. *Ich weiß, **dass sie morgen kommt**.* As they are typically used as complements to the verb they are sometimes termed COMPLEMENT CLAUSES.

(ii) **Adjective clauses** have the function of adjectives, e.g. *die Frau, **die morgen kommt**.* They are introduced by a relative pronoun and are often called RELATIVE CLAUSES.

(iii) **Adverbial clauses**, which have the same function as adverbs, i.e. they indicate time, cause, manner, etc., e.g. (for time): *Die Frau kam, **als die Sonne aufging**.* They can be classified according to their meaning in a similar way to adverbs (see Table 7.1).

This chapter gives details about the clauses of German and the conjunctions used in them as follows:

- **Coordinating conjunctions** (section 19.1)
- **Noun clauses** (section 19.2)
- **Adverbial clauses** (sections 19.3–19.7)
  - Conjunctions of **time** (section 19.3)
  - **Causal** conjunctions (section 19.4)
  - Conjunctions of **purpose** and **result** (section 19.5)
  - **Concessive** conjunctions (section 19.6)
  - Conjunctions of **manner** and **degree** (section 19.7)

Relative pronouns and **relative clauses** are dealt with in section 5.4. Conjunctions used to introduce **conditional clauses** (= 'if') are explained in section 16.5.

19.1 Coordinating conjunctions

Coordinating conjunctions link clauses of the same kind. If both the clauses they join are main clauses, they are followed by regular main clause word order, i.e. the verb is the second element, see 21.1.4:

> Er ist gestern Abend angekommen, **aber** ich **habe** ihn noch nicht gesehen.

They can also join subordinate clauses:

> Ich weiß, dass sie morgen kommt **und** dass sie mich sehen möchte.

Most of them can also link single words or phrases:

> Ich finde diese CD schön, **aber** etwas zu teuer.
> Sie hat ein Buch **und** zwei Zeitschriften gekauft.

A few, like *sowie*, are only used like this, i.e. they cannot link clauses.

Table 19.1 lists the coordinating conjunctions of German, with the section indicated in which their use is explained.

TABLE 19.1 *Coordinating conjunctions*

aber	but	19.1.1	nämlich	as, for	19.1.2
allein	but	19.1.1	oder	or	19.1.3
bald ... bald	now ... now	19.1.5	sondern	but	19.1.1
beziehungsweise	or	19.1.3	sowie	as well as	19.1.4
denn	as, for	19.1.2	sowohl ... als	as well as	19.1.4
doch	but	19.1.1	teils ... teils	partly ... partly	19.1.5
entweder ... oder	either ... or	19.1.3	und	and	19.1.4
jedoch	but	19.1.1	weder ... noch	neither ... nor	

19.1.1 *aber, allein, doch, jedoch, sondern* 'but'

These conjunctions all indicate restrictions of some kind.

(a) *aber* **is the usual equivalent of English 'but'**

> Er runzelte die Stirn, **aber** sie sagte noch   *He frowned, but she still didn't say*
> nichts   *anything*

NB: For *aber* with *zwar* in the preceding clause, see 19.6.1b.

(b) *allein, doch* **and** *jedoch* **are mainly literary alternatives to** *aber*
(i) *allein* is only used in formal literary German. It usually introduces a restriction which is unwelcome or unexpected:

> Ich hatte gehofft, ihn nach der Sitzung   *I had hoped to speak to him after the*
> zu sprechen, **allein** er war nicht   *meeting, but he wasn't present*
> zugegen

(ii) *jedoch* is rather more emphatic than *doch*:

> Der Lohn ist karg, **doch** man genießt   *The wages are meagre, but one enjoys the*
> die abendlichen Stunden (*Jens*)   *evening hours*
> Im Allgemeinen war er kein guter   *In general he was not a good pupil, but he*
> Schüler, **jedoch** in Latein war er allen   *was better than any in Latin*
> überlegen

(c) *aber, doch* **and** *jedoch* **are also used as modal particles or adverbs**

(For *aber*, see 10.1.2, for *doch*, see 10.7.1). They have much the same meaning when used like this as when they are used as conjunctions, but they form part of the clause rather than introduce it, and the word order is different. Compare these alternatives to the sentences in (a) and (b):

> Er runzelte die Stirn, sie **aber** sagte noch nichts
> Er runzelte die Stirn, sie sagte **aber** noch nichts
> Der Lohn ist karg, **doch** genießt man die abendlichen Stunden
> Der Lohn ist karg, man genießt **doch** die abendlichen Stunden
> ..., in Latein **jedoch** war er allen überlegen
> ..., in Latein war er **jedoch** allen überlegen

Constructions like this highlight the contrast rather more than when these words are used as conjunctions. *aber* is often used like this if the verbs in the two clauses have the same subject, and the subject is omitted in the second clause: *Er runzelte die Stirn, sagte aber noch nichts.*

(d) *sondern* **'but'**

(i) *sondern* contradicts a preceding negative

Er ist nicht reich, **sondern** arm	*He is not rich, but poor*
Wir sind nicht ins Kino gegangen, **sondern** wir haben im Garten gearbeitet	*We didn't go to the cinema, but worked in the garden*

sondern is distinct from *aber*, which is only used after a negative if it doesn't contradict, i.e. if **both** the linked elements are valid:

Er ist nicht reich, **aber** ehrlich (i.e. he is both 'not rich' *and* 'honest')	*He is not rich, but honest*

(ii) *nicht nur ... sondern auch* corresponds to 'not only ... but also':

Er ist **nicht nur** reich, **sondern auch** großzügig	*He is not only rich, but generous, too*
Sie besorgten **nicht nur** ihren Haushalt, **sondern** sie waren **auch** berufstätig	*They didn't only run the household, they had a job, too*

NB: (i) See 12.1.4 (d)/(e) for the agreement of the finite verb if the subject consists of more than one noun or pronoun linked by *nicht nur ... sondern auch*.

(ii) Initial *nicht nur* is followed immediately by the finite verb, e.g. **Nicht nur hat** Helmut kräftig *mitgeholfen, sondern Franziska hat auch ihren Teil dazu beigetragen.*

19.1.2 *denn, nämlich* 'as', 'because', 'for'

denn and *nämlich* are coordinating, not subordinating conjunctions, i.e. they introduce main clauses, with the verb in second position. Clauses with them give the reason for the event or action in the preceding clause, so these clauses are never in first position in the sentence.

(a) *denn*

Karsch räusperte sich, **denn** anderes fiel ihm nicht ein (*Johnson*)	*Karsch cleared his throat because he couldn't think of anything else to do*

denn is infrequent in colloquial speech, and *weil* is often heard in its place as a coordinating conjunction, followed by a main clause, even though this is regarded as substandard, see 19.4.1.

(b) *nämlich* **is always placed within the clause, after the verb**

Er konnte sie nicht verstehen, er war **nämlich** taub	*He couldn't understand her, as he was deaf*

19.1.3 *oder, beziehungsweise* 'or', *entweder . . . oder* 'either . . . or', *weder . . . noch* 'neither . . . nor'

These are **disjunctive** conjunctions, giving alternatives. See 12.1.4 for the agreement of the finite verb if the subject consists of two or more nouns or pronouns linked by them.

(a) *oder* **is the most usual equivalent for English 'or'**

Ich weiß, was passiert, wenn eine Warmfront **oder** eine Kaltfront vorbeiziehen (*Grzimek*)	*I know what happens when a warm front or a cold front go past*
Morgen können wir zu Hause bleiben, **oder** wir können einen Spaziergang machen, wenn du willst	*Tomorrow we can stay at home, or we can go for a walk if you want to*
Wir können in Heidelberg **oder** in Mannheim umsteigen	*We can change trains in Heidelberg or Mannheim*
Sie wollten das Haus aus- **oder** umbauen	*They wanted to extend or alter the house*

oder can be ambiguous, like English 'or', since the alternatives linked by it can be **exclusive** (one or the other, but not both) or **inclusive** (i.e. 'and/or', as in the last example above). In order to confirm that exclusion is meant, *aber (auch)* can be added to *oder* (see 10.1.2), e.g.: *Wir können in Heidelberg, oder aber (auch) in Mannheim umsteigen.* Alternatively, *beziehungsweise* or *entweder . . . oder* can be used to signal exclusion (see (b) and (c) below).

(b) *beziehungsweise* **indicates mutually exclusive alternatives**
In writing it is usually abbreviated to *bzw.*:

Sie haben lange in Deutschland gewohnt, **bzw.** sie haben dort oft Urlaub gemacht	*They lived a long time in Germany, or (else) they often took their holidays there*
Es kostet 300 Euro, **bzw.** 250 Euro mit Rabatt	*It costs 300 euro, or 250 euro with the discount*

beziehungsweise was originally restricted to formal registers, but it is now common in both speech and writing.

(c) *entweder ... oder* **'either ... or' signals mutually exclusive alternatives**

Entweder er wird entlassen, **oder** er findet gar keine Stellung (*BILD*)
He will either be dismissed or not find a job at all

Rather less commonly, *entweder* may be immediately followed by the verb, e.g. *Entweder wird er entlassen, oder ...*

(d) *weder ... noch* **'neither ... nor'**

Er liest **weder** Bücher **noch** Zeitungen
He reads neither books nor newspapers

Ich habe **weder** seinen Brief bekommen, **noch** habe ich sonst von ihm gehört
Neither have I received his letter, nor have I heard from him in any other way

A common alternative to *weder ... noch* is to use *und auch nicht/kein*. This is often felt to be less clumsy and more natural, especially in spoken German:

Er liest keine Bücher **und auch keine** Zeitungen.

Ich habe seinen Brief nicht bekommen, **und** ich habe **auch nicht** sonst von ihm gehört.

noch cannot be used on its own in the sense of 'nor' without a preceding *weder*. As an equivalent for English 'nor' without a preceding 'neither' (or 'or' preceded by a negative) German uses *und auch nicht/kein*:

Sie hat mir noch nicht geschrieben, **und** ich erwarte **auch nicht**, dass ich bald von ihr höre
She hasn't written to me yet, nor do I expect to hear from her soon

Ich höre die Nachrichten im Radio nicht **und** kaufe **auch keine** Zeitungen
I don't listen to the news on the radio or buy newspapers

19.1.4 *und* **'and';** *sowie, sowohl ... als* **'as well as'**

(a) *und* **is the common equivalent for English 'and'**

Angela **und** Gudrun wollen auch kommen
Angela and Gudrun want to come too

Einer der Verdächtigen durchbrach eine Straßensperre **und** konnte erst nach einer Verfolgungsjagd gestoppt werden (*NZZ*)
One of the suspects broke through a road block and could only be stopped after a chase

(b) *sowie, sowohl ... als* **'both ... and', 'as well as'**
These are frequent stylistic alternatives to *und*, especially in written German, although they are by no means unknown in speech. They emphasise the connection between the elements more than *und*, and they are often used with a following *auch*:

Dürrenmatt hat **sowohl** Dramen **als (auch)** Kriminalromane geschrieben
Dürrenmatt wrote both plays and detective novels

NB: Less commonly, *wie* is used for *als* with *sowohl*.

sowie puts rather more stress on the second element than *sowohl . . . als*, e.g.:

> Dürrenmatt hat Dramen **sowie (auch)** Kriminalromane geschrieben.

NB: See 12.1.4 for the agreement of the finite verb if the subject consists of more than one noun or pronoun linked by *sowohl . . . als* or *sowie*.

19.1.5 Less frequent coordinating conjunctions

(a) *bald . . . bald* **'one moment . . . the next, now . . . now'**
This is mainly found in formal writing. *bald* is followed immediately by the verb in both clauses:

Bald weinte das Kind, **bald** lachte es	*One moment the child was crying, the next it was laughing*

(b) *teils . . . teils* **'partly . . . partly'**

Wir haben unseren Urlaub **teils** in Italien verbracht, **teils** in der Schweiz	*We spent our holiday partly in Italy, partly in Switzerland*
teils heiter, **teils** wolkig	*cloudy with sunny intervals*

When clauses are linked with *teils*, the verb follows *teils* in both clauses:

Teils war man sehr zuvorkommend, **teils** hat man mich völlig ignoriert	*Sometimes people were very helpful, at others I was completely ignored*

19.2 Noun clauses

Noun clauses have the same function in the sentence as nouns or noun phrases. In particular, they are most often found as complements of a verb, and for this reason they are also called COMPLEMENT CLAUSES. They can be the subject (***Dass sie kommt**, freut mich*), object (*Sie sah, **wie er sich anstrengte***) or one of the other **complements** of a verb (see Table 18.1). Noun clauses in German can be introduced by *dass*, *ob*, *wenn* or the interrogative *w*-words (see 7.5).

NB: If a noun clause is the **subject** of a verb, it has the third person singular endings, see 12.1.4a.

19.2.1 *dass* 'that'

(a) *dass* **is the commonest conjunction used to introduce noun clauses**
In this respect it corresponds closely to English 'that':

subject:	**Dass sie morgen kommt**, erstaunt mich
accusative object:	Sie versicherte mir, **dass alles in Ordnung war**
genitive object:	Man klagt ihn an, **dass er das Geld gestohlen hat**
prepositional object:	Er wartete darauf, **dass Peter ihn grüßte**
predicate complement:	Tatsache ist, **dass er gelogen hat**

Noun clauses with *dass* can also depend on adjectives, e.g. *Ich bin froh, dass du kommen konntest* or on nouns related to verbs, e.g. *Ihn quälte die Angst, dass etwas passieren könnte*

(b) The omission of *dass*

The conjunction *dass* can be omitted in some contexts and some types of noun clause, in which case the dependent clause has the order of a main clause, with the verb second. Compare the following alternatives:

> Sie sagte, **dass** sie einen Brief **schreibe**
> Sie sagte, sie **schreibe** einen Brief

However, it is far less frequent for *dass* to be omitted in German than is the case for English that. It is possible to drop *dass*:

(i) after verbs (and other expressions) of saying, when introducing indirect speech (see 16.6):

Ich sagte, sie sei das einzige Mädchen, mit dem ich „diese Sache" tun wollte (*Böll*)	*I said she was the only girl I wanted to do "that" with*
Bei denen herrscht die Meinung vor, die Universitäten litten an der Überlast ungeeigneter Studenten (*Spiegel*)	*With these people the idea is dominant that universities are suffering from being overloaded with unsuitable students*

In practice, the alternative without *dass* is rather more frequent in both spoken and written German. However, *dass* <u>is</u> usually included if the main verb is negative. Thus *Er sagte nicht, dass er sie nach Hause fahren werde* is more usual than *Er sagte nicht, er werde sie nach Hause fahren*.

(ii) after verbs (and other expressions) of perceiving, feeling, hoping, thinking and believing (in the widest sense). The omission of *dass* here is more usual in spoken German than in formal writing

Ich hatte gehofft, er würde es auf zehn Mark abrunden (*Böll*)	*I had hoped he would round it down to ten marks*
die Ahnung, sie könnte noch unterwegs sein	*the idea that she could still be on her way*

(c) Initial *dass*-clauses are more frequent in German than in English

Especially in written German, it is much more usual to find sentences which begin with a subject or object *dass*-clause than is the case in English, where we tend to provide a noun (especially 'the fact') for the 'that'-clause to link to. Compare:

Dass die Wahlergebnisse der DDR gefälscht waren, bestreitet auch Modrow nicht (*Spiegel*)	*The fact that the election results in the GDR were falsified is not disputed even by Modrow*
Dass die SED-Führung da mauert, muss nicht überraschen (*Zeit*)	*The fact that the SED leadership is stalling shouldn't surprise us*
Dass er einmal nicht mehr wollen würde, wagte er nicht zu hoffen (*Walser*)	*The possibility that at some time he wouldn't want to any more, was something he didn't dare to hope*

(d) *dass* should not be followed immediately by another conjunction

It is considered poor style for another conjunction to come straight after *dass*, so that, for example:

> (i)　　Sie sagte, **dass** er, **wenn** er am Wochenende kommen sollte, bei ihrer Mutter übernachten könnte
> (ii)　Sie sagte, **dass** er bei ihrer Mutter übernachten könnte, **wenn** er am Wochenende kommen sollte

are considered preferable to the following construction (although it is not unknown, even in writing):

> (iii)　Sie sagte, **dass**, **wenn** er am Wochenende kommen sollte, er bei ihrer Mutter übernachten könnte

In English, an adverbial clause (especially one introduced by 'as', 'if' or 'when') often follows straight after 'that', e.g.: 'She said that if he were to come at the weekend he would be able to stay with her mother'. It is advisable for English learners to avoid this type of construction in German, and to use only type (i) or (ii).

(e) *dass*-clauses can be used in isolation
(i) in commands or wishes (often with an 'ethic' dative, see 2.5.3d):

> **Dass** du (mir) rechtzeitig nach Haus kommst!　　　　*Make sure you're not too late home!*

(ii) in exclamations:

> **Dass** die es heute so eilig haben!　　　　*They are in a hurry today!*

19.2.2 *ob* 'whether', 'if'

(a) *ob* typically indicates a question or a doubt
ob-clauses are all indirect questions of one kind or another. They can have the following functions:

subject:	**Ob sie morgen kommt**, ist mir gleich
accusative object:	Sie vergaß, **ob sie eine Karte gekauft hatte**
prepositional object:	Ich erinnere mich nicht daran, **ob ich eine gekauft habe**
predicate complement:	Die Frage ist, **ob wir eine Tankstelle erreichen**

(b) Isolated *ob*-clauses
ob-clauses are often used elliptically, especially in spoken German. They can be used to ask a question:

> **Ob** es in Schwerin noch Glocken gibt?　　*Are there still bells in Schwerin?*
> (*Surminski*)

They are particularly frequent to pick up or repeat a question, and they are also often used to express a general query or supposition:

> Ja, **ob** das wirklich stimmt?　　　　　*I wonder whether that's really right*

19.2.3 *wenn* 'when', 'if'

Noun clauses introduced by *wenn* can function as:

subject:	Mir ist es recht, **wenn sie heute nicht kommt**
accusative object:	Sie mag es nicht, **wenn ich sie bei der Arbeit störe**

The verb in noun clauses introduced by *wenn* can be in the *Konjunktiv II* form if an unreal condition is involved, see 16.5.1, e.g. *Mir* **wäre** *es recht, wenn sie heute nicht käme*. Noun clauses with *wenn* **always** have a correlating *es* in the main clause, see 19.2.5.

19.2.4 Interrogatives

All the *w*-words which can be used to ask questions (see 7.5) can also be used as conjunctions to introduce noun clauses. Noun clauses with *w*-words are all indirect questions of one kind or another and can function as:

subject:	**Was sie dort macht**, ist mir gleich
accusative object:	Sie vergaß, **wie man es macht**
prepositional object:	Ich erinnere mich nicht daran, **wann ich es hörte**
predicate complement:	Die Frage ist, **wo sie es gekauft hat**

19.2.5 Correlates to complement clauses

In German, a noun clause is often linked to a pronoun in the main clause which anticipates it. Such pronouns are called **correlates**, and their form differs depending on the function of the clause.

(a) The pronoun *es* functions as a correlate to subject and object clauses

Dann fiel **es** mir auf, dass sie plötzlich fehlte	*Then I noticed that all at once she wasn't there*
Ich bedaure **es**, dass sie nicht kommen konnte	*I regret that she couldn't come*

Further details on the use of this 'correlating' *es* are given in 3.6.2e and 3.6.3a.

(b) The prepositional adverb can act as a correlate to noun clauses functioning as prepositional objects
i.e. the form *da(r)* + preposition (see 3.5) can appear in the main clause:

die Angst **davor**, dass er vielleicht nicht entkommen könnte	*the fear of perhaps not being able to escape*
Er verlässt sich **darauf**, dass wir rechtzeitig kommen	*He's relying on us arriving on time*

With many nouns, adjectives and verbs this use of the prepositional adverb is optional. For further details, see 6.6.2 and 18.6.14.

(c) The pronoun *dessen* can function as a correlate to noun clauses with the function of a genitive object
These constructions are infrequent in modern German, and *dessen* is in all cases optional:

Ich bin mir (**dessen**) bewusst, dass ich ihn strafen sollte	*I am aware that I should punish him*

19.3 Conjunctions of time

The main conjunctions which introduce adverbial clauses of time in German are given in Table 19.2.

TABLE 19.2 *Conjunctions of time*

als	*when*	19.3.1	seit(dem)	*since*	19.3.5
bevor	*before*	19.3.2	sobald	*as soon as*	19.3.6
bis	*until, till; by the time*	19.3.2	solange	*as long as*	19.3.6
da	*when*	19.3.1	sooft	*as often as, whenever*	19.3.6
ehe	*before*	19.3.2	sowie	*as soon as*	19.3.6
indem	*as*	19.3.1	während	*while, whilst*	19.3.7
indes, indessen	*while, whilst*	19.3.7	wann, wenn	*when(ever)*	19.3.1
kaum dass	*hardly, scarcely*	19.3.3	wie	*as*	19.3.1
nachdem	*after*	19.3.4			

19.3.1 *als, da, indem, wann, wenn, wie* 'when', 'as'

(a) Clauses with *als* refer to a single event in the past
als corresponds to English 'when' or 'as':

Als ich in Passau ankam, habe ich sie auf dem Bahnsteig gesehen	*When I arrived in Passau, I saw her on the platform*
Als ich weiterging, wurde ich immer müder	*As I went on, I grew more and more tired*
Als die Frau später ihre Arbeitspapiere vorlegen musste, kam die Wahrheit an den Tag (*BILD*)	*When, later on, the woman had to show her work documents, the truth came to light*

A main clause following an *als*-clause is often introduced by a correlating *da*, e.g. *Als ich in Passau ankam,* **da** *habe ich sie auf dem Bahnsteig gesehen.* This *da* is always optional.

(b) *da* is a literary (and rather old-fashioned) alternative to *als*

Die Sonne schien an einem wolkenlosen Himmel, **da** er seinen Heimatort verließ (*Dürrenmatt*)	*The sun was shining in a cloudless sky as/when he left his home village*

(c) *wie* can be used for 'when' with a verb in the present tense referring to a past action
i.e. with a 'historic' present (see 14.2.4). *wie* is an alternative to *als* in such contexts:

Als/Wie ich das Fenster öffne, schlägt mir heftiger Lärm entgegen	*As/When I opened the window, I was confronted by an intense noise*

The use of *wie* in place of *als* with a past or perfect tense is common in colloquial spoken German, especially in the south, e.g. **Wie** *ich in Passau ankam/angekommen bin, . . .* This usage is occasionally found in writing, but it is generally considered substandard.

(d) *wann* is used in questions
wann is an interrogative adverb (= 'when?'), see 7.5. As such, it is used to introduce questions in direct speech, e.g. *Wann kommst du heute Abend nach Hause?* or
in indirect speech (see 19.2.4), e.g. *Er fragte mich, wann ich heute Abend nach Hause
komme.*

(e) *wenn* introduces clauses referring to the present, the future, or to repeated actions in the past

Ich bringe es, **wenn** ich morgen vorbeikomme	*I'll bring it when I drop by tomorrow*

A main clause following a *wenn*-clause is often introduced by *dann*. This *dann* is
always optional:

Wenn das Wasser ausgelaufen ist, (**dann**) schließt sich die Klappe automatisch	*When the water has run out, the valve shuts off automatically*

wenn often conveys the sense of English 'whenever', especially in the past, where
als must be used if a single action is involved (see (a) above):

Er empfand eine Art Ekel, **wenn** er daran dachte, mit wie viel Vergangenheit er schon angefüllt war (*Walser*)	*He felt a kind of disgust when(ever) he thought about how full of the past he was*

wenn, not *als*, is used if there is a sense of a future-in-the-past:

Ich wollte zu Hause sein, **wenn** Karl ankam	*I wanted to be at home when Karl arrived*

wenn is also used in conditional clauses, i.e. = 'If' (see 16.5). If there is a possibility
of ambiguity, *immer wenn* can be used to emphasise that the sense is that of 'whenever'. Alternatively, *falls* can be used to make it clear that 'if' is meant (see 16.5.3d).

(f) *indem* 'as' can only link simultaneous actions

Anna küsste ihre Mutter, **indem** sie die Palette und den nassen Pinsel in ihren Händen weit von ihr abhielt (*Th. Mann*)	*Anna kissed her mother, holding the palette and the wet brush well away from her in her hands*

This use of *indem*, where the *indem*-clause corresponds to an English participial
phrase, sounds old-fashioned. See 13.7 for German equivalents of English phrases
with an 'ing'-form. In modern German, *indem* is mainly used in the sense of
English 'by +...ing', see 19.7.3.

(g) Equivalents of English 'when' introducing relative clauses
e.g. *zu einer Zeit, wo* ... 'at a time **when** ...'. For these, see 5.4.6b.

19.3.2 *bevor, ehe* 'before'; *bis* 'until, till', 'by the time'

For the occasional use of the subjunctive in clauses introduced by these conjunctions, see 16.7.4.

(a) *bevor* and *ehe* 'before'
There is no real difference in meaning between these. *bevor* is far more frequent; *ehe* is typical of more formal registers, although it does occasionally occur in speech.

die Großmutter hatte angefangen Achim zu fragen, **bevor** sie etwas kaufte (*Johnson*)	*Grandmother had started asking Achim before she bought anything*
Es bestand, **ehe** die Erde geschieden war von den Himmeln (*Heym*)	*It existed before the earth was separated from the heavens*

bevor or *ehe* can be strengthened by *noch* to give the sense of '**even** before', e.g. *Noch bevor/ehe sie zurückkam* 'Even before she got back'.

(b) German equivalents for English 'not ... before', 'not ... until'
(i) The most straightforward equivalent is usually *erst ..., wenn/als*:

Ich will **erst** nach Hause gehen, **wenn** Mutter wieder da ist	*I don't want to go home before/until mother gets back*
Das Kind hörte **erst** zu weinen auf, **als** es vor Müdigkeit einschlief	*The child didn't stop crying until it was so tired that it fell asleep*

(ii) *Nicht ... bevor* (or *ehe*) and *nicht ... bis* are only used if the dependent clause implies a condition. An extra (redundant) *nicht* is often added:

Bevor er sich (nicht) entschuldigt hatte, wollte sie das Zimmer nicht verlassen	*She didn't want to leave the room before/until he had apologised*
Du darfst nicht gehen, **bis** du (nicht) deine Hausaufgaben fertig hast	*You can't go out until you've finished your homework*

The rule given by some authorities that this second *nicht* is only added if the subordinate clause precedes is not always followed in practice.

(c) *bis* **has two main English equivalents**
(i) 'until, till':

Ich warte hier, **bis** du zurückkommst	*I'll wait here till you get back*

(ii) 'by the time (when)', e.g.:

Bis du zurückkommst, habe ich das Fenster repariert	*I'll have fixed the window by the time you get back*

19.3.3 *kaum (dass)*, etc. 'hardly/scarcely ... when', 'no sooner ... than'

The most usual German equivalent for these English combinations is to use two main clauses, the first introduced by *kaum*, the second by *so* or *da*:

Kaum hatten wir das Wirtshaus erreicht, **so/da** begann es zu regnen	*We had hardly reached the inn when it began to rain/No sooner had we reached the inn, than it began to rain*

Alternatively, a main clause introduced by *kaum* followed by a subordinate clause with *als* can be used: **Kaum** *hatten wir das Wirtshaus erreicht,* **als** *es zu regnen begann.* In formal written German, the phrasal conjunction *kaum dass* is sometimes used, e.g. **Kaum dass** *wir das Wirtshaus erreicht hatten, begann es zu regnen.* This alternative now sounds rather old-fashioned.

19.3.4 *nachdem* 'after'

Genau eine Woche **nachdem** er die Bergeinsamkeit verlassen hatte, fand sich Grenouille auf einem Podest in der großen Aula der Universität von Montpellier (*Süßkind*)	*Exactly a week after he had left his mountain fastness Grenouille found himself on a platform in the great hall of the university of Montpellier*

nachdem is sometimes used in a causal sense, as an alternative to *da* (= 'as, since', see 19.4.1):

Er musste zurücktreten, **nachdem** ihm verschiedene Delikte nachgewiesen wurden	*He had to resign, as various offences had been proved against him*

This usage is typical of south Germany and Austria.

NB: For *je nachdem* 'according as', see 19.7.5

19.3.5 *seit, seitdem* 'since'

The shorter form *seit* was formerly restricted to colloquial registers, but it is now at least as frequent as *seitdem*, even in writing:

Seit(dem) er sein Haus verkauft hat, wohnt er in einem Hotel	*Since he sold his house, he's been living in a hotel*
Seit ich warte, sind mindestens dreißig Leute reingegangen (*Fallada*)	*Since I've been waiting, at least thirty people have gone in*

NB: For the use of tenses in sentences with *seit(dem)*, see 14.2.2 and 14.3.4a.

19.3.6 *sobald, sowie* 'as soon as', *solange* 'as long as', *sooft* 'as often as'

None of these conjunctions is normally followed by *als* or *wie*. They are always spelled as single words.

(a) *sobald* 'as soon as'

Sobald ich merkte, dass er gar nicht zuhörte, griff ich ihn am Ärmel (*Frisch*)	*As soon as I noticed he wasn't listening I grabbed him by the sleeve*

sowie is commonly used for *sobald* in colloquial registers, e.g. *Das tat sie auch,* **sowie** *sie nach Hause kam.*

(b) *solange* **'as long as'**
(i) *solange* can refer purely to time:

Wir haben gewartet, **solange** wir konnten	*We waited as long as we could*
Solange es Menschen auf der Erde gibt, haben sie immer in der Natur zwischen ihren Mitgeschöpfen gelebt (*Grzimek*)	*As long as there have been people on earth they have lived amongst their fellow creatures in natural surroundings*

NB: The sense of *solange* can approach that of *seit(dem)*, as in the second example, and tense use is similar, see 14.2.2 and 14.3.4a.

(ii) It may also have a conditional sense (= 'provided that'), e.g.:

Solange er sein Bestes tut, bin ich zufrieden	*As long as he does his best, I shall be satisfied*

(iii) The conjunction *solange* should be distinguished from the phrase *so lange* 'so long':

Du hast uns **so lange** warten lassen, dass wir den Zug verpasst haben	*You kept us waiting so long that we missed the train*
So lange er auch wartete, es kam kein Zug mehr	*However long he waited, no more trains came*

(c) *sooft* **corresponds to English 'as often as' or 'whenever'**

Du kannst kommen, **sooft** du willst	*You can come as often as you want to*
Sooft er kam, brachte er uns immer Geschenke mit	*Whenever he came, he always brought us presents*

19.3.7 *während* 'while, whilst' and alternatives

(a) *während* **is the usual equivalent of English 'while, whilst'**
Like 'while', it can express time **or** a contrast (i.e. = 'whereas'):

Die Zollprobleme löste Boris, **während** wir in Urlaub waren (*Bednarz*)	*Boris solved the problems with the customs while we were on holiday*
Klaus Buch müsste auch sechsundvierzig sein, **während** der vor ihm Stehende doch eher sechsundzwanzig war (*Walser*)	*Klaus Buch ought to be forty-two as well, whereas the man standing in front of him was more like twenty-six*

NB: (i) noch *während* is used for 'even as/whilst', e.g. **Noch während** sie schlief … 'Even as she slept …'
(ii) *während* is sometimes used with main clause word-order (i.e. with the verb second) in colloquial speech. This usage is substandard.

(b) *indes* and *indessen* are alternatives to *während* in both senses
They are restricted to literary registers:

seine Glieder zitterten, **indes** er diese grauenvolle Lust in sich erwürgte (*Süßkind*)	*His limbs were trembling as he throttled this terrible desire in himself*

(c) *wohingegen* **is an alternative to** *während* **to signal a contrast**
It occurs mainly in formal writing and stresses the contrast more strongly:

Er ist sehr zuvorkommend, **wohingegen** sein Bruder oft einen recht unfreundlichen Eindruck macht	*He is very obliging, whilst/whereas his brother often makes a very unpleasant impression*

19.4 Causal conjunctions

German conjunctions signalling a cause or a reason are given in Table 19.3.

TABLE 19.3 *Causal conjunctions*

da	*as, since*	19.4.1	weil	*because*	19.4.1
nun (da/wo)	*now that, seeing that*	19.4.2	zumal	*especially as*	19.4.3
umso mehr, als	*all the more because*	19.4.3			

19.4.1 *da* and *weil*

The distinction between *da* and *weil* parallels that between English 'as' (or 'since') 'because'. *da*-clauses, like those with 'as' or 'since', usually precede the main clause and typically indicate a reason which is already known.

Ich musste zu Fuß nach Hause gehen, weil ich die letzte Straßenbahn verpasst hatte	*I had to walk home because I had missed the last tram*
Da er getrunken hatte, wollte er nicht fahren	*As he'd had something to drink, he didn't want to drive*

A *weil*-clause can be anticipated by *darum*, *deshalb* or *deswegen* in the preceding main clause. This is particularly common in spoken German. The effect is to give greater emphasis to the reason given in the *weil*-clause:

Er konnte **darum/deshalb/deswegen** nicht kommen, **weil** er krank war	*He wasn't able to come because he was ill*

In colloquial German *weil* is frequently heard with main clause word order, i.e. with the finite verb second rather than at the end of the clause:

Du musst langsam sprechen, **weil** der **versteht** nicht viel	*You'll have to speak more slowly because he doesn't understand a lot*

This usage is increasingly common, but it is universally regarded as substandard and felt to be quite unacceptable in written German.

NB: *denn* and *nämlich* are also used to indicate a cause or a reason (i.e. in the sense of English 'because'). They are, however, **coordinating** conjunctions, with main clause word-order, see 19.1.2.

19.4.2 *nun da*, etc. 'now that', 'seeing that'

nun da is the usual equivalent for these English conjunctions:

Nun da wir alle wieder versammelt sind, können wir das Problem weiter besprechen	*Seeing/Now that we're all gathered together again, we can carry on talking about the problem*

There are a number of alternatives to *nun da*. Simple *nun* is occasionally found in formal written registers:

Nun alles geschehen ist, bleibt nur zu wünschen, dass ... (*FAZ*)	*Now that everything has been done, one can only wish that ...*

Other alternatives, i.e. *nun wo, wo ... (doch), da ... nun (mal)*, are in the main more typical of colloquial registers:

Nun wo du sowieso in die Stadt fährst, kannst du uns wohl mitnehmen, oder?	*Seeing as you're going into town anyway, you'll be able to take us with you, won't you?*
Ich muss es wohl tun, **wo** ich es dir (**doch**) versprochen habe	*I'll have to do it, seeing that I promised you*
Da er das **nun (mal)** schon weiß, (so) muss ich ihm wohl das Weitere erzählen	*Seeing that he already knows that, I'll have to tell him the rest*

19.4.3 Other causal conjunctions

(a) *zumal* is a stronger alternative to *da*
It corresponds to English 'especially as':

Sie wird uns sicher helfen, **zumal** sie dich so gern hat	*She's sure to help us, especially as she's so fond of you*
Mehr verriet sie nicht, **zumal** es Stiller gar nicht wunderte, warum sie dieses Bedürfnis hatte (*Frisch*)	*She didn't reveal any more, especially as Stiller was not at all surprised why she felt this need*

(b) *umso mehr ...*, *als/da/weil* correspond to 'all the more ... because'

Ich freute mich **umso mehr** über seinen Erfolg, **als/da/weil** er völlig unerwartet war	*I was all the more pleased about his success because it was totally unexpected*
Du musst früh ins Bett gehen, **umso mehr als** du morgen einen schweren Tag hast	*You've got to go to bed early, all the more because you've got a busy day tomorrow*

The construction with *umso ...*, *als* can be used with other comparatives:

Die Sache ist **umso** dringlicher, **als/da** die Iraker den Ölhahn zudrehen könnten	*The matter is all the more urgent because the Iraqis might turn off the oil tap*

19.5 Conjunctions of purpose and result

German conjunctions indicating purpose or result (also called **final conjunctions** and **consecutive conjunctions** respectively) are given in Table 19.4:

TABLE 19.4 *Conjunctions of purpose and result*

als dass	*for … to*	19.5.3	derart dass	*so that* (consecutive)	19.5.2
auf dass	*so that* (purpose)	19.5.1	so dass	*so that* (consecutive)	19.5.2
damit	*so that* (purpose)	19.5.1			

English learners need to be aware that 'so that' has two distinct senses, with different German equivalents, i.e.:

(i) Final 'so that' expresses purpose and is an alternative to 'in order that'. The usual German equivalent is *damit*, see 19.5.1.

(ii) Consecutive 'so that' expresses a result and has the sense of '(in) such (a way) that'. It usually corresponds to German *so dass*, see 19.5.2.

19.5.1 Clauses of purpose

(a) *damit* **is the most widely employed conjunction in final clauses**

Diese Tute ist aus Papier, **damit** sie nicht aus Kunststoff ist	*This bag is made of paper so that it shouldn't be made of plastic*
König Ludwig ließ Wagner 40 000 Gulden auszahlen, **damit** sich der total verschuldete Meister bei seinen Gläubigern freikaufen konnte (SZ)	*King Ludwig had 40,000 guilders paid to Wagner so that the totally debt-ridden maestro could pay off his creditors*

NB: (i) The verb in *damit*-clauses is usually in the indicative in modern German. For the occasional use of the subjunctive, see 16.7.2a.

(ii) Infinitive clauses with *um … zu* have a final meaning (= 'in order to'), see 13.2.7a.

(b) *auf dass* **is an old-fashioned sounding alternative to** *damit*

It has a formal and biblical ring and is used principally for stylistic effect. It is always followed by a subjunctive, see 16.7.2b:

Schenke du ihr ein reines Herz, **auf dass** sie einstmals eingehe in die Wohnungen des ewigen Friedens (Th. Mann)	*Give her a pure heart, so that she may some day enter into the dwellings of eternal peace*

(c) Simple *dass* **is sometimes used for** *damit*

This usage is most often encountered in colloquial speech, but it is not unknown in formal writing, where it is sometimes used with a subjunctive:

Ich mache dir noch ein paar Stullen, **dass** du unterwegs auch was zu essen hast	*I'll make you a couple of sandwiches so that you've got something to eat on the journey*
Er entfernte sich leise, **dass** niemand ihn sehe, niemand ihn höre (Süßkind)	*He withdrew quietly, so that no-one should see him, no-one should hear him*

NB: In colloquial German *so dass* is sometimes used to introduce clauses of purpose. This usage is considered substandard.

19.5.2 Clauses of result

(a) *so dass* is the most frequent conjunction introducing clauses of result

Sein Bein war steif, **so dass** er kaum gehen konnte	*His leg was stiff, so that he could hardly walk*
Das Wetter war schlecht, **so dass** wir wenig wandern konnten	*The weather was bad, so that we couldn't do much hiking*
Er schob den Ärmel zurück, **so dass** wir die Narbe sehen konnten	*He pushed his sleeve back, so that we were able to see the scar*

The difference between consecutive clauses and final clauses is clear if we replace *so dass* by *damit* in the last example. *Er schob die Ärmel zurück,* **damit** *wir die Narbe sehen konnten* implies that he did it with the express intention that we should see the scar. With *so dass*, the fact that we could see the scar is only the (possibly unintentional) result of his action.

NB: *so dass* can alternatively be written as a single word (i.e. *sodass*), and this is the usual form in Austria.

(b) In clauses with adjectives or adverbs, the *so* can precede these

These correspond to similar constructions in English. Compare the examples below to the first two examples in (a) above:

Sein Bein war **so** steif, **dass** er kaum gehen konnte	*His leg was so stiff that he could hardly walk*
Das Wetter war **so** schlecht, **dass** wir wenig wandern konnten	*The weather was so bad that we weren't able to do much hiking*

derart and (in some contexts) *dermaßen* are more emphatic alternatives to *so* in such contexts:

Er fuhr **so/derart/dermaßen** langsam, **dass** Frieda uns leicht einholte	*He drove so slowly that Frieda caught us up easily*
Es hat **so/derart/dermaßen** geregnet, **dass** wir schon Montag nach Hause gefahren sind	*It rained so much that we came home as early as Monday*

dermaßen is only possible if some idea of quantity is involved. Thus, only *derart* could replace *so* in: *Er hat den Ärmel* **so/derart** *zurückgeschoben, dass wir die Narbe sehen konnten.*

19.5.3 *als dass*

als dass is only used to introduce a clause after an adjective modified by *zu, nicht genug* or *nicht so*. The equivalent English sentences usually have an infinitive with 'for':

Er ist **zu** vernünftig, **als dass** ich das von ihm erwartet hätte	*He's too sensible for me to have expected that of him*
Es ist noch **nicht so** kalt, **als dass** wir jetzt schon die Heizung einschalten müssten	*It's not so cold for us to have to turn the heating on yet*
Das Kind ist **nicht** alt **genug, als dass** wir es auf einer so langen Reise mitnehmen könnten	*The child is not old enough for us to be able to take it with us on such a long journey*

In everyday speech, simpler constructions are preferred to sentences with *als dass*, e.g. *Es ist noch nicht so kalt, also brauchen wir die Heizung noch nicht einschalten.*

NB: (i)   If the subject of the two clauses is the same, an infinitive clause with *um ... zu* is used (see 13.2.7a).
    (ii)   *Konjunktiv II*, particularly of a modal verb, is commonly used in *als dass* clauses, see 16.7.5a.

19.6 Concessive conjunctions

Concessive conjunctions typically include the equivalents for English '(al)though' (see section 19.6.1), and the forms which correspond to English 'however', 'where(so)ever', etc. (see section 19.6.2). Conditional concessive conjunctions (*selbst wenn, auch wenn, sogar wenn, wenn ... auch* = English 'even if') are treated in 16.5.3d.

19.6.1 German equivalents for English '(al)though'

(a) *obwohl* is the commonest concessive conjunction in current usage

Obwohl sie Schwierigkeiten mit dem Reißverschluss hatte, stand ich nicht auf, ihr zu helfen (*Böll*)	*Although she was having difficulties with her zip, I didn't stand up to help her*

If the *obwohl*-clause comes first, the contrast can be emphasised by using (*so*) ... *doch* in the main clause:

Obwohl ich unterschrieben hatte, (**so**) blieb sie **doch** sehr skeptisch	*Although I had signed, she still remained very sceptical*

Less commonly, the contrast may be stressed by putting the verb second in the following main clause:

Obwohl er mein Vetter ist, ich **kann** nichts für ihn tun	*Although he is my cousin, I can't do anything for him*

NB: *obwohl* is occasionally used with the word order of a main clause, i.e. with the verb second: *Sie kann ihn sehen, obwohl es ist sehr dunkel.* This usage seems to be increasing, but it is regarded as substandard.

(b) Other concessive conjunctions
(i) *obschon* is quite common in Swiss usage:

Ivy hatte drei Stunden lang auf mich eingeschwätzt, **obschon** sie wusste, dass ich grundsätzlich nicht heirate (*Frisch*)	*Ivy had kept on at me for three hours although she knew that I wasn't getting married on principle*

(ii) *trotzdem* is sometimes used as a conjunction to mean 'although':

Ich hab die jungen Herrschaften auch gleich erkannt, **trotzdem** es ein bisschen dunkel ist (*Th. Mann*)	*I recognised the young master and mistress immediately although it is a little dark*

The use of *trotzdem* as a conjunction is chiefly colloquial, and many Germans avoid it in writing.

(iii) A common alternative way to express concession is a construction with *zwar ... aber*, i.e. with two main clauses. The first one contains the particle *zwar* (see 10.36.1), and the second is introduced by *aber*:

Offenbar war ihr meine Existenz **zwar** bekannt, **aber** sie hatte keine klaren Anweisungen mich betreffend (*Böll*)	*Although they were aware of my existence, they didn't have any clear instructions in respect of me*

(iv) Some other alternatives to *obwohl* are used occasionally in written German, roughly in the following descending order of frequency: *obgleich, wenngleich, wiewohl, obzwar.*

19.6.2 Clauses of the type 'however', 'whoever', 'whenever', etc.

(a) The usual German equivalent for these is *wie ... auch, wer ... auch*, etc.
i.e. the clause is introduced by one of the interrogative pronouns (see 5.3) or the interrogative adverbs (see 7.5), and the particle *auch* is placed later in the clause:

Wer er **auch** ist, ich kann nichts für ihn tun	*Whoever he is, I can't do anything for him*
Wann sie **auch** ankommt, ich will sie sofort sprechen	*Whenever she arrives, I want to speak to her immediately*
Wohin sie **auch** hingeht, ich werde ihr folgen	*Wherever she may go, I shall follow her*
Wo er sich **auch** zeigte, er wurde mit Beifall begrüßt	*Wherever he showed himself, he was greeted with applause*

As the examples show, a main clause following these concessive clauses usually has normal word order, with the verb second, see 21.2.1c. Other features of this type of concessive clause:

(i) The modal verb *mögen* often occurs in these clauses in more formal registers, e.g. *Wer er auch sein **mag**, ...; Wann sie auch ankommen **mag**, ...* etc. (see 17.4.3).

(ii) In modern German, the indicative mood is used in clauses of this type. The subjunctive still occurs occasionally, but it can sound affected, except in the set phrase *Wie dem auch sei* 'However that may be'.

(iii) *auch* can be strengthened by adding *immer*, e.g. *Wo er sich **auch immer** zeigte, ...* Alternatively, *immer* can be used on its own. It always follows the interrogative, e.g.: *Wo **immer** er sich zeigte...*

(b) *so/wie ... auch* corresponds to English 'however' followed by an adjective or an adverb

So/Wie gescheit er **auch** sein mag, für diese Stelle passt er nicht	*However clever he may be, he's not right for this job*
So/Wie teuer das Bild **auch** ist/sein mag, ich will es doch kaufen	*However dear the picture is, I'm still going to buy it*
So höhnisch die Antwort Vittlars **auch** sein mochte, gab sie mir dennoch mehr Gewissheit (*Grass*)	*However scornful Vittlar's answer may have been, it still gave me more certainty*

Similarly *sosehr ... auch* is usual for 'however much':

> **Sosehr** ich es **auch** bedaure, es wird mir nicht möglich sein
>
> *However much I regret it, I shan't be able to do it*

noch so can be used in a concessive sense with a following adjective. Compare the following alternative for the first example above: *Er mag **noch so** gescheit sein, für diese Stelle passt er nicht.*

(c) *was für (ein)* or *welcher ... auch* **corresponds to 'whatever' with a noun**

> **Was für** Schwierigkeiten du **auch** hast, es ist der Mühe wert
>
> *Whatever difficulties you may have, it's worth the trouble*
>
> diese Vorgänge, von **welcher** Seite man sie **auch** betrachtet (*SZ*)
>
> *these events, from whatever side one considers them*
>
> aus **welchem** Land **auch immer**
>
> *from whatever country*
>
> aus **welchem** Grund **auch immer**
>
> *for whatever reason*

19.7 Conjunctions of manner and degree

Table 19.5 lists the principal conjunctions of manner and degree.

TABLE 19.5 *Conjunctions of manner and degree*

als	*than*	19.7.1	insoweit (als)	*inasmuch as*	19.7.4
als ob/wenn	*as if*	16.7.1	je ... umso/desto	*the more ... the more*	8.3.5
(an)statt dass	*instead of*	13.2.7c	je nachdem (ob/wie)	*according to*	19.7.5
außer dass	*except that*	19.7.2	nur dass	*only that*	19.7.6
außer wenn	*except when*	19.7.2	ohne dass	*without + ...ing*	19.7.7
dadurch dass	*by + ...ing*	19.7.3	sofern/soviel	*provided that*	19.7.4
indem	*by + ...ing*	19.7.3	soweit	*as/so far as*	19.7.4
insofern (als)	*inasmuch as*	19.7.4	wie	*as, like*	19.7.1

19.7.1 *als* and *wie* introduce comparative clauses

For the use of *als* and *wie* generally in comparatives, see 8.3:

> Wir fahren schneller, **als** du denkst
>
> *We're travelling faster than you think*
>
> Der Vortrag war nicht so interessant, **wie** ich erwartet hatte
>
> *The lecture was not as interesting as I had expected*

Clauses expressing unreal comparisons with *als ob/wenn* (= 'as if') are explained in 16.7.1. For *je ... umso/desto* 'the more ... the more', see 8.3.5.

19.7.2 *außer dass* and *außer wenn*

(a) *außer dass* **corresponds to English 'except that'**

> Ich habe nichts herausfinden können, **außer dass** er erst im April zurückkommt
>
> *I didn't find anything out, except that he's not coming back till April*

NB: An infinitive clause with *außer ... zu* can be used if the subjects of the two clauses are the same, see 13.2.7d.

(b) *außer wenn* **corresponds to English 'except when' or 'unless'**

Wir gingen oft im Gebirge wandern, **außer wenn** es regnete	*We often used to go hiking in the mountains, except when/unless it was raining*
Du brauchst die Suppe nicht zu essen, **außer wenn** du sie wirklich magst	*You don't need to eat the soup, unless you really like it*

Especially in colloquial speech, *außer* can be used for *außer wenn*. It is followed by the word order of a main clause statement, with the verb second, e.g. *Wir gehen morgen im Gebirge wandern,* **außer** *es regnet.*

NB: (i) For other equivalents for English 'unless', see 16.5.3d.
    (ii) For *anstatt dass* 'instead of', see 13.2.7c.

19.7.3 *dadurch dass* and *indem* have instrumental meaning

Their usual English equivalent is 'by' followed by the 'ing-'form of the verb, see also 13.7.2a:

Er hat sich **dadurch** gerettet, **dass** er aus dem Fenster sprang/Er hat sich gerettet, **indem** er aus dem Fenster sprang	*He saved himself by jumping out of the window*
Man kann **dadurch** Unfälle vermeiden helfen, **dass** man die Verkehrsvorschriften beachtet/Man kann Unfälle vermeiden helfen, **indem** man die Verkehrsvorschriften beachtet	*One can help to avoid accidents by observing the highway code*

NB: This is the only current use of *indem* in modern German. Its use in time clauses, see 19.3.1f, is now obsolete.

19.7.4 *insofern (als), insoweit (als),* *sofern, soviel, soweit*

These are all quite close in meaning.

(a) *insofern (als)* **and** *insoweit (als)* **correspond to English '(in) so/as far as' or 'inasmuch as'**

Ich werde dir helfen, **insofern (als)** ich kann/**insoweit (als)** ich kann	*I'll help you in so far as I'm able to*

insofern and *insoweit* can be placed within a preceding main clause, especially qualifying an adjective or adverb. In this case they **must** be used with a following *als*:

Diese Verhandlungen werden **insofern**/**insoweit** schwierig sein, **als** es sich um ein ausgesprochen heikles Problem handelt	*These negotiations will be difficult, inasmuch as we're dealing with an extremely delicate problem*

(b) *soweit* **usually has the sense of '(in) so/as far as'**

In this sense *soweit* is an alternative to *insofern/insoweit (als)*:

Ich werde dir helfen, **soweit** ich kann	*I'll help you as far as I can*
Soweit ich die Lage beurteilen kann, muss ich ihm Recht geben	*In so far as I can judge the situation, I've got to admit he's right*

soweit can sometimes be used with a conditional sense. In such contexts it is an alternative to *sofern*, see (c) below and 16.5.3d:

Soweit/Sofern noch Interesse besteht, wollen wir schon morgen damit anfangen	*Provided there's still interest, we're going to make a start tomorrow*

NB: *soviel ich weiß* 'as far as I know'.

(c) *sofern* **usually has a clear conditional sense, corresponding to English 'provided that' or 'if'**

See also 16.5.3d.

Sofern wir es im Stadtrat durchsetzen können, wird die neue Straße bald gebaut	*Provided (that)/If we can get it through the town council, the new road will soon be built*

19.7.5 *je nachdem* 'according to', 'depending on'

je nachdem is normally used with a following *ob* or an interrogative:

Je nachdem ob es ihm besser geht oder nicht, wird er morgen verreisen	*Depending on whether he's better or not, he'll leave tomorrow*
Je nachdem wann wir fertig sind, werden wir hier oder in der Stadt essen	*Depending on when we get finished, we'll eat here or in town*
Je nachdem wie das Wetter wird, werden wir am Montag oder am Dienstag angeln gehen	*According to what the weather is like, we'll go sailing on Monday or Tuesday*

je nachdem often occurs in isolation, e.g.:

Kommst du morgen mit? – Na, **je nachdem**	*Are you coming tomorrow? – Well, it depends*

19.7.6 *nur dass* 'only (that)'

In der neuen Schule hat er sich gut eingelebt, **nur dass** seine Noten etwas besser sein könnten	*He's settled down well at his new school, only his marks could be a bit better*

Especially in spoken German, a construction with a main clause is often preferred to *nur dass*, e.g. . . . , **nur** *könnten seine Noten etwas besser sein.*

19.7.7 *ohne dass* 'without'

ohne dass must be used for English 'without' followed by an 'ing'-form if the subordinate clause has a different subject from the main clause:

Er verließ das Zimmer, **ohne dass** wir es merkten	*He left the room without our noticing*
Sie haben mir sofort geholfen, **ohne dass** ich sie darum bitten musste	*They helped me immediately without my having to ask them*

If the subjects of the two clauses are the same, an infinitive clause with *ohne . . . zu* can be used for English 'without' + 'ing', see 13.2.7b.

NB: The subjunctive is often used in *ohne dass* clauses, see 16.7.5a.

20

Prepositions

PREPOSITIONS are a small class of words which combine with a following **noun phrase** to form a PREPOSITIONAL PHRASE. Prepositional phrases often express notions of time, place and direction and are typically (but not only) used as **adverbials**.

In German, the noun phrase following each preposition is in a particular CASE – we say that the the preposition 'governs' a particular case. Most German prepositions govern the dative or the accusative case; prepositions governing the genitive are mainly confined to formal language. One important group of common prepositions is followed by the accusative **or** the dative case, with a difference in meaning.

All the prepositions of German are dealt with in this chapter, ordered according to the case they govern:

- prepositions with the **accusative** case (section 20.1)
- prepositions with the **dative** case (section 20.2)
- prepositions with the **dative** or the **accusative** case (section 20.3)
- prepositions with the **genitive** case (section 20.4)
- German equivalents for **English 'to'** (section 20.5)

The most important literal and figurative senses of each preposition are treated together. Some uses of prepositions are dealt with in more detail elsewhere in the book, as indicated below:

- the use of prepositions in **time phrases** (section 11.5)
- the use of prepositions after **adjectives** (section 6.6)
- prepositions with verbs – **prepositional objects** (section 18.6)
- the **contraction** of some prepositions with the definite article, e.g. *am*, *ins* (section 4.1.1c)
- the **prepositional adverb**, e.g. *darauf*, *damit* (section 3.5)

Table 20.1 lists the most frequent German prepositions with their cases.

20.1 Prepositions governing the accusative case

Six common prepositions are used with the accusative:

| bis | durch | für | gegen | ohne | um |

The following are less frequent and are treated together in 20.1.7:

| à | betreffend | eingerechnet | per | pro | wider |

TABLE 20.1 *German prepositions and their cases*

accusative	dative	accusative or dative	genitive
Prepositions governing the			
bis	aus	an	statt
durch	außer	auf	trotz
für	bei	hinter	während
gegen	gegenüber	in	wègen
ohne	mit	neben	
um	nach	über	
	seit	unter	
	von	vor	
	zu	zwischen	

20.1.1 *bis*

In practice, *bis* is rarely used as a preposition in its own right. It is **never** followed by an article (or any determiner), and it is used on its own only with names, adverbs and a few time words. Otherwise it is followed by another preposition which determines the case of the following noun.

(a) Referring to place, *bis* means 'as far as', '(up) to'
(i) Followed by names of places and adverbs *bis* is used **without an article**. In practice the case of the following noun is never obvious:

Ich fahre nur **bis** Frankfurt	*I'm only going as far as Frankfurt*
Bis dahin gehe ich mit	*I'll go that far with you*
bis hierher und nicht weiter	*so far and no further*

(ii) If the following noun has an article, an appropriate preposition must follow, usually the appropriate equivalent of English 'to', see 20.5:

Wir gingen **bis zum** Waldrand	*We went as far as the edge of the forest*
Sie ging **bis zur** Tür	*She went up to the door*
Sie ging **bis an** die Tür	*She went right up to the door*
Wir fuhren **bis an** die Grenze	*We went as far as/up to the border*
Sie standen im Wasser **bis an** die Knöchel (H. Mann)	*They were standing in water up to their ankles*
Sie standen im Wasser **bis über** die Knöchel	*They were standing in water coming up over their ankles*
bis hin zu den Wanzen im Gesicht (Borst)	*right down to the warts on his face*
Er stieg **bis aufs** Dach	*He climbed right onto the roof*
bis über die Ohren verschuldet	*up to one's ears in debt*

(iii) With names of towns, cities and countries, *bis* **or** *bis nach* can be used. The latter is more emphatic: *Wir fahren **bis (nach)** Freiburg, von Köln **bis (nach)** Aachen.*

(b) Referring to time, *bis* means 'until' or 'by'
e.g. *bis nächste Woche, bis nächstes Jahr*, see 11.5.4. If the noun is used with a determiner, *zu* (or another appropriate preposition) is inserted: ***bis zum** Abend, **bis zum** 4. Mai, **bis zu** seinem Tod, **bis zu** diesem Augenblick, **bis auf** den heutigen Tag.*

(c) *bis auf* **(+ acc.) means 'down to (and including)' or 'all but, except'**

Die Kabinen waren mit 447 Passagieren	*With 447 passengers, the cabins were full*
bis auf das letzte Klappbett belegt (*Zeit*)	*down to the last camp bed*
Die Insassen kamen alle um **bis auf** drei	*All but three of the passengers were killed*

bis auf can be ambiguous in some contexts. *Der Bus war* **bis auf** *den letzten Platz besetzt* can mean 'The bus was full down to the last seat' or 'The bus was full except for the last seat'.

20.1.2 *durch*

(a) *durch* **means 'through', referring to place**

Sie ging **durch** die Stadt	*She went through the city*
Er atmete **durch** den Mund	*He was breathing through his mouth*
mitten **durch** den Park (see 7.1.3)	*through the middle of the park*

durch is often strengthened by adding *hindurch*, see 7.2.4, e.g.: *Wir gingen* **durch** *den Wald* **hindurch** 'We went (right) through the forest'.

It can also be used for English 'across', especially with a preceding *quer*. This can give the sense of 'crosswise', 'diagonally', but it is often used simply to strengthen *durch* (i.e. = 'right through'):

Wir wateten (**quer**) **durch** den Fluss	*We waded across the river*
Neulich wurde ein Junge gebracht, dem	*Not long ago a boy was brought in; a*
ein Speer **quer durch** den Bauch	*spear had gone right through his belly*
gegangen war (*Grzimek*)	

(b) *durch* **can also be used for English 'throughout'**
(i) This is its usual sense when it refers to time, in which case it can be strengthened by adding *hindurch*, e.g. **durch** *viele Generationen* **(hindurch)** 'throughout many generations'.

(ii) *hindurch* can be used without a preceding *durch* for 'throughout' after an accusative phrase of time with *ganz*, see 11.4.1a:

den ganzen Winter **hindurch**	*throughout the winter*
die ganze Nacht **hindurch**	*throughout the whole night*

durch can also be used on its own after the noun in this meaning: *die ganze Nacht durch*.

(iii) A phrase with *ganz* and an appropriate preposition is needed to give the sense of English 'throughout' referring to place, e.g.:

im **ganzen** Land	*throughout the country*
durch die **ganze** Stadt	*throughout the town*

(c) *durch* **is used to express means**
(i) *durch* introduces the agent or means through whom or which an action is carried out:

Durch harte Arbeit hat er sein Ziel	*He attained his aim by (means of)*
erreicht	*hard work*
Er ist **durch** einen Unfall ums Leben	*He was killed through an accident*
gekommen	

durch seine eigene Schuld	*through his own fault*
Ich habe es **durch** Zufall erfahren	*I learnt of it by chance*

This use of *durch* is related to its use for 'by' in passive sentences, see 15.3.

(ii) *durch* in this sense corresponds to 'by' with a verbal noun:

die Annahme des Kaisertitels **durch** den König	*the assumption of the title of emperor by the king*
die Erfindung des Verbrennungsmotors **durch** Benz und Daimler	*the invention of the internal combustion engine by Benz and Daimler*

(iii) *durch* with a **verbal noun** often corresponds to English 'by' with an 'ing-'form, see 13.7.2a, e.g.: *durch Betätigung des Mechanismus* 'by activating the mechanism'

(iv) The prepositional adverb *dadurch* often has the sense of 'thereby':

Was willst du **dadurch** erreichen?	*What do you hope to gain by that?*
Meinst du, **dadurch** wird alles wieder gut?	*Do you think that will make everything all right again?*

NB: For the compound conjunction *dadurch, dass* 'by . . .ing' see 19.7.3.

20.1.3 *für*

(a) *für* **corresponds to English 'for' in a wide range of senses**
i.e. where 'for' has the meaning of 'on behalf of' and the like, e.g.:

Er hat viel **für** mich getan	Das ist kein Buch **für** Kinder
Das wäre genug **für** heute	Ich habe es **für** zehn Euro gekriegt
Das war sehr unangenehm **für** mich (6.5.1a)	
Für einen Ausländer spricht er recht gut Deutsch	

NB: (i) *für* is used idiomatically in *ein Sinn, ein Beispiel für etwas* 'a sense, an example **of** sth.'.
(ii) Where English 'for' expresses **purpose**, its usual German equivalent is *zu*, see 20.2.9d.

(b) *für* **indicates a period of time**
e.g. *für sechs Wochen* 'for six weeks'. For this, and other German equivalents for English 'for' referring to time, see 11.5.5.

20.1.4 *gegen*

(a) Referring to place or opposition, *gegen* means 'against'

Er warf den Ball **gegen** die Mauer	*He threw the ball against the wall*
gegen den Strom schwimmen	*swim against the current*
	(in literal <u>and</u> figurative senses)
Er verteidigte sich **gegen** diese Leute	*He defended himself against those people*

The prepositional adverb *dagegen* is commonly used to indicate opposition, e.g.:

Hast du was **dagegen**, wenn wir früher anfangen?	*Do you have any objection to our starting earlier?*

Note the different idiomatic usage between German and English in *Ich brauche Tabletten gegen Kopfschmerzen* 'I need tablets **for** a headache'.

(b) *gegen* can indicate direction

(i) *gegen* often corresponds to 'into':

Er fuhr **gegen** einen Baum	*He drove into a tree*
Wir müssen aufpassen, dass wir nicht **gegen** die Kraterwände fliegen (*Grzimek*)	*We've got to watch out that we don't fly into the sides of the crater*

(ii) In some contexts *gegen* has the sense of 'towards':

Michael will die Maschine mit dem Propeller **gegen** die flache Böschung am Seeufer drehen (*Grzimek*)	*Michael wants to turn the aeroplane with the propellor towards the slight incline on the lake shore*

The use of *gegen* in the sense of 'towards' with the points of the compass is now old-fashioned. For *gegen Norden fahren* one now finds **nach** *Norden fahren*, see 20.2.6. The form *gen* (e.g. *gen Norden fahren*) is even more restricted to elevated literary registers and sounds archaic and biblical.

NB: Note the difference from English usage in *etwas* **gegen** *das Licht halten* 'hold sth. **up to** the light'.

(c) *gegen* can express a contrast (= 'contrary to', 'compared with')

Ich handelte **gegen** seinen Befehl	*I acted against/contrary to his orders*
gegen alle Erwartungen	*against/contrary to all expectations*
Gegen meine Schwester bin ich groß	*I'm tall compared with my sister*
gegen früher	*compared with formerly*

(d) *gegen* can have the sense of '(in exchange/return) for'

Er gab mir das Geld **gegen** eine Quittung	*He gave me the money in exchange for a receipt*
Ich will meine Kamera **gegen** einen Camcorder eintauschen	*I want to exchange my camera for a camcorder*

(e) *gegen* can express approximation (= 'about')

Es waren **gegen** (*or* etwa, *or* an die) 500 Zuschauer im Saal	*There were about 500 spectators in the hall*

(f) *gegen* is used after a number of nouns and adjectives

See also 6.6.1. These nouns or adjectives mostly involve a mental attitude 'towards' something or someone, e.g.:

die Abneigung gegen	*aversion towards*	die Grausamkeit gegen	*cruelty towards*
der Hass gegen	*hatred of*	das Misstrauen gegen	*distrust of*
argwöhnisch gegen	*suspicious of*	gleichgültig gegen	*indifferent to*
gesichert gegen	*secure against*		

seine Pflicht gegen seine Eltern	*his duty towards his parents*
sein Verhalten gegen seinen Chef	*his attitude to(wards) his boss*
rücksichtslos/rücksichtsvoll gegen	*(in)considerate towards*

With these nouns and adjectives *gegenüber* is often a possible alternative to *gegen*, see 20.2.4d. Some adjectives can be followed by *zu* **or** *gegen*, see 20.2.9g.

(g) Referring to time, *gegen* means 'about', 'towards'
e.g. *Sie kam gegen Abend, gegen vier Uhr an.* For details, see 11.5.6.

20.1.5 *ohne*

In most contexts *ohne* corresponds almost exactly to English 'without':

> Das tat er **ohne** mein Wissen   Er geht selten **ohne** Hut
> Das haben wir **ohne** große Schwierigkeiten erledigt

ohne can be used idiomatically on its own in colloquial speech:

> Der Wein ist nicht **ohne**   *The wine's got quite a kick*
> Er ist gar nicht so **ohne**   *He's got what it takes*

NB: (i)   *ohne* is used with no determiner in many contexts where English has an indefinite article or a possessive, see 4.9.3b.
  (ii) For the use of *ohne* in infinitive clauses (i.e. *ohne . . . zu*), see 13.2.7b; for the conjunction *ohne dass*, see 19.7.7.

20.1.6 *um*

(a) Referring to place, *um* means '(a)round', 'about'

> Wir standen **um** den Teich   *We were standing (a)round the pond*
> Er kam **um** die Ecke   *He came (a)round the corner*
> Sie sah **um** sich   *She looked round (in all directions)*

um is often strengthened by adding *rund*, *rings* or *herum* (see 7.2.4b), e.g.:

> Wir standen **rings/rund um** den Tisch *or* **um** den Tisch **herum**
> Er kam **um** die Ecke **herum**   Sie sah um sich **herum**.

(b) *um* means 'at' with clock times, but 'about' with other time expressions
e.g. *Ich komme um zwei Uhr*, see 11.5.11. *um* can also be used adverbially with numerals in the sense of 'about', 'approximately', see 9.1.6. It is then often followed by a definite article, but a following adjective has **strong** endings, e.g. *um die vierzig ausländische Gäste.*

(c) *um* is used to denote the degree of difference
This usually corresponds to English 'by':

> Ich werde meinen Aufenthalt **um** zwei   *I shall extend my stay by two days*
>   Tage verlängern
> Sie hat sich **um** 20 Euro verrechnet   *She was 20 euro out in her calculations*
> **um** die Hälfte mehr   *half as much again*
> eine Erweiterung der EWG **um** England   *an expansion of the EEC by the inclusion*
>   (SZ)   *of England*

When *um* is used in this sense with a comparative adjective and a measurement phrase (see 8.3.1c), an alternative to *um* is simply to put the measurement phrase in the **accusative** case, e.g.: *Er ist (um) einen Kopf größer als ich.*

(d) *um* can convey the idea of 'in respect of', 'concerning'
This sense is common when *um* is used in a prepositional object, see 18.6.10, but it occurs in other constructions, especially after some nouns and adjectives, e.g.:

der Kampf **ums** Dasein	*the struggle for existence*
Er tat es nur **um** das Geld	*He only did it for the money*
Er wandte sich an mich **um** Rat	*He turned to me for advice*
Es ist schade **um** den Verlust	*It's a pity about the loss*
Es steht schlecht **um** ihren Bruder	*Her brother's in a bad way*
ein Streit **um** etwas	*an argument about sth.*
die Angst **ums** Leben	*fear for one's life*
Es ist recht still **um** ihn geworden	*You don't hear anything about him now*

Idiomatically also *Auge um Auge, Zahn um Zahn* 'an eye for an eye, a tooth for a tooth'

(e) The prepositional adverb *darum* is used in the meaning 'therefore', 'that's why'

It is an alternative to *deshalb*:

Darum habe ich nicht schreiben können	*That's why I couldn't write*
Sie hatte eine Panne, **darum** ist sie so spät gekommen	*She had a breakdown, that's why she was so late coming*

20.1.7 Less frequent prepositions which govern the accusative

(a) *à* is used in the sense of 'at' (i.e. @), with prices

e.g.: *zehn Paar Schuhe à 150 Mark.* This usage is now rather old-fashioned, and *zu* is now more frequent than *à*, see 20.2.9h.

(b) *betreffend* 'with regard to' is used mainly in commercial German

It is an alternative to *betreffs* (+ gen.) and may precede or follow the noun it governs: ***betreffend** Ihr Schreiben vom 23. Mai* or *Ihr Schreiben vom 23. Mai **betreffend***.

(c) *eingerechnet* 'including' is limited to commercial language

It follows the noun it governs: *meine Unkosten eingerechnet* 'including my expenses'.

(d) *per* 'per', 'by'

per was originally only used in commercial language, but it has increasingly come to be used in spoken registers. When used with a means of transport it is an alternative to more usual *mit*, see 20.2.5b:

per Post (= mit der Post)	*by post*	per Bahn (= mit der Bahn)	*by rail*
per Luftfracht	*by air*	per Einschreiben	*by recorded mail*
per Adresse (p.A.)	*c/o*	per Anhalter fahren	*to hitchhike*

mit jdm. per du sein	*be on first-name terms with sb.*
Sie bezahlen erst per 31. Dezember	*You do not pay until 31 December*
Die Waren sind per 1. Mai bestellt	*The goods are ordered for 1 May*

As *per* is used predominantly without a following determiner, the case it governs is often not discernible. This has given rise to uncertainty, and in practice, when a case is clear, *per* is actually used as often with the dative as with the accusative, e.g. *per zweitem Bildungsweg* (*Spiegel*).

(e) *pro* **'per'**

pro was originally restricted to commercial language, but, like *per*, it has increasingly come to be used in speech. A common alternative is *je*, see 9.4.1:

Die Pfirsiche kosten 80 Cent **pro** Stück	*The peaches cost 80 cents each*
Was ist der Preis **pro** Tag?	*What is the cost per day?*
zwanzig Euro **pro** Person	*twenty euro per person*
Unsere Reisekosten betragen 3000 Euro	*Our travel expenses amount to 3000*
pro/**je** Vertreter **pro**/**je** Monat	*euro per representative per month*

As with *per*, when the case of a following noun is clear, *pro* is seen to be used as frequently with the dative as with the accusative.

(f) *wider* **'against' is an obsolete alternative to** *gegen*

It is occasionally used in elevated registers, but most often in a few set phrases:

Diese Unterlassung relativiert alle	*This omission qualifies all the*
markigen Worte **wider** den	*vigorous speeches against*
Terrorismus (*Zeit*)	*terrorism*
wider (alles) Erwarten	*against (all) expectations*
wider Willen	*against my (his, her, etc) will*
wider besseres Wissen (*MM*)	*against my (his, her, etc) better judgement*

20.2 Prepositions governing the dative case

Nine common prepositions are used with the dative:

aus	außer	bei	gegenüber	mit	nach	seit	von	zu

The following are less frequent and are treated together in 20.2.10:

ab	binnen	dank	entgegen	entsprechend	fern	gemäß
laut	(mit)samt	nahe	nebst	zufolge	zuliebe	zuwider

20.2.1 *aus*

(a) *aus* **most commonly denotes direction 'out of' or 'from' a place**

(i) Examples of the use of *aus* in the sense of 'out of':

Er kam **aus** dem Haus	*He was coming out of the house*
Ich sah **aus** dem Fenster	*I looked out of the window*
(*or:* zum Fenster hinaus)	
Er trank **aus** einer Tasse	*He was drinking out of a cup*
Sie ging mir **aus** dem Weg	*She avoided me*
aus der Mode kommen/sein	*go/be out of fashion*
aus der Übung kommen	*get out of practice*

(ii) In practice, *aus* more often corresponds to English 'from'

English learners need to distinguish between *aus* and *von*, which can also mean 'from' (see 20.2.8a). *aus* is used with reference to places one has been **in**, with the idea of origin. Its opposite is *in* (+ acc.). *von*, by contrast, is used for 'from' with reference to places one has been **at**, i.e. it expresses the idea of direction. Its opposite is *zu*. Examples of *aus*:

Er kommt **aus** Hamburg	*He comes from Hamburg*

i.e. *Er wohnt in Hamburg. Er kommt **von** Hamburg* means 'He is travelling from Hamburg' (on this occasion).

aus dieser Richtung	*from that direction*

Compare: *in diese(r) Richtung* 'in that direction'

Dieser Schrank ist **aus** dem 18. Jahrhundert	*This cupboard is from the 18th century*

i.e. it was made **in** the 18th century

ein Mädchen **aus** unserer Klasse	*a girl from our class*

i.e. she is **in** our class

(b) *aus* denotes 'made of' referring to materials

Die Kaffeekanne war **aus** Silber	*The coffee pot was made of silver*
aus Holz, Stahl, Eisen	*made of wood, steel, iron*
ein Kleid **aus** Wolle	*a woollen dress*

(c) *aus* is used to denote a cause, a reason or a motive

Sie tat es **aus** Dankbarkeit, **aus** Mitleid, **aus** Überzeugung	*She did it out of gratitude, out of sympathy, from conviction*
Ich weiß es **aus** (der) Erfahrung	*I know it from experience*
Ich frage nur **aus** Interesse	*I'm only asking out of interest*
aus Furcht vor, Liebe zu etwas	*for fear, love of sth.*
aus diesem Grund(e)	*for that reason*

NB: For the distinction between *aus* and *vor* (+ dat) to indicate cause, see 20.3.15d.

(d) Some idiomatic uses of *aus*

aus erster Hand	*at first hand*
Daraus werde ich nicht klug	*I can't make it out*
Aus dir wird nichts werden	*You'll never come to anything*

20.2.2 *außer*

(a) *außer* usually expresses a restriction (= 'except (for)', 'besides')

Niemand hat ihn gesehen **außer** dem Nachtwächter	*No-one saw him except for the nightwatchman*
Niemand wird es machen können **außer** mir	*No-one will be able to do it except for me*
Ich konnte nichts sehen **außer** Straßenlichtern	*I couldn't see anything besides street lights*

außer can also be used with the same case as the word to which it refers back, rather than with the dative. The following are acceptable alternatives to the examples above:

Ich konnte **nichts** sehen außer **Lichter**
Niemand wird es machen können außer **ich**

In effect *außer* is used in such contexts to introduce a phrase in apposition (see 2.6) rather than as a preposition. It can also be used in a similar way to introduce another preposition, e.g.: *Außer bei Regen kann man hier spielen.*

(b) *außer* is used in the meaning 'out of', 'outside'
This sense now occurs chiefly in set phrases, in most of which *außer* is used without a following article:

Die Maschine ist **außer** Betrieb	*The machine is out of service*
außer Kontrolle sein/geraten	*be/get out of control*
etwas **außer** Acht lassen	*disregard sth.*
Ich war **außer** mir	*I was beside myself*
Aber dies war etwas, was ganz **außer** seiner Macht lag (*Musil*)	*But this was something which lay completely beyond his power*

Similarly:

außer Atem	*out of breath*	außer Gefahr	*out of danger*
außer Reichweite	*out of range*	außer Sicht	*out of sight*
außer Übung	*out of practice*	außer Zweifel	*beyond doubt*

In one or two obsolescent phrases *außer* is used with a genitive, notably in *außer Landes gehen* 'leave the country'. More usual for this would be *ins Ausland gehen*, or simply *auswandern*.

With verbs of motion, *außer* is used with the accusative, although this is only obvious in those rare contexts where a determiner or an adjective is used, e.g. *etwas außer jeden Zweifel setzen*.

20.2.3 *bei*

(a) Referring to place, *bei* usually corresponds to English 'by' or 'at'
(i) In this sense *bei* is less precise than *an* (+ dat.), see 20.3.2a, meaning 'in the vicinity of' rather than 'adjacent to':

Er stand **bei** mir (= Er stand in meiner Nähe)	*He was standing by/near me*
Bad Homburg liegt **bei** Frankfurt	*Bad Homburg is by/near Frankfurt*
(dicht) **bei** der Kirche	*(right) by the church*
Ich habe ihn neulich **beim** Fußballspiel gesehen	*I saw him recently at the football match*
Er saß **beim** Feuer	*He was sitting by the fire*

NB: *bei* is always used with battles, e.g. *die Schlacht bei Hastings*.

(ii) Used with reference to people, *bei* usually means 'at (the house of)'. It is also used to indicate place of employment:

Sie wohnt **bei** ihrer Tante	*She lives at her aunt's*
Ich habe dieses Fleisch **beim** neuen Metzger gekauft	*I bought this meat at the new butcher's*
Sie arbeitet **bei** der Post, **bei** Bayer	*She works at the post office, at Bayer's*
bei uns	*at our house*
bei uns in der Fabrik	*at our works*

bei cannot be used to indicate motion **to** somebody's house. Compare *Sie geht zu ihrer Tante* 'She's going to her aunt's house'.

(iii) *bei* is also used in a number of extended senses with reference to people. This often corresponds to English 'with':

Das hat ihm **bei** den Amerikanern sehr geschadet	*That did him a lot of harm with the Americans*
Ich habe mich **bei** ihm entschuldigt, beschwert	*I apologised, complained to him*
Er hat großen Einfluss **beim** Minister	*He has a lot of influence with the minister*

Mathe haben wir **bei** Frau Gerstner	*We have Frau Gerstner for maths*
Hast du deinen Ausweis **bei** dir/dabei?	*Have you got your identity card on you?*
Bei Goethe liest man ...	*In Goethe's works one reads ...*

(b) *bei* is frequently used to indicate attendant circumstances
This usage has a range of English equivalents, i.e.:

(i) *bei* can mean 'in view of', 'with', etc., e.g.:

bei den immer steigenden Preisen	*in view of the constantly rising prices*
Bei diesem Gehalt kann ich mir keinen neuen Wagen leisten	*With this salary I can't afford a new car*
Bei all seinen Verlusten bleibt er ein Optimist	*Despite all his losses he remains an optimist*

(ii) *bei* can mean 'on the occasion of', 'at'. This sense is related to its use in time expressions, see 11.5.3:

bei dieser Gelegenheit	*on this occasion*
bei dem bloßen Gedanken	*at the very thought*
Sie erblasste **bei** der Nachricht	*She turned pale at the news*
Acht Menschen kamen **bei** diesem Verkehrsunfall ums Leben (*FAZ*)	*Eight people were killed in this road accident*
bei diesem Anblick	*at the sight of this*
bei einem Glas Wein	*over a glass of wine*

Similarly:

bei der Arbeit	*at work*	beim Fußball	*when playing football*
bei Tisch	*at table*	bei seinem Tod	*at his death*
bei schönem Wetter	*if it's fine*	bei diesen Worten	*at these words*

Both *bei* and *auf* (see 20.3.4b), can be used for English 'at', referring to formal occasions, functions and the like, e.g.:

Ich habe sie **bei/auf** ihrer Hochzeit kennen gelernt	*I met her at their wedding*

The difference of meaning is often slight but in general *bei* points more clearly to the **time**, rather than the place, of the event in question.

(iii) *bei* is used with the infinitive or other verbal nouns in the sense of English 'on ...ing' or a subordinate time clause, see 13.4.3a and 13.7.2d. This usage is very frequent in non-literary written German, but it is not restricted to that register:

beim Schließen der Türen	*on shutting the doors*
beim Schlafen, **beim** Essen	*whilst sleeping, eating*
bei seiner Ankunft	*on arrival/when he arrived*
bei näherer Überlegung	*on closer consideration*

(c) Some idiomatic uses of *bei*

Sie war bei guter/schlechter Laune	*She was in a good/bad mood*
Sie nannte mich beim Vornamen	*She called me by my first name*
Sie nahm mich beim Wort	*She took me at my word*
Sie nahm mich bei der Hand	*She took me by the hand*

20.2.4 *gegenüber*

(a) The position of *gegenüber* before or after the noun or pronoun
(i) *gegenüber* always follows a pronoun, e.g.:

    Sie saß **mir gegenüber**   **Ihr gegenüber** stand ein alter Herr

(ii) *gegenüber* can come before **or** after a noun. It tends to follow words denoting people, otherwise it is commoner for it to precede, e.g.:

    Alten Menschen **gegenüber** soll man   *One ought always to be ready to*
      immer hilfsbereit sein   *help old people*
      (Less common: *Gegenüber alten Menschen ...*)
    Gegenüber dem Rathaus liegt ein   *Opposite the town hall there is a*
      Krankenhaus   *hospital*
      (Less common: *Dem Rathaus gegenüber ...*)

(b) Referring to place, *gegenüber* means 'opposite'

    Ich setzte mich ihr **gegenüber**   *I sat down opposite her*
    Ich wohne **gegenüber** dem Krankenhaus   *I live opposite the hospital*

In this sense, *gegenüber* is often used with a following *von*, especially in speech: *Ich saß* ***gegenüber von*** *ihr, Ich wohne* ***gegenüber vom*** *Krankenhaus.*

    gegenüber is often used on its own, as an adverb, e.g. *Sie wohnt gegenüber; das Haus gegenüber; die Leute von gegenüber.*

(c) *gegenüber* can express a comparison (= 'compared with')
Depending on the context, *gegen*, see 20.1.4c, or *neben*, see 20.3.10d, may be alternatives to *gegenüber* in this sense:

    Gegenüber meiner Schwester bin ich groß   *I'm tall compared with my sister*
    gegenüber dem Vorjahr   *compared with last year*

(d) *gegenüber* can mean 'in relation to', in respect of', 'towards'

    mein Verhalten Astrid **gegenüber**   *my attitude towards Astrid*
    Heinrich war vollkommen hilflos   *Heinrich was completely helpless in*
      Maries Ängsten **gegenüber** (*Böll*)   *the face of Marie's fears*

In this sense, *gegenüber* is particularly common after nouns and adjectives, where it is an (often more common) alternative to *gegen*, see 20.1.4f, or, in some contexts, *zu*, see 20.2.9g:

    Er handelte durchaus gerecht mir   *He acted absolutely fairly towards me*
      gegenüber (*or:* gegen mich)
    Seine Güte mir **gegenüber** (*or:* zu   *His kindness towards me was touching*
      mir) war rührend

Similarly:

    das Misstrauen gegenüber/gegen   *distrust of*
    eine Pflicht gegenüber/gegen   *a duty towards*
    gleichgültig gegenüber/gegen   *indifferent towards*
    rücksichtsvoll/-los gegenüber/gegen   *(in)considerate to*
    freundlich gegenüber/zu   *kind to(wards)*

20.2.5 *mit*

(a) In most uses *mit* corresponds to English 'with'

ein Paar Würstchen **mit** Kartoffelsalat	*a pair of sausages with potato salad*
Mit ihr spiele ich oft Tennis	*I often play tennis with her*
Was ist **mit** dir los?	*What's up with you?*
mit großer Freude	*with great pleasure*
mit meinem Bruder zusammen	*together with my brother*

(b) *mit* indicates the instrument with which an action is performed

This usually corresponds to English 'with':

Er hat **mit** einem Filzstift geschrieben	*He wrote with a felt-tip*
Er hat den Eber **mit** einem Messer getötet	*He killed the boar with a knife*

German usage is sometimes at variance with English:

mit Tinte schreiben	*write in ink*
mit leiser Stimme	*in a low voice*
mit der Maschine schreiben	*type*

To refer to a means of transport German has *mit* for English 'by':

mit der Bahn/dem Zug	*by rail/train*	mit dem Auto	*by car*
mit dem Flugzeug	*by plane*	mit der Post	*by post*
Ich bin mit dem Fahrrad gekommen	*I came by bike/on a bike*		

NB: Whereas *mit* indicates the **instrument**, the **means** by which an action is carried out is usually given by *durch*, see 20.1.2c

(c) *mit* is common in phrases involving parts of the body, where English does not have a preposition or uses a simple verb

Sie hat mich **mit** dem Fuß gestoßen	*She kicked me*
mit den Achseln zucken	*shrug one's shoulders*

(d) Some common idiomatic uses of *mit*

mit vierzig Jahren	*at the age of forty*
mit der Zeit	*in (the course of) time*
etwas mit Absicht tun	*do sth on purpose*
mit anderen Worten (m.a.W.)	*in other words*
Her damit! (coll.)	*Give it here!*
Schluss damit!	*That's enough!*

20.2.6 *nach*

(a) *nach* is used to denote direction, in the sense of English 'to'

See also 20.5.3. In this sense *nach* is only used with:

(i) neuter names of countries and towns used without an article:

Er ging **nach** Amerika, **nach** Irland, **nach** Bacharach.

NB: *in* is used with names of countries which have an article, see 4.4.1: *Sie ging in die Schweiz.*

(ii) points of the compass used without an article:

> Wir fuhren **nach** Norden, Süden, Westen, Osten.

NB: *in* is used if an article is present (normally when the noun is qualified by an adjective): *Wir fuhren in den sonnigen Süden.*

(iii) with adverbs of place:
> Sie ging **nach** oben, **nach** unten, **nach** vorne, **nach** rechts, links

NB: also *nach Hause gehen* 'go home'.

(iv) in north Germany *nach* is often used for *zu, an, auf* or *in*: *Ich gehe nach* (standard German: *zu*) *meiner Schwester; Wir gingen nach dem* (standard German: *auf den, zum*) *Bahnhof*. This usage is regional and non-standard, but north Germans sometimes use it in writing.

(b) *nach* **can be used in the sense of 'towards', 'in the direction of'**
It is frequently strengthened by adding *hin*, see 7.2.3, e.g.:

Er bewegte sich langsam **nach** der Tür	*He moved slowly towards the door*
Ich sah **nach** der Tür (hin)	*I looked towards the door*
Er richtete seine Schritte **nach** der alten Brücke	*He turned his steps in the direction of the old bridge*
nach allen Seiten (hin)	*in all directions*

NB: *auf . . . zu* is a frequent alternative for 'towards', see 20.3.5a.

(c) Referring to time, *nach* **means 'after'**
e.g. *nach vier Uhr, nach dem Sommer,* etc. Full details are given in 11.5.8. The prepositional adverb *danach* can be used to mean 'after(wards)' or 'later', see 11.6.4b.

(d) *nach* **can be used in the sense of 'according to', 'judging by'**

Nach meiner Uhr ist es schon halb elf	*By my watch it's already half past ten*
nach italienischer Art	*in the Italian manner*
nach Ansicht meines Bruders	*in my brother's view*
etwas **nach** dem Gewicht verkaufen	*sell sth. by weight*
nach besten Kräften	*to the best of one's ability*
nach Wunsch	*just as I (he, she, etc.) wanted*

In this sense, *nach* can **follow** the noun. In general, this is usual only with certain nouns (most of which it may precede **or** follow), in set phrases, and in the meaning 'judging by':

allem Anschein **nach**	*to all appearances*
diesem Bericht **nach**	*according to this report*
(in less formal language usually: *nach diesem Bericht*)	
der Größe **nach**	*according to size*
(also commonly: *nach der Größe*)	
meiner Meinung **nach**	*in my opinion*
(also: *nach meiner Meinung*)	
Ich kenne sie nur dem Namen **nach**	*I only know her by name*
der Reihe **nach**	*in turns*
Ihrer Aussprache **nach** kommt sie aus Schwaben	*Judging by her accent she comes from Swabia*

NB: A number of other prepositions are used in the meaning 'according to' in formal registers, i.e. *entsprechend, gemäß, laut* and *zufolge*. These are dealt with in 20.2.10e.

20.2.7 *seit*

seit is only used with reference to time, in the meaning of English 'since' (e.g. *seit dem achtzehnten Jahrhundert*) or 'for' (e.g. *Ich warte seit einer halben Stunde auf meine Schwester*). For full details, see 11.5.9. For the use of tenses in *seit* phrases, see 14.2.2 and 14.3.4a.

20.2.8 *von*

(a) *von* indicates direction 'from' a place

(i) In this sense, *von* is the opposite of *zu*, which indicates direction towards, see 20.2.9. For the difference between *von* and *aus* as equivalents of English 'from', see 20.2.1a:

Ich fuhr **von** Frankfurt nach München	*I travelled from Frankfurt to Munich*
Sie bekam einen Brief **von** mir	*She received a letter from me*
Sie kommt **von** ihrer Schwester	*She's coming from her sister's*
Ich wohne zehn Minuten **vom** Bahnhof (entfernt)	*I live ten minutes from the station*
Die Blätter fallen **von** den Bäumen	*The leaves are falling from the trees*

(ii) *von* can be strengthened by adding *aus* after the noun to emphasise the point of origin, e.g.:

Von meinem Fenster (**aus**) kann ich die Paulskirche sehen	*I can see St. Paul's church from my window*
Wir sind **von** Madrid (**aus**) mit der Bahn nach Barcelona gefahren	*We travelled by train from Madrid to Barcelona*

von . . . aus also occurs in a few idiomatic phrases:

Er war **von** Haus **aus** Lehrer	*He was originally a teacher*
von mir **aus**	*as far as I'm concerned*
von Natur **aus**	*by nature*
Das ist **von** Grund **aus** falsch	*That is completely wrong*

(iii) Direction from a point can be emphasised by adding *her* (see 7.2.3):

Eine Stimme kam **von** oben **her**	*A voice came from above*
Ich komme **von** meiner Schwester **her**	*I am coming from my sister's*

von . . . her is now commonly (and fashionably) used in the sense 'in respect of', 'from the point of view of', 'regarding'. In practice this represents a contraction of the phrase *von . . . her betrachtet*:

Von Beruf **her** ist er Schlosser	*As for his job, he's a mechanic*
Wir sind **von** der Technik **her** schon viel weiter	*We're now a lot further on from the point of view of the technology*
Besonders raffiniert **von** der Farbe **her**	*Particularly subtle in respect of the colouring*
Von der Zielsetzung **her** sind wir der gleichen Meinung	*We're of the same opinion in respect of our objectives*

Occasionally, *her* is omitted in these contexts: *Von der Zielsetzung sind wir der gleichen Meinung.*

(b) *von* also usually has the sense of 'from' referring to time
In this case it is often strengthened by *an* following the noun, e.g. *von neun Uhr (an).*
Details are given in 11.5.12.

(c) *von* is used to introduce the agent in passive constructions
Details about the use of *von* with the passive, and on the distinction between *von* and *durch* as equivalents of English 'by', are given in 15.3.

(d) A phrase with *von* is often used in place of a genitive
i.e. for English 'of', e.g. *ein Ereignis von weltgeschichtlicher Bedeutung.* This usage is fully treated in 2.4.

(e) *von* has a wide range of figurative uses
(i) It often corresponds to English 'of' in the sense of 'on the part of':

Das war sehr nett, liebenswürdig, vernünftig **von** ihr	*That was very nice, kind, sensible of her*
Das war doch dumm **von** mir	*That was silly of me, wasn't it?*
Er tat es **von** selbst	*He did it of his own accord*

(ii) Some common idiomatic phrases with *von*:

Das ist nicht von ungefähr passiert	*It didn't happen by accident*
Das kommt davon	*That's what comes of it*
Das gilt nicht von ihm	*That's not true of him*
Ich kenne sie nur vom Sehen	*I only know her by sight*
von ganzem Herzen	*with all one's heart*

20.2.9 zu

(a) *zu* expresses direction
It is a common equivalent for English 'to', particularly:

(i) for going to a person('s house):

Er ging **zu** seinem Onkel, **zu** Müllers, **zum** Frisör.

NB: For 'at (a person's house), *bei* is used, see 20.2.3.

(ii) for going to a place or an occasion:

Dieser Bus fährt **zum** Bahnhof	*This bus goes to the station*
Ich ging **zur** Kirche und wartete dort auf sie	*I went to the church and waited for her there*
Wir machten einen Ausflug **zum** Dorf	*We went on an outing to the village*
Ich war auf dem Weg **zu** einem einsamen Tal	*I was on my way to a secluded valley*
Sie kehrte **zu** ihrer Arbeit zurück	*She returned to her work*
Der Rauch stieg **zur** Decke	*The smoke rose to the ceiling*
eine Expedition **zum** Mond	*an expedition to the moon*
Sie geht morgen **zu** einem Kongress	*She's going to a conference tomorrow*
Wir alle trotten hinter den Eseln her **zu** einer Wellblechhütte (*Grzimek*)	*We're all trotting behind the donkeys towards a corrugated iron hut*

zu is the opposite of *von*, see 20.2.8a and puts the emphasis on the **general direction** rather than reaching the destination. For the distinction between it and the more specific prepositions *an*, *auf* or *in* (with the accusative) as an equivalent of 'to', see 20.5.

zu can be strengthened by adding *hin* after the noun, see 7.2.3, e.g. *Sie ging zur Post* (*hin*). *Er blickte zur Decke* (*hin*). The effect is to emphasise the direction, so that *zu . . . hin* is a common equivalent for English 'towards'.

(iii) in some idiomatic phrases:

Sie sah **zum** Fenster, **zur** Tür **hinaus**	*She looked out of the window, the door*
Setzen Sie sich doch **zu** uns!	*Do come and join us*

(b) *zu* sometimes refers to a place

i.e. with the meaning of English 'at' or 'in'. This sense of *zu* used to be common, especially with names of towns, but it is now only used in elevated styles, as modern German prefers *in*:

J.S. Bach wurde **zu** (more usually: *in*) Eisenach geboren	*J.S. Bach was born in Eisenach*
der Dom **zu** Köln (more usually: *der Kölner Dom*)	*Cologne cathedral*

However, *zu* still occurs in this sense in some common set phrases, e.g.:

zu Hause	*at home*
zu beiden Seiten	*on either side*

(c) *zu* is used in certain time expressions

It usually corresponds to English 'at', e.g. *zu Ostern*, *zu dieser Zeit*. Details are given in 11.5.15.

(d) *zu* is the usual equivalent of English 'for' to express purpose

(i) Examples of this usage:

zu diesem Zweck	*for this purpose*
Das ist kein Anlass **zur** Klage	*That is no cause for complaint*
Was gibt es heute **zum** Nachtisch?	*What's for dessert today?*
Stoff **zu** einem neuen Anzug	*material for a new suit*
Zum Geburtstag hat er mir eine Uhr geschenkt	*He bought me a watch for my birthday*
Wir hatten keine Gelegenheit **zu** einem Gespräch	*We didn't have a chance for a talk*

The prepositional adverb *dazu* is commonly used in the sense of 'for that purpose', e.g. ***Dazu** soll man ein scharfes Messer gebrauchen*. Compare also *Wozu?* 'To what purpose?', 'What for?'.

(ii) In this sense, *zu* is very common with an infinitive used as a noun, or with other verbal nouns, where English uses 'for . . .ing' or an infinitive with 'to'. More details on this usage are given in 13.4.3b and 13.7.2b. It is particularly frequent in written non-literary German, but it is by no means confined to that register. Examples:

Wozu gebraucht man dieses Messer? – **Zum** Kartoffelschälen.	*What do you use this knife for? – For peeling potatoes/To peel potatoes*

Hier gibt es viele Möglichkeiten **zum**   *There are lots of possibilities for*
   Schilaufen   *skiing here*
Ich sage dir das **zu** deiner Beruhigung   *I'm telling you this to reassure you*

(iii) In certain contexts, this sense of *zu* approaches that of *als*, i.e. 'by way of', 'as':

Er murmelte etwas **zur** Antwort   *He muttered something by way of reply*
Er tat es mir **zu** Gefallen   *He did it as a favour to me*

Similarly:

zur Abwechslung	*for a change*	zum Scherz	*as a joke*
zum Andenken an	*in memory of*	zum Spaß	*as a joke*
zum Beispiel	*for example*	zur Strafe	*as a punishment*
zur Not	*if necessary, at a pinch*	zum Vergnügen	*for pleasure*

(e) In some contexts *zu* can indicate a result or an effect
The English equivalent is most often 'to':

Zu meinem Erstaunen hat sie das   *To my surprise she passed her finals*
   Examen bestanden

Similarly:

zu meinem Ärger	*to my annoyance*
zu meiner Befriedigung	*to my satisfaction*
zu meiner großen Freude	*to my great pleasure*
Es ist zum Lachen, zum Heulen,	*It is laughable, enough to make one*
zum Verrücktwerden	*weep, enough to drive one mad*

NB: *zu* commonly occurs in this sense in the prepositional object of a number of verbs, see 18.6.13a.

(f) *zu* can express a change of state
This usage is associated with a small number of verbs or nouns with appropriate meanings:

Sie wählten ihn **zum** Präsidenten	*They elected him President*
Er wurde **zum** Major befördert	*He was promoted to major*
Ich habe es mir **zur** Regel gemacht,	*I've made it a rule to do this*
dies zu tun	
etwas **zu** Brei kochen	*cook sth. to a pulp*

Similarly with *bestimmen* 'destine to be', *degradieren* 'demote', *ernennen* 'appoint', *krönen* 'crown', *weihen* 'ordain', *werden* 'become' (see 18.8), etc. and the nouns *die Beförderung* 'promotion', *die Ernennung* 'appointment', *die Wahl* 'election', etc.

(g) *zu* can express a mental attitude towards someone or something
(i) This is frequent with adjectives, see 6.6.1, e.g.:

Sie war sehr freundlich **zu** mir   *She was very kind to me*

Similarly:

frech zu	*impudent towards*	nett zu	*nice to*
gut zu	*good, kind to*	respektvoll zu	*respectful to*
(un)höflich zu	*(im)polite to*	unfreundlich zu	*unkind to*

(ii) also with a number of nouns, e.g.:

Wir haben freundliche Beziehungen **zu** Müllers	*We're on friendly terms with the Müllers*
ihre Einstellung **zur** Wiedervereinigung	*her attitude to reunification*
seine Liebe **zu** ihr	*his love for her*
das Verhältnis des Einzelnen **zum** Staat	*the relationship of the individual to the state*

gegen (see 20.1.4f) and *gegenüber* (see 20.2.4d) can also denote attitude towards or relations with someone or something. Whether *gegen* or *zu* is used depends on the particular noun or adjective, though *gegen* tends to occur with those which denote hostile attitudes, *zu* with those which denote friendly attitudes. A few adjectives can be used with either, e.g.:

gerecht zu/gegen	*fair, just to*	hart zu/gegen	*hard towards*
grausam zu/gegen	*cruel to*		

gegen is used with some nouns although the related adjective has *zu*, e.g. *die Frechheit, die Gerechtigkeit, die Grausamkeit, die Härte, die (Un)höflichkeit gegen jdn. gegenüber* is a common alternative to *gegen* or *zu* with most adjectives or nouns which occur with these prepositions, see 20.2.4.

(h) Uses of *zu* with numbers

(i) to indicate price or measure:

10 Stück Seife **zu** je 4 Euro	*10 bars of soap at 4 euro each*
5 Päckchen Kaffee **zu** hundert Gramm	*5 hundred-gram packs of coffee*
zum halben Preis	*at half price*

Also with fractions, etc.: *zur Hälfte, zum Teil, zu einem Drittel fertig*

(ii) With the dative of the cardinal or the stem of the ordinal to indicate groups, e.g *zu zweien, zu zweit*, see 9.1.3b.

(iii) With the declined ordinal number for 'first(ly)', 'secondly', etc., e.g. *zum Ersten, zum Zweiten*, etc., see 9.2.3.

(i) Selected idiomatic uses of *zu*

jdn. zum Besten haben	*make a fool of sb.*
zu Boden fallen	*fall to the ground*
sich (dat.) etwas zu eigen machen	*adopt sth.*
zu Ende gehen	*draw to a close*
zu Fuß	*on foot*
jdn. zu Rate ziehen	*ask sb.'s advice*
jdn. zur Rechenschaft ziehen	*call sb. to account*
zur Sache kommen	*come to the point*
jdm. zur Seite stehen	*give sb. one's support*
zur Welt kommen	*be born*

20.2.10 Less frequent prepositions governing the dative

(a) *ab* 'from'

ab was originally restricted to commercial and official German, but it is now quite common in colloquial registers.

(i) Referring to place, it is an alternative to *von*, but it emphasises the starting point more strongly:

Ab Jericho folgten wir einer langen Kolonne israelischer Touristenbusse (*Zeit*)	*From Jericho we followed a long convoy of Israeli tourist buses*
Dieser Sondertarif gilt **ab** allen deutschen Flughäfen	*This special fare applies from all airports in Germany*
ab Fabrik	*ex works*

(ii) Referring to time, it is an alternative to *von ... an*, see 11.5.12. If is used without a following determiner (as is usually the case, see 4.9.3c), it can take the dative <u>or</u> (rather more frequently) the accusative:

ab neun Uhr, **ab** heute	*from nine o'clock, from today,*
ab sofort	*with immediate effect*
ab ersten (erstem) Mai	*from the first of May*
ab nächste(r) Woche	*from next week*
ab dem 21. Lebensjahr	*from the age of 21*

(b) *binnen* indicates a period of time (= 'within')

It is used mainly in formal registers to avoid the potential ambiguity of *in*, see 11.5.7:

binnen einem Jahr, drei Jahren	*within a year, three years*
binnen kurzem	*shortly*

NB: (i) In elevated literary usage *binnen* may still occasionally be found with a following genitive, e.g. *binnen eines Jahres*.
    (ii) In Switzerland *innert* is commonly used for *binnen*, with a following dative or (occasionally) a genitive, e.g. *innert einem/eines Jahres*.

(c) *dank* 'thanks to'

It is mainly found in formal German and is often used with a genitive, especially with a following plural noun:

dank seinem Einfluss/seines Einflusses	*thanks to his influence*
dank seiner Sprachkenntnisse (*Goes*)	*thanks to his knowledge of languages*

(d) *entgegen* 'contrary to'

It can occur before or (rather less frequently) after the noun:

entgegen allen Erwartungen/allen Erwartungen **entgegen**	*contrary to all expectations*

(e) *entsprechend, gemäß, laut, zufolge* 'according to'

These prepositions are used chiefly in formal German. They all mean 'according to', as does the more frequent *nach*, see. 20.2.6d, but they are not interchangeable in all contexts:

(i) *entsprechend* means 'in accordance with'. It can precede or (more commonly) follow the noun:

unseren Anordnungen **entsprechend**/ **entsprechend** unseren Anordnungen	*in accordance with our instructions*

(ii) *gemäß* usually follows the noun, but occasionally precedes it. It means 'in accordance with':

Die Maschine wurde den Anweisungen **gemäß** in Betrieb gesetzt	*The machine was put into operation in accordance with the instructions*

gemäß is occasionally heard with a genitive in spoken German. This usage is non-standard.

(iii) *laut* introduces a verbatim report of something said or written. It is commonly used without a following article, see 4.9.3:

Laut Berichten soll Saddam Hussein neue Verhandlungen vorgeschlagen haben	*According to reports Saddam Hussein has proposed fresh negotiations*
laut Gesetz	*according to the law*
laut Helmut Kohl	*according to Helmut Kohl*

If the following noun has an article (or an adjective) with it, *laut* often governs the genitive rather than the dative:

laut des Berichtes/dem Bericht aus Bonn	*according to the report from Bonn*
laut neuer Berichte/neuen Berichten	*according to recent reports*
laut ämtlichem Nachweis/ämtlichen Nachweises	*according to an official attestation*

(iv) *zufolge* follows the noun. In accepted usage it indicates a consequence:

Dem Vertrag **zufolge** werden nun große Mengen von Rohöl geliefert	*In accordance with the contract large quantities of crude oil are now being delivered*

zufolge is also used where there is no sense of a consequence or a result. This usage has been frowned on by purists, but it is very widespread:

unbestätigen Berichten **zufolge**	*according to unconfirmed reports*
einem Regierungssprecher **zufolge**	*according to a government spokesman*

The use of *zufolge* with a following noun in the genitive, e.g. *zufolge des Vertrages*, is now obsolete and *infolge* (+ gen.) is used in its stead.

(f) *fern* **'far from' is restricted to elevated registers**
It can occur before or (rather less frequently) after the noun:

Sie blieben **fern** der Heimat/der Heimat **fern**	*They remained far from home*
Europa liegt immer noch **fern** dem britischen Horizont (*Zeit*)	*Europe is still far removed from British horizons*

In practice, *fern von* or *weit von* are more frequent for English 'far from'.

(g) *mitsamt* **and** *samt* **'together with'**
These are restricted to elevated styles. The usual equivalent for 'together with' is *zusammen mit*, or often simply *mit*:

Das große Krögersche Haus stand **mitsamt** seiner würdigen Geschichte zum Verkaufe (*Th. Mann*)	*The great Kröger house, together with its stately history, was up for sale*

(h) *nahe* **'near (to)' is used chiefly in formal registers**

> ein altes Haus **nahe** dem freien Feld (*FR*)   *an old house near the open field*

(i) When used in an abstract sense *nahe* **commonly follows the noun:**

> Sie war der Verzweiflung **nahe**   *She was close to despair*

(j) *nebst* **'together with', 'in addition to' occurs in formal registers**

> Sie hatten das Haus **nebst** Obstgarten   *They had rented the house together with*
> gemietet   *the orchard*

(k) *zuliebe* **'for the sake of' follows the noun it governs**

> Ich habe es meiner Mutter **zuliebe** getan   *I did it for my mother's sake*
> Dir **zuliebe** gibt es Spargel   *Just for you, we're having asparagus*
> wahrscheinlich dem Wald **zuliebe**   *probably for the sake of the forest*
> (*Walser*)

(l) *zuwider* **'contrary to' follows the noun it governs**
It is an emphatic alternative to *gegen* in formal registers:

> Karl handelte seinem Befehl **zuwider**   *Karl acted contrary to his order*

20.3 Prepositions governing the accusative or the dative case

Ten prepositions govern the accusative *or* the dative, i.e.:

an	auf	entlang	hinter	in
neben	über	unter	vor	zwischen

General rules governing the use of the two cases are given in 20.3.1, and the individual prepositions are dealt with in the following sections. For the commoner ones (i.e. *an, auf, in, über, unter* and *vor*) the use with the accusative and the dative is treated separately.

20.3.1 These prepositions govern the accusative case if they express direction, but the dative if they express position

It is often claimed that the accusative case is used with these prepositions when motion is involved, but this is not really precise. The crucial principle is that the **accusative case** is used with a phrase expressing the **direction** in which someone or something is moving or being put.

> Ich hänge das Bild an **die** Wand   *I'm hanging the picture on the wall*
> Das Bild hängt an **der** Wand   *The picture is hanging on the wall*
> Wir gingen in **dieses** Zimmer hinein   *We went into this room*
> Wir essen in **diesem** Zimmer   *We eat in this room*

In some contexts the reason for the choice of case is less obvious, or usage is variable:

(a) Even if direction is involved, the dative case is used if there is no movement in relation to the person or thing denoted by the following noun

Er ging neben **seiner** Frau	*He was walking next to his wife*
Er ging zwischen **seinen** Eltern	*He was walking between his parents*

   (His position is constant in relation to his wife or his parents)

Ein Flugzeug kreiste über **der** Stadt	*A plane was circling over the town*

   (Though it was moving, it stayed over the town)

Usage where two prepositional phrases occur in the same sentence with a verb of motion follows the basic principle, e.g.: *Elke legte sich auf eine Bank im Schatten hin.* Elke is moving in the direction of the bench, but the bench is stationary in relation to the shadow.

(b) The dative is usual with verbs of arriving, appearing and disappearing
German does not consider that such verbs indicate a direction:

Sie kamen **am** Bahnhof an	*They arrived at the station*
Wir trafen in **der** Hauptstadt ein	*We arrived in the capital*
Sie kehrten in **einer** Gaststätte ein	*They turned in at an inn*
Sie landeten auf **dem** Mond	*They landed on the moon*
Er kroch unter **dem** Tisch hervor	*He crept out from under the table*
Sie erschien hinter **der** Theke	*She appeared behind the counter*
Der Reiter verschwand hinter **dem** Berg	*The horseman disappeared behind the hill*
Sie verbarg sich unter **der** Decke	*She hid under the sheet*

Occasionally with these verbs the sense of movement in a particular direction may be felt so strongly that the accusative is used, e.g. *Er verschwand über das Dach.* Nevertheless, this is quite infrequent.

(c) In a few contexts, these prepositions are used with the accusative after a simple verb, but with the dative after a related prefixed verb
With the prefixed verbs, the action is seen as already completed, whereas with the simple verbs it is visualised as continuing:

(an/fest)**binden** *tie, fasten*
   Das Pferd war an **einen** Baum gebunden
   Das Pferd war an **einem** Baum an-/festgebunden

(vor)**fahren** *drive up*
   Der Wagen fuhr vor **den** Bahnhof
   Der Wagen fuhr vor **dem** Schloss vor

(auf)**hängen** *hang (up)*
   Sie hängte das Bild an **die** Wand
   Sie hängte das Bild an **der** Wand auf

sich (fest)**klammern** *cling to*
   Er klammerte sich an **sie**
   Er klammerte sich an **ihr** fest

sich (nieder)**legen, -setzen** *lie, sit down*
   Sie legte/setzte sich auf **die** Bank
   Sie legte/setzte sich auf **der** Bank nieder

(auf)**schreiben** *write (down)*
   Ich schrieb ihre Adresse in **mein** Notizbuch
   Ich schrieb ihre Adresse in **meinem** Notizbuch auf

(d) Usage with verbs with the prefix *ein-*
(i) These verbs are often used with *in*, usually followed by a noun phrase in the accusative case:

> Sie stieg in **den** Zug ein   Wir weihten ihn in **das** Geheimnis ein
> Ich trug den Namen in **die** Liste ein   Er wickelte sich in **eine** Decke ein

(ii) A noun in the accusative case is used even in the *sein*-passive, although here usage is variable:

> Er war in **eine** Reisedecke eingehüllt   Sie ist in **das** Geheimnis eingeweiht
> Sein Name war in **die/der** Liste eingetragen

(iii) *sich einschließen* is used with either case depending on whether the movement in a particular direction is emphasised: *Sie schloss sich in **ihr/ihrem** Zimmer ein.*

(iv) *sich einfinden, einkehren* and *eintreffen* are followed by a preposition with a noun phrase in the dative case, as they denote arrival (see (a) above).

(e) With a few verbs usage is idiomatic
In the main these are verbs which do not denote movement as such. The choice of case depends on how native speakers envisage the action, and it can vary. If no preposition is indicated the verb is commonly used with more than one (e.g. *sehen* occurs with *an, auf, in*, etc.)

(i) A noun phrase in the dative case is usual in conjunction with the following verbs:

> anbringen *fix*   befestigen an *fasten*   drucken *print*   notieren *note*

(ii) A noun phrase in the accusative case is usual in conjunction with the following verbs:

anbauen an	*build on to*	kleiden in	*clothe in*	verteilen	*distribute*
anschließen	*add on*	münden in	*flow into*	vertieft in	*engrossed in*
gebeugt über	*bent over*	sehen, schauen	*look*	verwickelt in	*involved in*
grenzen an	*border on*	stützen auf	*support*		

(f) The dative and the accusative have different meanings with a few verbs
aufnehmen A noun phrase in the accusative case implies complete acceptance, in the dative case that the acceptance is temporary:

> Er ist **in den** Chor aufgenommen worden   *He was admitted into the choir*
> Ich wurde **in seiner** Familie sehr   *I was amicably received in his family*
>   freundlich aufgenommen

einführen   If there is an idea of direction, a noun phrase in the accusative case is used, whereas a noun phrase in the dative puts the stress on the place:

> Waren **in ein** Land einführen (i.e. **nach**   *import goods into a country*
>   Italien)
> Er will die Sitte **in diesem** Land einführen   *He wants to introduce the custom*
>   (i.e. **in** Italien)   *in that country*

halten　　If the gesture is emphasised, a noun phrase in the accusative is used, a noun phrase in the dative emphasises the position:

Er hielt das Buch in **die** Höhe　　*He held the book up in the air*
Er hielt das Buch in **der** Hand　　*He held the book in his hand*

klopfen　　A noun phrase in the accusative is the norm, but in the context of knocking on doors, etc., the dative can be used if the emphasis is on the place rather than the action:

Er klopfte **an die** Tür, **auf den** Tisch　　*He knocked on the door, the table*
Da klopfte es **an der** Haustür　　*There was a knock at the front door*
　　(i.e. the front door rather than somewhere else)

schreiben　　A noun phrase in the accusative case refers to the action of writing down, the dative case is used if the place where something is written is uppermost:

Er schrieb es **in sein** Heft　　*He wrote it (down) in his notebook*
In seinem Brief schreibt er, dass ...　　*He writes in his letter that ...*

(g) In contexts where these prepositions do not have their literal meaning, they are used only or predominantly with a single case
In idiomatic uses, *auf* and *über* are used only with the accusative, all the other prepositions mainly with the dative. This is particularly evident where these prepositions are used to refer to time, see 11.5, where they are used in prepositional objects, see 18.6, with adjectives, see 6.6, and in all other contexts where they are not used in their literal senses.

20.3.2　*an* (+ dative)

(a) The basic meaning of *an* with the dative is 'on (the side of)'
(i) This contrasts with *auf* (+ dat.), which means 'on (top of)'. *an* (+ dat.) can correspond to English 'on', or, if the person or thing is not actually touching, 'at', 'by' or 'along'. See 20.2.3a for the distinction between *an* (+ dat.) and *bei* in the sense of 'at':

Das Bild hing **an** der Wand　　*The picture was hanging on the wall*
am Berg　　*on the mountain(side)*
　　(Compare *auf dem Berg* 'on the mountain-top')
An der Grenze wird kontrolliert　　*There's a check at the border*
Wir warteten **an** der Bushaltestelle　　*We were waiting at/by the bus stop*
am Fluss　　*on the river(side)*
　　(Compare *auf dem Fluss* 'on the river' (i.e. in a boat))
Wir standen **an** der Kirche　　*We were standing by the church*
Ich stand **am** Fenster　　*I was standing by/at the window*
Sie wohnt **am** See　　*She lives by the lake*
die Bäume **am** Flusstal (*Grzimek*)　　*the trees along the river valley*

(ii) *an* (+ dat.) is also used for 'on (the underside of)':

Die Lampe hängt **an** der Decke　　*The lamp was hanging from the ceiling*
am Himmel　　*in the sky*
　　(Compare *im Himmel* 'in heaven')

(iii) In older German, *an* was commonly used in the sense of 'down on', and this is still apparent in phrases like *am Boden, an der Erde* 'on the ground', where *auf* is a possible alternative. Compare also *am Strand* 'on the beach', *am Ufer* 'on the bank', etc.

(iv) *an* (+ dat) is used in three phrases in conjunction with an adverb following the noun. In all these the dative is used since, although movement is involved, there is no indication of direction.

With a following *hin*, see 7.2.3, *an* expresses movement alongside:

Sie gingen **an** der Mauer **hin**   *They were walking along the wall*

an (+ dat.) ... *vorbei* means 'past':

Wir gingen **an** seinem Haus **vorbei**   *We walked past his house*

an (+ dat.) ... *entlang* means 'along', see 20.3.6c.

(b) *an* **(+ dat.) is used with academic and other institutions at which a person is employed**

Sie lehrt **an** der Universität Augsburg   *She teaches at the University of Augsburg*
Er ist Intendant **am** Staatstheater   *He is director at the State Theatre*
Er ist Pfarrer **an** der Peterskirche   *He is the pastor at S. Peter's*

(c) *an* **(+ dat.) is used in a number of time expressions**
In particular with dates and days of the week, e.g. *am Dienstag, am 31. August*, see 11.5.1.

(d) *an* **(+ dat.) is used with many nouns, adjectives and verbs meaning 'in respect of', 'in connection with'**
Further details of the use of *an* in this sense with adjectives are given in 6.6.1. For its use in the prepositional object of verbs, see 18.6.2a.

Der Bedarf **an** Arbeitskräften verringert sich   *The demand for labour is decreasing*
Wir haben mehrere Millionen Mark **an** Aufträgen vorliegen   *We have several million marks' worth of orders on the books*
Sie hat etwas Eigenartiges **an** sich   *There's something strange about her*
Das Schönste **an** der Sache ist, dass ...   *The best thing about it is that ...*
Sie waren siebzig **an** der Zahl   *They were seventy in number*
Das Land ist arm, reich **an** Bodenschätzen   *The country is poor, rich in natural resources*

an (+ dat.) often indicates the feature **by** which one recognises or notices something:

Ich bemerkte **an** seinem Benehmen, dass ...   *I noticed from his behaviour that ...*
Sie erkannte ihn **an** seinem Bart   *She recognised him by his beard*

(e) *an* **(+ dat.) indicates a partially completed action**
This often provides a way of indicating progressive action, see 14.6.2d:

Sie strickt **an** einem Pullover   *She's knitting a pullover*
Er arbeitet **an** seiner Dissertation   *He's working on his thesis*

(f) Other uses of *an* (+ dat.)

(i) *am* is used to form the superlative of adverbs and predicate adjectives, e.g. *am schönsten, am einfachsten*, see 8.4.1.

(ii) In north-west Germany *am* is used colloquially with the infinitive to express a continuous action, e.g. *Sie ist am Schreiben*, see 14.6.2c.

20.3.3 *an* (+ accusative)

(a) *an* (+ acc.) indicates direction if the destination is *an* (+ dat.)
i.e. in contexts where the ultimate goal of the person or thing will be a position 'on', 'at' or 'by' something.

(i) It most often corresponds to English 'to' (see 20.5.1c) or 'on':

Sie hängte ein Bild **an** die Wand	*She hung the picture on the wall*
Wir gingen **an** die Kirche	*We went to the church*
Sie fuhr **an** die Küste	*She drove to the coast*

Similarly:

Ich ging **ans** Fenster, **an** die Tür, **an** seinen Platz
Er kam **an** die Bushaltestelle, **an** den Waldrand

(ii) The idea of right up to somebody or something can be indicated by adding *heran*, see 7.2.4b. e.g.:

Sie trat **an** mich, **an** den Tisch **heran**   *She walked up to me, to the table*

(iii) *an* occurs commonly with the person to whom one addresses something:

Er richtete diese Frage **an** mich	*He addressed this question to me*
eine Bitte **an** den Bundeskanzler	*a request to the Federal Chancellor*
Ich werde mich **an** ihn um Rat wenden	*I shall turn to him for advice*

(b) Verbal nouns from verbs which take a dative usually govern *an* (+ acc.)
See 18.4. The dative object of the verb appears in a prepositional phrase with *an*:

die Anpassung **an** die neuen Verhältnisse   *adaptation to new circumstances*
    Compare: *Er passt sich den neuen Verhältnissen an.*
sein Befehl **an** die Truppen   *his order to the troops*
    Compare: *Er befahl den Truppen . . .*

Similarly:

eine Antwort **an** mich	ein Bericht **an** die Akademie
viele Grüße **an** Onkel Robert	die Kriegserklärung **an** Japan
der Verkauf des Hauses **an** meinen Sohn	sein Vermächtnis **an** seine Tochter
der Verrat von Geheimnissen **an** den Feind	

NB: For the use of *an* (+ acc.) in this sense with verbs in place of a dative, see 18.4.2d.

(c) *an* (+ acc.) is used to indicate indefinite quantity

Er verdient **an** die 5000 im Monat   *He earns getting on for 5000 a month*

an in this sense is often followed by the definite article. A following adjective has **strong** endings: *an die vierzig ausländische Gäste.*

(d) Some idiomatic uses of *an* **(+ acc.)**

etwas ans Licht, an den Tag bringen	*bring sth. to light*
an (und für) sich	*actually*
die Erinnerung an seine Jugend	*the memory of his youth*
der Glaube an den Sieg	*the belief in victory*

NB: For the use of *an* (+ acc.) in prepositional objects with verbs denoting mental processes, see 18.6.2b.

20.3.4 *auf* (+ dative)

(a) The basic meaning of *auf* **(+ dat.) is 'on (top of)'**
For the distinction between *auf* and *an* (+ dat.), see 20.3.2a.

Das Buch liegt **auf** dem Tisch	*The book is lying on the table*
Sie sind **auf** dem Mond gelandet	*They landed on the moon*
Die Katze spielt **auf** dem Rasen	*The cat is playing on the lawn*
auf dem Weg nach Stuttgart	*on the way to Stuttgart*

(b) *auf* **(+ dat.) is used for English 'at' or 'in' in some contexts**
(i) for formal occasions, e.g. weddings, conferences, parties, etc.:

Ich traf sie **auf** einem Empfang	*I met her at a reception*
Wir lernten uns **auf** ihrer Hochzeit kennen	*We met at their wedding*
Sie ist **auf** einer Tagung	*She's at a conference*

bei is a common alternative to *auf* in this sense, but there may be a slight difference in meaning, see 20.2.3b.

(ii) with a few other nouns, where idiomatic usage may differ from English:

Die Schafe sind **auf** der Wiese	*The sheep are in the meadow*
Er ist **auf** seinem Zimmer	*He is (up) in his room*
auf dem Land(e)	*in the country*
Die Kinder spielten **auf** der Straße	*The children were playing in the street*

NB: *in* (+ dat.) is used to refer to a particular street, e.g. *Wir wohnen in der Schillerstraße. Das Unglück ereignete sich in unserer Straße.*

Similarly:

auf dem (Bauern)hof	*on the farm*	auf dem Gang	*in the corridor*
auf ihrer Bude	*in her bedsit*	auf seinem Gut	*on his estate*
auf dem Feld	*in the field*	auf dem Hof	*in the yard*
auf dem Flur	*in the (entrance) hall*	auf der Toilette	*on the toilet*

(iii) with a few nouns denoting public buildings and places. With several of these *auf* is obsolescent, especially in spoken German. In this case, the preposition which is more frequently used nowadays is given in brackets:

auf dem Bahnhof (an)	auf dem Markt(platz)	auf dem Rathaus (in)
auf der Bank (in)	auf der Post	auf der Universität (an)
auf der Bibliothek (in)		

(c) Some idiomatic uses of *auf* **(+ dat.)**

blind auf einem Auge	*blind in one eye*
Das hat nichts, viel auf sich	*There's nothing, a lot to that*

etwas auf dem Herzen haben	*have sth. on one's mind*
Sie liefen auf dem Feld herum	*They were running all over the field*
auf der Jagd sein	*be hunting*
auf der anderen Seite	*on the other hand*
auf der Stelle	*immediately*

20.3.5 *auf* (+ accusative)

(a) *auf* **(+ acc.) indicates direction if the destination is** *auf* **(+ dat)**
i.e. in contexts where the ultimate goal of the person or thing will be a position 'on (top of)' or 'at' something.

(i) *auf* (+ acc.) usually corresponds to English 'on(to)':

Sie legte das Buch **auf** den Tisch	*She put the book on the table*
Die Katze sprang **auf** das Dach	*The cat leapt onto the roof*

(ii) Where German uses *auf* (+ dat.) for English 'at' or 'in', *auf* (+ acc.) usually corresponds to English 'into' or 'to':

Wir gingen **auf** das Feld	*We went into the field*
Er ging **auf** sein Zimmer	*He went (up) to his room*
Er geht **auf** die Toilette	*He's going to the toilet*

This use of *auf* (+ acc.) is rather restricted in modern German. More details are given in 20.5.1b.

(iii) *auf* (+ acc.) . . . *zu* indicates direction (i.e. = 'towards'):

Sie kam **auf** mich **zu**	*She came towards me/approached me*
Sie ging **auf** die Tore des Friedhofs **zu**	*She went towards the cemetery gates*

(b) *auf* **(+ acc.) indicates a period of time extending from 'now'**
e.g. *Ich fahre auf vier Wochen in die Schweiz.* For details see 11.5.2. The prepositional adverb *darauf* is used in the sense of 'after(wards)', see 11.6.4b, e.g. *am Tag darauf* 'the day after'.

NB: *auf* (+ acc.) is similarly used to indicate a distance **from** here, e.g.: *Kurven auf fünf Kilometer* 'bends for 5 kilometres'.

(c) *auf* **(+ acc.) is used after a large number of adjectives and verbs**
e.g.: *Sie ist neidisch auf ihn. Ich wartete vor dem Bahnhof auf sie.* For the use of *auf* with adjectives, see 6.6.1, with verbs in prepositional objects, see 18.6.3a.

(d) *auf* **(+ acc.) can denote 'in response to', 'as a result of'**
In this sense it is often strengthened by a following *hin*, see 7.2.3c:

Auf meine Bitte (**hin**) hat er die Sache für sich behalten	*At my request he kept the matter to himself*
Er hat sofort **auf** meinen Brief **hin** gehandelt	*He acted immediately following my letter*

Similarly:

auf Anfrage	*on application*
auf meine Empfehlung (hin)	*on my recommendation*
auf einen Verdacht hin	*on the strength of a suspicion*

auf Wunsch, auf meinen Wunsch (hin)	*by request, at my request*
daraufhin	*as a result, thereupon*

(e) Other uses of *auf* (+ acc.)
(i) with languages:

Sie hat mir **auf Deutsch** geantwortet	*She answered me in German*

in (+ dat.) is also used, especially with extended phrases:

Er hält seine Vorlesungen **in Deutsch/auf Deutsch**	*He gives his lectures in German*
Er sagte es **in gebrochenem Deutsch**	*He said it in broken German*
Wie heißt das **in Ihrer Sprache**?	*What's that called in your language?*

(ii) to form absolute superlatives, e.g. *aufs angenehmste/Angenehmste*. See 8.4.3 for further details.

(iii) Some common idiomatic expressions with *auf*:

jdn. auf den Arm (S.G.), auf die Schippe (N.G.) nehmen	*pull somebody's leg*
etwas auf die lange Bank schieben	*put sth. off*
auf den ersten Blick	*at first sight*
Das kommt, läuft auf dasselbe hinaus	*It comes down to the same thing*
auf jeden Fall, auf alle Fälle	*in any case*
auf eigene Gefahr	*at one's own risk*
auf eigene Kosten	*at one's own expense*
jdm. auf die Nerven gehen, auf den Wecker gehen, fallen	*get on somebody's nerves*
Das geht auf meine Rechnung	*This one's on me*
auf diese Weise	*in this way*

20.3.6 *entlang*

entlang (often shortened to *lang* in colloquial speech) corresponds to English 'along'. There is much variation in its use, both in respect of the position of the noun and the case used with it.

(a) Indicating POSITION alongside an extended object
The most frequent usage in this meaning is *entlang* followed by a noun phrase in the **dative** case:

im Sommer, wenn **entlang den** Boulevards und in den Vorgärten Rosen blühen (*Zeit*)	*in summer when roses are blooming along the boulevards and in the front gardens*
die Männer, die **entlang der** Küchenwand saßen (*Welt*)	*the men who were sitting along the kitchen wall*
Bäume standen **entlang der** Bahnlinie	*Trees stood along the railway line*

Alternatively, *entlang* is often used in written German with a **following** noun phrase in the **genitive** case to express position:

die Uferpromenade **entlang des** Rheins (*MM*)	*the promenade along the bank of the Rhine*

Very occasionally, *entlang* **follows** a noun phrase in the **dative** or **accusative** case to express position:

die Straße, die Mussolini **der Küste entlang** gebaut hat (*Grzimek*)	*the road which Mussolini built along the coast*
Flaschen und Gläser standen **die lange Tafel entlang** (*Welt*)	*Bottles and glasses were standing along the long table*

(b) Indicating movement alongside an extended object, or down the middle of a road or river

The most frequent usage in this meaning is for *entlang* to **follow** a noun phrase in the **accusative** case:

Gehst du die Reihen der Maschinen **entlang** (*ND*)	*If you walk along the rows of machines*
Sie gingen den Bach **entlang**	*They were walking along the stream*
Sie hastete den Flur **entlang** bis zum Ende des Ganges (*Johnson*)	*She hurried along the entrance hall to the end of the corridor*
Sie laufen die Feldwege **entlang** (*Stritmatter*)	*They are running along the tracks through the fields*

In Swiss usage, *entlang* can **follow** a noun phrase in the **dative** case in this meaning:

Wir flogen gar nicht der Küste **entlang** (*Frisch*)	*We were not flying along the coast at all*

(c) *an* (+ dat.) ... *entlang* is a common alternative to simple *entlang*

It can be used with reference to position or movement alongside an extended object, but not for 'down the middle' of roads, rivers, etc.:

Da gab es **an** der nördlichen Friedhofsmauer **entlang** den Bittweg (*Grass*)	*Along the north wall of the cemetery was the Bittweg*
Er steuerte **am** Ufer **entlang**, bis die Stelle gefunden war (*Frisch*)	*He steered along the bank until he had found the spot*

(d) Alternatives to *entlang* in the meaning 'along'

(i) *längs*, see 20.4.3, only expresses position. It governs a following genitive or (less commonly) a dative, e.g. *längs der Küste, längs des Flusses/dem Fluss*.

(ii) *an* (+ dat.), see 20.3.2a, often appears in contexts where English naturally uses 'along', e.g.:

An der Küste war das Wetter schön	*The weather was fine along the coast*

an (+ dat.) ... *hin* can refer to movement alongside something, especially when one is very close to it or in contact with it:

Sie ging **an der Mauer hin**	*She went along the wall*
Er rutschte **am Boden hin**	*He slid along the floor*

20.3.7 *hinter*

(a) *hinter* is used chiefly with reference to place and usually corresponds to English 'behind'

(i) Used with a following noun phrase in the dative case, *hinter* indicates position:

Der Wagen steht **hinter** der Garage	*The car is behind the garage*
Ich habe das Schlimmste **hinter** mir	*I've got the worst behind me*
100 Kilometer **hinter** der Grenze	*100 kilometres beyond the border*

(ii) Used with a following noun phrase in the accusative case, *hinter* indicates direction:

Er fuhr den Wagen **hinter** die Garage	*He drove the car round the back of the garage*
Sie trieben ihn **hinter** die Kirche	*They drove him round the back of the church*

(b) To indicate movement in relation to another person or thing, *hinter* is used with *her*

See also 7.2.3b. The noun phrase is always in the dative case:

Er rannte **hinter** ihr **her**	*He was running after her*
Ich ging **hinter** meinen Eltern **her**	*I was walking behind my parents*

(c) *hinter* is used in a few idiomatic expressions

Ich konnte nicht dahinter kommen	*I couldn't get to the bottom of it*
Es muss etwas dahinter stecken	*There must be something in it*
Schreib dir das hinter die Ohren!	*Will you get that into your thick head!*

20.3.8 *in* **(+ dative)**

(a) The basic meaning of *in* (+ dat) is 'in(side)'

Sie ist **im** Haus, **im** Freien, **in** der Kirche, **im** Kino, **in** der Stadt, **im** Wald, **im** Tal, **in** ihrem Zimmer	*She is in the house, in the open air, in the church, in the cinema, in town, in the forest, in the valley, in her room*
Sie sind **in** Bremen, **in** Deutschland, **in** der Schweiz, **im** Ausland	*They are in Bremen, in Germany, in Switzerland, abroad*
Die Milch ist **im** Kühlschrank	*The milk is in the fridge*
Die Sonne geht **im** Westen unter	*The sun sets in the west*

NB: In colloquial German *in* is often strengthened by adding *drin*, e.g.: *Die sind **in** der Hütte **drin**.*

In some contexts, German usage is at variance with English, e.g.:

Ihr Büro ist **im** vierten Stock	*Her office is on the fourth floor*
Das habe ich **im** Fernsehen gesehen, **im** Radio gehört	*I saw it on the television, heard it on the radio*

In particular, German uses *in* with reference to attendance at public buildings and the like, where English often uses 'at':

Die Kinder sind heute **in** der Schule	*The children are at school today*
Meine Eltern sind **in** der Kirche	*My parents are at church*
Elke ist **im** Kino, **im** Theater, **in** einem Konzert, **im** Rathaus, **in** der Bibliothek	*Elke is at the cinema, at the theatre, at a concert, at the town hall, at the library*

(b) *in* (+ dat.) indicates a period of time

e.g. *In drei Wochen sind wir wieder da.* Full details are given in 11.5.7.

(c) Some common idiomatic phrases with *in* (+ dat.)

in der Absicht, etwas zu tun	*with the intention of doing something*
im Allgemeinen	*in general*
Ist dein Chef im Bilde?	*Is your boss in the picture?*
im Durchschnitt	*on average*

nicht im Geringsten/Entferntesten   *not in the slightest*
in dieser Hinsicht   *in this respect*
in gewissem Maße   *to a certain extent*
in dieser Weise   *in this way*
  (also: **auf diese** Weise)
in diesem Zusammenhang   *in this context*

20.3.9 *in* (+ accusative)

(a) *in* **(+ acc.) indicates direction if the destination is** *in* **(+ dat.)**
i.e. in contexts where the ultimate goal of the person or thing will be a position 'in(side)' something.

(i) *in* often corresponds to English 'into':

Sie ging **ins** Haus, **in** die Kirche, **in** den Wald, **in** das Tal, **in** ihr Zimmer	*She went into the house, the church, the forest, the valley, her room*
Ich habe die Milch **in** den Kühlschrank gestellt	*I put the milk in the fridge*

NB: With *Richtung* the accusative or the dative case are equally acceptable: *in diese/dieser Richtung*.

(ii) *in* is a common equivalent of English 'to', if, on arrival, one will be in the place concerned, see 20.5.1a:

Sie ging **in** ein Konzert, **ins** Kino, **in** den vierten Stock	*She went to a concert, to the cinema, to the fourth floor*
Wir sind **in** die Schweiz, **ins** Ausland gefahren	*We went to Switzerland, abroad*
Die Kinder gehen heute **in** die Schule	*The children are going to school today*
Die Kinder gehen **in** die Schule	*The children go to school*

(b) Some frequent idiomatic phrases with *in* **(+ acc.):**

Der Vorteil springt ins Auge	*The advantage is obvious*
sich in Bewegung setzen	*begin to move*
mit jdm. ins Gespräch kommen	*get into conversation with sb.*
aus dem Französischen ins Deutsche übersetzen	*translate from French into German*
die Verhandlungen in die Länge ziehen	*drag out the negotiations*

20.3.10 *neben*

(a) *neben* **is most often used with reference to place**
It usually corresponds to English 'next to' or 'beside':

(i) Used with a following dative case, *neben* indicates position:

Die Blumen standen **neben** dem Schrank	*The flowers were next to the cupboard*
Das Geschäft ist **neben** dem Verkehrsverein	*The shop is next to the tourist information office*
Er saß **neben** seiner Frau	*He was sitting next to his wife*

(ii) Used with a following accusative case, *neben* indicates direction. It can be strengthened by adding *hin*, see 7.2.3a:

Er stellte die Blumen **neben** den Schrank (hin)	He put the flowers (down) next to the cupboard
Er setzte sich **neben** seine Frau (hin)	He sat down next to his wife

(b) To indicate relation of movement to another person or thing moving in the same direction, *neben* is used with a following *her*

See also 7.2.3b. The noun phrase is always in the dative case:

Er ging **neben** seiner Frau **her**	He was walking by the side of his wife

(c) *neben* (+ dat.) can be used in the sense of 'besides', 'apart from'

Its sense is close to that of *außer*, see 20.2.2a:

Neben zwei Franzosen waren alle Anwesenden aus Deutschland	Apart from two Frenchmen all those present were from Germany

(d) *neben* (+ dat.) can be used to express a comparison

It is a common alternative to *gegen* or *gegenüber*, see 20.2.4c:

Neben ihrer Mutter ist sie groß	She's tall compared with her mother

(e) The prepositional adverb *daneben* is used with verbs to express the idea of failing to hit a target

daneben is usually interpreted as a separable prefix, see 22.5.2, and written together with the verb:

Er hat danebengeschossen	He shot wide of the mark
Sie hat sich danebenbenommen	She behaved quite abominably

20.3.11 *über* (+ dative)

With a following noun phrase in the dative case, *über* is only used to refer to position. It corresponds to English 'over', 'above' or, in certain contexts, 'across' or 'beyond':

Das Bild hängt **über** meinem Tisch	The picture hangs over my desk
Briançon liegt 1400 Meter **über** dem Meeresspiegel	Briançon lies 1400 metres above sea level
Der Baum lag mir (quer) **über** dem Weg	The tree lay across my path
Er wohnt **über** der Grenze	He lives over/across the border
Sie wohnt **über** dem See	She lives across/beyond the lake

20.3.12 *über* (+ accusative)

(a) *über* (+ acc.) indicates movement over a person or object

über corresponds to English 'above', 'over', 'across' or (with reference to a journey) 'via':

Sie hängte das Bild **über** meinen Tisch	She hung the picture over/above my desk
Wir gingen **über** die Straße	We crossed the road
die neue Brücke **über** den Inn	the new bridge over/across the Inn
Der Baum fiel uns (quer) **über** den Weg	The tree fell across our path
Er ist **über** die Grenze geflüchtet	He fled over the border

Es lief mir eiskalt **über** den Rücken	*An ice-cold shiver went down my back*
Wir sind **über** die Schweiz nach Italien gefahren	*We drove to Italy through Switzerland*
Dieser Zug fährt nach Rostock **über** Potsdam	*This train goes to Rostock via Potsdam*
Der Kaiser herrschte **über** viele Länder	*The emperor ruled over many countries*

If the movement involved is parallel to a surface, *über* (+ acc.) can be strengthened by adding *hin*, see 7.2.3a:

Die Wildenten flogen **über** den See (**hin**)	*The wild ducks were flying over the lake*

(b) *über* (+ acc.) is used in more abstract senses of 'above' or 'beyond'
In the sense of going 'beyond' a limitation *über* can be strengthened by adding *hinaus*:

Diese Aufgabe geht **über** meine Fähigkeiten (**hinaus**)	*This task goes beyond my capabilities*
Er liebt die Ruhe **über** alles	*He likes quiet above all things*
darüber hinaus	*over and above that*

(c) *über* (+ acc.) occurs in a few time expressions in the sense of 'over'
For details, see 11.5.10.

(d) *über* (+ acc.) has the sense of 'over', 'more than' with quantities
e.g. *Es hat über tausend Euro gekostet; Kinder über zehn Jahre*, etc. See 9.1.6 for further details of this usage and the distinction between the adverbial and prepositional usage of *über* with quantities.

(e) *über* (+ acc.) is used in the sense of 'about', 'concerning'

seine Ansicht **über** eine mögliche Wiedervereinigung	*his views concerning a possible reunification*
ein Buch **über** die europäischen Vögelarten	*a book about European bird species*
meine Freude **über** ihren Erfolg	*my delight at her success*
Er beschwerte sich **über** den kaputten Fernsehapparat	*He complained about the broken television set*
Sie war ärgerlich **über** ihn	*She was annoyed at him*

This usage is particularly frequent with nouns, adjectives (see 6.6.1) and in the prepositional object of verbs of saying, etc. (see 18.6.9a).

20.3.13 *unter* (+ dative)

(a) With reference to place, *unter* (+ dat.) corresponds to English 'under(neath)', 'beneath', 'below'

Manfred lag **unter** dem Tisch	*Manfred was lying under(neath) the table*
200 Meter **unter** dem Gipfel	*200 metres below the summit*
Das Land steht **unter** Wasser	*The land is under water*
unter Tage	*below ground/underground* (of miners)

Sie trug die Tasche **unter** dem Arm	*She was carrying her bag under her arm*
unter dem Schutz der Dunkelheit	*under cover of darkness*
unter Zwang handeln	*act under duress*

(b) *unter* (+ dat.) is a common equivalent for English 'among(st)'

Hier bist du **unter** Freunden	*You're among friends here*
Ich fand das Rezept **unter** meinen Papieren	*I found the prescription among my papers*
Es waren viele Ausländer **unter** den Zuschauern	*There were a lot of foreigners among the spectators*
unter uns gesagt	*between ourselves*
unter vier Augen	*in private*
unter anderem (u.a.)	*amongst other things*

zwischen can also correspond to English 'among(st)', see 20.3.17a. It is preferred if *unter* could be understood to mean 'under'. Compare:

Das Haus steht **unter Bäumen**	*The house stands under some trees*
Das Haus steht **zwischen Bäumen**	*The house stands amongst some trees*

(c) *unter* (+ dat.) is used to indicate circumstances

unter diesen Umständen	*under these circumstances*
unter allen Umständen	*in any case*
unter den größten Schwierigkeiten	*with the greatest difficulty*
unter dieser Bedingung	*on this condition*
unter diesem Vorwand	*on this pretext*
Sie starb **unter** großen Schmerzen	*She died in great pain*
Er gestand **unter** Tränen	*He confessed amid tears*
unter Vorspiegelung falscher Tatsachen	*on false pretences*

(d) *unter* (+ dat.) has the sense of 'under', 'below' with reference to quantity

e.g. *Es hat unter tausend Euro gekostet*. See 9.1.6 for further details of this usage and the distinction between the adverbial and prepositional usage of *unter* with quantities.

20.3.14 *unter* (+ accusative)

(a) *unter* (+ acc.) indicates direction if the destination is *unter* (+ dat.)

i.e. where English has 'under(neath)', 'below', 'among':

Manfred kroch **unter** den Tisch	*Manfred crawled under the table*
Sie steckte die Tasche **unter** ihren Arm	*She put her bag under her arm*
Er tauchte den Kopf **unter** das Wasser	*He dipped his head under the water*
Wir gingen **unter** die Brücke hindurch	*We walked under the bridge*
Sie ging **unter** die Menge	*She went among the crowd*

(b) Some common idiomatic expressions with *unter* (+ acc.)

jdn. **unter** die Arme greifen	*come to sb.'s assistance*
sein Licht **unter** den Scheffel stellen	*hide one's light under a bushel*
etwas **unter** den Tisch fallen lassen	*let sth. go by the board*

20.3.15 vor (+ dative)

(a) With reference to place, vor (+ dat.) means 'in front of', 'ahead of'

Das Auto steht **vor** der Garage	The car is in front of the garage
Der Himalaja lag **vor** uns	The Himalayas lay before us
Der Nashorn hatte ein paar Meter **vor** dem Wagen gestoppt (*Grzimek*)	The rhinoceros had stopped within a few feet of the car
vor ihm in einiger Entfernung	some distance ahead of him
vor Gericht erscheinen	appear in court
Die Insel liegt **vor** der deutschen Ostseeküste	The island lies off the Baltic coast of Germany

(b) To indicate relation of movement to another person or thing moving in the same direction, vor (+ dat.) is used with her
See also 7.2.3b:

Vor uns **her** fuhr ein roter BMW	A red BMW was driving along ahead of us

(c) vor is used in time expressions with the sense of 'ago' or 'before'
e.g. *vor zwei Jahren, vor Weihnachten*. For details, see 11.5.13.

(d) vor can be used to indicate cause or reason
In this sense, *vor* (+ dat.) normally occurs without a following article:

Man konnte **vor** Lärm nichts hören	You couldn't hear anything for the noise
Ich war außer mir **vor** Wut	I was beside myself with rage
Ich konnte **vor** Aufregung nicht einschlafen	I couldn't get to sleep with the excitement
Vor Nebel war nichts zu sehen	You couldn't see anything for the fog
Sie gähnte **vor** Langeweile	She yawned from boredom
Sie warnte mich **vor** dem Hund	She warned me of the dog
blass **vor** Furcht, gelb **vor** Neid	pale with fear, green with envy

In contrast to *aus*, see 20.2.1c, which points to a voluntary cause or reason, *vor* (+ dat.) always expresses a cause which is involuntary. This use of *vor* (+ dat.) is very common with adjectives, see 6.6.1, and in the prepositional object of verbs, see 18.6.12.

20.3.16 vor (+ accusative)

(a) vor (+ acc.) indicates if the destination is vor (+ dat.)

Ich fuhr den Wagen **vor** die Garage	I drove up in front of the garage
Sie stellte sich **vor** mich	She stood in front of me
Alle traten **vor** den Vorhang	Everyone stepped out in front of the curtain
Die Sache kommt **vor** Gericht	The case is coming to court

(b) vor sich hin means 'to oneself'
See 7.2.5, e.g.:

Sie las **vor** sich **hin**	She was reading to herself
Ich murmelte etwas **vor** mich **hin**	I muttered something to myself

20.3.17 *zwischen*

(a) *zwischen* **is used with reference to place or time in the sense of English 'between'**

(i) *zwischen* (+ dat.) indicates position:

Ich saß **zwischen** dem Minister und seiner Frau	*I was sitting between the minister and his wife*
Das Geschäft liegt **zwischen** dem Kino und der Post	*The shop is between the cinema and the post office*
Die Tagung fand **zwischen** dem 4. und dem 11. Oktober statt	*The conference took place between the 4th and the 11th of October*
zwischen den Zeilen lesen	*read between the lines*

zwischen can also correspond to English 'among(st)' if more than two objects are involved:

Pilze wuchsen **zwischen** den Bäumen	*Toadstools were growing among(st) the trees*

NB: See 20.3.13b for the distinction between *unter* and *zwischen* to mean 'among'.

(ii) *zwischen* (+ acc.) indicates direction:

Ich setzte mich **zwischen** den Minister und seine Frau	*I sat down between the minister and his wife*
Wir legen die Tagung **zwischen** den 4. und den 11. Oktober	*We are putting the conference between the 4th and the 11th of October*

(b) To indicate relation of movement to another person or thing moving in the same direction, *zwischen* (+ dat.) is used with *her*
See also 7.2.3b. The noun phrase is always in the dative case:

Ich ging **zwischen** meinen Eltern **her**	*I was walking between my parents*

(c) *zwischen* (+ dat.) has the sense of 'between' with reference to quantity
e.g. *Kinder zwischen dem 10. und dem 15. Lebensjahr.* See 9.1.6 for further details of this usage and the distinction between the adverbial and prepositional usage of *zwischen* with expressions of quantity.

20.4 Prepositions governing the genitive case

The prepositions governing the genitive fall into three main groups:

(i) four common prepositions, dealt with in 20.4.1:

(an)statt	trotz	während	wegen

These are normally used with the genitive case in formal German, but are often found with a dative case in colloquial speech.

(ii) eight prepositions expressing place relationships, see 20.4.2:

außerhalb	oberhalb	diesseits	unweit
innerhalb	unterhalb	jenseits	
		beid(er)seits	

These are often used with a following *von* rather than a genitive.

(iii) a large number of prepositions with rather specialised meanings which are hardly used outside very formal (often official) registers. They are listed and explained in 20.4.3.

20.4.1 The four common prepositions which govern the genitive

(a) (an)statt 'instead of'

(i) Examples of the use of *(an)statt*:

Statt eines Fernsehers hat sie sich eine neue Stereoanlage gekauft	*Instead of a television she bought herself a new stereo system*
Statt eines Briefes schickte er ihr eine Postkarte	*Instead of a letter he sent her a postcard*
statt dessen	*instead (of that)*

(ii) *(an)statt* can be used as a conjunction rather than a preposition, i.e. as an alternative to *und nicht*. In this construction the noun or pronoun has the same case as the noun or pronoun immediately preceding *(an)statt* with which it is linked:

Ich besuchte meinen Onkel **statt** (= und nicht) meinen Bruder	*I visited my uncle instead of my brother*
Ihr Haus hat sie mir **statt** (= und nicht) ihm vermacht	*She left her house to me instead of to him*

(an)statt is always used in this way if it links prepositional phrases or personal pronouns:

Ich schreibe jetzt mit einem Filzstift **statt** mit einem Füller	*I write with a felt-tip now instead of with a fountain pen*

(iii) *anstelle von* is a common alternative to *(an)statt*. It often sounds less stilted:

Wir gebrauchen jetzt Margarine **anstelle von** Butter	*We use margarine instead of butter now*

NB: (i) The longer form *anstatt* is less frequent; it occurs chiefly in formal written German.
(ii) For infinitive phrases with *(an)statt . . . zu* and the conjunction *(an)statt dass* see 13.2.7c.

(b) trotz 'despite', 'in spite of'

Wir sind am Sonntag **trotz** des starken Regens nach Eulbach gewandert	*We walked to Eulbach on Sunday despite the heavy rain*

(c) während 'during'
e.g. *während des Sommers* 'during the summer'. Details on the use of *während* are given in 11.5.14.

(d) wegen 'because of', 'for the sake of'
(i) *wegen* normally precedes the noun it governs, but it sometimes follows in very formal registers:

Wir konnten **wegen** des Regens nicht kommen	*We couldn't come because of the rain*
Er musste **wegen** zu schnellen Fahrens eine Geldstrafe bezahlen	*He had to pay a fine because he had been driving too fast*

> Er wich jeder Schafherde aus, nicht
> der Schafe **wegen**, sondern um den
> Geruch der Hirten zu umgehen
> (*Süßkind*)

> *He kept away from all the flocks of sheep,*
> *not because of the sheep, but to*
> *avoid the smell of the shepherds*

(ii) *wegen* is sometimes used in the sense of 'about', 'concerning':

> **Wegen** deiner Reise muss ich noch mit
> Astrid sprechen

> *I've still got to talk to Astrid about*
> *your trip*

(iii) The combination *von* (+ gen.) ... *wegen* occurs in a few set phrases:

> von Amts wegen   *ex officio*
> von Berufs wegen   *by virtue of one's profession*
> von Rechts wegen   *legally, by rights*

(iv) The combination *von wegen* (+ dat.) is common in colloquial German to mean 'because of' or 'concerning'. It is regarded as substandard:

> Jetzt hört mir nur auf **von wegen**
> Idealismus (*Valentin*)

> *For goodness' sake stop talking about*
> *idealism*

It is very frequent in isolation to challenge a previous statement:

> Also, heute Abend bezahlst du alles –
> **Von wegen!**

> *So, you're paying for everything tonight –*
> *No way!*

NB: For the forms of personal pronouns with *wegen* (*meinetwegen, ihretwegen*, etc.), see 3.1.2c.

(e) The use of (*an*)*statt, trotz, während* and *wegen* with a dative
Although these prepositions are normally followed by a noun phrase in the genitive case in standard German, in certain conditions they are used with a following noun phrase in the dative case.

(i) They are very commonly used with a following dative in everyday colloquial speech. This reflects the general avoidance of the genitive in informal registers, see 2.3:

> Ich konnte **wegen dem Regen** nicht kommen
> **Während dem Mittagessen** hat sie uns etwas über ihren Urlaub erzählt

(ii) They are more often used with a following dative in written Swiss usage, e.g.:
*Die Koalition wird deshalb vorerst wahrscheinlich trotz **dem neuerlichen Scheitern** überleben* (NZZ).

(iii) Although the use of the dative case with these prepositions is generally considered substandard in written usage in Germany, it is accepted (or at least tolerated) in a number of constructions, i.e.:

- if they are followed by a plural noun which is not accompanied by a declined determiner or adjective: *während fünf **Jahren**, wegen ein paar **Hindernissen***
- if the noun they govern is preceded by a possessive genitive: *während Vaters **kurzem Urlaub**, wegen des ehemaligen Bundeskanzlers **langem Schweigen***

- to avoid the use of the genitive of the personal pronouns, see 3.1.2: *Langsam fahren – wegen uns!* (on a road sign outside a Kindergarten)
- to avoid consecutive genitives in *-(e)s*, see 2.4.2a: ***trotz dem Rollen*** *des Zuges* (Th. Mann)
- if the following noun has no determiner with it: *trotz Geldmangel(s), wegen Amtsmissbrauch(s)*
- to achieve a particular stylistic effect: *Freies Denken **statt starrem Lenken*** (election slogan)
- a relative pronoun with these prepositions can be in the dative: *seit dem Ende des Zweiten Weltkriegs, während **dem** die Stadt Salzburg zahlreiche Bombenangriffe erleiden musste* (Baedeker)

20.4.2 The eight prepositions denoting position

(a) Meaning and use

(i) *außerhalb* 'outside' and *innerhalb* 'inside', 'within' can be used with reference to place or time:

Sie wohnt **außerhalb** der Stadt	*She lives outside the city*
Das liegt **außerhalb/innerhalb** meines Fachgebietes	*That lies outside/within my specialist field*
Das kann sie **außerhalb** der Arbeitszeit erledigen	*She can finish that outside working hours*
Das wird **innerhalb** eines Jahres geändert werden	*That will be changed within a year*

NB: (i) *außerhalb* and *innerhalb* only denote position. Compare *Wir gingen aus der Hütte hinaus, in die Hütte hinein* 'We went outside, inside the hut'.
(ii) Like *binnen* (see 20.2.10b), *innerhalb* can be used to avoid any potential ambiguity with *in*, see 11.5.7c.

(ii) *oberhalb* 'above' and *unterhalb* 'below', 'underneath' refer to position and are more specific in meaning than *über* and *unter*:

Oberhalb der Straße war ein Felsenvorsprung	*Above the road there was a rocky ledge*
Ich habe mich **unterhalb** des Knies verletzt	*I injured myself below the knee*
der Rhein **oberhalb/unterhalb** der Stadt Basel	*the Rhine above/below the city of Basle*

(iii) *beid(er)seits* 'on either side of', *diesseits* 'on this side of', *jenseits* 'beyond', 'on the other side of':

in den Bauten **beidseits** des Flusses (FR)	*in the buildings on either side of the river*
diesseits, jenseits der niederländischen Grenze	*on this side, the other side of the Dutch border*

NB: *hinter* is more commonly used for 'beyond' than *jenseits*, especially in everyday German, e.g. *Das Dorf liegt hinter der Grenze, hinter Hannover*.

(iv) *unweit* 'not far from'

Wir standen auf einer Höhe **unweit** des Dorfes	*We were standing on a hill not far from the village*

NB: *unfern*, with the same meaning as *unweit*, is now obsolete. It could be used with the genitive or the dative case.

(b) All these prepositions are often used with *von* rather than the genitive
(i) This usage is usual in colloquial speech, but it is quite common in writing, too, although many Germans feel the genitive to be more appropriate in formal registers:

> Sie wohnt **außerhalb von** der Stadt
> **Innerhalb von** einem Jahr wir alles anders werden
> **Jenseits von** der Grenze standen vier Vopos
> ein Dorf **unweit von** Moskau (*Bednarz*)

(ii) The use of *von* is the norm even in written German in those contexts where the common prepositions taking the genitive are commonly used with the dative case (see 20.4.1e), e.g. *innerhalb **von** fünf Jahren*. A following relative pronoun is also often in the dative, e.g. *die Zone, innerhalb **der*** (less commonly: *derer*) *Autos verboten sind*.

20.4.3 Other prepositions governing the genitive

The large number of other prepositions with the genitive are effectively limited to use in formal written German, the majority in official and commercial language. Outside this register, they can sound very stilted. Many of them were originally adverbs, participles or phrases which have fairly recently come to be used as prepositions, and similar new ones are constantly entering the language. With this proviso, the following list is as complete as possible.

NB: The asterisked prepositions are used with a following dative case in the same contexts as the common preposi-
    tions, see 20.4.1e.

abseits *away from*
    eine Speisekarte abseits jeglicher Tradition (*Presse*)
***abzüglich** *deducting, less*:
    abzüglich der Unkosten
anfangs *at the beginning of*:
    anfangs dieses Jahres (or with the acc.: *anfangs nächsten Monat*)
angesichts *in view of*:
    angesichts der gegenwärtigen massenhaften Auswanderung von DDR-Bürgern
    (*Spiegel*)
anhand (also **an Hand**) *with the aid of, from*:
    anhand einiger Beispiele
anlässlich *on the occasion of*:
    anlässlich seines siebzigsten Geburtstages
anstelle (also **an Stelle**) *in place of, instead of*:
    anstelle einer Antwort (in speech often *anstelle **von***)
aufgrund (also **auf Grund**) *on the strength of*:
    aufgrund seiner juristischen Ausbildung (in speech often *aufgrund von*)
***ausschließlich** *exclusive of*
    die Miete ausschließlich der Heizungskosten
ausweislich *according to*
    Im Lesen sind die Deutschen ausweislich dieser Studie keineswegs Spitze (*SZ*)

behufs *for the purpose of*
  behufs einer Verhandlung
betreffs, bezüglich *with regard to*
  betreffs, bezüglich Ihres Angebotes
eingangs *at the beginning of*
  eingangs dieses Jahres
eingedenk *bearing in mind* (It may precede **or** follow the noun)
  eingedenk seiner beruflichen Fehlschläge
*****einschließlich** *including*
  einschließlich der Angehörigen (*SZ*)
*****exklusive** *excluding*
  exklusive Versandkosten
fernab *far from*
  fernab des Lärms der Städte
gelegentlich *on the occasion of*
  gelegentlich seines Besuches
halber (following the noun) *for the sake of*
  der Wahrheit halber

> NB: (i) *halber* is compounded with a few nouns to form adverbs, e.g. *sicherheitshalber* 'for safety's sake', *vorsichtshalber* 'as a precaution'.
> (ii) When used with pronouns *halber* appears as *-halben* and is compounded with forms of the pronoun in *-t*, e.g. *meinethalben* 'for my sake' 'for all me', see 3.1.1c.

hinsichtlich *with regard to*
  hinsichtlich Ihrer Anfrage
infolge *as a result of*
  infolge der neuen Steuergesetze (often with *von*: *infolge von den Steuergesetzen*)
*****inklusive** *including*
  inklusive Bedienung
inmitten *in the middle of*
  inmitten üppiger Blütenpracht (*HA*)
kraft *in virtue of*
  kraft seines Amtes
längs *along(side)*
  längs des Flusses (less frequently: *längs dem Fluss*)
links *on/to the left of*
  links der Donau
*****mangels** *for want of*
  Freispruch mangels Beweises
*****mittels** *by means of*
  mittels eines gefälschten Passes
namens *in the name of*
  Ich möchte Sie namens unseres Betriebes einladen
ob *on account of*
  die Besorgnisse des sowjetischen Staatspräsidenten ob der deutschen Frage (*Zeit*)
rechts *to/on the right of*
  rechts der Isar
seitens *on the part of*
  seitens der Bezirksverwaltung

seitlich *to/at the side of*
  seitlich der Hauptstraße
um ... willen *for the sake of*
  um meiner Mutter willen
> NB: *um ... willen* forms compounds with special forms of the personal pronouns, e.g. *um meinetwillen*, see
> 3.1.1c.

unbeschadet *regardless of* (It may precede **or** follow the noun)
  Heute ist London das kulturelle Zentrum der Welt, unbeachtet des Außen-
  handelsdefizits und des kränklichen Pfund Sterling (*Zeit*)
ungeachtet *notwithstanding* (It can precede **or** follow the noun)
  ungeachtet unserer üblichen Skepsis (*Dönhoff*)
vermöge *by dint of*
  vermöge seines unermüdlichen Fleißes
vorbehaltlich *subject to*
  vorbehaltlich seiner Zustimmung
zeit *during* (only used in set phrases with *das Leben*)
  zeit seines Lebens
zugunsten (*also* **zu Gunsten**) *for the benefit of*
  eine Sammlung zugunsten/zu Gunsten der Opfer des Faschismus
zuungunsten (*also* **zu Ungunsten**) *to the disadvantage of*
  Die Luftanschläge haben die Gegebenheiten auf dem Terrain zuungunsten/zu
  Ungunsten der bosnischen Serben geändert (*NZZ*)
*zuzüglich *plus*
  Es kostet 2000 Euro zuzüglich der Versandkosten
*zwecks *for the purpose of*
  Er besuchte sie zwecks einer gründlichen Erörterung der Situation

20.5 German equivalents for English 'to'

English 'to' has a number of possible German equivalents depending on context, and the use of each of these is summarised here. Fuller details and further
examples can be found in earlier sections under the relevant German prepositions.

20.5.1 *an, auf* or *in* (+ accusative) are frequent equivalents for 'to'

The choice between *an, auf* or *in* with a noun phrase in the accusative case to mean
'to' depends on which of these prepositions would be used with the dative to
express position 'in' or 'at' the place concerned after you arrive. Thus:

**(a) *in* (+ accusative) is used for going 'to' places which one will then be
inside, i.e. (*in* + dative)**

> Sie ging **ins** Büro, **ins** Dorf, **ins** Kino, **in** die Kirche, **in** ein Museum, **ins** Restaurant,
> **in** die Schule, **in** die Stadt, **in** den Zoo, etc.

In this way, *Ich gehe in die Kirche* means 'I am going to church' in the sense of going in to a service. If one is just going up to the church, one says *Ich gehe an die Kirche* or *Ich gehe zur Kirche*.

(b) *auf* **(+ accusative) is used for going 'to' certain places and events, presence 'at' which is indicated by** *auf* **(+ dative)**
(i) The use of *auf* is fixed with a number of nouns:

Die Schafe gingen **auf** die Wiese	*The sheep went into the meadow*
Wir fuhren **aufs** Land	*We went into the countryside*
Die Kinder gingen **auf** die Straße	*The children went into the street*

Similarly:

auf den Berg	*up the mountain*	auf sein Gut	*to his estate*
auf den (Bauern)hof	*to the farm*	auf den Hof	*into the yard*
auf ihre Bude	*to her bedsit*	auf die Jagd gehen	*go hunting*
auf den Flur	*into the hall*	auf die Toilette	*to the toilet*
auf den Gang	*into the corridor*		

With all these, *auf* (+ dative) is used to denote presence 'in' or 'on' them, see 20.3.4b.

(ii) *auf* (+ accusative) is also sometimes used for going 'to' formal occasions (e.g. weddings, conferences, parties, etc.):

Sie ging **auf** einen Empfang, **auf** eine Hochzeit, **auf** eine Party, **auf** eine Tagung.

Although *auf* (+ dative) is still used to denote presence 'at' such functions, see 20.3.4b, *zu* is now more usual than *auf* (+ acc.) to express going 'to' them, especially in less formal registers.

(iii) *auf* (+ accusative) is used for going 'to' certain public buildings:

Sie ging **auf** den Bahnhof, **auf** die Bank, **auf** die Bibliothek, **auf** die Post, **auf** das Rathaus, **auf** die Universität

With many of these words, *auf* occurs chiefly in more formal registers (see 20.3.4b and 20.3.5a). *zu* is regularly used in its place, although *an* (+ accusative) is frequent with *Universität*.

(c) *an* **expresses direction 'to' a precise spot or objects which extend lengthways (i.e. rivers, shores, etc.)**
an expresses movement to a point adjacent to the object concerned. One is then *an* (+ dative) that point, i.e. 'at' it, see 20.3.2a. Examples:

Er ging **an den** Tisch → Er steht an dem Tisch
Sie kam **an die** Bushaltestelle → Sie traf ihn an der Haltestelle
Sie ging **an die** Grenze → An der Grenze wurde kontrolliert
Wir fahren **ans** Meer → Wir verbringen unseren Urlaub am Meer

Similarly:

Er eilte **ans** Fenster	Er ging **an** die Kasse
Wir kamen **an** die Front	Sie ging **ans** Ufer

Sie geht **ans** Mikrophon, **an** ihren Platz, **an** die Straßenkreuzung, **an** die Tür, **an** die Tafel, **an** die Stelle, wo der Tote aufgefunden wurde

Sie gingen **an** den Fluss, **an** die Mosel, **an** den Strand, **an** den See, **an** die Theke, **an** den Zaun

20.5.2 *zu* commonly has the meaning of English 'to'

(a) *zu* **is used in many contexts in place of the more precise prepositions** *an,* *auf* **and** *in*

(see 20.5.1). It is rather vaguer than these three prepositions and tends to emphasise general direction rather than reaching the objective. It is particularly frequent in colloquial registers.

(i) *zu* is used rather than *in* if one is just going up to the place involved (but not necessarily going inside), or to emphasise the general direction rather than reaching the place:

Ich ging **zum** neuen Kino und wartete auf ihn
Die Straßenbahn fährt **zum** Zoo

(ii) *zu* is in practice more common than *auf* in current (especially informal) usage with reference to functions and public buildings:

Er geht **zu** einem Empfang, **zu** einer Tagung, **zu** einer Party
Wir gehen **zum** Bahnhof, **zur** Bank, **zur** Post, **zum** Rathaus, **zur** Universität

(iii) *zu* can be used rather than *an* if the emphasis is on general direction rather than arriving adjacent to the place concerned:

Ich begleitete sie **zur** Fabrik   Er ging **zum** Fenster, **zur** Tür
Sie ging **zu** ihrem Platz   Er schlenderte **zur** Theke

(b) *zu* **is always used with reference to people**
i.e. going up to someone, or to their house or shop

Sie ging **zu** ihrem Onkel, **zu** ihrer Freundin
Er ging **zu** Fleischers, **zu** seinem Chef
Wir gehen **zum** Bäcker frische Semmeln kaufen

20.5.3 Equivalents for English 'to' with geographical names

(a) *nach* **is used with neuter names of continents, countries and towns which are used without an article**

Wir fahren **nach** Amerika, **nach** Frankreich, **nach** Duisburg (see 20.2.6a)

(b) *in* **(+ accusative) is used with names of countries, etc. which are used with an article**

Most of these are feminine, but a few are masculine, neuter or plural, see 4.4.1:

Sie reist morgen **in** die Schweiz, **in** den Jemen (or **nach** Jemen), **in** das Elsass, **in** die USA

(c) Various prepositions are used with other geographical names

In particular *in, an* or *auf* (+ acc.) are used in the same way as with other nouns, see 20.5.1, depending on whether one will be *in, an* or *auf* (+ dat.) on arrival:

> Wir fahren **in** die Alpen, **in** den Harz
> Wir gingen **auf** den Feldberg, **auf** die Jungfrau
> Wir wollen im Sommer **an** den Bodensee, **an** die Riviera fahren

21

Word order

German **word order is different to English** and it has a different role in determining how sentences are constructed. English uses word order to identify the subject and the object(s) of the verb. In English, the SUBJECT must come first, before the verb, and the OBJECTS after it, in the order indirect object + direct object. In a sentence like

> *My father lent our neighbour the old lawnmower*

we cannot move the elements round without saying something quite different: *Our neighbour lent my father the old lawnmower* has another meaning. In German, various permutations are possible without changing the essential meaning:

(i)   **Mein Vater** hat *unserem Nachbarn den alten Rasenmäher* geliehen
(ii)   *Unserem Nachbarn* hat **mein Vater** *den alten Rasenmäher* geliehen
(iii) *Den alten Rasenmäher* hat **mein Vater** *unserem Nachbarn* geliehen
(iv) **Mein Vater** hat *den alten Rasenmäher unserem Nachbarn* geliehen

In German it is the **case endings,** not the word order, which tell us **who is doing what to whom**, i.e. what is the subject and what are the objects. The order of the words and phrases can be changed round to give a different emphasis to the elements without altering the basic meaning. Sentence (iv), for example, stresses who is being lent the lawnmower. In German, the position of the verb is relatively fixed, and the other elements can be moved in order to show different emphases.

Nevertheless, the various elements do tend to come in a particular order – but this is a tendency rather than a rule of grammar. This chapter shows first this 'neutral' basic order, and then how it can be varied to give a different emphasis:

- the **three basic clause structures**, with the finite verb in different positions (section 21.1)
- the use of **first position** in main clauses to highlight an important element (section 21.2)
- the position of the **other elements** in the clause (sections 21.3–21.8)
  - the position of **pronouns** (section 21.4)
  - the position of **noun subject** and **objects** (section 21.5)
  - the position of **adverbials** (section 21.6)
  - the position of *nicht* and other negative elements (section 21.7)
  - the position of other verb **complements** (section 21.8)
  - placing elements **after the verb** at the end of the clause (section 21.9)

Although we usually speak of '**word** order', what is involved is often a **phrase** of some kind rather than a single word. For example, time adverbials tend to come in a particular place whether they are single words, like *heute* or phrases like *den ganzen Tag* or *am kommenden Dienstag*. In order to cover these possibilities, we refer to these segments of the clause as **elements**. In German they are called *Satzglieder*.

21.1 Clause structure and the position of the verb

The basic feature of German word order is that the various parts of the verb have a fixed position in the clause.

21.1.1 The three basic clause structures of German

There are three clause types in German which differ in the place of the finite verb:

- (i) main clause statements: *Petra **kommt** aus Erfurt*
  The finite verb is the **second** element
- (ii) questions and commands: ***Kommt** Petra aus Erfurt?* *Grundform*
  The finite verb is the **first** element
- (iii) subordinate clauses: *Ich weiß, dass Petra aus Erfurt **kommt***
  The finite verb is the **last** element

(a) Main clause statements: the finite verb is the SECOND element

Only **one** element, whether it is a single word, a phrase, or a whole clause, can normally come before the finite verb in main clauses (see 21.2). All other parts of the verb, i.e. infinitives, past participles or separable prefixes, are placed at the end of the clause:

Initial position	Verb¹	Other elements	Verb²
Helga	kommt	eben aus der Bäckerei	
Morgen	muss	ich mit dem Zug nach Trier	fahren
Dann	blickte	sie zum Fenster	hinaus
In der Stadt	habe	ich eine neue CD	gekauft
Als er klein war,	hat	er oft mit Werner	gespielt

Noun clauses with *dass* omitted (see 19.2.1b) have the same structure as main clause statements: *Sie glaubt, **sie hat ihn gestern in der Stadt gesehen**.*

NB: (i) Exceptions to the rule that the finite verb must be the second element are explained in 21.2.1c.
    (ii) The order of infinitives and participles at the end of the clause when there is more than one of these is explained in 21.1.3.

(b) Questions and commands: the finite verb is the FIRST element

As in main clause statements, any other parts of the verb are in final position. In some questions, the verb is preceded by an interrogative (e.g. *was, was für ein* ..., etc.):

w-word	Verb¹	Other elements	Verb²
	Kommt	sie bald?	
	Musst	du schon	gehen?
	Hat	dich Peter schon	gesprochen?
	Fangen	Sie sofort	an!
	Pass	doch an der Kreuzung	auf!
Was	hast	du da schon wieder	angestellt?
Welches Buch	sollen	wir zuerst	lesen?
Was für eine Stadt	ist	Bochum?	

Conditional clauses with no *wenn* (see 16.5.3a), and comparative clauses introduced simply by *als*, see 16.7.1a, have a similar structure, with the finite verb in first position, e.g.: ***Hätte ich Zeit**, so würde ich gern mit Ihnen nach Italien fahren; Es war mir, **als wäre ich** hoch in der Luft.*

(c) Subordinate clauses: the finite verb is the FINAL element

The clause is introduced by a conjunction in first position, see Chapter 19. Other parts of the verb come immediately before the finite verb at the end of the clause (see 21.1.3):

Conjunction	Other elements	Verb²	Verb¹
weil	ich gestern krank		war
(der Mann), **der**	in der Ecke allein		steht
ob	sie eine neue Bluse	gekauft	hat?
dass	er den Brief sofort	tippen	soll
dass	er morgen		kommt
	den Besen in die Ecke		zu stellen
ohne	ihrem Freund	helfen	zu können

As the table shows, non-finite clauses with an infinitive with *zu* (see 13.2.1) have a similar structure to that of other subordinate clauses, with the verb last (although there is not necessarily a conjunction at the beginning of the clause). Clauses with participles follow the same pattern, with the verb last: ***Den Schildern folgend**, fanden sie das Krankenhaus* (Walser); *eine Betonburg, **wie von einem anderen Stern in diesen Wald gefallen*** (Walser).

NB: Exclamations introduced by an interrogative word may have the form of questions **or** subordinate clauses, e.g.: *Wie der Chef darüber geschimpft hat!* **or**: *Wie hat der Chef darüber geschimpft!*

21.1.2 The 'verbal bracket'

A typical feature of German is that most elements in the clause are sandwiched between the various parts of the verb in main clauses, or between the conjunction and the parts of the verb in subordinate clauses. This construction is known as the 'verbal bracket'. This bracket forms a framework for German clauses, and the order of all the other elements in the clause can be described in relation to it:

Vorfeld

Initial position	Bracket¹ [	Other elements *Mittelfeld*	Bracket²]
Heute	darf	sie mit uns ins Kino	kommen
Ich	habe	sie zufällig in der Stadt	gesehen
Ich	komme	morgen gegen zwei Uhr noch einmal	vorbei
Darf	sie heute mit uns ins Kino		kommen?
Hast	du sie zufällig in der Stadt		gesehen?
Komm	doch morgen gegen zwei Uhr noch einmal		vorbei
...,	ob	sie heute mit uns ins Kino	kommen darf?
...,	weil	ich sie heute zufällig in der Stadt	gesehen habe
...,	dass	du morgen gegen zwei Uhr noch einmal	vorbeikommst

More examples of verbal brackets can be seen in the tables in 21.1.1. The construction has some characteristic features:

(i)   In main clauses there is only **one element** in initial position before the first 'bracket' formed by the verb. This position is called the *Vorfeld* in German; its function is explained in 21.2.

(ii) All other elements (and this means all elements in questions, commands and subordinate clauses) are positioned within the bracket. In German, this is called the *Mittelfeld*. As the examples above show, the order of elements in the *Mittelfeld* is exactly the same for all clause types. The order of elements within it is explained in 21.3 to 21.8.

(iii) Under certain conditions elements can be placed after the closing bracket, i.e. after the part of the verb which is at the end, e.g. *Ich rufe an **aus London**; Hat sie dich angerufen **aus London?**; Ich weiß, dass sie dich angerufen hat **aus London**.* This position is called the *Nachfeld* in German. Its use is explained in section 21.9.

21.1.3 The order of verbs at the end of the clause

If there is more than one part of the verb at the end of the clause, the order of these is fixed.

(a) In main clause statements, questions and commands the auxiliary verb comes after the main verb

Initial	Finite verb	Other elements	Main verb	Auxiliary verb
Ich	werde	es ihr doch	sagen	müssen
Sie	hat	ihn voriges Jahr	schwimmen	gelernt
	Ist	dir das schon	erklärt	worden?
	Soll	dieser Brief heute noch	geschrieben	werden?

(b) In subordinate clauses the finite verb usually follows all infinitives and participles
The main verb comes before the infinitive or past participle of an auxiliary verb:

Conjunction	Other elements	Main verb	Auxiliary	Finite verb
Da	ich sie zufällig	gesehen		habe,...
..., dass	er mir das Geld	leihen		wird
..., dass	sie mit uns ins Kino	gehen		darf
..., wie	sie den Brief	fallen		ließ
(das Haus), das	sie	verkaufen		sollte
..., dass	mir das schon	erklärt	worden	ist
(das Haus), das	heute noch	verkauft	werden	muss

However, if there are two infinitives at the end of the clause (the 'double infinitive' construction, see 13.3.2), the finite verb comes before them both:

Conjunction	Other elements	Finite verb	Main verb	Auxiliary
(Ich weiß), dass	ich es bald	werde	erledigen	müssen
(der Brief), den	sie	hat	fallen	lassen
..., weil	er die Probleme	soll	lösen	können
(das Haus), das	sie	hätte	verkaufen	sollen
..., dass	Paul ihn	hat	kommen	hören

NB: (i) In Austrian usage, the finite verb is often placed **between** the main verb and the auxiliary: *der Brief, den sie fallen **hat** lassen.*

(ii) This rule only applies with *lassen, hören* and *sehen* **if** the infinitive is substituting for a past participle (see 13.3.2). Otherwise, the finite verb is placed at the end of the clause *Weil Norwegen die Isländer in einem Stück internationalen Gewässers nicht fischen lassen **will**, ...* (Presse).

21.1.4 Coordinated clauses have the same structure

Coordinated clauses are linked by a coordinating conjunction such as *aber*, *oder* or *und* (see 19.1).

(a) In coordinated main clauses, the verb is in second position in both

> Zu Hause **schreibt** Mutter Briefe und Vater **arbeitet** im Garten
> Am Abend **blieb** ich in meinem Zimmer, aber ich **konnte** nicht arbeiten
> Du **kannst** mit uns ins Kino kommen oder du **kannst** zu deiner Freundin gehen

If the subject of clauses linked by *sondern* or *und* is identical, it can be omitted ('understood'):

> Wir **gingen** nicht ins Kino, sondern **arbeiteten** im Garten
> Jürgen **kam** um vier Uhr in Soest an und **ging** sofort zu seiner Tante

However, if the second clause has another element in initial position, the subject **must** be inserted again after the verb and cannot be omitted. This is different from English, where the subject can still be understood even if another element comes before the verb. Compare:

> Ich schrieb ein paar Briefe und dann   *I wrote a few letters and then went to my*
>   ging **ich** zu meiner Tante   *aunt's*

If an element other than the subject comes in initial position, before the verb, it can be left out (and taken as understood) in following coordinated clauses. The following clauses begin with the verb, and the subject is repeated after it. This stresses that the initial element applies equally to all the clauses:

> **Schon im April** demonstrierten die   *As early as April the farmers*
>   Bauern, blockierten **sie** Straßen in   *demonstrated, blocked streets in East*
>   Ost-Berlin und protestierten **sie** vor   *Berlin and protested in front of the*
>   der Volkskammer (*Zeit*)   *Volkskammer*
> (*Schon im April* is here taken to apply to **all three** coordinated clauses)

However, if no need is felt to emphasise that the initial phrase also applies to the second clause, the subject is placed before the second verb. In practice this is more usual, especially outside formal written German:

> Am Abend blieb ich zu Hause und   *That night I stayed at home and my sister*
>   **meine Schwester ging** ins Kino   *went to the cinema*

(b) In parallel subordinate clauses linked by coordinating conjunctions the verb is in final position

> Ich weiß, dass sie gestern krank **war**   *I know that she was ill yesterday and that*
>   und dass ihr Mann deswegen zu   *her husband stayed at home because of*
>   Hause geblieben **ist**   *that*
> Wenn deine Familie dagegen **ist** oder   *If your family is against it or if you don't*
>   wenn du keine Zeit **hast**, dann wollen   *have time, then we'll drop the plan*
>   wir den Plan fallen lassen

If the two clauses have compound tenses with the same auxiliary, the auxiliary can be omitted in the first one:

Nachdem ich Tee **getrunken** und eine
Weile **gelesen hatte**, machte ich einen
kurzen Spaziergang

After I had had tea and read for a while, I
went for a short walk

21.2 Initial position in main clause statements

21.2.1 Only ONE element precedes the finite verb in main clause statements

This means that the finite verb is normally the **second element** in a main clause, forming the first part of the verbal bracket, see 21.1.1a and 21.1.2.

(a) This clause structure is quite different to English

In English the subject has to come before the verb, because that is the only way we can tell it is the subject. In English, too, other elements can come before the subject, so that there can be several elements in front of the verb:

(i)   *Then she began to read the letter*
(ii)   *Then, unwillingly, she began to read the letter*
(iii) *Then, unwillingly, when she had shut the door, she began to read the letter*

In the equivalent German sentences, all but one of these elements has to be moved to another position, so that the **verb stays in second place**, e.g. (among numerous possible permutations):

(i)   **Dann** begann sie den Brief zu lesen/**Sie** begann dann den Brief zu lesen
(ii)   **Widerwillig** begann sie dann den Brief zu lesen/ **Dann** begann sie widerwillig den Brief zu lesen
(iii) **Nachdem sie die Tür geschlossen hatte**, begann sie dann widerwillig den Brief zu lesen/**Dann** begann sie widerwillig den Brief zu lesen, nachdem sie die Tür geschlossen hatte

Because of this fundamental difference in clause structure, corresponding sentences in English and German often have a very different form.

(b) Many types of element can occur in initial position

The subject is often the most natural element to occur in initial position, and it has been estimated that two thirds of main clause statements in German in all registers begin with the subject:

Tobias zog heftig an seiner Pfeife. **Die Spucke im Mundstück** prasselte; **man** hörte es, obwohl jetzt, immer deutlicher, auch noch das Schießen der anderen hinzukam.... **Sie** waren am Kahn. **Tobias** bückte sich und ließ das Kettenschloss aufschnappen. **Die Luft überm See** flimmerte. **Der Milan hoch oben** tat keinen Flügelschlag. (*Schnurre*)

However, it is quite wrong to think of the order subject + finite verb as the 'normal' order (as it is in English), and thus imply that it is 'abnormal' for something else to come before the verb. Almost all types of element except the negative *nicht* and the modal particles (see Chapter 10) can naturally come first in a main clause. To demonstrate this, examples are given below of those elements, aside from the subject, which are common at the start of main clause.

(i) an accusative or dative object. This is occasionally a (stressed) pronoun, more usually a noun phrase:

> **Ihn** nahm er zuletzt nach Prag mit (*Hildesheimer*)
> **Ihr** war das Bett viel zu klein
> **Das Verfahren gegen ihn** deutet er als weiterer Beleg für die politische Verfolgung (*Spiegel*)
> **Mariken** hat es sehr Leid getan (*Surminski*)

(ii) an adverbial (a single adverb or a phrase):

> **Natürlich** kannte er sämtliche Parfum- und Drogenhandlungen der Stadt (*Süßkind*)
> **Trotz den feierlichen Londoner Erklärungen** wird weiter gekämpft (*NZZ*)

Time and **place adverbials** are especially frequent in initial position:

> **An dem Abend** kam ich mit Mahler in den „Kronenkeller" (*Bachmann*)
> **Am steilen Kreidefelsen** bricht sich das Meer (*Wiechert*)

(iii) another complement of the verb, i.e. a genitive object, a prepositional object, a place or direction complement or a predicate complement (see Table 18.1)

> **Zu einem bedauerlichen Zwischenfall** kam es, als ... (*Zwerenz*)
> **Ins Theater/Dahin** komme ich jetzt nur sehr selten
> **Ein guter Kerl** ist er trotz alledem

(iv) a prepositional phrase qualifying a noun later in the clause

> **Über den Ernst der Lage** hat aber auch er keinen Zweifel (*FR*)

(v) the non-finite part of a compound tense. This gives particularly strong emphasis to the verb:

> **Anzeigen** wird sie ihn (*Fallada*)
> **Abgefunden mit ihrer Lage** haben sich 16,6 Prozent der Frauen (*LV*)

(vi) a noun belonging with a quantifying determiner later in the clause. This gives particular emphasis to the noun:

> **Personen** wurden nach Polizeiangaben keine verletzt (*NZZ*)
> **Menschen** sind um diese Zeit wenige unterwegs (*Gaiser*)

Occasionally this construction is found with adjectives, e.g.:

> **Beweise** hat er äußerst triftige gebracht

(vii) part of a phrasal verb

> **Sehr Leid** hat es mir getan
> **Zur Abstimmung** ist dieser Vorschlag nicht gekommen

(viii) a subordinate clause. This can be a finite or non-finite clause

> **Wohin sie dich gebracht haben**, weiß ich nicht (*Surminski*)
> **Den Schildern folgend**, fanden sie das Krankenhaus (*Walser*)
> **Ihr Geld zu leihen**, habe ich doch nie versprochen

(c) Constructions with more than one element in initial position
There are a few possible exceptions to the rule that the verb is always the second element in main clauses. In practice, these are only apparent exceptions in special kinds of construction, i.e.:

(i) Interjections, the particles *ja* and *nein*, and names of persons addressed are regarded as standing outside the clause proper and are placed before the initial element and followed by a comma, e.g.:

> **Ach**, es regnet schon wieder
> **Du liebe Zeit**, da ist sie ja auch
> **Ja**, du hast Recht
> **Nein**, das darfst du nicht
> **Karl**, ich habe dein Buch gefunden
> **Lieber Freund**, ich kann nichts dafür

(ii) Some other words or phrases link up a clause with what has just been said or the general context. They are seen as standing outside the clause and placed before the initial element with a comma:

> **Kurzum**, die Lage ist nun kritisch
> **Wissen Sie**, ich habe sie nie richtig kennen gelernt

The most frequent of these words and phrases are:

das heißt (d.h.)	*that is (i.e.)*	so	*well now, well then*
im Gegenteil	*on the contrary*	unter uns gesagt	*between ourselves*
kurz, kurzum, kurz gesagt,	*in short*	weiß Gott	*Heaven knows*
kurz und gut		wie gesagt	*as I said*
mit anderen Worten	*in other words*	wissen Sie, weißt du	*you know*
nun, na	*well*	zugegeben	*admittedly*
sehen Sie, siehst du	*d'you see*		

A few such words or phrases can be used like the group above, or (more commonly) on their own in initial position as part of the clause, e.g.:

> Er ist unzuverlässig. **Zum Beispiel,** er kommt immer spät *or* **Zum Beispiel** kommt er immer spät.

The following words and phrases can be used like this:

zum Beispiel	*for instance*	natürlich	*of course*
erstens, zweitens, etc. (see 9.2.3)	*first, secondly, etc.*	offen gesagt	*to be frank*

(iii) A few adverbs and particles can be used together with another element in initial position, i.e.:

Am Ende **freilich** ist etwas Unerwartetes und etwas Neues da (*Borst*)	*To be sure at the end something new and unexpected is there*
Der Buchfink **jedoch** ist nur in den ersten Lebensmonaten lernfähig (*NZZ*)	*Chaffinches, on the other hand, are only able to learn in the first months of their life*
Selbst in den Chroniken der Städter **schließlich** hat sich die Stadt als revolutionäre Neuheit in die Feudalwelt gestellt (*Borst*)	*After all, even in the chronicles of the burghers the city appears as a revolutionary innovation in feudal society*

The following adverbs can be used in this way:

allerdings	*to be sure, admittedly*	jedenfalls	*at any rate*
also	*thus*	jedoch	*however*
freilich	*to be sure, admittedly*	wenigstens	*at least*
höchstens	*at most*	sozusagen	*so to speak*
immerhin	*all the same*	übrigens	*incidentally*

Alternatively, these can occur on their own in initial position in the usual way, e.g.
Freilich ist am Ende etwas Unerwartetes und etwas Neues da.

NB: The function of these adverbs is like that of a coordinating conjunction in such constructions, and the conjunctions *aber* and *doch* have a similar flexibility in their positioning, see 19.1.1c.

(iv) Some types of subordinate clause are seen as separate from the main clause and are followed by another element before the finite verb, in particular:

a *was*-clause which relates to the following clause as a whole:

Was so wichtig ist, das Buch verkauft sich gut	*What is so important, the book is selling well*

concessive clauses of the 'whatever' type, see 19.6.2:

Es mag noch so kalt sein, die Post muss ausgetragen werden
Wer er auch ist, ich kann nichts für ihn tun
Wie schnell er auch lief, der Polizist holte ihn ein

(v) Two (or more) elements of the same kind can occur together in initial position if they complement or extend one another. In effect, they are seen as a single element. This is most frequent with adverbials of time and place, e.g.:

Gestern um zwei Uhr wurde mein Mann operiert
Auf dem alten Marktplatz in der Marburger Stadtmitte findet diese Woche ein Fest statt
Gestern Abend in Leipzig fand eine große Demonstration statt

(vi) A highlighted element can occur in isolation from the clause and dislocated from it. It is usually picked up by a pronoun or the like in initial position in the clause proper, e.g.:

Nach Kanada auswandern, das haben sie ja immer gewollt
Die Gudrun, der traue ich ja alles zu
Der Nachbar, der hat uns ja immer davon abhalten wollen
Als ich davon hörte, da war es schon zu spät
Mit Andreas, da wird es bald Ärger geben

Alternatively, the highlighted element may be placed after the clause, with a pronoun within the clause which refers forward to it, e.g. *Der traue ich doch alles zu, der Gudrun*. These constructions are typical of everyday colloquial language and are rarely encountered in formal writing.

21.2.2 The initial element functions as the TOPIC of the clause

The topic is the element in a sentence which we mention first to say something more about it:

Der Kranke hat die ganze Nacht nicht geschlafen
    (Information is being given about the patient)
In Frankfurt findet jedes Jahr die internationale Buchmesse statt
    (We are being told what happens in Frankfurt)
In diesem Zimmer kannst du dich nicht richtig konzentrieren
    (We are given information about this room)
In zwei Tagen wird die Reparatur fertig sein
    (We are informed about what will be happening in two days)

The topic, in initial position, functions as a starting point for the clause. It comes first because we want to give the listener or reader some piece of new information about it. The following general observations can be made about the topic in a German main clause statement.

(a) The element in initial position is often known or familiar to both speaker and listener

A clause often starts off with something which is known in this way, and some piece of new information is given about it later in the clause. This is shown by the examples above and the following:

> **Trotz des Poststreiks** ist der Brief rechtzeitig angekommen
> (You knew about the postal strike, but it's news to you that the letter still got there on time)
> **An den meisten deutschen Gymnasien** ist Englisch die erste Fremdsprache
> (You know about German schools but this is something you didn't know about the curriculum)

It is because a clause often begins with an element which is familiar to both speaker and listener that time adverbials are so common in initial position.

(b) The initial element often refers back to something just mentioned

Very often we want to pick up something which has just been referred to and give further information about it. The initial element often takes up a preceding word or phrase in continuous texts or dialogue:

> Wir haben ihn im Garten gesucht, aber **im Garten** war niemand zu sehen
> Ich sehe ihn oft. **Seinen Bruder** aber sehe ich jetzt recht selten
> Ich war drei Wochen auf Sylt. – **Darum** siehst du auch so gut aus.

The answer to a question often repeats an element in the question in initial position and gives the answer later in the clause. Compare:

> Was ist gegen Kriegsende geschehen? – **Gegen Kriegsende** wurden viele Städte zerstört
> Wann wurden diese Städte zerstört?   – **Diese Städte** wurden gegen Kriegsende zerstört

(c) The element in initial position is seldom the main piece of new information in the clause

Most main clauses begin with something familiar and the new information appears later. In this way, the following sentences sound odd because they start off with an important piece of new information:

> ?? **In einem kleinen Dorf** in Böhmen ist Stifter im Jahre 1805 geboren
> ?? **Ein neues Schloss** kaufte dieser Mann gestern
> ?? **Scharlachrot** ist ihr neues Kleid

These examples show that it is not true that 'any' element can be placed first 'for emphasis'. The first element must be a suitable topic or starting point of the clause. The strongest emphasis is usually on the most important piece of new information which appears later in the clause, see 21.3.

(d) In many clauses, the subject may not be suitable for use in initial position
The subject is often a natural choice as topic of a clause. However, if the subject involves new information, it is often more natural to begin with another element which is known and delay the subject until later in the clause:

> Vor deiner Tür steht doch **ein neues Auto**   *But there's a new car by your front door*
>   (With strong emphasis on the surprise at seeing the new car)
> Zwei Tage darauf wurde gegen die   *Two days later the military was deployed*
>   Streikenden **Militär** eingesetzt (*Brecht*)   *against the strikers*
>   (*Militär* is the crucial new information; it would sound odd to begin the sentence with it)

It is unusual for a sentence to begin with an indefinite noun, as they normally involve new pieces of information. For similar reasons, the subject rarely occurs in initial position with verbs of happening, since the event is usually the main new information (see also 21.5.3), e.g.: *Gestern ereignete sich **ein schwerer Unfall** in der Mariahilfer Straße*.

A 'dummy subject' *es* (see 3.6.2d) is often used to shift the subject to later in the clause and give it heavier emphasis as important new information, e.g.:

> Es kamen **viele Gäste**   *There were many guests*
> Es möchte Sie **jemand** am Telefon   *There's somebody who wants to speak*
>   sprechen   *to you on the telephone*

(e) The topic of the sentence can be changed readily
The emphasis in a clause can be altered by changing the element in initial position. What we choose to place in first position depends on how we want to present the information and what we assume the listener already knows. Thus, if we say:

> **Das Konzert** findet heute Abend im Rathaus statt

we assume the listener knows that there is a concert on, and we are telling him or her where it is. On the other hand, if we say:

> **Heute Abend** findet ein Konzert im Rathaus statt

we are telling the listener what's happening tonight. We are assuming that he or she doesn't know that there's a concert on in the town hall, and we are giving him or her this information. We can begin with *heute Abend*, because that is information which the speaker and the listener share. Finally, if we say:

> **Im Rathaus** findet heute Abend ein Konzert statt

we are telling the listener something about the town hall, i.e. that there's a concert on there tonight.

21.2.3 English equivalents for German constructions with an element other than the subject in initial position

The ease with which an element can be moved into initial position German to serve as the topic of the clause, as shown in 21.2.2e, is not shared by English, where the order subject + verb is fixed. If we want to convert something other than the natural subject of the verb into the topic of a main clause in English we have to use one of a range of complex constructions which are not necessary in German. The following gives examples of these English constructions and their German equivalents.

(a) Cleft sentence constructions

If we want to bring an element other than the subject into first position in English, we often put it in a clause of its own with 'it' and the verb 'be', e.g. *It was Angela (who) I gave the book to*. These are called **cleft sentence** constructions. They are not needed in German, where the topic can simply be shifted into initial position before the verb:

Erst gestern habe ich es ihr gesagt	*It was only yesterday that I told her*
Dort habe ich sie getroffen	*It was there that I met her*
Weil sie oft schwimmt, ist sie fit	*It's because she swims a lot that she's fit*
Was man sagt, zählt	*It's what you say that counts*

There are many variants of this construction, all with simpler equivalents in German:

Diesen Wagen da muss ich kaufen	*That's the car I've got to buy*
Dort/Hier wohnt sie	*That/This is where she lives*
Das meine ich (auch)	*That's what I mean*
So macht man das	*That's the way to do it*
Dann ist es passiert	*That's when it happened*
Dem gehört es	*That's whose it is*
Im Frühjahr ist es hier am schönsten	*Spring is when it's loveliest here*
Zu diesem Schluss gelangt Haas in ihrer neusten Arbeit	*This is the conclusion reached by Haas in her most recent work*

With the exception of the type *Er war es, der mich davon abhielt*, see 3.6.2c, cleft sentence constructions sound unnatural in German and should be avoided.

(b) English often uses a passive construction where an active is possible or preferable in German

Passive constructions are often used in English to shift the object of the verb to initial position (as the subject of the verb) and function as its topic. Although passives are by not unusual in German, a construction using the active voice, with the object in initial position, is often preferred (see also 15.5). For example:

Meinem Vater hat der Chef sehr freundlich gratuliert	*My father was congratulated by the boss in a very kind manner*
Auf diese Worte müssen nun Taten folgen (*Zeit*)	*These words must now be followed by deeds*

(c) English can use a construction with 'have' and a participle

This construction brings the relevant element to the beginning of the sentence by making it the subject of 'have'. There is no equivalent construction in German, where the relevant element is simply placed in initial position:

In diesem Buch fehlen zwanzig Seiten	*This book has (got) twenty pages missing*
In diesem Wald haben voriges Jahr viele Nachtigalle genistet	*This wood had a lot of nightingales nesting in it last year*
Ihm wurde eine Golduhr gestohlen	*He had a gold watch stolen*
Ihnen wurden die Fenster eingeworfen	*They had their windows smashed*

21.3 The order of other elements in the sentence: general principles

Most elements in all clause types come within the verbal bracket explained in 21.1. The relative order of these elements inside the verbal bracket is the same for all clause types:

Initial position	Bracket[1] [	Other elements	Bracket[2]]
Sie	hat	ihn heute zufällig in der Stadt	gesehen
	Hat	sie ihn heute zufällig in der Stadt	gesehen?
...,	weil	sie ihn heute zufällig in der Stadt	gesehen hat

This order is determined by two main underlying principles:

(i) Elements which are more heavily stressed and convey important new information tend to follow elements which are less stressed
The elements inside the verbal bracket are usually put in order of increasing importance, passing from unstressed elements like pronouns to those elements which represent the main new information and are given most emphasis. The element nearest the end of the bracket is typically the most important piece of information and naturally carries the heaviest stress.

(ii) Elements which are more closely linked to the verb tend to come after elements with a less strong link *Prädikatsergänzung*
For instance, many verb complements usually appear immediately before the final part of the verbal bracket. Similarly, direct objects, if they are nouns, normally come after the indirect objects, whose link with the verb is less 'direct'.

Following these general principles, the elements within the verbal bracket tend to occur in the order given in Table 21.1.

The order given in Table 21.1 reflects general guidelines for the English-speaking learner, and it should not be taken to represent rigid rules of German word order. However, following these guidelines will almost always produce an acceptable German sentence, if they can be varied in certain ways for reasons of emphasis. Details on the position of each of the groups of elements are outlined in sections 21.4 to 21.8.

However, English-speaking learners need to be aware of the effect, in terms of emphasis and presentation, of changing the position of elements in a sentence. It is quite possible to end up saying something rather different to what you mean.

21.4 The position of the pronouns

21.4.1 Pronouns normally follow immediately after the finite verb or the conjunction

Pronouns refer to persons and things already mentioned, or well known to the speaker and listener. They are typically unstressed and occupy the least prominent position within the verbal bracket, before everything else:

TABLE 21.1 *Basic order of the elements in the German sentence*

secretly

	Topic	Bracket¹	Pronouns N A D	Noun subject	Dative noun object	Most adverbials	Accusative noun object	Manner adverbials	Complements	Bracket²
Main clause	Heute Jan Wir	hat soll wurden	ihr	mein Freund	dem Chef	heimlich jetzt nachher	eine E-Mail den Bericht	höflich		geschickt. bringen. erinnert.
Question/ command		Hat Soll Geben	sie es ihm er Ihnen Sie mir			denn trotzdem sofort	den Weg das Geld	richtig	daran	erklärt? zeigen? zurück!
Subordinate clause		..., weil ..., da ..., dass	sie	der alte Herr meine Tante	dem Mann	meistens	den Brief	vorsichtig schnell	für seine Hilfe in die Tasche	gedankt hat. fährt. stecken wollte.

> Gestern hat **ihn** mein Mann in der Stadt gesehen
> Hat **ihn** dein Mann gestern in der Stadt gesehen?
> Da **ihn** mein Mann gestern in der Stadt gesehen hat, ...
> Dann hat **es** mein Bruder meinem Vater gegeben
> Dann hat **mir** mein Bruder den Brief gegeben

The only exception to this rule is that pronouns can be placed **before or after a noun subject**. It is more common for them to come first, but the following are quite usual alternatives to the first three examples above:

> Gestern hat mein Mann **ihn** in der Stadt gesehen
> Hat dein Mann **ihn** gestern in der Stadt gesehen?
> Da dein Mann **ihn** gestern in der Stadt gesehen hat, ...

However, a pronoun does more usually follow a noun subject if the endings do not show nominative and accusative case unambiguously:

> Gestern hat meine Mutter **sie** in der   *My mother saw her in town yesterday*
> Stadt gesehen
> Da das Mädchen **sie** in der Stadt   *As the girl has seen her in town ...*
> gesehen hat, ...
>
> (*Da sie das Mädchen in der Stadt gesehen hat* would normally be taken to mean 'As she has seen the girl in town')

If there are two pronoun objects, it is more usual for them to follow a noun subject, e.g.:

> Weil der Lehrer **es ihnen** gezeigt hat, ...   *Because the teacher has shown it to them*

Nevertheless, other orders are also quite possible, e.g.: *Weil **es** der Lehrer **ihnen** gezeigt hat, ... Weil **es ihnen** der Lehrer gezeigt hat, ...*

21.4.2 Personal pronouns precede other pronouns

Thus, *er, dir, Ihnen, ihm*, etc. (and *man*) come before demonstrative pronouns such as *der, das, dieser*, etc., irrespective of case, e.g.:

> Wollen **Sie die** gleich mitnehmen?   *Do you want to take those away with you?*
> Hat **ihn dieser** denn nicht erkannt?   *Didn't that person recognise him, then?*
> Eben hat sie **mir das** gezeigt   *She's just shown me that*

21.4.3 Personal pronouns occur in the order nominative + accusative + dative

This order is usual if there is more than one personal pronoun within the verbal bracket:

> Da **sie dich ihm** nicht vorstellen   *As she didn't want to introduce you to*
> wollte, ...   *him ...*
> Hast **du es uns** nicht schon gesagt?   *Haven't you already told us that?*
> Gestern hat **er sie ihm** gegeben   *He gave them to him yesterday*
> Heute will **sie ihm** helfen   *She's going to help him today*
> Heinz hat **es mir** gezeigt   *Heinz showed it to me*

This order is relatively fixed. The only common variation on it is that the pronoun *es*, in the reduced form *'s*, often follows a dative pronoun in colloquial speech, e.g. *Heinz hat **mir's** gezeigt.*

21.4.4 The position of the reflexive pronoun *sich*

sich normally occurs in the same position as other accusative or dative pronouns, i.e. immediately after the finite verb or the conjunction (and after a pronoun in the nominative, if there is one):

> Gestern hat **sich** der Deutsche über das Essen beschwert
> Gestern hat **sich** jemand darüber beschwert
> Gestern hat er **sich** darüber beschwert *personal pronoun precedes others*
> Er hatte es **sich** (dat.!) so vorgestellt *N A D*
> Er hat **sich** (acc.!) mir vorgestellt — // —

However, it is occasionally placed after a noun subject, e.g.: *Gestern hat der Deutsche **sich** über das Essen beschwert.* Very occasionally, it is placed later in the clause, e.g.: *Gestern hat der Deutsche über das Essen **sich** beschwert.* In general, this is only possible with 'true' reflexive verbs used with an accusative reflexive, see 18.3.6a.

21.5 The position of noun subject and objects

21.5.1 The usual order for noun subject and objects within the verbal bracket is nominative + dative + accusative   *p. 482* ✱

This group of elements includes not only noun phrases in the nominative, accusative or dative case, but also indefinite pronouns such as *etwas, jemand, niemand, nichts.* As Table 21.1 shows, they usually follow personal and demonstrative pronouns (but see 21.4.1 for exceptions), and precede other verb complements. The position of adverbials in relation to them is explained in 21.6.1. Examples:

> Gestern hat **jemand meinem Vater eine Kettensäge** geliehen
> Warum hat **Manfred seiner Freundin nichts** gebracht?
> Ich weiß, dass **mein Freund seiner Frau diese Bitte** nicht verweigern konnte
> Heute hat **der Chef den Mitarbeitern** für ihre Mühe gedankt

Variations on this order usually involve special circumstances of some kind, as explained in 21.5.2 and 21.5.3

21.5.2 The dative object can sometimes follow the accusative object

(a) If the dative object refers to a person, this order indicates it is much more important in context and emphasises it very strongly
This possibility is used sparingly:

> Er hat sein ganzes Vermögen **seinem**   *He left his whole fortune to his nephew*
>   **Neffen** vermacht
>   (We already know about the fortune, what is surprising is who he left it to; *Neffen* is heavily stressed to indicate this)
> Er stellte seinen Neffen **dem Pfarrer** vor   *He introduced his nephew to the parson*
>   (**Who** the nephew was introduced to is the important fact. Compare *Er stellte dem Pfarrer seinen Neffen vor*)

✱ *Gestern hat mein mann (S) ihn ... gesehen.*
Hat dein mann ihn gestern ... gesehen?

als mein Vater diese merkwürdige
Geschichte **einem ihm völlig
unbekannten Herrn** erzählte

*when my father told this remarkable story
to a gentleman whom he didn't know
at all*

(The dative object is indefinite and thus previously unknown to the listener. It is
more newsworthy and significant in context than 'this story', which must have
been mentioned before)

**(b) If both accusative and dative objects refer to things, the more important of
them in context is placed second**

dass er uns nicht alle zwingt, unsere
höheren Zwecke **seinem Interesse** zu
unterwerfen (*Wolf*)

*that he's not forcing us all to subject our
higher aims to his personal interest*

Er hat sein Glück **seiner Karriere**
geopfert

He sacrificed his happiness to his career

(Compare the different emphasis in *Er hat seiner Karriere **sein ganzes Glück** geopfert*)

**(c) A dative object referring to a thing usually follows an accusative object
referring to a person**

It is rarely possible for the dative object to come first in such contexts:

Sie überantworteten die Verbrecher **der
Justiz**

They delivered up the criminal to justice

Sie haben den armen Jungen **der
Lächerlichkeit** preisgegeben

They exposed the poor boy to ridicule

**21.5.3 The noun subject can follow an accusative and/or a dative object (and
other elements) if it constitutes the major piece of new information**

see also 21.2.2d. In practice the subject in such contexts is usually a noun with an
indefinite article or no article, or an indefinite pronoun:

Glücklicherweise wartet nun in Wien an
jeder Ecke **ein Kaffeehaus** (*Zweig*)

*Luckily there is a coffee house waiting for
you on every corner in Vienna*

Nun begrüßte den Dirigenten und den
Virtuosen **lautes Händeklatschen**
(*Kapp*)

*Now the conductor and the virtuoso were
met with loud applause*

Gestern hat meinen Bruder Gott sei
dank **niemand** gestört

*Thank goodness nobody disturbed my
brother yesterday*

Er wusste, dass dieser Gruppe **etwas
Unangenehmes** bevorstand

*He knew that something unpleasant was in
store for this group*

Occasionally a subject with a definite article is placed late in the clause if it needs
strong emphasis:

Die Tatsache, dass der EG unausweichlich
1994 **das Geld** ausgeht (*Zeit*)

*The fact that the EC's money will
inevitably run out in 1994*

The late position of an indefinite subject is almost regular with verbs of happening
and the like, and it is also frequent in passive sentences:

Er wusste, dass seinem Chef **eine große Ehre** zuteil geworden war	*He knew that a great honour had been bestowed on his boss*
Zum Glück ist meinem Bruder da **nichts** passiert	*Luckily nothing happened to my brother*
Deshalb können den Asylbewerbern **keine Personalausweise** ausgestellt werden	*For this reason no identity cards can be issued to the asylum-seekers*

21.6 The place and order of adverbials

An adverbial can be a single word (e.g. *trotzdem, heute*), or a phrase with or without a preposition (e.g. *den ganzen Tag, mit großer Mühe*). This difference in form has no effect on word order. In practice, the classification of adverbs in Chapter 7 applies equally to all adverbials.

The placing of adverbials is more flexible than that of any other element in the clause. This reflects their general freedom of occurrence as elements optionally added to give additional information, see 18.1.4. This section deals first with the placing of adverbials in relation to other elements (chiefly the noun subject and objects), and then explains the ordering of adverbials where more than one is present.

21.6.1 The position of adverbials in relation to the noun subject and objects

As shown in Table 21.1, most adverbials occur after a noun subject and dative object, but before an accusative object. However, the relative position of adverbials and noun subjects and objects depends very much on their relative importance in the clause. Specifically, that element appears later in the clause which is most strongly stressed or conveys the most important new information.

(a) Unstressed adverbials (usually single words) can precede the noun subject and/or the dative object

This applies in particular to adverbs of attitude (and modal particles, see Chapter 10), e.g. *bestimmt, sicher, vielleicht*, etc. Unstressed short adverbs of time and place like *da, dort, hier, gestern, heute, morgen, dann, damals, daher* also often occur early in the clause, immediately after the personal pronouns, e.g.:

Sie wird es **wohl** ihrem Mann sagen	*She'll probably tell her husband*
Ich weiß, dass sie es **sicher** meinem Vater empfehlen wird	*I know she'll be sure to recommend it to my father*
Sie ist **heute** ihrem Freund aus Bonn begegnet	*She met her friend from Bonn today*
Hat sie **schon damals** ihrem Großvater die ganze Geschichte erzählt?	*Did she tell her grandfather the whole story at that time?*

In most of the above contexts the adverb can follow the noun subject or objects. It is then more strongly emphasised. Compare *Hat sie ihrem Großvater schon damals die ganze Geschichte erzählt?* However, such permutation is not possible in contexts where the noun subject or object is a vital piece of new information (it is indefinite) and needs to be placed where it carries most stress, e.g.:

important new info

Das hat **bisher** keiner gemerkt	*Nobody's noticed it up to now*
Da war **doch** niemand	*Nobody was there, though*
Ich bin **dort** einem Freund von deinem Bruder begegnet	*I ran into a friend of your brother's there*

A sentence like *Da war niemand doch* would sound quite odd.

(b) The order of adverbials and noun objects (accusative or dative) most frequently depends on emphasis

i.e. how important they are in the context of the whole clause or sentence. The element which is being presented as more important comes later. Compare the following:

> Er hat diesen neuen Wagen **im Sommer** gekauft
> (The stress is on **when** he bought the new car)
> Er hat im Sommer **diesen neuen Wagen** gekauft
> (The emphasis is on **what** he bought)

> Sie haben Fußball **im Park** gespielt
> (This tells us **where** they were playing)
> Sie haben im Park **Fußball** gespielt
> (This tells us **what** they were playing)

> Das hat **gestern** ihr Kollege meinem Verlobten erzählt
> (**Who** was told is the point at issue)
> Das hat ihr Kollege **gestern** meinem Verlobten erzahlt
> (Who did the telling is seen as relatively unimportant)
> Das hat ihr Kollege meinem Verlobten **gestern** erzählt
> (prominence is given to the time when the fiancé was told)

Although, from a grammatical point of view, there is flexibility in the order of these elements, in a particular context only one may be appropriate. Thus, in answer to the question *Wann hat er diesen neuen Wagen gekauft?* one would most naturally use the first of the alternatives above, and the second would sound weird. *Gestern hat er ...*

(c) Adverbials of manner follow the noun objects

(and **all** other adverbials, see 21.6.2). This is because they usually convey the most important new information:

Meiner Meinung nach hat das Quartett dieses Stück **viel zu schnell** gespielt	*In my opinion the quartet played that piece much too fast*
Er warf den Ball **sehr vorsichtig** über den Gartenzaun	*He threw the ball very carefully over the garden fence*

21.6.2 The relative order of adverbials

(a) If a clause contains more than one adverbial, they most frequently occur in the order:

> attitude – time – reason – viewpoint – place – manner

More detail on these groups, which correspond to the classification given in Chapter 7, is given below:

(i) Adverbials of **attitude.** This group includes all the modal particles (see Chapter 10) and other adverbials which express some attitude on the part of the speaker towards what is being said (see 7.3.2), e.g. *angeblich, leider, vermutlich, zum Glück, zweifellos*, etc.: *de; hiszen, bár, ugyan*

> Sie wollte **doch** vor zwei Uhr in Magdeburg sein
> Er ist **vielleicht** schon am Montag abgereist *(leave)*

(ii) **Time** adverbials. As explained in 11.6 these can indicate a point in time (e.g. *bald, voriges Jahr, am kommenden Sonntag*), frequency (e.g. *stündlich, jeden Tag*) or duration (e.g. *lange, seit Montag, ein ganzes Jahr*). If there is more than one time adverbial in a clause, they are usually placed in the order

| point of time – duration – frequency |

Within these categories the general precedes the particular, e.g. *jeden Tag um vier Uhr*. Examples:

> Sie ist **vor zwei Tagen** trotz des Sturms nach Reutte gewandert
> Die Streikenden blieben **vier Stunden lang** vor dem Rathaus versammelt

(iii) Adverbials of **reason** i.e. adverbials expressing circumstance (e.g. *zu unserem Erstaunen*), condition (e.g. *gegebenenfalls*), purpose (e.g. *zur Durchsicht*) or reason (e.g. *wegen des Unfalls*), see 7.3.3. The **passive agent** introduced by *von* or *durch* (see 15.3) also occurs in this position:

> Sie hat den Brief **trotzdem** mit der Maschine geschrieben
> Der Brand wurde **von der freiwilligen Feuerwehr** schnell gelöscht

(iv) **Viewpoint** adverbials e.g. *finanziell* 'from a financial point of view', see 7.3.1b. Phrases with *mit* and *ohne* also occur in this position:

> Deutschland ist in den letzten Jahren **wirtschaftlich** stärker geworden
> Pastor Grün hat ihn **mit dem Beil** in der Küche erschlagen

(v) **Place** adverbials. See 7.1. Place adverbials should be distinguished from place and direction complements, see (c) below.

> Pastor Grün hat ihn mit dem Beil **in der Küche** erschlagen
> Ich habe bis 18 Uhr **im Büro** gearbeitet

(vi) **Manner** adverbials i.e. those which indicate **how** an action is carried out, see 7.3.1. Adverbs of manner are almost always the final element in the clause before any complements:

> Sie ist heute mit ihrem Porsche **viel zu schnell** in die Kurve gefahren
> Der Vorschlag wurde von den Anwesenden **einstimmig** angenommen

(b) **The order of adverbials is subject to variation for reasons of emphasis**
The relative order given in (a) above is only a guide to a 'neutral' order of the adverbs, assuming they all have roughly similar emphasis, and it is not a rigid rule. As with the relative order of adverbials and the noun subject and objects, variation in the order of adverbials follows the general principle given in 21.3, i.e. an adverbial can be given more or less emphasis by being placed later or earlier in the clause. This often depends on what is regarded as the main new information in context, which needs to be emphasised, e.g.:

Paula ist zum Glück **gestern** nicht zu schnell gefahren
Paula ist gestern **zum Glück** nicht zu schnell gefahren
  (The adverbial in bold is made more prominent in each case by being placed
  later. The manner adverbial, as the major information, is the last element in both
  cases.)

Viele deutsche Städte wurden gegen Kriegsende **von den Allierten** zerstört
Viele deutsche Städte wurden von den Allierten **gegen Kriegsende** zerstört
  (Placing the time adverbial after the *von*-phrase in the second example gives it
  particular prominence, possibly in reply to a question about when it happened.)

Sie hat sehr lange **dort** auf ihre Mutter gewartet
Sie hat dort **sehr lange** auf ihre Mutter gewartet
  (Time adverbials usually precede place adverbials, but they can follow if they
  need to be given prominence. The prepositional object always follows both
  adverbials.)

**(c) The traditional rule that adverbials occur in the order time – manner –
place can be misleading**

As shown in (a) above, adverbials normally occur in the order **time – place –
manner**:

Der junge Tenor hat gestern in Berlin **gut** gesungen
Die Kinder wollten heute auf der Wiese **ungestört** spielen

Elements indicating place and direction at the end of the verbal bracket, immediately before the final part of the verb, are complements of the verb, not adverbials,
see 18.7 and 21.8.1. These complements follow **all** adverbials, including those of
manner:

Paula ist gestern viel zu schnell **in die Kurve** gefahren
Andreas wollte gestern mit seiner Freundin gemütlich **nach Freising** wandern
Sie hat die schöne Vase sehr vorsichtig **auf den Tisch** gestellt
Müllers wohnen einsam in einem großen Haus **im Wald**
Astrid lag erschöpft **auf der Couch**
Sie sind wegen des schlechten Wetters widerwillig **zu Hause** geblieben

The elements in bold in the above examples are **direction complements** depending on verbs of motion, or **place complements** depending on verbs of position. As
explained in 18.1.4, complements are much more closely linked to the verb than
adverbials, which simply give additional circumstantial information. Following
the principles given in 21.3, they are placed at the end of the verbal bracket.

21.7 The position of *nicht* and other negative elements

Other negative elements like *nie* 'never' and *kaum* 'hardly, scarcely' occupy the
same position in the clause as *nicht*, and the following applies equally to them.

21.7.1 The position of *nicht* if it negates the content of the whole clause

In this case, *nicht* is placed near the end of the clause, just **before any adverbs of
manner and verb complements**. *Nicht* is similar to an adverb of manner, and this
determines its position if it relates globally to the whole content of the clause.
However, it usually precedes other manner adverbials.

(a) *nicht* follows any noun objects

Er hat seinen Zweck **nicht** erwähnt	*He didn't mention his purpose*
Er hat mir das Buch **nicht** gegeben	*He didn't give me the book*
Verkaufe die Bücher **nicht**!	*Don't sell the books*
Ich weiß, dass sie ihren Bruder gestern **nicht** gesehen hat	*I know she didn't see her brother yesterday*

However, *nicht* precedes objects with no article which are part of a fixed verb phrase (see 21.8.2):

Sie hatte damals **nicht** Klavier gespielt	*She didn't play the piano then*

(b) *nicht* follows all adverbials except those of manner

Sie haben sich seit langem **nicht** gesehen	*They haven't seen each other for a long time*
Den Turm sieht man von hier aus **nicht**	*You can't see the tower from here*
Ich wollte es ihr trotzdem **nicht** geben	*I didn't want to give it to her all the same*
Das ist mir in diesem Zusammenhang **nicht** aufgefallen	*That didn't occur to me in that context*
Wir sind wegen des Regens **nicht** nach Bernau gewandert	*We didn't walk to Bernau because it was raining*
Sie haben gestern **nicht** gut gespielt	*They didn't play well yesterday*
Ich weiß es **nicht** ausführlich	*I don't know it in detail*

(c) *nicht* precedes most verb complements

i.e. all complements of the verb **except** the subject and the objects of the verb, see 21.8:

Sie sind gestern **nicht** nach Aalen gefahren	*They didn't go to Aalen yesterday*
Sie legte das Buch **nicht** auf den Tisch	*She didn't put the book on the table*
Wir konnten uns **nicht** an diesen Vorfall erinnern	*We couldn't remember the incident*
Er blieb **nicht** in Rostock	*He didn't stay in Rostock*
Sie ist sicher **nicht** dumm	*She's certainly not stupid*
Sie war heute **nicht** im Büro	*She wasn't at the office today*

nicht can follow prepositional objects or place and direction complements **if** it is relatively unstressed and the complement itself is to be emphasised. Compare:

Das kann ich doch **nicht von ihm** verlangen	*I can't ask that of him*
Das kann ich doch **von ihm nicht** verlangen	*I can't ask that of him*

21.7.2 The position of *nicht* if it applies to one particular element in the clause rather than the clause as a whole

In this case it comes **before** the element in question.

Sie hat mir **nicht** das Buch gegeben (not the book, but something else)	*She didn't give me the book*
Sie sind **nicht** am Freitag nach Kreta geflogen (not Friday, but some other day)	*They didn't fly to Crete on Friday*
Nicht mir hat er das Buch gegeben, sondern meiner Schwester	*It wasn't me he gave the book to, it was my sister*

Compare the 'partial' negation in the first example above with 'global' negation of the whole clause, with *nicht* in its usual position: *Sie hat mir das Buch **nicht** gegeben* means 'She didn't give me the book (or anything else)'.

NB: Alternatively, the stressed element can appear on its own in initial position, with the *nicht* later in the clause, e.g. *Mir hat er das Buch **nicht** gegeben*. This is common if the contrast is implicit, i.e. if there is no following *sondern* clause.

Unstressed *nicht* is often used in this way in tentative or rhetorical questions or exclamations, e.g.:

Hast du **nicht** die Königin gesehen?	*Didn't you see the Queen?*
War **nicht** dein Vater eigentlich etwas enttäuscht?	*Wasn't your father really a bit disappointed?*
Was du **nicht** alles weißt!	*Don't you know a lot!*

21.8 The position of complements

Apart from the subject and objects of the verb, which have their own position in the clause (see 21.4–21.5), the other complements of the verb (see 18.5–18.8) are invariably placed towards the end of the verbal bracket. This position is relatively fixed, irrespective of emphasis, and only very exceptionally are the complements found earlier in the clause.

21.8.1 The following complements are placed at the end of the verbal bracket

(a) genitive objects

weil der Verletzte dringend **eines Arztes** bedurfte	*because the injured man urgently needed a doctor*

(b) prepositional objects

Nun wird er sich sicher **um seine beiden Kinder** kümmern können	*Now he will certainly be able to look after his two children*
Sie hat in der Ankunftshalle lange **auf ihren Mann** gewartet	*She waited for her husband in the arrivals hall for a long time*
Wir haben uns vorgestern lange und ausführlich **darüber** unterhalten	*We talked about it in detail for a long time the day before yesterday*

(c) place complements with verbs of position

Er befand sich plötzlich **in einem dunklen Saal**	*He suddenly found himself in a dark room*
Er wollte unter keinen Umständen **in Duisburg** bleiben	*He didn't want to remain in Duisburg under any circumstances*
Sie haben lange **in dieser Hütte** gewohnt	*They lived in that hut for a long time*

(d) direction complements with verbs of motion

Warum hat Peter den Stein plötzlich **in den Bach** geworfen?	*Why did Peter suddenly throw the stone into the stream?*
Sie ist mit ihrem Porsche zu schnell **in die Kurve** gefahren	*She took the bend too fast in her Porsche*
Wir möchten nächste Woche **nach Emden zu meinen Eltern** fahren	*We want to go to my parents' in Emden next week*

(e) the predicate complement of copular verbs

i.e. *sein, werden, bleiben, scheinen, heißen*, see 18.8. This complement may be a noun or an adjective:

Herbert war immerhin längere Zeit **der beste Schuler** in unserer Klasse	*All the same, Herbert was top of our class for a long time*
Sie wurde plötzlich **blass**	*She suddenly turned pale*
Dann scheinen mir diese Bedingungen jedoch **etwas hart**	*In that case these conditions seem rather hard to me, though*

21.8.2 The position of the noun portions of phrasal verbs

Extended verb phrases can consist of a noun (often an infinitive or other verbal noun) used in a set phrase with a verb, e.g. *Abstand halten, Abschied nehmen, ins Rollen geraten.* The noun portion of these is always placed in the last position in the verbal bracket. They are similar to separable prefixes, and could be considered as forming part of the final portion of the verb bracket rather than as separate elements within the clause.

Er hat sie durch seine Unvorsichtigkeit **in die größte Gefahr** gebracht	*He brought her into very great danger through his carelessness*
Ich habe ihr alle meine Bücher **zur Verfügung** gestellt	*I put all my books at her disposal*
Gestern hat uns der Minister von seinem Entschluss **in Kenntnis** gesetzt	*The Minister informed us of his decision yesterday*
Sein Chef hat ihn vorige Woche sehr **unter Druck** gesetzt	*The boss put him under a lot of pressure last week*
Ich merkte, wie der Wagen langsam **ins Rollen** kam	*I noticed the car slowly starting to roll forwards*

21.9 Placing elements after the end of the verbal bracket

The last element in a German clause is usually the final part of the verb, whether this is a separable prefix, an infinitive or a past participle (in main clause statements, questions and commands) or the finite verb (in subordinate clauses).

However, there are some contexts where it is usual or possible to place an element after the final part of the verb. This construction is called *Ausklammerung* in German, and it is becoming increasingly frequent, even in formal writing. This section explains where *Ausklammerung* is preferable or acceptable in modern German.

21.9.1 Subordinate clauses are not normally enclosed within the verbal bracket

Sentences with clauses enclosed within one another and a cluster of verbs at the end (called *Schachtelsätze* because they are like sets of boxes inside each other) can be cumbersome and are best avoided. Taken to extremes they can be almost impenetrable, like the following example:

> Das „Vorsicht-Glatteis"-Verkehrszeichen, das letzte Nacht, die Frostbildung, was für den Autofahrer, der etwas getrunken und ein Auto gefahren, das abgefahrene Reifen hat, hat, erhöhte Gefahren mit sich bringt, brachte, total beschädigt wurde, wird nicht mehr aufgestellt.

As a general rule it is preferable to complete one clause, with the final part of its verbal bracket, before another is begun. In the following pair of sentences, the second alternative, though not ungrammatical, is regarded as clumsier:

> Ich konnte den Gedanken nicht loswerden, **dass wir ihn betrogen hatten**
> Ich konnte den Gedanken, **dass wir ihn betrogen hatten**, nicht loswerden

A relative clause can be separated from the noun it refers to in order to avoid enclosing it:

> Und wie dürfte man eine Zeitung verbieten, **die sich wiederholt und nachhaltig für die Wahl der staatstragenden Partei eingesetzt hat**? (*Spiegel*)

Enclosing the relative clause would result in an unwieldy sentence: *Und wie dürfte man eine Zeitung, **die sich wiederholt und nachhaltig fur die Wahl der staatstragenden Partei eingesetzt hat**, verbieten?*

21.9.2 Infinitive clauses

In general, infinitive clauses are not enclosed within the verbal bracket:

> Sie haben beschlossen **vor dem Rathaus zu warten**
> Er hat versucht **sein Geschäft zu verkaufen**

However, enclosure is usual or possible in some constructions, notably with some 'semi-auxiliary' verbs. Details are given in 13.2.2.

21.9.3 Comparative phrases introduced by *als* or *wie*

These are usually placed outside the verbal bracket:

> Gestern haben wir einen besseren Wein getrunken **als diesen**
> *Yesterday we drank a better wine than this one*
>
> Ich wusste, dass sie ebenso ärgerlich war **wie ich**
> *I knew she was just as annoyed as me*

However, enclosure of these phrases within the verbal bracket is not unusual:

> Die Volkstracht hat sich in Oberbayern stärker **als anderswo** in Deutschland erhalten (*Baedeker*)
> *Local costumes have been retained in Upper Bavaria longer than elsewhere in Germany*
>
> ein Mann, der **wie ein Italiener** aussah
> *a man who looked like an Italian*

Enclosure is especially frequent within longer clauses, especially in writing:

> da die Orangen und Zitronen von den Kindern **wie Schneebälle** über die Gartenmauern geworfen wurden (*Andres*)

21.9.4 Other elements are sometimes placed after the verbal bracket

There are three main reasons for such *Ausklammerung*:

(i)   to emphasise the element placed last:

> Du hebst das auf **bis nach dem Abendessen** (*Baum*)

(ii)   as an afterthought: *de listen*

> Ich habe sie doch heute gesehen **in der Stadt**

(iii)   In order not to overstretch the verbal bracket, e.g.:

> Seitdem Rodrigue seine Chronik begonnen hatte, freute er sich darauf, sie zu
> *decide* beschließen **mit der Darstellung der Regierung dieses seines lieben Schülers und Beichtkindes**

The following elements are commonly placed outside the verbal bracket:

(a) Adverbials which have the form of prepositional phrases
These are commonly excluded for the reasons given above:

> Hallo, ich rufe an **aus London** (*Telecom advert*)
> Vieles hatte Glum schon gesehen **auf seinem Weg von seiner Heimat bis über den Rhein hinweg** (*Böll*)

In general, these constructions are more typical of colloquial speech than formal writing. However, *Ausklammerung* is not uncommon in writing, especially if the prepositional phrase is lengthy or if a further clause (usually a relative clause) depends on the element excluded, e.g.: *Von hier aus konnte man noch wenig sehen von der kleinen Stadt, die am anderen Ufer im Nebel lag.*

(b) Prepositional objects
Prepositional objects are the only complement of the verb to be regularly excluded in standard German:

> Er hatte das merken können **an den gelegentlichen Rückblicken und dem Arm**, der entspannt auf der freien Vorderlehne lag (*Johnson*)
> Er darf sich entschädigt fühlen **für ganze Jahre Underdog-Dasein im Straßenverkehr** (*Zeit*) *Kárpótol*
> Du solltest dich nicht zu sehr freuen **auf diese Entwicklung** *fejlődés/fejlemény*

Not all prepositional objects can be excluded in this way and sentences like, e.g., *Ich habe vor dem Bahnhof gewartet auf meine Freundin* are unacceptable to many native speakers. No clear rules have yet been identified about the prepositional objects which can or cannot be excluded.

(c) Other verb complements
i.e. the subject or the accusative and dative objects, or place and direction complements. These are not usually excluded in standard German, although *Ausklammerung* of lengthy elements is occasionally found in writing, e.g.:

> Wir haben aus Steuergeldern gebaut **Wohnungen für nahezu zwanzigtausend Menschen**

Otherwise, such exclusions are restricted to substandard colloquial speech (and then only nouns, never pronouns), e.g.: *Gestern habe ich gesehen* **Manfred Schuhmacher und Angela Hartmann**.

(d) Adverbs

Exclusion of simple adverbs is common in colloquial speech, but generally avoided in formal written German:

> Bei uns hat es Spätzle gegeben **heute**
> Sie sollen leise reden **hier**
> Ich bin nach Trier gefahren **deshalb**
> Hat es euch gefallen **dort**?

22

Word formation

We can distinguish in German between **simple words** (or 'root words') like *Kind*, *dort* and *schön*, which cannot be broken down, and **complex words** like *kindisch*, *dortig* and *Schönheit*, which are obviously made up of more than one component and are derived from simple words in some way. Knowing about German word formation (often called derivation), i.e. how these complex words are made up, is invaluable for extending the learner's vocabulary. The importance of being able to work out the meaning of a whole word from its parts, and to recognise patterns like *Dank – danken – dankbar – Dankbarkeit – Undankbarkeit* cannot be overestimated. Such series of words are often much more transparent in German than in English, as we can see when we compare this set to English *thanks – to thank – grateful – gratitude – ingratitude*.

This chapter explains the most frequent means of word formation in German:

- methods of **word formation** (section 22.1)
- the formation of **nouns** (section 22.2)
- the formation of **adjectives** (section 22.3)
- the formation of **verbs** (sections 22.4–22.7)
  - with **inseparable prefixes** (section 22.4)
  - with **separable prefixes** (section 22.5)
  - with **variable prefixes** (section 22.6)
  - other means of **verb formation** (section 22.7)

22.1 Methods of word formation

22.1.1 Complex words are formed from simple words in three main ways

(a) by means of a prefix or suffix
In general, prefixes and suffixes do not occur as words in their own right, but are only used with root-words to form other words, e.g.:

(i) prefixes:

die Sprache	→ die **Ur**sprache	schön	→ **un**schön
stehen	→ **be**stehen	besser	→ **ver**bessern

(ii) suffixes:

gemein	→ die Gemein**heit**	bedeuten	→ die Bedeut**ung**
der Freund	→ freund**lich**	denken	→ denk**bar**
der Motor	→ motor**isieren**	die Kontrolle	→ kontroll**ieren**

Prefixes are most often used to create nouns from nouns, adjectives from adjectives, or verbs from other verbs or from nouns and adjectives. Suffixes are most common to make nouns from adjectives or verbs or adjectives from nouns or verbs; they are little used to form verbs.

(b) by means of vowel changes
These vowel changes are often linked with particular suffixes, but they can occur on their own. The following vowel changes are used in word formation:

(i) *Umlaut*:

    der Arzt   → die Ärztin   der Bart → bärtig
    der Druck → drücken   scharf   → schärfen

(ii) *Ablaut*, i.e. vowel changes like those of the strong verbs, see 12.1.2. *Ablaut* in word formation is chiefly restricted to use with strong verb roots:

    aufsteigen → der Aufstieg   werfen   → der Wurf
    beißen   → bissig   schließen → schlüssig

These vowel changes, especially *Ablaut*, are barely still productive (see 22.1.2) in modern German.

(c) by forming compound words
In compounding, a new word is made up from two (or more) existing words:

    der Staub + saugen → der Staubsauger   hell + blau → hellblau
    der Rat + das Haus → das Rathaus   die Brust + schwimmen →
                                       brustschwimmen

Sometimes there is a linking sound between the two words, e.g.:

    der Bauer + der Hof → der Bauernhof   das Land + der Mann → der
                                          Landsmann

The ease with which compounds can be formed is a distinctive feature of German (and the source of the notorious long words), and the extensive use of compounds is typical of modern German, especially in technical registers.

22.1.2 Productive and unproductive word formation patterns

If new words are still being created by means of a particular pattern (e.g. by adding a particular prefix or suffix), that pattern is called **productive**. For example, the suffix *-bar* is commonly used to make adjectives from nouns (= English '-able', '-ible', see 22.3.1a), and new words in *-bar* are regularly found, like *machbar* 'do-able'.
    On the other hand, many abstract nouns from adjectives are found with the suffix *-e*, and *Umlaut* of the root vowel where possible, see 22.2.1b, e.g.:

    groß → die Größe   gut → die Güte   hoch → die Höhe   lang → die Länge

However, no new nouns are created from adjectives in this way; the pattern is **unproductive**. Nevertheless, it is still important to know about it, because there are so many words in the language which have been formed with this pattern. This chapter deals with the commonest patterns of word formation in German, whether they are productive or unproductive.

22.2 The formation of nouns

22.2.1 Noun derivation by means of suffixes

The following suffixes are common, although not all of them are still fully productive. Most are linked to a particular gender, see 1.1.

(a) *-chen, -lein* (neuter)
These suffixes are very productive and used to form **diminutives** from nouns:

>   das Auge → das Äuglein *little eye*   die Karte → das Kärtchen *little card*
>   das Buch → das Büchlein *little book*   die Stadt → das Städtchen *little town*

The vowel of the stressed syllable usually has *Umlaut* if possible, although exceptions are common, especially with names, e.g. *Kurtchen*. *-chen* is commoner than *-lein*, which is mainly restricted to words ending in *-ch*, *-g* or *-ng*, and to archaic or poetic language. It was originally south German, but, in practice, colloquial south German speech now uses other forms from the local dialects to form diminutives, e.g. *-li* (Switzerland), *-(e)le* (Swabia), *-la* (Franconia), *-(er)l* (Austria and Bavaria).

In some cases, derivations with both *chen* and *lein* from the same noun are used with a difference in meaning, e.g. *Fräulein* 'girl', *Frauchen* 'mistress' (e.g. of a dog).

NB: In substandard colloquial speech, *-chen* is sometimes added to plurals in *-er*, e.g. *Kinderchen*.

(b) *-e* (feminine)
(i) Nouns in *-e* from verbs denote an **action** or an **instrument**. The latter is still productive, especially in technical registers:

>   absagen → die Absage *refusal*   bremsen → die Bremse *brake*
>   pflegen → die Pflege *care*   leuchten → die Leuchte *light*

(ii) Nouns in *-e* from adjectives denote a **quality**. The vowel has *Umlaut* if possible. This pattern is no longer productive, having been replaced by *-heit* or *-(ig)keit* (see (e) below):

>   groß → die Größe *size*   stark → die Stärke *strength*

(c) *-ei, -erei, -elei* (feminine)
These suffixes are productive and form nouns from verbs or from other nouns.

(i) Nouns in *-erei* from verbs are mainly **pejorative**, indicating a repeated, irritating action:

>   fragen → die Fragerei *lots of annoying questions*

The basis can be a whole phrase, e.g.:

> Rekorde haschen → die Rekordhasch**erei** *record hunting*.

-ei is used in the same sense from verbs in *-eln* and *-ern*, e.g.:

> lieben → die Liebel**ei** *flirtation*

-elei and *-erei* also have pejorative meaning if used with a noun base:

> Fremdwörter → die Fremdwört**elei** *using (too) many foreign words*
> die Sklave → die Sklav**erei** *slavery*

(ii) Nouns in *-ei* from nouns denote the **place** where something is done. The base is often a noun in *–er*:

> die Auskunft → die Auskunf**tei** *information bureau*
> der Bäcker → die Bäck**erei** *bakery*

(d) -er, -ler, -ner (masculine)
These productive suffixes form nouns from verbs or nouns. The root vowel occasionally has *Umlaut*, though this is rare with recent formations:

(i) Most nouns in *-er* from verbs denote the **person who does something**, often indicating a profession:

> einbrechen → der Einbrech**er** *burglar*   schreiben → der Schreib**er** *writer*
> lehren   → der Lehr**er** *teacher*   betteln   → der Bettl**er** *beggar*

The base may be a whole phrase:

> einen Auftrag geben → der Auftraggeb**er** *client, customer*

(ii) *-ler* (less commonly *-ner*) is used to derive nouns from other nouns to indicate the **person who does something**. Some are pejorative:

> das Bühnenbild → der Bühnenbild**ner**   die Rente   → der Rent**ner** *pensioner*
>   *stage designer*   der Sport   → der Sport**ler** *sportsman*
> die Kunst   → der Künst**ler** *artist*   die Wissenschaft → der Wissenschaft**ler**
> der Profit   → der Profit**ler** *profiteer*   *scientist*

In some instances *-er* is used rather than *-ler* to form nouns from other nouns:

> die Eisenbahn → der Eisenbahn**er**   die Taktik → der Taktik**er** *tactician*
>   *railway worker*

(iii) Some nouns in *-er* from verbs denote an **instrument**:

> bohren → der Bohr**er** *drill*   empfangen → der Empfäng**er** *receiver*

The base is often a whole phrase, especially in technical language:

> Staub saugen → der Staubsaug**er** *vacuum cleaner*

(iv) Nouns in *-er* from place names designate the **inhabitants**:

> Frankfurt → der Frankfurt**er**   Österreich → der Österreich**er**
> Hamburg → der Hamburg**er**   Wien   → der Wien**er**

Some of these are rather irregular:

Hannover → der Hannover**aner**   Zürich → der Zür**cher**

(e) *-heit, -(ig)keit* (feminine)
These suffixes are used productively to form **abstract nouns** from adjectives denoting a quality:

bitter	→ die Bitter**keit** *bitterness*	heftig	→ die Heft**igkeit** *violence*
gleich	→ die Gleich**heit** *similarity*	geschwind	→ die Geschwind**igkeit** *speed*
eitel	→ die Eitel**keit** *vanity*	genau	→ die Genau**igkeit** *precision*

The distribution of the forms *-heit, -keit* and *-igkeit* is not wholly regular. In general, *-heit* is the most common form. *-keit* is used with adjectives ending in *-bar, -ig, -lich* and *-sam* and with most in *-el* and *-er* (but not all, e.g. *die Dunkelheit, die Sicherheit*). *-igkeit* is used with adjectives ending in *-haft* and *-los* (e.g. *die Glaubhaftigkeit*) and a number of others, especially those which end in *-e* (e.g. *müde → die Müdigkeit*).

(f) *-in* (feminine)
The productive suffix *-in* forms nouns denoting the **feminine** of persons and animals. The root vowel usually has *Umlaut*:

der Arzt → die **Ärztin** *woman doctor*   der Fuchs → die Füchs**in** *vixen*

NB. For the use of these feminine forms in modern German, see 1.1.4a.

(g) *-ling* (masculine)
This productive suffix is used to form nouns from verbs or adjectives.

(i) Nouns in *-ling* from verbs denote persons who are the **object** of the action:

prüfen → der Prüf**ling** *examinee*   strafen → der Sträf**ling** *prisoner*

(ii) Nouns in *-ling* from adjectives designate **persons possessing that quality**, often (but not always) with a pejorative sense:

feige → der Feig**ling** *coward*   fremd → der Fremd**ling** *stranger*

Similar formations denoting plants and animals are common, e.g. *der Grünling* 'greenfinch', but they are no longer productive.

(h) *-nis* (neuter or feminine)
Nouns in *-nis* are **abstract nouns** from verbs or adjectives. Those from verbs (which often have irregular forms or use the past participle as a base) often denote the result of the verbal action. The suffix is no longer productive:

erleben	→ das Erleb**nis** *experience*	finster	→ die Finster**nis** *darkness*
ersparen	→ das Erspar**nis** *savings*	geheim	→ das Geheim**nis** *secret*
gestehen	→ das Geständ**nis** *confession*	wild	→ die Wild**nis** *wilderness*

(i) *-schaft* **(feminine)**
The productive use of this suffix is to form nouns from other nouns designating a
collective or a **state**:

> der Student → die Studenten**schaft** *student body*
> der Freund → die Freund**schaft** *friendship*

Other derivational patterns with *-schaft*, i.e. from adjectives (e.g. *die
Schwangerschaft* 'pregnancy') or from participles (e.g. *die Errungenschaft* 'achievement), are no longer productive.

(j) *-tum* **(neuter)**
-tum is used productively in modern German with nouns referring to persons to
form nouns denoting **institutions**, **collectives** or **characteristic features**:

> der Beamte → das Beamten**tum** *civil*   der König → das König**tum** *monarchy*
>   *servants*   der Papst → das Papst**tum** *papacy*
> der Deutsche → das Deutsch**tum**   das Volk → das Volks**tum** *national*
>   *German ethos*   *traditions*

(k) *-ung* **(feminine)**
This very productive suffix is used to form nouns from verbs referring simply to
the **action of the verb**:

> bedeuten *mean* → die Bedeut**ung**   bilden *form* → die Bild**ung** *formation*
>   *meaning*   töten *kill* → die Töt**ung** *killing*
> landen *land* → die Land**ung** *landing*

22.2.2 Noun derivation by means of prefixes

All these prefixes except *Ge-* are stressed. The gender of nouns with prefixes is the
same as that of the root noun, with the exception of those in *Ge-*, which are mostly
neuter, see 1.1.8c.

(a) *Erz-* **= 'arch-', 'out and out'**

> der Bischof → der **Erz**bischof *archbishop*
> der Gauner → der **Erz**gauner *out and out scoundrel*

(b) *Ge-*
Nouns in *Ge-* (often with the suffix *-e* in addition) can be formed from verbs or
from other nouns:

(i) Nouns in *Ge-* from verbs denote a **repeated** or **protracted activity**. They often
have a pejorative sense, like nouns in *-erei*, see 22.2.1c, to which those in *Ge-* are
often an alternative:

> laufen → das **Ge**laufe *running about, bustle* (esp. to no real purpose)
> schwätzen → das **Ge**schwätz *idle talk, gossip*

(ii) Nouns in *Ge-* from other nouns are collectives. The root vowel has *Umlaut* if possible (and *-e-* changes to *-i-*):

> der Ast → das **Ge**äst *branches*   der Berg → das **Ge**birge *mountain range*

(c) *Grund-* = 'basic', 'essential'

> die Tendenz → die **Grund**tendenz *basic tendency*

(d) *Haupt-* = 'main'

> der Bahnhof → der **Haupt**bahnhof *main station*

(e) *Miss-* **designates an opposite or a negative**
It sometimes has a pejorative sense:

> der Brauch → der **Miss**brauch *misuse*   der Erfolg → der **Miss**erfolg *failure*

Fehl- is now at least as productive than *Miss-* to express an opposite or a negative, e.g.:

> die Einschätzung → die **Fehl**einschätzung *false estimation*

(f) *Mit-* = co-, etc.

> der Arbeiter → der **Mit**arbeiter *colleague, collaborator*
> der Reisende → der **Mit**reisende *fellow traveller*

(g) *Nicht-* = non-

> der Raucher → der **Nicht**raucher *non-smoker*

(h) *Riesen-* **has an augmentative sense**

> der Erfolg → der **Riesen**erfolg *enormous success*

Riesen- is particularly common in speech, and colloquial German is rich in other augmentative prefixes, e.g.: *Superhit, Spitzenbelastung, Bombengeschäft, Heidenlärm, Höllendurst, Mordsapparat, Teufelskerl, Topmanager*, etc.

(i) *Rück-* **occurs with many nouns related to verbs in** *zurück-*

> die Fahrt → die **Rück**fahrt *return journey* (cf.: *zurückfahren*)

The full form *Zurück-* is usually retained with nouns in *-ung* from verbs, e.g. *zurückhalten* → die Zurückhaltung.

(j) *Un-* = opposite, abnormal

> der Mensch → der **Un**mensch *inhuman*   die Summe → die **Un**summe *vast sum*
>   *person*   das Wetter → das **Un**wetter *bad weather*
> die Ruhe   → die **Un**ruhe *unrest*

(k) *Ur-* = 'original'

> die Sprache → die **Ur**sprache *original language*

22.2.3 Other methods of noun formation

(a) Many nouns are formed from verb roots without a suffix

Most of these are masculine, see 1.1.5b. This means of derivation is no longer productive. It is most common with strong verbs (which may themselves be prefixed), and the root vowel is often changed:

ausgehen	→ der Ausgang *exit*	schließen	→ der Schluss *close*
brechen	→ der Bruch *break*	stechen	→ der Stich *stab, sting*
ersetzen	→ der Ersatz *replacement*	zurückfallen	→ der Rückfall *relapse*

(b) Verb infinitives can be used as nouns

e.g. *das Aufstehen* 'getting up', *das Reiten* 'riding'. These often correspond to English 'ing'-forms used as nouns and refer to the action as such. They are all neuter (see 1.1.3e) and further details about them are given in 13.4.

(c) Adjectives and participles can be used as nouns

e.g. *der/die Fremde* 'stranger', *der/die Vorsitzende* 'chair(person)' (see 6.4 for further examples). Such nouns from adjectives often co-exist with derived nouns:

fremd	→ der Fremde *and* der Fremdling
einbrechen	→ der Einbrechende *and* der Einbrecher

In these cases the noun derived by means of a suffix has a more developed sense than the adjective used as a noun. Both *der Fremde* and *der Fremdling* mean 'stranger', but the latter is rather pejorative. *der Einbrecher* means, specifically, 'burglar', but *der Einbrechende* simply means 'the person breaking in at present' (who may not necessarily be a criminal).

22.2.4 Compound nouns

The ease with which compound nouns can be formed is a characteristic feature of German, and the use of compounds has increased significantly in recent years. In particular, while two-part compounds like *Krankenhaus* and *Schreibtisch* have always been common, there has been an extension in the use of compounds with three or more elements over the last hundred years, especially in technical language, e.g. *Fahrpreisermäßigung*, *Autobahnraststätte*, *Roggenvollkornbrot*. Even so, compounds with more than four elements are (thankfully) still unusual.

NB: Compound nouns usually take the gender of the last part, see 1.1.9a.

(a) Types of noun compound

Almost any part of speech can combine with a noun to form a compound, e.g.:

(i)	**noun + noun:**	das Haar + die Bürste	→ die Haarbürste *hair brush*
(ii)	**adjective + noun:**	edel + der Stein	→ der Edelstein *gem*
(iii)	**numeral + noun:**	drei + der Fuß	→ der Dreifuß *tripod*
(iv)	**verb + noun:**	hören + der Saal	→ der Hörsaal *lecture theatre*
(v)	**preposition + noun:**	unter + die Tasse	→ die Untertasse *saucer*
(vi)	**adverb + noun:**	jetzt + die Zeit	→ die Jetztzeit *the present day*

(b) A linking element is inserted in many noun + noun compounds

e.g.: *die Lieblingsfarbe, die Straßenecke*. These linking elements (called *Fugenelemente* in German) occur in about a third of all compounds, and they are notoriously unpredictable. A few words form some compounds with a link and some without one, e.g. *der Lobgesang* **but** *die Lobeshymne*. Other words form some compounds with one link and others with a different one, e.g. *das Tagebuch* **but** *die Tageszeitung*. Austrian and Swiss usage often differs from that in Germany, e.g. Austrian *der Zugsführer* for German *der Zugführer*. In practice, each compound needs to be learnt with its link. These linking elements depend on the **first** part of the compound, and the following are found:

(i) *-e-* occurs with a few nouns, especially those with a plural in *-e*. The root vowel often has *Umlaut* if the plural has *Umlaut*, e.g. *der Pferdestall, der Gänsebraten*.

(ii) *-(e)s-* (i.e. the ending of the genitive) occurs with many masculine and neuter nouns (and a few feminines), e.g. *die Windeseile, das Kalbsleder, der Liebesbrief*.

(iii) *-(e)n-* is used with many feminine nouns, with 'weak' masculine nouns (see 1.3.2) and with adjectives used as nouns, e.g. *der Scheibenwischer, die Heldentat*.

(iv) *-er-* is found with some nouns which have a plural in *-er*. *Umlaut* is usually present if possible, e.g. *die Männerstimme, die Rinderzucht*.

(c) Restrictions on the formation of compound nouns

It seems easy to make up compound words in German, but there are restrictions on their formation which are not fully understood, and it is not possible to give clear rules. A few hints are given here for guidance, but it is good practice to be cautious in forming compounds which one has not actually seen or heard used.

(i) In a German compound noun the first element carries the main stress and usually defines the second. Thus, *Rathaus* is a type of *Haus* and *Tiefkühltruhe* is a kind of *Truhe*. A compound like *Blauhimmel* for 'blue sky', on the other hand, is not possible, because it is not a type of sky. We must say *der blaue Himmel*.

In particular, compounds whose first element is an individual person or place are not usually possible. We cannot say *Vatermitarbeiter* or *Ulmbesuch* because they are not 'types' of colleague or visit, we have to use a full phrase: *der Mitarbeiter meines Vaters* or *sein Besuch in Ulm*.

(ii) Adjective + noun compounds tend to be very restricted. In practice they always mean something rather different from when the relevant adjective is used as an epithet with the noun. Thus, *eine Großstadt* is more than *eine große Stadt*, and *ein Junggeselle* is not simply *ein junger Geselle*.

22.3 The formation of adjectives

22.3.1 Adjective derivation by means of suffixes

(a) *-bar*

This very productive suffix forms adjectives from verbs with the sense of English '-able', '-ible':

> brauchen → brauch**bar** *usable*   essen → ess**bar** *edible*

Adjectives in *-bar* are a frequent alternative to passive constructions, see 15.4.8.

(b) *-(e)n, -ern*

These suffixes are formed from nouns denoting a material, and the adjective indicates that the qualified noun is made from that material. The form *-ern* is normally associated with *Umlaut*:

das Gold	→ gold**en** *golden*	das Silber	→ silb**ern** *silver*
das Holz	→ hölz**ern** *wooden*	der Stahl	→ stähl**ern** *steel*

NB: Note the difference between adjectives in *-(e)n* or *-ern* and those in *-ig* (see (d) below) from the same noun, e.g. *silbern* '(made of) silver', *silbrig* 'silvery' (i.e. like silver).

(c) *-haft*

Adjectives formed from nouns with the suffix *-haft* indicate a quality like the person or thing denoted by the noun, e.g.:

der Greis → greisen**haft** *senile*	der Held → helden**haft** *heroic*

(d) *-ig*

-ig is a common and productive suffix, often associated with *Umlaut*. It is mainly used to form adjectives from nouns:

(i) with the idea of possessing what is denoted by the noun, e.g.:

das Haar → haar**ig** *hairy*	der Staub → staub**ig** *dusty*

(ii) indicating a quality like the person or thing denoted by the noun:

die Milch → milch**ig** *milky*	der Riese → ries**ig** *gigantic*

Adjectives in *-ig* can be formed from whole phrases. *blauäugig* 'blue-eyed', *heißblütig* 'hot-blooded'.

(iii) indicating duration (from time expressions):

zwei Stunden → zweistünd**ig** *lasting two hours*

Note the difference between these adjectives in *-ig* (which express duration) and those in *-lich* (which express frequency), e.g. *zweistündlich* 'every two hours', see (f) below.

(iv) *-ig* forms adjectives from adverbs, e.g.:

dort	→ dort**ig**	heute	→ heut**ig**
ehemals	→ ehemal**ig**	morgen	→ morg**ig**
hier	→ hies**ig**	sonst	→ sonst**ig**

(e) *-isch*

This is a productive suffix, often associated with *Umlaut*, used mainly to form adjectives from nouns:

(i) adjectives from proper names and geographical names:

England → engl**isch** *English*		Homer	→ homer**isch** *Homeric*
Europa → europä**isch** *European*		Sachsen → sächs**isch** *Saxon*	

(ii) adjectives which indicate a quality like that of the person or thing denoted by the noun. They are often pejorative:

der Held → held**isch** *heroic*	das Kind → kind**isch** *puerile*
der Herr → herr**isch** *imperious*	der Wähler → wähler**isch** *fastidious*

Compare the pejorative *kindisch* with the neutral *kindlich* 'childlike'.

(iii) adjectives from nouns of foreign origin:

die Biologie → biolog**isch** *biological*	die Musik → musikal**isch** *musical*
die Mode → mod**isch** *fashionable*	der Nomade → nomad**isch** *nomadic*

(f) -lich

A common suffix with a wide range of functions. Adjectives formed with *-lich* often have *Umlaut*:

(i) Adjectives from nouns in *-lich* indicate a relationship to that person or thing, or indicate the possession of the quality denoted by it:

der Arzt → ärzt**lich** *medical*	der Preis → preis**lich** *in respect of price*
der Buchstabe → buchstäb**lich** *literal*	der Tod → töd**lich** *fatal, deadly*
der Fürst → fürst**lich** *princely*	

This is the only use of *-lich* which is still productive in modern German.

(ii) Adjectives in *-lich* from time expressions denote frequency:

zwei Stunden → zweistünd**lich** *every two hours*

NB: For the difference between adjectives in *-ig* and *-lich* from time expressions, see (d) above.

(iii) Adjectives in *-lich* from verbs indicate ability:

bestechen → bestech**lich** *corruptible*	verkaufen → verkäuf**lich** *saleable*

This use of *-lich* is no longer productive, having been replaced by *-bar*, see (a) above.

(iv) Adjectives in *lich* from other adjectives usually indicate a lesser degree of the relevant quality:

arm → ärm**lich** *shabby; humble*	krank → kränk**lich** *sickly*
klein → klein**lich** *petty*	rot → röt**lich** *reddish*

(g) -los

-los is used to form adjectives from nouns and corresponds to English '-less':

die Hoffnung → hoffnungs**los** *hopeless*	die Wahl → wahl**los** *indiscriminate*

(h) -mäßig

This suffix is very productive in modern German, especially in formal registers, to derive adjectives from nouns:

(i) with the sense of 'in accordance with':

die Gewohnheit → gewohnheits**mäßig** *habitual*
der Plan → plan**mäßig** *according to plan*

-gemäß is an alternative to *-mäßig* in this sense, but it is less common, e.g. *plangemäß, ordnungsgemäß*.

(ii) with the sense of 'in respect of something', 'pertaining to':

der Instinkt → instinkt**mäßig** *instinctive*
der Verkehr → verkehrs**mäßig** *relating to traffic*

(iii) with the sense of 'like someone or something':

der Fürst → fürsten**mäßig** *princely*
das Lehrbuch → lehrbuch**mäßig** *like a textbook*

(i) *-sam*
This suffix is barely productive in modern German. Adjectives in *-sam* have two main sources:

(i) from verbs (especially reflexive verbs), expressing a possibility or a tendency:

sich biegen → bieg**sam** *flexible*   sparen → spar**sam** *thrifty*

(ii) from nouns, indicating a quality

die Furcht → furcht**sam** *timid*   die Gewalt → gewalt**sam** *violent*

22.3.2 Adjective derivation by means of prefixes

These prefixes are usually stressed and form adjectives from other adjectives.

(a) *erz-*, *grund-*, *hoch-* have intensifying meaning
erz- is mainly used with a rather negative sense, whereas *grund-* and *hoch-* tend to be more positive. Both *erz-* and *grund-* are rather limited in use:

reaktionär → **erz**reaktionär *very reactionary*
ehrlich → **grund**ehrlich *thoroughly honest*
verschieden → **grund**verschieden *totally different*
begabt → **hoch**begabt *highly talented*
intelligent → **hoch**intelligent *very intelligent*

(b) *un-* negates and/or produces an opposite meaning
It closely resembles English 'un-'. It is not always stressed.

artig → **un**artig *naughty*   wahrscheinlich → **un**wahrscheinlich
vorsichtig → **un**vorsichtig *incautious*   *improbable*

If an adjective already has a simple word as its opposite (e.g. *klug – dumm*), the form in *un-* gives a negative rather than an opposite. Thus, whilst *dumm* means 'stupid', *unklug* means 'unwise'. In general, only adjectives with a positive meaning can form an opposite with *un-*. Thus, whilst *unschön* (← *schön*) is fairly common, one does not find **unhäßlich* from *häßlich*.

(c) *ur-* with adjectives usually intensifies the sense

alt → **ur**alt *very old*   komisch → **ur**komisch *very comical*

Sometimes, it gives the idea of 'original' or 'typical', e.g. *urdeutsch* 'typically German'.

22.3.3 Adjective compounding

In general, adjective compounding is similar to noun compounding, see 22.2.4.

(a) Types of adjective compounds
In practice only the following are at all common:

- (i)   **noun + adjective:**   die Pflicht + treu → pflichttreu *dutiful*
- (ii) **verb + adjective:**   trinken + fest   → trinkfest *able to hold one's drink*
- (iii) **adjective + adjective:** klein + laut   → kleinlaut *meek*

Adjective + adjective compounds are often 'additive', i.e. the qualities of both adjectives apply, e.g. *nasskalt* 'cold and wet'.

(b) Many noun + adjective compounds have a linking element
These are similar to those in noun + noun compounds, see 22.2.4b. *-s-* and *-n-* are the most common, e.g. *geisteskrank, gesundheitsschädlich, seitenverkehrt.*

(c) Some compound elements forming adjectives have now become suffixes
A number of adjectives are so widely used in modern German as the basis for form compound adjectives that they can be considered as suffixes rather than as distinct words.

(i) with the sense of **having** or **possessing** something:

-**haltig** › koffeinhaltig   -**stark**   → charakterstark
-**reich** → erlebnisreich   -**(s)voll** → rucksichtsvoll

(ii) with the sense of **lacking** something:

-**arm** → nikotinarm   -**leer** → gedankenleer
-**frei** → alkoholfrei

(iii) with the sense of being **protected** from something:

-**dicht** → schalldicht   -**fest**   → hitzefest
-**echt** → kussecht   -**sicher** → kugelsicher

(iv) with the sense of being **similar** to something:

-**artig**   → kugelartig   -**gleich** → maskengleich
-**förmig** → plattenförmig

(v) with the sense of being **capable** of something:

-**fähig** → strapazierfähig

(vi) with the sense of being **worth(y of)** something:

-**wert** → lesens**wert**   -**würdig** → nachahmens**würdig**

(vii) with the sense of **needing** something:

-**bedürftig** → korrektur**bedürftig**

22.4 The formation of verbs: inseparable prefixes

New verbs are formed in German primarily by means of prefixes – largely because all verbs have to have inflectional suffixes to show categories like tense, person and number. There are three main types of verb prefix in German:

(i) inseparable prefixes like *be-, emp-, ent-, er-, ge-, ver- and zer-*, e.g. *bestellen, erstehen, verbringen*. They are called inseparable prefixes because they always remain fixed to the root, and they are always **unstressed**. Their past participle does not have the prefix *ge-*, (e.g. *bestellt, erstanden, verbracht*, see 12.2.1h). The formation of verbs with inseparable prefixes is treated in this section 22.4.

(ii) separable prefixes, of which there are a large number. The most typical are like prepositions, e.g. *ab-, an-, auf-*, etc., e.g. *abfahren, ankommen, aufmachen*, but they can also come from nouns, adverbs and other parts of speech, e.g. *teilnehmen, totschlagen, weglaufen*. They are called separable prefixes because they are separated from the root under certain conditions, e.g. *Sie kamen in München an* (see 12.2.1i), and they are always **stressed**. The formation of verbs with separable prefixes is dealt with in section 22.5.

(iii) variable prefixes are separable in some cases and inseparable in others, usually with a difference in meaning, e.g. *Sie übersetzte den Brief* 'She translated the letter' – *Sie setzten zum anderen Ufer über* 'They crossed over to the other bank'. The prefixes *durch-, über-, um-* and *unter-* and one or two less common ones are variable in this way. They are explained in section 22.6.

Many patterns of forming verbs with inseparable prefixes are common or productive. They are dealt with in the remainder of this section, in alphabetical order of the individual prefixes.

22.4.1 *be-*

(a) *be-* **makes intransitive verbs transitive**
See 18.3.5b. The simple intransitive verb may be used with a dative object or a prepositional object, which becomes the accusative object of the prefixed verb with *be-*, e.g.:

jdn. **be**dienen *serve sb.* (← jdm. dienen)
eine Frage **be**antworten *answer a question* (← auf eine Frage antworten)

(b) With transitive verbs *be-* **can change the action to a different object**

jdn. mit etwas **be**liefern *supply sb. with sth.* (← jdm. etwas liefern *deliver sth. to sb.*)

(c) *be-* forms verbs from nouns with the idea of providing with something
With some verbs the suffix *-ig-* is added:

das Wasser → **be**wässern *irrigate*   die Nachricht → **be**nachrichtigen *notify*
der Reifen → **be**reifen *put tyres on*

(d) *be-* makes verbs from adjectives with the sense of giving someone or something that quality
With some verbs the suffix *-ig-* is added:

feucht → **be**feuchten *moisten*   gerade → **be**gradigen *straighten*
frei   → **be**freien *liberate*   ruhig → **be**ruhigen *calm*

22.4.2 ent-

NB: The prefix *emp-* is a variant of *ent-*, used before some roots beginning with *f*, e.g. *empfehlen, empfinden.*

(a) Verbs in *ent-* from verbs of motion have the idea of escaping or going away
What is being escaped from usually appears as a dative object with these verbs, see 18.4.1c, e.g.:

gleiten → jdm. **ent**gleiten *slip away from sb.* (e.g. glass from hand)
laufen → jdm./etwas **ent**laufen *run away/escape from sb./sth.*
reißen → jdm. etwas **ent**reißen *snatch sth. from sb.*

(b) Verbs in *ent-* from nouns, adjectives or other verbs can have the sense of removing something
In this sense, *ent-* often corresponds to the English prefixes 'de-' or 'dis-':

das Gift → **ent**giften *decontaminate*   scharf   → **ent**schärfen *tone down*
der Mut → **ent**mutigen *discourage*   spannen → **ent**spannen *relax*

22.4.3 er-

(a) Verbs in *er-* from other verbs often express the achievement or conclusion of an action

bitten   → **er**bitten *get (sth.) by asking for it*
schießen → **er**schießen *shoot (sb.) dead*

A productive use of *er-* is to form verbs from verbs or nouns with the idea of acquiring something by the action expressed by the simple verb or the noun. Compare *erbitten* above and the following:

arbeiten → Er hat etwas **er**arbeitet   *He got sth. by working for it*
die List → Er hat etwas **er**listet   *He got sth. through cunning*

A handful of verbs in *er-* from other verbs point to the start of an action, e.g. *erklingen* 'ring out', *erbeben* 'tremble'.

(b) Verbs in *er-* formed from adjectives express a change of state
i.e. either intransitive verbs with the idea of becoming something, or transitive verbs with the idea of making somebody or something have the quality expressed by the adjective, e.g.:

blind → **er**blinden *become blind*	frisch → **er**frischen *refresh*
rot → **er**röten *turn red, blush*	leichter → **er**leichtern *make easier*

22.4.4 *ver-*

This is the most widely used inseparable prefix, with a range of meanings. The following are the most frequent or productive:

(a) Many verbs in *ver-* from verbs express the idea of finishing or 'away'

blühen → **ver**blühen *fade* (flowers)	hungern → **ver**hungern *starve to death*
brauchen → **ver**brauchen *consume*	klingen → **ver**klingen *fade away* (sounds)

(b) Some verbs in *ver-* from other verbs convey the notion of 'wrongly' or 'to excess'

biegen → **ver**biegen *bend out of shape*	salzen → **ver**salzen *put too much salt in*
lernen → **ver**lernen *unlearn, forget*	sth.

Some reflexive verbs in *ver-* have the idea of making a mistake, e.g.:

fahren → sich **ver**fahren *get lost, take a wrong turning*	wählen → sich **ver**wählen *misdial*

A few verbs in *ver-* are opposites, e.g.:

achten → **ver**achten *despise*	kaufen → **ver**kaufen *sell*

(c) Verbs in *ver-* formed from adjectives often express a change of state
As with *er-*, these can be intransitive verbs with the idea of becoming something., or transitive verbs with the idea of making somebody or something have the quality expressed by the adjective:

arm → **ver**armen *become poor*	länger → **ver**längern *make longer*
einfach → **ver**einfachen *simplify*	stumm → **ver**stummen *become silent*

Some verbs in *ver-* from nouns have a similar meaning, e.g.:

das Unglück → **ver**unglücken *have an accident*	
der Sklave → **ver**sklaven *enslave*	

(d) Many verbs formed from nouns with *ver-* convey the idea of providing with something

das Glas → **ver**glasen *glaze*	der Körper → **ver**körpern *embody*
das Gold → **ver**golden *gild*	der Zauber → **ver**zaubern *enchant*

22.4.5 zer-

Verbs in *zer-*, which are usually formed from other verbs, always convey the notion of 'in pieces':

beißen	→ **zer**beißen *bite into pieces*	fallen	→ **zer**fallen *distintegrate*
brechen	→ **zer**brechen *smash*	streuen	→ **zer**streuen *disperse*

22.5 The formation of verbs: separable prefixes

Separable prefixes are so called because they are separated from the root under certain conditions, e.g. *Sie kamen in München an* (see 12.2.1i). For the difference between them and inseparable prefixes, see 22.4. Most separable prefixes also exist as independent words, chiefly as adverbs, prepositions, nouns or adjectives. The forms of separable verbs, in particular the position of the prefix, are explained in 12.2.1i. Separable prefixes are always **stressed**.

22.5.1 Simple separable prefixes

The majority of these derive from prepositions or adverbs and their meanings are often transparent. The examples below illustrate some common and productive patterns of derivation.

NB: Prefixes from prepositions expressing direction (e g *ab-, an-, auf-*) often have a less transparent or figurative sense because direction can be indicated by using a prefix with *her-* or *hin-*, see 7.2.4d.

(a) *ab-*
(i) = 'away':

abfahren *depart, leave*	**ab**fliegen *take off*

(ii) = 'down':

absteigen *get down*	**ab**setzen *put, set down*

(iii) completing an action:

abdrehen *switch off*	**ab**laufen *wear out* (i.e. shoes)

(b) *an-*
(i) with the idea of approaching:

ankommen *arrive*	**an**reden *address (sb.)*

(ii) indicating the start of an action: partially:

andrehen *switch on*	**an**brennen *catch fire*

(c) *auf-*
(i) = 'up' or 'on':

aufbleiben *stay up*	**auf**setzen *put on* (hat, water)

(ii) with the idea of a sudden start:

auflachen *burst out laughing*	**auf**klingen *ring out*

(d) *aus-* = 'out' often pointing to the completion of an action:

ausbrennen *burn out*   **aus**dorren *dry up*

(e) *ein-* is related to the preposition *in*

It often conveys the idea of becoming used to something:

einfahren *run in* (i.e. new car)   sich **ein**leben *settle down*

(f) *los-* most often has the meaning of beginning something:

losgehen *set off; start*   **los**reißen *tear off, away*

(g) *mit-*
(i) accompanying or cooperating:

mitarbeiten *cooperate*   **mit**gehen *go with sb.*

(h) *vor-*
(i) going on or preceding:

vorgehen *go ahead; be fast* (clock) **vor**stoßen *push forward*

(ii) demonstrating:

vorlesen *read aloud*   **vor**machen *show sb. how to do sth.*

(i) *weg-* = 'away'

wegbleiben *stay away*   **weg**laufen *run away*

fort- is a less common (and more formal) alternative to *weg-* with some verbs: *fortbleiben, fortlaufen.*

(j) Other simple prefixes are less frequent or no longer productive

bei-:	**bei**treten	*join* (e.g. club)	**bei**tragen	*contribute*
da-:	**da**bleiben	*stay on/behind*	**da**stehen	*stand there*
dar-:	**dar**stellen	*depict, represent*	**dar**legen	*explain, expound*
fehl-:	**fehl**gehen	*miss one's way*	**fehl**greifen	*miss one's hold*
inne-:	**inne**haben	*occupy* (position)	**inne**halten	*pause*
nach-:	**nach**ahmen	*imitate*	**nach**gehen	*follow*
nieder-:	**nieder**brennen	*burn down*	**nieder**lassen	*lower, let down*
zu-:	**zu**drehen	*turn off* (tap)	**zu**steigen	*get on, board* (train)

22.5.2 Compound separable prefixes

Some compound elements, mainly from adverbs, are widely used as separable prefixes

dabei-	(indicating proximity):	**dabei**stehen	*stand close by*
daneben-	(indicating missing sth.):	**daneben**schießen	*miss* (a shot)
davon-	('away'):	**davon**eilen	*hurry away*
dazu-	(indicating an addition):	**dazu**kommen	*be added*
empor-	('upwards'):	**empor**blicken	*look up*
entgegen-	('towards'):	**entgegen**nehmen	*receive, accept*
überein-	(indicating agreement):	**überein**kommen	*agree*
voraus-	(= 'in advance'):	**voraus**sagen	*foretell, predict*
vorbei-, vorüber-	(= 'past')	**vorbei**gehen	*pass*
zurück-	(= 'back')	**zurück**fahren	*drive back, return*
zusammen-	(= 'together' or 'up')	**zusammen**rücken	*move together*
		zusammenfalten	*fold up*

The compound directional adverbs in *hin-* and *her-*, see 7.2.4, are also commonly used as separable prefixes, e.g. *hinausgehen, herunterkommen*. Other compound elements, e.g. *drauf-, hintan-, vorweg-, zuvor-* are used with one or two verbs only, e.g. *vorwegnehmen* 'anticipate'.

22.5.3 Separable prefix or separate word?

In the old spelling, some nouns, verbs and adjectives were treated as separable prefixes and written together with the verb according to the same rules as for separable prefixes, e.g. *achtgeben* 'pay heed', *radfahren* 'cycle', *fallenlassen* 'drop', *kennenlernen* 'get to know', *liebgewinnen* 'grow fond of', *offenlassen* 'leave open'. As there were no clear rules which combinations could be treated as separable verbs, there were many exceptions and anomalies, and the new spelling rules prescribe that most of these combinations should be spelled as separate words in all their forms, e.g. *Acht geben, Rad fahren, fallen lassen, kennen lernen, lieb gewinnen, offen lassen*.

The following rules now apply:

(a) Combinations of noun + verb are now normally spelled as separate words

> **Halt machen**: ich mache Halt, sie machte Halt, sie haben Halt gemacht
> **Maß halten**: ich halte Maß, sie hielt Maß, sie haben Maß gehalten
> **Ski laufen**: ich laufe Ski, sie lief Ski, sie sind Ski gelaufen

An exception is made of the following nouns, which are taken to have lost their full meaning in combinations with a verb and are seen as separable prefixes:

heim-	*irre-*	*preis-*	*stand-*	*statt-*	*teil-*	*wett-*	*wunder-*

heimgehen	*go home*		stattfinden	*take place*	
irreführen	*mislead*		teilnehmen	*participate*	
preisgeben	*expose*		wettmachen	*make up for*	
standhalten	*stand firm*		wundernehmen	*surprise*	

Forms which do not exist as separate words are also treated as separable prefixes, e.g. *fehlschlagen, feilbieten, kundgeben, weismachen*.

(b) Combinations of adjective or adverb + verb are normally written as separate words

aneinander fügen	*join together*	kurz treten	*go easy*
anheim fallen	*fall victim to*	leicht machen	*make sth. easy*
aufwärts gehen	*do better*	nahe legen	*suggest*
durcheinander bringen	*muddle up*	richtig machen	*do correctly*
fern liegen	*be far from*	überhand nehmen	*get out of hand*
gut gehen	*do well*	übrig bleiben	*be left over*

In particular, compound adjectives and adverbs, especially those with a preposition and *-einander*, and adjectives in *-ig* are always spelled as separate words.

However, adjectives and adverbs which cannot be used in the comparative in conjunction with the verb, or be modified by *sehr* or *ganz*, are seen to form fixed idiomatic combinations with the verb and thus considered to be separable prefixes:

bereithalten	*have ready*	gutschreiben	*credit*
bloßstellen	*show up*	schwarzarbeiten	*moonlight*
fernsehen	*watch TV*	totschlagen	*kill*
festsetzen	*fix*		

One can, for instance say *ich sehe fern*, but it is not possible to say **ich sehe ferner*, and *ich sehe sehr fern* can only have its literal meaning of 'I am looking a long way'.

(c) Combinations of verb or participle + verb are always written as separate words

fallen lassen	*drop*	spazieren gehen	*go for a walk*
gefangen nehmen	*take captive*	stehen bleiben	*stop*
liegen bleiben	*remain lying*	verloren gehen	*be lost*
kennen lernen	*get to know*		

There are no exceptions to this rule.

(d) All combinations with the verb *sein* are always written as separate words
This applies even with forms which are normally taken as separable prefixes:

da sein	*be there*	vorbei sein	*be past*
inne sein	*be conscious of*	zufrieden sein	*be satisfied*
los sein	*be up*	zurück sein	*be back*

NB: Some verbs look as if they have prefixes, but they are formed from compound nouns and the first element does not separate, e.g. *frühstücken* 'breakfast': *Ich frühstücke, ich habe gefrühstückt*, etc. Similarly: *handhaben* 'manipulate', *langweilen* 'bore', *liebkosen* 'caress', *wetteifern* 'compete'.

(e) Defective compound verbs are always written as a single word
These are verbs which have a special meaning and are only used in the form of the infinitive and/or the past participle. They are especially frequent in technical language.

(i) Some compounds only exist in the infinitive form:

brustschwimmen	*swim breast-stroke*	segelfliegen	*glide*
kettenrauchen	*chain-smoke*	wettlaufen	*race*

One can say, for instance *ich gehe morgen segelfliegen*, but not **ich segelfliege*

(ii) Some compounds are only used in the infinitive and past participle:

seiltanzen	*walk the tightrope*
uraufführen	*perform for the first time*

With these, one can say, for example, *Das neue Stück wird morgen uraufgeführt*, but not **Morgen uraufführt man das neue Stück*.

22.6 The formation of verbs: variable prefixes

A small number of prefixes can form both separable and inseparable verbs (for the difference between these, see 22.4). **If the verb is separable, the prefix is stressed, if it is inseparable, the prefix is unstressed.**

22.6.1 *durch-*

durch- always expresses the idea of 'through', whether separable or inseparable.

(a) A few compounds with *durch-* are only inseparable

durch`denken	*think through*
durch`leben	*experience*
durch`löchern	*make holes in*

NB: Separable `durchdenken is also found with the identical meaning to *durch`denken*, but it is less common.

(b) Many compounds with *durch-* are only separable

`durchblicken	*look through*	`durchführen	*carry out*
`durchkommen	*get through, succeed*	`durchrosten	*rust through*
`durchfallen	*fall through; fail*	`durchhalten	*hold out, survive*
`durchkriechen	*crawl through*	`durchsehen	*look through*

(c) Some verbs form separable and inseparable compounds with *durch-*

The separable compounds always mean 'right the way through'. The inseparable verbs emphasise penetration without necessarily reaching the other side. However, the distinction may be fine, especially with verbs of motion. Compare:

Er **eilte** durch die Vorhalle **durch**	*He hurried through the vestibule*
Er **durcheilte** die Vorhalle	*He hurried across the vestibule*
Er **ritt** durch den Wald **durch**	*He crossed the forest on horseback*
Er **durchritt** den Wald	*He rode through the forest*

Similarly:

durchbrechen	*break through*	durch`setzen	*infiltrate*
durchschauen	*see through*	durchlaufen	*run through*
durchdringen	*penetrate*	durchstoßen	*break through*
`durchsetzen	*carry through*	durchreisen	*travel through*
durchfahren	*travel through*	durchwachen	*stay awake*

22.6.2 *hinter-* normally forms inseparable compounds

hinter`gehen	*deceive*	hinter`legen	*deposit*
hinter`fragen	*analyse*	hinter`treiben	*foil, thwart*
hinter`lassen	*leave, bequeathe*		

Separable compounds with *hinter-* are substandard colloquial regionalisms, e.g. `hinterbringen 'take to the back', `hintergehen 'go to the back'.

22.6.3 *miss-* is generally inseparable

It has two main senses, i.e.:

(i) 'opposite':

missachten *despise, disdain*	**misstrauen** *distrust*

(ii) 'badly', 'wrongly':

    missdeuten *misinterpret*   **misshandeln** *ill-treat*

With a few verbs *miss-* can be treated as separable in the past participle and the infinitive with *zu*, e.g. *missgeachtet, misszuachten*, see 13.1.4b. These forms are alternatives to the regular inseparable forms *missachtet, zu missachten* and are generally less frequent, with the exception of *missverstehen*, where the extended infinitive most commonly has the form *misszuverstehen*.

22.6.4 *über-*

(a) A few compounds with *über-* are only separable
They are all intransitive and have the literal meaning 'over', e.g.:

`überhängen	*overhang*
`überkippen	*keel over*
`überkochen	*boil over*

(b) A large number of compounds with *über-* are only inseparable
They are all transitive and have a variety of meanings, i.e.:

(i) repetition:

    über`arbeiten *rework*          über`prüfen *check*

(ii) more than enough:

    über`fordern *overtax*          über`treiben *exaggerate*

(iii) failing to notice:

    über`hören *fail to hear*          über`sehen *overlook*

(iv) 'over':

    über`denken *think over*          über`fallen *attack*

(c) Many verbs form both separable and inseparable compounds with *über-*
The separable compounds are mostly intransitive. They all have the literal meaning 'over'. The inseparable verbs are mostly transitive, with a more figurative meaning often similar to those given under (b) above:

	separable	inseparable
überfahren	*cross over*	*run over*
überführen	*transfer*	*convict*
übergehen	*turn into sth.*	*leave out*
überlaufen	*overflow; desert*	*overrun*
überlegen	*put sth. over sb./sth.*	*consider*
übersetzen	*ferry over*	*translate*
überspringen	*jump over*	*skip*
übertreten	*change over*	*infringe*
überziehen	*put on*	*cover*

22.6.5 *um-*

(a) A large number of compounds in *um-* are only separable
Most express the idea of turning or changing a state:

`umblicken	*look round*	`umfallen	*fall over*
`umbringen	*kill*	`umschalten	*switch*
`umdrehen	*turn round*	`umsteigen	*change* (trains, etc.)

(b) Many compounds in *um-* are only inseparable
They all express encirclement or surrounding:

um`armen	*embrace*	um`ringen	*surround*
um`fassen	*embrace, encircle*	um`segeln	*sail round, circumnavigate*
um`geben	*surround*	um`zingeln	*surround, encircle*

(c) Many verbs form separable and inseparable compounds in *um-*
The difference in meaning corresponds to that given in (a) and (b) above:

	separable	inseparable
umbauen	*rebuild*	*enclose*
umbrechen	*break up*	*set* (i.e. type)
umfahren	*run over, knock down*	*travel round*
umgehen	*circulate*	*avoid*
umreißen	*tear down*	*outline*
umschreiben	*rewrite*	*paraphrase*
umstellen	*rearrange*	*surround*

22.6.6 *unter-*

(a) A large number of compounds in *unter-* are only separable
They generally have a literal meaning, i.e. 'under', e.g.:

`unterbringen *accommodate*	`unterkommen *find accommodation*
`untergehen *sink, decline*	`untersetzen *put underneath*

(b) Many compounds in *unter-* are only inseparable
They have a variety of meanings, i.e.:
(i) less than enough:

unter`bieten	*undercut*	unter`schreiten	*fall short*
unter`schätzen	*underestimate*	unter`steuern	*understeer*

(ii) 'under':

unter`drücken	*suppress; oppress*	unter`schreiben	*sign*
unter`liegen	*be defeated*	unter`stützen	*support*

(iii) other, miscellaneous meanings:

unter`bleiben	*cease*	unter`richten	*teach*
unter`brechen	*interrupt*	unter`sagen	*forbid, prohibit*
unter`lassen	*refrain from*	unter`suchen	*investigate*
unter`laufen	*occur*		

(c) Many verbs form separable and inseparable compounds with *unter*-
The separable verbs are mostly intransitive and have the meaning 'under'. The inseparable compounds are all transitive. Most have a more figurative meaning:

	separable	**inseparable**
unterbinden	*tie underneath*	*prevent*
untergraben	*dig in*	*undermine*
unterhalten	*hold underneath*	*entertain*
unterlegen	*put underneath*	*underlay*
unterschieben	*foist*	*insinuate*
unterschlagen	*cross* (e.g. legs)	*embezzle*
unterstellen	*keep, store*	*assume*
unterziehen	*put on underneath*	*undergo*

22.6.7 *voll-*

(a) Many verbs form compounds with *voll*- which are only separable
They all have the meaning 'full', e.g.:

`vollbekommen	*manage to fill*	`vollschreiben	*fill with writing*
`vollstopfen	*cram full*	`volltanken	*fill up* (car with fuel)

(b) A few compounds with *voll*- are only inseparable
Most of these are words used in formal registers with the meaning 'complete', 'finish' or 'accomplish':

voll`bringen	*achieve, accomplish*	voll`strecken	*execute, carry out*
voll`enden	*complete*	voll`ziehen	*execute, carry out*
voll`führen	*execute, perform*		

22.6.8 *wider-* usually forms inseparable verbs

wider`legen	*refute*	wider`stehen	*resist*

Only two verbs in *wider*- are separable, i.e.:

`widerhallen	*echo, reverberate*	`widerspiegeln	*reflect*

22.6.9 *wieder-* usually forms separable verbs

`wiederkehren *return*		`wiedersehen *see again*

Only **one** verb prefixed with *wieder*- is inseparable: *wieder`holen* 'repeat'.

22.7 Verb formation by means other than prefixes

By far the most productive means of creating verbs is by means of prefixes, as has been explained in 22.4–22.6. Nevertheless, a few other patterns are frequent or productive.

22.7.1 Many verbs are formed simply from nouns or adjectives

The simplest way to convert a noun or an adjective to a verb is to add verbal endings (i.e. those indicating person, number, tense, etc.) to the root of the noun or the adjective. These have a variety of meanings, and some add *Umlaut*, especially the verbs from adjectives which have the sense of giving something a particular quality:

der Dampf	→ dampfen *steam*	falsch	→ fälschen *forge, falsify*
der Donner	→ donnern *thunder*	krank	→ kranken *suffer*
die Feder	→ federn *be springy*	kurz	→ kürzen *shorten*
der Fluch	→ fluchen *curse*	leer	→ leeren *empty*
das Fohlen	→ fohlen *foal (of mare)*	reif	→ reifen *ripen*
der Hammer	→ hämmern *hammer*	scharf	→ schärfen *sharpen*
die Kachel	→ kacheln *tile*	schwarz	→ schwärzen *blacken*
der Kellner	→ kellnern *work as a waiter*	trocken	→ trocknen *dry*
der Löffel	→ löffeln *spoon*	wach	→ wachen *be awake*
der Splitter	→ splittern *splinter*	welk	→ welken *wilt*

22.7.2 Some verbs meaning 'cause to do' have been formed from strong verbs by means of a vowel change

This pattern is no longer productive, but its results are still common. In general, a transitive weak verb has been formed from an intransitive strong verb:

ertrinken *drown*	→ ertränken *drown*	sitzen *sit*	→ setzen *set*
(intr.)	(trans.)	springen *jump*	→ sprengen *blow up*
fallen *fall*	→ fällen *fell*		

22.7.3 Verbs in *-eln* express a weaker form of the action

They usually have *Umlaut*:

husten *cough*	→ hüsteln *cough slightly*	lachen *laugh* → lächeln *smile*
krank *ill, sick*	→ kränkeln *be sickly*	streichen *stroke* → streicheln *caress*

Some such verbs have a pejorative sense, e.g.: tanzen *dance* → tänzeln *prance*.

This formation is productive and can be based on nouns or adjectives as well as on other verbs:

fromm *pious*	→ frömmeln *affect piety*
der Schwabe *Swabian*	→ schwäbeln *talk like a Swabian*

22.7.4 The suffix *-ieren* is mainly used to form verbs from foreign words

The source of most verbs in *-ieren* (and its derivatives *-isieren* and *-ifizieren*) is French or Latin. Some have entered German directly from French verbs in *-er*, e.g. *arranger* → *arrangieren*. Others have been formed in German from the roots of words taken into German from these or other languages, e.g. *das Tabu* → *tabuisieren*. Only a very few are formed from German roots – *der Buchstabe* → *buchstabieren* is the most noteworthy exception.

23

Spelling and punctuation

German spelling and punctuation are relatively consistent (particularly in contrast to English!), but some rules are quite different to those for English. A selection of such problematic points is dealt with in this chapter. The rulings given are those accepted as authoritative throughout Germany; variations in the other German-speaking countries are relatively insignificant.

A uniform official spelling for German across all the German-speaking countries was first established in 1901/1902, and it had long been felt that the rulings made then had still left some unnecessary inconsistencies and anomalies which needed to be eliminated. For this reason, the countries where German is used as an official language agreed in 1994/95 on a set of fairly modest reforms which began to be introduced in primary schools in 1996. For a transitional period the old and the new spellings are permitted, but from 2005 only the new spellings will be regarded as correct.

This spelling reform turned out to be immensely controversial, and numerous steps were undertaken, even through the law courts, to reverse the decision to introduce it. However, these appear to have been unsuccessful, and the waves of protest have subsided somewhat, so that, with the exception of one or two leading newspapers (notably the *Frankfurter Allgemeine Zeitung* in Germany and *Die Presse* in Austria) which have retained the old spelling or reverted to it, all publications in the German-speaking countries now follow the new rules. Nevertheless, many books are of course still in circulation which use the old rules, and many people who finished their schooling before the new rules were introduced will probably adhere to the old spelling rules for private use for years to come.

In this edition the reformed spelling has been applied consistently, and the information given in this chapter relates exclusively to it. We deal in particular with the following:

- the use of **capital letters** (section 23.1)
- whether to write **one word or two** (section 23.2)
- the distribution of **ß and ss** (section 23.3)
- other **miscellaneous points** of spelling (section 23.4)
- the use of the **comma** (section 23.5)
- the use of other **punctuation marks** (section 23.6)

23.1 The use of capital letters

The basic rules are that initial capital letters are used:

(i) for the first word in a sentence (or a line of poetry)

(ii) for all nouns, e.g. *der Sack, die Schwierigkeit, das Bürgertum, die Pfirsiche.*

(iii) for the 'polite' second person pronoun *Sie* and all its forms (e.g. *Ihnen, Ihr,* etc., see 3.3)

(iv) for proper names, e.g. *Frankfurt, Deutschland, das Schwarze Meer*

All other words begin with a small letter. Some provisos are necessary in respect of these basic rules.

23.1.1 The use of capital letters with nouns and proper names

(a) Other parts of speech used as nouns are written with an initial capital letter

beim Lesen	das Für und Wider	das Ich	das Entweder-Oder
eine Drei	ein Drittel	der Vorsitzende	Bekanntes
alles Gute	nichts Schlechtes		

The exceptions to this rule which existed under the previous spelling rules have been largely eliminated, and all nouns are now spelled with an initial capital letter, e.g. *im Allgemeinen* 'in general', *alles Mögliche* 'everything possible', *aufs Neue* 'afresh'. However, small letters are still used in a number of idiomatic expressions which do not include distinct nouns. The most frequent are:

bei weitem	*by far*
durch dick und dünn	*through thick and thin*
gegen bar	*for cash*
ohne weiteres	*without thinking*
schwarz auf weiß	*in black and white*
seit langem	*for a long time*
über kurz oder lang	*sooner or later*
von klein auf	*from childhood*
von nah und fern	*from near and far*
von weitem	*from afar*

(b) Adjectives are spelled with an initial small letter if a preceding (or following) noun is understood

Das rote Kleid hat mir nicht gepasst, ich musste das **blaue** nehmen
Es ist wohl das **schnellste** von diesen drei Autos

(c) The determiners *ander, beide* and *ein* have small letters in most contexts
i.e. even in contexts where it would appear that they are being used as nouns, e.g. *etwas anderes, diese beiden, das eine und das andere.* However, *ander* can be used with an initial capital letter if it refers to something quite specific:

die Suche nach dem **Anderen**   *the search for otherness*

(d) Usage with geographical and other proper names
(i) Adjectives forming part of geographical or other names referring to something or somebody unique have an initial capital letter:

das Schwarze Meer	the Black Sea
das Neue Testament	the New Testament
das Auswärtige Amt	the Foreign Office
der Eiserne Vorhang	the Iron Curtain
Karl der Erste	Charles the First
die Olympischen Spiele	the Olympic Games
die Französische Revolution	the French Revolution

However, the following, and others like them, are not names of unique things, and they are spelled with a small letter:

die goldene Hochzeit	golden wedding
der schwarze Markt	the black market

(ii) Indeclinable adjectives in -*er* from the names of towns and countries have an initial capital:

der Kölner Dom   die Berliner Straßen   das Wiener Rathaus

(iii) Adjectives formed from proper names with the suffix -*isch* (or -*sch*) normally have a small letter:

die goetheschen Gedichte   das elisabethanische Drama   das ohmsche Gesetz

However, these adjectives can be used with an apostrophe after the name to emphasise the person involved, in which case they are written with an initial capital, e.g. *die Grimm'schen Märchen*.

(e) Usage with *deutsch* and other adjectives of nationality
(i) Adjectives of nationality are written with a capital letter when used as a noun to refer to the language or the school subject (see 6.4.6a):

Er kann kein Wort Deutsch   Das ist (kein) gutes Deutsch   auf Deutsch *in German*
Wir haben Deutsch in der Schule   Ich habe eine Drei in Deutsch
Sie spricht, kann, lernt, liest (kein, gut) Deutsch, Russisch, Englisch
Das Buch ist in Deutsch und Englisch erschienen

As an adjective used as a noun *der/die Deutsche* 'German' is also always spelled with a capital letter.

(ii) When used as adjectives they have a small letter:

das deutsche Volk	ein deutsches Lied	die deutsche Bundesrepublik
italienische Weine	ein britisches Schiff	dieser französische Käse

This runs counter to English usage, which requires a capital letter ('the German people', 'Italian wines', etc.). Only in names is a capital used in German, e.g. *die Österreichische Bundesbahn*.

(iii) They have a small letter when used as the equivalent of an adverb:

Der Minister hat mit ihr deutsch gesprochen
Redet sie jetzt deutsch oder niederländisch?

(f) Capital and small letters with superlatives
(i) Superlatives with *am* (see 8.4.1) are spelled with a small letter, e.g.:

am besten, am schönsten

(ii) Superlative forms used with the definite article are written with a capital letter, e.g.

> es ist das Beste, wenn wir ihr alles sagen.

(iii) Superlatives with the preposition *aufs* (see 8.4.3) can be written with a capital **or** a small letter:

> aufs Heftigste/heftigste

23.1.2 Nouns used as other parts of speech are written with a small letter

This applies in particular to:

(i) nouns used as **prepositions**, see 20.4, e.g.:

> angesichts, kraft, mittels, statt, trotz

(ii) nouns used as **adverbs**, e.g.:

> abends, anfangs, kreuz und quer, mitten, morgens, rechtens, rings, sonntags, teils, willens.

NB: Capital letters are used for words denoting a part of the day used in conjunction with *heute, gestern* and *morgen*, e.g. *gestern Abend, heute Mittag* (see 11.6.2).

(iii) nouns used in **indefinite expressions of number**, e.g.:

> ein bisschen   *a little*
> ein paar   *a few* (see 5.5.6. Compare *ein Paar* 'a pair')

(iv) Some nouns used as **adjectives** with the verbs *sein, bleiben* and *werden*. This applies to *Angst, Bange, Gram, Leid, Pleite, Schade* and *Schuld*.

> Mir ist, wird **angst**   *I am, am becoming afraid*
> Er blieb ihr **gram**   *He bore her ill-will*
> Die Firma ist **pleite**   *The firm is bankrupt*
> Es ist **schade**   *It's a pity*
> Sie war **schuld** daran   *It was her fault*

With other verbs, these words have an initial capital letter, e.g. *Ich habe Angst*.

(v) Nouns which have become idiomatic **separable prefixes** are spelled with a small letter, see 22.5.3a, e.g. stattfinden, teilnehmen.

23.1.3 Capitalisation of pronouns and related forms

All forms of the 'polite' second person pronoun Sie are spelled with a capital letter, see Table 3.1, e.g. *Sie, Ihnen, Ihre Frau*, etc.

No other pronouns have initial capital letters (except when they begin a sentence). According to the revised spelling the other second person pronouns *du, ihr* and their forms are to be spelled with small initial letters in letter-writing, not with capitals as previously, e.g. *Ich danke dir recht herzlich für deinen Brief*.

23.2 One word or two

The general rule is that **compounds are written as a single word if they are felt to be a single concept**. On the other hand, where the individual words are still felt to retain full meaning, they are written separately. The word stress often gives a clue to this, as a true compound only has one main stress, whereas separate words are still stressed independently. Compare:

`gut `schreiben *write well*	`gutschreiben *credit*
`so `weit *so far*	`soweit *on the whole*

Many uncertainties in respect of the writing of compound words were eliminated in the revised spelling, and the main principles are explained with examples in the remainder of this section.

NB: See 22.5.3 for a detailed explanation of the spelling of separable and compound verbs, e.g. *Rad fahren, kundgeben*.

23.2.1 Combinations of preposition + noun

These have the function of adverbs or prepositions and they are written separately if the individual words are still felt to retain independent meanings:

mit Bezug auf, unter Bezug auf	nach Hause gehen, zu Hause sein
zu Ende gehen	in/außer Kraft treten, sein

On the other hand, such adverbs or prepositions are written as single words if they are considered to be single entities, e.g. *beiseite, infolge, inmitten, vonnöten, vonstatten, vorderhand, zurzeit, zuzeiten*.

Alternative forms are permitted in some set phrases where it is debatable whether the words involved retain their separate meanings or not:

außerstand/außer Stand setzen, sein
imstande/im Stande sein
infrage/in Frage stellen
instand/in Stand setzen
zugrunde/zu Grunde gehen
zuleide/zu Leide tun
zumute/zu Mute sein
zurande/zu Rande kommen
zuschanden/zu Schanden machen, werden
sich etwas zuschulden/zu Schulden kommen lassen
zustande/zu Stande bringen
zutage/zu Tage bringen, fördern
zuwege/zu Wege bringen

Some prepositions from complex phrases also have alternative spellings, i.e. *aufgrund/auf Grund, zugunsten/zu Gunsten, anhand/an Hand, mithilfe/mit Hilfe, anstelle/an Stelle*.

23.2.2 Combinations of a noun or an adverb with a participle or an adjective

Compounds which involve an underlying phrase are written together.

das bahnbrechende Werk	*the pioneering work*
(from: *sich eine Bahn brechend*)	
der angsterfüllte alte Mann	*the terrified old man*
(from: *von Angst erfüllt*)	
ein himmelschreiendes Unrecht	*an outrageous injustice*
(from: *zum Himmel schreiend*)	
die staubbedeckten Bücher	*the books covered with dust*
(from: *mit Staub bedeckt*)	

All other such combinations are written as separate words: *ein Aufsehen erregendes Ereignis, die Eisen verarbeitende Industrie.*

23.2.3 Compound adverbs with *so-*, *wie-* and *wo-*

Note the difference between the following pairs (see 19.3.6 for details on the conjunctions in *so-*):

sobald *as soon as*	so bald *so soon*
solange *as long as*	so lange *so long*
sooft *as often as*	so oft *so often*
wieweit? *to what extent?*	wie weit? *how far, what distance?*
woanders *elsewhere* (see 7.1.5d)	wo anders? *where else?*
womöglich *possibly*	wo möglich *if possible*

NB: (i) *so dass* 'so that', see 19.5.2, may alternatively be spelled *sodass*.
(ii) Most combinations with *viel* and *wenig* are spelled as separate words, e.g. *so viel, wie viel, zu wenig*, see 5.5.25e, but when used as a conjunction *soviel* is written as a single word, see 19.7.4.

23.3 *ss* or *ß*?

The distinction between *ss* and *ß* (called *scharfes s* or *eszett*) is universally observed in Germany and Austria. In Switzerland, though, no distinction is made and *ss* is used in all cases. Foreign learners are strongly recommended to follow the majority practice.

(a) *-ss* is used if the preceding vowel is SHORT

dass, der Fluss, die Flüsse, gewiss, lassen, er lässt, müssen, es muss, wissen, ich wusste, das Wasser

(b) *-ß* is used if the preceding vowel is LONG or a DIPHTHONG

beißen, die Buße, der Fuß, die Füße, groß, der Gruß, der Maß, groß, die Maße, die Straße

The letter *ß* now fits consistently with the rule in German which stipulates that long vowels are followed by a single consonant in the spelling.

NB: (i) Some family names are spelled with a final *-ss*, e.g.: *Günther Grass, Theodor Heuss, Richard Strauss* (**but** *Johann Strauß*), *Carl Zeiss*.
(ii) *-ß-* was originally only a small letter, but its use as a capital is now tolerated, e.g. *BONNER STRAßE*. However, many people still always write *-SS-* in capitals: *STRASSE*.

23.4 Other points of spelling

23.4.1 The plural of nouns in *-ee* and *-ie*

These nouns do not add an extra *-e* in the spelling of the plural, even if the plural ending is pronounced as a distinct syllable, e.g.:

der See, die Seen [zeːən]   das Knie, die Knie [kniːə]
die Industrie, die Industrien [ɪndʊstriːən]

Similarly in verb forms, see 12.2.1d:

knien [kniːən] *kneel*   wir schrien [ʃriːən] *we cried*

23.4.2 Double vowels are simplified under *Umlaut*

(i) in plurals (see 1.2.2a):

der Saal *room* – die **Säle**

(ii) in diminutives (see 22.2.1a):

das Paar *pair* – das **Pär**chen

23.5 The use of the comma

Unlike English, the comma in German is used to mark off grammatical units, **not** to signal a pause when speaking. Germans adhere to the rules for inserting commas quite strictly, regarding deviations from them as seriously as spelling mistakes.

This principle that commas are used to mark off larger syntactic units means that, unlike English, adverbs and adverbial phrases within the sentence are **never** separated by commas. Compare:

Er konnte ihr jedoch helfen	*He was, however, able to help her*
Bringen Sie mir bitte eine Zeitung	*Bring me a newspaper, please*

23.5.1 The use of commas with coordinated clauses and phrases

i.e. those linked by one of the coordinating conjunctions, like *aber, oder* and *und*.

(a) Clauses and phrases joined by *und* or *oder* do not need a comma

Die alte Dame öffnete ihm die Tür und er ging in den Garten
Christa rief an und er erzählte ihr, was passiert war
Ich gehe morgen ins Theater oder besuche ein Konzert

Parallel subordinate clauses linked by *und* or *oder* do not have a comma between them:

Er sagte, dass ich sofort kommen müsste und dass er mir etwas sehr Wichtiges zu berichten hätte
Sie wird nicht kommen, weil sie nicht kann oder weil sie einfach keine Lust hat

A comma can be used if the writer feels the need to make the sentence clearer or avoid ambiguity:

Sie begegnete ihrem Trainer, und dessen Mannschaft musste lange auf ihn warten

No comma is necessary, either, before conjunctions with a similar meaning to *oder* and *und*, i.e. *beziehungsweise, sowie, weder… noch*, etc. (see 19.1.3 and 19.1.4).

(b) A comma is used before the conjunctions *aber, denn, doch, jedoch* and *sondern*

Er runzelte die Stirn, aber sie sagte nichts
Ich machte Licht, denn es war inzwischen dunkel geworden
Der Lohn ist karg, doch man genießt die abendlichen Stunden
Das Kleid war nicht grün, sondern hellblau

(c) A comma is used between parallel clauses and phrases which have no linking conjunction

> Das Licht geht aus, der Vorhang hebt auf, das Spiel beginnt
> Berlin, Paris, London, Madrid sind europäische Hauptstädte

23.5.2 The use of commas with subordinate clauses

In principle, all subordinate clauses are separated from the rest of the sentence by commas. This applies whether they are introduced by a conjunction or not:

> Er fragte, ob ich morgen nach Halberstadt fahren wollte
> Weil ich morgen arbeiten muss, werde ich keine Zeit haben
> Sie sagte, sie habe diesen Mann nie vorher gesehen
> Unsere Lage wäre unmöglich gewesen, hätte er diesen Plan nicht ausgedacht

23.5.3 The use of commas with participial clauses and infinitive clauses with *zu*

In principle, these do not need to be separated by commas from the rest of the sentence:

> Sie beschloss den Betrag möglichst bald zu überweisen
> Ich hoffte in der nächsten Runde zu gewinnen
> Diesen Vorgang wollen wir zu erklären versuchen
> Ich brauche heute nicht ins Geschäft zu gehen
> Ich konnte nichts tun um ihn zu beruhigen
> Er verließ das Haus ohne gesehen zu werden
> Aus vollem Halse lachend kam er auf mich zu
> Er sank zu Tode getroffen zu Boden.

However, a comma can be used if the writer feels the need to make the sense clear or avoid ambiguities, as with the following example, where the comma in each case shows which part of the sentence *heute* belongs to:

> Das Kind versprach heute, nichts mehr von dem Kuchen zu essen
> Das Kind versprach, heute nichts mehr von dem Kuchen zu essen

23.5.4 Interjections, exclamations, explanatory phrases, phrases in apposition and parenthetical words and phrases

If these are seen as separate from the structure of the clause they are normally divided from it by commas, e.g.:

> **Ach,** kannst du morgen wirklich nicht zu uns kommen?
> **Kurz und gut,** die Lage ist kritisch
> **Wissen Sie,** ich kann Ihnen da leider nicht mehr helfen
> **Sohn eines reichen Gutsbesitzers,** er hat in seiner Eigenschaft als Reserveoffizier mit den Regeln des Ehrenhandels Bekanntschaft geschlossen
> Das macht, **grob gerechnet,** vierzig Prozent von unserem Absatz aus
> Ich habe jetzt, **wie gesagt,** keine Zeit dazu
> Wir wurden durch Herrn Meiring, **den Direktor des Instituts,** aufs herzlichste empfangen

Comparative phrases introduced by *als* or *wie* are not normally separated by commas, e.g.:

> Sie ist jetzt wohl größer als ihre ältere Schwester
> Dieser Mann sah aus wie ein Schornsteinfeger

23.5.5 Two or more adjectives qualifying a noun are divided by commas if they are of equal importance

i.e. if they could be linked by *und*, e.g.:

> gute, billige Äpfel (the apples are good *and* cheap)

No comma is used if the second adjective forms a single idea with the noun:

> gute englische Äpfel (i.e. English apples which are good)

In practice, this rule is not always followed consistently (any more than the similar rule in English is) and many German writers use no commas in any series of adjectives.

23.6 Other punctuation marks

In some instances, German usage is at variance with English.

23.6.1 The semi-colon is little used in German

In principle, the semi-colon is used as in English. However, a comma or full stop, as appropriate, tends to be preferred in German. In particular, it is much more usual in German to have main clauses not linked by a conjunction, and these are commonly separated by commas:

> Geh in die Stadt und kaufe Mehl, unterdessen heize ich schon den Ofen an

23.6.2 A colon, not a comma, is used when direct speech is introduced by a verb of saying

> Dann sagte sie: „Ich kann es nicht"

Similarly with reported phrases and the like:

> Das Sprichwort heißt: Der Apfel fällt nicht weit vom Stamm

Note that when a colon introduces a full sentence of any kind it is always followed by a capital letter.

23.6.3 The first of a set of inverted commas is placed on the line

i.e. not above it as in English. This applies equally to single and double inverted commas:

> Dann sagte sie: „Ich kann ihn überhaupt nicht verstehen".
> Er fragte mich: „Kennen Sie Brechts Stück, Mutter Courage und ihre Kinder'?"

23.6.4 The exclamation mark

(a) The exclamation mark is used after interjections and exclamations

Ach!   Donnerwetter!   Pfui Teufel!   Guten Tag!

(b) Commands are followed by an exclamation mark:

Komm sofort zuruck!   Hören Sie sofort auf!
Seid doch vorsichtig, Kinder!   Einsteigen und die Türen schließen!

Standard usage has traditionally required the use of the exclamation mark with commands in German, but this rule is not always followed nowadays, and many Germans prefer to use a full stop, especially if the command is not felt to be particularly forceful.

(c) An exclamation mark can be used after the words of address at the beginning of a letter

Sehr geehrter Herr Dr. Fleischmann!   Liebe Petra!

This traditional usage has now largely been replaced by the use of the comma, as in English. However, if a comma is used, a capital letter should not be used for the first word of the letter proper, as, strictly speaking, it is not the beginning of a sentence, e.g.:

Lieber Martin,

es hat uns sehr gefreut, wieder mal von dir zu hören ...

Sources

The examples illustrating points of grammar and usage have been drawn from a wide range of sources and registers, spoken as well as written. Many of the unattributed examples which are new to this revised edition have been simplified or amended from modern texts, from phrases and sentences heard in conversation or on radio and television, etc. and in large number from the computerised corpus of modern spoken and written German set up by the Institut für deutsche Sprache in Mannheim. Longer examples quoted verbatim or with minor simplifications have been attributed wherever possible. The following sources have provided such material:

Authors

A. Andersch	M.L. Fleißer	E. Jünger	B. Schlink
S. Andres	U. Frevert	F. Kafka	P. Schneider
R. Augstein	M. Frisch	G. Kapp	W. Schnurre
I. Bachmann	F. Fühmann	E. Kästner	A. Seghers
V. Baum	G. Gaiser	A. Kolb	K. Sonnenberg
K. Bednarz	A. Goes	F.X. Kroetz	E. Strauß
W. Bergengruen	G. Grass	E. Langgässer	E. Strittmatter
T. Bernhard	M. von der Grün	S. Lenz	A. Surminski
P. Bichsel	B. Grzimek	K. Mann	P. Süßkind
O. Bollnow	S. Haffner	Th. Mann	Th. Valentin
K.H. Borst	E.W. Heine	I. Morgner	M. Walser
H. Böll	S. Hermlin	R. Musil	P. Weiß
H. Bollnow	Th. Heuss	T. Pinkwart	I. Wendt
B. Brecht	S. Heym	T. Plievier	U. Wickert
S. Brinkmann	P. Heyse	R. Pörtner	E. Wiechert
J. Bumke	W. Hildesheimer	E.M. Remarque	G. Wohmann
A. Döblin	M. Horbach	G. Reuter	C. Wolf
M. Dönhoff	E.H. Jacob	R.M. Rilke	C. Zuckmayer
F. Dürrenmatt	W. Jens	H. von Rimscha	S. Zweig
H. Fallada	U. Johnson	J. Roth	G. Zwerenz

Newspapers

The following newspapers or periodicals have provided material. Some titles have been abbreviated as indicated:

BILD	BILD-Zeitung	NZZ	Neue Zürcher Zeitung
BZ	Berliner Zeitung	OH	Odenwälder Heimatzeitung
FAZ	Frankfurter Allgemeine Zeitung		(Die) Presse
FR	Frankfurter Rundschau		Quick
HA	Hamburger Abendblatt		(Der) Spiegel
	Horizont		Stern
	Kurier	SZ	Süddeutsche Zeitung
LV	Leipziger Volkszeitung		(Die) Welt
MM	Mannheimer Morgen		(Die) Zeit
ND	Neues Deutschland		

In addition, the Baedeker series of travel guides, Knaur's encyclopedia, and Innsbruck university *Vorlesungsverzeichnis* provided some examples, as did the following radio and television stations: ARD, NDR, SWF, WDR, ZDF.

Bibliography and references

We list here the most important works which have been consulted for this and previous revisions of *Hammer's Grammar*. Major dictionaries and general accounts of German and English grammar are given first, followed by a selection of works containing more extensive accounts of specific points of grammar and usage, arranged according to the individual chapters of this book. In principle, the references have been limited to major recent books on each topic; users requiring more detailed bibliographical information are referred to: P. Eisenberg and B. Wiese, *Bibliographie zur deutschen Grammatik 1984–1994*. 3rd. ed. Tübingen: Stauffenburg Verlag, 1995.

Dictionaries

DUDEN, *Das große Wörterbuch der deutschen Sprache*. 3rd ed. 10 vols. Dudenverlag: Mannheim, 1999.

Farrell, R.B., *Dictionary of German Synonyms*. 3rd ed. CUP: Cambridge, 1977.

Götz, D., Haensch, G. and Wellmann, H. (eds), *Langenscheidts Großwörterbuch Deutsch als Fremdsprache*. Langenscheidt: Berlin, etc., 1993.

Scholze-Stubenrecht, W. and Sykes, J.B. (eds), *The Oxford Duden German Dictionary*. 2nd ed. OUP: Oxford, 2001.

Terrell, P. et al. (eds), *Collins German–English English–German Dictionary*. 4th ed. HarperCollins: Glasgow, 1999.

Trask, R.L., *A Dictionary of Grammatical Terms in Linguistics*. Routledge: London and New York, 1993.

Wahrig, G., *Deutsches Wörterbuch*. 2nd rev. ed. Bertelsmann: Gütersloh, 2000.

Works on German grammar and usage

Abraham, W., *Deutsche Syntax im Sprachvergleich: Grundlegung einer typologischen Syntax des Deutschen*. Narr: Tübingen, 1995.

Admoni, W., *Der deutsche Sprachbau*. 4th ed. Beck: Munich, 1982.

Askedal, J.O., *Innføring i tysk grammatikk*. Universitetsforlaget: Oslo, etc., 1976.

Berger, D., *Fehlerfreies Deutsch*. 2nd ed. Dudenverlag: Mannheim, etc., 1982.

Bresson, D., *Grammaire d'usage de l'allemand contemporain*. Hachette: Paris, 1988.

Buscha, J. et al., *Grammatik in Feldern. Ein Lehr- und Übungsbuch für Fortgeschrittene*. Verlag für Deutsch: Ismaning, 1998.

Clyne, M., *The German Language in a Changing Europe*. CUP: Cambridge, 1995.

Collinson, W.E., *The German Language Today. Its Patterns and Historical Background*. Hutchinson: London, 1953.

Curme, O., *A Grammar of the German Language*. Rev. ed. Macmillan: New York, 1922.

Dickens, E., *German for University Students*. Acme Publications: Stoke-on-Trent, 1990.

Dodd, W. et al., *Modern German Grammar. A Practical Guide*. Routledge: London, New York, 1996.

Dückert, J. and Kempcke, G. (eds), *Wörterbuch der Sprachschwierigkeiten*. Bibliographisches Institut: Leipzig, 1984.

DUDEN, *Richtiges und gutes Deutsch. Wörterbuch der sprachlichen Zweifelsfälle*. 4th ed. Dudenverlag: Mannheim, etc., 1997.

DUDEN, *Grammatik der deutschen Gegenwartssprache*. 6th ed. Dudenverlag: Mannheim, etc., 1998.

Eichhoff, J., *Wortatlas der deutschen Umgangssprachen*. Vols 1–2, Francke: Bern and Munich, 1977–78; Vols 3–4, Saur, Munich, 1998–2000.

Eisenberg, P., *Grundriß der deutschen Grammatik*. 2 vols. Metzler: Stuttgart, Weimar, 1998–99.

Engel, U., *Deutsche Grammatik*. 2nd. ed. Groos: Heidelberg, 1991.

Engel, U., *Syntax der deutschen Gegenwartssprache*. 3rd ed. Erich Schmidt: Berlin, 1994.

Engel, U. and Tertel, R.K., *Kommunikative Grammatik Deutsch als Fremdsprache*. iudicium: Munich, 1993.

Eroms, H.-W., *Syntax der deutschen Sprache*. de Gruyter: Berlin and New York, 2000.

Flämig, W., *Grammatik des Deutschen. Einführung in Struktur- und Wirkungszusammenhänge erarbeitet auf der theoretischen Grundlage der „Grundzüge einer deutschen Grammatik"*. Akademie: Berlin, 1991.

Fourquet, J., *Grammaire de l'allemand*. Hachette: Paris, 1952.

Fox, A., *The Structure of German*. Clarendon Press: Oxford, 1990.

Freund, F. and Sundqvist, B., *Tysk grammatik*. Natur och Kultur: Stockholm, 1988.

Genzmer, H., *Deutsche Grammatik*. Insel: Frankfurt/Main, 1995.

Glinz, H., *Grammatiken im Vergleich. Deutsch – Französisch – Englisch – Latein. Formen – Bedeutungen – Verstehen*. Niemeyer: Tübingen, 1994.

Glück, H. and Sauer, W., *Gegenwartsdeutsch*. 2nd ed. Metzler: Stuttgart, 1997.

Götze, L. and Hess-Lüttich, E.W.B., *Grammatik der deutschen Sprache. Sprachsystem und Sprachgebrauch*. Bertelsmann: Gütersloh, 1993.

Griesbach, H., *Neue deutsche Grammatik*. Langenscheidt: Berlin, etc., 1986.

Hartwig, H., *Besseres Deutsch – größere Chancen*. Heyne: Munich, 1985.

Hawkins, J.A., *A Comparative Typology of English and German. Unifying the Contrasts*. Croom Helm: London, Sydney, 1986.

Heidolph, K.E., Flämig, W. and Motsch, W. (eds), *Grundzüge einer deutschen Grammatik*. Akademie: Berlin, 1981.

Helbig, G., *Probleme der deutschen Grammatik für Ausländer*. 4th ed. Enzyklopädie: Leipzig, 1976.

Helbig, G., *Studien zur deutschen Syntax*. Enzyklopädie: Leipzig, 1983.

Helbig, G., *Deutsche Grammatik. Grundfragen und Abriß*. 2nd ed. iudicium: Munich, 1993.

Helbig, G. and Buscha, J., *Deutsche Grammatik. Ein Handbuch für den Ausländerunterricht*. 13th ed. Langenscheidt/Enzyklopädie: Leipzig, 1995.

Hentschel, E. and Weydt, H., *Handbuch der deutschen Grammatik*. 2nd ed. de Gruyter: Berlin and New York, 1994.

Herbst, T., Heath, D. and Dederding, H.-M., *Grimm's Grandchildren. Current Topics in German Linguistics*. Longman: London, 1980.

Jung, W., *Grammatik der deutschen Sprache*. Bibliographisches Institut: Leipzig, 1966.

Lang, E. and Zifonun, G. (eds), *Deutsch typologisch*. de Gruyter: Berlin and New York, 1996

Lockwood, W.B., *German Today: The Advanced Learner's Guide*. Clarendon Press: Oxford, 1987.

Sanders, W., *Gutes Deutsch – Besseres Deutsch. Praktische Stillehre der deutschen Gegenwartssprache*. Wissenschaftliche Buchgesellschaft: Darmstadt, 1986.

Sanders, W., *Sprachkritikastereien und was der „Fachler" dazu sagt*. Wissenschaftliche Buchgesellschaft: Darmstadt, 1992.

Schanen, F., *Grammatik Deutsch als Fremdsprache*. iudicium: Munich, 1995.

Schanen, F. and Confais, J.-P., *Grammaire de l'allemand. Formes et fonctions*. Nathan: Paris, 1986.

Schlobinski, P. *Syntax des gesprochenen Deutsch*. Westdeutscher Verlag: Opladen, 1997.

Schulz, D. and Griesbach, H., *Grammatik der deutschen Sprache*. 11th ed. Hueber: Munich, 1981.

Schwitalla, J., *Gesprochenes Deutsch. Eine Einführung*. Erich Schmidt: Berlin, 1997.

Skibitzi, B. and Wotjak, B. (eds), *Linguistik und Deutsch als Fremdsprache*. Niemeyer: Tübingen, 1999.

Sommerfeldt, K.-E. (ed.), *Entwicklungstendenzen in der deutschen Gegenwartssprache*. Niemeyer: Tübingen, 1988.

Sommerfeldt, K.-E. and Starke, G., *Einführung in die Grammatik der deutschen Gegenwartssprache*. 3rd ed. Niemeyer: Tübingen, 1998.

Thieroff, R. et al. (eds), *Deutsche Grammatik in Theorie und Praxis*. Niemeyer: Tübingen, 2000.

Toman, J. (ed.), *Studies in German Grammar*. Foris: Dordrecht, 1984.

Weinrich, H., *DUDEN – Textgrammatik der deutschen Sprache*. Dudenverlag: Mannheim, 1993.

West, J., *Progressive Grammar of German*. 6 vols. Authentik: Dublin, 1992–94.

Zifonun, G. et al., *Grammatik der deutschen Sprache*. de Gruyter: Berlin and New York, 1997.

Works on English grammar and usage

Graustein, G. et al. (eds), *English Grammar. A University Handbook*. 4th ed. Enzyklopädie: Leipzig, 1984.

Lamprecht, A., *Grammatik der englischen Sprache*. 5th ed. Cornelsen-Velhagen and Klasing: Berlin, 1977.

Quirk, R. et al., *A Comprehensive Grammar of the English Language*. Longman: London, 1985.

Swan, M., *Practical English Usage*. 2nd ed. OUP: Oxford, 1996.

1: Nouns

Corbett, G., *Gender*. CUP: Cambridge, 1991.

Doleschal, U., *Movierung im Deutschen. Eine Darstellung der Bildung und Verwendung weiblicher Personenbezeichnungen*. Lincom Europa: Unterschließheim/Munich, 1992.

Gregor, B., *Genuszuordnung. Das Genus englischer Lehnwörter im Deutschen*. Niemeyer: Tübingen, 1983.

Köpcke, K.-M., *Untersuchungen zum Genussystem der deutschen Gegenwartssprache*. Niemeyer: Tübingen, 1982.

Mills, A.E., *The Acquisition of Gender: A Study of English and German*. Springer: Berlin, etc., 1986.

Sieburg, H., *Sprache – Genus/Sexus*. Lang: Frankfurt/Main, etc., 1997.

Wegener, H., *Die Nominalflexion des Deutschen – verstanden als Lerngegenstand*. Niemeyer: Tübingen, 1995.

Wegera, K.-P., *Das Genus: Ein Beitrag zur Didaktik des Daf-Unterrichts*. iudicium: Munich, 1997.

2: Case

Blake, B.J., *Case*. 2nd ed. CUP: Cambridge, 2001.

Dürscheid, C., *Die verbalen Kasus des Deutschen. Untersuchungen zur Syntax, Semantik und Perspektive*. de Gruyter: Berlin and New York, 1999.

Helbig, G., *Die Funktion der substantivischen Kasus in der deutschen Gegenwartssprache*. Niemeyer: Halle/Saale, 1973.

Lauterbach, S., *Genitiv, Komposition und Präpositionalattribut – Zum System nominaler Relationen im Deutschen*. iudicium: Munich, 1993.

Wegener, H., *Der Dativ im heutigen Deutsch*. Narr: Tübingen, 1985.

3: Personal pronouns

Besch, W., *Duzen, Siezen, Titullieren. Zur Anrede im Deutschen heute und gestern*. Vandenhoeck and Ruprecht: Göttingen, 1996.

Kretzenbacher, H.L. and Segebrecht, W., *Vom Sie zum Du – mehr als eine Konvention?* Luchterhand: Hamburg and Zurich, 1991.

Marx-Moyse, J., *Untersuchungen zur deutschen Satzsyntax. 'Es' als vorausweisendes Element eines Subjektsatzes*. Steiner: Wiesbaden, 1983.

4: The articles

Bisle-Müller, H., *Artikelwörter im Deutschen. Semantische und pragmatische Aspekte ihrer Verwendung*. Niemeyer: Tübingen, 1991.

Grimm, H.-J., *Untersuchungen zum Artikelgebrauch im Deutschen*. Enzyklopädie: Leipzig, 1986.

Grimm, H.-J., *Lexikon zum Artikelgebrauch*. Enzyklopädie: Leipzig, 1987.

5: Other determiners and pronouns

Bethke, I., *'der', 'die', 'das' als Pronomen*. iudicium: Munich, 1990.

6: Adjectives

Sommerfeldt, K.-E. and Schreiber, H., *Wörterbuch zur Valenz und Distribution deutscher Adjektive*. 2nd ed. Bibliographisches Institut: Leipzig, 1977.

7: Adverbs

Renz, I., *Adverbiale im Deutschen*. Niemeyer: Tübingen, 1993.

10: Modal particles

Helbig, G., *Lexikon deutscher Partikeln*. Enzyklopädie: Leipzig, 1988.
Helbig, G. and Helbig, A., *Deutsche Partikeln – Richtig gebraucht?* Langenscheidt/ Enzyklopädie: Leipzig, etc., 1995.
Weydt, H. et al., *Kleine deutsche Partikellehre*. Klett: Stuttgart, 1983.

12: Verbs: conjugation

Jaeger, C., *Probleme der syntaktischen Kongruenz. Theorie und Normvergleich im Deutschen*. Niemeyer: Tübingen, 1992.

13: The infinitive and the participles

Bech, G., *Studien über das deutsche Verbum infinitum*. 2nd ed. Niemeyer: Tübingen, 1983.
Buscha, J. and Zoch, I., *Der Infinitiv*. Enzyklopädie: Leipzig, 1988.

14: Uses of the tenses

Comrie, B., *Tense*. CUP: Cambridge, 1985.
D'Alquen, R., *Time, Mood and Aspect in German Tense*. Lang: Frankfurt/Main, etc., 1997.
Dieling, K. and Kempter, F., *Die Tempora*. 2nd ed. Enzyklopädie: Leipzig, 1989.
Latzel, S., *Die deutschen Tempora Perfekt und Präteritum. Eine Darstellung mit Bezug auf die Erfordernisse des Faches „Deutsch als Fremdsprache"*. Hueber: Munich, 1977.
Thieroff, R., *Das finite Verb im Deutschen. Tempus – Modus – Distanz*. Narr: Tübingen, 1992.

15: The passive

Fagan, S.M.B., *The Syntax and Semantics of Middle Constructions. A Study with Special Reference to German*. CUP: Cambridge, 1992.
Helbig, G. and Heinrich, G., *Das Vorgangspassiv*. 4th ed. Bibliographisches Institut: Leipzig, 1983.

16: Mood: the imperative and the subjunctive

Bausch, K.-H., *Modalität und Konjunktivgebrauch in der gesprochenen deutschen Standardssprache. Sprachsystem, Sprachvariation und Sprachwandel im heutigen Deutsch*. Hueber: Munich, 1979.
Buscha, J. and Zoch, I., *Der Konjunktiv*. 2nd ed. Enzyklopädie: Leipzig, 1988.
Jäger, S., *Empfehlungen zum Gebrauch des Konjunktivs*. Schwann: Düsseldorf, 1970.

17: The modal auxiliaries

Öhlschläger, G., *Zur Syntax und Semantik der Modalverben des Deutschen*. Niemeyer: Tübingen, 1989.
Diewald, G., *Die Modalverben im Deutschen. Grammatikalisierung und Polyfunktionalität*. Niemeyer: Tübingen, 1999.

18: Verbs: valency

Ágel, V., *Valenztheorie*. Narr: Tübingen, 2000.

Bausewein, K., *Akkusativobjekt, Akkusativobjektsätze und Objektsprädikate im Deutschen*. Niemeyer: Tübingen, 1990.

Engel, U. and Schuhmacher, H., *Kleines Valenzlexikon deutscher Verben*. 2nd ed. Narr: Tübingen, 1978.

Helbig, G., *Valenz – Satzglieder – semantische Kasus – Satzmodelle*. Enzyklopädie: Leipzig, 1982.

Helbig, G. and Schenkel, W., *Wörterbuch zur Valenz und Distribution deutscher Verben*. 8th ed. Niemeyer: Tübingen, 1991.

Sommerfeldt, K.-E. and Schreiber, H., *Wörterbuch der Valenz etymologisch verwandter Wörter: Verben, Adjektive, Substantive*. Niemeyer: Tübingen, 1996.

Sonnenberg, B., *Korrelate im Deutschen. Beschreibung, Geschichte und Grammatiktheorie*. Niemeyer: Tübingen, 1992.

Storrer, A., *Verbvalenz. Theoretische und methodischer Grundlagen ihrer Beschreibung in Grammatographie und Lexikographie*. Niemeyer: Tübingen, 1992.

19: Conjunctions and subordination

Buscha, J., *Lexikon deutsche Konjunktionen*. Enzyklopädie: Leipzig, 1989.

20: Prepositions

Schmitz, W., *Der Gebrauch der deutschen Präpositionen*. 8th ed. Hueber: Munich, 1974.

Schröder, J., *Lexikon deutscher Präpositionen*. 2nd ed. Enzyklopädie: Leipzig, 1990.

21: Word order

Eroms, H.W., *Funktionale Satzperspektive*. Niemeyer: Tübingen, 1986.

Haftka, B., *Deutsche Wortstellung. Studienbibliographie*. Groos: Heidelberg, 2000.

Hoberg, U., *Die Wortstellung der geschriebenen deutschen Gegenwartssprache: Untersuchungen zur Elementenfolge im einfachen Verbalsatz*. Hueber: Munich, 1981.

22: Word formation

Eichinger, L. M., *Deutsche Wortbildung. Eine Einführung*. Narr: Tübingen, 1999.

Erben, J. *Einführung in die deutsche Wortbildungslehre*. 4th ed. Erich Schmidt: Berlin, etc., 2000.

Fleischer, W. and Barz, I., *Wortbildung der deutschen Gegenwartssprache*. 2nd rev. ed. Niemeyer: Tübingen, 1995.

Naumann, B. *Einführung in die Wortbildungslehre des Deutschen*. 3rd ed. Niemeyer: Tübingen, 2000.

23: Spelling and punctuation

Augst, G. et al., *Zur Neuregelung der deutschen Orthographie. Begründung und Kritik*. Niemeyer: Tübingen, 1997.

Bertelsmann, *Die neue deutsche Rechtschreibung*. Bertelsmann: Gütersloh, 1996.

DUDEN, *Rechtschreibung der deutschen Sprache und Fremdwörter*. 22nd ed. Dudenverlag: Mannheim, etc., 2000.

Eroms, H.-W. and Munske, H.H. (eds), *Die Rechtschreibreform. Pro und Contra*. Erich Schmidt: Berlin, etc., 1997.

Heller, K., *Rechtschreibung 2000. Die Reform auf einen Blick. Wörterliste der geänderten Schreibungen*. Klett: Stuttgart, etc. 1995.

Glossary

The explanations include references to sections or chapters where more detail is given. Words in small capitals are themselves explained in the glossary.

accusative a CASE (2.2) which indicates the DIRECT OBJECT of TRANSITIVE verbs (18.3): *Ich sehe* **den Hund**. It is also used after some PREPOSITIONS (20.1, 20.3): *Ich gehe durch* **den Wald**, as well as in some ADVERBIAL constructions (11.4.1): *Sie kommt* **jeden Tag**.

accusative object the DIRECT OBJECT of the verb, in the ACCUSATIVE case (18.3): *Der Wolf fraß* **den Esel**.

adjective a word which modifies, or describes a NOUN (Chapter 6). **Attributive** adjectives are used before a noun: *die* **schöne** *Stadt*; **predicative** adjectives are used after a COPULAR VERB: *die Stadt ist* **schön**.

adverb a word which modifies a VERB, an ADJECTIVE or a whole CLAUSE, often giving extra information on **how**, **when**, **where** or **why** (Chapter 7): *Sie singt* **gut**; *Sie war* **sehr** *freundlich*.

adverbial any part of a SENTENCE which has the **function** of an ADVERB (18.1.4). It can be a single word (an ADVERB), or a phrase, or a whole CLAUSE: *Sie sang* **gut**; *Sie sang* **mit einer hellen Stimme**; *Sie sang,* **als sie ins Zimmer kam**.

agreement copying a grammatical feature from one word to another, so that certain words have ENDINGS according to the words they are used with or refer to. In German, DETERMINERS and ADJECTIVES 'agree' with the NOUN (4.1, 6.1): **dieses** *Buch*; *mit* **meinem neuen** *Auto*, and VERBS 'agree' with their SUBJECT (12.1.4): *ich* **singe**, *du* **singst**.

apposition a phrase used to modify a NOUN PHRASE without a connecting preposition is **'in apposition'** to it (2.6): *Wilhelm,* **der letzte deutsche Kaiser**, *starb im Exil*.

article the most important of the DETERMINERS (Chapter 4). German has a **definite article** *der*, *die*, *das*, etc. (= English *the*) and an **indefinite article** *ein*, *eine*, etc. (= English *a*).

auxiliary verb	a VERB used in combination with the INFINITIVE or PAST PAR-TICIPLE of another verb to form a COMPOUND TENSE or the PASSIVE (12.3–4): *Karin* **hat** *einen Hund* **gekauft**, or, in the case of the MODAL AUXILIARIES (Chapter 17), to indicate the attitude of the speaker with regard to what is being said: *Sie* **muss** *sofort* **kommen**.
bracket	the **'bracket' construction** is typical of German CLAUSES, with most words and phrases in a CLAUSE bracketed between two parts of the VERB (21.1): *Wir [kommen um 17 Uhr in Innsbruck an]*.
cardinal number	the numerals used in counting (9.1): *eins, zwei, ... hundert*.
case	indicates the function of a NOUN PHRASE in the CLAUSE (Chapter 2). German has four **cases**: NOMINATIVE *der Igel*; ACCUSATIVE *den Igel*; GENITIVE *des Igels* and DATIVE *dem Igel*.
clause	a part of a SENTENCE with a VERB and its COMPLEMENTS (18.1). A **main clause** can stand on its own: *Dein Vater kommt*. A **subordinate clause** (Chapter 19) is dependent on another clause in the sentence and is usually introduced by a CONJUNCTION: *Ich weiß, dass dein Vater kommt*.
comparative	the form of an ADJECTIVE or ADVERB used to express a comparison (Chapter 8): *schneller, höher, weiter*.
complement	an element in a CLAUSE which is closely linked to the VERB and completes its meaning (18.1). The most important complements of the verb are its SUBJECT and OBJECTS.
complement clause	a **subordinate** CLAUSE which has the same role as a verb COMPLEMENT (19.2): *Dass sie gekommen war, hat mich erstaunt* (the clause is the SUBJECT of the verb); *Ich wusste, dass sie gekommen war* (the clause is the DIRECT OBJECT of the verb).
compound tense	a TENSE formed by using an AUXILIARY VERB with the INFINITIVE or PAST PARTICIPLE of another **verb** (12.3), e.g. the PERFECT tense: *Sie hat geschlafen*, or the FUTURE tense: *Sie wird kommen*.
compound word	a word formed by joining two or more words (22.1): *Kindergarten, dunkelrot*.
conditional	a compound form of KONJUNKTIV II formed from the **past subjunctive** form of the AUXILIARY VERB *werden*, i.e. *würde*, and the INFINITIVE of another verb (12.5.2, 16.4–5): *Ich würde gehen*.
conditional sentence	a SENTENCE which expresses a condition, i.e. 'If X, then Y' (16.5). The SUBJUNCTIVE **mood** is often used in conditional sentences in German.

conjugation	the forms of a verb, in particular the pattern of ENDINGS and/or **vowel changes** which show AGREEMENT with the SUBJECT and indicate the various TENSES or the MOOD, etc., (Chapter 12): *ich komme, du kommst, wir kamen, wir kämen*, etc.
conjunction	a word used to link CLAUSES within a SENTENCE (Chapter 19). **Coordinating conjunctions** link main clauses (e.g. *und, aber*), and **subordinating conjunctions** introduce subordinate clauses (e.g. *dass, obwohl, weil, wenn*).
copular verb	a **linking** VERB, which typically links the SUBJECT with a PREDICATE COMPLEMENT, i.e. an ADJECTIVE or a NOUN PHRASE in the NOMINATIVE case (18.8). The most frequent **copular verbs** in German are *sein, werden* and *scheinen*: *Er ist ein guter Lehrer; Die alte Frau wurde blass.*
count noun	a NOUN referring to a thing or object which can be counted. Count nouns, unlike MASS NOUNS, can be used in the PLURAL and with the **indefinite** ARTICLE.
dative	a CASE (2.5) used to mark some OBJECTS of the VERB: *Sie hat meiner Schwester die CD gegeben, Ich helfe meinem Bruder.* It can also indicate **possession**: *Sie zog dem Kind die Jacke aus*, it is used after some ADJECTIVES (6.5): *Er sieht meinem Vater ähnlich*, and after many PREPOSITIONS (20.2–3): *Er hat mit den Kindern gespielt.*
dative object	a COMPLEMENT of the VERB in the DATIVE case (18.4). With some verbs it is the only object: *Sie wollte dem kleinen Mädchen helfen*, with verbs which also have an ACCUSATIVE (DIRECT) OBJECT, it is the INDIRECT OBJECT: *Sie hat dem kleinen Mädchen das Heft gegeben.*
declension	the pattern of ENDINGS on a NOUN (1.3), an ADJECTIVE (6.1–2), or a DETERMINER (4.1, Chapter 5) which show CASE, NUMBER and GENDER: *der gute Hund, des guten Hundes, den guten Hunden.*
demonstrative	a DETERMINER or PRONOUN (5.1) which points to something specific, e.g. *dieser, jener.*
derivation	forming words from others, typically by using SUFFIXES and/or PREFIXES (Chapter 22): *beglaubigen (< Glaube), Gesundheit (< gesund).*
determiner	a function word used with NOUNS (Chapters 4 and 5). They include the ARTICLES (*der, ein*), the DEMONSTRATIVES (*dieser*, etc.), the POSSESSIVES, (*mein*, etc.) and INDEFINITES (*einige, viele*, etc.). They typically come **before** ADJECTIVES in the NOUN PHRASE.
direct object	a verb COMPLEMENT, typically a person or thing directly affected by the action (18.3). It is in the ACCUSATIVE case. *Der Löwe fraß den Esel; Die böse Frau schlug den Hund.*

direction complement	a COMPLEMENT used with VERBS of **motion**, indicating **where** the SUBJECT is going or where the DIRECT OBJECT is being put (18.7): *Sie fuhr **nach Ulm**; Er stellt den Besen **in die Ecke***.
ending	a SUFFIX which gives grammatical information, e.g. about CASE, NUMBER or TENSE. All the **endings** of a NOUN, ADJECTIVE or DETERMINER make up its DECLENSION; all the endings of a VERB make up its CONJUGATION.
feminine	one of the three GENDERS into which NOUNS are divided (1.1).
finite verb	a form of the VERB which has an ENDING in AGREEMENT with the SUBJECT (12.1): *Ich **komme**; Wir **haben** geschlafen; Sie **wurden** betrogen; Ihr **könnt** gehen*.
future tense	a TENSE formed with the AUXILIARY VERB *werden* and an INFINITIVE (12.3), and used to refer to future time (14.4): *Ich **werde** das Buch nicht **lesen***.
future perfect	a TENSE formed with the AUXILIARY VERB *werden* and a **compound** INFINITIVE (12.3), used to refer to an action or event which will occur before another in the future: *Sie **wird** das Buch **gelesen haben*** (14.4).
gender	a division of NOUNS into three classes in German, called MASCULINE, FEMININE and NEUTER (1.1). The **gender** of a noun is shown by the ENDINGS of the DETERMINER or ADJECTIVE in the NOUN PHRASE: ***der** Mann, **diese** Frau, **klares** Wasser*.
genitive	a CASE which is mainly used to show possession or to link NOUNS together (2.3): *das Buch **meines Vaters**; die Geschichte **dieser Stadt***. A few verbs have a **genitive** OBJECT (18.5), and it is used after a few PREPOSITIONS (see 20.4): *trotz **des Wetters***.
imperative	a MOOD of the VERB used to give commands or instructions, or to make a request (16.2): ***Komm** hierher! **Seid** vorsichtig! **Steigen** Sie bitte **ein***!
indefinite	an **indefinite** PRONOUN or DETERMINER is one which does not refer to a specific person or thing (5.5): *etwas, jemand, irgendwelcher*.
indicative	the most usual MOOD of the VERB, used to make statements and ask questions (Chapter 16): *Sie **kam** gestern. **Siehst** du das Licht?*
indirect object	a verb COMPLEMENT, typically a person indirectly affected by the action expressed by the VERB, especially someone being given something (the DIRECT OBJECT) or benefiting from the action (18.4.2). It is in the DATIVE case: *Sie gab **ihrem Vater** das Geld*.
indirect speech	a construction by which what was said is incorporated into a sentence rather than given in the speaker's original words (16.6). Compare **'direct speech'** *Er sagte: „Ich bin heute krank."* with the corresponding **'indirect speech'**: *Er sagte, dass er heute krank sei*.

infinitive	the basic form of a VERB, ending in *-en* or *-n* (12.1–2, 13.1–4): *kommen, betteln, tun*. It is the form of the **verb** given in dictionaries.
infinitive clause	a **subordinate** CLAUSE containing an INFINITIVE, typically preceded by the particle *zu* (13.2): *Sie hat mir geraten **nach Hause zu gehen**.*
inflection	changing the form of words, most often by ENDINGS, to indicate some grammatical idea, like CASE or TENSE. The **inflection** of NOUNS, ADJECTIVES and DETERMINERS is called DECLENSION, while the **inflection** of verbs is called CONJUGATION.
inseparable verb	a **prefixed** VERB whose PREFIX is not stressed and always remains attached to the **verb** (12.2.1, 22.4): *besuchen, erwarten, verstehen*.
interrogative	**interrogative** DETERMINERS, ADVERBS or PRONOUNS (5.3, 7.5) are used to ask a question: ***Welches** Hemd kaufst du? **Warum** geht er nicht? **Wem** sagst du das?*
intransitive verb	a VERB is **intransitive** if it does not have an ACCUSATIVE (DIRECT) OBJECT (18.3): *Wir **schwimmen**; Dort **stand** er und **wartete** auf Luise; Meine Schwester **hilft** mir.*
irregular verb	a VERB with a CONJUGATION which does not follow the pattern of the WEAK VERBS or the STRONG VERBS (12.1.3, 12.2.2): *wissen – ich weiß – ich wusste – gewusst*.
Konjunktiv	The German term for the SUBJUNCTIVE **mood** (12.5, 16.3–7). There are two main forms: *Konjunktiv I*, used mainly in INDIRECT SPEECH (16.6): *Sie sagte, er **sei** nicht gekommen*, and *Konjunktiv II*, which indicates **unreal conditions** (16.5): *Ich würde lachen, wenn sie käme*.
masculine	one of the three GENDERS into which NOUNS are divided (1.1).
mass noun	a NOUN referring to an indivisible entity, typically a substance or an abstract idea: *das Gold, der Frieden*. Mass nouns, unlike COUNT NOUNS, are not normally used with the indefinite article or in the plural.
modal auxiliaries	the verbs *dürfen, können, mögen, müssen, sollen* and *wollen*, which indicate the attitude of the speaker with regard to what is being said (Chapter 17). They are highly IRREGULAR (12.2.2), and as AUXILIARY VERBS they are normally only used with the INFINITIVE of another VERB (13.3.1): *Sie **darf** spielen; Ich **musste** gehen; Du **sollst** das Fenster **aufmachen**.*
modal particle	a small word which indicates the speaker's attitude to what is being said (Chapter 10): *Es gibt **ja** hier nur zwei gute Restaurants, Das Bier ist **aber** kalt!* (surprise).

mood	forms of the VERB which indicate the speaker's attitude (Chapter 16). German has three **moods**: INDICATIVE (neutral, factual): *Er **geht** nach Hause*; IMPERATIVE (commands, requests): ***Geh** nach Hause!* and SUBJUNCTIVE (possibly not factual): *Wenn er nach Hause **ginge**, . . .*
neuter	one of the three GENDERS into which NOUNS are divided (1.1).
nominative	a CASE (2.1) which most often indicates the SUBJECT of a VERB (18.2): ***Du** lügst*; ***Der Hund** bellt*. It is also used in the PREDICATE COMPLEMENT of COPULAR VERBS (18.8): *Ich bin **der neue Lehrer**.*
non-finite	a form of the VERB which does not have an ENDING in AGREEMENT with the SUBJECT (12.1–2), i.e. the INFINITIVE and the PARTICIPLES.
noun	a type of word which typically refers to a person, a living being, a thing, a place or an idea and can normally be used with a **definite** ARTICLE: ***der** Tisch, **die** Idee, **das** Pferd*.
noun phrase	A group of connected words containing a NOUN (or a PRONOUN) and any other words accompanying it, i.e. a DETERMINER and/or an ADJECTIVE: ***Brot, weißes Brot, das weiße Brot***.
number	the grammatical distinction between SINGULAR and PLURAL.
object	certain COMPLEMENTS of the VERB are known as its **objects** (Chapter 18), i.e. the DIRECT OBJECT, the INDIRECT OBJECT and the PREPOSITIONAL OBJECT.
ordinal number	a form of a numeral used as an ADJECTIVE: *sein **zwanzigster** Geburtstag*. (9.2)
participle	NON-FINITE forms of the VERB (12.1–2, 13.5–7). German has two **participles**: the PRESENT PARTICIPLE, e.g. ***spielend***, and the PAST PARTICIPLE, e.g. ***gespielt***.
passive voice	a form of a VERB where the doer of the action is not necessarily mentioned and the SUBJECT is typically a person or thing to which something happens (12.4, Chapter 15): German has two **passive** constructions, using the AUXILIARY VERBS ***werden*** or ***sein*** and the PAST PARTICIPLE: *Die Schlange **wurde** (von dem Jäger) **getötet***; *Die Stadt **war zerstört***. The **passive voice** contrasts with the (more frequently used) **active voice**: *Der Jäger tötet die Schlange.*
past tense	the **simple** (i.e. one-word) TENSE (12.2) used to relate an action, state or event in the **past** (14.3): *Ich **kam** an; Sie **sah** mich.*
past participle	a NON-FINITE form of the VERB, typically with the PREFIX *ge-* and the ENDING *-t* with WEAK verbs or *-en* with STRONG verbs (12.1–2): ***gekauft; gekommen***. It is most often used to form COMPOUND TENSES (12.3), or as an ADJECTIVE (13.5).

perfect tense	a COMPOUND TENSE formed with the PRESENT TENSE of the AUX-ILIARY VERBS *haben* or *sein* and the PAST PARTICIPLE (12.3), used to relate an action, state or event in the **past** (14.3): *Ich habe sie gesehen; Sie sind gekommen.*
person	a grammatical category indicating the person speaking, i.e. the **'first'** person: *ich, wir*; the person addressed, i.e. the **'second'** person: *du, ihr, Sie*; or other persons or things, i.e. the **'third'** person: *er, sie, es* (3.1). The FINITE VERB has ENDINGS in AGREEMENT with the PERSON and NUMBER of its SUBJECT (12.1).
personal pronoun	simple words standing for the various PERSONS or referring to a NOUN PHRASE (Chapter 3): *ich, mich, mir, du, sie*, etc.
place complement	a typical COMPLEMENT with VERBS that indicate **position**, indicating **where** something is situated (18.7): *Die Flasche steht auf dem Tisch; Ich wohne in Berlin.*
pluperfect tense	a COMPOUND TENSE formed with the PAST TENSE forms of the AUXILIARY VERBS *haben* or *sein* and the PAST PARTICIPLE (12.3), and used to relate actions or events further back in the past than the context (14.5): *Ich hatte sie gesehen; Sie waren gekommen.*
plural	a grammatical term referring to **more than one** person or thing, whereas SINGULAR refers to just one. German NOUNS have special ENDINGS to show the **plural** (1.2).
possessive	a word used to indicate **possession** (5.2), either as a DETER-MINER: *sein Fahrrad*, or as a PRONOUN: *das ist meines.*
predicate complement	the typical verb COMPLEMENT with a COPULAR VERB, normally an ADJECTIVE or a NOUN PHRASE in the NOMINATIVE CASE which describes the subject (18.8): *Mein neuer BMW ist rot; Er wird bestimmt ein guter Tennisspieler.*
prefix	an element added to the beginning of a word to form another word (Chapter 22): *Urwald, unglücklich, verbessern, weggehen.*
preposition	a word used to introduce a NOUN PHRASE and typically indicating position, direction, time, etc. (Chapter 20): *an, auf, aus, neben, ohne*, etc. All German **prepositions** are followed by a NOUN PHRASE in a particular CASE: *Er kam ohne seinen Hund* (acc.); *Er kam mit seinem Hund* (dat.); *Er kam wegen seines Hundes* (gen.).
prepositional adverb	a compound of *da(r)-* with a PREPOSITION, typically used as a PRONOUN referring to things (3.5, 18.6.14): *darauf* 'on it', 'on them', *damit* 'with it', 'with them'.

prepositional object a COMPLEMENT of the VERB introduced by a PREPOSITION (18.6). Typically, the **preposition** does not have its usual meaning, and the choice of **preposition** depends on the individual **verb**: *Wir warten **auf meine Mutter**; Sie warnte mich **vor dem großen Hund**.*

prepositional phrase the combination of a NOUN PHRASE with a PREPOSITION: *an diesem Tag, aus dem Haus, zwischen den Häusern.*

present participle a NON-FINITE form of the VERB, with the SUFFIX *-d* added to the INFINITIVE (12.1–2): *leidend, schlafend.* It is used most often as an ADJECTIVE (13.5): *das **schlafende** Kind.*

present tense the simple TENSE (12.2) used to relate something going on at the moment of speaking, or which takes place regularly or repeatedly (14.2): *Jetzt **kommt** sie; In Irland **regnet** es viel.*

principal parts the **three main forms** in the CONJUGATION of a VERB, i.e. the INFINITIVE, the PAST TENSE and the PAST PARTICIPLE (12.1–2): *machen – machte – gemacht* (WEAK verb); *kommen – kam – kommen* (STRONG verb). The other forms of most verbs are constructed on the basis of these three forms.

pronoun typically a little word which stands for a whole NOUN PHRASE, e.g. PERSONAL PRONOUNS (Chapter 3), e.g. *ich, mich, sie*; DEMONSTRATIVE **pronouns** (5.1), e.g. *dieser*, POSSESSIVE **pronouns** (5.2), e.g. *meiner, seines*; INDEFINITE **pronouns** (5.5), e.g. *man, niemand.*

reflexive pronoun a PRONOUN in the ACCUSATIVE or DATIVE case referring back to the SUBJECT of the VERB (3.2): *Sie wäscht **sich**; Ich habe es **mir** so vorgestellt.*

reflexive verb a VERB used in combination with a REFLEXIVE PRONOUN (18.3.6): *sich erinnern* (remember), *sich weigern* (refuse).

register differences of usage linked to different **situations** and **addressees**, typically associated with degrees of formality/informality, as found, for example, in differences between **spoken** and **written** language.

relative clause a **subordinate** CLAUSE used in the function of an ADJECTIVE to describe a NOUN: *der Mann, **der dort spielt**.* **Relative clauses** are introduced by a RELATIVE PRONOUN (5.4).

relative pronoun a PRONOUN which, like English 'who', 'which' or 'that', is used to introduce a RELATIVE CLAUSE: (5.4): *der Mann, **den** ich gegrüßt hatte, die Männer, **denen** ich helfen konnte.*

root the base form of a word, without PREFIXES and SUFFIXES: *wiederkommen, arbeiten, uninteressant.*

sentence the longest unit of grammar, ending with a full stop in writing. It must have at least one **main** CLAUSE: *Else hat mir* *geantwortet*, and the main clause(s) can have one or more dependent **subordinate clauses**: *Else hat mir geantwortet, dass Sie nicht nach New York gehen wollte.*

sentence pattern	A limited number of combinations of COMPLEMENTS occur commonly with German verbs, since many verbs have the same VALENCY. Such combinations are known as **sentence patterns** (18.1.3).
separable verb	a VERB with a **stressed** PREFIX which detaches from the FINITE VERB in MAIN CLAUSES and is placed at the **end** of the CLAUSE (12.2.1, 22.5), e.g. *ankommen*: *Wir **kommen** morgen um zwei Uhr in Dresden **an**.*
singular	a grammatical term referring to **one** person or thing, whereas PLURAL refers to more than one. The pronouns *ich, du, es* and the nouns *der kleine Hund* or *das Kind* are **singular**.
strong adjective declension	a set of ENDINGS used with ADJECTIVES which are like the **endings** of the **definite** ARTICLE and *dieser* (6.1–2). They are used when there is no DETERMINER in the NOUN PHRASE, or when the **determiner** has no **ending** of its own: *starkes Bier, mein alter Freund.*
strong verb	a VERB which changes its vowel in the PAST TENSE (and often in the PAST PARTICIPLE), and has the ending *-en* in the past participle (12.1.2, 12.2): *bitten – bat – gebeten.*
subject	the NOUN PHRASE in the NOMINATIVE CASE with which the FINITE VERB **agrees** for PERSON and NUMBER (12.1.4, 18.2): *Du **kommst** morgen; Die Leute beschwerten sich über die Preise.* Typically it is the person or thing carrying out the action expressed by the verb.
subjunctive mood	a MOOD of the VERB typically used to indicate that an action, event or state may not be factual (16.3–7). There are two forms of the **subjunctive** in German (12.5): KONJUNKTIV I is used most often to mark INDIRECT SPEECH (16.6): *Sie sagte, er sei nicht gekommen* and KONJUNKTIV II indicates **unreal conditions** (16.5): *Ich würde lachen, wenn sie käme.*
suffix	an element added to the end of a word or ROOT to form a new word by DERIVATION (Chapter 22): *freundlich, Freundlichkeit* or, as an INFLECTION in the form of an ENDING, to give grammatical information: *Kinder, machte.*
superlative	the form of an ADJECTIVE or ADVERB which expresses the highest degree of comparison (Chapter 8): *der höchste Baum, das Auto fährt am schnellsten.*
tense	a form of the VERB which indicates the **time** of an action, event or state in relation to the moment of speaking

(Chapter 14). German has **simple tenses**, of one word (12.2): PRESENT *ich warte*; PAST *ich wartete* and COMPOUND TENSES (12.3): FUTURE *ich werde warten*; PERFECT *ich habe gewartet*; PLUPERFECT *ich hatte gewartet*; FUTURE PERFECT *ich werde gewartet haben*.

topic
the **first element** in a **main** CLAUSE, before the FINITE VERB (21.2): *Max ist gestern nach Rom gefahren; Gestern ist Max nach Rom gefahren; Nach Rom ist Max gestern gefahren.* It is typically something we are emphasising because we want to say something about it.

transitive verb
a VERB is **transitive** if it can have a DIRECT OBJECT in the ACCUSATIVE CASE (18.3): *Sie sah mich; Ich grüsste meinen Freund; Meine Schwester kauft die Bücher.*

valency
the construction used with a particular VERB, i.e. the number and type of COMPLEMENTS which it requires to form a **fully grammatical** CLAUSE **or** SENTENCE (Chapter 18).

verb
a type of word which refers to an action, event, process or state: *schlagen, passieren, recyceln, schlafen.*

weak adjective declension
a set of ENDINGS used with ADJECTIVES when there is a DETERMINER with its own ENDING preceding it in the NOUN PHRASE (6.1–2): *das starke Bier, die jungen Frauen.*

weak masculine noun
one of a small set of MASCULINE NOUNS which have the ENDING *-(e)n* in the ACCUSATIVE, GENITIVE and DATIVE CASES in the SINGULAR as well as in the PLURAL (1.3.2): *der Affe, den Affen, des Affen, dem Affen, die Affen,* etc.

weak verb
the mainly regular VERBS of German, which form their PAST TENSE with the ENDING *-te* and their PAST PARTICIPLE with the ENDING *-t* (12.1.2, 12.2): *machen – machte – gemacht.*

Index

The index lists all the German and English words and the grammatical topics about which specific information is given in this book. However, individual words in lists illustrating points of grammar are not included. To facilitate finding particular entries, German words are given in regular type, English words in *italics* and grammatical topics in SMALL CAPITALS (with any German terms *ITALICISED*)

à 20.1.7a
ab 4.9.3c, 11.5.12, 20.2.10a
ab- 22.5.1a
ABBREVIATIONS:
  gender 1.1.9b; genitive singular 1.3.7d; plural 1.2.5c
Abdruck, der 1.2.8
Abend, der 11.5.14
abends 11.4.2, 23.1.2
aber (conjunction) 10.1.4, 10.7.7b, 10.30.1a, 10.35.3, 10.36.1, 19.1.1, 23.5.1b
aber (particle) 10.1, 10.2.1, 10.7.1, 10.19.2, 10.34.1
abfahren 18.3.5a
abfragen 18.3.3a
abhalten 18.6.14
abhängig 6.6.1a
abhold 6.5.1b
abhören 18.3.3a
ABLAUT:
  in word formation 22.1.1b, 22.2.3a; with strong verbs 12.1.2, Table 12.1
about 6.6.1b, 9.1.6, 11.5.6, 11.5.11b, 18.6.9a, 20.1.4e, 20.1.6, 20.3.12e, 20.4.1d
above 20.3.11, 20.3.12
abraten 18.4.1a, 18.6.14
Abscheu, der (die) 1.1.9, 1.1.11a
abseits 20.4.3
ABSOLUTE PHRASES:
  in accusative 2.2.6 ; in nominative 2.1.1
abstoßend 13.5.4a
ABSTRACT NOUNS:
  derived from adjectives 22.2.1e; derived from verbs 22.2.1k; use of articles with 4.2, 4.6.2, 4.8.2c

Abteil, das 1.1.11c
Abwasser, das 1.2.4d
abwesend 13.5.4a
abzüglich 20.4.3
accomplish 22.6.7
according to 19.7.5, 20.2.6d, 20.2.10e
ACCUSATIVE CASE (*see also:* accusative object) **2.2**, Table 2.1:
  adverbial use 2.2.5; governed by adjectives 6.5.2; governed by prepositions **20.1, 20.3**; in absolute constructions 2.2.6; in distance phrases 2.2.5c; in measurement phrases 2.2.5b; in predicate complement 18.3.3h; in time phrases 2.2.5a, 11.4.1; to indicate possession 2.5.4c; used in greetings 2.2.3
ACCUSATIVE OBJECT (*see also:* direct object) 2.2.1, **18.3**:
  becoming subject in passive 15.1.2; 'cognate' 2.2.2; double 18.3.3; in initial position 21.2.1b; position in verbal bracket 21.5, 21.6.1; reflexive 18.3.6; with dative object 18.4.2; with genitive object 18.5.3
Acht geben 18.6.3a, 18.6.14, 22.5.3
Acker, der 1.2.2c
across 20.1.2a, 20.3.11, 20.3.12
ACTIVE VOICE 12.1.1d, Ch. 15
actual(ly) 10.10
ADDRESSES 4.4.1e, 9.5
ADJECTIVE **Ch. 6** (*see also:* participles, word formation):

ADJECTIVE – *contd*
  agreement for gender 1.1.13c
  as part of geographical and other proper names 23.1.1d
  attributive adjective: 6.1: extended as phrase 6.6.3, 13.5.3; undeclined 6.2.7; use of commas with 23.5.5
  commas with more than one adjective 23.5.5
  comparative: **Ch. 8** (see also: comparison of adjectives and adverbs)
  declension **6.1, 6.2**, Tables **6.1–6.4**: after indefinite determiners and quantifiers 6.2.3; after personal pronouns 6.2.8; lack of declension 6.2.7; 'mixed' declension 6.2.1b; spelling changes in declined adjectives 6.3; 'strong' declension 6.1.2, 6.2.1; 'weak' declension 6.1.2, 6.2.2
  formation of abstract nouns from 22.2.1d
  formed from: adverbs 22.3.1d; cardinal numbers 6.2.7e; names of towns and countries 6.2.7d, 23.1.1d
  governing cases: **6.5**: accusative 6.5.2; dative 6.5.1; genitive 3.6.4, 6.5.3
  governing prepositions **6.6**
  of language and nationality 6.4.6a, 20.3.5e, 23.1.1e
  predicate adjective: as complement 18.8; in apposition 6.4.2b; in constructions with es and sein 3.6.4, 18.2.4d; in constructions with

ADJECTIVE – *contd*
predicate adjective – *contd*
genitive 6.5.3c; in
constructions with
personal dative 2.5.5c,
6.5.1b, 18.2.4e; not
declined 6.1.1; superlative
forms 8.4.1b; with
following infinitive clause
13.2.6
superlative **Ch. 8** (see:
comparison of adjectives
and adverbs)
used as adverb 6.2.7c
used as noun **6.4**, 22.2.3c,
Table **6.5**: after indefinites
5.5.1h, 5.5.9b, 5.5.15b,
5.5.22, 5.5.25b, 6.4.5; after
was 5.3.3e; declension
6.4.2; followed by relative
clause 5.4.3b; masculine
and feminine 6.4.3; neuter
6.4.4–5; spelling with
initial capital 23.1.1–2
use of initial capital or small
letters 23.1.1–2
ADJECTIVE CLAUSE (*see:* relative
clause)
admit 7.3.4
admittedly 10.2, 10.14
ADVERB **Ch. 7**:
as equivalent of English
clause 7.3.4
as equivalent of English
progressive tenses 14.6.2a
comparative: **Ch. 8** (see:
comparison of adjectives
and adverbs)
from adjectives: 6.2.7c, 7.3.1c
from nouns – no initial
capital 23.1.2
from participles 13.5.2c
from preposition plus noun
23.2.1
interrogative 7.5: as
conjunctions 19.2.4,
19.3.1c; in concessive
clauses 19.6.2
of attitude 7.3.2, 7.3.6b:
position 21.6.1a
of degree: 7.4: with numerals
9.1.6
of direction: 2.2.5c, **7.2**: used
as separable prefix 7.2.2–4,
22.5.1
of manner 7.3.1, 7.3.6a;
position 21.6.1c, 21.6.2c
of place **7.1**: used with
preposition 20.2.6a;
position 21.6.1a, 21.6.2c
of reason 7.3.3
of time 11.6: indicating
duration 11.6.1b;
indicating frequency

ADVERB – *contd*
of time – *contd*
11.6.1c; of point in time
11.6.1a; with bis 11.5.4;
position 21.6.1a, 21.6.2c
of viewpoint 7.3.1
position 21.2.1, **21.6**, 21.9.4d
prepositional 3.5 (see also:
prepositional adverb)
superlative **Ch. 8** (see:
comparison of adjectives
and adverbs)
types Table 7.1
used as separable verb
prefixes 22.5.2–3
Adverb, das 1.2.6d
ADVERBIAL (*see also:* adverb)
18.1.4:
word order 21.2.1b, **21.6**,
21.9.4
ADVERBIAL CLAUSE 19.3–19.8
afraid 7.3.4
after 11.5.8, 11.6.4b, 18.6.8a,
19.3.4
after all 10.29
against 20.1.4a, 20.1.7f
AGENT 15.3.1, 18.2.1, 18.2.3
ago 7.2.5e, 11.5.13
AGREEMENT:
for gender 1.1.13: of
possessives 5.2.1; of relative
pronoun 5.4.1a; of third
person pronouns 3.4.1
of subject and verb 12.1.1a,
12.1.4: with collective
nouns 12.1.4g; names of
festivals 1.2.10b; with
neuter indefinites and
pronouns 3.6.2b, 5.1.1h,
5.3.1a, 5.3.3b, 5.5.3d; with
subject clause 12.1.4a
ahead of 20.3.15a
ähneln 15.4.2b, 18.4.1a
ähnlich 6.5.1a, 23.1.1c
Album, das 1.2.6a
all 5.5.1, 5.5.23
all but 20.1.1c
all right 10.30.1b
all the same 10.2, 10.14, 10.18
all/alles/alle 5.3.3b, 5.4.3a,
5.5.1, 5.5.3a, 5.5.23, 6.2.3b,
6.4.5
allein 19.1.1b
allerdings 7.3.4, 10.2, 10.14,
21.2.1c
allmählich 7.3.4
allow 13.3.1c, 17.2.1
allzu 10.15a
along 20.3.2a, 20.3.6
already 10.30.5
als 'as' 18.3.3b, 20.2.9d
als 'than' 2.6, 4.8.3, 8.3.1,
8.3.6a, 10.6.2e, 13.2.8,
19.7.1, 21.9.3, 23.5.4

als 'when' 5.4.6b, 13.7.2d,
13.7.3a, 14.3.3b, 19.3.1
als dass 16.7.5a, 19.5.3
als ob 16.7.1
als wenn 16.7.1
also 10.3, 21.2.1c
also 10.4.5b
alt 8.3.3, 8.2.3a
although 10.36.1, 13.6.3, 19.6.1
am …sten 8.1.2, 8.4.1, 23.1.1f
am besten 7.3.4
am wenigsten 8.3.2
among(st) 20.3.13b, 20.3.14a,
20.3.17a
an 4.5.3, **11.5.1**, 11.5.15a, 18.6.2,
20.2.3a, 20.2.6a, **20.3.2**,
20.3.3, 20.5.1c
an- 22.5.1b
an … entlang 20.3.2a, 20.3.6c
an … hin 7.2.3a, 20.3.2a,
20.3.6d
an … vorbei 20.3.2a
anbauen 20.3.1e
anbelangt (was …) 20.4.3
anbieten 13.2.4b, 15.2.2f
anbinden 20.3.1c
anbringen 20.3.1e
and 19.1.4
andauernd 7.3.4
Andenken, das 13.4.4
ander 5.5.2, 5.5.15, 7.3.5, 9.1.2e,
23.1.1c
ändern (sich) 18.3.5c
anders 7.3.5
anderswo 7.1.5a
anderthalb 9.3.2e
aneignen, sich 18.4.3b
aneinander fügen 22.5.3b
Anfang, der 4.5.1, 11.4.1b
anfangen 12.3.2a, 13.2.2b,
18.6.14
anfangs 20.4.3, 23.1.2
angeblich 7.3.4
angebracht 13.5.4b
angehen 18.3.3a
angehören 18.4.1a
angenehm 6.5.1a
angenommen, dass 16.5.3d
angesehen 13.5.4b
angesichts 20.4.3, 23.1.2
Angestellte, der 6.4.2a
angewiesen 6.6.1a
angst 6.6.1c, 23.1.2
ängstigen, sich 18.6.10,
18.6.12a
anhand/an Hand 20.4.3, 23.2.1
anheben Table 12.12
anheim fallen 22.5.3b
anklagen 18.5.3
anlässlich 20.4.3
anmaßen, sich 18.4.3b
anmerken 18.4.2c
Anmut, die 1.1.9a
annehmen, sich 18.5.2

anordnen 13.2.4b
anregen 13.2.4b
ans 4.1.1c
anscheinend 7.3.4
anschließen 20.3.1e
ansehen 4.8.3
ansichtig 6.5.3c
(an)statt 20.4.1a, 23.1.2
(an)statt dass 13.2.7c, 13.7.2c
(an)statt ... zu 13.2.7c, 13.7.2c
ansteckend 13.5.4a
anstelle/an Stelle (von)
  20.4.1a, 20.4.3, 23.2.1
anstrengend 13.5.4a
answer 18.3.5b
Antarktis, die 1.1.3g
ANTICIPATORY *ES* 3.6.2c, 3.6.3a
Antwort, die 1.1.9
antworten 18.3.5b, 18.4.2b
anweisen 13.2.4b
anwesend 13.5.4a
any 4.2.2a, 4.8.7, 5.5.9, 5.5.11,
  5.5.12, 5.5.14b, 5.5.16,
  5.5.26
any ... at all 5.5.11
anyhow 5.5.11, 10.20.2, 10.32.1
anyone 5.5.4c, 5.5.11c
anything 5.5.9, 5.5.11c
anything but 8.2.4e
anyway 10.9, 10.27, 10.31
anywhere 5.5.11b, 7.1.5
apart from 20.3.10c
Aperitif, der (das) 1.1.11a
Apfel, der 1.2.2c
appear 20.3.1b
APPOSITION 2.6:
  in measurement phrases
  2.7; lack of article in 4.8.4;
  use of comma 23.5.4; with
  adjectives used as nouns
  6.4.2b
arg 8.2.3a
ärgerlich 6.6.1a
ärgern (sich) 18.6.14
Arktis, die 1.1.3g
arm 6.6.1a, 8.2.3a
Armut, die 1.1.9a
Aroma, das 1.2.6b
around 11.5.11b, 20.1.6
arrive 20.3.1b
Art, die 5.4.6c
ARTICLE **Ch. 4** (*see also:* definite
  article, indefinite article,
  zero article)
as (cause) 19.1.2, 19.3.4, 19.4.1
as (comparative) 4.8.3, 8.3.6,
  19.7.1
as (time) 13.4.3a, 19.3.1
as a result of 20.3.5d
as far as 20.1.1
as if 16.7.1
as long as 19.3.6
as often as 19.3.6
as soon as 19.3.6

as well as 19.1.4
assuming that 16.5.3d
at 11.5.11a, 20.1.7a, 20.2.3,
  20.3.2a, 20.3.4a, 20.3.8a
at all 10.32.1
at any rate 10.20.1
at least 10.20.1
(at) once 10.16
Atem, der 1.2.11
Atlas, der 1.2.6d
auch 10.4, 19.6.2
auch kein/nicht 10.4.5e,
  17.3.2b
auch nur 10.4.5c
auch wenn 16.5.3d
auf 6.6.1a, **11.5.2**, 11.5.5, 18.6.3,
  20.2.3b, 20.2.6a, 20.3.2a,
  20.3.4, **20.3.5**, 20.5.1b
auf- 22.5.1c
auf dass 16.7.2b, 19.5.1b
auf ... hin 7.2.3c, 20.3.5d
auf ... zu 20.3.5a
auffallen 18.4.1d
auffallend 13.5.4a
auffordern 13.2.4b
aufgebracht 6.6.1b, 13.5.4b
aufgehen 18.3.5a, 18.4.1d
aufgeregt 13.5.4b
aufgrund/auf Grund 20.4.3,
  23.2.1
aufhalten, sich 18.7.1
aufhängen 20.3.1c
aufhören 18.6.14
aufmachen 18.3.5a
aufmerksam 6.6.1a
aufnehmen 20.3.1f
aufpassen 18.6.14
aufregend 13.5.4a
aufs ...ste 8.4.3, 23.1.1f
aufschreiben 20.3.1c
aufwärts gehen 22.5.3b
aufweichen Table 12.12
Auge, das 1.1.8b, 1.2.4e
Augenblick, der 11.5.7a
aus- 22.5.1d
aus 18.6.4, **20.2.1**, 20.3.15d
ausbedingen, sich Table 12.12,
  18.4.3b
ausgezeichnet 13.5.4b
AUSKLAMMERUNG 21.9
Auskunft, die 1.2.12
ausschließlich 20.4.3
außen 7.1.4
außer 3.5.2, 4.2.3c, 5.3.3c,
  13.2.7d, 19.7.2, **20.2.2**,
  20.3.10c
außer dass 13.2.7d, 19.7.2a
außer wenn 19.7.2b
außer ... zu 13.2.7d
außerdem 3.5.2
Äußere, das 6.4.2b
äußere/äußerste 8.2.5
außerhalb 20.4.2
äußerlich 8.2.5

äußerst 8.4.4a
außerstande/außer Stande
  23.2.1
ausweichen 18.4.1a
ausweislich 20.4.3
AUXILIARY VERB 12.1.1b, 12.1.3
  (*see also:* verb, modal
  auxiliary):
  forms 12.2.2, Tables 12.3–4;
  in compound tenses 12.3;
  in passive 12.4; in perfect
  tense 12.3.2; position
  17.1.3, 21.1; semi-auxiliary
  verbs 13.2.5; understood in
  coordinated clauses
  21.1.4b; use in past and
  perfect tense 14.3.2b,
  14.3.3b

Backbord, das (der) 1.1.11a
backen Table 12.12
Bahnhof, der 20.3.4b, 20.5.1b
bald 8.2.4
bald ... bald 19.1.5a
Band, das 1.1.12, 1.2.8
Band, der 1.1.12
Band, die 1.1.12
bang(e) 2.5.5c, 8.2.3b, 23.1.2
bangen 18.2.2
Bank, die 1.2.8, 20.3.4b, 20.5.1b
bar 6.5.3a
-bar 15.4.8, 22.3.1a
Bär, der 1.3.2a
Barock, der & das 1.1.11a
Bau, der 1.2.2e
bauen 15.2.2f
Bauer, der 1.2.2b, 1.3.2
Bayer, der 1.2.2b, 1.3.2a
be able to 17.3.1
be meant/supposed to 17.6.1a,
  17.6.2a
be to 17.6.1a, 17.6.2a
be- 22.4.1
Beamte, der 6.4.3
Beamtin, die 6.4.3
beantragen Table 12.12,
  13.2.4b, 18.3.4
beantworten 18.3.5b
beauftragen Table 12.12
because 19.1.2, 19.4.1
because of 20.4.1d
bedauerlicherweise 7.3.4
bedeutend 7.4.2, 13.5.4a
bedienen, sich 18.5.2
Bedingung, die 4.8.2b
bedürfen 18.2.4g, 18.5.1
bedürftig 6.5.3c
beerben 18.3.4
befehlen Table 12.12, 13.2.4b
befestigen 20.3.1e
Beförderung, die 20.2.9f
before 10.12.2b, 11.5.13, 11.6.4a,
  16.7.4, 19.3.2
befragen 15.2.2f

befürchten 13.2.5, 15.4.5
befürworten 13.2.4b
begegnen 15.2.2f, 15.4.2b,
    18.4.1a
begeistert 6.6.1a
begierig 6.6.2
begin 7.3.4
beginnen 12.3.2a; Table 12.12,
    13.2.2b, 18.6.14
begraben 15.2.2f
begreiflich 6.5.1a
behaupten 13.2.4c
behilflich 6.5.1a
behind 20.3.7
behufs 20.4.3
bei 2.6.3, 11.5.3, 20.2.3, 20.3.4b
bei- 18.4.1c, 22.5.1j
bei weitem 7.4.2, 23.1.1a
beide 5.5.3, 6.2.3b, 9.1.1j,
    23.1.1c
beid(er)seits 20.4.2
beifügen 18.4.2c
beim 4.1.1c, 13.4.3a, 13.7.2d,
    14.6.2c, 20.2.3b
beinahe 16.7.5c
beinhalten Table 12.12
beiseite 23.2.1
beißen 2.5.4c; Table 12.12
bekannt 6.5.1a, 8.3.3, 13.5.4b
bekanntlich 7.3.4
beklagen, sich 18.6.14
bekommen 12.3.2c, 13.2.5,
    15.1.2b, 14.4.2, 18.4.1a
belegt 13.5.4b
beleibt 13.5.4b
belieben 13.2.5
beliebig 7.3.4
belong 18.4.1a
below 20.3.13, 20.3.14a, 20.4.2
bemächtigen, sich 18.5.2
bemerken 15.2.2f
bemühen, sich 18.6.14
benachbart 13.5.4b
beneath 20.3.13a, 20.3.14a,
    20.4.2
Benehmen, das 13.4.4
benötigen 18.5.1
bequem 6.5.1a
berauben 18.5.3
berechtigt 6.6.1a
bereit 6.6.1a, 6.6.2
bereithalten 22.5.3b
bergen Table 12.12
bersten Table 12.12
beruhigend 13.5.4a
beschämt 6.6.1b
beschuldigen 18.5.3
beschweren (sich) 18.6.14
beschwerlich 6.5.1a
beside 20.3.10
besides 13.2.7d, 20.2.2a, 20.3.10c
besitzen 15.1.2b
besorgt 6.6.1a
besser/best 8.2.4

bestehen 18.6.3b, 18.6.4,
    18.6.6b
besteigen 18.3.5b
bestens 8.4.4b
bestimmen 20.2.9f
bestimmt 7.3.4, 21.6.1a
bestürzt 6.6.1b
betrachten 4.8.3, 15.2.2f
beträchtlich 7.4.2
betreffend 20.1.7b
betreffs 20.1.7b, 20.4.3
betrifft (was...) 20.4.3
betroffen 6.6.1b
Bett, das 1.2.4e
better 7.3.4
between 20.3.17
beunruhigen 15.2.2f
bevor 16.7.4, 19.3.2a
bevorstehen 18.4.1b
bewegen 12.2.1e; Table 12.12,
    18.6.13a
bewundern 15.2.2f
bewusst 6.5.1a, 6.5.3a
beyond 20.3.11, 20.3.12, 20.4.2a
bezahlen 18.3.4
bezeichnend 6.6.1a
bezichtigen 18.5.3
beziehungsweise 19.1.3b,
    23.5.1a
bezüglich 20.4.3
Bibliothek, die 20.3.4b, 20.5.1b
biegen Table 12.12
bieten Table 12.12
binden Table 12.12
binnen 20.2.10b, 20.4.2a
bis (conjunction) 16.7.4, 19.3.2c
bis (preposition) 11.5.4, 20.1.1
bis auf 11.5.4, 20.1.1c
bis dahin 11.6.3b
bis wann? 7.5
bis zu 4.5.3, 9.1.6, 11.5.4,
    13.4.3b, 20.1.1
bisher 14.2.2, 14.3.4a
(ein) bisschen 5.5.5, 23.1.2
(a) bit 5.5.9c
bitten Table 12.12, 13.2.4b,
    18.3.3a, 18.6.10, 18.6.14
blasen Table 12.12
blass 6.6.1a, 8.2.3b
bleiben 2.1.3, 4.8.2, 12.3.2a;
    Table 12.12, 13.2.5, 13.3.1f,
    13.5.5d, 13.7.5c, 14.3.3b,
    15.2.2e, 15.4.5b, 18.7.1,
    18.8, 21.8.1e, 23.1.2
bleich 6.6.1a
bleichen Table 12.12
Blitz, der 1.2.12
blitzen 18.2.4a
blöd(e) 6.3.3
bloß 10.5, 10.12.1b, 10.26,
    16.7.6b
bloßstellen 22.5.3b
Boden, der 1.2.2c
Bogen, der 1.2.2c

Bonus, der 1.2.6a
born 15.2.2g
bös(e) 6.3.3, 6.5.1a, 6.6.1a, 6.6.2,
    8.2.4d
Bösewicht, der 1.2.2d
both 5.5.3
both ... and 19.1.4b
bottom 7.1.2
BRACKET (*see*: verbal bracket)
braten Table 12.12
brauchen 12.2.1j, 12.5.2b,
    13.2.5, 13.3.1a, 13.3.2a,
    15.2.2f, 17.5.1b, 17.5.2c,
    17.5.3a, 18.5.1
break 18.3.5
brechen 12.3.2c; Table 12.12,
    15.2.2f, 18.3.5
brennen Table 12.12
bringen Table 12.12, 13.4.3b
Brot, das 1.2.12
Bruder, der 1.2.2c
Brünette, die 6.4.3
brustschwimmen 22.5.3e
Bub, der 1.3.2a
Buchstabe, der 1.1.8b, 1.2.2e,
    1.3.3
Bulle, der & die 1.1.12
Bund, das & der 1.1.12
Bus, der 1.2.6a, 1.3.7g
but 10.1.2, 10.7.7b, 19.1.1
by 11.5.4, 15.3, 20.1.6c, 20.1.7d,
    20.2.3a, 20.2.5b, 20.3.2a
by ...-ing 13.7.2a, 19.7.3, 20.1.2c
by the way 10.33
by way of 20.2.9d

can 17.2.1, 17.3.1, 17.3.4,
    17.5.2d
CAPITAL LETTERS, use of **23.1**
CARDINAL NUMBERS **9.1**; Table
    9.1:
    adjectival forms 6.2.7e,
    9.1.4; adjective declension
    after 6.2.1b; form 9.1.1; in
    partitive constructions
    2.4.2d, 3.1.2a; inflection
    9.1.3; qualification of 9.1.6;
    used as nouns 1.1.2d,
    9.1.1n; with *zu* 20.2.9h
CASE **Ch. 2**, Table 2.1 (*see also*:
    accusative case, dative
    case, genitive case,
    nominative case):
    after adjectives 6.5; after
    prepositions **Ch. 20**; of
    relative pronoun 5.4.1a;
    with verbs **Ch. 18**
CAUSAL CLAUSE 19.4
CAUSATIVE:
    constructions with *lassen*
    13.3.1c, 13.3.2b, 18.3.5d,
    21.1.3b; formation of
    causative verbs 22.7.2
cause 13.3.1c

cease 7.3.4
chance 7.3.4
change 18.3.5c
Charakter, der 1.2.2b
charakteristisch 6.6.1a
Charme, der 1.1.8b, 1.3.2a
-chen 1.1.4c, 1.1.7, 1.1.13d, 1.2.4c, 22.2.1a
circa 9.1.6
claim 7.3.4, 17.7.2
CLAUSE (*see*: adverbial clause, infinitive clause, main clause, noun clause, relative clause, subordinate clause)
CLAUSES OF DEGREE 19.7
CLAUSES OF MANNER 19.7
CLAUSES OF RESULT 19.5.2
CLEFT SENTENCE 3.6.2c, 21.2.3a
climb 18.3.5b
cling to 20.3.1c
CLOCK TIMES 11.1; Tables 11.1–2
CLOTHING, articles of: use of definite article or possessive 4.6.1; use of singular 1.2.13; with possessive dative 2.5.4
COLON 23.6.2
COLOURS, nouns and adjectives denoting 6.4.6: gender 1.1.3c
come 13.7.5b, 14.2.2c
COMMA **23.5**: with coordinated main clauses 23.5.1; with infinitive clauses 23.5.3; with interjections and exclamations 23.5.4; with multiple adjectives 23.5.5; with participial clauses 23.5.3; with phrases in apposition 23.5.4; with subordinate clauses 23.5.2
COMMANDS (*see also*: imperative mood) **16.2**: in first person plural 16.2.2f, 16.7.6d
in form of dass-clause 16.2.2h, 19.2.1d
in third person 16.2.2g, 16.7.6c, 17.4.4a
indirect commands 16.6.4b, 17.4.4b, 17.6.1b
infinitive used in:13.3.3a, 16.2.2a
past participle used in 13.5.5a, 16.2.2b
use of exclamation mark 23.6.4b
use of modal particles in: auch 10.4.4; doch 10.7.3; eben 10.8.1b; einfach 10.11; ja 10.19.3; jedenfalls

COMMANDS – *contd*
use of modal particles in – *contd*
10.20.2; mal 10.22; nur 10.26.1a; ruhig 10.28; schon 10.30.4; überhaupt 10.32.1; wohl 10.35.4
with form of statements or questions 16.2.2d
with Konjunktiv I 16.2.2, 17.4.4
with mögen 17.4.4
with sollen 16.2.2, 17.6.1b
with subjectless passive 15.1.4d, 16.2.2c
word order 21.1.1b
COMPARATIVE **Ch. 8** (*see*: comparison of adjectives and adverbs)
COMPARATIVE CLAUSES: with *als ob*, etc. 16.7.1, 21.1.1b; with *als* or *wie* 3.4.3, 13.3.1b, 19.7.1; with *je ... desto* 8.3.5; with past participle 13.6.2
COMPARATIVE PHRASES with *als* or *wie*: 8.3.1, 8.3.6: enclosure within main clause 21.9.3; for English predicate complement 18.3.4b; lacking article 4.8.3; punctuation 23.5.4; with infinitive clauses 13.2.9a
compared with 20.1.4c, 20.2.4c, 20.3.10d
COMPARISON OF ADJECTIVES AND ADVERBS **Ch. 8**:
absolute comparative 8.3.3
absolute superlative ('elative') 8.4.2: of adverbs 8.4.3
comparative particle 8.3.1
degrees of comparison 8.3.1–2, 20.1.6c
equal comparison 8.3.6
formation of comparative and superlative 8.1–2: irregular forms 8.2; of adverbs 8.1.2, 8.4.1a, 8.4.4; of compound adjectives 8.2.6; of participles 8.2.7, 13.5.4; regular formation 8.1; with umlaut 8.2.3
lower degrees of comparison 8.3.2
positive degree 8
progressive comparison ('more and more') 8.3.4
proportionate comparison ('the more ... the more') 8.3.5

COMPARISON OF ADJECTIVES AND ADVERBS – *contd*
superlative, types and uses 8.4: absolute 8.4.2–3; compounded with numerals 9.2.1b; use of capital letters 23.1.1f; with am 8.4.1; with aufs 8.4.3
COMPLEMENT (of verb) **18.1** (*see also*: direction complement, place complement, predicate complement, prepositional object, subject, object)
COMPLEMENT CLAUSES 19.2 (*see also*: noun clauses)
complete 22.6.7
COMPOUND TENSE 12.1.1b, Table 12.5: formation 12.3; position of non-finite verb 21.1 (*see also*: tense)
COMPOUND WORDS: 22.1.1c: adjectives 22.3.3; linking element in 22.2.4b, 22.3.3b; nouns 22.2.4; spelling as single or separate words 23.2; verbs 22.5.3
concerning 18.6.10, 20.1.6d, 20.3.12e, 20.4.1d
CONCESSIVE CLAUSES AND SENTENCES **19.6**: concessive particles 10.2, 10.14, 10.30.1a, 10.35.3, 10.36.1; followed by main clause word order 21.2.1c; with *auch* 10.4.5f, 19.6.2a; with *mögen* 17.4.3, 19.6.2a
CONDITIONAL CLAUSES AND SENTENCES **16.5**, Table 16.2: alternative forms 16.5.3; expressing a wish 16.7.6b; open conditions 10.30.3, 16.5.2, 16.5.3d; use of *etwa* 10.13.3; use of indicative 16.5.2; use of subjunctive 16.5.1; with *sollen* 16.5.1d, 17.6.4d; word order if conjunction omitted 21.1.1b
CONDITIONAL (with *würde*) 12.5.2, 16.4.4–5 (*see also*: subjunctive)
CONJUGATION (*see*: verb)
CONJUNCTIONS **Ch. 19**: causal 19.4; comma use with coordinating conjunctions 23.5.1; comma use with subordinating conjunctions 23.5.2; concessive 19.6; conditional 16.5.3d; coordinating 19.1, 21.1.4;

CONJUNCTIONS – *contd*
degree 19.7; final 19.5.1;
introducing noun clauses
19.2; of manner 19.7; of
purpose 19.5.1; of result
19.5.2; of time 19.3; verb
agreement with
coordinating conjunctions
12.1.4
CONSECUTIVE CLAUSES (*see:*
clauses of result)
continue 7.3.4
contrary to 20.2.10
COPULAR VERB 18.8
CORRELATION 19.2.5:
in causal clauses 19.4.1; in
conditional clauses
16.5.3b, 19.2.3; in object
clauses 3.6.3a, 19.2.5a; in
time clauses 19.3.1a; in
subject clauses 3.6.2e,
19.2.5a; through
prepositional adverb 6.6.2,
18.6.14, 19.2.5b
could 17.3.2a, 17.3.7
COUNTRIES AND PROVINCES,
names of (*see also:*
geographical names):
adjectives derived from
22.3.1e, 23.1.1d; article use
with 4.4; gender 1.1.3g; in
form of adjective used as
noun 6.4.4; nouns derived
from 22.2.1d; prepositions
with 20.1.1a, 20.2.6a,
20.5.3
cut 18.3.5e

da 'as', 'since' 5.4.6b, 13.2.7e,
13.7.3b, 19.3.1a, 19.4.1
da 'there' 3.6.2d, 5.1.1e, 7.1.1c,
21.6.1a
da sein 22.5.3d
da- (verb prefix) 22.5.1j
da(r)- + prep. 3.5, 5.4.4b,
13.2.4e, 18.6.14, 19.2.5b
dabei 13.7.3a, 14.6.2a
dabei- 22.5.2
dadurch 20.1.2b
dadurch ..., dass 13.7.2a,
19.7.3
dagegen 20.1.4a
daher 7.2.1, 21.6.1a
dahin 7.2.1
damals 11.6.3a, 14.3.3b, 21.6.1a
damit 16.7.2a, 19.5.1
dämmern 18.2.4a
danach 11.6.4b
daneben- 22.5.2
dank 20.2.10c
dankbar 6.5.1a, 6.6.1a
danken 18.4.1a
dann 10.6.2c, 10.8.1b, 11.6.3b,
16.5.3b, 19.3.1d, 21.6.1a

dar- 22.5.1j
darauf 11.6.4b
darum 19.4.1, 20.1.6e
Dasein, das 13.4.4
dass 19.2
DASS-CLAUSE 19.2.1 (*see also:*
noun clause)
DATES 2.2.5a, 2.6.2a, **11.3**, 11.5.4
DATIVE CASE (*see also:* dative
object) **2.5**, Table 2.1:
benefactive dative 2.5.3a;
dative of advantage 2.5.3a;
dative of disadvantage
2.5.3b; dative of
possession 2.5.4; dative of
standpoint 2.5.3c; dative
plural of nouns in *-n*
1.3.1b; dative singular of
nouns in *-e* 1.3.5; 'free'
dative 2.5.3; ethic dative
2.5.3d, 16.2.2h; governed
by adjectives 2.5.5, 6.5.1;
governed by prepositions
20.2, 20.3; in place of
genitive after prepositions
20.4.1e; marked by definite
article 4.7.1b; reflexive
dative 2.5.3a, 2.5.4a, 18.4.3;
replaced by phrase with
für 2.5.3a
DATIVE OBJECT (*see also:* indirect
object) **18.4**:
corresponding to English
subject 18.4.1d; in initial
position 21.2.1b; position
21.5, 21.6.1; reflexive
18.4.3; replaced by phrase
with *an* 18.4.2d, 20.3.3b; in
passive 15.1.3, 15.4.2; with
verbal nouns 20.3.3c
dauern 'last' 15.1.2b
dauern 'regret' 18.3.4
davon 3.1.2b
davon- 22.5.2
DAYS OF THE WEEK 11.2.1, Table
11.3:
followed by dates 2.6.2a,
11.3.2, 11.5.4; gender
1.1.1b; in genitive case
1.3.7a; with *bis* 11.5.4; with
prepositions 11.5.1
dazu 20.2.9d
dazu- 22.5.2
DECIMALS 9.3.3
Deck, das 1.2.5d
DECLENSION OF NOUNS **1.3**,
Table **1.5**:
dative plural 1.3.1b; dative
singular 1.3.5; genitive
singular 1.3.1a, 1.3.6;
irregular nouns 1.3.3–1.3.4,
Table 1.7; of adjectives
used as nouns 6.4.2, Table
6.5; proper names and

DECLENSION OF NOUNS – *contd*
titles 1.3.8; weak
masculine nouns 1.3.2,
Table 1.6
DEFINITE ARTICLE **Ch. 4**:
contracted with
prepositions 4.1.1c;
declension and forms
4.1.1, Table **4.1**; declension
of following adjective
6.2.2, Table 6.3;
distributive use 4.7.2; in
generalisations 4.3; in
place of possessive 2.5.4a,
4.6; in time expressions
4.5; reduction in colloquial
speech 4.1.1a; use with
abstract nouns 4.2, 4.6.2,
4.8.2c; use with
prepositions 4.5.3, 4.9,
11.5.4; used to mark case
4.7.1; with geographical
and proper names 4.4
degradieren 20.2.9f
DEMONSTRATIVES **5.1**:
with following relative
clause 5.1.3c, 5.4.3c, 5.4.5b
demonstrative determiner
der 5.1.1: declension of
following adjective 6.2.2
demonstrative pronoun der
5.1.1, Table 5.1: followed
by relative pronoun 5.4.5b;
genitive 3.1.3, 5.1.1f; not
used with prepositions
5.1.1i; position 21.4.2;
replaced by prepositional
adverb 3.5.3b, 5.5.1j; used
for personal pronoun 3.4.2,
5.1.1d
other demonstratives
5.1.2–5.1.6, Table 5.2:
declension of following
adjective 6.2.2
Demut, die 1.1.9a
denkbar 7.4.2
denken Table 12.12, 18.5.1,
18.6.2b, 18.6.9a
denn (conjunction) 10.6.2d,
19.1.2a, 23.5.1b
denn (particle) 8.3.1b, 10.6,
10.10.1a, 11.6.3c, 16.5.3d
denn noch 10.6.1e
dennoch 10.7.1
DEPENDENT CLAUSE (*see:*
subordinate clause)
depending on 19.7.5
der (definite article) Chapter 4
der (demonstrative) 5.1
der (relative pronoun) 5.4
der eine ... der andere 5.5.4d
derart 19.5.2b
derartig 5.1.6f
derer 5.1.1g, 5.4.1c

dergleichen 5.1.6g
DERIVATION (*see:* word
    formation)
derjenige 5.1.4, 5.4.5b
derlei 5.1.6g
dermaßen 19.5.2b
derselbe 5.1.5, 9.1.2e
deshalb 19.4.1
despite 20.4.1b
desto 8.3.5
deswegen 3.1.2b, 19.4.1
DETERMINERS **Ch. 4 & Ch. 5**
    (*see also:* capital letters,
    definite article,
    demonstratives, indefinite
    article, indefinite
    determiners and
    pronouns, possessives,
    quantifiers)
deutsch 23.1.1e
Deutsche, der 6.4.2a
dick 8.3.3
dienen 15.2.2a, 18.4.1a
dies 5.1.2
dieser 5.1.1a, 5.1.2, 5.1.3a,
    5.5.1e, 6.2.2c, 6.2.3c
diesseits 20.4.2
different(ly) 7.3.5
Dilemma, das 1.2.6b
DIMINUTIVES:
    agreement 1.1.13;
    formation 22.2.1a; gender
    1.1.4, 1.1.7; spelling 23.4.2
Ding, das 1.2.8, 6.4.1
dingen Table 12.12
DIRECT OBJECT (*see also:*
    accusative object) 2.2.1,
    18.3:
    as subject in passive
    15.1.2a; in the form of a
    noun clause 18.3.2, 19.2; in
    the form of an infinitive
    clause 13.2.4, 18.3.2;
    position 21.5, 21.6.1
DIRECT SPEECH 16.6.1:
    introduced by colon in
    writing 23.6.2; use of
    inverted commas 23.6.3
DIRECTION COMPLEMENT
    18.7.2:
    position 21.6.2c, 21.8.1d
disappear 20.3.1b
do 3.6.3b
doch 10.1.2, 10.7, 10.11,
    10.19.1b, 10.26.1c, 16.2.1a,
    16.5.3d, 16.7.6b, 19.1.1,
    23.5.1b
doch gleich 10.7.4, 10.16
doch mal 10.22.1
doch nicht 10.13.1
doch wohl 10.35.1
Dock, das 1.2.5d
Doktor, der 1.3.8d
doppelt 8.3.6a, 9.4.2b

Dorn, der 1.2.2e
dort 7.1.1b, 21.6.1a
Dotter, der & das 1.1.11a
double 9.4.2b
doubt 7.3.4
down 7.2.5a
down to 20.1.1c
dozen 9.1.5
drängen 13.2.4b
draußen 7.1.4
drehen (sich) 18.3.5c
drei Viertel 9.3.1
dreier 6.2.1b, 9.1.3a
dreschen Table 12.12
drin 20.3.8a
dringen 12.3.2c; Table 12.12
dringend 13.5.4a
drinnen 7.1.4
drittens 9.2.3
drive up 20.3.1c
drohen 13.2.5, 18.4.1a
Drohne, die 1.1.4b
drop 18.3.5d
drown 18.3.5b
drucken 20.3.1e
drückend 13.5.4a
Dschungel, der (das, die)
    1.1.11a
du/ihr/Sie 3.3, 23.1.3
dumm 8.2.3a
dunkel 6.3.1a, 8.3.3
dünn 8.3.3
durch 13.7.2a, 15.3, 20.1.2
durch- 22.6.1
durch was? 5.3.3c
durcheinander bringen 22.5.3a
durchfallen 18.3.5d
dürfen 12.1.3c, 12.2.2; Table
    12.4, 13.3.1a, 13.3.2a,
    14.4.3, 16.4.4b, **17.2**
during 11.5.14
dürsten 18.2.2
durstig 6.6.1a
Dutzend, das 2.7.4, 9.1.5b

euch 5.5.12, 5.5.14, 9.4.1
each other 3.2.7
eben 10.8, 10.17, 10.22.1,
    14.6.2a
ebenso 8.3.6c
ebenso sehr 8.3.6c
Effekt, der 1.2.8
egal 6.5.1b
eh 10.9, 10.27
ehe 16.7.4, 19.3.2a
eher 8.2.4
-ei 1.1.6a, 22.2.1c
eifersüchtig 6.6.1a
eigen 4.6.3, 6.5.1a
eigentlich 10.10
eignen, sich 18.6.5, 18.6.13b
eiligst 8.4.4a
ein (indefinite article) Ch. 4
ein- 20.3.1d, 22.5.1e

einander 3.2.7, 22.5.3b
einbilden, sich 18.4.3b
einer 5.5.4, 5.5.15a, 5.5.18b,
    9.1.2c
einerlei 6.5.1b, 9.4.4
einfach 9.4.2a, 10.11, 13.2.6,
    13.7.5g, 17.3.6
einfallen 18.4.1a
einfältig 9.4.2d
einfinden, sich 20.3.1c
einführen 20.3.1f
eingangs 20.4.3
eingedenk 6.5.3c, 20.4.3
eingerechnet 20.1.7c
einige 5.4.3a, 5.5.6, 5.5.7, 5.5.8,
    5.5.26, 6.2.3b
einigen, sich 18.6.14
einkehren 20.3.1c
Einkommen, das 13.4.4
einladen Table 12.12
einleuchten 18.4.1d
einleuchtend 13.5.4a
einmal 9.4.3, 10.22.2
einmalig 9.4.3
einreden 13.2.4b
eins 9.1.2a
einschließen, sich 20.3.1c
einschließlich 20.4.3
eintreffen 20.3.1c
eintreten 13.2.4b
einverstanden 6.6.1a, 6.6.2
einweichen Table 12.12
einzeln 9.4.2e
Einzelteil, das 1.1.11c
einzig 6.2.7c, 9.4.2e
either 19.1.3c
Ekel, das & der 1.1.12
ekeln (sich) 18.2.2, 18.3.4,
    18.6.12a, 18.6.14
ELATIVE SUPERLATIVE 8.4.2
Elektrische, die 6.4.3b
elend 6.6.1c
Ell(en)bogen, der 1.2.2c
Elsass, das 4.4.1c
else 7.3.5, 10.4.5d
elsewhere 7.1.5d
Eltern, die 1.2.10a
emp- 22.4.2
empfänglich 6.6.1a
empfehlen Table 12.12, 13.2.4b
empfindlich 6.6.1a
empor- 22.5.2
empörend 13.5.4a
empört 6.6.1b
Ende, das 1.1.8b, 1.2.4e, 4.5.1,
    11.4.1b
endlich 10.7.3
Engadin, das 4.4.1c
ent- 18.4.1c, 22.4.2
entbehren 18.5.1
entbehrlich 6.5.1a
entfallen 18.4.1d
Entfernung, die 5.5.7a
entgegen 20.2.10d

entgegen- 18.4.1c, 22.5.2
enthalten 15.1.2b
entlang 20.3.6
entnehmen 18.6.4
entrüstet 6.6.1b
entscheiden, sich 18.6.14
entscheidend 13.5.4a
entschieden 7.4.2
entschließen, sich 18.6.14
entsinnen, sich 18.5.2
entsprechend 20.2.10e
entweder ... oder 12.1.4, 19.1.3c
entwenden Table 12.12
entzückt 6.6.1b
Epoche, die 11.5.7a
Epos, das 1.2.6d
er- 22.4.3
Erbe, das & der 1.1.8b, 1.1.12
erbittert 6.6.1b
erbleichen Table 12.12
erbost 6.6.1b
Erbteil, das 1.1.11c
-erei 22.2.1c
erfahren 13.5.4b, 15.4.4
erfreuen, sich 18.5.2
erfreulicherweise 7.3.4
erfreut 6.6.1b
ERGÄNZUNG 18.1.1 (*see also:* complement)
ergeben 6.5.1a
ergeben, sich 18.4.2e, 18.6.4, 18.6.6a
erhaben 13.5.4b
erhalten 15.1.2b, 15.4.2, 15.4.4
erheben 13.5.4b
erinnern (sich) 15.2.2f, 18.3.6b, 18.5.2, 18.6.2b, 18.6.14
erkiesen Table 12.12
erklimmen Table 12.12
erkundigen, sich 18.6.8
Erlass, der 1.2.2a
erlauben 18.4.2b
-erlei 9.4.4
erlöschen 12.2.1e; Table 12.12
ermöglichen 18.4.2c
-ern (adj. suffix) 22.3.1b
ernennen 20.2.9f
Ernennung, die 20.2.9f
Ersatzteil, das 1.1.11c
erschrecken Table 12.12
erschweren 18.4.2c
ersichtlich 6.6.1a
erst 10.12, 10.30.5, 11.5.4
erst recht 10.12.1a
erst ... wenn/als 19.3.2b
erstaunt 6.6.1b
Erste, der 9.2.2
ersteigen 18.3.5b
erstens 9.2.3, 21.2.1c
erstmals 9.4.3b
ersuchen 13.2.4b
ertränken 18.3.5b
ertrinken 18.3.5b
erwägen Table 12.12

erwarten 13.2.5, 15.4.5
erwehren (sich) 18.5.2
erwünscht 6.5.1a
erz- 22.2.2a, 22.3.2a
erzählen 18.6.9a
es sei denn, (dass) 10.6.2a, 16.5.3d
escape 18.4.1c
especially as 19.4.3a
Espresso, der 1.2.6d
essen Table 12.12
Essen, das 1.2.11, 13.4.4
etliche 5.5.8, 6.2.3b
etwa 10.13, 10.34.2
🖝 etwas 5.4.3a, 5.5.9, 5.5.26, 21.5.1
even 8.3.1c, 10.4.5
even if 16.5.3d
even so 10.18, 10.19.4, 10.22.2
-ever 10.4.5f, 19.6.2
every 5.5.12, 5.5.14
everyone 5.5.12, 5.5.13
everywhere 7.1.5
exactly 10.8.2a
Examen, das 1.2.6d
except (for) 13.2.7d, 20.1.1c, 20.2.2a, 20.3.10c
except that/when 19.7.2
EXCLAMATION MARK 23.6.4
EXCLAMATIONS:
  in form of *dass*-clause 19.2.1d
  use of commas 23.5.4
  use of modal particles in:
    aber 10.1.1, 10.1.3; doch 10.7.5; erst 10.12.1a; ja 10.19.2; nur 10.26.1b; vielleicht 10.34.1
  with infinitive clauses 13.2.9b
  with interrogatives 5.3.1c, 5.3.2c, 5.3.3d
  with subjunctive 10.7.6, 10.26.1c, 16.7.6b
exklusive 20.4.3
EXTENDED EPITHET 6.6.3, 13.5.3
external(ly) 8.2.5
extremely 8.4.2

-fach 9.4.2
fad(e) 6.3.3
Faden, der 1.2.2c
-fähig 15.4.8
fähig 6.5.3a, 6.6.1a
fahren Table 12.12, 13.3.1e, 13.7.5b, 20.3.1c
fail 7.3.4, 18.3.5d
Fakt, das (der) 1.1.11a, 1.2.4e, 4.8.2b
fallen Table 12.12, 18.3.5d
fallen lassen 18.3.5d, 22.5.3c
falls 16.5.3d, 19.3.1d
-fältig 9.4.2d
FAMILY NAMES (*see:* personal and proper names)
fangen Table 12.12
Fasan, der 1.2.2e

fast 16.7.5c
fasten 20.3.1
Feber 11.2.2
fechten Table 12.12
feel 13.3.1b, 13.7.5a, 17.3.5, 18.3.5c
Fehl- 22.2.2e
fehl- 22.5.1j
fehlen 18.4.1d, 18.6.2a
fehlschagen 22.5.3a
feilbieten 22.5.3a
feind 6.5.1b
FEMININE (*see:* gender)
fern 6.5.1a, 20.2.10f
fern liegen 22.5.3b
fernab 20.4.3
fernsehen 22.5.3b
fertig 6.6.1a
festbinden 20.3.1c
FESTIVALS AND PUBLIC HOLIDAYS 11.2.3:
    singular or plural? 1.2.10b;
    use of article with 4.5.2;
    with prepositions 11.5.15a
festklammern 20.3.1c
festsetzen 22.5.3b
(a) few 5.5.6, 5.5.7, 5.5.25
Filter, der (das) 1.1.11a
FINAL CLAUSES (*see:* purpose clauses)
find 13.5.5b, 13.7.5c
finden Table 12.12, 13.3.1f, 13.5.5b, 13.7.5c, 15.4.4, 16.4.4c
finish 22.6.7
FINITE VERB 12.1.1a, 12.1.4:
    position 21.1
Fink, der 1.3.2a
first 9.2.2, 9.2.3
fix 20.3.1e
flechten Table 12.12
Fleck, der 1.2.2c
fliegen Table 12.12
fliehen Table 12.12
fließen Table 12.12
Flitterwochen, die 1.2.10a
Floß, das 1.2.4f
Flur, der & die 1.1.12
folgen 12.3.2c, 18.4.1a
folgend 5.4.3a, 5.5.10, 6.2.3b
following 5.5.10
for (conjunction) 19.1.2a
for (preposition) 2.5.1, 2.5.3a, 11.5.5, 13.2.7e, 18.6.5, 18.6.8a, 20.1.3, 20.1.4
for ...-ing 13.4.3b, 13.7.2b, 20.2.9d
fordern 13.2.4b
FOREIGN WORDS:
    declension 1.3.2a, 1.3.7d;
    gender 1.1.10; plural 1.2.5–6
Fortschritt, der 1.2.12
Fossil, das 1.2.6d
Foto, das (die) 1.1.9c, 1.1.11a

FRACTIONS 9.3:
gender 1.1.7; with *zu* 20.2.9h
fragen Table 12.12, 18.3.3a,
18.6.8, 18.6.14
frau 5.5.18a
Fräulein, das 1.1.13a, 1.3.8d
free(ly) 10.14.2
frei 10.14.2
FREIE ANGABE 18.1.4 (*see also:*
adverbials)
freilich 7.3.4, 10.2, **10.14**, 21.2.1c
fremd 6.5.1a
Fresko, das 1.2.6d
fressen Table 12.12
freuen (sich) 18.3.4, 18.3.6b,
18.6.2a, 18.6.3a, 18.6.9,
18.6.14
freundlichst 8.4.4a
Friede(n), der 1.1.8b, 1.2.2e,
1.3.3
frieren 12.3.2c; Table 12.12,
18.2.2
froh 6.5.3a, 6.6.1b
from 11.5.12, 18.6.4, 18.6.11,
18.6.12b, 20.2.1a, 20.2.8a,
20.2.10a
fromm 8.2.3b
früher 11.6.4a
frühstens 8.4.4b
frühstücken 22.5.3d
fühlen (sich) 4.8.3, 13.3.1b,
13.3.2c, 13.7.5a, 15.1.2c,
18.3.5c
full 6.5.3b, 22.6.7
fully 10.35.5
fünfzehn 9.1.1k
fünfzig 9.1.1k
Funke, der 1.1.8b, 1.2.2e, 1.3.3
für 2.5.3a, 2.5.5b, 11.5.2, **11.5.5**,
13.2.7e, 18.6.5, **20.1.3**
Furcht, die 1.2.11
fürchten (sich) 18.3.4, 18.6.14
Fürst, der 1.3.2a
FUTURE-IN-THE-PAST:
conjunction used with
19.3.1d; indicated by
conditional with *würde*
16.4.5, 16.6.3b; indicated
by past tense 14.3.4b;
indicated by *sollen* 17.6.2c
FUTURE PERFECT TENSE:
formation 12.3, Table 12.5;
replaced by perfect
14.3.5a; use 14.4
FUTURE TENSE:
distinct from *wollen* 17.7.1a;
formation 12.3, Table 12.5;
present tense used instead
14.2.3, 15.1.1a; similarity to
dürfte 17.2.2; to express
commands 16.2.2d; use
14.4; use in *werden*-passive
15.1.1a; with *wohl* 10.35.1,
14.4.3

ganz 5.5.1g, 6.2.7g, 20.1.2b,
22.5.3b
Ganze, das 6.4.2b
gar 10.15, 10.32.3
gären Table 12.12
Garten, der 1.2.2c
Ge- 1.1.8c, 1.2.4c, 22.2.2b
Gebärde, die 1.1.8c
gebären Table 12.12
geben 12.2.1e; Table 12.12,
13.2.5, 15.4.2b, 16.4.4c
gebeugt 20.3.1e
geboren 15.2.2g
Gebrauch, der 1.1.8c
Gebühr, die 1.1.8c
Geburt, die 1.1.8c
Gedanke, der 1.1.8b, 1.1.8c,
1.2.2e, 1.3.3
gedeihen Table 12.12, 13.5.4b
gedenken 13.2.5, 15.1.3b, 18.5.1
gediegen 13.5.4b
Geduld, die 1.1.8c
geeignet 6.6.1a
Gefahr, die 1.1.8c
gefährlich 6.5.1a
gefallen 15.4.2b, 18.4.1d
Gefallen, das & der 1.1.8c,
1.1.12
gefällig 6.5.1a
gefälligst 8.4.4a
gefangen nehmen 22.5.3c
gefasst 6.6.1a
gegebenenfalls 7.3.4
gegen 9.1.6, 11.5.6, **20.1.4**,
20.2.4c, 20.2.9g, 20.3.10d
gegen bar 23.1.1a
Gegenstand, der 4.8.2b
Gegenteil, das 1.1.11c
gegenüber 3.5.2, 5.3.3c, 20.1.4f,
20.2.4, 20.2.9g, 20.3.10d
Gehalt, das & der 1.1.8c, 1.1.12
gehen 4.2.3d, 12.2.1e, 12.3.2b,
Table 12.12, 13.2.5, 13.3.1e,
13.7.5b, 14.3.3b, 15.4.4,
15.4.5c, 16.4.4c
geheuer 6.5.1a
gehorchen 18.4.1a
gehören 15.4.2b, 15.4.7, 18.4.1a,
18.6.13a
gehorsam 6.5.1a
Gehorsam, der 1.1.8c
Geisel, die 1.1.4c
Geist, der 1.2.2d
gelangen 15.4.4
geläufig 6.5.1a
Gelee, das & der 1.1.11a
gelegentlich 20.4.3
gelehrt 13.5.4b
gelingen Table 12.12, 18.4.1a
gelten 4.8.3; Table 12.12,
18.4.1a
-gemäß 22.3.1h
gemäß 4.9.3c, 20.2.10e
Gemeinde, die 1.1.8c

gemeinsam 6.5.1a
gen 20.1.4b
genau 10.8.2a
genauso 8.3.6c
GENDER **1.1**, Tables 1.1–1.2:
abbreviations 1.1.9b;
agreement for gender
1.1.13; anomalous 1.1.4c;
compound nouns 1.1.9a;
double 1.1.12; English
loan-words 1.1.10;
grammatical and natural
1.1.4; humans and
animals 1.1.4; linked to
form 1.1.5–8; linked to
meaning 1.1.1–3;
shortened words 1.1.9c;
varying 1.1.11
General, der 1.2.2a
genesen 12.2.1e; Table 12.12
Genie, das 1.1.4c
genießen Table 12.12
GENITIVE CASE **2.3–2.4**, Table
2.1:
adjective declension after
genitive phrases 6.2.1b
adverbial use 2.3.5, 4.8.8,
11.4.2
definite article used to mark
4.7.1a
genitive object **18.5**: in form
of clause 19.2.1; in passive
15.1.3b; position 21.8.1a
genitive singular ending of
noun: in -(e)s 1.3.1a, 1.3.6;
lacking 1.3.7
governed by adjectives 6.5.3
governed by prepositions
1.3.7e, 3.1.2, 3.1.2b, **20.4**;
replaced by dative
20.4.1e
in apposition 2.6.2
in measurement phrases 2.7
in predicate of sein 2.3.4
in time phrases 11.4.2
of personal pronouns 3.1.2
of reflexive pronoun 3.2.2
of relative pronoun 5.4.1c,
5.4.2a
position of genitive phrases
2.3.2
replaced by a phrase with
von **2.4**, 5.5.25b
genug 2.5.3c, 2.5.5b, 7.4.1a,
13.2.7a, 19.5.3
genügen 18.4.1d
Genuss, der 1.1.8c
GEOGRAPHICAL NAMES (*see also:*
countries and provinces,
rivers, towns and cities):
article use with 4.4;
declension 1.3.8; in
genitive case 2.3.2, 2.4.2e;
prepositions with 20.1.1,

GEOGRAPHICAL NAMES – *contd*
20.5.3; use of apposition
with 2.6.3; use of capital
letters with 23.1.1d; used
with *ganz* 5.5.1g, 6.2.7g
gerade 10.8.2c, 11.6.1a,
14.6.2a
Gerade, die 6.4.3
geraten 13.4.3c
gerecht 6.5.1a, 20.2.9g
gern 7.3.4, 8.2.4, 17.4.1a
Geruch, der 1.1.8c
Gesang, der 1.1.8c
geschehen Table 12.12, 18.4.1b
Geschichte, die 1.1.8c
geschickt 13.5.4b
Geschmack, der 1.1.8c
geschweige denn 10.6.2b
Geschwister, die 1.2.10a
Geschwulst, die 1.1.8c
gesinnt 6.5.1a
gespannt 6.6.1a, 6.6.2
Gestalt, die 1.1.8c
geständig 6.5.3c
Gestank, der 1.1.8c
gestern 11.6.2, 21.6.1a, 23.1.2
gesund 8.2.3b
get 15.4.2, 17.5.1a
gewahr werden 3.6.4, 6.5.2,
6.5.3a
Gewähr, die 1.1.8c
Gewalt, die 1.1.8c
gewärtig 6.5.3c
Gewinn, der 1.1.8c
gewinnen Table 12.12
gewiss 6.5.3a
gewogen 6.5.1a
gewohnt 3.6.4, 6.5.2
gewöhnt 6.6.1a, 6.6.2
gibt (es) 13.2.5, 15.4.5e, 18.2.5
gierig 6.6.1a
gießen Table 12.12
Gift, das 1.1.9
Gischt, der & die 1.1.11a
glad 7.3.4
glatt 8.2.3b
Glaube, der 1.1.8b, 1.3.3
glauben 3.6.3b, 13.2.2b, 13.2.4c,
13.3.1h, 18.4.2b, 18.6.2b,
18.6.14
gleich 5.1.5, 6.5.1b, 8.3.6d,
10.7.4, 10.16, 14.6.2a
gleichen Table 12.12, 18.4.1a
gleichgültig 6.6.1a
gleiten Table 12.12
glimmen Table 12.12
Globus, der 1.2.6a
glücklich 6.6.1b
glühend 13.5.4a
go 13.7.5b
Golf, das & der 1.1.12
Gott, der 1.2.2d
graben Table 12.12
Graben, der 1.2.2c

Graf, der 1.3.2a
gram 6.5.1b, 23.1.2
Grat, der 1.1.9a
gratulieren 18.4.1a
grauen 18.2.2
grausam 20.2.9g
greifen Table 12.12
grenzen 20.3.1e
grob 8.2.3a
groß 8.2.4, 8.3.3
Großmut, die 1.1.9a
grow 18.3.5a
Grund, der 5.4.6d
gründen (sich) 18.6.3b
Grundlage 4.8.2b
gruseln 13.3.1h
guilty 6.5.2
Gummi, das & der 1.1.12
günstig 6.5.1a
gut 2.5.5c, 8.2.4, 8.3.3
gut gehen 22.5.3b
Gutachten, das 13.4.4
Guthaben, das 13.4.4
gütigst 8.4.4a
gutschreiben 22.5.3b

haben 4.2.3e, 4.2.4c, 5.5.16b,
12.1.3d, 12.2.2a, 12.3;
Table 12.3, 13.1.2, 13.2.5,
13.3.1f, 13.7.5c, 14.3.3b,
15.1.2b, 16.4.4b
habhaft 6.5.3c
Hafen, der 1.2.2c
-haft 22.3.1c
hageln 18.2.4a
halb 6.2.7g, 9.3.2
Halb, das 9.3.2
halber 3.1.1d, 5.1.1b, 5.4.1c,
20.4.3
half 9.3.2
Hälfte, die 9.3.2
halt 10.8.1, 10.17
Halt machen 22.5.3a
halten 4.2.3d; Table 12.12,
16.4.4c, 20.3.1f
Hammer, der 1.2.2c
handhaben 22.5.3d
hang (up) 20.3.1c
hängen Table 12.12, 18.7.1,
20.3.1c
happen 7.3.4, 18.4.1b
hardly 19.3.3
harren 18.5.1
hart 8.2.3a, 20.2.9g
Harz, das & der 1.1.12
hauen 2.5.4c; Table 12.12
häufig 8.2.3a
Haupt, das 1.1.4c
Hausaufgabe, die 1.2.12
haushalten Table 12.12
have 13.7.5c, 21.2.3c
have to 17.5, 17.6.1a
hear 13.3.1b, 13.7.5a, 17.3.5
heben 12.2.1e; Table 12.12

Heide, der & die 1.1.12
heilig 6.5.1a
Heilige Abend, der 4.5.2,
11.2.3
heim- 22.5.3a
heiß 2.5.5c
heißen 2.1.3; Table 12.12,
13.3.1, 13.3.2d, 16.4.4c,
18.3.3b, 18.8, 21.8.1e
-heit 1.1.6a, 22.2.1e
Held, der 1.3.2a
helfen 12.5.2b; Table 12.12,
13.3.1g, 13.3.2d, 15.2.2a,
18.4.1a
hell 8.3.3
help 13.3.1g, 13.7.5g, 17.3.6
Hemd, das 1.2.4e
her 2.2.5c, 3.5.1f, **7.2**, 11.5.13,
20.3.7b, 20.3.10b, 20.3.15b,
20.3.17b
here 7.1.1
Herr, der 1.3.2
herum 7.2.4b, 11.5.11, 20.1.6a
Herz, das 1.2.4e, 1.3.4
herzlichst 8.4.4a
heute 11.6.2, 21.6.1a, 23.1.2
hier 5.1.1e, 7.1.1a, 21.6.1a
hier- 5.1.1i
HIGHLIGHTING (dislocation)
21.2.1c
highly 7.4.1b
hin 2.2.5c, 3.5.1f, **7.2**, 20.2.6b,
20.3.12a, 20.3.16b
hinderlich 6.5.1a
hindern 18.6.14
hindurch 7.2.4b, 11.4.1a,
20.1.2
hinsichtlich 20.4.3
hinter 5.3.3c, 7.2.3b, 20.3.7,
20.4.2a
hinter- 22.6.2
hintere/hinterste 8.2.5
hinterher 11.6.4b
Hirt, der 1.3.2a
hoch 6.3.2, 7.4.1b, 8.2.4
höchst 7.4.1a, 8.4.4a
höchstens 8.4.4b, 21.2.1c
hoffen 3.6.3b, 13.2.2b, 13.2.5,
18.6.14
hoffentlich 7.3.4
höflich 6.6.1a
höflichst 8.4.4a
höher 8.2.4
hold 6.5.1b
hope 7.3.4
hören 13.3.1b, 13.3.2c, 13.7.5a,
15.1.2c, 18.6.9a
Horizontale, die 6.4.3
however 19.1.1c, 19.6.2
hundert 9.1.1c, 9.1.5a
Hundert, das 2.7.4, 9.1.1m,
9.1.5b
hundred 9.1.5
hungern 18.2.2, 18.6.8

hungrig 6.6.1a
Hut, der & die 1.1.12
hüten, sich 18.6.14

-ieren 22.7.4
if 16.5
-ig (adjective suffix) 22.3.1d
ihr/du/Sie 3.3, 23.1.3
Illustrierte, die 6.4.3
im 4.1.1c
Image, das 1.1.8b
immediately 10.16
immer 8.3.4, 10.7.3, 10.24.2a,
    11.6.1c, 19.6.2
immerhin 10.18, 21.2.1c
IMPERATIVE MOOD (*see also:*
    commands):
    formation 12.2, Table 12.2;
    in passive 12.4.2, 15.1.1b,
    15.2.1; meaning 12.1.1c,
    16.1.2; use **16.2.1**
'IMPERFECT' TENSE 14.1.1 (*see:*
    past tense)
IMPERSONAL VERBS AND
    CONSTRUCTIONS (*see also:*
    subject) 3.6.2, **18.2.4**:
    passive 15.1.3; with *sich
    lassen* 15.4.6
imponieren 18.4.1a
imstande/ im Stande 23.2.1
in 11.5.1, 11.5.7, 20.2.10b,
    20.3.4b, 20.3.8a, 20.3.9a
in 4.2.3c, 4.5.3, **11.5.7**, 11.5.15b,
    18.6.6, 20.2.6a, **20.3.8**,
    20.3.9, 20.4.2a, 20.5.1a,
    20.5.3
-in (noun suffix) 1.1.4a, 1.1.6a,
    1.2.3a, 22.2.1f
in connection with 20.3.2d
in front of 20.3.15a, 20.3.16a
in order to 13.2.7a
in relation to 20.2.4d
in respect of 18.6.2, 18.6.10,
    20.1.6d, 20.2.4d, 20.2.8a,
    20.3.2d
in so/as far as 19.7.4
in spite of 20.4.1b
in that 19.7.3
in view of 20.2.3b
inasmuch as 19.7.4
including 20.1.7c
indeed 10.19.4
INDEFINITE ARTICLE **Ch. 4**:
    declension and forms
    4.1.2, Table 4.2; declension
    of following adjective
    6.2.1b, 6.2.2b, Table 6.4;
    distinct from numeral *ein*
    9.1.2b; negative 5.5.16;
    omission in certain
    contructions 4.8.2–3, 4.9.1;
    reduced forms in
    colloquial speech 4.1.2b;
    use with prepositions 4.9

INDEFINITE DETERMINERS AND
    PRONOUNS **5.5**
    declension of following
    adjective 6.2.3; declension
    when used with preceding
    determiner 6.2.3c; in
    partitive constructions
    2.4.1d, 2.4.2; spelling with
    initial small letter 23.1.1c
indem 13.7.2a, 13.7.3a, 19.3.1e,
    19.7.3
indes 19.3.7b
indessen 19.3.7b
Index, der 1.2.6d
INDICATIVE MOOD 12.1.1c, 16.1.1
INDIRECT OBJECT (*see also:*
    dative object) 18.4.2:
    in passive 15.1.3c, 15.4.2b
INDIRECT QUESTIONS 16.6.4a,
    19.2.2:
    introduced by interrogative
    adverbs 7.5, 19.2.4; with
    infinitive clauses in English
    13.2.8a
INDIRECT SPEECH **16.6**, Tables
    16.3–16.4:
    form of clause 19.2.1b;
    indirect and direct speech
    16.6.1; use of indicative
    16.6.3c; use of subjunctive
    16.6.2–4
Individuum, das 1.1.4c
Industrie, die 23.4.1
INFINITIVE **13.1–13.4** (*see also:*
    infinitive clause):
    bare infinitive (without *zu*)
    13.1.3, **13.3**: after modal
    auxiliaries 13.3.1a, 17.1.2;
    in future tense 12.3;
    position 13.3.1, 21.1,
    21.2.1b; replacing past
    participle 13.3.2; use of
    reflexive pronoun with
    3.2.4; verbs occurring with
    13.3.1
    compound infinitive 13.1.2:
    with zu 13.1.4c
    formation 12.2, 13.1
    in commands 13.3.3a, 16.2.2a
    in compound verbs 22.5.3c
    passive infinitive 13.1.2
    perfect infinitive 13.1.2
    simple infinitive 13.1.1
    used as noun **13.4**: for
    English 'ing'-form 13.7.1;
    from reflexive verbs
    13.4.1b; gender 1.1.3e,
    1.1.8a; indicating
    continuous action 14.6.2c;
    use of articles with 4.2.1b,
    4.2.3a; with prepositions
    13.4.3
    used in place of past
    participle 13.3.2, 17.1.4

INFINITIVE CLAUSE (with *zu*)
    13.1.3, **13.2**:
    after adjectives governing a
    preposition 6.6.2
    after verbs governing a
    preposition 13.2.4e, 18.6.14
    as object 13.2.4: anticipated
    by es 3.6.3, 13.2.4d
    as subject 13.2.3: agreement
    of verb 12.1.4a; anticipated
    by es 3.6.2e, 13.2.3c
    depending on predicate
    adjective 13.2.6
    depending on relative clause
    13.2.2d
    enclosure within main clause
    13.2.2, 21.9.2, 23.5.2b
    equivalent of clause with
    'ing'-form 13.2.3a, 13.2.4a,
    13.7.1b
    in comparative phrases
    13.2.9a
    incorporation within main
    clause 13.2.2c
    position of verbs 13.2.2,
    17.1.3b, 21.1.1c: with
    modal auxiliaries 17.1.3b
    subject of infinitive clause
    13.2.4b
    use of comma with 23.5.3
    use of reflexive pronoun
    with 3.2.5
    used with prepositions 13.2.7
    restrictions on use with
    passive infinitive 15.1.3d
    with passive sense 15.4.5
    with semi-auxiliary verbs
    13.2.5, 15.4.5
infolge 4.9.3c, 20.4.3, 23.2.1
infrage/in Frage 23.2.1
'ING' FORM (English) – German
    equivalents 13.2.3a,
    13.2.4a, 13.4.1a, 13.4.3, **13.7**
inklusive 20.4.3
inmitten 20.4.3, 23.2.1
inne- 22.5.1j
inne sein 22.5.3d
innen 7.1.4
Innere, das 6.4.2b
innere/innerste 8.2.5
innerhalb 20.4.2
innerlich 8.2.5
Insekt, das 1.2.4e
inside (adverb) 7.1.4
inside (preposition) 20.3.8a,
    20.3.9a, 20.4.2
insofern (als) 19.7.4a
insoweit (als) 19.7.4a
instand/in Stand 23.2.1
instead of 13.2.7c, 13.7.2c, 20.4.1
INSTRUMENT (of action) 20.2.5b
INTENSIFIERS 7.4.1, 10.12.1,
    10.13.2, 10.15, 10.19.3,
    10.26.1, 10.32.3

interessant 13.2.6
Interesse, das 1.1.8b, 1.2.4e
interessieren (sich) 18.6.5
interessiert 6.6.1a
INTERJECTIONS:
  use of comma: 23.5.4; use
  of exclamation mark 23.6.4
internal(ly) 8.2.5
INTERROGATIVE DETERMINERS
  AND PRONOUNS **5.3**:
  declension of following
  adjective 6.2.2
into 18.6.13a, 20.1.4b, 20.3.9a
INTRANSITIVE VERB (*see:* verb)
INVERTED COMMAS 23.6.3
Irak, der 1.1.3g, 4.4.1a
Iran, der 1.1.3g, 4.4.1a
irgend- 5.5.11
irgendwelche 5.5.11d, 6.2.3b
irgendwo 5.5.11b, 7.1.5a, 7.3.5a
irr(e) 6.3.3
irre- 22.5.3a
irren 12.3.2c
Irrtum, der 1.2.2d
-isch (adj. suffix) 22.3.1e
ist/sind (es) 3.6.2d, 18.2.5
it 3.4.1, 3.6

ja 10.1.1, 10.4.1, 10.7.5, 10.11,
  10.14.2, 10.19, 10.26.1a,
  10.34.1, 16.2.1a
ja wohl 10.35.1
Jahr, das 11.5.7a, 11.5.14
Jahrhundert, das 11.5.7a
Jänner 11.2.2
Januar 11.2.2
je 4.7.2, 8.3.5, 9.4.1, 11.6.1c,
  20.1.7e
je nachdem 19.7.5
jedenfalls 10.20, 21.2.1c
jeder 5.5.12, 5.5.13, 5.5.14,
  6.2.2c, 12.1.4c
jedermann 5.5.13
jedoch 19.1.1, 21.2.1c, 23.5.1b
jedweder 5.5.14
jeglicher 5.5.14, 6.2.2c
jemand 5.5.4c, 5.5.15, 7.3.5a,
  21.5.1
Jemen, der 1.1.3g, 4.4.1a
jener 5.1.3, 5.4.5b, 6.2.2c, 6.2.3c
jenseits 20.4.2
jetzt 10.25.3, 11.6.1a
judging by 20.2.6d
Juli 11.2.2
jung 8.2.3a, 8.3.3
Junge, das & der 1.1.12
jüngst 8.4.4a, 11.6.1a
Juni 11.2.2
just 10.8, 10.11, 10.22
Juwel, das 1.2.4e

Kai, der 1.2.5d
Kaktus, der 1.2.6a
kalt 2.5.5c, 8.2.3a

Karfreitag, der 4.5.2, 11.2.3
karg 8.2.3b
Käse, der 1.1.8b, 1.2.11, 1.3.2a
Kasten, der 1.2.2c
Katapult, das & der 1.1.11a
kaum (dass) 19.3.3
keep 13.7.5d
keep on 7.3.4, 13.7.5e
Kehricht, der & das 1.1.11a
kein 4.1.2a, 5.5.16, 6.2.1b,
  6.2.2b, 12.1.4c
keiner 5.5.4b, 5.5.16
-keit 1.1.6a, 22.2.1e
Keks, der (das) 1.1.11a
kennen Table 12.12, 15.1.2b
kennen lernen 13.3.1g, 22.5.3c
Kenntnis, die 1.2.12
kettenrauchen 22.5.3e
Kiefer, der & die 1.1.12
klagen 18.6.14
klammern 20.3.1c
klappen 12.3.2a
klar 3.6.2e, 6.5.1a
kleiden 20.3.1e
klein 8.3.3
Kleinod, das 1.2.4e
klimmen Table 12.12
klingen Table 12.12
klopfen 2.5.4c, 20.3.1f
Kloster, das 1.2.4d
klug 8.2.3a
knapp 9.1.6
Knäuel, der & das 1.1.11a
kneifen Table 12.12
Knie, das 1.2.4a, 23.4.1
knien 12.2.1d, 23.4.1
know 7.3.4, 17.3.3
Kohl, der 1.2.11
Komma, das 1.2.6b
kommen Table 12.12, 13.2.5,
  13.3.1e, 13.4.3, 13.5.5c,
  13.7.5b, 14.2.2c, 14.3.3b,
  15.4.4, 16.4.4c
Kompromiss, der (das) 1.1.11a
Kongo, der 1.1.3g, 4.4.1a
Kongress, der 1.3.7g
KONJUNKTIV I/II (*see:*
  subjunctive)
können 12.1.3c, 12.2.2; Table
  12.4, 13.3.1a, 13.3.2a,
  16.4.4b, 16.7.2a, **17.3**
Konto, das 1.2.6d
Korporal, der 1.2.2a
kosten 18.3.3a
Kosten, die 1.2.10a
kraft 4.9.3c, 20.4.3, 23.1.2
Kragen, der 1.2.2c
Kran, der 1.2.2a
krank 8.2.3a
kriechen Table 12.12
kriegen 15.1.2b, 15.4.2
Krokus, der 1.2.6a
krönen 20.2.9f
krumm 8.2.3b

Kummer, der 1.2.11
Kunde, der & die 1.1.12
kundgeben 22.5.3a
kundig 6.5.3c
kündigen 18.4.1a
küren Table 12.12
kurz 8.2.3a, 8.3.3, 21.2.1c
kurz treten 22.5.3b
kürzlich 11.6.5
kurzum 21.2.1c
Kurzwaren, die 1.2.10a
küssen 2.5.4c

lachen 13.3.1h, 15.2.2f
laden Table 12.12
Laden, der 1.2.2c
Lama, das & der 1.1.12
Land, das 1.2.8
lang 7.4.1c, 8.2.3a, 8.3.3,
  11.4.1a, 11.5.5b
Langmut, die 1.1.9a
längs 20.3.6d, 20.4.3
längst 7.4.1c, 8.4.4a
LANGUAGES, names of:
  article use with 4.2.4d;
  form 6.4.6a; gender 1.1.3e;
  initial capital letter 23.1.1e
langweilen 22.5.3a
lassen Table 12.12, 13.3.1c,
  13.3.2b, 13.7.1d, 13.7.5,
  15.4.6, 16.2.2f, 16.4.4c,
  18.3.5a
Laster, das & der 1.1.12
lästig 6.5.1a
later 11.5.8, 11.6.4b
laufen Table 12.12, 18.3.5d
Lausitz, die 1.1.3g, 4.4.1b
laut 4.9.3c, 20.2.10e
lauter 5.5.17
least 8.2.4b, 8.3.2, 8.4.4b,
  10.20.1
leave 18.3.5a, 13.7.5c
leben 18.7.1
Leben, das 13.4.4
Lebensmittel, die 1.2.10a
ledig 6.5.3c
lediglich 10.21
legen (sich) 13.3.1h, 20.3.1c
lehren 13.3.1g, 13.3.2d, 15.4.2c,
  18.3.3a
Leib, der 1.2.2d
leicht 3.6.2e, 6.5.1a, 13.2.6
leicht fallen 18.4.1d
leicht machen 22.5.3b
leid 23.1.2
Leid tun 18.4.1d
leiden Table 12.12
leider 7.3.4
leihen Table 12.12
-lein 1.1.4c, 1.1.7, 1.1.13d,
  1.2.4c, 22.2.1a
leis(e) 6.3.3
Leiter, der & die 1.1.12
-ler (noun suffix) 22.2.1d

lernen 13.3.1g, 13.3.2d
lesen Table 12.12, 18.6.9a
less 8.3.2
let 13.3.1c
let's 16.7.6d
LETTER WRITING:
addresses 4.4.1e, 9.5; dates
11.3.3; punctuation 23.6.4c
LETTERS OF ALPHABET:
gender 1.1.3d; used with
adjectives 6.2.7f
letzt 4.5.1, 23.7.2
letzthin 11.6.5
-leute 1.2.7
Leute, die 5.5.18a, 6.4.1
Lexikon, das 1.2.6d
Libanon, der 1.1.3g, 4.4.1a
-lich (adj. suffix) 15.4.8, 22.3.1f
lie down 20.3.1c
Liebe, die 1.2.11
lieber 7.3.4, 8.2.4
liebkosen 22.5.3a
liegen 12.3.2b; Table 12.12,
18.4.1d, 18.6.2a, 18.7.1
liegen bleiben 22.5.3c
like 7.3.4, 17.4.1
lila 6.2.7b
-ling (noun suffix) 1.1.5a,
22.2.1g
Linke, die 6.4.3
links 20.4.3
Liter, das & der 1.1.11b
(a) little 5.5.5, 5.5.7a, 5.5.9, 5.5.25
LOAN-WORDS (*see:* foreign
words)
loben 15.2.2f
Lorbeer, der 1.2.2e
-los 22.3.1g
los 3.6.4, 6.5.2
los- 22.5.1f
los sein 22.5.3d
löschen Table 12.12
a lot of 5.5.25
lügen Table 12.12
Luxus, der 1.2.11

machen 13.3.1h, 13.3.2d
mächtig 6.5.3a
made of 20.2.1b
Magen, der 1.2.2c
Magnet, der 1.3.2
mahlen Table 12.12
MAIN CLAUSE Ch. 19:
co-ordinated 21.1.4a,
23.5.1; initial position
21.1.2, 21.1.4a, **21.2**;
position of verbs at end
21.1.3a; structure and
word order 21.1.1a; two
elements permitted in
initial position 21.2.1c; use
of commas when
coordinated 23.5.1;'verb
second' rule 21.2

make 13.3.1c
-mal 9.4.3
mal 10.7.3, 10.11, **10.22**, 16.2.1a
Mal, das 9.4.3, 11.5.15c
man 4.3.1, 6.4.1
man (particle) 10.23
man (pronoun) 5.5.4c, 5.5.18,
15.4.1, 16.2.2g
manch(e) 5.4.3a, 5.5.19, 5.5.26,
6.2.3b
Mangel, der 1.1.12, 1.2.2c
Mangel, die 1.1.12
mangeln 18.4.1d
mangels 4.9.3c, 20.4.3
-mann 1.1.4a, 1.2.7
Mann, der 1.2.2d, 1.2.8
Männchen, das 1.1.4b
Mannequin, das 1.1.4c
mannigfaltig 9.4.2d
Mantel, der 1.2.2c
many 5.5.25
many a 5.5.19
Mark, das 1.1.12
Mark, die 1.1.12, 1.2.14
Markt, der 20.3.4b, 20.5.1b
Marsch, der & die 1.1.12
MASCULINE (*see:* gender)
Maß halten 22.5.3a
-mäßig 22.3.1h
Mast, der 1.2.2c
Match, das (der) 1.1.11a
Material, das 1.2.6d
MATHEMATICAL TERMS 9.4.5
may 17.2.1, 17.3.2, 17.4.2
MEASUREMENT PHRASES:
verb agreement with
12.1.4f; with accusative
2.2.5b; with genitive, *von*
or apposition? **2.7**; with
nouns used in singular
1.2.14, with *zu* 20.2.9h
mehr 8.2.4, 8.2.7
mehrere 5.5.20, 6.2.3b, 9.1.2e
mehrmalig 9.4.3a
meiden Table 12.12
meinen 13.2.2b, 13.2.4c
meinesgleichen 5.5.21
meist 4.7.3, 8.2.7, 8.4.4a
meistens 8.4.4b
melken 12.2.1e; Table 12.12
Mensch, das 1.1.12
Mensch, der 1.1.12, 1.3.2a,
4.3.1
merely 10.5
messen Table 12.12
Messer, das & der 1.1.12
Meteor, der (das) 1.1.11a
Meter, das (der) 1.1.11b
middle 7.1.3
might 17.3.2, 17.3.7
mild(e) 6.3.3
Militär, das & der 1.1.12
Milliarde, die 2.7.4, 9.1.1e
Million, die 2.7.4, 9.1.1e

minder/mindest 8.2.4, 8.3.2
mindestens 8.4.4b
Mineral, das 1.2.6d
Minute, die 11.5.7a
miss- 22.2.2f, 22.6.3
missachten 13.1.4b
misslingen Table 12.12
misstrauen 18.4.1a
missverstehen 13.1.4b, 22.6.3
mit 2.1.1, 2.2.6, 4.9.1, 4.9.3a,
15.3.4, 18.6.7, 20.1.7d,
20.2.5
mit- 22.2.2f, 22.5.1g
Mitgift, die 1.1.9a
Mitglied, das 1.1.4c
mithilfe/mit Hilfe 23.2.1
mitsamt 20.2.10g
Mitte, die 4.5.1, 11.4.1b
mitteilen 18.4.2c
mittels 20.4.3, 23.1.2
mitten 7.1.3, 23.1.2
mittlere/mittelste 8.2.5
Mittwoch, der 1.1.9a
Möbel, die 1.2.10a
MODAL AUXILIARY VERBS **Ch. 17**:
forms 12.1.3c, Table 12.4;
in conditional sentences
16.5.1d; in indirect
commands 16.6.4b; in
purpose clauses:16.7.2;
infinitive used instead of
past participle 13.3.2a,
17.1.4; omission of
following infinitive 17.1.5;
perfect auxiliary 12.3.2b;
position 21.6.1a, 21.6.2a;
use in past and perfect
tenses 14.3.3b; position
17.1.3, 21.1; subjunctive
forms 12.5.2b, 16.4.4b;
used with bare infinitive
13.3.1a
MODAL PARTICLES **Ch. 10**,
Table 10.1:
position 21.6.2a
mögen 12.1.3c, 12.2.2; Table
12.4, 13.3.1a, 13.3.2a,
16.2.2g, 16.4.4b, 16.6.4b,
16.7.6c, **17.4**, 19.6.2a
möglich 3.6.2e, 6.5.1a, 17.3.2b
möglicherweise 7.3.4, 17.3.2b
möglichst 8.4.4a
Moment, das & der 1.1.12
Monat, der 11.5.7a
MONTHS, names of 11.2.2,
Table 11.4:
gender 1.1.1b; lack of
ending in genitive 1.3.7a;
use of article with 4.5,
4.8.2c, 11.5.7a; with
prepositions 11.5.7a
MOOD (of verb) 12.1.1c, **Ch. 16**
(*see also:* imperative,
subjunctive)

more 8.1, 8.2, 8.3
more and more 8.3.4
morgen 11.6.2, 21.6.1a, 23.1.2
morgens 11.4.2, 23.1.2
most 4.7.3, 5.4.1c, 8.1, 8.2, 8.4
much 5.5.25, 7.4.3b
müd(e) 3.6.4, 6.3.3, 6.5.3a,
   6.6.1a
MULTIPLES 9.4.2
Mund, der 1.2.2d
Mündel, das (der) 1.1.4c,
   1.1.11a
münden 20.3.1e
Muskel, der 1.2.2b, 1.2.2e
müssen 12.1.3c, 12.2.2; Table
   12.4, 13.3.1a, 13.3.2a,
   13.7.5f, 16.4.4b, 16.6.4b,
   17.5
must 17.2.1b, 17.5.1, 17.5.2,
   17.6.1a
Mut, der 1.1.9a
Mutter, die 1.2.3d, 1.2.8
Mythos, der 1.2.6d

na 21.2.1c
nach 11.5.8, 18.6.8, **20.2.6**,
   20.2.10e, 20.5.3a
nach- 18.4.1c, 22.5.1j
Nachbar, der 1.3.2
nachdem 13.7.3a, 19.3.4
nachher 11.6.4b
Nachhinein (im) 11.6.4b
nachmittags 11.4.2
Nachricht, die 1.2.12
nächst 4.5.1, 8.2.4
nächstens 8.4.4b
Nacht, die 1.2.3b, 11.4.2, 11.5.1,
   11.5.7a, 11.5.14
nachts 11.4.2
nachweisen 18.4.2c
Nagel, der 1.2.2c
nah(e) 6.5.1a, 8.2.4
nahe (prep.) 20.2.10h
nahe legen 22.5.3b
nähern, sich 18.4.2e
Name, der 1.1.8b, 1.2.2e, 1.3.3
namely 10.36.2
namens 20.4.3
nämlich 19.1.2b
Narr, der 1.3.2a
nass 8.2.3b
natürlich 21.2.1c
nay 10.19.4
neben 5.3.3c, 7.2.3b, 20.2.4c,
   20.3.10
nebst 20.2.10i
need 13.7.5f, 17.5.1b, 17.5.3a,
   17.7.1c
NEGATION 5.5.16, 10.7.7a,
   10.13.2, 10.32.3:
   position 21.7
nehmen 5.5.16b, 12.2.1e; Table
   12.12
neidisch 6.6.1a

neither ... nor 10.4.5e, 19.1.3d
nennen 2.1.3; Table 12.12,
   13.3.1h, 18.3.3b
-ner (noun suffix) 22.2.1d
Nerv, der 1.2.2e
neu 8.3.3
neuerdings 11.6.5
neugierig 6.6.1a, 6.6.2
Neujahr 4.5.2, 11.2.3, 11.5.15a
neulich 11.6.5
NEUTER (*see*: gender)
next (to) 20.3.10
nicht 5.5.16b, 7.3.4, 21.7
nicht dass 16.7.5a
nicht (nur) ..., sondern (auch)
   12.1.4, 19.1.1d
nicht wahr? 10.7.2
nichts 5.4.3a, 5.5.22, 6.4.5,
   21.5.1
nichts weniger als 8.2.4e
nie 11.6.1c
nieder- 22.5.1j
niedere 8.2.5
Niederlande, die 4.4.1b
niederlegen, sich 20.3.1c
niedersetzen, sich 20.3.1c
niemand 5.5.15, 5.5.16d, 7.3.5a,
   21.5.1
nirgends 7.1.5c
nirgendwo 7.1.5c, 7.3.5a
-nis 1.1.8d, 1.2.3c, 1.2.4a,
   22.2.1h
no 5.5.16
no matter which/who 5.5.11d,
   5.5.12, 5.5.14b
nobody/no-one 5.5.15
noch 8.3.1d, 10.24, 11.6.4a,
   19.6.2b
noch bevor 19.3.2a
noch ein 5.5.2b
noch während 19.3.7a
NOMINATIVE CASE **2.1**, Table
   2.1:
   for verb subject 18.2.1a; for
   predicate complement 18.8
NON-FINITE VERB FORMS (*see
   also:* infinitive, participle)
   12.1.1e:
   formation 12.2; position in
   compound tenses 21.1,
   21.2.1b; use **Ch. 13**
not a 5.5.16
note 20.3.1e
nothing 5.5.22
nothing less than 8.2.4e
notieren 20.3.1e
nötig 6.5.1a
NOUN CLAUSE **19.2**:
   after adjectives 6.6.2,
   19.2.1; agreement of verb
   12.1.4a; anticipated by *es*
   3.6.2e, 3.6.3a; for English
   'ing'-form 13.7.1c; for
   prepositional object

NOUN CLAUSE – *contd*
   18.6.14; in initial position
   19.2.1c; omission of *dass*
   19.2.1b, 21.1.1a; used as
   command 16.2.2h
NOUNS (*see*: capital letters;
   declension of nouns,
   gender, plural of nouns,
   word formation)
now 10.25.3
now that 19.4.2
nowhere 7.1.5
NUMBER (of verb) 12.1.1a,
   12.1.4
(a) number of 5.5.8
NUMERALS **Ch. 9** (*see also:*
   cardinal numbers,
   decimals, fractions,
   ordinal numbers)
nun 10.25, 10.30.4, 11.6.1a,
   19.4.2, 21.2.1c
nun da 19.4.2
nur 10.5, 10.7.6, 10.12.1b,
   10.12.2c, 10.19.3, 10.21,
   10.26, 10.28, 10.30.1a,
   10.35.3, 16.2.1a, 16.7.6b
nur dass 19.7.6
nutzen/nützen 15.2.2a,
   18.4.1a
nützlich 6.5.1a

ob (conjunction) 19.2.2
ob (preposition) 20.4.3
oben 7.1.2
obere/oberste 8.2.5
oberhalb 20.4.2
Oberst, der 1.3.2
Oberteil, das & der 1.1.11c
obgleich 19.6.1b
OBJECT (*see*: accusative object,
   dative object, direct
   object, genitive object,
   indirect object,
   prepositional object)
OBJECT CLAUSES (*see*: noun
   clauses)
obschon 19.6.1b
Obst, das 1.2.11
obwohl 13.6.3, 19.6.1
obzwar 19.6.1b
OCCUPATIONS (*see*: professions)
occur 18.4.1b
Ochs, der 1.3.2a
öd(e) 6.3.3
oder 10.1.2, 10.7.2, 12.1.4,
   19.1.3a, 23.5.1a
oder auch 10.4.5d
of 2.3.1, 2.3.6, 2.6.3, 18.6.4,
   18.6.8b, 18.6.11, 18.6.12a,
   20.2.8e
Ofen, der 1.2.2c
öffnen (sich) 15.2.2f, 18.3.5c
oft 8.2.3a, 8.3.3, 11.6.1c

ohne 3.5.1a, 3.5.2, 4.9.3b,
5.3.3c, **20.1.5**
ohne dass 13.2.7b, 13.7.2f,
16.7.5a, 19.7.7
ohne weiteres 23.1.1a
ohne ... zu 13.2.7b, 13.7.2f
ohnehin 10.9, 10.27, 10.31
Ohr, das 1.2.4e
on 11.5.1, 20.3.2, 20.3.4a
on ...-ing 13.4.3a, 13.7.2d, 20.3.2
once 9.4.3a, 10.22.2,
one (numeral) 4.1.2b, 5.4.1c,
5.4.5, 5.5.4, 5.5.24, 9.1.2
one (pronoun) 5.5.18, 15.4.1
only 5.5.17, 10.5, 10.12.2, 10.21,
10.26
only that 19.7.6
onto 20.3.5a
open 18.3.5
opposite 20.2.4b
or 19.1.3
orange 6.2.7b
ORDINAL NUMBERS **9.2**, Table
9.2:
formation 9.2.1; indication
in writing 9.2.1c; use 9.2.2;
with *zu* 20.2.9h
Ostern 1.2.10b, 4.5.2, 11.2.3,
11.5.15a
other 5.5.2, 5.5.4d, 7.3.5
otherwise 7.3.5b
Otter, der & die 1.1.12
ought (not) 17.2.1b, 17.5.3b,
17.6.4
out of 20.2.1a, 20.2.2b
outside (adverb) 7.1.4
outside (preposition) 20.2.2b,
20.4.2
over 11.5.10, 20.3.11, 20.3.12
own (adjective) 4.6.3

Paar, das 5.5.6, 23.1.2, 23.4.2
paar (ein) 5.5.6, 5.5.7, 23.1.2
Pack, das & der 1.1.12
paddeln 12.3.2c
pair 5.5.6
Pantoffel, der 1.2.2b, 1.2.2e
Papagei, der 1.3.2
Paradigma, das 1.2.6b
Parallele, die 6.4.3
parent 1.2.10a
parken 18.7.1
PARTICIPIAL CLAUSES **13.6**:
position of participle 13.6.1,
21.1.1c; use of comma
23.5.3.3; with *obwohl* 13.6.3;
with *wie*-clause 13.6.2
PARTICIPIAL PHRASE, extended
6.6.3, 13.5.3
PARTICIPLES' 12.1.1e, **13.5** (*see
also:* 'ing'-form):
formation 12.2
lexicalisation 13.5.4
meanings 13.5.1

PARTICIPLES – *contd*
past participle: 13.5.1: in
commands 13.5.5a, 16.2.2b;
in passive 12.4, 15.2.2e; in
perfect 12.3; position in
passive and compound
tenses 21.1, 21.2.1b
present participle: 13.5.1:
used with -zu- 13.5.2e
used as adjectives or adverbs
7.3.1c, 13.5.2: in
comparative and
superlative 8.2.7
used as nouns: 6.4, 13.5.2a,
22.2.3c
used as separable verb prefix
22.5.3
Partisan, der 1.3.2a
PARTITIVE CONSTRUCTIONS:
use of genitive or *von*
2.4.1d, 2.4.2d; with *etwas*
5.5.9a; with *nichts* 5.5.22
PARTS OF THE BODY:
phrases with prepositions
20.2.5c; use of definite
article or possessive 4.6.1;
use of singular in German
1.2.13; with possessive
dative 2.5.4
passen 18.4.1a, 18.6.13a
passieren 18.4.1b
PASSIVE 12.1.1d, **Ch. 15**:
active preferred to 15.5,
21.2.3b
distinction between werden-
and sein-passive 15.2.2–3
formation 12.4, Tables
12.6–12.7
imperative 15.1.1b, 15.2.1
impersonal: (see: subjectless
passive)
infinitive 13.1.2: after
müssen 17.5.1b; with verbs
governing dative 15.1.3d
other passive constructions
15.4
sein-passive: formation
12.4.2b, Table 12.7; use **15.2**
subjectless 3.6.2a, 15.1.3–4,
18.2.4f: for English 'ing'-
form 13.7.1d; in
commands 15.1.4d, 16.2.2c
tense use 15.1.1, 15.2.1: past
and perfect 14.3.2b, 14.3.3b
von or durch with **15.3**:
position 21.6.2a
werden-passive: formation
12.4.2a, Table 12.6; use **15.1**
with bekommen or kriegen
15.4.2
with intransitive verbs
15.1.3–4
with transitive verbs 15.1.3
word order 21.5.3, 21.6.2a

past 20.3.2a
PAST TENSE:
for English pluperfect
14.3.4a; formation 12.2,
Table 12.2; in *sein*-passive
15.2.1; in sense of 'future
in the past' 14.3.4b;
overlap with perfect 14.3;
referring to present
14.3.4c; replacing
pluperfect 14.5.1c; term
14.1.1; use **14.3**
Pastor, der 1.2.2a
peinlich 6.5.1a
people 5.5.18, 5.5.21, 6.4.1
per 4.7.2, 20.1.7
per 4.9.3c, 20.1.7d
PERFECT TENSE:
auxiliary (*haben* or *sein*?)
12.3.2; formation 12.3,
Table 12.2; indicating
characteristic state 14.3.5b;
overlap with past tense
14.3; perfect infinitive
13.1.2; relation to *sein*-
passive 15.2.2d; replacing
future perfect tense
14.3.5a; replacing
pluperfect tense 14.5.1b;
use **14.3**; use in 'up-to-
now' contexts 14.2.2b
perhaps 10.34.3
Person, die 1.1.4c
PERSON (of verb) 12.1.1a, 12.1.4
PERSONAL AND PROPER NAMES:
adjectives derived from
22.3.1e, 23.1.1d; article use
with 4.4; declension 1.3.8;
gender 1.1.13d; in genitive
case 2.3.2; plural of family
names 1.2.5f; use of initial
capital letters 23.1
PERSONAL PRONOUN **Ch. 3**:
agreement for gender
1.1.13
declension 3.1, Table 3.1;
genitive forms 2.4.1c, 3.1.2
declension of following
adjective 6.2.8
followed by relative clause
5.4.1d
omission or reduction in
colloquial speech 3.1.1
position 21.4
second person: familiar and
polite 3.3; used in
commands 16.2.1b; use of
capital letters 23.1.3
third person 3.4: after
prepositions 3.5; use of
demonstrative for 3.4.2
Pfalz, die 1.1.3g, 4.4.1b
Pfau, der 1.2.2e
pfeifen Table 12.12

Pfingsten 1.2.10b, 4.5.2, 11.2.3, 11.5.15a
pflegen 13.2.5
PHRASAL VERBS:
  formation 13.4.3b; in negation 5.5.16b; use of articles with 4.2.3; with passive sense 15.4.4; word order 21.2.1b, 21.8.2
piepe 6.5.1b
Pizza, die 1.2.6c
PLACE COMPLEMENT 18.7.1: position 21.6.2c, 21.8.1c
plädieren 13.2.4b
pleite 23.1.2
PLUPERFECT TENSE:
  complex pluperfects 14.5.3; formation 12.3, Table 12.3; use 14.5
PLURAL OF NOUNS **1.2**:
  double plurals 1.2.8; German plural for English singular 1.2.10a; German singular for English plural 1.2.9, 1.2.11; nouns without plural forms 1.2.11–12; plural in -s 1.2.5; plural of feminine nouns 1.2.3; plural of masculine nouns 1.2.2; plural of neuter nouns 1.2.4; plural of nouns of measurement 1.2.14; plural of words in -*mann* 1.2.7; spelling of plural forms 23.4; unusual plural formation 1.2.6
Pocken, die 1.2.10a
Pony, das & der 1.1.12
POSSESSIVES **5.2**:
  formation Table 5.4
  possessive determiners: declension of following adjective 6.2.1b, 6.2.2b, Table 6.4; forms 5.2.2, Table 5.5; replaced by definite article 4.6; replaced by demonstrative in genitive 5.1.1f
  possessive pronouns: forms 5.2.3, Table 5.6
possible 7.3.4
Post, die 20.3.4b, 20.5.1b
Praxis, die 1.2.6d
precisely 10.8.2a
PREDICATE COMPLEMENT **18.8**:
  agreement of verb 12.1.4b; in accusative 18.3.3b; in form of clause 19.2.1; in genitive 2.3.4; in nominative 2.1.3, 18.8; position 21.8.1e; referred to by *es* 3.6.1b; use of article in 4.8.1
prefer 7.3.4

PREFIX 22.1.1a:
  adjective 22.3.2; noun 22.2.2; verb, inseparable 22.4, 22.6; verb, separable 7.2.2–4, 12.2.1i, 21.1, 22.5, 22.6; verb, variable 22.6
preis- 22.5.3a
preisen Table 12.12
PREPOSITIONAL ADVERB **3.5**:
  individual forms 20.1.2c, 20.1.6e, 20.2.9d, 20.3.5a, 20.3.10e; prepositions not forming 3.5.2; replacing demonstrative 3.5.3b, 5.1.1i; replacing third person pronoun 3.5.1; splitting 3.5.3a; used as interrogative 5.3.3c; used as relative pronoun 5.4.4b; used to anticipate *dass*-clause or infinitive clause 6.6.2, 13.2.4e, 18.6.14, 19.2.5b
PREPOSITIONAL OBJECT **18.6**:
  in form of clause 18.6.14; in passive 15.1.3b; position 21.8.1b, 21.9.4b
PREPOSITIONS **Ch. 20**:
  compounded with noun 23.2.1; contracted with definite article 4.1.1b; from nouns – spelling 23.1.2; governed by adjectives 6.6; governed by verbs 18.6; governing accusative **20.1**; governing accusative or dative **20.3**; governing dative **20.2**; governing genitive 3.1.2, 3.1.2b, 3.5.2, **20.4**; in time expressions 11.5; 'stranded' in English 5.4.4a; used as separable verb prefix 22.5.1; use of article with 4.9; with demonstrative 3.5.3b, 5.1.1j; with personal pronoun 3.5; with reflexive pronoun 3.2.3; with relative pronoun 5.4.4
PRESENT TENSE:
  formation 12.2, Table 12.2; 'historic' present 14.2.4, 19.3.1b; in 'up-to-now' contexts 14.2.2; referring to future 14.2.3, 15.1.1a; referring to past 14.2.4; use **14.2**
Prestige, das 1.1.8b
presume 7.3.4
PRINCIPAL PARTS (of verbs) 12.2.1:
  strong and irregular verbs Table 12.12
print 20.3.1e

Prinzip, das 1.2.6d
Privileg, das 1.2.6d
pro 4.7.2, 4.9.3c, 20.1.7e
probably 10.35.1
PROFESSIONS AND OCCUPATIONS, names of: derivation 22.2.1d; masculine and feminine forms 1.1.4, 22.2.1f; plural of those in -*mann* 1.2.7; used without article 4.8.2
PROGRESSIVE TENSES (English) 13.5.4b, 14.1.5, 14.2.2a, 14.3.4a, **14.6**, 15.2.2.c, 20.3.2e
PRONOMINAL ADVERB (*see:* prepositional adverb)
PRONOUN (*see:* demonstrative, indefinite pronoun, personal pronoun, possessive, reciprocal pronoun, reflexive pronoun, relative pronoun)
PRONOUNS OF ADDRESS 3.3: use of capitals 23.1.3
PROPER NAMES (*see:* personal and proper names)
provided that 16.5.3d, 19.3.6b, 19.7.4c
PROVINCES, names of (*see:* countries)
PUBLIC HOLIDAYS (*see also:* festivals): 11.2.3
Puff, der (das) 1.1.11a
PUNCTUATION **23.5–6** (*see also:* colon, comma, exclamation mark, inverted commas, semicolon)
PURPOSE CLAUSES 19.5.1: use of *sollen* 17.6.4d; use of subjunctive 16.7.2
Pyjama, der (das) 1.1.11a

QUANTIFIERS **5.5**:
  declension when used with preceding determiner 6.2.3c; declension of following adjective 6.2.2, 6.2.3; in initial position in main clause 21.2.3b; separated from noun in initial position 21.2.1b
quellen Table 12.12
quer 20.1.2a
QUESTIONS (*see also:* indirect questions, rhetorical questions):
  adverbs used to introduce 7.5
  determiners or pronouns used to introduce 5.3

QUESTIONS – *contd*
use of modal particles in:
auch 10.4.2–3; denn 10.6.1;
doch 10.7.4; eigentlich
10.10; etwa 10.13.1; gleich
10.16; mal 10.22; noch
10.24.3a; nun 10.25.1; nur
10.26.1b; schon 10.30.2;
überhaupt 10.32.7;
vielleicht 10.34.2; wohl
10.35.2
word order 21.1.1b

Rad fahren 22.5.3
Radio, das (der) 1.1.11a
Rand, der 1.2.2d
Ränke, die 1.2.10a
Rasen, der 1.2.11
Rat, der 1.2.8, 1.2.12
raten Table 12.12, 13.2.4b,
18.6.14
Rathaus, das 20.3.4b, 20.5.1b
rather 8.2.7
Raub, der 1.2.11
rauben 18.5.3
Razzia, die 1.2.6c
real 10.10.3
recent(ly) 11.6.5
Rechte, die 6.4.3
rechts 20.4.3
RECIPROCAL PRONOUN 3.2.7
reden 13.3.1h
REFLEXIVE CONSTRUCTIONS:
impersonal 3.6.2a, 15.4.3b,
18.2.4f
REFLEXIVE PRONOUN 3.2:
forms 3.2.1–2, Table 3.2; in
infinitive constructions
3.2.4–5; position 21.4.4;
referring to subject 3.2.3,
3.2.5
REFLEXIVE VERB 18.3.6,
Table 3.2:
for English intransitive
18.3.5c; for English passive
15.4.3, 18.3.6b; passive of
15.1.2d, 15.2.2c; perfect
auxiliary 12.3.2b; use of
infinitive in commands
16.2.2a; with accusative
reflexive 18.3.6, 18.4.2e;
with dative reflexive
18.4.3; with genitive object
18.5.2
refuse 17.7.1c
Regatta, die 1.2.6c
Regime, das 1.1.8b
regnen 18.2.4a
regret 7.3.4
reiben Table 12.12
reich 6.6.1a
reichen 18.4.1d
Reichtum, der 1.2.2d
reißen Table 12.12

reiten 12.3.2c; Table 12.12
reizend 13.5.4a
RELATIVE CLAUSE:
5.1.1g, 5.1.3c, **5.4:** for
English infinitive clauses
13.2.8b; for English 'ing'-
form 13.7.4; less used in
speech 5.4.1b; not enclosed
in main clause 21.9.1; with
dependent infinitive
clause 13.2.2d
RELATIVE PRONOUN: **5.4,**
Table 5.8:
after adjectives used as
nouns 5.4.3b; after
demonstratives 5.4.3c,
5.4.5b; after indefinite
pronouns 5.4.3a; after
personal pronouns 5.4.1d;
after prepositions 5.4.4,
20.4.1e; agreement for
gender 1.1.13; compound
5.4.5; genitive 5.4.1c,
6.2.1b, 20.4.1e; indicating
cause 5.4.6d; indicating
manner 5.4.6c; referring
back to whole clause
5.4.3d; referring to place
5.4.6a; referring to time
5.4.6b
remain 13.7.5c
rennen Table 12.12
reparieren 15.2.2f
Repertoire, das 1.1.8b
REPORTED SPEECH (*see:* indirect
speech)
Reptil, das 1.2.6d
Rest, der 1.2.2a
Rheinland, das 4.4.1c
RHETORICAL QUESTIONS 10.4.3,
10.6.1c
richtig machen 22.5.3b
Richtung, die 20.3.9a
riechen Table 12.12
Ries, das 4.4.1c
ringen Table 12.12
rings 20.1.6a
rinnen Table 12.12
Risiko, das 1.2.6d
RIVERS, names of:
gender 1.1.1g, 1.1.2c
rosa 6.2.7b
Ross, das 1.2.4b
rot 8.2.3a
round 20.1.6
Rück- 22.2.2i
Rückgrat, das 1.1.9a
rudern 12.3.2c
rufen Table 12.12
ruhig 7.3.4, 10.7.3, 10.26.1a,
10.28, 16.2.1a
rühmen, sich 18.5.2
rührend 13.5.4a
run 18.3.5d

rund 9.1.6, 20.1.6a

Saal, der 1.2.2a, 23.4.2
Sache, die 4.8.2b
sagen 3.6.3b, 18.4.2b, 18.6.9a
Sakko, der (das) 1.1.11a
-sal 1.1.8d, 1.2.3c
Saldo, der 1.2.6d
salzen Table 12.12
-sam 22.3.1i
same 5.1.5
Same, der 1.1.8b, 1.2.2e, 1.3.3
Samstag 11.2.1
samt 20.2.10g
sämtlich(e) 5.5.1g, 5.5.23,
6.2.3b
Sanftmut, die 1.1.9a
satt 3.6.4, 6.5.2
Sattel, der 1.2.2c
Saturday 11.2.1
SATZBAUPLAN 18.1.3
SATZKLAMMER (*see:* verbal
bracket)
Sau, die 1.2.3b
saufen Table 12.12
saugen 12.2.1f; Table 12.12
say 3.6.3b
SCALAR PARTICLES:
auch 10.4.5a; *erst* 10.12.2;
etwa 10.13.4; *ja* 10.19.4;
noch, 10.24.1; *nur* 10.26.2;
schon 10.30.5
scarcely 19.3.3
schade 23.1.2
SCHACHTELSATZ 21.9.1
schaden 15.2.2a, 15.4.2b,
18.4.1a
Schaden, der 1.2.2c, 1.2.12
schädlich 6.5.1a
schaffen 12.2.1f; Table 12.12
-schaft 1.1.6a, 22.2.1i
schämen, sich 18.5.2, 18.6.5,
18.6.12a, 18.6.14
scharf 6.6.1a, 8.2.3a
schaudern 18.2.2
schauen 20.3.1e
scheiden Table 12.12
scheinen 2.1.3; Table 12.12,
13.2.5, 13.5.5d, 15.2.2e,
18.8, 21.8.1e
scheißen Table 12.12
schelten Table 12.12
Schema, das 1.2.6b
scheren 12.2.1e; Table 12.12
Scheu, die 1.1.9a
scheuen, sich 18.6.14
schicken 13.3.1e, 13.7.5b
schieben Table 12.12
schießen 2.5.3c; Table 12.12
Schild, das & der 1.1.12
schimpfen 15.4.2c, 18.3.3b
schinden Table 12.12
schlafen Table 12.12, 13.3.1h
schlagen 2.5.3c; Table 12.12

schlecht 2.5.5c
schleichen Table 12.12
schleifen Table 12.12
schleunigst 8.4.4a
schließen Table 12.12
schließlich 10.29
schlingen Table 12.12
schmal 8.2.3b
schmecken 18.4.1d
schmeicheln 18.4.1a
schmeißen Table 12.12
schmelzen Table 12.12
Schmerz, der 1.2.2e
Schnabel, der 1.2.2c
schneiden 2.5.3c; Table 12.12, 18.3.5e
schneien 18.2.4a
schnellstens 8.4.4b
Schnur, die 1.2.3b
schon 10.6.1c, **10.30**, 10.35.3, 10.36.1, 11.5.9, 14.2.2, 14.3.4a, 14.6.2a, 16.2.1a
Schrecken, das 13.4.4
schreiben Table 12.12, 15.2.2f, 18.6.9a, 20.3.1
schreien 12.2.1d; Table 12.12, 23.4.1
schreiten Table 12.12
schuld 6.6.1a, 23.1.2
schuldig 6.5.1a, 6.5.2, 6.5.3a
schwach 8.2.3a
Schwager, der 1.2.2c
schwarz 8.2.3a
schwarz auf weiß 23.1.1a
schwarzarbeiten 22.5.3b
schweigen Table 12.12
Schweiz, die 1.1.3g, 4.4.1b
schwellen Table 12.12
schwer 3.6.2e, 6.5.1a, 13.2.6
schwer fallen 18.4.1d
Schwermut, die 1.1.9a
Schwerpunkt, der 4.8.2b
schwierig 13.2.6
schwimmen 12.3.2c; Table 12.12
schwindeln 13.3.1h, 18.2.2
schwinden Table 12.12
schwindlig 2.5.5c
schwingen Table 12.12
schwitzen 15.1.2b
schwören Table 12.12
see 13.3.1b, 13.7.5a, 17.3.5
See, der 1.1.12, 1.2.2e, 23.4.1
See, die 1.1.12
seeing that 19.4.2
seem 7.3.4
segelfliegen 22.5.3e
segeln 12.3.2c
sehen Table 12.12, 13.3.1b, 13.3.2c, 13.7.5a, 15.1.2c, 15.2.2f, 20.3.1e
sehnen, sich 18.6.14
Sehnsucht, die 1.2.11
sehr 7.4.3, 8.3.6c, 22.5.3b

seiltanzen 22.5.3e
sein (verb) 2.1.3, 2.3.4, 2.5.5c, 3.6.2, 3.6.4, 4.8.2, 8.4.1b, 12.1.3d, 12.1.4b, 12.2.2a, 12.3, 12.4; **Table 12.3**; Table 12.4, 13.1.2, 13.2.3b, 13.2.5, 13.2.6, 13.3.1e, 14.3.3b, 15.2, 15.4.5a, 16.4.4b, 16.7.6c, 18.2.4, 18.8, 21.8.1e, 22.5.3d, 23.1.2
SEIN-PASSIVE: 12.4.2b, 15.2, Table 12.7 (*see also:* passive)
seit 3.5.2, 5.3.3c, 11.5.5b, **11.5.9**, 14.2.2, 14.3.4a, 19.3.5, 20.2.7
seit kurzem 11.6.5
seit langem 23.1.1a
seit wann? 7.5
seitdem 11.6.3b, 14.2.2, 14.3.4a, 19.3.5
seitens 20.4.3
seither 3.5.2, 11.6.3b
seitlich 20.4.3
selber 3.2.6
selbst 3.2.2, 3.2.6, 10.4.5a
selbst wenn 16.5.3d
-self 3.2.6
SEMI-AUXILIARY VERB 13.2.5
SEMI-COLON 23.6.1
senden Table 12.12
SENTENCE PATTERN 18.1.3
SEPARABLE PREFIX (*see:* prefix)
SEPARABLE VERB (*see:* verb)
Service, das & der 1.1.10a
setzen (sich) 4.2.3d, 20.3.1c
several 5.5.8, 5.5.19, 5.5.20
shall 17.6.1a, 17.7.1b
should (not) 16.5.1d, 17.2.1b, 17.5.3b, 17.6.4
sicher 6.5.3a, 6.6.1a, 17.5.2a, 21.6.1a
Sie/du/ihr 3.3, 23.1.3
sieden Table 12.12
Silvester 4.5.2, 11.2.3
SIMPLE TENSE: 12.1.1b, 12.2, Table 12.2 (*see also:* tense)
simply 10.5, 10.11
Sims, der & das 1.1.11a
since (cause) 19.3.4, 19.4.1
since (time) 11.5.9, 14.2.2, 14.3.4a, 19.3.5
singen Table 12.12
single 9.4.2e
sink 18.3.5b
sinken Table 12.12, 18.3.5b
sinnen Table 12.12
sit down 20.3.1c
sitzen 12.3.2b; Table 12.12, 18.7.1, 22.7.2
sitzen bleiben 13.3.1f
Skala, die 1.2.6c
Ski, der 1.2.2d

Ski laufen 22.5.3a
smell 17.3.5
so 3.6.3b, 10.3.1
so 5.1.6, 10.6.1d, 16.5.3b, 19.5.2b, 19.6.2b, 21.2.1c, 23.2.3
so dass/sodass 19.5.1, 19.5.2, 23.2.3
so that 16.7.2, 19.5
so viel 5.5.25e, 23.2.3
so wenig 5.5.25e, 23.2.3
so ... wie 8.3.6
sobald 19.3.6a, 23.2.3
Soda, die & das 1.1.11a
sofern 16.5.3d, 19.7.4
sogar 10.4.5a, 10.15b, 10.19.4
sogar wenn 16.5.3d
solange 14.2.2, 14.3.4a, 19.3.6b, 23.2.3
solch(e) 5.1.6, 5.5.1b, 6.2.3b
sollen 12.1.3c, 12.2.2; Table 12.4, 13.3.1a, 13.3.2a, 16.2.2, 16.4.4b, 16.5.1d, 16.6.4b, 16.5.3d, 16.7.2a, **17.6**
Solo, das 1.2.6d
some 4.2.2a, 4.8.7, 5.4.1c, 5.5.4d, 5.5.7, 5.5.8, 5.5.9, 5.5.11, 5.5.19, 5.5.26
some ... or other 5.5.11
somehow 5.5.11
someone 5.5.4c, 5.5.11c, 5.5.15, 5.5.24, 5.5.27
something 5.5.9, 5.5.11c
somewhat 5.5.9c
somewhere 5.5.11b, 7.1.5
sondern 12.1.4, 19.1.1d, 23.5.1b
Sonnabend 11.2.1
sonst 7.3.5b
sooft 19.3.6c, 23.2.3
sorgen (sich) 15.2.2a, 18.6.5, 18.6.14
sorgfältigst 8.4.4a
soweit 16.5.3d, 19.7.4
sowie 12.1.4, 19.1.4b, 19.3.6a, 23.5.1a
sowieso 10.9, 10.27, 10.31
sowohl ... als/wie (auch) 8.3.6a, 12.1.4, 19.1.4b
sozusagen 21.2.1c
spalten Table 12.12
spannend 13.5.4a
Spargel, der (die) 1.1.11a
spätestens 8.4.4b
Spatz, der 1.3.2a
spazieren 13.3.1e
spazieren gehen 22.5.3c
speien Table 12.12
SPELLING **23.1–4**: one word or two? 5.5.25e, 22.5.3, 23.2; -*ss*- or -*ß*- 23.3; use of initial capital letters 23.1
spinnen Table 12.12

Sporn, der 1.2.2e
Sport, der 1.2.11
sprechen Table 12.12, 18.6.9a
sprießen Table 12.12
springen Table 12.12
spüren 13.3.1b, 13.3.2c, 13.7.5a,
   15.1.2c
Staat, der 1.2.2e
Stachel, der 1.2.2b, 1.2.2e
Stadion, das 1.2.6d
stand- 22.5.3a
stark 8.2.3a
starr 6.6.1c
statt (*see:* anstatt)
statt- 22.5.3a
statt dessen 3.1.2b
stattfinden 18.7.1, 22.5.3a
Statut, das 1.2.4e
staubsaugen Table 12.12
stay 13.7.5c
stechen Table 12.12
stehen 12.2.1e, 12.3.2b, 12.5.2b;
   Table 12.12, 13.2.5, 14.3.3b,
   15.4.4, 15.4.5d, 16.4.4c,
   18.7.1
stehen bleiben 13.3.1f, 22.5.3c
stehlen Table 12.12
steigen Table 12.12, 18.3.5b
-stens 8.4.4b
sterben 12.5.2b; Table 12.12
Steuer, die & das 1.1.12
Steuerbord, das (der) 1.1.11a
stieben Table 12.12
stießen 12.3.2c
Stift, das & der 1.1.12
still 10.24.2
stinken Table 12.12, 15.1.2b
Stock, der 1.2.8
stolz 6.6.1a, 6.6.2
stop 7.3.4
stoßen 2.5.3c, 12.2.1f; Table
   12.12
Strahl, der 1.2.2e
Strauch, der 1.2.2d
Strauß, der 1.2.8
streichen Table 12.12
streiten (sich) Table 12.12,
   18.6.14
strengstens 8.4.4b
STRONG ADJECTIVE DECLENSION
   Tables 6.1–6.2 (*see also:*
   adjective)
STRONG VERB Tables 12.1, 12.11,
   12.12 (*see also:* verb)
stumm 6.6.1c
Stunde, die 9.3.1, 11.5.15b
stützen 20.3.1e
SUBJECT (of verb) **18.2**:
   agreement of finite verb
   with 12.1.4; case 2.1.2,
   18.2.1a; noun clause used
   as 3.6.2e, 19.2; 'dummy'
   subject 3.6.2d, 21.2.2d;
   formal

SUBJECT (of verb) – *contd*
   3.6.2; impersonal 3.6.2,
   18.2.4; in passive 15.1.3–4;
   infinitive clause used as
   3.6.2e, 13.2.3; of infinitive
   clauses 3.2.5, 13.2.4b;
   position of noun subject
   21.2.1b, 21.2.2d, 21.4.1,
   21.5, 21.6.1; referred to by
   reflexive pronoun 3.2.3,
   3.2.5; restrictions on in
   German 18.2.3;
   understood in coordinated
   clauses 21.1.4a; verbs
   without subjects 18.2.2
SUBJECT CLAUSES (*see:* noun
   clauses)
SUBJUNCTIVE 12.5, **Ch. 16**:
   conditional (with *würde*)
   12.5.2, 16.4.4–5, Table
   12.10: in conditional
   sentences 16.5; in indirect
   speech 16.6.3b; in sense of
   future-in-the-past 16.4.5
   formation: 12.5, Tables 12.8,
   12.9, 12.10, 12.11
   general 16.1.3, 16.3
   in hypothetical comparisons
   16.7.1b
   in indirect speech 16.6.2–4
   in negative contexts 16.7.5
   in purpose clauses 16.7.2
   in time clauses 16.7.4
   in wishes, instructions and
   commands 10.7.6, 10.12.1b,
   10.26.1c, 16.7.6, 17.4.4
   Konjunktiv I 16.4.2, Tables
   12.8, 12.9: expressing a
   proposition 16.7.6c;
   expressing a wish 16.7.6a;
   forms 12.5.1, 16.4.1, use in
   commands 16.2.2, 16.7.6d,
   17.4.4
   Konjunktiv II 16.4.2, Tables
   12.8, 12.9, 12.11: expressing
   a wish 16.7.6b; forms
   12.5.2, 16.4.1; in
   conditional sentences 16.5;
   in time clauses 16.7.4;
   simple and compound
   form 16.4.4; to moderate
   tone of statements, etc.
   16.7.3
   past subjunctive 12.5.2b,
   16.4.2b, 16.4.4, Tables 12.8,
   12.9, 12.11 (see also:
   Konjunktiv II)
   pluperfect subjunctive
   16.5.1b, Table 12.10 (see
   also: Konjunktiv II)
   present subjunctive 12.5.1,
   16.4.2a, Tables 12.8, 12.9
   (see also: Konjunktiv I)
   simple tenses: Table 12.9

SUBJUNCTIVE – *contd*
   tenses of subjunctive 12.5,
   16.4, 16.5.1c, Table 12.8
SUBORDINATE CLAUSE **Ch. 19**:
   in initial position 21.2.1b;
   not enclosed in verbal
   bracket 21.9.1; structure
   and word order 21.1.1c,
   21.1.3b, 21.1.4b; use of
   comma 23.5.2 (*see also:*
   adverbial clause, causal
   clause, clause of degree,
   clause of manner, clause of
   result, comparative clause,
   concessive clause,
   conditional clause, noun
   clause, purpose clause,
   relative clause, time clause)
such 5.1.6
suchen 13.2.5
suchlike 5.1.6g
Sudan, der 1.1.3g, 4.4.1a
SUFFIX 22.1.1a:
   adjective 22.3.1; noun
   22.2.1; verb 22.7.2–3
SUPERLATIVE **Ch. 8** (*see also:*
   comparison of adjectives
   and adverbs)
sure 7.3.4

Tag, der 1.2.2d, 11.5.1, 11.5.14
TAG QUESTION (English) 10.4.2,
   10.7, 10.34.2, 10.35.1
tags 11.4.2
tanzen 12.3.2c
Tatsache, die 4.8.2b
Tau, das & der 1.1.12
täuschen, sich 18.6.6b, 18.6.9a
tausend 9.1.1c, 9.1.5a
Tausend, das 2.7.4, 9.1.1m,
   9.1.5b
Taxi, das (der) 1.1.11a
teil- 22.5.3a
Teil, der (das) 1.1.11c
teilhaftig 3.6.4, 6.5.3c
teilnehmen 22.5.3a
teils … teils 19.1.5b
Tempo, das 1.2.6d
Tempus, das 1.2.6a
TENSE 12.1.1b, **Ch. 14**, Table
   14.1 (*see also:* future tense,
   future perfect tense,
   passive, past tense,
   perfect tense, pluperfect
   tense, present tense,
   subjunctive)
Terminus, der 1.2.6a
teuer 6.5.1a
Textil, das 1.2.6d
than 8.3.1, 10.6.2e, 19.7.1
thanks to 20.2.10c
that (conjunction) 19.2.1
that (demonstrative) 4.1.1c,
   5.1.1, 5.1.2, 5.1.4

that (relative pronoun) 5.4
that kind of 5.1.6g
that sort of 5.1.6g
Thema, das 1.2.6b
then 10.3.1, 10.6.2c, 11.6.3
there 7.1.1
there is/are 18.2.5
thereby 20.1.2c
therefore 20.1.6e
thing(s) 6.4.1
this 5.1.1, 5.1.2
though 10.7, 19.1.1b, 19.6.1
thousand 9.1.5
through 13.7.2a, 20.1.2a
throughout 11.4.1a, 20.1.2b
thus 10.3.1
tie 20.3.1c
till (see: *until*)
TIME CLAUSE 19.3: with
    subjunctive 16.7.4
TIME EXPRESSIONS **Ch. 11**:
    article use in 4.5; telling
    the time 11.1; with
    accusative 2.2.5a, 11.4.1;
    with *erst* 10.12.2b; with
    ganz 5.5.1g; with genitive
    2.3.5b, 11.4.2; with *noch*
    10.24.2; with prepositions
    11.5; with *schon* 10.30.5
Tirol, das 4.4.1c
TITLES article use with 4.2.5c;
    declension 1.3.8
to 2.5.1, 18.6.13a, 20.1.1a,
    20.2.6a, 20.2.9, 20.3.3a,
    20.3.5a, 20.3.9a, 20.5
Tochter, die 1.2.3d
Tod, der 1.2.11
together with 20.2.10g
too 10.4.5b
top 7.1.2
TOPIC (of clause) 21.2.2
Tor, das 1.1.12
Tor, der 1.1.12, 1.3.2a
totschlagen 22.5.3b
towards 11.5.6, 20.1.4b, 20.2.4d,
    20.2.6b, 20.2.9, 20.3.5a
TOWNS AND CITIES, names of
    (*see also:* geographical
    names):
    adjectives derived from
    22.3.1e, 23.1.1d; article use
    with 4.4; gender 1.1.3g;
    nouns derived from
    22.2.1d; prepositions with
    20.1.1a, 20.2.6a, 20.5.3
trachten 13.2.2b
träg(e) 6.3.3
tragen Table 12.12
TRANSITIVE VERB (*see:* verb)
trauen 18.4.1a
träumen 18.2.2, 18.6.14
traurig 6.6.1b
treffen Table 12.12
treiben Table 12.12

treten 2.5.3c, 12.2.1e, 12.3.2c;
    Table 12.12
treu 6.5.1a
triefen Table 12.12
trinken Table 12.12
trotz 20.4.1b, 23.1.2
trotzdem 3.1.2b, 10.7.1, 19.6.1b
trotzen 18.4.1a
trüb(e) 6.3.3
trügen Table 12.12
Trümmer, die 1.2.10a
-tum 1.1.7, 1.2.4b, 22.2.1j
tun 3.6.3b, 12.2.1d; Table 12.12,
    13.3.1d, 16.4.4c, 16.5.1d,
    17.1.5b
tunlichst 8.4.4a
Türkei, die 4.4.1b
turn 18.3.5c
twice 9.4.3a
two 5.5.3b, 9.1.1k
Typ, der 1.2.2e, 1.3.2a
typisch 6.6.1a

übel 2.5.5c
über 6.6.1, 9.1.6, 11.4.1a,
    11.5.10, 18.6.9, **20.3.11**,
    20.3.12, 20.4.2a
über- 22.6.4
über ... hinaus 20.3.12b
über kurz oder lang 23.1.1a
überall 7.1.5b
überdrüssig 3.6.4, 6.5.3a
überein- 22.5.2
überführen 18.5.3
überhand nehmen 22.5.3b
überhaupt 10.32
überlegen 6.5.1a
übernachten 18.7.1
überraschend 13.5.4a
überzeugen 13.2.4c, 18.6.14
überzeugend 13.5.4a
überzeugt 6.6.1a, 6.6.2
übrig bleiben 22.5.3b
übrigens 10.33, 21.2.1c
um 9.1.6, 11.5.11, 18.6.10, 20.1.6
um- 22.6.5
um ... als 8.3.1c
um so 8.3.5
um so mehr ... als 19.4.3b
um ... willen 3.1.1d, 5.1.1b,
    5.4.1c, 20.4.3
um ... zu 13.2.7a, 13.7.2b
umfassen 15.1.2b
umfassend 13.5.4a
umher 7.2.4
UMLAUT:
    in adjective comparison
    8.2.3; in noun plurals 1.2;
    in *Konjunktiv II* of strong
    and irregular verbs
    12.5.2b, Table 12.11; in
    present tense of strong
    verbs 12.2.1f; in word
    formation 22.1.1b, 22.7.1,

UMLAUT – contd
    22.7.3; with double vowels
    23.4.2
umpteen 9.1.1m, 9.2.1a, 9.4.3b
un- 22.2.2j, 22.3.2b
unabhängig 6.6.1a
unbeschadet 20.4.3
und 12.1.4, 13.2.7e, 13.7.3a,
    19.1.4a, 23.5.1a
und auch nicht/kein 19.1.3d
und zwar 10.36.2
under(neath) 20.3.13, 20.3.14,
    20.4.2
-ung 1.1.6a, 22.2.1k
ungeachtet 20.4.3
ungefähr 9.1.6
Unglück, das 1.2.11
Universität, die 20.3.4b, 20.5.1b
unkundig 6.5.3c
unlängst 8.4.4a, 11.6.5
unless 10.6.2a, 16.5.3d, 19.7.2d
unser aller 3.1.2a
unsereiner 5.5.24
unten 7.1.2
unter 4.2.3c, 9.1.6, **20.3.13**,
    20.3.14, 20.4.2a
unter- 22.6.6
untere/unterste 8.2.5
unterhalb 20.4.2
unterliegen 18.4.1a
Unternehmen, das 13.4.4
untertan 6.5.1b
Untertan, der 1.2.2e
until 10.12.2b, 11.5.4, 13.4.3b,
    16.7.4, 19.3.2
unweit 20.4.2
unwohl 2.5.5c
up to 20.1.1a, 20.3.3a
ur- 22.2.2k, 22.3.2c
uraufführen 22.5.3e
Urteil, das 1.1.11c
urteilen 18.6.14
USA, die 4.4.1b
used (accustomed) to 6.5.2, 6.6.1
Utensil, das 1.2.6d

vag(e) 6.3.3
VALENCY (of verb) **Ch. 18:**
    changed by use of prefixes
    22.4.1
Vater, der 1.2.2c
ver- 22.4.4
Veranda, die 1.2.6c
veranlassen Table 12.12,
    13.2.4b
Verb, das 1.2.4e
VERB (*see also:* auxiliary verb,
    causative; imperative;
    infinitive, modal auxiliary,
    mood, participle, passive,
    phrasal verb, prefix,
    reflexive verb, subjunctive,
    tense, valency, word
    formation):

VERB – *contd*
abstract nouns derived from 22.2.1k
conjugation: **Ch. 12**: compound tenses 12.3, Table 12.5; imperative 12.2; irregular verbs Tables 12.3–12.4, 12.12; non-finite forms 12.2; passive 12.4, Tables 12.6–12.7; simple tenses 12.2, Table 12.2.; subjunctive 12.5, Tables 12.9, 12.10, 12.11
copular 18.8
grammatical categories of 12.1.1
impersonal 3.6.2, 18.2.4: perfect auxiliary 12.3.2b
inseparable 21.4, 21.6: formation of past participle 12.2.1h
intransitive 18.3.5: in reflexive constructions 15.4.3b; in subjectless passive 15.1.4b; meaning of past participle 13.5.1b; perfect auxiliary 12.3.2
irregular 12.1.3: formation of simple tenses and non-finite forms 12.2.2, Tables 12.3, 12.4, 12.12; Konjunktiv II forms 12.5.2b, 16.4.4, Table 12.11
of motion: governing direction complements 18.7.2; in progressive sense 14.6.2a; omission after modal auxiliaries 17.1.5a; used with bare infinitive 13.3.1e, 13.7.5b; with prepositions governing accusative or dative 20.3.1
of perception: used with bare infinitive 13.3.1b, 13.3.2c, 13.7.5a, 15.1.2c, 21.1.3b; with können 17.3.5
position 21.1–2: at end of clause 21.1.3; 'verb second' rule 21.2
principal parts 12.2.1; of strong and irregular verbs Table 12.12
root 12.1.1, 12.2.1
separable 21.5, 21.6: conjugation and forms 12.2.1i; infinitive with zu 13.1.4b
strong 12.1.2: formation of Konjunktiv II 12.5.2b, Table 12.11; formation of simple tenses and non-finite forms 12.2.1, Table 12.2; nouns formed from 1.1.5b, 22.2.3a; use of Konjunktiv II forms 16.4.4

VERB – *contd*
transitive 18.3.1: differences between English and German 18.3.5; formation from intransitive verbs 22.4.1a, 22.7.1; in reflexive constructions 15.4.3a; meaning of past participle 13.5.1b; perfect auxiliary 12.3.2; use in passive 15.1.2
weak 12.1.2: formation of simple tenses and non-finite forms 12.2.1, Table 12.2; use of Konjunktiv II forms 16.4.4a
VERBAL BRACKET 21.1.2, 21.2 (*see also:* word order)
verbitten 18.4.3b
verbleichen Table 12.12
verblüffend 13.5.4a
Verbrechen, das 13.4.4
Verdacht, der 1.2.11
verdächtig 6.5.3c
verdächtigen 18.5.3
verderben 12.3.2c; Table 12.12
Verdienst, das & der 1.1.12
verdrießen Table 12.12
vergangen 4.5.1
vergessen Table 12.12
vergewissern, sich 18.5.2
Vergnügen, das 13.4.4
verhasst 6.5.1a
verhehlen 13.5.4b
verheiratet 6.6.1a
verhohlen 13.5.4b
verlangen 13.2.4b
verlassen 18.3.5a
verleiden Table 12.12
verletzen 15.2.2f
verliebt 6.6.1a, 13.5.4b
verlieren (sich) Table 12.12, 18.7.1
verlockend 13.5.4a
verloren gehen 22.5.3c
verlustig 6.5.3c
vermöge 20.4.3
vermögen 13.2.2h
Vermögen, das 13.4.4
vermutlich 7.3.4
verrückt 13.5.4b
verschieden 6.6.1a
verschleißen Table 12.12
verschweigen 18.4.2c
versenken 18.3.5b
versessen 6.6.1a
versichern 18.5.3
versprechen (sich) 13.2.2b, 13.2.5, 18.3.6b
Versprechen, das 13.4.4
verständlich 6.5.1a
verstehen 13.2.5
versuchen 13.2.2b
verteilen 20.3.1e

vertieft 20.3.1e
Vertikale, die 6.4.3
vertrauen 18.4.1a
verwandt 6.6.1a
verwenden Table 12.12
verwickelt 20.3.1e
verwirren 13.5.4b
verworren 13.5.4b
verwundert 6.6.1b
very 7.4.3
verzeihen Table 12.12
Vetter, der 1.2.2b, 1.2.2e
via 20.3.12a
viel/vieles/viele 2.4.1d, 5.4.3a, **5.5.25**, 6.2.3b, 6.4.5, 7.4.2, 8.2.4, 23.2.3
vielleicht 10.1.1, 10.19.2, **10.34**, 17.3.2b, 21.6.1a
vielmals 9.4.3b
Villa, die 1.2.6c
Virus, der (das) 1.1.11a
Visum, das 1.2.6a
Vogel, der 1.2.2c
Vogtland, das 4.4.1c
VOICE (of verb) 12.1.1d (*see also:* passive)
voll 6.5.3b
voll- 22.6.7
von 2.4, 2.7, 3.1.2b, 4.7.1a, 11.5.12, 15.3, 18.6.9a, 18.6.11, 20.2.1a, **20.2.8**
von … an 11.5.12, 20.2.10a
von … aus 20.2.8a
von … her 7.2.3a, 20.2.8a
von klein auf 23.1.1a
von nah und fern 23.1.1a
von … wegen 4.9.3c, 20.4.1d
von weitem 23.1.1.a
von wo? 5.3.3c, 7.2.1, 7.5
vonnöten 23.2.1
vonstatten 23.2.1
vor 6.6.1c, 11.5.13, 18.6.12, 20.3.15, 20.3.16
vor- 22.5.1h
voraus- 22.5.2
vorausgesetzt, dass 16.5.3d
Voraussetzung, die 4.8.2b
vorbehaltlich 20.4.3
vorbei 20.3.2a, 22.5.2
vorbei sein 22.5.3d
vorbereitet 6.6.1a
vordere/vorderste 8.2.5
vorderhand 23.2.1
vorfahren 20.3.1c
VORGANGSPASSIV 12.4.1, 15.1 (*see also:* passive)
Vorhaben, das 13.4.4
vorher 11.6.4a
vorig 4.5.1
vorkommen 18.4.1b
vormittags 11.4.2
vornehmen, sich 18.4.3b
vorschlagen 13.2.4b
vorstellen, sich 18.4.3b

vorüber- 22.5.2

Wache, die 1.1.4c
wachsen Table 12.12, 18.3.5a
Wagen, der 1.2.2c
wagen 13.2.2b
wägen Table 12.12
Wahl, die 20.2.9f
während (conj.) 19.3.7
während (prep.) 11.5.14,
    20.4.1c
währenddessen 3.1.2b
Waise, die 1.1.4c
Wald, der 1.2.2d
Wallis, das 4.4.1c
wann 7.5, 19.3.1c
want 13.7.5f, 17.4.1, 17.7.1
warm 2.5.5c, 8.2.3a
wärmstens 8.4.4b
warnen 13.2.4b
warten 18.5.1
warum 5.4.6d, 7.5
was (interrogative) 5.3.3, 7.5,
    21.2.1c
was (relative pronoun) 5.4.3,
    5.4.5a
was für (ein[er]) 5.3.2, 19.6.2c
waschen Table 12.12, 15.2.2f
Wasser, das 1.2.4d
WEAK ADJECTIVE DECLENSION
    Tables 6.1, 6.3 (*see also:*
    adjective)
WEAK MASCULINE NOUNS 1.3.2,
    Table 1.6:
    adjective declension with
    6.1.1
WEAK VERB (*see:* verb)
weben 12.2.1e; Table 12.12
weder ... noch 10.24.3c, 12.1.4,
    19.1.3d, 23.5.1a
weg- 22.5.1i
wegen 3.1.1d, 5.1.1b, 5.4.1c,
    20.4.1d
weggehen 18.3.5a
Wehmut, die 1.1.9a
Wehr, die & das 1.1.12
wehtun 18.4.1a
Weib, das 1.1.4c
Weibchen, das 1.1.4b
weichen Table 12.12
weihen 20.2.9f
Weihnachten 1.2.10b, 4.5.2,
    11.2.3, 11.5.15
weil 13.2.7e, 13.7.3b, 19.4.1
weinen 13.3.1h
-weise 7.3.6
Weise, die 7.3.6
Weisel, der 1.1.4b
weisen Table 12.12
weismachen 22.5.3a
weit 7.4.2
weitaus 7.4.2
weiter 7.3.4, 13.7.5e
welcher (indefinite) 5.5.26

welcher (interrogative) 5.3.1,
    6.2.2c, 19.6.2c
welcher (relative pronoun)
    5.4.2, 5.4.5b
well 8.2.4c, 10.25.2, 10.35.5
wenden Table 12.12
wenig(es) 2.4.1d, 5.4.3a,
    5.5.25, 6.4.5, 7.4.1a, 8.2.4,
    23.2.3
wenig (ein) 5.5.5
wenige 6.2.3b
weniger 8.2.4, 8.3.2
wenigstens 8.4.4b, 10.20.1,
    21.2.1c
wenn 3.6.3a, 5.4.6b, 13.7.2d,
    13.7.3a, **16.5**, 16.7.6b,
    19.2.3, 19.3.1d
wenn ... auch 16.5.3d
wenn ... nicht 16.5.3d
wenngleich 19.6.1b
wer (indefinite) 5.5.15a
wer (interrogative) 5.3.3
wer (relative pronoun) 5.4.5a
wer ... auch 19.6.2
werben Table 12.12
werden 2.1.3, 2.5.5c, 3.6.1b,
    3.6.2b, 3.6.4, 4.8.2, 10.35.4,
    12.1.3d, 12.2.2b, 12.3, 12.4;
    Table 12.3; Table 12.4,
    13.1.2, 15.1, 18.2.4, 18.8,
    20.2.9f, 21.8.1e, 23.1.2
WERDEN-PASSIVE 12.4.2a, 15.1
    (*see also:* passive)
werfen Table 12.12
Werkstatt, die 1.2.3a
wert 3.6.4, 6.5.2, 6.5.3a
wesentlich 7.4.2
weshalb? 7.5
wett- 22.5.3a
wetteifern 22.5.3d
wettlaufen 22.5.3e
what (interrogative) 5.3.3
what (relative pronoun) 5.4.3c
what a ...! 5.3.1c, 5.3.2c
what for 5.3.3f, 7.5
what kind of 5.3.2
whatever 19.6.2
when 13.4.3a, 19.3.1
whenever 19.3.1d, 19.3.6b,
    19.6.2
whereas 19.3.7
which (interrogative) 5.3.1,
    5.3.2d
which (relative pronoun) 5.4
while/whilst 19.3.7
who (interrogative) 5.3.3
who (relative pronoun) 5.4
whoever 19.6.2
whose (interrogative) 5.3.3a
whose (relative pronoun) 5.4
why 5.3.3f, 7.5
wichtig 3.6.2e, 6.5.1a
wider 20.1.7f
wider- 18.4.1c, 22.6.8

widerfahren 18.4.1b
widerlich 6.5.1a
wie 'as', 'like' 2.6, 3.4.3, 8.3.1a,
    8.3.6, 13.6.2, 14.3.3b,
    19.3.1b, 19.7.1, 21.9.3,
    23.2.3, 23.5.4
wie 'how' 5.4.6c, 7.5, 13.3.1b
wie ... auch 19.6.2, 21.2.1c
wie viel 5.5.25e, 23.2.3
wie wenn 16.7.1
wieder- 22.6.9
wiegen Table 12.12
wieso 7.5
wieweit 23.2.3
wiewohl 19.6.1b
Wiking, der 1.2.2d
will 17.7.1a
Wille, der 1.1.8b, 1.3.3
willkommen 6.5.1a
winden Table 12.12
winken Table 12.12
Wirren, die 1.2.10a
wish 17.7.1
wissen 12.1.3c, 12.2.2d; Table
    12.4, 13.2.5, 15.1.2b,
    16.4.4c, 18.6.9a
with 13.2.7e, 13.7.2e, 18.6.7,
    20.2.3, 20.2.5
with regard to 20.1.7b
within 20.2.10b, 20.4.2
without 13.2.7b, 13.7.2f, 19.7.7,
    20.1.5
wo 5.4.6, 7.1.5a, 7.3.5a, 7.5,
    23.2.3
wo(r)- + preposition 5.3.3c,
    5.4.4b
woanders 7.1.5a, 7.3.5a,
    23.2.3
wobei 13.7.3a
Woche, die 1.1.9a, 11.5.7
wodurch 5.3.3c
woher 5.3.3c, 5.4.6a, 7.2.1,
    7.3.5a, 7.5
wohin 5.3.3c, 5.4.6a, 7.2.1,
    7.3.5a, 7.5
wohingegen 19.3.7c
wohl (adjective) 2.5.5c, 8.2.4
wohl (particle) 10.30.1a, **10.35**,
    10.36.1, 14.4.3, 17.2.2
wohnen 18.7.1
wollen 10.35.4, 12.1.3c, 12.2.2;
    Table 12.4, 13.3.1a, 13.3.2a,
    16.2.2f, 16.4.4b, 16.5.1d,
    17.7
woman 6.4.1
womöglich 23.2.3
wonach 5.3.3c
WORD FORMATION **Ch. 22**:
    adjective formation:
    compounding 22.3.3;
    prefixes 22.3.2; suffixes
    22.3.1
    methods of word formation
    21.1

WORD FORMATION – *contd*
noun formation: 22.2: by
vowel change 22.2.3a;
compounding 22.2.4; from
other parts of speech
23.1.1; prefixes 22.2.2;
suffixes 22.2.1
productive and
unproductive formations
22.1.2
verb formation:
adjective/adverb plus
verb 22.5.3b; causative
22.7.2; compound 22.5.3e;
inseparable prefixes 22.4,
22.6; noun plus verb
22.5.3a, 23.1.2; separable
prefixes 22.5–6; simple,
from nouns and adjectives
22.7.1; suffixes 22.7.3–4;
variable prefixes 22.6; verb
plus verb 22.5.3c
WORD ORDER **Ch. 21** (*see also*:
main clause, questions,
subordinate clause):
initial position: 21.1.2,
21.1.4a, **21.2**
position of elements after
verbal bracket 21.1.2, 21.9
position of elements within
verbal bracket 21.1.2
general principles: 21.3
position and order of
adverbials 21.6
position of complements 21.8
position of nicht 21.7
position of noun subject and
objects 21.5
position of pronouns 21.4
verb position 21.1–2
Wort, das 1.1.9a, 1.2.8
wovon 5.3.3c
wozu 5.3.3c, 7.5
Wrack, das 1.2.5d
wringen Table 12.12
write down 20.3.1c
wunder- 22.5.3a
wundern (sich) 18.2.2, 18.6.14
wünschen 13.2.2b
würdig 3.6.4, 6.5.3a
Wurm, der 1.2.2d

wurs(ch)t 6.5.1b
wütend 6.6.1a, 13.5.4a

x-mal 9.4.3b
x-te 9.2.1a

yes 10.19.5, 10.35.5
yet 10.24.2
you 3.3

zäh(e) 6.3.3
zart 8.2.3b
Zeh, der 1.2.2e
zeigen 15.2.2f
zeit 20.4.3
Zeit, die 5.5.7a, 11.5.15b
Zeitalter, das 11.5.7a
zelten 18.7.1
zer- 22.4.5
zerbrechen 12.3.2c
ZERO ARTICLE 4.8:
use with prepositions 4.9
zerstören 15.2.2f
ziehen Table 12.12
Ziel, das 4.8.2b
zig 9.1.1l
zigmal 9.1.1l, 9.4.3b
zigste 9.1.2a
Zinsen, die 1.2.10a
zirka 9.1.6
Zirkus, der 1.2.6a
zittern 13.3.1h
zornig 6.6.1a
zu (preposition) 4.2.3b, **11.5.15**,
18.3.3b, 18.6.13, 18.6.14,
20.1.4f, 20.2.4d, 20.2.6a,
20.2.9, 20.5.2
zu 'too' 2.5.3c, 2.5.5b, 7.4.1a,
13.2.7a, 19.5.3
zu- 18.4.1c, 22.5.1j
zu- -st 8.4.4c
zu viel 5.5.25e, 23.2.1
zu wenig 23.2.1
Zubehör, das & der 1.1.11a
züchten 18.3.5a
zufällig 7.3.4
zufolge 20.2.10e
zufrieden 3.6.4
zufrieden sein 22.5.3d
zugänglich 6.5.1a
zugegeben 21.2.1c

zugetan 6.5.1b
zugrunde/zu Grunde 23.2.1
zugunsten/zu Gunsten 20.4.3,
23.2.1
zuleide/zu Leide 23.2.1
zuliebe 20.2.10j
zumal 19.4.3a
zumindest 8.4.4c, 10.20.1
zunächst 8.4.4c
zuoberst 8.4.4c
zurande/zu Rande 23.2.1
zurück- 22.2.2i, 22.5.2
zurück sein 22.5.3d
zurzeit 23.2.1
zusammen- 22.5.2
zuschanden/zu Schanden
23.2.1
zuschulden/zu Schulden
23.2.1
zusichern 13.2.4b, 18.5.3
zustande/zu Stande 23.2.1
zuständig 6.6.1a
ZUSTANDSPASSIV 12.4.1, 15.2 (*see
also*: passive)
zustoßen 18.4.1b
zutage/zu Tage 23.2.1
zutiefst 8.4.4c
zuträglich 6.5.1a
zutrauen 18.4.2c
zuungunsten/zu Ungunsten
20.4.3
zuvor 11.6.4a
zuvorderst 8.4.4c
zuwege/zu Wege 23.2.1
zuwider 6.5.1b, 8.2.7, 20.2.10k
zuzeiten 23.2.1
zuzüglich 20.4.3
zwar 10.30.1a, 10.35.3, **10.36**,
19.6.1b
zwecks 4.9.3c, 20.4.3
zweier 6.2.1b, 9.1.3a
zweifach 9.4.2
zweifellos 7.3.4
zweifeln 18.6.14
zweitens 9.2.3, 21.2.1c
zwicken 2.5.3c
zwingen Table 12.12
zwischen 5.3.3c, 9.1.6, 20.3.13b,
20.3.17
zwo 9.1.1f

a LANGE medical book

Harper's Illustrated Biochemistry

twenty-seventh edition

Robert K. Murray, MD, PhD
Professor (Emeritus) of Biochemistry
University of Toronto
Toronto, Ontario

Daryl K. Granner, MD
Joe C. Davis Professor of Biomedical Science
Director, Vanderbilt Diabetes Center
Professor of Molecular Physiology and Biophysics
and of Medicine
Vanderbilt University
Nashville, Tennessee

Victor W. Rodwell, PhD
Professor of Biochemistry
Purdue University
West Lafayette, Indiana

Lange Medical Books/McGraw-Hill
Medical Publishing Division

New York   Chicago   San Francisco   Lisbon
Milan   New Delhi   San Juan   Seoul   Sing

Harper's Illustrated Biochemistry, Twenty-Seventh Edition

2 3 4 5 6 7 8 9 0 DOC/DOC 0 9 8 7 6

ISBN-13: 978-0-07-146197-9; ISBN-10: 0-07-146197-3

ISSN 1043-9811

Notice

Medicine is an ever-changing science. As new research and clinical experience broaden our knowledge, changes in treatment and drug therapy are required. The authors and the publisher of this work have checked with sources believed to be reliable in their efforts to provide information that is complete and generally in accord with the standards accepted at the time of publication. However, in view of the possibility of human error or changes in medical sciences, neither the authors nor the publisher nor any other party who has been involved in the preparation or publication of this work warrants that the information contained herein is in every respect accurate or complete, and they disclaim all responsibility for any errors or omissions or for the results obtained from use of the information contained in this work. Readers are encouraged to confirm the information contained herein with other sources. For example and in particular, readers are advised to check the product information sheet included in the package of each drug they plan to administer to be certain that the information contained in this work is accurate and that changes have not been made in the recommended dose or in the contraindications for administration. This recommendation is of particular importance in connection with new or infrequently used drugs.

This book was set in Garamond by Silverchair Science + Communications, Inc
The editors were Jason Malley, Karen G. Edmonson, and Karen Davis.
The production supervisor was Phil Galea.
The text designer was Eve Siegel.
The cover designer was Kelly Parr of Pehrsson Design.
The index was prepared by Kathrin Unger.
RR Donnelley was printer and binder.

This book is printed on acid-free paper.

Cover: Ribosome large subunit. Ribosomes catalyze the synthesis of polypeptides using the genetic coding information found in messenger RNA. Ribosomes are large macromolecular complexes comprised of two major subunits, termed large and small based upon their relative sizes, each of which is composed of several RNA and protein subunits. Shown is the structure of the large ribosomal subunit from the halophilic archaeon *Haloarcula marismortui,* which was determined by the research group of Dr. Thomas A. Steitz (Ban N et al: The complete atomic structure of the large ribosomal subunit at 2.4 Å resolution. Science 2000;289:905). Various colors are used to denote the individual RNA and protein molecules. Ribosomal RNA is represented by thin lines and polypeptide chains by ribbons. *Credit:* Protein Data Bank/Photo Researchers, Inc.

INTERNATIONAL EDITION ISBN-13: 978-0-07-125300-0; ISBN-10: 0-07-125300-9
Copyright © 2006. Exclusive rights by The McGraw-Hill Companies, Inc. for manufacture and export. This book cannot be re-exported from the country to which it is consigned by McGraw-Hill. The International Edition is not available in North America.

Authors

David A. Bender, PhD
Sub-Dean Royal Free and University College Medical School, Assistant Faculty Tutor and Tutor to Medical Students, Senior Lecturer in Biochemistry, Department of Biochemistry and Molecular Biology, University College London

Kathleen M. Botham, PhD, DSc
Reader in Veterinary Basic Sciences, Royal Veterinary College, University of London

Daryl K. Granner, MD
Joe C. Davis Professor of Biomedical Science, Director, Vanderbilt Diabetes Center, Professor of Molecular Physiology and Biophysics and of Medicine, Vanderbilt University, Nashville, Tennessee

Frederick W. Keeley, PhD
Associate Director and Senior Scientist, Research Institute, Hospital for Sick Children, Toronto, and Professor, Department of Biochemistry, University of Toronto

Peter J. Kennelly, PhD
Professor of Biochemistry, Virginia Polytechnic Institute and State University, Blacksburg, Virginia

Peter A. Mayes, PhD, DSc
Emeritus Professor of Veterinary Biochemistry, Royal Veterinary College, University of London

Robert K. Murray, MD, PhD
Professor (Emeritus) of Biochemistry, University of Toronto

Margaret L. Rand, PhD
Scientist, Research Institute, Hospital for Sick Children, Toronto, and Associate Professor, Departments of Laboratory Medicine and Pathobiology and Department of Biochemistry, University of Toronto

Victor W. Rodwell, PhD
Professor of Biochemistry, Purdue University, West Lafayette, Indiana

P. Anthony Weil, PhD
Professor of Molecular Physiology and Biophysics, Vanderbilt University School of Medicine, Nashville, Tennessee

Contents

Preface ix

1. Biochemistry & Medicine
Robert K. Murray, MD, PhD 1

2. Water & pH
Peter J. Kennelly, PhD, & Victor W. Rodwell, PhD 5

SECTION I. STRUCTURES & FUNCTIONS OF PROTEINS & ENZYMES 14

3. Amino Acids & Peptides
Peter J. Kennelly, PhD, & Victor W. Rodwell, PhD 14

4. Proteins: Determination of Primary Structure
Peter J. Kennelly, PhD, & Victor W. Rodwell, PhD 21

5. Proteins: Higher Orders of Structure
Peter J. Kennelly, PhD, & Victor W. Rodwell, PhD 30

6. Proteins: Myoglobin & Hemoglobin
Peter J. Kennelly, PhD, & Victor W. Rodwell, PhD 41

7. Enzymes: Mechanism of Action
Peter J. Kennelly, PhD, & Victor W. Rodwell, PhD 49

8. Enzymes: Kinetics
Peter J. Kennelly, PhD, & Victor W. Rodwell, PhD 61

9. Enzymes: Regulation of Activities
Peter J. Kennelly, PhD, & Victor W. Rodwell, PhD 73

10. Bioinformatics & Computational Biology
Peter J. Kennelly, PhD, & Victor W. Rodwell, PhD 82

SECTION II. BIOENERGETICS & THE METABOLISM OF CARBOHYDRATES & LIPIDS 88

11. Bioenergetics: The Role of ATP
Kathleen M. Botham, PhD, DSc, & Peter A. Mayes, PhD, DSc 88

12. Biologic Oxidation
Kathleen M. Botham, PhD, DSc, & Peter A. Mayes, PhD, DSc 94

13. The Respiratory Chain & Oxidative Phosphorylation
Kathleen M. Botham, PhD, DSc, & Peter A. Mayes, PhD, DSc 100

14. Carbohydrates of Physiologic Significance
David A. Bender, PhD, & Peter A. Mayes, PhD, DSc 112

15. Lipids of Physiologic Significance
Kathleen M. Botham, PhD, DSc, & Peter A. Mayes, PhD, DSc 121

16. Overview of Metabolism & the Provision of Metabolic Fuels
David A. Bender, PhD, & Peter A. Mayes, PhD, DSc 132

17. The Citric Acid Cycle: The Catabolism of Acetyl-CoA
David A. Bender, PhD, & Peter A. Mayes, PhD, DSc 145

18. Glycolysis & the Oxidation of Pyruvate
David A. Bender, PhD, & Peter A. Mayes, PhD, DSc 151

19. Metabolism of Glycogen
David A. Bender, PhD, & Peter A. Mayes, PhD, DSc 159

20. Gluconeogenesis & the Control of Blood Glucose
David A. Bender, PhD, & Peter A. Mayes, PhD, DSc 167

21. The Pentose Phosphate Pathway & Other Pathways of Hexose Metabolism
David A. Bender, PhD, & Peter A. Mayes, PhD, DSc 177

22. Oxidation of Fatty Acids: Ketogenesis
Kathleen M. Botham, PhD, DSc, & Peter A. Mayes, PhD, DSc 187

23. Biosynthesis of Fatty Acids & Eicosanoids
Kathleen M. Botham, PhD, DSc, & Peter A. Mayes, PhD, DSc 196

24. Metabolism of Acylglycerols & Sphingolipids
Kathleen M. Botham, PhD, DSc, & Peter A. Mayes, PhD, DSc 209

25. Lipid Transport & Storage
Kathleen M. Botham, PhD, DSc, & Peter A. Mayes, PhD, DSc 217

26. Cholesterol Synthesis, Transport, & Excretion
Kathleen M. Botham, PhD, DSc, & Peter A. Mayes, PhD, DSc 230

SECTION III. METABOLISM OF PROTEINS & AMINO ACIDS 241

27. Biosynthesis of the Nutritionally Nonessential Amino Acids
Victor W. Rodwell, PhD 241

28. Catabolism of Proteins & of Amino Acid Nitrogen
Victor W. Rodwell, PhD 246

29. Catabolism of the Carbon Skeletons of Amino Acids
Victor W. Rodwell, PhD. 254

30. Conversion of Amino Acids to Specialized Products
Victor W. Rodwell, PhD. 270

31. Porphyrins & Bile Pigments
Robert K. Murray, MD, PhD. 279

**SECTION IV. STRUCTURE, FUNCTION, & REPLICATION
OF INFORMATIONAL MACROMOLECULES** 294

32. Nucleotides
Victor W. Rodwell, PhD. 294

33. Metabolism of Purine & Pyrimidine Nucleotides
Victor W. Rodwell, PhD. 301

34. Nucleic Acid Structure & Function
P. Anthony Weil, PhD, & Daryl K. Granner, MD. 311

35. DNA Organization, Replication, & Repair
P. Anthony Weil, PhD, & Daryl K. Granner, MD. 322

36. RNA Synthesis, Processing, & Modification
P. Anthony Weil, PhD, & Daryl K. Granner, MD. 348

37. Protein Synthesis & the Genetic Code
Daryl K. Granner, MD, & P. Anthony Weil, PhD. 365

38. Regulation of Gene Expression
Daryl K. Granner, MD, & P. Anthony Weil, PhD. 380

39. Molecular Genetics, Recombinant DNA, & Genomic Technology
Daryl K. Granner, MD, & P. Anthony Weil, PhD. 402

**SECTION V. BIOCHEMISTRY OF EXTRACELLULAR
& INTRACELLULAR COMMUNICATION** 422

40. Membranes: Structure & Function
Robert K. Murray, MD, PhD, & Daryl K. Granner, MD 422

41. The Diversity of the Endocrine System
Daryl K. Granner, MD 442

42. Hormone Action & Signal Transduction
Daryl K. Granner, MD 464

SECTION VI. SPECIAL TOPICS 482

43. Nutrition, Digestion, & Absorption
David A. Bender, PhD, & Peter A. Mayes, PhD, DSc 482

44. Micronutrients: Vitamins & Minerals
David A. Bender, PhD, & Peter A. Mayes, PhD, DSc 489

45. Intracellular Traffic & Sorting of Proteins
Robert K. Murray, MD, PhD 506

46. Glycoproteins
Robert K. Murray, MD, PhD 523

47. The Extracellular Matrix
Robert K. Murray, MD, PhD, & Frederick W. Keeley, PhD. 545

48. Muscle & the Cytoskeleton
Robert K. Murray, MD, PhD 565

49. Plasma Proteins & Immunoglobulins
Robert K. Murray, MD, PhD 588

50. Hemostasis & Thrombosis
Margaret L. Rand, PhD, & Robert K. Murray, MD, PhD 606

51. Red & White Blood Cells
Robert K. Murray, MD, PhD 617

52. Metabolism of Xenobiotics
Robert K. Murray, MD, PhD 633

Appendix—Access to the Biomedical Literature 641

Index 643

Preface

The authors and publisher are pleased to present the twenty-seventh edition of *Harper's Illustrated Biochemistry*. First published as *Review of Physiological Chemistry* in 1939 and revised in 1944, it quickly gained a wide readership. In 1951, the third edition appeared with Harold A. Harper, University of California at San Francisco, as author. Dr. Harper remained the sole author until the ninth edition and co-authored eight subsequent editions. Peter Mayes and Victor Rodwell joined as authors in the tenth edition, Daryl Granner in the twentieth, and Rob Murray in the twenty-first edition. We now bid a fond and grateful farewell to our long-time colleague Peter Mayes, who retired from active authorship after the previous edition. Asked by Harold Harper to review portions of the ninth edition, Peter joined as an author for the tenth through twenty-sixth editions. Peter contributed a unique ability to design diagrams that integrate all key aspects of a metabolic pathway: the enzymes, intermediates, and the mechanisms that guide and regulate metabolic flow. Such skills, his concise and informative prose, and his collegial relationships with the other authors contributed significantly to the continued success of this text. He will be greatly missed by his fellow authors and by readers.

The ever-increasing complexity of biochemical knowledge has led to the addition of several co-authors in recent editions. Peter Mayes' responsibilities now pass to his former collaborators, David Bender and Kathleen Botham, continuing the long-standing trans-Atlantic ties in the authorship of this text. P. Anthony Weil, a co-author with Daryl Granner in the previous edition, continues his invaluable input. Additional co-authors for this and prior editions include Fred Keeley and Margaret Rand with Rob Murray and Peter Kennelly with Victor Rodwell. The senior authors are grateful to their new colleagues for bringing their expertise and fresh perspectives to the text.

CHANGES IN THE TWENTY-SEVENTH EDITION

A major goal continues to be to provide to students of medicine and the health sciences a text that describes and illustrates the basics of biochemistry in a concise, user-friendly, and interesting manner. Significant advances in biochemistry that are of importance in medicine continue to be emphasized. The twenty-sixth edition incorporated drastic revisions, motivated by the fact that many students expressed a desire for a shorter text. Important new features of the twenty-seventh edition include:

- All chapters have been revised, with the inclusion of many new figures and references.
- The origins of the term pH are clearly described.
- The completely new chapter on bioinformatics and computational biology, which emphasizes their impact on present and future medical practice provides valuable insight into these fast growing fields.
- Modern methods of drug discovery that build on advances in genomics and proteomics are emphasized.
- Introduction of the concept of the protein life cycle provides a unified framework for understanding the interrelated processes of the maturation, post-translational modification, regulation, and degradation of proteins.
- The role of mass spectrometry in identification of proteins and small molecules that facilitate the diagnosis of metabolic diseases is emphasized.
- Descriptions of the cell cycle and of the ubiquitin-proteasome pathway of protein degradation have been included.
- The chapter on the respiratory chain and oxidative phosphorylation has been extensively revised.
- Text relating to metabolic disorders of the urea cycle has been revised and updated, and the biosynthesis and metabolic roles of selenocysteine, the twenty-first amino acid, have been introduced.
- New material has been included on lipid rafts, ion channels and voltage-gated channels, glucose transport, and gap junctions.
- With regard to intracellular traffic and sorting of proteins, information on the unfolded protein response and ER-associated degradation has been added.
- The involvement of glycoproteins in many diseases, including peptic ulcer, certain congenital muscular dystrophies, and cystic fibrosis, has been discussed.
- The many newly discovered proteins involved in iron metabolism and hemochromatosis are described.
- Information on hemostasis, thrombosis, and platelet action has been updated.

ORGANIZATION OF THE BOOK

Following two introductory chapters ("Biochemistry & Medicine" and "Water & pH"), the text is divided into six main sections.

 Section I deals with the structures and functions of proteins and enzymes, the workhorses of organisms. Because almost all of the reactions in cells are catalyzed by enzymes, it is vital to understand the properties of enzymes before considering other topics. Section I also contains a new chapter on bioinformatics and computational biology, reflecting the increasing importance of these topics in modern biochemistry, biology, and medicine.

 Section II explains how various cellular reactions either utilize or release energy, and traces the pathways by which carbohydrates and lipids are synthesized and degraded. Also described are the many functions of these two classes of molecules.

 Section III deals with the amino acids, their many metabolic fates, certain key features of protein catabolism, and the biochemistry of the porphyrins and bile pigments.

 Section IV describes the structures and functions of the nucleotides and nucleic acids, and includes topics such as DNA replication and repair, RNA synthesis and modification, protein synthesis, the principles of recombinant DNA and genomic technology, and new understanding of how gene expression is regulated.

 Section V deals with aspects of extracellular and intracellular communication. Topics include membrane structure and function, the molecular bases of the actions of hormones, and the key field of signal transduction.

 Section VI discusses ten special topics: nutrition, digestion, and absorption; vitamins and minerals; intracellular trafficking and sorting of proteins; glycoproteins; the extracellular matrix; muscle and the cytoskeleton; plasma proteins and immunoglobulins; hemostasis and thrombosis; red and white blood cells; and the metabolism of xenobiotics.

 The **Appendix** contains a list of useful web sites and a list of biochemical journals or journals that contain considerable biochemical content. All of the Sections contain numerous illustrations of the medical relevance of biochemistry.

ACKNOWLEDGMENTS

The authors thank Jason Malley for his roles in the planning and actualization of this edition. It has been a pleasure to work with him. We are grateful to Karen Davis for her highly professional and courteous supervising of the editing, her superb skills, and those of her editorial colleagues that ensured that work on this edition proceeded smoothly. We thank Karen Edmonson, Susan Kelly, and Selina Connor for their various contributions to this text. We acknowledge the work of the artists, typesetters, and other individuals not known to us who participated in the production of the twenty-seventh edition of *Harper's Illustrated Biochemistry*. Suggestions from students and colleagues around the world have been most helpful in the formulation of this edition. We look forward to receiving similar input in the future.

Robert K. Murray, Toronto, Ontario, Canada
Daryl K. Granner, Nashville, Tennessee
Victor W. Rodwell, West Lafayette, Indiana

Biochemistry & Medicine

Robert K. Murray, MD, PhD

INTRODUCTION

Biochemistry can be defined as *the science concerned with the chemical basis of life* (Gk *bios* "life"). The **cell** is the structural unit of living systems. Thus, biochemistry can also be described as *the science concerned with the chemical constituents of living cells and with the reactions and processes they undergo.* By this definition, biochemistry encompasses large areas of **cell biology,** of **molecular biology,** and of **molecular genetics.**

The Aim of Biochemistry Is to Describe & Explain, in Molecular Terms, All Chemical Processes of Living Cells

The major objective of biochemistry is the complete understanding, at the molecular level, of all of the chemical processes associated with living cells. To achieve this objective, biochemists have sought to isolate the numerous molecules found in cells, determine their structures, and analyze how they function. Many techniques have been used for these purposes; some of them are summarized in Table 1–1.

A Knowledge of Biochemistry Is Essential to All Life Sciences

The biochemistry of the nucleic acids lies at the heart of **genetics;** in turn, the use of genetic approaches has been critical for elucidating many areas of biochemistry. **Physiology,** the study of body function, overlaps with biochemistry almost completely. **Immunology** employs numerous biochemical techniques, and many immunologic approaches have found wide use by biochemists. **Pharmacology** and **pharmacy** rest on a sound knowledge of biochemistry and physiology; in particular, most drugs are metabolized by enzyme-catalyzed reactions. Poisons act on biochemical reactions or processes; this is the subject matter of **toxicology.** Biochemical approaches are being used increasingly to study basic aspects of **pathology** (the study of disease), such as inflammation, cell injury, and cancer. Many workers in **microbiology, zoology,** and **botany** employ biochemical approaches almost exclusively. These relationships are not surprising, because life as we know it depends on biochemical reactions and processes. In fact, the old barriers among the life sciences are breaking down, and biochemistry is increasingly becoming their common language.

A Reciprocal Relationship Between Biochemistry & Medicine Has Stimulated Mutual Advances

The two major concerns for workers in the health sciences—and particularly physicians—are the understanding and maintenance of **health** and the understanding and effective treatment of **diseases.** Biochemistry impacts enormously on both of these fundamental concerns of medicine. In fact, the interrelationship of biochemistry and medicine is a wide, two-way street. Biochemical studies have illuminated many aspects of health and disease, and conversely, the study of various aspects of health and disease has opened up new areas of biochemistry. Some examples of this two-way street are shown in Figure 1–1. For instance, a knowledge of protein structure and function was necessary to elucidate the single biochemical difference between normal hemoglobin and sickle cell hemoglobin. On the other hand, analysis of sickle cell hemoglobin has contributed significantly to our understanding of the structure and function of both normal hemoglobin and other proteins. Analogous examples of reciprocal benefit between biochemistry and medicine could be cited for the other paired items shown in Figure 1–1. Another example is the pioneering work of Archibald Garrod, a physician in England during the early 1900s. He studied patients with a number of relatively rare disorders (alkaptonuria, albinism, cystinuria, and pentosuria; these are described in later chapters) and established that these conditions were genetically determined. Garrod designated these conditions as **inborn errors of metabolism.** His insights provided a major foundation for the development of the field of human biochemical genetics. More recent efforts to understand the basis of the genetic disease known as **familial hypercholesterolemia,** which results in severe atherosclerosis at an early age, have led to dramatic progress in understanding of cell receptors and of mechanisms of uptake of cholesterol into cells. Studies of **oncogenes** in cancer cells have directed

Table 1-1. The principal methods and preparations used in biochemical laboratories.

Methods for Separating and Purifying Biomolecules[1]
　Salt fractionation (eg, precipitation of proteins with ammonium sulfate)
　Chromatography: Paper; ion exchange; affinity; thin-layer; gas–liquid; high-pressure liquid; gel filtration
　Electrophoresis: Paper; high-voltage; agarose; cellulose acetate; starch gel; polyacrylamide gel; SDS-polyacrylamide gel
　Ultracentrifugation

Methods for Determining Biomolecular Structures
　Elemental analysis
　UV, visible, infrared, and NMR spectroscopy
　Use of acid or alkaline hydrolysis to degrade the biomolecule under study into its basic constituents
　Use of a battery of enzymes of known specificity to degrade the biomolecule under study (eg, proteases, nucleases, glycosidases)
　Mass spectrometry
　Specific sequencing methods (eg, for proteins and nucleic acids)
　X-ray crystallography

Preparations for Studying Biochemical Processes
　Whole animal (includes transgenic animals and animals with gene knockouts)
　Isolated perfused organ
　Tissue slice
　Whole cells
　Homogenate
　Isolated cell organelles
　Subfractionation of organelles
　Purified metabolites and enzymes
　Isolated genes (including polymerase chain reaction and site-directed mutagenesis)

---

[1]Most of these methods are suitable for analyzing the components present in cell homogenates and other biochemical preparations. The sequential use of several techniques will generally permit purification of most biomolecules. The reader is referred to texts on methods of biochemical research for details.

attention to the molecular mechanisms involved in the control of normal cell growth. These and many other examples emphasize how the study of disease can open up areas of cell function for basic biochemical research.

　The relationship between medicine and biochemistry has important implications for the former. As long as medical treatment is firmly grounded in a knowledge of biochemistry and other basic sciences, the practice of medicine will have a rational basis that can be adapted to accommodate new knowledge. This contrasts with unorthodox health cults and at least some "alternative medicine" practices that are often founded on little more than myth and wishful thinking and generally lack any intellectual basis.

NORMAL BIOCHEMICAL PROCESSES ARE THE BASIS OF HEALTH

The World Health Organization (WHO) defines health as a state of "complete physical, mental and social well-being and not merely the absence of disease and infirmity." From a strictly biochemical viewpoint, health may be considered that situation in which all of the many thousands of intra- and extracellular reactions that occur in the body are proceeding at rates commensurate with the organism's maximal survival in the physiologic state. However, this is an extremely reductionist view, and it should be apparent that caring for the health of patients requires not only a wide knowledge of biologic principles but also of psychologic and social principles.

Biochemical Research Has Impact on Nutrition & Preventive Medicine

One major prerequisite for the maintenance of health is that there be optimal dietary intake of a number of chemicals; the chief of these are **vitamins,** certain **amino acids,** certain **fatty acids,** various **minerals,** and **water.** Because much of the subject matter of both biochemistry and nutrition is concerned with the study of various aspects of these chemicals, there is a close relationship between these two sciences. Moreover, more emphasis is being placed on systematic attempts to maintain health and forestall disease, ie, on **preventive medicine.** Thus, nutritional approaches to—for example—the prevention of atherosclerosis and cancer are receiving increased emphasis. Understanding nutrition depends to a great extent on a knowledge of biochemistry.

Most & Perhaps All Disease Has a Biochemical Basis

We believe that most if not all diseases are manifestations of abnormalities of molecules, chemical reactions, or biochemical processes. The major factors responsible for causing diseases in animals and humans are listed in Table 1–2. All of them affect one or more critical chemical reactions or molecules in the body. Numerous examples of the biochemical bases of diseases will be encountered in this text. In most of these conditions, biochemical studies contribute to both the diagnosis and treatment. Some major uses of biochemical investigations and of laboratory tests in relation to diseases are summarized in Table 1–3.

　Additional examples of many of these uses are presented in various sections of this text.

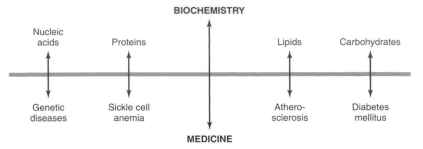

Figure 1–1. Examples of the two-way street connecting biochemistry and medicine. Knowlege of the biochemical molecules shown in the top part of the diagram has clarified our understanding of the diseases shown on the bottom half—and conversely, analyses of the diseases shown below have cast light on many areas of biochemistry. Note that sickle cell anemia is a genetic disease and that both atherosclerosis and diabetes mellitus have genetic components.

Impact of the Human Genome Project (HGP) on Biochemistry & Medicine

Remarkable progress was made in the late 1990s in sequencing the human genome. This culminated in July 2000, when leaders of the two groups involved in this effort (the International Human Genome Sequencing Consortium and Celera Genomics, a private company) announced that over 90% of the genome had been sequenced. Draft versions of the sequence were published in early 2001. With the exception of a few gaps, the sequence of the entire human genome was completed in 2003, 50 years after the description of the double-helical nature of DNA by Watson and Crick.

The implications of this work for biochemistry, all of biology, and for medicine are tremendous, and only a few points are mentioned here. Many previously unknown genes have been revealed; their protein products await characterization. New light has been thrown

Table 1–2. The major causes of diseases. All of the causes listed act by influencing the various biochemical mechanisms in the cell or in the body.[1]

1. Physical agents: Mechanical trauma, extremes of temperature, sudden changes in atmospheric pressure, radiation, electric shock.
2. Chemical agents, including drugs: Certain toxic compounds, therapeutic drugs, etc.
3. Biologic agents: Viruses, bacteria, fungi, higher forms of parasites.
4. Oxygen lack: Loss of blood supply, depletion of the oxygen-carrying capacity of the blood, poisoning of the oxidative enzymes.
5. Genetic disorders: Congenital, molecular.
6. Immunologic reactions: Anaphylaxis, autoimmune disease.
7. Nutritional imbalances: Deficiencies, excesses.
8. Endocrine imbalances: Hormonal deficiencies, excesses.

[1]Adapted, with permission, from Robbins SL, Cotram RS, Kumar V: *The Pathologic Basis of Disease,* 3rd ed. Saunders, 1984. Copyright © 1984 Elsevier Inc. Reprinted with permission from Elsevier.

Table 1–3. Some uses of biochemical investigations and laboratory tests in relation to diseases.

Use	Example
1. To reveal the fundamental causes and mechanisms of diseases	Demonstration of the nature of the genetic defects in cystic fibrosis.
2. To suggest rational treatments of diseases based on (1) above	A diet low in phenylalanine for treatment of phenylketonuria.
3. To assist in the diagnosis of specific diseases	Use of the plasma enzyme creatine kinase MB (CK-MB) in the diagnosis of myocardial infarction.
4. To act as screening tests for the early diagnosis of certain diseases	Use of measurement of blood thyroxine or thyroid-stimulating hormone (TSH) in the neonatal diagnosis of congenital hypothyroidism.
5. To assist in monitoring the progress (ie, recovery, worsening, remission, or relapse) of certain diseases	Use of the plasma enzyme alanine aminotransferase (ALT) in monitoring the progress of infectious hepatitis.
6. To assist in assessing the response of diseases to therapy	Use of measurement of blood carcinoembryonic antigen (CEA) in certain patients who have been treated for cancer of the colon.

on human evolution, and procedures for tracking disease genes have been greatly refined. The results are having major effects on areas such as proteomics, bioinformatics, biotechnology, and pharmacogenomics. Reference to the human genome will be made in various sections of this text.

SUMMARY

- Biochemistry is the science concerned with studying the various molecules that occur in living cells and organisms and with their chemical reactions. Because life depends on biochemical reactions, biochemistry has become the basic language of all biologic sciences.
- Biochemistry is concerned with the entire spectrum of life forms, from relatively simple viruses and bacteria to complex human beings.
- Biochemistry and medicine are intimately related. Health depends on a harmonious balance of biochemical reactions occurring in the body, and disease reflects abnormalities in biomolecules, biochemical reactions, or biochemical processes.
- Advances in biochemical knowledge have illuminated many areas of medicine. Conversely, the study of diseases has often revealed previously unsuspected aspects of biochemistry. The determination of the sequence of the human genome, nearly complete, will have a great impact on all areas of biology, including biochemistry, bioinformatics, and biotechnology.
- Biochemical approaches are often fundamental in illuminating the causes of diseases and in designing appropriate therapies.
- The judicious use of various biochemical laboratory tests is an integral component of diagnosis and monitoring of treatment.
- A sound knowledge of biochemistry and of other related basic disciplines is essential for the rational practice of medical and related health sciences.

- Results of the Human Genome Project will have a profound influence on the future of medicine and other health sciences.

REFERENCES

Burtis CA, Ashwood ER: *Tietz Fundamentals of Clinical Chemistry,* 5th ed. Saunders, 2001.

Encyclopedia of Life Sciences. John Wiley, 2001. (Contains some 3,000 comprehensive articles on various aspects of the life sciences. Accessible online at www.els.net via libraries with a subscription.)

Fruton JS: *Proteins, Enzymes, Genes: The Interplay of Chemistry and Biology.* Yale Univ Press, 1999. (Provides the historical background for much of today's biochemical research.)

Garrod AE: Inborn errors of metabolism. (Croonian Lectures.) Lancet 1908;2:1, 73, 142, 214.

Guttmacher AE, Collins FS: Genomic medicine—A Primer. N Engl J Med 2002;347:1512. (This article was the first of a series of eleven monthly articles published in the *New England Journal of Medicine* describing various aspects of genomic medicine.)

Kornberg A: Basic research: The lifeline of medicine. FASEB J 1992;6:3143.

Kornberg A: Centenary of the birth of modern biochemistry. FASEB J 1997;11:1209.

McKusick VA: *Mendelian Inheritance in Man. Catalogs of Human Genes and Genetic Disorders*, 12th ed. Johns Hopkins Univ Press, 1998. [Abbreviated MIM]

Online Mendelian Inheritance in Man (OMIM): Center for Medical Genetics, Johns Hopkins University and National Center for Biotechnology Information, National Library of Medicine, 1997. http://www.ncbi.nlm.nih.gov/omim/

(The numbers assigned to the entries in MIM and OMIM will be cited in selected chapters of this work. Consulting this extensive collection of diseases and other relevant entries—specific proteins, enzymes, etc—will greatly expand the reader's knowledge and understanding of various topics referred to and discussed in this text. The online version is updated almost daily.)

Scriver CR et al (editors): *The Metabolic and Molecular Bases of Inherited Disease,* 8th ed. McGraw-Hill, 2001.

Water & pH

Peter J. Kennelly, PhD, & Victor W. Rodwell, PhD

BIOMEDICAL IMPORTANCE

Water is the predominant chemical component of living organisms. Its unique physical properties, which include the ability to solvate a wide range of organic and inorganic molecules, derive from water's dipolar structure and exceptional capacity for forming hydrogen bonds. The manner in which water interacts with a solvated biomolecule influences the structure of each. An excellent nucleophile, water is a reactant or product in many metabolic reactions. Water has a slight propensity to dissociate into hydroxide ions and protons. The acidity of aqueous solutions is generally reported using the logarithmic pH scale. Bicarbonate and other buffers normally maintain the pH of extracellular fluid between 7.35 and 7.45. Suspected disturbances of acid-base balance are verified by measuring the pH of arterial blood and the CO_2 content of venous blood. Causes of acidosis (blood pH < 7.35) include diabetic ketosis and lactic acidosis. Alkalosis (pH > 7.45) may, for example, follow vomiting of acidic gastric contents. Regulation of water balance depends upon hypothalamic mechanisms that control thirst, on antidiuretic hormone (ADH), on retention or excretion of water by the kidneys, and on evaporative loss. Nephrogenic diabetes insipidus, which involves the inability to concentrate urine or adjust to subtle changes in extracellular fluid osmolarity, results from the unresponsiveness of renal tubular osmoreceptors to ADH.

WATER IS AN IDEAL BIOLOGIC SOLVENT

Water Molecules Form Dipoles

A water molecule is an irregular, slightly skewed tetrahedron with oxygen at its center (Figure 2–1). The two hydrogens and the unshared electrons of the remaining two sp^3-hybridized orbitals occupy the corners of the tetrahedron. The 105-degree angle between the hydrogens differs slightly from the ideal tetrahedral angle, 109.5 degrees. Ammonia is also tetrahedral, with a 107-degree angle between its hydrogens. Water is a **dipole,** a molecule with electrical charge distributed asymmetrically about its structure. The strongly electronegative oxygen atom pulls electrons away from the hydrogen nuclei, leaving them with a partial positive charge, while its two unshared electron pairs constitute a region of local negative charge.

Water, a strong dipole, has a high **dielectric constant.** As described quantitatively by Coulomb's law, the strength of interaction F between oppositely charged particles is inversely proportionate to the dielectric constant ε of the surrounding medium. The dielectric constant for a vacuum is unity; for hexane it is 1.9; for ethanol it is 24.3; and for water it is 78.5. Water therefore greatly decreases the force of attraction between charged and polar species relative to water-free environments with lower dielectric constants. Its strong dipole and high dielectric constant enable water to dissolve large quantities of charged compounds such as salts.

Water Molecules Form Hydrogen Bonds

An unshielded hydrogen nucleus covalently bound to an electron-withdrawing oxygen or nitrogen atom can interact with an unshared electron pair on another oxygen or nitrogen atom to form a **hydrogen bond.** Since water molecules contain both of these features, hydrogen bonding favors the self-association of water molecules into ordered arrays (Figure 2–2). Hydrogen bonding profoundly influences the physical properties of water and accounts for its exceptionally high viscosity, surface tension, and boiling point. On average, each molecule in liquid water associates through hydrogen bonds with 3.5 others. These bonds are both relatively weak and transient, with a half-life of about one microsecond. Rupture of a hydrogen bond in liquid water requires only about 4.5 kcal/mol, less than 5% of the energy required to rupture a covalent O—H bond.

Hydrogen bonding enables water to dissolve many organic biomolecules that contain functional groups which can participate in hydrogen bonding. The oxygen atoms of aldehydes, ketones, and amides provide pairs of electrons that can serve as hydrogen acceptors. Alcohols and amines can serve both as hydrogen acceptors and as donors of unshielded hydrogen atoms for formation of hydrogen bonds (Figure 2–3).

5

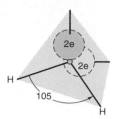

Figure 2–1. The water molecule has tetrahedral geometry.

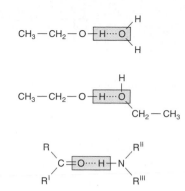

Figure 2–3. Additional polar groups participate in hydrogen bonding. Shown are hydrogen bonds formed between an alcohol and water, between two molecules of ethanol, and between the peptide carbonyl oxygen and the peptide nitrogen hydrogen of an adjacent amino acid.

INTERACTION WITH WATER INFLUENCES THE STRUCTURE OF BIOMOLECULES

Covalent & Noncovalent Bonds Stabilize Biologic Molecules

The covalent bond is the strongest force that holds molecules together (Table 2–1). Noncovalent forces, while of lesser magnitude, make significant contributions to the structure, stability, and functional competence of macromolecules in living cells. These forces, which can be either attractive or repulsive, involve interactions both within the biomolecule and between it and the water that forms the principal component of the surrounding environment.

Biomolecules Fold to Position Polar & Charged Groups on Their Surfaces

Most biomolecules are **amphipathic;** that is, they possess regions rich in charged or polar functional groups as well as regions with hydrophobic character. Proteins tend to fold with the R-groups of amino acids with hydrophobic side chains in the interior. Amino acids with charged or polar amino acid side chains (eg, arginine, glutamate, serine) generally are present on the surface in contact with water. A similar pattern prevails in a phospholipid bilayer, where the charged head groups

of phosphatidyl serine or phosphatidyl ethanolamine contact water while their hydrophobic fatty acyl side chains cluster together, excluding water. This pattern maximizes the opportunities for the formation of energetically favorable charge–dipole, dipole–dipole, and hydrogen bonding interactions between polar groups on the biomolecule and water. It also minimizes energetically unfavorable contact between water and hydrophobic groups.

Hydrophobic Interactions

Hydrophobic interaction refers to the tendency of nonpolar compounds to self-associate in an aqueous environment. This self-association is driven neither by mutual attraction nor by what are sometimes incorrectly referred to as "hydrophobic bonds." Self-association arises from the need to minimize energetically unfavorable interactions between nonpolar groups and water.

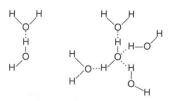

Figure 2–2. Left: Association of two dipolar water molecules by a hydrogen bond (dotted line). **Right:** Hydrogen-bonded cluster of four water molecules. Note that water can serve simultaneously both as a hydrogen donor and as a hydrogen acceptor.

Table 2–1. Bond energies for atoms of biologic significance.

Bond Type	Energy (kcal/mol)	Bond Type	Energy (kcal/mol)
O—O	34	O=O	96
S—S	51	C—H	99
C—N	70	C=S	108
S—H	81	O—H	110
C—C	82	C=C	147
C—O	84	C=N	147
N—H	94	C=O	164

While the hydrogens of nonpolar groups such as the methylene groups of hydrocarbons do not form hydrogen bonds, they do affect the structure of the water that surrounds them. Water molecules adjacent to a hydrophobic group are restricted in the number of orientations (degrees of freedom) that permit them to participate in the maximum number of energetically favorable hydrogen bonds. Maximal formation of multiple hydrogen bonds can be maintained only by increasing the order of the adjacent water molecules, with an accompanying decrease in entropy.

It follows from the second law of thermodynamics that the optimal free energy of a hydrocarbon–water mixture is a function of both maximal enthalpy (from hydrogen bonding) and minimum entropy (maximum degrees of freedom). Thus, nonpolar molecules tend to form droplets with minimal exposed surface area, reducing the number of water molecules affected. For the same reason, in the aqueous environment of the living cell the hydrophobic portions of biopolymers tend to be buried inside the structure of the molecule, or within a lipid bilayer, minimizing contact with water.

Electrostatic Interactions

Interactions between charged groups help shape biomolecular structure. Electrostatic interactions between oppositely charged groups within or between biomolecules are termed **salt bridges.** Salt bridges are comparable in strength to hydrogen bonds but act over larger distances. They thus often facilitate the binding of charged molecules and ions to proteins and nucleic acids.

Van der Waals Forces

Van der Waals forces arise from attractions between transient dipoles generated by the rapid movement of electrons on all neutral atoms. Significantly weaker than hydrogen bonds but potentially extremely numerous, van der Waals forces decrease as the sixth power of the distance separating atoms. Thus, they act over very short distances, typically 2–4 Å.

Multiple Forces Stabilize Biomolecules

The DNA double helix illustrates the contribution of multiple forces to the structure of biomolecules. While each individual DNA strand is held together by covalent bonds, the two strands of the helix are held together exclusively by noncovalent interactions. These noncovalent interactions include hydrogen bonds between nucleotide bases (Watson–Crick base pairing) and van der Waals interactions between the stacked purine and pyrimidine bases. The helix presents the charged phosphate groups and polar ribose sugars of the backbone to water while burying the relatively hydrophobic nucleotide bases inside. The extended backbone maximizes the distance between negatively charged backbone phosphates, minimizing unfavorable electrostatic interactions.

WATER IS AN EXCELLENT NUCLEOPHILE

Metabolic reactions often involve the attack by lone pairs of electrons on electron-rich molecules termed **nucleophiles** on electron-poor atoms called **electrophiles.** Nucleophiles and electrophiles do not necessarily possess a formal negative or positive charge. Water, whose two lone pairs of sp^3 electrons bear a partial negative charge, is an excellent nucleophile. Other nucleophiles of biologic importance include the oxygen atoms of phosphates, alcohols, and carboxylic acids; the sulfur of thiols; the nitrogen of amines; and the imidazole ring of histidine. Common electrophiles include the carbonyl carbons in amides, esters, aldehydes, and ketones and the phosphorus atoms of phosphoesters.

Nucleophilic attack by water generally results in the cleavage of the amide, glycoside, or ester bonds that hold biopolymers together. This process is termed **hydrolysis.** Conversely, when monomer units are joined together to form biopolymers such as proteins or glycogen, water is a product, as shown below for the formation of a peptide bond between two amino acids.

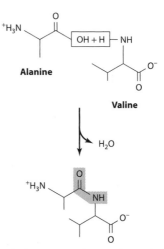

While hydrolysis is a thermodynamically favored reaction, the amide and phosphoester bonds of polypeptides and oligonucleotides are stable in the aqueous environment of the cell. This seemingly paradoxic behavior reflects the fact that the thermodynamics governing the equilibrium of a reaction do not determine the rate at which it will proceed. In the cell, protein catalysts called **enzymes** accelerate the rate of hydrolytic reactions when needed. **Proteases** catalyze the hydrolysis of proteins into their component amino

acids, while **nucleases** catalyze the hydrolysis of the phosphoester bonds in DNA and RNA. Careful control of the activities of these enzymes is required to ensure that they act only on appropriate target molecules at appropriate times.

Many Metabolic Reactions Involve Group Transfer

In group transfer reactions, a group G is transferred from a donor D to an acceptor A, forming an acceptor group complex A–G:

$$D-G + A \rightleftarrows A-G + D$$

The hydrolysis and phosphorolysis of glycogen represent group transfer reactions in which glucosyl groups are transferred to water or to orthophosphate. The equilibrium constant for the hydrolysis of covalent bonds strongly favors the formation of split products. The biosynthesis of macromolecules also involves group transfer reactions in which the thermodynamically unfavored formation of covalent bonds is coupled to favored reactions so that the overall change in free energy favors biopolymer synthesis. Given the nucleophilic character of water and its high concentration in cells, why are biopolymers such as proteins and DNA relatively stable? And how can synthesis of biopolymers occur in an aqueous environment? Central to both questions are the properties of enzymes. In the absence of enzymic catalysis, even thermodynamically highly favored reactions do not necessarily take place rapidly. Precise and differential control of enzyme activity and the sequestration of enzymes in specific organelles determine under what physiologic conditions a given biopolymer will be synthesized or degraded. Newly synthesized polymers are not immediately hydrolyzed, in part because the active sites of biosynthetic enzymes sequester substrates in an environment from which water can be excluded.

Water Molecules Exhibit a Slight But Important Tendency to Dissociate

The ability of water to ionize, while slight, is of central importance for life. Since water can act both as an acid and as a base, its ionization may be represented as an intermolecular proton transfer that forms a hydronium ion (H_3O^+) and a hydroxide ion (OH^-):

$$H_2O + H_2O \rightleftarrows H_3O^+ + OH^-$$

The transferred proton is actually associated with a cluster of water molecules. Protons exist in solution not only as H_3O^+, but also as multimers such as $H_5O_2^+$ and $H_7O_3^+$. The proton is nevertheless routinely represented as H^+, even though it is in fact highly hydrated.

Since hydronium and hydroxide ions continuously recombine to form water molecules, an *individual* hydrogen or oxygen cannot be stated to be present as an ion or as part of a water molecule. At one instant it is an ion; an instant later it is part of a molecule. Individual ions or molecules are therefore not considered. We refer instead to the *probability* that at any instant in time a hydrogen will be present as an ion or as part of a water molecule. Since 1 g of water contains 3.46×10^{22} molecules, the ionization of water can be described statistically. To state that the probability that a hydrogen exists as an ion is 0.01 means that at any given moment in time, a hydrogen atom has 1 chance in 100 of being an ion and 99 chances out of 100 of being part of a water molecule. The actual probability of a hydrogen atom in pure water existing as a hydrogen ion is approximately 1.8×10^{-9}. The probability of its being part of a water molecule thus is almost unity. Stated another way, for every hydrogen ion and hydroxide ion in pure water, there are 1.8 billion or 1.8×10^9 water molecules. Hydrogen ions and hydroxide ions nevertheless contribute significantly to the properties of water.

For dissociation of water,

$$K = \frac{[H^+][OH^-]}{[H_2O]}$$

where brackets represent molar concentrations (strictly speaking, molar activities) and K is the **dissociation constant.** Since 1 mole (mol) of water weighs 18 g, 1 liter (L) (1000 g) of water contains $1000 \div 18 = 55.56$ mol. Pure water thus is 55.56 molar. Since the probability that a hydrogen in pure water will exist as a hydrogen ion is 1.8×10^{-9}, the molar concentration of H^+ ions (or of OH^- ions) in pure water is the product of the probability, 1.8×10^{-9}, times the molar concentration of water, 55.56 mol/L. The result is 1.0×10^{-7} mol/L.

We can now calculate K for pure water:

$$K = \frac{[H^+][OH^-]}{[H_2O]} = \frac{[10^{-7}][10^{-7}]}{[55.56]}$$
$$= 0.018 \times 10^{-14} = 1.8 \times 10^{-16}\, mol/L$$

The molar concentration of water, 55.56 mol/L, is too great to be significantly affected by dissociation. It therefore is considered to be essentially constant. This constant may therefore be incorporated into the dissociation constant K to provide a useful new constant K_w termed the **ion product** for water. The relationship between K_w and K is shown below:

$$K = \frac{[H^+][OH^-]}{[H_2O]} = 1.8 \times 10^{-16} \text{ mol/L}$$

$$K_w = (K)[H_2O] = [H^+][OH^-]$$

$$= (1.8 \times 10^{-16} \text{ mol/L})(55.56 \text{ mol/L})$$

$$= 1.00 \times 10^{-14} \text{ (mol/L)}^2$$

Note that the dimensions of K are moles per liter and those of K_w are moles^2 per liter^2. As its name suggests, the ion product K_w is numerically equal to the product of the molar concentrations of H^+ and OH^-:

$$K_w = [H^+][OH^-]$$

At 25 °C, $K_w = (10^{-7})^2$, or 10^{-14} (mol/L)^2. At temperatures below 25 °C, K_w is somewhat less than 10^{-14}, and at temperatures above 25 °C it is somewhat greater than 10^{-14}. Within the stated limitations of the effect of temperature, K_w **equals 10^{-14} (mol/L)^2 for all aqueous solutions, even solutions of acids or bases.** We use K_w to calculate the pH of acidic and basic solutions.

pH IS THE NEGATIVE LOG OF THE HYDROGEN ION CONCENTRATION

The term **pH** was introduced in 1909 by Sörensen, who defined pH as the negative log of the hydrogen ion concentration:

$$pH = -\log [H^+]$$

This definition, while not rigorous, suffices for many biochemical purposes. To calculate the pH of a solution:

1. Calculate hydrogen ion concentration [H^+].
2. Calculate the base 10 logarithm of [H^+].
3. pH is the negative of the value found in step 2.

For example, for pure water at 25 °C,

$$pH = -\log [H^+] = -\log 10^{-7} = -(-7) = 7.0$$

This value is also known as the *power* (English), *puissant* (French), or *potennz* (German) of the exponent, hence the use of the term "p."

Low pH values correspond to high concentrations of H^+ and high pH values correspond to low concentrations of H^+.

Acids are **proton donors** and bases are **proton acceptors. Strong acids** (eg, HCl, H$_2$SO$_4$) completely dissociate into anions and cations even in strongly acidic solutions (low pH). **Weak acids** dissociate only partially in acidic solutions. Similarly, **strong bases** (eg, KOH, NaOH)—but not **weak bases** (eg, Ca[OH]$_2$)—are completely dissociated at high pH. Many biochemicals are weak acids. Exceptions include phosphorylated intermediates, whose phosphoryl group contains two dissociable protons, the first of which is strongly acidic.

The following examples illustrate how to calculate the pH of acidic and basic solutions.

Example 1: What is the pH of a solution whose hydrogen ion concentration is 3.2×10^{-4} mol/L?

$$pH = -\log [H^+]$$
$$= -\log (3.2 \times 10^{-4})$$
$$= -\log (3.2) - \log (10^{-4})$$
$$= -0.5 + 4.0$$
$$= 3.5$$

Example 2: What is the pH of a solution whose hydroxide ion concentration is 4.0×10^{-4} mol/L? We first define a quantity **pOH** that is equal to $-\log$ [OH$^-$] and that may be derived from the definition of K_w:

$$K_w = [H^+][OH^-] = 10^{-14}$$

Therefore:

$$\log [H^+] + \log [OH^-] = \log 10^{-14}$$

or

$$pH + pOH = 14$$

To solve the problem by this approach:

$$[OH^-] = 4.0 \times 10^{-4}$$
$$pOH = -\log [OH^-]$$
$$= -\log (4.0 \times 10^{-4})$$
$$= -\log (4.0) - \log (10^{-4})$$
$$= -0.60 + 4.0$$
$$= 3.4$$

Now:

$$pH = 14 - pOH = 14 - 3.4$$
$$= 10.6$$

Example 3: What are the pH values of (a) 2.0×10^{-2} mol/L KOH and of (b) 2.0×10^{-6} mol/L KOH? The OH$^-$ arises from two sources, KOH and water. Since pH is determined by the total [H^+] (and pOH by the total [OH$^-$]), both sources must be considered. In the first case (a), the contribution of water to the total [OH$^-$] is negligible. The same cannot be said for the second case (b):

	Concentration (mol/L)	
	(a)	(b)
Molarity of KOH	2.0×10^{-2}	2.0×10^{-6}
[OH$^-$] from KOH	2.0×10^{-2}	2.0×10^{-6}
[OH$^-$] from water	1.0×10^{-7}	1.0×10^{-7}
Total [OH$^-$]	2.00001×10^{-2}	2.1×10^{-6}

Once a decision has been reached about the significance of the contribution by water, pH may be calculated as above.

The above examples assume that the strong base KOH is completely dissociated in solution and that the concentration of OH$^-$ ions was thus equal to that of the KOH plus that present initially in the water. This assumption is valid for dilute solutions of strong bases or acids but not for weak bases or acids. Since weak electrolytes dissociate only slightly in solution, we must use the **dissociation constant** to calculate the concentration of [H$^+$] (or [OH$^-$]) produced by a given molarity of a weak acid (or base) before calculating total [H$^+$] (or total [OH$^-$]) and subsequently pH.

Functional Groups That Are Weak Acids Have Great Physiologic Significance

Many biochemicals possess functional groups that are weak acids or bases. Carboxyl groups, amino groups, and phosphate esters, whose second dissociation falls within the physiologic range, are present in proteins and nucleic acids, most coenzymes, and most intermediary metabolites. Knowledge of the dissociation of weak acids and bases thus is basic to understanding the influence of intracellular pH on structure and biologic activity. Charge-based separations such as electrophoresis and ion exchange chromatography also are best understood in terms of the dissociation behavior of functional groups.

We term the protonated species (eg, HA or R—NH$_3^+$) the **acid** and the unprotonated species (eg, A$^-$ or R—NH$_2$) its **conjugate base.** Similarly, we may refer to a **base** (eg, A$^-$ or R—NH$_2$) and its **conjugate acid** (eg, HA or R—NH$_3^+$). Representative weak acids (left), their conjugate bases (center), and the pK_a values (right) include the following:

R—CH$_2$—COOH	R—CH$_2$—COO$^-$	pK_a = 4–5
R—CH$_2$—NH$_3^+$	R—CH$_2$—NH$_2$	pK_a = 9–10
H$_2$CO$_3$	HCO$_3^-$	pK_a = 6.4
H$_2$PO$_4^-$	HPO$_4^{-2}$	pK_a = 7.2

We express the relative strengths of weak acids and bases in terms of their dissociation constants. Shown below are the expressions for the dissociation constant (K_a) for two representative weak acids, R—COOH and R—NH$_3^+$.

$$R—COOH \rightleftarrows R—COO^- + H^+$$

$$K_a = \frac{[R—COO^-][H^+]}{[R—COOH]}$$

$$R—NH_3^+ \rightleftarrows R—NH_2 + H^+$$

$$K_a = \frac{[R—NH_2][H^+]}{[R—NH_3^+]}$$

Since the numeric values of K_a for weak acids are negative exponential numbers, we express K_a as pK_a, where

$$pK_a = -\log K_a$$

Note that pK_a is related to K_a as pH is to [H$^+$]. The stronger the acid, the lower its pK_a value.

pK_a is used to express the relative strengths of both acids and bases. For any weak acid, its conjugate is a strong base. Similarly, the conjugate of a strong base is a weak acid. The relative strengths of bases are expressed in terms of the pK_a of their conjugate acids. For polyprotic compounds containing more than one dissociable proton, a numerical subscript is assigned to each in order of relative acidity. For a dissociation of the type

$$R—NH_3^+ \rightarrow R—NH_2 + H^+$$

the pK_a is the pH at which the concentration of the acid R—NH$_3^+$ equals that of the base R—NH$_2$.

From the above equations that relate K_a to [H$^+$] and to the concentrations of undissociated acid and its conjugate base, when

$$[R—COO^-] = [R—COOH]$$

or when

$$[R—NH_2] = [R—NH_3^+]$$

then

$$K_a = [H^+]$$

Thus, when the associated (protonated) and dissociated (conjugate base) species are present at equal concentrations, the prevailing hydrogen ion concentration [H$^+$] is numerically equal to the dissociation constant, K_a. If the logarithms of both sides of the above equation are

taken and both sides are multiplied by −1, the expressions would be as follows:

$$K_a = [H^+]$$

$$-\log K_a = -\log [H^+]$$

Since $-\log K_a$ is defined as pK_a, and $-\log [H^+]$ defines pH, the equation may be rewritten as

$$pK_a = pH$$

ie, the pK_a of an acid group is the pH at which the protonated and unprotonated species are present at equal concentrations. The pK_a for an acid may be determined by adding 0.5 equivalent of alkali per equivalent of acid. The resulting pH will be the pK_a of the acid.

The Henderson-Hasselbalch Equation Describes the Behavior of Weak Acids & Buffers

The Henderson-Hasselbalch equation is derived below.
A weak acid, HA, ionizes as follows:

$$HA \rightleftarrows H^+ + A^-$$

The equilibrium constant for this dissociation is

$$K_a = \frac{[H^+][A^-]}{[HA]}$$

Cross-multiplication gives

$$[H^+][A^-] = K_a[HA]$$

Divide both sides by $[A^-]$:

$$[H^+] = K_a \frac{[HA]}{[A^-]}$$

Take the log of both sides:

$$\log [H^+] = \log \left(K_a \frac{[HA]}{[A^-]} \right)$$

$$= \log K_a + \log \frac{[HA]}{[A^-]}$$

Multiply through by −1:

$$-\log [H^+] = -\log K_a - \log \frac{[HA]}{[A^-]}$$

Substitute pH and pK_a for $-\log [H^+]$ and $-\log K_a$, respectively; then:

$$pH = pK_a - \log \frac{[HA]}{[A^-]}$$

Inversion of the last term removes the minus sign and gives the Henderson-Hasselbalch equation:

$$pH = pK_a + \log \frac{[A^-]}{[HA]}$$

The Henderson-Hasselbalch equation has great predictive value in protonic equilibria. For example,

(1) When an acid is exactly half-neutralized, $[A^-]$ = $[HA]$. Under these conditions,

$$pH = pK_a + \log \frac{[A^-]}{[HA]} = pK_a + \log \frac{1}{1} = pK_a + 0$$

Therefore, at half-neutralization, pH = pK_a.

(2) When the ratio $[A^-]/[HA]$ = 100:1,

$$pH = pK_a + \log \frac{[A^-]}{[HA]}$$

$$pH = pK_a + \log 100/1 = pK_a + 2$$

(3) When the ratio $[A^-]/[HA]$ = 1:10,

$$pH = pK_a + \log 1/10 = pK_a + (-1)$$

If the equation is evaluated at ratios of $[A^-]/[HA]$ ranging from 10^3 to 10^{-3} and the calculated pH values are plotted, the resulting graph describes the titration curve for a weak acid (Figure 2–4).

Solutions of Weak Acids & Their Salts Buffer Changes in pH

Solutions of weak acids or bases and their conjugates exhibit buffering, the ability to resist a change in pH following addition of strong acid or base. Since many metabolic reactions are accompanied by the release or uptake of protons, most intracellular reactions are buffered. Oxidative metabolism produces CO_2, the anhydride of carbonic acid, which if not buffered would produce severe acidosis. Maintenance of a constant pH involves buffering by phosphate, bicarbonate, and proteins, which accept or release protons to resist a change in pH. For experiments using tissue extracts or enzymes,

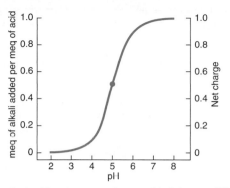

Figure 2–4. Titration curve for an acid of the type HA. The heavy dot in the center of the curve indicates the pK_a 5.0.

constant pH is maintained by the addition of buffers such as MES ([2-N-morpholino]ethanesulfonic acid, pK_a 6.1), inorganic orthophosphate (pK_{a2} 7.2), HEPES (N-hydroxyethylpiperazine-N'-2-ethanesulfonic acid, pK_a 6.8), or Tris (tris[hydroxymethyl] aminomethane, pK_a 8.3). The value of pK_a relative to the desired pH is the major determinant of which buffer is selected.

Buffering can be observed by using a pH meter while titrating a weak acid or base (Figure 2–4). We can also calculate the pH shift that accompanies addition of acid or base to a buffered solution. In the example, the buffered solution (a weak acid, pK_a = 5.0, and its conjugate base) is initially at one of four pH values. We will calculate the pH shift that results when 0.1 meq of KOH is added to 1 meq of each solution:

Initial pH	5.00	5.37	5.60	5.86
$[A^-]_{initial}$	0.50	0.70	0.80	0.88
$[HA]_{initial}$	0.50	0.30	0.20	0.12
$([A^-]/[HA])_{initial}$	1.00	2.33	4.00	7.33
Addition of 0.1 meq of KOH produces				
$[A^-]_{final}$	0.60	0.80	0.90	0.98
$[HA]_{final}$	0.40	0.20	0.10	0.02
$([A^-]/[HA])_{final}$	1.50	4.00	9.00	49.0
log $([A^-]/[HA])_{final}$	0.176	0.602	0.95	1.69
Final pH	5.18	5.60	5.95	6.69
ΔpH	0.18	0.60	0.95	1.69

Notice that the change in pH per milliequivalent of OH⁻ added depends on the initial pH. The solution resists changes in pH most effectively at pH values close to the pK_a. A solution of a weak acid and its conjugate base buffers most effectively in the pH range pK_a ± 1.0 pH unit.

Figure 2–4 also illustrates the net charge on one molecule of the acid as a function of pH. A fractional charge of –0.5 does not mean that an individual molecule bears

a fractional charge, but the *probability* is 0.5 that a given molecule has a unit negative charge at any given moment in time. Consideration of the net charge on macromolecules as a function of pH provides the basis for separatory techniques such as ion exchange chromatography and electrophoresis.

Acid Strength Depends on Molecular Structure

Many acids of biologic interest possess more than one dissociating group. The presence of adjacent negative charge hinders the release of a proton from a nearby group, raising its pK_a. This is apparent from the pK_a values for the three dissociating groups of phosphoric acid and citric acid (Table 2–2). The effect of adjacent charge decreases with distance. The second pK_a for succinic acid, which has two methylene groups between its carboxyl groups, is 5.6, whereas the second pK_a for glutaric acid, which has one additional methylene group, is 5.4.

pK_a Values Depend on the Properties of the Medium

The pK_a of a functional group is also profoundly influenced by the surrounding medium. The medium may

Table 2–2. Relative strengths of selected acids of biologic significance. Tabulated values are the pK_a values (–log of the dissociation constant) of selected monoprotic, diprotic, and triprotic acids.

Monoprotic Acids		
Formic	pK	3.75
Lactic	pK	3.86
Acetic	pK	4.76
Ammonium ion	pK	9.25
Diprotic Acids		
Carbonic	pK_1	6.37
	pK_2	10.25
Succinic	pK_1	4.21
	pK_2	5.64
Glutaric	pK_1	4.34
	pK_2	5.41
Triprotic Acids		
Phosphoric	pK_1	2.15
	pK_2	6.82
	pK_3	12.38
Citric	pK_1	3.08
	pK_2	4.74
	pK_3	5.40

either raise or lower the pK_a depending on whether the undissociated acid or its conjugate base is the charged species. The effect of dielectric constant on pK_a may be observed by adding ethanol to water. The pK_a of a carboxylic acid *increases,* whereas that of an amine *decreases* because ethanol decreases the ability of water to solvate a charged species. The pK_a values of dissociating groups in the interiors of proteins thus are profoundly affected by their local environment, including the presence or absence of water.

SUMMARY

- Water forms hydrogen-bonded clusters with itself and with other proton donors or acceptors. Hydrogen bonds account for the surface tension, viscosity, liquid state at room temperature, and solvent power of water.
- Compounds that contain O, N, or S can serve as hydrogen bond donors or acceptors.
- Macromolecules exchange internal surface hydrogen bonds for hydrogen bonds to water. Entropic forces dictate that macromolecules expose polar regions to an aqueous interface and bury nonpolar regions.
- Salt bonds, hydrophobic interactions, and van der Waals forces participate in maintaining molecular structure.
- pH is the negative log of $[H^+]$. A low pH characterizes an acidic solution, and a high pH denotes a basic solution.
- The strength of weak acids is expressed by pK_a, the negative log of the acid dissociation constant. Strong acids have low pK_a values and weak acids have high pK_a values.
- Buffers resist a change in pH when protons are produced or consumed. Maximum buffering capacity occurs ± 1 pH unit on either side of pK_a. Physiologic buffers include bicarbonate, orthophosphate, and proteins.

REFERENCES

Reese KM: Whence came the symbol pH. Chem & Eng News 2004;82:64.

Segel IM: *Biochemical Calculations.* Wiley, 1968.

Stillinger FH: Water revisited. Science 1980;209:451.

Suresh SJ, Naik VM: Hydrogen bond thermodynamic properties of water from dielectric constant data. J Chem Phys 2000;113:9727.

Wiggins PM: Role of water in some biological processes. Microbiol Rev 1990;54:432.

SECTION I
Structures & Functions of Proteins & Enzymes

Amino Acids & Peptides

3

Peter J. Kennelly, PhD, & Victor W. Rodwell, PhD

BIOMEDICAL IMPORTANCE

In addition to providing the monomer units from which the long polypeptide chains of proteins are synthesized, the L-α-amino acids and their derivatives participate in cellular functions as diverse as nerve transmission and the biosynthesis of porphyrins, purines, pyrimidines, and urea. Short polymers of amino acids called *peptides* perform prominent roles in the neuroendocrine system as hormones, hormone-releasing factors, neuromodulators, or neurotransmitters. While proteins contain only L-α-amino acids, microorganisms elaborate peptides that contain both D- and L-α-amino acids. Several of these peptides are of therapeutic value, including the antibiotics bacitracin and gramicidin A and the antitumor agent bleomycin. Certain other microbial peptides are toxic. The cyanobacterial peptides microcystin and nodularin are lethal in large doses, while small quantities promote the formation of hepatic tumors. Neither humans nor any other higher animals can synthesize 10 of the 20 common L-α-amino acids in amounts adequate to support infant growth or to maintain health in adults. Consequently, the human diet must contain adequate quantities of these nutritionally essential amino acids.

PROPERTIES OF AMINO ACIDS

The Genetic Code Specifies 20 L-α-Amino Acids

Of the over 300 naturally occurring amino acids, 20 constitute the monomer units of proteins. While a nonredundant three-letter genetic code could accommodate more than 20 amino acids, its redundancy limits the available codons to the 20 L-α-amino acids listed in Table 3–1, classified according to the polarity of their R groups. Both one- and three-letter abbreviations for each amino acid can be used to represent the amino acids in peptides (Table 3–1). Some proteins contain additional amino acids that arise by modification of an amino acid already present in a peptide. Examples include conversion of peptidyl proline and lysine to 4-hydroxyproline and 5-hydroxylysine; the conversion of peptidyl glutamate to γ-carboxyglutamate; and the methylation, formylation, acetylation, prenylation, and phosphorylation of certain aminoacyl residues. These modifications extend the biologic diversity of proteins by altering their solubility, stability, and interaction with other proteins.

Selenocysteine, the 21st L-α-Amino Acid?

Selenocysteine is an L-α-amino acid found in a handful of proteins. As its name implies, a selenium atom replaces the sulfur of its structural analog, cysteine. The pK_3 of selenocysteine, 5.2, is 3 units lower than that of cysteine. Since selenocysteine is inserted into polypeptides during translation, it is commonly referred to as the "21st amino acid." However, unlike the other 20 genetically encoded amino acids, selenocysteine is not specified by a simple three-letter codon (see Chapter 27).

Only L-α-Amino Acids Occur in Proteins

With the sole exception of glycine, the α-carbon of amino acids is chiral. Although some protein amino acids are dextrorotatory and some levorotatory, all share the absolute

Table 3–1. L-α-Amino acids present in proteins.

Name	Symbol	Structural Formula	pK_1	pK_2	pK_3
			α-COOH	α-NH$_3^+$	R Group
With Aliphatic Side Chains					
Glycine	Gly [G]		2.4	9.8	
Alanine	Ala [A]		2.4	9.9	
Valine	Val [V]		2.2	9.7	
Leucine	Leu [L]		2.3	9.7	
Isoleucine	Ile [I]		2.3	9.8	
With Side Chains Containing Hydroxylic (OH) Groups					
Serine	Ser [S]		2.2	9.2	about 13
Threonine	Thr [T]		2.1	9.1	about 13
Tyrosine	Tyr [Y]	See below.			
With Side Chains Containing Sulfur Atoms					
Cysteine	Cys [C]		1.9	10.8	8.3
Methionine	Met [M]		2.1	9.3	
With Side Chains Containing Acidic Groups or Their Amides					
Aspartic acid	Asp [D]		2.0	9.9	3.9
Asparagine	Asn [N]		2.1	8.8	
Glutamic acid	Glu [E]		2.1	9.5	4.1
Glutamine	Gln [Q]		2.2	9.1	

(continued)

Table 3–1. L-α-Amino acids present in proteins. (continued)

Name	Symbol	Structural Formula	pK_1 α-COOH	pK_2 α-NH$_3^+$	pK_3 R Group
With Side Chains Containing Basic Groups					
Arginine	Arg [R]		1.8	9.0	12.5
Lysine	Lys [K]		2.2	9.2	10.8
Histidine	His [H]		1.8	9.3	6.0
Containing Aromatic Rings					
Histidine	His [H]	See above.			
Phenylalanine	Phe [F]		2.2	9.2	
Tyrosine	Tyr [Y]		2.2	9.1	10.1
Tryptophan	Trp [W]		2.4	9.4	
Imino Acid					
Proline	Pro [P]		2.0	10.6	

configuration of L-glyceraldehyde and thus are L-α-amino acids. Several free L-α-amino acids fulfill important roles in metabolic processes. Examples include ornithine, citrulline, and argininosuccinate that participate in urea synthesis; tyrosine in formation of thyroid hormones; and glutamate in neurotransmitter biosynthesis. D-Amino acids that occur naturally include free D-serine and D-aspartate in brain tissue, D-alanine and D-glutamate in the cell walls of gram-positive bacteria, and D-amino acids in some nonmammalian peptides and certain antibiotics.

Amino Acids May Have Positive, Negative, or Zero Net Charge

Charged and uncharged forms of the ionizable —COOH and —NH$_3^+$ weak acid groups exist in solution in protonic equilibrium:

$$R—COOH \rightleftarrows R—COO^- + H^+$$

$$R—NH_3^+ \rightleftarrows R—NH_2 + H^+$$

While both R—COOH and R—NH$_3^+$ are weak acids, R—COOH is a far stronger acid than R—NH$_3^+$. At physiologic pH (pH 7.4), carboxyl groups exist almost entirely as R—COO$^-$ and amino groups predominantly as R—NH$_3^+$. Figure 3–1 illustrates the effect of pH on the charged state of aspartic acid.

Molecules that contain an equal number of ionizable groups of opposite charge and that therefore bear no net charge are termed **zwitterions.** Amino acids in blood and most tissues thus should be represented as in **A,** below.

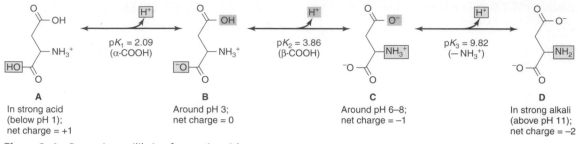

Figure 3–1. Protonic equilibria of aspartic acid.

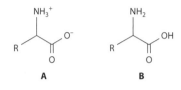

Structure **B** cannot exist in aqueous solution because at any pH low enough to protonate the carboxyl group, the amino group would also be protonated. Similarly, at any pH sufficiently high for an uncharged amino group to predominate, a carboxyl group will be present as R—COO⁻. The uncharged representation **B** (above) is, however, often used for reactions that do not involve protonic equilibria.

pK_a Values Express the Strengths of Weak Acids

The acid strengths of weak acids are expressed as their **pK_a**. For molecules with multiple dissociable protons, the pK_a for each acidic group is designated by replacing the subscript "a" with a number (Table 3–1). The imidazole group of histidine and the guanidino group of arginine exist as resonance hybrids with positive charge distributed between both nitrogens (histidine) or all three nitrogens (arginine) (Figure 3–2). The net charge

on an amino acid—the algebraic sum of all the positively and negatively charged groups present—depends upon the pK_a values of its functional groups and on the pH of the surrounding medium. Altering the charge on amino acids and their derivatives by varying the pH facilitates the physical separation of amino acids, peptides, and proteins (see Chapter 4).

At Its Isoelectric pH (pI), an Amino Acid Bears No Net Charge

The **isoelectric** species is the form of a molecule that has an equal number of positive and negative charges and thus is electrically neutral. The isoelectric pH, also called the pI, is the pH midway between pK_a values on either side of the isoelectric species. For an amino acid such as alanine that has only two dissociating groups, there is no ambiguity. The first pK_a (R—COOH) is 2.35 and the second pK_a (R—NH$_3^+$) is 9.69. The isoelectric pH (pI) of alanine thus is

$$pI = \frac{pK_1 + pK_2}{2} = \frac{2.35 + 9.69}{2} = 6.02$$

For polyfunctional acids, pI is also the pH midway between the pK_a values on either side of the isoionic species. For example, the pI for aspartic acid is

$$pI = \frac{pK_1 + pK_2}{2} = \frac{2.09 + 3.96}{2} = 3.02$$

For lysine, pI is calculated from:

$$pI = \frac{pK_2 + pK_3}{2}$$

Similar considerations apply to all polyprotic acids (eg, proteins), regardless of the number of dissociating groups present. In the clinical laboratory, knowledge of the pI guides selection of conditions for electrophoretic separations. For example, electrophoresis at pH 7.0 will separate two molecules with pI values of 6.0 and 8.0,

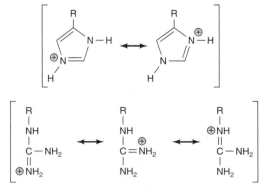

Figure 3–2. Resonance hybrids of the protonated forms of the R groups of histidine and arginine.

because at pH 7.0 the molecule with a pI of 6.0 will have a net positive charge, and that with pI of 8.0 a net negative charge. Similar considerations apply to understanding chromatographic separations on ionic supports such as DEAE cellulose (see Chapter 4).

pK_a Values Vary with the Environment

The environment of a dissociable group affects its pK_a. The pK_a values of the R groups of free amino acids in aqueous solution (Table 3–1) thus provide only an approximate guide to the pK_a values of the same amino acids when present in proteins. A polar environment favors the charged form (R—COO$^-$ or R—NH$_3^+$), and a nonpolar environment favors the uncharged form (R—COOH or R—NH$_2$). A nonpolar environment thus *raises* the pK_a of a carboxyl group (making it a weaker acid) but *lowers* that of an amino group (making it a stronger acid). The presence of adjacent charged groups can reinforce or counteract solvent effects. The pK_a of a functional group thus will depend upon its location within a given protein. Variations in pK_a can encompass whole pH units (Table 3–2). pK_a values that diverge from those listed by as much as 3 pH units are common at the active sites of enzymes. An extreme example, a buried aspartic acid of thioredoxin, has a pK_a above 9—a shift of more than 6 pH units!

The Solubility of Amino Acids Reflects Their Ionic Character

The charged functional groups of amino acids ensure that they are readily solvated by—and thus soluble in—polar solvents such as water and ethanol but insoluble in nonpolar solvents such as benzene, hexane, or ether.

Amino acids do not absorb visible light and thus are colorless. However, tyrosine, phenylalanine, and especially tryptophan absorb high-wavelength (250–290 nm) ultraviolet light. Tryptophan therefore makes the major contribution to the ability of most proteins to absorb light in the region of 280 nm.

Table 3–2. Typical range of pK_a values for ionizable groups in proteins.

Dissociating Group	pK_a Range
α-Carboxyl	3.5–4.0
Non-α COOH of Asp or Glu	4.0–4.8
Imidazole of His	6.5–7.4
SH of Cys	8.5–9.0
OH of Tyr	9.5–10.5
α-Amino	8.0–9.0
ε-Amino of Lys	9.8–10.4
Guanidinium of Arg	~12.0

THE α-R GROUPS DETERMINE THE PROPERTIES OF AMINO ACIDS

Since glycine, the smallest amino acid, can be accommodated in places inaccessible to other amino acids, it often occurs where peptides bend sharply. The hydrophobic R groups of alanine, valine, leucine, and isoleucine and the aromatic R groups of phenylalanine, tyrosine, and tryptophan typically occur primarily in the interior of cytosolic proteins. The charged R groups of basic and acidic amino acids stabilize specific protein conformations via ionic interactions, or salt bonds. These bonds also function in "charge relay" systems during enzymatic catalysis and electron transport in respiring mitochondria. Histidine plays unique roles in enzymatic catalysis. The pK_a of its imidazole proton permits it to function at neutral pH as either a base or an acid catalyst. The primary alcohol group of serine and the primary thioalcohol (—SH) group of cysteine are excellent nucleophiles and can function as such during enzymatic catalysis. However, the secondary alcohol group of threonine, while a good nucleophile, does not fulfill an analogous role in catalysis. The —OH groups of serine, tyrosine, and threonine also participate in regulation of the activity of enzymes whose catalytic activity depends on the phosphorylation state of these residues.

FUNCTIONAL GROUPS DICTATE THE CHEMICAL REACTIONS OF AMINO ACIDS

Each functional group of an amino acid exhibits all of its characteristic chemical reactions. For carboxylic acid groups, these reactions include the formation of esters, amides, and acid anhydrides; for amino groups, acylation, amidation, and esterification; and for —OH and —SH groups, oxidation and esterification. The most important reaction of amino acids is the formation of a peptide bond (shaded).

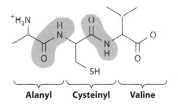

Alanyl **Cysteinyl** **Valine**

Amino Acid Sequence Determines Primary Structure

The number and order of all of the amino acid residues in a polypeptide constitute its primary structure. Amino acids present in peptides are called aminoacyl residues and are named by replacing the -*ate* or -*ine* suffixes of free amino acids with -*yl* (eg, alan*yl*, aspart*yl*, tyros*yl*). Peptides are then named as derivatives of the carboxyl

terminal aminoacyl residue. For example, Lys-Leu-Tyr-Gln is called lys*yl*-leuc*yl*-tyros*yl*-glutam*ine*. The *-ine* ending on glutamine indicates that its α-carboxyl group is *not* involved in peptide bond formation.

Peptide Structures Are Easy to Draw

Prefixes like *tri-* or *octa-* denote peptides with three or eight **residues,** respectively, not those with three or eight peptide **bonds.** By convention, peptides are written with the residue that bears the free α-amino group at the left. To draw a peptide, use a zigzag to represent the main chain or backbone. Add the main chain atoms, which occur in the repeating order: α-nitrogen, α-carbon, carbonyl carbon. Now add a hydrogen atom to each α-carbon and to each peptide nitrogen, and an oxygen to the carbonyl carbon. Finally, add the appropriate R groups (shaded) to each α-carbon atom.

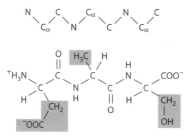

Three-letter abbreviations linked by straight lines represent an unambiguous primary structure. Lines are omitted for single-letter abbreviations.

Glu - Ala - Lys - Gly - Tyr - Ala
E   A   K   G   Y   A

Some Peptides Contain Unusual Amino Acids

In mammals, peptide hormones typically contain only the α-amino acids of proteins linked by standard peptide bonds. Other peptides may, however, contain nonprotein amino acids, derivatives of the protein amino acids, or amino acids linked by an atypical peptide bond. For example, the amino terminal glutamate of glutathione, which participates in protein folding and in the metabolism of xenobiotics (Chapter 52), is linked to cysteine by a non-α peptide bond (Figure 3–3). The amino terminal glutamate of thyrotropin-releasing hormone (TRH) is cyclized to pyroglutamic acid, and the carboxyl group of the carboxyl terminal prolyl residue is amidated. Peptides elaborated by fungi, bacteria, and lower animals can contain nonprotein amino acids. The antibiotics tyrocidin and gramicidin S are cyclic peptides that contain D-phenylalanine and ornithine. The heptapeptide opioids dermorphin and delto-

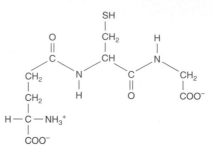

Figure 3–3. Glutathione (γ-glutamyl-cysteinyl-glycine). Note the non-α peptide bond that links Glu to Cys.

phorin in the skin of South American tree frogs contain D-tyrosine and D-alanine.

Peptides Are Polyelectrolytes

The peptide bond is uncharged at any pH of physiologic interest. Formation of peptides from amino acids is therefore accompanied by a net loss of one positive and one negative charge per peptide bond formed. Peptides nevertheless are charged at physiologic pH owing to their carboxyl and amino terminal groups and, where present, their acidic or basic R groups. As for amino acids, the net charge on a peptide depends on the pH of its environment and on the pK_a values of its dissociating groups.

The Peptide Bond Has Partial Double-Bond Character

Although peptides are written as if a single bond linked the α-carboxyl and α-nitrogen atoms, this bond in fact exhibits partial double-bond character:

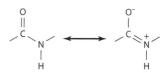

There thus is no freedom of rotation about the bond that connects the carbonyl carbon and the nitrogen of a peptide bond. Consequently, all four of the colored atoms of Figure 3–4 are coplanar. The imposed semirigidity of the peptide bond has important consequences for higher orders of protein structure. Encircling arrows (Figure 3–4) indicate free rotation about the remaining bonds of the polypeptide backbone.

Noncovalent Forces Constrain Peptide Conformations

Folding of a peptide probably occurs coincident with its biosynthesis (see Chapter 38). The physiologically

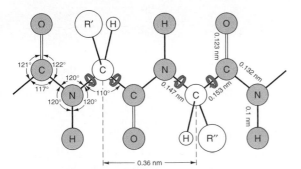

Figure 3–4. Dimensions of a fully extended polypeptide chain. The four atoms of the peptide bond (colored) are coplanar. The unshaded atoms are the α-carbon atom, the α-hydrogen atom, and the α-R group of the particular amino acid. Free rotation can occur about the bonds that connect the α-carbon with the α-nitrogen and with the α-carbonyl carbon (color arrows). The extended polypeptide chain is thus a semirigid structure with two-thirds of the atoms of the backbone held in a fixed planar relationship one to another. The distance between adjacent α-carbon atoms is 0.36 nm (3.6 Å). The interatomic distances and bond angles, which are not equivalent, are also shown. (Redrawn and reproduced, with permission, from Pauling L, Corey LP, Branson HR: The structure of proteins: Two hydrogen-bonded helical configurations of the polypeptide chain. Proc Natl Acad Sci U S A 1951;37:205.)

active conformation reflects the collective contributions of the amino acid sequence, steric hindrance, and noncovalent interactions (eg, hydrogen bonding, hydrophobic interactions) between residues. Common conformations include α-helices and β-pleated sheets (see Chapter 5).

ANALYSIS OF THE AMINO ACID CONTENT OF BIOLOGIC MATERIALS

In order to determine the identity and quantity of each amino acid in a sample of biologic material, it is first necessary to hydrolyze the peptide bonds that link the amino acids together by treatment with hot HCl. The resulting mixture of free amino acids is then treated with 6-amino-*N*-hydroxysuccinimidyl carbamate, which reacts with their α-amino groups to form fluorescent derivatives that are separated and identified using high-pressure liquid chromatography (see Chapter 4). Ninhydrin, also widely used for detecting amino acids,

forms a purple product with α-amino acids and a yellow adduct with the imine groups of proline and hydroxyproline.

SUMMARY

- Both D-amino acids and non-α-amino acids occur in nature, but only L-α-amino acids are present in proteins.
- All amino acids possess at least two weakly acidic functional groups, $R—NH_3^+$ and R—COOH. Many also possess additional weakly acidic functional groups such as —OH, —SH, guanidino, or imidazole moieties.
- The pK_a values of all functional groups of an amino acid dictate its net charge at a given pH. pI is the pH at which an amino acid bears no net charge and thus does not move in a direct current electrical field.
- Of the biochemical reactions of amino acids, the most important is the formation of peptide bonds.
- The R groups of amino acids determine their unique biochemical functions. Amino acids are classified as basic, acidic, aromatic, aliphatic, or sulfur-containing based on the properties of their R groups.
- Peptides are named for the number of amino acid residues present, and as derivatives of the carboxyl terminal residue. The primary structure of a peptide is its amino acid sequence, starting from the amino-terminal residue.
- The partial double bond character of the bond that links the carbonyl carbon and the nitrogen of a peptide renders four atoms of the peptide bond coplanar and restricts the number of possible peptide conformations.

REFERENCES

Doolittle RF: Reconstructing history with amino acid sequences. Protein Sci 1992;1:191.

Gladyshev VN, Hatfield DL. Selenocysteine-containing proteins in mammals. J Biomed Sci 1999;6:151.

Kreil G: D-Amino acids in animal peptides. Annu Rev Biochem 1997;66:337.

Nokihara K, Gerhardt J: Development of an improved automated gas-chromatographic chiral analysis system: application to non-natural amino acids and natural protein hydrolysates. Chirality 2001;13:431.

Sanger F: Sequences, sequences, and sequences. Annu Rev Biochem 1988;57:1.

Stadtman TC: Selenocysteine. Annu Rev Biochem 1996;65:83.

Wilson NA et al: Aspartic acid 26 in reduced *Escherichia coli* thioredoxin has a pK_a greater than 9. Biochemistry 1995;34:8931.

Proteins: Determination of Primary Structure

4

Peter J. Kennelly, PhD, & Victor W. Rodwell, PhD

BIOMEDICAL IMPORTANCE

Proteins are physically and functionally complex macromolecules that perform multiple critically important roles. An internal protein network, the cytoskeleton (Chapter 48), maintains cellular shape and physical integrity. Actin and myosin filaments form the contractile machinery of muscle (Chapter 48). Hemoglobin transports oxygen (Chapter 6), while circulating antibodies search out foreign invaders (Chapter 49). Enzymes catalyze reactions that generate energy, synthesize and degrade biomolecules, replicate and transcribe genes, process mRNAs, etc (Chapter 7). Receptors enable cells to sense and respond to hormones and other environmental cues (Chapters 41 and 42). Proteins are subject to physical and functional changes that mirror the life cycle of the organisms in which they reside. A typical protein is born at translation (Chapter 37), matures through posttranslational processing events such as partial proteolysis (Chapters 9 and 37), alternates between working and resting states through the intervention of regulatory factors (Chapter 9), ages through oxidation, deamidation, etc (Chapter 51), and dies when it is degraded to its component amino acids (Chapter 29). An important goal of molecular medicine is the identification of proteins and those events in their life cycle whose presence, absence, or deficiency is associated with specific physiologic states or diseases (Figure 4–1). The primary sequence of a protein provides both a molecular fingerprint for its identification and information that can be used to identify and clone the gene or genes that encode it.

PROTEINS & PEPTIDES MUST BE PURIFIED PRIOR TO ANALYSIS

Highly purified protein is essential for the detailed examination of its physical and functional properties. Cells contain thousands of different proteins, each in widely varying amounts. The isolation of a specific protein in quantities sufficient for analysis thus presents a formidable challenge that may require multiple successive purification techniques. Classic approaches exploit differences in relative solubility of individual proteins as a function of pH (isoelectric precipitation), polarity (precipitation with ethanol or acetone), or salt concentration (salting out with ammonium sulfate). Chromatographic separations partition molecules between two phases, one mobile and the other stationary. For separation of amino acids or sugars, the stationary phase, or matrix, may be a sheet of filter paper (paper chromatography) or a thin layer of cellulose, silica, or alumina (thin-layer chromatography; TLC).

Column Chromatography

Column chromatography of proteins employs as the stationary phase a column containing small spherical beads of modified cellulose, acrylamide, or silica whose surface typically has been coated with chemical functional groups. These stationary phase matrices interact with proteins based on their charge, hydrophobicity, and ligand-binding properties. A protein mixture is applied to the column and the liquid mobile phase is percolated through it. Small portions of the mobile phase or eluant are collected as they emerge (Figure 4–2).

Partition Chromatography

Column chromatographic separations depend on the relative affinity of different proteins for a given stationary phase and for the mobile phase. Association between each protein and the matrix is weak and transient. Proteins that interact more strongly with the stationary phase are retained longer. The length of time that a protein is associated with the stationary phase is a function of the composition of both the stationary and mobile phases. Optimal separation of the protein of interest from other proteins thus can be achieved by careful manipulation of the composition of the two phases.

Size Exclusion Chromatography

Size exclusion—or gel filtration—chromatography separates proteins based on their **Stokes radius,** the diameter

21

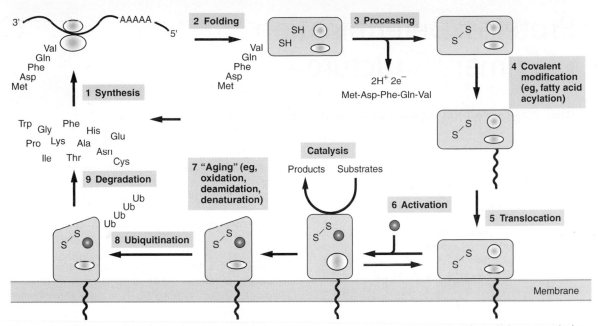

Figure 4–1. Diagrammatic representation of the life cycle of a hypothetical protein. (1) The life cycle begins with the synthesis on a ribosome of a polypeptide chain, whose primary structure is dictated by an mRNA. (2) As synthesis proceeds, the polypeptide begins to fold into its native conformation (light color). (3) Folding may be accompanied by processing events such as proteolytic cleavage of an *N*-terminal leader sequence (dark color) or the formation of disulfide bonds (S—S). (4) Subsequent covalent modification may, for example, attach a fatty acid molecule for (5) translocation of the modified peptide to a membrane. (6) Binding an allosteric effector (darkly colored circle) may trigger the adoption of a catalytically active conformation. (7) Over time, proteins become damaged by chemical attack, deamidation, or denaturation, and (8) may be "labeled" by the covalent attachment of several ubiquitin molecules (Ub). (9) The ubiquitinated protein is subsequently degraded to its component amino acids, which become available for the synthesis of new proteins.

of the sphere they occupy as they tumble in solution. The Stokes radius is a function of molecular mass and shape. A tumbling elongated protein occupies a larger volume than a spherical protein of the same mass. Size exclusion chromatography employs porous beads (Figure 4–3). The pores are analogous to indentations in a river bank. As objects move downstream, those that enter an indentation are retarded until they drift back into the main current. Similarly, proteins with Stokes radii too large to enter the pores (excluded proteins) remain in the flowing mobile phase and emerge before proteins that can enter the pores (included proteins). Proteins thus emerge from a gel filtration column in descending order of their Stokes radii.

Absorption Chromatography

For absorption chromatography, the protein mixture is applied to a column under conditions where the protein of interest associates with the stationary phase so tightly that its partition coefficient is essentially unity. Nonad-

hering molecules are first eluted and discarded. Proteins are then sequentially released by disrupting the forces that stabilize the protein-stationary phase complex, most often by using a gradient of increasing salt concentration. The composition of the mobile phase is altered gradually so that molecules are selectively released in descending order of their affinity for the stationary phase.

Ion Exchange Chromatography

In ion exchange chromatography, proteins interact with the stationary phase by charge-charge interactions. Proteins with a net positive charge at a given pH adhere to beads with negatively charged functional groups such as carboxylates or sulfates (cation exchangers). Similarly, proteins with a net negative charge adhere to beads with positively charged functional groups, typically tertiary or quaternary amines (anion exchangers). Proteins, which are polyanions, compete against monovalent ions for binding to the support—thus the term "ion exchange." For example, proteins

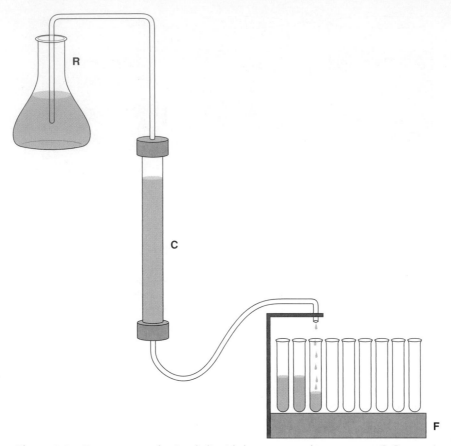

Figure 4–2. Components of a simple liquid chromatography apparatus. **R:** Reservoir of mobile phase liquid, delivered either by gravity or using a pump. **C:** Glass or plastic column containing stationary phase. **F:** Fraction collector for collecting portions, called *fractions,* of the eluant liquid in separate test tubes.

bind to diethylaminoethyl (DEAE) cellulose by replacing the counter-ions (generally Cl⁻ or CH_3COO^-) that neutralize the protonated amine. Bound proteins are selectively displaced by gradually raising the concentration of monovalent ions in the mobile phase. Proteins elute in inverse order of the strength of their interactions with the stationary phase.

Since the net charge on a protein is determined by the pH (see Chapter 3), sequential elution of proteins may be achieved by changing the pH of the mobile phase. Alternatively, a protein can be subjected to consecutive rounds of ion exchange chromatography, each at a different pH, such that proteins that co-elute at one pH elute at different salt concentrations at another pH.

Hydrophobic Interaction Chromatography

Hydrophobic interaction chromatography separates proteins based on their tendency to associate with a stationary phase matrix coated with hydrophobic groups (eg, phenyl Sepharose, octyl Sepharose). Proteins with exposed hydrophobic surfaces adhere to the matrix via hydrophobic interactions that are enhanced by a mobile phase of high ionic strength. Nonadherent proteins are first washed away. The polarity of the mobile phase is then decreased by gradually lowering the salt concentration. If the interaction between protein and stationary phase is particularly strong, ethanol or glycerol may be added to the mobile phase to decrease its polarity and further weaken hydrophobic interactions.

Affinity Chromatography

Affinity chromatography exploits the high selectivity of most proteins for their ligands. Enzymes may be purified by affinity chromatography using immobilized substrates, products, coenzymes, or inhibitors. In theory,

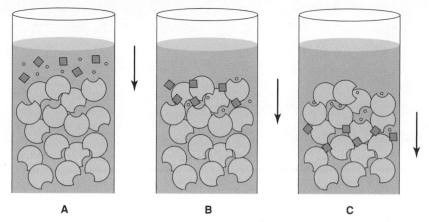

A   **B**   **C**

Figure 4–3. Size exclusion chromatography. **A:** A mixture of large molecules (diamonds) and small molecules (circles) are applied to the top of a gel filtration column. **B:** Upon entering the column, the small molecules enter pores in the stationary phase matrix from which the large molecules are excluded. **C:** As the mobile phase flows down the column, the large, excluded molecules flow with it, while the small molecules, which are temporarily sheltered from the flow when inside the pores, lag farther and farther behind.

only proteins that interact with the immobilized ligand adhere. Bound proteins are then eluted either by competition with soluble ligand or, less selectively, by disrupting protein-ligand interactions using urea, guanidine hydrochloride, mildly acidic pH, or high salt concentrations. Stationary phase matrices available commercially contain ligands such as NAD^+ or ATP analogs. Among the most powerful and widely applicable affinity matrices are those used for the purification of suitably modified recombinant proteins. These include a Ni^{2+} matrix that binds proteins with an attached polyhistidine "tag" and a glutathione matrix that binds a recombinant protein linked to glutathione *S*-transferase.

Peptides Are Purified by Reversed-Phase High-Pressure Chromatography

The stationary phase matrices used in classic column chromatography are spongy materials whose compressibility limits flow of the mobile phase. High-pressure liquid chromatography (HPLC) employs incompressible silica or alumina microbeads as the stationary phase and pressures of up to a few thousand psi. Incompressible matrices permit both high flow rates and enhanced resolution. HPLC can resolve complex mixtures of lipids or peptides whose properties differ only slightly. Reversed-phase HPLC exploits a hydrophobic stationary phase of aliphatic polymers 3–18 carbon atoms in length. Peptide mixtures are eluted using a gradient of a water-miscible organic solvent such as acetonitrile or methanol.

Protein Purity Is Assessed by Polyacrylamide Gel Electrophoresis (PAGE)

The most widely used method for determining the purity of a protein is SDS-PAGE—polyacrylamide gel electrophoresis (PAGE) in the presence of the anionic detergent sodium dodecyl sulfate (SDS). Electrophoresis separates charged biomolecules based on the rates at which they migrate in an applied electrical field. For SDS-PAGE, acrylamide is polymerized and cross-linked to form a porous matrix. SDS denatures and binds to proteins at a ratio of one molecule of SDS per two peptide bonds. When used in conjunction with 2-mercaptoethanol or dithiothreitol to reduce and break disulfide bonds (Figure 4–4), SDS separates the component polypeptides of multimeric proteins. The large number of anionic SDS molecules, each bearing a charge of −1, on each polypeptide overwhelms the charge contributions of the amino acid functional groups. Since the charge-to-mass ratio of each SDS-polypeptide complex is approximately equal, the physical resistance each peptide encounters as it moves through the acrylamide matrix determines the rate of migration. Since large complexes encounter greater resistance, polypeptides separate based on their relative molecular mass (M_r). Individual polypeptides trapped in the acrylamide gel are visualized by staining with dyes such as Coomassie blue (Figure 4–5).

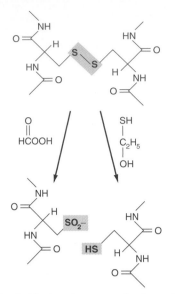

Figure 4–4. Oxidative cleavage of adjacent polypeptide chains linked by disulfide bonds (shaded) by performic acid **(left)** or reductive cleavage by β-mercaptoethanol **(right)** forms two peptides that contain cysteic acid residues or cysteinyl residues, respectively.

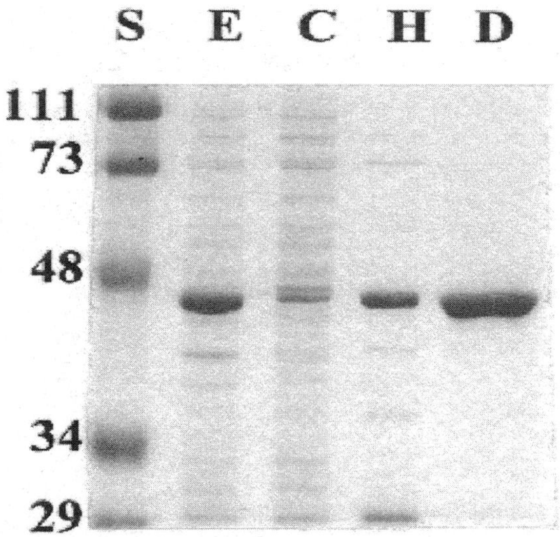

S E C H D

111
73

48

34

29

Figure 4–5. Use of SDS-PAGE to observe successive purification of a recombinant protein. The gel was stained with Coomassie blue. Shown are protein standards (lane **S**) of the indicated mass, crude cell extract **(E),** cytosol **(C),** high-speed supernatant liquid **(H),** and the DEAE-Sepharose fraction **(D).** The recombinant protein has a mass of about 45 kDa.

Isoelectric Focusing (IEF)

Ionic buffers called ampholytes and an applied electric field are used to generate a pH gradient within a polyacrylamide matrix. Applied proteins migrate until they reach the region of the matrix where the pH matches their isoelectric point (pI), the pH at which a molecule's net charge is zero. IEF is used in conjunction with SDS-PAGE for two-dimensional electrophoresis, which separates polypeptides based on pI in one dimension and based on M_r in the second (Figure 4–6). Two-dimensional electrophoresis is particularly well suited for separating the components of complex mixtures of proteins.

SANGER WAS THE FIRST TO DETERMINE THE SEQUENCE OF A POLYPEPTIDE

Mature insulin consists of the 21-residue A chain and the 30-residue B chain linked by disulfide bonds. Frederick Sanger reduced the disulfide bonds (Figure 4–4), separated the A and B chains, and cleaved each chain into smaller peptides using trypsin, chymotrypsin, and pepsin. The resulting peptides were then isolated and treated with acid to hydrolyze peptide bonds and generate peptides with as few as two or three amino acids. Each peptide was reacted with 1-fluoro-2,4-dinitrobenzene (Sanger's reagent), which derivatizes the exposed α-amino group of amino terminal residues. The amino acid content of each peptide was then determined. While the ε-amino group of lysine also reacts with Sanger's reagent, amino-terminal lysines can be distinguished from those at other positions because they react with 2 mol of Sanger's reagent. Working backward to larger fragments enabled Sanger to determine the complete sequence of insulin, an accomplishment for which he received a Nobel Prize in 1958.

THE EDMAN REACTION ENABLES PEPTIDES & PROTEINS TO BE SEQUENCED

Pehr Edman introduced phenylisothiocyanate (Edman's reagent) to selectively label the amino-terminal residue of a peptide. In contrast to Sanger's reagent, the phenylthiohydantoin (PTH) derivative can be removed under mild conditions to generate a new amino terminal residue (Figure 4–7). Successive rounds of derivatization with Edman's reagent can therefore be used to sequence many residues of a single sample of peptide. While the first 20–30 residues of a peptide can readily be determined by the Edman method, most polypeptides contain several hundred amino acids. Consequently, most polypeptides must first be cleaved into smaller peptides prior to Edman sequencing. Cleavage

pH = 3   pH = 10

⟵————————————— IEF —————————————⟶

SDS
PAGE

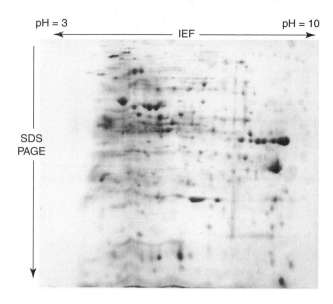

Figure 4–6. Two-dimensional IEF-SDS-PAGE. The gel was stained with Coomassie blue. A crude bacterial extract was first subjected to isoelectric focusing (IEF) in a pH 3–10 gradient. The IEF gel was then placed horizontally on the top of an SDS gel, and the proteins then further resolved by SDS-PAGE. Notice the greatly improved resolution of distinct polypeptides relative to ordinary SDS-PAGE gel (Figure 4–5).

also may be necessary to circumvent posttranslational modifications that render a protein's α-amino group "blocked," or unreactive with the Edman reagent.

It usually is necessary to generate several peptides using more than one method of cleavage. This reflects both inconsistency in the spacing of chemically or enzymatically susceptible cleavage sites and the need for sets of peptides whose sequences overlap so one can infer the sequence of the polypeptide from which they derive. Following cleavage, the resulting peptides are purified by reversed-phase HPLC and sequenced.

MOLECULAR BIOLOGY REVOLUTIONIZED THE DETERMINATION OF PRIMARY STRUCTURE

Knowledge of DNA sequences permits deduction of the primary structures of polypeptides. DNA sequencing requires only minute amounts of DNA and can readily yield the sequence of hundreds of nucleotides. To clone and sequence the DNA that encodes a particular protein, some means of identifying the correct clone—eg, knowledge of a portion of its nucleotide sequence—is essential. A hybrid approach thus has emerged. Edman sequencing is used to provide a partial amino acid sequence. Oligonucleotide primers modeled on this partial sequence can then be used to identify clones or to amplify the appropriate gene by the polymerase chain reaction (PCR) (see Chapter 39). Once an authentic DNA clone is obtained, its oligonucleotide sequence can be determined and the genetic code used to infer the primary structure of the encoded polypeptide.

The hybrid approach enhances the speed and efficiency of primary structure analysis and the range of proteins that can be sequenced. It also circumvents obstacles such as the presence of an amino-terminal blocking group or the lack of a key overlap peptide. Only a few segments of primary structure must be determined by Edman analysis.

DNA sequencing reveals the order in which amino acids are added to the nascent polypeptide chain as it is synthesized on the ribosome. However, it provides no information about posttranslational modifications such as proteolytic processing, methylation, glycosylation, phosphorylation, hydroxylation of proline and lysine, and disulfide bond formation that accompany maturation. While Edman sequencing can detect the presence of most posttranslational events, technical limitations often prevent identification of a specific modification.

MASS SPECTROMETRY DETECTS COVALENT MODIFICATIONS

On account of its superior sensitivity, speed, and versatility, mass spectrometry (MS) has replaced the Edman method as the principle method for determining the sequences of peptides and proteins. Similarly, the posttranslational modification of proteins by the addition or deletion of carbohydrate moieties, phosphoryl, hydroxyl, or other groups adds or subtracts specific and readily identified increments of mass (Table 4–1). Mass spectrometry, which discriminates molecules based solely on their mass, thus can detect the comparatively subtle physical changes in proteins that occur during the life cycle of a cell or organism. A sample in a vacuum is vaporized under conditions where protonation can occur, imparting positive charge. An electrical field then propels the cations through a magnetic field, which

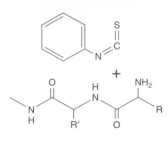

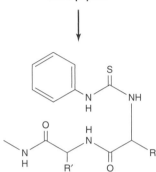

**Phenylisothiocyanate (Edman reagent)
and a peptide**

A phenylthiohydantoic acid

H^+, nitro-
methane H_2O

**A phenylthiohydantoin and a peptide
shorter by one residue**

Figure 4–7. The Edman reaction. Phenylisothiocyanate derivatizes the amino-terminal residue of a peptide as a phenylthiohydantoic acid. Treatment with acid in a non-hydroxylic solvent releases a phenylthiohydantoin, which is subsequently identified by its chromatographic mobility, and a peptide one residue shorter. The process is then repeated.

Table 4–1. Mass increases resulting from common posttranslational modifications.

Modification	Mass Increase (Da)
Phosphorylation	80
Hydroxylation	16
Methylation	14
Acetylation	42
Myristylation	210
Palmitoylation	238
Glycosylation	162

they are accelerated—and hence the time required to reach the detector—will be inversely proportionate to their mass.

Conventional mass spectrometers generally are used to determine the masses of molecules of 1000 Da or less, whereas time-of-flight mass spectrometers are suited for determining the large masses of proteins. The analysis of peptides and proteins by mass spectometry initially was hindered by difficulties in volatilizing large organic molecules. However, matrix-assisted laser-desorption (MALDI) and electrospray dispersion (eg, nanospray) permit the masses of even large polypeptides (> 100,000 Da) to be determined with extraordinary accuracy (± 1 Da). Using electrospray dispersion, peptides eluting from a reversed-phase HPLC column are

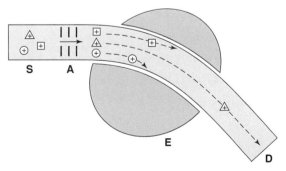

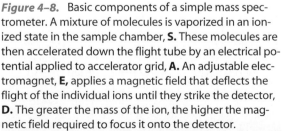

Figure 4–8. Basic components of a simple mass spectrometer. A mixture of molecules is vaporized in an ionized state in the sample chamber, **S.** These molecules are then accelerated down the flight tube by an electrical potential applied to accelerator grid, **A.** An adjustable electromagnet, **E,** applies a magnetic field that deflects the flight of the individual ions until they strike the detector, **D.** The greater the mass of the ion, the higher the magnetic field required to focus it onto the detector.

deflects them at a right angle to their original direction of flight and focuses them onto a detector (Figure 4–8). The magnetic force required to deflect the path of each ionic species onto the detector, measured as the current applied to the electromagnet, is recorded. For ions of identical net charge, this force is proportionate to their mass. In a time-of-flight mass spectrometer, a briefly applied electric field accelerates the ions towards a detector that records the time at which each ion arrives. For molecules of identical charge, the velocity to which

introduced directly into the mass spectrometer for immediate determination of their masses.

Peptides inside the mass spectrometer can be broken down into smaller units by collisions with neutral helium atoms (collision-induced dissociation), and the masses of the individual fragments determined. Since peptide bonds are much more labile than carbon-carbon bonds, the most abundant fragments will differ from one another by units equivalent to one or two amino acids. Since—with the exception of leucine and isoleucine—the molecular mass of each amino acid is unique, the sequence of the peptide can be reconstructed from the masses of its fragments.

Tandem Mass Spectrometry

Complex peptide mixtures can now be analyzed without prior purification by tandem mass spectrometry, which employs the equivalent of two mass spectrometers linked in series. The first spectrometer separates individual peptides based upon their differences in mass. By adjusting the field strength of the first magnet, a single peptide can be directed into the second mass spectrometer, where fragments are generated and their masses determined.

Tandem Mass Spectrometry Can Detect Metabolic Abnormalities

Tandem mass spectrometry can be used to screen blood samples from newborns for the presence and concentrations of amino acids, fatty acids, and other metabolites. Abnormalities in metabolite levels can serve as diagnostic indicators for a variety of genetic disorders, such as phenylketonuria, ethylmalonic encephalopathy, and glutaric acidemia type 1.

GENOMICS ENABLES PROTEINS TO BE IDENTIFIED FROM SMALL AMOUNTS OF SEQUENCE DATA

Primary structure analysis has been revolutionized by genomics, the application of automated oligonucleotide sequencing and computerized data retrieval and analysis to sequence an organism's entire genetic complement. Since the determination in 1995 of the complete genome sequence of *Haemophilus influenza,* the genomes of hundreds of organisms have been deciphered. Where genome sequence is known, the task of determining a protein's DNA-derived primary sequence is materially simplified. In essence, the second half of the hybrid approach has already been completed. All that remains is to acquire sufficient information to permit the open reading frame (ORF) that encodes the protein to be retrieved from an Internet-accessible genome database and identified. In some cases, a segment of amino acid sequence only four or five residues in length may be sufficient to identify the correct ORF.

Computerized search algorithms assist the identification of the gene encoding a given protein. In peptide mass profiling, for example, a peptide digest is introduced into the mass spectrometer and the sizes of the peptides are determined. A computer is then used to find an ORF whose predicted protein product would, if broken down into peptides by the cleavage method selected, produce a set of peptides whose masses match those observed by mass spectrometry.

PROTEOMICS & THE PROTEOME

The Goal of Proteomics Is to Identify the Entire Complement of Proteins Elaborated by a Cell under Diverse Conditions

While the sequence of the human genome is known, the picture provided by genomics alone is both static and incomplete. Proteomics aims to identify the entire complement of proteins elaborated by a cell under diverse conditions. As genes are switched on and off, proteins are synthesized in particular cell types at specific times of growth or differentiation and in response to external stimuli. Muscle cells express proteins not expressed by neural cells, and the type of subunits present in the hemoglobin tetramer undergo change pre- and postpartum. Many proteins undergo post-translational modifications during maturation into functionally competent forms or as a means of regulating their properties. Knowledge of the human genome therefore represents only the beginning of the task of describing living organisms in molecular detail and understanding the dynamics of processes such as growth, aging, and disease. As the human body contains thousands of cell types, each containing thousands of proteins, the proteome—the set of all the proteins expressed by an individual cell at a particular time—represents a moving target of formidable dimensions.

Two-Dimensional Electrophoresis & Gene Array Chips Are Used to Survey Protein Expression

One goal of proteomics is the identification of proteins whose levels of expression correlate with medically significant events. The presumption is that proteins whose appearance or disappearance is associated with a specific physiologic condition or disease will provide insights into root causes and mechanisms. Determination of the proteomes characteristic of each cell type requires the utmost efficiency in the isolation and identification of individual proteins. The contemporary approach utilizes robotic automation to speed sample preparation

and large two-dimensional gels to resolve cellular proteins. Individual polypeptides are then extracted and analyzed by Edman sequencing or mass spectroscopy. While only about 1000 proteins can be resolved on a single gel, two-dimensional electrophoresis has a major advantage in that it examines the proteins themselves. An alternative and complementary approach employs gene arrays, sometimes called DNA chips, to detect the expression of the mRNAs that encode proteins. While changes in the expression of the mRNA encoding a protein do not necessarily reflect comparable changes in the level of the corresponding protein, gene arrays are more sensitive probes than two-dimensional gels and thus can examine more gene products.

Bioinformatics Assists Identification of Protein Functions

The functions of a large proportion of the proteins encoded by the human genome are presently unknown. The development of protein arrays or chips for directly testing the potential functions of proteins on a mass scale remains in its infancy. However, recent advances in bioinformatics permit researchers to compare amino acid sequences to discover clues to potential properties, physiologic roles, and mechanisms of action of proteins. Algorithms exploit the tendency of nature to employ variations of a structural theme to perform similar functions in several proteins [eg, the Rossmann nucleotide binding fold to bind NAD(P)H, nuclear targeting sequences, and EF hands to bind Ca^{2+}]. These domains generally are detected in the primary structure by conservation of particular amino acids at key positions. Insights into the properties and physiologic role of a newly discovered protein thus may be inferred by comparing its primary structure with that of known proteins.

SUMMARY

- Long amino acid polymers or polypeptides constitute the basic structural unit of proteins, and the structure of a protein provides insight into how it fulfills its functions.

- Proteins undergo posttransitional alterations during their lifetime that influence their function and determine their fate.

- The Edman method has been largely replaced by mass spectrometry, a sensitive and versatile tool for determining primary structure, for identifying post-translational modifications, and for detecting metabolic abnormalities.

- DNA cloning and molecular biology coupled with protein chemistry provide a hybrid approach that greatly increases the speed and efficiency for determination of primary structures of proteins.

- Genomics—the analysis of the entire oligonucleotide sequence of an organism's complete genetic material—has provided further enhancements.

- Computer algorithms facilitate identification of the open reading frames that encode a given protein by using partial sequences and peptide mass profiling to search sequence databases.

- Scientists are now trying to determine the primary sequence and functional role of every protein expressed in a living cell, known as its proteome.

- A major goal is the identification of proteins and of their posttranslational modifications whose appearance or disappearance correlates with physiologic phenomena, aging, or specific diseases.

REFERENCES

Austin CP: The impact of the completed human genome sequence on the development of novel therapeutics for human disease. Annu Rev Med 2004;55:1.

Cutler P: Protein arrays: the current state-of-the-art. Proteomics 2003;3:3.

Deutscher MP (editor): *Guide to Protein Purification.* Methods Enzymol 1990;182. (Entire volume.)

Geveart K, Vandekerckhove J: Protein identification methods in proteomics. Electrophoresis 2000;21:1145.

Khan J et al: DNA microarray technology: the anticipated impact on the study of human disease. Biochim Biophys Acta 1999;1423:M17.

Patnaik SK, Blumenfeld OO: Use of on-line tools and databases for routine sequence analyses. Anal Biochem 2001;289:1.

Rinaldo P, Tortorelli S, Matern D: Recent developments and new applications of tandem mass spectrometry in newborn screening. Curr Opin Pediatrics 2004;16:427.

Rodland KD: Proteomics and cancer diagnosis: the potential of mass spectrometry. Clin Biochem 2004;37:579.

Schena M et al: Quantitative monitoring of gene expression patterns with a complementary DNA microarray. Science 1995;270:467.

Semsarian C, Seidman CE: Molecular medicine in the 21st century. Intern Med J 2001;31:53.

Temple LK et al: Essays on science and society: defining disease in the genomics era. Science 2001;293:807.

Wilkins MR et al: High-throughput mass spectrometric discovery of protein post-translational modifications. J Mol Biol 1999;289:645.

Woodage T, Broder S: The human genome and comparative genomics: understanding human evolution, biology, and medicine. J Gastroenterol 2003;15:68.

Proteins: Higher Orders of Structure

Peter J. Kennelly, PhD, & Victor W. Rodwell, PhD

BIOMEDICAL IMPORTANCE

In nature, form follows function. In order for a newly synthesized polypeptide to mature into a biologically functional protein capable of catalyzing a metabolic reaction, powering cellular motion, or forming the macromolecular rods and cables that provide structural integrity to hair, bones, tendons, and teeth, it must fold into a specific three dimensional arrangement, or **conformation.** In addition, during maturation **posttranslational modifications** may add new chemical groups or remove transiently needed peptide segments. Genetic or nutritional deficiencies that impede protein maturation are deleterious to health. Examples of the former include Creutzfeldt-Jakob disease, scrapie, Alzheimer's disease, and bovine spongiform encephalopathy ("mad cow disease"). Scurvy represents a nutritional deficiency that impairs protein maturation.

CONFORMATION VERSUS CONFIGURATION

The terms configuration and conformation are often confused. **Configuration** refers to the geometric relationship between a given set of atoms, for example, those that distinguish L- from D-amino acids. Interconversion of *configurational* alternatives requires breaking covalent bonds. **Conformation** refers to the spatial relationship of every atom in a molecule. Interconversion between conformers occurs without covalent bond rupture, with retention of configuration, and typically via rotation about single bonds.

PROTEINS WERE INITIALLY CLASSIFIED BY THEIR GROSS CHARACTERISTICS

Scientists initially approached structure-function relationships in proteins by separating them into classes based upon properties such as solubility, shape, or the presence of nonprotein groups. For example, the proteins that can be extracted from cells using aqueous solutions at physiologic pH and ionic strength are classified as **soluble.** Extraction of **integral membrane proteins** requires dissolution of the membrane with detergents. **Globular proteins** are compact, roughly spherical molecules that have **axial ratios** (the ratio of their shortest to longest dimensions) of not over 3. Most enzymes are globular proteins. By contrast, many structural proteins adopt highly extended conformations. These **fibrous proteins** possess axial ratios of 10 or more.

Lipoproteins and **glycoproteins** contain covalently bound lipid and carbohydrate, respectively. Myoglobin, hemoglobin, cytochromes, and many other **metalloproteins** contain tightly associated metal ions. More precise classification schemes have emerged based upon similarity, or **homology,** in amino acid sequence and three-dimensional structure. However, many early classification terms remain in use.

PROTEINS ARE CONSTRUCTED USING MODULAR PRINCIPLES

Proteins perform complex physical and catalytic functions by positioning specific chemical groups in a precise three-dimensional arrangement. The polypeptide scaffold containing these groups must adopt a conformation that is both functionally efficient and physically strong. At first glance, the biosynthesis of polypeptides comprised of tens of thousands of individual atoms would appear to be extremely challenging. When one considers that a typical polypeptide can adopt $\geq 10^{50}$ distinct conformations, folding into the conformation appropriate to their biologic function would appear to be even more difficult. As described in Chapters 3 and 4, synthesis of the polypeptide backbones of proteins employs a small set of common building blocks or modules, the amino acids, joined by a common linkage, the peptide bond. A stepwise modular pathway simplifies the folding and processing of newly synthesized polypeptides into mature proteins.

THE FOUR ORDERS OF PROTEIN STRUCTURE

The modular nature of protein synthesis and folding are embodied in the concept of orders of protein structure: **primary structure,** the sequence of the amino acids in a polypeptide chain; **secondary structure,** the folding of short (3- to 30-residue), contiguous segments of

polypeptide into geometrically ordered units; **tertiary structure,** the assembly of secondary structural units into larger functional units such as the mature polypeptide and its component domains; and **quaternary structure,** the number and types of polypeptide units of oligomeric proteins and their spatial arrangement.

SECONDARY STRUCTURE

Peptide Bonds Restrict Possible Secondary Conformations

Free rotation is possible about only two of the three covalent bonds of the polypeptide backbone: the α-carbon (Cα) to the carbonyl carbon (Co) bond, and the Cα to nitrogen bond (Figure 3–4). The partial double-bond character of the peptide bond that links Co to the α-nitrogen requires that the carbonyl carbon, carbonyl oxygen, and α-nitrogen remain coplanar, thus preventing rotation. The angle about the Cα—N bond is termed the phi (Φ) angle, and that about the Co—Cα bond the psi (ψ) angle. For amino acids other than glycine, most combinations of phi and psi angles are disallowed because of steric hindrance (Figure 5–1). The conformations of proline are even more restricted due to the absence of free rotation of the N—Cα bond.

Regions of ordered secondary structure arise when a series of aminoacyl residues adopt similar phi and psi angles. Extended segments of polypeptide (eg, loops) can possess a variety of such angles. The angles that define the two most common types of secondary structure, the α **helix** and the β **sheet,** fall within the lower and upper left-hand quadrants of a Ramachandran plot, respectively (Figure 5–1).

The Alpha Helix

The polypeptide backbone of an α helix is twisted by an equal amount about each α-carbon with a phi angle of approximately −57 degrees and a psi angle of approximately −47 degrees. A complete turn of the helix contains an average of 3.6 aminoacyl residues, and the distance it rises per turn (its *pitch*) is 0.54 nm (Figure 5–2). The R groups of each aminoacyl residue in an α helix face outward (Figure 5–3). Proteins contain only L-amino acids, for which a right-handed α helix is by far the more stable, and only right-handed α helices are present in proteins. Schematic diagrams of proteins represent α helices as cylinders.

The stability of an α helix arises primarily from hydrogen bonds formed between the oxygen of the peptide bond carbonyl and the hydrogen atom of the peptide bond nitrogen of the fourth residue down the polypeptide chain (Figure 5–4). The ability to form the maximum number of hydrogen bonds, supplemented by van der Waals interactions in the core of this tightly

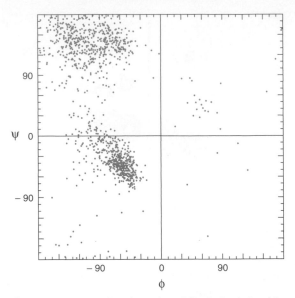

Figure 5–1. Ramachandran plot of the main chain phi (Φ) and psi (ψ) angles for approximately 1000 nonglycine residues in 8 proteins whose structures were solved at high resolution. The dots represent allowable combinations and the spaces prohibited combinations of phi and psi angles. (Reproduced, with permission, from Richardson JS: The anatomy and taxonomy of protein structures. Adv Protein Chem 1981;34:167. Copyright © 1981. Reprinted with permission from Elsevier.)

packed structure, provides the thermodynamic driving force for the formation of an α helix. Since the peptide bond nitrogen of proline lacks a hydrogen atom to contribute to a hydrogen bond, proline can only be stably accommodated within the first turn of an α helix. When present elsewhere, proline disrupts the conformation of the helix, producing a bend. Because of its small size, glycine also often induces bends in α helices.

Many α helices have predominantly hydrophobic R groups on one side of the axis of the helix and predominantly hydrophilic ones on the other. These **amphipathic helices** are well adapted to the formation of interfaces between polar and nonpolar regions such as the hydrophobic interior of a protein and its aqueous environment. Clusters of amphipathic helices can create a channel, or pore, that permits specific polar molecules to pass through hydrophobic cell membranes.

The Beta Sheet

The second (hence "beta") recognizable regular secondary structure in proteins is the β sheet. The amino acid residues of a β sheet, when viewed edge-on, form a zigzag or pleated pattern in which the R groups of

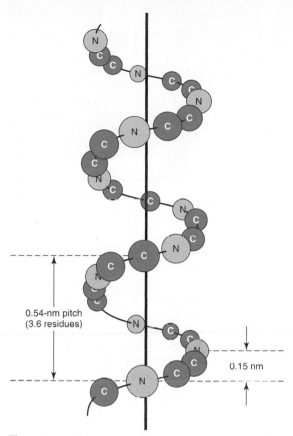

Figure 5–2. Orientation of the main chain atoms of a peptide about the axis of an α helix.

0.54-nm pitch
(3.6 residues)

0.15 nm

adjacent residues point in opposite directions. Unlike the compact backbone of the α helix, the peptide backbone of the β sheet is highly extended. But like the α helix, β sheets derive much of their stability from hydrogen bonds between the carbonyl oxygens and amide hydrogens of peptide bonds. However, in contrast to the α helix, these bonds are formed with adjacent segments of β sheet (Figure 5–5).

Interacting β sheets can be arranged either to form a **parallel** β sheet, in which the adjacent segments of the polypeptide chain proceed in the same direction amino to carboxyl, or an **antiparallel** sheet, in which they proceed in opposite directions (Figure 5–5). Either configuration permits the maximum number of hydrogen bonds between segments, or strands, of the sheet. Most β sheets are not perfectly flat but tend to have a right-handed twist. Clusters of twisted strands of β sheet form the core of many globular proteins (Figure 5–6). Schematic diagrams represent β sheets as arrows that point in the amino to carboxyl terminal direction.

Loops & Bends

Roughly half of the residues in a "typical" globular protein reside in α helices and β sheets and half in loops, turns, bends, and other extended conformational features. Turns and bends refer to short segments of amino acids that join two units of secondary structure, such as two adjacent strands of an antiparallel β sheet. A β turn involves four aminoacyl residues, in which the first residue is hydrogen-bonded to the fourth, resulting in a tight 180-degree turn (Figure 5–7). Proline and glycine often are present in β turns.

Loops are regions that contain residues beyond the minimum number necessary to connect adjacent regions of secondary structure. Irregular in conformation, loops nevertheless serve key biologic roles. For many enzymes, the loops that bridge domains responsible for binding substrates often contain aminoacyl residues that participate in catalysis. **Helix-loop-helix motifs** provide the oligonucleotide-binding portion of DNA-binding proteins such as repressors and transcription factors. Structural motifs such as the helix-loop-helix motif that are intermediate between secondary and tertiary structures are often termed **supersecondary structures.** Since many loops and bends reside on the surface of proteins and are thus exposed to solvent, they constitute readily accessible sites, or **epitopes,** for recognition and binding of antibodies.

While loops lack apparent structural regularity, they exist in a specific conformation stabilized through hydro-

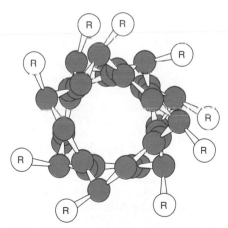

Figure 5–3. View down the axis of an α helix. The side chains (R) are on the outside of the helix. The van der Waals radii of the atoms are larger than shown here; hence, there is almost no free space inside the helix. (Slightly modified and reproduced, with permission, from Stryer L: *Biochemistry,* 3rd ed. Freeman, 1995. Copyright © 1995 W.H. Freeman and Company.)

spatially to one another. A **domain** is a section of protein structure sufficient to perform a particular chemical or physical task such as binding of a substrate or other ligand. Other domains may anchor a protein to a membrane or interact with a regulatory molecule that modulates its function. A small polypeptide such as triose phosphate isomerase (Figure 5–6) or myoglobin (Chapter 6) may consist of a single domain. By contrast, protein kinases contain two domains. Protein kinases catalyze the transfer of a phosphoryl group from ATP to a peptide or protein. The amino terminal portion of the polypeptide, which is rich in β sheet, binds ATP, while the carboxyl terminal domain, which is rich in α helix, binds the peptide or protein substrate (Figure 5–8). The groups that catalyze phosphoryl transfer reside in a loop positioned at the interface of the two domains.

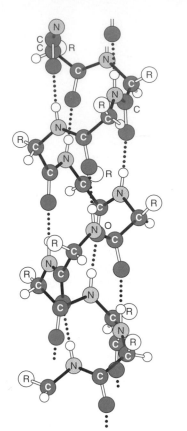

Figure 5–4. Hydrogen bonds (dotted lines) formed between H and O atoms stabilize a polypeptide in an α-helical conformation. (Reprinted, with permission, from Haggis GH et al: *Introduction to Molecular Biology.* Wiley, 1964. Reprinted with permission of Pearson Education Limited.)

gen bonding, salt bridges, and hydrophobic interactions with other portions of the protein. However, not all portions of proteins are necessarily ordered. Proteins may contain "disordered" regions, often at the extreme amino or carboxyl terminal, characterized by high conformational flexibility. In many instances, these disordered regions assume an ordered conformation upon binding of a ligand. This structural flexibility enables such regions to act as ligand-controlled switches that affect protein structure and function.

Tertiary & Quaternary Structure

The term "tertiary structure" refers to the entire three-dimensional conformation of a polypeptide. It indicates, in three-dimensional space, how secondary structural features—helices, sheets, bends, turns, and loops—assemble to form domains and how these domains relate

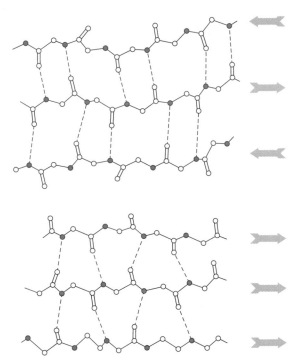

Figure 5–5. Spacing and bond angles of the hydrogen bonds of antiparallel and parallel pleated β sheets. Arrows indicate the direction of each strand. The hydrogen-donating α-nitrogen atoms are shown as color circles. Hydrogen bonds are indicated by dotted lines. For clarity in presentation, R groups and hydrogens are omitted. **Top:** Antiparallel β sheet. Pairs of hydrogen bonds alternate between being close together and wide apart and are oriented approximately perpendicular to the polypeptide backbone. **Bottom:** Parallel β sheet. The hydrogen bonds are evenly spaced but slant in alternate directions.

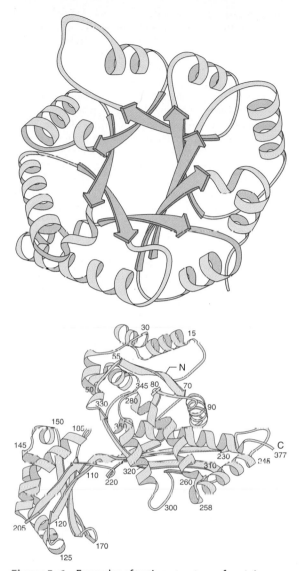

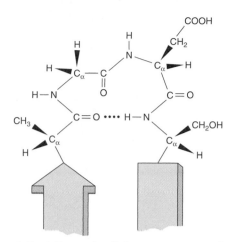

Figure 5–7. A β-turn that links two segments of anti-parallel β sheet. The dotted line indicates the hydrogen bond between the first and fourth amino acids of the four-residue segment Ala-Gly-Asp-Ser.

Figure 5–6. Examples of tertiary structure of proteins. **Top:** The enzyme triose phosphate isomerase. Note the elegant and symmetrical arrangement of alternating β sheets and α helices. (Courtesy of J Richardson.) **Bottom:** Two-domain structure of the subunit of a homodimeric enzyme, a bacterial class II HMG-CoA reductase. As indicated by the numbered residues, the single polypeptide begins in the large domain, enters the small domain, and ends in the large domain. (Courtesy of C Lawrence, V Rodwell, and C Stauffacher, Purdue University.)

In some cases, proteins are assembled from more than one polypeptide, or protomer. Quaternary structure defines the polypeptide composition of a protein and, for an oligomeric protein, the spatial relationships between its subunits or protomers. **Monomeric** proteins consist of a single polypeptide chain. **Dimeric** proteins contain two polypeptide chains. **Homodimers** contain two copies of the same polypeptide chain, while in a **heterodimer** the polypeptides differ. Greek letters (α, β, γ, etc) are used to distinguish different subunits of a heterooligomeric protein, and subscripts indicate the number of each subunit type. For example, α_4 designates a homotetrameric protein, and $\alpha_2\beta_2\gamma$ a protein with five subunits of three different types.

Since even small proteins contain many thousands of atoms, depictions of protein structure that indicate the position of every atom are generally too complex to be readily interpreted. Simplified schematic diagrams thus are used to depict key features of a protein's tertiary and quaternary structure. Ribbon diagrams (Figures 5–6 and 5–8) trace the conformation of the polypeptide backbone, with cylinders and arrows indicating regions of α helix and β sheet, respectively. In an even simpler representation, line segments that link the α carbons indicate the path of the polypeptide backbone. These schematic diagrams often include the side chains of selected amino acids that emphasize specific structure-function relationships.

MULTIPLE FACTORS STABILIZE TERTIARY & QUATERNARY STRUCTURE

Higher orders of protein structure are stabilized primarily—and often exclusively—by noncovalent interactions. Principal among these are hydrophobic interactions that drive most hydrophobic amino acid side chains into the interior of the protein, shielding them

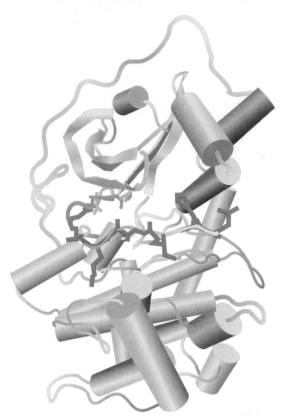

Figure 5–8. Domain structure. Protein kinases contain two domains. The upper, amino terminal domain binds the phosphoryl donor ATP (light color). The lower, carboxyl terminal domain is shown binding a synthetic peptide substrate (dark color).

from water. Other significant contributors include hydrogen bonds and salt bridges between the carboxylates of aspartic and glutamic acid and the oppositely charged side chains of protonated lysyl, argininyl, and histidyl residues. While individually weak relative to a typical covalent bond of 80–120 kcal/mol, collectively these numerous interactions confer a high degree of stability to the biologically functional conformation of a protein, just as a Velcro fastener harnesses the cumulative strength of multiple plastic loops and hooks.

Some proteins contain covalent disulfide (S—S) bonds that link the sulfhydryl groups of cysteinyl residues. Formation of disulfide bonds involves oxidation of the cysteinyl sulfhydryl groups and requires oxygen. Intrapolypeptide disulfide bonds further enhance the stability of the folded conformation of a peptide, while interpolypeptide disulfide bonds stabilize the quaternary structure of certain oligomeric proteins.

THREE-DIMENSIONAL STRUCTURE IS DETERMINED BY X-RAY CRYSTALLOGRAPHY OR BY NMR SPECTROSCOPY

X-Ray Crystallography

Following the solution in 1960 by John Kendrew of the three-dimensional structure of myoglobin, x-ray crystallography revealed the structures of thousands of proteins and of many viruses. For solution of its structure by x-ray crystallography, a protein is first precipitated under conditions that form large, well-ordered crystals. To establish appropriate conditions, crystallization trials use a few microliters of protein solution and a matrix of variables (temperature, pH, presence of salts or organic solutes such as polyethylene glycol) to establish optimal conditions for crystal formation. Crystals mounted in quartz capillaries are first irradiated with monochromatic x-rays of approximate wavelength 0.15 nm to confirm that they are protein, not salt. Protein crystals are then frozen in liquid nitrogen for subsequent collection of a high-resolution data set. The diffraction patterns formed as the x-rays are diffracted by the atoms in their path are recorded on a photographic plate or its computer equivalent as a circular pattern of spots of varying intensity. The data inherent in these spots is then analyzed using a mathematical approach termed a *Fourier synthesis,* which summates wave functions. The wave amplitudes are related to spot intensity, but since the waves are not in phase, the relationship between their phases must next be determined. The traditional approach to solution of the "phase problem" uses **isomorphous displacement.** Prior to irradiation, an atom with a distinctive x-ray "signature" is introduced into a crystal at known positions in the primary structure of the protein. Heavy atom isomorphous displacement generally uses mercury or uranium, which bind to cysteine residues. An alternative approach uses the expression of plasmid-encoded recombinant proteins in which selenium replaces the sulfur of methionine. Expression uses a bacterial host auxotrophic for methionine biosynthesis and a defined medium in which selenomethionine replaces methionine. The most recent approach exploits the ever-increasing numbers of published three-dimensional structures. If the unknown structure is similar to one that has been solved, **molecular replacement** on an existing model avoids the heavy atom approach and provides an attractive way to phase the data. Finally, the results from the phasing and Fourier summations provide an electron density profile or three-dimensional map of how the atoms are connected or related to one another.

Laue X-Ray Crystallography

The ability of some crystallized enzymes to catalyze chemical reactions strongly suggests that structures

determined by crystallography are indeed representative of the structures present in free solution. Classic crystallography provides, however, an essentially static picture of a protein that may undergo significant structural changes such as those that accompany enzymic catalysis. The Laue approach uses diffraction of polychromatic x-rays, and many crystals. The time-consuming process of rotating the crystal in the x-ray beam is avoided, which permits the use of extremely short exposure times. Detection of the motions of residues or domains of an enzyme during catalysis uses crystals that contain an inactive or "caged" substrate analog that becomes a substrate only after exposure to a flash of visible light. This initiates catalysis. The data collected over times as short as a few nanoseconds may then be analyzed to reveal structural changes that occur during catalysis.

Nuclear Magnetic Resonance Spectroscopy

Nuclear magnetic resonance (NMR) spectroscopy, a powerful complement to x-ray crystallography, measures the absorbance of radio frequency electromagnetic energy by certain atomic nuclei. "NMR-active" isotopes of biologically relevant elements include ^1H, ^{13}C, ^{15}N, and ^{31}P. The frequency, or chemical shift, at which a particular nucleus absorbs energy is a function of both the functional group within which it resides and the proximity of other NMR-active nuclei. Two-dimensional NMR spectroscopy permits a three-dimensional representation of a protein to be constructed by determining the proximity of these nuclei to one another. NMR spectroscopy analyzes proteins in aqueous solution, obviating the need to form crystals. It thus is possible to observe changes in conformation that accompany ligand binding or catalysis using NMR spectroscopy. However, only the spectra of relatively small proteins, ≤ 30 kDa in size, can be analyzed with current technology.

Molecular Modeling

An increasingly useful adjunct to the empirical determination of the three-dimensional structure of proteins is the use of computer technology for molecular modeling. When the three-dimensional structure is known, **molecular dynamics** programs can be used to simulate the conformational dynamics of a protein and the manner in which factors such as temperature, pH, ionic strength, or amino acid substitutions influence these motions. **Molecular docking** programs simulate the interactions that take place when a protein encounters a substrate, inhibitor, or other ligand. Virtual screening for molecules likely to interact with key sites on a protein of biomedical interest is extensively used to facilitate the discovery of new drugs. In **homology modeling,** the known three-dimensional structure of a protein

is used as a template to build a model of the probable structure of a related protein. Eventually, scientists hope to devise computer programs that can predict the three-dimensional conformation of a protein directly from its primary sequence.

PROTEIN FOLDING

Proteins are conformationally dynamic molecules that can fold and unfold in a time frame of milliseconds, and can undergo unfolding and refolding hundreds or thousands of times during their lifetime. How is this remarkable process of folding achieved? Folding into the native state does not involve an exhaustive search of all possible structures. Denatured proteins are not just random coils. Native contacts are favored, and regions of native structure persist even in the denatured state. Ribosomes may participate the first time the protein is folded, although not in subsequent folding or after a protein has been translocated into an organelle. The extremely high concentrations of proteins in cells can also affect the kinetics of protein folding. Discussed below are factors that facilitate folding and refolding, and the current concepts and proposed mechanisms based on more than 40 years of largely in vitro experimentation.

The Native Conformation of a Protein Is Thermodynamically Favored

The number of distinct combinations of phi and psi angles specifying potential conformations of even a relatively small—15-kDa—polypeptide is unbelievably vast. Proteins are guided through this vast labyrinth of possibilities by thermodynamics. Since the biologically relevant—or native—conformation of a protein generally is that which is most energetically favored, knowledge of the native conformation is specified in the primary sequence. However, if one were to wait for a polypeptide to find its native conformation by random exploration of all possible conformations, the process would require billions of years to complete. Clearly, protein folding in cells takes place in a more orderly and guided fashion.

Folding Is Modular

Protein folding generally occurs via a stepwise process. In the first stage, as the newly synthesized polypeptide emerges from the ribosomes, short segments fold into secondary structural units that provide local regions of organized structure. Folding is now reduced to the selection of an appropriate arrangement of this relatively small number of secondary structural elements. In the second stage, the forces that drive hydrophobic regions into the interior of the protein away from sol-

vent drive the partially folded polypeptide into a "molten globule" in which the modules of secondary structure rearrange to arrive at the mature conformation of the protein. This process is orderly, but not rigid. Considerable flexibility exists in the ways and in the order in which elements of secondary structure can be rearranged. In general, each element of secondary or supersecondary structure facilitates proper folding by directing the folding process toward the native conformation and away from unproductive alternatives. For oligomeric proteins, individual protomers tend to fold before they associate with other subunits.

Auxiliary Proteins Assist Folding

Under appropriate in vitro conditions, many proteins will spontaneously refold after being previously **denatured** (ie, unfolded) by treatment with acid or base, chaotropic agents, or detergents. However, unlike the folding process in vivo, refolding under laboratory conditions is a far slower process. Moreover, some proteins fail to spontaneously refold in vitro, often forming insoluble **aggregates,** disordered complexes of unfolded or partially folded polypeptides held together by hydrophobic interactions. Aggregates represent unproductive dead ends in the folding process. Cells employ auxiliary proteins to speed the process of folding and to guide it toward a productive conclusion.

Chaperones

Chaperone proteins participate in the folding of over half of mammalian proteins. The hsp70 (70-kDa heat shock protein) family of chaperones binds short sequences of hydrophobic amino acids in newly synthesized polypeptides, shielding them from solvent. Chaperones prevent aggregation, thus providing an opportunity for the formation of appropriate secondary structural elements and their subsequent coalescence into a molten globule. The hsp60 family of chaperones, sometimes called **chaperonins,** differ in sequence and structure from hsp70 and its homologs. Hsp60 acts later in the folding process, often together with an hsp70 chaperone. The central cavity of the donut-shaped hsp60 chaperone provides a sheltered environment in which a polypeptide can fold until all hydrophobic regions are buried in its interior, eliminating aggregation.

Protein Disulfide Isomerase

Disulfide bonds between and within polypeptides stabilize tertiary and quaternary structure. However, disulfide bond formation is nonspecific. Under oxidizing conditions, a given cysteine can form a disulfide bond with the —SH of any accessible cysteinyl resi-

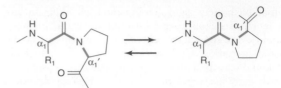

Figure 5–9. Isomerization of the *N*-α_1 prolyl peptide bond from a *cis* to a *trans* configuration relative to the backbone of the polypeptide.

due. By catalyzing disulfide exchange, the rupture of an S—S bond and its reformation with a different partner cysteine, protein disulfide isomerase facilitates the formation of disulfide bonds that stabilize a protein's native conformation.

Proline-*cis,trans*-Isomerase

All X-Pro peptide bonds—where X represents any residue—are synthesized in the *trans* configuration. However, of the X-Pro bonds of mature proteins, approximately 6% are *cis*. The *cis* configuration is particularly common in β-turns. Isomerization from *trans* to *cis* is catalyzed by the enzyme proline-*cis,trans*-isomerase (Figure 5–9).

Folding Is a Dynamic Process

Proteins are conformationally dynamic molecules that can fold and unfold hundreds or thousands of times in their lifetime. How do proteins, once unfolded, refold and restore their functional conformation? First, unfolding rarely leads to the complete randomization of the polypeptide chain inside the cell. Unfolded proteins thus retain a number of contacts and regions of secondary structure that facilitate the refolding process. Second, chaperone proteins can "rescue" unfolded proteins that have become thermodynamically trapped in a misfolded dead end by unfolding hydrophobic regions and providing a second chance to fold productively, and glutathione can reduce inappropriate disulfide bonds formed upon exposure to oxidizing agents such as O_2, hydrogen peroxide, or superoxide (Chapter 51).

PERTURBATION OF PROTEIN CONFORMATION MAY HAVE PATHOLOGIC CONSEQUENCES

Prions

The transmissible spongiform encephalopathies, or **prion diseases,** are fatal neurodegenerative diseases characterized by spongiform changes, astrocytic gliomas, and neuronal loss resulting from the deposition of

insoluble protein aggregates in neural cells. They include Creutzfeldt-Jakob disease in humans, scrapie in sheep, and bovine spongiform encephalopathy (mad cow disease) in cattle. vCJD, a variant form of Creutzfeldt-Jakob disease that afflicts younger patients, is associated with early-onset psychiatric and behavioral disorders. Prion diseases may manifest themselves as infectious, genetic, or sporadic disorders. Because no viral or bacterial gene encoding the pathologic prion protein could be identified, the source and mechanism of transmission of prion disease long remained elusive. Today it is recognized that prion diseases are protein conformation diseases transmitted by altering the conformation, and hence the physical properties, of proteins endogenous to the host. Human prion-related protein, PrP, a glycoprotein encoded on the short arm of chromosome 20, normally is monomeric and rich in α helix. Pathologic prion proteins serve as the templates for the conformational transformation of normal PrP, known as PrPc, into PrPsc. PrPsc is rich in β sheet with many hydrophobic aminoacyl side chains exposed to solvent. PrPsc molecules therefore associate strongly with one other, forming insoluble protease-resistant aggregates. Since one pathologic prion or prion-related protein can serve as template for the conformational transformation of many times its number of PrPc molecules, prion diseases can be transmitted by the protein alone without involvement of DNA or RNA.

Alzheimer's Disease

Refolding or misfolding of another protein endogenous to human brain tissue, β-amyloid, is a prominent feature of Alzheimer's disease. While the main cause of Alzheimer's disease remains elusive, the characteristic senile plaques and neurofibrillary bundles contain aggregates of the protein β-amyloid, a 4.3-kDa polypeptide produced by proteolytic cleavage of a larger protein known as amyloid precursor protein. In Alzheimer's disease patients, levels of β-amyloid become elevated, and this protein undergoes a conformational transformation from a soluble α helix–rich state to a state rich in β sheet and prone to self-aggregation. Apolipoprotein E has been implicated as a potential mediator of this conformational transformation.

Beta-Thalassemias

Thalassemias are caused by genetic defects that impair the synthesis of one of the polypeptide subunits of hemoglobin (Chapter 6). During the burst of hemoglobin synthesis that occurs during red cell development, a specific chaperone called α-hemoglobin-stabilizing protein (AHSP) binds to free hemoglobin α-subunits awaiting incorporation into the hemoglobin multimer. In the absence of this chaperone, free α-hemoglobin subunits aggregate, and the resulting precipitate has cytotoxic effects on the developing erythrocyte. Investigations using genetically modified mice suggest a role for AHSP in modulating the severity of β-thalassemia in human subjects.

COLLAGEN ILLUSTRATES THE ROLE OF POSTTRANSLATIONAL PROCESSING IN PROTEIN MATURATION

Protein Maturation Often Involves Making & Breaking Covalent Bonds

The maturation of proteins into their final structural state often involves the cleavage or formation (or both) of covalent bonds, a process of **posttranslational modification.** Many polypeptides are initially synthesized as larger precursors called **proproteins.** The "extra" polypeptide segments in these proproteins often serve as leader sequences that target a polypeptide to a particular organelle or facilitate its passage through a membrane. Other segments ensure that the potentially harmful activity of a protein such as the proteases trypsin and chymotrypsin remains inhibited until these proteins reach their final destination. However, once these transient requirements are fulfilled, the now superfluous peptide regions are removed by selective proteolysis. Other covalent modifications may take place that add new chemical functionalities to a protein. The maturation of collagen illustrates both of these processes.

Collagen Is a Fibrous Protein

Collagen is the most abundant of the fibrous proteins that constitute more than 25% of the protein mass in the human body. Other prominent fibrous proteins include keratin and myosin. These fibrous proteins represent a primary source of structural strength for cells (ie, the cytoskeleton) and tissues. Skin derives its strength and flexibility from a crisscrossed mesh of collagen and keratin fibers, while bones and teeth are buttressed by an underlying network of collagen fibers analogous to the steel strands in reinforced concrete. Collagen also is present in connective tissues such as ligaments and tendons. The high degree of tensile strength required to fulfill these structural roles requires elongated proteins characterized by repetitive amino acid sequences and a regular secondary structure.

Collagen Forms a Unique Triple Helix

Tropocollagen consists of three fibers, each containing about 1000 amino acids, bundled together in a unique conformation, the collagen triple helix (Figure 5–10). A mature collagen fiber forms an elongated rod with an

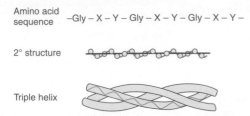

Amino acid sequence –Gly – X – Y – Gly – X – Y – Gly – X – Y –

2° structure

Triple helix

Figure 5–10. Primary, secondary, and tertiary structures of collagen.

axial ratio of about 200. Three intertwined polypeptide strands, which twist to the left, wrap around one another in a right-handed fashion to form the collagen triple helix. The opposing handedness of this superhelix and its component polypeptides makes the collagen triple helix highly resistant to unwinding—the same principle used in the steel cables of suspension bridges. A collagen triple helix has 3.3 residues per turn and a rise per residue nearly twice that of an α helix. The R groups of each polypeptide strand of the triple helix pack so closely that in order to fit, one must be glycine. Thus, every third amino acid residue in collagen is a glycine residue. Staggering of the three strands provides appropriate positioning of the requisite glycines throughout the helix. Collagen is also rich in proline and hydroxyproline, yielding a repetitive Gly-X-Y pattern (Figure 5–10) in which Y generally is proline or hydroxyproline.

Collagen triple helices are stabilized by hydrogen bonds between residues in *different* polypeptide chains. The hydroxyl groups of hydroxyprolyl residues also participate in interchain hydrogen bonding. Additional stability is provided by covalent cross-links formed between modified lysyl residues both within and between polypeptide chains.

Collagen Is Synthesized as a Larger Precursor

Collagen is initially synthesized as a larger precursor polypeptide, procollagen. Numerous prolyl and lysyl residues of procollagen are hydroxylated by prolyl hydroxylase and lysyl hydroxylase, enzymes that require ascorbic acid (vitamin C; see Chapters 27 & 44). Hydroxyprolyl and hydroxy-lysyl residues provide additional hydrogen bonding capability that stabilizes the mature protein. In addition, glucosyl and galactosyl transferases attach glucosyl or galactosyl residues to the hydroxyl groups of specific hydroxylysyl residues.

The central portion of the precursor polypeptide then associates with other molecules to form the characteristic triple helix. This process is accompanied by the removal of the globular amino terminal and carboxyl terminal extensions of the precursor polypeptide by selective proteolysis. Certain lysyl residues are modified by lysyl oxidase, a copper-containing protein that converts ε-amino groups to aldehydes. The aldehydes can either undergo an aldol condensation to form a C=C double bond or to form a Schiff base (eneimine) with the ε-amino group of an unmodified lysyl residue, which is subsequently reduced to form a C—N single bond. These covalent bonds cross-link the individual polypeptides and imbue the fiber with exceptional strength and rigidity.

Nutritional & Genetic Disorders Can Impair Collagen Maturation

The complex series of events in collagen maturation provide a model that illustrates the biologic consequences of incomplete polypeptide maturation. The best-known defect in collagen biosynthesis is scurvy, a result of a dietary deficiency of vitamin C required by prolyl and lysyl hydroxylases. The resulting deficit in the number of hydroxyproline and hydroxylysine residues undermines the conformational stability of collagen fibers, leading to bleeding gums, swelling joints, poor wound healing, and ultimately death. Menkes' syndrome, characterized by kinky hair and growth retardation, reflects a dietary deficiency of the copper required by lysyl oxidase, which catalyzes a key step in formation of the covalent cross-links that strengthen collagen fibers.

Genetic disorders of collagen biosynthesis include several forms of osteogenesis imperfecta, characterized by fragile bones. In Ehlers-Danlos syndrome, a group of connective tissue disorders that involve impaired integrity of supporting structures, defects in the genes that encode α collagen-1, procollagen N-peptidase, or lysyl hydroxylase result in mobile joints and skin abnormalities (see also Chapter 47).

SUMMARY

- Proteins may be classified based on their solubility, shape, or function or of the presence of a prosthetic group, such as heme.

- The gene-encoded primary structure of a polypeptide is the sequence of its amino acids. Its secondary structure results from folding of polypeptides into hydrogen-bonded motifs such as the α helix, the β-pleated sheet, β bends, and loops. Combinations of these motifs can form supersecondary motifs.

- Tertiary structure concerns the relationships between secondary structural domains. Quaternary structure of proteins with two or more polypeptides (oligomeric proteins) concerns the spatial relationships between various types of polypeptides.

- Primary structures are stabilized by covalent peptide bonds. Higher orders of structure are stabilized by weak

forces—multiple hydrogen bonds, salt (electrostatic) bonds, and association of hydrophobic R groups.

- The phi (Φ) angle of a polypeptide is the angle about the C_α—N bond; the psi (ψ) angle is that about the C_α—C_o bond. Most combinations of phi-psi angles are disallowed due to steric hindrance. The phi-psi angles that form the α helix and the α sheet fall within the lower and upper left-hand quadrants of a Ramachandran plot, respectively.

- Protein folding is a poorly understood process. Broadly speaking, short segments of newly synthesized polypeptide fold into secondary structural units. Forces that bury hydrophobic regions from solvent then drive the partially folded polypeptide into a "molten globule" in which the modules of secondary structure are rearranged to give the native conformation of the protein.

- Proteins that assist folding include protein disulfide isomerase, proline-*cis,trans*-isomerase, and the chaperones that participate in the folding of over half of mammalian proteins. Chaperones shield newly synthesized polypeptides from solvent and provide an environment for elements of secondary structure to emerge and coalesce into molten globules.

- Techniques for study of higher orders of protein structure include x-ray crystallography, NMR spectroscopy, analytical ultracentrifugation, gel filtration, and gel electrophoresis.

- Collagen illustrates the close linkage between protein structure and biologic function. Diseases of collagen maturation include Ehlers-Danlos syndrome and the vitamin C deficiency disease scurvy.

- Prions—protein particles that lack nucleic acid—cause fatal transmissible spongiform encephalopathies such as Creutzfeldt-Jakob disease, scrapie, and bovine spongiform encephalopathy. Prion diseases involve an altered secondary-tertiary structure of a naturally occurring protein, PrPc. When PrPc interacts with its pathologic isoform PrPSc, its conformation is transformed from a predominantly α-helical structure to the α-sheet structure characteristic of PrPSc.

REFERENCES

Branden C, Tooze J: *Introduction to Protein Structure*. Garland, 1991.

Burkhard P, Stetefeld J, Strelkov SV: Coiled coils: A highly versatile protein folding motif. Trends Cell Biol 2001;11:82.

Collinge J: Prion diseases of humans and animals: Their causes and molecular basis. Annu Rev Neurosci 2001;24:519.

Frydman J: Folding of newly translated proteins in vivo: The role of molecular chaperones. Annu Rev Biochem 2001;70:603.

Gothel SF, Marahiel MA: Peptidyl-prolyl *cis-trans* isomerases, a superfamily of ubiquitous folding catalysts. Cell Mol Life Sci 1999;55:423.

Hajdu J et al: Analyzing protein functions in four dimensions. Nat Struct Biol 2000;7:1006.

Hardy J: Toward Alzheimer therapies based on genetic knowledge. Annu Rev Med 2004;55:15.

Ho BK, Thomas A, Brasseur R: Revisiting the Ramachandran plot: Hard-sphere repulsion, electrostatics, and H-bonding in the α-helix. Protein Sci 2003;12:2508.

Ice GE et al: Polychromatic x-ray microdiffraction studies of mesoscale structure and dynamics. J Synchrotron Rad 2005;12:155.

Irani DN, Johnson RT: Diagnosis and prevention of bovine spongiform encephalopathy and variant Creutzfeldt-Jakob disease. Annu Rev Med 2003;54:305.

Jorgensen WL: The many roles of computation in drug discovery. Science 2004;303:1813.

Kong Y et al: Loss of alpha-hemoglobin-stabilizing protein impairs erythropoiesis and exacerbates beta thalassemia. J Clin Invest 2004;114:1457.

Myers JK, Oas TG. Mechanism of fast protein folding. Annu Rev Biochem 2002;71:783.

Myllyharju J: Prolyl 4-hydroxylases, the key enzymes of collagen biosynthesis. Matrix Biol 2003;22:15.

Radord S: Protein folding: Progress made and promises ahead. Trends Biochem Sci 2000;25:611.

Sadana A, Vo Dinh T. Biomedical implications of protein folding and misfolding. Biotechnol Appl Biochem 2001;33:7.

Segrest MP et al: The amphipathic alpha-helix: A multifunctional structural motif in plasma lipoproteins. Adv Protein Chem 1995;45:1.

Stoddard BL et al: Millisecond Laue structures of an enzyme-product complex using photocaged substrate analogs. Nat Struct Biol 1998;5:891.

Young JC, Moarefi I, Hartl FU: *Hsp*90: A specialized but essential protein-folding tool. J Cell Biol 2001;154:267.

Proteins: Myoglobin & Hemoglobin

Peter J. Kennelly, PhD, & Victor W. Rodwell, PhD

BIOMEDICAL IMPORTANCE

The heme proteins myoglobin and hemoglobin maintain a supply of oxygen essential for oxidative metabolism. Myoglobin, a monomeric protein of red muscle, stores oxygen as a reserve against oxygen deprivation. Hemoglobin, a tetrameric protein of erythrocytes, transports O_2 to the tissues and returns CO_2 and protons to the lungs. Cyanide and carbon monoxide kill because they disrupt the physiologic function of the heme proteins cytochrome oxidase and hemoglobin, respectively. The secondary-tertiary structure of the subunits of hemoglobin resembles myoglobin. However, the tetrameric structure of hemoglobin permits cooperative interactions that are central to its function. For example, 2,3-bisphosphoglycerate (BPG) promotes the efficient release of O_2 by stabilizing the quaternary structure of deoxyhemoglobin. Hemoglobin and myoglobin illustrate both protein structure-function relationships and the molecular basis of genetic diseases such as sickle cell disease and the thalassemias.

HEME & FERROUS IRON CONFER THE ABILITY TO STORE & TO TRANSPORT OXYGEN

Myoglobin and hemoglobin contain **heme,** a cyclic tetrapyrrole consisting of four molecules of pyrrole linked by α-methylene bridges. This planar network of conjugated double bonds absorbs visible light and colors heme deep red. The substituents at the β-positions of heme are methyl (M), vinyl (V), and propionate (Pr) groups arranged in the order M, V, M, V, M, Pr, Pr, M (Figure 6–1). One atom of ferrous iron (Fe_2^+) resides at the center of the planar tetrapyrrole. Other proteins with metal-containing tetrapyrrole prosthetic groups include the cytochromes (Fe and Cu) and chlorophyll (Mg) (see Chapter 31). Oxidation and reduction of the Fe and Cu atoms of cytochromes is essential to their biologic function as carriers of electrons. By contrast, oxidation of the Fe_2^+ of myoglobin or hemoglobin to Fe_3^+ destroys their biologic activity.

Myoglobin Is Rich in α Helix

Oxygen stored in red muscle myoglobin is released during O_2 deprivation (eg, severe exercise) for use in muscle mitochondria for aerobic synthesis of ATP (see Chapter 13). A 153-aminoacyl residue polypeptide (MW 17,000), myoglobin folds into a compact shape that measures $4.5 \times 3.5 \times 2.5$ nm (Figure 6–2). Unusually high proportions, about 75%, of the residues are present in eight right-handed, 7–20 residue α helices. Starting at the amino terminal, these are termed helices A–H. Typical of globular proteins, the surface of myoglobin is polar, while—with only two exceptions—the interior contains only nonpolar residues such as Leu, Val, Phe, and Met. The exceptions are His E7 and His F8, the seventh and eighth residues in helices E and F, which lie close to the heme iron where they function in O_2 binding.

Histidines F8 & E7 Perform Unique Roles in Oxygen Binding

The heme of myoglobin lies in a crevice between helices E and F oriented with its polar propionate groups facing the surface of the globin (Figure 6–2). The remainder resides in the nonpolar interior. The fifth coordination position of the iron is linked to a ring nitrogen of the **proximal histidine,** His F8. The **distal histidine,** His E7, lies on the side of the heme ring opposite to His F8.

The Iron Moves Toward the Plane of the Heme When Oxygen Is Bound

The iron of unoxygenated myoglobin lies 0.03 nm (0.3 Å) outside the plane of the heme ring, toward His F8. The heme therefore "puckers" slightly. When O_2 occupies the sixth coordination position, the iron moves to within 0.01 nm (0.1 Å) of the plane of the heme ring. Oxygenation of myoglobin thus is accompanied by motion of the iron, of His F8, and of residues linked to His F8.

Apomyoglobin Provides a Hindered Environment for Heme Iron

When O_2 binds to myoglobin, the bond between the first oxygen atom and the Fe_2^+ is perpendicular to the plane of the heme ring. The bond linking the first and second oxygen atoms lies at an angle of 121 degrees to the plane of the heme, orienting the second oxygen away from the distal histidine (Figure 6–3, left). Isolated

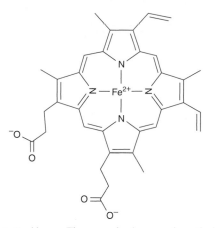

Figure 6–1. Heme. The pyrrole rings and methylene bridge carbons are coplanar, and the iron atom (Fe_2^+) resides in almost the same plane. The fifth and sixth coordination positions of Fe_2^+ are directed perpendicular to—and directly above and below—the plane of the heme ring. Observe the nature of the substituent groups on the β carbons of the pyrrole rings, the central iron atom, and the location of the polar side of the heme ring (at about 7 o'clock) that faces the surface of the myoglobin molecule.

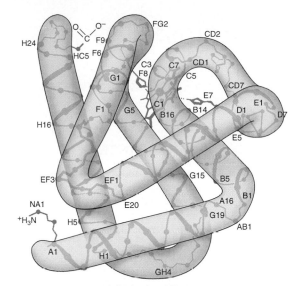

Figure 6–2. A model of myoglobin at low resolution. Only the α-carbon atoms are shown. The α-helical regions are named A through H. (Based on Dickerson RE in: *The Proteins*, 2nd ed. Vol 2. Neurath H [editor]. Academic Press, 1964. Reproduced with permission. Copyright © 1963. Reprinted with permission from Elsevier.)

heme binds carbon monoxide (CO) 25,000 times more strongly than oxygen. Since CO is present in small quantities in the atmosphere and arises in cells from the catabolism of heme, why is it that CO does not completely displace O_2 from heme iron? The accepted explanation is that the apoproteins of myoglobin and hemoglobin create a **hindered environment.** While CO can bind to isolated heme in its preferred orientation, ie, with all three atoms (Fe, C, and O) perpendicular to the plane of the heme, in myoglobin and hemoglobin the distal histidine sterically precludes this orientation. Binding at a less favored angle reduces the strength of the heme-CO bond to about 200 times that of the heme-O_2 bond (Figure 6–3, right) at which level the great excess of O_2 over CO normally present dominates. Nevertheless, about 1% of myoglobin typically is present combined with carbon monoxide.

THE OXYGEN DISSOCIATION CURVES FOR MYOGLOBIN & HEMOGLOBIN SUIT THEIR PHYSIOLOGIC ROLES

Why is myoglobin unsuitable as an O_2 transport protein but well suited for O_2 storage? The relationship between the concentration, or partial pressure, of O_2 (PO_2) and the quantity of O_2 bound is expressed as an O_2 saturation isotherm (Figure 6–4). The oxygen-binding curve for myoglobin is hyperbolic. Myoglobin therefore loads O_2 readily at the PO_2 of the lung capillary bed (100 mm Hg). However, since myoglobin releases only a small fraction of its bound O_2 at the PO_2 values typically encountered in active muscle (20 mm Hg) or other tissues (40 mm Hg), it represents an ineffective vehicle for delivery of O_2. However, when strenuous exercise lowers the PO_2 of muscle tissue to about 5 mm Hg, myoglobin releases O_2 for mitochondrial synthesis of ATP, permitting continued muscular activity.

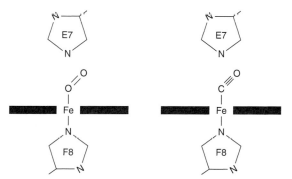

Figure 6–3. Angles for bonding of oxygen and carbon monoxide to the heme iron of myoglobin. The distal E7 histidine hinders bonding of CO at the preferred (180-degree) angle to the plane of the heme ring.

THE ALLOSTERIC PROPERTIES OF HEMOGLOBINS RESULT FROM THEIR QUATERNARY STRUCTURES

The properties of individual hemoglobins are consequences of their quaternary as well as of their secondary and tertiary structures. The quaternary structure of hemoglobin confers striking additional properties, absent from monomeric myoglobin, which adapts it to its unique biologic roles. The **allosteric** (Gk *allos* "other," *steros* "space") properties of hemoglobin provide, in addition, a model for understanding other allosteric proteins (see Chapter 18).

Hemoglobin Is Tetrameric

Hemoglobins are tetramers composed of pairs of two different polypeptide subunits. Greek letters are used to designate each subunit type. The subunit composition of the principal hemoglobins are $\alpha_2\beta_2$ (HbA; normal adult hemoglobin), $\alpha_2\gamma_2$ (HbF; fetal hemoglobin), α_2S_2 (HbS; sickle cell hemoglobin), and $\alpha_2\delta_2$ (HbA$_2$; a minor adult hemoglobin). The primary structures of the β, γ, and δ chains of human hemoglobin are highly conserved.

Myoglobin & the β Subunits of Hemoglobin Share Almost Identical Secondary and Tertiary Structures

Despite differences in the kind and number of amino acids present, myoglobin and the β polypeptide of hemoglobin A have almost identical secondary and tertiary structures. Similarities include the location of the heme and the eight helical regions and the presence of amino acids with similar properties at comparable locations. Although it possesses seven rather than eight helical regions, the α polypeptide of hemoglobin also closely resembles myoglobin.

Oxygenation of Hemoglobin Triggers Conformational Changes in the Apoprotein

Hemoglobins bind four molecules of O_2 per tetramer, one per heme. A molecule of O_2 binds to a hemoglobin tetramer more readily if other O_2 molecules are already bound (Figure 6–4). Termed **cooperative binding,** this phenomenon permits hemoglobin to maximize both the quantity of O_2 loaded at the PO_2 of the lungs and the quantity of O_2 released at the PO_2 of the peripheral tissues. Cooperative interactions, an exclusive property of multimeric proteins, are critically important to aerobic life.

P$_{50}$ Expresses the Relative Affinities of Different Hemoglobins for Oxygen

The quantity P_{50}, a measure of O_2 concentration, is the partial pressure of O_2 that half-saturates a given hemo-

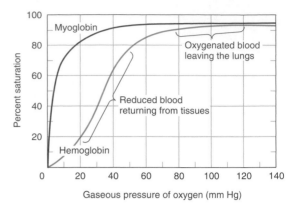

Figure 6–4. Oxygen-binding curves of both hemoglobin and myoglobin. Arterial oxygen tension is about 100 mm Hg; mixed venous oxygen tension is about 40 mm Hg; capillary (active muscle) oxygen tension is about 20 mm Hg; and the minimum oxygen tension required for cytochrome oxidase is about 5 mm Hg. Association of chains into a tetrameric structure (hemoglobin) results in much greater oxygen delivery than would be possible with single chains. (Modified, with permission, from Scriver CR et al [editors]: *The Molecular and Metabolic Bases of Inherited Disease*, 7th ed. McGraw-Hill, 1995.)

globin. Depending on the organism, P_{50} can vary widely, but in all instances it will exceed the PO_2 of the peripheral tissues. For example, values of P_{50} for HbA and fetal HbF are 26 and 20 mm Hg, respectively. In the placenta, this difference enables HbF to extract oxygen from the HbA in the mother's blood. However, HbF is suboptimal postpartum since its high affinity for O_2 dictates that it can deliver less O_2 to the tissues.

The subunit composition of hemoglobin tetramers undergoes complex changes during development. The human fetus initially synthesizes a $\zeta_2\varepsilon_2$ tetramer. By the end of the first trimester, ζ and ε subunits have been replaced by α and γ subunits, forming HbF ($\alpha_2\gamma_2$), the hemoglobin of late fetal life. While synthesis of β subunits begins in the third trimester, β subunits do not completely replace γ subunits to yield adult HbA ($\alpha_2\beta_2$) until some weeks postpartum (Figure 6–5).

Oxygenation of Hemoglobin Is Accompanied by Large Conformational Changes

The binding of the first O_2 molecule to deoxyHb shifts the heme iron toward the plane of the heme ring from a position about 0.6 nm beyond it (Figure 6–6). This motion is transmitted to the proximal (F8) histidine and to the residues attached thereto, which in turn causes the rupture of salt bridges between the carboxyl

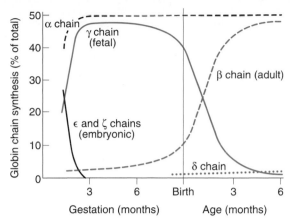

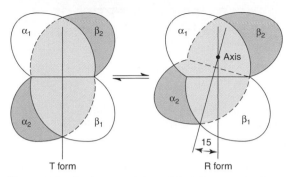

Figure 6–5. Developmental pattern of the quaternary structure of fetal and newborn hemoglobins. (Reproduced, with permission, from Ganong WF: *Review of Medical Physiology*, 20th ed. McGraw-Hill, 2001.)

Figure 6–7. During transition of the T form to the R form of hemoglobin, one pair of subunits (α_2/β_2) rotates through 15 degrees relative to the other pair (α_1/β_1). The axis of rotation is eccentric, and the α_2/β_2 pair also shifts toward the axis somewhat. In the diagram, the unshaded α_1/β_1 pair is shown fixed while the colored α_2/β_2 pair both shifts and rotates.

terminal residues of all four subunits. As a consequence, one pair of α/β subunits rotates 15 degrees with respect to the other, compacting the tetramer (Figure 6–7). Profound changes in secondary, tertiary, and quater-

nary structure accompany the high-affinity O_2-induced transition of hemoglobin from the low-affinity **T (taut) state** to the high-affinity **R (relaxed) state.** These changes significantly increase the affinity of the remaining unoxygenated hemes for O_2, as subsequent binding events require the rupture of fewer salt bridges (Figure 6–8). The terms T and R also are used to refer to the low-affinity and high-affinity conformations of allosteric enzymes, respectively.

After Releasing O_2 at the Tissues, Hemoglobin Transports CO_2 & Protons to the Lungs

In addition to transporting O_2 from the lungs to peripheral tissues, hemoglobin transports CO_2, the by-product of respiration, and protons from peripheral tissues to the lungs. Hemoglobin carries CO_2 as carbamates formed with the amino terminal nitrogens of the polypeptide chains.

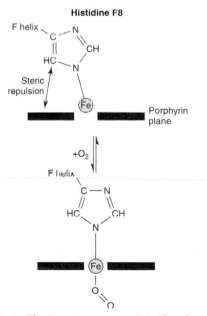

Figure 6–6. The iron atom moves into the plane of the heme on oxygenation. Histidine F8 and its associated residues are pulled along with the iron atom. (Slightly modified and reproduced, with permission, from Stryer L: *Biochemistry*, 4th ed. Freeman, 1995. Copyright © 1995 W. H. Freeman and Company.)

$$CO_2 + Hb\text{—}NH_3^+ \rightleftharpoons 2H^+ + Hb\text{—}\overset{H}{N}\text{—}\overset{\overset{O}{\|}}{C}\text{—}O^-$$

Carbamates change the charge on amino terminals from positive to negative, favoring salt bond formation between the α and β chains.

Hemoglobin carbamates account for about 15% of the CO_2 in venous blood. Much of the remaining CO_2 is carried as bicarbonate, which is formed in erythrocytes by the hydration of CO_2 to carbonic acid (H_2CO_3), a process catalyzed by carbonic anhydrase. At the pH of venous blood, H_2CO_3 dissociates into bicarbonate and a proton.

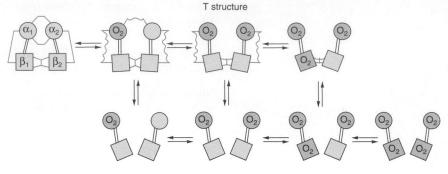

T structure

R structure

Figure 6–8. Transition from the T structure to the R structure. In this model, salt bridges (thin lines) linking the subunits in the T structure break progressively as oxygen is added, and even those salt bridges that have not yet ruptured are progressively weakened (wavy lines). The transition from T to R does not take place after a fixed number of oxygen molecules have been bound but becomes more probable as each successive oxygen binds. The transition between the two structures is influenced by protons, carbon dioxide, chloride, and BPG; the higher their concentration, the more oxygen must be bound to trigger the transition. Fully oxygenated molecules in the T structure and fully deoxygenated molecules in the R structure are not shown because they are unstable. (Modified and redrawn, with permission, from Perutz MF: Hemoglobin structure and respiratory transport. Sci Am [Dec] 1978;239:92.)

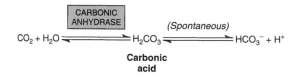

$$CO_2 + H_2O \rightleftharpoons H_2CO_3 \rightleftharpoons HCO_3^- + H^+$$

Carbonic anhydrase   (Spontaneous)

Carbonic acid

Deoxyhemoglobin binds one proton for every two O_2 molecules released, contributing significantly to the buffering capacity of blood. The somewhat lower pH of peripheral tissues, aided by carbamation, stabilizes the T state and thus enhances the delivery of O_2. In the lungs, the process reverses. As O_2 binds to deoxyhemoglobin, protons are released and combine with bicarbonate to form carbonic acid. Dehydration of H_2CO_3, catalyzed by carbonic anhydrase, forms CO_2, which is exhaled. Binding of oxygen thus drives the exhalation of CO_2 (Figure 6–9). This reciprocal coupling of proton and O_2 binding is termed the **Bohr effect.** The Bohr effect is dependent upon **cooperative interactions between the hemes of the hemoglobin tetramer.** Myoglobin, a monomer, exhibits no Bohr effect.

Protons Arise from Rupture of Salt Bonds When O_2 Binds

Protons responsible for the Bohr effect arise from rupture of salt bridges during the binding of O_2 to T state hemoglobin. Conversion to the oxygenated R state breaks salt bridges involving β-chain residue His 146. The subsequent dissociation of protons from His 146 drives the conversion of bicarbonate to carbonic acid (Figure 6–9). Upon the release of O_2, the T structure and its salt bridges re-form. This conformational change increases the pK_a of the β-chain His 146 residues, which bind protons. By facilitating the re-formation of salt bridges, an increase in proton concentration enhances the release of O_2 from oxygenated (R state) hemoglobin. Conversely, an increase in PO_2 promotes proton release.

2,3-Bisphosphoglycerate (BPG) Stabilizes the T Structure of Hemoglobin

A low PO_2 in peripheral tissues promotes the synthesis in erythrocytes of 2,3-bisphosphoglycerate (BPG) from the glycolytic intermediate 1,3-bisphosphoglycerate.

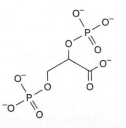

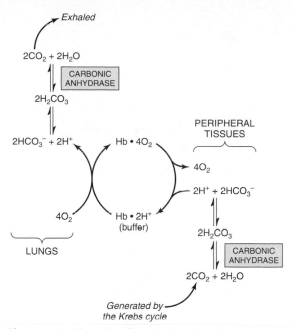

Figure 6–9. The Bohr effect. Carbon dioxide generated in peripheral tissues combines with water to form carbonic acid, which dissociates into protons and bicarbonate ions. Deoxyhemoglobin acts as a buffer by binding protons and delivering them to the lungs. In the lungs, the uptake of oxygen by hemoglobin releases protons that combine with bicarbonate ion, forming carbonic acid, which when dehydrated by carbonic anhydrase becomes carbon dioxide, which then is exhaled.

The hemoglobin tetramer binds one molecule of BPG in the central cavity formed by its four subunits. However, the space between the H helices of the β chains lining the cavity is sufficiently wide to accommodate BPG only when hemoglobin is in the T state. BPG forms salt bridges with the terminal amino groups of both β chains via Val NA1 and with Lys EF6 and His H21 (Figure 6–10). BPG therefore stabilizes deoxygenated (T state) hemoglobin by forming additional salt bridges that must be broken prior to conversion to the R state.

Residue H21 of the γ subunit of fetal hemoglobin (HbF) is Ser rather than His. Since Ser cannot form a salt bridge, BPG binds more weakly to HbF than to HbA. The lower stabilization afforded to the T state by BPG accounts for HbF having a higher affinity for O_2 than HbA.

Adaptation to High Altitude

Physiologic changes that accompany prolonged exposure to high altitude include an increase in the number of erythrocytes and in their concentrations of hemoglobin and of BPG. Elevated BPG lowers the affinity of HbA for O_2 (decreases P_{50}), which enhances release of O_2 at the tissues.

NUMEROUS MUTANT HUMAN HEMOGLOBINS HAVE BEEN IDENTIFIED

Mutations in the genes that encode the α or β subunits of hemoglobin potentially can affect its biologic function. However, almost all of the over 900 known mutant human hemoglobins are both extremely rare and benign, presenting no clinical abnormalities. When a mutation does compromise biologic function, the condition is termed a **hemoglobinopathy.** The URL http://globin.cse.psu.edu/ (Globin Gene Server) provides information about—and links for—normal and mutant hemoglobins. Selected examples are described below.

Methemoglobin & Hemoglobin M

In methemoglobinemia, the heme iron is ferric rather than ferrous. Methemoglobin thus can neither bind nor transport O_2. Normally, the enzyme methemoglobin reductase reduces the Fe_3^+ of methemoglobin to Fe_2^+. Methemoglobin can arise by oxidation of Fe_2^+ to Fe_3^+ as a side effect of agents such as sulfonamides, from hereditary hemoglobin M, or consequent to reduced activity of the enzyme methemoglobin reductase.

In hemoglobin M, histidine F8 (His F8) has been replaced by tyrosine. The iron of HbM forms a tight

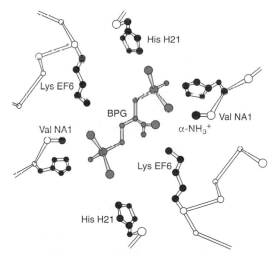

Figure 6–10. Mode of binding of 2,3-bisphosphoglycerate to human deoxyhemoglobin. BPG interacts with three positively charged groups on each β chain. (Based on Arnone A: X-ray diffraction study of binding of 2,3-diphosphoglycerate to human deoxyhemoglobin. Nature 1972;237:146. Reproduced with permission. Copyright © 1972. Adapted by permission from Macmillan Publishers Ltd.)

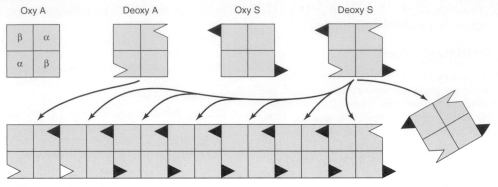

Figure 6–11. Representation of the sticky patch (▲) on hemoglobin S and its "receptor" (△) on deoxyhemoglobin A and deoxyhemoglobin S. The complementary surfaces allow deoxyhemoglobin S to polymerize into a fibrous structure, but the presence of deoxyhemoglobin A will terminate the polymerization by failing to provide sticky patches. (Modified and reproduced, with permission, from Stryer L: *Biochemistry*, 4th ed. Freeman, 1995. Copyright © 1995 W. H. Freeman and Company.)

ionic complex with the phenolate anion of tyrosine that stabilizes the Fe_3^+ form. In α-chain hemoglobin M variants, the R-T equilibrium favors the T state. Oxygen affinity is reduced, and the Bohr effect is absent. β-Chain hemoglobin M variants exhibit R-T switching, and the Bohr effect is therefore present.

Mutations that favor the R state (eg, hemoglobin Chesapeake) increase O_2 affinity. These hemoglobins therefore fail to deliver adequate O_2 to peripheral tissues. The resulting tissue hypoxia leads to **polycythemia,** an increased concentration of erythrocytes.

Hemoglobin S

In HbS, the nonpolar amino acid valine has replaced the polar surface residue Glu6 of the β subunit, generating a hydrophobic **"sticky patch"** on the surface of the β subunit of both oxyHbS and deoxyHbS. Both HbA and HbS contain a complementary sticky patch on their surfaces that is exposed only in the deoxygenated, R state. Thus, at low PO_2, deoxyHbS can polymerize to form long, insoluble fibers. Binding of deoxyHbA terminates fiber polymerization, since HbA lacks the second sticky patch necessary to bind another Hb molecule (Figure 6–11). These twisted helical fibers distort the erythrocyte into a characteristic sickle shape, rendering it vulnerable to lysis in the interstices of the splenic sinusoids. They also cause multiple secondary clinical effects. A low PO_2 such as that at high altitudes exacerbates the tendency to polymerize. Emerging treatments for sickle cell disease include inducing fetal hemoglobin expression to inhibit the polymerization of HbS, stem cell transplantation, and in the future, gene therapy.

BIOMEDICAL IMPLICATIONS

Myoglobinuria

Following massive crush injury, myoglobin released from damaged muscle fibers colors the urine dark red. Myoglobin can be detected in plasma following a myocardial infarction, but assay of serum enzymes (see Chapter 7) provides a more sensitive index of myocardial injury.

Anemias

Anemias, reductions in the number of red blood cells or of hemoglobin in the blood, can reflect impaired synthesis of hemoglobin (eg, in iron deficiency; Chapter 49) or impaired production of erythrocytes (eg, in folic acid or vitamin B_{12} deficiency; Chapter 44). Diagnosis of anemias begins with spectroscopic measurement of blood hemoglobin levels.

Thalassemias

The genetic defects known as thalassemias result from the partial or total absence of one or more α or β chains of hemoglobin. Over 750 different mutations have been identified, but only three are common. Either the α chain (alpha thalassemias) or β chain (beta thalassemias) can be affected. A superscript indicates whether a subunit is completely absent ($α^0$ or $β^0$) or whether its synthesis is reduced ($α^+$ or $β^+$). Apart from marrow transplantation, treatment is symptomatic.

Certain mutant hemoglobins are common in many populations, and a patient may inherit more than one type. Hemoglobin disorders thus present a complex

pattern of clinical phenotypes. The use of DNA probes for their diagnosis is considered in Chapter 39.

Glycosylated Hemoglobin (HbA$_{1c}$)

When blood glucose enters the erythrocytes it glycosylates the ε-amino group of lysine residues and the amino terminals of hemoglobin. The fraction of hemoglobin glycosylated, normally about 5%, is proportionate to blood glucose concentration. Since the half-life of an erythrocyte is typically 60 days, the level of glycosylated hemoglobin (HbA$_{1c}$) reflects the mean blood glucose concentration over the preceding 6–8 weeks. Measurement of HbA$_{1c}$ therefore provides valuable information for management of diabetes mellitus.

SUMMARY

- Myoglobin is monomeric; hemoglobin is a tetramer of two subunit types ($\alpha_2\beta_2$ in HbA). Despite having different primary structures, myoglobin and the subunits of hemoglobin have nearly identical secondary and tertiary structures.

- Heme, an essentially planar, slightly puckered, cyclic tetrapyrrole, has a central Fe^{2+} linked to all four nitrogen atoms of the heme, to histidine F8, and, in oxyMb and oxyHb, also to O_2.

- The O_2-binding curve for myoglobin is hyperbolic, but for hemoglobin it is sigmoidal, a consequence of cooperative interactions in the tetramer. Cooperativity maximizes the ability of hemoglobin both to load O_2 at the PO_2 of the lungs and to deliver O_2 at the PO_2 of the tissues.

- Relative affinities of different hemoglobins for oxygen are expressed as P_{50}, the PO_2 that half-saturates them with O_2. Hemoglobins saturate at the partial pressures of their respective respiratory organ, eg, the lung or placenta.

- On oxygenation of hemoglobin, the iron, histidine F8, and linked residues move toward the heme ring. Conformational changes that accompany oxygenation include rupture of salt bonds and loosening of quaternary structure, facilitating binding of additional O_2.

- 2,3-Bisphosphoglycerate (BPG) in the central cavity of deoxyHb forms salt bonds with the β subunits that stabilize deoxyHb. On oxygenation, the central cavity contracts, BPG is extruded, and the quaternary structure loosens.

- Hemoglobin also functions in CO_2 and proton transport from tissues to lungs. Release of O_2 from oxyHb at the tissues is accompanied by uptake of protons due to lowering of the pK_a of histidine residues.

- In sickle cell hemoglobin (HbS), Val replaces the $\beta6$ Glu of HbA, creating a "sticky patch" that has a complement on deoxyHb (but not on oxyHb). DeoxyHbS polymerizes at low O_2 concentrations, forming fibers that distort erythrocytes into sickle shapes.

- Alpha and beta thalassemias are anemias that result from reduced production of α and β subunits of HbA, respectively.

REFERENCES

Bettati S et al: Allosteric mechanism of haemoglobin: Rupture of salt-bridges raises the oxygen affinity of the T-structure. J Mol Biol 1998;281:581.

Frauenfelder H, McMahon BH, Fenimore PW: Myoglobin: The hydrogen atom of biology and a paradigm of complexity. Proc Natl Acad Sci USA 2003;100:8615.

Hardison RC et al: Databases of human hemoglobin variants and other resources at the globin gene server. Hemoglobin 2001;25:183.

Lukin JA, Ho C: The structure-function relationship of hemoglobin in solution at atomic resolution. Chem Rev 2004;104:1219.

Ordway GA, Garry DJ: Myoglobin: An essential hemoprotein in striated muscle. J Exp Biol 2004;207:3441.

Persons DA: Update on gene therapy for hemoglobin disorders. Curr Opin Mol Ther 2003;5:508.

Schrier SL, Angelucci E: New strategies in the treatment of the thalassemias. Annu Rev Med 2005;56:157.

Steinberg MH, Brugnara C: Pathophysiological-based approaches to treatment of sickle-cell disease. Annu Rev Med 2003;54:89.

Weatherall DJ et al: The hemoglobinopathies. Chapter 181 in *The Metabolic and Molecular Bases of Inherited Disease*, 8th ed. Scriver CR et al (editors). McGraw-Hill, 2000.

Enzymes: Mechanism of Action

7

Peter J. Kennelly, PhD, & Victor W. Rodwell, PhD

BIOMEDICAL IMPORTANCE

Enzymes are biologic polymers that catalyze the chemical reactions that make life as we know it possible. The presence and maintenance of a complete and balanced set of enzymes is essential for the breakdown of nutrients to supply energy and chemical building blocks; the assembly of those building blocks into proteins, DNA, membranes, cells, and tissues; and the harnessing of energy to power cell motility, neural function, and muscle contraction. With the exception of catalytic RNA molecules, or ribozymes, enzymes are proteins. Deficiencies in the quantity or catalytic activity of key enzymes can result from genetic defects, nutritional deficits, or toxins. Defective enzymes can result from genetic mutations or infection by viral or bacterial pathogens (eg, *Vibrio cholerae*). Medical scientists address imbalances in enzyme activity by using pharmacologic agents to inhibit specific enzymes and are investigating gene therapy as a means to remedy deficits in enzyme level or function.

ENZYMES ARE EFFECTIVE & HIGHLY SPECIFIC CATALYSTS

The enzymes that catalyze the conversion of one or more compounds (**substrates**) into one or more different compounds (**products**) enhance the rates of the corresponding noncatalyzed reaction by factors of at least 10^6. Like all catalysts, enzymes are neither consumed nor permanently altered as a consequence of their participation in a reaction.

In addition to being highly efficient, enzymes are also extremely selective catalysts. Unlike most catalysts used in synthetic chemistry, enzymes are specific both for the type of reaction catalyzed and for a single substrate or a small set of closely related substrates. Enzymes are also stereospecific catalysts and typically catalyze reactions only of one stereoisomer of a given compound—for example, D- but not L-sugars, L- but not D-amino acids. Since they bind substrates through at least "three points of attachment," enzymes can even convert nonchiral substrates to chiral products. Figure 7–1 illustrates why the enzyme-catalyzed reduction of the nonchiral substrate pyruvate produces L-lactate

rather a racemic mixture of D- and L-lactate. The exquisite specificity of enzyme catalysts imbues living cells with the ability to simultaneously conduct and independently control a broad spectrum of chemical processes.

ENZYMES ARE CLASSIFIED BY REACTION TYPE

The commonly used names for most enzymes describe the type of reaction catalyzed, followed by the suffix *-ase*. For example, dehydrogen*ases* remove hydrogen atoms, prote*ases* hydrolyze proteins, and isomer*ases* catalyze rearrangements in configuration. Modifiers may precede the name to indicate the substrate (*xanthine* oxidase), the source of the enzyme (*pancreatic* ribonuclease), its regulation (*hormone-sensitive* lipase), or a feature of its mechanism of action (*cysteine* protease). Where needed, alphanumeric designators are added to identify multiple forms of an enzyme (eg, RNA polymerase *III*; protein kinase *C*β).

To address ambiguities, the International Union of Biochemists (IUB) developed an unambiguous system of enzyme nomenclature in which each enzyme has a unique name and code number that identify the type of reaction catalyzed and the substrates involved. Enzymes are grouped into six classes:

1. **Oxidoreductases** (catalyze oxidations and reductions)
2. **Transferases** (catalyze transfer of moieties such as glycosyl, methyl, or phosphoryl groups)
3. **Hydrolases** (catalyze *hydrolytic* cleavage of C—C, C—O, C—N, and other bonds)
4. **Lyases** catalyze cleavage of C—C, C—O, C—N, and other bonds by *atom elimination*, leaving double bonds
5. **Isomerases** (catalyze geometric or structural changes within a molecule)
6. **Ligases** (catalyze the joining together of two molecules coupled to the hydrolysis of ATP)

Despite the clarity of the IUB system, the names are lengthy and relatively cumbersome, so we generally

49

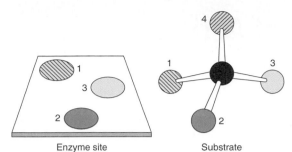

Figure 7–1. Planar representation of the "three-point attachment" of a substrate to the active site of an enzyme. Although atoms 1 and 4 are identical, once atoms 2 and 3 are bound to their complementary sites on the enzyme, only atom 1 can bind. Once bound to an enzyme, apparently identical atoms thus may be distinguishable, permitting a stereospecific chemical change.

continue to refer to enzymes by their traditional, albeit sometimes ambiguous names. The IUB name for hexokinase illustrates both the clarity of the IUB system and its complexities. The IUB name of hexokinase is ATP:D-hexose 6-phosphotransferase E.C. 2.7.1.1. This name identifies hexokinase as a member of class 2 (transferases), subclass 7 (transfer of a phosphoryl group), sub-subclass 1 (alcohol is the phosphoryl acceptor), and "hexose-6" indicates that the alcohol phosphorylated is on carbon six of a hexose. However, we continue to call it hexokinase.

PROSTHETIC GROUPS, COFACTORS, & COENZYMES PLAY IMPORTANT ROLES IN CATALYSIS

Many enzymes contain small nonprotein molecules and metal ions that participate directly in substrate binding or catalysis. Termed **prosthetic groups, cofactors,** and **coenzymes,** these extend the repertoire of catalytic capabilities beyond those afforded by the limited number of functional groups present on the aminoacyl side chains of peptides.

Prosthetic Groups Are Tightly Integrated into an Enzyme's Structure

Prosthetic groups are distinguished by their tight, stable incorporation into a protein's structure by covalent or noncovalent forces. Examples include pyridoxal phosphate, flavin mononucleotide (FMN), flavin adenine dinucleotide (FAD), thiamin pyrophosphate, biotin, and the metal ions of Co, Cu, Mg, Mn, and Zn. Metals are the most common prosthetic groups. The roughly one-third of all enzymes that contain tightly bound

metal ions are termed **metalloenzymes.** Metal ions that participate in redox reactions generally are complexed to prosthetic groups such as heme (Chapter 6) or iron-sulfur clusters (Chapter 12). Metals also may facilitate the binding and orientation of substrates, the formation of covalent bonds with reaction intermediates (Co^{2+} in coenzyme B_{12}), or interact with substrates to render them more **electrophilic** (electron-poor) or **nucleophilic** (electron-rich).

Cofactors Associate Reversibly with Enzymes or Substrates

Cofactors serve functions similar to those of prosthetic groups but bind in a transient, dissociable manner either to the enzyme or to a substrate such as ATP. Unlike the stably associated prosthetic groups, cofactors therefore must be present in the medium surrounding the enzyme for catalysis to occur. The most common cofactors also are metal ions. Enzymes that require a metal ion cofactor are termed **metal-activated enzymes** to distinguish them from the **metalloenzymes** for which metal ions serve as prosthetic groups.

Coenzymes Serve As Substrate Shuttles

Coenzymes serve as recyclable shuttles—or group transfer agents—that transport many substrates from their point of generation to their point of utilization. Association with the coenzyme also stabilizes substrates such as hydrogen atoms or hydride ions that are unstable in the aqueous environment of the cell. Other chemical moieties transported by coenzymes include methyl groups (folates), acyl groups (coenzyme A), and oligosaccharides (dolichol).

Many Coenzymes, Cofactors, & Prosthetic Groups Are Derivatives of B Vitamins

The water-soluble B vitamins supply important components of numerous coenzymes. Several coenzymes contain, in addition, the adenine, ribose, and phosphoryl moieties of AMP or ADP (Figure 7–2). Nicotinamide is a component of the redox coenzymes NAD and NADP, whereas riboflavin is a component of the redox coenzymes FMN and FAD. **Pantothenic acid** is a component of the acyl group carrier coenzyme A. As its pyrophosphate, **thiamin** participates in decarboxylation of α-keto acids and **folic acid** and **cobamide** coenzymes function in one-carbon metabolism.

CATALYSIS OCCURS AT THE ACTIVE SITE

The extreme substrate specificity and high catalytic efficiency of enzymes reflect the existence of an envi-

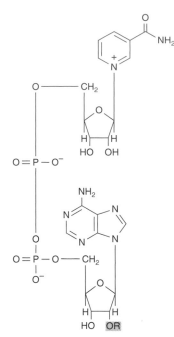

Figure 7–2. Structure of NAD^+ and $NADP^+$. For NAD^+, R = H. For $NADP^+$, R = PO_3^{2-}.

ronment that is exquisitely tailored to a single reaction. Termed the **active site,** this environment generally takes the form of a cleft or pocket. The active sites of multimeric enzymes often are located at the interface between subunits and recruit residues from more than one monomer. The three-dimensional active site both shields substrates from solvent and facilitates catalysis. Substrates bind to the active site at a region complementary to a portion of the substrate that will *not* undergo chemical change during the course of the reaction. This simultaneously aligns those portions of the substrate that *will* undergo change with the functional groups of peptidyl aminoacyl residues. The active site also binds and orients cofactors or prosthetic groups. Many amino acyl residues drawn from diverse portions of the polypeptide chain (Figure 7–3) contribute to the extensive size and three-dimensional character of the active site.

ENZYMES EMPLOY MULTIPLE MECHANISMS TO FACILITATE CATALYSIS

Enzymes use various combinations of four general mechanisms to achieve dramatic catalytic enhancement of the rates of chemical reactions.

Catalysis by Proximity

For molecules to react, they must come within bond-forming distance of one another. The higher their concentration, the more frequently they will encounter one another and the greater will be the rate of their reaction. When an enzyme binds substrate molecules at its active site, it creates a region of high local substrate concentration. This environment also orients the substrate molecules spatially in a position ideal for them to interact, resulting in rate enhancements of at least a thousandfold.

Acid-Base Catalysis

The ionizable functional groups of aminoacyl side chains and (where present) of prosthetic groups contribute to catalysis by acting as acids or bases. Acid-base catalysis can be either specific or general. By "specific" we mean only protons (H_3O^+) or OH^- ions. In **specific acid** or **specific base catalysis,** the rate of reaction is sensitive to changes in the concentration of protons but independent of the concentrations of other acids (proton donors) or bases (proton acceptors) present in solution or at the active site. Reactions whose rates are responsive to *all* the acids or bases present are said to be subject to **general acid** or **general base catalysis.**

Catalysis by Strain

Enzymes that catalyze lytic reactions that involve breaking a covalent bond typically bind their substrates in a conformation slightly unfavorable for the bond that will undergo cleavage. The resulting strain stretches or

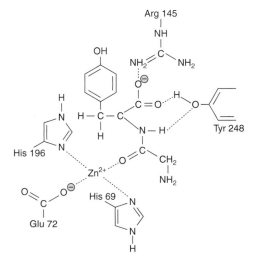

Figure 7–3. Two-dimensional representation of a dipeptide substrate, glycyl-tyrosine, bound within the active site of carboxypeptidase A.

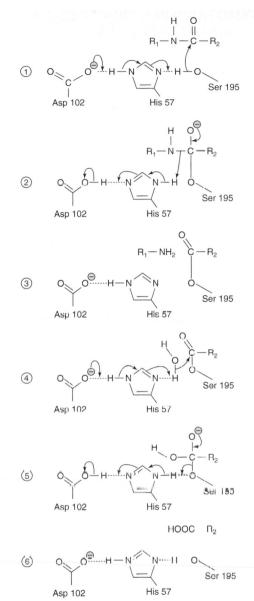

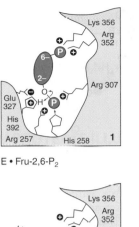

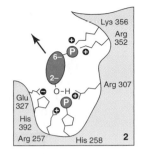

E • Fru-2,6-P₂   E-P • Fru-6-P

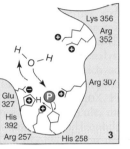

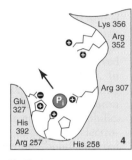

E-P • H₂O   E • Pᵢ

Figure 7–8. Catalysis by fructose-2,6-bisphosphatase. (1) Lys 356 and Arg 257, 307, and 352 stabilize the quadruple negative charge of the substrate by charge-charge interactions. Glu 327 stabilizes the positive charge on His 392. (2) The nucleophile His 392 attacks the C-2 phosphoryl group and transfers it to His 258, forming a phosphoryl-enzyme intermediate. Fructose 6-phosphate leaves the enzyme. (3) Nucleophilic attack by a water molecule, possibly assisted by Glu 327 acting as a base, forms inorganic phosphate. (4) Inorganic orthophosphate is released from Arg 257 and Arg 307. (Reproduced, with permission, from Pilkis SJ et al: 6-Phosphofructo-2-kinase/fructose-2,6 bisphosphatase: A metabolic signaling enzyme. Annu Rev Biochem 1995;64:799. © 1995 by Annual Reviews, www.annualreviews.org. Reprinted with permission.)

Figure 7–7. Catalysis by chymotrypsin. ① The charge-relay system removes a proton from Ser 195, making it a stronger nucleophile. ② Activated Ser 195 attacks the peptide bond, forming a transient tetrahedral intermediate. ③ Release of the amino terminal peptide is facilitated by donation of a proton to the newly formed amino group by His 57 of the charge-relay system, yielding an acyl-Ser 195 intermediate. ④ His 57 and Asp 102 collaborate to activate a water molecule, which attacks the acyl-Ser 195, forming a second tetrahedral intermediate. ⑤ The charge-relay system donates a proton to Ser 195, facilitating breakdown of tetrahedral intermediate to release the carboxyl terminal peptide ⑥.

encodes a particular enzyme. The proteins encoded by the two genes can then evolve independently to recognize different substrates—resulting, for example, in chymotrypsin, which cleaves peptide bonds on the carboxyl terminal side of large hydrophobic amino acids; and trypsin, which cleaves peptide bonds on the carboxyl terminal side of basic amino acids. The common ancestry of enzymes can be inferred from the presence of specific amino acids in the same position in each family member. These residues are said to be **conserved residues.** Proteins that share a large number of conserved residues are said to be **homologous** to one another. Table 7–1 illustrates the primary structural conservation

Table 7–1. Amino acid sequences in the neighborhood of the catalytic sites of several bovine proteases. Regions shown are those on either side of the catalytic site seryl (S) and histidyl (H) residues.

Enzyme	Sequence Around Serine Ⓢ														Sequence Around Histidine Ⓗ									
Trypsin	D	S	C	Q	D	G	Ⓢ	G	G	P	V	V	C	S	G	K	V	V	S	A	A	Ⓗ	C	Y	K	S	G
Chymotrypsin A	S	S	C	M	G	D	Ⓢ	G	G	P	L	V	C	K	K	N	V	V	T	A	A	Ⓗ	G	G	V	T	T
Chymotrypsin B	S	S	C	M	G	D	Ⓢ	G	G	P	L	V	C	Q	K	N	V	V	T	A	A	Ⓗ	C	G	V	T	T
Thrombin	D	A	C	E	G	D	Ⓢ	G	G	P	F	V	M	K	S	P	V	L	T	A	A	Ⓗ	C	L	L	Y	P

of two components of the charge-relay network for several serine proteases. Among the most highly conserved residues are those that participate directly in catalysis.

ISOZYMES ARE DISTINCT ENZYME FORMS THAT CATALYZE THE SAME REACTION

Higher organisms often elaborate several physically distinct versions of a given enzyme, each of which catalyzes the same reaction. Like the members of other protein families, these protein catalysts or **isozymes** arise through gene duplication. Isozymes may exhibit subtle differences in properties such as sensitivity to particular regulatory factors (Chapter 9) or substrate affinity (eg, hexokinase and glucokinase) that adapt them to specific tissues or circumstances. Some isozymes may also enhance survival by providing a "backup" copy of an essential enzyme.

THE CATALYTIC ACTIVITY OF ENZYMES FACILITATES THEIR DETECTION

The relatively small quantities of enzymes present in cells complicate determination of their presence and concentration. However, the ability to rapidly transform thousands of molecules of a specific substrate into products imbues each enzyme with the ability to reveal its presence. Assays of the catalytic activity of enzymes are frequently used in research and clinical laboratories. Under appropriate conditions (see Chapter 8), the rate of the catalytic reaction being monitored is proportionate to the amount of enzyme present, which allows its concentration to be inferred.

Single Molecule Enzymology

The limited sensitivity of traditional enzyme assays necessitates using a large group, or ensemble, of enzyme molecules in order to produce measurable quantities of product. The data obtained thus reflects the average catalytic capability of individual molecules. Recent advances in **nanotechnology** have made it possible to observe, usually by fluorescence microscopy, catalysis

by individual enzyme and substrate molecules. Consequently, scientists can now measure the rate of single catalytic events and sometimes the individual steps in catalysis by a process called **single molecule enzymology** (Figure 7–9).

Drug Discovery Requires Enzyme Assays Suitable for "High-Throughput" Screening

Enzymes constitute one of the primary classes of biomolecules targeted for the development of drugs and

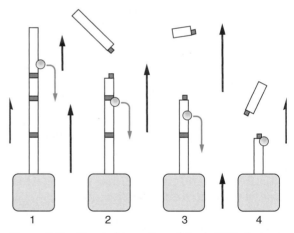

Figure 7–9. Direct observation of single DNA cleavage events catalyzed by a restriction endonuclease. DNA molecules immobilized to beads (gray) are placed in a flowing stream of buffer (thick arrows), which causes them to assume an extended conformation. Cleavage at one of the restriction sites (labeled in color) by an endonuclease leads to a shortening of the DNA molecule, which can be observed directly in a microscope since the nucleotide bases in DNA are fluorescent. Although the endonuclease (open circle) does not fluoresce, and hence is invisible, the progressive manner in which the DNA molecule is shortened (1→4) reveals that the endonuclease binds to the free end of the DNA molecule and moves along it from site to site.

other therapeutic agents. Many antibiotics, for example, inhibit enzymes that are unique to microbial pathogens. The discovery of new drugs is greatly facilitated when a large number of potential pharmacophores can be assayed in a rapid, automated fashion—a process referred to as **high-throughput screening.** High-throughput screening is ideal for surveying the numerous products of **combinatorial chemistry,** the simultaneous synthesis of large libraries of chemical compounds that contain all possible combinations of a set of chemical precursors. Enzyme assays that produce a chromagenic or fluorescent product are ideal for high-throughput screening since optical detectors are readily engineered to permit the rapid analysis of multiple samples.

Enzyme-Linked Immunoassays

The sensitivity of enzyme assays can be exploited to detect proteins that lack catalytic activity. **Enzyme-linked immunoassays** (ELISAs) use antibodies covalently linked to a "reporter enzyme" such as alkaline phosphatase or horseradish peroxidase whose products are readily detected, generally by the absorbance of light or by fluorescence. Serum or other biologic samples to be tested are placed in a plastic microtiter plate, where the proteins adhere to the plastic surface and are immobilized. Any remaining absorbing areas of the well are then "blocked" by adding a non-antigenic protein such as bovine serum albumin. A solution of antibody covalently linked to a reporter enzyme is then added. The antibodies adhere to the immobilized antigen and are themselves immobilized. Excess free antibody molecules are then removed by washing. The presence and quantity of bound antibody is then determined by adding the substrate for the reporter enzyme.

NAD(P)$^+$-Dependent Dehydrogenases Are Assayed Spectrophotometrically

The physicochemical properties of the reactants in an enzyme-catalyzed reaction dictate the options for the assay of enzyme activity. Spectrophotometric assays exploit the ability of a substrate or product to absorb light. The reduced coenzymes NADH and NADPH, written as NAD(P)H, absorb light at a wavelength of 340 nm, whereas their oxidized forms NAD(P)$^+$ do not (Figure 7–10). When NAD(P)$^+$ is reduced, the absorbance at 340 nm therefore increases in proportion to—and at a rate determined by—the quantity of NAD(P)H produced. Conversely, for a dehydrogenase that catalyzes the oxidation of NAD(P)H, a decrease in absorbance at 340 nm will be observed. In each case, the rate of change in optical density at 340 nm will be proportionate to the quantity of enzyme present.

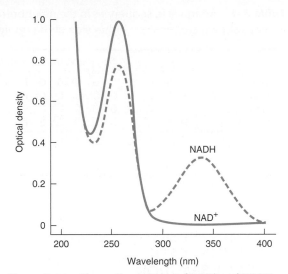

Figure 7–10. Absorption spectra of NAD$^+$ and NADH. Densities are for a 44 mg/L solution in a cell with a 1 cm light path. NADP$^+$ and NADPH have spectrums analogous to NAD$^+$ and NADH, respectively.

Many Enzymes Are Assayed by Coupling to a Dehydrogenase

The assay of enzymes whose reactions are not accompanied by a change in absorbance or fluorescence is generally more difficult. In some instances, the product or remaining substrate can be transformed into a more readily detected compound. In other instances, the reaction product may have to be separated from unreacted substrate prior to measurement. An alternative strategy is to devise a synthetic substrate whose product absorbs light or fluoresces. For example, *p*-nitrophenyl phosphate is an artificial substrate for certain phosphatases and for chymotrypsin that does not absorb visible light. However, following hydrolysis, the resulting *p*-nitrophenylate anion absorbs light at 419 nm.

Another quite general approach is to employ a "coupled" assay (Figure 7–11). Typically, a dehydrogenase whose substrate is the product of the enzyme of interest is added in catalytic excess. The rate of appearance or disappearance of NAD(P)H then depends on the rate of the enzyme reaction to which the dehydrogenase has been coupled.

THE ANALYSIS OF CERTAIN ENZYMES AIDS DIAGNOSIS

Of the thousands of different enzymes present in the human body, those that fulfill functions indispensable to cell vitality are present throughout the body tissues. Other enzymes or isozymes are expressed only in specific cell

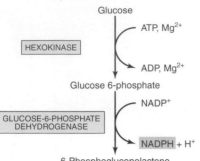

Figure 7–11. Coupled enzyme assay for hexokinase activity. The production of glucose 6-phosphate by hexokinase is coupled to the oxidation of this product by glucose-6-phosphate dehydrogenase in the presence of added enzyme and $NADP^+$. When an excess of glucose-6-phosphate dehydrogenase is present, the rate of formation of NADPH, which can be measured at 340 nm, is governed by the rate of formation of glucose-6-phosphate by hexokinase.

Table 7–2. Principal serum enzymes used in clinical diagnosis.

Serum Enzyme	Major Diagnostic Use
Aminotransferases	
Aspartate aminotrans- ferase (AST, or SGOT)	Myocardial infarction
Alanine aminotransfer- ase (ALT, or SGPT)	Viral hepatitis
Amylase	Acute pancreatitis
Ceruloplasmin	Hepatolenticular degenera- tion (Wilson's disease)
Creatine kinase	Muscle disorders and myo- cardial infarction
γ-Glutamyl transpeptidase	Various liver diseases
Lactate dehydrogenase (isozymes)	Myocardial infarction
Lipase	Acute pancreatitis
Phosphatase, acid	Metastatic carcinoma of the prostate
Phosphatase, alkaline (isozymes)	Various bone disorders, ob- structive liver diseases

Note: Many of the enzymes are not specific for the disease listed.

types, during certain periods of development, or in response to specific physiologic or pathophysiologic changes. Analysis of the presence and distribution of enzymes and isozymes—whose expression is normally tissue-, time-, or circumstance-specific—often aids diagnosis.

Nonfunctional Plasma Enzymes Aid Diagnosis & Prognosis

Certain enzymes, proenzymes, and their substrates are present at all times in the circulation of normal individuals and perform a physiologic function in the blood. Examples of these **functional plasma enzymes** include lipoprotein lipase, pseudocholinesterase, and the proenzymes of blood coagulation and blood clot dissolution (Chapter 50). The majority of these enzymes are synthesized in and secreted by the liver.

Plasma also contains numerous other enzymes that perform no known physiologic function in blood. These apparently **nonfunctional plasma enzymes** arise from the routine normal destruction of erythrocytes, leukocytes, and other cells. Tissue damage or necrosis resulting from injury or disease is generally accompanied by increases in the levels of several nonfunctional plasma enzymes. Table 7–2 lists several enzymes used in diagnostic enzymology.

Isozymes of Lactate Dehydrogenase Are Used to Detect Myocardial Infarctions

L-Lactate dehydrogenase is a tetrameric enzyme whose four subunits occur in two isoforms, designated H (for

heart) and M (for muscle). The subunits can combine as shown below to yield catalytically active isozymes of L-lactate dehydrogenase:

Lactate Dehydrogenase Isozyme	Subunits
I_1	HHHH
I_2	HHHM
I_3	HHMM
I_4	HMMM
I_5	MMMM

Distinct genes whose expression is differentially regulated in various tissues encode the H and M subunits. Since heart expresses the H subunit almost exclusively, isozyme I_1 predominates in this tissue. By contrast, isozyme I_5 predominates in liver. Small quantities of lactate dehydrogenase are normally present in plasma. Following a myocardial infarction or in liver disease, the damaged tissues release characteristic lactate dehydrogenase isoforms into the blood. The resulting elevation in the levels of the I_1 or I_5 isozymes is detected by separating the different oligomers of lactate dehydrogenase by electrophoresis and assaying their catalytic activity (Figure 7–12).

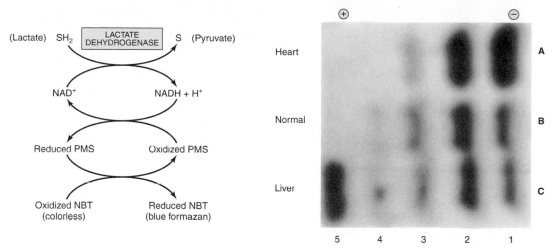

Figure 7–12. Normal and pathologic patterns of lactate dehydrogenase (LDH) isozymes in human serum. LDH isozymes of serum were separated by electrophoresis and visualized using the coupled reaction scheme shown on the left. (NBT, nitroblue tetrazolium; PMS, phenazine methylsulfate). At right is shown the stained electropherogram. Pattern A is serum from a patient with a myocardial infarct; B is normal serum; and C is serum from a patient with liver disease. Arabic numerals denote specific LDH isozymes.

ENZYMES FACILITATE DIAGNOSIS OF GENETIC DISEASES

While many diseases have long been known to result from alterations in an individual's DNA, tools for the detection of genetic mutations have only recently become widely available. These techniques rely upon the catalytic efficiency and specificity of enzyme catalysts. For example, the **polymerase chain reaction (PCR)** relies upon the ability of enzymes to serve as catalytic amplifiers to analyze the DNA present in biologic and forensic samples. In the PCR technique, a thermostable DNA polymerase, directed by appropriate oligonucleotide primers, produces thousands of copies of a sample of DNA that was present initially at levels too low for direct detection.

The detection of **restriction fragment length polymorphisms (RFLPs)** facilitates prenatal detection of hereditary disorders such as sickle cell trait, beta-thalassemia, infant phenylketonuria, and Huntington's disease. Detection of RFLPs involves cleavage of double-stranded DNA by restriction endonucleases, which can detect subtle alterations in DNA that affect their recognized sites. Chapter 39 provides further details concerning the use of PCR and restriction enzymes for diagnosis.

RECOMBINANT DNA PROVIDES AN IMPORTANT TOOL FOR STUDYING ENZYMES

Recombinant DNA technology has emerged as an important asset in the study of enzymes. Highly puri-

fied samples of enzymes are necessary for the study of their structure and function. The isolation of an individual enzyme, particularly one present in low concentration, from among the thousands of proteins present in a cell can be extremely difficult. If the gene for the enzyme of interest has been cloned, it generally is possible to produce large quantities of its encoded protein in *Escherichia coli* or yeast. However, not all animal proteins can be expressed in active form in microbial cells, nor do microbes perform certain posttranslational processing tasks. For these reasons, a gene may be expressed in cultured animal cell systems employing the baculovirus expression vector to transform cultured insect cells. For more details concerning recombinant DNA techniques, see Chapter 39.

Recombinant Fusion Proteins Are Purified by Affinity Chromatography

Recombinant DNA technology can also be used to create modified proteins that are readily purified by affinity chromatography. The gene of interest is linked to an oligonucleotide sequence that encodes a carboxyl or amino terminal extension to the encoded protein. The resulting modified protein, termed a **fusion protein,** contains a domain tailored to interact with a specific affinity support. One popular approach is to attach an oligonucleotide that encodes six consecutive histidine residues. The expressed "His tag" protein binds to chromatographic supports that contain an immobilized divalent metal ion such as Ni^{2+}. Alternatively, the substrate-binding domain

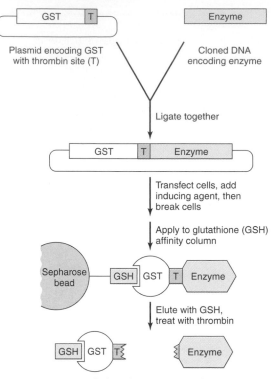

Figure 7–13. Use of glutathione S-transferase (GST) fusion proteins to purify recombinant proteins. (GSH, glutathione.)

of glutathione S-transferase (GST) can serve as a "GST tag." Figure 7–13 illustrates the purification of a GST-fusion protein using an affinity support containing bound glutathione. Fusion proteins also often encode a cleavage site for a highly specific protease such as thrombin in the region that links the two portions of the protein. This permits removal of the added fusion domain following affinity purification.

Site-Directed Mutagenesis Provides Mechanistic Insights

Once the ability to express a protein from its cloned gene has been established, it is possible to employ **site-directed mutagenesis** to change specific aminoacyl residues by altering their codons. Used in combination with kinetic analyses and x-ray crystallography, this approach facilitates identification of the specific roles of given aminoacyl residues in substrate binding and catalysis. For example, the inference that a particular aminoacyl residue functions as a general acid can be tested by replacing it with an aminoacyl residue incapable of donating a proton.

SUMMARY

- Enzymes are highly effective and extremely specific catalysts.
- Organic and inorganic prosthetic groups, cofactors, and coenzymes play important roles in catalysis. Co-enzymes, many of which are derivatives of B vitamins, serve as "shuttles."
- Catalytic mechanisms employed by enzymes include the introduction of strain, approximation of reactants, acid-base catalysis, and covalent catalysis.
- Aminoacyl residues that participate in catalysis are highly conserved among all classes of a given enzyme.
- Substrates and enzymes induce mutual conformational changes in one another that facilitate substrate recognition and catalysis.
- The catalytic activity of enzymes reveals their presence, facilitates their detection, and provides the basis for enzyme-linked immunoassays.
- Many enzymes can be assayed spectrophotometrically by coupling them to an NAD(P)$^+$-dependent dehydrogenase.
- Combinatorial chemistry generates extensive libraries of potential enzyme activators and inhibitors that can be tested by high-throughput screening.
- Assay of plasma enzymes aids diagnosis and prognosis. For example, a myocardial infarction elevates serum levels of lactate dehydrogenase isozyme I_1.
- Restriction endonucleases facilitate diagnosis of genetic diseases by revealing restriction fragment length polymorphisms.
- Site-directed mutagenesis, used to change residues suspected of being important in catalysis or substrate binding, provides insights into the mechanisms of enzyme action.
- Recombinant fusion proteins such as His-tagged or GST fusion enzymes are readily purified by affinity chromatography.

REFERENCES

Brik A, Wong C-H: HIV-1 protease: Mechanism and drug discovery. Org Biomol Chem 2003;1:5.

Conyers GB et al: Metal requirements of a diadenosine pyrophosphatase from *Bartonella bacilliformis*. Magnetic resonance and kinetic studies of the role of Mn^{2+}. Biochemistry 2000;39:2347.

Fersht A: *Structure and Mechanism in Protein Science: A Guide to Enzyme Catalysis and Protein Folding.* Freeman, 1999.

Frank RAW, et al: A molecular switch and proton wire synchronize the active sites in thiamine enzymes. Science 2004;306:872.

Geysen HM, Schoenen F, Wagner D, Wagner R: Combinatorial compound libraries for drug discovery: An ongoing challenge. Nature Rev Drug Disc 2003;2:222.

Goddard J-P, Reymond J-L: Enzyme assays for high-throughput screening. Curr Opin Biotech 2004;15:314.

Hedstrom L: Serine protease mechanism and specificity. Chem Rev 2002;102:4501.

Ishijima A, Yanagida T: Single molecule nanobioscience. Trends Biochem Sci 2001;26:438.

Schafer B, Gemeinhardt H, Greulich KO: Direct microscopic observation of the time course of single-molecule DNA restriction reactions. Agnew Chem Int Ed 2001;40:4663

Silverman RB: *The Organic Chemistry of Enzyme-Catalyzed Reactions.* Academic Press, 2002.

Suckling CJ: *Enzyme Chemistry.* Chapman & Hall, 1990.

Sundaresan V, Abrol R: Towards a general model for protein-substrate stereoselectivity. Protein Sci 2002;11:1330.

Todd AE, Orengo CA, Thornton JM: Plasticity of enzyme active sites. Trends Biochem Sci 2002;27:419.

Walsh CT: *Enzymatic Reaction Mechanisms.* Freeman, 1979.

Enzymes: Kinetics

Peter J. Kennelly, PhD, & Victor W. Rodwell, PhD

BIOMEDICAL IMPORTANCE

Enzyme kinetics is the field of biochemistry concerned with the quantitative measurement of the rates of enzyme-catalyzed reactions and the systematic study of factors that affect these rates. A complete, balanced set of enzyme activities is of fundamental importance for maintaining homeostasis. An understanding of enzyme kinetics thus is important to understanding how physiologic stresses such as anoxia, metabolic acidosis or alkalosis, toxins, and pharmacologic agents affect that balance. Kinetic analysis can reveal the number and order of the individual steps by which enzymes transform substrates into products. Together with site-directed mutagenesis and other techniques that probe protein structure, kinetic analyses can also reveal details of the catalytic mechanism of a given enzyme. The involvement of enzymes in virtually all physiologic processes makes them the targets of choice for drugs that cure or ameliorate human disease. Applied enzyme kinetics therefore represents the principal way by which scientists identify and characterize therapeutic agents that selectively inhibit the rates of specific enzyme-catalyzed processes. Enzyme kinetics thus plays a central and critical role in drug discovery, comparative pharmacodynamics, and determining the mode of action of drugs.

CHEMICAL REACTIONS ARE DESCRIBED USING BALANCED EQUATIONS

A **balanced chemical equation** lists the initial chemical species (substrates) present and the new chemical species (products) formed for a particular chemical reaction, all in their correct proportions or **stoichiometry.** For example, balanced equation (1) below describes the reaction of one molecule each of substrates A and B to form one molecule each of products P and Q.

$$A + B \rightleftarrows P + Q \qquad (1)$$

The double arrows indicate reversibility, an intrinsic property of all chemical reactions. Thus, for reaction (1), if A and B can form P and Q, then P and Q can also form A and B. Designation of a particular reactant as a "substrate" or "product" is therefore somewhat arbitrary since the products for a reaction written in one direction are the substrates for the reverse reaction. The term "products" is, however, often used to designate the reactants whose formation is thermodynamically favored. Reactions for which thermodynamic factors strongly favor formation of the products to which the arrow points often are represented with a single arrow as if they were "irreversible":

$$A + B \rightarrow P + Q \qquad (2)$$

Unidirectional arrows are also used to describe reactions in living cells where the products of reaction (2) are immediately consumed by a subsequent enzyme-catalyzed reaction. The rapid removal of product P or Q therefore effectively precludes occurrence of the reverse reaction, rendering equation (2) **functionally irreversible under physiologic conditions.**

CHANGES IN FREE ENERGY DETERMINE THE DIRECTION & EQUILIBRIUM STATE OF CHEMICAL REACTIONS

The Gibbs free energy change ΔG (also called either the free energy or Gibbs energy) describes both the *direction* in which a chemical reaction will tend to proceed and the concentrations of reactants and products that will be present at equilibrium. ΔG for a chemical reaction equals the sum of the free energies of formation of the reaction products ΔG_p minus the sum of the free energies of formation of the substrates ΔG_s. ΔG^0 denotes the change in free energy that accompanies transition from the standard state, one-molar concentrations of substrates and products, to equilibrium. A more useful biochemical term is $\Delta G^{0'}$, which defines ΔG^0 at a standard state of 10^{-7} M protons, pH 7.0 (Chapter 11). If the free energy of formation of the products is lower than that of the substrates, the signs of ΔG^0 and $\Delta G^{0'}$ will be negative, indicating that the reaction as written is favored in the direction left to right. Such reactions are referred to as **spontaneous.** The **sign** and the **magnitude** of the free energy change determine how far the reaction will proceed. Equation (3)

$$\Delta G^0 = -RT \ln K_{eq} \qquad (3)$$

illustrates the relationship between the equilibrium constant K_{eq} and ΔG^0, where R is the gas constant (1.98 cal/mol/K or 8.31 J/mol/K) and T is the absolute temperature in degrees Kelvin. K_{eq} is equal to the product of the concentrations of the reaction products, each raised to the power of their stoichiometry, divided by the product of the substrates, each raised to the power of their stoichiometry.

For the reaction $A + B \rightleftarrows P + Q$

$$K_{eq} = \frac{[P][Q]}{[A][B]} \qquad (4)$$

and for reaction (5)

$$A + A \rightleftarrows P \qquad (5)$$

$$K_{eq} = \frac{[P]}{[A]^2} \qquad (6)$$

ΔG^0 may be calculated from equation (3) if the concentrations of substrates and products present at equilibrium are known. If ΔG^0 is a negative number, K_{eq} will be greater than unity and the concentration of products at equilibrium will exceed that of the substrates. If ΔG^0 is positive, K_{eq} will be less than unity and the formation of substrates will be favored.

Notice that, since ΔG^0 is a function exclusively of the initial and final states of the reacting species, it can provide information only about the *direction* and *equilibrium state* of the reaction. ΔG^0 is independent of the mechanism of the reaction and therefore provides no information concerning **rates** of reactions. Consequently—and as explained below—although a reaction may have a large negative ΔG^0 or $\Delta G^{0'}$, it may nevertheless take place at a negligible rate.

THE RATES OF REACTIONS ARE DETERMINED BY THEIR ACTIVATION ENERGY

Reactions Proceed via Transition States

The concept of the **transition state** is fundamental to understanding the chemical and thermodynamic basis of catalysis. Equation (7) depicts a displacement reaction in which an entering group E displaces a leaving group L, attached initially to R.

$$E + R - L \rightleftarrows E - R + L \qquad (7)$$

Midway through the displacement, the bond between R and L has weakened but has not yet been completely

severed, and the new bond between E and R is as yet incompletely formed. This transient intermediate—in which neither free substrate nor product exists—is termed the **transition state, E···R···L.** Dotted lines represent the "partial" bonds that are undergoing formation and rupture.

Reaction (7) can be thought of as consisting of two "partial reactions," the first corresponding to the formation (F) and the second to the subsequent decay (D) of the transition state intermediate. As for all reactions, characteristic changes in free energy, ΔG_F and ΔG_D are associated with each partial reaction.

$$E + R - L \rightleftarrows E \cdots R \cdots L \quad \Delta G_F \qquad (8)$$

$$E \cdots R \cdots L \rightleftarrows E - R + L \quad \Delta G_D \qquad (9)$$

$$E + R - L \rightleftarrows E - R + L \quad \Delta G = \Delta G_F + \Delta G_D \qquad (10)$$

For the overall reaction (10), ΔG is the sum of ΔG_F and ΔG_D. As for any equation of two terms, it is not possible to infer from ΔG either the sign or the magnitude of ΔG_F or ΔG_D.

Many reactions involve multiple transition states, each with an associated change in free energy. For these reactions, the overall ΔG represents the sum of *all* of the free energy changes associated with the formation and decay of *all* of the transition states. **Therefore, it is not possible to infer from the overall ΔG the number or type of transition states through which the reaction proceeds.** Stated another way: overall thermodynamics tells us nothing about kinetics.

ΔG_F Defines the Activation Energy

Regardless of the sign or magnitude of ΔG, ΔG_F for the overwhelming majority of chemical reactions has a positive sign. The formation of transition state intermediates therefore requires surmounting of energy barriers. For this reason, ΔG_F is often termed the **activation energy,** E_{act}, the energy required to surmount a given energy barrier. The ease—and hence the frequency—with which this barrier is overcome is inversely related to E_{act}. The thermodynamic parameters that determine how *fast* a reaction proceeds thus are the ΔG_F values for formation of the transition states through which the reaction proceeds. For a simple reaction, where $\propto$ means "proportionate to,"

$$Rate \propto e^{-E_{act}/RT} \qquad (11)$$

The activation energy for the reaction proceeding in the opposite direction to that drawn is equal to $-\Delta G_D$.

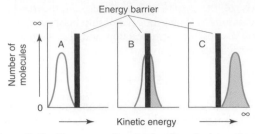

Figure 8–1. The energy barrier for chemical reactions.

NUMEROUS FACTORS AFFECT THE REACTION RATE

The **kinetic theory**—also called the **collision theory**—of chemical kinetics states that for two molecules to react they must (1) approach within bond-forming distance of one another, or "collide"; and (2) must possess sufficient kinetic energy to overcome the energy barrier for reaching the transition state. It therefore follows that anything that increases the *frequency* or *energy* of collision between substrates will increase the rate of the reaction in which they participate.

Temperature

Raising the temperature increases the kinetic energy of molecules. As illustrated in Figure 8–1, the total number of molecules whose kinetic energy exceeds the energy barrier E_{act} (vertical bar) for formation of products increases from low (A), through intermediate (B), to high (C) temperatures. Increasing the kinetic energy of molecules also increases their motion and therefore the frequency with which they collide. This combination of more frequent and more highly energetic and productive collisions increases the reaction rate.

Reactant Concentration

The frequency with which molecules collide is directly proportionate to their concentrations. For two different molecules A and B, the frequency with which they collide will double if the concentration of either A or B is doubled. If the concentrations of both A and B are doubled, the probability of collision will increase fourfold.

For a chemical reaction proceeding at constant temperature that involves one molecule each of A and B,

$$A + B \rightarrow P \tag{12}$$

the number of molecules that possess kinetic energy sufficient to overcome the activation energy barrier will be a constant. The number of collisions with sufficient energy to produce product P therefore will be directly proportionate to the number of collisions between A

and B and thus to their molar concentrations, denoted by square brackets.

$$\text{Rate} \propto [A][B] \tag{13}$$

Similarly, for the reaction represented by

$$A + 2B \rightarrow P \tag{14}$$

which can also be written as

$$A + B + B \rightarrow P \tag{15}$$

the corresponding rate expression is

$$\text{Rate} \propto [A][B][B] \tag{16}$$

or

$$\text{Rate} \propto [A][B]^2 \tag{17}$$

For the general case when n molecules of A react with m molecules of B,

$$nA + mB \rightarrow P \tag{18}$$

the rate expression is

$$\text{Rate} \propto [A]^n[B]^m \tag{19}$$

Replacing the proportionality constant with an equals sign by introducing a proportionality or **rate constant k** characteristic of the reaction under study gives equations (20) and (21), in which the subscripts 1 and −1 refer to the forward and reverse reactions, respectively.

$$\text{Rate}_1 = k_1[A]^n[B]^m \tag{20}$$

$$\text{Rate}_{-1} = k_{-1}[P] \tag{21}$$

K_{eq} Is a Ratio of Rate Constants

While all chemical reactions are to some extent reversible, at equilibrium the *overall* concentrations of reactants and products remain constant. At equilibrium, the rate of conversion of substrates to products therefore equals the rate at which products are converted to substrates.

$$\text{Rate}_1 = \text{Rate}_{-1} \tag{22}$$

Therefore,

$$k_1[A]^n[B]^m = k_{-1}[P] \tag{23}$$

and

$$\frac{k_1}{k_{-1}} = \frac{[P]}{[A]^n[B]^m} \tag{24}$$

The ratio of k_1 to k_{-1} is termed the equilibrium constant, K_{eq}. The following important properties of a system at equilibrium must be kept in mind:

(1) The equilibrium constant is a ratio of the reaction *rate constants* (not the reaction *rates*).
(2) At equilibrium, the reaction *rates* (not the *rate constants*) of the forward and back reactions are equal.
(3) Equilibrium is a *dynamic* state. Although there is no *net* change in the concentration of substrates or products, individual substrate and product molecules are continually being interconverted.
(4) The numeric value of the equilibrium constant K_{eq} can be calculated either from the concentrations of substrates and products at equilibrium or from the ratio k_1/k_{-1}.

THE KINETICS OF ENZYMATIC CATALYSIS

Enzymes Lower the Activation Energy Barrier for a Reaction

All enzymes accelerate reaction rates by providing transition states with a lowered ΔG_F for formation of the transition states. However, they may differ in the way this is achieved. Where the mechanism or the sequence of chemical steps at the active site is essentially the same as those for the same reaction proceeding in the absence of a catalyst, **the environment of the active site lowers ΔG_F by** stabilizing the transition state intermediates. As discussed in Chapter 7, stabilization can involve (1) acid-base groups suitably positioned to transfer protons to or from the developing transition state intermediate, (2) suitably positioned charged groups or metal ions that stabilize developing charges, or (3) the imposition of steric strain on substrates so that their geometry approaches that of the transition state. HIV protease (see Figure 7–6) illustrates catalysis by an enzyme that lowers the activation barrier by stabilizing a transition state intermediate.

Catalysis by enzymes that proceeds via a *unique* reaction mechanism typically occurs when the transition state intermediate forms a covalent bond with the enzyme **(covalent catalysis).** The catalytic mechanism of the serine protease chymotrypsin (see Figure 7–7) illustrates how an enzyme utilizes covalent catalysis to provide a unique reaction pathway.

ENZYMES DO NOT AFFECT K_{eq}

Enzymes accelerate reaction rates by lowering the activation barrier ΔG_F. While they may undergo transient modification during the process of catalysis, enzymes emerge unchanged at the completion of the reaction. **The presence of an enzyme therefore has no effect on ΔG^0 for the *overall* reaction,** which is a function

solely of the *initial and final states* of the reactants. Equation (25) shows the relationship between the equilibrium constant for a reaction and the standard free energy change for that reaction:

$$\Delta G^0 = -RT \ln K_{eq} \qquad (25)$$

If we include the presence of the enzyme (Enz) in the calculation of the equilibrium constant for a reaction,

$$A + B + Enz \rightleftarrows P + Q + Enz \qquad (26)$$

the expression for the equilibrium constant,

$$K_{eq} = \frac{[P][Q][Enz]}{[A][B][Enz]} \qquad (27)$$

reduces to one identical to that for the reaction in the absence of the enzyme:

$$K_{eq} = \frac{[P][Q]}{[A][B]} \qquad (28)$$

Enzymes therefore have no effect on K_{eq}.

MULTIPLE FACTORS AFFECT THE RATES OF ENZYME-CATALYZED REACTIONS

Temperature

Raising the temperature increases the rate of both uncatalyzed and enzyme-catalyzed reactions by increasing the kinetic energy and the collision frequency of the reacting molecules. However, heat energy can also increase the kinetic energy of the enzyme to a point that exceeds the energy barrier for disrupting the noncovalent interactions that maintain the enzyme's three-dimensional structure. The polypeptide chain then begins to unfold, or **denature,** with an accompanying loss of catalytic activity. The temperature range over which an enzyme maintains a stable, catalytically competent conformation depends upon—and typically moderately exceeds—the normal temperature of the cells in which it resides. Enzymes from humans generally exhibit stability at temperatures up to 45–55 °C. By contrast, enzymes from the thermophilic microorganisms that reside in volcanic hot springs or undersea hydrothermal vents may be stable up to or even above 100 °C.

The **Q_{10}, or temperature coefficient,** is the factor by which the rate of a biologic process increases for a 10 °C increase in temperature. For the temperatures over which enzymes are stable, the rates of most biologic processes typically double for a 10 °C rise in temperature ($Q_{10} = 2$). Changes in the rates of enzyme-catalyzed reactions that accompany a rise or fall in body temperature constitute a prominent survival feature for "cold-blooded" life forms such as lizards or fish, whose

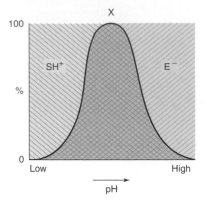

Figure 8–2. Effect of pH on enzyme activity. Consider, for example, a negatively charged enzyme (EH⁻) that binds a positively charged substrate (SH⁺). Shown is the proportion (%) of SH⁺ [\\\] and of EH⁻ [///] as a function of pH. Only in the cross-hatched area do both the enzyme and the substrate bear an appropriate charge.

body temperatures are dictated by the external environment. However, for mammals and other homeothermic organisms, changes in enzyme reaction rates with temperature assume physiologic importance only in circumstances such as fever or hypothermia.

Hydrogen Ion Concentration

The rate of almost all enzyme-catalyzed reactions exhibits a significant dependence on hydrogen ion concentration. Most intracellular enzymes exhibit optimal activity at pH values between 5 and 9. The relationship of activity to hydrogen ion concentration (Figure 8–2) reflects the balance between enzyme denaturation at high or low pH and effects on the charged state of the enzyme, the substrates, or both. For enzymes whose mechanism involves acid-base catalysis, the residues involved must be in the appropriate state of protonation for the reaction to proceed. The binding and recognition of substrate molecules with dissociable groups also typically involves the formation of salt bridges with the enzyme. The most common charged groups are the negative carboxylate groups and the positively charged groups of protonated amines. Gain or loss of critical charged groups thus will adversely affect substrate binding and thus will retard or abolish catalysis.

ASSAYS OF ENZYME-CATALYZED REACTIONS TYPICALLY MEASURE THE INITIAL VELOCITY

Most measurements of the rates of enzyme-catalyzed reactions employ relatively short time periods, condi-

tions that approximate **initial rate conditions.** Under these conditions, since only traces of product accumulate, the rate of the reverse reaction is negligible. The **initial velocity** (v_i) of the reaction thus is essentially that of the rate of the forward reaction. Assays of enzyme activity almost always employ a large (10^3–10^7) molar excess of substrate over enzyme. Under these conditions, v_i is proportionate to the concentration of enzyme. Measuring the initial velocity therefore permits one to estimate the quantity of enzyme present in a biologic sample.

SUBSTRATE CONCENTRATION AFFECTS REACTION RATE

In what follows, enzyme reactions are treated as if they had only a single substrate and a single product. While most enzymes have more than one substrate, the principles discussed below apply with equal validity to enzymes with multiple substrates.

For a typical enzyme, as substrate concentration is increased, v_i increases until it reaches a maximum value V_{max} (Figure 8–3). When further increases in substrate concentration do not further increase v_i, the enzyme is said to be "saturated" with substrate. Note that the shape of the curve that relates activity to substrate concentration (Figure 8–3) is hyperbolic. At any given instant, only substrate molecules that are combined with the enzyme as an ES complex can be transformed into product. Second, the equilibrium constant for the formation of the enzyme-substrate complex is not infinitely large. Therefore, even when the substrate is present in excess (points A and B of Figure 8–4), only a fraction of the enzyme may be present as an ES complex. At points A or B, increasing or decreasing [S] therefore will increase or decrease the number of ES complexes with a corresponding change in v_i. At point C (Figure 8–4), essentially all the enzyme is present as the ES complex. Since no free enzyme remains available for forming ES, further increases in [S] cannot increase the rate of the reaction. Under these saturating conditions, v_i depends

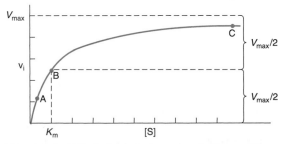

Figure 8–3. Effect of substrate concentration on the initial velocity of an enzyme-catalyzed reaction.

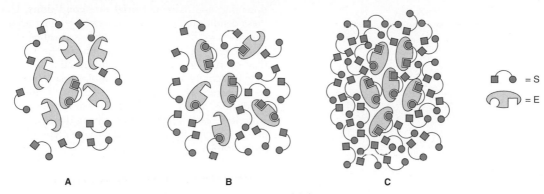

Figure 8–4. Representation of an enzyme at low **(A)**, at high **(C)**, and at a substrate concentration equal to K_m **(B)**. Points A, B, and C correspond to those points in Figure 8–3.

solely on—and thus is limited by—the rapidity with which product dissociates from the enzyme so that it may combine with more substrate.

THE MICHAELIS-MENTEN & HILL EQUATIONS MODEL THE EFFECTS OF SUBSTRATE CONCENTRATION

The Michaelis-Menten Equation

The Michaelis-Menten equation (29) illustrates in mathematical terms the relationship between initial reaction velocity v_i and substrate concentration [S], shown graphically in Figure 8–3.

$$v_i = \frac{V_{max}[S]}{K_m + [S]} \qquad (29)$$

The Michaelis constant K_m is the substrate concentration at which v_i is half the maximal velocity ($V_{max}/2$) attainable at a particular concentration of enzyme. K_m thus has the dimensions of substrate concentration. The dependence of initial reaction velocity on [S] and K_m may be illustrated by evaluating the Michaelis-Menten equation under three conditions.

(1) When [S] is much less than K_m (point A in Figures 8–3 and 8–4), the term $K_m + [S]$ is essentially equal to K_m. Replacing $K_m + [S]$ with K_m reduces equation (29) to

$$v_1 = \frac{V_{max}[S]}{K_m + [S]} \qquad v_1 \approx \frac{V_{max}[S]}{K_m} \approx \left(\frac{V_{max}}{K_m}\right)[S] \qquad (30)$$

where ≈ means "approximately equal to." Since V_{max} and K_m are both constants, their ratio is a constant. In other words, when [S] is considerably below K_m, v_i is proportionate to k[S]. The initial reaction velocity therefore is directly proportional to [S].

(2) When [S] is much greater than K_m (point C in Figures 8–3 and 8–4), the term $K_m + [S]$ is essentially equal to [S]. Replacing $K_m + [S]$ with [S] reduces equation (29) to

$$v_i = \frac{V_{max}[S]}{K_m + [S]} \qquad v_i \approx \frac{V_{max}[S]}{[S]} \approx V_{max} \qquad (31)$$

Thus, when [S] greatly exceeds K_m, the reaction velocity is maximal (V_{max}) and unaffected by further increases in substrate concentration.

(3) When [S] = K_m (point B in Figures 8–3 and 8–4).

$$v_i = \frac{V_{max}[S]}{K_m + [S]} = \frac{V_{max}[S]}{2[S]} = \frac{V_{max}}{2} \qquad (32)$$

Equation (32) states that when [S] equals K_m, the initial velocity is half-maximal. Equation (32) also reveals that K_m is—and may be determined experimentally from—the substrate concentration at which the initial velocity is half-maximal.

A Linear Form of the Michaelis-Menten Equation Is Used to Determine K_m & V_{max}

The direct measurement of the numeric value of V_{max} and therefore the calculation of K_m often requires impractically high concentrations of substrate to achieve saturating conditions. A linear form of the Michaelis-Menten equation circumvents this difficulty and permits V_{max} and K_m to be extrapolated from initial velocity data obtained at less than saturating concentrations of substrate. Starting with equation (29),

$$v_i = \frac{V_{max}[S]}{K_m + [S]} \qquad (29)$$

invert

$$\frac{1}{v_i} = \frac{K_m + [S]}{V_{max}[S]} \qquad (33)$$

factor

$$\frac{1}{v_i} = \frac{K_m}{V_{max}[S]} + \frac{[S]}{V_{max}[S]} \qquad (34)$$

and simplify

$$\frac{1}{v_i} = \left(\frac{K_m}{V_{max}}\right)\frac{1}{[S]} + \frac{1}{V_{max}} \qquad (35)$$

Equation (35) is the equation for a straight line, $y = ax + b$, where $y = 1/v_i$ and $x = 1/[S]$. A plot of $1/v_i$ as y as a function of $1/[S]$ as x therefore gives a straight line whose y intercept is $1/V_{max}$ and whose slope is K_m/V_{max}. Such a plot is called a **double reciprocal** or **Lineweaver-Burk plot** (Figure 8–5). Setting the y term of equation (36) equal to zero and solving for x reveals that the x intercept is $-1/K_m$.

$$0 = ax + b; \quad \text{therefore,} \quad x = \frac{-b}{a} = \frac{-1}{K_m} \qquad (36)$$

K_m is thus most readily calculated from the negative x intercept.

K_m May Approximate a Binding Constant

The affinity of an enzyme for its substrate is the inverse of the dissociation constant K_d for dissociation of the enzyme substrate complex ES.

$$E + S \underset{k_{-1}}{\overset{k_1}{\rightleftarrows}} ES \qquad (37)$$

$$K_d = \frac{k_{-1}}{k_1} \qquad (38)$$

Stated another way, the smaller the tendency of the enzyme and its substrate to *dissociate*, the *greater* the affinity of the enzyme for its substrate. While the Michaelis constant K_m often approximates the dissociation constant K_d, this is by no means always the case. For a typical enzyme-catalyzed reaction,

$$E + S \underset{k_{-1}}{\overset{k_1}{\rightleftarrows}} ES \overset{k_2}{\longrightarrow} E + P \qquad (39)$$

the value of [S] that gives $v_i = V_{max}/2$ is

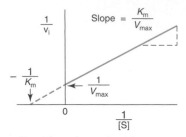

Figure 8–5. Double reciprocal or Lineweaver-Burk plot of $1/v_i$ versus $1/[S]$ used to evaluate K_m and V_{max}.

$$[S] = \frac{k_{-1} + k_2}{k_1} = K_m \qquad (40)$$

When $k_{-1} \gg k_2$, then

$$k_{-1} + k_2 \approx k_{-1} \qquad (41)$$

and

$$[S] \approx \frac{k_1}{k_{-1}} \approx K_d \qquad (42)$$

Hence, $1/K_m$ only approximates $1/K_d$ under conditions where the association and dissociation of the ES complex is rapid relative to the rate-limiting step in catalysis. For the many enzyme-catalyzed reactions for which $k_{-1} + k_2$ is *not* approximately equal to k_{-1}, $1/K_m$ will underestimate $1/K_d$.

The Hill Equation Describes the Behavior of Enzymes That Exhibit Cooperative Binding of Substrate

While most enzymes display the simple **saturation kinetics** depicted in Figure 8–3 and are adequately described by the Michaelis-Menten expression, some enzymes bind their substrates in a *cooperative* fashion analogous to the binding of oxygen by hemoglobin (Chapter 6). Cooperative behavior is an exclusive property of multimeric enzymes that bind substrate at multiple sites.

For enzymes that display positive cooperativity in binding substrate, the shape of the curve that relates changes in v_i to changes in [S] is sigmoidal (Figure 8–6). Neither the Michaelis-Menten expression nor its derived double-reciprocal plots can be used to evaluate cooperative saturation kinetics. Enzymologists therefore employ a graphic representation of the **Hill equation** originally derived to describe the cooperative binding of O_2 by hemoglobin. Equation (43) represents the Hill equation arranged in a form that predicts a straight line, where k′ is a complex constant.

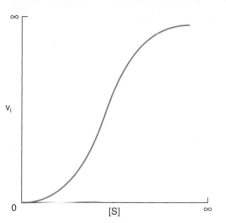

Figure 8–6. Representation of sigmoid substrate saturation kinetics.

$$\frac{\log v_1}{V_{max} - v_1} = n \log[S] - \log k' \qquad (43)$$

Equation (43) states that when [S] is low relative to k′, the initial reaction velocity increases as the nth power of [S].

A graph of $\log v_i/(V_{max} - v_i)$ versus $\log[S]$ gives a straight line (Figure 8–7), where the slope of the line **n** is the **Hill coefficient,** an empirical parameter whose value is a function of the number, kind, and strength of the interactions of the multiple substrate-binding sites on the enzyme. When n = 1, all binding sites behave independently, and simple Michaelis-Menten kinetic behavior is observed. If n is greater than 1, the enzyme is said to exhibit positive cooperativity. Binding of substrate to one site then enhances the affinity of the

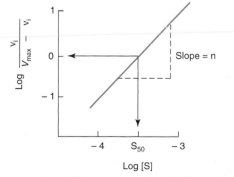

Figure 8–7. A graphic representation of a linear form of the Hill equation is used to evaluate S_{50}, the substrate concentration that produces half-maximal velocity, and the degree of cooperativity **n.**

remaining sites to bind additional substrate. The greater the value for n, the higher the degree of cooperativity and the more sigmoidal will be the plot of v_i versus [S]. A perpendicular dropped from the point where the *y* term $\log v_i/(V_{max} - v_i)$ is zero intersects the *x* axis at a substrate concentration termed S_{50}, the substrate concentration that results in half-maximal velocity. S_{50} thus is analogous to the P_{50} for oxygen binding to hemoglobin (Chapter 6).

KINETIC ANALYSIS DISTINGUISHES COMPETITIVE FROM NONCOMPETITIVE INHIBITION

Inhibitors of the catalytic activities of enzymes provide both pharmacologic agents and research tools for study of the mechanism of enzyme action. Inhibitors can be classified based upon their site of action on the enzyme, on whether they chemically modify the enzyme, or on the kinetic parameters they influence. Kinetically, we distinguish two classes of inhibitors based upon whether raising the substrate concentration does or does not overcome the inhibition.

Competitive Inhibitors Typically Resemble Substrates

The effects of competitive inhibitors can be overcome by raising the concentration of the substrate. Most frequently, in competitive inhibition the inhibitor, **(I)**, binds to the substrate-binding portion of the active site and blocks access by the substrate. The structures of most classic competitive inhibitors therefore tend to resemble the structures of a substrate, and thus are termed **substrate analogs.** Inhibition of the enzyme succinate dehydrogenase by malonate illustrates competitive inhibition by a substrate analog. Succinate dehydrogenase catalyzes the removal of one hydrogen atom from each of the two methylene carbons of succinate (Figure 8–8). Both succinate and its structural analog malonate ($^-OOC—CH_2—COO^-$) can bind to the active site of succinate dehydrogenase, forming an ES or an EI complex, respectively. However, since malonate contains only one methylene carbon, it cannot undergo dehydrogenation. The forma-

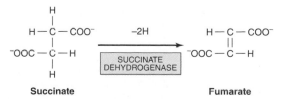

Figure 8–8. The succinate dehydrogenase reaction.

tion and dissociation of the EI complex is a dynamic process described by

$$EnzI \underset{k_{-1}}{\overset{k_1}{\rightleftarrows}} Enz + I \tag{44}$$

for which the equilibrium constant K_i is

$$K_1 = \frac{[Enz][I]}{[EnzI]} = \frac{k_1}{k_{-1}} \tag{45}$$

In effect, **a competitive inhibitor acts by decreasing the number of free enzyme molecules available to bind substrate, ie, to form ES, and thus eventually to form product,** as described below:

$$
\begin{array}{c}
\overset{+I}{\longrightarrow} \text{E-I} \\
\text{E} \underset{\overset{+S}{\longrightarrow}}{\overset{}{}} \\
\text{E-S} \\
\downarrow \\
\text{E + P}
\end{array}
\tag{46}
$$

A competitive inhibitor and substrate exert reciprocal effects on the concentration of the EI and ES complexes. Since binding substrate removes free enzyme available to combine with inhibitor, increasing [S] decreases the concentration of the EI complex and raises the reaction velocity. The extent to which [S] must be increased to completely overcome the inhibition depends upon the concentration of inhibitor present, its affinity for the enzyme K_i, and the K_m of the enzyme for its substrate.

Double Reciprocal Plots Facilitate the Evaluation of Inhibitors

Double reciprocal plots distinguish between competitive and noncompetitive inhibitors and simplify evaluation of inhibition constants. v_i is determined at several substrate concentrations both in the presence and in the absence of inhibitor. For classic competitive inhibition, the lines that connect the experimental data points meet at the y axis (Figure 8–9). Since the y intercept is equal to $1/V_{max}$, this pattern indicates that **when 1/[S] approaches 0, v_i is independent of the presence of inhibitor.** Note, however, that the intercept on the x axis does vary with *inhibitor* concentration—and that since $-1/K'_m$ is smaller than $1/K_m$, K'_m (the "apparent K_m") becomes larger in the presence of increasing concentrations of inhibitor. Thus, **a competitive inhibitor has no effect on V_{max} but raises K'_m, the apparent K_m for the substrate.** For simple competitive inhibition, the intercept on the x axis is

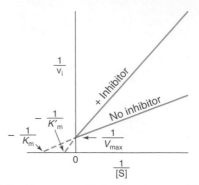

Figure 8–9. Lineweaver-Burk plot of competitive inhibition. Note the complete relief of inhibition at high [S] (ie, low 1/[S]).

$$x = \frac{-1}{K_m}\left(1 + \frac{[I]}{K_i}\right) \tag{47}$$

Once K_m has been determined in the absence of inhibitor, K_i can be calculated from equation (47). K_i values are used to compare different inhibitors of the same enzyme. The lower the value for K_i, the more effective the inhibitor. For example, the statin drugs that act as competitive inhibitors of HMG-CoA reductase (Chapter 26) have K_i values several orders of magnitude lower than the K_m for the substrate HMG-CoA.

Simple Noncompetitive Inhibitors Lower V_{max} But Do Not Affect K_m

In noncompetitive inhibition, binding of the inhibitor does not affect binding of substrate. Formation of both EI and EIS complexes is therefore possible. However, while the enzyme-inhibitor complex can still bind substrate, its efficiency at transforming substrate to product, reflected by V_{max}, is decreased. Noncompetitive inhibitors bind enzymes at sites distinct from the substrate-binding site and generally bear little or no structural resemblance to the substrate.

For simple noncompetitive inhibition, E and EI possess identical affinity for substrate, and the EIS complex generates product at a negligible rate (Figure 8–10). More complex noncompetitive inhibition occurs when binding of the inhibitor *does* affect the apparent affinity of the enzyme for substrate, causing the lines to intercept in either the third or fourth quadrants of a double reciprocal plot (not shown). While certain inhibitors exhibit characteristics of a mixture of competitive and noncompetitive inhibition, the evaluation of these inhibitors exceeds the scope of this chapter.

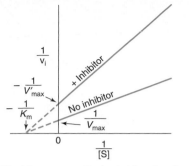

Figure 8–10. Lineweaver-Burk plot for simple non-competitive inhibition.

Irreversible Inhibitors "Poison" Enzymes

In the above examples, the inhibitors form a dissociable, dynamic complex with the enzyme. Fully active enzyme can therefore be recovered simply by removing the inhibitor from the surrounding medium. However, a variety of other inhibitors act irreversibly by chemically modifying the enzyme. These modifications generally involve making or breaking covalent bonds with aminoacyl residues essential for substrate binding, catalysis, or maintenance of the enzyme's functional conformation. Since these covalent changes are relatively stable, an enzyme that has been "poisoned" by an irreversible inhibitor such as a heavy metal atom or an acylating reagent remains inhibited even after removal of the remaining inhibitor from the surrounding medium.

MOST ENZYME-CATALYZED REACTIONS INVOLVE TWO OR MORE SUBSTRATES

While many enzymes have a single substrate, many others have two—and sometimes more than two—substrates and products. The fundamental principles discussed above, while illustrated for single-substrate enzymes, apply also to multisubstrate enzymes. The mathematical expressions used to evaluate multisubstrate reactions are, however, complex. While detailed kinetic analysis of multisubstrate reactions exceeds the scope of this chapter, two-substrate, two-product reactions (termed "Bi-Bi" reactions) are considered below.

Sequential or Single Displacement Reactions

In **sequential reactions,** both substrates must combine with the enzyme to form a ternary complex before catalysis can proceed (Figure 8–11, top). Sequential reactions are sometimes referred to as single displacement reactions because the group undergoing transfer is usually passed directly, in a single step, from one sub-

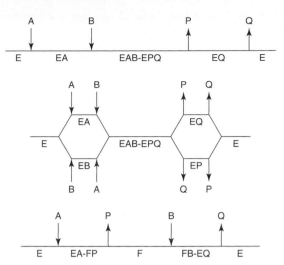

Figure 8–11. Representations of three classes of Bi-Bi reaction mechanisms. Horizontal lines represent the enzyme. Arrows indicate the addition of substrates and departure of products. **Top:** An ordered Bi-Bi reaction, characteristic of many NAD(P)H-dependent oxidoreductases. **Center:** A random Bi-Bi reaction, characteristic of many kinases and some dehydrogenases. **Bottom:** A ping-pong reaction, characteristic of aminotransferases and **serine proteases.**

strate to the other. Sequential Bi-Bi reactions can be further distinguished based on whether the two substrates add in a **random** or in a **compulsory** order. For random-order reactions, either substrate A or substrate B may combine first with the enzyme to form an EA or an EB complex (Figure 8–11, center). For compulsory-order reactions, A must first combine with E before B can combine with the EA complex. One explanation for a compulsory-order mechanism is that the addition of A induces a conformational change in the enzyme that aligns residues that recognize and bind B.

Ping-Pong Reactions

The term **"ping-pong"** applies to mechanisms in which one or more products are released from the enzyme before all the substrates have been added. Ping-pong reactions involve covalent catalysis and a transient, modified form of the enzyme (see Figure 7–4). Ping-pong Bi-Bi reactions are **double displacement reactions.** The group undergoing transfer is first displaced from substrate A by the enzyme to form product P and a modified form of the enzyme (F). The subsequent group transfer from F to the second substrate B, forming product Q and regenerating E, constitutes the second displacement (Figure 8–11, bottom).

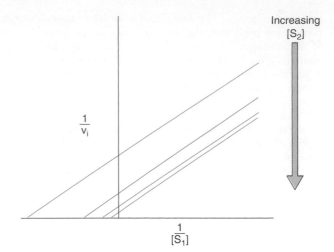

Figure 8–12. Lineweaver-Burk plot for a two-substrate ping-pong reaction. An increase in concentration of one substrate (S_1) while that of the other substrate (S_2) is maintained constant changes both the *x* and *y* intercepts, but not the slope.

Most Bi-Bi Reactions Conform to Michaelis-Menten Kinetics

Most Bi-Bi reactions conform to a somewhat more complex form of Michaelis-Menten kinetics in which V_{max} refers to the reaction rate attained when both substrates are present at saturating levels. Each substrate has its own characteristic K_m value that corresponds to the concentration that yields half-maximal velocity when the second substrate is present at saturating levels. As for single-substrate reactions, double-reciprocal plots can be used to determine V_{max} and K_m. v_i is measured as a function of the concentration of one substrate (the variable substrate) while the concentration of the other substrate (the fixed substrate) is maintained constant. If the lines obtained for several fixed-substrate concentrations are plotted on the same graph, it is possible to distinguish between a ping-pong enzyme, which yields parallel lines, and a sequential mechanism, which yields a pattern of intersecting lines (Figure 8–12).

Product inhibition studies are used to complement kinetic analyses and to distinguish between ordered and random Bi-Bi reactions. For example, in a random-order Bi-Bi reaction, each product will be a competitive inhibitor regardless of which substrate is designated the variable substrate. However, for a sequential mechanism (Figure 8–11, top), only product Q will give the pattern indicative of competitive inhibition when A is the variable substrate, while only product P will produce this pattern with B as the variable substrate. The other combinations of product inhibitor and variable substrate will produce forms of complex noncompetitive inhibition.

KNOWLEDGE OF ENZYME KINETICS, MECHANISM, AND INHIBITION AIDS DRUG DEVELOPMENT

Many Drugs Act as Enzyme Inhibitors

The goal of pharmacology is to identify agents that can

1. Destroy or impair the growth, invasiveness, or development of invading pathogens
2. Stimulate endogenous defense mechanisms
3. Halt or impede aberrant molecular processes triggered by genetic, environmental, or biologic stimuli with minimal perturbation of the host's normal cellular functions

By virtue of their diverse physiologic roles and high degree of substrate selectivity, enzymes constitute natural targets for the development of pharmacologic agents that are both potent and specific. Statin drugs, for example, lower cholesterol production by inhibiting 3-hydroxy-3-methylglutaryl coenzyme A reductase (Chapter 26), while emtricitabine and tenofovir disoproxil fumarate block replication of the human immunodeficiency virus by inhibiting the viral reverse transcriptase (Chapter 34). Pharmacologic treatment of hypertension often includes the administration of an inhibitor of angiotensin-converting enzyme, thus lowering the level of angiotensin II, a vasoconstrictor (Chapter 42).

Enzyme Kinetics Define Appropriate Screening Conditions

Enzyme kinetics play a crucial role in drug discovery. Knowledge of the kinetic behavior of the enzyme of

interest is necessary, first and foremost to select appropriate assay conditions that readily detect the presence of an inhibitor. The concentration of substrate, for example, must be adjusted such that sufficient product is generated to permit facile detection of the enzyme's activity without being so high that it masks the presence of an inhibitor. Second, enzyme kinetics provide the means for quantifying and comparing the potency of different inhibitors and defining their mode of action. Noncompetitive inhibitors are particularly desirable, because by contrast to competitive inhibitors, their effects can never be completely overcome by increases in substrate concentration.

Many Drugs Are Metabolized In Vivo

Drug development often involves more than the kinetic evaluation of the interaction of inhibitors with the target enzyme. Drugs are acted upon by enzymes present in the patient or pathogen, a process termed **drug metabolism.** For example, penicillin and other β-lactam antibiotics block cell wall synthesis in bacteria by irreversibly poisoning the enzyme alanyl alanine carboxy-peptidase-transpeptidase. Many bacteria, however, produce β-lactamases that hydrolyze the critical β-lactam function. One strategy for overcoming the resulting antibiotic resistance is to simultaneously administer a β-lactamase inhibitor and a β-lactam antibiotic.

Metabolic transformation is also required to convert an inactive drug precursor, or **prodrug,** into its biologically active form (Chapter 52). 2′-Deoxy-5-fluorouridylic acid, a potent inhibitor of thymidylate synthase, a common target of cancer chemotherapy, is produced from 5-fluorouracil via a series of enzymatic transformations catalyzed by a phosphorobosyl transferase and the enzymes of the deoxyribonucleoside salvage pathway (Chapter 33). Effective design and administration of prodrugs requires knowledge of the kinetics and mechanisms of the enzymes responsible for transforming them into their biologically active forms.

SUMMARY

- The study of enzyme kinetics—the factors that affect the rates of enzyme-catalyzed reactions—reveals the individual steps by which enzymes transform substrates into products.

- ΔG, the overall change in free energy for a reaction, is independent of reaction mechanism and provides no information concerning *rates* of reactions.

- Enzymes do not affect K_{eq}. K_{eq}, a ratio of reaction *rate constants*, may be calculated from the concentrations of substrates and products at equilibrium or from the ratio k_1/k_{-1}.

- Reactions proceed via transition states in which ΔG_F is the activation energy. Temperature, hydrogen ion concentration, enzyme concentration, substrate concentration, and inhibitors all affect the rates of enzyme-catalyzed reactions.

- A measurement of the rate of an enzyme-catalyzed reaction generally employs initial rate conditions, for which the essential absence of product precludes the reverse reaction.

- A linear form of the Michaelis-Menten equation simplifies determination of K_m and V_{max}.

- A linear form of the Hill equation is used to evaluate the cooperative substrate-binding kinetics exhibited by some multimeric enzymes. The slope **n**, the Hill coefficient, reflects the number, nature, and strength of the interactions of the substrate-binding sites. A value of **n** greater than 1 indicates positive cooperativity.

- The effects of competitive inhibitors, which typically resemble substrates, are overcome by raising the concentration of the substrate. Noncompetitive inhibitors lower V_{max} but do not affect K_m.

- Substrates may add in a random order (either substrate may combine first with the enzyme) or in a compulsory order (substrate A must bind before substrate B).

- In ping-pong reactions, one or more products are released from the enzyme before all the substrates have added.

- Applied enzyme kinetics facilitates the identification and characterization of drugs that selectively inhibit specific enzymes. Enzyme kinetics thus plays a central and critical role in drug discovery, in comparative pharmacodynamics, and in determining the mode of action of drugs.

REFERENCES

Fersht A: *Structure and Mechanism in Protein Science: A Guide to Enzyme Catalysis and Protein Folding.* Freeman, 1999.

Fraser CM, Rappuoli R: Application of microbial genomic science to advanced therapeutics. Annu Rev Med 2005;56:459.

Schultz AR: *Enzyme Kinetics: From Diastase to Multi-enzyme Systems.* Cambridge Univ Press, 1994.

Segel IH: *Enzyme Kinetics.* Wiley Interscience, 1975.

Wlodawer A: Rational approach to AIDS drug design through structural biology. Annu Rev Med 2002;53:595.

Enzymes: Regulation of Activities

9

Peter J. Kennelly, PhD, & Victor W. Rodwell, PhD

BIOMEDICAL IMPORTANCE

The 19th-century physiologist Claude Bernard enunciated the conceptual basis for metabolic regulation. He observed that living organisms respond in ways that are both quantitatively and temporally appropriate to permit them to survive the multiple challenges posed by changes in their external and internal environments. Walter Cannon subsequently coined the term "homeostasis" to describe the ability of animals to maintain a constant intracellular environment despite changes in their external environment. We now know that organisms respond to changes in their external and internal environment by balanced, coordinated changes in the rates of specific metabolic reactions. Many human diseases, including cancer, diabetes, cystic fibrosis, and Alzheimer's disease, are characterized by regulatory dysfunctions triggered by pathogenic agents or genetic mutations. For example, many oncogenic viruses elaborate protein-tyrosine kinases that modify the regulatory events that control patterns of gene expression, contributing to the initiation and progression of cancer. The toxin from *Vibrio cholerae,* the causative agent of cholera, disables sensor-response pathways in intestinal epithelial cells by ADP-ribosylating the GTP-binding proteins (G-proteins) that link cell surface receptors to adenylyl cyclase. The consequent activation of the cyclase triggers the flow of water into the intestines, resulting in massive diarrhea and dehydration. *Yersinia pestis,* the causative agent of plague, elaborates a protein-tyrosine phosphatase that hydrolyzes phosphoryl groups on key cytoskeletal proteins. Dysfunctions in the systems responsible for the degradation of defective or abnormal proteins are believed to play a role in neurodegenerative diseases such as Alzheimer's and Parkinson's. Knowledge of factors that control the rates of enzyme-catalyzed reactions thus is essential to an understanding of the molecular basis of disease. This chapter outlines the patterns by which metabolic processes are controlled and provides illustrative examples. Subsequent chapters provide additional examples.

REGULATION OF METABOLITE FLOW CAN BE ACTIVE OR PASSIVE

Enzymes that operate at their maximal rate cannot respond to an increase in substrate concentration, and can respond only to a precipitous decrease in substrate concentration. For most enzymes, therefore, the average intracellular concentration of their substrate tends to be close to the K_m value, so that changes in substrate concentration generate corresponding changes in metabolite flux (Figure 9–1). Responses to changes in substrate level represent an important but *passive* means for coordinating metabolite flow and maintaining homeostasis in quiescent cells. However, they offer limited scope for responding to changes in environmental variables. The mechanisms that regulate enzyme activity in an *active* manner in response to internal and external signals are discussed below.

Metabolite Flow Tends to Be Unidirectional

Despite the existence of short-term oscillations in metabolite concentrations and enzyme levels, living cells exist in a dynamic steady state in which the mean concentrations of metabolic intermediates remain relatively constant over time (Figure 9–2). While all chemical reactions are to some extent reversible, in living cells the reaction products serve as substrates for—and are removed by—other enzyme-catalyzed reactions. Many nominally reversible reactions thus occur unidirectionally. This succession of coupled metabolic reactions is accompanied by an overall change in free energy that favors unidirectional metabolite flow (Chapter 11). The unidirectional flow of metabolites through a pathway with a large overall negative change in free energy is analogous to the flow of water through a pipe in which one end is lower than the other. Bends or kinks in the pipe simulate individual enzyme-catalyzed steps with a small negative or positive change in free energy. Flow of water through the pipe nevertheless remains unidirectional due to the overall change in height, which corresponds to the overall change in free energy in a pathway (Figure 9–3).

COMPARTMENTATION ENSURES METABOLIC EFFICIENCY & SIMPLIFIES REGULATION

In eukaryotes, anabolic and catabolic pathways that interconvert common products may take place in specific subcellular compartments. For example, many of

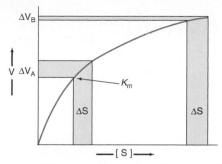

Figure 9–1. Differential response of the rate of an enzyme-catalyzed reaction, ΔV, to the same incremental change in substrate concentration at a substrate concentration of K_m (ΔV_A) or far above K_m (ΔV_B).

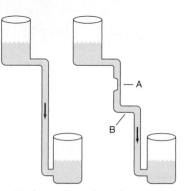

Figure 9–3. Hydrostatic analogy for a pathway with a rate-limiting step **(A)** and a step with a ΔG value near zero **(B)**.

the enzymes that degrade proteins and polysaccharides reside inside organelles called lysosomes. Similarly, fatty acid biosynthesis occurs in the cytosol, whereas fatty acid oxidation takes place within mitochondria (Chapters 22 and 23). Segregation of certain metabolic pathways within specialized cell types can provide further physical compartmentation. Alternatively, possession of one or more *unique intermediates* can permit apparently opposing pathways to coexist even in the absence of physical barriers. For example, despite many shared intermediates and enzymes, both glycolysis and gluconeogenesis are favored energetically. This cannot be true if *all* the reactions were the same. If one pathway was favored energetically, the other would be accompanied by a change in free energy ΔG equal in magnitude but opposite in sign. Simultaneous spontaneity of both pathways results from substitution of one or more reactions by different reactions favored thermodynamically in the opposite direction. The glycolytic enzyme phosphofructokinase (Chapter 18) is replaced by the gluconeogenic enzyme fructose-1,6 bisphosphatase (Chapter 20). The ability of enzymes to discriminate between the structurally similar coenzymes NAD+ and NADP+ also

results in a form of compartmentation, since it segregates the electrons of NADH that are destined for ATP generation from those of NADPH that participate in the reductive steps in many biosynthetic pathways.

Controlling an Enzyme That Catalyzes a Rate-Limiting Reaction Regulates an Entire Metabolic Pathway

While the flux of metabolites through metabolic pathways involves catalysis by numerous enzymes, active control of homeostasis is achieved by regulation of only a small number of enzymes. The ideal enzyme for regulatory intervention is one whose quantity or catalytic efficiency dictates that the reaction it catalyzes is slow relative to all others in the pathway. Decreasing the catalytic efficiency or the quantity of the catalyst for the "bottleneck" or **rate-limiting reaction** therefore reduces metabolite flux through the entire pathway. Conversely, an increase in either its quantity or catalytic efficiency enhances flux through the pathway as a whole. For example, acetyl-CoA carboxylase catalyzes the synthesis of malonyl-CoA, the first committed reaction of fatty acid biosynthesis (Chapter 23). When synthesis of malonyl-CoA is inhibited, subsequent reactions of fatty acid synthesis cease due to lack of substrates. Enzymes that catalyze rate-limiting steps serve as natural "governors" of metabolic flux. Thus, they constitute efficient targets for regulatory intervention by drugs. For example, inhibition by "statin" drugs of HMG-CoA reductase, which catalyzes the rate-limiting reaction of cholesterogenesis, curtails synthesis of cholesterol.

REGULATION OF ENZYME QUANTITY

The catalytic capacity of the rate-limiting reaction in a metabolic pathway is the product of the concentration of enzyme molecules and their intrinsic catalytic efficiency. It therefore follows that catalytic capacity can be

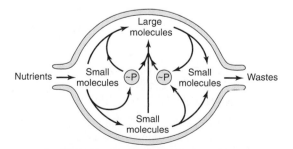

Figure 9–2. An idealized cell in steady state. Note that metabolite flow is unidirectional.

influenced both by changing the quantity of enzyme present and by altering its intrinsic catalytic efficiency.

Proteins Are Continually Synthesized and Degraded

By measuring the rates of incorporation of ^{15}N-labeled amino acids into protein and the rates of loss of ^{15}N from protein, Schoenheimer deduced that body proteins are in a state of "dynamic equilibrium" in which they are continuously synthesized and degraded—a process referred to as **protein turnover.** While the steady-state concentrations of some enzymes and other proteins remain essentially constant, or **constitutive,** over time; the concentrations of many enzymes are influenced by a wide range of physiologic, hormonal, or dietary factors.

The absolute quantity of an enzyme reflects the net balance between its rate of synthesis and its rate of degradation. In human subjects, alterations in the levels of specific enzymes can be affected by a change in the rate constant for the overall processes of synthesis (k_s), degradation (k_{deg}) or both.

Control of Enzyme Synthesis

The synthesis of certain enzymes depends upon the presence of **inducers,** typically substrates or structurally related compounds, that initiate their synthesis. *Escherichia coli* grown on glucose will, for example, only catabolize lactose after addition of a β-galactoside, an inducer that initiates synthesis of a β-galactosidase and a galactoside permease (Figure 38–3). Inducible enzymes of humans include tryptophan pyrrolase, threonine dehydrase, tyrosine-α-ketoglutarate aminotransferase, enzymes of the urea cycle, HMG-CoA reductase, and cytochrome P450. Conversely, an excess of a metabolite may curtail synthesis of its cognate enzyme via **repression.** Both induction and repression involve cis elements, specific DNA sequences located upstream of regulated genes, and trans-acting regulatory proteins. The molecular mechanisms of induction and repression are discussed in Chapter 38. The synthesis of other enzymes can be stimulated by the binding to specific cell receptors of hormones and other extracellular signals. Detailed information on the control of protein synthesis in response to hormonal stimuli can be found in Chapter 42.

Control of Enzyme Degradation

In animals, many proteins are degraded by the ubiquitin proteasome pathway, the discovery of which earned Aaron Ciechanover, Avram Hershko, and Irwin Roose a Nobel Prize. The 26S proteasome is comprised of more than 30 polypeptide subunits arranged in the form of a hollow cylinder. The active sites of its proteolytic subunits face the interior of the cylinder, thus preventing indiscriminate degradation of cellular proteins. Proteins are targeted to the proteasome by "ubiquitination," the covalent attachment of one or more ubiquitin molecules. Ubiquitin is a small, approximately 75 residue protein that is highly conserved among eukaryotes. Ubiquitination is catalyzed by a large family of enzymes called E3 ligases, which attach ubiquitin to the side-chain amino group of lysyl residues.

The ubiquitin-proteasome pathway is responsible both for the regulated degradation of selected cellular proteins, for example cyclins, in response to specific intra- or extra-cellular signals, and for the removal of defective or aberrant protein species. The key to the versatility and selectivity of the ubiquitin-proteasome system resides in both the variety of intracellular E3 ligases and their ability to discriminate between different physical or conformational states of a target protein. Thus, the ubiquitin-proteasome pathway can selectively degrade proteins whose physical integrity and functional competency has been compromised by the loss of or damage to a prosthetic group, oxidation of cysteine or histidine residues, or deamidation of asparagine or glutamine residues. Recognition by proteolytic enzymes also can be regulated by covalent modifications such as phosphorylation; binding of substrates or allosteric effectors; or association with membranes, oligonucleotides, or other proteins. A growing body of evidence suggests that dysfunctions of the ubiquitin-proteasome pathway contribute to the accumulation of aberrantly folded protein species characteristic of several neurodegenerative diseases.

MULTIPLE OPTIONS ARE AVAILABLE FOR REGULATING CATALYTIC ACTIVITY

In humans, the induction of protein synthesis is a complex multistep process that typically requires hours to produce significant changes in overall enzyme level. By contrast, changes in intrinsic catalytic efficiency effected by binding of dissociable ligands (**allosteric regulation**) or by **covalent modification** achieve regulation of enzymic activity within seconds. Changes in protein level serve long-term adaptive requirements, whereas changes in catalytic efficiency are best suited for rapid and transient alterations in metabolite flux.

ALLOSTERIC EFFECTORS REGULATE CERTAIN ENZYMES

Feedback inhibition refers to inhibition of an enzyme in a biosynthetic pathway by an end product of that

pathway. In the following example, for the biosynthesis of D from A catalyzed by enzymes Enz_1 through Enz_3,

$$Enz_1 \quad Enz_2 \quad Enz_3$$
$$A \;\rightarrow\; B \;\rightarrow\; C \;\rightarrow\; D$$

high concentrations of D inhibit the conversion of A to B. Inhibition results not from the "backing up" of intermediates but from the ability of D to bind to and inhibit Enz_1. Typically, D binds at an **allosteric site** spatially distinct from the catalytic site of the target enzyme. Feedback inhibitors thus are allosteric effectors that typically bear little or no structural similarity to the substrates of the enzymes they inhibit. In this example, the feedback inhibitor D acts as a **negative allosteric effector** of Enz_1.

In a branched biosynthetic pathway, the initial reactions participate in the synthesis of several products. Figure 9–4 shows a hypothetical branched biosynthetic pathway in which curved arrows lead from feedback inhibitors to the enzymes whose activity they inhibit. The sequences $S_3 \rightarrow A$, $S_4 \rightarrow B$, $S_4 \rightarrow C$, and $S_3 \rightarrow \rightarrow D$ each represent linear reaction sequences that are feedback-inhibited by their end products. The pathways of nucleotide biosynthesis (Chapter 33) provide specific examples.

The kinetics of feedback inhibition may be competitive, noncompetitive, partially competitive, or mixed. Feedback inhibitors, which frequently are the small molecule building blocks of macromolecules (eg, amino acids for proteins, nucleotides for nucleic acids), typically inhibit the first committed step in a particular biosynthetic sequence. A much-studied example is inhibition of bacterial aspartate transcarbamoylase by CTP (see below and Chapter 33).

Multiple feedback loops can provide additional fine control. For example, as shown in Figure 9–5, the presence of excess product B decreases the requirement for substrate S_2. However, S_2 is also required for synthesis of A, C, and D. Excess B should therefore also curtail

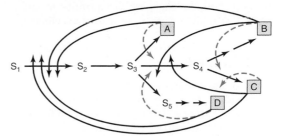

Figure 9–5. Multiple feedback inhibition in a branched biosynthetic pathway. Superimposed on simple feedback loops (dashed curved arrows) are multiple feedback loops (solid curved arrows) that regulate enzymes common to biosynthesis of several end products.

synthesis of all four end products. To circumvent this potential difficulty, each end product typically only partially inhibits catalytic activity. The effect of an excess of two or more end products may be strictly additive or, alternatively, may be greater than their individual effect (cooperative feedback inhibition).

Aspartate Transcarbamoylase Is a Model Allosteric Enzyme

Aspartate transcarbamoylase (ATCase), the catalyst for the first reaction unique to pyrimidine biosynthesis (Figure 33–7), is feedback-inhibited by cytidine triphosphate (CTP) and adenosine triphosphate. CTP, an end product of the pyrimidine biosynthetic pathway, inhibits the enzyme, whereas ATP activates the enzyme. Moreover, high levels of ATP can overcome the inhibition by CTP, enabling synthesis of pyrimidine nucleotides to proceed when purine nucleotide levels are elevated.

Allosteric & Catalytic Sites Are Spatially Distinct

The lack of structural similarity between a feedback inhibitor and the substrate for the enzyme whose activity it regulates suggests that these effectors are not **isosteric** with a substrate but **allosteric** ("occupy another space"). Jacques Monod therefore proposed the existence of allosteric sites that are physically distinct from the catalytic site. **Allosteric enzymes** thus are those whose activity at the active site may be modulated by the presence of effectors at an allosteric site. This hypothesis has been confirmed by many lines of evidence, including x-ray crystallography and site-directed mutagenesis, demonstrating the existence of spatially distinct active and allosteric sites on a variety of enzymes. For example, the ATCase of *Escherichia coli* is a dodecamer consisting of six catalytic subunits and six regulatory subunits that bind the nucleotide tri-

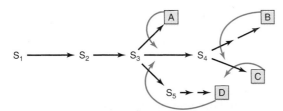

Figure 9–4. Sites of feedback inhibition in a branched biosynthetic pathway. S_1–S_5 are intermediates in the biosynthesis of end products A–D. Straight arrows represent enzymes catalyzing the indicated conversions. Curved arrows represent feedback loops and indicate sites of feedback inhibition by specific end products.

phosphates that modulate activity. In general, binding of an allosteric regulator induces a conformational change in the enzyme that encompasses the active site. These changes may have an impact on the catalytic efficiency of the enzyme (V-series enzymes), the apparent affinity of the enzyme for its substrates (K-series enzymes), or both catalysis and substrate affinity.

Allosteric Effects May Be on K_m or on V_{max}

To refer to the kinetics of allosteric inhibition as "competitive" or "noncompetitive" with substrate carries misleading mechanistic implications. We refer instead to two classes of regulated enzymes: K-series and V-series enzymes. For K-series allosteric enzymes, the substrate saturation kinetics are competitive in the sense that K_m is raised without an effect on V_{max}. For V-series allosteric enzymes, the allosteric inhibitor lowers V_{max} without affecting the K_m. Alterations in K_m or V_{max} probably result from conformational changes at the catalytic site induced by binding of the allosteric effector at the allosteric site. For a K-series allosteric enzyme, this conformational change may weaken the bonds between substrate and substrate-binding residues. For a V-series allosteric enzyme, the primary effect may be to alter the orientation or charge of catalytic residues, lowering V_{max}. Intermediate effects on K_m and V_{max}, however, may be observed consequent to these conformational changes.

FEEDBACK REGULATION IS NOT SYNONYMOUS WITH FEEDBACK INHIBITION

In both mammalian and bacterial cells, end products "feed back" and control their own synthesis, in many instances by feedback inhibition of an early biosynthetic enzyme. We must, however, distinguish between **feedback regulation,** a phenomenologic term devoid of mechanistic implications, and **feedback inhibition,** a mechanism for regulation of enzyme activity. For example, while dietary cholesterol decreases hepatic synthesis of cholesterol, this feedback **regulation** does not involve feedback **inhibition.** HMG-CoA reductase, the rate-limiting enzyme of cholesterologenesis, is affected, but cholesterol does not feedback-inhibit its activity. Regulation in response to dietary cholesterol involves curtailment by cholesterol or a cholesterol metabolite of the expression of the gene that encodes HMG-CoA reductase (enzyme repression) (Chapter 26).

MANY HORMONES ACT THROUGH ALLOSTERIC SECOND MESSENGERS

Nerve impulses—and binding of hormones to cell surface receptors—elicit changes in the rate of enzyme-catalyzed reactions within target cells by inducing the release or synthesis of specialized allosteric effectors called **second messengers.** The primary, or "first," messenger is the hormone molecule or nerve impulse. Second messengers include 3′,5′-cAMP, synthesized from ATP by the enzyme adenylyl cyclase in response to the hormone epinephrine, and Ca^{2+}, which is stored inside the endoplasmic reticulum of most cells. Membrane depolarization resulting from a nerve impulse opens a membrane channel that releases calcium ion into the cytoplasm, where it binds to and activates enzymes involved in the regulation of contraction and the mobilization of stored glucose from glycogen. Glucose then supplies the increased energy demands of muscle contraction. Other second messengers include 3′,5′-cGMP and polyphosphoinositols, produced by the hydrolysis of inositol phospholipids by hormone-regulated phospholipases.

REGULATORY COVALENT MODIFICATIONS CAN BE REVERSIBLE OR IRREVERSIBLE

In mammalian cells, the two most common forms of covalent modification are **partial proteolysis** and **phosphorylation.** Because cells lack the ability to reunite the two portions of a protein produced by hydrolysis of a peptide bond, proteolysis constitutes an irreversible modification. By contrast, phosphorylation is a reversible modification process. The phosphorylation of proteins on seryl, threonyl, or tyrosyl residues, catalyzed by protein kinases, is thermodynamically favored. Equally favored is the hydrolytic removal of these phosphoryl groups by enzymes called protein phosphatases. The activities of protein kinases and protein phosphatases are themselves regulated, for if they were not, their concerted action would be both thermodynamically and biologically unproductive.

PROTEASES MAY BE SECRETED AS CATALYTICALLY INACTIVE PROENZYMES

Certain proteins are synthesized and secreted as inactive precursor proteins known as **proproteins.** The proproteins of enzymes are termed **proenzymes** or **zymogens.** Selective proteolysis converts a proprotein by one or more successive proteolytic "clips" to a form that exhibits the characteristic activity of the mature protein, eg, its enzymatic activity. Proteins synthesized as proproteins include the hormone insulin (proprotein = proinsulin), the digestive enzymes pepsin, trypsin, and chymotrypsin (proproteins = pepsinogen, trypsinogen, and chymotrypsinogen, respectively), several factors of the blood clotting and blood clot dissolution cascades (see Chapter 50), and the connective tissue protein collagen (proprotein = procollagen).

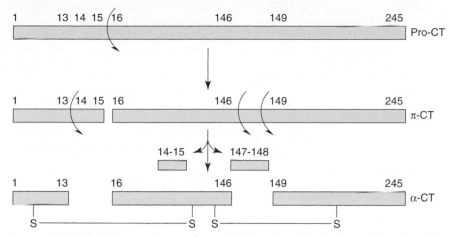

Figure 9–6. Selective proteolysis and associated conformational changes form the active site of chymotrypsin, which includes the Asp102-His57-Ser195 catalytic triad. Successive proteolysis forms prochymotrypsin (pro-CT), π-chymotrypsin (π-CT), and ultimately α-chymotrypsin (α-CT), an active protease whose three peptides remain associated by covalent inter-chain disulfide bonds.

Proenzymes Facilitate Rapid Mobilization of an Activity in Response to Physiologic Demand

The synthesis and secretion of proteases as catalytically inactive proenzymes protects the tissue of origin (eg, the pancreas) from autodigestion, such as can occur in pancreatitis. Certain physiologic processes such as digestion are intermittent but fairly regular and predictable. Others such as blood clot formation, clot dissolution, and tissue repair are brought "on line" only in response to pressing physiologic or pathophysiologic need. The processes of blood clot formation and dissolution clearly must be temporally coordinated to achieve homeostasis. Enzymes needed intermittently but rapidly often are secreted in an initially inactive form since the secretion process or new synthesis of the required proteins might be insufficiently rapid for response to a pressing pathophysiologic demand such as the loss of blood (see Chapter 50).

Activation of Prochymotrypsin Requires Selective Proteolysis

Selective proteolysis involves one or more highly specific proteolytic clips that may or may not be accompanied by separation of the resulting peptides. Most importantly, selective proteolysis often results in conformational changes that "create" the catalytic site of an enzyme. Note that while His 57 and Asp 102 reside on the B peptide of α-chymotrypsin, Ser 195 resides on the C peptide (Figure 9–6). The conformational changes that accompany selective proteolysis of prochymotrypsin (chymotrypsinogen) align the three residues of the charge-relay network, forming the catalytic site. Note also that contact and catalytic residues can be located on different peptide chains but still be within bond-forming distance of bound substrate.

REVERSIBLE COVALENT MODIFICATION REGULATES KEY MAMMALIAN ENZYMES

Mammalian proteins are the targets of a wide range of covalent modification processes. Modifications such as prenylation, glycosylation, hydroxylation, and fatty acid acylation introduce unique structural features into newly synthesized proteins that tend to persist for the lifetime of the protein. Among the covalent modifications that regulate protein function (eg, methylation, adenylylation), the most common by far is phosphorylation-dephosphorylation. **Protein kinases** phosphorylate proteins by catalyzing transfer of the terminal phosphoryl group of ATP to the hydroxyl groups of seryl, threonyl, or tyrosyl residues, forming O-phosphoseryl, O-phosphothreonyl, or O-phosphotyrosyl residues, respectively (Figure 9–7). Some protein kinases target the side chains of histidyl, lysyl, arginyl, and aspartyl residues. The unmodified form of the protein can be regenerated by hydrolytic removal of phosphoryl groups, catalyzed by **protein phosphatases.**

A typical mammalian cell possesses thousands of phosphorylated proteins and several hundred protein kinases and protein phosphatases that catalyze their interconver-

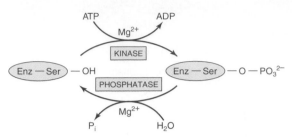

Figure 9–7. Covalent modification of a regulated enzyme by phosphorylation-dephosphorylation of a seryl residue.

PROTEIN PHOSPHORYLATION IS EXTREMELY VERSATILE

Protein phosphorylation-dephosphorylation is a highly versatile and selective process. Not all proteins are subject to phosphorylation, and of the many hydroxyl groups on a protein's surface, only one or a small subset are targeted. While the most common enzyme function affected is the protein's catalytic efficiency, phosphorylation can also alter its location within the cell, susceptibility to proteolytic degradation, or responsiveness to regulation by allosteric ligands. Phosphorylation can increase an enzyme's catalytic efficiency, converting it to its active form in one protein, while phosphorylation of another converts it into an intrinsically inefficient, or inactive, form (Table 9–1).

Many proteins can be phosphorylated at multiple sites or are subject to regulation both by phosphorylation-dephosphorylation and by the binding of allosteric ligands. Phosphorylation-dephosphorylation at any one site can be catalyzed by multiple protein kinases or protein phosphatases. Many protein kinases and most protein phosphatases act on more than one protein and are themselves interconverted between active and inactive forms by the binding of second messengers or by covalent modification by phosphorylation-dephosphorylation.

The interplay between protein kinases and protein phosphatases, between the functional consequences of phosphorylation at different sites, or between phosphorylation sites and allosteric sites provides the basis for regulatory networks that integrate multiple environmental input signals to evoke an appropriate coordinated cellular response. In these sophisticated regulatory networks, individual enzymes respond to different environmental signals. For example, if an enzyme can be phosphorylated at a single site by more than one protein kinase, it can be converted from a catalytically efficient to an inefficient

sion. The ease of interconversion of enzymes between their phospho- and dephospho- forms in part accounts for the frequency of phosphorylation-dephosphorylation as a mechanism for regulatory control. Phosphorylation-dephosphorylation permits the functional properties of the affected enzyme to be altered only for as long as it serves a specific need. Once the need has passed, the enzyme can be converted back to its original form, poised to respond to the next stimulatory event. A second factor underlying the widespread use of protein phosphorylation-dephosphorylation lies in the chemical properties of the phosphoryl group itself. In order to alter an enzyme's functional properties, any modification of its chemical structure must influence the protein's three-dimensional configuration. The high charge density of protein-bound phosphoryl groups—generally −2 at physiologic pH—and their propensity to form salt bridges with arginyl residues make them potent agents for modifying protein structure and function. Phosphorylation generally targets amino acids distant from the catalytic site itself. Consequent conformational changes then influence an enzyme's intrinsic catalytic efficiency or other properties.

Covalent Modification Regulates Metabolite Flow

In many respects, sites of protein phosphorylation and other covalent modifications can be considered another form of allosteric site. However, in this case, the "allosteric ligand" binds covalently to the protein. Both phosphorylation-dephosphorylation and feedback inhibition provide for short-term, readily reversible regulation of metabolite flow in response to specific physiologic signals. Both act without altering gene expression. Both act on early enzymes of a protracted and often biosynthetic metabolic sequence, and both act at allosteric rather than catalytic sites. Feedback inhibition, however, involves a single protein and lacks hormonal and neural features. By contrast, regulation of mammalian enzymes by phosphorylation-dephosphorylation involves several proteins and ATP, and is under direct neural and hormonal control.

Table 9–1. Examples of mammalian enzymes whose catalytic activity is altered by covalent phosphorylation-dephosphorylation.

Enzyme	Activity State[1]	
	Low	High
Acetyl-CoA carboxylase	EP	E
Glycogen synthase	EP	E
Pyruvate dehydrogenase	EP	E
HMG-CoA reductase	EP	E
Glycogen phosphorylase	E	EP
Citrate lyase	E	EP
Phosphorylase b kinase	E	EP
HMG-CoA reductase kinase	E	EP

[1]E, dephosphoenzyme; EP, phosphoenzyme.

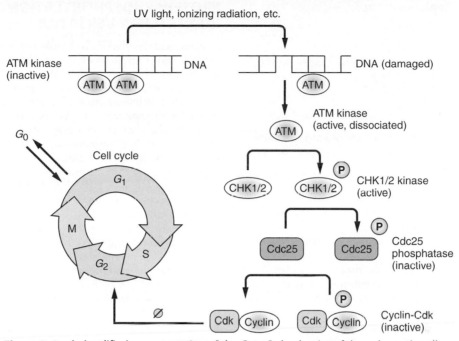

Figure 9–8. A simplified representation of the G_1 to S checkpoint of the eukaryotic cell cycle. The circle shows the various stages in the eukaryotic cell cycle. The genome is replicated during S phase, while the two copies of the genome are segregated and cell division occurs during M phase. Each of these phases are separated by a G, or growth, phase characterized by an increase in cell size and the accumulation of the precursors required for the assembly of the large macromolecular complexes formed during S and M phase.

(inactive) form, or vice versa, in response to any one of several signals. If the protein kinase is activated in response to a signal different from the signal that activates the protein phosphatase, the phosphoprotein becomes a decision node. The functional output, generally catalytic activity, reflects the phosphorylation state. This state or degree of phosphorylation is determined by the relative activities of the protein kinase and protein phosphatase, a reflection of the presence and relative strength of the environmental signals that act through each.

The ability of many protein kinases and protein phosphatases to target more than one protein provides a means for an environmental signal to coordinately regulate multiple metabolic processes. For example, the enzymes 3-hydroxy-3-methylglutaryl-CoA reductase and acetyl-CoA carboxylase—the rate-controlling enzymes for cholesterol and fatty acid biosynthesis, respectively—are phosphorylated and inactivated by the AMP-activated protein kinase. When this protein kinase is activated either through phosphorylation by yet another protein kinase or in response to the binding of its allosteric activator 5′-AMP, the two major pathways responsible for the synthesis of lipids from acetyl-CoA both are inhibited.

Interconvertible enzymes and the enzymes responsible for their interconversion do not act as mere on and off switches working independently of one another. They form the building blocks of regulatory networks that maintain homeostasis in cells that carry out a complex array of metabolic processes that must be regulated in response to a broad spectrum of environmental factors.

The best-studied example of such a network is the eukaryotic cell cycle that controls cell division. Upon emergence from the quiescent, or G_0, state, the extremely complex process of cell division proceeds through a series of specific phases designated G_1, S, G_2, and M (Figure 9–8). Elaborate monitoring systems, called checkpoints, assess key indicators of progress to ensure that no phase of the cycle is initiated until the prior phase is complete. Figure 9–8 outlines, in simplified form, part of the checkpoint that controls the initiation of DNA replication, called the S phase. A protein kinase called ATM is associated with the genome. If the DNA contains a double-stranded break, the resulting change in the conformation of the chromatin activates ATM. Upon activation, one subunit of the activated ATM dimer dissociates and initiates a series, or cascade,

of protein phosphorylation-dephosphorylation events mediated by the CHK1 and CHK2 protein kinases, the Cdc25 protein phosphatase, and finally a complex between a cyclin and a cyclin-dependent protein kinase, or Cdk. Activation of the Cdk-cyclin complex blocks the G_1 to S transition, thus preventing the replication of damaged DNA. Failure at this checkpoint can lead to mutations in DNA that may lead to cancer or other diseases. Each step in the cascade provides a conduit for monitoring additional indicators of cell status prior to entering S phase.

SUMMARY

- Homeostasis involves maintaining a relatively constant intracellular and intra-organ environment despite wide fluctuations in the external environment via appropriate changes in the rates of biochemical reactions in response to physiologic need.

- The substrates for most enzymes are usually present at a concentration close to K_m. This facilitates passive control of the rates of product formation in response to changes in levels of metabolic intermediates.

- Active control of metabolite flux involves changes in the concentration, catalytic activity, or both of an enzyme that catalyzes a committed, rate-limiting reaction.

- Selective proteolysis of catalytically inactive proenzymes initiates conformational changes that form the active site. Secretion as an inactive proenzyme facilitates rapid mobilization of activity in response to injury or physiologic need and may protect the tissue of origin (eg, autodigestion by proteases).

- Binding of metabolites and second messengers to sites distinct from the catalytic site of enzymes triggers conformational changes that alter V_{max} or K_m.

- Phosphorylation by protein kinases of specific seryl, threonyl, or tyrosyl residues—and subsequent dephosphorylation by protein phosphatases—regulates the activity of many human enzymes. The protein kinases and phosphatases that participate in regulatory cascades that respond to hormonal or second messenger signals constitute regulatory networks that can process and integrate complex environmental information to produce an appropriate and comprehensive cellular response.

REFERENCES

Bray D: Protein molecules as computational elements in living cells. Nature 1995;376:307.

Ciechanover A, Schwartz AL: The ubiquitin system: Pathogenesis of human diseases and drug targeting. Biochim Biophys Acta 2004;1695:3.

Graves DJ, Martin BL, Wang JH: *Co- and Post-translational Modification of Proteins: Chemical Principles and Biological Effects.* Oxford Univ Press, 1994.

Johnson LN, Lewis RJ: Structural basis for control by phosphorylation. Chem Rev 2001;101:2209.

Pilkis SJ et al: 6-Phosphofructo-2-kinase/fructose-2,6-bisphosphatase: A metabolic signaling enzyme. Annu Rev Biochem 1995;64:799.

Scriver CR et al (editors): *The Metabolic and Molecular Bases of Inherited Disease,* 8th ed. McGraw-Hill, 2000.

Sitaramayya A (editor): *Introduction to Cellular Signal Transduction.* Birkhauser, 1999.

Stadtman ER, Chock PB (editors): *Current Topics in Cellular Regulation.* Academic Press, 1969 to the present.

Stieglitz K et al: Monitoring the transition from the T to the R state in *E. coli* aspartate transcarbamoylase by x-ray crystallography: Crystal structures of the E50A mutant enzyme in four distinct allosteric states. J Mol Biol 2004;341:853.

Weber G (editor): *Advances in Enzyme Regulation.* Pergamon Press, 1963 to the present.

Bioinformatics & Computational Biology

10

Peter J. Kennelly, PhD, & Victor W. Rodwell, PhD

BIOMEDICAL IMPORTANCE

The first scientific models of pathogenesis, such as Louis Pasteur's seminal germ theory of disease, were binary in nature: each disease possessed a single, definable causal agent. Malaria was caused by the amoeba *Plasmodium falciparum*, tuberculosis by the bacterium *Mycobacterium tuberculosis*, sickle cell disease by a mutation in a gene encoding one of the subunits of hemoglobin, poliomyelitis by poliovirus, and scurvy by a deficiency in ascorbic acid. The strategy for treating or preventing disease thus could be reduced to a straightforward process of tracing the causal agent and then devising some means of eliminating it, neutralizing its effects, or blocking its route of transmission. This basic approach has been successfully employed to understand and treat a wide range of infectious and genetic diseases. However, it has become clear that the determinants of many pathologies—including cancer, coronary heart disease, type II diabetes, and Alzheimer's disease—are **multifactorial** in nature. Rather than having a specific causal agent or agents whose presence is both necessary and sufficient, the appearance and progression of the aforementioned diseases reflect the complex interplay between each individual's genetic makeup, diet, and lifestyle, as well as a range of environmental factors such as the presence of toxins, viruses, or bacteria.

The challenge posed by multifactorial diseases demands a quantum increase in the breadth and depth of our knowledge of living organisms capable of matching their sophistication and complexity. We must identify the many as-yet unknown proteins encoded within the genomes of humans and the organisms with which they interact, the relationships between these proteins, and the impact of dietary, genetic, and environmental factors thereupon. The sheer mass of information that must be processed to understand, as completely and comprehensively as possible, the molecular mechanisms that underlie the behavior of living organisms, as well as the manner in which perturbations can lead to disease or dysfunction, lies well beyond the ability of the human mind to review and analyze. Biomedical scientists therefore have turned to sophisticated computational tools to collect and evaluate biologic information on a mass scale.

WHAT ARE BIOINFORMATICS AND COMPUTATIONAL BIOLOGY?

Bioinformatics exploits the formidable information storage and processing capabilities of the computer to develop tools for the collection, collation, retrieval, and analysis of biologic data on a mass scale. Many bioinformatic resources (see below) can be accessed via the Internet, which provides them with global reach and impact. The central objective of a typical bioinformatics project is to assemble all of the available information relevant to a particular topic in a single location, often referred to as a library or **database**, in a uniform format that renders the data amenable to manipulation and analysis by computer algorithms.

The size and capabilities of bioinformatic databases can vary widely depending upon the scope and nature of their objectives. The PubMed database, for example, compiles citations for all articles published in journals devoted to biomedical and biological research. The number of journals tracked by PubMed is in the hundreds, each of which typically publishes a few hundred to several thousand papers a year. By contrast, the Cytochrome P450 Home page (http://drnelson.utmem.edu/CytochromeP450.html) confines itself to the approximately 2000 members of the cytochrome P450 family of enzymes that are involved in the metabolism of many drugs and other xenobiotics (see Chapter 52).

The construction of a comprehensive and user-friendly database presents many challenges. First, biomedical information comes in a wide variety of forms. For example, the coding information in a genome, although voluminous, is composed of simple linear sequences of four nucleotide bases. While the number of amino acid residues that define a protein's primary structure is much, much smaller than the number of base pairs in a genome, a description of a protein's x-ray structure requires that the location of each of its com-

82

ponent atoms be specified in three-dimensional space. A diverse range of criteria may apply when describing the subjects of a biomedical study: height; weight; age; gender; body mass index; diet; ethnicity; medical history; profession; use of drugs, alcohol, or tobacco products; exercise; blood pressure; habitat; marital status; blood type; serum cholesterol level; etc.

Second, anticipating the manner in which users may wish to search or analyze the information within a database and devising algorithms for coping with these variables can prove extremely challenging. For example, even the simple task of searching a gene database commonly employs, alone or in various combinations, criteria as diverse as the name of the gene, the name of the protein that it encodes, the biologic function of the gene product, a nucleotide sequence within the gene, a sequence of amino acids within the protein it encodes, the organism in which it is present, or the name of an investigator who works on that gene. Researchers wishing to determine whether the impact of a genetic polymorphism on longevity is influenced by the nature of the climate where a person lives may need to compare data from multiple databases.

The primary objective of **computational biology** is to develop computer algorithms that enable scientists to construct models mimicking the behavior of novel biologic molecules and processes through the application of physical, chemical, and biological principles. While the major focus of bioinformatics is the collection and evaluation of existing data, computational biology is experimental and exploratory in nature. A major goal of computational biologists is to utilize knowledge of the sequence and structure of well-studied proteins to develop computer algorithms capable of predicting from the primary sequence of novel proteins their three-dimensional structure and potential function. Computer-aided drug design uses the three-dimensional structure of a protein as a template against which to screen prospective ligands. Other computational biologists are developing algorithms describing at a global or systems level the entire range of metabolic activities that take place in a cell. These virtual cells can then be utilized to predict the effects of toxins, pathogens, or potential pharmacologic agents upon cellular functions. By enabling scientists to perform sophisticated experiments "in silico," computational biology promises to greatly accelerate the pace of biomedical research and the development of new treatments for human pathologies.

THE HUMAN GENOME PROJECT

The successful completion of the Human Genome Project represents the culmination of more than six decades of monumental achievements in molecular biology, genetics, and biochemistry. The chronology below enumerates several of the milestone events that led to the determination of the entire sequence of the human genome.

1944—DNA is shown to be the hereditary material
1953—Concept of the double helix is posited
1966—The genetic code is solved
1972—Recombinant DNA technology is developed
1977—Practical DNA sequencing technology emerges
1983—The gene for Huntington's disease is mapped
1985—The Polymerase Chain Reaction (PCR) is invented
1986—DNA sequencing becomes automated
1986—The gene for Duchenne muscular dystrophy is identified
1989—The gene for cystic fibrosis is identified
1990—The Human Genome Project is launched in the United States
1994—Human genetic mapping is completed
1996—The first human gene map is established
1999—The Single Nucleotide Polymorphism Initiative is started
1999—The first sequence of a human chromosome, number 22, is completed
2000—"First draft" of the human genome is completed
2003—Sequencing of the first human genome is completed

Coincident with these advances were the sequencing of the genomes of hundreds of other organisms including *Haemophilus influenzae* (1995), yeast (1996), *Escherichia coli* (1997), *Caenorhabditis elegans* (1998), *Mycobacterium tuberculosis* (1998), rice (2000), *Listeria monocytogenes* (2001), draft versions of the mouse and rat genomes (2002), and the SARS coronavirus (2003).

Two groups were responsible for sequencing the human genome. The Human Genome Sequencing Consortium employed hierarchical shotgun sequencing. The entire genome was fragmented into approximately 100–200 kb pieces and inserted into bacterial artificial chromosomes (BACs). The BACs were then positioned on individual chromosomes by looking for marker sequences known as sequence-tagged sites (short unique genomic loci for which a PCR assay is available) whose locations were known. Clones of the BACs were then broken into small fragments (shotgunning), sequenced, and computer algorithms used to identify matching sequence information from overlapping fragments to piece together the complete sequence. The team from Celera used the whole genome shotgun approach. Shotgun fragments were assembled on scaffolds, sets of contigs (sets of DNA that possess overlapping sequences) in the correct order but not necessarily connected in one continuous sequence. The correct positions of these

scaffolds were then determined by using sequence-tagged sites. High-throughput sequenators, powerful computer programs, and the element of competition each contributed to the rapid progress made by both groups that culminated in the rapid completing of the Human Genome Project. A more detailed description of the two approaches can be found at www.genomenewsnetwork.org/articles/06_00/sequence_primer.shtml.

THE GENOMICS REVOLUTION

The early decades of the 21st century will witness a "Genomics Revolution" as physicians and scientists exploit the genetic information implicit in the Human Genome Project and in the genomes of the organisms that colonize, feed, and infect *Homo sapiens*. In this new era, the task of identifying the genes responsible for human genetic diseases has been vastly simplified by the availability of detailed genetic information over the Internet and the ability to obtain and analyze DNA using rapid, highly sensitive techniques such as the PCR and automated DNA sequencing. The sheer size of these genomes renders bioinformatics and computational biology indispensable for assessing the factors that underlie disease susceptibility, aging, and other health-related issues.

It is already apparent that even subtle, apparently minor genetic differences can be highly significant. For example, while human and chimpanzee genes are 98.8% identical, primates other than humans are not susceptible to AIDS or to malaria. Comparative genomics thus should provide clues to these differences in susceptibility. The mouse represents an additional useful model mammal by virtue of its availability and experimental tractability. While more phylogenetically and phenotypically divergent from humans than are primates, 90% of the genes in mice have a corresponding human homolog. Moreover, mice possess short generation times and can be genetically engineered using "transgenic" technology.

CHALLENGES TO MEDICINE

The potential and challenges of genomics research were presented with admirable clarity in a recent review by FS Collins and associates entitled "A vision for the future of genomic research. A blueprint for the genomic era" (*Nature* 2003;422;6934) that identifies the challenges that physicians, scientists, and policy makers will face as the genomic revolution progresses. While the general societal implications are of unquestioned significance, this chapter focuses on the challenges to medicine and to biology set forth in the above-cited article:

- To develop robust strategies for identifying the genetic contributions to disease and drug response.
- To identify gene variants that contribute to good health and resistance to disease.

- To develop genome-based approaches for the prediction of disease susceptibility and drug response, the early detection of illness, and the delineation of the molecular taxonomy of disease states.
- To exploit new insights into genes and pathways for the development of more effective therapeutic approaches to disease.
- To determine how genetic risk information should be conveyed in clinical settings and how that information should guide health strategies and behavior.

Present and forthcoming advances in our understanding of genomes and the functions of their encoded elements will vastly accelerate the advance of medicine and the biological sciences. An immediate goal is the compilation of an "encyclopedia" that encompasses all the proteins encoded by the human genome. Long-term challenges include elucidating the manner in which these proteins are integrated to fulfill physiologic functions and understanding the mechanisms by which genomes change and assume new functions. While the DNA sequence of the human genome is well understood, its functional architecture is exceedingly complex and largely undefined. Because of its vast size, only 1–2% of human DNA is devoted to storing the amino acid sequences of its 30,000 encoded proteins. A further 1–2% of the remaining, noncoding DNA is, however, under active selection and would appear to be essential. However, apart from the small segments that serve as genes or regulatory elements for the control of gene expression and replication, the function of the vast majority of the human genome remains to be determined.

The continued accumulation of genome sequences from diverse organisms is crucial to the functional understanding of the human genome. The ability to compare and contrast genome sequences across a diverse range of organisms will aid in the identification of presently uncharacterized genes and gene products. The application of increasingly powerful computational tools will permit scientists to reconstruct the development of the human genome, and thus provide insights into its functional architecture.

The advancing genomic revolution presents society with challenges beyond the arena of human health. The first harbingers of these challenges can be glimpsed in the ongoing controversies regarding genetically modified foods, the cloning of whole animals, and the utilization of human embryonic stem cells in research. Forthcoming insights into the molecular and genetic contributions to human traits and behavior, as well as to physical health or to disease, require the development of a new generation of national and international policies in the areas of law, medicine, agriculture, etc.

CHALLENGES TO BIOLOGY

Its impact on medicine makes up only one aspect of the genomic revolution. Genome sequences from diverse

organisms are crucial to understanding the functional roles of all genomes. Advances in bioinformatics, computational biology, comparative genomics, and high-throughput biochemistry have expanded and enhanced the research tools available to biologists for the investigation and analysis of health and disease at a previously unattainable level of molecular detail. Biochemical advances now allow simultaneous study of the patterns of expression of thousands of mRNAs and the proteins they encode using microarray and proteomics technology.

Ready access via the Internet to genome sequences from organisms spanning all three phylogenetic domains, the *Archaea*, *Bacteria*, and *Eukarya*, coupled with access to powerful algorithms for manipulating and transforming data derived from these sequences, has already effected major transformations in biology and biochemistry. As noted above for the human genome, the comparison of genome sequences from evolutionarily diverse species constitutes a powerful tool for identifying functionally important genomic elements in all forms of life. Investigations into the molecular aspects of comparative biochemistry are yielding novel insights into diverse metabolic processes. An early application of bioinformatics was the use of computer-generated multiple sequence alignments of the amino acid sequences of proteins to identify conserved amino acid residues that serve critical functional or structural roles (see Table 7–1), and to provide clues to the catalytic, regulatory, and other capabilities of novel proteins and gene products (see Chapter 42).

As set forth in the above-cited article, the challenges to biology are as follows:

- To comprehensively identify the structural and functional components encoded in a biologically diverse range of organisms.

- To elucidate the organization of genetic networks and protein pathways and establish how they contribute to cellular and organismal phenotypes.

- To develop a detailed understanding of the heritable variation in genomes.

- To understand evolutionary variation across species and the mechanisms that underlie this variation.

- To develop policy options that facilitate appropriate widespread use of genomics in both research and clinical settings.

BIOINFORMATIC AND GENOMIC RESOURCES

Single Nucleotide Polymorphisms

While the genome sequence of any two individuals is 99.9% identical, human DNA contains approximately 10 million sites where individuals differ by a single nucleotide base. These sites are called **single nucleotide polymorphisms** or **SNPs.** One approach to the detection of SNPs is Transgenomic Wave Denaturing High Performance Liquid Chromatography (DHPLC, or WAVE/DHPLC), a variant of HPLC that can detect single base-pair differences between otherwise identical 750 bp fragments of DNA.

When sets of SNPs localized to the same chromosome are inherited together in blocks, the pattern of SNPs in each block is termed a **haplotype.** By comparing the haplotype distributions in groups of individuals with or without a given disease or response, biomedical scientists can identify SNPs that are associated with specific phenotypic traits. This process can be facilitated by focusing on **Tag SNPs,** a subset of the SNPs in a given block sufficient to provide a unique signature for a given haplotype. Detailed study of each region should reveal variants in genes that contribute to a specific disease or response. The identification of such genes should lead to more early diagnosis, and hopefully also to improved prevention and patient management. Knowledge of an individual's genetic profile also will be used to guide the selection of safe and effective drugs or vaccines, a process termed **pharmacogenomics.**

As the principal agency responsible for human health research in the United States, the National Institutes of Health, through its **National Center for Biotechnology Information (NCBI)**, provides free and ready access to a sophisticated arsenal of molecular, genomic, structural and literature databases, and to algorithms for their analysis through its Entrez site (http://www.ncbi.nlm.nih.gov/gquery/gquery.fcgi). While its primary focus is on biomedicine, Entrez resources are of equal value for the systematic investigation of molecular aspects of biology and biochemistry. Discussed below are selected examples of these resources.

The ENCODE Project

Identification of all the *functional elements* of the genome will vastly expand our understanding of the molecular events underlying human development, health, and disease. To address this goal, in late 2003 the National Human Genome Research Institute (NHGRI) initiated the ENCODE Project. ENCODE (**E**ncyclopedia **O**f **D**NA **E**lements) combines laboratory and computational approaches in an open consortium–based effort to comprehensively identify every functional element in the human genome. Consortium investigators with diverse backgrounds and expertise will collaborate in the development and evaluation of new high-throughput techniques, technologies, and strategies that will address current deficiencies in our ability to identify functional elements.

During its pilot phase, ENCODE will target approximately 1% (30 Mb) of the human genome for rigorous computational and experimental analysis. The challenges faced by the consortium are many. In addition

to the sheer size of the human genome and the cryptic nature of much of its sequence, scientists must cope with the variations in genome function that characterize different cell types and developmental stages. Given the complexity of the issues, it is clear that no single experimental approach or cell type will suffice to provide a complete overview of the interrelationships between genome sequence, architecture, and function.

BLAST

BLAST (Basic Local Alignment Search Tool) and other sequence comparison/alignment algorithms trace their origins to the efforts of early molecular biologists to determine whether the observed patterns of similarities among proteins that performed common metabolic functions were indicative of progressive change from a common origin. The major evolutionary question addressed was whether the similarities reflected (a) descent from a common ancestral protein (divergent evolution), or (b) the independent selection of a common mechanism for meeting some specific cellular need (convergent evolution), as would be anticipated if one particular solution was overwhelmingly superior to the alternatives. By comparing sequences to calculate the minimum number of nucleotide changes necessary to interconvert the putative protein isoforms, it could be determined whether the similarities and differences exhibited a pattern indicative of progressive change from a shared starting point.

BLAST has evolved into a family of programs optimized to address specific needs and data sets. **blastp** compares an *amino acid* query sequence against a *protein* sequence database, **blastn** compares a *nucleotide* query sequence against a *nucleotide* sequence database, **blastx** compares a *nucleotide* query sequence translated in all reading frames against a *protein* sequence database to reveal potential translation products, **tblastn** compares a *protein* query sequence against a *nucleotide* sequence database dynamically translated in all six reading frames, and **tblastx** compares the six-frame translations of a *nucleotide* query sequence against the six-frame translations of a *nucleotide* sequence database. Unlike multiple sequence alignment programs that rely on *global* alignments, the **BLAST** algorithms emphasize regions of *local* alignment to detect relationships among sequences with only isolated regions of similarity, and thus provide speed and increased sensitivity for distant sequence relationships. Input or "query" sequences are broken into "words" (default size 11 for nucleotides, 3 for amino acids). Word hits to databases are then extended in both directions.

Entrez Gene

Entrez Gene provides a variety of information about individual human genes. These include the sequence of the genome in and around the gene, gene structure (exon-intron boundaries), the sequence of the mRNA(s) produced from the gene, and any phenotypes associated with a given mutation. Entrez Gene also lists, where known, the function of the encoded protein and the impact of known single nucleotide polymorphisms in the coding region.

The HapMap Project

The HapMap Project is a cooperative effort by scientists from the United States, Canada, China, Japan, Nigeria, and the United Kingdom to identify genes associated with human disease and differential responses to pharmaceuticals. The resulting **haplotype map (HapMap)** of the human genome will provide a powerful resource for elucidating the genetic factors that contribute to variations in human sensitivity to environmental factors, susceptibility to infection, and responsiveness, either salutary or adverse, to drugs and vaccines.

CDD

Just as some words are formed by the fusion of individual root words or syllables—eg superhighway, crystallography, mainspring—many proteins contain multiple domains, each possessing a distinct evolutionary origin and function. Computational biologists classify conserved domains (CDs) based upon recurring sequence patterns or motifs. These conserved motifs can be identified and defined by comparing and contrasting the sequences of multiple proteins thought to possess a shared domain, a process referred to as multiple sequence alignment (Figure 10–1). The NCBI **CDD (Conserved Domain Database)** contains a library of such multiple sequence alignments for both individual domains and full-length proteins.

CDART

The **Conserved Domain Architecture Retrieval Tool (CDART)** employs the domain definitions and annotations from the CDD database to search for proteins that display similar domain architectures—the sequential order of conserved domains—suggestive of shared functions and common evolutionary origins. **CDART** uses **RPS-BLAST (Reverse-Position-Specific BLAST)**, a fast algorithm that locates similarities across significant evolutionary distances using sensitive protein domain profiles rather than direct, residue for residue, sequence comparisons. The domain architecture is then used to query the CDD for proteins with similar domain organizations. Since CDART relies on domain profiles and annotated functional domains, it is fast and informative. Domain profiles include functional annotation and are linked to available three-dimensional

Language	Word	Alignment
English	PHYSIOLOGICAL	PHYSIOLOGI-CAL
French	PHYSIOLOGIQUE	PHYSIOLOGI-QUE
German	PHYSIOLOGISCH	PHYSIOLOGISCH
Dutch	FYSIOLOGISCH	F-YSIOLOGISCH
Spanish	FYSIOLOGICO	F-YSIOLOGI-CO
Polish	FIZJOLOGICZNY	F-IZJOLOGI-CZNY

Figure 10–1. Representation of a multiple sequence alignment. Languages evolve in a fashion that mimics that of genes and proteins. Shown is the English word "physiological" in several Romance languages. The alignment demonstrates their conserved features. Identities with the English word are shown in dark color; linguistic similarities in light color. Multiple sequence alignment algorithms identify conserved nucleotide and amino acid letters in DNA, RNA, and polypeptides in an analogous fashion.

structures. Searches can be further refined by taxonomy and by selecting domains of interest.

Molecular Modeling Database & Cn3D

The three-dimensional structures of more than 28,000 proteins and polynucleotides are stored in the **Molecular Modeling Database (MMDB).** The file for each structure is linked to relevant bibliographic citations, taxonomic classifications, and sequence and structure neighbors in other NCBI databases. Structures may be retrieved by a *keyword*, such as the name of an enzyme; by *protein sequence*; or by *nucleotide sequence*. Structures may then be viewed, rotated, and manipulated using **Cn3D**, downloadable freeware for viewing three-dimensional structures accessed from Entrez. Cn3D simultaneously displays structure, sequence, and alignment, and has powerful annotation and alignment editing features.

VAST

The computer algorithm **VAST (Vector Alignment Search Tool)** identifies structural neighbors of a protein as specified by a set of user-supplied three-dimensional coordinates. Since precomputed structural neighbors for proteins already in the MMDB are accessible through Entrez, VAST is used to identify neighbors of protein structures not yet in the MMDB.

CONCLUSION

The rapidly evolving fields of bioinformatics and computational biology hold unparalleled promise for the future both of medicine and of basic biology. Some promises are at present perceived clearly, others dimly, while yet others remain unimagined. Yet there seems little doubt that the impact on medical practice in the 21st century will equal or surpass that of the discovery of bacterial pathogenesis in the 19th century.

SUMMARY

- Bioinformatics utilizes the computer to collect, organize, and analyze biomedical data.
- Computational biology uses the computer algorithms to perform simulations that serve as virtual experiments.
- The information storage and processing capabilities of the computer enable research scientists to analyze massive sets of data, such as genome sequences and protein structures.
- The ability to perform complex comparisons of multiple data sets makes bioinformatics an important tool for identifying protein domains and deciphering the causes of multifactorial diseases.
- BLAST is used to compare short sequences of proteins and nucleic acids.
- Entrez Gene and HapMap are used to identify single nucleotide polymorphisms that may contribute to pathological conditions.
- CDART, MMDB, and VAST are used to analyze the domain architecture and three-dimensional structure of proteins.

REFERENCES

Altschul, SF et al: Basic local alignment search tool. J Mol Biol 1990;215:403.

Butcher SC, Berg EL, Kunkel EJ: Systems biology in drug discovery. Nature Biotechnol 2004;22:1253.

Carroll SB: Genetics and the making of *Homo sapiens*. Nature 2003;422:849.

Collins FS et al: A vision for the future of genomics research. A blueprint for the genomic era. Nature 2003;422:835.

Debes JD, Urrutia R: Bioinformatics tools to understand human diseases. Surgery 2004;135:579.

Doolittle RF: Similar amino acid sequences: Chance or common ancestry? Science 1981;214:149.

Kim JH: Bioinformatics and genomic medicine. Genet Med 2002; 4:62S.

Koonin EV, Galperin MY: *Sequence—Evolution—Function. Computational Approaches to Comparative Genomics.* Kluwer Academic Publishers, 2003.

Slepchencko BM et al: Quantitative cell biology with the Virtual Cell. Trends Cell Biol 2003;13:570.

SECTION II
Bioenergetics & the Metabolism of Carbohydrates & Lipids

Bioenergetics: The Role of ATP | 11

Kathleen M. Botham, PhD, DSc, & Peter A. Mayes, PhD, DSc

BIOMEDICAL IMPORTANCE

Bioenergetics, or biochemical thermodynamics, is the study of the energy changes accompanying biochemical reactions. Biologic systems are essentially **isothermic** and use chemical energy to power living processes. How an animal obtains suitable fuel from its food to provide this energy is basic to the understanding of normal nutrition and metabolism. Death from **starvation** occurs when available energy reserves are depleted, and certain forms of malnutrition are associated with energy imbalance **(marasmus).** Thyroid hormones control the rate of energy release (metabolic rate), and disease results when they malfunction. Excess storage of surplus energy causes **obesity,** one of the most common diseases of Western society.

FREE ENERGY IS THE USEFUL ENERGY IN A SYSTEM

Gibbs change in free energy (ΔG) is that portion of the total energy change in a system that is available for doing work—ie, the useful energy, also known as the chemical potential.

Biologic Systems Conform to the General Laws of Thermodynamics

The first law of thermodynamics states that **the total energy of a system, including its surroundings, remains constant.** It implies that within the total system, energy is neither lost nor gained during any change. However, energy may be transferred from one part of the system to another or may be transformed into another form of energy. In living systems, chemical energy may be transformed into heat or into electrical, radiant, or mechanical energy.

The second law of thermodynamics states that **the total entropy of a system must increase if a process is to occur spontaneously. Entropy** is the extent of disorder or randomness of the system and becomes maximum as equilibrium is approached. Under conditions of constant temperature and pressure, the relationship between the free energy change (ΔG) of a reacting system and the change in entropy (ΔS) is expressed by the following equation, which combines the two laws of thermodynamics:

$$\Delta G = \Delta H - T\Delta S$$

where ΔH is the change in **enthalpy** (heat) and T is the absolute temperature.

In biochemical reactions, because ΔH is approximately equal to ΔE, the total change in internal energy of the reaction, the above relationship may be expressed in the following way:

$$\Delta G = \Delta E - T\Delta S$$

If ΔG is negative, the reaction proceeds spontaneously with loss of free energy; ie, it is **exergonic.** If, in

addition, ΔG is of great magnitude, the reaction goes virtually to completion and is essentially irreversible. On the other hand, if ΔG is positive, the reaction proceeds only if free energy can be gained; ie, it is **endergonic.** If, in addition, the magnitude of ΔG is great, the system is stable, with little or no tendency for a reaction to occur. If ΔG is zero, the system is at equilibrium and no net change takes place.

When the reactants are present in concentrations of 1.0 mol/L, ΔG^0 is the standard free energy change. For biochemical reactions, a standard state is defined as having a pH of 7.0. The standard free energy change at this standard state is denoted by $\Delta G^{0'}$.

The standard free energy change can be calculated from the equilibrium constant K_{eq}.

$$\Delta G^{0'} = -RT \ln K'_{eq}$$

where R is the gas constant and T is the absolute temperature (Chapter 8). It is important to note that the actual ΔG may be larger or smaller than $\Delta G^{0'}$ depending on the concentrations of the various reactants, including the solvent, various ions, and proteins.

In a biochemical system, an enzyme only speeds up the attainment of equilibrium; it never alters the final concentrations of the reactants at equilibrium.

ENDERGONIC PROCESSES PROCEED BY COUPLING TO EXERGONIC PROCESSES

The vital processes—eg, synthetic reactions, muscular contraction, nerve impulse conduction, active transport—obtain energy by chemical linkage, or **coupling,** to oxidative reactions. In its simplest form, this type of coupling may be represented as shown in Figure 11–1. The conversion of metabolite A to metabolite B occurs with release of free energy and is coupled to another reaction in which free energy is required to convert metabolite C to metabolite D. The terms **exergonic** and **endergonic** rather than the normal chemical terms "exothermic" and "endothermic" are used to indicate that a process is accompanied by loss or gain, respectively, of free energy in any form, not necessarily as heat. In practice, an endergonic process cannot exist independently, but must be a component of a coupled exergonic–endergonic system where the overall net change is exergonic. The exergonic reactions are termed **catabolism** (generally, the breakdown or oxidation of fuel molecules), whereas the synthetic reactions that build up substances are termed **anabolism.** The combined catabolic and anabolic processes constitute **metabolism.**

If the reaction shown in Figure 11–1 is to go from left to right, then the overall process must be accompanied by loss of free energy as heat. One possible mechanism of

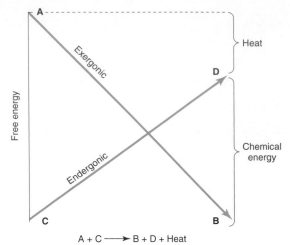

Figure 11–1. Coupling of an exergonic to an endergonic reaction.

coupling could be envisaged if a common obligatory intermediate (I) took part in both reactions, ie,

$$A + C \rightarrow I \rightarrow B + D$$

Some exergonic and endergonic reactions in biologic systems are coupled in this way. This type of system has a built-in mechanism for biologic control of the rate of oxidative processes since the common obligatory intermediate allows the rate of utilization of the product of the synthetic path (D) to determine by mass action the rate at which A is oxidized. Indeed, these relationships supply a basis for the concept of **respiratory control,** the process that prevents an organism from burning out of control. An extension of the coupling concept is provided by dehydrogenation reactions, which are coupled to hydrogenations by an intermediate carrier (Figure 11–2).

An alternative method of coupling an exergonic to an endergonic process is to synthesize a compound of high-energy potential in the exergonic reaction and to incorporate this new compound into the endergonic reaction, thus effecting a transference of free energy from the exergonic to the endergonic pathway (Figure 11–3). The biologic advantage of this mechanism is

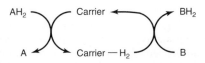

Figure 11–2. Coupling of dehydrogenation and hydrogenation reactions by an intermediate carrier.

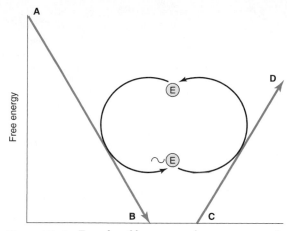

Figure 11–3. Transfer of free energy from an exergonic to an endergonic reaction via a high-energy intermediate compound (~Ⓔ).

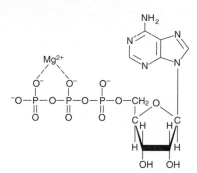

Figure 11–4. Adenosine triphosphate (ATP) shown as the magnesium complex. ADP forms a similar complex with Mg^{2+}.

that the compound of high potential energy, ~Ⓔ, unlike I in the previous system, need not be structurally related to A, B, C, or D, allowing Ⓔ to serve as a transducer of energy from a wide range of exergonic reactions to an equally wide range of endergonic reactions or processes, such as biosyntheses, muscular contraction, nervous excitation, and active transport. In the living cell, the principal high-energy intermediate or carrier compound (designated ~Ⓔ in Figure 11–3) is **adenosine triphosphate (ATP).**

HIGH-ENERGY PHOSPHATES PLAY A CENTRAL ROLE IN ENERGY CAPTURE AND TRANSFER

In order to maintain living processes, all organisms must obtain supplies of free energy from their environment. **Autotrophic** organisms utilize simple exergonic processes; eg, the energy of sunlight (green plants), the reaction $Fe^{2+} \rightarrow Fe^{3+}$ (some bacteria). On the other hand, **heterotrophic** organisms obtain free energy by coupling their metabolism to the breakdown of complex organic molecules in their environment. In all these organisms, ATP plays a central role in the transference of free energy from the exergonic to the endergonic processes (Figure 11–3). ATP is a nucleoside triphosphate containing adenine, ribose, and three phosphate groups. In its reactions in the cell, it functions as the Mg^{2+} complex (Figure 11–4).

The importance of phosphates in intermediary metabolism became evident with the discovery of the role of ATP, adenosine diphosphate (ADP), and inorganic phosphate (P_i) in glycolysis (Chapter 18).

The Intermediate Value for the Free Energy of Hydrolysis of ATP Has Important Bioenergetic Significance

The standard free energy of hydrolysis of a number of biochemically important phosphates is shown in Table 11–1. An estimate of the comparative tendency of each of the phosphate groups to transfer to a suitable acceptor may be obtained from the $\Delta G^{0'}$ of hydrolysis at 37 °C. The value for the hydrolysis of the terminal

Table 11–1. Standard free energy of hydrolysis of some organophosphates of biochemical importance.[1,2]

Compound	$\Delta G^{0'}$	
	kJ/mol	kcal/mol
Phosphoenolpyruvate	–61.9	–14.8
Carbamoyl phosphate	–51.4	–12.3
1,3-Bisphosphoglycerate (to 3-phosphoglycerate)	–49.3	–11.8
Creatine phosphate	–43.1	–10.3
ATP → AMP + PP_i	–32.2	–7.7
ATP → ADP + P_i	–30.5	–7.3
Glucose 1-phosphate	–20.9	–5.0
PP_i	–19.2	–4.6
Fructose 6-phosphate	–15.9	–3.8
Glucose 6-phosphate	–13.8	–3.3
Glycerol 3-phosphate	–9.2	–2.2

[1] PP_i, pyrophosphate; P_i, inorganic orthophosphate.
[2] All values taken from Jencks (1976), except that for PP_i which is from Frey and Arabshahi (1995). Values differ between investigators depending on the precise conditions under which the measurements were made.

phosphate of ATP divides the list into two groups. **Low-energy phosphates,** exemplified by the ester phosphates found in the intermediates of glycolysis, have $\Delta G^{0'}$ values smaller than that of ATP, while in **high-energy phosphates** the value is higher than that of ATP. The components of this latter group, including ATP, are usually anhydrides (eg, the 1-phosphate of 1,3-bisphosphoglycerate), enolphosphates (eg, phosphoenolpyruvate), and phosphoguanidines (eg, creatine phosphate, arginine phosphate). The intermediate position of ATP allows it to play an important role in energy transfer. The high free-energy change on hydrolysis of ATP is due to relief of charge repulsion of adjacent negatively charged oxygen atoms and to stabilization of the reaction products, especially phosphate, as resonance hybrids. Other "high-energy compounds" are thiol esters involving coenzyme A (eg, acetyl-CoA), acyl carrier protein, amino acid esters involved in protein synthesis, *S*-adenosylmethionine (active methionine), UDPGlc (uridine diphosphate glucose), and PRPP (5-phosphoribosyl-1-pyrophosphate).

High-Energy Phosphates Are Designated by ~Ⓟ

The symbol ~Ⓟ indicates that the group attached to the bond, on transfer to an appropriate acceptor, results in transfer of the larger quantity of free energy. For this reason, the term **group transfer potential** rather than "high-energy bond" is preferred by some. Thus, ATP contains two high-energy phosphate groups and ADP contains one, whereas the phosphate in AMP (adenosine monophosphate) is of the low-energy type, since it is a normal ester link (Figure 11–5).

HIGH-ENERGY PHOSPHATES ACT AS THE "ENERGY CURRENCY" OF THE CELL

ATP is able to act as a donor of high-energy phosphate to form those compounds below it in Table 11–1. Likewise, with the necessary enzymes, ADP can accept high-energy phosphate to form ATP from those compounds above ATP in the table. In effect, an **ATP/ADP cycle** connects those processes that generate ~Ⓟ to those processes that utilize ~Ⓟ (Figure 11–6), continuously consuming and regenerating ATP. This occurs at a very rapid rate, since the total ATP/ADP pool is extremely small and sufficient to maintain an active tissue for only a few seconds.

There are three major sources of ~Ⓟ taking part in **energy conservation** or **energy capture:**

(1) **Oxidative phosphorylation:** The greatest quantitative source of ~Ⓟ in aerobic organisms. Free energy comes from respiratory chain oxidation using molecular O_2 within mitochondria (Chapter 12).

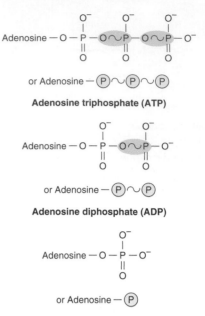

Figure 11–5. Structure of ATP, ADP, and AMP showing the position and the number of high-energy phosphates (~Ⓟ).

(2) **Glycolysis:** A net formation of two ~Ⓟ results from the formation of lactate from one molecule of glucose, generated in two reactions catalyzed by phosphoglycerate kinase and pyruvate kinase, respectively (Figure 18–2).

(3) **The citric acid cycle:** One ~Ⓟ is generated directly in the cycle at the succinyl thiokinase step (Figure 17–3).

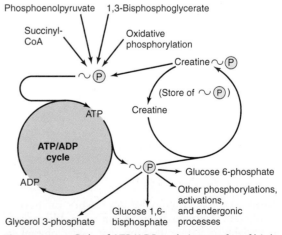

Figure 11–6. Role of ATP/ADP cycle in transfer of high-energy phosphate.

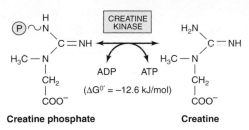

Creatine phosphate   **Creatine**

Figure 11–7. Transfer of high-energy phosphate between ATP and creatine.

Phosphagens act as storage forms of high-energy phosphate and include creatine phosphate, occurring in vertebrate skeletal muscle, heart, spermatozoa, and brain; and arginine phosphate, occurring in invertebrate muscle. When ATP is rapidly being utilized as a source of energy for muscular contraction, phosphagens permit its concentrations to be maintained, but when the ATP/ADP ratio is high, their concentration can increase to act as a store of high-energy phosphate (Figure 11–7).

When ATP acts as a phosphate donor to form those compounds of lower free energy of hydrolysis (Table 11–1), the phosphate group is invariably converted to one of low energy, eg,

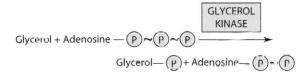

ATP Allows the Coupling of Thermodynamically Unfavorable Reactions to Favorable Ones

The phosphorylation of glucose to glucose 6-phosphate, the first reaction of glycolysis (Figure 18–2), is highly endergonic and cannot proceed under physiologic conditions.

$$(1) \text{ Glucose} + P_i \rightarrow \text{Glucose 6-phosphate} + H_2O$$

$$(\Delta G^{0'} = +13.8 \text{ kJ/mol})$$

To take place, the reaction must be coupled with another—more exergonic—reaction such as the hydrolysis of the terminal phosphate of ATP.

$$(2) \text{ ATP} \rightarrow \text{ADP} + P_i \ (\Delta G^{0'} = -30.5 \text{ kJ/mol})$$

When (1) and (2) are coupled in a reaction catalyzed by hexokinase, phosphorylation of glucose readily proceeds in a highly exergonic reaction that under physiologic conditions is irreversible. Many "activation" reactions follow this pattern.

Adenylyl Kinase (Myokinase) Interconverts Adenine Nucleotides

This enzyme is present in most cells. It catalyzes the following reaction:

$$\text{ATP} + \text{AMP} \rightleftharpoons 2\text{ADP}$$

This allows:

(1) High-energy phosphate in ADP to be used in the synthesis of ATP.

(2) AMP, formed as a consequence of several activating reactions involving ATP, to be recovered by rephosphorylation to ADP.

(3) AMP to increase in concentration when ATP becomes depleted and act as a metabolic (allosteric) signal to increase the rate of catabolic reactions, which in turn lead to the generation of more ATP (Chapter 20).

When ATP Forms AMP, Inorganic Pyrophosphate (PP$_i$) Is Produced

ATP can also be hydrolyzed directly to AMP, with the release of PP$_i$ (Table 11–1). This occurs, for example, in the activation of long-chain fatty acids (Chapter 22):

$$\boxed{\begin{array}{c}\text{ACYL CoA}\\\text{SYNTHETASE}\end{array}}$$

$$\text{ATP} + \text{CoA} \cdot \text{SH} + R \cdot \text{COOH} \longrightarrow \text{AMP} + \text{PP}_i + R \cdot \text{CO} - \text{SCoA}$$

This reaction is accompanied by loss of free energy as heat, which ensures that the activation reaction will go to the right; and is further aided by the hydrolytic splitting of PP$_i$, catalyzed by **inorganic pyrophosphatase,** a reaction that itself has a large $\Delta G^{0'}$ of −19.2 kJ/mol. Note that activations via the pyrophosphate pathway result in the loss of two ~Ⓟ rather than one, as occurs when ADP and P$_i$ are formed.

$$\boxed{\begin{array}{c}\text{INORGANIC}\\\text{PYROPHOSPHATASE}\end{array}}$$

$$\text{PP}_i + H_2O \longrightarrow 2 P_i$$

A combination of the above reactions makes it possible for phosphate to be recycled and the adenine nucleotides to interchange (Figure 11–8).

Other Nucleoside Triphosphates Participate in the Transfer of High-Energy Phosphate

By means of the enzyme **nucleoside diphosphate kinase,** UTP, GTP, and CTP can be synthesized from their diphosphates, eg,

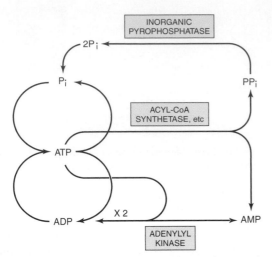

Figure 11–8. Phosphate cycles and interchange of adenine nucleotides.

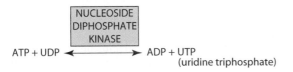

All of these triphosphates take part in phosphorylations in the cell. Similarly, specific nucleoside monophosphate kinases catalyze the formation of nucleoside diphosphates from the corresponding monophosphates.

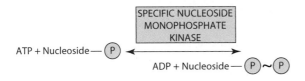

Thus, adenylyl kinase is a specialized monophosphate kinase.

SUMMARY

- Biologic systems use chemical energy to power the living processes.

- Exergonic reactions take place spontaneously with loss of free energy (ΔG is negative). Endergonic reactions require the gain of free energy (ΔG is positive) and occur only when coupled to exergonic reactions.

- ATP acts as the "energy currency" of the cell, transferring free energy derived from substances of higher energy potential to those of lower energy potential.

REFERENCES

de Meis L: The concept of energy-rich phosphate compounds: Water, transport ATPases, and entropy energy. Arch Biochem Biophys 1993;306:287.

Frey PA, Arabshahi A: Standard free energy change for the hydrolysis of the alpha, beta-phosphoanhydride bridge in ATP. Biochemistry 1995;34:11307.

Harold FM: *The Vital Force: A Study of Bioenergetics.* Freeman, 1986.

Harris DA: *Bioenergetics at a Glance: An Illustrated Introduction.* Blackwell Publishing, 1995.

Jencks WP: Free energies of hydrolysis and decarboxylation. In: *Handbook of Biochemistry and Molecular Biology,* vol 1. *Physical and Chemical Data.* Fasman GD (editor). CRC Press, 1976.

Klotz IM: *Introduction to Biomolecular Energetics.* Academic Press, 1986.

Nicholls D, Ferguson F: *Bioenergetics.* Elsevier, 2003.

Biologic Oxidation

Kathleen M. Botham, PhD, DSc, & Peter A. Mayes, PhD, DSc

BIOMEDICAL IMPORTANCE

Chemically, **oxidation** is defined as the removal of electrons and **reduction** as the gain of electrons. Thus, oxidation is always accompanied by reduction of an electron acceptor. This principle of oxidation-reduction applies equally to biochemical systems and is an important concept underlying understanding of the nature of biologic oxidation. Note that many biologic oxidations can take place without the participation of molecular oxygen, eg, dehydrogenations. The life of higher animals is absolutely dependent upon a supply of oxygen for **respiration,** the process by which cells derive energy in the form of ATP from the controlled reaction of hydrogen with oxygen to form water. In addition, molecular oxygen is incorporated into a variety of substrates by enzymes designated as **oxygenases;** many drugs, pollutants, and chemical carcinogens (xenobiotics) are metabolized by enzymes of this class, known as the **cytochrome P450 system.** Administration of oxygen can be lifesaving in the treatment of patients with respiratory or circulatory failure.

FREE ENERGY CHANGES CAN BE EXPRESSED IN TERMS OF REDOX POTENTIAL

In reactions involving oxidation and reduction, the free energy change is proportionate to the tendency of reactants to donate or accept electrons. Thus, in addition to expressing free energy change in terms of $\Delta G^{0\prime}$ (Chapter 11), it is possible, in an analogous manner, to express it numerically as an **oxidation-reduction** or **redox potential** (E'_0). The redox potential of a system (E_0) is usually compared with the potential of the hydrogen electrode (0.0 volts at pH 0.0). However, for biologic systems, the redox potential (E'_0) is normally expressed at pH 7.0, at which pH the electrode potential of the hydrogen electrode is −0.42 volts. The redox potentials of some redox systems of special interest in mammalian biochemistry are shown in Table 12–1. The relative positions of redox systems in the table allows prediction of the direction of flow of electrons from one redox couple to another.

Enzymes involved in oxidation and reduction are called **oxidoreductases** and are classified into four groups: **oxidases, dehydrogenases, hydroperoxidases,** and **oxygenases.**

OXIDASES USE OXYGEN AS A HYDROGEN ACCEPTOR

Oxidases catalyze the removal of hydrogen from a substrate using oxygen as a hydrogen acceptor.* They form water or hydrogen peroxide as a reaction product (Figure 12–1).

Some Oxidases Contain Copper

Cytochrome oxidase is a hemoprotein widely distributed in many tissues, having the typical heme prosthetic group present in myoglobin, hemoglobin, and other cytochromes (Chapter 6). It is the terminal component of the chain of respiratory carriers found in mitochondria and transfers electrons resulting from the oxidation of substrate molecules by dehydrogenases to their final acceptor, oxygen. The enzyme is poisoned by carbon monoxide, cyanide, and hydrogen sulfide. It has also been termed "cytochrome a_3." It is now known that cytochromes a and a_3 are combined in a single protein, and the cytochrome oxidase enzyme complex is known as **cytochrome aa_3.** It contains two molecules of heme, each having one Fe atom that oscillates between Fe^{3+} and Fe^{2+} during oxidation and reduction. Furthermore, two atoms of Cu are present, each associated with a heme unit.

Other Oxidases Are Flavoproteins

Flavoprotein enzymes contain **flavin mononucleotide (FMN)** or **flavin adenine dinucleotide (FAD)** as prosthetic groups. FMN and FAD are formed in the body from the vitamin **riboflavin** (Chapter 44). FMN and FAD are usually tightly—but not covalently—bound to their respective apoenzyme proteins. Metalloflavoproteins contain one or more metals as essential cofactors. Examples of flavoprotein enzymes include **L-amino acid oxidase,** an FMN-linked enzyme found

---

* The term "oxidase" is sometimes used collectively to denote all enzymes that catalyze reactions involving molecular oxygen.

Table 12–1. Some redox potentials of special interest in mammalian oxidation systems.

System	E'_0 Volts
H^+/H_2	−0.42
$NAD^+/NADH$	−0.32
Lipoate; ox/red	−0.29
Acetoacetate/3-hydroxybutyrate	−0.27
Pyruvate/lactate	−0.19
Oxaloacetate/malate	−0.17
Fumarate/succinate	+0.03
Cytochrome b; Fe^{3+}/Fe^{2+}	+0.08
Ubiquinone; ox/red	+0.10
Cytochrome c_1; Fe^{3+}/Fe^{2+}	+0.22
Cytochrome a; Fe^{3+}/Fe^{2+}	+0.29
Oxygen/water	+0.82

in kidney with general specificity for the oxidative deamination of the naturally occurring L-amino acids; **xanthine oxidase,** which contains molybdenum and plays an important role in the conversion of purine bases to uric acid (Chapter 33), and is of particular significance in uricotelic animals (Chapter 28); and **aldehyde dehydrogenase,** an FAD-linked enzyme present in mammalian livers, which contains molybdenum and nonheme iron and acts upon aldehydes and N-heterocyclic substrates. The mechanisms of oxidation and reduction of these enzymes are complex. Evidence suggests a two-step reaction as shown in Figure 12–2.

DEHYDROGENASES CANNOT USE OXYGEN AS A HYDROGEN ACCEPTOR

There are a large number of enzymes in this class. They perform two main functions:

(1) Transfer of hydrogen from one substrate to another in a coupled oxidation-reduction reaction (Figure 12–3). These dehydrogenases are specific for their substrates but often utilize common coenzymes or hydrogen carriers, eg, NAD^+. Since the reactions are reversible, these properties enable reducing equivalents to be freely transferred within the cell. This type of reaction, which

enables one substrate to be oxidized at the expense of another, is particularly useful in enabling oxidative processes to occur in the absence of oxygen, such as during the anaerobic phase of glycolysis (Figure 18–2).

(2) As components in the **respiratory chain** of electron transport from substrate to oxygen (Figure 13–3).

Many Dehydrogenases Depend on Nicotinamide Coenzymes

These dehydrogenases use **nicotinamide adenine dinucleotide (NAD^+)** or **nicotinamide adenine dinucleotide phosphate ($NADP^+$)**—or both—which are formed in the body from the vitamin **niacin** (Chapter 44). The coenzymes are reduced by the specific substrate of the dehydrogenase and reoxidized by a suitable electron acceptor (Figure 12–4). They may freely and reversibly dissociate from their respective apoenzymes.

Generally, NAD-linked dehydrogenases catalyze oxidoreduction reactions in the oxidative pathways of metabolism, particularly in glycolysis, in the citric acid cycle, and in the respiratory chain of mitochondria. NADP-linked dehydrogenases are found characteristically in reductive syntheses, as in the extramitochondrial pathway of fatty acid synthesis and steroid synthesis—and also in the pentose phosphate pathway.

Other Dehydrogenases Depend on Riboflavin

The flavin groups associated with these dehydrogenases are similar to FMN and FAD occurring in oxidases. They are generally more tightly bound to their apoenzymes than are the nicotinamide coenzymes. Most of the riboflavin-linked dehydrogenases are concerned with electron transport in (or to) the respiratory chain (Chapter 13). **NADH dehydrogenase** acts as a carrier of electrons between NADH and the components of higher redox potential (Figure 13–3). Other dehydrogenases such as **succinate dehydrogenase, acyl-CoA dehydrogenase,** and **mitochondrial glycerol-3-phosphate dehydrogenase** transfer reducing equivalents directly from the substrate to the respiratory chain (Figure 13–5). Another role of the flavin-dependent dehydrogenases is in the dehydrogenation (by **dihydrolipoyl dehydrogenase**) of reduced lipoate, an intermediate in the oxidative decarboxylation of pyruvate and α-ketoglutarate (Figures 13–5 and 18–5). The **electron-transferring flavoprotein** is an intermediary carrier of electrons between acyl-CoA dehydrogenase and the respiratory chain (Figure 13–5).

Cytochromes May Also Be Regarded As Dehydrogenases

The cytochromes are iron-containing hemoproteins in which the iron atom oscillates between Fe^{3+} and Fe^{2+}

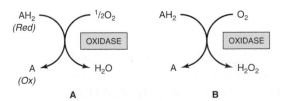

Figure 12–1. Oxidation of a metabolite catalyzed by an oxidase **(A)** forming H_2O, **(B)** forming H_2O_2.

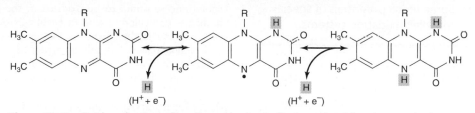

Figure 12–2. Oxidoreduction of isoalloxazine ring in flavin nucleotides via a semiquinone (free radical) intermediate (center).

during oxidation and reduction. Except for cytochrome oxidase (previously described), they are classified as dehydrogenases. In the respiratory chain, they are involved as carriers of electrons from flavoproteins on the one hand to cytochrome oxidase on the other (Figure 13–5). Several identifiable cytochromes occur in the respiratory chain, ie, cytochromes b, c_1, c, and a, + a_3 (cytochrome oxidase). Cytochromes are also found in other locations, eg, the endoplasmic reticulum (cytochromes P450 and b_5), and in plant cells, bacteria, and yeasts.

HYDROPEROXIDASES USE HYDROGEN PEROXIDE OR AN ORGANIC PEROXIDE AS SUBSTRATE

Two type of enzymes found both in animals and plants fall into this category: **peroxidases** and **catalase.**

Hydroperoxidases protect the body against harmful peroxides. Accumulation of peroxides can lead to generation of free radicals, which in turn can disrupt membranes and perhaps cause diseases including cancer and atherosclerosis. (See Chapters 15 and 44.)

Peroxidases Reduce Peroxides Using Various Electron Acceptors

Peroxidases are found in milk and in leukocytes, platelets, and other tissues involved in eicosanoid metabolism (Chapter 23). The prosthetic group is protoheme. In the reaction catalyzed by peroxidase, hydrogen peroxide is reduced at the expense of several substances that will act as electron acceptors, such as ascorbate, quinones, and

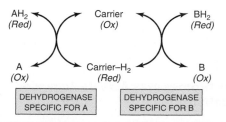

Figure 12–3. Oxidation of a metabolite catalyzed by coupled dehydrogenases.

cytochrome c. The reaction catalyzed by peroxidase is complex, but the overall reaction is as follows:

$$\boxed{\text{PEROXIDASE}}$$
$$H_2O_2 + AH_2 \longrightarrow 2H_2O + A$$

In erythrocytes and other tissues, the enzyme **glutathione peroxidase,** containing **selenium** as a prosthetic group, catalyzes the destruction of H_2O_2 and lipid hydroperoxides through the conversion of reduced to oxidized glutathione, protecting membrane lipids and hemoglobin against oxidation by peroxides (Chapter 21).

Catalase Uses Hydrogen Peroxide as Electron Donor & Electron Acceptor

Catalase is a hemoprotein containing four heme groups. In addition to possessing peroxidase activity, it is able to use one molecule of H_2O_2 as a substrate electron donor and another molecule of H_2O_2 as an oxidant or electron acceptor.

$$\boxed{\text{CATALASE}}$$
$$2H_2O_2 \longrightarrow 2H_2O + O_2$$

Under most conditions in vivo, the peroxidase activity of catalase seems to be favored. Catalase is found in blood, bone marrow, mucous membranes, kidney, and liver. Its function is assumed to be the destruction of hydrogen peroxide formed by the action of oxidases. **Peroxisomes** are found in many tissues, including liver. They are rich in oxidases and in catalase, Thus, the enzymes that produce H_2O_2 are grouped with the enzyme that destroys it. However, mitochondrial and microsomal electron transport systems as well as xanthine oxidase must be considered as additional sources of H_2O_2.

OXYGENASES CATALYZE THE DIRECT TRANSFER & INCORPORATION OF OXYGEN INTO A SUBSTRATE MOLECULE

Oxygenases are concerned with the synthesis or degradation of many different types of metabolites. They cat-

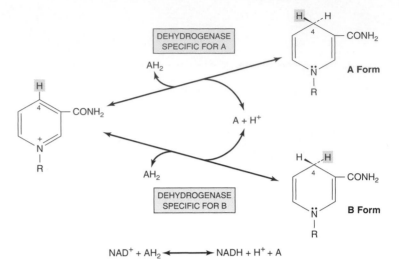

Figure 12–4. Mechanism of oxidation and reduction of nicotinamide coenzymes. There is stereospecificity about position 4 of nicotinamide when it is reduced by a substrate AH_2. One of the hydrogen atoms is removed from the substrate as a hydrogen nucleus with two electrons (hydride ion, H^-) and is transferred to the 4 position, where it may be attached in either the A or the B position according to the specificity determined by the particular dehydrogenase catalyzing the reaction. The remaining hydrogen of the hydrogen pair removed from the substrate remains free as a hydrogen ion.

alyze the incorporation of oxygen into a substrate molecule in two steps: (1) oxygen is bound to the enzyme at the active site, and (2) the bound oxygen is reduced or transferred to the substrate. Oxygenases may be divided into two subgroups, as follows.

Dioxygenases Incorporate Both Atoms of Molecular Oxygen into the Substrate

The basic reaction is shown below:

$$A + O_2 \rightarrow AO_2$$

Examples include the liver enzymes, **homogentisate dioxygenase** (oxidase) and **3-hydroxyanthranilate dioxygenase** (oxidase), that contain iron; and **L-tryptophan dioxygenase** (tryptophan pyrolase) (Chapter 29), that utilizes heme.

Monooxygenases (Mixed-Function Oxidases, Hydroxylases) Incorporate Only One Atom of Molecular Oxygen into the Substrate

The other oxygen atom is reduced to water, an additional electron donor or cosubstrate (Z) being necessary for this purpose.

$$A-H + O_2 + ZH_2 \rightarrow A-OH + H_2O + Z$$

Cytochromes P450 Are Monooxygenases Important for the Detoxification of Many Drugs & for the Hydroxylation of Steroids

Cytochromes P450 are an important superfamily of heme-containing monooxgenases, and more than

1000 such enzymes are known. Both NADH and NADPH donate reducing equivalents for the reduction of these cytochromes (Figure 12–5), which in turn are oxidized by substrates in a series of enzymatic reactions collectively known as the **hydroxylase cycle** (Figure 12–6). In liver microsomes, cytochromes P450 are found together with **cytochrome b_5** and have an important role in detoxification. Benzpyrene, aminopyrine, aniline, morphine, and benzphetamine are hydroxylated, increasing their solubility and aiding their excretion. Many drugs such as phenobarbital have the ability to induce the formation of microsomal enzymes and of cytochromes P450.

Mitochondrial cytochrome P450 systems are found in steroidogenic tissues such as adrenal cortex, testis, ovary, and placenta and are concerned with the biosynthesis of steroid hormones from cholesterol (hydroxylation at C_{22} and C_{20} in side-chain cleavage and at the 11β and 18 positions). In addition, renal systems catalyzing 1α- and 24-hydroxylations of 25-hydroxycholecalciferol in vitamin D metabolism—and cholesterol 7α-hydroxylase and sterol 27-hydroxylase involved in bile acid biosynthesis in the liver (Chapter 26)—are P450 enzymes.

SUPEROXIDE DISMUTASE PROTECTS AEROBIC ORGANISMS AGAINST OXYGEN TOXICITY

Transfer of a single electron to O_2 generates the potentially damaging **superoxide anion free radical (O_2^{-})**, the destructive effects of which are amplified by its giving rise to free-radical chain reactions (Chapter 15). The ease with which superoxide can be formed from

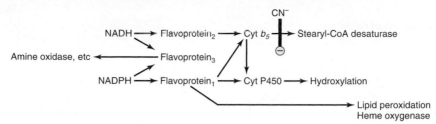

Figure 12–5. Electron transport chain in microsomes. Cyanide (CN^-) inhibits the indicated step.

oxygen in tissues and the occurrence of **superoxide dismutase,** the enzyme responsible for its removal in all aerobic organisms (although not in obligate anaerobes) indicate that the potential toxicity of oxygen is due to its conversion to superoxide.

Superoxide is formed when reduced flavins—present, for example, in xanthine oxidase—are reoxidized univalently by molecular oxygen.

$$Enz-Flavin-H_2 + O_2 \rightarrow Enz-Flavin-H + O_2^- + H^+$$

Superoxide can reduce oxidized cytochrome c

$$O_2^- + Cyt\ c\ (Fe^{3+}) \rightarrow O_2 + Cyt\ c\ (Fe^{2+})$$

or be removed by superoxide dismutase.

$$O_2^- + O_2^- + 2H^+ \xrightarrow{\boxed{\text{SUPEROXIDE DISMUTASE}}} H_2O_2 + O_2$$

In this reaction, superoxide acts as both oxidant and reductant. Thus, superoxide dismutase protects aerobic organisms against the potential deleterious effects of superoxide. The enzyme occurs in all major aerobic tissues in the mitochondria and the cytosol. Although exposure of animals to an atmosphere of 100% oxygen causes an adaptive increase in superoxide dismutase, particularly in the lungs, prolonged exposure leads to lung damage and death. Antioxidants, eg, α-tocopherol (vitamin E), act as scavengers of free radicals and reduce the toxicity of oxygen (Chapter 44).

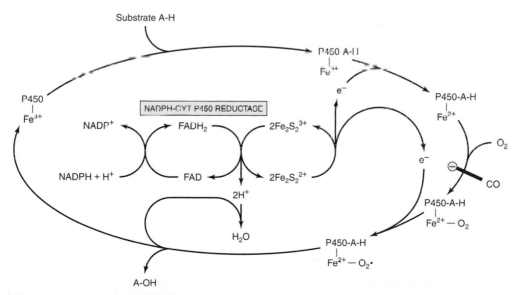

Figure 12–6. Cytochrome P450 hydroxylase cycle in microsomes. The system shown is typical of steroid hydroxylases of the adrenal cortex. Liver microsomal cytochrome P450 hydroxylase does not require the iron-sulfur protein Fe_2S_2. Carbon monoxide (CO) inhibits the indicated step.

SUMMARY

- In biologic systems, as in chemical systems, oxidation (loss of electrons) is always accompanied by reduction of an electron acceptor.
- Oxidoreductases have a variety of functions in metabolism; oxidases and dehydrogenases play major roles in respiration; hydroperoxidases protect the body against damage by free radicals; and oxygenases mediate the hydroxylation of drugs and steroids.
- Tissues are protected from oxygen toxicity caused by the superoxide free radical by the specific enzyme superoxide dismutase.

REFERENCES

Babcock GT, Wikstrom M: Oxygen activation and the conservation of energy in cell respiration. Nature 1992;356:301.

Coon MJ: Cytochrome P450: Nature's most versatile biological catalyst. Annu Rev Pharmacol Toxicol 2005;4:1.

Harris DA: *Bioenergetics at a Glance: An Illustrated Introduction.* Blackwell Publishing, 1995.

Nicholls D, Ferguson F: *Bioenergetics.* Elsevier, 2003.

Raha S, Robinson BH: Mitochondria, oxygen free radicals, disease and aging. Trends Biochem Sci 2000;25:502.

Tyler DD: *The Mitochondrion in Health and Disease.* VCH Publishers, 1992.

The Respiratory Chain & Oxidative Phosphorylation

Kathleen M. Botham, PhD, DSc, & Peter A. Mayes, PhD, DSc

BIOMEDICAL IMPORTANCE

Aerobic organisms are able to capture a far greater proportion of the available free energy of respiratory substrates than anaerobic organisms. Most of this takes place inside mitochondria, which have been termed the "powerhouses" of the cell. Respiration is coupled to the generation of the high-energy intermediate, ATP, by **oxidative phosphorylation.** A number of drugs (eg, **amobarbital**) and poisons (eg, **cyanide, carbon monoxide**) inhibit oxidative phosphorylation, usually with fatal consequences. Several inherited defects of mitochondria involving components of the respiratory chain and oxidative phosphorylation have been reported. Patients present with **myopathy** and **encephalopathy** and often have **lactic acidosis.**

SPECIFIC ENZYMES ACT AS MARKERS OF COMPARTMENTS SEPARATED BY THE MITOCHONDRIAL MEMBRANES

Mitochondria have an **outer membrane** that is permeable to most metabolites, an **inner membrane** that is selectively permeable, enclosing a **matrix** within (Figure 13–1). The outer membrane is characterized by the presence of various enzymes, including acyl-CoA synthetase and glycerolphosphate acyltransferase. Adenylyl kinase and creatine kinase are found in the intermembrane space. The phospholipid cardiolipin is concentrated in the inner membrane together with the enzymes of the respiratory chain, ATP synthase and various membrane transporters.

THE RESPIRATORY CHAIN OXIDIZES REDUCING EQUIVALENTS & ACTS AS A PROTON PUMP

Most of the energy liberated during the oxidation of carbohydrate, fatty acids, and amino acids is made available within mitochondria as reducing equivalents (—H or electrons) (Figure 13–2). Note that the enzymes of the citric acid cycle and β-oxidation (Chapters 22 and 17) are contained in mitochondria, together with the respiratory chain, which collects and transports reducing equivalents, directing them to their final reaction with oxygen to form water, and the machinery for oxidative phosphorylation, the process by which the liberated free energy is trapped as high-energy phosphate.

Components of the Respiratory Chain Are Contained in Four Large Protein Complexes Embedded in the Inner Mitochondrial Membrane

Electrons flow through the respiratory chain through a redox span of 1.1 V from NAD$^+$/NADH to O$_2$/2H$_2$O (Table 12–1), passing through three large protein complexes; **NADH-Q oxidoreductase (Complex I),** where electrons are transferred from NADH to coenzyme Q (Q) (also called **ubiquinone**); **Q-cytochrome *c* oxidoreductase (Complex III),** which passes the electrons on to cytochrome *c*; and **cytochrome *c* oxidase (Complex IV),** which completes the chain, passing the electrons to O$_2$ and causing it to be reduced to H$_2$O (Figure 13–3). Some substrates with more positive redox potentials than NAD$^+$/NADH (eg, succinate) pass electrons to Q via a fourth complex, **succinate Q reductase (Complex II),** rather than Complex I. The four complexes are embedded in the inner mitochondrial membrane, but Q and cytochrome *c* are mobile. Q diffuses rapidly within the membrane, while cytochrome *c* is a soluble protein. The flow of electrons through Complexes I, III, and IV results in the pumping of protons from the matrix across the inner mitochondrial membrane into the intermembrane space (Figure 13–7).

Flavoproteins and Iron-Sulfur Proteins (Fe-S) Are Components of the Respiratory Chain Complexes

Flavoproteins (Chapter 12) are important components of Complexes I and II. The oxidized flavin nucleotide (FMN or FAD) can be reduced in reactions involving the transfer of two electrons (to form FMNH$_2$ or FADH$_2$), but they can also accept one electron to form the semiquinone (Figure 12–2). **Iron-sulfur proteins (non-heme iron proteins, Fe-S)** are found in Complexes I, II, and

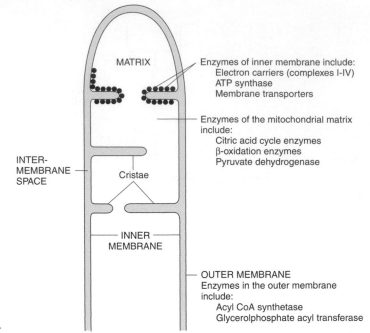

Figure 13–1. Structure of the mitochondrial membranes. Note that the inner membrane contains many folds, or cristae.

III. These may contain one, two, or four Fe atoms linked to inorganic sulfur atoms and/or via cysteine-SH groups to the protein (Figure 13-4). The Fe-S take part in single electron transfer reactions in which one Fe atom undergoes oxidoreduction between Fe^{2+} and Fe^{3+}.

Q Accepts Electrons Via Complex I and Complex II

NADH-Q oxidoreductase or Complex I is a large L-shaped multi-subunit protein that catalyzes electron transfer

from NADH to Q, coupled with the transfer of four H^+ across the membrane:

$$NADH + Q + 5H^+_{matrix} \rightarrow$$

$$NAD + QH_2 + 4H^+_{intermembrane\ space}$$

Electrons are transferred from NADH to FMN initially, then to a series of Fe-S centers, and finally to Q (Figure 13–5). In Complex II (succinate -Q reductase), $FADH_2$ is formed during the conversion of succinate to

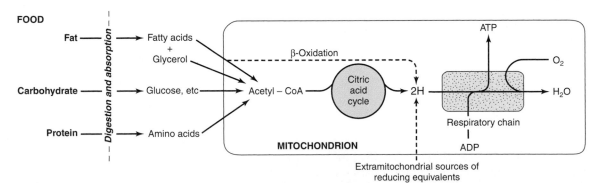

Figure 13–2. Role of the respiratory chain of mitochondria in the conversion of food energy to ATP. Oxidation of the major foodstuffs leads to the generation of reducing equivalents (2H) that are collected by the respiratory chain for oxidation and coupled generation of ATP.

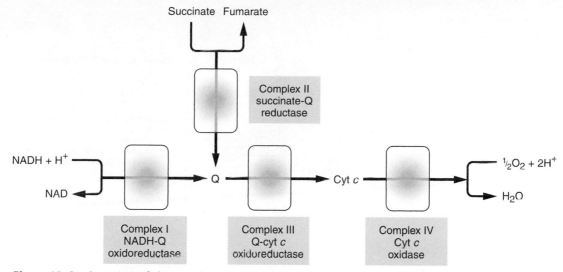

Figure 13–3. Overview of electron flow through the respiratory chain. Q, co-enzyme Q or ubiquinone; cyt, cytochrome.

fumarate in the citric acid cycle (Figure 17–3) and electrons are then passed via several Fe-S centers to Q (Figure 13–5). Glycerol-3-phosphate (generated in the break-

down of triacylglycerols or from glycolysis, Figure 18–2) and acyl CoA also pass electrons to Q via different pathways involving flavoproteins (Figure 13–5).

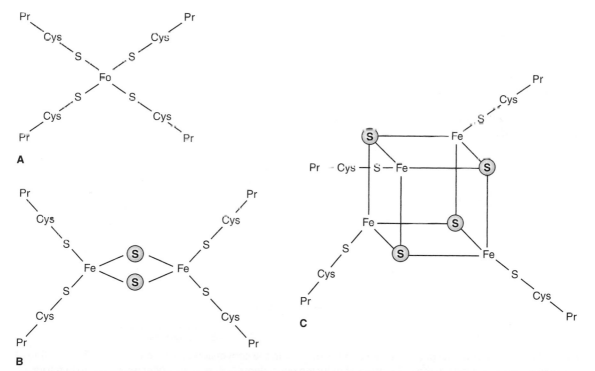

Figure 13–4. Iron sulfur proteins (Fe-S). **(A)** The simplest Fe-S with one Fe bound by four cysteines. **(B)** 2Fe-2S center. **(C)** 4Fe-4S center. Ⓢ, Inorganic sulfur; Pr, apoprotein; Cys, cysteine.

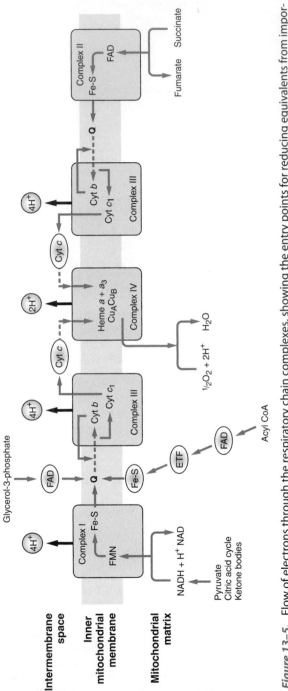

Figure 13–5. Flow of electrons through the respiratory chain complexes, showing the entry points for reducing equivalents from important substrates. Q and cyt c are mobile components of the system as indicated by the dotted arrow. The flow through Complex III (the Q cycle) is shown in more detail in Figure 13–6. Fe-S, iron sulfur protein; ETF, electron transferring flavoprotein; Q, co-enzyme Q or ubiquinone; cyt, cytochrome.

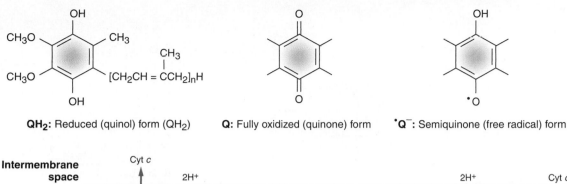

QH₂: Reduced (quinol) form (QH₂)   **Q: Fully oxidized (quinone) form**   **˙Q⁻: Semiquinone (free radical) form**

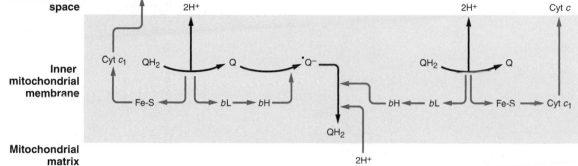

Figure 13–6. The Q cycle. During the oxidation of QH_2 to Q, one electron is donated to cyt c via a Rieske Fe-S and cyt c_1 and the second to a Q to form the semiquinone via cyt b_L and cyt b_H, with $2H^+$ being released into the intermembrane space. A similar process then occurs with a second QH_2, but in this case the second electron is donated to the semiquinone, reducing it to QH_2 and $2H^+$ are taken up from the matrix. Fe-S, iron-sulfur protein; Q, co-enzyme Q or ubiquinone; cyt, cytochrome.

The Q Cycle Couples Electron Transfer to Proton Transport in Complex III

Electrons are passed from QH_2 to cytochrome c via Complex III (Q-cytochrome c oxidoreductase):

$$QH_2 + 2Cyt\ c_{oxidized} + 2H^+_{matrix} \rightarrow$$
$$Q + 2Cyt\ c_{reduced} + 4H^+_{intermembrane\ space}$$

The process is believed to involve **cytochromes c_1, b_1, and b_H** and a **Rieske Fe-S** (an unusual Fe-S in which one of the Fe atoms is linked to two histidine-SH groups rather than two cysteine-SH groups) (Figure 13–5), and is known as the **Q cycle** (Figure 13–6). Q may exist in three forms, the oxidized quinone, the reduced quinol, or the semiquinone (Figure 13–6). The semiquinone is formed transiently during the cycle, one turn of which results in the oxidation of $2QH_2$ to Q, releasing $4H^+$ into the intermembrane space, and the reduction of one Q to QH_2, causing $2H^+$ to be taken up from the matrix (Figure 13–6). Note that while Q carries two electrons, the cytochromes carry only one, thus the oxidation of one QH_2 is coupled to the reduction of two molecules of cytochrome c via the Q cycle.

Molecular Oxygen Is Reduced to Water Via Complex IV

Reduced cytochrome c is oxidized by Complex IV (cytochrome c oxidase), with the concomitant reduction of O_2 to two molecules of water:

$$4Cyt\ c_{reduced} + O_2 + 8H^+_{matrix} \rightarrow$$
$$4Cyt\ c_{oxidized} + 2H_2O + 4H^+_{intermembrane\ space}$$

This transfer of four electrons from cytochrome c to O_2 involves two heme groups, a and a_3, and Cu (Figure 13–5). Electrons are passed initially to a Cu center (Cu_A), which contains 2Cu atoms linked to two protein cysteine-SH groups (resembling an Fe-S), then in sequence to heme a, heme a_3, a second Cu center, Cu_B, which is linked to heme a_3, and finally to O_2. Of the eight H^+ removed from the matrix, four are used to form two water molecules and four are pumped into the intermembrane space. Thus, for every pair of electrons passing down the chain from NADH or $FADH_2$, $2H^+$ are pumped across the membrane by Complex IV. O_2 remains tightly bound to Complex IV until it is fully reduced, and this minimizes the release of poten-

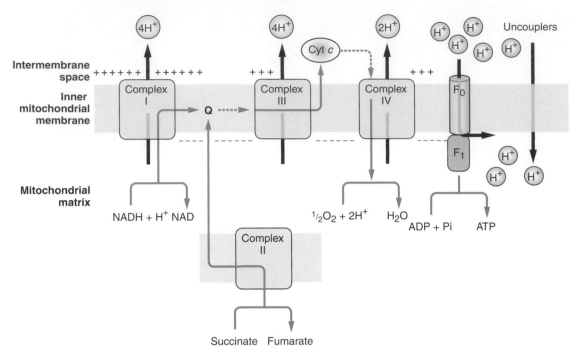

Figure 13–7. The chemiosmotic theory of oxidative phosphorylation. Complexes I, III, and IV act as proton pumps creating a proton gradient across the membrane, which is negative on the matrix side. The proton motive force created drives the synthesis of ATP as the protons flow back into the matrix through the ATP synthase enzyme (see Figure 13–8). Uncouplers increase the permeability of the membrane to ions, collapsing the proton gradient by allowing the H^+ to pass across without going through the ATP synthase and thus uncouple electron flow through the respiratory complexes from ATP synthesis. Q, co-enzyme Q or ubiquinone; cyt, cytochrome.

tially damaging intermediates such as superoxide anions or peroxide which are formed when O_2 accepts one or two electrons, respectively (Chapter 12).

ELECTRON TRANSPORT VIA THE RESPIRATORY CHAIN CREATES A PROTON GRADIENT WHICH DRIVES THE SYNTHESIS OF ATP

The flow of electrons through the respiratory chain generates ATP by the process of **oxidative phosphorylation. The chemiosmotic theory,** proposed by Peter Mitchell in 1961, postulates that the two processes are coupled by a proton gradient across the inner mitochondrial membrane so that **the proton motive force** caused by the electrochemical potential difference (negative on the matrix side) drives the mechanism of ATP synthesis. As we have seen, Complexes I, III, and IV act as **proton pumps.** Since the inner mitochondrial membrane is impermeable to ions in general and particularly to protons, these accumulate in the intermembrane space, creating the proton motive force predicted by the chemiosmotic theory.

A Membrane-Located ATP Synthase Functions As a Rotary Motor to Form ATP

The proton motive force drives a membrane-located **ATP synthase** that in the presence of P_i + ADP forms ATP. ATP synthase is embedded in the inner membrane, together with the respiratory chain complexes (Figure 13–7). Several subunits of the protein form a ball-like shape arranged around an axis known as F_1, which projects into the matrix and contains the phosphorylation mechanism (Figure 13–8). F_1 is attached to a membrane protein complex known as F_0, which also consists of several protein subunits. F_0 spans the membrane and forms a proton channel. The flow of protons through F_0 causes it to rotate, driving the production of ATP in the F_1 complex (Figures 13–7 and 13–8). This is thought to occur by a **binding change mechanism** in which the conformation of the β-subunits in F_1 is changed as the axis rotates from one which binds ATP tightly to one which releases ATP and binds ADP and P_i so that the next ATP can be formed. Estimates suggest that for each NADH oxidized, Complexes I and III translocate four protons each and Complex IV translocates two.

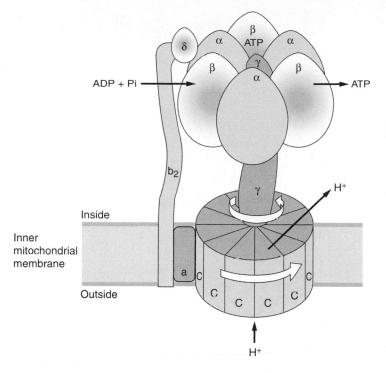

Figure 13-8. Mechanism of ATP production by ATP synthase. The enzyme complex consists of an F_0 subcomplex which is a disk of "C" protein subunits. Attached is a γ subunit in the form of a "bent axle." Protons passing through the disk of "C" units cause it and the attached γ subunit to rotate. The γ subunit fits inside the F_1 subcomplex of three α and three β subunits, which are fixed to the membrane and do not rotate. ADP and P_i are taken up sequentially by the β subunits to form ATP, which is expelled as the rotating γ subunit squeezes each β subunit in turn and changes its conformation. Thus, three ATP molecules are generated per revolution. For clarity, not all the subunits that have been identified are shown— eg, the "axle" also contains an ε subunit.

THE RESPIRATORY CHAIN PROVIDES MOST OF THE ENERGY CAPTURED DURING CATABOLISM

ADP captures, in the form of high-energy phosphate, a significant proportion of the free energy released by catabolic processes. The resulting ATP has been called the energy "currency" of the cell because it passes on this free energy to drive those processes requiring energy (Figure 11-6)

There is a net direct capture of two high-energy phosphate groups in the glycolytic reactions (Table 18-1). Two more high-energy phosphates per mole of glucose are captured in the citric acid cycle during the conversion of succinyl CoA to succinate. All of these phosphorylations occur at the **substrate level**. When substrates are oxidized via Complexes I, III, and IV in the respiratory chain (ie, via NADH), 2.5 mol of ATP are formed per half mol of O_2 consumed; ie, the P:O ratio = 2.5 (Figure 13-7). On the other hand, when a substrate (eg, succinate or 3-phosphoglycerate) is oxidized via Complexes II, III, and IV, only 1.5 mol of ATP are formed; ie, P:O = 1.5. These reactions are known as **oxidative phosphorylation at the respiratory chain level.** Taking these values into account, it can be estimated that nearly 90% of the high energy phosphates produced from the complete oxidation of 1 mol glucose is obtained via oxidative phosphorylation coupled to the respiratory chain (Table 18-1).

Respiratory Control Ensures a Constant Supply of ATP

The rate of respiration of mitochondria can be controlled by the availability of ADP. This is because oxidation and phosphorylation are tightly coupled; ie, oxidation cannot proceed via the respiratory chain without concomitant phosphorylation of ADP. Table 13-1 shows the five conditions controlling the rate of respiration in mitochondria. Most cells in the resting state are in state 4, and respiration is controlled by the availability of ADP. When work is performed, ATP is converted to ADP, allowing more respiration to occur, which in turn replenishes the store of ATP. Under certain conditions, the concentration of inorganic phosphate can also affect the rate of functioning of the respiratory chain. As respiration increases (as in exercise), the cell approaches state 3 or state 5 when either

Table 13-1. States of respiratory control.

	Conditions Limiting the Rate of Respiration
State 1	Availability of ADP and substrate
State 2	Availability of substrate only
State 3	The capacity of the respiratory chain itself, when all substrates and components are present in saturating amounts
State 4	Availability of ADP only
State 5	Availability of oxygen only

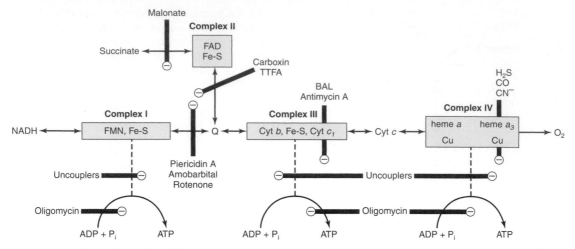

Figure 13–9. Sites of inhibition (⊖) of the respiratory chain by specfic drugs, chemicals, and antibiotics. BAL, dimercaprol. TTFA, an Fe-chelating agent. Other abbreviations as in Figure 13–5.

the capacity of the respiratory chain becomes saturated or the PO_2 decreases below the K_m for heme a_3. There is also the possibility that the ADP/ATP transporter, which facilitates entry of cytosolic ADP into and ATP out of the mitochondrion, becomes rate-limiting.

Thus, the manner in which biologic oxidative processes allow the free energy resulting from the oxidation of foodstuffs to become available and to be captured is stepwise, efficient, and controlled—rather than explosive, inefficient, and uncontrolled, as in many nonbiologic processes. The remaining free energy that is not captured as high-energy phosphate is liberated as **heat.** This need not be considered "wasted," since it ensures that the respiratory system as a whole is sufficiently exergonic to be removed from equilibrium, allowing continuous unidirectional flow and constant provision of ATP. It also contributes to maintenance of body temperature.

MANY POISONS INHIBIT THE RESPIRATORY CHAIN

Much information about the respiratory chain has been obtained by the use of inhibitors, and, conversely, this has provided knowledge about the mechanism of action of several poisons (Figure 13–9). They may be classified as inhibitors of the respiratory chain, inhibitors of oxidative phosphorylation, and uncouplers of oxidative phosphorylation.

Barbiturates such as amobarbital inhibit electron transport via Complex I by blocking the transfer from Fe-S to Q. At sufficient dosage, they are fatal in vivo. **Antimycin A** and **dimercaprol** inhibit the respiratory chain at Complex III. The classic poisons **H_2S, carbon monoxide,** and **cyanide** inhibit Complex IV and can therefore totally arrest respiration. **Malonate** is a competitive inhibitor of Complex II.

Atractyloside inhibits oxidative phosphorylation by inhibiting the transporter of ADP into and ATP out of the mitochondrion (Figure 13–10).

Uncouplers dissociate oxidation in the respiratory chain from phosphorylation (Figure 13–7). These compounds are toxic in vivo, causing respiration to become uncontrolled, since the rate is no longer limited by the concentration of ADP or P_i. The uncoupler that has been used most frequently is **2,4-dinitrophenol,** but other compounds act in a similar manner. **Thermogenin (or the uncoupling protein)** is a physiological uncoupler found in brown adipose tissue that functions to generate body heat, particularly for the newborn and during hibernation in animals (Chapter 25). The antibiotic **oligomycin** completely blocks oxidation and phosphorylation by blocking the flow of protons through ATP synthase (Figure 13–9).

THE CHEMIOSMOTIC THEORY CAN ACCOUNT FOR RESPIRATORY CONTROL AND THE ACTION OF UNCOUPLERS

The electrochemical potential difference across the membrane, once established as a result of proton translocation, inhibits further transport of reducing equivalents through the respiratory chain unless discharged by back-translocation of protons across the membrane through the ATP synthase. This in turn depends on availability of ADP and P_i.

Uncouplers (eg, dinitrophenol) are amphipathic (Chapter 15) and increase the permeability of the lipoid inner mitochondrial membrane to protons, thus reducing the electrochemical potential and short-circuiting the ATP synthase (Figure 13–7). In this way, oxidation can proceed without phosphorylation.

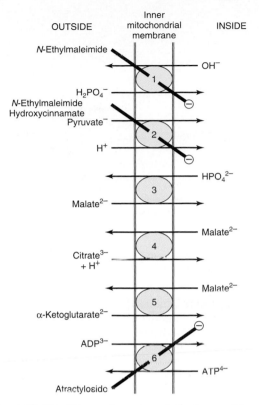

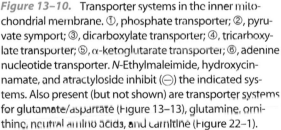

Figure 13–10. Transporter systems in the inner mitochondrial membrane. ①, phosphate transporter; ②, pyruvate symport; ③, dicarboxylate transporter; ④, tricarboxylate transporter; ⑤, α-ketoglutarate transporter; ⑥, adenine nucleotide transporter. N-Ethylmaleimide, hydroxycinnamate, and atractyloside inhibit (⊖) the indicated systems. Also present (but not shown) are transporter systems for glutamate/aspartate (Figure 13–13), glutamine, ornithine, neutral amino acids, and carnitine (Figure 22–1).

THE RELATIVE IMPERMEABILITY OF THE INNER MITOCHONDRIAL MEMBRANE NECESSITATES EXCHANGE TRANSPORTERS

Exchange diffusion systems involving transporter proteins that span the membrane are present in the membrane for exchange of anions against OH^- ions and cations against H^+ ions. Such systems are necessary for uptake and output of ionized metabolites while preserving electrical and osmotic equilibrium. The inner mitochondrial membrane is freely permeable to uncharged small molecules, such as oxygen, water, CO_2, NH_3, and to monocarboxylic acids, such as 3-hydroxybutyric, acetoacetic, and acetic. Long-chain fatty acids are transported into mitochondria via the carnitine system (Figure 22–1), and there is also a special carrier for pyruvate involving a symport that utilizes the H^+ gradient from outside to inside the mitochondrion (Figure 13–10). However, dicarboxylate and tricarboxylate anions and amino acids require specific transporter or carrier systems to facilitate their passage across the membrane. Monocarboxylic acids penetrate more readily in their undissociated and more lipid-soluble form.

The transport of di- and tricarboxylate anions is closely linked to that of inorganic phosphate, which penetrates readily as the $H_2PO_4^-$ ion in exchange for OH^-. The net uptake of malate by the dicarboxylate transporter requires inorganic phosphate for exchange in the opposite direction. The net uptake of citrate, isocitrate, or cis-aconitate by the tricarboxylate transporter requires malate in exchange. α-Ketoglutarate transport also requires an exchange with malate. The adenine nucleotide transporter allows the exchange of ATP and ADP but not AMP. It is vital in allowing ATP exit from mitochondria to the sites of extramitochondrial utilization and in allowing the return of ADP for ATP production within the mitochondrion (Figure 13–11). Since in this translocation four negative charges are removed from the matrix for every three taken in, the electrochemical gradient across the membrane (the proton motive force) favors the export of ATP. Na^+ can be exchanged for H^+, driven by the proton gradient. It is believed that active uptake of Ca^{2+} by mitochondria occurs with a net charge transfer of 1 (Ca^+ uniport), possibly through a Ca^{2+}/H^+ antiport. Calcium release from mitochondria is facilitated by exchange with Na^+.

Ionophores Permit Specific Cations to Penetrate Membranes

Ionophores are lipophilic molecules that complex specific cations and facilitate their transport through biologic

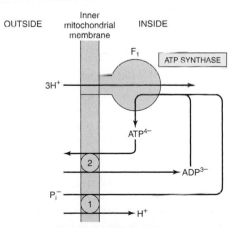

Figure 13–11. Combination of phosphate transporter (①) with the adenine nucleotide transporter (②) in ATP synthesis. The H^+/P_i symport shown is equivalent to the P_i/OH^- antiport shown in Figure 13–10.

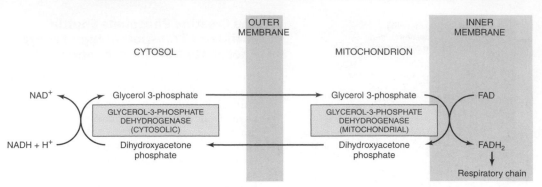

Figure 13–12. Glycerophosphate shuttle for transfer of reducing equivalents from the cytosol into the mitochondrion.

membranes, eg, **valinomycin** (K⁺). The classic uncouplers such as dinitrophenol are, in fact, proton ionophores.

A Proton-Translocating Transhydrogenase Is a Source of Intramitochondrial NADPH

Energy-linked transhydrogenase, a protein in the inner mitochondrial membrane, couples the passage of protons down the electrochemical gradient from outside to inside the mitochondrion with the transfer of H from intramitochondrial NADH to NADPH for intramitochondrial enzymes such as glutamate dehydrogenase and hydroxylases involved in steroid synthesis.

Oxidation of Extramitochondrial NADH Is Mediated by Substrate Shuttles

NADH cannot penetrate the mitochondrial membrane, but it is produced continuously in the cytosol by 3-phos-phoglyceraldehyde dehydrogenase, an enzyme in the glycolysis sequence (Figure 18–2). However, under aerobic conditions, extramitochondrial NADH does not accumulate and is presumed to be oxidized by the respiratory chain in mitochondria. The transfer of reducing equivalents through the mitochondrial membrane requires substrate pairs, linked by suitable dehydrogenases on each side of the mitochondrial membrane. The mechanism of transfer using the **glycerophosphate shuttle** is shown in Figure 13–12. Since the mitochondrial enzyme is linked to the respiratory chain via a flavoprotein rather than NAD, only 1.5 mol rather than 2.5 mol of ATP are formed per atom of oxygen consumed. Although this shuttle is present in some tissues (eg, brain, white muscle), in others (eg, heart muscle) it is deficient. It is therefore believed that the **malate shuttle** system (Figure 13–13) is of more universal utility. The complexity of this system is due to the impermeability of the mitochondrial mem-

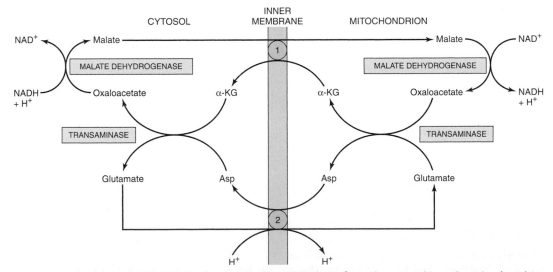

Figure 13–13. Malate shuttle for transfer of reducing equivalents from the cytosol into the mitochondrion. ①, α-Ketoglutarate transporter; ②, glutamate/aspartate transporter (note the proton symport with glutamate).

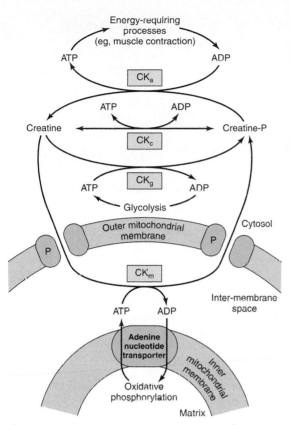

Figure 13–14. The creatine phosphate shuttle of heart and skeletal muscle. The shuttle allows rapid transport of high-energy phosphate from the mitochondrial matrix into the cytosol. CK_a, creatine kinase concerned with large requirements for ATP, eg, muscular contraction; CK_c, creatine kinase for maintaining equilibrium between creatine and creatine phosphate and ATP/ADP; CK_g, creatine kinase coupling glycolysis to creatine phosphate synthesis; CK_m, mitochondrial creatine kinase mediating creatine phosphate production from ATP formed in oxidative phosphorylation; P, pore protein in outer mitochondrial membrane.

brane to oxaloacetate, which must react with glutamate to form aspartate and α-ketoglutarate by transamination before transport through the mitochondrial membrane and reconstitution to oxaloacetate in the cytosol.

Ion Transport in Mitochondria Is Energy Linked

Mitochondria maintain or accumulate cations such as K^+, Na^+, Ca^{2+}, and Mg^{2+}, and P_i. It is assumed that a primary proton pump drives cation exchange.

The Creatine Phosphate Shuttle Facilitates Transport of High-Energy Phosphate from Mitochondria

This shuttle (Figure 13–14) augments the functions of creatine phosphate as an energy buffer by acting as a dynamic system for transfer of high-energy phosphate from mitochondria in active tissues such as heart and skeletal muscle. An isoenzyme of creatine kinase (CK_m) is found in the mitochondrial intermembrane space, catalyzing the transfer of high-energy phosphate to creatine from ATP emerging from the adenine nucleotide transporter. In turn, the creatine phosphate is transported into the cytosol via protein pores in the outer mitochondrial membrane, becoming available for generation of extramitochondrial ATP.

CLINICAL ASPECTS

The condition known as **fatal infantile mitochondrial myopathy and renal dysfunction** involves severe diminution or absence of most oxidoreductases of the respiratory chain. **MELAS** (mitochondrial encephalopathy, lactic acidosis, and stroke) is an inherited condition due to NADH:Q oxidoreductase (Complex I) or cytochrome oxidase (Complex IV) deficiency. It is caused by a mutation in mitochondrial DNA and may be involved in Alzheimer's disease and diabetes mellitus. A number of drugs and poisons act by inhibition of oxidative phosphorylation.

SUMMARY

- Virtually all energy released from the oxidation of carbohydrate, fat, and protein is made available in mitochondria as reducing equivalents (—H or e⁻). These are funneled into the respiratory chain, where they are passed down a redox gradient of carriers to their final reaction with oxygen to form water.

- The redox carriers are grouped into four respiratory chain complexes in the inner mitochondrial membrane. Three of the four complexes are able to use the energy released in the redox gradient to pump protons to the outside of the membrane, creating an electrochemical potential between the matrix and the inner membrane space.

- ATP synthase spans the membrane and acts like a rotary motor using the potential energy of the proton gradient or proton motive force to synthesize ATP from ADP and P_i. In this way, oxidation is closely coupled to phosphorylation to meet the energy needs of the cell.

- Because the inner mitochondrial membrane is impermeable to protons and other ions, special exchange

transporters span the membrane to allow ions such as OH^-, ATP^{4-}, ADP^{3-}, and metabolites to pass through without discharging the electrochemical gradient across the membrane.

- Many well-known poisons such as cyanide arrest respiration by inhibition of the respiratory chain.

REFERENCES

Hinkle PC et al: P/O ratios of mitochondrial oxidative phosphorylation. Biochem Biophys Acta 2005;1706:1.

Mitchell P: Keilin's respiratory chain concept and its chemiosmotic consequences. Science 1979;206:1148.

Schultz BE, Chan SI: Structures and proton-pumping strategies of mitochondrial respiratory enzymes. Annu Rev Biophys Biomol Struct 2001;30:23.

Smeitink J et al: The genetics and pathology of oxidative phosphorylation. Nat Rev Genet 2001;2:342.

Tyler DD: *The Mitochondrion in Health and Disease*. VCH Publishers, 1992.

Wallace DC: Mitochondrial DNA in aging and disease. Sci Am 1997;277:22.

Yoshida M et al: ATP synthase—a marvellous rotary engine of the cell. Nat Rev Mol Cell Biol 2001;2:669.

Carbohydrates of Physiologic Significance

14

David A. Bender, PhD, & Peter A. Mayes, PhD, DSc

BIOMEDICAL IMPORTANCE

Carbohydrates are widely distributed in plants and animals; they have important structural and metabolic roles. In plants, glucose is synthesized from carbon dioxide and water by photosynthesis and stored as starch or used to synthesize the cellulose of the plant cell walls. Animals can synthesize carbohydrates from amino acids, but most animal carbohydrate is derived ultimately from plants. **Glucose** is the most important carbohydrate; most dietary carbohydrate is absorbed into the bloodstream as glucose, and other sugars are converted to glucose in the liver. Glucose is the major metabolic fuel of mammals (except ruminants) and a universal fuel of the fetus. It is the precursor for synthesis of all the other carbohydrates in the body, including **glycogen** for storage; **ribose** and **deoxyribose** in nucleic acids; **galactose** in lactose of milk, in glycolipids, and in combination with protein in glycoproteins and proteoglycans. Diseases associated with carbohydrate metabolism include **diabetes mellitus, galactosemia, glycogen storage diseases,** and **lactose intolerance.**

CARBOHYDRATES ARE ALDEHYDE OR KETONE DERIVATIVES OF POLYHYDRIC ALCOHOLS

Carbohydrates are classified as follows:

(1) **Monosaccharides** are those carbohydrates that cannot be hydrolyzed into simpler carbohydrates. They may be classified as **trioses, tetroses, pentoses, hexoses, or heptoses,** depending upon the number of carbon atoms; and as **aldoses** or **ketoses** depending upon whether they have an aldehyde or ketone group. Examples are listed in Table 14–1. In addition to aldehydes and ketones, the polyhydric alcohols (sugar alcohols or **polyols**), in which the aldehyde or ketone group has been reduced to an alcohol group, also occur naturally in foods. They are manufactured by reduction of monosaccharides for use in the manufacture of foods for weight reduction and for diabetics. They are poorly absorbed, and have about half the energy yield of sugars.

(2) **Disaccharides** are condensation products of two monosaccharide units; examples are maltose and sucrose.

(3) **Oligosaccharides** are condensation products of three to ten monosaccharides. Most are not digested by human enzymes.

(4) **Polysaccharides** are condensation products of more than ten monosaccharide units; examples are the starches and dextrins, which may be linear or branched polymers. Polysaccharides are sometimes classified as hexosans or pentosans, depending on the identity of the constituent monosaccharides. In addition to starches and dextrins, foods contain a wide variety of other polysaccharides that are collectively known as nonstarch polysaccharides; they are not digested by human enzymes, and are the major component of dietary fiber. Examples are cellulose from plant cell walls (a glucose polymer) and inulin, the storage carbohydrate in some plants (a fructose polymer).

BIOMEDICALLY, GLUCOSE IS THE MOST IMPORTANT MONOSACCHARIDE

The Structure of Glucose Can Be Represented in Three Ways

The straight-chain structural formula (aldohexose; Figure 14–1A) can account for some of the properties of glucose, but a cyclic structure (a **hemiacetal** formed by reaction between the aldehyde group and a hydroxyl group) is thermodynamically favored and accounts for other properties. The cyclic structure is normally drawn as shown in Fig 14–1B, the Haworth projection, in which the molecule is viewed from the side and above the plane of the ring; the bonds nearest to the viewer are bold and thickened, and the hydroxyl groups are above or below the plane of the ring. The six-membered ring containing one oxygen atom is actually in the form of a chair (Figure 14–1C).

Sugars Exhibit Various Forms of Isomerism

Glucose, with four asymmetric carbon atoms, can form 16 isomers. The more important types of isomerism found with glucose are:

(1) **D and L isomerism:** The designation of a sugar isomer as the D form or of its mirror image as the L form

Table 14–1. Classification of important sugars.

	Aldoses	Ketoses
Trioses ($C_3H_6O_3$)	Glycerose (glycer-aldehyde)	Dihydroxyacetone
Tetroses ($C_4H_8O_4$)	Erythrose	Erythrulose
Pentoses ($C_5H_{10}O_5$)	Ribose	Ribulose
Hexoses ($C_6H_{12}O_6$)	Glucose	Fructose
Heptoses ($C_7H_{14}O_7$)	—	Sedoheptulose

is determined by its spatial relationship to the parent compound of the carbohydrates, the three-carbon sugar glycerose (glyceraldehyde). The L and D forms of this sugar, and of glucose, are shown in Figure 14–2. The orientation of the —H and —OH groups around the carbon atom adjacent to the terminal primary alcohol carbon (carbon 5 in glucose) determines whether the sugar belongs to the D or L series. When the —OH group on this carbon is on the right (as seen in Figure 14–2), the sugar is the D isomer; when it is on the left, it is the L isomer. Most of the monosaccharides occurring in mammals are D sugars, and the enzymes responsible for their metabolism are specific for this configuration.

The presence of asymmetric carbon atoms also confers **optical activity** on the compound. When a beam of plane-

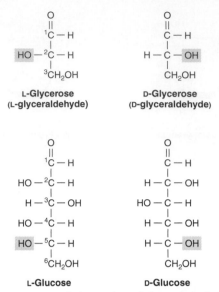

Figure 14–2. D- and L-isomerism of glycerose and glucose.

polarized light is passed through a solution of an **optical isomer,** it rotates either to the right, dextrarotatory (+), or to the left, levorotatory (–). The direction of rotation of polarized light is independent of the stereochemistry of the sugar, so it may be designated D(–), D(+), L(–), or L(+). For example, the naturally occurring form of fructose is the D(–) isomer. In solution, glucose is dextrarotatory, and glucose solutions are sometimes known as **dextrose.**

(2) **Pyranose and furanose ring structures:** The ring structures of monosaccharides are similar to the ring structures of either pyran (a six-membered ring) or furan (a five-membered ring) (Figures 14–3 and 14–4).

Pyran　　　　　**Furan**

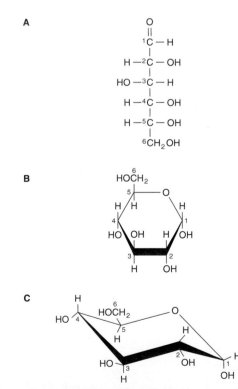

Figure 14–1. D-Glucose. **(A)** Straight chain form. **(B)** α-D-glucose; Haworth projection. **(C)** α-D-glucose; chair form.

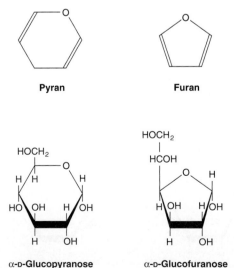

α-D-Glucopyranose　　　**α-D-Glucofuranose**

Figure 14–3. Pyranose and furanose forms of glucose.

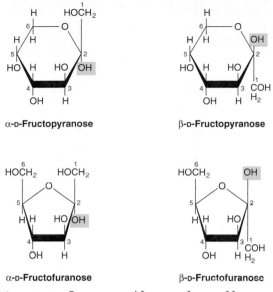

α-D-**Fructopyranose**   β-D-**Fructopyranose**

α-D-**Fructofuranose**   β-D-**Fructofuranose**

Figure 14–4. Pyranose and furanose forms of fructose.

For glucose in solution, more than 99% is in the pyranose form.

(3) **Alpha and beta anomers:** The ring structure of an aldose is a hemiacetal, since it is formed by combination of an aldehyde and an alcohol group. Similarly, the ring structure of a ketose is a hemiketal. Crystalline glucose is α-D-glucopyranose. The cyclic structure is retained in solution, but isomerism occurs about position 1, the carbonyl or **anomeric carbon atom,** to give a mixture of α-glucopyranose (38%) and β-glucopyranose (62%). Less than 0.3% is represented by α and β anomers of glucofuranose.

(4) **Epimers:** Isomers differing as a result of variations in configuration of the —OH and —H on carbon atoms 2, 3, and 4 of glucose are known as epimers. Biologically, the most important epimers of glucose are mannose and galactose, formed by epimerization at carbons 2 and 4, respectively (Figure 14–5).

(5) **Aldose-ketose isomerism:** Fructose has the same molecular formula as glucose but differs in its structural formula, since there is a potential keto group in position 2, the anomeric carbon of fructose (Figures 14–4 and 14–6), whereas there is a potential aldehyde group in position 1, the anomeric carbon of glucose (Figures 14–2 and 14–7).

Many Monosaccharides Are Physiologically Important

Derivatives of trioses, tetroses, and pentoses and of a seven-carbon sugar (sedoheptulose) are formed as metabolic intermediates in glycolysis and the pentose phosphate pathway. Pentoses are important in nucleotides, nucleic acids, and several coenzymes (Table 14–2). Glucose, galactose, fructose, and mannose are physiologically the most important hexoses (Table 14–3). The biochemically important ketoses are shown in Figure 14–6, and important aldoses in Figure 14–7.

In addition, carboxylic acid derivatives of glucose are important, including D-glucuronate (for glucuronide formation and in glycosaminoglycans) and its metabolic derivative, L-iduronate (in glycosaminoglycans) (Figure 14–8) and L-gulonate (an intermediate in the uronic acid pathway; see Figure 21–4).

Sugars Form Glycosides with Other Compounds & with Each Other

Glycosides are formed by condensation between the hydroxyl group of the anomeric carbon of a monosaccharide, and a second compound that may or may not (in the case of an **aglycone**) be another monosaccharide. If the second group is a hydroxyl, the O-glycosidic bond is an **acetal** link because it results from a reaction between a hemiacetal group (formed from an aldehyde and an —OH group) and another —OH group. If the hemiacetal portion is glucose, the resulting compound is a **glucoside;** if galactose, a **galactoside;** and so on. If the second group is an amine, an N-glycosidic bond is formed, eg, between adenine and ribose in nucleotides such as ATP (Figure 11–4).

Glycosides are widely distributed in nature; the aglycone may be methanol, glycerol, a sterol, a phenol, or a base such as adenine. The glycosides that are important in medicine because of their action on the heart (**cardiac glycosides**) all contain steroids as the aglycone. These

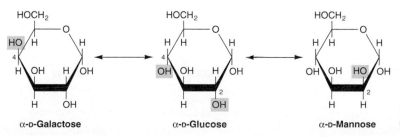

α-D-**Galactose**   α-D-**Glucose**   α-D-**Mannose**

Figure 14–5. Epimerization of glucose.

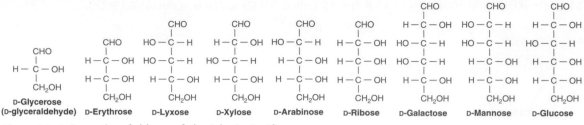

Figure 14–6. Examples of aldoses of physiologic significance.

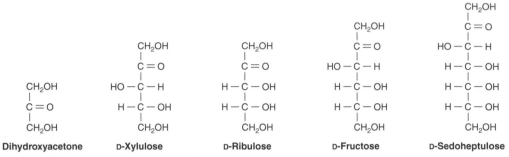

Figure 14–7. Examples of ketoses of physiologic significance.

Table 14–2. Pentoses of physiologic importance.

Sugar	Source	Biochemical and Clinical Importance
D-Ribose	Nucleic acids and metabolic intermediate	Structural component of nucleic acids and coenzymes, including ATP, NAD(P), and flavin coenzymes
D-Ribulose	Metabolic intermediate	Intermediate in the pentose phosphate pathway
D-Arabinose	Plant gums	Constituent of glycoproteins
D-Xylose	Plant gums, proteoglycans, glycosaminoglycans	Constituent of glycoproteins
L-Xylulose	Metabolic intermediate	Excreted in the urine in essential pentosuria

Table 14–3. Hexoses of physiologic importance.

Sugar	Source	Biochemical Importance	Clinical Significance
D-Glucose	Fruit juices, hydrolysis of starch, cane or beet sugar, maltose and lactose	The main metabolic fuel for tissues; "blood sugar"	Excreted in the urine (glucosuria) in poorly controlled diabetes mellitus as a result of hyperglycemia
D-Fructose	Fruit juices, honey, hydrolysis of cane or beet sugar and inulin, enzymic isomerization of glucose syrups for food manufacture	Readily metabolized either via glucose or directly	Hereditary fructose intolerance leads to fructose accumulation and hypoglycemia
D-Galactose	Hydrolysis of lactose	Readily metabolized to glucose; synthesized in the mammary gland for synthesis of lactose in milk. A constituent of glycolipids and glycoproteins	Hereditary galactosemia as a result of failure to metabolize galactose leads to cataracts
D-Mannose	Hydrolysis of plant mannan gums	Constituent of glycoproteins	

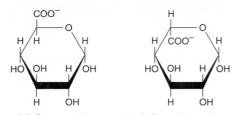

Figure 14–8. α-D-Glucuronate (left) and β-L-iduronate (right).

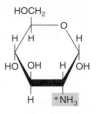

Figure 14–10. Glucosamine (2-amino-D-glucopyranose) (α form). Galactosamine is 2-amino-D-galactopyranose. Both glucosamine and galactosamine occur as *N*-acetyl derivatives in more complex carbohydrates, eg, glycoproteins.

include derivatives of digitalis and strophanthus such as **ouabain,** an inhibitor of the Na⁺-K⁺ ATPase of cell membranes. Other glycosides include antibiotics such as **streptomycin.**

Deoxy Sugars Lack an Oxygen Atom

Deoxy sugars are those in which one hydroxyl group has been replaced by hydrogen. An example is **deoxyribose** (Figure 14–9) in DNA. The deoxy sugar L-fucose (Figure 14–13) occurs in glycoproteins; 2-deoxyglucose is used experimentally as an inhibitor of glucose metabolism.

Amino Sugars (Hexosamines) Are Components of Glycoproteins, Gangliosides, & Glycosaminoglycans

The amino sugars include D-glucosamine, a constituent of hyaluronic acid (Figure 14–10), D-galactosamine (also known as chondrosamine), a constituent of chondroitin, and D-mannosamine. Several **antibiotics** (eg, erythromycin) contain amino sugars, which are important for their antibiotic activity.

Maltose, Sucrose, & Lactose Are Important Disaccharides

The disaccharides are sugars composed of two monosaccharide residues linked by a glycoside bond (Figure 14–11). The physiologically important disaccharides are maltose, sucrose, and lactose (Table 14–4). Hydrolysis of sucrose yields a mixture of glucose and

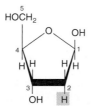

Figure 14–9. 2-Deoxy-D-ribofuranose (β form).

fructose called "invert sugar" because fructose is strongly levorotatory and changes (inverts) the weaker dextrarotatory action of sucrose.

POLYSACCHARIDES SERVE STORAGE & STRUCTURAL FUNCTIONS

Polysaccharides include the following physiologically important carbohydrates.

Starch is a homopolymer of glucose forming an α-glucosidic chain, called a **glucosan** or **glucan.** It is the most important dietary source of carbohydrate in cereals, potatoes, legumes, and other vegetables. The two main constituents are **amylose** (13–20%), which has a nonbranching helical structure, and **amylopectin** (80–85%), which consists of branched chains composed of 24–30 glucose residues united by $\alpha 1 \rightarrow 4$ linkages in the chains and by $\alpha 1 \rightarrow 6$ linkages at the branch points (Figure 14–12).

The extent to which starch in foods is hydrolyzed by amylase is determined by its structure, the degree of crystallization or hydration (the result of cooking), and whether it is enclosed in intact (and indigestible) plant cells walls. The **glycemic index** of a starchy food is a measure of its digestibility, based on the extent to which it raises the blood concentration of glucose compared with an equivalent amount of glucose or a reference food such as white bread or boiled rice.

Glycogen (Figure 14–13) is the storage polysaccharide in animals and is sometimes called animal starch. It is a more highly branched structure than amylopectin with chains of 12–14 α-D-glucopyranose residues (in $\alpha 1 \rightarrow 4$ glucosidic linkage) with branching by means of $\alpha 1 \rightarrow 6$ glucosidic bonds. **Inulin** is a polysaccharide of fructose (and hence a fructosan) found in tubers and roots of dahlias, artichokes, and dandelions. It is readily soluble in water and is used to determine the glomerular filtration rate, but it is not hydrolyzed by intestinal enzymes. **Dextrins** are intermediates in the hydrolysis of starch. **Cellulose** is the chief constituent of plant cell walls. It is insoluble and consists of β-D-glucopyranose

Maltose

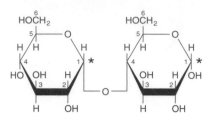

O-α-D-Glucopyranosyl-(1 → 4)-α-D-glucopyranose

Lactose

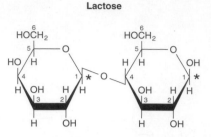

O-β-D-Galactopyranosyl-(1 → 4)-β-D-glucopyranose

Sucrose

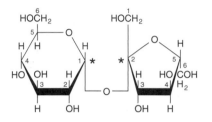

O-α-D-Glucopyranosyl-(1 → 2)-β-D-fructofuranoside

Figure 14–11. Structures of important disaccharides. The α and β refer to the configuration at the anomeric carbon atom (*). When the anomeric carbon of the second residue takes part in the formation of the glycosidic bond, as in sucrose, the residue becomes a glycoside known as a furanoside or a pyranoside. As the disaccharide no longer has an anomeric carbon with a free potential aldehyde or ketone group, it no longer exhibits reducing properties. The configuration of the β-fructofuranose residue in sucrose results from turning the β-fructofuranose molecule depicted in Figure 14–4 through 180 degrees and inverting it.

units linked by β1 → 4 bonds to form long, straight chains strengthened by cross-linking hydrogen bonds. Mammals lack any enzyme that hydrolyzes the β1 → 4 bonds, and so cannot digest cellulose. It is an important source of "bulk" in the diet, and the major component of dietary fiber. Microorganisms in the gut of rumi-nants and other herbivores can hydrolyze the β linkage and ferment the products to short-chain fatty acids as a major energy source. There is some bacterial metabolism of cellulose in the human colon. **Chitin** is a structural polysaccharide in the exoskeleton of crustaceans and insects, and also in mushrooms. It consists

Table 14–4. Disaccharides of physiologic importance.

Sugar	Composition	Source	Clinical Significance
Isomaltose	*O*-α-D-glucopyranosyl-(1→6)-α-D-glucopyranose	Enzymic hydrolysis of starch (the branch points in amylopectin)	
Maltose	*O*-α-D-glucopyranosyl-(1→4)-α-D-glucopyranose	Enzymic hydrolysis of starch (amylase); germinating cereals and malt	
Lactose	*O*-α-D-galactopyranosyl-(1→4)-β-D-glucopyranose	Milk (and many pharmaceutical preparations as a filler)	Lack of lactase (alactasia) leads to lactose intolerance—diarrhea and flatulence; may be excreted in the urine in pregnancy
Lactulose	*O*-α-D-galactopyranosyl-(1→4)-β-D-fructofuranose	Heated milk (small amounts), mainly synthetic	Not hydrolyzed by intestinal enzymes, but fermented by intestinal bacteria; used as a mild osmotic laxative
Sucrose	*O*-α-D-glucopyranosyl-(1→2)-β-D-fructofuranoside	Cane and beet sugar, sorghum and some fruits and vegetables	Rare genetic lack of sucrase leads to sucrose intolerance—diarrhea and flatulence
Trehalose	*O*-α-D-glucopyranosyl-(1→1)-α-D-glucopyranoside	Yeasts and fungi; the main sugar of insect hemolymph	

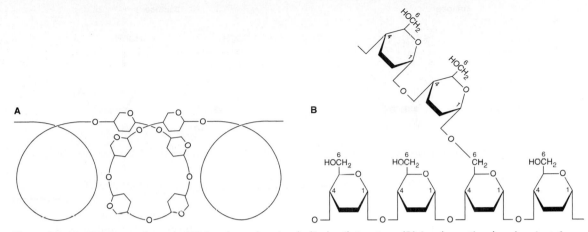

Figure 14–12. Structure of starch. **(A)** Amylose, showing helical coil structure. **(B)** Amylopectin, showing 1 → 6 branch point.

of *N*-acetyl-D-glucosamine units joined by β1 → 4 glycosidic bonds (Figure 14–14).

Glycosaminoglycans (mucopolysaccharides) are complex carbohydrates containing **amino sugars** and **uronic acids.** They may be attached to a protein molecule to form a **proteoglycan.** Proteoglycans provide the ground or packing substance of connective tissue. They hold large quantities of water and occupy space, thus cushioning or lubricating other structures, because of the large number of —OH groups and negative charges

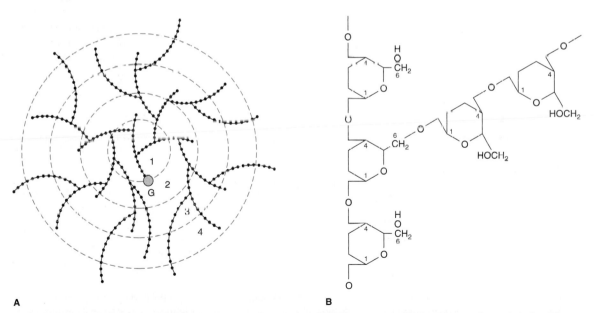

Figure 14–13. The glycogen molecule. **(A)** General structure. **(B)** Enlargement of structure at a branch point. The molecule is a sphere approximately 21 nm in diameter that can be seen in electron micrographs. It has a molecular mass of 10^7 Da and consists of polysaccharide chains, each containing about 13 glucose residues. The chains are either branched or unbranched and are arranged in 12 concentric layers (only four are shown in the figure). The branched chains (each has two branches) are found in the inner layers and the unbranched chains in the outer layer. (G, glycogenin, the primer molecule for glycogen synthesis.)

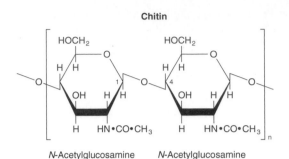

Chitin

N-Acetylglucosamine   N-Acetylglucosamine

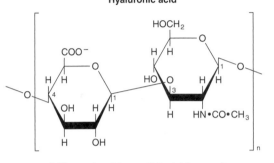

Hyaluronic acid

β-Glucuronic acid   N-Acetylglucosamine

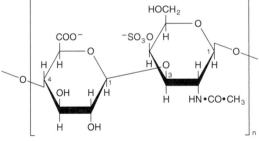

Chondroitin 4-sulfate
(Note: There is also a 6-sulfate)

β-Glucuronic acid   N-Acetylgalactosamine sulfate

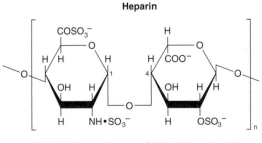

Heparin

Sulfated glucosamine   Sulfated iduronic acid

Figure 14–14. Structure of some complex polysaccharides and glycosaminoglycans.

Table 14–5. Carbohydrates found in glycoproteins.

Hexoses	Mannose (Man), galactose (Gal)
Acetyl hexosa-mines	N-Acetylglucosamine (GlcNAc), N-acetyl-galactosamine (GalNAc)
Pentoses	Arabinose (Ara), Xylose (Xyl)
Methyl pentose	L-Fucose (Fuc, see Fig. 14–15)
Sialic acids	N-Acyl derivatives of neuraminic acid; the predominant sialic acid is N-acetyl-neuraminic acid (NeuAc, see Fig. 14–16)

on the molecule which, by repulsion, keep the carbohydrate chains apart. Examples are **hyaluronic acid, chondroitin sulfate,** and **heparin** (Figure 14–16).

Glycoproteins (also known as mucoproteins) are proteins containing branched or unbranched oligosaccharide chains (Table 14–5, Figure 14–15); they occur in cell membranes (Chapters 40 and 46) and many other situations; serum albumin is a glycoprotein. The **sialic acids** are N- or O-acyl derivatives of neuraminic acid (Figure 14–16). **Neuraminic acid** is a nine-carbon sugar derived from mannosamine (an epimer of glucosamine) and pyruvate. Sialic acids are constituents of both **glycoproteins** and **gangliosides**. Gangliosides are also glycolipids.

CARBOHYDRATES OCCUR IN CELL MEMBRANES & IN LIPOPROTEINS

Approximately 5% of the weight of cell membranes is carbohydrate, in glycoproteins and glycolipids. Their presence on the outer surface of the plasma membrane (the **glycocalyx**) has been shown with the use of plant **lectins,** protein agglutinins that bind specific glycosyl residues. For example, **concanavalin A** binds α-glucosyl and α-mannosyl residues. **Glycophorin** is a major integral membrane glycoprotein of human erythrocytes. It has 130 amino acid residues and spans the lipid membrane, with polypeptide regions outside both the exter-

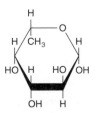

Figure 14–15. β-L-Fucose (6-deoxy-β-L-galactose).

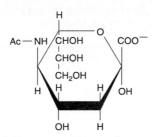

Figure 14–16. Structure of *N*-acetylneuraminic acid, a sialic acid (Ac = CH₃—CO—).

nal and internal (cytoplasmic) surfaces. Carbohydrate chains are attached to the amino terminal portion outside the external surface. Carbohydrates are also present in apo-protein B of plasma lipoproteins.

SUMMARY

- Carbohydrates are major constituents of animal food and animal tissues. They are characterized by the type and number of monosaccharide residues in their molecules.
- Glucose is the most important carbohydrate in mammalian biochemistry because nearly all carbohydrate in food is converted to glucose for metabolism.
- Sugars have large numbers of stereoisomers because they contain several asymmetric carbon atoms.

- The physiologically important monosaccharides include glucose, the "blood sugar," and ribose, an important constituent of nucleotides and nucleic acids.
- The important disaccharides include maltose (glucosyl glucose), an intermediate in the digestion of starch; sucrose (glucosyl fructose), important as a dietary constituent containing fructose; and lactose (galactosyl glucose), in milk.
- Starch and glycogen are storage polymers of glucose in plants and animals, respectively. Starch is the major source of energy in the diet.
- Complex carbohydrates contain other sugar derivatives such as amino sugars, uronic acids, and sialic acids. They include proteoglycans and glycosaminoglycans, which are associated with structural elements of the tissues, and glycoproteins, which are proteins containing oligosaccharide chains; they are found in many situations including the cell membrane.

REFERENCES

Boons J-G: *Carbohydrate Chemistry.* Blackie Academic and Professional, 1998.

Davis BG, Fairbanks AJ: *Carbohydrate Chemistry.* Oxford University Press, 2002.

Ernst B, Hart GW, Sinay P: *Carbohydrates in Chemistry and Biology.* Wiley-VCH, 2000.

Lindhorst TK, Thisbe K: *Essentials of Carbohydrate Chemistry and Biochemistry.* Wiley, 2003.

Lipids of Physiologic Significance

Kathleen M. Botham, PhD, DSc, & Peter A. Mayes, PhD, DSc

BIOMEDICAL IMPORTANCE

The lipids are a heterogeneous group of compounds, including fats, oils, steroids, waxes, and related compounds, that are related more by their physical than by their chemical properties. They have the common property of being (1) relatively **insoluble in water** and (2) **soluble in nonpolar solvents** such as ether and chloroform. They are important dietary constituents not only because of their high energy value, but also because of the fat-soluble vitamins and the essential fatty acids contained in the fat of natural foods. Fat is stored in **adipose tissue,** where it also serves as a thermal insulator in the subcutaneous tissues and around certain organs. Nonpolar lipids act as **electrical insulators,** allowing rapid propagation of depolarization waves along **myelinated nerves.** Combinations of lipid and protein (lipoproteins) are important cellular constituents, occurring both in the cell **membrane** and in the mitochondria, and serving also as the means of **transporting lipids** in the blood. Knowledge of lipid biochemistry is necessary in understanding many important biomedical areas, eg, **obesity, diabetes mellitus, atherosclerosis,** and the role of various **polyunsaturated fatty acids** in nutrition and health.

LIPIDS ARE CLASSIFIED AS SIMPLE OR COMPLEX

1. **Simple lipids:** Esters of fatty acids with various alcohols.
   a. **Fats:** Esters of fatty acids with glycerol. **Oils** are fats in the liquid state.
   b. **Waxes:** Esters of fatty acids with higher molecular weight monohydric alcohols.
2. **Complex lipids:** Esters of fatty acids containing groups in addition to an alcohol and a fatty acid.
   a. **Phospholipids:** Lipids containing, in addition to fatty acids and an alcohol, a phosphoric acid residue. They frequently have nitrogen-containing bases and other substituents, eg, in **glycerophospholipids** the alcohol is glycerol and in **sphingophospholipids** the alcohol is sphingosine.
   b. **Glycolipids (glycosphingolipids):** Lipids containing a fatty acid, sphingosine, and carbohydrate.
   c. **Other complex lipids:** Lipids such as sulfolipids and aminolipids. Lipoproteins may also be placed in this category.
3. **Precursor and derived lipids:** These include fatty acids, glycerol, steroids, other alcohols, fatty aldehydes, and ketone bodies (Chapter 22), hydrocarbons, lipid-soluble vitamins, and hormones.

Because they are uncharged, acylglycerols (glycerides), cholesterol, and cholesteryl esters are termed **neutral lipids.**

FATTY ACIDS ARE ALIPHATIC CARBOXYLIC ACIDS

Fatty acids occur mainly as esters in natural fats and oils but do occur in the unesterified form as **free fatty acids,** a transport form found in the plasma. Fatty acids that occur in natural fats are usually straight-chain derivatives containing an even number of carbon atoms. The chain may be **saturated** (containing no double bonds) or **unsaturated** (containing one or more double bonds).

Fatty Acids Are Named after Corresponding Hydrocarbons

The most frequently used systematic nomenclature names the fatty acid after the hydrocarbon with the same number and arrangement of carbon atoms, with **-oic** being substituted for the final **-e** (Genevan system). Thus, saturated acids end in **-anoic,** eg, octanoic acid, and unsaturated acids with double bonds end in **-enoic,** eg, octadecenoic acid (oleic acid).

Carbon atoms are numbered from the carboxyl carbon (carbon No. 1). The carbon atoms adjacent to the carboxyl carbon (Nos. 2, 3, and 4) are also known as the α, β, and γ carbons, respectively, and the terminal methyl carbon is known as the ω or n-carbon.

Various conventions use Δ for indicating the number and position of the double bonds (Figure 15–1); eg, Δ^9 indicates a double bond between carbons 9 and 10 of the fatty acid; ω9 indicates a double bond on

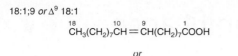

Figure 15–1. Oleic acid. n – 9 (n minus 9) is equivalent to ω9.

the ninth carbon counting from the ω carbon. In animals, additional double bonds are introduced only between the existing double bond (eg, ω9, ω6, or ω3) and the carboxyl carbon, leading to three series of fatty acids known as the ω9, ω6, and ω3 families, respectively.

Saturated Fatty Acids Contain No Double Bonds

Saturated fatty acids may be envisaged as based on acetic acid (CH_3 —COOH) as the first member of the series in which —CH_2 — is progressively added between the terminal CH_3— and —COOH groups. Examples are shown in Table 15–1. Other higher members of the series are known to occur, particularly in waxes. A few branched-chain fatty acids have also been isolated from both plant and animal sources.

Table 15–1. Saturated fatty acids.

Common Name	Number of C Atoms	
Acetic	2	Major end product of carbohydrate fermentation by rumen organisms
Butyric	4	In certain fats in small amounts (especially butter). An end product of carbohydrate fermentation by rumen organisms[1]
Valeric	5	
Caproic	6	
Lauric	12	Spermaceti, cinnamon, palm kernel, coconut oils, laurels, butter
Myristic	14	Nutmeg, palm kernel, coconut oils, myrtles, butter
Palmitic	16	Common in all animal and plant fats
Stearic	18	

[1]Also formed in the cecum of herbivores and to a lesser extent in the colon of humans.

Unsaturated Fatty Acids Contain One or More Double Bonds

Unsaturated fatty acids (Table 15–2) may be further subdivided as follows:

(1) **Monounsaturated** (monoethenoid, monoenoic) acids, containing one double bond.
(2) **Polyunsaturated** (polyethenoid, polyenoic) acids, containing two or more double bonds.
(3) **Eicosanoids:** These compounds, derived from eicosa (20-carbon) polyenoic fatty acids, comprise the **prostanoids, leukotrienes (LTs),** and **lipoxins (LXs).** Prostanoids include **prostaglandins (PGs), prostacyclins (PGIs),** and **thromboxanes (TXs).**

Prostaglandins exist in virtually every mammalian tissue, acting as local hormones; they have important physiologic and pharmacologic activities. They are synthesized in vivo by cyclization of the center of the carbon chain of 20-carbon (eicosanoic) polyunsaturated fatty acids (eg, arachidonic acid) to form a cyclopentane ring (Figure 15–2). A related series of compounds, the **thromboxanes,** have the cyclopentane ring interrupted with an oxygen atom (oxane ring) (Figure 15–3). Three different eicosanoic fatty acids give rise to three groups of eicosanoids characterized by the number of double bonds in the side chains, eg, PG_1, PG_2, PG_3. Different substituent groups attached to the rings give rise to series of prostaglandins and thromboxanes, labeled A, B, etc—eg, the "E" type of prostaglandin (as in PGE_2) has a keto group in position 9, whereas the "F" type has a hydroxyl group in this position. The **leukotrienes** and **lipoxins** are a third group of eicosanoid derivatives formed via the lipoxygenase pathway (Figure 15–4). They are characterized by the presence of three or four conjugated double bonds, respectively. Leukotrienes cause bronchoconstriction as well as being potent proinflammatory agents and play a part in **asthma.**

Most Naturally Occurring Unsaturated Fatty Acids Have *cis* Double Bonds

The carbon chains of saturated fatty acids form a zigzag pattern when extended, as at low temperatures. At higher temperatures, some bonds rotate, causing chain shortening, which explains why biomembranes become thinner with increases in temperature. A type of **geometric isomerism** occurs in unsaturated fatty acids, depending on the orientation of atoms or groups around the axes of double bonds, which do not allow rotation. If the acyl chains are on the same side of the bond, it is *cis-,* as in oleic acid; if on opposite sides, it is *trans-,* as in elaidic acid, the *trans* isomer of oleic acid (Figure 15–5). Naturally occurring unsaturated long-chain fatty acids are nearly all of the *cis* configuration, the molecules being "bent" 120 degrees at the double

Table 15–2. Unsaturated fatty acids of physiologic and nutritional significance.

Number of C Atoms and Number and Position of Double Bonds	Family	Common Name	Systematic Name	Occurrence
Monoenoic acids (one double bond)				
16:1;9	ω7	Palmitoleic	*cis*-9-Hexadecenoic	In nearly all fats.
18:1;9	ω9	Oleic	*cis*-9-Octadecenoic	Possibly the most common fatty acid in natural fats.
18:1;9	ω9	Elaidic	*trans*-9-Octadecenoic	Hydrogenated and ruminant fats.
Dienoic acids (two double bonds)				
18:2;9,12	ω6	Linoleic	all-*cis*-9,12-Octadecadienoic	Corn, peanut, cottonseed, soybean, and many plant oils.
Trienoic acids (three double bonds)				
18:3;6,9,12	ω6	γ-Linolenic	all-*cis*-6,9,12-Octadecatrienoic	Some plants, eg, oil of evening primrose, borage oil; minor fatty acid in animals.
18:3;9,12,15	ω3	α-Linolenic	all-*cis*-9,12,15-Octadecatrienoic	Frequently found with linoleic acid but particularly in linseed oil.
Tetraenoic acids (four double bonds)				
20:4;5,8,11,14	ω6	Arachidonic	all-*cis*-5,8,11,14-Eicosatetraenoic	Found in animal fats; important component of phospholipids in animals.
Pentaenoic acids (five double bonds)				
20:5;5,8,11,14,17	ω3	Timnodonic	all-*cis*-5,8,11,14,17-Eicosapentaenoic	Important component of fish oils, eg, cod liver, mackerel, menhaden, salmon oils.
Hexaenoic acids (six double bonds)				
22:6;4,7,10,13,16,19	ω3	Cervonic	all-*cis*-4,7,10,13,16,19-Docosahexaenoic	Fish oils, phospholipids in brain.

bond. Thus, oleic acid has an L shape, whereas elaidic acid remains "straight." Increase in the number of *cis* double bonds in a fatty acid leads to a variety of possible spatial configurations of the molecule—eg, arachidonic acid, with four *cis* double bonds, has "kinks" or a U shape. This has profound significance for molecular packing in membranes and on the positions occupied by fatty acids in more complex molecules such as phospholipids. *Trans* double bonds alter these spatial relationships. *Trans* fatty acids are present in certain foods, arising as a by-product of the saturation of fatty acids during hydrogenation, or "hardening," of natural oils in the manufacture of margarine. An additional small contribution comes from the ingestion of ruminant fat that

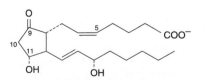

Figure 15–2. Prostaglandin E$_2$ (PGE$_2$).

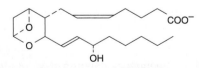

Figure 15–3. Thromboxane A$_2$ (TXA$_2$).

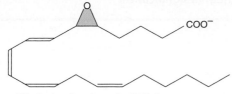

Figure 15–4. Leukotriene A$_4$ (LTA$_4$).

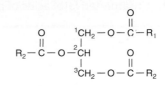

Figure 15–6. Triacylglycerol.

contains *trans* fatty acids arising from the action of microorganisms in the rumen.

Physical and Physiologic Properties of Fatty Acids Reflect Chain Length and Degree of Unsaturation

The melting points of even-numbered carbon fatty acids increase with chain length and decrease according to unsaturation. A triacylglycerol containing three saturated fatty acids of 12 carbons or more is solid at body temperature, whereas if the fatty acid residues are 18:2, it is liquid to below 0 °C. In practice, natural acylglycerols contain a mixture of fatty acids tailored to suit their functional roles. The membrane lipids, which must be fluid at all environmental temperatures, are more unsaturated than storage lipids. Lipids in tissues that are subject to cooling, eg, in hibernators or in the extremities of animals, are more unsaturated.

TRIACYLGLYCEROLS (TRIGLYCERIDES)* ARE THE MAIN STORAGE FORMS OF FATTY ACIDS

The triacylglycerols (Figure 15–6) are esters of the trihydric alcohol glycerol and fatty acids. Mono- and diacylglycerols, wherein one or two fatty acids are esterified with glycerol, are also found in the tissues. These are of particular significance in the synthesis and hydrolysis of triacylglycerols.

Carbons 1 & 3 of Glycerol Are Not Identical

To number the carbon atoms of glycerol unambiguously, the *-sn* (stereochemical numbering) system is used. It is important to realize that carbons 1 and 3 of glycerol are not identical when viewed in three dimensions (shown as a projection formula in Figure 15–7). Enzymes readily distinguish between them and are nearly always specific for one or the other carbon; eg, glycerol is always phosphorylated on *sn*-3 by glycerol kinase to give glycerol 3-phosphate and not glycerol 1 phosphate.

PHOSPHOLIPIDS ARE THE MAIN LIPID CONSTITUENTS OF MEMBRANES

Phospholipids may be regarded as derivatives of **phosphatidic acid** (Figure 15–8), in which the phosphate is esterified with the —OH of a suitable alcohol. Phosphatidic acid is important as an intermediate in the synthesis of triacylglycerols as well as phosphoglycerols but is not found in any great quantity in tissues.

Phosphatidylcholines (Lecithins) Occur in Cell Membranes

Phosphoacylglycerols containing choline (Figure 15–8) are the most abundant phospholipids of the cell membrane and represent a large proportion of the body's store of choline. Choline is important in nervous transmission,

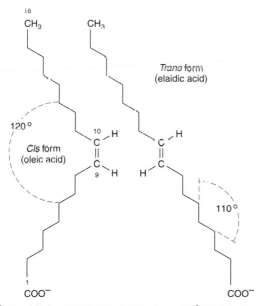

Figure 15–5. Geometric isomerism of Δ^9, 18:1 fatty acids (oleic and elaidic acids).

---

* According to the standardized terminology of the International Union of Pure and Applied Chemistry (IUPAC) and the International Union of Biochemistry (IUB), the monoglycerides, diglycerides, and triglycerides should be designated monoacylglycerols, diacylglycerols, and triacylglycerols, respectively. However, the older terminology is still widely used, particularly in clinical medicine.

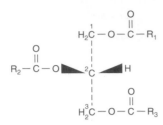

Figure 15–7. Triacyl-*sn*-glycerol.

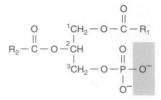

Phosphatidic acid

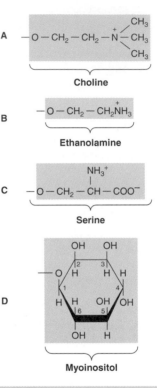

as acetylcholine, and as a store of labile methyl groups. **Dipalmitoyl lecithin** is a very effective surface-active agent and a major constituent of the **surfactant** preventing adherence, due to surface tension, of the inner surfaces of the lungs. Its absence from the lungs of premature infants causes **respiratory distress syndrome.** Most phospholipids have a saturated acyl radical in the *sn*-1 position but an unsaturated radical in the *sn*-2 position of glycerol.

Phosphatidylethanolamine (cephalin) and **phosphatidylserine** (found in most tissues) differ from phosphatidylcholine only in that ethanolamine or serine, respectively, replaces choline (Figure 15–8).

Phosphatidylinositol Is a Precursor of Second Messengers

The inositol is present in **phosphatidylinositol** as the stereoisomer, myoinositol (Figure 15–8). **Phosphatidylinositol 4,5-bisphosphate** is an important constituent of cell membrane phospholipids; upon stimulation by a suitable hormone agonist, it is cleaved into **diacylglycerol** and **inositol trisphosphate,** both of which act as internal signals or second messengers.

Cardiolipin Is a Major Lipid of Mitochondrial Membranes

Phosphatidic acid is a precursor of **phosphatidylglycerol** which, in turn, gives rise to **cardiolipin** (Figure 15–8).

Lysophospholipids Are Intermediates in the Metabolism of Phosphoglycerols

These are phosphoacylglycerols containing only one acyl radical, eg, **lysophosphatidylcholine (lysolecithin),** important in the metabolism and interconversion of phospholipids (Figure 15–9). It is also found in oxidized lipoproteins and has been implicated in some of their effects in promoting **atherosclerosis.**

Plasmalogens Occur in Brain & Muscle

These compounds constitute as much as 10% of the phospholipids of brain and muscle. Structurally, the

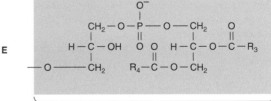

Phosphatidylglycerol

Figure 15–8. Phosphatidic acid and its derivatives. The O⁻ shown shaded in phosphatidic acid is substituted by the substituents shown to form in **(A)** 3-phosphatidylcholine, **(B)** 3-phosphatidylethanolamine, **(C)** 3-phosphatidylserine, **(D)** 3-phosphatidylinositol, and **(E)** cardiolipin (diphosphatidylglycerol).

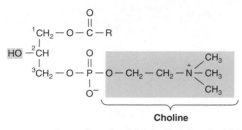

Figure 15–9. Lysophosphatidylcholine (lysolecithin).

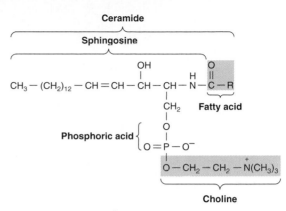

Figure 15–11. A sphingomyelin.

plasmalogens resemble phosphatidylethanolamine but possess an ether link on the *sn*-1 carbon instead of the ester link found in acylglycerols. Typically, the alkyl radical is an unsaturated alcohol (Figure 15–10). In some instances, choline, serine, or inositol may be substituted for ethanolamine.

Sphingomyelins Are Found in the Nervous System

Sphingomyelins are found in large quantities in brain and nerve tissue. On hydrolysis, the sphingomyelins yield a fatty acid, phosphoric acid, choline, and a complex amino alcohol, **sphingosine** (Figure 15–11). No glycerol is present. The combination of sphingosine plus fatty acid is known as **ceramide,** a structure also found in the glycosphingolipids (see below).

GLYCOLIPIDS (GLYCOSPHINGOLIPIDS) ARE IMPORTANT IN NERVE TISSUES & IN THE CELL MEMBRANE

Glycolipids are widely distributed in every tissue of the body, particularly in nervous tissue such as brain. They occur particularly in the outer leaflet of the plasma membrane, where they contribute to **cell surface carbohydrates.**

The major glycolipids found in animal tissues are glycosphingolipids. They contain ceramide and one or more sugars. **Galactosylceramide** is a major glycosphingolipid of brain and other nervous tissue, found in relatively low amounts elsewhere. It contains a number of characteristic C_{24} fatty acids, eg, cerebronic acid.

Galactosylceramide (Figure 15–12) can be converted to sulfogalactosylceramide (**sulfatide**), present in high amounts in myelin. Glucosylceramide is the predominant simple glycosphingolipid of extraneural tissues, also occurring in the brain in small amounts. **Gangliosides** are complex glycosphingolipids derived from glucosylceramide that contain in addition one or more molecules of a **sialic acid.** Neuraminic acid (NeuAc; see Chapter 14) is the principal sialic acid found in human tissues. Gangliosides are also present in nervous tissues in high concentration. They appear to have receptor and other functions. The simplest ganglioside found in tissues is G_{M3}, which contains ceramide, one molecule of glucose, one molecule of galactose, and one molecule of NeuAc. In the shorthand nomenclature used, G represents ganglioside; M is a monosialo-containing species; and the subscript 3 is a number assigned on the basis of chromatographic migration. G_{M1} (Figure 15–13), a more complex ganglioside derived from G_{M3}, is of considerable biologic interest, as it is known to be the receptor in human intestine for cholera toxin. Other gangliosides can contain anywhere from one to five molecules of sialic acid, giving rise to di-, trisialo gangliosides, etc.

STEROIDS PLAY MANY PHYSIOLOGICALLY IMPORTANT ROLES

Cholesterol is probably the best known steroid because of its association with **atherosclerosis** and heart disease. However, biochemically it is also of significance because it is the precursor of a large number of equally important steroids that include the bile acids, adrenocortical hormones, sex hormones, D vitamins, cardiac glycosides, sitosterols of the plant kingdom, and some alkaloids.

All steroids have a similar cyclic nucleus resembling phenanthrene (rings A, B, and C) to which a cyclopen-

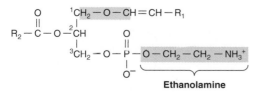

Figure 15–10. Plasmalogen.

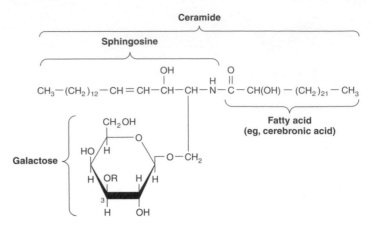

Figure 15–12. Structure of galactosylce-ramide (galactocerebroside, R = H), and sulfogalactosylceramide (a sulfatide, R = SO_4^{2-}).

tane ring (D) is attached. The carbon positions on the steroid nucleus are numbered as shown in Figure 15–14. It is important to realize that in structural formulas of steroids, a simple hexagonal ring denotes a completely saturated six-carbon ring with all valences satisfied by hydrogen bonds unless shown otherwise; ie, it is not a benzene ring. All double bonds are shown as such. Methyl side chains are shown as single bonds unattached at the farther (methyl) end. These occur typically at positions 10 and 13 (constituting C atoms 19 and 18). A side chain at position 17 is usual (as in cholesterol). If the compound has one or more hydroxyl groups and no carbonyl or carboxyl groups, it is a **sterol,** and the name terminates in -ol.

Because of Asymmetry in the Steroid Molecule, Many Stereoisomers Are Possible

Each of the six-carbon rings of the steroid nucleus is capable of existing in the three-dimensional conformation either of a "chair" or a "boat" (Figure 15–15). In naturally occurring steroids, virtually all the rings are in the "chair" form, which is the more stable conformation. With respect to each other, the rings can be either *cis* or *trans* (Figure 15–16). The junction between the A and B rings can be *cis* or *trans* in natu-

rally occurring steroids. That between B and C is *trans,* as is usually the C/D junction. Bonds attaching substituent groups above the plane of the rings (β bonds) are shown with bold solid lines, whereas those bonds attaching groups below (α bonds) are indicated with broken lines. The A ring of a 5α steroid is always *trans* to the B ring, whereas it is *cis* in a 5β steroid. The methyl groups attached to C_{10} and C_{13} are invariably in the β configuration.

Cholesterol Is a Significant Constituent of Many Tissues

Cholesterol (Figure 15–17) is widely distributed in all cells of the body but particularly in nervous tissue. It is a major constituent of the plasma membrane and of plasma lipoproteins. It is often found as **cholesteryl ester,** where the hydroxyl group on position 3 is esterified with a long-chain fatty acid. It occurs in animals but not in plants or bacteria.

Ergosterol Is a Precursor of Vitamin D

Ergosterol occurs in plants and yeast and is important as a precursor of vitamin D (Figure 15–18). When irradiated with ultraviolet light, it acquires antirachitic properties consequent to the opening of ring B.

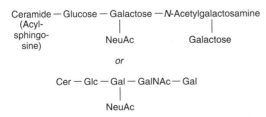

Figure 15–13. G_{M1} ganglioside, a monosialoganglioside, the receptor in human intestine for cholera toxin.

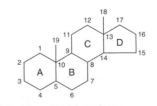

Figure 15–14. The steroid nucleus.

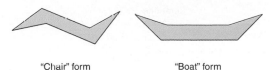

"Chair" form   "Boat" form

Figure 15–15. Conformations of stereoisomers of the steroid nucleus.

Polyprenoids Share the Same Parent Compound as Cholesterol

Although not steroids, these compounds are related because they are synthesized, like cholesterol (Figure 26–2), from five-carbon isoprene units (Figure 15–19). They include **ubiquinone** (Chapter 13), which participates in the respiratory chain in mitochondria, and the long-chain alcohol **dolichol** (Figure 15–20), which takes part in glycoprotein synthesis by transferring carbohydrate residues to asparagine residues of the polypeptide (Chapter 46). Plant-derived isoprenoid compounds include rubber, camphor, the fat-soluble vitamins A, D, E, and K, and β-carotene (provitamin A).

LIPID PEROXIDATION IS A SOURCE OF FREE RADICALS

Peroxidation (**auto-oxidation**) of lipids exposed to oxygen is responsible not only for deterioration of foods (**rancidity**) but also for damage to tissues in vivo, where it may be a cause of cancer, inflammatory diseases, atherosclerosis, and aging. The deleterious effects are considered to be caused by free radicals ($ROO^\bullet$, $RO^\bullet$, $OH^\bullet$) produced during peroxide formation from fatty acids

containing methylene-interrupted double bonds, ie, those found in the naturally occurring polyunsaturated fatty acids (Figure 15–21). Lipid peroxidation is a chain reaction providing a continuous supply of free radicals that initiate further peroxidation. The whole process can be depicted as follows:

(1) Initiation:

$$ROOH + Metal^{(n)+} \rightarrow ROO^\bullet + Metal^{(n-1)+} + H^+$$

$$X^\bullet + RH \rightarrow R^\bullet + XH$$

(2) Propagation:

$$R^\bullet + O_2 \rightarrow ROO^\bullet$$

$$ROO^\bullet + RH \rightarrow ROOH + R^\bullet, \text{ etc}$$

(3) Termination:

$$ROO^\bullet + ROO^\bullet \rightarrow ROOR + O_2$$

$$ROO^\bullet + R^\bullet \rightarrow ROOR$$

$$R^\bullet + R^\bullet \rightarrow RR$$

Since the molecular precursor for the initiation process is generally the hydroperoxide product ROOH, lipid peroxidation is a chain reaction with potentially devastating effects. To control and reduce lipid peroxidation, both humans in their activities and nature invoke the use of **antioxidants.** Propyl gallate, butylated hydroxyanisole (BHA), and butylated hydroxytoluene (BHT) are antioxidants used as food additives. Naturally occurring antioxidants include vitamin E (tocopherol), which is lipid-soluble, and urate and vitamin C, which are water-soluble. Beta-carotene is an antioxidant

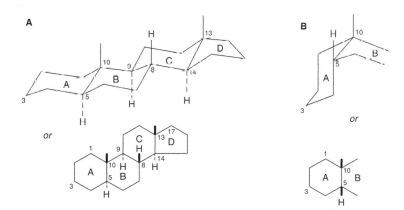

Figure 15–16. Generalized steroid nucleus, showing **(A)** an all-*trans* configuration between adjacent rings and **(B)** a *cis* configuration between rings A and B.

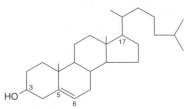

Figure 15–17. Cholesterol, 3-hydroxy-5,6-cholestene.

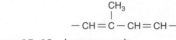

Figure 15–19. Isoprene unit.

at low PO_2. Antioxidants fall into two classes: (1) preventive antioxidants, which reduce the rate of chain initiation; and (2) chain-breaking antioxidants, which interfere with chain propagation. Preventive antioxidants include catalase and other peroxidases such as glutathione peroxidase that react with ROOH; selenium, which is an essential component of glutathione peroxidase and regulates its activity and chelators of metal ions such as EDTA (ethylenediaminetetraacetate) and DTPA (diethylenetriaminepentaacetate). In vivo, the principal chain-breaking antioxidants are superoxide dismutase, which acts in the aqueous phase to trap superoxide free radicals (O_2^-); urate; and vitamin E, which acts in the lipid phase to trap ROO• radicals (Figure 44–6).

Peroxidation is also catalyzed in vivo by heme compounds and by **lipoxygenases** found in platelets and leukocytes. Other products of auto-oxidation or enzymic oxidation of physiologic significance include **oxysterols** (formed from cholesterol) and **isoprostanes** (prostanoids).

AMPHIPATHIC LIPIDS SELF-ORIENT AT OIL:WATER INTERFACES

They Form Membranes, Micelles, Liposomes, & Emulsions

In general, lipids are insoluble in water since they contain a predominance of nonpolar (hydrocarbon) groups. However, fatty acids, phospholipids, sphingolipids, bile salts, and, to a lesser extent, cholesterol

contain polar groups. Therefore, part of the molecule is **hydrophobic,** or water-insoluble; and part is **hydrophilic,** or water-soluble. Such molecules are described as **amphipathic** (Figure 15–22). They become oriented at oil:water interfaces with the polar group in the water phase and the nonpolar group in the oil phase. A bilayer of such amphipathic lipids is the basic structure in biologic membranes (Chapter 40). When a critical concentration of these lipids is present in an aqueous medium, they form **micelles.** Liposomes may be formed by sonicating an amphipathic lipid in an aqueous medium. They consist of spheres of lipid bilayers that enclose part of the aqueous medium. Aggregations of bile salts into micelles and liposomes and the formation of mixed micelles with the products of fat digestion are important in facilitating absorption of lipids from the intestine. Liposomes are of potential clinical use—particularly when combined with tissue-specific antibodies—as carriers of drugs in the circulation, targeted to specific organs, eg, in cancer therapy. In addition, they are used for gene transfer into vascular cells and as carriers for topical and transdermal delivery of drugs and cosmetics. **Emulsions** are much larger particles, formed usually by nonpolar lipids in an aqueous medium. These are stabilized by emulsifying agents such as amphipathic lipids (eg, lecithin), which form a surface layer separating the main bulk of the nonpolar material from the aqueous phase (Figure 15–22).

SUMMARY

- Lipids have the common property of being relatively insoluble in water (hydrophobic) but soluble in nonpolar solvents. Amphipathic lipids also contain one or more polar groups, making them suitable as constituents of membranes at lipid:water interfaces.

- The lipids of major physiologic significance are fatty acids and their esters, together with cholesterol and other steroids.

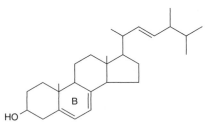

Figure 15–18. Ergosterol.

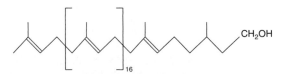

Figure 15–20. Dolichol—a C_{95} alcohol.

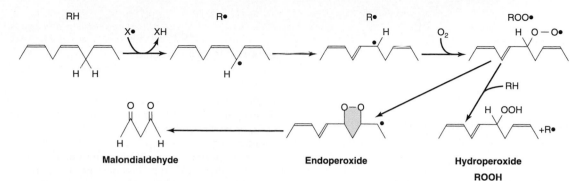

Figure 15–21. Lipid peroxidation. The reaction is initiated by an existing free radical (X'), by light, or by metal ions. Malondialdehyde is only formed by fatty acids with three or more double bonds and is used as a measure of lipid peroxidation together with ethane from the terminal two carbons of ω3 fatty acids and pentane from the terminal five carbons of ω6 fatty acids.

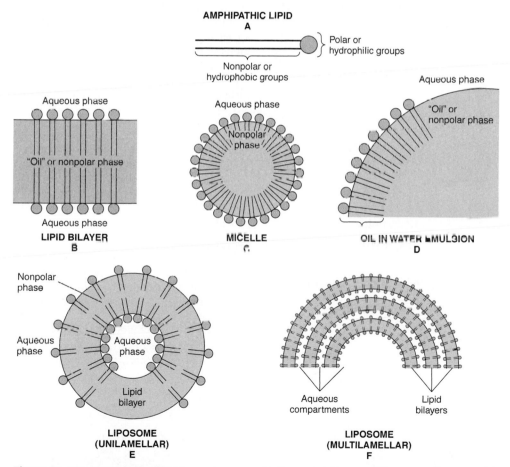

Figure 15–22. Formation of lipid membranes, micelles, emulsions, and liposomes from amphipathic lipids, eg, phospholipids.

- Long-chain fatty acids may be saturated, monounsaturated, or polyunsaturated, according to the number of double bonds present. Their fluidity decreases with chain length and increases according to degree of unsaturation.

- Eicosanoids are formed from 20-carbon polyunsaturated fatty acids and make up an important group of physiologically and pharmacologically active compounds known as prostaglandins, thromboxanes, leukotrienes, and lipoxins.

- The esters of glycerol are quantitatively the most significant lipids, represented by triacylglycerol ("fat"), a major constituent of lipoproteins and the storage form of lipid in adipose tissue. Phosphoacylglycerols are amphipathic lipids and have important roles—as major constituents of membranes and the outer layer of lipoproteins, as surfactant in the lung, as precursors of second messengers, and as constituents of nervous tissue.

- Glycolipids are also important constituents of nervous tissue such as brain and the outer leaflet of the cell membrane, where they contribute to the carbohydrates on the cell surface.

- Cholesterol, an amphipathic lipid, is an important component of membranes. It is the parent molecule from which all other steroids in the body, including major hormones such as the adrenocortical and sex hormones, D vitamins, and bile acids, are synthesized.

- Peroxidation of lipids containing polyunsaturated fatty acids leads to generation of free radicals that damage tissues and cause disease.

REFERENCES

Benzie IFF: Lipid peroxidation: a review of causes, consequences, measurement and dietary influences. Int J Food Sci Nutr 1996;47:233.

Christie WW: *Lipid Analysis,* 3rd ed. The Oily Press, 2003.

Dowhan W, Bodanov H: Functional roles of lipids in membranes. In: *Biochemistry of Lipids, Lipoproteins and Membranes,* 4th ed. Vance DE, Vance JE (editors). Elsevier, 2002.

Gurr MI: *Lipids in Nutrition and Health: A Reappraisal.* The Oily Press, 1999.

Gurr MI, Harwood JL, Frayn K: *Lipid Biochemistry.* Blackwell Publishing, 2002.

Overview of Metabolism & the Provision of Metabolic Fuels

16

David A. Bender, PhD, & Peter A. Mayes, PhD, DSc

BIOMEDICAL IMPORTANCE

Metabolism is the term used to describe the interconversion of chemical compounds in the body, the pathways taken by individual molecules, their interrelationships and the mechanisms that regulate the flow of metabolites through the pathways. Metabolic pathways fall into three categories: (1) **Anabolic pathways,** which are those involved in the synthesis of larger and more complex compounds from smaller precursors—eg, the synthesis of protein from amino acids and the synthesis of reserves of triacylglycerol and glycogen. Anabolic pathways are endothermic. (2) **Catabolic pathways,** which are involved in the breakdown of larger molecules, commonly involving oxidative reactions; they are exothermic, producing reducing equivalents, and, mainly via the respiratory chain, ATP. (3) **Amphibolic pathways,** which occur at the "crossroads" of metabolism, acting as links between the anabolic and catabolic pathways, eg, the citric acid cycle.

A knowledge of normal metabolism is essential for an understanding of abnormalities underlying disease. Normal metabolism includes adaptation to periods of starvation, exercise, pregnancy, and lactation. Abnormal metabolism may result from nutritional deficiency, enzyme deficiency, abnormal secretion of hormones, or the actions of drugs and toxins.

A 70-kg adult human being requires about 10–12 MJ (2400–2900 kcal) from metabolic fuels each day; larger animals require less, and smaller animals more, per kg body weight, and growing children and animals have a proportionally higher requirement to allow for the energy cost of growth. For human beings this requirement is met from carbohydrates (40–60%), lipids (mainly triacylglycerol, 30–40%), and protein (10–15%), as well as alcohol. The mix of carbohydrate, lipid, and protein being oxidized varies depending on whether the subject is in the fed or fasting state, and on the intensity of physical work.

The requirement for metabolic fuels is relatively constant throughout the day, since average physical activity increases metabolic rate only by about 40–50% over the basal metabolic rate. However, most people consume their daily intake of metabolic fuels in two or three meals, so there is a need to form reserves of carbohydrate (glycogen in liver and muscle) and lipid (triacylglycerol in adipose tissue) in the period following a meal, for use during the intervening time when there is no intake of food.

If the intake of metabolic fuels is consistently greater than energy expenditure, the surplus is stored, largely as triacylglycerol in adipose tissue, leading to the development of **obesity** and its associated health hazards. By contrast, if the intake of metabolic fuels is consistently lower than energy expenditure, there is negligible fat and carbohydrate reserves, and amino acids arising from protein turnover are used for energy-yielding metabolism rather than replacement protein synthesis, leading to **emaciation,** wasting, and, eventually, death.

In the fed state, after a meal, there is an ample supply of carbohydrate, and the metabolic fuel for most tissues is glucose. In the fasting state glucose must be spared for use by the central nervous system (which is largely dependent on glucose) and the red blood cells (which are wholly reliant on glucose). Therefore, tissues that can use fuels other than glucose do so; muscle and liver oxidize fatty acids and the liver synthesizes ketone bodies from fatty acids to export to muscle and other tissues. As glycogen reserves become depleted, so amino acids arising from protein turnover are used for **gluconeogenesis.**

The formation and utilization of reserves of triacylglycerol and glycogen, and the extent to which tissues take up and oxidize glucose, are largely controlled by the hormones **insulin** and **glucagon.** In **diabetes mellitus,** there is either impaired synthesis and secretion of insulin (juvenile onset, or type I diabetes) or impaired sensitivity of tissues to insulin action (adult onset, or type II diabetes), leading to severe metabolic derangement. In cattle, the demands of heavy lactation can lead to ketosis, as can the demands of twin pregnancy in sheep.

PATHWAYS THAT PROCESS THE MAJOR PRODUCTS OF DIGESTION

The nature of the diet sets the basic pattern of metabolism. There is a need to process the products of diges-

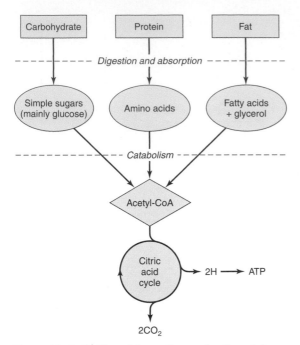

Figure 16–1. Outline of the pathways for the catabolism of dietary carbohydrate, protein, and fat. All the pathways lead to the production of acetyl-CoA, which is oxidized in the citric acid cycle, ultimately yielding ATP by the process of oxidative phosphorylation.

tion of dietary carbohydrate, lipid, and protein. These are mainly glucose, fatty acids and glycerol, and amino acids, respectively. In ruminants (and, to a lesser extent, other herbivores), dietary cellulose is fermented by symbiotic microorganisms to short-chain fatty acids (acetic, propionic, butyric), and metabolism in these animals is adapted to use these fatty acids as major substrates. All the products of digestion are metabolized to a **common product, acetyl-CoA,** which is then oxidized by the **citric acid cycle** (Figure 16–1).

Carbohydrate Metabolism Is Centered on the Provision & Fate of Glucose

Glucose is the major fuel of most tissues (Figure 16–2). It is metabolized to pyruvate by the pathway of **glycolysis.** Aerobic tissues metabolize pyruvate to **acetyl-CoA,** which can enter the **citric acid cycle** for complete oxidation to CO_2 and H_2O, linked to the formation of ATP in the process of **oxidative phosphorylation** (Figure 13–2). Glycolysis can also occur anaerobically (in the absence of oxygen), when the end product is lactate.

Glucose and its metabolites also take part in other processes, eg, (1) Synthesis of the storage polymer **gly-**

cogen in skeletal muscle and liver. (2) The **pentose phosphate pathway,** an alternative to part of the pathway of glycolysis. It is a source of reducing equivalents (NADPH) for fatty acid synthesis and the source of **ribose** for nucleotide and nucleic acid synthesis. (3) Triose phosphates gives rise to the **glycerol moiety** of triacylglycerols. (4) Pyruvate and intermediates of the citric acid cycle provide the carbon skeletons for the synthesis of **amino acids,** and acetyl-CoA is the precursor of **fatty acids** and **cholesterol** (and hence of all steroids synthesized in the body). **Gluconeogenesis** is the process of forming glucose from noncarbohydrate precursors, eg, lactate, amino acids, and glycerol.

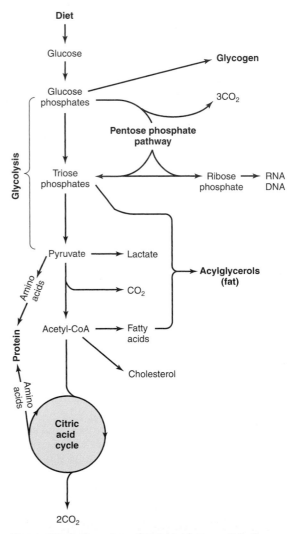

Figure 16–2. Overview of carbohydrate metabolism showing the major pathways and end products. Gluconeogenesis is not shown.

Lipid Metabolism Is Concerned Mainly with Fatty Acids & Cholesterol

The source of long-chain fatty acids is either dietary lipid or de novo synthesis from acetyl-CoA derived from carbohydrate or amino acids (Figure 16–3). Fatty acids may be oxidized to **acetyl-CoA (β-oxidation)** or esterified with glycerol, forming **triacylglycerol** (fat) as the body's main fuel reserve.

Acetyl-CoA formed by β-oxidation may undergo several fates.

(1) As with acetyl-CoA arising from glycolysis, it is **oxidized** to $CO_2 + H_2O$ via the citric acid cycle.

(2) It is the precursor for synthesis of **cholesterol** and other **steroids.**

(3) In the liver, it is used to form **ketone bodies** (acetoacetate and 3-hydroxybutyrate) that are important fuels in prolonged fasting.

Much of Amino Acid Metabolism Involves Transamination

The amino acids are required for protein synthesis (Figure 16–4). Some must be supplied in the diet (the **essential amino acids**), since they cannot be synthesized in the body. The remainder are **nonessential amino acids,** which are supplied in the diet, but can also be formed from metabolic intermediates by **transamination** using the amino nitrogen from other amino acids. After **deamination,** amino nitrogen is excreted as **urea,** and the carbon skeletons that remain after transamination may (1) be oxidized to CO_2 via the citric acid cycle; (2) be used to synthesize glucose (gluconeogenesis); or (3) form ketone bodies.

Several amino acids are also the precursors of other compounds, eg, purines, pyrimidines, hormones such as epinephrine and thyroxine, and neurotransmitters.

METABOLIC PATHWAYS MAY BE STUDIED AT DIFFERENT LEVELS OF ORGANIZATION

In addition to studies in the whole organism, the location and integration of metabolic pathways is revealed by studies at several levels of organization. (1) At the **tissue and organ level** the nature of the substrates entering and metabolites leaving tissues and organs is defined. (2) At the **subcellular level** each cell organelle (eg, the mitochondrion) or compartment (eg, the cytosol) has specific roles that form part of a subcellular pattern of metabolic pathways.

At the Tissue & Organ Level, the Blood Circulation Integrates Metabolism

Amino acids resulting from the digestion of dietary protein and **glucose** resulting from the digestion of carbohy-

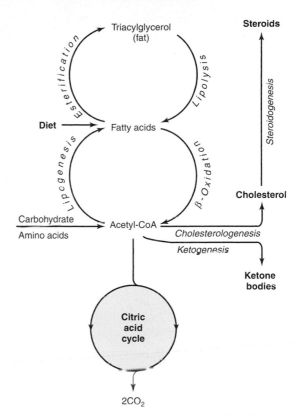

Figure 16–3. Overview of fatty acid metabolism showing the major pathways and end products. The ketone bodies are acetoacetate, 3-hydroxybutyrate, and acetone.

drate are absorbed via the **hepatic portal vein.** The liver has the role of regulating the blood concentration of water soluble metabolites (Figure 16–5). In the case of glucose, this is achieved by taking up glucose in excess of immediate requirements and converting it to glycogen (**glycogenesis**) or to fatty acids (**lipogenesis**). Between meals, the liver acts to maintain the blood glucose concentration from glycogen (**glycogenolysis**) and, together with the kidney, by converting noncarbohydrate metabolites such as lactate, glycerol, and amino acids to glucose (**gluconeogenesis**). The maintenance of an adequate concentration of blood glucose is vital for those tissues in which it is the major fuel (the brain) or the only fuel (erythrocytes). The liver also **synthesizes the major plasma proteins** (eg, albumin) and **deaminates amino acids** that are in excess of requirements, forming urea, which is transported to the kidney and excreted.

Skeletal muscle utilizes glucose as a fuel, both aerobically, forming CO_2, and anaerobically, forming lactate. It stores glycogen as a fuel for its use in muscular contraction and synthesizes muscle protein from plasma amino acids. Muscle accounts for approximately 50%

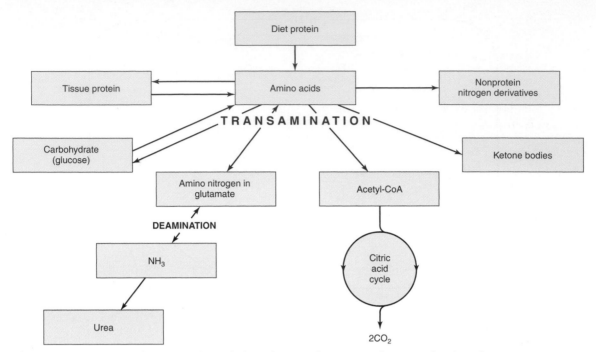

Figure 16–4. Overview of amino acid metabolism showing the major pathways and end products.

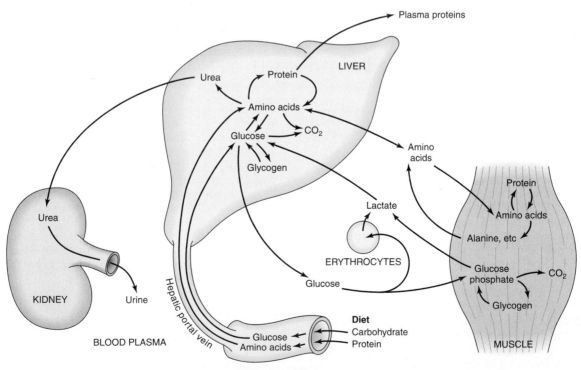

Figure 16–5. Transport and fate of major carbohydrate and amino acid substrates and metabolites. Note that there is little free glucose in muscle, since it is rapidly phosphorylated upon entry.

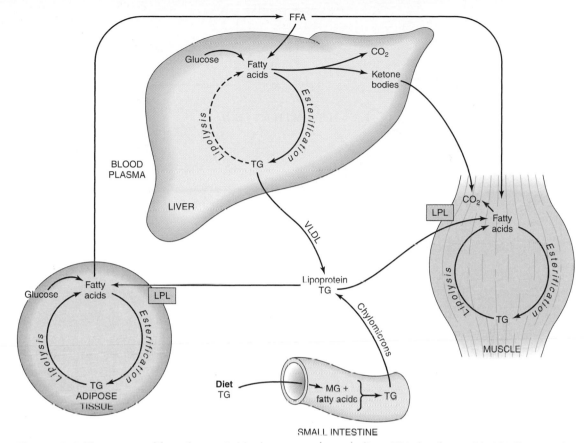

Figure 16–6. Transport and fate of major lipid substrates and metabolites. (FFA, free fatty acids; LPL, lipoprotein lipase; MG, monoacylglycerol; TG, triacylglycerol; VLDL, very low density lipoprotein.)

of body mass and consequently represents a considerable store of protein that can be drawn upon to supply amino acids for gluconeogenesis in starvation.

Lipids in the diet (Figure 16–6) are mainly triacylglycerol, and are hydrolyzed to monoacylglycerols and fatty acids in the gut, then re-esterified in the intestinal mucosa. Here they are packaged with protein and secreted into the lymphatic system and thence into the bloodstream as **chylomicrons,** the largest of the plasma **lipoproteins.** Chylomicrons also contain other lipid-soluble nutrients. Unlike glucose and amino acids, chylomicron triacylglycerol is not taken up directly by the liver. It is first metabolized by tissues that have **lipoprotein lipase,** which hydrolyzes the triacylglycerol, releasing fatty acids that are incorporated into tissue lipids or oxidized as fuel. The chylomicron remnants are cleared by the liver. The other major source of long-chain fatty acids is synthesis (**lipogenesis**) from carbohydrate, in adipose tissue and the liver.

Adipose tissue triacylglycerol is the main fuel reserve of the body. It is hydrolyzed (**lipolysis**) and glycerol and free fatty acids are released into the circulation. Glycerol is a substrate for gluconeogenesis. The fatty acids are transported bound to serum albumin; they are taken up by most tissues (but not brain or erythrocytes) and either esterified to acylglycerols or oxidized as a fuel. In the liver, triacylglycerol arising from lipogenesis, free fatty acids, and chylomicron remnants (see Figure 25–3) is secreted into the circulation in **very low density lipoprotein (VLDL).** This triacylglycerol undergoes a fate similar to that of chylomicrons. Partial oxidation of fatty acids in the liver leads to **ketone body** production (**ketogenesis).** Ketone bodies are transported to extrahepatic tissues, where they act as a fuel in prolonged fasting and starvation.

At the Subcellular Level, Glycolysis Occurs in the Cytosol & the Citric Acid Cycle in the Mitochondria

Compartmentation of pathways in separate subcellular compartments or organelles permits integration and regulation of metabolism. Not all pathways are of equal importance in all cells. Figure 16–7 depicts the subcel-

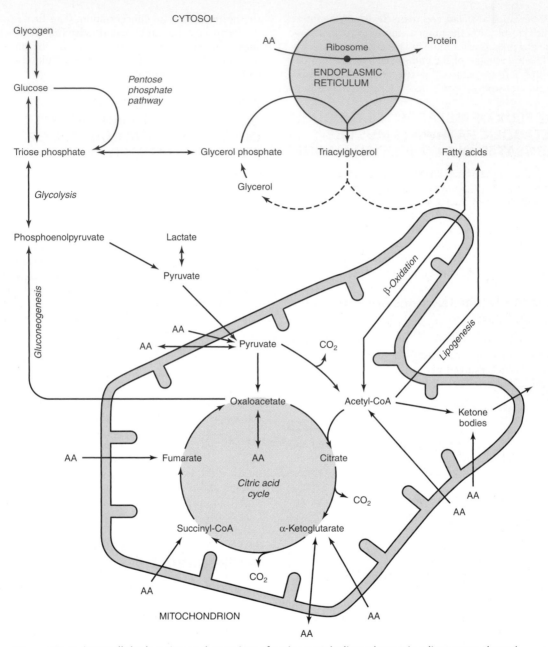

Figure 16–7. Intracellular location and overview of major metabolic pathways in a liver parenchymal cell. (AA →, metabolism of one or more essential amino acids; AA ↔, metabolism of one or more non-essential amino acids.)

lular compartmentation of metabolic pathways in a liver parenchymal cell.

The central role of the **mitochondrion** is immediately apparent, since it acts as the focus of carbohydrate, lipid, and amino acid metabolism. It contains the enzymes of the citric acid cycle, β-oxidation of fatty acids and ketogenesis, as well as the respiratory chain and ATP synthase.

Glycolysis, the pentose phosphate pathway, and fatty acid synthesis all occur in the cytosol. In gluconeogenesis,

substrates such as lactate and pyruvate, which are formed in the cytosol, enter the mitochondrion to yield **oxaloacetate** as a precursor for the synthesis of glucose.

The membranes of the **endoplasmic reticulum** contain the enzyme system for **triacylglycerol synthesis,** and the **ribosomes** are responsible for **protein synthesis.**

THE FLUX OF METABOLITES THROUGH METABOLIC PATHWAYS MUST BE REGULATED IN A CONCERTED MANNER

Regulation of the overall flux through a pathway is important to ensure an appropriate supply of the products of that pathway. It is achieved by control of one or more key reactions in the pathway, catalyzed by **regulatory enzymes.** The physicochemical factors that control the rate of an enzyme-catalyzed reaction, such as substrate concentration, are of primary importance in the control of the overall rate of a metabolic pathway (Chapter 9).

Nonequilibrium Reactions Are Potential Control Points

In a reaction at equilibrium, the forward and reverse reactions occur at equal rates, and there is therefore no net flux in either direction.

$$A \leftrightarrow B \leftrightarrow C \leftrightarrow D$$

In vivo, under "steady-state" conditions, there is a net flux from left to right because there is a continuous supply of A and removal of D. In practice, there are invariably one or more **nonequilibrium** reactions in a metabolic pathway, where the reactants are present in concentrations that are far from equilibrium. In attempting to reach equilibrium, large losses of free energy occur, making this type of reaction essentially irreversible.

$$A \leftrightarrow B \overset{\text{Heat}}{\to} C \leftrightarrow D$$

Such a pathway has both flow and direction. The enzymes catalyzing nonequilibrium reactions are usually present in low concentration and are subject to a variety of regulatory mechanisms. However, most reactions in metabolic pathways cannot be classified as equilibrium or nonequilibrium, but fall somewhere between the two extremes.

The Flux-Generating Reaction Is the First Reaction in a Pathway That Is Saturated with Substrate

It may be identified as a nonequilibrium reaction in which the K_m of the enzyme is considerably lower than

the normal substrate concentration. The first reaction in glycolysis, catalyzed by **hexokinase** (Figure 18–2), is such a flux-generating step because its K_m for glucose of 0.05 mmol/L is well below the normal blood glucose concentration of 5 mmol/L.

ALLOSTERIC & HORMONAL MECHANISMS ARE IMPORTANT IN THE METABOLIC CONTROL OF ENZYME-CATALYZED REACTIONS

A hypothetical metabolic pathway is shown in Figure 16–8, in which reactions A ↔ B and C ↔ D are equilibrium reactions and B → C is a nonequilibrium reaction. The flux through such a pathway can be regulated by the availability of substrate A. This depends on its supply from the blood, which in turn depends on either food intake or key reactions that release substrates from tissue reserves into the bloodstream, eg, glycogen phosphorylase in liver (Figure 19–1) and hormone-sensitive lipase in adipose tissue (Figure 25–8). It also depends on the transport of substrate A into the cell. Flux is also determined by removal of the end product D and the availability of cosubstrates or cofactors represented by X and Y. Enzymes catalyzing nonequilibrium reactions are often allosteric proteins subject to the rapid actions of "feed-back" or "feed-forward" control by **allosteric modifiers,** in immediate response to the needs of the cell (Chapter 9). Frequently, the product of a biosynthetic pathway inhibits the enzyme catalyzing the first reaction in the pathway. Other control mechanisms depend on the action of **hormones** responding to the needs of the body as a whole; they may act rapidly by altering the activity of existing enzyme molecules, or slowly by altering the rate of enzyme synthesis (see Chapter 42).

MANY METABOLIC FUELS ARE INTERCONVERTIBLE

Carbohydrate in excess of requirements for immediate energy-yielding metabolism and formation of glycogen reserves in muscle and liver can readily be used for synthesis of fatty acids, and hence triacylglycerol in both adipose tissue and liver (whence it is exported in very low density lipoprotein). The importance of lipogenesis in humans is unclear; in Western countries dietary fat provides 35–45% of energy intake, while in less-developed countries, where carbohydrate may provide 60–75% of energy intake, the total intake of food is so low that there is little surplus for lipogenesis anyway. A high intake of fat inhibits lipogenesis in adipose tissue and liver.

Fatty acids (and ketone bodies formed from them) cannot be used for the synthesis of glucose. The reaction of pyruvate dehydrogenase, forming acetyl-CoA, is irre-

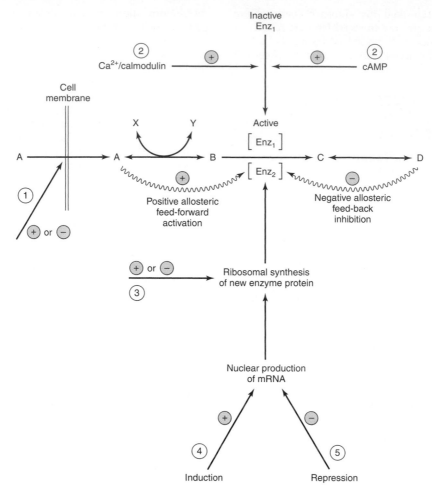

Figure 16–8. Mechanisms of control of an enzyme-catalyzed reaction. Circled numbers indicate possible sites of action of hormones. ① Alteration of membrane permeability; ② conversion of an inactive to an active enzyme, usually involving phosphorylation/dephosphorylation reactions; ③ alteration of the rate of translation of mRNA at the ribosomal level; ④ induction of new mRNA formation; and ⑤ repression of mRNA formation. ① and ② are rapid, whereas ③ through ⑤ are slower ways of regulating enzyme activity.

versible, and for every two-carbon unit from acetyl-CoA that enters the citric acid cycle, there is a loss of two carbon atoms as carbon dioxide before oxaloacetate is reformed. This means that that acetyl-CoA (and hence any substrates that yield acetyl-CoA) can never be used for gluconeogenesis. The (relatively rare) fatty acids with an odd number of carbon atoms yield propionyl CoA as the product of the final cycle of β-oxidation, and this can be a substrate for gluconeogenesis, as can the glycerol released by lipolysis of adipose tissue triacylglycerol reserves.

Most of the amino acids in excess of requirements for protein synthesis (arising from the diet or from tis-

sue protein turnover) yield pyruvate, or four- and five-carbon intermediates of the citric acid cycle. Pyruvate can be carboxylated to oxaloacetate, which is the primary substrate for gluconeogenesis, and the other intermediates of the cycle also result in a net increase in the formation of oxaloacetate, which is then available for gluconeogenesis. These amino acids are classified as **glucogenic.** Two amino acids (lysine and leucine) yield only acetyl-CoA on oxidation, and hence cannot be used for gluconeogenesis, and four others (ie, phenylalanine, tyrosine, tryptophan, and isoleucine) give rise to both acetyl-CoA and intermediates of the citric acid

cycle that can be used for gluconeogenesis. Those amino acids that give rise to acetyl-CoA are referred to as **ketogenic,** because in prolonged fasting and starvation much of the acetyl-CoA is used for synthesis of ketone bodies in the liver.

A SUPPLY OF METABOLIC FUELS IS PROVIDED IN BOTH THE FED & FASTING STATES

Glucose Is Always Required by the Central Nervous System and Erythrocytes

Erythrocytes lack mitochondria and hence are wholly reliant on (anaerobic) glycolysis and the pentose phosphate pathway at all times. The brain can metabolize ketone bodies to meet about 20% of its energy requirements; the remainder must be supplied by glucose. The metabolic changes that occur in the fasting state and starvation are the consequences of the need to preserve glucose and the limited reserves of glycogen in liver and muscle for use by the brain and red blood cells, and to ensure the provision of alternative metabolic fuels for other tissues. In pregnancy the fetus requires a significant amount of glucose, as does the synthesis of lactose in lactation (Figure 16–9).

In the Fed State, Metabolic Fuel Reserves Are Laid Down

For several hours after a meal, while the products of digestion are being absorbed, there is an abundant supply of metabolic fuels. Under these conditions, glucose is the major fuel for oxidation in most tissues; this is observed as an increase in the respiratory quotient (the ratio of carbon dioxide produced / oxygen consumed) from about 0.8 in the fasting state to near 1 (Table 16–1).

Glucose uptake into muscle and adipose tissue is controlled by **insulin,** which is secreted by the β-islet cells of the pancreas in response to an increased concentration of glucose in the portal blood. In the fasting state the glucose transporter of muscle and adipose tissue (GLUT-4) is in intracellular vesicles. An early response to insulin is the migration of these vesicles to the cell surface, where they fuse with the plasma membrane, exposing active glucose transporters. These insulin sensitive tissues only take up glucose from the bloodstream to any significant extent in the presence of the hormone. As insulin secretion falls in the fasting state, so the receptors are internalized again, reducing glucose uptake.

The uptake of glucose into the liver is independent of insulin, but liver has an isoenzyme of hexokinase (glucokinase) with a high K_m, so that as the concentration of glucose entering the liver increases, so does the rate of synthesis of glucose 6-phosphate. This is in excess of the liver's requirement for energy-yielding metabolism, and is used mainly for synthesis of **glycogen.** In both liver and skeletal muscle, insulin acts to stimulate glycogen synthetase and inhibit glycogen phosphorylase. Some of the additional glucose entering the liver may also be used for lipogenesis and hence triacylglycerol synthesis. In adipose tissue, insulin stimulates glucose uptake, its conversion to fatty acids and their esterification to triacylglycerol. It inhibits intracellular lipolysis and the release of free fatty acids.

The products of lipid digestion enter the circulation as **chylomicrons,** the largest of the plasma lipoproteins, especially rich in triacylglycerol (see Chapter 25). In adipose tissue and skeletal muscle, extracellular lipoprotein lipase is synthesized and activated in response to insulin; the resultant nonesterified fatty acids are largely taken up by the tissue and used for synthesis of triacylglycerol, while the glycerol remains in the bloodstream and is taken up by the liver and used for either gluconeogenesis and glycogen synthesis or lipogenesis. Fatty acids remaining in the bloodstream are taken up by the liver and reesterified. The lipid-depleted chylomicron remnants are cleared by the liver, and the remaining triacylglycerol is exported, together with that synthesized in the liver, in **very low density lipoprotein.**

Under normal conditions, the rate of tissue protein catabolism is more or less constant throughout the day; it is only in **cachexia** associated with advanced cancer and other diseases that there is an increased rate of protein catabolism. There is net protein catabolism in the fasting state, and net protein synthesis in the fed state, when the rate of synthesis increases by 20–25%. The increased rate of protein synthesis in response to increased availability of amino acids and metabolic fuel is again a response to insulin action. Protein synthesis is an energy expensive process; it may account for up to 20% of resting energy expenditure after a meal, but only 9% in the fasting state.

Metabolic Fuel Reserves Are Mobilized in the Fasting State

There is a small fall in plasma glucose in the fasting state, then little change as fasting is prolonged into starvation. Plasma free fatty acids increase in fasting, but then rise little more in starvation; as fasting is prolonged, so the plasma concentration of ketone bodies (acetoacetate and β-hydroxybutyrate) increases markedly (Table 16–2, Figure 16–10).

In the fasting state, as the concentration of glucose in the portal blood falls, so insulin secretion decreases, and skeletal muscle and adipose tissue take up less glucose. The increase in secretion of **glucagon** by the α-cells of the pancreas inhibits glycogen synthetase, and activates glycogen phosphorylase in the liver. The resulting glucose 6-phosphate is hydrolyzed by glucose 6-phosphatase, and glucose is released into the bloodstream for use by the brain and erythrocytes.

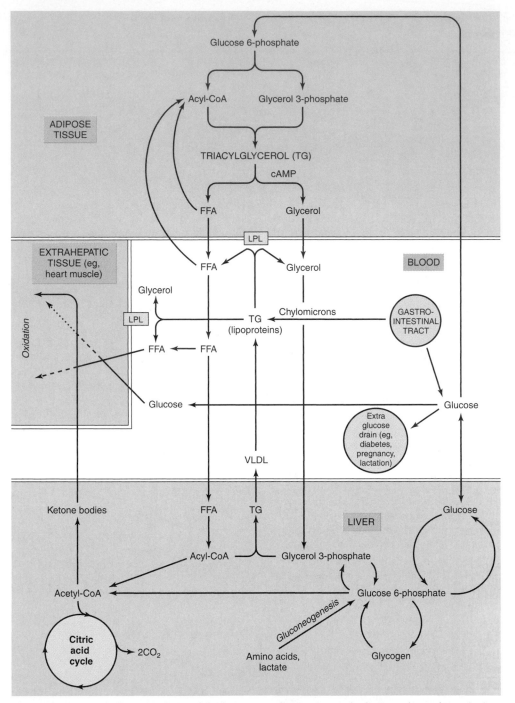

Figure 16-9. Metabolic interrelationships between adipose tissue, the liver, and extrahepatic tissues. In tissues such as heart, metabolic fuels are oxidized in the following order of preference: ketone bodies > fatty acids > glucose. (LPL, lipoprotein lipase; FFA, free fatty acids; VLDL, very low density lipoproteins.)

Table 16–1. Energy yields, oxygen consumption, and carbon dioxide production in the oxidation of metabolic fuels.

	Energy Yield (kJ/g)	O_2 Consumed (L/g)	CO_2 Produced (L/g)	RQ (CO_2 Produced/ O_2 Consumed)	Energy (kJ)/L O_2
Carbohydrate	16	0.829	0.829	1.00	20
Protein	17	0.966	0.782	0.81	20
Fat	37	2.016	1.427	0.71	20
Alcohol	29	1.429	0.966	0.66	20

Muscle glycogen cannot contribute directly to plasma glucose, since muscle lacks glucose 6-phosphatase, and the primary purpose of muscle glycogen is to provide a source of glucose 6-phosphate for energy-yielding metabolism in the muscle itself. However, acetyl-CoA formed by oxidation of fatty acids in muscle inhibits pyruvate dehydrogenase, leading to an accumulation of pyruvate. Most of this is transaminated to alanine, at the expense of amino acids arising from breakdown of "labile" protein reserves synthesized in the fed state. The alanine, and much of the keto-acids resulting from this transamination are exported from muscle, and taken up by the liver, where the alanine is transaminated to yield pyruvate. The resultant amino acids are largely exported back to muscle, to provide amino groups for formation of more alanine, while the pyruvate is a major substrate for gluconeogenesis in the liver.

In adipose tissue the decrease in insulin and increase in glucagon results in inhibition of lipogenesis, inactivation of lipoprotein lipase, and activation of intracellular hormone-sensitive lipase (Chapter 25). This leads to release from adipose tissue of increased amounts of glycerol (which is a substrate for gluconeogenesis in the liver) and free fatty acids, which are used by liver, heart, and skeletal muscle as their preferred metabolic fuel, therefore sparing glucose.

Although muscle preferentially takes up and metabolizes free fatty acids in the fasting state, it cannot meet all of its energy requirements by β-oxidation. By contrast, the liver has a greater capacity for β-oxidation than it requires to meet its own energy needs, and as fasting becomes more prolonged, it forms more acetyl-CoA than can be oxidized. This acetyl-CoA is used to synthesize the **ketone bodies** (Chapter 22), which are major metabolic fuels for skeletal and heart muscle and can meet some of the brain's energy needs. In prolonged starvation, glucose may represent less than 10% of whole body energy-yielding metabolism.

Were there no other source of glucose, liver and muscle glycogen would be exhausted after about 18 hours fasting. As fasting becomes more prolonged, so an increasing amount of the amino acids released as a

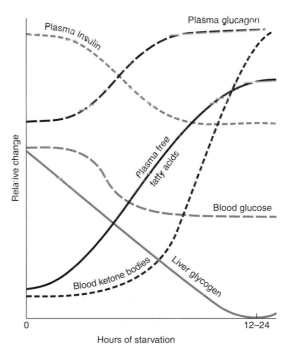

Figure 16–10. Relative changes in metabolic parameters during the onset of starvation.

Table 16–2. Plasma concentrations of metabolic fuels (mmol/L) in the fed and fasting states.

	Fed	40 Hours Fasting	7 Days Starvation
Glucose	5.5	3.6	3.5
Free fatty acids	0.30	1.15	1.19
Ketone bodies	Negligible	2.9	4.5

Table 16–3. Summary of the major metabolic features of the principal organs.

Organ	Major Pathways	Main Substrates	Major Products Exported	Specialist Enzymes
Liver	Glycolysis, gluconeogenesis, lipogenesis, β-oxidation, citric acid cycle, ketogenesis, lipoprotein metabolism, drug metabolism, synthesis of bile salts, urea, uric acid, cholesterol, plasma proteins	Free fatty acids, glucose (in fed state), lactate, glycerol, fructose, amino acids, alcohol	Glucose, triacylglycerol in VLDL, ketone bodies, urea, uric acid, bile salts, cholesterol, plasma proteins	Glucokinase, glucose 6-phosphatase, glycerol kinase, phosphoenolpyruvate carboxykinase, fructokinase, arginase, HMG CoA synthase, HMG CoA lyase, alcohol dehydrogenase
Brain	Glycolysis, amino acid metabolism, neurotransmitter synthesis	Glucose, amino acids, ketone bodies in prolonged starvation	Lactate, end products of neurotransmitter metabolism	Those for synthesis and catabolism of neurotransmitters
Heart	β-Oxidation and citric acid cycle	Ketone bodies, free fatty acids, lactate, chylomicron and VLDL triacylglycerol, some glucose	—	Lipoprotein lipase, very active electron transport chain
Adipose tissue	Lipogenesis, esterification of fatty acids, lipolysis (in fasting)	Glucose, chylomicron and VLDL triacylglycerol	Free fatty acids, glycerol	Lipoprotein lipase, hormone-sensitive lipase, enzymes of pentose phosphate pathway
Fast twitch muscle	Glycolysis	Glucose, glycogen	Lactate, (alanine and ketoacids in fasting)	—
Slow twitch muscle	β-Oxidation and citric acid cycle	Ketone bodies, chylomicron, and VLDL triacylglycerol	—	Lipoprotein lipase, very active electron transport chain
Kidney	Gluconeogenesis	Free fatty acids, lactate, glycerol, glucose	Glucose	Glycerol kinase, phosphoenolpyruvate carboxykinase
Erythrocytes	Anaerobic glycolysis, pentose phosphate pathway	Glucose	Lactate	Hemoglobin, enzymes of pentose phosphate pathway

VLDL, very low density lipoproteins.

result of protein catabolism is utilized in the liver and kidneys for gluconeogenesis (Table 16–3).

CLINICAL ASPECTS

In prolonged starvation, as adipose tissue reserves are depleted, there is a very considerable increase in the net rate of protein catabolism to provide amino acids, not only as substrates for gluconeogenesis, but also as the main metabolic fuel of all tissues. Death results when essential tissue proteins are catabolized and not replaced. In patients with **cachexia** as a result of release of **cytokines** in response to tumors and a number of other pathologic conditions, there is an increase in the rate of tissue protein catabolism, as well as a considerably increased metabolic rate, so they are in a state of

advanced starvation. Again, death results when essential tissue proteins are catabolized and not replaced.

The high demand for glucose by the fetus, and for lactose synthesis in lactation, can lead to ketosis. This may be seen as mild ketosis with hypoglycemia in human beings; in lactating cattle and in ewes carrying a twin pregnancy, there may be very pronounced ketoacidosis and profound hypoglycemia.

In poorly controlled type 1 **diabetes mellitus,** patients may become hyperglycemic, partly as a result of lack of insulin to stimulate uptake and utilization of glucose, and partly because in the absence of insulin there is increased gluconeogenesis from amino acids in the liver. At the same time, the lack of insulin results in increased lipolysis in adipose tissue, and the resultant free fatty acids are substrates for ketogenesis in the liver.

Utilization of these ketone bodies in muscle (and other tissues) may be impaired because of the lack of oxaloacetate (all tissues have a requirement for some glucose metabolism to maintain an adequate amount of oxaloacetate for citric acid cycle activity). In uncontrolled diabetes, the ketosis may be severe enough to result in pronounced acidosis (**ketoacidosis**) since acetoacetate and β-hydroxybutyrate are relatively strong acids. Coma results from both the acidosis and also the considerably increased osmolality of extracellular fluid (mainly as a result of the hyperglycemia).

SUMMARY

- The products of digestion provide the tissues with the building blocks for the biosynthesis of complex molecules and also with the fuel to power the living processes.
- Nearly all products of digestion of carbohydrate, fat, and protein are metabolized to a common metabolite, acetyl-CoA, before oxidation to CO_2 in the citric acid cycle.
- Acetyl-CoA is also the precursor for synthesis of long-chain fatty acids and steroids, including cholesterol and ketone bodies.
- Glucose provides carbon skeletons for the glycerol of triacylglycerols and nonessential amino acids.
- Water-soluble products of digestion are transported directly to the liver via the hepatic portal vein. The liver regulates the blood concentrations of glucose and amino acids.
- Pathways are compartmentalized within the cell. Glycolysis, glycogenesis, glycogenolysis, the pentose phosphate pathway, and lipogenesis occur in the cytosol. The mitochondria contain the enzymes of the citric acid cycle, β-oxidation of fatty acids, and the respiratory chain and ATP synthase. The membranes of the endoplasmic reticulum contain the enzymes for a number of other processes, including triacylglycerol synthesis and drug metabolism.

- Metabolic pathways are regulated by rapid mechanisms affecting the activity of existing enzymes, ie, allosteric and covalent modification (often in response to hormone action) and slow mechanisms affecting the synthesis of enzymes.
- Dietary carbohydrate and amino acids in excess of requirements can be used for fatty acid and hence triacylglycerol synthesis.
- In fasting and starvation, glucose must be provided for the brain and red blood cells; in the early fasting state, this is supplied from glycogen reserves. In order to spare glucose, muscle and other tissues do not take up glucose when insulin secretion is low; they utilize fatty acids (and later ketone bodies) as their preferred fuel.
- Adipose tissue releases free fatty acids in the fasting state. In prolonged fasting and starvation these are used by the liver for synthesis of ketone bodies, which are exported to provide the major fuel for muscle.
- Most amino acids, arising from the diet or from tissue protein turnover, can be used for gluconeogenesis, as can the glycerol from triacylglycerol.
- Neither fatty acids, arising from the diet or from lipolysis of adipose tissue triacylglycerol, nor ketone bodies, formed from fatty acids in the fasting state, can provide substrates for gluconeogenesis.

REFERENCES

Bender DA: *Introduction to Nutrition and Metabolism*, 3rd ed. Taylor & Francis, London, 2002.

Brosnan JT: Comments on the metabolic needs for glucose and the role of gluconeogenesis. European Journal of Clinical Nutrition 1999;53:Suppl 1, S107–S111.

Fell D: *Understanding the Control of Metabolism*. Portland Press, 1997.

Frayn KN: Integration of substrate flow in vivo: some insights into metabolic control. Clinical Nutrition 1997;16:277–282.

Frayn KN: *Metabolic Regulation: A Human Perspective*, 2nd ed. Blackwell Science, 2003.

Zierler K: Whole body metabolism of glucose. American Journal of Physiology 1999;276:E409–E426.

The Citric Acid Cycle: The Catabolism of Acetyl-CoA

17

David A. Bender, PhD, & Peter A. Mayes, PhD, DSc

BIOMEDICAL IMPORTANCE

The citric acid cycle (Krebs cycle, tricarboxylic acid cycle) is a sequence of reactions in mitochondria that oxidizes the acetyl moiety of acetyl-CoA and reduces coenzymes that are reoxidized through the electron transport chain, linked to the formation of ATP.

The citric acid cycle is the final common pathway for the oxidation of carbohydrate, lipid, and protein because glucose, fatty acids, and most amino acids are metabolized to acetyl-CoA or intermediates of the cycle. It also has a central role in gluconeogenesis, lipogenesis, and interconversion of amino acids. Many of these processes occur in most tissues, but the liver is the only tissue in which all occur to a significant extent. The repercussions are therefore profound when, for example, large numbers of hepatic cells are damaged as in acute **hepatitis** or replaced by connective tissue (as in **cirrhosis**). The few genetic defects of citric acid cycle enzymes that have been reported are associated with severe neurological damage as a result of very considerably impaired ATP formation in the central nervous system.

THE CITRIC ACID CYCLE PROVIDES SUBSTRATE FOR THE RESPIRATORY CHAIN

The cycle starts with reaction between the acetyl moiety of acetyl-CoA and the four-carbon dicarboxylic acid oxaloacetate, forming a six-carbon tricarboxylic acid, citrate. In the subsequent reactions, two molecules of CO_2 are released and oxaloacetate is regenerated (Figure 17–1). Only a small quantity of oxaloacetate is needed for the oxidation of a large quantity of acetyl-CoA; it can be considered as playing a **catalytic role.**

The citric acid cycle is an integral part of the process by which much of the free energy liberated during the oxidation of fuels is made available. During the oxidation of acetyl-CoA, coenzymes are reduced and subsequently reoxidized in the respiratory chain, linked to the formation of ATP (oxidative phosphorylation, Figure 17–2; see also Chapter 13). This process is **aerobic,** requiring oxygen as the final oxidant of the reduced coenzymes. The enzymes of the citric acid cycle are located in the **mitochondrial matrix,** either free or attached to the inner mitochondrial membrane and the crista membrane, where the enzymes of the respiratory chain are also found.

REACTIONS OF THE CITRIC ACID CYCLE LIBERATE REDUCING EQUIVALENTS & CO_2

The initial reaction between acetyl-CoA and oxaloacetate to form citrate is catalyzed by **citrate synthase,** which forms a carbon-carbon bond between the methyl carbon of acetyl-CoA and the carbonyl carbon of oxaloacetate (Figure 17–3). The thioester bond of the resultant citryl-CoA is hydrolyzed, releasing citrate and CoASH—an exothermic reaction.

Citrate is isomerized to isocitrate by the enzyme **aconitase** (aconitate hydratase); the reaction occurs in two steps: dehydration to *cis*-aconitate and rehydration to isocitrate. Although citrate is a symmetric molecule, aconitase reacts with citrate asymmetrically, so that the two carbon atoms that are lost in subsequent reactions of the cycle are not those that were added from acetyl-CoA. This asymmetric behavior is the result of **channelling**—transfer of the product of citrate synthase directly onto the active site of aconitase, without entering free solution. This provides integration of citric acid cycle activity and the provision of citrate in the cytosol as a source of acetyl-CoA for fatty acid synthesis. The poison **fluoroacetate** is toxic, because fluoroacetyl-CoA condenses with oxaloacetate to form fluorocitrate, which inhibits aconitase, causing citrate to accumulate.

Isocitrate undergoes dehydrogenation catalyzed by **isocitrate dehydrogenase** to form, initially, oxalosuccinate, which remains enzyme-bound and undergoes decarboxylation to α-ketoglutarate. The decarboxylation requires Mg^{++} or Mn^{++} ions. There are three isoenzymes of isocitrate dehydrogenase. One, which uses NAD^+, is found only in mitochondria. The other two use $NADP^+$ and are found in mitochondria and the

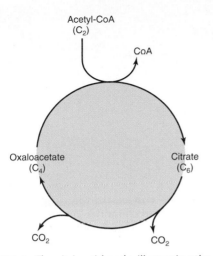

Figure 17–1. The citric acid cycle, illustrating the catalytic role of oxaloacetate.

cytosol. Respiratory chain-linked oxidation of isocitrate proceeds almost completely through the NAD$^+$-dependent enzyme.

α-Ketoglutarate undergoes **oxidative decarboxylation** in a reaction catalyzed by a multi-enzyme complex similar to that involved in the oxidative decarboxylation of pyruvate (Figure 18–5). The **α-ketoglutarate dehydrogenase complex** requires the same cofactors as the pyruvate dehydrogenase complex—thiamin diphosphate, lipoate, NAD$^+$, FAD, and CoA—and results in the formation of succinyl-CoA. The equilibrium of this reaction is so much in favor of succinyl-CoA formation that it must be considered to be physiologically unidirectional. As in the case of pyruvate oxidation (Chapter 18), arsenite inhibits the reaction, causing the substrate, α-ketoglutarate, to accumulate.

Succinyl-CoA is converted to succinate by the enzyme **succinate thiokinase (succinyl-CoA synthetase).** This is the only example in the citric acid cycle of substrate level phosphorylation. Tissues in which gluconeogenesis occurs (the liver and kidney) contain two isoenzymes of succinate thiokinase, one specific for GDP and the other for ADP. The GTP formed is used for the decarboxylation of oxaloacetate to phosphoenolpyruvate in gluconeogenesis, and provides a regulatory link between citric acid cycle activity and the withdrawal of oxaloacetate for gluconeogenesis. Nongluconeogenic tissues have only the isoenzyme that uses ADP.

When ketone bodies are being metabolized in extrahepatic tissues there is an alternative reaction catalyzed by **succinyl-CoA-acetoacetate-CoA transferase (thiophorase),** involving transfer of CoA from succinyl-CoA to acetoacetate, forming acetoacetyl-CoA (Chapter 22).

The onward metabolism of succinate, leading to the regeneration of oxaloacetate, is the same sequence of

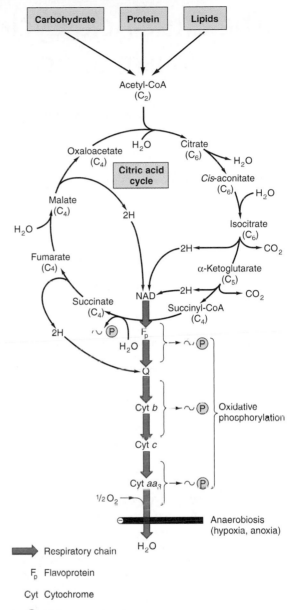

Figure 17–2. The citric acid cycle: the major catabolic pathway for acetyl-CoA in aerobic organisms. Acetyl-CoA, the product of carbohydrate, protein, and lipid catabolism, is taken into the cycle and oxidized to CO_2 with the release of reducing equivalents (2H). Subsequent oxidation of 2H in the respiratory chain leads to phosphorylation of ADP to ATP. For one turn of the cycle, 11 ATP are generated via oxidative phosphorylation and 1 ATP arises at substrate level from the conversion of succinyl-CoA to succinate.

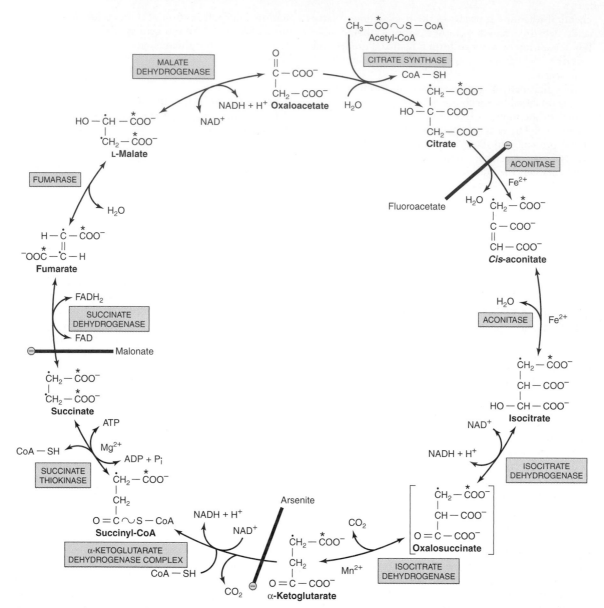

Figure 17–3. The citric acid (Krebs) cycle. Oxidation of NADH and FADH$_2$ in the respiratory chain leads to the formation of ATP via oxidative phosphorylation. In order to follow the passage of acetyl-CoA through the cycle, the two carbon atoms of the acetyl radical are shown labeled on the carboxyl carbon (*) and on the methyl carbon (•). Although two carbon atoms are lost as CO$_2$ in one turn of the cycle, these atoms are not derived from the acetyl-CoA that has immediately entered the cycle, but from that portion of the citrate molecule that was derived from oxaloacetate. However, on completion of a single turn of the cycle, the oxaloacetate that is regenerated is now labeled, which leads to labeled CO$_2$ being evolved during the second turn of the cycle. Because succinate is a symmetric compound, "randomization" of label occurs at this step so that all four carbon atoms of oxaloacetate appear to be labeled after one turn of the cycle. During gluconeogenesis, some of the label in oxaloacetate is incorporated into glucose and glycogen (Figure 20–1). The sites of inhibition (⊖) by fluoroacetate, malonate, and arsenite are indicated.

chemical reactions as occurs in the β-oxidation of fatty acids: dehydrogenation to form a carbon-carbon double bond, addition of water to form a hydroxyl group, and a further dehydrogenation to yield the oxo-group of oxaloacetate.

The first dehydrogenation reaction, forming fumarate, is catalyzed by **succinate dehydrogenase,** which is bound to the inner surface of the inner mitochondrial membrane. The enzyme contains FAD and iron-sulfur (Fe:S) protein, and directly reduces ubiquinone in the electron transport chain. **Fumarase (fumarate hydratase)** catalyzes the addition of water across the double bond of fumarate, yielding malate. Malate is converted to oxaloacetate by **malate dehydrogenase,** a reaction requiring NAD^+. Although the equilibrium of this reaction strongly favors malate, the net flux is to oxaloacetate because of the continual removal of oxaloacetate (to form citrate, as a substrate for gluconeogenesis, or to undergo transamination to aspartate) and also the continual reoxidation of NADH.

TWELVE ATP ARE FORMED PER TURN OF THE CITRIC ACID CYCLE

As a result of oxidations catalyzed by the dehydrogenases of the citric acid cycle, three molecules of NADH and one of $FADH_2$ are produced for each molecule of acetyl-CoA catabolized in one turn of the cycle. These reducing equivalents are transferred to the respiratory chain (see Figure 13–3), where reoxidation of each NADH results in formation of ~3 ATP, and of $FADH_2$, ~2 ATP. In addition, 1 ATP (or GTP) is formed by substrate level phosphorylation catalyzed by succinate thiokinase.

VITAMINS PLAY KEY ROLES IN THE CITRIC ACID CYCLE

Four of the B vitamins are essential in the citric acid cycle and hence energy-yielding metabolism: (1) **riboflavin,** in the form of flavin adenine dinucleotide (FAD), a cofactor for succinate dehydrogenase; (2) **niacin,** in the form of nicotinamide adenine dinucleotide (NAD), the electron acceptor for isocitrate dehydrogenase, α-ketoglutarate dehydrogenase, and malate dehydrogenase; (3) **thiamin (vitamin B_1),** as thiamin diphosphate, the coenzyme for decarboxylation in the α-ketoglutarate dehydrogenase reaction; and (4) **pantothenic acid,** as part of coenzyme A, the cofactor attached to "active" carboxylic acid residues such as acetyl-CoA and succinyl-CoA.

THE CITRIC ACID CYCLE PLAYS A PIVOTAL ROLE IN METABOLISM

The citric acid cycle is not only a pathway for oxidation of two-carbon units, but is also a major pathway for interconversion of metabolites arising from **transami-**nation and **deamination** of amino acids, and providing the substrates for **amino acid synthesis** by transamination, as well as for **gluconeogenesis** and **fatty acid synthesis.** Because it functions in both oxidative and synthetic processes, it is **amphibolic** (Figure 17–4).

The Citric Acid Cycle Takes Part in Gluconeogenesis, Transamination, & Deamination

All the intermediates of the cycle are potentially **glucogenic,** since they can give rise to oxaloacetate, and hence net production of glucose (in the liver and kidney, the organs that carry out gluconeogenesis; see Chapter 20). The key enzyme that catalyzes net transfer out of the cycle into gluconeogenesis is **phosphoenolpyruvate carboxykinase,** which catalyzes the decarboxylation of oxaloacetate to phosphoenolpyruvate, with GTP acting as the phosphate donor (see Figure 20–1).

Net transfer into the cycle occurs as a result of several reactions. Among the most important of such **anaplerotic** reactions is the formation of oxaloacetate by the carboxylation of pyruvate, catalyzed by **pyruvate carboxylase.** This reaction is important in maintaining an adequate concentration of oxaloacetate for the condensation reaction with acetyl-CoA. If acetyl-CoA accumulates, it acts as both an allosteric activator of pyruvate carboxylase and an inhibitor of pyruvate dehydrogenase, thereby ensuring a supply of oxaloacetate. Lactate, an important substrate for gluconeogenesis, enters the cycle via oxidation to pyruvate and then carboxylation to oxaloacetate.

Aminotransferase (transaminase) reactions form pyruvate from alanine, oxaloacetate from aspartate, and α-ketoglutarate from glutamate. Because these reactions are reversible, the cycle also serves as a source of carbon skeletons for the synthesis of these amino acids. Other amino acids contribute to gluconeogenesis because their carbon skeletons give rise to citric acid cycle intermediates. Alanine, cysteine, glycine, hydroxyproline, serine, threonine, and tryptophan yield pyruvate; arginine, histidine, glutamine, and proline yield α-ketoglutarate; isoleucine, methionine, and valine yield succinyl-CoA; tyrosine and phenylalanine yield fumarate (see Figure 17–4).

In ruminants, whose main metabolic fuel is short-chain fatty acids formed by bacterial fermentation, the conversion of propionate, the major glucogenic product of rumen fermentation, to succinyl-CoA via the methylmalonyl-CoA pathway (Figure 20–2) is especially important.

The Citric Acid Cycle Takes Part in Fatty Acid Synthesis

Acetyl-CoA, formed from pyruvate by the action of pyruvate dehydrogenase, is the major substrate for long-chain fatty acid synthesis in nonruminants (Figure

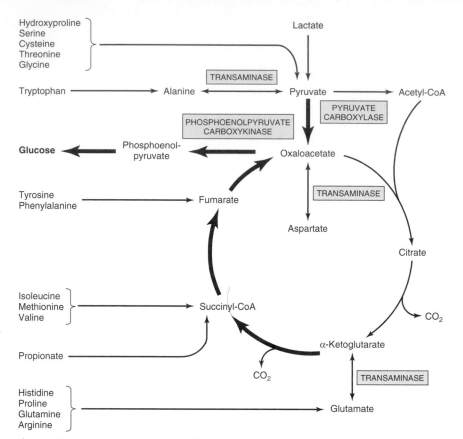

Figure 17–4. Involvement of the citric acid cycle in transamination and gluconeogenesis. The bold arrows indicate the main pathway of gluconeogenesis.

17–5). (In ruminants, acetyl-CoA is derived directly from acetate.) Pyruvate dehydrogenase is a mitochondrial enzyme, and fatty-acid synthesis is a cytosolic pathway; the mitochondrial membrane is impermeable to acetyl-CoA. Acetyl-CoA is made available in the cytosol from citrate synthesized in the mitochondrion, transported into the cytosol, and cleaved in a reaction catalyzed by **ATP-citrate lyase.** Citrate is only available for transport out of the mitochondrion when aconitase is saturated with its substrate, and citrate cannot be channelled directly from citrate synthase onto aconitase. This ensures that citrate is used for fatty acid synthesis only when there is an adequate amount to ensure continued activity of the cycle.

Regulation of the Citric Acid Cycle Depends Primarily on a Supply of Oxidized Cofactors

In most tissues, where the primary role of the citric acid cycle is in energy-yielding metabolism, **respiratory control** via the respiratory chain and oxidative phosphorylation regulates citric acid cycle activity (Chapter 13). Thus, activity is immediately dependent on the supply of NAD$^+$, which in turn, because of the tight coupling between oxidation and phosphorylation, is dependent on the availability of ADP and hence, ultimately on the rate of utilization of ATP in chemical and physical work. In addition, individual enzymes of the cycle are regulated. The most likely sites for regulation are the nonequilibrium reactions catalyzed by pyruvate dehydrogenase, citrate synthase, isocitrate dehydrogenase, and α-ketoglutarate dehydrogenase. The dehydrogenases are activated by Ca^{2+}, which increases in concentration during muscular contraction and secretion, when there is increased energy demand. In a tissue such as brain, which is largely dependent on carbohydrate to supply acetyl-CoA, control of the citric acid cycle may occur at pyruvate dehydrogenase. Several enzymes are responsive to the energy status as shown by the [ATP]/[ADP] and [NADH]/[NAD$^+$] ratios. Thus, there is allosteric inhibition of citrate

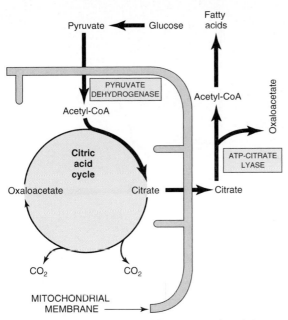

Figure 17–5. Participation of the citric acid cycle in fatty acid synthesis from glucose. See also Figure 23–5.

synthase by ATP and long-chain fatty acyl-CoA. Allosteric activation of mitochondrial NAD-dependent isocitrate dehydrogenase by ADP is counteracted by ATP and NADH. The α-ketoglutarate dehydrogenase complex is regulated in the same way as is pyruvate dehydrogenase (Figure 18–6). Succinate dehydrogenase is inhibited by oxaloacetate, and the availability of oxaloacetate, as controlled by malate dehydrogenase, depends on the [NADH]/[NAD$^+$] ratio. Since the K_m for oxaloacetate of citrate synthase is of the same order of magnitude as the intramitochondrial concentration, it is likely that the concentration of oxaloacetate controls the rate of citrate formation. Which of these mechanisms are important in vivo is still to be resolved.

SUMMARY

- The citric acid cycle is the final pathway for the oxidation of carbohydrate, lipid, and protein. Their common end-metabolite, acetyl-CoA, reacts with oxaloacetate to form citrate. By a series of dehydrogenations and decarboxylations, citrate is degraded, reducing coenzymes, releasing $2CO_2$, and regenerating oxaloacetate.

- The reduced coenzymes are oxidized by the respiratory chain linked to formation of ATP. Thus, the cycle is the major route for the formation of ATP and is located in the matrix of mitochondria adjacent to the enzymes of the respiratory chain and oxidative phosphorylation.

- The citric acid cycle is amphibolic, since in addition to oxidation it is important in the provision of carbon skeletons for gluconeogenesis, fatty acid synthesis, and interconversion of amino acids.

REFERENCES

Baldwin JE, Krebs HA. The evolution of metabolic cycles. Nature 1981;291:381.

Bowtell JL, Bruce M. Glutamine: an anaplerotic precursor. Nutrition 2002;18:222.

De Meirleir L: Defects of pyruvate metabolism and the Krebs cycle. Journal of Childhood Neurology 2002;Suppl 3:3S26.

Gibala MJ, Young ME. Anaplerosis of the citric acid cycle: role in energy metabolism of heart and skeletal muscle. Acta Physiologica Scandinavica 2000;168:657.

Kay J, Weitzman PDJ (editors): *Krebs' Citric Acid Cycle—Half a Century and Still Turning.* Biochemical Society, London, 1987.

Kornberg H. Krebs and his trinity of cycles. Nature Review of Molecular Cell Biology 2000;1:225.

Owen OE, Kalhan SC. The key role of anaplerosis and cataplerosis for citric acid cycle function. Journal of Biological Chemistry 2002;277:30409

Rustin P, Bourgeron T. Inborn errors of the Krebs cycle: A group of unusual mitochondrial diseases in humans. Biochimica et Biophysica Acta 1997;1361:185.

Sumegi B, Sherry AD. Is there tight channelling in the tricarboxylic acid cycle metabolon? Biochemical Society Transactions 1991;19:1002.

Glycolysis & the Oxidation of Pyruvate

18

David A. Bender, PhD, & Peter A. Mayes, PhD, DSc

BIOMEDICAL IMPORTANCE

Most tissues have at least some requirement for glucose. In brain, the requirement is substantial. Glycolysis, the major pathway for glucose metabolism, occurs in the cytosol of all cells. It is unique, in that it can function either aerobically or anaerobically, depending on the availability of oxygen and the electron transport chain. Erythrocytes, which lack mitochondria, are completely reliant on glucose as their metabolic fuel, and metabolize it by anaerobic glycolysis. However, to oxidize glucose beyond pyruvate (the end product of glycolysis) requires both oxygen and mitochondrial enzyme systems such as the pyruvate dehydrogenase complex, the citric acid cycle, and the respiratory chain.

Glycolysis is both the principal route for glucose metabolism and also the main pathway for the metabolism of fructose, galactose, and other carbohydrates derived from the diet. The ability of glycolysis to provide ATP in the absence of oxygen is especially important, because this allows skeletal muscle to perform at very high levels when oxygen supply is insufficient, and it allows tissues to survive anoxic episodes. However, heart muscle, which is adapted for aerobic performance, has relatively low glycolytic activity and poor survival under conditions of **ischemia.** Diseases in which enzymes of glycolysis (eg, pyruvate kinase) are deficient are mainly seen as **hemolytic anemias** or, if the defect affects skeletal muscle (eg, phosphofructokinase), as **fatigue.** In fast-growing cancer cells, glycolysis proceeds at a high rate, forming large amounts of pyruvate, which is reduced to lactate and exported. This produces a relatively acidic local environment in the tumor, which may have implications for cancer therapy. The lactate is used for gluconeogenesis in the liver, an energy-expensive process, which is responsible for much of the **hypermetabolism** seen in **cancer cachexia.** **Lactic acidosis** results from several causes, including impaired activity of pyruvate dehydrogenase.

GLYCOLYSIS CAN FUNCTION UNDER ANAEROBIC CONDITIONS

Early in the investigations of glycolysis it was realized that fermentation in yeast was similar to the breakdown of glycogen in muscle. It was noted that when a muscle contracts in an anaerobic medium, ie, one from which oxygen is excluded, **glycogen disappears** and **lactate appears.** When oxygen is admitted, aerobic recovery takes place and lactate disappears. However, if contraction occurs under aerobic conditions, lactate does not accumulate and pyruvate is the major end product of glycolysis. Pyruvate is oxidized further to CO_2 and water (Figure 18–1). When oxygen is in short supply, mitochondrial reoxidation of NADH formed during glycolysis is impaired, and NADH is reoxidized by reducing pyruvate to lactate, so permitting glycolysis to proceed (Figure 18–1). While glycolysis can occur under anaerobic conditions, this has a price, for it limits the amount of ATP formed per mole of glucose oxidized, so that much more glucose must be metabolized under anaerobic than aerobic conditions. In yeast and some other microorganisms, pyruvate formed in anaerobic glycolysis is not reduced to lactate, but is decarboxylated and reduced to ethanol.

THE REACTIONS OF GLYCOLYSIS CONSTITUTE THE MAIN PATHWAY OF GLUCOSE UTILIZATION

The overall equation for glycolysis from glucose to lactate is as follows:

$$\text{Glucose} + 2\,\text{ADP} + 2\,\text{P}_i \rightarrow 2\,\text{Lactate} + 2\,\text{ATP} + 2\,\text{H}_2\text{O}$$

All of the enzymes of glycolysis (Figure 18–2) are found in the cytosol. Glucose enters glycolysis by phosphorylation to glucose 6-phosphate, catalyzed by **hexokinase,** using ATP as the phosphate donor. Under physiologic conditions, the phosphorylation of glucose to glucose 6-phosphate can be regarded as irreversible. Hexokinase is inhibited allosterically by its product, glucose 6-phosphate.

In tissues other than the liver (and pancreatic β-islet cells), the availability of glucose for glycolysis (or glycogen synthesis in muscle and lipogenesis in adipose tissue) is controlled by transport into the cell, which in turn is

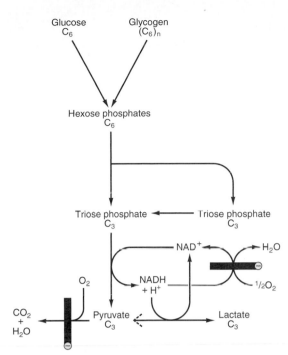

Figure 18–1. Summary of glycolysis. ⊖, blocked by anaerobic conditions or by absence of mitochondria containing key respiratory enzymes, eg, as in erythrocytes.

regulated by **insulin.** Hexokinase has a high affinity (low K_m) for glucose, and in the liver it is saturated under normal conditions, and so acts at a constant rate to provide glucose 6-phosphate to meet the cell's need. Liver cells also contain an isoenzyme of hexokinase, **glucokinase,** which has a K_m very much higher than the normal intracellular concentration of glucose. The function of glucokinase in the liver is to remove glucose from the blood following a meal, providing glucose 6-phosphate in excess of requirements for glycolysis, which is used for glycogen synthesis and lipogenesis.

Glucose 6-phosphate is an important compound at the junction of several metabolic pathways: glycolysis, gluconeogenesis, the pentose phosphate pathway, glycogenesis, and glycogenolysis. In glycolysis it is converted to fructose 6-phosphate by **phosphohexose isomerase,** which involves an aldose-ketose isomerization. This reaction is followed by another phosphorylation catalyzed by the enzyme **phosphofructokinase (phosphofructokinase-1)** forming fructose 1,6-bisphosphate. The phosphofructokinase reaction may be considered to be functionally irreversible under physiologic conditions; it is both inducible and subject to allosteric regulation, and has a major role in regulating the rate of glycolysis. Fructose 1,6-bisphosphate is cleaved by **aldolase** (fructose

1,6-bisphosphate aldolase) into two triose phosphates, glyceraldehyde 3-phosphate and dihydroxyacetone phosphate. Glyceraldehyde 3-phosphate and dihydroxyacetone phosphate are interconverted by the enzyme **phosphotriose isomerase.**

Glycolysis continues with the oxidation of glyceraldehyde 3-phosphate to 1,3-bisphosphoglycerate. The enzyme catalyzing this oxidation, **glyceraldehyde 3-phosphate dehydrogenase,** is NAD-dependent. Structurally, it consists of four identical polypeptides (monomers) forming a tetramer. Four —SH groups are present on each polypeptide, derived from cysteine residues within the polypeptide chain. One of the —SH groups is found at the active site of the enzyme (Figure 18–3). The substrate initially combines with this —SH group, forming a thiohemiacetal that is oxidized to a thiol ester; the hydrogens removed in this oxidation are transferred to NAD^+. The thiol ester then undergoes phosphorolysis; inorganic phosphate (P_i) is added, forming 1,3-bisphosphoglycerate, and the —SH group is reconstituted. In the next reaction, catalyzed by **phosphoglycerate kinase,** phosphate is transferred from 1,3-bisphosphoglycerate onto ADP, forming ATP (substrate-level phosphorylation) and 3-phosphoglycerate.

Since two molecules of triose phosphate are formed per molecule of glucose undergoing glycolysis, two molecules of ATP are formed at this stage per molecule of glucose undergoing glycolysis. The toxicity of arsenic is the result of competition of arsenate with inorganic phosphate (P_i) in the above reactions to give 1-arseno-3-phosphoglycerate, which hydrolyzes spontaneously to 3-phosphoglycerate without forming ATP. 3-Phosphoglycerate is isomerized to 2-phosphoglycerate by **phosphoglycerate mutase.** It is likely that 2,3-bisphosphoglycerate (diphosphoglycerate, DPG) is an intermediate in this reaction.

The subsequent step is catalyzed by **enolase** and involves a dehydration, forming phosphoenolpyruvate. Enolase is inhibited by **fluoride,** and when blood samples are taken for measurement of glucose, it is collected in tubes containing fluoride to inhibit glycolysis. The enzyme is also dependent on the presence of either Mg^{2+} or Mn^{2+}. The phosphate of phosphoenolpyruvate is transferred to ADP by **pyruvate kinase** to form two molecules of ATP per molecule of glucose oxidized.

The redox state of the tissue now determines which of two pathways is followed. Under **anaerobic** conditions, the NADH cannot be reoxidized through the respiratory chain to oxygen. Pyruvate is reduced by the NADH to lactate, catalyzed by **lactate dehydrogenase.** There are different tissue specific isoenzymes lactate dehydrogenase that have clinical significance (Chapter 7). The reoxidation of NADH via lactate formation allows glycolysis to proceed in the absence of oxygen by regenerating sufficient NAD^+ for another cycle of the reaction catalyzed by glyceraldehyde-3-phosphate dehydrogenase. Under

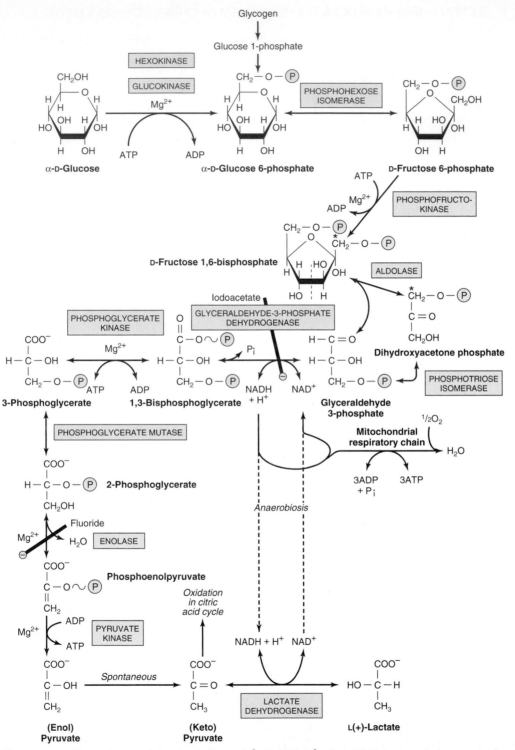

Figure 18–2. The pathway of glycolysis. (P), $-PO_3^{2-}$; P_i, $HOPO_3^{2-}$; $\ominus$, inhibition. At *: Carbons 1–3 of fructose bisphosphate form dihydroxyacetone phosphate, and carbons 4–6 form glyceraldehyde 3-phosphate. The term "bis-," as in bisphosphate, indicates that the phosphate groups are separated, whereas the term "di-," as in adenosine diphosphate, indicates that they are joined.

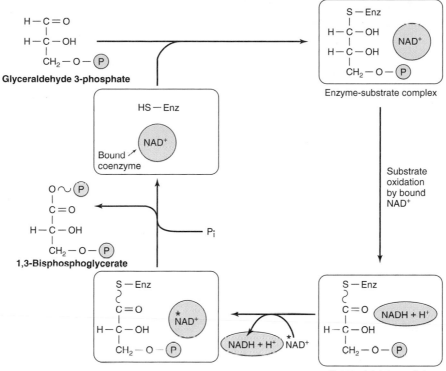

Figure 18–3. Mechanism of oxidation of glyceraldehyde 3-phosphate. (Enz, glyceraldehyde 3-phosphate dehydrogenase.) The enzyme is inhibited by the —SH poison iodoacetate, which is thus able to inhibit glycolysis. The NADH produced on the enzyme is not so firmly bound to the enzyme as is NAD⁺. Consequently, NADH is easily displaced by another molecule of NAD⁺.

aerobic conditions, pyruvate is taken up into mitochondria, and after oxidative decarboxylation to acetyl-CoA is oxidized to CO_2 by the citric acid cycle. The reducing equivalents from the NADH formed in glycolysis are taken up into mitochondria for oxidation via one of the two shuttles described in Chapter 13.

Tissues That Function under Hypoxic Conditions Produce Lactate

This is true of skeletal muscle, particularly the white fibers, where the rate of work output, and hence the need for ATP formation, may exceed the rate at which oxygen can be taken up and utilized (Figure 18–2). Glycolysis in erythrocytes always terminates in lactate, because the subsequent reactions of pyruvate oxidation are mitochondrial, and erythrocytes lack mitochondria. Other tissues that normally derive much of their energy from glycolysis and produce lactate include brain, gastrointestinal tract, renal medulla, retina, and skin. The

liver, kidneys, and heart usually take up lactate and oxidize it but will produce it under hypoxic conditions.

GLYCOLYSIS IS REGULATED AT THREE STEPS INVOLVING NONEQUILIBRIUM REACTIONS

Although most of the reactions of glycolysis are reversible, three are markedly exergonic and must therefore be considered physiologically irreversible. These reactions, catalyzed by **hexokinase** (and glucokinase), **phosphofructokinase,** and **pyruvate kinase,** are the major sites of regulation of glycolysis. Phosphofructokinase is significantly inhibited at normal intracellular concentrations of ATP; as discussed in Chapter 20, this inhibition can be rapidly relieved by 5′AMP that is formed as ADP begins to accumulate, signaling the need for an increased rate of glycolysis. Cells that are capable of **gluconeogenesis** (reversing the glycolytic pathway) have different enzymes that catalyze reactions to reverse these irreversible steps; glucose

6-phosphatase, fructose 1,6-bisphosphatase and, to reverse the reaction of pyruvate kinase, pyruvate carboxylase and phosphoenolpyruvate carboxykinase. **Fructose** enters glycolysis by phosphorylation to fructose 1-phosphate, and bypasses the main regulatory steps, so resulting in formation of more pyruvate (and acetyl-CoA) than is required for ATP formation. In the liver and adipose tissue, this leads to increased lipogenesis, and a high intake of fructose may be a factor in the development of obesity.

In Erythrocytes, the First Site in Glycolysis for ATP Formation May Be Bypassed

In erythrocytes, the reaction catalyzed by **phosphoglycerate kinase** may be bypassed to some extent by the reaction of **bisphosphoglycerate mutase,** which catalyzes the conversion of 1,3-bisphosphoglycerate to 2,3-bisphosphoglycerate, followed by hydrolysis to 3-phosphoglycerate and P_i, catalyzed by **2,3-bisphosphoglycerate phosphatase** (Figure 18–4). This alternative pathway involves no net yield of ATP from glycolysis. However, it does serve to provide 2,3-bisphosphoglycerate, which binds to hemoglobin, decreasing its affinity for oxygen, and so making oxygen more readily available to tissues (see Chapter 6).

THE OXIDATION OF PYRUVATE TO ACETYL-CoA IS THE IRREVERSIBLE ROUTE FROM GLYCOLYSIS TO THE CITRIC ACID CYCLE

Pyruvate, formed in the cytosol, is transported into the mitochondrion by a proton symporter (Figure 13–10). Inside the mitochondrion, it is oxidatively decarboxylated to acetyl-CoA by a multienzyme complex that is associated with the inner mitochondrial membrane. This **pyruvate dehydrogenase complex** is analogous to the α-ketoglutarate dehydrogenase complex of the citric acid cycle (Figure 17–3). Pyruvate is decarboxylated by the **pyruvate dehydrogenase** component of the enzyme complex to a hydroxyethyl derivative of the thiazole ring of enzyme-bound **thiamin diphosphate,** which in turn reacts with oxidized lipoamide, the prosthetic group of **dihydrolipoyl transacetylase,** to form acetyl lipoamide (Figure 18–5). Thiamin is vitamin B_1 (Chapter 44) and in deficiency, glucose metabolism is impaired, and there is significant (and potentially life-threatening) lactic and pyruvic acidosis. Acetyl lipoamide reacts with coenzyme A to form acetyl-CoA and reduced lipoamide. The reaction is completed when the reduced lipoamide is reoxidized by a flavoprotein, **dihydrolipoyl dehydrogenase,** containing FAD. Finally, the reduced flavoprotein is oxidized by NAD^+, which in turn transfers reducing equivalents to the respiratory chain.

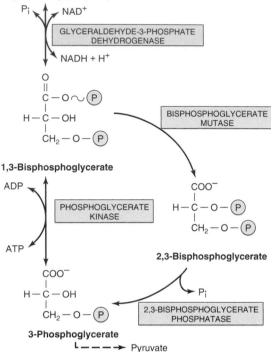

Figure 18–4. 2,3-Bisphosphoglycerate pathway in erythrocytes.

$$Pyruvate + NAD^+ + CoA \rightarrow Acetyl-CoA + NADH + H^+ + CO_2$$

The pyruvate dehydrogenase complex consists of a number of polypeptide chains of each of the three component enzymes, and the intermediates do not dissociate, but remain bound to the enzymes. Such a complex of enzymes, in which the substrates are handed on from one enzyme to the next, increases the reaction rate and eliminates side reactions, increasing overall efficiency.

Pyruvate Dehydrogenase Is Regulated by End-Product Inhibition & Covalent Modification

Pyruvate dehydrogenase is inhibited by its products, acetyl-CoA and NADH (Figure 18–6). It is also regulated by phosphorylation by a kinase of three serine residues on the pyruvate dehydrogenase component of the multienzyme complex, resulting in decreased activity,

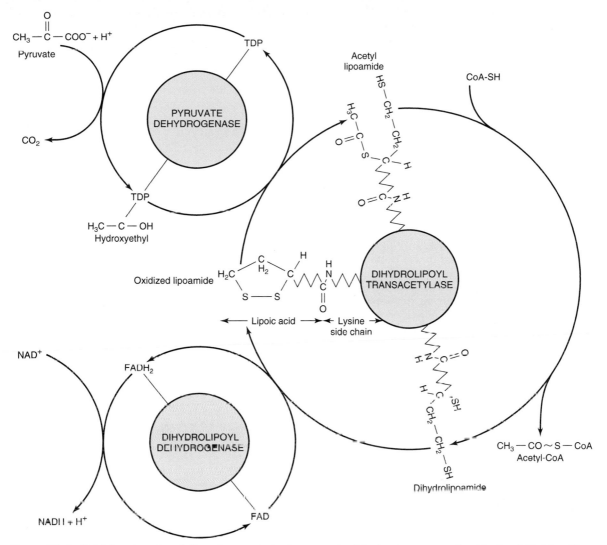

Figure 18–5. Oxidative decarboxylation of pyruvate by the pyruvate dehydrogenase complex. Lipoic acid is joined by an amide link to a lysine residue of the transacetylase component of the enzyme complex. It forms a long flexible arm, allowing the lipoic acid prosthetic group to rotate sequentially between the active sites of each of the enzymes of the complex. (NAD+, nicotinamide adenine dinucleotide; FAD, flavin adenine dinucleotide; TDP, thiamin diphosphate.)

and by dephosphorylation by a phosphatase that causes an increase in activity. The kinase is activated by increases in the [ATP]/[ADP], [acetyl-CoA]/[CoA], and [NADH]/[NAD+] ratios. Thus, pyruvate dehydrogenase, and therefore glycolysis, is inhibited both when there is adequate ATP (and reduced coenzymes for ATP formation) available, and also when fatty acids are being oxidized. In fasting, when free fatty acid concentrations increase, there is a decrease in the proportion of the enzyme in the active form, leading to a sparing of carbohydrate. In adipose tissue, where glucose provides acetyl-CoA for lipogenesis, the enzyme is activated in response to insulin.

Oxidation of Glucose Yields Up to 38 Mol of ATP under Aerobic Conditions, But Only 2 Mol When O₂ Is Absent

When 1 mol of glucose is combusted in a calorimeter to CO_2 and water, approximately 2870 kJ are liberated as heat. When oxidation occurs in the tissues, approximately 38 mol of ATP are generated per molecule of

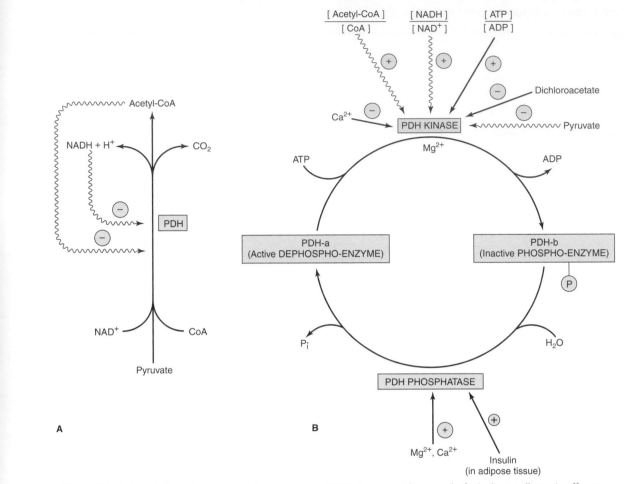

Figure 18–6. Regulation of pyruvate dehydrogenase (PDH). Arrows with wavy shafts indicate allosteric effects. **(A)** Regulation by end-product inhibition. **(B)** Regulation by interconversion of active and inactive forms.

glucose oxidized to CO_2 and water. In vivo, ΔG for the ATP synthase reaction has been calculated as approximately 51.6 kJ. It follows that the total energy captured in ATP per mole of glucose oxidized is 1761 kJ, or approximately 68% of the energy of combustion. Most of the ATP is formed by oxidative phosphorylation resulting from the reoxidation of reduced coenzymes by the respiratory chain. The remainder is formed by substrate level phosphorylation (Table 18–1).

CLINICAL ASPECTS

Inhibition of Pyruvate Metabolism Leads to Lactic Acidosis

Arsenite and mercuric ions react with the —SH groups of lipoic acid and inhibit pyruvate dehydrogenase, as does a **dietary deficiency of thiamin,** allowing pyruvate to accumulate. Many alcoholics are thiamin-deficient (both because of a poor diet and also because alcohol inhibits thiamin absorption), and may develop potentially fatal pyruvic and lactic acidosis. Patients with **inherited pyruvate dehydrogenase deficiency,** which can be the result of defects in one or more of the components of the enzyme complex, also present with lactic acidosis, particularly after a glucose load. Because of the dependence of the brain on glucose as a fuel, these metabolic defects commonly cause neurologic disturbances.

Inherited aldolase A deficiency and pyruvate kinase deficiency in erythrocytes cause **hemolytic anemia.** The exercise capacity of patients with **muscle phosphofructokinase deficiency** is low, particularly if they are on high-carbohydrate diets. By providing lipid as an alternative fuel, eg, during starvation, when blood

Table 18–1. ATP formation in the catabolism of glucose.

Pathway	Reaction Catalyzed by	Method of ATP Formation	ATP per Mol of Glucose
Glycolysis	Glyceraldehyde 3-phosphate dehydrogenase	Respiratory chain oxidation of 2 NADH	6[*]
	Phosphoglycerate kinase	Substrate level phosphorylation	2
	Pyruvate kinase	Substrate level phosphorylation	2
			10
	Consumption of ATP for reactions of hexokinase and phosphofructokinase		−2
			Net 8
Citric acid cycle	Pyruvate dehydrogenase	Respiratory chain oxidation of 2 NADH	6
	Isocitrate dehydrogenase	Respiratory chain oxidation of 2 NADH	6
	α-Ketoglutarate dehydrogenase	Respiratory chain oxidation of 2 NADH	6
	Succinate thiokinase	Substrate level phosphorylation	2
	Succinate dehydrogenase	Respiratory chain oxidation of 2 $FADH_2$	4
	Malate dehydrogenase	Respiratory chain oxidation of 2 NADH	6
			Net 30
	Total per mol of glucose under aerobic conditions		38
	Total per mol of glucose under anaerobic conditions		2

[*]This assumes that NADH formed in glycolysis is transported into mitochondria by the malate shuttle (Figure 13–13). If the glycerophosphate shuttle is used, then only 2 ATP will be formed per mol of NADH. Note that there is a considerable advantage in using glycogen rather than glucose for anaerobic glycolysis in muscle, since the product of glycogen phosphorylase is glucose 1-phosphate (Figure 19–1), which is interconvertible with glucose 6-phosphate. This saves the ATP that would otherwise be used by hexokinase, increasing the net yield of ATP from 2 to 3 per glucose.

free-fatty acid and ketone bodies are increased, work capacity is improved.

SUMMARY

- Glycolysis is the cytosolic pathway of all mammalian cells for the metabolism of glucose (or glycogen) to pyruvate and lactate.
- It can function anaerobically by regenerating oxidized NAD^+ (required in the glyceraldehyde-3-phosphate dehydrogenase reaction), by reducing pyruvate to lactate.
- Lactate is the end product of glycolysis under anaerobic conditions (eg, in exercising muscle) or when the metabolic machinery is absent for the further oxidation of pyruvate (eg, in erythrocytes).
- Glycolysis is regulated by three enzymes catalyzing nonequilibrium reactions: hexokinase, phosphofructokinase, and pyruvate kinase.
- In erythrocytes, the first site in glycolysis for generation of ATP may be bypassed, leading to the formation of 2,3-bisphosphoglycerate, which is important in decreasing the affinity of hemoglobin for O_2.
- Pyruvate is oxidized to acetyl-CoA by a multienzyme complex, pyruvate dehydrogenase, which is

dependent on the vitamin-derived cofactor thiamin diphosphate.
- Conditions that involve an impairment of pyruvate metabolism frequently lead to lactic acidosis.

REFERENCES

Behal RH, Buxton DB, Robertson JG, Olson MS. Regulation of the pyruvate dehydrogenase multienzyme complex. Annual Review of Nutrition 1993;13:497.

Boiteux A, Hess B. Design of glycolysis. Philosophical Transactions of the Royal Society of London Series B 1981;293:5.

Fothergill-Gilmore LA. The evolution of the glycolytic pathway. Trends in Biochemical Sciences 1986;11:47.

Gladden LB. Lactate metabolism: A new paradigm for the third millennium. Journal of Physiology 2004;558:5.

Hers HG, Hue L. Gluconeogenesis and related aspects of glycolysis. Annual Review of Biochemistry 1983;52:617.

Kim J-W, Dang CV. Multifaceted roles of glycolytic enzymes. Trends in Biochemical Sciences 2005;30:142.

Robergs RA, Ghiasvand F, Parker D. Biochemistry of exercise-induced metabolic acidosis. American Journal of Physiology 2004;287:R502.

Wang YM, Eys J. Nutritional significance of fructose and sugar alcohols. Annual Review of Nutrition 1981;1:437.

Wasserman DH. Regulation of glucose fluxes during exercise in the postabsorptive state. Annual Review of Physiology 1995;57:191.

Metabolism of Glycogen

19

David A. Bender, PhD, & Peter A. Mayes, PhD, DSc

BIOMEDICAL IMPORTANCE

Glycogen is the major storage carbohydrate in animals, corresponding to starch in plants; it is a branched polymer of α-D-glucose (Figure 14–13). It occurs mainly in liver and muscle; although the liver content of glycogen is greater than that of muscle, because the muscle mass of the body is considerably greater than that of the liver, about three-quarters of total body glycogen is in muscle (Table 19–1).

Muscle glycogen provides a readily available source of glucose for glycolysis within the muscle itself. Liver glycogen functions to store and export glucose to maintain **blood glucose** between meals. After 12–18 hours of fasting, liver glycogen is almost totally depleted. Although muscle glycogen does not directly yield free glucose (because muscle lacks glucose 6-phosphatase), pyruvate formed by glycolysis in muscle can undergo transamination to alanine, which is exported from muscle and used for gluconeogenesis in the liver. **Glycogen storage diseases** are a group of inherited disorders characterized by deficient mobilization of glycogen or deposition of abnormal forms of glycogen, leading to muscle weakness; some glycogen storage diseases result in early death.

The highly branched structure of glycogen provides a large number of sites for glycogenolysis, permitting rapid release of glucose 1-phosphate for muscle activity. Endurance athletes require a slower, more sustained release of glucose 1-phosphate. The formation of branch points in glycogen is slower than the addition of glucose units to a linear chain, and some endurance athletes practice carbohydrate loading—exercise to exhaustion (when muscle glycogen in largely depleted) followed by a high carbohydrate meal, which results in rapid glycogen synthesis, with fewer branch points than normal.

GLYCOGENESIS OCCURS MAINLY IN MUSCLE & LIVER

The Pathway of Glycogen Biosynthesis Involves a Special Nucleotide of Glucose

As in glycolysis, glucose is phosphorylated to glucose 6-phosphate, catalyzed by **hexokinase** in muscle and **glucokinase** in liver (Figure 19–1). Glucose 6-phosphate is isomerized to glucose 1-phosphate by **phosphoglucomu-tase.** The enzyme itself is phosphorylated, and the phospho-group takes part in a reversible reaction in which glucose 1,6-bisphosphate is an intermediate. Next, glucose 1-phosphate reacts with uridine triphosphate (UTP) to form the active nucleotide **uridine diphosphate glucose (UDPGlc)** and pyrophosphate (Figure 19–2), catalyzed by **UDPGlc pyrophosphorylase.** The reaction proceeds in the direction of UDPGlc formation because **pyrophosphatase** catalyzes hydrolysis of pyrophosphate to 2 x phosphate, so removing one of the reaction products.

Glycogen synthase catalyzes the formation of a glycoside bond between C_1 of the glucose of UDPGlc and C_4 of a terminal glucose residue of glycogen, liberating uridine diphosphate (UDP). A preexisting glycogen molecule, or "glycogen primer," must be present to initiate this reaction. The glycogen primer may in turn be formed on a protein primer known as **glycogenin.** Glycogenin is a 37 kDa protein that is glucosylated on a specific tyrosine residue by UDPGlc. Further glucose residues are attached in the 1→4 position to form a short chain that is a substrate for glycogen synthase. In skeletal muscle, glycogenin remains attached in the center of the glycogen molecule (Figure 14–13); in liver the number of glycogen molecules is greater than the number of glycogenin molecules.

Branching Involves Detachment of Existing Glycogen Chains

The addition of a glucose residue to a preexisting glycogen chain, or "primer," occurs at the nonreducing, outer end of the molecule, so that the branches of the glycogen molecule become elongated as successive 1→4 linkages are formed (Figure 19–3). When the chain is at least 11 glucose residues long, **branching enzyme** transfers a part of the 1→4-chain (at least 6 glucose residues) to a neighboring chain to form a 1→6 linkage, establishing a **branch point.** The branches grow by further additions of 1→4-glucosyl units and further branching.

GLYCOGENOLYSIS IS NOT THE REVERSE OF GLYCOGENESIS, BUT IS A SEPARATE PATHWAY

Glycogen phosphorylase catalyzes the rate-limiting step in glycogenolysis by catalyzing the phosphoroylytic

159

Table 19–1. Storage of carbohydrate in a 70-kg human.

	Percentage of Tissue Weight	Tissue Weight	Body Content
Liver glycogen	5.0	1.8 kg	90 g
Muscle glycogen	0.7	35 kg	245 g
Extracellular glucose	0.1	10 L	10 g

cleavage (phosphorolysis; cf hydrolysis) of the 1→4 linkages of glycogen to yield glucose 1-phosphate (Figure 19–4). The terminal glucosyl residues from the outermost chains of the glycogen molecule are removed sequentially until approximately four glucose residues remain on either side of a 1→6 branch (Figure 19–4). Another enzyme (**α-[1 → 4] → α-[1 → 4] glucan transferase**) transfers a trisaccharide unit from one branch to the other, exposing the 1→6 branch point. **Hydrolysis** of the 1→6 linkages requires the **debranching enzyme;** glucan transferase and the debranching enzyme are probably both activities of a

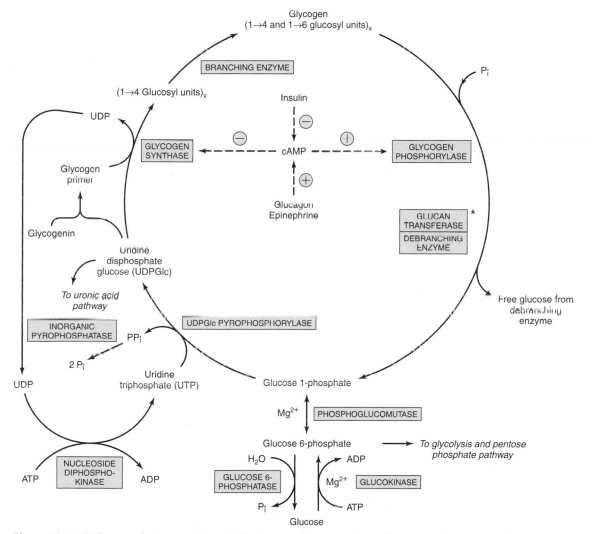

Figure 19–1. Pathways of glycogenesis and of glycogenolysis in the liver. ⊕, Stimulation; ⊖, inhibition. Insulin decreases the level of cAMP only after it has been raised by glucagon or epinephrine; ie, it antagonizes their action. Glucagon is active in heart muscle but not in skeletal muscle. At *: Glucan transferase and debranching enzyme appear to be two separate activities of the same enzyme.

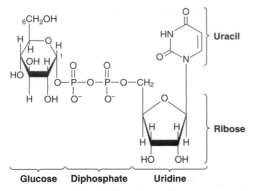

Figure 19–2. Uridine diphosphate glucose (UDPGlc).

single protein. Further phosphorylase action can then proceed. The combined action of phosphorylase and these other enzymes leads to the complete breakdown of glycogen. The reaction catalyzed by phosphogluco-mutase is reversible, so that glucose 6-phosphate can be formed from glucose 1-phosphate. In **liver** (and **kidney**), but not in muscle, **glucose 6-phosphatase** hydrolyzes glucose 6-phosphate, yielding glucose that is exported, leading to an increase in the blood glucose concentration.

CYCLIC AMP INTEGRATES THE REGULATION OF GLYCOGENOLYSIS & GLYCOGENESIS

The principal enzymes controlling glycogen metabolism—glycogen phosphorylase and glycogen synthase—are regulated by allosteric mechanisms and covalent modifications due to reversible phosphorylation and

dephosphorylation of enzyme protein in response to hormone action (Chapter 9).

Cyclic AMP (cAMP) (Figure 19–5) is formed from ATP by **adenylyl cyclase** at the inner surface of cell membranes and acts as an intracellular **second messenger** in response to hormones such as **epinephrine, norepinephrine,** and **glucagon.** cAMP is hydrolyzed by **phosphodiesterase,** so terminating hormone action; in liver insulin increases the activity of phosphodiesterase.

The Control of Phosphorylase Differs between Liver & Muscle

In the liver the role of glycogen is to provide free glucose for export to maintain the blood concentration of glucose; in muscle the role of glycogen is to provide a source of glucose 6-phosphate for glycolysis in response to the need for ATP for muscle contraction. In both tissues, the enzyme is activated by phosphorylation catalyzed by phosphorylase kinase (to yield phosphorylase a) and inactivated by dephosphorylation catalyzed by phosphoprotein phosphatase (to yield phosphorylase b), in response to hormonal and other signals.

Active phosphorylase a in both tissues is allosterically inhibited by ATP and glucose 6-phosphate; in liver, but not muscle, free glucose is also an inhibitor. Muscle phosphorylase differs from the liver isoenzyme in having a binding site for 5'AMP, which acts as an allosteric activator of the (inactive) dephosphorylated b-form of the enzyme. 5'AMP acts as a potent signal of the energy state of the muscle cell; it is formed as the concentration of ADP begins to increase (indicating the need for increased substrate metabolism to permit ATP formation), as a result of the reaction of adenylate kinase: $2 \times ADP \leftrightarrow ATP + 5'AMP$.

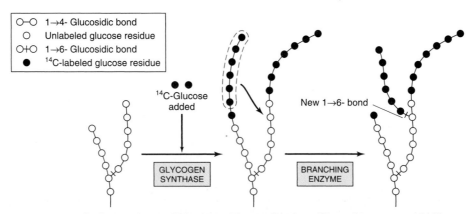

Figure 19–3. The biosynthesis of glycogen. The mechanism of branching as revealed by feeding ^{14}C-labeled glucose and examining liver glycogen at intervals.

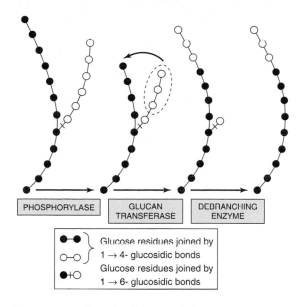

Figure 19–4. Steps in glycogenolysis.

cAMP Activates Phosphorylase

Phosphorylase kinase is activated in response to cAMP (Figure 19–6). Increasing the concentration of cAMP activates **cAMP-dependent protein kinase,** which catalyzes the phosphorylation by ATP of inactive **phosphorylase kinase b** to active **phosphorylase kinase a,** which in turn, phosphorylates phosphorylase b to phosphorylase a. In the liver, cAMP is formed in response to glucagon, which is secreted in response to falling blood glucose; muscle is insensitive to glucagon. In muscle, the signal for increased cAMP formation is the action of norepinephrine, which is secreted in response to fear or fright, when there is a need for increased glycogenolysis to permit rapid muscle activity.

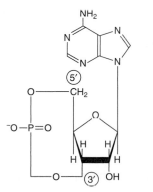

Figure 19–5. 3′,5′-Adenylic acid (cyclic AMP; cAMP).

Ca²⁺ Synchronizes the Activation of Phosphorylase with Muscle Contraction

Glycogenolysis in muscle increases several hundred-fold at the same time as the onset of contraction; the same signal (increased intracellular Ca^{2+} ion concentration) is responsible for initiation of both contraction and glycogenolysis. Muscle phosphorylase kinase, which activates glycogen phosphorylase, is a tetramer of four different subunits, α, β, γ, and δ. The α and β subunits contain serine residues that are phosphorylated by cAMP-dependent protein kinase. The δ subunit is identical to the Ca^{2+}-binding protein **calmodulin** (Chapter 42), and binds four Ca^{2+}. The binding of Ca^{2+} activates the catalytic site of the γ subunit even while the enzyme is in the dephosphorylated b state; the phosphorylated a form is only fully activated in the presence of Ca^{2+}.

Glycogenolysis in Liver Can Be cAMP-Independent

In the liver, there is a cAMP-independent activation of glycogenolysis in response to stimulation of α_1 **adrenergic** receptors by epinephrine and norepinephrine. This involves mobilization of Ca^{2+} from mitochondria into the cytosol, followed by the stimulation of a **Ca^{2+}/calmodulin-sensitive phosphorylase kinase.** cAMP-independent glycogenolysis is also caused by vasopressin, oxytocin, and angiotensin II acting through calcium or the phosphatidylinositol bisphosphate pathway (Figure 42–10).

Protein Phosphatase-1 Inactivates Phosphorylase

Both phosphorylase a and phosphorylase kinase a are dephosphorylated and inactivated by **protein phosphatase-1.** Protein phosphatase-1 is inhibited by a protein, **inhibitor-1,** which is active only after it has been phosphorylated by cAMP-dependent protein kinase. Thus, cAMP controls both the activation and inactivation of phosphorylase (Figure 19–6). **Insulin** reinforces this effect by inhibiting the activation of phosphorylase b. It does this indirectly by increasing uptake of glucose, leading to increased formation of glucose 6-phosphate, which is an inhibitor of phosphorylase kinase.

Glycogen Synthase & Phosphorylase Activity Are Reciprocally Regulated

Like phosphorylase, glycogen synthase exists in both phosphorylated or nonphosphorylated states; however, the effect of phosphorylation is the reverse of that seen in phosphorylase (Figure 19–7). Active **glycogen synthase a** is dephosphorylated and inactive **glycogen synthase b** is phosphorylated.

Six different protein kinases act on glycogen synthase. Two are Ca^{2+}/calmodulin-dependent (one of these is phos-

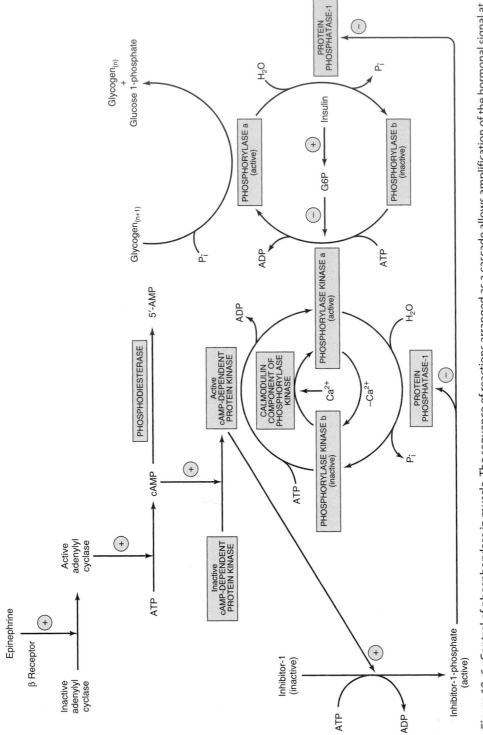

Figure 19–6. Control of phosphorylase in muscle. The sequence of reactions arranged as a cascade allows amplification of the hormonal signal at each step. (n = number of glucose residues; G6P = glucose 6-phosphate)

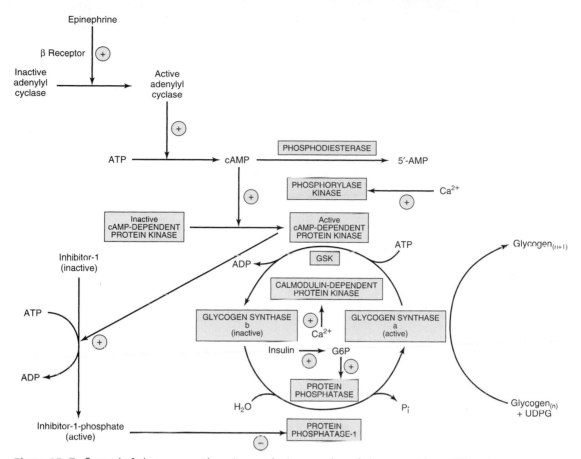

Figure 19–7. Control of glycogen synthase in muscle. (n = number of glucose residues; GSK = glycogen synthase kinase; G6P = glucose 6-phosphate)

phorylase kinase). Another kinase is cAMP dependent protein kinase, which allows cAMP-mediated hormonal action to inhibit glycogen synthesis synchronously with the activation of glycogenolysis. Insulin also promotes glycogenesis in muscle at the same time as inhibiting glycogenolysis by raising glucose 6-phosphate concentrations, which stimulates the dephosphorylation and activation of glycogen synthase. Dephosphorylation of glycogen synthase b is carried out by protein phosphatase-1, which is under the control of cAMP-dependent protein kinase.

REGULATION OF GLYCOGEN METABOLISM IS EFFECTED BY A BALANCE IN ACTIVITIES BETWEEN GLYCOGEN SYNTHASE & PHOSPHORYLASE

At the same time as phosphorylase is activated by a rise in concentration of cAMP (via phosphorylase kinase), glycogen synthase is converted to the inactive form; both effects are mediated via **cAMP-dependent protein kinase (Figure 19–8).** Thus, inhibition of glycogenolysis enhances net glycogenesis, and inhibition of glycogenesis enhances net glycogenolysis. Also, the dephosphorylation of phosphorylase a, phosphorylase kinase, and glycogen synthase b is catalyzed by a single enzyme with broad specificity—**protein phosphatase-1.** In turn, protein phosphatase-1 is inhibited by cAMP-dependent protein kinase via inhibitor-1. Thus, glycogenolysis can be terminated and glycogenesis can be stimulated synchronously, or vice versa, because both processes are dependent on the activity of cAMP-dependent protein kinase. Both phosphorylase kinase and glycogen synthase may be reversibly phosphorylated in more than one site by separate kinases and phosphatases. These secondary phosphorylations modify the sensitivity of the primary sites to phosphorylation and dephosphorylation (**multisite phosphorylation).** Also, they allow insulin, via glucose 6-phosphate elevation, to have effects that act reciprocally to those of cAMP (see Figures 19–6 and 19–7).

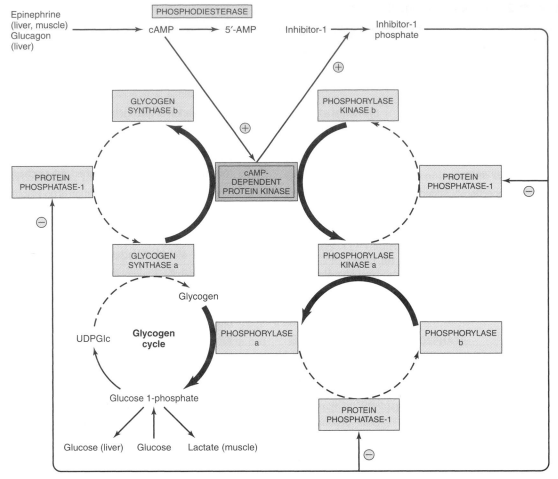

Figure 19–8. Coordinated control of glycogenolysis and glycogenesis by cAMP-dependent protein kinase. The reactions that lead to glycogenolysis as a result of an increase in cAMP concentrations are shown with bold arrows, and those that are inhibited by activation of protein phosphatase-1 are shown as dashed arrows. The reverse occurs when cAMP concentrations decrease as a result of phosphodiesterase activity, leading to glycogenesis.

CLINICAL ASPECTS

Glycogen Storage Diseases Are Inherited

"Glycogen storage disease" is a generic term to describe a group of inherited disorders characterized by deposition of an abnormal type or quantity of glycogen in tissues, or failure to mobilize glycogen. The principal diseases are summarized in Table 19–2.

SUMMARY

- Glycogen represents the principal storage form of carbohydrate in the body, mainly in the liver and muscle.

- In the liver, its major function is to provide glucose for extrahepatic tissues. In muscle, it serves mainly as a ready source of metabolic fuel for use in muscle.

- Glycogen is synthesized from glucose by the pathway of glycogenesis. It is broken down by a separate pathway, glycogenolysis. Glycogenolysis leads to glucose formation in liver and lactate formation in muscle owing to the respective presence or absence of glucose 6-phosphatase.

- Cyclic AMP integrates the regulation of glycogenolysis and glycogenesis by promoting the simultaneous activation of phosphorylase and inhibition of glycogen synthase. Insulin acts reciprocally by inhibiting glycogenolysis and stimulating glycogenesis.

Table 20–1. Regulatory and adaptive enzymes associated with carbohydrate metabolism.

	Activity in					
	Carbo-hydrate Feeding	Fasting and Diabetes	Inducer	Repressor	Activator	Inhibitor
Glycogenolysis, glycolysis, and pyruvate oxidation						
Glycogen synthase	↑	↓			Insulin, glucose 6-phosphate	Glucagon
Hexokinase						Glucose 6-phosphate
Glucokinase	↑	↓	Insulin	Glucagon		
Phosphofructokinase-1	↑	↓	Insulin	Glucagon	5'AMP, fructose 6-phosphate, fructose 2,6-bisphosphate, P_i	Citrate, ATP, glucagon
Pyruvate kinase	↑	↓	Insulin, fructose	Glucagon	Fructose 1,6-bisphosphate, insulin	ATP, alanine, glucagon, nor-epinephrine
Pyruvate dehydro-genase	↑	↓			CoA, NAD^+, insulin, ADP, pyruvate	Acetyl CoA, NADH, ATP (fatty acids, ketone bodies)
Gluconeogenesis						
Pyruvate carboxylase	↓	↑	Glucocorticoids, glucagon, epinephrine	Insulin	Acetyl CoA	ADP
Phosphoenolpyru-vate carboxykinase	↓	↑	Glucocorticoids, glucagon, epinephrine	Insulin	Glucagon?	
Glucose 6-phospha-tase	↓	↑	Glucocorticoids, glucagon, epinephrine	Insulin		

also affect the concentration of fructose 2,6-bisphosphate and therefore glycolysis and gluconeogenesis, as described below.

Allosteric Modification Is Instantaneous

In gluconeogenesis, pyruvate carboxylase, which catalyzes the synthesis of oxaloacetate from pyruvate, requires acetyl-CoA as an **allosteric activator.** The addition of acetyl-CoA results in a change in the tertiary structure of the protein, lowering the K_m for bicarbonate. This means that as acetyl-CoA is formed from pyruvate, it automatically ensures the provision of oxaloacetate and, therefore, its further oxidation in the citric acid cycle, by activating pyruvate carboxylase. The activation of pyruvate carboxylase and the reciprocal inhibition of pyruvate dehydrogenase by acetyl-CoA derived from the oxidation of fatty acids explain the action of fatty acid oxidation in sparing the oxidation of pyruvate and in stimulating gluconeogenesis.

The reciprocal relationship between these two enzymes alters the metabolic fate of pyruvate as the tissue changes from carbohydrate oxidation (glycolysis) to gluconeogenesis during the transition from the fed to fasting state (see Figure 20–1). A major role of fatty acid oxidation in promoting gluconeogenesis is to supply the ATP required.

Phosphofructokinase (phosphofructokinase-1) occupies a key position in regulating glycolysis and is also subject to feedback control. It is inhibited by citrate and by normal intracellular concentrations of ATP and is activated by 5'AMP. 5'AMP acts as an indicator of the energy status of the cell. The presence of **adenylyl kinase** in liver and many other tissues allows rapid equilibration of the reaction

$$2ADP \leftrightarrow ATP + 5'AMP$$

Thus, when ATP is used in energy-requiring processes resulting in formation of ADP, [AMP] increases. A rel-

atively small decrease in [ATP] causes a several-fold increase in [AMP], so that [AMP] acts as a metabolic amplifier of a small change in [ATP], and hence a sensitive signal of the energy state of the cell. The activity of phosphofructokinase-1 is thus regulated in response to the energy status of the cell to control the quantity of carbohydrate undergoing glycolysis prior to its entry into the citric acid cycle. Simultaneously, AMP activates phosphorylase, increasing glycogenolysis. A consequence of the inhibition of phosphofructokinase-1 is an accumulation of glucose 6-phosphate, which in turn inhibits further uptake of glucose in extrahepatic tissues by inhibition of hexokinase.

Fructose 2,6-Bisphosphate Plays a Unique Role in the Regulation of Glycolysis & Gluconeogenesis in Liver

The most potent positive allosteric activator of phosphofructokinase-1 and inhibitor of fructose 1,6-bisphosphatase in liver is **fructose 2,6-bisphosphate.** It relieves inhibition of phosphofructokinase-1 by ATP and increases the affinity for fructose 6-phosphate. It inhibits fructose 1,6-bisphosphatase by increasing the K_m for fructose 1,6-bisphosphate. Its concentration is under both substrate (allosteric) and hormonal control (covalent modification) (Figure 20–3).

Fructose 2,6-bisphosphate is formed by phosphorylation of fructose 6-phosphate by **phosphofructokinase-2.** The same enzyme protein is also responsible for its breakdown, since it has **fructose 2,6-bisphosphatase** activity. This **bifunctional enzyme** is under the allosteric control of fructose 6-phosphate, which stimulates the kinase and inhibits the phosphatase. Hence, when there is an abundant supply of glucose, the concentration of fructose 2,6-bisphosphate increases, stimulating glycolysis by activating phosphofructokinase-1 and inhibiting fructose 1,6-bisphosphatase. In the fasting state, glucagon stimulates the production of cAMP, activating cAMP-dependent protein kinase, which in turn inactivates phosphofructokinase-2 and activates fructose 2,6-bisphosphatase by phosphorylation. Hence, gluconeogenesis is stimulated by a decrease in the concentration of fructose 2,6-bisphosphate, which inactivates phosphofructokinase-1 and relieves the inhibition of fructose 1,6-bisphosphatase.

Substrate (Futile) Cycles Allow Fine Tuning & Rapid Response

The control points in glycolysis and glycogen metabolism involve a cycle of phosphorylation and dephosphorylation catalyzed by glucokinase and glucose 6-phosphatase; phosphofructokinase-1 and fructose 1,6-bisphosphatase; pyruvate kinase, pyruvate carboxylase, and phosphoenolpyruvate carboxykinase; and glycogen synthase and phosphorylase. It would seem obvious

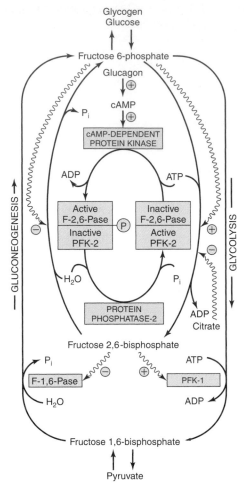

Figure 20–3. Control of glycolysis and gluconeogenesis in the liver by fructose 2,6-bisphosphate and the bifunctional enzyme PFK-2/F-2,6-Pase (6-phospho-fructo-2-kinase/fructose 2,6-bisphosphatase). (PFK-1, phosphofructokinase-1 [6-phosphofructo-1-kinase]; F-1,6-Pase, fructose 1,6-bisphosphatase. Arrows with wavy shafts indicate allosteric effects.)

that these opposing enzymes are regulated in such a way that when those involved in glycolysis are active, those involved in gluconeogenesis are inactive, since otherwise there would be cycling between phosphorylated and nonphosphorylated intermediates, with net hydrolysis of ATP. While this is so, in muscle, both phosphofructokinase and fructose 1,6-bisphosphatase have some activity at all times, so that there is indeed some measure of (wasteful) substrate cycling. This permits the very rapid increase in the rate of glycolysis necessary for muscle contraction. At rest the rate of phosphofructokinase activity is some tenfold higher

than that of fructose 1,6-bisphosphatase; in anticipation of muscle contraction, the activity of both enzymes increases, fructose 1,6-bisphosphatase ten times more than phosphofructokinase, maintaining the same net rate of glycolysis. At the start of muscle contraction, the activity of phosphofructokinase increases further, and that of fructose 1,6-bisphosphatase falls, so increasing the net rate of glycolysis (and hence ATP formation) as much as a thousandfold.

THE CONCENTRATION OF BLOOD GLUCOSE IS REGULATED WITHIN NARROW LIMITS

In the postabsorptive state, the concentration of blood glucose in most mammals is maintained between 4.5–5.5 mmol/L. After the ingestion of a carbohydrate meal, it may rise to 6.5–7.2 mmol/L, and in starvation, it may fall to 3.3–3.9 mmol/L. A sudden decrease in blood glucose (eg, in response to insulin overdose) causes convulsions, because of the dependence of the brain on a supply of glucose. However, much lower concentrations can be tolerated if hypoglycemia develops slowly enough for adaptation to occur. The blood glucose level in birds is considerably higher (14.0 mmol/L) and in ruminants considerably lower (approximately 2.2 mmol/L in sheep and 3.3 mmol/L in cattle). These lower normal levels appear to be associated with the fact that ruminants ferment virtually all dietary

carbohydrate to short-chain fatty acids, and these largely replace glucose as the main metabolic fuel of the tissues in the fed state.

BLOOD GLUCOSE IS DERIVED FROM THE DIET, GLUCONEOGENESIS, & GLYCOGENOLYSIS

The digestible dietary carbohydrates yield glucose, galactose, and fructose that are transported to the liver via the **hepatic portal vein.** Galactose and fructose are readily converted to glucose in the liver (Chapter 21).

Glucose is formed from two groups of compounds that undergo gluconeogenesis (see Figures 17–4 and 20–1): (1) those which involve a direct net conversion to glucose, including most **amino acids** and **propionate;** and (2) those which are the products of the metabolism of glucose in tissues. Thus **lactate,** formed by glycolysis in skeletal muscle and erythrocytes, is transported to the liver and kidney where it reforms glucose, which again becomes available via the circulation for oxidation in the tissues. This process is known as the **Cori cycle,** or the **lactic acid cycle** (Figure 20–4).

In the fasting state, there is a considerable output of alanine from skeletal muscle, far in excess of its concentration in the muscle proteins that are being catabolized. It is formed by transamination of pyruvate produced by glycolysis of muscle glycogen, and is exported to the liver, where, after transamination back to pyru-

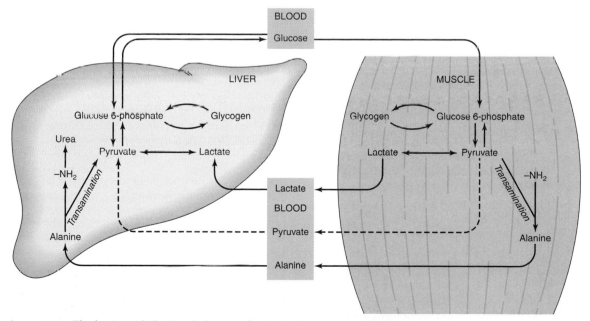

Figure 20–4. The lactic acid (Cori) and glucose-alanine cycles.

Table 20–2. Major glucose transporters.

	Tissue Location	Functions
Facilitative bidirectional transporters		
GLUT 1	Brain, kidney, colon, placenta, erythrocytes	Glucose uptake
GLUT 2	Liver, pancreatic β-cell, small intestine, kidney	Rapid uptake or release of glucose
GLUT 3	Brain, kidney, placenta	Glucose uptake
GLUT 4	Heart and skeletal muscle, adipose tissue	Insulin-stimulated glucose uptake
GLUT 5	Small intestine	Absorption of glucose
Sodium-dependent unidirectional transporter		
SGLT 1	Small intestine and kidney	Active uptake of glucose against a concentration gradient

vate, it is a substrate for gluconeogenesis. This **glucose-alanine cycle** (see Figure 20–4) thus provides an indirect way of utilizing muscle glycogen to maintain blood glucose in the fasting state. The ATP required for the hepatic synthesis of glucose from pyruvate is derived from the oxidation of fatty acids.

Glucose is also formed from liver glycogen by glycogenolysis (Chapter 19).

Metabolic & Hormonal Mechanisms Regulate the Concentration of Blood Glucose

The maintenance of stable levels of glucose in the blood is one of the most finely regulated of all homeostatic mechanisms, involving the liver, extrahepatic tissues, and several hormones. Liver cells are freely permeable to glucose (via the GLUT 2 transporter), whereas cells of extrahepatic tissues (apart from pancreatic β-islets) are relatively impermeable, and their glucose transporters are regulated by insulin. As a result, uptake from the bloodstream is the rate-limiting step in the utilization of glucose in extrahepatic tissues. The role of various glucose transporter proteins found in cell membranes is shown in Table 20–2.

Glucokinase Is Important in Regulating Blood Glucose after a Meal

Hexokinase has a low K_m for glucose, and in the liver is saturated and acting at a constant rate under all normal conditions. Glucokinase has a considerably higher K_m (lower affinity) for glucose, so that its activity increases with increases in the concentration of glucose in the hepatic portal vein (Figure 20–5). It promotes hepatic uptake of large amounts of glucose after a carbohydrate meal. It is absent from the liver of ruminants, which have little glucose entering the portal circulation from the intestines.

At normal systemic-blood glucose concentrations (4.5–5.5 mmol/L), the liver is a net producer of glu-

cose. However, as the glucose level rises, the output of glucose ceases, and there is a net uptake.

Insulin Plays a Central Role in Regulating Blood Glucose

In addition to the direct effects of hyperglycemia in enhancing the uptake of glucose into the liver, the hormone insulin plays a central role in regulating blood glucose. It is produced by the β-cells of the islets of Langerhans in the pancreas in response to hyperglycemia. The β-islet cells are freely permeable to glucose via the GLUT 2 transporter, and the glucose is phosphorylated by glucokinase. Therefore, increasing blood glucose increases metabolic flux through glycolysis, the citric acid cycle, and the generation of ATP. The increase in [ATP] inhibits ATP-sensitive K^+ channels, causing depolarization of

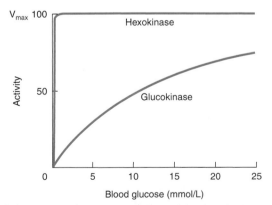

Figure 20–5. Variation in glucose phosphorylating activity of hexokinase and glucokinase with increasing blood glucose concentration. The K_m for glucose of hexokinase is 0.05 mmol/L and of glucokinase is 10 mmol/L.

Table 20–3. Tissue responses to insulin and glucagon.

	Liver	Adipose Tissue	Muscle
Increased by insulin	Fatty acid synthesis Glycogen synthesis Protein synthesis	Glucose uptake Fatty acid synthesis	Glucose uptake Glycogen synthesis Protein synthesis
Decreased by insulin	Ketogenesis Gluconeogenesis	Lipolysis	
Increased by glucagon	Glycogenolysis Gluconeogenesis Ketogenesis	Lipolysis	

the cell membrane, which increases Ca^{2+} influx via voltage-sensitive Ca^{2+} channels, stimulating exocytosis of insulin. Thus, the concentration of insulin in the blood parallels that of the blood glucose. Other substances causing release of insulin from the pancreas include amino acids, free fatty acids, ketone bodies, glucagon, secretin, and the sulfonylurea drugs tolbutamide and glyburide. These drugs are used to stimulate insulin secretion in type 2 diabetes mellitus (NIDDM, non–insulin-dependent diabetes mellitus); they act by inhibiting the ATP-sensitive K^+ channels. Epinephrine and norepinephrine block the release of insulin. Insulin lowers blood glucose immediately by enhancing glucose transport into adipose tissue and muscle by recruitment of glucose transporters (GLUT 4) from the interior of the cell to the plasma membrane. Although it does not affect glucose uptake into the liver directly, insulin does enhance long-term uptake as a result of its actions on the enzymes controlling glycolysis, glycogenesis, and gluconeogenesis. (Chapter 19 and Table 20–1).

Glucagon Opposes the Actions of Insulin

Glucagon is the hormone produced by the α-cells of the pancreatic islets. Its secretion is stimulated by hypoglycemia. In the liver it stimulates glycogenolysis by activating phosphorylase. Unlike epinephrine, glucagon does not have an effect on muscle phosphorylase. Glucagon also enhances gluconeogenesis from amino acids and lactate. In all these actions, glucagon acts via generation of cAMP (see Table 20–1). Both hepatic glycogenolysis and gluconeogenesis contribute to the **hyperglycemic effect** of glucagon, whose actions oppose those of insulin. Most of the endogenous glucagon (and insulin) is cleared from the circulation by the liver (Table 20–3).

Other Hormones Affect Blood Glucose

The **anterior pituitary gland** secretes hormones that tend to elevate the blood glucose and therefore antagonize the action of insulin. These are growth hormone, ACTH (corticotropin), and possibly other "diabetogenic" hormones. Growth hormone secretion is stimulated by hypoglycemia; it decreases glucose uptake in muscle. Some of this effect may be indirect, since it stimulates mobilization of free fatty acids from adipose tissue, which themselves inhibit glucose utilization. The **glucocorticoids** (11-oxysteroids) are secreted by the adrenal cortex, and are also synthesized in an unregulated manner in adipose tissue. They act to increase gluconeogenesis as a result of enhanced hepatic catabolism of amino acids, due to induction of aminotransferases (and other enzymes such as tryptophan dioxygenase) and key enzymes of gluconeogenesis. In addition, glucocorticoids inhibit the utilization of glucose in extrahepatic tissues. In all these actions, glucocorticoids act in a manner antagonistic to insulin. A number of **cytokines** secreted by macrophages infiltrating adipose tissue also have insulin-antagonistic actions; together with glucocorticoids secreted by adipose tissue, this explains the insulin resistance that commonly occurs in obese people.

Epinephrine is secreted by the adrenal medulla as a result of stressful stimuli (fear, excitement, hemorrhage, hypoxia, hypoglycemia, etc) and leads to glycogenolysis in liver and muscle owing to stimulation of phosphorylase via generation of cAMP. In muscle, glycogenolysis results in increased glycolysis, whereas in liver it results in the release of glucose into the bloodstream.

FURTHER CLINICAL ASPECTS

Glucosuria Occurs When the Renal Threshold for Glucose Is Exceeded

When the blood glucose rises to relatively high levels, the kidney also exerts a regulatory effect. Glucose is continuously filtered by the glomeruli, but is normally completely reabsorbed in the renal tubules by active transport. The capacity of the tubular system to reabsorb glucose is limited to a rate of about 350 mg/min, and in hyperglycemia (as occurs in poorly controlled diabetes mellitus), the glomerular filtrate may contain

more glucose than can be reabsorbed, resulting in **glucosuria.** Glucosuria occurs when the venous blood glucose concentration exceeds 9.5–10.0 mmol/L; this is termed the **renal threshold** for glucose.

Hypoglycemia May Occur During Pregnancy & in the Neonate

During pregnancy, fetal glucose consumption increases and there is a risk of maternal and possibly fetal hypoglycemia, particularly if there are long intervals between meals or at night. Furthermore, premature and low-birth-weight babies are more susceptible to hypoglycemia, since they have little adipose tissue to provide alternative fuels such as free fatty acids or ketone bodies during the transition from fetal dependency to the free-living state. The enzymes of gluconeogenesis may not be completely functional at this time, and gluconeogenesis is anyway dependent on a supply of free fatty acids for energy. Little glycerol, which would normally be released from adipose tissue, is available for gluconeogenesis.

The Body's Ability to Utilize Glucose May Be Ascertained by Measuring Glucose Tolerance

Glucose tolerance is the ability to regulate the blood glucose concentration after the administration of a test dose of glucose (normally 1 g/kg body weight) (Figure 20–6). **Diabetes mellitus** (type 1, or insulin-dependent diabetes mellitus; IDDM) is characterized by decreased glucose tolerance as a result of decreased secretion of insulin as a result of progressive destruction of pancreatic β-islet cells. Glucose tolerance is also impaired in type 2 diabetes mellitus (NIDDM) as a result of impaired sensitivity of tissues to insulin action. Insulin resistance associated with obesity (and especially abdominal obesity) leading to the development of hyperlipidemia, then atherosclerosis and coronary heart disease, as well as overt diabetes, is known as the **metabolic syndrome.** Impaired glucose tolerance also occurs in conditions where the liver is damaged, in some infections, and in response to some drugs, as well as in conditions that lead to hyperactivity of the pituitary or adrenal cortex because of the antagonism of the hormones secreted by these glands to the action of insulin.

Administration of insulin (as in the treatment of diabetes mellitus) lowers the blood glucose concentration and increases its utilization and storage in the liver and muscle as glycogen. An excess of insulin may cause **hypoglycemia,** resulting in convulsions and even in death unless glucose is administered promptly. Increased tolerance to glucose is observed in pituitary or adrenocortical insufficiency, attributable to a decrease in the antagonism to insulin by the hormones normally secreted by these glands.

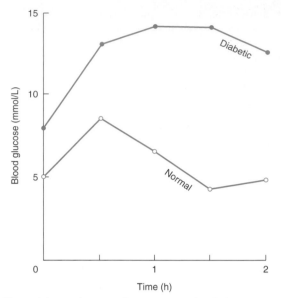

Figure 20–6. Glucose tolerance test. Blood glucose curves of a normal and a diabetic person after oral administration of 1 g of glucose/kg body weight. Note the initial raised concentration in the fasting diabetic. A criterion of normality is the return of the curve to the initial value within 2 hours.

The Energy Cost of Gluconeogenesis Explains Why Very Low Carbohydrate Diets Promote Weight Loss

Very low carbohydrate diets, providing only 20 g per day of carbohydrate or less (compared with a desirable intake of 100–120 g/day), but permitting unlimited consumption of fat and protein, have been promoted as an effective regime for weight loss, although such diets are counter to all advice on a prudent diet for health. Since there is a continual demand for glucose, there will be a considerable amount of gluconeogenesis from amino acids; the associated high ATP cost must then be met by oxidation of fatty acids.

SUMMARY

- Gluconeogenesis is the process of synthesizing glucose or glycogen from noncarbohydrate precursors. It is of particular importance when carbohydrate is not available from the diet. Significant substrates are amino acids, lactate, glycerol, and propionate.
- The pathway of gluconeogenesis in the liver and kidney utilizes those reactions in glycolysis that are reversible plus four additional reactions that circumvent the irreversible nonequilibrium reactions.

- Since glycolysis and gluconeogenesis share the same pathway but operate in opposite directions, their activities must be regulated reciprocally.
- The liver regulates the blood glucose after a meal because it contains the high-K_m glucokinase that promotes increased hepatic utilization of glucose.
- Insulin is secreted as a direct response to hyperglycemia; it stimulates the liver to store glucose as glycogen and facilitates uptake of glucose into extrahepatic tissues.
- Glucagon is secreted as a response to hypoglycemia and activates both glycogenolysis and gluconeogenesis in the liver, causing release of glucose into the blood.

REFERENCES

Brosnan JT: Comments on metabolic needs for glucose and the role of gluconeogenesis. European Journal of Clinical Nutrition 1999;53 Suppl 1:S107.

Klover PJ, Mooney RA: Hepatocytes: Critical for glucose homeostasis. International Journal of Biochemistry and Cell Biology 2004;36:753.

Nordlie RC, Foster JD, Lange AJ: Regulation of glucose production by the liver. Annual Review of Nutrition 1999;19:379.

Pilkis SJ, Claus TH: Hepatic gluconeogenesis/glycolysis: Regulation and structure/function relationships of substrate cycle enzymes. Annual Review of Nutrition. 1991; 11:465.

Pilkis SJ, Granner DK: Molecular physiology of the regulation of hepatic gluconeogenesis and glycolysis. Annual Review of Physiology. 1992;54:885.

Postic C, Shiota M, Magnuson MA: Cell-specific roles of glucokinase in glucose homeostasis. Recent Progress in Hormone Research 2001;56:195.

Schuit FC, Huypens P, Heimberg H, Pipeleers DG: Glucose sensing in pancreatic beta-cells: A model for the study of other glucose-regulated cells in gut, pancreas, and hypothalamus. Diabetes 2001;50:1.

The Pentose Phosphate Pathway & Other Pathways of Hexose Metabolism

21

David A Bender, PhD, & Peter A. Mayes, PhD, DSc

BIOMEDICAL IMPORTANCE

The pentose phosphate pathway is an alternative route for the metabolism of glucose. It does not lead to formation of ATP but has two major functions: (1) The formation of **NADPH** for synthesis of fatty acids and steroids, and (2) the synthesis of **ribose** for nucleotide and nucleic acid formation. Glucose, fructose, and galactose are the main hexoses absorbed from the gastrointestinal tract, derived from dietary starch, sucrose, and lactose, respectively. Fructose and galactose can be converted to glucose, mainly in the liver.

Genetic deficiency of **glucose 6-phosphate dehydrogenase,** the first enzyme of the pentose phosphate pathway, is a major cause of hemolysis of red blood cells, resulting in **hemolytic anemia,** affecting some 100 million persons worldwide. Glucuronic acid is synthesized from glucose via the **uronic acid pathway,** of minor quantitative importance, but of major significance for the excretion of metabolites and foreign chemicals (xenobiotics) as **glucuronides.** A deficiency in the pathway leads to the condition of **essential pentosuria.** The lack of one enzyme of the pathway (gulonolactone oxidase) in primates and some other animals explains why **ascorbic acid** (vitamin C) is a dietary requirement for humans but not most other mammals. Deficiencies in the enzymes of fructose and galactose metabolism lead to metabolic diseases such as **essential fructosuria** and the **galactosemias.**

THE PENTOSE PHOSPHATE PATHWAY GENERATES NADPH & RIBOSE PHOSPHATE

The pentose phosphate pathway (hexose monophosphate shunt) is a more complex pathway than glycolysis (Figure 21–1). Three molecules of glucose 6-phosphate give rise to three molecules of CO_2 and three five-carbon sugars. These are rearranged to regenerate two molecules of glucose 6-phosphate and one molecule of the glycolytic intermediate, glyceraldehyde 3-phosphate.

Since two molecules of glyceraldehyde 3-phosphate can regenerate glucose 6-phosphate, the pathway can account for the complete oxidation of glucose.

REACTIONS OF THE PENTOSE PHOSPHATE PATHWAY OCCUR IN THE CYTOSOL

Like glycolysis, the enzymes of the pentose phosphate pathway are cytosolic. Unlike glycolysis, oxidation is achieved by dehydrogenation using **NADP+,** not **NAD+,** as the hydrogen acceptor. The sequence of reactions of the pathway may be divided into two phases: an **oxidative nonreversible phase** and a **nonoxidative reversible phase.** In the first phase, glucose 6-phosphate undergoes dehydrogenation and decarboxylation to yield a pentose, ribulose 5-phosphate. In the second phase, ribulose 5-phosphate is converted back to glucose 6-phosphate by a series of reactions involving mainly two enzymes: **transketolase** and **transaldolase** (see Figure 21–1).

The Oxidative Phase Generates NADPH

Dehydrogenation of glucose 6-phosphate to 6-phosphogluconate occurs via the formation of 6-phosphogluconolactone catalyzed by **glucose 6-phosphate dehydrogenase,** an NADP-dependent enzyme (Figures 21–1 and 21–2). The hydrolysis of 6-phosphogluconolactone is accomplished by the enzyme **gluconolactone hydrolase.** A second oxidative step is catalyzed by **6-phosphogluconate dehydrogenase,** which also requires NADP+ as hydrogen acceptor. Decarboxylation follows with the formation of the ketopentose ribulose 5-phosphate.

The Nonoxidative Phase Generates Ribose Precursors

Ribulose 5-phosphate is the substrate for two enzymes. **Ribulose 5-phosphate 3-epimerase** alters the configuration about carbon 3, forming the epimer xylulose

177

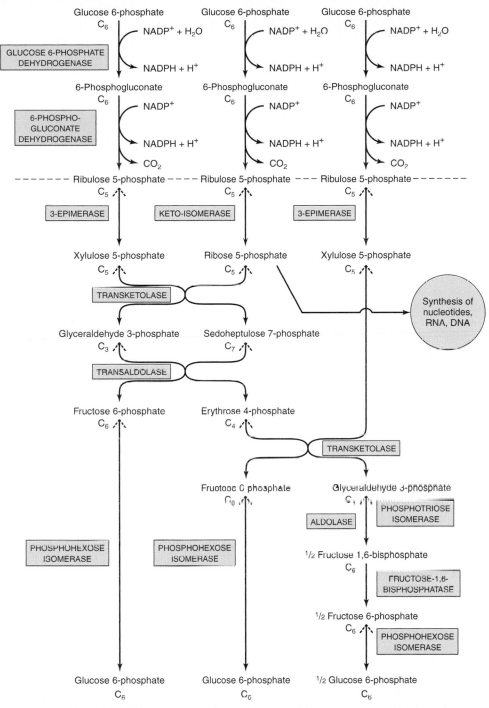

Figure 21–1. Flow chart of pentose phosphate pathway and its connections with the pathway of glycolysis. The full pathway, as indicated, consists of three interconnected cycles in which glucose 6-phosphate is both substrate and end-product. The reactions above the broken line are nonreversible, whereas all reactions under that line are freely reversible apart from that catalyzed by fructose 1,6-bisphosphatase.

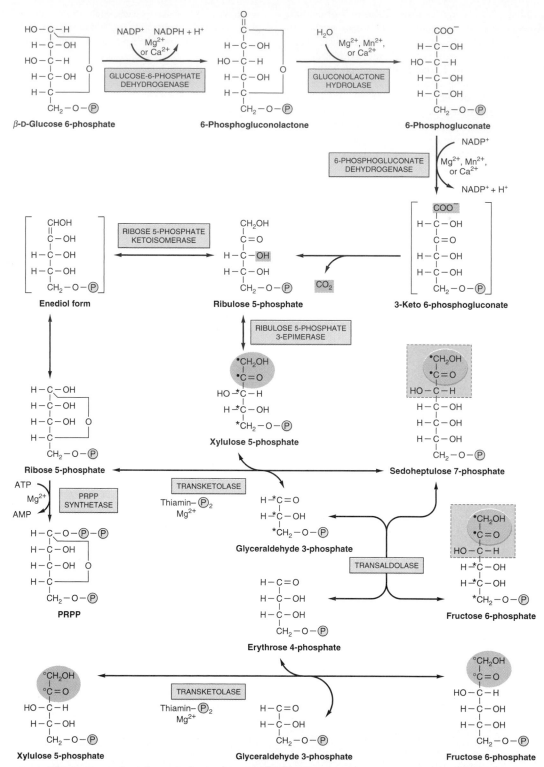

Figure 21–2. The pentose phosphate pathway. (P, —PO$_3^{2-}$; PRPP, 5-phosphoribosyl 1-pyrophosphate.)

5-phosphate, also a ketopentose. **Ribose 5-phosphate ketoisomerase** converts ribulose 5-phosphate to the corresponding aldopentose, ribose 5-phosphate, which is the precursor of the ribose required for nucleotide and nucleic acid synthesis. **Transketolase** transfers the two-carbon unit comprising carbons 1 and 2 of a ketose onto the aldehyde carbon of an aldose sugar. It therefore effects the conversion of a ketose sugar into an aldose with two carbons less and an aldose sugar into a ketose with two carbons more. The reaction requires Mg^{2+} and **thiamin diphosphate** (vitamin B_1) as coenzyme. The two-carbon moiety transferred is probably glycolaldehyde bound to thiamin diphosphate. Thus, transketolase catalyzes the transfer of the two-carbon unit from xylulose 5-phosphate to ribose 5-phosphate, producing the seven-carbon ketose sedoheptulose 7-phosphate and the aldose glyceraldehyde 3-phosphate. These two products then undergo transaldolation. **Transaldolase** catalyzes the transfer of a three-carbon dihydroxyacetone moiety (carbons 1–3) from the ketose sedoheptulose 7-phosphate onto the aldose glyceraldehyde 3-phosphate to form the ketose fructose 6-phosphate and the four-carbon aldose erythrose 4-phosphate. In a further reaction catalyzed by **transketolase,** xylulose 5-phosphate serves as a donor of glycolaldehyde. In this case erythrose 4-phosphate is the acceptor, and the products of the reaction are fructose 6-phosphate and glyceraldehyde 3-phosphate.

In order to oxidize glucose completely to CO_2 via the pentose phosphate pathway, there must be enzymes present in the tissue to convert glyceraldehyde 3-phosphate to glucose 6-phosphate. This involves reversal of glycolysis and the gluconeogenic enzyme **fructose 1,6-bisphosphatase.** In tissues that lack this enzyme, glyceraldehyde 3-phosphate follows the normal pathway of glycolysis to pyruvate.

The Two Major Pathways for the Catabolism of Glucose Have Little in Common

Although glucose 6-phosphate is common to both pathways, the pentose phosphate pathway is markedly different from glycolysis. Oxidation utilizes NADP rather than NAD, and CO_2, which is not produced in glycolysis, is a characteristic product. No ATP is generated in the pentose phosphate pathway, whereas it is a major product of glycolysis.

Reducing Equivalents Are Generated in Those Tissues Specializing in Reductive Syntheses

The pentose phosphate pathway is active in liver, adipose tissue, adrenal cortex, thyroid, erythrocytes, testis, and lactating mammary gland. Its activity is low in nonlactating mammary gland and skeletal muscle. Those tissues in which the pathway is active use NADPH in reductive

syntheses, eg, of fatty acids, steroids, amino acids via glutamate dehydrogenase, and reduced glutathione. The synthesis of glucose 6-phosphate dehydrogenase and 6-phosphogluconate dehydrogenase may also be induced by insulin in the fed state, when lipogenesis increases.

Ribose Can Be Synthesized in Virtually All Tissues

Little or no ribose circulates in the bloodstream, so tissues have to synthesize the ribose they require for nucleotide and nucleic acid synthesis using the pentose phosphate pathway (see Figure 21–2). It is not necessary to have a completely functioning pentose phosphate pathway for a tissue to synthesize ribose 5-phosphate. Muscle has only low activity of glucose 6-phosphate dehydrogenase and 6-phosphogluconate dehydrogenase, but, like most other tissues, it is capable of synthesizing ribose 5-phosphate by reversal of the nonoxidative phase of the pentose phosphate pathway utilizing fructose 6-phosphate.

THE PENTOSE PHOSPHATE PATHWAY & GLUTATHIONE PEROXIDASE PROTECT ERYTHROCYTES AGAINST HEMOLYSIS

In red blood cells the pentose phosphate pathway provides NADPH for the reduction of oxidized glutathione catalyzed by **glutathione reductase,** a flavoprotein containing FAD. Reduced glutathione removes H_2O_2 in a reaction catalyzed by **glutathione peroxidase,** an enzyme that contains the **selenium** analogue of cysteine (selenocysteine) at the active site (Figure 21–3). The reaction is important, since accumulation of H_2O_2 may decrease the life span of the erythrocyte by causing oxidative damage to the cell membrane, leading to hemolysis.

GLUCURONATE, A PRECURSOR OF PROTEOGLYCANS & CONJUGATED GLUCURONIDES, IS A PRODUCT OF THE URONIC ACID PATHWAY

In liver, the **uronic acid pathway** catalyzes the conversion of glucose to glucuronic acid, ascorbic acid (except in human beings and other species for which ascorbate is a vitamin), and pentoses (Figure 21–4). It is also an alternative oxidative pathway for glucose that, like the pentose phosphate pathway, does not lead to the formation of ATP. Glucose 6-phosphate is isomerized to glucose 1-phosphate, which then reacts with uridine triphosphate (UTP) to form uridine diphosphate glucose (UDPGlc) in a reaction catalyzed by **UDPGlc pyrophosphorylase,** as occurs in glycogen synthesis (Chapter 19). UDPGlc is oxidized at carbon 6 by NAD-dependent **UDPGlc dehydrogenase** in a two-step reaction to yield UDP-glucuronate.

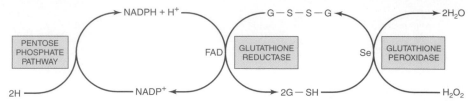

Figure 21–3. Role of the pentose phosphate pathway in the glutathione peroxidase reaction of erythrocytes. (G-S-S-G, oxidized glutathione; G-SH, reduced glutathione; Se, selenium-containing enzyme.)

UDP-glucuronate is the source of glucuronate for reactions involving its incorporation into proteoglycans or for reactions of substrates such as steroid hormones, bilirubin, and a number of drugs that are excreted in urine or bile as glucuronide conjugates (Figure 31–13).

Glucuronate is reduced to L-gulonate, the direct precursor of **ascorbate** in those animals capable of synthesizing this vitamin, in an NADPH-dependent reaction. In humans and other primates, as well as guinea pigs, bats, and some birds and fishes, ascorbic acid cannot be synthesized because of the absence of L-**gulonolactone oxidase.** L-Gulonate is oxidized to 3-keto-L-gulonate, which is then decarboxylated to L-xylulose. L-Xylulose is converted to the D isomer by an NADPH-dependent reduction to xylitol, followed by oxidation in an NAD-dependent reaction to D-xylulose. After conversion to D-xylulose 5-phosphate, it is metabolized via the pentose phosphate pathway.

INGESTION OF LARGE QUANTITIES OF FRUCTOSE HAS PROFOUND METABOLIC CONSEQUENCES

Diets high in sucrose or in high-fructose syrups (HFS) used in manufactured foods and beverages lead to large amounts of fructose (and glucose) entering the hepatic portal vein.

Fructose undergoes more rapid glycolysis in the liver than does glucose, because it bypasses the regulatory step catalyzed by phosphofructokinase (Figure 21–5). This allows fructose to flood the pathways in the liver, leading to enhanced fatty acid synthesis, increased esterification of fatty acids, and increased VLDL secretion, which may raise serum triacylglycerols and ultimately raise LDL cholesterol concentrations. A specific kinase, **fructokinase,** in liver, kidney, and intestine, catalyzes the phosphorylation of fructose to fructose 1-phosphate. This enzyme does not act on glucose, and, unlike glucokinase, its activity is not affected by fasting or by insulin, which may explain why fructose is cleared from the blood of diabetic patients at a normal rate. Fructose 1-phosphate is cleaved to D-glyceraldehyde and dihydroxyacetone phosphate by **aldolase B,** an enzyme found in the liver, which also functions in glycolysis in the liver by cleaving fructose 1,6-bisphosphate.

D-Glyceraldehyde enters glycolysis via phosphorylation to glyceraldehyde 3-phosphate catalyzed by **triokinase.** The two triose phosphates, dihydroxyacetone phosphate and glyceraldehyde 3-phosphate, may be degraded by glycolysis or may be substrates for aldolase and hence gluconeogenesis, which is the fate of much of the fructose metabolized in the liver.

In extrahepatic tissues, hexokinase catalyzes the phosphorylation of most hexose sugars, including fructose, but glucose inhibits the phosphorylation of fructose, since it is a better substrate for hexokinase. Nevertheless, some fructose can be metabolized in adipose tissue and muscle. Fructose is found in seminal plasma and in the fetal circulation of ungulates and whales. Aldose reductase is found in the placenta of the ewe and is responsible for the secretion of sorbitol into the fetal blood. The presence of sorbitol dehydrogenase in the liver, including the fetal liver, is responsible for the conversion of sorbitol into fructose. This pathway is also responsible for the occurrence of fructose in seminal fluid.

GALACTOSE IS NEEDED FOR THE SYNTHESIS OF LACTOSE, GLYCOLIPIDS, PROTEOGLYCANS, & GLYCOPROTEINS

Galactose is derived from intestinal hydrolysis of the disaccharide **lactose,** the sugar of milk. It is readily converted in the liver to glucose. **Galactokinase** catalyses the phosphorylation of galactose, using ATP as phosphate donor (Figure 21–6). Galactose 1-phosphate reacts with uridine diphosphate glucose (UDPGlc) to form uridine diphosphate galactose (UDPGal) and glucose 1-phosphate, in a reaction catalyzed by **galactose 1-phosphate uridyl transferase.** The conversion of UDPGal to UDPGlc is catalyzed by **UDPGal 4-epimerase.** The reaction involves oxidation, then reduction, at carbon 4, with NAD+ as coenzyme. The UDPGlc is then incorporated into glycogen (Chapter 19).

Since the epimerase reaction is freely reversible, glucose can be converted to galactose, so that galactose is not a dietary essential. Galactose is required in the body not only in the formation of lactose but also as a constituent of glycolipids (cerebrosides), proteoglycans, and glycoproteins.

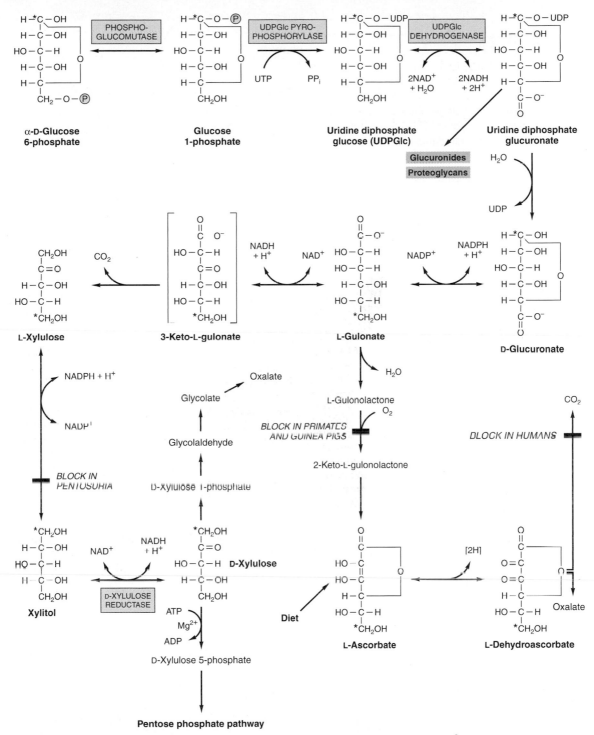

Figure 21–4. Uronic acid pathway. (* indicates the fate of carbon 1 of glucose; Ⓟ, —PO₃²⁻.)

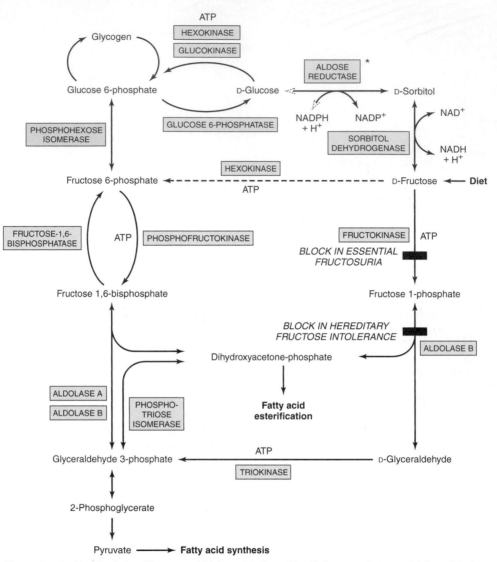

Figure 21–5. Metabolism of fructose. Aldolase A is found in all tissues, whereas aldolase B is the predominant form in liver. (*, not found in liver.)

In the synthesis of lactose in the mammary gland, UDPGal condenses with glucose to yield lactose, catalyzed by **lactose synthase** (see Figure 21–6).

Glucose Is the Precursor of All Amino Sugars (Hexosamines)

Amino sugars are important components of **glycoproteins** (Chapter 46), of certain **glycosphingolipids** (eg, gangliosides; Chapter 15), and of **glycosaminoglycans** (Chapter 47). The major amino sugars are the hexosamines **glucosamine, galactosamine,** and **mannosamine,** and the nine-carbon compound **sialic acid.** The principal sialic acid found in human tissues is *N*-acetylneuraminic acid (NeuAc). A summary of the metabolic interrelationships among the amino sugars is shown in Figure 21–7.

CLINICAL ASPECTS

Impairment of the Pentose Phosphate Pathway Leads to Erythrocyte Hemolysis

Genetic defects of glucose 6-phosphate dehydrogenase, with consequent impairment of the generation of

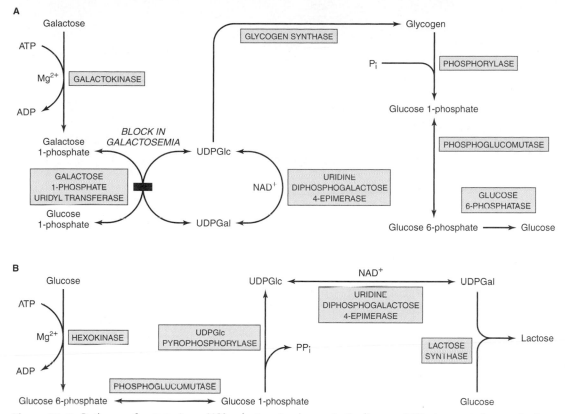

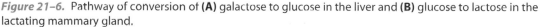

Figure 21–6. Pathway of conversion of **(A)** galactose to glucose in the liver and **(B)** glucose to lactose in the lactating mammary gland.

NADPH, are common in populations of Mediterranean and Afro-Caribbean origin. The defect is manifested as red cell hemolysis (**hemolytic anemia**) when susceptible individuals are subjected to oxidants, such as the antimalarial primaquine, aspirin, or sulfonamides, or when they have eaten fava beans (*Vicia fava*—hence the name of the disease, **favism**). Glutathione peroxidase is dependent upon a supply of NADPH, which in erythrocytes can be formed only via the pentose phosphate pathway. It reduces organic peroxides and H_2O_2, as part of the body's defense against lipid peroxidation (Figure 15–21). Measurement of erythrocyte **transketolase,** and its activation by thiamin diphosphate is used to assess thiamin nutritional status (Chapter 44).

Disruption of the Uronic Acid Pathway Is Caused by Enzyme Defects & Some Drugs

In the rare hereditary condition **essential pentosuria,** considerable quantities of **L-xylulose** appear in the urine, because of absence of the enzyme necessary to reduce L-xylulose to xylitol. Various drugs increase the rate at which glucose enters the uronic acid pathway. For example, administration of barbital or chlorobutanol to rats results in a significant increase in the conversion of glucose to glucuronate, L-gulonate, and ascorbate. Aminopyrine and antipyrine increase the excretion of L-xylulose in pentosuric subjects.

Loading of the Liver with Fructose May Potentiate Hypertriacylglycerolemia, Hypercholesterolemia, & Hyperuricemia

In the liver, fructose increases triacylglycerol synthesis and VLDL secretion, leading to hypertriacylglycerolemia— and increased LDL cholesterol—which can be regarded as potentially atherogenic (Chapter 26). In addition, acute loading of the liver with fructose, as can occur with intravenous infusion or following very high fructose intakes, causes sequestration of inorganic phosphate in fructose 1-phosphate and diminished ATP synthesis. As a result there is less inhibition of de novo purine synthesis by ATP, and uric acid formation is increased, causing hyperuricemia, which is a cause of gout (Chapter 33).

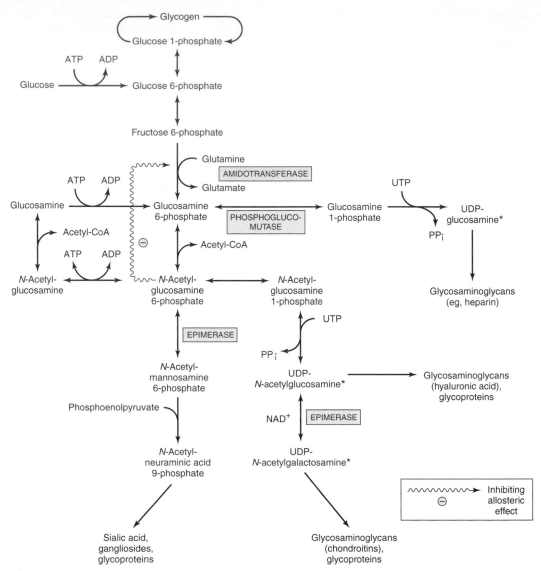

Figure 21–7. Summary of the interrelationships in metabolism of amino sugars. (At *: Analogous to UDPGlc.) Other purine or pyrimidine nucleotides may be similarly linked to sugars or amino sugars. Examples are thymidine diphosphate (TDP)-glucosamine and TDP-*N*-acetylglucosamine.

Defects in Fructose Metabolism Cause Disease

A lack of hepatic fructokinase causes **essential fructosuria,** and absence of aldolase B, which cleaves fructose 1-phosphate, leads to **hereditary fructose intolerance** (Figure 21–5). Diets low in fructose, sorbitol, and sucrose are beneficial for both conditions. One consequence of hereditary fructose intolerance and of a related condition as a result of **fructose 1,6-bisphosphatase deficiency** is fructose-induced **hypoglycemia** despite the presence of high glycogen reserves, because of fructose

1-phosphate and 1,6-bisphosphate allosterically inhibit liver phosphorylase. The sequestration of inorganic phosphate also leads to depletion of ATP and hyperuricemia.

Fructose & Sorbitol in the Lens Are Associated With Diabetic Cataract

Both fructose and sorbitol are found in the lens of the eye in increased concentrations in diabetes mellitus, and may be involved in the pathogenesis of **diabetic cataract.** The **sorbitol (polyol) pathway** (not found in

liver) is responsible for fructose formation from glucose (see Figure 21–5) and increases in activity as the glucose concentration rises in those tissues that are not insulin-sensitive, ie, the lens, peripheral nerves, and renal glomeruli. Glucose is reduced to sorbitol by **aldose reductase,** followed by oxidation of sorbitol to fructose in the presence of NAD^+ and sorbitol dehydrogenase (polyol dehydrogenase). Sorbitol does not diffuse through cell membranes, but accumulates, causing osmotic damage. Simultaneously, myoinositol levels fall. Sorbitol accumulation and myoinositol depletion, as well as diabetic cataract, can be prevented by aldose reductase inhibitors in experimental animals, but to date there is no evidence that inhibitors are effective in preventing cataract or diabetic neuropathy in humans.

Enzyme Deficiencies in the Galactose Pathway Cause Galactosemia

Inability to metabolize galactose occurs in the **galactosemias,** which may be caused by inherited defects of galactokinase, uridyl transferase, or 4-epimerase (Figure 21–6A), though deficiency of **uridyl transferase** is the best known. Galactose is a substrate for aldose reductase, forming galactitol, which accumulates in the lens of the eye, causing cataract. The general condition is more severe if it is the result of a defect in the uridyl transferase, since galactose 1-phosphate accumulates and depletes the liver of inorganic phosphate. Ultimately, liver failure and mental deterioration result. In uridyl transferase deficiency, the epimerase is present in adequate amounts, so that the galactosemic individual can still form UDPGal from glucose. This explains how it is possible for normal growth and development of affected children to occur regardless of the galactose-free diets used to control the symptoms of the disease.

SUMMARY

- The pentose phosphate pathway, present in the cytosol, can account for the complete oxidation of glucose, producing NADPH and CO_2 but not ATP.

- The pathway has an oxidative phase, which is irreversible and generates NADPH, and a nonoxidative phase, which is reversible and provides ribose precursors for nucleotide synthesis. The complete pathway is present only in those tissues having a requirement for NADPH for reductive syntheses, eg, lipogenesis or steroidogenesis, whereas the nonoxidative phase is present in all cells requiring ribose.

- In erythrocytes, the pathway has a major function in preventing hemolysis by providing NADPH to maintain glutathione in the reduced state as the substrate for glutathione peroxidase.

- The uronic acid pathway is the source of glucuronic acid for conjugation of many endogenous and exogenous substances before excretion as glucuronides in urine and bile.

- Fructose bypasses the main regulatory step in glycolysis, catalyzed by phosphofructokinase, and stimulates fatty acid synthesis and hepatic triacylglycerol secretion.

- Galactose is synthesized from glucose in the lactating mammary gland and in other tissues where it is required for the synthesis of glycolipids, proteoglycans, and glycoproteins

REFERENCES

Ali M, Rellos P, Cox TM: Hereditary fructose intolerance. Journal of Medical Genetics 1998;35:353.

Bron AJ, Sparrow J, Brown NA, Harding JJ, Blakytny R: The lens in diabetes. Eye 1993;7:260.

Dunlop M: Aldose reductase and the role of the polyol pathway in diabetic nephropathy. Kidney International 2000;77:S3.

Horecker BL: The pentose phosphate pathway. Journal of Biological Chemistry 2002;277:47965.

Mayes PA: Intermediary metabolism of fructose. American Journal of Clinical Nutrition 1993;58:754.

Mehta A, Mason PJ, Vulliamy II: Glucose 6-phosphate dehydrogenase deficiency. Ballière's Clinical Haematology 2000;13:21.

OMIM, On-line Mendelian Inheritance in Man, a reference work for all genetic diseases. Retrieved at http:// www.ncbi.nlm.nih.gov/entrez/query.fcgi?db=OMIM

Van den Berghe G: Inborn errors of fructose metabolism. Annual Review of Nutrition 1994;14:41.

Oxidation of Fatty Acids: Ketogenesis | 22

Kathleen M. Botham, PhD, DSc, & Peter A. Mayes, PhD, DSc

BIOMEDICAL IMPORTANCE

Although fatty acids are both oxidized to acetyl-CoA and synthesized from acetyl-CoA, fatty acid oxidation is not the simple reverse of fatty acid biosynthesis but an entirely different process taking place in a separate compartment of the cell. The separation of fatty acid oxidation in mitochondria from biosynthesis in the cytosol allows each process to be individually controlled and integrated with tissue requirements. Each step in fatty acid oxidation involves acyl-CoA derivatives catalyzed by separate enzymes, utilizes NAD$^+$ and FAD as coenzymes, and generates ATP. It is an aerobic process, requiring the presence of oxygen.

Increased fatty acid oxidation is a characteristic of starvation and of diabetes mellitus, leading to **ketone body** production by the liver **(ketosis).** Ketone bodies are acidic and when produced in excess over long periods, as in diabetes, cause **ketoacidosis,** which is ultimately fatal. Because gluconeogenesis is dependent upon fatty acid oxidation, any impairment in fatty acid oxidation leads to **hypoglycemia.** This occurs in various states of **carnitine deficiency** or deficiency of essential enzymes in fatty acid oxidation, eg, **carnitine palmitoyltransferase,** or inhibition of fatty acid oxidation by poisons, eg, **hypoglycin.**

OXIDATION OF FATTY ACIDS OCCURS IN MITOCHONDRIA

Fatty Acids Are Transported in the Blood As Free Fatty Acids (FFA)

Free fatty acids—also called unesterified (UFA) or non-esterified (NEFA) fatty acids—are fatty acids that are in the **unesterified state.** In plasma, longer-chain FFA are combined with **albumin,** and in the cell they are attached to a **fatty acid-binding protein,** so that in fact they are never really "free." Shorter-chain fatty acids are more water-soluble and exist as the un-ionized acid or as a fatty acid anion.

Fatty Acids Are Activated before Being Catabolized

Fatty acids must first be converted to an active intermediate before they can be catabolized. This is the only step in the complete degradation of a fatty acid that requires energy from ATP. In the presence of ATP and coenzyme A, the enzyme **acyl-CoA synthetase (thiokinase)** catalyzes the conversion of a fatty acid (or free fatty acid) to an "active fatty acid" or acyl-CoA, which uses one high-energy phosphate with the formation of AMP and PP$_i$ (Figure 22–1). The PP$_i$ is hydrolyzed by **inorganic pyrophosphatase** with the loss of a further high-energy phosphate, ensuring that the overall reaction goes to completion. Acyl-CoA synthetases are found in the endoplasmic reticulum, peroxisomes, and inside and on the outer membrane of mitochondria.

Long-Chain Fatty Acids Penetrate the Inner Mitochondrial Membrane As Carnitine Derivatives

Carnitine (β-hydroxy-γ-trimethylammonium butyrate), $(CH_3)_3N^+$—CH_2—$CH(OH)$—CH_2—COO^-, is widely distributed and is particularly abundant in muscle. Long-chain acyl-CoA (or FFA) will not penetrate the inner membrane of mitochondria. However, **carnitine palmitoyltransferase-I,** present in the outer mitochondrial membrane, converts long-chain acyl-CoA to acylcarnitine, which is able to penetrate the inner membrane and gain access to the β-oxidation system of enzymes (Figure 22–1). **Carnitine-acylcarnitine translocase** acts as an inner membrane exchange transporter. Acylcarnitine is transported in, coupled with the transport out of one molecule of carnitine. The acylcarnitine then reacts with CoA, catalyzed by **carnitine palmitoyltransferase-II,** located on the inside of the inner membrane. Acyl-CoA is re-formed in the mitochondrial matrix, and carnitine is liberated.

β-OXIDATION OF FATTY ACIDS INVOLVES SUCCESSIVE CLEAVAGE WITH RELEASE OF ACETYL-CoA

In β-oxidation (Figure 22–2), two carbons at a time are cleaved from acyl-CoA molecules, starting at the carboxyl end. The chain is broken between the α(2)- and β(3)-carbon atoms—hence the name β-oxidation. The

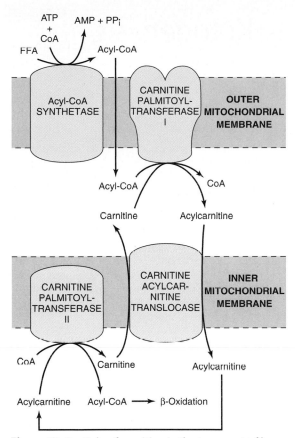

Figure 22–1. Role of carnitine in the transport of long-chain fatty acids through the inner mitochondrial membrane. Long-chain acyl-CoA cannot pass through the inner mitochondrial membrane, but its metabolic product, acylcarnitine, can.

two-carbon units formed are acetyl-CoA; thus, palmitoyl-CoA forms eight acetyl-CoA molecules.

The Cyclic Reaction Sequence Generates FADH$_2$ & NADH

Several enzymes, known collectively as "fatty acid oxidase," are found in the mitochondrial matrix or inner membrane adjacent to the respiratory chain. These catalyze the oxidation of acyl-CoA to acetyl-CoA, the system being coupled with the phosphorylation of ADP to ATP (Figure 22–3).

The first step is the removal of two hydrogen atoms from the 2(α)- and 3(β)-carbon atoms, catalyzed by **acyl-CoA dehydrogenase** and requiring FAD. This results in the formation of Δ^2-*trans*-enoyl-CoA and FADH$_2$. The reoxidation of FADH$_2$ by the respiratory chain requires the mediation of another flavoprotein,

termed **electron-transferring flavoprotein** (Chapter 12). Water is added to saturate the double bond and form 3-hydroxyacyl-CoA, catalyzed by Δ^2-**enoyl-CoA hydratase.** The 3-hydroxy derivative undergoes further dehydrogenation on the 3-carbon catalyzed by L(+)-3-**hydroxyacyl-CoA dehydrogenase** to form the corresponding 3-ketoacyl-CoA compound. In this case, NAD$^+$ is the coenzyme involved. Finally, 3-ketoacyl-CoA is split at the 2,3- position by **thiolase** (3-ketoacyl-CoA-thiolase), forming acetyl-CoA and a new acyl-CoA two carbons shorter than the original acyl-CoA molecule. The acyl-CoA formed in the cleavage reaction reenters the oxidative pathway at reaction 2 (Figure 22–3). In this way, a long-chain fatty acid may be degraded completely to acetyl-CoA (C$_2$ units). Since acetyl-CoA can be oxidized to CO$_2$ and water via the citric acid cycle (which is also found within the mitochondria), the complete oxidation of fatty acids is achieved.

Oxidation of a Fatty Acid with an Odd Number of Carbon Atoms Yields Acetyl-CoA Plus a Molecule of Propionyl-CoA

Fatty acids with an odd number of carbon atoms are oxidized by the pathway of β-oxidation, producing acetyl-CoA, until a three-carbon (propionyl-CoA) residue remains. This compound is converted to succinyl-CoA, a constituent of the citric acid cycle (Figure 20–2). Hence, **the propionyl residue from an odd-chain fatty acid is the only part of a fatty acid that is glucogenic.**

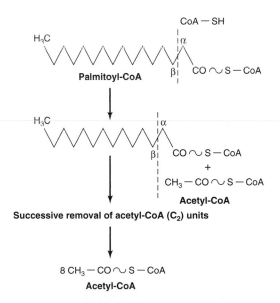

Figure 22–2. Overview of β-oxidation of fatty acids.

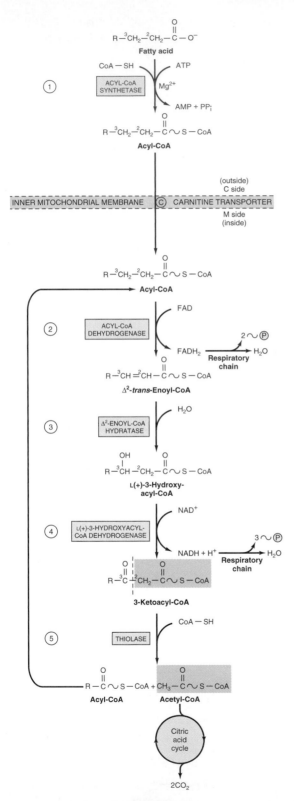

Figure 22–3. β-Oxidation of fatty acids. Long-chain acyl-CoA is cycled through reactions 2–5, acetyl-CoA being split off, each cycle, by thiolase (reaction 5). When the acyl radical is only four carbon atoms in length, two acetyl-CoA molecules are formed in reaction 5.

Oxidation of Fatty Acids Produces a Large Quantity of ATP

Transport in the respiratory chain of electrons from $FADH_2$ and NADH leads to the synthesis of four high-energy phosphates (Chapter 13) for each of the first seven acetyl-CoA molecules formed by β-oxidation of palmitate ($7 \times 4 = 28$). A total of 8 mol of acetyl-CoA is formed, and each gives rise to 10 mol of ATP on oxidation in the citric acid cycle, making $8 \times 10 = 80$ mol. Two must be subtracted for the initial activation of the fatty acid, yielding a net gain of 106 mol of ATP per mole of palmitate, or $106 \times 51.6^* = 5470$ kJ. This represents 68% of the free energy of combustion of palmitic acid.

Peroxisomes Oxidize Very Long Chain Fatty Acids

A modified form of β-oxidation is found in peroxisomes and leads to the formation of acetyl-CoA and H_2O_2 (from the flavoprotein-linked dehydrogenase step), which is broken down by catalase. Thus, this dehydrogenation in peroxisomes is not linked directly to phosphorylation and the generation of ATP. The system facilitates the oxidation of very long chain fatty acids (eg, C_{20}, C_{22}). These enzymes are induced by high-fat diets and in some species by hypolipidemic drugs such as clofibrate.

The enzymes in peroxisomes do not attack shorter chain fatty acids; the β-oxidation sequence ends at octanoyl-CoA. Octanoyl and acetyl groups are both further oxidized in mitochondria. Another role of peroxisomal β-oxidation is to shorten the side chain of cholesterol in bile acid formation (Chapter 26). Peroxisomes also take part in the synthesis of ether glycerolipids (Chapter 24), cholesterol, and dolichol (Figure 26–2).

OXIDATION OF UNSATURATED FATTY ACIDS OCCURS BY A MODIFIED β-OXIDATION PATHWAY

The CoA esters of these acids are degraded by the enzymes normally responsible for β-oxidation until either a Δ^3-*cis*-acyl-CoA compound or a Δ^4-*cis* acyl-CoA compound is formed, depending upon the position of the double bonds (Figure 22–4). The former compound is isomerized ($\Delta^3cis \rightarrow \Delta^2$-*trans*-enoyl-CoA isomerase)

---

* ΔG for the ATP reaction, as explained in Chapter 18.

Figure 22–4. Sequence of reactions in the oxidation of unsaturated fatty acids, eg, linoleic acid. Δ^4-*cis*-fatty acids or fatty acids forming Δ^4-*cis*-enoyl-CoA enter the pathway at the position shown. NADPH for the dienoyl-CoA reductase step is supplied by intramitochondrial sources such as glutamate dehydrogenase, isocitrate dehydrogenase, and NAD(P)H transhydrogenase.

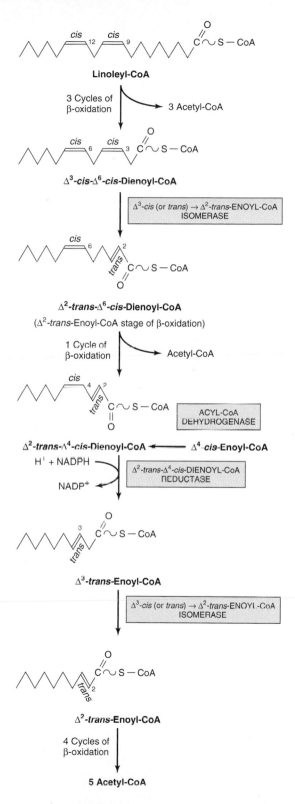

to the corresponding Δ^2-*trans*-CoA stage of β-oxidation for subsequent hydration and oxidation. Any Δ^4-*cis*-acyl-CoA either remaining, as in the case of linoleic acid, or entering the pathway at this point after conversion by acyl-CoA dehydrogenase to Δ^2-*trans*-Δ^4-*cis*-dienoyl-CoA, is then metabolized as indicated in Figure 22–4.

KETOGENESIS OCCURS WHEN THERE IS A HIGH RATE OF FATTY ACID OXIDATION IN THE LIVER

Under metabolic conditions associated with a high rate of fatty acid oxidation, the liver produces considerable quantities of **acetoacetate** and D(–)-**3-hydroxybutyrate** (β-hydroxybutyrate). Acetoacetate continually undergoes spontaneous decarboxylation to yield **acetone.** These three substances are collectively known as the **ketone bodies** (also called acetone bodies or [incorrectly*] "ketones") (Figure 22–5). Acetoacetate and 3-hydroxybutyrate are interconverted by the mitochondrial enzyme D(–)-**3-hydroxybutyrate dehydrogenase;** the equilibrium is controlled by the mitochondrial [NAD+]/[NADH] ratio, ie, the **redox state.** The concentration of total ketone bodies in the blood of well-fed mammals does not normally exceed 0.2 mmol/L except in ruminants, where 3-hydroxybutyrate is formed continuously from butyric acid (a product of ruminal fermentation) in the rumen wall. In vivo, the liver appears to be the only organ in nonruminants to add significant quantities of ketone bodies to the blood. Extrahepatic tissues utilize them as respiratory substrates. The net flow of ketone bodies from the liver to the extrahepatic tissues results from active hepatic synthesis coupled with very low utilization. The reverse situation occurs in extrahepatic tissues (Figure 22–6).

3-Hydroxy-3-Methylglutaryl-CoA (HMG-CoA) Is an Intermediate in the Pathway of Ketogenesis

Enzymes responsible for ketone body formation are associated mainly with the mitochondria. Two acetyl-

* The term "ketones" should not be used because 3-hydroxybutyrate is not a ketone and there are ketones in blood that are not ketone bodies, eg, pyruvate, fructose.

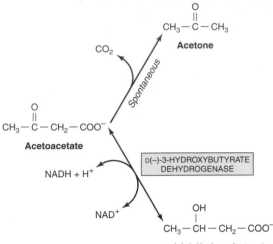

Figure 22–5. Interrelationships of the ketone bodies. D(−)-3-hydroxybutyrate dehydrogenase is a mitochondrial enzyme.

CoA molecules formed in β-oxidation condense with one another to form acetoacetyl-CoA by a reversal of the **thiolase** reaction. Acetoacetyl-CoA, which is the starting material for ketogenesis, also arises directly from the ter-

minal four carbons of a fatty acid during β-oxidation (Figure 22–7). Condensation of acetoacetyl-CoA with another molecule of acetyl-CoA by **3-hydroxy-3-methylglutaryl-CoA synthase** forms 3-hydroxy-3-methylglutaryl-CoA **(HMG-CoA). 3-Hydroxy-3-methylglutaryl-CoA lyase** then causes acetyl-CoA to split off from the HMG-CoA, leaving free acetoacetate. The carbon atoms split off in the acetyl-CoA molecule are derived from the original acetoacetyl-CoA molecule. **Both enzymes must be present in mitochondria for ketogenesis to take place.** This occurs solely in liver and rumen epithelium. D(−)-3-Hydroxybutyrate is quantitatively the predominant ketone body present in the blood and urine in ketosis.

Ketone Bodies Serve As a Fuel for Extrahepatic Tissues

While an active enzymatic mechanism produces acetoacetate from acetoacetyl-CoA in the liver, acetoacetate once formed cannot be reactivated directly except in the cytosol, where it is used in a much less active pathway as a precursor in cholesterol synthesis. This accounts for the net production of ketone bodies by the liver.

In extrahepatic tissues, acetoacetate is activated to acetoacetyl-CoA by **succinyl-CoA-acetoacetate CoA transferase.** CoA is transferred from succinyl-CoA to form acetoacetyl-CoA (Figure 22–8). The acetoacetyl-

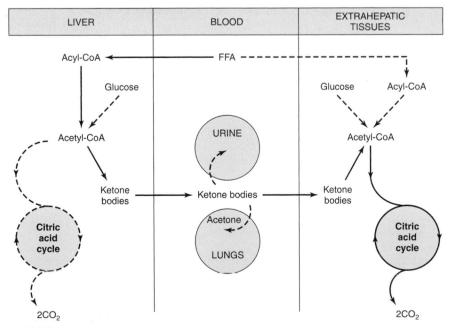

Figure 22–6. Formation, utilization, and excretion of ketone bodies. (The main pathway is indicated by the solid arrows.)

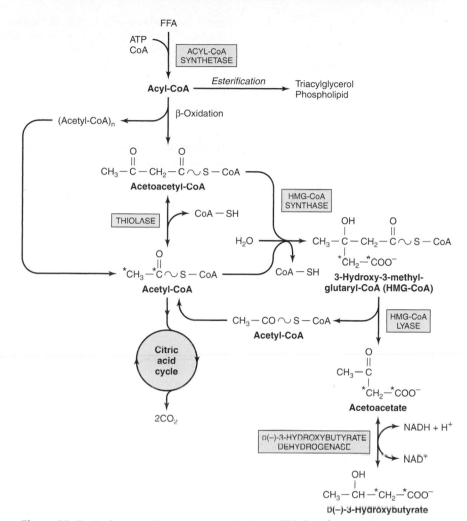

Figure 22–7. Pathways of ketogenesis in the liver. (FFA, free fatty acids.)

CoA is split to acetyl-CoA by thiolase and oxidized in the citric acid cycle. If the blood level is raised, oxidation of ketone bodies increases until, at a concentration of approximately 12 mmol/L, they saturate the oxidative machinery. When this occurs, a large proportion of the oxygen consumption may be accounted for by the oxidation of ketone bodies.

In most cases, **ketonemia is due to increased production of ketone bodies** by the liver rather than to a deficiency in their utilization by extrahepatic tissues. While acetoacetate and D(−)-3-hydroxybutyrate are readily oxidized by extrahepatic tissues, acetone is difficult to oxidize in vivo and to a large extent is volatilized in the lungs.

In moderate ketonemia, the loss of ketone bodies via the urine is only a few percent of the total ketone body production and utilization. Since there are renal thresh-

old-like effects (there is not a true threshold) that vary between species and individuals, measurement of the ketonemia, not the ketonuria, is the preferred method of assessing the severity of ketosis.

KETOGENESIS IS REGULATED AT THREE CRUCIAL STEPS

(1) Ketosis does not occur in vivo unless there is an increase in the level of circulating free fatty acids that arise from lipolysis of triacylglycerol in adipose tissue. **Free fatty acids are the precursors of ketone bodies in the liver.** The liver, both in fed and in fasting conditions, extracts about 30% of the free fatty acids passing through it, so that at high concentrations the flux passing into the liver is substantial. **Therefore, the factors regulating mobilization of free fatty acids from adi-**

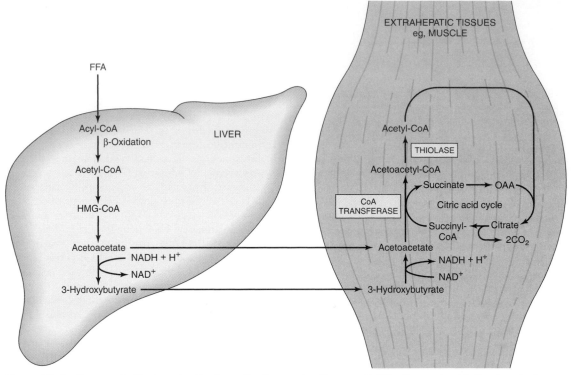

Figure 22–8. Transport of ketone bodies from the liver and pathways of utilization and oxidation in extrahepatic tissues.

pose tissue are important in controlling ketogenesis (Figures 22–9 and 25–8).

(2) After uptake by the liver, free fatty acids are either **β-oxidized** to CO_2 or ketone bodies or **esterified** to triacylglycerol and phospholipid. There is regulation of entry of fatty acids into the oxidative pathway by **carnitine palmitoyltransferase-I** (CPT-I), and the remainder of the fatty acid taken up is esterified. CPT-I activity is low in the fed state, leading to depression of fatty acid oxidation, and high in starvation, allowing fatty acid oxidation to increase. Malonyl-CoA, the initial intermediate in fatty acid biosynthesis (Figure 23–1), formed by acetyl-CoA carboxylase in the fed state, is a potent inhibitor of CPT-I (Figure 22–10). Under these conditions, free fatty acids enter the liver cell in low concentrations and are nearly all esterified to acylglycerols and transported out of the liver in very low density lipoproteins (VLDL). However, as the concentration of free fatty acids increases with the onset of starvation, acetyl-CoA carboxylase is inhibited directly by acyl-CoA, and [malonyl-CoA] decreases, releasing the inhibition of CPT-I and allowing more acyl-CoA to be β-oxidized. These events are reinforced in starvation by decrease in the **[insulin]/[glucagon] ratio.** Thus, β-oxidation from free fatty acids is controlled by the

CPT-I gateway into the mitochondria, and the balance of the free fatty acid uptake not oxidized is esterified.

(3) In turn, the acetyl-CoA formed in β-oxidation is oxidized in the citric acid cycle, or it enters the pathway of ketogenesis to form ketone bodies. As the level of serum free fatty acids is raised, proportionately more free fatty acid is converted to ketone bodies and less is oxidized via the citric acid cycle to CO_2. The partition of acetyl-CoA between the ketogenic pathway and the pathway of oxidation to CO_2 is so regulated that the total free energy captured in ATP which results from the oxidation of free fatty acids remains constant as their concentration in the serum changes. This may be appreciated when it is realized that complete oxidation of 1 mol of palmitate involves a net production of 106 mol of ATP via β-oxidation and CO_2 production in the citric acid cycle (see above), whereas only 26 mol of ATP are produced when acetoacetate is the end product and only 21 mol when 3-hydroxybutyrate is the end product. Thus, ketogenesis may be regarded as a mechanism that allows the liver to oxidize increasing quantities of fatty acids within the constraints of a tightly coupled system of oxidative phosphorylation.

Theoretically, a fall in concentration of oxaloacetate, particularly within the mitochondria, could impair the

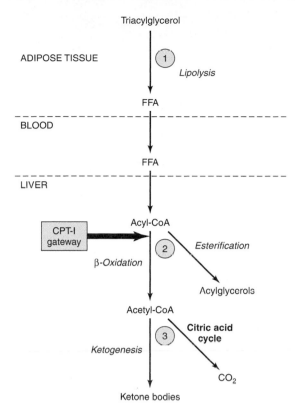

Figure 22–9. Regulation of ketogenesis. ①–③ show three crucial steps in the pathway of metabolism of free fatty acids (FFA) that determine the magnitude of ketogenesis. (CPT-I, carnitine palmitoyltransferase-I.)

ability of the citric acid cycle to metabolize acetyl-CoA and divert fatty acid oxidation toward ketogenesis. Such a fall may occur because of an increase in the [NADH]/[NAD+] ratio caused by increased β-oxidation affecting the equilibrium between oxaloacetate and malate, leading to a decrease in the concentration of oxaloacetate. However, pyruvate carboxylase, which catalyzes the conversion of pyruvate to oxaloacetate, is activated by acetyl-CoA. Consequently, when there are significant amounts of acetyl-CoA, there should be sufficient oxaloacetate to initiate the condensing reaction of the citric acid cycle.

CLINICAL ASPECTS

Impaired Oxidation of Fatty Acids Gives Rise to Diseases Often Associated with Hypoglycemia

Carnitine deficiency can occur particularly in the newborn—and especially in preterm infants—owing to inadequate biosynthesis or renal leakage. Losses can also occur in hemodialysis. This suggests a vitamin-like

dietary requirement for carnitine in some individuals. Symptoms of deficiency include hypoglycemia, which is a consequence of impaired fatty acid oxidation and lipid accumulation with muscular weakness. Treatment is by oral supplementation with carnitine.

Inherited **CPT-I deficiency** affects only the liver, resulting in reduced fatty acid oxidation and ketogenesis, with hypoglycemia. **CPT-II deficiency** affects primarily skeletal muscle and, when severe, the liver. The sulfonylurea drugs (**glyburide [glibenclamide]** and **tolbutamide),** used in the treatment of type 2 diabetes mellitus, reduce fatty acid oxidation and, therefore, hyperglycemia by inhibiting CPT-I.

Inherited defects in the enzymes of β-oxidation and ketogenesis also lead to nonketotic hypoglycemia, coma, and fatty liver. Defects are known in long- and short-chain 3-hydroxyacyl-CoA dehydrogenase (deficiency of the long-chain enzyme may be a cause of **acute fatty liver of pregnancy**). **3-Ketoacyl-CoA thiolase** and **HMG-CoA lyase deficiency** also affect the degradation of leucine, a ketogenic amino acid (Chapter 29).

Jamaican vomiting sickness is caused by eating the unripe fruit of the akee tree, which contains the toxin **hypoglycin,** which inactivates medium- and short-chain acyl-CoA dehydrogenase, inhibiting β-oxidation and causing hypoglycemia. **Dicarboxylic aciduria** is characterized by the excretion of C_6–C_{10} ω-dicarboxylic acids and by nonketotic hypoglycemia, and is caused by a lack of mitochondrial **medium-chain acyl-CoA dehydrogenase. Refsum's disease** is a rare neurologic disorder due to a metabolic defect that results in the accumulation of phytanic acid, which is found in dairy products and ruminant fat and meat. Phytanic acid is thought to have pathological effects on membrane function, protein prenylation, and gene expression. **Zellweger's (cerebrohepatorenal) syndrome** occurs in individuals with a rare inherited absence of peroxisomes in all tissues. They accumulate C_{26}–C_{38} polyenoic acids in brain tissue and also exhibit a generalized loss of peroxisomal functions. The disease causes severe neurological symptoms, and most patients die in the first year of life.

Ketoacidosis Results from Prolonged Ketosis

Higher than normal quantities of ketone bodies present in the blood or urine constitute **ketonemia** (hyperketonemia) or **ketonuria,** respectively. The overall condition is called **ketosis.** The basic form of ketosis occurs in **starvation** and involves depletion of available carbohydrate coupled with mobilization of free fatty acids. This general pattern of metabolism is exaggerated to produce the pathologic states found in **diabetes mellitus, the type 2 form of which is increasingly common in Western countries; twin lamb disease;** and **ketosis in lactating cattle.** Nonpathologic forms of ketosis are found under conditions of high-fat feeding and after severe exercise in the postabsorptive state.

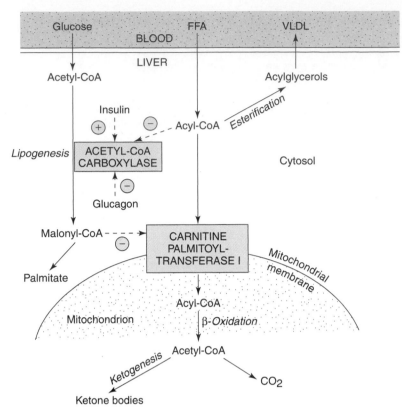

Figure 22–10. Regulation of long-chain fatty acid oxidation in the liver. (FFA, free fatty acids; VLDL, very low density lipoprotein.) Positive (⊕) and negative (⊖) regulatory effects are represented by broken arrows and substrate flow by solid arrows.

Acetoacetic and 3-hydroxybutyric acids are both moderately strong acids and are buffered when present in blood or other tissues. However, their continual excretion in quantity progressively depletes the alkali reserve, causing **ketoacidosis.** This may be fatal in uncontrolled **diabetes mellitus.**

SUMMARY

- Fatty acid oxidation in mitochondria leads to the generation of large quantities of ATP by a process called β-oxidation that cleaves acetyl-CoA units sequentially from fatty acyl chains. The acetyl-CoA is oxidized in the citric acid cycle, generating further ATP.

- The ketone bodies (acetoacetate, 3-hydroxybutyrate, and acetone) are formed in hepatic mitochondria when there is a high rate of fatty acid oxidation. The pathway of ketogenesis involves synthesis and breakdown of 3-hydroxy-3-methylglutaryl-CoA (HMG-CoA) by two key enzymes, HMG-CoA synthase and HMG-CoA lyase.

- Ketone bodies are important fuels in extrahepatic tissues.

- Ketogenesis is regulated at three crucial steps: (1) control of free fatty acid mobilization from adipose tissue;

(2) the activity of carnitine palmitoyltransferase-I in liver, which determines the proportion of the fatty acid flux that is oxidized rather than esterified; and (3) partition of acetyl-CoA between the pathway of ketogenesis and the citric acid cycle.

- Diseases associated with impairment of fatty acid oxidation lead to hypoglycemia, fatty infiltration of organs, and hypoketonemia.

- Ketosis is mild in starvation but severe in diabetes mellitus and ruminant ketosis.

REFERENCES

Eaton S, Bartlett K, Pourfarzam M: Mammalian mitochondrial β-oxidation. Biochem J 1996;320:345.

Fukao T, Lopaschuk GD, Mitchell GA: Pathways and control of ketone body metabolism: on the fringe of lipid metabolism. Prostaglandins Leukot Essent Fatty Acids 2004;70:243.

Gurr MI, Harwood JL, Frayn K: *Lipid Biochemistry.* Blackwell Publishing, 2002.

Reddy JK, Mannaerts GP: Peroxisomal lipid metabolism. Annu Rev Nutr 1994;14:343.

Scriver CR et al (editors): *The Metabolic and Molecular Bases of Inherited Disease,* 8th ed. McGraw-Hill, 2001.

Wood PA: Defects in mitochondrial beta-oxidation of fatty acids. Curr Opin Lipidol 1999;10:107.

Biosynthesis of Fatty Acids & Eicosanoids

23

Kathleen M. Botham, PhD, DSc, & Peter A. Mayes, PhD, DSc

BIOMEDICAL IMPORTANCE

Fatty acids are synthesized by an **extramitochondrial system,** which is responsible for the complete synthesis of palmitate from acetyl-CoA in the cytosol. In most mammals, glucose is the primary substrate for lipogenesis, but in ruminants it is acetate, the main fuel molecule produced by the diet. Critical diseases of the pathway have not been reported in humans. However, inhibition of lipogenesis occurs in type 1 (insulin-dependent) **diabetes mellitus,** and variations in its activity affect the nature and extent of **obesity.**

Unsaturated fatty acids in phospholipids of the cell membrane are important in maintaining membrane fluidity. A high ratio of polyunsaturated fatty acids to saturated fatty acids (P:S ratio) in the diet is considered to be beneficial in preventing coronary heart disease. Animal tissues have limited capacity for desaturating fatty acids, and require certain dietary polyunsaturated fatty acids derived from plants. These **essential fatty acids** are used to form eicosanoic (C_{20}) fatty acids, which give rise to the **eicosanoids** prostaglandins, thromboxanes, leukotrienes, and lipoxins. Prostaglandins mediate **inflammation, pain,** and induce **sleep** and also regulate **blood coagulation and reproduction.** Nonsteroidal anti-inflammatory drugs such as **aspirin** act by inhibiting prostaglandin synthesis. Leukotrienes have muscle contractant and chemotactic properties and are important in allergic reactions and inflammation.

THE MAIN PATHWAY FOR DE NOVO SYNTHESIS OF FATTY ACIDS (LIPOGENESIS) OCCURS IN THE CYTOSOL

This system is present in many tissues, including liver, kidney, brain, lung, mammary gland, and adipose tissue. Its cofactor requirements include NADPH, ATP, Mn^{2+}, biotin, and HCO_3^- (as a source of CO_2). **Acetyl-CoA** is the immediate substrate, and **free palmitate** is the end product.

Production of Malonyl-CoA Is the Initial & Controlling Step in Fatty Acid Synthesis

Bicarbonate as a source of CO_2 is required in the initial reaction for the carboxylation of acetyl-CoA to **malonyl-CoA** in the presence of ATP and **acetyl-CoA carboxylase.** Acetyl-CoA carboxylase has a requirement for the vitamin **biotin** (Figure 23–1). The enzyme is a **multi-enzyme protein** containing a variable number of identical subunits, each containing biotin, biotin carboxylase, biotin carboxyl carrier protein, and transcarboxylase, as well as a regulatory allosteric site. The reaction takes place in two steps: (1) carboxylation of biotin involving ATP and (2) transfer of the carboxyl to acetyl-CoA to form malonyl-CoA.

The Fatty Acid Synthase Complex Is a Polypeptide Containing Seven Enzyme Activities

In bacteria and plants, the individual enzymes of the **fatty acid synthase** system are separate, and the acyl radicals are found in combination with a protein called the **acyl carrier protein (ACP).** However, in yeast, mammals, and birds, the synthase system is a multienzyme polypeptide complex that incorporates ACP, which takes over the role of CoA. It contains the vitamin **pantothenic acid** in the form of 4'-phosphopantetheine (Figure 44–18). The use of one multienzyme functional unit has the advantages of achieving the effect of compartmentalization of the process within the cell without the erection of permeability barriers, and synthesis of all enzymes in the complex is coordinated since it is encoded by a single gene.

In mammals, the fatty acid synthase complex is a dimer comprising two identical monomers, each containing all seven enzyme activities of fatty acid synthase on one polypeptide chain (Figure 23–2). Initially, a priming molecule of acetyl-CoA combines with a cysteine —SH group catalyzed by **acetyl transacylase** (Figure 23–3, reaction 1a). Malonyl-CoA combines with the adjacent —SH on the 4'-phosphopantetheine of ACP of the other monomer, catalyzed by **malonyl**

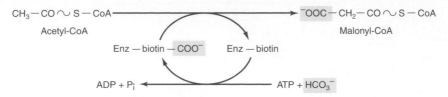

Figure 23–1. Biosynthesis of malonyl-CoA. (Enz, acetyl-CoA carboxylase.)

transacylase (reaction 1b), to form **acetyl (acyl)-malonyl enzyme.** The acetyl group attacks the methylene group of the malonyl residue, catalyzed by **3-ketoacyl synthase,** and liberates CO_2, forming 3-ketoacyl enzyme (acetoacetyl enzyme) (reaction 2), freeing the cysteine —SH group. Decarboxylation allows the reaction to go to completion, pulling the whole sequence of reactions in the forward direction. The 3-ketoacyl group is reduced, dehydrated, and reduced again (reactions 3, 4, 5) to form the corresponding saturated acyl-S-enzyme. A new malonyl-CoA molecule combines with the —SH of 4'-phosphopantetheine, displacing the saturated acyl residue onto the free cysteine —SH group. The sequence of reactions is repeated six more times until a saturated 16-carbon acyl radical (palmityl) has been assembled. It is liberated from the enzyme com-

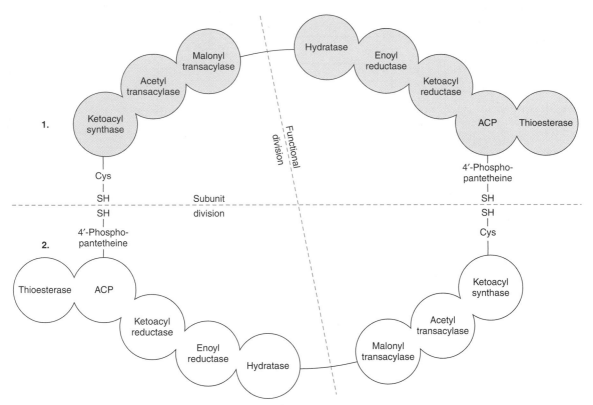

Figure 23–2. Fatty acid synthase multienzyme complex. The complex is a dimer of two identical polypeptide monomers, 1 and 2, each consisting of seven enzyme activities and the acyl carrier protein (ACP). (Cys—SH, cysteine thiol.) The —SH of the 4'-phosphopantetheine of one monomer is in close proximity to the —SH of the cysteine residue of the ketoacyl synthase of the other monomer, suggesting a "head-to-tail" arrangement of the two monomers. Though each monomer contains all the partial activities of the reaction sequence, the actual functional unit consists of one-half of one monomer interacting with the complementary half of the other. Thus, two acyl chains are produced simultaneously. The sequence of the enzymes in each monomer is based on Wakil.

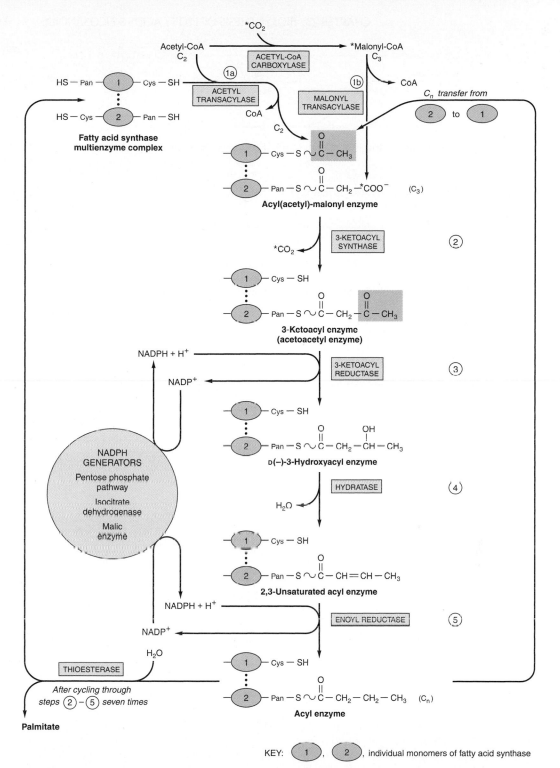

Figure 23–3. Biosynthesis of long-chain fatty acids. Details of how addition of a malonyl residue causes the acyl chain to grow by two carbon atoms. (Cys, cysteine residue; Pan, 4′-phosphopante-theine.) The blocks shown in dark color contain initially a C_2 unit derived from acetyl-CoA (as illustrated) and subsequently the C_n unit formed in reaction 5.

plex by the activity of a seventh enzyme in the complex, **thioesterase** (deacylase). The free palmitate must be activated to acyl-CoA before it can proceed via any other metabolic pathway. Its usual fate is esterification into acylglycerols, chain elongation or desaturation, or esterification to cholesteryl ester. In mammary gland, there is a separate thioesterase specific for acyl residues of C_8, C_{10}, or C_{12}, which are subsequently found in milk lipids.

The equation for the overall synthesis of palmitate from acetyl-CoA and malonyl-CoA is

$$CH_3CO \cdot S \cdot CoA + 7HOOC \cdot CH\ CO \cdot S \cdot CoA + 14NADPH + 14H^+$$

$$\rightarrow CH_3(CH_2)_{14}COOH + 7CO_2 + 6H_2O + 8CoA \cdot SH + 14NADP^+$$

The acetyl-CoA used as a primer forms carbon atoms 15 and 16 of palmitate. The addition of all the subsequent C_2 units is via malonyl-CoA. Propionyl-CoA acts as primer for the synthesis of long-chain fatty acids having an odd number of carbon atoms, found particularly in ruminant fat and milk.

The Main Source of NADPH for Lipogenesis Is the Pentose Phosphate Pathway

NADPH is involved as donor of reducing equivalents in both the reduction of the 3-ketoacyl and of the 2,3-unsaturated acyl derivatives (Figure 23–3, reactions 3 and 5). The oxidative reactions of the pentose phosphate pathway (see Chapter 21) are the chief source of the hydrogen required for the reductive synthesis of fatty acids. Significantly, tissues specializing in active lipogenesis—ie, liver, adipose tissue, and the lactating mammary gland—also possess an active pentose phosphate pathway. Moreover, both metabolic pathways are found in the cytosol of the cell, so there are no membranes or permeability barriers against the transfer of NADPH. Other sources of NADPH include the reaction that converts malate to pyruvate catalyzed by the "**malic enzyme**" (NADP malate dehydrogenase) (Figure 23–4) and the extramitochondrial **isocitrate dehydrogenase** reaction (probably not a substantial source, except in ruminants).

Acetyl-CoA Is the Principal Building Block of Fatty Acids

Acetyl-CoA is formed from glucose via the oxidation of pyruvate within the mitochondria. However, it does not diffuse readily into the extramitochondrial cytosol, the principal site of fatty acid synthesis. Citrate, formed after condensation of acetyl-CoA with oxaloacetate in the citric acid cycle within mitochondria, is translocated into the extramitochondrial compartment via the tricarboxylate transporter, where in the presence of CoA and ATP it undergoes cleavage to acetyl-CoA and

oxaloacetate catalyzed by **ATP-citrate lyase,** which increases in activity in the well-fed state. The acetyl-CoA is then available for malonyl-CoA formation and synthesis to palmitate (Figure 23–4). The resulting oxaloacetate can form malate via NADH-linked malate dehydrogenase, followed by the generation of NADPH via the malic enzyme. The NADPH becomes available for lipogenesis, and the pyruvate can be used to regenerate acetyl-CoA after transport into the mitochondrion. This pathway is a means of transferring reducing equivalents from extramitochondrial NADH to NADP. Alternatively, malate itself can be transported into the mitochondrion, where it is able to re-form oxaloacetate. Note that the citrate (tricarboxylate) transporter in the mitochondrial membrane requires malate to exchange with citrate (see Figure 13-10). There is little ATP-citrate lyase or malic enzyme in ruminants, probably because in these species acetate (derived from the rumen and activated to acetyl-CoA extramitochondrially) is the main source of acetyl-CoA.

Elongation of Fatty Acid Chains Occurs in the Endoplasmic Reticulum

This pathway (the "microsomal system") elongates saturated and unsaturated fatty acyl-CoAs (from C_{10} upward) by two carbons, using malonyl-CoA as the acetyl donor and NADPH as the reductant, and is catalyzed by the microsomal **fatty acid elongase** system of enzymes (Figure 23–5). Elongation of stearyl-CoA in brain increases rapidly during myelination in order to provide C_{22} and C_{24} fatty acids for sphingolipids.

THE NUTRITIONAL STATE REGULATES LIPOGENESIS

Excess carbohydrate is stored as fat in many animals in anticipation of periods of caloric deficiency such as starvation, hibernation, etc, and to provide energy for use between meals in animals, including humans, that take their food at spaced intervals. Lipogenesis converts surplus glucose and intermediates such as pyruvate, lactate, and acetyl-CoA to fat, assisting the anabolic phase of this feeding cycle. The nutritional state of the organism is the main factor regulating the rate of lipogenesis. Thus, the rate is high in the well-fed animal whose diet contains a high proportion of carbohydrate. It is depressed by restricted caloric intake, high fat diet, or a deficiency of insulin, as in diabetes mellitus. These latter conditions are associated with increased concentrations of plasma free fatty acids, and an inverse relationship has been demonstrated between hepatic lipogenesis and the concentration of serum-free fatty acids. Lipogenesis is increased when sucrose is fed instead of glucose because fructose bypasses the phosphofructokinase control point in glycolysis and floods the lipogenic pathway (Figure 21–5).

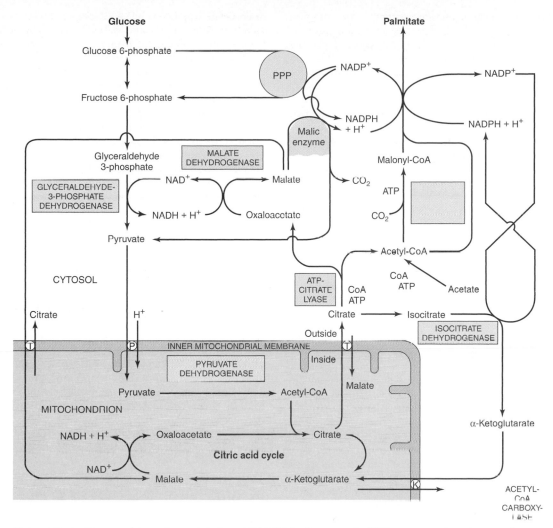

Figure 23–4. The provision of acetyl-CoA and NADPH for lipogenesis. (PPP, pentose phosphate pathway; T, tricarboxylate transporter; K, α-ketoglutarate transporter; P, pyruvate transporter.)

SHORT- & LONG-TERM MECHANISMS REGULATE LIPOGENESIS

Long-chain fatty acid synthesis is controlled in the short term by allosteric and covalent modification of enzymes and in the long term by changes in gene expression governing rates of synthesis of enzymes.

Acetyl-CoA Carboxylase Is the Most Important Enzyme in the Regulation of Lipogenesis

Acetyl-CoA carboxylase is an allosteric enzyme and is activated by **citrate,** which increases in concentration in the well-fed state and is an indicator of a plentiful supply of

acetyl-CoA. Citrate converts the enzyme from an inactive dimer to an active polymeric form, with a molecular mass of several million. Inactivation is promoted by phosphorylation of the enzyme and by long-chain acyl-CoA molecules, an example of negative feedback inhibition by a product of a reaction. Thus, if acyl-CoA accumulates because it is not esterified quickly enough or because of increased lipolysis or an influx of free fatty acids into the tissue, it will automatically reduce the synthesis of new fatty acid. Acyl-CoA also inhibits the mitochondrial **tricarboxylate transporter,** thus preventing activation of the enzyme by egress of citrate from the mitochondria into the cytosol.

Acetyl-CoA carboxylase is also regulated by hormones such as **glucagon, epinephrine,** and **insulin** via changes in its phosphorylation state (details in Figure 23–6).

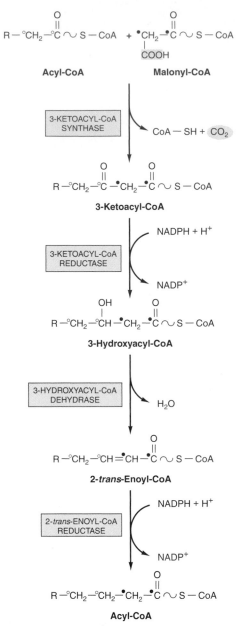

Figure 23–5. Microsomal elongase system for fatty acid chain elongation. NADH is also used by the reductases, but NADPH is preferred.

Pyruvate Dehydrogenase Is Also Regulated by Acyl-CoA

Acyl-CoA causes an inhibition of pyruvate dehydrogenase by inhibiting the ATP-ADP exchange transporter of the inner mitochondrial membrane, which leads to increased intramitochondrial [ATP]/[ADP] ratios and therefore to conversion of active to inactive pyruvate dehydrogenase (see Figure 18–6), thus regulating the availability of acetyl-CoA for lipogenesis. Furthermore, oxidation of acyl-CoA due to increased levels of free fatty acids may increase the ratios of [acetyl-CoA]/[CoA] and [NADH]/[NAD+] in mitochondria, inhibiting pyruvate dehydrogenase.

Insulin Also Regulates Lipogenesis by Other Mechanisms

Insulin stimulates lipogenesis by several other mechanisms as well as by increasing acetyl-CoA carboxylase activity. It increases the transport of glucose into the cell (eg, in adipose tissue), increasing the availability of both pyruvate for fatty acid synthesis and glycerol

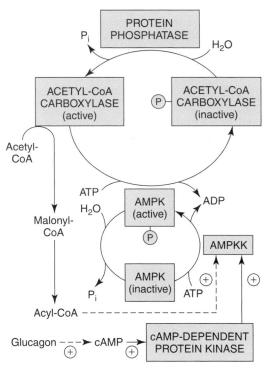

Figure 23–6. Regulation of acetyl-CoA carboxylase by phosphorylation/dephosphorylation. The enzyme is inactivated by phosphorylation by AMP-activated protein kinase (AMPK), which in turn is phosphorylated and activated by AMP-activated protein kinase kinase (AMPKK). Glucagon (and epinephrine) increase cAMP, and thus activate this latter enzyme via cAMP-dependent protein kinase. The kinase kinase enzyme is also believed to be activated by acyl-CoA. Insulin activates acetyl-CoA carboxylase, probably through an "activator" protein and an insulin-stimulated protein kinase.

3-phosphate for esterification of the newly formed fatty acids, and also converts the inactive form of pyruvate dehydrogenase to the active form in adipose tissue but not in liver. Insulin also—by its ability to depress the level of intracellular cAMP—**inhibits lipolysis** in adipose tissue and thereby reduces the concentration of plasma free fatty acids and therefore long-chain acyl-CoA, an inhibitor of lipogenesis.

The Fatty Acid Synthase Complex & Acetyl-CoA Carboxylase Are Adaptive Enzymes

These enzymes adapt to the body's physiologic needs by increasing in total amount in the fed state and by decreasing in starvation, feeding of fat, and in diabetes. **Insulin** is an important hormone causing gene expression and induction of enzyme biosynthesis, and glucagon (via cAMP) antagonizes this effect. Feeding fats containing polyunsaturated fatty acids coordinately regulates the inhibition of expression of key enzymes of glycolysis and lipogenesis. These mechanisms for longer-term regulation of lipogenesis take several days to become fully manifested and augment the direct and immediate effect of free fatty acids and hormones such as insulin and glucagon.

SOME POLYUNSATURATED FATTY ACIDS CANNOT BE SYNTHESIZED BY MAMMALS & ARE NUTRITIONALLY ESSENTIAL

Certain long-chain unsaturated fatty acids of metabolic significance in mammals are shown in Figure 23–7. Other C_{20}, C_{22}, and C_{24} polyenoic fatty acids may be derived from oleic, linoleic, and α-linolenic acids by chain elongation. Palmitoleic and oleic acids are not essential in the diet because the tissues can introduce a double bond at the Δ^9 position of a saturated fatty acid. **Linoleic and α-linolenic acids** are the only fatty acids known to be essential for the complete nutrition of many species of animals, including humans, and are known as the **nutritionally essential fatty acids.** In most mammals, **arachidonic acid** can be formed from linoleic acid (Figure 23–10). Double bonds can be introduced at the Δ^4, Δ^5, Δ^6, and Δ^9 positions (see Chapter 15) in most animals, but never beyond the Δ^9 position. In contrast, plants are able to synthesize the nutritionally essential fatty acids by introducing double bonds at the Δ^{12} and Δ^{15} positions.

MONOUNSATURATED FATTY ACIDS ARE SYNTHESIZED BY A Δ^9 DESATURASE SYSTEM

Several tissues including the liver are considered to be responsible for the formation of nonessential monounsaturated fatty acids from saturated fatty acids. The first

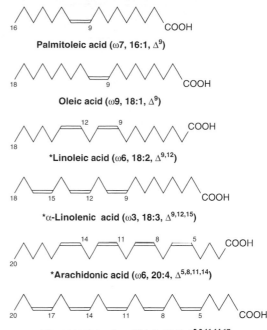

Figure 23–7. Structure of some unsaturated fatty acids. Although the carbon atoms in the molecules are conventionally numbered—ie, numbered from the carboxyl terminal—the ω numbers (eg, ω7 in palmitoleic acid) are calculated from the reverse end (the methyl terminal) of the molecules. The information in parentheses shows, for instance, that α-linolenic acid contains double bonds starting at the third carbon from the methyl terminal, has 18 carbons and 3 double bonds, and has these double bonds at the 9th, 12th, and 15th carbons from the carboxyl terminal. (Asterisks: Classified as "essential fatty acids.")

double bond introduced into a saturated fatty acid is nearly always in the Δ^9 position. An enzyme system—Δ^9 **desaturase** (Figure 23–8)—in the endoplasmic reticulum will catalyze the conversion of palmitoyl-CoA or stearoyl-CoA to palmitoleoyl-CoA or oleoyl-CoA, respectively. Oxygen and either NADH or NADPH are necessary for the reaction. The enzymes appear to be similar to a monooxygenase system involving cytochrome b_5 (Chapter 12).

SYNTHESIS OF POLYUNSATURATED FATTY ACIDS INVOLVES DESATURASE & ELONGASE ENZYME SYSTEMS

Additional double bonds introduced into existing monounsaturated fatty acids are always separated from

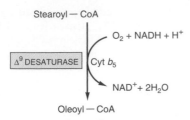

Figure 23–8. Microsomal Δ^9 desaturase.

each other by a methylene group (methylene interrupted) except in bacteria. Since animals have a Δ^9 desaturase, they are able to synthesize the ω9 (oleic acid) family of unsaturated fatty acids completely by a combination of chain elongation and desaturation (Figure 23–9). However, as indicated above, linoleic (ω6) or α-linolenic (ω3) acids required for the synthesis of the other members of the ω6 or ω3 families must be supplied in the diet. Linoleate may be converted to arachidonate via **γ-lino-lenate** by the pathway shown in Figure 23–10. The nutritional requirement for arachidonate may thus be dispensed with if there is adequate linoleate in the diet. The desaturation and chain elongation system is greatly diminished in the starving state, in response to glucagon and epinephrine administration, and in the absence of insulin as in type 1 diabetes mellitus.

DEFICIENCY SYMPTOMS ARE PRODUCED WHEN THE ESSENTIAL FATTY ACIDS (EFA) ARE ABSENT FROM THE DIET

Rats fed a purified nonlipid diet containing vitamins A and D exhibit a reduced growth rate and reproductive deficiency which may be cured by the addition of linoleic, α-linolenic, and arachidonic acids to the diet. These fatty acids are found in high concentrations in vegetable oils (Table 15–2) and in small amounts in animal carcasses. Essential fatty acids are required for prostaglandin, thromboxane, leukotriene, and lipoxin formation (see below), and they also have various other functions which are less well defined. They are found in the structural lipids of the cell, often in the 2 position of phospholipids, and are concerned with the structural integrity of the mitochondrial membrane.

Arachidonic acid is present in membranes and accounts for 5–15% of the fatty acids in phospholipids. Docosahexaenoic acid (DHA; ω3, 22:6), which is synthesized from α-linolenic acid or obtained directly from fish oils, is present in high concentrations in retina, cerebral cortex, testis, and sperm. DHA is particularly needed for development of the brain and retina and is supplied via the placenta and milk. Patients with **retinitis pigmentosa** are reported to have low blood levels of DHA. In **essential fatty acid deficiency,** nonessential polyenoic acids of the ω9 family, particularly $\Delta^{5,8,11}$-eicosatrienoic acid (ω9 20:3) (Figure 23–9), replace the essential fatty acids in phospholipids, other complex lipids, and membranes. The triene:tetraene ratio in plasma lipids can be used to diagnose the extent of essential fatty acid deficiency.

Trans Fatty Acids Are Implicated in Various Disorders

Small amounts of trans-unsaturated fatty acids are found in ruminant fat (eg, butter fat has 2–7%), where they arise from the action of microorganisms in the rumen, but the main source in the human diet is from partially hydrogenated vegetable oils (eg, margarine). Trans fatty acids compete with essential fatty acids and may exacerbate

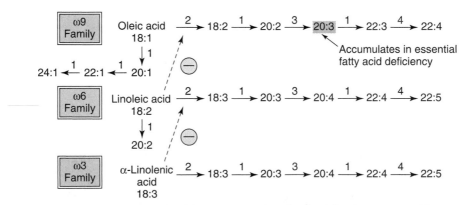

Figure 23–9. Biosynthesis of the ω9, ω6, and ω3 families of polyunsaturated fatty acids. Each step is catalyzed by the microsomal chain elongation or desaturase system: 1, elongase; 2, Δ^6 desaturase; 3, Δ^5 desaturase; 4, Δ^4 desaturase. (⊖, Inhibition.)

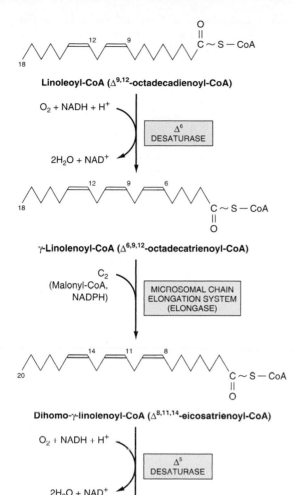

Linoleoyl-CoA ($\Delta^{9,12}$-octadecadienoyl-CoA)

$O_2 + NADH + H^+$

Δ^6 DESATURASE

$2H_2O + NAD^+$

γ-Linolenoyl-CoA ($\Delta^{6,9,12}$-octadecatrienoyl-CoA)

C_2 (Malonyl-CoA, NADPH)

MICROSOMAL CHAIN ELONGATION SYSTEM (ELONGASE)

Dihomo-γ-linolenoyl-CoA ($\Delta^{8,11,14}$-eicosatrienoyl-CoA)

$O_2 + NADH + H^+$

Δ^5 DESATURASE

$2H_2O + NAD^+$

Arachidonoyl-CoA ($\Delta^{5,8,11,14}$-eicosatetraenoyl-CoA)

Figure 23–10. Conversion of linoleate to arachidonate. Cats cannot carry out this conversion owing to absence of Δ^6 desaturase and must obtain arachidonate in their diet.

essential fatty acid deficiency. Moreover, they are structurally similar to saturated fatty acids (Chapter 15) and have comparable effects in the promotion of hypercholesterolemia and atherosclerosis (Chapter 26).

EICOSANOIDS ARE FORMED FROM C$_{20}$ POLYUNSATURATED FATTY ACIDS

Arachidonate and some other C_{20} polyunsaturated fatty acids give rise to **eicosanoids,** physiologically and pharma-

cologically active compounds known as **prostaglandins (PG), thromboxanes (TX), leukotrienes (LT),** and **lipoxins (LX)** (Chapter 15). Physiologically, they are considered to act as local hormones functioning through G-protein-linked receptors to elicit their biochemical effects.

There are three groups of eicosanoids that are synthesized from C_{20} eicosanoic acids derived from the essential fatty acids **linoleate** and **α-linolenate,** or directly from dietary arachidonate and eicosapentaenoate (Figure 23–11). Arachidonate, which may be obtained from the diet, but is usually derived from the 2 position of phospholipids in the plasma membrane by the action of phospholipase A_2 (Figure 24–6), is the substrate for the synthesis of the PG_2, TX_2 series **(prostanoids)** by the **cyclooxygenase pathway,** or the LT_4 and LX_4 series by the **lipoxygenase pathway,** with the two pathways competing for the arachidonate substrate (Figure 23–11).

THE CYCLOOXYGENASE PATHWAY IS RESPONSIBLE FOR PROSTANOID SYNTHESIS

Prostanoid synthesis (Figure 23–12) involves the consumption of two molecules of O_2 catalyzed by cyclooxygenase (COX) (also called **prostaglandin H synthase),** an enzyme that has two activities, a **cyclooxygenase** and **peroxidase.** COX is present as two isoenzymes, COX-1 and COX-2. The product, an endoperoxide (PGH), is converted to prostaglandins D and E as well as to a thromboxane (TXA_2) and prostacyclin (PGI_2). Each cell type produces only one type of prostanoid. **Aspirin,** a nonsteroidal anti-inflammatory drug (NSAID), inhibits COX-1 and COX-2. Other NSAIDs include indomethacin and ibuprofen, and usually inhibit cyclooxygenases by competing with arachidonate. Since inhibition of COX-1 causes the stomach irritation often associated with taking NSAIDs, new drugs which selectively inhibit COX-2 are being developed. Transcription of COX-2— but not of COX-1— is completely inhibited by **anti-inflammatory corticosteroids.**

Essential Fatty Acids Do Not Exert All Their Physiologic Effects Via Prostaglandin Synthesis

The role of essential fatty acids in membrane formation is unrelated to prostaglandin formation. Prostaglandins do not relieve symptoms of essential fatty acid deficiency, and an essential fatty acid deficiency is not caused by inhibition of prostaglandin synthesis.

Cyclooxygenase Is a "Suicide Enzyme"

"Switching off" of prostaglandin activity is partly achieved by a remarkable property of cyclooxygenase— that of self-catalyzed destruction; ie, it is a "suicide

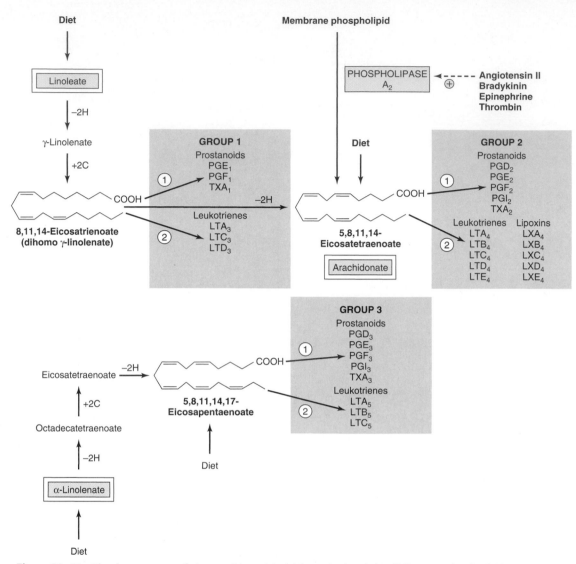

Figure 23–11. The three groups of eicosanoids and their biosynthetic origins. (PG, prostaglandin; PGI, prostacyclin; TX, thromboxane; LT, leukotriene; LX, lipoxin; ①, cyclooxygenase pathway; ②, lipoxygenase pathway.) The subscript denotes the total number of double bonds in the molecule and the series to which the compound belongs.

enzyme." Furthermore, the inactivation of prostaglandins by **15-hydroxyprostaglandin dehydrogenase** is rapid. Blocking the action of this enzyme with sulfasalazine or indomethacin can prolong the half-life of prostaglandins in the body.

LEUKOTRIENES & LIPOXINS ARE FORMED BY THE LIPOXYGENASE PATHWAY

The leukotrienes are a family of conjugated trienes formed from eicosanoic acids in leukocytes, masto-cytoma cells, platelets, and macrophages by the **lipoxygenase pathway** in response to both immunologic and nonimmunologic stimuli. Three different lipoxygenases (dioxygenases) insert oxygen into the 5, 12, and 15 positions of arachidonic acid, giving rise to hydroperoxides (HPETE). Only **5-lipoxygenase** forms leukotrienes (details in Figure 23–13). Lipoxins are a family of conjugated tetraenes also arising in leukocytes. They are formed by the combined action of more than one lipoxygenase (Figure 23–13).

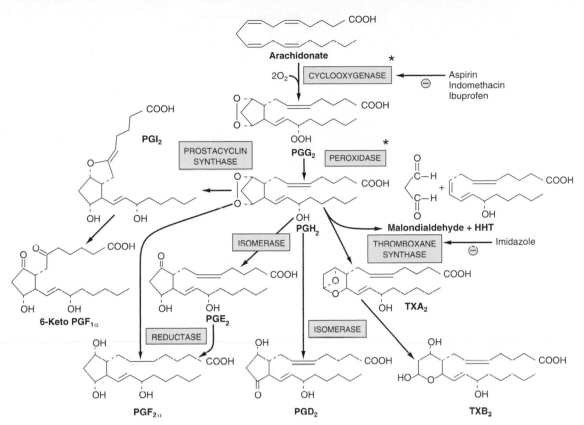

Figure 23–12. Conversion of arachidonic acid to prostaglandins and thromboxanes of series 2. (PG, prostaglandin; TX, thromboxane; PGI, prostacyclin; HHT, hydroxyheptadecatrienoate.) (Asterisk: Both of these starred activities are attributed to one enzyme: prostaglandin H synthase. Similar conversions occur in prostaglandins and thromboxanes of series 1 and 3.)

CLINICAL ASPECTS

Symptoms of Essential Fatty Acid Deficiency in Humans Include Skin Lesions & Impairment of Lipid Transport

In adults subsisting on ordinary diets, no signs of essential fatty acid deficiencies have been reported. However, infants receiving formula diets low in fat and patients maintained for long periods exclusively by intravenous nutrition low in essential fatty acids show deficiency symptoms that can be prevented by an essential fatty acid intake of 1–2% of the total caloric requirement.

Abnormal Metabolism of Essential Fatty Acids Occurs in Several Diseases

Abnormal metabolism of essential fatty acids, which may be connected with dietary insufficiency, has been noted in cystic fibrosis, acrodermatitis enteropathica, hepatore-

nal syndrome, Sjögren-Larsson syndrome, multisystem neuronal degeneration, Crohn's disease, cirrhosis and alcoholism, and Reye's syndrome. Elevated levels of very long chain polynoic acids have been found in the brains of patients with Zellweger's syndrome (Chapter 22). Diets with a high P:S (polyunsaturated:saturated fatty acid) ratio reduce serum cholesterol levels and are considered to be beneficial in terms of the risk of development of coronary heart disease.

Prostanoids Are Potent Biologically Active Substances

Thromboxanes are synthesized in platelets and upon release cause vasoconstriction and platelet aggregation. Their synthesis is specifically inhibited by low-dose aspirin. **Prostacyclins (PGI₂)** are produced by blood vessel walls and are potent inhibitors of platelet aggregation. Thus, thromboxanes and prostacyclins are antagonistic. PG₃ and TX₃, formed from eicosapentaenoic acid (EPA),

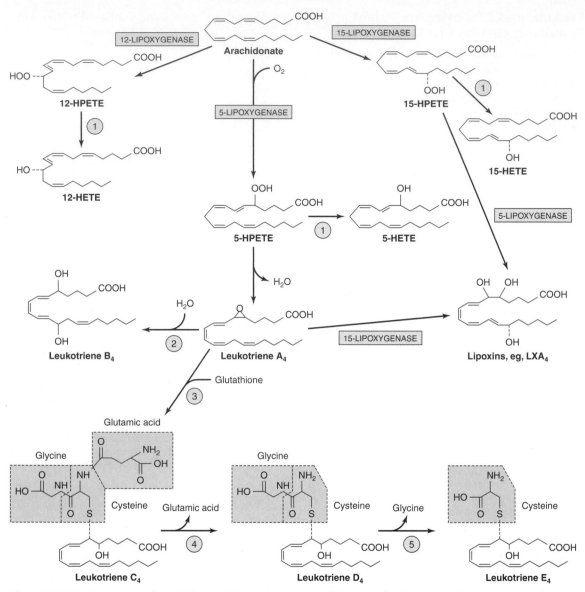

Figure 23–13. Conversion of arachidonic acid to leukotrienes and lipoxins of series 4 via the lipoxygenase pathway. Some similar conversions occur in series 3 and 5 leukotrienes. (HPETE, hydroperoxyeicosatetraenoate; HETE, hydroxy-eicosatetraenoate; ①, peroxidase; ②, leukotriene A_4 epoxide hydrolase; ③, glutathione S-transferase; ④, γ-glutamyl-transpeptidase; ⑤, cysteinyl-glycine dipeptidase.)

inhibit the release of arachidonate from phospholipids and the formation of PG_2 and TX_2. PGI_3 is as potent an antiaggregator of platelets as PGI_2, but TXA_3 is a weaker aggregator than TXA_2, changing the balance of activity and favoring longer clotting times. As little as 1 ng/mL of plasma prostaglandins causes contraction of smooth muscle in animals. Potential therapeutic uses include prevention of conception, induction of labor at

term, termination of pregnancy, prevention or alleviation of gastric ulcers, control of inflammation and of blood pressure, and relief of asthma and nasal congestion. In addition, PGD_2 is a potent sleep-promoting substance. Prostaglandins increase cAMP in platelets, thyroid, corpus luteum, fetal bone, adenohypophysis, and lung but reduce cAMP in renal tubule cells and adipose tissue (Chapter 25).

Leukotrienes & Lipoxins Are Potent Regulators of Many Disease Processes

Slow-reacting substance of anaphylaxis (**SRS-A**) is a mixture of leukotrienes C_4, D_4, and E_4. This mixture of leukotrienes is a potent constrictor of the bronchial airway musculature. These leukotrienes together with leukotriene B_4 also cause vascular permeability and attraction and activation of leukocytes and are important regulators in many diseases involving inflammatory or immediate hypersensitivity reactions, such as asthma. Leukotrienes are vasoactive, and 5-lipoxygenase has been found in arterial walls. Evidence supports an anti-inflammatory role for lipoxins in vasoactive and immunoregulatory function, eg, as counterregulatory compounds (chalones) of the immune response.

SUMMARY

- The synthesis of long-chain fatty acids (lipogenesis) is carried out by two enzyme systems: acetyl-CoA carboxylase and fatty acid synthase.
- The pathway converts acetyl-CoA to palmitate and requires NADPH, ATP, Mn^{2+}, biotin, pantothenic acid, and HCO_3^- as cofactors.
- Acetyl-CoA carboxylase converts acetyl-CoA to malonyl-CoA, then fatty acid synthase, a multienzyme complex of one polypeptide chain with seven separate enzymatic activities, catalyzes the formation of palmitate from one acetyl-CoA and seven malonyl-CoA molecules.
- Lipogenesis is regulated at the acetyl-CoA carboxylase step by allosteric modifiers, phosphorylation/dephosphorylation, and induction and repression of enzyme synthesis. The enzyme is allosterically activated by citrate and deactivated by long-chain acyl-CoA. Dephosphorylation (eg, by insulin) promotes its activity, while phosphorylation (eg, by glucagon or epinephrine) is inhibitory.

- Biosynthesis of unsaturated long-chain fatty acids is achieved by desaturase and elongase enzymes, which introduce double bonds and lengthen existing acyl chains, respectively.
- Higher animals have Δ^4, Δ^5, Δ^6, and Δ^9 desaturases but cannot insert new double bonds beyond the 9 position of fatty acids. Thus, the essential fatty acids linoleic ($\omega6$) and α-linolenic ($\omega3$) must be obtained from the diet.
- Eicosanoids are derived from C_{20} (eicosanoic) fatty acids synthesized from the essential fatty acids and make up important groups of physiologically and pharmacologically active compounds, including the prostaglandins, thromboxanes, leukotrienes, and lipoxins.

REFERENCES

Cook HW, McMaster CR: Fatty acid desaturation and chain elongation in eukaryotes. In: *Biochemistry of Lipids, Lipoproteins and Membranes.* Vance DE, Vance JE (editors). Elsevier, 2002.

Fischer S: Dietary polyunsaturated fatty acids and eicosanoid formation in humans. Adv Lipid Res 1989;23:169.

Fitzpatrick FA: Cyclooxygenase enzymes: regulation and function. Curr Pharm Des 2004;10:577.

Kim KH: Regulation of mammalian acetyl coenzyme A carboxylase. Annu Rev Nutr 1997;17:77.

McMahon B et al: Lipoxins: revelations on resolution. Trends Pharmacol Sci 1001;22:391.

Rangan VS, Smith S: Fatty acid synthesis in eukaryotes. In: *Biochemistry of Lipids, Lipoproteins and Membranes.* Vance DE, Vance JE (editors). Elsevier, 2002.

Sith S, Witkowski A, Joshi AK: Structural and functional organisation of the animal fatty acid synthase. Prog Lipid Res 2003;42:289.

Smith WL, Murphy RC: The eicosanoids: cyclooxygenase, lipoxygenase, and epoxygenase pathways. In: *Biochemistry of Lipids, Lipoproteins and Membranes.* Vance DE, Vance JE (editors). Elsevier, 2002.

Wijendran V, Hayes KC: Dietary n-6 and n-3 fatty acid balance and cardiovascular health. Annu Rev Nutr 2004;24:597.

Metabolism of Acylglycerols & Sphingolipids

24

Kathleen M. Botham, PhD, DSc, & Peter A. Mayes, PhD, DSc

BIOMEDICAL IMPORTANCE

Acylglycerols constitute the majority of lipids in the body. Triacylglycerols are the major lipids in fat deposits and in food, and their roles in lipid transport and storage and in various diseases such as obesity, diabetes, and hyperlipoproteinemia will be described in subsequent chapters. The amphipathic nature of phospholipids and sphingolipids makes them ideally suitable as the main lipid component of cell membranes. Phospholipids also take part in the metabolism of many other lipids. Some phospholipids have specialized functions; eg, dipalmitoyl lecithin is a major component of **lung surfactant,** which is lacking in respiratory distress syndrome of the newborn. Inositol phospholipids in the cell membrane act as precursors of **hormone second messengers,** and **platelet-activating factor** is an alkylphospholipid. Glycosphingolipids, containing sphingosine and sugar residues as well as fatty acid and found in the outer leaflet of the plasma membrane with their oligosaccharide chains facing outward, form part of the glycocalyx of the cell surface and are important (1) in cell adhesion and cell recognition; (2) as receptors for bacterial toxins (eg, the toxin that causes cholera); and (3) as ABO blood group substances. A dozen or so **glycolipid storage diseases** have been described (eg, Gaucher's disease, Tay-Sachs disease), each due to a genetic defect in the pathway for glycolipid degradation in the lysosomes.

HYDROLYSIS INITIATES CATABOLISM OF TRIACYLGLYCEROLS

Triacylglycerols must be hydrolyzed by a **lipase** to their constituent fatty acids and glycerol before further catabolism can proceed. Much of this hydrolysis (lipolysis) occurs in adipose tissue with release of free fatty acids into the plasma, where they are found combined with serum albumin. This is followed by free fatty acid uptake into tissues (including liver, heart, kidney, muscle, lung, testis, and adipose tissue, but not readily by brain), where they are oxidized or reesterified. The utilization of glycerol depends upon whether such tissues possess **glycerol kinase,** found in significant amounts in liver, kidney, intestine, brown adipose tissue, and lactating mammary gland.

TRIACYLGLYCEROLS & PHOSPHOGLYCEROLS ARE FORMED BY ACYLATION OF TRIOSE PHOSPHATES

The major pathways of triacylglycerol and phosphoglycerol biosynthesis are outlined in Figure 24–1. Important substances such as triacylglycerols, phosphatidylcholine, phosphatidylethanolamine, phosphatidylinositol, and cardiolipin, a constituent of mitochondrial membranes, are formed from glycerol-3-phosphate. Significant branch points in the pathway occur at the phosphatidate and diacylglycerol steps. From dihydroxyacetone phosphate are derived phosphoglycerols containing an ether link (—C—O—C—), the best-known of which are plasmalogens and platelet-activating factor (PAF). Glycerol 3-phosphate and dihydroxyacetone phosphate are intermediates in glycolysis, making a very important connection between carbohydrate and lipid metabolism.

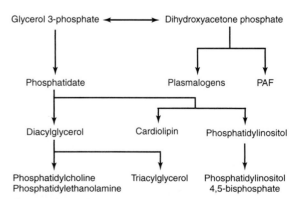

Figure 24–1. Overview of acylglycerol biosynthesis. (PAF, platelet-activating factor.)

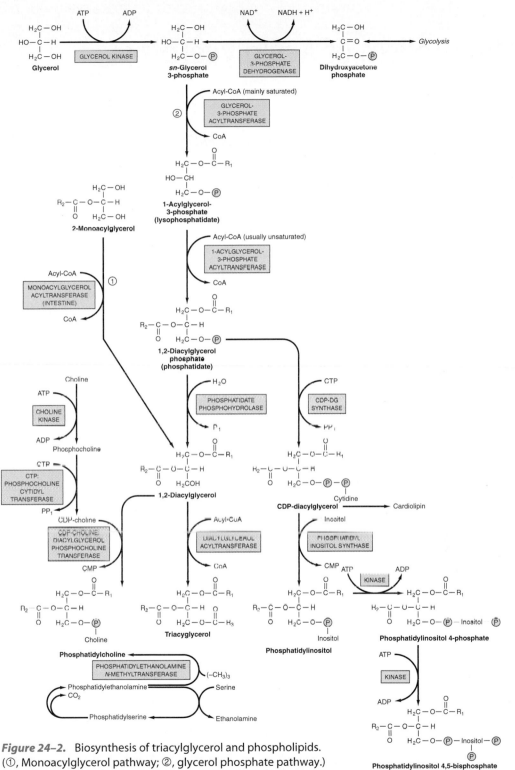

Figure 24–2. Biosynthesis of triacylglycerol and phospholipids. (①, Monoacylglycerol pathway; ②, glycerol phosphate pathway.) Phosphatidylethanolamine may be formed from ethanolamine by a pathway similar to that shown for the formation of phosphatidylcholine from choline.

Phosphatidate Is the Common Precursor in the Biosynthesis of Triacylglycerols, Many Phosphoglycerols, & Cardiolipin

Both glycerol and fatty acids must be activated by ATP before they can be incorporated into acylglycerols. Glycerol kinase catalyzes the activation of glycerol to *sn*-glycerol 3-phosphate. If the activity of this enzyme is absent or low, as in muscle or adipose tissue, most of the glycerol 3-phosphate is formed from dihydroxyace-tone phosphate by **glycerol-3-phosphate dehydrogenase** (Figure 24–2).

A. BIOSYNTHESIS OF TRIACYLGLYCEROLS

Two molecules of acyl-CoA, formed by the activation of fatty acids by **acyl-CoA synthetase** (Chapter 22), combine with glycerol 3-phosphate to form **phosphatidate** (1,2-diacylglycerol phosphate). This takes place in two stages, catalyzed by **glycerol-3-phosphate acyltransferase** and **1-acylglycerol-3-phosphate acyltransferase.** Phosphatidate is converted by **phosphatidate phosphohydrolase** and **diacylglycerol acyltransferase (DGAT)** to 1,2-diacylglycerol and then triacylglycerol. DGAT catalyzes the only step specific for triacylglycerol synthesis and is thought to be rate limiting in most circumstances. In intestinal mucosa, **monoacylglycerol acyltransferase** converts **monoacylglycerol** to 1,2-diacylglycerol in the **monoacylglycerol pathway.** Most of the activity of these enzymes resides in the endoplasmic reticulum, but some is found in mitochondria. Phosphatidate phosphohydrolase is found mainly in the cytosol, but the active form of the enzyme is membrane-bound.

In the biosynthesis of phosphatidylcholine and phosphatidylethanolamine (Figure 24–2), choline or ethanolamine must first be activated by phosphorylation by ATP followed by linkage to CTP. The resulting CDP-choline or CDP-ethanolamine reacts with 1,2-diacylglycerol to form either phosphatidylcholine or phosphatidylethanolamine, respectively. Phosphatidylserine is formed from phosphatidylethanolamine directly by reaction with serine (Figure 24–2). Phosphatidylserine may re-form phosphatidylethanolamine by decarboxylation. An alternative pathway in liver enables phosphatidylethanolamine to give rise directly to phosphatidylcholine by progressive methylation of the ethanolamine residue. In spite of these sources of choline, it is considered to be an essential nutrient in many mammalian species, but this has not been established in humans.

The regulation of triacylglycerol, phosphatidylcholine, and phosphatidylethanolamine biosynthesis is driven by the availability of free fatty acids. Those that escape oxidation are preferentially converted to phospholipids, and when this requirement is satisfied they are used for triacylglycerol synthesis.

A phospholipid present in mitochondria is **cardiolipin** (diphosphatidylglycerol; Figure 15–8). It is formed from phosphatidylglycerol, which in turn is synthesized from CDP-diacylglycerol (Figure 24–2) and glycerol 3-phosphate according to the scheme shown in Figure 24–3. Cardiolipin, found in the inner membrane of mitochondria, has a key role in mitochondrial structure and function, and is also thought to be involved in programmed cell death (apoptosis).

B. BIOSYNTHESIS OF GLYCEROL ETHER PHOSPHOLIPIDS

This pathway is located in peroxisomes. Dihydroxyace-tone phosphate is the precursor of the glycerol moiety of glycerol ether phospholipids (Figure 24–4). This compound combines with acyl-CoA to give 1-acyldihydroxy-acetone phosphate. The ether link is formed in the next reaction, producing 1-alkyldihydroxyacetone phosphate, which is then converted to 1-alkylglycerol 3-phosphate. After further acylation in the 2 position, the resulting 1-alkyl-2-acylglycerol 3-phosphate (analogous to phosphatidate in Figure 24–2) is hydrolyzed to give the free glycerol derivative. **Plasmalogens,** which comprise much of the phospholipid in mitochondria, are formed by desaturation of the analogous 3-phosphoethanolamine derivative (Figure 24–4). **Platelet-activating factor (PAF)** (1-alkyl-2-acetyl-*sn*-glycerol-3-phosphocholine) is synthesized from the corresponding 3-phosphocholine derivative. It is formed by many blood cells and other tissues and aggregates platelets at concentrations as low as 10^{-11} mol/L. It also has hypotensive and ulcerogenic properties and is involved in a variety of biologic responses, including inflammation, chemotaxis, and protein phosphorylation.

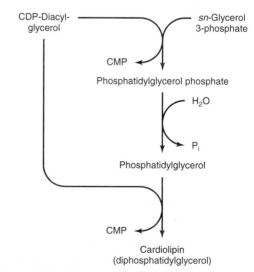

Figure 24–3. Biosynthesis of cardiolipin.

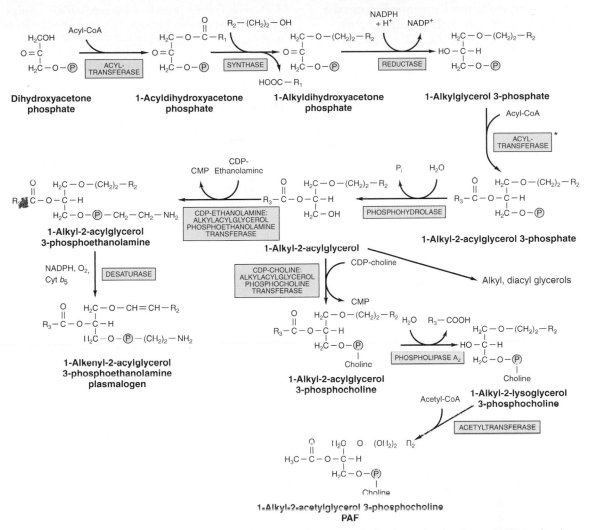

Figure 24–4. Biosynthesis of ether lipids, including plasmalogens, and platelet-activating factor (PAF). In the de novo pathway for PAF synthesis, acetyl-CoA is incorporated at stage *, avoiding the last two steps in the pathway shown here.

Phospholipases Allow Degradation & Remodeling of Phosphoglycerols

Although phospholipids are actively degraded, each portion of the molecule turns over at a different rate—eg, the turnover time of the phosphate group is different from that of the 1-acyl group. This is due to the presence of enzymes that allow partial degradation followed by resynthesis (Figure 24–5). **Phospholipase A_2** catalyzes the hydrolysis of glycerophospholipids to form a free fatty acid and lysophospholipid, which in turn may be reacylated by acyl-CoA in the presence of an acyltransfer-

ase. Alternatively, lysophospholipid (eg, lysolecithin) is attacked by **lysophospholipase,** forming the corresponding glyceryl phosphoryl base, which in turn may be split by a hydrolase liberating glycerol 3-phosphate plus base. **Phospholipases A_1, A_2, B, C, and D** attack the bonds indicated in Figure 24–6. **Phospholipase A_2** is found in pancreatic fluid and snake venom as well as in many types of cells; **phospholipase C** is one of the major toxins secreted by bacteria; and **phospholipase D** is known to be involved in mammalian signal transduction.

Lysolecithin (lysophosphatidylcholine) may be formed by an alternative route that involves **leci-**

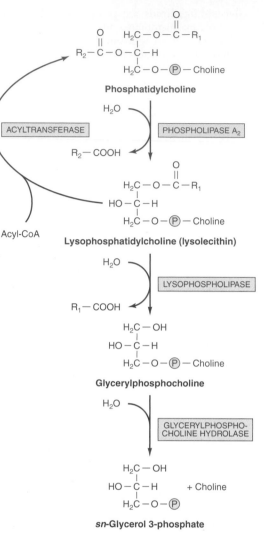

Figure 24–5. Metabolism of phosphatidylcholine (lecithin).

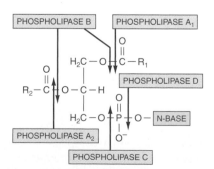

Figure 24–6. Sites of the hydrolytic activity of phospholipases on a phospholipid substrate.

thin:cholesterol acyltransferase (LCAT). This enzyme, found in plasma, catalyzes the transfer of a fatty acid residue from the 2 position of lecithin to cholesterol to form cholesteryl ester and lysolecithin and is considered to be responsible for much of the cholesteryl ester in plasma lipoproteins. Long-chain saturated fatty acids are found predominantly in the 1 position of phospholipids, whereas the polyunsaturated acids (eg, the precursors of prostaglandins) are incorporated more frequently into the 2 position. The incorporation of fatty acids into lecithin occurs by complete synthesis of the phospholipid, by transacylation between cholesteryl ester and lysolecithin, and by direct acylation of lysolecithin by acyl-CoA. Thus, a continuous exchange of the fatty acids is possible, particularly with regard to introducing essential fatty acids into phospholipid molecules.

ALL SPHINGOLIPIDS ARE FORMED FROM CERAMIDE

Ceramide is synthesized in the endoplasmic reticulum from the amino acid serine according to Figure 24–7. Ceramide is an important signaling molecule (second messenger) regulating pathways including programmed cell death **(apoptosis),** the cell cycle and cell differentiation and senescence.

Sphingomyelins (Figure 15–11) are phospholipids and are formed when ceramide reacts with phosphatidylcholine to form sphingomyelin plus diacylglycerol (Figure 24–8A). This occurs mainly in the Golgi apparatus and to a lesser extent in the plasma membrane.

Glycosphingolipids Are a Combination of Ceramide with One or More Sugar Residues

The simplest glycosphingolipids **(cerebrosides)** are **galactosylceramide (GalCer)** and **glucosylceramide (GlcCer).** GalCer is a major lipid of myelin, whereas GlcCer is the major glycosphingolipid of extraneural tissues and a precursor of most of the more complex glycosphingolipids. GalCer (Figure 24–8B) is formed in a reaction between ceramide and UDPGal (formed by epimerization from UDPGlc—Figure 21–6). **Sulfogalactosylceramide** and other sulfolipids such as the **sulfo(galacto)-glycerolipids** and the **steroid sulfates** are formed after further reactions involving 3′-phosphoadenosine-5′-phosphosulfate (PAPS; "active sulfate"). **Gangliosides** are synthesized from ceramide by the stepwise addition of activated sugars (eg, UDPGlc and UDPGal) and a **sialic acid,** usually **N-acetylneuraminic acid** (Figure 24–9). A large number of gangliosides of increasing molecular weight may be formed. Most of the enzymes transferring sugars from nucleotide sugars (glycosyl transferases) are found in the Golgi apparatus.

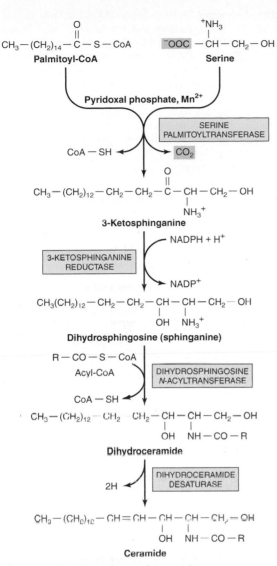

Figure 24–7. Biosynthesis of ceramide.

Glycosphingolipids are constituents of the outer leaflet of plasma membranes and are important in **cell adhesion** and **cell recognition.** Some are antigens, eg, ABO blood group substances. Certain gangliosides function as receptors for bacterial toxins (eg, for cholera toxin, which subsequently activates adenylyl cyclase).

CLINICAL ASPECTS

Deficiency of Lung Surfactant Causes Respiratory Distress Syndrome

Lung surfactant is composed mainly of lipid with some proteins and carbohydrate and prevents the alveoli from collapsing. The phospholipid **dipalmitoylphosphatidylcholine** decreases surface tension at the air-liquid interface and thus greatly reduces the work of breathing, but other surfactant lipid and protein components are also important in surfactant function. Deficiency of lung surfactant in the lungs of many preterm newborns gives rise to **infant respiratory distress syndrome (IRDS).** Administration of either natural or artificial surfactant is of therapeutic benefit.

Phospholipids & Sphingolipids Are Involved in Multiple Sclerosis and Lipidoses

Certain diseases are characterized by abnormal quantities of these lipids in the tissues, often in the nervous system. They may be classified into two groups: (1) true demyelinating diseases and (2) sphingolipidoses.

In **multiple sclerosis,** which is a demyelinating disease, there is loss of both phospholipids (particularly ethanolamine plasmalogen) and of sphingolipids from white matter. Thus, the lipid composition of white matter resembles that of gray matter. The cerebrospinal fluid shows raised phospholipid levels.

The **sphingolipidoses (lipid storage diseases)** are a group of inherited diseases that are caused by a genetic defect in the catabolism of lipids containing sphingosine. They are part of a larger group of lysosomal disorders and exhibit several constant features: (1) Complex lipids containing ceramide accumulate in cells, particularly neurons, causing neurodegeneration and shortening the life span. (2) The rate of **synthesis** of the

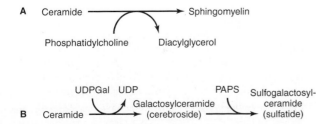

Figure 24–8. Biosynthesis of sphingomyelin (A), galactosylceramide and its sulfo derivative (B). (PAPS, "active sulfate," adenosine 3'-phosphate-5'-phosphosulfate.)

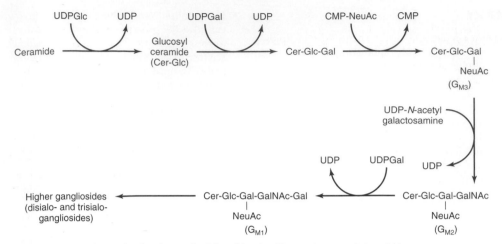

Figure 24–9. Biosynthesis of gangliosides. (NeuAc, *N*-acetylneuraminic acid.)

stored lipid is normal. (3) The enzymatic defect is in the **lysosomal degradation pathway** of sphingolipids. (4) The extent to which the activity of the affected enzyme is decreased is similar in all tissues. There is no effective treatment for many of the diseases, although some success has been achieved with enzyme replacement therapy and bone marrow transplantation in the treatment of Gaucher's and Fabry's diseases. Other promising approaches are substrate deprivation therapy

to inhibit the synthesis of sphingolipids and chemical chaperone therapy. Gene therapy for lysosomal disorders is also currently under investigation. Some examples of the more important lipid storage diseases are shown in Table 24–1.

Multiple sulfatase deficiency results in accumulation of sulfogalactosylceramide, steroid sulfates, and proteoglycans owing to a combined deficiency of arylsulfatases A, B, and C and steroid sulfatase.

Table 24–1. Examples of sphingolipidoses.

Disease	Enzyme Deficiency	Lipid Accumulating[1]	Clinical Symptoms
Tay-Sachs disease	Hexosaminidase A	Cer—Glc—Gal(NeuAc)$\div$GalNAc G_{M2} Ganglioside	Mental retardation, blindness, muscular weakness.
Fabry's disease	α-Galactosidase	Cer—Glc—Gal$\div$Gal Globotriaosylceramide	Skin rash, kidney failure (full symptoms only in males; X-linked recessive).
Metachromatic leukodystrophy	Arylsulfatase A	Cer—Gal$\div$OSO$_3$ 3-Sulfogalactosylceramide	Mental retardation and psychologic disturbances in adults; demyelination.
Krabbe's disease	β-Galactosidase	Cer$\div$Gal Galactosylceramide	Mental retardation; myelin almost absent.
Gaucher's disease	β-Glucosidase	Cer$\div$Glc Glucosylceramide	Enlarged liver and spleen, erosion of long bones, mental retardation in infants.
Niemann-Pick disease	Sphingomyelinase	Cer$\div$P—choline Sphingomyelin	Enlarged liver and spleen, mental retardation; fatal in early life.
Farber's disease	Ceramidase	Acyl$\div$Sphingosine Ceramide	Hoarseness, dermatitis, skeletal deformation, mental retardation; fatal in early life.

[1]NeuAc, *N*-acetylneuraminic acid; Cer, ceramide; Glc, glucose; Gal, galactose. $\div$, site of deficient enzyme reaction.

SUMMARY

- Triacylglycerols are the major energy-storing lipids, whereas phosphoglycerols, sphingomyelin, and glycosphingolipids are amphipathic and have structural functions in cell membranes as well as other specialized roles.

- Triacylglycerols and some phosphoglycerols are synthesized by progressive acylation of glycerol 3-phosphate. The pathway bifurcates at phosphatidate, forming inositol phospholipids and cardiolipin on the one hand and triacylglycerol and choline and ethanolamine phospholipids on the other.

- Plasmalogens and platelet-activating factor (PAF) are ether phospholipids formed from dihydroxyacetone phosphate.

- Sphingolipids are formed from ceramide (*N*-acylsphingosine). Sphingomyelin is present in membranes of organelles involved in secretory processes (eg, Golgi apparatus). The simplest glycosphingolipids are a combination of ceramide plus a sugar residue (eg, GalCer in myelin). Gangliosides are more complex glycosphingolipids containing more sugar residues plus sialic acid. They are present in the outer layer of the plasma membrane, where they contribute to the glycocalyx and are important as antigens and cell receptors.

- Phospholipids and sphingolipids are involved in several disease processes, including infant respiratory distress syndrome (lack of lung surfactant), multiple sclerosis (demyelination), and sphingolipidoses (inability to break down sphingolipids in lysosomes due to inherited defects in hydrolase enzymes).

REFERENCES

McPhail LC: Glycerolipid in signal transduction. In: *Biochemistry of Lipids, Lipoproteins and Membranes,* 4th ed. Vance DE, Vance JE (Eds.). Elsevier, 2002.

Merrill AH, Sandhoff K: Sphingolipids: metabolism and cell signaling. In: *Biochemistry of Lipids, Lipoproteins and Membranes,* 4th ed. Vance DE, Vance JE (Eds.). Elsevier, 2002.

Meyer KC, Zimmerman JJ: Inflammation and surfactant. Paediatric Respiratory Reviews 2002;3:308.

Prescott SM et al: Platelet-activating factor and related lipid mediators. Annu Rev Biochem 2000;69:419.

Ruvolo PP: Intracellular signal transduction pathways activated by ceramide and its metabolites. Pharmacol Res 2003;47:383.

Scriver CR et al (editors): *The Metabolic and Molecular Bases of Inherited Disease,* 8th ed. McGraw-Hill, 2001.

Vance DE: Phospholipid biosynthesis in eukaryotes. In: *Biochemistry of Lipids, Lipoproteins and Membranes,* 4th ed. Vance DE, Vance JE (Eds.). Elsevier, 2002.

van Echten G, Sandhoff K: Ganglioside metabolism. Enzymology, topology, and regulation. J Biol Chem 1993;268:5341.

Lipid Transport & Storage

25

Kathleen M. Botham, PhD, DSc, & Peter A. Mayes, PhD, DSc

BIOMEDICAL IMPORTANCE

Fat absorbed from the diet and lipids synthesized by the liver and adipose tissue must be transported between the various tissues and organs for utilization and storage. Since lipids are insoluble in water, the problem of how to transport them in the aqueous blood plasma is solved by associating nonpolar lipids (triacylglycerol and cholesteryl esters) with amphipathic lipids (phospholipids and cholesterol) and proteins to make water-miscible lipoproteins.

In a meal-eating omnivore such as the human, excess calories are ingested in the anabolic phase of the feeding cycle, followed by a period of negative caloric balance when the organism draws upon its carbohydrate and fat stores. Lipoproteins mediate this cycle by transporting lipids from the intestines as chylomicrons—and from the liver as very low density lipoproteins (VLDL)—to most tissues for oxidation and to adipose tissue for storage. Lipid is mobilized from adipose tissue as free fatty acids (FFA) attached to serum albumin. Abnormalities of lipoprotein metabolism cause various **hypo-** or **hyperlipoproteinemias.** The most common of these is **diabetes mellitus,** where insulin deficiency causes excessive mobilization of FFA and underutilization of chylomicrons and VLDL, leading to **hypertriacylglycerolemia.** Most other pathologic conditions affecting lipid transport are due primarily to inherited defects, some of which cause **hypercholesterolemia,** and premature **atherosclerosis. Obesity**—particularly abdominal obesity—is a risk factor for increased mortality, hypertension, type 2 diabetes mellitus, hyperlipidemia, hyperglycemia, and various endocrine dysfunctions.

LIPIDS ARE TRANSPORTED IN THE PLASMA AS LIPOPROTEINS

Four Major Lipid Classes Are Present in Lipoproteins

Plasma lipids consist of **triacylglycerols** (16%), **phospholipids** (30%), **cholesterol** (14%), and **cholesteryl esters** (36%) and a much smaller fraction of unesterified long-chain fatty acids (free fatty acids) (4%). This latter fraction, the **free fatty acids (FFA),** is metabolically the most active of the plasma lipids.

Four Major Groups of Plasma Lipoproteins Have Been Identified

Because fat is less dense than water, the density of a lipoprotein decreases as the proportion of lipid to protein increases (Table 25–1). Four major groups of lipoproteins have been identified that are important physiologically and in clinical diagnosis. These are (1) **chylomicrons,** derived from intestinal absorption of triacylglycerol and other lipids; (2) **very low density lipoproteins** (VLDL, or pre-β-lipoproteins), derived from the liver for the export of triacylglycerol; (3) **low-density lipoproteins** (LDL, or β-lipoproteins), representing a final stage in the catabolism of VLDL; and (4) **high-density lipoproteins** (HDL, or α-lipoproteins), involved in cholesterol transport and also in VLDL and chylomicron metabolism. Triacylglycerol is the predominant lipid in chylomicrons and VLDL, whereas cholesterol and phospholipid are the predominant lipids in LDL and HDL, respectively (Table 25–1). Lipoproteins may be separated according to their electrophoretic properties into **α-, β-,** and **pre-β-lipoproteins.**

Lipoproteins Consist of a Nonpolar Core & a Single Surface Layer of Amphipathic Lipids

The **nonpolar lipid core** consists of mainly **triacylglycerol** and **cholesteryl ester** and is surrounded by a **single surface layer** of amphipathic **phospholipid** and **cholesterol** molecules (Figure 25–1). These are oriented so that their polar groups face outward to the aqueous medium, as in the cell membrane (Chapter 15). The protein moiety of a lipoprotein is known as an **apolipoprotein** or **apoprotein,** constituting nearly 70% of some HDL and as little as 1% of chylomicrons. Some apolipoproteins are integral and cannot be removed, whereas others are free to transfer to other lipoproteins.

The Distribution of Apolipoproteins Characterizes the Lipoprotein

One or more apolipoproteins (proteins or polypeptides) are present in each lipoprotein. The major apolipoproteins of HDL (α-lipoprotein) are designated A (Table 25–1). The main apolipoprotein of LDL (β-lipoprotein)

217

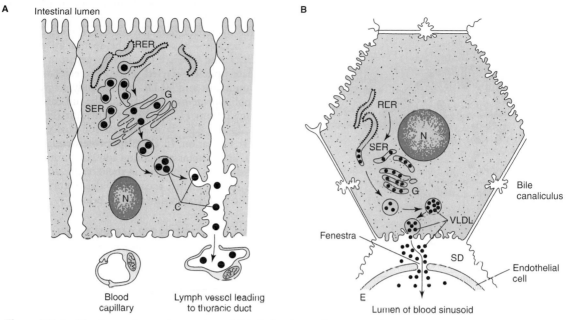

Figure 25–2. The formation and secretion of **(A)** chylomicrons by an intestinal cell and **(B)** very low density lipoproteins by a hepatic cell. (RER, rough endoplasmic reticulum; SER, smooth endoplasmic reticulum; G, Golgi apparatus; N, nucleus; C, chylomicrons; VLDL, very low density lipoproteins; E, endothelium; SD, space of Disse, containing blood plasma.) Apolipoprotein B, synthesized in the RER, is incorporated into lipoproteins in the SER, the main site of synthesis of triacylglycerol. After addition of carbohydrate residues in G, they are released from the cell by reverse pinocytosis. Chylomicrons pass into the lymphatic system. VLDL are secreted into the space of Disse and then into the hepatic sinusoids through fenestrae in the endothelial lining.

25–4). Heart lipoprotein lipase has a low K_m for triacylglycerol, about one-tenth of that for the enzyme in adipose tissue. This enables the delivery of fatty acids from triacylglycerol to be **redirected from adipose tissue to the heart in the starved state** when the plasma triacylglycerol decreases. A similar redirection to the mammary gland occurs during lactation, allowing uptake of lipoprotein triacylglycerol fatty acid for milk fat synthesis. The **VLDL receptor** plays an important part in the delivery of fatty acids from VLDL triacylglycerol to adipocytes by binding VLDL and bringing it into close contact with lipoprotein lipase. In adipose tissue, insulin enhances lipoprotein lipase synthesis in adipocytes and its translocation to the luminal surface of the capillary endothelium.

The Action of Lipoprotein Lipase Forms Remnant Lipoproteins

Reaction with lipoprotein lipase results in the loss of approximately 90% of the triacylglycerol of chylomicrons and in the loss of apo C (which returns to HDL) but not apo E, which is retained. The resulting **chylomicron remnant** is about half the diameter of the parent chylomicron and is relatively enriched in cholesterol and cholesteryl esters because of the loss of triacylglycerol (Figure 25–3). Similar changes occur to VLDL, with the formation of VLDL remnants or IDL (intermediate-density lipoprotein) (Figure 25–4).

The Liver Is Responsible for the Uptake of Remnant Lipoproteins

Chylomicron remnants are taken up by the liver by receptor-mediated endocytosis, and the cholesteryl esters and triacylglycerols are hydrolyzed and metabolized. Uptake is mediated by **apo E** (Figure 25–3), via two apo E-dependent receptors, the **LDL (apo B-100, E) receptor** and the **LRP (LDL receptor-related protein).** Hepatic lipase has a dual role: (1) it acts as a ligand to facilitate remnant uptake and (2) it hydrolyzes remnant triacylglycerol and phospholipid.

After metabolism to IDL, VLDL may be taken up by the liver directly via the LDL (apo B-100, E) receptor, or it may be converted to LDL. Only one molecule of apo B-100 is present in each of these lipoprotein particles, and this is conserved during the transformations. Thus, each LDL particle is derived from a single precursor VLDL particle (Figure 25–4). In humans, a rela-

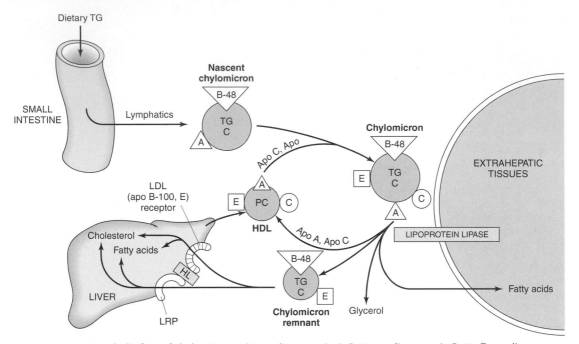

Figure 25–3. Metabolic fate of chylomicrons. (A, apolipoprotein A; B-48, apolipoprotein B-48; ©, apolipoprotein C; E, apolipoprotein E; HDL, high-density lipoprotein; TG, triacylglycerol; C, cholesterol and cholesteryl ester; P, phospholipid; HL, hepatic lipase; LRP, LDL receptor-related protein.) Only the predominant lipids are shown.

tively large proportion of IDL forms LDL, accounting for the increased concentrations of LDL in humans compared with many other mammals.

LDL IS METABOLIZED VIA THE LDL RECEPTOR

The liver and many extrahepatic tissues express the **LDL (apo B-100, E) receptor.** It is so designated because it is specific for apo B-100 but not B-48, which lacks the carboxyl terminal domain of B-100 containing the LDL receptor ligand, and it also takes up lipoproteins rich in apo E. This receptor is defective in **familial hypercholesterolemia.** Approximately 30% of LDL is degraded in extrahepatic tissues and 70% in the liver. A positive correlation exists between the incidence of **coronary atherosclerosis** and the plasma concentration of LDL cholesterol. For further discussion of the regulation of the LDL receptor, see Chapter 26.

HDL TAKES PART IN BOTH LIPOPROTEIN TRIACYLGLYCEROL & CHOLESTEROL METABOLISM

HDL is synthesized and secreted from both liver and intestine (Figure 25–5). However, apo C and apo E are synthesized in the liver and transferred from liver HDL to intestinal HDL when the latter enters the plasma. A major function of HDL is to act as a repository for the apo C and apo E required in the metabolism of chylomicrons and VLDL. Nascent HDL consists of discoid phospholipid bilayers containing apo A and free cholesterol. These lipoproteins are similar to the particles found in the plasma of patients with a deficiency of the plasma enzyme **lecithin:cholesterol acyltransferase (LCAT)** and in the plasma of patients with obstructive jaundice. LCAT—and the LCAT activator apo A-I—bind to the discoidal particles, and the surface phospholipid and free cholesterol are converted into cholesteryl esters and lysolecithin (Chapter 24). The nonpolar cholesteryl esters move into the hydrophobic interior of the bilayer, whereas lysolecithin is transferred to plasma albumin. Thus, a nonpolar core is generated, forming a spherical, pseudomicellar HDL covered by a surface film of polar lipids and apolipoproteins. This aids the removal of excess unesterified cholesterol from lipoproteins and tissues as described below. The **class B scavenger receptor B1 (SR-B1)** has been identified as an **HDL receptor with a dual role in HDL metabolism.** In the liver and in steroidogenic tissues, it binds HDL via apo A-I, and cholesteryl ester is selectively delivered to the cells, although the particle itself, including apo A-I, is not taken up. In the tissues, on the other hand, SR-B1 mediates the acceptance of cholesterol from the cells by HDL,

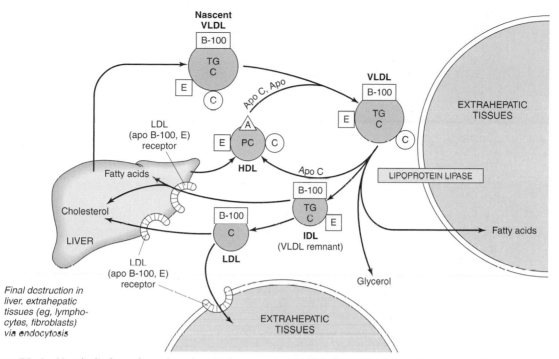

Figure 25–4. Metabolic fate of very low density lipoproteins (VLDL) and production of low-density lipoproteins (LDL). (A, apolipoprotein A; B-100, apolipoprotein B-100; ©, apolipoprotein C; E, apolipoprotein E; HDL, high-density lipoprotein; TG, triacylglycerol; IDL, intermediate-density lipoprotein; C, cholesterol and cholesteryl ester; P, phospholipid.) Only the predominant lipids are shown. It is possible that some IDL is also metabolized via the LRP.

which then transports it to the liver for excretion via the bile (either as cholesterol or after conversion to bile acids) in the process known as **reverse cholesterol transport** (Figure 25–5). HDL$_3$, generated from discoidal HDL by the action of LCAT, accepts cholesterol from the tissues via the **SR-B1** and the cholesterol is then esterified by LCAT, increasing the size of the particles to form the less dense HDL$_2$. HDL$_3$ is then reformed, either after selective delivery of cholesteryl ester to the liver via the SR-B1 or by hydrolysis of HDL$_2$ phospholipid and triacylglycerol by hepatic lipase. This interchange of HDL$_2$ and HDL$_3$ is called the HDL cycle (Figure 25–5). Free apo A-I is released by these processes and forms **preβ-HDL** after associating with a minimum amount of phospholipid and cholesterol. Surplus apo A-I is destroyed in the kidney. A second important mechanism for reverse cholesterol transport involves the **ATP-binding cassette transporter A1 (ABCA1).** ABCA1 is a member of a family of transporter proteins that couple the hydrolysis of ATP to the binding of a substrate, enabling it to be transported across the membrane. ABCA1 preferentially transfer cholesterol from cells to poorly lipidated particles such as preβ-HDL or apo A-1, which are then converted to HDL$_3$ via discoidal HDL (Figure 25–5). Preβ-HDL

is the most potent form of HDL inducing cholesterol efflux from the tissues.

HDL concentrations vary reciprocally with plasma triacylglycerol concentrations and directly with the activity of lipoprotein lipase. This may be due to surplus surface constituents, eg, phospholipid and apo A-I being released during hydrolysis of chylomicrons and VLDL and contributing toward the formation of preβ-HDL and discoidal HDL. HDL$_2$ concentrations are **inversely related to the incidence of coronary atherosclerosis,** possibly because they reflect the efficiency of reverse cholesterol transport. HDL$_c$ (HDL$_1$) is found in the blood of diet-induced hypercholesterolemic animals. It is rich in cholesterol, and its sole apolipoprotein is apo E. It appears that all plasma lipoproteins are interrelated components of one or more metabolic cycles that together are responsible for the complex process of plasma lipid transport.

THE LIVER PLAYS A CENTRAL ROLE IN LIPID TRANSPORT & METABOLISM

The liver carries out the following major functions in lipid metabolism: (1) It facilitates the digestion and

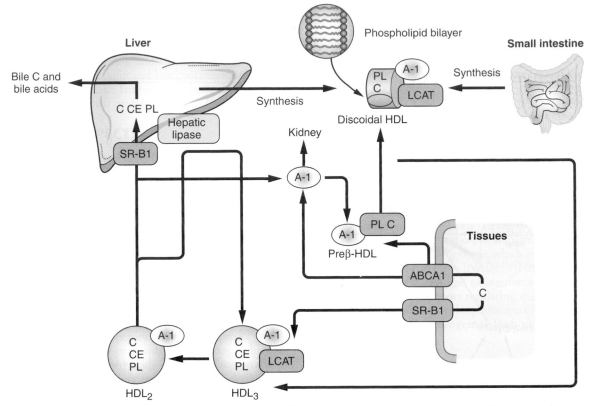

Figure 25–5. Metabolism of high-density lipoprotein (HDL) in reverse cholesterol transport. (LCAT, lecithin:cholesterol acyltransferase; C, cholesterol; CE, cholesteryl ester; PL, phospholipid; A-I, apolipoprotein A-I; SR-B1, scavenger receptor B1; ABCA 1, ATP binding cassette transporter A1.) Preβ-HDL, HDL$_2$, HDL$_3$—see Table 25–1. Surplus surface constituents from the action of lipoprotein lipase on chylomicrons and VLDL are another source of preβ-HDL. Hepatic lipase activity is increased by androgens and decreased by estrogens, which may account for higher concentrations of plasma HDL$_2$ in women.

absorption of lipids by the production of bile, which contains cholesterol and bile salts synthesized within the liver de novo or from uptake of lipoprotein cholesterol (Chapter 26). (2) It actively synthesizes and oxidizes fatty acids (Chapters 22 and 23) and also synthesizes triacylglycerols and phospholipids (Chapter 24). (3) It converts fatty acids to ketone bodies (ketogenesis) (Chapter 22). (4) It plays an integral part in the synthesis and metabolism of plasma lipoproteins (this chapter).

Hepatic VLDL Secretion Is Related to Dietary & Hormonal Status

The cellular events involved in VLDL formation and secretion have been described above (Figure 25–2) and are shown in Figure 25–6. Hepatic triacylglycerol synthesis provides the immediate stimulus for the formation

and secretion of VLDL. The fatty acids used are derived from two possible sources: (1) synthesis within the liver from acetyl-CoA derived mainly from carbohydrate (perhaps not so important in humans) and (2) uptake of free fatty acids from the circulation. The first source is predominant in the well-fed condition, when fatty acid synthesis is high and the level of circulating free fatty acids is low. As triacylglycerol does not normally accumulate in the liver under this condition, it must be inferred that it is transported from the liver in VLDL as rapidly as it is synthesized and that the synthesis of apo B-100 is not rate-limiting. Free fatty acids from the circulation are the main source during starvation, the feeding of high-fat diets, or in diabetes mellitus, when hepatic lipogenesis is inhibited. Factors that enhance both the synthesis of triacylglycerol and the secretion of VLDL by the liver include (1) the fed state rather than

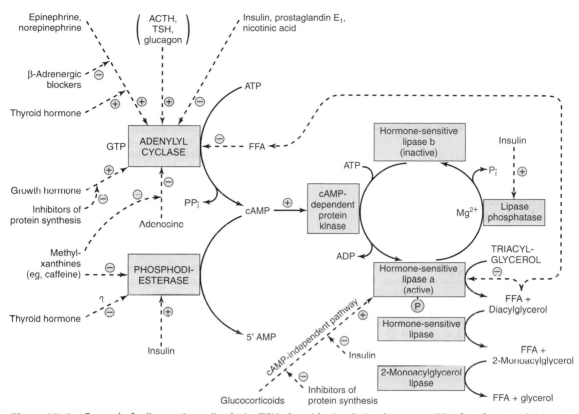

Figure 25–8. Control of adipose tissue lipolysis. (TSH, thyroid-stimulating hormone; FFA, free fatty acids.) Note the cascade sequence of reactions affording amplification at each step. The lipolytic stimulus is "switched off" by removal of the stimulating hormone; the action of lipase phosphatase; the inhibition of the lipase and adenylyl cyclase by high concentrations of FFA; the inhibition of adenylyl cyclase by adenosine; and the removal of cAMP by the action of phosphodiesterase. ACTH, TSH, and glucagon may not activate adenylyl cyclase in vivo, since the concentration of each hormone required in vitro is much higher than is found in the circulation. Positive ($\oplus$) and negative ($\ominus$) regulatory effects are represented by broken lines and substrate flow by solid lines.

On consideration of the profound derangement of metabolism in **diabetes mellitus** (due in large part to increased release of free fatty acids from the depots) and the fact that insulin to a large extent corrects the condition, it must be concluded that insulin plays a prominent role in the regulation of adipose tissue metabolism.

BROWN ADIPOSE TISSUE PROMOTES THERMOGENESIS

Brown adipose tissue is involved in metabolism, particularly at times when heat generation is necessary. Thus, the tissue is extremely active in some species in arousal from hibernation, in animals exposed to cold (nonshivering thermogenesis), and in heat production in the newborn animal. Though not a prominent tissue in humans, it is present in normal individuals, where it could be responsible for **"diet-induced thermogenesis."** It is

noteworthy that brown adipose tissue is reduced or absent in obese persons. The tissue is characterized by a well-developed blood supply and a high content of mitochondria and cytochromes but low activity of ATP synthase. Metabolic emphasis is placed on oxidation of both glucose and fatty acids. **Norepinephrine** liberated from sympathetic nerve endings is important in increasing lipolysis in the tissue and increasing synthesis of lipoprotein lipase to enhance utilization of triacylglycerol-rich lipoproteins from the circulation. Oxidation and phosphorylation are not coupled in mitochondria of this tissue, and the phosphorylation that does occur is at the substrate level, eg, at the succinate thiokinase step and in glycolysis. Thus, **oxidation produces much heat, and little free energy is trapped in ATP.** A thermogenic uncoupling protein, **thermogenin,** acts as a proton conductance pathway dissipating the electrochemical potential across the mitochondrial membrane (Figure 25–9).

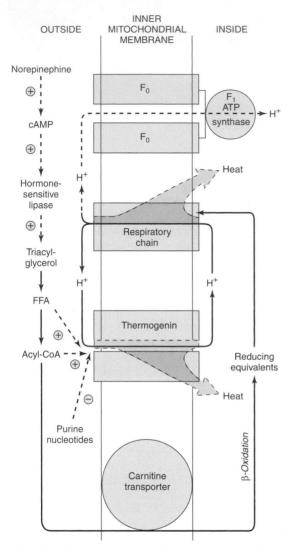

OUTSIDE — **INNER MITOCHONDRIAL MEMBRANE** — **INSIDE**

Figure 25–9. Thermogenesis in brown adipose tissue. Activity of the respiratory chain produces heat in addition to translocating protons (Chapter 13). These protons dissipate more heat when returned to the inner mitochondrial compartment via thermogenin instead of via the F_1 ATP synthase, the route that generates ATP. The passage of H^+ via thermogenin is inhibited by purine nucleotides when brown adipose tissue is unstimulated. Under the influence of norepinephrine, the inhibition is removed by the production of free fatty acids (FFA) and acyl-CoA. Note the dual role of acyl-CoA in both facilitating the action of thermogenin and supplying reducing equivalents for the respiratory chain. $\oplus$ and $\ominus$ signify positive or negative regulatory effects.

SUMMARY

- Since nonpolar lipids are insoluble in water, for transport between the tissues in the aqueous blood plasma they are combined with amphipathic lipids and proteins to make water-miscible lipoproteins.

- Four major groups of lipoproteins are recognized: Chylomicrons transport lipids resulting from digestion and absorption. Very low density lipoproteins (VLDL) transport triacylglycerol from the liver. Low-density lipoproteins (LDL) deliver cholesterol to the tissues, and high-density lipoproteins (HDL) remove cholesterol from the tissues and return it to the liver for excretion in the process known as reverse cholesterol transport.

- Chylomicrons and VLDL are metabolized by hydrolysis of their triacylglycerol, and lipoprotein remnants are left in the circulation. These are taken up by liver, but some of the remnants (IDL), resulting from VLDL form LDL, which is taken up by the liver and other tissues via the LDL receptor.

- Apolipoproteins constitute the protein moiety of lipoproteins. They act as enzyme activators (eg, apo C-II and apo A-I) or as ligands for cell receptors (eg, apo A-I, apo E, and apo B-100).

- Triacylglycerol is the main storage lipid in adipose tissue. Upon mobilization, free fatty acids and glycerol are released. Free fatty acids are an important fuel source.

- Brown adipose tissue is the site of "nonshivering thermogenesis." It is found in hibernating and newborn animals and is present in small quantity in humans. Thermogenesis results from the presence of an uncoupling protein, thermogenin, in the inner mitochondrial membrane.

REFERENCES

Eaton S et al: Multiple biochemical effects in the pathogenesis of fatty liver. Eur J Clin Invest 1997;27:719.

Goldberg IJ, Merkel M: Lipoprotein lipase: physiology, biochemistry and molecular biology. Front Biosci 2001;6:D388.

Holm C et al: Molecular mechanisms regulating hormone sensitive lipase and lipolysis. Annu Rev Nutr 2000;20:365.

Kershaw EE, Flier JS: Adipose tissue as an endocrine organ. J Clin Endocrinol Metab 2004;89:2548.

Lardy H, Shrago E: Biochemical aspects of obesity. Annu Rev Biochem 1990;59:689.

Redgrave TG: Chylomicron metabolism. Biochem Soc Trans 2004;32:79.

Rye K-A et al: Overview of plasma lipid transport. In: *Plasma Lipids and Their Role in Disease.* Barter PJ, Rye K-A (editors). Harwood Academic Publishers, 1999.

Sell H, Deshaies Y, Richard D: The brown adipocyte: update on its metabolic role. Int J Biochem Cell Biol. 2004;36:2098.

Shelness GS, Sellers JA: Very-low-density lipoprotein assembly and secretion. Curr Opin Lipidol 2001;12:151.

Various authors: *Biochemistry of Lipids, Lipoproteins and Membranes,* 4th ed. Vance DE, Vance JE (editors). Elsevier, 2002.

Cholesterol Synthesis, Transport, & Excretion

26

Kathleen M. Botham, PhD, DSc, & Peter A. Mayes, PhD, DSc

BIOMEDICAL IMPORTANCE

Cholesterol is present in tissues and in plasma either as free cholesterol or as a storage form, combined with a long-chain fatty acid as cholesteryl ester. In plasma, both forms are transported in lipoproteins (Chapter 25). Cholesterol is an amphipathic lipid and as such is an essential structural component of membranes and of the outer layer of plasma lipoproteins. It is synthesized in many tissues from acetyl-CoA and is the precursor of all other steroids in the body, including corticosteroids, sex hormones, bile acids, and vitamin D. As a typical product of animal metabolism, cholesterol occurs in foods of animal origin such as egg yolk, meat, liver, and brain. Plasma low-density lipoprotein (LDL) is the vehicle of uptake of cholesterol and cholesteryl ester into many tissues. Free cholesterol is removed from tissues by plasma high-density lipoprotein (HDL) and transported to the liver, where it is eliminated from the body either unchanged or after conversion to bile acids in the process known as **reverse cholesterol transport** (Chapter 25). Cholesterol is a major constituent of **gallstones.** However, its chief role in pathologic processes is as a factor in the genesis of **atherosclerosis** of vital arteries, causing cerebrovascular, coronary, and peripheral vascular disease.

CHOLESTEROL IS DERIVED ABOUT EQUALLY FROM THE DIET & FROM BIOSYNTHESIS

A little more than half the cholesterol of the body arises by synthesis (about 700 mg/d), and the remainder is provided by the average diet. The liver and intestine account for approximately 10% each of total synthesis in humans. Virtually all tissues containing nucleated cells are capable of cholesterol synthesis, which occurs in the endoplasmic reticulum and the cytosol.

Acetyl-CoA Is the Source of All Carbon Atoms in Cholesterol

The biosynthesis of cholesterol may be divided into five steps: (1) Synthesis of mevalonate from acetyl-CoA (Figure 26–1). (2) Formation of isoprenoid units from mevalonate by loss of CO_2 (Figure 26–2). (3) Condensation of six isoprenoid units form squalene. (4) Cyclization of squalene give rise to the parent steroid, lanosterol. (5) Formation of cholesterol from lanosterol (Figure 26–3).

Step 1—Biosynthesis of Mevalonate: HMG-CoA (3-hydroxy-3-methylglutaryl-CoA) is formed by the reactions used in mitochondria to synthesize ketone bodies (Figure 22–7). However, since cholesterol synthesis is extramitochondrial, the two pathways are distinct. Initially, two molecules of acetyl-CoA condense to form acetoacetyl-CoA catalyzed by cytosolic **thiolase.** Acetoacetyl-CoA condenses with a further molecule of acetyl-CoA catalyzed by **HMG-CoA synthase** to form HMG-CoA, which is reduced to **mevalonate** by NADPH catalyzed by **HMG-CoA reductase.** This is the principal regulatory step in the pathway of cholesterol synthesis and is the site of action of the most effective class of cholesterol-lowering drugs, the HMG-CoA reductase inhibitors (statins) (Figure 26–1).

Step 2—Formation of Isoprenoid Units: Mevalonate is phosphorylated sequentially by ATP by three kinases, and after decarboxylation (Figure 26–2) the active isoprenoid unit, **isopentenyl diphosphate,** is formed.

Step 3—Six Isoprenoid Units Form Squalene: Isopentenyl diphosphate is isomerized by a shift of the double bond to form **dimethylallyl diphosphate,** then condensed with another molecule of isopentenyl diphosphate to form the ten-carbon intermediate **geranyl diphosphate** (Figure 26–2). A further condensation with isopentenyl diphosphate forms **farnesyl diphosphate.** Two molecules of farnesyl diphosphate condense at the diphosphate end to form **squalene.** Initially, inorganic pyrophosphate is eliminated, forming presqualene diphosphate, which is then reduced by NADPH with elimination of a further inorganic pyrophosphate molecule.

Step 4—Formation of Lanosterol: Squalene can fold into a structure that closely resembles the steroid

230

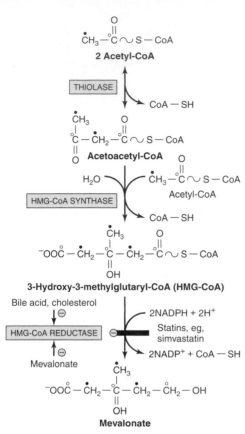

Figure 26–1. Biosynthesis of mevalonate. HMG-CoA reductase is inhibited by atorvastatin, pravastatin, and simvastatin. The open and solid circles indicate the fate of each of the carbons in the acetyl moiety of acetyl-CoA.

Farnesyl Diphosphate Gives Rise to Dolichol & Ubiquinone

The polyisoprenoids **dolichol** (Figure 15–20 and Chapter 46) and **ubiquinone** (Figure 13–5) are formed from farnesyl diphosphate by the further addition of up to 16 (dolichol) or 3–7 (ubiquinone) isopentenyl diphosphate residues, respectively. Some GTP-binding proteins in the cell membrane are prenylated with farnesyl or geranylgeranyl (20 carbon) residues. Protein prenylation is believed to facilitate the anchoring of proteins into lipoid membranes and may also be involved in protein-protein interactions and membrane-associated protein trafficking.

CHOLESTEROL SYNTHESIS IS CONTROLLED BY REGULATION OF HMG-CoA REDUCTASE

Regulation of cholesterol synthesis is exerted near the beginning of the pathway, at the HMG-CoA reductase step. The reduced synthesis of cholesterol in starving animals is accompanied by a decrease in the activity of the enzyme. However, it is only hepatic synthesis that is inhibited by dietary cholesterol. HMG-CoA reductase in liver is inhibited by mevalonate, the immediate product of the pathway, and by cholesterol, the main product. Cholesterol and metabolites repress transcription of the HMG-CoA reductase via activation of a **sterol regulatory element-binding protein (SREBP)** transcription factor. SREBPs are a family of proteins that regulate the transcription of a range of genes involved in the cellular uptake and metabolism of cholesterol and other lipids. A **diurnal variation** occurs in both cholesterol synthesis and reductase activity. In addition to these mechanisms regulating the rate of protein synthesis, the enzyme activity is also modulated more rapidly by posttranslational modification (Figure 26–4). Insulin or thyroid hormone increases HMG-CoA reductase activity, whereas glucagon or glucocorticoids decrease it. Activity is reversibly modified by phosphorylation-dephosphorylation mechanisms, some of which may be cAMP-dependent and therefore immediately responsive to glucagon. Attempts to lower plasma cholesterol in humans by reducing the amount of cholesterol in the diet produce variable results. Generally, a decrease of 100 mg in dietary cholesterol causes a decrease of approximately 0.13 mmol/L of serum.

MANY FACTORS INFLUENCE THE CHOLESTEROL BALANCE IN TISSUES

In tissues, cholesterol balance is regulated as follows (Figure 26–5): Cell cholesterol increase is due to uptake of cholesterol-containing lipoproteins by receptors, eg, the

nucleus (Figure 26–3). Before ring closure occurs, squalene is converted to squalene 2,3-epoxide by a mixed-function oxidase in the endoplasmic reticulum, **squalene epoxidase.** The methyl group on C_{14} is transferred to C_{13} and that on C_8 to C_{14} as cyclization occurs, catalyzed by **oxidosqualene:lanosterol cyclase.**

  Step 5—Formation of Cholesterol: The formation of cholesterol from **lanosterol** takes place in the membranes of the endoplasmic reticulum and involves changes in the steroid nucleus and side chain (Figure 26–3). The methyl groups on C_{14} and C_4 are removed to form 14-desmethyl lanosterol and then zymosterol. The double bond at C_8–C_9 is subsequently moved to C_5–C_6 in two steps, forming **desmosterol.** Finally, the double bond of the side chain is reduced, producing cholesterol. The exact order in which the steps described actually take place is not known with certainty.

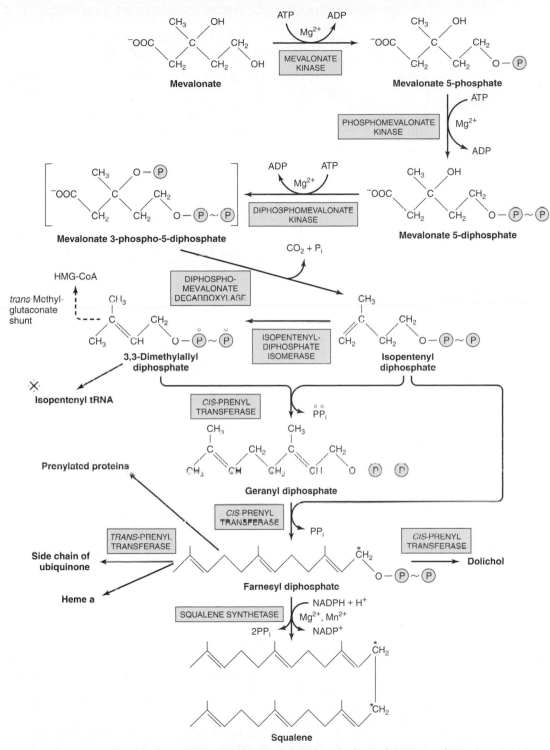

Figure 26–2. Biosynthesis of squalene, ubiquinone, dolichol, and other polyisoprene derivatives. (HMG, 3-hydroxy-3-methylglutaryl; ⁒, cytokinin.) A farnesyl residue is present in heme a of cytochrome oxidase. The carbon marked with asterisk becomes C_{11} or C_{12} in squalene. Squalene synthetase is a microsomal enzyme; all other enzymes indicated are soluble cytosolic proteins, and some are found in peroxisomes.

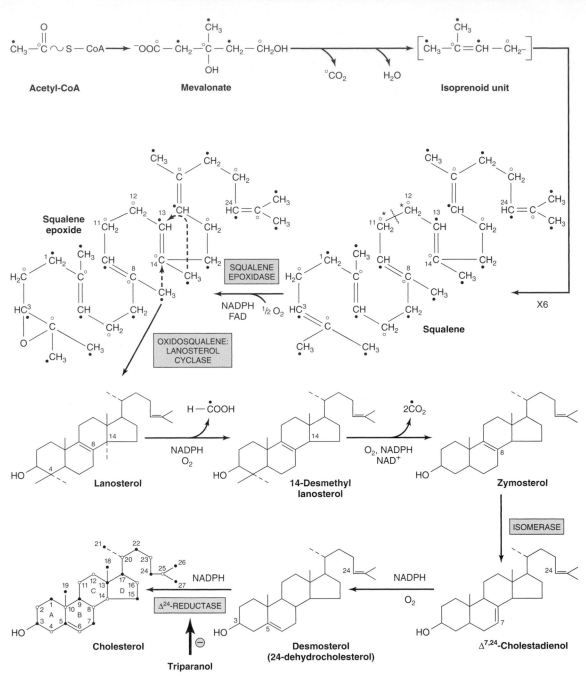

Figure 26–3. Biosynthesis of cholesterol. The numbered positions are those of the steroid nucleus and the open and solid circles indicate the fate of each of the carbons in the acetyl moiety of acetyl-CoA. Asterisks: Refer to labeling of squalene in Figure 26–2.

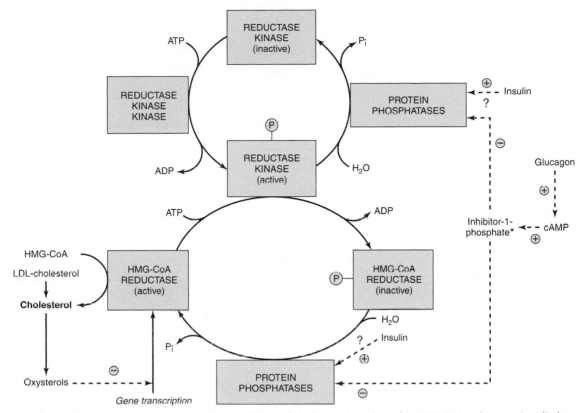

Figure 26–4. Possible mechanisms in the regulation of cholesterol synthesis by HMG-CoA reductase. Insulin has a dominant role compared with glucagon. Asterisk: See Figure 19–6.

LDL receptor or the scavenger receptor; uptake of free cholesterol from cholesterol-rich lipoproteins to the cell membrane; cholesterol synthesis; and hydrolysis of cholesteryl esters by the enzyme **cholesteryl ester hydrolase.** Decrease is due to efflux of cholesterol from the membrane to HDL via the ABCA-1 or SR-B1 (Chapter 25); esterification of cholesterol by **ACAT** (acyl-CoA:cholesterol acyltransferase); and utilization of cholesterol for synthesis of other steroids, such as hormones, or bile acids in the liver.

The LDL Receptor Is Highly Regulated

LDL (apo B-100, E) receptors occur on the cell surface in pits that are coated on the cytosolic side of the cell membrane with a protein called clathrin. The glycoprotein receptor spans the membrane, the B-100 binding region being at the exposed amino terminal end. After binding, LDL is taken up intact by endocytosis. The apoprotein and cholesteryl ester are then hydrolyzed in the lysosomes, and cholesterol is translocated into the cell. The receptors are recycled to the cell surface. This influx of cholesterol inhibits the transcription of the genes encoding HMG-CoA synthase—HMG-CoA reductase and other enzymes involved in cholesterol synthesis as well as the LDL receptor itself via the SREBP pathway, and thus coordinately suppresses cholesterol synthesis and uptake. In addition, ACAT activity is stimulated, promoting cholesterol esterification. In this way, LDL receptor activity on the cell surface is regulated by the cholesterol requirement for membranes, steroid hormones, or bile acid synthesis (Figure 26–5).

CHOLESTEROL IS TRANSPORTED BETWEEN TISSUES IN PLASMA LIPOPROTEINS

The normal range for total plasma cholesterol in humans is considered to be <5.2 mmol/L, with the greater part found in the esterified form. Cholesterol is transported in plasma in lipoproteins (Figure 26–6), and in humans the highest proportion is found in LDL. Dietary cholesterol equilibrates with plasma cholesterol in days and with tissue cholesterol in weeks. Cholesteryl ester in the diet is hydrolyzed to cholesterol, which is then absorbed by the intestine together with dietary

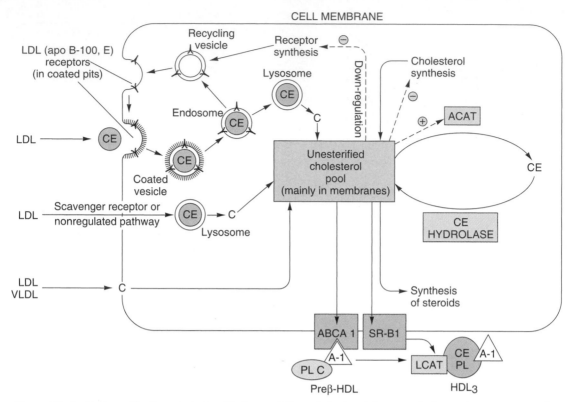

Figure 26–5. Factors affecting cholesterol balance at the cellular level. Reverse cholesterol transport may be mediated via the ABCA 1 transporter protein (with preβ-HDL as the exogenous acceptor) or the SR-B1 (with HDL_3 as the exogenous acceptor). (C, cholesterol; CE, cholesteryl ester; PL, phospholipid; ACAT, acyl-CoA:cholesterol acyltransferase; LCAT, lecithin:cholesterol acyltransferase; A-I, apolipoprotein A-I; LDL, low-density lipoprotein; VLDL, very low density lipoprotein.) LDL and HDL are not shown to scale.

unesterified cholesterol and other lipids. With cholesterol synthesized in the intestines, it is then incorporated into chylomicrons. Of the cholesterol absorbed, 80–90% is esterified with long-chain fatty acids in the intestinal mucosa. Ninety-five percent of the chylomicron cholesterol is delivered to the liver in chylomicron remnants, and most of the cholesterol secreted by the liver in VLDL is retained during the formation of IDL and ultimately LDL, which is taken up by the LDL receptor in liver and extrahepatic tissues (Chapter 25).

Plasma LCAT Is Responsible for Virtually All Plasma Cholesteryl Ester in Humans

LCAT activity is associated with HDL containing apo A-I. As cholesterol in HDL becomes esterified, it creates a concentration gradient and draws in cholesterol from tissues and from other lipoproteins (Figures 26–5 and 26–6), thus enabling HDL to function in **reverse cholesterol transport** (Figure 25–5).

Cholesteryl Ester Transfer Protein Facilitates Transfer of Cholesteryl Ester from HDL to Other Lipoproteins

This protein, associated with HDL, is found in plasma of humans and many other species. It facilitates transfer of cholesteryl ester from HDL to VLDL, IDL, and LDL in exchange for triacylglycerol, relieving product inhibition of LCAT activity in HDL. Thus, in humans, much of the cholesteryl ester formed by LCAT finds its way to the liver via VLDL remnants (IDL) or LDL (Figure 26–6). The triacylglycerol-enriched HDL_2 delivers its cholesterol to the liver in the HDL cycle (Figure 25–5).

CHOLESTEROL IS EXCRETED FROM THE BODY IN THE BILE AS CHOLESTEROL OR BILE ACIDS (SALTS)

About 1 g of cholesterol is eliminated from the body per day. Approximately half is excreted in the feces after conver-

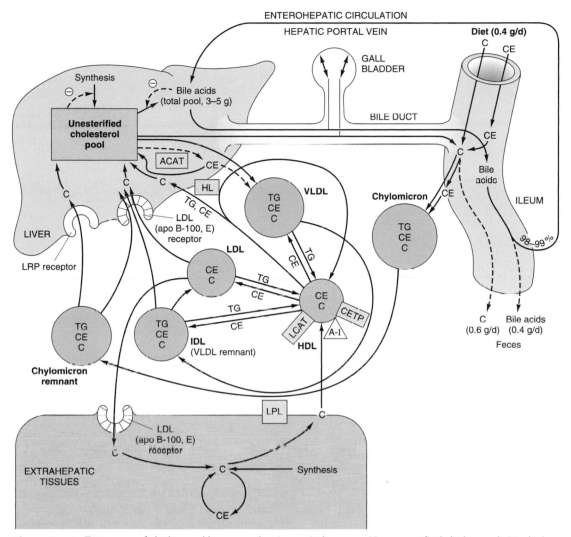

Figure 26–6. Transport of cholesterol between the tissues in humans. (C, unesterified cholesterol; CE, cholesteryl ester; TG, triacylglycerol; VLDL, very low density lipoprotein; IDL, intermediate-density lipoprotein; LDL, low-density lipoprotein; HDL, high-density lipoprotein; ACAT, acyl-CoA:cholesterol acyltransferase; LCAT, lecithin:cholesterol acyltransferase; A-I, apolipoprotein A-I; CETP, cholesteryl ester transfer protein; LPL, lipoprotein lipase; HL, hepatic lipase; LRP, LDL receptor-related protein.)

sion to bile acids. The remainder is excreted as cholesterol. **Coprostanol** is the principal sterol in the feces; it is formed from cholesterol by the bacteria in the lower intestine.

Bile Acids Are Formed from Cholesterol

The **primary bile acids** are synthesized in the liver from cholesterol. These are **cholic acid** (found in the largest amount) and **chenodeoxycholic acid** (Figure 26–7). The 7α-hydroxylation of cholesterol is the first and principal regulatory step in the biosynthesis of bile acids and is cata-

lyzed by **cholesterol 7α-hydroxylase,** a microsomal enzyme. A typical monooxygenase, it requires oxygen, NADPH, and cytochrome P450. Subsequent hydroxylation steps are also catalyzed by monooxygenases. The pathway of bile acid biosynthesis divides early into one subpathway leading to **cholyl-CoA,** characterized by an extra α-OH group on position 12, and another pathway leading to **chenodeoxycholyl-CoA** (Figure 26–7). A second pathway in mitochondria involving the 27-hydroxylation of cholesterol by **sterol 27-hydroxylase** as the first step is responsible for a significant proportion of the primary bile

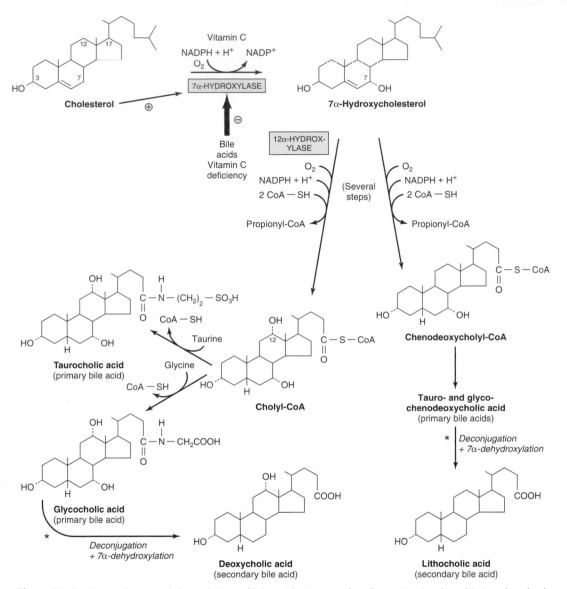

Figure 26–7. Biosynthesis and degradation of bile acids. A second pathway in mitochondria involves hydroxylation of cholesterol by sterol 27-hydroxylase. Asterisk: Catalyzed by microbial enzymes.

acids synthesized. The primary bile acids (Figure 26–7) enter the bile as glycine or taurine conjugates. Conjugation takes place in peroxisomes. In humans, the ratio of the glycine to the taurine conjugates is normally 3:1. In the alkaline bile, the bile acids and their conjugates are assumed to be in a salt form—hence the term "bile salts."

A portion of the primary bile acids in the intestine is subjected to further changes by the activity of the intestinal bacteria. These include deconjugation and 7α-dehydroxylation, which produce the **secondary bile acids,** deoxycholic acid and lithocholic acid.

Most Bile Acids Return to the Liver in the Enterohepatic Circulation

Although products of fat digestion, including cholesterol, are absorbed in the first 100 cm of small intestine, the primary and secondary bile acids are absorbed almost exclusively in the ileum, and 98–99% are returned to the liver via the portal circulation. This is known as the **enterohepatic circulation** (Figure 26–6). However, lithocholic acid, because of its insolubility, is not reabsorbed to any significant extent. Only a small fraction of the bile salts

escapes absorption and is therefore eliminated in the feces. Nonetheless, this represents a major pathway for the elimination of cholesterol. Each day the small pool of bile acids (about 3–5 g) is cycled through the intestine six to ten times and an amount of bile acid equivalent to that lost in the feces is synthesized from cholesterol, so that a pool of bile acids of constant size is maintained. This is accomplished by a system of feedback controls.

Bile Acid Synthesis Is Regulated at the 7α-Hydroxylase Step

The principal rate-limiting step in the biosynthesis of bile acids is at the **cholesterol 7α-hydroxylase reaction** (Figure 26–7). The activity of the enzyme is feedback-regulated via the nuclear bile acid-binding receptor **farnesoid X receptor (FXR).** When the size of the bile acid pool in the enterohepatic circulation increases, FXR is activated and transcription of the cholesterol 7α-hydroxylase gene is suppressed. Chenodeoxycholic acid is particularly important in activating FXR. Cholesterol 7α-hydroxylase activity is also enhanced by cholesterol of endogenous and dietary origin and regulated by insulin, glucagon, glucocorticoids, and thyroid hormone.

CLINICAL ASPECTS

The Serum Cholesterol Is Correlated with the Incidence of Atherosclerosis & Coronary Heart Disease

While elevated plasma cholesterol levels are believed to be a major factor in promoting atherosclerosis, it is now recognized that triacylglycerols are an independent risk factor. Atherosclerosis is characterized by the deposition of cholesterol and cholesteryl ester from the plasma lipoproteins into the artery wall. Diseases in which prolonged elevated levels of VLDL, IDL, chylomicron remnants, or LDL occur in the blood (eg, diabetes mellitus, lipid nephrosis, hypothyroidism, and other conditions of hyperlipidemia) are often accompanied by premature or more severe atherosclerosis. There is also an inverse relationship between HDL (HDL$_2$) concentrations and coronary heart disease, making the **LDL:HDL cholesterol ratio a good predictive parameter.** This is consistent with the function of HDL in reverse cholesterol transport. Susceptibility to atherosclerosis varies widely among species, and humans are one of the few in which the disease can be induced by diets high in cholesterol.

Diet Can Play an Important Role in Reducing Serum Cholesterol

Hereditary factors play the greatest role in determining individual serum cholesterol concentrations; however, dietary and environmental factors also play a part, and the most beneficial of these is the substitution in the diet of **polyunsaturated and monounsaturated fatty acids** for saturated fatty acids. Plant oils such as corn oil and sunflower seed oil contain a high proportion of polyunsaturated fatty acids, while olive oil contains a high concentration of monounsaturated fatty acids. On the other hand, butter fat, beef fat, and palm oil contain a high proportion of saturated fatty acids. Sucrose and fructose have a greater effect in raising blood lipids, particularly triacylglycerols, than do other carbohydrates.

The reason for the cholesterol-lowering effect of polyunsaturated fatty acids is still not fully understood. It is clear, however, that one of the mechanisms involved is the up-regulation of LDL receptors by poly- and monounsaturated as compared with saturated fatty acids, causing an increase in the catabolic rate of LDL, the main atherogenic lipoprotein. In addition, saturated fatty acids cause the formation of smaller VLDL particles that contain relatively more cholesterol, and they are utilized by extrahepatic tissues at a slower rate than are larger particles—tendencies that may be regarded as atherogenic.

Lifestyle Affects the Serum Cholesterol Level

Additional factors considered to play a part in coronary heart disease include high blood pressure, smoking, male gender, obesity (particularly abdominal obesity), lack of exercise, and drinking soft as opposed to hard water. Factors associated with elevation of plasma FFA followed by increased output of triacylglycerol and cholesterol into the circulation in VLDL include emotional stress and coffee drinking. Premenopausal women appear to be protected against many of these deleterious factors, and this is thought to be related to the beneficial effects of estrogen. There is an association between moderate alcohol consumption and a lower incidence of coronary heart disease. This may be due to elevation of HDL concentrations resulting from increased synthesis of apo A-I and changes in activity of cholesteryl ester transfer protein. It has been claimed that red wine is particularly beneficial, perhaps because of its content of antioxidants. Regular exercise lowers plasma LDL but raises HDL. Triacylglycerol concentrations are also reduced, due most likely to increased insulin sensitivity, which enhances the expression of lipoprotein lipase.

When Diet Changes Fail, Hypolipidemic Drugs Will Reduce Serum Cholesterol & Triacylglycerol

A family of drugs known as statins have proved highly efficacious in lowering plasma cholesterol and preventing heart disease. Statins act by inhibiting HMG-CoA reductase and up-regulating LDL receptor activity. Examples currently in use include **atorvastatin, simvastatin, fluvastatin,** and **pravastatin.** Other drugs used include fibrates such as **clofibrate** and **gemfibrozil and nicotinic acid,**

which act mainly to lower plasma triacylglycerols by decreasing the secretion of triacylglycerol and cholesterol-containing VLDL by the liver. In addition, a new drug, ezetimibe, which reduces blood cholesterol levels by inhibiting the absorption of cholesterol by the intestine, has recently been introduced. Ezetimibe belongs to the azetidinone class of cholesterol absorption inhibitors.

Primary Disorders of the Plasma Lipoproteins (Dyslipoproteinemias) Are Inherited

Inherited defects in lipoprotein metabolism lead to the primary condition of either **hypo-** or **hyperlipoproteinemia** (Table 26–1). In addition, diseases such as diabetes mellitus, hypothyroidism, kidney disease (nephrotic

Table 26–1. Primary disorders of plasma lipoproteins (dyslipoproteinemias).

Name	Defect	Remarks
Hypolipoproteinemias Abetalipoproteinemia	No chylomicrons, VLDL, or LDL are formed because of defect in the loading of apo B with lipid.	Rare; blood acylglycerols low; intestine and liver accumulate acylglycerols. Intestinal malabsorption. Early death avoidable by administration of large doses of fat-soluble vitamins, particularly vitamin E.
Familial alpha-lipoprotein deficiency Tangier disease Fish-eye disease Apo-A-I deficiencies	All have low or near absence of HDL.	Tendency toward hypertriacylglycerolemia as a result of absence of apo C-II, causing inactive LPL. Low LDL levels. Atherosclerosis in the elderly.
Hyperlipoproteinemias Familial lipoprotein lipase deficiency (type I)	Hypertriacylglycerolemia due to deficiency of LPL, abnormal LPL, or apo C-II deficiency causing inactive LPL.	Slow clearance of chylomicrons and VLDL. Low levels of LDL and HDL. No increased risk of coronary disease.
Familial hypercholesterolemia (type IIa)	Defective LDL receptors or mutation in ligand region of apo B-100.	Elevated LDL levels and hypercholesterolemia, resulting in atherosclerosis and coronary disease.
Familial type III hyperlipoproteinemia (broad beta disease, remnant removal disease, familial dysbetalipoproteinemia)	Deficiency in remnant clearance by the liver is due to abnormality in apo E. Patients lack isoforms E3 and E4 and have only E2, which does not react with the E receptor.[1]	Increase in chylomicron and VLDL remnants of density < 1.019 (β-VLDL). Causes hypercholesterolemia, xanthomas, and atherosclerosis.
Familial hypertriacylglycerolemia (type IV)	Overproduction of VLDL often associated with glucose intolerance and hyperinsulinemia.	Cholesterol levels rise with the VLDL concentration. LDL and HDL tend to be subnormal. This type of pattern is commonly associated with coronary heart disease, type II diabetes mellitus, obesity, alcoholism, and administration of progestational hormones.
Familial hyperalphalipoproteinemia	Increased concentrations of HDL.	A rare condition apparently beneficial to health and longevity.
Hepatic lipase deficiency	Deficiency of the enzyme leads to accumulation of large triacylglycerol-rich HDL and VLDL remnants.	Patients have xanthomas and coronary heart disease.
Familial lecithin:cholesterol acyltransferase (LCAT) deficiency	Absence of LCAT leads to block in reverse cholesterol transport. HDL remains as nascent disks incapable of taking up and esterifying cholesterol.	Plasma concentrations of cholesteryl esters and lysolecithin are low. Present is an abnormal LDL fraction, lipoprotein X, found also in patients with cholestasis. VLDL is abnormal (β-VLDL).
Familial lipoprotein(a) excess	Lp(a) consists of 1 mol of LDL attached to 1 mol of apo(a). Apo(a) shows structural homologies to plasminogen.	Premature coronary heart disease due to atherosclerosis, plus thrombosis due to inhibition of fibrinolysis.

[1]There is an association between patients possessing the apo E4 allele and the incidence of Alzheimer's disease. Apparently, apo E4 binds more avidly to β-amyloid found in neuritic plaques.

syndrome), and atherosclerosis are associated with secondary abnormal lipoprotein patterns that are very similar to one or another of the primary inherited conditions. Virtually all of the primary conditions are due to a defect at a stage in lipoprotein formation, transport, or destruction (see Figures 25–4, 26–5, and 26–6). Not all of the abnormalities are harmful.

SUMMARY

- Cholesterol is the precursor of all other steroids in the body, eg, corticosteroids, sex hormones, bile acids, and vitamin D. It also plays an important structural role in membranes and in the outer layer of lipoproteins.

- Cholesterol is synthesized in the body entirely from acetyl-CoA. Three molecules of acetyl-CoA form mevalonate via the important regulatory reaction for the pathway, catalyzed by HMG-CoA reductase. Next, a five-carbon isoprenoid unit is formed, and six of these condense to form squalene. Squalene undergoes cyclization to form the parent steroid lanosterol, which, after the loss of three methyl groups, forms cholesterol.

- Cholesterol synthesis in the liver is regulated partly by cholesterol in the diet. In tissues, cholesterol balance is maintained between the factors causing gain of cholesterol (eg, synthesis, uptake via the LDL or scavenger receptors) and the factors causing loss of cholesterol (eg, steroid synthesis, cholesteryl ester formation, excretion). The activity of the LDL receptor is modulated by cellular cholesterol levels to achieve this balance. In reverse cholesterol transport, HDL takes up cholesterol from the tissues and LCAT esterifies it and deposits it in the core of the particles. The cholesteryl ester in HDL is taken up by the liver, either directly or after transfer to VLDL, IDL, or LDL via the cholesteryl ester transfer protein.

- Excess cholesterol is excreted from the liver in the bile as cholesterol or bile salts. A large proportion of bile salts is absorbed into the portal circulation and returned to the liver as part of the enterohepatic circulation.

- Elevated levels of cholesterol present in VLDL, IDL, or LDL are associated with atherosclerosis, whereas high levels of HDL have a protective effect.

- Inherited defects in lipoprotein metabolism lead to a primary condition of hypo- or hyperlipoproteinemia. Conditions such as diabetes mellitus, hypothyroidism, kidney disease, and atherosclerosis exhibit secondary abnormal lipoprotein patterns that resemble certain primary conditions.

REFERENCES

Chiang JL: Regulation of bile acid synthesis: pathways, nuclear receptors and mechanisms. J Hepatol 2004;40:539.

Illingworth DR: Management of hypercholesterolemia. Med Clin North Am 2000;84:23.

Ness GC, Chambers CM: Feedback and hormonal regulation of hepatic 3-hydroxy-3-methylglutaryl coenzyme A reductase: the concept of cholesterol buffering capacity. Proc Soc Exp Biol Med 2000;224:8.

Parks DJ et al: Bile acids: natural ligands for a nuclear orphan receptor. Science 1999;284:1365.

Russell DW: Cholesterol biosynthesis and metabolism. Cardiovascular Drugs Therap 1992;6:103.

Spady DK, Woollett LA, Dietschy JM: Regulation of plasma LDL cholesterol levels by dietary cholesterol and fatty acids. Annu Rev Nutr 1993;13:355.

Tall A: Plasma lipid transfer proteins. Annu Rev Biochem 1993;64:235.

Various authors: *Biochemistry of Lipids, Lipoproteins and Membranes*, 4th ed. Vance DE, Vance JE (editors). Elsevier, 2002.

Various authors: The cholesterol facts. A summary of the evidence relating dietary fats, serum cholesterol, and coronary heart disease. Circulation 1990;81:1721.

Zhang FL, Casey PJ: Protein prenylation: Molecular mechanisms and functional consequences. Annu Rev Biochem 1996;65:241.

SECTION III
Metabolism of Proteins & Amino Acids

Biosynthesis of the Nutritionally Nonessential Amino Acids

Victor W. Rodwell, PhD

BIOMEDICAL IMPORTANCE

All 20 of the amino acids present in proteins are essential for health. While comparatively rare in the Western world, amino acid deficiency states are endemic in certain regions of West Africa where the diet relies heavily on grains that are poor sources of amino acids such as tryptophan and lysine. These disorders include kwashiorkor, which results when a child is weaned onto a starchy diet poor in protein; and marasmus, in which both caloric intake and specific amino acids are deficient.

Humans can synthesize 12 of the 20 common amino acids from the amphibolic intermediates of glycolysis and of the citric acid cycle (Table 27–1). While *nutritionally* nonessential, these 12 amino acids are not "nonessential." All 20 amino acids are *biologically* essential. Of the 12 nutritionally nonessential amino acids, 9 are formed from amphibolic intermediates and 3 (cysteine, tyrosine and hydroxylysine) from nutritionally essential amino acids. Identification of the 12 amino acids that humans can synthesize rested primarily on data derived from feeding diets in which purified amino acids replaced protein. This chapter considers only the biosynthesis of the twelve amino acids that are synthesized in human tissues, not the other 8 that are synthesized by plants, lower eukaryotes, or prokaryotes.

NUTRITIONALLY NONESSENTIAL AMINO ACIDS HAVE SHORT BIOSYNTHETIC PATHWAYS

The enzymes glutamate dehydrogenase, glutamine synthetase, and aminotransferases occupy central positions in amino acid biosynthesis. The combined effect of those three enzymes is to transform ammonium ion into the α-amino nitrogen of various amino acids.

Glutamate and Glutamine. Reductive amination of α-ketoglutarate is catalyzed by glutamate dehydrogenase (Figure 27–1). Amination of glutamate to glutamine is catalyzed by glutamine synthetase (Figure 27–2).

Alanine. Transamination of pyruvate forms alanine (Figure 27–3).

Aspartate and Asparagine. Transamination of oxaloacetate forms aspartate. The conversion of aspartate to asparagine is catalyzed by asparagine synthetase (Figure 27–4), which resembles glutamine synthetase (Figure 27–2) except that glutamine, not ammonium ion, provides the nitrogen. Bacterial asparagine synthetases can, however, also use ammonium ion. Coupled hydrolysis of PP_i to P_i by pyrophosphatase ensures that the reaction is strongly favored.

Serine. Oxidation of the α-hydroxyl group of the glycolytic intermediate 3-phosphoglycerate converts it to an oxo acid, whose subsequent transamination and dephosphorylation leads to serine (Figure 27–5).

Glycine. Glycine aminotransferases can catalyze the synthesis of glycine from glyoxylate and glutamate or alanine. Unlike most aminotransferase reactions, these strongly favor glycine synthesis. Additional important mammalian routes for glycine formation are from choline (Figure 27–6) and from serine (Figure 27–7).

Proline. Proline is formed from glutamate by reversal of the reactions of proline catabolism (Figure 27–8).

Table 27–1. Amino acid requirements of humans.

Nutritionally Essential	Nutritionally Nonessential
Arginine[1]	Alanine
Histidine	Asparagine
Isoleucine	Aspartate
Leucine	Cysteine
Lysine	Glutamate
Methionine	Glutamine
Phenylalanine	Glycine
Threonine	Hydroxyproline[2]
Tryptophan	Hydroxylysine[2]
Valine	Proline
	Serine
	Tyrosine

[1]"Nutritionally semiessential." Synthesized at rates inadequate to support growth of children.
[2]Not necessary for protein synthesis but formed during post-translational processing of collagen.

Cysteine. Cysteine, while not nutritionally essential, is formed from methionine, which is nutritionally essential. Following conversion of methionine to homocysteine (see Figure 29–18), homocysteine and serine form cystathionine, whose hydrolysis forms cysteine and homoserine (Figure 27–9).

Tyrosine. Phenylalanine hydroxylase converts phenylalanine to tyrosine (Figure 27–10). Provided that the diet contains adequate nutritionally essential phenylalanine, tyrosine is nutritionally nonessential. But since the phenylalanine hydroxylase reaction is irreversible, dietary tyrosine cannot replace phenylalanine. Catalysis by this mixed-function oxygenase incorporates one atom of O_2 into phenylalanine and reduces the other atom to water. Reducing power, provided as tetrahydrobiopterin, derives ultimately from NADPH.

Hydroxyproline and Hydroxylysine. Hydroxyproline and hydroxylysine are present principally in collagen. Since there is no tRNA for either hydroxylated amino acid, neither dietary hydroxyproline nor hydroxylysine is incorporated into protein. Both are completely degraded (see Chapter 29). Hydroxyproline and hydroxylysine arise from proline and lysine, but only after these amino acids have been incorporated into peptides. Hydroxylation of peptide-bound prolyl and lysyl residues is catalyzed by prolyl hydroxylase and lysyl hydroxylase of tissues, including skin and skeletal muscle, and of granulating wounds (Figure 27–11). The hydroxylases are mixed-function oxygenases that require substrate, molecular O_2, ascorbate, Fe^{2+}, and α-ketoglutarate. For every mole of proline or lysine hydroxylated, one mole of α-ketoglutarate is decarboxylated to succinate. One atom of O_2 is incorporated into proline or lysine, the other into succinate (Figure 27–11). A defi-

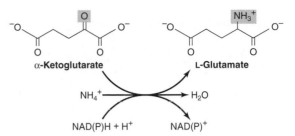

Figure 27–1. The glutamate dehydrogenase reaction.

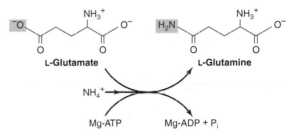

Figure 27–2. The glutamine synthetase reaction.

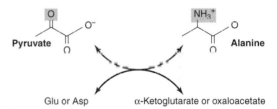

Figure 27–3. Formation of alanine by transamination of pyruvate. The amino donor may be glutamate or aspartate. The other product thus is α-ketoglutarate or oxaloacetate.

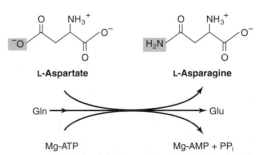

Figure 27–4. The asparagine synthetase reaction. Note similarities to and differences from the glutamine synthetase reaction (Figure 27–2).

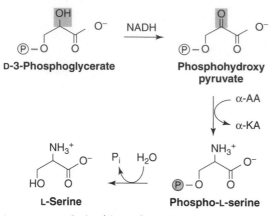

Figure 27–5. Serine biosynthesis. (α-AA, α-amino acids; α-KA, α-keto acids.)

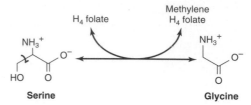

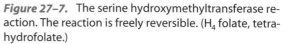

Figure 27–7. The serine hydroxymethyltransferase reaction. The reaction is freely reversible. (H$_4$ folate, tetrahydrofolate.)

ciency of the vitamin C required for these hydroxylases results in scurvy.

Valine, Leucine, and Isoleucine. While leucine, valine, and isoleucine are all nutritionally essential amino acids, tissue aminotransferases reversibly interconvert all three amino acids and their corresponding α-keto acids. These α-keto acids thus can replace their amino acids in the diet.

Seleoncysteine, the 21st Amino Acid. While its occurrence in proteins is uncommon, seleoncysteine is present at the active site of several human enzymes that catalyze redox reactions. Examples include thioredoxin reductase, glutathione peroxidase, and the deiodinase that converts thyroxine to triiodothyronine. Where present, selenocysteine participates in the catalytic mechanism of these enzymes, and replacement of selenocysteine by cysteine can result in significantly decreased catalytic activity. Impairments in human selenoproteins have been implicated in tumorigenesis and atherosclerosis, and are associated with selenium deficiency cardiomyopathy (Keshan disease).

Biosynthesis of selenocysteine requires L-cysteine, selenate (SeO$_4^{2-}$), ATP, a specific tRNA, and several enzymes. L-Serine provides the carbon skeleton of selenocysteine. Selenophosphate, formed from ATP and selenate (Figure 27–12), serves as the selenium donor. Unlike hydroxyproline or hydroxylysine, selenocysteine

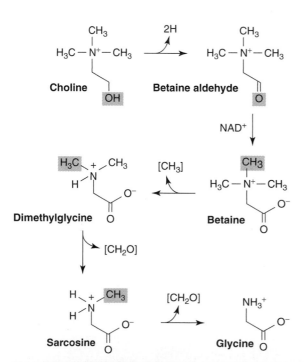

Figure 27–6. Formation of glycine from choline.

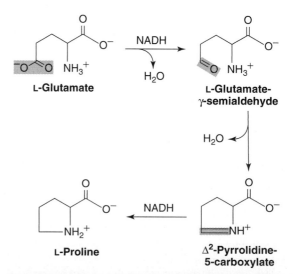

Figure 27–8. Biosynthesis of proline from glutamate by reversal of reactions of proline catabolism.

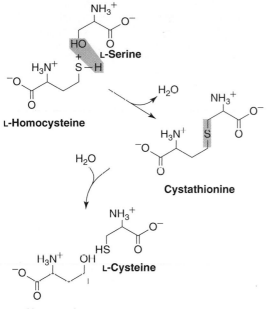

Figure 27–9. Conversion of homocysteine and serine to homoserine and cysteine. The sulfur of cysteine derives from methionine and the carbon skeleton from serine.

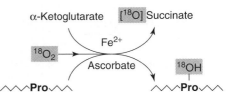

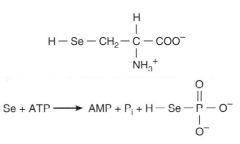

Figure 27–11. The prolyl hydroxylase reaction. The substrate is a proline-rich peptide. During the course of the reaction, molecular oxygen is incorporated into both succinate and proline. Lysyl hydroxylase catalyzes an analogous reaction.

$$H-Se-CH_2-\overset{\overset{\displaystyle H}{|}}{\underset{\underset{\displaystyle NH_3^+}{|}}{C}}-COO^-$$

$$Se + ATP \longrightarrow AMP + P_i + H-Se-\overset{\overset{\displaystyle O}{\|}}{\underset{\underset{\displaystyle O^-}{|}}{P}}-O^-$$

Figure 27–12. Selenocysteine *(top)* and the reaction catalyzed by selenophosphate synthetase *(bottom)*.

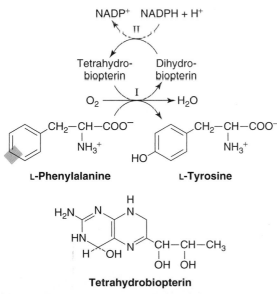

Figure 27–10. The phenylalanine hydroxylase reaction. Two distinct enzymatic activities are involved. Activity II catalyzes reduction of dihydrobiopterin by NADPH, and activity I the reduction of O_2 to H_2O and of phenylalanine to tyrosine. This reaction is associated with several defects of phenylalanine metabolism discussed in Chapter 29.

arises co-translationally during its incorporation into peptides. The UGA anticodon of the unusual tRNA designated tRNA^{Sec} normally signals STOP. The ability of the protein synthetic apparatus to identify a selenocysteine-specific UGA codon involves the selenocysteine insertion element, a stem-loop structure in the untranslated region of the mRNA. Selenocysteine tRNA^{Sec} is first charged with serine by the ligase that charges tRNA^{Ser}. Subsequent replacement of the serine oxygen by selenium involves selenophosphate formed by selenophosphate synthase (Figure 27–12). Successive enzyme-catalyzed reactions convert cysteyl-tRNA^{Sec} to aminoacryl-tRNA^{Sec} and then to selenocysteyl-tRNA^{Sec}. In the presence of a specific elongation factor that recognizes selenocysteyl-tRNA^{Sec}, selenocysteine can then be incorporated into proteins.

SUMMARY

- All vertebrates can form certain amino acids from amphibolic intermediates or from other dietary amino acids. The intermediates and the amino acids to which they give rise are α-ketoglutarate (Glu, Gln, Pro, Hyp), oxaloacetate (Asp, Asn), and 3-phosphoglycerate (Ser, Gly).
- Cysteine, tyrosine, and hydroxylysine are formed from nutritionally essential amino acids. Serine provides the carbon skeleton, and homocysteine the sulfur for cysteine biosynthesis. Phenylalanine hydroxylase converts phenylalanine to tyrosine.

- Neither dietary hydroxyproline nor hydroxylysine is incorporated into proteins because no codon or tRNA dictates their insertion into peptides.
- Peptidyl hydroxyproline and hydroxylysine are formed by hydroxylation of peptidyl proline or lysine in reactions catalyzed by mixed-function oxidases that require vitamin C as cofactor. The nutritional disease scurvy reflects impaired hydroxylation due to a deficiency of vitamin C.
- Selenocysteine, an essential active site residue in several mammalian enzymes, arises by co-translational insertion from a previously modified tRNA.

REFERENCES

Beckett GJ, Arthur JR: Selenium and endocrine systems. J Endocrinol 2005;184:455.

Brown KM, Arthur JR: Selenium, selenoproteins and human health: a review. Public Health Nutr 2001;4:593.

Kohrl J et al: Selenium in biology: facts and medical perspectives. Biol Chem 2000;381:849.

Nordberg J et al: Mammalian thioredoxin reductase is irreversibly inhibited by dinitrohalobenzenes by alkylation of both the redox active selenocysteine and its neighboring cysteine residue. J Biol Chem 1998;273:10835.

Scriver CR et al (editors): *The Metabolic and Molecular Bases of Inherited Disease,* 8th ed. McGraw-Hill, 2001.

Catabolism of Proteins & of Amino Acid Nitrogen

Victor W. Rodwell, PhD

BIOMEDICAL IMPORTANCE

This chapter describes how the nitrogen of amino acids is converted to urea and the rare disorders that accompany defects in urea biosynthesis. In normal adults, nitrogen intake matches nitrogen excreted. Positive nitrogen balance, an excess of ingested over excreted nitrogen, accompanies growth and pregnancy. Negative nitrogen balance, where output exceeds intake, may follow surgery, advanced cancer, and kwashiorkor or marasmus.

While ammonia, derived mainly from the α-amino nitrogen of amino acids, is highly toxic, tissues convert ammonia to the amide nitrogen of nontoxic glutamine. Subsequent deamination of glutamine in the liver releases ammonia, which is then converted to nontoxic urea. If liver function is compromised, as in cirrhosis or hepatitis, elevated blood ammonia levels generate clinical signs and symptoms. Each enzyme of the urea cycle provides examples of metabolic defects and their physiologic consequences, and the cycle as a whole serves as a molecular model for the study of human metabolic defects.

PROTEIN TURNOVER OCCURS IN ALL FORMS OF LIFE

The continuous degradation and synthesis of cellular proteins occur in all forms of life. Each day, humans turn over 1–2% of their total body protein, principally muscle protein. High rates of protein degradation occur in tissues undergoing structural rearrangement—eg, uterine tissue during pregnancy, tadpole tail tissue during metamorphosis, or skeletal muscle in starvation. Of the liberated amino acids, approximately 75% are reutilized. The excess nitrogen forms urea. Since excess amino acids are not stored, those not immediately incorporated into new protein are rapidly degraded to amphibolic intermediates.

PROTEASES & PEPTIDASES DEGRADE PROTEINS TO AMINO ACIDS

The susceptibility of a protein to degradation is expressed as its half-life ($t_{1/2}$), the time required to lower its con-

centration to half the initial value. Half-lives of liver proteins range from under 30 minutes to over 150 hours. Typical "housekeeping" enzymes have $t_{1/2}$ values of over 100 hours. By contrast, many key regulatory enzymes have a $t_{1/2}$ of 0.5–2 hours. PEST sequences, regions rich in proline (P), glutamate (E), serine (S), and threonine (T), target some proteins for rapid degradation. Intracellular proteases hydrolyze internal peptide bonds. The resulting peptides are then degraded to amino acids by endopeptidases that cleave internal bonds and by aminopeptidases and carboxypeptidases that remove amino acids sequentially from the amino and carboxyl terminals, respectively. Degradation of circulating peptides such as hormones follows loss of a sialic acid moiety from the nonreducing ends of their oligosaccharide chains. Asialoglycoproteins are internalized by liver cell asialoglycoprotein receptors and degraded by lysosomal proteases termed cathepsins.

Extracellular, membrane-associated, and long-lived intracellular proteins are degraded in lysosomes by ATP-independent processes. By contrast, degradation of abnormal and other short-lived proteins occurs in the cytosol and requires ATP and ubiquitin. Ubiquitin, so named because it is present in all eukaryotic cells, is a small (8.5 kDa) protein that targets many intracellular proteins for degradation. The primary structure of ubiquitin is highly conserved. Only 3 of 76 residues differ between yeast and human ubiquitin. Several molecules of ubiquitin are attached by non-α-peptide bonds formed between the carboxyl terminal of ubiquitin and the ε-amino groups of lysyl residues in the target protein (Figure 28–1). The residue present at its amino terminal affects whether a protein is ubiquitinated. Amino terminal Met or Ser retards whereas Asp or Arg accelerates ubiquitination. Degradation occurs in a multicatalytic complex of proteases known as the proteasome.

ANIMALS CONVERT α-AMINO NITROGEN TO VARIED END PRODUCTS

Different animals excrete excess nitrogen as ammonia, uric acid, or urea. The aqueous environment of teleo-

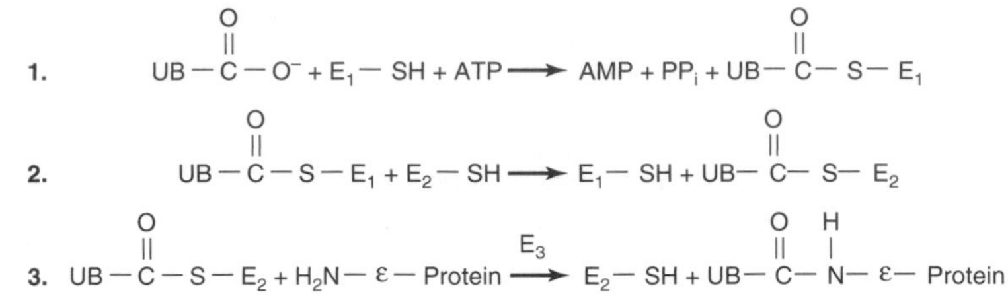

1. $$UB-\overset{\overset{\displaystyle O}{\|}}{C}-O^- + E_1-SH + ATP \longrightarrow AMP + PP_i + UB-\overset{\overset{\displaystyle O}{\|}}{C}-S-E_1$$

2. $$UB-\overset{\overset{\displaystyle O}{\|}}{C}-S-E_1 + E_2-SH \longrightarrow E_1-SH + UB-\overset{\overset{\displaystyle O}{\|}}{C}-S-E_2$$

3. $$UB-\overset{\overset{\displaystyle O}{\|}}{C}-S-E_2 + H_2N-\varepsilon-Protein \overset{E_3}{\longrightarrow} E_2-SH + UB-\overset{\overset{\displaystyle O}{\|}}{C}-\overset{\overset{\displaystyle H}{|}}{N}-\varepsilon-Protein$$

Figure 28–1. Partial reactions in the attachment of ubiquitin (UB) to proteins. (1) The terminal COOH of ubiquitin forms a thioester bond with an –SH of E_1 in a reaction driven by conversion of ATP to AMP and PP_i. Subsequent hydrolysis of PP_i by pyrophosphatase ensures that reaction 1 will proceed readily. (2) A thioester exchange reaction transfers activated ubiquitin to E_2. (3) E_3 catalyzes transfer of ubiquitin to ε-amino groups of lysyl residues of target proteins.

stean fish, which are ammonotelic (excrete ammonia), compels them to excrete water continuously, facilitating excretion of highly toxic ammonia. Birds, which must conserve water and maintain low weight, are uricotelic and excrete uric acid as semisolid guano. Many land animals, including humans, are ureotelic and excrete nontoxic, water-soluble urea. High blood urea levels in renal disease are a consequence—not a cause—of impaired renal function.

BIOSYNTHESIS OF UREA

Urea biosynthesis occurs in four stages: (1) transamination, (2) oxidative deamination of glutamate, (3) ammonia transport, and (4) reactions of the urea cycle (Figure 28–2).

Transamination Transfers α-Amino Nitrogen to α-Ketoglutarate, Forming Glutamate

Transamination interconverts pairs of α-amino acids and α-keto acids (Figure 28–3). All the protein amino acids except lysine, threonine, proline, and hydroxyproline participate in transamination. Transamination is readily reversible, and aminotransferases also function in amino acid biosynthesis. The coenzyme pyridoxal phosphate (PLP) is present at the catalytic site of aminotransferases and of many other enzymes that act on amino acids. PLP, a derivative of vitamin B_6, forms an enzyme-bound Schiff base intermediate that can rearrange in various ways. During transamination, bound PLP serves as a carrier of amino groups. Rearrangement forms an α-keto acid and enzyme-bound pyridoxamine phosphate, which forms a Schiff base with a second keto acid. Following removal of α-amino nitrogen by transamination, the remaining carbon "skeleton" is degraded by pathways discussed in Chapter 29.

Alanine-pyruvate aminotransferase (alanine aminotransferase) and glutamate-α-ketoglutarate aminotransferase (glutamate aminotransferase) catalyze the transfer of amino groups to pyruvate (forming alanine) or to α-ketoglutarate (forming glutamate) (Figure 28–4). Each aminotransferase is specific for one pair of substrates but nonspecific for the other pair. Since alanine is also a substrate for glutamate aminotransferase, all the amino nitrogen from

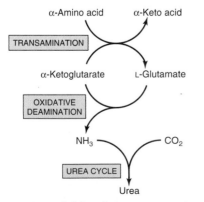

Figure 28–2. Overall flow of nitrogen in amino acid catabolism.

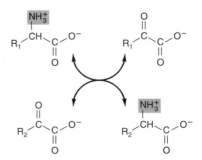

Figure 28–3. Transamination. The reaction is freely reversible with an equilibrium constant close to unity.

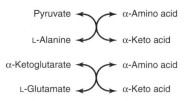

Figure 28–4. Alanine aminotransferase *(top)* and glutamate aminotransferase *(bottom)*.

amino acids that undergo transamination can be concentrated in glutamate. This is important because L-glutamate is the only amino acid that undergoes oxidative deamination at an appreciable rate in mammalian tissues. The formation of ammonia from α-amino groups thus occurs mainly via the α-amino nitrogen of L-glutamate.

Transamination is not restricted to α-amino groups. The δ-amino group of ornithine—but not the ε-amino group of lysine—readily undergoes transamination. Serum levels of aminotransferases are elevated in some disease states (see Table 7–2).

L-GLUTAMATE DEHYDROGENASE OCCUPIES A CENTRAL POSITION IN NITROGEN METABOLISM

Transfer of amino nitrogen to α-ketoglutarate forms L-glutamate. Release of this nitrogen as ammonia is then catalyzed by hepatic **L-glutamate dehydrogenase (GDH)**, which can use either NAD^+ or $NADP^+$ (Figure 28–5). Conversion of α-amino nitrogen to ammonia by the concerted action of glutamate aminotransferase and GDH is often termed "transdeamination." Liver GDH activity is allosterically inhibited by ATP, GTP, and NADH and activated by ADP. The reaction catalyzed by GDH is freely reversible and functions also in amino acid biosynthesis (see Figure 27–1).

Amino Acid Oxidases Also Remove Nitrogen as Ammonia

While their physiologic role is uncertain, L-amino acid oxidases of liver and kidney convert amino acids to an

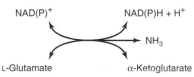

Figure 28–5. The L-glutamate dehydrogenase reaction. $NAD(P)^+$ means that either NAD^+ or $NADP^+$ can serve as co-substrate. The reaction is reversible but favors glutamate formation.

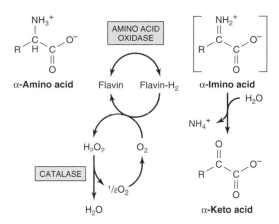

Figure 28–6. Oxidative deamination catalyzed by L-amino acid oxidase (L-α-amino acid:O_2 oxidoreductase). The α-imino acid, shown in brackets, is not a stable intermediate.

α-imino acid that decomposes to an α-keto acid with release of ammonium ion (Figure 28–6). The reduced flavin is reoxidized by molecular oxygen, forming hydrogen peroxide (H_2O_2), which then is split to O_2 and H_2O by **catalase.**

Ammonia Intoxication Is Life-Threatening

The ammonia produced by enteric bacteria and absorbed into portal venous blood and the ammonia produced by tissues are rapidly removed from circulation by the liver and converted to urea. Thus, only traces (10–20 μg/dL) normally are present in peripheral blood. This is essential, since ammonia is toxic to the central nervous system. Should portal blood bypass the liver, systemic blood ammonia levels may rise to toxic levels. This occurs in severely impaired hepatic function or the development of collateral links between the portal and systemic veins in cirrhosis. Symptoms of **ammonia intoxication** include tremor, slurred speech, blurred vision, coma, and ultimately death. Ammonia may be toxic to the brain in part because it reacts with α-ketoglutarate to form glutamate. The resulting depleted levels of α-ketoglutarate then impair function of the tricarboxylic acid (TCA) cycle in neurons.

Glutamine Synthase Fixes Ammonia as Glutamine

Formation of glutamine is catalyzed by mitochondrial **glutamine synthase** (Figure 28–7). Since amide bond synthesis is coupled to the hydrolysis of ATP to ADP and P_i, the reaction strongly favors glutamine synthesis. One function of glutamine is to sequester ammonia in a nontoxic form.

reaction requ[...]
tion of citr[...]
AMP by asp[...]

Cleavage [...]
Arginine & [...]

Cleavage of [...]
succinase, pr[...]
ine and rele[...]
(reaction 4, [...]
rate forms L-[...]
oxidation of [...]
tions are anal[...]
(see Figure 17[...]
and malate [...]
acetate by g[...]
aspartate. Th[...]
thus acts as a [...]
precursor of u[...]

Cleavage [...]
& Re-form[...]

Hydrolytic cl[...]
catalyzed by [...]
Figure 28–9) [...]
liver mitocho[...]
thesis. Ornitl[...]
arginase, com[...]
as the precur[...]
oxide (NO) i[...]
NO synthase [...]

Carbamoyl [...]
Pacemaker [...]

The activity o[...]
mined by N-a[...]
dictated by it[...]
glutamate and[...]
glutamate. Tł[...]
glutamate syr[...]
respectively. N[...]
centrations of i[...]
Starvation, for[...]
ably to cope w[...]
that accompan[...]

METABOL[...]
OF THE UF[...]

The compara[...]
metabolic dis[...]
illustrate the f[...]
diseases:

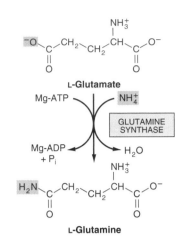

Figure 28–7. The glutamine synthase reaction strongly favors glutamine synthesis.

Glutaminase & Asparaginase Deamidate Glutamine & Asparagine

Hydrolytic release of the amide nitrogen of glutamine as ammonia, catalyzed by **glutaminase** (Figure 28–8), strongly favors glutamate formation. The concerted action of glutamine synthase and glutaminase thus catalyzes the interconversion of free ammonium ion and glutamine. An analogous reaction is catalyzed by L-asparaginase.

Formation & Secretion of Ammonia Maintains Acid-Base Balance

Excretion into urine of ammonia produced by renal tubular cells facilitates cation conservation and regulation of acid-base balance. Ammonia production from intracellular renal amino acids, especially glutamine, increases in **metabolic acidosis** and decreases in **metabolic alkalosis.**

UREA IS THE MAJOR END PRODUCT OF NITROGEN CATABOLISM IN HUMANS

Synthesis of 1 mol of urea requires 3 mol of ATP plus 1 mol each of ammonium ion and of the α-amino nitrogen of aspartate. Five enzymes catalyze the numbered reactions of Figure 28–9. Of the six participating amino acids, N-acetylglutamate functions solely as an enzyme activator. The others serve as carriers of the atoms that ultimately become urea. The major metabolic role of **ornithine, citrulline,** and **argininosuccinate** in mammals is urea synthesis. Urea synthesis is a cyclic process. Since the ornithine consumed in reaction 2 is regenerated in reaction 5, there is no net loss or gain of ornithine, citrulline, argininosuccinate, or arginine. Ammo-

nium ion, CO_2, ATP, and aspartate are, however, consumed. Some reactions of urea synthesis occur in the matrix of the mitochondrion, other reactions in the cytosol (Figure 28–9).

Carbamoyl Phosphate Synthase I Initiates Urea Biosynthesis

Condensation of CO_2, ammonia, and ATP to form **carbamoyl phosphate** is catalyzed by mitochondrial **carbamoyl phosphate synthase I** (reaction 1, Figure 28–9). A cytosolic form of this enzyme, carbamoyl phosphate synthase II, uses glutamine rather than ammonia as the nitrogen donor and functions in pyrimidine biosynthesis (see Chapter 33). Carbamoyl phosphate synthase I, the rate-limiting enzyme of the urea cycle, is active only in the presence of its allosteric activator **N-acetylglutamate,** which enhances the affinity of the synthase for ATP. Formation of carbamoyl phosphate requires 2 mol of ATP, one of which serves as a phosphoryl donor. Conversion of the second ATP to AMP and pyrophosphate, coupled to the hydrolysis of pyrophosphate to orthophosphate, provides the driving force for synthesis of the amide bond and the mixed acid anhydride bond of carbamoyl phosphate. The concerted action of GDH and carbamoyl phosphate synthase I thus shuttles nitrogen into carbamoyl phosphate, a compound with high group transfer potential. The reaction proceeds stepwise. Reaction of bicarbonate with ATP forms carbonyl phosphate and ADP. Ammonia then displaces ADP, forming carbamate and orthophosphate. Phosphorylation of carbamate by the second ATP then forms carbamoyl phosphate.

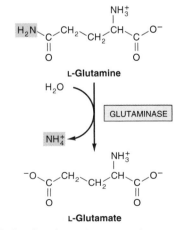

Figure 28–8. The glutaminase reaction proceeds essentially irreversibly in the direction of glutamate and NH_4^+ formation. Note that the *amide* nitrogen, not the α-amino nitrogen, is removed.

CO₂

2 Mg

H₂

Carl
pho

Figure 28
tribute to
and react
enter the
mitochon

Carbamoyl
Forms Citru

L-Ornithine
the carbamoyl
thine, forming
2, Figure 28–9
chondrial matr
the subsequen
the cytosol. E

The Ornithine Transporter

Hyperornithinemia, hyperammonemia, and homocitrullinuria syndrome (HHH syndrome) results from mutation of the ORNT1 gene that encodes the mitochondrial membrane ornithine transporter. The failure to import cytosolic ornithine into the mitochondrial matrix renders the urea cycle inoperable, with consequent hyperammonemia, and the accompanying accumulation of cytosolic ornithine results in hyperornithinemia. In the absence of its normal acceptor ornithine, mitochondrial carbamoyl phosphate carbamoylates lysine to homocitrulline with a resulting homocitrullinuria.

Ornithine Transcarbamoylase

The X-chromosome linked deficiency termed "hyperammonemia type 2" reflects a defect in ornithine transcarbamoylase (reaction 2, Figure 28–9). The mothers also exhibit hyperammonemia and an aversion to high-protein foods. Levels of glutamine are elevated in blood, cerebrospinal fluid, and urine, probably as a result of enhanced glutamine synthesis in response to elevated levels of tissue ammonia.

Argininosuccinate Synthase

In addition to patients that lack detectable argininosuccinate synthase activity (reaction 3, Figure 28–9), a 25-fold elevated K_m for citrulline has been reported. These examples illustrate the first principle listed above. In the resulting citrullinemia, plasma and cerebrospinal fluid citrulline levels are elevated, and 1–2 g of citrulline are excreted daily.

Argininosuccinase (Argininosuccinate Lyase)

Argininosuccinicaciduria, accompanied by elevated levels of argininosuccinate in blood, cerebrospinal fluid, and urine, is associated with friable, tufted hair (trichorrhexis nodosa). Both early- and late-onset types are known. The metabolic defect is in argininosuccinase (argininosuccinate lyase; reaction 4, Figure 28–9). Diagnosis by measurement of erythrocyte argininosuccinase activity can be performed in utero on umbilical cord blood or amniotic fluid cells.

Arginase

Hyperargininemia is an autosomal recessive defect in the gene for arginase (reaction 5, Figure 28–9). Unlike other urea cycle disorders, the first symptoms of hyperargininemia typically do not appear until age 2 to 4 years. Blood and cerebrospinal fluid levels of arginine are elevated. The urinary amino acid pattern, which resembles that of lysine-cystinuria, may reflect competition by arginine with lysine and cysteine for reabsorption in the renal tubule.

Analysis of Neonate Blood by Tandem Mass Spectrometry Can Detect Metabolic Diseases

Metabolic diseases caused by the absence or functional impairment of metabolic enzymes can be devastating. Early dietary intervention, however, can in many instances ameliorate the otherwise inevitable dire effects. The early detection of such metabolic diseases is thus is of primary importance. Since the initiation in the United States of newborn screening programs in the 1960s, all states now conduct metabolic screening of newborns, but the scope of screen employed varies among states. The immensely powerful and sensitive technique of **tandem mass spectrometry** (see Chapter 4) can screen for over two dozen metabolic diseases using only drops of neonate blood. Most states, and presumably soon all states, employ tandem MS to screen newborns to detect metabolic disorders such as organic acidemias, aminoacidemias, disorders of fatty acid oxidation, and defects in the enzymes of the urea cycle.

Gene Therapy Offers Promise for Correcting Defects in Urea Biosynthesis

Gene therapy for rectification of defects in the enzymes of the urea cycle is an area of active investigation. Encouraging preliminary results have been obtained, for example, in animal models using an adenoviral vector to treat citrullinemia.

SUMMARY

- Human subjects degrade 1–2% of their body protein daily at rates that vary widely between proteins and with physiologic state. Key regulatory enzymes often have short half-lives.

- Proteins are degraded by both ATP-dependent and ATP-independent pathways. Ubiquitin targets many intracellular proteins for degradation. Liver cell surface receptors bind and internalize circulating asialoglycoproteins destined for lysosomal degradation.

- Ammonia is highly toxic. Fish excrete NH_3 directly; birds convert NH_3 to uric acid. Higher vertebrates convert NH_3 to urea.

- Transamination channels α-amino acid nitrogen into glutamate. L-Glutamate dehydrogenase (GDH) occupies a central position in nitrogen metabolism.

- Glutamine synthase converts NH_3 to nontoxic glutamine. Glutaminase releases NH_3 for use in urea synthesis.

- NH_3, CO_2, and the amide nitrogen of aspartate provide the atoms of urea.
- Hepatic urea synthesis takes place in part in the mitochondrial matrix and in part in the cytosol. Inborn errors of metabolism are associated with each reaction of the urea cycle.
- Changes in enzyme levels and allosteric regulation of carbamoyl phosphate synthase by N-acetylglutamate regulate urea biosynthesis.
- Metabolic diseases are associated with defects in each enzyme of the urea cycle, of the membrane-associated ornithine transporter, and of N-acetylglutamate synthetase.
- Tandem mass spectrometry is the technique of choice for screening neonates for over two dozen metabolic diseases.

REFERENCES

Brooks P et al: Subcellular localization of proteasomes and their regulatory complexes in mammalian cells. Biochem J 2000;346:155.

Caldovic L et al: Late onset N-acetylglutamate synthase deficiency caused by hypomorphic alleles. Hum Mutat 2005;25:293.

Crombez EA, Cederbaum SD: Hyperargininemia due to liver arginase deficiency. Mol Genet Metab 2005;84:243.

Elpeleg O et al: N-acetylglutamate synthase deficiency and the treatment of hyperammonemic encephalopathy. Ann Neurol 2002;52:845.

Gyato K et al: Metabolic and neuropsychological phenotype in women heterozygous for ornithine transcarbamylase deficiency. Ann Neurol 2004;55:80.

Haberle J et al: Diagnosis of N-acetylglutamate synthase deficiency by use of cultured fibroblasts and avoidance of nonsense-mediated mRNA decay. J Inherit Metab Dis 2003;26:601.

Haberle J et al: Mild citrullinemia in caucasians is an allelic variant of argininosuccinate synthetase deficiency (citrullinemia type 1). Mol Genet Metab 2003;80:302.

Iyer R et al: The human arginases and arginase deficiency. J Inherit Metab Dis 1998;21:86.

Pickart CM. Mechanisms underlying ubiquitination. Annu Rev Biochem 2001;70:503.

Scriver CR et al (editors): *The Metabolic and Molecular Bases of Inherited Disease,* 8th ed. McGraw-Hill, 2001.

Catabolism of the Carbon Skeletons of Amino Acids

29

Victor W. Rodwell, PhD

BIOMEDICAL IMPORTANCE

This chapter considers conversion of the carbon skeletons of the common L-amino acids to amphibolic intermediates and the metabolic diseases or "inborn errors of metabolism" associated with these processes. Left untreated, these disorders can result in irreversible brain damage and early mortality. Prenatal or early postnatal detection and timely initiation of treatment thus are essential. Many of the enzymes concerned can be detected in cultured amniotic fluid cells, which facilitates prenatal diagnosis by amniocentesis. Almost all states conduct screening tests for up to as many as 30 metabolic diseases. These include, but are not limited to, disorders that result from defects in the catabolism of amino acids. The screens employ tandem mass spectrometry to detect, in a few drops of neonate blood, catabolites suggestive of a metabolic defect. Treatment consists primarily of feeding diets low in the amino acids whose catabolism is impaired. While many changes in the primary structure of enzymes have no adverse effects, others modify the three-dimensional structure of catalytic or regulatory sites, lower catalytic efficiency (lower V_{max} or elevate K_m), or alter the affinity for an allosteric regulator of activity. A variety of mutations thus may give rise to the same clinical signs and symptoms.

TRANSAMINATION TYPICALLY INITIATES AMINO ACID CATABOLISM

Removal of α-amino nitrogen by transamination (see Figure 28–3) is the first catabolic reaction of amino acids except for proline, hydroxyproline, threonine, and lysine. The hydrocarbon skeleton that remains is then degraded to amphibolic intermediates as outlined in Figure 29–1.

Asparagine, Aspartate, Glutamine, and Glutamate. All four carbons of asparagine and aspartate form **oxaloacetate** (Figure 29–2, top). Analogous reactions convert glutamine and glutamate to **α-ketoglutarate** (Figure 29–2, bottom). Since the enzymes also fulfill anabolic func-

tions, no metabolic defects are associated with the catabolism of these four amino acids.

Proline. Since proline does not participate in transamination, the nitrogen of this imino acid is retained throughout its oxidation to dehydroproline, ring opening to glutamate-γ-semialdehyde, and oxidation to glutamate, and is only removed during transamination of glutamate to α-ketoglutarate (Figure 29–3, top). The metabolic block in **type I hyperprolinemia** is at **proline dehydrogenase.** There is no associated impairment of hydroxyproline catabolism. The metabolic block in **type II hyperprolinemia** is at **glutamate-γ-semialdehyde dehydrogenase,** which also functions in hydroxyproline catabolism. Both proline and hydroxyproline catabolism thus are affected and Δ^1-pyrroline-3-hydroxy-5-carboxylate (see Figure 29–11) is excreted.

Arginine and Ornithine. Arginine is converted to ornithine, then to glutamate γ-semialdehyde, which is converted to **α-ketoglutarate,** as for proline (Figure 29–3, bottom). Mutations in **ornithine δ-aminotransferase** elevate plasma and urinary ornithine and cause **gyrate atrophy of the retina.** Treatment involves restricting dietary arginine. In **hyperornithinemia-hyperammonemia syndrome,** a defective mitochondrial **ornithine-citrulline antiporter** (see Figure 28–9) impairs transport of ornithine into mitochondria for use in urea synthesis.

Histidine. Catabolism of histidine proceeds via urocanate, 4-imidazolone-5-propionate, and *N*-formiminoglutamate (Figlu). Formimino group transfer to tetrahydrofolate forms glutamate, then **α-ketoglutarate** (Figure 29–4). In folic acid deficiency, group transfer is impaired and Figlu is excreted. Excretion of Figlu following a dose of histidine thus can be used to detect folic acid deficiency. Benign disorders of histidine catabolism include **histidinemia** and **urocanic aciduria** associated with impaired **histidase.**

SIX AMINO ACIDS FORM PYRUVATE

All of the carbons of glycine, serine, alanine, and cysteine and two carbons of threonine form pyruvate and subsequently acetyl-CoA.

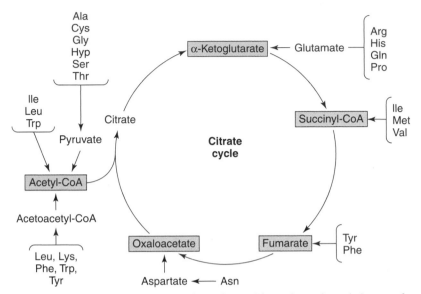

Figure 29–1. Amphibolic intermediates formed from the carbon skeletons of amino acids.

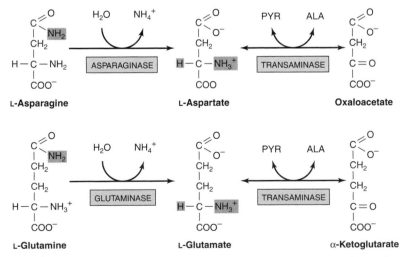

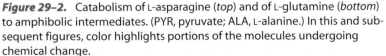

Figure 29–2. Catabolism of L-asparagine (*top*) and of L-glutamine (*bottom*) to amphibolic intermediates. (PYR, pyruvate; ALA, L-alanine.) In this and subsequent figures, color highlights portions of the molecules undergoing chemical change.

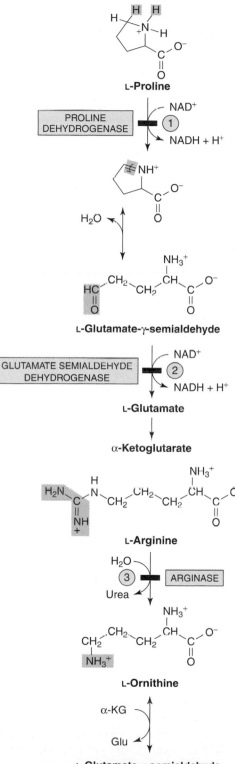

Figure 29–3. **Top:** Catabolism of proline. Numerals indicate sites of the metabolic defects in ① type I and ② type II hyperprolinemias. **Bottom:** Catabolism of arginine. Glutamate-γ-semialdehyde forms α-ketoglutarate as shown above. ③, site of the metabolic defect in hyperargininemia.

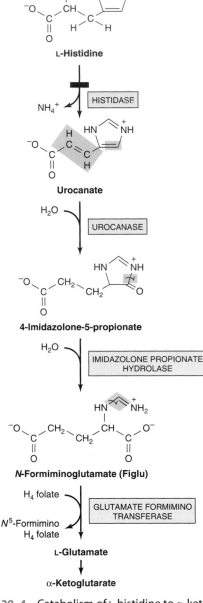

Figure 29–4. Catabolism of L-histidine to α-ketoglutarate. (H$_4$ folate, tetrahydrofolate.) Histidase is the probable site of the metabolic defect in histidinemia.

Glycine. The **glycine synthase complex** of liver mitochondria splits glycine to CO_2 and NH_4^+ and forms N^5, N^{10}-methylene tetrahydrofolate (Figure 29–5). **Glycinuria** results from a defect in renal tubular reabsorption. The defect in **primary hyperoxaluria** is the failure to catabolize glyoxylate formed

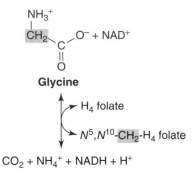

Figure 29–5. Reversible cleavage of glycine by the mitochondrial glycine synthase complex. (PLP, pyridoxal phosphate.)

by deamination of glycine. Subsequent oxidation of glyoxylate to oxalate results in urolithiasis, nephrocalcinosis, and early mortality from renal failure or hypertension.

Serine. Following conversion to glycine, catalyzed by **serine hydroxymethyltransferase** (Figure 29–6), serine catabolism merges with that of glycine.

Alanine. Transamination of alanine forms pyruvate. Perhaps for the reason advanced under glutamate and aspartate catabolism, there is no known metabolic defect of alanine catabolism.

Cysteine. Cystine is first reduced to cysteine by **cystine reductase** (Figure 29–7). Two different pathways then convert cysteine to pyruvate (Figure 29–8).

There are numerous abnormalities of cysteine metabolism. Cystine, lysine, arginine, and ornithine are excreted in **cystine-lysinuria (cystinuria),** a defect in renal reabsorption of these amino acids. Apart from cystine calculi, cystinuria is benign. The mixed disulfide of L-cysteine and L-homocysteine (Figure 29–9) excreted by cystinuric patients is more soluble than cystine and reduces formation of cystine calculi. Several metabolic defects result in vitamin

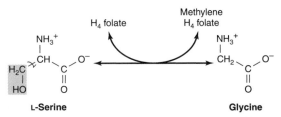

Figure 29–6. Interconversion of serine and glycine catalyzed by serine hydroxymethyltransferase. (H$_4$ folate, tetrahydrofolate.)

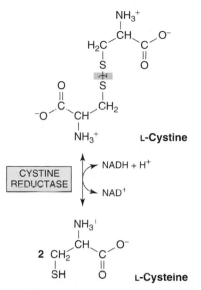

Figure 29–7. The cystine reductase reaction.

B_6-responsive or -unresponsive **homocystinurias.** Defective carrier-mediated transport of cystine results in **cystinosis (cystine storage disease)** with deposition of cystine crystals in tissues and early mortality from acute renal failure. Despite epidemiologic data suggesting a relationship between plasma homocysteine and cardiovascular disease, whether homocysteine represents a causal cardiovascular risk factor remains controversial.

Threonine. Threonine is cleaved to acetaldehyde and glycine. Oxidation of acetaldehyde to acetate is followed by formation of acetyl-CoA (Figure 29–10). Catabolism of glycine is discussed above.

4-Hydroxyproline. Catabolism of 4-hydroxy-L-proline forms, successively, L-Δ^1-pyrroline-3-hydroxy-5-carboxylate, γ-hydroxy-L-glutamate-γ-semialdehyde, erythro-γ-hydroxy-L-glutamate, and α-keto-γ-hydroxy-glutarate. An aldol-type cleavage then forms glyoxylate plus pyruvate (Figure 29–11). A defect in **4-hydroxyproline dehydrogenase** results in **hyperhydroxyprolinemia,** which is benign. There is no associated impairment of proline catabolism.

TWELVE AMINO ACIDS FORM ACETYL-CoA

Tyrosine. Figure 29–12 diagrams the conversion of tyrosine to amphibolic intermediates. Since ascorbate is the reductant for conversion of *p*-hydroxyphenylpyruvate to homogentisate, scorbutic patients excrete incompletely oxidized products of tyrosine catabolism.

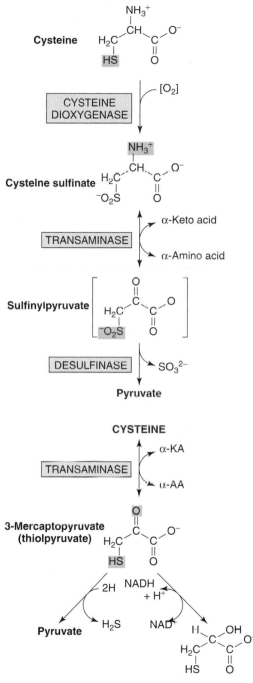

Figure 29–8. Catabolism of L-cysteine via the cysteine sulfinate pathway *(top)* and by the 3-mercaptopyruvate pathway *(bottom)*.

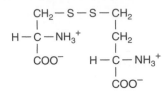

(Cysteine)   (Homocysteine)

Figure 29–9. Mixed disulfide of cysteine and homocysteine.

Subsequent catabolism forms maleylacetoacetate, fumarylacetoacetate, fumarate, acetoacetate, and ultimately **acetyl-CoA.**

The probable metabolic defect in **type I tyrosinemia (tyrosinosis)** is at **fumarylacetoacetate hydrolase** (reaction 4, Figure 29–12). Therapy employs a diet low in tyrosine and phenylalanine. Untreated acute and chronic tyrosinosis leads to death from liver failure. Alternate metabolites of tyrosine are also excreted in **type II tyrosinemia (Richner-Hanhart syndrome),** a defect in **tyrosine aminotransferase** (reaction 1, Figure 29–12), and in **neonatal tyrosinemia,** due to lowered *p*-hydroxyphenylpyruvate hydroxylase activity (reaction 2, Figure 29–12). Therapy employs a diet low in protein.

Alkaptonuria was first recognized and described in the 16th century. Characterized in 1859, it provided the basis for Garrod's classic ideas concerning heritable metabolic disorders. The defect is lack of **homogentisate oxidase** (reaction 3, Figure 29–12). The urine darkens on exposure to air due to oxidation of excreted homogentisate. Late in the disease, there is arthritis and connective tissue pigmentation (ochronosis) due to oxidation of homogentisate to benzoquinone acetate, which polymerizes and binds to connective tissue.

Phenylalanine. Phenylalanine is first converted to tyrosine (see Figure 27–10). Subsequent reactions are those of tyrosine (Figure 29–12). **Hyperphenylalaninemias** arise from defects in phenylalanine hydroxylase itself (**type I, classic phenylketonuria** or **PKU**), in dihydrobiopterin reductase (**types II and III**), or in dihydrobiopterin biosynthesis (**types IV and V**) (Figure 27–10). Alternative catabolites are excreted (Figure 29–13). DNA probes facilitate prenatal diagnosis of defects in phenylalanine hydroxylase or dihydrobiopterin reductase. A diet low in phenylalanine can prevent the mental retardation of PKU (frequency 1:10,000 births). Elevated blood phenylalanine may not be detectable until 3–4 days postpartum. False-positives in premature infants may reflect delayed maturation of enzymes of phenylalanine catabolism. An older and less reliable screening

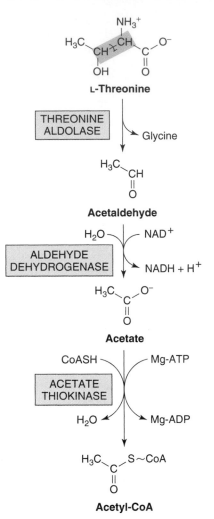

Figure 29–10. Conversion of threonine to glycine and acetyl-CoA.

test employs $FeCl_3$ to detect urinary phenylpyruvate. $FeCl_3$ screening for PKU of the urine of newborn infants is compulsory in many countries, but in the United States has been largely supplanted by screening by tandem mass spectrometry.

Lysine. The first six reactions of L-lysine catabolism in human liver form crotonyl-CoA, which is then degraded to acetyl-CoA and CO_2 by the reactions of fatty acid catabolism. In what follows, circled numerals refer to the corresponding numbered reactions of Figure 29–14.

Reactions ① and ② convert the Schiff base formed between α-ketoglutarate and the ε-amino group of lysine to L-α-aminoadipate-δ-semialdehde. Both reactions are catalyzed by a single bifunctional

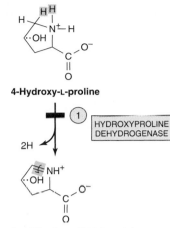

4-Hydroxy-L-proline

① HYDROXYPROLINE
DEHYDROGENASE

2H

L-Δ¹-Pyrroline-3-hydroxy-5-carboxylate

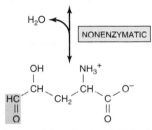

H_2O

NONENZYMATIC

γ-Hydroxy-L-glutamate-γ-scmialdehyde

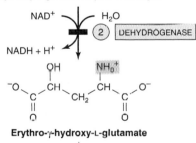

NAD^+ H_2O

② DEHYDROGENASE

$NADH + H^+$

Erythro-γ-hydroxy-L-glutamate

α-KA

TRANSAMINASE

α-AA

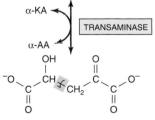

α-Keto-γ-hydroxyglutarate

AN ALDOLASE

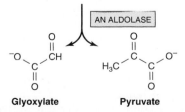

Glyoxylate   **Pyruvate**

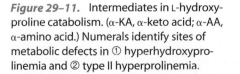

Figure 29–11. Intermediates in L-hydroxy-proline catabolism. (α-KA, α-keto acid; α-AA, α-amino acid.) Numerals identify sites of metabolic defects in ① hyperhydroxypro-linemia and ② type II hyperprolinemia.

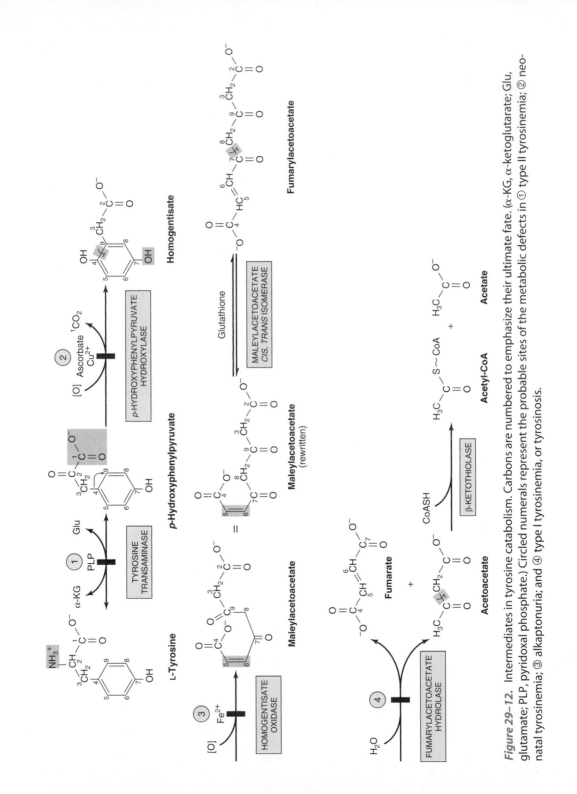

Figure 29–12. Intermediates in tyrosine catabolism. Carbons are numbered to emphasize their ultimate fate. (α-KG, α-ketoglutarate; Glu, glutamate; PLP, pyridoxal phosphate.) Circled numerals represent the probable sites of the metabolic defects in ① type I tyrosinemia; ② neonatal tyrosinemia; ③ alkaptonuria; and ④ type I tyrosinemia, or tyrosinosis.

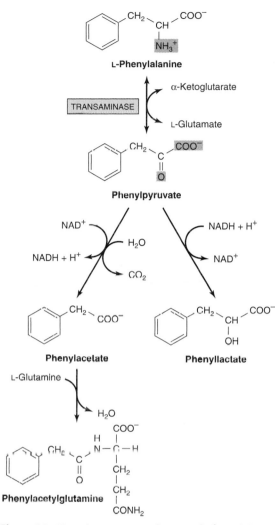

Figure 29–13. Alternative pathways of phenylalanine catabolism in phenylketonuria. The reactions also occur in normal liver tissue but are of minor significance.

enzyme, aminoadipate semialdehde synthase (also called lysine 2-oxoglutarate reductase-saccharopine dehydrogenase). Reduction of L-α-aminoadipate-δ-semialdehde to L-α-aminoadipate (reaction ③) is followed by transamination to α-ketoadipate (reaction ④). Conversion to the thioester glutaryl-CoA (reaction ⑤) is followed by the decarboxylation of glutaryl-CoA to crotonyl-CoA (reaction ⑥). The subsequent reactions are those of the catabolism of α-unsaturated fatty acids with an odd number of carbons.

Metabolic defects associated with reactions of the lysine catabolic pathway include hyperlysinemias. Hyperlysinemia can result from a defect in either activity ① **or** ② of the bifunctional enzyme aminoadipate semialdehde synthase. Hyperlysinemia is accompanied by elevated levels of blood saccharopine only if the defect involves activity ②. A metabolic defect at reaction ⑥ results in an inherited metabolic disease that is associated with striatal and cortical degeneration, and characterized by elevated concentrations of glutaric acid and its metabolites, glutaconic acid and 3-hydroxy-glutaric acid. The challenge in management of these metabolic defects is to restrict dietary intake of L-lysine without accompanying malnutrition.

Tryptophan. Tryptophan is degraded to amphibolic intermediates via the kynurenine-anthranilate pathway (Figure 29–15). **Tryptophan oxygenase (tryptophan pyrrolase)** opens the indole ring, incorporates molecular oxygen, and forms N-formylkynurenine. An iron porphyrin metalloprotein that is inducible in liver by adrenal corticosteroids and by tryptophan, tryptophan oxygenase is feedback-inhibited by nicotinic acid derivatives, including NADPH. Hydrolytic removal of the formyl group of N-formylkynurenine, catalyzed by **kynurenine formylase,** produces kynurenine. Since **kynureninase** requires pyridoxal phosphate, excretion of xanthurenate (Figure 29–16) in response to a tryptophan load is diagnostic of vitamin B_6 deficiency. **Hartnup disease** reflects impaired intestinal and renal transport of tryptophan and other neutral amino acids. Indole derivatives of unabsorbed tryptophan formed by intestinal bacteria are excreted. The defect limits tryptophan availability for niacin biosynthesis and accounts for the pellagra-like signs and symptoms.

Methionine. Methionine reacts with ATP forming S-adenosylmethionine, "active methionine" (Figure 29–17). Subsequent reactions form propionyl-CoA (Figure 29–18) and ultimately succinyl-CoA (see Figure 20–2).

THE INITIAL REACTIONS ARE COMMON TO ALL THREE BRANCHED-CHAIN AMINO ACIDS

Reactions 1–3 of Figure 29–19 are analogous to those of fatty acid catabolism. Following transamination, all three α-keto acids undergo oxidative decarboxylation catalyzed by mitochondrial **branched-chain α-keto acid dehydrogenase.** This multimeric enzyme complex of a decarboxylase, a transacylase, and a dihydrolipoyl dehydrogenase closely resembles pyruvate dehydrogenase

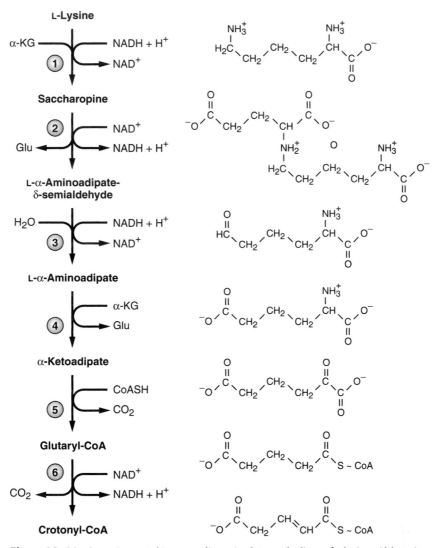

Figure 29–14. Reactions and intermediates in the catabolism of L-lysine. Abbreviations: α-KT, α-ketoglutarate; Glu, L-glutamate. Shown on the left are the reactions and at the right the structures of the intermediates. The numbered reactions and the metabolic defects associated with lysine catabolism are discussed in the accompanying text.

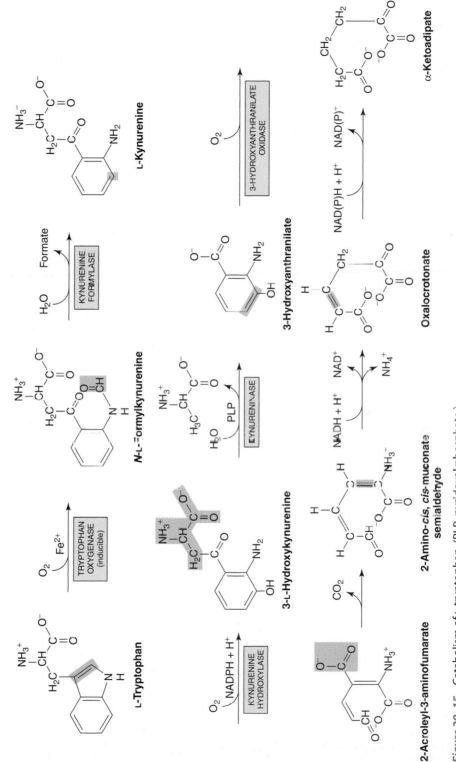

Figure 29–15. Catabolism of L-tryptophan. (PLP, pyridoxal phosphate.)

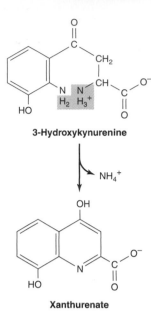

3-Hydroxykynurenine

NH$_4^+$

Xanthurenate

Figure 29–16. Formation of xanthurenate in vitamin B$_6$ deficiency. Conversion of the tryptophan metabolite 3-hydroxykynurenine to 3-hydroxyanthranilate is impaired (see Figure 29–15). A large portion is therefore converted to xanthurenate.

(see Figure 18–5). Its regulation also parallels that of pyruvate dehydrogenase, being inactivated by phosphorylation and reactivated by dephosphorylation (see Figure 18–6).

Reaction 3 is analogous to the dehydrogenation of fatty acyl-CoA thioesters (see Figure 22–3). In

isovaleric acidemia, ingestion of protein-rich foods elevates isovalerate, the deacylation product of isovaleryl-CoA. Figures 29–20, 29–21, and 29–22 illustrate the subsequent reactions unique to each amino acid skeleton.

METABOLIC DISORDERS OF BRANCHED-CHAIN AMINO ACID CATABOLISM

As the name implies, the odor of urine in **maple syrup urine disease (branched-chain ketonuria)** suggests maple syrup or burnt sugar. The biochemical defect involves the **α-keto acid decarboxylase complex** (reaction 2, Figure 29–19). Plasma and urinary levels of leucine, isoleucine, valine, α-keto acids, and α-hydroxy acids (reduced α-keto acids) are elevated. The mechanism of toxicity is unknown. Early diagnosis, especially prior to 1 week of age, employs enzymatic analysis. Prompt replacement of dietary protein by an amino acid mixture that lacks leucine, isoleucine, and valine averts brain damage and early mortality.

Mutation of the dihydrolipoate reductase component impairs decarboxylation of branched-chain α-keto acids, of pyruvate, and of α-ketoglutarate. In **intermittent branched-chain ketonuria,** the α-keto acid decarboxylase retains some activity, and symptoms occur later in life. The impaired enzyme in **isovaleric acidemia** is **isovaleryl-CoA dehydrogenase** (reaction 3, Figure 29–19). Vomiting, acidosis, and coma follow ingestion of excess protein. Accumulated isovaleryl-CoA is hydrolyzed to isovalerate and excreted.

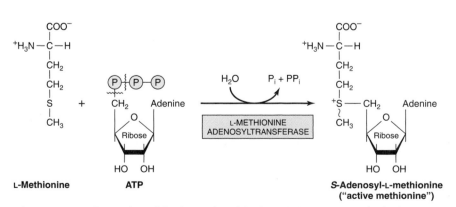

L-Methionine   ATP

L-METHIONINE ADENOSYLTRANSFERASE

S-Adenosyl-L-methionine ("active methionine")

Figure 29–17. Formation of *S*-adenosylmethionine. ~CH$_3$ represents the high group transfer potential of "active methionine."

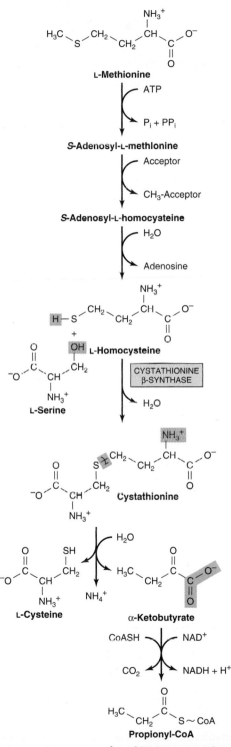

Figure 29–18. Conversion of methionine to propionyl-CoA.

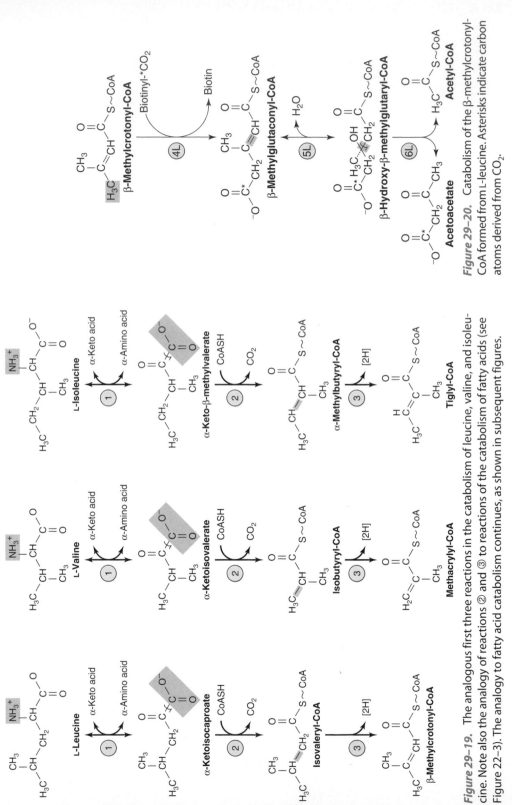

Figure 29–20. Catabolism of the β-methylcrotonyl-CoA formed from L-leucine. Asterisks indicate carbon atoms derived from CO₂.

Figure 29–19. The analogous first three reactions in the catabolism of leucine, valine, and isoleucine. Note also the analogy of reactions ② and ③ to reactions of the catabolism of fatty acids (see Figure 22–3). The analogy to fatty acid catabolism continues, as shown in subsequent figures.

267

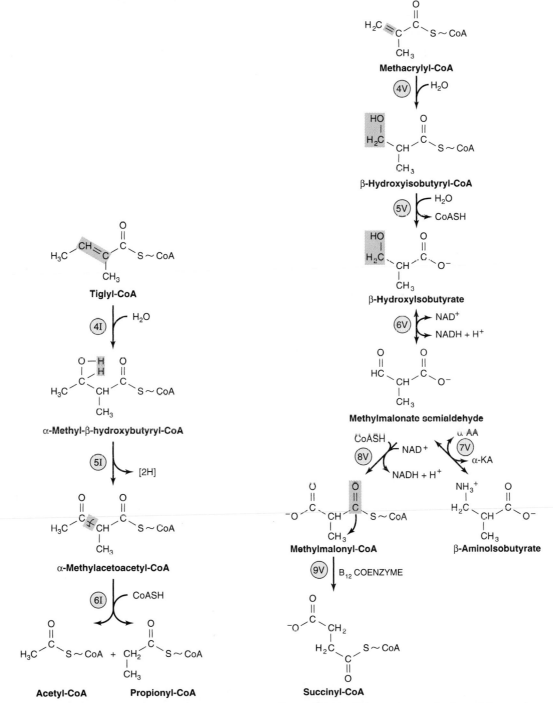

Figure 29–21. Subsequent catabolism of the tiglyl-CoA formed from L-isoleucine.

Figure 29–22. Subsequent catabolism of the methacrylyl-CoA formed from L-valine (see Figure 29–19). (α-KA, α-keto acid; α-AA, α-amino acid.)

SUMMARY

- Excess amino acids are catabolized to amphibolic intermediates used as sources of energy or for carbohydrate and lipid biosynthesis.

- Transamination is the most common initial reaction of amino acid catabolism. Subsequent reactions remove any additional nitrogen and restructure the hydrocarbon skeleton for conversion to oxaloacetate, α-ketoglutarate, pyruvate, and acetyl-CoA.

- Metabolic diseases associated with glycine catabolism include glycinuria and primary hyperoxaluria.

- Two distinct pathways convert cysteine to pyruvate. Metabolic disorders of cysteine catabolism include cystine-lysinuria, cystine storage disease, and the homocystinurias.

- Threonine catabolism merges with that of glycine after threonine aldolase cleaves threonine to glycine and acetaldehyde.

- Following transamination, the carbon skeleton of tyrosine is degraded to fumarate and acetoacetate. Metabolic diseases of tyrosine catabolism include tyrosinosis, Richner-Hanhart syndrome, neonatal tyrosinemia, and alkaptonuria.

- Metabolic disorders of phenylalanine catabolism include phenylketonuria (PKU) and several hyperphenylalaninemias.

- Neither nitrogen of lysine undergoes transamination. Metabolic diseases of lysine catabolism include periodic and persistent forms of hyperlysinemia-ammonemia.

- The catabolism of leucine, valine, and isoleucine presents many analogies to fatty acid catabolism. Metabolic disorders of branched-chain amino acid catabolism include hypervalinemia, maple syrup urine disease, intermittent branched-chain ketonuria, isovaleric acidemia, and methylmalonic aciduria.

REFERENCES

Blacher J, Safar ME: Homocysteine, folic acid, B vitamins and cardiovascular risk. J Nutr Health Aging 2001;5:196.

Bliksrud YT et al: Tyrosinemia type I, de novo mutation in liver tissue suppressing an inborn splicing defect. J Mol Med 2005;83:406.

Cooper AJL: Biochemistry of the sulfur-containing amino acids. Annu Rev Biochem 1983;52:187.

Gerstner B et al: Glutaric acid and its metabolites cause apoptosis in immature oligodendrocytes: a novel mechanism of white matter degeneration in glutaryl-CoA dehydrogenase deficiency. Pediatr Res 2005;57;771.

Gjetting T et al: A phenylalanine hydroxylase amino acid polymorphism with implications for molecular diagnostics. Mol Genet Metab 2001;73:280.

Harris RA et al: Molecular cloning of the branched-chain α-ketoacid dehydrogenase kinase and the CoA-dependent methylmalonate semialdehyde dehydrogenase. Adv Enzyme Regul 1993;33:255.

Heldt K et al: Diagnosis of maple syrup urine disease by newborn screening allows early intervention without extraneous detoxification. Mol Genet Metab 2005;84:313.

Muller E, Kolker S: Reduction of lysine intake while avoiding malnutrition: major goals and major problems in dietary treatment of glutaryl-CoA dehydrogenase deficiency. J Inherit Metab Dis 2004;27:903.

Sacksteder KA et al: Identification of the alpha-aminoadipic semialdehyde synthase gene which is defective in familial hyperlysinemia. Am J Hum Genet 2000;66:1736.

Scriver CR: Garrod's foresight; our hindsight. J Inherit Metab Dis 2001;24:93.

Scriver CR et al (editors): *The Metabolic and Molecular Bases of Inherited Disease,* 8th ed. McGraw-Hill, 2001.

Waters PJ, Scriver CR, Parniak MA: Homomeric and heteromeric interactions between wild-type and mutant phenylalanine hydroxylase subunits: evaluation of two-hybrid approaches for functional analysis of mutations causing hyperphenylalaninemia. Mol Genet Metab 2001;73:230.

Conversion of Amino Acids to Specialized Products

Victor W. Rodwell, PhD

30

BIOMEDICAL IMPORTANCE

Important products derived from amino acids that are discussed in other chapters include heme, purines, pyrimidines, hormones, neurotransmitters, and biologically active peptides. In addition, many proteins contain amino acids that have been posttranslationally modified for a specific function. The amino acid residues in those proteins serve as precursors for these modified residues. Examples include the carboxylation of glutamate to form γ-carboxyglutamate, which functions in Ca^{2+} binding, the hydroxylation of proline for incorporation into the collagen triple helix, and the formation of hydroxylysine, whose subsequent modification and cross-linking stabilizes maturing collagen fibers. Small peptides or peptide-like molecules not synthesized on ribosomes fulfill specific functions in cells. Histamine plays a central role in many allergic reactions. Neurotransmitters derived from amino acids include γ-aminobutyrate, 5-hydroxytryptamine (serotonin), dopamine, norepinephrine, and epinephrine. Many drugs used to treat neurologic and psychiatric conditions affect the metabolism of these neurotransmitters.

Glycine

Metabolites and pharmaceuticals excreted as water-soluble glycine conjugates include glycocholic acid (Chapter 26) and hippuric acid formed from the food additive benzoate (Figure 30–1). Many drugs, drug metabolites, and other compounds with carboxyl groups are excreted in the urine as glycine conjugates. Glycine is incorporated into creatine (see Figure 30–8), the nitrogen and α-carbon of glycine are incorporated into the pyrrole rings and the methylene bridge carbons of heme (Chapter 31), and the entire glycine molecule becomes atoms 4, 5, and 7 of purines (Figure 33–1).

α-Alanine

Together with glycine, α-alanine constitutes a major fraction of the free amino acids in plasma.

β-Alanine

β-Alanine, a metabolite of cysteine (Figure 33–9), is present in coenzyme A (Figure 44–18) and as β-alanyl dipeptides, principally carnosine (see below). Mammalian tissues form β-alanine from cytosine (Figure 33–9), carnosine, and anserine (Figure 30–2). Mammalian tissues transaminate β-alanine, forming malonate semialdehyde. Body fluid and tissue levels of β-alanine, taurine, and β-aminoisobutyrate are elevated in the rare metabolic disorder hyper β-alaninemia.

β-Alanyl Dipeptides

The β-alanyl dipeptides carnosine and anserine (N-methylcarnosine) (Figure 30–2) activate myosin ATPase, chelate copper, and enhance copper uptake. β-Alanyl-imidazole buffers the pH of anaerobically contracting skeletal muscle. Biosynthesis of carnosine is catalyzed by carnosine synthetase in a two-stage reaction that involves initial formation of an enzyme-bound acyl-adenylate of β-alanine and subsequent transfer of the β-alanyl moiety to L-histidine.

$$ATP + \beta\text{-Alanine} \rightarrow \beta\text{-Alanyl}-AMP \rightarrow +PP_i$$
$$\beta\text{-Alanyl}-AMP + L\text{-Histidine} \rightarrow Carnosine + AMP$$

Hydrolysis of carnosine to β-alanine and L-histidine is catalyzed by carnosinase. The heritable disorder carnosinase deficiency is characterized by carnosinuria.

Homocarnosine (Figure 30–2), present in human brain at higher levels than carnosine, is synthesized in brain tissue by carnosine synthetase. Serum carnosinase does not hydrolyze homocarnosine. Homocarnosinosis, a rare genetic disorder, is associated with progressive spastic paraplegia and mental retardation.

Serine

Serine participates in the biosynthesis of sphingosine (Chapter 24), and of purines and pyrimidines, where it provides carbons 2 and 8 of purines and the methyl group of thymine (Chapter 33).

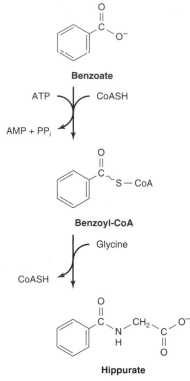

Figure 30–1. Biosynthesis of hippurate. Analogous reactions occur with many acidic drugs and catabolites.

Phosphorylated Serine, Threonine, & Tyrosine

The phosphorylation and dephosphorylation of seryl, threonyl, and tyrosyl residues regulate the activity of certain enzymes of lipid and carbohydrate metabolism and the properties of proteins that participate in signal transduction cascades.

Methionine

S-Adenosylmethionine, the principal source of methyl groups in the body, also contributes its carbon skeleton for the biosynthesis of the 3-diaminopropane portions of the polyamines spermine and spermidine (Figure 30–4).

Cysteine

L-Cysteine is a precursor of the thioethanolamine portion of coenzyme A and of the taurine that conjugates with bile acids such as taurocholic acid (Chapter 26).

Histidine

Decarboxylation of histidine to histamine is catalyzed by a broad-specificity aromatic L-amino acid decarboxylase that also catalyzes the decarboxylation of dopa, 5-hydroxytryptophan, phenylalanine, tyrosine, and tryptophan. α-Methyl amino acids, which inhibit decarboxylase activity, find application as antihypertensive agents. Histidine compounds present in the human body include ergothioneine, carnosine, and dietary anserine (Figure 30–2). Urinary levels of 3-methylhistidine are unusually low in patients with Wilson's disease.

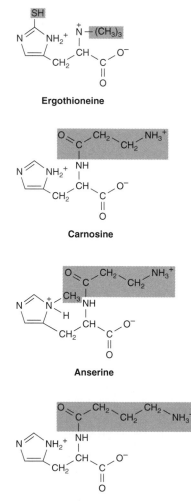

Figure 30–2. Compounds related to histidine. Colored boxes surround the components not derived from histidine. The SH group of ergothioneine derives from cysteine.

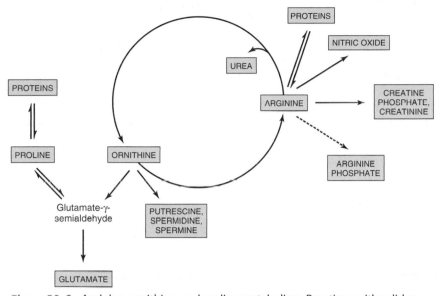

Figure 30–3. Arginine, ornithine, and proline metabolism. Reactions with solid arrows all occur in mammalian tissues. Putrescine and spermine synthesis occurs in both mammals and bacteria. Arginine phosphate of invertebrate muscle functions as a phosphagen analogous to creatine phosphate of mammalian muscle.

Ornithine & Arginine

Arginine is the formamidine donor for creatine synthesis (Figure 30–8) and via ornithine to putrescine, spermine, and spermidine (Figure 30–3). Arginine is also the precursor of the intercellular signaling molecule nitric oxide (NO) that serves as a neurotransmitter, smooth muscle relaxant, and vasodilator. Synthesis of NO, catalyzed by NO synthase, involves the NADPH-dependent reaction of L-arginine with O_2 to yield L-citrulline and NO (Figure 48–15).

Polyamines

The polyamines spermidine and spermine function in cell proliferation and growth, are growth factors for cultured mammalian cells, and stabilize intact cells, subcellular organelles, and membranes. Pharmacologic doses of polyamines are hypothermic and hypotensive. Since they bear multiple positive charges, polyamines associate readily with DNA and RNA. Figure 30–4 summarizes polyamine biosynthesis, and Figure 30–5 shows the catabolism of polyamines.

Tryptophan

Following hydroxylation of tryptophan to 5-hydroxytryptophan by liver tyrosine hydroxylase, subsequent decarboxylation forms serotonin (5-hydroxytryptamine), a potent vasoconstrictor and stimulator of smooth muscle contraction. Catabolism of serotonin is initiated by monoamine oxidase-catalyzed oxidative deamination to 5-hydroxyindole-3-acetate (Figure 30–6). The psychic stimulation that follows administration of iproniazid results from its ability to prolong the action of serotonin by inhibiting monoamine oxidase. In carcinoid (argentaffinoma), tumor cells overproduce serotonin. Urinary metabolites of serotonin in patients with carcinoid include N-acetylserotonin glucuronide and the glycine conjugate of 5-hydroxyindoleacetate. Serotonin and 5-methoxytryptamine are metabolized to the corresponding acids by monoamine oxidase. N-Acetylation of serotonin, followed by O-methylation in the pineal body, forms melatonin. Circulating melatonin is taken up by all tissues, including brain, but is rapidly metabolized by hydroxylation followed by conjugation with sulfate or with glucuronic acid.

Kidney tissue, liver tissue, and fecal bacteria all convert tryptophan to tryptamine, then to indole 3-acetate. The principal normal urinary catabolites of tryptophan are 5-hydroxyindoleacetate and indole 3-acetate.

Tyrosine

Neural cells convert tyrosine to epinephrine and norepinephrine (Figure 30–7). While dopa is also an inter-

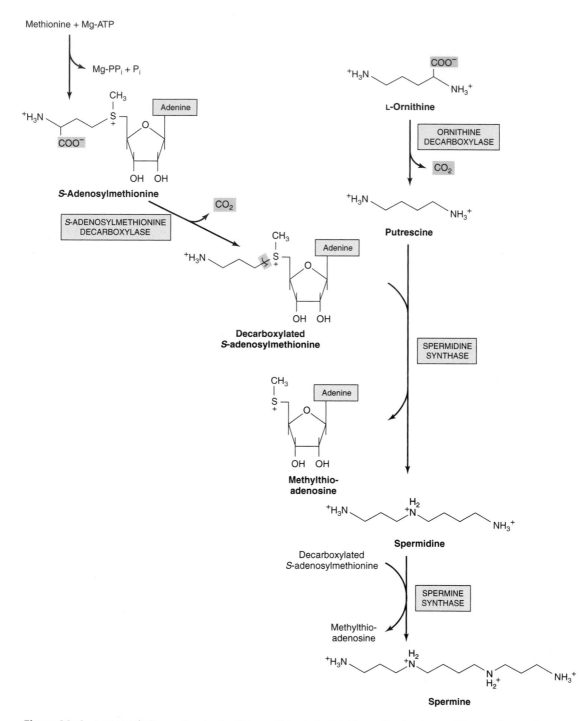

Figure 30–4. Intermediates and enzymes that participate in the biosynthesis of spermidine and spermine. Methylene groups are abbreviated to facilitate visualization of the overall process.

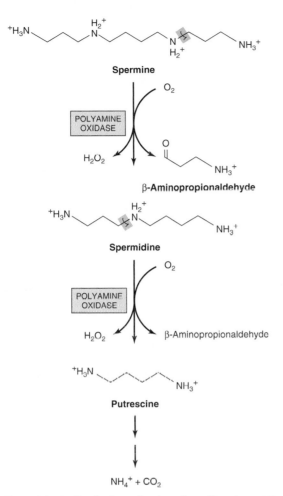

Figure 30–5. Catabolism of polyamines. Structures are abbreviated to facilitate presentation.

tion of creatinine is proportionate to muscle mass. Glycine, arginine, and methionine all participate in creatine biosynthesis. Synthesis of creatine is completed by methylation of guanidoacetate by *S*-adenosylmethionine (Figure 30–8).

γ-Aminobutyrate

γ-Aminobutyrate (GABA) functions in brain tissue as an inhibitory neurotransmitter by altering transmembrane potential differences. It is formed by decarboxylation of L-glutamate, a reaction catalyzed by L-glutamate decarboxylase (Figure 30–9). Transamination of γ-aminobutyrate forms succinate semialdehyde (Figure 30–9), which may then undergo reduction to γ-hydroxybutyrate, a reaction catalyzed by L-lactate dehydrogenase, or oxidation to succinate and thence via the citric acid cycle to CO_2 and H_2O. A rare genetic disorder of GABA metabolism involves a defective GABA aminotransferase, an enzyme that participates in the catabolism of GABA subsequent to its postsynaptic release in brain tissue. Defects in succinic semialdehyde dehydrogenase (Figure 30–9) are responsible for another rare metabolic disorder of γ-aminobutyrate catabolism characterized by 4-hydroxybutyric aciduria.

SUMMARY

- In addition to their roles in proteins and polypeptides, amino acids participate in a wide variety of additional biosynthetic processes.
- Glycine participates in the biosynthesis of heme, purines, and creatine and is conjugated to bile acids and to the urinary metabolites of many drugs.
- In addition to its roles in phospholipid and sphingosine biosynthesis, serine provides carbons 2 and 8 of purines and the methyl group of thymine.
- *S*-Adenosylmethionine, the methyl group donor for many biosynthetic processes, also participates directly in spermine and spermidine biosynthesis.
- Glutamate and ornithine form the neurotransmitter γ-aminobutyrate (GABA).
- The thioethanolamine of coenzyme A and the taurine of taurocholic acid arise from cysteine.
- Decarboxylation of histidine forms histamine, and several dipeptides are derived from histidine and β-alanine.
- Arginine serves as the formamidine donor for creatine biosynthesis, participates in polyamine biosynthesis, and provides the nitrogen of nitric oxide (NO).
- Important tryptophan metabolites include serotonin and melatonin.
- Tyrosine forms both epinephrine and norepinephrine, and its iodination forms thyroid hormone.

mediate in the formation of melanin, different enzymes hydroxylate tyrosine in melanocytes. Dopa decarboxylase, a pyridoxal phosphate-dependent enzyme, forms dopamine. Subsequent hydroxylation by dopamine β-oxidase then forms norepinephrine. In the adrenal medulla, phenylethanolamine-*N*-methyltransferase utilizes *S*-adenosylmethionine to methylate the primary amine of norepinephrine, forming epinephrine (Figure 30–7). Tyrosine is also a precursor of triiodothyronine and thyroxine (Chapter 41).

Creatinine

Creatinine is formed in muscle from creatine phosphate by irreversible, nonenzymatic dehydration and loss of phosphate (Figure 30–8). The 24-hour urinary excre-

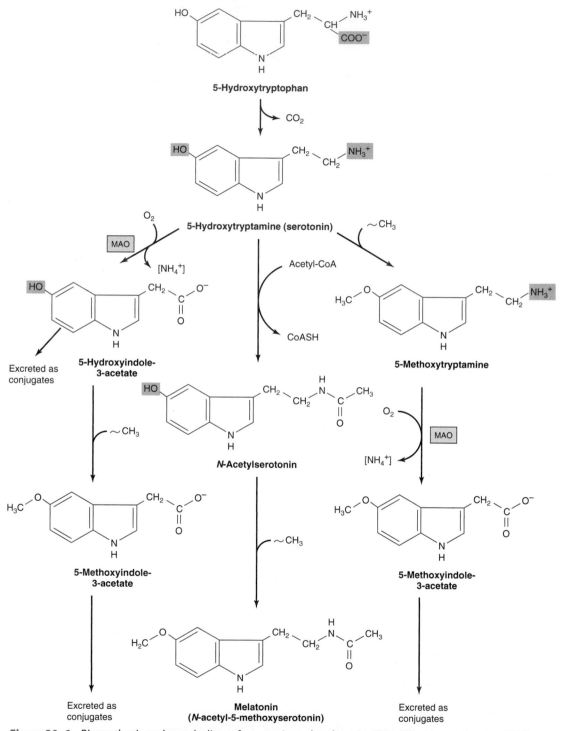

Figure 30–6. Biosynthesis and metabolism of serotonin and melatonin. ($[NH_4^+]$ by transamination; MAO, monoamine oxidase; ~CH_3, from S-adenosylmethionine.)

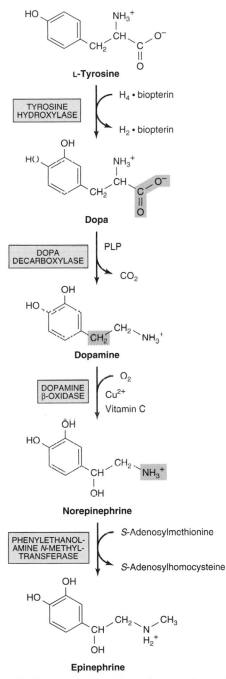

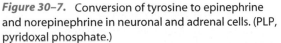

Figure 30–7. Conversion of tyrosine to epinephrine and norepinephrine in neuronal and adrenal cells. (PLP, pyridoxal phosphate.)

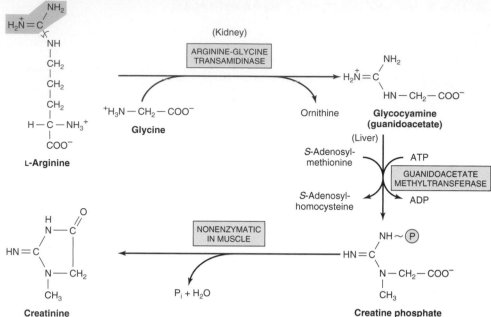

Figure 30–8. Biosynthesis and metabolism of creatine and creatinine.

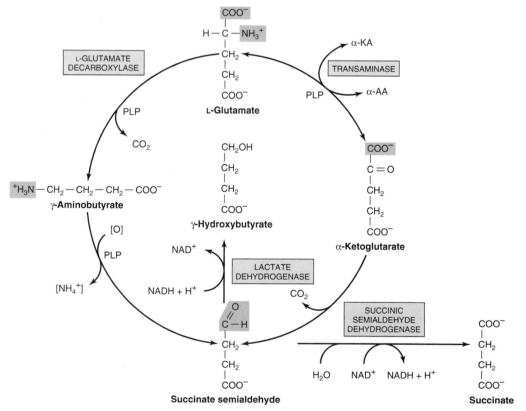

Figure 30–9. Metabolism of γ-aminobutyrate. (α-KA, α-keto acids; α-AA, α-amino acids; PLP, pyridoxal phosphate.)

REFERENCES

Lindemose S, Nielsen PE, Mollegaard NE: Polyamines preferentially interact with bent adenine tracts in double-stranded DNA. Nucleic Acids Res 2005;33:1790.

Moinard C, Cynober L, de Bandt JP: Polyamines: metabolism and implications in human diseases. Clin Nutr 2005;24:184.

Pearl PL, Gibson KM: Clinical aspects of the disorders of GABA metabolism in children. Curr Opin Neurol 2004;17:107.

Pearl PL et al: Succinic semialdehyde dehydrogenase deficiency in children and adults. Ann Neurol 2003;54 Suppl 6:S73.

Scriver CR et al (editors): *The Metabolic and Molecular Bases of Inherited Disease,* 8th ed. McGraw-Hill, 2001.

Porphyrins & Bile Pigments

Robert K. Murray, MD, PhD

BIOMEDICAL IMPORTANCE

The biochemistry of the porphyrins and of the bile pigments is presented in this chapter. These topics are closely related, because heme is synthesized from porphyrins and iron, and the products of degradation of heme are the bile pigments and iron.

Knowledge of the biochemistry of the porphyrins and of heme is basic to understanding the varied functions of **hemoproteins** (see below) in the body. The **porphyrias** are a group of diseases caused by abnormalities in the pathway of biosynthesis of the various porphyrins. Although porphyrias are not very prevalent, physicians must be aware of them. A much more prevalent clinical condition is **jaundice,** due to elevation of bilirubin in the plasma. This elevation is due to overproduction of bilirubin or to failure of its excretion and is seen in numerous diseases ranging from hemolytic anemias to viral hepatitis and to cancer of the pancreas.

METALLOPORPHYRINS & HEMOPROTEINS ARE IMPORTANT IN NATURE

Porphyrins are cyclic compounds formed by the linkage of four pyrrole rings through methyne (—HC=) bridges (Figure 31–1). A characteristic property of the porphyrins is the formation of complexes with metal ions bound to the nitrogen atom of the pyrrole rings. Examples are the **iron porphyrins** such as **heme** of hemoglobin and the **magnesium**-containing porphyrin **chlorophyll,** the photosynthetic pigment of plants.

Proteins that contain heme (hemoproteins) are widely distributed in nature. Examples of their importance in humans and animals are listed in Table 31–1.

Natural Porphyrins Have Substituent Side Chains on the Porphin Nucleus

The porphyrins found in nature are compounds in which various **side chains** are substituted for the eight hydrogen atoms numbered in the porphyrin nucleus shown in Figure 31–1. As a simple means of showing these substitutions, Fischer proposed a shorthand formula in which the methine bridges are omitted and each pyrrole ring is

shown as indicated with the eight substituent positions numbered as shown in Figure 31–2. Various porphyrins are represented in Figures 31–2, 31–3, and 31–4.

The arrangement of the acetate (A) and propionate (P) substituents in the uroporphyrin shown in Figure 31–2 is asymmetric (in ring IV, the expected order of the A and P substituents is reversed). A porphyrin with this type of **asymmetric substitution** is classified as a type III porphyrin. A porphyrin with a completely symmetric arrangement of the substituents is classified as a type I porphyrin. Only types I and III are found in nature, and the type III series is far more abundant (Figure 31–3)—and more important because it includes heme.

Heme and its immediate precursor, protoporphyrin IX (Figure 31–4), are both type III porphyrins (ie, the methyl groups are asymmetrically distributed, as in type III coproporphyrin). However, they are sometimes identified as belonging to series IX, because they were designated ninth in a series of isomers postulated by Hans Fischer, the pioneer worker in the field of porphyrin chemistry.

HEME IS SYNTHESIZED FROM SUCCINYL-CoA & GLYCINE

Heme is synthesized in living cells by a pathway that has been much studied. The two starting materials are **succinyl-CoA,** derived from the citric acid cycle in mitochondria, and the amino acid **glycine.** Pyridoxal phosphate is also necessary in this reaction to "activate" glycine. The product of the condensation reaction between succinyl-CoA and glycine is α-amino-β-ketoadipic acid, which is rapidly decarboxylated to form α-aminolevulinate (ALA) (Figure 31–5). This reaction sequence is catalyzed by ALA synthase, the rate-controlling enzyme in porphyrin biosynthesis in mammalian liver. Synthesis of ALA occurs in **mitochondria.** In the cytosol, two molecules of ALA are condensed by the enzyme **ALA dehydratase** to form two molecules of water and one of **porphobilinogen** (PBG) (Figure 31–5). ALA dehydratase is a zinc-containing enzyme and is sensitive to inhibition by **lead,** as can occur in lead poisoning.

The formation of a cyclic tetrapyrrole—ie, a porphyrin—occurs by condensation of four molecules of PBG

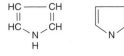

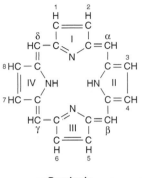

Porphyrin
$(C_{20}H_{14}N_4)$

Figure 31–1. The porphyrin molecule. Rings are labeled I, II, III, and IV. Substituent positions on the rings are labeled 1, 2, 3, 4, 5, 6, 7, and 8. The methyne bridges (—HC—) are labeled α, β, γ, and δ. The numbering system used is that of Hans Fischer.

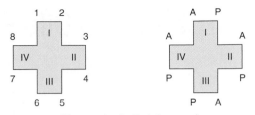

Figure 31–2. Uroporphyrin III. A (acetate) = —CH₂COOH; P (propionate) = —CH₂CH₂COOH. Note the asymmetry of substituents in ring IV (see text).

(Figure 31–6). These four molecules condense in a head-to-tail manner to form a linear tetrapyrrole, hydroxymethylbilane (HMB). The reaction is catalyzed by uroporphyrinogen I synthase, also named PBG deaminase or HMB synthase. HMB cyclizes spontaneously to form **uroporphyrinogen I** (left-hand side of Figure 31–6) or is converted to **uroporphyrinogen III** by the action of uroporphyrinogen III synthase (right-hand side of Figure 31–6). Under normal conditions, the uroporphyrinogen formed is almost exclusively the III isomer, but

Table 31–1. Examples of some important human and animal hemoproteins.[1]

Protein	Function
Hemoglobin	Transport of oxygen in blood
Myoglobin	Storage of oxygen in muscle
Cytochrome *c*	Involvement in electron transport chain
Cytochrome P450	Hydroxylation of xenobiotics
Catalase	Degradation of hydrogen peroxide
Tryptophan pyrrolase	Oxidation of tryptophan

[1]The functions of the above proteins are described in various chapters of this text.

in certain of the porphyrias (discussed below), the type I isomers of porphyrinogens are formed in excess.

Note that both of these uroporphyrinogens have the pyrrole rings connected by methylene bridges (—CH₂—), which do not form a conjugated ring system. Thus, these compounds are colorless (as are all porphyrinogens). However, the porphyrinogens are readily auto-oxidized to their respective colored porphyrins. These oxidations are catalyzed by light and by the porphyrins that are formed.

Uroporphyrinogen III is converted to coproporphyrinogen III by decarboxylation of all of the acetate (A) groups, which changes them to methyl (M) substituents. The reaction is catalyzed by **uroporphyrinogen decarboxylase,** which is also capable of converting uroporphyrinogen I to coproporphyrinogen I (Figure 31–7). Coproporphyrinogen III then enters the mitochondria, where it is converted to **protoporphyrinogen III** and then to **protoporphyrin III.** Several steps are involved in this conversion. The mitochondrial enzyme **coproporphyrinogen oxidase** catalyzes the decarboxylation and oxidation of two propionic side chains to form protoporphyrinogen. This enzyme is able to act only on type III coproporphyrinogen, which would explain why type I protoporphyrins do not generally occur in nature. The oxidation of protoporphyrinogen to protoporphyrin is catalyzed by another mitochondrial enzyme, **protoporphyrinogen oxidase.** In mammalian liver, the conversion of coproporphyrinogen to protoporphyrin requires molecular oxygen.

Formation of Heme Involves Incorporation of Iron into Protoporphyrin

The final step in heme synthesis involves the incorporation of ferrous iron into protoporphyrin in a reaction catalyzed by **ferrochelatase (heme synthase),** another mitochondrial enzyme (Figure 31–4).

A summary of the steps in the biosynthesis of the porphyrin derivatives from PBG is given in Figure 31–8. The last three enzymes in the pathway and ALA synthase are located in the mitochondrion, whereas the other enzymes are cytosolic. Both erythroid and non-

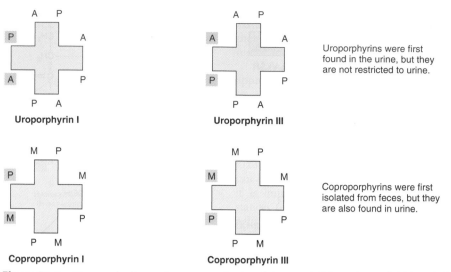

Figure 31–3. Uroporphyrins and coproporphyrins. A (acetate); P (propionate); M (methyl).

erythroid ("housekeeping") forms of the first four enzymes are found. Heme biosynthesis occurs in most mammalian cells with the exception of mature erythrocytes, which do not contain mitochondria. However, approximately 85% of heme synthesis occurs in erythroid precursor cells in the **bone marrow** and the majority of the remainder in **hepatocytes.**

The porphyrinogens described above are colorless, containing six extra hydrogen atoms as compared with the corresponding colored porphyrins. These **reduced porphyrins** (the porphyrinogens) and not the corresponding porphyrins are the actual intermediates in the biosynthesis of protoporphyrin and of heme.

ALA Synthase Is the Key Regulatory Enzyme in Hepatic Biosynthesis of Heme

ALA synthase occurs in both hepatic (ALAS1) and erythroid (ALAS2) forms. The rate-limiting reaction in the synthesis of heme in liver is that catalyzed by ALAS1

(Figure 31–5), a regulatory enzyme. It appears that heme, probably acting through an aporepressor molecule, acts as a negative regulator of the synthesis of ALAS1. This repression-derepression mechanism is depicted diagrammatically in Figure 31–9. Thus, the rate of synthesis of ALAS1 increases greatly in the absence of heme and is diminished in its presence. The turnover rate of ALAS1 in rat liver is normally rapid (half-life about 1 hour), a common feature of an enzyme catalyzing a rate-limiting reaction. Heme also affects translation of the enzyme and its transfer from the cytosol to the mitochondrion.

Many **drugs** when administered to humans can result in a marked increase in ALAS1. Most of these drugs are metabolized by a system in the liver that utilizes a specific hemoprotein, **cytochrome P450** (see Chapter 52). During their metabolism, the utilization of heme by cytochrome P450 is greatly increased, which in turn diminishes the intracellular heme concentration. This latter event effects a derepression of

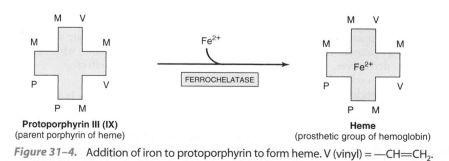

Protoporphyrin III (IX)
(parent porphyrin of heme)

Heme
(prosthetic group of hemoglobin)

Figure 31–4. Addition of iron to protoporphyrin to form heme. V (vinyl) = —CH=CH₂.

(left margin column:)

8. FERRO

7. PROTOPORP
   OXI

6. COPROPOR
   OXI

5. UROPORP
   DECARB

4. UROPORPH
   SYN

3. UROPORPI
   SYN

DE

Figure 31–9
The enzyme
zymes 1, 6, 7
Mutations ir
anemia. Mu
rias, though
ported. Reg
(ALAS1) by
its hypothe
regulation b
nase or hyd

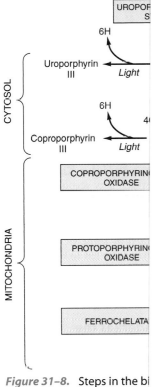

UROPOR
S

6H

Uroporphyrin III ← *Light*

CYTOSOL

6H

Coproporphyrin III ← *Light*

COPROPORPHYRIN OXIDASE

MITOCHONDRIA

PROTOPORPHYRIN OXIDASE

FERROCHELATA

Figure 31–8. Steps in the bi
rinogen I synthase is also call

Assay of the activity of one or m
using an appropriate source (eg, r
important in making a definitive
pected case of porphyria. Individu
of enzyme 1 (ALAS2) develop an
(see Table 31–2). Patients with lov
2 (ALA dehydratase) have been
rarely; the resulting condition i
dratase-deficient porphyria.

In general, the porphyrias desc
an autosomal dominant manner,
congenital erythropoietic porphyria
a recessive mode. The precise abno
directing synthesis of the enzymes
synthesis have been determined in
the use of appropriate gene probes
prenatal diagnosis of some of the p

As is true of most **inborn e**
symptoms of porphyria result fro

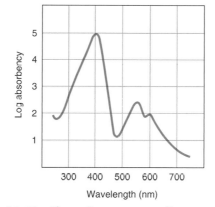

Figure 31–10. Absorption spectrum of hematopor-
phyrin (0.01% solution in 5% HCl).

radicals. These latter species injure lysosomes and other
organelles. Damaged lysosomes release their degradative
enzymes, causing variable degrees of skin damage,
including scarring.

The porphyrias can be **classified** on the basis of the
organs or cells that are most affected. These are generally organs or cells in which synthesis of heme is particularly active. The bone marrow synthesizes considerable

Mutations in DNA
↓
Abnormalities of the enzymes of heme synthesis
↓
Accumulation of ALA and PBG and/or decrease in heme in cells and body fluids → Neuropsychiatric signs and symptoms

Accumulation of porphyrinogens in skin and tissues → Spontaneous oxidation of porphyrinogens to porphyrins → Photosensitivity

Figure 31–11. Biochemical causes of the major signs
and symptoms of the porphyrias.

hemoglobin, and the liver is active in the synthesis of
another hemoprotein, cytochrome P450. Thus, one
classification of the porphyrias is to designate them as
predominantly either **erythropoietic** or **hepatic;** the

Table 31–2. Summary of major findings in the porphyrias.[1]

Enzyme Involved[2]	Type, Class, and MIM Number	Major Signs and Symptoms	Results of Laboratory Tests
1. ALA synthase (erythroid form)	X-linked sideroblastic anemia[3] (erythropoietic) (MIM 301300)	Anemia	Red cell counts and hemoglobin decreased
2. ALA dehydratase	ALA dehydratase deficiency (hepatic) (MIM 125270)	Abdominal pain, neuropsychiatric symptoms	Urinary ALA and coproporphyrin III increased
3. Uroporphyrinogen I synthase[4]	Acute intermittent porphyria (hepatic) (MIM 176000)	Abdominal pain, neuropsychiatric symptoms	Urinary ALA and PBG increased
4. Uroporphyrinogen III synthase	Congenital erythropoietic (erythropoietic) (MIM 263700)	No photosensitivity	Urinary, fecal, and red cell uroporphyrin I increased
5. Uroporphyrinogen decarboxylase	Porphyria cutanea tarda (hepatic) (MIM 176100)	Photosensitivity	Urinary uroporphyrin I increased
6. Coproporphyrinogen oxidase	Hereditary coproporphyria (hepatic) (MIM 121300)	Photosensitivity, abdominal pain, neuropsychiatric symptoms	Urinary ALA, PBG, and coproporphyrin III and fecal coproporphyrin III increased
7. Protoporphyrinogen oxidase	Variegate porphyria (hepatic) (MIM 176200)	Photosensitivity, abdominal pain, neuropsychiatric symptoms	Urinary ALA, PBG, and coproporphyrin III and fecal protoporphyrin IX increased
8. Ferrochelatase	Protoporphyria (erythropoietic) (MIM 177000)	Photosensitivity	Fecal and red cell protoporphyrin IX increased

ALA, δ-aminolevulinic acid; PBG, porphobilinogen.
[1]Only the biochemical findings in the active stages of these diseases are listed. Certain biochemical abnormalities are detectable in the latent stages of some of the above conditions. Conditions 3, 5, and 8 are generally the most prevalent porphyrias. Condition 2 is rare.
[2]The numbering of the enzymes in this table corresponds to that used in Figure 31–9.
[3]X-linked sideroblastic anemia is not a porphyria but is included here because ALA synthase is involved.
[4]This enzyme is also called PBG deaminase or hydroxymethylbilane synthase.

types of porphyrias that fall into these two classes are so characterized in Table 31–2. Porphyrias can also be classified as acute or cutaneous on the basis of their clinical features. Why do specific types of porphyria affect certain organs more markedly than others? A partial answer is that the levels of metabolites that cause damage (eg, ALA, PBG, specific porphyrins, or lack of heme) can vary markedly in different organs or cells depending upon the differing activities of their heme-forming enzymes.

As described above, **ALAS1** is the key regulatory enzyme of the heme biosynthetic pathway in liver. A large number of **drugs** (eg, barbiturates, griseofulvin) induce the enzyme. Most of these drugs do so by inducing cytochrome P450 (see Chapter 52), which uses up heme and thus derepresses (induces) ALAS1. In patients with porphyria, increased activities of ALAS1 result in increased levels of potentially harmful heme precursors prior to the metabolic block. Thus, taking drugs that cause induction of cytochrome P450 (so-called microsomal inducers) can precipitate attacks of porphyria.

The **diagnosis** of a specific type of porphyria can generally be established by consideration of the clinical and family history, the physical examination, and appropriate laboratory tests. The major findings in the six principal types of porphyria are listed in Table 31–2.

High levels of **lead** can affect heme metabolism by combining with SH groups in enzymes such as ferrochelatase and ALA dehydratase. This affects porphyrin metabolism. Elevated levels of protoporphyrin are found in red blood cells, and elevated levels of ALA and of coproporphyrin are found in urine.

It is hoped that **treatment** of the porphyrias at the gene level will become possible. In the meantime, treatment is essentially symptomatic. It is important for patients to avoid drugs that cause induction of cytochrome P450. Ingestion of large amounts of carbohydrates (glucose loading) or administration of hematin (a hydroxide of heme) may repress ALAS1, resulting in diminished production of harmful heme precursors. Patients exhibiting photosensitivity may benefit from administration of β-carotene; this compound appears to lessen production of free radicals, thus diminishing photosensitivity. Sunscreens that filter out visible light can also be helpful to such patients.

CATABOLISM OF HEME PRODUCES BILIRUBIN

Under physiologic conditions in the human adult, $1–2 \times 10^8$ erythrocytes are destroyed per hour. Thus, in 1 day, a 70-kg human turns over approximately 6 g of hemoglobin. When hemoglobin is destroyed in the body, **globin** is degraded to its constituent amino acids, which are reused, and the **iron** of heme enters the iron pool, also for reuse. The iron-free **porphyrin** portion of heme is also degraded, mainly in the reticuloendothelial cells of the liver, spleen, and bone marrow.

The catabolism of heme from all of the heme proteins appears to be carried out in the microsomal fractions of cells by a complex enzyme system called **heme oxygenase.** By the time the heme derived from heme proteins reaches the oxygenase system, the iron has usually been oxidized to the ferric form, constituting **hemin.** The heme oxygenase system is substrate-inducible. As depicted in Figure 31–12, the hemin is reduced to heme with NADPH, and, with the aid of more NADPH, oxygen is added to the α-methyne bridge between pyrroles I and II of the porphyrin. The ferrous iron is again oxidized to the ferric form. With the further addition of oxygen, **ferric ion** is released, **carbon monoxide** is produced, and an equimolar quantity of **biliverdin** results from the splitting of the tetrapyrrole ring.

In birds and amphibia, the green biliverdin IX is excreted; in mammals, a soluble enzyme called **biliverdin reductase** reduces the methyne bridge between pyrrole III and pyrrole IV to a methylene group to produce **bilirubin,** a yellow pigment (Figure 31–12).

It is estimated that 1 g of hemoglobin yields 35 mg of bilirubin. The daily bilirubin formation in human adults is approximately 250–350 mg, deriving mainly from hemoglobin but also from ineffective erythropoiesis and from various other heme proteins such as cytochrome P450.

The chemical conversion of heme to bilirubin by reticuloendothelial cells can be observed in vivo as the purple color of the heme in a hematoma is slowly converted to the yellow pigment of bilirubin.

Bilirubin formed in peripheral tissues is **transported to the liver** by plasma albumin. The **further metabolism** of bilirubin occurs primarily in the liver. It can be divided into three processes: (1) uptake of bilirubin by liver parenchymal cells, (2) conjugation of bilirubin with glucuronate in the endoplasmic reticulum, and (3) secretion of conjugated bilirubin into the bile. Each of these processes will be considered separately.

THE LIVER TAKES UP BILIRUBIN

Bilirubin is only **sparingly soluble** in water, but its solubility in plasma is increased by noncovalent binding to albumin. Each molecule of albumin appears to have one high-affinity site and one low-affinity site for bilirubin. In 100 mL of plasma, approximately 25 mg of bilirubin can be tightly bound to albumin at its high-affinity site. Bilirubin in excess of this quantity can be bound only loosely and thus can easily be detached and diffuse into tissues. A number of compounds such as antibiotics and other drugs compete with bilirubin for the high-affinity binding site on albumin. Thus, these compounds can displace bilirubin from albumin and have significant clinical effects.

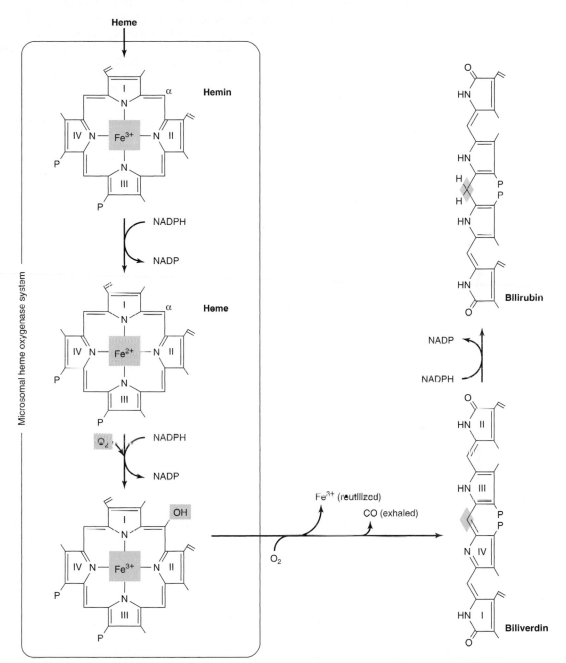

Figure 31–12. Schematic representation of the microsomal heme oxygenase system. (Modified from Schmid R, McDonough AF in: *The Porphyrins*. Dolphin D [editor]. Academic Press, 1978. Copyright © 1978. Reprinted with permission from Elsevier.)

In the liver, the bilirubin is removed from albumin and taken up at the sinusoidal surface of the hepatocytes by a carrier-mediated saturable system. This **facilitated transport system** has a very large capacity, so that even under pathologic conditions the system does not appear to be rate-limiting in the metabolism of bilirubin.

Since this facilitated transport system allows the equilibrium of bilirubin across the sinusoidal membrane of the hepatocyte, the net uptake of bilirubin will

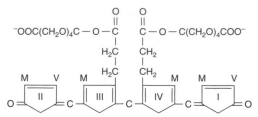

Figure 31–13. Structure of bilirubin diglucuronide (conjugated, "direct-reacting" bilirubin). Glucuronic acid is attached via ester linkage to the two propionic acid groups of bilirubin to form an acylglucuronide.

be dependent upon the removal of bilirubin via subsequent metabolic pathways.

Once bilirubin enters the hepatocytes, it can **bind to certain cytosolic proteins,** which help to keep it solubilized prior to conjugation. Ligandin (a member of the family of glutathione S-transferases) and protein Y are the involved proteins. They may also help to prevent efflux of bilirubin back into the blood stream.

Conjugation of Bilirubin with Glucuronic Acid Occurs in the Liver

Bilirubin is **nonpolar** and would persist in cells (eg, bound to lipids) if not rendered water-soluble. Hepatocytes convert bilirubin to a **polar** form, which is readily excreted in the bile, by adding glucuronic acid molecules to it. This process is called **conjugation** and can employ polar molecules other than glucuronic acid (eg, sulfate). Many steroid hormones and drugs are also converted to water-soluble derivatives by conjugation in preparation for excretion (see Chapter 52).

The conjugation of bilirubin is catalyzed by a specific **glucuronosyltransferase.** The enzyme is mainly located in the endoplasmic reticulum, uses UDP-glucuronic acid

as the glucuronosyl donor, and is referred to as bilirubin-UGT. Bilirubin monoglucuronide is an intermediate and is subsequently converted to the diglucuronide (Figures 31–13 and 31–14). Most of the bilirubin excreted in the bile of mammals is in the form of bilirubin diglucuronide. However, when bilirubin conjugates exist abnormally in human plasma (eg, in obstructive jaundice), they are predominantly monoglucuronides. Bilirubin-UGT activity can be **induced** by a number of clinically useful drugs, including phenobarbital. More information about glucuronosylation is presented below in the discussion of inherited disorders of bilirubin conjugation.

Bilirubin Is Secreted into Bile

Secretion of conjugated bilirubin into the bile occurs by an active transport mechanism, which is probably rate-limiting for the entire process of hepatic bilirubin metabolism. The protein involved is MRP-2 (multidrug resistance-like protein 2), also called multispecific organic anion transporter (MOAT). It is located in the plasma membrane of the bile canalicular membrane and handles a number of organic anions. It is a member of the family of ATP-binding cassette (ABC) transporters. The hepatic transport of conjugated bilirubin into the bile is inducible by those same drugs that are capable of inducing the conjugation of bilirubin. Thus, the conjugation and excretion systems for bilirubin behave as a coordinated functional unit.

Figure 31–15 summarizes the three major processes involved in the *transfer of bilirubin* from blood to bile. Sites that are affected in a number of conditions causing jaundice (see below) are also indicated.

Conjugated Bilirubin Is Reduced to Urobilinogen by Intestinal Bacteria

As the conjugated bilirubin reaches the terminal ileum and the large intestine, the glucuronides are removed by

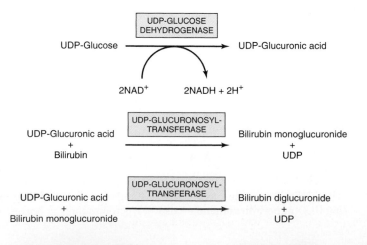

Figure 31–14. Conjugation of bilirubin with glucuronic acid. The glucuronate donor, UDP-glucuronic acid, is formed from UDP-glucose as depicted. The UDP-glucuronosyltransferase is also called bilirubin-UGT.

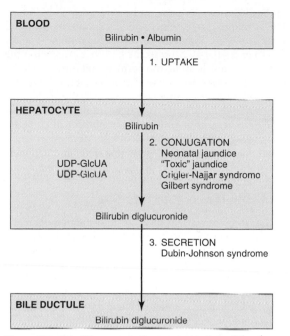

Figure 31–15. Diagrammatic representation of the three major processes (uptake, conjugation, and secretion) involved in the transfer of bilirubin from blood to bile. Certain proteins of hepatocytes, such as ligandin (a member of the glutathione *S*-transferase family of enzymes) and Y protein, bind intracellular bilirubin and may prevent its efflux into the blood stream. The process affected in a number of conditions causing jaundice is also shown.

specific bacterial enzymes (**β-glucuronidases**), and the pigment is subsequently **reduced** by the fecal flora to a group of colorless tetrapyrrolic compounds called **urobilinogens.** In the terminal ileum and large intestine, a small fraction of the urobilinogens is reabsorbed and reexcreted through the liver to constitute the **enterohepatic urobilinogen cycle.** Under abnormal conditions, particularly when excessive bile pigment is formed or liver disease interferes with this intrahepatic cycle, urobilinogen may also be excreted in the urine.

Normally, most of the colorless urobilinogens formed in the colon by the fecal flora are oxidized there to urobilins (colored compounds) and are excreted in the feces. Darkening of feces upon standing in air is due to the oxidation of residual urobilinogens to urobilins.

HYPERBILIRUBINEMIA CAUSES JAUNDICE

When bilirubin in the blood exceeds 1 mg/dL (17.1 μmol/L), **hyperbilirubinemia** exists. Hyperbilirubin-emia may be due to the production of more bilirubin than the normal liver can excrete, or it may result from the failure of a damaged liver to excrete bilirubin produced in normal amounts. In the absence of hepatic damage, obstruction of the excretory ducts of the liver—by preventing the excretion of bilirubin—will also cause hyperbilirubinemia. In all these situations, bilirubin accumulates in the blood, and when it reaches a certain concentration (approximately 2–2.5 mg/dL), it diffuses into the tissues, which then become yellow. That condition is called **jaundice** or **icterus.**

In clinical studies of jaundice, measurement of bilirubin in the serum is of great value. A method for quantitatively assaying the bilirubin content of the serum was first devised by **van den Bergh** by application of **Ehrlich's test** for bilirubin in urine. The Ehrlich reaction is based on the coupling of diazotized sulfanilic acid (Ehrlich's diazo reagent) and bilirubin to produce a reddish-purple azo compound. In the original procedure as described by Ehrlich, methanol was used to provide a solution in which both bilirubin and the diazo regent were soluble. Van den Bergh inadvertently omitted the methanol on an occasion when assay of bile pigment in human bile was being attempted. To his surprise, normal development of the color occurred "directly." This form of bilirubin that would react without the addition of methanol was thus termed **"direct-reacting."** It was then found that this same direct reaction would also occur in serum from cases of jaundice due to biliary obstruction. However, it was still necessary to add methanol to detect bilirubin in normal serum or that which was present in excess in serum from cases of hemolytic jaundice where no evidence of obstruction was to be found. To that form of bilirubin which could be measured only after the addition of methanol, the term **"indirect-reacting"** was applied.

It was subsequently discovered that the **indirect bilirubin is "free"** (unconjugated) bilirubin en route to the liver from the reticuloendothelial tissues, where the bilirubin was originally produced by the breakdown of heme porphyrins. Since this bilirubin is not water-soluble, it requires methanol to initiate coupling with the diazo reagent. In the liver, the free bilirubin becomes conjugated with glucuronic acid, and the conjugate, predominantly bilirubin diglucuronide, can then be excreted into the bile. Furthermore, conjugated bilirubin, being water-soluble, can react directly with the diazo reagent, so that the "direct bilirubin" of van den Bergh is actually a bilirubin conjugate (bilirubin glucuronide).

Depending on the type of bilirubin present in plasma—ie, unconjugated or conjugated—hyperbilirubinemia may be classified as **retention hyperbilirubinemia,** due to overproduction, or **regurgitation hyperbilirubinemia,** due to reflux into the bloodstream because of biliary obstruction.

Separation and quantitation of unconjugated bilirubin and the conjugated species can be performed using high-pressure liquid chromatography.

Because of its hydrophobicity, only unconjugated bilirubin can cross the blood-brain barrier into the central nervous system; thus, encephalopathy due to hyperbilirubinemia (**kernicterus**) can occur only in connection with unconjugated bilirubin, as found in retention hyperbilirubinemia. On the other hand, because of its water-solubility, only conjugated bilirubin can appear in urine. Accordingly, **choluric jaundice** (choluria is the presence of bile pigments in the urine) occurs only in regurgitation hyperbilirubinemia, and **acholuric jaundice** occurs only in the presence of an excess of unconjugated bilirubin.

Elevated Amounts of Unconjugated Bilirubin in Blood Occur in a Number of Conditions

A. HEMOLYTIC ANEMIAS

Hemolytic anemias are important causes of unconjugated hyperbilirubinemia, though unconjugated hyperbilirubinemia is usually only slight (< 4 mg/dL; < 68.4 μmol/L) even in the event of extensive hemolysis because of the healthy liver's large capacity for handling bilirubin.

B. NEONATAL "PHYSIOLOGIC JAUNDICE"

This transient condition is the most common cause of unconjugated hyperbilirubinemia. It results from an accelerated hemolysis around the time of **birth** and an immature hepatic system for the uptake, conjugation, and secretion of bilirubin. Not only is the bilirubin-UGT activity reduced, but there probably is reduced synthesis of the substrate for that enzyme, UDP-glucuronic acid. Since the increased amount of bilirubin is unconjugated, it is capable of penetrating the blood-brain barrier when its concentration in plasma exceeds that which can be tightly bound by albumin (20–25 mg/dL). This can result in a hyperbilirubinemic toxic encephalopathy, or **kernicterus,** which can cause mental retardation. Because of the recognized inducibility of this bilirubin-metabolizing system, phenobarbital has been administered to jaundiced neonates and is effective in this disorder. In addition, exposure to blue light (phototherapy) promotes the hepatic excretion of unconjugated bilirubin by converting some of the bilirubin to other derivatives such as maleimide fragments and geometric isomers that are excreted in the bile.

C. CRIGLER-NAJJAR SYNDROME, TYPE I; CONGENITAL NONHEMOLYTIC JAUNDICE

Type I Crigler-Najjar syndrome is a rare autosomal recessive disorder. It is characterized by severe congenital jaundice (serum bilirubin usually exceeds 20 mg/dL) due to mutations in the gene encoding bilirubin-UGT activity in hepatic tissues. The disease is often fatal within the first 15 months of life. Children with this condition have been treated with phototherapy, resulting in some reduction in plasma bilirubin levels. Phenobarbital has no effect on the formation of bilirubin glucuronides in patients with type I Crigler-Najjar syndrome. A liver transplant may be curative.

It should be noted that the gene encoding human bilirubin-UGT is part of a large UGT gene complex situated on chromosome 2. Many different substrates are subjected to glucuronosylation, so many glucuronosyltransferases are required. The complex contains some 13 substrate-specific first exons, each with its own promoter. Four are pseudogenes, so nine different isoforms with differing glucuronosyltransferase activities are encoded. Exon A1 is that involved with conjugation of bilirubin. In the case of bilirubin, exon A1 is spliced to DNA containing exons 2–5, producing bilirubin-UGT. Other transferases are produced by splicing other first exons (members of A 2–13) to exons 2–5.

D. CRIGLER-NAJJAR SYNDROME, TYPE II

This rare inherited disorder also results from mutations in the gene encoding bilirubin-UGT, but some activity of the enzyme is retained and the condition has a more benign course than type I. Serum bilirubin concentrations usually do not exceed 20 mg/dL. Patients with this condition can respond to treatment with large doses of phenobarbital.

E. GILBERT SYNDROME

Again, this relatively prevalent condition is caused by mutations in the gene encoding bilirubin-UGT. It is more common among males. Approximately 30% of the enzyme's activity is preserved and the condition is entirely harmless.

F. TOXIC HYPERBILIRUBINEMIA

Unconjugated hyperbilirubinemia can result from toxin-induced liver dysfunction such as that caused by chloroform, arsphenamines, carbon tetrachloride, acetaminophen, hepatitis virus, cirrhosis, and *Amanita* mushroom poisoning. These acquired disorders are due to hepatic parenchymal cell damage, which impairs conjugation.

Obstruction in the Biliary Tree Is the Most Common Cause of Conjugated Hyperbilirubinemia

A. OBSTRUCTION OF THE BILIARY TREE

Conjugated hyperbilirubinemia commonly results from blockage of the hepatic or common bile ducts, most often due to a gallstone or to cancer of the head

of the pancreas. Because of the obstruction, bilirubin diglucuronide cannot be excreted. It thus regurgitates into the hepatic veins and lymphatics, and conjugated bilirubin appears in the blood and urine (choluric jaundice).

The term **cholestatic jaundice** is used to include all cases of extrahepatic obstructive jaundice. It also covers those cases of jaundice that exhibit conjugated hyperbilirubinemia due to micro-obstruction of intrahepatic biliary ductules by swollen, damaged hepatocytes (eg, as may occur in infectious hepatitis).

B. DUBIN-JOHNSON SYNDROME

This benign autosomal recessive disorder consists of conjugated hyperbilirubinemia in childhood or during adult life. The hyperbilirubinemia is caused by mutations in the gene encoding **MRP-2** (see above), the protein involved in the secretion of conjugated bilirubin into bile. The centrilobular hepatocytes contain an abnormal black pigment that may be derived from epinephrine.

C. ROTOR SYNDROME

This is a rare benign condition characterized by chronic conjugated hyperbilirubinemia and normal liver histology. Its precise cause has not been identified.

Some Conjugated Bilirubin Can Bind Covalently to Albumin

When levels of conjugated bilirubin remain high in plasma, a fraction can **bind covalently to albumin** (delta bilirubin). Because it is bound covalently to albumin, this fraction has a longer half-life in plasma than does conventional conjugated bilirubin. Thus, it remains elevated during the recovery phase of obstructive jaundice after the remainder of the conju-

gated bilirubin has declined to normal levels; this explains why some patients continue to appear jaundiced after conjugated bilirubin levels have returned to normal.

Urobilinogen & Bilirubin in Urine Are Clinical Indicators

Normally, there are mere traces of urobilinogen in the urine. In **complete obstruction of the bile duct,** no urobilinogen is found in the urine, since bilirubin has no access to the intestine, where it can be converted to urobilinogen. In this case, the presence of bilirubin (conjugated) in the urine without urobilinogen suggests obstructive jaundice, either intrahepatic or posthepatic.

In **jaundice secondary to hemolysis,** the increased production of bilirubin leads to increased production of urobilinogen, which appears in the urine in large amounts. Bilirubin is not usually found in the urine in hemolytic jaundice (because unconjugated bilirubin does not pass into the urine), so that the combination of increased urobilinogen and absence of bilirubin is suggestive of hemolytic jaundice. Increased blood destruction from any cause brings about an increase in urine urobilinogen.

Table 31–3 summarizes **laboratory results** obtained on patients with three different causes of jaundice—hemolytic anemia (a prehepatic cause), hepatitis (a hepatic cause), and obstruction of the common bile duct (a posthepatic cause). Laboratory tests on blood (evaluation of the possibility of a hemolytic anemia and measurement of prothrombin time) and on serum (eg, electrophoresis of proteins; activities of the enzymes ALT, AST, and alkaline phosphatase) are also important in helping to distinguish between prehepatic, hepatic, and posthepatic causes of jaundice.

Table 31–3. Laboratory results in normal patients and patients with three different causes of jaundice.

Condition	Serum Bilirubin	Urine Urobilinogen	Urine Bilirubin	Fecal Urobilinogen
Normal	Direct: 0.1–0.4 mg/dL Indirect: 0.2–0.7 mg/dL	0–4 mg/24 h	Absent	40–280 mg/24 h
Hemolytic anemia	↑Indirect	Increased	Absent	Increased
Hepatitis	↑Direct and indirect	Decreased if micro-obstruction is present	Present if micro-obstruction occurs	Decreased
Obstructive jaundice[1]	↑Direct	Absent	Present	Trace to absent

[1]The most common causes of obstructive (posthepatic) jaundice are cancer of the head of the pancreas and a gallstone lodged in the common bile duct. The presence of bilirubin in the urine is sometimes referred to as choluria—therefore, hepatitis and obstruction of the common bile duct cause choluric jaundice, whereas the jaundice of hemolytic anemia is referred to as acholuric. The laboratory results in patients with hepatitis are variable, depending on the extent of damage to parenchymal cells and the extent of micro obstruction to bile ductules. Serum levels of ALT and AST are usually markedly elevated in hepatitis, whereas serum levels of alkaline phosphatase are elevated in obstructive liver disease.

SUMMARY

- Hemoproteins, such as hemoglobin and the cytochromes, contain heme. Heme is an iron-porphyrin compound (Fe^{2+}-protoporphyrin IX) in which four pyrrole rings are joined by methine bridges. The eight side groups (methyl, vinyl, and propionyl substituents) on the four pyrrole rings of heme are arranged in a specific sequence.

- Biosynthesis of the heme ring occurs in mitochondria and cytosol via eight enzymatic steps. It commences with formation of δ-aminolevulinate (ALA) from succinyl-CoA and glycine in a reaction catalyzed by ALA synthase, the regulatory enzyme of the pathway.

- Genetically determined abnormalities of seven of the eight enzymes involved in heme biosynthesis result in the inherited porphyrias. Red blood cells and liver are the major sites of metabolic expression of the porphyrias. Photosensitivity and neurologic problems are common complaints. Intake of certain compounds (such as lead) can cause acquired porphyrias. Increased amounts of porphyrins or their precursors can be detected in blood and urine, facilitating diagnosis.

- Catabolism of the heme ring is initiated by the enzyme heme oxygenase, producing a linear tetrapyrrole.

- Biliverdin is an early product of catabolism and on reduction yields bilirubin. The latter is transported by albumin from peripheral tissues to the liver, where it is taken up by hepatocytes. The iron of heme and the amino acids of globin are conserved and reutilized.

- In the liver, bilirubin is made water-soluble by conjugation with two molecules of glucuronic acid and is secreted into the bile. The action of bacterial enzymes in the gut produces urobilinogen and urobilin, which are excreted in the feces and urine.

- Jaundice is due to elevation of the level of bilirubin in the blood. The causes of jaundice can be classified as prehepatic (eg, hemolytic anemias), hepatic (eg, hepatitis), and posthepatic (eg, obstruction of the common bile duct). Measurements of plasma total and nonconjugated bilirubin, of urinary urobilinogen and bilirubin, and of certain serum enzymes as well as inspection and analysis of stool samples help distinguish between these causes.

REFERENCES

Anderson KE et al: Disorders of heme biosynthesis: X-linked sideroblastic anemia and the porphyrias. In: *The Metabolic and Molecular Bases of Inherited Disease,* 8th ed. Scriver CR et al (editors). McGraw-Hill, 2001.

Chowdhury JR et al: Hereditary jaundice and disorders of bilirubin metabolism. In: *The Metabolic and Molecular Bases of Inherited Disease,* 8th ed. Scriver CR et al (editors). McGraw-Hill, 2001.

Desnick RJ: The porphyrias. In: *Harrison's Principles of Internal Medicine,* 16th ed. Kaspar DL et al (editors). McGraw-Hill, 2005.

Nuttall KL, Klee GG. Analytes of hemoglobin metabolism—porphyrins, iron and bilirubin. In: *Tietz Fundamentals of Clinical Chemistry,* 5th ed. Burtis, CA, Ashwood ER (editors). Saunders, 2001.

Pratt DS, Kaplan MM: Jaundice. In: *Harrison's Principles of Internal Medicine,* 16th ed. Kasper DL et al (editors). McGraw-Hill, 2005.

Wolkoff AW: The hyperbilirubinemias. In: *Harrison's Principles of Internal Medicine,* 16th ed. Kasper DL et al (editors). McGraw-Hill, 2005.

SECTION IV
Structure, Function, & Replication of Informational Macromolecules

Nucleotides

Victor W. Rodwell, PhD

BIOMEDICAL IMPORTANCE

Nucleotides—the monomer units or building blocks of nucleic acids—serve multiple additional functions. They form a part of many coenzymes and serve as donors of phosphoryl groups (eg, ATP or GTP), of sugars (eg, UDP- or GDP-sugars), or of lipid (eg, CDP-acylglycerol). Regulatory nucleotides include the second messengers cAMP and cGMP, the control by ADP of oxidative phosphorylation, and allosteric regulation of enzyme activity by ATP, AMP, and CTP. Synthetic purine and pyrimidine analogs that contain halogens, thiols, or additional nitrogen are employed for chemotherapy of cancer and AIDS and as suppressors of the immune response during organ transplantation.

PURINES, PYRIMIDINES, NUCLEOSIDES, & NUCLEOTIDES

Purines and pyrimidines are nitrogen-containing heterocycles, cyclic compounds whose rings contain both carbon and other elements (hetero atoms). Note that the smaller pyrimidine has the *longer* name and the larger purine the *shorter* name and that their six-atom rings are numbered in opposite directions (Figure 32–1). The planar character of purines and pyrimidines facilitates their close association, or "stacking," which stabilizes double-stranded DNA (Chapter 34). The oxo and amino groups of purines and pyrimidines exhibit keto-enol and amine-imine tautomerism (Figure 32–2), but physiologic conditions strongly favor the amino and oxo forms.

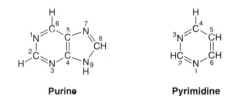

Figure 32–1. Purine and pyrimidine. The atoms are numbered according to the international system.

Nucleosides & Nucleotides

Nucleo**sides** are derivatives of purines and pyrimidines that have a sugar linked to a ring nitrogen of a heterocycle called heterocyclic "base," even though many lack significant basic character. Numerals with a prime (eg, 2′ or 3′) distinguish atoms of the sugar from those of the heterocyclic base. The sugar in **ribonucleosides** is D-ribose, and in **deoxyribonucleosides** it is 2-deoxy-D-ribose. The sugar is linked to the heterocyclic base via a **β-N-glycosidic bond,** almost always to N-1 of a pyrimidine or to N-9 of a purine (Figure 32–3).

Figure 32–2. Tautomerism of the oxo and amino functional groups of purines and pyrimidines.

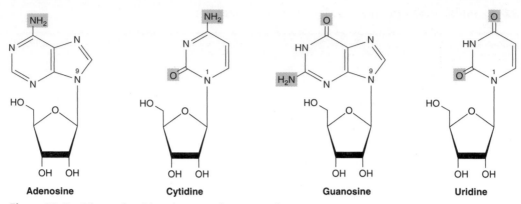

Figure 32–3. Ribonucleosides, drawn as the syn conformers.

Mononucleo**tides** are nucleo**sides** with a phosphoryl group esterified to a hydroxyl group of the sugar. The 3′- and 5′-nucleo**tides** are nucleo**sides** with a phosphoryl group on the 3′- or 5′-hydroxyl group of the sugar, respectively. Since most nucleotides are 5′-, the prefix "5′-" is usually omitted when naming them. UMP and dAMP thus represent nucleotides with a phosphoryl group on C-5 of the pentose. Additional phosphoryl groups linked by **acid anhydride bonds** to the phosphoryl group of a mononucleotide form nucleoside **diphosphates** and **triphosphates** (Figure 32–4).

Steric hindrance by the heterocyclic base restricts rotation about the β-N-glycosidic bond of nucleosides

and nucleotides. Both therefore exist as *syn* or *anti* conformers (Figure 32–5). While both conformers occur in nature, *anti* conformers predominate. Table 32–1 lists the major purines and pyrimidines and their nucleoside and nucleotide derivatives. Single-letter abbreviations are used to identify adenine (A), guanine (G), cytosine (C), thymine (T), and uracil (U), whether free or present in nucleosides or nucleotides. The prefix "d" (deoxy) indicates that the sugar is 2′-deoxy-D-ribose (eg, dGTP) (Figure 32–6).

Nucleic Acids Also Contain Additional Heterocyclic Bases

Small quantities of additional purines and pyrimidines occur in DNA and RNAs. Examples include 5-methylcytosine of bacterial and human DNA, 5-hydroxymethylcytosine of bacterial and viral nucleic acids, and mono- and di-N-methylated adenine and guanine of mammalian messenger RNAs (Figure 32–7), bases that

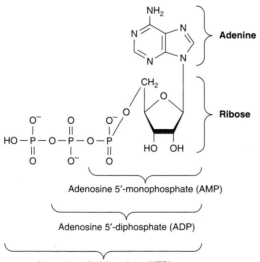

Figure 32–4. ATP, its diphosphate, and its monophosphate.

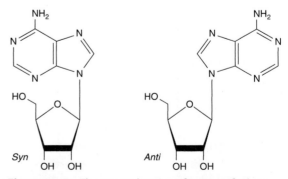

Figure 32–5. The syn and anti conformers of adenosine differ with respect to orientation about the N-glycosidic bond.

Table 32–1. Purine bases, ribonucleosides, and ribonucleotides.

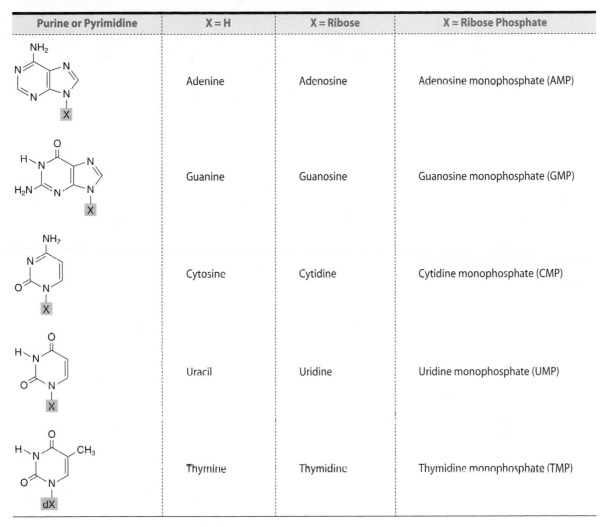

Purine or Pyrimidine	X = H	X = Ribose	X = Ribose Phosphate
	Adenine	Adenosine	Adenosine monophosphate (AMP)
	Guanine	Guanosine	Guanosine monophosphate (GMP)
	Cytosine	Cytidine	Cytidine monophosphate (CMP)
	Uracil	Uridine	Uridine monophosphate (UMP)
	Thymine	Thymidine	Thymidine monophosphate (TMP)

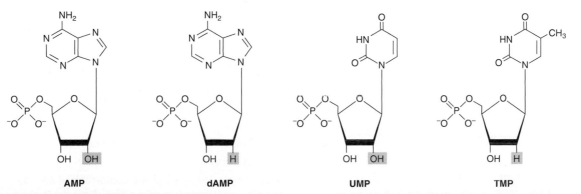

AMP   dAMP   UMP   TMP

Figure 32–6. AMP, dAMP, UMP, and TMP.

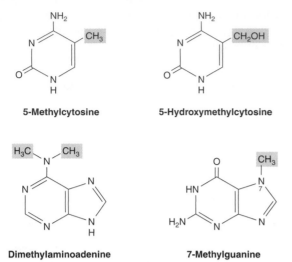

5-Methylcytosine · 5-Hydroxymethylcytosine

Dimethylaminoadenine · 7-Methylguanine

Figure 32–7. Four uncommon but naturally occurring pyrimidines and purines.

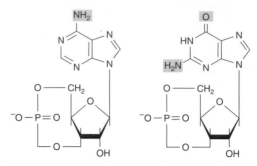

Figure 32–9. cAMP, 3′,5′-cyclic AMP, and cGMP.

Nucleotides Serve Diverse Physiologic Functions

Nucleotides participate in reactions that fulfill physiologic functions as diverse as protein synthesis, nucleic acid synthesis, regulatory cascades, and signal transduction pathways.

Nucleoside Triphosphates Have High Group Transfer Potential

Acid anhydrides, unlike phosphate esters, have high group transfer potential. $\Delta G^{0\prime}$ for the hydrolysis of each of the two terminal (β and γ) phosphoryl groups of nucleoside triphosphates is about −7 kcal/mol (−30 kJ/mol). The high group transfer potential of purine and pyrimidine nucleoside triphosphates permits them to function as group transfer reagents, most frequently of the γ-phosphoryl group. Cleavage of an acid anhydride bond typically is coupled with a highly endergonic process such as covalent bond synthesis—eg, polymerization of nucleoside triphosphates to form a nucleic acid.

In addition to their roles as precursors of nucleic acids, ATP, GTP, UTP, CTP, and their derivatives each serve unique physiologic functions discussed in other chapters. Selected examples include the role of ATP as the principal biologic transducer of free energy; the second messenger cAMP (Figure 32–9); adenosine 3′-phosphate-5′-phosphosulfate (Figure 32–10), the sulfate donor for sulfated proteoglycans (Chapter 47) and for sulfate conjugates of drugs; and the methyl group donor S-adenosylmethionine (Figure 32–11). GTP serves as an allosteric regulator and as

function in oligonucleotide recognition and in regulating the half-lives of RNAs. Free nucleotides include hypoxanthine, xanthine, and uric acid (see Figure 33–8), intermediates in the catabolism of adenine and guanine (Chapter 33). Methylated heterocyclic bases of plants include the xanthine derivatives caffeine of coffee, theophylline of tea, and theobromine of cocoa (Figure 32–8).

Posttranslational modification of preformed polynucleotides can generate additional bases such as pseudouridine, in which D-ribose is linked to C-5 of uracil by a carbon-to-carbon bond rather than by a β-N-glycosidic bond. The nucleotide pseudouridylic acid (ψ) arises by rearrangement of a UMP of a preformed tRNA. Similarly, methylation by S-adenosylmethionine of a UMP of preformed tRNA forms TMP (thymidine monophosphate), which contains ribose rather than deoxyribose.

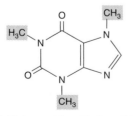

Figure 32–8. Caffeine, a trimethylxanthine. The dimethylxanthines theobromine and theophylline are similar but lack the methyl group at N-1 and at N-7, respectively.

Figure 32–10. Adenosine 3′-phosphate-5′-phosphosulfate.

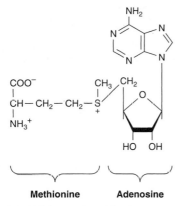

Figure 32–11. S-Adenosylmethionine.

Table 32–2. Many coenzymes and related compounds are derivatives of adenosine monophosphate.

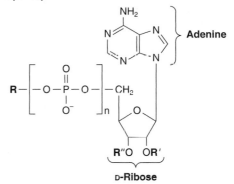

Coenzyme	R	R'	R"	n
Active methionine	Methionine[a]	H	H	0
Amino acid adenylates	Amino acid	H	H	1
Active sulfate	SO_3^{2-}	H	PO_3^{2-}	1
3',5'-Cyclic AMP		H	PO_3^{2-}	1
NAD[a]	[b]	H	H	2
NADP[a]	[b]	PO_3^{2-}	H	2
FAD	[b]	H	H	2
CoASH	[b]	H	PO_3^{2-}	2

[a]Replaces phosphoryl group.
[b]R is a B vitamin derivative.

an energy source for protein synthesis, and cGMP (Figure 32–9) serves as a second messenger in response to nitric oxide (NO) during relaxation of smooth muscle (Chapter 48). UDP-sugar derivatives participate in sugar epimerizations and in biosynthesis of glycogen, glucosyl disaccharides, and the oligosaccharides of glycoproteins and proteoglycans (Chapters 46 and 47). UDP-glucuronic acid forms the urinary glucuronide conjugates of bilirubin (Chapter 31) and of many drugs such as aspirin. CTP participates in biosynthesis of phosphoglycerides, sphingomyelin, and other substituted sphingosines (Chapter 24). Finally, many coenzymes incorporate nucleotides as well as structures similar to purine and pyrimidine nucleotides (see Table 32–2).

Nucleotides Are Polyfunctional Acids

Nucleosides or free purine or pyrimidine bases are uncharged at physiologic pH. By contrast, the pK_a values of the primary and secondary phosphoryl groups of nucleotides are about 1.0 and 6.2, respectively. Nucleotides therefore bear a negative charge at physiologic pH. Nucleotides can, however, act as proton donors or acceptors at pH values two or more units above or below neutrality.

Nucleotides Absorb Ultraviolet Light

The conjugated double bonds of purine and pyrimidine derivatives absorb ultraviolet light. The mutagenic effect of ultraviolet light results from its absorption by nucleotides in DNA with accompanying chemical changes. While spectra are pH-dependent, at pH 7.0 all the common nucleotides absorb light at a wavelength close to 260 nm. The concentration of nucleotides and nucleic acids thus often is expressed in terms of "absorbance at 260 nm."

SYNTHETIC NUCLEOTIDE ANALOGS ARE USED IN CHEMOTHERAPY

Synthetic analogs of purines, pyrimidines, nucleosides, and nucleotides altered in either the heterocyclic ring or the sugar moiety have numerous applications in clinical medicine. Their toxic effects reflect either inhibition of enzymes essential for nucleic acid synthesis or their incorporation into nucleic acids with resulting disruption of base-pairing. Oncologists employ 5-fluoro- or 5-iodouracil, 3-deoxyuridine, 6-thioguanine and 6-mercaptopurine, 5- or 6-azauridine, 5- or 6-azacytidine, and 8-azaguanine (Figure 32–12), which are incorporated into DNA prior to cell division. The purine analog allopurinol, used in treatment of hyperuricemia and gout, inhibits purine biosynthesis and xanthine oxidase activity. Cytarabine is used in chemotherapy of cancer. Finally, azathioprine, which is catabolized to 6-mercaptopurine, is employed during organ transplantation to suppress immunologic rejection.

Nonhydrolyzable Nucleoside Triphosphate Analogs Serve As Research Tools

Synthetic nonhydrolyzable analogs of nucleoside triphosphates (Figure 32–13) allow investigators to distin-

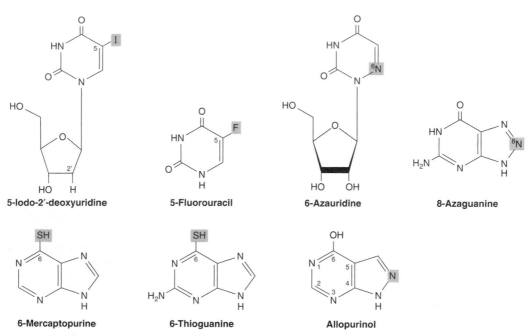

Figure 32–12. Selected synthetic pyrimidine and purine analogs.

guish the effects of nucleotides due to phosphoryl transfer from effects mediated by occupancy of allosteric nucleotide-binding sites on regulated enzymes.

POLYNUCLEOTIDES

The 5′-phosphoryl group of a mononucleotide can esterify a second —OH group, forming a **phosphodiester.** Most commonly, this second —OH group is the 3′-OH of the pentose of a second nucleotide. This forms a **dinucleotide** in which the pentose moieties are linked by a 3′ → 5′ phosphodiester bond to form the "backbone" of RNA and DNA.

The formation of a dinucleotide may be represented as the elimination of water between two mononucleotides. Biologic formation of dinucleotides does not, however, occur in this way because the reverse reaction, hydrolysis of the phosphodiester bond, is strongly favored on thermodynamic grounds. However, despite an extremely favorable ΔG, in the absence of catalysis by **phosphodiesterases,** hydrolysis of the phosphodiester bonds of DNA occurs only over long periods of time. Consequently, DNA persists for considerable periods and has been detected even in fossils. RNAs are far less stable than DNA since the 2′-hydroxyl group of RNA (absent from DNA) functions as a nucleophile during hydrolysis of the 3′,5′-phosphodiester bond.

Polynucleotides Are Directional Macromolecules

Phosphodiester bonds link the 3′- and 5′-carbons of adjacent monomers. Each end of a nucleotide polymer thus is distinct. We therefore refer to the "5′-end" or the "3′- end" of polynucleotides, the 5′- end being the one with a free or phosphorylated 5′-hydroxyl.

Polynucleotides Have Primary Structure

The base sequence or **primary structure** of a polynucleotide can be represented as shown below. The phosphodiester bond is represented by P or p, bases by a single letter, and pentoses by a vertical line.

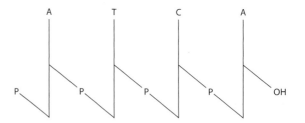

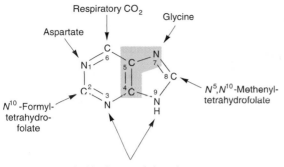

Figure 33–1. Sources of the nitrogen and carbon atoms of the purine ring. Atoms 4, 5, and 7 (shaded) derive from glycine.

"SALVAGE REACTIONS" CONVERT PURINES & THEIR NUCLEOSIDES TO MONONUCLEOTIDES

Conversion of purines, their ribonucleo**sides,** and their deoxyribonucleo**sides** to mononucleo**tides** involves so-called "salvage reactions" that require far less energy than de novo synthesis. The more important mechanism involves phosphoribosylation by PRPP (structure II, Figure 33–2) of a free purine (Pu) to form a purine 5'-mononucleotide (Pu-RP).

$$Pu + PR - PP \rightarrow PRP + PP_i$$

Two phosphoribosyl transferases then convert adenine to AMP and hypoxanthine and guanine to IMP or GMP (Figure 33–4). A second salvage mechanism involves phosphoryl transfer from ATP to a purine ribonucleo**side** (PuR):

$$PuR + ATP \rightarrow PuR - P + ADP$$

Adenosine kinase catalyzes phosphorylation of adenosine and deoxyadenosine to AMP and dAMP, and deoxycytidine kinase phosphorylates deoxycytidine and 2'-deoxyguanosine to dCMP and dGMP.

Liver, the major site of purine nucleotide biosynthesis, provides purines and purine nucleosides for salvage and for utilization by tissues incapable of their biosynthesis. For example, human brain has a low level of PRPP glutamyl amidotransferase (reaction ②, Figure 33–2) and hence depends in part on exogenous purines. Erythrocytes and polymorphonuclear leukocytes cannot synthesize 5-phosphoribosylamine (structure III, Figure 33–2) and therefore utilize exogenous purines to form nucleotides.

AMP & GMP Feedback-Regulate PRPP Glutamyl Amidotransferase

Since biosynthesis of IMP consumes glycine, glutamine, tetrahydrofolate derivatives, aspartate, and ATP, it is advantageous to regulate purine biosynthesis. The major determinant of the rate of de novo purine nucleotide biosynthesis is the concentration of PRPP, a function of its rates of synthesis, utilization, and degradation. The rate of PRPP synthesis depends on the availability of ribose 5-phosphate and on the activity of PRPP synthase, an enzyme sensitive to feedback inhibition by AMP, ADP, GMP, and GDP.

AMP & GMP Feedback-Regulate Their Formation from IMP

Two mechanisms regulate conversion of IMP to GMP and AMP. AMP and GMP feedback-inhibit adenylosuccinate synthase and IMP dehydrogenase (reactions ⑫ and ⑭, Figure 33–3), respectively. Furthermore, conversion of IMP to adenylosuccinate en route to AMP requires GTP, and conversion of xanthinylate (XMP) to GMP requires ATP. This cross-regulation between the pathways of IMP metabolism thus serves to decrease synthesis of one purine nucleotide when there is a deficiency of the other nucleotide. AMP and GMP also inhibit hypoxanthine-guanine phosphoribosyltransferase, which converts hypoxanthine and guanine to IMP and GMP (Figure 33–4), and GMP feedback-inhibits PRPP glutamyl amidotransferase (reaction ②, Figure 33–2).

REDUCTION OF RIBONUCLEOSIDE DIPHOSPHATES FORMS DEOXYRIBONUCLEOSIDE DIPHOSPHATES

Reduction of the 2'-hydroxyl of purine and pyrimidine ribonucleotides, catalyzed by the **ribonucleotide reductase complex** (Figure 33–5), forms deoxyribonucleoside diphosphates (dNDPs). The enzyme complex is active only when cells are actively synthesizing DNA. Reduction requires thioredoxin, thioredoxin reductase, and NADPH. The immediate reductant, reduced thioredoxin, is produced by NADPH:thioredoxin reductase (Figure 33–5). Reduction of ribonucleoside diphosphates (NDPs) to deoxyribonucleoside diphosphates (dNDPs) is subject to complex regulatory controls that achieve balanced production of deoxyribonucleotides for synthesis of DNA (Figure 33–6).

BIOSYNTHESIS OF PYRIMIDINE NUCLEOTIDES

Figure 33–7 illustrates the intermediates and enzymes of pyrimidine nucleotide biosynthesis. The catalyst for

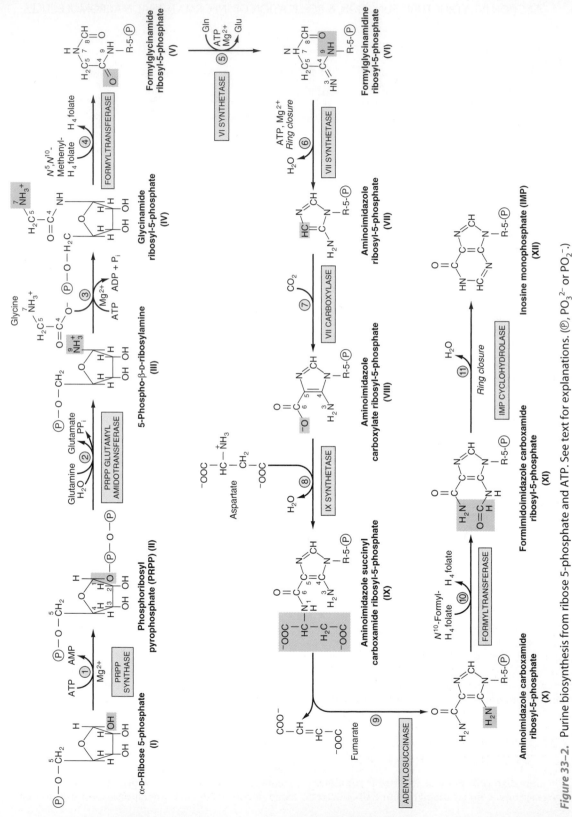

Figure 33–2. Purine biosynthesis from ribose 5-phosphate and ATP. See text for explanations. (Ⓟ, PO_3^{2-} or PO_2^{-}.)

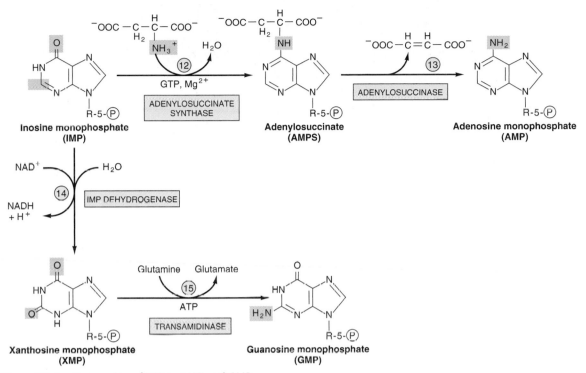

Figure 33–3. Conversion of IMP to AMP and GMP.

the initial reaction is *cytosolic carbamoyl phosphate synthase II*, a different enzyme from the *mitochondrial carbamoyl phosphate synthase I* of urea synthesis (Figure 28–9). Compartmentation thus provides two independent pools of carbamoyl phosphate. PRPP, an early participant in purine nucleotide synthesis (Figure 33–2), is a much later participant in pyrimidine biosynthesis.

Multifunctional Proteins Catalyze the Early Reactions of Pyrimidine Biosynthesis

Five of the first six enzyme activities of pyrimidine biosynthesis reside on multifunctional polypeptides. One such polypeptide catalyzes the first three reactions of Figure 33–7 and ensures efficient channeling of carbamoyl phosphate to pyrimidine biosynthesis. A second bifunctional enzyme catalyzes reactions ⑤ and ⑥.

THE DEOXYRIBONUCLEOSIDES OF URACIL & CYTOSINE ARE SALVAGED

While mammalian cells reutilize few free pyrimidines, "salvage reactions" convert the pyrimidine ribonucleo-

sides uridine and cytidine and the pyrimidine deoxyribonucleosides thymidine and deoxycytidine to their respective nucleotides. ATP-dependent phosphoryltransferases (kinases) catalyze the phosphorylation of the diphosphates of 2′-deoxycytidine, 2′-deoxyguanosine, and 2′-deoxyadenosine to their corresponding nucleoside triphosphates. In addition, orotate phosphoribosyltransferase (reaction ⑤, Figure 33–7), an enzyme of pyrimidine nucleotide synthesis, salvages orotic acid by converting it to orotidine monophosphate (OMP).

Methotrexate Blocks Reduction of Dihydrofolate

Reaction ⑫ of Figure 33–7 is the only reaction of pyrimidine nucleotide biosynthesis that requires a tetrahydrofolate derivative. The methylene group of N^5, N^{10}-methylene-tetrahydrofolate is reduced to the methyl group that is transferred, and tetrahydrofolate is oxidized to dihydrofolate. For further pyrimidine synthesis to occur, dihydrofolate must be reduced back to tetrahydrofolate, a reaction catalyzed by dihydrofolate reductase. Dividing cells, which must generate TMP and dihydrofolate, thus are especially sensitive to inhib-

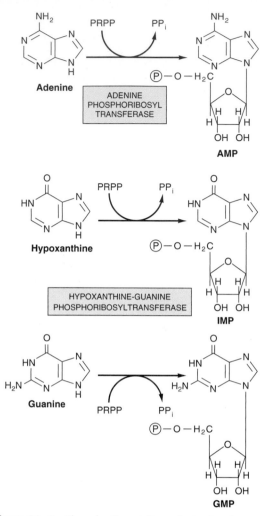

Figure 33–4. Phosphoribosylation of adenine, hypoxanthine, and guanine to form AMP, IMP, and GMP, respectively.

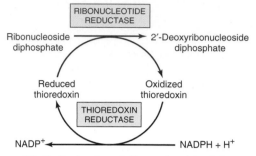

Figure 33–5. Reduction of ribonucleoside diphosphates to 2′-deoxyribonucleoside diphosphates.

REGULATION OF PYRIMIDINE NUCLEOTIDE BIOSYNTHESIS

Gene Expression & Enzyme Activity Both Are Regulated

The activities of the first and second enzymes of pyrimidine nucleotide biosynthesis are controlled by allosteric regulation. Carbamoyl phosphate synthase II (reaction ①, Figure 33–7) is inhibited by UTP and purine nucleotides but activated by PRPP. Aspartate transcarbamoylase (reaction ②, Figure 33–7) is inhibited by CTP but activated by ATP. In addition, the first three and the

itors of dihydrofolate reductase such as the anticancer drug **methotrexate.**

Certain Pyrimidine Analogs Are Substrates for Enzymes of Pyrimidine Nucleotide Biosynthesis

Orotate phosphoribosyltransferase (reaction ⑤, Figure 33–7) converts the drug **allopurinol** (Figure 32–12) to a nucleotide in which the ribosyl phosphate is attached to N-1 of the pyrimidine ring. The anticancer drug **5-fluorouracil** (Figure 32–12) is also phosphoribosylated by orotate phosphoribosyl transferase.

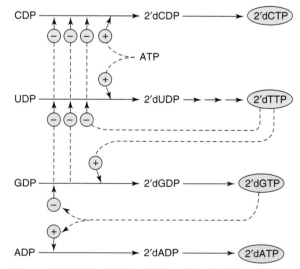

Figure 33–6. Regulation of the reduction of purine and pyrimidine ribonucleotides to their respective 2′-deoxyribonucleotides. Solid lines represent chemical flow. Broken lines show negative (⊖) or positive (⊕) feedback regulation.

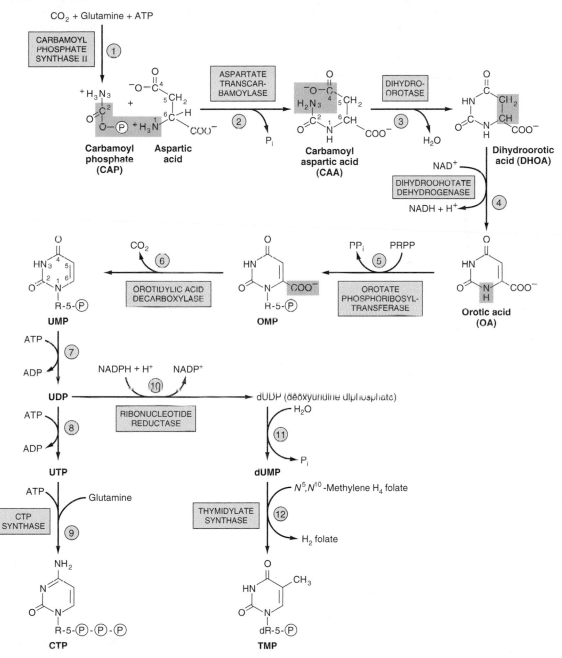

Figure 33–7. The biosynthetic pathway for pyrimidine nucleotides.

last two enzymes of the pathway are regulated by coordinate repression and derepression.

Purine & Pyrimidine Nucleotide Biosynthesis Are Coordinately Regulated

Purine and pyrimidine biosynthesis parallel one another mole for mole, suggesting coordinated control of their biosynthesis. Several sites of cross-regulation characterize purine and pyrimidine nucleotide biosynthesis. PRPP synthase (reaction ①, Figure 33–2), which forms a precursor essential for both processes, is feedback-inhibited by both purine and pyrimidine nucleotides.

HUMANS CATABOLIZE PURINES TO URIC ACID

Humans convert adenosine and guanosine to uric acid (Figure 33–8). Adenosine is first converted to inosine by adenosine deaminase. In mammals other than higher primates, uricase converts uric acid to the water-soluble product allantoin. However, since humans lack uricase, the end product of purine catabolism in humans is uric acid.

GOUT IS A METABOLIC DISORDER OF PURINE CATABOLISM

Various genetic defects in PRPP synthetase (reaction ①, Figure 33–2) present clinically as gout. Each defect—eg, an elevated V_{max}, increased affinity for ribose 5-phosphate, or resistance to feedback inhibition—results in overproduction and overexcretion of purine catabolites. When serum urate levels exceed the solubility limit, sodium urate crystalizes in soft tissues and joints and causes an inflammatory reaction, **gouty arthritis.** However, most cases of gout reflect abnormalities in renal handling of uric acid.

OTHER DISORDERS OF PURINE CATABOLISM

While purine deficiency states are rare in human subjects, there are numerous genetic disorders of purine catabolism. **Hyperuricemias** may be differentiated based on whether patients excrete normal or excessive quantities of total urates. Some hyperuricemias reflect specific enzyme

Figure 33–8. Formation of uric acid from purine nucleosides by way of the purine bases hypoxanthine, xanthine, and guanine. Purine deoxyribonucleosides are degraded by the same catabolic pathway and enzymes, all of which exist in the mucosa of the mammalian gastrointestinal tract.

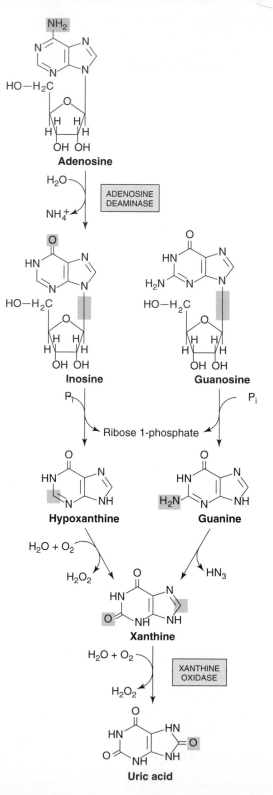

defects. Others are secondary to diseases such as cancer or psoriasis that enhance tissue turnover.

Lesch-Nyhan Syndrome

Lesch-Nyhan syndrome, an overproduction hyperuricemia characterized by frequent episodes of uric acid lithiasis and a bizarre syndrome of self-mutilation, reflects a defect in **hypoxanthine-guanine phosphoribosyl transferase,** an enzyme of purine salvage (Figure 33–4). The accompanying rise in intracellular PRPP results in purine overproduction. Mutations that decrease or abolish hypoxanthine-guanine phosphoribosyltransferase activity include deletions, frameshift mutations, base substitutions, and aberrant mRNA splicing.

Von Gierke's Disease

Purine overproduction and hyperuricemia in von Gierke's disease **(glucose-6-phosphatase deficiency)** occurs secondary to enhanced generation of the PRPP precursor ribose 5-phosphate. An associated lactic acidosis elevates the renal threshold for urate, elevating total body urates.

Hypouricemia

Hypouricemia and increased excretion of hypoxanthine and xanthine are associated with **xanthine oxidase deficiency** (Figure 33–8) due to a genetic defect or to severe liver damage. Patients with a severe enzyme deficiency may exhibit xanthinuria and xanthine lithiasis.

Adenosine Deaminase & Purine Nucleoside Phosphorylase Deficiency

Adenosine deaminase deficiency (Figure 33–8) is associated with an immunodeficiency disease in which both thymus-derived lymphocytes (T cells) and bone marrow-derived lymphocytes (B cells) are sparse and dysfunctional. **Purine nucleoside phosphorylase deficiency** is associated with a severe deficiency of T cells but apparently normal B cell function. Immune dysfunctions appear to result from accumulation of dGTP and dATP, which inhibit ribonucleotide reductase and thereby deplete cells of DNA precursors.

CATABOLISM OF PYRIMIDINES PRODUCES WATER-SOLUBLE METABOLITES

Unlike the end products of purine catabolism, the end products of pyrimidine catabolism are highly water-soluble: CO_2, NH_3, β-alanine, and β-aminoisobutyrate (Figure 33–9). Excretion of β-aminoisobutyrate increases in leukemia and severe x-ray radiation exposure due to increased destruction of DNA. However, many persons of

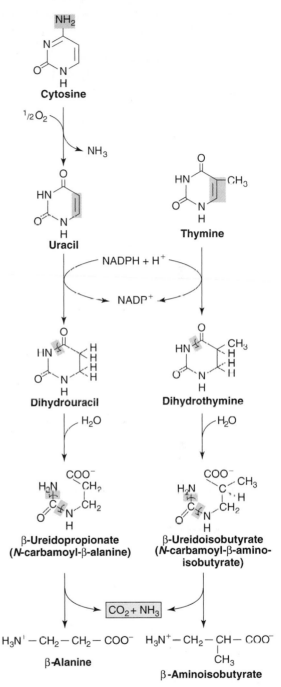

Figure 33–9. Catabolism of pyrimidines.

Chinese or Japanese ancestry routinely excrete β-aminoisobutyrate. Humans probably transaminate β-aminoisobutyrate to methylmalonate semialdehyde, which then forms succinyl-CoA (see Figure 20–2).

Pseudouridine Is Excreted Unchanged

Since no human enzyme catalyzes hydrolysis or phosphorolysis of pseudouridine, this unusual nucleoside is excreted unchanged in the urine of normal subjects, and was indeed first isolated from urine.

OVERPRODUCTION OF PYRIMIDINE CATABOLITES IS ONLY RARELY ASSOCIATED WITH CLINICALLY SIGNIFICANT ABNORMALITIES

Since the end products of pyrimidine catabolism are highly water-soluble, pyrimidine overproduction results in few clinical signs or symptoms. In hyperuricemia associated with severe overproduction of PRPP, there is overproduction of pyrimidine nucleotides and increased excretion of β-alanine. Since N^5,N^{10}-methylene-tetrahydrofolate is required for thymidylate synthesis, disorders of folate and vitamin B_{12} metabolism result in deficiencies of TMP.

Orotic Acidurias

The orotic aciduria that accompanies **Reye syndrome** probably is a consequence of the inability of severely damaged mitochondria to utilize carbamoyl phosphate, which then becomes available for cytosolic overproduction of orotic acid. **Type I orotic aciduria** reflects a deficiency of both orotate phosphoribosyltransferase and orotidylate decarboxylase (reactions ⑤ and ⑥, Figure 33–7); the rarer **type II orotic aciduria** is due to a deficiency only of orotidylate decarboxylase (reaction ⑥, Figure 33–7).

Deficiency of a Urea Cycle Enzyme Results in Excretion of Pyrimidine Precursors

Increased excretion of orotic acid, uracil, and uridine accompanies a deficiency in liver mitochondrial ornithine transcarbamoylase (reaction ②, Figure 28–9). Excess carbamoyl phosphate exits to the cytosol, where it stimulates pyrimidine nucleotide biosynthesis. The resulting mild **orotic aciduria** is increased by high-nitrogen foods.

Drugs May Precipitate Orotic Aciduria

Allopurinol (Figure 32–12), an alternative substrate for orotate phosphoribosyltransferase (reaction ⑤, Figure 33–7), competes with orotic acid. The resulting nucleotide product also inhibits orotidylate decarboxylase (reaction ⑥, Figure 33–7), resulting in **orotic aciduria** and **orotidinuria.** 6-Azauridine, following conversion to 6-azauridylate, also competitively inhibits orotidylate decarboxylase (reaction ⑥, Figure 33–7), enhancing excretion of orotic acid and orotidine.

SUMMARY

- Ingested nucleic acids are degraded to purines and pyrimidines. New purines and pyrimidines are formed from amphibolic intermediates and thus are dietarily nonessential.

- Several reactions of IMP biosynthesis require folate derivatives and glutamine. Consequently, antifolate drugs and glutamine analogs inhibit purine biosynthesis.

- Oxidation and amination of IMP forms AMP and GMP, and subsequent phosphoryl transfer from ATP forms ADP and GDP. Further phosphoryl transfer from ATP to GDP forms GTP. ADP is converted to ATP by oxidative phosphorylation. Reduction of NDPs forms dNDPs.

- Hepatic purine nucleotide biosynthesis is stringently regulated by the pool size of PRPP and by feedback inhibition of PRPP-glutamyl amidotransferase by AMP and GMP.

- Coordinated regulation of purine and pyrimidine nucleotide biosynthesis ensures their presence in proportions appropriate for nucleic acid biosynthesis and other metabolic needs.

- Humans catabolize purines to uric acid (pK_a 5.8), present as the relatively insoluble acid at acidic pH or as its more soluble sodium urate salt at a pH near neutrality. Urate crystals are diagnostic of gout. Other disorders of purine catabolism include Lesch-Nyhan syndrome, von Gierke's disease, and hypouricemias.

- Since pyrimidine catabolites are water-soluble, their overproduction does not result in clinical abnormalities. Excretion of pyrimidine precursors can, however, result from a deficiency of ornithine transcarbamoylase because excess carbamoyl phosphate is available for pyrimidine biosynthesis.

REFERENCES

Brooks EM et al: Molecular description of three macro-deletions and an Alu-Alu recombination-mediated duplication in the HPRT gene in four patients with Lesch-Nyhan disease. Mutat Res 2001;476:43.

Chow EL et al: Reassessing Reye syndrome. Arch Pediatr Adolesc Med 2003;157:1241.

Christopherson RI, Lyons SD, Wilson PK: Inhibitors of de novo nucleotide biosynthesis as drugs. Acc Chem Res 2002;35:961.

Curto R, Voit EO, Cascante M: Analysis of abnormalities in purine metabolism leading to gout and to neurological dysfunctions in man. Biochem J 1998;329:477.

Kamal MA, Christopherson RI: Accumulation of 5-phosphoribosyl-1-pyrophosphate in human CCRF-CEM leukemia cells treated with antifolates. Int J Biochem Cell Biol 2004;36:957.

Lipkowitz MS et al: Functional reconstitution, membrane targeting, genomic structure, and chromosomal localization of a human urate transporter. J Clin Invest 2001;107:1103.

Martinez J et al: Human genetic disorders, a phylogenetic perspective. J Mol Biol 2001;308:587.

Moyer RA, John DS: Acute gout precipitated by total parenteral nutrition. J Rheumatol 2003;30:849.

Neychev VK, Mitev VI: The biochemical basis of the neurobehavioral abnormalities in the Lesch-Nyhan syndrome: a hypothesis. Med Hypotheses 2004;63:131.

Olsen DB et al: A 7-deaza-adenosine analog is a potent and selective inhibitor of hepatitis C virus replication with excellent pharmacokinetic properties. Antimicrob Agents Chemother 2004;48:3944.

Scriver CR et al (editors): *The Metabolic and Molecular Bases of Inherited Disease,* 8th ed. McGraw-Hill, 2001.

Wu VC et al: Renal hypouricemia is an ominous sign in patients with severe acute respiratory syndrome. Am J Kidney Dis 2005;45:88.

Nucleic Acid Structure & Function

P. Anthony Weil, PhD, & Daryl K. Granner, MD

BIOMEDICAL IMPORTANCE

The discovery that genetic information is coded along the length of a polymeric molecule composed of only four types of monomeric units was one of the major scientific achievements of the twentieth century. This polymeric molecule, **deoxyribonucleic acid (DNA),** is the chemical basis of heredity and is organized into genes, the fundamental units of genetic information. The basic information pathway—ie, DNA directs the synthesis of RNA, which in turn directs protein synthesis—has been elucidated. Genes do not function autonomously; their replication and function are controlled by various gene products, often in collaboration with components of various signal transduction pathways. Knowledge of the structure and function of nucleic acids is essential in understanding genetics and many aspects of pathophysiology as well as the genetic basis of disease.

DNA CONTAINS THE GENETIC INFORMATION

The demonstration that DNA contained the genetic information was first made in 1944 in a series of experiments by Avery, MacLeod, and McCarty. They showed that the genetic determination of the character (type) of the capsule of a specific pneumococcus could be transmitted to another of a different capsular type by introducing purified DNA from the former coccus into the latter. These authors referred to the agent (later shown to be DNA) accomplishing the change as "transforming factor." Subsequently, this type of genetic manipulation has become commonplace. Similar experiments have recently been performed utilizing yeast, cultured plant and mammalian cells, and insect and mammalian embryos as recipients and molecularly cloned DNA as the donor of genetic information.

DNA Contains Four Deoxynucleotides

The chemical nature of the monomeric deoxynucleotide units of DNA—**deoxyadenylate, deoxyguanylate, deoxycytidylate,** and **thymidylate**—is described in Chapter 32. These monomeric units of DNA are held in polymeric form by 3′,5′-phosphodiester bridges constituting a single strand, as depicted in Figure 34–1. The informational content of DNA (the genetic code)

resides in the sequence in which these monomers—purine and pyrimidine deoxyribonucleotides—are ordered. The polymer as depicted possesses a polarity; one end has a 5′-hydroxyl or phosphate terminal while the other has a 3′-phosphate or hydroxyl terminal. The importance of this polarity will become evident. Since the genetic information resides in the order of the monomeric units within the polymers, there must exist a mechanism of reproducing or replicating this specific information with a high degree of fidelity. That requirement, together with x-ray diffraction data from the DNA molecule and the observation of Chargaff that in DNA molecules the concentration of deoxyadenosine (A) nucleotides equals that of thymidine (T) nucleotides (A = T), while the concentration of deoxyguanosine (G) nucleotides equals that of deoxycytidine (C) nucleotides (G = C), led Watson, Crick, and Wilkins to propose in the early 1950s a model of a double-stranded DNA molecule. The model they proposed is depicted in Figure 34–2. The two strands of this double-stranded helix are held in register by both **hydrogen bonds** between the purine and pyrimidine bases of the respective linear molecules and by van der Waals and hydrophobic interactions between the stacked adjacent base pairs. The pairings between the purine and pyrimidine nucleotides on the opposite strands are very specific and are dependent upon hydrogen bonding of **A with T** and **G with C** (Figure 34–2).

This common form of DNA is said to be right-handed because as one looks down the double helix, the base residues form a spiral in a clockwise direction. In the double-stranded molecule, restrictions imposed by the rotation about the phosphodiester bond, the favored anticonfiguration of the glycosidic bond (Figure 32–5), and the predominant tautomers (see Figure 32–2) of the four bases (A, G, T, and C) allow A to pair only with T and G only with C, as depicted in Figure 34–3. This base-pairing restriction explains the earlier observation that in a double-stranded DNA molecule the content of A equals that of T and the content of G equals that of C. The two strands of the double-helical molecule, each of which possesses a polarity, are **antiparallel;** ie, one strand runs in the 5′ to 3′ direction and the other in the 3′ to 5′ direction. This is analogous to two parallel streets, each running one way but carrying traffic in opposite direc-

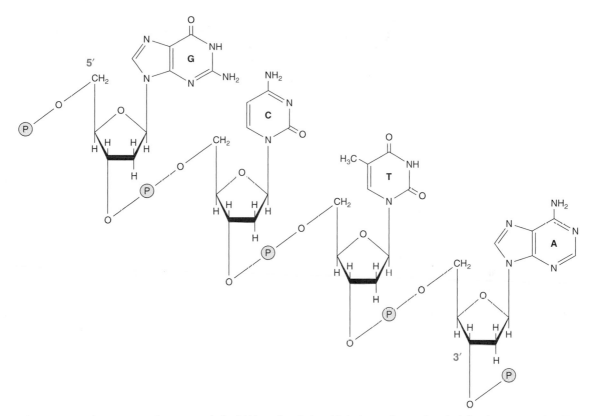

Figure 34–1. A segment of one strand of a DNA molecule in which the purine and pyrimidine bases guanine (G), cytosine (C), thymine (T), and adenine (A) are held together by a phosphodiester backbone between 2′-deoxyribosyl moieties attached to the nucleobases by an *N*-glycosidic bond. Note that the backbone has a polarity (ie, a direction). Convention dictates that a single-stranded DNA sequence is written in the 5′ to 3′ direction (ie, pGpCpTpA, where G, C, T, and A represent the four bases and p represents the interconnecting phosphates).

tions. In the double-stranded DNA molecules, the genetic information resides in the sequence of nucleotides on one strand, the **template strand.** This is the strand of DNA that is copied during **ribonucleic acid (RNA)** synthesis. It is sometimes referred to as the **noncoding strand.** The opposite strand is considered the **coding strand** because it matches the sequence of the RNA transcript (but containing uracil in place of thymine; see Figure 34–8) that encodes the protein.

The two strands, in which opposing bases are held together by interstrand hydrogen bonds, wind around a central axis in the form of a **double helix.** Double-stranded DNA exists in at least six forms (A–E and Z). The B form is usually found under physiologic conditions (low salt, high degree of hydration). A single turn of B-DNA about the axis of the molecule contains ten base pairs. The distance spanned by one turn of B-DNA is 3.4 nm (34 Å). The width (helical diameter) of the double helix in B-DNA is 2 nm (20 Å).

As depicted in Figure 34–3, three hydrogen bonds hold the deoxyguanosine nucleotide to the deoxycytidine nucleotide, whereas the other pair, the A–T pair, is held together by two hydrogen bonds. Thus, the G–C bonds are much more resistant to denaturation, or "melting," than A–T-rich regions.

The Denaturation (Melting) of DNA Is Used to Analyze Its Structure

The double-stranded structure of DNA can be separated into two component strands (melted) in solution by increasing the temperature or decreasing the salt concentration. Not only do the two stacks of bases pull apart but the bases themselves unstack while still connected in the polymer by the phosphodiester backbone. Concomitant with this denaturation of the DNA molecule is an increase in the optical absorbance of the purine and pyrimidine bases—a phenomenon referred

lowering the T_m. This allows the strands of DNA or DNA-RNA hybrids to be separated at much lower temperatures and minimizes the phosphodiester bond breakage that can occur at higher temperatures.

Renaturation of DNA Requires Base Pair Matching

Separated strands of DNA renature or reassociate when appropriate physiologic temperature and salt conditions are achieved, a process often referred to as **hybridization.** The rate of reassociation depends upon the concentration of the complementary strands. Reassociation of the two complementary DNA strands of a chromosome after DNA replication is a physiologic example of renaturation (see below). At a given temperature and salt concentration, a particular nucleic acid strand will associate tightly only with a complementary strand. Hybrid molecules will also form under appropriate conditions. For example, DNA will form a hybrid with a complementary DNA (cDNA) or with a cognate messenger RNA (mRNA; see below). When combined with gel electrophoresis techniques that separate hybrid molecules by size and radioactive or fluorescent labeling to provide a detectable signal, the resulting analytic techniques are called **Southern**

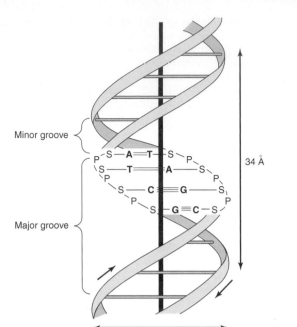

Figure 34–2. A diagrammatic representation of the Watson and Crick model of the double-helical structure of the B form of DNA. The horizontal arrow indicates the width of the double helix (20 Å), and the vertical arrow indicates the distance spanned by one complete turn of the double helix (34 Å). One turn of B-DNA includes 10 base pairs (bp), so the rise is 3.4 Å per bp. The central axis of the double helix is indicated by the vertical rod. The short arrows designate the polarity of the antiparallel strands. The major and minor grooves are depicted. (A, adenine; C, cytosine; G, guanine; T, thymine; P, phosphate; S, sugar [deoxyribose].) Hydrogen bonds between A/T and G/C bases indicated by short, colored, horizontal lines.

to as **hyperchromicity** of denaturation. Because of the stacking of the bases and the hydrogen bonding between the stacks, the double-stranded DNA molecule exhibits properties of a rigid rod and in solution is a viscous material that loses its viscosity upon denaturation.

The strands of a given molecule of DNA separate over a temperature range. The midpoint is called the **melting temperature, or T_m.** The T_m is influenced by the base composition of the DNA and by the salt concentration of the solution. DNA rich in G–C pairs, which have three hydrogen bonds, melts at a higher temperature than that rich in A–T pairs, which have two hydrogen bonds. A tenfold increase of monovalent cation concentration increases the T_m by 16.6 °C. Formamide, which is commonly used in recombinant DNA experiments, destabilizes hydrogen bonding between bases, thereby

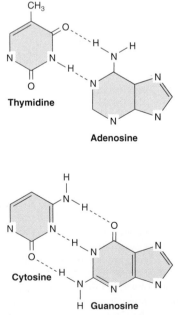

Figure 34–3. Base pairing between deoxyadenosine and thymidine involves the formation of two hydrogen bonds. Three such bonds form between deoxycytidine and deoxyguanosine. The broken lines represent hydrogen bonds.

(DNA/cDNA) and **Northern (RNA/DNA) blotting,** respectively. These procedures allow for very specific, high-sensitivity identification of hybrids from mixtures of DNA or RNA (see Chapter 39).

There Are Grooves in the DNA Molecule

Careful examination of the model depicted in Figure 34–2 reveals a **major groove** and a **minor groove** winding along the molecule parallel to the phosphodiester backbones. In these grooves, proteins can interact specifically with exposed atoms of the nucleotides (via specific hydrophobic and ionic interactions) thereby recognizing and binding to specific nucleotide sequences without disrupting the base pairing of the double-helical DNA molecule. As discussed in Chapters 36 and 38, regulatory proteins control the expression of specific genes via such interactions.

DNA Exists in Relaxed & Supercoiled Forms

In some organisms such as bacteria, bacteriophages, many DNA-containing animal viruses, as well as organelles such as mitochondria (see Figure 35–8), the ends of the DNA molecules are joined to create a closed circle with no covalently free ends. This of course does not destroy the polarity of the molecules, but it eliminates all free 3' and 5' hydroxyl and phosphoryl groups. Closed circles exist in relaxed or supercoiled forms. Supercoils are introduced when a closed circle is twisted around its own axis or when a linear piece of duplex DNA, whose ends are fixed, is twisted. This energy requiring process puts the molecule under torsional stress, and the greater the number of supercoils, the greater the stress or torsion (test this by twisting a rubber band). **Negative supercoils** are formed when the molecule is twisted in the direction opposite from the clockwise turns of the right-handed double helix found in B-DNA. Such DNA is said to be underwound. The energy required to achieve this state is, in a sense, stored in the supercoils. The transition to another form that requires energy is thereby facilitated by the underwinding. One such transition is strand separation, which is a prerequisite for DNA replication and transcription. Supercoiled DNA is therefore a preferred form in biologic systems. Enzymes that catalyze topologic changes of DNA are called **topoisomerases.** Topoisomerases can relax or insert supercoils. The best-characterized example is **bacterial gyrase,** which induces negative supercoiling in DNA using ATP as energy source. Homologs of this enzyme exist in all organisms and are important targets for cancer chemotherapy.

DNA PROVIDES A TEMPLATE FOR REPLICATION & TRANSCRIPTION

The genetic information stored in the nucleotide sequence of DNA serves two purposes. It is the source of information for the synthesis of all protein molecules of the cell and organism, and it provides the information inherited by daughter cells or offspring. Both of these functions require that the DNA molecule serve as a template—in the first case for the transcription of the information into RNA and in the second case for the replication of the information into daughter DNA molecules.

The complementarity of the Watson and Crick double-stranded model of DNA strongly suggests that replication of the DNA molecule occurs in a semiconservative manner. Thus, when each strand of the double-stranded parental DNA molecule separates from its complement during replication, each serves as a template on which a new complementary strand is synthesized (Figure 34–4). The two newly formed double-stranded daughter DNA molecules, each containing one strand (but complementary rather than identical) from the parent double-stranded DNA molecule, are then sorted between the two daughter cells (Figure 34–5). Each daughter cell contains DNA molecules with information identical to that which the parent possessed; yet in each daughter cell the DNA molecule of the parent cell has been only semiconserved.

THE CHEMICAL NATURE OF RNA DIFFERS FROM THAT OF DNA

Ribonucleic acid (RNA) is a polymer of purine and pyrimidine ribonucleotides linked together by 3',5'-phosphodiester bridges analogous to those in DNA (Figure 34–6). Although sharing many features with DNA, RNA possesses several specific differences:

(1) In RNA, the sugar moiety to which the phosphates and purine and pyrimidine bases are attached is ribose rather than the 2'-deoxyribose of DNA.

(2) The pyrimidine components of RNA differ from those of DNA. Although RNA contains the ribonucleotides of adenine, guanine, and cytosine, it does not possess thymine except in the rare case mentioned below. Instead of thymine, RNA contains the ribonucleotide of uracil.

(3) RNA exists as a single strand, whereas DNA exists as a double-stranded helical molecule. However, given the proper complementary base sequence with opposite polarity, the single strand of RNA—as demonstrated in Figure 34–7—is capable of folding back on itself like a hairpin and thus acquiring double-stranded characteristics.

(4) Since the RNA molecule is a single strand complementary to only one of the two strands of a gene, its guanine content does not necessarily equal its cytosine content, nor does its adenine content necessarily equal its uracil content.

(5) RNA can be hydrolyzed by alkali to 2',3' cyclic diesters of the mononucleotides, compounds that cannot be formed from alkali-treated DNA because of the

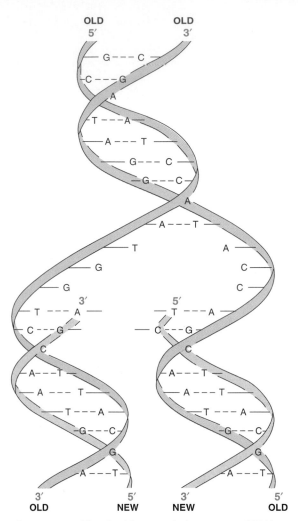

Figure 34–4. The double-stranded structure of DNA and the template function of each old strand (dark shading) on which a new complementary strand (light shading) is synthesized.

Nearly All of the Several Species of RNA Are Involved in Some Aspect of Protein Synthesis

Those cytoplasmic RNA molecules that serve as templates for protein synthesis (ie, that transfer genetic information from DNA to the protein-synthesizing machinery) are designated **messenger RNAs,** or **mRNAs.** Many other cytoplasmic RNA molecules (**ribosomal RNAs; rRNAs**) have structural roles wherein they contribute to the formation and function of ribosomes (the organellar machinery for protein synthesis) or serve as adapter molecules (**transfer RNAs; tRNAs**) for the translation of RNA information into specific sequences of polymerized amino acids.

Some RNA molecules have intrinsic catalytic activity. The activity of these **ribozymes** often involves the cleavage of a nucleic acid. An example is the role of RNA in catalyzing the processing of the primary transcript of a gene into mature messenger RNA.

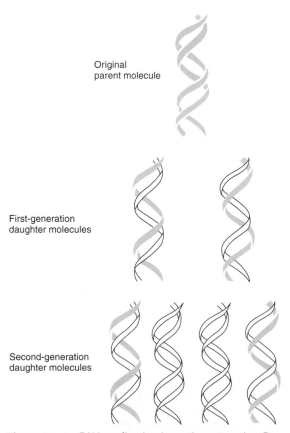

Figure 34–5. DNA replication is semiconservative. During a round of replication, each of the two strands of DNA is used as a template for synthesis of a new, complementary strand.

absence of a 2′-hydroxyl group. The alkali lability of RNA is useful both diagnostically and analytically.

Information within the single strand of RNA is contained in its sequence ("primary structure") of purine and pyrimidine nucleotides within the polymer. The sequence is complementary to the template strand of the gene from which it was transcribed. Because of this complementarity, an RNA molecule can bind specifically via the base-pairing rules to its template DNA strand; it will not bind ("hybridize") with the other (coding) strand of its gene. The sequence of the RNA molecule (except for U replacing T) is the same as that of the coding strand of the gene (Figure 34–8).

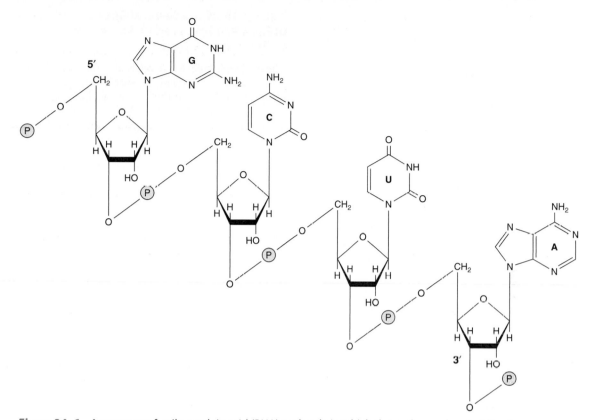

Figure 34–6. A segment of a ribonucleic acid (RNA) molecule in which the purine and pyrimidine bases—guanine (G), cytosine (C), uracil (U), and adenine (A)—are held together by phosphodiester bonds between ribosyl moieties attached to the nucleobases by N-glycosidic bonds. Note that the polymer has a polarity as indicated by the labeled 3′- and 5′-attached phosphates.

Much of the RNA synthesized from DNA templates in eukaryotic cells, including mammalian cells, is degraded within the nucleus, and it never serves as either a structural or an informational entity within the cellular cytoplasm.

In all eukaryotic cells there are **small nuclear RNA (snRNA)** species that are not directly involved in protein synthesis but play pivotal roles in RNA processing. These relatively small molecules vary in size from 90 to about 300 nucleotides (Table 34–1).

The genetic material for some animal and plant viruses is RNA rather than DNA. Although some RNA viruses never have their information transcribed into a DNA molecule, many animal RNA viruses—specifically, the retroviruses (the HIV virus, for example)—are transcribed by an RNA-dependent DNA polymerase, the so-called **reverse transcriptase,** to produce a double-stranded DNA copy of their RNA genome. In many cases, the resulting double-stranded DNA transcript is integrated into the host genome and subsequently serves as a template for gene expression and from which new viral RNA genomes can be transcribed.

RNA Is Organized in Several Distinct Classes

In all prokaryotic and eukaryotic organisms, three main classes of RNA molecules exist: messenger RNA (mRNA), transfer RNA (tRNA), and ribosomal RNA (rRNA). Each differs from the others by size, function, and general stability.

A. MESSENGER RNA (mRNA)

This class is the most heterogeneous in size and stability. All members of the class function as messengers conveying the information in a gene to the protein-synthesizing machinery, where each serves as a template on which a specific sequence of amino acids is polymerized to form a specific protein molecule, the ultimate gene product (Figure 34–9).

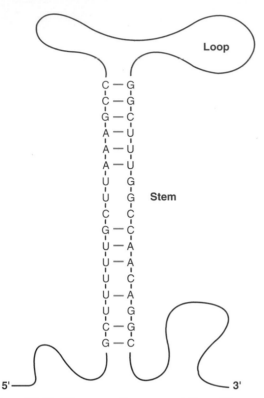

Figure 34–7. Diagrammatic representation of the secondary structure of a single-stranded RNA molecule in which a stem loop, or "hairpin," has been formed. Formation of this structure is dependent upon the indicated intramolecular base pairing (colored horizontal lines between bases). Note that A forms hydrogen bonds with U in RNA.

Table 34–1. Some of the species of small stable RNAs found in mammalian cells.

Name	Length (nucleotides)	Molecules per Cell	Localization
U1	165	1×10^6	Nucleoplasm/hnRNA
U2	188	5×10^5	Nucleoplasm
U3	216	3×10^5	Nucleolus
U4	139	1×10^5	Nucleoplasm
U5	118	2×10^5	Nucleoplasm
U6	106	3×10^5	Perichromatin granules
4.5S	95	3×10^5	Nucleus and cytoplasm
7SK	280	5×10^5	Nucleus and cytoplasm

methylated nucleotides. The cap is involved in the recognition of mRNA by the translation machinery, and it probably also helps stabilize the mRNA by preventing the attack of 5′-exonucleases. The protein-synthesizing machinery begins translating the mRNA into proteins beginning downstream of the 5′ or capped terminal. The other end of most mRNA molecules, the 3′-hydroxyl terminal, has an attached polymer of adenylate residues 20–250 nucleotides in length. The specific function of the **poly(A) "tail"** at the 3′-hydroxyl terminal of mRNAs is not fully understood, but it seems that it maintains the intracellular stability of the specific mRNA by preventing the attack of 3′-exonucleases. Some mRNAs, including those for some histones, do not contain poly(A). The poly(A) tail, because it will form a base pair with oligodeoxythymidine polymers attached to a solid substrate like cellulose, can be used to separate mRNA from other species of RNA, including mRNA molecules that lack this tail. Both the mRNA "cap" and "poly(A) tail" are added posttranscriptionally by nontemplate-directed enzymes.

In mammalian cells, including cells of humans, the mRNA molecules present in the cytoplasm are not the RNA products immediately synthesized from the DNA template but must be formed by processing from a precursor molecule before entering the cytoplasm. Thus, in mammalian nuclei, the immediate products of gene transcription constitute a fourth class of RNA mole-

Messenger RNAs, particularly in eukaryotes, have some unique chemical characteristics. The 5′ terminal of mRNA is "capped" by a 7-methylguanosine triphosphate that is linked to an adjacent 2′-O-methyl ribonucleoside at its 5′-hydroxyl through the three phosphates (Figure 34–10). The mRNA molecules frequently contain internal 6-methyladenylates and other 2′-O-ribose

DNA strands:

Coding → **5′** —TGGAATTGTGAGCGGATAACAATTTCACACAGGAAACAGCTATGACCATG—**3′**
Template → **3′** —ACCTTAACACTCGCCTATTGTTAAAGTGTGTCCTTTGTCGATACTGGTAC—**5′**

RNA transcript   **5′** p AUUGUGAGCGGAUAACAAUUUCACACAGGAAACAGCUAUGACCAUG   **3′**

Figure 34–8. The relationship between the sequences of an RNA transcript and its gene, in which the coding and template strands are shown with their polarities. The RNA transcript with a 5′ to 3′ polarity is complementary to the template strand with its 3′ to 5′ polarity. Note that the sequence in the RNA transcript and its polarity is the same as that in the coding strand, except that the U of the transcript replaces the T of the gene.

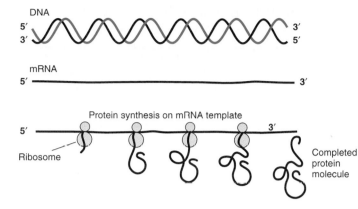

Figure 34–9. The expression of genetic information in DNA into the form of an mRNA transcript. This is subsequently translated by ribosomes into a specific protein molecule.

cules. These nuclear RNA molecules, precursors to the mature, fully processed mRNAs, are very heterogeneous in size and are quite large. The **heterogeneous nuclear RNA (hnRNA)** molecules may have a molecular weight in excess of 10^7, whereas the molecular weight of mRNA molecules is generally less than 2×10^6. As discussed in Chapter 36, hnRNA molecules are processed to generate the mRNA molecules which then enter the cytoplasm to serve as templates for protein synthesis.

B. TRANSFER RNA (tRNA)

tRNA molecules vary in length from 74 to 95 nucleotides. They also are generated by nuclear processing of a precursor molecule (Chapter 36). The tRNA molecules serve as adapters for the translation of the information in the sequence of nucleotides of the mRNA into specific amino acids. There are at least 20 species of tRNA molecules in every cell, at least one (and often several) corresponding to each of the 20 amino acids required for protein synthesis. Although each specific tRNA differs from the others in its sequence of nucleotides, the tRNA molecules as a class have many features in common. The primary structure—ie, the nucleotide sequence—of all tRNA molecules allows extensive folding and intrastrand complementarity to generate a secondary structure that appears in two dimensions like a cloverleaf (Figure 34–11).

All tRNA molecules contain four main arms. The **acceptor arm** terminates in the nucleotides CpCpAOH. These three nucleotides are added posttranscriptionally by a specific nucleotidyl transferase enzyme. The tRNA-appropriate amino acid is attached, or "charged" onto, the 3′-OH group of the A moiety of the acceptor arm (see Figure 37–1). The **D, TψC,** and **extra arms** help define a specific tRNA.

Although tRNAs are quite stable in prokaryotes, they are somewhat less stable in eukaryotes. The opposite is true for mRNAs, which are quite unstable in prokaryotes but generally more stable in eukaryotic organisms.

C. RIBOSOMAL RNA (rRNA)

A ribosome is a cytoplasmic nucleoprotein structure that acts as the machinery for the synthesis of proteins from the mRNA templates. On the ribosomes, the mRNA and tRNA molecules interact to translate into a specific protein molecule information transcribed from the gene. In active protein synthesis, many ribosomes are associated with an mRNA molecule in an assembly called the **polysome.**

The components of the mammalian ribosome, which has a molecular weight of about 4.2×10^6 and a sedimentation velocity of 80S (Svedberg units), are shown in Table 34–2. The mammalian ribosome contains two major nucleoprotein subunits—a larger one with a molecular weight of 2.8×10^6 (60S) and a smaller subunit with a molecular weight of 1.4×10^6 (40S). The 60S subunit contains a 5S ribosomal RNA (rRNA), a 5.8S rRNA, and a 28S rRNA; there are also probably more than 50 specific polypeptides. The 40S subunit is smaller and contains a single 18S rRNA and approximately 30 distinct polypeptide chains. All of the ribosomal RNA molecules except the 5S rRNA are processed from a single 45S precursor RNA molecule in the nucleolus (Chapter 36). 5S rRNA is independently transcribed. The highly methylated ribosomal RNA molecules are packaged in the nucleolus with the specific ribosomal proteins. In the cytoplasm, the ribosomes remain quite stable and capable of many translation cycles. The functions of the ribosomal RNA molecules in the ribosomal particle are not fully understood, but they are necessary for ribosomal assembly and seem to play key roles in the binding of mRNA to ribosomes and its translation. Recent studies suggest that an rRNA component performs the peptidyl transferase activity and thus is an enzyme (a ribozyme).

D. SMALL RNA

A large number of discrete, highly conserved, and small stable RNA species are found in eukaryotic cells. Most of these molecules are complexed with proteins to form

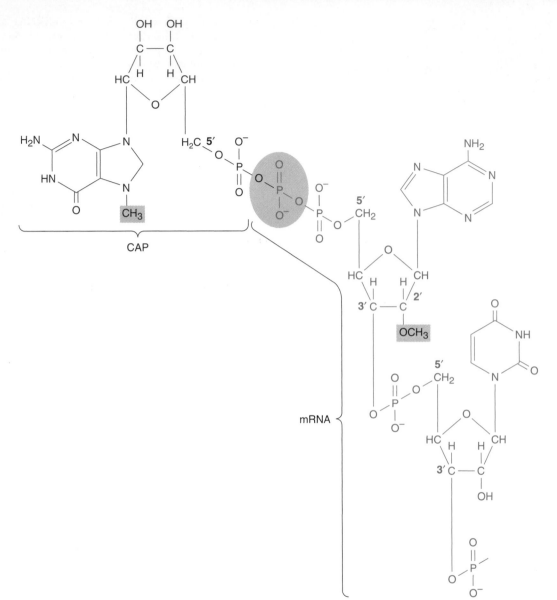

Figure 34–10. The cap structure attached to the 5′ terminal of most eukaryotic messenger RNA molecules. A 7-methylguanosine triphosphate (black) is attached at the 5′ terminal of the mRNA (shown in color), which usually also contains a 2′-O-methylpurine nucleotide. These modifications (the cap and methyl group) are added after the mRNA is transcribed from DNA.

ribonucleoproteins and are distributed in the nucleus, in the cytoplasm, or in both. They range in size from 20 to 300 nucleotides and are present in 100,000–1,000,000 copies per cell.

1. Small Nuclear RNAs (snRNAs). snRNAs, a subset of the small RNAs, are significantly involved in mRNA processing and gene regulation. Of the several snRNAs, U1, U2, U4, U5, and U6 are involved in intron removal and the processing of hnRNA into mRNA (Chapter 36). The U7 snRNA is involved in production of the correct 3′ ends of histone mRNA—which lacks a poly(A) tail. 7SK RNA associates with several proteins to form a ribonucleoprotein complex

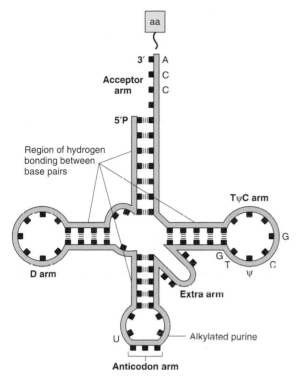

Figure 34–11. Typical aminoacyl tRNA in which the amino acid (aa) is attached to the 3′ CCA terminal. The anticodon, TψC, and dihydrouracil (D) arms are indicated, as are the positions of the intramolecular hydrogen bonding between these base pairs. (From Watson JD: *Molecular Biology of the Gene*, 3rd ed. Copyright © 1976, 1970, 1965, by W.A. Benjamin, Inc., Menlo Park, California.)

that modulates miRNA gene transcription elongation by RNA polymerase II (see Chapter 36).

2. Micro RNAs, miRNAs, and Small Interfering RNAs, siRNAs. These two classes of RNAs represent a subset of small RNAs; both play important roles in gene regulation. Presently, all known **miRNAs and siRNAs cause inhibition of gene expression** by decreasing specific protein production albeit apparently via distinct mechanisms. miRNAs are typically 21–25 nucleotides in length and are generated by nucleolytic processing of the products of distinct genes/transcription units (see Figure 36–5). miRNA precursors are single stranded but have extensive intramolecular secondary structure. These precursors range in size from about 500 to 1000 nucleotides; the small processed mature **miRNAs typically hybridize, via the formation of imperfect RNA-RNA duplexes within the 3′-untranslated regions** (3′UTR's; see Figure 38–19) of specific target mRNAs, **leading via unknown mechanisms to translation arrest.** To date, hundreds of distinct miRNAs have been described in humans. siRNAs are derived by the specific nucleolytic cleavage of larger, double-stranded RNAs to again form small 21–25 nucleotide-long products. These short **siRNAs usually form perfect RNA-RNA hybrids** with their distinct targets potentially anywhere within the length of the mRNA where the complementary sequence exists. Formation of such RNA-RNA duplexes between siRNA and mRNA results in reduced specific protein production because the **siRNA-mRNA complexes are degraded** by dedicated nucleolytic machinery; some or all of this mRNA degradation occurs in specific organelles termed P bodies. Both miRNAs and siRNAs represent exciting new **potential targets for therapeutic drug development in humans.** In addition, siRNAs are frequently used to decrease or "knock-down" specific protein levels (via siRNA homology–directed mRNA degradation) in experimental contexts in the laboratory, an extremely useful and powerful alternative to gene-knockout technology (Chapter 39).

SPECIFIC NUCLEASES DIGEST NUCLEIC ACIDS

Enzymes capable of degrading nucleic acids have been recognized for many years. These nucleases can be clas-

Table 34–2. Components of mammalian ribosomes.[1]

| Component | Mass (MW) | Protein | | RNA | | |
		Number	Mass	Size	Mass	Bases
40S subunit	1.4×10^6	33	7×10^5	18S	7×10^5	1900
60S subunit	2.8×10^6	50	1×10^6	5S	35,000	120
				5.8S	45,000	160
				28S	1.6×10^6	4700

[1]The ribosomal subunits are defined according to their sedimentation velocity in Svedberg units (40S or 60S). The number of unique proteins and their total mass (MW) and the RNA components of each subunit in size (Svedberg units), mass, and number of bases are listed.

sified in several ways. Those which exhibit specificity for deoxyribonucleic acid are referred to as **deoxyribonucleases.** Those which specifically hydrolyze ribonucleic acids are **ribonucleases.** Within both of these classes are enzymes capable of cleaving internal phosphodiester bonds to produce either 3'-hydroxyl and 5'-phosphoryl terminals or 5'-hydroxyl and 3'-phosphoryl terminals. These are referred to as **endonucleases.** Some are capable of hydrolyzing both strands of a **double-stranded** molecule, whereas others can only cleave **single strands** of nucleic acids. Some nucleases can hydrolyze only unpaired single strands, while others are capable of hydrolyzing single strands participating in the formation of a double-stranded molecule. There exist classes of endonucleases that recognize specific sequences in DNA; the majority of these are the **restriction endonucleases,** which have in recent years become important tools in molecular genetics and medical sciences. A list of some currently recognized restriction endonucleases is presented in Table 39–2.

Some nucleases are capable of hydrolyzing a nucleotide only when it is present at a terminal of a molecule; these are referred to as **exonucleases.** Exonucleases act in one direction ($3' \rightarrow 5'$ or $5' \rightarrow 3'$) only. In bacteria, a $3' \rightarrow 5'$ exonuclease is an integral part of the DNA replication machinery and there serves to edit—or proofread—the most recently added deoxynucleotide for base-pairing errors.

SUMMARY

- DNA consists of four bases—A, G, C, and T—that are held in linear array by phosphodiester bonds through the 3' and 5' positions of adjacent deoxyribose moieties.
- DNA is organized into two strands by the pairing of bases A to T and G to C on complementary strands. These strands form a double helix around a central axis.
- The 3×10^9 base pairs of DNA in humans are organized into the haploid complement of 23 chromosomes. The exact sequence of these 3 billion nucleotides defines the uniqueness of each individual.
- DNA provides a template for its own replication and thus maintenance of the genotype and for the transcription of the roughly 30,000 human genes into a variety of RNA molecules.
- RNA exists in several different single-stranded structures, most of which are directly or indirectly involved in protein synthesis or its regulation. The linear array of nucleotides in RNA consists of A, G, C, and U, and the sugar moiety is ribose.
- The major forms of RNA include messenger RNA (mRNA), ribosomal RNA (rRNA), transfer RNA (tRNA), and small nuclear RNAs (snRNAs; miRNAs). Certain RNA molecules act as catalysts (ribozymes).

REFERENCES

Green R, Noller HF: Ribosomes and translation. Annu Rev Biochem 1997;66:689.

Guthrie C, Patterson B: Spliceosomal snRNAs. Ann Rev Genet 1988;22:387.

Hunt T: *DNA Makes RNA Makes Protein.* Elsevier, 1983.

Moore M: From birth to death: the complex lives of eukaryotic mRNAs. Science 2005;309:1514.

Watson JD, Crick FHC: Molecular structure of nucleic acids. Nature 1953;171:737.

Watson JD: *The Double Helix.* Atheneum, 1968.

Watson JD et al: *Molecular Biology of the Gene,* 5th ed. Benjamin-Cummings, 2000.

Zamore PD, Haley B: Ribo-gnome: the big world of small RNAs. Science 2005;309:1519.

DNA Organization, Replication, & Repair

35

P. Anthony Weil, PhD, & Daryl K. Granner, MD

BIOMEDICAL IMPORTANCE*

The genetic information in the DNA of a chromosome can be transmitted by exact replication or it can be exchanged by a number of processes, including crossing over, recombination, transposition, and conversion. These provide a means of ensuring adaptability and diversity for the organism but, when these processes go awry, can also result in disease. A number of enzyme systems are involved in DNA replication, alteration, and repair. Mutations are due to a change in the base sequence of DNA and may result from the faulty replication, movement, or repair of DNA and occur with a frequency of about one in every 10^6 cell divisions. Abnormalities in gene products (either in protein function or amount) can be the result of mutations that occur in coding or regulatory-region DNA. A mutation in a germ cell is transmitted to offspring (so-called vertical transmission of hereditary disease). A number of factors, including viruses, chemicals, ultraviolet light, and ionizing radiation, increase the rate of mutation. Mutations often affect somatic cells and so are passed on to successive generations of cells, but only within an organism. It is becoming apparent that a number of diseases—and perhaps most cancers—are due to the combined effects of vertical transmission of mutations as well as horizontal transmission of induced mutations.

CHROMATIN IS THE CHROMOSOMAL MATERIAL EXTRACTED FROM NUCLEI OF CELLS OF EUKARYOTIC ORGANISMS

Chromatin consists of very long double-stranded **DNA molecules** and a nearly equal mass of rather small basic proteins termed **histones** as well as a smaller amount of **nonhistone proteins** (most of which are acidic and

*So far as is possible, the discussion in this chapter and in Chapters 36, 37, and 38 will pertain to mammalian organisms, which are, of course, among the higher eukaryotes. At times it will be necessary to refer to observations in prokaryotic organisms such as bacteria and viruses, but in such cases the information will be of a kind that can be extrapolated to mammalian organisms.

larger than histones) and a small quantity of **RNA.** The nonhistone proteins include enzymes involved in DNA replication, such as DNA topoisomerases. Also included are proteins involved in transcription, such as the RNA polymerase complex. The double-stranded DNA helix in each chromosome has a length that is thousands of times the diameter of the cell nucleus. One purpose of the molecules that comprise chromatin, particularly the histones, is to condense the DNA. Electron microscopic studies of chromatin have demonstrated dense spherical particles called **nucleosomes,** which are approximately 10 nm in diameter and connected by DNA filaments (Figure 35–1). Nucleosomes are composed of DNA wound around a collection of histone molecules.

Histones Are the Most Abundant Chromatin Proteins

The histones are a small family of closely related basic proteins. H1 histones are the ones least tightly bound to chromatin (Figure 35–1) and are, therefore, easily removed with a salt solution, after which chromatin becomes soluble. The organizational unit of this soluble chromatin is the nucleosome. Nucleosomes contain four types of histones: **H2A, H2B, H3,** and **H4.** The structures of all four histones—H2A, H2B, H3, and H4, the so-called core histones forming the nucleosome—have been highly conserved between species. This extreme conservation implies that the function of histones is identical in all eukaryotes and that the entire molecule is involved quite specifically in carrying out this function. The carboxyl terminal two-thirds of the molecules have a typical random amino acid composition, while their amino terminal thirds are particularly rich in basic amino acids. **These four core histones are subject to at least six types of covalent modification:** acetylation, methylation, phosphorylation, ADP-ribosylation, monoubiquitylation, and sumoylation. These histone modifications play an important role in chromatin structure and function, as illustrated in Table 35–1.

The histones interact with each other in very specific ways. **H3 and H4 form a tetramer** containing two molecules of each $(H3/H4)_2$, while **H2A and H2B form**

322

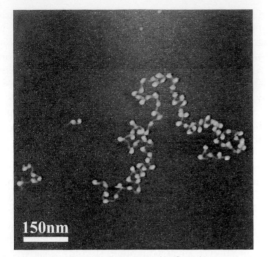

Figure 35–1. Electron micrograph of nucleosomes (white, ball-shaped) attached to strands of DNA (thin, gray line); see Figure 35–2. (Reproduced, with permission, from Shao Z. Probing nanometer structures with atomic force microscopy. News Physiol Sci, 1999, Aug.;14:142–149. Courtesy of Professor Zhifeng Shao, University of Virginia.)

dimers (H2A-H2B). Under physiologic conditions, these histone oligomers associate to form the **histone octamer** of the composition (H3/H4)$_2$-(H2A-H2B)$_2$.

The Nucleosome Contains Histone & DNA

When the histone octamer is mixed with purified, double-stranded DNA, the same x-ray diffraction pattern is formed as that observed in freshly isolated chromatin. Electron microscopic studies confirm the existence of reconstituted nucleosomes. Furthermore, the reconstitution of nucleosomes from DNA and histones H2A, H2B, H3, and H4 is independent of the organismal or

cellular origin of the various components. The histone H1 and the nonhistone proteins are not necessary for the reconstitution of the nucleosome core.

In the nucleosome, the DNA is supercoiled in a left-handed helix over the surface of the disk-shaped histone octamer (Figure 35–2). The majority of core histone proteins interact with the DNA on the inside of the supercoil without protruding, though the amino terminal tails of all the histones probably protrude outside of this structure and are available for regulatory covalent modifications (see Table 35–1).

The (H3/H4)$_2$ tetramer itself can confer nucleosome-like properties on DNA and thus has a central role in the formation of the nucleosome. The addition of two H2A-H2B dimers stabilizes the primary particle and firmly binds two additional half-turns of DNA previously bound only loosely to the (H3/H4)$_2$. Thus, 1.75 superhelical turns of DNA are wrapped around the surface of the histone octamer, protecting 146 base pairs of DNA and forming the nucleosome core particle (Figure 35–2). The core particles are separated by an about 30-bp linker region of DNA. Most of the DNA is in a repeating series of these structures, giving the so-called "beads-on-a-string" appearance when examined by electron microscopy (see Figure 35–1).

The assembly of nucleosomes is mediated by one of several chromatin assembly factors facilitated by histone chaperones, a group of proteins that exhibit high-affinity histone binding. As the nucleosome is assembled, histones are released from the histone chaperones. Nucleosomes appear to exhibit preference for certain regions on

Table 35–1. Possible roles of modified histones.

1. Acetylation of histones H3 and H4 is associated with the activation or inactivation of gene transcription (Chapter 36).
2. Acetylation of core histones is associated with chromosomal assembly during DNA replication.
3. Phosphorylation of histone H1 is associated with the condensation of chromosomes during the replication cycle.
4. ADP-ribosylation of histones is associated with DNA repair.
5. Methylation of histones is correlated with activation and repression of gene transcription.
6. Monoubiquitylation is associated with gene activation, repression, and heterochromatic gene silencing.
7. Sumoylation of histones (SUMO; small ubiquitin-related modifier) leads to transcription repression.

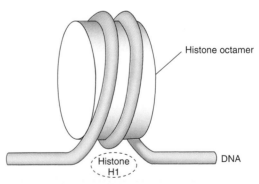

Figure 35–2. Model for the structure of the nucleosome, in which DNA is wrapped around the surface of a flat protein cylinder consisting of two each of histones H2A, H2B, H3, and H4 that form the histone octamer. The 146 base pairs of DNA, consisting of 1.75 superhelical turns, are in contact with the histone octamer. This protects the DNA from digestion by a nuclease. The position of histone H1, when it is present, is indicated by the dashed outline at the bottom of the figure.

specific DNA molecules, but the basis for this nonrandom distribution, termed **phasing,** is not completely understood. It is probably related to the relative physical flexibility of certain nucleotide sequences that are able to accommodate the regions of kinking within the supercoil as well as the presence of other DNA-bound factors that limit the sites of nucleosome deposition.

The super-packing of nucleosomes in nuclei is seemingly dependent upon the interaction of the H1 histones with adjacent nucleosomes.

HIGHER-ORDER STRUCTURES PROVIDE FOR THE COMPACTION OF CHROMATIN

Electron microscopy of chromatin reveals two higher orders of structure—the 10-nm fibril and the 30-nm chromatin fiber—beyond that of the nucleosome itself. The disk-like nucleosome structure has a 10-nm diameter and a height of 5 nm. The **10-nm fibril** consists of nucleosomes arranged with their edges separated by a small distance (30 bp of DNA) with their flat faces parallel with the fibril axis (Figure 35–3). The 10-nm fibril is probably further supercoiled with six or seven nucleosomes per turn to form the **30-nm chromatin fiber** (Figure 35–3). Each turn of the supercoil is relatively flat, and the faces of the nucleosomes of successive turns would be nearly parallel to each other. H1 histones appear to stabilize the 30-nm fiber, but their position and that of the variable length spacer DNA are not clear. It is probable that nucleosomes can form a variety of packed structures. In order to form a mitotic chromosome, the 30-nm fiber must be compacted in length another 100-fold (see below).

In **interphase chromosomes,** chromatin fibers appear to be organized into 30,000–100,000 bp **loops or domains** anchored in a scaffolding (or supporting matrix) within the nucleus. Within these domains, some DNA sequences may be located nonrandomly. It has been suggested that each looped domain of chromatin corresponds to one or more separate genetic functions, containing both coding and noncoding regions of the cognate gene or genes. This nuclear architecture is likely dynamic, having important regulatory effects upon gene regulation.

SOME REGIONS OF CHROMATIN ARE "ACTIVE" & OTHERS ARE "INACTIVE"

Generally, every cell of an individual metazoan organism contains the same genetic information. Thus, the differences between cell types within an organism must be explained by differential expression of the common genetic information. Chromatin containing active genes (ie, transcriptionally active chromatin) has been shown to differ in several ways from that of inactive regions. The nucleosome structure of active chromatin appears to be altered, sometimes quite extensively, in highly active regions. DNA in active chromatin contains large regions (about 100,000 bases long) that are relatively more **sensitive to digestion by a nuclease** such as DNase I. DNase I makes single-strand cuts in any segment of DNA (no sequence specificity). It will digest DNA not protected by protein into its component deoxynucleotides. The sensitivity to DNase I of chromatin regions being actively transcribed reflects only a potential for transcription rather than transcription itself and in several systems can be correlated with a relative lack of 5-methyldeoxycytidine in the DNA and particular histone covalent modifications (phosphorylation, acetylation, etc; see Table 35–1).

Within the large regions of active chromatin there exist shorter stretches of 100–300 nucleotides that exhibit an even greater (another 10-fold) sensitivity to DNase I. These **hypersensitive sites** probably result from a structural conformation that favors access of the nuclease to the DNA. These regions are often located immediately upstream from the active gene and are the location of interrupted nucleosomal structure caused by the binding of nonhistone regulatory transcription factor proteins. (See Chapters 36 and 38.) In many cases, it seems that if a gene is capable of being transcribed, it very often has a DNase-hypersensitive site(s) in the chromatin immediately upstream. As noted above, nonhistone regulatory proteins involved in transcription control and those involved in maintaining access to the template strand lead to the formation of hypersensitive sites. Hypersensitive sites often provide the first clue about the presence and location of a transcription control element.

Transcriptionally inactive chromatin is densely packed during interphase as observed by electron microscopic studies and is referred to as **heterochromatin;** transcriptionally active chromatin stains less densely and is referred to as **euchromatin.** Generally, euchromatin is replicated earlier than heterochromatin in the mammalian cell cycle (see below).

There are two types of heterochromatin: constitutive and facultative. **Constitutive heterochromatin** is always condensed and thus inactive. It is found in the regions near the chromosomal centromere and at chromosomal ends (telomeres). **Facultative heterochromatin** is at times condensed, but at other times it is actively transcribed and, thus, uncondensed and appears as euchromatin. Of the two members of the X chromosome pair in mammalian females, one X chromosome is almost completely inactive transcriptionally and is heterochromatic. However, the heterochromatic X chromosome decondenses during gametogenesis and becomes transcriptionally active during early embryogenesis—thus, it is facultative heterochromatin.

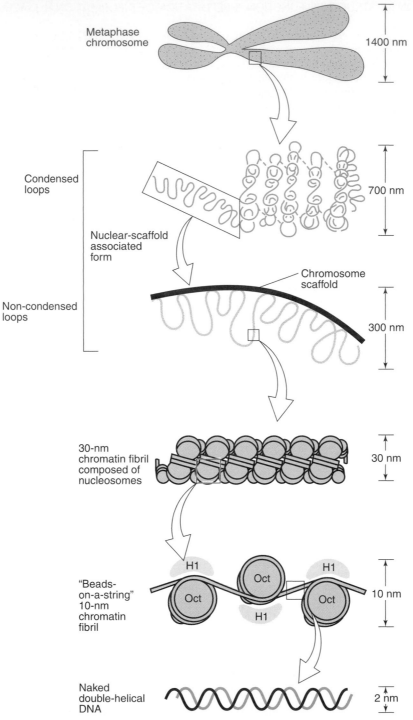

Figure 35–3. Shown is the extent of DNA packaging in metaphase chromosomes (*top*) to noted duplex DNA (*bottom*). Chromosomal DNA is packaged and organized at several levels as shown (see Table 35–2). Each phase of condensation or compaction and organization (*bottom to top*) decreases overall DNA accessibility to an extent that the DNA sequences in metaphase chromosomes are almost totally transcriptionally inert. In toto, these five levels of DNA compaction result in nearly a 10^4-fold linear decrease in end-to-end DNA length. Complete condensation and decondensation of the linear DNA in chromosomes occur in the space of hours during the normal replicative cell cycle (see Figure 35–20).

Certain cells of insects, eg, *Chironomus,* contain giant chromosomes that have been replicated for ten cycles without separation of daughter chromatids. These copies of DNA line up side by side in precise register and produce a banded chromosome containing regions of condensed chromatin and lighter bands of more extended chromatin. Transcriptionally active regions of these **polytene chromosomes** are especially decondensed into **"puffs"** that can be shown to contain the enzymes responsible for transcription and to be the sites of RNA synthesis (Figure 35–4).

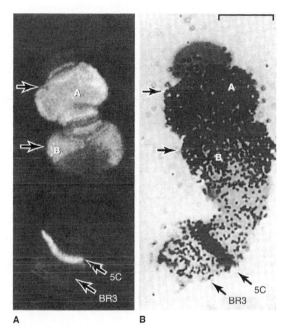

A   **B**

Figure 35–4. Illustration of the tight correlation between the presence of RNA polymerase II and messenger RNA synthesis. A number of genes, labeled A, B (*top*), and 5C, but not genes at locus (band) BR3 (5C, BR3, *bottom*) are activated when *Chironomus tentans* larvae are subjected to heat shock (39 °C for 30 minutes). **(A)** Distribution of RNA polymerase II in isolated chromosome IV from the salivary gland (at arrows). The enzyme was detected by immunofluorescence using an antibody directed against the polymerase. The 5C and BR3 are specific bands of chromosome IV, and the arrows indicate puffs. **(B)** Autoradiogram of a chromosome IV that was incubated in ^{3}H-uridine to label the RNA. Note the correspondence of the immunofluorescence and presence of the radioactive RNA (black dots). Bar = 7 μm. (Reproduced, with permission, from Sass H: RNA polymerase B in polytene chromosomes. Cell 1982;28:274. Copyright © 1982. Reprinted with permission from Elsevier.)

DNA IS ORGANIZED INTO CHROMOSOMES

At metaphase, mammalian **chromosomes** possess a twofold symmetry, with the identical duplicated **sister chromatids** connected at a **centromere,** the relative position of which is characteristic for a given chromosome (Figure 35–5). The centromere is an adenine-thymine (A–T) rich region ranging in size from 10^2 (brewers' yeast) to 10^6 (mammals) base pairs. It binds several proteins with high affinity. This complex, called the **kinetochore,** provides the anchor for the mitotic spindle. It thus is an essential structure for chromosomal segregation during mitosis.

The ends of each chromosome contain structures called **telomeres.** Telomeres consist of short, repeat TG-rich sequences. Human telomeres have a variable number of repeats of the sequence 5′-TTAGGG-3′, which can extend for several kilobases. **Telomerase,** a multisubunit RNA-containing complex related to viral RNA-dependent DNA polymerases (reverse transcriptases), is the enzyme responsible for telomere synthesis and thus for maintaining the length of the telomere. Since telomere shortening has been associated with both malignant transformation and aging, telomerase has become an attractive target for cancer chemotherapy and drug development. Each sister chromatid contains one double-stranded DNA molecule. During interphase, the packing of the DNA molecule is less dense than it is in the condensed chromosome during metaphase. Metaphase chromosomes are nearly completely transcriptionally inactive.

The human haploid genome consists of about 3×10^9 bp and about 1.7×10^7 nucleosomes. Thus, each of the 23 chromatids in the human haploid genome would contain on the average 1.3×10^8 nucleotides in one double-stranded DNA molecule. The length of each DNA molecule must be compressed about 8000-fold to generate the structure of a condensed metaphase chromosome! In metaphase chromosomes, the 30-nm chromatin fibers are also folded into a series of **looped domains,** the proximal portions of which are anchored to a nonhistone proteinaceous scaffolding within the nucleus (Figure 35–3). The packing ratios of each of the orders of DNA structure are summarized in Table 35–2.

The packaging of nucleoproteins within chromatids is not random, as evidenced by the characteristic patterns observed when chromosomes are stained with specific dyes such as quinacrine or Giemsa's stain (Figure 35–6).

From individual to individual within a single species, the pattern of staining (banding) of the entire chromosome complement is highly reproducible; nonetheless, it differs significantly from other species, even those closely related. Thus, the packaging of the nucleoproteins in chromosomes of higher eukaryotes must in

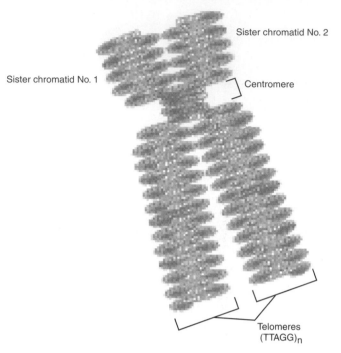

Sister chromatid No. 2

Sister chromatid No. 1

Centromere

Telomeres
(TTAGG)$_n$

Figure 35–5. The two sister chromatids of human chromosome 12. The location of the A+T-rich centromeric region connecting sister chromatids is indicated, as are two of the four telomeres residing at the very ends of the chromatids that are attached one to the other at the centromere.

some way be dependent upon species-specific characteristics of the DNA molecules.

A combination of specialized staining techniques and high-resolution microscopy has allowed geneticists to quite precisely map thousands of genes to specific regions of mouse and human chromosomes. With the recent elucidation of the human and mouse genome sequences, it has become clear that many of these visual mapping methods were remarkably accurate.

Coding Regions Are Often Interrupted by Intervening Sequences

The **protein coding regions of DNA,** the transcripts of which ultimately appear in the cytoplasm as single mRNA molecules, are usually **interrupted in the eukary-**

Table 35–2. The packing ratios of each of the orders of DNA structure.

Chromatin Form	Packing Ratio
Naked double-helical DNA	~1.0
10-nm fibril of nucleosomes	7–10
30-nm chromatin fiber of superhelical nucleosomes	40–60
Condensed metaphase chromosome of loops	8000

otic genome by large intervening sequences of nonprotein coding DNA. Accordingly, the primary transcripts of DNA (mRNA precursors, originally termed hnRNA because this species of RNA was quite heterogeneous in size [length] and mostly restricted to the nucleus), contain noncoding intervening sequences of RNA that must be removed in a process which also joins together the appropriate coding segments to form the mature mRNA. Most coding sequences for a single mRNA are interrupted in the genome (and thus in the primary transcript) by at least one—and in some cases as many as 50—noncoding intervening sequences **(introns).** In most cases, the introns are much longer than the continuous coding regions **(exons).** The processing of the primary transcript, which involves removal of introns and splicing of adjacent exons, is described in detail in Chapter 36.

The function of the intervening sequences, or introns, is not clear. They may serve to separate functional domains (exons) of coding information in a form that permits genetic rearrangement by recombination to occur more rapidly than if all coding regions for a given genetic function were contiguous. Such an enhanced rate of genetic rearrangement of functional domains might allow more rapid evolution of biologic function. The relationships among chromosomal DNA, gene clusters on the chromosome, the exon-intron structure of genes, and the final mRNA product are illustrated in Figure 35–7.

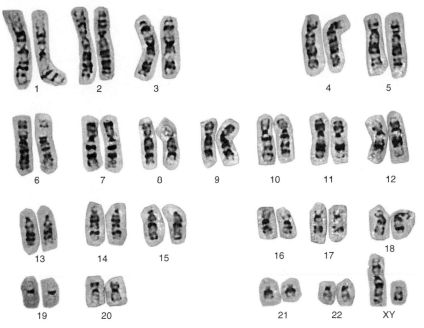

Figure 35–6. A human karyotype (of a man with a normal 46,XY constitution), in which the metaphase chromosomes have been stained by the Giemsa method and aligned according to the Paris Convention. (Courtesy of H Lawce and F Conte.)

MUCH OF THE MAMMALIAN GENOME IS REDUNDANT & MUCH IS NOT TRANSCRIBED

The haploid genome of each human cell consists of 3×10^9 base pairs of DNA subdivided into 23 chromosomes. The entire haploid genome contains sufficient DNA to code for nearly 1.5 million average sized genes. However, studies of mutation rates and of the complexities of the genomes of higher organisms strongly suggest that humans have < 100,000 proteins encoded by the ~1% of the human genome that is composed of exonic DNA. This implies that most of the DNA is non-protein coding—ie, its information is never translated into an amino acid sequence of a protein molecule. Certainly, some of the excess DNA sequences serve to regulate the expression of genes during development, differentiation, and adaptation to the environment, either by serving as binding sites for regulatory proteins or by encoding regulatory RNAs (ie, miRNAs). Some excess clearly makes up the intervening sequences or introns (24% of the total human genome) that split the coding regions of genes, but much of the excess appears to be composed of many families of repeated sequences for which no functions have been clearly defined. A summary of the salient features of the human genome is presented in Chapter 39.

The DNA in a eukaryotic genome can be divided into different "sequence classes." These are **unique-sequence, or nonrepetitive, DNA** and **repetitive-sequence DNA.** In the haploid genome, unique-sequence DNA generally includes the single copy genes that code for proteins. The repetitive DNA in the haploid genome includes sequences that vary in copy number from 2 to as many as 10^7 copies per cell.

More Than Half the DNA in Eukaryotic Organisms Is in Unique or Nonrepetitive Sequences

This estimation (and the distribution of repetitive-sequence DNA) is based on a variety of DNA-RNA hybridization techniques and, more recently, on direct DNA sequencing. Similar techniques are used to estimate the number of active genes in a population of unique-sequence DNA. In brewers' yeast (*Saccharomyces cerevisiae,* a lower eukaryote), about two thirds of its 6200 genes are expressed. In typical tissues in a higher eukaryote (eg, mammalian liver and kidney), between 10,000 and 15,000 genes are expressed. Different combinations of genes are expressed in each tissue, of course, and how this is accomplished is one of the major unanswered questions in biology.

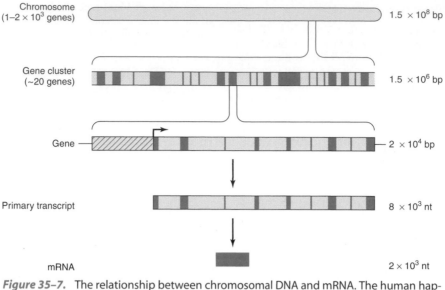

Figure 35–7. The relationship between chromosomal DNA and mRNA. The human haploid DNA complement of 3×10^9 base pairs (bp) is distributed between 23 chromosomes. Genes are clustered on these chromosomes. An average gene is 2×10^4 bp in length, including the regulatory region (hatched area), which is usually located at the 5′ end of the gene. The regulatory region is shown here as being adjacent to the transcription initiation site (arrow). Most eukaryotic genes have alternating exons and introns. In this example, there are nine exons (dark colored areas) and eight introns (light colored areas). The introns are removed from the primary transcript by the processing reaction, and the exons are ligated together in sequence to form the mature mRNA. (nt, nucleotides.)

In Human DNA, at Least 30% of the Genome Consists of Repetitive Sequences

Repetitive-sequence DNA can be broadly classified as moderately repetitive or as highly repetitive. The highly repetitive sequences consist of 5–500 base pair lengths repeated many times in tandem. These sequences are usually clustered in centromeres and telomeres of the chromosome and are present in about 1–10 million copies per haploid genome. These sequences are transcriptionally inactive and may play a structural role in the chromosome (see Chapter 39).

The moderately repetitive sequences, which are defined as being present in numbers of less than 10^6 copies per haploid genome, are not clustered but are interspersed with unique sequences. In many cases, these long interspersed repeats are transcribed by RNA polymerase II and contain caps indistinguishable from those on mRNA.

Depending on their length, moderately repetitive sequences are classified as **long interspersed repeat sequences (LINEs)** or **short interspersed repeat sequences (SINEs).** Both types appear to be **retroposons,** ie, they arose from movement from one location to another (**transposition**) through an RNA intermediate by the action of reverse transcriptase that transcribes an RNA template into DNA. Mammalian genomes contain 20,000–50,000 copies of the 6–7 kb LINEs. These represent species-specific families of repeat elements. SINEs are shorter (70–300 bp), and there may be more than 100,000 copies per genome. Of the SINEs in the human genome, one family, the **Alu family,** is present in about 500,000 copies per haploid genome and accounts for at least 5–6% of the human genome. Members of the human Alu family and their closely related analogs in other animals are transcribed as integral components of hnRNA or as discrete RNA molecules, including the well-studied 4.5S RNA and 7S RNA. These particular family members are highly conserved within a species as well as between mammalian species. Components of the short interspersed repeats, including the members of the Alu family, may be mobile elements, capable of jumping into and out of various sites within the genome (see below). This can have disastrous results, as exemplified by the insertion of Alu sequences into a gene, which, when so mutated, causes neurofibromatosis.

Microsatellite Repeat Sequences

One category of repeat sequences exists as both dispersed and grouped tandem arrays. The sequences consist of 2–6 bp repeated up to 50 times. These **microsatellite sequences** most commonly are found as dinucleotide repeats of AC on one strand and TG on the opposite strand, but several other forms occur, including CG, AT, and CA. The AC repeat sequences are estimated to occur at 50,000–100,000 locations in the genome. At any locus, the number of these repeats may vary on the two chromosomes, thus providing heterozygosity of the number of copies of a particular microsatellite number in an individual. This is a heritable trait, and, because of their number and the ease of detecting them using the polymerase chain reaction (PCR) (Chapter 39), AC repeats are very useful in constructing genetic linkage maps. Most genes are associated with one or more microsatellite markers, so the relative position of genes on chromosomes can be assessed, as can the association of a gene with a disease. Using PCR, a large number of family members can be rapidly screened for a certain **microsatellite polymorphism.** The association of a specific polymorphism with a gene in affected family members—and the lack of this association in unaffected members—may be the first clue about the genetic basis of a disease.

Trinucleotide sequences that increase in number (microsatellite instability) can cause disease. The unstable $p(CGG)_n$ repeat sequence is associated with the fragile X syndrome. Other trinucleotide repeats that undergo dynamic mutation (usually an increase) are associated with Huntington's chorea (CAG), myotonic dystrophy (CTG), spinobulbar muscular atrophy (CAG), and Kennedy's disease (CAG).

ONE PERCENT OF CELLULAR DNA IS IN MITOCHONDRIA

The majority of the peptides in mitochondria (about 54 out of 67) are coded by nuclear genes. The rest are coded by genes found in mitochondrial (mt) DNA. Human mitochondria contain two to ten copies of a small circular double-stranded DNA molecule that makes up approximately 1% of total cellular DNA. This mtDNA codes for mt ribosomal and transfer RNAs and for 13 proteins that play key roles in the respiratory chain. The linearized structural map of the human mitochondrial genes is shown in Figure 35–8. Some of the features of mtDNA are shown in Table 35–3.

An important feature of human mitochondrial mtDNA is that—because all mitochondria are contributed by the ovum during zygote formation—it is transmitted by maternal nonmendelian inheritance. Thus, in diseases resulting from mutations of mtDNA, an affected mother would in theory pass the disease to all of her children but only her daughters would transmit the trait. However, in some cases, deletions in mtDNA occur during oogenesis and thus are not inherited from the mother. A number of diseases have now been shown to be due to mutations of mtDNA. These include a variety of myopathies, neurologic disorders, and some cases of diabetes mellitus.

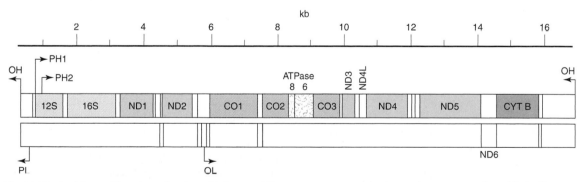

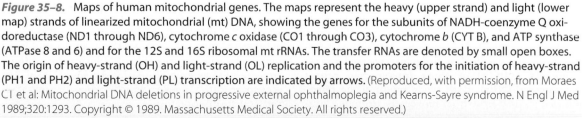

Figure 35–8. Maps of human mitochondrial genes. The maps represent the heavy (upper strand) and light (lower map) strands of linearized mitochondrial (mt) DNA, showing the genes for the subunits of NADH-coenzyme Q oxidoreductase (ND1 through ND6), cytochrome *c* oxidase (CO1 through CO3), cytochrome *b* (CYT B), and ATP synthase (ATPase 8 and 6) and for the 12S and 16S ribosomal mt rRNAs. The transfer RNAs are denoted by small open boxes. The origin of heavy-strand (OH) and light-strand (OL) replication and the promoters for the initiation of heavy-strand (PH1 and PH2) and light-strand (PL) transcription are indicated by arrows. (Reproduced, with permission, from Moraes CT et al: Mitochondrial DNA deletions in progressive external ophthalmoplegia and Kearns-Sayre syndrome. N Engl J Med 1989;320:1293. Copyright © 1989. Massachusetts Medical Society. All rights reserved.)

Table 35–3. Some major features of the structure and function of human mitochondrial DNA.[1]

- Is circular, double-stranded, and composed of heavy (H) and light (L) chains or strands
- Contains 16,569 bp
- Encodes 13 protein subunits of the respiratory chain (of a total of about 67)
    - Seven subunits of NADH dehydrogenase (complex I)
    - Cytochrome *b* of complex III
    - Three subunits of cytochrome oxidase (complex IV)
    - Two subunits of ATP synthase
- Encodes large (16s) and small (12s) mt ribosomal RNAs
- Encodes 22 mt tRNA molecules
- Genetic code differs slightly from the standard code
    - UGA (standard stop codon) is read as Trp
    - AGA and AGG (standard codons for Arg) are read as stop codons
- Contains very few untranslated sequences
- High mutation rate (five to ten times that of nuclear DNA)
- Comparisons of mtDNA sequences provide evidence about evolutionary origins of primates and other species

---

[1]Adapted from Harding AE: Neurological disease and mitochondrial genes. Trends Neurol Sci 1991;14:132. Copyright © 1991. Reprinted with permission from Elsevier.

GENETIC MATERIAL CAN BE ALTERED & REARRANGED

An alteration in the sequence of purine and pyrimidine bases in a gene due to a change—a removal or an insertion—of one or more bases may result in an altered gene product. Such alteration in the genetic material results in a **mutation** whose consequences are discussed in detail in Chapter 37.

Chromosomal Recombination Is One Way of Rearranging Genetic Material

Genetic information can be exchanged between similar or homologous chromosomes. The exchange or **recombination** event occurs primarily during meiosis in mammalian cells and requires alignment of homologous metaphase chromosomes, an alignment that almost always occurs with great exactness. A process of crossing over occurs as shown in Figure 35–9. This usually results in an equal and reciprocal exchange of genetic information between homologous chromosomes. If the homologous chromosomes possess different alleles of the same genes, the crossover may produce noticeable and heritable genetic linkage differences. In the rare case where the alignment of homologous chromosomes is not exact, the crossing over or recombination event may result in an unequal exchange of information. One chromosome may receive less genetic material and thus a deletion, while the other partner of the chromosome pair receives more genetic material and thus an insertion or duplication (Figure 35–9). Unequal crossing over does occur in humans, as evidenced by the existence of hemoglobins designated Lepore and anti-Lepore (Figure 35–10). The farther apart two sequences are on an individual chromosome, the greater the likelihood of a crossover recombination event. This is the basis for genetic mapping methods. **Unequal crossover** affects tandem arrays of repeated DNAs whether they are related globin genes, as in Figure 35–10, or more abundant repetitive DNA. Unequal crossover through slippage in the pairing can result in expansion or contraction in the copy number of the repeat family and may contribute to the expansion and fixation of variant members throughout the array.

Chromosomal Integration Occurs with Some Viruses

Some bacterial viruses (bacteriophages) are capable of recombining with the DNA of a bacterial host in such a

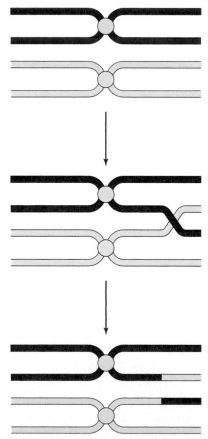

Figure 35–9. The process of crossing-over between homologous metaphase chromosomes to generate recombinant chromosomes. See also Figure 35–12.

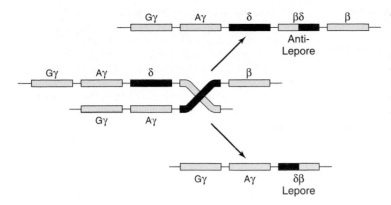

Figure 35–10. The process of unequal crossover in the region of the mammalian genome that harbors the structural genes encoding hemoglobins and the generation of the unequal recombinant products hemoglobin delta-beta Lepore and beta-delta anti-Lepore. The examples given show the locations of the crossover regions between amino acid residues. (Redrawn and reproduced, with permission, from Clegg JB, Weatherall DJ: β⁰ Thalassemia: Time for a reappraisal? Lancet 1974;2:133. Copyright © 1974. Reprinted with permission from Elsevier.)

way that the genetic information of the bacteriophage is incorporated in a linear fashion into the genetic information of the host. This integration, which is a form of recombination, occurs by the mechanism illustrated in Figure 35–11. The backbone of the circular bacteriophage genome is broken, as is that of the DNA molecule of the host; the appropriate ends are resealed with the proper polarity. The bacteriophage DNA is figuratively straightened out ("linearized") as it is integrated into the bacterial DNA molecule—frequently a closed circle as well. The site at which the bacteriophage genome integrates or recombines with the bacterial genome is chosen by one of two mechanisms. If the bacteriophage contains a DNA sequence **homologous** to a sequence in the host DNA molecule, then a recombination event analogous to that occurring between homologous chromosomes can occur. However, some bacteriophages synthesize proteins that bind specific sites on bacterial chromosomes to a **nonhomologous** site characteristic of the bacteriophage DNA molecule. Integration occurs at the site and is said to be **"site-specific."**

Many animal viruses, particularly the oncogenic viruses—either directly or, in the case of RNA viruses such as HIV that causes AIDS, their DNA transcripts generated by the action of the viral RNA-dependent DNA polymerase, or reverse transcriptase—can be integrated into chromosomes of the mammalian cell. The integration of the animal virus DNA into the animal genome generally is not "site-specific" but does display site preferences.

Transposition Can Produce Processed Genes

In eukaryotic cells, small DNA elements that clearly are not viruses are capable of transposing themselves in and out of the host genome in ways that affect the function of neighboring DNA sequences. These mobile elements, sometimes called "jumping DNA," can carry flanking regions of DNA and, therefore, profoundly affect evolution. As mentioned above, the Alu family of moderately repeated DNA sequences has structural characteristics similar to the termini of retroviruses, which would account for the ability of the latter to move into and out of the mammalian genome.

Direct evidence for the transposition of other small DNA elements into the human genome has been provided by the discovery of "processed genes" for immunoglobulin molecules, α-globin molecules, and several others. These **processed genes** consist of DNA sequences identical or nearly identical to those of the messenger RNA for the appropriate gene product. That

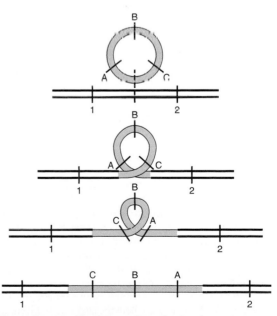

Figure 35–11. The integration of a circular genome from a virus (with genes A, B, and C) into the DNA molecule of a host (with genes 1 and 2) and the consequent ordering of the genes.

is, the 5′ nontranscribed region, the coding region without intron representation, and the 3′ poly(A) tail are all present contiguously. This particular DNA sequence arrangement must have resulted from the reverse transcription of an appropriately processed messenger RNA molecule from which the intron regions had been removed and the poly(A) tail added. The only recognized mechanism this reverse transcript could have used to integrate into the genome would have been a transposition event. In fact, these "processed genes" have short terminal repeats at each end, as do known transposed sequences in lower organisms. In the absence of their transcription and thus genetic selection for function, many of the processed genes have been randomly altered through evolution so that they now contain nonsense codons which preclude their ability to encode a functional, intact protein (see Chapter 37). Thus, they are referred to as **"pseudogenes."**

Gene Conversion Produces Rearrangements

Besides unequal crossover and transposition, a third mechanism can effect rapid changes in the genetic material. Similar sequences on homologous or nonhomologous chromosomes may occasionally pair up and eliminate any mismatched sequences between them. This may lead to the accidental fixation of one variant or another throughout a family of repeated sequences and thereby homogenize the sequences of the members of repetitive DNA families. This latter process is referred to as **gene conversion.**

Sister Chromatids Exchange

In diploid eukaryotic organisms such as humans, after cells progress through the S phase they contain a tetraploid content of DNA. This is in the form of sister chromatids of chromosome pairs (Figure 35–6). Each of these sister chromatids contains identical genetic information since each is a product of the semiconservative replication of the original parent DNA molecule of that chromosome. Crossing over occurs between these genetically identical sister chromatids. Of course, these **sister chromatid exchanges** (Figure 35–12) have no genetic consequence as long as the exchange is the result of an equal crossover.

Immunoglobulin Genes Rearrange

In mammalian cells, some interesting gene rearrangements occur normally during development and differentiation. For example, in mice the V_L and C_L genes for a single immunoglobulin molecule (see Chapter 38) are widely separated in the germ line DNA. In the DNA of a differentiated immunoglobulin-producing (plasma)

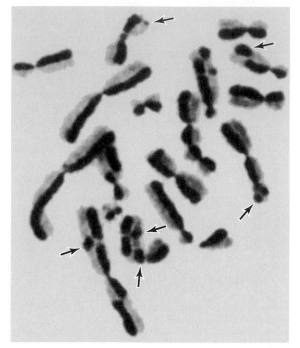

Figure 35–12. Sister chromatid exchanges between human chromosomes. These are detectable by Giemsa staining of the chromosomes of cells replicated for two cycles in the presence of bromodeoxyuridine. The arrows indicate some regions of exchange. (Courtesy of S Wolff and J Bodycote.)

cell, the same V_L and C_L genes have been moved physically closer together in the genome and into the same transcription unit. However, even then, this rearrangement of DNA during differentiation does not bring the V_L and C_L genes into contiguity in the DNA. Instead, the DNA contains an interspersed or interruption sequence of about 1200 base pairs at or near the junction of the V and C regions. The interspersed sequence is transcribed into RNA along with the V_L and C_L genes, and the interspersed information is removed from the RNA during its nuclear processing (Chapters 36 and 38).

DNA SYNTHESIS & REPLICATION ARE RIGIDLY CONTROLLED

The primary function of DNA replication is understood to be the provision of progeny with the genetic information possessed by the parent. Thus, the replication of DNA must be complete and carried out in such a way as to maintain genetic stability within the organism and the species. The process of DNA replication is

complex and involves many cellular functions and several verification procedures to ensure fidelity in replication. About 30 proteins are involved in the replication of the *E coli* chromosome, and this process is more complex in eukaryotic organisms. The first enzymologic observations on DNA replication were made in *E coli* by Kornberg, who described in that organism the existence of an enzyme now called DNA polymerase I. This enzyme has multiple catalytic activities, a complex structure, and a requirement for the triphosphates of the four deoxyribonucleosides of adenine, guanine, cytosine, and thymine. The polymerization reaction catalyzed by DNA polymerase I of *E coli* has served as a prototype for all DNA polymerases of both prokaryotes and eukaryotes, even though it is now recognized that the major role of this polymerase is to complete replication on the lagging strand.

In all cells, replication can occur only from a single-stranded DNA (ssDNA) template. Mechanisms must exist to target the site of initiation of replication and to unwind the double-stranded DNA (dsDNA) in that region. The replication complex must then form. After replication is complete in an area, the parent and daughter strands must re-form dsDNA. In eukaryotic cells, an additional step must occur. The dsDNA must precisely re-form the chromatin structure, including nucleosomes, that existed prior to the onset of replication. Although this entire process is not well understood in eukaryotic cells, replication has been quite precisely described in prokaryotic cells, and the general principles are thought to be the same in both. The major steps are listed in Table 35–4, illustrated in Figure 35–13, and discussed, in sequence, below. A number of proteins, most with specific enzymatic action, are involved in this process (Table 35–5).

The Origin of Replication

At the **origin of replication (ori),** there is an association of sequence-specific dsDNA-binding proteins with a series of direct repeat DNA sequences. In bacteriophage λ, the oriλ is bound by the λ-encoded O protein to four adjacent sites. In *E coli,* the oriC is bound by the protein dnaA. In both cases, a complex is formed consisting of 150–250 bp of DNA and multimers of the DNA-binding protein. This leads to the local denaturation and unwinding of an adjacent A+T-rich region of DNA. Functionally similar **autonomously replicating sequences (ARS) or replicators** have been identified in yeast cells. The ARS contains a somewhat degenerate 11-bp sequence called the **origin replication element (ORE).** The ORE binds a set of proteins, analogous to the dnaA protein of *E coli,* which is collectively called the **origin recognition complex (ORC).** ORC homologs have been found in all eukaryotes examined. The ORE is located adjacent to an approximately 80-bp A+T-rich sequence that is easy to unwind. This is called the **DNA unwinding element (DUE).** The DUE is the origin of replication in yeast.

Consensus sequences similar to ori or ARS in structure or function have not been precisely defined in mammalian cells, though several of the proteins that participate in ori recognition and function have been identified and appear quite similar to their yeast counterparts in both amino acid sequence and function.

Unwinding of DNA

The interaction of proteins with ori defines the start site of replication and provides a short region of ssDNA essential for initiation of synthesis of the nascent DNA strand. This process requires the formation of a number of protein-protein and protein-DNA interactions. A critical step is provided by a DNA helicase that allows for processive unwinding of DNA. In uninfected *E coli,* this function is provided by a complex of dnaB helicase and the dnaC protein. Single-stranded DNA-binding proteins (SSBs) stabilize this complex. In λ phage-infected *E coli,* the phage protein P binds to dnaB and the P/dnaB complex binds to oriλ by interacting with the O protein. dnaB is not an active helicase when in the P/dnaB/O complex. Three *E coli* heat shock proteins (dnaK, dnaJ, and GrpE) cooperate to remove the P protein and activate the dnaB helicase. In cooperation with SSB, this leads to DNA unwinding and active replication. In this way, the replication of the λ phage is accomplished at the expense of replication of the host *E coli* cell.

Formation of the Replication Fork

A replication fork consists of four components that form in the following sequence: (1) the DNA helicase unwinds a short segment of the parental duplex DNA; (2) a primase initiates synthesis of an RNA molecule that is essential for priming DNA synthesis; (3) the DNA polymerase initiates nascent, daughter strand synthesis; and (4) SSBs bind to ssDNA and prevent prema-

Table 35–4. Steps involved in DNA replication in eukaryotes.

1. Identification of the origins of replication
2. Unwinding (denaturation) of dsDNA to provide an ssDNA template
3. Formation of the replication fork
4. Initiation of DNA synthesis and elongation
5. Formation of replication bubbles with ligation of the newly synthesized DNA segments
6. Reconstitution of chromatin structure

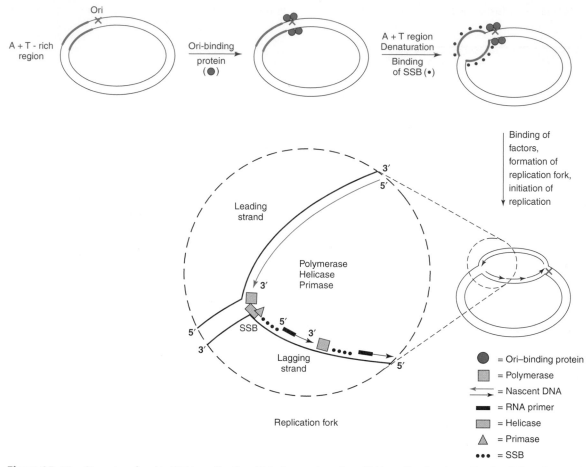

Figure 35–13. Steps involved in DNA replication. This figure describes DNA replication in an *E coli* cell, but the general steps are similar in eukaryotes. A specific interaction of a protein (the O protein) to the origin of replication (ori) results in local unwinding of DNA at an adjacent A+T-rich region. The DNA in this area is maintained in the single-strand conformation (ssDNA) by single-strand-binding proteins (SSBs). This allows a variety of proteins, including helicase, primase, and DNA polymerase, to bind and to initiate DNA synthesis. The replication fork proceeds as DNA synthesis occurs continuously (long arrow) on the leading strand and discontinuously (short arrows) on the lagging strand. The nascent DNA is always synthesized in the 5′ to 3′ direction, as DNA polymerases can add a nucleotide only to the 3′ end of a DNA strand.

ture reannealing of ssDNA to dsDNA. These reactions are illustrated in Figure 35–13.

The polymerase III holoenzyme (the *dnaE* gene product in *E coli*) binds to template DNA as part of a multiprotein complex that consists of several polymerase accessory factors (β, γ, δ, δ', and τ). DNA polymerases only synthesize DNA in the 5′ to 3′ direction, and only one of the several different types of polymerases is involved at the replication fork. Because the DNA strands are antiparallel (Chapter 34), the polymerase functions asymmetrically. On the **leading (forward) strand,** the DNA is synthesized continuously.

On the **lagging (retrograde) strand,** the DNA is synthesized in short (1–5 kb; see Figure 35–16) fragments, the so-called **Okazaki fragments.** Several Okazaki fragments (up to 250) must be sequentially synthesized for each replication fork. To ensure that this happens, the helicase acts on the lagging strand to unwind dsDNA in a 5′ to 3′ direction. The helicase associates with the primase to afford the latter proper access to the template. This allows the RNA primer to be made and, in turn, the polymerase to begin replicating the DNA. This is an important reaction sequence since DNA polymerases cannot initiate DNA synthesis de novo. The

Table 35–5. Classes of proteins involved in replication.

Protein	Function
DNA polymerases	Deoxynucleotide polymerization
Helicases	Processive unwinding of DNA
Topoisomerases	Relieve torsional strain that results from helicase-induced unwinding
DNA primase	Initiates synthesis of RNA primers
Single-strand binding proteins	Prevent premature reannealing of dsDNA
DNA ligase	Seals the single strand nick between the nascent chain and Okazaki fragments on lagging strand

mobile complex between helicase and primase has been called a **primosome.** As the synthesis of an Okazaki fragment is completed and the polymerase is released, a new primer has been synthesized. The same polymerase molecule remains associated with the replication fork and proceeds to synthesize the next Okazaki fragment.

The DNA Polymerase Complex

A number of different DNA polymerase molecules engage in DNA replication. These share three important properties: (1) **chain elongation,** (2) **processivity,** and (3) **proofreading.** Chain elongation accounts for the rate (in nucleotides per second) at which polymerization occurs. Processivity is an expression of the number of nucleotides added to the nascent chain before the polymerase disengages from the template. The proofreading function identifies copying errors and corrects them. In *E coli*, polymerase III (pol III) functions at the replication fork. Of all polymerases, it catalyzes the highest rate of chain elongation and is the most processive. It is capable of polymerizing 0.5 Mb of DNA during one cycle on the leading strand. Pol III is a large (> 1 MDa), ten-subunit protein complex in *E coli*. The two identical β subunits of pol III encircle the DNA template in a sliding "clamp," which accounts for the stability of the complex and for the high degree of processivity the enzyme exhibits.

Polymerase II (pol II) is mostly involved in proofreading and DNA repair. Polymerase I (pol I) completes chain synthesis between Okazaki fragments on the lagging strand. Eukaryotic cells have counterparts for each of these enzymes plus some additional ones. A comparison is shown in Table 35–6.

In mammalian cells, the polymerase is capable of polymerizing about 100 nucleotides per second, a rate

at least tenfold slower than the rate of polymerization of deoxynucleotides by the bacterial DNA polymerase complex. This reduced rate may result from interference by nucleosomes. It is not known how the replication complex negotiates nucleosomes.

Initiation & Elongation of DNA Synthesis

The initiation of DNA synthesis (Figure 35–14) requires **priming by a short length of RNA,** about 10–200 nucleotides long. This priming process involves the nucleophilic attack by the 3′-hydroxyl group of the RNA primer on the α phosphate of the first entering deoxynucleoside triphosphate (N in Figure 35–14) with the splitting off of pyrophosphate. The 3′-hydroxyl group of the recently attached deoxyribonucleoside monophosphate is then free to carry out a **nucleophilic attack** on the next entering deoxyribonucleoside triphosphate (N + 1 in Figure 35–14), again at its α phosphate moiety, with the splitting off of pyrophosphate. Of course, selection of the proper deoxyribonucleotide whose terminal 3′-hydroxyl group is to be attacked is dependent upon **proper base pairing with the other strand** of the DNA molecule according to the rules proposed originally by Watson and Crick (Figure 35–15). When an adenine deoxyribonucleoside monophosphoryl moiety is in the template position, a thymidine triphosphate will enter and its α phosphate will be attacked by the 3′-hydroxyl group of the deoxyribonucleoside monophosphoryl most recently added to the polymer. By this stepwise process, the template dictates which deoxyribonucleoside triphosphate is complementary and by hydrogen bonding holds it in place while the 3′-hydroxyl group of the growing strand attacks and incorporates the new nucleotide into the polymer. These segments of DNA attached to an RNA initiator component are the **Okazaki fragments** (Figure 35–16). In mammals, after many Okazaki fragments are generated, the replication complex begins to remove the RNA primers, to fill in the gaps left by their removal

Table 35–6. A comparison of prokaryotic and eukaryotic DNA polymerases.

E coli	Mammalian	Function
I	α	Gap filling and synthesis of lagging strand
II	ε	DNA proofreading and repair
	β	DNA repair
	γ	Mitochondrial DNA synthesis
III	δ	Processive, leading strand synthesis

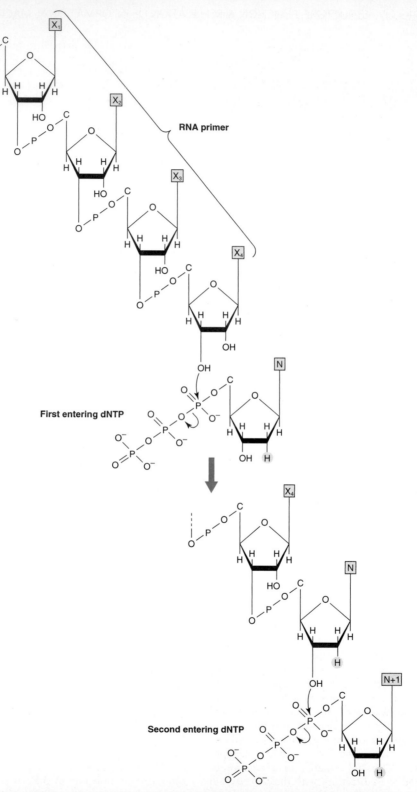

Figure 35–14. The initiation of DNA synthesis upon a primer of RNA and the subsequent attachment of the second deoxyribonucleoside triphosphate.

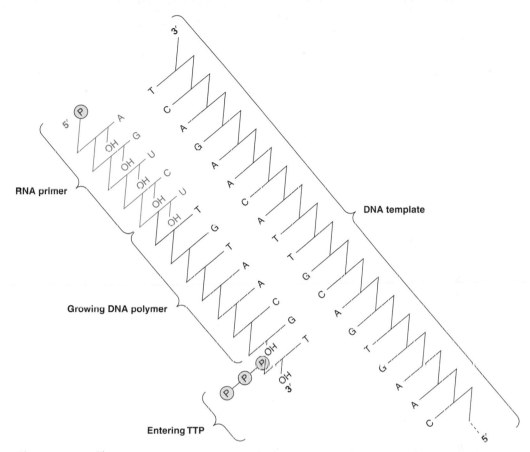

Figure 35–15. The RNA-primed synthesis of DNA demonstrating the template function of the complementary strand of parental DNA.

with the proper base-paired deoxynucleotide, and then to seal the fragments of newly synthesized DNA by enzymes referred to as **DNA ligases.**

Replication Exhibits Polarity

As has already been noted, DNA molecules are double-stranded and the two strands are antiparallel, ie, running in opposite directions. The replication of DNA in prokaryotes and eukaryotes occurs on both strands simultaneously. However, an enzyme capable of polymerizing DNA in the 3′ to 5′ direction does not exist in any organism, so that both of the newly replicated DNA strands cannot grow in the same direction simultaneously. Nevertheless, the same enzyme does replicate both strands at the same time. The single enzyme replicates one strand ("leading strand") in a continuous manner in the 5′ to 3′ direction, with the same overall forward direction. It replicates the other strand ("lagging strand") discontinuously while polymerizing the

nucleotides in short spurts of 150–250 nucleotides, again in the 5′ to 3′ direction, but at the same time it faces toward the back end of the preceding RNA primer rather than toward the unreplicated portion. This process of **semidiscontinuous DNA synthesis** is shown diagrammatically in Figures 35–13 and 35–16.

In the mammalian nuclear genome, most of the RNA primers are eventually removed as part of the replication process, whereas after replication of the mitochondrial genome the small piece of RNA remains as an integral part of the closed circular DNA structure.

Formation of Replication Bubbles

Replication proceeds from a single ori in the circular bacterial chromosome, composed of roughly 6×10^6 bp of DNA. This process is completed in about 30 minutes, a replication rate of 3×10^5 bp/min. The entire mammalian genome replicates in approximately 9 hours, the average period required for formation of a

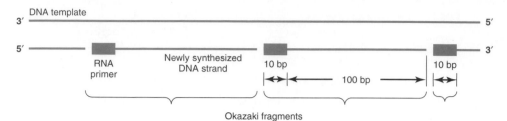

Figure 35–16. The discontinuous polymerization of deoxyribonucleotides on the lagging strand; formation of Okazaki fragments during lagging strand DNA synthesis is illustrated. Okazaki fragments are 100–250 nt long in eukaryotes, 1000–2000 bp in prokaryotes.

tetraploid genome from a diploid genome in a replicating cell. If a mammalian genome (3×10^9 bp) replicated at the same rate as bacteria (ie, 3×10^5 bp/min) from but a single ori, replication would take over 150 hours! Metazoan organisms get around this problem using two strategies. First, replication is bidirectional. Second, replication proceeds from multiple origins in each chromosome (a total of as many as 100 in humans). Thus, replication occurs in both directions along all of the chromosomes, and both strands are replicated simultaneously. This replication process generates **"replication bubbles"** (Figure 35–17).

The multiple sites that serve as origins for DNA replication in eukaryotes are poorly defined except in a few animal viruses and in yeast. However, it is clear that initiation is regulated both spatially and temporally, since clusters of adjacent sites initiate replication synchronously. Replication firing, or DNA replication initiation at a replicator/ori, is influenced by a number of distinct properties of chromatin structure that are just beginning to be understood. It is clear, however, that there are more replicators and excess ORC than needed to replicate the mammalian genome within the time of a typical S-phase. Therefore, mechanisms for control-

ling the excess ORC-bound replicators must exist. Understanding the control of this process is a major challenge.

During the replication of DNA, there must be a separation of the two strands to allow each to serve as a template by hydrogen bonding its nucleotide bases to the incoming deoxynucleoside triphosphate. The separation of the DNA double helix is promoted by SSBs, specific protein molecules that stabilize the single-stranded structure as the replication fork progresses. These stabilizing proteins bind cooperatively and stoichiometrically to the single strands without interfering with the abilities of the nucleotides to serve as templates (Figure 35–13). In addition to separating the two strands of the double helix, there must be an unwinding of the molecule (once every 10 nucleotide pairs) to allow strand separation. This must happen in segments, given the time during which DNA replication occurs. There are multiple "swivels" interspersed in the DNA molecules of all organisms. The swivel function is provided by specific enzymes that introduce **"nicks" in one strand of the unwinding double helix,** thereby allowing the unwinding process to proceed. The nicks are quickly resealed without requiring energy input,

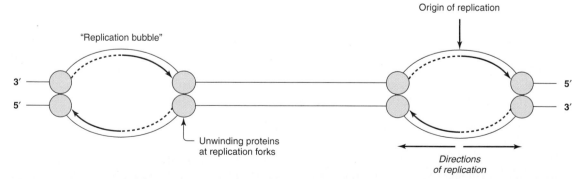

Figure 35–17. The generation of "replication bubbles" during the process of DNA synthesis. The bidirectional replication and the proposed positions of unwinding proteins at the replication forks are depicted.

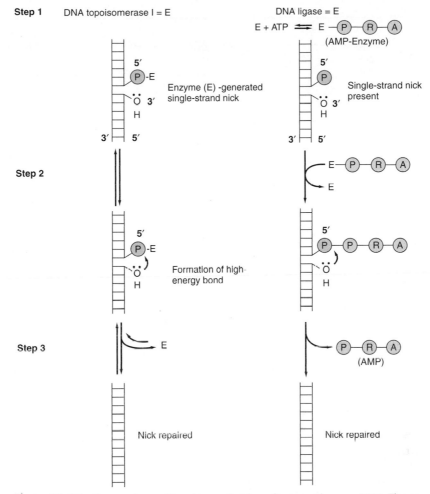

Figure 35–18. Comparison of two types of nick-sealing reactions on DNA. The series of reactions at left is catalyzed by DNA topoisomerase I, that at right by DNA ligase; P = phosphate, R = ribose, A = adenine. (Slightly modified and reproduced, with permission, from Lehninger AL: *Biochemistry*, 2nd ed. Worth, 1975. Copyright © 1975 by Worth Publishers. Used with permission from W. H. Freeman and Company.)

because of the formation of a high-energy covalent bond between the nicked phosphodiester backbone and the nicking-sealing enzyme. The nicking-resealing enzymes are called **DNA topoisomerases.** This process is depicted diagrammatically in Figure 35–18 and there compared with the ATP-dependent resealing carried out by the DNA ligases. Topoisomerases are also capable of unwinding supercoiled DNA. Supercoiled DNA is a higher-ordered structure occurring in circular DNA molecules wrapped around a core, as depicted in Figure 35–19.

There exists in one species of animal viruses (retroviruses) a class of enzymes capable of synthesizing a single-stranded and then a double-stranded DNA molecule from a single-stranded RNA template. This polymerase,

RNA-dependent DNA polymerase, or **"reverse transcriptase,"** first synthesizes a DNA-RNA hybrid molecule utilizing the RNA genome as a template. A specific virus-encoded nuclease, RNase H, degrades the RNA strand, and the remaining DNA strand in turn serves as a template to form a double-stranded DNA molecule containing the information originally present in the RNA genome of the animal virus.

Reconstitution of Chromatin Structure

There is evidence that nuclear organization and chromatin structure are involved in determining the regulation and initiation of DNA synthesis. As noted above,

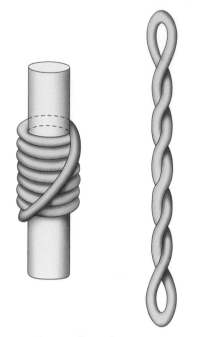

Figure 35–19. Supercoiling of DNA. A left-handed toroidal (solenoidal) supercoil, at left, will convert to a right-handed interwound supercoil, at right, when the cylindric core is removed. Such a transition is analogous to that which occurs when nucleosomes are disrupted by the high salt extraction of histones from chromatin.

the rate of polymerization in eukaryotic cells, which have chromatin and nucleosomes, is tenfold slower than that in prokaryotic cells, which have naked DNA. It is also clear that chromatin structure must be re-formed

after replication. Newly replicated DNA is rapidly assembled into nucleosomes, and the preexisting and newly assembled histone octamers are randomly distributed to each arm of the replication fork.

DNA Synthesis Occurs during the S Phase of the Cell Cycle

In animal cells, including human cells, the replication of the DNA genome occurs only at a specified time during the life span of the cell. This period is referred to as the synthetic or S phase. This is usually temporally separated from the mitotic phase by nonsynthetic periods referred to as gap 1 (G1) and gap 2 (G2), occurring before and after the S phase, respectively (Figure 35–20). Among other things, the cell prepares for DNA synthesis in G1 and for mitosis in G2. The cell regulates its DNA synthesis grossly by allowing it to occur only at specific times and mostly in cells preparing to divide by a mitotic process.

It appears that all eukaryotic cells have gene products that govern the transition from one phase of the cell cycle to another. The **cyclins** are a family of proteins whose concentration increases and decreases throughout the cell cycle—thus their name. The cyclins turn on, at the appropriate time, different **cyclin-dependent protein kinases (CDKs)** that phosphorylate substrates essential for progression through the cell cycle (Figure 35–21). For example, cyclin D levels rise in late G1 phase and allow progression beyond the **start (yeast)** or **restriction point (mammals),** the point beyond which cells irrevocably proceed into the S or DNA synthesis phase.

The D cyclins activate CDK4 and CDK6. These two kinases are also synthesized during G1 in cells undergoing active division. The D cyclins and CDK4 and CDK6 are nuclear proteins that assemble as a complex in

Figure 35–20. Mammalian cell cycle and cell cycle checkpoints. DNA, chromosome, and chromosome segregation integrity is continuously monitored throughout the cell cycle. If DNA damage is detected in either the G1 or the G2 phase of the cell cycle, if the genome is incompletely replicated, or if normal chromosome segregation machinery is incomplete (ie, a defective spindle), cells will not progress through the phase of the cycle in which defects are detected. In some cases, if the damage cannot be repaired, such cells undergo programmed cell death (apoptosis).

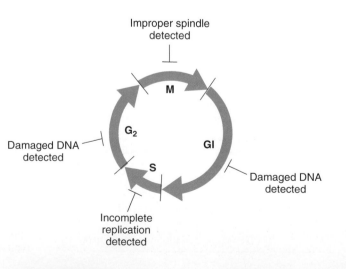

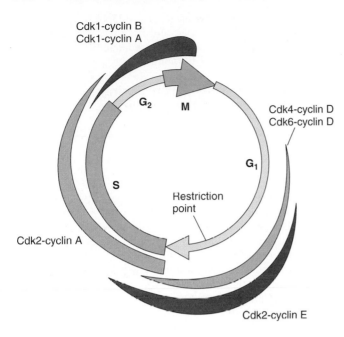

Figure 35–21. Schematic illustration of the points during the mammalian cell cycle during which the indicated cyclins and cyclin-dependent kinases are activated. The thickness of the various colored lines is indicative of the extent of activity.

late G1 phase. The complex is an active serine-threonine protein kinase. One substrate for this kinase is the retinoblastoma (Rb) protein. Rb is a cell cycle regulator because it binds to and inactivates a transcription factor (E2F) necessary for the transcription of certain genes (histone genes, DNA replication proteins, etc) needed for progression from G1 to S phase. The phosphorylation of Rb by CDK4 or CDK6 results in the release of E2F from Rb-mediated transcription repression—thus, gene activation ensues and cell cycle progression takes place.

Other cyclins and CDKs are involved in different aspects of cell cycle progression (Table 35–7). Cyclin E and CDK2 form a complex in late G1. Cyclin E is rapidly degraded, and the released CDK2 then forms a complex with cyclin A. This sequence is necessary for the initiation of DNA synthesis in S phase. A complex between cyclin B and CDK1 is rate-limiting for the G2/M transition in eukaryotic cells.

Many of the cancer-causing viruses (oncoviruses) and cancer-inducing genes (oncogenes) are capable of alleviating or disrupting the apparent restriction that normally controls the entry of mammalian cells from G1 into the S phase. From the foregoing, one might have surmised that excessive production of a cyclin—or production at an inappropriate time—might result in abnormal or unrestrained cell division. In this context it is noteworthy that the *bcl* oncogene associated with B cell lymphoma appears to be the cyclin D1 gene. Similarly, the oncoproteins (or transforming proteins) produced by several DNA viruses target the Rb transcription repressor for inactivation, inducing cell division inappropriately.

During the S phase, mammalian cells contain greater quantities of DNA polymerase than during the nonsynthetic phases of the cell cycle. Furthermore, those enzymes responsible for formation of the substrates for DNA synthesis—ie, deoxyribonucleoside triphosphates—are also increased in activity, and their activity will diminish following the synthetic phase until the reappearance of the signal for renewed DNA synthesis. During the S phase, the nuclear DNA is **completely replicated once and only once.** It seems that once chromatin has been replicated, it is marked so as to prevent its further replication until it again passes through mitosis. The molecular mechanisms for this phenomenon have yet to be elucidated.

In general, a given pair of chromosomes will replicate simultaneously and within a fixed portion of the S phase upon every replication. On a chromosome, clusters of replication units replicate coordinately. The nature of the

Table 35–7. Cyclins and cyclin-dependent kinases involved in cell cycle progression.

Cyclin	Kinase	Function
D	CDK4, CDK6	Progression past restriction point at G1/S boundary
E, A	CDK2	Initiation of DNA synthesis in early S phase
B	CDK1	Transition from G2 to M

signals that regulate DNA synthesis at these levels is unknown, but the regulation does appear to be an intrinsic property of each individual chromosome.

Enzymes Repair Damaged DNA

The maintenance of the integrity of the information in DNA molecules is of utmost importance to the survival of a particular organism as well as to survival of the species. Thus, it can be concluded that surviving species have evolved mechanisms for repairing DNA damage occurring as a result of either replication errors or environmental insults.

As described in Chapter 34, the major responsibility for the fidelity of replication resides in the specific pairing of nucleotide bases. Proper pairing is dependent upon the presence of the favored tautomers of the purine and pyrimidine nucleotides, but the equilibrium whereby one tautomer is more stable than another is only about 10^4 or 10^5 in favor of that with the greater stability. Although this is not favorable enough to ensure the high fidelity that is necessary, favoring of the preferred tautomers—and thus of the proper base pairing—could be ensured by monitoring the base pairing twice. Such double monitoring does appear to occur in both bacterial and mammalian systems: once at the time of insertion of the deoxyribonucleoside triphosphates, and later by a follow-up energy-requiring mechanism that removes all improper bases which may occur in the newly formed strand. This "proofreading" prevents tautomer-induced misincorporation from occurring more frequently than once every 10^8–10^{10} base pairs of DNA synthesized. The mechanisms responsible for this monitoring mechanism in *E coli* include the 3' to 5' exonuclease activities of one of the subunits of the pol III complex and of the pol I molecule. The analogous mammalian enzymes (δ and α) do not seem to possess such a nuclease proofreading function. Other enzymes provide this repair function.

Replication errors, even with a very efficient repair system, lead to the accumulation of mutations. A human has 10^{14} nucleated cells each with 3×10^9 base pairs of DNA. If about 10^{16} cell divisions occur in a lifetime and 10^{-10} mutations per base pair per cell generation escape repair, there may eventually be as many as one mutation per 10^6 bp in the genome. Fortunately, most of these will probably occur in DNA that does not encode proteins or will not affect the function of encoded proteins and so are of no consequence. In addition, spontaneous and chemically induced damage to DNA must be repaired.

Damage to DNA by environmental, physical, and chemical agents may be classified into four types (Table 35–8). Abnormal regions of DNA, either from copying errors or DNA damage, are replaced by four mechanisms: (1) mismatch repair, (2) base excision-repair, (3) nucleo-

Table 35–8. Types of damage to DNA.

I. Single-base alteration
  A. Depurination
  B. Deamination of cytosine to uracil
  C. Deamination of adenine to hypoxanthine
  D. Alkylation of base
  E. Insertion or deletion of nucleotide
  F. Base-analog incorporation
II. Two-base alteration
  A. UV light–induced thymine-thymine (pyrimidine) dimer
  B. Bifunctional alkylating agent cross-linkage
III. Chain breaks
  A. Ionizing radiation
  B. Radioactive disintegration of backbone element
  C. Oxidative free radical formation
IV. Cross-linkage
  A. Between bases in same or opposite strands
  B. Between DNA and protein molecules (eg, histones)

tide excision-repair, and (4) double-strand break repair (Table 35–9). These mechanisms exploit the redundancy of information inherent in the double helical DNA structure. The defective region in one strand can be returned to its original form by relying on the complementary information stored in the unaffected strand.

Mismatch Repair

Mismatch repair corrects errors made when DNA is copied. For example, a C could be inserted opposite an A, or the polymerase could slip or stutter and insert two

Table 35–9. Mechanism of DNA repair.

Mechanism	Problem	Solution
Mismatch repair	Copying errors (single base or two- to five-base unpaired loops)	Methyl-directed strand cutting, exonuclease digestion, and replacement
Base excision–repair	Spontaneous, chemical, or radiation damage to a single base	Base removal by *N*-glycosylase, abasic sugar removal, replacement
Nucleotide excision–repair	Spontaneous, chemical, or radiation damage to a DNA segment	Removal of an approximately 30-nucleotide oligomer and replacement
Double-strand break repair	Ionizing radiation, chemotherapy, oxidative free radicals	Synapsis, unwinding, alignment, ligation

to five extra unpaired bases. Specific proteins scan the newly synthesized DNA, using adenine methylation within a GATC sequence as the point of reference (Figure 35–22). The template strand is methylated, and the newly synthesized strand is not. This difference allows the repair enzymes to identify the strand that contains the errant nucleotide which requires replacement. If a mismatch or small loop is found, a GATC endonuclease cuts the strand bearing the mutation at a site corresponding to the GATC. An exonuclease then digests this strand from the GATC through the mutation, thus removing the faulty DNA. This can occur from either end if the defect is bracketed by two GATC sites. This defect is then filled in by normal cellular enzymes according to base pairing rules. In *E coli,* three proteins (Mut S, Mut C, and Mut H) are required for recognition of the mutation and nicking of the strand. Other cellular enzymes, including ligase, polymerase, and SSBs, remove and replace the strand. The process is somewhat more complicated in mammalian cells, as about six proteins are involved in the first steps.

Faulty mismatch repair has been linked to hereditary nonpolyposis colon cancer (HNPCC), one of the most common inherited cancers. Genetic studies linked HNPCC in some families to a region of chromosome 2. The gene located, designated *hMSH2,* was subsequently shown to encode the human analog of the *E coli* MutS protein that is involved in mismatch repair (see above). Mutations of *hMSH2* account for 50–60% of HNPCC cases. Another gene, *hMLH1,* is associated with most of the other cases. *hMLH1* is the human analog of the bacterial mismatch repair gene *MutL.* How does faulty mismatch repair result in colon cancer? The human genes were localized because microsatellite instability was detected. That is, the cancer cells had a microsatellite of a length different from that found in the normal cells of the individual. It appears that the affected cells, which harbor a mutated *hMSH2* or *hMLH1* mismatch repair enzyme, are unable to remove small loops of unpaired DNA, and the microsatellite thus increases in size. Ultimately, microsatellite DNA expansion must affect either the expression or the function of a protein critical in surveillance of the cell cycle in these colon cells.

Base Excision-Repair

The **depurination of DNA,** which happens spontaneously owing to the thermal lability of the purine N-glycosidic bond, occurs at a rate of 5000–10,000/cell/d at 37 °C. Specific enzymes recognize a depurinated site and replace the appropriate purine directly, without interruption of the phosphodiester backbone.

Cytosine, adenine, and guanine bases in DNA spontaneously form uracil, hypoxanthine, or xanthine, respectively. Since none of these normally exist in DNA, it is not surprising that specific **N-glycosylases** can recognize these abnormal bases and remove the base itself from the DNA. This removal marks the site of the defect and allows an **apurinic or apyrimidinic endonuclease** to excise the abasic sugar. The proper base is then replaced by a repair DNA polymerase, and a **ligase** returns the DNA to its original state (Figure 35–23). This series of events is called **base excision-repair.** By a similar series of steps involving initially the recognition of the defect, alkylated bases and base analogs can be removed from DNA and the DNA returned to its original informational content. This mechanism is suitable for replacement of a single base but is not effective at replacing regions of damaged DNA.

Nucleotide Excision-Repair

This mechanism is used to replace regions of damaged DNA up to 30 bases in length. Common causes of

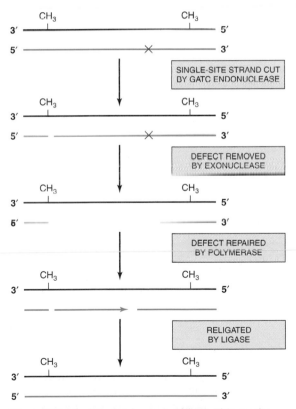

Figure 35–22. Mismatch repair of DNA. This mechanism corrects a single mismatch base pair (eg, C to A rather than T to A) or a short region of unpaired DNA. The defective region is recognized by an endonuclease that makes a single-strand cut at an adjacent methylated GATC sequence. The DNA strand is removed through the mutation, replaced, and religated.

```
3' ─────────────────── 5'
  A T C G G C T [C] A T C C G A T
  | | | | | | | | | | | | | | | |
5' T A G C C G A G T A G G C T A 3'
  ───────────────────
```

↓ Heat energy

```
  A T C G G C T [U] A T C C G A T
  | | | | | | | | | | | | | | | |
  T A G C C G A G T A G G C T A
  ───────────────────
```

U ← | URACIL DNA GLYCOSYLASE |

```
  A T C G G C T [*] A T C C G A T
  | | | | | | | | | | | | | | | |
  T A G C C G A G T A G G C T A
  ───────────────────
```

↓ | NUCLEASES |

```
  A T C G G C          T C C G A T
  | | | | | |          | | | | | |
  T A G C C G A G T A G G C T A
  ───────────────────
```

↓ | DNA POLYMERASE + DNA LIGASE |

```
  A T C G G C T [C] A T C C G A T
  | | | | | | | | | | | | | | | |
  T A G C C G A G T A G G C T A
  ───────────────────
```

Figure 35–23. Base excision-repair of DNA. The enzyme uracil DNA glycosylase removes the uracil created by spontaneous deamination of cytosine in the DNA. An endonuclease cuts the backbone near the defect; then, after an endonuclease removes a few bases, the defect is filled in by the action of a repair polymerase and the strand is rejoined by a ligase. (Courtesy of B Alberts.)

such DNA damage include ultraviolet (UV) light, which induces the formation of cyclobutane pyrimidine-pyrimidine dimers, and smoking, which causes formation of benzo[*a*]pyrene-guanine adducts. Ionizing radiation, cancer chemotherapeutic agents, and a variety of chemicals found in the environment cause base modification, strand breaks, cross-linkage between bases on opposite strands or between DNA and protein, and numerous other defects. These are repaired by a process called nucleotide excision-repair (Figure 35–24). This complex process, which involves more gene products than the two other types of repair, essentially involves the hydrolysis of two phosphodiester bonds on the strand containing the defect. A special excision nuclease (exinuclease), consisting of at least three subunits in *E coli* and 16 polypeptides in humans, accomplishes this task. In eukaryotic cells the enzymes cut between the third to fifth phosphodiester bond 3' from the lesion, and on the 5' side the cut is somewhere between the

twenty-first and twenty-fifth bonds. Thus, a fragment of DNA 27–29 nucleotides long is excised. After the strand is removed it is replaced, again by exact base pairing, through the action of yet another polymerase (δ/ε in humans), and the ends are joined to the existing strands by DNA ligase.

Xeroderma pigmentosum (XP) is an autosomal recessive genetic disease. The clinical syndrome includes marked sensitivity to sunlight (ultraviolet) with subsequent formation of multiple skin cancers and premature death. The risk of developing skin cancer is increased 1000- to 2000-fold. The inherited defect seems to involve the repair of damaged DNA, particularly thymine dimers. Cells cultured from patients with xeroderma pigmentosum exhibit low activity for the nucleotide excision-repair process. Seven complementation groups have been identified using hybrid cell analyses, so at least seven gene products (XPA–XPG) are involved. Two of these (XPA and XPC) are involved in recognition and excision. XPB and XPD are helicases and, interestingly, are subunits of the transcription factor TFIIH (see Chapter 36).

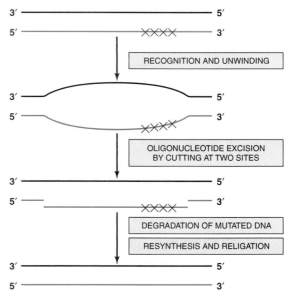

Figure 35–24. Nucleotide excision-repair. This mechanism is employed to correct larger defects in DNA and generally involves more proteins than either mismatch or base excision-repair. After defect recognition (indicated by XXXX) and unwinding of the DNA encompassing the defect, an excision nuclease (exinuclease) cuts the DNA upstream and downstream of the defective region. This gap is then filled in by a polymerase (δ/ε in humans) and religated.

second conformational change leading to **promoter clearance.** Once this transition occurs, RNAP physically moves away from the promoter, transcribing down the transcription unit, leading to the next phase of the process, elongation.

As the **elongation** complex containing the core RNA polymerase progresses along the DNA molecule, **DNA unwinding** must occur in order to provide access for the appropriate base pairing to the nucleotides of the coding strand. The extent of this transcription bubble (ie, DNA unwinding) is constant throughout transcription and has been estimated to be about 20 base pairs per polymerase molecule. Thus, it appears that the size of the unwound DNA region is dictated by the polymerase and is independent of the DNA sequence in the complex. This suggests that RNA polymerase has associated with it an "unwindase" activity that opens the DNA helix. The fact that the DNA double helix must unwind and the strands part at least transiently for transcription implies some disruption of the nucleosome structure of eukaryotic cells. Topoisomerase both precedes and follows the progressing RNAP to prevent the formation of superhelical complexes.

Termination of the synthesis of the RNA molecule in bacteria is signaled by a sequence in the template strand of the DNA molecule—a signal that is recognized by a termination protein, the rho (ρ) factor. Rho is an ATP-dependent RNA-stimulated helicase that disrupts the nascent RNA-DNA complex. After termination of synthesis of the RNA molecule, the enzyme separates from the DNA template and probably dissociates to free core enzyme and free σ factor. With the assistance of another σ factor, the core enzyme then recognizes a promoter at which the synthesis of a new RNA molecule commences. In eukaryotic cells, termination is less well defined. It appears to be somehow linked both to initiation and to addition of the 3′ polyA tail of mRNA and could involve destabilization of the RNA-DNA complex at a region of A–U base pairs. More than one RNA polymerase molecule may transcribe the same template strand of a gene simultaneously, but the process is phased and spaced in such a way that at any one moment each is transcribing a different portion of the DNA sequence (Figures 36–1 and 36–4).

THE FIDELITY & FREQUENCY OF TRANSCRIPTION IS CONTROLLED BY PROTEINS BOUND TO CERTAIN DNA SEQUENCES

The DNA sequence analysis of specific genes has allowed the recognition of a number of sequences important in gene transcription. From the large number of bacterial genes studied it is possible to construct consensus models of transcription initiation and termination signals.

The question, "How does RNAP find the correct site to initiate transcription?" is not trivial when the complexity of the genome is considered. E $coli$ has 4×10^3 transcription initiation sites in 4×10^6 base pairs (bp) of DNA. The situation is even more complex in humans, where as many as 10^5 transcription initiation sites are distributed throughout in 3×10^9 bp of DNA. RNAP can bind to many regions of DNA, but it scans the DNA sequence—at a rate of $\geq 10^3$ bp/s—until it recognizes certain specific regions of DNA to which it binds with higher affinity. This region is called the promoter, and it is the association of RNAP with the promoter that ensures accurate initiation of transcription. The promoter recognition-utilization process is the target for regulation in both bacteria and humans.

Bacterial Promoters Are Relatively Simple

Bacterial promoters are approximately 40 nucleotides (40 bp or four turns of the DNA double helix) in length, a region small enough to be covered by an E $coli$ RNA holopolymerase molecule. In this consensus promoter region are two short, conserved sequence elements. Approximately 35 bp upstream of the transcription start site there is a consensus sequence of eight nucleotide pairs (5′-TGTTGACA-3′) to which the RNAP binds to form the so-called **closed complex.** More proximal to the transcription start site—about ten nucleotides upstream—is a six-nucleotide-pair A+T-rich sequence (5′-TATAAT-3′). These conserved sequence elements comprising the promoter are shown schematically in Figure 36–5. The latter sequence has a low melting temperature because of its deficiency of GC nucleotide pairs. Thus, the **TATA box** is thought to ease the dissociation between the two DNA strands so that RNA polymerase bound to the promoter region can have access to the nucleotide sequence of its immediately downstream template strand. Once this process occurs, the combination of RNA polymerase plus promoter is called the **open complex.** Other bacteria have slightly different consensus sequences in their promoters, but all generally have two components to the promoter; these tend to be in the same position relative to the transcription start site, and in all cases the sequences between the boxes have no similarity but still provide critical spacing functions facilitating recognition of −35 and −10 sequence by RNA polymerase holoenzyme. Within a bacterial cell, different sets of genes are often coordinately regulated. One important way that this is accomplished is through the fact that these co-regulated genes share unique −35 and −10 promoter sequences. These unique promoters are recognized by different σ factors bound to core RNA polymerase.

Rho-dependent transcription **termination signals** in E $coli$ also appear to have a distinct consensus

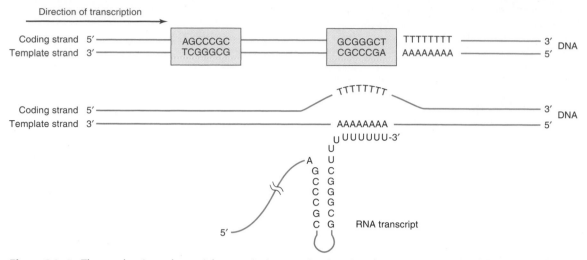

Figure 36–6. The predominant bacterial transcription termination signal contains an inverted, hyphenated repeat (the two boxed areas) followed by a stretch of AT base pairs (top). The inverted repeat, when transcribed into RNA, can generate the secondary structure in the RNA transcript shown at the bottom of the figure. Formation of this RNA hairpin causes RNA polymerase to pause and subsequently the ρ termination factor interacts with the paused polymerase and somehow induces chain termination.

sequence, as shown in Figure 36–6. The conserved consensus sequence, which is about 40 nucleotide pairs in length, can be seen to contain a hyphenated or interrupted inverted repeat followed by a series of AT base pairs. As transcription proceeds through the hyphenated, inverted repeat, the generated transcript can form the intramolecular hairpin structure, also depicted in Figure 36–6.

Transcription continues into the AT region, and with the aid of the ρ termination protein the RNA polymerase stops, dissociates from the DNA template, and releases the nascent transcript.

Eukaryotic Promoters Are More Complex

It is clear that the signals in DNA which control transcription in eukaryotic cells are of several types. Two types of sequence elements are promoter-proximal. One of these defines **where transcription is to commence** along the DNA, and the other contributes to the mechanisms that control **how frequently** this event is to occur. For example, in the thymidine kinase gene of the herpes simplex virus, which utilizes transcription factors of its mammalian host for gene expression, there is a single unique transcription start site, and accurate transcription from this start site depends upon a nucleotide sequence located 32 nucleotides upstream from the start site (ie, at −32) (Figure 36–7). This region has the sequence of **TATAAAAG** and bears remarkable similarity to the functionally related TATA box that is located

about 10 bp upstream from the prokaryotic mRNA start site (Figure 36–5). Mutation or inactivation of the TATA box markedly reduces transcription of this and many other genes that contain this consensus *cis* element (see Figures 36–7, 36–8). Most mammalian genes have a TATA box that is usually located 25–30 bp upstream from the transcription start site. The consensus sequence for a TATA box is TATAAA, though numerous variations have been characterized. The TATA box is bound by 34 kDa **TATA binding protein (TBP),** which in turn binds several other proteins called **TBP-associated factors (TAFs).** This complex of TBP and TAFs is referred to as TFIID. Binding of TFIID to the TATA box sequence is thought to represent the first step in the formation of the transcription complex on the promoter.

A small number of genes lack a TATA box. In such instances, two additional *cis* elements, an **initiator sequence (Inr)** and the so-called **downstream promoter element (DPE),** direct RNA polymerase II to the promoter and in so doing provide basal transcription starting from the correct site. The Inr element spans the start site (from −3 to +5) and consists of the general consensus sequence TCA_{+1} G/T T T/C which is similar to the initiation site sequence per se. (A+1 indicates the first nucleotide transcribed.) The proteins that bind to Inr in order to direct pol II binding include TFIID. Promoters that have both a TATA box and an Inr may be stronger than those that have just one of these elements. The DPE has the consensus

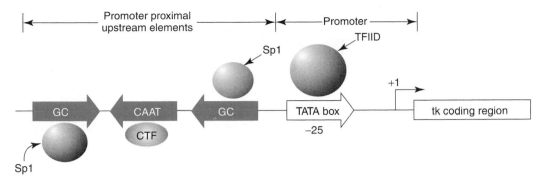

Figure 36–7. Transcription elements and binding factors in the herpes simplex virus thymidine kinase *(tk)* gene. DNA-dependent RNA polymerase II (not shown) binds to the region of the TATA box (which is bound by transcription factor TFIID) to form a multicomponent preinitiation complex capable of initiating transcription at a single nucleotide (+1). The frequency of this event is increased by the presence of upstream *cis*-acting elements (the GC and CAAT boxes). These elements bind *trans*-acting transcription factors, in this example Sp1 and CTF (also called C/EBP, NF1, NFY). These *cis* elements can function independently of orientation *(arrows)*.

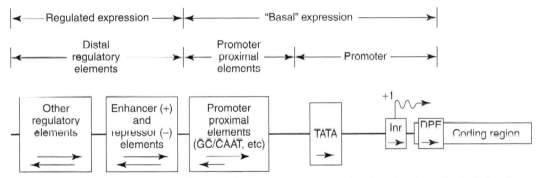

Figure 36–8. Schematic diagram showing the transcription control regions in a hypothetical class II mRNA-producing, eukaryotic gene transcribed by RNA polymerase II. Such a gene can be divided into its coding and regulatory regions, as defined by the transcription start site *(arrow;* +1). The coding region contains the DNA sequence that is transcribed into mRNA, which is ultimately translated into protein. The regulatory region consists of two classes of elements. One class is responsible for ensuring basal expression. These elements generally have two components. The proximal component, generally the TATA box, or Inr or DPE elements direct RNA polymerase II to the correct site (fidelity). In TATA-less promoters, an initiator (Inr) element that spans the initiation site (+1) may direct the polymerase to this site. Another component, the upstream elements, specifies the frequency of initiation. Among the best studied of these is the CAAT box, but several other elements (bound by the transactivator proteins Sp1, NF1, AP1, etc) may be used in various genes. Typically, a second class of regulatory *cis*-acting elements is responsible for regulated expression. This class consists of elements that enhance or repress expression and of others that mediate the response to various signals, including hormones, heat shock, heavy metals, and chemicals. Tissue-specific expression also involves specific sequences of this sort. The orientation dependence of all the elements is indicated by the arrows within the boxes. For example, the proximal element (the TATA box) must be in the 5′ to 3′ orientation. The upstream elements work best in the 5′ to 3′ orientation, but some of them can be reversed. The locations of some elements are not fixed with respect to the transcription start site. Indeed, some elements responsible for regulated expression can be located either interspersed with the upstream elements, or they can be located downstream from the start site.

sequence A/GGA/T CGTG and is localized about 25 bp downstream of the +1 start site. Like the Inr, DPE sequences are also bound by the TAF subunits of TFIID. In a survey of over 200 eukaryotic genes, roughly 30% contained a TATA box and Inr, 25% contained Inr and DPE, 15% contained all three elements, while ~30% contained just the Inr.

Sequences farther upstream from the start site determine how frequently the transcription event occurs. Mutations in these regions reduce the frequency of transcriptional starts tenfold to twentyfold. Typical of these DNA elements are the GC and CAAT boxes, so named because of the DNA sequences involved. As illustrated in Figure 36–7, each of these boxes binds a specific protein, Sp1 in the case of the GC box and CTF (or C/EPB,NF1,NFY) by the CAAT box; both bind through their distinct DNA binding domains (DBDs). The frequency of transcription initiation is a consequence of these protein-DNA interactions and complex interactions between particular domains of the transcription factors (distinct from the DBD domains—so-called activation domains; ADs) of these proteins and the rest of the transcription machinery (RNA polymerase II and the basal factors TFIIA, B, D, E, F). (See below and Figures 36–9 and 36–10.) The protein-DNA interaction at the TATA box involving RNA polymerase II and other components of the basal transcription machinery ensures the fidelity of initiation.

Together, then, the promoter and promoter-proximal *cis*-active upstream elements confer fidelity and frequency of initiation upon a gene. The TATA box has a particularly rigid requirement for both position and orientation. Single-base changes in any of these *cis* elements have dramatic effects on function by reducing the binding affinity of the cognate *trans* factors (either TFIID/TBP or Sp1, CTF, and similar factors). The spacing of these elements with respect to the transcription start site can also be critical. This is particularly true for the TATA box Inr and DPE.

A third class of sequence elements can either increase or decrease the rate of transcription initiation of eukaryotic genes. These elements are called either **enhancers** or **repressors (or silencers),** depending on which effect they have. They have been found in a variety of locations both upstream and downstream of the transcription start site and even within the transcribed portions of some genes. In contrast to proximal and upstream promoter elements, enhancers and silencers can exert their effects when located hundreds or even thousands of bases away from transcription units located on the same chromosome. Surprisingly, enhancers and silencers can function in an orientation-independent fashion. Literally hundreds of these elements have been described. In some cases, the sequence requirements for binding are rigidly constrained; in others, considerable sequence variation is allowed. Some sequences bind only a single protein, but the majority bind several different proteins. Similarly, a single protein can bind to more than one element.

Hormone response elements (for steroids, T_3, retinoic acid, peptides, etc) act as—or in conjunction with—enhancers or silencers (Chapter 42). Other processes that enhance or silence gene expression—such as the response to heat shock, heavy metals (Cd^{2+} and

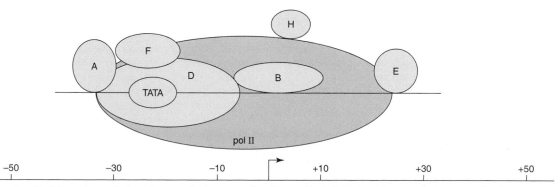

Figure 36–9. The eukaryotic basal transcription complex. Formation of the basal transcription complex begins when TFIID binds to the TATA box. It directs the assembly of several other components by protein-DNA and protein-protein interactions. The entire complex spans DNA from position −30 to +30 relative to the initiation site (+1, marked by bent arrow). The atomic level, x-ray-derived structures of RNA polymerase II alone and of TBP bound to TATA promoter DNA in the presence of either TFIIB or TFIIA have all been solved at 3 Å resolution. The structures of TFIID and TFIIH complexes have been determined by electron microscopy at 30 Å resolution. Thus, the molecular structures of the transcription machinery are beginning to be elucidated. Much of this structural information is consistent with the models presented here.

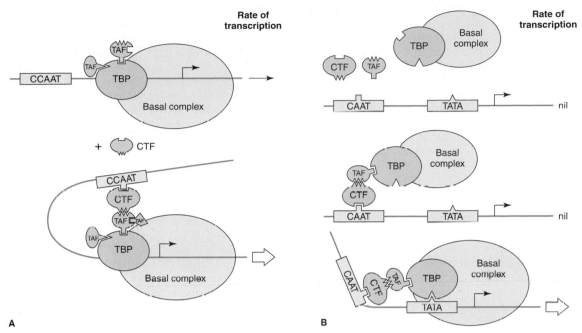

Figure 36–10. Two models for assembly of the active transcription complex and for how activators and coactivators might enhance transcription. Shown here as a large oval are all the components of the basal transcription complex illustrated in Figure 36–9 (ie, RNAP II and TFIIA, TFIIB, TFIIE, TFIIF, and TFIIH). **(A)** The basal transcription complex is assembled on the promoter after the TBP subunit of TFIID is bound to the TATA box. Several TAFs (coactivators) are associated with TBP. In this example, a transcription activator, CTF, is shown bound to the CAAT box, forming a loop complex by interacting with a TAF bound to TBP. **(B)** The recruitment model. The transcription activator CTF binds to the CAAT box and interacts with a coactivator (TAF in this case). This allows for an interaction with the preformed TBP-basal transcription complex. TBP can now bind to the TATA box, and the assembled complex is fully active.

Zn^{2+}), and some toxic chemicals (eg, dioxin)—are mediated through specific regulatory elements. Tissue-specific expression of genes (eg, the albumin gene in liver, the hemoglobin gene in reticulocytes) is also mediated by specific DNA sequences.

Specific Signals Regulate Transcription Termination

The **signals for the termination of transcription** by eukaryotic RNA polymerase II are very poorly understood. However, it appears that the termination signals exist far downstream of the coding sequence of eukaryotic genes. For example, the transcription termination signal for mouse β-globin occurs at several positions 1000–2000 bases beyond the site at which the poly(A) tail will eventually be added. Little is known about the termination process or whether specific termination factors similar to the bacterial ρ factor are involved. However, it is known that the mRNA 3' terminal is generated posttranscriptionally, is somehow coupled to

events or structures formed at the time and site of initiation, depends on a special structure in one of the subunits of RNA polymerase II (the CTD; see below), and appears to involve at least two steps. After RNA polymerase II has traversed the region of the transcription unit encoding the 3' end of the transcript, an RNA endonuclease cleaves the primary transcript at a position about 15 bases 3' of the consensus sequence **AAUAAA** that serves in eukaryotic transcripts as a cleavage signal. Finally, this newly formed 3' terminal is polyadenylated in the nucleoplasm, as described below.

THE EUKARYOTIC TRANSCRIPTION COMPLEX

A complex apparatus consisting of as many as 50 unique proteins provides accurate and regulatable transcription of eukaryotic genes. The RNA polymerase enzymes (pol I, pol II, and pol III for class I, II, and III genes, respectively) transcribe information contained in the template strand of DNA into RNA. These poly-

merases must recognize a specific site in the promoter in order to initiate transcription at the proper nucleotide. In contrast to the situation in prokaryotes, eukaryotic RNA polymerases alone are not able to discriminate between promoter sequences and other regions of DNA; thus, other proteins known as **general transcription factors or GTFs** facilitate promoter-specific binding of these enzymes and formation of the preinitiation complex (PIC). This combination of components can catalyze basal or (non)-unregulated transcription in vitro. Another set of proteins—coactivators—help regulate the rate of transcription initiation by interacting with transcription activators that bind to upstream DNA elements (see below).

Formation of the Basal Transcription Complex

In bacteria, a σ factor–polymerase complex selectively binds to DNA in the promoter forming the PIC. The situation is more complex in eukaryotic genes. Class II genes—those transcribed by pol II to make mRNA—are described as an example. In class II genes, the function of σ factors is assumed by a number of proteins. **Basal transcription requires, in addition to pol II, a number of GTFs called TFIIA, TFIIB, TFIID, TFIIE, TFIIF, and TFIIH.** These GTFs serve to promote RNA polymerase II transcription on essentially all genes. Some of these GTFs are composed of multiple subunits. **TFIID, which binds to the TATA box promoter element, is the only one of these factors capable of binding to specific sequences of DNA.** As described above, TFIID consists of TATA binding protein (TBP) and 14 TBP-associated factors (TAFs).

TBP binds to the TATA box in the minor groove of DNA (most transcription factors bind in the major groove) and causes an approximately 100-degree bend or kink of the DNA helix. This bending is thought to facilitate the interaction of TBP-associated factors with other components of the transcription initiation complex and possibly with factors bound to upstream elements. Although defined as a component of class II gene promoters, TBP, by virtue of its association with distinct, polymerase-specific sets of TAFs, is also an important component of class I and class III initiation complexes even if they do not contain TATA boxes.

The binding of TBP marks a specific promoter for transcription and is the only step in the assembly process that is entirely dependent on specific, high-affinity protein-DNA interaction. Of several subsequent in vitro steps, the first is the binding of TFIIA, then TFIIB to the TFIID-promoter complex. This results in a stable ternary complex which is then more precisely located and more tightly bound at the transcription ini-

tiation site. This complex then attracts and tethers the pol II-TFIIF complex to the promoter. TFIIF is structurally and functionally similar to the bacterial σ factor and is required for the delivery of pol II to the promoter. Addition of TFIIE and TFIIH is the final step in the assembly of the PIC. TFIIE appears to join the complex with pol II-TFIIF, and TFIIH is then recruited. Each of these binding events extends the size of the complex so that finally about 60 bp (from −30 to +30 relative to +1, the nucleotide from which transcription commences) are covered (Figure 36–9). The PIC is now complete and capable of basal transcription initiated from the correct nucleotide. In genes that lack a TATA box, the same factors, including TBP, are required. In such cases, an Inr or the DPEs (see Figure 36–8) position the complex for accurate initiation of transcription.

Phosphorylation Activates Pol II

Eukaryotic pol II consists of 12 subunits. The two largest subunits, both about 200 kDa, are homologous to the bacterial β and β′ subunits. In addition to the increased number of subunits, eukaryotic pol II differs from its prokaryotic counterpart in that it has a series of heptad repeats with consensus sequence Tyr-Ser-Pro-Thr-Ser-Pro-Ser at the carboxyl terminal of the largest pol II subunit. This **carboxyl terminal repeat domain (CTD)** has 26 repeated units in brewers' yeast and 52 units in mammalian cells. The CTD is both a substrate for several kinases, including the kinase component of TFIIH, and a binding site for a wide array of proteins. The CTD has been shown to interact with RNA processing enzymes; such binding may be involved with RNA polyadenylation. The association of the factors with the CTD of RNA polymerase II (and other components of the basal machinery) somehow serves to couple initiation with mRNA 3′ end formation. Pol II is activated when phosphorylated on the Ser and Thr residues and displays reduced activity when the CTD is dephosphorylated. CTD phosphorylation is critical for promoter clearance, elongation, termination, and even appropriate mRNA processing. Pol II lacking the CTD tail is incapable of activating transcription, which underscores the importance of this domain.

Pol II associates with other proteins termed Med or Mediator proteins to form a holoenzyme complex; this complex can form on the promoter or in solution prior to PIC formation. In yeast, at least 25 gene products bind to the CTD. The Med proteins are essential for appropriate regulation of pol II transcription, though their exact role in this process remains to be defined. Related proteins comprising even more complex forms of RNA polymerase II have been described in human cells (>30 proteins, Med1–Med31).

The Role of Transcription Activators & Coactivators

TFIID was originally considered to be a single protein. However, several pieces of evidence led to the important discovery that TFIID is actually a complex consisting of TBP and the 14 TAFs. The first evidence that TFIID was more complex than just the TBP molecules came from the observation that TBP binds to a 10-bp segment of DNA, immediately over the TATA box of the gene, whereas native holo-TFIID covers a 35 bp or larger region (Figure 36–9). Second, TBP has a molecular mass of 20–40 kDa (depending on the species), whereas the TFIID complex has a mass of about 1000 kDa. Finally, and perhaps most importantly, TBP supports basal transcription but not the augmented transcription provided by certain activators, eg, Sp1 bound to the GC box. TFIID, on the other hand, supports both basal and enhanced transcription by Sp1, Oct1, AP1, CTF, ATF, etc (Table 36–3). The TAFs are essential for this activator-enhanced transcription. It is not yet clear whether there are one or several forms of TFIID that might differ slightly in their complement of TAFs. It is conceivable that different combinations of TAFs with TBP—or one of several recently discovered TBP-like factors (TLFs)—may bind to different promoters, and recent reports suggest that this may account for selective activation noted in various promoters and for the different strengths of certain promoters. **TAFs, since they are required for the action of activators, are often called coactivators.** There are thus three classes of transcription factors involved in the regulation of class II genes: basal factors, coactivators, and activator-repressors (Table 36–4). How these classes of proteins interact to

Table 36–3. Some of the transcription control elements, their consensus sequences, and the factors that bind to them which are found in mammalian genes transcribed by RNA polymerase II.

Element	Consensus Sequence	Factor
TATA box	TATAAA	TBP/TFIID
CAAT box	CCAATC	C/EBP*, NF-Y*
GC box	GGGCGG	Sp1*
	CAACTGAC	Myo D
	T/CGGA/CN$_5$GCCAA	NF1*
Ig octamer	ATGCAAAT	Oct1, 2, 4, 6*
AP1	TGAG/CTC/AA	Jun, Fos, ATF*
Serum response	GATGCCCATA	SRF
Heat shock	(NGAAN)$_3$	HSF

A complete list would include dozens of examples. The asterisks mean that there are several members of this family.

Table 36–4. Three classes of transcription factors in class II genes.

General Mechanisms	Specific Components
Basal components	TBP, TFIIA, B, E, F, and H
Coactivators	TAFs (TBP + TAFs) = TFIID; Meds
Activators	SP1, ATF, CTF, AP1, etc

govern both the site and frequency of transcription is a question of central importance.

Two Models Explain the Assembly of the Preinitiation Complex

The formation of the PIC described above is based on the sequential addition of purified components in in vitro experiments. An essential feature of this model is that the assembly takes place on the DNA template. Accordingly, transcription activators, which have autonomous DNA binding and activation domains (see Chapter 38), are thought to function by stimulating either PIC formation or PIC function. The TAF coactivators are viewed as bridging factors that communicate between the upstream activators, the proteins associated with pol II, or the many other components of TFIID. This view, which assumes that there is **stepwise assembly** of the PIC—promoted by various interactions between activators, coactivators, and PIC components—is illustrated in panel A of Figure 36–10. This model was supported by observations that many of these proteins could indeed bind to one another in vitro.

Recent evidence suggests that there is another possible mechanism of PIC formation and transcription regulation. First, large preassembled complexes of GTFs and pol II are found in cell extracts, and this complex can associate with a promoter in a single step. Second, the rate of transcription achieved when activators are added to limiting concentrations of pol II holoenzyme can be matched by increasing the concentration of the pol II holoenzyme in the absence of activators. Thus, activators are not in themselves absolutely essential for PIC formation. These observations led to the **"recruitment" hypothesis,** which has now been tested experimentally. Simply stated, the role of activators and coactivators may be solely to recruit a preformed holoenzyme-GTF complex to the promoter. The requirement for an activation domain is circumvented when either a component of TFIID or the pol II holoenzyme is artificially tethered, using recombinant DNA techniques, to the DNA binding domain (DBD) of an activator. This anchoring, through the DBD component of the activator molecule, leads to a transcriptionally competent structure, and

there is no further requirement for the activation domain of the activator. In this view, the role of activation domains and TAFs is to form an assembly that directs the preformed holoenzyme-GTF complex to the promoter; they do not assist in PIC assembly (see panel B, Figure 36–10). In this model, the efficiency of the recruitment process directly determines the rate of transcription at a given promoter.

Hormones—and other effectors that serve to transmit information related to the extracellular environment—modulate gene expression by influencing the assembly and activity of the activator and coactivator complexes and the subsequent formation of the PIC at the promoter of target genes (see Chapter 42). The numerous components involved provide for an abundance of possible combinations and therefore a range of transcriptional activity of a given gene. It is important to note that the two models are not mutually exclusive—stepwise versus holoenzyme-mediated PIC formation. Indeed, one can envision various more complex scenarios invoking elements of both models operating on a gene.

RNA MOLECULES ARE USUALLY PROCESSED BEFORE THEY BECOME FUNCTIONAL

In prokaryotic organisms, the primary transcripts of mRNA-encoding genes begin to serve as translation templates even before their transcription has been completed. This is because the site of transcription is not compartmentalized into a nucleus as it is in eukaryotic organisms. Thus, transcription and translation are coupled in prokaryotic cells. Consequently, prokaryotic mRNAs are subjected to little processing prior to carrying out their intended function in protein synthesis. Indeed, appropriate regulation of some genes (eg, the *Trp* operon) relies upon this coupling of transcription and translation. Prokaryotic rRNA and tRNA molecules are transcribed in units considerably longer than the ultimate molecule. In fact, many of the tRNA transcription units contain more than one molecule. Thus, in prokaryotes the processing of these rRNA and tRNA precursor molecules is required for the generation of the mature functional molecules.

Nearly all eukaryotic RNA primary transcripts undergo extensive processing between the time they are synthesized and the time at which they serve their ultimate function, whether it be as mRNA or as a component of the translation machinery such as rRNA, 5S RNA, or tRNA or RNA processing machinery, snRNAs. Processing occurs primarily within the nucleus and includes nucleolytic cleavage to smaller molecules and coupled **nucleolytic and ligation reactions (splicing of exons)**. However, the processes of **transcription,** **RNA processing, and even RNA transport from the nucleus are highly coordinated.** Indeed, a transcriptional coactivator termed SAGA in yeasts and P/CAF in human cells is thought to link transcription activation to RNA processing by recruiting a second complex termed TREX to transcription elongation, splicing, and nuclear export. TREX (transcription-export) represents a likely molecular link between transcription elongation complexes, the RNA splicing machinery, and nuclear export (see Figure 36–11). This coupling presumably dramatically increases both the fidelity and rate of movement of mRNA to the cytoplasm for translation.

In mammalian cells, 50–75% of the nuclear RNA does not contribute to the cytoplasmic mRNA. This nuclear RNA loss is significantly greater than can be reasonably accounted for by the loss of intervening sequences alone (see below). Thus, the exact function of the seemingly excessive transcripts in the nucleus of a mammalian cell is not known, although the recently discovered miRNAs may account for a significant fraction of this transcription.

The Coding Portions (Exons) of Most Eukaryotic Genes Are Interrupted by Introns

Interspersed within the amino acid-coding portions **(exons)** of many genes are long sequences of DNA that do not contribute to the genetic information ultimately translated into the amino acid sequence of a protein molecule (see Chapter 35). In fact, these sequences actually interrupt the coding region of structural genes. These **intervening sequences (introns)** exist within most but not all mRNA encoding genes of higher eukaryotes. The primary transcripts of most mRNA (protein) encoding genes contain RNA complementary to the interspersed sequences. However, the intron RNA sequences are cleaved out of the transcript, and the exons of the transcript are appropriately spliced together in the nucleus before the resulting mRNA molecule appears in the cytoplasm for translation (Figures 36–12 and 36–13). One speculation for this exon-intron gene organization is that exons, which often encode an activity domain of a protein, represent a convenient means of shuffling genetic information, permitting organisms to quickly test the results of combining novel protein functional domains.

Introns Are Removed & Exons Are Spliced Together

The mechanisms whereby introns are removed from the primary transcript in the nucleus, exons are ligated to form the mRNA molecule, and the mRNA molecule is transported to the cytoplasm are being elucidated. Four

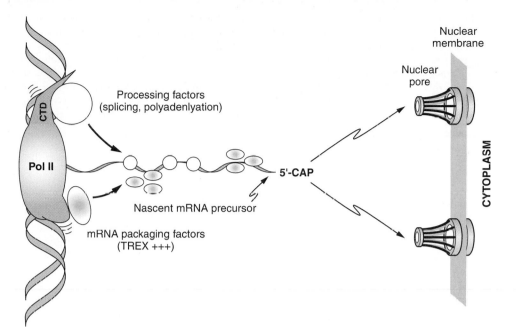

Figure 36–11. RNA Polymerase II–mediated mRNA gene transcription is cotranscriptionally coupled to RNA processing and transport. Shown is RNA Pol II actively transcribing an mRNA encoding gene (elongation top to bottom of figure). RNA processing factors (i.e., SR/RNP-motif-containing splicing factors as well as polyadenylation and termination factors) interact with the CTD domain of Pol II, while mRNA packaging factors such as THO/TREX complex are recruited to the nascent mRNA primary transcript either through direct Pol II interactions as shown or through interactions with SR/splicing factors resident on the nascent mRNA. In both cases, nascent mRNA chains are thought to be more rapidly and accurately processed due to the rapid recruitment of these many factors to the growing mRNA (precursor) chain. Following appropriate mRNA processing, the mature mRNA is delivered to the nuclear pores dotting the nuclear membrane, where, upon transport through the pores, the mRNAs can be engaged by ribosomes and translated into protein. (Adapted from Jensen et al. (2005). *Molecular Cell* 11:1129–1138.)

different splicing reaction mechanisms have been described. The one most frequently used in eukaryotic cells is described below. Although the sequences of nucleotides in the introns of the various eukaryotic transcripts—and even those within a single transcript—are quite heterogeneous, there are reasonably conserved sequences at each of the two exon-intron (splice) junctions and at the branch site, which is located 20–40 nucleotides upstream from the 3′ splice site (see consensus sequences in Figure 36–13). A special multicomponent complex, the **spliceosome,** is involved in converting the primary transcript into mRNA. Spliceosomes consist of the primary transcript, five small nuclear RNAs (U1, U2, U5, U4, and U6) and more than 60 proteins, many of which contain conserved "RNP" and "SR" protein motifs. Collectively, these form a **small ribonucleoprotein (snRNP) complex,** sometimes called a **"snurp."** It is likely that this penta-snRNP spliceosome forms prior to interaction with

mRNA precursors. Snurps are thought to position the RNA segments for the necessary splicing reactions. The splicing reaction starts with a cut at the junction of the 5′ exon (donor or left) and intron (Figure 36–12). This is accomplished by a nucleophilic attack by an adenylyl residue in the branch point sequence located just upstream from the 3′ end of this intron. The free 5′ terminal then forms a loop or lariat structure that is linked by an unusual 5′–2′ phosphodiester bond to the reactive A in the PyNPyPyPuAPy branch site sequence (Figure 36–13). This adenylyl residue is typically located 28–37 nucleotides upstream from the 3′ end of the intron being removed. The branch site identifies the 3′ splice site. A second cut is made at the junction of the intron with the 3′ exon (donor on right). In this second transesterification reaction, the 3′ hydroxyl of the upstream exon attacks the 5′ phosphate at the downstream exon-intron boundary, and the lariat structure containing the intron is released

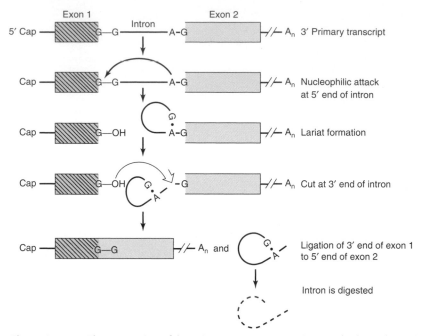

Figure 36–12. The processing of the primary transcript to mRNA. In this hypothetical transcript, the 5′ (left) end of the intron is cut (↓) and a lariat forms between the G at the 5′ end of the intron and an A near the 3′ end, in the consensus sequence UACUAAC. This sequence is called the branch site, and it is the 3′ most A that forms the 5′–2′ bond with the G. The 3′ (right) end of the intron is then cut (⇓). This releases the lariat, which is digested, and exon 1 is joined to exon 2 at G residues.

and hydrolyzed. The 5′ and 3′ exons are ligated to form a continuous sequence.

The snRNAs and associated proteins are required for formation of the various structures and intermediates. U1 within the snRNP complex binds first by base pairing to the 5′ exon-intron boundary. U2 within the snRNP complex then binds by base pairing to the branch site, and this exposes the nucleophilic A residue. U5/U4/U6 within the snRNP complex mediates an ATP-dependent protein-mediated unwinding that results in disruption of the base-paired U4-U6 complex

with the release of U4. U6 is then able to interact first with U2, then with U1. These interactions serve to approximate the 5′ splice site, the branch point with its reactive A, and the 3′ splice site. This alignment is enhanced by U5. This process also results in the formation of the loop or lariat structure. **The two ends are cleaved, probably by the U2-U6 within the snRNP complex.** U6 is certainly essential, since yeasts deficient in this snRNA are not viable. It is important to note that RNA serves as the catalytic agent. This sequence is then repeated in genes containing multiple introns. In

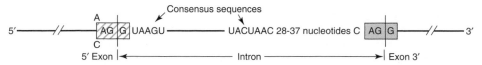

Figure 36–13. Consensus sequences at splice junctions. The 5′ (donor or left) and 3′ (acceptor or right) sequences are shown. Also shown is the yeast consensus sequence (UACUAAC) for the branch site. In mammalian cells, this consensus sequence is PyNPyPyPuAPy, where Py is a pyrimidine, Pu is a purine, and N is any nucleotide. The branch site is located 20–40 nucleotides upstream from the 3′ site. (Copyright © 2005. Reprinted with permission from Elsevier.)

such cases, a definite pattern is followed for each gene, and the introns are not necessarily removed in sequence—1, then 2, then 3, etc.

The relationship between hnRNA and the corresponding mature mRNA in eukaryotic cells is now apparent. The hnRNA molecules are the primary transcripts plus their early processed products, which, after the addition of caps and poly(A) tails and removal of the portion corresponding to the introns, are transported to the cytoplasm as mature mRNA molecules.

Alternative Splicing Provides for Different mRNAs

The processing of hnRNA molecules is a site for regulation of gene expression. Alternative patterns of RNA splicing result from tissue-specific adaptive and developmental control mechanisms. As mentioned above, the sequence of exon-intron splicing events generally follows a hierarchical order for a given gene. The fact that very complex RNA structures are formed during splicing and that a number of snRNAs and proteins are involved—affords numerous possibilities for a change of this order and for the generation of different mRNAs. Similarly, the use of alternative termination-cleavage-polyadenylation sites also results in mRNA variability. Some schematic examples of these processes, all of which occur in nature, are shown in Figure 36–14.

Faulty splicing can cause disease. At least one form of β-thalassemia, a disease in which the β-globin gene of hemoglobin is severely underexpressed, appears to result from a nucleotide change at an exon-intron junction, precluding removal of the intron and therefore leading to diminished or absent synthesis of the β-chain protein. This is a consequence of the fact that the normal translation reading frame of the mRNA is disrupted—a defect in this fundamental process (splicing) that underscores the accuracy which the process of RNA-RNA splicing must achieve.

Alternative Promoter Utilization Provides a Form of Regulation

Tissue-specific regulation of gene expression can be provided by control elements in the promoter or by the use of alternative promoters. The glucokinase *(GK)* gene consists of ten exons interrupted by nine introns. The sequence of exons 2–10 is identical in liver and pancreatic B cells, the primary tissues in which GK protein is expressed. Expression of the *GK* gene is regulated very differently—by two different promoters—in these two tissues. The liver promoter and exon 1L are located near exons 2–10; exon 1L is ligated directly to exon 2. In contrast, the pancreatic B cell promoter is located about 30 kbp upstream. In this case, the 3′ boundary of exon 1B is ligated to the 5′ boundary of exon 2. The

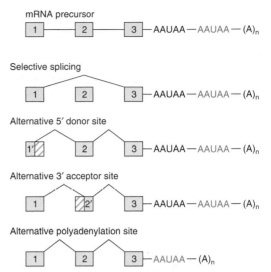

Figure 36–14. Mechanisms of alternative processing of mRNA precursors. This form of RNA processing involves the selective inclusion or exclusion of exons, the use of alternative 5′ donor or 3′ acceptor sites, and the use of different polyadenylation sites.

liver promoter and exon 1L are excluded and removed during the splicing reaction (see Figure 36–15). The existence of multiple distinct promoters allows for cell- and tissue-specific expression patterns of a particular gene (mRNA).

Both Ribosomal RNAs & Most Transfer RNAs Are Processed from Larger Precursors

In mammalian cells, the three rRNA molecules are transcribed as part of a single large precursor molecule. **The precursor is subsequently processed in the nucleolus** to provide the RNA component for the ribosome subunits found in the cytoplasm. The rRNA genes are located in the nucleoli of mammalian cells. Hundreds of copies of these genes are present in every cell. This large number of genes is required to synthesize sufficient copies of each type of rRNA to form the 10^7 ribosomes required for each cell replication. Whereas a single mRNA molecule may be copied into 10^5 protein molecules, providing a large amplification, the rRNAs are end products. This lack of amplification requires both a large number of genes and a high transcription rate, typically synchronized with cell growth rate. Similarly, transfer RNAs are often synthesized as precursors, with extra sequences both 5′ and 3′ of the sequences comprising the mature tRNA. A small fraction of tRNAs even contain introns.

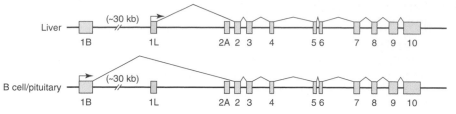

Figure 36–15. Alternative promoter use in the liver and pancreatic B cell glucokinase genes. Differential regulation of the glucokinase (*GK*) gene is accomplished by the use of tissue-specific promoters. The B cell *GK* gene promoter and exon 1B are located about 30 kbp upstream from the liver promoter and exon 1L. Each promoter has a unique structure and is regulated differently. Exons 2–10 are identical in the two genes, and the GK proteins encoded by the liver and B cell mRNAs have identical kinetic properties.

RNAS CAN BE EXTENSIVELY MODIFIED

Essentially all RNAs are covalently modified after transcription. It is clear that at least some of these modifications are regulatory.

Messenger RNA (mRNA) Is Modified at the 5′ & 3′ Ends

As mentioned above, mammalian mRNA molecules contain a 7-methylguanosine cap structure at their 5′ terminal, and most have a poly(A) tail at the 3′ terminal. The cap structure is added to the 5′ end of the newly transcribed mRNA precursor in the nucleus prior to transport of the mRNA molecule to the cytoplasm. The **5′ cap** of the RNA transcript is required both for efficient translation initiation and protection of the 5′ end of mRNA from attack by 5′ → 3′ exonucleases. The secondary methylations of mRNA molecules, those on the 2′-hydroxy and the N^6 of adenylyl residues, occur after the mRNA molecule has appeared in the cytoplasm.

Poly(A) tails are added to the 3′ end of mRNA molecules in a posttranscriptional processing step. The mRNA is first cleaved about 20 nucleotides downstream from an AAUAA recognition sequence. Another enzyme, poly(A) polymerase, adds a poly(A) tail which is subsequently extended to as many as 200 A residues. The **poly(A) tail** appears to protect the 3′ end of mRNA from 3′ → 5′ exonuclease attack. The presence or absence of the poly(A) tail does not determine whether a precursor molecule in the nucleus appears in the cytoplasm, because all poly(A)-tailed hnRNA molecules do not contribute to cytoplasmic mRNA, nor do all cytoplasmic mRNA molecules contain poly(A) tails (histone mRNAs are most notable in this regard). Cytoplasmic enzymes in mammalian cells can both add and remove adenylyl residues from the poly(A) tails; this process has been associated with an alteration of mRNA stability and translatability.

The size of some cytoplasmic mRNA molecules, even after the poly(A) tail is removed, is still considerably greater than the size required to code for the specific protein for which it is a template, often by a factor of 2 or 3. **The extra nucleotides occur in untranslated (non-protein coding) regions** both 5′ and 3′ of the coding region; the longest untranslated sequences are usually at the 3′ end. The exact function of **5′ UTR and 3′ UTR** sequences is unknown, but they have been implicated in RNA processing, transport, degradation, and translation; each of these reactions potentially contributes additional levels of control of gene expression.

RNA Editing Changes mRNA after Transcription

The central dogma states that for a given gene and gene product there is a linear relationship between the coding sequence in DNA, the mRNA sequence, and the protein sequence (Figure 35–7). Changes in the DNA sequence should be reflected in a change in the mRNA sequence and, depending on codon usage, in protein sequence. However, exceptions to this dogma have been recently documented. Coding information can be changed at the mRNA level by **RNA editing.** In such cases, the coding sequence of the mRNA differs from that in the cognate DNA. An example is the apolipoprotein B *(apoB)* gene and mRNA. In liver, the single *apoB* gene is transcribed into an mRNA that directs the synthesis of a 100-kDa protein, apoB100. In the intestine, the same gene directs the synthesis of the primary transcript; however, a cytidine deaminase converts a CAA codon in the mRNA to UAA at a single specific site. Rather than encoding glutamine, this codon becomes a termination signal, and a 48-kDa protein (apoB48) is the result. ApoB100 and apoB48 have different functions in the two organs. A growing number of other examples include a glutamine to arginine change in the glutamate receptor and several changes in trypanosome mitochondrial mRNAs, generally involving the addition or deletion of uridine. The exact extent of RNA editing is unknown, but current estimates suggest that < 0.01% of mRNAs are edited in this fashion.

Transfer RNA (tRNA) Is Extensively Processed & Modified

As described in Chapter 34 and Chapter 37, the tRNA molecules serve as adapter molecules for the translation of mRNA into protein sequences. The tRNAs contain many modifications of the standard bases A, U, G, and C, including methylation, reduction, deamination, and rearranged glycosidic bonds. Further modification of the tRNA molecules includes nucleotide alkylations and the attachment of the characteristic CpCpAOH terminal at the 3′ end of the molecule by the enzyme nucleotidyl transferase. The 3′ OH of the A ribose is the point of attachment for the specific amino acid that is to enter into the polymerization reaction of protein synthesis. The methylation of mammalian tRNA precursors probably occurs in the nucleus, whereas the cleavage and attachment of CpCpAOH are cytoplasmic functions, since the terminals turn over more rapidly than do the tRNA molecules themselves. Enzymes within the cytoplasm of mammalian cells are required for the attachment of amino acids to the CpCpAOH residues. (See Chapter 37.)

RNA CAN ACT AS A CATALYST

In addition to the catalytic action served by the snRNAs in the formation of mRNA, several other enzymatic functions have been attributed to RNA. **Ribozymes** are RNA molecules with catalytic activity. These generally involve transesterification reactions, and most are concerned with RNA metabolism (splicing and endoribonuclease). Recently, a ribosomal RNA component was noted to hydrolyze an aminoacyl ester and thus to play a central role in peptide bond function (peptidyl transferases; see Chapter 37). These observations, made in organelles from plants, yeast, viruses, and higher eukaryotic cells, show that RNA can act as an enzyme. This has revolutionized thinking about enzyme action and the origin of life itself.

SUMMARY

- RNA is synthesized from a DNA template by the enzyme RNA polymerase.
- There are three distinct nuclear DNA-dependent RNA polymerases in mammals: RNA polymerases I, II, and III. These enzymes control the transcriptional function—the transcription of rRNA, mRNA, and small RNA (tRNA/5S rRNA, snRNA) genes, respectively.
- RNA polymerases interact with unique *cis*-active regions of genes, termed promoters, in order to form preinitiation complexes (PICs) capable of initiation. In eukaryotes the process of PIC formation is facilitated by multiple general transcription factors (GTFs), TFIIA, B, D, E, F, and H.
- Eukaryotic PIC formation can occur either stepwise—by the sequential, ordered interactions of GTFs and RNA polymerase with promoters—or in one step by the recognition of the promoter by a preformed GTF-RNA polymerase holoenzyme complex.
- Transcription exhibits three phases: initiation, elongation, and termination. All are dependent upon distinct DNA *cis*-elements and can be modulated by distinct *trans*-acting protein factors.
- Most eukaryotic RNAs are synthesized as precursors that contain excess sequences which are removed prior to the generation of mature, functional RNA.
- Eukaryotic mRNA synthesis results in a pre-mRNA precursor that contains extensive amounts of excess RNA (introns) that must be precisely removed by RNA splicing to generate functional, translatable mRNA composed of exonic coding and noncoding sequences.
- All steps—from changes in DNA template, sequence, and accessibility in chromatin to RNA stability—are subject to modulation and hence are potential control sites for eukaryotic gene regulation.

REFERENCES

Bourbon H-M et al: A unified nomenclature for protein subunits of mediator complexes linking transcriptional regulators to RNA polymerase II. Mol Cell 2004;14:553.

Busby S, Ebright RH: Promoter structure, promoter recognition, and transcription activation in prokaryotes. Cell 1994;79:743.

Cramer P, Bushnell DA, Kornberg R: Structural basis of transcription: RNA polymerase II at 2.8 angstrom resolution. Science 2001;292:1863.

Fedor MJ: Ribozymes. Curr Biol 1998;8:R441.

Gott IM, Emeson RB: Functions and mechanisms of RNA editing. Ann Rev Genet 2000;34:499.

Hirose Y, Manley JL: RNA polymerase II and the integration of nuclear events. Genes Dev 2000;14:1415.

Keaveney M, Struhl K: Activator-mediated recruitment of the RNA polymerase machinery is the predominant mechanism for transcriptional activation in yeast. Mol Cell 1998;1:917.

Kornblihtt AR et al: Multiple links between transcription and splicing. RNA 2004;10:1489.

Lemon B, Tjian R: Orchestrated response: a symphony of transcription factors for gene control. Genes Dev 2000;14:2551.

Maniatis T, Reed R: An extensive network of coupling among gene expression machines. Nature 2002;416:499.

Orphanides G, Reinberg D: A unified theory of gene expression. Cell 2002;108:439.

Reed R, Cheng H: TREX, SR proteins and export of mRNA. Curr Opin Cell Biol 2005;17:269.

Shatkin AJ, Manley JL: The ends of the affair: capping and polyadenylation. Nat Struct Biol 2000;7:838.

Sims RJ, Belotserkovskaya R, Reinberg D: Elongation by RNA polymerase II: the short and long of it. Gene Dev 2004;18:2437.

Stevens SW et al: Composition and functional characterization of the yeast spliceosomal penta-snRNP. Mol Cell 2002;9:31.

Tucker M, Parker R: Mechanisms and control of mRNA decapping in *Saccharomyces cerevisiae*. Ann Rev Biochem 2000;69:571.

Woychik NA, Hampsey M: The RNA polymerase II machinery: structure illuminates function. Cell 2002;108:453.

Protein Synthesis & the Genetic Code

37

Daryl K. Granner, MD, & P. Anthony Weil, PhD

BIOMEDICAL IMPORTANCE

The letters A, G, T, and C correspond to the nucleotides found in DNA. They are organized into three-letter code words called **codons,** and the collection of these codons makes up the **genetic code.** It was impossible to understand protein synthesis—or to explain mutations—before the genetic code was elucidated. The code provides a foundation for explaining the way in which protein defects may cause genetic disease and for the diagnosis and perhaps the treatment of these disorders. In addition, the pathophysiology of many viral infections is related to the ability of these agents to disrupt host cell protein synthesis. Many antibacterial agents are effective because they selectively disrupt protein synthesis in the invading bacterial cell but do not affect protein synthesis in eukaryotic cells.

GENETIC INFORMATION FLOWS FROM DNA TO RNA TO PROTEIN

The genetic information within the nucleotide sequence of DNA is transcribed in the nucleus into the specific nucleotide sequence of an RNA molecule. The sequence of nucleotides in the RNA transcript is complementary to the nucleotide sequence of the template strand of its gene in accordance with the base-pairing rules. Several different classes of RNA combine to direct the synthesis of proteins.

In prokaryotes there is a linear correspondence between the gene, the **messenger RNA (mRNA)** transcribed from the gene, and the polypeptide product. The situation is more complicated in higher eukaryotic cells, in which the primary transcript is much larger than the mature mRNA. The large mRNA precursors contain coding regions **(exons)** that will form the mature mRNA and long intervening sequences **(introns)** that separate the exons. The mRNA is processed within the nucleus, and the introns, which often make up much more of this RNA than the exons, are removed. Exons are spliced together to form mature mRNA, which is transported to the cytoplasm, where it is translated into protein.

The cell must possess the machinery necessary to translate information accurately and efficiently from the nucleotide sequence of an mRNA into the sequence of amino acids of the corresponding specific protein. Clarification of our understanding of this process, which is termed **translation,** awaited deciphering of the genetic code. It was realized early that mRNA molecules themselves have no affinity for amino acids and, therefore, that the translation of the information in the mRNA nucleotide sequence into the amino acid sequence of a protein requires an intermediate adapter molecule. This adapter molecule must recognize a specific nucleotide sequence on the one hand as well as a specific amino acid on the other. With such an adapter molecule, the cell can direct a specific amino acid into the proper sequential position of a protein during its synthesis as dictated by the nucleotide sequence of the specific mRNA. In fact, the functional groups of the amino acids do not themselves actually come into contact with the mRNA template.

THE NUCLEOTIDE SEQUENCE OF AN mRNA MOLECULE CONSISTS OF A SERIES OF CODONS THAT SPECIFY THE AMINO ACID SEQUENCE OF THE ENCODED PROTEIN

Twenty different amino acids are required for the synthesis of the cellular complement of proteins; thus, there must be at least 20 distinct codons that make up the genetic code. Since there are only four different nucleotides in mRNA, each codon must consist of more than a single purine or pyrimidine nucleotide. Codons consisting of two nucleotides each could provide for only 16 (4^2) specific codons, whereas codons of three nucleotides could provide 64 (4^3) specific codons.

It is now known that each codon consists of a sequence of three nucleotides; ie, **it is a triplet code** (see Table 37–1). The deciphering of the genetic code depended heavily on the chemical synthesis of nucleotide polymers, particularly triplets in repeated sequence. These synthetic triplet ribonucleotides were used to

Table 37–1. The genetic code (codon assignments in mammalian messenger RNA).[1]

First Nucleotide	Second Nucleotide				Third Nucleotide
	U	C	A	G	
U	Phe	Ser	Tyr	Cys	U
	Phe	Ser	Tyr	Cys	C
	Leu	Ser	Term	Term[2]	A
	Leu	Ser	Term	Trp	G
C	Leu	Pro	His	Arg	U
	Leu	Pro	His	Arg	C
	Leu	Pro	Gln	Arg	A
	Leu	Pro	Gln	Arg	G
A	Ile	Thr	Asn	Ser	U
	Ile	Thr	Asn	Ser	C
	Ile[2]	Thr	Lys	Arg[2]	A
	Met	Thr	Lys	Arg[2]	G
G	Val	Ala	Asp	Gly	U
	Val	Ala	Asp	Gly	C
	Val	Ala	Glu	Gly	A
	Val	Ala	Glu	Gly	G

[1]The terms first, second, and third nucleotide refer to the individual nucleotides of a triplet codon. U, uridine nucleotide; C, cytosine nucleotide; A, adenine nucleotide; G, guanine nucleotide; Term, chain terminator codon. AUG, which codes for Met, serves as the initiator codon in mammalian cells and encodes for internal methionines in a protein. (Abbreviations of amino acids are explained in Chapter 3.)
[2]In mammalian mitochondria, AUA codes for Met and UGA for Trp, and AGA and AGG serve as chain terminators.

program protein synthesis, allowing investigators to deduce the genetic code.

THE GENETIC CODE IS DEGENERATE, UNAMBIGUOUS, NONOVERLAPPING, WITHOUT PUNCTUATION, & UNIVERSAL

Three of the 64 possible codons do not code for specific amino acids; these have been termed **nonsense codons.** These nonsense codons are utilized in the cell as **termination signals;** they specify where the polymerization of amino acids into a protein molecule is to stop. The remaining 61 codons code for 20 amino acids (Table 37–1). Thus, there must be **"degeneracy"** in the genetic code—ie, multiple codons must decode the same amino acid. Some amino acids are encoded by several codons; for example, six different codons specify serine. Other amino acids, such as methionine and tryptophan, have a single codon. In general, the third nucleotide in a codon is less important than the first two in determining the specific amino acid to be incorporated, and this accounts for most of the degeneracy

of the code. However, for any specific codon, only a single amino acid is indicated; with rare exceptions, the genetic code is **unambiguous**—ie, given a specific codon, only a single amino acid is indicated. **The distinction between ambiguity and degeneracy is an important concept.**

The unambiguous but degenerate code can be explained in molecular terms. The recognition of specific codons in the mRNA by the tRNA adapter molecules is dependent upon their **anticodon region** and specific base-pairing rules. Each tRNA molecule contains a specific sequence, complementary to a codon, which is termed its anticodon. For a given codon in the mRNA, only a single species of tRNA molecule possesses the proper anticodon. Since each tRNA molecule can be charged with only one specific amino acid, each codon therefore specifies only one amino acid. However, some tRNA molecules can utilize the anticodon to recognize more than one codon. **With few exceptions, given a specific codon, only a specific amino acid will be incorporated—although, given a specific amino acid, more than one codon may be used.**

As discussed below, the reading of the genetic code during the process of protein synthesis does not involve any overlap of codons. **Thus, the genetic code is nonoverlapping.** Furthermore, once the reading is commenced at a specific codon, there is **no punctuation** between codons, and the message is read in a continuing sequence of nucleotide triplets until a translation stop codon is reached.

Until recently, the genetic code was thought to be universal. It has now been shown that the set of tRNA molecules in mitochondria (which contain their own separate and distinct set of translation machinery) from lower and higher eukaryotes, including humans, reads four codons differently from the tRNA molecules in the cytoplasm of even the same cells. As noted in Table 37–1, the codon AUA is read as Met, and UGA codes for Trp in mammalian mitochondria. In addition, in mitochondria, the codons AGA and AGG are read as stop or chain terminator codons rather than as Arg. As a result, mitochondria require only 22 tRNA molecules to read their genetic code, whereas the cytoplasmic translation system possesses a full complement of 31 tRNA species. These exceptions noted, **the genetic code is universal.** The frequency of use of each amino acid codon varies considerably between species and among different tissues within a species. The specific tRNA levels generally mirror these codon usage biases. Thus, a particular abundantly used codon is decoded by a similarly abundant specific tRNA which recognizes that particular codon. Tables of **codon usage** are becoming more accurate as more genes are sequenced. This is of considerable importance because investigators often need to

Table 37–2. Features of the genetic code.

• Degenerate
• Unambiguous
• Nonoverlapping
• Not punctuated
• Universal

deduce mRNA structure from the primary sequence of a portion of protein in order to synthesize an oligonucleotide probe and initiate a recombinant DNA cloning project. The main features of the genetic code are listed in Table 37–2.

AT LEAST ONE SPECIES OF TRANSFER RNA (tRNA) EXISTS FOR EACH OF THE 20 AMINO ACIDS

tRNA molecules have extraordinarily similar functions and three-dimensional structures. The adapter function of the tRNA molecules requires the charging of each specific tRNA with its specific amino acid. Since there is no affinity of nucleic acids for specific functional groups of amino acids, this recognition must be carried out by a protein molecule capable of recognizing both a specific tRNA molecule and a specific amino acid. At least 20 specific enzymes are required for these specific recognition functions and for the proper attachment of the 20 amino acids to specific tRNA molecules. The process of **recognition and attachment (charging)** proceeds in two steps by one enzyme for each of the 20 amino acids. These enzymes are termed **aminoacyl-tRNA synthetases.** They form an activated intermediate of aminoacyl-AMP-enzyme complex (Figure 37–1). The specific aminoacyl-AMP-enzyme complex then

recognizes a specific tRNA to which it attaches the aminoacyl moiety at the 3′-hydroxyl adenosyl terminal. The charging reactions have an error rate of less than 10^{-4} and so are extremely accurate. The amino acid remains attached to its specific tRNA in an ester linkage until it is polymerized at a specific position in the fabrication of a polypeptide precursor of a protein molecule.

The regions of the tRNA molecule referred to in Chapter 34 (and illustrated in Figure 34–11) now become important. The ribothymidine pseudouridine-cytidine (TψC) arm is involved in binding of the aminoacyl-tRNA to the ribosomal surface at the site of protein synthesis. The D arm is one of the sites important for the proper recognition of a given tRNA species by its proper aminoacyl-tRNA synthetase. The acceptor arm, located at the 3′-hydroxyl adenosyl terminal, is the site of attachment of the specific amino acid.

The anticodon region consists of seven nucleotides, and it recognizes the three-letter codon in mRNA (Figure 37–2). The sequence read from the 3′ to 5′ direction in that anticodon loop consists of a variable base–modified purine–XYZ–pyrimidine–pyrimidine-5′. Note that this direction of reading the anticodon is 3′ to 5′, whereas the genetic code in Table 37–1 is read 5′ to 3′, since the codon and the anticodon loop of the mRNA and tRNA molecules, respectively, are **antiparallel** in their complementarity just like all other intermolecular interactions between nucleic acid strands.

The degeneracy of the genetic code resides mostly in the last nucleotide of the codon triplet, suggesting that the base pairing between this last nucleotide and the corresponding nucleotide of the anticodon is not strictly by the Watson-Crick rule. This is called **wobble;** the pairing of the codon and anticodon can "wobble" at this specific nucleotide-to-nucleotide pairing site. For example, the two codons for arginine, AGA

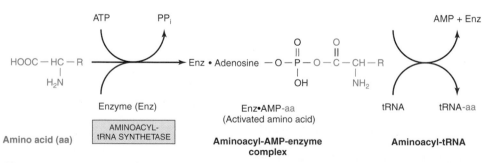

Figure 37–1. Formation of aminoacyl-tRNA. A two-step reaction, involving the enzyme aminoacyl-tRNA synthetase, results in the formation of aminoacyl-tRNA. The first reaction involves the formation of an AMP-amino acid-enzyme complex. This activated amino acid is next transferred to the corresponding tRNA molecule. The AMP and enzyme are released, and the latter can be reutilized. The charging reactions have an error rate of less than 10^{-4} and so are extremely accurate.

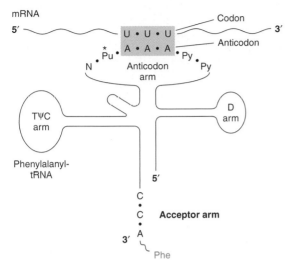

Figure 37–2. Recognition of the codon by the anticodon. One of the codons for phenylalanine is UUU. tRNA charged with phenylalanine (Phe) has the complementary sequence AAA; hence, it forms a base-pair complex with the codon. The anticodon region typically consists of a sequence of seven nucleotides: variable (N), modified purine (Pu*), X, Y, Z (here, A•A•A), and two pyrimidines (Py) in the 3′ to 5′ direction.

and AGG, can bind to the same anticodon having a uracil at its 5′ end (UCU). Similarly, three codons for glycine—GGU, GGC, and GGA—can form a base pair from one anticodon, CCI. I is an inosine nucleotide (see Figure 33–2 for structure), another of the peculiar bases appearing in tRNA molecules.

MUTATIONS RESULT WHEN CHANGES OCCUR IN THE NUCLEOTIDE SEQUENCE

Although the initial change may not occur in the template strand of the double-stranded DNA molecule for that gene, after replication, daughter DNA molecules with mutations in the template strand will segregate and appear in the population of organisms.

Some Mutations Occur by Base Substitution

Single-base changes (**point mutations**) may be **transitions** or **transversions.** In the former, a given pyrimidine is changed to the other pyrimidine or a given purine is changed to the other purine. Transversions are changes from a purine to either of the two pyrimidines or the change of a pyrimidine into either of the two purines, as shown in Figure 37–3.

If the nucleotide sequence of the gene containing the mutation is transcribed into an RNA molecule,

then the RNA molecule will possess a complementary base change at this corresponding locus.

Single-base changes in the mRNA molecules may have one of several effects when translated into protein:

(1) There may be no detectable effect because of the degeneracy of the code; such mutations are often referred to as **silent mutations.** This would be more likely if the changed base in the mRNA molecule were to be at the third nucleotide of a codon. Because of wobble, the translation of a codon is least sensitive to a change at the third position.

(2) A **missense effect** will occur when a different amino acid is incorporated at the corresponding site in the protein molecule. This mistaken amino acid—or missense, depending upon its location in the specific protein—might be acceptable, partially acceptable, or unacceptable to the function of that protein molecule. From a careful examination of the genetic code, one can conclude that most single-base changes would result in the replacement of one amino acid by another with rather similar functional groups. This is an effective mechanism to avoid drastic change in the physical properties of a protein molecule. If an acceptable missense effect occurs, the resulting protein molecule may not be distinguishable from the normal one. A partially acceptable missense will result in a protein molecule with partial but abnormal function. If an unacceptable missense effect occurs, then the protein molecule will not be capable of functioning in its assigned role.

(3) A **nonsense** codon may appear that would then result in the **premature termination** of amino acid incorporation into a peptide chain and the production of only a fragment of the intended protein molecule. The probability is high that a prematurely terminated protein molecule or peptide fragment will not function in its assigned role.

Hemoglobin Illustrates the Effects of Single-Base Changes in Structural Genes

Some mutations have no apparent effect. The gene system that encodes hemoglobin is one of the best-studied in humans. The lack of effect of a single-base change is demonstrable only by sequencing the nucleo-

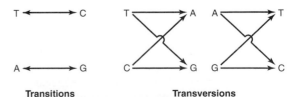

Figure 37–3. Diagrammatic representation of transition mutations and transversion mutations.

tides in the mRNA molecules or structural genes. The sequencing of a large number of hemoglobin mRNAs and genes from many individuals has shown that the codon for valine at position 67 of the β chain of hemoglobin is not identical in all persons who possess a normally functional β chain of hemoglobin. Hemoglobin Milwaukee has at position 67 a glutamic acid; hemoglobin Bristol contains aspartic acid at position 67. In order to account for the amino acid change by the change of a single nucleotide residue in the codon for amino acid 67, one must infer that the mRNA encoding hemoglobin Bristol possessed a GUU or GUC codon prior to a later change to GAU or GAC, both codons for aspartic acid. However, the mRNA encoding hemoglobin Milwaukee would have to possess at position 67 a codon GUA or GUG in order that a single nucleotide change could provide for the appearance of the glutamic acid codons GAA or GAG. Hemoglobin Sydney, which contains an alanine at position 67, could have arisen by the change of a single nucleotide in any of the four codons for valine (GUU, GUC, GUA, or GUG) to the alanine codons (GCU, GCC, GCA, or GCG, respectively).

Substitution of Amino Acids Causes Missense Mutations

A. ACCEPTABLE MISSENSE MUTATIONS

An example of an acceptable missense mutation (Figure 37–4, top) in the structural gene for the β chain of hemoglobin could be detected by the presence of an electrophoretically altered hemoglobin in the red cells of an apparently healthy individual. Hemoglobin Hikari has been found in at least two families of Japanese people. This hemoglobin has asparagine substituted for lysine at the 61 position in the β chain. The corresponding transversion might be either AAA or AAG changed to either AAU or AAC. The replacement of the specific lysine with asparagine apparently does not alter the normal function of the β chain in these individuals.

B. PARTIALLY ACCEPTABLE MISSENSE MUTATIONS

A partially acceptable missense mutation (Figure 37–4, center) is best exemplified by **hemoglobin S,** which is found in sickle cell anemia. Here glutamic acid, the normal amino acid in position 6 of the β chain, has

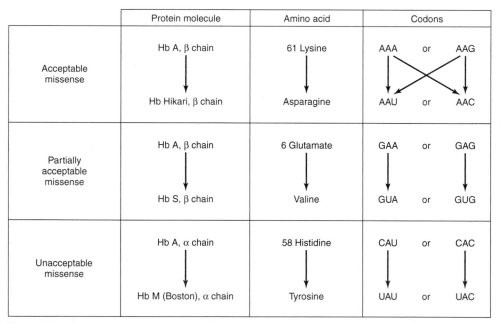

Figure 37–4. Examples of three types of missense mutations resulting in abnormal hemoglobin chains. The amino acid alterations and possible alterations in the respective codons are indicated. The hemoglobin Hikari β-chain mutation has apparently normal physiologic properties but is electrophoretically altered. Hemoglobin S has a β-chain mutation and partial function; hemoglobin S binds oxygen but precipitates when deoxygenated. Hemoglobin M Boston, an α-chain mutation, permits the oxidation of the heme ferrous iron to the ferric state and so will not bind oxygen at all.

been replaced by valine. The corresponding single nucleotide change within the codon would be GAA or GAG of glutamic acid to GUA or GUG of valine. Clearly, this missense mutation hinders normal function and results in sickle cell anemia when the mutant gene is present in the homozygous state. The glutamate-to-valine change may be considered to be partially acceptable because hemoglobin S does bind and release oxygen, although abnormally.

C. Unacceptable Missense Mutations

An unacceptable missense mutation (Figure 37–4, bottom) in a hemoglobin gene generates a nonfunctioning hemoglobin molecule. For example, the hemoglobin M mutations generate molecules that allow the Fe^{2+} of the heme moiety to be oxidized to Fe^{3+}, producing methemoglobin. Methemoglobin cannot transport oxygen (see Chapter 6).

Frameshift Mutations Result from Deletion or Insertion of Nucleotides in DNA That Generates Altered mRNAs

The deletion of a single nucleotide from the coding strand of a gene results in an altered reading frame in the mRNA. The machinery translating the mRNA does not recognize that a base was missing, since there is no punctuation in the reading of codons. Thus, a major alteration in the sequence of polymerized amino acids, as depicted in example 1, Figure 37–5, results. Altering the reading frame results in a garbled translation of the mRNA distal to the single nucleotide deletion. Not only is the sequence of amino acids distal to this deletion garbled, but reading of the message can also result in the appearance of a nonsense codon and thus the production of a polypeptide both garbled and prematurely terminated (example 3, Figure 37–5).

If three nucleotides or a multiple of three are deleted from a coding region, the corresponding mRNA when translated will provide a protein from which is missing the corresponding number of amino acids (example 2, Figure 37–5). Because the reading frame is a triplet, the reading phase will not be disturbed for those codons distal to the deletion. If, however, deletion of one or two nucleotides occurs just prior to or within the normal termination codon (nonsense codon), the reading of the normal termination signal is disturbed. Such a deletion might result in reading through a termination signal until another nonsense codon is encountered (example 1, Figure 37–5). Examples of this phenomenon are described in discussions of hemoglobinopathies.

Insertions of one or two or nonmultiples of three nucleotides into a gene result in an mRNA in which the reading frame is distorted upon translation, and the same effects that occur with deletions are reflected in the mRNA translation. This may result in garbled amino acid sequences distal to the insertion and the generation of a **nonsense codon** at or distal to the insertion, or perhaps reading through the normal termination codon. Following a deletion in a gene, an insertion (or vice versa) can reestablish the proper reading frame (example 4, Figure 37–5). The corresponding mRNA, when translated, would contain a garbled amino acid sequence between the insertion and deletion. Beyond the reestablishment of the reading frame, the amino acid sequence would be correct. One can imagine that different combinations of deletions, of insertions, or of both would result in formation of a protein wherein a portion is abnormal, but this portion is surrounded by the normal amino acid sequences. Such phenomena have been demonstrated convincingly in a number of diseases.

Suppressor Mutations Can Counteract Some of the Effects of Missense, Nonsense, & Frameshift Mutations

The above discussion of the altered protein products of gene mutations is based on the presence of normally functioning tRNA molecules. However, in prokaryotic and lower eukaryotic organisms, abnormally functioning tRNA molecules have been discovered that are themselves the results of mutations. Some of these abnormal tRNA molecules are capable of binding to and decoding altered codons, thereby suppressing the effects of mutations in distant structural genes. These **suppressor tRNA molecules,** usually formed as the result of alterations in their anticodon regions, are capable of suppressing missense mutations, nonsense mutations, and frameshift mutations. However, since the suppressor tRNA molecules are not capable of distinguishing between a normal codon and one resulting from a gene mutation, their presence in a cell usually results in decreased viability. For instance, the nonsense suppressor tRNA molecules can suppress the normal termination signals to allow a read-through when it is not desirable. Frameshift suppressor tRNA molecules may read a normal codon plus a component of a juxtaposed codon to provide a frameshift, also when it is not desirable. Suppressor tRNA molecules may exist in mammalian cells, since read-through transcription occurs.

LIKE TRANSCRIPTION, PROTEIN SYNTHESIS CAN BE DESCRIBED IN THREE PHASES: INITIATION, ELONGATION, & TERMINATION

The general structural characteristics of ribosomes and their self-assembly process are discussed in Chapter 36. These particulate entities serve as the machinery on which the mRNA nucleotide sequence is translated into

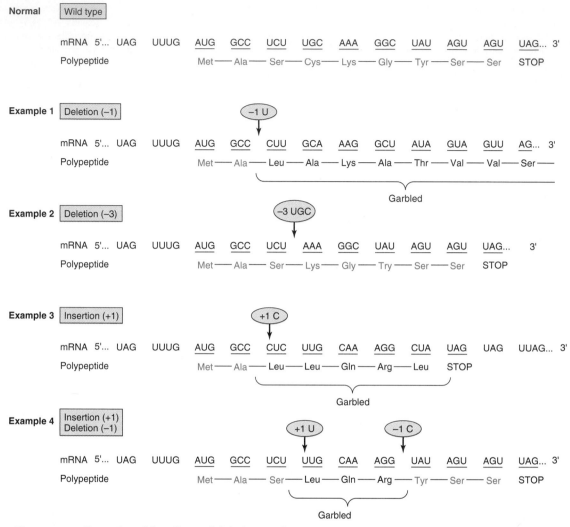

Figure 37–5. Examples of the effects of deletions and insertions in a gene on the sequence of the mRNA transcript and of the polypeptide chain translated therefrom. The arrows indicate the sites of deletions or insertions, and the numbers in the ovals indicate the number of nucleotide residues deleted or inserted. Color type indicates amino acids in correct order.

the sequence of amino acids of the specified protein. The translation of the mRNA commences near its 5′ terminal with the formation of the corresponding amino terminal of the protein molecule. The message is read from 5′ to 3′, concluding with the formation of the carboxyl terminal of the protein. Again, the concept of **polarity** is apparent. As described in Chapter 36, the transcription of a gene into the corresponding mRNA or its precursor first forms the 5′ terminal of the RNA molecule. In prokaryotes, this allows for the beginning of mRNA translation before the transcription of the gene is completed. In eukaryotic organisms, the process of transcription is a nuclear one; mRNA translation occurs in the cytoplasm. This precludes simultaneous transcription and translation in eukaryotic organisms and makes possible the processing necessary to generate mature mRNA from the primary transcript—hnRNA.

Initiation Involves Several Protein-RNA Complexes

Initiation of protein synthesis requires that an mRNA molecule be selected for translation by a ribosome (Figure 37–6). Once the mRNA binds to the ribosome, the

latter finds the correct reading frame on the mRNA, and translation begins. This process involves tRNA, rRNA, mRNA, and at least ten eukaryotic initiation factors (eIFs), some of which have multiple (three to eight) subunits. Also involved are GTP, ATP, and amino acids. Initiation can be divided into four steps: (1) dissociation of the ribosome into its 40S and 60S subunits; (2) binding of a ternary complex consisting of met-tRNA^i, GTP, and eIF-2 to the 40S ribosome to form a preinitiation complex; (3) binding of mRNA to the 40S preinitiation complex to form a 43S initiation complex; and (4) combination of the 43S initiation complex with the 60S ribosomal subunit to form the 80S initiation complex.

A. RIBOSOMAL DISSOCIATION

Two initiation factors, eIF-3 and eIF-1A, bind to the newly dissociated 40S ribosomal subunit. This delays its reassociation with the 60S subunit and allows other translation initiation factors to associate with the 40S subunit.

B. FORMATION OF THE 43S PREINITIATION COMPLEX

The first step in this process involves the binding of GTP by eIF-2. This binary complex then binds to met-tRNA^i, a tRNA specifically involved in binding to the initiation codon AUG. (There are two tRNAs for methionine. One specifies methionine for the initiator codon, the other for internal methionines. Each has a unique nucleotide sequence.) This ternary complex binds to the 40S ribosomal subunit to form the 43S preinitiation complex, which is stabilized by association with eIF-3 and eIF-1A.

eIF-2 is one of two control points for protein synthesis initiation in eukaryotic cells. eIF-2 consists of α, β, and γ subunits. eIF-2α is phosphorylated (on serine 51) by at least four different protein kinases (HCR, PKR, PERK, and GCN2) that are activated when a cell is under stress and when the energy expenditure required for protein synthesis would be deleterious. Such conditions include amino acid and glucose starvation, virus infection, misfolded proteins, serum deprivation, hyperosmolality, and heat shock. PKR is particularly interesting in this regard. This kinase is activated by viruses and provides a host defense mechanism that decreases protein synthesis, thereby inhibiting viral replication. Phosphorylated eIF-2α binds tightly to and inactivates the GTP-GDP recycling protein eIF-2B. This prevents formation of the 43S preinitiation complex and blocks protein synthesis.

C. FORMATION OF THE 43S INITIATION COMPLEX

The 5′ terminals of most mRNA molecules in eukaryotic cells are "capped," as described in Chapter 36. This methyl-guanosyl triphosphate cap facilitates the binding of mRNA to the 43S preinitiation complex. A cap binding protein complex, eIF-4F (4F), which consists of eIF-

4E and the eIF-4G (4G)-eIF4A (4A) complex, binds to the cap through the 4E protein. Then eIF-4A (4A) and eIF-4B (4B) bind and reduce the complex secondary structure of the 5′ end of the mRNA through ATPase and ATP-dependent helicase activities. The association of mRNA with the 43S preinitiation complex to form the 48S initiation complex requires ATP hydrolysis. eIF-3 is a key protein because it binds with high affinity to the 4G component of 4F, and it links this complex to the 40S ribosomal subunit. Following association of the 43S preinitiation complex with the mRNA cap and reduction ("melting") of the secondary structure near the 5′ end of the mRNA, the complex scans the mRNA for a suitable initiation codon. Generally this is the 5′-most AUG, but the precise initiation codon is determined by so-called **Kozak consensus sequences** that surround the AUG:

$$\overset{-3}{\underset{|}{}} \quad \overset{-1}{\underset{|}{}} \quad \overset{+4}{}$$

GCCA / GCC**AUG**G

Most preferred is the presence of a purine at positions −3 and +4 relative to the AUG.

D. ROLE OF THE POLY(A) TAIL IN INITIATION

Biochemical and genetic experiments in yeast have revealed that the 3′ poly(A) tail and its binding protein, Pab1p, are required for efficient initiation of protein synthesis. Further studies showed that the poly(A) tail stimulates recruitment of the 40S ribosomal subunit to the mRNA through a complex set of interactions. Pab1p, bound to the poly(A) tail, interacts with eIF-4G, which in turn binds to eIF-4E that is bound to the cap structure. It is possible that a circular structure is formed and that this helps direct the 40S ribosomal subunit to the 5′ end of the mRNA. This helps explain how the cap and poly(A) tail structures have a synergistic effect on protein synthesis. It appears that a similar mechanism is at work in mammalian cells.

E. FORMATION OF THE 80S INITIATION COMPLEX

The binding of the 60S ribosomal subunit to the 48S initiation complex involves hydrolysis of the GTP bound to eIF-2 by eIF-5. This reaction results in release of the initiation factors bound to the 48S initiation complex (these factors then are recycled) and the rapid association of the 40S and 60S subunits to form the 80S ribosome. At this point, the met-tRNA^i is on the P site of the ribosome, ready for the elongation cycle to commence.

The Regulation of eIF-4E Controls the Rate of Initiation

The 4F complex is particularly important in controlling the rate of protein translation. As described above, 4F is a complex consisting of 4E, which binds to the m^{7}G

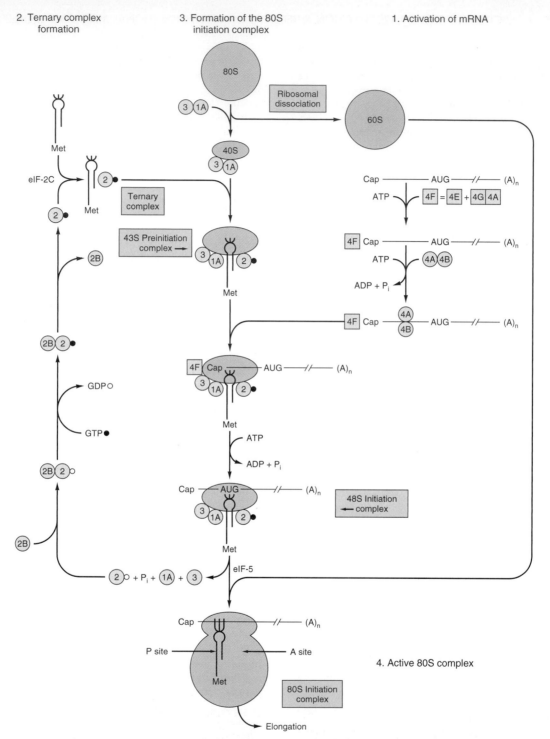

Figure 37–6. Diagrammatic representation of the initiation of protein synthesis on the mRNA template containing a 5′ cap (Cap) and 3′ poly(A) terminal [(A)$_n$]. This process proceeds in several steps: (1) activation of mRNA; (2) formation of the ternary complex consisting of tRNAmet^i, initiation factor eIF-2, and GTP; (3) scanning in the 43S complex to locate the AUG initiator coding, forming the 48S initiation complex; and (4) formation of the active 80S initiation complex. (See text for details.) GTP, ●; GDP, ○. The various initiation factors appear in abbreviated form as circles or squares, eg, eIF-3 (③), eIF-4F ([4F]). 4·F is a complex consisting of 4E and 4A bound to 4G (see Figure 37–7). The constellation of protein factors and the 40S ribosomal subunit comprise the 43S preinitiation complex. When bound to mRNA, this forms the 48S preinitiation complex.

cap structure at the 5' end of the mRNA, and 4G, which serves as a scaffolding protein. In addition to binding 4E, 4G binds to eIF-3, which links the complex to the 40S ribosomal subunit. It also binds 4A and 4B, the ATPase-helicase complex that helps unwind the RNA (Figure 37–7).

4E is responsible for recognition of the mRNA cap structure, which is a rate-limiting step in translation. This process is regulated at two levels. Insulin and mitogenic growth factors result in the phosphorylation of 4E on ser 209 (or thr 210). Phosphorylated 4E binds to the cap much more avidly than does the nonphosphorylated form, thus enhancing the rate of initiation. A component of the MAP kinase pathway (see Figure 42–8) appears to be involved in this phosphorylation reaction.

The activity of 4E is regulated in a second way, and this also involves phosphorylation. A recently discovered set of proteins bind to and inactivate 4E. These proteins include 4E-BP1 (BP1, also known as PHAS-1) and the closely related proteins 4E-BP2 and 4E-BP3. BP1 binds with high affinity to 4E. The [4E]•[BP1] association prevents 4E from binding to 4G (to form 4F). Since this interaction is essential for the binding of 4F to the ribosomal 40S subunit and for correctly positioning this on the capped mRNA, BP-1 effectively inhibits translation initiation.

Insulin and other growth factors result in the phosphorylation of BP-1 at five unique sites. Phosphorylation of BP-1 results in its dissociation from 4E, and it cannot rebind until critical sites are dephosphorylated. The protein kinase responsible has not been identified, but it appears to be different from the one that phosphorylates 4E. A kinase in the mammalian target of rapamycin (mTOR) pathway, perhaps mTOR itself, is involved. These effects on the activation of 4E explain in part how insulin causes a marked posttranscriptional increase of protein synthesis in liver, adipose tissue, and muscle.

Elongation Also Is a Multistep Process

Elongation is a cyclic process on the ribosome in which one amino acid at a time is added to the nascent peptide chain (Figure 37–8). The peptide sequence is determined by the order of the codons in the mRNA. Elongation involves several steps catalyzed by proteins called elongation factors (EFs). These steps are (1) binding of aminoacyl-tRNA to the A site, (2) peptide bond formation, and (3) translocation.

A. Binding of Aminoacyl-tRNA to the A Site

In the complete 80S ribosome formed during the process of initiation, the A site (aminoacyl or acceptor site) is free. The binding of the proper aminoacyl-tRNA in the A site requires proper codon recognition. **Elongation factor EF1A** forms a ternary complex with GTP and the entering aminoacyl-tRNA (Figure 37–8). This complex then allows the aminoacyl-tRNA to enter the A site with the release of EF1A•GDP and phosphate. GTP hydrolysis is catalyzed by an active site on the ribosome. As shown in Figure 37–8, EF1A-GDP then recycles to EF1A-GTP with the aid of other soluble protein factors and GTP.

B. Peptide Bond Formation

The α-amino group of the new aminoacyl-tRNA in the A site carries out a nucleophilic attack on the esterified carboxyl group of the peptidyl-tRNA occupying the P site (peptidyl or polypeptide site). At initiation, this site is occupied by aminoacyl-tRNA met[i]. This reaction is catalyzed by a **peptidyltransferase,** a component of the 28S RNA of the 60S ribosomal subunit. This is another

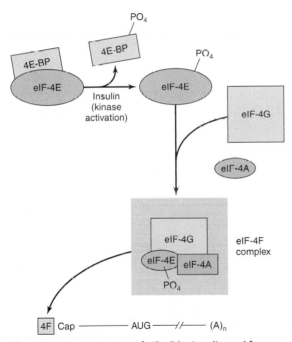

Figure 37–7. Activation of eIF-4E by insulin and formation of the cap binding eIF-4F complex. The 4F-cap mRNA complex is depicted as in Figure 37–6. The 4F complex consists of eIF-4E (4E), eIF-4A, and eIF-4G. 4E is inactive when bound by one of a family of binding proteins (4E-BPs). Insulin and mitogenic factors (eg, IGF-1, PDGF, interleukin-2, and angiotensin II) activate a serine protein kinase in the mTOR pathway, and this results in the phosphorylation of 4E-BP. Phosphorylated 4E-BP dissociates from 4E, and the latter is then able to form the 4F complex and bind to the mRNA cap. These growth peptides also phosphorylate 4E itself by activating a component of the MAP kinase pathway. Phosphorylated 4E binds much more avidly to the cap than does nonphosphorylated 4E.

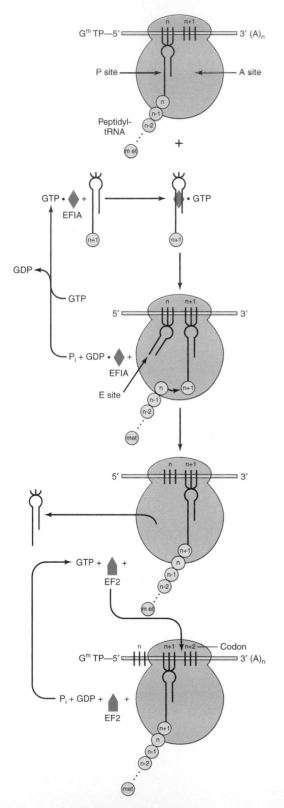

Table 37–3. Evidence that rRNA is peptidyltransferase.

- Ribosomes can make peptide bonds even when proteins are removed or inactivated.
- Certain parts of the rRNA sequence are highly conserved in all species.
- These conserved regions are on the surface of the RNA molecule.
- RNA can be catalytic.
- Mutations that result in antibiotic resistance at the level of protein synthesis are more often found in rRNA than in the protein components of the ribosome.
- X-ray crystal structure of large subunit bound to tRNAs suggest detailed mechanism.

example of ribozyme activity and indicates an important—and previously unsuspected—direct role for RNA in protein synthesis (Table 37–3). Because the amino acid on the aminoacyl-tRNA is already "activated," no further energy source is required for this reaction. The reaction results in attachment of the growing peptide chain to the tRNA in the A site.

C. TRANSLOCATION

The now deacylated tRNA is attached by its anticodon to the P site at one end and by the open CCA tail to an **exit (E) site** on the large ribosomal subunit (middle portion of Figure 37–8). At this point, **elongation factor 2 (EF2)** binds to and displaces the peptidyl tRNA from the A site to the P site. In turn, the deacylated tRNA is on the E site, from which it leaves the ribosome. The EF2-GTP complex is hydrolyzed to EF2-GDP, effectively moving the mRNA forward by one codon and leaving the A site open for occupancy by another ternary complex of amino acid tRNA-EF1A-GTP and another cycle of elongation.

The charging of the tRNA molecule with the aminoacyl moiety requires the hydrolysis of an ATP to an AMP, equivalent to the hydrolysis of two ATPs to two ADPs and phosphates. The entry of the aminoacyl-tRNA into the A site results in the hydrolysis of one GTP to GDP. Translocation of the newly formed peptidyl-tRNA in the A site into the P site by EF2 similarly

Figure 37–8. Diagrammatic representation of the peptide elongation process of protein synthesis. The small circles labeled n – 1, n, n + 1, etc, represent the amino acid residues of the newly formed protein molecule. EFIA and EF2 represent elongation factors 1 and 2, respectively. The peptidyl-tRNA, aminoacyl-tRNA, and Exit sites on the ribosome are represented by P site, A site, and E site, respectively.

results in hydrolysis of GTP to GDP and phosphate. Thus, the energy requirements for the formation of one peptide bond include the equivalent of the hydrolysis of two ATP molecules to ADP and of two GTP molecules to GDP, or the hydrolysis of four high-energy phosphate bonds. A eukaryotic ribosome can incorporate as many as six amino acids per second; prokaryotic ribosomes incorporate as many as 18 per second. Thus, the process of peptide synthesis occurs with great speed and accuracy until a termination codon is reached.

Termination Occurs When a Stop Codon Is Recognized

In comparison to initiation and elongation, termination is a relatively simple process (Figure 37–9). After multiple cycles of elongation culminating in polymerization of the specific amino acids into a protein molecule, the stop or terminating codon of mRNA (UAA, UAG, UGA) appears in the A site. Normally, there is no tRNA with an anticodon capable of recognizing such a termination signal. **Releasing factor RF1** recognizes that a stop codon resides in the A site (Figure 37–9). RF1 is bound by a complex consisting of **releasing factor RF3** with bound GTP. This complex, with the peptidyl transferase, promotes hydrolysis of the bond between the peptide and the tRNA occupying the P site. Thus, a water molecule rather than an amino acid is added. This hydrolysis releases the protein and the tRNA from the P site. Upon hydrolysis and release, the **80S ribosome dissociates** into its 40S and 60S subunits, which are then recycled. Therefore, the releasing factors are proteins that hydrolyze the peptidyl-tRNA bond when a stop codon occupies the A site. The mRNA is then released from the ribosome, which dissociates into its component 40S and 60S subunits, and another cycle can be repeated.

Polysomes Are Assemblies of Ribosomes

Many ribosomes can translate the same mRNA molecule simultaneously. Because of their relatively large size, the ribosome particles cannot attach to an mRNA any closer than 35 nucleotides apart. Multiple ribosomes on the same mRNA molecule form a **polyribosome,** or "polysome." In an unrestricted system, the number of ribosomes attached to an mRNA (and thus the size of polyribosomes) correlates positively with the length of the mRNA molecule. The mass of the mRNA molecule is, of course, quite small compared with the mass of even a single ribosome.

Polyribosomes actively synthesizing proteins can exist as free particles in the cellular cytoplasm or may be attached to sheets of membranous cytoplasmic material referred to as **endoplasmic reticulum.** Attachment of the particulate polyribosomes to the endoplasmic reticu-

lum is responsible for its "rough" appearance as seen by electron microscopy. The proteins synthesized by the attached polyribosomes are extruded into the cisternal space between the sheets of rough endoplasmic reticulum and are exported from there. Some of the protein products of the rough endoplasmic reticulum are packaged by the Golgi apparatus into zymogen particles for eventual export (see Chapter 45). The polyribosomal particles free in the cytosol are responsible for the synthesis of proteins required for intracellular functions.

The Machinery of Protein Synthesis Can Respond to Environmental Threats

Ferritin, an iron-binding protein, prevents ionized iron (Fe^{2+}) from reaching toxic levels within cells. Elemental iron stimulates ferritin synthesis by causing the release of a cytoplasmic protein that binds to a specific region in the 5′ nontranslated region of ferritin mRNA. Disruption of this protein-mRNA interaction activates ferritin mRNA and results in its translation. This mechanism provides for rapid control of the synthesis of a protein that sequesters Fe^{2+}, a potentially toxic molecule.

Many Viruses Co-Opt the Host Cell Protein Synthesis Machinery

The protein synthesis machinery can also be modified in deleterious ways. **Viruses replicate by using host cell processes,** including those involved in protein synthesis. Some viral mRNAs are translated much more efficiently than those of the host cell (eg, encephalomyocarditis virus). Others, such as reovirus and vesicular stomatitis virus, replicate abundantly, and their mRNAs have a competitive advantage over host cell mRNAs for limited translation factors. Other viruses inhibit host cell protein synthesis by preventing the association of mRNA with the 40S ribosome.

Poliovirus and other picornaviruses gain a selective advantage by disrupting the function of the 4F complex to their advantage. The mRNAs of these viruses do not have a cap structure to direct the binding of the 40S ribosomal subunit (see above). Instead, the 40S ribosomal subunit contacts an **internal ribosomal entry site (IRES)** in a reaction that requires 4G but not 4E. The virus gains a selective advantage by having a protease that attacks 4G and removes the amino terminal 4E binding site. Now the 4E-4G complex (4F) cannot form, so the 40S ribosomal subunit cannot be directed to capped mRNAs. Host cell translation is thus abolished. The 4G fragment can direct binding of the 40S ribosomal subunit to IRES-containing mRNAs, so viral mRNA translation is very efficient (Figure 37–10). These viruses also promote the dephosphorylation of BP1 (PHAS-1), thereby decreasing cap (4E)-dependent translation.

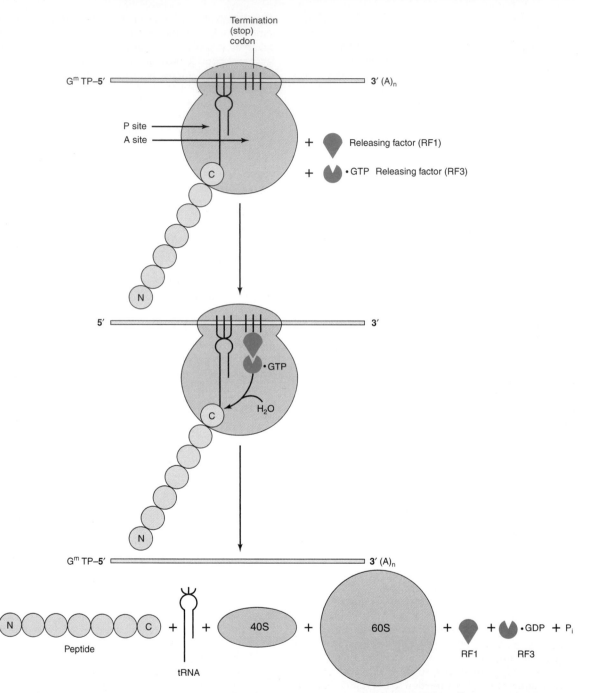

Figure 37–9. Diagrammatic representation of the termination process of protein synthesis. The peptidyl-tRNA and aminoacyl-tRNA sites are indicated as P site and A site, respectively. The termination (stop) codon is indicated by the three vertical bars. Releasing factor RF1 binds to the stop codon. Releasing factor RF3, with bound GTP, binds to RF1. Hydrolysis of the peptidyl-tRNA complex is shown by the entry of H_2O. N and C indicate the amino and carboxyl terminal amino acids of the nascent polypeptide chain, respectively, and illustrate the polarity of protein synthesis.

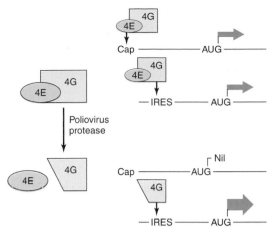

Figure 37–10. Picornaviruses disrupt the 4F complex. The 4E-4G complex (4F) directs the 40S ribosomal subunit to the typical capped mRNA (see text). 4G alone is sufficient for targeting the 40S subunit to the internal ribosomal entry site (IRES) of viral mRNAs. To gain selective advantage, certain viruses (eg, poliovirus) have a protease that cleaves the 4E binding site from the amino terminal end of 4G. This truncated 4G can direct the 40S ribosomal subunit to mRNAs that have an IRES but not to those that have a cap. The widths of the arrows indicate the rate of translation initiation from the AUG codon in each example.

POSTTRANSLATIONAL PROCESSING AFFECTS THE ACTIVITY OF MANY PROTEINS

Some animal viruses, notably HIV, poliovirus, and hepatitis A virus, synthesize long polycistronic proteins from one long mRNA molecule. The protein molecules translated from these long mRNAs are subsequently cleaved at specific sites to provide the several specific proteins required for viral function. In animal cells, many proteins are synthesized from the mRNA template as a precursor molecule, which then must be modified to achieve the active protein. The prototype is insulin, which is a low-molecular-weight protein having two polypeptide chains with interchain and intrachain disulfide bridges. The molecule is synthesized as a single chain precursor, or **prohormone,** which folds to allow the disulfide bridges to form. A specific protease then clips out the segment that connects the two chains which form the functional insulin molecule (see Figure 41–12).

Many other peptides are synthesized as proproteins that require modifications before attaining biologic activity. Many of the posttranslational modifications involve the removal of amino terminal amino acid residues by specific aminopeptidases. Collagen, an abundant protein in the extracellular spaces of higher eukaryotes, is synthesized as procollagen. Three procollagen polypeptide molecules, frequently not identical in sequence, align themselves in a particular way that is dependent upon the existence of specific amino terminal peptides. Specific enzymes then carry out hydroxylations and oxidations of specific amino acid residues within the procollagen molecules to provide cross-links for greater stability. Amino terminal peptides are cleaved off the molecule to form the final product—a strong, insoluble collagen molecule. Many other posttranslational modifications of proteins occur. Covalent modification by acetylation, phosphorylation, methylation, ubiquitinylation, and glycosylation is common, for example.

MANY ANTIBIOTICS WORK BECAUSE THEY SELECTIVELY INHIBIT PROTEIN SYNTHESIS IN BACTERIA

Ribosomes in bacteria and in the mitochondria of higher eukaryotic cells differ from the mammalian ribosome described in Chapter 34. The bacterial ribosome is smaller (70S rather than 80S) and has a different, somewhat simpler complement of RNA and protein molecules. This difference is exploited for clinical purposes because many effective antibiotics interact specifically with the proteins and RNAs of prokaryotic ribosomes and thus inhibit protein synthesis. This results in growth arrest or death of the bacterium. The most useful members of this class of antibiotics (eg, tetracyclines, lincomycin, erythromycin, and chloramphenicol) do not interact with components of eukaryotic ribosomal particles and thus are not toxic to eukaryotes. Tetracycline prevents the binding of aminoacyl-tRNAs to the A site. Chloramphenicol and the macrolide class of antibiotics work by binding to 23S rRNA, which is interesting in view of the newly appreciated role of rRNA in peptide bond formation through its peptidyltransferase activity. It should be mentioned that the close similarity between prokaryotic and mitochondrial ribosomes can lead to complications in the use of some antibiotics.

Other antibiotics inhibit protein synthesis on all ribosomes **(puromycin)** or only on those of eukaryotic cells **(cycloheximide).** Puromycin (Figure 37–11) is a structural analog of tyrosinyl-tRNA. Puromycin is incorporated via the A site on the ribosome into the carboxyl terminal position of a peptide but causes the premature release of the polypeptide. Puromycin, as a tyrosinyl-tRNA analog, effectively inhibits protein synthesis in both prokaryotes and eukaryotes. Cycloheximide inhibits peptidyltransferase in the 60S ribosomal subunit in eukaryotes, presumably by binding to an rRNA component.

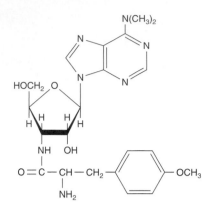

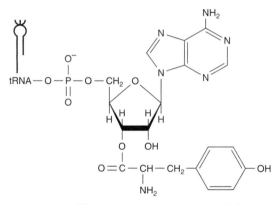

Figure 37–11. The comparative structures of the antibiotic puromycin (*top*) and the 3′ terminal portion of tyrosinyl-tRNA (*bottom*).

Diphtheria toxin, an exotoxin of *Corynebacterium diphtheriae* infected with a specific lysogenic phage, catalyzes the ADP-ribosylation of EF-2 on the unique amino acid diphthamide in mammalian cells. This modification inactivates EF-2 and thereby specifically inhibits mammalian protein synthesis. Many animals (eg, mice) are resistant to diphtheria toxin. This resistance is due to inability of diphtheria toxin to cross the cell membrane rather than to insensitivity of mouse EF-2 to diphtheria toxin-catalyzed ADP-ribosylation by NAD.

Ricin, an extremely toxic molecule isolated from the castor bean, inactivates eukaryotic 28S ribosomal RNA by providing the N-glycolytic cleavage or removal of a single adenine.

Many of these compounds—puromycin and cycloheximide in particular—are not clinically useful but have been important in elucidating the role of protein

synthesis in the regulation of metabolic processes, particularly enzyme induction by hormones.

SUMMARY

- The flow of genetic information follows the sequence DNA → RNA → protein.
- The genetic information in the structural region of a gene is transcribed into an RNA molecule such that the sequence of the latter is complementary to that in the DNA.
- Several different types of RNA, including ribosomal RNA (rRNA), transfer RNA (tRNA), and messenger RNA (mRNA), are involved in protein synthesis.
- The information in mRNA is in a tandem array of codons, each of which is three nucleotides long.
- The mRNA is read continuously from a start codon (AUG) to a termination codon (UAA, UAG, UGA).
- The open reading frame of the mRNA is the series of codons, each specifying a certain amino acid, that determines the precise amino acid sequence of the protein.
- Protein synthesis, like DNA and RNA synthesis, follows a 5′ to 3′ polarity and can be divided into three processes: initiation, elongation, and termination. Mutant proteins arise when single-base substitutions result in codons that specify a different amino acid at a given position, when a stop codon results in a truncated protein, or when base additions or deletions alter the reading frame, so different codons are read.
- A variety of compounds, including several antibiotics, inhibit protein synthesis by affecting one or more of the steps involved in protein synthesis.

REFERENCES

Crick F et al: The genetic code. Nature 1961;192:1227.

Green R, Noller HF: Ribosomes and translation. Annu Rev Biochem 1997;66:679.

Kapp LD, Lorsch JR: The molecular mechanics of eukaryotic translation. Ann Rev Biochem 2004;73:657.

Kozak M: Structural features in eukaryotic mRNAs that modulate the initiation of translation. J Biol Chem 1991;266:1986.

Lawrence JC, Abraham RT: PHAS/4E-BPs as regulators of mRNA translation and cell proliferation. Trends Biochem Sci 1997;22:345.

Sachs AB, Buratowski S: Common themes in translational and transcriptional regulation. Trends Biochem Sci 1997;22:189.

Sachs AB, Sarnow P, Hentze MW: Starting at the beginning, middle and end: translation initiation in eukaryotes. Cell 1997;98:831.

Steitz TA, Moore PB: RNA, the first macromolecular catalyst: the ribosome is a ribozyme. Trends Biochem Sci 2003;28:411.

Weatherall DJ et al: The hemoglobinopathies. In: *The Metabolic and Molecular Bases of Inherited Disease,* 8th ed. Scriver CR et al (editors). McGraw-Hill, 2001.

Regulation of Gene Expression

Daryl K. Granner, MD, & P. Anthony Weil, PhD

BIOMEDICAL IMPORTANCE

Organisms adapt to environmental changes by altering gene expression. The process of alteration of gene expression has been studied in detail and often involves modulation of gene transcription. Control of transcription ultimately results from changes in the interaction of specific binding regulatory proteins with various regions of DNA in the controlled gene. This can have a positive or negative effect on transcription. Transcription control can result in tissue-specific gene expression, and gene regulation is influenced by hormones, heavy metals, and chemicals. In addition to transcription level controls, gene expression can also be modulated by gene amplification, gene rearrangement, posttranscriptional modifications, and RNA stabilization. Many of the mechanisms that control gene expression are used to respond to hormones and therapeutic agents. Thus, a molecular understanding of these processes will lead to development of agents that alter pathophysiologic mechanisms or inhibit the function or arrest the growth of pathogenic organisms.

REGULATED EXPRESSION OF GENES IS REQUIRED FOR DEVELOPMENT, DIFFERENTIATION, & ADAPTATION

The genetic information present in each somatic cell of a metazoan organism is practically identical. The exceptions are found in those few cells that have amplified or rearranged genes in order to perform specialized cellular functions. Expression of the genetic information must be regulated during ontogeny and differentiation of the organism and its cellular components. Furthermore, in order for the organism to adapt to its environment and to conserve energy and nutrients, the expression of genetic information must be cued to extrinsic signals and respond only when necessary. As organisms have evolved, more sophisticated regulatory mechanisms have appeared which provide the organism and its cells with the responsiveness necessary for survival in a complex environment. Mammalian cells possess about 1000 times more genetic information than does the bacterium *Escherichia coli*. Much of this additional genetic information is probably involved in regulation of gene expression during the differentiation of tissues and biologic processes in the multi-cellular organism and in ensuring that the organism can respond to complex environmental challenges.

In simple terms, there are only two types of gene regulation: **positive regulation** and **negative regulation** (Table 38–1). When the expression of genetic information is quantitatively increased by the presence of a specific regulatory element, regulation is said to be positive; when the expression of genetic information is diminished by the presence of a specific regulatory element, regulation is said to be negative. The element or molecule mediating negative regulation is said to be a negative regulator or **repressor;** that mediating positive regulation is a positive regulator or **activator.** However, a **double negative** has the effect of acting as a positive. Thus, an effector that inhibits the function of a negative regulator will appear to bring about a positive regulation. Many regulated systems that appear to be induced are in fact **derepressed** at the molecular level. (See Chapter 9 for explanation of these terms.)

BIOLOGIC SYSTEMS EXHIBIT THREE TYPES OF TEMPORAL RESPONSES TO A REGULATORY SIGNAL

Figure 38–1 depicts the extent or amount of gene expression in three types of temporal response to an inducing signal. A **type A response** is characterized by an increased extent of gene expression that is dependent upon the continued presence of the inducing signal. When the inducing signal is removed, the amount of gene expression diminishes to its basal level, but the amount repeatedly increases in response to the reappearance of the specific signal. This type of response is commonly observed in prokaryotes in response to sudden changes of the intracellular concentration of a nutrient. It is also observed in many higher organisms after exposure to inducers such as hormones, nutrients, or growth factors (Chapter 42).

A **type B response** exhibits an increased amount of gene expression that is transient even in the continued presence of the regulatory signal. After the regulatory signal has terminated and the cell has been allowed to recover, a second transient response to a subsequent regulatory signal may be observed. This phenomenon of response-desensitization-recovery characterizes the action

Table 38–1. Effects of positive and negative regulation on gene expression.

	Rate of Gene Expression	
	Negative Regulation	Positive Regulation
Regulator present	Decreased	Increased
Regulator absent	Increased	Decreased

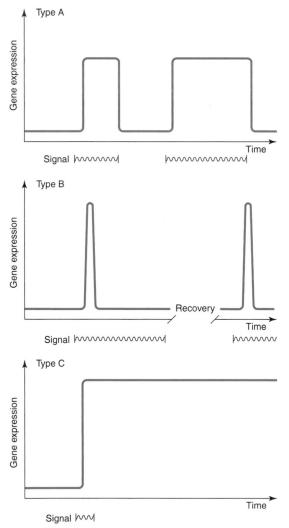

Figure 38–1. Diagrammatic representations of the responses of the extent of expression of a gene to specific regulatory signals such as a hormone.

of many pharmacologic agents, but it is also a feature of many naturally occurring processes. This type of response commonly occurs during development of an organism, when only the transient appearance of a specific gene product is required although the signal persists.

The **type C response** pattern exhibits, in response to the regulatory signal, an increased extent of gene expression that persists indefinitely even after termination of the signal. The signal acts as a trigger in this pattern. Once expression of the gene is initiated in the cell, it cannot be terminated even in the daughter cells; it is therefore an irreversible and inherited alteration. This type of response typically occurs during the development of differentiated function in a tissue or organ.

Prokaryotes Provide Models for the Study of Gene Expression in Mammalian Cells

Analysis of the regulation of gene expression in prokaryotic cells helped establish the principle that information flows from the gene to a messenger RNA to a specific protein molecule. These studies were aided by the advanced genetic analyses that could be performed in prokaryotic and lower eukaryotic organisms. In recent years, the principles established in these early studies, coupled with a variety of molecular biology techniques, have led to remarkable progress in the analysis of gene regulation in higher eukaryotic organisms, including mammals. In this chapter, the initial discussion will center on prokaryotic systems. The impressive genetic studies will not be described, but the physiology of gene expression will be discussed. However, nearly all of the conclusions about this physiology have been derived from genetic studies and confirmed by molecular genetic and biochemical studies.

Some Features of Prokaryotic Gene Expression Are Unique

Before the physiology of gene expression can be explained, a few specialized genetic and regulatory terms must be defined for prokaryotic systems. In prokaryotes, the genes involved in a metabolic pathway are often present in a linear array called an **operon,** eg, the *lac* operon. An operon can be regulated by a single promoter or regulatory region. The **cistron** is the smallest unit of genetic expression. As described in Chapter 9, some enzymes and other protein molecules are composed of two or more nonidentical subunits. Thus, the "one gene, one enzyme" concept is not necessarily valid. The cistron is the genetic unit coding for the structure of the subunit of a protein molecule, acting as it does as the smallest unit of genetic expression. Thus, the one gene, one enzyme idea might more accurately be regarded as a **one cistron, one subunit** concept. A single mRNA that encodes more than one separately translated protein

is referred to as a **polycistronic mRNA.** For example, the polycistronic *lac* operon mRNA is translated into three separate proteins (see below). Operons and polycistronic mRNAs are common in bacteria but not in eukaryotes.

An **inducible gene** is one whose expression increases in response to an **inducer** or **activator,** a specific positive regulatory signal. In general, inducible genes have relatively low basal rates of transcription. By contrast, genes with high basal rates of transcription are often subject to down-regulation by repressors.

The expression of some genes is **constitutive,** meaning that they are expressed at a reasonably constant rate and not known to be subject to regulation. These are often referred to as **housekeeping genes.** As a result of mutation, some inducible gene products become constitutively expressed. A mutation resulting in constitutive expression of what was formerly a regulated gene is called a **constitutive mutation.**

Analysis of Lactose Metabolism in *E coli* Led to the Operon Hypothesis

Jacob and Monod in 1961 described their **operon model** in a classic paper. Their hypothesis was to a large extent based on observations on the regulation of lactose metabolism by the intestinal bacterium *E coli.* The molecular mechanisms responsible for the regulation of the genes involved in the metabolism of lactose are now among the best-understood in any organism. β-Galactosidase hydrolyzes the β-galactoside lactose to galactose and glucose. The structural gene for β-galactosidase *(lacZ)* is clustered with the genes responsible for the permeation of galactose into the cell *(lacY)* and for thiogalactoside transacetylase *(lacA).* The structural genes for these three enzymes, along with the *lac* promoter and *lac* operator (a regulatory region), are physically associated to constitute the **lac** operon as depicted in Figure 38–2. This genetic arrangement of the structural genes and their regulatory genes allows for **coordinate expression** of the three enzymes concerned with lactose metabolism. Each of these linked genes is transcribed into one large mRNA molecule that contains multiple independent translation start (AUG) and stop (UAA) codons for each cistron. Thus, each protein is translated separately, and they are not processed from a single large precursor protein. This type of mRNA molecule is called a **polycistronic mRNA.** Polycistronic mRNAs are predominantly found in prokaryotic organisms.

It is now conventional to consider that a gene includes regulatory sequences as well as the region that encodes the primary transcript. Although there are many historical exceptions, a gene is generally italicized in lower case and the encoded protein, when abbreviated, is expressed in roman type with the first letter capitalized. For example, the gene *lacI* encodes the repressor protein LacI. When *E coli* is presented with lactose or some specific lactose analogs under appropriate nonrepressing conditions (eg, high

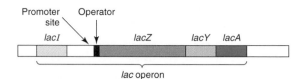

Figure 38–2. The positional relationships of the structural and regulatory genes of the *lac* operon. *lacZ* encodes β-galactosidase, *lacY* encodes a permease, and *lacA* encodes a thiogalactoside transacetylase. *lacI* encodes the *lac* operon repressor protein.

logs under appropriate nonrepressing conditions (eg, high concentrations of lactose, no or very low glucose in media; see below), the expression of the activities of β-galactosidase, galactoside permease, and thiogalactoside transacetylase is increased 100-fold to 1000-fold. This is a type A response, as depicted in Figure 38–1. The kinetics of induction can be quite rapid; *lac*-specific mRNAs are fully induced within 5–6 minutes after addition of lactose to a culture; β-galactosidase protein is maximal within 10 minutes. Under fully induced conditions, there can be up to 5000 β-galactosidase molecules per cell, an amount about 1000 times greater than the basal, uninduced level. Upon removal of the signal, ie, the inducer, the synthesis of these three enzymes declines.

When *E coli* is exposed to both lactose and glucose as sources of carbon, the organisms first metabolize the glucose and then temporarily stop growing until the genes of the *lac* operon become induced to provide the ability to metabolize lactose as a usable energy source. Although lactose is present from the beginning of the bacterial growth phase, the cell does not induce those enzymes necessary for catabolism of lactose until the glucose has been exhausted. This phenomenon was first thought to be attributable to repression of the *lac* operon by some catabolite of glucose; hence, it was termed catabolite repression. It is now known that catabolite repression is in fact mediated by a **catabolite gene activator protein (CAP)** in conjunction with **cAMP** (Figure 17–5). This protein is also referred to as the cAMP regulatory protein (CRP). The expression of many inducible enzyme systems or operons in *E coli* and other prokaryotes is sensitive to catabolite repression, as discussed below.

The physiology of induction of the *lac* operon is well understood at the molecular level (Figure 38–3). Expression of the normal *lacI* gene of the *lac* operon is constitutive; it is expressed at a constant rate, resulting in formation of the subunits of the **lac repressor.** Four identical subunits with molecular weights of 38,000 assemble into a *lac* repressor molecule. The LacI repressor protein molecule, the product of *lacI*, has a high affinity (K_d about 10^{-13} mol/L) for the operator locus. The **operator locus** is a region of double-stranded

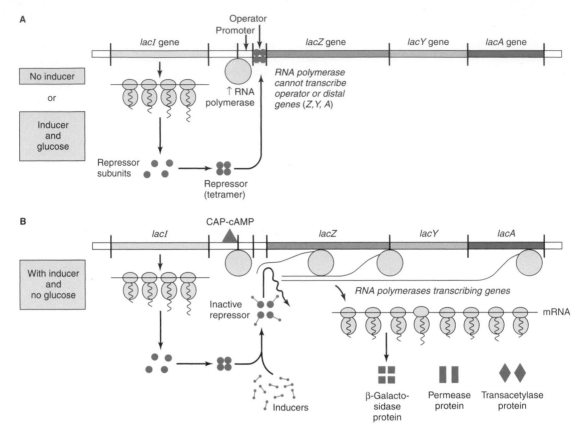

Figure 38–3. The mechanism of repression and derepression of the *lac* operon. When either no inducer is present or inducer is present with glucose **(A),** the *lacI* gene products that are synthesized constitutively form a repressor tetramer molecule which binds at the operator locus to prevent the efficient initiation of transcription by RNA polymerase at the promoter locus and thus to prevent the subsequent transcription of the *lacZ, lacY,* and *lacA* structural genes. When inducer is present **(B),** the constitutively expressed *lacI* gene forms tetrameric repressor molecules that are conformationally altered by the inducer and cannot efficiently bind to the operator locus (affinity of binding reduced > 1000-fold). In the presence of cAMP and its binding protein (CAP), the RNA polymerase can transcribe the structural genes *lacZ, lacY,* and *lacA,* and the polycistronic mRNA molecule formed can be translated into the corresponding protein molecules β-galactosidase, permease, and transacetylase, allowing for the catabolism of lactose.

DNA 27 base pairs long with a twofold rotational symmetry and an inverted palindrome (indicated by arrows about the dotted axis) in a region that is 21 base pairs long, as shown below:

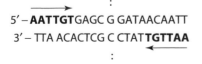

At any one time, only two subunits of the repressors appear to bind to the operator, and within the 21-base-

pair region nearly every base of each base pair is involved in LacI recognition and binding. The binding occurs mostly in the **major groove** without interrupting the base-paired, double-helical nature of the operator DNA. The **operator locus** is between the **promoter site,** at which the DNA-dependent RNA polymerase attaches to commence transcription, and the transcription initiation site of the ***lacZ* gene,** the structural gene for β-galactosidase (Figure 38–2). When attached to the operator locus, the LacI repressor molecule prevents transcription of the operator locus as well as of the distal structural genes, *lacZ, lacY,* and *lacA.* Thus, the LacI repressor molecule is a **negative regulator;** in its presence

(and in the absence of inducer; see below), expression from the *lacZ*, *lacY*, and *lacA* genes is prevented. There are normally 20–40 repressor tetramer molecules in the cell, a concentration of tetramer sufficient to effect, at any given time, > 95% occupancy of the one *lac* operator element in a bacterium, thus ensuring low (but not zero) basal *lac* operon gene transcription in the absence of inducing signals.

A lactose analog that is capable of inducing the *lac* operon while not itself serving as a substrate for β-galactosidase is an example of a **gratuitous inducer.** An example is isopropylthiogalactoside (IPTG). The addition of lactose or of a gratuitous inducer such as IPTG to bacteria growing on a poorly utilized carbon source (such as succinate) results in prompt induction of the *lac* operon enzymes. Small amounts of the gratuitous inducer or of lactose are able to enter the cell even in the absence of permease. The LacI repressor molecules—both those attached to the operator loci and those free in the cytosol—have a high affinity for the inducer. Binding of the inducer to a repressor molecule attached to the operator locus induces a conformational change in the structure of the repressor and causes it to dissociate from the DNA because its affinity for the operator is now 10^3 times lower (K_d about 10^{-9} mol/L) than that of LacI in the absence of IPTG. If DNA-dependent RNA polymerase has already attached to the coding strand at the promoter site, transcription will begin. The polymerase generates a polycistronic mRNA whose 5′ terminal is complementary to the template strand of the operator. In such a manner, **an inducer derepresses the *lac* operon** and allows transcription of the structural genes for β-galactosidase, galactoside permease, and thiogalactoside transacetylase. Translation of the polycistronic mRNA can occur even before transcription is completed. Derepression of the *lac* operon allows the cell to synthesize the enzymes necessary to catabolize lactose as an energy source. Based on the physiology just described, IPTG-induced expression of transfected plasmids bearing the *lac* operator-promoter ligated to appropriate bioengineered constructs is commonly used to express mammalian recombinant proteins in *E coli*.

In order for the RNA polymerase to efficiently form a PIC at the promoter site, there must also be present the **catabolite gene activator protein (CAP)** to which cAMP is bound. By an independent mechanism, the bacterium accumulates cAMP only when it is starved for a source of carbon. In the presence of glucose—or of glycerol in concentrations sufficient for growth—the bacteria will lack sufficient cAMP to bind to CAP because the glucose inhibits adenylyl cyclase, the enzyme that converts ATP to cAMP (see Chapter 41). Thus, in the presence of glucose or glycerol, cAMP-saturated CAP is lacking, so that the DNA-dependent

RNA polymerase cannot initiate transcription of the *lac* operon. In the presence of the CAP-cAMP complex, which binds to DNA just upstream of the promoter site, transcription then occurs (Figure 38–3). Studies indicate that a region of CAP contacts the RNA polymerase α subunit and facilitates binding of this enzyme to the promoter. Thus, the CAP-cAMP regulator is acting as a **positive regulator** because its presence is required for gene expression. The *lac* operon is therefore controlled by two distinct, ligand-modulated DNA binding trans factors; one that acts positively (cAMP-CRP complex) and one that acts negatively (LacI repressor). Maximal activity of the *lac* operon occurs when glucose levels are low (high cAMP with CAP activation) and lactose is present (LacI is prevented from binding to the operator).

When the *lacI* gene has been mutated so that its product, LacI, is not capable of binding to operator DNA, the organism will exhibit **constitutive expression** of the *lac* operon. In a contrary manner, an organism with a *lacI* gene mutation that produces a LacI protein which prevents the binding of an inducer to the repressor will remain repressed even in the presence of the inducer molecule, because the inducer cannot bind to the repressor on the operator locus in order to derepress the operon. Similarly, bacteria harboring mutations in their *lac* operator locus such that the operator sequence will not bind a normal repressor molecule constitutively express the *lac* operon genes. Mechanisms of positive and negative regulation comparable to those described here for the *lac* system have been observed in eukaryotic cells (see below).

The Genetic Switch of Bacteriophage Lambda (λ) Provides a Paradigm for Protein-DNA Interactions in Eukaryotic Cells

Like some eukaryotic viruses (eg, herpes simplex, HIV), some bacterial viruses can either reside in a dormant state within the host chromosomes or can replicate within the bacterium and eventually lead to lysis and killing of the bacterial host. Some *E coli* harbor such a "temperate" virus, bacteriophage lambda (λ). When lambda infects an organism of that species it injects its 45,000-bp, double-stranded, linear DNA genome into the cell (Figure 38–4). Depending upon the nutritional state of the cell, the lambda DNA will either **integrate** into the host genome **(lysogenic pathway)** and remain dormant until activated (see below), or it will commence **replicating** until it has made about 100 copies of complete, protein-packaged virus, at which point it causes lysis of its host **(lytic pathway).** The newly generated virus particles can then infect other susceptible hosts.

When integrated into the host genome in its dormant state, lambda will remain in that state until acti-

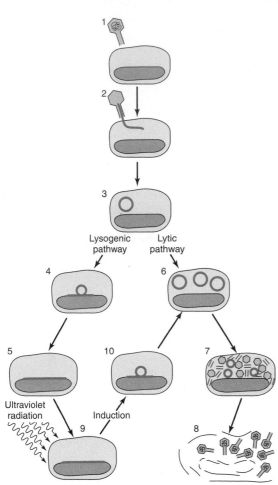

Figure 38–4. Infection of the bacterium *E coli* by phage lambda begins when a virus particle attaches itself to specific receptors on the bacterial cell (1) and injects its DNA (shaded line) into the cell (2, 3). Infection can take either of two courses depending on which of two sets of viral genes is turned on. In the lysogenic pathway, the viral DNA becomes integrated into the bacterial chromosome (4, 5), where it replicates passively as the bacterial cell divides. The dormant virus is called a prophage, and the cell that harbors it is called a lysogen. In the alternative lytic mode of infection, the viral DNA replicates itself (6) and directs the synthesis of viral proteins (7). About 100 new virus particles are formed. The proliferating viruses lyse, or burst, the cell (8). A prophage can be "induced" by a DNA damaging agent such as ultraviolet radiation (9). The inducing agent throws a switch, so that a different set of genes is turned on. Viral DNA loops out of the chromosome (10) and replicates; the virus proceeds along the lytic pathway. (Reproduced, with permission, from Ptashne M, Johnson AD, Pabo CO: A genetic switch in a bacterial virus. Sci Am [Nov] 1982;247:128.)

vated by exposure of its lysogenic bacterial host to DNA-damaging agents. In response to such a noxious stimulus, the dormant bacteriophage becomes "induced" and begins to transcribe and subsequently translate those genes of its own genome which are necessary for its excision from the host chromosome, its DNA replication, and the synthesis of its protein coat and lysis enzymes. This event acts like a trigger or type C (Figure 38–1) response; ie, once lambda has committed itself to induction, there is no turning back until the cell is lysed and the replicated bacteriophage released. This switch from a dormant or **prophage state** to a **lytic infection** is well understood at the genetic and molecular levels and will be described in detail here.

The switching event in lambda is centered around an 80-bp region in its double-stranded DNA genome referred to as the "right operator" (O_R) (Figure 38–5A). The **right operator** is flanked on its left side by the structural gene for the lambda repressor protein, the **cI protein,** and on its right side by the structural gene encoding another regulatory protein called **Cro.** When lambda is in its prophage state—ie, integrated into the host genome—the cI repressor gene is the *only* lambda gene that is expressed. When the bacteriophage is undergoing lytic growth, the cI repressor gene is not expressed, but the *cro* gene—as well as many other genes in lambda—is expressed. That is, **when the repressor gene is on, the *cro* gene is off, and when the *cro* gene is on, the repressor gene is off.** As we shall see, these two genes regulate each other's expression and thus, ultimately, the decision between lytic and lysogenic growth of lambda. **This decision between repressor gene transcription and *cro* gene transcription is a paradigmatic example of a molecular transcriptional switch.**

The 80-bp λ right operator, O_R, can be subdivided into three discrete, evenly spaced, 17-bp cis-active DNA elements that represent the binding sites for either of two bacteriophage λ regulatory proteins. Importantly, the nucleotide sequences of these three tandemly arranged sites are similar but not identical (Figure 38–5B). The three related cis elements, termed operators O_R1, O_R2, and O_R3, can be bound by either cI or Cro proteins. However, the relative affinities of cI and Cro for each of the sites varies, and this differential binding affinity is central to the appropriate operation of the λ phage lytic or lysogenic "molecular switch." The DNA region between the *cro* and repressor genes also contains two promoter sequences that direct the binding of RNA polymerase in a specified orientation, where it commences transcribing adjacent genes. One promoter directs RNA polymerase to transcribe in the **rightward direction** and, thus, to transcribe *cro* and other distal genes, while the other promoter directs the transcription of the **repressor** gene in the **leftward direction** (Figure 38–5B).

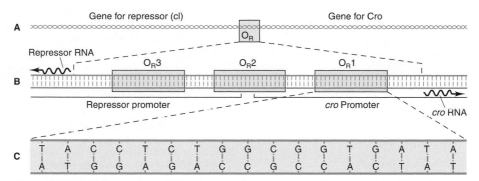

Figure 38–5. Right operator (O_R) is shown in increasing detail in this series of drawings. The operator is a region of the viral DNA some 80 base pairs long **(A)**. To its left lies the gene encoding lambda repressor (cI), to its right the gene *(cro)* encoding the regulator protein Cro. When the operator region is enlarged **(B)**, it is seen to include three subregions, O_R1, O_R2, and O_R3, each 17 base pairs long. They are recognition sites to which both repressor and Cro can bind. The recognition sites overlap two promoters—sequences of bases to which RNA polymerase binds in order to transcribe these genes into mRNA (wavy lines), that are translated into protein. Site O_R1 is enlarged **(C)** to show its base sequence. Note that in the O_R region of the λ chromosome, both strands of DNA act as a template for transcription (Chapter 36). (Reproduced, with permission, from Ptashne M, Johnson AD, Pabo CO: A genetic switch in a bacterial virus. Sci Am [Nov] 1982;247:128.)

The product of the repressor gene, the 236-amino-acid, 27 kDa **repressor protein,** exists as a **two-domain** molecule in which the **amino terminal domain binds to operator DNA** and the **carboxyl terminal domain promotes the association** of one repressor protein with another to form a dimer. A **dimer** of repressor molecules binds to **operator DNA** much more tightly than does the monomeric form (Figure 38–6A to 38–6C).

The product of the *cro* gene, the 66-amino-acid, 9 kDa **Cro protein,** has a single domain but also binds the operator DNA more tightly as a **dimer** (Figure 38–6D). The Cro protein's single domain mediates both operator binding and dimerization.

In a lysogenic bacterium—ie, a bacterium containing a lambda prophage—the lambda repressor dimer binds **preferentially to O_R1** but in so doing, by a cooperative interaction, enhances the binding (by a factor of 10) of another repressor dimer to O_R2 (Figure 38–7). The affinity of repressor for O_R3 is the least of the three operator subregions. The binding of repressor to O_R1 has two major effects. The occupation of O_R1 by repressor **blocks the binding of RNA polymerase to the rightward promoter** and in that way prevents expression of *cro*. Second, as mentioned above, repressor dimer bound to O_R1 enhances the binding of repressor dimer to O_R2. The binding of repressor to O_R2 has the important added effect of **enhancing the binding of RNA polymerase to the leftward promoter** that overlaps O_R2 and thereby enhances transcription

and subsequent expression of the repressor gene. This enhancement of transcription is apparently mediated through direct protein-protein interactions between promoter-bound RNA polymerase and O_R2-bound repressor. Thus, the lambda repressor is both a **negative regulator,** by preventing transcription of *cro,* and a **positive regulator,** by enhancing transcription of its own gene, the repressor gene. This dual effect of repressor is responsible for the stable state of the dormant lambda bacteriophage; not only does the repressor prevent expression of the genes necessary for lysis, but it also promotes expression of itself to stabilize this state of differentiation. In the event that intracellular repressor protein concentration becomes very high, this excess repressor will bind to O_R3 and by so doing diminish transcription of the repressor gene from the leftward promoter until the repressor concentration drops and repressor dissociates itself from O_R3.

With such a stable, repressive, cI-mediated, lysogenic state, one might wonder how the lytic cycle could ever be entered. However, this process does occur quite efficiently. When a DNA-damaging signal, such as ultraviolet light, strikes the lysogenic host bacterium, fragments of single-stranded DNA are generated that activate a specific **protease** coded by a bacterial gene and referred to as **recA** (Figure 38–7). The activated recA protease hydrolyzes the portion of the repressor protein that connects the amino terminal and carboxyl terminal domains of that molecule (see Figure 38–6A). Such cleavage of the repressor domains causes the **repressor dimers to dissociate,** which in turn causes

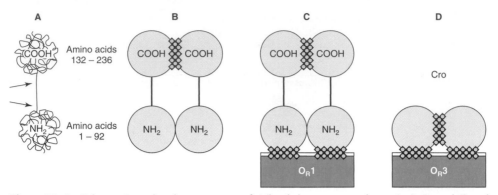

Figure 38–6. Schematic molecular structures of cI (lambda repressor, shown in **A, B,** and **C**) and Cro **(D)**. Lambda repressor protein is a polypeptide chain 236 amino acids long. The chain folds itself into a dumbbell shape with two substructures: an amino terminal (NH$_2$) domain and a carboxyl terminal (COOH) domain. The two domains are linked by a region of the chain that is susceptible to cleavage by proteases (indicated by the two arrows in **A**). Single repressor molecules (monomers) tend to associate to form dimers **(B);** a dimer can dissociate to form monomers again. A dimer is held together mainly by contact between the carboxyl terminal domains (hatching). Repressor dimers bind to (and can dissociate from) the recognition sites in the operator region; they display the greatest affinity for site O$_R$1 **(C).** It is the amino terminal domain of the repressor molecule that makes contact with the DNA (hatching). Cro **(D)** has a single domain with sites that promote dimerization and other sites that promote binding of dimers to operator, preferentially to O$_R$3. (Reproduced, with permission, from Ptashne M, Johnson AD, Pabo CO: A genetic switch in a bacterial virus. Sci Am [Nov] 1982;247:128.)

dissociation of the repressor molecules from O$_R$2 and eventually from O$_R$1. The effects of removal of repressor from O$_R$1 and O$_R$2 are predictable. RNA polymerase immediately has access to the rightward promoter and commences transcribing the **cro gene,** and the enhancement effect of the repressor at O$_R$2 on leftward transcription is lost (Figure 38–7).

The resulting newly synthesized Cro protein also binds to the operator region as a dimer, but its order of preference is opposite to that of repressor (Figure 38–7). That is, **Cro binds most tightly to O$_R$3,** but there is no cooperative effect of Cro at O$_R$3 on the binding of Cro to O$_R$2. At increasingly higher concentrations of Cro, the protein will bind to O$_R$2 and eventually to O$_R$1.

Occupancy of O$_R$3 by Cro immediately turns off transcription from the leftward promoter and in that way **prevents any further expression of the repressor gene.** The molecular switch is thus completely "thrown" in the lytic direction. The *cro* gene is now expressed, and the repressor gene is fully turned off. This event is irreversible, and the expression of other lambda genes begins as part of the lytic cycle. When Cro repressor concentration becomes quite high, it will eventually occupy O$_R$1 and in so doing reduce the expression of its own gene, a process that is necessary in order to effect the final stages of the lytic cycle.

The three-dimensional structures of Cro and of the lambda repressor protein have been determined by x-ray crystallography, and models for their binding and effecting the above-described molecular and genetic events have been proposed and tested. Both bind to DNA using helix-turn-helix DNA binding domain motifs (see below). To date, this system provides the best understanding of the molecular events involved in gene regulation.

Detailed analysis of the lambda repressor led to the important concept that transcription regulatory proteins have several functional domains. For example, lambda repressor binds to DNA with high affinity. Repressor monomers form dimers, dimers interact with each other, and repressor interacts with RNA polymerase. The protein-DNA interface and the three protein-protein interfaces all involve separate and distinct domains of the repressor molecule. As will be noted below (see Figure 38–17), this is a characteristic shared by most (perhaps all) molecules that regulate transcription.

SPECIAL FEATURES ARE INVOLVED IN REGULATION OF EUKARYOTIC GENE TRANSCRIPTION

Most of the DNA in prokaryotic cells is organized into genes, and the templates can always be transcribed. A very different situation exists in mammalian cells, in

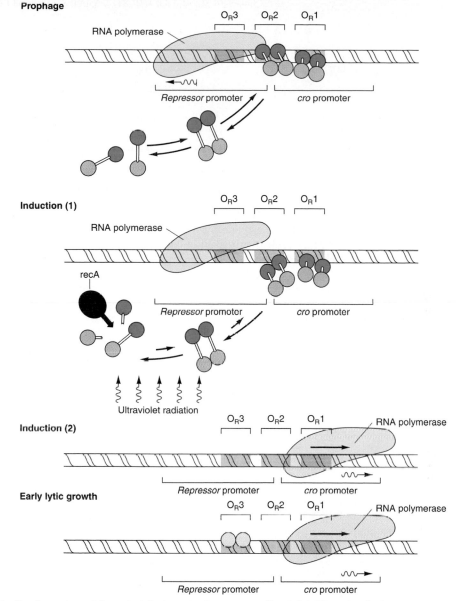

Figure 38–7. Configuration of the switch is shown at four stages of lambda's life cycle. The lysogenic pathway (in which the virus remains dormant as a prophage) is selected when a repressor dimer binds to O_R1, thereby making it likely that O_R2 will be filled immediately by another dimer. In the prophage (top), the repressor dimers bound at O_R1 and O_R2 prevent RNA polymerase from binding to the rightward promoter and so block the synthesis of Cro (negative control). The repressors also enhance the binding of polymerase to the leftward promoter (positive control), with the result that the repressor gene is transcribed into RNA (wavy line) and more repressor is synthesized, maintaining the lysogenic state. The prophage is induced when ultraviolet radiation activates the protease recA, which cleaves repressor monomers. The equilibrium of free monomers, free dimers, and bound dimers is thereby shifted, and dimers leave the operator sites. RNA polymerase is no longer encouraged to bind to the leftward promoter, so that repressor is no longer synthesized. As induction proceeds, all the operator sites become vacant, and so polymerase can bind to the rightward promoter and Cro is synthesized. During early lytic growth, a single Cro dimer binds to O_R3 shaded circles, the site for which it has the highest affinity. Consequently, RNA polymerase cannot bind to the leftward promoter, but the rightward promoter remains accessible. Polymerase continues to bind there, transcribing *cro* and other early lytic genes. Lytic growth ensues. (Reproduced, with permission, from Ptashne M, Johnson AD, Pabo CO: A genetic switch in a bacterial virus. Sci Am [Nov] 1982;247:128.)

which relatively little of the total DNA is organized into genes and their associated regulatory regions. The function of the extra DNA is unknown. In addition, as described in Chapter 35, the DNA in eukaryotic cells is extensively folded and packed into the protein-DNA complex called chromatin. Histones are an important part of this complex since they both form the structures known as nucleosomes (see Chapter 35) and also factor significantly into gene regulatory mechanisms as outlined below.

Chromatin Remodeling Is an Important Aspect of Eukaryotic Gene Expression

Chromatin structure provides an additional level of control of gene transcription. As discussed in Chapter 35, large regions of chromatin are transcriptionally inactive while others are either active or potentially active. With few exceptions, each cell contains the same complement of genes (antibody-producing cells are a notable exception). The development of specialized organs, tissues, and cells and their function in the intact organism depend upon the differential expression of genes.

Some of this differential expression is achieved by having different regions of chromatin available for transcription in cells from various tissues. For example, the DNA containing the β-globin gene cluster is in **"active" chromatin** in the reticulocyte but in **"inactive" chromatin** in muscle cells. All the factors involved in the determination of active chromatin have not been elucidated. The presence of nucleosomes and of complexes of histones and DNA (see Chapter 35) certainly provides a barrier against the ready association of transcription factors with specific DNA regions. The dynamics of the formation and disruption of nucleosome structure are therefore an important part of eukaryotic gene regulation.

Histone acetylation and deacetylation is an important determinant of gene activity. The surprising discovery that histone acetylase activity is associated with TAFs and the coactivators involved in hormonal regulation of gene transcription (see Chapter 42) has provided a new concept of gene regulation. Acetylation is known to occur on lysine residues in the amino terminal tails of histone molecules. This modification reduces the positive charge of these tails and decreases the binding affinity of histone for the negatively charged DNA. Accordingly, the acetylation of histones could result in disruption of nucleosomal structure and allow readier access of transcription factors to cognate regulatory DNA elements. As discussed previously, this would enhance binding of the basal transcription machinery to the promoter. Histone deacetylation would have the opposite effect. Different proteins with specific acetylase and deacetylase activities are associated with various components of the transcription apparatus. The

specificity of these processes is under investigation, as are a variety of mechanisms of action. Some specific examples are illustrated in Chapter 42.

There is evidence that the **methylation of deoxycytidine residues** (in the sequence 5′-^{m}CpG-3′) in DNA may effect gross changes in chromatin so as to preclude its active transcription, as described in Chapter 35. For example, in mouse liver, only the unmethylated ribosomal genes can be expressed, and there is evidence that many animal viruses are not transcribed when their DNA is methylated. Acute demethylation of deoxycytidine residues in a specific region of the tyrosine aminotransferase gene—in response to glucocorticoid hormones—has been associated with an increased rate of transcription of the gene. However, it is not possible to generalize that methylated DNA is transcriptionally inactive, that all inactive chromatin is methylated, or that active DNA is not methylated.

Finally, the binding of specific transcription factors to cognate DNA elements may result in disruption of nucleosomal structure. Many eukaryotic genes have multiple protein-binding DNA elements. The serial binding of transcription factors to these elements—in a combinatorial fashion—may either directly disrupt the structure of the nucleosome or prevent its re-formation or recruit, via protein-protein interactions, multiprotein coactivator complexes that have the ability to covalently modify or remodel nucleosomes. These reactions result in chromatin-level structural changes that in the end increase DNA accessibility to other factors and the transcription machinery.

Eukaryotic DNA that is in an "active" region of chromatin can be transcribed. As in prokaryotic cells, a **promoter** dictates where the RNA polymerase will initiate transcription, but this promoter cannot be neatly defined as containing a −35 and −10 box, particularly in mammalian cells (Chapter 36). In addition, the trans-acting factors generally come from other chromosomes (and so act in trans), whereas this consideration is moot in the case of the single chromosome-containing prokaryotic cells. Additional complexity is added by elements or factors that enhance or repress transcription, define tissue-specific expression, and modulate the actions of many effector molecules. Finally, recent results suggest that gene activation and repression might occur when particular genes move into or out of different subnuclear compartments.

Certain DNA Elements Enhance or Repress Transcription of Eukaryotic Genes

In addition to gross changes in chromatin affecting transcriptional activity, certain DNA elements facilitate or enhance initiation at the promoter. For example, in simian virus 40 (SV40) there exists about 200 bp upstream from the promoter of the early genes a region

of two identical, tandem 72-bp lengths that can greatly increase the expression of genes in vivo. Each of these 72-bp elements can be subdivided into a series of smaller elements; therefore, some enhancers have a very complex structure. **Enhancer elements** differ from the promoter in two remarkable ways. They can exert their positive influence on transcription even when separated by thousands of base pairs from a promoter; they work when oriented in either direction; and they can work upstream (5′) or downstream (3′) from the promoter. Enhancers are promiscuous; they can stimulate any promoter in the vicinity and may act on more than one promoter. The SV40 enhancer element can exert an influence on, for example, the transcription of β-globin by increasing its transcription 200-fold in cells containing both the enhancer and the β-globin gene on the same plasmid (see below and Figure 38–8). The enhancer element does not produce a product that in turn acts on the promoter, since it is active only when it exists within the same DNA molecule as (ie, cis to) the promoter. Enhancer binding proteins are responsible for this effect. The exact mechanisms by which these transcription activators work are subject to much debate. Certainly, enhancer binding trans factors have been shown to interact with a plethora of other transcription proteins. These interactions include chromatin-modifying coactivators as well as the individual components of the basal RNA polymerase II transcription machinery. Ultimately, trans-factor-enhancer DNA binding events result in an increase in the binding of the basal transcription machinery to the promoter. Enhancer elements and associated binding proteins often convey nuclease hypersensitivity to those regions where they reside (Chapter 35). A summary of the properties of enhancers is presented in Table 38–2.

One of the best-understood mammalian enhancer systems is that of the β-interferon gene. This gene is induced upon viral infection of mammalian cells. One goal of the cell, once virally infected, is to attempt to mount an antiviral response—if not to save the infected cell, then to help to save the entire organism from viral infection. Interferon production is one mechanism by which this is accomplished. This family of proteins is secreted by virally infected cells. They interact with neighboring cells to cause an inhibition of viral replication by a variety of mechanisms, thereby limiting the extent of viral infection. The enhancer element controlling induction of this gene, located between nucleotides −110 and −45 of the β-interferon gene, is well characterized. This enhancer is composed of four distinct clustered cis elements, each of which is bound by distinct trans factors. One cis element is bound by the trans-acting factor NF-κB, one by a member of the IRF (interferon regulatory factor) family of trans factors, and a third by the heterodimeric leucine zipper factor

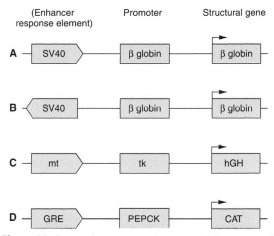

Figure 38–8. A schematic explanation of the action of enhancers and other cis-acting regulatory elements. These model chimeric genes, all constructed by recombinant DNA techniques (Chapter 39) in vitro, consist of a reporter (structural) gene that encodes a protein which can be readily assayed, a promoter that ensures accurate initiation of transcription, and the putative regulatory elements. In all cases, high-level transcription from the indicated chimeras depends upon the presence of enhancers, which stimulate transcription > 100-fold over basal transcriptional levels (ie, transcription of the same chimeric genes containing just promoters fused to the structural genes). Examples **(A)** and **(B)** illustrate the fact that enhancers (eg, SV40) work in either orientation and upon a heterologous promoter. Example **(C)** illustrates that the metallothionein (mt) regulatory element (which under the influence of cadmium or zinc induces transcription of the endogenous mt gene and hence the metal-binding mt protein) will work through the thymidine kinase (tk) promoter to enhance transcription of the human growth hormone (hGH) gene. The engineered genetic constructions were introduced into the male pronuclei of single-cell mouse embryos and the embryos placed into the uterus of a surrogate mother to develop as transgenic animals. Offspring have been generated under these conditions, and in some the addition of zinc ions to their drinking water effects an increase in liver growth hormone. In this case, these transgenic animals have responded to the high levels of growth hormone by becoming twice as large as their normal litter mates. Example **(D)** illustrates that a glucocorticoid response element (GRE) will work through homologous (PEPCK gene) or heterologous promoters (not shown; ie, tk) promoter, SV40 promoter, β-globin promoter, etc).

Table 38–2. Summary of the properties of enhancers.

- Work when located long distances from the promoter
- Work when upstream or downstream from the promoter
- Work when oriented in either direction
- Can work with homologous or heterologous promoters
- Work by binding one or more proteins
- Work by facilitating binding of the basal transcription complex to the promoter

ATF-2/c-Jun. The fourth factor is the ubiquitous, architectural transcription factor known as HMG I(Y). Upon binding to its degenerate, A+T-rich binding sites, HMG I(Y) induces a significant bend in the DNA. There are four such HMG I(Y) binding sites interspersed throughout the enhancer. These sites play a critical role in forming the enhanceosome, along with the aforementioned three trans factors, by inducing a series of critically spaced DNA bends. Consequently, HMG I(Y) induces the cooperative formation of a unique, stereospecific, three dimensional structure within which all four factors are active when viral infection signals are sensed by the cell. The structure formed by the cooperative assembly of these four factors is termed the β-interferon enhanceosome (see Figure 38–9), so named because of its obvious structural similarity to the nucleosome, also a unique three-dimensional protein DNA structure that wraps DNA about an assembly of proteins (see Figures 35–1 and 35–2). The enhanceosome, once formed, induces a large increase in β-interferon gene transcription upon virus infection. It is not simply the protein occupancy of the linearly apposed cis element sites that induces β-interferon gene transcription—rather, it is the formation of the enhanceosome proper that provides appropriate surfaces for the recruitment of coactivators that results in the enhanced formation of the PIC on the cis-linked promoter and thus transcription activation.

The cis-acting elements that decrease or **repress** the expression of specific genes have also been identified. Because fewer of these elements have been studied, it is not possible to formulate generalizations about their mechanism of action—though again, as for gene activation, chromatin level covalent modifications of histones and other proteins by (repressor)-recruited multisubunit corepressors have been implicated.

Tissue-Specific Expression May Result from the Action of Enhancers or Repressors

Many genes are now recognized to harbor enhancer or activator elements in various locations relative to their coding regions. In addition to being able to enhance gene

transcription, some of these enhancer elements clearly possess the ability to do so in a tissue-specific manner. Thus, the enhancer element associated with the immunoglobulin genes between the J and C regions enhances the expression of those genes preferentially in lymphoid cells. Similarly to the SV40 enhancer, which is capable of promiscuously activating a variety of cis-linked genes, enhancer elements associated with the genes for pancreatic enzymes are capable of enhancing even unrelated but physically linked genes preferentially in the pancreatic cells of mice into which the specifically engineered gene constructions were introduced microsurgically at the single-cell embryo stage. This **transgenic animal** approach has proved useful in studying tissue-specific gene expression. For example, DNA containing a pancreatic B cell tissue-specific enhancer (from the insulin gene), when ligated in a vector to polyoma large-T antigen, an oncogene, produced B cell tumors in transgenic mice. Tumors did not develop in any other tissue. Tissue-specific gene expression is mediated by enhancers or enhancer-like elements.

Reporter Genes Are Used to Define Enhancers & Other Regulatory Elements

By ligating regions of DNA suspected of harboring regulatory sequences to various reporter genes (the **reporter** or **chimeric gene approach**) (Figures 38–8, 38–10, and 38–11), one can determine which regions in the vicinity of structural genes have an influence on their expression. Pieces of DNA thought to harbor regulatory elements are ligated to a suitable reporter gene and introduced into a host cell (Figure 38–10). Basal expression of the reporter gene will be increased if the DNA contains an enhancer. Addition of a hormone or heavy metal to the culture medium will increase expression of the reporter gene if the DNA contains a hormone or metal response element (Figure 38–11). The location of the element can be pinpointed by using progressively shorter pieces of DNA, deletions, or point mutations (Figure 38–11).

This strategy, **using transfected cells in culture and transgenic animals,** has led to the identification of dozens of enhancers, repressors, tissue-specific elements, and hormone, heavy metal, and drug-response elements. The activity of a gene at any moment reflects the interaction of these numerous cis-acting DNA elements with their respective trans-acting factors. The challenge now is to figure out how this occurs.

Combinations of DNA Elements & Associated Proteins Provide Diversity in Responses

Prokaryotic genes are often regulated in an on-off manner in response to simple environmental cues. Some

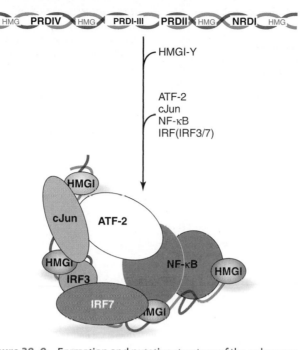

Figure 38–9. Formation and putative structure of the enhanceosome formed on the human β-interferon gene enhancer. Diagram matically represented at the top is the distribution of the multiple cis-elements (HMG, PRDIV, PRDI-III, PRDII, NRDI) composing the β-interferon gene enhancer. The intact enhancer mediates tran scriptional induction of the β-interferon gene (over 100-fold) upon virus infection of human cells. The cis-elements of this modular enhancer represent the binding sites for the trans-factors HMG I(Y), cJun-ATF-2, IRF3, IRF7, and NF-κB, respectively. The factors interact with these DNA elements in an obligatory, ordered, and highly cooperative fashion as indicated by the arrow. Initial binding of four HMG I(Y) proteins induces sharp DNA bends in the enhancer, causing the entire 70 80 bp region to assume a high level of curvature. This curvature is integral to the subsequent highly cooperative binding of the other trans-factors since this enables the DNA-bound factors to make important, direct protein-protein interactions that both contribute to the formation and stability of the enhanceosome and generate a unique three-dimensional surface that serves to recruit chromatin-modifying activities (eg, Swi/Snf and P/CAF) as well as the general transcription machinery (RNA polymerase II and GTFs). Although four of the five cis-elements (PRDIV, PRDI-III, PRDII, NRDI) independently can modestly stimulate (~tenfold) transcription of a reporter gene in transfected cells (see Figures 38–10 and 38–12), all five cis-elements, in appropriate order, are required to form an enhancer that can appropriately stimulate mRNA gene transcription (ie, ≥ 100-fold) in response to viral infection of a human cell. This distinction indicates the strict requirement for appropriate enhanceosome architecture for efficient trans-activation. Similar enhanceosomes, involving distinct cis- and trans-factors, are proposed to form on many other mammalian genes.

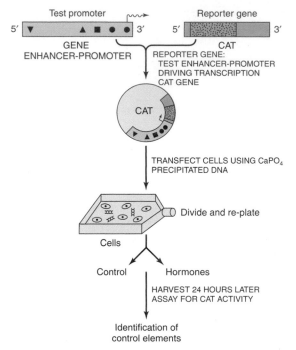

Figure 38–10. The use of reporter genes to define DNA regulatory elements. A DNA fragment from the gene in question—in this example, approximately 2 kb of 5′-flanking DNA and cognate promoter—is ligated into a plasmid vector that contains a suitable reporter gene—in this case, the bacterial enzyme chloramphenicol transferase (CAT). The enzyme luciferase (abbreviated LUC) is another popular reporter gene. Neither LUC nor CAT is present in mammalian cells; hence, detection of these activities in a cell extract means that the cell was successfully transfected by the plasmid. An increase of CAT activity over the basal level, eg, after addition of one or more hormones, means that the region of DNA inserted into the reporter gene plasmid contains functional hormone response elements (HRE). Progressively shorter pieces of DNA, regions with internal deletions, or regions with point mutations can be constructed and inserted to pinpoint the response element (see Figure 38–11 for deletion mapping of the relevant HREs).

eukaryotic genes are regulated in the simple on-off manner, but the process in most genes, especially in mammals, is much more complicated. Signals representing a number of complex environmental stimuli may converge on a single gene. The response of the gene to these signals can have several physiologic characteristics. First, the response may extend over a considerable range. This is accomplished by having additive and synergistic positive responses counterbalanced by negative or repressing effects. In some cases, either the positive or the negative response can be dominant. Also required is a mechanism whereby an effector such as a hormone can activate some genes in a cell while repressing others and leaving still others unaffected. When all of these processes are coupled with tissue-specific element factors, considerable flexibility is afforded. These physiologic variables obviously require an arrangement much more complicated than an on-off switch. The array of DNA elements in a promoter specifies—with associated factors—how a given gene will respond. Some simple examples are illustrated in Figure 38–12.

Transcription Domains Can Be Defined by Locus Control Regions & Insulators

The large number of genes in eukaryotic cells and the complex arrays of transcription regulatory factors presents an organizational problem. Why are some genes available for transcription in a given cell whereas others are not? If enhancers can regulate several genes and are not position- and orientation-dependent, how are they prevented from triggering transcription randomly? Part of the solution to these problems is arrived at by having the chromatin arranged in functional units that restrict patterns of gene expression. This may be achieved by having the chromatin form a structure with the nuclear matrix or other physical entity, or compartments within the nucleus. Alternatively, some regions are controlled by complex DNA elements called **locus control regions (LCRs).** An LCR—with associated bound proteins—controls the expression of a cluster of genes. The best-defined LCR regulates expression of the globin gene family over a large region of DNA. Another mechanism is provided by **insulators.** These DNA elements, also in association with one or more proteins, prevent an enhancer from acting on a promoter on the other side of an insulator in another transcription domain.

SEVERAL MOTIFS MEDIATE THE BINDING OF REGULATORY PROTEINS TO DNA

The specificity involved in the control of transcription requires that regulatory proteins bind with high affinity to the correct region of DNA. Three unique motifs—the **helix-turn-helix,** the **zinc finger,** and the **leucine zipper**—account for many of these specific protein-DNA interactions. Examples of proteins containing these motifs are given in Table 38–3.

Comparison of the binding activities of the proteins that contain these motifs leads to several important generalizations.

(1) Binding must be of high affinity to the specific site and of low affinity to other DNA.

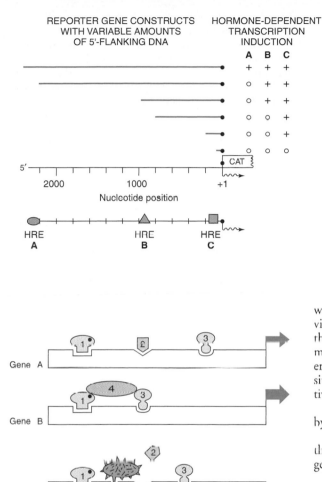

REPORTER GENE CONSTRUCTS
WITH VARIABLE AMOUNTS
OF 5'-FLANKING DNA

HORMONE-DEPENDENT
TRANSCRIPTION
INDUCTION

Figure 38–11. Location of hormone response elements (HREs) **(A)**, **(B)**, and **(C)** using the reporter gene–transfection approach. A family of reporter genes, constructed as described in Figure 38–10, can be transfected individually into a recipient cell. By analyzing when certain hormone responses are lost in comparison to the 5' deletion, specific hormone-responsive elements can be located.

(2) Small regions of the protein make direct contact with DNA; the rest of the protein, in addition to providing the trans-activation domains, may be involved in the dimerization of monomers of the binding protein, may provide a contact surface for the formation of heterodimers, may provide one or more ligand-binding sites, or may provide surfaces for interaction with coactivators or corepressors.

(3) The protein-DNA interactions are maintained by hydrogen bonds and van der Waals forces.

(4) The motifs found in these proteins are unique; their presence in a protein of unknown function suggests that the protein may bind to DNA.

Figure 38–12. Combinations of DNA elements and proteins provide diversity in the response of a gene. Gene A is activated (the width of the arrow indicates the extent) by the combination of activators 1, 2, and 3 (probably with coactivators, as shown in Figure 36–10). Gene B is activated, in this case more effectively, by the combination of 1, 3, and 4; note that 4 does not contact DNA directly in this example. The activators could form a linear bridge that links the basal machinery to the promoter, or this could be accomplished by looping out of the DNA. In either case, the purpose is to direct the basal transcription machinery to the promoter. Gene C is inactivated by the combination of 1, 5, and 3; in this case, factor 5 is shown to preclude the essential binding of factor 2 to DNA, as occurs in example A. If activator 1 helps repressor 5 bind and if activator 1 binding requires a ligand (solid dot), it can be seen how the ligand could activate one gene in a cell (gene A) and repress another (gene C).

Table 38–3. Examples of transcription regulatory proteins that contain the various binding motifs.

Binding Motif	Organism	Regulatory Protein
Helix-turn-helix	E coli	lac repressor CAP
	Phage	λcl, cro, and tryptophan and 434 repressors
	Mammals	homeo box proteins Pit-1, Oct1, Oct2
Zinc finger	E coli	Gene 32 protein
	Yeast	Gal4
	Drosophila	Serendipity, Hunchback
	Xenopus	TFIIIA
	Mammals	steroid receptor family, Sp1
Leucine zipper	Yeast	GCN4
	Mammals	C/EBP, fos, Jun, Fra-1, CRE binding protein, c-*myc*, n-*myc*, l-*myc*

(5) Proteins with the helix-turn-helix or leucine zipper motifs form symmetric dimers, and their respective DNA binding sites are symmetric palindromes. In proteins with the zinc finger motif, the binding site is repeated two to nine times. These features allow for cooperative interactions between binding sites and enhance the degree and affinity of binding.

The Helix-Turn-Helix Motif

The first motif described—and the one studied most extensively—is the helix-turn-helix. Analysis of the three-dimensional structure of the λ Cro transcription regulator has revealed that each monomer consists of three antiparallel β sheets and three α helices (Figure 38–13). The dimer forms by association of the antiparallel β_3 sheets. The α_3 helices form the DNA recognition surface, and the rest of the molecule appears to be involved in stabilizing these structures. The average diameter of an α helix is 1.2 nm, which is the approximate width of the major groove in the B form of DNA.

The DNA recognition domain of each Cro monomer interacts with 5 bp and the dimer binding sites span 3.4 nm, allowing fit into successive half turns of the major groove on the same surface (Figure 38–13). X-ray analyses of the λ cI repressor, CAP (the cAMP receptor protein of *E coli*), tryptophan repressor, and phage 434 repressor all also display this dimeric helix-turn-helix structure that is present in eukaryotic DNA binding proteins as well (see Table 38–3).

The Zinc Finger Motif

The zinc finger was the second DNA binding motif whose atomic structure was elucidated. It was known that the protein TFIIIA, a positive regulator of 5S RNA transcription, required zinc for activity. Structural and biophysical analyses revealed that each TFIIIA molecule contains nine zinc ions in a repeating coordination complex formed by closely spaced cysteine-cysteine residues followed 12–13 amino acids later by a histidine-histidine pair (Figure 38–14). In some instances—notably the

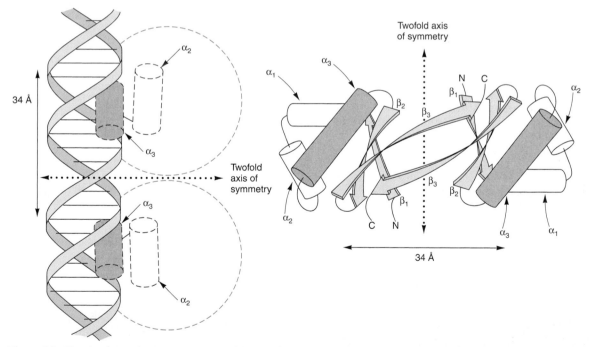

Figure 38–13. A schematic representation of the three-dimensional structure of Cro protein and its binding to DNA by its helix-turn-helix motif. The Cro monomer consists of three antiparallel β sheets (β_1–β_3) and three α-helices (α_1–α_3). The helix-turn-helix motif is formed because the α_3 and α_2 helices are held at about 90 degrees to each other by a turn of four amino acids. The α_3 helix of Cro is the DNA recognition surface (shaded). Two monomers associate through the antiparallel β_3 sheets to form a dimer that has a twofold axis of symmetry (right). A Cro dimer binds to DNA through its α_3 helices, each of which contacts about 5 bp on the same surface of the major groove. The distance between comparable points on the two DNA α-helices is 34 Å, which is the distance required for one complete turn of the double helix. (Courtesy of B Mathews.)

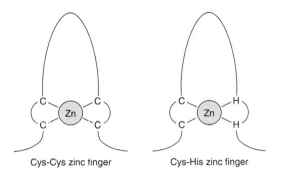

Cys-Cys zinc finger   Cys-His zinc finger

Figure 38–14. Zinc fingers are a series of repeated domains (two to nine) in which each is centered on a tetrahedral coordination with zinc. In the case of TFIIIA, the coordination is provided by a pair of cysteine residues (C) separated by 12–13 amino acids from a pair of histidine (H) residues. In other zinc finger proteins, the second pair also consists of C residues. Zinc fingers bind in the major groove, with adjacent fingers making contact with 5 bp along the same face of the helix.

steroid-thyroid nuclear hormone receptor family the His-His doublet is replaced by a second Cys-Cys pair. The protein containing zinc fingers appears to lie on one face of the DNA helix, with successive fingers alternatively positioned in one turn in the major groove. As is the case with the recognition domain in the helix-turn-helix protein, each TFIIIA zinc finger contacts about 5 bp of DNA. The importance of this motif in the action of steroid hormones is underscored by an "experiment of nature." A single amino acid mutation in either of the two zinc fingers of the $1,25(OH)_2$-D_3 receptor protein results in resistance to the action of this hormone and the clinical syndrome of rickets.

The Leucine Zipper Motif

Careful analysis of a 30-amino-acid sequence in the carboxyl terminal region of the enhancer binding protein C/EBP revealed a novel structure. As illustrated in Figure 38–15, this region of the protein forms an α helix in which there is a periodic repeat of leucine residues at every seventh position. This occurs for eight helical turns and four leucine repeats. Similar structures have been found in a number of other proteins associated with the regulation of transcription in mammalian and yeast cells. It is thought that this structure allows two identical monomers or heterodimers (eg, Fos-Jun or Jun-Jun) to "zip together" in a coiled coil and form a tight dimeric complex (Figure 38–15). This protein-protein interaction may serve to enhance the association of the separate DNA binding domains with their target (Figure 38–15).

THE DNA BINDING & TRANS-ACTIVATION DOMAINS OF MOST REGULATORY PROTEINS ARE SEPARATE & NONINTERACTIVE

DNA binding could result in a general conformational change that allows the bound protein to activate transcription, or these two functions could be served by separate and independent domains. Domain swap experiments suggest that the latter is the case.

The *GAL1* gene product is involved in galactose metabolism in yeast. Transcription of this gene is positively regulated by the GAL4 protein, which binds to an upstream activator sequence (UAS), or enhancer, through an amino terminal domain. The amino terminal 73-amino-acid DNA-binding domain (DBD) of GAL4 was removed and replaced with the DBD of LexA, an *E coli* DNA-binding protein. This domain swap resulted in a molecule that did not bind to the *GAL1* UAS and, of course, did not activate the *GAL1* gene (Figure 38–16). If, however, the *lexA* operator—the DNA sequence normally bound by the *lexA* DBD—was inserted into the promoter region of the *GAL* gene, the hybrid protein bound to this promoter (at the *lexA* operator) and it activated transcription of *GAL1*. This experiment, which has been repeated a number of times, affords solid evidence that the carboxyl terminal region of GAL4 causes transcriptional activation. These data also demonstrate that the DNA-binding DBD and trans-activation domains (ADs) are independent and noninteractive. The hierarchy involved in assembling gene transcription activating complexes includes proteins that bind DNA and transactivate; others that form protein-protein complexes which bridge DNA-binding proteins to trans-activating proteins; and others that form protein-protein complexes with components of the basal transcription apparatus. A given protein may thus have several surfaces or domains that serve different functions (see Figure 38–17). As described in Chapter 36, the primary purpose of these complex assemblies is to facilitate the assembly and/or activity of the basal transcription apparatus on the cis-linked promoter.

GENE REGULATION IN PROKARYOTES & EUKARYOTES DIFFERS IN IMPORTANT RESPECTS

In addition to transcription, eukaryotic cells employ a variety of mechanisms to regulate gene expression (Table 38–4). The nuclear membrane of eukaryotic cells physically segregates gene transcription from translation, since ribosomes exist only in the cytoplasm. Many more steps, especially in RNA processing, are involved in the expression of eukaryotic genes than of

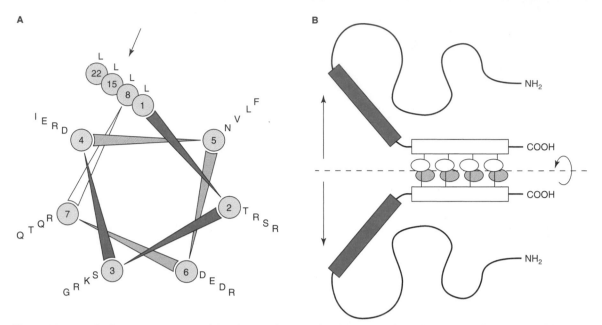

Figure 38–15. The leucine zipper motif. **(A)** shows a helical wheel analysis of a carboxyl terminal portion of the DNA binding protein C/EBP. The amino acid sequence is displayed end-to-end down the axis of a schematic α-helix. The helical wheel consists of seven spokes that correspond to the seven amino acids that comprise every two turns of the α-helix. Note that leucine residues (L) occur at every seventh position (in this schematic C/EBP amino acid residues 1, 8, 15, 22; see arrow). Other proteins with "leucine zippers" have a similar helical wheel pattern. **(B)** is a schematic model of the DNA binding domain of C/EBP. Two identical C/EBP polypeptide chains are held in dimer formation by the leucine zipper domain of each polypeptide (denoted by the rectangles and attached ovals). This association is apparently required to hold the DNA binding domains of each polypeptide (the shaded rectangles) in the proper conformation for DNA binding. (Courtesy of S McKnight.)

prokaryotic genes, and these steps provide additional sites for regulatory influences that cannot exist in prokaryotes. These RNA processing steps in eukaryotes, described in detail in Chapter 36, include capping of the 5′ ends of the primary transcripts, addition of a polyadenylate tail to the 3′ ends of transcripts, and excision of intron regions to generate spliced exons in the mature mRNA molecule. To date, analyses of eukaryotic gene expression provide evidence that regulation occurs at the level of **transcription, nuclear RNA processing,** and **mRNA stability.** In addition, gene amplification and rearrangement influence gene expression.

Owing to the advent of recombinant DNA technology, much progress has been made in recent years in the understanding of eukaryotic gene expression. However, because most eukaryotic organisms contain so much more genetic information than do prokaryotes and because manipulation of their genes is so much more limited, molecular aspects of eukaryotic gene regulation are less well understood than the examples discussed earlier in this chapter. This section briefly describes a few different types of eukaryotic gene regulation.

Eukaryotic Genes Can Be Amplified or Rearranged during Development or in Response to Drugs

During early development of metazoans, there is an abrupt increase in the need for specific molecules such as ribosomal RNA and messenger RNA molecules for proteins that make up such organs as the eggshell. One way to increase the rate at which such molecules can be formed is to increase the number of genes available for transcription of these specific molecules. Among the repetitive DNA sequences are hundreds of copies of ribosomal RNA genes and tRNA genes. These genes preexist repetitively in the genomic material of the gametes and thus are transmitted in high copy numbers from generation to generation. In some specific organisms such as the fruit fly (drosophila), there occurs during oogenesis an amplification of a few preexisting genes such as those for the chorion (eggshell) proteins. Subsequently, these amplified genes, presumably generated by a process of repeated initiations during DNA synthesis, provide multiple sites for gene transcription (Figures 36–4 and 38–18).

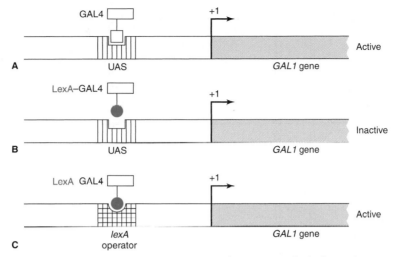

Figure 38–16. Domain-swap experiments demonstrate the independent nature of DNA binding and transcription activation domains. The *GAL1* gene promoter contains an upstream activating sequence (UAS) or enhancer that binds the regulatory protein GAL4 **(A).** This interaction results in a stimulation of *GAL1* gene transcription. A chimeric protein, in which the amino terminal DNA binding domain of GAL4 is removed and replaced with the DNA binding region of the *E coli* protein LexA, fails to stimulate *GAL1* transcription because the LexA domain cannot bind to the UAS **(B).** The LexA–GAL4 fusion protein does increase *GAL1* transcription when the *lexA* operator (its natural target) is inserted into the *GAL1* promoter region **(C),** replacing the normal GAL1 UAS.

As noted in Chapter 36, the coding sequences responsible for the generation of specific protein molecules are frequently not contiguous in the mammalian genome. In the case of antibody encoding genes, this is particularly true. As described in detail in Chapter 49, immunoglobulins are composed of two polypeptides, the so-called heavy (about 50 kDa) and light (about 25 kDa) chains. The mRNAs encoding these two protein subunits are encoded by gene sequences that are subjected to extensive DNA sequence-coding changes. These DNA coding changes are integral to generating the requisite recognition diversity central to appropriate immune function.

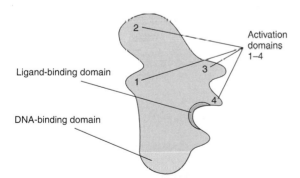

Figure 38–17. Proteins that regulate transcription have several domains. This hypothetical transcription factor has a DNA-binding domain (DBD) that is distinct from a ligand-binding domain (LBD) and several activation domains (ADs) (1–4). Other proteins may lack the DBD or LBD and all may have variable numbers of domains that contact other proteins, including co-regulators and those of the basal transcription complex (see also Chapters 41 and 42).

Table 38–4. Gene expression is regulated by transcription and in numerous other ways at the RNA level in eukaryotic cells.

- Gene amplification
- Gene rearrangement
- RNA processing
- Alternate mRNA splicing
- Transport of mRNA from nucleus to cytoplasm
- Regulation of mRNA stability

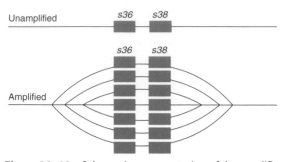

Figure 38–18. Schematic representation of the amplification of chorion protein genes *s36* and *s38*. (Reproduced, with permission, from Chisholm R: Gene amplification during development. Trends Biochem Sci 1982;7:161. Copyright © 1982. Reprinted with permission from Elsevier.)

IgG heavy and light chain mRNAs are encoded by several different segments that are tandemly repeated in the germline. Thus, for example, the IgG light chain is composed of variable (V_L), joining (J_L), and constant (C_L) domains or segments. For particular subsets of IgG light chains, there are roughly 300 tandemly repeated V_L gene coding segments, five tandemly arranged J_L coding sequences, and roughly ten C_L gene coding segments. All of these multiple, distinct coding regions are located in the same region of the same chromosome, and each type of coding segment (V_L, J_L, and C_L) is tandemly repeated in head-to-tail fashion within the segment repeat region. By having multiple V_L, J_L, and C_L segments to choose from, an immune cell has a greater repertoire of sequences to work with to develop both immunologic flexibility and specificity. However, a given functional IgG light chain transcription unit—like all other "normal" mammalian transcription units—contains only the coding sequences for a single protein. Thus, before a particular IgG light chain can be expressed, *single* V_L, J_L, and C_L coding sequences must be recombined to generate a *single,* contiguous transcription unit excluding the multiple nonutilized segments (ie, the other approximately 300 unused V_L segments, the other four unused J_L segments, and the other nine unused C_L segments). This deletion of unused genetic information is accomplished by selective DNA recombination that removes the unwanted coding DNA while retaining the required coding sequences: one V_L, one J_L, and one C_L sequence. (V_L sequences are subjected to additional point mutagenesis to generate even more variability—hence the name.) The newly recombined sequences thus form a single transcription unit that is competent for RNA polymerase II-mediated transcription. Although the IgG genes represent one of the best-studied instances of directed DNA rearrangement modulating gene expression, other

cases of gene regulatory DNA rearrangement have been described in the literature. Indeed, as detailed below, drug-induced gene amplification is an important complication of cancer chemotherapy.

In recent years, it has been possible to promote the amplification of specific genetic regions in cultured mammalian cells. In some cases, a several thousand-fold increase in the copy number of specific genes can be achieved over a period of time involving increasing doses of selective drugs. In fact, it has been demonstrated in patients receiving methotrexate for cancer that malignant cells can develop **drug resistance** by increasing the number of genes for dihydrofolate reductase, the target of methotrexate. Gene amplification events such as these occur spontaneously in vivo—ie, in the absence of exogenously supplied selective agents—and these unscheduled extra rounds of replication can become "frozen" in the genome under appropriate selective pressures.

Alternative RNA Processing Is Another Control Mechanism

In addition to affecting the efficiency of promoter utilization, eukaryotic cells employ alternative RNA processing to control gene expression. This can result when alternative promoters, intron-exon splice sites, or polyadenylation sites are used. Occasionally, heterogeneity within a cell results, but more commonly the same primary transcript is processed differently in different tissues. A few examples of each of these types of regulation are presented below.

The use of alternative **transcription start sites** results in a different 5′ exon on mRNAs corresponding to mouse amylase and myosin light chain, rat glucokinase, and drosophila alcohol dehydrogenase and actin. **Alternative polyadenylation sites** in the μ immunoglobulin heavy chain primary transcript result in mRNAs that are either 2700 bases long (μ_m) or 2400 bases long (μ_s). This results in a different carboxyl terminal region of the encoded proteins such that the μ_m protein remains attached to the membrane of the B lymphocyte and the μ_s immunoglobulin is secreted. **Alternative splicing and processing** results in the formation of seven unique α-tropomyosin mRNAs in seven different tissues. It is not clear how these processing-splicing decisions are made or whether these steps can be regulated.

Regulation of Messenger RNA Stability Provides Another Control Mechanism

Although most mRNAs in mammalian cells are very stable (half-lives measured in hours), some turn over very rapidly (half-lives of 10–30 minutes). In certain instances, mRNA stability is subject to regulation. This has important implications since there is usually a direct

relationship between mRNA amount and the translation of that mRNA into its cognate protein. Changes in the stability of a specific mRNA can therefore have major effects on biologic processes.

Messenger RNAs exist in the cytoplasm as ribonucleoprotein particles (RNPs). Some of these proteins protect the mRNA from digestion by nucleases, while others may under certain conditions promote nuclease attack. It is thought that mRNAs are stabilized or destabilized by the interaction of proteins with these various structures or sequences. Certain effectors, such as hormones, may regulate mRNA stability by increasing or decreasing the amount of these proteins.

It appears that **the ends of mRNA molecules are involved in mRNA stability** (Figure 38–19). The 5′ cap structure in eukaryotic mRNA prevents attack by 5′ exonucleases, and the poly(A) tail prohibits the action of 3′ exonucleases. In mRNA molecules with those structures, it is presumed that a single endonucleolytic cut allows exonucleases to attack and digest the entire molecule. Other structures (sequences) in the 5′ untranslated region (5′ UTR), the coding region, and the 3′ UTR are thought to promote or prevent this initial endonucleolytic action (Figure 38–19). A few illustrative examples will be cited.

Deletion of the 5′ UTR results in a threefold to fivefold prolongation of the half-life of *c-myc* mRNA. Shortening the coding region of histone mRNA results in a prolonged half-life. A form of autoregulation of mRNA stability indirectly involves the coding region. Free tubulin binds to the first four amino acids of a nascent chain of tubulin as it emerges from the ribosome. This appears to activate an RNase associated with the ribosome (RNP) which then digests the tubulin mRNA.

Structures at the 3′ end, including the poly(A) tail, enhance or diminish the stability of specific mRNAs. The absence of a poly(A) tail is associated with rapid degradation of mRNA, and the removal of poly(A) from some RNAs results in their destabilization. Histone mRNAs lack a poly(A) tail but have a sequence near the 3′ terminal that can form a stem-loop structure, and this appears to provide resistance to exonucleolytic attack. Histone H4 mRNA, for example, is degraded in the 3′ to 5′ direction but only after a single endonucleolytic cut occurs about nine nucleotides from the 3′ end in the region of the putative stem-loop structure. Stem-loop structures in the 3′ noncoding sequence are also critical for the regulation, by iron, of the mRNA encoding the transferrin receptor. Stem-loop structures are also associated with mRNA stability in bacteria, suggesting that this mechanism may be commonly employed.

Other sequences in the 3′ ends of certain eukaryotic mRNAs appear to be involved in the destabilization of these molecules. Of particular interest are AU-rich regions, many of which contain the sequence AUUUA. This sequence appears in mRNAs that have a very short half-life, including some encoding oncogene proteins and cytokines. The importance of this region is underscored by an experiment in which a sequence corresponding to the 3′ UTR of the short-half-life colony-stimulating factor (CSF) mRNA, which contains the AUUUA motif, was added to the 3′ end of the β-globin mRNA. Instead of becoming very stable, this hybrid β-globin mRNA now had the short-half-life characteristic of CSF mRNA. Finally, the recently discovered miRNAs (Chapter 34) target mRNAs for degradation as well. Much of this mRNA metabolism occurs in specific cytoplasmic structures termed **P-bodies.**

From the few examples cited, it is clear that a number of mechanisms are used to regulate mRNA stability—just as several mechanisms are used to regulate the synthesis of mRNA. Coordinate regulation of these two processes confers on the cell remarkable adaptability.

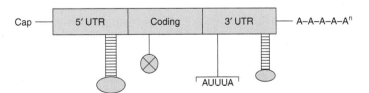

Figure 38–19. Structure of a typical eukaryotic mRNA showing elements that are involved in regulating mRNA stability. The typical eukaryotic mRNA has a 5′ noncoding sequence (5′ NCS), a coding region, and a 3′ NCS. All are capped at the 5′ end, and most have a polyadenylate sequence at the 3′ end. The 5′ cap and 3′ poly(A) tail protect the mRNA against exonuclease attack. Stem-loop structures in the 5′ and 3′ NCS, features in the coding sequence, and the AU-rich region in the 3′ NCS are thought to play roles in mRNA stability.

SUMMARY

- The genetic constitutions of nearly all metazoan somatic cells are identical.
- Phenotype (tissue or cell specificity) is dictated by differences in gene expression of this complement of genes.
- Alterations in gene expression allow a cell to adapt to environmental changes.
- Gene expression can be controlled at multiple levels by changes in transcription, RNA processing, localization, and stability or utilization. Gene amplification and rearrangements also influence gene expression.
- Transcription controls operate at the level of protein-DNA and protein-protein interactions. These interactions display protein domain modularity and high specificity.
- Several different classes of DNA-binding domains have been identified in transcription factors.
- Chromatin modifications are important in eukaryotic transcription control.

REFERENCES

Albright SR, Tjian R: TAFs revisited: more data reveal new twists and confirm old ideas. Gene 2000;242:1.

Berger SL, Felsenfeld G: Chromatin goes global. Mol Cell 2001;8:263.

Bird AP, Wolffe AP: Methylation-induced repression—belts, braces and chromatin. Cell 1999;99:451.

Busby S, Ebright RH: Promoter structure, promoter recognition, and transcription activation in prokaryotes. Cell 1994;79:743.

Busby S, Ebright RH: Transcription activation by catabolite activator protein (CAP). J Mol Biol 1999;293:199.

Cowell IG: Repression versus activation in the control of gene transcription. Trends Biochem Sci 1994;1:38.

Ebright RH: RNA polymerase: structural similarities between bacterial RNA polymerase and eukaryotic RNA polymerase II. J Mol Biol 2000;304:687.

Fugman SD: RAG1 and RAG2 in V(D)J recombination and transposition. Immunol Res 2001;23:23.

Jacob F, Monod J: Genetic regulatory mechanisms in protein synthesis. J Mol Biol 1961;3:318.

Lemon B, Tjian R: Orchestrated response: a symphony of transcription factors for gene control. Genes Dev 2000;14:2551.

Letchman DS: Transcription factor mutations and disease. N Engl J Med 1996;334:28.

Merika M, Thanos D: Enhanceosomes. Curr Opin Genet Dev 2001;11:205.

Naar AM, Lemon BD, Tjian R: Transcriptional coactivator complexes. Annu Rev Biochem 2001;70:475.

Narlikar GJ, Fan HY, Kingston RE: Cooperation between complexes that regulate chromatin structure and transcription. Cell 2002;108:475.

Oltz EM: Regulation of antigen receptor gene assembly in lymphocytes. Immunol Res 2001;23:121.

Ptashne M: A Genetic Switch, 2nd ed. Cell Press and Blackwell Scientific Publications, 1992.

Roeder RG: Transcriptional regulation and the role of diverse coactivators in animal cells. FEBS Lett 2005;579:909.

Sterner DE, Berger SL: Acetylation of histones and transcription-related factors. Microbiol Mol Biol Rev 2000;64:435.

Valencia-Sanchez ME, Liu J, Hannon GJ, Parker R: Control of translation and mRNA degradation by miRNAs and SiRNAs. Genes Dev 2006;20:515.

Wu R, Bahl CP, Narang SA: Lactose operator-repressor interaction. Curr Top Cell Regul 1978;13:137.

Molecular Genetics, Recombinant DNA, & Genomic Technology

39

Daryl K. Granner, MD, & P. Anthony Weil, PhD

BIOMEDICAL IMPORTANCE*

The development of recombinant DNA, high-density, high-throughput screening, and other molecular genetic methodologies has revolutionized biology and is having an increasing impact on clinical medicine. Much has been learned about human genetic disease from pedigree analysis and study of affected proteins, but in many cases where the specific genetic defect is unknown, these approaches cannot be used. The new technologies circumvent these limitations by going directly to the DNA molecule for information. Manipulation of a DNA sequence and the construction of chimeric molecules—so-called genetic engineering—provides a means of studying how a specific segment of DNA works. Novel molecular genetic tools allow investigators to query and manipulate genomic sequences as well as to examine both cellular mRNA and protein profiles at the molecular level.

Understanding this technology is important for several reasons: (1) It offers a rational approach to understanding the molecular basis of a number of diseases (eg, familial hypercholesterolemia, sickle cell disease, the thalassemias, cystic fibrosis, muscular dystrophy). (2) Human proteins can be produced in abundance for therapy (eg, insulin, growth hormone, tissue plasminogen activator). (3) Proteins for vaccines (eg, hepatitis B) and for diagnostic testing (eg, AIDS tests) can be obtained. (4) This technology is used to diagnose existing diseases and predict the risk of developing a given disease. (5) Special techniques have led to remarkable advances in forensic medicine. (6) Gene therapy for sickle cell disease, the thalassemias, adenosine deaminase deficiency, and other diseases may be devised.

---

* See glossary of terms at the end of this chapter.

ELUCIDATION OF THE BASIC FEATURES OF DNA LED TO RECOMBINANT DNA TECHNOLOGY

DNA Is a Complex Biopolymer Organized as a Double Helix

The fundamental organizational element is the sequence of purine (adenine [A] or guanine [G]) and pyrimidine (cytosine [C] or thymine [T]) bases. These bases are attached to the C-1' position of the sugar deoxyribose, and the bases are linked together through joining of the sugar moieties at their 3' and 5' positions via a phosphodiester bond (Figure 34–1). The alternating deoxyribose and phosphate groups form the backbone of the double helix (Figure 34–2). These 3',5' linkages also define the orientation of a given strand of the DNA molecule, and, since the two strands run in opposite directions, they are said to be antiparallel.

Base Pairing Is a Fundamental Concept of DNA Structure & Function

Adenine and thymine always pair, by hydrogen bonding, as do guanine and cytosine (Figure 34–3). These base pairs are said to be **complementary,** and the guanine content of a fragment of double-stranded DNA will always equal its cytosine content; likewise, the thymine and adenine contents are equal. Base pairing and hydrophobic base-stacking interactions hold the two DNA strands together. These interactions can be reduced by heating the DNA to denature it. The laws of base pairing predict that two complementary DNA strands will reanneal exactly in register upon renaturation, as happens when the temperature of the solution is slowly reduced to normal. Indeed, the degree of base-pair matching (or mismatching) can be estimated from the temperature required for denaturation-renaturation. Segments of DNA with high degrees of base-pair

matching require more energy input (heat) to accomplish denaturation—or, to put it another way, a closely matched segment will withstand more heat before the strands separate. This reaction is used to determine whether there are significant differences between two DNA sequences, and it underlies the concept of **hybridization,** which is fundamental to the processes described below.

There are about 3×10^9 base pairs (bp) in each human haploid genome. If an average gene length is 3 $\times 10^3$ bp (3 kilobases [kb]), the genome could consist of 10^6 genes, assuming that there is no overlap and that transcription proceeds in only one direction. It is thought that there are $< 10^5$ genes in the human and that only 1–2% of the DNA codes for proteins. The exact function of the remaining ~98% of the human genome has not yet been defined.

The double-helical DNA is packaged into a more compact structure by a number of proteins, most notably the basic proteins called histones. This condensation may serve a regulatory role and certainly has a practical purpose. The DNA present within the nucleus of a cell, if simply extended, would be about 1 meter long. The chromosomal proteins compact this long strand of DNA so that it can be packaged into a nucleus with a volume of a few cubic micrometers.

DNA Is Organized into Genes

In general, prokaryotic genes consist of a small regulatory region (100–500 bp) and a large protein-coding segment (500–10,000 bp). Several genes are often controlled by a single regulatory unit. Most mammalian genes are more complicated in that the coding regions are interrupted by noncoding regions that are eliminated when the primary RNA transcript is processed into mature **messenger RNA (mRNA).** The **coding regions** (those regions that appear in the mature RNA species) are called exons, and the **noncoding regions,** which interpose or intervene between the exons, are called introns (Figure 39–1). Introns are always removed from precursor RNA before transport into the cytoplasm occurs. The process by which introns are removed from precursor RNA and by which exons are ligated together is called **RNA splicing.** Incorrect processing of the primary transcript into the mature mRNA can result in disease in humans (see below); this underscores the importance of these posttranscriptional processing steps. The variation in size and complexity of some human genes is illustrated in Table 39–1. Although there is a 300-fold difference in the sizes of the genes illustrated, the mRNA sizes vary only about 20-fold. This is because most of the DNA in genes is present as introns, and introns tend to be much larger than exons. Regulatory regions for specific eukaryotic genes are usually located in the DNA that flanks the transcription initiation site at its 5′ end (**5′ flanking-sequence DNA).** Occasionally, such sequences are found within the gene itself or in the region that flanks the 3′ end of the gene. In mammalian cells, each gene has its own regulatory region. Many eukaryotic genes (and some viruses that replicate in mammalian cells) have special regions, called **enhancers,** that increase the rate of transcription. Some genes also have DNA sequences, known as **silencers,** that repress transcription. Mammalian genes are obviously complicated, multicomponent structures.

Genes Are Transcribed into RNA

Information generally flows from DNA to mRNA to protein, as illustrated in Figure 39–1 and discussed in more detail in Chapter 38. This is a rigidly controlled process involving a number of complex steps, each of which no doubt is regulated by one or more enzymes or factors; faulty function at any of these steps can cause disease.

RECOMBINANT DNA TECHNOLOGY INVOLVES ISOLATION & MANIPULATION OF DNA TO MAKE CHIMERIC MOLECULES

Isolation and manipulation of DNA, including end-to-end joining of sequences from very different sources to make chimeric molecules (eg, molecules containing both human and bacterial DNA sequences in a sequence-independent fashion), is the essence of recombinant DNA research. This involves several unique techniques and reagents.

Restriction Enzymes Cut DNA Chains at Specific Locations

Certain endonucleases—enzymes that cut DNA at specific DNA sequences within the molecule (as opposed to exonucleases, which digest from the ends of DNA molecules)—are a key tool in recombinant DNA research. These enzymes were called **restriction enzymes** because their presence in a given bacterium restricted the growth of certain bacterial viruses called bacteriophages. Restriction enzymes cut DNA of any source into short pieces in a sequence-specific manner—in contrast to most other enzymatic, chemical, or physical methods, which break DNA randomly. These defensive enzymes (hundreds have been discovered) protect the host bacterial DNA from DNA from foreign organisms (primarily infective phages). However, they are present only in cells that also have a companion enzyme which methylates the host DNA, rendering it an unsuitable substrate for digestion by the restriction enzyme. Thus, **site-specific DNA methylases** and restriction enzymes always exist in pairs in a bacterium.

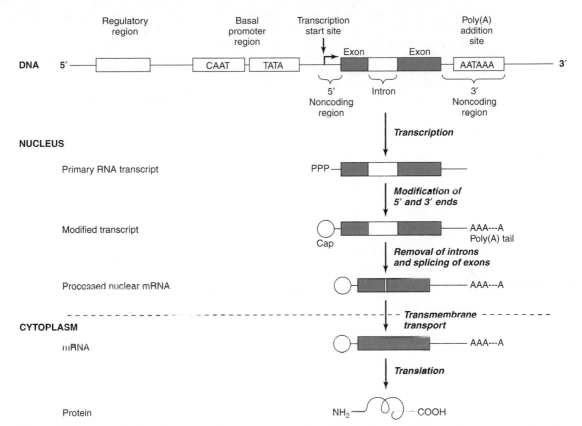

Figure 39–1. Organization of a eukaryotic transcription unit and the pathway of eukaryotic gene expression. Eukaryotic genes have structural and regulatory regions. The structural region consists of the coding DNA and 5′ and 3′ noncoding DNA sequences. The coding regions are divided into two parts: (1) exons, which eventually are ligated together to become mature RNA, and (2) introns, which are processed out of the primary transcript. The structural region is bounded at its 5′ end by the transcription initiation site and at its 3′ end by the polyadenylate addition or termination site. The promoter region, which contains specific DNA sequences that interact with various protein factors to regulate transcription, is discussed in detail in Chapters 36 and 38. The primary transcript has a special structure, a cap, at the 5′ end and a stretch of As at the 3′ end. This transcript is processed to remove the introns; and the mature mRNA is then transported to the cytoplasm, where it is translated into protein.

Restriction enzymes are named after the bacterium from which they are isolated. For example, *EcoRI* is from *Escherichia coli*, and *BamHI* is from *Bacillus amyloliquefaciens* (Table 39–2). The first three letters in the restriction enzyme name consist of the first letter of the genus (E) and the first two letters of the species (co). These may be followed by a strain designation (R) and a roman numeral (I) to indicate the order of discovery (eg, *EcoRI, EcoRII*). Each enzyme recognizes and cleaves a specific double-stranded DNA sequence that is 4–7 bp long. These DNA cuts result in **blunt ends** (eg, *HpaI*) or overlapping **(sticky) ends** (eg, *BamHI*) (Figure 39–2), depending on the mechanism used by the enzyme. Sticky ends are particularly useful in constructing hybrid or chimeric DNA molecules (see

below). If the four nucleotides are distributed randomly in a given DNA molecule, one can calculate how frequently a given enzyme will cut a length of DNA. For each position in the DNA molecule, there are four possibilities (A, C, G, and T); therefore, a restriction enzyme that recognizes a 4-bp sequence cuts, on average, once every 256 bp (4^4), whereas another enzyme that recognizes a 6-bp sequence cuts once every 4096 bp (4^6). A given piece of DNA has a characteristic linear array of sites for the various enzymes dictated by the linear sequence of its bases; hence, a **restriction map** can be constructed. When DNA is digested with a given enzyme, the ends of all the fragments have the same DNA sequence. The fragments produced can be isolated by electrophoresis on agarose or polyacrylamide

Table 39–1. Variations in the size and complexity of some human genes and mRNAs.[1]

Gene	Gene Size (kb)	Number of Introns	mRNA Size (kb)
β-Globin	1.5	2	0.6
Insulin	1.7	2	0.4
β-Adrenergic receptor	3	0	2.2
Albumin	25	14	2.1
LDL receptor	45	17	5.5
Factor VIII	186	25	9.0
Thyroglobulin	300	36	8.7

[1]The sizes are given in kilobases (kb). The sizes of the genes include some proximal promoter and regulatory region sequences; these are generally about the same size for all genes. Genes vary in size from about 1500 base pairs (bp) to over 2×10^6 bp. There is also great variation in the number of introns and exons. The β-adrenergic receptor gene is intronless, and the thyroglobulin gene has 36 introns. As noted by the smaller difference in mRNA sizes, introns comprise most of the gene sequence.

gels (see the discussion of blot transfer, below); this is an essential step in cloning and a major use of these enzymes.

A number of other enzymes that act on DNA and RNA are an important part of recombinant DNA technology. Many of these are referred to in this and subsequent chapters (Table 39–3).

Restriction Enzymes & DNA Ligase Are Used to Prepare Chimeric DNA Molecules

Sticky-end ligation is technically easy, but some special techniques are often required to overcome problems inherent in this approach. Sticky ends of a vector may reconnect with themselves, with no net gain of DNA. Sticky ends of fragments can also anneal, so that tandem heterogeneous inserts form. Also, sticky-end sites may not be available or in a convenient position. To circumvent these problems, an enzyme that generates blunt ends is used, and new ends are added using the enzyme terminal transferase. If poly d(G) is added to the 3′ ends of the vector and poly d(C) is added to the 3′ ends of the foreign DNA, the two molecules can only anneal to each other, thus circumventing the problems listed above. This procedure is called homopolymer tailing. Sometimes, synthetic blunt-ended duplex oligonucleotide linkers with a convenient restriction enzyme sequence are ligated to the blunt-ended DNA. Direct blunt-end ligation is accomplished using the enzyme bacteriophage T4 DNA ligase. This technique, though less efficient than sticky-end ligation, has the advantage of joining together any pairs of ends. The disadvantages

Table 39–2. Selected restriction endonucleases and their sequence specificities.[1]

Endonuclease	Sequence Recognized Cleavage Sites Shown	Bacterial Source
BamHI	↓ GGATCC CCTAGG ↑	Bacillus amyloliquefaciens H
BglII	↓ AGATCT TCTAGA ↑	Bacillus glolbigii
EcoRI	↓ GAATTC CTTAAG ↑	Escherichia coli RY13
EcoRII	↓ CCTGG GGACC ↑	Escherichia coli R245
HindIII	↓ AAGCTT TTCGAA ↑	Haemophilus influenzae R_d
HhaI	↓ GCGC CGCG ↑	Haemophilus haemolyticus
HpaI	↓ GTTAAC CAATTG ↑	Haemophilus parainfluenzae
MstII	↓ CCTNAGG GGANTCC ↑	Microcoleus strain
PstI	↓ CTGCAG GACGTC ↑	Providencia stuartii 164
TaqI	↓ TCGA AGCT ↑	Thermus aquaticus YTI

[1]A, adenine; C, cytosine; G, guanine; T, thymine. Arrows show the site of cleavage; depending on the site, sticky ends (BamHI) or blunt ends (HpaI) may result. The length of the recognition sequence can be 4 bp (TaqI), 5 bp (EcoRII), 6 bp (EcoRI), or 7 bp (MstII) or longer. By convention, these are written in the 5′ or 3′ direction for the upper strand of each recognition sequence, and the lower strand is shown with the opposite (ie, 3′ or 5′) polarity. Note that most recognition sequences are palindromes (ie, the sequence reads the same in opposite directions on the two strands). A residue designated N means that any nucleotide is permitted.

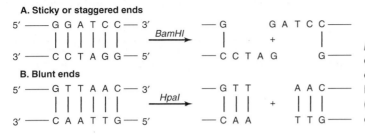

Figure 39–2. Results of restriction endonuclease digestion. Digestion with a restriction endonuclease can result in the formation of DNA fragments with sticky, or cohesive, ends **(A)** or blunt ends **(B).** This is an important consideration in devising cloning strategies.

are that there is no control over the orientation of insertion or the number of molecules annealed together, and there is no easy way to retrieve the insert.

Cloning Amplifies DNA

A **clone** is a large population of identical molecules, bacteria, or cells that arise from a common ancestor. Molecular cloning allows for the production of a large number of identical DNA molecules, which can then be characterized or used for other purposes. This technique is based on the fact that chimeric or hybrid DNA molecules can be constructed in **cloning vectors**—typically bacterial plasmids, phages, or cosmids—which then continue to replicate in a host cell under their own control systems. In this way, the chimeric DNA is amplified. The general procedure is illustrated in Figure 39–3.

Bacterial **plasmids** are small, circular, duplex DNA molecules whose natural function is to confer antibiotic resistance to the host cell. Plasmids have several properties that make them extremely useful as cloning vectors. They exist as single or multiple copies within the bacterium and replicate independently from the bacterial DNA. The complete DNA sequence of many plasmids is known; hence, the precise location of restriction enzyme cleavage sites for inserting the foreign DNA is available. Plasmids are smaller than the host chromosome and are therefore easily separated from the latter, and the desired plasmid-inserted DNA is readily removed by cutting the plasmid with the enzyme specific for the restriction site into which the original piece of DNA was inserted.

Table 39–3. Some of the enzymes used in recombinant DNA research.[1]

Enzyme	Reaction	Primary Use
Alkaline phosphatase	Dephosphorylates 5′ ends of RNA and DNA	Removal of 5′-PO_4 groups prior to kinase labeling; also used to prevent self-ligation
BAL 31 nuclease	Degrades both the 3′ and 5′ ends of DNA	Progressive shortening of DNA molecules
DNA ligase	Catalyzes bonds between DNA molecules	Joining of DNA molecules
DNA polymerase I	Synthesizes double-stranded DNA from single-stranded DNA	Synthesis of double-stranded cDNA; nick translation; generation of blunt ends from sticky ends
DNase I	Under appropriate conditions, produces single-stranded nicks in DNA	Nick translation; mapping of hypersensitive sites; mapping protein-DNA interactions
Exonuclease III	Removes nucleotides from 3′ ends of DNA	DNA sequencing; mapping of DNA-protein interactions
λ Exonuclease	Removes nucleotides from 5′ ends of DNA	DNA sequencing
Polynucleotide kinase	Transfers terminal phosphate (γ position) from ATP to 5′-OH groups of DNA or RNA	^{32}P end-labeling of DNA or RNA
Reverse transcriptase	Synthesizes DNA from RNA template	Synthesis of cDNA from mRNA; RNA (5′ end) mapping studies
S1 nuclease	Degrades single-stranded DNA	Removal of "hairpin" in synthesis of cDNA; RNA mapping studies (both 5′ and 3′ ends)
Terminal transferase	Adds nucleotides to the 3′ ends of DNA	Homopolymer tailing

[1]Adapted and reproduced, with permission, from Emery AEH: Page 41 in: *An Introduction to Recombinant DNA.* Wiley, 1984. Copyright © 1984 John Wiley & Sons Limited. Reproduced with permission.

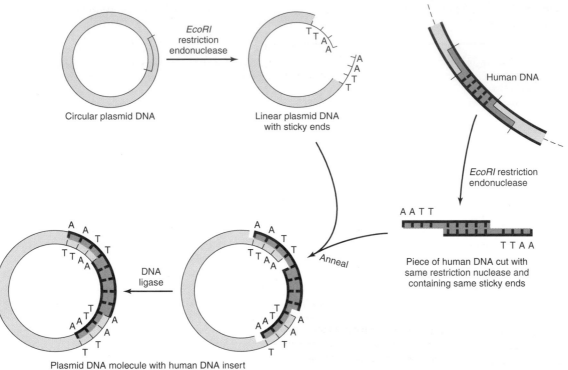

Figure 39–3. Use of restriction nucleases to make new recombinant or chimeric DNA molecules. When inserted back into a bacterial cell (by the process called transformation), typically only a single plasmid is taken up by a single cell, and the plasmid DNA replicates not only itself but also the physically linked new DNA insert. Since recombining the sticky ends, as indicated, regenerates the same DNA sequence recognized by the original restriction enzyme, the cloned DNA insert can be cleanly cut back out of the recombinant plasmid circle with this endonuclease. If a mixture of all of the DNA pieces created by treatment of total human DNA with a single restriction nuclease is used as the source of human DNA, a million or so different types of recombinant DNA molecules can be obtained, each pure in its own bacterial clone. (Modified and reproduced, with permission, from Cohen SN: The manipulation of genes. Sci Am [July] 1975;233:25. Copyright © The Estate of Bunji Tagawa.)

Phages usually have linear DNA molecules into which foreign DNA can be inserted at several restriction enzyme sites. The chimeric DNA is collected after the phage proceeds through its lytic cycle and produces mature, infective phage particles. A major advantage of phage vectors is that while plasmids accept DNA pieces about 6–10 kb long, phages can accept DNA fragments 10–20 kb long, a limitation imposed by the amount of DNA that can be packed into the phage head.

Larger fragments of DNA can be cloned in **cosmids,** which combine the best features of plasmids and phages. Cosmids are plasmids that contain the DNA sequences, so-called **cos sites,** required for packaging lambda DNA into the phage particle. These vectors grow in the plasmid form in bacteria, but since much of the unnecessary lambda DNA has been removed, more chimeric DNA can be packaged into the particle head. It is not unusual for cosmids to carry inserts of chimeric DNA that are 35–

50 kb long. Even larger pieces of DNA can be incorporated into bacterial artificial chromosome (**BAC**), yeast artificial chromosome (**YAC**), or *E. coli* bacteriophage P1-based (**PAC**) vectors. These vectors will accept and propagate DNA inserts of several hundred kilobases or more and have largely replaced the plasmid, phage, and cosmid vectors for some cloning and gene mapping applications. A comparison of these vectors is shown in Table 39–4.

Because insertion of DNA into a functional region of the vector will interfere with the action of this region, care must be taken not to interrupt an essential function of the vector. This concept can be exploited, however, to provide a selection technique. For example, the common plasmid vector **pBR322** has both **tetracycline (tet)** and **ampicillin (amp)** resistance genes. A single *PstI* restriction enzyme site within the amp resistance gene is commonly used as the insertion site for a piece of foreign DNA. In addition to having sticky ends (Table 39–2 and

Table 39–4. Cloning capacities of common cloning vectors.

Vector	DNA Insert Size (kb)
Plasmid pBR322	0.01–10
Lambda charon 4A	10–20
Cosmids	35–50
BAC, P1	50–250
YAC	500–3000

Figure 39–2), the DNA inserted at this site disrupts the amp resistance gene and makes the bacterium carrying this plasmid amp-sensitive (Figure 39–4). Thus, the parental plasmid, which provides resistance to both antibiotics, can be readily separated from the chimeric plasmid, which is resistant only to tetracycline. YACs contain selection, replication, and segregation functions that work in both bacteria and yeast cells and therefore can be propagated in either organism.

In addition to the vectors described in Table 39–4 that are designed primarily for propagation in bacterial cells,

vectors for mammalian cell propagation and insert gene (cDNA)/protein expression have also been developed. These vectors are all based upon various eukaryotic viruses that are composed of RNA or DNA genomes. Notable examples of such viral vectors are those utilizing adenoviral (DNA-based) and retroviral (RNA-based) genomes. Though somewhat limited in the size of DNA sequences that can be inserted, such mammalian viral cloning vectors make up for this shortcoming because they will efficiently infect a wide range of different cell types. For this reason, various mammalian viral vectors are being investigated for use in gene therapy experiments.

A Library Is a Collection of Recombinant Clones

The combination of restriction enzymes and various cloning vectors allows the entire genome of an organism to be packed into a vector. A collection of these different recombinant clones is called a library. A **genomic library** is prepared from the total DNA of a cell line or tissue. A **cDNA library** comprises complementary DNA copies of the population of mRNAs in a tissue. Genomic DNA

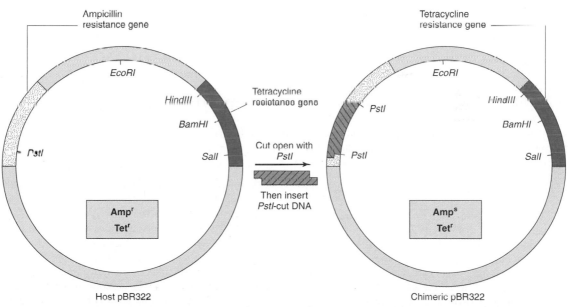

Figure 39–4. A method of screening recombinants for inserted DNA fragments. Using the plasmid pBR322, a piece of DNA is inserted into the unique *PstI* site. This insertion disrupts the gene coding for a protein that provides ampicillin resistance to the host bacterium. Hence, the chimeric plasmid will no longer survive when plated on a substrate medium that contains this antibiotic. The differential sensitivity to tetracycline and ampicillin can therefore be used to distinguish clones of plasmid that contain an insert. A similar scheme relying upon production of an in-frame fusion of a newly inserted DNA producing a peptide fragment capable of complementing an inactive, deleted form of the enzyme β-galactosidase allows for blue-white colony formation on agar plates containing a dye hydrolyzable by β-galactoside. β-Galactosidase-positive colonies are blue; such colonies contain plasmids in which a DNA was successfully inserted.

libraries are often prepared by performing partial digestion of total DNA with a restriction enzyme that cuts
DNA frequently (eg, a four base cutter such as *TaqI*).
The idea is to generate rather large fragments so that
most genes will be left intact. The BAC, YAC, and P1
vectors are preferred since they can accept very large fragments of DNA and thus offer a better chance of isolating
an intact gene on a single DNA fragment.

A vector in which the protein coded by the gene
introduced by recombinant DNA technology is actually
synthesized is known as an **expression vector.** Such vectors are now commonly used to detect specific cDNA
molecules in libraries and to produce proteins by genetic
engineering techniques. These vectors are specially constructed to contain very active inducible promoters,
proper in-phase translation initiation codons, both transcription and translation termination signals, and appropriate protein processing signals, if needed. Some expression vectors even contain genes that code for protease
inhibitors, so that the final yield of product is enhanced.

Probes Search Libraries for Specific Genes or cDNA Molecules

A variety of molecules can be used to "probe" libraries in
search of a specific gene or cDNA molecule or to define
and quantitate DNA or RNA separated by electrophoresis
through various gels. Probes are generally pieces of DNA
or RNA labeled with a ^{32}P-containing nucleotide—or fluorescently labeled nucleotides (more commonly now).
Importantly, neither modification (^{32}P or fluorescent-
label) affects the hybridization properties of the resulting
labeled nucleic acid probes. The probe must recognize a
complementary sequence to be effective. A cDNA synthesized from a specific mRNA can be used to screen either a
cDNA library for a longer cDNA or a genomic library for
a complementary sequence in the coding region of a gene.
A popular technique for finding specific genes entails taking a short amino acid sequence and, employing the
codon usage for that species (see Chapter 37), making an
oligonucleotide probe that will detect the corresponding
DNA fragment in a genomic library. If the sequences
match exactly, probes 15–20 nucleotides long will hybridize. cDNA probes are used to detect DNA fragments on
Southern blot transfers and to detect and quantitate RNA
on Northern blot transfers. Specific antibodies can also be
used as probes provided that the vector used synthesizes
protein molecules that are recognized by them.

Blotting & Hybridization Techniques Allow Visualization of Specific Fragments

Visualization of a specific DNA or RNA fragment among
the many thousands of "contaminating" molecules requires
the convergence of a number of techniques, collectively
termed **blot transfer.** Figure 39–5 illustrates the **Southern**

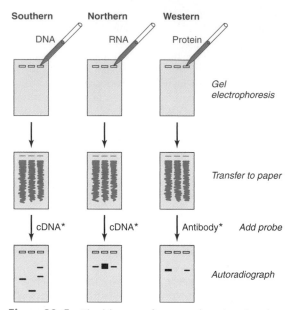

Figure 39–5. The blot transfer procedure. In a Southern, or DNA, blot transfer, DNA isolated from a cell line
or tissue is digested with one or more restriction enzymes. This mixture is pipetted into a well in an agarose
or polyacrylamide gel and exposed to a direct electrical
current. DNA, being negatively charged, migrates toward the anode; the smaller fragments move the most
rapidly. After a suitable time, the DNA is denatured by
exposure to mild alkali and transferred to nitrocellulose
or nylon paper, in an exact replica of the pattern on the
gel, by the blotting technique devised by Southern.
The DNA is bound to the paper by exposure to heat,
and the paper is then exposed to the labeled cDNA
probe, which hybridizes to complementary fragments
on the filter. After thorough washing, the paper is exposed to x-ray film, which is developed to reveal several
specific bands corresponding to the DNA fragment that
recognized the sequences in the cDNA probe. The RNA,
or Northern, blot is conceptually similar. RNA is subjected to electrophoresis before blot transfer. This requires some different steps from those of DNA transfer,
primarily to ensure that the RNA remains intact, and is
generally somewhat more difficult. In the protein, or
Western, blot, proteins are electrophoresed and transferred to nitrocellulose and then probed with a specific
antibody or other probe molecule. (Asterisks signify labeling, either radioactive or fluorescent.) In the case of
Southwestern blotting (see text; not shown), a protein
blot similar to that shown above under "Western" is exposed to labeled nucleic acid, and protein-nucleic acid
complexes formed are detected by autoradiography.

(DNA), **Northern** (RNA), and **Western** (protein) blot transfer procedures. (The first is named for the person who devised the technique, and the other names began as laboratory jargon but are now accepted terms.) These procedures are useful in determining how many copies of a gene are in a given tissue or whether there are any gross alterations in a gene (deletions, insertions, or rearrangements). Occasionally, if a specific base is changed and a restriction site is altered, these procedures can detect a point mutation. The Northern and Western blot transfer techniques are used to size and quantitate specific RNA and protein molecules, respectively. A fourth hybridization technique, the **Southwestern** blot, examines protein•DNA interactions. Proteins are separated by electrophoresis, renatured, and analyzed for an interaction by hybridization with a specific labeled DNA probe.

Colony or **plaque hybridization** is the method by which specific clones are identified and purified. Bacteria are grown as colonies on an agar plate and overlaid with nitrocellulose filter paper. Cells from each colony stick to the filter and are permanently fixed thereto by heat, which with NaOH treatment also lyses the cells and denatures the DNA so that it will hybridize with the probe. A radioactive probe is added to the filter, and (after washing) the hybrid complex is localized by exposing the filter to x-ray film. By matching the spot on the autoradiograph to a colony, the latter can be picked from the plate. A similar strategy is used to identify fragments in phage libraries. Successive rounds of this procedure result in a clonal isolate (bacterial colony) or individual phage plaque.

All of the hybridization procedures discussed in this section depend on the specific base-pairing properties of complementary nucleic acid strands described above. Perfect matches hybridize readily and withstand high temperatures in the hybridization and washing reactions. Specific complexes also form in the presence of low salt concentrations. Less than perfect matches do not tolerate these **stringent conditions** (ie, elevated temperatures and low salt concentrations); thus, hybridization either never occurs or is disrupted during the washing step. Gene families, in which there is some degree of homology, can be detected by varying the stringency of the hybridization and washing steps. Cross-species comparisons of a given gene can also be made using this approach. Hybridization conditions capable of detecting just a single base pair mismatch between probe and target have been devised.

Manual & Automated Techniques Are Available to Determine the Sequence of DNA

The segments of specific DNA molecules obtained by recombinant DNA technology can be analyzed to determine their nucleotide sequence. This method depends upon having a large number of identical DNA molecules.

This requirement can be satisfied by cloning the fragment of interest, using the techniques described above. The **manual enzymatic method (Sanger)** employs specific dideoxynucleotides that terminate DNA strand synthesis at specific nucleotides as the strand is synthesized on purified template nucleic acid. The reactions are adjusted so that a population of DNA fragments representing termination at every nucleotide is obtained. By having a radioactive label incorporated at the end opposite the termination site, one can separate the fragments according to size using polyacrylamide gel electrophoresis. An autoradiograph is made, and each of the fragments produces an image (band) on an x-ray film. These are read in order to give the DNA sequence (Figure 39–6). Another manual method, that of **Maxam and Gilbert,** employs **chemical methods** to cleave the DNA molecules where they contain the specific nucleotides. Techniques that do not require the use of radioisotopes are employed in automated DNA sequencing. Most commonly employed is an automated procedure in which four different fluorescent labels—one representing each nucleotide—are used. Each emits a specific signal upon excitation by a laser beam, and this can be recorded by a computer.

Oligonucleotide Synthesis Is Now Routine

The automated chemical synthesis of moderately long oligonucleotides (about 100 nucleotides) of precise sequence is now a routine laboratory procedure. Each synthetic cycle takes but a few minutes, so an entire molecule can be made by synthesizing relatively short segments that can then be ligated to one another. Oligonucleotides are now indispensable for DNA sequencing, library screening, protein-DNA binding, DNA mobility shift assays, the polymerase chain reaction (see below), site-directed mutagenesis, synthetic gene synthesis, and numerous other applications.

The Polymerase Chain Reaction (PCR) Amplifies DNA Sequences

The polymerase chain reaction (PCR) is a method of amplifying a target sequence of DNA. PCR provides a sensitive, selective, and extremely rapid means of amplifying a desired sequence of DNA. Specificity is based on the use of two oligonucleotide primers that hybridize to complementary sequences on opposite strands of DNA and flank the target sequence (Figure 39–7). The DNA sample is first heated to separate the two strands; the primers are allowed to bind to the DNA; and each strand is copied by a DNA polymerase, starting at the primer site. The two DNA strands each serve as a template for the synthesis of new DNA from the two primers. Repeated cycles of heat denaturation, annealing of the primers to their complementary sequences, and extension of the annealed

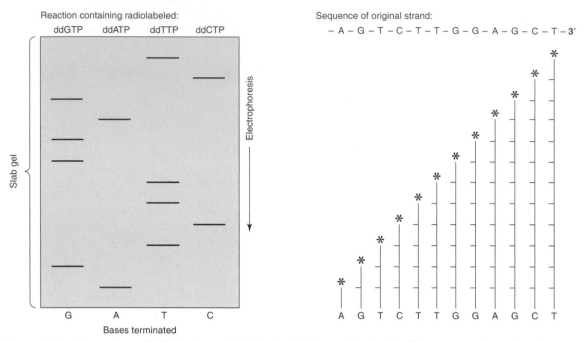

Figure 39–6. Sequencing of DNA by the method devised by Sanger. The ladder-like arrays represent from bottom to top all of the successively longer fragments of the original DNA strand. Knowing which specific dideoxynucleotide reaction was conducted to produce each mixture of fragments, one can determine the sequence of nucleotides from the unlabeled end toward the labeled end (*) by reading up the gel. Automated sequencing involves the reading of chemically modified deoxynucleotides. The base-pairing rules of Watson and Crick (A–T, G–C) dictate the sequence of the other (complementary) strand. (Asterisks signify site of radiolabeling.)

primers with DNA polymerase result in the exponential amplification of DNA segments of defined length. Early PCR reactions used an *E coli* DNA polymerase that was destroyed by each heat denaturation cycle. Substitution of a heat-stable DNA polymerase from *Thermus aquaticus* (or the corresponding DNA polymerase from other thermophilic bacteria), an organism that lives and replicates at 70–80 °C, obviates this problem and has made possible automation of the reaction, since the polymerase reactions can be run at 70 °C. This has also improved the specificity and the yield of DNA.

DNA sequences as short as 50–100 bp and as long as 10 kb can be amplified. Twenty cycles provide an amplification of 10^6 and 30 cycles of 10^9. The PCR allows the DNA in a single cell, hair follicle, or spermatozoon to be amplified and analyzed. Thus, the applications of PCR to forensic medicine are obvious. The PCR is also used (1) to detect infectious agents, especially latent viruses; (2) to make prenatal genetic diagnoses; (3) to detect allelic polymorphisms; (4) to establish precise tissue types for transplants; and (5) to study evolution, using DNA from archeological samples or (6) using RNA analyses after RNA copying and mRNA quantitation by the so-

called RT-PCR method (cDNA copies of mRNA generated by a retroviral reverse transcriptase). There are an equal number of applications of PCR to problems in basic science, and new uses are developed every year.

PRACTICAL APPLICATIONS OF RECOMBINANT DNA TECHNOLOGY ARE NUMEROUS

The isolation of a specific gene from an entire genome requires a technique that will discriminate one part in a million. The identification of a regulatory region that may be only 10 bp in length requires a sensitivity of one part in 3×10^8; a disease such as sickle cell anemia is caused by a single base change, or one part in 3×10^9. Recombinant DNA technology is powerful enough to accomplish all these things.

Gene Mapping Localizes Specific Genes to Distinct Chromosomes

Gene localizing thus can define a map of the human genome. This is already yielding useful information in

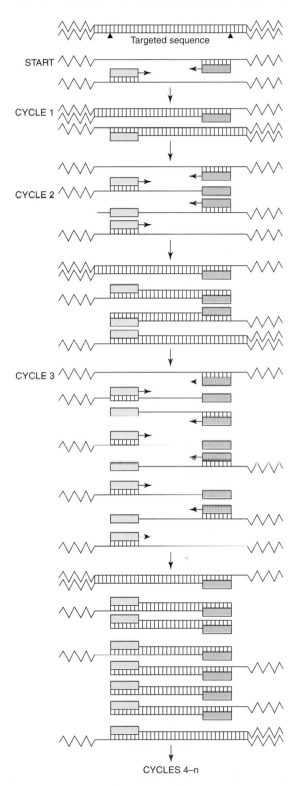

the definition of human disease. Somatic cell hybridization and in situ hybridization are two techniques used to accomplish this. In **in situ hybridization,** the simpler and more direct procedure, a radioactive probe is added to a metaphase spread of chromosomes on a glass slide. The exact area of hybridization is localized by layering photographic emulsion over the slide and, after exposure, lining up the grains with some histologic identification of the chromosome. **Fluorescence in situ hybridization (FISH)** is a very sensitive technique that is also used for this purpose. This often places the gene at a location on a given band or region on the chromosome. Some of the human genes localized using these techniques are listed in Table 39–5. This table represents only a sampling, since thousands of genes have been mapped as a result of the recent sequencing of the human genome. Once the defect is localized to a region of DNA that has the characteristic structure of a gene (Figure 39–1), a synthetic gene can be constructed and expressed in an appropriate vector and its function can be assessed—or the putative peptide, deduced from the open reading frame in the coding region, can be synthesized. Antibodies directed against this peptide can be used to assess whether this peptide is expressed in normal persons and whether it is absent in those with the genetic syndrome.

Proteins Can Be Produced for Research & Diagnosis

A practical goal of recombinant DNA research is the production of materials for biomedical applications. This technology has two distinct merits: (1) It can supply large amounts of material that could not be obtained by conventional purification methods (eg, interferon, tissue plasminogen activating factor). (2) It can provide human material (eg, insulin, growth hormone). The advantages in both cases are obvious. Although the primary aim is to supply products—generally proteins—for treatment (insulin) and diagnosis (AIDS testing) of human and other animal diseases and for disease prevention (hepatitis B vaccine), there are other

---

Figure 39–7. The polymerase chain reaction is used to amplify specific gene sequences. Double-stranded DNA is heated to separate it into individual strands. These bind two distinct primers that are directed at specific sequences on opposite strands and that define the segment to be amplified. DNA polymerase extends the primers in each direction and synthesizes two strands complementary to the original two. This cycle is repeated several times, giving an amplified product of defined length and sequence. Note that the two primers are present in excess.

Table 39–5. Localization of human genes.[1]

Gene	Chromosome	Disease
Insulin	11p15	
Prolactin	6p23-q12	
Growth hormone	17q21-qter	Growth hormone deficiency
α-Globin	16p12-pter	α-Thalassemia
β-Globin	11p12	β-Thalassemia, sickle cell
Adenosine deaminase	20q13-qter	Adenosine deaminase deficiency
Phenylalanine hydroxylase	12q24	Phenylketonuria
Hypoxanthine-guanine phosphoribosyltransferase	Xq26-q27	Lesch-Nyhan syndrome
DNA segment G8	4p	Huntington's chorea

[1]This table indicates the chromosomal location of several genes and the diseases associated with deficient or abnormal production of the gene products. The chromosome involved is indicated by the first number or letter. The other numbers and letters refer to precise localizations, as defined in McKusick, Victor A., MD, *Mendelian Inheritance in Man: Catalogs of Autosomal Dominant, Autosomal Recessive, and X-Linked Phenotypes.* Copyright © 1983 Johns Hopkins University Press. Reprinted with permission from the Johns Hopkins University Press.

potential commercial applications, especially in agriculture. An example of the latter is the attempt to engineer plants that are more resistant to drought or temperature extremes, more efficient at fixing nitrogen, or that produce seeds containing the complete complement of essential amino acids (rice, wheat, corn, etc).

Recombinant DNA Technology Is Used in the Molecular Analysis of Disease

A. Normal Gene Variations

There is a normal variation of DNA sequence just as is true of more obvious aspects of human structure. Variations of DNA sequence, **polymorphisms,** occur approximately once in every 500 nucleotides, or about 10^7 times per genome. There are without doubt deletions and insertions of DNA as well as single-base substitutions. In healthy people, these alterations obviously occur in noncoding regions of DNA or at sites that cause no change in function of the encoded protein. This heritable polymorphism of DNA structure can be associated with certain diseases within a large kindred and can be used to search for the specific gene involved, as is illustrated below. It can also be used in a variety of applications in forensic medicine.

B. Gene Variations Causing Disease

Classic genetics taught that most genetic diseases were due to point mutations which resulted in an impaired protein. This may still be true, but if on reading the initial sections of this chapter one predicted that genetic disease could result from derangement of any of the steps illustrated in Figure 39–1, one would have made a proper assessment. This point is nicely illustrated by examination of the β-globin gene. This gene is located in a cluster on chromosome 11

(Figure 39–8), and an expanded version of the gene is illustrated in Figure 39–9. Defective production of β-globin results in a variety of diseases and is due to many different lesions in and around the β-globin gene (Table 39–6).

C. Point Mutations

The classic example is **sickle cell disease,** which is caused by mutation of a single base out of the 3×10^9 in the genome, a T-to-A DNA substitution, which in turn results in an A-to-U change in the mRNA corresponding to the sixth codon of the β-globin gene. The altered codon specifies a different amino acid (valine rather than glutamic acid), and this causes a structural abnormality of the β-globin molecule. Other point mutations in and around the β-globin gene result in decreased production or, in some instances, no production of β-globin; β-thalassemia is the result of these mutations. (The thalassemias are characterized by defects in the synthesis of hemoglobin subunits, and so β-thalassemia results when there is insufficient production of β-globin.) Figure 39–9 illustrates that point mutations affecting each of the many processes involved in generating a normal mRNA (and therefore a normal protein) have been implicated as a cause of β-thalassemia.

D. Deletions, Insertions, & Rearrangements of DNA

Studies of bacteria, viruses, yeasts, and fruit flies show that pieces of DNA can move from one place to another within a genome. The deletion of a critical piece of DNA, the rearrangement of DNA within a gene, or the insertion of a piece of DNA within a coding or regulatory region can all cause changes in gene expression resulting in disease. Again, a molecular analysis of β-thalassemia produces numerous examples of these processes—particularly

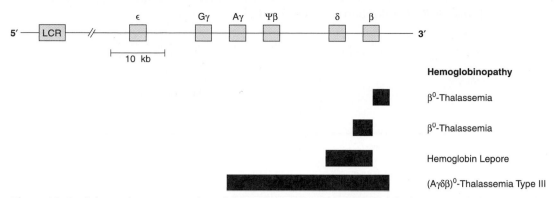

Figure 39–8. Schematic representation of the β-globin gene cluster and of the lesions in some genetic disorders. The β-globin gene is located on chromosome 11 in close association with the two γ-globin genes and the δ-globin gene. The β-gene family is arranged in the order 5'-ε-Gγ-Aγ-Ψβ-δ-β-3'. The ε locus is expressed in early embryonic life (as $\alpha_2\varepsilon_2$). The γ genes are expressed in fetal life, making fetal hemoglobin (HbF, $\alpha_2\gamma_2$). Adult hemoglobin consists of HbA ($\alpha_2\beta_2$) or HbA$_2$($\alpha_2\delta_2$). The Ψβ is a pseudogene that has sequence homology with β but contains mutations that prevent its expression. A locus control region (LCR) located upstream (5') from the ε gene controls the rate of transcription of the entire β-globin gene cluster. Deletions (solid bar) of the β locus cause β-thalassemia (deficiency or absence [β^0] of β-globin). A deletion of δ and β causes hemoglobin Lepore (only hemoglobin α is present). An inversion $(A\gamma\delta\beta)^0$ in this region (largest bar) disrupts gene function and also results in thalassemia (type III). Each type of thalassemia tends to be found in a certain group of people, eg, the $(A\gamma\delta\beta)^0$ deletion inversion occurs in persons from India. Many more deletions in this region have been mapped, and each causes some type of thalassemia.

deletions—as causes of disease (Figure 39–8). The globin gene clusters seem particularly prone to this lesion. Deletions in the α-globin cluster, located on chromosome 16, cause α-thalassemia. There is a strong ethnic association for many of these deletions, so that northern Europeans, Filipinos, blacks, and Mediterranean peoples have different lesions all resulting in the absence of hemoglobin A and α-thalassemia.

A similar analysis could be made for a number of other diseases. Point mutations are usually defined by sequencing the gene in question, though occasionally, if the mutation destroys or creates a restriction enzyme site, the technique of restriction fragment analysis can be used to pinpoint the lesion. Deletions or insertions of DNA larger than 50 bp can often be detected by the Southern blotting procedure.

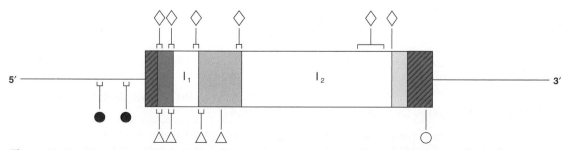

Figure 39–9. Mutations in the β-globin gene causing β-thalassemia. The β-globin gene is shown in the 5' to 3' orientation. The cross-hatched areas indicate the 5' and 3' nontranslated regions. Reading from the 5' to 3' direction, the shaded areas are exons 1–3 and the clear spaces are introns 1 (I$_1$) and 2 (I$_2$). Mutations that affect transcription control (●) are located in the 5' flanking-region DNA. Examples of nonsense mutations (△), mutations in RNA processing (◇), and RNA cleavage mutations (○) have been identified and are indicated. In some regions, many distinct mutations have been found. These are indicated by the brackets.

Table 39–6. Structural alterations of the β-globin gene.

Alteration	Function Affected	Disease
Point mutations	Protein folding	Sickle cell disease
	Transcriptional control	β-Thalassemia
	Frameshift and non-sense mutations	β-Thalassemia
	RNA processing	β-Thalassemia
Deletion	mRNA production	β⁰-Thalassemia Hemoglobin Lepore
Rearrangement	mRNA production	β-Thalassemia type III

E. PEDIGREE ANALYSIS

Sickle cell disease again provides an excellent example of how recombinant DNA technology can be applied to the study of human disease. The substitution of T for A in the template strand of DNA in the β-globin gene changes the sequence in the region that corresponds to the sixth codon from

```
        ↓
      CCTGAGG    Coding strand
      GGACⓉCC    Template strand
            ↑
```
to
```
      CCTGTGG    Coding strand
      GGACⒶCC    Template strand
```

and destroys a recognition site for the restriction enzyme *MstII* (CCTNAGG; denoted by the small vertical arrows; Table 39–2). Other *MstII* sites 5′ and 3′ from this site (Figure 39–10) are not affected and so will be cut. Therefore, incubation of DNA from normal (AA), heterozygous (AS), and homozygous (SS) individuals results in three different patterns on Southern blot transfer (Figure 39–10). This illustrates how a DNA pedigree can be established using the principles discussed in this chapter. Pedigree analysis has been applied to a number of genetic diseases and is most useful in those caused by deletions and insertions or the rarer instances in which a restriction endonuclease cleavage site is affected, as in the example cited here. The analysis is facilitated by the PCR reaction, which can provide sufficient DNA for analysis from just a few nucleated red blood cells.

F. PRENATAL DIAGNOSIS

If the genetic lesion is understood and a specific probe is available, prenatal diagnosis is possible. DNA from cells collected from as little as 10 mL of amniotic fluid (or by chorionic villus biopsy) can be analyzed by Southern blot trans-

fer. A fetus with the restriction pattern AA in Figure 39–10 does not have sickle cell disease, nor is it a carrier. A fetus with the SS pattern will develop the disease. Probes are now available for this type of analysis of many genetic diseases.

G. RESTRICTION FRAGMENT LENGTH POLYMORPHISM (RFLP) AND SINGLE NUCLEOTIDE POLYMORPHISMS (SNPs)

The differences in DNA sequence cited above can result in variations of restriction sites and thus in the length of restriction fragments. Similarly, single nucleotide polymorphisms, or **SNPs,** can be detected by the sensitive PCR method. An inherited difference in the pattern of restriction (eg, a DNA variation occurring in more than 1% of the general population) is known as a restriction fragment length polymorphism, or RFLP. Extensive RFLP and SNP maps of the human genome are being constructed. This is proving useful in the Human Genome Sequencing Project and is an important component of the effort to understand various single-gene and multigenic diseases. RFLPs result from single-base changes (eg, sickle cell disease) or from deletions or insertions of DNA into a restriction fragment (eg, the thalassemias) and have proved to be useful diagnostic tools. They have been found at known gene loci and in sequences that have no known function; thus, RFLPs may disrupt the function of the gene or may have no biologic consequences.

RFLPs and SNPs are inherited, and they segregate in a mendelian fashion. A major use of RFLPs (thousands are now known) is in the definition of inherited diseases in which the functional deficit is unknown. SNPs/RFLPs can be used to establish linkage groups, which in turn, by the process of **chromosome walking,** will eventually define the disease locus. In chromosome walking (Figure 39–11), a fragment representing one end of a long piece of DNA is used to isolate another that overlaps but extends the first. The direction of extension is determined by restriction mapping, and the procedure is repeated sequentially until the desired sequence is obtained. The X chromosome-linked disorders are particularly amenable to this approach, since only a single allele is expressed. Hence, 20% of the defined RFLPs are on the X chromosome, and a reasonably complete linkage map of this chromosome exists. The gene for the X-linked disorder, Duchenne-type muscular dystrophy, was found using RFLPs. Likewise, the defect in Huntington's disease was localized to the terminal region of the short arm of chromosome 4, and the defect that causes polycystic kidney disease is linked to the α-globin locus on chromosome 16.

H. MICROSATELLITE DNA POLYMORPHISMS

Short (2–6 bp), inherited, tandem repeat units of DNA occur about 50,000–100,000 times in the human genome (Chapter 35). Because they occur more frequently—and in view of the routine application of

A. *MstII* restriction sites around and in the β-globin gene

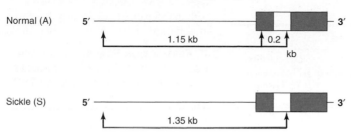

B. Pedigree analysis

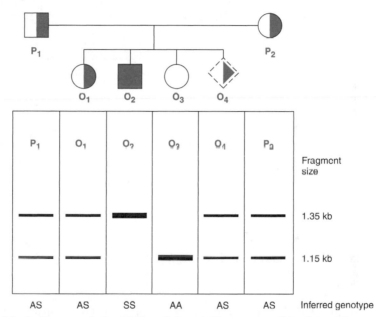

Figure 39–10. Pedigree analysis of sickle cell disease. The top part of the figure **(A)** shows the first part of the β-globin gene and the *MstII* restriction enzyme sites in the normal (A) and sickle cell (S) β-globin genes. Digestion with the restriction enzyme *MstII* results in DNA fragments 1.15 kb and 0.2 kb long in normal individuals. The T-to-A change in individuals with sickle cell disease abolishes one of the three *MstII* sites around the β-globin gene; hence, a single restriction fragment 1.35 kb in length is generated in response to *MstII*. This size difference is easily detected on a Southern blot. (The 0.2-kb fragment would run off the gel in this illustration.) **(B)** Pedigree analysis shows three possibilities: AA = normal (open circle); AS = heterozygous (half-solid circles, half-solid square); SS = homozygous (solid square). This approach can allow for prenatal diagnosis of sickle cell disease (dash-sided square). See text.

sensitive PCR methods—they are replacing RFLPs as the marker loci for various genome searches.

I. RFLPs & VNTRs in Forensic Medicine

Variable numbers of tandemly repeated (VNTR) units are one common type of "insertion" that results in an RFLP. The VNTRs can be inherited, in which case they are use-

ful in establishing genetic association with a disease in a family or kindred; or they can be unique to an individual and thus serve as a molecular fingerprint of that person.

J. Gene Therapy

Diseases caused by deficiency of a gene product (Table 39–5) are amenable to replacement therapy. The strat-

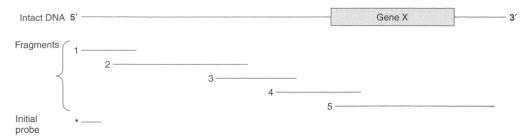

Figure 39–11. The technique of chromosome walking. Gene X is to be isolated from a large piece of DNA. The exact location of this gene is not known, but a probe (*———) directed against a fragment of DNA (shown at the 5′ end in this representation) is available, as is a library of clones containing a series of overlapping DNA insert fragments. For the sake of simplicity, only five of these are shown. The initial probe will hybridize only with clones containing fragment 1, which can then be isolated and used as a probe to detect fragment 2. This procedure is repeated until fragment 4 hybridizes with fragment 5, which contains the entire sequence of gene X.

egy is to clone a gene (eg, the gene that codes for adenosine deaminase) into a vector that will readily be taken up and incorporated into the genome of a host cell. Bone marrow precursor cells are being investigated for this purpose because they presumably will resettle in the marrow and replicate there. The introduced gene would begin to direct the expression of its protein product, and this would correct the deficiency in the host cell.

K. Transgenic Animals

The somatic cell gene replacement therapy described above would obviously not be passed on to offspring. Other strategies to alter germ cell lines have been devised but have been tested only in experimental animals. A certain percentage of genes injected into a fertilized mouse ovum will be incorporated into the genome and found in both somatic and germ cells. Hundreds of transgenic animals have been established, and these are useful for analysis of tissue-specific effects on gene expression and effects of overproduction of gene products (eg, those from the growth hormone gene or oncogenes) and in discovering genes involved in development—a process that heretofore has been difficult to study. The transgenic approach has recently been used to correct a genetic deficiency in mice. Fertilized ova obtained from mice with genetic hypogonadism were injected with DNA containing the coding sequence for the gonadotropin-releasing hormone (GnRH) precursor protein. This gene was expressed and regulated normally in the hypothalamus of a certain number of the resultant mice, and these animals were in all respects normal. Their offspring also showed no evidence of GnRH deficiency. This is, therefore, evidence of somatic cell expression of the transgene and of its maintenance in germ cells.

Targeted Gene Disruption or Knockout

In transgenic animals, one is adding one or more copies of a gene to the genome, and there is no way to control where that gene eventually resides. A complementary—and much more difficult—approach involves the selective removal of a gene from the genome. Gene knockout animals (usually mice) are made by creating a mutation that totally disrupts the function of a gene. This is then used to replace one of the two genes in an embryonic stem cell that can be used to create a heterozygous transgenic animal. The mating of two such animals will, by mendelian genetics, result in a homozygous mutation in 25% of offspring. Several hundred strains of mice with knockouts of specific genes have been developed. Techniques for disrupting genes in specific cells, tissues, or organs have been developed, so-called conditional, or directed, knockouts. This can be accomplished by taking advantage of particular promoter-enhancer combinations driving expression of DNA recombinases or SiRNAs, both of which inactivate gene expression. These methods are particularly useful in cases where gene ablation during early development causes embryonic lethality.

RNA Transcript & Protein Profiling

The "-omic" revolution of the last several years has culminated in the determination of the nucleotide sequences of entire genomes, including those of budding and fission yeasts, various bacteria, the fruit fly, the worm *Caenorhabditis elegans,* the mouse and, most notably, humans. Additional genomes are being sequenced at an accelerating pace. The availability of all of this DNA sequence information, coupled with engineering advances, has lead to the development of several revolutionary methodologies, most of which are based upon **high-density microarray technology.** We now have the ability to deposit thousands of specific, known, definable DNA sequences (more typically now synthetic oligonucleotides) on a glass microscope-style slide in the space of a few square centimeters. By coupling such DNA microarrays with highly sensitive detection of hybridized fluorescently labeled nucleic acid probes

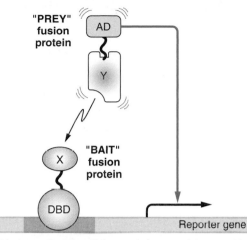

Figure 39–12. Outline of two hybrid system for identifying and characterizing protein-protein interactions. Shown are the basic components and operation of the two hybrid system, originally devised by Fields and Song [*Nature* 340:245–246 (1989)] to function in the Bakers yeast system. **(1)** A reporter gene, either a selectable marker (ie, a gene conferring prototrophic growth on selective media, or producing an enzyme for which a colony colorimetric assay exists, such as β-galactosidase) that is expressed only when a transcription factor binds upstream to a *cis*-linked enhancer (dark gray bar). **(2)** A "Bait" fusion protein **(DBD-X)** produced from a chimeric gene expressing a modular DNA binding domain **(DBD**; often derived from the yeast Ga14 protein or the bacterial LexA protein, both high-affinity, high-specificity DNA binding proteins) fused in-frame to a protein of interest, here X. In two hybrid experiments, one is testing whether any protein can interact with protein X. Prey protein X may be fused in its entirety or often alternatively just a portion of protein X is expressed in frame with the DBD. **(3)** A "Prey" protein **(Y-AD),** which represents a fusion of a specific protein fused in-frame to a transcriptional activation domain **(AD**; often derived from either the *Herpes simplex* virus VP16 protein or the yeast Ga14 protein). This system serves as a useful test of protein-protein interactions between proteins X and Y because in the absence of a functional transactivator binding to the indicated enhancer, no transcription of the reporter gene occurs. Thus, one observes transcription only if protein X-protein Y interaction occurs thereby bringing a functional AD to the *cis*-linked transcription unit, in this case activating transcription of the reporter gene. In this scenario, protein DBD-X alone fails to activate reporter transcription because the X-domain fused to the DBD does not contain an AD. Similarly, protein Y-AD alone fails to activate reporter gene transcription because it lacks a DBD to target the Y-AD protein to the enhancer. Only when both proteins are expressed in a single cell and bind the enhancer and, via DBD-X–Y-AD protein-protein interactions, regenerate a functional transactivator binary "protein" does reporter gene transcription result in activation and mRNA synthesis (colored line from AD to reporter gene).

derived from mRNA, investigators can rapidly and accurately generate profiles of gene expression (eg, specific cellular mRNA content) from cell and tissue samples as small as 1 gram or less. Thus entire **transcriptome information** (the entire collection of cellular mRNAs) for such cell or tissue sources can readily be obtained in only a few days. Transcriptome information allows one to predict the collection of proteins that might be expressed in a particular cell, tissue, or organ in normal and disease states based upon the mRNAs present in those cells. Complementing this high-throughput, transcript-profiling method is the recent development of high-sensitivity, high-throughput **mass spectrometry of complex protein samples.** Newer mass spectrometry methods allow one to identify hundreds to thousands of proteins in proteins extracted from very small numbers of cells (< 1 g). This critical information tells investigators which of the many mRNAs detected in transcript microarray mapping studies are actually translated into protein, generally the ultimate dictator of phenotype. New genetic means for identifying protein-protein interactions and protein function have also been devised. Systematic genome-wide gene expression knockdown, using SiRNAs, or synthetic lethal genetic interaction screens, have been applied to assess the contribution of individual genes to a variety of processes in model systems (yeast, worms, flies) and mammalian cells (human and mouse). Specific network mappings of protein-protein interactions on a genome-wide basis have been identified using high throughput variants of the two hybrid interaction test (Figure 39–12). This simple yet powerful method can be performed in bacteria, yeast, or metazoan cells, and allows for detecting

specific protein-protein interactions in living cells. Reconstruction experiments indicate that protein-protein interactions of affinity $K_d \sim 1\ \mu M$ or tighter can readily be detected with this method. Together, these technologies provide powerful new tools with which to dissect the intricacies of human biology.

Microarray techniques, high throughput two hybrid, genetic knockdown, and mass spectrometric protein identification experiments have led to the generation of huge amounts of data. Appropriate data management and interpretation of the deluge of information forthcoming from such studies has relied upon statistical methods; and this new technology, coupled with the flood of DNA sequence information, has led to the development of the fields of **bioinformatics and systems biology,** new disciplines whose goals are to help manage, analyze, and integrate this flood of biologically important information. Future work at the intersection of bioinformatics, transcript-protein profiling, and systems biology will revolutionize our understanding of physiology and medicine.

SUMMARY

- A variety of very sensitive techniques can now be applied to the isolation and characterization of genes and to the quantitation of gene products.

- In DNA cloning, a particular segment of DNA is removed from its normal environment using PCR or one of many restriction endonucleases. This is then ligated into a vector in which the DNA segment can be amplified and produced in abundance.

- Cloned DNA can be used as a probe in one of several types of hybridization reactions to detect other related or adjacent pieces of DNA, or it can be used to quantitate gene products such as mRNA.

- Manipulation of the DNA to change its structure, so-called genetic engineering, is a key element in cloning (eg, the construction of chimeric molecules) and can also be used to study the function of a certain fragment of DNA and to analyze how genes are regulated.

- Chimeric DNA molecules are introduced into cells to make transfected cells or into the fertilized oocyte to make transgenic animals.

- Techniques involving cloned DNA are used to locate genes to specific regions of chromosomes, to identify the genes responsible for diseases, to study how faulty gene regulation causes disease, to diagnose genetic diseases, and increasingly to treat genetic diseases.

GLOSSARY

ARS: Autonomously replicating sequence; the origin of replication in yeast.

Autoradiography: The detection of radioactive molecules (eg, DNA, RNA, protein) by visualization of their effects on photographic film.

Bacteriophage: A virus that infects a bacterium.

Blunt-ended DNA: Two strands of a DNA duplex having ends that are flush with each other.

cDNA: A single-stranded DNA molecule that is complementary to an mRNA molecule and is synthesized from it by the action of reverse transcriptase.

Chimeric molecule: A molecule (eg, DNA, RNA, protein) containing sequences derived from two different species.

Clone: A large number of organisms, cells or molecules that are identical with a single parental organism cell or molecule.

Cosmid: A plasmid into which the DNA sequences from bacteriophage lambda that are necessary for the packaging of DNA (cos sites) have been inserted; this permits the plasmid DNA to be packaged in vitro.

Endonuclease: An enzyme that cleaves internal bonds in DNA or RNA.

Excinuclease: The excision nuclease involved in nucleotide exchange repair of DNA.

Exon: The sequence of a gene that is represented (expressed) as mRNA.

Exonuclease: An enzyme that cleaves nucleotides from either the 3′ or 5′ ends of DNA or RNA.

Fingerprinting: The use of RFLPs or repeat sequence DNA to establish a unique pattern of DNA fragments for an individual.

Footprinting: DNA with protein bound is resistant to digestion by DNase enzymes. When a sequencing reaction is performed using such DNA, a protected area, representing the "footprint" of the bound protein, will be detected.

Hairpin: A double-helical stretch formed by base pairing between neighboring complementary sequences of a single strand of DNA or RNA.

Hybridization: The specific reassociation of complementary strands of nucleic acids (DNA with DNA, DNA with RNA, or RNA with RNA).

Insert: An additional length of base pairs in DNA, generally introduced by the techniques of recombinant DNA technology.

Intron: The sequence of a gene that is transcribed but excised before translation.

Library: A collection of cloned fragments that represents the entire genome. Libraries may be either genomic DNA (in which both introns and exons are represented) or cDNA (in which only exons are represented).

Ligation: The enzyme-catalyzed joining in phosphodiester linkage of two stretches of DNA or RNA into one; the respective enzymes are DNA and RNA ligases.

Lines: Long interspersed repeat sequences.

Microsatellite polymorphism: Heterozygosity of a certain microsatellite repeat in an individual.

Microsatellite repeat sequences: Dispersed or group repeat sequences of 2–5 bp repeated up to 50 times. May occur at 50–100 thousand locations in the genome.

miRNAs: MicroRNAs, 21–25 nucleotide long RNA species derived from RNA polymerase II transcription units, 500–1500 bp in length via RNA processing. These RNAs, recently discovered, are thought to play crucial roles in gene regulation.

Nick translation: A technique for labeling DNA based on the ability of the DNA polymerase from *E coli* to degrade a strand of DNA that has been nicked and then to resynthesize the strand; if a radioactive nucleoside triphosphate is employed, the rebuilt strand becomes labeled and can be used as a radioactive probe.

Northern blot: A method for transferring RNA from an agarose gel to a nitrocellulose filter, on which the RNA can be detected by a suitable probe.

Oligonucleotide: A short, defined sequence of nucleotides joined together in the typical phosphodiester linkage.

Ori: The origin of DNA replication.

PAC: A high-capacity (70–95 kb) cloning vector based upon the lytic *E coli* bacteriophage P1 that replicates in bacteria as an extrachromosomal element.

Palindrome: A sequence of duplex DNA that is the same when the two strands are read in opposite directions.

Plasmid: A small, extrachromosomal, circular molecule of DNA that replicates independently of the host DNA.

Polymerase chain reaction (PCR): An enzymatic method for the repeated copying (and thus amplification) of the two strands of DNA that make up a particular gene sequence.

Primosome: The mobile complex of helicase and primase that is involved in DNA replication.

Probe: A molecule used to detect the presence of a specific fragment of DNA or RNA in, for instance, a bacterial colony that is formed from a genetic library or during analysis by blot transfer techniques; common probes are cDNA molecules, synthetic oligodeoxynucleotides of defined sequence, or antibodies to specific proteins.

Proteome: The entire collection of expressed proteins in an organism.

Pseudogene: An inactive segment of DNA arising by mutation of a parental active gene.

Recombinant DNA: The altered DNA that results from the insertion of a sequence of deoxynucleotides not previously present into an existing molecule of DNA by enzymatic or chemical means.

Restriction enzyme: An endodeoxynuclease that causes cleavage of both strands of DNA at highly specific sites dictated by the base sequence.

Reverse transcription: RNA-directed synthesis of DNA, catalyzed by reverse transcriptase.

RT-PCR: A method used to quantitate mRNA levels that relies upon a first step of cDNA copying of mRNAs catalyzed by reverse transcriptase prior to PCR amplification and quantitation.

Signal: The end product observed when a specific sequence of DNA or RNA is detected by autoradiography or some other method. Hybridization with a complementary radioactive polynucleotide (eg, by Southern or Northern blotting) is commonly used to generate the signal.

Sines: Short interspersed repeat sequences.

SiRNAs: Silencing RNAs, 21–25 nt in length generated by selective nucleolytic degradation of double-stranded RNAs of cellular or viral origin. SiRNAs anneal to various specific sites within target in RNAs leading to mRNA degradation, hence gene "knockdown."

SNP: Single nucleotide polymorphism. Refers to the fact that single nucleotide genetic variation in genome sequence exists at discrete loci throughout the chromosomes. Measurement of allelic SNP differences is useful for gene mapping studies.

snRNA: Small nuclear RNA. This family of RNAs is best known for its role in mRNA processing.

Southern blot: A method for transferring DNA from an agarose gel to nitrocellulose filter, on which the DNA can be detected by a suitable probe (eg, complementary DNA or RNA).

Southwestern blot: A method for detecting protein-DNA interactions by applying a labeled DNA probe to a transfer membrane that contains a renatured protein.

Spliceosome: The macromolecular complex responsible for precursor mRNA splicing. The spliceosome consists of at least five small nuclear RNAs (snRNA; U1, U2, U4, U5, and U6) and many proteins.

Splicing: The removal of introns from RNA accompanied by the joining of its exons.

Sticky-ended DNA: Complementary single strands of DNA that protrude from opposite ends of a DNA duplex or from the ends of different duplex molecules (see also Blunt-ended DNA, above).

Tandem: Used to describe multiple copies of the same sequence (eg, DNA) that lie adjacent to one another.

Terminal transferase: An enzyme that adds nucleotides of one type (eg, deoxyadenonucleotidyl residues) to the 3′ end of DNA strands.

Transcription: Template DNA-directed synthesis of nucleic acids; typically DNA-directed synthesis of RNA.

Transcriptome: The entire collection of expressed mRNAs in an organism.

Transgenic: Describing the introduction of new DNA into germ cells by its injection into the nucleus of the ovum.

Translation: Synthesis of protein using mRNA as template.

Vector: A plasmid or bacteriophage into which foreign DNA can be introduced for the purposes of cloning.

Western blot: A method for transferring protein to a nitrocellulose filter, on which the protein can be detected by a suitable probe (eg, an antibody).

REFERENCES

Friedman A, Perrimon N: Genome-wide high-throughput screens in functional genomics. Curr Opin Gen Dev 2004;14:470.

Lewin B: *Genes VII.* Oxford Univ Press, 1999.

Martin JB, Gusella JF: Huntington's disease: pathogenesis and management. N Engl J Med 1986:315:1267.

Sambrook J, Fritsch EF, Maniatis T: *Molecular Cloning: A Laboratory Manual.* Cold Spring Harbor Laboratory Press, 1989.

Spector DL, Goldman RD, Leinwand LA: *Cells: A Laboratory Manual.* Cold Spring Harbor Laboratory Press, 1998.

Watson JD et al: *Recombinant DNA,* 2nd ed. Scientific American Books. Freeman, 1992.

Weatherall DJ: *The New Genetics and Clinical Practice,* 3rd ed. Oxford Univ Press, 1991.

SECTION V
Biochemistry of Extracellular & Intracellular Communication

Membranes: Structure & Function

Robert K. Murray, MD, PhD, & Daryl K. Granner, MD

BIOMEDICAL IMPORTANCE

Membranes are highly viscous, plastic structures. **Plasma membranes** form closed compartments around cellular protoplasm to separate one cell from another and thus permit cellular individuality. The plasma membrane has **selective permeabilities** and acts as a barrier, thereby maintaining differences in composition between the inside and outside of the cell. The selective permeabilities are provided mainly by **channels** and **pumps** for ions and substrates. The plasma membrane also exchanges material with the extracellular environment by exocytosis and endocytosis, and there are special areas of membrane structure—the gap junctions—through which adjacent cells exchange material. In addition, the plasma membrane plays key roles in **cell-cell interactions** and in **transmembrane signaling.**

Membranes also form **specialized compartments** within the cell. Such intracellular membranes help shape many of the morphologically distinguishable structures (organelles), eg, mitochondria, ER, sarcoplasmic reticulum, Golgi complexes, secretory granules, lysosomes, and the nuclear membrane. Membranes localize **enzymes,** function as integral elements in **excitation-response coupling,** and provide sites of **energy transduction,** such as in photosynthesis and oxidative phosphorylation.

Changes in membrane structure (eg caused by ischemia) can affect water balance and ion flux and therefore every process within the cell. Specific deficiencies or alterations of certain membrane components lead to a variety of **diseases** (see Table 40–5). In short, normal cellular function depends on normal membranes.

MAINTENANCE OF A NORMAL INTRA- & EXTRACELLULAR ENVIRONMENT IS FUNDAMENTAL TO LIFE

Life originated in an aqueous environment; enzyme reactions, cellular and subcellular processes, and so forth have therefore evolved to work in this milieu. Since mammals live in a gaseous environment, how is the aqueous state maintained? Membranes accomplish this by internalizing and compartmentalizing body water.

The Body's Internal Water Is Compartmentalized

Water makes up about 60% of the lean body mass of the human body and is distributed in two large compartments.

A. INTRACELLULAR FLUID (ICF)

This compartment constitutes two-thirds of total body water and provides the environment for the cell (1) to make, store, and utilize energy; (2) to repair itself; (3) to replicate; and (4) to perform special functions.

B. EXTRACELLULAR FLUID (ECF)

This compartment contains about one-third of total body water and is distributed between the plasma and interstitial compartments. The extracellular fluid is a delivery system. It brings to the cells nutrients (eg, glucose, fatty acids, amino acids), oxygen, various ions and trace minerals, and a variety of regulatory molecules (hormones) that coordinate the functions of widely sep-

arated cells. Extracellular fluid removes CO_2, waste products, and toxic or detoxified materials from the immediate cellular environment.

The Ionic Compositions of Intracellular & Extracellular Fluids Differ Greatly

As illustrated in Table 40–1, the **internal environment** is rich in K^+ and Mg^{2+}, and phosphate is its major anion. **Extracellular fluid** is characterized by high Na^+ and Ca^{2+} content, and Cl^- is the major anion. Note also that the concentration of glucose is higher in extracellular fluid than in the cell, whereas the opposite is true for proteins. Why is there such a difference? It is thought that the primordial sea in which life originated was rich in K^+ and Mg^{2+}. It therefore follows that enzyme reactions and other biologic processes evolved to function best in that environment—hence the high concentration of these ions within cells. Cells were faced with strong selection pressure as the sea gradually changed to a composition rich in Na^+ and Ca^{2+}. Vast changes would have been required for evolution of a completely new set of biochemical and physiologic machinery; instead, as it happened, cells developed barriers—membranes with associated "pumps"—to maintain the internal microenvironment.

MEMBRANES ARE COMPLEX STRUCTURES COMPOSED OF LIPIDS, PROTEINS, & CARBOHYDRATES

We shall mainly discuss the membranes present in eukaryotic cells, although many of the principles described also apply to the membranes of prokaryotes. The various cellular membranes have **different compositions**, as reflected in the ratio of protein to lipid (Figure 40–1). This is not surprising, given their divergent functions. Membranes are asymmetric sheet-like

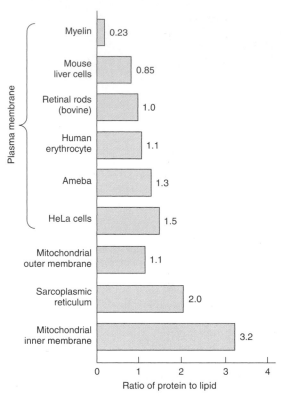

Figure 40–1. Ratio of protein to lipid in different membranes. Proteins equal or exceed the quantity of lipid in nearly all membranes. The outstanding exception is myelin, an electrical insulator found on many nerve fibers.

enclosed structures with distinct inner and outer surfaces. These sheet-like structures are **noncovalent assemblies** that are thermodynamically stable and metabolically active. Numerous proteins are located in membranes, where they carry out specific functions of the organelle, the cell, or the organism.

The Major Lipids in Mammalian Membranes Are Phospholipids, Glycosphingolipids, & Cholesterol

A. PHOSPHOLIPIDS

Of the two major phospholipid classes present in membranes, **phosphoglycerides** are the more common and consist of a glycerol backbone to which are attached two fatty acids in ester linkage and a phosphorylated alcohol (Figure 40–2). The fatty acid constituents are usually even-numbered carbon molecules, most commonly containing 16 or 18 carbons. They are unbranched and can be saturated or unsaturated. The simplest phosphoglyceride is phosphatidic acid, which

Table 40–1. Comparison of the mean concentrations of various molecules outside and inside a mammalian cell.

Substance	Extracellular Fluid	Intracellular Fluid
Na^+	140 mmol/L	10 mmol/L
K^+	4 mmol/L	140 mmol/L
Ca^{2+} (free)	2.5 mmol/L	0.1 μmol/L
Mg^{2+}	1.5 mmol/L	30 mmol/L
Cl^-	100 mmol/L	4 mmol/L
HCO_3^-	27 mmol/L	10 mmol/L
PO_4^{3-}	2 mmol/L	60 mmol/L
Glucose	5.5 mmol/L	0–1 mmol/L
Protein	2 g/dL	16 g/dL

Fatty acids

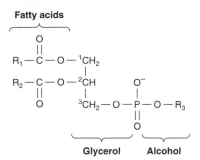

Figure 40–2. A phosphoglyceride showing the fatty acids (R_1 and R_2), glycerol, and phosphorylated alcohol components. In phosphatidic acid, R_3 is hydrogen.

is 1,2-diacylglycerol 3-phosphate, a key intermediate in the formation of all other phosphoglycerides (Chapter 24). In other phosphoglycerides, the 3-phosphate is esterified to an alcohol such as ethanolamine, choline, serine, glycerol, or inositol (Chapter 15).

The second major class of phospholipids is composed of **sphingomyelin,** which contains a sphingosine backbone rather than glycerol. A fatty acid is attached by an amide linkage to the amino group of sphingosine, forming ceramide. The primary hydroxyl group of sphingosine is esterified to phosphorylcholine. Sphingomyelin, as the name implies, is prominent in myelin sheaths.

The amounts and fatty acid compositions of the various phospholipids vary among the different cellular membranes.

B. Glycosphingolipids

The glycosphingolipids (GSLs) are sugar-containing lipids built on a backbone of ceramide; they include galactosyl- and glucosylceramide (cerebrosides) and the gangliosides. Their structures are described in Chapter 15. They are mainly located in the plasma membranes of cells.

C. Sterols

The most common sterol in membranes is **cholesterol** (Chapter 15), which resides mainly in the plasma membranes of mammalian cells but can also be found in lesser quantities in mitochondria, Golgi complexes, and nuclear membranes. Cholesterol intercalates among the phospholipids of the membrane, with its hydroxyl group at the aqueous interface and the remainder of the molecule within the leaflet. Its effect on the fluidity of membranes is discussed subsequently.

All of the above lipids can be separated from one another by techniques such as column, thin layer, and gas-liquid chromatography and their structures established by mass spectrometry.

Each eukaryotic cell membrane has a somewhat different lipid composition, though phospholipids are the major class in all.

Membrane Lipids Are Amphipathic

All major lipids in membranes contain both hydrophobic and hydrophilic regions and are therefore termed **"amphipathic."** Membranes themselves are thus amphipathic. If the hydrophobic regions were separated from the rest of the molecule, it would be insoluble in water but soluble in oil. Conversely, if the hydrophilic region were separated from the rest of the molecule, it would be insoluble in oil but soluble in water. The amphipathic nature of a phospholipid is represented in Figure 40–3. Thus, the polar head groups of the phospholipids and the hydroxyl group of cholesterol interface with the aqueous environment; a similar situation applies to the sugar moieties of the GSLs (see below).

Saturated fatty acids have straight tails, whereas **unsaturated fatty acids,** which generally exist in the cis form in membranes, make kinked tails (Figure 40–3). As more kinks are inserted in the tails, the membrane becomes less tightly packed and therefore more fluid.

Detergents are amphipathic molecules that are important in biochemistry as well as in the household. The molecular structure of a detergent is not unlike that of a phospholipid. Certain detergents are widely used to solubilize membrane proteins as a first step in their purification. The hydrophobic end of the detergent binds to hydrophobic regions of the proteins, displacing most of their bound lipids. The polar end of the detergent is free, bringing the proteins into solution as

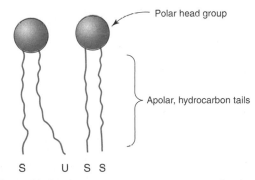

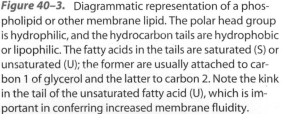

Figure 40–3. Diagrammatic representation of a phospholipid or other membrane lipid. The polar head group is hydrophilic, and the hydrocarbon tails are hydrophobic or lipophilic. The fatty acids in the tails are saturated (S) or unsaturated (U); the former are usually attached to carbon 1 of glycerol and the latter to carbon 2. Note the kink in the tail of the unsaturated fatty acid (U), which is important in conferring increased membrane fluidity.

The phospholipids of cellular membranes generally contain at least one unsaturated fatty acid with at least one cis double bond.

Cholesterol modifies the fluidity of membranes. At temperatures below the T_m, it interferes with the interaction of the hydrocarbon tails of fatty acids and thus increases fluidity. At temperatures above the T_m, it limits disorder because it is more rigid than the hydrocarbon tails of the fatty acids and cannot move in the membrane to the same extent, thus limiting fluidity. At high cholesterol:phospholipid ratios, transition temperatures are altogether indistinguishable.

The **fluidity** of a membrane significantly affects its **functions.** As membrane fluidity increases, so does its permeability to water and other small hydrophilic molecules. The lateral mobility of integral proteins increases as the fluidity of the membrane increases. If the active site of an integral protein involved in a given function is exclusively in its hydrophilic regions, changing lipid fluidity will probably have little effect on the activity of the protein; however, if the protein is involved in a transport function in which transport components span the membrane, lipid phase effects may significantly alter the transport rate. The insulin receptor is an excellent example of altered function with changes in fluidity. As the concentration of unsaturated fatty acids in the membrane is increased (by growing cultured cells in a medium rich in such molecules), fluidity increases. This alters the receptor so that it binds more insulin.

Lipid Rafts, Caveolae, & Tight Junctions Are Specialized Features of Plasma Membranes

Plasma membranes contain certain specialized structures whose biochemical natures have been investigated in some detail.

Lipid rafts are dynamic areas of the exoplasmic leaflet of the lipid bilayer enriched in cholesterol, sphingolipids, and certain proteins (see Figure 40–8). They appear to be involved in signal transduction and other processes. It is thought that clustering certain components of signaling systems closely together may increase the efficiency of their function.

Caveolae may derive from lipid rafts. Many, if not all, contain the protein **caveolin-1,** which may be involved in their formation from rafts. Caveolae are observable by electron microscopy as flask-shaped indentations of the cell membrane (Figure 40–9). Proteins detected in caveolae include various components of the signal transduction system (eg, the insulin receptor and some G proteins), the folate receptor, and endothelial nitric oxide synthase (eNOS). Caveolae and lipid rafts are active areas of research, and ideas concerning them and their possible roles in various disorders are rapidly evolving.

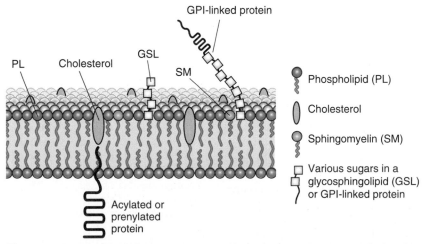

Figure 40–8. Schematic diagram of a lipid raft. Lipid rafts are somewhat thicker than the remainder of the bilayer. They are enriched in sphingolipids (eg, sphingomyelin), glycosphingolipids (eg, the ganglioside GM₁), saturated phospholipids, and cholesterol. They also contain certain GPI-linked proteins (outer leaflet) and acylated and prenylated proteins (inner leaflet). GPI-linked proteins are discussed in Chapter 46. Acylation and prenylations are post-translational modifications of certain membrane proteins.

detergent-protein complexes, usually also containing some residual lipids.

Membrane Lipids Form Bilayers

The amphipathic character of phospholipids suggests that the two regions of the molecule have incompatible solubilities; however, in a solvent such as water, phospholipids organize themselves into a form that thermodynamically serves the solubility requirements of both regions. A **micelle** (Figure 40–4) is such a structure; the hydrophobic regions are shielded from water, while the hydrophilic polar groups are immersed in the aqueous environment. However, micelles are usually relatively small in size (eg, approximately 200 nm) and thus are limited in their potential to form membranes.

As was recognized in 1925 by Gorter and Grendel, a **bimolecular layer,** or **lipid bilayer,** can also satisfy the thermodynamic requirements of amphipathic molecules in an aqueous environment. **Bilayers,** not micelles, are indeed the key structures in biologic membranes. A bilayer exists as a sheet in which the hydrophobic regions of the phospholipids are protected from the aqueous environment, while the hydrophilic regions are immersed in water (Figure 40–5). Only the ends or edges of the bilayer sheet are exposed to an unfavorable environment, but even these exposed edges can be eliminated by folding the sheet back upon itself to form an enclosed vesicle with no edges. A bilayer can extend over relatively large distances (eg, 1 mm). The closed

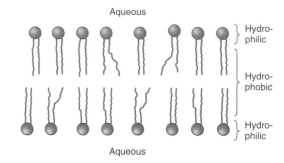

Figure 40–5. Diagram of a section of a bilayer membrane formed from phospholipid molecules. The unsaturated fatty acid tails are kinked and lead to more spacing between the polar head groups, hence to more room for movement. This in turn results in increased membrane fluidity. (Slightly modified and reproduced, with permission, from Stryer L: *Biochemistry*, 2nd ed. Freeman, 1981. Copyright © 1981 by W.H. Freeman and Company.)

bilayer provides one of the most essential properties of membranes. It is impermeable to most water-soluble molecules, since they would be insoluble in the hydrophobic core of the bilayer.

Lipid bilayers are formed by **self-assembly,** driven by the **hydrophobic effect** (Chapter 2). When lipid molecules come together in a bilayer, the entropy of the surrounding solvent molecules increases.

Two questions arise from consideration of the above. First, how many biologic materials are **lipid-soluble** and can therefore readily enter the cell? Gases such as oxygen, CO_2, and nitrogen—small molecules with little interaction with solvents—readily diffuse through the hydrophobic regions of the membrane. The permeability coefficients of several ions and of a number of other molecules in a lipid bilayer are shown in Figure 40–6. The three electrolytes shown (Na^+, K^+, and Cl^-) cross the bilayer much more slowly than water. In general, the permeability coefficients of small molecules in a lipid bilayer correlate with their solubilities in nonpolar solvents. For instance, steroids more readily traverse the lipid bilayer compared with electrolytes. The high permeability coefficient of water itself is surprising but is partly explained by its small size and relative lack of charge.

The second question concerns **molecules that are not lipid-soluble:** How are the transmembrane concentration gradients for non-lipid-soluble molecules maintained? The answer is that membranes contain proteins, and proteins are also amphipathic molecules that can be inserted into the correspondingly amphipathic lipid bilayer. Proteins form **channels** for the movement of ions and small molecules and serve as **transporters** for larger molecules that otherwise could not pass the bilayer. These processes are described below.

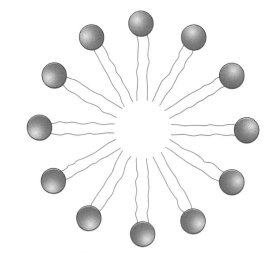

Figure 40–4. Diagrammatic cross-section of a micelle. The polar head groups are bathed in water, whereas the hydrophobic hydrocarbon tails are surrounded by other hydrocarbons and thereby protected from water. Micelles are relatively small (compared with lipid bilayers) spherical structures.

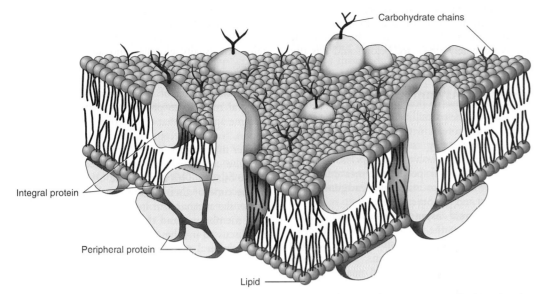

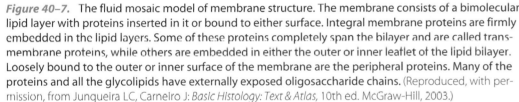

Figure 40–7. The fluid mosaic model of membrane structure. The membrane consists of a bimolecular lipid layer with proteins inserted in it or bound to either surface. Integral membrane proteins are firmly embedded in the lipid layers. Some of these proteins completely span the bilayer and are called transmembrane proteins, while others are embedded in either the outer or inner leaflet of the lipid bilayer. Loosely bound to the outer or inner surface of the membrane are the peripheral proteins. Many of the proteins and all the glycolipids have externally exposed oligosaccharide chains. (Reproduced, with permission, from Junqueira LC, Carneiro J: *Basic Histology: Text & Atlas,* 10th ed. McGraw-Hill, 2003.)

and isolated genes. There is interest in using liposomes to distribute drugs to certain tissues, and if components (eg, antibodies to certain cell surface molecules) could be incorporated into liposomes so that they would be targeted to specific tissues or tumors, the therapeutic impact would be considerable. DNA entrapped inside liposomes appears to be less sensitive to attack by nucleases; this approach may prove useful in attempts at gene therapy.

THE FLUID MOSAIC MODEL OF MEMBRANE STRUCTURE IS WIDELY ACCEPTED

The **fluid mosaic model** of membrane structure proposed in 1972 by Singer and Nicolson (Figure 40–7) is now widely accepted. The model is often likened to icebergs (membrane proteins) floating in a sea of predominantly phospholipid molecules. Early evidence for the model was the finding that certain species-specific integral proteins (detected by fluorescent labeling techniques) rapidly and randomly redistributed in the plasma membrane of an interspecies hybrid cell formed by the artificially induced fusion of two different parent cells. It has subsequently been demonstrated that phospholipids also undergo rapid redistribution in the plane

of the membrane. This diffusion within the plane of the membrane, termed lateral diffusion, can be quite rapid for a phospholipid; in fact, within the plane of the membrane, one molecule of phospholipid can move several micrometers per second.

The phase changes—and thus the **fluidity** of membranes—are largely dependent upon the lipid composition of the membrane. In a lipid bilayer, the hydrophobic chains of the fatty acids can be highly aligned or ordered to provide a rather stiff structure. As the temperature increases, the hydrophobic side chains undergo a transition from the ordered state (more gel-like or crystalline phase) to a disordered one, taking on a more liquid-like or fluid arrangement. The temperature at which the structure undergoes the transition from ordered to disordered (ie, melts) is called the "**transition temperature**" (T_m). The longer and more saturated fatty acid chains interact more strongly with each other via their longer hydrocarbon chains and thus cause higher values of T_m—ie, higher temperatures are required to increase the fluidity of the bilayer. On the other hand, unsaturated bonds that exist in the cis configuration tend to increase the fluidity of a bilayer by decreasing the compactness of the side chain packing without diminishing hydrophobicity (Figure 40–3).

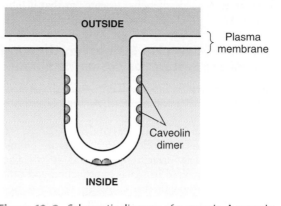

Figure 40–9. Schematic diagram of a caveola. A caveola is an invagination in the plasma membrane. The protein caveolin appears to play an important role in the formation of caveolae, and occurs as a dimer. Each caveolin monomer is anchored to the inner leaflet of the plasma membrane by three palmitoyl molecules (not shown).

Tight junctions are other structures found in surface membranes. They are often located below the apical surfaces of epithelial cells and prevent the diffusion of macromolecules between cells. They are composed of various proteins, including occludin, various claudins, and junctional adhesion molecules.

Yet other specialized structures found in surface membranes include desmosomes, adherens junctions, and microvilli; their chemical natures and functions are not discussed here. The nature of **gap junctions** is described below.

MEMBRANE SELECTIVITY ALLOWS ADJUSTMENTS OF CELL COMPOSITION & FUNCTION

If the plasma membrane is relatively impermeable, how do most molecules enter a cell? How is **selectivity** of this movement established? Answers to such questions are important in understanding how cells adjust to a constantly changing extracellular environment. Metazoan organisms also must have **means of communicating** between adjacent and distant cells, so that complex biologic processes can be coordinated. These signals must arrive at and be transmitted by the membrane, or they must be generated as a consequence of some interaction with the membrane. Some of the major mechanisms used to accomplish these different objectives are listed in Table 40–3.

Passive Mechanisms Move Some Small Molecules Across Membranes

Molecules can passively traverse the bilayer down electrochemical gradients by **simple diffusion** or by **facili-**

Table 40–3. Transfer of material and information across membranes.

Cross-membrane movement of small molecules
Diffusion (passive and facilitated)
Active transport
Cross-membrane movement of large molecules
Endocytosis
Exocytosis
Signal transmission across membranes
Cell surface receptors
1. Signal transduction (eg, glucagon → cAMP)
2. Signal internalization (coupled with endocytosis, eg, the LDL receptor)
Movement to intracellular receptors (steroid hormones; a form of diffusion)
Intercellular contact and communication

tated diffusion. This spontaneous movement toward equilibrium contrasts with **active transport,** which requires energy because it constitutes movement against an electrochemical gradient. Figure 40–10 provides a schematic representation of these mechanisms.

As described above, some solutes such as gases can enter the cell by diffusing down an electrochemical gradient across the membrane and do not require metabolic energy. The simple **passive diffusion** of a solute across the membrane is limited by the thermal agitation of that specific molecule, by the concentration gradient across the membrane, and by the solubility of that solute (the permeability coefficient, Figure 40–6) in the hydrophobic core of the membrane bilayer. Solubility is inversely proportional to the number of hydrogen bonds that must be broken in order for a solute in the external aqueous phase to become incorporated in the hydrophobic bilayer. Electrolytes, poorly soluble in lipid, do not form hydrogen bonds with water, but they do acquire a shell of water from hydration by electrostatic interaction. The size of the shell is directly proportionate to the **charge density** of the electrolyte. Electrolytes with a large charge density have a larger shell of hydration and thus a slower diffusion rate. Na^+, for example, has a higher charge density than K^+. Hydrated Na^+ is therefore larger than hydrated K^+; hence, the latter tends to move more easily through the membrane.

The following factors affect **net diffusion** of a substance: (1) Its concentration gradient across the membrane. Solutes move from high to low concentration. (2) The electrical potential across the membrane. Solutes move toward the solution that has the opposite charge. The inside of the cell usually has a negative charge. (3) The permeability coefficient of the substance for the membrane. (4) The hydrostatic pressure gradient across the membrane. Increased pressure will

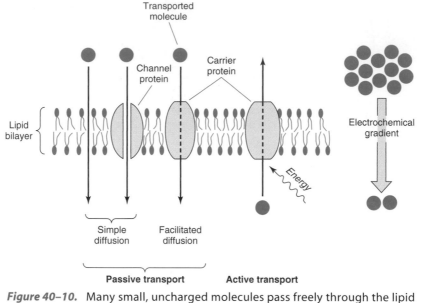

Figure 40–10. Many small, uncharged molecules pass freely through the lipid bilayer. Charged molecules, larger uncharged molecules, and some small uncharged molecules are transferred through channels or pores or by specific carrier proteins. Passive transport is always down an electrochemical gradient, toward equilibrium. Active transport is against an electrochemical gradient and requires an input of energy, whereas passive transport does not. (Redrawn and reproduced, with permission, from Alberts B et al: *Molecular Biology of the Cell.* Garland, 1983.)

increase the rate and force of the collision between the molecules and the membrane. (5) Temperature. Increased temperature will increase particle motion and thus increase the frequency of collisions between external particles and the membrane. In addition, a multitude of **channels** exist in membranes that route the entry of ions into cells.

Ion Channels Are Transmembrane Proteins That Allow the Selective Entry of Various Ions

Natural membranes contain transmembrane channels, pore-like structures composed of proteins that constitute selective **ion channels.** Cation-conductive channels have an average diameter of about 5–8 nm. The **permeability** of a channel depends upon the size, the extent of hydration, and the extent of charge density on the ion. **Specific channels** for Na^+, K^+, Ca^{2+}, and Cl^- have been identified; one such channel is illustrated in Figure 40–11. It is seen to consist of four subunits. Each subunit consists of six α-helical transmembrane domains. The amino and carboxyl terminals are located in the cytoplasm, with both extracellular and intracellu-

lar loops being present. The actual pore in the channel through which the ions pass is not shown. A pore constitutes the center (diameter about 5–8 nm) of a structure formed by apposition of the subunits. Ion channels are very **selective,** in most cases permitting the passage of only one type of ion (Na^+, Ca^{2+}, etc). Many variations on the above structural theme are found, but all ion channels are basically made up of transmembrane subunits that come together to form a central pore through which ions pass selectively.

The membranes of **nerve cells** contain well-studied ion channels that are responsible for the generation of action potentials. The activity of some of these channels is controlled by neurotransmitters; hence, channel activity can be **regulated.**

Ion channels are open transiently and thus are "gated." Gates can be controlled by opening or closing. In **ligand-gated channels,** a specific molecule binds to a receptor and opens the channel. **Voltage-gated channels** open (or close) in response to changes in membrane potential.

Some properties of ion channels are listed in Table 40–4; other aspects of ion channels are discussed briefly in Chapter 48.

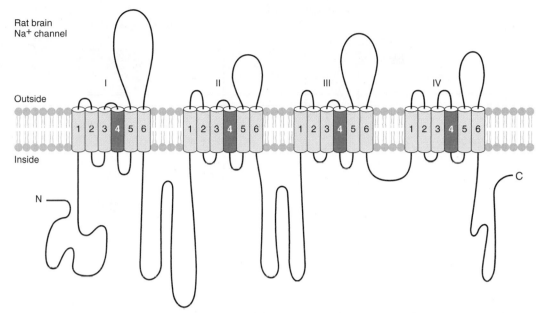

Figure 40–11. Diagrammatic representation of the structures of an ion channel (a Na+ channel of rat brain). The Roman numerals indicate the four subunits of the channel and the Arabic numerals the α-helical transmembrane domains of each subunit. The actual pore through which the ions (Na+) pass is not shown, but is formed by apposition of the various subunits. The specific areas of the subunits involved in the opening and closing of the channel are also not indicated. (After WK Catterall. Modified and reproduced from Hall ZW: *An Introduction to Molecular Neurobiology.* Sinauer, 1992.)

DETAILED STUDIES OF A K+ CHANNEL & OF A VOLTAGE-GATED CHANNEL HAVE YIELDED MAJOR INSIGHTS INTO THEIR ACTIONS

There are at least four features of ion channels that must be elucidated: (1) their overall structures; (2) how they conduct ions so rapidly; (3) their selectivity; and (4) their gating properties. As described below, considerable progress in tackling these difficult problems has been made.

Especial progress has been made by MacKinnon and colleagues elucidating the structure and function of a K+ channel (KvAP) present in *Streptomyces lividans*. A variety of techniques were used, including site-directed mutagenesis and x-ray crystallography. The channel is an integral membrane protein composed of four identical subunits, each with two transmembrane segments, creating an inverted teepee-like structure (Figure 40–12). The part of the channels that confers ion selectivity (the **selectivity filter**) measures 12 Å long (a relatively short length of the membrane, so K+ does not have far to travel in the membrane) and is situated at the wide end of the inverted teepee. The large, water-filled cavity and helical dipoles shown in Figure 40–12 help overcome

the relatively large electrostatic energy barrier for a cation to cross the membrane. The **selectivity filter** is lined with carbonyl oxygen atoms (contributed by a TVGYG sequence), providing a number of sites with which K+ can interact. K+ ions, which dehydrate as they enter the narrow selectivity filter, fit with proper coordination into the filter, but Na+ is too small to interact

Table 40–4. Some properties of ion channels.

- They are composed of transmembrane protein subunits.
- Most are highly selective for one ion; a few are nonselective.
- They allow impermeable ions to cross membranes at rates approaching diffusion limits.
- They can permit ion fluxes of 10^6–10^7/s.
- Their activities are regulated.
- The two main types are voltage-gated and ligand-gated.
- They are usually highly conserved across species.
- Most cells have a variety of Na+, K+, Ca^{2+}, and Cl$^-$ channels.
- Mutations in genes encoding them can cause specific diseases.[1]
- Their activities are affected by certain drugs.

[1]Some diseases caused by mutations of ion channels are briefly discussed in Chapter 48.

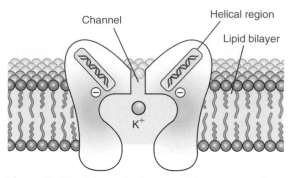

Figure 40–12. Schematic diagram of the structure of a K⁺ channel (KvAP) from *Streptomyces lividans*. A single K⁺ is shown in a large aqueous cavity inside the membrane interior. Two helical regions of the channel protein are oriented with their carboxylate ends pointing to where the K⁺ is located. The channel is lined by carboxyl oxygens. (Modified from Doyle DA et al: Science 1998;280:69. Copyright © 1998 AAAS. Adapted with permission.)

with the carbonyl oxygen atoms in correct alignment and is rejected. Two K^+ ions, when close to each other in the filter, repel one another. This repulsion overcomes interactions between K^+ and the surrounding protein molecule and allows very rapid conduction of K^+ with high selectivity.

Other studies on a **voltage-gated ion channel** (HvAP) in *Aeropyrum pernix* have revealed many features of its voltage-sensing and -gating mechanisms. This channel is made up of four subunits, each with six transmembrane segments. One of the six segments (S4 and part of S3) is the voltage sensor. It behaves like a **charged paddle** (Figure 40–13), in that it can move through the interior of the membrane transferring four positive charges (due to 4 Arg residues in each subunit) from one membrane surface to the other in response to changes in voltage. There are four voltage sensors in each channel, linked to the gate. The gate part of the channel is constructed from S6 helices (one from each of the subunits). Movements of this part of the channel in response to changing voltage effectively close the channel or reopen it, in the latter case allowing a current of ions to cross.

Ionophores Are Molecules That Act as Membrane Shuttles for Various Ions

Certain microbes synthesize small organic molecules, **ionophores,** that function as shuttles for the movement of ions across membranes. These ionophores contain hydrophilic centers that bind specific ions and are surrounded by peripheral hydrophobic regions; this arrangement allows the molecules to dissolve effectively in the

membrane and diffuse transversely therein. Others, like the well-studied polypeptide gramicidin, form channels.

Microbial toxins such as diphtheria toxin and activated **serum complement components** can produce large pores in cellular membranes and thereby provide macromolecules with direct access to the internal milieu.

Aquaporins Are Proteins That Form Water Channels in Certain Membranes

In certain cells (eg, red cells, cells of the collecting ductules of the kidney), the movement of water by simple diffusion is augmented by movement through water channels. These channels are composed of tetrameric transmembrane proteins named aquaporins. Some 10 distinct aquaporins (AP-1 to AP-10) have been identified. Mutations in the gene encoding AP-2 have been shown to be the cause of one type of nephrogenic diabetes insipidus.

PLASMA MEMBRANES ARE INVOLVED IN FACILITATED DIFFUSION, ACTIVE TRANSPORT, & OTHER PROCESSES

Transport systems can be described in a functional sense according to the number of molecules moved and the direction of movement (Figure 40–14) or according to whether movement is toward or away from equilibrium. A **uniport** system moves one type of molecule bidirectionally. In **cotransport** systems, the transfer of

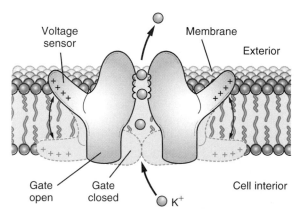

Figure 40–13. Schematic diagram of the voltage-gated K⁺ channel of *Aeorpyrum pernix*. The voltage sensors behave like charged paddles that move through the interior of the membrane. Four voltage sensors (only two are shown here) are linked mechanically to the gate of the channel. Each sensor has four positive charges contributed by arginine residues. (Modified from Sigworth FJ: Nature 2003;423:21. Copyright © 2003. Adapted by permission from Macmillan Publishers Ltd.)

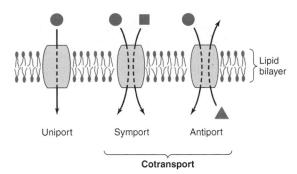

Figure 40–14. Schematic representation of types of transport systems. Transporters can be classified with regard to the direction of movement and whether one or more unique molecules are moved. A uniport can also allow movement in the opposite direction, depending on the concentrations inside and outside a cell of the molecule transported. (Redrawn and reproduced, with permission, from Alberts B et al: *Molecular Biology of the Cell.* Garland, 1983.)

one solute depends upon the stoichiometric simultaneous or sequential transfer of another solute. A **symport** moves two solutes in the same direction. Examples are the proton-sugar transporter in bacteria and the Na^+-sugar transporters (for glucose and certain other sugars) and Na^+-amino acid transporters in mammalian cells. **Antiport** systems move two molecules in opposite directions (eg, Na^+ in and Ca^{2+} out).

Molecules that cannot pass freely through the lipid bilayer membrane by themselves do so in association with carrier proteins. This involves two processes—**facilitated diffusion** and **active transport**—and highly specific transport systems.

Facilitated diffusion and active transport share many features. Both involve **carrier proteins,** and both show **specificity** for ions, sugars, and amino acids. Mutations in bacteria and mammalian cells (including some that result in human disease) have supported these conclusions. Facilitated diffusion and active transport **resemble a substrate-enzyme reaction** except that no covalent interaction occurs. Points of resemblance between the two processes are as follows: (1) There is a specific binding site for the solute. (2) The carrier is saturable, so it has a maximum rate of transport (V_{max}; Figure 40–15). (3) There is a binding constant (K_m) for the solute, and so the whole system has a K_m (Figure 40–15). (4) Structurally similar competitive inhibitors block transport.

Major **differences** are the following: (1) Facilitated diffusion can operate bidirectionally, whereas active transport is usually unidirectional. (2) Active transport always occurs against an electrical or chemical gradient, and so it requires energy.

Facilitated Diffusion

Some specific solutes diffuse down electrochemical gradients across membranes more rapidly than might be expected from their size, charge, or partition coefficients. This **facilitated diffusion** exhibits properties distinct from those of simple diffusion. The rate of facilitated diffusion, a uniport system, can be saturated; ie, the number of sites involved in diffusion of the specific solutes appears finite. Many facilitated diffusion systems are stereospecific but, like simple diffusion, require no metabolic energy.

A **"Ping-Pong" mechanism** (Figure 40–16) explains facilitated diffusion. In this model, the carrier protein exists in two principal conformations. In the "pong" state, it is exposed to high concentrations of solute, and molecules of the solute bind to specific sites on the carrier protein. Transport occurs when a conformational change exposes the carrier to a lower concentration of solute ("ping" state). This process is completely reversible, and net flux across the membrane depends upon the concentration gradient. The rate at which solutes enter a cell by facilitated diffusion is determined by the following factors: (1) The concentration gradient across the membrane. (2) The amount of carrier available (this is a key control step). (3) The rapidity of the solute-carrier interaction. (4) The rapidity of the conformational change for both the loaded and the unloaded carrier.

Hormones regulate facilitated diffusion by changing the number of transporters available. **Insulin** increases

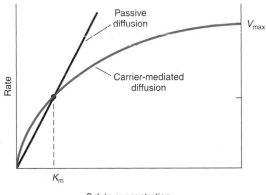

Figure 40–15. A comparison of the kinetics of carrier-mediated (facilitated) diffusion with passive diffusion. The rate of movement in the latter is directly proportionate to solute concentration, whereas the process is saturable when carriers are involved. The concentration at half-maximal velocity is equal to the binding constant (K_m) of the carrier for the solute. (V_{max}, maximal rate.)

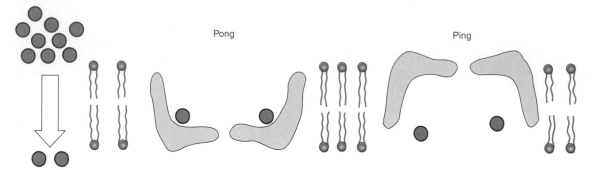

Figure 40–16. The "Ping-Pong" model of facilitated diffusion. A protein carrier (gray structure) in the lipid bilayer associates with a solute in high concentration on one side of the membrane. A conformational change ensues ("pong" to "ping"), and the solute is discharged on the side favoring the new equilibrium. The empty carrier then reverts to the original conformation ("ping" to "pong") to complete the cycle.

glucose transport in fat and muscle by recruiting transporters from an intracellular reservoir. Insulin also enhances amino acid transport in liver and other tissues. One of the coordinated actions of **glucocorticoid hormones** is to enhance transport of amino acids into liver, where the amino acids then serve as a substrate for gluconeogenesis. **Growth hormone** increases amino acid transport in all cells, and **estrogens** do this in the uterus. There are at least five different carrier systems for amino acids in animal cells. Each is specific for a group of closely related amino acids, and most operate as Na^+-symport systems (Figure 40–14).

Active Transport

The process of active transport differs from diffusion in that molecules are transported away from thermodynamic equilibrium; hence, **energy is required.** This energy can come from the hydrolysis of **ATP,** from **electron movement,** or from **light.** The maintenance of electrochemical gradients in biologic systems is so important that it consumes approximately 30% of the total energy expenditure in a cell.

In general, cells maintain a low intracellular Na^+ concentration and a high intracellular K^+ concentration (Table 40–1), along with a net negative electrical potential inside. The pump that maintains these gradients is an **ATPase** that is activated by Na^+ and K^+ (Na^+-K^+ ATPase; see Figure 40–17). The ATPase is an integral membrane protein and requires phospholipids for activity. The ATPase has catalytic centers for both ATP and Na^+ on the cytoplasmic side of the membrane, but the K^+ binding site is located on the extracellular side of the membrane. **Ouabain** or **digitalis** inhibits this ATPase by binding to the extracellular domain. Inhibition of the ATPase by ouabain can be antagonized by extracellular K^+.

Nerve Impulses Are Transmitted Up & Down Membranes

The membrane forming the surface of **neuronal cells** maintains an asymmetry of inside-outside voltage (electrical potential) and is electrically excitable. When appropriately stimulated by a chemical signal mediated by a specific synaptic membrane receptor (see discussion of the transmission of biochemical signals, below), gates in the membrane are opened to allow the rapid influx of Na^+ or Ca^{2+} (with or without the efflux of K^+), so that the voltage difference rapidly collapses and that segment of the membrane is depolarized. However, as a result of the action of the ion pumps in the membrane, the gradient is quickly restored.

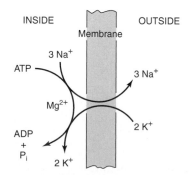

Figure 40–17. Stoichiometry of the Na^+-K^+ ATPase pump. This pump moves three Na^+ ions from inside the cell to the outside and brings two K^+ ions from the outside to the inside for every molecule of ATP hydrolyzed to ADP by the membrane-associated ATPase. Ouabain and other cardiac glycosides inhibit this pump by acting on the extracellular surface of the membrane. (Courtesy of R Post.)

When large areas of the membrane are **depolarized** in this manner, the electrochemical disturbance propagates in wave-like form down the membrane, generating a **nerve impulse. Myelin sheets,** formed by Schwann cells, wrap around nerve fibers and provide an electrical insulator that surrounds most of the nerve and greatly speeds up the propagation of the wave (signal) by allowing ions to flow in and out of the membrane only where the membrane is free of the insulation. The myelin membrane is composed of phospholipids, cholesterol, proteins, and GSLs. Relatively few proteins are found in the myelin membrane; those present appear to hold together multiple membrane bilayers to form the hydrophobic insulating structure that is impermeable to ions and water. **Certain diseases,** eg, multiple sclerosis and the Guillain-Barré syndrome, are characterized by demyelination and impaired nerve conduction.

Glucose Transport Involves Several Mechanisms

A discussion of the **transport of glucose** summarizes many of the points made in this chapter. Glucose must enter cells as the first step in energy utilization. In adipocytes and muscle, glucose enters by a specific transport system that is enhanced by insulin. Changes in transport are primarily due to alterations of V_{max} (presumably from more or fewer active transporters), but changes in K_m may also be involved. Glucose transport involves different aspects of the principles of transport discussed above. Glucose and Na^+ bind to different sites on the glucose transporter. Na^+ moves into the cell down its electrochemical gradient and "drags" glucose with it (Figure 40–18). Therefore, the greater the Na^+ gradient, the more glucose enters; and if Na^+ in extracellular fluid is low, glucose transport stops. To maintain a steep Na^+ gradient, this Na^+-glucose symport is dependent on gradients generated by the Na^+K^+ ATPase, which maintains a low intracellular Na^+ concentration. Similar mechanisms are used to transport other sugars as well as amino acids.

The transcellular movement of sugars involves one additional component: a uniport (Figure 40–18) that allows the glucose accumulated within the cell to move across a different surface toward a new equilibrium; this occurs in intestinal cells, for example, and involves a glucose uniporter (GLUT2).

The treatment of severe cases of **diarrhea** (such as is found in cholera) makes use of the above information. In **cholera,** massive amounts of fluid can be passed as watery stools in a very short time, resulting in severe dehydration and possibly death. Oral rehydration therapy, consisting primarily of NaCl and glucose, has been developed by the World Health Organization (WHO). The transport of glucose and Na^+ across the intestinal epithelium forces (via osmosis) movement of water

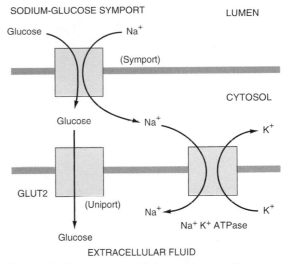

Figure 40–18. The transcellular movement of glucose in an intestinal cell. Glucose follows Na^+ across the luminal epithelial membrane. The Na^+ gradient that drives this symport is established by Na^+-K^+ exchange, which occurs at the basal membrane facing the extracellular fluid compartment via the action of the Na^+ K^+ ATPase. Glucose at high concentration within the cell moves "downhill" into the extracellular fluid by facilitated diffusion (a uniport mechanism), via GLUT2 (a glucose transporter). The sodium-glucose symport actually carries 2 Na^+ for each glucose.

from the lumen of the gut into intestinal cells, resulting in rehydration. Glucose alone or NaCl alone would not be effective.

Cells Transport Certain Macromolecules Across the Plasma Membrane

The process by which cells take up large molecules is called **"endocytosis."** Some of these molecules (eg, polysaccharides, proteins, and polynucleotides), when hydrolyzed inside the cell, yield nutrients. Endocytosis provides a mechanism for regulating the content of certain membrane components, hormone receptors being a case in point. Endocytosis can be used to learn more about how cells function. DNA from one cell type can be used to transfect a different cell and alter the latter's function or phenotype. A specific gene is often employed in these experiments, and this provides a unique way to study and analyze the regulation of that gene. **DNA transfection** depends upon endocytosis; endocytosis is responsible for the entry of DNA into the cell. Such experiments commonly use calcium phosphate, since Ca^{2+} stimulates endocytosis and precipitates DNA, which makes the DNA a better object

for endocytosis. Cells also release macromolecules by **exocytosis.** Endocytosis and exocytosis both involve vesicle formation with or from the plasma membrane.

A. ENDOCYTOSIS

All eukaryotic cells are continuously ingesting parts of their plasma membranes. Endocytotic vesicles are generated when segments of the plasma membrane invaginate, enclosing a minute volume of extracellular fluid and its contents. The vesicle then pinches off as the fusion of plasma membranes seals the neck of the vesicle at the original site of invagination (Figure 40–19). This vesicle fuses with other membrane structures and thus achieves the transport of its contents to other cellular compartments or even back to the cell exterior. Most endocytotic vesicles fuse with **primary lysosomes** to form **secondary lysosomes,** which contain hydrolytic enzymes and are therefore specialized organelles for intracellular disposal. The macromolecular contents are digested to yield amino acids, simple sugars, or nucleotides, and they diffuse out of the vesicles to be reused in the cytoplasm. Endocytosis requires (1) energy, usually from the hydrolysis of ATP; (2) Ca^{2+} in extracellular fluid; and (3) contractile elements in the cell (probably the microfilament system) (Chapter 48).

There are two general types of endocytosis. **Phagocytosis** occurs only in specialized cells such as macrophages and granulocytes. Phagocytosis involves the ingestion of large particles such as viruses, bacteria, cells, or debris. Macrophages are extremely active in this regard and may ingest 25% of their volume per hour. In so doing, a macrophage may internalize 3% of its plasma membrane each minute or the entire membrane every 30 minutes.

Pinocytosis is a property of all cells and leads to the cellular uptake of fluid and fluid contents. There are two types. **Fluid-phase pinocytosis** is a nonselective process in which the uptake of a solute by formation of small vesicles is simply proportionate to its concentration in the surrounding extracellular fluid. The formation of these vesicles is an extremely active process. Fibroblasts, for example, internalize their plasma membrane at about one-third the rate of macrophages. This process occurs more rapidly than membranes are made. The surface area and volume of a cell do not change much, so membranes must be replaced by exocytosis or by being recycled as fast as they are removed by endocytosis.

The other type of pinocytosis, **absorptive pinocytosis,** is a receptor-mediated selective process primarily responsible for the uptake of macromolecules for which there are a finite number of binding sites on the plasma membrane. These high-affinity receptors permit the selective concentration of ligands from the medium, minimize the uptake of fluid or soluble unbound macromolecules, and markedly increase the rate at which

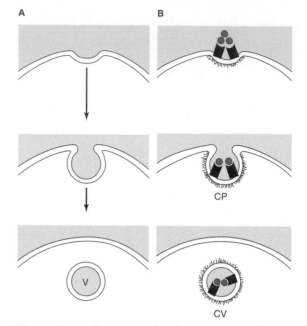

Figure 40–19. Two types of endocytosis. An endocytotic vesicle (V) forms as a result of invagination of a portion of the plasma membrane. Fluid-phase endocytosis **(A)** is random and nondirected. Receptor-mediated endocytosis **(B)** is selective and occurs in coated pits (CP) lined with the protein clathrin (the fuzzy material). Targeting is provided by receptors (black symbols) specific for a variety of molecules. This results in the formation of a coated vesicle (CV).

specific molecules enter the cell. The vesicles formed during absorptive pinocytosis are derived from invaginations (pits) that are coated on the cytoplasmic side with a filamentous material and are appropriately named **coated pits.** In many systems, the protein **clathrin** is the filamentous material. It has a three-limbed structure (called a triskelion), with each limb being made up of one light and one heavy chain of clathrin. The polymerization of clathrin into a vesicle is directed by **assembly particles,** composed of four **adapter proteins.** These interact with certain amino acid sequences in the receptors that become cargo, ensuring selectivity of uptake. The lipid **PIP_2** also plays an important role in vesicle assembly. In addition, the protein **dynamin,** which both binds and hydrolyzes GTP, is necessary for the pinching off of clathrin-coated vesicles from the cell surface. Coated pits may constitute as much as 2% of the surface of some cells.

As an example, the low-density lipoprotein (LDL) molecule and its receptor (Chapter 25) are internalized by means of coated pits containing the LDL receptor.

Figure 40–20. A comparison of the mechanisms of endocytosis and exocytosis. Exocytosis involves the contact of two inside surface (cytoplasmic side) monolayers, whereas endocytosis results from the contact of two outer surface monolayers.

These endocytotic vesicles containing LDL and its receptor fuse to lysosomes in the cell. The receptor is released and recycled back to the cell surface membrane, but the apoprotein of LDL is degraded and the cholesteryl esters metabolized. Synthesis of the LDL receptor is regulated by secondary or tertiary consequences of pinocytosis, eg, by metabolic products—such as cholesterol—released during the degradation of LDL. Disorders of the LDL receptor and its internalization are medically important and are discussed in Chapter 25.

Absorptive pinocytosis of **extracellular glycoproteins** requires that the glycoproteins carry specific carbohydrate recognition signals. These recognition signals are bound by membrane receptor molecules, which play a role analogous to that of the LDL receptor. A galactosyl receptor on the surface of hepatocytes is instrumental in the absorptive pinocytosis of asialoglycoproteins from the circulation (Chapter 46). Acid hydrolases taken up by absorptive pinocytosis in fibroblasts are recognized by their mannose 6-phosphate moieties. Interestingly, the mannose 6-phosphate moiety also seems to play an important role in the intracellular targeting of the acid hydrolases to the lysosomes of the cells in which they are synthesized (Chapter 46).

There is a **dark side** to receptor-mediated endocytosis in that viruses which cause such diseases as hepatitis (affecting liver cells), poliomyelitis (affecting motor neurons), and AIDS (affecting T cells) initiate their damage by this mechanism. Iron toxicity also begins with excessive uptake due to endocytosis.

B. EXOCYTOSIS

Most cells **release** macromolecules to the exterior by exocytosis. This process is also involved in membrane remodeling, when the components synthesized in the Golgi apparatus are carried in vesicles to the plasma membrane. The signal for exocytosis is often a hormone which, when it binds to a cell-surface receptor, induces a local and transient change in Ca^{2+} concentration. Ca^{2+} triggers exocytosis. Figure 40–20 provides a comparison of the mechanisms of exocytosis and endocytosis.

Molecules released by exocytosis have at least three fates: (1) They can attach to the cell surface and become peripheral proteins, eg, antigens. (2) They can become part of the extracellular matrix, eg, collagen and glycosaminoglycans. (3) They can enter extracellular fluid and signal other cells. Insulin, parathyroid hormone, and the catecholamines are all packaged in granules and processed within cells, to be released upon appropriate stimulation.

Some Signals Are Transmitted Across Membranes

Specific biochemical signals such as neurotransmitters, hormones, and immunoglobulins bind to specific **receptors** (integral proteins) exposed to the outside of cellular membranes and transmit information through these membranes to the cytoplasm. This process, called **transmembrane signaling,** involves the generation of a number of signals, including cyclic nucleotides, calcium, phosphoinositides, and diacylglycerol. It is discussed in detail in Chapter 42.

Gap Junctions Allow Direct Flow of Molecules from One Cell to Another

Gap junctions are structures that permit direct transfer of small molecules (up to ~ 1200 Da) from one cell to its neighbor. They are composed of a family of proteins called connexins that form a hexagonal structure consisting of 12 such proteins. Six connexins form a connexin hemichannel and join to a similar structure in a neighboring cell to make a complete connexon channel (Figure 40–21). One gap junction contains several connexons. Different connexins are found in different tissues. Mutations in genes encoding connexins have been found to be associated with a number of conditions, including cardiovascular abnormalities, one type of deafness, and the X-linked form of Charcot-Marie-Tooth disease (a demyelinating neurologic disorder).

MUTATIONS AFFECTING MEMBRANE PROTEINS CAUSE DISEASES

In view of the fact that membranes are located in so many organelles and are involved in so many processes, it is not surprising that **mutations** affecting their pro-

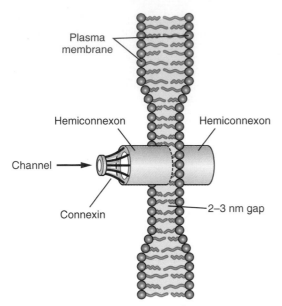

Figure 40–21. Schematic diagram of a gap junction. One connexon is made from two hemiconnexons. Each hemiconnexon is made from six connexin molecules. Small solutes are able to diffuse through the central channel, providing a direct mechanism of cell-cell communication.

tein constituents should result in many diseases or disorders. Proteins in membranes can be classified as **receptors, transporters, ion channels, enzymes,** and **structural components.** Members of all of these classes are often **glycosylated,** so that mutations affecting this process may alter their function. Examples of diseases or disorders due to abnormalities in membrane proteins are listed in Table 40–5; these mainly reflect mutations in proteins of the **plasma membrane,** with one affecting lysosomal function (I-cell disease). Over 30 genetic diseases or disorders have been ascribed to mutations affecting various proteins involved in the transport of amino acids, sugars, lipids, urate, anions, cations, water, and vitamins across the plasma membrane. Mutations in genes encoding proteins in other membranes can also have harmful consequences. For example, mutations in genes encoding **mitochondrial membrane proteins** involved in oxidative phosphorylation can cause neurologic and other problems (eg, Leber's hereditary optic neuropathy; LHON). Membrane proteins can also be affected by conditions other than mutations. Formation of **autoantibodies** to the acetylcholine receptor in skeletal muscle causes myasthenia gravis. **Ischemia** can quickly affect the integrity of various ion channels in membranes. Abnormalities of membrane constituents other than proteins can also be harmful. With regard to **lipids,** excess of cholesterol (eg, in familial hypercholes-

terolemia), of lysophospholipid (eg, after bites by certain snakes, whose venom contains phospholipases), or of glycosphingolipids (eg, in a sphingolipidosis) can all affect membrane function.

Cystic Fibrosis Is Due to Mutations in the Gene Encoding a Chloride Channel

Cystic fibrosis (CF) is a recessive genetic disorder prevalent among whites in North America and certain parts of northern Europe. It is characterized by chronic bacterial infections of the airways and sinuses, fat maldigestion due to pancreatic exocrine insufficiency,

Table 40–5. Some diseases or pathologic states resulting from or attributed to abnormalities of membranes.[1]

Disease	Abnormality
Achondroplasia (MIM 100800)	Mutations in the gene encoding the fibroblast growth factor receptor 3
Familial hypercholesterolemia (MIM 143890)	Mutations in the gene encoding the LDL receptor
Cystic fibrosis (MIM 219700)	Mutations in the gene encoding the CFTR protein, a Cl^- transporter
Congenital long QT syndrome (MIM 192500)	Mutations in genes encoding ion channels in the heart
Wilson disease (MIM 277900)	Mutations in the gene encoding a copper-dependent ATPase
I-cell disease (MIM 252500)	Mutations in the gene encoding GlcNAc phosphotransferase, resulting in absence of the Man 6-P signal for lysosomal localization of certain hydrolases
Hereditary spherocytosis (MIM 182900)	Mutations in the genes encoding spectrin or other structural proteins in the red cell membrane
Metastasis	Abnormalities in the oligosaccharide chains of membrane glycoproteins and glycolipids are thought to be of importance
Paroxysmal nocturnal hemoglobinuria (MIM 311770)	Mutation resulting in deficient attachment of the GPI anchor to certain proteins of the red cell membrane

[1]The disorders listed are discussed further in other chapters. The table lists examples of mutations affecting receptors, a transporter, an ion channel, an enzyme, and a structural protein. Examples of altered or defective glycosylation of glycoproteins are also presented. Most of the conditions listed affect the plasma membrane.

infertility in males due to abnormal development of the vas deferens, and elevated levels of chloride in sweat (> 60 mmol/L).

After a Herculean landmark endeavor, the gene for CF was identified in 1989 on chromosome 7. It was found to encode a protein of 1480 amino acids, named cystic fibrosis transmembrane regulator (CFTR), a cyclic AMP-regulated Cl^- channel (see Figure 40–22). An abnormality of membrane Cl^- permeability is believed to result in the increased viscosity of many bodily secretions, though the precise mechanisms are still under investigation. The commonest mutation (~70% in certain Caucasian populations) is deletion of three bases, resulting in loss of residue 508, a phenylalanine (ΔF_{508}). However, more than 1000 other mutations have been identified. These mutations affect CFTR in at least four ways: (1) its amount is reduced; (2) depending upon the particular mutation, it may be susceptible to misfolding and retention within the ER or Golgi apparatus; (3) mutations in the nucleotide-binding domains may affect the ability of the Cl^- channel to open, an event affected by ATP; (4) the mutations may also reduce the rate of ion flow through a channel, generating less of a Cl^- current.

The most serious and life-threatening complication is recurrent pulmonary infections due to overgrowth of various pathogens in the viscous secretions of the respiratory tract. Poor nutrition as a result of pancreatic insufficiency worsens the situation. The treatment of CF thus requires a comprehensive effort to maintain nutritional status, to prevent and combat pulmonary infections, and to maintain physical and psychologic health. Advances in molecular genetics mean that mutation analysis can be performed for prenatal diagnosis and for carrier testing in families in which one child already has the condition. Efforts are in progress to use gene therapy to restore the activity of CFTR. An aerosolized preparation of human DNase that digests the DNA of microorganisms in the respiratory tract has proved helpful in therapy.

SUMMARY

- Membranes are complex structures composed of lipids, carbohydrates, and proteins.

- The basic structure of all membranes is the lipid bilayer. This bilayer is formed by two sheets of phospholipids in which the hydrophilic polar head groups are directed away from each other and are exposed to the aqueous environment on the outer and inner surfaces of the membrane. The hydrophobic nonpolar tails of these molecules are oriented toward each other, in the direction of the center of the membrane.

- Membranes are dynamic structures. Lipids and certain proteins show rapid lateral diffusion. Flip-flop is very slow for lipids and nonexistent for proteins.

- The fluid mosaic model forms a useful basis for thinking about membrane structure.

- Membrane proteins are classified as integral if they are firmly embedded in the bilayer and as peripheral if they are loosely attached to the outer or inner surface.

- The 20 or so different membranes in a mammalian cell have intrinsic functions (eg, enzymatic activity), and they define compartments, or specialized environments, within the cell that have specific functions (eg, lysosomes).

- Certain molecules freely diffuse across membranes, but the movement of others is restricted because of size, charge, or solubility.

- Various passive and active mechanisms are employed to maintain gradients of such molecules across different membranes.

- Certain solutes, eg, glucose, enter cells by facilitated diffusion, along a downhill gradient from high to low concentration. Specific carrier molecules, or transporters, are involved in such processes.

- Ligand- or voltage-gated ion channels are often employed to move charged molecules (Na^+, K^+, Ca^{2+}, etc) across membranes.

- Large molecules can enter or leave cells through mechanisms such as endocytosis or exocytosis. These processes often require binding of the molecule to a receptor, which affords specificity to the process.

- Receptors may be integral components of membranes (particularly the plasma membrane). The in-

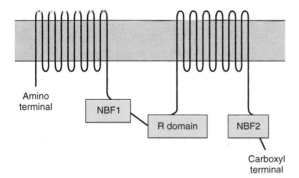

Figure 40–22. Diagram of the structure of the CFTR protein (not to scale). The protein contains twelve transmembrane segments (probably helical), two nucleotide-binding folds or domains (NBF1 and NBF2), and one regulatory (R) domain. NBF1 and NBF2 probably bind ATP and couple its hydrolysis to transport of Cl^-. Phe 508, the major locus of mutations in cystic fibrosis, is located in NBF1.

teraction of a ligand with its receptor may not involve the movement of either into the cell, but the interaction results in the generation of a signal that influences intracellular processes (transmembrane signaling).

• Mutations that affect the structure of membrane proteins (receptors, transporters, ion channels, enzymes, and structural proteins) may cause diseases; examples include cystic fibrosis and familial hypercholesterolemia.

REFERENCES

Alberts B et al: *Molecular Biology of the Cell.* 4th ed. Garland Science, 2002.

Clapham DE: Symmetry, selectivity and the 2003 Nobel Prize. Cell 2003;115:641.

Holland IB et al: *ABC Proteins: From Bacteria to Man.* Academic Press/Elsevier Science, 2003.

Le Roy C, Wrana JL: Clathrin- and non-clathrin-mediated endocytic regulation of cell signaling. Nat Rev Mol Cell Biol 2005;6:112.

Lodish H et al: *Molecular Cell Biology.* 5th ed. WH Freeman & Co., 2004.

Longo N: Inherited defects of membrane transport. In: *Harrison's Principles of Internal Medicine.* 16th ed. Kasper DL et al (editors). McGraw-Hill, 2005.

Lucero HA, Robbins PW: Lipid rafts: protein association and the regulation of protein activity. Arch Biochem Biophys 2004;426:208.

Riordan JR: Assembly of functional CFTR chloride channels. Annu Rev Physiol 2005;67:701.

Singer SJ: Some early history of membrane molecular biology. Annu Rev Physiol 2004;66:1.

Vance DE, Vance JE: *Biochemistry of Lipids, Lipoproteins and Membranes.* 4th ed. Elsevier, 2002.

Yeagle PL. *The Structure of Biological Membranes.* 2nd ed. CRC Press, 2004.

The Diversity of the Endocrine System

41

Daryl K. Granner, MD

ACTH	Adrenocorticotropic hormone		**GH**	Growth hormone
ANF	Atrial natriuretic factor		**IGF-I**	Insulin-like growth factor-I
cAMP	Cyclic adenosine monophosphate		**LH**	Luteotropic hormone
CBG	Corticosteroid-binding globulin		**LPH**	Lipotropin
CG	Chorionic gonadotropin		**MIT**	Monoiodotyrosine
cGMP	Cyclic guanosine monophosphate		**MSH**	Melanocyte-stimulating hormone
CLIP	Corticotropin-like intermediate lobe peptide		**OHSD**	Hydroxysteroid dehydrogenase
DBH	Dopamine β-hydroxylase		**PNMT**	Phenylethanolamine-N-methyltransferase
DHEA	Dehydroepiandrosterone		**POMC**	Pro-opiomelanocortin
DHT	Dihydrotestosterone		**SHBG**	Sex hormone-binding globulin
DIT	Diiodotyrosine		**StAR**	Steroidogenic acute regulatory (protein)
DOC	Deoxycorticosterone		**TBG**	Thyroxine-binding globulin
EGF	Epidermal growth factor		**TEBG**	Testosterone-estrogen-binding globulin
FSH	Follicle-stimulating hormone		**TRH**	Thyrotropin-releasing hormone
			TSH	Thyrotropin-stimulating hormone

BIOMEDICAL IMPORTANCE

The survival of multicellular organisms depends on their ability to adapt to a constantly changing environment. Intercellular communication mechanisms are necessary requirements for this adaptation. The nervous system and the endocrine system provide this intercellular, organism-wide communication. The nervous system was originally viewed as providing a fixed communication system, whereas the endocrine system supplied hormones, which are mobile messages. In fact, there is a remarkable convergence of these regulatory systems. For example, neural regulation of the endocrine system is important in the production and secretion of some hormones; many neurotransmitters resemble hormones in their synthesis, transport, and mechanism of action; and many hormones are synthesized in the nervous system. The word "hormone" is derived from a Greek term that means to arouse to activity. As classically defined, a hormone is a substance that is synthesized in one organ and transported by the circulatory system to act on another tissue. However, this original description is too restrictive because hormones can act on adjacent cells (paracrine action) and on the cell in which they were synthesized (autocrine action) without entering the systemic circulation. A diverse array of hormones—each with distinctive mechanisms of action and properties of biosynthesis, storage, secretion, transport, and metabolism—has evolved to provide homeostatic responses. This biochemical diversity is the topic of this chapter.

THE TARGET CELL CONCEPT

There are about 200 types of differentiated cells in humans. Only a few produce hormones, but virtually all of the 75 trillion cells in a human are targets of one or more of the over 50 known hormones. The concept of the target cell is a useful way of looking at hormone action. It was thought that hormones affected a single cell type—or only a few kinds of cells—and that a hormone elicited a unique biochemical or physiologic action. We now know that a given hormone can affect several different cell types; that more than one hormone can affect a given cell type; and that hormones can exert many different effects in one cell or in different cells. With the discovery of specific cell-surface and

442

intracellular hormone receptors, the definition of a target has been expanded to include any cell in which the hormone (ligand) binds to its receptor, whether or not a biochemical or physiologic response has yet been determined.

Several factors determine the response of a target cell to a hormone. These can be thought of in two general ways: (1) as factors that affect the concentration of the hormone at the target cell (see Table 41–1) and (2) as factors that affect the actual response of the target cell to the hormone (see Table 41–2).

HORMONE RECEPTORS ARE OF CENTRAL IMPORTANCE

Receptors Discriminate Precisely

One of the major challenges faced in making the hormone-based communication system work is illustrated in Figure 41–1. Hormones are present at very low concentrations in the extracellular fluid, generally in the range of 10^{-15} to 10^{-9} mol/L. This concentration is much lower than that of the many structurally similar molecules (sterols, amino acids, peptides, proteins) and other molecules that circulate at concentrations in the 10^{-5} to 10^{-3} mol/L range. Target cells, therefore, must distinguish not only between different hormones present in small amounts but also between a given hormone and the 10^6- to 10^9-fold excess of other similar molecules. This high degree of discrimination is provided by cell-associated recognition molecules called receptors. Hormones initiate their biologic effects by binding to specific receptors, and since any effective control system also must provide a means of stopping a response, hormone-induced actions generally terminate when the effector dissociates from the receptor.

A target cell is defined by its ability to selectively bind a given hormone to its cognate receptor. Several biochemical features of this interaction are important in order for hormone-receptor interactions to be physiologically relevant: (1) binding should be specific, ie,

Table 41–1. Determinants of the concentration of a hormone at the target cell.

The rate of synthesis and secretion of the hormones.
The proximity of the target cell to the hormone source (dilution effect).
The dissociation constants of the hormone with specific plasma transport proteins (if any).
The conversion of inactive or suboptimally active forms of the hormone into the fully active form.
The rate of clearance from plasma by other tissues or by digestion, metabolism, or excretion.

Table 41–2. Determinants of the target cell response.

The number, relative activity, and state of occupancy of the specific receptors on the plasma membrane or in the cytoplasm or nucleus.
The metabolism (activation or inactivation) of the hormone in the target cell.
The presence of other factors within the cell that are necessary for the hormone response.
Up- or down-regulation of the receptor consequent to the interaction with the ligand.
Postreceptor desensitzation of the cell, including down-regulation of the receptor.

displaceable by agonist or antagonist; (2) binding should be saturable; and (3) binding should occur within the concentration range of the expected biologic response.

Both Recognition & Coupling Domains Occur on Receptors

All receptors have at least two functional domains. A recognition domain binds the hormone ligand and a second region generates a signal that couples hormone recognition to some intracellular function. Coupling (signal transduction) occurs in two general ways. Polypeptide and protein hormones and the catecholamines bind to receptors located in the plasma membrane and thereby generate a signal that regulates various intracellular functions, often by changing the activity of an enzyme. In contrast, steroid, retinoid, and thyroid hormones interact with intracellular receptors, and it is this ligand-receptor complex that directly provides the signal, generally to specific genes whose rate of transcription is thereby affected.

The domains responsible for hormone recognition and signal generation have been identified in the protein polypeptide and catecholamine hormone receptors. Steroid, thyroid, and retinoid hormone receptors have several functional domains: one site binds the hormone; another binds to specific DNA regions; a third is involved in the interaction with other coregulator proteins that result in the activation (or repression) of gene transcription; and a fourth may specify binding to one or more other proteins that influence the intracellular trafficking of the receptor.

The dual functions of binding and coupling ultimately define a receptor, and it is the coupling of hormone binding to signal transduction—so-called **receptor-effector coupling**—that provides the first step in amplification of the hormonal response. This dual purpose also distinguishes the target cell receptor from the plasma

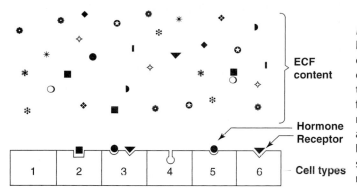

Figure 41–1. Specificity and selectivity of hormone receptors. Many different molecules circulate in the extracellular fluid (ECF), but only a few are recognized by hormone receptors. Receptors must select these molecules from among high concentrations of the other molecules. This simplified drawing shows that a cell may have no hormone receptors (1), have one receptor (2+5+6), have receptors for several hormones (3), or have a receptor but no hormone in the vicinity (4).

carrier proteins that bind hormone but do not generate a signal (see Table 41–6).

Receptors Are Proteins

Several classes of peptide hormone receptors have been defined. For example, the insulin receptor is a heterotetramer ($\alpha_2\beta_2$) linked by multiple disulfide bonds in which the extracellular α subunit binds insulin and the membrane-spanning β subunit transduces the signal through the tyrosine protein kinase domain located in the cytoplasmic portion of this polypeptide. The receptors for insulin-like growth factor I (IGF-I) and epidermal growth factor (EGF) are generally similar in structure to the insulin receptor. The growth hormone and prolactin receptors also span the plasma membrane of target cells but do not contain intrinsic protein kinase activity. Ligand binding to these receptors, however, results in the association and activation of a completely different protein kinase pathway, the Jak-Stat pathway. Polypeptide hormone and catecholamine receptors, which transduce signals by altering the rate of production of cAMP through G-proteins, are characterized by the presence of seven domains that span the plasma membrane. Protein kinase activation and the generation of cyclic AMP (cAMP, 3'5'-adenylic acid; see Figure 19–5) is a downstream action of this class of receptor (see Chapter 42 for further details).

A comparison of several different steroid receptors with thyroid hormone receptors revealed a remarkable conservation of the amino acid sequence in certain regions, particularly in the DNA-binding domains. This led to the realization that receptors of the steroid or thyroid type are members of a large superfamily of nuclear receptors. Many related members of this family have no known ligand at present and thus are called orphan receptors. The nuclear receptor superfamily plays a critical role in the regulation of gene transcription by hormones, as described in Chapter 42.

HORMONES CAN BE CLASSIFIED IN SEVERAL WAYS

Hormones can be classified according to chemical composition, solubility properties, location of receptors, and the nature of the signal used to mediate hormonal action within the cell. A classification based on the last two properties is illustrated in Table 41–3, and general features of each group are illustrated in Table 41–4.

The hormones in group I are lipophilic. After secretion, these hormones associate with plasma transport or carrier proteins, a process that circumvents the problem of solubility while prolonging the plasma half-life of the hormone. The relative percentages of bound and free hormone are determined by the binding affinity and binding capacity of the transport protein. The free hormone, which is the biologically active form, readily traverses the lipophilic plasma membrane of all cells and encounters receptors in either the cytosol or nucleus of target cells. The ligand-receptor complex is assumed to be the intracellular messenger in this group.

The second major group consists of water-soluble hormones that bind to the plasma membrane of the target cell. Hormones that bind to the surfaces of cells communicate with intracellular metabolic processes through intermediary molecules called **second messengers** (the hormone itself is the first messenger), which are generated as a consequence of the ligand-receptor interaction. The second messenger concept arose from an observation that epinephrine binds to the plasma membrane of certain cells and increases intracellular cAMP. This was followed by a series of experiments in which cAMP was found to mediate the effects of many hormones. Hormones that clearly employ this mechanism are shown in group II.A of Table 41–3. To date, only one hormone, atrial natriuretic factor (ANF), uses cGMP as its second messenger, but other hormones will probably be added to group II.B. Several hormones, many of which were previously thought to affect cAMP, appear to use ionic calcium (Ca^{2+}) or metabolites of complex phosphoinositides (or both) as the intracellular signal. These are shown

Table 41–3. Classification of hormones by mechanism of action.

I. Hormones that bind to intracellular receptors
Androgens
Calcitriol (1,25[OH]$_2$-D$_3$)
Estrogens
Glucocorticoids
Mineralocorticoids
Progestins
Retinoic acid
Thyroid hormones (T$_3$ and T$_4$)
II. Hormones that bind to cell surface receptors
A. The second messenger is cAMP
α_2-Adrenergic catecholamines
β-Adrenergic catecholamines
Adrenocorticotropic hormone
Antidiuretic hormone
Calcitonin
Chorionic gonadotropin, human
Corticotropin-releasing hormone
Follicle-stimulating hormone
Glucagon
Lipotropin
Luteinizing hormone
Melanocyte-stimulating hormone
Parathyroid hormone
Somatostatin
Thyroid-stimulating hormone
B. The second messenger is cGMP
Atrial natriuretic factor
Nitric oxide
C. The second messenger is calcium or phosphatidyl-inositols (or both)
Acetylcholine (muscarinic)
α_1-Adrenergic catecholamines
Angiotensin II
Antidiuretic hormone (vasopressin)
Cholecystokinin
Gastrin
Gonadotropin-releasing hormone
Oxytocin
Platelet-derived growth factor
Substance P
Thyrotropin-releasing hormone
D. The second messenger is a kinase or phosphatase cascade
Adiponectin
Chorionic somatomammotropin
Epidermal growth factor
Erythropoietin
Fibroblast growth factor
Growth hormone
Insulin
Insulin-like growth factors I and II
Leptin
Nerve growth factor
Platelet-derived growth factor
Prolactin

Table 41–4. General features of hormone classes.

	Group I	Group II
Types	Steroids, iodothyronines, calcitriol, retinoids	Polypeptides, proteins, glycoproteins, catecholamines
Solubility	Lipophilic	Hydrophilic
Transport proteins	Yes	No
Plasma half-life	Long (hours to days)	Short (minutes)
Receptor	Intracellular	Plasma membrane
Mediator	Receptor-hormone complex	cAMP, cGMP, Ca^{2+}, metabolites of complex phosphoinositols, kinase cascades

in group II.C of the table. The intracellular messenger for group II.D is a protein kinase-phosphatase cascade. Several of these have been identified, and a given hormone may use more than one kinase cascade. A few hormones fit into more than one category, and assignments change as new information is brought forward.

DIVERSITY OF THE ENDOCRINE SYSTEM

Hormones Are Synthesized in a Variety of Cellular Arrangements

Hormones are synthesized in discrete organs designed solely for this specific purpose, such as the thyroid (triiodothyronine), adrenal (glucocorticoids and mineralocorticoids), and the pituitary (TSH, FSH, LH, growth hormone, prolactin, ACTH). Some organs are designed to perform two distinct but closely related functions. For example, the ovaries produce mature oocytes and the reproductive hormones estradiol and progesterone. The testes produce mature spermatozoa and testosterone. Hormones are also produced in specialized cells within other organs such as the small intestine (glucagon-like peptide), thyroid (calcitonin), and kidney (angiotensin II). Finally, the synthesis of some hormones requires the parenchymal cells of more than one organ—eg, the skin, liver, and kidney are required for the production of 1,25(OH)$_2$-D$_3$ (calcitriol). Examples of this diversity in the approach to hormone synthesis, each of which has evolved to fulfill a specific purpose, are discussed below.

Hormones Are Chemically Diverse

Hormones are synthesized from a wide variety of chemical building blocks. A large series is derived from cholesterol. These include the glucocorticoids, mineralo-

corticoids, estrogens, progestins, and $1,25(OH)_2\text{-}D_3$ (see Figure 41–2). In some cases, a steroid hormone is the precursor molecule for another hormone. For example, progesterone is a hormone in its own right but is also a precursor in the formation of glucocorticoids, mineralocorticoids, testosterone, and estrogens. Testosterone is an obligatory intermediate in the biosynthesis of estradiol and in the formation of dihydrotestosterone (DHT). In these examples, described in detail below, the final product is determined by the cell type and the associated set of enzymes in which the precursor exists.

The amino acid tyrosine is the starting point in the synthesis of the catecholamines and of the thyroid hormones tetraiodothyronine (thyroxine; T_4) and triiodothyronine (T_3) (Figure 41–2). T_3 and T_4 are unique in that they require the addition of iodine (as I^-) for bioactivity. Because dietary iodine is very scarce in many parts of the world, an intricate mechanism for accumulating and retaining I^- has evolved.

Many hormones are polypeptides or glycoproteins. These range in size from thyrotropin-releasing hormone (TRH), a tripeptide, to single-chain polypeptides like adrenocorticotropic hormone (ACTH; 39 amino acids), parathyroid hormone (PTH; 84 amino acids), and growth hormone (GH; 191 amino acids) (Figure 41–2). Insulin is an AB chain heterodimer of 21 and 30 amino acids, respectively. Follicle-stimulating hormone (FSH), luteinizing hormone (LH), thyroid stimulating hormone (TSH), and chorionic gonadotropin (CG) are glycoprotein hormones of αβ heterodimeric structure. The α chain is identical in all of these hormones, and distinct β chains impart hormone uniqueness. These hormones have a molecular mass in the range of 25–30 kDa depending on the degree of glycosylation and the length of the β chain.

Hormones Are Synthesized & Modified for Full Activity in a Variety of Ways

Some hormones are synthesized in final form and secreted immediately. Included in this class are the hormones derived from cholesterol. Others such as the catecholamines are synthesized in final form and stored in the producing cells. Others are synthesized from precursor molecules in the producing cell, then are processed and secreted upon a physiologic cue (insulin). Finally, still others are converted to active forms from precursor molecules in the periphery (T_3 and DHT). All of these examples are discussed in more detail below.

MANY HORMONES ARE MADE FROM CHOLESTEROL

Adrenal Steroidogenesis

The adrenal steroid hormones are synthesized from cholesterol. Cholesterol is mostly derived from the plasma, but a small portion is synthesized in situ from acetyl-CoA via mevalonate and squalene. Much of the cholesterol in the adrenal is esterified and stored in cytoplasmic lipid droplets. Upon stimulation of the adrenal by ACTH, an esterase is activated, and the free cholesterol formed is transported into the mitochondrion, where a **cytochrome P450 side chain cleavage enzyme (P450scc)** converts cholesterol to pregnenolone. Cleavage of the side chain involves sequential hydroxylations, first at C_{22} and then at C_{20}, followed by side chain cleavage (removal of the six-carbon fragment isocaproaldehyde) to give the 21-carbon steroid (Figure 41–3, top). An ACTH-dependent **steroidogenic acute regulatory (StAR) protein** is essential for the transport of cholesterol to P450scc in the inner mitochondrial membrane.

All mammalian steroid hormones are formed from cholesterol via pregnenolone through a series of reactions that occur in either the mitochondria or endoplasmic reticulum of the producing cell. Hydroxylases that require molecular oxygen and NADPH are essential, and dehydrogenases, an isomerase, and a lyase reaction are also necessary for certain steps. There is cellular specificity in adrenal steroidogenesis. For instance, 18-hydroxylase and 19-hydroxysteroid dehydrogenase, which are required for aldosterone synthesis, are found only in the zona glomerulosa cells (the outer region of the adrenal cortex), so that the biosynthesis of this mineralocorticoid is confined to this region. A schematic representation of the pathways involved in the synthesis of the three major classes of adrenal steroids is presented in Figure 41–4. The enzymes are shown in the rectangular boxes, and the modifications at each step are shaded.

A. MINERALOCORTICOID SYNTHESIS

Synthesis of aldosterone follows the mineralocorticoid pathway and occurs in the zona glomerulosa. Pregnenolone is converted to progesterone by the action of two smooth endoplasmic reticulum enzymes, **3β-hydroxysteroid dehydrogenase (3β-OHSD)** and **$\Delta^{5,4}$-isomerase.** Progesterone is hydroxylated at the C_{21} position to form 11-deoxycorticosterone (DOC), which is an active (Na^+-retaining) mineralocorticoid. The next hydroxylation, at C_{11}, produces corticosterone, which has glucocorticoid activity and is a weak mineralocorticoid (it has less than 5% of the potency of aldosterone). In some species (eg, rodents), it is the most potent glucocorticoid. C_{21} hydroxylation is necessary for both mineralocorticoid and glucocorticoid activity, but most steroids with a C_{17} hydroxyl group have more glucocorticoid and less mineralocorticoid action. In the zona glomerulosa, which does not have the smooth endoplasmic reticulum enzyme 17α-hydroxylase, a mitochondrial 18-hydroxylase is present. The **18-hydroxylase (aldosterone synthase)** acts

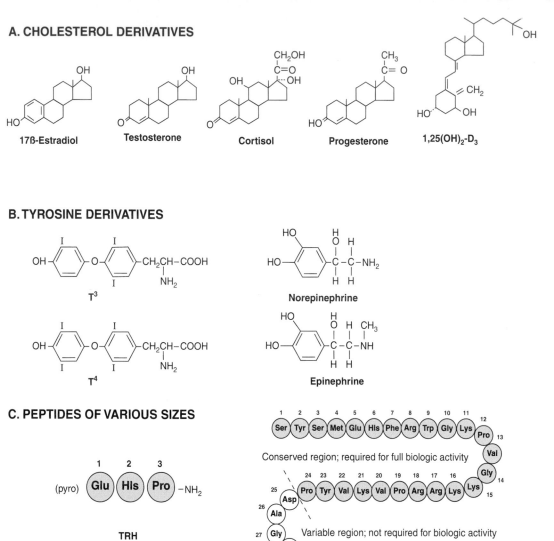

A. CHOLESTEROL DERIVATIVES

17ß-Estradiol   Testosterone   Cortisol   Progesterone   1,25(OH)₂-D₃

B. TYROSINE DERIVATIVES

T³   Norepinephrine

T⁴   Epinephrine

C. PEPTIDES OF VARIOUS SIZES

(pyro) Glu His Pro –NH₂

TRH

ACTH

D. GLYCOPROTEINS (TSH, FSH, LH)

common α subunits

unique β subunits

Figure 41–2. Chemical diversity of hormones. **(A)** Cholesterol derivatives. **(B)** Tyrosine derivatives. **(C)** Peptides of various sizes. **(D)** Glycoproteins (TSH, FSH, LH) with common α subunits and unique β subunits.

on corticosterone to form 18-hydroxycorticosterone, which is changed to aldosterone by conversion of the 18-alcohol to an aldehyde. This unique distribution of enzymes and the special regulation of the zona glomerulosa by K⁺ and angiotensin II have led some investigators to suggest that, in addition to the adrenal being

two glands, the adrenal cortex is actually two separate organs.

B. GLUCOCORTICOID SYNTHESIS

Cortisol synthesis requires three hydroxylases located in the fasciculata and reticularis zones of the adrenal cor-

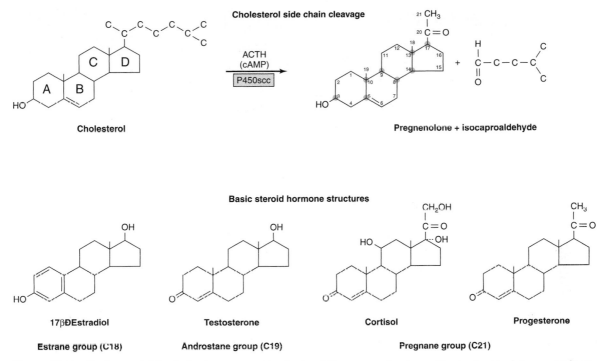

Figure 41–3. Cholesterol side-chain cleavage and basic steroid hormone structures. The basic sterol rings are identified by the letters A–D. The carbon atoms are numbered 1–21, starting with the A ring. Note that the estrane group has 18 carbons (C18), etc.

tex that act sequentially on the C_{17}, C_{21}, and C_{11} positions. The first two reactions are rapid, while C_{11} hydroxylation is relatively slow. If the C_{11} position is hydroxylated first, the action of **17α-hydroxylase** is impeded and the mineralocorticoid pathway is followed (forming corticosterone or aldosterone, depending on the cell type). 17α-Hydroxylase is a smooth endoplasmic reticulum enzyme that acts upon either progesterone or, more commonly, pregnenolone. 17α-Hydroxyprogesterone is hydroxylated at C_{21} to form 11-deoxycortisol, which is then hydroxylated at C_{11} to form cortisol, the most potent natural glucocorticoid hormone in humans. 21-Hydroxylase is a smooth endoplasmic reticulum enzyme, whereas 11β-hydroxylase is a mitochondrial enzyme. Steroidogenesis thus involves the repeated shuttling of substrates into and out of the mitochondria.

C. ANDROGEN SYNTHESIS

The major androgen or androgen precursor produced by the adrenal cortex is dehydroepiandrosterone (DHEA). Most 17-hydroxypregnenolone follows the glucocorticoid pathway, but a small fraction is subjected to oxidative fission and removal of the two-carbon side chain through the action of 17,20-lyase. The lyase activity is

actually part of the same enzyme (P450c17) that catalyzes 17α-hydroxylation. This is therefore a **dual function protein.** The lyase activity is important in both the adrenals and the gonads and acts exclusively on 17α-hydroxy containing molecules. Adrenal androgen production increases markedly if glucocorticoid biosynthesis is impeded by the lack of one of the hydroxylases (**adrenogenital syndrome**). DHEA is really a prohormone, since the actions of 3β-OHSD and $\Delta^{5,4}$-isomerase convert the weak androgen DHEA into the more potent **androstenedione.** Small amounts of androstenedione are also formed in the adrenal by the action of the lyase on 17α-hydroxyprogesterone. Reduction of androstenedione at the C_{17} position results in the formation of **testosterone,** the most potent adrenal androgen. Small amounts of testosterone are produced in the adrenal by this mechanism, but most of this conversion occurs in the testes.

Testicular Steroidogenesis

Testicular androgens are synthesized in the interstitial tissue by the Leydig cells. The immediate precursor of the gonadal steroids, as for the adrenal steroids, is cholesterol. The rate-limiting step, as in the adrenal, is

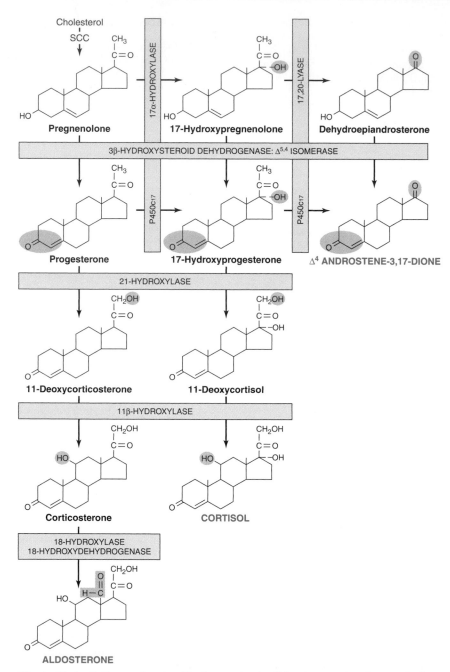

Figure 41–4. Pathways involved in the synthesis of the three major classes of adrenal steroids (mineralocorticoids, glucocorticoids, and androgens). Enzymes are shown in the rectangular boxes, and the modifications at each step are shaded. Note that the 17α-hydroxylase and 17,20-lyase activities are both part of one enzyme, designated P450c17. (Slightly modified and reproduced, with permission, from Harding BW: In: *Endocrinology*, vol 2. DeGroot LJ [editor]. Grune & Stratton, 1979. Copyright © 1979 Elsevier Inc. Reprinted with permission from Elsevier.)

delivery of cholesterol to the inner membrane of the mitochondria by the transport protein StAR. Once in the proper location, cholesterol is acted upon by the side chain cleavage enzyme P450scc. The conversion of cholesterol to pregnenolone is identical in adrenal, ovary, and testis. In the latter two tissues, however, the reaction is promoted by LH rather than ACTH.

The conversion of pregnenolone to testosterone requires the action of five enzyme activities contained in three proteins: (1) 3β-hydroxysteroid dehydrogenase (3β-OHSD) and $\Delta^{5,4}$-isomerase; (2) 17α-hydroxylase and 17,20-lyase; and (3) 17β-hydroxysteroid dehydrogenase (17β-OHSD). This sequence, referred to as the **progesterone (or Δ^4) pathway,** is shown on the right side of Figure 41–5. Pregnenolone can also be converted to testosterone by the **dehydroepiandrosterone (or Δ^5) pathway,** which is illustrated on the left side of Figure 41–5. The Δ^5 route appears to be most used in human testes.

The five enzyme activities are localized in the microsomal fraction in rat testes, and there is a close functional association between the activities of 3β-OHSD and $\Delta^{5,4}$-isomerase and between those of a 17α-hydroxylase and 17,20-lyase. These enzyme pairs, both contained in a single protein, are shown in the general reaction sequence in Figure 41–5.

Dihydrotestosterone Is Formed from Testosterone in Peripheral Tissues

Testosterone is metabolized by two pathways. One involves oxidation at the 17 position, and the other involves reduction of the A ring double bond and the 3-ketone. Metabolism by the first pathway occurs in many tissues, including liver, and produces 17-ketosteroids that are generally inactive or less active than the parent compound. Metabolism by the second pathway, which is less efficient, occurs primarily in target tissues and produces the potent metabolite dihydrotestosterone (DHT).

The most significant metabolic product of testosterone is DHT, since in many tissues, including prostate, external genitalia, and some areas of the skin, this is the active form of the hormone. The plasma content of DHT in the adult male is about one-tenth that of testosterone, and approximately 400 μg of DHT is produced daily as compared with about 5 mg of testosterone. About 50–100 μg of DHT are secreted by the testes. The rest is produced peripherally from testosterone in a reaction catalyzed by the NADPH-dependent **5α-reductase** (Figure 41–6). Testosterone can thus be considered a prohormone, since it is converted into a much more potent compound (dihydrotestosterone) and since most of this conversion occurs outside the testes. Some estradiol is formed from the peripheral aromatization of testosterone, particularly in males.

Ovarian Steroidogenesis

The estrogens are a family of hormones synthesized in a variety of tissues. 17β-Estradiol is the primary estrogen of ovarian origin. In some species, estrone, synthesized in numerous tissues, is more abundant. In pregnancy, relatively more estriol is produced, and this comes from the placenta. The general pathway and the subcellular localization of the enzymes involved in the early steps of estradiol synthesis are the same as those involved in androgen biosynthesis. Features unique to the ovary are illustrated in Figure 41–7.

Estrogens are formed by the aromatization of androgens in a complex process that involves three hydroxylation steps, each of which requires O_2 and NADPH. The **aromatase enzyme complex** is thought to include a P450 monooxygenase. Estradiol is formed if the substrate of this enzyme complex is testosterone, whereas estrone results from the aromatization of androstenedione.

The cellular source of the various ovarian steroids has been difficult to unravel, but a transfer of substrates between two cell types is involved. Theca cells are the source of androstenedione and testosterone. These are converted by the aromatase enzyme in granulosa cells to estrone and estradiol, respectively. Progesterone, a precursor for all steroid hormones, is produced and secreted by the corpus luteum as an end-product hormone because these cells do not contain the enzymes necessary to convert progesterone to other steroid hormones (Figure 41–8).

Significant amounts of estrogens are produced by the peripheral aromatization of androgens. In human males, the peripheral aromatization of testosterone to estradiol (E_2) accounts for 80% of the production of the latter. In females, adrenal androgens are important substrates, since as much as 50% of the E_2 produced during pregnancy comes from the aromatization of androgens. Finally, conversion of androstenedione to estrone is the major source of estrogens in postmenopausal women. Aromatase activity is present in adipose cells and also in liver, skin, and other tissues. Increased activity of this enzyme may contribute to the "estrogenization" that characterizes such diseases as cirrhosis of the liver, hyperthyroidism, aging, and obesity. Aromatase inhibitors show promise as therapeutic agents in breast cancer and possibly in other female reproductive tract malignancies.

1,25(OH)$_2$-D$_3$ (Calcitriol) Is Synthesized from a Cholesterol Derivative

1,25(OH)$_2$-D$_3$ is produced by a complex series of enzymatic reactions that involve the plasma transport of precursor molecules to a number of different tissues (Figure 41–9). One of these precursors is vitamin D—really not a vitamin, but this common name persists. The active

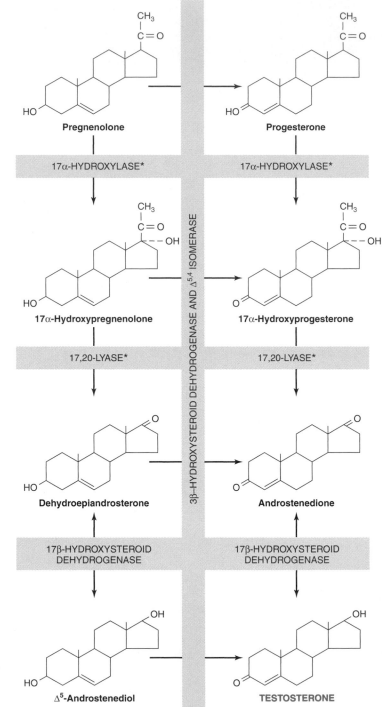

Figure 41–5. Pathways of testosterone biosynthesis. The pathway on the left side of the figure is called the Δ^5 or dehydroepiandrosterone pathway; the pathway on the right side is called the Δ^4 or progesterone pathway. The asterisk indicates that the 17α-hydroxylase and 17,20-lyase activities reside in a single protein, P450c17.

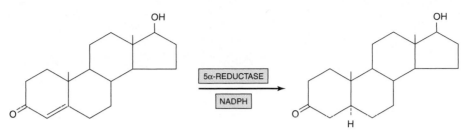

Figure 41–6. Dihydrotestosterone is formed from testosterone through action of the enzyme 5α-reductase.

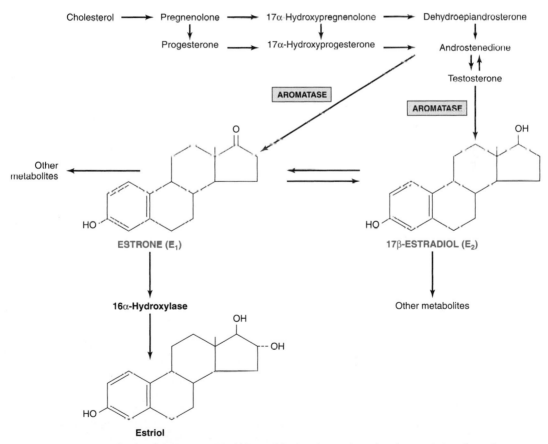

Figure 41–7. **Biosynthesis of estrogens.** (Slightly modified and reproduced, with permission, from Ganong WF: *Review of Medical Physiology,* 20th ed. McGraw-Hill, 2001.)

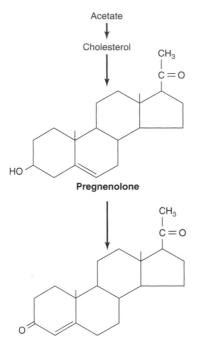

Acetate

Cholesterol

Pregnenolone

Progesterone

Figure 41–8. Biosynthesis of progesterone in the corpus luteum.

molecule, $1,25(OH)_2$-D_3, is transported to other organs where it activates biologic processes in a manner similar to that employed by the steroid hormones.

A. Skin

Small amounts of the precursor for $1,25(OH)_2$-D_3 synthesis are present in food (fish liver oil, egg yolk), but most of the precursor for $1,25(OH)_2$-D_3 synthesis is produced in the malpighian layer of the epidermis from 7-dehydrocholesterol in an ultraviolet light-mediated, nonenzymatic **photolysis** reaction. The extent of this conversion is related directly to the intensity of the exposure and inversely to the extent of pigmentation in the skin. There is an age-related loss of 7-dehydrocholesterol in the epidermis that may be related to the negative calcium balance associated with old age.

B. Liver

A specific transport protein called the **vitamin D-binding protein** binds vitamin D_3 and its metabolites and moves vitamin D_3 from the skin or intestine to the liver, where it undergoes 25-hydroxylation, the first obligatory reaction in the production of $1,25(OH)_2$-D_3. 25-Hydroxylation occurs in the endoplasmic reticulum in a reaction that requires magnesium, NADPH, molec-

ular oxygen, and an uncharacterized cytoplasmic factor. Two enzymes are involved: an NADPH-dependent cytochrome P450 reductase and a cytochrome P450. This reaction is not regulated, and it also occurs with low efficiency in kidney and intestine. The $25(OH)_2$-D_3 enters the circulation, where it is the major form of vitamin D found in plasma, and is transported to the kidney by the vitamin D-binding protein.

C. Kidney

$25(OH)_2$-D_3 is a weak agonist and must be modified by hydroxylation at position C_1 for full biologic activity. This is accomplished in mitochondria of the renal proximal convoluted tubule by a three-component monooxygenase reaction that requires NADPH, Mg^{2+}, molecular oxygen, and at least three enzymes: (1) a flavoprotein, renal ferredoxin reductase; (2) an iron sulfur protein, renal ferredoxin; and (3) cytochrome P450. This system produces $1,25(OH)_2$-D_3, which is the most potent naturally occurring metabolite of vitamin D.

CATECHOLAMINES & THYROID HORMONES ARE MADE FROM TYROSINE

Catecholamines Are Synthesized in Final Form & Stored in Secretion Granules

Three amines—dopamine, norepinephrine, and epinephrine—are synthesized from tyrosine in the chromaffin cells of the adrenal medulla. The major product of the adrenal medulla is epinephrine. This compound constitutes about 80% of the catecholamines in the medulla, and it is not made in extramedullary tissue. In contrast, most of the norepinephrine present in organs innervated by sympathetic nerves is made in situ (about 80% of the total), and most of the rest is made in other nerve endings and reaches the target sites via the circulation. Epinephrine and norepinephrine may be produced and stored in different cells in the adrenal medulla and other chromaffin tissues.

The conversion of tyrosine to epinephrine requires four sequential steps: (1) ring hydroxylation; (2) decarboxylation; (3) side chain hydroxylation to form norepinephrine; and (4) N-methylation to form epinephrine. The biosynthetic pathway and the enzymes involved are illustrated in Figure 41–10.

A. Tyrosine Hydroxylase Is Rate-Limiting for Catecholamine Biosynthesis

Tyrosine is the immediate precursor of catecholamines, and **tyrosine hydroxylase** is the rate-limiting enzyme in catecholamine biosynthesis. Tyrosine hydroxylase is found in both soluble and particle-bound forms only in tissues that synthesize catecholamines; it functions as an oxidoreductase, with tetrahydropteridine as a cofactor,

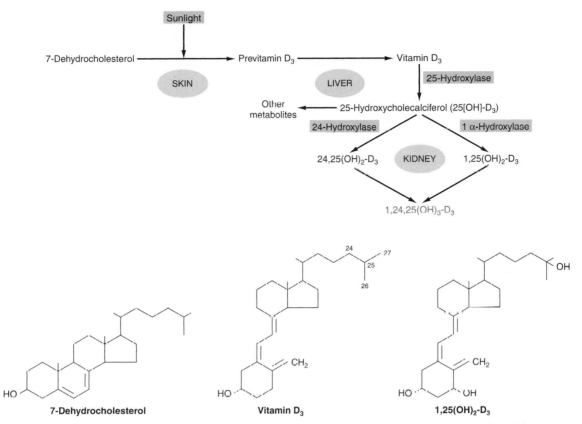

Figure 41–9. Formation and hydroxylation of vitamin D_3. 25-Hydroxylation takes place in the liver, and the other hydroxylations occur in the kidneys. 25,26(OH)$_2$-D$_3$ and 1,25,26(OH)$_3$-D$_3$ are probably formed as well. The formulas of 7-dehydrocholesterol, vitamin D$_3$, and 1,25(OH)$_2$-D$_3$ are also shown. (Modified and reproduced, with permission, from Ganong WF. *Review of Medical Physiology*, 20th ed. McGraw-Hill, 2001.)

to convert L-tyrosine to L-dihydroxyphenylalanine (**L-dopa**). As the rate-limiting enzyme, tyrosine hydroxylase is regulated in a variety of ways. The most important mechanism involves feedback inhibition by the catecholamines, which compete with the enzyme for the pteridine cofactor. Catecholamines cannot cross the blood-brain barrier; hence, in the brain they must be synthesized locally. In certain central nervous system diseases (eg, Parkinson's disease), there is a local deficiency of dopamine synthesis. L-Dopa, the precursor of dopamine, readily crosses the blood-brain barrier and so is an important agent in the treatment of Parkinson's disease.

B. DOPA DECARBOXYLASE IS PRESENT IN ALL TISSUES

This soluble enzyme requires pyridoxal phosphate for the conversion of L-dopa to 3,4-dihydroxyphenylethylamine (**dopamine**). Compounds that resemble L-dopa,

such as α-methyldopa, are competitive inhibitors of this reaction. α-Methyldopa is effective in treating some kinds of hypertension.

C. DOPAMINE β-HYDROXYLASE (DBH) CATALYZES THE CONVERSION OF DOPAMINE TO NOREPINEPHRINE

DBH is a monooxygenase and uses ascorbate as an electron donor, copper at the active site, and fumarate as modulator. DBH is in the particulate fraction of the medullary cells, probably in the secretion granule; thus, the conversion of dopamine to **norepinephrine** occurs in this organelle.

D. PHENYLETHANOLAMINE-*N*-METHYLTRANSFERASE (PNMT) CATALYZES THE PRODUCTION OF EPINEPHRINE

PNMT catalyzes the N-methylation of norepinephrine to form **epinephrine** in the epinephrine-forming cells of the adrenal medulla. Since PNMT is soluble, it is

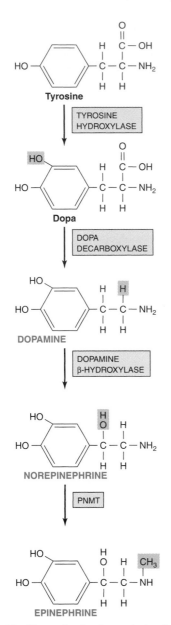

Figure 41–10. Biosynthesis of catecholamines. (PNMT, phenylethanolamine-*N*-methyltransferase.)

T$_3$ & T$_4$ Illustrate the Diversity in Hormone Synthesis

The formation of **triiodothyronine (T$_3$)** and **tetraiodothyronine (thyroxine; T$_4$)** (see Figure 41–2) illustrates many of the principles of diversity discussed in this chapter. These hormones require a rare element (iodine) for bioactivity; they are synthesized as part of a very large precursor molecule (thyroglobulin); they are stored in an intracellular reservoir (colloid); and there is peripheral conversion of T$_4$ to T$_3$, which is a much more active hormone.

The thyroid hormones T$_3$ and T$_4$ are unique in that iodine (as iodide) is an essential component of both. In most parts of the world, iodine is a scarce component of soil, and for that reason there is little in food. A complex mechanism has evolved to acquire and retain this crucial element and to convert it into a form suitable for incorporation into organic compounds. At the same time, the thyroid must synthesize thyronine from tyrosine, and this synthesis takes place in thyroglobulin (Figure 41–11).

Thyroglobulin is the precursor of T$_4$ and T$_3$. It is a large iodinated, glycosylated protein with a molecular mass of 660 kDa. Carbohydrate accounts for 8–10% of the weight of thyroglobulin and iodide for about 0.2–1%, depending upon the iodine content in the diet. Thyroglobulin is composed of two large subunits. It contains 115 tyrosine residues, each of which is a potential site of iodination. About 70% of the iodide in thyroglobulin exists in the inactive precursors, **monoiodotyrosine (MIT)** and **diiodotyrosine (DIT),** while 30% is in the **iodothyronyl residues,** T$_4$ and T$_3$. When iodine supplies are sufficient, the T$_4$:T$_3$ ratio is about 7:1. In **iodine deficiency,** this ratio decreases, as does the DIT:MIT ratio. Thyroglobulin, a large molecule of about 5000 amino acids, provides the conformation required for tyrosyl coupling and iodide organification necessary in the formation of the diaminoacid thyroid hormones. It is synthesized in the basal portion of the cell and moves to the lumen, where it is a storage form of T$_3$ and T$_4$ in the colloid; several weeks' supply of these hormones exist in the normal thyroid. Within minutes after stimulation of the thyroid by TSH, colloid reenters the cell and there is a marked increase of phagolysosome activity. Various acid proteases and peptidases hydrolyze the thyroglobulin into its constituent amino acids, including T$_4$ and T$_3$, which are discharged from the basal portion of the cell (see Figure 41–11). Thyroglobulin is thus a very large prohormone.

Iodide Metabolism Involves Several Discrete Steps

The thyroid is able to concentrate I$^-$ against a strong electrochemical gradient. This is an energy-dependent

assumed that norepinephrine-to-epinephrine conversion occurs in the cytoplasm. The synthesis of PNMT is induced by glucocorticoid hormones that reach the medulla via the intra-adrenal portal system. This special system provides for a 100-fold steroid concentration gradient over systemic arterial blood, and this high intra-adrenal concentration appears to be necessary for the induction of PNMT.

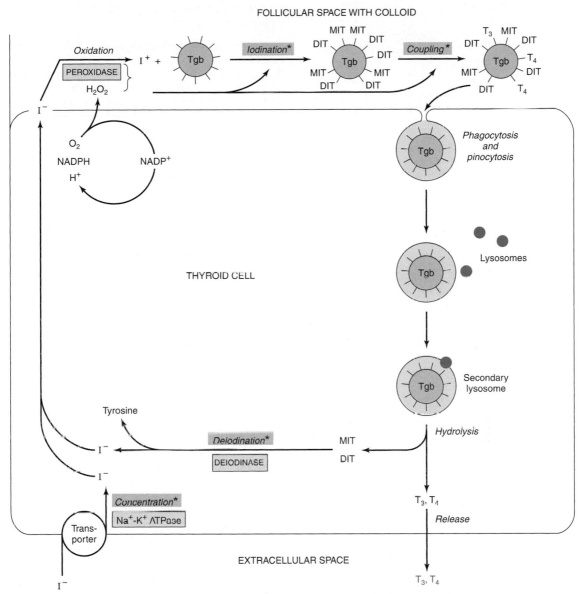

Figure 41–11. Model of iodide metabolism in the thyroid follicle. A follicular cell is shown facing the follicular lumen (top) and the extracellular space (at bottom). Iodide enters the thyroid primarily through a transporter (bottom left). Thyroid hormone synthesis occurs in the follicular space through a series of reactions, many of which are peroxidase-mediated. Thyroid hormones, stored in the colloid in the follicular space, are released from thyroglobulin by hydrolysis inside the thyroid cell. (Tgb, thyroglobulin; MIT, monoiodotyrosine; DIT, diiodotyrosine; T_3, triiodothyronine; T_4, tetraiodothyronine.) Asterisks indicate steps or processes that are inherited enzyme deficiencies that cause congenital goiter and often result in hypothyroidism.

process and is linked to the Na^+-K^+ ATPase-dependent thyroidal I^- transporter. The ratio of iodide in thyroid to iodide in serum (T:S ratio) is a reflection of the activity of this transporter. This activity is primarily con-trolled by TSH and ranges from 500:1 in animals chronically stimulated with TSH to 5:1 or less in hypophysectomized animals (no TSH). The T:S ratio in humans on a normal iodine diet is about 25:1.

The thyroid is the only tissue that can oxidize I^- to a higher valence state, an obligatory step in I^- organification and thyroid hormone biosynthesis. This step involves a heme-containing peroxidase and occurs at the luminal surface of the follicular cell. Thyroperoxidase, a tetrameric protein with a molecular mass of 60 kDa, requires hydrogen peroxide as an oxidizing agent. The H_2O_2 is produced by an NADPH-dependent enzyme resembling cytochrome c reductase. A number of compounds inhibit I^- oxidation and therefore its subsequent incorporation into MIT and DIT. The most important of these are the thiourea drugs. They are used as antithyroid drugs because of their ability to inhibit thyroid hormone biosynthesis at this step. Once iodination occurs, the iodine does not readily leave the thyroid. Free tyrosine can be iodinated, but it is not incorporated into proteins since no tRNA recognizes iodinated tyrosine.

The coupling of two DIT molecules to form T_4—or of an MIT and DIT to form T_3—occurs within the thyroglobulin molecule. A separate coupling enzyme has not been found, and since this is an oxidative process it is assumed that the same thyroperoxidase catalyzes this reaction by stimulating free radical formation of iodotyrosine. This hypothesis is supported by the observation that the same drugs which inhibit I^- oxidation also inhibit coupling. The formed thyroid hormones remain as integral parts of thyroglobulin until the latter is degraded, as described above.

A deiodinase removes I^- from the inactive mono- and diiodothyronine molecules in the thyroid. This mechanism provides a substantial amount of the I^- used in T_3 and T_4 biosynthesis. A peripheral deiodinase in target tissues such as pituitary, kidney, and liver selectively removes I^- from the 5' position of T_4 to make T_3 (see Figure 41–2), which is a much more active molecule. In this sense, T_4 can be thought of as a prohormone, though it does have some intrinsic activity.

Several Hormones Are Made from Larger Peptide Precursors

Formation of the critical disulfide bridges in insulin requires that this hormone be first synthesized as part of a larger precursor molecule, proinsulin. This is conceptually similar to the example of the thyroid hormones, which can only be formed in the context of a much larger molecule. Several other hormones are synthesized as parts of large precursor molecules, not because of some special structural requirement but rather as a mechanism for controlling the available amount of the active hormone. PTH and angiotensin II are examples of this type of regulation. Another interesting example is the POMC protein, which can be processed into many different hormones in a tissue-specific manner. These examples are discussed in detail below.

Insulin Is Synthesized as a Preprohormone & Modified Within the β Cell

Insulin has an AB heterodimeric structure with one intrachain (A6–A11) and two interchain disulfide bridges (A7–B7 and A20–B19) (Figure 41–12). The A and B chains could be synthesized in the laboratory, but attempts at a biochemical synthesis of the mature insulin molecule yielded very poor results. The reason for this became apparent when it was discovered that insulin is synthesized as a **preprohormone** (molecular weight approximately 11,500), which is the prototype for peptides that are processed from larger precursor molecules. The hydrophobic 23-amino-acid pre-, or leader, sequence directs the molecule into the cisternae of the endoplasmic reticulum and then is removed. This results in the 9000-MW proinsulin molecule, which provides the conformation necessary for the proper and efficient formation of the disulfide bridges. As shown in Figure 41–12, the sequence of proinsulin, starting from the amino terminal, is B chain—connecting (C) peptide—A chain. The proinsulin molecule undergoes a series of site-specific peptide cleavages that result in the formation of equimolar amounts of mature insulin and C peptide. These enzymatic cleavages are summarized in Figure 41–12.

Parathyroid Hormone (PTH) Is Secreted as an 84-Amino-Acid Peptide

The immediate precursor of PTH is **proPTH,** which differs from the native 84-amino-acid hormone by having a highly basic hexapeptide amino terminal extension. The primary gene product and the immediate precursor for proPTH is the 115-amino-acid **preproPTH.** This differs from proPTH by having an additional 25-amino-acid amino terminal extension that, in common with the other leader or signal sequences characteristic of secreted proteins, is hydrophobic. The complete structure of preproPTH and the sequences of proPTH and PTH are illustrated in Figure 41–13. PTH_{1-34} has full biologic activity, and the region 25–34 is primarily responsible for receptor binding.

The biosynthesis of PTH and its subsequent secretion are regulated by the plasma ionized calcium (Ca^{2+}) concentration through a complex process. An acute decrease of Ca^{2+} results in a marked increase of PTH mRNA, and this is followed by an increased rate of PTH synthesis and secretion. However, about 80–90% of the proPTH synthesized cannot be accounted for as intact PTH in cells or in the incubation medium of experimental systems. This finding led to the conclusion that most of the proPTH synthesized is quickly degraded. It was later discovered that this rate of degradation decreases when Ca^{2+} concentrations are low, and it increases when Ca^{2+} concentrations are high. A Ca^{2+}

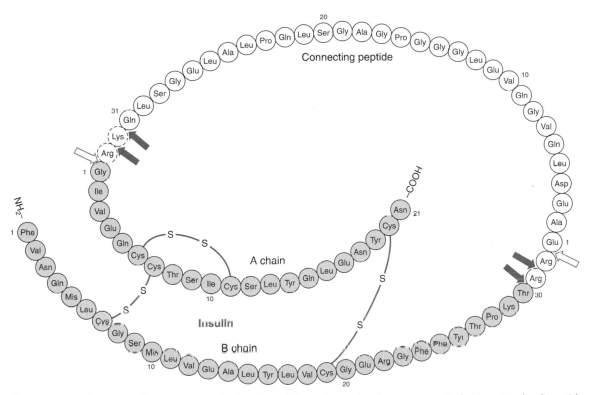

Figure 41–12. Structure of human proinsulin. Insulin and C-peptide molecules are connected at two sites by dipeptide links. An initial cleavage by a trypsin-like enzyme (open arrows) followed by several cleavages by a carboxypeptidase-like enzyme (solid arrows) results in the production of the heterodimeric (AB) insulin molecule (light color) and the C peptide.

receptor on the surface of the parathyroid cell mediates these effects. Very specific fragments of PTH are generated during its proteolytic digestion (Figure 41–13). A number of proteolytic enzymes, including cathepsins B and D, have been identified in parathyroid tissue. Cathepsin B cleaves PTH into two fragments: PTH_{1-36} and PTH_{37-84}. PTH_{37-84} is not further degraded; however, PTH_{1-36} is rapidly and progressively cleaved into di- and tripeptides. Most of the proteolysis of PTH occurs within the gland, but a number of studies confirm that PTH, once secreted, is proteolytically degraded in other tissues, especially the liver, by similar mechanisms.

Angiotensin II Is Also Synthesized from a Large Precursor

The renin-angiotensin system is involved in the regulation of blood pressure and electrolyte metabolism (through production of aldosterone). The primary hormone involved in these processes is angiotensin II, an octapeptide made from angiotensinogen (Figure 41–14). Angiotensinogen, a large α_2-globulin made in liver, is the substrate for renin, an enzyme produced in the juxtaglomerular cells of the renal afferent arteriole. The position of these cells makes them particularly sensitive to blood pressure changes, and many of the physiologic regulators of renin release act through renal baroreceptors. The juxtaglomerular cells are also sensitive to changes of Na^+ and Cl^- concentration in the renal tubular fluid; therefore, any combination of factors that decreases fluid volume (dehydration, decreased blood pressure, fluid or blood loss) or decreases NaCl concentration stimulates renin release. Renal sympathetic nerves that terminate in the juxtaglomerular cells mediate the central nervous system and postural effects on renin release independently of the baroreceptor and salt effects, a mechanism that involves the β-adrenergic receptor. Renin acts upon the substrate angiotensinogen to produce the decapeptide angiotensin I.

Angiotensin-converting enzyme, a glycoprotein found in lung, endothelial cells, and plasma, removes two carboxyl terminal amino acids from the decapeptide angiotensin I to form angiotensin II in a step that is not thought to be rate-limiting. Various nonapeptide analogs of angiotensin I and other compounds act as competitive

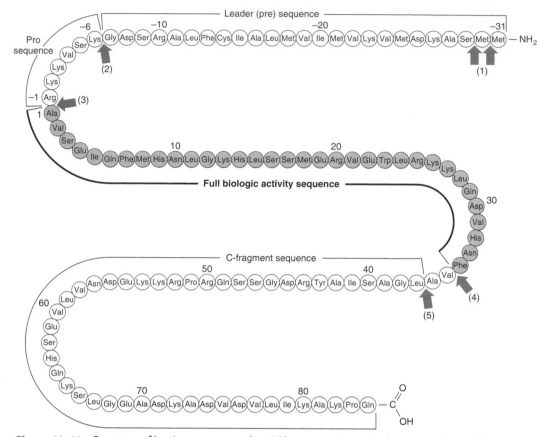

Figure 41–13. Structure of bovine preproparathyroid hormone. Arrows indicate sites cleaved by processing enzymes in the parathyroid gland (1–5) and in the liver after secretion of the hormone (4–5). The biologically active region of the molecule is flanked by sequence not required for activity on target receptors. (Slightly modified and reproduced, with permission, from Habener JF: Recent advances in parathyroid hormone research. Clin Biochem 1981;14:223. Copyright © 1981. Reprinted with permission from Elsevier.)

inhibitors of converting enzyme and are used to treat renin-dependent hypertension. These are referred to as **angiotensin-converting enzyme (ACE) inhibitors.** Angiotensin II increases blood pressure by causing vasoconstriction of the arteriole and is a very potent vasoactive substance. It inhibits renin release from the juxtaglomerular cells and is a potent stimulator of aldosterone production. This results in Na^+ retention, volume expansion, and increased blood pressure.

In some species, angiotensin II is converted to the heptapeptide angiotensin III (Figure 41–14), an equally potent stimulator of aldosterone production. In humans, the plasma level of angiotensin II is four times greater than that of angiotensin III, so most effects are exerted by the octapeptide. Angiotensins II and III are rapidly inactivated by angiotensinases.

Angiotensin II binds to specific adrenal cortex glomerulosa cell receptors. The hormone-receptor interaction does not activate adenylyl cyclase, and cAMP does not appear to mediate the action of this hormone. The actions of angiotensin II, which are to stimulate the conversion of cholesterol to pregnenolone and of corticosterone to 18-hydroxycorticosterone and aldosterone, may involve changes in the concentration of intracellular calcium and of phospholipid metabolites by mechanisms similar to those described in Chapter 42.

Complex Processing Generates the Pro-Opiomelanocortin (POMC) Peptide Family

The POMC family consists of peptides that act as hormones (ACTH, LPH, MSH) and others that may serve as neurotransmitters or neuromodulators (endorphins) (see Figure 41–15). POMC is synthesized as a precursor molecule of 285 amino acids and is processed differently in various regions of the pituitary.

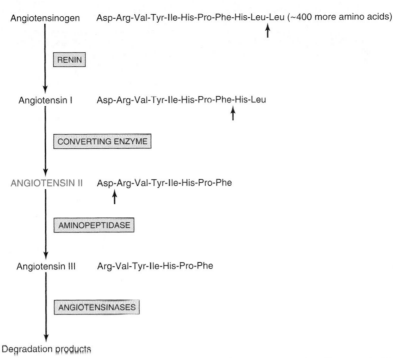

Figure 41–14. Formation and metabolism of angiotensins. Small arrows indicate cleavage sites.

The POMC gene is expressed in the anterior and intermediate lobes of the pituitary. The most conserved sequences between species are within the amino terminal fragment, the ACTH region, and the β-endorphin region. POMC or related products are found in several other vertebrate tissues, including the brain, placenta, gastrointestinal tract, reproductive tract, lung, and lymphocytes.

The POMC protein is processed differently in the anterior lobe than in the intermediate lobe. The intermediate lobe of the pituitary is rudimentary in adult

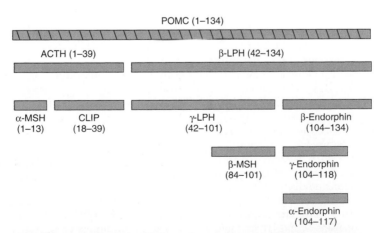

Figure 41–15. Products of pro-opiomelanocortin (POMC) cleavage. (MSH, melanocyte-stimulating hormone; CLIP, corticotropin-like intermediate lobe peptide; LPH, lipotropin.)

humans, but it is active in human fetuses and in pregnant women during late gestation and is also active in many animal species. Processing of the POMC protein in the peripheral tissues (gut, placenta, male reproductive tract) resembles that in the intermediate lobe. There are three basic peptide groups: (1) ACTH, which can give rise to α-MSH and corticotropin-like intermediate lobe peptide (CLIP); (2) β-lipotropin (β-LPH), which can yield γ-LPH, β-MSH, and β-endorphin (and thus α- and γ-endorphins); and (3) a large amino terminal peptide, which generates γ-MSH. The diversity of these products is due to the many dibasic amino acid clusters that are potential cleavage sites for trypsin-like enzymes. Each of the peptides mentioned is preceded by Lys-Arg, Arg-Lys, Arg-Arg, or Lys-Lys residues. After the prehormone segment is cleaved, the next cleavage, in both anterior and intermediate lobes, is between ACTH and β-LPH, resulting in an amino terminal peptide with ACTH and a β-LPH segment (Figure 41–15). $ACTH_{1-39}$ is subsequently cleaved from the amino terminal peptide, and in the anterior lobe essentially no further cleavages occur. In the intermediate lobe, $ACTH_{1-39}$ is cleaved into α-MSH (residues 1–13) and CLIP (18–39); β-LPH (42–134) is converted to γ-LPH (42–101) and β-endorphin (104–134). β-MSH (84–101) is derived from γ-LPH.

There are extensive additional tissue-specific modifications of these peptides that affect activity. These modifications include phosphorylation, acetylation, glycosylation, and amidation.

Mutations of the α-MSH receptor are linked to a common, early-onset form of obesity. This observation has redirected attention to the POMC peptide hormones.

THERE IS VARIATION IN THE STORAGE & SECRETION OF HORMONES

As mentioned above, the steroid hormones and $1,25(OH)_2$-D_3 are synthesized in their final active form. They are also secreted as they are made, and thus there is no intracellular reservoir of these hormones. The catecholamines, also synthesized in active form, are stored in granules in the chromaffin cells in the adrenal medulla. In response to appropriate neural stimulation, these granules are released from the cell through exocytosis, and the catecholamines are released into the circulation. A several-hour reserve supply of catecholamines exists in the chromaffin cells.

Parathyroid hormone also exists in storage vesicles. As much as 80–90% of the proPTH synthesized is degraded before it enters this final storage compartment, especially when Ca^{2+} levels are high in the parathyroid cell (see above). PTH is secreted when Ca^{2+} is low in the parathyroid cells, which contain a several-hour supply of the hormone.

Table 41–5. Diversity in the storage of hormones.

Hormone	Supply Stored in Cell
Steroids and $1,25(OH)_2$-D_3	None
Catecholamines and PTH	Hours
Insulin	Days
T_3 and T_4	Weeks

The human pancreas secretes about 40–50 units of insulin daily, which represents about 15–20% of the hormone stored in the B cells. Insulin and the C-peptide (see Figure 41–12) are normally secreted in equimolar amounts. Stimuli such as glucose, which provokes insulin secretion, therefore trigger the processing of proinsulin to insulin as an essential part of the secretory response.

A several-week supply of T_3 and T_4 exists in the thyroglobulin that is stored in colloid in the lumen of the thyroid follicles. These hormones can be released upon stimulation by TSH. This is the most exaggerated example of a prohormone, as a molecule containing approximately 5000 amino acids must be first synthesized, then degraded, to supply a few molecules of the active hormones T_4 and T_3.

The diversity in storage and secretion of hormones is illustrated in Table 41–5.

SOME HORMONES HAVE PLASMA TRANSPORT PROTEINS

The class I hormones are hydrophobic in chemical nature and thus are not very soluble in plasma. These hormones, principally the steroids and thyroid hormones, have specialized plasma transport proteins that serve several purposes. First, these proteins circumvent the solubility problem and thereby deliver the hormone to the target cell. They also provide a circulating reservoir of the hormone that can be substantial, as in the case of the thyroid hormones. Hormones, when bound to the transport proteins, cannot be metabolized, thereby prolonging their plasma half-life ($t_{1/2}$). The binding affinity of a given hormone to its transporter determines the bound versus free ratio of the hormone. This is important because only the free form of a hormone is biologically active. In general, the concentration of free hormone in plasma is very low, in the range of 10^{-15} to 10^{-9} mol/L. It is important to distinguish between plasma transport proteins and hormone receptors. Both bind hormones but with very different characteristics (Table 41–6).

The hydrophilic hormones—generally class II and of peptide structure—are freely soluble in plasma and do not require transport proteins. Hormones such as

Table 41–6. Comparison of receptors with transport proteins.

Feature	Receptors	Transport Proteins
Concentration	Very low (thousands/cell)	Very high (billions/μL)
Binding affinity	High (pmol/L to nmol/L range)	Low (μmol/L range)
Binding specificity	Very high	Low
Saturability	Yes	No
Reversibility	Yes	Yes
Signal transduction	Yes	No

Table 41–8. Approximate affinities of steroids for serum-binding proteins.

	SHBG[1]	CBG[1]
Dihydrotestosterone	1	> 100
Testosterone	2	> 100
Estradiol	5	>10
Estrone	> 10	> 100
Progesterone	> 100	~ 2
Cortisol	> 100	~ 3
Corticosterone	> 100	~ 5

[1]Affinity expressed as K_d (nmol/L).

insulin, growth hormone, ACTH, and TSH circulate in the free, active form and have very short plasma half-lives. A notable exception is IGF-I, which is transported bound to members of a family of binding proteins.

Thyroid Hormones Are Transported by Thyroid-Binding Globulin

Many of the principles discussed above are illustrated in a discussion of thyroid-binding proteins. One-half to two-thirds of T_4 and T_3 in the body is in an extrathyroidal reservoir. Most of this circulates in bound form, ie, bound to a specific binding protein, **thyroxine-binding globulin (TBG).** TBG, a glycoprotein with a molecular mass of 50 kDa, binds T_4 and T_3 and has the capacity to bind 20 μg/dL of plasma. Under normal circumstances, TBG binds—noncovalently—nearly all of the T_4 and T_3 in plasma, and it binds T_4 with greater affinity than T_3 (Table 41–7). The plasma half-life of T_4 is correspondingly four to five times that of T_3. The small, unbound (free) fraction is responsible for the biologic activity. Thus, in spite of the great difference in total amount, the free fraction of T_3 approximates that of T_4, and given that T_3 is intrinsically more active than T_4, most biologic activity is attributed to T_3. TBG does not bind any other hormones.

Table 41–7. Comparison of T_4 and T_3 in plasma.

Total Hormone (μg/dL)	Free Hormone			$t^{1/_2}$ in Blood (days)
	Percentage of Total	ng/dL	Molarity	
T_4 8	0.03	~2.24	3.0×10^{-11}	6.5
T_3 0.15	0.3	~0.4	$~0.6 \times 10^{-11}$	1.5

Glucocorticoids Are Transported by Corticosteroid-Binding Globulin

Hydrocortisone (cortisol) also circulates in plasma in protein-bound and free forms. The main plasma binding protein is an α-globulin called **transcortin,** or **corticosteroid-binding globulin (CBG).** CBG is produced in the liver, and its synthesis, like that of TBG, is increased by estrogens. CBG binds most of the hormone when plasma cortisol levels are within the normal range; much smaller amounts of cortisol are bound to albumin. The avidity of binding helps determine the biologic half-lives of various glucocorticoids. Cortisol binds tightly to CBG and has a $t_{1/2}$ of 1.5–2 hours, while corticosterone, which binds less tightly, has a $t_{1/2}$ of less than 1 hour (Table 41–8). The unbound (free) cortisol constitutes about 8% of the total and represents the biologically active fraction. Binding to CBG is not restricted to glucocorticoids. Deoxycorticosterone and progesterone interact with CBG with sufficient affinity to compete for cortisol binding. Aldosterone, the most potent natural mineralocorticoid, does not have a specific plasma transport protein. Gonadal steroids bind very weakly to CBG (Table 41–8).

Gonadal Steroids Are Transported by Sex Hormone-Binding Globulin

Most mammals, humans included, have a plasma β-globulin that binds testosterone with specificity, relatively high affinity, and limited capacity (Table 41–8). This protein, usually called **sex hormone-binding globulin (SHBG)** or testosterone-estrogen-binding globulin (TEBG), is produced in the liver. Its production is increased by estrogens (women have twice the serum concentration of SHBG as men), certain types of liver disease, and hyperthyroidism; it is decreased by androgens, advancing age, and hypothyroidism. Many of these conditions also affect the production of CBG and TBG. Since SHBG and albumin bind 97–99% of circulating testosterone, only a small fraction of the hormone in circulation is in the free (biologically active)

form. The primary function of SHBG may be to restrict the free concentration of testosterone in the serum. Testosterone binds to SHBG with higher affinity than does estradiol (Table 41–8). Therefore, a change in the level of SHBG causes a greater change in the free testosterone level than in the free estradiol level.

Estrogens are bound to SHBG and progestins to CBG. SHBG binds estradiol about five times less avidly than it binds testosterone or DHT, while progesterone and cortisol have little affinity for this protein (Table 41–8). In contrast, progesterone and cortisol bind with nearly equal affinity to CBG, which in turn has little avidity for estradiol and even less for testosterone, DHT, or estrone.

These binding proteins also provide a circulating reservoir of hormone, and because of the relatively large binding capacity they probably buffer against sudden changes in the plasma level. Because the metabolic clearance rates of these steroids are inversely related to the affinity of their binding to SHBG, estrone is cleared more rapidly than estradiol, which in turn is cleared more rapidly than testosterone or DHT.

SUMMARY

- The presence of a specific receptor defines the target cells for a given hormone.
- Receptors are proteins that bind specific hormones and generate an intracellular signal (receptor-effector coupling).
- Some hormones have intracellular receptors; others bind to receptors on the plasma membrane.
- Hormones are synthesized from a number of precursor molecules, including cholesterol, tyrosine per se, and all the constituent amino acids of peptides and proteins.

- A number of modification processes alter the activity of hormones. For example, many hormones are synthesized from larger precursor molecules.
- The complement of enzymes in a particular cell type allows for the production of a specific class of steroid hormone.
- Most of the lipid-soluble hormones are bound to rather specific plasma transport proteins.

REFERENCES

Bartalina L: Thyroid hormone-binding proteins: update 1994. Endocr Rev 1994;13:140.

Beato M et al: Steroid hormone receptors: many actors in search of a plot. Cell 1995;83:851.

Dai G, Carrasco L, Carrasco N: Cloning and characterization of the thyroid iodide transporter. Nature 1996;379:458.

DeLuca HR: The vitamin D story: a collaborative effort of basic science and clinical medicine. FASEB J 1988;2:224.

Douglass J, Civelli O, Herbert E: Polyprotein gene expression: Generation of diversity of neuroendocrine peptides. Annu Rev Biochem 1984;53:665.

Farooqi IS, O'Rahilly S: Monogenic obesity in humans. Ann Rev Med 2005;56:443.

Miller WL: Molecular biology of steroid hormone biosynthesis. Endocr Rev 1988;9:295.

Nagatsu T: Genes for human catecholamine-synthesizing enzymes. Neurosci Res 1991;12:315.

Russell DW, Wilson JD: Steroid 5 alpha-reductase: two genes/two enzymes. Annu Rev Biochem 1994;63:25.

Russell J et al: Interaction between calcium and 1,25-dihydroxy-vitamin D_3 in the regulation of preproparathyroid hormone and vitamin D receptor mRNA in avian parathyroids. Endocrinology 1993;132:2639.

Steiner DF et al: The new enzymology of precursor processing endoproteases. J Biol Chem 1992;267:23435.

Hormone Action & Signal Transduction

Daryl K. Granner, MD

BIOMEDICAL IMPORTANCE

The homeostatic adaptations an organism makes to a constantly changing environment are in large part accomplished through alterations of the activity and amount of proteins. Hormones provide a major means of facilitating these changes. A hormone-receptor interaction results in generation of an intracellular signal that can either regulate the activity of a select set of genes, thereby altering the amount of certain proteins in the target cell, or affect the activity of specific proteins, including enzymes and transporter or channel proteins. The signal can influence the location of proteins in the cell and can affect general processes such as protein synthesis, cell growth, and replication, perhaps through effects on gene expression. Other signaling molecules—including cytokines, interleukins, growth factors, and metabolites—use some of the same general mechanisms and signal transduction pathways. Excessive, deficient, or inappropriate production and release of hormones and of these other regulatory molecules are major causes of disease. Many pharmacotherapeutic agents are aimed at correcting or otherwise influencing the pathways discussed in this chapter.

HORMONES TRANSDUCE SIGNALS TO AFFECT HOMEOSTATIC MECHANISMS

The general steps involved in producing a coordinated response to a particular stimulus are illustrated in Figure 42–1. The stimulus can be a challenge or a threat to the organism, to an organ, or to the integrity of a single cell within that organism. Recognition of the stimulus is the first step in the adaptive response. At the organismic level, this generally involves the nervous system and the special senses (sight, hearing, pain, smell, touch). At the organismic or cellular level, recognition involves physicochemical factors such as pH, O_2 tension, temperature, nutrient supply, noxious metabolites, and osmolarity. Appropriate recognition results in the release of one or more hormones that will govern generation of the necessary adaptive response. For purposes of this discussion, the hormones are categorized as

described in Chapter 41, ie, based on the location of their specific cellular receptors and the type of signals generated. Group I hormones interact with an intracellular receptor and group II hormones with receptor recognition sites located on the extracellular surface of the plasma membrane of target cells. The cytokines, interleukins, and growth factors should also be considered in this latter category. These molecules, of critical importance in homeostatic adaptation, are hormones in the sense that they are produced in specific cells, have the equivalent of autocrine, paracrine, and endocrine actions, bind to cell surface receptors, and activate many of the same signal transduction pathways employed by the more traditional group II hormones.

SIGNAL GENERATION

The Ligand-Receptor Complex Is the Signal for Group I Hormones

The lipophilic group I hormones diffuse through the plasma membrane of all cells but only encounter their specific, high-affinity intracellular receptors in target cells. These receptors can be located in the cytoplasm or in the nucleus of target cells. The hormone-receptor complex first undergoes an **activation reaction.** As shown in Figure 42–2, receptor activation occurs by at least two mechanisms. For example, glucocorticoids diffuse across the plasma membrane and encounter their cognate receptor in the cytoplasm of target cells. Ligand-receptor binding results in the dissociation of heat shock protein 90 (hsp90) from the receptor. This step appears to be necessary for subsequent nuclear localization of the glucocorticoid receptor. This receptor also contains nuclear localization sequences that assist in the translocation from cytoplasm to nucleus. The now activated receptor moves into the nucleus (Figure 42–2) and binds with high affinity to a specific DNA sequence called the **hormone response element (HRE).** In the case illustrated, this is a glucocorticoid response element, or GRE. Consensus sequences for HREs are shown in Table 42–1. The DNA-bound, liganded receptor serves as a high-affinity binding site

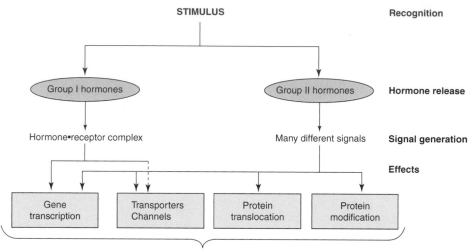

Figure 42–1. Hormonal involvement in responses to a stimulus. A challenge to the integrity of the organism elicits a response that includes the release of one or more hormones. These hormones generate signals at or within target cells, and these signals regulate a variety of biologic processes which provide for a coordinated response to the stimulus or challenge. See Figure 42–8 for a specific example.

for one or more coactivator proteins, and accelerated gene transcription typically ensues when this occurs. By contrast, certain hormones such as the thyroid hormones and retinoids diffuse from the extracellular fluid across the plasma membrane and go directly into the nucleus. In this case, the cognate receptor is already bound to the HRE (the thyroid hormone response element [TRE], in this example). However, this DNA-bound receptor fails to activate transcription because it exists in a corepressor complex. Indeed, this receptor-corepressor complex serves as an active repressor of gene transcription. The association of ligand with these receptors results in dissociation of the corepressor(s). The liganded receptor is now capable of binding one or more coactivators with high affinity, resulting in the activation of gene transcription. The relationship of hormone receptors to other nuclear receptors and to coregulators is discussed in more detail below.

By selectively affecting gene transcription and the consequent production of appropriate target mRNAs, the amounts of specific proteins are changed and metabolic processes are influenced. The influence of each of these hormones is quite specific; generally, the hormone affects less than 1% of the genes, mRNA, or proteins in a target cell; sometimes only a few are affected. The nuclear actions of steroid, thyroid, and retinoid hormones are quite well defined. Most evidence suggests that these hormones exert their dominant effect on

modulating gene transcription, but they—and many of the hormones in the other classes discussed below—can act at any step of the "information pathway" illustrated in Figure 42–3. Direct actions of steroids in the cytoplasm and on various organelles and membranes have also been described.

GROUP II (PEPTIDE & CATECHOLAMINE) HORMONES HAVE MEMBRANE RECEPTORS & USE INTRACELLULAR MESSENGERS

Many hormones are water-soluble, have no transport proteins (and therefore have a short plasma half-life), and initiate a response by binding to a receptor located in the plasma membrane (see Tables 41–3 and 41–4). The mechanism of action of this group of hormones can best be discussed in terms of the **intracellular signals** they generate. These signals include cAMP (cyclic AMP; 3′,5′-adenylic acid; see Figure 19–5), a nucleotide derived from ATP through the action of adenylyl cyclase; cGMP, a nucleotide formed by guanylyl cyclase; Ca^{2+}; and phosphatidylinositides. Many of these second messengers affect gene transcription, as described in the previous paragraph; but they also influence a variety of other biologic processes, as shown in Figure 42–1.

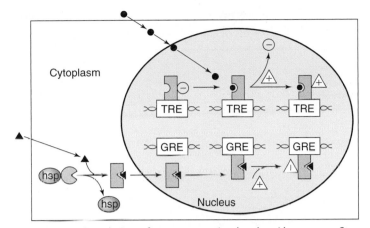

Figure 42–2. Regulation of gene expression by class I hormones. Steroid hormones readily gain access to the cytoplasmic compartment of target cells. Glucocorticoid hormones (solid triangles) encounter their cognate receptor in the cytoplasm, where it exists in a complex with heat shock protein 90 (hsp). Ligand binding causes dissociation of hsp and a conformational change of the receptor. The receptor·ligand complex then traverses the nuclear membrane and binds to DNA with specificity and high affinity at a glucocorticoid response element (GRE). This event triggers the assembly of a number of transcription coregulators (△), and enhanced transcription ensues. By contrast, thyroid hormones and retinoic acid (●) directly enter the nucleus, where their cognate receptors are already bound to the appropriate response elements with an associated transcription repressor complex (⊖). This complex, which consists of molecules such as N-CoR or SMRT (see Table 42–6) in the absence of ligand, actively inhibits transcription. Ligand binding results in dissociation of the repressor complex from the receptor, allowing an activator complex to assemble. The gene is then actively transcribed.

G Protein-Coupled Receptors (GPCR)

Many of the group II hormones bind to receptors that couple to effectors through a GTP-binding protein intermediary. These receptors typically have seven hydrophobic plasma membrane-spanning domains. This is illustrated by the seven interconnected cylinders extending through the lipid bilayer in Figure 42–4. Receptors of this class, which signal through guanine nucleotide-bound protein intermediates, are known as **G protein-coupled receptors,** or **GPCRs.** To date, over 130 G protein-linked receptor genes have been cloned from various mammalian species. A wide variety of responses are mediated by the GPCRs.

cAMP Is the Intracellular Signal for Many Responses

Cyclic AMP was the first intracellular signal identified in mammalian cells. Several components comprise a system for the generation, degradation, and action of cAMP.

A. Adenylyl Cyclase

Different peptide hormones can either stimulate (s) or inhibit (i) the production of cAMP from adenylyl cyclase, which is encoded by at least nine different genes (Table 42–2). Two parallel systems, a stimulatory (s) one and an inhibitory (i) one, converge upon a catalytic molecule (C). Each consists of a receptor, R_s or R_i, and a regulatory complex, G_s and G_i. G_s and G_i are each trimers composed of α, β, and γ subunits. Because the α subunit in G_s differs from that in G_i, the proteins, which are distinct gene products, are designated α_s and α_i. The α subunits bind guanine nucleotides. The β and γ subunits are always associated ($\beta\gamma$) and appear to function as a heterodimer. The binding of a hormone to R_s or R_i results in a receptor-mediated activation of G, which entails the exchange

Table 42–1. The DNA sequences of several hormone response elements (HREs).[1]

Hormone or Effector	HRE	DNA Sequence
Glucocorticoids	GRE	
Progestins	PRE	GGTACA NNN TGTTCT
Mineralocorticoids	MRE	$\longleftarrow \qquad \longrightarrow$
Androgens	ARE	
Estrogens	ERE	AGGTCA --- TGA/TCCT
		$\longleftarrow \qquad \longrightarrow$
Thyroid hormone	TRE	AGGTCA N3,4,5 AGGTCA
Retinoic acid	RARE	$\longrightarrow \qquad \longrightarrow$
Vitamin D	VDRE	
cAMP	CRE	TGACGTCA

[1]Letters indicate nucleotide; N means any one of the four can be used in that position. The arrows pointing in opposite directions illustrate the slightly imperfect inverted palindromes present in many HREs; in some cases these are called "half binding sites" because each binds one monomer of the receptor. The GRE, PRE, MRE, and ARE consist of the same DNA sequence. Specificity may be conferred by the intracellular concentration of the ligand or hormone receptor, by flanking DNA sequences not included in the consensus, or by other accessory elements. A second group of HREs includes those for thyroid hormones, estrogens, retinoic acid, and vitamin D. These HREs are similar except for the orientation and spacing between the half palindromes. Spacing determines the hormone specificity. VDRE (N = 3), TRE (N = 4), and RARE (N = 5) bind to direct repeats rather than to inverted repeats. Another member of the steroid receptor superfamily, the retinoid X receptor (RXR), forms heterodimers with VDR, TR, and RARE, and these constitute the *trans*-acting factors. cAMP affects gene transcription through the CRE.

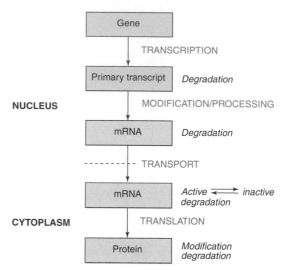

Figure 42–3. The "information pathway." Information flows from the gene to the primary transcript to mRNA to protein. Hormones can affect any of the steps involved and can affect the rates of processing, degradation, or modification of the various products.

of GDP by GTP on α and the concomitant dissociation of βγ from α.

The α_s protein has intrinsic GTPase activity. The active form, $\alpha_s \cdot$GTP, is inactivated upon hydrolysis of the GTP to GDP; the trimeric G_s complex (αβγ) is then re-formed and is ready for another cycle of activation. Cholera and pertussis toxins catalyze the ADP-ribosylation of α_s and α_{i-2} (see Table 42–3), respectively. In the case of α_s, this modification disrupts the intrinsic GTP-ase activity; thus, α_s cannot reassociate with βγ and is therefore irreversibly activated. ADP-ribosylation of α_{i-2} prevents the dissociation of α_{i-2} from βγ, and free α_{i-2} thus cannot be formed. α_s activity in such cells is therefore unopposed.

There is a large family of G proteins, and these are part of the superfamily of GTPases. The G protein family is classified according to sequence homology into four subfamilies, as illustrated in Table 42–3. There are 21 α, 5 β, and 8 γ subunit genes. Various combinations of these subunits provide a large number of possible αβγ and cyclase complexes.

The α subunits and the βγ complex have actions independent of those on adenylyl cyclase (see Figure 42–4 and Table 42–3). Some forms of α_i stimulate K[+] channels and inhibit Ca[2+] channels, and some α_s molecules have the opposite effects. Members of the G_q family activate the phospholipase C group of enzymes. The βγ complexes have been associated with K[+] channel stimulation and phospholipase C activation. G proteins are involved in many important biologic processes in addition to hormone action. Notable examples include olfaction (α_{OLF}) and vision (α_t). Some examples are listed in Table 42–3. GPCRs are implicated in a number of diseases and are major targets for pharmaceutical agents.

B. PROTEIN KINASE

In prokaryotic cells, cAMP binds to a specific protein called catabolite regulatory protein (CRP) that binds directly to DNA and influences gene expression. In eukaryotic cells, cAMP binds to a protein kinase called **protein kinase A (PKA)** that is a heterotetrameric molecule consisting of two regulatory subunits (R) and two catalytic subunits (C). cAMP binding results in the following reaction:

$$4\,cAMP + R_2C_2 \rightleftarrows R_2 \cdot (4\,cAMP) + 2C$$

The R_2C_2 complex has no enzymatic activity, but the binding of cAMP by R dissociates R from C, thereby activating the latter (Figure 42–5). The active

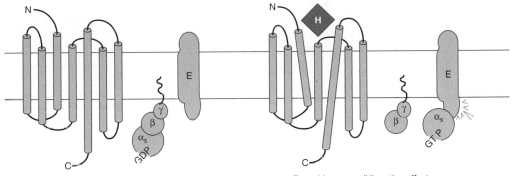

No hormone: inactive effector   Bound hormone (H): active effector

Figure 42–4. Components of the hormone receptor–G protein effector system. Receptors that couple to effectors through G proteins (GPCR) typically have seven membrane-spanning domains. In the absence of hormone (left), the heterotrimeric G-protein complex (α, β, γ) is in an inactive guanosine diphosphate (GDP)-bound form and is probably not associated with the receptor. This complex is anchored to the plasma membrane through prenylated groups on the βγ subunits (wavy lines) and perhaps by myristoylated groups on α subunits (not shown). On binding of hormone (⟨H⟩) to the receptor, there is a presumed conformational change of the receptor—as indicated by the tilted membrane spanning domains—and activation of the G-protein complex. This results from the exchange of GDP with guanosine triphosphate (GTP) on the α subunit, after which α and βγ dissociate. The α subunit binds to and activates the effector (E). E can be adenylyl cyclase, Ca^{2+}, Na^+, or Cl^- channels (α_s), or it could be a K^+ channel (α_i), phospholipase Cβ (α_q), or cGMP phosphodiesterase (α_t). The βγ subunit can also have direct actions on E. (Modified and reproduced, with permission, from Granner DK in: *Principles and Practice of Endocrinology and Metabolism*, 2nd ed. Becker KL [editor]. Lippincott, 1995.)

C subunit catalyzes the transfer of the γ phosphate of ATP to a serine or threonine residue in a variety of proteins. The consensus phosphorylation sites are -Arg-Arg/Lys-X-Ser/Thr- and Arg-Lys-X-X-Ser-, where X can be any amino acid.

Table 42–2. Subclassification of group II.A hormones.

Hormones That Stimulate Adenylyl Cyclase (H_s)	Hormones That Inhibit Adenylyl Cyclase (H_i)
ACTH	Acetylcholine
ADH	α_2-Adrenergics
β-Adrenergics	Angiotensin II
Calcitonin	Somatostatin
CRH	
FSH	
Glucagon	
hCG	
LH	
LPH	
MSH	
PTH	
TSH	

Protein kinase activities were originally described as being "cAMP-dependent" or "cAMP-independent." This classification has changed, as protein phosphorylation is now recognized as being a major regulatory mechanism. Several hundred protein kinases have now been described. The kinases are related in sequence and structure within the catalytic domain, but each is a unique molecule with considerable variability with respect to subunit composition, molecular weight, autophosphorylation, K_m for ATP, and substrate specificity.

C. PHOSPHOPROTEINS

The effects of cAMP in eukaryotic cells are all thought to be mediated by protein phosphorylation-dephosphorylation, principally on serine and threonine residues. The control of any of the effects of cAMP, including such diverse processes as steroidogenesis, secretion, ion transport, carbohydrate and fat metabolism, enzyme induction, gene regulation, synaptic transmission, and cell growth and replication, could be conferred by a specific protein kinase, by a specific phosphatase, or by specific substrates for phosphorylation. These substrates help define a target tissue and are involved in defining the extent of a particular response within a given cell. For example, the effects of cAMP on gene transcription are mediated by the protein **cyclic AMP response ele-**

Table 42–3. Classes and functions of selected G proteins.[1,2]

Class or Type	Stimulus	Effector	Effect
G_s			
α_s	Glucagon, β-adrenergics	↑Adenylyl cyclase ↑Cardiac Ca^{2+}, Cl^-, and Na^+ channels	Gluconeogenesis, lipolysis, glycogenolysis
α_{olf}	Odorant	↑Adenylyl cyclase	Olfaction
G_i			
$\alpha_{i-1,2,3}$	Acetylcholine, α_2-adrenergics	↓ Adenylyl cyclase ↑Potassium channels	Slowed heart rate
	M_2 cholinergics	↓ Calcium channels	
α_0	Opioids, endorphins	↑Potassium channels	Neuronal electrical activity
α_t	Light	↑cGMP phosphodiesterase	Vision
G_q			
α_q	M_1 cholinergics α_1-Adrenergics	↑Phospholipase C-β1	↑Muscle contraction and
α_{11}	α_1-Adrenergics	↑Phospholipase c-β2	↑Blood pressure
G_{12}			
α_{12}	?	Cl^- channel	?

[1]Modified and reproduced, with permission, from Granner DK in: *Principles and Practice of Endocrinology and Metabolism,* 2nd ed. Becker KL (editor). Lippincott, 1995.
[2]The four major classes or families of mammalian G proteins (G_s, G_i, G_q, and G_{12}) are based on protein sequence homology. Representative members of each are shown, along with known stimuli, effectors, and well-defined biologic effects. Nine isoforms of adenylyl cyclase have been identified (isoforms I–IX). All isoforms are stimulated by α_s; α_i isoforms inhibit types V and VI, and α_0 inhibits types I and V. At least 16 different α subunits have been identified.

ment binding protein (CREB). CREB binds to a cAMP responsive element (CRE) (see Table 42–1) in its nonphosphorylated state and is a weak activator of transcription. When phosphorylated by PKA, CREB binds the coactivator **CREB-binding protein CBP/p300** (see below) and as a result is a much more potent transcription activator.

D. PHOSPHODIESTERASES

Actions caused by hormones that increase cAMP concentration can be terminated in a number of ways, including the hydrolysis of cAMP to 5′-AMP by phosphodiesterases (see Figure 42–5). The presence of these hydrolytic enzymes ensures a rapid turnover of the signal (cAMP) and hence a rapid termination of the biologic process once the hormonal stimulus is removed. There are at least 11 known members of the phosphodiesterase family of enzymes. These are subject to regulation by their substrates, cAMP and cGMP; by hormones; and by intracellular messengers such as calcium, probably acting through calmodulin. Inhibitors of phosphodiesterase, most notably methylated xanthine derivatives such as caffeine, increase intracellular cAMP and mimic or prolong the actions of hormones through this signal.

E. PHOSPHOPROTEIN PHOSPHATASES

Given the importance of protein phosphorylation, it is not surprising that regulation of the protein dephosphorylation reaction is another important control mechanism (see Figure 42–5). The phosphoprotein phosphatases are themselves subject to regulation by phosphorylation-dephosphorylation reactions and by a variety of other mechanisms, such as protein-protein interactions. In fact, the substrate specificity of the phosphoserine-phosphothreonine phosphatases may be dictated by distinct regulatory subunits whose binding is regulated hormonally. The best-studied role of regulation by the dephosphorylation of proteins is that of glycogen metabolism in muscle. Two major types of phosphoserine-phosphothreonine phosphatases have been described. Type I preferentially dephosphorylates the β subunit of phosphorylase kinase, whereas type II dephosphorylates the α subunit. Type I phosphatase is implicated in the regulation of glycogen synthase, phosphorylase, and phosphorylase kinase. This phosphatase is itself regulated by phosphorylation of certain of its subunits, and these reactions are reversed by the action of one of the type II phosphatases. In addition, two heat-stable protein inhibitors regulate type I phosphatase activity. Inhibitor-1 is phosphorylated and activated

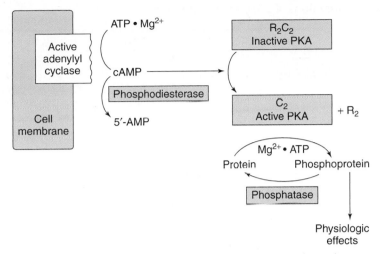

Figure 42–5. Hormonal regulation of cellular processes through cAMP-dependent protein kinase (PKA). PKA exists in an inactive form as an R_2C_2 heterotetramer consisting of two regulatory and two catalytic subunits. The cAMP generated by the action of adenylyl cyclase (activated as shown in Figure 42–4) binds to the regulatory (R) subunit of PKA. This results in dissociation of the regulatory and catalytic subunits and activation of the latter. The active catalytic subunits phosphorylate a number of target proteins on serine and threonine residues. Phosphatases remove phosphate from these residues and thus terminate the physiologic response. A phosphodiesterase can also terminate the response by converting cAMP to 5′-AMP.

by cAMP-dependent protein kinases; and inhibitor-2, which may be a subunit of the inactive phosphatase, is also phosphorylated, possibly by glycogen synthase kinase 3. Phosphatases that attack phosphotyrosine are also important in signal transduction (see Figure 42–8).

cGMP Is Also an Intracellular Signal

Cyclic GMP is made from GTP by the enzyme guanylyl cyclase, which exists in soluble and membrane-bound forms. Each of these isozymes has unique physiologic properties. The atriopeptins, a family of peptides produced in cardiac atrial tissues, cause natriuresis, diuresis, vasodilation, and inhibition of aldosterone secretion. These peptides (eg, atrial natriuretic factor) bind to and activate the membrane-bound form of guanylyl cyclase. This results in an increase of cGMP by as much as 50-fold in some cases, and this is thought to mediate the effects mentioned above. Other evidence links cGMP to vasodilation. A series of compounds, including nitroprusside, nitroglycerin, nitric oxide, sodium nitrite, and sodium azide, all cause smooth muscle relaxation and are potent vasodilators. These

agents increase cGMP by activating the soluble form of guanylyl cyclase, and inhibitors of cGMP phosphodiesterase (the drug sildenafil [Viagra], for example) enhance and prolong these responses. The increased cGMP activates cGMP-dependent protein kinase (PKG), which in turn phosphorylates a number of smooth muscle proteins. Presumably, this is involved in relaxation of smooth muscle and vasodilation.

Several Hormones Act Through Calcium or Phosphatidylinositols

Ionized calcium is an important regulator of a variety of cellular processes, including muscle contraction, stimulus-secretion coupling, the blood clotting cascade, enzyme activity, and membrane excitability. It is also an intracellular messenger of hormone action.

A. CALCIUM METABOLISM

The extracellular calcium (Ca^{2+}) concentration is about 5 mmol/L and is very rigidly controlled. Although substantial amounts of calcium are associated with intracellular organelles such as mitochondria and the endoplasmic reticulum, the intracellular concentration of free or ion-

ized calcium (Ca^{2+}) is very low: 0.05–10 μmol/L. In spite of this large concentration gradient and a favorable trans-membrane electrical gradient, Ca^{2+} is restrained from entering the cell. A considerable amount of energy is expended to ensure that the intracellular Ca^{2+} is controlled, as a prolonged elevation of Ca^{2+} in the cell is very toxic. A Na^+/Ca^{2+} exchange mechanism that has a high capacity but low affinity pumps Ca^{2+} out of cells. There also is a Ca^{2+}/proton ATPase-dependent pump that extrudes Ca^{2+} in exchange for H^+. This has a high affinity for Ca^{2+} but a low capacity and is probably responsible for fine-tuning cytosolic Ca^{2+}. Furthermore, Ca^{2+} ATPases pump Ca^{2+} from the cytosol to the lumen of the endoplasmic reticulum. There are three ways of changing cytosolic Ca^{2+}: (1) Certain hormones (class II.C, Table 41–3) by binding to receptors that are themselves Ca^{2+} channels, enhance membrane permeability to Ca^{2+} and thereby increase Ca^{2+} influx. (2) Hormones also indirectly promote Ca^{2+} influx by modulating the membrane potential at the plasma membrane. Membrane depolarization opens voltage-gated Ca^{2+} channels and allows for Ca^{2+} influx. (3) Ca^{2+} can be mobilized from the endoplasmic reticulum, and possibly from mitochondrial pools.

An important observation linking Ca^{2+} to hormone action involved the definition of the intracellular targets of Ca^{2+} action. The discovery of a Ca^{2+}-dependent regulator of phosphodiesterase activity provided the basis for a broad understanding of how Ca^{2+} and cAMP interact within cells.

B. CALMODULIN

The calcium-dependent regulatory protein is calmodulin, a 17-kDa protein that is homologous to the muscle protein troponin C in structure and function. Calmodulin has four Ca^{2+} binding sites, and full occupancy of these sites leads to a marked conformational change, which allows calmodulin to activate enzymes and ion channels. The interaction of Ca^{2+} with calmodulin (with the resultant change of activity of the latter) is conceptually similar to the binding of cAMP to PKA and the subsequent activation of this molecule. Calmodulin can be one of numerous subunits of complex proteins and is particularly involved in regulating various kinases and enzymes of cyclic nucleotide generation and degradation. A partial list of the enzymes regulated directly or indirectly by Ca^{2+}, probably through calmodulin, is presented in Table 42–4.

In addition to its effects on enzymes and ion transport, Ca^{2+}/calmodulin regulates the activity of many structural elements in cells. These include the actin-myosin complex of smooth muscle, which is under β-adrenergic control, and various microfilament-mediated processes in noncontractile cells, including cell motility, cell conformation changes, mitosis, granule release, and endocytosis.

Table 42–4. Enzymes and proteins regulated by calcium or calmodulin.

Adenylyl cyclase
Ca^{2+}-dependent protein kinases
Ca^{2+}-Mg^{2+} ATPase
Ca^{2+}-phospholipid-dependent protein kinase
Cyclic nucleotide phosphodiesterase
Some cytoskeletal proteins
Some ion channels (eg, L-type calcium channels)
Nitric oxide synthase
Phosphorylase kinase
Phosphoprotein phosphatase 2B
Some receptors (eg, NMDA-type glutamate receptor)

C. CALCIUM IS A MEDIATOR OF HORMONE ACTION

A role for Ca^{2+} in hormone action is suggested by the observations that the effect of many hormones is (1) blunted by Ca^{2+}-free media or when intracellular calcium is depleted; (2) can be mimicked by agents that increase cytosolic Ca^{2+}, such as the Ca^{2+} ionophore A23187; and (3) influences cellular calcium flux. The regulation of glycogen metabolism in liver by vasopressin and α-adrenergic catecholamines provides a good example. This is shown schematically in Figures 19–6 and 19–7.

A number of critical metabolic enzymes are regulated by Ca^{2+}, phosphorylation, or both, including glycogen synthase, pyruvate kinase, pyruvate carboxylase, glycerol-3-phosphate dehydrogenase, and pyruvate dehydrogenase.

D. PHOSPHATIDYLINOSITIDE METABOLISM AFFECTS Ca^{2+}-DEPENDENT HORMONE ACTION

Some signal must provide communication between the hormone receptor on the plasma membrane and the intracellular Ca^{2+} reservoirs. This is accomplished by products of phosphatidylinositol metabolism. Cell surface receptors such as those for acetylcholine, antidiuretic hormone, and $α_1$-type catecholamines are, when occupied by their respective ligands, potent activators of phospholipase C. Receptor binding and activation of phospholipase C are coupled by the G_q isoforms (Table 42–3 and Figure 42–6). Phospholipase C catalyzes the hydrolysis of phosphatidylinositol 4,5-bisphosphate to inositol trisphosphate (IP_3) and 1,2-diacylglycerol (Figure 42–7). Diacylglycerol is itself capable of activating **protein kinase C (PKC),** the activity of which also depends upon Ca^{2+}. IP_3, by interacting with a specific intracellular receptor, is an effective releaser of Ca^{2+} from intracellular storage sites in the endoplasmic reticulum. Thus, the hydrolysis of phosphatidylinositol 4,5-bisphosphate leads to activation of PKC and promotes an increase of cyto-

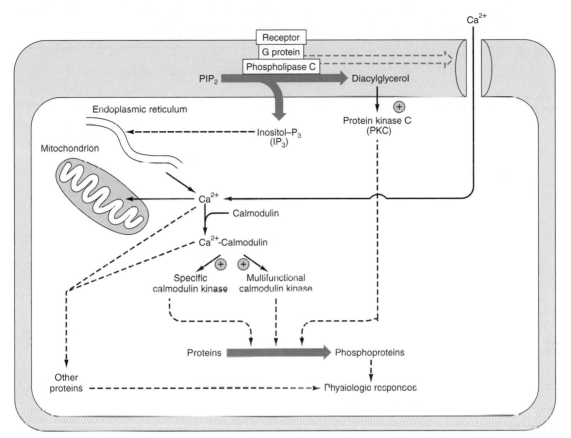

Figure 42–6. Certain hormone-receptor interactions result in the activation of phospholipase C. This appears to involve a specific G protein, which also may activate a calcium channel. Phospholipase C results in generation of inositol trisphosphate (IP$_3$), which liberates stored intracellular Ca^{2+}, and diacylglycerol (DAG), a potent activator of protein kinase C (PKC). In this scheme, the activated PKC phosphorylates specific substrates, which then alter physiologic processes. Likewise, the Ca^{2+}-calmodulin complex can activate specific kinases, two of which are shown here. These actions result in phosphorylation of substrates, and this leads to altered physiologic responses. This figure also shows that Ca^{2+} can enter cells through voltage- or ligand-gated Ca^{2+} channels. The intracellular Ca^{2+} is also regulated through storage and release by the mitochondria and endoplasmic reticulum. (Courtesy of JH Exton.)

plasmic Ca^{2+}. As shown in Figure 42–4, the activation of G proteins can also have a direct action on Ca^{2+} channels. The resulting elevations of cytosolic Ca^{2+} activate Ca^{2+}–calmodulin-dependent kinases and many other Ca^{2+}–calmodulin-dependent enzymes.

Steroidogenic agents—including ACTH and cAMP in the adrenal cortex; angiotensin II, K$^+$, serotonin, ACTH, and cAMP in the zona glomerulosa of the adrenal; LH in the ovary; and LH and cAMP in the Leydig cells of the testes—have been associated with increased amounts of phosphatidic acid, phosphatidylinositol, and polyphosphoinositides (see Chapter 15) in the respective target tissues. Several other examples could be cited.

The roles that Ca^{2+} and polyphosphoinositide breakdown products might play in hormone action are presented in Figure 42–6. In this scheme the activated protein kinase C can phosphorylate specific substrates, which then alter physiologic processes. Likewise, the Ca^{2+}-calmodulin complex can activate specific kinases. These then modify substrates and thereby alter physiologic responses.

Some Hormones Act Through a Protein Kinase Cascade

Single protein kinases such as PKA, PKC, and Ca^{2+}-calmodulin (CaM)-kinases, which result in the phos-

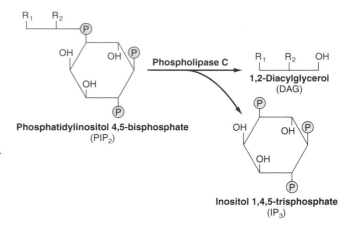

Figure 42–7. Phospholipase C cleaves PIP_2 into diacylglycerol and inositol trisphosphate. R_1 generally is stearate, and R_2 is usually arachidonate. IP_3 can be dephosphorylated (to the inactive $I-1,4-P_2$) or phosphorylated (to the potentially active $I-1,3,4,5-P_4$).

phorylation of serine and threonine residues in target proteins, play a very important role in hormone action. The discovery that the EGF receptor contains an intrinsic tyrosine kinase activity that is activated by the binding of the ligand EGF was an important breakthrough. The insulin and IGF-I receptors also contain intrinsic ligand-activated tyrosine kinase activity. Several receptors—generally those involved in binding ligands involved in growth control, differentiation, and the inflammatory response—either have intrinsic tyrosine kinase activity or are associated with proteins that are tyrosine kinases. Another distinguishing feature of this class of hormone action is that these kinases preferentially phosphorylate tyrosine residues, and tyrosine phosphorylation is infrequent (< 0.03% of total amino acid phosphorylation) in mammalian cells. A third distinguishing feature is that the ligand-receptor interaction that results in a tyrosine phosphorylation event initiates a cascade that may involve several protein kinases, phosphatases, and other regulatory proteins.

A. INSULIN TRANSMITS SIGNALS BY SEVERAL KINASE CASCADES

The insulin, epidermal growth factor (EGF), and IGF-I receptors have intrinsic protein tyrosine kinase activities located in their cytoplasmic domains. These activities are stimulated when the receptor binds ligand. The receptors are then autophosphorylated on tyrosine residues, and this initiates a complex series of events (summarized in simplified fashion in Figure 42–8). The phosphorylated insulin receptor next phosphorylates insulin receptor substrates (there are at least four of these molecules, called IRS 1–4) on tyrosine residues. Phosphorylated IRS binds to the Src homology 2 (SH2) domains of a variety of proteins that are directly involved in mediating different effects of insulin. One of these proteins, PI-3 kinase, links insulin receptor activation to insulin action through activation of a

number of molecules, including the kinase PDK1 (phosphoinositide-dependent kinase-1). This enzyme propagates the signal through several other kinases, including PKB (akt), SKG, and aPKC (see legend to Figure 42–8 for definitions and expanded abbreviations). An alternative pathway downstream from PKD1 involves p70S6K and perhaps other as yet unidentified kinases. A second major pathway involves mTOR. This enzyme is directly regulated by amino acids and insulin and is essential for p70S6K activity. This pathway provides a distinction between the PKB and p70S6K branches downstream from PKD1. These pathways are involved in protein translocation, enzyme activity, and the regulation, by insulin, of genes involved in metabolism (Figure 42–8). Another SH2 domain-containing protein is GRB2, which binds to IRS-1 and links tyrosine phosphorylation to several proteins, the result of which is activation of a cascade of threonine and serine kinases. A pathway showing how this insulin-receptor interaction activates the mitogen-activated protein (MAP) kinase pathway and the anabolic effects of insulin is illustrated in Figure 42–8. The exact roles of many of these docking proteins, kinases, and phosphatases remain to be established.

B. THE JAK/STAT PATHWAY IS USED BY HORMONES AND CYTOKINES

Tyrosine kinase activation can also initiate a phosphorylation and dephosphorylation cascade that involves the action of several other protein kinases and the counterbalancing actions of phosphatases. Two mechanisms are employed to initiate this cascade. Some hormones, such as growth hormone, prolactin, erythropoietin, and the cytokines, initiate their action by activating a tyrosine kinase, but this activity is not an integral part of the hormone receptor. The hormone-receptor interaction promotes binding and activation of **cytoplasmic protein tyrosine kinases,** such as **Tyk-2, Jak1,** or **Jak2.**

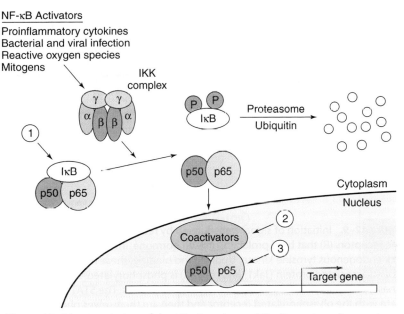

Figure 42–10. Regulation of the NF-κB pathway. NF-κB consists of two sub-units, p50 and p65, which regulate transcription of many genes when in the nucleus. NF-κB is restricted from entering the nucleus by IκB, an inhibitor of NF-κB. IκB binds to—and masks—the nuclear localization signal of NF-κB. This cytoplasmic protein is phosphorylated by an IKK complex which is activated by cytokines, reactive oxygen species, and mitogens. Phosphorylated IκB can be ubiquitinylated and degraded, thus releasing its hold on NF-κB. Glucocorti-coids affect many steps in this process, as described in the text.

HORMONES CAN INFLUENCE SPECIFIC BIOLOGIC EFFECTS BY MODULATING TRANSCRIPTION

The signals generated as described above have to be trans-lated into an action that allows the cell to effectively adapt to a challenge (Figure 42–1). Much of this adaptation is accomplished through alterations in the rates of transcrip-tion of specific genes. Many different observations have led to the current view of how hormones affect transcrip-tion. Some of these are as follows: (1) Actively transcribed genes are in regions of "open" chromatin (defined by a susceptibility to the enzyme DNase I), which allows for the access of transcription factors to DNA. (2) Genes have regulatory regions, and transcription factors bind to these to modulate the frequency of transcription initia-tion. (3) The hormone-receptor complex can be one of these transcription factors. The DNA sequence to which this binds is called a hormone response element (HRE; see Table 42–1 for examples). (4) Alternatively, other hormone-generated signals can modify the location, amount, or activity of transcription factors and thereby influence binding to the regulatory or response element.

(5) Members of a large superfamily of nuclear receptors act with—or in a manner analogous to—hormone recep-tors. (6) These nuclear receptors interact with another large group of coregulatory molecules to effect changes in the transcription of specific genes.

Several Hormone Response Elements (HREs) Have Been Defined

Hormone response elements resemble enhancer elements in that they are not strictly dependent on position and location. They generally are found within a few hundred nucleotides upstream (5′) of the transcription initiation site, but they may be located within the coding region of the gene, in introns. HREs were defined by the strategy illustrated in Figure 38–11. The consensus sequences illustrated in Table 42–1 were arrived at through analysis of several genes regulated by a given hormone using sim-ple, heterologous reporter systems (see Figure 38–10). Although these simple HREs bind the hormone-receptor complex more avidly than surrounding DNA—or DNA from an unrelated source—and confer hormone respon-siveness to a reporter gene, it soon became apparent that

Figure 42–11. The hormone response transcription unit. The hormone response transcription unit is an assembly of DNA elements and bound proteins that interact, through protein-protein interactions, with a number of coactivator or corepressor molecules. An essential component is the hormone response element which binds the ligand (▲)-bound receptor (R). Also important are the accessory factor elements (AFEs) with bound transcription factors. More than two dozen of these accessory factors (AFs), which are often members of the nuclear receptor superfamily, have been linked to hormone effects on transcription. The AFs can interact with each other, with the liganded nuclear receptors, or with coregulators. These components communicate with the basal transcription complex through a coregulator complex that can consist of one or more members of the p160, corepressor, mediator-related, or CBP/p300 families (see Table 42–6).

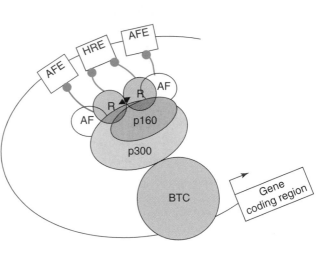

the regulatory circuitry of natural genes must be much more complicated. Glucocorticoids, progestins, mineralocorticoids, and androgens have vastly different physiologic actions. How could the specificity required for these effects be achieved through regulation of gene expression by the same HRE (Table 42–1)? Questions like this have led to experiments which have allowed for elaboration of a very complex model of transcription regulation. For example, the HRE must associate with other DNA elements (and associated binding proteins) to function optimally. The extensive sequence similarity noted between steroid hormone receptors, particularly in their DNA-binding domains, led to discovery of the **nuclear receptor superfamily** of proteins. These—and a large number of **coregulator proteins**—allow for a wide variety of DNA-protein and protein-protein interactions and the specificity necessary for highly regulated physiologic control. A schematic of such an assembly is illustrated in Figure 42–11.

There Is a Large Family of Nuclear Receptor Proteins

The nuclear receptor superfamily consists of a diverse set of transcription factors that were discovered because of a sequence similarity in their DNA-binding domains. This family, now with more than 50 members, includes the nuclear hormone receptors discussed above, a number of other receptors whose ligands were discovered after the receptors were identified, and many putative or orphan receptors for which a ligand has yet to be discovered.

These nuclear receptors have several common structural features (Figure 42–12). All have a centrally located **DNA-binding domain (DBD)** that allows the receptor

to bind with high affinity to a response element. The DBD contains two zinc finger binding motifs (see Figure 38–14) that direct binding either as homodimers, as heterodimers (usually with a retinoid X receptor [RXR] partner), or as monomers. The target response element consists of one or two DNA half-site consensus sequences arranged as an inverted or direct repeat. The spacing between the latter helps determine binding specificity. Thus, in general, a direct repeat with three, four, or five nucleotide spacer regions specifies the binding of the vitamin D, thyroid, and retinoic acid receptors, respectively, to the same consensus response element (Table 42–1). A multifunctional **ligand-binding domain (LBD)** is located in the carboxyl terminal half of the receptor. The LBD binds hormones or metabolites with selectivity and thus specifies a particular biologic response. The LBD also contains domains that mediate the binding of heat shock proteins, dimerization, nuclear localization, and transactivation. The latter function is facilitated by the carboxyl terminal transcription activation function **(AF-2 domain),** which forms a surface required for the interaction with coactivators. A highly variable **hinge region** separates the DBD from the LBD. This region provides flexibility to the receptor, so it can assume different DNA-binding conformations. Finally, there is a highly variable amino terminal region that contains another transactivation domain referred to as **AF-1.** Less well defined, the AF-1 domain may provide for distinct physiologic functions through the binding of different coregulator proteins. This region of the receptor, through the use of different promoters, alternative splice sites, and multiple translation initiation sites, provides for receptor isoforms that share DBD and LBD identity but exert different physiologic responses because of the asso-

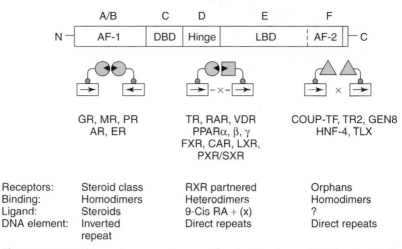

Figure 42–12. The nuclear receptor superfamily. Members of this family are divided into six structural domains (A–F). Domain A/B is also called AF-1, or the modulator region, because it is involved in activating transcription. The C domain consists of the DNA-binding domain (DBD). The D region contains the hinge, which provides flexibility between the DBD and the ligand-binding domain (LBD, region E). The amino (N) terminal part of region E contains AF-2, another domain important for transactivation. The F region is poorly defined. The functions of these domains are discussed in more detail in the text. Receptors with known ligands, such as the steroid hormones, bind as homodimers on inverted repeat half-sites. Other receptors form heterodimers with the partner RXR on direct repeat elements. There can be nucleotide spacers of one to five bases between these direct repeats (DR1–5). Another class of receptors for which ligands have not been determined (orphan receptors) bind as homodimers to direct repeats and occasionally as monomers to a single half-site.

ciation of various coregulators with this variable amino terminal AF-1 domain.

It is possible to sort this large number of receptors into groups in a variety of ways. Here they are discussed according to the way they bind to their respective DNA elements (Figure 42–12). Classic hormone receptors for glucocorticoids (GR), mineralocorticoids (MR), estrogens (ER), androgens (AR), and progestins (PR) bind as homodimers to inverted repeat sequences. Other hormone receptors such as thyroid (TR), retinoic acid (RAR), and vitamin D (VDR) and receptors that bind various metabolite ligands such as PPAR α, β, and γ, FXR, LXR, PXR/SXR, and CAR bind as heterodimers, with retinoid X receptor (RXR) as a partner, to direct repeat sequences (see Figure 42–12 and Table 42–5). Another group of orphan receptors that as yet have no known ligand bind as homodimers or monomers to direct repeat sequences.

As illustrated in Table 42–5, the discovery of the nuclear receptor superfamily has led to an important understanding of how a variety of metabolites and xenobiotics regulate gene expression and thus the metabolism, detoxification, and elimination of normal body products and exogenous agents such as pharmaceuticals. Not surprisingly, this area is a fertile field for investigation of new therapeutic interventions.

A Large Number of Nuclear Receptor Coregulators Also Participate in Regulating Transcription

Chromatin remodeling, transcription factor modification by various enzyme activities, and the communication between the nuclear receptors and the basal transcription apparatus are accomplished by protein-protein interactions with one or more of a class of coregulator molecules. The number of these coregulator molecules now exceeds 100, not counting species variations and splice variants. The first of these to be described was the **CREB-binding protein, CBP.** CBP, through an amino terminal domain, binds to phosphorylated serine 137 of CREB and mediates transactivation in response to cAMP. It thus is described as a coactivator. CBP and its close relative, p300, interact directly or indirectly with a number of signaling molecules, including activator pro-

Table 42–5. Nuclear receptors with special ligands.[1]

Receptor		Partner	Ligand	Process Affected
Peroxisome Proliferator- activated	PPARα PPARβ PPARγ	RXR (DR1)	Fatty acids Fatty acids Fatty acids Eicosanoids, thiazolidinediones	Peroxisome proliferation Lipid and carbohydrate metabolism
Farnesoid X	FXR	RXR (DR4)	Farnesol, bile acids	Bile acid metabolism
Liver X	LXR	RXR (DR4)	Oxysterols	Cholesterol metabolism
Xenobiotic X	CAR	RXR (DR5)	Androstanes Phenobarbital Xenobiotics	Protection against certain drugs, toxic metab- olites, and xenobiotics
	PXR	RXR (DR3)	Pregnanes Xenobiotics	

[1]Many members of the nuclear receptor superfamily were discovered by cloning, and the corresponding ligands were then identified. These ligands are not hormones in the classic sense, but they do have a similar function in that they activate specific members of the nuclear receptor superfamily. The receptors described here form heterodimers with RXR and have variable nucleotide sequences separating the direct repeat binding elements (DR1–5). These receptors regulate a variety of genes encoding cytochrome p450s (CYP), cytosolic binding proteins, and ATP-binding cassette (ABC) transporters to influence metabolism and protect cells against drugs and noxious agents.

tein-1 (AP-1), signal transducers and activators of transcription (STATs), nuclear receptors, and CREB (Figure 42–13). **CBP/p300** also binds to the p160 family of coactivators described below and to a number of other proteins, including viral transcription factor Ela, the p90rsk protein kinase, and RNA helicase A. It is important to note that **CBP/p300 also has intrinsic histone acetyltransferase (HAT) activity.** The importance of this is described below. Some of the many actions of

CBP/p300, which appear to depend on intrinsic enzyme activities and its ability to serve as a scaffold for the binding of other proteins, are illustrated in Figure 42–11. Other coregulators may serve similar functions.

Several other families of coactivator molecules have been described. Members of the **p160 family of coactivators,** all of about 160 kDa, include (1) SRC-1 and NCoA-1; (2) GRIP 1, TIF2, and NCoA-2; and (3) p/CIP, ACTR, AIB1, RAC3, and TRAM-1 (Table 42–6). The

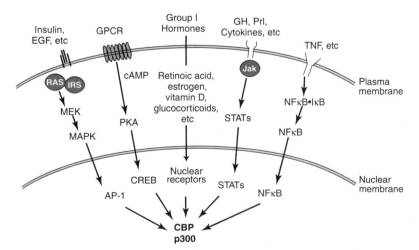

Figure 42–13. Several signal transduction pathways converge on CBP/p300. Ligands that associate with membrane or nuclear receptors eventually converge on CBP/p300. Several different signal transduction pathways are employed. EGF, epidermal growth factor; GH, growth hormone; Prl, prolactin; TNF, tumor necrosis factor; other abbreviations are expanded in the text.

Table 42–6. Some mammalian coregulator proteins.

I.	**300-kDa family of coactivators**	
	A. CBP	CREB-binding protein
	B. p300	Protein of 300 kDa
II.	**160-kDa family of coactivators**	
	A. SRC-1	Steroid receptor coactivator 1
	NCoA-1	Nuclear receptor coactivator 1
	B. TIF2	Transcriptional intermediary factor 2
	GRIP1	Glucocorticoid receptor-interacting protein
	NCoA-2	Nuclear receptor coactivator 2
	C. p/CIP	p300/CBP cointegrator-associated protein 1
	ACTR	Activator of the thyroid and retinoic acid receptors
	AIB	Amplified in breast cancer
	RAC3	Receptor-associated coactivator 3
	TRAM-1	TR activator molecule 1
III.	**Corepressors**	
	A. NCoR	Nuclear receptor corepressor
	B. SMRT	Silencing mediator for RXR and TR
IV.	**Mediator-related proteins**	
	A. TRAPs	Thyroid hormone receptor-associated proteins
	B. DRIPs	Vitamin D receptor–interacting proteins
	C. ARC	Activator-recruited cofactor

different names for members within a subfamily often represent species variations or minor splice variants. There is about 35% amino acid identity between members of the different subfamilies. The p160 coactivators share several properties. They (1) bind nuclear receptors in an agonist and AF-2 transactivation domain-dependent manner; (2) have a conserved amino terminal basic helix-loop-helix (bHLH) motif (see Chapter 38); (3) have a weak carboxyl terminal transactivation domain and a stronger amino terminal transactivation domain in a region that is required for the CBP/p160 interaction; (4) contain at least three of the **LXXLL motifs** required for protein-protein interaction with other coactivators; and (5) often have HAT activity. The role of HAT is particularly interesting, as mutations of the HAT domain disable many of these transcription factors. Current thinking holds that these HAT activities acetylate histones and result in remodeling of chromatin into a transcription-efficient environment; however, other protein substrates for HAT-mediated acetylation have been reported. Histone acetylation/deacetylation is proposed to play a critical role in gene expression.

A small number of proteins, including NCoR and SMRT, comprise the **corepressor family.** They function, at least in part, as described in Figure 42–2. Another family includes the TRAPs, DRIPs, and ARC (Table 42–6). These so-called **mediator-related proteins** range in size from 80 kDa to 240 kDa and are thought to be involved in linking the nuclear receptor-coactivator complex to RNA polymerase II and the other components of the basal transcription apparatus.

The exact role of these coactivators is presently under intensive investigation. Many of these proteins have intrinsic enzymatic activities. This is particularly interesting in view of the fact that acetylation, phosphorylation, methylation, sumoylation, and ubiquitination—as well as proteolysis and cellular translocation—have been proposed to alter the activity of some of these coregulators and their targets.

It appears that certain combinations of coregulators—and thus different combinations of activators and inhibitors—are responsible for specific ligand-induced actions through various receptors. Furthermore, these interactions on a given promoter are dynamic. In some cases, complexes consisting of as many as 47 transcription factors have been observed on a single gene.

SUMMARY

- Hormones, cytokines, interleukins, and growth factors use a variety of signaling mechanisms to facilitate cellular adaptive responses.

- The ligand-receptor complex serves as the initial signal for members of the nuclear receptor family.

- Class II hormones, which bind to cell surface receptors, generate a variety of intracellular signals. These include cAMP, cGMP, Ca^{2+}, phosphatidylinositides, and protein kinase cascades.

- Many hormone responses are accomplished through alterations in the rate of transcription of specific genes.

- The nuclear receptor superfamily of proteins plays a central role in the regulation of gene transcription.

- These receptors, which may have hormones, metabolites, or drugs as ligands, bind to specific DNA elements as homodimers or as heterodimers with RXR. Some—orphan receptors—have no known ligand but bind DNA and influence transcription.

- Another large family of coregulator proteins remodel chromatin, modify other transcription factors, and bridge the nuclear receptors to the basal transcription apparatus.

REFERENCES

Arvanitakis L et al: Constitutively signaling G-protein-coupled receptors and human disease. Trends Endocrinol Metab 1998;9:27.

Darnell JE Jr, Kerr IM, Stark GR: Jak-STAT pathways and transcriptional activation in response to IFNs and other extracellular signaling proteins. Science 1994;264:1415.

Fantl WJ, Johnson DE, Williams LT: Signalling by receptor tyrosine kinases. Annu Rev Biochem 1993;62:453.

Hanoune J, Defer N: Regulation and role of adenylyl cyclase isoforms. Annu Rev Pharmacol Toxicol 2001;41:145.

Jaken S: Protein kinase C isozymes and substrates. Curr Opin Cell Biol 1996;8:168.

Lee C-H, Olson P, Evans RM: Mini-review: Lipid metabolism, metabolic diseases and peroxisome proliferators-activated receptor. Endocrinology 2003;144:2201.

Lonard DM, O'Malley BW: Expanding functional diversity of the coactivators. Trends Biochem Sci 2005;30:126.

Montminy M: Transcriptional regulation by cyclic AMP. Annu Rev Biochem 1997;66:807

Morris AJ, Malbon CC: Physiological regulation of G protein-linked signaling. Physiol Rev 1999;79:1373.

Perissi V, Rosenfield MG: Controlling nuclear receptors: the circular logic of cofactor cycles. Nat Rev Mol Cell Biol 2005;6:542.

Walton KM, Dixon JE: Protein tyrosine phosphatases. Annu Rev Biochem 1993;62:101.

SECTION VI
Special Topics

Nutrition, Digestion, & Absorption

David A. Bender, PhD, & Peter A. Mayes, PhD, DSc

BIOMEDICAL IMPORTANCE

In addition to water, the diet must provide metabolic fuels (mainly carbohydrates and lipids), protein (for growth and turnover of tissue proteins), fiber (for bulk in the intestinal lumen), minerals (containing elements with specific metabolic functions), and vitamins and essential fatty acids (organic compounds needed in smaller amounts for other metabolic and physiologic functions). The polysaccharides, triacylglycerols, and proteins that make up the bulk of the diet must be hydrolyzed to their constituent monosaccharides, fatty acids, and amino acids, respectively, before absorption and utilization. Minerals and vitamins must be released from the complex matrix of food before they can be absorbed and utilized.

Globally, **undernutrition** is widespread, leading to impaired growth, defective immune systems, and reduced work capacity. By contrast, in developed countries, there is excessive food consumption (especially of fat), leading to obesity, and the development of cardiovascular disease and some forms of cancer. Deficiencies of vitamin A, iron, and iodine pose major health concerns in many countries, and deficiencies of other vitamins and minerals are a major cause of ill health. In developed countries nutrient deficiency is rare, although there are vulnerable sections of the population at risk. Intakes of minerals and vitamins that are adequate to prevent deficiency may be inadequate to promote optimum health and longevity.

Excessive secretion of gastric acid, associated with *Helicobacter pylori* infection, can result in the development of gastric and duodenal **ulcers;** small changes in the composition of bile can result in crystallization of

cholesterol as **gallstones;** failure of exocrine pancreatic secretion (as in **cystic fibrosis**) leads to undernutrition and steatorrhea. **Lactose intolerance** is the result of lactase deficiency, leading to diarrhea and intestinal discomfort. Absorption of intact peptides that stimulate antibody responses cause **allergic reactions** and **celiac disease** is an allergic reaction to wheat gluten.

DIGESTION & ABSORPTION OF CARBOHYDRATES

The digestion of carbohydrates is by hydrolysis to liberate oligosaccharides, then free mono- and disaccharides. The increase in blood glucose after a test dose of a carbohydrate compared with that after an equivalent amount of glucose is known as the **glycemic index.** Glucose and galactose have an index of 1, as do lactose, maltose, isomaltose, and trehalose, which give rise to these monosaccharides on hydrolysis. Fructose and the sugar alcohols are absorbed less rapidly and have a lower glycemic index, as does sucrose. The glycemic index of starch varies between near 1 to near 0 as a result of variable rates of hydrolysis, and that of nonstarch polysaccharides is 0. Foods that have a low glycemic index are considered to be more beneficial since they cause less fluctuation in insulin secretion.

Amylases Catalyze the Hydrolysis of Starch

The hydrolysis of starch is catalyzed by salivary and pancreatic amylases, which catalyze random hydrolysis of $\alpha(1\rightarrow4)$ glycoside bonds, yielding dextrins, then a mixture of glucose, maltose, and isomaltose (from the branchpoints in amylopectin).

Disaccharidases Are Brush Border Enzymes

The disaccharidases, maltase, sucrase-isomaltase (a bifunctional enzyme catalyzing hydrolysis of sucrose and isomaltose), lactase, and trehalase are located on the brush border of the intestinal mucosal cells, where the resultant monosaccharides and others arising from the diet are absorbed. In most people, apart from those of northern European origin, lactase is gradually lost through adolescence, leading to **lactose intolerance.** Lactose remains in the intestinal lumen, where it is a substrate for bacterial fermentation to lactate, resulting in discomfort and diarrhea.

There Are Two Separate Mechanisms for the Absorption of Monosaccharides in the Small Intestine

Glucose and galactose are absorbed by a sodium-dependent process. They are carried by the same transport protein (SGLT 1), and compete with each other for intestinal absorption (Figure 43–1). Other monosaccharides are absorbed by carrier-mediated diffusion. Because they are not actively transported, fructose and sugar alcohols are only absorbed down their concentration gradient, and after a moderately high intake, some may remain in the intestinal lumen, acting as a substrate for bacterial fermentation.

DIGESTION & ABSORPTION OF LIPIDS

The major lipids in the diet are triacylglycerols and, to a lesser extent, phospholipids. These are hydrophobic molecules, and have to be hydrolyzed and emulsified to very small droplets (micelles) before they can be absorbed. The fat-soluble vitamins, A, D, E, and K, and a variety of other lipids (including cholesterol) are absorbed dissolved in the lipid micelles. Absorption of the fat-soluble vitamins is impaired on a very low fat diet.

Hydrolysis of triacylglycerols is initiated by lingual and gastric lipases, which attack the *sn-3* ester bond forming 1,2-diacylglycerols and free fatty acids, aiding emulsification. Pancreatic lipase is secreted into the small intestine, and requires a further pancreatic protein, colipase, for activity. It is specific for the primary ester links—ie, positions 1 and 3 in triacylglycerols—resulting in 2-monoacylglycerols and free fatty acids as the major end products of luminal triacylglycerol digestion. Monoacylglycerols are poor substrates for hydrolysis, so that less than 25% of ingested triacylglycerol is completely hydrolyzed to glycerol and fatty acids (Figure 43–2). Bile salts, formed in the liver and secreted in the bile, permit emulsification of the products of lipid digestion into micelles together with phospholipids and cholesterol from the bile. Because the micelles are soluble, they allow the products of digestion, including the fat-soluble vitamins, to be transported through the aqueous environment of the intestinal lumen

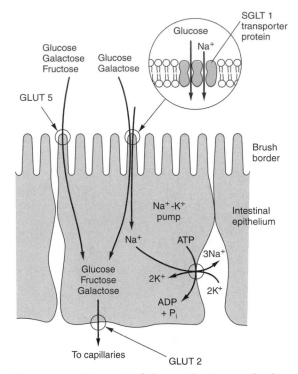

Figure 43–1. Transport of glucose, fructose, and galactose across the intestinal epithelium. The SGLT 1 transporter is coupled to the Na^+-K^+ pump, allowing glucose and galactose to be transported against their concentration gradients. The GLUT 5 Na^+-independent facilitative transporter allows fructose, as well as glucose and galactose, to be transported down their concentration gradients. Exit from the cell for all sugars is via the GLUT 2 facilitative transporter.

and permit close contact with the brush border of the mucosal cells, allowing uptake into the epithelium. The bile salts pass on to the ileum, where most are absorbed into the **enterohepatic circulation** (Chapter 26). Within the intestinal epithelium, 1-monoacylglycerols are hydrolyzed to fatty acids and glycerol and 2-monoacylglycerols are re-acylated to triacylglycerols via the **monoacylglycerol pathway.** Glycerol released in the intestinal lumen is not reutilized but passes into the portal vein; glycerol released within the epithelium is reutilized for triacylglycerol synthesis via the normal phosphatidic acid pathway (Chapter 24). Long-chain fatty acids are esterified to yield to triacylglycerol in the mucosal cells and together with the other products of lipid digestion, secreted as chylomicrons into the lymphatics, entering the bloodstream via the thoracic duct (Chapter 25). Short- and medium-chain fatty acids are mainly absorbed into the hepatic portal vein as free fatty acids.

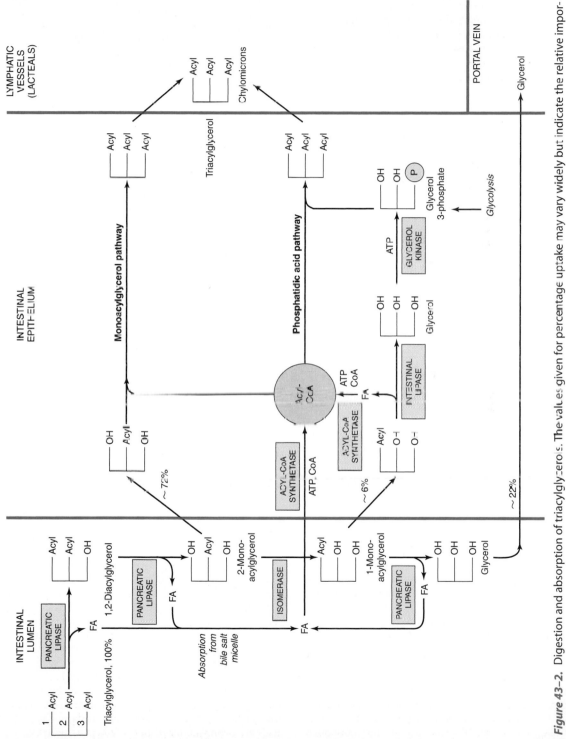

Figure 43–2. Digestion and absorption of triacylglycerols. The values given for percentage uptake may vary widely but indicate the relative importance of the three routes shown.

DIGESTION & ABSORPTION OF PROTEINS

Few bonds are accessible to the proteolytic enzymes that catalyze hydrolysis of peptide bonds, without prior denaturation of dietary proteins (by heat in cooking and by the action of gastric acid).

Several Groups of Enzymes Catalyze the Digestion of Proteins

There are two main classes of proteolytic digestive enzymes (**proteases**), with different specificities for the amino acids forming the peptide bond to be hydrolyzed. **Endopeptidases** hydrolyze peptide bonds between specific amino acids throughout the molecule. They are the first enzymes to act, yielding a larger number of smaller fragments: eg, pepsin in the gastric juice; trypsin, chymotrypsin, and elastase secreted into the small intestine by the pancreas. **Exopeptidases** catalyze the hydrolysis of peptide bonds, one at a time, from the ends of peptides. **Carboxypeptidases,** secreted in the pancreatic juice, release amino acids from the free carboxyl terminal; **aminopeptidases,** secreted by the intestinal mucosal cells, release amino acids from the amino terminal. **Dipeptidases** in the brush border of intestinal mucosal cells catalyze the hydrolysis of dipeptides, which are not substrates for amino- and carboxypeptidases.

The proteases are secreted as inactive **zymogens;** the active site of the enzyme is masked by a small region of the peptide chain that is removed by hydrolysis of a specific peptide bond. Pepsinogen is activated to pepsin by gastric acid and by activated pepsin (autocatalysis). In the small intestine, trypsinogen, the precursor of trypsin, is activated by enteropeptidase, which is secreted by the duodenal epithelial cells; trypsin can then activate chymotrypsinogen to chymotrypsin, proelastase to elastase, procarboxypeptidase to carboxypeptidase, and proaminopeptidase to aminopeptidase.

Free Amino Acids & Small Peptides Are Absorbed by Different Mechanisms

The end product of the action of endopeptidases and exopeptidases is a mixture of free amino acids, di- and tripeptides, and oligopeptides, all of which are absorbed. Free amino acids are absorbed across the intestinal mucosa by sodium-dependent active transport. There are several different amino acid transporters, with specificity for the nature of the amino acid side-chain (large or small, neutral, acidic or basic). The various amino acids carried by any one transporter compete with each other for absorption and tissue uptake. Dipeptides and tripeptides enter the brush border of the intestinal mucosal cells, where they are hydrolyzed to free amino acids, which are then transported into the hepatic portal vein.

Relatively large peptides may be absorbed intact, either by uptake into mucosal epithelial cells (transcellular) or by passing between epithelial cells (paracellular). Many such peptides are large enough to stimulate antibody formation—this is the basis of allergic reactions to foods.

DIGESTION & ABSORPTION OF VITAMINS & MINERALS

Vitamins and minerals are released from food during digestion, although this is not complete, and the availability of vitamins and minerals depends on the type of food and, especially for minerals, the presence of chelating compounds. The fat-soluble vitamins are absorbed in the lipid micelles that are the result of fat digestion; water-soluble vitamins and most mineral salts are absorbed from the small intestine either by active transport or by carrier-mediated diffusion followed by binding to intracellular proteins to achieve concentrative uptake. Vitamin B_{12} absorption requires a specific transport protein, intrinsic factor; calcium absorption is dependent on vitamin D; zinc absorption probably requires a zinc-binding ligand secreted by the exocrine pancreas, and the absorption of iron is limited.

Calcium Absorption Is Dependent on Vitamin D

In addition to its role in regulating calcium homeostasis, vitamin D is required for the intestinal absorption of calcium. Synthesis of the intracellular calcium binding protein, **calbindin,** required for calcium absorption, is induced by vitamin D, which also affects the permeability of the mucosal cells to calcium, an effect that is rapid and independent of protein synthesis.

Phytic acid (inositol hexaphosphate) in cereals binds calcium in the intestinal lumen, preventing its absorption. Other minerals, including zinc, are also chelated by phytate. This is mainly a problem among people who consume large amounts of unleavened wholewheat products; yeast contains an enzyme, **phytase,** that dephosphorylates phytate, so rendering it inactive. High concentrations of fatty acids in the intestinal lumen, as a result of impaired fat absorption, can also reduce calcium absorption, by forming insoluble calcium salts; a high intake of oxalate can sometimes cause deficiency, since calcium oxalate is insoluble.

Iron Absorption Is Limited and Strictly Controlled, but Enhanced by Vitamin C and Alcohol

Although iron deficiency is a common problem, about 10% of the population are genetically at risk of iron overload (**hemochromatosis),** and in order to reduce the risk of adverse effects of nonenzymic generation of free radi-

cals by elemental iron, absorption is strictly regulated. Inorganic iron is accumulated in intestinal mucosal cells bound to an intracellular protein, **ferritin.** Once the ferritin in the cell is saturated with iron, no more can enter. Iron can leave the mucosal cell only if there is **transferrin** in plasma to bind to. Once transferrin is saturated with iron, any that has accumulated in the mucosal cells is lost when the cells are shed. As a result of this mucosal barrier, only about 10% of dietary iron is absorbed, and only 1–5% from many plant foods (Chapter 50).

Inorganic iron is absorbed in the Fe^{2+} (reduced) state, hence the presence of reducing agents enhances absorption. The most effective compound is **vitamin C,** and while intakes of 40–80 mg of vitamin C/day are more than adequate to meet requirements, an intake of 25–50 mg per meal enhances iron absorption, especially when iron salts are used to treat iron deficiency anemia. Alcohol and fructose also enhance iron absorption. Heme iron from meat is absorbed separately, and is considerably more available than inorganic iron. However, the absorption of both inorganic and heme iron is impaired by calcium—a glass of milk with a meal significantly reduces availability.

ENERGY BALANCE: OVER- & UNDERNUTRITION

After the provision of water, the body's first requirement is for metabolic fuels—fats, carbohydrates, amino acids from proteins (Table 16–1). Food intake in excess of energy expenditure leads to **obesity,** while intake less than expenditure leads to emaciation and wasting, **marasmus,** and **kwashiorkor.** Both obesity and severe undernutrition are associated with increased mortality. The body mass index = weight (in kg)/height^2 (in m) is commonly used as a way of expressing relative obesity; a desirable range is between 20 and 25.

Energy Requirements Are Estimated by Measurement of Energy Expenditure

Energy expenditure can be determined directly by measuring heat output from the body, but is normally estimated indirectly from the consumption of oxygen. There is an energy expenditure of 20 kJ/liter of oxygen consumed, regardless of whether the fuel being metabolized is carbohydrate, fat, or protein (Table 16–1).

Measurement of the ratio of the volume of carbon dioxide produced:volume of oxygen consumed (**respiratory quotient, RQ**) is an indication of the mixture of metabolic fuels being oxidized (Table 16–1).

A more recent technique permits estimation of total energy expenditure over a period of 1–2 weeks, using dual isotopically labeled water, $^2H_2^{18}O$. ^2H is lost from the body only in water, while ^{18}O is lost in both water

and carbon dioxide; the difference in the rate of loss of the two labels permits estimation of total carbon dioxide production, and hence oxygen consumption and energy expenditure.

Basal metabolic rate (BMR) is the energy expenditure by the body when at rest, but not asleep, under controlled conditions of thermal neutrality, measured about 12 hours after the last meal, and depends on weight, age, and gender. Total energy expenditure depends on the basal metabolic rate, the energy required for physical activity and the energy cost of synthesizing reserves in the fed state. It is therefore possible to calculate an individual's energy requirement from body weight, age, gender, and level of physical activity. Body weight affects BMR because there is a greater amount of active tissue in a larger body. The decrease in BMR with increasing age, even when body weight remains constant, is the result of muscle tissue replacement by adipose tissue, which is metabolically less active. Similarly, women have a significantly lower BMR than do men of the same body weight because women's bodies contain proportionally more adipose tissue.

Energy Requirements Increase with Activity

The most useful way of expressing the energy cost of physical activities is as a multiple of BMR. Sedentary activities use only about 1.1–1.2 × BMR. By contrast, vigorous exertion, such as climbing stairs, cross-country walking uphill, etc, may use 6–8 × BMR.

Ten Percent of the Energy Yield of a Meal May Be Expended in Forming Reserves

There is a considerable increase in metabolic rate after a meal (**diet-induced thermogenesis**). A small part of this is the energy cost of secreting digestive enzymes and of active transport of the products of digestion; the major part is the result of synthesizing reserves of glycogen, triacylglycerol, and protein.

There Are Two Extreme Forms of Undernutrition

Marasmus can occur in both adults and children, and occurs in vulnerable groups of all populations. **Kwashiorkor** affects only children, and has been reported only in developing countries. The distinguishing feature of kwashiorkor is that there is fluid retention, leading to edema. Marasmus is a state of extreme emaciation; it is the outcome of prolonged negative energy balance. Not only have the body's fat reserves been exhausted, but there is wastage of muscle as well, and as the condition progresses there is loss of protein from the heart, liver, and kidneys. The amino acids released by the catabolism of tissue proteins are used as a source of metabolic

fuel and as substrates for gluconeogenesis to maintain a supply of glucose for the brain and red blood cells (Chapter 20). As a result of the reduced synthesis of proteins, there is impaired immune response and more risk from infections. Impairment of cell proliferation in the intestinal mucosa occurs, resulting in reduction in surface area of the intestinal mucosa, and reduction in absorption of such nutrients as are available.

Patients with Advanced Cancer and AIDS Are Malnourished

Patients with advanced cancer, HIV infection and AIDS, and a number of other chronic diseases are frequently undernourished, a condition called **cachexia.** Physically, they show all the signs of marasmus, but there is considerably more loss of body protein than occurs in starvation. The secretion of cytokines in response to infection and cancer increases the catabolism of tissue protein. This differs from marasmus, in which protein synthesis is reduced, but catabolism in unaffected. Patients are **hypermetabolic,** ie, a considerable increase in basal metabolic rate. Many tumors metabolize glucose anaerobically to release lactate. This is then used for gluconeogenesis in the liver, which is energy consuming with a net cost of 6 ATP for each mol of glucose cycled (see Figure 20–4). There is increased stimulation of **uncoupling proteins** by **cytokines** leading to thermogenesis and increased oxidation of metabolic fuels. Futile cycling of lipids occurs because hormone sensitive lipase is activated by a proteoglycan secreted by tumors resulting in liberation of fatty acids from adipose tissue and ATP-expensive reesterification to triacylglycerols in the liver, which are exported in VLDL.

Kwashiorkor Affects Undernourished Children

In addition to the wasting of muscle tissue, loss of intestinal mucosa and impaired immune responses seen in marasmus, children with **kwashiorkor** show a number of characteristic features. The defining characteristic is **edema,** associated with a decreased concentration of plasma proteins. In addition, there is enlargement of the liver as a result of accumulation of fat. It was formerly believed that the cause of kwashiorkor was a lack of protein, with a more or less adequate energy intake, however, analysis of the diets of affected children shows that this is not so. Children with kwashiorkor are less stunted than those with marasmus and the edema begins to improve early in treatment, when the child is still receiving a low protein diet.

Very commonly, an infection precipitates kwashiorkor. Superimposed on general food deficiency, there is probably a deficiency of the antioxidant nutrients such as zinc, copper, carotene, and vitamins C and E. The **respiratory burst** in response to infection leads to the production of oxygen and halogen **free radicals** as part of the cytotoxic action of stimulated macrophages. This added oxidant stress may well trigger the development of kwashiorkor.

PROTEIN & AMINO ACID REQUIREMENTS

Protein Requirements Can Be Determined by Measuring Nitrogen Balance

The state of protein nutrition can be determined by measuring the dietary intake and output of nitrogenous compounds from the body. Although nucleic acids also contain nitrogen, protein is the major dietary source of nitrogen and measurement of total nitrogen intake gives a good estimate of protein intake (mg $N \times 6.25$ = mg protein, as N is 16% of most proteins). The output of N from the body is mainly in urea and smaller quantities of other compounds in urine, undigested protein in feces; significant amounts may also be lost in sweat and shed skin. The difference between intake and output of nitrogenous compounds is known as **nitrogen balance.** Three states can be defined. In a healthy adult, nitrogen balance is in **equilibrium,** when intake equals output, and there is no change in the total body content of protein. In a growing child, a pregnant woman, or a person in recovery from protein loss, the excretion of nitrogenous compounds is less than the dietary intake and there is net retention of nitrogen in the body as protein—**positive nitrogen balance.** In response to trauma or infection, or if the intake of protein is inadequate to meet requirements, there is net loss of protein nitrogen from the body—**negative nitrogen balance.**

The continual catabolism of tissue proteins creates the requirement for dietary protein, even in an adult who is not growing; although some of the amino acids released can be reutilized, much is used for gluconeogenesis in the fasting state. Nitrogen balance studies show that the average daily requirement is 0.6 g of protein/kg body weight (0.75 allowing for individual variation), or approximately 50 g/day. Average intakes of protein in developed countries are of the order of 80–100 g/day, ie, 14–15% of energy intake. Because growing children are increasing the protein in the body, they have a proportionally greater requirement than adults and should be in positive nitrogen balance. Even so, the need is relatively small compared with the requirement for protein turnover. In some countries, protein intake may be inadequate to meet these requirements, resulting in stunting of growth.

There Is a Loss of Body Protein in Response to Trauma & Infection

One of the metabolic reactions to a major trauma, such as a burn, a broken limb, or surgery, is an increase in

the net catabolism of tissue proteins. As much as 6–7% of the total body protein may be lost over 10 days. Prolonged bed rest results in considerable loss of protein because of atrophy of muscles. Protein is catabolized as normal, but without the stimulus of exercise, it is not completely replaced. Lost protein is replaced during **convalescence,** when there is positive nitrogen balance. A normal diet is adequate to permit this replacement.

The Requirement Is Not Just for Protein, But for Specific Amino Acids

Not all proteins are nutritionally equivalent. More of some is needed to maintain nitrogen balance than others because different proteins contain different amounts of the various amino acids. The body's requirement is for amino acids in the correct proportions to replace the body proteins. The amino acids can be divided into two groups: **essential** and **nonessential.** There are nine essential or indispensable amino acids, which cannot be synthesized in the body: histidine, isoleucine, leucine, lysine, methionine, phenylalanine, threonine, tryptophan, and valine. If one of these is lacking or inadequate, then regardless of the total intake of protein, it will not be possible to maintain nitrogen balance, since there will not be enough of that amino acid for protein synthesis.

Two amino acids, cysteine and tyrosine, can be synthesized in the body, but only from essential amino acid precursors—cysteine from methionine and tyrosine from phenylalanine. The dietary intakes of cysteine and tyrosine thus affect the requirements for methionine and phenylalanine. The remaining 11 amino acids in proteins are considered to be nonessential or dispensable, since they can be synthesized as long as there is enough total protein in the diet. If one of these amino acids is omitted from the diet, nitrogen balance can still be maintained. However, only three amino acids, alanine, aspartate, and glutamate, can be considered to be truly dispensable; they are synthesized from common metabolic intermediates (pyruvate, oxaloacetate, and α-ketoglutarate respectively). The remaining amino acids are considered as nonessential, but under some circumstances the requirement may outstrip the capacity for synthesis.

SUMMARY

- Digestion involves hydrolyzing food molecules into smaller molecules for absorption through the gastrointestinal epithelium. Polysaccharides are absorbed as monosaccharides, triacylglycerols as 2-monoacylglycerols, fatty acids and glycerol, and proteins as amino acids.

- Digestive disorders arise as a result of (1) enzyme deficiency, eg, lactase and sucrase; (2) malabsorption, eg, of glucose and galactose as a result of defects in the Na^+-glucose cotransporter (SGLT 1); (3) absorption of unhydrolyzed polypeptides leading to immune responses, eg, as in celiac disease; and (4) precipitation of cholesterol from bile as gallstones.

- In addition to water, the diet must provide metabolic fuels (carbohydrate and fat) for body growth and activity, protein for synthesis of tissue proteins, fiber for roughage, minerals for specific metabolic functions, certain polyunsaturated fatty acids of the n-3 and n-6 families, and vitamins, organic compounds needed in small amounts for other essential functions.

- Twenty different amino acids are required for protein synthesis, of which nine are essential in the human diet. The quantity of protein required is affected by protein quality, energy intake, and physical activity.

- Undernutrition occurs in two extreme forms: marasmus, in adults and children, and kwashiorkor in children. Overnutrition is concerned with excess energy intake, and is associated with diseases such as obesity, non-insulin-dependent diabetes mellitus, atherosclerosis, cancer, and hypertension.

REFERENCES

Bender DA, Bender AE: *Nutrition: A Reference Handbook.* Oxford University Press, 1997.

Fuller MF, Garllick PJ: Human amino acid requirements: can the controversy be resolved? Ann Rev Nutr 1994;14:217.

Geissler C, Powers HJ: *Human Nutrition.* 11th edition. Elsevier, 2005.

Institute of Medicine: *Dietary Reference Intakes for Energy, Carbohydrate, Fiber, Fat, Fatty Acids, Cholesterol, Protein, and Amino Acids (Macronutrients).* National Academies Press, 2002.

Pencharz PB, Ball RO: Different approaches to define individual amino acid requirements. Ann Rev Nutr 2003;23:101.

Micronutrients: Vitamins & Minerals | 44

David A. Bender, PhD, & Peter A. Mayes, PhD, DSc

BIOMEDICAL IMPORTANCE

Vitamins are a group of organic nutrients, required in small quantities for a variety of biochemical functions that, generally, cannot be synthesized by the body and must therefore be supplied in the diet.

The lipid-soluble vitamins are hydrophobic compounds that can be absorbed efficiently only when there is normal fat absorption. Like other lipids, they are transported in the blood in lipoproteins or attached to specific binding proteins. They have diverse functions—eg, vitamin A, vision and cell differentiation; vitamin D, calcium and phosphate metabolism and cell differentiation; vitamin E, antioxidant; and vitamin K, blood clotting. As well as dietary inadequacy, conditions affecting the digestion and absorption of the lipid-soluble vitamins, such as steatorrhea and disorders of the biliary system, can all lead to deficiency syndromes, including night blindness and xerophthalmia (vitamin A); rickets in young children and osteomalacia in adults (vitamin D); neurologic disorders and hemolytic anemia of the newborn (vitamin E); and hemorrhage of the newborn (vitamin K). Toxicity can result from excessive intake of vitamins A and D. Vitamin A and the carotenes (many of which are precursors of vitamin A), and vitamin E are antioxidants and have possible roles in prevention of atherosclerosis and cancer.

The water-soluble vitamins are composed of the B vitamins and vitamin C; they function mainly as enzyme cofactors. Folic acid acts as a carrier of one-carbon units. Deficiency of a single vitamin of the B complex is rare, since poor diets are most often associated with **multiple deficiency states.** Nevertheless, specific syndromes are characteristic of deficiencies of individual vitamins, eg, beriberi (thiamin); cheilosis, glossitis, seborrhea (riboflavin); pellagra (niacin); megaloblastic anemia, methylmalonic aciduria, and pernicious anemia (vitamin B_{12}); megaloblastic anemia (folic acid); and scurvy (vitamin C).

Inorganic mineral elements that have a function in the body must be provided in the diet. When the intake is insufficient, deficiency signs may arise, eg, anemia (iron), and cretinism and goiter (iodine). If present in excess, then there may be signs of toxicity.

The Determination of Micronutrient Requirements Depends on the Criteria of Adequacy Chosen

For any nutrient, there is a range of intakes between that which is clearly inadequate, leading to **clinical deficiency disease,** and that which is so much in excess of the body's metabolic capacity that there may be signs of **toxicity.** Between these two extremes is a level of intake that is adequate for normal health and the maintenance of metabolic integrity. Individuals do not all have the same requirement for nutrients, even when calculated on the basis of body size or energy expenditure. There is a range of individual requirements of up to 25% around the mean. Therefore, in order to assess the adequacy of diets, it is necessary to set a reference level of intake high enough to ensure that no one either suffers from deficiency or is at risk of toxicity. If it is assumed that individual requirements are distributed in a statistically normal fashion around the observed mean requirement, then a range of $\pm 2 \times$ the standard deviation (SD) around the mean includes the requirements of 95% of the population. Reference intakes are therefore set at the average requirement plus $2 \times$ SD, and so meet or exceed the requirements of 97.5% of the population.

THE VITAMINS ARE A DISPARATE GROUP OF COMPOUNDS WITH A VARIETY OF METABOLIC FUNCTIONS

A vitamin is defined as an organic compound that is required in the diet in small amounts for the maintenance of normal metabolic integrity. Deficiency causes a specific disease, which is cured or prevented only by restoring the vitamin to the diet (Table 44–1). However, **vitamin D,** which is formed in the skin after exposure to sunlight, and **niacin,** which can be formed from the essential amino acid tryptophan, do not strictly comply with this definition.

Table 44–1. The vitamins.

	Vitamin	Functions	Deficiency disease
A	Retinol, β-carotene	Visual pigments in the retina; regulation of gene expression and cell differentiation (β-carotene is an antioxidant)	Night blindness, xerophthalmia; keratinization of skin
D	Calciferol	Maintenance of calcium balance; enhances intestinal absorption of Ca^{2+} and mobilizes bone mineral; regulation of gene expression and cell differentiation	Rickets = poor mineralization of bone; osteomalacia = bone demineralization
E	Tocopherols, tocotrienols	Antioxidant, especially in cell membranes; roles in cell signaling	Extremely rare—serious neurologic dysfunction
K	Phylloquinone: menaquinones	Coenzyme in formation of γ-carboxyglutamate in enzymes of blood clotting and bone matrix	Impaired blood clotting, hemorrhagic disease
B_1	Thiamin	Coenzyme in pyruvate and α-ketoglutarate dehydrogenases, and transketolase; regulates Cl^- channel in nerve conduction	Peripheral nerve damage (beriberi) or central nervous system lesions (Wernicke-Korsakoff syndrome)
B_2	Riboflavin	Coenzyme in oxidation and reduction reactions; prosthetic group of flavoproteins	Lesions of corner of mouth, lips, and tongue, seborrheic dermatitis
Niacin	Nicotinic acid, nicotinamide	Coenzyme in oxidation and reduction reactions, functional part of NAD and NADP; role in intracellular calcium regulation and cell signaling	Pellagra—photosensitive dermatitis, depressive psychosis
B_6	Pyridoxine, pyridoxal, pyridoxamine	Coenzyme in transamination and decarboxylation of amino acids and glycogen phosphorylase; modulation of steroid hormone action	Disorders of amino acid metabolism, convulsions
	Folic acid	Coenzyme in transfer of one-carbon fragments	Megaloblastic anemia
B_{12}	Cobalamin	Coenzyme in transfer of one-carbon fragments and metabolism of folic acid	Pernicious anemia = megaloblastic anemia with degeneration of the spinal cord
	Pantothenic acid	Functional part of CoA and acyl carrier protein: fatty acid synthesis and metabolism	Peripheral nerve damage (nutritional melalgia or "burning foot syndrome")
H	Biotin	Coenzyme in carboxylation reactions in gluconeogenesis and fatty acid synthesis; role in regulation of cell cycle	Impaired fat and carbohydrate metabolism, dermatitis
C	Ascorbic acid	Coenzyme in hydroxylation of proline and lysine in collagen synthesis; antioxidant; enhances absorption of iron	Scurvy—impaired wound healing, loss of dental cement, subcutaneous hemorrhage

■ LIPID-SOLUBLE VITAMINS

TWO GROUPS OF COMPOUNDS HAVE VITAMIN A ACTIVITY

Retinoids comprise **retinol, retinaldehyde,** and **retinoic acid** (preformed vitamin A, found only in foods of animal origin); carotenoids, found in plants, are composed of carotenes and related compounds; many are precursors of vitamin A, as they can be cleaved to yield retinaldehyde, then retinol and retinoic acid (Figure 44–1). The α-, β-, and γ-carotenes and cryptoxanthin are quantitatively the most important provitamin A carotenoids. Although it would appear that one molecule of β-carotene should yield two of retinol, this is not so in practice; 6 μg of β-carotene is equivalent to 1 μg of preformed retinol. The total amount of vitamin A in foods is therefore expressed as micrograms of retinol equivalents. β-Carotene and other provitamin A carotenoids are cleaved in the intestinal mucosa by carotene dioxygenase, yielding retinaldehyde, which is reduced to retinol, esterified and secreted in chylomicrons together

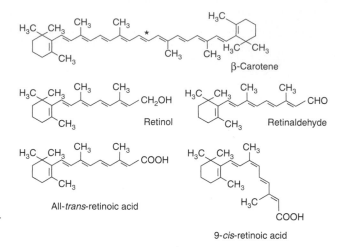

Figure 44–1. β-Carotene and the major vitamin A vitamers. Asterisk shows the site of cleavage of β-carotene by carotene dioxygenase, to yield retinaldehyde.

with esters formed from dietary retinol. The intestinal activity of carotene dioxygenase is low, so that a relatively large proportion of ingested β-carotene may appear in the circulation unchanged. While the principal site of carotene dioxygenase attack is the central bond of β-carotene, asymmetric cleavage may also occur, leading to the formation of 8'-, 10'-, and 12'-apo-carotenals, which are oxidized to retinoic acid, but cannot be used as sources of retinol or retinaldehyde.

Vitamin A Has a Function in Vision

In the retina, retinaldehyde functions as the prosthetic group of the light-sensitive opsin proteins, forming **rhodopsin** (in rods) and **iodopsin** (in cones). Any one cone cell contains only one type of opsin, and is sensitive to only one color. In the pigment epithelium of the retina, all-*trans*-retinol is isomerized to 11-*cis*-retinol and oxidized to 11-*cis*-retinaldehyde. This reacts with a lysine residue in opsin, forming the holo-protein rhodopsin. As shown in Figure 44–2, the absorption of light by rhodopsin causes isomerization of the retinaldehyde from 11-*cis* to all-*trans*, and a conformational change in opsin. This results in the release of retinaldehyde from the protein, and the initiation of a nerve impulse. The formation of the initial excited form of rhodopsin, bathorhodopsin, occurs within picoseconds of illumination. There is then a series of conformational changes leading to the formation of metarhodopsin II, which initiates a guanine nucleotide amplification cascade and then a nerve impulse. The final step is hydrolysis to release all-*trans*-retinaldehyde and opsin. The key to initiation of the visual cycle is the availability of 11-*cis*-retinaldehyde, and hence vitamin A. In deficiency, both the time taken to adapt to darkness and the ability to see in poor light are impaired.

Retinoic Acid Has a Role in the Regulation of Gene Expression and Tissue Differentiation

A major role of vitamin A is in the control of cell differentiation and turnover. All-*trans*-retinoic acid and 9-*cis*-retinoic acid (Figure 44–1) regulate growth, development, and tissue differentiation; they have different actions in different tissues. Like the thyroid and steroid hormones and vitamin D, retinoic acid binds to nuclear receptors that bind to response elements of DNA and regulate the transcription of specific genes. There are two families of nuclear retinoid receptors: the retinoic acid receptors (RAR) bind all-*trans*-retinoic acid or 9-*cis*-retinoic acid, and the retinoid X receptors (RXR) bind 9-*cis*-retinoic acid. Retinoid X receptors also form active dimers with a variety of other nuclear acting hormone receptors.

Vitamin A Deficiency Is a Major Public Health Problem Worldwide

Vitamin A deficiency is the most important preventable cause of blindness. The earliest sign of deficiency is a loss of sensitivity to green light, followed by impairment to adapt to dim light, followed by night blindness. More prolonged deficiency leads to **xerophthalmia:** keratinization of the cornea and blindness. Vitamin A also has an important role in differentiation of immune system cells, and even mild deficiency leads to increased susceptibility to infectious diseases. Also, the synthesis of retinol binding protein is reduced in response to infection (it is a negative **acute phase protein**), decreasing the circulating concentration of the vitamin, and further impairing immune responses.

Vitamin A Is Toxic in Excess

There is only a limited capacity to metabolize vitamin A, and excessive intakes lead to accumulation beyond

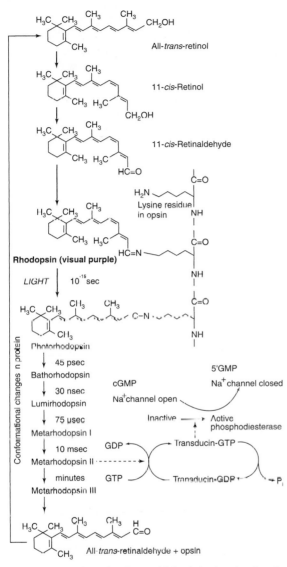

Figure 44–2. The role of retinaldehyde in the visual cycle.

the capacity of binding proteins, so that unbound vitamin A causes tissue damage. Symptoms of toxicity affect the central nervous system (headache, nausea, ataxia, and anorexia, all associated with increased cere-brospinal fluid pressure); the liver (hepatomegaly with histologic changes and hyperlipidemia); calcium homeostasis (thickening of the long bones, hypercalcemia, and calcification of soft tissues); and the skin (excessive dryness, desquamation, and alopecia).

VITAMIN D IS REALLY A HORMONE

Vitamin D is not strictly a vitamin, since it can be synthesized in the skin, and under most conditions that is the major source of the vitamin. Only when sunlight exposure is inadequate is a dietary source required. Its main function is in the regulation of calcium absorption and homeostasis; most of its actions are mediated by way of nuclear receptors that regulate gene expression. Deficiency, leading to rickets in children and osteomalacia in adults, continues to be a problem in northern latitudes, where sunlight exposure is inadequate.

Vitamin D Is Synthesized in the Skin

7-Dehydrocholesterol (an intermediate in the synthesis of cholesterol that accumulates in the skin) undergoes a nonenzymic reaction on exposure to ultraviolet light, yielding previtamin D (Figure 44–3). This undergoes a further reaction over a period of hours to form cholecalciferol, which is absorbed into the bloodstream. In temperate climates, the plasma concentration of vitamin D is highest at the end of summer and lowest at the end of winter. Beyond latitudes about 40° north or south there is very little ultraviolet radiation of the appropriate wavelength in winter.

Vitamin D Is Metabolized to the Active Metabolite, Calcitriol, in Liver & Kidney

Cholecalciferol, either synthesized in the skin or from food, undergoes two hydroxylations to yield the active metabolite, 1,25-dihydroxyvitamin D or calcitriol (Figure 44–4). Ergocalciferol from fortified foods undergoes similar hydroxylation to yield ercalcitriol. In the liver, cholecalciferol is hydroxylated to form the 25-hydroxy-derivative, calcidiol. This is released into the circulation bound to a vitamin D binding globulin, which is the main storage form of the vitamin. In the kidney, calcidiol undergoes either 1-hydroxylation to yield the active metabolite 1,25-dihydroxy-vitamin D (calcitriol), or 24-

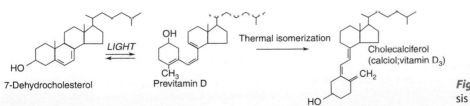

Figure 44–3. The synthesis of vitamin D in the skin.

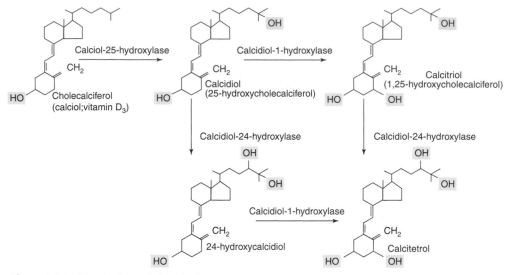

Figure 44–4. Metabolism of vitamin D.

hydroxylation to yield a probably inactive metabolite, 24,25-dihydroxyvitamin D (24-hydroxycalcidiol).

Vitamin D Metabolism Is Both Regulated by and Regulates Calcium Homeostasis

The main function of vitamin D is in the control of calcium homeostasis, and in turn, vitamin D metabolism is regulated by factors that respond to plasma concentrations of calcium and phosphate. Calcitriol acts to reduce its own synthesis by inducing the 24-hydroxylase and repressing the 1-hydroxylase in the kidney. The principal function of vitamin D is to maintain the plasma calcium concentration. Calcitriol achieves this in three ways: it increases intestinal absorption of calcium; it reduces excretion of calcium (by stimulating resorption in the distal renal tubules); and it mobilizes bone mineral. In addition, calcitriol is involved in insulin secretion, synthesis and secretion of parathyroid and thyroid hormones, inhibition of production of interleukin by activated T-lymphocytes and of immunoglobulin by activated B-lymphocytes, differentiation of monocyte precursor cells, and modulation of cell proliferation. In most of these actions, it acts like a steroid hormone, binding to nuclear receptors and enhancing gene expression, although it also has rapid effects on calcium transporters in the intestinal mucosa. For further details of the role of calcitriol in calcium homeostasis, see Chapter 47.

Vitamin D Deficiency Affects Children & Adults

In the vitamin D deficiency disease **rickets,** the bones of children are undermineralized as a result of poor absorption of calcium. Similar problems occur as a result of deficiency during the adolescent growth spurt. **Osteomalacia** in adults results from the demineralization of bone, especially in women who have little exposure to sunlight, often after several pregnancies. Although vitamin D is essential for prevention and treatment of osteomalacia in the elderly, there is little evidence that it is beneficial in treating **osteoporosis.**

Vitamin D Is Toxic in Excess

Some infants are sensitive to intakes of vitamin D as low as 50 μg/day, resulting in an elevated plasma concentration of calcium. This can lead to contraction of blood vessels, high blood pressure, and **calcinosis**—the calcification of soft tissues. Although excess dietary vitamin D is toxic, excessive exposure to sunlight does not lead to vitamin D poisoning, because there is a limited capacity to form the precursor, 7-dehydrocholesterol, and prolonged exposure of previtamin D to sunlight leads to formation of inactive compounds.

VITAMIN E DOES NOT HAVE A PRECISELY DEFINED METABOLIC FUNCTION

No unequivocal unique function for vitamin E has been defined. It acts as a lipid-soluble antioxidant in cell membranes, where many of its functions can be provided by synthetic antioxidants, and is important in maintaining the fluidity of cell membranes. It also has a (relatively poorly defined) role in cell signaling. Vitamin E is the generic descriptor for two families of compounds, the **tocopherols** and the **tocotrienols** (Figure 44–5). The different vitamers have different biologic

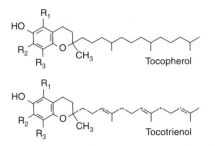

Figure 44–5. Vitamin E vitamers. In α-tocopherol and tocotrienol R_1, R_2, and R_3 are all —CH_3 groups. In the β-vitamers R_2 is H, in the γ-vitamers R_1 is H, and in the δ-vitamers R_1 and R_2 are both H.

potency; the most active is D-α-tocopherol, and it is usual to express vitamin E intake in terms of milligrams D-α-tocopherol equivalents. Synthetic DL-α-tocopherol does not have the same biologic potency as the naturally occurring compound.

Vitamin E Is the Major Lipid-Soluble Antioxidant in Cell Membranes and Plasma Lipoproteins

The main function of vitamin E is as a chain-breaking, free-radical trapping antioxidant in cell membranes and plasma lipoproteins by reacting with the lipid peroxide radicals formed by peroxidation of polyunsaturated fatty acids. The tocopheroxyl radical product is relatively unreactive, and ultimately forms nonradical compounds. Commonly, the tocopheroxyl radical is reduced back to tocopherol by reaction with vitamin C from plasma (Figure 44–6). The resultant monodehy-

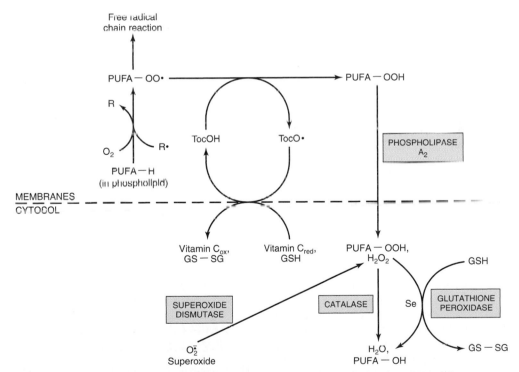

Figure 44–6. Interaction between antioxidants in the lipid phase (cell membranes) and the aqueous phase (cytosol). (R•, free radical; PUFA—OO•, peroxyl radical of polyunsaturated fatty acid in membrane phospholipid; PUFA-OOH, hydroxyperoxy polyunsaturated fatty acid in membrane phospholipid, released into the cytosol as hydroxyperoxy polyunsaturated fatty acid by the action of phospholipase A_2; PUFA-OH, hydroxy polyunsaturated fatty acid; Toc-OH vitamin E (α-tocopherol); TocO•, tocopheroxyl radical; Se, selenium; SSH, reduced glutathione; GS-SG, oxidized glutathione, which is reduced to GSH after reaction with NADPH, catalyzed by glutathione reductase; PUFA-H, polyunsaturated fatty acid).

droascorbate radical then undergoes enzymic or nonenzymic reaction to yield ascorbate and dehydroascorbate, neither of which is a radical.

The stability of the tocopheroxyl free radical means that it can penetrate further into cells and, potentially, propagate a chain reaction. Therefore, vitamin E may, like other antioxidants, also have pro-oxidant actions, especially at high concentrations. This may explain why, although studies have shown an association between high blood concentrations of vitamin E and lower incidence of atherosclerosis, trials of high doses of vitamin E have been disappointing.

Vitamin E Deficiency

In experimental animals, vitamin E deficiency results in resorption of fetuses and testicular atrophy. Dietary deficiency of vitamin E in humans is unknown, although patients with severe fat malabsorption, cystic fibrosis, and some forms of chronic liver disease suffer deficiency because they are unable to absorb the vitamin or transport it, exhibiting nerve and muscle membrane damage. Premature infants are born with inadequate reserves of the vitamin. The erythrocyte membranes are abnormally fragile as a result of peroxidation, leading to hemolytic anemia.

VITAMIN K IS REQUIRED FOR SYNTHESIS OF BLOOD CLOTTING PROTEINS

Vitamin K was discovered as a result of investigations into the cause of a bleeding disorder, hemorrhagic (sweet clover) disease of cattle and of chickens fed on a fat-free diet. The missing factor in the diet of the chickens was vitamin K, while the cattle feed contained **dicumarol,** an antagonist of the vitamin. Antagonists of vitamin K are used to reduce blood coagulation in patients at risk of thrombosis; the most widely used is **warfarin.**

Three compounds have the biological activity of vitamin K (Figure 44–7): **phylloquinone,** the normal dietary source, found in green vegetables; **menaquinones,** synthesized by intestinal bacteria, with differing lengths of side-chain; and **menadione** and menadiol diacetate, synthetic compounds that can be metabolized to phylloquinone. Menaquinones are absorbed to some extent, but it is not clear to what extent they are biologically active as it is possible to induce signs of vitamin K deficiency simply by feeding a phylloquinone-deficient diet, without inhibiting intestinal bacterial action.

Vitamin K Is the Coenzyme for Carboxylation of Glutamate in Postsynthetic Modification of Calcium Binding Proteins

Vitamin K is the cofactor for the carboxylation of glutamate residues in the post-synthetic modification of proteins to form the unusual amino acid γ-carboxy-

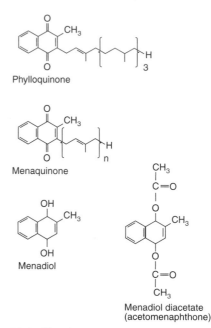

Figure 44–7. The vitamin K vitamers. Menadiol (or menadione) and menadiol diacetate are synthetic compounds that are converted to menaquinone in the liver.

glutamate (Gla) (Figure 44–8). Initially, vitamin K hydroquinone is oxidized to the epoxide, which activates a glutamate residue in the protein substrate to a carbanion, which reacts nonenzymically with carbon dioxide to form γ-carboxyglutamate. Vitamin K epoxide is reduced to the quinone by a warfarin-sensitive reductase, and the quinone is reduced to the active hydroquinone by either the same warfarin-sensitive reductase or a warfarin-insensitive quinone reductase. In the presence of warfarin, vitamin K epoxide cannot be reduced, but accumulates and is excreted. If enough vitamin K (as the quinone) is provided in the diet, it can be reduced to the active hydroquinone by the warfarin-insensitive enzyme, and carboxylation can continue, with stoichiometric utilization of vitamin K and excretion of the epoxide. A high dose of vitamin K is the antidote to an overdose of warfarin.

Prothrombin and several other proteins of the blood clotting system (Factors VII, IX, and X, and proteins C and S) each contain 4–6 γ-carboxyglutamate residues. γ-Carboxyglutamate chelates calcium ions, and so permits the binding of the blood clotting proteins to membranes. In vitamin K deficiency, or in the presence of warfarin, an abnormal precursor of prothrombin (preprothrombin) containing little or no γ-carboxyglutamate, and incapable of chelating calcium, is released into the circulation.

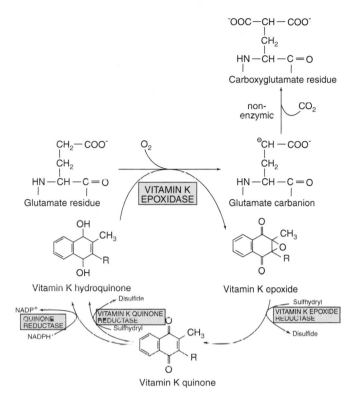

Figure 44–8. The role of vitamin K in the synthesis of γ-carboxyglutamate.

Vitamin K Is Also Important in Synthesis of Bone Calcium-Binding Proteins

Treatment of pregnant women with warfarin can lead to fetal bone abnormalities (fetal warfarin syndrome). Two proteins that contain γ-carboxyglutamate are present in bone, osteocalcin, and bone matrix Gla protein. Osteocalcin also contains hydroxyproline, so its synthesis is dependent on both vitamins K and C; in addition, its synthesis is induced by vitamin D. The release into the circulation of osteocalcin provides an index of vitamin D status.

■ WATER-SOLUBLE VITAMINS

VITAMIN B₁ (THIAMIN) HAS A KEY ROLE IN CARBOHYDRATE METABOLISM

Thiamin has a central role in energy-yielding metabolism, and especially the metabolism of carbohydrates (Figure 44–9). **Thiamin diphosphate** is the coenzyme for three multi-enzyme complexes that catalyze oxidative decarboxylation reactions: pyruvate dehydrogenase in carbohydrate metabolism (Chapter 17); α-ketoglu-

tarate dehydrogenase in the citric acid cycle (Chapter 17); and the branched-chain keto-acid dehydrogenase involved in the metabolism of leucine, isoleucine, and valine (Chapter 29). In each case, the thiamin diphosphate provides a reactive carbon on the thiazole moiety that forms a carbanion, which then adds to the carbonyl group of, for instance, pyruvate. The addition compound then decarboxylates, eliminating CO_2. Thiamin diphosphate is also the coenzyme for transketolase, in the pentose phosphate pathway (Chapter 21).

Thiamin triphosphate has a role in nerve conduction; it phosphorylates, and so activates, a chloride channel in the nerve membrane.

Thiamin Deficiency Affects the Nervous System & the Heart

Thiamin deficiency can result in three distinct syndromes: a chronic peripheral neuritis, **beriberi,** which may or may not be associated with **heart failure** and **edema;** acute pernicious (fulminating) beriberi (shoshin beriberi), in which heart failure and metabolic abnormalities predominate, without peripheral neuritis; and **Wernicke's encephalopathy** with **Korsakoff's psychosis,** which is associated especially with alcohol and narcotic abuse. The role of thiamin diphosphate in pyruvate dehydrogenase means that in deficiency there is impaired

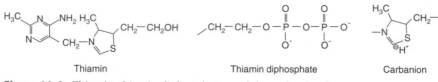

Figure 44–9. Thiamin, thiamin diphosphate, and the carbanion form.

conversion of pyruvate to acetyl CoA. In subjects on a relatively high carbohydrate diet, this results in increased plasma concentrations of lactate and pyruvate, which may cause life-threatening **lactic acidosis.**

Thiamin Nutritional Status Can Be Assessed by Erythrocyte Transketolase Activation

The activation of apo-transketolase (the enzyme protein) in erythrocyte lysate by thiamin diphosphate added in vitro has become the accepted index of thiamin nutritional status.

VITAMIN B$_2$ (RIBOFLAVIN) HAS A CENTRAL ROLE IN ENERGY-YIELDING METABOLISM

Riboflavin provides the reactive moieties of the coenzymes **flavin mononucleotide (FMN)** and **flavin adenine dinucleotide (FAD)** (Figure 44–10). FMN is formed by ATP-dependent phosphorylation of riboflavin, whereas FAD is synthesized by further reaction with ATP in which its AMP moiety is transferred to FMN. The main dietary sources of riboflavin are milk and dairy products. In addition, because of its intense yellow color, riboflavin is widely used as a food additive.

Flavin Coenzymes Are Electron Carriers in Oxidoreduction Reactions

These include the mitochondrial respiratory chain, key enzymes in fatty acid and amino acid oxidation, and the citric acid cycle. Reoxidation of the reduced flavin in oxygenases and mixed-function oxidases proceeds by way of formation of the flavin radical and flavin hydroperoxide, with the intermediate generation of superoxide and perhydroxyl radicals and hydrogen peroxide. Because of this, flavin oxidases make a significant contribution to the total oxidant stress in the body.

Riboflavin Deficiency Is Widespread But Not Fatal

Although riboflavin is centrally involved in lipid and carbohydrate metabolism, and deficiency occurs in many countries, it is not fatal, because there is very efficient conservation of tissue riboflavin. Riboflavin deficiency is characterized by cheilosis, desquamation and inflammation of the tongue, and a seborrheic dermatitis. Riboflavin nutritional status is assessed by measurement of the activation of erythrocyte glutathione reductase by FAD added in vitro.

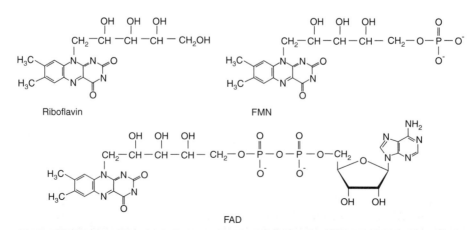

Figure 44–10. Riboflavin and the coenzymes flavin mononucleotide (FMN) and flavin adenine dinucleotide (FAD).

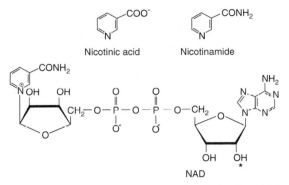

Figure 44–11. Niacin (nicotinic acid and nicotinamide) and nicotinamide adenine dinucleotide (NAD). Asterisk shows the site of phosphorylation in NADP.

NIACIN IS NOT STRICTLY A VITAMIN

Niacin was discovered as a nutrient during studies of **pellagra.** It is not strictly a vitamin since it can be synthesized in the body from the essential amino acid tryptophan. Two compounds, **nicotinic acid** and **nicotinamide,** have the biologic activity of niacin; its metabolic function is as the nicotinamide ring of the coenzymes **NAD** and **NADP** in oxidation/reduction reactions (Figure 44–11). Some 60 mg of tryptophan is equivalent to 1 mg of dietary niacin. The niacin content of foods is expressed as

mg niacin equivalents = mg preformed niacin
+ 1/60 × mg tryptophan

Because most of the niacin in cereals is biologically unavailable, this is discounted.

NAD Is the Source of ADP-Ribose

In addition to its coenzyme role, NAD is the source of ADP-ribose for the **ADP-ribosylation** of proteins and polyADP-ribosylation of nucleoproteins involved in the **DNA repair mechanism.**

Pellagra Is Caused by Deficiency of Tryptophan & Niacin

Pellagra is characterized by a photosensitive dermatitis. As the condition progresses, there is dementia and possibly diarrhea. Untreated pellagra is fatal. Although the nutritional etiology of pellagra is well established, and tryptophan or niacin prevents or cures the disease, additional factors, including deficiency of riboflavin or vitamin B_6, both of which are required for synthesis of nicotinamide from tryptophan, may be important. In most outbreaks of pellagra, twice as many women as men are affected, probably the result of inhibition of tryptophan metabolism by estrogen metabolites.

Pellagra Can Occur as a Result of Disease Despite an Adequate Intake of Tryptophan & Niacin

A number of genetic diseases that result in defects of tryptophan metabolism are associated with the development of pellagra, despite an apparently adequate intake of both tryptophan and niacin. **Hartnup disease** is a rare genetic condition in which there is a defect of the membrane transport mechanism for tryptophan, resulting in large losses as a result of intestinal malabsorption and failure of the renal resorption mechanism. In **carcinoid syndrome,** there is metastasis of a primary liver tumor of enterochromaffin cells, which synthesize 5-hydroxytryptamine. Overproduction of 5-hydroxytryptamine may account for as much as 60% of the body's tryptophan metabolism, causing pellagra because of the diversion away from NAD synthesis.

Niacin Is Toxic in Excess

Nicotinic acid has been used to treat hyperlipidemia when of the order of 1–6 g/day are required, causing dilatation of blood vessels and flushing, along with skin irritation. Intakes of both nicotinic acid and nicotinamide in excess of 500 mg/day also cause liver damage.

VITAMIN B_6 IS IMPORTANT IN AMINO ACID & GLYCOGEN METABOLISM & IN STEROID HORMONE ACTION

Six compounds have vitamin B_6 activity (Figure 44–12): **pyridoxine, pyridoxal, pyridoxamine,** and their 5'-phosphates. The active coenzyme is pyridoxal 5'-phosphate. Some 80% of the body's total vitamin B_6 is pyridoxal phosphate in muscle, mostly associated with glycogen phosphorylase. This is not available in deficiency, but is released in starvation, when glycogen reserves become depleted, and is then available, especially in liver and kidney, to meet increased requirement for gluconeogenesis from amino acids.

Vitamin B_6 Has Several Roles in Metabolism

Pyridoxal phosphate is a coenzyme for many enzymes involved in amino acid metabolism, especially transamination and decarboxylation. It is also the cofactor of glycogen phosphorylase, where the phosphate group is catalytically important. In addition, B_6 is important in steroid hormone action. Pyridoxal phosphate removes the hormone-receptor complex from DNA binding, terminating the action of the hormones. In vitamin B_6 deficiency, there is increased sensitivity to the actions of

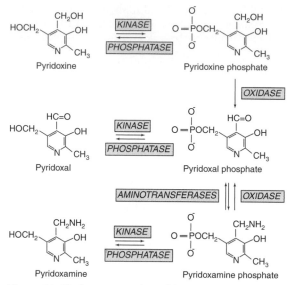

Figure 44–12. Interconversion of the vitamin B_6 vitamers.

low concentrations of estrogens, androgens, cortisol, and vitamin D.

Vitamin B_6 Deficiency Is Rare

Although clinical deficiency disease is rare, there is evidence that a significant proportion of the population have marginal vitamin B_6 status. Moderate deficiency results in abnormalities of tryptophan and methionine metabolism. Increased sensitivity to steroid hormone action may be important in the development of **hormone-dependent cancer** of the breast, uterus, and prostate, and vitamin B_6 status may affect the prognosis.

Vitamin B_6 Status Is Assessed by Assaying Erythrocyte Transaminases

The most widely used method of assessing vitamin B_6 status is by the activation of erythrocyte transaminases by pyridoxal phosphate added in vitro, expressed as the activation coefficient.

In Excess, Vitamin B_6 Causes Sensory Neuropathy

The development of sensory neuropathy has been reported in patients taking 2–7 g of pyridoxine per day for a variety of reasons (there is some slight evidence that it is effective in treating **premenstrual syndrome**). There was some residual damage after withdrawal of these high doses; other reports suggest that intakes in excess of 200 mg/d are associated with neurologic damage.

VITAMIN B_12 IS FOUND ONLY IN FOODS OF ANIMAL ORIGIN

The term "vitamin B_12" is used as a generic descriptor for the **cobalamins**—those **corrinoids** (cobalt-containing compounds possessing the corrin ring) having the biologic activity of the vitamin (Figure 44–13). Some corrinoids that are growth factors for microorganisms not only have no vitamin B_12 activity, but may also be antimetabolites of the vitamin. Although it is synthesized exclusively by microorganisms, for practical purposes vitamin B_12 is found only in foods of animal origin, there being no plant sources of this vitamin. This means that strict vegetarians (Vegans) are at risk of developing B_12 deficiency. The small amounts of the vitamin formed by bacteria on the surface of fruits may be adequate to meet requirements, but preparations of vitamin B_12 made by bacterial fermentation are available.

Vitamin B_12 Absorption Requires Two Binding Proteins

Vitamin B_12 is absorbed bound to **intrinsic factor,** a small glycoprotein secreted by the parietal cells of the gastric mucosa. Gastric acid and pepsin release the vita-

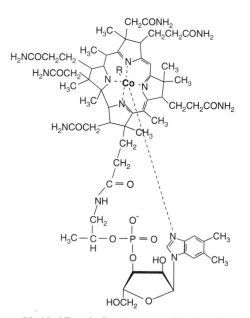

Figure 44–13. Vitamin B_12. Four coordination sites on the central cobalt atom are chelated by the nitrogen atoms of the corrin ring, and one by the nitrogen of the dimethylbenzimidazole nucleotide. The sixth coordination site may be occupied by: CN⁻ (cyanocobalamin), OH⁻ (hydroxocobalamin), H_2O (aquocobalamin, —CH_3 (methyl cobalamin) or 5'-deoxyadenosine (adenosylcobalamin).

min from protein binding in food and make it available to bind to **cobalophilin,** a binding protein secreted in the saliva. In the duodenum, cobalophilin is hydrolyzed, releasing the vitamin for binding to intrinsic factor. **Pancreatic insufficiency** can therefore be a factor in the development of vitamin B_{12} deficiency, resulting in the excretion of cobalophilin-bound vitamin B_{12}. Intrinsic factor binds only the active vitamin B_{12} vitamers and not other corrinoids. Vitamin B_{12} is absorbed from the distal third of the ileum via receptors that bind the intrinsic factor-vitamin B_{12} complex, but not free intrinsic factor or free vitamin.

There Are Three Vitamin B₁₂–Dependent Enzymes

Methylmalonyl CoA mutase, leucine aminomutase, and **methionine synthase** (Figure 44–14) are vitamin B_{12}–dependent enzymes. Methylmalonyl CoA is formed as an intermediate in the catabolism of valine and by the carboxylation of propionyl CoA arising in the catabolism of isoleucine, cholesterol, and, rarely, fatty acids with an odd number of carbon atoms or directly from propionate, a major product of microbial fermentation in the rumen. It undergoes a vitamin B_{12}–dependent rearrangement to succinyl CoA, catalyzed by methylmalonyl CoA mutase (Figure 20–2). The activity of this enzyme is greatly reduced in vitamin B_{12} deficiency, leading to an accumulation of methylmalonyl CoA and urinary excretion of methylmalonic acid, which provides a means of assessing vitamin B_{12} nutritional status.

Vitamin B₁₂ Deficiency Causes Pernicious Anemia

Pernicious anemia arises when vitamin B_{12} deficiency impairs the metabolism of folic acid, leading to func-

tional folate deficiency that disturbs erythropoiesis, causing immature precursors of erythrocytes to be released into the circulation (megaloblastic anemia). The most common cause of pernicious anemia is failure of the absorption of vitamin B_{12} rather than dietary deficiency. This can be the result of failure of intrinsic factor secretion caused by autoimmune disease affecting parietal cells or from production of anti-intrinsic factor antibodies.

THERE ARE MULTIPLE FORMS OF FOLATE IN THE DIET

The active form of folic acid (pteroyl glutamate) is tetrahydrofolate (Figure 44–15). The folates in foods may have up to seven additional glutamate residues linked by γ-peptide bonds. In addition, all of the one-carbon substituted folates in Figure 44–15 may also be present in foods. The extent to which the different forms of folate can be absorbed varies, and folate intakes are calculated as dietary folate equivalents – the sum of μg food folates + 1.7 × μg of folic acid (used in food enrichment).

Tetrahydrofolate Is a Carrier of One-Carbon Units

Tetrahydrofolate can carry one-carbon fragments attached to N-5 (formyl, formimino, or methyl groups), N-10 (formyl) or bridging N-5–N-10 (methylene or methenyl groups). 5-Formyl-tetrahydrofolate is more stable than folate, and is therefore used pharmaceutically (known as **folinic acid**), and the synthetic (racemic) compound (**leucovorin**). The major point of entry for one-carbon fragments into substituted folates is methylene-tetrahydrofolate (Figure 44–16), which is formed by the reaction of glycine, serine, and choline with tetrahydrofolate. Serine is the most important source of substituted folates for biosynthetic reactions, and the activity of serine hydroxymethyltransferase is regulated by the state of folate substitution and the availability of folate. The reaction is reversible, and in liver it can form serine from glycine as a substrate for gluconeogenesis. Methylene-, methenyl-, and 10-formyl-tetrahydrofolates are interconvertible. When one-carbon folates are not required, the oxidation of formyl-tetrahydrofolate to yield carbon dioxide provides a means of maintaining a pool of free folate.

Inhibitors of Folate Metabolism Provide Cancer Chemotherapy, Antibacterial, & Antimalarial Drugs

The methylation of deoxyuridine monophosphate (dUMP) to thymidine monophosphate (TMP), catalyzed by thymidylate synthase, is essential for the synthesis of DNA.

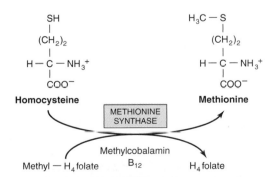

Figure 44–14. Homocysteine and the "folate trap." Vitamin B_{12} deficiency leads to impairment of methionine synthase, resulting in accumulation of homocysteine and trapping folate as methyltetrahydrofolate.

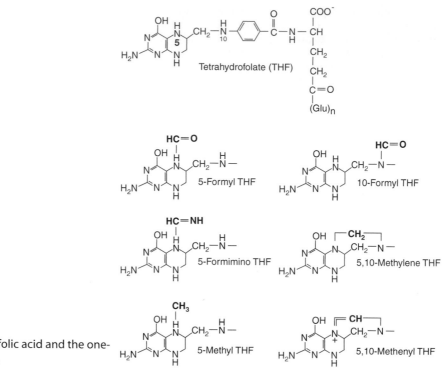

Figure 44–15. Tetrahydrofolic acid and the one-carbon substituted folates.

The one-carbon fragment of methylene-tetrahydrofolate is reduced to a methyl group with release of dihydrofolate, which is then reduced back to tetrahydrofolate by **dihydrofolate reductase.** Thymidylate synthase and dihydrofolate reductase are especially active in tissues with a high rate of cell division. **Methotrexate,** an analog of 10-methyl-tetrahydrofolate, inhibits dihydrofolate reductase and has been exploited as an anticancer drug. The dihydrofolate reductases of some bacteria and parasites differ from the human enzyme;

inhibitors of these enzymes can be used as antibacterial drugs (eg, **trimethoprim**) and antimalarial drugs (eg, **pyrimethamine**).

Vitamin B₁₂ Deficiency Causes Functional Folate Deficiency—the "Folate Trap"

When acting as a methyl donor, S-adenosyl methionine forms homocysteine, which may be remethylated by methyl-tetrahydrofolate catalyzed by methionine syn-

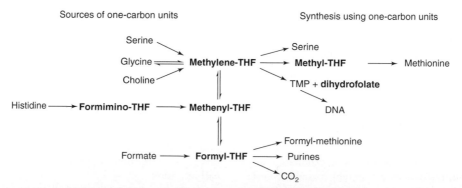

Figure 44–16. Sources and utilization of one-carbon substituted folates.

thase, a vitamin B_{12}–dependent enzyme (Figure 44–14). As the reduction of methylene-tetrahydrofolate to methyl-tetrahydrofolate is irreversible and the major source of tetrahydrofolate for tissues is methyl-tetrahydrofolate, the role of methionine synthase is vital, and provides a link between the functions of folate and vitamin B_{12}. Impairment of methionine synthase in vitamin B_{12} deficiency results in the accumulation of methyl-tetrahydrofolate—the "folate trap." There is therefore functional deficiency of folate, secondary to the deficiency of vitamin B_{12}.

Folate Deficiency Causes Megaloblastic Anemia

Deficiency of folic acid itself or deficiency of vitamin B_{12}, which leads to functional folic acid deficiency, affects cells that are dividing rapidly because they have a large requirement for thymidine for DNA synthesis. Clinically, this affects the bone marrow, leading to megaloblastic anemia.

Folic Acid Supplements Reduce the Risk of Neural Tube Defects & Hyperhomocysteinemia, & May Reduce the Incidence of Cardiovascular Disease & Some Cancers

Supplements of 400 μg/day of folate begun before conception result in a significant reduction in the incidence of **spina bifida** and other **neural tube defects.** Elevated blood homocysteine is a significant risk factor for **atherosclerosis, thrombosis,** and **hypertension.** The condition is the result of an impaired ability to form methyl-tetrahydrofolate by methylene-tetrahydrofolate reductase, causing functional folate deficiency, resulting in failure to remethylate homocysteine to methionine. People with the abnormal variant of methylene-tetrahydrofolate reductase do not develop hyperhomocysteinemia if they have a relatively high intake of folate, but it is not yet known whether this affects the incidence of cardiovascular disease.

There is also evidence that low folate status results in impaired methylation of CpG islands in DNA, which is a factor in the development of colorectal and other cancers. A number of studies suggest that folate supplementation or food enrichment may reduce the risk of developing some cancers.

Folate Enrichment of Foods May Put Some People at Risk

Folate supplements will rectify the megaloblastic anemia of vitamin B_{12} deficiency but may hasten the development of the (irreversible) nerve damage found in vitamin B_{12} deficiency. There is also antagonism between

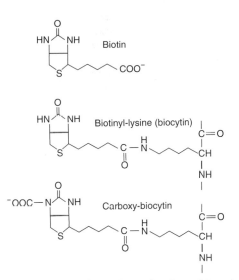

Figure 44–17. Biotin, biocytin, and carboxy-biocytin.

folic acid and the anticonvulsants used in the treatment of epilepsy.

DIETARY BIOTIN DEFICIENCY IS UNKNOWN

The structures of biotin, biocytin, and carboxybiotin (the active metabolic intermediate) are shown in Figure 44–17. Biotin is widely distributed in many foods as biocytin (ε-amino-biotinyllysine), which is released on proteolysis. It is synthesized by intestinal flora in excess of requirements. Deficiency is unknown, except among people maintained for many months on total parenteral nutrition, and a very small number who eat abnormally large amounts of uncooked egg white, which contains avidin, a protein that binds biotin and renders it unavailable for absorption.

Biotin Is a Coenzyme of Carboxylase Enzymes

Biotin functions to transfer carbon dioxide in a small number of carboxylation reactions (acetyl-CoA, pyruvate, propionyl-CoA, and methylcrotonyl-CoA carboxylases). A holocarboxylase synthetase catalyzes the transfer of biotin onto a lysine residue of the apo-enzyme to form the biocytin residue of the holoenzyme. The reactive intermediate is 1-N-carboxy-biocytin, formed from bicarbonate in an ATP-dependent reaction. The carboxy group is then transferred to the substrate for carboxylation.

Biotin also has a role in regulation of the cell cycle, acting to biotinylate key nuclear proteins.

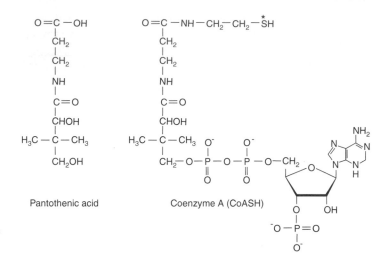

Pantothenic acid   Coenzyme A (CoASH)

Figure 44–18. Pantothenic acid and coenzyme A. Asterisk shows site of acylation by fatty acids.

AS PART OF CoA & ACP, PANTOTHENIC ACID ACTS AS A CARRIER OF ACYL RADICALS

Pantothenic acid has a central role in acyl group metabolism when acting as the pantetheine functional moiety of coenzyme A or acyl carrier protein (ACP) (Figure 44–18). The pantetheine moiety is formed after combination of pantothenate with cysteine, which provides the –SH prosthetic group of CoA and ACP. CoA takes part in reactions of the citric acid cycle (Chapter 17), fatty acid oxidation (Chapter 22), acetylations and cholesterol synthesis (Chapter 26). ACP participates in fatty acid synthesis (Chapter 23). The vitamin is widely distributed in all food-stuffs, and deficiency has not been unequivocally reported in humans except in specific depletion studies.

ASCORBIC ACID IS A VITAMIN FOR ONLY SOME SPECIES

Vitamin C (Figure 44–19) is a vitamin for humans and other primates, the guinea pig, bats, passeriform birds, and most fishes and invertebrates; other animals synthesize it as an intermediate in the uronic acid pathway of glucose metabolism (Chapter 21). In those species for

which it is a vitamin, there is a block in the pathway as a result of absence of gulonolactone oxidase. Both ascorbic acid and dehydroascorbic acid have vitamin activity.

Vitamin C Is the Coenzyme for Two Groups of Hydroxylases

Ascorbic acid has specific roles in the copper-containing hydroxylases and the α-ketoglutarate-linked iron-containing hydroxylases. It also increases the activity of a number of other enzymes in vitro, although this is a nonspecific reducing action. In addition, it has a number of nonenzymic effects as a result of its action as a reducing agent and oxygen radical quencher.

Dopamine β-hydroxylase is a copper-containing enzyme involved in the synthesis of the catecholamines, norepinephrine, and epinephrine, from tyrosine in the adrenal medulla and central nervous system. During hydroxylation the Cu^+ is oxidized to Cu^{2+}; reduction back to Cu^+ specifically requires ascorbate, which is oxidized to monodehydroascorbate.

A number of peptide hormones have a carboxy terminal amide that is derived from a terminal glycine residue. This glycine is hydroxylated on the α-carbon by a copper-containing enzyme, **peptidylglycine hydroxylase,** which, again, requires ascorbate for reduction of Cu^{2+}.

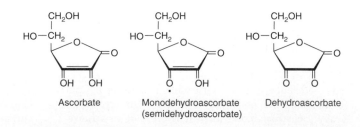

Ascorbate   Monodehydroascorbate   Dehydroascorbate
                     (semidehydroascorbate)

Figure 44–19. Vitamin C.

A number of iron-containing, ascorbate-requiring hydroxylases share a common reaction mechanism, in which hydroxylation of the substrate is linked to decarboxylation of α-ketoglutarate. Many of these enzymes are involved in the modification of precursor proteins. **Proline** and **lysine hydroxylases** are required for the postsynthetic modification of **procollagen** to **collagen,** and proline hydroxylase is also required in formation of **osteocalcin** and the C1q component of **complement.** Aspartate β-hydroxylase is required for the postsynthetic modification of the precursor of protein C, the vitamin K–dependent protease that hydrolyzes activated factor V in the blood-clotting cascade. Trimethyllysine and γ-butyrobetaine hydroxylases are required for the synthesis of carnitine.

Vitamin C Deficiency Causes Scurvy

Signs of vitamin C deficiency include skin changes, fragility of blood capillaries, gum decay, tooth loss, and bone fracture, many of which can be attributed to deficient collagen synthesis.

There May Be Benefits from Higher Intakes of Vitamin C

At intakes above about 100 mg/day, the body's capacity to metabolize vitamin C is saturated, and any further intake is excreted in the urine. However, in addition to its other roles, vitamin C enhances the absorption of iron, and this depends on the presence of the vitamin in the gut. Therefore, increased intakes may be beneficial. There is very little good evidence that high doses of vitamin C prevent the common cold, although they may reduce the duration and severity of symptoms.

MINERALS ARE REQUIRED FOR BOTH PHYSIOLOGIC & BIOCHEMICAL FUNCTIONS

Many of the essential minerals (Table 44–2) are widely distributed in foods, and most people eating a mixed diet are likely to receive adequate intakes. The amounts required vary from grams per day for sodium and calcium, through milligrams per day (eg, iron, zinc), to micrograms per day for the trace elements. In general, mineral deficiencies occur when foods come from one region where the soil may be deficient in some minerals (eg, iodine and selenium, deficiencies of both of which occur in many areas of the world); when foods come from a variety of regions, mineral deficiency is less likely to occur. However, iron deficiency is a general problem, because if iron losses from the body are relatively high (eg, from heavy menstrual blood loss), it is difficult to achieve

Table 44–2. Classification of minerals according to their function.

Function	Mineral
Structural function	Calcium, magnesium, phosphate
Involved in membrane function	Sodium, potassium
Function as prosthetic groups in enzymes	Cobalt, copper, iron, molybdenum, selenium, zinc
Regulatory role or role in hormone action	Calcium, chromium, iodine, magnesium, manganese, sodium, potassium
Known to be essential, but function unknown	Silicon, vanadium, nickel, tin
Have effects in the body, but essentiality is not established	Fluoride, lithium
May occur in foods and known to be toxic in excess	Aluminum, arsenic, antimony, boron, bromine, cadmium, cesium, germanium, lead, mercury, silver, strontium

an adequate intake to replace losses. Foods grown on soil containing high levels of selenium cause toxicity, and excessive intakes of sodium cause hypertension in susceptible people.

SUMMARY

- Vitamins are organic nutrients with essential metabolic functions, generally required in small amounts in the diet because they cannot be synthesized by the body. The lipid-soluble vitamins (A, D, E, and K) are hydrophobic molecules requiring normal fat absorption for their efficient absorption and the avoidance of deficiency symptoms.
- Vitamin A (retinol), present in meat, and the provitamin (β-carotene), found in plants, form retinaldehyde, utilized in vision, and retinoic acid, which acts in the control of gene expression.
- Vitamin D is a steroid prohormone yielding the active hormone derivative calcitriol, which regulates calcium and phosphate metabolism; deficiency leads to rickets and osteomalacia.
- Vitamin E (tocopherol) is the most important antioxidant in the body, acting in the lipid phase of membranes protecting against the effects of free radicals.
- Vitamin K functions as cofactor to a carboxylase that acts on glutamate residues of precursor proteins of clotting factors and bone proteins to enable them to chelate calcium.

- The water-soluble vitamins of the B complex act as enzyme cofactors. Thiamin is a cofactor in oxidative decarboxylation of α-keto acids and of transketolase in the pentose phosphate pathway. Riboflavin and niacin are important cofactors in oxidoreduction reactions, present in flavoprotein enzymes and in NAD and NADP, respectively.
- Pantothenic acid is present in coenzyme A and acyl carrier protein, which act as carriers for acyl groups in metabolic reactions.
- Pyridoxine as pyridoxal phosphate, is the coenzyme for several enzymes of amino acid metabolism, including the transaminases, and of glycogen phosphorylase. Biotin is the coenzyme for several carboxylase enzymes.
- Besides other functions, vitamin B_{12} and folic acid take part in providing one-carbon residues for DNA synthesis; deficiency results in megaloblastic anemia.
- Vitamin C is a water-soluble antioxidant that maintains vitamin E and many metal cofactors in the reduced state.
- Inorganic mineral elements that have a function in the body must be provided in the diet. When intake is insufficient, deficiency may develop, and excessive intakes may be toxic.

REFERENCES

Bender DA, Bender AE: *Nutrition: A Reference Handbook.* Oxford University Press, 1997.

Bender DA: *Nutritional Biochemistry of the Vitamins,* 2nd edition. Cambridge University Press, 2003.

Department of Health: *Dietary Reference Values for Food Energy and Nutrients for the United Kingdom.* Her Majesty's Stationery Office, 1991.

Department of Health: *Folic Acid and the Prevention of Disease.* The Stationery Office, 2000.

FAO/WHO: *Human Vitamin and Mineral Requirements: Report of a Joint FAO/WHO Expert Consultation: Bankok, Thailand.* Food and Nutrition Division of the United Nations Food and Agriculture Organization, 2000.

Geissler C, Powers HJ: *Human Nutrition,* 11th edition, Elsevier, 2005.

Institute of Medicine: *Dietary Reference Intakes for Calcium, Phosphorus, Magnesium, Vitamin D and Fluoride.* National Academy Press, 1997.

Institute of Medicine: *Dietary Reference Values for Thiamin, Riboflavin, Niacin, Vitamin B_6, Folate, Vitamin B_{12}, Pantothenic Acid, Biotin and Choline.* National Academy Press, 2000.

Institute of Medicine: *Dietary Reference Values for Vitamin C, Vitamin E, Selenium and Carotenoids.* National Academy Press, 2000.

Institute of Medicine: *Dietary Reference Intakes for Vitamin A, Vitamin K, Arsenic, Boron, Chromium, Copper, Iodine, Iron, Manganese, Molybdenum, Nickel, Silicon, Vanadium and Zinc.* National Academy Press, 2001.

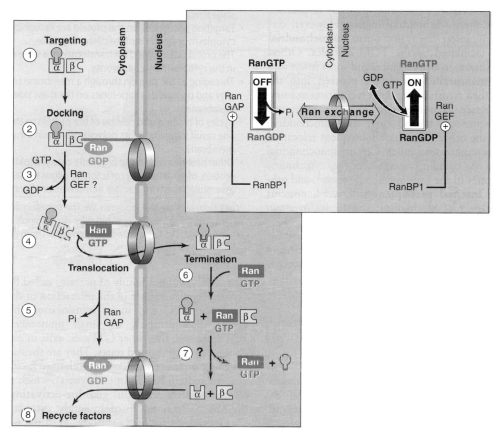

Figure 45–3. Schematic representation of the proposed role of Ran in the import of cargo carrying an NLS signal. (1) The targeting complex forms when the NLS receptor (α, an importin) binds NLS cargo and the docking factor (β). (2) Docking occurs at filamentous sites that protrude from the NPC. Ran-GDP docks independently. (3) Transfer to the translocation channel is triggered when a RanGEF converts Ran-GDP to Ran-GTP. (4) The NPC catalyzes translocation of the targeting complex. (5) Ran-GTP is recycled to Ran-GDP by docked RanGAP. (6) Ran-GTP disrupts the targeting complex by binding to a site on β that overlaps with a binding site. (7) NLS cargo dissociates from α, and Ran-GTP may dissociate from β. (8) α and β factors are recycled to the cytoplasm. *Inset:* The Ran translocation switch is off in the cytoplasm and on in the nucleus. Ran-GTP promotes NLS- and NES-directed translocation. However, cytoplasmic Ran is enriched in Ran-GDP (OFF) by an active RanGAP, and nuclear pools are enriched in Ran-GTP (ON) by an active GEF. RanBP1 promotes the contrary activities of these two factors. Direct linkage of nuclear and cytoplasmic pools of Ran occurs through the NPC by an unknown shuttling mechanism. P_i, inorganic phosphate; NLS, nuclear localization signal; NPC, nuclear pore complex; GEF, guanine nucleotide exchange factor; GAP, guanine-activating protein; NES, nuclear export signal; BP, binding protein. (Reprinted, with permission, from Goldfarb DS: Whose finger is on the switch? Science 1997;276:1814. Copyright © 1997 AAAS. Reprinted with permission.)

Proteins similar to importins, referred to as **exportins,** are involved in export of many macromolecules from the nucleus. Cargo molecules for export carry **nuclear export signals (NESs).** Ran proteins are involved in this process also, and it is now established that the processes of import and export share a number of common features.

MOST CASES OF ZELLWEGER SYNDROME ARE DUE TO MUTATIONS IN GENES INVOLVED IN THE BIOGENESIS OF PEROXISOMES

The **peroxisome** is an important organelle involved in aspects of the metabolism of many molecules, including fatty acids and other lipids (eg, plasmalogens, cholesterol, bile acids), purines, amino acids, and hydrogen peroxide. The peroxisome is bounded by a single membrane and contains more than 50 enzymes; catalase and urate oxidase are marker enzymes for this organelle. Its proteins are **synthesized on cytosolic polyribosomes** and fold prior to import. The pathways of import of a number of its proteins and enzymes have been studied, some being **matrix components** and others **membrane components.** At least two **peroxisomal-matrix targeting sequences (PTSs)** have been discovered. One, PTS1, is a tripeptide (ie, Ser-Lys-Leu [SKL], but variations of this sequence have been detected) located at the carboxyl terminal of a number of matrix proteins, including catalase. Another, PTS2, consisting of about 26–36 amino acids, has been found in at least four matrix proteins (eg, thiolase) and, unlike PTS1, is cleaved after entry into the matrix. Proteins containing PTS1 sequences form complexes with a soluble receptor protein (PTS1R) and proteins containing PTS2 sequences complex with another, PTS2R. The resulting complexes then interact with a membrane receptor, Pex14p. Proteins involved in further transport of proteins into the matrix are also present. Most peroxisomal membrane proteins have been found to contain neither of the above two targeting sequences, but apparently contain others. The import system can handle **intact oligomers** (eg, tetrameric catalase). Import of matrix proteins requires ATP, whereas import of membrane proteins does not.

Interest in import of proteins into peroxisomes has been stimulated by studies on **Zellweger syndrome.** This condition is apparent at birth and is characterized by profound neurologic impairment, victims often dying within a year. The number of peroxisomes can vary from being almost normal to being virtually absent in some patients. Biochemical findings include an accumulation of very long chain fatty acids, abnormalities of the synthesis of bile acids, and a marked reduction of plasmalogens. The condition is believed to be due to

Table 45–2. Disorders due to peroxisomal abnormalities.[1]

	MIM Number[2]
Zellweger syndrome	214100
Neonatal adrenoleukodystrophy	202370
Infantile Refsum disease	266510
Hyperpipecolic acidemia	239400
Rhizomelic chondrodysplasia punctata	215100
Adrenoleukodystrophy	300100
Pseudoneonatal adrenoleukodystrophy	264470
Pseudo-Zellweger syndrome	261515
Hyperoxaluria type 1	259900
Acatalasemia	115500
Glutaryl-CoA oxidase deficiency	231690

[1]Reproduced, with permission, from Seashore MR, Wappner RS: *Genetics in Primary Care & Clinical Medicine.* Appleton & Lange, 1996.
[2]MIM = *Mendelian Inheritance in Man.* Each number specifies a reference in which information regarding each of the above conditions can be found.

mutations in genes encoding certain proteins—so called **peroxins**—involved in various steps of **peroxisome biogenesis** (such as the import of proteins described above), or in genes encoding certain peroxisomal enzymes themselves. Two closely related conditions are **neonatal adrenoleukodystrophy** and **infantile Refsum disease.** Zellweger syndrome and these two conditions represent a spectrum of overlapping features, with Zellweger syndrome being the most severe (many proteins affected) and infantile Refsum disease the least severe (only one or a few proteins affected). Table 45–2 lists some features of these and related conditions.

THE SIGNAL HYPOTHESIS EXPLAINS HOW POLYRIBOSOMES BIND TO THE ENDOPLASMIC RETICULUM

As indicated above, the rough ER branch is the second of the two branches involved in the synthesis and sorting of proteins. In this branch, proteins are synthesized on membrane-bound polyribosomes and translocated into the lumen of the rough ER prior to further sorting (Figure 45–2).

The **signal hypothesis** was proposed by Blobel and Sabatini partly to explain the distinction between free and membrane-bound polyribosomes. They found that proteins synthesized on membrane-bound polyribosomes contained a peptide extension (**signal peptide**) at their amino terminals which mediated their attachment to the membranes of the ER. As noted above, proteins whose entire synthesis occurs on free polyribosomes lack this signal peptide. An important aspect of

Table 45–3. Some properties of signal peptides.

- Usually, but not always, located at the amino terminal
- Contain approximately 12–35 amino acids
- Methionine is usually the amino terminal amino acid
- Contain a central cluster of hydrophobic amino acids
- Contain at least one positively charged amino acid near their amino terminal
- Usually cleaved off at the carboxyl terminal end of an Ala residue by signal peptidase

the signal hypothesis was that it suggested—as turns out to be the case—that **all ribosomes have the same structure** and that the distinction between membrane-bound and free ribosomes depends solely on the former's carrying proteins that have signal peptides. Much evidence has confirmed the original hypothesis. Because many membrane proteins are synthesized on membrane-bound polyribosomes, the signal hypothesis plays an important role in concepts of membrane assembly. Some characteristics of signal peptides are summarized in Table 45–3.

Figure 45–4 illustrates the principal features in relation to the passage of a secreted protein through the membrane of the ER. It incorporates features from the original signal hypothesis and from subsequent work. The mRNA for such a protein encodes an amino terminal **signal peptide** (also variously called a leader sequence, a transient insertion signal, a signal sequence, or a presequence). The signal hypothesis proposed that the protein is inserted into the ER membrane at the same time as its mRNA is being translated on polyribosomes, so called **cotranslational insertion.** As the signal peptide emerges from the large subunit of the ribosome, it is recognized by a **signal recognition particle (SRP)** that blocks further translation after about 70 amino acids have been polymerized (40 buried in the large ribosomal subunit and 30 exposed). The block is referred to as **elongation arrest.** The SRP contains six proteins and has a 7S RNA associated with it that is closely related to the Alu family of highly repeated DNA sequences (Chapter 35). The SRP-imposed block is not released until the SRP-signal peptide-polyribosome complex has bound to the so-called **docking protein** (SRP-R, a receptor for the SRP) on the ER membrane; the SRP thus guides the signal peptide to the SRP-R and prevents premature folding and expulsion of the protein being synthesized into the cytosol.

The **SRP-R** is an integral membrane protein composed of α and β subunits. The α subunit binds GDP and the β subunit spans the membrane. When the SRP-signal peptide complex interacts with the receptor, the exchange of GDP for GTP is stimulated. This form of the receptor (with GTP bound) has a high affinity for the SRP and thus releases the signal peptide, which binds to

the translocation machinery (translocon) also present in the ER membrane. The α subunit then hydrolyzes its bound GTP, restoring GDP and completing a GTP-GDP cycle. The **unidirectionality** of this cycle helps drive the interaction of the polyribosome and its signal peptide with the ER membrane in the forward direction.

The **translocon** consists of three membrane proteins (the **Sec61 complex**) that form a protein-conducting channel in the ER membrane through which the newly synthesized protein may pass. The channel appears to be open only when a signal peptide is present, preserving conductance across the ER membrane when it closes. The conductance of the channel has been measured experimentally.

The insertion of the signal peptide into the conducting channel, while the other end of the parent protein is still attached to ribosomes, is termed "cotranslational insertion." The process of elongation of the remaining portion of the protein probably facilitates passage of the nascent protein across the lipid bilayer as the ribosomes remain attached to the membrane of the ER. Thus, the rough (or ribosome-studded) ER is formed. It is important that the protein be kept in an **unfolded state** prior to entering the conducting channel—otherwise, it may not be able to gain access to the channel.

Ribosomes remain attached to the ER during synthesis of signal peptide-containing proteins but are released and dissociated into their two types of subunits when the process is completed. The signal peptide is hydrolyzed by **signal peptidase,** located on the luminal side of the ER membrane (Figure 45–4), and then is apparently rapidly degraded by proteases.

Cytochrome P450 (Chapter 52), an integral ER membrane protein, does not completely cross the membrane. Instead, it resides in the membrane with its signal peptide intact. Its passage through the membrane is prevented by a sequence of amino acids called a **halt-** or **stop-transfer signal.**

Secretory proteins and proteins destined for **membranes distal to the ER** completely traverse the membrane bilayer and are discharged into the lumen of the ER. **N-Glycan chains,** if present, are added (Chapter 46) as these proteins traverse the inner part of the ER membrane—a process called **"cotranslational glycosylation."** Subsequently, the proteins are found in the **lumen of the Golgi apparatus,** where further changes in glycan chains occur (Figure 46–9) prior to intracellular distribution or secretion. There is strong evidence that the **signal peptide** is involved in the process of protein **insertion into ER membranes.** Mutant proteins, containing altered signal peptides in which a hydrophobic amino acid is replaced by a hydrophilic one, are not inserted into ER membranes. Nonmembrane proteins (eg, α-globin) to which signal peptides have been attached by genetic engineering can be inserted into the lumen of the ER or even secreted.

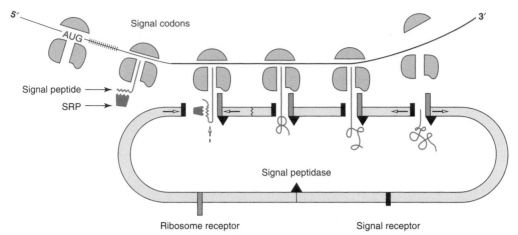

Figure 45–4. Diagram of the signal hypothesis for the transport of secreted proteins across the ER membrane. The ribosomes synthesizing a protein move along the messenger RNA specifying the amino acid sequence of the protein. (The messenger is represented by the line between 5′ and 3′.) The codon AUG marks the start of the message for the protein; the hatched lines that follow AUG represent the codons for the signal sequence. As the protein grows out from the larger ribosomal subunit, the signal sequence is exposed and bound by the signal recognition particle (SRP). Translation is blocked until the complex binds to the "docking protein," also designated SRP-R (represented by the solid bar) on the ER membrane. There is also a receptor (open bar) for the ribosome itself. The interaction of the ribosome and growing peptide chain with the ER membrane results in the opening of a channel through which the protein is transported to the interior space of the ER. During translocation, the signal sequence of most proteins is removed by an enzyme called the "signal peptidase," located at the luminal surface of the ER membrane. The completed protein is eventually released by the ribosome, which then separates into its two components, the large and small ribosomal subunits. The protein ends up inside the ER. See text for further details. (Slightly modified and reproduced, with permission, from Marx JL: Newly made proteins zip through the cell. Science 1980;207:164. Copyright © 1980 by the American Association for the Advancement of Science.)

There is evidence that the transposon in the ER membrane is involved in **retrograde transport** of various molecules from the ER lumen to the cytosol. These molecules include unfolded or misfolded glycoproteins, glycopeptides, and oligosaccharides. Some at least of these molecules are degraded in proteasomes (see below). Thus, there is two-way traffic across the ER membrane.

PROTEINS FOLLOW SEVERAL ROUTES TO BE INSERTED INTO OR ATTACHED TO THE MEMBRANES OF THE ENDOPLASMIC RETICULUM

The routes that proteins follow to be inserted into the membranes of the ER include the following.

A. COTRANSLATIONAL INSERTION

Figure 45–5 shows a variety of ways in which proteins are distributed in the plasma membrane. In particular, the **amino terminals** of certain proteins (eg, the LDL

receptor) can be seen to be on the extracytoplasmic face, whereas for other proteins (eg, the asialoglycoprotein receptor) the **carboxyl terminals** are on this face. To explain these dispositions, one must consider the initial biosynthetic events at the ER membrane. The **LDL receptor** enters the ER membrane in a manner analogous to a secretory protein (Figure 45–4); it partly traverses the ER membrane, its signal peptide is cleaved, and its amino terminal protrudes into the lumen. However, it is retained in the membrane because it contains a highly hydrophobic segment, the **halt- or stop-transfer signal.** This sequence forms the single transmembrane segment of the protein and is its membrane-anchoring domain. The small patch of ER membrane in which the newly synthesized LDL receptor is located subsequently buds off as a component of a transport vesicle, probably from the transitional elements of the ER (Figure 45–2). As described below in the discussion of asymmetry of proteins and lipids in membrane assembly, the disposition of the receptor in the ER membrane is preserved in the vesicle, which eventually fuses with the plasma

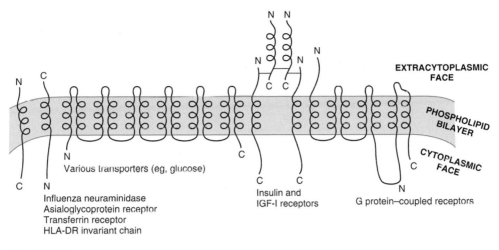

Figure 45–5. Variations in the way in which proteins are inserted into membranes. This schematic representation, which illustrates a number of possible orientations, shows the segments of the proteins within the membrane as α-helices and the other segments as lines. The LDL receptor, which crosses the membrane once and has its amino terminal on the exterior, is called a type I transmembrane protein. The asialoglycoprotein receptor, which also crosses the membrane once but has its carboxyl terminal on the exterior, is called a type II transmembrane protein. Cytochrome P450 (not shown) is an example of a type III transmembrane protein; its disposition is similar to type I proteins, but does not contain a cleavable signal sequence. The various transporters indicated (eg, glucose) cross the membrane a number of times and are called type IV transmembrane proteins; they are also referred to as polytopic membrane proteins. (N, amino terminal; C, carboxyl terminal.) (Adapted, with permission, from Wickner WT, Lodish HF: Multiple mechanisms of protein insertion into and across membranes. Science 1985;230:400. Copyright © 1985 by the American Association for the Advancement of Science.)

membrane. In contrast, the **asialoglycoprotein receptor** possesses an **internal insertion sequence,** which inserts into the membrane but is **not cleaved.** This acts as an anchor, and its carboxyl terminal is extruded through the membrane. The more complex disposition of the **transporters** (eg, for glucose) can be explained by the fact that alternating transmembrane α-helices act as uncleaved insertion sequences and as halt-transfer signals, respectively. Each pair of helical segments is inserted as a hairpin. Sequences that determine the structure of a protein in a membrane are called **topogenic sequences.** As explained in the legend to Figure 45–5, the above three proteins are examples of **type I, type II,** and **type IV** transmembrane proteins.

B. SYNTHESIS ON FREE POLYRIBOSOMES & SUBSEQUENT ATTACHMENT TO THE ENDOPLASMIC RETICULUM MEMBRANE

An example is cytochrome b_5, which enters the ER membrane spontaneously.

C. RETENTION AT THE LUMINAL ASPECT OF THE ENDOPLASMIC RETICULUM BY SPECIFIC AMINO ACID SEQUENCES

A number of proteins possess the amino acid sequence **KDEL** (Lys-Asp-Glu-Leu) at their carboxyl terminal. This sequence specifies that such proteins will be **attached to the inner aspect of the ER** in a relatively loose manner. The chaperone BiP (see below) is one such protein. Actually, KDEL-containing proteins first travel to the Golgi, interact there with a specific KDEL receptor protein, and then return in transport vesicles to the ER, where they dissociate from the receptor.

D. RETROGRADE TRANSPORT FROM THE GOLGI APPARATUS

Certain other **non-KDEL-containing proteins** destined for the membranes of the ER also pass to the Golgi and then return, by **retrograde vesicular transport,** to the ER to be inserted therein (see below).

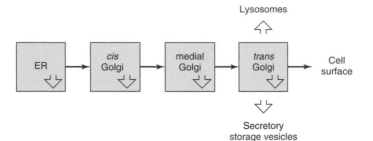

Figure 45–6. Flow of membrane proteins from the endoplasmic reticulum (ER) to the cell surface. Horizontal arrows denote steps that have been proposed to be signal independent and thus represent bulk flow. The open vertical arrows in the boxes denote retention of proteins that are resident in the membranes of the organelle indicated. The open vertical arrows outside the boxes indicate signal-mediated transport to lysosomes and secretory storage granules. (Reproduced, with permission, from Pfeffer SR, Rothman JE: Biosynthetic protein transport and sorting by the endoplasmic reticulum and Golgi. Annu Rev Biochem 1987;56:829. Copyright © by Annual Reviews, www.annualreviews.org. Reprinted with permission.)

The foregoing paragraphs demonstrate that a **variety of routes** are involved in assembly of the proteins of the ER membranes; a similar situation probably holds for other membranes (eg, the mitochondrial membranes and the plasma membrane). Precise targeting sequences have been identified in some instances (eg, KDEL sequences).

The topic of membrane biogenesis is discussed further later in this chapter.

PROTEINS MOVE THROUGH CELLULAR COMPARTMENTS TO SPECIFIC DESTINATIONS

A scheme representing the possible flow of proteins along the ER → Golgi apparatus → plasma membrane route is shown in Figure 45–6. The horizontal arrows denote transport steps that may be independent of targeting signals, whereas the vertical open arrows represent steps that depend on specific signals. Thus, flow of certain proteins (including membrane proteins) from the ER to the plasma membrane (designated **"bulk flow,"** as it is nonselective) probably occurs without any targeting sequences being involved, ie, **by default.** On the other hand, insertion of resident proteins into the ER and Golgi membranes is **dependent upon specific signals** (eg, KDEL or halt-transfer sequences for the ER). Similarly, transport of many enzymes to **lysosomes** is dependent upon the **Man 6-P signal** (Chapter 46), and a signal may be involved for entry of proteins into **secretory granules.** Table 45–4 summarizes information on sequences that are

known to be involved in targeting various proteins to their correct intracellular sites.

CHAPERONES ARE PROTEINS THAT PREVENT FAULTY FOLDING & UNPRODUCTIVE INTERACTIONS OF OTHER PROTEINS

Exit from the ER may be the rate-limiting step in the secretory pathway. In this context, it has been found that certain proteins play a role in the assembly or

Table 45–4. Some sequences or compounds that direct proteins to specific organelles.

Targeting Sequence or Compound	Organelle Targeted
Signal peptide sequence	Membrane of ER
Amino terminal KDEL sequence (Lys-Asp-Glu-Leu)	Luminal surface of ER
Amino terminal sequence (20–80 residues)	Mitochondrial matrix
NLS (eg, Pro$_2$-Lys$_2$-Ala-Lys-Val)	Nucleus
PTS (eg, Ser-Lys-Leu)	Peroxisome
Mannose 6-phosphate	Lysosome

NLS, nuclear localization signal; PTS, peroxisomal-matrix targeting sequence.

Table 45–5. Some properties of chaperone proteins.

- Present in a wide range of species from bacteria to humans
- Many are so-called heat shock proteins (Hsp)
- Some are inducible by conditions that cause unfolding of newly synthesized proteins (eg, elevated temperature and various chemicals)
- They bind to predominantly hydrophobic regions of unfolded and aggregated proteins
- They act in part as a quality control or editing mechanism for detecting misfolded or otherwise defective proteins
- Most chaperones show associated ATPase activity, with ATP or ADP being involved in the protein-chaperone interaction
- Found in various cellular compartments such as cytosol, mitochondria, and the lumen of the endoplasmic reticulum

---

proper folding of other proteins without themselves being components of the latter. Such proteins are called **molecular chaperones;** a number of important properties of these proteins are listed in Table 45–5, and the names of some of particular importance in the ER are listed in Table 45–6. Basically, they stabilize unfolded or partially folded intermediates, allowing them time to fold properly, and prevent inappropriate interactions, thus combating the formation of nonfunctional structures. Most chaperones exhibit **ATPase activity** and bind ADP and ATP. This activity is important for their effect on folding. The ADP-chaperone complex often has a high affinity for the unfolded protein, which, when bound, stimulates release of ADP with replacement by ATP. The ATP-chaperone complex, in turn, releases segments of the protein that have folded properly, and the **cycle** involving ADP and ATP binding is repeated until the folded protein is released.

Several examples of chaperones were introduced above when the sorting of mitochondrial proteins was discussed. The **immunoglobulin heavy chain binding protein (BiP)** is located in the lumen of the ER. This protein will bind abnormally folded immunoglobulin

Table 45–6. Some chaperones and enzymes involved in folding that are located in the rough endoplasmic reticulum.

- BiP (immunoglobulin heavy chain binding protein)
- GRP94 (glucose-regulated protein)
- Calnexin
- Calreticulin
- PDI (protein disulfide isomerase)
- PPI (peptidyl prolyl cis-trans isomerase)

---

heavy chains and certain other proteins and prevent them from leaving the ER, in which they are degraded. Another important chaperone is **calnexin,** a calcium-binding protein located in the ER membrane. This protein binds a wide variety of proteins, including mixed histocompatibility (MHC) antigens and a variety of serum proteins. As mentioned in Chapter 46, calnexin binds the monoglycosylated species of glycoproteins that occur during processing of glycoproteins, retaining them in the ER until the glycoprotein has folded properly. **Calreticulin,** which is also a calcium-binding protein, has properties similar to those of calnexin; it is not membrane-bound. Chaperones are not the only proteins in the ER lumen that are concerned with proper folding of proteins. Two enzymes are present that play an active role in folding. **Protein disulfide isomerase (PDI)** promotes rapid reshuffling of disulfide bonds until the correct set is achieved. **Peptidyl prolyl isomerase (PPI)** accelerates folding of proline-containing proteins by catalyzing the cis-trans isomerization of X-Pro bonds, where X is any amino acid residue.

ACCUMULATION OF MISFOLDED PROTEINS IN THE ENDOPLASMIC RETICULUM CAN CAUSE THE UNFOLDED PROTEIN RESPONSE

Homeostasis in the ER is important for normal cell function. When protein folding in the ER is affected by various factors (eg, abnormal levels of Ca^{2+}, alterations of redox status, mutations, various diseases), the ER can sense this situation. Signaling mechanisms are activated in the ER that include increasing its folding capacity (eg, increased synthesis of chaperones and proteins involved in folding mentioned above), and other responses to restore cellular homeostasis. If sustained impairment of folding occurs, cell death pathways (apoptosis) are activated. This overall process is named the **unfolded protein response.** It is different in scope to the next topic to be discussed.

MISFOLDED PROTEINS UNDERGO ENDOPLASMIC RETICULUM–ASSOCIATED DEGRADATION (ERAD)

Misfolded proteins occur in many genetic diseases (eg, CFTR in cystic fibrosis; see Chapter 39). Proteins that misfold in the ER are selectively transported back across the ER to enter **proteasomes** present in the cytosol. **Retrograde transport** across the ER membrane probably occurs through the translocon (Sec 61 complex) described above. It may be powered by ATPases present in proteasomes, as these structures can be found in close proximity to the ER. Chaperones present in the lumen of the ER and in the cytosol target misfolded proteins to

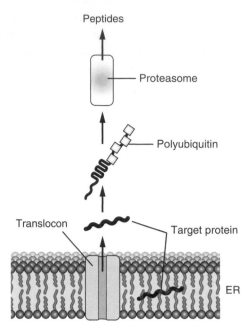

Figure 45–7. Schematic diagram of the events in ERAD. A target protein (which may be misfolded or normally folded) undergoes retrograde transport through the translocon into the cytosol, where it is subjected to polyubiquitination. Following polyubiquitination, it enters a proteasome, inside which it is degraded to small peptides that exit and may have several fates. Liberated ubiquitin molecules are recycled.

proteasomes. Prior to entering proteasomes, most proteins are **ubiquitinated** and are escorted to proteasomes by polyubiquitin-binding proteins. The above process is referred to as ERAD and is outlined in Figure 45–7.

UBIQUITIN IS A KEY MOLECULE IN PROTEIN DEGRADATION

There are two major pathways of protein degradation in eukaryotes. One involves **lysosomal proteases** and does not require ATP. The other pathway involves **ubiquitin** and is ATP-dependent. It plays the major role in the degradation of proteins, and is particularly associated with disposal of misfolded proteins and regulatory enzymes that have short half-lives. Research on ubiquitin has expanded rapidly, and it is known to be involved in cell cycle regulation (degradation of cyclins), DNA repair, activation of NFκB (see Chapter 49), muscle wasting, viral infections, and many other important physiologic and pathologic processes. Ubiquitin is a small (76 amino acids), highly conserved protein that plays a key role in marking various proteins for

subsequent degradation in proteasomes. The mechanism of attachment of ubiquitin to a target protein (eg, a misfolded form of CFTR, the protein involved in the causation of cystic fibrosis; see Chapter 40) is shown in Figure 45–8 and involves three enzymes: an activating enzyme, a conjugating enzyme, and a ligase. There are a number of types of conjugating enzymes, and, surprisingly, some 500 different ligases. It is the latter enzyme that confers substrate specificity. Once the molecule of ubiquitin is attached to the protein, a number of others are also attached, resulting in a polyubiquitinated target protein. It is estimated that a minimum of four ubiquitin molecules must be attached to commit a target molecule to degradation in a proteasome. Ubiquitin can be cleaved from a target protein by deubiquitinating enzymes and the liberated ubiquitin can be reused.

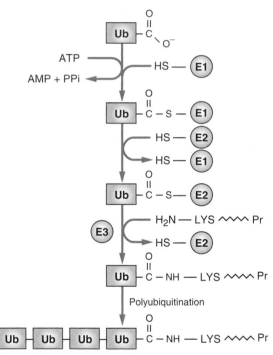

Figure 45–8. Sequence of reactions in addition of ubiquitin to a target protein. (Ub, ubiquitin; E1, activating enzyme; E2, conjugating enzyme; E3, ligase; LYS ∿∿ Pr, target protein.) In the reaction catalyzed by E1, the C-terminal COO⁻ group of ubiquitin is linked in a thioester bond to an SH group of E1. In the reaction catalyzed by E2, the activated ubiquitin is transferred to an SH group of E2. In the reaction catalyzed by E3, ubiquitin is transferred from E2 to an ε-amino group on a lysine of the target protein. Additional rounds of ubiquitination then build up the polyubiquitin chain.

UBIQUITINATED PROTEINS ARE DEGRADED IN PROTEASOMES

Polyubiquitinated target proteins enter the proteasomes, located in the cytosol. The proteasome is a relatively large cylindrical structure and is composed of some 28 subunits arranged in four stacked rings of 7 subunits. It has a hollow core, which is lined by at least three different proteases. Target proteins pass to its core to be degraded to small peptides, which then exit the proteasome (Figure 45–7). Both normally and abnormally folded proteins are substrates for the proteasome. Liberated ubiquitin molecules are recycled. The proteasome plays an important role in presenting small peptides produced by degradation of various viruses and other molecules to major histocompatibility class I molecules, a key step in antigen presentation to T lymphocytes.

TRANSPORT VESICLES ARE KEY PLAYERS IN INTRACELLULAR PROTEIN TRAFFIC

Most proteins that are synthesized on membrane-bound polyribosomes and are destined for the Golgi apparatus or plasma membrane reach these sites inside **transport vesicles.** The precise mechanisms by which proteins synthesized in the rough ER are inserted into these vesicles are not known. Those involved in transport from the ER to the Golgi apparatus and vice versa—and from the Golgi to the plasma membrane—are **mainly clathrin-free,** unlike the coated vesicles involved in endocytosis (see discussions of the LDL receptor in Chapters 25 and 26). For the sake of clarity, the **non-clathrin-coated vesicles** are referred to in this text as **transport vesicles.** There is evidence that proteins destined for the **membranes of the Golgi apparatus** contain specific **signal sequences.** On the other hand, most proteins destined for the **plasma membrane** or for **secretion** do not appear to contain specific signals, reaching these destinations by **default.**

The Golgi Apparatus Is Involved in Glycosylation & Sorting of Proteins

The **Golgi apparatus** plays two important roles in membrane synthesis. First, it is involved in the **processing of the oligosaccharide chains** of membrane and other N-linked glycoproteins and also contains enzymes involved in O-glycosylation (see Chapter 46). Second, it is involved in the **sorting** of various proteins prior to their delivery to their appropriate intracellular destinations. All parts of the Golgi apparatus participate in the first role, whereas the trans-Golgi is particularly involved in the second and is very rich in vesicles. Because of their central role in protein transport, considerable research has been conducted in recent years concerning the formation and fate of transport vesicles.

Table 45–7. Factors involved in the formation of non-clathrin-coated vesicles and their transport.

- ARF: ADP-ribosylation factor, a GTPase
- Coatomer: A family of at least seven coat proteins (α, β, γ, δ, ε, β', and ζ). Different transport vesicles have different complements of coat proteins.
- SNAP: Soluble NSF attachment factor
- SNARE: SNAP receptor
- v-SNARE: Vesicle SNARE
- t-SNARE: Target SNARE
- GTP-γ-S: A nonhydrolyzable analog of GTP, used to test the involvement of GTP
- NEM: N-Ethylmaleimide, a chemical that alkylates sulfhydryl groups
- NSF: NEM-sensitive factor, an ATPase
- Rab proteins: A family of ras-related proteins first observed in rat brain; they are GTPases and are active when GTP is found
- Sec1: A member of a family of proteins that attach to t-SNAREs and are displaced from them by Rab proteins, thereby allowing v-SNARE–t-SNARE interactions to occur.

A Model of Non-Clathrin-Coated Vesicles Involves SNAREs & Other Factors

Vesicles lie at the heart of intracellular transport of many proteins. Recently, significant progress has been made in understanding the events involved in vesicle formation and transport. This has transpired because of the use of a number of approaches. These include establishment of **cell-free systems** with which to study vesicle formation. For instance, it is possible to observe, by electron microscopy, budding of vesicles from Golgi preparations incubated with cytosol and ATP. The development of genetic approaches for studying vesicles in yeast has also been crucial. The picture is complex, with its own nomenclature (Table 45–7), and involves a variety of cytosolic and membrane proteins, GTP, ATP, and accessory factors.

Based largely on a proposal by Rothman and colleagues, anterograde vesicular transport can be considered to occur in eight steps (Figure 45–9). The basic concept is that each transport vesicle bears a unique address marker consisting of one or more **v-SNARE proteins,** while each target membrane bears one or more **complementary t-SNARE proteins** with which the former interact specifically.

Step 1: **Coat assembly** is initiated when ARF is activated by binding GTP, which is exchanged for GDP. This leads to the association of GTP-bound ARF with its putative receptor (hatched in Figure 45–9) in the donor membrane.

Step 2: Membrane-associated ARF **recruits the coat proteins** that comprise the coatomer shell from the cytosol, forming a coated bud.

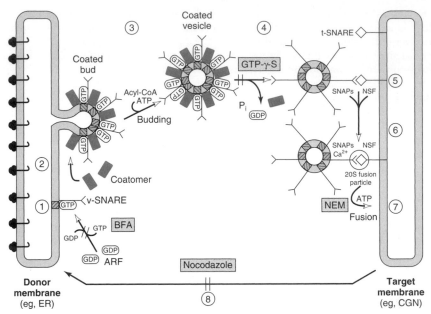

Figure 45–9. Model of the steps in a round of anterograde vesicular transport. The cycle starts in the bottom left-hand side of the figure, where two molecules of ARF are represented as small ovals containing GDP. The steps in the cycle are described in the text. Most of the abbreviations used are explained in Table 45–7. The roles of Rab and Sec1 proteins (see text) in the overall process are not dealt with in this figure. (CGN, cis-Golgi network; BFA, Brefeldin A.) (Adapted from Rothman JE: Mechanisms of intracellular protein transport. Nature 1994;372:55.) (Courtesy of E Degen.)

Step 3: The **bud pinches off** in a process involving acyl-CoA—and probably ATP—to complete the formation of the coated vesicle.

Step 4: **Coat disassembly** (involving dissociation of ARF and coatomer shell) follows hydrolysis of bound GTP; uncoating is necessary for fusion to occur.

Step 5: **Vesicle targeting** is achieved via members of a family of integral proteins, termed v-SNAREs, that tag the vesicle during its budding. v-SNAREs pair with cognate t-SNAREs in the target membrane to dock the vesicle.

It is presumed that steps 4 and 5 are closely coupled and that step 4 may follow step 5, with ARF and the coatomer shell rapidly dissociating after docking.

Step 6: The **general fusion machinery** then assembles on the paired SNARE complex; it includes an ATPase (NSF; NEM-sensitive factor) and the SNAP (soluble NSF attachment factor) proteins. SNAPs bind to the SNARE (SNAP receptor) complex, enabling NSF to bind.

Step 7: **Hydrolysis of ATP by NSF** is essential for fusion, a process that can be inhibited by NEM

(*N*-ethylmaleimide). Certain other proteins and calcium are also required.

Step 8: **Retrograde transport** occurs to restart the cycle. This last step may retrieve certain proteins or recycle v-SNAREs. Nocodazole, a microtubule-disrupting agent, inhibits this step.

Brefeldin A Inhibits the Coating Process

The following points expand and clarify the above.

(a) To participate in step 1, ARF must first be modified by addition of **myristic acid** (C14:0), employing myristoyl-CoA as the acyl donor. **Myristoylation** is one of a number of enzyme-catalyzed posttranslational modifications, involving addition of certain lipids to specific residues of proteins, that facilitate the binding of proteins to the cytosolic surfaces of membranes or vesicles. Others are addition of **palmitate, farnesyl,** and **geranylgeranyl;** the two latter molecules are polyisoprenoids containing 15 and 20 carbon atoms, respectively.

(b) At least three different types of coated vesicles have been distinguished: **COPI, COPII,** and **clathrin-coated vesicles;** the first two are referred to here as **transport vesicles.** Many other types of vesicles no

doubt remain to be discovered. **COPI vesicles** are involved in bidirectional transport from the ER to the Golgi and in the reverse direction, whereas **COPII vesicles** are involved mainly in transport in the former direction. **Clathrin-containing vesicles** are involved in transport from the trans-Golgi network to prelysosomes and from the plasma membrane to endosomes, respectively. Regarding **selection** of cargo molecules by vesicles, this appears to be primarily a function of the coat proteins of vesicles. **Cargo molecules** may interact with coat proteins either directly or via intermediary proteins that attach to coat proteins, and they then become enclosed in their appropriate vesicles.

(c) The fungal metabolite **brefeldin A** prevents GTP from binding to ARF in step 1 and thus inhibits the entire coating process. In its presence, the Golgi apparatus appears to disintegrate, and fragments are lost. It may do this by inhibiting the guanine nucleotide exchanger involved in step 1.

(d) GTP-γ-S (a nonhydrolyzable analog of GTP often used in investigations of the role of GTP in biochemical processes) blocks disassembly of the coat from coated vesicles, leading to a build up of coated vesicles.

(e) A family of Ras-like proteins, called the **Rab protein family,** are required in several steps of intracellular protein transport, regulated secretion, and endocytosis. They are small monomeric GTPases that attach to the cytosolic faces of membranes via geranylgeranyl chains. They attach in the GTP-bound state (not shown in Figure 45–9) to the budding vesicle. Another family of proteins (**Sec1**) binds to t-SNAREs and prevents interaction with them and their complementary v-SNAREs. When a vesicle interacts with its target membrane, Rab proteins displace Sec1 proteins and the v-SNARE-t-SNARE interaction is free to occur. It appears that the Rab and Sec1 families of proteins **regulate the speed of vesicle formation,** opposing each other. Rab proteins have been likened to **throttles** and Sec1 proteins to **dampers** on the overall process of vesicle formation.

(f) Studies using v- and t-SNARE proteins reconstituted into separate lipid bilayer vesicles have indicated that they form **SNAREpins,** ie, SNARE complexes that link two membranes (vesicles). SNAPs and NSF are required for formation of SNAREpins, but once they have formed they can apparently lead to spontaneous fusion of membranes at physiologic temperature, suggesting that they are the minimal machinery required for membrane fusion.

(g) The fusion of synaptic vesicles with the plasma membrane of **neurons** involves a series of events similar to that described above. For example, one v-SNARE is designated **synaptobrevin** and two t-SNAREs are designated **syntaxin** and **SNAP 25** (synaptosome-associated protein of 25 kDa). **Botulinum B toxin** is one of

the most lethal toxins known and the most serious cause of food poisoning. One component of this toxin is a protease that appears to cleave only synaptobrevin, thus inhibiting release of acetylcholine at the neuromuscular junction and possibly proving fatal, depending on the dose taken.

(h) Although the above model **describes nonclathrin-coated vesicles,** it appears likely that many of the events described above apply, at least in principle, to clathrin-coated vesicles.

THE ASSEMBLY OF MEMBRANES IS COMPLEX

There are many cellular membranes, each with its own specific features. No satisfactory scheme describing the assembly of any one of these membranes is available. How various proteins are initially inserted into the membrane of the ER has been discussed above. The transport of proteins, including membrane proteins, to various parts of the cell inside vesicles has also been described. Some general points about membrane assembly remain to be addressed.

Asymmetry of Both Proteins & Lipids Is Maintained during Membrane Assembly

Vesicles formed from membranes of the ER and Golgi apparatus, either naturally or pinched off by homogenization, exhibit **transverse asymmetries** of both lipid and protein. These asymmetries are maintained during fusion of transport vesicles with the plasma membrane. The inside of the vesicles after fusion becomes the outside of the plasma membrane, and the cytoplasmic side of the vesicles remains the cytoplasmic side of the membrane (Figure 45–10). Since the transverse asymmetry of the membranes already exists in the vesicles of the ER well before they are fused to the plasma membrane, a major problem of membrane assembly becomes understanding how the integral proteins are inserted into the lipid bilayer of the ER. This problem was addressed earlier in this chapter.

Phospholipids are the major class of lipid in membranes. The enzymes responsible for the synthesis of phospholipids reside in the cytoplasmic surface of the cisternae of the ER. As phospholipids are synthesized at that site, they probably self-assemble into thermodynamically stable bimolecular layers, thereby expanding the membrane and perhaps promoting the detachment of so-called lipid vesicles from it. It has been proposed that these vesicles travel to other sites, donating their lipids to other membranes; however, little is known about this matter. As indicated above, cytosolic proteins that take up phospholipids from one membrane and release them to another (ie, **phospholipid exchange**

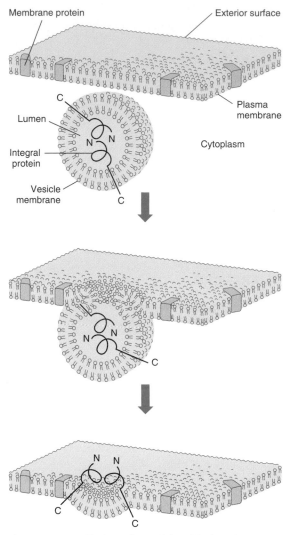

Figure 45–10. Fusion of a vesicle with the plasma membrane preserves the orientation of any integral proteins embedded in the vesicle bilayer. Initially, the amino terminal of the protein faces the lumen, or inner cavity, of such a vesicle. After fusion, the amino terminal is on the exterior surface of the plasma membrane. That the orientation of the protein has not been reversed can be perceived by noting that the other end of the molecule, the carboxyl terminal, is always immersed in the cytoplasm. The lumen of a vesicle and the outside of the cell are topologically equivalent. (Redrawn and modified, with permission, from Lodish HF, Rothman JE: The assembly of cell membranes. Sci Am [Jan] 1979;240:43.)

proteins) have been demonstrated; they probably play a role in contributing to the specific lipid composition of various membranes.

Lipids & Proteins Undergo Turnover at Different Rates in Different Membranes

It has been shown that the half-lives of the lipids of the ER membranes of rat liver are generally shorter than those of its proteins, so that the **turnover rates of lipids and proteins are independent.** Indeed, different lipids have been found to have different half-lives. Furthermore, the half-lives of the proteins of these membranes vary quite widely, some exhibiting short (hours) and others long (days) half-lives. Thus, individual lipids and proteins of the ER membranes appear to be inserted into it relatively independently; this is the case for many other membranes.

The biogenesis of membranes is thus a complex process about which much remains to be learned. One indication of the complexity involved is to consider the number of **posttranslational modifications** that membrane proteins may be subjected to prior to attaining their mature state. These include proteolysis, assembly into multimers, glycosylation, addition of a glycophosphatidylinositol (GPI) anchor, sulfation on tyrosine or carbohydrate moieties, phosphorylation, acylation, and prenylation—a list that is undoubtedly not complete. Nevertheless, significant progress has been made; Table 45–8 summarizes some of the major features of membrane assembly that have emerged to date.

Various Disorders Result from Mutations in Genes Encoding Proteins Involved in Intracellular Transport

Some of these are listed in Table 45–9; the majority affect **lysosomal function.** A number of other muta-

Table 45–8. Major features of membrane assembly.

- Lipids and proteins are inserted independently into membranes.
- Individual membrane lipids and proteins turn over independently and at different rates.
- Topogenic sequences (eg, signal [amino terminal or internal] and stop-transfer) are important in determining the insertion and disposition of proteins in membranes.
- Membrane proteins inside transport vesicles bud off the endoplasmic reticulum on their way to the Golgi; final sorting of many membrane proteins occurs in the trans-Golgi network.
- Specific sorting sequences guide proteins to particular organelles such as lysosomes, peroxisomes, and mitochondria.

Table 45–9. Some disorders due to mutations in genes encoding proteins involved in intracellular membrane transport.[1]

Disorder[2]	Protein Involved
Chédiak-Higashi syndrome, 214500	Lysosomal trafficking regulator
Combined deficiency of factors V and VIII, 227300	ERGIC53, a mannose-binding lectin, multiple coagulation factor deficiency protein 2 (MCFD2)
Hermansky-Pudlak syndrome, 203300	AP-3 adaptor complex β3A subunit
I-cell disease, 252500	N-Acetylglucosamine 1-phosphotransferase
Oculocerebrorenal syndrome, 309000	OCRL-1, a PIP_2 5-phosphatase

[1]Modified from Olkonnen VM, Ikonen E: Genetic defects of intracellular-membrane transport. N Eng J Med 2000;343:1095. Certain related conditions not listed here are also described in this publication. I-cell disease is described in Chapter 46. The majority of the disorders listed above affect lysosomal function; readers should consult a textbook of medicine for information on the clinical manifestations of these conditions.
[2]The numbers after each disorder are the OMIM numbers.

tions affecting intracellular protein transport have been reported but are not included here.

SUMMARY

- Many proteins are targeted to their destinations by signal sequences. A major sorting decision is made when proteins are partitioned between cytosolic and membrane-bound polyribosomes by virtue of the absence or presence of a signal peptide.
- The pathways of protein import into mitochondria, nuclei, peroxisomes, and the endoplasmic reticulum are described.
- Many proteins synthesized on membrane-bound polyribosomes proceed to the Golgi apparatus and the plasma membrane in transport vesicles.
- A number of glycosylation reactions occur in compartments of the Golgi, and proteins are further sorted in the trans-Golgi network.

- Most proteins destined for the plasma membrane and for secretion appear to lack specific signals—a default mechanism.
- The role of chaperone proteins in the folding of proteins is presented and the unfolded protein response is described.
- Endoplasmic reticulum–associated degradation is described and the key role of ubiquitin in protein degradation is shown.
- A model describing budding and attachment of transport vesicles to a target membrane is summarized.
- Membrane assembly is discussed and shown to be complex. Asymmetry of both lipids and proteins is maintained during membrane assembly.
- A number of disorders have been shown to be due to mutations in genes encoding proteins involved in various aspects of protein traffic and sorting.

REFERENCES

Alder NN, Johnson AE: Cotranslational membrane protein biogenesis at the endoplasmic reticulum. J Biol Chem 2004;279:22787.

Dalbey RE, von Heijne G (editors): *Protein Targeting, Transport and Translocation.* Academic Press, 2002.

Ellgaard L, Helenius A: Quality control in the endoplasmic reticulum. Nat Rev Mol Cell Biol 2003;4:181.

Koehler CM: New developments in mitochondrial assembly. Ann Rev Cell Dev Biol 2004;20:309.

Lee MCS et al: Bi-directional protein transport between the ER and Golgi. Ann Rev Cell Dev Biol 2004;20:87.

Lodish H et al: *Molecular Cell Biology,* 5th ed. WH Freeman & Co., 2004.

Owen DJ, Collins BM, Evans PR: Adaptors for clathrin coats: structure and function. Ann Rev Cell Dev Biol 2004;20:153.

Romisch K: Endoplasmic-reticulum–associated degradation. Ann Rev Cell Dev Biol 2005;21:435.

Schroder M, Kaufman RJ: The mammalian unfolded protein response. Ann Rev Biochem 2005;74:739.

Trombetta ES, Parodi AJ: Quality control and protein folding in the secretory pathway. Ann Rev Cell Dev Biol 2003;19:649.

Van Meer G, Sprong H: Membrane lipids and vesicular traffic. Curr Opin Cell Biol 2004;16:373.

Vance DE, Vance J: *Biochemistry of Lipids, Lipoproteins and Membranes,* 4th ed. Elsevier, 2002.

Wiedemann N, Frazier AE, Pfanner N: The protein import machinery of mitochondria. J Biol Chem 2004;279:14473.

Zaidiu SK et al: Intranuclear trafficking: organization and assembly of regulatory machinery for combinatorial biological control. J Biol Chem 2004;279:43363.

Glycoproteins

46

Robert K. Murray, MD, PhD

BIOMEDICAL IMPORTANCE

Glycobiology is the study of the roles of sugars in health and disease. The **glycome** is the entire complement of sugars, whether free or present in more complex molecules, of an organism. **Glycomics,** an analogous term to genomics and proteomics, is the comprehensive study of glycomes, including genetic, physiologic, pathologic, and other aspects.

One major class of molecules included in the glycome is **glycoproteins.** These are proteins that contain oligosaccharide chains (glycans) covalently attached to their polypeptide backbones. It has been estimated that approximately 50% of eukaryotic proteins have sugars attached, so that **glycosylation** (enzymic attachment of sugars) is the most frequent post-translational modification of proteins. Nonenzymic attachment of sugars to proteins can also occur, and is referred to as **glycation.** This process can have serious pathologic consequences (eg, in uncontrolled diabetes mellitus). Glycoproteins are one class of **glycoconjugate** or **complex carbohydrate**—equivalent terms used to denote molecules containing one or more carbohydrate chains covalently linked to protein (to form glycoproteins or proteoglycans) or lipid (to form glycolipids). (**Proteoglycans** are discussed in Chapter 47 and **glycolipids** in Chapter 15.) Almost all the **plasma proteins** of humans—except albumin—are glycoproteins. Many **proteins of cellular membranes** (Chapter 40) contain substantial amounts of carbohydrate. A number of the **blood group substances** are glycoproteins, whereas others are glycosphingolipids. Certain **hormones** (eg, chorionic gonadotropin) are glycoproteins. A major problem in cancer is **metastasis,** the phenomenon whereby cancer cells leave their tissue of origin (eg, the breast), migrate through the bloodstream to some distant site in the body (eg, the brain), and grow there in an unregulated manner, with catastrophic results for the affected individual. Many cancer researchers think that alterations in the structures of glycoproteins and other glycoconjugates on the surfaces of cancer cells are important in the phenomenon of metastasis.

GLYCOPROTEINS OCCUR WIDELY & PERFORM NUMEROUS FUNCTIONS

Glycoproteins occur in most organisms, from bacteria to humans. Many viruses also contain glycoproteins, some of which have been much investigated, in part because they often play key roles in viral attachment to cells (eg, HIV-1 and influenza A virus). Numerous proteins with diverse functions are glycoproteins (Table 46–1); their carbohydrate content ranges from 1% to over 85% by weight.

Many studies have been conducted in an attempt to define the precise roles oligosaccharide chains play in the functions of glycoproteins. Table 46–2 summarizes results from such studies. Some of the functions listed are firmly established; others are still under investigation.

OLIGOSACCHARIDE CHAINS ENCODE BIOLOGIC INFORMATION

An enormous number of glycosidic linkages can be generated between sugars. For example, three different hexoses may be linked to each other to form over 1000 different trisaccharides. The conformations of the sugars in oligosaccharide chains vary depending on their linkages and proximity to other molecules with which the oligosaccharides may interact. It is now established that certain oligosaccharide chains encode considerable **biologic information** and that this depends upon their constituent sugars, their sequences, and their linkages. For instance, mannose 6-phosphate residues target newly synthesized lysosomal enzymes to that organelle (see later). Utilizing the biologic information that sugars contain involves interactions between specific sugars, either free or in glycoconjugates, and proteins (such as lectins; see below) or other sugar-containing molecules. These interactions lead to changes of cellular activity. Thus, deciphering the so-called sugar code entails elucidating all of the interactions that sugars and sugar-containing molecules participate in, and also the results of these interactions on cellular behavior. This will not be an easy task, considering the diversity of glycans found in cells.

Table 46–1. Some functions served by glycoproteins.

Function	Glycoproteins
Structural molecule	Collagens
Lubricant and protective agent	Mucins
Transport molecule	Transferrin, ceruloplasmin
Immunologic molecule	Immunoglobulins, histocompatibility antigens
Hormone	Chorionic gonadotropin, thyroid-stimulating hormone (TSH)
Enzyme	Various, eg, alkaline phosphatase
Cell attachment-recognition site	Various proteins involved in cell-cell (eg, sperm-oocyte), virus-cell, bacterium-cell, and hormone-cell interactions
Antifreeze	Certain plasma proteins of cold-water fish
Interact with specific carbohydrates	Lectins, selectins (cell adhesion lectins), antibodies
Receptor	Various proteins involved in hormone and drug action
Affect folding of certain proteins	Calnexin, calreticulin
Regulation of development	Notch and its analogs, key proteins in development
Hemostasis (and thrombosis)	Specific glycoproteins on the surface membranes of platelets

Table 46–2. Some functions of the oligosaccharide chains of glycoproteins.[1]

- Modulate physicochemical properties, eg, solubility, viscosity, charge, conformation, denaturation, and binding sites for bacteria and viruses
- Protect against proteolysis, from inside and outside of cell
- Affect proteolytic processing of precursor proteins to smaller products
- Are involved in biologic activity, eg, of human chorionic gonadotropin (hCG)
- Affect insertion into membranes, intracellular migration, sorting and secretion
- Affect embryonic development and differentiation
- May affect sites of metastases selected by cancer cells

[1]Adapted from Schachter H: Biosynthetic controls that determine the branching and heterogeneity of protein-bound oligosaccharides. Biochem Cell Biol 1986;64:163.

TECHNIQUES ARE AVAILABLE FOR DETECTION, PURIFICATION, STRUCTURAL ANALYSIS, & SYNTHESIS OF GLYCOPROTEINS

A variety of methods used in the detection, purification, and structural analysis of glycoproteins are listed in Table 46–3. The conventional methods used to purify proteins and enzymes are also applicable to the purification of glycoproteins. Once a glycoprotein has been purified, the use of **mass spectrometry** and **high-resolution NMR spectroscopy** can often identify the structures of its glycan chains. Analysis of glycoproteins can be complicated by the fact that they often exist as **glycoforms;** these are proteins with identical amino acid sequences but somewhat different oligosaccharide compositions. Although linkage details are not stressed in this chapter, it is critical to appreciate that the precise natures of the linkages between the sugars of glycoproteins are of fundamental importance in determining the structures and functions of these molecules.

Impressive advances are also being made in **synthetic chemistry,** allowing synthesis of complex glycans that can be tested for biologic and pharmacologic activity. In addition, methods have been developed that use simple organisms, such as yeasts, to secrete human glycoproteins of therapeutic value (eg, erythropoietin) into their surrounding medium.

EIGHT SUGARS PREDOMINATE IN HUMAN GLYCOPROTEINS

About 200 monosaccharides are found in nature; however, only eight are commonly found in the oligosaccharide chains of glycoproteins (Table 46–4). Most of these sugars were described in Chapter 14. N-Acetylneuraminic acid (NeuAc) is usually found at the termini of oligosaccharide chains, attached to subterminal galactose (Gal) or N-acetylgalactosamine (GalNAc) residues. The other sugars listed are generally found in more internal positions. **Sulfate** is often found in glycoproteins, usually attached to Gal, GalNAc, or GlcNAc.

The sugars other than glucose listed in Table 46–4 have been thought to be able to be synthesized from glucose in amounts adequate to sustain body needs. There are enzymes in human tissue that can make these sugars from glucose. However, there is evidence that the other sugars may be beneficial in some circumstances when added to the diet. This has led to the development of **glyconutrient supplements,** containing either members of the sugars listed in Table 46–4 (excluding glucose) or precursors of them. The efficacy of such supplements is under study.

Table 46–3. Some important methods used to study glycoproteins.

Method	Use
Periodic acid–Schiff reagent	Detects glycoproteins as pink bands after electrophoretic separation.
Incubation of cultured cells with glycoproteins as radioactive bands	Leads to detection of a radioactive sugar after electrophoretic separation.
Treatment with appropriate endo- or exoglycosidase or phospholipases	Resultant shifts in electrophoretic migration help distinguish among proteins with N-glycan, O-glycan, or GPI linkages and also between high mannose and complex N-glycans.
Sepharose-lectin column chromatography	To purify glycoproteins or glycopeptides that bind the particular lectin used.
Compositional analysis following acid hydrolysis	Identifies sugars that the glycoprotein contains and their stoichiometry.
Mass spectrometry	Provides information on molecular mass, composition, sequence, and sometimes branching of a glycan chain.
NMR spectroscopy	To identify specific sugars, their sequence, linkages, and the anomeric nature of glycosidic linkages.
Methylation (linkage) analysis	To determine linkages between sugars.
Amino acid or cDNA sequencing	Determination of amino acid sequence.

NUCLEOTIDE SUGARS ACT AS SUGAR DONORS IN MANY BIOSYNTHETIC REACTIONS

It is important to understand that in most biosynthetic reactions, it is not the free sugar or phosphorylated sugar that is involved in such reactions, but rather the corresponding nucleotide sugar. The first nucleotide sugar to be reported was uridine diphosphate glucose (UDP-Glc); its structure is shown in Figure 19–2. The common nucleotide sugars involved in the biosynthesis of glycoproteins are listed in Table 46–4; the reasons some contain UDP and others guanosine diphosphate (GDP) or cytidine monophosphate (CMP) are obscure. Many of the glycosylation reactions involved in the biosynthesis of glycoproteins utilize these compounds (see

below). The anhydro nature of the linkage between the phosphate group and the sugars is of the high-energy, high-group-transfer-potential type (Chapter 11). The sugars of these compounds are thus "activated" and can be transferred to suitable acceptors provided appropriate transferases are available.

Most nucleotide sugars are formed in the cytosol, generally from reactions involving the corresponding nucleoside triphosphate. CMP-sialic acids are formed in the nucleus. Formation of uridine diphosphate galactose (UDP-Gal) requires the following two reactions in mammalian tissues:

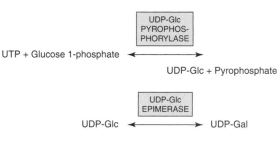

Because many glycosylation reactions occur within the lumen of the Golgi apparatus, **carrier systems** (permeases, transporters) are necessary to transport nucleotide sugars across the Golgi membrane. Systems transporting UDP-Gal, GDP-Man, and CMP-NeuAc into the cisternae of the Golgi apparatus have been described. They are **antiport** systems; ie, the influx of one molecule of nucleotide sugar is balanced by the efflux of one molecule of the corresponding nucleotide (eg, UMP, GMP, or CMP) formed from the nucleotide sugars. This mechanism ensures an adequate concentration of each nucleotide sugar inside the Golgi apparatus. UMP is formed from UDP-Gal in the above process as follows:

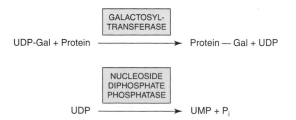

EXO- & ENDOGLYCOSIDASES FACILITATE STUDY OF GLYCOPROTEINS

A number of **glycosidases** of defined specificity have proved useful in examining structural and functional aspects of glycoproteins (Table 46–5). These enzymes act at either external (exoglycosidases) or internal (endoglycosidases) positions of oligosaccharide chains. Examples of exoglycosidases are **neuraminidases** and **galactosidases;**

Table 46–4. The principal sugars found in human glycoproteins. Their structures are illustrated in Chapter 14.

Sugar	Type	Abbreviation	Nucleotide Sugar	Comments
Galactose	Hexose	Gal	UDP-Gal	Often found subterminal to NeuAc in N-linked glycoproteins. Also found in core trisaccharide of proteoglycans.
Glucose	Hexose	Glc	UDP-Glc	Present during the biosynthesis of N-linked glycoproteins but not usually present in mature glycoproteins. Present in some clotting factors.
Mannose	Hexose	Man	GDP-Man	Common sugar in N-linked glycoproteins.
N-Acetylneuraminic acid	Sialic acid (nine C atoms)	NeuAc	CMP-NeuAc	Often the terminal sugar in both N- and O-linked glycoproteins. Other types of sialic acid are also found, but NeuAc is the major species found in humans. Acetyl groups may also occur as O-acetyl species as well as N-acetyl.
Fucose	Deoxyhexose	Fuc	GDP-Fuc	May be external in both N- and O-linked glycoproteins or internal, linked to the GlcNAc residue attached to Asn in N-linked species. Can also occur internally attached to the OH of Ser (eg, in t-PA and certain clotting factors).
N-Acetylgalactosamine	Aminohexose	GalNAc	UDP-GalNAc	Present in both N- and O-linked glycoproteins.
N-Acetylglucosamine	Aminohexose	GlcNAc	UDP-GlcNAc	The sugar attached to the polypeptide chain via Asn in N-linked glycoproteins; also found at other sites in the oligosaccharides of these proteins. Many nuclear proteins have GlcNAc attached to the OH of Ser or Thr as a single sugar.
Xylose	Pentose	Xyl	UDP-Xyl	Xyl is attached to the OH of Ser in many proteoglycans. Xyl in turn is attached to two Gal residues, forming a link trisaccharide. Xyl is also found in t-PA and certain clotting factors.

their sequential use removes terminal NeuAc and subterminal Gal residues from most glycoproteins. **Endoglycosidases F and H** are examples of the latter class; these enzymes cleave the oligosaccharide chains at specific GlcNAc residues close to the polypeptide backbone (ie, at internal sites; Figure 46–5) and are thus useful in releasing large oligosaccharide chains for structural analyses. A glycoprotein can be treated with one or more of the above glycosidases to analyze the effects on its biologic behavior of removal of specific sugars.

Table 46–5. Some glycosidases used to study the structure and function of glycoproteins.[1]

Enzymes	Type
Neuraminidases	Exoglycosidase
Galactosidases	Exo- or endoglycosidase
Endoglycosidase F	Endoglycosidase
Endoglycosidase H	Endoglycosidase

[1]The enzymes are available from a variety of sources and are often specific for certain types of glycosidic linkages and also for their anomeric natures. The sites of action of endoglycosidases F and H are shown in Figure 46–5. F acts on both high-mannose and complex oligosaccharides, whereas H acts on the former.

THE MAMMALIAN ASIALOGLYCOPROTEIN RECEPTOR IS INVOLVED IN CLEARANCE OF CERTAIN GLYCOPROTEINS FROM PLASMA BY HEPATOCYTES

Experiments performed by Ashwell and his colleagues in the early 1970s played an important role in focusing attention on the functional significance of the oligosaccharide chains of glycoproteins. They treated rabbit ceruloplasmin (a plasma protein; see Chapter 49) with neuraminidase in vitro. This procedure exposed subterminal Gal residues that were normally masked by termi-

nal NeuAc residues. Neuraminidase-treated radioactive ceruloplasmin was found to disappear rapidly from the circulation, in contrast to the slow clearance of the untreated protein. Very significantly, when the Gal residues exposed to treatment with neuraminidase were removed by treatment with a galactosidase, the clearance rate of the protein returned to normal. Further studies demonstrated that liver cells contain a **mammalian asialoglycoprotein receptor** that recognizes the Gal moiety of many desialylated plasma proteins and leads to their endocytosis. This work indicated that an individual sugar, such as Gal, could play an important role in governing at least one of the biologic properties (ie, time of residence in the circulation) of certain glycoproteins. This greatly strengthened the concept that oligosaccharide chains could contain biologic information.

LECTINS CAN BE USED TO PURIFY GLYCOPROTEINS & TO PROBE THEIR FUNCTIONS

Lectins are carbohydrate-binding proteins that agglutinate cells or precipitate glycoconjugates; a number of lectins are themselves glycoproteins. Immunoglobulins that react with sugars are not considered lectins. Lectins contain at least two sugar-binding sites; proteins with a single sugar-binding site will not agglutinate cells or precipitate glycoconjugates. The specificity of a lectin is usually defined by the sugars that are best at inhibiting its ability to cause agglutination or precipitation. Enzymes, toxins, and transport proteins can be classified as lectins if they bind carbohydrate. Lectins were first discovered in plants and microbes, but many lectins of animal origin are now known. The mammalian asialoglycoprotein receptor described above is an important example of an animal lectin. Some important lectins are listed in Table 46–6. Much current research is centered on the roles of various animal lectins in the mechanisms of action of glycoproteins, some of which are discussed below (eg, with regard to the selectins).

Numerous lectins have been purified and are commercially available; three plant lectins that have been widely used experimentally are listed in Table 46–7. Among many uses, lectins have been employed to purify specific glycoproteins, as tools for probing the glycoprotein profiles of cell surfaces, and as reagents for generating mutant cells deficient in certain enzymes involved in the biosynthesis of oligosaccharide chains.

THERE ARE THREE MAJOR CLASSES OF GLYCOPROTEINS

Based on the nature of the linkage between their polypeptide chains and their oligosaccharide chains, glycoproteins can be divided into three major classes (Figure

Table 46–6. Some important lectins.

Lectins	Examples or Comments
Legume lectins	Concanavalin A, pea lectin
Wheat germ agglutinin	Widely used in studies of surfaces of normal cells and cancer cells
Ricin	Cytotoxic glycoprotein derived from seeds of the castor plant
Bacterial toxins	Heat-labile enterotoxin of *E coli* and cholera toxin
Influenza virus hemagglutinin	Responsible for host-cell attachment and membrane fusion
C-type lectins	Characterized by a Ca^{2+}-dependent carbohydrate recognition domain (CRD); includes the mammalian asialoglycoprotein receptor, the selectins, and the mannose-binding protein
S-type lectins	β-Galactoside-binding animal lectins with roles in cell-cell and cell-matrix interactions
P-type lectins	Mannose 6-P receptor
I-type lectins	Members of the immunoglobulin superfamily, eg, sialoadhesin mediating adhesion of macrophages to various cells

46–1): (1) those containing an O-glycosidic linkage (ie, O-linked), involving the hydroxyl side chain of serine or threonine and a sugar such as *N*-acetylgalactosamine (GalNAc-Ser[Thr]); (2) those containing an N-glycosidic linkage (ie, N-linked), involving the amide nitrogen of asparagine and *N*-acetylglucosamine (GlcNAc-Asn); and (3) those linked to the carboxyl terminal amino acid of a protein via a phosphoryl-ethanolamine moiety joined to an oligosaccharide (glycan), which in turn is linked via glucosamine to phosphatidylinositol (PI). This latter class is referred to as **glycosylphosphatidylinositol-anchored** (**GPI-anchored,** or **GPI-linked**) glycoproteins. Other minor classes of glycoproteins also exist.

Table 46–7. Three plant lectins and the sugars with which they interact.[1]

Lectin	Abbreviation	Sugars
Concanavalin A	ConA	Man and Glc
Soybean lectin		Gal and GalNAc
Wheat germ agglutinin	WGA	Glc and NeuAc

[1]In most cases, lectins show specificity for the anomeric nature of the glycosidic linkage (α or β); this is not indicated in the table.

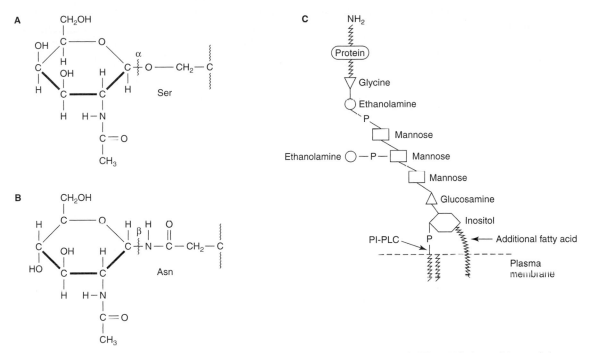

Figure 46–1. Depictions of **(A)** an O-linkage (*N*-acetylgalactosamine to serine); **(B)** an N-linkage (*N*-acetylglu-cosamine to asparagine) and **(C)** a glycosylphosphatidylinositol (GPI) linkage. The GPI structure shown is that linking acetylcholinesterase to the plasma membrane of the human red blood cell. The carboxyl terminal amino acid is glycine joined in amide linkage via its COOH group to the NH₂ group of phosphorylethanolamine, which in turn is joined to a mannose residue. The core glycan contains three mannose and one glucosamine residues. The glucosamine is linked to inositol, which is attached to phosphatidic acid. The site of action of PI-phospholi-pase C (PI-PLC) is indicated. The structure of the core glycan is shown in the text. This particular GPI contains an extra fatty acid attached to inositol and also an extra phosphorylethanolamine moiety attached to the middle of the three mannose residues. Variations found among different GPI structures include the identity of the carboxyl terminal amino acid, the molecules attached to the mannose residues, and the precise nature of the lipid moiety. (Republished with permission conveyed through Copyright Clearance Center, Inc.)

The number of oligosaccharide chains attached to one protein can vary from one to 30 or more, with the sugar chains ranging from one or two residues in length to much larger structures. Many proteins contain more than one type of linkage; for instance, **glycophorin,** an important red cell membrane glycoprotein (Chapter 51), contains both O- and N-linked oligosaccharides.

GLYCOPROTEINS CONTAIN SEVERAL TYPES OF O-GLYCOSIDIC LINKAGES

At least four subclasses of O-glycosidic linkages are found in human glycoproteins: (1) The **GalNAc-Ser(Thr)** linkage shown in Figure 46–1 is the predominant linkage. Two typical oligosaccharide chains found in members of this subclass are shown in Figure 46–2. Usually a Gal or a NeuAc residue is attached to the Gal-NAc, but many variations in the sugar compositions and lengths of such oligosaccharide chains are found. This

type of linkage is found in **mucins** (see below). (2) **Pro-teoglycans** contain a **Gal-Gal-Xyl-Ser** trisaccharide (the so-called link trisaccharide). (3) **Collagens** contain a **Gal-hydroxylysine (Hyl)** linkage. (Subclasses [2] and [3] are discussed further in Chapter 47.) (4) Many **nuclear proteins** (eg, certain transcription factors) and **cytosolic proteins** contain side chains consisting of a single GlcNAc attached to a serine or threonine residue **(GlcNAc-Ser[Thr]).**

Mucins Have a High Content of O-Linked Oligosaccharides & Exhibit Repeating Amino Acid Sequences

Mucins are glycoproteins with two major characteristics: (1) a high content of **O-linked oligosaccharides** (the carbohydrate content of mucins is generally more than 50%); and (2) the presence of **repeating amino acid sequences** (tandem repeats) in the center of their poly-

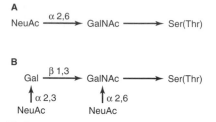

Figure 46–2. Structures of two O-linked oligosaccharides found in **(A)** submaxillary mucins and **(B)** fetuin and in the sialoglycoprotein of the membrane of human red blood cells. (Modified and reproduced, with permission, from Lennarz WJ: *The Biochemistry of Glycoproteins and Proteoglycans.* Plenum Press, 1980. Reproduced with kind permission from Springer Science and Business Media.)

peptide backbones, to which the O-glycan chains are attached in clusters (Figure 46–3). These sequences are rich in serine, threonine, and proline. Although O-glycans predominate, mucins often contain a number of N-glycan chains. Both **secretory** and **membrane-bound** mucins occur. The former are found in the mucus present in the secretions of the gastrointestinal, respiratory, and reproductive tracts. **Mucus** consists of about 94% water and 5% mucins, with the remainder being a mixture of various cell molecules, electrolytes, and remnants of cells. Secretory mucins generally have an oligomeric structure and thus often have a very high molecular mass. The oligomers are composed of monomers linked by disulfide bonds. Mucus exhibits a high **viscosity** and often forms a

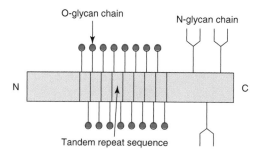

Figure 46–3. Schematic diagram of a mucin. O-glycan chains are shown attached to the central region of the extended polypeptide chain and N-glycan chains to the carboxyl terminal region. The narrow rectangles represent a series of tandem repeat amino acid sequences. Many mucins contain cysteine residues whose SH groups form interchain linkages; these are not shown in the figure. (Adapted from Strous GJ, Dekker J: Mucin-type glycoproteins. Crit Rev Biochem Mol Biol 1992;27:57. Copyright © 1992. Reproduced by permission of Taylor & Francis Group, LLC., http://www.taylorandfrancis.com.)

gel. These qualities are functions of its content of mucins. The high content of O-glycans confers an extended structure on mucins. This is in part explained by steric interactions between their GalNAc moieties and adjacent amino acids, resulting in a chain-stiffening effect so that the conformations of mucins often become those of rigid rods. Intermolecular noncovalent interactions between various sugars on neighboring glycan chains contribute to gel formation. The high content of **NeuAc** and **sulfate** residues found in many mucins confers a negative charge on them. With regard to function, mucins help **lubricate** and form a **protective physical barrier** on epithelial surfaces. Membrane-bound mucins participate in various **cell-cell interactions** (eg, involving selectins; see below). The density of oligosaccharide chains makes it difficult for **proteases** to approach their polypeptide backbones, so that mucins are often resistant to their action. Mucins also tend to "mask" certain surface antigens. Many cancer cells form excessive amounts of mucins; perhaps the mucins may mask certain surface antigens on such cells and thus protect the cells from immune surveillance. Mucins also carry cancer-specific peptide and carbohydrate epitopes (an epitope is a site on an antigen recognized by an antibody, also called an antigenic determinant). Some of these epitopes have been used to stimulate an immune response against cancer cells.

The **genes** encoding the polypeptide backbones of a number of mucins derived from various tissues (eg, pancreas, small intestine, trachea and bronchi, stomach, and salivary glands) have been cloned and sequenced. These studies have revealed new information about the polypeptide backbones of mucins (size of tandem repeats, potential sites of N-glycosylation, etc) and ultimately should reveal aspects of their genetic control. Some important properties of mucins are summarized in Table 46–8.

The Biosynthesis of O-Linked Glycoproteins Uses Nucleotide Sugars

The polypeptide chains of O-linked and other glycoproteins are encoded by mRNA species; because most

Table 46–8. Some properties of mucins.

- Found in secretions of the gastrointestinal, respiratory, and reproductive tracts and also in membranes of various cells.
- Exhibit high content of O-glycan chains, usually containing NeuAc.
- Contain repeating amino acid sequences rich in serine, threonine, and proline.
- Extended structure contributes to their high viscoelasticity.
- Form protective physical barrier on epithelial surfaces, are involved in cell-cell interactions, and may contain or mask certain surface antigens.

Table 46–9. Summary of main features of O-glycosylation.

- Involves a battery of membrane-bound glycoprotein glycosyltransferases acting in a stepwise manner; each transferase is generally specific for a particular type of linkage.
- The enzymes involved are located in various subcompartments of the Golgi apparatus.
- Each glycosylation reaction involves the appropriate nucleotide-sugar.
- Dolichol-P-P-oligosaccharide is not involved, nor are glycosidases; and the reactions are not inhibited by tunicamycin.
- O-Glycosylation occurs posttranslationally at certain Ser and Thr residues.

glycoproteins are membrane-bound or secreted, they are generally translated on membrane-bound polyribosomes (Chapter 37). Hundreds of different oligosaccharide chains of the O-glycosidic type exist. These glycoproteins are built up by the **stepwise donation of sugars from nucleotide sugars,** such as UDP-GalNAc, UDP-Gal, and CMP-NeuAc. The enzymes catalyzing this type of reaction are membrane-bound **glycoprotein glycosyltransferases.** Generally, synthesis of one specific type of linkage requires the activity of a correspondingly specific transferase. The factors that determine which specific serine and threonine residues are glycosylated have not

been identified but are probably found in the peptide structure surrounding the glycosylation site. The enzymes assembling O-linked chains are located in the Golgi apparatus, sequentially arranged in an assembly line with terminal reactions occurring in the trans-Golgi compartments.

The major features of the biosynthesis of O-linked glycoproteins are summarized in Table 46–9.

N-LINKED GLYCOPROTEINS CONTAIN AN Asn-GlcNAc LINKAGE

N-Linked glycoproteins are distinguished by the presence of the Asn-GlcNAc linkage (Figure 46–1). It is the major class of glycoproteins and has been much studied, since the most readily accessible glycoproteins (eg, plasma proteins) mainly belong to this group. It includes both **membrane-bound** and **circulating** glycoproteins. The principal difference between this and the previous class, apart from the nature of the amino acid to which the oligosaccharide chain is attached (Asn versus Ser or Thr), concerns their biosynthesis.

Complex, Hybrid, & High-Mannose Are the Three Major Classes of N-Linked Oligosaccharides

There are three major classes of N-linked oligosaccharides: **complex, hybrid,** and **high-mannose** (Figure 46–4). Each type shares a common pentasaccharide,

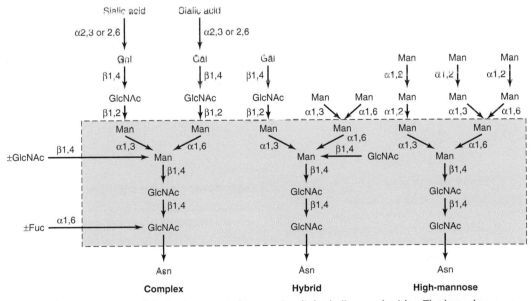

Figure 46–4. Structures of the major types of asparagine-linked oligosaccharides. The boxed area encloses the pentasaccharide core common to all N-linked glycoproteins. (Reproduced, with permission, from Kornfeld R, Kornfeld S: Assembly of asparagine-linked oligosaccharides. Annu Rev Biochem 1985;54:631. Copyright © 1985 by Annual Reviews, www.annualreviews.org. Reprinted with permission.)

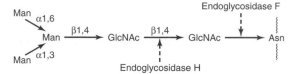

Figure 46–5. Schematic diagram of the pentasaccharide core common to all N-linked glycoproteins and to which various outer chains of oligosaccharides may be attached. The sites of action of endoglycosidases F and H are also indicated.

Man$_3$GlcNAc$_2$—shown within the boxed area in Figure 46–4 and depicted also in Figure 46–5—but they differ in their outer branches. The presence of the **common pentasaccharide** is explained by the fact that all three classes share an initial common mechanism of biosynthesis. Glycoproteins of the complex type generally contain terminal NeuAc residues and underlying Gal and GlcNAc residues, the latter often constituting the disaccharide *N*-acetyllactosamine. Repeating ***N*-acetyllactosamine units**—[Galβ1–3/4GlcNAcβ1–3]$_n$ (poly-*N*-acetyllactosaminoglycans)—are often found on N-linked glycan chains. I/i blood group substances belong to this class. The majority of complex-type oligosaccharides contain two, three, or four outer branches (Figure 46–4), but structures containing five branches have also been described. The oligosaccharide branches are often referred to as **antennae,** so that bi-, tri-, tetra-, and penta-antennary structures may all be found. A bewildering number of chains of the complex type exist, and that indicated in Figure 46–4 is only one of many. Other complex chains may terminate in Gal or Fuc. High-mannose oligosaccharides typically have two to six additional Man residues linked to the pentasaccharide core. Hybrid molecules contain features of both of the two other classes.

The Biosynthesis of N-Linked Glycoproteins Involves Dolichol-P-P-Oligosaccharide

Leloir and his colleagues described the occurrence of a **dolichol-pyrophosphate-oligosaccharide (Dol-P-P-oligosaccharide),** which subsequent research showed to play a key role in the biosynthesis of N-linked glycopro-

teins. The oligosaccharide chain of this compound generally has the structure R-GlcNAc$_2$Man$_9$Glc$_3$ (R = Dol-P-P). The sugars of this compound are first assembled on the Dol-P-P backbone, and the oligosaccharide chain is then transferred en bloc to suitable Asn residues of acceptor apoglycoproteins during their synthesis on membrane-bound polyribosomes. All N-glycans have a common pentasaccharide core structure (Figure 46–5).

To form **high-mannose** chains, only the Glc residues plus certain of the peripheral Man residues are removed. To form an oligosaccharide chain of the **complex type,** the Glc residues and four of the Man residues are removed by glycosidases in the endoplasmic reticulum and Golgi. The sugars characteristic of complex chains (GlcNAc, Gal, NeuAc) are added by the action of individual glycosyltransferases located in the Golgi apparatus. The phenomenon whereby the glycan chains of N-linked glycoproteins are first partially degraded and then in some cases rebuilt is referred to as **oligosaccharide processing. Hybrid chains** are formed by partial processing, forming complex chains on one arm and Man structures on the other arm.

Thus, the initial steps involved in the biosynthesis of the N-linked glycoproteins differ markedly from those involved in the biosynthesis of the O-linked glycoproteins. The former involves Dol-P-P-oligosaccharide; the latter, as described earlier, does not.

The process of N-glycosylation can be broken down into two stages: (1) assembly of Dol-P-P-oligosaccharide and transfer of the oligosaccharide; and (2) processing of the oligosaccharide chain.

A. ASSEMBLY & TRANSFER OF DOLICHOL-P-P-OLIGOSACCHARIDE

Polyisoprenol compounds exist in both bacteria and eukaryotic cells. They participate in the synthesis of bacterial polysaccharides and in the biosynthesis of N-linked glycoproteins and GPI anchors. The polyisoprenol used in eukaryotic tissues is **dolichol,** which is, next to rubber, the longest naturally occurring hydrocarbon made up of a single repeating unit. Dolichol is composed of 17–20 repeating isoprenoid units (Figure 46–6).

Before it participates in the biosynthesis of Dol-P-P-oligosaccharide, dolichol must first be phosphorylated to form dolichol phosphate (Dol-P) in a reaction catalyzed by **dolichol kinase** and using ATP as the phosphate donor.

Figure 46–6. The structure of dolichol. The phosphate in dolichol phosphate is attached to the primary alcohol group at the left-hand end of the molecule. The group within the brackets is an isoprene unit (n = 17–20 isoprenoid units).

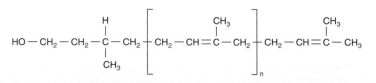

Dolichol-P-P-GlcNAc (Dol-P-P-GlcNAc) is the key lipid that acts as an acceptor for other sugars in the assembly of Dol-P-P-oligosaccharide. It is synthesized in the membranes of the endoplasmic reticulum from Dol-P and UDP-GlcNAc in the following reaction, catalyzed by GlcNAc-P transferase:

$$Dol\text{-}P + UDP\text{-}GlcNAc \rightarrow Dol\text{-}P\text{-}P\text{-}GlcNAc + UMP$$

The above reaction—which is the first step in the assembly of Dol-P-P-oligosaccharide—and the other later reactions are summarized in Figure 46–7. The essential features of the subsequent steps in the assembly of Dol-P-P-oligosaccharide are as follows:

(1) A second GlcNAc residue is added to the first, again using UDP-GlcNAc as the donor.

(2) Five Man residues are added, using GDP-mannose as the donor.

(3) Four additional Man residues are next added, using Dol-P-Man as the donor. Dol-P-Man is formed by the following reaction:

$$Dol\text{-}P + GDP\text{-}Man \rightarrow Dol\text{-}P\text{-}Man + GDP$$

(4) Finally, the three peripheral glucose residues are donated by Dol-P-Glc, which is formed in a reaction analogous to that just presented except that Dol-P and UDP-Glc are the substrates.

It should be noted that the first seven sugars (two GlcNAc and five Man residues) are donated by nucleotide sugars, whereas the last seven sugars (four Man and three Glc residues) added are donated by dolichol-P-sugars. The net result is assembly of the compound illustrated in Figure 46–8 and referred to in shorthand as Dol-P-P-GlcNAc$_2$Man$_9$Glc$_3$.

The oligosaccharide linked to dolichol-P-P is transferred en bloc to form an N-glycosidic bond with one or more specific Asn residues of an acceptor protein emerging from the luminal surface of the membrane of the endoplasmic reticulum. The reaction is catalyzed by **oligosaccharide:protein transferase,** a membrane-associated enzyme complex. The transferase will recognize and transfer any substrate with the general structure Dol-P-P-(GlcNAc)$_2$-R, but it has a strong preference for the Dol-P-P-GlcNAc$_2$Man$_9$Glc$_3$ structure. Glycosylation occurs at the Asn residue of an Asn-X-Ser/Thr tripeptide sequence, where X is any amino acid except proline, aspartic acid, or glutamic acid. A tripeptide site contained within a β turn is favored. Only about one-third of the Asn residues that are potential acceptor sites are actually glycosylated, suggesting that factors other than the tripeptide are also important.

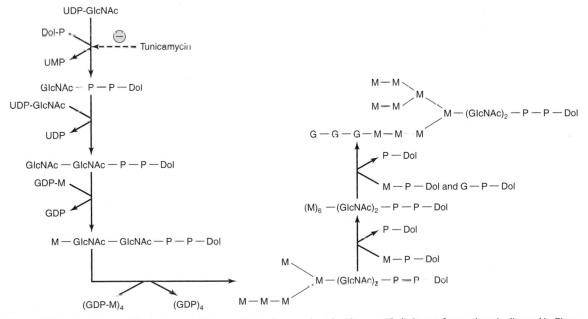

Figure 46–7. Pathway of biosynthesis of dolichol-P-P-oligosaccharide. The specific linkages formed are indicated in Figure 46–8. Note that the first five internal mannose residues are donated by GDP-mannose, whereas the more external mannose residues and the glucose residues are donated by dolichol-P-mannose and dolichol-P-glucose. (UDP, uridine diphosphate; Dol, dolichol; P, phosphate; UMP, uridine monophosphate; GDP, guanosine diphosphate; M, mannose; G, glucose.)

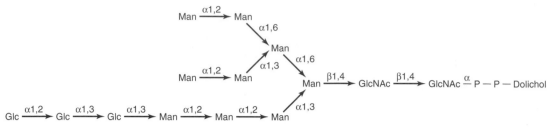

Figure 46–8. Structure of dolichol-P-P-oligosaccharide. (From Li E, et al: Structure of the lipid-linked oligosaccharide precursor of the complex-type oligosaccharides of the vesicular stomatitis virus G protein. J Biol Chem 1978;253:7762. Republished with permission conveyed through Copyright Clearance Center, Inc.)

The acceptor proteins are of both the secretory and integral membrane class. Cytosolic proteins are rarely glycosylated. The transfer reaction and subsequent processes in the glycosylation of N-linked glycoproteins, along with their subcellular locations, are depicted in Figure 46–9. The other product of the oligosaccharide:protein transferase reaction is dolichol-P-P, which is subsequently converted to dolichol-P by a phosphatase. The dolichol-P can serve again as an acceptor for the synthesis of another molecule of Dol-P-P-oligosaccharide.

B. PROCESSING OF THE OLIGOSACCHARIDE CHAIN

1. Early Phase—The various reactions involved are indicated in Figure 46–9. The oligosaccharide:protein transferase catalyzes reaction 1 (see above). Reactions 2 and 3 involve the removal of the terminal Glc residue by glucosidase I and of the next two Glc residues by glucosidase II, respectively. In the case of **high-mannose** glycoproteins, the process may stop here, or up to four Man residues may also be removed. However, to form **complex** chains, additional steps are necessary, as follows. Four external Man residues are removed in reactions 4 and 5 by at least two different mannosidases. In reaction 6, a GlcNAc residue is added to the Man residue of the Manα1–3 arm by GlcNAc transferase I. The action of this latter enzyme permits the occurrence of reaction 7, a reaction catalyzed by yet another mannosidase (Golgi α-mannosidase II) and which results in a reduction of the Man residues to the core number of three (Figure 46–5).

An important additional pathway is indicated in reactions I and II of Figure 46–9. This involves enzymes destined for **lysosomes.** Such enzymes are targeted to the lysosomes by a specific chemical marker. In reaction I, a residue of GlcNAc-1-P is added to carbon 6 of one or more specific Man residues of these enzymes. The reaction is catalyzed by a GlcNAc phosphotransferase, which uses UDP-GlcNAc as the donor and generates UMP as the other product:

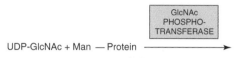

In reaction II, the GlcNAc is removed by the action of a phosphodiesterase, leaving the Man residues phosphorylated in the 6 position:

Man 6-P receptors, located in the Golgi apparatus, bind the Man 6-P residue of these enzymes and direct them to the lysosomes. Fibroblasts from patients with **I-cell disease** (see below) are severely deficient in the activity of the GlcNAc phosphotransferase.

2. Late Phase—To assemble a typical complex oligosaccharide chain, additional sugars must be added to the structure formed in reaction 7. Hence, in reaction 8, a second GlcNAc is added to the peripheral Man residue of the other arm of the bi-antennary structure shown in Figure 46–9; the enzyme catalyzing this step is GlcNAc transferase II. Reactions 9, 10, and 11 involve the addition of Fuc, Gal, and NeuAc residues at the sites indicated, in reactions catalyzed by fucosyl, galactosyl, and sialyl transferases, respectively. The assembly of poly-*N*-acetyllactosamine chains requires additional GlcNAc transferases.

The Endoplasmic Reticulum & Golgi Apparatus Are the Major Sites of Glycosylation

As indicated in Figure 46–9, the endoplasmic reticulum and the Golgi apparatus are the major sites involved in glycosylation processes. The assembly of Dol-P-P-oligosaccharide occurs on both the cytoplasmic and luminal surfaces of the ER membranes. Addition of

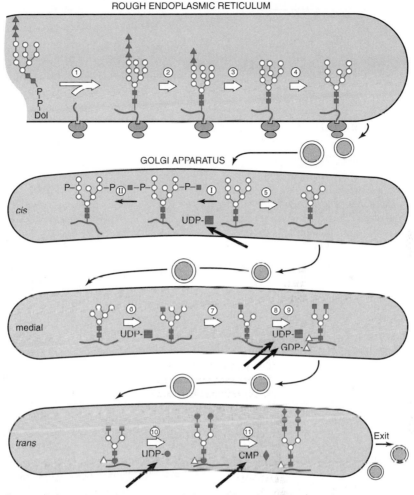

Figure 46–9. Schematic pathway of oligosaccharide processing. The reactions are catalyzed by the following enzymes: ①, oligosaccharide:protein transferase; ②, α-glucosidase I; ③, α-glucosidase II; ④, endoplasmic reticulum α1,2-mannosidase; Ⓘ, N-acetylglucosaminylphosphotransferase; Ⓘ, N-acetylglucosamine-1-phosphodiester α-N-acetylglucosaminidase; ⑤, Golgi apparatus α-mannosidase I; ⑥, N-acetylglucosaminyltransferase I; ⑦, Golgi apparatus α-mannosidase II; ⑧, N-acetylglucosaminyltransferase II; ⑨, fucosyltransferase; ⑩, galactosyltransferase; ⑪, sialyltransferase. The thick arrows indicate various nucleotide sugars involved in the overall scheme. (Solid square, N-acetylglucosamine; open circle, mannose; solid triangle, glucose; open triangle, fucose; solid circle, galactose; solid diamond, sialic acid.) (Reproduced, with permission, from Kornfeld R, Kornfeld S: Assembly of asparagine-linked oligosaccharides. Annu Rev Biochem 1985;54:631. Copyright © 1985 by Annual Reviews, www.annualreviews.org. Reprinted with permission.)

the oligosaccharide to protein occurs in the rough endoplasmic reticulum during or after translation. Removal of the Glc and some of the peripheral Man residues also occurs in the endoplasmic reticulum. The Golgi apparatus is composed of cis, medial, and trans cisternae; these can be separated by appropriate centrifugation procedures. Vesicles containing glycoproteins appear to bud off in the endoplasmic reticulum and are transported to the cis Golgi. Various studies have shown that the enzymes involved in glycoprotein

Table 46–10. Summary of main features of N-glycosylation.

- The oligosaccharide $Glc_3Man_9(GlcNAc)_2$ is transferred from dolichol-P-P-oligosaccharide in a reaction catalyzed by oligosaccharide:protein transferase, which is inhibited by tunicamycin.
- Transfer occurs to specific Asn residues in the sequence Asn-X-Ser/Thr, where X is any residue except Pro, Asp, or Glu.
- Transfer can occur cotranslationally in the endoplasmic reticulum.
- The protein-bound oligosaccharide is then partially processed by glucosidases and mannosidases; if no additional sugars are added, this results in a high-mannose chain.
- If processing occurs down to the core heptasaccharide ($Man_5[GlcNAc]_2$), complex chains are synthesized by the addition of GlcNAc, removal of two Man, and the stepwise addition of individual sugars in reactions catalyzed by specific transferases (eg, GlcNAc, Gal, NeuAc transferases) that employ appropriate nucleotide sugars.

processing show differential locations in the cisternae of the Golgi. As indicated in Figure 46–9, Golgi α-mannosidase I (catalyzing reaction 5) is located mainly in the cis Golgi, whereas GlcNAc transferase I (catalyzing reaction 6) appears to be located in the medial Golgi, and the fucosyl, galactosyl, and sialyl transferases (catalyzing reactions 9, 10, and 11) are located mainly in the trans Golgi. The major features of the biosynthesis of N-linked glycoproteins are summarized in Table 46–10 and should be contrasted with those previously listed (Table 46–9) for O-linked glycoproteins.

Some Glycan Intermediates Formed during N-Glycosylation Have Specific Functions

The following are a number of specific functions of N-glycan chains that have been established or are under investigation. (1) The involvement of the **mannose 6-P signal** in targeting of certain lysosomal enzymes is clear (see above and discussion of I-cell disease, below). (2) It is likely that the large N-glycan chains present on newly synthesized glycoproteins may assist in keeping these proteins in a soluble state inside the lumen of the endoplasmic reticulum. (3) One species of N-glycan chains has been shown to play a role in the folding and retention of certain glycoproteins in the lumen of the endoplasmic reticulum. **Calnexin** is a protein present in the endoplasmic reticulum membrane that acts as a "chaperone" (Chapter 45). It has been found that calnexin will bind specifically to a number of glycoproteins (eg, the influenza virus hemagglutinin [HA]) that possess the **monoglycosylated core structure.** This species is the product of reaction 2 shown in Figure 46–9 but from which the terminal glucose residue has been

removed, leaving only the innermost glucose attached. The release of fully folded HA from calnexin requires the enzymatic removal of this last glucosyl residue by α-glucosidase II. In this way, calnexin retains certain partly folded (or misfolded) glycoproteins and releases them when proper folding has occurred; it is thus an important component of the **quality control systems** operating in the lumen of the ER. The soluble protein **calreticulin** appears to play a similar function.

Several Factors Regulate the Glycosylation of Glycoproteins

It is evident that glycosylation of glycoproteins is a complex process involving a large number of enzymes. It has been estimated that some 1% of the human genome may be involved with glycosylation events. Another index of its complexity is that more than ten distinct GlcNAc transferases involved in glycoprotein biosynthesis have been reported, and many others are theoretically possible. Multiple species of the other glycosyltransferases (eg, sialyltransferases) also exist. Controlling factors of the first stage of N-linked glycoprotein biosynthesis (ie, **oligosaccharide assembly and transfer**) include (1) the presence of suitable acceptor sites in proteins, (2) the tissue level of Dol-P, and (3) the activity of the oligosaccharide:protein transferase.

Some factors known to be involved in the regulation of **oligosaccharide processing** are listed in Table 46–11. Two of the points listed merit further comment. First, **species variations** among processing enzymes have assumed importance in relation to production of glycoproteins of therapeutic use by means of recombinant DNA technology. For instance, **recombinant erythropoietin** (epoetin alfa; EPO) is sometimes administered to patients with certain types of chronic anemia in order to stimulate erythropoiesis. The half-life of EPO in plasma is influenced by the nature of its glycosylation pattern, with certain patterns being associated with a short half-life, appreciably limiting its period of therapeutic effectiveness. It is thus important to harvest EPO from host cells that confer a pattern of glycosylation consistent with a normal half-life in plasma. Second, there is great interest in analysis of the activities of glycoprotein-processing enzymes in various types of **cancer cells.** These cells have often been found to synthesize different oligosaccharide chains (eg, they often exhibit greater branching) from those made in control cells. This could be due to cancer cells containing different patterns of glycosyltransferases from those exhibited by corresponding normal cells, due to specific gene activation or repression. The differences in oligosaccharide chains could affect adhesive interactions between cancer cells and their normal parent tissue cells, contributing to metastasis. If a correlation could be found between the activity of particular processing enzymes and the **metastatic properties** of cancer cells, this could be important

Table 46–11. Some factors affecting the activities of glycoprotein processing enzymes.

Factor	Comment
Cell type	Different cell types contain different profiles of processing enzymes.
Previous enzyme	Certain glycosyltransferases act only on an oligosaccharide chain if it has already been acted upon by another processing enzyme.[1]
Development	The cellular profile of processing enzymes may change during development if their genes are turned on or off.
Intracellular location	For instance, if an enzyme is destined for insertion into the membrane of the ER (eg, HMG-CoA reductase), it may never encounter Golgi-located processing enzymes.
Protein conformation	Differences in conformation of different proteins may facilitate or hinder access of processing enzymes to identical oligosaccharide chains.
Species	Same cells (eg, fibroblasts) from different species may exhibit different patterns of processing enzymes.
Cancer	Cancer cells may exhibit processing enzymes different from those of corresponding normal cells.

[1]For example, prior action of GlcNAc transferase I is necessary for the action of Golgi α-mannosidase II.

as it might permit synthesis of drugs to inhibit these enzymes and, secondarily, metastasis.

The genes encoding many glycosyltransferases have already been cloned, and others are under study. Cloning has revealed new information on both protein and gene structures. The latter should also cast light on the mechanisms involved in their transcriptional control, and gene knockout studies are being used to evaluate the biologic importance of various glycosyltransferases.

Tunicamycin Inhibits N- But Not O-Glycosylation

A number of compounds are known to inhibit various reactions involved in glycoprotein processing. **Tunicamycin, deoxynojirimycin,** and **swainsonine** are three such agents. The reactions they inhibit are indicated in Table 46–12. These agents can be used experimentally to inhibit various stages of glycoprotein biosynthesis and to study the effects of specific alterations upon the process. For instance, if cells are grown in the presence of tunicamycin, no glycosylation of their normally N-linked glycoproteins

will occur. In certain cases, lack of glycosylation has been shown to increase the susceptibility of these proteins to proteolysis. Inhibition of glycosylation does not appear to have a consistent effect upon the secretion of glycoproteins that are normally secreted. The inhibitors of glycoprotein processing listed in Table 46–12 do not affect the biosynthesis of O-linked glycoproteins. The extension of O-linked chains can be prevented by GalNAc-benzyl. This compound competes with natural glycoprotein substrates and thus prevents chain growth beyond GalNAc.

SOME PROTEINS ARE ANCHORED TO THE PLASMA MEMBRANE BY GLYCOSYLPHOSPHATIDYL-INOSITOL STRUCTURES

Glycosylphosphatidylinositol (GPI)-linked glycoproteins comprise the third major class of glycoprotein. The GPI structure (sometimes called a "sticky foot") involved in linkage of the enzyme acetylcholinesterase (ACh esterase) to the plasma membrane of the red blood cell is shown in Figure 46–1. GPI-linked proteins are anchored to the outer leaflet of the plasma membrane by the fatty acids of phosphatidylinositol (PI). The PI is linked via a GlcN moiety to a glycan chain that contains various sugars (eg, Man, GlcN). In turn, the oligosaccharide chain is linked via phosphorylethanolamine in an amide linkage to the carboxyl terminal amino acid of the attached protein. The core of most GPI structures contains one molecule of phosphorylethanolamine, three Man residues, one molecule of GlcN, and one molecule of phosphatidylinositol, as follows:

$$\text{Ethanolamine - phospho} \rightarrow 6\text{Man}\alpha 1 \rightarrow$$
$$2\text{Man}\alpha 1 \rightarrow 6\text{Man}\alpha 1 \rightarrow \text{GlcN}\alpha 1 \rightarrow$$
$$6 — \textit{myo} \text{ - inositol - 1 - phospholipid}$$

Additional constituents are found in many GPI structures; for example, that shown in Figure 46–1 contains an extra

Table 46–12. Three inhibitors of enzymes involved in the glycosylation of glycoproteins and their sites of action.

Inhibitor	Site of Action
Tunicamycin	Inhibits GlcNAc-P transferase, the enzyme catalyzing addition of GlcNAc to dolichol-P, the first step in the biosynthesis of oligosaccharide-P-P-dolichol
Deoxynojirimycin	Inhibitor of glucosidases I and II
Swainsonine	Inhibitor of mannosidase II

Table 46–13. Some GPI-linked proteins.

- Acetylcholinesterase (red cell membrane)
- Alkaline phosphatase (intestinal, placental)
- Decay-accelerating factor (red cell membrane)
- 5′-Nucleotidase (T lymphocytes, other cells)
- Thy-1 antigen (brain, T lymphocytes)
- Variable surface glycoprotein (*Trypanosoma brucei*)

phosphorylethanolamine attached to the middle of the three Man moieties of the glycan and an extra fatty acid attached to GlcN. The functional significance of these variations among structures is not understood. This type of linkage was first detected by the use of bacterial PI-specific phospholipase C (PI-PLC), which was found to release certain proteins from the plasma membrane of cells by splitting the bond indicated in Figure 46–1. Examples of some proteins that are anchored by this type of linkage are given in Table 46–13. At least three possible functions of this type of linkage have been suggested: (1) The GPI anchor may allow greatly enhanced **mobility** of a protein in the plasma membrane compared with that observed for a protein that contains transmembrane sequences. This is perhaps not surprising, as the GPI anchor is attached only to the outer leaflet of the lipid bilayer, so that it is freer to diffuse than a protein anchored via both leaflets of the bilayer. Increased mobility may be important in facilitating rapid responses to appropriate stimuli. (2) Some GPI anchors may connect with **signal transduction** pathways. (3) It has been shown that GPI structures can **target** certain proteins to apical domains of the plasma membrane of certain epithelial cells. The biosynthesis of GPI anchors is complex and begins in the endoplasmic reticulum. The GPI anchor is assembled independently by a series of enzyme-catalyzed reactions and then transferred to the carboxyl terminal end of its acceptor protein, accompanied by cleavage of the preexisting carboxyl terminal hydrophobic peptide from that protein. This process is sometimes called **glypiation.** An acquired defect in an early stage of the biosynthesis of the GPI structure has been implicated in the causation of **paroxysmal nocturnal hemoglobinuria** (see later).

GLYCOPROTEINS ARE INVOLVED IN MANY BIOLOGIC PROCESSES & IN MANY DISEASES

As listed in Table 46–1, glycoproteins have many different functions; some have already been addressed in this chapter and others are described elsewhere in this text (eg, transport molecules, immunologic molecules, and hormones). Here, their involvement in two specific processes—fertilization and inflammation—will be briefly described. In addition, the bases of a number of diseases that are due to abnormalities in the synthesis and degradation of glycoproteins will be summarized.

Glycoproteins Are Important in Fertilization

To reach the plasma membrane of an oocyte, a sperm has to traverse the **zona pellucida (ZP),** a thick, transparent, noncellular envelope that surrounds the oocyte. The zona pellucida contains three glycoproteins of interest, ZP1–3. Of particular note is ZP3, an O-linked glycoprotein that functions as a receptor for the sperm. A protein on the sperm surface, possibly galactosyl transferase, interacts specifically with oligosaccharide chains of ZP3; in at least certain species (eg, the mouse), this interaction, by transmembrane signaling, induces the **acrosomal reaction,** in which enzymes such as proteases and hyaluronidase and other contents of the acrosome of the sperm are released. Liberation of these enzymes helps the sperm to pass through the zona pellucida and reach the plasma membrane (PM) of the oocyte. In hamsters, it has been shown that another glycoprotein, PH-30, is important in both the binding of the PM of the sperm to the PM of the oocyte and also in the subsequent fusion of the two membranes. These interactions enable the sperm to enter and thus fertilize the oocyte. It may be possible to inhibit fertilization by developing drugs or antibodies that interfere with the normal functions of ZP3 and PH-30 and which would thus act as contraceptive agents.

Selectins Play Key Roles in Inflammation & in Lymphocyte Homing

Leukocytes play important roles in many inflammatory and immunologic phenomena. The first steps in many of these phenomena are interactions between circulating leukocytes and endothelial cells prior to passage of the former out of the circulation. Work done to identify specific molecules on the surfaces of the cells involved in such interactions has revealed that leukocytes and endothelial cells contain on their surfaces specific lectins, called **selectins,** that participate in their intercellular adhesion. Features of the three major classes of selectins are summarized in Table 46–14. Selectins are single-chain Ca^{2+}-binding transmembrane proteins that contain a number of domains (Figure 46–10). Their amino terminal ends contain the lectin domain, which is involved in binding to specific carbohydrate ligands.

The adhesion of neutrophils to endothelial cells of postcapillary venules can be considered to occur in four stages, as shown in Figure 46–11. The initial baseline stage is succeeded by slowing or rolling of the neutrophils, mediated by selectins. Interactions between L-selectin on the neutrophil surface and CD34 and Gly-CAM-1 or other glycoproteins on the endothelial surface

Table 46–14. Some molecules involved in leukocyte-endothelial cell interactions.[1]

Molecule	Cell	Ligands
Selectins		
L-selectin	PMN, lymphs	CD34, Gly-CAM-1[2] Sialyl-Lewis[x] and others
P-selectin	EC, platelets	P-selectin glycoprotein ligand-1 (PSGL-1) Sialyl-Lewis[x] and others
E-selectin	EC	Sialyl-Lewis[x] and others
Integrins		
LFA-1	PMN, lymphs	ICAM-1, ICAM-2 (CD11a/CD18)
Mac-1	PMN	ICAM-1 and others (CD11b/CD18)
Immunoglobulin superfamily		
ICAM-1	Lymphs, EC	LFA-1, Mac-1
ICAM-2	Lymphs, EC	LFA-1
PECAM-1	EC, PMN, lymphs	Various platelets

[1]Modified from Albelda SM, Smith CW, Ward PA: Adhesion molecules and inflammatory injury. FASEB J 1994;8:504. Republished with permission conveyed through Copyright Clearance Center, Inc.
[2]These are ligands for lymphocyte L-selectin; the ligands for neutrophil L-selectin have not been identified.
PMN, polymorphonuclear leukocytes; EC, endothelial cell; lymphs, lymphocytes, CD, cluster of differentiation; ICAM, intercellular adhesion molecule; LFA-1, lymphocyte function-associated antigen-1; PECAM-1, platelet endothelial cell adhesion cell molecule-1.

L-selectin

Figure 46–10. Schematic diagram of the structure of human L-selectin. The extracellular portion contains an amino terminal domain homologous to C-type lectins and an adjacent epidermal growth factor-like domain. These are followed by a variable number of complement regulatory-like modules (numbered circles) and a transmembrane sequence (black diamond). A short cytoplasmic sequence (open rectangle) is at the carboxyl terminal. The structures of P- and E-selectin are similar to that shown except that they contain more complement-regulatory modules. The numbers of amino acids in L-, P-, and E- selectins, as deduced from the cDNA sequences, are 385, 789, and 589, respectively. (Reproduced, with permission, from Bevilacqua MP, Nelson RM: Selectins. J Clin Invest 1993;91:370. Republished with permission conveyed through Copyright Clearance Center, Inc.)

are involved. These particular interactions are initially short-lived, and the overall binding is of relatively low affinity, permitting rolling. However, during this stage, activation of the neutrophils by various chemical mediators (discussed below) occurs, resulting in a change of shape of the neutrophils and firm adhesion of these cells to the endothelium. An additional set of adhesion molecules is involved in firm adhesion, namely, LFA-1 and Mac-1 on the neutrophils and ICAM-1 and ICAM-2 on endothelial cells. LFA-1 and Mac-1 are CD11/CD18 integrins (see Chapter 51 for a discussion of integrins), whereas ICAM-1 and ICAM-2 are members of the immunoglobulin superfamily. The fourth stage is transmigration of the neutrophils across the endothelial wall. For this to occur, the neutrophils insert pseudopods into the junctions between endothelial cells, squeeze through these junctions, cross the basement membrane, and then are free to migrate in the extravascular space. Platelet-endothelial cell adhesion molecule-1 (PECAM-1) has been found to be localized at the junctions of endothelial cells and thus may have a role in transmigration. A variety of biomolecules have been found to be involved in activation of neutrophil and endothelial cells, including tumor necrosis factor α, various interleukins, platelet activating factor (PAF), leukotriene B$_4$, and certain complement fragments. These compounds stimulate various signaling pathways, resulting in changes in cell shape and function, and some are also chemotactic. One important functional change is recruitment of selectins to the cell surface, as in some cases selectins are stored in granules (eg, in endothelial cells and platelets).

The precise chemical nature of some of the ligands involved in selectin-ligand interactions has been determined. All three selectins bind **sialylated and fucosylated oligosaccharides,** and in particular all three bind **sialyl-Lewis^x** (Figure 46–12), a structure present on both glycoproteins and glycolipids. Whether this compound is the actual ligand involved in vivo is not established. Sulfated molecules, such as the sulfatides (Chapter 15), may be ligands in certain instances. This basic knowledge is being used in attempts to synthesize compounds that block selectin-ligand interactions and thus may inhibit the inflammatory response. Approaches include administration of specific monoclonal antibodies or of chemically synthesized analogs of sialyl-Lewis^x, both of which bind selectins. Cancer cells often exhibit sialyl-Lewis^x and other selectin ligands on their surfaces. It is thought that these ligands play a role in the invasion and metastasis of cancer cells.

Abnormalities in the Synthesis of Glycoproteins Underlie Certain Diseases

Table 46–15 lists a number of conditions in which abnormalities in the synthesis of glycoproteins are of importance. As mentioned above, many **cancer cells** exhibit dif-

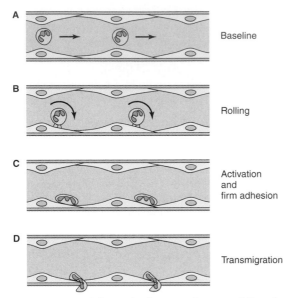

Figure 46–11. Schematic diagram of neutrophil-endothelial cell interactions. **A:** Baseline conditions: Neutrophils do not adhere to the vessel wall. **B:** The first event is the slowing or rolling of the neutrophils within the vessel (venule) mediated by selectins. **C:** Activation occurs, resulting in neutrophils firmly adhering to the surfaces of endothelial cells and also assuming a flattened shape. This requires interaction of activated CD18 integrins on neutrophils with ICAM-1 on the endothelium. **D:** The neutrophils then migrate through the junctions of endothelial cells into the interstitial tissue; this requires involvement of PECAM-1. Chemotaxis is also involved in this latter stage. (Reproduced, with permission, from Albelda SM, Smith CW, Ward PA: Adhesion molecules and inflammatory injury. FASEB J 1994;8;504.)

Table 46–15. Some diseases due to or involving abnormalities in the biosynthesis of glycoproteins.

Disease	Abnormality
Cancer	Increased branching of cell surface glycans or presentation of selectin ligands may be important in metastasis.
Congenital disorders of glycosylation[1]	See Table 46–16.
HEMPAS[2] (MIM 224100)	Abnormalities in certain enzymes (eg, mannosidase II and others) involved in the biosynthesis of N-glycans, particularly affecting the red blood cell membrane.
Leukocyte adhesion deficiency, type II (MIM 266265)	Probably mutations affecting a Golgi-located GDP-fucose transporter, resulting in defective fucosylation.
Paroxysmal nocturnal hemoglobinuria (MIM 311770)	Acquired defect in biosynthesis of the GPI[3] structures of decay accelerating factor (DAF) and CD59.
I-cell disease (MIM 252500)	Deficiency of GlcNAc phosphotransferase, resulting in abnormal targeting of certain lysosomal enzymes.

[1]The MIM number for congenital disorder of glycosylation type Ia is 212065.
[2]Hereditary erythroblastic multinuclearity with a positive acidified serum lysis test (congenital dyserythropoietic anemia type II). This is a relatively mild form of anemia. It reflects at least in part the presence in the red cell membranes of various glycoproteins with abnormal N-glycan chains, which contribute to the susceptibility to lysis.
[3]Glycosylphosphatidylinositol.

ferent profiles of oligosaccharide chains on their surfaces, some of which may contribute to metastasis.

The **congenital disorders of glycosylation (CDG)** are a group of disorders of considerable current interest. The major features of these conditions are summarized in Table 46–16.

Leukocyte adhesion deficiency (LAD) II is a rare condition probably due to mutations affecting the activity of a Golgi-located GDP-fucose transporter. It

Figure 46–12. Schematic representation of the structure of sialyl-Lewis^x.

can be considered a congenital disorder of glycosylation. The absence of fucosylated ligands for selectins leads to a marked decrease in neutrophil rolling. Subjects suffer life-threatening, recurrent bacterial infections and also psychomotor and mental retardation. The condition appears to respond to oral fucose.

Hereditary erythroblastic multinuclearity with a positive acidified lysis test (HEMPAS)—congenital dyserythropoietic anemia type II—is another disorder due to abnormalities in the processing of N-glycans. Some cases have been claimed to be due to defects in alpha–mannosidase II.

Paroxysmal nocturnal hemoglobinuria is an acquired mild anemia characterized by the presence of hemoglobin in urine due to hemolysis of red cells, particularly during sleep. This latter phenomenon may reflect a slight drop in plasma pH during sleep, which increases susceptibility to lysis by the complement system (Chapter 49). The basic defect in paroxysmal nocturnal hemoglobinuria is the acquisition of somatic

Table 46–16. Major features of the congenital disorders of glycosylation.

- Autosomal recessive disorders
- Multisystem disorders that have probably not been recognized in the past
- Generally affect the central nervous system, resulting in psychomotor retardation and other features
- Type I disorders are due to mutations in genes encoding enzymes (eg, phosphomannomutase-2 [PMM-2], causing CDG Ia) involved in the synthesis of dolichol-P-P-oligosaccharide
- Type II disorders are due to mutations in genes encoding enzymes (eg, GlcNAc transferase-2, causing CDG IIa) involved in the processing of N-glycan chains
- About 11 distinct disorders have been recognized
- Isoelectric focusing of transferrin is a useful biochemical test for assisting in the diagnosis of these conditions; truncation of the oligosaccharide chains of this protein alters its isoelectric focusing pattern
- Oral mannose has proved of benefit in the treatment of CDG Ia

CDG, congenital disorder of glycosylation.

mutations in the *PIG-A* (for phosphatidylinositol glycan class A) gene of certain hematopoietic cells. The product of this gene appears to be the enzyme that links glucosamine to phosphatidylinositol in the GPI structure (Figure 46–1). Thus, proteins that are anchored by a GPI linkage are deficient in the red cell membrane. Two proteins are of particular interest: **decay accelerating factor (DAF)** and another protein designated **CD59**. They normally interact with certain components of the complement system (Chapter 49) to prevent the hemolytic actions of the latter. However, when they are deficient, the complement system can act on the red cell membrane to cause hemolysis. Paroxysmal nocturnal hemoglobinuria can be diagnosed relatively simply, as the red cells are much more sensitive to hemolysis in normal serum acidified to pH 6.2 (Ham's test); the complement system is activated under these conditions, but normal cells are not affected. Figure 46–13 summarizes the etiology of paroxysmal nocturnal hemoglobinuria.

Study of the **congenital muscular dystrophies (CMDs)** has revealed that certain of them (eg, the Walker-Warburg syndrome, muscle-eye-brain disease, Fukuyama CMD) are the result of defects in the synthesis of glycans in the protein α-dystroglycan (α-DG). This protein protrudes from the surface membrane of muscle cells and interacts with laminin-2 (merosin) in the basal lamina (see Figure 48–12). If the glycans of α-DG are not correctly formed (as a result of mutations in genes encoding certain glycosyl transferases), this results in defective interaction of α-DG with laminin, which in turn leads to the development of a CMD.

Rheumatoid arthritis is associated with an alteration in the glycosylation of circulating immunoglobulin G (IgG) molecules (Chapter 49), such that they lack galactose in their Fc regions and terminate in GlcNAc. **Mannose-binding protein** (MBP, not to be confused with the mannose 6-P receptor), a C-lectin synthesized by liver cells and secreted into the circulation, binds mannose, GlcNAc, and certain other sugars. It can thus bind agalactosyl IgG molecules, which subsequently activate the complement system, contributing to chronic inflammation in the synovial membranes of joints.

MBP can also bind the above sugars when they are present on the surfaces of certain bacteria, fungi, and viruses, preparing these pathogens for opsonization or for destruction by the complement system. This is an example of **innate immunity,** not involving immunoglobulins. Deficiency of this protein in young infants as a result of mutation renders them very susceptible to recurrent infections.

I-Cell Disease Results from Faulty Targeting of Lysosomal Enzymes

As indicated above, Man 6-P serves as a chemical marker to target certain lysosomal enzymes to that organelle. Analysis of cultured fibroblasts derived from patients with I-cell (inclusion cell) disease played a large part in revealing the above role of Man 6-P. I-cell disease is an uncommon condition characterized by severe progressive psychomotor retardation and a variety of physical signs, with death often occurring in the first decade. Cultured cells from patients with I-cell disease were found to lack almost all of the normal lysosomal enzymes; the lysosomes thus accumulate many different types of undegraded molecules, forming inclusion bodies. Samples of plasma from patients

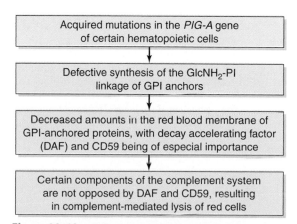

Acquired mutations in the *PIG-A* gene of certain hematopoietic cells

↓

Defective synthesis of the GlcNH$_2$-PI linkage of GPI anchors

↓

Decreased amounts in the red blood membrane of GPI-anchored proteins, with decay accelerating factor (DAF) and CD59 being of especial importance

↓

Certain components of the complement system are not opposed by DAF and CD59, resulting in complement-mediated lysis of red cells

Figure 46–13. Scheme of causation of paroxysmal nocturnal hemoglobinuria (MIM 311770).

with the disease were observed to contain very high activities of lysosomal enzymes; this suggested that the enzymes were being synthesized but were failing to reach their proper intracellular destination and were instead being secreted. Cultured cells from patients with the disease were noted to take up exogenously added lysosomal enzymes obtained from normal subjects, indicating that the cells contained a normal receptor on their surfaces for endocytic uptake of lysosomal enzymes. In addition, this finding suggested that lysosomal enzymes from patients with I-cell disease might lack a recognition marker. Further studies revealed that lysosomal enzymes from normal individuals carried the Man 6-P recognition marker described above, which interacted with a specific intracellular protein, the Man 6-P receptor. Cultured cells from patients with I-cell disease were then found to be deficient in the activity of the cis Golgi-located GlcNAc phosphotransferase, explaining how their lysosomal enzymes failed to acquire the Man 6-P marker. It is now known that there are two Man 6-P receptor proteins, one of high (275 kDa) and one of low (46 kDa) molecular mass. These proteins are lectins, recognizing Man 6-P. The former is cation-independent and also binds IGF-II (hence it is named the Man 6-P–IGF-II receptor), whereas the latter is cation-dependent in some species and does not bind IGF-II. It appears that both receptors function in the intracellular sorting of lysosomal enzymes into clathrin-coated vesicles, which occurs in the trans Golgi subsequent to synthesis of Man 6-P in the cis Golgi. These vesicles then leave the Golgi and fuse with a prelysosomal compartment. The low pH in this compartment causes the lysosomal enzymes to dissociate from their receptors and subsequently enter into lysosomes. The receptors are recycled and reused. Only the smaller receptor functions in the endocytosis of extracellular lysosomal enzymes, which is a minor pathway for lysosomal location. Not all cells employ the Man 6-P receptor to target their lysosomal enzymes (eg, hepatocytes use a different but undefined pathway); furthermore, not all lysosomal enzymes are targeted by this mechanism. Thus, biochemical investigations of I-cell disease not only led to elucidation of its basis but also contributed significantly to knowledge of how newly synthesized proteins are targeted to specific organelles, in this case the lysosome. Figure 46–14 summarizes the causation of I-cell disease.

Pseudo-Hurler polydystrophy is another genetic disease closely related to I-cell disease. It is a milder condition, and patients may survive to adulthood. Studies have revealed that the GlcNAc phosphotransferase involved in I-cell disease has several domains, including a catalytic domain and a domain that specifically recognizes and interacts with lysosomal enzymes. It has been

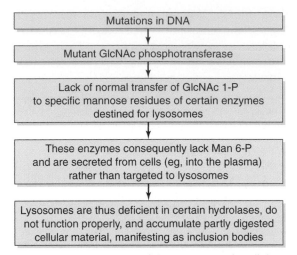

Mutations in DNA

↓

Mutant GlcNAc phosphotransferase

↓

Lack of normal transfer of GlcNAc 1-P to specific mannose residues of certain enzymes destined for lysosomes

↓

These enzymes consequently lack Man 6-P and are secreted from cells (eg, into the plasma) rather than targeted to lysosomes

↓

Lysosomes are thus deficient in certain hydrolases, do not function properly, and accumulate partly digested cellular material, manifesting as inclusion bodies

Figure 46–14. Summary of the causation of I-cell disease (MIM 252500).

proposed that the defect in pseudo-Hurler polydystrophy lies in the latter domain, and the retention of some catalytic activity results in a milder condition.

Genetic Deficiencies of Glycoprotein Lysosomal Hydrolases Cause Diseases Such As α-Mannosidosis

Glycoproteins, like most other biomolecules, undergo both synthesis and degradation (ie, turnover). Degradation of the oligosaccharide chains of glycoproteins involves a battery of lysosomal hydrolases, including α-neuraminidase, β-galactosidase, β-hexosaminidase, α- and β-mannosidases, α-N-acetylgalactosaminidase, α-fucosidase, endo-β-N-acetylglucosaminidase, and aspartylglucosaminidase. The sites of action of the last two enzymes are indicated in the legend to Figure 46–5. Genetically determined defects of the activities of these enzymes can occur, resulting in abnormal degradation of glycoproteins. The accumulation in tissues of such abnormally degraded glycoproteins can lead to various diseases. Among the best-recognized of these diseases are mannosidosis, fucosidosis, sialidosis, aspartylglycosaminuria, and Schindler disease, due respectively to deficiencies of α-mannosidase, α-fucosidase, α-neuraminidase, aspartylglucosaminidase, and α-N-acetyl-galactosaminidase. These diseases, which are relatively uncommon, have a variety of manifestations; some of their major features are listed in Table 46–17. The fact that patients affected by these disorders all show signs referable to the central nervous system reflects the importance of glycoproteins in the development and normal function of that system.

Table 46–17. Major features of some diseases (eg, α-mannosidosis, β-mannosidosis, fucosidosis, sialidosis, aspartylglycosaminuria, and Schindler disease) due to deficiencies of glycoprotein hydrolases.[1]

- Usually exhibit mental retardation or other neurologic abnormalities, and in some disorders coarse features or visceromegaly (or both)
- Variations in severity from mild to rapidly progressive
- Autosomal recessive inheritance
- May show ethnic distribution (eg, aspartylglycosaminuria is common in Finland)
- Vacuolization of cells observed by microscopy in some disorders
- Presence of abnormal degradation products (eg, oligosaccharides that accumulate because of the enzyme deficiency) in urine, detectable by TLC and characterizable by GLC-MS
- Definitive diagnosis made by assay of appropriate enzyme, often using leukocytes
- Possibility of prenatal diagnosis by appropriate enzyme assays
- No definitive treatment at present

[1]MIM numbers: α-mannosidosis, 248500; β-mannosidosis, 248510; fucosidosis, 230000; sialidosis, 256550; aspartylglycosaminuria, 208400; Schindler disease, 609241.

MANY GLYCANS BIND VIRUSES & BACTERIA

A principal feature of glycans, and one that explains many of their biologic actions, is that they **bind** specifically to a variety of molecules such as proteins or other glycans. One reflection of this is their ability to bind certain viruses and many bacteria.

Influenza virus A binds to cell surface receptor molecules containing NeuAc via a protein named **hemagglutinin.** It also possesses a **neuraminidase** that plays a key role in allowing elution of newly synthesized progeny from infected cells. If this process is inhibited, spread of the viruses is markedly diminished. Inhibitors of this enzyme (eg, zanamivir, oseltamivir) are now available for use in treating patients with influenza.

HIV-1, thought by most to be the cause of AIDS, attaches to cells via one of its surface glycoproteins (gp 120) and uses another surface glycoprotein (gp 41) to fuse with the host cell membrane.

Helicobacter pylori is believed to be the major cause of peptic ulcers. Studies have shown that this bacterium binds to at least two different glycans present on the surfaces of epithelial cells in the stomach (see Figure 46–15). This allows it to establish a stable attachment site to the stomach lining, and subsequent secretion of ammonia and other molecules by the bacterium are believed to initiate ulceration.

Similarly, many **bacteria that cause diarrhea** are also known to attach to surface cells of the intestine via glycans present in glycoproteins or glycolipids.

The basic cause of **cystic fibrosis** (CF) is mutations in the gene encoding CFTR (see Chapter 40). A major problem in this disease is recurring lung infections by bacteria such as *Pseudomonas aeruginosa*. In CF, a relative dehydration of respiratory secretions occurs secondary to changes in electrolyte composition in the airway as a result of mutations in CFTR. Bacteria such as *P. aeruginosa* attach to the sugar chains of mucins and find the dehydrated environment in the bronchioles a favorable location in which to multiply.

NEW EXAMPLES OF THE IMPORTANCE OF GLYCOPROTEINS IN BIOLOGIC PROCESSES ARE BEING REVEALED BY GLYCOMICS

Recent research in many areas has shown the importance of glycoproteins in diverse areas. Only three examples are cited here.

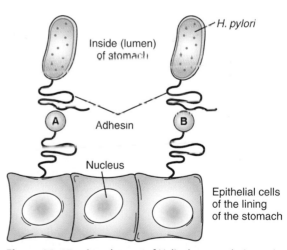

Figure 46–15. Attachment of *Helicobacter pylori* to epithelial cells of the stomach. Adhesin, a protein present in the tail of *H. pylori*, interacts with two different glycans (structures shown below) present in glycoproteins on the surface of gastric epithelial cells. This provides an attachment site for the bacterium. Subsequently it liberates molecules, such as ammonia, that contribute to initiating peptic ulceration. (A) NeuAcα2,3Galβ1,4—Protein (Neuraminyl-galactose); (B) Fucα1,2Galβ1,3GlcNAc—Protein (Lewis[B] substance). (Reproduced with permission from Murray RK. Glycoproteins: Crucial molecules in many diseases. Glycoscience & Nutrition 2003;4(8):3.)

The **Notch glycoprotein,** which is O-fucosylated on serine and threonine residues, plays a key role in certain developmental processes.

Transfusion of platelets is often important in certain clinical situations. Unfortunately, the life of platelets in the circulation after collection, chilling, and transfusion is shortened. This has been shown to be the result of clustering of the von Willebrand factor receptor complex on the platelet surface, leading to rapid clearance of transfused platelets. Enzymic galactosylation of chilled platelets has been found to prevent clustering, thereby prolonging the life of platelets.

The pig is a suitable animal as a source of organs (eg, hearts) for transplantation to humans (**xenotransplantation**). Unfortunately, the presence of galactose → α-1,3-galactose residues on the surface of pig cells is a major obstacle to xenotransplantation, because humans, who do not possess this epitope, form antibodies to it. Thus attempts are being made to rear pigs in which the α-1,3-galactosyltransferase responsible for addition of this epitope has been knocked out by genetic techniques.

The pace of research in **glycomics** is accelerating markedly. Research in the past has been hampered by the lack of availability of suitable technics to determine the structures of glycans. However, appropriate technics are now available (see Table 46–3). Along with powerful new genetic technics (eg, knock-outs and knock-downs using RNAi molecules), it is certain that research in this area will uncover many new important biologic interactions that are sugar-dependent and will provide targets for drug and other therapies.

SUMMARY

- Glycoproteins are widely distributed proteins—with diverse functions—that contain one or more covalently linked carbohydrate chains.

- The carbohydrate components of a glycoprotein range from 1% to more than 85% of its weight and may be simple or very complex in structure.

- At least certain of the oligosaccharide chains of glycoproteins encode biologic information; they are also important to glycoproteins in modulating their solubility and viscosity, in protecting them against proteolysis, and in their biologic actions.

- The structures of many oligosaccharide chains can be elucidated by gas-liquid chromatography, mass spectrometry, and high-resolution NMR spectrometry.

- Glycosidases hydrolyze specific linkages in oligosaccharides and are used to explore both the structures and functions of glycoproteins.

- Lectins are carbohydrate-binding proteins involved in cell adhesion and many other biologic processes.

- The major classes of glycoproteins are O-linked (involving an OH of serine or threonine), N-linked (involving the N of the amide group of asparagine), and glycosylphosphatidylinositol (GPI)-linked.

- Mucins are a class of O-linked glycoproteins that are distributed on the surfaces of epithelial cells of the respiratory, gastrointestinal, and reproductive tracts.

- The endoplasmic reticulum and Golgi apparatus play a major role in glycosylation reactions involved in the biosynthesis of glycoproteins.

- The oligosaccharide chains of O-linked glycoproteins are synthesized by the stepwise addition of sugars donated by nucleotide sugars in reactions catalyzed by individual specific glycoprotein glycosyltransferases.

- In contrast, the biosynthesis of N-linked glycoproteins involves a specific dolichol-P-P-oligosaccharide and various glycosidases. Depending on the glycosidases and precursor proteins synthesized by a tissue, it can synthesize complex, hybrid, or high-mannose types of N-linked oligosaccharides.

- Glycoproteins are implicated in many biologic processes. For instance, they have been found to play key roles in fertilization and inflammation.

- A number of diseases involving abnormalities in the synthesis and degradation of glycoproteins have been recognized. Glycoproteins are also involved in many other diseases, including influenza, AIDS, and rheumatoid arthritis.

- Developments in the new field of glycomics are likely to provide much new information on the roles of sugars in health and disease and also indicate targets for drug and other types of therapies.

REFERENCES

Brockhausen I, Kuhns W: *Glycoproteins and Human Disease.* Chapman & Hall, 1997.

Helenius A, Aebi M: Roles of N-linked glycans in the endoplasmic reticulum. Ann Rev Biochem 2004;73:1019.

Hoffmeister KM et al: Glycosylation restores survival of chilled blood platelets. Science 2003;301:1531.

Kornfeld R, Kornfeld S: Assembly of asparagine-linked oligosaccharides. Ann Rev Biochem 1985;54:631.

Lowe JB, Marth JD: A genetic approach to mammalian glycan function. Ann Rev Biochem 2003;72:643.

Michele DE, Campbell KP: Dystrophin-glycoproteins complex: post-translational processing and dystroglycan function. J Biol Chem 2003;278:15457.

Ramasamy R et al: Advanced glycation end products and RAGE: a common thread in aging, diabetes, neurodegeneration, and inflammation. Glycobiology 2005;15:16R.

Roseman S: Reflections on glycobiology. J Biol Chem 2001;276:41527.

Schachter H: The clinical relevance of glycobiology. J Clin Invest 2001;108:1579.

Science 2001;21(5512):2263. (This issue contains a special section entitled Carbohydrates and Glycobiology. It contains articles on the synthesis, structural determination, and functions of sugar-containing molecules and the roles of glycosylation in the immune system.)

Scriver CR et al (editors): *The Metabolic and Molecular Bases of Inherited Disease*, 8th ed. McGraw-Hill, 2001. (Various chapters in this text give in-depth coverage of topics such as I-cell disease and disorders of glycoprotein degradation.)

Sharon N, Lis H: History of lectins: from hemagglutinins to biological recognition molecules. Glycobiology 2004;14:53R.

Spiro RG: Protein glycosylation: nature, distribution, enzymatic formation, and disease implications of glycopeptide bonds. Glycobiology 2002;12:43R.

Taylor ME, Drickamer K: *Introduction to Glycobiology*. Oxford University Press, 2003.

Varki A et al (editors): *Essentials of Glycobiology*. Cold Spring Harbor Laboratory Press, 1999.

Winchester B: Lysosomal metabolism of glycoproteins. Glycobiology 2005;15:1R.

The Extracellular Matrix

47

Robert K. Murray, MD, PhD, & Frederick W. Keeley, PhD

BIOMEDICAL IMPORTANCE

Most mammalian cells are located in tissues where they are surrounded by a complex **extracellular matrix (ECM)** often referred to as **"connective tissue."** The ECM contains three major classes of biomolecules: (1) the **structural proteins,** collagen, elastin, and fibrillin; (2) certain **specialized proteins** such as fibrillin, fibronectin, and laminin; and (3) **proteoglycans,** whose chemical natures are described below. The ECM has been found to be involved in many normal and pathologic processes—eg, it plays important roles in development, in inflammatory states, and in the spread of cancer cells. Involvement of certain components of the ECM has been documented in both **rheumatoid arthritis** and **osteoarthritis.** Several diseases (eg, osteogenesis imperfecta and a number of types of the Ehlers-Danlos syndrome) are due to genetic disturbances of the synthesis of collagen. Specific components of proteoglycans (the glycosaminoglycans; GAGs) are affected in the group of genetic disorders known as the **mucopolysaccharidoses.** Changes occur in the ECM during the **aging process.** This chapter describes the basic biochemistry of the three major classes of biomolecules found in the ECM and illustrates their biomedical significance. Major biochemical features of two specialized forms of ECM—bone and cartilage—and of a number of diseases involving them are also briefly considered.

COLLAGEN IS THE MOST ABUNDANT PROTEIN IN THE ANIMAL WORLD

Collagen, the major component of most connective tissues, constitutes approximately 25% of the protein of mammals. It provides an extracellular framework for all metazoan animals and exists in virtually every animal tissue. At least 25 distinct types of collagen made up of over 30 distinct polypeptide chains (each encoded by a separate gene) have been identified in human tissues. Although several of these are present only in small proportions, they may play important roles in determining the physical properties of specific tissues. In addition, a number of proteins (eg, the C1q component of the complement system, pulmonary surfactant proteins SP-A and SP-D) that are not classified as collagens have collagen-like domains in their structures; these proteins are sometimes referred to as "noncollagen collagens."

Table 47–1 summarizes the types of collagens found in human tissues; the nomenclature used to designate types of collagen and their genes is described in the footnote.

In Table 47–2, 19 of the types of collagen mentioned above are subdivided into a number of classes based primarily on the structures they form. In this chapter, we shall be primarily concerned with the fibril-forming **collagens I and II,** the major collagens of skin and bone and of cartilage, respectively. However, mention will be made of some of the other collagens.

COLLAGEN TYPE I IS COMPOSED OF A TRIPLE HELIX STRUCTURE & FORMS FIBRILS

All collagen types have a **triple helical structure.** In some collagens, the entire molecule is triple helical, whereas in others the triple helix may involve only a fraction of the structure. Mature collagen type I, containing approximately 1000 amino acids, belongs to the former type; in it, each polypeptide subunit or alpha chain is twisted into a left-handed helix of three residues per turn (Figure 47–1). Three of these alpha chains are then wound into a **right-handed superhelix,** forming a rod-like molecule 1.4 nm in diameter and about 300 nm long. A striking characteristic of collagen is the occurrence of **glycine** residues at every third position of the triple helical portion of the alpha chain. This is necessary because glycine is the only amino acid small enough to be accommodated in the limited space available down the central core of the triple helix. This **repeating structure,** represented as $(Gly-X-Y)_n$, is an absolute requirement for the formation of the triple helix. While X and Y can be any other amino acids, about 100 of the X positions are proline and about 100 of the Y positions are hydroxyproline. Proline and hydroxyproline confer **rigidity** on the collagen molecule. **Hydroxyproline** is formed by the posttranslational hydroxylation of peptide-bound proline residues catalyzed by the enzyme **prolyl hydroxylase,** whose cofactors are **ascorbic acid** (vitamin C) and α-ketoglutarate. Lysines in the Y posi-

tion are also posttranslationally modified.

Table 47–1. Types of collagen and their genes.[1,2]

Type	Genes	Tissue
I	COL1A1, COL1A2	Most connective tissues, including bone
II	COL2A1	Cartilage, vitreous humor
III	COL3A1	Extensible connective tissues such as skin, lung, and the vascular system
IV	COL4A1–COL4A6	Basement membranes
V	COL5A1–COL5A3	Minor component in tissues containing collagen I
VI	COL6A1–COL6A3	Most connective tissues
VII	COL7A1	Anchoring fibrils
VIII	COL8A1–COL8A2	Endothelium, other tissues
IX	COL9A1–COL9A3	Tissues containing collagen II
X	COL10A1	Hypertrophic cartilage
XI	COL11A1, COL11A2, COL2A1	Tissues containing collagen II
XII	COL12A1	Tissues containing collagen I
XIII	COL13A1	Many tissues
XIV	COL14A1	Tissues containing collagen I
XV	COL15A1	Many tissues
XVI	COL16A1	Many tissues
XVII	COL17A1	Skin hemidesmosomes
XVIII	COL18A1	Many tissues (eg, liver, kidney)
XIX	COL19A1	Rhabdomyosarcoma cells

[1]Adapted slightly from Prockop DJ, Kivirikko KI: Collagens: molecular biology, diseases, and potentials for therapy. Annu Rev Biochem 1995;64:403. Copyright © 1995 by Annual Reviews, www.annualreviews.org. Reprinted with permission.
[2]The types of collagen are designated by Roman numerals. Constituent procollagen chains, called proα chains, are numbered using Arabic numerals, followed by the collagen type in parentheses. For instance, type I procollagen is assembled from two proα1(I) and one proα2(I) chain. It is thus a heterotrimer, whereas type 2 procollagen is assembled from three proα1(II) chains and is thus a homotrimer. The collagen genes are named according to the collagen type, written in Arabic numerals for the gene symbol, followed by an A and the number of the proα chain that they encode. Thus, the COL1A1 and COL1A2 genes encode the α1 and α2 chains of type I collagen, respectively. At least 25 types of collagen have now been recognized.

tion may also be posttranslationally modified to hydroxylysine through the action of **lysyl hydroxylase,** an enzyme with similar cofactors. Some of these hydroxylysines may be further modified by the addition of galac-

Table 47–2. Classification of collagens, based primarily on the structures that they form.[1]

Class	Type
Fibril-forming	I, II, III, V, and XI
Network-like	IV, VIII, X
FACITs[2]	IX, XII, XIV, XVI, XIX
Beaded filaments	VI
Anchoring fibrils	VII
Transmembrane domain	XIII, XVII
Others	XV, XVIII

[1]Based on Prockop DJ, Kivirikko KI: Collagens: molecular biology, diseases, and potentials for therapy. Annu Rev Biochem 1995;64:403. Copyright © 1995 by Annual Reviews, www.annualreviews.org. Reprinted with permission.
[2]FACITs = fibril-associated collagens with interrupted triple helices. Additional collagens to these listed above have been recognized.

tose or galactosyl-glucose through an **O glycosidic linkage,** a glycosylation site that is unique to collagen.

Collagen types that form long rod-like fibers in tissues are assembled by lateral association of these triple helical units into a *"quarter staggered" alignment* such that each is displaced longitudinally from its neighbor by slightly less than one-quarter of its length (Figure 47–1, upper part). This arrangement is responsible for the banded appearance of these fibers in connective tissues. Collagen fibers are further stabilized by the formation of **covalent cross-links,** both within and between the triple helical units. These cross-links form through the action of **lysyl oxidase,** a copper-dependent enzyme that oxidatively deaminates the ε-amino groups of certain lysine and hydroxylysine residues, yielding reactive aldehydes. Such aldehydes can form aldol condensation products with other lysine- or hydroxylysine-derived aldehydes or form Schiff bases with the ε-amino groups of unoxidized lysines or hydroxylysines. These reactions, after further chemical rearrangements, result in the stable covalent cross-links that are important for the tensile strength of the fibers. Histidine may also be involved in certain cross-links.

Several collagen types do not form fibrils in tissues (Table 47–2). They are characterized by interruptions of the triple helix with stretches of protein lacking Gly-X-Y repeat sequences. These non-Gly-X-Y sequences result in areas of globular structure interspersed in the triple helical structure.

Type IV collagen, the best-characterized example of a collagen with discontinuous triple helices, is an important component of **basement membranes,** where it forms a mesh-like network.

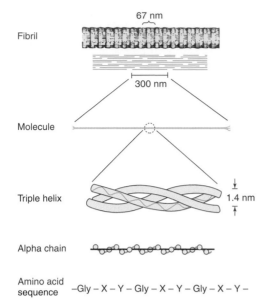

Fibril

67 nm

300 nm

Molecule

Triple helix

1.4 nm

Alpha chain

Amino acid sequence —Gly — X — Y — Gly — X — Y — Gly — X — Y —

Figure 47–1. Molecular features of collagen structure from primary sequence up to the fibril. Each individual polypeptide chain is twisted into a left-handed helix of three residues (Gly-X-Y) per turn, and all of these chains are then wound into a right-handed superhelix. (Slightly modified and reproduced, with permission, from Eyre DR: Collagen: Molecular diversity in the body's protein scaffold. Science 1980;207:1315. Copyright © 1980 by the American Association for the Advancement of Science. Adapted with permission.)

Collagen Undergoes Extensive Posttranslational Modifications

Newly synthesized collagen undergoes extensive **posttranslational modification** before becoming part of a mature extracellular collagen fiber (Table 47–3). Like most secreted proteins, collagen is synthesized on ribosomes in a precursor form, **preprocollagen,** which contains a leader or signal sequence that directs the polypeptide chain into the lumen of the endoplasmic reticulum. As it enters the endoplasmic reticulum, this leader sequence is enzymatically removed. **Hydroxylation** of proline and lysine residues and **glycosylation** of hydroxylysines in the **procollagen** molecule also take place at this site. The procollagen molecule contains polypeptide extensions (**extension peptides**) of 20–35 kDa at both its amino and carboxyl terminal ends, neither of which is present in mature collagen. Both extension peptides contain cysteine residues. While the amino terminal propeptide forms only intrachain disulfide bonds, the carboxyl terminal propeptides form both intrachain and interchain disulfide bonds. Formation of these disulfide bonds assists in the **registration**

of the three collagen molecules to form the triple helix, winding from the carboxyl terminal end. After formation of the triple helix, no further hydroxylation of proline or lysine or glycosylation of hydroxylysines can take place. **Self-assembly** is a cardinal principle in the biosynthesis of collagen.

Following **secretion** from the cell by way of the Golgi apparatus, extracellular enzymes called **procollagen aminoproteinase** and **procollagen carboxyproteinase** remove the extension peptides at the amino and carboxyl terminal ends, respectively. Cleavage of these propeptides may occur within crypts or folds in the cell membrane. Once the propeptides are removed, the triple helical collagen molecules, containing approximately 1000 amino acids per chain, **spontaneously assemble** into collagen fibers. These are further stabilized by the formation of **inter- and intrachain cross-links** through the action of lysyl oxidase, as described previously.

The same cells that secrete collagen also secrete **fibronectin,** a large glycoprotein present on cell surfaces, in the extracellular matrix, and in blood (see below). Fibronectin binds to aggregating precollagen fibers and alters the kinetics of fiber formation in the pericellular matrix. Associated with fibronectin and procollagen in this matrix are the **proteoglycans** heparan sulfate and chondroitin sulfate (see below). In fact, **type IX collagen,** a minor collagen type from cartilage, contains attached proteoglycan chains. Such interactions may serve to regulate the formation of collagen fibers and to determine their orientation in tissues.

Once formed, collagen is relatively **metabolically stable.** However, its breakdown is increased during starvation and various inflammatory states. Excessive production of collagen occurs in a number of conditions, eg, hepatic cirrhosis.

Table 47–3. Order and location of processing of the fibrillar collagen precursor.

Intracellular
1. Cleavage of signal peptide
2. Hydroxylation of prolyl residues and some lysyl residues; glycosylation of some hydroxylysyl residues
3. Formation of intrachain and interchain S–S bonds in extension peptides
4. Formation of triple helix

Extracellular
1. Cleavage of amino and carboxyl terminal propeptides
2. Assembly of collagen fibers in quarter-staggered alignment
3. Oxidative deamination of ε-amino groups of lysyl and hydroxylysyl residues to aldehydes
4. Formation of intra- and interchain cross-links via Schiff bases and aldol condensation products

A Number of Genetic Diseases Result from Abnormalities in the Synthesis of Collagen

About 30 genes encode collagen, and its pathway of biosynthesis is complex, involving at least eight enzyme-catalyzed posttranslational steps. Thus, it is not surprising that a number of diseases (Table 47–4) are due to **mutations in collagen genes** or in **genes encoding some of the enzymes** involved in these posttranslational modifications. The diseases affecting bone (eg, osteogenesis imperfecta) and cartilage (eg, the chondrodysplasias) will be discussed later in this chapter.

Ehlers-Danlos syndrome comprises a group of inherited disorders whose principal clinical features are

Table 47–4. Diseases caused by mutations in collagen genes or by deficiencies in the activities of posttranslational enzymes involved in the biosynthesis of collagen.[1]

Gene or Enzyme	Disease[2]
COL1A1, COL1A2	Osteogenesis imperfecta, type 1[3] (MIM 166200) Osteoporosis[4] (MIM 166710) Ehlers-Danlos syndrome type VII autosomal dominant (130060)
COL2A1	Severe chondrodysplasias Osteoarthritis[4] (MIM 165720)
COL3A1	Ehlers-Danlos syndrome type IV (MIM 130050)
COL4A3–COL4A6	Alport syndrome (including both autosomal and X-linked forms) (MIM 104200)
COL7A1	Epidermolysis bullosa, dystrophic (MIM 131750)
COL10A1	Schmid metaphysial chondrodysplasia (MIM 156500)
Lysyl hydroxylase	Ehlers-Danlos syndrome type VI (MIM 225400)
Procollagen N-proteinase	Ehlers-Danlos syndrome type VII autosomal recessive (MIM 225410)
Lysyl hydroxylase	Menkes disease[5] (MIM 309400)

[1]Adapted from Prockop DJ, Kivirrikko KI: Collagens: molecular biology, diseases, and potentials for therapy. Annu Rev Biochem 1995;64:403. Copyright © 1995 by Annual Reviews, www.annualreviews.org. Reprinted with permission.
[2]Genetic linkage to collagen genes has been shown for a few other conditions not listed here.
[3]At least four types of osteogenesis imperfecta are recognized; the great majority of mutations in all types are in the COL1A1 and COL1A2 genes.
[4]At present applies to only a relatively small number of such patients.
[5]Secondary to a deficiency of copper (Chapter 49).

hyperextensibility of the skin, abnormal tissue fragility, and increased joint mobility. The clinical picture is variable, reflecting underlying extensive genetic heterogeneity. At least 10 types have been recognized, most but not all of which reflect a variety of lesions in the synthesis of collagen. **Type IV** is the most serious because of its tendency for spontaneous rupture of arteries or the bowel, reflecting abnormalities in type III collagen. Patients with **type VI**, due to a deficiency of lysyl hydroxylase, exhibit marked joint hypermobility and a tendency to ocular rupture. A deficiency of procollagen N-proteinase, causing formation of abnormal thin, irregular collagen fibrils, results in **type VIIC**, manifested by marked joint hypermobility and soft skin.

Alport syndrome is the designation applied to a number of genetic disorders (both X-linked and autosomal) affecting the structure of **type IV** collagen fibers, the major collagen found in the basement membranes of the renal glomeruli (see discussion of laminin, below). Mutations in several genes encoding type IV collagen fibers have been demonstrated. The presenting sign is hematuria, and patients may eventually develop end-stage renal disease. Electron microscopy reveals characteristic abnormalities of the structure of the basement membrane and lamina densa.

In **epidermolysis bullosa,** the skin breaks and blisters as a result of minor trauma. The dystrophic form is due to mutations in COL7A1, affecting the structure of **type VII** collagen. This collagen forms delicate fibrils that anchor the basal lamina to collagen fibrils in the dermis. These anchoring fibrils have been shown to be markedly reduced in this form of the disease, probably resulting in the blistering. Epidermolysis bullosa simplex, another variant, is due to mutations in keratin 5 (Chapter 48).

Scurvy affects the structure of collagen. However, it is due to a deficiency of ascorbic acid (Chapter 44) and is not a genetic disease. Its major signs are bleeding gums, subcutaneous hemorrhages, and poor wound healing. These signs reflect impaired synthesis of collagen due to deficiencies of prolyl and lysyl hydroxylases, both of which require ascorbic acid as a cofactor.

ELASTIN CONFERS EXTENSIBILITY & RECOIL ON LUNG, BLOOD VESSELS, & LIGAMENTS

Elastin is a connective tissue protein that is responsible for properties of extensibility and elastic recoil in tissues. Although not as widespread as collagen, elastin is present in large amounts, particularly in tissues that require these physical properties, eg, lung, large arterial blood vessels, and some elastic ligaments. Smaller quantities of elastin are also found in skin, ear cartilage, and several other tissues. In contrast to collagen, there

appears to be only one genetic type of elastin, although variants arise by alternative splicing (Chapter 36) of the hnRNA for elastin. Elastin is synthesized as a soluble monomer of 70 kDa called **tropoelastin.** Some of the prolines of tropoelastin are hydroxylated to **hydroxyproline** by prolyl hydroxylase, though hydroxylysine and glycosylated hydroxylysine are not present. Unlike collagen, tropoelastin is not synthesized in a pro- form with extension peptides. Furthermore, elastin does not contain repeat Gly-X-Y sequences, triple helical structure, or carbohydrate moieties.

After secretion from the cell, certain lysyl residues of tropoelastin are oxidatively deaminated to aldehydes by **lysyl oxidase,** the same enzyme involved in this process in collagen. However, the major cross-links formed in elastin are the **desmosines,** which result from the condensation of three of these lysine-derived aldehydes with an unmodified lysine to form a tetrafunctional cross-link unique to elastin. Once cross-linked in its mature, extracellular form, elastin is highly insoluble and **extremely stable** and has a very low turnover rate. Elastin exhibits a variety of random coil conformations that permit the protein to stretch and subsequently recoil during the performance of its physiologic functions.

Table 47–5 summarizes the main differences between collagen and elastin.

Deletions in the elastin gene (located at 7q11.23) have been found in approximately 90% of subjects with **Williams syndrome,** a developmental disorder affecting connective tissue and the central nervous system. The mutations, by affecting synthesis of elastin, probably play a causative role in the **supravalvular aortic stenosis** often found in this condition. A number of **skin diseases** (eg, scleroderma) are associated with accumulation

Table 47–5. Major differences between collagen and elastin.

Collagen	Elastin
1. Many different genetic types	One genetic type
2. Triple helix	No triple helix; random coil conformations permitting stretching
3. $(Gly-X-Y)_n$ repeating structure	No $(Gly-X-Y)_n$ repeating structure
4. Presence of hydroxylysine	No hydroxylysine
5. Carbohydrate-containing	No carbohydrate
6. Intramolecular aldol cross-links	Intramolecular desmosine cross-links
7. Presence of extension peptides during biosynthesis	No extension peptides present during biosynthesis

of elastin. Fragmentation or, alternatively, a decrease of elastin is found in conditions such as pulmonary emphysema, cutis laxa, and aging of the skin.

MARFAN SYNDROME IS DUE TO MUTATIONS IN THE GENE FOR FIBRILLIN, A PROTEIN PRESENT IN MICROFIBRILS

Marfan syndrome is a relatively prevalent inherited disease affecting connective tissue; it is inherited as an autosomal dominant trait. It affects the **eyes** (eg, causing dislocation of the lens, known as ectopia lentis), the **skeletal system** (most patients are tall and exhibit long digits [arachnodactyly] and hyperextensibility of the joints), and the **cardiovascular system** (eg, causing weakness of the aortic media, leading to dilation of the ascending aorta). Abraham Lincoln may have had this condition. Most cases are caused by mutations in the gene (on chromosome 15) for fibrillin; missense mutations have been detected in several patients with Marfan syndrome.

Fibrillin is a large glycoprotein (about 350 kDa) that is a structural component of microfibrils, 10- to 12-nm fibers found in many tissues. Fibrillin is secreted (subsequent to a proteolytic cleavage) into the extracellular matrix by fibroblasts and becomes incorporated into the insoluble **microfibrils,** which appear to provide a **scaffold** for deposition of elastin. Of special relevance to Marfan syndrome, fibrillin is found in the zonular fibers of the **lens,** in the **periosteum,** and associated with elastin fibers in the **aorta** (and elsewhere); these locations respectively explain the ectopia lentis, arachnodactyly, and cardiovascular problems found in the syndrome. Other proteins (eg, emelin and two microfibril-associated proteins) are also present in these microfibrils, and it appears likely that abnormalities of them may cause other connective tissue disorders. Another gene for fibrillin exists on chromosome 5; mutations in this gene are linked to causation of congenital contractural arachnodactyly but not to Marfan syndrome. The probable sequence of events leading to Marfan syndrome is summarized in Figure 47–2.

FIBRONECTIN IS AN IMPORTANT GLYCOPROTEIN INVOLVED IN CELL ADHESION & MIGRATION

Fibronectin is a major glycoprotein of the extracellular matrix, also found in a soluble form in plasma. It consists of two identical subunits, each of about 230 kDa, joined by two disulfide bridges near their carboxyl terminals. The gene encoding fibronectin is very large, containing some 50 exons; the RNA produced by its transcription is subject to considerable alternative splicing, and as many as 20 different mRNAs have been detected in various tissues. Fibronectin contains three types of repeating motifs

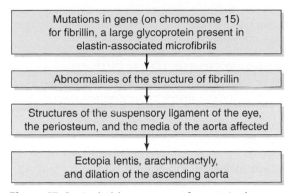

Figure 47–2. Probable sequence of events in the causation of the major signs exhibited by patients with Marfan syndrome (MIM 154700).

(I, II, and III), which are organized into functional **domains** (at least seven); functions of these domains include binding **heparin** (see below) and fibrin, collagen, DNA, and cell surfaces (Figure 47–3). The amino acid sequence of the fibronectin receptor of fibroblasts has been derived, and the protein is a member of the transmembrane integrin class of proteins (Chapter 50). The **integrins** are heterodimers, containing various types of α and β polypeptide chains. Fibronectin contains an Arg-Gly-Asp (RGD) sequence that binds to the receptor. The **RGD sequence** is shared by a number of other proteins present in the ECM that bind to integrins present in cell surfaces. Synthetic peptides containing the RGD sequence inhibit the binding of fibronectin to cell surfaces. Figure 47–4 illustrates the interaction of collagen, fibronectin, and laminin, all major proteins of the ECM, with a typical cell (eg, fibroblast) present in the matrix.

The fibronectin receptor interacts indirectly with **actin** microfilaments (Chapter 48) present in the cytosol (Figure 47–5). A number of proteins, collectively known as **attachment proteins,** are involved; these include talin, vinculin, an actin-filament capping protein, and α-actinin. Talin interacts with the receptor and vinculin, whereas the latter two interact with actin. The interaction of fibronectin with its receptor provides one route whereby the **exterior of the cell can communicate with the interior** and thus affect cell behavior. Via the interaction with its cell receptor, fibronectin plays an important role in the **adhesion** of cells to the ECM. It is also involved in **cell migration** by providing a binding site for cells and thus helping them to steer their way through the ECM. The amount of fibronectin around many **transformed cells** is sharply reduced, partly explaining their faulty interaction with the ECM.

LAMININ IS A MAJOR PROTEIN COMPONENT OF RENAL GLOMERULAR & OTHER BASAL LAMINAS

Basal laminas are specialized areas of the ECM that surround epithelial and some other cells (eg, muscle cells); here we discuss only the laminas found in the **renal glomerulus.** In that structure, the basal lamina is contributed by two separate sheets of cells (one endothelial and one epithelial), each disposed on opposite sides of the lamina; these three layers make up the **glomerular membrane.** The primary components of the basal lamina are three proteins—laminin, entactin, and type IV collagen—and the GAG **heparin** or **heparan sulfate.** These components are synthesized by the underlying cells.

Laminin (about 850 kDa, 70 nm long) consists of three distinct elongated polypeptide chains (A, B₁, and

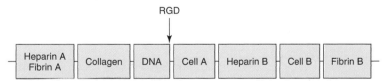

Figure 47–3. Schematic representation of fibronectin. Seven functional domains of fibronectin are represented; two different types of domain for heparin, cell-binding, and fibrin are shown. The domains are composed of various combinations of three structural motifs (I, II, and III), not depicted in the figure. Also not shown is the fact that fibronectin is a dimer joined by disulfide bridges near the carboxyl terminals of the monomers. The approximate location of the RGD sequence of fibronectin, which interacts with a variety of fibronectin integrin receptors on cell surfaces, is indicated by the arrow. (Redrawn after Yamada KM: Adhesive recognition sequences. J Biol Chem 1991;266:12809. Republished with permission conveyed through Copyright Clearance Center, Inc.)

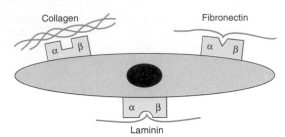

Figure 47–4. Schematic representation of a cell interacting through various integrin receptors with collagen, fibronectin, and laminin present in the ECM. (Specific subunits are not indicated.) (Redrawn after Yamada KM: Adhesive recognition sequences. J Biol Chem 1991;266:12809. Republished with permission conveyed through Copyright Clearance Center, Inc.)

B_2) linked together to form an elongated cruciform shape. It has binding sites for type IV collagen, heparin, and integrins on cell surfaces. The collagen interacts with laminin (rather than directly with the cell surface), which in turn interacts with integrins or other laminin

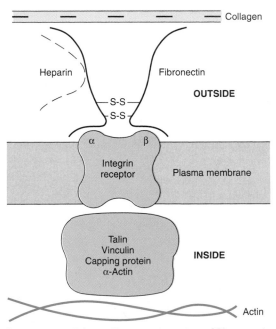

Figure 47–5. Schematic representation of fibronectin interacting with an integrin fibronectin receptor situated in the exterior of the plasma membrane of a cell of the ECM and of various attachment proteins interacting indirectly or directly with an actin microfilament in the cytosol. For simplicity, the attachment proteins are represented as a complex.

receptor proteins, thus anchoring the lamina to the cells. **Entactin,** also known as "nidogen," is a glycoprotein containing an RGD sequence; it binds to laminin and is a major cell attachment factor. The relatively thick basal lamina of the renal glomerulus has an important role in **glomerular filtration,** regulating the passage of large molecules (most plasma proteins) across the glomerulus into the renal tubule. The glomerular membrane allows small molecules, such as **inulin** (5.2 kDa), to pass through as easily as water. On the other hand, only a small amount of the protein **albumin** (69 kDa), the major plasma protein, passes through the normal glomerulus. This is explained by two sets of facts: (1) The **pores** in the glomerular membrane are large enough to allow molecules up to about 8 nm to pass through. (2) Albumin is smaller than this pore size, but it is prevented from passing through easily by the **negative charges** of heparan sulfate and of certain sialic acid-containing glycoproteins present in the lamina. These negative charges repel albumin and most plasma proteins, which are negatively charged at the pH of blood. The normal structure of the glomerulus may be severely damaged in certain types of **glomerulonephritis** (eg, caused by antibodies directed against various components of the glomerular membrane). This alters the pores and the amounts and dispositions of the negatively charged macromolecules referred to above, and relatively massive amounts of albumin (and of certain other plasma proteins) can pass through into the urine, resulting in severe **albuminuria.**

PROTEOGLYCANS & GLYCOSAMINOGLYCANS

The Glycosaminoglycans Found in Proteoglycans Are Built Up of Repeating Disaccharides

Proteoglycans are proteins that contain covalently linked glycosaminoglycans. At least 30 have been characterized and given names such as syndecan, betaglycan, serglycin, perlecan, aggrecan, versican, decorin, biglycan, and fibromodulin. They vary in tissue distribution, nature of the core protein, attached glycosaminoglycans, and function. The proteins bound covalently to glycosaminoglycans are called **"core proteins";** they have proved difficult to isolate and characterize, but the use of recombinant DNA technology is beginning to yield important information about their structures. The amount of **carbohydrate** in a proteoglycan is usually much greater than is found in a glycoprotein and may comprise up to 95% of its weight. Figures 47–6 and 47–7 show the general structure of one particular proteoglycan, **aggrecan,** the major type found in cartilage. It is very large (about 2×10^3 kDa), with its overall structure resembling that of a bottle

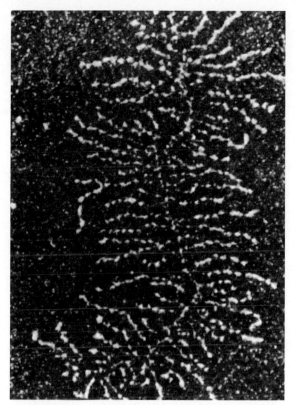

Figure 47–6. Darkfield electron micrograph of a proteoglycan aggregate in which the proteoglycan subunits and filamentous backbone are particularly well extended. (Reproduced, with permission, from Rosenberg L, Hellman W, Kleinschmidt AK: Electron microscopic studies of proteoglycan aggregates from bovine articular cartilage. J Biol Chem 1975;250:1877. Republished with permission conveyed through Copyright Clearance Center, Inc.)

brush. It contains a long strand of hyaluronic acid (one type of GAG) to which link proteins are attached **noncovalently.** In turn, these latter interact noncovalently with core protein molecules from which chains of other GAGs (keratan sulfate and chondroitin sulfate in this case) project. More details on this macromolecule are given when cartilage is discussed below.

There are at least seven **glycosaminoglycans (GAGs):** hyaluronic acid, chondroitin sulfate, keratan sulfates I and II, heparin, heparan sulfate, and dermatan sulfate. A GAG is an unbranched polysaccharide made up of repeating disaccharides, one component of which is always an **amino sugar** (hence the name GAG), either D-glucosamine or D-galactosamine. The other component of the repeating disaccharide (except in the case of keratan sulfate) is a **uronic acid,** either L-glucuronic acid (GlcUA)

or its 5′-epimer, L-iduronic acid (IdUA). With the exception of hyaluronic acid, all the GAGs contain **sulfate groups,** either as O-esters or as N-sulfate (in heparin and heparan sulfate). Hyaluronic acid affords another exception because there is no clear evidence that it is attached covalently to protein, as the definition of a proteoglycan given above specifies. Both GAGs and proteoglycans have proved difficult to work with, partly because of their complexity. However, they are major components of the ground substance; they have a number of important biologic roles; and they are involved in a number of disease processes—so that interest in them is increasing rapidly.

Biosynthesis of Glycosaminoglycans Involves Attachment to Core Proteins, Chain Elongation, & Chain Termination

A. ATTACHMENT TO CORE PROTEINS

The linkage between GAGs and their core proteins is generally one of three types.

1. An **O-glycosidic bond** between **xylose** (Xyl) and **Ser,** a bond that is unique to proteoglycans. This linkage is formed by transfer of a Xyl residue to Ser from UDP-xylose. Two residues of Gal are then added to the

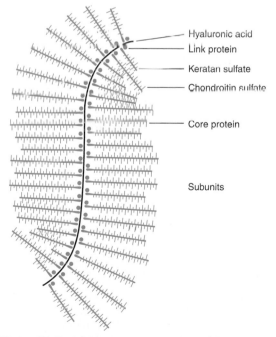

- Hyaluronic acid
- Link protein
- Keratan sulfate
- Chondroitin sulfate
- Core protein

Subunits

Figure 47–7. Schematic representation of the proteoglycan aggrecan. (Reproduced, with permission, from Lennarz WJ: *The Biochemistry of Glycoproteins and Proteoglycans.* Plenum Press, 1980. Reproduced with kind permission from Springer Science and Business Media.)

Xyl residue, forming a **link trisaccharide,** Gal-Gal-Xyl-Ser. Further chain growth of the GAG occurs on the terminal Gal.

2. An **O-glycosidic bond** forms between **GalNAc** (*N*-acetylgalactosamine) and **Ser (Thr)** (Figure 46–1A), present in keratan sulfate II. This bond is formed by donation to Ser (or Thr) of a GalNAc residue, employing UDP-GalNAc as its donor.

3. An **N-glycosylamine bond** between **GlcNAc** (*N*-acetylglucosamine) and the amide nitrogen of **Asn,** as found in N-linked glycoproteins (Figure 46–1B). Its synthesis is believed to involve dolichol-P-P-oligosaccharide.

The synthesis of the core proteins occurs in the **endoplasmic reticulum,** and formation of at least some of the above linkages also occurs there. Most of the later steps in the biosynthesis of GAG chains and their subsequent modifications occur in the **Golgi apparatus.**

B. CHAIN ELONGATION

Appropriate **nucleotide sugars** and highly specific Golgi-located **glycosyltransferases** are employed to synthesize the oligosaccharide chains of GAGs. The **"one enzyme, one linkage"** relationship appears to hold here, as in the case of certain types of linkages found in glycoproteins. The enzyme systems involved in chain elongation are capable of high-fidelity reproduction of complex GAGs.

C. CHAIN TERMINATION

This appears to result from (1) **sulfation,** particularly at certain positions of the sugars, and (2) the **progression** of the growing GAG chain away from the membrane site where catalysis occurs.

D. FURTHER MODIFICATIONS

After formation of the GAG chain, **numerous chemical modifications** occur, such as the introduction of sulfate groups onto GalNAc and other moieties and the epimerization of GlcUA to IdUA residues. The enzymes catalyzing sulfation are designated **sulfotransferases** and use 3′-phosphoadenosine-5′-phosphosulfate (PAPS; active sulfate) as the sulfate donor. These Golgi-located enzymes are highly specific, and distinct enzymes catalyze sulfation at different positions (eg, carbons 2, 3, 4, and 6) on the acceptor sugars. An **epimerase** catalyzes conversions of glucuronyl to iduronyl residues.

The Various Glycosaminoglycans Exhibit Differences in Structure & Have Characteristic Distributions

The seven GAGs named above **differ** from each other in a number of the following properties: amino sugar composition, uronic acid composition, linkages between these components, chain length of the disaccharides, the presence or absence of sulfate groups and their positions of attachment to the constituent sugars, the nature of the core proteins to which they are attached, the nature of the linkage to core protein, their tissue and subcellular distribution, and their biologic functions.

The structures (Figure 47–8) and the distributions of each of the GAGs will now be briefly discussed. The major features of the seven GAGs are summarized in Table 47–6.

A. HYALURONIC ACID

Hyaluronic acid consists of an unbranched chain of repeating disaccharide units containing GlcUA and GlcNAc. Hyaluronic acid is present in bacteria and is widely distributed among various animals and tissues, including synovial fluid, the vitreous body of the eye, cartilage, and loose connective tissues.

B. CHONDROITIN SULFATES (CHONDROITIN 4-SULFATE & CHONDROITIN 6-SULFATE)

Proteoglycans linked to **chondroitin sulfate** by the Xyl-Ser O-glycosidic bond are prominent components of **cartilage** (see below). The repeating disaccharide is similar to that found in hyaluronic acid, containing GlcUA but with **GalNAc** replacing GlcNAc. The GalNAc is substituted with *sulfate* at either its 4′ or its 6′ position, with approximately one sulfate being present per disaccharide unit.

C. KERATAN SULFATES I & II

As shown in Figure 47–8, the keratan sulfates consist of repeating **Gal-GlcNAc** disaccharide units containing **sulfate** attached to the 6′ position of GlcNAc or occasionally of Gal. Type I is abundant in **cornea,** and type II is found along with chondroitin sulfate attached to hyaluronic acid in **loose connective tissue.** Types I and II have different attachments to protein (Figure 47–8).

D. HEPARIN

The repeating disaccharide contains **glucosamine** (GlcN) and either of the two uronic acids (Figure 47–9). Most of the amino groups of the GlcN residues are **N-sulfated,** but a few are acetylated. The GlcN also carries a C_6 sulfate ester.

Approximately 90% of the uronic acid residues are **IdUA.** Initially, all of the uronic acids are GlcUA, but a 5′-epimerase converts approximately 90% of the GlcUA residues to IdUA after the polysaccharide chain is formed. The protein molecule of the heparin proteoglycan is unique, consisting exclusively of serine and glycine residues. Approximately two-thirds of the serine residues contain GAG chains, usually of 5–15 kDa but occasionally much larger. Heparin is found in the granules of **mast cells** and also in liver, lung, and skin.

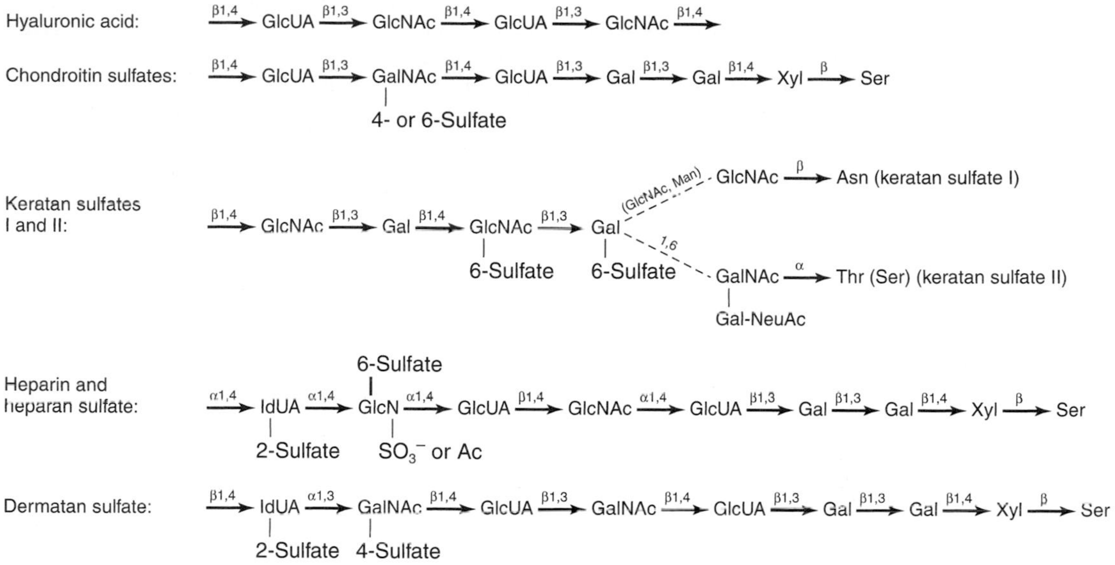

Hyaluronic acid: $\xrightarrow{\beta1,4}$ GlcUA $\xrightarrow{\beta1,3}$ GlcNAc $\xrightarrow{\beta1,4}$ GlcUA $\xrightarrow{\beta1,3}$ GlcNAc $\xrightarrow{\beta1,4}$

Chondroitin sulfates: $\xrightarrow{\beta1,4}$ GlcUA $\xrightarrow{\beta1,3}$ GalNAc $\xrightarrow{\beta1,4}$ GlcUA $\xrightarrow{\beta1,3}$ Gal $\xrightarrow{\beta1,3}$ Gal $\xrightarrow{\beta1,4}$ Xyl $\xrightarrow{\beta}$ Ser
|
4- or 6-Sulfate

Keratan sulfates I and II: $\xrightarrow{\beta1,4}$ GlcNAc $\xrightarrow{\beta1,3}$ Gal $\xrightarrow{\beta1,4}$ GlcNAc $\xrightarrow{\beta1,3}$ Gal $\xrightarrow{(GlcNAc, Man)}$ · GlcNAc $\xrightarrow{\beta}$ Asn (keratan sulfate I)
| |
6-Sulfate   6-Sulfate $\xrightarrow{1,6}$ GalNAc $\xrightarrow{\alpha}$ Thr (Ser) (keratan sulfate II)
|
Gal-NeuAc

Heparin and heparan sulfate: $\xrightarrow{\alpha1,4}$ IdUA $\xrightarrow{\alpha1,4}$ GlcN $\xrightarrow{\alpha1,4}$ GlcUA $\xrightarrow{\beta1,4}$ GlcNAc $\xrightarrow{\alpha1,4}$ GlcUA $\xrightarrow{\beta1,3}$ Gal $\xrightarrow{\beta1,3}$ Gal $\xrightarrow{\beta1,4}$ Xyl $\xrightarrow{\beta}$ Ser
| | 6-Sulfate
2-Sulfate SO_3^- or Ac

Dermatan sulfate: $\xrightarrow{\beta1,4}$ IdUA $\xrightarrow{\alpha1,3}$ GalNAc $\xrightarrow{\beta1,4}$ GlcUA $\xrightarrow{\beta1,3}$ GalNAc $\xrightarrow{\beta1,4}$ GlcUA $\xrightarrow{\beta1,3}$ Gal $\xrightarrow{\beta1,3}$ Gal $\xrightarrow{\beta1,4}$ Xyl $\xrightarrow{\beta}$ Ser
| |
2-Sulfate 4-Sulfate

Figure 47–8. Summary of structures of glycosaminoglycans and their attachments to core proteins. (GlcUA, D-glucuronic acid; IdUA, L-iduronic acid; GlcN, D-glucosamine; GalN, D-galactosamine; Ac, acetyl; Gal, D-galactose; Xyl, D-xylose; Ser, L-serine; Thr, L-threonine; Asn, L-asparagine; Man, D-mannose; NeuAc, N-acetylneuraminic acid.) The summary structures are qualitative representations only and do not reflect, for example, the uronic acid composition of hybrid glycosaminoglycans such as heparin and dermatan sulfate, which contain both L-iduronic and D-glucuronic acid. Neither should it be assumed that the indicated substituents are always present, eg, whereas most iduronic acid residues in heparin carry a 2′-sulfate group, a much smaller proportion of these residues are sulfated in dermatan sulfate. The presence of link trisaccharides (Gal-Gal-Xyl) in the chondroitin sulfates, heparin, and heparan and dermatan sulfates is shown. (Slightly modified and reproduced, with permission, from Lennarz WJ: *The Biochemistry of Glycoproteins and Proteoglycans.* Plenum Press, 1980. Reproduced with kind permission from Springer Science and Business Media.)

Table 47–6. Major properties of the glycosaminoglycans.

GAG	Sugars	Sulfate[1]	Linkage of Protein	Location
HA	GlcNAc, GlcUA	Nil	No firm evidence	Synovial fluid, vitreous humor, loose connective tissue
CS	GalNAc, GlcUA	GalNAc	Xyl-Ser; associated with HA via link proteins	Cartilage, bone, cornea
KS I	GlcNAc, Gal	GlcNAc	GlcNAc-Asn	Cornea
KS II	GlcNAc, Gal	Same as KS I	GalNAc-Thr	Loose connective tissue
Heparin	GlcN, IdUA	GlcN GlcN IdUA	Ser	Mast cells
Heparan sulfate	GlcN, GlcUA	GlcN	Xyl-Ser	Skin fibroblasts, aortic wall
Dermatan sulfate	GalNAc, IdUA, (GlcUA)	GalNAc IdUa	Xyl-Ser	Wide distribution

[1]The sulfate is attached to various positions of the sugars indicated (see Figure 47–7).
Note that all of the GAGs (except the keratan sulfates) contain a uronic acid (glucuronic or iduronic acid).

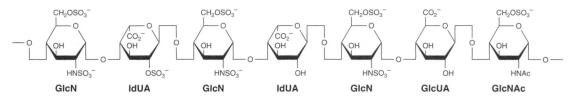

Figure 47–9. Structure of heparin. The polymer section illustrates structural features typical of heparin; however, the sequence of variously substituted repeating disaccharide units has been arbitrarily selected. In addition, non-O-sulfated or 3-O-sulfated glucosamine residues may also occur. (Modified, redrawn, and reproduced, with permission, from Lindahl U et al: Structure and biosynthesis of heparin-like polysaccharides. Fed Proc 1977;36:19.)

E. HEPARAN SULFATE

This molecule is present on many **cell surfaces** as a proteoglycan and is extracellular. It contains **GlcN** with fewer N-sulfates than heparin, and, unlike heparin, its predominant uronic acid is **GlcUA.**

F. DERMATAN SULFATE

This substance is widely distributed in animal tissues. Its structure is similar to that of chondroitin sulfate, except that in place of a GlcUA in β-1,3 linkage to Gal-NAc it contains an **IdUA** in an α-1,3 linkage to **Gal-NAc.** Formation of the IdUA occurs, as in heparin and heparan sulfate, by 5'-epimerization of GlcUA. Because this is regulated by the degree of sulfation and because sulfation is incomplete, dermatan sulfate contains **both** IdUA-GalNAc and GlcUA-GalNAc disaccharides.

Deficiencies of Enzymes That Degrade Glycosaminoglycans Result in Mucopolysaccharidoses

Both **exo-** and **endoglycosidases** degrade GAGs. Like most other biomolecules, GAGs are subject to **turnover,** being both synthesized and degraded. In adult tissues, GAGs generally exhibit relatively **slow** turnover, their half-lives being days to weeks.

Understanding of the degradative pathways for GAGs, as in the case of glycoproteins (Chapter 46) and glycosphingolipids (Chapter 24), has been greatly aided by elucidation of the specific enzyme deficiencies that occur in certain **inborn errors of metabolism.** When GAGs are involved, these inborn errors are called **mucopolysaccharidoses** (Table 47–7).

Degradation of GAGs is carried out by a battery of **lysosomal hydrolases.** These include certain endoglycosidases, various exoglycosidases, and sulfatases, generally acting in sequence to degrade the various GAGs. A number of them are indicated in Table 47–7.

The **mucopolysaccharidoses** share a common mechanism of causation, as illustrated in Figure 47–10. They are inherited in an **autosomal recessive** manner, with **Hurler** and **Hunter syndromes** being perhaps the most widely studied. None are common. In some cases, a family history of a mucopolysaccharidosis is obtained. Specific **laboratory investigations** of help in their diagnosis are urine testing for the presence of increased amounts of GAGs and assays of suspected enzymes in white cells, fibroblasts, or sometimes in serum. In certain cases, a tissue biopsy is performed and the GAG that has accumulated can be determined by electrophoresis. DNA tests are increasingly available. Prenatal diagnosis can be made using amniotic cells or chorionic villus biopsy.

The term **"mucolipidosis"** was introduced to denote diseases that combined features common to both mucopolysaccharidoses and sphingolipidoses (Chapter 24). Three mucolipidoses are listed in Table 47–7. In **sialidosis** (mucolipidosis I, ML-I), various oligosaccharides derived from glycoproteins and certain gangliosides can accumulate in tissues. **I-cell disease** (ML-II) and **pseudo-Hurler polydystrophy** (ML-III) are described in Chapter 46. The term "mucolipidosis" is retained because it is still in relatively widespread clinical usage, but it is not appropriate for these two latter diseases since the mechanism of their causation involves **mislocation** of certain lysosomal enzymes. Genetic defects of the catabolism of the oligosaccharide chains of glycoproteins (eg, mannosidosis, fucosidosis) are also described in Chapter 46. Most of these defects are characterized by increased excretion of various fragments of glycoproteins in the urine, which accumulate because of the metabolic block, as in the case of the mucolipidoses.

Hyaluronidase is one important enzyme involved in the catabolism of both hyaluronic acid and chondroitin sulfate. It is a widely distributed endoglycosidase that cleaves hexosaminidic linkages. From hyaluronic acid, the enzyme will generate a tetrasaccharide with the structure $(GlcUA-\beta-1,3-GlcNAc-\beta-1,4)_2$, which can be degraded further by a β-glucuronidase and β-*N*-acetylhexosaminidase. Surprisingly, only one

Table 47–7. Biochemical defects and diagnostic tests in mucopolysaccharidoses (MPS) and mucolipidoses (ML).[1]

Name	Alternative Designation[2,3]	Enzymatic Defect	Urinary Metabolites
Mucopolysaccharidoses			
Hurler (MIM 607014), Scheie (MIM 607016), Hurler-Scheie (MIM 607015)	MPS I	α-L-Iduronidase	Dermatan sulfate, heparan sulfate
Hunter (MIM 309900)	MPS II	Iduronate sulfatase	Dermatan sulfate, heparan sulfate
Sanfilippo A (MIM 252900)	MPS IIIA	Heparan sulfate N-sulfatase (sulfamidase)	Heparan sulfate
Sanfilippo B (MIM 252920)	MPS IIIB	α-N-Acetylglucosaminidase	Heparan sulfate
Sanfilippo C (MIM 252930)	MPS IIIC	Acetyltransferase	Heparan sulfate
Sanfilippo D (MIM 252940)	MPS IIID	N-Acetylglucosamine 6-sulfatase	Heparan sulfate
Morquio A (MIM 253000)	MPS IVA	Galactosamine 6-sulfatase	Keratan sulfate, chondroitin 6-sulfate
Morquio B (MIM 253010)	MPS IVB	β-Galactosidase	Keratan sulfate
Maroteaux-Lamy (MIM 253200)	MPS VI	N-Acetylgalactosamine 4-sulfatase (arylsulfatase B)	Dermatan sulfate
Sly (MIM 253220)	MPS VII	β-Glucuronidase	Dermatan sulfate, heparan sulfate, chondroitin 4-sulfate, chondroitin 6-sulfate
Mucolipidoses			
Sialidosis (MIM 256550)	ML I	Sialidase (neuraminidase)	Glycoprotein fragments
I-cell disease (MIM 252500)	ML II	UDP-N-acetylglucosamine: glyco-protein N-acetylglucosamini-nylphosphotransferase (acid hydrolases thus lack phospho-mannosyl residues)	Glycoprotein fragments
Pseudo-Hurler polydystro-phy (MIM 252600)	ML III	As for ML II but deficiency is incomplete	Glycoprotein fragments

[1]Modified and reproduced, with permission, from DiNatale P, Neufeld EF: The biochemical diagnosis of mucopolysaccharidoses, mucolip-idoses and related disorders. In: *Perspectives in Inherited Metabolic Diseases*, vol 2. Barr B et al (editors). Editiones Ermes (Milan), 1979.
[2]Fibroblasts, leukocytes, tissues, amniotic fluid cells, or serum can be used for the assay of many of the above enzymes. Patients with these disorders exhibit a variety of clinical findings that may include cloudy corneas, mental retardation, stiff joints, cardiac abnormalities, hepatosplenomegaly, and short stature, depending on the specific disease and its severity.
[3]The term MPS V is no longer used. The existence of MPS VIII (suspected glucosamine 6-sulfatase deficiency: MIM 253230) has not been confirmed. At least one case of hyaluronidase deficiency (MPS IX; MIM 601492) has been reported.

case of an apparent genetic deficiency of this enzyme appears to have been reported.

Proteoglycans Have Numerous Functions

As indicated above, **proteoglycans** are remarkably complex molecules and are found in **every tissue** of the body, mainly in the ECM or "ground substance." There they are associated with each other and also with the other major structural components of the matrix, collagen and elastin, in quite specific manners. Some proteoglycans bind to collagen and others to elastin. These interactions are important in determining the structural organization of the matrix. Some proteoglycans (eg, decorin) can also

bind growth factors such as TGF-β, modulating their effects on cells. In addition, some of them interact with certain **adhesive proteins** such as fibronectin and laminin (see above), also found in the matrix. The GAGs present in the proteoglycans are **polyanions** and hence bind polycations and cations such as Na^+ and K^+. This latter ability attracts water by osmotic pressure into the extracellular matrix and contributes to its turgor. GAGs also **gel** at relatively low concentrations. Because of the long extended nature of the polysaccharide chains of GAGs and their ability to gel, the proteoglycans can act as **sieves**, restricting the passage of large macromolecules into the ECM but allowing relatively free diffusion of small molecules. Again, because of their extended struc-

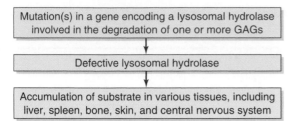

Figure 47–10. Simplified scheme of causation of a mucopolysaccharidosis, such as Hurler syndrome (MIM 607014), in which the affected enzyme is α-L-iduronidase. Marked accumulation of the GAGs in the tissues mentioned in the figure could cause hepatomegaly, splenomegaly, disturbances of growth, coarse facies, and mental retardation, respectively.

tures and the huge macromolecular aggregates they often form, they occupy a **large volume** of the matrix relative to proteins.

A. Some Functions of Specific GAGs & Proteoglycans

Hyaluronic acid is especially high in concentration in embryonic tissues and is thought to play an important role in permitting **cell migration** during morphogenesis and wound repair. Its ability to attract water into the extracellular matrix and thereby "loosen it up" may be important in this regard. The high concentrations of hyaluronic acid and chondroitin sulfates present in **cartilage** contribute to its compressibility (see below).

Chondroitin sulfates are located at sites of calcification in endochondral **bone** and are also found in **cartilage.** They are also located inside certain **neurons** and may provide an endoskeletal structure, helping to maintain their shape.

Both **keratan sulfate I** and **dermatan sulfate** are present in the **cornea.** They lie between collagen fibrils and play a critical role in corneal transparency. Changes in proteoglycan composition found in corneal scars disappear when the cornea heals. The presence of dermatan sulfate in the **sclera** may also play a role in maintaining the overall shape of the eye. Keratan sulfate I is also present in **cartilage.**

Heparin is an important **anticoagulant.** It binds with factors IX and XI, but its most important interaction is with **plasma antithrombin** (discussed in Chapter 50). Heparin can also bind specifically to **lipoprotein lipase** present in capillary walls, causing a release of this enzyme into the circulation.

Certain proteoglycans (eg, **heparan sulfate**) are associated with the plasma membrane of cells, with their core proteins actually spanning that membrane. In it they may act as **receptors** and may also participate in the

mediation of **cell growth** and **cell-cell communication.** The attachment of cells to their substratum in culture is mediated at least in part by heparan sulfate. This proteoglycan is also found in the **basement membrane of the kidney** along with type IV collagen and laminin (see above), where it plays a major role in determining the charge selectiveness of glomerular filtration.

Proteoglycans are also found in **intracellular locations** such as the nucleus; their function in this organelle has not been elucidated. They are present in some storage or secretory granules, such as the chromaffin granules of the adrenal medulla. It has been postulated that they play a role in release of the contents of such granules. The various functions of GAGs are summarized in Table 47–8.

B. Associations with Major Diseases & with Aging

Hyaluronic acid may be important in permitting **tumor cells to migrate** through the ECM. Tumor cells can induce fibroblasts to synthesize greatly increased amounts of this GAG, thereby perhaps facilitating their own spread. Some tumor cells have less heparan sulfate at their surfaces, and this may play a role in the **lack of adhesiveness** that these cells display.

The intima of the **arterial wall** contains hyaluronic acid and chondroitin sulfate, dermatan sulfate, and heparan sulfate proteoglycans. Of these proteoglycans, dermatan sulfate binds plasma low-density lipoproteins. In addition, dermatan sulfate appears to be the major GAG

Table 47–8. Some functions of glycosaminoglycans and proteoglycans.

- Act as structural components of the ECM
- Have specific interactions with collagen, elastin, fibronectin, laminin, and other proteins such as growth factors
- As polyanions, bind polycations and cations
- Contribute to the characteristic turgor of various tissues
- Act as sieves in the ECM
- Facilitate cell migration (HA)
- Have role in compressibility of cartilage in weight-bearing (HA, CS)
- Play role in corneal transparency (KS I and DS)
- Have structural role in sclera (DS)
- Act as anticoagulant (heparin)
- Are components of plasma membranes, where they may act as receptors and participate in cell adhesion and cell-cell interactions (eg, HS)
- Determine charge-selectiveness of renal glomerulus (HS)
- Are components of synaptic and other vesicles (eg, HS)

ECM, extracellular matrix; HA, hyaluronic acid; CS, chondroitin sulfate; KS I, keratan sulfate I; DS, dermatan sulfate; HS, heparan sulfate.

synthesized by arterial smooth muscle cells. Because it is these cells that proliferate in **atherosclerotic lesions** in arteries, dermatan sulfate may play an important role in development of the atherosclerotic plaque.

In various types of **arthritis,** proteoglycans may act as **autoantigens,** thus contributing to the pathologic features of these conditions. The amount of chondroitin sulfate in cartilage diminishes with age, whereas the amounts of keratan sulfate and hyaluronic acid increase. These changes may contribute to the development of **osteoarthritis,** as may increased activity of the enzyme aggrecanase, which acts to degrade aggrecan. Changes in the amounts of certain GAGs in the skin are also observed with **aging** and help to account for the characteristic changes noted in this organ in the elderly.

An exciting new phase in proteoglycan research is opening up with the findings that mutations that affect individual proteoglycans or the enzymes needed for their synthesis alter the regulation of **specific signaling pathways** in *Drosophila* and *Caenorhabditis elegans,* thus affecting **development;** it already seems likely that similar effects exist in mice and humans.

BONE IS A MINERALIZED CONNECTIVE TISSUE

Bone contains both **organic** and **inorganic** material. The **organic** matter is mainly **protein.** The principal proteins of bone are listed in Table 47–9; **type I collagen** is the major protein, comprising 90–95% of the organic material. Type V collagen is also present in small amounts, as are a number of noncollagen proteins, some of which are relatively specific to bone. The **inorganic** or mineral component is mainly crystalline **hydroxyapatite**—$Ca_{10}(PO_4)_6(OH)_2$—along with sodium, magnesium, carbonate, and fluoride; approximately 99% of the body's calcium is contained in bone (Chapter 44). Hydroxyapatite confers on bone the strength and resilience required by its physiologic roles.

Bone is a **dynamic structure** that undergoes continuing cycles of remodeling, consisting of resorption followed by deposition of new bone tissue. This remodeling permits bone to adapt to both physical (eg, increases in weight-bearing) and hormonal signals.

The major cell types involved in bone resorption and deposition are **osteoclasts** and **osteoblasts** (Figure 47–11). The former are associated with resorption and the latter with deposition of bone. Osteocytes are descended from osteoblasts; they also appear to be involved in maintenance of bone matrix but will not be discussed further here.

Osteoclasts are multinucleated cells derived from pluripotent hematopoietic stem cells. Osteoclasts possess an apical membrane domain, exhibiting a ruffled border that plays a key role in bone resorption (Figure 47–12).

Table 47–9. The principal proteins found in bone.[1]

Proteins	Comments
Collagens	
Collagen type I	Approximately 90% of total bone protein. Composed of two $\alpha1(I)$ and one $\alpha2(I)$ chains.
Collagen type V	Minor component.
Noncollagen proteins	
Plasma proteins	Mixture of various plasma proteins.
Proteoglycans[2] CS-PG I (biglycan)	Contains two GAG chains; found in other tissues.
CS-PG II (decorin)	Contains one GAG chain; found in other tissues.
CS-PG III	Bone-specific.
Bone SPARC[3] protein (osteonectin)	Not bone-specific.
Osteocalcin (bone Gla protein)	Contains γ-carboxyglutamate residues that bind to hydroxyapatite. Bone-specific.
Osteopontin	Not bone-specific. Glycosylated and phosphorylated.
Bone sialoprotein	Bone-specific. Heavily glycosylated, and sulfated on tyrosine.
Bone morphogenetic proteins (BMPs)	A family (eight or more) of secreted proteins with a variety of actions on bone; many induce ectopic bone growth.
Osteoprotegerin	Inhibits osteoclastogenesis

[1]Various functions have been ascribed to the noncollagen proteins, including roles in mineralization; however, most of them are still speculative. It is considered unlikely that the noncollagen proteins that are not bone-specific play a key role in mineralization. A number of other proteins are also present in bone, including a tyrosine-rich acidic matrix protein (TRAMP), some growth factors (eg, TGFβ), and enzymes involved in collagen synthesis (eg, lysyl oxidase).
[2]CS-PG, chondroitin sulfate–proteoglycan; these are similar to the dermatan sulfate PGs (DS-PGs) of cartilage (Table 47–11).
[3]SPARC, secreted protein acidic and rich in cysteine.

A proton-translocating **ATPase** expels protons across the ruffled border into the resorption area, which is the microenvironment of low pH shown in the figure. This lowers the local pH to 4.0 or less, thus increasing the solubility of hydroxyapatite and allowing demineralization to occur. Lysosomal acid proteases are released that digest the now accessible matrix proteins. **Osteoblasts**—

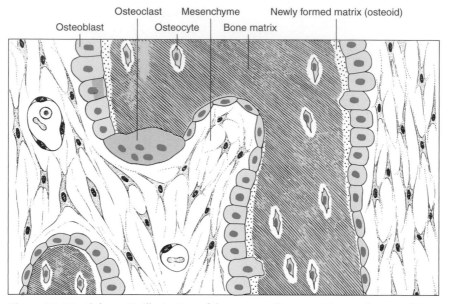

Figure 47–11. Schematic illustration of the major cells present in membranous bone. Osteoblasts (lighter color) are synthesizing type I collagen, which forms a matrix that traps cells. As this occurs, osteoblasts gradually differentiate to become osteocytes. (Reproduced, with permission, from Junqueira LC, Carneiro J: *Basic Histology: Text & Atlas*, 10th ed. McGraw-Hill, 2003.)

mononuclear cells derived from pluripotent mesenchymal precursors—synthesize most of the proteins found in bone (Table 47–9) as well as various growth factors and cytokines. They are responsible for the deposition of new bone matrix (osteoid) and its subsequent mineralization. Osteoblasts **control mineralization** by regulating the passage of calcium and phosphate ions across their surface membranes. The latter contain **alkaline phosphatase,** which is used to generate phosphate ions from organic phosphates. The mechanisms involved in mineralization are not fully understood, but several factors have been implicated. Alkaline phosphatase contributes to mineralization but in itself is not sufficient. Small vesicles (matrix vesicles) containing calcium and phosphate have been described at sites of mineralization, but their role is not clear. **Type I collagen** appears to be necessary, with mineralization being first evident in the gaps between successive molecules. Recent interest has focused on **acidic phosphoproteins,** such as bone sialoprotein, acting as sites of nucleation. These proteins contain motifs (eg, poly-Asp and poly-Glu stretches) that bind calcium and may provide an initial scaffold for mineralization. Some macromolecules, such as certain proteoglycans and glycoproteins, can also act as **inhibitors** of nucleation.

It is estimated that approximately 4% of compact bone is **renewed annually** in the typical healthy adult, whereas approximately 20% of trabecular bone is replaced.

Many factors are involved in the **regulation of bone metabolism,** only a few of which will be mentioned here. Some **stimulate osteoblasts** (eg, parathyroid hormone and 1,25-dihydroxycholecalciferol) and others **inhibit** them (eg, corticosteroids). Parathyroid hormone and 1,25-dihydroxycholecalciferol also stimulate osteoclasts, whereas calcitonin and estrogens inhibit them.

MANY METABOLIC & GENETIC DISORDERS INVOLVE BONE

A number of the more important examples of metabolic and genetic disorders that affect bone are listed in Table 47–10.

Osteogenesis imperfecta (brittle bones) is characterized by abnormal fragility of bones. The scleras are often abnormally thin and translucent and may appear blue owing to a deficiency of connective tissue. Four types of this condition (mild, extensive, severe, and variable) have been recognized, of which the extensive type occurring in the newborn is the most ominous. Affected infants may be born with multiple fractures and not survive. Over 90% of patients with osteogenesis imperfecta have mutations in the *COL1A1* and *COL1A2* genes, encoding proα1(I) and proα2(I) chains, respectively. Over 100 mutations in these

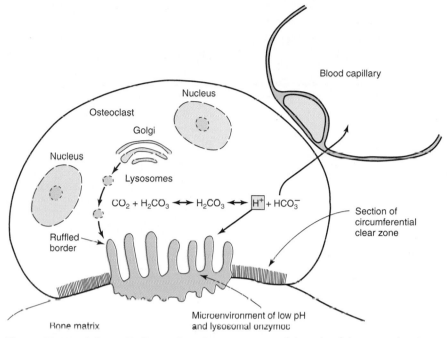

Figure 47–12. Schematic illustration of some aspects of the role of the osteoclast in bone resorption. Lysosomal enzymes and hydrogen ions are released into the confined microenvironment created by the attachment between bone matrix and the peripheral clear zone of the osteoclast. The acidification of this confined space facilitates the dissolution of calcium phosphate from bone and is the optimal pH for the activity of lysosomal hydrolases. Bone matrix is thus removed, and the products of bone resorption are taken up into the cytoplasm of the osteoclast, probably digested further, and transferred into capillaries. The chemical equation shown in the figure refers to the action of carbonic anhydrase II, described in the text. (Reproduced, with permission, from Junqueira LC, Carneiro J: *Basic Histology: Text & Atlas,* 10th ed. McGraw-Hill, 2003.)

two genes have been documented and include partial gene deletions and duplications. Other mutations affect RNA splicing, and the most frequent type results in the replacement of glycine by another bulkier amino acid, affecting formation of the triple helix. In general, these mutations result in decreased expression of collagen or in structurally abnormal proα chains that assemble into abnormal fibrils, weakening the overall structure of bone. When one abnormal chain is present, it may interact with two normal chains, but folding may be prevented, resulting in enzymatic degradation of all of the chains. This is called **"procollagen suicide"** and is an example of a dominant negative mutation, a result often seen when a protein consists of multiple different subunits.

Osteopetrosis (marble bone disease), characterized by increased bone density, is due to inability to resorb bone. One form occurs along with renal tubular acidosis and cerebral calcification. It is due to mutations in the gene (located on chromosome 8q22) encoding **carbonic anhydrase II** (CA II), one of four isozymes of carbonic anhydrase present in human tissues. The reaction catalyzed by carbonic anhydrase is shown below:

$$CO_2 + H_2O \leftrightarrow H_2CO_3 \leftrightarrow H^+ + HCO_3^-$$

In osteoclasts involved in bone resorption, CA II apparently provides protons to neutralize the OH^- ions left inside the cell when H^+ ions are pumped across their ruffled borders (see above). Thus, **if CA II is deficient in activity** in osteoclasts, normal bone resorption does not occur, and osteopetrosis results. The mechanism of the cerebral calcification is not clear, whereas the renal tubular acidosis reflects deficient activity of CA II in the renal tubules.

Osteoporosis is a generalized progressive reduction in bone tissue mass per unit volume causing skeletal weakness. The ratio of mineral to organic elements is unchanged in the remaining normal bone. Fractures of

Table 47–10. Some metabolic and genetic diseases affecting bone and cartilage.

Disease	Comments
Dwarfism	Often due to a deficiency of growth hormone, but has many other causes.
Rickets	Due to a deficiency of vitamin D during childhood.
Osteomalacia	Due to a deficiency of vitamin D during adulthood.
Hyperparathyroidism	Excess parathormone causes bone resorption.
Osteogenesis imperfecta (eg, MIM 166200)	Due to a variety of mutations in the COL1A1 and COL1A2 genes affecting the synthesis and structure of type I collagen.
Osteoporosis	Commonly postmenopausal or in other cases is more gradual and related to age; a small number of cases are due to mutations in the COL1A1 and COL1A2 genes and possibly in the vitamin D receptor gene (MIM 166710)
Osteoarthritis	A small number of cases are due to mutations in the COL1A genes.
Several chondro-dysplasias	Due to mutations in COL2A1 genes.
Pfeiffer syndrome[1] (MIM 101600)	Mutations in the gene encoding fibroblast growth receptor 1 (FGFR1).
Jackson-Weiss (MIM 123150) and Crouzon (MIM 123500) syndromes[1]	Mutations in the gene encoding FGFR2.
Achondroplasia (MIM 100800) and thanatophoric dysplasia[2] (MIM 187600)	Mutations in the gene encoding FGFR3.

[1]The Pfeiffer, Jackson-Weiss, and Crouzon syndromes are craniosynostosis syndromes; craniosynostosis is a term signifying premature fusion of sutures in the skull.

[2]Thanatophoric (Gk *thanatos* "death" + *phoros* "bearing") dysplasia is the most common neonatal lethal skeletal dysplasia, displaying features similar to those of homozygous achondroplasia.

various bones, such as the head of the femur, occur very easily and represent a huge burden to both the affected patients and to the health care budget of society. Among other factors, *estrogens* and *interleukins-1* and *-6* appear to be intimately involved in the causation of osteoporosis.

THE MAJOR COMPONENTS OF CARTILAGE ARE TYPE II COLLAGEN & CERTAIN PROTEOGLYCANS

The **principal proteins** of hyaline cartilage (the major type of cartilage) are listed in Table 47–11. **Type II collagen** is the principal protein (Figure 47–13), and a number of other minor types of collagen are also present. In addition to these components, elastic cartilage contains elastin and fibroelastic cartilage contains type I collagen. Cartilage contains a number of **proteoglycans,** which play an important role in its compressibility. **Aggrecan** (about 2×10^3 kDa) is the major proteoglycan. As shown in Figure 47–14, it has a very complex structure, containing several GAGs (hyaluronic acid, chondroitin sulfate, and keratan sulfate) and both link and core proteins. The core protein contains three domains: A, B, and C. The hyaluronic acid binds noncovalently to domain A of the core protein as well as to the link protein, which stabilizes the hyaluronate–core protein interactions. The keratan sulfate chains are located in domain B, whereas the chondroitin sulfate chains are located in domain C; both of these types of GAGs are bound covalently to the core protein. The

Table 47–11. The principal proteins found in cartilage.

Proteins	Comments
Collagen proteins	
Collagen type II	90–98% of total articular cartilage collagen. Composed of three α1(II) chains.
Collagens V, VI, IX, X, XI	Type IX cross-links to type II collagen. Type XI may help control diameter of type II fibrils.
Noncollagen proteins	
Proteoglycans	
Aggrecan	The major proteoglycan of cartilage.
Large non-aggregating proteoglycan	Found in some types of cartilage.
DS-PG I (biglycan)[1]	Similar to CS-PG I of bone.
DS-PG II (decorin)	Similar to CS-PG II of bone.
Chondronectin	May play role in binding type II collagen to surface of cartilage.
Anchorin C II	May bind type II collagen to surface of chondrocyte.

[1]The core proteins of DS-PG I and DS-PG II are homologous to those of CS-PG I and CS-PG II found in bone (Table 47–9). A possible explanation is that osteoblasts lack the epimerase required to convert glucuronic acid to iduronic acid, the latter of which is found in dermatan sulfate.

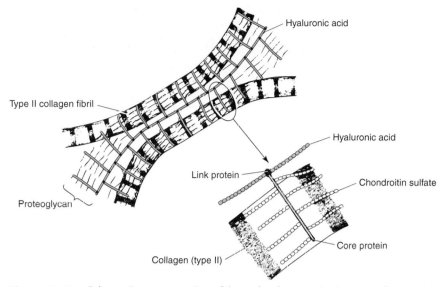

Figure 47–13. Schematic representation of the molecular organization in cartilage matrix. Link proteins noncovalently bind the core protein (lighter color) of proteoglycans to the linear hyaluronic acid molecules (darker color). The chondroitin sulfate side chains of the proteoglycan electrostatically bind to the collagen fibrils, forming a cross-linked matrix. The oval outlines the area enlarged in the lower part of the figure. (Reproduced, with permission, from Junqueira LC, Carneiro J: *Basic Histology: Text & Atlas,* 10th ed. McGraw-Hill, 2003.)

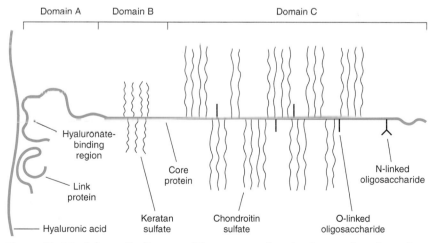

Figure 47–14. Schematic diagram of the aggrecan from bovine nasal cartilage. A strand of hyaluronic acid is shown on the left. The core protein (about 210 kDa) has three major domains. Domain A, at its amino terminal end, interacts with approximately five repeating disaccharides in hyaluronate. The link protein interacts with both hyaluronate and domain A, stabilizing their interactions. Approximately 30 keratan sulfate chains are attached, via GalNAc-Ser linkages, to domain B. Domain C contains about 100 chondroitin sulfate chains attached via Gal-Gal-Xyl-Ser linkages and about 40 O-linked oligosaccharide chains. One or more N-linked glycan chains are also found near the carboxyl terminal of the core protein. (Reproduced, with permission, from Moran LA et al: *Biochemistry,* 2nd ed. Neil Patterson Publishers, 1994. Copyright © 1994. Reprinted with permission of Pearson Education, Inc., Upper Saddle River, New Jersey.)

core protein also contains both O- and N-linked oligosaccharide chains.

The other proteoglycans found in cartilage have simpler structures than aggrecan.

Chondronectin is involved in the attachment of type II collagen to chondrocytes.

Cartilage is an avascular tissue and obtains most of its nutrients from synovial fluid. It exhibits slow but continuous **turnover.** Various **proteases** (eg, collagenases and stromalysin) synthesized by chondrocytes can **degrade collagen** and the other proteins found in cartilage. Interleukin-1 (IL-1) and tumor necrosis factor α (TNFα) appear to stimulate the production of such proteases, whereas transforming growth factor β (TGFβ) and insulin-like growth factor 1 (IGF-I) generally exert an anabolic influence on cartilage.

THE MOLECULAR BASES OF THE CHONDRODYSPLASIAS INCLUDE MUTATIONS IN GENES ENCODING TYPE II COLLAGEN & FIBROBLAST GROWTH FACTOR RECEPTORS

Chondrodysplasias are a mixed group of hereditary disorders affecting cartilage. They are manifested by short-limbed dwarfism and numerous skeletal deformities. A number of them are due to a variety of mutations in the *COL2A1* gene, leading to abnormal forms of type II collagen. One example is **Stickler syndrome,** manifested by degeneration of joint cartilage and of the vitreous body of the eye.

The best-known of the chondrodysplasias is **achondroplasia,** the most common cause of short-limbed dwarfism. Affected individuals have short limbs, normal trunk size, macrocephaly, and a variety of other skeletal abnormalities. The condition is often inherited as an autosomal dominant trait, but many cases are due to new mutations. The molecular basis of achondroplasia is outlined in Figure 47–15. Achondroplasia is not a collagen disorder but is due to mutations in the gene encoding **fibroblast growth factor receptor 3 (FGFR3). Fibroblast growth factors** are a family of at least nine proteins that affect the growth and differentiation of cells of mesenchymal and neuroectodermal origin. Their **receptors** are transmembrane proteins and form a subgroup of the family of receptor tyrosine kinases. FGFR3 is one member of this subgroup and mediates the actions of FGF3 on cartilage. In almost all cases of achondroplasia that have been investigated, the mutations were found to involve nucleotide 1138 and resulted in substitution of arginine for glycine (residue number 380) in the transmembrane domain of the protein, rendering it inactive. No such mutation was found in unaffected individuals. As indicated in Table 47–10, **other skele-**

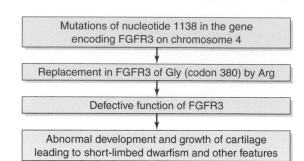

Figure 47–15. Simplified scheme of the causation of achondroplasia (MIM 100800). In most cases studied so far, the mutation has been a G to A transition at nucleotide 1138. In a few cases, the mutation was a G to C transversion at the same nucleotide. This particular nucleotide is a real "hot spot" for mutation. Both mutations result in replacement of a Gly residue by an Arg residue in the transmembrane segment of the receptor. A few cases involving replacement of Gly by Cys at codon 375 have also been reported.

tal dysplasias (including certain craniosynostosis syndromes) are also due to mutations in genes encoding FGF receptors. Another type of skeletal dysplasia (diastrophic dysplasia) has been found to be due to mutation in a sulfate transporter. Thus, thanks to recombinant DNA technology, a new era in understanding of skeletal dysplasias has begun.

SUMMARY

- The major components of the ECM are the structural proteins collagen, elastin, and fibrillin; a number of specialized proteins (eg, fibronectin and laminin); and various proteoglycans.

- Collagen is the most abundant protein in the animal kingdom; approximately 25 types have been isolated. All collagens contain greater or lesser stretches of triple helix and the repeating structure $(Gly-X-Y)_n$.

- The biosynthesis of collagen is complex, featuring many posttranslational events, including hydroxylation of proline and lysine.

- Diseases associated with impaired synthesis of collagen include scurvy, osteogenesis imperfecta, Ehlers-Danlos syndrome (many types), and Menkes disease.

- Elastin confers extensibility and elastic recoil on tissues. Elastin lacks hydroxylysine, Gly-X-Y sequences, triple helical structure, and sugars but contains desmosine and isodesmosine cross-links not found in collagen.

- Fibrillin is located in microfibrils. Mutations in the gene for fibrillin cause Marfan syndrome.

- The glycosaminoglycans (GAGs) are made up of repeating disaccharides containing a uronic acid (glucuronic or iduronic) or hexose (galactose) and a hexosamine (galactosamine or glucosamine). Sulfate is also frequently present.

- The major GAGs are hyaluronic acid, chondroitin 4- and 6-sulfates, keratan sulfates I and II, heparin, heparan sulfate, and dermatan sulfate.

- The GAGs are synthesized by the sequential actions of a battery of specific enzymes (glycosyltransferases, epimerases, sulfotransferases, etc) and are degraded by the sequential action of lysosomal hydrolases. Genetic deficiencies of the latter result in mucopolysaccharidoses (eg, Hurler syndrome).

- GAGs occur in tissues bound to various proteins (linker proteins and core proteins), constituting proteoglycans. These structures are often of very high molecular weight and serve many functions in tissues.

- Many components of the ECM bind to proteins of the cell surface named integrins; this constitutes one pathway by which the exteriors of cells can communicate with their interiors.

- Bone and cartilage are specialized forms of the ECM. Collagen I and hydroxyapatite are the major constituents of bone. Collagen II and certain proteoglycans are major constituents of cartilage.

- The molecular causes of a number of heritable diseases of bone (eg, osteogenesis imperfecta) and of cartilage (eg, the chondrodystrophies) are being revealed by the application of recombinant DNA technology.

REFERENCES

Brodsky B, Persikov AV: Molecular structure of the collagen triple helix. Adv Prot Chem 2005;70:301.

Chen D, Zhao M, Mundy GR: Bone morphogenetic proteins. Growth Fact 2004;22:233.

Deftos LJ: Treatment of Paget's disease—taming the wild osteoclast. N Engl J Med 2005;353:872.

Farach-Carson MC, Hecht JT, Carson DD: Heparan sulfate proteoglycans: key players in cartilage biology. Crit Rev Eukaryot Gene Expr 2005;15:29.

Hacker U, Nybakken K, Perrimon N: Heparan sulfate proteoglycans: the sweet side of development. Nat Rev Mol Cell Biol 2005;6:530.

Handel TM et al: Regulation of protein function by glycosaminoglycans—as exemplified by chemokines. Ann Rev Biochem 2005;74:385.

Iozzo RV: Basement membrane proteoglycans: from cellar to ceiling. Nat Rev Mol Cell Biol 2005;6:645.

Prockop DJ, Ala-Kokko L: Inherited disorders of connective tissue. In: *Harrison's Principles of Internal Medicine,* 16th ed. McGraw-Hill, 2005.

Sage E: Regulation of interactions between cells and extracellular matrix: a command performance on several stages. J Clin Invest 2001;107:781. (This article introduces a series of six articles on cell-matrix interaction. The topics covered are cell adhesion and de-adhesion, thrombospondins, syndecan, SPARC, osteopontin, and Ehlers-Danlos syndrome. All of the articles can be accessed at http://www.jci.org.)

Scriver CR et al (editors): *The Metabolic and Molecular Bases of Inherited Disease,* 8th ed. McGraw-Hill, 2001. (This comprehensive four-volume text contains chapters on disorders of collagen biosynthesis and structure, Marfan syndrome, the mucopolysaccharidoses, achondroplasia, Alport syndrome, and craniosynostosis syndromes.)

Yoon JH, Halper J: Tendon proteoglycans: biochemistry and function. J Musculoskelet Neuronal Interact 2005;5:350.

Muscle & the Cytoskeleton

Robert K. Murray, MD, PhD

BIOMEDICAL IMPORTANCE

Proteins play an important role in **movement** at both the organ (eg, skeletal muscle, heart, and gut) and cellular levels. In this chapter, the roles of specific proteins and certain other key molecules (eg, Ca^{2+}) in **muscular contraction** are described. A brief coverage of **cytoskeletal proteins** is also presented.

Knowledge of the molecular bases of a number of conditions that affect muscle has advanced greatly in recent years. Understanding of the molecular basis of **Duchenne-type muscular dystrophy** was greatly enhanced when it was found that it was due to mutations in the gene encoding dystrophin. Significant progress has also been made in understanding the molecular basis of **malignant hyperthermia,** a serious complication for some patients undergoing certain types of anesthesia. **Heart failure** is a very common medical condition, with a variety of causes; its rational therapy requires understanding of the biochemistry of heart muscle. One group of conditions that cause heart failure are the **cardiomyopathies,** some of which are genetically determined. **Nitric oxide** (NO) has been found to be a major regulator of smooth muscle tone. Many widely used **vasodilators**—such as nitroglycerin, used in the treatment of angina pectoris—act by increasing the formation of NO. Muscle, partly because of its mass, plays major roles in the **overall metabolism** of the body.

MUSCLE TRANSDUCES CHEMICAL ENERGY INTO MECHANICAL ENERGY

Muscle is the major biochemical **transducer** (machine) that converts potential (chemical) energy into kinetic (mechanical) energy. Muscle, the largest single tissue in the human body, makes up somewhat less than 25% of body mass at birth, more than 40% in the young adult, and somewhat less than 30% in the aged adult. We shall discuss aspects of the three types of muscle found in vertebrates: **skeletal, cardiac,** and **smooth.** Both skeletal and cardiac muscle appear **striated** upon microscopic observation; smooth muscle is **nonstriated.** Although skeletal muscle is under voluntary nervous control, the control of both cardiac and smooth muscle is involuntary.

The Sarcoplasm of Muscle Cells Contains ATP, Phosphocreatine, & Glycolytic Enzymes

Striated muscle is composed of multinucleated muscle fiber cells surrounded by an electrically excitable plasma membrane, the **sarcolemma.** An individual muscle fiber cell, which may extend the entire length of the muscle, contains a bundle of many **myofibrils** arranged in parallel, embedded in intracellular fluid termed **sarcoplasm.** Within this fluid is contained glycogen, the high-energy compounds ATP and phosphocreatine, and the enzymes of glycolysis.

The Sarcomere Is the Functional Unit of Muscle

An overall view of voluntary muscle at several levels of organization is presented in Figure 48–1.

When the **myofibril** is examined by electron microscopy, alternating dark and light bands (anisotropic bands, meaning birefringent in polarized light; and isotropic bands, meaning not altered by polarized light) can be observed. These bands are thus referred to as **A and I bands,** respectively. The central region of the A band (the H band) appears less dense than the rest of the band. The I band is bisected by a very dense and narrow **Z line** (Figure 48–2).

The **sarcomere** is defined as the region between two Z lines (Figures 48–1 and 48–2) and is repeated along the axis of a fibril at distances of 1500–2300 nm depending upon the state of contraction.

The **striated** appearance of voluntary and cardiac muscle in light microscopic studies results from their high degree of organization, in which most muscle fiber cells are aligned so that their sarcomeres are in parallel register (Figure 48–1).

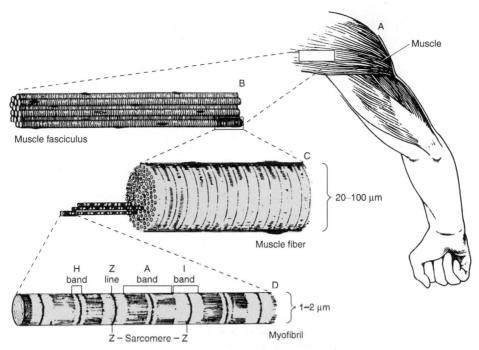

Figure 48–1. The structure of voluntary muscle. The sarcomere is the region between the Z lines. (Drawing by Sylvia Colard Keene. Reproduced, with permission, from Bloom W, Fawcett DW: *A Textbook of Histology,* 10th ed. Saunders, 1975.)

Thick Filaments Contain Myosin; Thin Filaments Contain Actin, Tropomyosin, & Troponin

When *myofibrils* are examined by electron microscopy, it appears that each one is constructed of two types of longitudinal filaments. One type, the **thick filament,** confined to the A band, contains chiefly the protein myosin. These filaments are about 16 nm in diameter and arranged in cross-section as a hexagonal array (Figure 48–2, center; right-hand cross-section).

The **thin filament** (about 7 nm in diameter) lies in the I band and extends into the A band but not into its H zone (Figure 48–2). Thin filaments contain the proteins actin, tropomyosin, and troponin (Figure 48–3). In the A band, the thin filaments are arranged around the thick (myosin) filament as a secondary hexagonal array. Each thin filament lies symmetrically between three thick filaments (Figure 48–2, center; mid cross-section), and each thick filament is surrounded symmetrically by six thin filaments.

The thick and thin filaments interact via **cross-bridges** that emerge at intervals of 14 nm along the thick filaments. As depicted in Figure 48–2, the cross-bridges (drawn as arrowheads at each end of the myosin filaments, but not shown extending fully across to the thin filaments) have opposite polarities at the two ends

of the thick filaments. The two poles of the thick filaments are separated by a 150-nm segment (the M band, not labeled in the figure) that is free of projections.

The Sliding Filament Cross-Bridge Model Is the Foundation on Which Current Thinking About Muscle Contraction Is Built

This model was proposed independently in the 1950s by Henry Huxley and Andrew Huxley and their colleagues. It was largely based on careful morphologic observations on resting, extended, and contracting muscle. Basically, when muscle contracts, there is no change in the lengths of the thick and thin filaments, but the H zones and the I bands shorten (see legend to Figure 48–2). Thus, the arrays of interdigitating filaments must **slide past one another** during contraction. **Cross-bridges** that link thick and thin filaments at certain stages in the contraction cycle generate and sustain the tension. The tension developed during muscle contraction is proportionate to the filament overlap and to the number of cross-bridges. Each cross-bridge head is connected to the thick filament via a flexible fibrous segment that can bend outward from the thick filament. This flexible segment facilitates contact of the head with the thin filament when necessary but is also sufficiently pliant to be accommodated in the interfilament spacing.

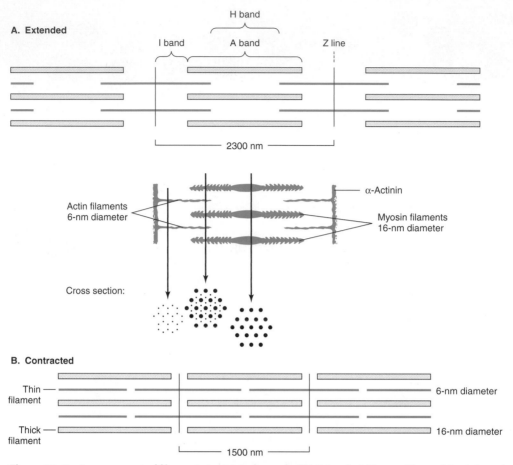

Figure 48–2. Arrangement of filaments in striated muscle. **(A)** Extended. The positions of the I, A, and H bands in the extended state are shown. The thin filaments partly overlap the ends of the thick filaments, and the thin filaments are shown anchored in the Z lines (often called Z disks). In the lower part of Figure 48–2A, "arrowheads," pointing in opposite directions, are shown emanating from the myosin (thick) filaments. Four actin (thin) filaments are shown attached to two Z lines via α-actinin. The central region of the three myosin filaments, free of arrowheads, is called the M band (not labeled). Cross-sections through the M bands, through an area where myosin and actin filaments overlap and through an area in which solely actin filaments are present, are shown. **(B)** Contracted. The actin filaments are seen to have slipped along the sides of the myosin fibers toward each other. The lengths of the thick filaments (indicated by the A bands) and the thin filaments (distance between Z lines and the adjacent edges of the H bands) have not changed. However, the lengths of the sarcomeres have been reduced (from 2300 nm to 1500 nm), and the lengths of the H and I bands are also reduced because of the overlap between the thick and thin filaments. These morphologic observations provided part of the basis for the sliding filament model of muscle contraction.

ACTIN & MYOSIN ARE THE MAJOR PROTEINS OF MUSCLE

The mass of a muscle is made up of 75% water and more than 20% protein. The two major proteins are actin and myosin.

Monomeric **G-actin** (43 kDa; G, globular) makes up 25% of muscle protein by weight. At physiologic ionic strength and in the presence of Mg^{2+}, G-actin polymerizes noncovalently to form an insoluble double helical filament called F-actin (Figure 48–3). The **F-actin** fiber is 6–7 nm thick and has a pitch or repeating structure every 35.5 nm.

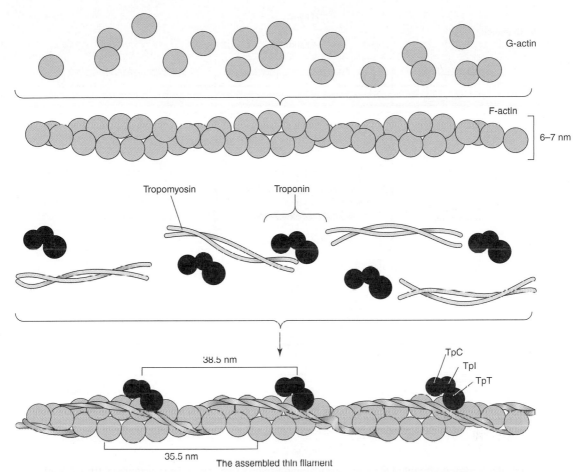

G-actin

F-actin

6–7 nm

Tropomyosin   Troponin

TpC
TpI
TpT

38.5 nm

35.5 nm
The assembled thin filament

Figure 48–3. Schematic representation of the thin filament, showing the spatial configuration of its three major protein components: actin, myosin, and tropomyosin. The upper panel shows individual molecules of G-actin. The middle panel shows actin monomers assembled into F-actin. Individual molecules of tropomyosin (two strands wound around one another) and of troponin (made up of its three subunits) are also shown. The lower panel shows the assembled thin filament, consisting of F-actin, tropomyosin, and the three subunits of troponin (TpC, TpI, and TpT).

Myosins constitute a family of proteins, with at least 12 classes having been identified in the human genome. The myosin discussed in this chapter is **myosin-II,** and when myosin is referred to in this text, it is this species that is meant unless otherwise indicated. Myosin-I is a monomeric species that binds to cell membranes. It may serve as a linkage between microfilaments and the cell membrane in certain locations.

Myosin contributes 55% of muscle protein by weight and forms the **thick filaments.** It is an asymmetric hexamer with a molecular mass of approximately 460 kDa. Myosin has a fibrous tail consisting of two intertwined helices. Each helix has a globular head portion attached at one end (Figure 48–4). The

hexamer consists of one pair of **heavy (H) chains** each of approximately 200 kDA molecular mass, and two pairs of **light (L) chains** each with a molecular mass of approximately 20 kDa. The L chains differ, one being called the **essential** light chain and the other the **regulatory** light chain. Skeletal muscle myosin binds actin to form **actomyosin** (actin-myosin), and its intrinsic ATPase activity is markedly enhanced in this complex. Isoforms of myosin exist whose amounts can vary in different anatomic, physiologic, and pathologic situations.

The structures of actin and of the head of myosin have been determined by x-ray crystallography; these studies have confirmed a number of earlier findings

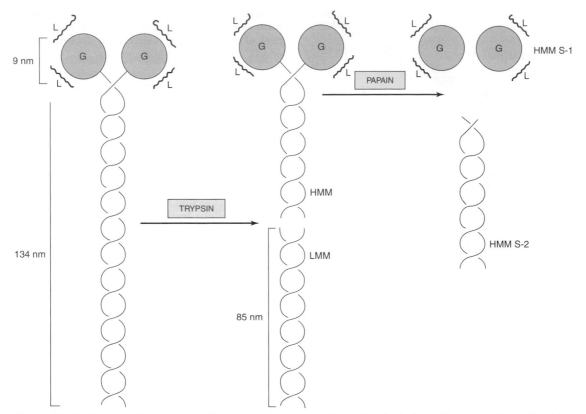

Figure 48–4. Diagram of a myosin molecule showing the two intertwined α-helices (fibrous portion), the globular region or head (G), the light chains (L), and the effects of proteolytic cleavage by trypsin and papain. The globular region (myosin head) contains an actin-binding site and an L chain-binding site and also attaches to the remainder of the myosin molecule.

concerning their structures and have also given rise to much new information.

Limited Digestion of Myosin with Proteases Has Helped to Elucidate Its Structure & Function

When myosin is digested with **trypsin,** two myosin fragments (meromyosins) are generated. **Light meromyosin** (LMM) consists of aggregated, insoluble α-helical fibers from the tail of myosin (Figure 48–4). LMM exhibits no ATPase activity and does not bind to F-actin.

   Heavy meromyosin (HMM; molecular mass about 340 kDa) is a soluble protein that has both a fibrous portion and a globular portion (Figure 48–4). It exhibits its **ATPase** activity and binds to F-actin. Digestion of HMM with **papain** generates two subfragments, S-1 and S-2. The S-2 fragment is fibrous in character, has no ATPase activity, and does not bind to F-actin.

   S-1 (molecular mass approximately 115 kDa) does exhibit ATPase activity, binds L chains, and in the absence of ATP will bind to and decorate actin with "arrowheads" (Figure 48–5). Both S-1 and HMM exhibit **ATPase** activity, which is accelerated 100- to 200-fold by complexing with F-actin. As discussed below, F-actin greatly enhances the rate at which myosin ATPase releases its products, ADP and P_i. Thus, although **F-actin** does not affect the hydrolysis step per se, its ability to **promote release** of the products produced by the ATPase activity greatly accelerates the overall rate of catalysis.

CHANGES IN THE CONFORMATION OF THE HEAD OF MYOSIN DRIVE MUSCLE CONTRACTION

How can hydrolysis of ATP produce macroscopic movement? Muscle contraction essentially consists of the cyclic **attachment and detachment** of the S-1 head

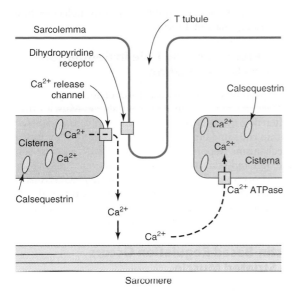

Figure 48–8. Diagram of the relationships among the sarcolemma (plasma membrane), a T tubule, and two cisternae of the sarcoplasmic reticulum of skeletal muscle (not to scale). The T tubule extends inward from the sarcolemma. A wave of depolarization, initiated by a nerve impulse, is transmitted from the sarcolemma down the T tubule. It is then conveyed to the Ca^{2+} release channel (ryanodine receptor), perhaps by interaction between it and the dihydropyridine receptor (slow Ca^{2+} voltage channel), which are shown in close proximity. Release of Ca^{2+} from the Ca^{2+} release channel into the cytosol initiates contraction. Subsequently, Ca^{2+} is pumped back into the cisternae of the sarcoplasmic reticulum by the Ca^{2+} ATPase (Ca^{2+} pump) and stored there, in part bound to calsequestrin.

Ca^{2+} is bound to a specific Ca^{2+}-binding protein designated **calsequestrin.** The sarcomere is surrounded by an excitable membrane (the T tubule system) composed of transverse (T) channels closely associated with the sarcoplasmic reticulum.

When the sarcolemma is excited by a **nerve impulse,** the signal is transmitted into the T tubule system and a **Ca^{2+} release channel** in the nearby sarcoplasmic reticulum opens, releasing Ca^{2+} from the sarcoplasmic reticulum into the sarcoplasm. The concentration of Ca^{2+} in the sarcoplasm rises rapidly to 10^{-5} mol/L. The Ca^{2+} binding sites on TpC in the thin filament are quickly occupied by Ca^{2+}. The TpC-4Ca^{2+} interacts with TpI and TpT to alter their interaction with tropomyosin. Accordingly, tropomyosin moves out of the way or alters the conformation of F-actin so that the myosin head-ADP-P_i (Figure 48–6) can interact with F-actin to start the contraction cycle.

The Ca^{2+} release channel is also known as the **ryanodine receptor** (RYR). There are two isoforms of this receptor, RYR1 and RYR2, the former being present in skeletal muscle and the latter in heart muscle and brain. **Ryanodine** is a plant alkaloid that binds to RYR1 and RYR2 specifically and modulates their activities. The Ca^{2+} release channel is a homotetramer made up of four subunits of kDa 565. It has transmembrane sequences at its carboxyl terminal, and these probably form the Ca^{2+} channel. The remainder of the protein protrudes into the cytosol, bridging the gap between the sarcoplasmic reticulum and the transverse tubular membrane. The channel is ligand-gated, Ca^{2+} and ATP working synergistically in vitro, although how it operates in vivo is not clear. A possible sequence of events leading to opening of the channel is shown in Figure 48–9. The channel lies very close to the **dihydropyridine receptor** (DHPR; a voltage-gated slow K type Ca^{2+} channel) of the transverse tubule system (Figure 48–8). Experiments in vitro employing an affinity column chromatography approach have indicated that a 37-amino-acid stretch in RYR1 interacts with one specific loop of DHPR.

Relaxation occurs when sarcoplasmic Ca^{2+} falls below 10^{-7} mol/L owing to its resequestration into the sarcoplasmic reticulum by **Ca^{2+} ATPase.** TpC-4Ca^{2+} thus loses its Ca^{2+}. Consequently, **troponin,** via interaction with tropomyosin, **inhibits** further myosin head and F-actin interaction, and in the presence of ATP the myosin head detaches from the F-actin.

Thus, Ca^{2+} controls skeletal muscle contraction and relaxation by an allosteric mechanism mediated by TpC, TpI, TpT, tropomyosin, and F-actin.

A **decrease** in the concentration of ATP in the sarcoplasm (eg, by excessive usage during the cycle of contrac-

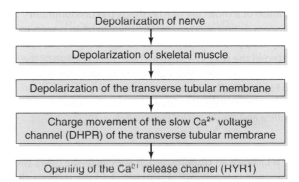

Figure 48–9. Possible chain of events leading to opening of the Ca^{2+} release channel. As indicated in the text, the Ca^{2+} voltage channel and the Ca^{2+} release channel have been shown to interact with each other in vitro via specific regions in their polypeptide chains. (DHPR, dihydropyridine receptor; RYR1, ryanodine receptor 1.)

tion-relaxation or by diminished formation, such as might occur in ischemia) has two major effects: (1) The **Ca^{2+} ATPase** (Ca^{2+} pump) in the sarcoplasmic reticulum ceases to maintain the low concentration of Ca^{2+} in the sarcoplasm. Thus, the interaction of the myosin heads with F-actin is promoted. (2) The ATP-dependent **detachment of myosin heads** from F-actin cannot occur, and rigidity (contracture) sets in. The condition of **rigor mortis,** following death, is an extension of these events.

Muscle contraction is a delicate dynamic balance of the attachment and detachment of myosin heads to F-actin, subject to fine regulation via the nervous system.

Table 48–1 summarizes the overall events in contraction and relaxation of skeletal muscle.

Mutations in the Gene Encoding the Ca^{2+} Release Channel Are One Cause of Human Malignant Hyperthermia

Some genetically predisposed patients experience a severe reaction, designated **malignant hyperthermia,** on exposure to certain anesthetics (eg, halothane) and depolarizing skeletal muscle relaxants (eg, succinylcholine). The reaction consists primarily of rigidity of skeletal muscles, hypermetabolism, and high fever. A **high cytosolic concentration of Ca^{2+}** in skeletal muscle is a major factor in its causation. Unless malignant hyperthermia is recognized and treated immediately, patients

may die acutely of ventricular fibrillation or survive to succumb subsequently from other serious complications. Appropriate treatment is to stop the anesthetic and administer the drug **dantrolene** intravenously. Dantrolene is a skeletal muscle relaxant that acts to inhibit release of Ca^{2+} from the sarcoplasmic reticulum into the cytosol, thus preventing the increase of cytosolic Ca^{2+} found in malignant hyperthermia.

Malignant hyperthermia also occurs in **swine.** Susceptible animals homozygous for malignant hyperthermia respond to stress with a fatal reaction (**porcine stress syndrome**) similar to that exhibited by humans. If the reaction occurs prior to slaughter, it affects the quality of the pork adversely, resulting in an inferior product. Both events can result in considerable economic losses for the swine industry.

The finding of a high level of cytosolic Ca^{2+} in muscle in malignant hyperthermia suggested that the condition might be caused by abnormalities of the Ca^{2+} ATPase or of the **Ca^{2+} release channel.** No abnormalities were detected in the former, but sequencing of cDNAs for the latter protein proved insightful, particularly in swine. All cDNAs from **swine** with malignant hyperthermia so far examined have shown a substitution of T for C1843, resulting in the substitution of Cys for Arg^{615} in the Ca^{2+} release channel. The mutation affects the function of the channel in that it opens more easily and remains open longer; the net result is massive release of Ca^{2+} into the cytosol, ultimately causing sustained muscle contraction.

The picture is more complex in **humans,** since malignant hyperthermia exhibits **genetic heterogeneity.** Members of a number of families who suffer from malignant hyperthermia have not shown genetic linkage to the *RYR1* gene. Some humans susceptible to malignant hyperthermia have been found to exhibit the same mutation found in swine, and others have a variety of point mutations at different loci in the *RYR1* gene. Certain families with malignant hypertension have been found to have mutations affecting the **DHPR.** Figure 48–10 summarizes the probable chain of events in malignant hyperthermia. The major promise of these findings is that, once additional mutations are detected, it will be possible to **screen,** using suitable DNA probes, for individuals at risk of developing malignant hyperthermia during anesthesia. Current screening tests (eg, the in vitro caffeine-halothane test) are relatively unreliable. Affected individuals could then be given **alternative anesthetics,** which would not endanger their lives. It should also be possible, if desired, to eliminate malignant hyperthermia from swine populations using suitable breeding practices.

Another condition due to mutations in the *RYR1* gene is **central core disease.** This is a rare myopathy presenting in infancy with hypotonia and proximal muscle weakness. Electron microscopy reveals an absence of

Table 48–1. Sequence of events in contraction and relaxation of skeletal muscle.[1]

Steps in contraction

(1) Discharge of motor neuron
(2) Release of transmitter (acetylcholine) at motor endplate
(3) Binding of acetylcholine to nicotinic acetylcholine receptors
(4) Increased Na$^+$ and K$^+$ conductance in endplate membrane
(5) Generation of endplate potential
(6) Generation of action potential in muscle fibers
(7) Inward spread of depolarization along T tubules
(8) Release of Ca^{2+} from terminal cisterns of sarcoplasmic reticulum and diffusion to thick and thin filaments
(9) Binding of Ca^{2+} to troponin C, uncovering myosin binding sites of actin
(10) Formation of cross-linkages between actin and myosin and sliding of thin on thick filaments, producing shortening

Steps in relaxation

(1) Ca^{2+} pumped back into sarcoplasmic reticulum
(2) Release of Ca^{2+} from troponin
(3) Cessation of interaction between actin and myosin

[1]Reproduced, with permission, from Ganong WF: *Review of Medical Physiology,* 21st ed. McGraw-Hill, 2003.

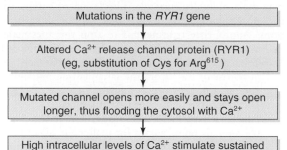

Figure 48–10. Simplified scheme of the causation of malignant hyperthermia (MIM 145600). At least 17 different point mutations have been detected in the *RYR1* gene, some of which are associated with central core disease (MIM 117000). It is estimated that at least 50% of families with members who have malignant hyperthermia are linked to the *RYR1* gene. Some individuals with mutations in the gene encoding DHPR have also been detected; it is possible that mutations in other genes for proteins involved in certain aspects of muscle metabolism will also be found.

mitochondria in the center of many type I (see below) muscle fibers. Damage to mitochondria induced by high intracellular levels of Ca^{2+} secondary to abnormal functioning of *RYR1* appears to be responsible for the morphologic findings.

MUTATIONS IN THE GENE ENCODING DYSTROPHIN CAUSE DUCHENNE MUSCULAR DYSTROPHY

A number of *additional proteins* play various roles in the structure and function of muscle. They include titin (the largest protein known), nebulin, α-actinin, desmin, dystrophin, and calcineurin. Some properties of these proteins are summarized in Table 48–2.

Dystrophin is of special interest. Mutations in the gene encoding this protein have been shown to be the cause of Duchenne muscular dystrophy and the milder Becker muscular dystrophy (see Figure 48–11). They are also implicated in some cases of dilated cardiomyopathy (see below). The gene encoding dystrophin is the largest gene known ($\approx$ 2300 kb) and is situated on the **X chromosome,** accounting for the maternal inheritance pattern of Duchenne and Becker muscular dystrophies. As shown in Figure 48–12, dystrophin forms part of a large complex of proteins that attach to or interact with the plasmalemma. Dystrophin links the

Table 48–2. Some other important proteins of muscle.

Protein	Location	Comment or Function
Titin	Reaches from the Z line to the M line	Largest protein in body. Role in relaxation of muscle.
Nebulin	From Z line along length of actin filaments	May regulate assembly and length of actin filaments.
α-Actinin	Anchors actin to Z lines	Stabilizes actin filaments.
Desmin	Lies alongside actin filaments	Attaches to plasma membrane (plasmalemma).
Dystrophin	Attached to plasmalemma	Deficient in Duchenne muscular dystrophy. Mutations of its gene can also cause dilated cardiomyopathy.
Calcineurin	Cytosol	A calmodulin-regulated protein phosphatase. May play important roles in cardiac hypertrophy and in regulating amounts of slow and fast twitch muscles.
Myosin-binding protein C	Arranged transversely in sarcomere A-bands	Binds myosin and titin. Plays a role in maintaining the structural integrity of the sarcomere.

actin cytoskeleton to the ECM and appears to be needed for assembly of the synaptic junction. Impairment of these processes by formation of defective dystrophin is presumably critical in the causation of Duchenne muscular dystrophy. Mutations in the genes

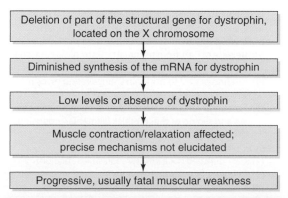

Figure 48–11. Summary of the causation of Duchenne muscular dystrophy (MIM 310200).

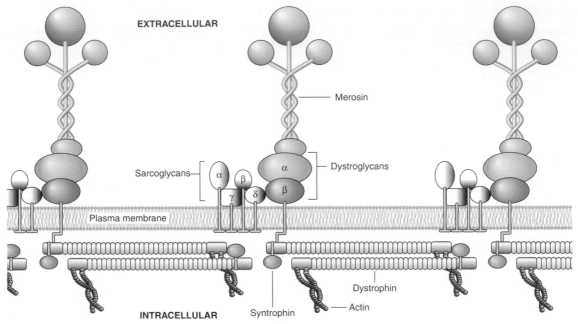

Figure 48–12. Organization of dystrophin and other proteins in relation to the plasma membrane of muscle cells. Dystrophin is part of a large oligomeric complex associated with several other protein complexes. The dystroglycan complex consists of α-dystroglycan, which associates with the basal lamina protein merosin (also named laminin-2), and β-dystroglycan, which binds α-dystroglycan and dystrophin. Syntrophin binds to the carboxyl terminal of dystrophin. The sarcoglycan complex consists of four transmembrane proteins: α-, β-, γ-, and δ-sarcoglycan. The function of the sarcoglycan complex and the nature of the interactions within the complex and between it and the other complexes are not clear. The sarcoglycan complex is formed only in striated muscle, and its subunits preferentially associate with each other, suggesting that the complex may function as a single unit. Mutations in the gene encoding dystrophin cause Duchenne and Becker muscular dystrophy; mutations in the genes encoding the various sarcoglycans have been shown to be responsible for limb-girdle dystrophies (eg, MIM 604286). (Reproduced, with permission, from Duggan DJ et al: Mutations in the sarcoglycan genes in patients with myopathy. N Engl J Med 1997;336:618. Copyright © 1997 Massachusetts Medical Society. All rights reserved.)

encoding some of the components of the sarcoglycan complex shown in Figure 48–12 are responsible for limb-girdle and certain other congenital forms of muscular dystrophy.

Mutations in genes encoding several glycosyltransferases involved in the synthesis of the sugar chains of α-dystroglycan have been found to be the cause of certain types of congenital muscular dystrophy (see Chapter 46).

CARDIAC MUSCLE RESEMBLES SKELETAL MUSCLE IN MANY RESPECTS

The general picture of muscle contraction in the heart resembles that of skeletal muscle. Cardiac muscle, like skeletal muscle, is **striated** and uses the actin-myosin-tropomyosin-troponin system described above. Unlike skeletal muscle, cardiac muscle exhibits **intrinsic rhythmicity,** and individual myocytes communicate with each other because of its syncytial nature. The **T tubular**

system is more developed in cardiac muscle, whereas the **sarcoplasmic reticulum** is less extensive and consequently the intracellular supply of Ca^{2+} for contraction is less. Cardiac muscle thus relies on **extracellular Ca^{2+}** for contraction; if isolated cardiac muscle is deprived of Ca^{2+}, it ceases to beat within approximately 1 minute, whereas skeletal muscle can continue to contract without an extracellular source of Ca^{2+}. **Cyclic AMP** plays a more prominent role in cardiac than in skeletal muscle. It modulates intracellular levels of Ca^{2+} through the activation of protein kinases; these enzymes phosphorylate various transport proteins in the sarcolemma and sarcoplasmic reticulum and also in the troponin-tropomyosin regulatory complex, affecting intracellular levels of Ca^{2+} or responses to it. There is a rough correlation between the phosphorylation of TpI and the increased contraction of cardiac muscle induced by catecholamines. This may account for the **inotropic effects** (increased contractility) of β-adrenergic

Table 48–3. Some differences between skeletal, cardiac, and smooth muscle.

Skeletal Muscle	Cardiac Muscle	Smooth Muscle
1. Striated.	1. Striated.	1. Nonstriated.
2. No syncytium.	2. Syncytial.	2. Syncytial.
3. Small T tubules.	3. Large T tubules.	3. Generally rudimentary T tubules.
4. Sarcoplasmic reticulum well developed and Ca^{2+} pump acts rapidly.	4. Sarcoplasmic reticulum present and Ca^{2+} pump acts relatively rapidly.	4. Sarcoplasmic reticulum often rudimentary and Ca^{2+} pump acts slowly.
5. Plasmalemma lacks many hormone receptors.	5. Plasmalemma contains a variety of receptors (eg, α- and β-adrenergic).	5. Plasmalemma contains a variety of receptors (eg, α- and β-adrenergic).
6. Nerve impulse initiates contraction.	6. Has intrinsic rhythmicity.	6. Contraction initiated by nerve impulses, hormones, etc.
7. Extracellular fluid Ca^{2+} not important for contraction.	7. Extracellular fluid Ca^{2+} important for contraction.	7. Extracellular fluid Ca^{2+} important for contraction.
8. Troponin system present.	8. Troponin system present.	8. Lacks troponin system; uses regulatory head of myosin.
9. Caldesmon not involved.	9. Caldesmon not involved.	9. Caldesmon is important regulatory protein.
10. Very rapid cycling of the cross-bridges.	10. Relatively rapid cycling of the cross-bridges.	10. Slow cycling of the cross-bridges permits slow, prolonged contraction and less utilization of ATP.

compounds on the heart. Some differences among skeletal, cardiac, and smooth muscle are summarized in Table 48–3.

Ca^{2+} Enters Myocytes Via Ca^{2+} Channels & Leaves Via the Na^+-Ca^{2+} Exchanger & the Ca^{2+} ATPase

As stated above, **extracellular Ca^{2+}** plays an important role in contraction of cardiac muscle but not in skeletal muscle. This means that Ca^{2+} both enters and leaves myocytes in a regulated manner. We shall briefly consider three transmembrane proteins that play roles in this process.

A. Ca^{2+} CHANNELS

Ca^{2+} enters myocytes via these channels, which allow entry only of Ca^{2+} ions. The major portal of entry is the L-type (long-duration current, large conductance) or **slow Ca^{2+} channel,** which is voltage-gated, opening during depolarization induced by spread of the cardiac action potential and closing when the action potential declines. These channels are equivalent to the dihydropyridine receptors of skeletal muscle (Figure 48–8). Slow Ca^{2+} channels are **regulated** by cAMP-dependent protein kinases (stimulatory) and cGMP-protein kinases (inhibitory) and are blocked by so-called calcium channel blockers (eg, verapamil). **Fast** (or T, transient) Ca^{2+}

channels are also present in the plasmalemma, though in much lower numbers; they probably contribute to the early phase of increase of myoplasmic Ca^{2+}.

The resultant increase of Ca^{2+} in the myoplasm acts on the Ca^{2+} release channel of the sarcoplasmic reticulum to open it. This is called **Ca^{2+}-induced Ca^{2+} release** (CICR). It is estimated that approximately 10% of the Ca^{2+} involved in contraction enters the cytosol from the extracellular fluid and 90% from the sarcoplasmic reticulum. However, the former 10% is important, as the rate of increase of Ca^{2+} in the myoplasm is important, and entry via the Ca^{2+} channels contributes appreciably to this.

B. Ca^{2+}-Na^+ EXCHANGER

This is the principal route of **exit** of Ca^{2+} from myocytes. In resting myocytes, it helps to maintain a low level of free intracellular Ca^{2+} by exchanging one Ca^{2+} for three Na^+. The energy for the uphill movement of Ca^{2+} out of the cell comes from the downhill movement of Na^+ into the cell from the plasma. This exchange contributes to relaxation but may run in the reverse direction during excitation. Because of the Ca^{2+}-Na^+ exchanger, anything that causes intracellular Na^+ (Na^+_i) to rise will secondarily cause Ca^{2+}_i to rise, causing more forceful contraction. This is referred to as a **positive inotropic effect.** One example is when the drug **digitalis** is used to treat heart failure. Digitalis inhibits

the sarcolemmal Na^+-K^+ ATPase, diminishing exit of Na^+ and thus increasing Na^+_i. This in turn causes Ca^{2+} to increase, via the Ca^{2+}-Na^+ exchanger. The increased Ca^{2+}_i results in increased force of cardiac contraction, of benefit in heart failure.

C. Ca^{2+} ATPASE

This Ca^{2+} pump, situated in the sarcolemma, also contributes to Ca^{2+} **exit** but is believed to play a relatively minor role as compared with the Ca^{2+}-Na^+ exchanger.

It should be noted that there are a variety of **ion channels** (Chapter 40) in most cells, for Na^+, K^+, Ca^{2+}, etc. Many of them have been cloned in recent years and their dispositions in their respective membranes worked out (number of times each one crosses its membrane, location of the actual ion transport site in the protein, etc). They can be classified as indicated in Table 48–4. Cardiac muscle is rich in ion channels, and they are also important in skeletal muscle. Mutations in genes encoding ion channels have been shown to be responsible for a number of relatively rare conditions affecting muscle. These and other diseases due to mutations of ion channels have been termed **channelopathies;** some are listed in Table 48–5.

Inherited Cardiomyopathies Are Due to Disorders of Cardiac Energy Metabolism or to Abnormal Myocardial Proteins

An **inherited cardiomyopathy** is any structural or functional abnormality of the ventricular myocardium due to an inherited cause. There are nonheritable types of cardiomyopathy, but these will not be described here. As shown in Table 48–6, the causes of inherited cardiomyopathies fall into two broad classes: (1) disorders of **cardiac energy metabolism,** mainly reflecting mutations in genes encoding enzymes or proteins involved in fatty acid oxidation (a major source of

Table 48–4. Major types of ion channels found in cells.

Type	Comment
External ligand-gated	Open in response to a specific extracellular molecule, eg, acetylcholine.
Internal ligand-gated	Open or close in response to a specific intracellular molecule, eg, a cyclic nucleotide.
Voltage-gated	Open in response to a change in membrane potential, eg, Na^+, K^+, and Ca^{2+} channels in heart.
Mechanically gated	Open in response to change in mechanical pressure.

Table 48–5. Some disorders (channelopathies) due to mutations in genes encoding polypeptide constituents of ion channels.[1]

Disorder[2]	Ion Channel and Major Organs Involved
Central core disease (MIM 117000)	Ca^{2+} release channel (RYR1) Skeletal muscle
Cystic fibrosis (MIM 219700)	CFTR (Cl^- channel) Lungs, pancreas
Hyperkalemic periodic paralysis (MIM 170500)	Sodium channel Skeletal muscle
Hypokalemic periodic paralysis (MIM 170400)	Slow Ca^{2+} voltage channel (DHPR) Skeletal muscle
Malignant hyperthermia (MIM 145600)	Ca^{2+} release channel (RYR1) Skeletal muscle
Myotonia congenita (MIM 160800)	Chloride channel Skeletal muscle

[1]Data in part from Ackerman NJ, Clapham DE: Ion channels—basic science and clinical disease. N Engl J Med 1997;336:1575.
[2]Other channelopathies include the long QT syndrome (MIM 192500); pseudoaldosteronism (Liddle syndrome, MIM 177200); persistent hyperinsulinemic hypoglycemia of infancy (MIM 601820); hereditary X-linked recessive type II nephrolithiasis of infancy (Dent syndrome, MIM 300009); and generalized myotonia, recessive (Becker disease, MIM 255700). The term "myotonia" signifies any condition in which muscles do not relax after contraction.

energy for the myocardium) and oxidative phosphorylation; and (2) mutations in genes encoding proteins involved in or **affecting myocardial contraction,** such as myosin, tropomyosin, the troponins, and cardiac myosin-binding protein C. Mutations in the genes encoding these latter proteins cause familial hypertrophic cardiomyopathy, which will now be discussed.

Mutations in the Cardiac β-Myosin Heavy Chain Gene Are One Cause of Familial Hypertrophic Cardiomyopathy

Familial hypertrophic cardiomyopathy is one of the most frequent hereditary cardiac diseases. Patients exhibit hypertrophy—often massive—of one or both ventricles, starting early in life, and not related to any extrinsic cause such as hypertension. Most cases are transmitted in an autosomal dominant manner; the rest are sporadic. Until recently, its cause was obscure. However, this situation changed when studies of one affected family showed that a **missense mutation** (ie, substitution of one amino acid by another) in the β-**myosin heavy chain gene** was responsible for the condition. Subsequent studies have shown a number of

Table 48–6. Biochemical causes of inherited cardiomyopathies.[1,2]

Cause	Proteins or Process Affected
Inborn errors of fatty acid oxidation	Carnitine entry into cells and mitochondria Certain enzymes of fatty acid oxidation
Disorders of mitochondrial oxidative phosphorylation	Proteins encoded by mitochondrial genes Proteins encoded by nuclear genes
Abnormalities of myocardial contractile and structural proteins	β-Myosin heavy chains, troponin, tropomyosin, dystrophin

[1]Based on Kelly DP, Strauss AW: Inherited cardiomyopathies. N Engl J Med 1994;330:913.
[2]Mutations (eg, point mutations, or in some cases deletions) in the genes (nuclear or mitochondrial) encoding various proteins, enzymes, or tRNA molecules are the fundamental causes of the inherited cardiomyopathies. Some conditions are mild, whereas others are severe and may be part of a syndrome affecting other tissues.

missense mutations in this gene, all coding for highly conserved residues. Some individuals have shown other mutations, such as formation of an α/β-myosin heavy chain hybrid gene. Patients with familial hypertrophic cardiomyopathy can show great variation in clinical picture. This in part reflects **genetic heterogeneity;** ie, mutation in a number of **other genes** (eg, those encoding cardiac actin, tropomyosin, cardiac troponins I and T, essential and regulatory myosin light chains, cardiac myosin-binding protein C, titin, and mitochondrial tRNA-glycine and tRNA-isoleucine) may also cause familial hypertrophic cardiomyopathy. In addition, mutations at different sites in the gene for β-myosin heavy chain may affect the function of the protein to a greater or lesser extent. The missense mutations are clustered in the head and head-rod regions of myosin heavy chain. One hypothesis is that the mutant polypeptides ("poison polypeptides") cause formation of abnormal myofibrils, eventually resulting in compensatory hypertrophy. Some mutations alter the **charge** of the amino acid (eg, substitution of arginine for glutamine), presumably affecting the **conformation** of the protein more markedly and thus affecting its function. Patients with these mutations have a significantly shorter life expectancy than patients in whom the mutation produced no alteration in charge. Thus, definition of the precise mutations involved in the genesis of FHC may prove to be of important prognostic value; it can be accomplished by appropriate use of the polymerase chain reaction on genomic DNA obtained from one sample of blood lymphocytes. Figure 48–13 is a simplified scheme of the events causing familial hypertrophic cardiomyopathy.

Another type of cardiomyopathy is termed **dilated cardiomyopathy.** Mutations in the genes encoding dystrophin, muscle LIM protein (so called because it was found to contain a cysteine-rich domain originally detected in three proteins: Lin-II, Isl-1, and Mec-3), the cyclic response-element binding protein (CREB), desmin and lamin have been implicated in the causation of this condition. The first two proteins help organize the contractile apparatus of cardiac muscle cells, and CREB is involved in the regulation of a number of genes in these cells. Current research is not only elucidating the molecular causes of the cardiomyopathies but is also disclosing mutations that cause **cardiac developmental disorders** (eg, septal defects) and arrhythmias (eg, due to mutations affecting ion channels).

Ca²⁺ Also Regulates Contraction of Smooth Muscle

While all muscles contain actin, myosin, and tropomyosin, only vertebrate **striated** muscles contain the **troponin system.** Thus, the mechanisms that regulate contraction must differ in various contractile systems.

Smooth muscles have molecular structures similar to those in striated muscle, but the sarcomeres are not aligned so as to generate the striated appearance. Smooth muscles contain α actinin and tropomyosin molecules, as do skeletal muscles. They **do not have the troponin system,** and the light chains of smooth muscle myosin molecules differ from those of striated muscle myosin. Regulation of smooth muscle contraction is **myosin-based,** unlike striated muscle, which is

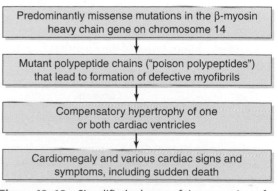

Figure 48–13. Simplified scheme of the causation of familial hypertrophic cardiomyopathy (MIM 192600) due to mutations in the gene encoding β-myosin heavy chain. Mutations in genes encoding other proteins (see text) can also cause this condition.

actin-based. However, like striated muscle, smooth muscle contraction is regulated by Ca^{2+}.

Phosphorylation of Myosin Light Chains Initiates Contraction of Smooth Muscle

When smooth muscle myosin is bound to F-actin in the absence of other muscle proteins such as tropomyosin, there is **no detectable ATPase activity.** This absence of activity is quite unlike the situation described for striated muscle myosin and F-actin, which has abundant ATPase activity. Smooth muscle myosin contains **light chains** that prevent the binding of the myosin head to F-actin; they **must be phosphorylated** before they allow F-actin to activate myosin ATPase. The ATPase activity then attained hydrolyzes ATP about tenfold more slowly than the corresponding activity in skeletal muscle. The phosphate on the myosin light chains may form a chelate with the Ca^{2+} bound to the tropomyosin-TpC-actin complex, leading to an increased rate of formation of cross-bridges between the myosin heads and actin. The phosphorylation of light chains **initiates** the attachment-detachment contraction cycle of smooth muscle.

Myosin Light Chain Kinase Is Activated by Calmodulin-4Ca²⁺ & Then Phosphorylates the Light Chains

Smooth muscle sarcoplasm contains a **myosin light chain kinase** that is calcium-dependent. The Ca^{2+} activation of myosin light chain kinase requires binding of **calmodulin-4Ca²⁺** to its kinase subunit (Figure 48–14). The calmodulin-4Ca²⁺-activated light chain kinase phosphorylates the light chains, which then ceases to inhibit the myosin–F-actin interaction. The contraction cycle then begins.

Another non-Ca^{2+}-dependent pathway exists in smooth muscle for initiating contraction. This involves **Rho kinase,** which is activated by a variety of stimuli. This enzyme phosphorylates myosin light chain phosphatase, inhibiting it, and thus increasing the phosphorylation of the light chain. Rho kinase also directly phosphorylates the light chain of myosin. Both of these actions (Figure 48–14) increase the contraction of smooth muscle.

Smooth Muscle Relaxes When the Concentration of Ca²⁺ Falls below 10⁻⁷ Molar

Relaxation of smooth muscle occurs when sarcoplasmic Ca^{2+} falls below 10^{-7} mol/L. The **Ca^{2+} dissociates** from calmodulin, which in turn dissociates from the myosin light chain kinase, inactivating the kinase. No new phosphates are attached to the p-light chain, and **light chain protein phosphatase,** which is continually active and calcium-independent, removes the existing phosphates from the light chains. Dephosphorylated myosin p-light

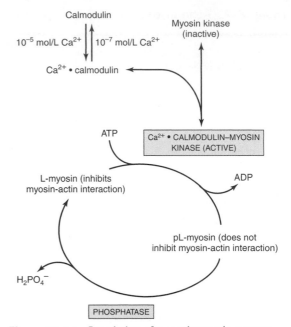

Figure 48–14. Regulation of smooth muscle contraction by Ca^{2+}. pL-myosin is the phosphorylated light chain of myosin; L-myosin is the dephosphorylated light chain. (Adapted from Adelstein RS, Eisenberg R: Regulation and kinetics of actin-myosin ATP interaction. Annu Rev Biochem 1980;49:921. Copyright © 1980 by Annual Reviews, www.annualreviews.org. Reprinted with permission.)

chain then inhibits the binding of myosin heads to F-actin and the ATPase activity. The myosin head detaches from the F-actin in the presence of ATP, but it cannot reattach because of the presence of dephosphorylated p-light chain; hence, **relaxation** occurs.

Table 48–7 summarizes and compares the regulation of actin-myosin interactions (activation of myosin ATPase) in striated and smooth muscles.

The myosin light chain kinase is not directly affected or activated by **cAMP.** However, cAMP-activated protein kinase can phosphorylate the myosin light chain kinase (not the light chains themselves). The phosphorylated myosin light chain kinase exhibits a significantly lower affinity for calmodulin-Ca^{2+} and thus is less sensitive to activation. Accordingly, an **increase in cAMP dampens the contraction response** of smooth muscle to a given elevation of sarcoplasmic Ca^{2+}. This molecular mechanism can explain the relaxing effect of β-adrenergic stimulation on smooth muscle.

Another protein that appears to play a Ca^{2+}-dependent role in the regulation of smooth muscle contraction is **caldesmon** (87 kDa). This protein is ubiquitous in smooth muscle and is also found in nonmuscle tissue. At low concentrations of Ca^{2+}, it binds to tropomyosin and

Table 48–7. Actin-myosin interactions in striated and smooth muscle.

	Striated Muscle	Smooth Muscle (and Nonmuscle Cells)
Proteins of muscle filaments	Actin Myosin Tropomyosin Troponin (TpI, TpT, TpC)	Actin Myosin[1] Tropomyosin
Spontaneous interaction of F-actin and myosin alone (spontaneous activation of myosin ATPase by F-actin)	Yes	No
Inhibitor of F-actin–myosin interaction (inhibitor of F-actin–dependent activation of ATPase)	Troponin system (TpI)	Unphosphorylated myosin light chain
Contraction activated by	Ca^{2+}	Ca^{2+}
Direct effect of Ca^{2+}	$4Ca^{2+}$ bind to TpC	$4Ca^{2+}$ bind to calmodulin
Effect of protein-bound Ca^{2+}	$TpC \cdot 4Ca^{2+}$ antagonizes TpI inhibition of F-actin–myosin interaction (allows F-actin activation of ATPase)	Calmodulin $\cdot 4Ca^{2+}$ activates myosin light chain kinase that phosphorylates myosin p-light chain. The phosphorylated p-light chain no longer inhibits F-actin–myosin interaction (allows F-actin activation of ATPase)

[1]Light chains of myosin are different in striated and smooth muscles.

actin. This **prevents interaction of actin with myosin,** keeping muscle in a relaxed state. At higher concentrations of Ca^{2+}, Ca^{2+} calmodulin binds caldesmon, **releasing it from actin.** The latter is then free to bind to myosin, and contraction can occur. Caldesmon is also subject to phosphorylation-dephosphorylation; when phosphorylated, it cannot bind actin, again freeing the latter to interact with myosin. Caldesmon may also participate in organizing the structure of the contractile apparatus in smooth muscle. Many of its effects have been demonstrated in vitro, and its physiologic significance is still under investigation.

As noted in Table 48–3, slow cycling of the cross-bridges permits slow prolonged contraction of smooth muscle (eg, in viscera and blood vessels) with less utilization of ATP compared with striated muscle. The ability of smooth muscle to maintain force at reduced velocities of contraction is referred to as the **latch state;** this is an important feature of smooth muscle, and its precise molecular bases are under study.

Nitric Oxide Relaxes the Smooth Muscle of Blood Vessels & Also Has Many Other Important Biologic Functions

Acetylcholine is a vasodilator that acts by causing relaxation of the smooth muscle of blood vessels. However, it does not act directly on smooth muscle. A key observation was that if **endothelial cells** were stripped away from underlying smooth muscle cells, acetylcholine no longer exerted its vasodilator effect. This finding indicated that vasodilators such as acetylcholine initially interact with the endothelial

cells of small blood vessels via receptors. The receptors are coupled to the phosphoinositide cycle, leading to the intracellular release of Ca^{2+} through the action of inositol trisphosphate. In turn, the elevation of Ca^{2+} leads to the liberation of **endothelium-derived relaxing factor (EDRF),** which diffuses into the adjacent smooth muscle. There, it reacts with the heme moiety of a soluble guanylyl cyclase, resulting in activation of the latter, with a consequent elevation of intracellular levels of **cGMP** (Figure 48–15). This in turn stimulates the activities of certain cGMP-dependent protein kinases, which probably phosphorylate specific muscle proteins, causing relaxation; however, the details are still being clarified. The important coronary artery vasodilator **nitroglycerin,** widely used to relieve angina pectoris, acts to increase intracellular release of EDRF and thus of cGMP.

Quite unexpectedly, EDRF was found to be the gas **nitric oxide (NO).** NO is formed by the action of the enzyme NO synthase, which is cytosolic. The endothelial and neuronal forms of NO synthase are activated by Ca^{2+} (Table 48–8). The substrate is **arginine,** and the products are citrulline and NO:

Arginine $\xrightarrow{\text{NO SYNTHASE}}$ Citrulline + NO

NO synthase catalyzes a five-electron oxidation of an amidine nitrogen of arginine. L-Hydroxyarginine is an intermediate that remains tightly bound to the enzyme. NO synthase is a very complex enzyme, employing five redox cofactors: NADPH, FAD, FMN, heme, and tetrahydrobiopterin. NO can also be formed from **nitrite,** derived

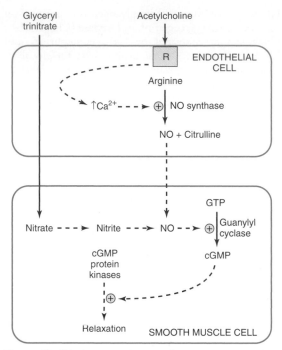

Figure 48–15. Diagram showing formation in an endothelial cell of nitric oxide (NO) from arginine in a reaction catalyzed by NO synthase. Interaction of an agonist (eg, acetylcholine) with a receptor (R) probably leads to intracellular release of Ca^{2+} via inositol trisphosphate generated by the phosphoinositide pathway, resulting in activation of NO synthase. The NO subsequently diffuses into adjacent smooth muscle, where it leads to activation of guanylyl cyclase, formation of cGMP, stimulation of cGMP-protein kinases, and subsequent relaxation. The vasodilator nitroglycerin is shown entering the smooth muscle cell, where its metabolism also leads to formation of NO.

from vasodilators such as glyceryl trinitrate during their metabolism. NO has a very short half-life (approximately 3–4 seconds) in tissues because it reacts with oxygen and superoxide. The product of the reaction with superoxide is **peroxynitrite** ($ONOO^-$), which decomposes to form the highly reactive $OH^{\bullet}$ radical. NO is inhibited by hemoglobin and other heme proteins, which bind it tightly. **Chemical inhibitors of NO synthase** are now available that can markedly decrease formation of NO. Administration of such inhibitors to animals and humans leads to vasoconstriction and a marked elevation of blood pressure, indicating that NO is of major importance in the maintenance of blood pressure in vivo. Another important cardiovascular effect is that by increasing synthesis of cGMP, it acts as an **inhibitor of platelet aggregation** (Chapter 50).

Since the discovery of the role of NO as a vasodilator, there has been intense experimental interest in this substance. It has turned out to have a variety of physiologic roles, involving virtually every tissue of the body (Table 48–9). Three major isoforms of NO synthase have been identified, each of which has been cloned, and the chromosomal locations of their genes in humans have been determined. Gene knockout experiments have been performed on each of the three isoforms and have helped establish some of the postulated functions of NO.

To summarize, research in the past decade has shown that NO plays an important role in many physiologic and pathologic processes.

SEVERAL MECHANISMS REPLENISH STORES OF ATP IN MUSCLE

The **ATP** required as the constant energy source for the contraction-relaxation cycle of muscle can be generated (1) by glycolysis, using blood glucose or muscle glycogen, (2) by oxidative phosphorylation, (3) from creatine phosphate, and (4) from two molecules of ADP in a

Table 48–8. Summary of the nomenclature of the NO synthases and of the effects of knockout of their genes in mice.[1]

Subtype	Name[2]	Comments	Result of Gene Knockout in Mice[3]
1	nNOS	Activity depends on elevated Ca^{2+}; first identified in neurons; calmodulin-activated	Pyloric stenosis, resistant to vascular stroke, aggressive sexual behavior (males)
2	iNOS[4]	Independent of elevated Ca^{2+}; prominent in macrophages	More susceptible to certain types of infection
3	eNOS	Activity depends on elevated Ca^{2+}; first identified in endothelial cells	Elevated mean blood pressure

[1]Adapted from Snyder SH: No endothelial NO. Nature 1995;377:196.
[2]n, neuronal; i, inducible; e, endothelial.
[3]Gene knockouts were performed by homologous recombination in mice. The enzymes are characterized as neuronal, inducible (macrophage), and endothelial because these were the sites in which they were first identified. However, all three enzymes have been found in other sites, and the neuronal enzyme is also inducible. Each gene has been cloned, and its chromosomal location in humans has been determined.
[4]iNOS is Ca^{2+}-independent but binds calmodulin very tightly.

Table 48–9. Some physiologic functions and pathologic involvements of nitric oxide (NO).

- Vasodilator, important in regulation of blood pressure
- Involved in penile erection; sildenafil citrate (Viagra) affects this process by inhibiting a cGMP phosphodiesterase
- Neurotransmitter in the brain and peripheral autonomic nervous system
- Role in long-term potentiation
- Role in neurotoxicity
- Low level of NO involved in causation of pylorospasm in infantile hypertrophic pyloric stenosis
- May have role in relaxation of skeletal muscle
- May constitute part of a primitive immune system
- Inhibits adhesion, activation, and aggregation of platelets

reaction catalyzed by adenylyl kinase (Figure 48–16). The amount of ATP in skeletal muscle is only sufficient to provide energy for contraction for a few seconds, so that ATP must be constantly renewed from one or more of the above sources, depending upon metabolic conditions. As discussed below, there are at least **two distinct types of fibers** in skeletal muscle, one predominantly active in **aerobic** conditions and the other in **anaerobic** conditions; not unexpectedly, they use each of the above sources of energy to different extents.

Skeletal Muscle Contains Large Supplies of Glycogen

The sarcoplasm of skeletal muscle contains large stores of **glycogen,** located in granules close to the I bands.

The release of glucose from glycogen is dependent on a specific muscle **glycogen phosphorylase** (Chapter 19), which can be activated by Ca^{2+}, epinephrine, and AMP. To generate glucose 6-phosphate for glycolysis in skeletal muscle, glycogen phosphorylase b must be activated to phosphorylase a via phosphorylation by phosphorylase b kinase (Chapter 19). Ca^{2+} promotes the activation of phosphorylase b kinase, also by phosphorylation. Thus, Ca^{2+} both initiates muscle contraction and activates a pathway to provide necessary energy. The hormone *epinephrine* also activates glycogenolysis in muscle. *AMP*, produced by breakdown of ADP during muscular exercise, can also activate phosphorylase b without causing phosphorylation. Muscle glycogen phosphorylase b is inactive in **McArdle disease,** one of the glycogen storage diseases (Chapter 19).

Under Aerobic Conditions, Muscle Generates ATP Mainly by Oxidative Phosphorylation

Synthesis of ATP via **oxidative phosphorylation** requires a supply of oxygen. Muscles that have a high demand for oxygen as a result of sustained contraction (eg, to maintain posture) store it attached to the heme moiety of **myoglobin.** Because of the heme moiety, muscles containing myoglobin are red, whereas muscles with little or no myoglobin are white. **Glucose,** derived from the blood glucose or from endogenous glycogen, and **fatty acids** derived from the triacylglycerols of adipose tissue are the principal substrates used for aerobic metabolism in muscle.

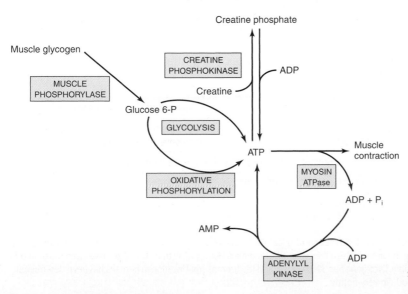

Figure 48–16. The multiple sources of ATP in muscle.

Creatine Phosphate Constitutes a Major Energy Reserve in Muscle

Creatine phosphate prevents the rapid depletion of ATP by providing a readily available high-energy phosphate that can be used to regenerate ATP from ADP. Creatine phosphate is formed from ATP and creatine (Figure 48–16) at times when the muscle is relaxed and demands for ATP are not so great. The enzyme catalyzing the phosphorylation of creatine is **creatine kinase** (CK), a muscle-specific enzyme with clinical utility in the detection of acute or chronic diseases of muscle.

SKELETAL MUSCLE CONTAINS SLOW (RED) & FAST (WHITE) TWITCH FIBERS

Different types of fibers have been detected in skeletal muscle. One classification subdivides them into type I (slow twitch), type IIA (fast twitch-oxidative), and type IIB (fast twitch-glycolytic). For the sake of simplicity, we shall consider only two types: type I (slow twitch, oxidative) and type II (fast twitch, glycolytic) (Table 48–10). The **type I** fibers are red because they contain myoglobin and mitochondria; their metabolism is aerobic, and they maintain relatively sustained contractions. The **type II** fibers, lacking myoglobin and containing few mitochondria, are white: they derive their energy from anaerobic glycolysis and exhibit relatively short durations of contraction. The **proportion** of these two types of fibers varies among the muscles of the body, depending on function (eg, whether or not a muscle is involved in sustained contraction, such as maintaining posture). The proportion also varies with **training;** for example, the number of type I fibers in certain leg muscles increases in athletes training for marathons, whereas the number of type II fibers increases in sprinters.

A Sprinter Uses Creatine Phosphate & Anaerobic Glycolysis to Make ATP, Whereas a Marathon Runner Uses Oxidative Phosphorylation

In view of the two types of fibers in skeletal muscle and of the various energy sources described above, it is of interest to compare their involvement in a sprint (eg, 100 meters) and in the marathon (42.2 km; just over 26 miles) (Table 48–11).

The major sources of energy in the **100-m sprint** are **creatine phosphate** (first 4–5 seconds) and then **anaerobic glycolysis,** using muscle glycogen as the source of glucose. The two main sites of metabolic control are at **glycogen phosphorylase** and at **PFK-1.** The former is activated by Ca^{2+} (released from the sarcoplasmic reticulum during contraction), epinephrine, and AMP. PFK-1 is activated by AMP, P_i, and NH_3.

Table 48–10. Characteristics of type I and type II fibers of skeletal muscle.

	Type I Slow Twitch	Type II Fast Twitch
Myosin ATPase	Low	High
Energy utilization	Low	High
Mitochondria	Many	Few
Color	Red	White
Myoglobin	Yes	No
Contraction rate	Slow	Fast
Duration	Prolonged	Short

Attesting to the efficiency of these processes, the flux through glycolysis can increase as much as 1000-fold during a sprint.

In contrast, in the **marathon, aerobic metabolism** is the principal source of ATP. The major fuel sources are **blood glucose** and **free fatty acids,** largely derived from the breakdown of triacylglycerols in adipose tissue, stimulated by epinephrine. Hepatic glycogen is degraded to maintain the level of blood glucose. Muscle glycogen is also a fuel source, but it is degraded much more gradually than in a sprint. It has been calculated that the amounts of glucose in the blood, of glycogen in the liver, of glycogen in muscle, and of triacylglycerol in adipose tissue are sufficient to supply muscle with energy during a marathon for 4 minutes, 18 minutes, 70 minutes, and approximately 4000 minutes, respectively. However, the rate of oxidation of fatty acids by muscle is slower than that of glucose, so that oxidation of glucose and of fatty acids are both major sources of energy in the marathon.

Table 48–11. Types of muscle fibers and major fuel sources used by a sprinter and by a marathon runner.

Sprinter (100 m)	Marathon Runner
Type II (glycolytic) fibers are used predominantly	Type I (oxidative) fibers are used predominantly
Creatine phosphate is the major energy source during the first 4–5 seconds	ATP is the major energy source throughout
Glucose derived from muscle glycogen and metabolized by anaerobic glycolysis is the major fuel source	Blood glucose and free fatty acids are the major fuel sources
Muscle glycogen is rapidly depleted	Muscle glycogen is slowly depleted

A number of procedures have been used by athletes to counteract muscle fatigue and inadequate strength. These include **carbohydrate loading, soda (sodium bicarbonate) loading, blood doping** (administration of red blood cells), and ingestion of **creatine** and **androstenedione.** Their rationales and efficacies will not be discussed here.

SKELETAL MUSCLE CONSTITUTES THE MAJOR RESERVE OF PROTEIN IN THE BODY

In humans, **skeletal muscle protein** is the major non-fat source of stored energy. This explains the very large losses of muscle mass, particularly in adults, resulting from prolonged caloric undernutrition.

The study of **tissue protein breakdown** in vivo is difficult, because amino acids released during intracellular breakdown of proteins can be extensively reutilized for protein synthesis within the cell, or the amino acids may be transported to other organs where they enter anabolic pathways. However, actin and myosin are methylated by a posttranslational reaction, forming **3-methylhistidine.** During intracellular breakdown of actin and myosin, 3-methylhistidine is released and excreted into the urine. The urinary output of the methylated amino acid provides a reliable index of the rate of myofibrillar protein breakdown in the musculature of human subjects.

Various features of muscle metabolism, most of which are dealt with in other chapters of this text, are summarized in Table 48–12.

THE CYTOSKELETON PERFORMS MULTIPLE CELLULAR FUNCTIONS

Nonmuscle cells perform mechanical work, including self-propulsion, morphogenesis, cleavage, endocytosis, exocytosis, intracellular transport, and changing cell shape. These cellular functions are carried out by an extensive intracellular network of filamentous structures constituting the **cytoskeleton.** The cell cytoplasm is not a sac of fluid, as once thought. Essentially all eukaryotic cells contain three types of filamentous structures: **actin filaments** (also known as microfilaments), **microtubules,** and **intermediate filaments.** Each type of filament can be distinguished biochemically and by the electron microscope.

Some properties of these 3 structures are summarized in Tables 48–13 and 48–14.

Nonmuscle Cells Contain Actin That Forms Microfilaments

G-actin is present in most if not all cells of the body. With appropriate concentrations of magnesium and

Table 48–12. Summary of major features of the biochemistry of skeletal muscle related to its metabolism.[1]

- Skeletal muscle functions under both aerobic (resting) and anaerobic (eg, sprinting) conditions, so both aerobic and anaerobic glycolysis operate, depending on conditions.
- Skeletal muscle contains myoglobin as a reservoir of oxygen.
- Skeletal muscle contains different types of fibers primarily suited to anaerobic (fast twitch fibers) or aerobic (slow twitch fibers) conditions.
- Actin, myosin, tropomyosin, troponin complex (TpT, TpI, and TpC), ATP, and Ca^{2+} are key constituents in relation to contraction.
- The Ca^{2+} ATPase, the Ca^{2+} release channel, and calsequestrin are proteins involved in various aspects of Ca^{2+} metabolism in muscle.
- Insulin acts on skeletal muscle to increase uptake of glucose.
- In the fed state, most glucose is used to synthesize glycogen, which acts as a store of glucose for use in exercise; "preloading" with glucose is used by some long-distance athletes to build up stores of glycogen.
- Epinephrine stimulates glycogenolysis in skeletal muscle, whereas glucagon does not because of absence of its receptors.
- Skeletal muscle cannot contribute directly to blood glucose because it does not contain glucose-6-phosphatase.
- Lactate produced by anaerobic metabolism in skeletal muscle passes to liver, which uses it to synthesize glucose, which can then return to muscle (the Cori cycle).
- Skeletal muscle contains phosphocreatine, which acts as an energy store for short-term (seconds) demands.
- Free fatty acids in plasma are a major source of energy, particularly under marathon conditions and in prolonged starvation.
- Skeletal muscle can utilize ketone bodies during starvation.
- Skeletal muscle is the principal site of metabolism of branched-chain amino acids, which are used as an energy source.
- Proteolysis of muscle during starvation supplies amino acids for gluconeogenesis.
- Major amino acids emanating from muscle are alanine (destined mainly for gluconeogenesis in liver and forming part of the glucose-alanine cycle) and glutamine (destined mainly for the gut and kidneys).

[1]This table brings together material from various chapters in this book.

potassium chloride, it spontaneously polymerizes to form double helical **F-actin** filaments like those seen in muscle. There are at least two types of actin in non-muscle cells: β-actin and γ-actin. Both types can coexist in the same cell and probably even copolymerize in the same filament. In the cytoplasm, **F-actin** forms **microfilaments** of 7–9.5 nm that frequently exist as bundles of a tangled-appearing meshwork. These bundles are prominent just underlying the plasma mem-

Table 48–13. Some properties of microfilaments and microtubules.

	Microfilaments	Microtubules
Protein(s)	Actin	α- and β-tubulins
Diameter	8–9 nm	25 nm
Functions	Structural, motility	Structural, motility, polarity

Some properties of intermediate filaments are described in Table 48–14.

brane of many cells and are there referred to as **stress fibers.** The stress fibers disappear as cell motility increases or upon malignant transformation of cells by chemicals or oncogenic viruses.

Although not organized as in muscle, actin filaments in nonmuscle cells interact with **myosin** to cause cellular movements.

Microtubules Contain α- & β-Tubulins

Microtubules, an integral component of the cellular cytoskeleton, consist of cytoplasmic tubes 25 nm in

Table 48–14. Classes of intermediate filaments of eukaryotic cells and their distributions.

Proteins	Molecular Mass	Distributions
Keratins		
Type I (acidic)	40–60 kDa	Epithelial cells,
Type II (basic)	50–70 kDa	hair, nails
Vimentin-like		
Vimentin	54 kDa	Various mesen-chymal cells
Desmin	53 kDa	Muscle
Glial fibrillary acid protein	50 kDa	Glial cells
Peripherin	66 kDa	Neurons
Neurofilaments		
Low (L), medium (M), and high (H)[1]	60–130 kDa	Neurons
Lamins		
A, B, and C	65–75 kDa	Nuclear lamina

[1]Refers to their molecular masses.
Intermediate filaments have an approximate diameter of 10 nm and have various functions. For example, keratins are distributed widely in epithelial cells and adhere via adapter proteins to desmosomes and hemidesmosomes. Lamins provide support for the nuclear membrane.

diameter and often of extreme length. Microtubules are necessary for the formation and function of the **mitotic spindle** and thus are present in all eukaryotic cells. They are also involved in the intracellular movement of endocytic and exocytic **vesicles** and form the major structural components of **cilia** and **flagella.** Microtubules are a major component of **axons** and **dendrites,** in which they maintain structure and participate in the axoplasmic flow of material along these neuronal processes.

Microtubules are cylinders of 13 longitudinally arranged protofilaments, each consisting of dimers of **α-tubulin** and **β-tubulin,** closely related proteins of approximately 50 kDa molecular mass. The tubulin dimers assemble into protofilaments and subsequently into sheets and then cylinders. A microtubule-organizing center, located around a pair of centrioles, nucleates the growth of new microtubules. A third species of tubulin, **γ-tubulin,** appears to play an important role in this assembly. **GTP** is required for assembly. A variety of proteins are associated with microtubules (**microtubule-associated proteins [MAPs],** one of which is **tau**) and play important roles in microtubule assembly and stabilization. Microtubules are in a state of dynamic instability, constantly assembling and disassembling. They exhibit **polarity** (plus and minus ends); this is important in their growth from centrioles and in their ability to direct intracellular movement. For instance, in axonal transport, the protein **kinesin,** with a myosin-like ATPase activity, uses hydrolysis of ATP to move vesicles down the axon toward the positive end of the microtubular formation. Flow of materials in the opposite direction, toward the negative end, is powered by **cytosolic dynein,** another protein with ATPase activity. Similarly, **axonemal dyneins** power ciliary and flagellar movement. Another protein, **dynamin,** uses GTP and is involved in endocytosis. Kinesins, dyneins, dynamin, and myosins are referred to as **molecular motors.**

An absence of dynein in cilia and flagella results in immotile cilia and flagella, leading to male sterility and chronic respiratory infection, a condition known as **Kartagener syndrome.**

Certain **drugs** bind to microtubules and thus interfere with their assembly or disassembly. These include colchicine (used for treatment of acute gouty arthritis), vinblastine (a vinca alkaloid used for treating certain types of cancer), paclitaxel (Taxol) (effective against ovarian cancer), and griseofulvin (an antifungal agent).

Intermediate Filaments Differ from Microfilaments & Microtubules

An intracellular fibrous system exists of filaments with an axial periodicity of 21 nm and a diameter of 8–10 nm that is intermediate between that of microfilaments (6 nm) and microtubules (23 nm). Four classes of **intermediate filaments** are found, as indicated in Table 48–14.

They are all elongated, fibrous molecules, with a central rod domain, an amino terminal head, and a carboxyl terminal tail. They form a structure like a rope, and the mature filaments are composed of tetramers packed together in a helical manner. They are important structural components of cells, and most are relatively *stable* components of the cytoskeleton, not undergoing rapid assembly and disassembly and not disappearing during mitosis, as do actin and many microtubular filaments. An important exception to this is provided by the *lamins*, which, subsequent to phosphorylation, disassemble at mitosis and reappear when it terminates. Mutations in the gene encoding lamin A cause progeria, characterized by striking premature aging and other features.

Keratins form a large family, with about 30 members being distinguished. As indicated in Table 48–14, two major types of keratins are found; all individual keratins are **heterodimers** made up of one member of each class.

Vimentins are widely distributed in mesodermal cells, and desmin, glial fibrillary acidic protein, and peripherin are related to them. All members of the vimentin-like family can copolymerize with each other. Intermediate filaments are very prominent in nerve cells; neurofilaments are classified as low, medium, and high on the basis of their molecular masses. **Lamins** form a meshwork in apposition to the inner nuclear membrane. The **distribution of intermediate filaments** in normal and abnormal (eg, cancer) cells can be studied by the use of immunofluorescent techniques, using antibodies of appropriate specificities. These antibodies to specific intermediate filaments can also be of use to pathologists in helping to decide the origin of certain dedifferentiated malignant tumors. These tumors may still retain the type of intermediate filaments found in their cell of origin.

A number of **skin diseases,** mainly characterized by blistering, have been found to be due to mutations in genes encoding **various keratins.** Three of these disorders are epidermolysis bullosa simplex, epidermolytic hyperkeratosis, and epidermolytic palmoplantar keratoderma. The blistering probably reflects a diminished capacity of various layers of the skin to resist mechanical stresses due to abnormalities in microfilament structure.

SUMMARY

- The myofibrils of skeletal muscle contain thick and thin filaments. The thick filaments contain myosin. The thin filaments contain actin, tropomyosin, and the troponin complex (troponins T, I, and C).
- The sliding filament cross-bridge model is the foundation of current thinking about muscle contraction. The basis of this model is that the interdigitating filaments slide past one another during contraction and cross-bridges between myosin and actin generate and sustain the tension.

- The hydrolysis of ATP is used to drive movement of the filaments. ATP binds to myosin heads and is hydrolyzed to ADP and P_i by the ATPase activity of the actomyosin complex.

- Ca^{2+} plays a key role in the initiation of muscle contraction by binding to troponin C. In skeletal muscle, the sarcoplasmic reticulum regulates distribution of Ca^{2+} to the sarcomeres, whereas inflow of Ca^{2+} via Ca^{2+} channels in the sarcolemma is of major importance in cardiac and smooth muscle.

- Many cases of malignant hyperthermia in humans are due to mutations in the gene encoding the Ca^{2+} release channel.

- A number of differences exist between skeletal and cardiac muscle; in particular, the latter contains a variety of receptors on its surface.

- Some cases of familial hypertrophic cardiomyopathy are due to missense mutations in the gene coding for β-myosin heavy chain. Mutations in genes encoding a number of other proteins have also been detected.

- Smooth muscle, unlike skeletal and cardiac muscle, does not contain the troponin system; instead, phosphorylation of myosin light chains initiates contraction.

- Nitric oxide is a regulator of vascular smooth muscle; blockage of its formation from arginine causes an acute elevation of blood pressure, indicating that regulation of blood pressure is one of its many functions.

- Duchenne-type muscular dystrophy is due to mutations in the gene, located on the X chromosome, encoding the protein dystrophin.

- Two major types of muscle fibers are found in humans: white (anaerobic) and red (aerobic). The former are particularly used in sprints and the latter in prolonged aerobic exercise. During a sprint, muscle uses creatine phosphate and glycolysis as energy sources; in the marathon, oxidation of fatty acids is of major importance during the later phases.

- Nonmuscle cells perform various types of mechanical work carried out by the structures constituting the cytoskeleton. These structures include actin filaments (microfilaments), microtubules (composed primarily of α-tubulin and β-tubulin), and intermediate filaments. The latter include keratins, vimentin-like proteins, neurofilaments, and lamins.

REFERENCES

Bruckdorfer R: The basics about nitric oxide. Mol Aspects Med 2005;26:3.

De La Cruz EM, Ostap EM: Relating biochemistry and function in the myosin superfamily. Curr Opin Cell Biol 2004;16:61.

Herrman H, Aebi U: Intermediate filaments: molecular structure, assembly mechanism, and integration into functionally distinct intracellular scaffolds. Annu Rev Biochem 2004;73:749.

Lodish H et al (editors): *Molecular Cell Biology,* 5th ed. WH Freeman & Co., 2004. (This excellent text contains extensive coverage of molecular motors, muscle contraction, microfilaments, microtubules, and intermediate filaments.)

Matthews KD, Moore SA: Multicore myopathy, central core disease, malignant hyperthermia susceptibility, and RYR1 mutations: one disease with many faces? Arch Neurol 2004;61:106.

Murphy RT, Starling RC: Genetics and cardiomyopathy: where are we now? Cleve Clin J Med 2005;72:465.

Nowak KJ, Davies KE: Duchenne muscular dystrophy and dystrophin: pathogenesis and opportunities for treatment. EMBO Rep 2004;5:872.

Palmer KJ, Watson P, Stephens DJ: The role of microtubules in transport between the endoplasmic reticulum and Golgi apparatus in mammalian cells. Biochem Soc Symp 2005;72:1.

Scriver CR et al (editors): *The Metabolic and Molecular Bases of Inherited Disease,* 8th ed. McGraw-Hill, 2001. (This comprehensive four-volume text contains chapters on malignant hyperthermia, channelopathies, hypertrophic cardiomyopathy, the muscular dystrophies, and disorders of intermediate filaments.)

Webb RC: Smooth muscle contraction and relaxation. Adv Physiol Educ 2003;27:201.

Wehrens XHT, Lehnart SE, Marks AR: Intracellular calcium release and cardiac disease. Annu Rev Physiol 2005;67:69.

Plasma Proteins & Immunoglobulins 49

Robert K. Murray, MD, PhD

BIOMEDICAL IMPORTANCE

The fundamental role of blood in the maintenance of **homeostasis** and the ease with which blood can be obtained have meant that the study of its constituents has been of central importance in the development of biochemistry and clinical biochemistry. The basic properties of a number of **plasma proteins,** including the **immunoglobulins** (antibodies), are described in this chapter. Changes in the amounts of various plasma proteins and immunoglobulins occur in many diseases and can be monitored by electrophoresis or other suitable procedures. As indicated in an earlier chapter, alterations of the activities of certain **enzymes** found in plasma are of diagnostic use in a number of pathologic conditions.

THE BLOOD HAS MANY FUNCTIONS

The functions of blood—except for specific cellular ones such as oxygen transport and cell-mediated immunologic defense—are carried out by plasma and its constituents (Table 49–1).

Plasma consists of water, electrolytes, metabolites, nutrients, proteins, and hormones. The water and electrolyte composition of plasma is practically the same as that of all extracellular fluids. Laboratory determinations of levels of Na^+, K^+, Ca^{2+}, Cl^-, HCO_3^-, $PaCO_2$, and of blood pH are important in the management of many patients.

PLASMA CONTAINS A COMPLEX MIXTURE OF PROTEINS

The concentration of total protein in human plasma is approximately 7.0–7.5 g/dL and comprises the major part of the solids of the plasma. The proteins of the plasma are actually a complex mixture that includes not only simple proteins but also conjugated proteins such as **glycoproteins** and various types of **lipoproteins.** Use of proteomic techniques is allowing the isolation and characterization of previously unknown plasma proteins, some present in very small amounts (eg, detected in hemodialysis fluid and in the plasma of patients with cancer), thus expanding **the plasma proteome.** Thousands of **antibodies** are present in human plasma, though the amount of any one antibody is usually quite low under normal circumstances. The relative dimensions and molecular masses of some of the most important plasma proteins are shown in Figure 49–1.

The **separation** of individual proteins from a complex mixture is frequently accomplished by the use of solvents or electrolytes (or both) to remove different protein fractions in accordance with their solubility characteristics. This is the basis of the so-called saltingout methods, which find some usage in the determination of protein fractions in the clinical laboratory. Thus, one can separate the proteins of the plasma into three major groups—**fibrinogen, albumin,** and **globulins**—by the use of varying concentrations of sodium or ammonium sulfate.

The most common method of analyzing plasma proteins is by **electrophoresis.** There are many types of electrophoresis, each using a different supporting medium. In clinical laboratories, **cellulose acetate** is widely used as a supporting medium. Its use permits resolution, after staining, of plasma proteins into five bands, designated albumin, α_1, α_2, β, and γ fractions, respectively (Figure 49–2). The stained strip of cellulose acetate (or other supporting medium) is called an electrophoretogram. The amounts of these five bands can be conveniently quantified by use of densitometric scanning machines. Characteristic changes in the amounts of one or more of these five bands are found in many diseases.

The Concentration of Protein in Plasma Is Important in Determining the Distribution of Fluid between Blood & Tissues

In arterioles, the **hydrostatic pressure** is about 37 mm Hg, with an interstitial (tissue) pressure of 1 mm Hg opposing it. The **osmotic pressure** (oncotic pressure) exerted by the plasma proteins is approximately 25 mm Hg. Thus, a net outward force of about 11 mm Hg drives fluid out into the interstitial spaces. In venules, the hydrostatic pressure is about 17 mm Hg, with the oncotic and interstitial pressures as described above; thus, a net force of about 9 mm Hg attracts water back into the circulation. The above pressures are often referred to as the **Starling forces.** If the concentration

Table 49–1. Major functions of blood.

1. **Respiration**—transport of oxygen from the lungs to the tissues and of CO_2 from the tissues to the lungs
2. **Nutrition**—transport of absorbed food materials
3. **Excretion**—transport of metabolic waste to the kidneys, lungs, skin, and intestines for removal
4. Maintenance of the normal **acid-base balance** in the body
5. Regulation of **water balance** through the effects of blood on the exchange of water between the circulating fluid and the tissue fluid
6. Regulation of **body temperature** by the distribution of body heat
7. **Defense** against infection by the white blood cells and circulating antibodies
8. Transport of **hormones** and regulation of metabolism
9. Transport of **metabolites**
10. **Coagulation**

of plasma proteins is markedly diminished (eg, due to severe protein malnutrition), fluid is not attracted back into the intravascular compartment and accumulates in the extravascular tissue spaces, a condition known as **edema.** Edema has many causes; protein deficiency is one of them.

Plasma Proteins Have Been Studied Extensively

Because of the relative ease with which they can be obtained, plasma proteins have been studied extensively in both humans and animals. Considerable information is available about the biosynthesis, turnover, structure, and functions of the major plasma proteins. Alterations of their amounts and of their metabolism in many disease states have also been investigated. In recent years, many of the genes for plasma proteins have been cloned and their structures determined.

The preparation of **antibodies** specific for the individual plasma proteins has greatly facilitated their study, allowing the precipitation and isolation of pure proteins from the complex mixture present in tissues or plasma. In addition, the use of **isotopes** has made possible the determination of their pathways of biosynthesis and of their turnover rates in plasma.

The following generalizations have emerged from studies of plasma proteins.

A. MOST PLASMA PROTEINS ARE SYNTHESIZED IN THE LIVER

This has been established by experiments at the whole-animal level (eg, hepatectomy) and by use of the isolated perfused liver preparation, of liver slices, of liver homogenates, and of in vitro translation systems using preparations of mRNA extracted from liver. However, the γ-globulins are synthesized in plasma cells and certain plasma proteins are synthesized in other sites, such as endothelial cells.

B. PLASMA PROTEINS ARE GENERALLY SYNTHESIZED ON MEMBRANE-BOUND POLYRIBOSOMES

They then traverse the major secretory route in the cell (rough endoplasmic membrane → smooth endoplasmic membrane → Golgi apparatus → secretory vesicles) prior to entering the plasma. Thus, most plasma proteins are synthesized as **preproteins** and initially contain amino terminal signal peptides (Chapter 45). They are usually subjected to various posttranslational modifications (proteolysis, glycosylation, phosphorylation, etc) as they travel through the cell. Transit times through the hepatocyte from the site of synthesis to the plasma vary from 30 minutes to several hours or more for individual proteins.

C. MOST PLASMA PROTEINS ARE GLYCOPROTEINS

Accordingly, they generally contain either N- or O-linked oligosaccharide chains, or both (Chapter 46). Albumin is the major exception; it does not contain sugar residues. The oligosaccharide chains have various

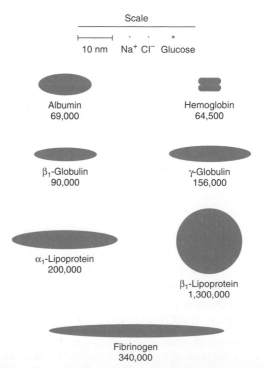

Figure 49–1. Relative dimensions and approximate molecular masses of protein molecules in the blood (Oncley).

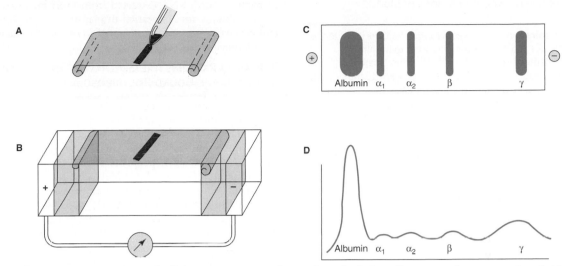

Figure 49–2. Technique of cellulose acetate zone electrophoresis. **A:** A small amount of serum or other fluid is applied to a cellulose acetate strip. **B:** Electrophoresis of sample in electrolyte buffer is performed. **C:** Separated protein bands are visualized in characteristic positions after being stained. **D:** Densitometer scanning from cellulose acetate strip converts bands to characteristic peaks of albumin, α_1-globulin, α_2-globulin, β-globulin, and γ-globulin. (Reproduced, with permission, from Parslow TG et al [editors]: *Medical Immunology,* 10th ed. McGraw-Hill, 2001.)

functions (Table 46–2). Removal of terminal sialic acid residues from certain plasma proteins (eg, ceruloplasmin) by exposure to neuraminidase can markedly shorten their half-lives in plasma (Chapter 46).

D. MANY PLASMA PROTEINS EXHIBIT POLYMORPHISM

A **polymorphism** is a mendelian or monogenic trait that exists in the population in at least two phenotypes, neither of which is rare (ie, neither of which occurs with frequency of less than 1–2%). The ABO blood group substances (Chapter 51) are the best-known examples of human polymorphisms. Human plasma proteins that exhibit polymorphism include α_1-antitrypsin, haptoglobin, transferrin, ceruloplasmin, and immunoglobulins. The polymorphic forms of these proteins can be distinguished by different procedures (eg, various types of electrophoresis or isoelectric focusing), in which each form may show a characteristic migration. Analyses of these human polymorphisms have proved to be of genetic, anthropologic, and clinical interest.

E. EACH PLASMA PROTEIN HAS A CHARACTERISTIC HALF-LIFE IN THE CIRCULATION

The **half-life** of a plasma protein can be determined by labeling the isolated pure protein with ^{131}I under mild, nondenaturing conditions. This isotope unites covalently with tyrosine residues in the protein. The labeled protein is freed of unbound ^{131}I and its specific activity (disinte-

grations per minute per milligram of protein) determined. A known amount of the radioactive protein is then injected into a normal adult subject, and samples of blood are taken at various time intervals for determinations of radioactivity. The values for radioactivity are plotted against time, and the half-life of the protein (the time for the radioactivity to decline from its peak value to one-half of its peak value) can be calculated from the resulting graph, discounting the times for the injected protein to equilibrate (mix) in the blood and in the extravascular spaces. The half-lives obtained for albumin and haptoglobin in normal healthy adults are approximately 20 and 5 days, respectively. In certain diseases, the half-life of a protein may be markedly altered. For instance, in some gastrointestinal diseases such as regional ileitis (Crohn's disease), considerable amounts of plasma proteins, including albumin, may be lost into the bowel through the inflamed intestinal mucosa. Patients with this condition have a **protein-losing gastroenteropathy,** and the half-life of injected iodinated albumin in these subjects may be reduced to as little as 1 day.

F. THE LEVELS OF CERTAIN PROTEINS IN PLASMA INCREASE DURING ACUTE INFLAMMATORY STATES OR SECONDARY TO CERTAIN TYPES OF TISSUE DAMAGE

These proteins are called **"acute phase proteins"** (or reactants) and include **C-reactive protein** (CRP, so-named because it reacts with the C polysaccharide of

Table 49–2. Some functions of plasma proteins.

Function	Plasma Proteins
Antiproteases	Antichymotrypsin α_1-Antitrypsin (α_1-antiproteinase) α_2-Macroglobulin Antithrombin
Blood clotting	Various coagulation factors, fibrinogen
Enzymes	Function in blood, eg, coagulation factors, cholinesterase Leakage from cells or tissues, eg, amino-transferases
Hormones	Erythropoietin[1]
Immune defense	Immunoglobulins, complement proteins, β_2-microglobulin
Involvement in inflammatory responses	Acute phase response proteins (eg, C-reactive protein, α_1-acid glycoprotein [orosomucoid])
Oncofetal	α_1-Fetoprotein (AFP)
Transport or binding proteins	Albumin (various ligands, including bilirubin, free fatty acids, ions [Ca^{2+}], metals [eg, Cu^{2+}, Zn^{2+}], metheme, steroids, other hormones, and a variety of drugs) Ceruloplasmin (contains Cu^{2+}; albumin probably more important in physiologic transport of Cu^{2+}) Corticosteroid-binding globulin (transcortin) (binds cortisol) Haptoglobin (binds extracorpuscular hemoglobin) Lipoproteins (chylomicrons, VLDL, LDL, HDL) Hemopexin (binds heme) Retinol-binding protein (binds retinol) Sex hormone-binding globulin (binds testosterone, estradiol) Thyroid-binding globulin (binds T_4, T_3) Transferrin (transport iron) Transthyretin (formerly prealbumin; binds T_4 and forms a complex with retinol-binding protein)

[1]Various other protein hormones circulate in the blood but are not usually designated as plasma proteins. Similarly, ferritin is also found in plasma in small amounts, but it too is not usually characterized as a plasma protein.

pneumococci), **α_1-antitrypsin, haptoglobin, α_1-acid glycoprotein,** and **fibrinogen.** The elevations of the levels of these proteins vary from as little as 50% to as much as 1000-fold in the case of CRP. Their levels are also usually elevated during chronic inflammatory states and in patients with cancer. These proteins are believed to play a role in the body's response to inflammation. For example, C-reactive protein can stimulate the classic complement pathway, and α_1-antitrypsin can neutralize certain proteases released during the acute inflammatory state. CRP is used as a marker of tissue injury, infection, and inflammation, and there is considerable interest in its use as a predictor of certain types of cardiovascular conditions secondary to atherosclerosis. Interleukin-1 (IL-1), a polypeptide released from mononuclear phagocytic cells, is the principal—but not the sole—stimulator of the synthesis of the majority of acute phase reactants by hepatocytes. Additional molecules such as IL-6 are involved, and they as well as IL-1 appear to work at the level of gene transcription.

Nuclear factor kappa-B (NFκB) is a transcription factor that has been involved in the stimulation of synthesis of certain of the acute phase proteins. This important factor is also involved in the expression of many cytokines, chemokines, growth factors, and cell adhesion molecules implicated in immunologic phenomena. Normally it exists in an inactive form in the cytosol but is activated and translocated to the nucleus via the action of a number of molecules (eg, interleukin-1) produced in processes such as inflammation, infection, and radiation injury.

Table 49–2 summarizes the functions of many of the plasma proteins. The remainder of the material in this chapter presents basic information regarding selected plasma proteins: albumin, haptoglobin, transferrin, ceruloplasmin, α_1-antitrypsin, α_2-macroglobulin, the immunoglobulins, and the complement system. The lipoproteins are discussed in Chapter 25.

Albumin Is the Major Protein in Human Plasma

Albumin (69 kDa) is the major protein of human plasma (3.4–4.7 g/dL) and makes up approximately 60% of the total plasma protein. About 40% of albumin is present in the plasma, and the other 60% is present in the extracellular space. The liver produces about 12 g of albumin per day, representing about 25% of total hepatic protein synthesis and half its secreted protein. Albumin is initially synthesized as a **preproprotein.** Its **signal peptide** is removed as it passes into the cisternae of the rough endoplasmic reticulum, and a **hexapeptide** at the resulting amino terminal is subsequently cleaved off farther along the secretory pathway. The synthesis of albumin is depressed in a variety of diseases, particularly those of the liver. The plasma of patients with **liver disease** often shows a decrease in the ratio of albumin to globulins (decreased albumin-globulin ratio). The synthesis of albumin decreases relatively early in conditions of protein malnutrition, such as kwashiorkor.

Mature human albumin consists of one polypeptide chain of 585 amino acids and contains 17 disulfide

bonds. By the use of proteases, albumin can be subdivided into three **domains,** which have different functions. Albumin has an ellipsoidal shape, which means that it does not increase the viscosity of the plasma as much as an elongated molecule such as fibrinogen does. Because of its relatively low molecular mass (about 69 kDa) and high concentration, albumin is thought to be responsible for 75–80% of the **osmotic pressure** of human plasma. Electrophoretic studies have shown that the plasma of certain humans lacks albumin. These subjects are said to exhibit **analbuminemia.** One cause of this condition is a mutation that affects splicing. Subjects with analbuminemia show only moderate edema, despite the fact that albumin is the major determinant of plasma osmotic pressure. It is thought that the amounts of the other plasma proteins increase and compensate for the lack of albumin.

Another important function of albumin is its ability to **bind various ligands.** These include free fatty acids (FFA), calcium, certain steroid hormones, bilirubin, and some of the plasma tryptophan. In addition, albumin appears to play an important role in transport of copper in the human body (see below). A variety of drugs, including sulfonamides, penicillin G, dicumarol, and aspirin, are bound to albumin; this finding has important pharmacologic implications.

Preparations of human albumin have been widely used in the treatment of hemorrhagic shock and of burns. However, some recent studies question the value of this therapy.

Haptoglobin Binds Extracorpuscular Hemoglobin, Preventing Free Hemoglobin from Entering the Kidney

Haptoglobin (Hp) is a plasma glycoprotein that binds extracorpuscular hemoglobin (Hb) in a tight noncovalent complex (Hb-Hp). The amount of haptoglobin in human plasma ranges from 40 mg to 180 mg of hemoglobin-binding capacity per deciliter. Approximately 10% of the hemoglobin that is degraded each day is released into the circulation and is thus extracorpuscular. The other 90% is present in old, damaged red blood cells, which are degraded by cells of the histiocytic system. The molecular mass of hemoglobin is approximately 65 kDa, whereas the molecular mass of the simplest polymorphic form of haptoglobin (Hp 1-1) found in humans is approximately 90 kDa. Thus, the Hb-Hp complex has a molecular mass of approximately 155 kDa. Free hemoglobin passes through the glomerulus of the kidney, enters the tubules, and tends to precipitate therein (as can happen after a massive incompatible blood transfusion, when the capacity of haptoglobin to bind hemoglobin is grossly exceeded) (Figure 49–3). However, the Hb-Hp complex is too large to pass through the glomerulus. The function of

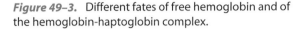

A. Hb → Kidney → Excreted in urine or precipitates in
(MW 65,000) tubules; iron is lost to body

B. Hb + Hp → Hb : Hp complex ↛ Kidney
(MW 65,000) (MW 90,000) ↓ (MW 155,000)

Catabolized by liver cells;
iron is conserved and reused

Figure 49–3. Different fates of free hemoglobin and of the hemoglobin-haptoglobin complex.

Hp thus appears to be to prevent loss of free hemoglobin into the kidney. This conserves the valuable iron present in hemoglobin, which would otherwise be lost to the body.

Human haptoglobin exists in **three polymorphic forms,** known as Hp 1-1, Hp 2-1, and Hp 2-2. Hp 1-1 migrates in starch gel electrophoresis as a single band, whereas Hp 2-1 and Hp 2-2 exhibit much more complex band patterns. Two genes, designated Hp^1 and Hp^2, direct these three phenotypes, with Hp 2-1 being the heterozygous phenotype. It has been suggested that the haptoglobin polymorphism may be associated with the prevalence of many inflammatory diseases.

The levels of haptoglobin in human plasma vary and are of some diagnostic use. Low levels of haptoglobin are found in patients with **hemolytic anemias.** This is explained by the fact that whereas the half life of haptoglobin is approximately 5 days, the half life of the Hb Hp complex is about 90 minutes, the complex being rapidly removed from plasma by hepatocytes. Thus, when haptoglobin is bound to hemoglobin, it is cleared from the plasma about 80 times faster than normally. Accordingly, the level of haptoglobin falls rapidly in situations where hemoglobin is constantly being released from red blood cells, such as occurs in hemolytic anemias. Haptoglobin is an acute phase protein, and its plasma level is elevated in a variety of inflammatory states.

Certain other plasma proteins bind heme but not hemoglobin. **Hemopexin** is a β_1-globulin that binds free heme. **Albumin** will bind some metheme (ferric heme) to form methemalbumin, which then transfers the metheme to hemopexin.

Absorption of Iron from the Small Intestine Is Tightly Regulated

Transferrin (Tf) is a plasma protein that plays a central role in transporting iron around the body to sites where it is needed. Before we discuss it further, certain aspects of iron metabolism will be reviewed.

Iron is important in the human body because of its occurrence in many hemoproteins such as hemoglobin, myoglobin, and the cytochromes. It is ingested in the

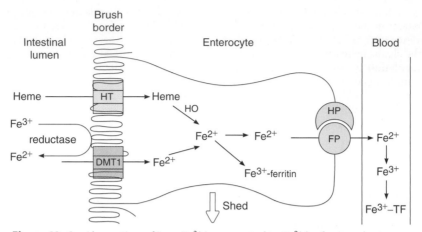

Figure 49–4. Absorption of iron. Fe^{3+} is converted to Fe^{2+} by ferric reductase, and Fe^{2+} is transported into the enterocyte by the apical membrane iron transporter DMT1. Heme is transported into the enterocyte by a separate heme transporter (HT), and heme oxidase (HO) releases Fe^{2+} from the heme. Some of the intracellular Fe^{2+} is converted to Fe^{3+} and bound by ferritin. The remainder binds to the basolateral Fe^{2+} transporter (FP) and is transported into the bloodstream, aided by hephaestin (HP). In plasma, Fe^{3+} is bound to the iron transport protein transferrin (TF). (Reproduced, with permission, from Ganong WF: *Review of Medical Physiology*, 21st ed. McGraw-Hill, 2003.)

diet either as heme or nonheme iron (Figure 49–4); as shown, these different forms involve separate pathways. Absorption of iron in the proximal duodenum is tightly regulated, as there is no physiologic pathway for its excretion from the body. Under normal circumstances, the body guards its content of iron zealously, so that a healthy adult male loses only about 1 mg/d, which is replaced by absorption. Adult females are more prone to states of iron deficiency because some may lose excessive blood during menstruation. The amounts of iron in various body compartments are shown in Table 49–3.

Enterocytes in the proximal duodenum are responsible for absorption of iron. Incoming iron in the Fe^{3+} state is reduced to Fe^{2+} by a **ferrireductase** present on the surface of enterocytes (Figure 49–4). Vitamin C in food also favors reduction of ferric iron to ferrous iron. The transfer of iron from the apical surfaces of enterocytes into their interiors is performed by a proton-coupled **divalent metal transporter (DMT1).** This protein is not specific for iron, as it can transport a wide variety of divalent cations.

A recently discovered peptide (25 amino acids, synthesized by liver cells) named **hepcidin** appears to play an important role in iron metabolism. It down-regulates the intestinal absorption and placental transfer of iron and also the release of iron from macrophages, possibly by interaction with ferroportin. When plasma levels of iron are high, synthesis of hepcidin increases; the oppo-

site occurs when plasma levels of iron are low. It may play an important role in hemochromatosis (see below) and also in the iron deficiency anemia seen in chronic inflammatory conditions. Another recently discovered protein named **hemojuvelin** may act by modulating the expression of hepcidin.

Once inside an enterocyte, iron can either be stored as **ferritin** or transferred across the basolateral membrane into the plasma, where it is carried by transferrin (see below). Passage across the basolateral membrane appears to be carried out by another protein, **ferroportin.** This protein may interact with the copper-containing protein **hephaestin,** a protein similar to ceruloplasmin (see

Table 49–3. Distribution of iron in a 70-kg adult male.[1]

Transferrin	3–4 mg
Hemoglobin in red blood cells	2500 mg
In myoglobin and various enzymes	300 mg
In stores (ferritin and hemosiderin)	1000 mg
Absorption	1 mg/d
Losses	1 mg/d

[1]In an adult female of similar weight, the amount in stores would generally be less (100–400 mg) and the losses would be greater (1.5–2 mg/d).

below). Hephaestin is thought to have a ferroxidase activity, which is important in the release of iron from cells. Thus, Fe^{2+} is converted back to Fe^{3+}, the form in which it is transported in the plasma by transferrin.

The **overall regulation** of iron absorption is complex and not well understood; although it appears that **hepcidin** plays a key role. Regulation occurs at the level of the enterocyte, where further absorption of iron is blocked (likely by hepcidin) if a sufficient amount has been taken up (so-called dietary regulation exerted by "mucosal block"). It also appears to be responsive to the overall requirement of erythropoiesis for iron (erythropoietic regulation). Absorption is excessive in hereditary hemochromatosis (see below).

Transferrin Shuttles Iron to Sites Where It Is Needed

Transferrin (Tf) is a β_1-globulin with a molecular mass of approximately 76 kDa. It is a glycoprotein and is synthesized in the liver. About 20 polymorphic forms of transferrin have been found. It plays a central role in the body's metabolism of iron because it transports iron (2 mol of Fe^{3+} per mole of Tf) in the circulation to sites where iron is required, eg, from the gut to the bone marrow and other organs. Approximately 200 billion red blood cells (about 20 mL) are catabolized per day, releasing about 25 mg of iron into the body—most of which will be transported by transferrin.

There are **receptors (TfR1 and TfR2)** on the surfaces of many cells for transferrin. It binds to these receptors and is internalized by receptor-mediated endocytosis (compare the fate of LDL; Chapter 25). The acid pH inside the lysosome causes the iron to dissociate from the protein. The dissociated iron leaves the endosome via DMT1 to enter the cytoplasm. Unlike the protein component of LDL, apoTf is not degraded within the lysosome. Instead, it remains associated with its receptor, returns to the plasma membrane, dissociates from its receptor, reenters the plasma, picks up more iron, and again delivers the iron to needy cells. Normally, the iron bound to Tf turns over 10–20 times a day.

Abnormalities of the glycosylation of transferrin occur in the **congenital disorders of glycosylation** (Chapter 46) and in **chronic alcohol abuse.** Their detection by, for example, isoelectric focusing is used to help diagnose these conditions.

Iron Deficiency Anemia Is Extremely Prevalent

Attention to iron metabolism is **particularly important in women** for the reason mentioned above. Additionally, in **pregnancy,** allowances must be made for the growing fetus. **Older people** with poor dietary habits ("tea and toasters") may develop iron deficiency.

Iron deficiency anemia due to inadequate intake, inadequate utilization, or excessive loss of iron is one of the most prevalent conditions seen in medical practice.

The concentration of transferrin in plasma is approximately 300 mg/dL. This amount of transferrin can bind 300 μg of iron per deciliter, so that this represents the **total iron-binding capacity** of plasma. However, the protein is normally only one-third saturated with iron. In **iron deficiency anemia,** the protein is even less saturated with iron, whereas in conditions of storage of excess iron in the body (eg, hemochromatosis) the saturation with iron is much greater than one-third.

Ferritin Stores Iron in Cells

Ferritin is another protein that is important in the metabolism of iron. Under normal conditions, it stores iron that can be called upon for use as conditions require. In conditions of excess iron (eg, hemochromatosis), body stores of iron are greatly increased and much more ferritin is present in the tissues, such as the liver and spleen. Ferritin contains approximately 23% iron, and **apoferritin** (the protein moiety free of iron) has a molecular mass of approximately 440 kDa. Ferritin is composed of 24 subunits of 18.5 kDa, which surround in a micellar form some 3000–4500 ferric atoms. Normally, there is a little ferritin in human plasma. However, in patients with excess iron, the amount of ferritin in plasma is markedly elevated. The amount of ferritin in plasma can be conveniently measured by a sensitive and specific radioimmunoassay and serves as an index of body iron stores.

Synthesis of the **transferrin receptor (TfR)** and that of **ferritin** are reciprocally linked to cellular iron content. Specific untranslated sequences of the mRNAs for both proteins (named **iron response elements**) interact with a cytosolic protein sensitive to variations in levels of cellular iron (**iron-responsive element-binding protein**). When iron levels are high, cells use stored ferritin mRNA to synthesize ferritin, and the TfR mRNA is degraded. In contrast, when iron levels are low, the TfR mRNA is stabilized and increased synthesis of receptors occurs, while ferritin mRNA is apparently stored in an inactive form. This is an important example of control of expression of proteins at the **translational** level.

Hemosiderin is a somewhat ill-defined molecule; it appears to be a partly degraded form of ferritin but still containing iron. It can be detected by histologic stains (eg, Prussian blue) for iron, and its presence is determined histologically when excessive storage of iron occurs.

Hereditary Hemochromatosis Is Due to Mutations in the *HFE* Gene

Hereditary (primary) hemochromatosis is a very prevalent autosomal recessive disorder in certain parts of the world (eg, Scotland, Ireland, and North America). It is

characterized by excessive storage of iron in tissues, leading to tissue damage. Total body iron ranges between 2.5 g and 3.5 g in normal adults; in primary hemochromatosis it usually exceeds 15 g. The accumulated iron damages organs and tissues such as the liver, pancreatic islets, and heart, perhaps in part due to effects on free radical production (Chapter 51). Melanin and various amounts of iron accumulate in the skin, accounting for the slate-gray color often seen. The precise cause of melanin accumulation is not clear. The frequent coexistence of diabetes mellitus (due to islet damage) and the skin pigmentation led to use of the term **bronze diabetes** for this condition. In 1995, Feder and colleagues isolated a gene, now known as *HFE,* located on chromosome 6 close to the major histocompatibility complex genes. The encoded protein (HFE) was found to be related to MHC class 1 antigens. Initially, two different missense mutations were found in *HFE* in individuals with hereditary hemochromatosis. The more frequent mutation was one that changed cysteinyl residue 282 to a tyrosyl residue (CY282Y), disrupting the structure of the protein. The other mutation changed histidyl residue 63 to an aspartyl residue (H63D). Other mutations in *HFE* may also be involved in the causation of hereditary hemochromatosis. Genetic screening for this condition has been evaluated but is not presently recommended. However, testing for *HFE* mutations in individuals with elevated serum iron concentrations may be useful.

HFE has been shown to be **located in cells in the crypts** of the small intestine, the site of iron absorption. There is evidence that it associates with β_2-**microglobulin,** an association that may be necessary for its stability, intracellular processing, and cell surface expression. The complex interacts with the **transferrin receptor (TfR);** how this leads to excessive storage of iron when *HFE* is altered by mutation is under close study. The mouse homolog of *HFE* has been knocked out, resulting in a potentially useful animal model of hemochromatosis.

A scheme of the likely main events in the causation of hereditary hemochromatosis is set forth in Figure 49–5.

Several **other types** of hemochromatosis have been found to be due to mutations in genes encoding hemojuvelin, hepcidin, tranferrin receptor 2, and ferroportin (Table 49–4).

Secondary hemochromatosis can occur after repeated transfusions (eg, for treatment of sickle cell anemia), excessive oral intake of iron (eg, by African Bantu peoples who consume alcoholic beverages fermented in containers made of iron), or a number of other conditions.

Table 49–5 summarizes laboratory tests useful in the assessment of patients with abnormalities of iron metabolism and Table 49–6 lists many of the proteins involved in iron metabolism.

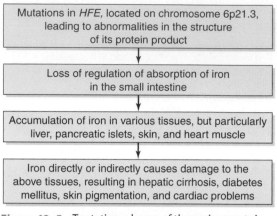

Figure 49–5. Tentative scheme of the main events in causation of hereditary hemochromatosis (MIM 235200). The two principal mutations are CY282Y and H63D (see text). Other mutations in *HFE* have been detected.

Ceruloplasmin Binds Copper, & Low Levels of This Plasma Protein Are Associated with Wilson Disease

Ceruloplasmin (about 160 kDa) is an α_2-globulin. It has a blue color because of its high copper content and carries 90% of the copper present in plasma. Each molecule of ceruloplasmin binds six atoms of copper very tightly, so that the copper is not readily exchangeable. **Albumin** carries the other 10% of the plasma copper but binds the metal less tightly than does ceruloplasmin. Albumin thus donates its copper to tissues more readily than ceruloplasmin and appears to be more important than ceruloplasmin in copper transport in the human body. Ceruloplasmin exhibits a copper-

Table 49–4. Types of hemochromatosis.

Type	Protein Involved
Hemochromatosis, hereditary	HFE
Hemochromatosis, juvenile Type 2A Type 2B	 Hemojuvelin Hepcidin
Hemochromatosis, type 3 (TfR2-related hereditary hemochromatosis)	Transferrin receptor 2
Hemochromatosis, type 4 (Ferroportin-related iron overload)	Ferroportin

Further information on these conditions can be accessed in OMIM.

There is also a neonatal type of hemochromatosis, cause unknown.

Table 49–5. Laboratory tests for assessing patients with disorders of iron metabolism.

- Red blood cell count and estimation of hemoglobin
- Determinations of plasma iron, total iron-binding capacity (TIBC), and % transferrin saturation
- Determination of ferritin in plasma by radioimmunoassay
- Prussian blue stain of tissue sections
- Determination of amount of iron (μg/g) in a tissue biopsy

dependent **oxidase** activity, but its physiologic significance has not been clarified apart from possible involvement in the oxidation of Fe^{2+} in transferrin to Fe^{3+}. The amount of ceruloplasmin in plasma is decreased in liver disease. In particular, low levels of ceruloplasmin are found in **Wilson disease** (hepatolenticular degeneration), a disease due to abnormal metabolism of copper. In order to clarify the description of Wilson disease, we shall first consider **the metabolism of copper** in the human body and then **Menkes disease,** another condition involving abnormal copper metabolism.

Copper Is a Cofactor for Certain Enzymes

Copper is an essential trace element. It is required in the diet because it is the metal cofactor for a variety of enzymes (see Table 49–7). Copper accepts and donates electrons and is involved in reactions involving dismutation, hydroxylation, and oxygenation. However, **excess copper** can cause problems because it can oxidize proteins and lipids, bind to nucleic acids, and enhance the production of free radicals. It is thus important to have mechanisms that will maintain the amount of copper in the body within normal limits. The body of the normal adult contains about 100 mg of copper, located mostly

Table 49–6. Some proteins involved in iron metabolism.

- Ceruloplasmin (ferroxidase activity)
- DMT1
- Ferrireductase (cytochrome b reductase I)
- Ferritin
- Ferroportin
- Heme transporter
- Hemojuvelin
- Hepcidin
- Hephaestin
- HFE
- Iron-responsive element-binding protein
- Transferrin
- Transferrin receptors 1 and 2

Further information on these proteins can be accessed in OMIM.

Table 49–7. Some important enzymes that contain copper.

- Amine oxidase
- Copper-dependent superoxide dismutase
- Cytochrome oxidase
- Tyrosinase

in bone, liver, kidney, and muscle. The daily intake of copper is about 2–4 mg, with about 50% being absorbed in the stomach and upper small intestine and the remainder excreted in the feces. Copper is carried to the liver **bound to albumin,** taken up by liver cells, and part of it is excreted in the bile. Copper also leaves the liver attached to **ceruloplasmin,** which is synthesized in that organ.

The Tissue Levels of Copper & of Certain Other Metals Are Regulated in Part by Metallothioneins

Metallothioneins are a group of small proteins (about 6.5 kDa), found in the cytosol of cells, particularly of liver, kidney, and intestine. They have a high content of cysteine and can **bind copper, zinc, cadmium,** and **mercury.** The SH groups of cysteine are involved in binding the metals. Acute intake (eg, by injection) of copper and of certain other metals increases the amount (induction) of these proteins in tissues, as does administration of certain hormones or cytokines. These proteins may function to store the above metals in a nontoxic form and are involved in their overall metabolism in the body. Sequestration of copper also diminishes the amount of this metal available to generate free radicals.

Menkes Disease Is Due to Mutations in the Gene Encoding a Copper-Binding P-Type ATPase

Menkes disease ("kinky" or "steely" hair disease) is a disorder of copper metabolism. It is X-linked, affects only male infants, involves the nervous system, connective tissue, and vasculature, and is usually fatal in infancy. In 1993, it was reported that the basis of Menkes disease was mutations in the gene (the *ATP7A* gene) for a **copper-binding P-type ATPase** (the ATP7A protein). Interestingly, the enzyme showed structural similarity to certain metal-binding proteins in microorganisms. This ATPase is thought to be responsible for directing the efflux of copper from cells. When altered by mutation, copper is not mobilized normally from the intestine, in which it accumulates, as it does in a variety of other cells and tissues, from which it cannot exit. Despite the accumulation of copper, the activities of

many copper-dependent enzymes are decreased, perhaps because of a defect of its incorporation into the apoenzymes. Normal liver expresses very little of the ATPase, which explains the absence of hepatic involvement in Menkes disease. This work led to the suggestion that liver might contain a different copper-binding ATPase, which could be involved in the causation of Wilson disease. As described below, this turned out to be the case.

Wilson Disease Is Also Due to Mutations in a Gene Encoding a Copper-Binding P-Type ATPase

Wilson disease is a genetic disease in which copper fails to be excreted in the bile and accumulates in liver, brain, kidney, and red blood cells. It can be regarded as an inability to maintain a near-zero copper balance, resulting in **copper toxicosis.** The increase of copper in liver cells appears to inhibit the coupling of copper to apoceruloplasmin and leads to low levels of ceruloplasmin in plasma. As the amount of copper accumulates, patients may develop a hemolytic anemia, chronic liver disease (cirrhosis, hepatitis), and a neurologic syndrome owing to accumulation of copper in the basal ganglia and other centers. A frequent clinical finding is the **Kayser-Fleischer ring.** This is a green or golden pigment ring around the cornea due to deposition of copper in Descemet's membrane. The major laboratory tests of copper metabolism are listed in Table 49–8. If Wilson disease is suspected, a **liver biopsy** should be performed; a value for liver copper of over 250 μg per gram dry weight along with a plasma level of ceruloplasmin of under 20 mg/dL is diagnostic.

The cause of Wilson disease was also revealed in 1993, when it was reported that a variety of mutations in a gene encoding a **copper-binding P-type ATPase** (ATP7B protein) were responsible. The gene (*ATP7B*) is estimated to encode a protein of 1411 amino acids, which is highly homologous to the product of the gene affected in Menkes disease. In a manner not yet fully explained, a nonfunctional ATPase causes defective excretion of copper into the bile, a reduction of incorporation of copper into apoceruloplasmin, and the accumulation of copper in liver and subsequently in other organs such as brain.

Treatment for Wilson disease consists of a diet low in copper along with lifelong administration of **penicillamine,** which chelates copper, is excreted in the urine, and thus depletes the body of the excess of this mineral.

Another condition involving ceruloplasmin is **aceruloplasminemia.** In this genetic disorder, levels of ceruloplasmin are very low and consequently its ferroxidase activity is markedly deficient. This leads to failure of release of iron from cells, and iron accumulates in certain brain cells, hepatocytes, and pancreatic islet cells. Affected individuals show severe neurologic signs and have diabetes mellitus. Use of a chelating agent or administration of plasma or ceruloplasmin concentrate may be beneficial.

Deficiency of α_1-Antiproteinase (α_1-Antitrypsin) Is Associated with Emphysema & One Type of Liver Disease

α_1-**Antiproteinase** (about 52 kDa) was formerly called α_1-**antitrypsin,** and this name is retained here. It is a single-chain protein of 394 amino acids, contains three oligosaccharide chains, and is the major component (> 90%) of the α_1 fraction of human plasma. It is synthesized by hepatocytes and macrophages and is the principal **serine protease inhibitor** (serpin, or Pi) of human plasma. It inhibits trypsin, elastase, and certain other proteases by forming complexes with them. At least 75 **polymorphic forms** occur, many of which can be separated by electrophoresis. The major genotype is MM, and its phenotypic product is PiM. There are two areas of clinical interest concerning α_1-antitrypsin. A deficiency of this protein has a role in certain cases (approximately 5%) of **emphysema.** This occurs mainly in subjects with the **ZZ genotype,** who synthesize PiZ, and also in PiSZ heterozygotes, both of whom secrete considerably less protein than PiMM individuals. Considerably less of this protein is secreted as compared with PiM. When the amount of α_1-antitrypsin is deficient and polymorphonuclear white blood cells increase in the lung (eg, during pneumonia), the affected individual lacks a countercheck to proteolytic damage of the lung by proteases such as elastase (Figure 49–6). It is of considerable interest that a particular **methionine** (residue 358) of α_1-antitrypsin is involved in its binding to proteases. **Smoking** oxidizes this methionine to methionine sulfoxide and thus inactivates it. As a result, affected molecules of α_1-antitrypsin no longer neutralize proteases. This is particularly devastating in patients (eg, PiZZ phenotype) who already have low levels of α_1-antitrypsin. The further diminution in α_1-antitrypsin

Table 49–8. Major laboratory tests used in the investigation of diseases of copper metabolism.[1]

Test	Normal Adult Range
Serum copper	10–22 μmol/L
Ceruloplasmin	200–600 mg/L
Urinary copper	< 1 μmol/24 h
Liver copper	20–50 μg/g dry weight

[1]Based on Gaw A et al: *Clinical Biochemistry.* Churchill Livingstone, 1995. Copyright © 1995 Elsevier Ltd. Reprinted with permission from Elsevier.

A. Active elastase + α_1–AT → Inactive elastase: α_1–AT complex → No proteolysis of lung → No tissue damage

B. Active elastase + ↓ or no α_1–AT → Active elastase → Proteolysis of lung → Tissue damage

Figure 49–6. Scheme illustrating **(A)** normal inactivation of elastase by α_1-antitrypsin and **(B)** situation in which the amount of α_1-antitrypsin is substantially reduced, resulting in proteolysis by elastase and leading to tissue damage.

brought about by smoking results in increased proteolytic destruction of lung tissue, accelerating the development of emphysema. **Intravenous administration of α_1-antitrypsin** (augmentation therapy) has been used as an adjunct in the treatment of patients with emphysema due to α_1-antitrypsin deficiency. Attempts are being made, using the techniques of protein engineering, to replace methionine 358 by another residue that would not be subject to oxidation. The resulting "mutant" α_1-antitrypsin would thus afford protection against proteases for a much longer period of time than would native α_1-antitrypsin. Attempts are also being made to develop **gene therapy** for this condition. One approach is to use a modified adenovirus (a pathogen of the respiratory tract) into which the gene for α_1-antitrypsin has been inserted. The virus would then be introduced into the respiratory tract (eg, by an aerosol). The hope is that pulmonary epithelial cells would express the gene and secrete α_1-antitrypsin locally. Experiments in animals have indicated the feasibility of this approach.

Deficiency of α_1-antitrypsin is also implicated in one type of **liver disease** (α_1-antitrypsin deficiency liver disease). In this condition, molecules of the **ZZ phenotype** accumulate and aggregate in the cisternae of the endoplasmic reticulum of hepatocytes. Aggregation is due to formation of **polymers** of mutant α_1-antitrypsin, the polymers forming via a strong interaction between a specific loop in one molecule and a prominent β-pleated sheet in another (loop-sheet polymerization). By mechanisms that are not understood, **hepatitis** results with consequent **cirrhosis** (accumulation of massive amounts of collagen, resulting in fibrosis). It is possible that administration of a synthetic peptide resembling the loop sequence could inhibit loop-sheet polymerization. Diseases such as α_1-antitrypsin deficiency, in which cellular pathology is primarily caused by the presence of aggregates of aberrant forms of individual proteins, have been named **conformational diseases.** Most appear to be due to the formation by conformationally unstable proteins of β sheets, which in turn leads to formation of aggregates. Other members of this group of conditions include Alzheimer disease, Parkinson disease, and Huntington disease.

At present, severe α_1-antitrypsin deficiency liver disease can be successfully treated by **liver transplantation.** In the future, introduction of the gene for normal α_1-antitrypsin into hepatocytes may become possible, but this would not stop production of the PiZ protein. Figure 49–7 is a scheme of the causation of this disease.

α_2-Macroglobulin Neutralizes Many Proteases & Targets Certain Cytokines to Tissues

α_2-Macroglobulin is a large plasma glycoprotein (720 kDa) made up of four identical subunits of 180 kDa. It comprises 8–10% of the total plasma protein in humans. Approximately 10% of the **zinc** in plasma is transported by α_2-macroglobulin, the remainder being transported by albumin. The protein is synthesized by a variety of cell types, including monocytes, hepatocytes, and astrocytes. It is the major member of a group of plasma proteins that include complement proteins C3 and C4. These proteins contain a unique **internal cyclic thiol ester bond** (formed between a cysteine and a glutamine residue) and for this reason have been designated as the **thiol ester plasma protein family**.

α_2-Macroglobulin binds many proteinases and is thus an important **panproteinase inhibitor.** The α_2-macroglobulin-proteinase complexes are rapidly cleared from the plasma by a receptor located on many cell types. In addition, α_2-macroglobulin binds many **cytokines** (platelet-derived growth factor, transforming

GAG to AAG mutation in exon 5 of gene for α_1-AT on chromosome 14

↓

Results in Glu^{342} to Lys^{342} substitution in α_1-AT, causing formation of PiZZ

↓

PiZZ accumulates in cisternae of endoplasmic reticulum and aggregates via loop-sheet polymerization

↓

Leads to hepatitis (mechanism unknown) and cirrhosis in ~10% of ZZ homozygotes

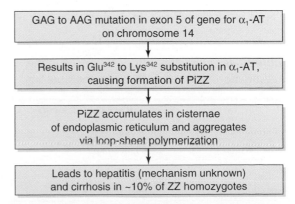

Figure 49–7. Scheme of causation of α_1-antitrypsin-deficiency liver disease. The mutation shown causes formation of PiZZ (MIM 107400). (α_1-AT, α_1-antitrypsin.)

growth factor-β, etc) and appears to be involved in targeting them toward particular tissues or cells. Once taken up by cells, the cytokines can dissociate from α_2-macroglobulin and subsequently exert a variety of effects on cell growth and function. The binding of proteinases and cytokines by α_2-macroglobulin involves different mechanisms that will not be considered here.

Amyloidosis Occurs by the Deposition of Fragments of Various Plasma Proteins in Tissues

Amyloidosis is the accumulation of various insoluble fibrillar proteins between the cells of tissues to an extent that affects function. The fibrils generally represent proteolytic fragments of various plasma proteins and possess a **β-pleated sheet structure.** The term "amyloidosis" is a misnomer, as it was originally thought that the fibrils were starch-like in nature. Among the most common **precursor proteins** are immunoglobulin light chains (see below), amyloid-associated protein derived from serum amyloid-associated protein (a plasma glycoprotein), and transthyretin (Table 49–2). The precursor proteins in plasma are generally either **increased in amount** (eg, immunoglobulin light chains in multiple myeloma or β_2-microglobulin in patients being maintained on chronic dialysis) or **mutant forms** (eg, of transthyretin in familial amyloidotic neuropathies). The precise factors that determine the deposition of proteolytic fragments in tissues await elucidation. Other proteins have been found in amyloid fibrils, such as calcitonin and amyloid β protein (not derived from a plasma protein) in Alzheimer disease; a total of about 15 different proteins have been found. All fibrils have a **P component** associated with them, which is derived from **serum amyloid P component,** a plasma protein closely related to C-reactive protein. Tissue sections containing amyloid fibrils interact with Congo red stain and display striking green birefringence when viewed by polarizing microscopy. Deposition of amyloid occurs in patients with a variety of disorders; treatment of the underlying disorder should be provided if possible. Several **small ligands** bind avidly to amyloid fibrils. For example, iodinated anthracycline binds specifically and with high affinity to all natural amyloid fibrils and promotes their disaggregation in vitro. It is possible that such compounds may prove useful in the treatment of amyloidosis.

PLASMA IMMUNOGLOBULINS PLAY A MAJOR ROLE IN THE BODY'S DEFENSE MECHANISMS

The immune system of the body consists of two major components: **B lymphocytes** and **T lymphocytes.** The B lymphocytes are mainly derived from bone marrow cells in higher animals and from the bursa of Fabricius in birds. The T lymphocytes are of thymic origin. The **B cells** are responsible for the synthesis of circulating, humoral antibodies, also known as **immunoglobulins.** The **T cells** are involved in a variety of important **cell-mediated immunologic processes** such as graft rejection, hypersensitivity reactions, and defense against malignant cells and many viruses. This section considers only the plasma immunoglobulins, which are synthesized mainly in **plasma cells.** These are specialized cells of B cell lineage that synthesize and secrete immunoglobulins into the plasma in response to exposure to a variety of **antigens.**

All Immunoglobulins Contain a Minimum of Two Light & Two Heavy Chains

Immunoglobulins contain a minimum of two identical light (L) chains (23 kDa) and two identical heavy (H) chains (53–75 kDa), held together as a tetramer (L_2H_2) by disulfide bonds. The structure of IgG is shown in Figure 49–8; it is **Y-shaped,** with binding of antigen occurring at both tips of the Y. Each chain can be divided conceptually into specific domains, or regions, that have structural and functional significance. The half of the light (L) chain toward the carboxyl terminal is referred to as the **constant region (C_L),** while the amino terminal half is the **variable region** of the light chain (V_L). Approximately one-quarter of the heavy (H) chain at the amino terminals is referred to as its **variable region** (V_H), and the other three-quarters of the heavy chain are referred to as the **constant regions (C_H1, C_H2, C_H3)** of that H chain. The portion of the immunoglobulin molecule that binds the specific antigen is formed by the amino terminal portions (variable regions) of both the H and L chains—ie, the V_H and V_L domains. The domains of the protein chains consist of two sheets of antiparallel distinct stretches of amino acids that bind antigen.

As depicted in Figure 49–8, digestion of an immunoglobulin by the enzyme **papain** produces two antigen-binding fragments **(Fab)** and one crystallizable fragment **(Fc),** which is responsible for functions of immunoglobulins other than direct binding of antigens. Because there are two Fab regions, IgG molecules bind two molecules of antigen and are termed **divalent.** The site on the antigen to which an antibody binds is termed an **antigenic determinant,** or **epitope.** The area in which papain cleaves the immunoglobulin molecule—ie, the region between the C_H1 and C_H2 domains—is referred to as the **"hinge region."** The hinge region confers **flexibility** and allows both Fab arms to move independently, thus helping them to bind to antigenic sites that may be variable distances apart (eg, on bacterial surfaces). Fc and hinge regions differ in the different

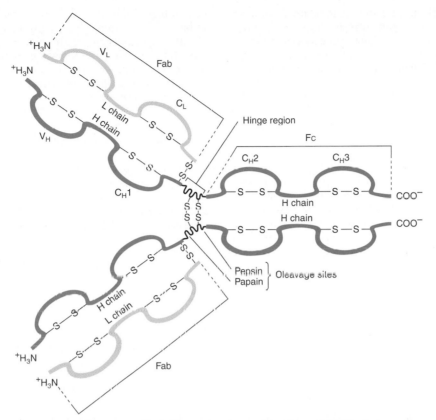

Figure 49–8. Structure of IgG. The molecule consists of two light (L) chains and two heavy (H) chains. Each light chain consists of a variable (V_L) and a constant (C_L) region. Each heavy chain consists of a variable region (V_H) and a constant region that is divided into three domains (C_H1, C_H2, and C_H3). The C_H2 domain contains the complement-binding site and the C_H3 domain contains a site that attaches to receptors on neutrophils and macrophages. The antigen-binding site is formed by the hypervariable regions of both the light and heavy chains, which are located in the variable regions of these chains (see Figure 49–9). The light and heavy chains are linked by disulfide bonds, and the heavy chains are also linked to each other by disulfide bonds. (Reproduced, with permission, from Parslow TG et al [editors]: *Medical Immunology*, 10th ed. McGraw-Hill, 2001.)

classes of antibodies, but the overall model of antibody structure for each class is similar to that shown in Figure 49–8 for IgG.

All Light Chains Are Either Kappa or Lambda in Type

There are two general types of light chains, **kappa (κ)** and **lambda (λ),** which can be distinguished on the basis of structural differences in their C_L regions. A given immunoglobulin molecule always contains two κ or two λ light chains—never a mixture of κ and λ. In humans, the κ chains are more frequent than λ chains in immunoglobulin molecules.

The Five Types of Heavy Chain Determine Immunoglobulin Class

Five classes of H chain have been found in humans (Table 49–9), distinguished by differences in their C_H **regions.** They are designated γ, α, μ δ, and ε. The μ and ε chains each have four C_H domains rather than the usual three. The type of H chain determines the class of immunoglobulin and thus its

Table 49–9. Properties of human immunoglobulins.[1]

Property	IgG	IgA	IgM	IgD	IgE
Percentage of total immunoglobulin in serum (approximate)	75	15	9	0.2	0.004
Serum concentration (mg/dL) (approximate)	1000	200	120	3	0.05
Sedimentation coefficient	7S	7S or 11S[2]	19S	7S	8S
Molecular weight ($\times$ 1000)	150	170 or 400[2]	900	180	190
Structure	Monomer	Monomer or dimer	Monomer or dimer	Monomer	Monomer
H-chain symbol	γ	α	μ	δ	ϵ
Complement fixation	+	—	+	—	—
Transplacental passage	+	—	—	?	—
Mediation of allergic responses	—	—	—	—	+
Found in secretions	—	+	—	—	—
Opsonization	+	—	—[3]	—	—
Antigen receptor on B cell	—	—	+	?	—
Polymeric form contains J chain	—	+	+	—	—

[1]Reproduced, with permission, from Levinson W, Jawetz E: *Medical Microbiology and Immunology*, 7th ed. McGraw-Hill, 2002.
[2]The 11S form is found in secretions (eg, saliva, milk, tears) and fluids of the respiratory, intestinal, and genital tracts.
[3]IgM opsonizes indirectly by activating complement. This produces C3b, which is an opsonin.

effector function. There are thus five immunoglobulin classes: **IgG, IgA, IgM, IgD,** and **IgE.** The biologic functions of these five classes are summarized in Table 49–10.

No Two Variable Regions Are Identical

The **variable regions** of immunoglobulin molecules consist of the V_L and V_H domains and are quite heterogeneous. In fact, no two variable regions from different humans have been found to have identical amino acid sequences. However, amino acid analyses have shown that the variable regions are comprised of **relatively invariable regions** and other **hypervariable regions** (Figure 49–9). L chains have three hypervariable regions (in V_L) and H chains have four (in V_H). These **hypervariable regions** comprise the **antigen-binding site** (located at the tips of the Y shown in Figure 49–8) and dictate the amazing specificity of antibodies. For this reason, hypervariable regions are also termed **complementarity-determining regions (CDRs).** About five to ten amino acids in each hypervariable region (CDR) contribute to the antigen-binding site. CDRs are located on small loops of the variable domains, the surrounding polypeptide regions between the hypervariable regions being termed **framework regions.** CDRs from both V_H and V_L domains, brought together by folding of the polypeptide chains in which they are contained, form a single hypervariable surface comprising the **antigen-binding site.** Various combinations of H and L chain CDRs can give rise to many antibodies of different specificities, a feature that contributes to the tremendous diversity of antibody molecules and is termed **combinatorial diversity.** Large antigens interact with all of the CDRs of an antibody, whereas small ligands may interact with only one or a few CDRs that form a pocket or groove in the antibody molecule. The essence of antigen-antibody interactions is **mutual complementarity** between the surfaces of CDRs and epitopes. The interactions between antibodies and antigens involve **noncovalent forces and bonds** (electrostatic and van der Waals forces and hydrogen and hydrophobic bonds).

The Constant Regions Determine Class-Specific Effector Functions

The **constant regions** of the immunoglobulin molecules, particularly the C_H2 and C_H3 (and C_H4 of IgM and IgE), which constitute the Fc fragment, are responsible for the **class-specific effector functions**

Table 49–10. Major functions of immunoglobulins.[1]

Immunoglobulin	Major Functions
IgG	Main antibody in the secondary response. Opsonizes bacteria, making them easier to phagocytose. Fixes complement, which enhances bacterial killing. Neutralizes bacterial toxins and viruses. Crosses the placenta.
IgA	Secretory IgA prevents attachment of bacteria and viruses to mucous membranes. Does not fix complement.
IgM	Produced in the primary response to an antigen. Fixes complement. Does not cross the placenta. Antigen receptor on the surface of B cells.
IgD	Uncertain. Found on the surface of many B cells as well as in serum.
IgE	Mediates immediate hypersensitivity by causing release of mediators from mast cells and basophils upon exposure to antigen (allergen). Defends against worm infections by causing release of enzymes from eosinophils. Does not fix complement. Main host defense against helminthic infections.

[1]Reproduced, with permission, from Levinson W, Jawetz E: *Medical Microbiology and Immunology*, 7th ed. McGraw-Hill, 2002.

of the different immunoglobulin molecules (Table 49–9, bottom part), eg, complement fixation or transplacental passage.

Some immunoglobulins such as immune IgG exist only in the basic tetrameric structure, while others such as IgA and IgM can exist as higher order polymers of two, three (IgA), or five (IgM) tetrameric units (Figure 49–10).

The L chains and H chains are synthesized as separate molecules and are subsequently assembled within the B cell or plasma cell into mature immunoglobulin molecules, all of which are **glycoproteins.**

Both Light & Heavy Chains Are Products of Multiple Genes

Each immunoglobulin **light chain** is the product of at least three separate structural genes: a **variable region** (V_L) gene, a **joining region** (*J*) gene (bearing no relationship to the J chain of IgA or IgM), and a **constant region** (C_L) gene. Each **heavy chain** is the product of at least **four** different genes: a **variable**

region (V_H) gene, a **diversity region** (*D*) gene, a **joining region** (*J*) gene, and a **constant region** (C_H) gene. Thus, the "one gene, one protein" concept is not valid. The molecular mechanisms responsible for the generation of the single immunoglobulin chains from multiple structural genes are discussed in Chapters 35 and 38.

Antibody Diversity Depends on Gene Rearrangements

Each person is capable of generating antibodies directed against perhaps 1 million different antigens. The generation of such immense **antibody diversity** depends upon a number of factors including the existence of multiple gene segments (V, C, J, and D segments), their recombinations (see Chapters 35 and 38), the combinations of different L and H chains, a high frequency of somatic mutations in immunoglobulin genes, and **junctional diversity.** The latter reflects the addition or deletion of a random number of nucleotides when certain gene segments are joined together, and

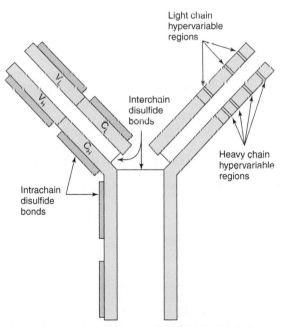

Figure 49–9. Schematic model of an IgG molecule showing approximate positions of the hypervariable regions in heavy and light chains. The antigen-binding site is formed by these hypervariable regions. The hypervariable regions are also called complementarity-determining regions (CDRs). (Modified and reproduced, with permission, from Parslow TG et al [editors]: *Medical Immunology*, 10th ed. McGraw-Hill, 2001.)

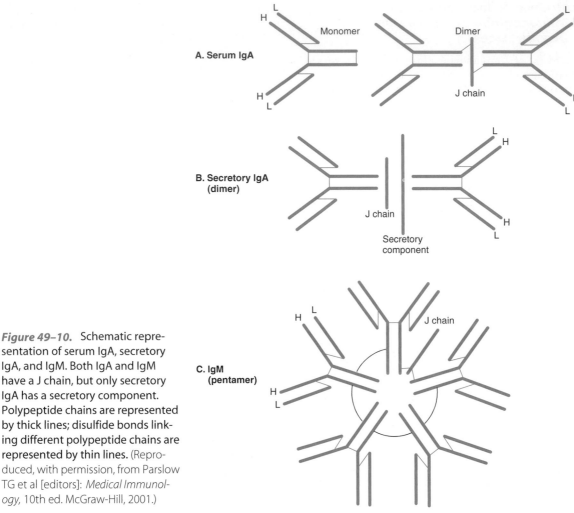

A. Serum IgA

Monomer

Dimer

H · L

J chain

B. Secretory IgA (dimer)

J chain

Secretory component

C. IgM (pentamer)

J chain

Figure 49–10. Schematic representation of serum IgA, secretory IgA, and IgM. Both IgA and IgM have a J chain, but only secretory IgA has a secretory component. Polypeptide chains are represented by thick lines; disulfide bonds linking different polypeptide chains are represented by thin lines. (Reproduced, with permission, from Parslow TG et al [editors]: *Medical Immunology*, 10th ed. McGraw-Hill, 2001.)

introduces an additional degree of diversity. Thus, the above factors ensure that **a vast number of antibodies** can be synthesized from several hundred gene segments.

Class (Isotype) Switching Occurs during Immune Responses

In most humoral immune responses, antibodies with identical specificity but of different classes are generated in a specific chronologic order in response to the immunogen (immunizing antigen). For instance, antibodies of the IgM class normally precede molecules of the IgG class. The switch from one class to another is designated **"class or isotype switching,"** and its molecular basis has been investigated extensively. A single type of immunoglobulin light chain can combine with an antigen-specific μ chain to generate a specific IgM

molecule. Subsequently, the same antigen-specific light chain combines with a γ chain with an identical V_H region to generate an IgG molecule with antigen specificity identical to that of the original IgM molecule. The same light chain can also combine with an α heavy chain, again containing the identical V_H region, to form an IgA molecule with identical antigen specificity. These three classes (IgM, IgG, and IgA) of immunoglobulin molecules against the same antigen have **identical variable domains** of both their light (V_L) chains and heavy (V_H) chains and are said to share an **idiotype.** (Idiotypes are the antigenic determinants formed by the specific amino acids in the hypervariable regions.) The **different classes** of these three immunoglobulins (called **isotypes**) are thus determined by their **different C_H regions,** which are combined with the same antigen-specific V_H regions.

Both Over- & Underproduction of Immunoglobulins May Result in Disease States

Disorders of immunoglobulins include **increased production** of specific classes of immunoglobulins or even specific immunoglobulin molecules, the latter by clonal tumors of plasma cells called myelomas. **Multiple myeloma** is a neoplastic condition; electrophoresis of serum or urine will usually reveal a large increase of one particular immunoglobulin or one particular light chain (the latter termed a Bence Jones protein). **Decreased production** may be restricted to a single class of immunoglobulin molecules (eg, IgA or IgG) or may involve underproduction of all classes of immunoglobulins (IgA, IgD, IgE, IgG, and IgM). A severe reduction in synthesis of an immunoglobulin class due to a genetic abnormality can result in a serious immunodeficiency disease—eg, **agammaglobulinemia,** in which production of IgG is markedly affected—because of impairment of the body's defense against microorganisms.

Hybridomas Provide Long-Term Sources of Highly Useful Monoclonal Antibodies

When an antigen is injected into an animal, the resulting antibodies are **polyclonal,** being synthesized by a mixture of B cells. Polyclonal antibodies are directed against a number of different sites (epitopes or determinants) on the antigen and thus are **not monospecific.** However, by means of a method developed by Kohler and Milstein, large amounts of a single monoclonal antibody specific for one epitope can be obtained.

The method involves **cell fusion,** and the resulting permanent cell line is called a **hybridoma.** Typically, B cells are obtained from the spleen of a mouse (or other suitable animal) previously injected with an antigen or mixture of antigens (eg, foreign cells). The B cells are mixed with mouse **myeloma cells** and exposed to polyethylene glycol, which causes cell fusion. A summary of the principles involved in generating hybridoma cells is given in Figure 49–11. Under the conditions used, only the hybridoma cells multiply in cell culture. This involves plating the hybrid cells into hypoxanthine-aminopterin-thymidine (HAT)-containing medium at a concentration such that each dish contains approximately one cell. Thus, a **clone** of hybridoma cells multiplies in each dish. The culture medium is harvested and screened for antibodies that react with the original antigen or antigens. If the immunogen is a mixture of many antigens (eg, a cell membrane preparation), an individual culture dish will contain a clone of hybridoma cells synthesizing a monoclonal antibody to one specific antigenic determinant of the mixture. By harvesting the media from many culture dishes, a battery

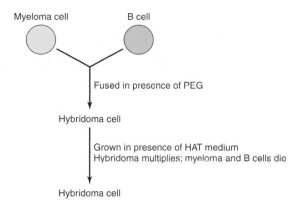

Figure 49–11. Scheme of production of a hybridoma cell. The myeloma cells are immortalized, do not produce antibody, and are HGPRT⁻ (rendering the salvage pathway of purine synthesis [Chapter 33] inactive). The B cells are not immortalized, each produces a specific antibody, and they are HGPRT⁺. Polyethylene glycol (PEG) stimulates cell fusion. The resulting hybridoma cells are immortalized (via the parental myeloma cells), produce antibody, and are HGPRT⁺ (both latter properties gained from the parental B cells). The B cells will die in the medium because they are not immortalized. In the presence of HAT, the myeloma cells will also die, since the aminopterin in HAT suppresses purine synthesis by the de novo pathway by inhibiting reutilization of tetrahydrofolate (Chapter 33). However, the hybridoma cells will survive, grow (because they are HGPRT⁺), and—if cloned—produce monoclonal antibody. (HAT, hypoxanthine, aminopterin, and thymidine; HGPRT, hypoxanthine-guanine phosphoribosyl transferase.)

of monoclonal antibodies can be obtained, many of which are specific for individual components of the immunogenic mixture. The hybridoma cells can be frozen and stored and subsequently thawed when more of the antibody is required; this ensures its long-term supply. The hybridoma cells can also be grown in the abdomen of mice, providing relatively large supplies of antibodies.

Because of their **specificity,** monoclonal antibodies have become **useful reagents** in many areas of biology and medicine. For example, they can be used to measure the amounts of many individual proteins (eg, plasma proteins), to determine the nature of infectious agents (eg, types of bacteria), and to subclassify both normal (eg, lymphocytes) and tumor cells (eg, leukemic cells). In addition, they are being used to direct therapeutic agents to tumor cells and also to accelerate removal of drugs from the circulation when they reach toxic levels (eg, digoxin).

The Complement System Comprises About 20 Plasma Proteins & Is Involved in Cell Lysis, Inflammation, & Other Processes

Plasma contains approximately 20 proteins that are members of the complement system. This system was discovered when it was observed that addition of fresh serum containing antibodies directed to a bacterium caused its lysis. Unlike antibodies, the factor was labile when heated at 56 °C. Subsequent work has resolved the proteins of the system and how they function; most have been cloned and sequenced. The major protein components are designated C1–9, with C9 associated with the C5–8 complex (together constituting the **membrane attack complex**) being involved in generating a lipid-soluble pore in the cell membrane that causes **osmotic lysis.**

The details of this system are relatively complex, and a textbook of immunology should be consulted. The basic concept is that the normally inactive proteins of the system, when triggered by a stimulus, become activated by proteolysis and interact in a specific sequence with one or more of the other proteins of the system. This results in cell lysis and generation of **peptide or polypeptide fragments** that are involved in various aspects of inflammation (chemotaxis, phagocytosis, etc). The system has other functions, such as clearance of antigen-antibody complexes from the circulation. Activation of the complement system is triggered by one of two routes, called the **classic** and the **alternative pathways.** The first involves interaction of C1 with antigen-antibody complexes, and the second (not involving antibody) involves direct interaction of bacterial cell surfaces or polysaccharides with a component designated C3b.

The complement system resembles blood coagulation (Chapter 50) in that it involves both conversion of inactive precursors to active products by proteases and a cascade with amplification.

SUMMARY

- Plasma contains many proteins with a variety of functions. Most are synthesized in the liver and are glycosylated.
- Albumin, which is not glycosylated, is the major protein and is the principal determinant of intravascular osmotic pressure; it also binds many ligands, such as drugs and bilirubin.
- Haptoglobin binds extracorpuscular hemoglobin, prevents its loss into the kidney and urine, and hence preserves its iron for reutilization.
- Transferrin binds iron, transporting it to sites where it is required. Ferritin provides an intracellular store of iron. Iron deficiency anemia is a very prevalent disorder. Hereditary hemochromatosis has been shown to be due to mutations in *HFE,* a gene encoding the protein HFE, which appears to play an important role in absorption of iron. Other types of hemochromatosis have been shown to be due to mutations in genes encoding hemojuvelin, hepcidin, transferrin receptor 2, and ferroportin.
- Ceruloplasmin contains substantial amounts of copper, but albumin appears to be more important with regard to its transport. Both Wilson disease and Menkes disease, which reflect abnormalities of copper metabolism, have been found to be due to mutations in genes encoding copper-binding P-type ATPases.
- α_1-Antitrypsin is the major serine protease inhibitor of plasma, in particular inhibiting the elastase of neutrophils. Genetic deficiency of this protein is a cause of emphysema and can also lead to liver disease.
- α_2-Macroglobulin is a major plasma protein that neutralizes many proteases and targets certain cytokines to specific organs.
- Immunoglobulins play a key role in the defense mechanisms of the body, as do proteins of the complement system. Some of the principal features of these proteins are described.

REFERENCES

Adamson JW: Iron deficiency and hypoproliferative anemias, Chapter 90, p. 586. In: Kasper DL et al (editors): *Harrison's Principles of Internal Medicine,* 16th ed. McGraw-Hill, 2005.

Adamson JW, Longo DL: Anemia and polycythemia, Chapter 52, p. 329. In: Kasper DL et al (editors): *Harrison's Principles of Internal Medicine,* 16th ed. McGraw-Hill, 2005.

Beutler E: "Pumping" iron: The proteins. Science 2004;306:2051.

Fleming RE, Bacon BR: Orchestration of iron homeostasis. N Engl J Med 2005;352:1741.

Janeway CA Jr et al: *Immunobiology,* 6th ed. Garland Science Publishing, 2005.

Johnson AM et al: Proteins. In: Burtis CA, Ashwood EA (editors): *Tietz Fundamentals of Clinical Chemistry,* 5th ed. Saunders, 2001.

Kelly JW: Attacking amyloid. N Engl J Med 2005;352:722.

Levinson W, Jawetz E: *Medical Microbiology and Immunology,* 6th ed. Appleton & Lange, 2000.

Merlini G, Belloti V: Molecular mechanisms of amyloidosis. N Engl J Med 2003;349:583.

Parslow TG et al (editors): *Medical Immunology,* 10th ed. Appleton & Lange, 2001.

Pietrangelo A: Hereditary hemochromatosis: A new look at an old disease. N Engl J Med 2004;350:2383.

Tall AR: C-reactive protein reassessed. N Engl J Med 2004;350:1450.

The SAFE Study Investigators: A comparison of albumin and saline for fluid resuscitation in the intensive care unit. N Engl J Med 2004;350:2247.

Hemostasis & Thrombosis

50

Margaret L. Rand, PhD, & Robert K. Murray, MD, PhD

BIOMEDICAL IMPORTANCE

Basic aspects of the proteins of the blood coagulation system and of fibrinolysis are described in this chapter. Some fundamental aspects of platelet biology are also presented. Hemorrhagic and thrombotic states can cause serious medical emergencies, and thromboses in the coronary and cerebral arteries are major causes of death in many parts of the world. Rational management of these conditions requires a clear understanding of the bases of blood coagulation, fibrinolysis, and platelet aggregation.

HEMOSTASIS & THROMBOSIS HAVE THREE COMMON PHASES

Hemostasis is the cessation of bleeding from a cut or severed vessel, whereas thrombosis occurs when the endothelium lining blood vessels is damaged or removed (eg, upon rupture of an atherosclerotic plaque). These processes encompass blood clotting (coagulation) and involve blood vessels, platelet aggregation, and plasma proteins that cause formation or dissolution of platelet aggregates.

In hemostasis, there is initial vasoconstriction of the injured vessel, causing diminished blood flow distal to the injury. Then hemostasis and thrombosis share three phases:

(1) Formation of a loose and temporary platelet aggregate at the site of injury. Platelets bind to collagen at the site of vessel wall injury, and release ADP and form thromboxane A_2, which activate other platelets flowing by the vicinity of the injury. (The mechanism of platelet activation is described below.) Thrombin, formed during coagulation at the same site, causes further platelet activation. Upon activation, platelets change shape and, in the presence of fibrinogen, aggregate to form the hemostatic plug (in hemostasis) or thrombus (in thrombosis).

(2) Formation of a fibrin mesh that binds to the platelet aggregate, forming a more stable hemostatic plug or thrombus.

(3) Partial or complete dissolution of the hemostatic plug or thrombus by plasmin.

There Are Three Types of Thrombi

Three types of thrombi or clots are distinguished. All three contain **fibrin** in various proportions.

(1) The **white** thrombus is composed of platelets and fibrin and is relatively poor in erythrocytes. It forms at the site of an injury or abnormal vessel wall, particularly in areas where blood flow is rapid (arteries).

(2) The **red** thrombus consists primarily of red cells and fibrin. It morphologically resembles the clot formed in a test tube and may form in vivo in areas of retarded blood flow or stasis (eg, veins) with or without vascular injury, or it may form at a site of injury or in an abnormal vessel in conjunction with an initiating platelet plug.

(3) A third type is a disseminated **fibrin deposit** in very small blood vessels or capillaries.

We shall first describe the coagulation pathway leading to the formation of fibrin. Then we shall briefly describe some aspects of the involvement of platelets and blood vessel walls in the overall process. This separation of clotting factors and platelets is artificial, since both play intimate and often mutually interdependent roles in hemostasis and thrombosis, but it facilitates description of the overall processes involved.

Both Intrinsic & Extrinsic Pathways Result in the Formation of Fibrin

Two pathways lead to fibrin clot formation: the intrinsic and the extrinsic pathways. These pathways are not independent, as previously thought. However, this artificial distinction is retained in the following text to facilitate their description.

Initiation of the fibrin clot in response to tissue injury is carried out by the extrinsic pathway. The intrinsic pathway is activated by negatively charged surfaces in vitro, eg, glass. Both pathways lead to activation of prothrombin to thrombin and the thrombin-catalyzed cleavage of fibrinogen to form the fibrin clot. The pathways are complex and involve many different proteins (Figure 50–1 and Table 50–1). In general, as shown in Table 50–2, these proteins can be

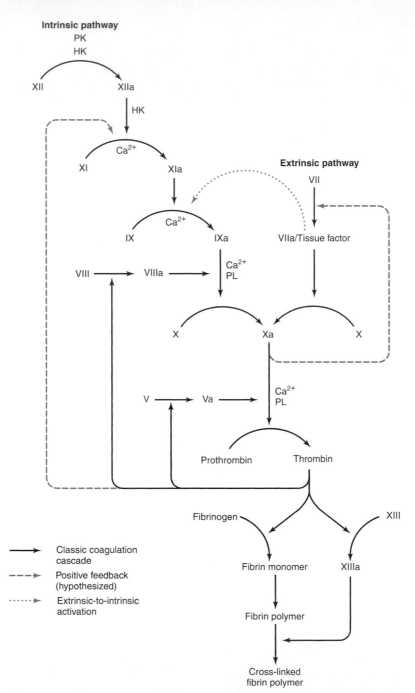

Figure 50–1. The pathways of blood coagulation. The intrinsic and extrinsic pathways are indicated. The pathways converge in the activation of factor Xa and culminate in the formation of cross-linked fibrin. Complexes of tissue factor and factor VIIa activate not only factor X (in the extrinsic pathway) but also factor IX in the intrinsic pathway (dotted arrow). In addition, thrombin and factor Xa feedback activate at the two sites indicated (dashed arrows). In vivo, blood coagulation is initiated by formation of the tissue factor-factor VIIa complex of the extrinsic pathway. (PK, prekallikrein; HK, HMW kininogen; PL, phospholipids.) (Reproduced, with permission, from Roberts HR, Lozier JN: New perspectives on the coagulation cascade. Hosp Pract [Off Ed] 1992 Jan;27:97.)

Table 50–1. Numerical system for nomenclature of blood clotting factors. The numbers indicate the order in which the factors have been discovered and bear no relationship to the order in which they act.

Factor	Common Name
I	Fibrinogen } These factors are usually referred
II	Prothrombin } to by their common names.
III	Tissue factor } These factors are usually not re-
IV	Ca^{2+} } ferred to as coagulation factors.
V	Proaccelerin, labile factor, accelerator (Ac-) globulin
VII[1]	Proconvertin, serum prothrombin conversion accelerator (SPCA), cothromboplastin
VIII	Antihemophilic factor A, antihemophilic globulin (AHG)
IX	Antihemophilic factor B, Christmas factor, plasma thromboplastin component (PTC)
X	Stuart-Prower factor
XI	Plasma thromboplastin antecedent (PTA)
XII	Hageman factor
XIII	Fibrin stabilizing factor (FSF), fibrinoligase

[1]There is no factor VI.

classified into five types: (1) zymogens of serine-dependent proteases, which become activated during the process of coagulation; (2) cofactors; (3) fibrinogen; (4) a transglutaminase, which stabilizes the fibrin clot; and (5) regulatory and other proteins.

The Intrinsic Pathway Leads to Activation of Factor X

The intrinsic pathway (Figure 50–1) involves factors XII, XI, IX, VIII, and X as well as prekallikrein, high-molecular-weight (HMW) kininogen, Ca^{2+}, and phospholipid. It results in the production of factor Xa (by convention, activated clotting factors are referred to by use of the suffix a).

This pathway commences with the "contact phase" in which prekallikrein, HMW kininogen, factor XII, and factor XI are exposed to a negatively charged activating surface. Kaolin can be used for in vitro tests as an initiator of the intrinsic pathway. When the components of the contact phase assemble on the activating surface, factor XII is activated to factor XIIa upon proteolysis by kallikrein. This factor XIIa, generated by kallikrein, attacks prekallikrein to generate more kallikrein, setting up a reciprocal activation. Factor XIIa, once formed, activates factor XI to XIa and also releases bradykinin (a nonapeptide with potent vasodilator action) from HMW kininogen.

Table 50–2. The functions of the proteins involved in blood coagulation.

Zymogens of serine proteases	
Factor XII	Binds to negatively charged surface, eg, kaolin, glass; activated by high-MW kininogen and kallikrein
Factor XI	Activated by factor XIIa
Factor IX	Activated by factor XIa in presence of Ca^{2+}
Factor VII	Activated thrombin in presence of Ca^{2+}
Factor X	Activated on surface of activated platelets by tenase complex (Ca^{2+}, factors VIIIa and IXa) and by factor VIIa in presence of tissue factor and Ca^{2+}
Factor II	Activated on surface of activated platelets by prothrombinase complex (Ca^{2+}, factors Va and Xa)
	[Factors II, VII, IX, and X are Gla-containing zymogens] (Gla = γ-carboxyglutamate)
Cofactors	
Factor VIII	Activated by thrombin; factor VIIIa is a cofactor in the activation of factor X by factor IXa
Factor V	Activated by thrombin; factor Va is a cofactor in the activation of prothrombin by factor Xa
Tissue factor (factor III)	A glycoprotein expressed on the surface of stimulated endothelial cells and monocytes to act as a cofactor for factor VIIa
Fibrinogen	
Factor I	Cleaved by thrombin to form fibrin clot
Thiol-dependent transglutaminase	
Factor XIII	Activated by thrombin in presence of Ca^{2+}; stabilizes fibrin clot by covalent cross-linking
Regulatory and other proteins	
Protein C	Activated to protein Ca by thrombin bound to thrombomodulin; then degrades factors VIIIa and Va
Protein S	Acts as a cofactor of protein C; both proteins contain Gla (γ-carboxyglutamate) residues
Thrombo-modulin	Protein on the surface of endothelial cells; binds thrombin, which then activates protein C

Factor XIa in the presence of Ca^{2+} activates factor IX (55 kDa, a zymogen containing vitamin K-dependent γ-carboxyglutamate [Gla] residues; see Chapter 44), to the serine protease, factor IXa. This in turn cleaves an Arg-Ile bond in factor X (56 kDa) to produce the two-chain serine protease, factor Xa. This latter reaction requires the assembly of components, called **the tenase complex,**

on a membrane surface: Ca^{2+} and factor VIIIa, as well as factors IXa and X. It should be noted that in all reactions involving the Gla-containing zymogens (factors II, VII, IX, and X), the Gla residues in the amino terminal regions of the molecules serve as high-affinity binding sites for Ca^{2+}. Factor VIII (330 kDa), a glycoprotein, is not a protease precursor but a cofactor that serves as a receptor for factors IXa and X on the platelet surface. Factor VIII is activated by minute quantities of thrombin to form factor VIIIa, which is in turn inactivated upon further cleavage by thrombin.

The Extrinsic Pathway Also Leads to Activation of Factor X But by a Different Mechanism

Factor Xa occurs at the site where the intrinsic and extrinsic pathways converge (Figure 50–1). The extrinsic pathway involves tissue factor, factors VII and X, and Ca^{2+} and results in the production of factor Xa. It is initiated at the site of tissue injury with the exposure of **tissue factor** (Figure 50–1) on activated endothelial cells and monocytes. Tissue factor interacts with and activates factor VII (53 kDa), a circulating Gla-containing glycoprotein synthesized in the liver. Tissue factor acts as a cofactor for factor VIIa, enhancing its enzymatic activity to activate factor X. The association of tissue factor and factor VIIa is called **tissue factor complex.** Factor VIIa cleaves the same Arg-Ile bond in factor X that is cleaved by the tenase complex of the intrinsic pathway. Activation of factor X provides an important link between the intrinsic and extrinsic pathways.

Another important interaction between the extrinsic and intrinsic pathways is that complexes of tissue factor and factor VIIa also activate factor IX in the intrinsic pathway. Indeed, **the formation of complexes between tissue factor and factor VIIa is now considered to be the key process involved in initiation of blood coagulation in vivo.** The physiologic significance of the initial steps of the intrinsic pathway, in which factor XII, prekallikrein, and HMW kininogen are involved, has been called into question because

patients with a hereditary deficiency of these components do not exhibit bleeding problems. Similarly, patients with a deficiency of factor XI may not have bleeding problems. The intrinsic pathway may actually be more important in **fibrinolysis** (see below) than in coagulation, since kallikrein, factor XIIa, and factor XIa can cleave plasminogen and kallikrein can activate single-chain urokinase.

Tissue factor pathway inhibitor (TFPI) is a major physiologic inhibitor of coagulation. It is a protein that circulates in the blood associated with lipoproteins. TFPI directly inhibits factor Xa by binding to the enzyme near its active site. This factor Xa-TFPI complex then inhibits the factor VIIa-tissue factor complex.

Factor Xa Leads to Activation of Prothrombin to Thrombin

Factor Xa, produced by either the intrinsic or the extrinsic pathway, activates **prothrombin** (factor II) to **thrombin** (factor IIa), which then converts fibrinogen to fibrin (Figure 50–1).

The activation of prothrombin, like that of factor X, occurs on a membrane surface and requires the assembly of a **prothrombinase complex,** consisting of Ca^{2+}, factor Va, factor Xa, and prothrombin. The assembly of the prothrombinase and tenase complexes takes place on the membrane surface of platelets activated to expose the acidic (anionic) phospholipid **phosphatidylserine,** which is normally on the internal side of the plasma membrane of resting, nonactivated platelets.

Factor V (330 kDa), a glycoprotein with homology to factor VIII and ceruloplasmin, is synthesized in the liver, spleen, and kidney and is found in platelets as well as in plasma. It functions as a cofactor in a manner similar to that of factor VIII in the tenase complex. When activated to factor Va by traces of thrombin, it binds to specific receptors on the platelet membrane (Figure 50–2) and forms a complex with factor Xa and prothrombin. It is subsequently inactivated by further action of thrombin, thereby providing a means of limiting the activation of prothrombin to thrombin. **Prothrombin**

Figure 50–2. Diagrammatic representation (not to scale) of the binding of factors Va, Xa, Ca^{2+}, and prothrombin to the plasma membrane of the activated platelet. The sites of cleavage of prothrombin by factor Xa are indicated by two arrows. The part of prothrombin destined to form thrombin is labeled prethrombin. The Ca^{2+} is bound to anionic phospholipids of the plasma membrane of the activated platelet.

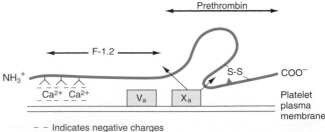

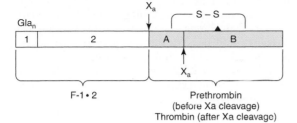

Figure 50–3. Diagrammatic representation (not to scale) of prothrombin. The amino terminal is to the left; region 1 contains all ten Gla residues. The sites of cleavage by factor Xa are shown and the products named. The site of the catalytically active serine residue is indicated by the solid triangle. The A and B chains of active thrombin (shaded) are held together by the disulfide bridge.

(72 kDa; Figure 50–3) is a single-chain glycoprotein synthesized in the liver. The amino terminal region of prothrombin (1 in Figure 50–3) contains ten Gla residues, and the serine-dependent active protease site (indicated by the arrowhead) is in the carboxyl terminal region of the molecule. Upon binding to the complex of factors Va and Xa on the platelet membrane, prothrombin is cleaved by factor Xa at two sites (Figure 50–2) to generate the active, two-chain thrombin molecule, which is then released from the platelet surface. The A and B chains of thrombin are held together by a disulfide bond.

Conversion of Fibrinogen to Fibrin Is Catalyzed by Thrombin

Fibrinogen (factor I, 340 kDa; see Figures 50–1 and 50–4; Tables 50–1 and 50–2) is a soluble plasma glycoprotein that consists of three nonidentical pairs of polypeptide chains $(A\alpha, B\beta\gamma)_2$ covalently linked by disulfide bonds. The $B\beta$ and γ chains contain asparagine-linked complex oligosaccharides. All three chains are synthesized in the liver; the three structural genes involved are on the same chromosome, and their expression is coordinately regulated in humans. The amino terminal regions of the six chains are held in close proximity by a

number of disulfide bonds, while the carboxyl terminal regions are spread apart, giving rise to a highly asymmetric, elongated molecule (Figure 50–4). The A and B portions of the $A\alpha$ and $B\beta$ chains, designated **fibrinopeptides A (FPA) and B (FPB),** respectively, at the amino terminal ends of the chains, bear excess negative charges as a result of the presence of aspartate and glutamate residues, as well as an unusual tyrosine O-sulfate in FPB. These negative charges contribute to the solubility of fibrinogen in plasma and also serve to prevent aggregation by causing electrostatic repulsion between fibrinogen molecules.

Thrombin (34 kDa), a serine protease formed by the prothrombinase complex, hydrolyzes the four Arg-Gly bonds between the fibrinopeptides and the α and β portions of the $A\alpha$ and $B\beta$ chains of fibrinogen (Figure 50–5A). The release of the fibrinopeptides by thrombin generates fibrin monomer, which has the subunit structure $(\alpha, \beta, \gamma)_2$. Since FPA and FPB contain only 16 and 14 residues, respectively, the fibrin molecule retains 98% of the residues present in fibrinogen. The removal of the fibrinopeptides exposes binding sites that allow the molecules of fibrin monomers to aggregate spontaneously in a regularly staggered array, forming an insoluble fibrin clot. It is the formation of this insoluble fibrin polymer that traps platelets, red cells, and other components to form the white or red thrombi. This initial fibrin clot is rather weak, held together only by the noncovalent association of fibrin monomers.

In addition to converting fibrinogen to fibrin, thrombin also converts factor XIII to factor XIIIa. This factor is a highly specific **transglutaminase** that covalently cross-links fibrin molecules by forming peptide bonds between the amide groups of glutamine and the ε-amino groups of lysine residues (Figure 50–5B), yielding a more stable fibrin clot with increased resistance to proteolysis.

Levels of Circulating Thrombin Must Be Carefully Controlled or Clots May Form

Once active thrombin is formed in the course of hemostasis or thrombosis, its concentration must be carefully controlled to prevent further fibrin formation

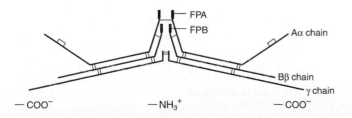

Figure 50–4. Diagrammatic representation (not to scale) of fibrinogen showing pairs of $A\alpha$, $B\beta$, and γ chains linked by disulfide bonds. (FPA, fibrinopeptide A; FPB, fibrinopeptide B.)

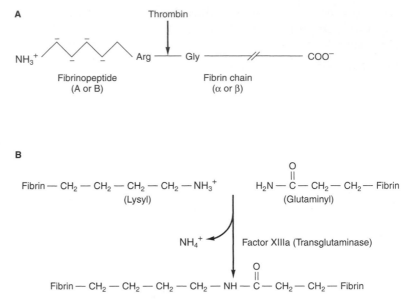

A

Figure 50–5. Formation of a fibrin clot. **(A)** Thrombin-induced cleavage of Arg-Gly bonds of the Aα and Bβ chains of fibrinogen to produce fibrinopeptides (left-hand side) and the α and β chains of fibrin monomer (right-hand side). **(B)** Cross-linking of fibrin molecules by activated factor XIII (factor XIIIa).

or platelet activation. This is achieved in two ways. Thrombin circulates as its inactive precursor, prothrombin, which is activated as the result of a cascade of enzymatic reactions, each converting an inactive zymogen to an active enzyme and leading finally to the conversion of prothrombin to thrombin (Figure 50–1). At each point in the cascade, **feedback mechanisms** produce a delicate balance of activation and inhibition. The concentration of factor XII in plasma is approximately 30 μg/mL, while that of fibrinogen is 3 mg/mL, with intermediate clotting factors increasing in concentration as one proceeds down the cascade, showing that the clotting cascade provides amplification. The second means of controlling thrombin activity is the inactivation of any thrombin formed by **circulating inhibitors,** the most important of which is antithrombin (see below).

The Activity of Antithrombin, an Inhibitor of Thrombin, Is Increased by Heparin

Four naturally occurring thrombin inhibitors exist in normal plasma. The most important is **antithrombin**, which contributes approximately 75% of the antithrombin activity. Antithrombin can also inhibit the activities of factors IXa, Xa, XIa, XIIa, and VIIa complexed with tissue factor. **α₂-Macroglobulin** contributes most of the remainder of the antithrombin activity, with **heparin cofactor II** and **α₁-antitrypsin** acting as minor inhibitors under physiologic conditions.

The endogenous activity of antithrombin is greatly potentiated by the presence of acidic proteoglycans such as **heparin** (Chapter 47). These bind to a specific cationic site of antithrombin, inducing a conformational change and promoting its binding to thrombin as well as to its other substrates. This is the basis for the use of heparin in clinical medicine to inhibit coagulation. The anticoagulant effects of heparin can be antagonized by strongly cationic polypeptides such as **protamine,** which bind strongly to heparin, thus inhibiting its binding to antithrombin.

Low molecular weight heparins (LMWHs), derived from enzymatic or chemical cleavage of unfractionated heparin, are finding increasing clinical use. They can be administered subcutaneously at home, have greater bioavailability than unfractionated heparin, and do not need frequent laboratory monitoring.

Individuals with inherited deficiencies of antithrombin are prone to develop venous thrombosis, providing evidence that antithrombin has a physiologic function and that the coagulation system in humans is normally in a dynamic state.

Thrombin is involved in an additional regulatory mechanism that operates in coagulation. It combines with **thrombomodulin,** a glycoprotein present on the surfaces of endothelial cells. The complex activates **protein C.** In combination with **protein S,** activated protein C (APC) degrades factors Va and VIIIa, limiting their actions in coagulation. A genetic deficiency of either protein C or protein S can cause venous thrombosis. Furthermore, patients with **factor V Leiden** (which has a glutamine residue in place of an arginine at position 506) have an increased risk of venous thrombotic disease because factor V Leiden is resistant to inactivation by APC. This condition is termed APC resistance.

Coumarin Anticoagulants Inhibit the Vitamin K-Dependent Carboxylation of Factors II, VII, IX, & X

The coumarin drugs (eg, warfarin), which are used as anticoagulants, inhibit the vitamin K-dependent carboxylation of Glu to Gla residues (see Chapter 44) in the amino terminal regions of factors II, VII, IX, and X and also proteins C and S. These proteins, all of which are synthesized in the liver, are dependent on the Ca^{2+}-binding properties of the Gla residues for their normal function in the coagulation pathways. The coumarins act by inhibiting the reduction of the quinone derivatives of vitamin K to the active hydroquinone forms (Chapter 44). Thus, the administration of vitamin K will bypass the coumarin-induced inhibition and allow maturation of the Gla-containing factors. Reversal of coumarin inhibition by vitamin K requires 12–24 hours, whereas reversal of the anticoagulant effects of heparin by protamine is almost instantaneous.

Heparin and warfarin are widely used in the treatment of thrombotic and thromboembolic conditions, such as deep vein thrombosis and pulmonary embolus. Heparin is administered first, because of its prompt onset of action, whereas warfarin takes several days to reach full effect. Their effects are closely monitored by use of appropriate tests of coagulation (see below) because of the risk of producing hemorrhage.

There Are Several Hereditary Bleeding Disorders, Including Hemophilia A

Inherited deficiencies of the clotting system that result in bleeding are found in humans. The most common is deficiency of factor VIII, causing **hemophilia A,** an X chromosome-linked disease that has played a major role in the history of the royal families of Europe. **Hemophilia B** is due to a deficiency of factor IX; its clinical features are almost identical to those of hemophilia A, but the conditions can be separated on the basis of specific assays that distinguish between the two factors.

The gene for human factor VIII has been cloned and is one of the largest so far studied, measuring 186 kb in length and containing 26 exons. A variety of mutations in the factor VIII and IX genes have been detected leading to diminished activities of the factor VIII and IX proteins; these include partial gene deletions and point and missense mutations. **Prenatal diagnosis** by DNA analysis after chorionic villus sampling is now possible.

In the past, treatment for patients with hemophilia A and B consisted of administration of **cryoprecipitates** (enriched in factor VIII) prepared from individual donors or lyophilized factor VIII or IX **concentrates** prepared from very large plasma pools. It is now possible to prepare factors VIII and IX by **recombinant DNA technology.** Such preparations are free of contaminating viruses (eg, hepatitis A, B, C, or HIV-1) found in human plasma, but are expensive; their use may increase if cost of production decreases.

The most common hereditary bleeding disorder is **von Willebrand disease,** with a prevalence of up to 1% of the population. It results from a deficiency or defect in **von Willebrand factor,** a large multimeric glycoprotein that is secreted by endothelial cells into the plasma, where it stabilizes factor VIII. von Willebrand factor also promotes platelet adhesion at sites of vessel wall injury (see below).

Fibrin Clots Are Dissolved by Plasmin

As stated above, the coagulation system is normally in a state of dynamic equilibrium in which fibrin clots are constantly being laid down and dissolved. This latter process is termed **fibrinolysis. Plasmin,** the serine protease mainly responsible for degrading fibrin and fibrinogen, circulates in the form of its inactive zymogen, **plasminogen** (90 kDa), and any small amounts of plasmin that are formed in the fluid phase under physiologic conditions are rapidly inactivated by the fast-acting plasmin inhibitor, α_2-antiplasmin. Plasminogen binds to fibrin and thus becomes incorporated in clots as they are produced; since plasmin that is formed when bound to fibrin is protected from α_2-antiplasmin, it remains active. **Activators of plasminogen** of various types are found in most body tissues, and all cleave the same Arg-Val bond in plasminogen to produce the two-chain serine protease, plasmin (Figure 50–6).

Tissue plasminogen activator (alteplase; t-PA) is a serine protease that is released into the circulation from vascular endothelium under conditions of injury or

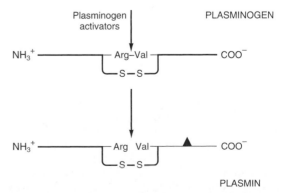

Figure 50–6. Activation of plasminogen. The same Arg-Val bond is cleaved by all plasminogen activators to give the two-chain plasmin molecule. The solid triangle indicates the serine residue of the active site. The two chains of plasmin are held together by a disulfide bridge.

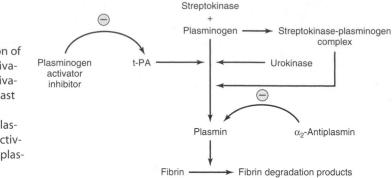

Figure 50–7. Scheme of sites of action of streptokinase, tissue plasminogen activator (t-PA), urokinase, plasminogen activator inhibitor, and α_2-antiplasmin (the last two proteins exert inhibitory actions). Streptokinase forms a complex with plasminogen, which exhibits proteolytic activity; this cleaves some plasminogen to plasmin, initiating fibrinolysis.

stress and is catalytically inactive unless bound to fibrin. Upon binding to fibrin, t-PA cleaves plasminogen within the clot to generate plasmin, which in turn digests the fibrin to form soluble degradation products and thus dissolves the clot. Neither plasmin nor the plasminogen activator can remain bound to these degradation products, and so they are released into the fluid phase, where they are inactivated by their natural inhibitors. Prourokinase is the precursor of a second activator of plasminogen, **urokinase.** Originally isolated from urine, it is now known to be synthesized by cell types such as monocytes and macrophages, fibroblasts, and epithelial cells. Its main action is probably in the degradation of extracellular matrix. Figure 50–7 indicates the sites of action of five proteins that influence the formation and action of plasmin.

Recombinant t-PA & Streptokinase Are Used As Clot Busters

Alteplase (t-PA), produced by recombinant DNA technology, is used therapeutically as a fibrinolytic agent, as is **streptokinase.** However, the latter is less selective than t-PA, activating plasminogen in the fluid phase (where it can degrade circulating fibrinogen) as well as plasminogen that is bound to a fibrin clot. The amount of plasmin produced by therapeutic doses of streptokinase may exceed the capacity of the circulating α_2-antiplasmin, causing fibrinogen as well as fibrin to be degraded and resulting in the bleeding often encountered during fibrinolytic therapy. Because of its relative **selectivity** for degrading fibrin, recombinant t-PA has been widely used to restore the patency of coronary arteries following thrombosis. If administered early enough, before irreversible damage of heart muscle occurs (about 6 hours after onset of thrombosis), t-PA can significantly reduce the mortality rate from myocardial damage following coronary thrombosis. Streptokinase has also been widely used in the treatment of coronary thrombosis, but has the disadvantage of being antigenic.

t-PA has also been used in the treatment of ischemic stroke, peripheral arterial occlusion, and pulmonary embolism.

There are a number of disorders, including cancer and shock, in which **the concentrations of plasminogen activators increase.** In addition, the antiplasmin activities contributed by α_1-antitrypsin and α_2-antiplasmin may be impaired in diseases such as cirrhosis. Since certain bacterial products, such as streptokinase, are capable of activating plasminogen, they may be responsible for the diffuse hemorrhage sometimes observed in patients with disseminated bacterial infections.

Activation of Platelets Involves Stimulation of the Polyphosphoinositide Pathway

Platelets normally circulate in an unstimulated disk-shaped form. During hemostasis or thrombosis, they become activated and help form hemostatic plugs or thrombi. Three major steps are involved: (1) adhesion to exposed collagen in blood vessels, (2) release of the contents of their granules, and (3) aggregation.

Platelets adhere to collagen via specific receptors on the platelet surface, including the glycoprotein complexes GPIa–IIa ($\alpha2\beta1$ integrin; Chapter 51) and GPIb–IX–V, and GPVI. The binding of GPIb–IX–V to collagen is mediated via von Willebrand factor; this interaction is especially important in platelet adherence to the subendothelium under conditions of high shear stress that occur in small vessels and partially stenosed arteries.

Platelets adherent to collagen change shape and spread out on the subendothelium. They release the contents of their storage granules (the dense granules and the alpha granules); secretion is also stimulated by thrombin.

Thrombin, formed from the coagulation cascade, is the most potent activator of platelets and initiates platelet activation by interacting with its receptors PAR (protease activated receptor)-1, PAR-4, and GPIb–IX–V on the plasma membrane (Figure 50–8A). The further events leading to platelet activation upon binding to PAR-1 and

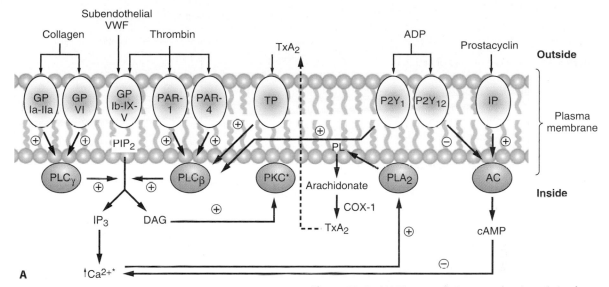

A

B

Figure 50–8. **(A)** Diagrammatic representation of platelet activation by collagen, thrombin, thromboxane A_2 and ADP, and inhibition by prostacyclin. The external environment, the plasma membrane, and the inside of a platelet are depicted from top to bottom. *Elevation of Ca^{2+} levels inside the platelet and activation of protein kinase C result in further signaling events, leading to change of platelet shape, release of the contents of the storage granules, and aggregation. (AC, adenylyl cyclase; cAMP, cyclic AMP; DAG, 1,2-diacylglycerol; GP, glycoprotein; IP, prostacyclin receptor; IP_3, inositol 1,4,5-trisphosphate; P2Y$_1$, P2Y$_{12}$, purinoceptors; PAR, protease activated receptor; PIP_2, phosphatidylinositol 4,5-bisphosphate; PKC, protein kinase C; PL, phospholipid; PI A_2, phospholipase A_2; PLCβ, phospholipase Cβ; PLCγ, phospholipase Cγ; TP, thromboxane A_2 receptor; TxA_2, thromboxane A_2; VWF, von Willebrand factor.) The G proteins that are involved are not shown. **(B)** Diagrammatic representation of platelet aggregation mediated by fibrinogen binding to activated GPIIb-IIIa molecules on adjacent platelets. Signaling events initiated by all aggregating agents transform GPIIb-IIIa from its resting state to an activated form that can bind fibrinogen.

PAR-4 are examples of **transmembrane signaling,** in which a chemical messenger outside the cell generates effector molecules inside the cell. In this instance, thrombin acts as the external chemical messenger (stimulus or agonist). The interaction of thrombin with its G protein–coupled receptors stimulates the activity of an intracellular **phospholipase Cβ.** This enzyme hydrolyzes the membrane phospholipid phosphatidylinositol 4,5-bisphosphate (PIP_2, a polyphosphoinositide) to form the two internal effector molecules, 1,2-diacylglycerol and 1,4,5-inositol trisphosphate.

Hydrolysis of PIP_2 is also involved in the action of many hormones and drugs. Diacylglycerol stimulates **protein kinase C,** which phosphorylates the protein **pleckstrin** (47 kDa). This results in aggregation and release of the contents of the storage granules. ADP released from dense granules can also activate platelets, resulting in aggregation of additional platelets. IP_3 causes release of Ca^{2+} into the cytosol mainly from the dense tubular system (or residual smooth endoplasmic reticulum from the megakaryocyte), which then interacts with calmodulin and myosin light chain kinase,

leading to phosphorylation of the light chains of myosin. These chains then interact with actin, causing changes of platelet shape.

Collagen-induced activation of a platelet phospholipase A_2 by increased levels of cytosolic Ca^{2+} results in liberation of arachidonic acid from platelet phospholipids, leading to the formation of **thromboxane A_2** (Chapter 23), which in turn, in a G protein–coupled receptor-mediated fashion, can further activate phospholipase C, promoting platelet aggregation.

Activated platelets, besides forming a platelet aggregate, are required, via the newly expressed anionic phospholipid phosphatidylserine on the membrane surface, for acceleration of the activation of coagulation factors X and II (Figure 50–1).

All of the aggregating agents, including thrombin, collagen, ADP, and others such as platelet-activating factor, modify via transmembrane signaling the platelet surface glycoprotein complex GPIIb-IIIa (αIIbβ3; Chapter 51) so that fibrinogen can bind to it on the activated platelet surface (Figure 50–8B). Molecules of divalent fibrinogen then link adjacent activated platelets to each other, forming a platelet aggregate. Some agents, including epinephrine, serotonin, and vasopressin, exert synergistic effects with other aggregating agents.

Endothelial Cells Synthesize Prostacyclin & Other Compounds That Affect Clotting & Thrombosis

The endothelial cells in the walls of blood vessels make important contributions to the overall regulation of hemostasis and thrombosis. As described in Chapter 23, these cells synthesize **prostacyclin** (PGI_2), a potent inhibitor of platelet aggregation, opposing the action of thromboxane A_2. Prostacyclin acts by stimulating the activity of adenylyl cyclase in the surface membranes of platelets. The resulting increase of intraplatelet cAMP opposes the increase in the level of intracellular Ca^{2+} produced by IP_3 and thus inhibits platelet activation (Figure 50–8). Endothelial cells play other roles in the regulation of thrombosis. For instance, these cells possess an ADPase, which hydrolyzes ADP, and thus opposes its aggregating effect on platelets. In addition, these cells appear to synthesize heparan sulfate, an anticoagulant, and they also synthesize plasminogen activators, which may help dissolve thrombi. Table 50–3 lists some molecules produced by endothelial cells that affect thrombosis and fibrinolysis. Endothelium-derived relaxing factor (nitric oxide) is discussed in Chapter 48.

Analysis of the mechanisms of uptake of atherogenic lipoproteins, such as LDL, by endothelial, smooth muscle, and monocytic cells of arteries, along with detailed studies of how these lipoproteins damage such cells is a

Table 50–3. Molecules synthesized by endothelial cells that play a role in the regulation of thrombosis and fibrinolysis.[1]

Molecule	Action
ADPase (an ecto-enzyme)	Degrades ADP (an aggregating agent of platelets) to AMP + Pi
Nitric oxide (NO)	Inhibits platelet adhesion and aggregation by elevating levels of cGMP
Heparan sulfate (a glycosaminoglycan)	Anticoagulant; combines with antithrombin to inhibit thrombin
Prostacyclin (PGI₂, a prostaglandin)	Inhibits platelet aggregation by increasing levels of cAMP
Thrombomodulin (a glycoprotein)	Binds protein C, which is then cleaved by thrombin to yield activated protein C; this in combination with protein S degrades factors Va and VIIIa, limiting their actions
Tissue plasminogen activator (t-PA, a protease)	Activates plasminogen to plasmin, which digests fibrin; the action of t-PA is opposed by plasminogen activator inhibitor-1 (PAI-1)

[1]Adapted from Wu KK: Endothelial cells in hemostasis, thrombosis and inflammation. Hosp Pract (Off Ed) 1992 Apr; 27:145.

key area of study in elucidating the mechanisms of **atherosclerosis** (Chapter 26).

Aspirin Is an Effective Antiplatelet Drug

Certain drugs (antiplatelet drugs) inhibit platelet responses. The most commonly used antiplatelet drug is aspirin (acetylsalicylic acid), which irreversibly acetylates and thus inhibits the platelet cyclooxygenase system (COX-1) involved in formation of thromboxane A_2 (Chapter 15), a potent aggregator of platelets and also a vasoconstrictor. Platelets are very sensitive to aspirin; as little as 30 mg/d (one aspirin tablet usually contains 325 mg) effectively eliminates the synthesis of thromboxane A_2. Aspirin also inhibits production of prostacyclin (PGI_2, which opposes platelet aggregation and is a vasodilator) by endothelial cells, but unlike platelets, these cells regenerate cyclooxygenase within a few hours. Thus, the overall balance between thromboxane A_2 and prostacyclin can be shifted in favor of the latter, opposing platelet aggregation. Indications for treatment with aspirin thus include management of angina, evolving myocardial infarction, transient cerebral ischemic attacks, acute ischemic stroke, and severe carotid artery stenosis.

Other antiplatelet drugs include clopidogrel, a specific inhibitor of the $P2Y_{12}$ receptor for ADP, and antagonists of ligand binding to GPIIb–IIIa (eg, abciximab) that interfere with fibrinogen binding and thus platelet aggregation.

Laboratory Tests Measure Coagulation, Thrombolysis, & Platelet Aggregation

A number of laboratory tests are available to measure the phases of hemostasis described above. The tests include platelet count, bleeding time, platelet aggregation, activated partial thromboplastin time (aPTT or PTT), prothrombin time (PT), thrombin time (TT), concentration of fibrinogen, fibrin clot stability, and measurement of fibrin degradation products. The platelet count quantitates the number of platelets, the bleeding time is an overall test of platelet function, and platelet aggregation measures responses to specific aggregating agents. aPTT is a measure of the intrinsic pathway and PT of the extrinsic pathway. PT is used to measure the effectiveness of oral anticoagulants such as warfarin, and aPTT is used to monitor heparin therapy. The reader is referred to a textbook of hematology for a discussion of these tests.

SUMMARY

- Hemostasis and thrombosis are complex processes involving coagulation factors, platelets, and blood vessels.
- Many coagulation factors are zymogens of serine proteases, becoming activated during the overall process.
- Both intrinsic and extrinsic pathways of coagulation exist, the latter initiated in vivo by tissue factor. The pathways converge at factor Xa, ultimately resulting in thrombin-catalyzed conversion of fibrinogen to fibrin, which is strengthened by cross-linking, catalyzed by factor XIII.
- Genetic disorders that lead to bleeding occur; the principal disorders involve factor VIII (hemophilia A), factor IX (hemophilia B), and von Willebrand factor (von Willebrand disease).
- Antithrombin is an important natural inhibitor of coagulation; genetic deficiency of this protein can result in thrombosis.
- For activity, factors II, VII, IX, and X and proteins C and S require vitamin K-dependent γ-carboxylation of certain glutamate residues, a process that is inhibited by the anticoagulant warfarin.
- Fibrin is dissolved by plasmin. Plasmin exists as an inactive precursor, plasminogen, which can be activated by tissue plasminogen activator (t-PA). Both t-PA and streptokinase are widely used to treat early thrombosis in the coronary arteries.
- Thrombin and other agents cause platelet aggregation, which involves a variety of biochemical and morphologic events. Stimulation of phospholipase C and the polyphosphoinositide pathway is a key event in platelet activation, but other processes are also involved.
- Aspirin is an important antiplatelet drug that acts by inhibiting production of thromboxane A_2.

REFERENCES

Hoffman R et al (editors): *Hematology: Basic Principles and Practice,* 4th ed. Elsevier Churchill Livingston, 2005.

Israels LG, Israels ED: *Mechanisms in Hematology,* 3rd ed. Core Health Sciences Inc, 2002. (This text has many excellent illustrations of basic mechanisms in hematology.)

Kasper DL et al (editors): *Harrison's Principles of Internal Medicine,* 16th ed. McGraw-Hill, 2005.

Red & White Blood Cells

51

Robert K. Murray, MD, PhD

BIOMEDICAL IMPORTANCE

Blood cells have been studied intensively because they are obtained easily, because of their functional importance, and because of their involvement in many disease processes. The structure and function of **hemoglobin,** the **porphyrias, jaundice,** and aspects of **iron metabolism** are discussed in previous chapters. Reduction of the number of red blood cells and of their content of hemoglobin is the cause of the **anemias,** a diverse and important group of conditions, some of which are seen very commonly in clinical practice. Certain of the **blood group systems,** present on the membranes of erythrocytes and other blood cells, are of extreme importance in relation to blood transfusion and tissue transplantation. Table 51–1 summarizes the causes of a number of important diseases affecting red blood cells; some are discussed in this chapter, and the remainder are discussed elsewhere in this text. Every organ in the body can be affected by **inflammation;** neutrophils play a central role in acute inflammation, and other white blood cells, such as lymphocytes, play important roles in chronic inflammation. **Leukemias,** defined as malignant neoplasms of blood-forming tissues, can affect precursor cells of any of the major classes of white blood cells; common types are acute and chronic myelocytic leukemia, affecting precursors of the neutrophils; and acute and chronic lymphocytic leukemias. Knowledge of the molecular mechanisms involved in the causation of the leukemias is increasing rapidly, but is not discussed in this text. **Combination chemotherapy,** using combinations of various chemotherapeutic agents, all of which act at one or more biochemical loci, has been remarkably effective in the treatment of certain of these types of leukemias. Understanding the role of red and white cells in health and disease requires a knowledge of certain fundamental aspects of their biochemistry.

THE RED BLOOD CELL IS SIMPLE IN TERMS OF ITS STRUCTURE & FUNCTION

The **major functions of the red blood cell** are relatively simple, consisting of delivering oxygen to the tissues and of helping in the disposal of carbon dioxide and protons formed by tissue metabolism. Thus, it has a much simpler structure than most human cells, being essentially composed of a membrane surrounding a solution of hemoglobin (this protein forms about 95% of the intracellular protein of the red cell). There are no intracellular organelles, such as mitochondria, lysosomes, or Golgi apparatus. Human red blood cells, like most red cells of animals, are nonnucleated. However, the red cell is not metabolically inert. **ATP** is synthesized from **glycolysis** and is important in processes that help the red blood cell maintain its biconcave shape and also in the regulation of the **transport of ions** (eg, by the Na^+-K^+ ATPase and the anion exchange protein [see below]) and of **water** in and out of the cell. The biconcave shape increases the surface-to-volume ratio of the red blood cell, thus facilitating gas exchange. The red cell contains cytoskeletal components (see below) that play an important role in determining its shape.

About Two Million Red Blood Cells Enter the Circulation Per Second

The **life span** of the normal red blood cell is 120 days; this means that slightly less than 1% of the population of red cells (200 billion cells, or 2 million per second) is replaced daily. The new red cells that appear in the circulation still contain ribosomes and elements of the endoplasmic reticulum. The RNA of the ribosomes can be detected by suitable stains (such as cresyl blue), and cells containing it are termed reticulocytes; they normally number about 1% of the total red blood cell count. The life span of the red blood cell can be dramatically shortened in a variety of **hemolytic anemias.** The number of reticulocytes is markedly increased in these conditions, as the bone marrow attempts to compensate for rapid breakdown of red blood cells by increasing the amount of new, young red cells in the circulation.

Erythropoietin Regulates Production of Red Blood Cells

Human **erythropoietin** is a glycoprotein of 166 amino acids (molecular mass about 34 kDa). Its amount in plasma can be measured by radioimmunoassay. It is the major regulator of human erythropoiesis. Erythropoietin

Table 51–1. Summary of the causes of some important disorders affecting red blood cells.

Disorder	Sole or Major Cause
Iron deficiency anemia	Inadequate intake or excessive loss of iron
Methemoglobinemia	Intake of excess oxidants (various chemicals and drugs) Genetic deficiency in the NADH-dependent methemoglobin reductase system (MIM 250800) Inheritance of HbM (MIM 141800)
Sickle cell anemia (MIM 603903)	Sequence of codon 6 of the β chain changed from GAG in the normal gene to GTG in the sickle cell gene, resulting in substitution of valine for glutamic acid
α-Thalassemias (MIM 141800)	Mutations in the α-globin genes, mainly unequal crossing-over and large deletions and less commonly nonsense and frameshift mutations
β-Thalassemia (MIM 141900)	A very wide variety of mutations in the β-globin gene, including deletions, nonsense and frameshift mutations, and others affecting every aspect of its structure (eg, splice sites, promoter mutants)
Megaloblastic anemias Deficiency of vitamin B_{12}	Decreased absorption of B_{12}, often due to a deficiency of intrinsic factor, normally secreted by gastric parietal cells
Deficiency of folic acid	Decreased intake, defective absorption, or increased demand (eg, in pregnancy) for folate
Hereditary spherocytosis[1] (MIM 182900)	Deficiencies in the amount or in the structure of α or β spectrin, ankyrin, band 3 or band 4.1
Glucose-6-phosphate dehydrogenase (G6PD) deficiency[1] (MIM 305900)	A variety of mutations in the gene (X-linked) for G6PD, mostly single point mutations
Pyruvate kinase (PK) deficiency[1] (MIM 266200)	Presumably a variety of mutations in the gene for the R (red cell) isozyme of PK
Paroxysmal nocturnal hemoglobinemia[1] (MIM 311770)	Mutations in the PIG-A gene, affecting synthesis of GPI-anchored proteins

[1]The last four disorders cause hemolytic anemias, as do a number of the other disorders listed. Most of the above conditions are discussed in other chapters of this text. MIM numbers apply only to disorders with a genetic basis.

is synthesized mainly by the kidney and is released in response to hypoxia into the bloodstream, in which it travels to the bone marrow. There it interacts with progenitors of red blood cells via a specific receptor. The receptor is a transmembrane protein consisting of two different subunits and a number of domains. It is not a tyrosine kinase, but it stimulates the activities of specific members of this class of enzymes involved in downstream signal transduction. Erythropoietin interacts with a red cell progenitor, known as the burst-forming unit-erythroid (BFU-E), causing it to proliferate and differentiate. In addition, it interacts with a later progenitor of the red blood cell, called the colony-forming unit-erythroid (CFU-E), also causing it to proliferate and further differentiate. For these effects, erythropoietin requires the cooperation of other factors (eg, interleukin-3 and insulin-like growth factor; Figure 51–1).

The availability of a cDNA for erythropoietin has made it possible to produce substantial amounts of this hormone for analysis and for therapeutic purposes; previously the isolation of erythropoietin from human urine yielded very small amounts of the protein. The major use of **recombinant erythropoietin** has been in the treatment of a small number of **anemic states,** such as that due to renal failure.

MANY GROWTH FACTORS REGULATE PRODUCTION OF WHITE BLOOD CELLS

A large number of **hematopoietic growth factors** have been identified in recent years in addition to erythropoietin. This area of study adds to knowledge about the differentiation of blood cells, provides factors that may be useful in treatment, and also has implications for understanding of the abnormal growth of blood cells (eg, the leukemias). Like erythropoietin, most of the growth factors isolated have been glycoproteins, are very active in vivo and in vitro, interact with their target cells via specific cell surface receptors, and ultimately (via intracellular signals) affect gene expression, thereby promoting differentiation. Many have been cloned, permitting their production in relatively large amounts. Two of particular interest are **granulocyte-** and **granulocyte-macrophage colony-stimulating factors** (G-CSF and GM-CSF, respectively). G-CSF is relatively specific, inducing mainly granulocytes. GM-CSF affects a variety of progenitor cells and induces granulocytes, macrophages, and eosinophils. When the production of neutrophils is severely depressed, this condition is referred to as **neutropenia.** It is particularly likely to occur in patients treated with certain chemotherapeutic regimens and after bone marrow transplantation. These patients are liable to develop overwhelming infections. G-CSF has been administered to such patients to boost production of neutrophils.

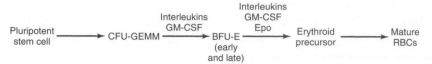

Figure 51–1. Greatly simplified scheme of differentiation of stem cells to red blood cells. Various interleukins (ILs), such as IL-3, IL-4, IL-9, and IL-11, are involved at different steps of the overall process. Erythroid precursors include the pronormoblast, basophilic, polychromatophilic, and orthochromatophilic normoblasts, and the reticulocyte. Epo acts on basophilic normoblasts but not on later erythroid cells. (CFU-GEMM, colony-forming unit whose cells give rise to granulocytes, erythrocytes, macrophages, and megakaryocytes; BFU-E, burst-forming unit-erythroid; GM-CSF, granulocyte-macrophage colony-stimulating factor; Epo, erythropoietin; RBC, red blood cell.)

THE RED BLOOD CELL HAS A UNIQUE & RELATIVELY SIMPLE METABOLISM

Various aspects of the **metabolism of the red cell,** many of which are discussed in other chapters of this text, are summarized in Table 51–2.

The Red Blood Cell Has a Glucose Transporter in Its Membrane

The entry rate of glucose into red blood cells is far greater than would be calculated for simple diffusion. Rather, it is an example of **facilitated diffusion** (Chapter 40). The specific protein involved in this process is called the **glucose transporter** (GLUT1) or glucose permease. Some of its properties are summarized in Table 51–3. The process of entry of glucose into red blood cells is of major importance because it is the major fuel supply for these cells. About twelve different but related glucose transporters have been isolated from various human tissues; unlike the red cell transporter, some of these are insulin-dependent (eg, in muscle and adipose tissue). There is considerable interest in the latter types of transporter because defects in their recruitment from intracellular sites to the surface of skeletal muscle cells may help explain the **insulin resistance** displayed by patients with type 2 diabetes mellitus.

Reticulocytes Are Active in Protein Synthesis

The mature red blood cell cannot synthesize protein. **Reticulocytes** are active in protein synthesis. Once reticulocytes enter the circulation, they lose their intracellular organelles (ribosomes, mitochondria, etc) within about 24 hours, becoming young red blood cells and concomitantly losing their ability to synthesize protein. Extracts of rabbit reticulocytes (obtained by injecting rabbits with a chemical—phenylhydrazine—that causes a severe hemolytic anemia, so that the red cells are almost completely replaced by reticulocytes) are widely used as an in

Table 51–2. Summary of important aspects of the metabolism of the red blood cell.

- The RBC is highly dependent upon glucose as its energy source; its membrane contains high affinity glucose transporters.
- Glycolysis, producing lactate, is the site of production of ATP.
- Because there are no mitochondria in RBCs, there is no production of ATP by oxidative phosphorylation.
- The RBC has a variety of transporters that maintain ionic and water balance.
- Production of 2,3-bisphosphoglycerate, by reactions closely associated with glycolysis, is important in regulating the ability of Hb to transport oxygen.
- The pentose phosphate pathway is operative in the RBC (it metabolizes about 5–10% of the total flux of glucose) and produces NADPH; hemolytic anemia due to a deficiency of the activity of glucose-6-phosphate dehydrogenase is common.
- Reduced glutathione (GSH) is important in the metabolism of the RBC, in part to counteract the action of potentially toxic peroxides; the RBC can synthesize GSH and requires NADPH to return oxidized glutathione (G-S-S-G) to the reduced state.
- The iron of Hb must be maintained in the ferrous state; ferric iron is reduced to the ferrous state by the action of an NADH-dependent methemoglobin reductase system involving cytochrome b_5 reductase and cytochrome b_5.
- Synthesis of glycogen, fatty acids, protein, and nucleic acids does not occur in the RBC; however, some lipids (eg, cholesterol) in the red cell membrane can exchange with corresponding plasma lipids.
- The RBC contains certain enzymes of nucleotide metabolism (eg, adenosine deaminase, pyrimidine nucleotidase, and adenylyl kinase); deficiencies of these enzymes are involved in some cases of hemolytic anemia.
- When RBCs reach the end of their life span, the globin is degraded to amino acids (which are reutilized in the body), the iron is released from heme and also reutilized, and the tetrapyrrole component of heme is converted to bilirubin, which is mainly excreted into the bowel via the bile.

Table 51–3. Some properties of the glucose transporter of the membrane of the red blood cell (GLUT1).

- It accounts for about 2% of the protein of the membrane of the RBC.
- It exhibits specificity for glucose and related D-hexoses (L-hexoses are not transported).
- The transporter functions at approximately 75% of its V_{max} at the physiologic concentration of blood glucose, is saturable and can be inhibited by certain analogs of glucose.
- At least seven similar but distinct glucose transporters have been detected to date in mammalian tissues, of which the red cell transporter is one.
- It is not dependent upon insulin, unlike the corresponding carrier in muscle and adipose tissue.
- Its complete amino acid sequence (492 amino acids) has been determined.
- It transports glucose when inserted into artificial liposomes.
- It is estimated to contain 12 transmembrane helical segments.
- It functions by generating a gated pore in the membrane to permit passage of glucose; the pore is conformationally dependent on the presence of glucose and can oscillate rapidly (about 900 times/s).

vitro system for synthesizing proteins. Endogenous mRNAs present in these reticulocytes are destroyed by use of a nuclease, whose activity can be inhibited by addition of Ca^{2+}. The system is then programmed by adding purified mRNAs or whole-cell extracts of mRNAs, and radioactive proteins are synthesized in the presence of ^{35}S-labeled L-methionine or other radiolabeled amino acids. The radioactive proteins synthesized are separated by SDS-PAGE and detected by radioautography.

Superoxide Dismutase, Catalase, & Glutathione Protect Blood Cells from Oxidative Stress & Damage

Several powerful **oxidants** are produced during the course of metabolism, in both blood cells and most

other cells of the body. These include superoxide (O_2^{-}), hydrogen peroxide (H_2O_2), peroxyl radicals ($ROO^{\bullet}$), and hydroxyl radicals ($OH^{\bullet}$) and are referred to as **reactive oxygen species (ROS). Free radicals** are atoms or groups of atoms that have an unpaired electron (see Chapter 15). $OH^{\bullet}$ is a particularly reactive molecule and can react with proteins, nucleic acids, lipids, and other molecules to alter their structure and produce tissue damage. The reactions listed in Table 51–4 play an important role in forming these oxidants and in disposing of them; each of these reactions will now be considered in turn.

Superoxide is formed (reaction 1) in the red blood cell by the auto-oxidation of hemoglobin to methemoglobin (approximately 3% of hemoglobin in human red blood cells has been calculated to auto-oxidize per day); in other tissues, it is formed by the action of enzymes such as cytochrome P450 reductase and xanthine oxidase. When stimulated by contact with bacteria, **neutrophils** exhibit a **respiratory burst** (see below) and produce superoxide in a reaction catalyzed by NADPH oxidase (reaction 2). Superoxide spontaneously dismutates to form H_2O_2 and O_2; however, the rate of this same reaction is speeded up tremendously by the action of the enzyme **superoxide dismutase** (reaction 3). **Hydrogen peroxide** is subject to a number of fates. The enzyme **catalase,** present in many types of cells, converts it to H_2O and O_2 (reaction 4). Neutrophils possess a unique enzyme, **myeloperoxidase,** that uses H_2O_2 and halides to produce hypohalous acids (reaction 5); this subject is discussed further below. The selenium-containing enzyme **glutathione peroxidase** (Chapter 21) will also act on reduced glutathione (GSH) and H_2O_2 to produce oxidized glutathione (GSSG) and H_2O (reaction 6); this enzyme can also use other peroxides as substrates. $OH^{\bullet}$ and OH^- can be formed from H_2O_2 in a nonenzymatic reaction catalyzed by Fe^{2+} (the **Fenton reaction,** reaction 7). O_2^{-} and H_2O_2 are the substrates in the iron-catalyzed **Haber-Weiss reaction** (reaction 8), which also produces $OH^{\bullet}$ and OH^-. Superoxide can release iron ions from ferritin. Thus, production of $OH^{\bullet}$ may be one of the mechanisms involved in tissue injury due to iron overload (eg, hemochromatosis; Chapter 49).

Table 51–4. Reactions of importance in relation to oxidative stress in blood cells and various tissues.

(1) Production of superoxide (by-product of various reactions)	$O_2 + e^- \rightarrow O_2^{-}$
(2) NADPH-oxidase	$2 O_2 + NADPH \rightarrow 2 O_2^{-} + NADP + H^+$
(3) Superoxide dismutase	$O_2^{-} + O_2^{-} + 2 H^+ \rightarrow H_2O_2 + O_2$
(4) Catalase	$H_2O_2 \rightarrow 2 H_2O + O_2$
(5) Myeloperoxidase	$H_2O_2 + X^- + H^+ \rightarrow HOX + H_2O$ ($X^- = Cl^-, Br^-, SCN^-$)
(6) Glutathione peroxidase (Se-dependent)	$2 GSH + R\text{-}O\text{-}OH \rightarrow GSSG + H_2O + ROH$
(7) Fenton reaction	$Fe^{2+} + H_2O_2 \rightarrow Fe^{3+} + OH^{\bullet} + OH^-$
(8) Iron-catalyzed Haber-Weiss reaction	$O_2^{-} + H_2O_2 \rightarrow O_2 + OH^{\bullet} + OH^-$
(9) Glucose-6-phosphate dehydrogenase (G6PD)	$G6P + NADP \rightarrow 6 \text{ Phosphogluconate} + NADPH + H^+$
(10) Glutathione reductase	$G\text{-}S\text{-}S\text{-}G + NADPH + H^+ \rightarrow 2 GSH + NADP$

Chemical compounds and reactions capable of generating potential toxic oxygen species can be referred to as **pro-oxidants.** On the other hand, compounds and reactions disposing of these species, scavenging them, suppressing their formation, or opposing their actions are **antioxidants** and include compounds such as NADPH, GSH, ascorbic acid, and vitamin E. In a normal cell, there is an appropriate pro-oxidant:antioxidant balance. However, this balance can be shifted toward the pro-oxidants when production of oxygen species is increased greatly (eg, following ingestion of certain chemicals or drugs) or when levels of antioxidants are diminished (eg, by inactivation of enzymes involved in disposal of oxygen species and by conditions that cause low levels of the antioxidants mentioned above). This state is called **"oxidative stress"** and can result in serious cell damage if the stress is massive or prolonged.

ROS are now thought to play an important role in many types of **cellular injury** (eg, resulting from administration of various toxic chemicals or from ischemia), some of which can result in cell death. Indirect evidence supporting a role for these species in generating cell injury is provided if administration of an enzyme such as superoxide dismutase or catalase is found to protect against cell injury in the situation under study.

Deficiency of Glucose-6-Phosphate Dehydrogenase Is Frequent in Certain Areas & Is an Important Cause of Hemolytic Anemia

NADPH, produced in the reaction catalyzed by the X-linked glucose-6-phosphate dehydrogenase (Table 51–4, reaction 9) in the **pentose phosphate pathway** (Chapter 21), plays a key role in supplying reducing equivalents in the red cell and in other cells such as the hepatocyte. Because the pentose phosphate pathway is virtually its sole means of producing NADPH, the red blood cell is very sensitive to oxidative damage if the function of this pathway is impaired (eg, by enzyme deficiency). One function of NADPH is to reduce GSSG to GSH, a reaction catalyzed by glutathione reductase (reaction 10).

Deficiency of the activity of **glucose-6-phosphate dehydrogenase,** owing to mutation, is extremely frequent in some regions of the world (eg, tropical Africa, the Mediterranean, certain parts of Asia, and in North America among blacks). It is the most common of all enzymopathies (diseases caused by abnormalities of enzymes), and over 300 genetic variants of the enzyme have been distinguished; at least 100 million people are deficient in this enzyme owing to these variants. The disorder resulting from deficiency of glucose-6-phosphate dehydrogenase is **hemolytic anemia.** Consumption of

broad beans *(Vicia faba)* by individuals deficient in activity of the enzyme can precipitate an attack of hemolytic anemia because they contain potential oxidants. In addition, a number of drugs (eg, the antimalarial drug **primaquine** [the condition caused by intake of primaquine is called **primaquine-sensitive hemolytic anemia**] and **sulfonamides**) and chemicals (eg, naphthalene) precipitate an attack, because their intake leads to generation of H_2O_2 or O_2^-. Normally, H_2O_2 is disposed of by **catalase** and **glutathione peroxidase** (Table 51–4, reactions 4 and 6), the latter causing increased production of GSSG. GSH is regenerated from GSSG by the action of the enzyme **glutathione reductase,** which depends on the availability of NADPH (reaction 10). The red blood cells of individuals who are deficient in the activity of glucose-6-phosphate dehydrogenase cannot generate sufficient NADPH to regenerate GSH from GSSG, which in turn impairs their ability to dispose of H_2O_2 and of oxygen radicals. These compounds can cause oxidation of critical SH groups in proteins and possibly peroxidation of lipids in the membrane of the red cell, causing lysis of the red cell membrane. Some of the SH groups of hemoglobin become oxidized, and the protein precipitates inside the red blood cell, forming **Heinz bodies,** which stain purple with cresyl violet. The presence of Heinz bodies indicates that red blood cells have been subjected to oxidative stress. Figure 51–2 summarizes the possible chain of events in hemolytic anemia due to deficiency of glucose-6-phosphate dehydrogenase.

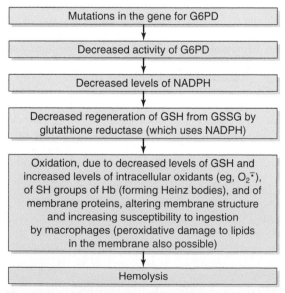

Figure 51–2. Summary of probable events causing hemolytic anemia due to deficiency of the activity of glucose-6-phosphate dehydrogenase (G6PD) (MIM 305900).

Methemoglobin Is Useless in Transporting Oxygen

The ferrous iron of hemoglobin is susceptible to oxidation by superoxide and other oxidizing agents, forming **methemoglobin,** which cannot transport oxygen. Only a very small amount of methemoglobin is present in normal blood, as the red blood cell possesses an effective system (the NADH-cytochrome b_5 methemoglobin reductase system) for reducing heme Fe^{3+} back to the Fe^{2+} state. This system consists of NADH (generated by glycolysis), a flavoprotein named cytochrome b_5 reductase (also known as methemoglobin reductase), and cytochrome b_5. The Fe^{3+} of methemoglobin is reduced back to the Fe^{2+} state by the action of reduced cytochrome b_5:

$$Hb\text{-}Fe^{3+} + Cyt\ b_{5\ red} \rightarrow Hb\text{-}Fe^{2+} + Cyt\ b_{5\ ox}$$

Reduced cytochrome b_5 is then regenerated by the action of cytochrome b_5 reductase:

$$Cyt\ b_{5\ ox} + NADH \rightarrow Cyt\ b_{5\ red} + NAD$$

Methemoglobinemia Is Inherited or Acquired

Methemoglobinemia can be classified as either **inherited** or **acquired** by ingestion of certain drugs and chemicals. Neither type occurs frequently, but physicians must be aware of them. The inherited form is usually due to deficient activity of **methemoglobin reductase,** transmitted in an autosomal recessive manner. Certain **abnormal hemoglobins** (eg, HbM) are also rare causes of methemoglobinemia. In HbM, mutation changes the amino acid residue to which heme is attached, thus altering its affinity for oxygen and favoring its oxidation. Ingestion of **certain drugs** (eg, sulfonamides) or **chemicals** (eg, aniline) can cause acquired methemoglobinemia. Cyanosis (bluish discoloration of the skin and mucous membranes due to increased amounts of deoxygenated hemoglobin in arterial blood, or in this case due to increased amounts of methemoglobin) is usually the presenting sign in both types and is evident when over 10% of hemoglobin is in the "met" form. Diagnosis is made by spectroscopic analysis of blood, which reveals the characteristic absorption spectrum of methemoglobin. Additionally, a sample of blood containing methemoglobin cannot be fully reoxygenated by flushing oxygen through it, whereas normal deoxygenated blood can. Electrophoresis can be used to confirm the presence of an abnormal hemoglobin. Ingestion of **methylene blue** or **ascorbic acid** (reducing agents) is used to treat mild methemoglobinemia due to enzyme deficiency. Acute massive methemoglobinemia (due to ingestion of chemicals) should be treated by intravenous injection of methylene blue.

MORE IS KNOWN ABOUT THE MEMBRANE OF THE HUMAN RED BLOOD CELL THAN ABOUT THE SURFACE MEMBRANE OF ANY OTHER HUMAN CELL

A variety of biochemical approaches have been used to study the membrane of the red blood cell. These include analysis of membrane proteins by SDS-PAGE, the use of specific enzymes (proteinases, glycosidases, and others) to determine the location of proteins and glycoproteins in the membrane, and various techniques to study both the lipid composition and disposition of individual lipids. Morphologic (eg, electron microscopy, freeze-fracture electron microscopy) and other techniques (eg, use of antibodies to specific components) have also been widely used. When red blood cells are lysed under specific conditions, their membranes will reseal in their original orientation to form **ghosts** (right side-out ghosts). By altering the conditions, ghosts can also be made to reseal with their cytosolic aspect exposed on the exterior (inside-out ghosts). Both types of ghosts have been useful in analyzing the disposition of specific proteins and lipids in the membrane. In recent years, cDNAs for many proteins of this membrane have become available, permitting the deduction of their amino sequences and domains. All in all, more is known about the membrane of the red blood cell than about any other membrane of human cells (Table 51–5).

Analysis by SDS-PAGE Resolves the Proteins of the Membrane of the Red Blood Cell

When the membranes of red blood cells are analyzed by **SDS-PAGE,** about ten major proteins are resolved (Figure 51–3), several of which have been shown to be **glycoproteins.** Their migration on SDS-PAGE was used to name these proteins, with the slowest migrating (and hence highest molecular mass) being designated band 1 or **spectrin.** All these major proteins have been isolated, most of them have been identified, and considerable insight has been obtained about their functions (Table 51–6). Many of their amino acid sequences also have been established. In addition, it has been determined which are integral or peripheral membrane proteins, which are situated on the external surface, which are on the cytosolic surface, and which span the membrane (Figure 51–4). Many minor components can also be detected in the red cell membrane by use of sensitive staining methods or two-dimensional

Table 51–5. Summary of biochemical information about the membrane of the human red blood cell.

- The membrane is a bilayer composed of about 50% lipid and 50% protein.
- The major lipid classes are phospholipids and cholesterol; the major phospholipids are phosphatidylcholine (PC), phosphatidylethanolamine (PE), and phosphatidylserine (PS) along with sphingomyelin (Sph).
- The choline-containing phospholipids, PC and Sph, predominate in the outer leaflet and the amino-containing phospholipids (PE and PS) in the inner leaflet.
- Glycosphingolipids (GSLs) (neutral GSLs, gangliosides, and complex species, including the ABO blood group substances) constitute about 5–10% of the total lipid.
- Analysis by SDS-PAGE shows that the membrane contains about 10 major proteins and more than 100 minor species.
- The major proteins (which include spectrin, ankyrin, the anion exchange protein, actin, and band 4.1) have been studied intensively, and the principal features of their disposition (eg, integral or peripheral), structure, and function have been established.
- Many of the proteins are glycoproteins (eg, the glycophorins) containing O- or N-linked (or both) oligosaccharide chains located on the external surface of the membrane.

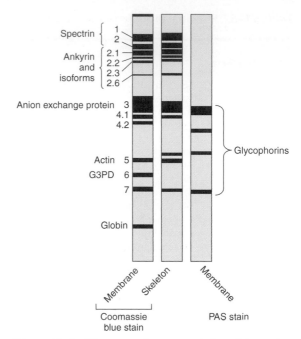

Figure 51–3. Diagrammatic representation of the major proteins of the membrane of the human red blood cell separated by SDS-PAGE. The bands detected by staining with Coomassie blue are shown in the two left-hand channels, and the glycoproteins detected by staining with periodic acid-Schiff (PAS) reagent are shown in the right-hand channel. (Reproduced, with permission, from Beck WS, Tepper RI: Hemolytic anemias III: membrane disorders. In: *Hematology*, 5th ed. Beck WS [editor]. The MIT Press, 1991.)

gel electrophoresis. One of these is the glucose transporter described above.

The Major Integral Proteins of the Red Blood Cell Membrane Are the Anion Exchange Protein & the Glycophorins

The **anion exchange protein (band 3)** is a transmembrane glycoprotein, with its carboxyl terminal end on the external surface of the membrane and its amino terminal end on the cytoplasmic surface. It is an example of a **multipass** membrane protein, extending across the bilayer at least ten times. It probably exists as a dimer in the membrane, in which it forms a tunnel, permitting the exchange of chloride for bicarbonate. Carbon dioxide, formed in the tissues, enters the red cell as bicarbonate, which is exchanged for chloride in the lungs, where carbon dioxide is exhaled. The amino terminal end binds many proteins, including hemoglobin, proteins 4.1 and 4.2, ankyrin, and several glycolytic enzymes. Purified band 3 has been added to lipid vesicles in vitro and has been shown to perform its transport functions in this reconstituted system.

Glycophorins A, B, and C are also transmembrane glycoproteins but of the **single-pass** type, extending across the membrane only once. A is the major glycophorin, is made up of 131 amino acids, and is heavily glycosylated (about 60% of its mass). Its amino terminal

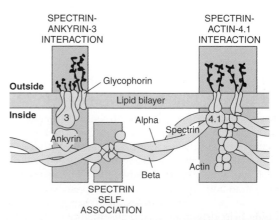

Figure 51–4. Diagrammatic representation of the interaction of cytoskeletal proteins with each other and with certain integral proteins of the membrane of the red blood cell. (Reproduced, with permission, from Beck WS, Tepper RI: Hemolytic anemias III: membrane disorders. In: *Hematology*, 5th ed. Beck WS [editor]. The MIT Press, 1991.)

Table 51–6. Principal proteins of the red cell membrane.[1]

Band Number[2]	Protein	Integral (I) or Peripheral (P)	Approximate Molecular Mass (kDa)
1	Spectrin (α)	P	240
2	Spectrin (β)	P	220
2.1	Ankyrin	P	210
2.2	Ankyrin	P	195
2.3	Ankyrin	P	175
2.6	Ankyrin	P	145
3	Anion exchange protein	I	100
4.1	Unnamed	P	80
5	Actin	P	43
6	Glyceraldehyde-3-phosphate dehydrogenase	P	35
7	Tropomyosin	P	29
8	Unnamed	P	23
	Glycophorins A, B, and C	I	31, 23, and 28

[1]Adapted from Lux DE, Becker PS: Disorders of the red cell membrane skeleton: hereditary spherocytosis and hereditary elliptocytosis. Chapter 95 in: *The Metabolic Basis of Inherited Disease,* 6th ed. Scriver CR et al (editors). McGraw-Hill, 1989.
[2]The band number refers to the position of migration on SDS-PAGE (see Figure 51–3). The glycophorins are detected by staining with the periodic acid-Schiff reagent. A number of other components (eg, 4.2 and 4.9) are not listed. Native spectrin is $\alpha_2\beta_2$.

end, which contains 16 oligosaccharide chains (15 of which are O-glycans), extrudes out from the surface of the red blood cell. Approximately 90% of the sialic acid of the red cell membrane is located in this protein. Its transmembrane segment (23 amino acids) is α-helical. The carboxyl terminal end extends into the cytosol and binds to protein 4.1, which in turn binds to spectrin. **Polymorphism** of this protein is the basis of the MN blood group system (see below). Glycophorin A contains binding sites for influenza virus and for *Plasmodium falciparum,* the cause of one form of malaria. Intriguingly, the function of red blood cells of individuals who lack glycophorin A does not appear to be affected.

Spectrin, Ankyrin, & Other Peripheral Membrane Proteins Help Determine the Shape & Flexibility of the Red Blood Cell

The red blood cell must be able to squeeze through some tight spots in the microcirculation during its numerous passages around the body; the sinusoids of the spleen are of special importance in this regard. For the red cell to be easily and reversibly **deformable,** its membrane must be both fluid and flexible; it should also preserve its biconcave shape, since this facilitates gas exchange. Membrane **lipids** help determine membrane fluidity. Attached to the inner aspect of the membrane of the red blood cell are a number of **peripheral cytoskeletal proteins** (Table 51–6) that play important roles in respect to preserving shape and flexibility; these will now be described.

Spectrin is the major protein of the cytoskeleton. It is composed of two polypeptides: spectrin 1 (α chain) and spectrin 2 (β chain). These chains, measuring approximately 100 nm in length, are aligned in an antiparallel manner and are loosely intertwined, forming a dimer. Both chains are made up of segments of 106 amino acids that appear to fold into triple-stranded α-helical coils joined by nonhelical segments. One dimer interacts with another, forming a head-to-head tetramer. The overall shape confers **flexibility** on the protein and in turn on the membrane of the red blood cell. At least four **binding sites** can be defined in spectrin: (1) for self-association, (2) for ankyrin (bands 2.1, etc), (3) for actin (band 5), and (4) for protein 4.1.

Ankyrin is a pyramid-shaped protein that **binds spectrin.** In turn, ankyrin binds tightly to band 3, securing attachment of spectrin to the membrane. Ankyrin is sensitive to proteolysis, accounting for the appearance of bands 2.2, 2.3, and 2.6, all of which are derived from band 2.1.

Actin (band 5) exists in red blood cells as short, double-helical filaments of F-actin. The tail end of spectrin dimers binds to actin. Actin also binds to protein 4.1.

Protein 4.1, a globular protein, binds tightly to the tail end of spectrin, near the actin-binding site of the latter, and thus is part of a protein 4.1-spectrin-actin ternary complex. Protein 4.1 also binds to the integral proteins, glycophorins A and C, thereby attaching the ternary complex to the membrane. In addition, protein 4.1 may interact with certain membrane phospholipids, thus connecting the lipid bilayer to the cytoskeleton.

Certain other proteins (4.9, adducin, and tropomyosin) also participate in **cytoskeletal assembly.**

Abnormalities in the Amount or Structure of Spectrin Cause Hereditary Spherocytosis & Elliptocytosis

Hereditary spherocytosis is a genetic disease, transmitted as an autosomal dominant, that affects about 1:5000 North Americans. It is characterized by the presence of spherocytes (spherical red blood cells, with a low surface-to-volume ratio) in the peripheral blood, by a hemolytic anemia, and by splenomegaly. The spherocytes are not as deformable as are normal red blood cells, and they are subject to destruction in the spleen, thus greatly shortening their life in the circulation. Hereditary spherocytosis is **curable by splenectomy** because the spherocytes can persist in the circulation if the spleen is absent.

The spherocytes are much more susceptible to osmotic lysis than are normal red blood cells. This is assessed in the **osmotic fragility test,** in which red blood cells are exposed in vitro to decreasing concentrations of NaCl. The physiologic concentration of NaCl is 0.85 g/dL. When exposed to a concentration of NaCl of 0.5 g/dL, very few normal red blood cells are hemolyzed, whereas approximately 50% of spherocytes would lyse under these conditions. The explanation is that the spherocyte, being almost circular, has little potential extra volume to accommodate additional water and thus lyses readily when exposed to a slightly lower osmotic pressure than is normal.

One cause of hereditary spherocytosis (Figure 51–5) is a deficiency in the amount of **spectrin** or abnormalities of its structure, so that it no longer tightly binds the other proteins with which it normally interacts. This weakens the membrane and leads to the spherocytic shape. Abnormalities of **ankyrin** and of **bands 3, 4.1,** and **4.2** are involved in other cases.

Hereditary elliptocytosis is a genetic disorder that is similar to hereditary spherocytosis except that affected red blood cells assume an elliptic, disk-like shape, recognizable by microscopy. It is also due to abnormalities in **spectrin;** some cases reflect abnormalities of band **4.1** or of **glycophorin C.**

THE BIOCHEMICAL BASES OF THE ABO BLOOD GROUP SYSTEM HAVE BEEN ESTABLISHED

Approximately 25 human **blood group systems** have been recognized, the best known of which are the **ABO, Rh (Rhesus),** and **MN** systems. The term "blood group" applies to a defined system of red blood cell antigens (blood group substances) controlled by a genetic locus having a variable number of alleles (eg, A, B, and O in the ABO system). The term **"blood type"** refers to the antigenic phenotype, usually recognized by

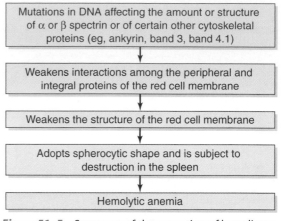

Figure 51–5. Summary of the causation of hereditary spherocytosis (MIM 182900). Approximately 50% of cases are due to abnormalities in ankyrin and 25% to abnormalities in spectrin.

the use of appropriate antibodies. For purposes of blood transfusion, it is particularly important to know the basics of the **ABO** and **Rh** systems. However, knowledge of blood group systems is also of biochemical, genetic, immunologic, anthropologic, obstetric, pathologic, and forensic interest. Here, we shall discuss only some key features of the **ABO system.** From a biochemical viewpoint, the major interests in the ABO substances have been in isolating and determining their structures, elucidating their pathways of biosynthesis, and determining the natures of the products of the A, B, and O genes.

The ABO System Is of Crucial Importance in Blood Transfusion

This system was first discovered by Landsteiner in 1900 when investigating the basis of compatible and incompatible transfusions in humans. The membranes of the red blood cells of most individuals contain one blood group substance of type A, type B, type AB, or type O. Individuals of **type A** have anti-B antibodies in their plasma and will thus agglutinate type B or type AB blood. Individuals of **type B** have anti-A antibodies and will agglutinate type A or type AB blood. **Type AB** blood has neither anti-A nor anti-B antibodies and has been designated the **universal recipient. Type O** blood has neither A nor B substances and has been designated the **universal donor.** The explanation of these findings is related to the fact that the body does not usually produce antibodies to its own constituents. Thus, individuals of type A do not produce antibodies to their own blood group substance, A, but do possess antibodies to the foreign blood group substance, B, possibly because

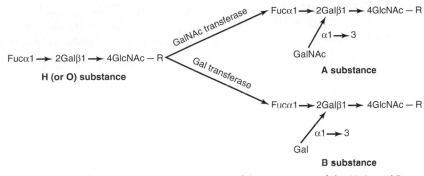

Figure 51–6. Diagrammatic representation of the structures of the H, A, and B blood group substances. R represents a long complex oligosaccharide chain, joined either to ceramide where the substances are glycosphingolipids, or to the polypeptide backbone of a protein via a serine or threonine residue where the substances are glycoproteins. Note that the blood group substances are biantennary; ie, they have two arms, formed at a branch point (not indicated) between the GlcNAc—R, and only one arm of the branch is shown. Thus, the H, A, and B substances each contain two of their respective short oligosaccharide chains shown above. The AB substance contains one type A chain and one type B chain.

similar structures are present in microorganisms to which the body is exposed early in life. Since individuals of type O have neither A nor B substances, they possess antibodies to both these foreign substances. The above description has been simplified considerably; eg, there are two subgroups of type A: A_1 and A_2.

The genes responsible for production of the ABO substances are present on the long arm of chromosome 9. There are **three alleles,** two of which are codominant (A and B) and the third (O) recessive; these ultimately determine the four phenotypic products: the A, B, AB, and O substances.

The ABO Substances Are Glycosphingolipids & Glycoproteins Sharing Common Oligosaccharide Chains

The **ABO substances** are complex oligosaccharides present in most cells of the body and in certain secretions. On membranes of red blood cells, the oligosaccharides that determine the specific natures of the ABO substances appear to be mostly present in **glycosphingolipids,** whereas in secretions the same oligosaccharides are present in **glycoproteins.** Their presence in secretions is determined by a gene designated *Se* (for **secretor**), which codes for a specific **fucosyl (Fuc) transferase** in secretory organs, such as the exocrine glands, but which is not active in red blood cells. Individuals of *SeSe* or *Sese* genotypes secrete A or B antigens (or both), whereas individuals of the *sese* genotype do not secrete A or B substances, but their red blood cells can express the A and B antigens.

H Substance Is the Biosynthetic Precursor of Both the A & B Substances

The ABO substances have been isolated and their structures determined; simplified versions, showing only their nonreducing ends, are presented in Figure 51–6. It is important to first appreciate the structure of the **H substance,** since it is the precursor of both the A and B substances and is the blood group substance found in persons of type O. H substance itself is formed by the action of a **fucosyltransferase,** which catalyzes the addition of the terminal fucose in $\alpha 1 \rightarrow 2$ linkage onto the terminal Gal residue of its precursor:

$$\text{GDP-Fuc} + \text{Gal-}\beta\text{-R} \rightarrow \text{Fuc-}\alpha 1,2\text{-Gal-}\beta\text{-R} + \text{GDP}$$
$$\text{Precursor} \qquad\qquad \text{H substance}$$

The H locus codes for this fucosyltransferase. The *h* allele of the H locus codes for an inactive fucosyltransferase; therefore, individuals of the *hh* genotype cannot generate H substance, the precursor of the A and B antigens. Thus, individuals of the *hh* genotype will have red blood cells of type O, even though they may possess the enzymes necessary to make the A or B substances (see below). They are referred to as being Bombay phenotype (O_h).

The *A* Gene Encodes a GalNAc Transferase, the *B* Gene a Gal Transferase, & the *O* Gene an Inactive Product

In comparison with H substance (Figure 51–6), **A substance** contains an additional GalNAc and **B substance** an

additional Gal, linked as indicated. Anti-A antibodies are directed to the additional GalNAc residue found in the A substance, and anti-B antibodies are directed toward the additional Gal residue found in the B substance. Thus, GalNAc is the **immunodominant sugar** (ie, the one determining the specificity of the antibody formed) of blood group A substance, whereas Gal is the immunodominant sugar of the B substance. In view of the structural findings, it is not surprising that A substance can be synthesized in vitro from O substance in a reaction catalyzed by a GalNAc transferase, employing UDP-GalNAc as the sugar donor. Similarly, blood group B can be synthesized from O substance by the action of a Gal transferase, employing UDP-Gal. It is crucial to appreciate that the product of the *A* gene is the **GalNAc transferase** that adds the terminal GalNAc to the O substance. Similarly, the product of the *B* gene is the **Gal transferase** adding the Gal residue to the O substance. Individuals of **type AB** possess both enzymes and thus have two oligosaccharide chains (Figure 51–6), one terminated by a GalNAc and the other by a Gal. Individuals of type O apparently synthesize an inactive protein, detectable by immunologic means; thus, H substance is their ABO blood group substance.

In 1990, a study using cloning and sequencing technology described the nature of the differences between the glycosyltransferase products of the *A, B,* and *O* genes. A difference of four nucleotides is apparently responsible for the distinct specificities of the A and B glycosyltransferases. On the other hand, the *O* allele has a single base-pair mutation, causing a **frameshift mutation** resulting in a protein lacking transferase activity.

HEMOLYTIC ANEMIAS ARE CAUSED BY ABNORMALITIES OUTSIDE, WITHIN, OR INSIDE THE RED BLOOD CELL MEMBRANE

Causes **outside the membrane** include hypersplenism, a condition in which the spleen is enlarged from a variety of causes and red blood cells become sequestered in it. **Immunologic abnormalities** (eg, transfusion reactions, the presence in plasma of warm and cold antibodies that lyse red blood cells, and unusual sensitivity to complement) also fall in this class, as do **toxins** released by various infectious agents, such as certain bacteria (eg, clostridium). Some snakes release **venoms** that act to lyse the red cell membrane (eg, via the action of phospholipases or proteinases).

Causes **within the membrane** include abnormalities of proteins. The most important conditions are hereditary spherocytosis and hereditary elliptocytosis, principally caused by abnormalities in the amount or structure of spectrin (see above).

Causes **inside the red blood cell** include **hemoglobinopathies** and **enzymopathies**. Sickle cell anemia is

Table 51–7. Laboratory investigations that assist in the diagnosis of hemolytic anemia.

General tests and findings
Increased nonconjugated (indirect) bilirubin
Shortened red cell survival time as measured by injection of autologous ^{51}Cr-labeled red cells
Reticulocytosis
Hemoglobinemia
Low level of plasma haptoglobin
Specific tests and findings
Hb electrophoresis (eg, HbS)
Red cell enzymes (eg, G6PD or PK deficiency)
Osmotic fragility (eg, hereditary spherocytosis)
Coombs test[1]
Cold agglutinins

[1]The direct Coombs test detects the presence of antibodies on red cells, whereas the indirect test detects the presence of circulating antibodies to antigens present on red cells.

the most important hemoglobinopathy. Abnormalities of enzymes in the pentose phosphate pathway and in glycolysis are the most frequent enzymopathies involved, particularly the former. Deficiency of **glucose-6-phosphate dehydrogenase** is prevalent in certain parts of the world and is a frequent cause of hemolytic anemia (see above). Deficiency of **pyruvate kinase** is not frequent, but it is the second commonest enzyme deficiency resulting in hemolytic anemia; the mechanism appears to be due to impairment of glycolysis, resulting in decreased formation of ATP, affecting various aspects of membrane integrity.

Laboratory investigations that aid in the diagnosis of hemolytic anemia are listed in Table 51–7.

NEUTROPHILS HAVE AN ACTIVE METABOLISM & CONTAIN SEVERAL UNIQUE ENZYMES & PROTEINS

The major biochemical features of **neutrophils** are summarized in Table 51–8. Prominent features are active aerobic glycolysis, active pentose phosphate pathway, moderately active oxidative phosphorylation (because mitochondria are relatively sparse), and a high content of lysosomal enzymes. Many of the enzymes listed in Table 51–4 are also of importance in the oxidative metabolism of neutrophils (see below). Table 51–9 summarizes the functions of some proteins that are relatively unique to neutrophils.

Neutrophils Are Key Players in the Body's Defense Against Bacterial Infection

Neutrophils are motile phagocytic cells that play a key role in acute inflammation. When bacteria enter tissues,

The process of **activation of neutrophils** is essentially similar. They are activated, via specific receptors, by interaction with bacteria, binding of chemotactic factors, or antibody-antigen complexes. The resultant **rise in intracellular Ca^{2+}** affects many processes in neutrophils, such as assembly of microtubules and the actin-myosin system. These processes are respectively involved in secretion of contents of granules and in motility, which enables neutrophils to seek out the invaders. The activated neutrophils are now ready to destroy the invaders by mechanisms that include production of active derivatives of oxygen.

The Respiratory Burst of Phagocytic Cells Involves NADPH Oxidase & Helps Kill Bacteria

When neutrophils and other phagocytic cells engulf bacteria, they exhibit a rapid increase in oxygen consumption known as **the respiratory burst.** This phenomenon reflects the rapid utilization of oxygen (following a lag of 15–60 seconds) and production from it of large amounts of **reactive derivatives,** such as O_2^-, H_2O_2, OH$^\bullet$, and OCl$^-$ (hypochlorite ion). Some of these products are potent microbicidal agents.

The **electron transport chain system** responsible for the respiratory burst (named NADPH oxidase) is composed of several components. One is **cytochrome b_{558},** located in the plasma membrane; it is a heterodimer, containing two polypeptides of 91 kDa and 22 kDa. When the system is activated (see below), two cytoplasmic polypeptides of 47 kDa and 67 kDa are recruited to the plasma membrane and, together with cytochrome b_{558}, form **the NADPH oxidase** responsible for the respiratory burst. The reaction catalyzed by NADPH oxidase, involving formation of superoxide anion, is shown in Table 51–4 (reaction 2). This system catalyzes the one-electron reduction of oxygen to superoxide anion. The NADPH is generated mainly by the pentose phosphate cycle, whose activity increases markedly during phagocytosis.

The above reaction is followed by the spontaneous production (by spontaneous dismutation) of **hydrogen peroxide** from two molecules of superoxide:

$$O_2^- + O_2^- + 2\ H^+ \rightarrow H_2O_2 + O_2$$

The **superoxide ion** is discharged to the outside of the cell or into phagolysosomes, where it encounters ingested bacteria. Killing of bacteria within phagolysosomes appears to depend on the combined action of elevated pH, superoxide ion, or further oxygen derivatives (H_2O_2, OH$^\bullet$, and HOCl [hypochlorous acid; see below]) and on the action of certain bactericidal peptides (defensins) and other proteins (eg, cathepsin G and certain cationic proteins) present in phagocytic cells. Any superoxide that enters the cytosol of the phagocytic cell is converted to H_2O_2 by the action of **superoxide dismutase,** which catalyzes the same reaction as the spontaneous dismutation shown above. In turn, H_2O_2 is used by myeloperoxidase (see below) or disposed of by the action of glutathione peroxidase or catalase.

NADPH oxidase is inactive in resting phagocytic cells and is **activated** upon contact with various ligands (complement fragment C5a, chemotactic peptides, etc) with receptors in the plasma membrane. The events resulting in activation of the oxidase system have been much studied and are similar to those described above for the process of activation of neutrophils. They involve **G proteins,** activation of **phospholipase C,** and generation of **inositol 1,4,5-triphosphate** (IP$_3$). The last mediates a transient increase in the level of cytosolic Ca^{2+}, which is essential for induction of the respiratory burst. **Diacylglycerol** is also generated and induces the translocation of protein kinase C into the plasma membrane from the cytosol, where it catalyzes the **phosphorylation** of various proteins, some of which are components of the oxidase system. A second pathway of activation not involving Ca^{2+} also operates.

Mutations in the Genes for Components of the NADPH Oxidase System Cause Chronic Granulomatous Disease

The importance of the **NADPH oxidase system** was clearly shown when it was observed that the respiratory burst was defective in **chronic granulomatous disease,** a relatively uncommon condition characterized by recurrent infections and widespread granulomas (chronic inflammatory lesions) in the skin, lungs, and lymph nodes. The granulomas form as attempts to wall off bacteria that have not been killed, owing to genetic deficiencies in the NADPH oxidase system. The disorder is due to mutations in the genes encoding the four polypeptides that constitute the NADPH oxidase system. Some patients have responded to treatment with gamma interferon, which may increase transcription of the 91-kDa component if it is affected. The probable sequence of events involved in the causation of chronic granulomatous disease is shown in Figure 51–7.

Neutrophils Contain Myeloperoxidase, Which Catalyzes the Production of Chlorinated Oxidants

The enzyme **myeloperoxidase,** present in large amounts in neutrophil granules and responsible for the green color of pus, can act on H_2O_2 to produce hypohalous acids:

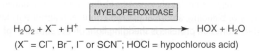

$$H_2O_2 + X^- + H^+ \xrightarrow{\text{MYELOPEROXIDASE}} HOX + H_2O$$

(X$^-$ = Cl$^-$, Br$^-$, I$^-$ or SCN$^-$; HOCl = hypochlorous acid)

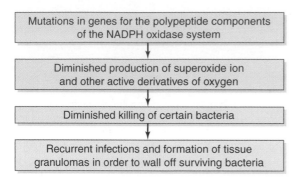

Figure 51–7. Simplified scheme of the sequence of events involved in the causation of chronic granulomatous disease (MIM 306400). Mutations in any of the genes for the four polypeptides involved (two are components of cytochrome b_{558} and two are derived from the cytoplasm) can cause the disease. The polypeptide of 91 kDa is encoded by a gene in the X chromosome; approximately 60% of cases of chronic granulomatous disease are X-linked, with the remainder being inherited in an autosomal recessive fashion.

The H_2O_2 used as substrate is generated by the NADPH oxidase system. Cl^- is the halide usually employed, since it is present in relatively high concentration in plasma and body fluids. **HOCl,** the active ingredient of household liquid bleach, is a powerful oxidant and is highly microbicidal. When applied to normal tissues, its potential for causing damage is diminished because it reacts with primary or secondary amines present in neutrophils and tissues to produce various nitrogen-chlorine derivatives; these **chloramines** are also oxidants, though less powerful than HOCl, and act as microbicidal agents (eg, in sterilizing wounds) without causing tissue damage.

The Proteinases of Neutrophils Can Cause Serious Tissue Damage If Their Actions Are Not Checked

Neutrophils contain a number of proteinases (Table 51–12) that can hydrolyze elastin, various types of collagens, and other proteins present in the extracellular matrix. Such enzymatic action, if allowed to proceed unopposed, can result in serious damage to tissues. Most of these proteinases are **lysosomal enzymes** and exist mainly as inactive precursors in normal neutrophils. Small amounts of these enzymes are released into normal tissues, with the amounts increasing markedly during inflammation. The activities of elastase and other proteinases are normally kept in check by a number of **antiproteinases** (also

listed in Table 51–12) present in plasma and the extracellular fluid. Each of them can combine—usually forming a noncovalent complex—with one or more specific proteinases and thus cause inhibition. In Chapter 49 it was shown that a genetic deficiency of α_1-**antiproteinase inhibitor** (α_1-antitrypsin) permits elastase to act unopposed and digest pulmonary tissue, thereby participating in the causation of emphysema. α_2-**Macroglobulin** is a plasma protein that plays an important role in the body's defense against excessive action of proteases; it combines with and thus neutralizes the activities of a number of important proteases (Chapter 49).

When increased amounts of chlorinated oxidants are formed during inflammation, they affect the proteinase:antiproteinase equilibrium, tilting it in favor of the former. For instance, certain of the proteinases listed in Table 51–12 are **activated** by HOCl, whereas certain of the antiproteinases are **inactivated** by this compound. In addition, the tissue inhibitor of metalloproteinases and α_1-antichymotrypsin can be hydrolyzed by activated elastase, and α_1-antiproteinase inhibitor can be hydrolyzed by activated collagenase and gelatinase. In most circumstances, **an appropriate balance** of proteinases and antiproteinases is achieved. However, in certain instances, such as in the lung when α_1-antiproteinase inhibitor is deficient or when large amounts of neutrophils accumulate in tissues because of inadequate drainage, considerable **tissue damage** can result from the unopposed action of proteinases.

Table 51–12. Proteinases of neutrophils and antiproteinases of plasma and tissues.[1]

Proteinases	Antiproteinases
Elastase	α_1-Antiproteinase (α_1-antitrypsin)
Collagenase	α_2-Macroglobulin
Gelatinase	Secretory leukoproteinase inhibitor
Cathepsin G	α_1-Antichymotrypsin
Plasminogen activator	Plasminogen activator inhibitor–1
	Tissue inhibitor of metalloproteinase

[1]The table lists some of the important proteinases of neutrophils and some of the proteins that can inhibit their actions. Most of the proteinases listed exist inside neutrophils as precursors. Plasminogen activator is not a proteinase, but it is included because it influences the activity of plasmin, which is a proteinase. The proteinases listed can digest many proteins of the extracellular matrix, causing tissue damage. The overall balance of proteinase:antiproteinase action can be altered by activating the precursors of the proteinases, or by inactivating the antiproteinases. The latter can be caused by proteolytic degradation or chemical modification, eg, Met-358 of α_1-antiproteinase inhibitor is oxidized by cigarette smoke.

RECOMBINANT DNA TECHNOLOGY HAS HAD A PROFOUND IMPACT ON HEMATOLOGY

Recombinant DNA technology has had a major impact on many aspects of hematology. The bases of the **thalassemias** and of many **disorders of coagulation** (Chapter 50) have been greatly clarified by investigations using cloning and sequencing. The study of oncogenes and chromosomal translocations has advanced understanding of the **leukemias.** As discussed above, cloning techniques have made available therapeutic amounts of **erythropoietin** and **other growth factors.** Deficiency of **adenosine deaminase,** which affects lymphocytes particularly, is the first disease to be treated by gene therapy. Like many other areas of biology and medicine, hematology has been and will continue to be revolutionized by this technology.

SUMMARY

- The red blood cell is simple in terms of its structure and function, consisting principally of a concentrated solution of hemoglobin surrounded by a membrane.

- The production of red cells is regulated by erythropoietin, whereas other growth factors (eg, granulocyte- and granulocyte-macrophage colony-stimulating factors) regulate the production of white blood cells.

- The red cell contains a battery of cytosolic enzymes, such as superoxide dismutase, catalase, and glutathione peroxidase, to dispose of powerful oxidants (ROS) generated during its metabolism.

- Genetically determined deficiency of the activity of glucose-6-phosphate dehydrogenase, which produces NADPH, is an important cause of hemolytic anemia.

- Methemoglobin is unable to transport oxygen; both genetic and acquired causes of methemoglobinemia are recognized. Considerable information has accumulated concerning the proteins and lipids of the red cell membrane. A number of cytoskeletal proteins, such as spectrin, ankyrin, and actin, interact with specific integral membrane proteins to help regulate the shape and flexibility of the membrane.

- Deficiency of spectrin results in hereditary spherocytosis, another important cause of hemolytic anemia.

- The ABO blood group substances in the red cell membrane are complex glycosphingolipids; the immunodominant sugar of A substance is N-acetyl-galactosamine, whereas that of the B substance is galactose.

- Neutrophils play a major role in the body's defense mechanisms. Integrins on their surface membranes determine specific interactions with various cell and tissue components.

- Leukocytes are activated on exposure to bacteria and other stimuli; NADPH oxidase plays a key role in the process of activation (the respiratory burst). Mutations in this enzyme and associated proteins cause chronic granulomatous disease.

- The proteinases of neutrophils can digest many tissue proteins; normally, this is kept in check by a battery of antiproteinases. However, this defense mechanism can be overcome in certain circumstances, resulting in extensive tissue damage.

- The application of recombinant DNA technology is revolutionizing the field of hematology.

REFERENCES

Ffrench-Constant C, Colognato H: Integrins: versatile integrators of extracellular signals. Trends Cell Biol 2004;14:678.

Hoffman R et al (editors): *Hematology: Basic Principles and Practice,* 4th ed. Elsevier Churchill Livingston, 2005.

Israels LG, Israels ED: *Mechanism in Hematology,* 3rd ed. Core Health Sciences Inc, 2002.

Kasper DL et al (editors): *Harrison's Principles of Internal Medicine,* 16th ed. McGraw-Hill, 2005.

Scriver CR et al (editors): *The Molecular Bases of Inherited Disease,* 8th ed. McGraw-Hill, 2001.

Yonekawa K, Harlan JM: Targeting leukocyte integrins in human diseases. J Leukoc Biol 2005;77:129.

Metabolism of Xenobiotics 52

Robert K. Murray, MD, PhD

BIOMEDICAL IMPORTANCE

Increasingly, humans are subjected to exposure to various foreign chemicals (**xenobiotics**)—drugs, food additives, pollutants, etc. The situation is well summarized in the following quotation from Rachel Carson: "As crude a weapon as the cave man's club, the chemical barrage has been hurled against the fabric of life." Understanding how xenobiotics are handled at the cellular level is important in learning how to cope with the chemical onslaught.

Knowledge of the metabolism of xenobiotics is basic to a rational understanding of pharmacology and therapeutics, pharmacy, toxicology, management of cancer, and drug addiction. All these areas involve administration of, or exposure to, xenobiotics.

HUMANS ENCOUNTER THOUSANDS OF XENOBIOTICS THAT MUST BE METABOLIZED BEFORE BEING EXCRETED

A **xenobiotic** (Gk *xenos* "stranger") is a compound that is foreign to the body. The principal classes of xenobiotics of medical relevance are drugs, chemical carcinogens, and various compounds that have found their way into our environment by one route or another, such as polychlorinated biphenyls (PCBs) and certain insecticides. More than 200,000 manufactured environmental chemicals exist. Most of these compounds are subject to metabolism (chemical alteration) in the human body, with the liver being the main organ involved; occasionally, a xenobiotic may be excreted unchanged. At least 30 different enzymes catalyze reactions involved in xenobiotic metabolism; however, this chapter will only cover a selected group of them.

It is convenient to consider the metabolism of xenobiotics in two phases. In **phase 1,** the major reaction involved is **hydroxylation,** catalyzed by members of a class of enzymes referred to as **monooxygenases** or **cytochrome P450s.** Hydroxylation may terminate the action of a drug, though this is not always the case. In addition to hydroxylation, these enzymes catalyze a wide range of reactions, including those involving deamination, dehalogenation, desulfuration, epoxidation, peroxygenation, and reduction. Reactions involving hydrolysis (eg, cata-

lyzed by esterases) and certain other non-P450-catalyzed reactions also occur in phase 1.

In **phase 2,** the hydroxylated or other compounds produced in phase 1 are converted by specific enzymes to various polar metabolites by **conjugation** with glucuronic acid, sulfate, acetate, glutathione, or certain amino acids, or by **methylation.**

The overall purpose of the two phases of metabolism of xenobiotics is to increase their **water solubility (polarity)** and thus **excretion** from the body. Very hydrophobic xenobiotics would persist in adipose tissue almost indefinitely if they were not converted to more polar forms. In certain cases, phase 1 metabolic reactions convert xenobiotics from **inactive** to **biologically active** compounds. In these instances, the original xenobiotics are referred to as **"prodrugs"** or **"procarcinogens."** In other cases, additional phase 1 reactions (eg, further hydroxylation reactions) convert the active compounds to less active or inactive forms prior to conjugation. In yet other cases, it is the conjugation reactions themselves that convert the active products of phase 1 reactions to less active or inactive species, which are subsequently excreted in the urine or bile. In a very few cases, conjugation may actually increase the biologic activity of a xenobiotic.

The term **"detoxification"** is sometimes used for many of the reactions involved in the metabolism of xenobiotics. However, the term is not always appropriate because, as mentioned above, in some cases the reactions to which xenobiotics are subject actually increase their biologic activity and toxicity.

ISOFORMS OF CYTOCHROME P450 HYDROXYLATE A MYRIAD OF XENOBIOTICS IN PHASE 1 OF THEIR METABOLISM

Hydroxylation is the chief reaction involved in phase 1. The responsible enzymes are called **monooxygenases** or **cytochrome P450s.** It is estimated that there are approximately 60 cytochrome P450 genes present in humans. The reaction catalyzed by a monooxygenase (cytochrome P450) is as follows:

$$RH + O_2 + NADPH + H^+ \rightarrow R-OH + H_2O + NADP$$

RH above can represent a very wide variety of xenobiotics, including drugs, carcinogens, pesticides, petroleum products, and pollutants (such as a mixture of PCBs). In addition, **endogenous compounds,** such as certain steroids, eicosanoids, fatty acids, and retinoids, are also substrates. The substrates are generally **lipophilic** and are rendered more **hydrophilic** by hydroxylation.

Cytochrome P450 is considered the **most versatile biocatalyst** known. The actual reaction mechanism is complex and has been briefly described previously (Figure 12–6). It has been shown by the use of $^{18}O_2$ that one atom of oxygen enters R–OH and one atom enters water. This dual fate of the oxygen accounts for the former naming of monooxygenases as **"mixed-function oxidases."** The reaction catalyzed by cytochrome P450 can also be represented as follows:

$$\text{Reduced cytochrome P450} \quad \text{Oxidized cytochrome P450}$$

$$RH + O_2 \rightarrow R\text{–}OH + H_2O$$

Cytochrome P450 is so named because the enzyme was discovered when it was noted that preparations of microsomes that had been chemically reduced and then exposed to carbon monoxide exhibited a distinct peak at 450 nm. Among reasons that this enzyme is important is the fact that approximately 50% of the common drugs humans ingest are metabolized by isoforms of cytochrome P450; these enzymes also act on various carcinogens and pollutants. The major cytochrome P450s in drug metabolism are members of the CYP1, CYP2, and CYP3 families (see below).

Isoforms of Cytochrome P450 Make Up a Superfamily of Heme-Containing Enzymes

The following are important points concerning cytochrome P450s.

(1) Because of the large number of isoforms (about 150) that have been discovered, it became important to have a **systematic nomenclature** for isoforms of P450 and for their genes. This is now available and in wide use and is based on structural homology. The abbreviated root symbol CYP denotes a cytochrome P450. This is followed by an Arabic number designating the **family;** cytochrome P450s are included in the same family if they exhibit 40% or more amino acid sequence identity. The Arabic number is followed by a capital letter indicating the **subfamily,** if two or more members exist; P450s are in the same subfamily if they exhibit greater than 55% sequence identity. The **individual** P450s are then arbitrarily assigned Arabic numerals. Thus, CYP1A1 denotes a cytochrome P450 that is a member of family 1 and subfamily A and is the first individual member of that subfamily. The

nomenclature for the **genes** encoding cytochrome P450s is identical to that described above except that italics are used; thus, the gene encoding CYP1A1 is *CYP1A1.*

CYP3A is the most important cytochrome P450 involved in drug metabolism, because of its abundance in liver and intestine. It can act on a wide variety of drugs from almost every class. Also its activity is somewhat unpredictable, because it can vary by almost 400-fold due to inhibition and induction, thus leading to problems with drug dosage.

(2) Like **hemoglobin,** they are hemoproteins.

(3) They are widely distributed across species, including bacteria.

(4) They are present in highest amount in **liver cells** and enterocytes but are probably present in all tissues. In liver and most other tissues, they are present mainly in the **membranes of the smooth endoplasmic reticulum,** which constitute part of the **microsomal fraction** when tissue is subjected to subcellular fractionation. In hepatic microsomes, cytochrome P450s can comprise as much as 20% of the total protein. P450s are found in most tissues, though often in low amounts compared with liver. In the **adrenal,** they are found in **mitochondria** as well as in the endoplasmic reticulum; the various hydroxylases present in that organ play an important role in cholesterol and steroid biosynthesis. The mitochondrial cytochrome P450 system differs from the microsomal system in that it uses an NADPH-linked flavoprotein, **adrenodoxin reductase,** and a nonheme iron sulfur protein, **adrenodoxin.** In addition, the specific P450 isoforms involved in steroid biosynthesis are generally much more restricted in their substrate specificity.

(5) At least six isoforms of cytochrome P450 are present in the endoplasmic reticulum of human liver, each with wide and somewhat overlapping **substrate specificities** and acting on both xenobiotics and endogenous compounds. The genes for many isoforms of P450 (from both humans and animals such as the rat) have been isolated and studied in detail in recent years.

(6) **NADPH,** not NADH, is involved in the reaction mechanism of cytochrome P450. The enzyme that uses NADPH to yield the reduced cytochrome P450, shown at the left-hand side of the above equation, is called **NADPH-cytochrome P450 reductase.** Electrons are transferred from NADPH to NADPH-cytochrome P450 reductase and then to cytochrome P450. This leads to the **reductive activation of molecular oxygen,** and one atom of oxygen is subsequently inserted into the substrate. **Cytochrome b_5,** another hemoprotein found in the membranes of the smooth endoplasmic reticulum (Chapter 12), may be involved as an electron donor in some cases.

(7) **Lipids** are also components of the cytochrome P450 system. The preferred lipid is **phosphatidylcho-**

line, which is the major lipid found in membranes of the endoplasmic reticulum.

(8) Most isoforms of cytochrome P450 are **inducible.** For instance, the administration of phenobarbital or of many other drugs causes hypertrophy of the smooth endoplasmic reticulum and a three- to fourfold increase in the amount of cytochrome P450 within 4–5 days. The mechanism of induction has been studied extensively and in most cases involves increased transcription of mRNA for cytochrome P450. However, certain cases of induction involve stabilization of mRNA, enzyme stabilization, or other mechanisms (eg, an effect on translation).

Induction of cytochrome P450 has important clinical implications, since it is a biochemical mechanism of **drug interaction.** A drug interaction has occurred when the effects of one drug are altered by prior, concurrent, or later administration of another. As an illustration, consider the situation when a patient is taking the anticoagulant **warfarin** to prevent blood clotting. This drug is metabolized by CYP2C9. Concomitantly, the patient is started on **phenobarbital** (an inducer of this P450) to treat a certain type of epilepsy, but the dose of warfarin is not changed. After 5 days or so, the level of CYP2C9 in the patient's liver will be elevated three- to fourfold. This in turn means that warfarin will be metabolized much more quickly than before, and its dosage will have become inadequate. Therefore, the dose must be increased if warfarin is to be therapeutically effective. To pursue this example further, a problem could arise later on if the phenobarbital is discontinued but the increased dosage of warfarin stays the same. The patient will be at risk of bleeding, since the high dose of warfarin will be even more active than before, because the level of CYP2C9 will decline once phenobarbital has been stopped.

Another example of enzyme induction involves **CYP2E1,** which is induced by consumption of **ethanol.** This is a matter for concern, because this P450 metabolizes certain widely used solvents and also components found in tobacco smoke, many of which are established **carcinogens.** Thus, if the activity of CYP2E1 is elevated by induction, this may increase the risk of carcinogenicity developing from exposure to such compounds.

(9) Certain isoforms of cytochrome P450 (eg, CYP1A1) are particularly involved in the metabolism of polycyclic aromatic hydrocarbons (PAHs) and related molecules; for this reason they were formerly called **aromatic hydrocarbon hydroxylases (AHHs).** This enzyme is important in the metabolism of PAHs and in carcinogenesis produced by these agents. For example, in the lung it may be involved in the conversion of inactive PAHs (procarcinogens), inhaled by smoking, to active carcinogens by hydroxylation reactions. Smokers have higher levels of this enzyme in some of their cells and tissues than do nonsmokers. Some reports have indicated that the activity of this enzyme may be elevated (induced) in the placenta of a woman who smokes, thus potentially altering the quantities of metabolites of PAHs (some of which could be harmful) to which the fetus is exposed.

(10) Certain cytochrome P450s exist in **polymorphic forms** (genetic isoforms), some of which exhibit low catalytic activity. These observations are one important explanation for the variations in drug responses noted among many patients. One P450 exhibiting polymorphism is CYP2D6, which is involved in the metabolism of debrisoquin (an antihypertensive drug; see Table 52–2) and sparteine (an antiarrhythmic and oxytocic drug). Certain polymorphisms of CYP2D6 cause poor metabolism of these and a variety of other drugs so that they can accumulate in the body, resulting in untoward consequences. Another interesting polymorphism is that of CYP2A6, which is involved in the metabolism of nicotine to conitine. Three *CYP2A6* alleles have been identified: a wild type and two null or inactive alleles. It has been reported that individuals with the null alleles, who have impaired metabolism of nicotine, are apparently protected against becoming tobacco-dependent smokers (Table 52–2). These individuals smoke less, presumably because their blood and brain concentrations of nicotine remain elevated longer than those of individuals with the wild-type allele. It has been speculated that inhibiting CYP2A6 may be a novel way to help prevent and to treat smoking.

Table 52–1 summarizes some principal features of cytochrome P450s.

CONJUGATION REACTIONS PREPARE XENOBIOTICS FOR EXCRETION IN PHASE 2 OF THEIR METABOLISM

In phase 1 reactions, xenobiotics are generally converted to more polar, hydroxylated derivatives. In phase 2 reactions, these derivatives are conjugated with molecules such as glucuronic acid, sulfate, or glutathione. This renders them even more water-soluble, and they are eventually excreted in the urine or bile.

Five Types of Phase 2 Reactions Are Described Here

A. GLUCURONIDATION

The glucuronidation of bilirubin is discussed in Chapter 31; the reactions whereby xenobiotics are glucuronidated are essentially similar. UDP-glucuronic acid is the glucuronyl donor, and a variety of glucuronosyltransferases, present in both the endoplasmic reticulum and cytosol, are

Table 52–1. Some properties of human cytochrome P450s.

- Involved in phase I of the metabolism of innumerable xenobiotics, including perhaps 50% of the drugs administered to humans
- Involved in the metabolism of many endogenous compounds (eg, steroids)
- All are hemoproteins
- Often exhibit broad substrate specificity, thus acting on many compounds; consequently, different P450s may catalyze formation of the same product
- Extremely versatile catalysts, perhaps catalyzing about 60 types of reactions
- However, basically they catalyze reactions involving introduction of one atom of oxygen into the substrate and one into water
- Their hydroxylated products are more water-soluble than their generally lipophilic substrates, facilitating excretion
- Liver contains highest amounts, but found in most if not all tissues, including small intestine, brain, and lung
- Located in the smooth endoplasmic reticulum or in mitochondria (steroidogenic hormones)
- In some cases, their products are mutagenic or carcinogenic
- Many have a molecular mass of about 55 kDa
- Many are inducible, resulting in one cause of drug interactions
- Many are inhibited by various drugs or their metabolic products, providing another cause of drug interactions
- Some exhibit genetic polymorphisms, which can result in atypical drug metabolism
- Their activities may be altered in diseased tissues (eg, cirrhosis), affecting drug metabolism
- Genotyping the P450 profile of patients (eg, to detect polymorphisms) may in the future permit individualization of drug therapy

the catalysts. Molecules such as 2-acetylaminofluorene (a carcinogen), aniline, benzoic acid, meprobamate (a tranquilizer), phenol, and many steroids are excreted as glucuronides. The glucuronide may be attached to oxygen, nitrogen, or sulfur groups of the substrates. Glucuronidation is probably the most frequent conjugation reaction.

B. SULFATION

Some alcohols, arylamines, and phenols are sulfated. The **sulfate donor** in these and other biologic sulfation reactions (eg, sulfation of steroids, glycosaminoglycans, glycolipids, and glycoproteins) is **adenosine 3′-phosphate-5′-phosphosulfate (PAPS)** (Chapter 24); this compound is called "active sulfate."

C. CONJUGATION WITH GLUTATHIONE

Glutathione (γ-glutamyl-cysteinylglycine) is a **tripeptide** consisting of glutamic acid, cysteine, and glycine (Figure 3–3). Glutathione is commonly abbreviated

GSH (because of the sulfhydryl group of its cysteine, which is the business part of the molecule). A number of potentially toxic electrophilic xenobiotics (such as certain carcinogens) are conjugated to the nucleophilic GSH in reactions that can be represented as follows:

$$R + GSH \rightarrow R - S - G$$

where R = an electrophilic xenobiotic. The enzymes catalyzing these reactions are called **glutathione S-transferases** and are present in high amounts in liver cytosol and in lower amounts in other tissues. A variety of glutathione S-transferases are present in human tissue. They exhibit different substrate specificities and can be separated by electrophoretic and other techniques. If the potentially toxic xenobiotics were not conjugated to GSH, they would be free to combine covalently with DNA, RNA, or cell protein and could thus lead to serious cell damage. GSH is therefore an important **defense mechanism** against certain toxic compounds, such as some drugs and carcinogens. If the levels of GSH in a tissue such as liver are lowered (as can be achieved by the administration to rats of certain compounds that react with GSH), then that tissue can be shown to be more susceptible to injury by various chemicals that would normally be conjugated to GSH. Glutathione conjugates are subjected to further metabolism before excretion. The glutamyl and glycinyl groups belonging to glutathione are removed by specific enzymes, and an acetyl group (donated by acetyl-CoA) is added to the amino group of the remaining cysteinyl moiety. The resulting compound is a **mercapturic acid,** a conjugate of L-acetylcysteine, which is then excreted in the urine.

Glutathione has other important functions in human cells apart from its role in xenobiotic metabolism.

1. It participates in the decomposition of potentially toxic **hydrogen peroxide** in the reaction catalyzed by glutathione peroxidase (Chapter 21).
2. It is an important **intracellular reductant,** helping to maintain essential SH groups of enzymes in their reduced state. This role is discussed in Chapter 21, and its involvement in the hemolytic anemia caused by deficiency of glucose-6-phosphate dehydrogenase is discussed in Chapters 21 and 51.
3. A metabolic cycle involving GSH as a carrier has been implicated in the **transport of certain amino acids** across membranes in the kidney. The first reaction of the cycle is shown below.

$$\text{Amino acid} + GSH \rightarrow \gamma\text{-Glutamyl amino acid} + \text{Cysteinylglycine}$$

This reaction helps transfer certain amino acids across the plasma membrane, the amino acid being subse-

quently hydrolyzed from its complex with GSH and the GSH being resynthesized from cysteinylglycine. The enzyme catalyzing the above reaction is **γ-glutamyl-transferase (GGT).** It is present in the plasma membrane of renal tubular cells and bile ductule cells, and in the endoplasmic reticulum of hepatocytes. The enzyme has diagnostic value because it is released into the blood from hepatic cells in various hepatobiliary diseases.

D. OTHER REACTIONS

The two most important other reactions are acetylation and methylation.

1. Acetylation—Acetylation is represented by

$$X + Acetyl\text{-}CoA \rightarrow Acetyl\text{-}X + CoA$$

where X represents a xenobiotic. As for other acetylation reactions, **acetyl-CoA** (active acetate) is the acetyl donor. These reactions are catalyzed by **acetyltransferases** present in the cytosol of various tissues, particularly liver. The drug **isoniazid,** used in the treatment of tuberculosis, is subject to acetylation. **Polymorphic types** of acetyltransferases exist, resulting in individuals who are classified as **slow or fast acetylators,** and influence the rate of clearance of drugs such as isoniazid from blood. Slow acetylators are more subject to certain toxic effects of isoniazid because the drug persists longer in these individuals.

2. Methylation—A few xenobiotics are subject to methylation by methyltransferases, employing *S*-adenosylmethionine (Figure 29–17) as the methyl donor.

THE ACTIVITIES OF XENOBIOTIC-METABOLIZING ENZYMES ARE AFFECTED BY AGE, SEX, & OTHER FACTORS

Various factors affect the activities of the enzymes metabolizing xenobiotics. The activities of these enzymes may differ substantially among **species.** Thus, for example, the possible **toxicity** or **carcinogenicity** of xenobiotics cannot be extrapolated freely from one species to another. There are significant differences in enzyme activities among individuals, many of which appear to be due to **genetic factors.** The activities of some of these enzymes vary according to **age** and **sex.**

Intake of various xenobiotics such as phenobarbital, PCBs, or certain hydrocarbons can cause **enzyme induction.** It is thus important to know whether or not an individual has been exposed to these inducing agents in evaluating biochemical responses to xenobiotics. Metabolites of certain xenobiotics can **inhibit** or **stimulate** the activities of xenobiotic-metabolizing enzymes. Again, this can affect the doses of certain drugs that are administered

to patients. Various **diseases** (eg, cirrhosis of the liver) can affect the activities of drug-metabolizing enzymes, sometimes necessitating adjustment of dosages of various drugs for patients with these disorders.

RESPONSES TO XENOBIOTICS INCLUDE PHARMACOLOGIC, TOXIC, IMMUNOLOGIC, & CARCINOGENIC EFFECTS

Xenobiotics are metabolized in the body by the reactions described above. When the xenobiotic is a drug, phase 1 reactions may produce its active form or may diminish or terminate its action if it is pharmacologically active in the body without prior metabolism. The diverse effects produced by drugs comprise the area of study of pharmacology; here it is important to appreciate that drugs act primarily through biochemical mechanisms. Table 52–2 summarizes four important reactions to drugs that reflect **genetically determined differences** in enzyme and protein structure among individuals—part of the field of study known as **pharmacogenetics** (see below).

Polymorphisms that affect drug metabolism can occur in any of the **enzymes** involved in drug metabolism (including cytochrome P450s), in **transporters** and in **receptors.**

Table 52–2. Some important drug reactions due to mutant or polymorphic forms of enzymes or proteins.[1]

Enzyme or Protein Affected	Reaction or Consequence
Glucose-6-phosphate dehydrogenase (G6PD) [mutations] (MIM 305900)	Hemolytic anemia following ingestion of drugs such as primaquine
Ca^{2+} release channel (ryanodine receptor) in the sarcoplasmic reticulum [mutations] (MIM 180901)	Malignant hyperthermia (MIM 145600) following administration of certain anesthetics (eg, halothane)
CYP2D6 [polymorphisms] (MIM 124030)	Slow metabolism of certain drugs (eg, debrisoquin), resulting in their accumulation
CYP2A6 [polymorphisms] (MIM 122720)	Impaired metabolism of nicotine, resulting in protection against becoming a tobacco-dependent smoker

[1]G6PD deficiency is discussed in Chapters 21 and 51 and malignant hyperthermia in Chapter 48. At least one gene other than that encoding the ryanodine receptor is involved in certain cases of malignant hypertension. Many other examples of drug reactions based on polymorphism or mutation are available.

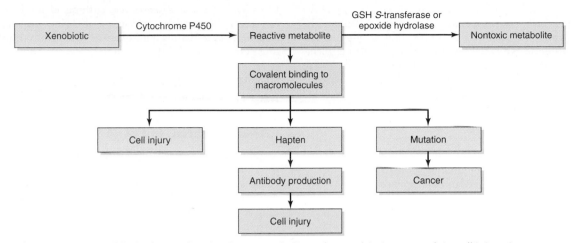

Figure 52–1. Simplified scheme showing how metabolism of a xenobiotic can result in cell injury, immunologic damage, or cancer. In this instance, the conversion of the xenobiotic to a reactive metabolite is catalyzed by a cytochrome P450, and the conversion of the reactive metabolite (eg, an epoxide) to a nontoxic metabolite is catalyzed either by a GSH S-transferase or by epoxide hydrolase.

Certain xenobiotics are very toxic even at low levels (eg, cyanide). On the other hand, there are few xenobiotics, including drugs, that do not exert some toxic effects if sufficient amounts are administered. The **toxic effects of xenobiotics** cover a wide spectrum, but the major effects can be considered under three general headings (Figure 52–1).

The first is **cell injury** (cytotoxicity), which can be severe enough to result in cell death. There are many mechanisms by which xenobiotics injure cells. The one considered here is **covalent binding to cell macromolecules** of reactive species of xenobiotics produced by metabolism. These macromolecular targets include **DNA, RNA,** and **protein.** If the macromolecule to which the reactive xenobiotic binds is essential for short-term cell survival, eg, a protein or enzyme involved in some critical cellular function such as oxidative phosphorylation or regulation of the permeability of the plasma membrane, then severe effects on cellular function could become evident quite rapidly.

Second, the reactive species of a xenobiotic may bind to a protein, altering its **antigenicity.** The xenobiotic is said to act as a **hapten,** ie, a small molecule that by itself does not stimulate antibody synthesis but will combine with antibody once formed. The resulting **antibodies** can then damage the cell by several immunologic mechanisms that grossly perturb normal cellular biochemical processes.

Third, reactions of activated species of chemical carcinogens with **DNA** are thought to be of great importance in **chemical carcinogenesis.** Some chemicals (eg, benzo[α]pyrene) require activation by monooxygenases in the endoplasmic reticulum to become carcinogenic

(they are thus called **indirect carcinogens**). The activities of the monooxygenases and of other xenobiotic-metabolizing enzymes present in the endoplasmic reticulum thus help to determine whether such compounds become carcinogenic or are "detoxified." Other chemicals (eg, various alkylating agents) can react directly (direct carcinogens) with DNA without undergoing intracellular chemical activation.

The enzyme **epoxide hydrolase** is of interest because it can exert a protective effect against certain carcinogens. The products of the action of certain monooxygenases on some procarcinogen substrates are **epoxides.** Epoxides are highly reactive and mutagenic or carcinogenic or both. Epoxide hydrolase—like cytochrome P450, also present in the membranes of the endoplasmic reticulum—acts on these compounds, converting them into much less reactive dihydrodiols. The reaction catalyzed by epoxide hydrolase can be represented as follows:

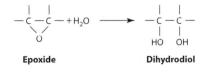

Epoxide   **Dihydrodiol**

PHARMACOGENOMICS WILL DRIVE THE DEVELOPMENT OF NEW & SAFER DRUGS

As indicated above, **pharmacogenetics** is the study of the roles of genetic variations in the responses to drugs. As a result of the progress made in sequencing the

human genome, a new field of study—**pharmacogenomics**—has developed recently. It includes pharmacogenetics but covers a much wider sphere of activity. Information from genomics, proteomics, bioinformatics, and other disciplines such as biochemistry and toxicology will be integrated to make possible the synthesis of newer and safer drugs. As the sequences of all our genes and their encoded proteins are determined, this will reveal many new **targets for drug actions.** It will also reveal **polymorphisms** (this term is briefly discussed in Chapter 49) of enzymes and proteins related to drug metabolism, action, and toxicity. Microarrays capable of detecting them will be constructed, permitting screening of individuals for potentially harmful polymorphisms prior to the start of drug therapy. Already gene chips are available for analyzing certain P450 genotypes (eg, for CYP2D6, whose gene product is involved in the metabolism of many antidepressants, antipsychotics, β-blockers, and some chemotherapeutic agents). Figure 52–2 summarizes some approaches to developing new drugs. Major thrusts of new drug development are to enhance treatment and to provide safer, personalized drugs, taking into account polymorphisms and other factors. It has been estimated that some 100,000 deaths from adverse drug reactions occur each year in the United States alone. Hopefully, new information provided by studies in the various areas indicated in Figure 52–2 and in other areas will translate into successful therapies and also eventually into a new era of personalized therapeutics.

SUMMARY

- Xenobiotics are chemical compounds foreign to the body, such as drugs, food additives, and environmental pollutants; more than 200,000 have been identified.

- Xenobiotics are metabolized in two phases. The major reaction of phase 1 is hydroxylation catalyzed by a variety of monooxygenases, also known as the cytochrome P450s. In phase 2, the hydroxylated species are conjugated with a variety of hydrophilic compounds such as glucuronic acid, sulfate, or glutathione. The combined operation of these two phases renders lipophilic compounds into water-soluble compounds that can be eliminated from the body.

- Cytochrome P450s catalyze reactions that introduce one atom of oxygen derived from molecular oxygen into the substrate, yielding a hydroxylated product. NADPH and NADPH-cytochrome P450 reductase are involved in the complex reaction mechanism.

- All cytochrome P450s are hemoproteins and generally have a wide substrate specificity, acting on many exogenous and endogenous substrates. They represent the most versatile biocatalyst known.

- Approximately 60 cytochrome P450 genes are found in human tissue.

- Cytochrome P450s are generally located in the endoplasmic reticulum of cells and are particularly enriched in liver.

- Many cytochrome P450s are inducible. This has important implications in phenomena such as drug interaction.

- Mitochondrial cytochrome P450s also exist and are involved in cholesterol and steroid biosynthesis. They use a nonheme iron-containing sulfur protein, adrenodoxin, not required by microsomal isoforms.

- Cytochrome P450s, because of their catalytic activities, play major roles in the reactions of cells to chemical compounds and in chemical carcinogenesis.

- Phase 2 reactions are catalyzed by enzymes such as glucuronosyltransferases, sulfotransferases, and glutathione S-transferases, using UDP-glucuronic acid, PAPS (active sulfate), and glutathione, respectively, as donors.

- Glutathione not only plays an important role in phase 2 reactions but is also an intracellular reducing agent and is involved in the transport of certain amino acids into cells.

- Xenobiotics can produce a variety of biologic effects, including pharmacologic responses, toxicity, immunologic reactions, and cancer.

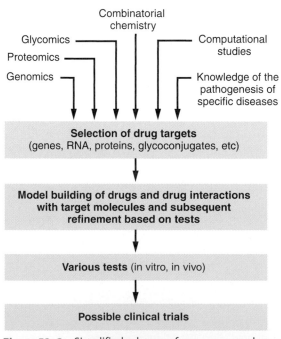

Figure 52–2. Simplified scheme of some approaches to the development of new drugs.

- Catalyzed by the progress made in sequencing the human genome, the new field of pharmacogenomics offers the promise of being able to make available a host of new rationally designed, safer drugs.

REFERENCES

Austin CP: The impact of the completed human genome sequence on the development of novel therapeutics for human disease. Annu Rev Med 2004;55:1.

Borst P, Elferink RO: Mammalian ABC transporters in health and disease. Annu Rev Biochem 2002;71:537.

Evans WE, McLeod HL: Pharmacogenomics—drug disposition, drug targets, and side effects. N Engl J Med 2003;348:538.

Human Cytochrome P450 (CYP) Allele Nomenclature Committee. http://www.imm.ki.se/CYPalleles/

Kalow W, Grant DM: Pharmacogenetics. In: *The Metabolic and Molecular Bases of Inherited Disease,* 8th ed. Scriver CR et al (editors). McGraw-Hill, 2001.

Katzung BG (editor): *Basic & Clinical Pharmacology,* 9th ed. McGraw-Hill, 2004.

Lee WM: Drug-induced hepatotoxicity. N Engl J Med 2003;349:474.

Szuromi P et al: Revisiting drug discovery. Science 2004;303:1795. (This is the introduction to a series of articles on drug development in this particular issue of Science.)

Weinshilboum R: Inheritance and drug response. N Engl J Med 2003;348:529.

Wilkinson GR: Drug metabolism and variability among patients in drug response. N Engl J Med 2005;350:2211.

Appendix

SELECTED WORLDWIDE WEB SITES

The following is a list of web sites that readers may find useful. The sites have been visited at various times by one or more of the authors. Most are located in the United States, but many provide extensive links to international sites and to databases (eg, for protein and nucleic acid sequences) and online journals. RKM would be grateful if readers who find other useful sites would notify him of their URLs by e-mail (rmurray6745@rogers.com) so that they may be considered for inclusion in future editions of this text.

Readers should note that URLs may change or cease to exist.

■ ACCESS TO THE BIOMEDICAL LITERATURE

High Wire Press: http://highwire.stanford.edu/
(Extensive lists of various classes of journals—biology, medicine, etc—and offers also the most extensive list of journals with free online access.)
National Library of Medicine: http://www.nlm.nih.gov/
(Free access to Medline via PubMed.)

GENERAL RESOURCE SITES

The Biology Project (from the University of Arizona): http://www.biology.arizona.edu/default.html
(Contains excellent biochemical coverage of enzymes, membranes, etc.)
Harvard University Department of Molecular & Cellular Biology Links: http://mcb.harvard.edu/BioLinks.html
(Contains many useful links.)

SITES ON SPECIFIC TOPICS

American Heart Association: http://www.americanheart.org/
(Useful information on nutrition, on the role of various biomolecules—eg, cholesterol, lipoproteins—in heart disease, and on the major cardiovascular diseases.)

Cancer Genome Anatomy Project (CGAP): http://www.cgap.nci.nih.gov.
(An interdisciplinary program to generate the information and technical tools to decipher the molecular anatomy of the cancer cell.)
Carbohydrate Chemistry and Glycobiology: A Web Tour: http://sciencemag.org/feature/data/carbohydrates.shl
(Contains links to organic chemistry, carbohydrate chemistry and glycobiology.)
European Bioinformatics Institute: http://ebi.ac.uk/index.html
(Maintains the EMBL Nucleotide and SWISS-PROT databases as well as other databases.)
GeneCards: http://www.genecards.org/
(A database of human genes, their products, and their involvements in disease; from the Weizmann Institute of Science.)
GeneTests: http://www.geneclinics.org/
(A medical genetics information resource with comprehensive articles on many genetic diseases.)
Genes and Disease: http://www.ncbi.nlm.nih.gov/disease/
(Coverage of the genetic bases of many different diseases.)
Howard Hughes Medical Institute: http://www.hhmi.org/
(An excellent site for following current biomedical research. Contains a comprehensive Research News Archive.)
Human Gene Mutation Database: http://www.hgmd.cf.ac.uk/hgmd0.html
(An extensive tabulation of mutations in human genes from the Institute of Medical Genetics in Cardiff, Wales.)
Human Genome Project Information: http://www.doegenomes.org/
(From the U.S. Department of Energy; also contains general information on genomics and on microbial genomes.)
Karolinska Institute: Diseases and Disorders: http://www.mic.ki.se/Diseases/C18.html
(Contains extensive links pertaining to nutritional and metabolic diseases.)
Lipids Online: http://lipidsonline.org/
(A resource from Baylor College of Medicine for health care practitioners with an interest in atherosclerosis, dyslipidemias, and lipid management.)
MITOMAP: http://www.mitomap.org/
(A human mitochondrial genome database.)
National Center for Biotechnology Information: http://ncbi.nlm.nih.gov/
(Information on molecular biology and how molecular processes affect human health and disease.)

National Human Genome Research Institute: http://www.genome.gov/

(Extensive information about the Human Genome Project and subsequent work.)

National Institutes of Health: http://www.nih.gov/

(Includes links to the separate Institutes and Centers that constitute NIH, covering a wide range of biomedical research.)

Office of Rare Diseases: http://rarediseases.info.nih.gov

(Access to information on more than 7,000 rare diseases, including current research.)

OMIM (Online Mendelian Inheritance in Man): http://www.ncbi.nlm.nih.gov/entrez/query.fcgi?db=OMIM

(A fantastically comprehensive resource on human genetic diseases, initiated by Dr Victor A. McKusick, considered by many to be the father of modern human genetics.)

Protein Data Bank: http://www.rcsb.org/pdb/

(A worldwide repository for the processing and distribution of three-dimensional biologic macromolecular structure data.)

Society for Endocrinology: http://www.endocrinology.org/default.htm

(The site aims to advance education and research in endocrinology for the public benefit.)

Society for Neuroscience: http://web.sfn.org

(Contains useful information on a variety of topics in neuroscience.)

The Broad Institute: http://www.broad.mit.edu/

(The Broad Institute is a research collaboration of MIT, Harvard and its affiliated hospitals, and the Whitehead Institute and was created to bring the power of genomics to medicine.)

The Institute for Genetic Research: http://www.tigr.org/

(Contains sequences of various bacterial genomes and other information.)

The Protein Kinase Resource: http://www.kinasenet.org/

(Information on the protein kinase family of enzymes.)

The Signaling Gateway: http://www.signalling-gateway.org/

(A comprehensive resource for anyone interested in signal transduction.)

The Wellcome Trust Sanger Institute: http://www.sanger.ac.uk/

(A genome research center whose purpose is to increase knowledge of genomes, particularly through large-scale sequencing and analysis.)

BIOCHEMICAL JOURNALS AND REVIEWS

The following is a partial list of biochemistry journals and review series and of some biomedical journals that contain biochemical articles. Biochemistry and biology journals now usually have Web sites, often with useful links, and some journals are fully accessible without charge. The reader can obtain the URLs for the following by using a search engine.

Annual Reviews of Biochemistry, Cell and Developmental Biology, Genetics, Genomics and Human Genetics

Archives of Biochemistry and Biophysics (Arch Biochem Biophys)

Biochemical and Biophysical Research Communications (Biochem Biophys Res Commun)

Biochemical Journal (Biochem J)

Biochemistry (Biochemistry)

Biochemistry (Moscow) (Biochemistry [Mosc])

Biochimica et Biophysica Acta (Biochim Biophys Acta)

Biochimie (Biochimie)

European Journal of Biochemistry (Eur J Biochem)

Indian Journal of Biochemistry and Biophysics (Indian J Biochem Biophys)

Journal of Biochemistry (Tokyo) (J Biochem [Tokyo])

Journal of Biological Chemistry (J Biol Chem)

Journal of Clinical Investigation (J Clin Invest)

Journal of Lipid Research (J Lipid Res)

Nature (Nature)

Nature Genetics (Nat Genet)

Proceedings of the National Academy of Sciences USA (Proc Natl Acad Sci USA)

Science (Science)

Trends in Biochemical Sciences (Trends Biochem Sci)

Index

Note: Page numbers followed by f indicate figures; and page numbers followed by t indicate tables.

A bands, 565, 566f, 567f
A blood group substance, 626, 626f
A cyclins, 342, 342f, 342t
A gene, GalNAc transferase encoded by, 626–627
A (aminoacyl/acceptor) site, aminoacyl-tRNA binding to, in protein synthesis, 374, 375f
ABC-1. *See* ATP-binding cassette transporter-1
Abetalipoproteinemia, 219, 239t
ABO blood group system, biochemical basis of, 625–627, 626f
Absorption, 482–488
Absorption chromatography, for protein/peptide purification, 22
Absorption spectra, of porphyrins, 282–283, 286f
Absorptive pinocytosis, 437
ACAT (acyl-CoA:cholesterol acyltransferase), 234
Accelerator (Ac-) globulin (factor V), 608t, 609, 609f
Acceptor arm, of tRNA, 318, 320f, 367, 368f
Acceptor (A/aminoacyl) site, aminoacyl-tRNA binding to, in protein synthesis, 374, 375f
Accessory factor elements (AFEs), 477f
Aceruloplasminemia, 597
ACEs. *See* Angiotensin-converting enzyme inhibitors
Acetal links, 114
Acetic acid, 122t
    p*K*/p*K*$_a$ value of, 12t
Acetoacetate, 190, 191f
    in tyrosine catabolism, 257, 261f
Acetoacetyl-CoA synthetase, in mevalonate synthesis, 230, 231f
Acetone, 190
Acetone bodies. *See* Ketone bodies
Acetyl (acyl)-malonyl enzyme, 197, 198f
Acetyl-CoA, 133, 133f, 138–139
    carbohydrate metabolism and, 133, 133f
    catabolism of, 145–148, 146f, 147f. *See also* Citric acid cycle
    cholesterol synthesis and, 230–231, 231f, 232f, 233f
    fatty acid oxidation to, 134, 134f, 187–189, 188f, 189f
    formation of, 257–262, 261f–266f

lipogenesis and, 197f, 198f, 199
    as fatty acid building block, 199
    in lipogenesis regulation, 196
    in platelet-activating factor synthesis, 212f
    pyruvate dehydrogenase regulated by, 155–156, 157f, 201
    pyruvate oxidation to, 148–149, 150f, 155–157, 156f, 157f, 158t
    xenobiotic metabolism and, 637
Acetyl-CoA carboxylase, 202
    in lipogenesis regulation, 196, 197f, 200, 201f, 202
Acetyl hexosamines, in glycoproteins, 119t
N-Acetyl lactosamines, on N-linked glycan chains, 520
Acetyl transacylase, 196, 197f, 198f
Acetylation
    in covalent modification, mass increases and, 27t
    of xenobiotics, 637
N-Acetylgalactosamine (GalNAc), in glycoproteins, 524, 526t
N-Acetylglucosamine (GlcNAc), in glycoproteins, 526t
N-Acetylglucosamine phosphotransferase (GlcNAc phosphotransferase)
    in I-cell disease, 541
    in pseudo-Hurler polydystrophy, 541
N-Acetylglutamate, in urea biosynthesis, 249, 250
N-Acetylneuraminic acid, 119, 120f, 183, 185f
    in gangliosides, 213, 215f
    in glycoproteins, 183, 185f, 524, 526t
    in mucins, 529, 529f
Acetyltransferases, xenobiotic metabolism and, 637
Acholuric jaundice, 291
Achondroplasia, 439t, 561t, 563, 563f
Acid anhydride bonds, 295
Acid anhydrides, group transfer potential for, 297–298, 297f, 298f, 298t
Acid-base balance, ammonia metabolism in, 249
Acid-base catalysis, 51
    HIV protease in, 52–53, 53f
Acid phosphatase, diagnostic significance of, 57t

Acidemia, isovaleric, 265, 266
Acidosis
    lactic. *See* Lactic acidosis
    metabolic, ammonia in, 249
Acids
    conjugate, 10
    molecular structure affecting strength of, 12, 12t
    polyfunctional, nucleotides as, 298
    as proton donors, 9
    strong, 9
    weak. *See* Weak acids
Aciduria
    dicarboxylic, 194
    methylmalonic, 169
    orotic, 309
    urocanic, 254
Aconitase (aconitate hydratase), 145
ACP. *See* Acyl carrier protein
Acrosomal reaction, glycoproteins in, 537
ACTH. *See* Adrenocorticotropic hormone
Actin, 566, 567
    decoration of, 569, 570f
    fibronectin receptor interacting with, 550, 551f
    in muscle contraction, 566, 567f, 570, 570f, 571f
        regulation of striated muscle and, 571
    in nonmuscle cells, 584–585
    in red cell membranes, 623f, 624, 624t
    in striated *vs.* smooth muscle, 580t
    structure of, 568–569
F-Actin, 567, 568f, 570
    in nonmuscle cells, 584
G-Actin, 567, 568f, 584
    in nonmuscle cells, 584
Actin-filament capping protein, 550, 551f
Actin (thin) filaments, 566, 567f, 568f
Activated protein C, in blood coagulation, 611
Activation energy, 62, 64
Activation energy barrier, enzymes affecting, 64
Activation reaction, 464, 466f
Activator-recruited cofactor (ARC), 480, 480t
Activators
    in regulation of gene expression, 380, 382. *See also* Enhancers/enhancer elements
    transcription, 358, 358t

Active chromatin, 324–326, 326f, 389
Active site, 51, 51f. *See also* Catalytic site
Active sulfate (adenosine 3′-phosphate-5′-phosphosulfate), 297, 297f, 636
Active transport, 430, 430t, 431f, 434, 435, 435f
  in bilirubin secretion, 289, 290f
Actomyosin, 568
ACTR coactivator, 479, 480t
Acute fatty liver of pregnancy, 194
Acute inflammatory response, neutrophils in, 628
Acute phase proteins, 590–591, 591t
  negative, vitamin A as, 491
Acyl carrier protein (ACP), 196, 197f
  synthesis of, from pantothenic acid, 196, 503
Acyl-CoA dehydrogenase, 95, 188, 189f
  medium-chain, deficiency of, 194
Acyl-CoA synthetase (thiokinase)
  in fatty acid activation, 187, 188f
  in triacylglycerol synthesis, 211, 226, 226f
Acyl-CoA:cholesterol acyltransferase (ACAT), 234
Acylcarnitine, 187, 188f
Acylglycerol, 209
Acylglycerol metabolism, 209–213
  catabolism, 209
  clinical aspects of, 214
  synthesis, 209–213, 210f
    in endoplasmic reticulum, 137f, 138
Adapter proteins, in absorptive pinocytosis, 437
Adenine, 296f, 296t
Adenine nucleotide transporter, 108, 108f
Adenosine, 295f, 296t
  base pairing of in DNA, 311, 312, 313f
  in uric acid formation, 307, 307f
Adenosine 3′-phosphate-5′-phosphosulfate, 297, 297f, 636
Adenosine deaminase
  deficiency of, 308, 632
  localization of gene for, 413t
Adenosine diphosphate. *See* ADP
Adenosine monophosphate. *See* AMP
Adenosine triphosphate. *See* ATP
S-Adenosylmethionine, 262, 265f, 271, 273f, 297, 298f, 298t
Adenylic acid, as second messenger, 465
Adenylyl cyclase
  in cAMP-dependent signal transduction, 466–467, 468t
  cAMP derived from, 161
  in lipolysis, 227, 228f
Adenylyl kinase (myokinase), 92
  in gluconeogenesis regulation, 170
  as source of ATP in muscle, 582, 582f
Adhesion molecules, 537–538, 538t. *See also* Cell adhesion
Adipose tissue, 121, 132, 226–227, 226f
  brown, 228, 229f

  in fasting state, 142
  glucose uptake into, 140
  metabolism in, 141f, 143t, 226–227, 226f
    control of, 227–228
ADP, 295f
  free energy of catabolism capture by, 91f, 106
  free energy of hydrolysis of, 90t
  myosin, muscle contraction and, 570, 570f
  in platelet activation, 614f, 615
  in respiratory control, 149–150
  structure of, 91f
ADP-chaperone complex, 516. *See also* Chaperones
ADP-ribose, NAD as source of, 498
ADP-ribosylation, 498
ADPase, 615, 615t
Adrenal cortical hormones. *See also* Mineralocorticoids; specific hormone and Glucocorticoids
  synthesis of, 446–448, 448f, 449f
Adrenal gland, cytochrome P450 isoforms in, 634
Adrenal medulla, catecholamines produced in, 453
Adrenergic receptors, in glycogenolysis, 162
Adrenocorticotropic hormone (ACTH), 445, 446, 447f, 460f, 461
Adrenodoxin, 634
Adrenodoxin reductase, 634
Adrenogenital syndrome, 448
Adrenoleukodystrophy, neonatal, 511, 511t
Aerobic glycolysis, 154
  as muscle ATP source, 582f, 583, 583t
Aerobic respiration, citric acid cycle and, 145
AF-2 domain, 470
Affinity chromatography
  for protein/peptide purification, 23–24
  in recombinant fusion protein purification, 58–59, 59f
AFP. *See* Alpha-fetoprotein
Agammaglobulinemia, 604
Age, xenobiotic-metabolizing enzymes affected by, 637
Aggrecan, 551, 561, 561t, 562f
Aggregates, formation of after denaturation, 37
Aging, glycosaminoglycans and, 557–558
Aging process, extracellular matrix in, 545
Aglycone, 114
AHG. *See* Antihemophilic factor A/globulin
AIB1 coactivator, 479, 480t
ALA. *See* Aminolevulinate
ALA synthase, 281–282
Alanine, 15t
  pI of, 17
  in pyruvate formation, 257
  synthesis of, 241, 242f
α-Alanine, 270
β-Alanine, 270

Alanine (alanine-pyruvate) aminotransferase (ALT/SGPT)
  diagnostic significance of, 57t
  in urea synthesis, 247–248, 248f
Albumin, 588, 589f, 591–592, 591t
  conjugated bilirubin binding to, 292
  copper binding to, 596
  free fatty acids in combination with, 187, 218, 218t, 592
  glomerular membrane permeability to, 551
Albuminuria, 551
Alcohol, ethyl. *See* Ethanol
Alcohol dehydrogenase, in fatty liver, 225
Alcoholism
  cirrhosis and, 225
  fatty liver and, 225–226
  transferrin glycosylation in, 594
Aldehyde dehydrogenase, 95
  in fatty liver, 225
Aldolase A, deficiency of, 157
Aldolase B, 181, 182f
  deficiency of, 185
Aldolases, in glycolysis, 152, 153f
Aldose-ketose isomerism, 113t, 114f, 115f
Aldose reductase, 181, 183f, 186
Aldoses, 112, 113t, 115f
  ring structure of, 114f
Aldosterone
  binding of, 462
  synthesis of, 446–447, 449f
    angiotensin affecting, 459
Aldosterone synthase (18-hydroxylase), in steroid synthesis, 446–447, 449f
Alkaline phosphatase
  in bone mineralization, 559
  isozymes of, diagnostic significance of, 57t
  in recombinant DNA technology, 406t
Alkalosis, metabolic, ammonia in, 249
Alkaptonuria, 257–258
Allergic reactions, peptide absorption causing, 482
Allopurinol, 298, 305
Allosteric activators, 170
Allosteric effectors/modifiers, 22f, 138
  in gluconeogenesis regulation, 170–171
  negative, 76. *See also* Feedback inhibition
  second messengers as, 77
Allosteric enzymes, 76, 138
  aspartate transcarbamoylase as model of, 76
Allosteric properties of hemoglobin, 43–46
Allosteric regulation, of enzymatic catalysis, 75–77, 76f, 138, 139f
  gluconeogenesis regulation and, 170
Allosteric site, 76
Alpha-adrenergic receptors, in glycogenolysis, 162
Alpha-amino acids. *See also* Amino acids
  genetic code specifying, 14, 15t–16t
  in proteins, 14

Alpha-amino nitrogen. *See* Amino acid nitrogen
Alpha anomers, 114
Alpha-fetoprotein, 591t
Alpha-globin gene, localization of, 413t
Alpha helix, 31
Alpha-lipoproteins, 217. *See also* High-density lipoproteins
   familial deficiency of, 239t
Alpha-R groups, amino acid properties affected by, 18
Alpha thalassemias, 47
Alpha-tocopherol. *See* Tocopherol
α-Alanine, 270
7α-Hydroxylase, sterol, 236
α-Linolenic acid, for essential fatty acid deficiency, 203
α$_1$-Antiproteinase, for emphysema, 597–598
α$_1$-Antitrypsin, for emphysema, 597–598
α$_1$-Antitrypsin liver disease, 597–598
α$_2$-Macroglobulin, 598–599
Alport syndrome, 548, 548t
ALT. *See* Alanine aminotransferase
Alteplase (tissue plasminogen activator/t-PA), 612–613, 613f, 615t
Alternative pathway, of complement activation, 605
Altitude, high, adaptation to, 46
Alu family, 329
Alzheimer disease, amyloid in, 38, 599
Ambiguity, genetic code and, 366
Amino acid carbon skeletons, catabolism of, 254–269
   acetyl-CoA formation and, 257–262, 261f–266f, 265f, 266f
   branched-chain, 265–266, 267f, 268f, 269f
      disorders of, 265–266
   pyruvate formation and, 254–257, 257f–260f
   transamination in initiation of, 254, 254f, 255f, 256f
Amino acid nitrogen
   catabolism of, 246–252
      in amino acid carbon skeleton catabolism, 254, 255f
      end products of, 246–247
         urea as, 249–251, 250
      L-glutamate dehydrogenase in, 248–249, 248f
      transamination of, 247–248, 247f
   L-Amino acid oxidase, 94–95
   in nitrogen metabolism, 248, 248f
Amino acid sequences. *See also* Protein sequencing
   determination of, for glycoproteins, 525t
   primary structure determined by, 18–19
   repeating, in mucins, 528–529, 529f
Amino acids, 2, 14–20, 15t–16t. *See also* Peptides
   absorption of, 485
   ammonia removal from, 248, 248f
   analysis/identification of, 20

blood glucose and, 172
branched chain, catabolism of, 267f, 268f, 269f
   disorders of, 265–266
in catalysis, conservation of, 53–55, 55t
chemical reactions of, functional groups dictating, 18–20
in citric acid cycle, 139
deamination of. *See* Deamination
deficiency of, 241, 488
excitatory. *See* Aspartate; Glutamate
glucogenic, 139–140
in gluconeogenesis, 148, 149f
interconvertability of, 139–140
keto acid replacement of in diet, 243
ketogenic, 140
melting point of, 18
metabolism of, 133f, 134, 135f. *See also* Amino acid carbon skeletons; Amino acid nitrogen
   pyridoxal phosphate in, 498–499
net charge of, 16–17, 17f
nutritionally essential, 134
nutritionally nonessential, 134
   synthesis of, 241–244
in peptides, 14, 19, 19f
pK/pK_a values of, 15t–16t, 17–18, 17f
   environment affecting, 18, 18t
products derived from, 270–277. *See also* specific product
properties of, 14–18
protein degradation and, 246, 247f
in proteins, 14
requirements for, 488
sequence of, in primary structure, 18–19
solubility point of, 18
substitutions of, missense mutations caused by, 369–370, 369f
synthesis of, 241–244
   in carbohydrate metabolism, 133
   citric acid cycle in, 148, 149f
transamination of. *See* Transamination
transporter/carrier systems for
   glutathione and, 636–637
   hormones affecting, 435
Amino sugars (hexosamines), 116, 116f
   glucose as precursor of, 183, 185f
   in glycosaminoglycans, 118, 183, 185f
   in glycosphingolipids, 183, 185f
   interrelationships in metabolism of, 185f
Aminoacyl residues, 18–19
   peptide structure and, 19
Aminoacyl (A/acceptor) site, aminoacyl-tRNA binding to, 374, 375f
Aminoacyl-tRNA, in protein synthesis, 374
Aminoacyl-tRNA synthetases, 367, 367f
Aminolevulinate (ALA), 279, 282f
   in porphyria, 287
Aminolevulinate dehydratase, 279, 282f
   in porphyria, 284, 286t
Aminolevulinate synthase, 279, 282f, 285f
   in porphyria, 284, 286f, 287
Aminolevulinate (ALA) synthase, 281–282

Aminopeptidases, 485
Aminophospholipids, membrane asymmetry and, 427
Aminoproteinase, procollagen, 547
Aminotransferases (transaminases), 148, 149f
   diagnostic significance of, 57t
   in urea biosynthesis, 247–248, 248f
Ammonia
   in acid-base balance, 249
   detoxification of, 246
   excess of, 251
   glutamine synthase fixing, 248f, 249
   nitrogen removed as, 248, 248f
Ammonia intoxication, 248
Ammonium ion, pK/pK_a value of, 12t
Amobarbital, on oxidative phosphorylation, 100
AMP, 295f, 296f, 296t, 305f
   coenzyme derivatives of, 298t
   cyclic. *See* Cyclic AMP
   free energy of hydrolysis of, 90t
   IMP conversion to, 301, 304f
      feedback regulation of, 302, 304f
   PRPP glutamyl amidotransferase regulated by, 302
   structure of, 91f, 296f
Amp resistance genes, 407, 408f
Amphibolic pathways/processes, 132
   citric acid cycle and, 148
Amphipathic helices, 31
Amphipathic lipids, 129, 130f
   in lipoproteins, 217, 219f
   in membranes, 129, 130f, 424–425, 424f
Amphipathic molecules, folding and, 6
Ampicillin resistance genes, 407, 408f
Amplification, gene, in gene expression regulation, 397–399, 399f
Amylases
   diagnostic significance of, 57t
   in hydrolysis of starch, 482
Amyloid-associated protein, 599
Amyloid precursor proteins, 599
   in Alzheimer disease, 38, 599
Amyloidosis, 599
Amylopectin, 116, 118f
Amylopectinosis, 166t
Amylose, 116, 118f
Anabolic pathways/anabolism, 89, 132. *See also* Endergonic reaction; Metabolism
Anaerobic glycolysis, 151, 152, 152f
   as muscle ATP source, 582f, 583–584, 583t
Analbuminemia, 592
Anaphylaxis, slow-reacting substance of, 208
Anaplerotic reactions, in citric acid cycle, 148
Anchorin, in cartilage, 561t
Andersen's disease, 166t
Androgen response element, 467t

Androgens
estrogens produced from, 450, 452f
receptors for, 478
synthesis of, 448–450, 449f, 451f
Androstenedione
estrone produced from, 450, 452f
synthesis of, 448, 451f
Anemias, 47, 617
Fanconi's, 346
hemolytic, 151, 157, 617, 627, 627t
glucose-6-phosphate dehydrogenase
deficiency causing, 177,
183–184, 621, 621f, 627
haptoglobin levels in, 592
hyperbilirubinemia/jaundice in, 291,
292t
pentose phosphate pathway/glu-
tathione peroxidase and,
180, 181f, 183–184
primaquine-sensitive, 621
red cell membrane abnormalities causing, 627
iron deficiency, 485–486, 504, 594, 618t
megaloblastic
folate deficiency causing, 490t, 500,
502
vitamin B_{12} deficiency causing, 490t,
500, 618t
pernicious, 490t, 500
recombinant erythropoietin for, 535,
618
sickle cell. See Sickle cell disease
Angiotensin-converting enzyme, 458–459,
460f
Angiotensin-converting enzyme inhibitors,
459
Angiotensin II, 445, 458–459, 460f
synthesis of, 458–459, 460f
Angiotensin III, 459, 460f
Angiotensinogen, 458, 460f
Anion exchange protein, 623, 623f, 624t
Ankyrin, 623f, 624, 624t
Anomeric carbon atom, 114
Anserine, 270, 271, 271f
Antennae (oligosaccharide branches), 531
Anterior pituitary gland hormones, blood
glucose affected by, 174
Anti conformers, 295, 295f
Antibiotics
amino sugars in, 116
bacterial protein synthesis affected by,
378–379
folate inhibitors as, 500–501
Antibodies, 588, 589. See also Immunoglob-
ulins
monoclonal, hybridomas in production
of, 604, 604f
in xenobiotic cell injury, 638, 638f
Antibody diversity, 599
DNA/gene rearrangement and, 602–603
Antichymotrypsin, 591t
Anticoagulants, coumarin, 612
Anticodon region, of tRNA, 366, 367, 367f

Antifolate drugs, purine nucleotide synthesis affected by, 301
Antigenic determinant (epitope), 32, 599
Antigenicity, xenobiotics altering, cell injury
and, 638, 638f
Antigens, 599
Antihemophilic factor A/globulin (factor
VIII), 607f, 608, 608t
deficiency of, 608
Antihemophilic factor B (factor IX), 607f,
608, 608t
coumarin drugs affecting, 612
deficiency of, 612
Antimalarial drugs, folate inhibitors as,
500–501
Antimycin A, on respiratory chain, 107, 107f
Antioxidants, 98, 128–129, 620t, 621
retinoids and carotenoids as, 128–129,
490t
vitamin C as, 128
vitamin E as, 98, 128, 494–495, 494f
Antiparallel beta sheet, 32, 33f
Antiparallel loops, mRNA and tRNA, 367
Antiparallel strands, DNA, 311
Antiport systems, 434, 434f
for nucleotide sugars, 525
α_1-Antiproteinase, in emphysema and liver
disease, 597–598
Antiproteinases, 631, 631t
Antithrombin/antithrombin III, 591t, 611
heparin binding to, 557, 611
α_1-Antitrypsin, in emphysema, 597–598
α_1-Antitrypsin liver disease, 598
APC. See Activated protein C
APC resistance, 611
Apo A-I, 218, 218t, 235
deficiencies of, 239t
Apo A-II, 218t
lipoprotein lipase affected by, 219
Apo A-IV, 218, 218t
Apo B-48, 218, 218t
Apo B-100, 217–218, 218t
in LDL metabolism, 221, 222f
regulation of, 234
Apo B-100 receptor
in LDL metabolism, 220
Apo C-I, 218, 218t
Apo C-II, 218, 218t
in lipoprotein lipase activity, 219–220
Apo C-III, 218, 218t
lipoprotein lipase affected by, 220
Apo D, 218, 218t
Apo E, 218, 218t, 220
Apo E receptor
in chylomicron remnant uptake, 220,
221f
in LDL metabolism, 220, 221, 222f
Apo-transketolase activation, in thiamin
nutritional status assess-
ment, 497
Apoferritin, 594
Apolipoproteins/apoproteins, 217–229
distribution of, 217–218, 218t

hemoglobin; oxygenation affecting, 43
Apomyoglobin, hindered environment for
heme iron and, 41–42, 42f
Apoproteins. See Apolipoproteins/apopro-
teins
Apoptosis, 213
p53 and, 347
APP. See Amyloid precursor proteins
Apurinic endonuclease, in base excision-
repair, 344
Apyrimidinic endonuclease, in base excision-repair, 344
Aquaporins, 433
D-Arabinose, 115f, 115t
Arabinosyl cytosine (cytarabine), 298
Arachidonic acid/arachidonate, 123, 123t,
202, 202f
eicosanoid formation and, 204, 205f,
206f, 207f
for essential fatty acid deficiency, 203
ARC, 480, 480t
ARE. See Androgen response element
Argentaffinoma (carcinoid), serotonin in,
272
Arginase
disorders of, 252
in periodic hyperlysinemia, 262
in urea synthesis, 250, 251
Arginine, 16t, 272
catabolism of, 254, 256f
metabolism of, 272f
in urea synthesis, 250, 251
Argininosuccinase
deficiency of, 252
in urea synthesis, 250, 251
Arginosuccinate, in urea synthesis, 249,
250–251
Arginosuccinate lyase deficiency, 252
Arginosuccinate synthase, 250–251
deficiency of, 252
Arginosuccinicaciduria, 252
Aromatase enzyme complex, 450, 452f
ARS (autonomously replicating sequences),
334, 419
Arsenate, oxidation and phosphorylation
affected by, 152
Arsenite, oxidation and phosphorylation
affected by, 157
Arterial wall intima, proteoglycans in,
557–558
Arthritis
gouty, 307
proteoglycans in, 558
rheumatoid, glycosylation alterations in,
540
Artificial membranes, 427–428
Ascorbate, 181, 182f
Ascorbic acid (vitamin C), 177, 490t,
503–504, 503f
as antioxidant, 128
in collagen synthesis, 39, 504, 545
deficiency of, 490t, 504
collagen affected in, 39, 504, 548

iron absorption and, 486, 504
supplemental, 504
Asialoglycoprotein receptors
in cotranslational insertion, 514, 514f
in glycoprotein clearance, 526–527
Asn-GlcNAc linkage
in glycoproteins, 530
in glycosaminoglycans, 553
Asparaginase, in amino acid nitrogen catabolism, 248f, 249
Asparagine, 15t
in amino acid nitrogen catabolism, 249
catabolism of, 254, 254f
synthesis of, 241, 242f
Asparagine synthetase, 241, 242f
Aspartate
catabolism of, 254, 254f
synthesis of, 241, 242f
in urea synthesis, 250–251
Aspartate 102, in covalent catalysis, 53, 54f
Aspartate aminotransferase (AST/SGOT), diagnostic significance of, 57t
Aspartate transcarbamoylase, 76
in pyrimidine synthesis, 305, 306f
Aspartic acid, 15t
pI of, 17
Aspartic protease family, in acid-base catalysis, 52–53, 53f
Aspartylglycosaminuria, 541, 542t
Aspirin
antiplatelet actions of, 615
cyclooxygenase affected by, 204
prostaglandins affected by, 196
Assembly particles, in absorptive pinocytosis, 437
AST. See Aspartate aminotransferase
Asthma, leukotrienes in, 122
Asymmetric substitution, in porphyrins, 279, 280f
Asymmetry
importin binding and, 509
inside-outside, 427
lipid and protein, membrane assembly and, 520–521, 521f
in membranes, 423, 427
Ataxia-telangiectasia, 346
ATCase. See Aspartate transcarbamoylase
Atherosclerosis, 217, 615
cholesterol and, 126, 230, 238
HDL and, 221–222
hyperhomocysteinemia and, folic acid supplements in prevention of, 502
LDL plasma concentration and, 221
lysophosphatidylcholine (lysolecithin) and, 125
Atorvastatin, 238
ATP, 90–93, 295f, 297
in active transport, 435, 435f
in coupling, 90, 92
fatty acid oxidation producing, 189
from free energy of catabolism, 91f, 106

free energy of hydrolysis of, 90–91, 90t
in free energy transfer from exergonic to endergonic processes, 90–91, 90f
hydrolysis of
in muscle contraction, 570, 570f
by NSF, 519, 519f
inorganic pyrophosphate production and, 92–93
in mitochondrial protein synthesis and import, 507
in muscle/muscle contraction, 565, 570, 570f
decrease in availability of, 572–573
sources of, 581–583, 582f, 583, 583t
in purine synthesis, 301–302, 303f
from respiratory control, 106–107, 106t
respiratory control in maintenance of supply of, 149–150
structure of, 91f
synthesis of
in citric acid cycle, 146f, 148, 156–157, 158t
glucose oxidation yielding, 156–157, 158t
respiratory chain electron transport in, 105, 105f, 106f
ATP/ADP cycle, 91, 92f
ATP-binding cassette transporter-1, 222, 223f
ATP-chaperone complex, 516. See also Chaperones
ATP-citrate lyase, 149, 150f
acetyl-CoA for lipogenesis and, 199
ATP synthase, 105, 105f, 106f
ATPase
in active transport, 435, 435f
chaperones exhibiting activity of, 516
copper-binding P-type, mutations in gene for
Menkes disease caused by, 596–597
Wilson disease caused by, 597
Atractyloside, on respiratory chain, 107, 108f
Attachment proteins, 550, 551f
Auto-oxidation. See Peroxidation
Autoantibodies, in myasthenia gravis, 439
Autonomously replicating sequences (ARS), 334, 419
Autoradiography, definition of, 419
Autotrophic organisms, 90
Avidin, biotin deficiency caused by, 502
Axial ratios, 30
Axonemal dyneins, 585
5- or 6-Azacytidine, 298
8-Azaguanine, 298, 299f
Azathioprine, 298
5- or 6-Azauridine, 298, 299f

B blood group substance, 626, 626f
B cyclins, 342, 342f, 342t
B gene, Gal transferase encoded by, 626–627

B lymphocytes, 599
in hybridoma production, 604, 604f
B vitamins. See Vitamin B complex
BAC vector. See Bacterial artificial chromosome (BAC) vector
Bacteria
intestinal, in bilirubin deconjugation, 281
transcription cycle in, 349f, 350
Bacterial artificial chromosome (BAC) vector, 407, 408t
Bacterial artificial chromosomes (BACs), 83
Bacterial gyrase, 314
Bacterial promoters, in transcription, 352–353, 353f
Bacteriophage, definition of, 419
BAL. See Dimercaprol
BAL 31 nuclease, in recombinant DNA technology, 406t
Balanced chemical equations, 61
BamHI, 404, 405t
Barbiturates, on respiratory chain, 107, 107f
Basal lamina, laminin as component of, 550–551
Basal metabolic rate, 486
Base excision-repair of DNA, 343t, 344, 345f
Base pairing in DNA, 7, 311–312, 313f
matching of for renaturation, 313–314
recombinant DNA technology and, 402–403
replication/synthesis and, 336, 338f
Base substitution, mutations occurring by, 368, 368f
Basement membranes, collagen in, 546
Bases
conjugate, 10
as proton acceptors, 9
strong, 9
weak, 9
Basic Local Alignment Search Tool (BLAST), 86
Bence Jones protein, 604
Bends (protein conformation), 32, 34f
Beriberi, 490t, 496
Beta anomers, 114
Beta-endorphins, 460f, 461
Beta-globin gene
localization of, 413t
recombinant DNA technology in detection of variations in, 413, 414f, 415t
Beta-lipoproteins, 217. See also Low-density lipoproteins
Beta-oxidation of fatty acids, 187–189, 188f, 189f
ketogenesis regulation and, 193, 194f
modified, 189–190, 190f
Beta sheet, 31–32
Beta subunits of hemoglobin, myoglobin and, 43
Beta thalassemias, 47

β-Alanine, 270
β₂-Microglobulin, 595
BFU-E. *See* Burst-forming unit-erythroid
BgIII, 405t
BHA. *See* Butylated hydroxyanisole
BHT. *See* Butylated hydroxytoluene
Bi-Bi reactions, 70–71, 70f, 71f
    Michaelis-Menten kinetics and, 71, 71f
Bicarbonate, in extracellular and intracellular fluid, 423t
Biglycan
    in bone, 558t
    in cartilage, 561t
Bilayers, lipid, 425, 425f, 426f
    membrane proteins and, 426
Bile, bilirubin secretion into, 289, 290f
Bile acids (salts), 235–238
    enterohepatic circulation of, 237–238
    in lipid digestion and absorption, 483, 484f
    secondary, 237, 237f
    synthesis of, 236–237, 237f
        regulation of, 237, 237f
Bile pigments, 287–292. *See also* Bilirubin
Biliary obstruction, hyperbilirubinemia/jaundice caused by, 291–292, 292t
Bilirubin
    accumulation of (hyperbilirubinemia), 290–292, 292t
    conjugated
        binding to albumin and, 292
        reduction of to urobilinogen, 289–290
    conjugation of, 289, 289f, 290f
    fecal, in jaundice, 292t
    heme catabolism producing, 287, 288f
    liver uptake of, 287–290, 289f, 290f
    normal values for, 292t
    secretion of into bile, 289, 290f
    unconjugated, disorders occurring in, 291
    urine, in jaundice, 291, 292t
Biliverdin, 287, 288f
Biliverdin reductase, 287
Bimolecular membrane layer, 425. *See also* Lipid bilayer
Binding constant, Michaelis constant (K_m) approximating, 67
Binding proteins, 461t, 462–463, 462t, 591t
Biochemistry
    as basis of health/disease, 2–4, 3t
    definition of, 1
    Human Genome Project and, 3–4
    methods and preparations used in, 1, 2t
    relationship of to medicine, 1–4, 3f
Biocytin, 502, 502f
Bioenergetics, 88–93. *See also* ATP
Bioinformatics, 82–87, 419
    challenges to biology in, 84–85
    challenges to medicine in, 84
    definition of, 82–83

genomic resources for, 85–87
genomics revolution in, 84
Human Genome Project in, 83–84
protein function and, 29
Biologic oxidation. *See* Oxidation
Biomolecules. *See also* specific type
    stabilization of, 7
    water affecting structure of, 6–7, 6t
Biotin, 490t, 502, 502f
    deficiency of, 490t, 502
    in malonyl-CoA synthesis, 196, 197f
    as prosthetic group, 50
BiP. *See* Immunoglobulin heavy chain binding protein
1,3-Bisphosphoglycerate (BPG), free energy of hydrolysis of, 90t
2,3-Bisphosphoglycerate (BPG), T structure of hemoglobin stabilized by, 45–46, 46f
Bisphosphoglycerate mutase, in glycolysis in erythrocytes, 155, 155f
2,3-Bisphosphoglycerate phosphatase, in erythrocytes, 155, 155f
BLAST, 86
blastn, 86
blastp, 86
blastx, 86
Blindness, vitamin A deficiency causing, 491
Blood, functions of, 588, 589t
Blood cells, 617–632. *See also* Erythrocytes; Neutrophils; Platelets
Blood clotting. *See* Coagulation
Blood coagulation. *See* Coagulation (blood); Coagulation factors
Blood glucose. *See* Glucose, blood
Blood group substances, 626, 626f
    glycoproteins as, 523, 626
Blood group systems, 617, 625–627, 626f
Blood plasma. *See* Plasma
Blood type, 625–627
Blood vessels, nitric oxide affecting, 580–581, 581f, 582t
Blot transfer techniques, 409–410, 409f
Blunt end ligation/blunt-ended DNA, 404, 405–406, 406f, 419
BMR. *See* Basal metabolic rate
Body mass index, 486
Body water. *See* Water
Bohr effect, 45, 46f
    in hemoglobin M, 47
Bonds. *See* specific types
Bone, 558–559, 559f, 560f
    metabolic and genetic disorders involving, 559–560, 561t
    proteins in, 558, 558t
Bone Gla protein, 558t
Bone marrow, heme synthesis in, 281
Bone matrix Gla protein, 496
Bone morphogenetic proteins, 558t
Bone sialoprotein, 558t
Bone SPARC protein, 558t
Botany, 1

Botulinum B toxin, 520
Bovine spongiform encephalopathy, 38
BPG. *See* 1,3-Bisphosphoglycerate (BPG); 2,3-Bisphosphoglycerate (BPG)
Bradykinin, in inflammation, 629t
Brain, metabolism in, 143t
    glucose as necessity for, 140
Branch point, 159
Branched chain amino acids, catabolism of, 267f, 268f, 269f
    disorders of, 265–266
Branched chain ketonuria (maple syrup urine disease), 265
Branching enzymes
    absence of, 166t
    in glycogen biosynthesis, 159, 161f
Brefeldin A, 519–520
Brittle bones (osteogenesis imperfecta), 561t
Broad beta disease, 239t
Bronze diabetes, 595
Brown adipose tissue, 228, 229f
Brush border enzymes, 483
BSE. *See* Bovine spongiform encephalopathy
Buffers
    Henderson-Hasselbalch equation describing behavior of, 11, 12f
    weak acids and their salts as, 11–12, 12f
"Bulk flow," of membrane proteins, 515
Burst-forming unit-erythroid, 618, 619f
Butylated hydroxyanisole (BHA), as antioxidant/food preservative, 128
Butylated hydroxytoluene (BHT), as antioxidant/food preservative, 128
Butyric acid, 122t

c oxidoreductase, 100, 102f, 103f, 104
C-peptide, 457, 458f
C-reactive protein, 590–591, 591t
C regions/segments. *See* Constant regions/segments
C1-9 (complement proteins), 605
C20 polyunsaturated acids, eicosanoids formed from, 202, 204, 205f, 206f
Ca^{2+} ATPase, 471
Ca^{2+}-Na^+ exchanger, 471, 576–577
Cachexia, 140
    cancer, 143, 151, 487
Caffeine, 297, 297f
    hormonal regulation of lipolysis and, 227
Calbindin, 485
Calcidiol (25-hydroxycholecalciferol), in vitamin D metabolism, 492, 493f
Calciferol. *See* Vitamin D
Calcineurin, 574t
Calcinosis, 493
Calcitonin, 445

Calcitriol (1,25(OH)$_2$-D$_3$), 445, 447f, 493
  calcium concentration regulated by, 493
  storage/secretion of, 461, 461t
  synthesis of, 450–453, 454f, 492–493, 493f
Calcium, 504t
  absorption of, 485
    vitamin D metabolism and, 485, 492–493
  in blood coagulation, 607f, 608–609, 608t
  in bone, 558
  in extracellular fluid, 423, 423t
  in intracellular fluid, 423, 423t
  iron absorption affected by, 486
  in malignant hyperthermia, 573–574, 574f
  metabolism of, 470–471
    vitamin D metabolism and, 492–493
  in muscle contraction, 571
    in cardiac muscle, 576–577
    phosphorylase activation and, 162
    sarcoplasmic reticulum and, 572, 572f
    in smooth muscle, 578–580
  in platelet activation, 614, 614f
  as second messenger, 444–445, 445t, 465, 471–472, 471t
    phosphatidylinositide metabolism affecting, 471–472, 472f, 473f
  vitamin D metabolism affected by, 493
Calcium ATPase, 471, 577
Calcium-binding proteins, vitamin K and glutamate carboxylation and postsynthetic modification and, 496, 496f
  synthesis and, 496, 612
Calcium/calmodulin, 471
Calcium/calmodulin-sensitive phosphorylase kinase, in glycogenolysis, 162
Calcium channels, 471. See also Calcium release channel
  in cardiac muscle, 576
Calcium-induced calcium release, in cardiac muscle, 576
Calcium pump, 471, 577
Calcium release channel, 572, 572f
  dihydropyridine receptor and, 572, 572f
  mutations in gene for, malignant hyperthermia caused by, 573–574, 574f, 637t
Calcium-sodium exchanger, 471
Caldesmon, 579–580
Calmodulin, 471, 471t, 571
  muscle phosphorylase and, 162, 163f
Calmodulin-4 Ca^{2+}, in smooth muscle contraction, 579, 579f
Calnexin, 516, 535
Calreticulin, 516, 535
Calsequestrin, 572, 572f
cAMP. See Cyclic AMP

Cancer cachexia, 151, 487
Cancer/cancer cells. See also Carcinogenesis/ carcinogens
  cyclins and, 342
  glycoproteins and, 523, 535, 538–539, 539f
  hormone-dependent, vitamin B$_6$ deficiency and, 499
  membrane abnormalities and, 439t
  mucins produced by, 529
Cancer chemotherapy
  combination, 617
  folate inhibitors in, 500–501
  neutropenia caused by, 618
  synthetic nucleotide analogs in, 298–299, 299f
Cancer phototherapy, porphyrins in, 282
CAP. See Catabolite gene activator protein
Caproic acid, 122t
Carbamates, hemoglobin, 44
Carbamoyl phosphate
  excess, 309
  free energy of hydrolysis of, 90t
  in urea synthesis, 249, 250, 251
Carbamoyl phosphate synthase I, 249
  deficiency of, 251
  in urea synthesis, 249, 250
Carbamoyl phosphate synthase II, in pyrimidine synthesis, 305, 306f
Carbohydrate complex. See specific types
Carbohydrates, 112–120. See also Glucose; Sugars; specific types
  in cell membranes, 119–120
  cell surface, glycolipids and, 126
  classification of, 112, 113t
  complex (glycoconjugate). See also specific types
    glycoproteins as, 523
  digestion and absorption of, 482–483, 483f
  in fatty acid synthesis, 138
  interconvertibility of, 138
  isomerism of, 112–114, 113f
  in lipoproteins, 119–120
  metabolism of, 133–134, 133f, 135f
    diseases associated with, 112
    vitamin B$_1$ (thiamin) in, 496–497, 497f
  in proteoglycans, 551, 552
  very low, weight loss from diets with, 175
Carbon dioxide
  citric acid cycle in production of, 145–148, 147f
  transport of, by hemoglobin, 44–45, 46f
Carbon monoxide
  heme catabolism producing, 287
  on oxidative phosphorylation, 100
  on respiratory chain, 107, 107f
Carbon skeleton, amino acid. See Amino acid carbon skeletons
Carbonic acid, pK/pK_a value of, 12t
Carbonic anhydrase, in osteopetrosis, 560
Carboxybiotin, 502, 502f
Carboxyl terminal repeat domain, 357

Carboxylase enzymes, biotin as coenzyme of, 502
Carboxypeptidases, 485
Carboxyproteinase, procollagen, 547
Carcinogenesis/carcinogens, 638
  chemical, 638
  cytochrome P450 induction and, 635
  indirect, 638
Carcinoid (argentaffinoma), serotonin in, 272
Carcinoid syndrome, 498
Cardiac developmental defects, 578
Cardiac glycosides, 114–116
Cardiac muscle, 565, 575–581, 576t, 578t
Cardiolipin, 125, 125f
  synthesis of, 209, 210f, 211, 211f
Cardiomyopathies, 565, 577, 578t
Cargo proteins/molecules, 520
  in export, 511
  in import, 509, 510f
Carnitine
  deficiency of, 187, 194
  in fatty acid transport, 187, 188f
Carnitine-acylcarnitine translocase, 187, 188f
Carnitine palmitoyltransferase, deficiency of, 187
Carnitine palmitoyltransferase-I, 187, 188f
  deficiency of, 194
  in ketogenesis regulation, 193, 194f
Carnitine palmitoyltransferase-II, 187, 188f
  deficiency of, 194
Carnitine system, 108
Carnosinase deficiency, 270
Carnosine, 270, 271, 271f
Carnosinuria, 270
Carotene dioxygenase, 490–491, 491f
Carotenoids, 490–491, 491f, 492f. See also Vitamin A
Carrier proteins/systems, 434, 434f
  for nucleotide sugars, 525
Cartilage, 553, 561–563, 561t, 562f
  chondrodysplasia affecting, 563
Catabolic pathways/catabolism, 89, 132. See also Exergonic reaction; Metabolism; specific substances
  energy captured in, from respiratory chain, 91f, 105–106, 158t
Catabolite gene activator protein (cyclic AMP regulatory protein), 382, 384
Catabolite regulatory protein, 467
Catalase, 96, 620
  as antioxidant, 129, 620t
  in nitrogen metabolism, 248, 248f
Catalysis/catalytic reactions (enzymatic). See also Metabolism
  acid-base, 51
    HIV protease in, 52–53, 53f
  at active site, 51–52, 51f
  Bi-Bi, 70–71, 70f, 71f
    Michaelis-Menten kinetics and, 71, 71f

Catalysis/catalytic reactions (enzymatic)—*continued*
  coenzymes/cofactors in, 50, 51f
  conservation of residues and, 53–55, 55t
  covalent, 52, 52f, 64
    chymotrypsin in, 53, 54f, 64
    fructose-2,6-bisphosphatase in, 53, 54f
  double displacement, 70, 70f
  enzyme detection facilitated by, 55–56, 57f
  equilibrium constant and, 64
  isozymes and, 55
  kinetics of, 64–72
    activation energy and, 62, 64
    balanced equations and, 61
    competitive *vs.* noncompetitive inhibition and, 68–70, 68f, 69f, 70f
    in drug development, 71–72
    factors affecting rates of, 63–65, 63f, 65f
    free energy changes and, 61–62
    initial velocity and, 65
    multiple substrates and, 70–71, 70f, 71f
    substrate concentration and, 65–66, 65f, 66f
      models of, 66–68, 67t, 68f
    transition states and, 62
  mechanisms of, 51–52, 52f
    prosthetic groups/cofactors/coenzymes in, 50, 51f
    site-directed mutagenesis in study of, 59
  oxaloacetate and, 145
  ping-pong, 70, 70f
  prosthetic groups in, 50, 51f
  by proximity, 51
  regulation of, 73–81, 138, 139t
    active and passive processes in, 73, 74f
    allosteric, 75–77, 76f, 138, 139f
    compartmentation in, 73–74
    covalent, 75, 77, 78–79, 79f
    enzyme quantity and, 74–75
    feedback inhibition and, 75–77, 76f, 138
    feedback regulation and, 77, 138
    metabolite flow and, 73, 74f
    Michaelis constant (K_m) in, 73, 74f
    phosphorylation-dephosphorylation in, 79f, 79t
    proteolysis in, 77, 78f
    second messengers in, 77
  RNA and, 364
  sequential (single) displacement, 70, 70f
  specificity of, 49, 50f
  by strain, 51–52
  substrate concentration affecting rate of, 65–66, 65f, 66f
    Hill model of, 67–68, 68f
    Michaelis-Menten model of, 66–67, 67f
Catalytic residues, conserved, 53–55, 55t
Catalytic site, 76. *See also* Active site

Cataracts, diabetic, 185–186
Catecholamines. *See also* specific type
  receptors for, 444
  storage/secretion of, 461, 461t
  synthesis of, 453–461, 455f
Cathepsins, in acid-base catalysis, 52
Cation. *See also* specific cations
  membrane penetration by, 108
Caveolae, 429
Caveolin-1, 429
CBG. *See* Corticosteroid-binding globulin
CBP/CBP/p300 (CREB-binding protein), 468–469, 475, 477f, 478–479, 480t
CD11a-c/CD18, in neutrophils, 628t, 629
CD18, 629
CD49a/e/f, 629t
CD59, 540
CDART, 86, 87f
CDD, 86, 87f
CDK-cyclin inhibitor/CDKI, DNA/chromosome integrity and, 347
CDKs. *See* Cyclin-dependent protein kinases
cDNA, 419
cDNA library, 408–409, 419
cDNA sequencing, in glycoprotein analysis, 525t
CDRs. *See* Complementarity-determining regions
Celiac disease, 482
Cell, 1
  in macromolecule transport, 436–438, 437f, 438f
Cell adhesion
  fibronectin in, 549–550, 551f
  glycosphingolipids in, 214
  integrins in, 628–629, 629t
  selectins in, 537–538, 538t, 539f
Cell biology, 1
Cell-cell communication, via gap junctions, 438, 439f
Cell-cell interactions, 422
  mucins in, 529
Cell cycle, S phase of, DNA synthesis during, 341–343, 341f, 342f, 342t
Cell death, 213
Cell-free systems, vesicles studied in, 518
Cell fusion, 604
Cell injury
  oxygen species causing, 620t, 621
  xenobiotics causing, 638, 638f
Cell lysis, complement in, 605
Cell-mediated immunity, 599
Cell membrane. *See* Plasma membrane
Cell migration, fibronectin in, 549–550
Cell recognition, glycosphingolipids in, 214
Cell sap. *See* Cytosol
Cell surface carbohydrates, glycolipids and, 126
Cell surfaces, heparan sulfate on, 555
Cellulose, 116–117

Cellulose acetate zone electrophoresis, 588, 590f
Central core disease, 573–574, 577t
Central nervous system, glucose as metabolic necessity for, 140
Centromere, 326, 327f
Cephalin (phosphatidylethanolamine), 125, 125f
  membrane asymmetry and, 427
  synthesis of, 209, 210f
Ceramide, 126, 126f, 213–214, 214f, 215f
  synthesis of, 213–214, 214f
Cerebrohepatorenal (Zellweger) syndrome, 194, 511, 511t
Cerebrosides, 213
Ceruloplasmin, 591t, 595–596
  deficiency of, 597
  diagnostic significance of, 57t, 596
Cervonic acid, 123t
CFTR. *See* Cystic fibrosis transmembrane regulator
CFU-E. *See* Colony-forming unit-erythroid
Chain elongation. *See also* Elongation
  by DNA polymerase, 336
  in glycosaminoglycan synthesis, 553
  in transcription cycle, 349, 349f
Chain initiation. *See also* Initiation
  in transcription cycle, 349, 349f
Chain termination. *See also* Termination
  in glycosaminoglycan synthesis, 553
  in transcription cycle, 349, 349f
Channeling, in citric acid cycle, 145
Channelopathies, 577, 577t
Channels, membrane, 425
Chaperones, 37, 515–516, 516t
  ATP-dependent protein binding to, 507, 516
  ATPase activity of, 516
  histone, 323
  in protein sorting, 507, 516t
Chaperonins, 37
Charged paddle, 433, 433f
Charging, in protein synthesis, 367, 367f
Checkpoint controls, 346
Chédiak-Higashi syndrome, 522t
Chemical carcinogenesis/carcinogens, 638
Chemiosmotic theory, 105
  on respiratory control, 107, 107f
Chemotactic factors, 628
Chemotherapy, cancer
  combination, 617
  folate inhibitors in, 500–501
  neutropenia caused by, 618
  synthetic nucleotide analogs in, 298–299, 299t
Chenodeoxycholic acid, 236, 237f
Chenodeoxycholyl CoA, 236, 237f
Chimeric gene approach, 391, 393f, 394f
Chimeric molecules, 403–406, 419
  restriction enzymes and DNA ligase in preparation of, 405–406, 407f
Chips, gene array, protein expression and, 28–29

Chitin, 117–118, 119f
Chloramines, 631
Chloride
  in extracellular and intracellular fluid, 423, 423t
  permeability coefficient of, 426f
Chlorophyll, 279
Cholecalciferol (vitamin D$_3$)
  skin synthesis of, 450–453, 454f, 492, 492f
  in vitamin D metabolism, 492, 492f, 493f
Cholera, glucose transport in treatment of, 436
Cholestatic jaundice, 292
Cholesterol, 126, 127, 129f, 217, 230–240
  in bile acid synthesis, 235–238, 237f
  in calcitriol (1,25(OH)$_2$-D$_3$) synthesis, 453, 454f
  dietary, 230
  excess of. *See* Hypercholesterolemia
  excretion of, 235–238, 237f
  in hormone synthesis, 446–448, 447f, 448f
  in lipoprotein, 217, 219f
  in membranes, 424
    fluid mosaic model and, 429
  metabolism of, 134, 134f
    clinical aspects of, 238–240, 239t
    diurnal variations in, 231
    high-density lipoproteins in, 221–222, 223f
  plasma levels of
    atherosclerosis and coronary heart disease and, 238
    dietary changes affecting, 238
    drug therapy affecting, 238–239
    lifestyle changes affecting, 238
    normal, 234
  synthesis of, 230–231, 231f, 232f, 233f
    acetyl-CoA in, 134, 134f, 230–231, 231f, 232f, 233f
    carbohydrate metabolism and, 133
    HMG-CoA reductase in regulation of, 231, 234f
  in tissues, 127, 129f
    factors affecting balance of, 231–234, 235f
  transport of, 234–235, 236f
    reverse, 222, 223f, 230, 235
Cholesteryl ester hydrolase, 234
Cholesteryl ester transfer protein, 235, 236f
Cholesteryl esters, 127, 217, 235
  in lipoprotein core, 217, 219f
Cholic acid, 236
Choline, 124–125, 125f
  deficiency of, fatty liver and, 225
  in glycine synthesis, 241, 243f
  membrane asymmetry and, 427
Choluric jaundice, 291
Cholyl CoA, in bile acid synthesis, 236, 237f
Chondrodysplasias, 561t, 563, 563f

Chondroitin sulfates, 119, 119f, 547, 553, 554f, 554t
  functions of, 557
Chondronectin, 561t, 563
Chorionic gonadotropin, human (hCG), 446
Christmas factor (factor IX), 607f, 608, 608t
  coumarin drugs affecting, 612
  deficiency of, 612
Chromatids
  nucleoprotein packing in, 326, 327t, 328f
  sister, 326, 327f
    exchanges between, 333, 333f
Chromatin, 322–326, 323f, 323t
  active *vs.* inactive regions of, 324–326, 326f
  higher order structure/compaction of, 324, 325f
  reconstitution of, in DNA replication, 341
  remodeling of in gene expression, 389
Chromatography. *See also* specific type
  affinity
    for protein/peptide purification, 23–24
    for recombinant fusion protein purification, 58–59, 59f
  for protein/peptide purification, 21–24
  Sepharose-lectin column, for glycoprotein analysis, 525t
Chromium, 504t
Chromosomal integration, 331–332, 332f
Chromosomal recombination, 331, 331f, 332f
Chromosomal transposition, 332–333
Chromosome walking, 415, 417f
Chromosomes, 326–327, 327f, 327t, 328f, 329f
  integrity of, monitoring, 346–347
  interphase, chromatin fibers in, 324
  metaphase, 325f, 326, 327t
  polytene, 326, 326f
Chronic granulomatous disease, 630, 631f
Chyle, 219
Chylomicron remnants, 218t, 220, 221f
  liver uptake of, 220
Chylomicrons, 136, 140, 217, 218t
  apolipoproteins of, 218, 218t
  metabolism of, 136, 136f, 219–220, 221f
  in triacylglycerol transport, 219, 220f, 221f
Chymotrypsin, 485
  conserved residues and, 55t
  in covalent catalysis, 53, 54f
  in digestion, 485
Chymotrypsinogen, 485
cI repressor protein/cI repressor gene, 385, 386f, 387f, 388f
CICR. *See* Calcium-induced calcium release
Cirrhosis of liver, 145, 225
Cistron, 381–382

Citrate
  in citric acid cycle, 145, 146f
  in lipogenesis regulation, 200
Citrate synthase, 145, 147f
Citric acid, p*K*/pK_a value of, 12t
Citric acid cycle (Krebs/tricarboxylic acid cycle), 91, 102, 139, 145–148, 146f, 147f
  ATP generated by, 146f, 148, 156–157, 158t
  carbon dioxide liberated by, 145–148, 147f
  deamination and, 148
  gluconeogenesis and, 148, 149f, 167–169, 168f
  in metabolism, 133, 133f, 134f, 135f, 136–138, 137f, 145, 148–150, 149f
    amino acid, 133f, 135f
    carbohydrate, 133, 133f, 148, 149f
    lipid/fatty acid, 133, 133f, 134f, 148–149, 150f
    at subcellular level, 136–138, 137f
  in mitochondria, 137–138, 137f
  reducing equivalents liberated by, 145–148, 147f
  regulation of, 149–150
  respiratory chain substrates provided by, 145, 146f
  transamination and, 148, 149f
  vitamins in, 148
Citrulline, in urea synthesis, 249, 250–251
Citrullinemia, 252
CJD. *See* Creutzfeldt-Jakob disease
Cl. *See* Chloride
Class B scavenger receptor B1, 221–222, 223f
Class (isotype) switching, 603
Classic pathway, of complement activation, 605
Clathrin, 437, 437f
Clathrin-coated vesicles, 520
Clathrin-free vesicles, 518
Cleavage, in protein sequencing, 25–26
Clinical deficiency disease. *See also* specific diseases
  vitamin, 489
CLIP, 460f, 461
Clofibrate, 238–239
Clones
  definition of, 419
  library of, 408–409, 419
  in monoclonal antibody production, 604
Cloning, 406–408, 407f, 408f, 408t
Cloning vectors, 406–408, 407f, 408f, 408t, 421
Closed complex, 352
Clotting factors, 608t. *See also* specific type under Factor
  vitamin K in synthesis of, 495, 495f
CMP, 296t
CMP-NeuAc, 525, 526t
Cn3D, 87

CO. *See* Carbon monoxide
CO_2. *See* Carbon dioxide
CoA. *See* Coenzyme A
Coactivators, transcription, 358, 358t
Coagulation (blood), 606–616
    endothelial cell products in, 615, 615t
    extrinsic pathway of, 606–608, 607f, 609
    fibrin formation in, 606–608, 607f
    final common pathway in, 609f
    intrinsic pathway of, 606–609, 607f
    laboratory tests in evaluation of, 616
    pathways of, 607f
    prostaglandins in, 196
    proteins involved in, 608, 608t. *See also*
            Coagulation factors
    vitamin K in, 495, 495f
        coumarin anticoagulants affecting,
            612
Coagulation factors, 608t. *See also* specific
            type under Factor
    vitamin K in synthesis of, 495, 495f
Coat proteins, recruitment of, 518, 519f
Coated pits, in absorptive pinocytosis, 437,
            437f
Coating, vesicle, 518–519, 519f
    brefeldin A affecting, 519–520
Cobalamin (vitamin B_{12}), 490t, 499–500,
            499f
    absorption of, 499–500
        intrinsic factor in, 485, 499
    deficiency of, 490t, 500
        functional folate deficiency and, 500,
            501–502
    in methylmalonic aciduria, 169
Cobalophilin, 500
Cobalt, 504t
    in vitamin B_{12}, 499
Cobamide, coenzymes derived from, 50
Coding regions, 327, 329f
    in recombinant DNA technology, 403,
            404f
Coding strand, 312
    in RNA synthesis, 348
Codon usage tables, 366–367
Codons, 365–366, 366t
    amino acid sequence of encoded protein
            specified by, 365–366
    nonsense, 366
Coenzyme A, synthesis of from pantothenic
            acid, 503, 503f
Coenzymes, 50
    in catalysis, 50, 51f
    nucleotide derivatives, 298, 298t
Cofactors, 50
    in blood coagulation, 608, 608t, 611
    in catalysis, 50, 51f
    in citric acid cycle regulation, 149–150
Colipase, 483
Collagen, 38–39, 378, 545–548, 546t
    in bone, 558, 558t
    in cartilage, 561–563, 561t, 562f
    classification of, 545, 546t
    elastin differentiated from, 549t

fibril formation by, 545–548, 547f, 547t
genes for, 545, 546t
    diseases caused by mutations in, 39,
            548, 548t
        chondrodysplasias, 561t, 563
        osteogenesis imperfecta, 559–560
maturation/synthesis of, 38–39
    ascorbic acid (vitamin C) in, 39, 504
    disorders of, 39
O-glycosidic linkage in, 527
in platelet activation, 613, 614f, 615
posttranslational modification of, 547,
            547t
triple helix structure of, 38–39, 39f,
            545–548, 547f
type I, 545–547, 546t
type II, 545
type IV, 546, 546t, 548t
type V, 546, 546t, 548t
type VI, 546, 546t, 548t
type VII, 546, 546t, 548t
type IX, 546t, 547
types of, 545, 546t
Collision-induced dissociation, in mass
            spectrometry, 28
Collision (kinetic) theory, 63
Colon cancer. *See* Colorectal cancer
Colony-forming unit-erythroid, 618, 619f
Colony hybridization, 410. *See also* Hybrid-
            ization
Colorectal cancer, mismatch repair genes in,
            344
Column chromatography, for protein/pep-
            tide purification, 21, 23f
Combination chemotherapy, 617
Combinatorial chemistry, 56
Combinatorial diversity, 601
Compartmentation, 73–74
Competitive inhibition, noncompetitive
            inhibition differentiated
            from, 68–70, 68f, 69f, 70f
Complement, 591t, 605
    in inflammation, 605, 628t
Complementarity
    of DNA, 314, 315f
        recombinant DNA technology and,
            402–403
    of RNA, 314, 317f
Complementarity-determining regions,
            601, 602f
Complementary DNA (cDNA), 419
Complementary DNA (cDNA) library,
            408–409, 419
Complex carbohydrate, 523
Complex (glycoconjugate) carbohydrates,
            glycoproteins as, 523
Complex oligosaccharide chains, 530–531,
            530f
    formation of, 531, 533
Computational biology, 82–87
    challenges to biology in, 84–85
    challenges to medicine in, 84
    definition of, 83

genomic resources for, 85–87
    Human Genome Project in, 83–84
Computer-aided drug design, 82
Concanavalin A (ConA), 119, 527t
Conformation. *See also* specific substances
    polypeptide/protein, 22f
    native, 36
Conformational diseases, 598
Congenital disorders of glycosylation
            (CDG), 539, 539t, 594
Congenital long QT syndrome, 439t
Congenital nonhemolytic jaundice (type I
            Crigler-Najjar syndrome),
            291
Conjugate acid, 10
Conjugate base, 10
Conjugation
    of bilirubin, 289, 289f, 290f
    of xenobiotics, 633, 634–636
Connecting (C) peptide, 457, 458f
Connective tissue, 545
    bone as, 558–559
    keratan sulfate I in, 553
Connexin, 438, 439f
Consensus sequences, 360, 361f
    Kozak, 372
Conservation of energy, 91
Conserved Domain Architecture Retrieval
            Tool (CDART), 86–87
Conserved Domain Database (CDD), 86, 87f
Conserved residues, 53–55, 55t
Constant regions/segments, 601–602
    gene for, 602
        DNA rearrangement and, 333, 399,
            602–603
        immunoglobulin heavy chain, 599–600,
            600f
        immunoglobulin light chain, 333, 399,
            599–600, 600f
Constitutive gene expression, 382, 384
Constitutive heterochromatin, 324
Constitutive mutation, 382
Constitutive secretion, 506
Contractility/contraction. *See* Muscle con-
            traction
Cooperative binding
    hemoglobin, 43
        Bohr effect and, 45, 46f
        Hill equation describing, 67–68, 68f
COPI vesicles, 519, 520
COPII vesicles, 519, 520
Coplanar atoms, partial double-bond char-
            acter and, 19, 20f
Copper, 504t
    ceruloplasmin in binding of, 595–596
    as cofactor, 596, 596t
    enzymes containing, 596t
    excess, 596
    in Menkes disease, 596–597
    metallothioneins in regulation of, 596
    in oxidases, 94
    tests for disorders of metabolism of, 597t
    in Wilson disease, 596, 597

Copper-binding P-type ATPase, mutations in gene for
  Menkes diseases caused by, 596
  Wilson disease caused by, 597
Copper toxicosis, 597. See also Wilson disease
Coproporphyrinogen I, 280, 283f, 284f
Coproporphyrinogen III, 280, 283, 284
Coproporphyrinogen oxidase, 280, 284f, 285f
  in porphyria, 286t
Coproporphyrins, 281f
  spectrophotometry in detection of, 282–283
Coprostanol (coprosterol), 236
Core proteins, 551, 552–553
  in glycosaminoglycan synthesis, 551
Coregulator proteins, 477, 478–480, 480t
Corepressors, 480, 480t
Cori cycle, 172, 172f
Cori's disease, 166t
Cornea, keratan sulfate I in, 553, 557
Coronary (ischemic) heart disease. See also Atherosclerosis
  cholesterol and, 238
Corrinoids, 499. See also Cobalamin
Corticosteroid-binding globulin (CBG/transcortin), 462, 462t, 591t
Corticosterone
  binding of, 462, 462t
  synthesis of, 446, 447–448, 449f
Corticotropin. See Adrenocorticotropic hormone
Cortisol, 447f, 448f
  binding of, 462, 462t
  synthesis of, 447–448, 449f
Cos sites, 407
Cosmids, 407, 408t, 419
Cothromboplastin (factor VII), 607f, 608t, 609
  coumarin drugs affecting, 612
Cotranslational glycosylation, 512
Cotranslational insertion, 512, 513–514
Cotransport systems, 433–434, 434f
Coulomb's law, 5
Coumarin, 612
Coupling, 89–90, 89f, 90f
  ATP in, 90, 92
  hormone receptor-effector, 443–444
Coupling domains, on hormone receptors, 443–444
Covalent bonds
  biologic molecules stabilized by, 6, 6t
  membrane lipid-protein interaction and, 426
  xenobiotic cell injury and, 638, 638f
Covalent catalysis, 52, 52f, 64
  chymotrypsin in, 53, 54f, 64
  fructose-2,6-bisphosphatase in, 53, 54f
Covalent cross-links, collagen, 546
Covalent modification
  mass spectrometry in detection of, 26–28, 27f, 27t

in protein maturation, 38
in regulation of enzymatic catalysis, 75, 77, 78–79, 79f. See also Phosphorylation; Proteolysis
  gluconeogenesis regulation and, 169–170
  irreversible, 77, 79f
  metabolite flow and, 79
  reversible, 78–79, 79f, 79t
CPT-I. See Carnitine palmitoyltransferase-I
CRE. See Cyclic AMP response element
Creatine, 274, 277f
Creatine kinase, diagnostic significance of, 57t
Creatine phosphate, 274, 277f
  free energy of hydrolysis of, 90t
  in muscle, 582f, 583, 583t
Creatine phosphate shuttle, 110, 110f
Creatinine, 274, 277f
CREB, 468–469
CREB-binding protein, 468–469, 477f, 478–479
Creutzfeldt-Jakob disease, 38
Crigler-Najjar syndrome
  type I (congenital nonhemolytic jaundice), 291
  type II, 291
Cro protein/cro gene, 385, 386f, 387f, 388f
  binding of to DNA, by helix-turn-helix motif, 395, 395f
Cross-bridges, 566, 567f, 571f
Cross-links, covalent in collagen, 546
Crossing-over, in chromosomal recombination, 331, 331f, 332f
Crouzon syndrome, 561t
CRP. See C-reactive protein; Catabolite regulatory protein; Cyclic AMP regulatory protein
Cryoprecipitates, recombinant DNA technology in production of, 612
Cryptoxanthin, 490
Crystallography, x-ray, protein structure demonstrated by, 35–36
CS-PG I/II/III, in bone, 558t
CT. See Calcitonin
CTD. See Carboxyl terminal repeat domain
CTP, 298
  in phosphorylation, 92–93
CY282Y mutation, in hemochromatosis, 595
Cyanide
  on oxidative phosphorylation, 100
  on respiratory chain, 107, 107f
Cyclic AMP, 161, 162f, 297, 297f, 298t, 466–470, 468t, 470f
  adenylyl cyclase affecting, 161, 466–467, 468t
  in cardiac muscle regulation, 575
  in gluconeogenesis, 171, 171f
  in glycogen metabolism regulation, 162–164, 162f, 163f, 164f
  as second messenger, 161, 444, 445t, 465, 466–470, 468t, 470f

smooth muscle contraction affected by, 579
Cyclic AMP-dependent protein kinase. See Protein kinases
Cyclic AMP regulatory protein (catabolite gene activator protein), 382, 384
Cyclic AMP response element, 467t, 468–469
Cyclic AMP response element binding protein, 468–469
Cyclic GMP, 297f, 298
  role in smooth muscle, 581f
  as second messenger, 298, 444, 445t, 465, 470
Cyclic 3′,5′-nucleotide phosphodiesterase, in lipolysis, 227
Cyclin-dependent protein kinases, 341, 342f, 342t
  inhibition of, DNA/chromosome integrity and, 347
Cyclins, 341–343, 342f, 342t
Cycloheximide, 378
Cyclooxygenase, 204
  as "suicide enzyme," 204–205
Cyclooxygenase pathway, 204–205, 205f, 206f
CYP nomenclature, for cytochrome P450 isoforms, 634
CYP2A6, polymorphism of, 635, 637t
CYP2C9, in warfarin-phenobarbital interaction, 635
CYP2D6, polymorphism of, 635, 637t, 639
CYP2E1, enzyme induction and, 635
Cysteine, 15t, 271
  metabolism of, 257, 259f, 260f
    abnormalities of, 254–257, 260f
  in pyruvate formation, 257, 259f, 260f
  requirements for, 488
  synthesis of, 242, 244f
Cystic fibrosis, 439–440, 439t, 482, 542, 577t
Cystic fibrosis transmembrane regulator (CFTR), 439–440, 439t, 542
  degradation of, 517
Cystine reductase, 257, 259f
Cystinosis (cystine storage disease), 254–257
Cystinuria (cystine-lysinuria), 257
Cytarabine (arabinosyl cytosine), 298
Cytidine, 295f, 296t
Cytidine monophosphate (CMP), 296t
Cytidine monophosphate N-acetyl-neuraminic acid (CMP-NeuAc), 525, 526t
Cytidine triphosphate (CTP), 298
  in phosphorylation, 92–93
Cytochrome b_5, 97, 630, 634
Cytochrome b_H, 104
Cytochrome b_L, 104
Cytochrome c oxidase, 100, 102f, 103f
Cytochrome c_1, 104

Cytochrome oxidase/cytochrome aa3, 94
Cytochrome P450, 512
Cytochrome P450-dependent microsomal
    ethanol oxidizing system,
    225–226
Cytochrome P450 side chain cleavage
    enzyme (P450scc), 446,
    448f, 450
Cytochrome P450 system, 94, 97, 98f,
    633
    ALA synthase affected by, 281, 287
    enzyme induction and, 281–282, 635
    genes encoding, nomenclature for, 634
    isoforms of, 634–635
    membrane insertion, 512
    in metabolism of xenobiotics, 633–635,
        636t
    mitochondrial, 97
    nomenclature system for, 634
    in xenobiotic cell injury, 638, 638f
Cytochromes, as dehydrogenases, 95–96
Cytokines
    α_2-macroglobulin binding of, 598–599
    in cachexia, 143
Cytosine, 296t
    base pairing of in DNA, 311, 312, 313f
    deoxyribonucleosides of, in pyrimidine
        synthesis, 304–305, 306f
Cytoskeleton/cytoskeletal proteins, 565,
    584–586
    red cell, 623f, 624, 624t
Cytosol
    ALA synthesis in, 279, 282f
    glycolysis in, 137f, 138, 151
    lipogenesis in, 196–199, 197f, 198f
    pentose phosphate pathway reactions in,
        177
    pyrimidine synthesis in, 304, 306f
Cytosolic branch, for protein sorting, 507,
    507f
Cytosolic dynein, 585
Cytosolic proteins, O-glycosidic linkages in,
    527
Cytotoxicity, xenobiotic, 638, 638f

D-amino acids, free, 14
D arm, of tRNA, 318, 320f, 367, 368f
D cyclins, 341–342, 342f, 342t
    cancer and, 341–342
D isomerism, 112–113, 113f
DAF. See Decay accelerating factor
dAMP, 296f
Dantrolene, for malignant hyperthermia,
    573
Databases, 82–83
DBD. See DNA binding domains
Deamination, 134, 135f
    citric acid cycle in, 148
    liver in, 134
Debranching enzymes
    absence of, 166t
    in glycogenolysis, 160–161, 162f

Debrisoquin, CYP2D6 in metabolism of,
    635
Decay accelerating factor, 540
Decorin
    in bone, 558t
    in cartilage, 561t
Defensins, 628t
Degeneracy, of genetic code, 366
Dehydrocholesterol, in vitamin D metabo-
    lism, 492, 492f
Dehydroepiandrosterone (DHEA), synthe-
    sis of, 448, 449f
Dehydrogenases, 94, 95–96, 96f
    in enzyme detection, 56, 57f
    nicotinamide coenzyme-dependent, 95,
        97f
    in respiratory chain, 95
    riboflavin-dependent, 95
Deletions, DNA, recombinant DNA tech-
    nology in detection of,
    413–414, 415t
Denaturation
    DNA structure analysis and, 312–313
    protein refolding and, 37
    temperature and, 64
Deoxynojirimycin, 536, 536t
Deoxy sugars, 116, 116f
Deoxyadenylate, 311
Deoxycholic acid, synthesis of, 237
Deoxycorticosterone
    binding of, 462
    synthesis of, 446, 449f
11-Deoxycortisol, synthesis of, 448, 449f
Deoxycytidine residues, methylation of,
    gene expression affected by,
    389
Deoxycytidylate, 311
Deoxyguanylate, 311
Deoxyhemoglobin, proton binding by, 45,
    46f
Deoxyhemoglobin A, "sticky patch" recep-
    tor on, 47
Deoxyhemoglobin S, "sticky patch" receptor
    on, 47
Deoxynucleotides, 311–312, 312f, 313f
Deoxyribonucleases (DNase)/DNase I,
    321
    active chromatin and, 324
Deoxyribonucleic acid. See DNA
Deoxyribonucleoside diphosphates
    (dNDPs), reduction of
    NDPs to, 302, 305f
Deoxyribonucleosides, 294
    in pyrimidine synthesis, 304
Deoxyribose, 112, 116, 116f
3-Deoxyuridine, 298
Dephosphorylation. See also Phosphoryla-
    tion
    in covalent modification, 79–80, 79t
Depolarization, in nerve impulse transmis-
    sion, 436
Depurination, DNA, base excision-repair
    and, 344

Dermatan sulfate, 554f, 554t, 555
    functions of, 557
Desmin, 574t, 585t
Desmosines, 549
Desmosterol, in cholesterol synthesis, 231,
    233f
Detergents, 424–425
Detoxification, 633
    cytochrome P450 system in, 97, 98f,
        633–635, 636t
Dextrinosis, limit, 166t
Dextrins, 116
Dextrose, 113
DHA. See Docosahexaenoic acid
DHEA. See Dehydroepiandrosterone
DHPR. See Dihydropyridine receptor
DHT. See Dihydrotestosterone
Diabetes mellitus, 112, 175
    fatty liver and, 225
    free fatty acid levels in, 218
    hemochromatosis and, 595
    hyperglycemia in, 143–144
    insulin resistance and, 619
    ketosis/ketoacidosis in, 194
    lipid transport and storage disorders and,
        217
    lipogenesis in, 196
    as metabolic disease, 132
Diabetic cataract, 185–186
Diacylglycerol, 125, 483, 484f
    in calcium-dependent signal transduc-
        tion, 471, 473f
    formation of, 210f
    in platelet activation, 614, 614f
    in respiratory burst, 630
Diacylglycerol acyltransferase, 210f, 211
Diagnostic enzymology, 56–57, 57t
Diarrhea
    bacteria causing, glycan binding of, 542
    severe, glucose transport in treatment of,
        436
Dicarboxylic aciduria, 194
Dicumarol (4-hydroxydicoumarin), 495
Dielectric constant, of water, 5
Diet. See also Nutrition
    blood glucose regulation and, 173
    cholesterol levels affected by, 238
    hepatic VLDL secretion and, 223–225,
        224f
    high-fat, fatty liver and, 225
    very low carbohydrate, weight loss from,
        175
Diet-induced thermogenesis, 228, 486
Diethylenetriaminepentaacetate (DTPA),
    as preventive antioxidant,
    129
Diffusion
    facilitated, 430, 430t, 431f, 434–435,
        435f
    of bilirubin, 288–289
    of glucose. See also Glucose transporters
        insulin affecting, 434–435
        in red cell membrane, 619

hormones in regulation of, 434–435
"Ping-Pong" model of, 434, 435f
net, 430, 431f
passive, 430, 430t, 431f
simple, 430, 430t, 431f
Digestion, 482–488
Digitalis
Ca^{2+}-Na$^+$ exchanger in action of, 576–577
Na$^+$-K$^+$ ATPase affected by, 435, 576–577
Dihydrobiopterin, defect in synthesis of, 259
Dihydrobiopterin reductase, defect in, 259
Dihydrofolate/dihydrofolate reductase, methotrexate affecting, 304–305, 501
Dihydrolipoyl dehydrogenase, 155, 156f
Dihydrolipoyl transacetylase, 155, 156f
Dihydropyridine receptor, 572, 572f
Dihydrotestosterone, 450, 452f
binding of, 462t
Dihydroxyacetone, 116f
Dihydroxyacetone phosphate, in glycolysis, 209, 210f
1,25-Dihydroxyvitamin D$_3$. See Calcitriol
24,25-Dihydroxyvitamin D$_3$ (24-hydroxy-calcidiol), in vitamin D metabolism, 493, 493f
Diiodotyrosine (DIT), 455, 456f, 457
Dilated cardiomyopathy, 578
Dimercaprol, on respiratory chain, 107, 107f
Dimeric proteins, 34
Dimers
Cro protein, 386, 387f
histone, 323
lambda repressor (cI) protein, 386, 387f
Dimethylallyl diphosphate, in cholesterol synthesis, 230, 232f
Dimethylaminoadenine, 297f
2,4-Dinitrophenol, 107
Dinucleotide, 299
Dioxygenases, 97
Dipalmitoyl lecithin, 125
Dipeptidases, 485
Diphosphates, nucleoside, 295, 295f
Diphosphatidylglycerol. See Cardiolipin
Diphtheria toxin, 379, 433
Dipoles, water forming, 5, 6f
Disaccharidases, 112, 483
Disaccharides, 116, 117f, 117t. See also specific type
Disease, 1. See also specific diseases
biochemical basis of, 2, 3t
Human Genome Project and, 3–4
major causes of, 3t
Displacement reactions
double, 70, 70f
sequential (single), 70, 70f
Dissociation, of water, 8–9
Dissociation constant, 8–9
Michaelis constant (K_m) and, 67

in pH calculation, 10
of weak acids, 10–11, 12
Distal histidine (histidine E7), in oxygen binding, 40, 42f
Disulfide bonds, protein folding and, 37
DIT. See Diiodotyrosine
Diurnal rhythm, in cholesterol synthesis, 231
Divalent metal transporter (DMT1), 593
Diversity
antibody, 601, 602–603
combinatorial, 601
in gene expression, 391–393, 394f
junctional, 602–603
Diversity segment, DNA rearrangement and, 602–603
DNA, 311–314, 322–347
base excision-repair of, 343t, 344, 345f
base pairing in, 7, 311–312, 313f
matching of for renaturation, 313–314
recombinant DNA technology and, 402–403
replication/synthesis and, 336, 338f
binding to regulatory proteins of, motifs for, 393–396, 394t, 395f, 396f, 397f
blunt-ended, 404, 405–406, 406f, 419
in chromatin, 322–326, 323f, 323t, 325f, 326f
chromosomal, 326–327, 327f, 327t, 328f, 329f
relationship of to mRNA, 329f
coding regions of, 327, 329f
complementarity of, 314, 315f
recombinant DNA technology and, 402–403
damage to, 343, 343t
repair of, 343–347, 343t
ADP-ribosylation for, 498
deletions in, recombinant DNA technology in detection of, 413–414, 415t
depurination of, base excision-repair and, 344
double-strand break repair of, 343t, 346, 346f
double-stranded, 311–312
flanking sequence, 403
genetic information contained in, 311–314
grooves in, 313f, 314
insertions in, recombinant DNA technology in detection of, 413–414
integrity of, monitoring, 346–347
"jumping," 332
mismatch repair of, 343–344, 343t, 344f
mitochondrial, 330, 330f, 331t
mutations in, 322, 331–333, 331f, 332f, 333f. See also Mutations
in nucleosomes, 323–324, 325f
nucleotide excision-repair of, 344–345, 345f

rearrangements of
in antibody diversity, 333, 399, 602–603
recombinant DNA technology in detection of, 413–414, 415t
recombinant. See Recombinant DNA/recombinant DNA technology
relaxed form of, 314
renaturation of, base pair matching and, 313–314
repair of, 343–347, 343t
repetitive-sequence, 328
replication/synthesis of, 314, 315f, 333–347, 334t, 335f, 336t, 342t
DNA polymerase complex in, 335, 336t
DNA primer in, 335, 336, 337f, 338f
initiation of, 336, 337f, 338f, 339f
origin of, 334
polarity of, 338
proteins involved in, 336t
reconstitution of chromatin structure and, 341
repair during, 343–347, 343t
replication bubble formation and, 338–339, 339f, 340f, 341f
replication fork formation and, 334–336, 335f
ribonucleoside diphosphate reduction and, 302, 305f
in S phase of cell cycle, 341–343, 341f, 342f
semiconservative nature of, 314, 315f
semidiscontinuous, 335f, 338, 339f
unwinding and, 334
in RNA synthesis, 348–351, 349f, 351t
stabilization of, 7
structure of, 311–314, 312f, 313f
denaturation in analysis of, 312–313
double-helical, 7, 311–312, 313f
recombinant DNA technology and, 402, 403
supercoiled, 314, 340, 341f
transcription of, 314
transposition of, 332–333
unique-sequence (nonrepetitive), 328
unwinding of, 334
RNA synthesis and, 352
xenobiotic cell injury and, 638
DNA binding domains, 396, 398f, 477
DNA binding motifs, 393–396, 394t, 395f, 396f, 397f
DNA-dependent protein kinase, in double-strand break repair, 346
DNA-dependent RNA polymerases, 349–350, 349f, 351t
DNA elements, gene expression affected by, 389–390, 390f, 391t, 392f
diversity and, 391–393, 394f

DNA fingerprinting, 419
DNA footprinting, 419
DNA helicase, 334, 335, 335f, 336t
DNA ligase, 336t, 338
  in recombinant DNA technology, 405–406, 406t, 407f
DNA-PK. See DNA-dependent protein kinase
DNA polymerases, 334–336, 335f, 336t
  in recombinant DNA technology, 406t
DNA primase, 334, 335–336, 335f, 336t
DNA probes, 409, 420
  library searched with, 409
  in porphyria diagnosis, 274
DNA-protein interactions, bacteriophage lambda as paradigm for, 384–387, 385f, 386f, 387f, 388f
DNA sequences
  amplification of by PCR, 410–411, 412f
  determination of, 410, 411f
  protein sequencing and, 26
DNA topoisomerases, 314, 336t, 340, 340f
DNA transfection, endocytosis in, 436
DNA transfection, identification of enhancers/regulatory elements and, 391
DNA unwinding element, 334
DNase (deoxyribonuclease)/DNase I, 321
  active chromatin and, 324
  in recombinant DNA technology, 406t
dNDPs. See Deoxyribonucleoside diphosphates
DOC. See Deoxycorticosterone
Docking, in nuclear import, 509, 510f
Docking programs, molecular, 36
Docking protein, 512
Docosahexaenoic acid, 203
Dolichol, 128, 129f, 531, 531f
  in cholesterol synthesis, 231, 232f
  in N-glycosylation, 532
Dolichol kinase, 531
Dolichol P P GlcNAc, 532–533
Dolichol-P-P-oligosaccharide (dolichol-pyrophosphate-oligosaccharide), 531, 533f
  in N-glycosylation, 531, 532f
Dolichol phosphate, 531
Domains. See also specific type
  albumin, 592
  carboxyl terminal repeat, 357
  chromatin, 324, 326, 327f
  coupling, on hormone receptors, 443–444
  DNA binding, 396, 398f, 477
  fibronectin, 550, 550f
  protein, 33
  Src homology 2 (SH2)
    in insulin signal transmission, 473, 474f
    in Jak/STAT pathway, 475
  trans-activation, of regulatory proteins, 396, 398f
  transcription, 393

L-Dopa, 454, 455f
Dopa decarboxylase, 274, 276f, 454, 455f
Dopamine, 454, 455f. See also Catecholamines
  synthesis of, 274, 276f, 453–454, 455f
Dopamine β-hydroxylase, 503
Double displacement reactions, 70, 70f
Double helix, of DNA structure, 7, 311–312, 313f
  recombinant DNA technology and, 402, 403
Double reciprocal plot
  inhibitor evaluation and, 69, 69f, 70f
  K_m and V_{max} estimated from, 67, 67f
Double-strand break repair of DNA, 343t, 346, 346f
Double-stranded DNA, 311–312, 322
  unwinding
    for replication, 334
    RNA synthesis and, 352
Downstream promoter element, 353–355, 354f
DPE. See Downstream promoter element
DRIPs, 480, 480t
Drug detoxification/interactions, cytochromes P450 and, 97, 98f, 635
Drug development
  enzyme kinetics, mechanism, and inhibition in, 71–72
  pharmacogenetics and, 638–639
  RNA targets for, 320
Drug discovery, enzyme assays suitable for "high-throughput" screening in, 55–56
Drug metabolism, in vivo, 72
Drug resistance, gene amplification in, 399
Drugs, as enzyme inhibitors, 71
dsDNA. See Double-stranded DNA
DS-PG I/DS-PG II, in cartilage, 561t
DTPA, as preventive antioxidant, 129
Dubin-Johnson syndrome, 292
Duchenne muscular dystrophy, 565, 574–575, 574f
DUE. See DNA unwinding element
Dwarfism, 561t, 563
Dynamin, in absorptive pinocytosis, 437, 585
Dyneins, 585
Dysbetalipoproteinemia, familial, 239t
Dyslipoproteinemias, 239–240, 239t
Dystrophin, 565, 574–575, 574t, 575f
  mutation in gene for, in muscular dystrophy, 574–575, 574f

E coli, lactose metabolism in, operon hypothesis and, 382–384, 382f, 383f
E coli bacteriophage P1-based (PAC) vector, 407, 408t, 420
E cyclins, 342, 342f, 342t
E-selectin, 538t

E (exit) site, in protein synthesis, 39f, 375
E0. See Redox (oxidation-reduction) potential
Eact. See Activation energy
ECF. See Extracellular fluid
ECM. See Extracellular matrix
EcoRI, 404, 405t, 407f
EcoRII, 405t
Edema
  in kwashiorkor, 486, 487
  plasma protein concentration and, 589
  in thiamin deficiency, 496
Edman reaction, for peptide/protein sequencing, 25–26, 27f
Edman reagent (phenylisothiocyanate), in protein sequencing, 25–26, 27f
EDRF. See Endothelium-derived relaxing factor
EDTA, as preventive antioxidant, 129
EFA. See Essential fatty acids
EFs. See Elongation factors
EGF. See Epidermal growth factor
Egg white, uncooked, biotin deficiency caused by, 502
Ehlers-Danlos syndrome, 548, 548t
Eicosanoids, 122, 196, 204, 205f, 206f, 628t
Eicosapentaenoic acid, 202f
eIF-4E complex, in protein synthesis, 372–374
eIFs, in protein synthesis, 372
80S initiation complex, in protein synthesis, 372, 373f
Elaidic acid, 122, 123t, 124f
Elastase, in digestion, 485
Elastin, 548–549, 549t
Electron carriers, flavin coenzymes as, 497
Electron flow, through respiratory chain, 101 102, 102f, 103f
Electron movement, in active transport, 435
Electron-transferring flavoprotein, 95, 188
Electron transport chain system, 630. See also Respiratory chain
Electrophiles, 7
Electrophoresis
  for plasma protein analysis, 588
  polyacrylamide, for protein/peptide purification, 24, 25f, 26f
  two-dimensional, protein expression and, 28–29
Electrospray dispersion, in mass spectrometry, 27–28
Electrostatic bonds/interactions, 7. See also Salt (electrostatic) bonds
  oxygen binding rupturing, Bohr effect
  protons and, 45, 46f
ELISAs. See Enzyme-linked immunoassays
Elliptocytosis, hereditary, 625
Elongase, 200, 201f
  in polyunsaturated fatty acid synthesis, 202–203, 203f, 204f

Elongation
chain
in fatty acid synthesis, 200, 201f
in transcription cycle, 349, 349f
in DNA synthesis, 336–338
in glycosaminoglycan synthesis, 553
in protein synthesis, 374–376, 375f
in RNA synthesis, 349, 349f, 352
Elongation arrest, 512
Elongation factor 2, in protein synthesis, 375, 375f
Elongation factor EF1A, in protein synthesis, 374, 375f
Elongation factors, in protein synthesis, 374–375, 375f
Emaciation, 132
Emelin, 549
Emphysema
α_1-antitrypsin deficiency in, 597
α_1-antitrypsin (α_1-antiproteinase) for, 597–598
Emulsions, amphipathic lipids forming, 129, 130f
Encephalopathies
hyperbilirubinemia causing (kernicterus), 291
from inherited mitochondrial defects, 100
spongiform (prion diseases), 38
Wernicke's, 496
ENCODE Project, 85–86
Endergonic reaction, 89
coupling and, 89–90, 89f, 90f
ATP in, 90, 92
Endocrine system, 442–463. See also Hormones
diversity of, 445–446
Endocytosis, 436, 437–438, 437f
receptor-mediated, 437–438, 437f
Endoglycosidase F, 526
Endoglycosidase H, 526
Endoglycosidases, in glycoprotein analysis, 525–526, 525t, 526t
Endonucleases, 321, 419
apurinic and apyrimidinic, in base excision-repair, 344
restriction, 321, 403–406, 405t, 406f, 419, 420
in recombinant DNA technology, 405–406, 405t, 406f, 406t, 407f
Endopeptidases, 485
Endoplasmic reticulum, 376
accumulation of misfolded proteins in, 516
acylglycerol synthesis and, 137f, 138
core protein synthesis in, 553
fatty acid chain elongation in, 200, 201f
rough
glycosylation in, 533–535, 534f
in protein sorting, 506, 507f, 508f
protein synthesis and, 376
routes of protein insertion into, 513–515, 514f

signal hypothesis of polyribosome binding to, 511–513, 512t, 513f
smooth, cytochrome P450 isoforms in, 634
Endoplasmic reticulum–associated degradation (ERAD)
of misfolded proteins, 516–517, 517f
Endorphins, 460f, 461
Endothelial cells
in clotting and thrombosis, 615, 615t
neutrophil interaction and
integrins in, 538t, 628–629, 629t
selectins in, 537–538, 538t, 539f
Endothelium-derived relaxing factor, 580, 615t. See also Nitric oxide
Energy
activation, 62, 64
conservation of, 91
free. See Free energy
in muscle, creatine phosphate as reserve for, 582f, 583
nutritional requirement for, 486
transduction of
membranes in, 422
in muscle, 565–566
Energy balance, 486–487
Energy capture, 90–91, 90f, 91
Energy expenditure, 486
Energy transfer, 90–91, 90f
Enhanceosome, 391, 392f
Enhancers/enhancer elements, 355
in gene expression, 389–390, 390f, 391t
tissue-specific expression and, 391
recombinant DNA technology and, 403
reporter genes in definition of, 389–391, 393f, 394f
Enolase, in glycolysis, 152, 153f
Entactin, in basal lamina, 551
Enterocytes, iron absorption in, 593
Enterohepatic circulation, 237–238
lipid absorption and, 483
Enterohepatic urobilinogen cycle, 290
Enteropeptidase, 485
Enthalpy, 88
Entrez Gene, 86
Entropy, 88
Enzyme induction, 637
cytochrome P450 and, 281–282, 635
in gluconeogenesis regulation, 169, 170t
Enzyme inhibitors, drugs as, 71
Enzyme-linked immunoassays (ELISAs), 56
Enzymes, 7
active sites of, 50–51, 51f
assay of, 56, 57f
branching, in glycogen biosynthesis, 159, 161f
catalytic activity of, 49, 50f. See also Catalysis/catalytic reactions (enzymatic)
detection facilitated by, 55–56, 57f
kinetics of, 64–72. See also Kinetics (enzyme)
in drug development, 71–72

regulation of, 73–81, 138, 139f
RNA and, 364
specificity of, 49, 50f
classification of, 49–50
debranching
absence of, 166t
in glycogenolysis, 160–161, 162f
degradation of, control of, 75
in disease diagnosis/prognosis, 56–57, 57t, 58f, 588
in DNA repair, 343, 343t, 346
hydrolysis rate affected by, 7
irreversible inhibition ("poisoning") of, 70
isosteric, 76
isozymes and, 55
kinetics of, 61–72. See also Kinetics (enzyme)
mechanisms of action of, 49–59
membranes in localization of, 422
metal-activated, 50
plasma, diagnostic significance of, 56–57, 57t
quantity of, catalytic capacity affected by, 74–75
recombinant DNA technology in study of, 58–59, 59f
regulatory, 138, 139f
restriction. See Restriction endonucleases/enzymes
specificity of, 49, 50f
substrates affecting conformation of, 52, 52f
Enzymology, single molecule, 55, 55f
Enzymopathies, 627
Epidermal growth factor (EGF), receptor for, 444
Epidermolysis bullosa, 548, 548t
Epimerases
in galactose metabolism, 181, 184f
in glycosaminoglycan synthesis, 553
in pentose phosphate pathway, 177, 179f
Epimers, 114, 114f
Epinephrine, 447f, 454–455, 455f. See also Catecholamines
blood glucose affected by, 174
in gluconeogenesis regulation, 169–170
in lipogenesis regulation, 200
synthesis of, 272–274, 276f, 453–455, 455f
Epitope (antigenic determinant), 32, 599
Epoxide hydrolase, 638
Epoxides, 638
Equilibrium constant (K_{eq}), 63–64
in enzymatic catalysis, 64
free energy changes and, 62
ER. See Estrogens
Ercalcitriol, 492
ERE. See Estrogen response element
eRF. See Releasing factors
Ergocalciferol (vitamin D_2), 492
Ergosterol, 127, 129f
Erythrocyte aminotransferases, in vitamin B_6 status assessment, 499

Erythrocyte transketolase activation, in thiamin nutritional status assessment, 497
Erythrocytes, 617–618, 619–625
  2,3-bisphosphoglycerate pathway in, 155, 155f
  disorders affecting, 617, 618t
  erythropoietin in regulation of, 617–618, 619f
  glucose-6-phosphate dehydrogenase deficiency affecting, 621, 621f, 627
  glucose as metabolic necessity for, 140
  glycolysis in, 155, 155f
  hemoglobin S "sticky patch" affecting, 47
  hemolysis of, pentose phosphate pathway/glutathione peroxidase and, 180, 181f, 183–184
  life span of, 617
  membranes of, 622–625, 623f, 623t, 624t
    glucose transporter of, 619, 620t
    hemolytic anemias and, 627, 627t
  metabolism of, 143t, 619–622, 619t
    oxidants produced during, 620–621, 620t
  recombinant DNA technology in study of, 632
  structure and function of, 617–618
Erythroid ALA synthase (ALAS2), 281, 282
  in porphyria, 274, 286t
Erythropoiesis, 617–618, 619f
Erythropoietin/recombinant erythropoietin (epoetin alfa/EPO), 535, 591t, 617–618, 619f
  cloning of, 632
D-Erythrose, 115f
Escherichia coli, lactose metabolism in, operon hypothesis and, 382–384, 382f, 383f
Escherichia coli bacteriophage P1-based (PAC) vector, 407, 408t, 420
Essential amino acids. *See* Nutritionally essential amino acids
Essential fatty acids, 196, 202, 202f, 204
  abnormal metabolism of, 206
  deficiency of, 203–204, 206
  prostaglandin production and, 196
Essential fructosuria, 177, 185
Essential pentosuria, 177, 184
Estriol, synthesis of, 450, 452f
Estrogen response element, 467t
Estrogens
  on amino acid transport, 435
  binding of, 462t, 463
  receptors for, 478
  synthesis of, 450, 452f, 453f
Estrone
  binding of, 462t
  synthesis of, 450, 452f
Ethanol
  CYP2E1 induction and, 635
  fatty liver and, 225–226

iron absorption and, 486
thiamin deficiency and, 496
transferrin glycosylation with chronic abuse of, 594
Ether lipids, biosynthesis of, 212f
Ethylenediaminetetraacetate (EDTA), as preventive antioxidant, 129
Euchromatin, 324
Eukaryotic cell cycle, versatility of, 80–81, 80f
Eukaryotic gene expression, 387–393, 396–400, 398t. *See also* Gene expression
  chromatin remodeling in, 389
  diversity of, 391–393, 394f
  DNA elements affecting, 389–390, 390f, 391t, 392f
  DNA-protein interactions in, bacteriophage lambda as paradigm for, 384–387, 385f, 386f, 387f, 388f
  locus control regions and insulators in, 393
  prokaryotic gene expression compared with, 396–400, 398t
  reporter genes and, 391, 393f, 394f
  tissue-specific, 391
Eukaryotic promoters, in transcription, 353–356, 354f, 355f, 356f
Eukaryotic transcription complex, 356–359, 358t
Exchange diffusion systems, 107–108
Exchange transporters, 107–110, 108t–110t
Excitation-response coupling, membranes in, 422
Exergonic reaction, 88, 89
  coupling and, 89–90, 89f, 90f
  ATP in, 90, 92
Exinuclease, in DNA repair, 345, 345f
Exit (E) site, in protein synthesis, 375, 375f
Exocytosis, 437, 438, 438f
Exocytotic (secretory) pathway, 506
Exoglycosidases, in glycoprotein analysis, 525–526, 525t, 526t
Exons, 327, 365, 419
  interruptions in. *See* Introns
  in recombinant DNA technology, 403, 404f
  splicing, 359–362, 419
    alternative, in regulation of gene expression, 362, 362f, 399
    recombinant DNA technology and, 403, 404f
Exonucleases, 321, 419
  in recombinant DNA technology, 406t
Exopeptidases, 485
Exportins, 511
Expression vector, 409
Extra arm, of tRNA, 318, 320f
Extracellular environment, membranes in maintenance of, 422–423, 423t

Extracellular fluid (ECF), 422–423, 423t
Extracellular matrix, 545–563. *See also* Matrix; specific components
Extramitochondrial system, fatty acid synthesis in, 196
Extrinsic pathway of blood coagulation, 606–608, 607f, 609
Eye, fructose and sorbitol in, diabetic cataract and, 185–186
Ezetimibe, for hypercholesterolemia, 239

F-Actin, 567, 568f, 570
  in nonmuscle cells, 584
Fab region, 599, 600f
Fabry's disease, 215t
Facilitated diffusion/transport system, 430, 430t, 431f, 434–435, 435f
  for bilirubin, 288–289
  for glucose. *See also* Glucose transporters
    insulin affecting, 434–435
    in red cell membrane, 619
    hormones in regulation of, 434–435
  "Ping-Pong" model of, 434, 435f
Factor I (fibrinogen), 588, 608, 608t
  conversion of to fibrin, 610
Factor II (prothrombin), 608t, 609
  coumarin drugs affecting, 495, 612
  vitamin K in synthesis of, 495
Factor III (tissue factor), 607f, 608t, 609
Factor IV. *See* Calcium
Factor IX (antihemophilic factor B/Christmas factor/plasma thromboplastin component), 607f, 608, 608t
  coumarin drugs affecting, 612
  deficiency of, 612
Factor V (proaccelerin/labile factor/accelerator globulin), 608t, 609, 609f
Factor V Leiden, 611
Factor VII (proconvertin/serum prothrombin conversion accelerator/cothromboplastin), 607f, 608t, 609
  coumarin drugs affecting, 612
Factor VIII (antihemophilic factor A/globulin), 607f, 608, 608t
  deficiency of, 612
Factor VIII concentrates, recombinant DNA technology in production of, 612
Factor X (Stuart-Prower factor), 607f, 608, 608t
  activation of, 607f, 608–609
  coumarin drugs affecting, 612
Factor Xa, prothrombin to thrombin activation by, 609–610
Factor XI (plasma thromboplastin antecedent), 607f, 608, 608t
  deficiency of, 609
Factor XII (Hageman factor), 607f, 608, 608t

Factor XIII (fibrin stabilizing factor/fibrino-ligase), 608t
Facultative heterochromatin, 324
FAD. *See* Flavin adenine dinucleotide
FADH2, fatty acid oxidation yielding, 188
Familial hypertrophic cardiomyopathy, 577–578, 578f
Fanconi's anemia, 346
Farber's disease, 215t
Farnesoid X receptor, in bile acid synthesis regulation, 238
Farnesyl diphosphate, in cholesterol/poly-isoprenoid synthesis, 230, 231, 232f
in vesicle coating, 519
Fast acetylators, 637
Fast (white) twitch fibers, 583, 583t
Fasting state, metabolic fuels in, 132, 140–143, 142f, 142t
Fat tissue. *See* Adipose tissue
Fatal infantile mitochondrial myopathy and renal dysfunction, 110
Fatigue (muscle), 151
Fats, 121. *See also* Lipids
diets high in, fatty liver and, 225
metabolism of, 133f, 134, 134f, 136, 136f
Fatty acid-binding protein, 187, 219
Fatty acid chains, elongation of, 200, 201f
Fatty acid elongase system, 199, 201f
in polyunsaturated fatty acid synthesis, 202–203, 203f, 204f
Fatty acid oxidase, 188, 189f
Fatty acid synthase, 196
Fatty acid synthase complex, 196–199, 197f, 198f, 202
Fatty acid synthesis, carbohydrates in, 138
Fatty acid-transport protein, membrane, 219
Fatty acids, 2, 121–124
activation of, 187, 188f
calcium absorption affected by, 485
eicosanoids formed from, 196, 204, 205f, 206f
essential, 196, 202, 202f, 204
abnormal metabolism of, 206
deficiency of, 203–204, 206
prostaglandin production and, 196
free. *See* Free fatty acids
interconvertibility of, 138–139
in membranes, 424, 425f
metabolism of, 134, 134f
nomenclature of, 121–122, 121f
oxidation of, 187. *See also* Ketogenesis
acetyl-CoA release and, 134, 134f, 187–189, 188f, 189f
clinical aspects of, 194–195
hypoglycemia caused by impairment of, 194
in mitochondria, 187, 188f
physical/physiologic properties of, 124
saturated, 121, 122, 122t

synthesis of, 196–202, 197f, 198f. *See also* Lipogenesis
carbohydrate metabolism and, 133
citric acid cycle in, 148–149, 150f
extramitochondrial, 196
trans, 122–123, 203–204
transport of, carnitine in, 187, 188f
triacylglycerols (triglycerides) as storage form of, 124, 124f, 125f
unesterified (free). *See* Free fatty acids
unsaturated. *See* Unsaturated fatty acids
Fatty liver
alcoholism and, 225–226
of pregnancy, 194
triacylglycerol metabolism imbalance and, 225
Favism, 184
Fc fragment, 599, 600f
receptors for, in neutrophils, 628t
Fe. *See* Iron
Fed state, metabolic fuels in, 132, 140, 142t
Feedback inhibition, in allosteric regulation, 75–77, 76f, 77, 138
Feedback regulation
in allosteric regulation, 77, 138
of circulating thrombin levels, 611
Fenton reaction, 620
Ferric iron, 287
in methemoglobinemia, 46
Ferrireductase, 593
Ferritin, 486, 593, 594
protein synthesis affected by, 376
Ferritin receptor, 594
Ferrochelatase (heme synthase), 280, 281f
in porphyria, 286t
Ferroprotein, 593
Ferrous iron
incorporation of into protoporphyrin, 280–281, 281f
in oxygen transport, 40–41
Fertilization, glycoproteins in, 537
Fetal hemoglobin, P_{50} of, 43
Fetal warfarin syndrome, 496
FFA. *See* Free fatty acids
FGFs. *See* Fibroblast growth factors
Fibrillin, 545, 549
Marfan syndrome caused by mutations in gene for, 549, 550f
Fibrils, collagen, 545–548, 547f, 547t
Fibrin
dissolution of by plasmin, 612–613, 612f
formation of, 606–608, 607f
thrombin in, 610, 611f
in thrombi, 606
Fibrin deposit, 606
Fibrin mesh, formation of, 606
Fibrin split products, in inflammation, 628t
Fibrin stabilizing factor (factor XIII), 608t
Fibrinogen, 610f
Fibrinogen (factor I), 588, 608, 608t
conversion of to fibrin, 610
Fibrinoligase (factor XIII), 608t

Fibrinolysis, 612–613
Fibrinopeptides A and B, 610, 611f
Fibroblast growth factor receptor 3, achon-droplasia caused by mutation in gene for, 561t, 563, 563f
Fibroblast growth factor receptors, chondro-dysplasias caused by muta-tion in gene for, 561t, 563, 563f
Fibroblast growth factors (FGFs), 563
Fibronectin, 545, 547, 549–550, 550f
Fibrous proteins, 30
collagen as, 38
Figlu. *See* Formiminoglutamate
Final common pathway of blood coagula-tion, 609f
Fingerprinting, DNA, 419
FISH. *See* Fluorescence in situ hybridization
Fish-eye disease, 239t
5′ cap, mRNA modification and, 363
Flanking-sequence DNA, 403
Flavin adenine dinucleotide (FAD), 94, 298t, 497
in citric acid cycle, 148
Flavin mononucleotide (FMN), 50, 94, 497
Flavoproteins
electron-transferring, 95
as oxidases, 94–95, 96f
in respiratory chain complexes, 96f, 100
Flip-flop, 427
Flip-flop, phospholipid, membrane asym-metry and, 427
Flippases, membrane asymmetry and, 427
Fluid mosaic model, 428–430, 428f
Fluid-phase pinocytosis, 437, 437f
Fluidity, membrane, 428–430
Fluorescence, of porphyrins, 282–283, 286f
Fluorescence in situ hybridization (FISH), 412
in gene mapping, 413t
Fluoride, 504t
in glycolysis, 152
1-Fluoro-2,4-dinitrobenzene (Sanger's reagent), for polypeptide sequencing, 25
Fluoroacetate, 145, 147f
5-Fluorouracil, 298, 299f, 305
Fluvastatin, 238
Flux-generating reaction, 138
FMN. *See* Flavin mononucleotide
Folate. *See* Folic acid
Folate trap, 500f, 501–502
Folding
polar and charged group positioning and, 6
protein, 22f, 36–37, 37f
after denaturation, 37
Folic acid (folate/pteroylglutamic acid), 490t, 500–502, 501f
coenzymes derived from, 50
deficiency of, 254, 490t, 502
functional, 500, 502
forms of in diet, 500–501, 501f

Folic acid—*continued*
　　inhibitors of metabolism of, 500–501
　　supplemental, 502
Folinic acid, 500
Follicle-stimulating hormone (FSH), 445, 446, 447f
Footprinting, DNA, 419
Forbes' disease, 166t
Forensic medicine
　　polymerase chain reaction (PCR) in, 411
　　restriction fragment length polymorphisms (RFLPs) in, 416
　　variable numbers of tandemly repeated units (VNTRs) in, 416
Formic acid, pK/pK_a value of, 12t
Formiminoglutamate, in histidine catabolism, 254, 256f
Formyl-tetrahydrofolate, 500, 501f
Fourier synthesis, 35
43S initiation complex, in protein synthesis, 372, 373f
43S preinitiation complex, in protein synthesis, 372, 373f
FPA/FPB. *See* Fibrinopeptides A and B
Fractions, 23f
Frameshift mutations, 370, 371f
　　ABO blood group and, 627
Framework regions, 601
Free amino acids, absorption of, 485
Free energy
　　changes in, 88
　　　　chemical reaction direction and, 61–62
　　　　coupling and, 89–90, 89f, 90f
　　　　enzymes affecting, 64
　　　　equilibrium state and, 61–62
　　　　redox potential and, 94, 95t
　　　　transition states and, 62
　　of hydrolysis of ATP, 90–91, 90t
Free fatty acids, 121, 187, 217, 218t
　　in fatty liver, 225
　　glucose metabolism affecting, 226–227
　　insulin affecting, 227
　　ketogenesis regulation and, 192–194, 194f
　　lipogenesis affected by, 200, 201f
　　metabolism of, 218–219
　　　　starvation and, 140–142, 142f, 142t
Free polyribosomes, protein synthesis on, 506, 514. *See also* Polyribosomes
Free radicals (reactive oxygen species). *See also* Antioxidants
　　hydroperoxidases in protection against, 96
　　in kwashiorkor, 487
　　lipid peroxidation producing, 128–129, 130f
　　in oxygen toxicity, 97–98, 620, 620t
　　xenobiotic cell injury and, 638, 638f
D-Fructofuranose, 114f
Fructokinase, 181, 183f
　　deficiency of, 185
D-Fructopyranose, 114f

Fructose
　　absorption of, 483, 483f
　　in diabetic cataract, 185–186
　　glycemic index of, 482
　　hepatic
　　　　hypertriacylglycerolemia/hypercholesterolemia/hyperuricemia and, 184
　　　　metabolism affected by, 181, 183f
　　iron absorption affected by, 486
　　metabolism of, 181, 183f
　　　　defects in, 185
　　pyranose and furanose forms of, 114f
D-Fructose, 115t, 116f
Fructose-1 deficiency, 185
Fructose-1,6-bisphosphatase, 180
Fructose-1,6-bisphosphate
　　in gluconeogenesis, 167, 168f
　　in glycolysis, 152, 153f
Fructose-2,6-bisphosphatase, 171, 171f
　　in covalent catalysis, 53, 54f
Fructose-2,6-bisphosphate, 171, 171f
Fructose 6-phosphate
　　free energy of hydrolysis of, 90t
　　in gluconeogenesis, 167, 168f
　　in glycolysis, 152, 153f
Fructose intolerance, hereditary, 185
Fructosuria, essential, 177, 185
FSF. *See* Fibrin stabilizing factor
FSH. *See* Follicle-stimulating hormone
Fucose, in glycoproteins, 526t
Fucosidosis, 541, 542t
Fucosylated oligosaccharides, selectins binding, 538
Fucosyltransferase/fucosyl (Fuc) transferase, 626
Fuels, metabolic. *See* Metabolic fuels
Fumarase (fumarate hydratase), 147f, 148
Fumarate, 147f, 148
　　in tyrosine catabolism, 261f, 262f
　　in urea synthesis, 250, 251
Fumarylacetoacetate, in tyrosine catabolism, 257, 261f
Fumarylacetoacetate hydrolase, defect at, in tyrosinemia, 257
Functional groups
　　amino acid chemical reactions affected by, 18–20
　　amino acid properties affected by, 18
　　physiologic significance of, 10–11
　　pK of, medium affecting, 12–13
Functional plasma enzymes, 57. *See also* Enzymes
Furanose ring structures, 113–114, 114f
Fusion proteins, recombinant, in enzyme study, 58–59, 59f
FXR. *See* Farnesoid X receptor

G-Actin, 567, 568f, 584
　　in nonmuscle cells, 584
G-CSF. *See* Granulocyte colony-stimulating factor

G protein-coupled receptors (GPCRs), 466, 468f
G proteins, 467, 469t
　　in calcium-dependent signal transduction, 472, 472f
　　in cAMP-dependent signal transduction, 444, 467, 469t
　　in Jak/STAT pathway, 475
　　in respiratory burst, 630
GAGs. *See* Glycosaminoglycans
Gal-Gal-Xyl-Ser trisaccharide, 528
Gal-hydroxylysine (Hyl) linkage, 528
Gal transferase, 626–627, 626f
Galactokinase, 181, 184f
　　inherited defects in, 186
Galactosamine, 183, 185f
D-Galactosamine (chondrosamine), 116
Galactose, 112, 181–183, 184f
　　absorption of, 483, 483f
　　glycemic index of, 482
　　in glycoproteins, 526t
　　metabolism of, 181–183, 184f
　　　　enzyme deficiencies and, 186
D-Galactose, 114f, 115t
Galactose 1-phosphate uridyl transferase, 181, 184f
Galactosemia, 112, 177, 186
Galactosidases, in glycoprotein analysis, 525
Galactoside, 114
Galactosylceramide, 126, 127f, 213, 215f
GalCer. *See* Galactosylceramide
Gallstones, 482
　　cholesterol, 230
GalNAc, in glycoproteins, 524, 526t
GalNAc-Ser(Thr) linkage
　　in glycoproteins, 528, 528f
　　in glycosaminoglycans, 553
GalNAc transferase, in ABO system, 626–627, 626f
Gamma-globulin, 589f
γ-Hydroxybutyrate
　　metabolism of, 274, 277f
Gangliosides, 126
　　amino sugars in, 116, 185f
　　sialic acids in, 119
　　synthesis of, 213, 215f
Gap junctions, 438
　　schematic diagram of, 439f
GAPs. *See* Guanine activating proteins
Gastric lipase, 483
Gastroenteropathy, protein-losing, 590
Gated ion channels, 431, 432–433
Gaucher's disease, 215t
GDH. *See* Glutamate dehydrogenase/L-glutamate dehydrogenase
GDP-Fuc, 526t
GDP-Man, 525, 526t
GEFs. *See* Guanine nucleotide exchange factors
Gel electrophoresis, polyacrylamide, for protein/peptide purification, 24, 25f, 26f

Gel filtration, for protein/peptide purification, 21–22, 24f
Gemfibrozil, 238–239
Gender, xenobiotic-metabolizing enzymes affected by, 637
Gene. See Genes; Genome
Gene amplification, in gene expression regulation, 397–399, 399f
Gene array chips, protein expression and, 28–29
Gene conversion, 333
Gene disruption/knockout, targeted, 417
Gene expression
    constitutive, 382, 384
    miRNA and siRNA inhibition of, 320
    in pyrimidine nucleotide synthesis, regulation of, 305–307
    regulation of, 380–400
        alternative splicing and, 362, 362f, 399
        eukaryotic transcription and, 387–393
        hormones in, 466f
        negative vs. positive, 380, 381t, 383–384, 386
        in prokaryotes vs. eukaryotes, 396–400, 398t
        regulatory protein DNA binding and trans-activation domains and, 396, 398f
        regulatory protein-DNA binding motifs and, 393–396, 394t, 395f, 396f, 397f
        retinoic acid in, 491
        temporal responses and, 380–381, 381f
Gene mapping, 327, 411–412, 413t
Gene products, diseases associated with deficiency of, 413t
Gene therapy, 416–417
    for urea biosynthesis defects, 252
Gene transcription. See Transcription
General acid/base catalysis, 51
Genes
    alteration of, 331–333, 332f, 333f
    amplification of, in gene expression regulation, 331–333, 332f, 333f
    disease causing, recombinant DNA technology in detection of, 413, 414f, 415t
    heterogeneous nuclear RNA processing in regulation of, 362
    housekeeping, 382
    immunoglobulin, DNA rearrangement and, 333, 399, 602–603
        double-strand break repair and, 346
    inducible, 382
    knockout, 417
    processed, 332–333
    reporter, 391, 393f, 394f
    targeted disruption of, 417
    variations in
        normal, recombinant DNA techniques for identification of, 413
        size/complexity and, 403, 405t

Genetic code, 311, 365–379, 366t
    features of, 366–367, 367t
Genetic diseases. See also specific diseases
    diagnosis of
        enzymes in, 58
        recombinant DNA technology in, 413–417, 414f, 415t, 416f, 417f
    gene therapy for, 416–417
Genetic linkage. See Linkage analysis
Genetics, 1
    molecular, 1
    xenobiotic-metabolizing enzymes affected by, 637
Genevan system, for fatty acid nomenclature, 121
Genome
    redundancy in, 328–330
    removal of gene from (targeted gene disruption/knockout), 417
Genomic library, 408, 419
Genomic resources, 85–87
Genomic technology, 402. See also Recombinant DNA/recombinant DNA technology
Genomics, protein sequencing and, 28
Genomics revolution, 84
Geometric isomerism, of unsaturated fatty acids, 122–124, 124f
Geranyl diphosphate, in cholesterol synthesis, 230, 232f
Geranylgeranyl, in vesicle coating, 519
Ghosts, red cell membrane analysis and, 622
Gibbs change in free energy, 88
Gibbs free energy/Gibbs energy. See Free energy
Gilbert syndrome, 291
GK (glucokinase) gene, regulation of, 362, 363f
GlcCer. See Glucosylceramide
GlcNAc. See N-Acetylglucosamine (GlcNAc)
Glial fibrillary acid protein, 585t
Glibenclamide. See Glyburide
Globin, 287
Globular proteins, 30
Globulins, 588
Glomerular filtration, basal lamina in, 551
Glomerular membrane, laminin in, 550–551
Glomerulonephritis, 551
Glomerulus, renal, laminin in, 550–551
Glucagon, 132, 162, 174
    in fasting state, 140
    in gluconeogenesis regulation, 169–170
    in lipogenesis regulation, 200, 201f
Glucagon/insulin ratio, in ketogenesis regulation, 193
Glucagon-like peptide, 445
Glucan (glucosan), 116
Glucan transferase, in glycogenolysis, 160, 160f, 162f

Glucocorticoid receptor-interacting protein (GRIP1 coactivator), 479, 480t
Glucocorticoid response element (GRE), 464, 466f, 467t
Glucocorticoids, 445. See also specific type
    in amino acid transport, 435
    blood glucose affected by, 174
    in lipolysis, 227, 228f
    receptors for, 478
    synthesis of, 447–448, 449f
    transport of, 462, 462t
D-Glucofuranose, 113f
Glucogenic amino acids, 139–140
Glucokinase, 170t
    in blood glucose regulation, 173, 173f
    in glycogen biosynthesis, 159, 160f, 170t
    in glycolysis, 152, 153f, 170t
Glucokinase gene, regulation of, 362, 363f
Gluconeogenesis, 132, 133, 134, 167–175, 168f
    blood glucose regulation and, 172–174, 172f, 173f
    citric acid cycle in, 148, 149f, 167–169, 168f
    energy cost of, in weight loss from very low carbohydrate diets, 175
    in glycolysis, 151–155, 153f, 154f, 167–169, 168f
        regulation of, 154–155
    regulation of, 169–172, 170t, 171f
        allosteric modification in, 170–171
        covalent modification in, 169–170
        enzyme induction/repression in, 169, 170t
        fructose 2,6-bisphosphate in, 171, 171f
        substrate (futile) cycles in, 171–172
        thermodynamic barriers to glycolysis and, 167–169, 168f
Gluconolactone hydrolase, 177, 179f
D-Glucopyranose, 113f
Glucosamine, 116f, 183, 185f
    in heparin, 553
Glucosan (glucan), 116
Glucose, 112–116
    absorption of, 482, 483, 483f
    as amino sugar precursor, 183, 185f
    epimers of, 114, 114f
    in extracellular and intracellular fluid, 423, 423t
    furanose forms of, 113–114, 113f
    galactose conversion to, 181–183, 184f
    glycemic index of, 482
    in glycogen biosynthesis, 159, 160f
    in glycoproteins, 526t
    insulin secretion and, 173–174, 175
    interconvertibility of, 138
    isomers of, 112–114, 113f
    as metabolic necessity, 140
    permeability coefficient of, 426f
    pyranose forms of, 113–114, 113f
    renal threshold for, 174–175

Glucose—*continued*
structure of, 112, 113f
transport of, 172, 173t, 436, 436f, 483, 483f
insulin affecting, 434–435
uptake of, 140
D-Glucose, 113f, 114f, 115t
L-Glucose, 113f
Glucose-alanine cycle, 173
Glucose, blood
normal, 159
regulation of
clinical aspects of, 174–175, 175f
diet/gluconeogenesis/glycogenolysis in, 172–174, 172f, 173f
glucagon in, 174
glucokinase in, 173, 173f
glycogen in, 159
insulin in, 173–174
limits of, 172
metabolic and hormonal mechanisms in, 173, 173t, 174
Glucose metabolism, 133–134, 133f, 135f, 151–155, 153f, 154f, 155f, 172, 172f. *See also* Gluconeogenesis; Glycolysis
ATP generated by, 156–157, 158t
in fed state, 140
free fatty acids and, 226–227
insulin affecting, 173–174, 175
by pentose phosphate pathway, 133, 177–180, 178f, 179f, 181f
starvation and, 140–142, 142f, 142t, 143
Glucose 1-phosphate
free energy of hydrolysis of, 90t
in gluconeogenesis, 167–169, 168f
Glucose-6-phosphatase
deficiency of, 166t, 308
in gluconeogenesis, 170t
in glycogenolysis, 161
Glucose 6-phosphate
free energy of hydrolysis of, 90t
in gluconeogenesis, 167, 168f
in glycogen biosynthesis, 159, 160f
in glycolysis, 152, 153f
Glucose-6-phosphate dehydrogenase
deficiency of, 177, 183–184, 621, 621f, 627, 637t
in pentose phosphate pathway, 177, 178f, 179f
Glucose synthesis, fatty acids and, 138–139
Glucose tolerance, 175, 175f
Glucose transporters, 173, 173t
in blood glucose regulation, 173, 174
insulin affecting, 434–435
red cell membrane, 619, 619t
Glucoside, 114
Glucosuria, 175
Glucosylceramide, 126, 213, 215f
D-Glucuronate, 114, 116f
Glucuronate/glucuronic acid, 180–181, 182f
bilirubin conjugation with, 289, 289f

Glucuronidation
of bilirubin, 289, 289f
of xenobiotics, 635–636
Glucuronides, 177
GLUT 1–4. *See* Glucose transporters
Glutamate
carboxylation of, vitamin K as cofactor for, 496, 496f
catabolism of, 254, 254f
in proline synthesis, 241, 243f
synthesis of, 241, 242f
transamination and, 247–248, 247f, 248f
in urea biosynthesis, 247–248, 247f, 248f
Glutamate aminotransferase, 247–248
Glutamate/aspartate transporter, 109–110, 109f
L-Glutamate decarboxylase, 274, 277f
Glutamate dehydrogenase/L-glutamate dehydrogenase, 241, 242f
in nitrogen metabolism, 248–249, 248f
Glutamic acid, 15t
Glutaminase, in amino acid nitrogen catabolism, 248f, 249
Glutamine, 15t
in amino acid nitrogen catabolism, 248f, 249
catabolism of, 254, 254f
synthesis of, 241, 242f
Glutamine analogs, purine nucleotide synthesis affected by, 301
Glutamine synthetase/synthase, 241, 242f, 248f, 249
Glutamyl amidotransferase, PRPP, regulation of, 302, 303f
Glutaric acid, pK/pK_a value of, 12t
Glutathione
as antioxidant, 620, 620t
in conjugation of xenobiotics, 636–637
as defense mechanism, 636
functions of, 636–637
Glutathione peroxidase, 96, 180, 181f, 184, 620, 620t
Glutathione reductase, erythrocyte
pentose phosphate pathway and, 180, 181f
riboflavin status and, 497
Glutathione S-transferases, 636
in enzyme study, 59, 59f
Glyburide (glibenclamide), 194
N-Glycan chains, 512
Glycan intermediates, formation of during N-glycosylation, 535
Glycans, virus and bacteria bound by, 542
Glycation, 523
Glycemic index, 116, 482
Glyceraldehyde (glycerose), D and L isomers of, 113f
Glyceraldehyde 3-phosphate
in glycolysis, 152, 153f
oxidation of, 152, 154f

Glyceraldehyde 3-phosphate dehydrogenase
in glycolysis, 152, 153f
in red cell membranes, 623f, 624t
Glycerol, 124
permeability coefficient of, 426f
synthesis of, 169
Glycerol-3-phosphate
acylglycerol biosynthesis and, 209, 210f
electron transfer via, 102
free energy of hydrolysis of, 90t
triacylglycerol esterification and, 226, 226f
Glycerol-3-phosphate acyltransferase, 210f, 211
Glycerol-3-phosphate dehydrogenase, 210f, 211
mitochondrial, 95
Glycerol ether phospholipids, synthesis of, 211, 212f
Glycerol kinase, 209, 210f, 226
Glycerol moiety, of triacylglycerols, 134
Glycerol phosphate pathway, 210f
Glycerophosphate shuttle, 109, 109f
Glycerophospholipids, 121
Glycerose (glyceraldehyde), D and L isomers of, 113f
Glycine, 15t, 270
catabolism of, pyruvate formation and, 255, 258f
in collagen, 545
in heme synthesis, 270, 279–282, 282f, 283f, 285f
synthesis of, 241, 243f
Glycine synthase complex, 255
Glycinuria, 255
Glycobiology, 523
Glycocalyx, 119
Glycochenodeoxycholic acid, synthesis of, 237f
Glycocholic acid, synthesis of, 237f
Glycoconjugate, 523
Glycoconjugate (complex) carbohydrates, glycoproteins as, 523
Glycoforms, 524
Glycogen, 112, 116, 118f
in carbohydrate metabolism, 133, 133f, 167–169
carbohydrate storage and, 159, 160t
metabolism of, 159–161. *See also* Glycogenesis; Glycogenolysis
branching in, 159, 161f
clinical aspects of, 165, 166t
regulation of
cyclic AMP in, 162–164, 162f, 163f, 164f
glycogen synthase and phosphorylase in, 164, 165f
in starvation, 143
muscle, 141, 159, 160t, 582, 582f
synthesis of, 140
Glycogen phosphorylase, 159–160, 160f, 582
pyridoxal phosphate as cofactor for, 498
regulation of, 162–164, 164f, 165f

Glycogen storage diseases, 112, 159, 165, 166t
Glycogen synthase, in glycogen metabolism, 159, 160f, 167, 170t
    regulation of, 162–164, 164, 164f, 165f
Glycogen synthase a, 162, 164f
Glycogen synthase b, 162, 164f
Glycogenesis, 133–134, 159, 160f
    regulation of
        cyclic AMP in, 162–164, 162f, 163f, 164f
        enzymes in, 170t
        glycogen synthase and phosphorylase in, 162–164, 164, 164f, 165f
Glycogenin, 159, 160f
Glycogenolysis, 134, 159–161, 160f
    blood glucose regulation and, 172–174, 172f, 173f
    cyclic AMP in regulation of, 162–164, 162f, 163f, 164f
    cyclic AMP-independent, 162
    debranching enzymes in, 160–161, 162f
    glycogen synthase and phosphorylase in regulation of, 162–164, 164, 164f, 165f
Glycolipid storage diseases, 209
Glycolipids (glycosphingolipids), 121, 126, 127f
    ABO blood group and, 626
    amino sugars in, 183, 185f
    galactose in synthesis of, 181–183, 184f
Glycolysis, 91, 133, 133f, 151–158, 152f
    aerobic, 154
    anaerobic, 151, 152, 152f
        as muscle ATP source, 582f, 583–584, 583t
    ATP generated by, 156–157, 158t
    clinical aspects of, 157–158
    in erythrocytes, 155, 155f
    glucose utilization/gluconeogenesis and, 151–155, 153f, 154f, 167–169, 168f. See also Gluconeogenesis
    pathway of, 151–155, 153f, 154f, 155f
    pyruvate oxidation and, 148–149, 150f, 155–157, 156f, 157f, 158t
    regulation of, 155
        enzymes in, 170t
        fructose 2,6-bisphosphate in, 171, 171f
        gluconeogenesis and, 154–155, 169–172, 170t, 171f
    at subcellular level, 136–138, 137f
    thermodynamic barriers to reversal of, 167–169
Glycolytic enzymes, in muscle, 565
Glycome, 523
Glycomics, 523, 542–543
Glycophorins, 119, 528, 623–624, 623f, 624t
Glycoprotein glycosyltransferases, 530
Glycoprotein IIb-IIIa, in platelet activation, 615, 629t

Glycoproteins, 30, 119, 119t, 447f, 523–543, 588, 589–590. See also specific type and Plasma proteins
    amino sugars in, 116, 183, 185f
    asialoglycoprotein receptor in clearance of, 526–527
    in biologic processes, glycomics of, 542–543
    as blood group substances, 523, 626
    carbohydrates in, 119t
    classes of, 527–528, 528f
    complex, 530–531, 530f
        formation of, 531, 533
    diseases associated with abnormalities of, 538–540, 539t, 540f, 540t, 541f, 542t
    extracellular, absorptive pinocytosis of, 438
    in fertilization, 537
    functions of, 523, 524t, 537–542, 538t
    galactose in synthesis of, 181–183, 184f
    glycosylphosphatidylinositol-anchored, 527, 528f, 536–537, 537t
    high-mannose, 530–531, 530f
        formation of, 531, 533
    hybrid, 530–531, 530f
        formation of, 531
    immunoglobulins as, 602
    membrane asymmetry and, 427
    N-linked, 528, 528f, 530–536
    nucleotide sugars, 525, 526t
    O-linked, 528–530, 528f, 529f, 529t, 530t
    oligosaccharide chains of, 523
    red cell membrane, 622, 623f
    sugars in, 524, 526t
    techniques for study of, 524, 525t
        asialoglycoprotein receptor in, 526–527
        glycosidases in, 525–526, 526t
        lectins in, 527, 527t
    in zona pellucida, 537
Glycosaminoglycans, 118, 119f, 552–556. See also specific type
    amino sugars in, 116
    deficiencies of enzymes in degradation of, 555–556, 557f
    disease associations of, 557–558
    distributions of, 553–555, 554f, 554t
    functions of, 556–558, 557t
    structural differences among, 553–555, 554t, 554t, 555f
    synthesis of, 551–553
Glycosidases, in glycoprotein analysis, 525–526
Glycosides, 114–116
Glycosphingolipids (glycolipids), 121, 126, 127f, 213–214, 215f
    ABO blood group and, 626
    amino sugars in, 183, 185f
    galactose in synthesis of, 181–183, 184f
    in membranes, 424
        membrane asymmetry and, 427

N-Glycosylases, in base excision-repair, 344, 345f
Glycosylated hemoglobin (HbA$_{1c}$), 48
Glycosylation, 523
    of collagen, 546
    congenital disorders of, 539, 540t, 594
    cotranslational, 512
    in covalent modification, mass increases and, 27t
    Golgi apparatus in, 518
    inhibitors of, 536, 536t
    nucleotide sugars in, 525, 526t
N-Glycosylation, 530–536, 531f, 532f, 534f, 535t
    dolichol-P-P-oligosaccharide in, 531–533, 532f
    in endoplasmic reticulum, 533–535, 534f
    glycan intermediates formed during, 535
    in Golgi apparatus, 533–535, 534f
    inhibition of, 536, 536t
    regulation of, 535–536, 536t
    tunicamycin affecting, 536, 536t
O-Glycosylation, 529–530, 530t
Glycosylphosphatidylinositol-anchored (GPI-anchored/GPI-linked) glycoproteins, 527, 528f, 536–537, 537t
    in paroxysmal nocturnal hemoglobinuria, 539–540, 540f
Glycosyltransferases, glycoprotein, 530, 536
Glypiation, 537
GM-CSF. See Granulocyte-macrophage colony-stimulating factor
GM$_1$ ganglioside, 126, 127f
GM$_3$ ganglioside, 126
GMP, 296t, 305f
    cyclic, 297f, 298
        as second messenger, 298, 444, 445t, 465, 470
    IMP conversion to, 301, 304f
        feedback-regulation of, 302, 304f
    PRPP glutamyl amidotransferase regulated by, 302
Golgi apparatus
    core protein synthesis in, 553
    glycosylation and, 518, 533–535, 534f
    lumen of, 512
    in membrane synthesis, 518
    in protein sorting, 506, 508f, 518
    proteins destined for membrane of, 518
    retrograde transport from, 514–515
    in VLDL formation, 224f
Gout/gouty arthritis, 307
GPCRs. See G protein-coupled receptors
GPI-anchored/linked glycoproteins, 527, 528f, 536–537, 537t
    in paroxysmal nocturnal hemoglobinuria, 540, 540f
GPIIb-IIIa, in platelet activation, 615, 629t
Granulocyte-colony stimulating factor, 618
Granulocyte-macrophage colony-stimulating factor, 618

Granulomatous disease, chronic, 630, 631f
Granulosa cells, hormones produced by, 450
Gratuitous inducers, 384
GRE. *See* Glucocorticoid response element
GRIP1 coactivator, 479, 480t
Group transfer potential, 91, 91f
  of nucleoside triphosphates, 297–298, 297f, 298f, 298t
Group transfer reactions, 8
Growth factors, hematopoietic, 618, 632. *See also* specific growth factors
Growth hormone, 445, 446
  amino acid transport affected by, 435
  localization of gene for, 413t
  receptor for, 444
GSH. *See* Glutathione
GSLs. *See* Glycosphingolipids
GST (glutathione S-transferase) tag, in enzyme study, 59, 59f
GTP, 297–298
  cyclic GMP formed from, 470
  in phosphorylation, 92–93
GTPases, 467
  small monomeric, 509
Guanine, 296t
Guanine activating proteins, 509, 510f
Guanine nucleotide exchange factors, 509, 510f
Guanosine, 295f, 296t
  base pairing of in DNA, 311, 312, 313f
  in uric acid formation, 307, 307f
Guanosine diphosphate fucose (GDP-Fuc), 526t
Guanosine diphosphate mannose (GDP-Man), 525, 526t
Guanosine monophosphate. *See* GMP
Guanylyl cyclase, 470
L-Gulonolactone oxidase, 181
Gyrase, bacterial, 314
Gyrate atrophy of retina, 254

H bands, 565, 566f, 567f
H blood group substance, 626, 626f
H chains. *See* Heavy chains
H substance, ABO blood group and, 626
H1 histones, 322, 323f
H2A histones, 322–323, 323
H2B histones, 322–323, 323
H$_2$S. *See* Hydrogen sulfide
H3 histones, 322–323
H4 histones, 322–323
Haber-Weiss reaction, 620
Hageman factor (factor XII), 607f, 608, 608t
Hairpin, 314, 317f, 419
Half-life
  enzyme, 246
  protein, 246
    plasma protein, 590
Halt-transfer signal, 512, 513

Haplotype, 85
Haplotype map (HapMap), 86
HapMap Project, 86
Hapten, in xenobiotic cell injury, 638, 638f
Haptoglobin, 591t, 592, 592f
Hartnup disease, 262, 498
HAT activity. *See* Histone acetyltransferase activity
Haworth projection, 112, 113f
HbA (hemoglobin A), P$_{50}$ of, 43
HbA$_{1c}$ (glycosylated hemoglobin), 48
HbF (fetal hemoglobin), P$_{50}$ of, 43
HbM (hemoglobin M), 46–47, 370, 622
HbS (hemoglobin S), 47, 47f, 369–370
hCG. *See* Human chorionic gonadotropin
HDL. *See* High-density lipoproteins
Health, 1
  normal biochemical processes as basis of, 2–4, 3t
Heart
  developmental defects of, 578
  metabolism in, 143t
  thiamin deficiency affecting, 496
Heart disease, coronary (ischemic). *See also* Atherosclerosis
  cholesterol and, 238
Heart failure, 565
  in thiamin deficiency, 496
Heat, from respiratory chain, 106–107
Heat-shock proteins, as chaperones, 37
Heavy chains
  immunoglobulin, 599–600, 600f
    genes producing, 602
  myosin, 568
    familial hypertrophic cardiomyopathy caused by mutations in gene for, 577–578, 578f
Heavy meromyosin, 569, 569f, 570f
Heinz bodies, 621
Helicases, DNA, 334, 335, 335f, 336t
Helicobacter pylori
  glycan binding of, 542, 542f
  ulcers associated with, 482
Helix
  double, of DNA structure, 7, 311–312, 313f
    recombinant DNA technology and, 402, 403
  triple, of collagen structure, 38–39, 39f, 545–548, 547f
Helix-loop-helix motifs, 32
Helix-turn-helix motif, 393, 394t, 395, 395f
Hemagglutinin, influenza virus, 542
  calnexin binding to, 535
Hematology, recombinant DNA technology affecting, 632
Hematopoietic growth factors, 618
Heme, 40, 42f, 279
  catabolism of, bilirubin produced by, 287, 288f
  in proteins, 279. *See also* Heme proteins

synthesis of, 279–282, 282f, 283f, 284f, 285f
  disorders of (porphyrias), 274, 278, 286f, 286t
Heme iron, 287, 593
  absorption of, 486, 593–594, 593f
  hindered environment for, 41–42, 42f
Heme oxygenase system, 287, 288f
Heme proteins (hemoproteins), 279, 280t. *See also* Hemoglobin; Myoglobin
  cytochrome P450 isoforms as, 634
Heme synthase (ferrochelatase), 280, 281f
  in porphyria, 286t
Hemiacetal, 112
Hemiconnexin, 438, 439f
Hemin, 287, 288f
Hemochromatosis, 485–486, 594–595, 595f
  types of, 595t
Hemoglobin, 40–48, 589f
  allosteric properties of, 43–46
  bilirubin synthesis and, 287, 288f
  in carbon dioxide transport, 44–45, 46f
  extracorpuscular, haptoglobin binding of, 591t, 592
  glycosylated (HbA$_{1c}$), 48
  mutant, 46–47, 368–369
  oxygen affinities (P$_{50}$) and, 43, 44f
  oxygen dissociation curve for, 42, 43f
  in oxygen transport, 40–41
  oxygenation of
    conformational changes and, 43–44, 44f, 45f
    2,3 bisphosphoglycerate stabilizing, 45–46, 46f
    apoprotein, 43
    high altitude adaptation and, 46
    mutant hemoglobins and, 46–47
  in proton transport, 44–45
  tetrameric structure of, 43
  changes in during development, 43, 44f
Hemoglobin A (HbA), P$_{50}$ of, 43
Hemoglobin A$_{1c}$ (glycosylated hemoglobin), 48
Hemoglobin Bristol, 369
Hemoglobin Chesapeake, 47
Hemoglobin F (fetal hemoglobin), P$_{50}$ of, 43
Hemoglobin Hikari, 369
Hemoglobin M, 46–47, 370, 622
Hemoglobin Milwaukee, 369
Hemoglobin S, 47, 47f, 369–370
Hemoglobin Sydney, 369
Hemoglobinopathies, 46–47, 627
Hemoglobinuria, paroxysmal nocturnal, 439t, 537, 539–540, 539t, 540f
Hemojuvelin, 593
Hemolytic anemias, 151, 157, 617, 627, 627t
  glucose-6-phosphate dehydrogenase deficiency causing, 177, 183–184, 621, 621f, 627

haptoglobin levels in, 592
hyperbilirubinemia/jaundice in, 291, 292t
pentose phosphate pathway/glutathione peroxidase and, 180, 181f, 183–184
primaquine-sensitive, 621
red cell membrane abnormalities causing, 627
Hemopexin, 591t
Hemophilia A, 612
Hemophilia B, 612
Hemoproteins. *See* Heme proteins
Hemosiderin, 594
Hemostasis, 606–616. *See also* Coagulation
laboratory tests in evaluation of, 616
pathways of, 607f
phases of, 606
HEMPAS. *See* Hereditary erythroblastic multinuclearity with a positive acidified lysis test
Henderson-Hasselbalch equation, 11
Heparan sulfate, 547, 554f, 554t, 555, 557
in basal lamina, 550
clotting/thrombosis affected by, 615, 615t
Heparin, 119, 119f, 553, 554f, 554t, 555f, 611
antithrombin III activity affected by, 557, 611
in basal lamina, 550
binding of, fibronectin in, 550f, 551
functions of, 557
lipoprotein and hepatic lipases affected by, 219
Heparin cofactor II, as thrombin inhibitor, 611
Hepatic ALA synthase (ALAS1), 281
in porphyria, 286t, 287
Hepatic lipase, 219
in chylomicron remnant uptake, 221, 221f
deficiency of, 239t
Hepatic portal system, 172
in metabolite circulation, 134, 135f
Hepatitis, 145
jaundice in, 292t
Hepatocytes
glycoprotein clearance from, asialoglycoprotein receptor in, 527
heme synthesis in, 281
ALA synthase in regulation of, 281–282, 285f
Hepatolenticular degeneration (Wilson disease), 439t, 596, 597
ceruloplasmin levels in, 596
gene mutations in, 439t, 597
Hepcidin, 594
Hephaestin, 593–594
Heptoses, 112, 113t
Hereditary elliptocytosis, 625
Hereditary erythroblastic multinuclearity with a positive acidified lysis test (HEMPAS), 539, 539t

Hereditary hemochromatosis, 594–595, 595f
Hereditary nonpolyposis colon cancer, mismatch repair genes in, 344
Hereditary spherocytosis, 439t, 625, 625f
Hermansky-Pudlak syndrome, 522t
Hers' disease, 166t
Heterochromatin, 324
Heterodimer, 34
Heterogeneous nuclear RNA (hnRNA), 318
processing of, gene regulation and, 362
Heterotrophic organisms, 90
Hexapeptide, in albumin synthesis, 591
Hexokinase, 170t
in blood glucose regulation, 173, 173f
in fructose metabolism, 181, 183f
in glycogen biosynthesis, 159, 170t
in glycolysis, 151–152, 153f, 170t
as flux-generating reaction, 138
regulation and, 154
Hexosamines (amino sugars), 116, 116f
glucose as precursor of, 183, 185f
in glycosaminoglycans, 118, 183, 185f
in glycosphingolipids, 183, 185f
interrelationships in metabolism of, 185f
Hexose monophosphate shunt. *See* Pentose phosphate pathway
Hexoses, 112, 113t
in glycoproteins, 119t
metabolism of, 177–180, 178f, 179f, 181f. *See also* Pentose phosphate pathway
clinical aspects of, 183–184
physiologic importance of, 114, 115t
HFE mutations, in hemochromatosis, 594–595
HGP. *See* Human Genome Project
HhaI, 405t
High altitude, adaptation to, 46
High-density lipoproteins, 217, 218t
apolipoproteins of, 217–229, 218t
atherosclerosis and, 221–222, 238
metabolism of, 221–222, 223f
ratio of to low-density lipoproteins, 238
receptor for, 221–222, 223f
High-density microarray technology, 417–418
High-energy phosphates, 91. *See also* ATP
in energy capture and transfer, 90–91, 90f, 90t, 91f
as "energy currency" of cell, 91–93, 92f, 93f, 106
symbol designating, 91
High-mannose oligosaccharides, 520–531, 530f
formation of, 531, 533
High-molecular-weight kininogen, 607f, 608
High-performance liquid chromatography, reversed phase, for protein/peptide purification, 24
"High-throughput" screening, 56

Hill coefficient, 68
Hill equation, 67–68, 68f
Hindered environment, for heme iron, 41–42, 42f
HindIII, 405t
Hinge region, 471
immunoglobulin, 599, 600f
Hippuric acid/hippurate, synthesis of, 270, 271f
Histamine, 628t
formation of, 271
Histidase, impaired, 254
Histidine, 16t, 271, 271f
catabolism of, 254, 256f
conserved residues and, 55t
decarboxylation of, 271
in oxygen binding, 40, 42f
requirements for, 488
Histidine E7, in oxygen binding, 40, 42f
Histidine F8
in oxygen binding, 40, 42f
replacement of in hemoglobin M, 46–47
Histidine 57, in covalent catalysis, 53, 54f
Histidinemia, 254
Histone acetyltransferase activity, of coactivators, 389, 479, 480
Histone chaperones, 323
Histone dimer, 323
Histone octamer, 323, 323f
Histone tetramer, 322–323, 323
Histones, 322–323, 323f, 323t
acetylation and deacetylation of, gene expression affected by, 389
HIV-I, glycoproteins in attachment of, 542
HIV protease, in acid-base catalysis, 52–53, 53f
HMG-CoA. *See* 3-Hydroxy-3-methylglutaryl-CoA (HMG-CoA)
HMM. *See* Heavy meromyosin
hMSH1/hMSH2, in colon cancer, 344
HNCC. *See* Hereditary nonpolyposis colon cancer
hnRNA. *See* Heterogeneous nuclear RNA
Holocarboxylase synthetase, biotin as coenzyme of, 502
Homeostasis
blood in maintenance of, 588
hormone signal transduction in regulation of, 464, 465f
Homocarnosine, 270, 271f
Homocarnosinosis, 270
Homocysteine
in cysteine and homoserine synthesis, 242, 244f
functional folate deficiency and, 500f, 502
Homocystinurias, 257
vitamin B_{12} deficiency/functional folate deficiency and, 500f, 502
Homodimers, 34
Homogentisate, in tyrosine catabolism, 259, 261f
Homogentisate dioxygenase/oxidase, 97
deficiency of, in alkaptonuria, 259

Homology
conserved residues and, 53–55, 55t
in protein classification, 30
Homology modeling, 36
Homopolymer tailing, 405
Homoserine, synthesis of, 242, 244f
Hormone-dependent cancer, vitamin B$_6$ deficiency and, 499
Hormone response elements, 355–356, 391, 394f, 464–465, 467t, 476–477, 478f
Hormone response transcription unit, 477f
Hormone-sensitive lipase, 226, 226f
insulin affecting, 227
Hormones. *See also* specific hormones
in blood glucose regulation, 173
classification of, 444–445, 445t
facilitated diffusion regulated by, 434–435
glycoproteins as, 523
lipid metabolism regulated by, 227–228, 228f
in metabolic control, 138, 139f
receptors for, 443–444, 444f, 478
proteins as, 444
recognition and coupling domains on, 443–444
specificity/selectivity of, 443, 444f
signal transduction and, 464–480
intracellular messengers and, 465–466, 469t, 471t
response to stimulus and, 464, 465f
signal generation and, 464–465, 466f, 467f, 467t
transcription modulation and, 476–480, 478f, 479f, 480t
stimulus recognition by, 464, 465f
storage/secretion of, 461, 461t
synthesis of
chemical diversity of, 445–446, 447f
cholesterol in, 446–448, 447f, 448f
peptide precursors and, 457
specialization of, 445
tyrosine in, 438, 446, 447f
target cells for, 442–443, 443t
transport of, 461t, 462–463, 462t
vitamin D as, 492–493
Housekeeping genes, 382
Hp. *See* Haptoglobin
HpaI, 405t
HPETE. *See* Hydroperoxides
HPLC. *See* High-performance liquid chromatography
HREs. *See* Hormone response elements
HRPT. *See* Hypoxanthine-guanine phosphoribosyl transferase
hsp60/hsp70, as chaperones, 37
5-HT (5-hydroxytryptamine). *See* Serotonin
Human chorionic gonadotropin (hCG), 446
Human Genome Project, 3–4
Human immunodeficiency virus (HIV-I), glycoproteins in attachment of, 542
Hunter syndrome, 556t

Hurler-Scheie syndrome, 556t
Hurler syndrome, 556t
Hyaluronic acid, 119, 119f, 553, 554f, 554t
disease associations and, 557–558
functions of, 557
Hyaluronidase, 555–556
Hybrid glycoproteins, 530–531, 530f
formation of, 531
Hybridization, 313, 403, 409–410, 419
in situ, in gene mapping, 411–412, 413t
Hybridomas, 604, 604f
Hydrocortisone. *See* Cortisol
Hydrogen bonds, 5, 6f
in DNA, 311, 312, 313f
Hydrogen ion concentration. *See also* pH
enzyme-catalyzed reaction rate affected by, 65, 65f
Hydrogen peroxide
glutathione in decomposition of, 636
as hydroperoxidase substrate, 96
production of in respiratory burst, 630
Hydrogen sulfide, on respiratory chain, 107, 107f
Hydrolases, 49
cholesteryl ester, 234
fumarylacetoacetate, defect at, in tyrosinemia, 257
gluconolactone, 177, 179f
lysosomal, deficiencies of, 541, 542t
Hydrolysis (hydrolytic reactions), 7–8. *See also* specific reaction
free energy of, 90–91, 90t
in glycogenolysis, 160, 160f, 162f
of triacylglycerols, 209
Hydropathy plot, 426
Hydroperoxidases, 94, 96
Hydroperoxides, formation of, 205, 207f
Hydrophilic compounds, hydroxylation producing, 634
Hydrophilic portion of lipid molecule, 129, 130f
Hydrophobic effect, in lipid bilayer self-assembly, 425
Hydrophobic interaction chromatography, for protein/peptide purification, 23
Hydrophobic interactions, 6–7
Hydrophobic portion of lipid molecule, 129, 130f
Hydrostatic pressure, 588
3-Hydroxy-3-methylglutaryl-CoA (HMG-CoA)
in ketogenesis, 190–191, 192f
in mevalonate synthesis, 230, 231f
3-Hydroxy-3-methylglutaryl-CoA (HMG-CoA) lyase
deficiency of, 194
in ketogenesis, 191, 192f
3-Hydroxy-3-methylglutaryl-CoA (HMG-CoA) reductase
cholesterol synthesis controlled by, 231, 234f
in mevalonate synthesis, 230, 231f

3-Hydroxy-3-methylglutaryl-CoA (HMG-CoA) synthase
in ketogenesis, 191, 192f
in mevalonate synthesis, 230, 231f
l(+)-3-Hydroxyacyl-CoA dehydrogenase, 188, 189f
3-Hydroxyanthranilate dioxygenase/oxygenase, 97
Hydroxyapatite, 558
d-3-Hydroxybutyrate dehydrogenase, 190, 191f
24-Hydroxycalcidiol (24,25-dihydroxyvitamin D$_3$), in vitamin D metabolism, 493, 493f
25-Hydroxycholecalciferol (calcidiol), in vitamin D metabolism, 492, 493f
4-Hydroxydicoumarin (dicumarol), 495
18-Hydroxylase, in steroid synthesis, 446–448, 449f
21-Hydroxylase, in steroid synthesis, 448, 449f
27-Hydroxylase, sterol, 235
Hydroxylase cycle, 97, 98f
Hydroxylases, 97
in steroid synthesis, 446–447, 446–448, 449f
Hydroxylation
in collagen processing, 546
in covalent modification, mass increases and, 27t
of xenobiotics, 633–635, 636t
Hydroxylysine, synthesis of, 242–243
5-Hydroxymethylcytosine, 295, 297f
17-Hydroxypregnenolone, 448, 449f
17-Hydroxyprogesterone, 449f
17α-Hydroxyprogesterone, 448
Hydroxyproline
catabolism of, 257, 260f
synthesis of, 242–243, 244f, 545–546
tropoelastin hydroxylation and, 549
4-Hydroxyproline dehydrogenase, defect in, in hyperhydroxyprolinemia, 257
15-Hydroxyprostaglandin dehydrogenase, 205
5-Hydroxytryptamine. *See* Serotonin
Hyper-β-alaninemia, 270
Hyperalphalipoproteinemia, familial, 239t
Hyperammonemia type 2, 250f, 252
Hyperargininemia, 252
Hyperbilirubinemia, 290–292, 292t
Hypercholesterolemia, 217
familial, 1, 239t, 439t
LDL receptor deficiency in, 221, 439t
from fructose loading of liver, 184
Hyperchromicity of denaturation, 313
Hyperglycemia. *See also* Diabetes mellitus
in diabetes mellitus, 143
glucagon causing, 174
insulin release in response to, 474f
Hyperhomocysteinemia, folic acid supplements in prevention of, 502

Hyperhydroxyprolinemia, 257
Hyperkalemic periodic paralysis, 577t
Hyperlacticacidemia, 225
Hyperlipidemia, niacin for, 498
Hyperlipoproteinemias, 217, 239–240, 239t
  familial, 239t
Hyperlysinemia, periodic, 262
Hypermetabolism, 151, 487
Hyperornithinemia, hyperammonemia, and homocitrullinuria syndrome (HHH syndrome), 252
Hyperornithinemia-hyperammonemia syndrome, 254
Hyperoxaluria, primary, 255
Hyperparathyroidism, bone and cartilage affected in, 561t
Hyperphenylalaninemias, 259
Hyperprolinemias, types I and II, 254
Hypersensitive sites, chromatin, 324
Hypersplenism, in hemolytic anemia, 627
Hypertension, hyperhomocysteinemia and, folic acid supplements in prevention of, 502
Hyperthermia, malignant, 565, 573–574, 574f, 577t
Hypertriacylglycerolemia
  in diabetes mellitus, 217
  familial, 239t
  from fructose loading of liver, 184
Hypertrophic cardiomyopathy, familial, 577–578, 578f
Hyperuricemia, 307–308
  from fructose loading of liver, 184
Hypervariable regions, 601, 602f
Hypoglycemia, 167
  fatty acid oxidation and, 187, 194
  fructose-induced, 185
  insulin excess causing, 175
  during pregnancy and in neonate, 175
Hypoglycemic effect
  of glucagon, 174
Hypoglycin, 187, 194
Hypokalemic periodic paralysis, 577t
Hypolipidemic drugs, 238–239
Hypolipoproteinemia, 217, 239–240, 239t
Hypouricemia, 308
Hypoxanthine, 297
Hypoxanthine-guanine phosphoribosyl transferase (HRPT)
  defect of in Lesch-Nyhan syndrome, 308
  localization of gene for, 413t
Hypoxia, lactate production and, 151, 152f, 154

I. See Iodine/iodide
I bands, 565, 566f, 567f
I-cell disease, 439, 439t, 522t, 533, 539t, 540–541, 541f, 555, 556t
  causation of, 541f
Ibuprofen, cyclooxygenases affected by, 204
ICAM-1, 538, 538t

ICAM-2, 538, 538t
ICF. See Intracellular fluid
Icterus (jaundice), 279, 290–292, 292t
IDDM. See Insulin-dependent diabetes mellitus
Idiotypes, 603
IDL. See Intermediate-density lipoproteins
IEF. See Isoelectric focusing
IgA, 601, 602t, 603f
IgD, 601, 602t
IgE, 601, 602t
IGF-I receptor, 444
IgG, 600f, 601, 602t
  deficiency of, 604
  hypervariable regions of, 601, 602f
IgM, 601, 602t, 603f
Immune response, class/isotype switching and, 603
Immunity, innate, 540
Immunoglobulin genes, 602
  DNA rearrangement and, 333, 399, 602–603
    double-strand break repair and, 346
Immunoglobulin heavy chain binding protein, 516
Immunoglobulin heavy chains, 599–600, 600f
  genes producing, 602
Immunoglobulin light chains, 599–600, 600f
  in amyloidosis, 599
  genes producing, 602
    DNA rearrangement and, 333, 399, 602–603
Immunoglobulins, 588, 591t, 599–605, 601t. See also specific type under Ig
  class switching and, 603
  classes of, 600–601, 601t, 602t
  diseases caused by over- and underproduction of, 604
  functions of, 601–602, 602t
  genes for. See Immunoglobulin genes
  hybridomas as sources of, 604, 604f
  structure of, 599–600, 600f, 602f, 603f
Immunology, 1
IMP (inosine monophosphate)
  conversion of to AMP and GMP, 301, 304f
    feedback regulation of, 302, 304f
  synthesis of, 301–302, 303f, 304f, 305f
Importins, 509, 510f
In situ hybridization, 412
In situ hybridization/fluorescence in situ hybridization, 412
  in gene mapping, 413t
Inactive chromatin, 324–326, 389
Inborn errors of metabolism, 1, 254, 555
Inclusion cell (I-cell) disease, 439, 439t, 522t, 533, 539t, 540–541, 541f
Indole, permeability coefficient of, 426f
Indomethacin, cyclooxygenases affected by, 204

Induced fit model, 52, 52f
Inducers
  enzyme synthesis affected by, 75
    in gluconeogenesis regulation, 169
  gratuitous, 384
  in regulation of gene expression, 382
Inducible gene, 382
Infantile Refsum disease, 194, 511, 511t
Infection
  neutrophils in, 627–628, 628t
  protein loss and, 487–488
  respiratory burst in, 630
Inflammation, 196, 617
  acute phase proteins in, 590–591, 591t
  complement in, 605
  neutrophils in, 627–628, 628t
    integrins and, 538t, 628–629, 629t
    selectins and, 537–538, 538t, 539f
  prostaglandins in, 196
  selectins in, 537–538, 538f, 538t, 539f
Influenza virus
  hemagglutinin in, calnexin binding to, 535
  neuraminidase in, 542
Information pathway, 465, 467f
Inhibition
  competitive vs. noncompetitive, 68–70, 68f, 69f, 70f
  feedback, in allosteric regulation, 75–77, 76f
  irreversible, 70
Inhibitor-1, 162, 163f, 164, 165f
Initial velocity, 65
  inhibitors affecting, 69, 69f, 70f
Initiation
  in DNA synthesis, 336, 337f, 338f, 339f
  in protein synthesis, 371–372, 373f
  in RNA synthesis, 349, 349f, 351–352
Initiation complexes, in protein synthesis, 372–374, 373f
Initiator sequence, 353–355, 354f
Innate immunity, 540
Inner mitochondrial membrane, 100
  protein insertion in, 509
  relative impermeability of, exchange transporters and, 107–110, 108f–110f
Inorganic pyrophosphatase, in fatty acid activation, 92
Inosine monophosphate (IMP)
  conversion of to AMP and GMP, 301, 304f
    feedback-regulation of, 302, 304f
  synthesis of, 301–302, 303f, 304f, 305f
Inositol hexaphosphate (phytic acid), calcium absorption affected by, 485
Inositol trisphosphate, 125, 471–472, 472f, 473f
  in platelet activation, 614, 614f
  in respiratory burst, 630
Inotropic effects, 575–576

Inr. *See* Initiator sequence
Insert/insertions, DNA, 419
  recombinant DNA technology in detection of, 413–414
Inside-outside asymmetry, membrane, 427
Insulators, 393
  nonpolar lipids as, 121
Insulin, 132, 446, 457, 458f
  adipose tissue metabolism affected by, 227–228
  in blood glucose regulation, 174
  deficiency of, 175. *See also* Diabetes mellitus
  free fatty acids affected by, 227
  gene for, localization of, 413t
  glucagon opposing actions of, 174
  in glucose transport, 434–435
  in glycolysis, 152, 169
  initiation of protein synthesis affected by, 374, 374f
  in lipogenesis regulation, 200, 201–202
  in lipolysis regulation, 202, 227, 228f
  on metabolic fuel reserves, 140
  phosphorylase b affected by, 162
  receptor for, 444, 473, 474f
  signal transmission by, 473, 474f
  storage/secretion of, 461, 461t
  synthesis of, 457, 458f
Insulin-dependent diabetes mellitus (IDDM/type 1), 175. *See also* Diabetes mellitus
Insulin/glucagon ratio, in ketogenesis regulation, 193
Insulin-like growth factor 1 receptor, 444
Insulin resistance, 619
Integral proteins, 30, 427, 428f
  as receptors, 438
  red cell membrane, 623–624, 623f, 624t
Integration, chromosomal, 331–332, 332f
Integrins, neutrophil interactions and, 538t, 628–629, 629f
Intermediate-density lipoproteins, 218t
Intermediate filaments, 585–586, 585t
Intermembrane space, proteins in, 509
Intermittent branched-chain ketonuria, 266
Internal presequences, 509
Internal ribosomal entry site, 376, 378f
Interphase chromosomes, chromatin fibers in, 324
Intervening sequences. *See* Introns
Intestinal bacteria, in bilirubin conjugation, 290
Intracellular environment, membranes in maintenance of, 422–423, 423t
Intracellular fluid (ICF), 422, 423, 423t
Intracellular membranes, 422
Intracellular messengers, 465–476, 469t, 471t. *See also* specific type and Second messengers
Intracellular signals, 465–475

Intracellular traffic, 506–522. *See also* Protein sorting
  disorders due to mutations in genes encoding, 521–522, 522t
  transport vesicles in, 518
Intrinsic factor, 485, 499
  in pernicious anemia, 500
Intrinsic pathway of blood coagulation, 606–609, 607f
Introns (intervening sequences), 327, 359–362, 361f, 365, 419
  in recombinant DNA technology, 403, 404f
  removal of from primary transcript, 359–362, 361f
Inulin, 116
Inulin, glomerular membrane permeability to, 551
"Invert sugar," 116
Iodine/iodide, 504t
  deficiency of, 455
  in thyroid hormone synthesis, 455–457, 456f
5-Iodo-2′-deoxyuridine, 299f
Iodopsin, 491
Iodothyronyl residues, 455. *See also* Thyroxine; Triiodothyronine
5-Iodouracil, 298
Ion channels, 422, 431, 432f, 432t, 577t
  in cardiac muscle, 576, 577, 577t
  diseases associated with disorders of, 577, 577t
Ion exchange, 22
Ion exchange chromatography, for protein/peptide purification, 22–23
Ion product, 8–9
Ionizing radiation, nucleotide excision-repair of DNA damage caused by, 345
Ionophores, 108, 433
IP₃. *See* Inositol trisphosphate
IPTG. *See* Isopropylthiogalactoside
IRES. *See* Internal ribosomal entry site
Iron, 504t
  absorption of, 485–486, 592–594, 593f, 593t
    in hemochromatosis, 485–486
    vitamin C and ethanol affecting, 486, 504
  deficiency of, 504
  distribution of, 593t
  ferrous, in oxygen transport, 40–41
  heme, 287, 592–593
    absorption of, 486, 593–594, 593f
    hindered environment for, 41–42, 42f
    in methemoglobinemia, 46
  incorporation of into protoporphyrin, 280–281, 281f
  metabolism of, 593, 593f
    disorders of, 594–595
  nonheme, 593
  transferrin in transport of, 592, 593f, 593t
Iron-binding capacity, total, 594

Iron deficiency/iron deficiency anemia, 485, 504, 594
Iron overload, 485–486
Iron porphyrins, 279
Iron response elements, 594
Iron-responsive element-binding protein, 594
Iron-sulfur proteins, in respiratory chain complexes, 100–101, 102f
Irreversible covalent modifications, 77, 79f
Irreversible inhibition, enzyme, 70
IRS 1-4, in insulin signal transmission, 473, 474f
Ischemia, 151, 439
Islets of Langerhans, insulin produced by, 173
Isocitrate dehydrogenase, 145–146, 147f
  in NADPH production, 199, 199f
Isoelectric focusing, for protein/peptide purification, 25, 26f
Isoelectric pH (pI), amino acid net charge and, 17–18
Isoenzymes. *See* Isozymes
Isoleucine, 15t
  catabolism of, 265, 267f, 268f
  interconversion of, 243
  requirements for, 488
Isomaltose, 117t
Isomerases, 49
  in steroid synthesis, 446, 449f, 450, 451f
Isomerism
  geometric, of unsaturated fatty acids, 122–124, 124f
  of steroids, 127, 128f
  of sugars, 112–114, 113f, 114f
Isomorphous displacement, 35
Isoniazid, acetylation of, 637
Isopentenyl diphosphate, in cholesterol synthesis, 230, 232f
Isoprene units, polyprenoids synthesized from, 128, 129f
Isoprenoids, synthesis of, 230, 233f
  in cholesterol synthesis, 232f
Isopropylthiogalactoside, 384
Isoprostanes (prostanoids), 122, 129
  cyclooxygenase pathway in synthesis of, 204–205, 205f, 206f
Isosteric enzymes, 76
Isothermic systems, biologic systems as, 88
Isotopes. *See also* specific types
  in plasma protein analysis, 589
Isotype (class) switching, 603
Isotypes, 603
Isovaleric acidemia, 266
Isovaleryl-CoA dehydrogenase, in isovaleric acidemia, 266
Isozymes, 55

J chain, 603f
Jackson-Weiss syndrome, 561t
JAK kinases, 444, 473–475, 475f
Jak-STAT pathway, 444, 473–475, 475f

Jamaican vomiting sickness, 194
Jaundice (icterus), 279, 290–292, 292t
Joining region, gene for, 602
    DNA rearrangement and, 399, 602–603
"Jumping DNA," 332
Junctional diversity, 602–603
Juxtaglomerular cells, in renin-angiotensin
        system, 458

K. See Dissociation constant; Potassium
k. See Rate constant
K^+ channel, 432–433
Kappa light chains, 600
Kartagener syndrome, 585
Karyotype, 328f
Kayser-Fleischer ring, 597
K_d. *See* Dissociation constant
KDEL-containing proteins, 514, 515t
K_{eq}. *See* Equilibrium constant
Keratan sulfates, 553, 554t
    functions of, 557
Keratins, 585t, 586
Kernicterus, 291
Ketoacidosis, 187, 194–195
    in diabetes mellitus, 144
3-Ketoacyl-CoA thiolase deficiency, 194
3-Ketoacyl synthase, 197, 198f
Ketogenesis, 136, 136f, 187–195. *See also*
    Fatty acids, oxidation of
    high rates of fatty acid oxidation and,
        190–192, 191f
    HMG-CoA in, 190–191, 192f
    regulation of, 192–194, 194f
Ketogenic amino acids, 140
α-Ketoglutarate, in amino acid carbon skel-
        eton catabolism, 254f
Ketoglutarate transporter, 109–110, 109f
Ketone bodies, 134, 136, 136f, 187, 190,
    191f
    in fasting state, 142
    free fatty acids as precursors of, 192
    as fuel for extrahepatic tissues, 191–192,
        193f
    in starvation, 140–142, 142f, 142t
Ketonemia, 193, 194
Ketonuria, 194
    branched chain (maple syrup urine dis-
        ease), 265
Ketoses (sugars), 112, 113t
Ketosis, 187, 192, 194
    in cattle
        fatty liver and, 225
        lactation and, 194
    in diabetes mellitus, 144, 194
    ketoacidosis caused by, 194–195
    in lactation, 143
    nonpathologic, 194
    in starvation, 194
Kidney
    in fasting state, 143
    glycogenolysis in, 161
    metabolism in, 143t

    in renin-angiotensin system, 458
    vitamin D metabolism in, 492
    vitamin D_3 synthesis in, 453, 454f
Kinases, protein. *See* Protein kinases
Kinesin, 585
Kinetic (collision) theory, 63
Kinetics (enzyme), 61–72. *See also* Cataly-
        sis/catalytic reactions (enzy-
        matic)
    activation energy affecting, 62, 64
    balanced equations and, 61
    competitive *vs.* noncompetitive inhibi-
        tion and, 68–70, 68f, 69f,
        70f
    in drug development, 71–72
    factors affecting reaction rate and,
        63–65, 63f, 65f
    free energy changes affecting, 61–62
    initial velocity and, 65
    multisubstrate enzymes and, 70–71, 70f,
        71f
    saturation, 65f, 67
        sigmoid (Hill equation), 67–68, 68f
    substrate concentration and, 65–66, 65f,
        66f
        models of effects of, 66–68, 67f, 68f
    transition states and, 62
Kinetochore, 326
Kininogen, high-molecular-weight, 607f,
    608
Kinky hair disease (Menkes disease),
    596–597
K_m. *See* Michaelis constant
Knockout genes, 417
Korsakoff's psychosis, 496
Kozak consensus sequences, 372
Krabbe's disease, 215t
Krebs cycle. *See* Citric acid cycle
Ku, in double-strand break repair, 346,
    346f
K_w. *See* Ion product
Kwashiorkor, 241, 486–487
Kynureninase, 262, 264f
Kynurenine-anthranilate pathway, for tryp-
        tophan catabolism, 262,
        264f
Kynurenine formylase, 262, 264f

L-amino acids
    in proteins, 14–16
L chains. *See* Light chains
L-Dopa, 454, 455f
L-Iduronate, 114, 116f
L isomerism, 112–113, 113f
L-tryptophan dioxygenase (tryptophan pyr-
        rolase), 97
l-type calcium channel, 576
Labile factor (factor V), 608t, 609, 609f
lac operon, 381, 382–384, 382f, 383f
lac repressor, 382, 383f
lacA gene, 382, 382f, 383, 383f
lacI gene, 382, 383–384, 383f

Lactase, 483
    deficiency of (lactose/milk intolerance),
        112, 482, 483
Lactate
    anaerobic glycolysis and, 151, 152f, 154
    hypoxia and, 152f, 154
Lactate dehydrogenase, in anaerobic glycol-
        ysis, 152
Lactate dehydrogenase isozymes, 57, 152
    diagnostic significance of, 57, 57t, 58f
Lactation, ketosis in, 143
Lactic acid, p*K*/pK_a value of, 12t
Lactic acid cycle, 172, 172f
Lactic acidosis, 151
    from inherited mitochondrial defects,
        100
    pyruvate metabolism and, 157–158
    thiamin deficiency and, 497
Lactoferrin, 628t
Lactogenic hormone. *See* Prolactin
Lactose, 116, 117f, 117t, 181
    galactose in synthesis of, 181–183,
        184f
    metabolism of, operon hypothesis and,
        382–384, 382f, 383f
Lactose (milk) intolerance, 112, 482, 483
Lactose synthase, 183, 184f
Lactulose, 117t
lacY gene, 382, 382f, 383, 383f
lacZ gene, 382, 382f, 383, 383f
Lagging (retrograde) strand, in DNA repli-
        cation, 335, 335f, 338
Lambda light chains, 600
Lambda repressor (cI) protein/gene,
        384–387, 386f, 387f, 388f
Laminin, 545, 550–551, 551f
Lamins, 585t, 586
Langerhans, islets of, insulin produced by,
    173
Lanosterol, in cholesterol synthesis,
    230–231, 233f
Latch state, 580
Laue x-ray crystallography, 35–36
Lauric acid, 122t
Laws of thermodynamics, 88–89
    hydrophobic interactions and, 7
LBD. *See* Ligand-binding domain
LCAT. *See* Lecithin:cholesterol acyltransferase
LCRs. *See* Locus control regions
LDH. *See* Lactate dehydrogenase isozymes
LDL. *See* Low-density lipoproteins
LDL:HDL cholesterol ratio, 238
Lead poisoning, ALA dehydratase inhibi-
        tion and, 279, 287
Leader sequence. *See* Signal peptide
Leading (forward) strand, in DNA replica-
        tion, 335, 335f, 338
Lecithin. *See also* Phosphatidylcholine
    metabolism of, 213f
Lecithin:cholesterol acyltransferase (LCAT),
        212–213, 221, 223f, 234,
        235
    familial deficiency of, 239t

Lecithins (phosphatidylcholines), 124–125, 125f
  membrane asymmetry and, 427
  synthesis of, 209, 210f
Lectins, 119, 527, 527t
  in glycoprotein analysis, 525t, 527, 527t
Leiden factor V, 611
Lens of eye, fructose and sorbitol in, diabetic cataract and, 185–186
Leptin, 227
Lesch-Nyhan syndrome, 308
Leucine, 15t
  catabolism of, 265, 267f, 268f
  interconversion of, 243
  requirements for, 488
Leucine aminomutase, 500
Leucine zipper motif, 393, 394t, 396, 397f
Leucovorin, 500
Leukemias, 617, 632
Leukocyte adhesion deficiency
    type I, 629
    type II, 539, 539t
Leukocytes, 628–631
  growth factors regulating production of, 618
  recombinant DNA technology in study of, 632
Leukodystrophy, metachromatic, 215t
Leukotriene A$_4$, 124f
Leukotrienes, 122, 124f, 196, 204
  clinical significance of, 208
  lipoxygenase pathway in formation of, 204, 205, 205f, 207f
LFA-1, 538, 538t, 629, 629t
LH. See Luteinizing hormone
Library, 408–409, 419
Lifestyle changes, cholesterol levels affected by, 238
Ligand-binding domain, 477
Ligand-gated channels, 431, 577t
Ligand-receptor complex, in signal generation, 464–465
Ligases, 49
  DNA, 336t, 338, 340, 340f
Ligation, 420
  in RNA processing, 359
Light, in active transport, 435
Light chains
  immunoglobulin, 600, 600f
    in amyloidosis, 599
    genes producing, 602
      DNA rearrangement and, 333, 399, 602–603
  myosin, 568
    in smooth muscle contraction, 578
Light meromyosin, 569, 569f
Limit dextrinosis, 166t
LINEs. See Long interspersed repeat sequences
Lines, definition of, 420
Lineweaver-Burk plot
  inhibitor evaluation and, 69, 69f, 70f
  K_m and V_{max} estimated from, 67, 67f
Lingual lipase, 483

Link trisaccharide, in glycosaminoglycan synthesis, 553
Linkage analysis, in glycoprotein study, 525t
N-linked glycoproteins synthesis, dolichol-P-P-oligosaccharide in, 531–533, 532f
Linoleic acid/linoleate, 123t, 202, 202f, 204
  in essential fatty acid deficiency, 203
  synthesis of, 203f
α-Linolenic acid, for essential fatty acid deficiency, 203
Lipases
  diagnostic significance of, 57t
  in digestion, 483, 484f
  in triacylglycerol metabolism, 209, 226, 226f, 483, 484f
Lipid bilayer, 425, 425f, 426f
  membrane proteins and, 426
Lipid core, of lipoprotein, 217
Lipid rafts, 429
Lipid storage disorders (lipidoses), 214–215, 215t
Lipids, 121–131. See also specific type
  amphipathic, 129, 130f
  asymmetry of, membrane assembly and, 520–521, 521f
  classification of, 121
  complex, 121
  in cytochrome P450 system, 634–635
  derived, 121
  digestion and absorption of, 483, 484f
  disorders associated with abnormalities of, 439
  fatty acids, 121–124
  glycolipids, 121, 126, 127f
  interconvertibility of, 138–139
  in membranes, 423–424
    ratio of to protein, 423, 423f
  metabolism of, 133f, 134, 134f, 136, 136f. See also Lipolysis
    in fed state, 140
    in liver, 222–225, 224f
  neutral, 121
  peroxidation of, 128–129, 130f
  phospholipids, 121, 124–126, 125f
  precursor, 121
  simple, 121
  steroids, 126–128, 127f, 128f, 129f
  transport and storage of, 217–229
    adipose tissue and, 226–227, 226f
    brown adipose tissue and, 228, 229f
    clinical aspects of, 225–226
    fatty acid deficiency and, 206
    as lipoproteins, 217–218, 218t, 219f
    liver in, 222–225, 224f
  triacylglycerols (triglycerides), 124, 124f, 125f
  turnover of, membranes and, 521
Lipogenesis, 134, 136, 138, 196–202, 197f, 198f
  acetyl-CoA for, 199
  fatty acid synthase complex in, 196–199, 197f, 198f

  malonyl-CoA production in, 196, 197f
  NADPH for, 198f, 199, 199f
  regulation of, 199–202, 201f
    enzymes in, 170t, 196–199, 197f, 200–202, 201f
    nutritional state in, 199
    short- and long-term mechanisms in, 200–202
Lipolysis, 136, 136f, 227, 228f. See also Lipids
  hormone-sensitive lipase in, 226, 226f
  hormones affecting, 227, 228f
  insulin affecting, 202
  triacylglycerol, 209
Lipophilic compounds, cytochrome P450 isoforms in hydroxylation of, 634
Lipoprotein lipase, 136, 136f, 219–220, 221f, 222f
  familial deficiency of, 239t
  involvement in remnant uptake, 220, 221f
Lipoprotein(a) excess, familial, 239t
Lipoproteins, 30, 121, 136, 217–229, 218t, 219f, 588, 591t. See also specific type
  carbohydrates in, 119–120
  in cholesterol transport, 234–235, 236f
  classification of, 217, 218t
  deficiency of, fatty liver and, 225
  disorders of, 239–240, 239t
  remnant, 218t, 220, 221f
  liver uptake of, 220–221
Liposomes, 427
  amphipathic lipids forming, 129, 130f
  artificial membranes and, 427–428
Lipotropic factor, 225
Lipoxins, 122, 124f, 196, 204
  clinical significance of, 208
  lipoxygenase pathway in formation of, 204, 205, 205f, 207f
Lipoxygenase, 129, 205, 207f
  reactive species produced by, 129
5-Lipoxygenase, 205, 207f
Lipoxygenase pathway, 204, 205, 205f, 207f
Liquid chromatography, 21, 23f
  high-performance reversed-phase, for peptide separation, 24
Lithium, 504t
Lithocholic acid, synthesis of, 237f
Liver
  angiotensinogen made in, 458
  bilirubin uptake by, 287–290, 289f, 290f
  cirrhosis of, 145, 225
  cytochrome P450 isoforms in, 634
  in fasting state, 140, 143
  fatty
    alcoholism and, 225–226
    of pregnancy, 194
    triacylglycerol metabolism imbalance and, 225
  fructose overload and, 184
  glucose uptake into, 140

glycogen in, 159, 160t
glycogenolysis in, 161
heme synthesis in, 281
    ALA synthase in regulation of, 281–282, 285f
ketone bodies produced by, 190, 191f, 192
metabolism in, 134, 135f, 136f, 143t, 145
    fatty acid oxidation, ketogenesis and, 190–192, 191f
    fructose, 181, 183f
    glucose, 168f, 172–173, 172f
        fructose 2,6-bisphosphate in regulation of, 171, 171f
    glycogen, 159–161, 160f, 162
    lipid, 222–225, 224f
phosphorylase in, control of, 161
plasma protein synthesis in, 134, 589
vitamin D metabolism in, 492
vitamin D_3 synthesis in, 453, 454f, 493f
Liver phosphorylase deficiency, 166t
LMM. *See* Light meromyosin
Lock and key model, 52
Locus control regions, 393
Long interspersed repeat sequences (LINEs), 329
Looped domains, chromatin, 324, 326, 327f
Loops (protein conformation), 32–33
Loose connective tissue, keratan sulfate I in, 553
Low-density lipoprotein receptor-related protein, 218
    in chylomicron remnant uptake, 221f
Low-density lipoprotein receptor-related protein (LRP)
    in chylomicron remnant uptake, 220
Low-density lipoproteins, 217, 218t
apolipoproteins of, 217–218, 218t
metabolism of, 221, 222f
ratio of to high-density lipoproteins, atherosclerosis and, 238
receptors for, 221
    in chylomicron remnant uptake, 220, 221f
    in cotranslational insertion, 513, 514f
    regulation of, 234
Low-energy phosphates, 91
Low molecular weight heparins (LMWHs), 611
LRP. *See* Low-density lipoprotein receptor-related protein
LTs. *See* Leukotrienes
Lung surfactant, 125, 209
deficiency of, 125, 214
Luteinizing hormone (LH), 445, 446, 447f
LXs. *See* Lipoxins
LXXLL motifs, nuclear receptor coregulators, 480
Lyases, 49
    in steroid synthesis, 448, 449f, 451f

Lymphocyte homing, selectins in, 537–538, 538f, 538t, 539f
Lymphocytes. *See also* B lymphocytes; T lymphocytes
    recombinant DNA technology in study of, 632
Lysine, 16t
catabolism of, 262, 263f
pI of, 17
requirements for, 488
Lysine hydroxylase, vitamin C as coenzyme for, 504
Lysis, cell, complement in, 605
Lysogenic pathway, 384, 385f
Lysolecithin (lysophosphatidylcholine), 125, 126f
metabolism of, 212–213, 213f
Lysophosphatidylcholine. *See* Lysolecithin
Lysophospholipase, 212, 213f
Lysophospholipids, 125, 126f
Lysosomal degradation pathway, defect in lipidoses, 215
Lysosomal enzymes, 631
    in I-cell disease, 439, 439t, 540–541, 541f
Lysosomal hydrolases, deficiencies of, 541, 542t
Lysosomal proteases, in protein degradation, 517
Lysosomes
    in endocytosis, 437
    in oligosaccharide processing, 533
    protein entry into, 515, 515f, 515t
        disorders associated with defects in, 521–522, 522t
Lysozyme, 628t
Lysyl hydroxylase
    diseases caused by deficiency of, 548t
    in hydroxylysine synthesis, 242, 546
Lysyl oxidase, 546, 549
Lytic pathway, 384, 385f
D-Lyxose, 115f, 115t

Mac-1, 538, 538t
α_2-Macroglobulin, 598–599
Macromolecules, cellular transport of, 436–437, 437f, 438f
Mad cow disease (bovine spongiform encephalopathy), 38
Magnesium, 504t
    in chlorophyll, 279
    in extracellular and intracellular fluid, 423, 423t
Major groove, in DNA, 313f, 314
    operon model and, 383
Malate, 147f, 148
Malate dehydrogenase, 147f, 148
Malate shuttle, 109–110, 109f
MALDI. *See* Matrix-assisted laser-desorption
Maleylacetoacetate, in tyrosine catabolism, 257, 261f

Malic enzyme, in NADPH production, 199, 199f
Malignancy/malignant cells. *See* Cancer/cancer cells
Malignant hyperthermia, 565, 573–574, 574f, 577t
Malonate
    on respiratory chain, 107, 107f
    succinate dehydrogenase inhibition by, 68–69, 68f
Malonyl-CoA, in fatty acid synthesis, 196, 197f
Malonyl transacylase, 196–197, 197f, 198f
Maltase, 483
Maltose, 116, 117f, 117t
Mammalian target of rapamycin (mTOR), in insulin signal transmission, 473, 474f
Mammotropin. *See* Prolactin
Manganese, 504t
Mannosamine, 183, 185f
D-Mannosamine, 116
D-Mannose, 115f, 115t
Mannose, in glycoproteins, 526t
Mannose 6-phosphate/mannose 6-P signal, 535
    in I-cell disease, 540–541, 541, 541f
    in protein flow, 515, 515t
Mannose-binding protein, deficiency of, 540
Mannosidosis, 541, 542t
Manual enzymatic method
    for DNA sequencing, 410
MAP (mitogen-activated protein) kinase
    in insulin signal transmission, 473, 474f
    in Jak/STAT pathway, 475
Maple syrup urine disease (branched-chain ketonuria), 265
Marasmus, 88, 241, 486–487
Marble bone disease (osteopetrosis), 560
Marfan syndrome, fibrillin mutations causing, 549, 550f
Maroteaux-Lamy syndrome, 556t
Mass spectrometry, 26–28, 27f
    covalent modifications detected by, 26–28, 27f, 27t
    for glycoprotein analysis, 524, 525t
    tandem, 28
    transcript-protein profiling and, 418
Mast cells, heparin in, 553
Matrix
    extracellular, 545–563. *See also* specific component
    mitochondrial, 100, 145
Matrix-assisted laser-desorption (MALDI), in mass spectrometry, 27
Matrix-processing peptidase, 507
Matrix proteins, 507
    diseases caused by defects in import of, 511
Maxam and Gilbert's method, for DNA sequencing, 410

Maximal velocity (V_{max})
  allosteric effects on, 77
  inhibitors affecting, 69, 69f, 70f
  Michaelis-Menten equation in determination of, 66–67, 67f
  substrate concentration and, 65, 65f
McArdle's disease/syndrome, 166t, 582
Mechanically gated ion channels, 577t
Mediator-related proteins, 480, 480t
Medicine
  preventive, biochemical research affecting, 2
  relationship of to biochemistry, 1–4, 3f
Medium-chain acyl-CoA dehydrogenase, deficiency of, 194
Megaloblastic anemia
  folate deficiency causing, 490t, 500, 618t
  vitamin B_{12} deficiency causing, 490t, 500, 502, 618t
Melanocyte-stimulating hormone (MSH), 460f, 461
MELAS, 110
Melatonin, biosynthesis and metabolism of, 275f
Melting point, of amino acids, 18
Melting temperature/transition temperature, 313, 428
Membrane attack complex, 605
Membrane fatty acid-transport protein, 219
Membrane proteins, 426, 426t, 523. See also Glycoproteins
  association of with lipid bilayer, 426
  flow of, 515, 515f, 515t
  integral, 30, 427, 428f
  mutations affecting, diseases caused by, 438–440, 439t, 440f
  peripheral, 427, 428f
  red cell, 622–625, 623f, 624t
  structure of, dynamic, 426–427
Membrane transport, 430, 430t, 431f, 433–438, 434f. See also specific mechanism
Membranes, 422–440
  artificial, 427–428
  assembly of, 520–522, 521f, 521t
  asymmetry of, 423, 427
  bilayers of, 425, 425f, 426f
    membrane protein association and, 426
  biogenesis of, 520–522, 521f, 521t
  cholesterol in, 424
    fluid mosaic model and, 429
  depolarization of, in nerve impulse transmission, 436
  function of, 422–428
    fluidity affecting, 428
  glycosphingolipids in, 424
  Golgi apparatus in synthesis of, 518
  intracellular, 422
  lipids in, 423–424
    amphipathic, 129, 130f, 424–425, 424f

mutations affecting, diseases caused by, 438–440, 439t, 440f
  phospholipids in, 124–126, 125f, 423–424, 424f
  plasma. See Plasma membrane
  protein:lipid ratio in, 423, 423f
  proteins in, 426, 426t. See also Membrane proteins
  red cell, 622–625, 623f, 623t, 624t
    hemolytic anemias and, 627, 627t
  selectivity of, 422, 430–431, 430t, 431f, 432f, 432t
  sterols in, 424
  structure of, 423–427, 423f
    asymmetry and, 427
    fluid mosaic model of, 428–430, 428f
Menadiol, 495, 495f
Menadiol diacetate, 495, 495f
Menadione, 495. See also Vitamin K
Menaquinone, 490t, 495, 495f. See also Vitamin K
Menkes disease, 596–597
MEOS. See Cytochrome P450-dependent microsomal ethanol oxidizing system
6-Mercaptopurine, 298, 299f
Mercapturic acid, 636
Mercuric ions, pyruvate metabolism affected by, 157
Meromyosin
  heavy, 569, 569f, 570f
  light, 569, 569f
Messenger RNA (mRNA), 315, 316–318, 318f, 319f, 348, 349t, 366. See also RNA
  alternative splicing and, 362, 362f, 399
  codon assignments in, 365–366, 366t
  editing of, 363
  modification of, 363–364
  nucleotide sequence of, 365–366
    mutations caused by changes in, 368–370, 368f, 369f, 371f
  polycistronic, 382
  recombinant DNA technology and, 403
  relationship of to chromosomal DNA, 329f
  stability of, regulation of gene expression and, 399–400, 400f
  transcription starting point and, 350
  variations in size/complexity of, 403, 405t
Metabolic acidosis, ammonia in, 249
Metabolic alkalosis, ammonia in, 249
Metabolic fuels, 138–144. See also Digestion
  clinical aspects of, 143–144
  diet providing, 482, 486
  diurnal requirements for, 132
  in fed and starving states, 140–142, 141f, 142f, 142t, 144
  interconvertability of, 138–140
  in normal adult, 132
  provision of, 132–144. See also Metabolism

Metabolic pathway/metabolite flow, 133. See also specific type and Metabolism
  flux-generating reactions in, 138
  nonequilibrium reactions in, 138
  regulation of, 73, 74f, 138, 139f
    covalent modification in, 79
  unidirectional nature of, 73, 74f
Metabolism, 89, 132–144, 143t. See also Catalysis/catalytic reactions (enzymatic); Metabolic pathway/metabolite flow; specific types
  blood circulation and, 134–136, 135f, 136f
  of drugs, in vivo, 72
  group transfer reactions in, 8
  inborn errors of, 1, 254
  integration of, metabolic fuels and, 138–144
  regulation of, 73, 74f, 138, 139f
    allosteric and hormonal mechanisms in, 75–77, 76f, 138, 139f
    enzymes in, 138, 139f
      allosteric regulation and, 75–77, 76f, 138, 139f
      compartmentation and, 73–74
      control of quantity and, 74–75
      covalent modification and, 75, 77, 78–79, 79f
      rate-limiting reactions and, 74
    at subcellular level, 136–138, 137f
    at tissue and organ levels, 134–136, 135f, 136f, 143t
  of xenobiotics, 633–639
Metabolite flow, 73
Metachromatic leukodystrophy, 215t
Metal-activated enzymes, 50
Metal ions, in enzymatic reactions, 50
Metalloenzymes, 50
Metalloflavoproteins, 94
Metalloproteins, 30
Metallothioneins, 596
Metaphase chromosomes, 325f, 326, 327t
Metastasis
  glycoproteins and, 523, 535–536, 538–539, 539t
  membrane abnormalities and, 439t
Methacrylyl-CoA, catabolism of, 269f
Methemoglobin, 46, 370, 622
Methemoglobinemia, 46–47, 622
Methionine, 15t, 271, 273f
  of α_1-antitrypsin, 597
  active (S-adenosylmethionine), 262, 265f, 271, 273f, 297, 298f, 298t
  catabolism of, 262, 265f, 266f
  in folate trap, 500f
  requirements for, 488
Methionine synthase, 500, 500f, 501–502
Methotrexate, 304–305, 501
  dihydrofolate/dihydrofolate reductase affected by, 304–305, 501

Methyl pentose, in glycoproteins, 119t
Methyl-tetrahydrofolate, in folate trap, 501–502, 501f
Methylation
  in covalent modification, mass increases and, 27t
  of deoxycytidine residues, gene expression affected by, 389
  in glycoprotein analysis, 525t
  of xenobiotics, 633, 637
5-Methylcytosine, 295, 297f
Methylene tetrahydrofolate, 500, 501f
  in folate trap, 500f, 502
7-Methylguanine, 297f
Methylhistidine, 584
  in Wilson's disease, 271
Methylmalonicaciduria, 169
Methylmalonyl-CoA, accumulation of in vitamin B_{12} deficiency, 500
Methylmalonyl-CoA isomerase (mutase), in propionate metabolism, 169, 169f, 500
Methylmalonyl-CoA mutase (isomerase), 169, 169f, 500
Methylmalonyl-CoA racemase, in propionate metabolism, 169, 169f
Mevalonate, synthesis of, 230, 233f
  in cholesterol synthesis, 231f, 232f
Mg. See Magnesium
mi and small interfering (si) RNA, 320
Micelles, 425, 425f
  amphipathic lipids forming, 129, 130f, 425, 425f
  in lipid absorption, 483
Michaelis constant (K_m), 66
  allosteric effects on, 77
  binding constant approximated by, 67
  enzymatic catalysis rate and, 66–67, 67f, 73, 74f
  inhibitors affecting, 69, 70f
  Michaelis-Menten equation in determination of, 66–67, 67f
Michaelis-Menten equation, 66
  Bi-Bi reactions and, 71, 71f
  regulation of metabolite flow and, 73, 74f
Micro (mi) RNAs, 320
Microbial toxins, 433
Microbiology, 1
Microfilaments, 584–585, 585t
Micronutrients. See also specific micronutrients
  determination of requirements for, 489
  minerals, 504–505, 504t
    digestion and absorption of, 485–486
  vitamins. See Vitamins
Microsatellite instability, 330
Microsatellite polymorphisms (DNA), 330, 415–416, 420
Microsatellite repeat sequences, 330, 420
Microsomal elongase system, 200, 201f
Microsomal fraction, cytochrome P450 isoforms in, 634

Microtubules, 585, 585t
Migration, cell, fibronectin in, 550
Milk (lactose) intolerance, 112, 482, 483
Mineralocorticoid response element, 467t
Mineralocorticoids, 445
  receptors for, 478
  synthesis of, 446–447, 449f
Minerals, 2, 504–505, 504t
  digestion and absorption of, 485–486
Minor groove, in DNA, 313f, 314
Misfolded proteins, accumulation of in endoplasmic reticulum, 516
Mismatch repair of DNA, 343–344, 343t, 344f
  colon cancer and, 344
Missense mutations, 368, 369–370, 369f
  familial hypertrophic cardiomyopathy caused by, 577–578, 578f
MIT. See Monoiodotyrosine
Mitchell's chemiosmotic theory. See Chemiosmotic theory
Mitochondria
  ALA synthesis in, 279, 282f
  citric acid cycle in, 133, 133f, 135f, 137, 137f, 145, 148–150, 149f
  fatty acid oxidation in, 187, 188f
  high-energy phosphate transport from, 110, 110f
  ion transport in, 110
  protein synthesis and import by, 507–509, 509t
  respiratory chain in. See Respiratory chain
Mitochondrial cytochrome P450, 97, 634. See also Cytochrome P450 system
Mitochondrial DNA, 330, 330f, 331t
Mitochondrial encephalopathy, lactic acidosis, and stroke (MELAS), 110
Mitochondrial genome, 507
Mitochondrial glycerol-3-phosphate dehydrogenase, 95
Mitochondrial membrane proteins, mutations of, 439
Mitochondrial membranes
  enzymes as markers of compartment separated by, 100
  protein insertion in, 509
  structure of, 100, 101f
Mitochondrial protein complexes, in respiratory chain, 95t, 100, 102f, 103f
Mitogen-activated protein (MAP) kinase
  in insulin signal transmission, 473, 474f
  in Jak/STAT pathway, 473–475
Mitotic spindle, microtubules in formation of, 585
Mixed-function oxidases, 97, 634. See also Cytochrome P450 system
ML. See Mucolipidoses
MOAT. See Multispecific organic anion transporter

Modeling, molecular, in protein structure analysis, 36
Molecular biology, 1. See also Recombinant DNA/recombinant DNA technology
  in primary structure determination, 26
Molecular chaperones. See Chaperones
Molecular docking programs, 36
Molecular dynamics, 36
Molecular genetics, 1, 402. See also Recombinant DNA/recombinant DNA technology
Molecular modeling, in protein structure analysis, 36
Molecular Modeling Database (MMDB), 87
Molecular motors, 585
Molecular replacement, 35
Molybdenum, 504t
Monoacylglycerol acyltransferase, 210f, 211
Monoacylglycerol pathway, 210f, 211, 483, 484f
2-Monoacylglycerols, 210f, 211
Monoclonal antibodies, hybridomas in production of, 604, 604f
Monoglycosylated core structure, calnexin binding and, 535
Monoiodotyrosine (MIT), 455, 456f, 457
Monomeric proteins, 34
Mononucleotides, 295
  "salvage" reactions and, 302, 303f, 305f
Monooxygenases, 97. See also Cytochrome P450 system
  in metabolism of xenobiotics, 633
Monosaccharides, 112. See also specific type and Glucose
  absorption of, 483, 483f
  physiologic importance of, 114, 115t
Monounsaturated fatty acids, 122, 123t. See also Fatty acids; Unsaturated fatty acids
  dietary, cholesterol levels affected by, 238
  synthesis of, 202, 203f
Morquio syndrome, 556t
MPP. See Matrix-processing peptidase
MPS. See Mucopolysaccharidoses
MRE. See Mineralocorticoid response element
mRNA. See Messenger RNA
MRP-2, in bilirubin secretion, 289
MSH. See Melanocyte-stimulating hormone
MstII, 405t
  in sickle cell disease, 415, 416f
mtDNA. See Mitochondrial DNA
mTOR, in insulin signal transmission, 473, 474f
Mucins, 528–529, 529t
  genes for, 529
  O-glycosidic linkages in, 528–529, 529f
  repeating amino acid sequences in, 528–529, 529f
Mucolipidoses, 555, 556t
Mucopolysaccharides, 118, 119f

Mucopolysaccharidoses, 555–556, 556t, 557f
  extracellular matrix in, 545
Mucoproteins. *See* Glycoproteins
Mucus, 529
Multidrug resistance-like protein 2 (MRP-2), in bilirubin secretion, 289
Multifactorial diseases, bioinformatics and, 82
Multipass membrane protein, anion exchange protein as, 623, 623f, 624t
Multiple deficiency states, vitamin, 489
Multiple myeloma, 604
Multiple sclerosis, 214
Multiple sequence alignment, 85
Multiple sulfatase deficiency, 215
Multisite phosphorylation, in glycogen metabolism, 164
Multispecific organic anion transporter (MOAT), in bilirubin secretion, 289
Muscle, 566f. *See also* Cardiac muscle; Skeletal muscle
  ATP in, 565, 570, 582f, 583
  contraction of. *See* Muscle contraction
  in energy transduction, 565–566, 566f, 567f, 568f
  in fasting state, 142
  fibers in, 565
  glucose uptake into, 140
  glycogen in, 159, 160t
    in fasting state, 141
  metabolism in, 134–136, 135f, 143t, 584t
    glycogen, 159
    lactate production and, 154
  phosphorylase in, control of, 161
  as protein reserve, 584
  proteins of, 574t. *See also* Actin; Myosin; Titin
  striated, 565
Muscle contraction, 565, 567f, 569–574, 573t
  ATP hydrolysis in, 570, 570f
  in cardiac muscle, 575–577
  regulation of
    actin-based, 571
    calcium in, 571
      in cardiac muscle, 575–577
      sarcoplasmic reticulum and, 571–573, 572f
      in smooth muscle, 579, 579f
    myosin-based, 579
    myosin light chain kinase in, 579, 579f
  relaxation phase of, 570, 572, 573t
    in smooth muscle
      calcium in, 579
      nitric oxide in, 580–581, 581f
  sliding filament cross-bridge model of, 566, 567f
  in smooth muscle, 579–581
  tropomyosin and troponin in, 570–571

Muscle fatigue, 151
Muscle phosphorylase
  absence of, 166t
  activation of
    calcium/muscle contraction and, 162
    cAMP and, 162, 163f
Muscular dystrophy, Duchenne, 565, 574–575, 574f
Mutagenesis, site-directed, in enzyme study, 59
Mutations, 322, 331–333, 331f, 332f, 333f
  base substitution, 368–369, 368f
  constitutive, 382
  frameshift, 370, 371f
    ABO blood group and, 627
  gene conversion and, 333
  integration and, 331–332, 332f
  of membrane proteins, diseases caused by, 438–440, 439t, 440f
  missense, 368, 369–370, 369f
    familial hypertrophic cardiomyopathy caused by, 577–578, 578f
  mRNA nucleotide sequence changes causing, 368–370, 368f, 369f, 371f
  nonsense, 368–369
  point, 368
    recombinant DNA technology in detection of, 413, 414f
  recombination and, 331, 331f, 332f
  silent, 368
  sister chromatid exchanges and, 333, 333f
  suppressor, 370
  transition, 368, 368f
  transposition and, 332–333
  transversion, 368, 368f
Myasthenia gravis, 439
Myelin sheets, 436
Myeloma, 604
Myeloma cells, hybridomas grown from, 604, 604f
Myeloperoxidase, 620, 628t, 630–631
Myocardial infarction, lactate dehydrogenase isoenzymes in diagnosis of, 57, 57t, 58f
Myofibrils, 565, 566, 566f, 567f
Myoglobin, 40–48
  oxygen dissociation curve for, 42, 43f
  oxygen stored by, 40, 42, 43f, 582
Myoglobinuria, 47
Myokinase (adenylyl kinase), 92
  in gluconeogenesis regulation, 170
  as source of ATP in muscle, 582, 582f
Myopathy, from inherited mitochondrial defects, 100
Myophosphorylase deficiency, 166t
Myosin, 566, 567–569, 569f
  in muscle contraction, 566, 567f, 570, 570f, 571f
    regulation of smooth muscle contraction and, 579
  in striated *vs.* smooth muscle, 580t

structure and function of, 568–569, 569f
Myosin-binding protein C, 574t
Myosin (thick) filaments, 566, 567f
Myosin head, 568, 569f
  conformational changes in, in muscle contraction, 569–574
Myosin heavy chains, 568
  familial hypertrophic cardiomyopathy caused by mutations in gene for, 577–578, 578f
Myosin light chain kinase, 579, 579f
Myosin light chains, 568
  in smooth muscle contraction, 579
Myotonia congenita, 577t
Myristic acid, 122t, 519
Myristylation, 519
  in covalent modification, mass increases and, 27t

N-acetylneuraminic acid, 119, 120f, 183, 185f
  in gangliosides, 213, 215f
  in glycoproteins, 183, 185f, 526t
  in mucins, 528t, 529
N-glycan chains, 512
N-linked glycoproteins, 527, 528f, 530–536
  classes of, 530–531, 530f
  synthesis of, 531–533, 531f, 532f, 534f, 535t
    in endoplasmic reticulum and Golgi apparatus, 533–535, 535t
    glycan intermediates formed during, 535
  regulation of, 535–536, 536t
  tunicamycin affecting, 536, 536t
Na. *See* Sodium
Na⁺-Ca²⁺ exchanger, 471
Na⁺-K⁺ ATPase, 435, 435f
  in glucose transport, 436, 436f
NAD⁺ (nicotinamide adenine dinucleotide), 95, 498, 498f
  absorption spectrum of, 56, 56f
  in citric acid cycle, 148
  as coenzyme, 95, 97f, 298t
NAD(P)⁺-dependent dehydrogenases, in enzyme detection, 56
NADH
  absorption spectrum of, 56, 56f
  extramitochondrial oxidation of, substrate shuttles in, 109–110, 109f
  fatty acid oxidation yielding, 188
  in pyruvate dehydrogenase regulation, 155–156, 157f
NADH dehydrogenase, 95
NADH-Q oxidoreductase, 100, 102f, 103f
  as electron acceptor, 101–102, 103f, 147f
NADP⁺ (nicotinamide adenine dinucleotide phosphate), 95, 498
  as coenzyme, 95, 97f, 298t

in pentose phosphate pathway, 177, 178f, 179f
NADPH
  in cytochrome P450 reactions, 98f, 634
  intramitochondrial, proton-translocating transhydrogenase in, 109
  for lipogenesis, 198f, 199, 199f
  pentose phosphate pathway and, 177, 178f, 179f, 184
NADPH-cytochrome P450 reductase, 634
NADPH oxidase, 628t, 630
  chronic granulomatous disease associated with mutations in, 630, 631f
Nanotechnology, 55
National Center for Biotechnology Information (NCBI), 85
Native conformation, protein, 36
NCoA-1/NCoA-2 coactivators, 479, 480t
NCoR, 480, 480t
NDPs. See Ribonucleoside diphosphates
Nebulin, 574t
NEFA (nonesterified fatty acids). See Free fatty acids
Negative nitrogen balance, 487
Negative regulators, of gene expression, 380, 381t, 383, 386
Negative supercoils, DNA, 314
NEM-sensitive factor (NSF), 519, 519f
Neonatal adrenoleukodystrophy, 511, 511t
Neonatal (physiologic) jaundice, 291
Neonatal tyrosinemia, 257
Neonate, hypoglycemia in, 165
Nerve cells. See Neurons
Nerve impulses, 435–436
Nervous system
  glucose as metabolic necessity for, 140
  thiamin deficiency affecting, 496
NESs. See Nuclear export signals
Net charge, of amino acid, 16–17, 17f
Net diffusion, 430
NeuAc. See N-Acetylneuraminic acid
Neural tube defects, folic acid supplements in prevention of, 502
Neuraminic acid, 119, 126
Neuraminidases
  deficiency of, 541, 542t
  in glycoprotein analysis, 526–527
  influenza virus, 542
Neurofilaments, 585t
Neurologic diseases, protein conformation alterations and, 37–38
Neurons, membranes of
  impulses transmitted along, 435–436
  ion channels in, 431, 432f
  synaptic vesicle fusion with, 520
Neuropathy, sensory, in vitamin B_6 excess, 499
Neutral lipids, 121
Neutropenia, 618
Neutrophils, 628–631
  activation of, 629–630
  biochemical features of, 627t
  enzymes and proteins of, 628t

in infection, 627–628
in inflammation, 627–628, 628t
  integrins and, 628–629, 629t
  selectins and, 537–538, 538t, 539f
proteinases of, 631, 631t
respiratory burst and, 630
Niacin, 489, 490t, 498, 498f. See also Nicotinamide; Nicotinic acid
  in citric acid cycle, 148
  deficiency of, 490t, 498
  excess/toxicity of, 498
Nick translation, 420
Nickel, 504t
Nicks/nick-sealing, in DNA replication, 339–340, 340f
Nicotinamide, 490t, 498, 498f. See also Niacin
  coenzymes derived from, 50
  dehydrogenases and, 95, 97f
  excess/toxicity of, 498
Nicotinamide adenine dinucleotide (NAD⁺), 95, 498, 498f
  absorption spectrum of, 56, 56f
  in citric acid cycle, 148
  as coenzyme, 95, 97f, 298t
Nicotinamide adenine dinucleotide phosphate (NADP⁺), 95, 498
  as coenzyme, 95, 97f, 298t
  in pentose phosphate pathway, 177, 178f, 179f
Nicotinic acid, 490t, 498, 498f. See also Niacin
  as hypolipidemic drug, 238–239
NIDDM. See Non-insulin dependent diabetes mellitus
Nidogen (entactin), in basal lamina, 551
Niemann-Pick disease, 215t
Night blindness, vitamin A deficiency causing, 490t, 491
Nitric oxide, 565, 580–581, 581f, 582t, 615t
  clotting/thrombosis affected by, 615, 615t
Nitric oxide synthases, 580–581, 581f, 581t
Nitrite, nitric oxide formation from, 580–581
Nitrogen balance, 487
Nitroglycerin, 580
NLS. See Nuclear localization signal
NMR. See Nuclear magnetic resonance (NMR) spectroscopy
NO. See Nitric oxide
NO synthase, 580–581, 581f, 581t
Non–clathrin-coated vesicles, 518
Noncoding regions, in recombinant DNA technology, 403, 404f
Noncoding strand, 312
Noncompetitive inhibition, competitive inhibition differentiated from, 68–70, 68f, 69f, 70f
Noncovalent assemblies, in membranes, 423
Noncovalent forces
  in biomolecule stabilization, 6
  peptide conformation and, 19–20

Nonequilibrium reactions, 138
  citric acid cycle regulation and, 149
  glycolysis regulation and, 154–155, 167–169
Nonesterified fatty acids. See Free fatty acids
Nonfunctional plasma enzymes, 57. See also Enzymes
  in diagnosis and prognosis, 57, 57t
Nonheme iron, 593
Nonhistone proteins, 322
Non-insulin dependent diabetes mellitus (NIDDM/type 2), 175
Nonoxidative phase, of pentose phosphate pathway, 177–180
Nonrepetitive (unique-sequence) DNA, 328
Nonsense codons, 366, 368, 370
Nonsense mutations, 368
Nonsteroidal anti-inflammatory drugs
  cyclooxygenase affected by, 204
  prostaglandins affected by, 196
Norepinephrine, 447f, 454, 455f. See also Catecholamines
  synthesis of, 272–274, 276f, 453–454, 455f
  in thermogenesis, 228, 229f
Northern blot transfer procedure, 314, 409–410, 409f, 420
NOS, 580–581, 581f, 581t
Notch glycoprotein, 543
NPCs. See Nuclear pore complexes
NSF. See NEM-sensitive factor
Nuclear export signals, 511
Nuclear genes, proteins encoded by, 507
Nuclear localization signal (NLS), 509, 510f, 515t
Nuclear magnetic resonance (NMR) spectroscopy
  for glycoprotein analysis, 524, 525t
  protein structure demonstrated by, 36
Nuclear pore complexes, 509
Nuclear proteins, O-glycosidic linkages in, 527
Nuclear receptor coactivators (NCoA-1/NCoA-2), 479, 480t
Nuclear receptor corepressor (NCoR), 480, 480t
Nuclear receptor superfamily, 444, 477–478, 479f, 479t
Nucleases, 8, 320–321
  active chromatin and, 324
Nucleic acids. See also DNA; RNA
  bases of, 295–297, 296t
  dietary nonessential, 301
  digestion of, 320–321
  structure and function of, 311–321
Nucleolytic processing, of RNA, 359
Nucleophile, water as, 7–8
Nucleophilic attack, in DNA synthesis, 336, 337f
Nucleoproteins, packing of, 326, 327t, 328f

Nucleosidases (nucleoside phosphorylases), purine, deficiency of, 308
Nucleoside diphosphate kinase, 92–93
Nucleoside triphosphates
  group transfer potential of, 297–298, 297f, 298f, 298t
  nonhydrolyzable analogs of, 298–299, 300f
  in phosphorylation, 92–93
  in transfer of high-energy phosphate, 92–93
Nucleosides, 294–298, 296t
Nucleosomes, 322, 323–324, 323f
Nucleotide excision-repair of DNA, 344–345, 345f
Nucleotide sugars, in glycoprotein biosynthesis, 525, 526t, 529–530, 530f
Nucleotides, 294–298, 296t. *See also* Purine; Pyrimidines/pyrimidine nucleotides
  adenylyl kinase (myokinase) in interconversion of, 92
  as coenzymes, 298, 298t
  DNA, deletion/insertion of, frameshift mutations and, 370, 371f
  metabolism of, 301–309
  in mRNA, 365–366
    mutations caused by changes in, 368–370, 368f, 369f, 371f
  physiologic functions of, 297
  as polyfunctional acids, 298
  polynucleotides, 299–300
  synthetic analogs of, in chemotherapy, 298–299, 299f
  ultraviolet light absorbed by, 298
Nucleus (cell), importins and exportins in transport and, 509–511, 510f
Nutrition, 482–488. *See also* Diet
  biochemical research affecting, 2
  lipogenesis regulated by, 199
Nutritional deficiencies, 482
  in AIDS and cancer, 487
Nutritionally essential amino acids, 134, 242t, 488. *See also* Amino acids
Nutritionally essential fatty acids, 202. *See also* Fatty acids
  abnormal metabolism of, 206
  deficiency of, 203–204, 206
Nutritionally nonessential amino acids, 134, 241, 242t, 488
  synthesis of, 241–244

O blood group substance, 626f, 627
O gene, 627
O-glycosidic linkage
  of collagen, 546
  of proteoglycans, 552–553
O-linked glycoproteins, 527, 528–530, 528f, 529f, 529t
  synthesis of, 529–530, 530f

O-linked oligosaccharides, in mucins, 528–529, 529f
1,25(OH)₂-D₃. *See* Calcitriol
Obesity, 88, 132, 217, 482, 486
  lipogenesis and, 196
Octamers, histone, 323, 323f
Oculocerebrorenal syndrome, 522t
Okazaki fragments, 335–336, 339f
Oleic acid, 122–123, 122f, 123t, 124f, 202f
  synthesis of, 202, 203f
Oligomers, import of by peroxisomes, 511
Oligomycin, on oxidation and phosphorylation, 107, 107f
Oligonucleotide
  definition of, 420
  in primary structure determination, 26
Oligosaccharide branches (antennae), 531
Oligosaccharide chains
  glycoprotein, 523, 525t, 589–590
    in N-glycosylation, 533, 534f
    regulation of, 535–536
    sugars in, 524, 526t
  glycosaminoglycans, 552
Oligosaccharide processing, 518, 531, 533, 534f
  Golgi apparatus in, 518
  regulation of, 535–536, 536t
Oligosaccharide:protein transferase, 532
Oligosaccharides, 112
  O-linked, in mucins, 528–529, 529f
OMP (orotidine monophosphate), 304, 306f
Oncogenes, 1
  cyclins and, 342
Oncoproteins, Rb protein and, 342
Oncotic (osmotic) pressure, 588, 592
Oncoviruses, cyclins and, 342
Open complex, 352
Operator locus, 382–383, 383f
Operon/operon hypothesis, 381, 382–384, 382f, 383f
Optical activity/isomer, 113
OR. *See* Right operator
ORC. *See* Origin replication complex
ORE. *See* Origin replication element
Ori (origin of replication), 334, 335f, 420
Origin of replication (ori), 334, 335f, 420
Origin replication complex, 334
Origin replication element, 334
Ornithine, 272
  catabolism of, 254, 256f
  metabolism of, 272f
  in urea synthesis, 249, 250, 251
Ornithine-citrulline antiporter, defective, 254
Ornithine transcarbamoylase/L-ornithine transcarbamoylase
  deficiency of, 252, 309
  in urea synthesis, 250
Ornithine transporter disorders, 252
Orotate phosphoribosyltransferase, 304, 305, 306f
Orotic aciduria, 309

Orotidine monophosphate (OMP), 304, 306f
Orotidinuria, 309
Orphan receptors, 444, 478
Osmotic fragility test, 625
Osmotic lysis, complement in, 605
Osmotic (oncotic) pressure, 588, 592
Osteoarthritis, 545, 561t
  proteoglycans in, 558
Osteoblasts, 558–559, 559f
Osteocalcin, 496, 504, 558t
Osteoclasts, 558, 559f, 560f
Osteocytes, 559f
Osteogenesis imperfecta (brittle bones), 559–560, 561t
Osteoid, 559, 559f
Osteomalacia, 490t, 492, 493, 561t
Osteonectin, 558t
Osteopetrosis (marble bone disease), 560
Osteopontin, 558t
Osteoporosis, 493, 560–561, 561t
Ouabain, 116
  Na⁺-K⁺ ATPase affected by, 435
Outer mitochondrial membrane, 100
  protein insertion in, 509
Ovary, hormones produced by, 445, 450, 452t, 453f
Overnutrition, 486
Oxaloacetate
  in amino acid carbon skeleton catabolism, 254, 254f
  in aspartate synthesis, 241, 242f
  in citric acid cycle, 137f, 138, 145, 146f, 148, 149f, 150
Oxidases, 94–95, 95f. *See also* specific type
  ceruloplasmin as, 595–596
  copper in, 94
  flavoproteins as, 94–95, 96f
  mixed-function, 97, 634. *See also* Cytochrome P450 system
Oxidation, 94
  definition of, 94
  dehydrogenases in, 95–96, 96f, 97f
  fatty acid, 187. *See also* Ketogenesis
    acetyl-CoA release and, 134, 134f, 187–189, 188f, 189f
    clinical aspects of, 194–195
    hypoglycemia caused by impairment of, 194
    in mitochondria, 187, 188f
  hydroperoxidases in, 96
  oxidases in, 94, 95f, 96f
  oxygen toxicity and, 97–98, 620–621, 620t
  oxygenases in, 97, 98f
  redox potential and, 94, 95t
Oxidation-reduction (redox) potential, 94, 95t
Oxidative phase, of pentose phosphate pathway, 177, 178f, 179f
Oxidative phosphorylation, 91, 133. *See also* Phosphorylation; Respiratory chain
  ATP generation by, 105

enzymes as markers of compartments separated by mitochondrial membranes in, 100
    muscle generation of ATP by, 582, 582f, 583–584, 583t
    respiration and, via ATP, 100
    at respiratory chain level, 106, 158t
Oxidative stress, 621
Oxidoreductase
    c, 100, 102f, 103f, 104
    NADH-Q, 100, 102f, 103f
        as electron acceptor, 101–102, 103f, 147f
Oxidoreductases, 49, 94. *See also* specific type
Oxidosqualene:lanosterol cyclase, 231, 233f
Oxygen
    binding, 43, 43f. *See also* Oxygenation
        Bohr effect and, 45, 46f
        histidines F8 and E7 in, 40, 42f
        hemoglobin affinities (P_{50}) for, 43, 44f
        myoglobin in storage of, 40, 42, 43f, 582
    reductive activation of, 634
    transport of, ferrous iron in, 40–41
Oxygen dissociation curve, for myoglobin and hemoglobin, 42, 43f
Oxygen radicals. *See* Free radicals
Oxygen toxicity, superoxide free radical and, 97–98, 620, 620t. *See also* Free radicals
Oxygenases, 94, 96–97
Oxygenation of hemoglobin
    conformational changes and, 43, 44f, 45f
    2,3-bisphosphoglycerate stabilizing, 45–46, 46f
        apoprotein, 43
    high altitude adaptation and, 46
    mutant hemoglobins and, 46–47
Oxysterols, 129

P bodies, 400
p/CIP coactivator, 479, 480t
P component, in amyloidosis, 599
p-Hydroxyphenylpyruvate, in tyrosine catabolism, 257, 261f
P-selectin, 538t
P_{50}, hemoglobin affinity for oxygen and, 43, 44f
p53 protein/p53 gene, 346–347
p160 coactivators, 479, 480t
p300 coactivator/CPB/p300, 469, 475, 477f, 479, 480t
P450 cytochrome. *See* Cytochrome P450 system
P450scc (cytochrome P450 side chain cleavage enzyme), 446, 448f, 450
PAC (P1-based) vector, 407, 408t, 420
Paddle, charged, 433, 433f
PAF. *See* Platelet-activating factor
PAGE. *See* Polyacrylamide gel electrophoresis
Pain, prostaglandins in, 196
Palindrome, 420

Palmitate, 196
    in vesicle coating, 519
Palmitic acid, 122t
Palmitoleic acid, 123t, 202f
    synthesis of, 202
Palmitoylation, in covalent modification, mass increases and, 27t
Pancreatic insufficiency, in vitamin B_{12} deficiency, 500
Pancreatic islets, insulin produced by, 173
Pancreatic lipase, 483, 484f
Panproteinase inhibitor, 598
Pantothenic acid, 196, 490t, 503, 503f
    in citric acid cycle, 148
    coenzymes derived from, 50
    deficiency of, 490t
Papain, immunoglobulin digestion by, 599
PAPS. *See* Adenosine 3′-phosphate-5′-phosphosulfate
Parallel beta sheet, 32, 33f
Parathyroid hormone (PTH), 446, 457–458, 459f
    storage/secretion of, 461, 461t
    synthesis of, 457–458, 459f
Paroxysmal nocturnal hemoglobinuria, 439t, 537, 539–540, 539t, 540f
Partition chromatography, for protein/peptide purification, 21
Passive diffusion/transport, 430, 430t, 431f
Pathology, 1
pBR322, 407, 408f, 408t
PCR. *See* Polymerase chain reaction
PDH. *See* Pyruvate dehydrogenase
PDI. *See* Protein disulfide isomerase
PECAM-1, 538, 538t
Pedigree analysis, 415, 416f
Pellagra, 490t, 498
Penicillamine, for Wilson disease, 597
Pentasaccharide, in N-linked glycoproteins, 530f, 531, 531f
Pentose phosphate pathway, 133, 177–180, 178f, 179f, 181f
    cytosol as location for reactions of, 177
    enzymes of, 170t
    erythrocyte hemolysis and, 183–184, 621
    impairment of, 183–184
    NADPH produced by, 177, 178f, 179f
        for lipogenesis, 198f, 199, 199f
    nonoxidative phase of, 177–180
    oxidative phase of, 177, 178f, 179f
    ribose produced by, 177, 178f
Pentoses, 112, 113t
    in glycoproteins, 119t
    physiologic importance of, 114, 115t
Pentosuria, essential, 177, 184
PEPCK. *See* Phosphoenolpyruvate carboxykinase
Pepsin, 485
    in acid-base catalysis, 52
Pepsinogen, 485

Peptic ulcers
    Helicobacter pylori in, 482
    glycan binding of, 542, 542f
Peptidases, in protein degradation, 246, 247f
Peptide bonds, 19. *See also* Peptides
    formation of, 7, 374–375
    partial double-bond character of, 19, 20f
    on secondary conformations, 31
Peptides, 14–20, 447f. *See also* Amino acids; Proteins
    absorption of, 485
    amino acids in, 14, 19, 19f
    as hormone precursors, 457
    intracellular messengers used by, 465–476, 469t, 471t
    as polyelectrolytes, 19
    purification of, 21–24
Peptidyl prolyl isomerase, 516
Peptidylglycine hydroxylase, vitamin C as coenzyme for, 503
Peptidyltransferase, 374, 375t
Periodic acid-Schiff reagent, in glycoprotein analysis, 525t
Periodic hyperlysinemia, 262
Periodic paralysis
    hyperkalemic, 577t
    hypokalemic, 577t
Peripheral proteins, 427, 428f
Peripherin, 585t
Permeability coefficients, of substances in lipid bilayer, 425, 426f
Pernicious anemia, 490t, 500
Peroxidases, 96, 204
Peroxidation, lipid, free radicals produced by, 128–129, 130f
Peroxins, 511
Peroxisomal-matrix targeting sequences (PTS), 511, 515t
Peroxisomes, 96, 511
    absence/abnormalities of, 511, 511t
        in Zellweger's syndrome, 194, 511
    biogenesis of, 511
    in fatty acid oxidation, 189
Pfeiffer syndrome, 561t
PFK-1. *See* Phosphofructokinase (phosphofructokinase-1)
PGHS. *See* Prostaglandin H synthase
PGIs. *See* Prostacyclins
PGs. *See* Prostaglandins
pH, 9–13. *See also* Acid-base balance
    amino acid net charge and, 16, 17f
    buffering and, 11–12, 12f. *See also* Buffers
    calculation of, 9–10
    definition of, 9
    enzyme-catalyzed reaction rate affected by, 65, 65f
    isoelectric, amino acid net charge and, 17–18
Phage lambda, 384–387, 385f, 386f, 387f, 388f
Phages, in recombinant DNA technology, 407

Phagocytic cells, respiratory burst of, 630
Phagocytosis, 437
Pharmacogenetics, 85, 637, 638–639
Pharmacogenomics, 638–639
Pharmacology, 1
Pharmacy, 1
Phasing, nucleosome, 324
Phenobarbital, warfarin interaction and, cytochrome P450 induction affecting, 635
Phenylalanine, 16t
  catabolism of, 259, 262, 262f
  in phenylketonuria, 259, 262f
  requirements for, 488
  in tyrosine synthesis, 242, 244f
Phenylalanine hydroxylase
  defect in, 259
  localization of gene for, 413t
  in tyrosine synthesis, 242, 244f
Phenylethanolamine-N-methyltransferase (PNMT), 454–455, 455f
Phenylisothiocyanate (Edman reagent), in protein sequencing, 25–26, 27f
Phenylketonuria, 259
Phi angle, 31, 31f
Phosphagens, 92, 92f
Phosphatases
  acid, diagnostic significance of, 57t
  alkaline
    in bone mineralization, 559
    isozymes of, diagnostic significance of, 57t
    in recombinant DNA technology, 406t
Phosphate transporter, 108, 108f
Phosphates/phosphorus, 504t
  in extracellular and intracellular fluid, 423t
  free energy of hydrolysis of, 90–91, 90t
  high-energy, 91. See also ATP
    in energy capture and transfer, 90–91, 90f, 90t, 91f
    as "energy currency" of cell, 91–93, 92f, 93f, 106
    symbol designating, 91
  low-energy, 91
Phosphatidate, 210f, 211
  in triacylglycerol synthesis, 209, 210f, 211
Phosphatidate phosphohydrolase, 210f, 211
Phosphatidic acid, 124, 125f, 423–424, 424f
Phosphatidic acid pathway, 484f, 485
Phosphatidylcholines (lecithins), 124–125, 125f
  membrane asymmetry and, 427
  synthesis of, 209, 210f
Phosphatidylethanolamine (cephalin), 125, 125f
  membrane asymmetry and, 427
  synthesis of, 209, 210f

Phosphatidylglycerol, 125, 125f
Phosphatidylinositol 3-kinase (PI-3 kinase)
  in insulin signal transmission, 473, 474f
  in Jak/STAT pathway, 475
Phosphatidylinositol 4
  in platelet activation, 614f
Phosphatidylinositol 4,5-bisphosphate (PIP$_2$), 125, 471–472, 473f
  in absorptive pinocytosis, 437
  in platelet activation, 614
Phosphatidylinositol bisphosphate, in neutrophil activation, 629–630
Phosphatidylinositol/phosphatidylinositide, 125, 125f
  GPI-linked glycoproteins and, 536. See also Glycosylphosphatidylinositol-anchored (GPI-anchored/GPI-linked) glycoproteins
  metabolism of, 471–472, 472f, 473f
  as second messenger/second messenger precursor, 125, 125f, 445, 445t, 465, 471–472, 471t, 472t, 473t
  synthesis of, 209, 210f
Phosphatidylserine, 125, 125f
  membrane asymmetry and, 427
Phosphocreatine, in muscle, 565
Phosphodiester, 299
Phosphodiesterases, 299
  in calcium-dependent signal transduction, 471
  in cAMP-dependent signal transduction, 469, 470f
  cAMP hydrolyzed by, 161
Phosphoenolpyruvate
  free energy of hydrolysis of, 90t
  in gluconeogenesis, 148, 149f
Phosphoenolpyruvate carboxykinase (PEPCK), 148, 149f
  in gluconeogenesis regulation, 148, 149f, 167, 168f
Phosphoenolpyruvate carboxylase, 170t
  in gluconeogenesis, 170t
Phosphofructokinase (phosphofructokinase-1), 170t
  in gluconeogenesis regulation, 170
  in glycolysis, 152, 153f, 170t
    regulation and, 154
  muscle, deficiency of, 157–158, 166t
Phosphofructokinase-2, 171, 171f
Phosphoglucomutase, in glycogen biosynthesis, 159, 160f
6-Phosphogluconate dehydrogenase, 177, 178f, 179f
3-Phosphoglycerate
  in glycolysis, 152, 153f
  in serine synthesis, 241, 243f
Phosphoglycerate kinase, in glycolysis, 152, 153f
  in erythrocytes, 155, 155f

Phosphoglycerate mutase, in glycolysis, 152, 153f
Phosphoglycerides, in membranes, 423–424, 424f
Phosphoglycerols
  lysophospholipids in metabolism of, 125, 126f
  synthesis of, 210f, 211
Phosphohexoseisomerase, in glycolysis, 152, 153f
Phosphoinositide-dependent kinase-1 (PDK1), in insulin signal transmission, 473
Phospholipase A$_1$, 212, 213f
Phospholipase A$_2$, 212, 213f
  in platelet activation, 614f, 615
Phospholipase C, 212, 213f
  in calcium-dependent signal transduction, 471–472, 472f, 473f
  in Jak/STAT pathway, 475
  in respiratory burst, 630
Phospholipase Cβ, 614
Phospholipase D, 212, 213f
Phospholipases
  in glycoprotein analysis, 525t
  in phosphoglycerol degradation and remodeling, 212–213, 213f
Phospholipids, 121, 217
  digestion and absorption of, 483, 484f
  glycerol ether, synthesis of, 211, 212f
  in lipoprotein lipase activity, 219–220
  in membranes, 124–126, 125f, 423–424, 424f, 426, 520–521
    membrane asymmetry and, 427, 520–521
  in multiple sclerosis, 214
  as second messenger precursors, 209
  synthesis of, 210f
Phosphoprotein phosphatases, in cAMP-dependent signal transduction, 469–470, 470f
Phosphoproteins, in cAMP-dependent signal transduction, 470f
Phosphoproteins phosphatases, in cAMP-dependent signal transduction, 469–470
Phosphoric acid, pK/pK_a value of, 12t
Phosphorus. See Phosphates/phosphorus
Phosphorylase
  activation of, cAMP and, 162
  in glycogen metabolism, 159–160, 160f
    regulation of, 162–164, 164f, 165f
  liver, 161
    deficiency of, 166t
  muscle, 161
    absence of, 166t
    activation of
      calcium/muscle contraction and, 162
      cAMP and, 163f
Phosphorylase a, 162, 163f
Phosphorylase b, 162, 163f

Phosphorylase kinase
   calcium/calmodulin-sensitive, in glyco-
      genolysis, 162
   deficiency of, 166t
   protein phosphatase-1 affecting, 162
Phosphorylase kinase a, 162, 163f
Phosphorylase kinase b, 162, 163f
Phosphorylation, protein
   in covalent modification, 77, 78–79, 79f,
      79t
      mass increases and, 27t
   multisite, in glycogen metabolism, 164
   oxidative. See Oxidative phosphorylation
   in respiratory burst, 630
   at substrate level, 105f, 106
   versatility of, 79–81, 79t, 80f
Phosphatidylcholine metabolism, 213f
Phosphotriose isomerase, 152
Photolysis reaction, in vitamin D synthesis,
      453
Photosensitivity, in porphyria, 283
Phototherapy, cancer, porphyrins in, 282
Phylloquinone, 490t, 495, 495f. See also
      Vitamin K
Physiologic (neonatal) jaundice, 291
Physiology, 1
Phytanic acid, Refsum's disease caused by
      accumulation of, 194
Phytase, 485
Phytic acid (inositol hexaphosphate), cal-
      cium absorption affected by,
      485
P_i, 597
   in muscle contraction, 570, 570f
pI (isoelectric pH), amino acid net charge
      and, 17–18
PI-3 kinase
   in insulin signal transmission, 473, 474f
   in Jak/STAT pathway, 475
PIC. See Preinitiation complex
PIG-A gene, mutations of in paroxysmal
      nocturnal hemoglobinuria,
      540, 540f
"Ping-Pong" mechanism, in facilitated dif-
      fusion, 434, 435f
Ping-pong reactions, 70, 70f
Pinocytosis, 437
PIP_2 (phosphatidylinositol 4,5-bisphos-
      phate), 125, 471–472, 473f
   in absorptive pinocytosis, 437
   in platelet activation, 614
Pitch, 31
Pituitary hormones, 445. See also specific
      type
   blood glucose affected by, 174
pK/pK_a
   of amino acids, 15t–16t, 17–18, 17f, 18
   environment affecting, 18, 18t
   medium affecting, 12–13
   of weak acids, 10–13, 12t, 17
PKA. See Protein kinase A
PKB. See Protein kinase B
PKC. See Protein kinase C

PKU. See Phenylketonuria
Placenta, estriol synthesis by, 450
Plaque hybridization, 410. See also Hybrid-
      ization
Plasma, 588
Plasma cells, immunoglobulins synthesized
      in, 599
Plasma enzymes. See also Enzymes
   diagnostic significance of, 57, 57t
Plasma lipoproteins. See Lipoproteins
Plasma membrane, 422, 433–438, 434f. See
      also Membranes
   carbohydrates in, 119–120
   mutations in, diseases caused by,
      438–440, 439t
Plasma proteins, 523, 588–599, 589f, 591t.
      See also specific type and Gly-
      coproteins
   in bone, 558t
   concentration of, 588
   electrophoresis for analysis of, 588, 590f
   functions of, 591, 591t
   half-life of, 590
   in inflammation, 628t
   polymorphism of, 590
   synthesis of
      in liver, 134, 589
      on polyribosomes, 589
   transport, 461t, 462–463, 462t, 591t
Plasma proteome, 588
Plasma thromboplastin antecedent (PTA/
      factor XI), 607f, 608, 608t
   deficiency of, 609
Plasma thromboplastin component (PTC/
      factor IX), 607f, 608, 608t
   coumarin drugs affecting, 612
   deficiency of, 612
Plasmalogens, 125–126, 126f, 211, 212f
   biosynthesis of, 212f
Plasmids, 406, 407f, 408f, 408t, 420
Plasmin, 612–613, 612f
Plasminogen, 612
   activators of, 612–613, 612f, 613f, 615t
Platelet-activating factor, 209, 628t
   synthesis of, 210f, 211, 212f
Platelet transfusion, 543
Platelets, activation/aggregation of, 606,
      613–615, 614f
   aspirin affecting, 615
Pleckstrin, in platelet activation, 614
PLP. See Pyridoxal phosphate
PNMT. See Phenylethanolamine-N-methyl-
      transferase
pOH, in pH calculation, 9
Point mutations, 368
   recombinant DNA technology in detec-
      tion of, 413, 414f, 415t
Pol II
   phosphorylation of, 357
   in preinitiation complex formation, 358
   in transcription, 357
Polarity
   of DNA replication/synthesis, 338

   of protein synthesis, 371
   of xenobiotics, metabolism and, 633
Polyacrylamide gel electrophoresis, for pro-
      tein/peptide purification, 24,
      25f, 26f
Polyadenylation sites, alternative, 399
Polyamines, synthesis of, 272, 273f, 274f
Polycistronic mRNA, 382
Polycythemia, 47
Polydystrophy, pseudo-Hurler, 541, 556t
Polyelectrolytes, peptides as, 19
Polyfunctional acids, nucleotides as, 298
Polyisoprenoids, in cholesterol synthesis,
      231, 232f
Polyisoprenol, in N-glycosylation, 531
Polymerase chain reaction (PCR), 58,
      410–411, 412f, 420
   in microsatellite repeat sequence detec-
      tion, 330
   in primary structure determination, 26
Polymerases
   DNA, 334–335, 335f, 336, 336t
      in recombinant DNA technology,
         406t
   RNA, DNA-dependent, in RNA synthe-
      sis, 349–351, 349f, 351t
Polymorphisms, 413
   acetyltransferase, 637
   cytochrome P450, 635, 637t
   microsatellite, 330, 420
   microsatellite DNA, 415–416
   plasma protein, 590
   restriction fragment length. See Restric-
      tion fragment length poly-
      morphisms
   single nucleotide, 420
Polynucleotide kinase, in recombinant
      DNA technology, 406t
Polynucleotides, 299–300
   posttranslational modification of, 297
Polyol (sorbitol) pathway, 185–186
Polypeptides
   protein synthesis on, 22f
   receptors for, 444
   sequencing of
      cleavage in, 25–26
      Sanger's determination of, 25
Polyphosphoinositide pathway, platelet acti-
      vation and, 613–615
Polyprenoids, 128, 129f
Polyribosomes (polysomes), 318, 376
   cytosolic, synthesis on, 51
   protein synthesis on, 506, 507f, 508f,
      514
   plasma proteins, 589
   signal hypothesis of binding of,
      511–513, 512t, 513f
Polysaccharides, 112, 116–119, 118f, 119f.
      See also specific type
Polysomes. See Polyribosomes
Poly(A) tail, of mRNA, 317, 363
   in initiation of protein synthesis, 372
Polytene chromosomes, 326, 326f

Polyunsaturated fatty acids, 122, 123t. *See also* Fatty acids; Unsaturated fatty acids
    dietary, cholesterol levels affected by, 238
    eicosanoids formed from, 202, 204, 205f, 206f
    essential, 202, 202f
    synthesis of, 202–203, 203f, 204f
POMC. *See* Pro-opiomelanocortin (POMC) peptide family
Pompe's disease, 166t
Porcine stress syndrome, 573
Porphobilinogen, 279, 282f, 284f
Porphyrias, 274, 278, 283–287, 285f, 286f, 286t
Porphyrinogens, 281
    accumulation of in porphyria, 274, 278
Porphyrins, 279–280, 280f, 281f
    absorption spectra of, 282–283, 286f
    heme synthesis and, 279–282, 282f, 283f, 284f, 285f
    reduced, 281
    spectrophotometry in detection of, 282–283
Positive nitrogen balance, 487
Positive regulators, of gene expression, 380, 381t, 384, 386
Posttranslational processing, 30, 38–39, 39f, 378
    of collagen, 547, 547t
    in membrane assembly, 521
Posttranslational translocation, 507
Potassium, 504t
    in extracellular and intracellular fluid, 423, 423t
    permeability coefficient of, 426f
Power stroke, 570
PPI. *See* Peptidyl prolyl isomerase
PPi. *See* Pyrophosphate
PR. *See* Progesterone
Pravastatin, 238
PRE. *See* Progestin response element
Precursor proteins, amyloid, 599
Pregnancy
    estriol synthesis in, 450
    fatty liver of, 194
    hypoglycemia during, 175
    iron needs during, 594
Pregnancy toxemia of ewes (twin lamb disease)
    fatty liver and, 225
    ketosis in, 194
Pregnenolone, 448f
    in adrenal steroidogenesis, 446, 448f, 449f
    in testicular steroidogenesis, 450, 451f
Preinitiation complex, 350, 351, 358–359
    assembly of, 358–359
    in protein synthesis, 372, 373f
Prekallikrein, 607f, 608
Premenstrual syndrome, vitamin B_6 in management of, sensory neuropathy and, 499

Prenatal diagnosis, recombinant DNA technology in, 415
Preprocollagen, 547
Preprohormone, insulin synthesized as, 457, 458f
Preproparathyroid hormone (preproPTH), 457, 459f
Preproprotein, albumin synthesized as, 591
Preproteins, 506, 589
Presequence. *See* Signal peptide
Preventive medicine, biochemical research affecting, 2
Primaquine-sensitive hemolytic anemia, 621
Primary structure, 21–29, 30. *See* Protein sequencing
    amino acid sequence determining, 18–19
    Edman reaction in determination of, 25–26, 27f
    genomics in analysis of, 28
    molecular biology in determination of, 26
    of polynucleotides, 299–300
    proteomics and, 28–29
    Sanger's technique in determination of, 25
Primary transcript, 349
Primases, DNA, 334, 335–336, 335f, 336t
Primosome, 336, 420
Prion diseases (transmissible spongiform encephalopathies), 37–38
Prion-related protein (PrP), 38
Prions, 37–38
Pro-opiomelanocortin (POMC) peptide family, 459–461, 460f. *See also* specific type
Pro-oxidants, 621. *See also* Free radicals
Proaccelerin (factor V), 608t, 609, 609f
Proaminopeptidase, 485
Probes, 409, 420. *See also* DNA probes
Procarcinogens, 633
Processivity, DNA polymerase, 336
Prochymotrypsin, activation of, 78, 78f
Procollagen, 378, 504, 547
Procollagen aminoproteinase, 547
Procollagen carboxyproteinase, 547
Procollagen N-proteinase, disease caused by deficiency of, 548t
Proconvertin (factor VII), 607f, 608t, 609
    coumarin drugs affecting, 612
Prodrugs, 72, 633
    metabolic transformation of, 72
Products, 49
Proelastase, 485
Proenzymes, 77
    rapid response to physiologic demand and, 78
Profiling, protein, RNA transcript and, 417–419
Progesterone, 447f, 448f
    binding of, 462t, 463
    receptors for, 478
    synthesis of, 446, 450, 453f

Progestin response element, 467t
Progestins, binding of, 463
Prohormones, 378
Proinsulin, 457, 458f
Prokaryotic gene expression. *See also* Gene expression
    eukaryotic gene expression compared with, 396–400, 398t
    as model for study, 381
    unique features of, 381–382
Prolactin, 445
    localization of gene for, 413t
    receptor for, 444
Proline, 16t
    accumulation of (hyperprolinemia), 254
    catabolism of, 254, 256f
    metabolism of, 272f
    synthesis of, 241, 243f
Proline-*cis*, *trans*-isomerase, protein folding and, 37, 37f
Proline dehydrogenase, block of proline catabolism at, 254
Proline hydroxylase, vitamin C as coenzyme for, 504
Prolyl hydroxylase reaction, 242, 244f, 545
Promoter recognition specificity, 350
Promoters, in transcription, 349, 349f
    alternative use of in regulation, 362, 363f, 399
    bacterial, 352–353, 353f
    eukaryotic, 353–356, 354f, 355f, 356f, 389
Promoter site, in operon model, 383, 383f
Proofreading, DNA polymerase, 336
Proparathyroid hormone (proPTH), 457, 458f
Propionate
    blood glucose and, 172
    in gluconeogenesis, 168f, 169
    metabolism of, 169, 169f
Propionic acid, 122t
Propionyl-CoA
    fatty acid oxidation yielding, 188
    methionine in formation of, 262, 266f
Propionyl-CoA carboxylase, 169, 169f
Proproteins, 38, 77, 378
Propyl gallate, as antioxidant/food preservative, 128
Prostacyclins, 122
    clinical significance of, 206–207
    clotting/thrombosis affected by, 615, 615t
Prostaglandin E_2, 122, 123f
Prostaglandin H synthase, 204
Prostaglandins, 122, 123f, 196, 204
    cyclooxygenase pathway in synthesis of, 204–205, 205f, 206f
Prostanoids, 122, 129
    clinical significance of, 206–207
    cyclooxygenase pathway in synthesis of, 204–205, 205f, 206f
Prosthetic groups, 50
    in catalysis, 50, 51f

Protamine, 611
Proteases/proteinases, 7, 485, 631t. *See also* specific type
    in cartilage, 563
    as catalytically inactive proenzymes, 77–78
    mucin resistance to, 529
    of neutrophils, 631, 631t
    in protein degradation, 246, 247f, 485
Proteasomes, misfolded proteins in, 516–517
    ubiquination in, 517–518, 517f
Protein. *See also* specific proteins
    life cycle of, 22f
    translocation of, 22f
Protein 4.1, in red cell membranes, 623f, 624, 624t
Protein C, in blood coagulation, 608t, 611
Protein degradation, ubiquitin in, 517–518, 517f
Protein disulfide isomerase, protein folding and, 37, 516
Protein-DNA interactions, bacteriophage lambda as paradigm for, 384–387, 385f, 386f, 387f, 388f
Protein folding, 22f, 36–37, 37f
    after denaturation, 37
    chaperones and, 507, 515–516, 516t
    misfolding in, 516–517
        endoplasmic reticulum–associated degradation of, 516–517, 517f
        ubiquination in, 517–518, 517f
Protein kinase A (PKA), 467, 470f
Protein kinase B (PKB), in insulin signal transmission, 473, 474f
Protein kinase C (PKC)
    in calcium-dependent signal transduction, 471, 472f
    in platelet activation, 614, 614f
Protein kinase D1, in insulin signal transmission, 473, 474f
Protein kinase-phosphatase cascade, as second messenger, 445, 445t
Protein kinases, 78
    in cAMP-dependent signal transduction, 467–468, 470f
    in cGMP-dependent signal transduction, 471
    DNA-dependent, in double-strand break repair, 346
    in glycogen metabolism, 162, 163f, 164, 165f
    in hormonal regulation, 444, 472–475
        of lipolysis, 227, 228f
    in initiation of protein synthesis, 372
    in insulin signal transmission, 472–475, 474f
    in Jak/STAT pathway, 473–475, 475f
    in protein phosphorylation, 78–81, 79f, 80f
Protein-losing gastroenteropathy, 590

Protein misfolding
    accumulation in endoplasmic reticulum in, 516
    endoplasmic reticulum–associated degradation of, 516–517, 517f
    ubiquination in, 517, 517f
Protein phosphatase-1, 162, 163f, 164, 165f
Protein phosphatases, 78–81, 80f. *See also* Phosphatases
Protein phosphorylation. *See* Phosphorylation, protein
Protein profiling, RNA transcript and, 417–419
Protein-RNA complexes, in initiation, 371–372, 373f
Protein S, in blood coagulation, 608t, 611
Protein sequencing
    Edman reaction in, 25–26, 27f
    genomics and, 28
    mass spectrometry in, 26–28, 27f, 27t
    molecular biology in, 26
    peptide purification for, 21–24
    polypeptide cleavage and, 25–26
    proteomics and, 28–29
    purification for, 21–24, 24f, 25f, 26f
    Sanger's method of, 25
Protein sorting, 506–522
    chaperones and, 515–516, 516t
    cotranslational insertion and, 513–514, 514f
    disorders due to mutations in genes encoding, 521–522, 522t
    Golgi apparatus in, 506, 508f, 514–515, 518
    importins and exportins in, 509–511, 510f
    KDEL amino acid sequence and, 514, 515t
    membrane assembly and, 520–522, 521f, 521t
    mitochondria in, 507–509, 509f
    peroxisomes/peroxisome disorders and, 511, 511t
    protein destination and, 515, 515f, 515t
    retrograde transport and, 514–515
    signal hypothesis of polyribosome binding and, 511–513, 512t, 513f
    signal sequences and, 507, 507f
    transport vesicles and, 518–520, 518t, 519f
    unfolded protein response in, 516
Protein structure
    primary, 21–29. *See also* Primary structure
    quaternary, 31, 34, 35f
        of hemoglobins, allosteric properties and, 43–46
        stabilizing factors and, 34–35
    secondary, 30–33, 32f, 33f, 34f
        peptide bonds affecting, 31, 31f
        supersecondary, 32
    tertiary, 31, 33, 35f
        stabilizing factors and, 34–35

Protein synthesis
    amino acids in, 134, 135f
    on ribosomes, 22f
Protein turnover, 75, 246
    membranes affecting, 521
    rate of enzyme degradation and, 75
Proteinases. *See* Proteases/proteinases
Proteins. *See also* specific type and Peptides
    acute phase, 590–591, 591t
        negative, vitamin A as, 491
    L-amino acids in, 14–16
    asymmetry of, membrane assembly and, 520–521, 521f
    binding, 461t, 462–463, 462t
    catabolism of, 246–252
    classification of, 30
    configuration of, 30
    conformation of, 30
        peptide bonds affecting, 19–20
    core, 551, 552
        in glycosaminoglycan synthesis, 552–553
    degradation of, to amino acids, 246, 247f
    denaturation of
        protein refolding and, 37
        temperature and, 64
    dietary
        digestion and absorption of, 485
        metabolism of, in fed state, 140
        requirements for, 487–488
    dimeric, 34
    domains of, 33
    in extracellular and intracellular fluid, 423, 423t
    fibrous, 30
        collagen as, 38
    function of, bioinformatics in identification of, 29
    fusion, in enzyme study, 58–59, 59f
    globular, 30
    Golgi apparatus in glycosylation and sorting of, 518
    import of, by mitochondria, 507–509, 509t
    loss of in trauma/infection, 487–488
    in membranes, 426, 426t, 523. *See also* Glycoproteins; Membrane proteins
    ratio of to lipids, 423, 423f
    modular principles in construction of, 30, 36–37
    monomeric, 34
    phosphorylation of, 77, 78–79, 79f, 79t. *See also* Phosphorylation
    posttranslational modification of, 30, 38–39, 39f, 378
    purification of, 21–24
    receptors as, 438, 444
    soluble, 30
    structure of, 31–36
        diseases associated with disorders of, 37–38
        folding and, 36–37, 37f

Proteins—*continued*
    higher orders of, 30–39
    molecular modeling and, 36
    nuclear magnetic resonance spectros-
        copy in analysis of, 36
    primary, 21–29, 30. *See also* Primary
        structure
    prion diseases associated with alter-
        ation of, 37 38
    quaternary, 31, 34, 35f
    secondary, 30–33, 31f, 32f, 33f, 34f
    supersecondary, 32
    tertiary, 31, 33, 35f
    x-ray crystallography in analysis of, 35
    synthesis of, 140, 365–379. *See also* Pro-
        tein sorting
      elongation in, 374–376, 375f
      environmental threats affecting, 376
      in fed state, 140
      genetic code/RNA and, 314–315,
        317t, 366–367. *See also*
        Genetic code
      inhibition of by antibiotics, 378–379,
        379f
      initiation of, 371–372, 373f, 374f
      by mitochondria, 507–509, 509t
      modular principles in, 30, 36 37
      polysomes in, 376, 506, 507f
      posttranslational processing and, 378
      recognition and attachment (charg-
        ing) in, 367, 367f
      recombinant DNA techniques for,
        412–413
      reticulocytes in, 619
      in ribosomes, 137f, 138
      termination of, 376, 377f
      translocation and, 375–376
      viruses affecting, 376, 378f
    transmembrane
      ion channels as, 431, 432f, 432t
      in red cells, 623–624, 623f, 624t
    transport, 461t, 462–463, 462t
    xenobiotic cell injury and, 638
Proteoglycans, 118, 545, 547, 551–552,
      552f, 556–558. *See also* Gly-
      cosaminoglycans
    in bone, 558t
    carbohydrates in, 551, 552, 552f
    in cartilage, 561–563
    disease associations and, 557–558
    functions of, 556–558, 557t
    galactose in synthesis of, 181–183, 184f
    link trisaccharide in, 528
Proteolysis
    in covalent modification, 77, 78f
    in prochymotrypsin activation, 78, 78f
Proteolytic cleavage, 22f
Proteome/proteomics, 28–29, 420
    plasma, 588
Prothrombin (factor II), 608t, 609–610, 609f
    activation of, 609
    coumarin drugs affecting, 495, 612
    in vitamin K deficiency, 495

Prothrombin to thrombin activation, by fac-
      tor Xa, 609–610
Proton acceptors, bases as, 9
Proton donors, acids as, 9
Proton motive force, 105
Proton pumps, 105
    respiratory chain as, 100
Proton-translocating transhydrogenase, 109
Protons, transport of, by hemoglobin,
      44–45, 46f
Protoporphyrin, 279, 281f
    incorporation of iron into, 280–281,
      281f
Protoporphyrin III, 280, 285f
Protoporphyrinogen III, 280, 285f
Protoporphyrinogen oxidase, 280, 284f,
      285f
Provitamin A carotenoids, 490–491
Proximal histidine (histidine F8)
    in oxygen binding, 40, 42f
    replacement of in hemoglobin M, 46–47
Proximity, catalysis by, 50
PrP (prion-related protein), 38
PRPP
    in purine synthesis, 302, 303f
    in pyrimidine synthesis, 304, 305, 306f,
      307
PRPP glutamyl amidotransferase, 302,
      303f
PRPP synthetase, defect in, gout caused by,
      307
Pseudo-Hurler polydystrophy, 541, 555,
      556t
Pseudogenes, 333, 420
Pseudomonas aeruginosa infection, in cystic
      fibrosis, 542
Psi angle, 31, 31f
PstI, 405t
PstI site, insertion of DNA at, 407, 408f
PTA. *See* Plasma thromboplastin antecedent
PTC. *See* Plasma thromboplastin compo-
      nent
Pteroylglutamic acid. *See* Folic acid
PTH. *See* Parathyroid hormone
PTSs. *See* Peroxisomal-matrix targeting
      sequences
PubMed, 82
"Puffs," polytene chromosome, 326, 326f
Pumps, 422
    in active transport, 435, 435f
Purification, protein/peptide, 21 24
Purine nucleoside phosphorylase deficiency,
      308
Purines/purine nucleotides, 294–298, 294f,
      297f
    dietary nonessential, 301
    metabolism of, 301–309
      disorders of, 307–308
      gout as, 307
      uric acid formation and, 307, 307f
    synthesis of, 301–302, 302f, 303f, 304f,
      305f
      catalysts in, 301, 302f

pyrimidine synthesis coordinated
      with, 307
    "salvage" reactions in, 302, 303f, 305f
    ultraviolet light absorbed by, 298
Puromycin, 378, 379f
Putrescine, in polyamine synthesis, 273f
Pyranose ring structures, 113–114, 113f,
      114f
Pyridoxal phosphate, 50, 498–499, 499f
    in heme synthesis, 279
    in urea biosynthesis, 247
Pyridoxine/pyridoxal/pyridoxamine (vitamin
      B$_6$), 490t, 498–499, 499f
    deficiency of, 490t, 499
    xanthurenate excretion in, 262, 265f
    excess/toxicity of, 499
Pyrimethamine, 501
Pyrimidine analogs, in pyrimidine nucle-
      otide biosynthesis, 305
Pyrimidines/pyrimidine nucleotides,
      294–298, 294f, 297f
    dietary nonessential, 301
    metabolism of, 301–309, 308f
      diseases caused by catabolite overpro-
        duction and, 309
      water-soluble metabolites and,
        308 309, 308f
    precursors of, deficiency of, 309
    synthesis of, 294–298, 306f
      catalysts in, 304
      purine synthesis coordinated with, 307
      regulation of, 305–307, 306f
    ultraviolet light absorbed by, 298
Pyrophosphatase, inorganic
    in fatty acid activation, 92, 187
    in glycogen biosynthesis, 159, 160f
Pyrophosphate
    free energy of hydrolysis of, 90t
    inorganic, 92, 93f
Pyrrole, 40, 42f
Pyruvate, 133
    formation of, in amino acid carbon skele-
      ton catabolism, 254–257,
      257f–260f
    in gluconeogenesis, 139
    oxidation of, 148–149, 150f, 155–157,
      156f, 157f, 158t. *See also*
      Acetyl-CoA; Glycolysis
    clinical aspects of, 157–158
    enzymes in, 170t
    gluconeogenesis and, 167, 168f
Pyruvate carboxylase, 148, 149f, 170t
    in gluconeogenesis regulation, 148, 149f,
      167, 170t
Pyruvate dehydrogenase, 148–149, 150f,
      155, 156f, 170t
    deficiency of, 157
    regulation of, 155–156, 157f
      acetyl-CoA in, 155–156
      acyl-CoA in, 157f, 201
    thiamin diphosphate as coenzyme for,
      496
Pyruvate dehydrogenase complex, 155

Pyruvate kinase, 170t
  deficiency of, 157, 627
  gluconeogenesis regulation and, 169–170
  in glycolysis, 152, 153f, 170t
    regulation and, 154

Q cycle, 100, 103f, 104, 104f
Q-cytochrome, 100, 102f, 103f, 104
Q_{10} (temperature coefficient), enzyme-catalyzed reactions and, 64–65
QT interval, congenitally long, 439t
Quaternary structure, 31, 34, 35f
  of hemoglobins, allosteric properties and, 43–46
  stabilizing factors and, 34–35

R groups, amino acid properties affected by, 18, 18t
  pK/pK_a, 18
R (relaxed) state, of hemoglobin, oxygenation and, 44, 44f, 45f
Rab protein family, 520
RAC3 coactivator, 479, 480t
Radiation, nucleotide excision-repair of DNA damage caused by, 345
Ran protein, 509, 510f, 511
Rancidity, peroxidation causing, 128
Rapamycin, mammalian target of (mTOR), in insulin signal transmission, 473, 474f
RAR. See Retinoic acid receptor
RARE. See Retinoic acid response element
Rate constant, 63–64
  K_{eq} as ratio of, 63–64
Rate-limiting reaction, metabolism regulated by, 74
Rb protein. See Retinoblastoma protein
Reactant concentration, chemical reaction rate affected by, 63
Reactive oxygen species. See Free radicals
Rearrangements, DNA
  in antibody diversity, 333, 399, 602–603
  recombinant DNA technology in detection of, 413–414, 415t
recA, 386, 388f
Receptor-associated coactivator 3 (RAC3 coactivator), 479, 480t
Receptor-effector coupling, 443–444
Receptor-mediated endocytosis, 437–438, 437f
Receptors, 438, 444. See also specific type
  activation of in signal generation, 464–465, 466f
  nuclear, 444, 477–478, 479f, 479t
Recognition domains, on hormone receptors, 443
Recombinant DNA/recombinant DNA technology, 402–419
  base pairing and, 402–403

blotting techniques in, 409–410, 409f
chimeric molecules in, 403–406
cloning in, 406–408, 407f, 408f, 408t
definition of, 420
DNA ligase in, 405–406
DNA sequencing in, 410, 411f
double helix structure and, 402, 403
in enzyme study, 58–59, 59f
gene mapping and, 411–412, 413t
in genetic disease diagnosis, 413–417, 414f, 415t, 416f, 417f
hybridization techniques in, 409–410
libraries and, 408–409
oligonucleotide synthesis in, 410
organization of DNA into genes and, 403, 404f, 405t
polymerase chain reaction in, 410–411, 412f
practical applications of, 411–419
restriction enzymes and, 403–406, 405t, 406f, 406t, 407f
terminology used in, 419–421
transcription and, 403, 404f
Recombinant erythropoietin (epoetin alfa/EPO), 535, 618
Recombinant fusion proteins, in enzyme study, 58–59, 59f
Recombination, chromosomal, 331, 331f, 332f
Recruitment hypothesis, of preinitiation complex formation, 358
Red blood cells, 617–618, 619–625. See also Erythrocytes
Red thrombus, 606
Red (slow) twitch fibers, 583, 583t
Redox (oxidation-reduction) potential, 94, 95t
Redox state, 190
Reduced porphyrins, 281
Reducing equivalents
  in citric acid cycle, 145–148, 147f
  in mitochondria, 100, 101f
  in pentose phosphate pathway, 180
Reduction, definition of, 94
Reductive activation, of molecular oxygen, 634
Refsum's disease, 194, 511, 511t
Regional asymmetries, membrane, 427
Regulated secretion, 506
Regulatory proteins, binding of to DNA, motifs for, 393–396, 394t, 395f, 396f, 397f
Regurgitation hyperbilirubinemia, 290
Relaxation phase
  of skeletal muscle contraction, 570, 572
  of smooth muscle contraction
    calcium in, 579
    nitric oxide in, 580–581, 581f
Relaxed (R) state, of hemoglobin, oxygenation and, 44, 44f, 45f
Releasing factors (RF1/RF3), in protein synthesis termination, 376, 377f

Remnant removal disease, 239t
Renal glomerulus, laminin in basal lamina of, 550–551
Renal threshold for glucose, 174–175
Renaturation, DNA, base pair matching and, 313–314
Renin, 458, 460f
Renin-angiotensin system, 458–459, 460f
Repeat sequences
  amino acid, 528–529, 529f
  short interspersed (SINEs), 329, 420
Repetitive-sequence DNA, 328, 329
Replication bubbles, 338–339, 339f, 340f, 341f
Replication fork, 334–336, 335f
Replication/synthesis. See DNA; RNA
Reporter genes, 391, 393f, 394f
Repression, enzyme
  enzyme synthesis control and, 75
  in gluconeogenesis regulation, 169
Repressor protein/gene, lambda (cI), 384–387, 386f, 387f, 388f
Repressors, 355
  in gene expression, 380, 382–383, 384, 391
  tissue-specific expression and, 391
Reproduction, prostaglandins in, 196
Residues, peptide, 19
Respiration, oxygen for, 94
Respiratory burst, 487, 630
Respiratory chain, 100–107. See also Oxidative phosphorylation
  chemiosmotic theory on respiratory control and uncouplers in, 107, 107f
  clinical aspects of, 110
  complex I and II in, 100, 101–102, 102f, 103f
  complex III (Q cycle) in, 100, 104, 104f
  complex IV in, 100, 103f, 104–105
  dehydrogenases in, 95
  energy captured in catabolism from, 91f, 105–106, 158t
  exchange transporters in, 107–110, 108f–110f
  flavoproteins and iron-sulfur proteins in, 100–101
  in mitochondria, 101f
  mitochondrial protein complexes in, 95t, 100, 102f, 103f
  NADH-Q oxidoreductase as electron acceptor in, 101–102, 103f, 147f
  oxidation of reducing equivalents in, 100, 101f
  oxidative phosphorylation at, 106, 158t
  poison inhibition of, 107, 107f
  protein gradient driving ATP synthesis from electron transport in, 105, 105f, 106f
  as proton pump, 100
  substrates for, citric acid cycle providing, 146, 146f

Respiratory control, 89, 149–150
    ATP supply from, 106–107, 106t
    chemiosmotic theory on, 107, 107f
Respiratory distress syndrome, surfactant
            deficiency causing, 125, 214
Restriction endonucleases/enzymes, 321,
            403–406, 405t, 406f, 420
    in recombinant DNA technology,
            405–406, 405t, 406f, 406t,
            407f
Restriction enzymes. *See* Restriction endo-
            nucleases/enzymes
Restriction fragment length polymor-
            phisms (RFLPs), 58, 415,
            417f
    in forensic medicine, 416
Restriction map, 404
Retention hyperbilirubinemia, 290
Reticulocytes, in protein synthesis, 619
Retina
    gyrate atrophy of, 254
    retinaldehyde in, 491, 492f
Retinal. *See* Retinol
Retinaldehyde, 490, 491f
Retinitis pigmentosa, essential fatty acid
            deficiency and, 203
Retinoblastoma protein, 342
Retinoic acid, 490, 491f. *See also* Retinol
    functions of, 491
    receptors for, 478, 491
Retinoic acid receptor (RAR), 478, 491
Retinoic acid response element, 467t
Retinoid X receptor (RXR), 477, 478, 478f,
            491
Retinoids, 490–491, 491f, 492f. *See also*
            Retinol
Retinol, 490, 490t, 491f, 492f. *See also* Vita-
            min A
    deficiency of, 490t
    functions of, 490t, 491, 492f
Retinol-binding protein, 591t
Retrograde strand, in DNA replication, 335
Retrograde transport, 513, 519
    from Golgi apparatus, 514–515
    of misfolded proteins, 516
Retroposons/retrotransposons, 329
Retroviruses, reverse transcriptases in, 316,
            340
Reverse cholesterol transport, 222, 223f,
            230, 235
Reverse transcriptase/reverse transcription,
            316, 340, 420
    in recombinant DNA technology, 406t
Reversed-phase high-pressure chromatogra-
            phy, for protein/peptide
            purification, 24
Reversible covalent modifications, 78–79,
            79f, 79t. *See also* Phosphory-
            lation
Reye's syndrome, orotic aciduria in, 309
RFLPs. *See* Restriction fragment length
            polymorphisms
RFs. *See* Releasing factors

Rheumatoid arthritis
    extracellular matrix in, 545
    glycosylation alterations in, 540
Rho-dependent termination signals,
            352–353, 353f
Rhodopsin, 491, 492f
Riboflavin (vitamin B$_2$), 94, 490t, 497–498
    in citric acid cycle, 148
    coenzymes derived from, 50, 497
    deficiency of, 490t, 497
    dehydrogenases dependent on, 95
Ribonucleases, 321
Ribonucleic acid. *See* RNA
Ribonucleoside diphosphates (NDPs),
            reduction of, 302, 305f
Ribonucleosides, 294, 295f
Ribonucleotide reductase complex, 302,
            305f
Ribose, 112
    in nucleosides, 294, 295f
    pentose phosphate pathway in produc-
            tion of, 133, 177, 180
D-Ribose, 115f, 115t, 294
Ribose 5-phosphate, in purine synthesis,
            301–302, 303f
Ribose 5-phosphate ketoisomerase,
            177–180, 179f
Ribose phosphate, pentose phosphate path-
            way in production of,
            177–180, 178f
Ribosomal dissociation, in protein synthe-
            sis, 372, 373f
Ribosomal RNA (rRNA), 315, 318, 348,
            349t. *See also* RNA
    as peptidyltransferase, 374–375, 375t
    processing of, 362
Ribosomes, 318, 320t
    bacterial, 378
    protein synthesis in, 22f, 137f, 138
    dissociation and, 376
Ribozymes, 315, 318, 364
D-Ribulose, 115t, 116f
Ribulose 5-phosphate 3-epimerase, 177,
            179f
Richner-Hanart syndrome, 257
Ricin, 379, 527t
Rickets, 490t, 492, 561t
Rieske Fe-S, 104
Right operator, 384–387, 386f, 388f
Rigor mortis, 570, 573
RNA, 311, 314–320, 348–364
    as catalyst, 364
    in chromatin, 322
    classes/species of, 315–316, 317t, 348,
            349t
    complementarity of, 314, 317f
    heterogeneous nuclear (hnRNA), 318
        gene regulation and, 362
    messenger (mRNA), 315, 316–318,
            318f, 319f, 348, 349t, 366
        alternative splicing and, 362, 362f,
            399
        codon assignments in, 365–366, 366t

    editing of, 363
    modification of, 363
    nucleotide sequence of, 365–366
        mutations caused by changes in,
            368–370, 368f, 369f, 371f
    polycistronic, 382
    recombinant DNA technology and,
            403
    relationship of to chromosomal DNA,
            329f
    stability of, regulation of gene expres-
            sion and, 399–400, 400f
    variations in size/complexity of, 403,
            405t
    micro (mi) and small interfering (si),
            320
    modification of, 363
    processing of, 359–362
        alternative, in regulation of gene
            expression, 362, 363f, 399
    in protein synthesis, 315–316, 317t
    ribosomal (rRNA), 315, 318, 348, 349t
        as peptidyltransferase, 374–375, 375t
        processing of, 362
    silencing, 420
    small, 318–320
    small nuclear (snRNA), 316, 317t,
            319–320, 348, 349t, 420
    splicing, 359–362, 420
        alternative, in regulation of gene
            expression, 362, 362f, 399
        recombinant DNA technology and,
            403, 404f
    structure of, 314–320, 316f, 317f, 319f,
            320f
    synthesis of, 312, 348–364
        initiation/elongation/termination in,
            349–350, 349f, 350f,
            351–352
    transfer (tRNA), 315, 318, 320f, 348,
            349t, 367–368, 368f
        aminoacyl, in protein synthesis, 374
        anticodon region of, 366
        processing and modification of, 362,
            364
        suppressor, 370
    xenobiotic cell injury and, 638
RNA editing, 363
RNA polymerase III, 351t
RNA polymerases, DNA-dependent, in
            RNA synthesis, 349–351,
            349f, 351t
RNA primer, in DNA synthesis, 336, 337f,
            338f
RNA probes, 409, 420
RNA-RNA duplexes, imperfect, 320
RNA-RNA hybrids, 320
RNA transcript, and protein profiling,
            417–419
RNAP. *See* RNA polymerases
RNase. *See* Ribonucleases
ROS (reactive oxygen species). *See* Free radi-
            cals

Rotor syndrome, 292
Rough endoplasmic reticulum
	glycosylation in, 533–535, 534f
	in protein sorting, 506, 507f, 508f
	protein synthesis and, 376
	routes of protein insertion into,
		513–515, 514f
	signal hypothesis of polyribosome
		binding to, 511–513, 512t,
		513f
rRNA. *See* Ribosomal RNA
RT-PCR, 420
RXR. *See* Retinoid X receptor
Ryanodine, 572
Ryanodine receptor, 572, 572f
	mutations in gene for, diseases caused by,
		573–574, 574f, 637t
RYR. *See* Ryanodine receptor

S phase of cell cycle, DNA synthesis during,
		341–343, 341f, 342t
S_{50}, 68
Saccharopine, in lysine catabolism, 262,
		263f
Salt (electrostatic) bonds (salt bridges/link-
		ages), 7
	oxygen binding rupturing, Bohr effect
		protons and, 45, 46f
"Salvage" reactions
	in purine synthesis, 302, 303f, 305f
	in pyrimidine synthesis, 304
Sanfilippo syndrome, 556t
Sanger's method
	for DNA sequencing, 410, 411f
	for polypeptide sequencing, 25
Sanger's reagent (1-fluoro-2,4-dinitro-ben-
		zene), for polypeptide
		sequencing, 25
Sarcolemma, 565
Sarcomere, 565, 566f
Sarcoplasm, 565
	of cardiac muscle, 575
Sarcoplasmic reticulum, calcium level in
		skeletal muscle and,
		571–573, 572f
Saturated fatty acids, 121, 122, 122t
	in membranes, 424, 425f
Saturation kinetics, 65f, 67
	sigmoid substrate, Hill equation in evalu-
		ation of, 67–68, 68f
Scavenger receptor B_1, 221, 223f
Scheie syndrome, 556t
Schindler disease, 541, 542t
Scrapie, 38
Screening conditions, drug, enzyme kinetics
		on, 71–72
Scurvy, 490t, 504
	collagen affected in, 39, 504, 548
SDS-PAGE. *See* Sodium dodecyl sulfate-
		polyacrylamide gel electro-
		phoresis
Se gene, 626

Sec1 proteins, 520
Sec61p complex, 512
Second messengers, 77, 444–445, 445t,
		465–476, 469t, 471t. *See also*
		specific type
	calcium as, 444–445, 445t, 465
	cAMP as, 161, 444, 445t, 465,
		466–470, 468t, 470f
	cGMP as, 298, 444, 445t, 465, 470
	diacylglycerol as, 471, 473f
	inositol trisphosphate as, 471–472, 472f,
		473f
	precursors of
		phosphatidylinositol as, 125, 125f
		phospholipids as, 209
Secondary structure, 30–33, 32f, 33f, 34f
	peptide bonds affecting, 31, 31f
	supersecondary, 32
Secretor (Se) gene, 626
Secretory component, of IgA, 603f
Secretory granules, protein entry into, 515,
		515f
Secretory (exocytotic) pathway, 506
Secretory proteins, 512
Secretory vesicles, 506, 508f
D-Sedoheptulose, 116f
L-Selectin, 538f, 538t
Selectins, 537–538, 538f, 538t, 539f
Selectivity filter, 432–433
Selectivity/selective permeability, mem-
		brane, 422, 430–431, 430t,
		431f, 432f, 432t
Selenium, 504t
	in glutathione peroxidase, 96, 180
Selenocysteine, synthesis of, 243–244, 244f
Selenophosphate synthetase/synthase, 244,
		244f
Self-assembly
	in collagen synthesis, 547
	of lipid bilayer, 425
Self-association, hydrophobic interactions
		and, 6–7
Sensory neuropathy, in vitamin B_6 excess,
		499
Sepharose-lectin column chromatography,
		in glycoprotein analysis, 525t
Sequential displacement reactions, 70, 70f
Serine, 15t
	catabolism of, pyruvate formation and,
		257, 257f
	conserved residues and, 55, 55t
	in cysteine and homoserine synthesis,
		242, 244f
	in glycine synthesis, 241, 243f
	phosphorylated, 271
	synthesis of, 241, 243f
	tetrahydrofolate and, 500, 501f
Serine 195, in covalent catalysis, 53, 54f
Serine hydroxymethyltransferase, 257, 257f,
		500
Serine protease inhibitor, 597
Serine proteases. *See also* specific type
	conserved residues and, 55, 55t

	in covalent catalysis, 53, 54f
	zymogens of, in blood coagulation, 608,
		608t, 609
Serotonin, 272, 628t
	biosynthesis and metabolism of, 275f
Serpin, 597
Serum complement, 433
Serum prothrombin conversion accelerator
		(SPCA/factor VII), 607f,
		608t, 609
	coumarin drugs affecting, 612
Sex (gender), xenobiotic-metabolizing
		enzymes affected by, 637
Sex hormone-binding globulin (testoster-
		one-estrogen-binding globu-
		lin), 462–463, 462t, 591t
SGLT 1 transporter protein, 483, 483f
SGOT. *See* Aspartate aminotransferase
SGPT. *See* Alanine aminotransferase
SH2 domains. *See* Src homology 2 (SH2)
		domains
SHBG. *See* Sex hormone-binding globulin
Short interspersed repeat sequences
		(SINEs), 329, 420
Shoshin beriberi, 496
SI nuclease, in recombinant DNA technol-
		ogy, 406t
si RNAs, 320
Sialic acids, 119, 120f, 126, 183, 185f
	in gangliosides, 185f, 213, 215f
	in glycoproteins, 119t, 526t
Sialidosis, 541, 542t, 555, 556t
Sialoprotein, bone, 558t, 559
Sialyl-Lewis^x, selectins binding, 538, 539f
Sialylated oligosaccharides, selectins bind-
		ing, 538
Sickle cell disease, 369–370, 627
	pedigree analysis of, 415, 416f
	recombinant DNA technology in detec-
		tion of, 413
Side chain cleavage enzyme P450 (P450scc),
		446, 448f, 450
Side chains, in porphyrins, 279, 280f
Sigmoid substrate saturation kinetics, Hill
		equation in evaluation of,
		67–68, 68f
Signal. *See also* Signal peptide
	generation of, 464–465, 466f, 467f, 467t
	in recombinant DNA technology, 420
	transmission of. *See also* Signal transduc-
		tion
	across membrane, 422, 438
Signal hypothesis, of polyribosome binding,
		511–513, 512t, 513f
Signal peptidase, 512, 513f
Signal peptide, 506, 511–512, 515t
	albumin, 591
	in protein sorting, 507, 507f, 508f,
		511–512, 513f
	in proteins destined for Golgi apparatus
		membrane, 518
Signal recognition particle, 512
Signal sequence. *See* Signal peptide

Signal transducers and activators of transcription (STATs), 475, 475f
Signal transduction, 464–480
  GPI-anchors in, 537
  hormone response to stimulus and, 464, 465f
  intracellular messengers in, 465–476, 469t, 471t. *See also* specific type
  in platelet activation, 614, 614f
  signal generation and, 464–465, 466f, 467f, 467t
  transcription modulation and, 476–480, 478f, 479f, 479t
Silencers, 355
  recombinant DNA technology and, 403
Silencing mediator for RXR and TR (SMRT), 480, 480t
Silencing sRNA, 420
Silent mutations, 368
Silicon, 504t
Simple diffusion, 430, 430t, 431f
Simvastatin, 238
SINEs. *See* Short interspersed repeat sequences
Single displacement reactions, 70, 70f
Single molecule enzymology, 55, 55f
Single nucleotide polymorphism (SNP), 85, 420
Single-pass membrane proteins, glycophorins as, 623–624, 623f, 624t
Single-stranded DNA, replication from, 334. *See also* DNA
Single-stranded DNA-binding proteins (SSBs), 334–335, 335f, 336t
siRNA-miRNA complexes, 320
Sister chromatid exchanges, 333, 333f
Sister chromatids, 326, 327f
Site-directed mutagenesis, in enzyme study, 59
Site-specific DNA methylases, 403
Site specific integration, 331–332
Size exclusion chromatography, for protein/peptide purification, 21–22, 24f
SK. *See* Streptokinase
Skeletal muscle, 565, 576t. *See also* Muscle; Muscle contraction
  glycogen stores in, 582
  metabolism in, 134–136, 135f
    lactate production and, 154
  as protein reserve, 584
  slow (red) and fast (white) twitch fibers in, 583, 583t
Skin
  essential fatty acid deficiency affecting, 206
  mutant keratins and, 586
  vitamin D_3 synthesis in, 453, 454f, 492, 492f
Sleep, prostaglandins in, 196
Sliding filament cross-bridge model, of muscle contraction, 566, 567f

Slow acetylators, 637
Slow-reacting substance of anaphylaxis, 208
Slow (red) twitch fibers, 583, 583t
Sly syndrome, 556t
Small interfering (si) RNAs, 320
Small intestine
  cytochrome P450 isoforms in, 634
  monosaccharide digestion in, 483, 483f
Small monomeric GTPases, 509
Small nuclear RNA (snRNA), 316, 317t, 319–320, 348, 349t, 420
Small nucleoprotein complex ("snurp"), 360
Small RNA, 318–320
Smoking
  CYP2A6 metabolism of nicotine and, 635
  cytochrome P450 induction and, 635
  on methionine, 597
  nucleotide excision-repair of DNA damage, 345
Smooth endoplasmic reticulum, cytochrome P450 isoforms in, 634
Smooth muscle, 565, 576t
  actin myosin interactions in, 580t
  contraction of
    calcium in, 579, 579f
    myosin-based regulation of, 579
    myosin light chain phosphorylation in, 579
  relaxation of
    calcium in, 579
    nitric oxide in, 580–581, 581f
SMRT, 480, 480t
SNAP 25, 520
SNAP (soluble NSF attachment factor) proteins, 519, 519f
SNARE proteins, 518–519, 519f, 520
SNAREpins, 520
SNP. *See* Single nucleotide polymorphism
snRNA. *See* Small nuclear RNA
"Snurp" (small nucleoprotein [snRNP] complex), 360
Sodium, 504t
  in extracellular and intracellular fluid, 423, 423t
  permeability coefficient of, 426f
Sodium-calcium exchanger, 471
Sodium dodecyl sulfate-polyacrylamide gel electrophoresis
  for protein/peptide purification, 24, 25f, 26f
  red cell membrane proteins determined by, 622–623, 623f
Sodium-potassium pump (Na^+-K^+ ATPase), 435, 435f
  in glucose transport, 436, 436f
Solubility point, of amino acids, 18
Soluble NSF attachment factor (SNAP) proteins, 519, 519f, 520
Solutions, aqueous, K_w of, 9
Solvent, water as, 5, 6f
Sorbitol, in diabetic cataract, 185–186

Sorbitol dehydrogenase, 181, 183f
Sorbitol intolerance, 186
Sorbitol (polyol) pathway, 185–186
Soret band, 282
Southern blot transfer procedure, 313–314, 409–410, 409f, 420
Southwestern blot transfer procedure, 410, 420
SPARC (bone) protein, 558t
Sparteine, CYP2D6 in metabolism of, 635
SPCA. *See* Serum prothrombin conversion accelerator
Specific acid/base catalysis, 51
Specificity, enzyme, 49, 50f
Spectrin, 622, 623f, 624, 624t
  abnormalities of, 625
Spectrometry
  covalent modifications detected by, 26–28, 27f, 27t
  for glycoprotein analysis, 524, 525t
Spectrophotometry
  for NAD(P)$^+$-dependent dehydrogenases, 56, 56f
  for porphyrins, 282–283
Spectroscopy, nuclear magnetic resonance (NMR)
  for glycoprotein analysis, 524, 525t
  protein structure demonstrated by, 36
Spermidine, synthesis of, 272, 273f
Spermine, synthesis of, 272, 273f
Spherocytosis, hereditary, 439t, 625, 625f
Sphingolipidoses, 214–215, 215t
Sphingolipids, 209
  metabolism of, 213–214, 214f, 215f
    clinical aspects of, 214–215, 215t
  in multiple sclerosis, 214
Sphingomyelins, 126, 126f, 213, 214f
  in membranes, 424
  membrane asymmetry and, 427
Sphingophospholipids, 121
Sphingosine, 126, 126f
Spina bifida, folic acid supplements in prevention of, 502
Spliceosome, 360, 420
Spongiform encephalopathies, transmissible (prion diseases), 38
Squalene
  in cholesterol synthesis, 230, 232f
  synthesis of, 233f
Squalene epoxidase, in cholesterol synthesis, 231, 233f
SR-B1. *See* Scavenger receptor B1
SRC-1 coactivator, 479, 480t
Src homology 2 (SH2) domains
  in insulin signal transmission, 473, 474f
  in Jak/STAT pathway, 475, 475f
SRP. *See* Signal recognition particle
SRP-R, 512
SRS-A. *See* Slow-reacting substance of anaphylaxis
ssDNA. *See* Single-stranded DNA
STAR. *See* Steroidogenic acute regulatory protein

Starch, 116, 118f
  glycemic index of, 482
  hydrolysis of, 482
Starling forces, 588
Starvation, 88
  clinical aspects of, 143
  fatty liver and, 225
  ketosis in, 194
  metabolic fuel mobilization in, 140–142,
      142f, 142t
  triacylglycerol redirection and, 220
Statin drugs, 238
STATs (signal transducers and activators of
      transcription), 475, 475f
Stearic acid, 122t
Steely hair disease (Menkes disease), 596–597
Stem cells, differentiation of to red blood
      cells, erythropoietin in regu-
      lation of, 618, 619f
Stereochemical (-sn-) numbering system,
      124, 125f
Stereoisomers. See also Isomerism
  of steroids, 127, 128f
Steroid nucleus, 126–127, 127f, 128f
Steroid receptor coactivator 1 (SRC-1 coac-
      tivator), 479, 480t
Steroid sulfates, 213
Steroidogenesis. See Steroids
Steroidogenic acute regulatory protein
      (StAR), 450
Steroids, 126–128, 127f, 128f, 129f. See also
      specific type
  adrenal. See also Glucocorticoids; Miner-
      alocorticoids
      synthesis of, 446–448, 448f, 449f
  receptors for, 444
  stereoisomers of, 127, 128f
  storage/secretion of, 461, 461t
  synthesis of, 134, 134f, 446–453, 447f,
      448f, 449f
  transport of, 462–463, 462t
Sterol 27-hydroxylase, 236
Sterols, 127
  in membranes, 424
Stickler syndrome, 563
Sticky end ligation/sticky-ended DNA, 404,
      406f, 407f, 442
"Sticky foot," 536
"Sticky patch," in hemoglobin S, 47, 47f
Stoichiometry, 61
Stokes radius, in size exclusion chromatog-
      raphy, 21–22
Stop codon, 376, 377f
Stop-transfer signal, 512, 513
Strain, catalysis by, 51–52
Streptokinase, 613, 613f
Streptomycin, 116
Striated muscle, 565, 566f. See also Cardiac
      muscle; Skeletal muscle
  actin-myosin interactions in, 580t
Strong acids, 9
Strong bases, 9
Structural proteins, 545

Stuart-Prower factor (factor X), 607f, 608,
      608t
  activation of, 607f, 608–609
  coumarin drugs affecting, 612
Substrate analogs, competitive inhibition by,
      68–69, 68f
Substrate level, phosphorylations at, 105f,
      106
Substrate shuttles, 109–110, 109f
  coenzymes as, 50
Substrate specificity, of cytochrome P450
      isoforms, 634
Substrates, 49
  competitive inhibitors resembling,
      68–69, 68f
  concentration of, enzyme-catalyzed reac-
      tion rate affected by, 65–66,
      65f, 66f
      Hill model of, 67–68, 68f
      Michaelis-Menten model of, 66–67,
      67f
  conformational changes in enzymes
      caused by, 52, 52f
  multiple, 70–71
Succinate, 146–148, 147f
Succinate dehydrogenase, 95, 147f, 148
  inhibition of, 68–69, 68f
Succinate Q reductase, 100, 101–102, 102f,
      103f
Succinate semialdehyde, 274, 277f
Succinate thiokinase (succinyl-CoA syn-
      thetase), 146, 147f
Succinic acid, pK/pK_a value of, 12t
Succinyl-CoA, in heme synthesis, 279–282,
      282f, 283f, 285f
Succinyl-CoA-acetoacetate-CoA transferase
      (thiophorase), 146,
      191–192, 193f
Succinyl-CoA synthetase (succinate thio-
      kinase), 146, 147f
Sucrase-isomaltase complex, 483
Sucrose, 116, 117f, 117t
  glycemic index of, 482
Sugars. See also Carbohydrates
  amino (hexosamines), 116, 116f
      glucose as precursor of, 183, 185f
      in glycosaminoglycans, 118, 183, 185f
      in glycosphingolipids, 183, 185f
      interrelationships in metabolism of,
      185f
  classification of, 112, 113t
  deoxy, 116, 116f
  "invert," 116
  isomerism of, 112–114, 113f, 114f
  nucleotide, in glycoprotein biosynthesis,
      525, 526t
"Suicide enzyme," cyclooxygenase as,
      204–205
Sulfate
  active (adenosine 3'-phosphate-5'-phos-
      phosulfate), 297, 297f, 636
  in glycoproteins, 524
  in mucins, 529

Sulfatide, 126
Sulfation, of xenobiotics, 636
Sulfo(galacto)-glycerolipids, 213
Sulfogalactosylceramide, 213
  accumulation of, 215
Sulfonamides, hemolytic anemia precipi-
      tated by, 621
Sulfonylurea drugs, 194
Sulfotransferases, in glycosaminoglycan syn-
      thesis, 553
Sunlight. See Ultraviolet light
Supercoils, DNA, 314, 340, 341f
Superoxide anion free radical, 97–98, 620,
      620t. See also Free radicals
  production of in respiratory burst, 630
Superoxide dismutase, 98, 129, 620, 620t,
      630
Supersecondary structures, 32
Suppressor mutations, 370
Suppressor tRNA, 370
Surfactant, 125, 209
  deficiency of, 125, 214
Swainsonine, 536, 536t
Symport systems, 434, 434f
Syn conformers, 295, 295f
Synaptobrevin, 520
Syntaxin, 520

T lymphocytes, 599
t-PA. See Tissue plasminogen activator
t-SNARE proteins, 518, 520
T (taut) state, of hemoglobin
  2,3-bisphosphoglycerate stabilizing,
      45–46, 46f
  oxygenation and, 44, 44f, 45f
T tubular system, in cardiac muscle, 575
T-type calcium channel, 576
$t_{1/2}$. See Half-life
T_3. See Triiodothyronine
T_4. See Thyroxine
TAFs. See TBP-associated factors
Tag SNPs, 85
Talin, 550, 551f
Tandem, 421
Tandem mass spectrometry, 28
  neonatal blood analysis with, 252
Tangier disease, 239t
TaqI, 405t
Target cells, 442–443, 443t
  receptors for, 443, 444f
Targeted gene disruption/knockout, 417
Tarui's disease, 166t
TATA binding protein, 353, 356f, 357, 358
TATA box, in transcription control, 352,
      353, 353f, 354f, 355, 355f,
      358t
Taurochenodeoxycholic acid, synthesis of,
      237f
Taut (T) state, of hemoglobin
  2,3-bisphosphoglycerate stabilizing,
      45–46, 46f
  oxygenation and, 44, 44f, 45f

Tay-Sachs disease, 215t
TBG. *See* Thyroxine-binding globulin
tblastn, 86
tblastx, 86
TBP. *See* TATA binding protein
TBP-associated factors, 353, 357, 358
TEBG. *See* Testosterone-estrogen-binding globulin
Telomerase, 326
Telomeres, 326, 327f
Temperature
   chemical reaction rate affected by, 63, 63f
   enzyme-catalyzed reaction rate affected by, 64–65
   in fluid mosaic model of membrane structure, 428
Temperature coefficient (Q_{10}), enzyme-catalyzed reactions and, 64–65
Template binding, in transcription, 349, 349f
Template strand DNA, 312, 314, 315f
   transcription of in RNA synthesis, 348–350, 349f
Tenase complex, 608–609
Terminal transferase, 406t, 421
Termination
   chain
      in glycosaminoglycan synthesis, 553
      in transcription cycle, 349, 349f
   of protein synthesis, 376, 377f
   of RNA synthesis, 349, 349f, 350f, 352
Termination signals, 366
   for bacterial transcription, 352–353, 353f
   for eukaryotic transcription, 356
Tertiary structure, 31, 33, 35f
   stabilizing factors and, 34–35
Testes, hormones produced by, 445, 448–450, 451f. *See also* specific type
Testosterone, 447f, 448f
   binding of, 462t, 463
   metabolism of, 450, 452f
   synthesis of, 448, 450, 451f
Testosterone-estrogen-binding globulin (sex hormone-binding globulin), 462, 462t, 591t
Tetracycline (tet) resistance genes, 407, 408f
Tetrahedral transition state intermediate, in acid-base catalysis, 52, 53f
Tetrahydrofolate, 500, 501f
Tetraiodothyronine (thyroxine/T_4), 446, 455
   storage/secretion of, 461, 461t
   synthesis of, 455, 456f
   transport of, 461t, 462
Tetramers
   hemoglobin as, 43
   histone, 322–323, 323
Tetroses, 112, 113t
Tf. *See* Transferrin
TFIIA, 357

TFIIB, 357
TFIID, 353, 357, 358
   in preinitiation complex formation, 358
TFIIE, 357
TFIIF, 357
TFIIH, 357
TFPI. *See* Tissue factor pathway inhibitor
TfR. *See* Transferrin receptor
Thalassemias, 47–48
Thanatophoric dysplasia, 561t
Theca cells, hormones produced by, 450
Theobromine, 297
Theophylline, 297
   hormonal regulation of lipolysis and, 227
Thermodynamics
   biochemical (bioenergetics), 88–93. *See also* ATP
   glycolysis reversal and, 167–169
   laws of, 88–89
   hydrophobic interactions and, 7
Thermogenesis, 228, 229f
   diet-induced, 228, 486
Thermogenin, 107, 228, 229f
Thiamin (vitamin B_1), 490t, 497f
   in citric acid cycle, 148
   coenzymes derived from, 50
   deficiency of, 490t, 496–497
      pyruvate metabolism affected by, 155, 157, 496–497
Thiamin diphosphate, 155, 180, 496, 497f
Thiamin pyrophosphate, 50
Thiamin triphosphate, 496
Thick (myosin) filaments, 566, 567f
Thin (actin) filaments, 566, 567f, 568f
Thioesterase, 199
6-Thioguanine, 298, 299f
Thiokinase (acyl-CoA synthetase)
   in fatty acid activation, 187, 188f
   in triacylglycerol synthesis, 211, 226, 226f
Thiol-dependent transglutaminase. *See* Transglutaminase
Thiol ester plasma protein family, 598
Thiolase, 188, 189f, 191
   in mevalonate synthesis, 230, 231f
Thiophorase (succinyl-CoA-acetoacetate-CoA transferase), 146, 192, 192f
Thioredoxin, 302
Thioredoxin reductase, 302, 305f
Threonine, 15t
   catabolism of, 257
   phosphorylated, 271
   requirements for, 488
Thrombin, 609, 610, 611f
   antithrombin III affecting, 611
   circulating levels of, 610–611
   conserved residues and, 55t
   formation of fibrin and, 610, 611f
   in platelet activation, 613–614, 614f
   from prothrombin, factor Xa activation of, 609–610

Thrombolysis
   laboratory tests in evaluation of, 616
   t-PA and streptokinase in, 613, 613f
Thrombomodulin, in blood coagulation, 608t, 611, 615, 615t
Thrombosis, 606–616. *See also* Coagulation
   antithrombin III in prevention of, 611
   circulating thrombin levels and, 610–611
   endothelial cell products in, 615, 615t
   hyperhomocysteinemia and, folic acid supplements in prevention of, 502
   phases of, 606
   in protein C or protein S deficiency, 611
   t-PA and streptokinase in management of, 613, 613f
   types of thrombi and, 606
Thromboxane A_2, 123f
   in platelet activation, 614f, 615
Thromboxanes, 122, 123f, 196, 204
   clinical significance of, 2–6
   cyclooxygenase pathway in formation of, 204, 205f
Thymidine, 296t
   base pairing of in DNA, 311, 312, 313f
Thymidine monophosphate (TMP), 296t
Thymidylate, 311
Thymine, 296t
Thyroglobulin, 455
Thyroid-binding globulin, 462, 591t
Thyroid hormone receptor-associated proteins (TRAPs), 480, 480t
Thyroid hormone response element, 467t
   storage/secretion of, 461, 461t
Thyroid hormones, 445, 446
   in lipolysis, 227, 228f
   receptors for, 444, 478
   synthesis of, 455, 456f
   transport of, 461t, 462
Thyroid-stimulating hormone (TSH), 445, 446, 447f, 455, 456
Thyroperoxidase, 457
Thyrotropin-releasing hormone (TRH), 446, 447f
Thyroxine (T_4), 446, 455
   storage/secretion of, 461, 461t
   synthesis of, 455, 456f
   transport of, 461t, 462
Thyroxine-binding globulin, 461t, 462
TIF2 coactivator, 479, 480t
Tiglyl-CoA, catabolism of, 268f
TIM. *See* Translocase-of-the-inner membrane
Timnodonic acid, 123t
Tin, 504t
Tissue differentiation, retinoic acid in, 491
Tissue factor (factor III), 607f, 608t, 609
Tissue factor complex, 609
Tissue factor pathway inhibitor, 609
Tissue plasminogen activator (alteplase/t-PA), 612–613, 613f, 615t
Tissue-specific gene expression, 391

Titin, 574t
Tm. *See* Melting temperature/transition temperature
TMP (thymidine monophosphate), 296f, 296t
Tocopherol, 490t, 493–495, 494f. *See also* Vitamin E
  as antioxidant, 98, 128, 494–495, 494f
  deficiency of, 490t
Tocotrienol, 493–495, 494f. *See also* Vitamin E
Tolbutamide, 194
TOM. *See* Translocase-of-the-outer membrane
Topogenic sequences, 514
Topoisomerases, DNA, 314, 336t, 340, 340f
Total iron-binding capacity, 594
Toxemia of pregnancy of ewes, ketosis and, 194
Toxic hyperbilirubinemia, 291
Toxicity, vitamin, 489
Toxicology, 1
Toxins, microbial, 433
Toxopheroxyl free radical, 494–495
TpC. *See* Troponin C
TpI. *See* Troponin I
TpT. *See* Troponin T
TR activator molecule 1 (TRAM-1 coactivator), 479, 480t
TRAM (translocating chain-associated membrane) protein, 512
TRAM-1 coactivator, 479, 480t
Trans fatty acids, 122–123, 203–204
Transaldolase, 177, 180
Transaminases. *See* Aminotransferases
Transamination, 134, 135f
  in amino acid carbon skeleton catabolism, 254, 254f, 255f, 256f
  citric acid cycle in, 148, 149f
  in urea biosynthesis, 247–248, 247f
Transcortin (corticosteroid-binding globulin), 462, 462t
Transcript profiling, 417–418
Transcription, 314, 356–359, 358t, 421
  activators and coactivators in control of, 358, 358t
  bacterial promoters in, 352–353, 353f
  control of fidelity and frequency of, 352–356
  eukaryotic promoters in, 353–356, 354f, 355f, 356f
  in gene expression regulation, 387–393, 397, 398t. *See also* Gene expression
  hormonal regulation of, 465, 466f, 476–480, 478f, 479f, 480t
  initiation of, 349–350, 349f
  nuclear receptor coregulators in, 478–480, 479t
  recombinant DNA technology and, 403, 404f
  retinoic acid in regulation of, 491

reverse, 420
  in retroviruses, 316, 340
  in RNA synthesis, 314, 315f, 348–350, 349f
Transcription complex, eukaryotic, 314, 356–359, 358f
Transcription control elements, 358, 358t
Transcription domains, definition of, 393
Transcription factors, 358, 358t
  nuclear receptor superfamily, 477–478, 479f, 479t
Transcription start sites, alternative, 399
Transcription unit, 349, 353f
Transcriptional intermediary factor 2 (TIF2 coactivator), 479, 480t
Transcriptome information, 418, 421
Transfection, identification of enhancers/regulatory elements and, 391
Transfer RNA (tRNA), 315, 318, 348, 349t, 367–368, 368f. *See also* RNA
  aminoacyl, in protein synthesis, 374
  anticodon region of, 366
  processing and modification of, 362, 364
  suppressor, 370
Transferases, 49
Transferrin, 486, 591t, 592, 593f, 593t, 594
Transferrin receptor, 595
Transfusion, ABO blood group and, 625–626
Transgenic animals, 391, 417, 421
  enhancers/regulatory elements identified in, 391
Transglutaminase, in blood coagulation, 608, 608t, 610, 611f
Transhydrogenase, proton-translocating, 109
Transient insertion signal. *See* Signal peptide
Transition mutations, 368, 368f
Transition state intermediate, tetrahedral, in acid-base catalysis, 52, 53f
Transition states, 62
Transition temperature/melting temperature (T_m), 313, 428
Transketolase, 177, 179f, 180, 184
  erythrocyte, in thiamin nutritional status assessment, 497
  thiamin diphosphate in reactions involving, 180, 184, 497
Translation, 365, 421
Translation arrest, 320
Translocase-of-the-inner membrane, 507
Translocase-of-the-outer membrane, 507
Translocating chain-associated membrane (TRAM) protein, 512
Translocation, protein, 22f, 507
Translocation complexes, 507
Translocon, 512
Transmembrane proteins, 426
  ion channels as, 431, 432f, 432t
  in red cells, 623–624, 623f, 624t
Transmembrane signaling, 422, 438, 614
  in platelet activation, 614, 614f
Transmissible spongiform encephalopathies (prion diseases), 38

Transport proteins, 461t, 462t, 469–470, 591t
Transport systems/transporters. *See also* specific type
  active, 430, 430t, 431f, 434, 435, 435f
  ATP-binding cassette, 222, 223f
  in cotranslational insertion, 514, 514f
  disorders associated with mutations in genes encoding, 521–522, 522t
  facilitated diffusion, 430, 430t, 431f, 434–435, 435f
  glucose. *See* Glucose transporters
  in inner mitochondrial membrane, 107–110, 108f–110f
  membrane, 433–438, 434f
  for nucleotide sugars, 525
Transport vesicles, 506, 518–520, 518t, 519f
  defined, 518
  in intracellular traffic, 518
  in vesicle coating, 519–520
Transporters, 425
Transposition, 332–333
  retroposons/retrotransposons and, 329
Transthyretin, 591t, 599
Transverse asymmetry, 520
Transverse movement, of lipids across membrane, 427
Transversion mutations, 368, 368f
TRAPs, 480, 480t
Trauma, protein loss and, 487–488
TRE. *See* Thyroid hormone response element
Trehalase, 483
Trehalose, 117t
TRH. *See* Thyrotropin-releasing hormone
Triacylglycerols (triglycerides), 124, 125f, 217
  in adipose tissue, 132
  digestion and absorption of, 483, 484f
  excess of. *See* Hypertriacylglycerolemia
  interconvertability of, 138–139
  in lipoprotein core, 217, 219f
  metabolism of, 134, 134f, 136, 136f
    in adipose tissue, 226–227, 226f
    fatty liver and, 224f, 225
    hepatic, 222–225, 224f
    high-density lipoproteins in, 221–222, 223f
    hydrolysis in, 209
    reduction of serum levels of, drugs for, 238–239
    synthesis of, 210f, 211
    transport of, 219–220, 220f, 221f, 222f
Tricarboxylate anions, transporter systems for lipogenesis regulation and, 200
Tricarboxylic acid cycle. *See* Citric acid cycle
Triglycerides. *See* Triacylglycerols
Triiodothyronine (T_3), 446, 455
  storage/secretion of, 461, 461t
  synthesis of, 455, 456f
  transport of, 461t, 462

Trimethoprim, 501
Trinucleotide repeat expansions, 330
Triokinase, 181, 183f
Triose phosphates, acylation of, 133
Trioses, 112, 113t
Triphosphates, nucleoside, 295, 295f
Triple helix structure, of collagen, 38–39, 39f, 545–548, 547f
Triplet code, genetic code as, 365, 366t
tRNA. *See* Transfer RNA
Tropocollagen, 38, 39f
Tropoelastin, 549
Tropomyosin, 566, 568f, 570–571
    in red cell membranes, 624t
    as striated muscle inhibitor, 571
Troponin C, 570–571
Troponin I, 570–571
Troponin T, 570–571
Troponin/troponin complex, 566, 568f, 570–571
    as striated muscle inhibitor, 571
Trypsin, 485
    conserved residues and, 55t
    in digestion, 485
Trypsinogen, 485
Tryptophan, 16t, 272, 498
    catabolism of, 262, 264f, 265f
    deficiency of, 498
    niacin synthesized from, 498
    permeability coefficient of, 426f
    requirements for, 488
L-Tryptophan dioxygenase (tryptophan pyrrolase), 97
Tryptophan oxygenase/L-tryptophan oxygenase (tryptophan pyrrolase), 97, 262, 264f
TSEs. *See* Transmissible spongiform encephalopathies
TSH. *See* Thyroid-stimulating hormone
Tumor cells, migration of, hyaluronic acid and, 557
Tumor suppressor genes, p53, 346–347
Tunicamycin, 536, 536t
Twin lamb disease. *See* Pregnancy toxemia of ewes
Twitch fibers, slow (red) and fast (white), 583, 583t
Two-dimensional electrophoresis, protein expression and, 28–29
TXs. *See* Thromboxanes
Tyk-2, in Jak-STAT pathway, 473–475
Type A response, in gene expression, 380, 381f
Type B response, in gene expression, 380–381, 381f
Type C response, in gene expression, 381, 381f
L-type calcium channel, 576
Tyrosine, 15t, 16t, 272–274, 276f
    catabolism of, 257–259, 261f
    epinephrine and norepinephrine formed from, 276f
    in hemoglobin M, 46–47

in hormone synthesis, 438, 446, 447f
    phosphorylated, 271
    requirements for, 488
    synthesis of, 242, 244f
Tyrosine aminotransferase, defect in, in tyrosinemia, 257
Tyrosine hydroxylase, catecholamine biosynthesis and, 453–454, 455f
Tyrosine kinase
    in insulin signal transmission, 472–475, 474f
    in Jak/STAT pathway, 473–475, 475f
Tyrosinemia, 257
Tyrosinosis, 257

Ubiquination, 22f
    of misfolded proteins, 517, 517f
Ubiquinone (Q/coenzyme Q), 128
    in cholesterol synthesis, 231, 232f
    in respiratory chain, 100, 102f, 103f
Ubiquitin, in protein degradation, 517–518, 517f
UDP-glucose. *See* Uridine diphosphate glucose
UDPGal. *See* Uridine diphosphate galactose
UDPGlc. *See* Uridine diphosphate glucose
UFA (unesterified fatty acids). *See* Free fatty acids
Ulcers, 482
Ultraviolet light
    nucleotide absorption of, 298
    nucleotide excision repair of DNA damage caused by, 345
    vitamin D synthesis and, 492, 492f
UMP (uridine monophosphate), 296f, 296t
Uncouplers/uncoupling proteins
    on respiratory chain, 107, 107f
    undernutrition and, 487
Uncoupling protein, 107
Undernutrition, 482, 486–487
Unequal crossover, 331, 332f
Unesterified fatty acids. *See* Free fatty acids
Unfolded protein response, 516
Uniport systems, 433, 434f
Unique-sequence (nonrepetitive) DNA, 328
Universal donor/universal recipient, 625
Unsaturated fatty acids, 121, 122, 123t. *See also* Fatty acids
    cis double bonds in, 122–124, 124f
    dietary, cholesterol levels affected by, 238
    eicosanoids formed from, 196, 204, 205f, 206f
    essential, 202, 202f, 204
        abnormal metabolism of, 206
        deficiency of, 203–204, 206
        prostaglandin production and, 196
    in membranes, 424, 425f
    metabolism of, 202–204
    oxidation of, 189–190
    structures of, 202f
    synthesis of, 202–203, 203f

Unwinding, DNA, 334
    RNA synthesis and, 352
Uracil, 296t
    deoxyribonucleosides of, in pyrimidine synthesis, 304–305, 306f
Urate, as antioxidant, 128
Urea
    amino acid metabolism and, 134, 135f
    nitrogen catabolism producing, 246–247, 249–251
    permeability coefficient of, 426f
    synthesis of, 247–248, 247f, 248f
        metabolic disorders associated with, 251–252
        gene therapy for, 252
Uric acid, 297
    purine catabolism in formation of, 307, 307f
Uridine, 295f, 296t
Uridine diphosphate galactose (UDPGal), 181, 525, 526t
Uridine diphosphate galactose (UDPGal) 4-epimerase, 181, 184f
    inherited defects in, 186
Uridine diphosphate glucose (UDP/UDPGlc), 159, 161f, 525, 526t
    in glycogen biosynthesis, 159, 160f
Uridine diphosphate glucose dehydrogenase, 180, 182f
Uridine diphosphate glucose pyrophosphorylase, 180, 182f
    in glycogen biosynthesis, 159, 160f
Uridine diphosphate-glucuronate/glucuronic acid, 180–181, 182f, 298
Uridine diphosphate N-acetylgalactosamine (UDP-GalNAc), 526t
Uridine diphosphate N-acetylglucosamine (UDP-GlcNAc), 526t
Uridine diphosphate xylose (UDP-Xyl), 526t
Uridine monophosphate (UMP), 296f, 296t
Uridine triphosphate (UTP), in glycogen biosynthesis, 159, 160f
Uridyl transferase deficiency, 186
Urobilinogens
    conjugated bilirubin reduced to, 289–290
    in jaundice, 292, 292t
    normal values for, 292t
Urocanic aciduria, 254
Urokinase, 613, 613f
Uronic acid pathway, 177, 180–181, 182f
    disruption of, 184
Uronic acids, 118
    in heparin, 553, 555f
Uroporphyrinogen decarboxylase, 280, 283f, 284f
    in porphyria, 286t
Uroporphyrinogen I, 280, 283f, 284f

Uroporphyrinogen I synthase, in porphyria, 286t
Uroporphyrinogen III, 280, 283f, 284f
Uroporphyrins, 279, 280f, 281f
  spectrophotometry in detection of, 282–283
UTP, in phosphorylation, 92–93

V region/segment. See Variable regions/segments
v-SNARE proteins, 518, 520
Valeric acid, 122t
Valine, 15t
  catabolism of, 265, 267f, 269f
  interconversion of, 243
  requirements for, 488
Valinomycin, 108
Vanadium, 504t
Van der Waals forces, 7
Variable numbers of tandemly repeated units (VNTRs), in forensic medicine, 416
Variable regions/segments, 602f
  gene for, 602
    DNA rearrangement and, 333, 399, 602–603
    immunoglobulin heavy chain, 600f, 601, 602f
    immunoglobulin light chain, 333, 399, 600f, 601, 602f
  of immunoglobulins, 601
Vascular system, nitric oxide affecting, 580–581, 581f, 582t
Vasodilators, 565
  nitric oxide as, 580–581, 581f, 582t
VAST, 87
VDRE. See Vitamin D response element
Vector, 421
  cloning, 406–408, 407f, 408f, 408t, 421
  expression, 409
Vector Alignment Research Tool (VAST), 87
Vegetarian diet, vitamin B_{12} deficiency and, 499
Velocity
  initial, 65
    inhibitors affecting, 69, 69f, 70f
  maximal (V_{max})
    allosteric effects on, 77
    inhibitors affecting, 69, 69f, 70f
    Michaelis-Menten equation in determination of, 66–67, 67f
    substrate concentration and, 65, 65f
Very low carbohydrate diets, weight loss from, 175
Very low density lipoprotein receptor, 219, 220
Very low density lipoproteins, 136, 217, 218t
  in fed state, 140
  hepatic secretion of, dietary and hormonal status and, 223–225, 224f

metabolism of, 136, 136f, 219–220, 222f
  in triacylglycerol transport, 220, 220f, 222f
Vesicles
  coating, 518–519, 519f
    brefeldin A affecting, 519–520
  secretory, 506, 508f
  targeting, 518–519, 519f
  transport, 506, 518–520, 518t, 519f
v_i. See Initial velocity
Vimentins, 585t, 586
Vinculin, 550, 551f
Viral oncogenes. See Oncogenes
Viruses
  glycan binding of, 542
  host cell protein synthesis affected by, 376, 378f
Vision, vitamin A in, 490t, 491, 492f
Vitamin A, 490–492, 490t, 491f, 492f
  deficiency of, 490t, 491
  excess/toxicity of, 491–492
  functions of, 490t, 491
  in vision, 490t, 491
Vitamin B complex. See also specific vitamin
  in citric acid cycle, 148
  coenzymes derived from, 50, 51f
Vitamin B_1 (thiamin), 490t, 496–497, 497f
  in citric acid cycle, 148
  coenzymes derived from, 50
  deficiency of, 490t, 496–497
    pyruvate metabolism affected by, 155, 157, 496–497
Vitamin B_2 (riboflavin), 94, 490t, 497–498
  in citric acid cycle, 148
  coenzymes derived from, 50, 497
  deficiency of, 490t, 497
  dehydrogenases dependent on, 95
Vitamin B_6 (pyridoxine/pyridoxal/pyridoxamine), 490t, 498–499, 499f
  deficiency of, 490t, 499
    xanthurenate excretion in, 262, 265f
  excess/toxicity of, 499
Vitamin B_{12} (cobalamin), 490t, 499–500, 499f
  absorption of, 499–500
    intrinsic factor in, 485, 499
  deficiency of, 490t, 500
    functional folate deficiency and, 500, 501–502
  in methylmalonic aciduria, 169
Vitamin B_{12}-dependent enzymes, 500, 500f
Vitamin C (ascorbic acid), 177, 490t, 503–504, 503f
  as antioxidant, 128
  in collagen synthesis, 39, 504, 545
  deficiency of, 490t, 504
    collagen affected in, 39, 504, 548
  iron absorption and, 486, 504
  supplemental, 504
Vitamin D, 489, 490t, 492–493
  in calcium absorption, 485, 492–493
  deficiency of, 490t, 492, 493

ergosterol as precursor for, 127, 129f
  excess/toxicity of, 493
  metabolism of, 492–493, 493f
  receptor for, 478
Vitamin D-binding protein, 453
Vitamin D receptor-interacting proteins (DRIPs), 480, 480t
Vitamin D response element, 467t
Vitamin D_2 (ergocalciferol), 492
Vitamin D_3 (cholecalciferol)
  synthesis of in skin, 453, 454f, 492, 492f
  in vitamin D metabolism, 492, 492f, 493f
Vitamin E, 490t, 493–495, 494f
  as antioxidant, 98, 128, 494–495, 494f
  deficiency of, 490t, 495
Vitamin H. See Biotin
Vitamin K, 490t, 495–496, 495f, 496f, 612
  calcium-binding proteins and, 496, 496f
  in coagulation, 495, 495f
    coumarin anticoagulants affecting, 612
  deficiency of, 490t
Vitamin K hydroquinone, 495, 496f
Vitamins, 2, 489–504, 490t. See also specific vitamins
  in citric acid cycle, 148
  digestion and absorption of, 485–486
  lipid- (fat-) soluble, 489, 490–496
    absorption of, 483
  metabolic functions of, 489, 490t
  water-soluble, 489, 496–504
VLA-1/VLA-5/VLA-6, 629t
VLDL. See Very low density lipoproteins
V_{max}. See Maximal velocity
VNTRs. See Variable numbers of tandemly repeated units
Voltage-gated channels, 431, 432–433, 577t
von Gierke's disease, 166t, 308
von Willebrand disease, 612
von Willebrand factor, 612
  in platelet activation, 613

Warfarin, 495, 612
  phenobarbital interaction and, cytochrome P450 induction affecting, 635
  vitamin K affected by, 495
Water, 2, 5–9
  as biologic solvent, 5, 6f
  biomolecular structure and, 6–7, 6t
  dissociation of, 8–9
  in hydrogen bonds, 5, 6f
  as nucleophile, 7–9
  permeability coefficient of, 426f
  structure of, 5, 6f
Water solubility, of xenobiotics, metabolism and, 633
Watson-Crick base pairing, 7, 311
Waxes, 121
Weak acids, 9
  buffering capacity of, 11–12, 12f
  dissociation constants for, 10–11, 12

Weak acids—*continued*
  Henderson-Hasselbalch equation describing behavior of, 11, 12f
  physiologic significance of, 10–11
  p*K*/p*K*$_a$ values of, 10–13, 12t
Weak bases, 9
Wernicke-Korsakoff syndrome, 490t
Wernicke's encephalopathy, 496
Western blot transfer procedure, 409–410, 409f, 421
White blood cells, 628–631. *See also* specific type
  growth factors regulating production of, 618
  recombinant DNA technology in study of, 632
White thrombus, 606
White (fast) twitch fibers, 583, 583t
Williams syndrome, 549
Wilson disease, 439t, 596
  ceruloplasmin levels in, 596
  gene mutations in, 439t, 597
  methylhistidine in, 271
Wobble, 367–368
Women, iron needs of, 594

X-linked disorders, RFLPs in diagnosis of, 415

X-ray crystallography, Laue, 35–36
X-ray diffraction and crystallography, protein structure demonstrated by, 35
Xanthine, 297
Xanthine oxidase, 95
  deficiency of, hypouricemia and, 308
Xanthurenate, excretion of in vitamin B$_6$ deficiency, 262, 265f
Xenobiotics, metabolism of, 633–639
  conjugation in, 633, 634–636
  cytochrome P450 system/hydroxylation in, 633–635, 636t
  factors affecting, 637
  pharmacogenetics in drug research and, 638–639
  responses to, 637–638, 637t, 638t
    toxic, 638, 638f
Xenotransplantation, 543
Xeroderma pigmentosum, 345
Xerophthalmia, vitamin A deficiency in, 490t, 491
XP. *See* Xeroderma pigmentosum
D-Xylose, 115f, 115t
Xylose, in glycoproteins, 526t
D-Xylulose, 116f
L-Xylulose, 115t
  accumulation of in essential pentosuria, 184

Yeast artificial chromosome (YAC) vector, 407, 408t
Yeast cells, mitochondrial protein import studied in, 507

Z line, 565, 566f, 567f
Zellweger's (cerebrohepatorenal) syndrome, 194, 511, 511t
Zinc, 504t
  α_2-macroglobulin transport of, 598
Zinc finger motif, 393, 394t, 395–396, 396f
  in DNA-binding domain, 477
Zona fasciculata, steroid synthesis in, 447
Zona glomerulosa, mineralocorticoid synthesis in, 446
Zona pellucida, glycoproteins in, 537
Zona reticularis, steroid synthesis in, 447
Zoology, 1
ZP. *See* Zona pellucida
ZP1-3 proteins, 537
Zwitterions, 16–17
Zymogens, 77, 485
  in blood coagulation, 608, 608t, 609
  rapid response to physiologic demand and, 78
ZZ genotype, 597